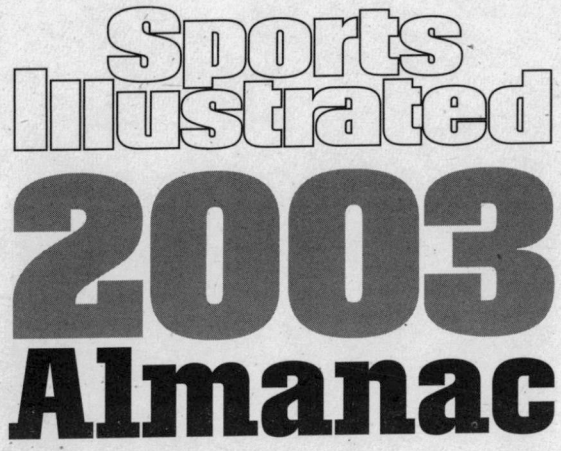

Sports Illustrated
2003
Almanac

By the Editors of Sports Illustrated

Sports Illustrated
2003
Almanac

SPORTS ILLUSTRATED is a registered trademark of Time Inc. Used under license.

First Edition
ISBN 1-929049-55-2

Sports Illustrated 2003 Almanac was prepared by Bishop Books of New York City.

Cover photography credits :
Tom Brady: Damian Strohmeyer
Alfonso Soriano: Chuck Solomon
Shaquille O'Neal: John W. McDonough

Back cover photography credits (left to right):
Sue Bird: Stephen Slade
Landon Donovan: Masakazu Watanabe/Aflo Sport/Newsport
Steve Yzerman: Dave Sandford/Getty Images/NHLI

Spine photography credit: Robert Beck

Title page photography credit: Reuters NewMedia Inc.Corbis

10 9 8 7 6 5 4 3 2 1
COM
PRINTED IN THE UNITED STATES OF AMERICA

TIME INC. HOME ENTERTAINMENT

President . . . . Rob Gursha
Vice President, Branded Businesses . . . . David Arfine
Executive Director, Marketing Services . . . . Carol Pittard
Director, Retail & Special Sales . . . . Tom Mifsud
Director of Finance . . . . .Tricia Griffin
Marketing Director . . . . Kenneth Maehlum
Associate Director . . . . Peter Harper
Assistant Marketing Director . . . . .Vanessa Cunningham
Prepress Manager . . . . Emily Rabin
Associate Book Production Manager . . . . Suzanne DeBenedetto
Associate Product Manager . . . . .Victoria Alfonso
Associate Product Manager . . . . Michelle Kuhr

Special thanks: Robert Dente, Gina Di Meglio, Anne-Michelle Gallero, Natalie McCrea, Jessica McGrath, Jonathan Polsky, Mary Jane Rigoroso, Steven Sandonato, Bozena Szwagulinski, Niki Whelan

Watch for the Sports Illustrated 2004 Trivia Calendar, available in stores August 2003

CONTENTS

In compiling the *Sports Illustrated 2003 Almanac*, the editors would like to extend their gratitude to the media relations offices of the following organizations for their help in providing information and materials relating to their sports: Major League Baseball; the Canadian Football League; the National Football League; the National Collegiate Athletic Association; the National Basketball Association; the National Hockey League; the Association of Tennis Professionals; the Women's Tennis Association; the U.S. Tennis Association; the U.S. Golf Association; the Ladies Professional Golf Association; the Professional Golfers Association; National Thoroughbred Racing Association; the U.S. Trotting Association; the Breeders' Cup; Churchill Downs; the New York Racing Association, Inc.; the Jockey's Guild, Inc.; Championship Auto Racing Teams; the National Hot Rod Association; the International Motor Sports Association; the National Association for Stock Car Auto Racing; the Professional Bowlers Association; the Ladies Professional Bowlers Tour; the United Soccer Leagues; Major League Soccer; the Women's United Soccer Association; the *Fédération Internationale de Football Association*; the U.S. Soccer Federation; the U.S. Olympic Committee; USA Track & Field; U.S. Swimming; U.S. Diving; U.S. Skiing; U.S. Figure Skating Association; the U.S. Chess Federation; U.S. Curling; the Iditarod Trail Committee; the International Game Fish Association; the USA Gymnastics; U.S. Handball Association; the Lacrosse Foundation; the American Power Boat Association; the Unlimited Hydroplane Racing Association; the Professional Rodeo Cowboys Association; U.S. Rowing; the American Amateur Softball Association; the U.S. Speed Skating ; U.S. Rugby Football Union; USA Triathlon; the National Archery Association; USA Wrestling; the U.S. Squash Racquets Association; the U.S. Polo Association; ABC Sports; and the U.S. Volleyball Association.

The following sources were consulted in gathering information:

Baseball   *The Baseball Encyclopedia*, Macmillan Publishing Co., 1990; *Total Baseball*, Viking Penguin, 1995; *Baseballistics*, St. Martin's Press, 1990; *The Book of Baseball Records*, Seymour Siwoff, publisher, 1991; *The Complete Baseball Record Book*, The Sporting News Publishing Co., 1992; *The Sporting News Baseball Guide*, The Sporting News Publishing Co., 1996; *The Sporting News Official Baseball Register*, The Sporting News Publishing Co., 1996; *National League Green Book—1994*, The Sporting News Publishing Co., 1993; *American League Red Book—1994*, The Sporting News Publishing Co., 1993; *The Scouting Report: 1996,* Harper Perennial, 1996.

Pro Football   *The Official 1997 National Football League Record & Fact Book*, The National Football League, 1997; *The Official National Football League Encyclopedia*, New American Library, 1990; *The Sporting News Football Guide*, The Sporting News Publishing Co., 1996; *The Sporting News Football Register*, The Sporting News Publishing Co., 1996; *The 1993 National Football League Record & Fact Book,* Workman Publishing, 1993; *The Football Encyclopedia,* David Neft and Richard Cohen, St. Martin's Press, 1991.

Pro Football Venues   *Ticketmaster*

College Football   *1997 NCAA Football*, The National Collegiate Athletic Association, 1997.

Pro Basketball   *The Official NBA Basketball Encyclopedia*, Villard Books, 1994; *The Sporting News Official NBA Guide*, The Sporting News Publishing Co., 1996; *The Sporting News Official NBA Register*, The Sporting News Publishing Co., 1996.

College Basketball   *1997 NCAA Basketball*, The National Collegiate Athletic Association, 1996.

Hockey   *The National Hockey League Official Guide & Record Book 1997–98*, The National Hockey League, 1997; *The Sporting News Complete Hockey Book,* The Sporting News Publishing Co., 1993; *The Complete Encyclopedia of Hockey,* Visible Ink Press, 1993.

Tennis   *1997 Official USTA Tennis Yearbook*, H.O. Zimman, Inc., 1997; *IBM/ATP Tour 1997 Player Guide*, Association of Tennis Professionals, 1997; *1997 Corel WTA Tour Media Guide*, Corel WTA Tour, 1997.

Golf   *PGA Tour Book 1997*, PGA Tour Creative Services, 1997; *LPGA 1997 Player Guide*, LPGA Communications Department, 1997; *Senior PGA Tour Book 1997*, PGA Tour Creative Services, 1997; *USGA Yearbook 1997*, U.S. Golf Association, 1997.

Boxing   *The Ring 1986–87 Record Book and Boxing Encyclopedia*, The Ring Publishing Corp., 1987. *Computer Boxing Update*, Ralph Citro, Inc., 1992; Bob Yalen, boxing statistician.

Horse Racing   *The American Racing Manual 1994*, Daily Racing Form, Inc., 1994; *1994 Directory and Record Book*, The Thoroughbred Racing Association, 1994; *The Trotting and Pacing Guide 1994*, United States Trotting Association, 1994; *Breeders' Cup 1993 Statistics*, Breeders' Cup Limited, 1993; *NYRA Media Guide 1993*, The New York Racing Association, 1994; *The 120th Kentucky Derby Media Guide, 1994*, Churchill Downs Public Relations Dept., 1994; *The 120th Preakness Press Guide, 1994*, Maryland Jockey Club, 1994; *Harness Racing News,* Harness Racing Communications.

Motor Sports   *The Official NASCAR Yearbook and Press Guide 1997*, UMI Publications, Inc., 1997; *1994 Indianapolis 500 Media Fact Book*, Indy 500 Publications, 1994; *IMSA Yearbook 1995 Season Review*, International Motor Sports Association, 1995; *1994 Winston Drag Racing Series Media Guide*, Sports Marketing Enterprises, 1994.

Bowling   *1994 Professional Bowlers Association Press, Radio and Television Guide*, Professional Bowlers Association, Inc., 1994; *The Professional Women's Bowling Association Tour Guide 1997.*

Soccer   *Rothmans Football Yearbook 1993–94*, Headline Book Publishing, 1993; *American Professional Soccer League 1992 Media Guide*, APSL Media Relations Department, 1992; *The European Football Yearbook*, Facer Publications Limited, 1988; *Soccer America,* Burling Communications; Dan Goldstein, editor of *Football Europe.*

NCAA Sports   *1997–98 National Collegiate Championships*, The National Collegiate Athletic Association, 1998; *1993–94 National Directory of College Athletics,* Collegiate Directories Inc., 1993.

Olympics   *The Complete Book of the Olympics*, Little, Brown and Co., 1991; *The Complete Book of the Summer Olympics,* Little, Brown and Co., 1996.

Track and Field   *American Athletics Annual 1996*, The Athletics Congress/USA, 1996.

Swimming   *6th World Swimming Championships Media Guide*, The World Swimming Championships Organizing Committee, 1991.

Skiing   *U.S. Ski Team 1994 Media Guide / USSA Directory*, U.S. Ski Association, 1993; *Ski Racing Annual Competition Guide 1993–94*, Ski Racing International, 1993; *Ski Magazine's Encyclopedia of Skiing*, Harper & Row, 1974; *Caffe Lavazza Ski World Cup Press Kit*, Biorama, 1991.

The Year In Sports

The Opening Ceremonies in Salt Lake City

Rebuilding Year

The sports world struggled to redefine itself as the shadow of the Sept. 11, 2001, terrorist attacks still loomed

BY MERRELL NODEN

IN THE PALINDROMIC year just past, sports fans, like everyone else, found themselves in the uncomfortable position of looking simultaneously forward and backward. The terrorist attacks of Sept. 11, 2001, cast a long, frightening shadow over the world of sports. Even as the basic question posed by all games—Who's going to win?—beckoned us to look toward the future, it was impossible not to remember what happened on that awful morning and to worry that it might happen again.

The sports world had extra reason to worry. Our games, which in happier times are the closest things we have to communal rallies, seemed to be all too obvious targets for cold-blooded terrorists. So, from the moment we resumed playing games in September 2001 through the one-year anniversary of the attacks and beyond, security became at least as important a goal as selling tickets. It became standard practice at stadiums to search fans' bags and to wave a metal-detecting wand over their bodies,

And patriotism, like the New England Patriots, made a comeback in 2001–02, intertwined with the new emphasis on security. American flags were ubiquitous additions to uniforms and caps, and the stars and stripes became the preferred formation for marching bands everywhere. At Yankee Stadium, where armed law enforcement personnel patrolled the roofs during the 2001 World Series, live renditions of "God Bless America" replaced "Take Me Out to the Ballgame" as the soundtrack for the 7th inning stretch.

The first major event in a year top-heavy with them was the Super Bowl, which kicked off on Feb. 3 at the Superdome in New Orleans. President Bush accepted an invitation to perform the pregame coin toss, sending security preparations to an entirely new level: The air space over the Superdome was declared a No-Fly Zone. An eight-foot high fence and concrete barricades were erected around the stadium, and all spectators, including NFL Commissioner Paul Tagliabue, were required to walk the final few blocks to the stadium. Awaiting them were

BOB ROSATO

Showing surprising poise for an unheralded backup, Brady led the Patriots to victory in Super Bowl XXXVI.

2,000 security personnel, twice the normal number. Fans were forbidden to bring banners, noisemakers, and, yes, foam fingers. After what happened last year, no one considered these measures unreasonable.

Hard on the heels of the Super Bowl came the Winter Olympics in Salt Lake City, and then, four months later, the World Cup in South Korea and Japan. Both of those events commanded huge, global audiences, and were therefore potentially inviting targets for terrorists. Organizers took extraordinary security measures, and, we are happy to report, succeeded unequivocally.

Still, uncertainty was a prevailing mood in the post-Sept 11 world, and it was a theme that touched the world of sports as well. So many things were up in the air: Would a strike end the baseball season in August, just as playoff races were starting to heat up? Just how sullied would the sport of figure skating be once investigators chased down all

of the leads in the Olympic pairs judging scandal? What really happened to retired NBA forward Bison Dele, whose empty catamaran was discovered in Tahiti, showing traces of blood? And, in a happier line of inquiry, would Dele's former Bulls teammate Michael Jordan return for another season of what must surely be the final act of his NBA career?

We witnessed the final act for two other legends of sport, former Baltimore Colts quarterback Johnny Unitas and Boston Red Sox outfielder Ted Williams. Unitas, who died at 69, was a square-jawed and crew-cutted graduate of the Pittsburgh sandlots. He threw touchdown passes in a record 47 straight games and led the Colts to victory in the game that still gets credit for transforming pro football into the cultural force it is today—Baltimore's overtime defeat of the New York Giants in the 1958 NFL championship game.

Williams, who passed away at 83, is the last man to hit .400 for an entire season. He hit .406 in 1941, won the Triple Crown the following year and retired in 1960 with a lifetime average of .344, sixth best ever. He also belted 521 homers despite losing nearly five seasons to military service.

The Splendid Splinter's legacy took a hit, however, from the bizarre events that followed his death on July 5, 2002. In the year's strangest family feud, two of Williams's children battled over what to do with his remains. His oldest daughter, Bobby Jo Williams Ferrell, produced one will in which her father requested that he be cremated, his ashes scattered off Florida. Her half brother, John Henry Williams, claimed that a later, handwritten will requesting that Williams be frozen cryogenically ought to prevail. While this bickering was going on, the body of the greatest Red Sox hitter of all time reposed in a Scottsdale, Ariz., cryogenics lab.

The year was marked by several other unseemly disputes: the baseball labor struggle, of course; a civil suit to determine the rightful owner of Barry Bonds' 73rd home run ball from 2001; and a tussle between Martha Burk, head of the National Council of Women's Organizations, and Hootie Johnson, chairman of the venerable Augusta National Golf Club, over Augusta's exclusion of women from its membership rolls.

While all of this posturing was going on, an eventful year of actual sports was unfolding on the playing field. Along with routinely sensational champions like cyclist Lance Armstrong, who won his fourth straight Tour de France, omnipotent hoop giant Shaquille O'Neal and sprinter Marion Jones, the year was rich in comebacks (Pete Sampras, Ronaldo and Jordan); in dominant teams (the Miami Hurricanes in college football and the UConn Huskies in women's college basketball); and wonderful surprises (the U.S. soccer team, Olympic figure skater Sarah Hughes, New England quarterback Tom Brady and PGA champion Rich Beem).

The college football season ended with as dominating a national champion as we've had in some time. The Miami Hurricanes, rejuvenated under rookie coach Larry Coker, and led by stars at nearly every position, pulled off a perfect season. On their way to going 12–0, they snapped Florida State's 54-game home winning streak, beating the Seminoles 49–27 in Tallahassee, and, on consecutive weekends beat No. 14 Syracuse 59–0 and No. 12 Washington 65–7. By the time the Hurricanes blew into the Rose Bowl to play Nebraska for the national title, they were already being touted as perhaps the school's greatest team ever.

Nebraska, whose only loss had been a 62–36 pounding at the hands of Colorado, was led by multitalented Eric Crouch, who'd won the Heisman Trophy, edging Florida's sophomore quarterback, Rex Grossman, in the closest race since 1962. Crouch ran for 1,115 yards and 18 touchdowns in the regular season. He also passed for 1,150 yards and made a 63-yard touchdown *reception* during a key win over Oklahoma. All of that failed to impress Miami, which ran up a 34–0 halftime

Quarterback Ken Dorsey guided Miami to a 12–0 season and the national championship.

Shea won the gold medal in skeleton to become the first third-generation Olympian in the history of the Games.

lead en route to a 37–14 trouncing.

In the 2001–02 pro football season, the defending champion St. Louis Rams produced the season's best record (14–2) and reached the Super Bowl for the second time in three years. Quarterback Kurt Warner completed 68.7% of his passes for 4,830 yards and 36 touchdowns and was named league MVP. Still, the most amazing player may have been 39-year-old Jerry Rice. Playing for a new team, the Oakland Raiders, he was the same old Rice, catching 83 passes and raising his career TD total to 195.

In the conference championships, the Rams' Marshall Faulk rushed for 159 yards to lead St. Louis past Philadelphia 29–24, and New England, which started the season 0–2, rode Drew Bledsoe's passing to a 24–17 win over Pittsburgh. And therein lies the surprising story of the Pats' season. In the second game of the year, Bledsoe took a vicious hit from the Jets' Mo Lewis and spent four days in the hospital recovering. His backup, Tom Brady, played so well that coach Bill Belichick kept Brady as the starter even when Bledsoe was ready to play again. Belichick made the right call, as the Pats went 11–3 the rest of the way. But when Brady went down in the first half of the AFC title game, Bledsoe came in to rally New England to victory and present Belichick with a dilemma: Who would start the Super Bowl? Belichick went with Brady, who justified his coach's faith by winning the MVP award and leading the Patriots to an exciting 20–17 victory. The winning margin came on a 48-yard field goal by Adam Vinatieri as time expired.

The Winter Olympics began just six days later, with President Bush seated among the U.S. athletes at the Opening Ceremonies as the American flag that had flown over the World Trade Center was carried in by an honor guard of athletes. These Games would feature the usual complement of outstanding Europeans, including Simon Amman, a baby-faced Swiss ski jumper who won two gold medals, and Janica Kostelic of Croatia, who became the first Alpine skier to win four medals in a single Games, but they were perhaps most notable for the number of outstanding performances by U.S. athletes. Americans won 34 medals, 10 of them gold, easily surpassing the country's previous best of 13. And while the U.S. was undoubtedly boosted by the recent inclusion of newfangled events like snowboarding, Americans also did well in traditional events like speed skating and bodsledding. The U.S. won both the silver and bronze medals in the four-man bobsled, as two ex-football players, Garrett Hines and Todd Hays, made history by becoming the first black medalists in a Winter Olympics. They were topped a few days later by Vonetta Flowers, an African American who teamed with Jill Bakken to win the gold medal in the two-person bobsled.

The U.S. also had its best Olympics in speed skating, with Casey FitzRandolph winning the men's 500 and Chris Witty coming back from a bout with mononucleosis to set a world record in the women's 1,000. Derek Parra won the 5,000 in world record time, and earned a silver in the 1500. Another noteworthy American was Jim Shea, gold medalist in the men's skeleton, and the first third-generation Winter Olympian.

On the down side, the Games were tainted by several positive drug tests, and by a judging scandal in pairs skating. In that competition, to the amazement of fans everywhere, the gold medal first went to the Russian pair of Yelena Berezhnaya and Anton Sikharulidze, who skated well but clearly not as gracefully or flawlessly as the Canadien pair of Jamie Salé and David Pelletier.

Widespread suspicion turned to loud accusation after the French judge, Marie-Reine La Gougne, broke down, complaining tearfully that "no one knows the pressure we are under." SKATEGATE! screamed the headlines. While an investigation revealed contradictory details, it seemed certain that the French had swapped votes with the Russians. The immediate upshot was that Salé and Pelletier were named co-gold medalists and received a second pair of medals. Thoroughly embarrassed, the International Skating Union spent the rest of the spring searching for a better judging system.

A welcome antidote to this story came in the form of Sara Hughes, a 16-year-old high school senior from Great Neck, Long Island. Standing fourth after the short program, Hughes, figuring she had nothing to lose, skated with graceful abandon, nailing every one of her jumps and playing to the rapturous crowd. When the ice chips settled, Hughes had vaulted from fourth to first.

At the skating rink in West Valley City, Canada won its first gold medal in men's hockey in 50 years. The presence of NHLers, in midseason form, made for a compelling tournament and several superb games. The U.S. tied Russia 2–2 in a preliminary round thriller, then beat its former Cold War rival 3–2 in the semis. Belarus pulled off the biggest upset since the U.S.'s "Miracle on Ice" in 1980, beating Sweden 4–3 in the quarterfinals, and Canada, which started slowly, put it all together in the gold medal game, downing the U.S. 5–2. Canada's women's team took the gold as well, beating the U.S. in the final.

When the hockey stars returned to the NHL, which had interrupted its season for the Olympics, the Detroit Red Wings sailed to their third Stanley Cup in six years. The title was a perfect sendoff for Detroit's legendary coach, Scotty Bowman, who

announced his retirement after the Wings knocked off Carolina in Game 5.

The most dominant college basketball team was the UConn women's squad, four of whose players were first round WNBA picks. Led by women's Player of the Year Sue Bird and Swin Cash, who was named the MVP of the Final Four, the Huskies marched through 39 games without a loss, capping the run with an 82–70 triumph over Oklahoma in the NCAA championship game.

Men's college basketball was a bit more balanced. Duke and Kansas finished the regular season at No. 1 and No. 2, respectively, each with 29–3 records. But in the NCAA tournament, Duke fell in a shocker to Indiana, which was not even in the Top 25 at the end of the regular season. The Hoosiers reached the championship game, and even took a 44–42 lead over Maryland, which had eliminated Kansas in the semis. But the Terps reeled off a 22–5 run and won 64–52.

In the professional ranks, the Lakers juggernaut rolled on as Kobe Bryant and Shaquille O'Neal led Los Angeles to a third straight NBA championship. Their toughest competition came from the Sacramento Kings, led by Chris Webber, Peja Stojakovic and Mike Bibby. Sacramento stretched the Lakers to overtime of Game 7 in the Western Conference finals before giving way. By comparison, the Finals were a cakewalk for Los Angeles, which dispatched point guard Jason Kidd and the New Jersey Nets—champions of the much weaker Eastern Conference—in four games.

If the balance of power remained tilted toward the West in the NBA, it has shifted significantly in the wider world of international hoops, a fact driven home at the World Basketball Championships in Indianapolis in September. A team of NBAers—albeit one lacking O'Neal, Bryant, Allen Iverson, and other stars—lost to Argentina, Yugoslavia and Spain at the worlds to finish a dismal sixth.

A world tournament with a much broader range of participants, the World Cup, began on May 31 in Seoul, South Korea, and it didn't take long for American fans to get excited. On June 5, the U.S. team beat highly

Ronaldo scored eight goals in seven games to lead Brazil to a record fifth World Cup.

JERRY LAMPEN/REUTERS

regarded Portugal 3–2 in arguably the biggest win in U.S. World Cup history. After giving up a late goal to allow host South Korea a 1–1 tie, the U.S. team needed only to tie disappointing Poland to move to the final 16. They stumbled, but got into the next round through the back door when South Korea held on to beat Portugal 1–0.

The Americans didn't squander their good fortune, producing an excellent performance to blank Mexico 2–0 in the Round of 16 and book a spot in the quarterfinals against Germany. It was the farthest the U.S. had advanced in the World Cup since 1930. But the Yanks would lose the quarterfinal meeting 1–0 in a game German legend Franz Beckebauer said his country was "lucky" to have won. Lucky or not, the Germans defeated South Korea by the same score in the semis to reach the final against Brazil, which defeated Turkey in the other semifinal. In Yokohama, before 69,029 fans and a worldwide television audience of close to 1.5 billion, the tournament's leading scorer, Ronaldo—back from injuries that had dogged him since 1998—scored two second-half goals to deliver Brazil its unprecedented

fifth World Cup title.

The Ronaldo of the PGA, Tiger Woods, won the Masters and the U.S. Open and sailed into the British Open with many people assuming he would easily claim the third leg of the Grand Slam. But a winter squall blew into Muirfield on Saturday and doused Woods's hopes. He shot an 81, his worst round as a professional, and finished 28th on Sunday as Ernie Els won the tournament.

Woods was eager to bounce back at the PGA, but the unheralded Rich Beem stared him down over the last nine holes at Hazeltine, outside Minneapolis. The unassuming Beem, who as recently as 1995 had been working as a $7-an-hour stereo salesman, was a very popular champion.

In track and field, Marion Jones went undefeated for the season while her training partner, Tim Montgomery, became the world's fastest man, running 9.78 at the Grand Prix Final in Paris. Both the men's and women's marathon world records fell as Khalid Kannouchi ran 2:05:38 in London, and Paula Radcliffe, a 28-year-old from Great Britain, ran 2:17:18 in Chicago in only the second marathon of her career.

Once again, the Williams sisters dominated women's tennis as they met in the finals of three of the year's four Grand Slam events. Serena won them all, and she might have swept the majors had she not hurt her ankle at the Australian Open. Serena's performance aside, the year's best tennis story was the back-to-the-future men's final at the U.S. Open, in which 31-year-old Pete Sampras, winner of 13 previous Grand Slam titles, beat 32-year-old rival Andre Aggasi in four sets. It was one of the sweetest moments of Sampras's fabulous career.

One of the greatest baseball careers of all time belongs to San Francisco slugger Barry

TOM DiPACE

set the tone. Despite being pitched around so often that he had only 403 official at bats, he hit 46 home runs, drove in 110 runs and led the league with a .370 batting average. He was walked a major league record 198 times and generated an on-base percentage of .580, another record. Bonds finished the season with a career home run total of 613, fourth on the alltime list behind his godfather, Willie Mays.

In the American League, Alex Rodriguez led the majors with 57 homers and 142 RBIs. But Rodriguez's Texas Rangers finished dead last in the American League West, so Alfonso Soriano, the Yankees' whippet-like leadoff hitter, who finished the season with 39 homers and 40 stolen bases, was frequently mentioned as the league's most "valuable" player, as was Oakland Athletics shortstop Miguel Tejada, who batted .308 with 34 homers and 131 RBIS. Tejada paced the A's during their AL-record streak of 20 consecutive wins in August and September.

In the end, though, none of the teams who won their divisions reached the World Series. Scrappy Anaheim beat the Yankees and the Twins, while Bonds and the Giants beat Atlanta and the St. Louis Cardinals.

The playoffs were full of exciting games, and two wild-card teams reached the World Series, but the specter of Sept. 11, 2001, never fully receded as the first anniversary of attacks came and went. Many games were halted to mark the date, and then resumed. Two yahoos invaded the field during a White Sox–Royals game in September, attacking a first-base coach. And in October, in the Washington, D.C. area, a sniper executed a series of lethal attacks that caused the cancellation of dozens of youth games in several sports.

Not so long ago, the world of sports seemed a protected place, governed by its own rules, where the worst that could happen would be that you picked up an injury or lost a game. But this year, the wall between the world of sports and the troubling "real" world was eroded, if not torn down. One hopes it can be rebuilt.

Bonds, and like Sampras, he achieved something to savor in his twilight as a player, advancing to the World Series for the first time in 17 seasons. But baseball came perilously close to depriving him of that glory. The players—at odds with the owners over everything from revenue sharing and drug testing to the so-called competitive balance tax—set a strike date of August 30. With two separate fan advocacy groups calling for a Nationwide Walkout on Baseball on August 28, and polls showing that two-thirds of fans said a strike would make them lose interest in the game, things did not look good. "It's a scary moment for baseball," said Detroit pitcher Jose Lima.

But mere hours before the strike deadline, the two sides reached a deal that would last until 2006. No one was fooled by the toothless new drug testing policy, but everyone breathed a sigh of relief at the settlement. And fans got to see the end of a fine season.

Bonds continued to bang out startling numbers despite his advancing age (he's 38). He hit two homers in the Giants' opener to

compiled by John Bolster

Baseball

Nov 6, 2001—On the day before its collective bargaining agreement with the players union is to end, Major League Baseball management announces plans to eliminate, for economic reasons, two franchises before the 2002 season begins. Commissioner Bud Selig's staff will determine which two of the four teams on management's list—which includes the Montreal Expos, the Minnesota Twins, the Florida Marlins and the Tampa Bay Devil Rays—will get the axe.

Nov 8—Accusing owners of unfair labor practices, the Major League Baseball Players Association files a grievance to block management's plan to eliminate two franchises before the 2002 season.

Nov 11—St. Louis Cardinals slugger Mark McGwire, who broke Roger Maris's 37-year-old single-season home run record in 1998, announces his retirement. McGwire belted 70 homers in '98, only to see his record eclipsed in 2001 by Barry Bonds. McGwire's 583 career home runs place him fifth on the alltime list at the time of his retirement.

JOHN IACONO

Nov 12—Ichiro Suzuki of the Seattle Mariners and Albert Pujols of the Cardinals are named rookies of the year in the American and National leagues, respectively. Suzuki, who rapped out 242 hits and won the batting title, received 27 of 28 first-place votes, while Pujols, who drove in 130 runs, was a unanimous choice.

Nov 13—Arizona Diamondbacks lefthander Randy Johnson wins the NL Cy Young Award, his third straight. Johnson went 21–6 with a 2.49 ERA and 372 strikeouts in 2001.

Nov 14—Lou Piniella, who led the Mariners to a record-tying 116 regular-season victories, is named AL manager of the year, while in the National League, the award goes to the Philadelphia Phillies' rookie skipper Larry Bowa, who kept the Phillies in the pennant chase until September.

Nov 15—After a season in which he went 20–3 with 213 strikeouts and a 3.51 ERA, Roger Clemens of the New York Yankees wins the AL Cy Young Award. It is his sixth Cy Young, a record.

Nov 19—Barry Bonds, who hit .328 with 137 RBIs, a record 73 homers and a record .863 slugging percentage, is named MVP of the National League. The honor makes the San Francisco Giants leftfielder baseball's first four-time MVP.

Nov 20—Seattle rightfielder Ichiro Suzuki wins the AL MVP award to join former Boston outfielder Fred Lynn (1975) as the only players to be named rookie of the year and MVP in the same season.

Nov 26—A San Francisco judge rules that Barry Bonds's 73rd home run ball, which fans fought over on Oct. 7 at Pacific Bell Park, must be locked away until its rightful owner can be determined.

Nov 27—Yankees third baseman Scott Brosius, who played on three championship teams in New York, announces his retirement.

Dec 2—The Atlanta Braves re-sign John Smoltz, who saved 10 games in 11 chances as a reliever in 2001, to a three-year contract to be their closer.

Dec 6—After his Nov. 6 announcement of baseball's plan to eliminate two teams provokes a court injunction, a grievance by the players' union and legislation in both the House and the Senate, Commissioner Bud Selig appears before Congress to plead his case for contraction in baseball. He gets a decidedly cool reception from lawmakers.

Big Mac retired with 583 career home runs, fifth place on the alltime list.

Dec 11—The Cleveland Indians and the New York Mets complete a blockbuster trade that sends second baseman Roberto Alomar—who batted .336 with 100 RBIs in 2001—to the Mets in exchange for outfielders Matt Lawton and Alex Escobar, reliever Jerrod Riggan and two players to be named later.

Dec 13—The Yankees sign free-agent first baseman Jason Giambi to a seven-year, $120 million contract. Giambi played for Oakland in 2001. New York also agrees to a two-year, $10 million deal with leftfielder Rondell White, formerly of the Chicago Cubs.

Dec 18—Free agents Tino Martinez and Chuck Knoblauch depart the Yankees, with whom they won three straight titles, signing with the Cardinals and the Kansas City Royals, respectively.

Dec 20—Only six weeks after Commissioner Bud Selig announced that baseball franchises are in such dire financial straits that two of them will have to be cut before the 2002 season, the Boston Red Sox are sold for $700 million to a group led by Florida Marlins owner John Henry and television producer Tom Werner. The price doubles the record amount for sale of a baseball franchise.

The Yankees picked up Giambi in December but he couldn't prevent their October demise.

CHUCK SOLOMON

Dec 27—The Mets and the Anaheim Angels complete a trade that sends pitcher Kevin Appier to Anaheim in exchange for first baseman Mo Vaughn.

Jan 4, 2002—Defying plans to eliminate them from the game, the Minnesota Twins announce that they've hired former Mets infielder Ron Gardenhire as manager.

Jan 7—Spurning offers from the Mets and the Baltimore Orioles, free-agent slugger Juan Gonzalez returns to the Texas Rangers—who had traded him to Detroit in 1999—signing a two-year, $24 million deal.

Jan 7—Former All-Star shortstop Ozzie Smith is elected to the baseball Hall of Fame on the first ballot.

Jan 9—Citing "irreparable conflicts of interest" arising from a loan that Commissioner Bud Selig obtained from an institution owned by Twins owner Carl Pohlad, Michigan Rep. John Conyers Jr., the House Judiciary Committee's ranking Democrat, calls for Selig's resignation.

Jan 14—Future Hall of Fame slugger Barry Bonds re-signs with the Giants for five years and $90 million.

Jan 15—The Dodgers trade disgruntled outfielder Gary Sheffield to the Braves in exchange for outfielder Brian Jordan, pitcher Odalis Perez and minor league pitcher Andy Brown.

Feb 5—One day after the Minnesota Court of Appeals upholds another court's order requiring the Twins—one of two MLB teams targeted for elimination—to play in the Metrodome in 2002, baseball Commissioner Bud Selig announces that the league's plans for contraction will be postponed until 2003.

Feb 12—In an unprecedented move to address its economic issues, Major League Baseball purchases the Montreal Expos, while former Expos owner Jeffrey Loria buys the struggling Florida Marlins.

Feb 20—The Philadelphia Phillies re-sign Bobby Abreu to the most lucrative contract in franchise history, securing the outfielder for five years and $64 million.

Feb 25—Diamondbacks third baseman Matt Williams breaks his left leg during a spring training drill and will miss the first three months of the season.

Feb 28—Twenty-four hours after taking control of the team, the Red Sox new ownership group dismisses general manager Dan Duquette.

March 11—The Red Sox hire former Cleveland bench coach Grady Little as manager, replacing Joe Kerrigan, who was fired on March 5.

March 26—Commissioner Bud Selig announces

that management will not lock out the players or impose new labor conditions through the 2002 World Series.

March 31—The 2002 Major League Baseball season gets under way as the Indians defeat the Angels 6–0 in Anaheim.

April 1—Ten teams kick off their 2002 seasons and two pitching aces, Roger Clemens and Pedro Martinez, get off to rough starts. Martinez gives up eight runs in three innings as the Red Sox fall to Toronto 12–11, and Clemens, the 2001 AL Cy Young Award winner, has the shortest opening-day outing of his career, giving up seven hits in 4 ⅓ innings as the Yankees lose to Baltimore 10–3. The 2001 NL Cy Young Award winner, Randy Johnson, picks up where he left off, pitching a six-hitter and leading the Diamondbacks to a 2–0 blanking of the San Diego Padres.

April 2—Giants outfielder Barry Bonds, who hit a record 73 home runs in 2001, starts his 2002 season with a bang, smashing two roundtrippers in San Francisco's 9–2 opening-day rout of the Dodgers. He hits two more the following day as the Giants trounce the Dodgers again, 12–0.

April 7—Diamondbacks ace Curt Schilling pitches a one-hitter and strikes out a career-high 17 batters as Arizona blanks Milwaukee 2–0.

April 8—After starting the season 0–6, the Tigers fire manager Phil Garner and general manager Randy Smith.

April 8—Houston second baseman Craig Biggio hits for the cycle during the Astros' 8–4 win over Colorado.

April 12—In a show of support for their team, which was threatened with elimination during the offseason, Minnesota fans fill the Metrodome for the Twins' home opener, a 4–2 victory over Detroit. It is the first opening-day sellout at the Metrodome since 1992.

April 27—Derek Lowe of Boston pitches the first no-hitter of the season, as the Red Sox blank the Devil Rays 10–0.

May 2—Seattle's Bret Boone and Mike Cameron make history as the first players to hit back-to-back home runs twice in one inning as they turn the trick in the 10-run first inning of the Mariners' 15–4 drubbing of the Chicago White Sox. Cameron also homers in the third and fifth innings to become just the fifth major leaguer to homer in four consecutive at bats and to complete the first four-homer game of his career.

May 9—The Yankees defeat Tampa Bay 3-1, sending the Devil Rays to their 14th consecutive defeat, which matches the longest losing streak in baseball since 1988.

May 22—With a home run in the sixth inning of the Giants's 12–5 victory over Arizona, Barry Bonds ties Mark McGwire for fifth place on the career home

run list. Both sluggers have 583 career homers.

May 23—Dodgers outfielder Shawn Green goes 6 for 6 with four homers, a double and a single during Los Angeles's 16–3 rout of the Brewers. Green's 19 total bases break the major league record set by Joe Adcock in 1954, and he becomes the 14th player since 1894 to hit four homers in a game.

June 2—Philadelphia pitcher Robert Person belts a grand slam and a three-run homer to help the Phillies shellack the Expos 18–3.

June 5—The Astros rename their home field Minute Maid Park after team owner Drayton McLane had bought out the 30-year, $100 million naming rights from the previous sponsor, the disgraced corporation Enron, in February.

June 6—The Metropolitan Sports Facilities Commission, which runs the Twins' home field, the Metrodome, drops its lawsuit against the team and Major League Baseball over the league's contraction plans. The move clears the way for the Twins to remain in existence through 2003.

June 15—In his first at bat at Shea Stadium since he beaned Mets catcher Mike Piazza on July 8, 2000, giving him a concussion, Yankees pitcher Roger Clemens faces New York's Shawn Estes. In an apparent attempt to hit Clemens, Estes throws a fastball behind the Yankees ace, missing him altogether. Both Piazza and Estes hit homers off Clemens as the Mets win 8–0.

June 18—Recent reports of widespread steroid use by baseball players prompts the U.S. senate to summon MLBPA head Don Fehr to Washington for a hearing. Following the hearing, Byron Dorgan, D-S.D., says, "I think the message to baseball was that it ought to do mandatory testing."

June 22—St. Louis righthander Darryl Kile is found dead in his Chicago hotel room the day before he is to start for the Cardinals against the Cubs. The Cook County medical examiner later determines that atherosclerosis, or hardening of the arteries, is the cause of death.

June 22—Florida second baseman Luis Castillo sees his hitting streak stopped at 35 games—the 10th longest run in baseball history—when he goes 0 for 4 in the Marlins' 5–4 win over Detroit.

July 9—While talk of a strike and rising concerns about steroid use among players weigh down the game, baseball suffers another setback as its All-Star game in Milwaukee ends in an anticlimactic 7–7 tie. Commissioner Bud Selig made the decision to halt the game in the 11th inning after both teams ran out of pitchers, prompting calls of "Let them play!" and "Refund!" from the sellout crowd of 41,871.

July 22—The Red Sox hold a two-hour tribute to Hall of Fame slugger Ted Williams at Fenway Park. Twenty-five thousand five hundred fans turn out to pay their respects to Williams—the last man to hit .400 for a season—who died on July 5.

July 29—The Phillies send third baseman Scott Rolen to the Cardinals in a five-player trade.

Aug 9—Barry Bonds becomes one of four major leaguers—the others are Hank Aaron, Babe Ruth and Willie Mays, Bonds's godfather—to have hit 600 career home runs, belting his 600th off Kip Wells in the sixth inning of the Giants 4–3 loss to the Pittsburgh Pirates.

Aug 11—With a grand slam and a run-scoring double during the Cubs' 12–9 win over Colorado, Sammy Sosa sets a National League record by driving in at least one run in 14 straight games.

Aug 16—After weeklong talks between management and player representatives hit another snag, the MLBPA announces that players will strike on Aug. 30 if the labor issues are not resolved by then.

Aug 25—Five days before the players' strike date, major league owners produce a counterproposal focusing on key economic issues, the most prominent of which is revenue sharing.

Aug 30—Slightly less than four hours before players are to go on strike, negotiators for baseball's owners and players reach a new collective bargaining agreement, good through 2006. The agreement averts what would have been baseball's ninth work stoppage since 1971.

Sept 3—Mets fans may be disappointed that the season will continue, as their team falls to Florida 3–2 for its 15th consecutive defeat at home, a National League record.

Sept 4—The Oakland A's set an American League record when they defeat the Royals 12–11 for their 20th straight victory.

Sept 9—With the Phillies' 6–4 loss to the Mets in Philadelphia, the Atlanta Braves clinch their 11th consecutive division title.

Sept 15—Threatened by the league's plans for contraction before the season began, the Minnesota Twins clinch the AL Central title with a 5–0 win over the Cleveland Indians.

Sept 24—The defending champion Diamondbacks learn they will be without star leftfielder Luis Gonzalez for the rest of the season. Gonzalez requires surgery on a separated left shoulder suffered on Sept. 23.

Sept 26—The Angels end a four-game skid and clinch a playoff spot for the first time since 1986 with a 10–5 rout of Texas. The win also eliminates Seattle from playoff contention. The following day Oakland defeats Seattle 5–2 to clinch the AL West title and leave the wild-card to Anaheim.

Sept 28—The Giants defeat Houston 5–2 at home to clinch the NL wild-card berth, eliminating the Dodgers, who began the day 2 ½ games back. Arizona clinches the AL West title with a 17–8 win over Colorado in Phoenix.

Oct 1—Bobby Valentine (Mets) and Jerry Narron (Rangers) join Hal McRae (Royals) and Luis Pujols (Tigers) in the ranks of dismissed managers. McRae and Pujols led their teams to 55–106 records, tied for the worst in the majors. Valentine failed to get New York in the playoffs despite an offseason spending binge that brought Roberto Alomar and Mo Vaughn to the team; and Narron went 72–90 in his first full season in Texas.

Oct 5—The previous year's World Series contestants are eliminated from the playoffs as the Angels knock out the Yankees with a 9–5 win in Game 4 of their division series, and the Cardinals sweep the defending champion Diamondbacks, taking Game 3 of their division series 6–3.

Oct 6—Minnesota extends its improbably successful season, defeating the A's 5–4 in Oakland in Game 5 of their division series to advance to the ALCS against Anaheim.

Oct 7—Barry Bonds erases the only blemish on his career—his poor performances in the playoffs—with a homer (his third of the series) and two runs scored to help San Francisco defeat Atlanta 3–1 in Game 5 and clinch the NL division series. The Giants will face the St. Louis in the NLCS.

Oct 9—The Detroit Tigers hire their former star shortstop Alan Trammell as manager.

Oct 13—After dropping the first game of the series 2–1, the Angels reel off four victories over Minnesota, including a 13–5 rout in Game 5, to win the ACLS and advance to the World Series for the first time in their 42-year history.

Oct 14—San Francisco steals Games 1 and 2 in St. Louis then returns home to Pac Bell Park and clinches the NLCS with a 2–1 win over the Cards in Game 5. Kenny Lofton drives in the winning run with a two-out single in the bottom of the ninth.

Oct 20—The Giants and the Angels split the first two games of the World Series in Anaheim as San Francisco takes the opener 4–3 on home runs by Barry Bonds and J.T. Snow, and Anaheim wins the wild second game 11–10 on Tim Salmon's two-run shot—his second of the game—in the eighth.

Oct 23—David Bell hits a run-scoring single in the eighth off the Angels' 20-year-old reliever Francisco Rodriguez—who pitched in eight of Anaheim's previous 12 playoff games and Anaheim won all eight—to give the Giants a 4–3 victory in Game 4 and even the series at 2–2. The Angels were 10–4 winners in Game 3.

Oct 27—After rallying from a 5–0 deficit in the seventh-inning of Game 6 to win 6–5, the Angels touch San Francisco starter Livan Hernandez for three runs in the third inning of Game 7 and hold on for a 4–1 victory and their first World Series title.

BRENT SMITH/REUTERS

Forrest (left) proved his mettle with victories over Mosley in January and July.

Nov 2, 2001—Kostya Tszyu wins the undisputed junior welterweight title with a TKO of Zab Judah in the second round of their fight in Las Vegas.

Nov 8—Oscar De La Hoya, the WBC super welterweight champion, undergoes surgery to remove bone spurs from his left hand and to repair cartilage in his left wrist. He will be sidelined for three months.

Nov 10—Junior lightweight champion Floyd Mayweather Jr. defends his title for the eighth and final time, stopping Jesus Chavez after the ninth round in San Francisco. At 24, Mayweather has difficulty making the 130-pound weight, and will move up to challenge Jose Luis Castillo for the lightweight belt.

Nov 17—Lennox Lewis avenges his April 2001 loss to Hasim Rahman, decking the IBF and WBC champ in the fourth round of their title fight in Las Vegas.

Dec 15—John Ruiz retains his WBA heavyweight title after a lackluster draw with Evander Holyfield in Mashantucket, Conn.

Jan 22, 2002—At a press conference in New York to announce a heavyweight title bout, scheduled for April 6 in Las Vegas, between Mike Tyson and champion Lennox Lewis, Tyson triggers a melee when he strides swiftly across the stage toward Lewis and is confronted by one of the champ's bodyguards. Lewis later claims that Tyson bit him in the ensuing pileup, after which Tyson spews a threatening, profanity laced diatribe at a reporter in the audience.

Jan 26—Vernon Forrest upsets Shane Mosley in the theater at Madison Square Garden to win the welterweight title by a unanimous decision.

Jan 29—By a 4–1 vote, the Nevada Athletic Commission denies Mike Tyson a license to box in the state of Nevada, putting his prospective title fight with Lennox Lewis, which had been set for April 6, in doubt.

Feb 2—Bernard Hopkins retains the undisputed middleweight title when Carl Daniels refuses to come out for the 11th round of their bout in Reading, Pa. The victory is Hopkins's 15th consecutive title defense, a middleweight record. In Miami Roy Jones Jr. defends his light heavyweight title with a seventh-round knockout of Glen Kelly.

Feb 21—Citing the inability of their evidence to withstand the rigors of a courtroom, Las Vegas prosecutors announce that they will not charge heavyweight Mike Tyson after two women lodged sexual assault complaints against him in September and December.

Feb 23—Paulie Ayala wins a unanimous decison over Clarence (Bones) Adams in their junior featherweight bout in Las Vegas.

Boxing (Cont.)

March 5—Mike Tyson is licensed to box in the state of Tennessee, clearing the way for a fight with Lennox Lewis at The Pyramid in Memphis on June 8. Twenty days later the fighters sign a contract finalizing the matchup.

April 20—In his debut as a lightweight, former junior lightweight champ Floyd Mayweather Jr. wins a controversial decision over Jose Luis Castillo in Las Vegas.

April 27—Despite being outpunched 1,466 to 772, Johnny Tapia wins a questionable decision over Manuel Medina at the theater in Madison Square Garden. The victory gives Tapia his fifth title in three weight classes.

May 11—Felix Trinidad dispatches former middleweight titlist Hacine Cherifi with a fourth-round TKO in San Juan, Puerto Rico.

June 1—After an accidental head butt produces a grotesque, softball-sized knot on Hasim Rahman's head, his heavyweight bout with Evander Holyfield in Atlantic City is stopped in the eighth round. Holyfield is awarded a technical split decision.

June 8—Dominating almost from the opening bell, Lennox Lewis knocks out Mike Tyson in the eighth round of their heavyweight title fight in Memphis.

June 22—In a rematch of their February 2000 bout, which was named fight of the year, top featherweights Marco Antonio Barrera and Erik Morales mix it up in Las Vegas. Like their first meeting, the fight ends with a disputed decision, this time in favor of Barrera.

July 2—Former welterweight and middleweight champion Felix Trinidad announces his retirement.

July 21—Vernon Forrest runs his record to 35–0 and retains his welterweight title with a unanimous decision over Shane Mosley in Indianapolis.

July 27—John Ruiz retains his share of the heavyweight title after challenger Kirk Johnson is disqualified for a low blow in the 10th round of their bout in Las Vegas.

Aug 17—Heavyweight contender David Tua floors former champ Michael Moorer in 30 seconds in Atlantic City.

Sept 14—In an impressive return to form, Oscar De La Hoya drops Fernando Vargas in the 11th round of their bout in Las Vegas to win the WBC and WBA junior middleweight titles.

Oct 1—The IBF strips Johnny Tapia of his featherweight belt after he schedules a bout with Marco Antonio Barrera instead of agreeing to a rematch with Manuel Medina.

College Basketball

Nov 5, 2001—Texas Christian coach Billy Tubbs announces that this season, his 28th, will be his last.

Nov 6—Duke guard Jason Williams is unanimously named to the AP preseason All-America team, the first such selection since Wake Forest center Tim Duncan in 1996.

Nov 9—Defeating a Top 10 team for the second game in a row, Arizona knocks off No. 6 Florida 75–71 to win the season-opening Coaches vs. Cancer Classic at Madison Square Garden. The Wildcats beat second-ranked Maryland 71–67 the previous night to reach the final.

Nov 18—Rick Pitino, who led Kentucky to a national title in 1996, makes a successful debut as head coach of the Wildcats' fierce in-state rival, Louisville, leading the Cardinals to a 92–38 rout of South Alabama.

Nov 20—North Carolina falls to Davidson 58–54 to go 0–2 at home for the first time in school history.

Nov 21—Duke defeats Ball State 83–71 to win the season-opening Maui Invitational.

Nov 27—The top two teams in women's basketball, Connecticut and Tennessee, run their records to 6–0 and 4–0, respectively, as No. 1 Connecticut crushes Wake Forest 88–38 in Winston Salem, N.C., and second-ranked Tennessee hands No. 22 George Washington its worst home defeat in 23 years, routing the Colonials 88–57.

Dec 18—A jury awards former Smith College coach James Babyak $1.65 million in damages as a result of his sex and age discrimination complaint against the Northampton, Mass., school, which fired him in 1997.

Dec 21—The Michigan women's team trounces in-state rival Oakland 71–42 to run its record to 10–1 and move to No. 12 in the national rankings. The Wolverines began the season with a loss to Louisana Tech and have reeled off 10 straight victories, a school record.

Dec 29—With first year coach Todd Lickliter at the helm, Butler defeats Indiana 66–64 to win the Hoosier Classic and run its record to 13–0. The Bulldogs are ranked 20th in the nation.

Jan 2, 2002—Miami opens its Big East schedule with a 79–71 victory over Georgetown to run its record to 14–0. The Hurricanes are one of four Division I schools still unbeaten; the others are Duke, Virginia and Oklahoma State.

Jan 5—Connecticut firmly establishes itself as

the top women's team in the country, routing second-ranked Tennessee 86–72 in Knoxville.

Jan 6—Defending national champion Duke, the nation's last remaining unbeaten Division I team, tumbles to its first loss of the season, a 77–76 defeat by unranked Florida State in Tallahassee.

Jan 15—Twelfth-ranked Kentucky rebounds from back-to-back losses with its second straight victory, downing Mississippi 87–64 in Lexington.

Jan 28—Former Indiana coach Bob Knight makes his first appearance in the Top 25 with his new team, Texas Tech, as the Red Raiders knocked off No. 6 Oklahoma two days earlier to move in to the 23rd spot in the national poll. Duke holds on to the No. 1 ranking after its 92–79 blowout of fifth-ranked Virginia.

Jan 31—Rallying from an 83–74 deficit with 3:22 to play, third-ranked Maryland edges No. 5 Virginia 91–87 in Charlottesville, Va.

Feb 15—Without its best player, Linda Frohlich of Germany, who sat out due to eligibility concerns arising from her play with German club teams, the UNLV women's team (20–4) defeats Colorado State 71–59 to secure its first 20-win season since 1994.

Sue Bird ran the show for the Huskies, who went 39–0 and won the national title.

ROBERT BECK

Feb 17—Maryland avenges its bitter defeat at Duke a month earlier, dispatching the Blue Devils 87–73 in College Park, Md., to take over first place in the Atlantic Coast Conference and knock Duke out of the top spot in the national rankings.

Feb 24—Kansas and Maryland hold on to the No. 1 and No. 2 spots, respectively, in the national rankings—but just barely. The Jayhawks (25–2) trail for most of the second half before rallying to nip Nebraska 88–87, and Mayland edges Wake Forest 90–89 on guard Juan Dixon's technical foul shot with 1.3 seconds remaining.

Feb 26—East Carolina (12–16) pulls off one of the biggest upsets of the season, stunning ninth-ranked Marquette 51–46 in Greenville, N.C.

March 1—Following a series of controversial remarks, including an invitation to the school to buy out the remaining years of his contract, Nolan Richardson is dismissed as coach of Arkansas.

March 5—In the most one-sided championship game in Big East tournament history, the Connecticut women's team crushes their counterparts from Boston College, 96–54.

March 10—Cincinnati, Duke, Kansas and Maryland are the No. 1 seeds as the NCAA tournament pairings are announced. But Kansas, which lost to Oklahoma in the Big 12 tournament final, relinquishes the top spot in the national rankings to Duke, which won the ACC tournament.

March 14—The opening day of the NCAA tournament almost always produces notable upsets, and this year is no exception as sixth-seeded Gonzaga, usually on the other end of these exchanges, is eliminated 73–66 by No. 11 seed Wyoming, No. 5 seeds Marquette and Miami, fall to twelfth-seeded Tulsa and Missouri, respectively, and 10th-seeded Kent State upends No. 7 Oklahoma State.

March 17—In the women's tournament, seventh-seeded Drake upsets No. 2 seed Baylor 76–72 to advance to the Sweet 16 and prevent the Big 12 conference from having seven of its teams advancing in the tournament.

March 21—Top-ranked Duke's quest to repeat as national champion comes to a stunning end as fifth-seeded Indiana rallies from a 17-point deficit to defeat the Blue Devils 74–73 in the South regional semifinal in Lexington, Ky.

March 24—The pairings for the men's Final Four are set as Maryland defeats Connecticut 90–82 to advance for the second year in a row to the semis, where it will face Kansas, which routed Oregon 104–86. The other semifinalists are rugged No. 2 seed Oklahoma, which downed Missouri 81–75, and surprise entrant Indiana, a fifth seed that beat Kent State 81–69 to reach the Final Four in Mike Davis's second season as coach.

College Basketball *(Cont.)*

March 25—Tennessee downs Vanderbilt 68–63 to advance to the women's Final Four, where it will face Connecticut, 85–64 winners over Old Dominion. In the other semifinal, Duke, which knocked off South Carolina 77–68 in the East Regional final, will face Oklahoma, 94–60 winners over Colorado.

March 31—The Connecticut Huskies complete a 39–0 season with a 82–70 victory over Oklahoma in the national championship game in San Antonio. Connecticut becomes just the fourth team to finish a season unbeaten since women's basketball became an NCAA sport in 1982.

April 1—Maryland wins the first basketball national title in school history, grinding out a 64–52 victory over Indiana in the NCAA final in Atlanta. Terrapins guard Juan Dixon, who scores 18 points in the final, and averages 25.5 in the semis, is named MVP of the Final Four.

April 7—Jason Williams of Duke, who will graduate the following month after three years

at the school, wins the John R. Wooden Award as the nation's top player.

May 2—Fewer than 24 hours after accepting the job, Tom Collen resigns as coach of the Vanderbilt women's team, citing "a mistake that was never caught" on his résumé that claims, incorrectly, that he holds two master's degrees.

Aug 23—Leon Barmore retires as coach of the Louisiana Tech women's team after 28 seasons at the school as a player, assistant and head coach. His .860 winning percentage is tops among Division I women's coaches.

Sept 23—*The Baltimore Sun* reports that D.J. Strawberry, son of former major league All-Star Darryl Strawberry, will sign a letter of intent in November to play basketball at Maryland.

Sept 29—Cincinnati coach Bob Huggins, 49, is in serious but stable condition at Medical Center in Beaver, Pa., one day after suffering a heart attack at Pittsburgh International Airport.

College Football

Paterno's charges carried him past Bryant in October 2001.

Oct 27, 2001—Penn State's Joe Paterno becomes the Division I college coach with the most career wins, surpassing Alabama legend Bear Bryant with his 324th career victory, a 29–27 come-from-behind triumph over Ohio State.

Oct 29—Miami and Nebraska top all three national polls after the Cornhuskers (9–0) defeat Oklahoma 20–10, ending the Sooners 20-game winning streak, and the Hurricanes (6–0) trounce West Virginia 45–3.

Nov 3—Arkansas outscores Mississippi 58–56 after seven overtimes to win the longest game in Division I history. The game ends when the Razorbacks' Jermaine Petty stops Mississippi's Doug Ziegler on a two-point conversion attempt that, had it been successful, would have sent the game into an eighth overtime.

Nov 10—Nebraska and Miami remain unbeaten and at the top of the rankings, but switch places in the coaches' poll as the Cornhuskers' 31–21 victory over Kansas State vaults them over the Hurricanes, who got by Boston College 18–7.

Nov 17—Maryland completes a remarkable turnaround from its 5–6 performance the previous year, topping North Carolina State 23–19 to finish the season at 10–1 and win its first ACC title in 16 years.

Nov 20—After steamrollering Syracuse 59–0, Miami strengthens its grip on second place in the Bowl Championship Series (BCS) standings, distancing itself from third-place Oklahoma. Unbeaten Nebraska continues to hold onto first. The top two teams in the final BCS poll on Dec. 9 will meet in the Rose Bowl for the national championship.

Nov 23—Colorado rambles to a 62–36 home

victory over second-ranked Nebraska, scrambling the national title picture and handing the Cornhuskers their first loss of the season.

Nov 24—With a 65–7 obliteration of 12th-ranked Washington in Miami, the undefeated Miami Hurricanes inch closer to a bid in the national title game in Pasadena. In the BCS rankings released two days later, the Hurricanes, as expected, are ranked No. 1 followed by Florida (9–1), and Texas (10–1).

Dec 2—Notre Dame fires coach Bob Davie after his team finishes the season at 5–6.

Dec 3—The BCS national title picture gets cloudier instead of clearer as the season nears its end. The No. 2 and No. 3 teams in the rankings fall from contention as Tennessee stuns Florida 34–32 in Gainesville, and Colorado nips Texas 39–37 in the Big 12 championship game. The Vols, now second in the BCS, squander their good position with a loss the following week against LSU in the SEC title game. Oregon moves to No. 3 in the rankings after a come-from-behind 17–14 win over archrival Oregon State.

Dec 8—Nebraska's Eric Crouch, who became the 13th quarterback in NCAA history to top 1,000 yards in both rushing and passing in a season, wins the Heisman Trophy by 62 points over Florida's Rex Grossman.

Dec 8—With 29 seconds remaining in the Division II national title game, North Dakota halfback Jed Perkerewiez plunges into the end zone from one yard out to give his team a 17–14 victory over Grand Valley State (Mich.).

Dec 9—The final BCS standings are set, but not without controversy. The system produces a Rose Bowl matchup for the national title between Miami (11–0)—a choice no one disputes—and Nebraska (11–1), a team that at least two other schools believe is undeserving. Those two are Colorado (10–2), which trounced Nebraska on Nov. 23, and Oregon (10–1), which finished the regular season ranked second in the media and coaches' polls. Oregon and Colorado will meet in the Fiesta Bowl.

Dec 14—Fomer Georgia Tech coach George O'Leary resigns as coach of Notre Dame after five days on the job following revelations that he fabricated portions of his résumé. Among O'Leary's false claims is his assertion that he earned a master's degree from New York University.

Dec 15—Mount Union wins its sixth Division III national title in nine years, edging Bridgewater 30–27 in Salem, Va.

Dec 15—North Texas, which lost its first five games of the season, recovers to finish 5–6 and win the Sun Belt Conference with a 5–1 league record. The conference title gives the Mean Green a bid in the inaugural New Orleans Bowl against Colorado State (6–5), making North Texas

the first team with a losing record to play in a bowl game since 1970. The Mean Green falls to Colorado State 45–20 on Dec. 18.

Dec 19—Led by quarterback Byron Leftwich, who passes for 576 yards and four touchdowns, including the game winner in double overtime, Marshall rallies from a 30-point halftime deficit to defeat East Carolina 64–61 in the GMAC Bowl.

Dec 21—Montana defeats Furman 13–6 in Chattanooga, Tenn., to win the Division I-AA national title.

Dec 29—Syracuse romps 26–3 over Kansas State in the Insight.com Bowl in Phoenix. In San Antonio, Nat Kaeding kicks a 47-yard field goal with 44 seconds left to lift Iowa to a 19–16 victory over Texas Tech in the Alamo Bowl. A pair of in-state rivals square off in the Motor City Bowl as Toledo tops Cincinnati 23–16 in Pontiac, Mich.

Jan 1, 2002—Notre Dame introduces Tyrone Willingham, formerly of Stanford, as its new coach. Willingham is the first African American head coach in the storied program's history.

Jan 1—Six bowl games kick off on New Year's Day as Oklahoma ties a school record with nine sacks in its 10–3 victory over Arkansas in the Cotton Bowl; South Carolina jumps out to a 28–0 lead against Ohio State and holds on for 31–28 win in the Outback Bowl; quarterback Casey Clausen throws for three touchdowns and runs for two to lead Tennessee to a 45–17 drubbing of Michigan in the Citrus Bowl; Florida State defeats Virginia Tech 30–17 in the Gator Bowl to give Seminoles coach Bobby Bowden his 323rd career victory, tying him with Bear Bryant for second on the Division I-A wins list; Oregon quarterback Joey Harrington produces a career day in the Fiesta Bowl, passing for 500 yards and five touchdowns to lead the Ducks over Colorado, 38–16; and Louisiana State outguns Illinois 47–34 in the Sugar Bowl.

Jan 2—In the Orange Bowl, Florida trounces Maryland 56–23 to run its record to 10–2. The Gators will finish the year ranked third in the polls.

Jan 3—Led by quarterback Ken Dorsey, who throws for a career high 362 yards and three touchdowns, Miami explodes for 27 points in the second quarter to take a 34–0 halftime lead against Nebraska in the Rose Bowl. The Hurricanes coast to a 37–14 victory and an undisputed national title.

Jan 9—Two high-profile programs introduce new coaches as Florida names former New Orleans Saints defensive coordinator Ron Zook to succeed Steve Spurrier, who left after the season to become head coach of the NFL's Washington Redskins, and Stanford hires Buddy Teevens, who was a member of Spurrier's staff at Florida, to replace the departed Tyrone Willingham.

Jan 31—The NCAA levies stiff penalties against Kentucky for a variety of violations. The sanctions include a ban on bowl games next season. The following day Alabama suffers an even harsher fate as the NCAA strips the Crimson Tide of more than 25% of its scholarships and bans it from bowl games for two years.

May 7—Fomer Pittsburgh star Dan Marino and Southern California standouts Ronnie Lott and Kellen Winslow lead a class of 13 elected to the College Football Hall of Fame.

June 24—The BCS tweaks its formula once again, eliminating margin of victory as a criterion for its rankings.

Aug 23—The 2002–03 college football season kicks off as No. 23 Wisconsin edges Fresno State 23–21 in the John Thompson Foundation Classic in Madison, Wisc. The following day, fourth-ranked Florida State struggles but gets by Iowa Sate 38–31 in the Eddie Robinson Classic in Kansas City, Mo.

The victory vaults Seminoles coach Bobby Bowden past Bear Bryant and into second place on the career coaching victories list with 324.

Sept 21—New coach Tyrone Willingham leads Notre Dame to a 4–0 start as the Irish top Michigan State 21–17 in East Lansing, Mich. Unranked at the start of the season, Notre Dame climbs to No. 10. In Knoxville, Florida rebounds from its 41–16 drubbing by No. 1 Miami (4–0) on Sept. 7 to defeat Tennessee 30–13 and move to No. 9 in the coaches' poll.

Oct 12—Top ranked Miami (6–0) gets a scare at home against 12th-ranked Florida State (5–2) as the Hurricanes must rally from a 13-point, fourth-quarter deficit and then watch as Seminoles kicker Xavier Beitia's 43-yard field goal attempt sails wide left as time expires before they can claim a 28–27 victory. In Dallas, third-ranked Oklahoma wins a battle of unbeatens, defeating No. 2 Texas 35–24.

Golf

Nov 4, 2001—In Houston, Mike Weir of Canada holes a five-foot birdie putt to win the Tour Championship on the first hole of a four-man playoff. Weir is the first non-American to win the Tour Championship.

Nov 18—At the LPGA's season-ending event, the Tyco/ADT Championship in West Palm Beach, Fla., Karrie Webb holds off Annika Sorenstam to win by two strokes, but Sorenstam's final-round 65 earns her the Vare Trophy for the season's lowest average (69.42), and her second-place finish pushes her over the $2 million mark in earnings for the season, an LPGA first.

Dec 3—Seventeen-year-old Ty Tryon shoots a 6-under-par 66 at Bear Lakes Golf Club to finish 23rd in the tournament and become the youngest player to earn a PGA Tour card, which went to the low 35 scorers in the event.

Dec 16—Tiger Woods wins the Williams World Challenge at Thousand Oaks, Calif.—an event he hosts—by three strokes, birdieing five straight holes on the back nine on Sunday.

Dec 23—Miami teenager James Vargas, 17, becomes the first golfer to win three consecutive Doral Publix Junior Golf Classics, when he shoots even par in the final round to take the event at Miami's Doral Resort and Spa.

Dec 27—After a season in which he tops the PGA Tour's non-member money list with $1,520,632 in earnings, Charles Howell III is named PGA rookie of the year.

Jan 6, 2002—Sergio Garcia makes a birdie on the first playoff hole to defeat David Toms and win the Mercedes Championships in Kapalua, Hawaii.

Jan 13—After playing in 200 PGA tournaments, Jerry Kelly gets his first Tour victory, birdieing the final hole to win Sony Open in Honolulu.

Jan 20—Phil Mickelson returns to the PGA Tour after a five-month layoff and wins the Bob Hope Chrysler Classic in Palm Springs, Calif.

Jan 21—Brad Faxon is the wire-to-wire winner at the Sony Open in Honolulu, taking the lead on the first day and shooting a 5-under-par 65 in the final round to win by four strokes over runner-up Tom Lehman.

Jan 24—At the Phoenix Open, Ty Tryon makes his professional debut, shooting a 6-over-par 77 in the first round. Three days later, Chris DiMarco finishes 69–267 to win the tournament by one stroke over Kenny Perry and Kaname Yokoo.

Feb 3—Matt Gogel takes advantage of a back nine collapse by Pat Perez, who hits three balls out of play on the final five holes, to pick up his first tour victory at the Pebble Beach (Calif.) Golf Links, shooting a 3-under-par 69 in the final round.

Feb 17—Len Mattiace gets his first PGA tour victory after 219 starts, winning the Nissan Open in Pacific Palisades, Calif., with a 3-under-par 68 in the final round.

Feb 24—With a 1-up victory over Scott McCarron in the 36-hole final, Kevin Sutherland wins the Match Play Championships in Carlsbad, Calif.

March 3—Ernie Els holds off a charging Tiger Woods to win the Genuity Chamionship in Miami by two strokes.

March 10—Birdieing five of the last nine holes, 1997 U.S. Amateur champion Matt Kuchar takes the Honda Classic in Coral Springs, Fla., for his first PGA Tour victory.

March 17—Tiger Woods wins the Bay Hill Invitational for the third consecutive year, shooting a final round 3-under-par 69 to win by four strokes over New Zealand's Michael Campbell.

March 31—Firing a 4-under-par 68 on Sunday, Annika Sorenstam defeats Liselotte Neumann by a stroke to win the LPGA's first major of the year, the Kraft Nabisco Championship in Rancho Mirage, Calif.

April 14—Tiger Woods wins the Masters for the second year in a row and third time in six years, shooting a 1-under-par 71 on Sunday to defeat Retief Goosen by three strokes.

April 21—After setting the tournament's 54-hole scoring record, Justin Leonard shoots a 2-over-par 73 in the final round of the WorldCom Classic on Hilton Head Island, S.C., but still holds on to win the event by a stroke over Heath Slocum.

May 5—Twenty-two-year-old K.J. Choi becomes the first golfer from South Korea to win a PGA Tour event as he takes the Compaq Classic in New Orleans.

May 16—Michelle Wie, a 12-year-old from Honolulu, makes her LPGA debut, shooting a 9-over-par 81 at the Asahi Ryokuken in North Augusta, Ga.

June 2—One season after she shot the first 59 in LPGA history, Annika Sorenstam ties the LPGA's 54-hole record, shooting 195 en route to winning the Kellogg-Keebler Classic in Aurora, Ill., by 11 strokes.

June 9—Se Ri Pak becomes the youngest woman to win four majors in her career, taking the LPGA Championships in Wilmington, Del.,

when she shoots a final-round, 1-under-par 70.

June 16—Tiger Woods leads from wire to wire to win his second major of the year, the U.S. Open, by three strokes over Phil Mickelson.

July 7—In Hutchinson, Kan., Juli Inkster wins the U.S. Women's Open by two strokes over Annika Sorenstam. Inkster, 42, came within months of being the oldest winner of the Women's Open, a distinction belonging to Babe Didrikson.

July 21—In the first sudden-death finish in the 142-year history of the tournament, Ernie Els defeats Thomas Levet to win the British Open in Muirfield, Scotland.

Aug 11—Karrie Webb rallies from three strokes down with a 6-under-par 66 to win the Women's British Open in Turnberry, Scotland, beating Michelle Ellis and Paula Marti by two strokes.

Aug 18—Rich Beem withstands a final-round charge by Tiger Woods to win the PGA Championship in Chaska, Minn. Woods trails Beem by two strokes at the start of the last round, but can only cut the margin to one as Beem shoots a 68.

Sept 8—Annika Sorenstam birdies four of the final six holes to win the Williams Championship in Tulsa for her seventh LPGA victory of the season.

Sept 23—Routing the team from Europe 8½–3½ in singles play the U.S. women win the Solheim Cup 15½–12½ in Edina, Minn.

Sept 29—Europe goes 5-2-5 in singles play on Sunday, picking up 7½ points to defeat the United States 15½–12½ in the Ryder Cup at Sutton Coldfield, England.

Oct 6—Breaking the LPGA record she set in 2001, Annika Sorenstam wins her ninth Tour event of the year, the Samsung World Championship in Vallejo, Calif.

Nov 6, 2001—Chirs Osgood makes 29 saves for his third shutout of the year and Michael Peca scores a shorthanded goal as the New York Islanders defeat the Tampa Bay Lightning 3–0 to run their record to 11-1-1. In the 2000–01 season, It took the Islanders until Dec. 29 to get their 11th win.

Nov 12—Leading a class of seven into the Hockey Hall of Fame in Toronto are former Edmonton Oiler winger Jari Kurri, the highest scoring European-born NHLer of all time (1,398 points), former rugged right wing Mike Gartner, who is fourth on the alltime goals list 708, and former Winnipeg Jets forward Dale Hawerchuk, who has 518 career goals.

Nov 20—The NHL suspends Florida Panthers center Jason Wiemer for seven games for hitting Toronto Maple Leafs center Darcy Tucker with the

butt end of his stick during a game on Nov. 19, giving Tucker a Grade 3 concussion that sidelines him for a week.

Dec 3—The Panthers introduce Mike Keenan as their new head coach, replacing Duane Sutter, who was 6-15-2 in 2001. The Florida job is Keenan's seventh NHL head coaching position.

Jan 2, 2002—Carolina center Ron Francis becomes the fifth player in league history with at least 500 goals and 1,000 assists when he scores in the first period of the Hurricanes' 6–3 loss to the Boston Bruins in Raleigh, N.C.

Jan 10—On the verge of returning to the NHL following a medical leave to recover from emergency spleen surgery last season and injuries to his feet, Colorado Avalanche center Peter Forsberg learns that he has further problems in his feet and undergoes surgery. He will be out for four months.

Jan 28—Three days after the Dallas Stars dismiss coach Ken Hitchcock, the New Jersey Devils fire coach Larry Robinson, who led the team to the Stanley Cup title in 2000 and to the Stanley Cup finals in 2001.

Feb 2—The World team tops the North America team 8–5 in the NHL All-Star game in Los Angeles. Chicago Blackhawks forward Eric Daze, who has two goals and an assist for the North America team, is named MVP of the game. World team goalie Nikolai Khabibulin makes 20 saves and doesn't give up a goal in 20 minutes of work.

Feb 7—Montreal Canadiens center Saku Koivu announces that the cancer that has kept him out of action this season is in remission. Koivu plans to resume workouts, and hopes to rejoin the Canadiens in April.

Feb 26—The NHL resumes play after a 12-day break to allow its stars to compete in the Olympics.

Feb 28—Mario Lemieux announces he will sit out the remainder of the season to rehabilitate his chronically painful hip injury, a combination of tendonitis and swelling of the hip capsule.

March 10—Eighteen-year-old Iya Kovalchuk, a star left wing for the Atlanta Thrashers and a leading candidate for rookie of the year, suffers a season-ending dislocated shoulder during Atlanta's 6–1 loss to the Islanders.

March 18—The Rangers acquire All-Star winger Pavel Bure from Florida in return for defensemen Igor Ulanov and Filip Novak, and three draft picks.

March 18—Thirteen-year-old Brittanie Cecil of West Alexandria, Ohio, dies as a result of injuries sustained when she was hit by a puck while watching the Columbus Blue Jackets–Calgary Flames game on March 16.

April 9—Saku Koivu returns to the ice after being diagnosed with non-Hodgkin's lymphoma in September, 2001.

April 14—The regular season ends and Calgary's Jarome Iginla becomes the first black player to win the scoring title as he finishes with 52 goals

Hasek got the only thing missing from his career—a Stanley Cup—then retired.

and 44 assists for 96 points, six more than Vancouver's Markus Naslund. Iginla is also the first player other than Wayne Gretzky, Mario Lemieux, Jaromir Jagr to win the scoring title since Marcel Dionne in 1980.

April 27—Carolina eliminates the defending Eastern Conference champion Devils with a 1–0 victory in Game 6 of their first-round series.

April 28—The NHL suspends Bruins defenseman Kyle McLaren for the remainder of Boston's first-round series with Montreal after he clotheslines Canadiens forward Richard Zednik during the Bruins' 5–2 victory in Game 4, leaving Zednik with a concussion, a broken nose, a bruised throat and a cut under his eyelid.

May 28—Underdogs in every round of the playoffs, the Carolina Hurricanes, who struggled for two decades as the Hartford Whalers before relocating in 1997, make their first trip to the Stanley Cup finals, defeating the Maple Leafs 2–1 in overtime of Game 6 of the Eastern Conference finals.

May 31—A classic Western Conference final series comes to an anticlimactic end in Game 7 as Detroit trounces the Avalanche 7–0 to advance to the Stanley Cup finals. The series featured three overtime games and no games, apart from the last one, decided by more than two goals.

June 3—Continuing to thrive in the role of underdog, the Hurricanes stun the Red Wings with a 3–2 overtime victory in Game 1 of the Stanley Cup finals in Detroit.

DAVID E. KLUTHO

June 6—The Rangers introduce Bryan Trottier, who starred for their archrivals the Islanders in the 1980s, as their new head coach.

June 13—Ending Carolina's darkhorse run through the playoffs, the Red Wings reel off four straight victories, including a 3–1 triumph in Game 5, to win the Stanley Cup, their third title in six years. After the game, Detroit coach Scotty Bowman, who has now won nine Stanley Cups, announces his retirement. The Cup is the first for Wings goalie Dominik Hasek, who follows Bowman into retirement on June 25.

June 13—The Devils name three-time NHL coach of the year Pat Burns as their head coach, replacing Kevin Constantine.

June 19—Former Washington Capitals defenseman Rod Langway joins ex-St. Louis star Bernie Federko, four-time Stanley Cup winner Clark Gilles, and veteran coach Roger Nielsen in the Hockey Hall of Fame's class of 2002.

June 20—The NHL announces it will add protective netting behind the goals in all of its rinks for the 2002–03 season. At the NHL awards ceremony in Toronto, the Canadiens' goalie Jose Theodore wins both the Hart (MVP) and the Vezina (top goalie) trophies.

July 1—The free-agent signing period kicks off as the Rangers sign former New Jersey center Bobby Holik for five years and $45 million, and the Mighty Ducks of Anaheim sign 2001–02 assists leader Adam Oates, formerly of the Flyers, for two years and $7 million.

July 2—Two of the NHL's top free-agent goaltenders join new teams as Detroit lures Curtis Joseph, 35, from his hometown of Toronto with a three-year, $24 million deal, and Ed Belfour, 37, departs Dallas for an incentive-laden, two year, $13.5 million deal with the Maple Leafs. Two days later the Ranger re-sign goalie Mike Richter for two more years.

July 31—All-Star winger Paul Kariya accepts a one-year $10 million qualifying offer from his team, the Mighty Ducks of Anaheim

Aug 13—The Bruins sign defenseman Brian Berard, who returned to hockey with the Rangers in 2001–02 after suffering a career-threatening eye injury in March 2000.

Sept 10—Four-time All-Star defenseman Gary Suter, 38, announces his retirement.

Oct 1—Calgary and Colorado complete a five-player trade that sends Avalanche center Chris Drury and Stephane Yelle in return for Derek Morris, Dean McAmmond, and Jeff Shantz.

Oct 8—Oft-troubled winger Theo Fleury, signed in the offseason by Chicago, voluntarily enters NHL-PA's substance-abuse program.

Oct 9—The 2002–03 season kicks off as Mark Messier, 41, helps make new Rangers coach Bryan Trottier's debut a success, scoring two goals to lead New York to a 4–1 victory over Caolina. In Dallas, the Stars and Colorado skate to a 1–1 tie.

Oct 27, 2001—For the second year in a row, Tiznow wins the $4 million Breeders' Cup Classic. In other Breeders' Cup races at Belmont Park, Unbridled Elaine takes the $2.4 million Distaff, Fantastic Light wins the $2.1 million Turf, and Banks Hill wins the Filly & Mare Turf, worth $1.4 million.

Nov 19—In Los Angeles, a federal judge dismisses a case against trainer Bob Baffert over a positive urine test for morphine for his filly Nautical Look. The test, taken after Nautical Look won a race at Hollywood Park in May 2000, was thrown out after the judge determined that the lab threw away Nautical Look's blood sample, which could have exonerated Baffert.

Nov 25—Spook Express, the second place finisher in the 2001 Breeders' Cup Filly & Mare Turf, is euthanized after falling at the end of The Matriarch at Hollywood Park.

Dec 22—Jockey Arnold Ruiz, 33, of Arlington Heights, Ill. is killed at Beulah Park in Columbus, Ohio, after his horse, Winds of Sonora, falls and he is trampled by two other horses.

Jan 7, 2002—On the first day of the Keeneland January Horses of All Ages Sale in Lexington, Ky., 242 horses are sold for a total of $17.9 million, a 53.6% increase over the previous year's opening. Former Breeders' Cup Sprint champion Desert Stormer is the top sale going to Live Oak Stud for $3.6 million.

Jan 28—Monarchos, the 2001 Kentucky Derby winner, is retired to stud with an ankle injury.

Feb 18—After a season in which he won the Preakness and the Belmont, 3-year-old Point Given receives the Eclipse Award as 2001 Horse of the Year.

March 16—Harlan's Holiday romps to a 3½-length victory in the $1 million Florida Derby, establishing himself as a Kentucky Derby favorite.

April 6—Taking the lead at the top of the stretch, Came Home breaks away from the field to win the $750,000 Santa Anita Derby by 2¼ lengths.

May 4—Despite having never ridden or even worked the horse before, jockey Victor Espinoza rides 20–1 long shot War Emblem to victory in the

128th Kentucky Derby, beating runner-up Proud Citizen by four lengths.

May 7—Seattle Slew, the last living Triple Crown winner, dies in his sleep at Hill 'n' Dale Farm near Lexington, Ky. The stallion was 28 years old.

May 18—Derby winner War Emblem takes the second leg of the Triple Crown, holding off 45–1 long shot Magic Weisner by ¾ of a length to win the Preakness at Pimlico Race Course.

May 29—Our Emblem, sire of Kentucky Derby and Preakness winner War Emblem, is sold to WinStar Farm and Taylor Made Farm, near Lexington, Ky., where he will stand at stud.

June 8—A record crowd of 103,222 turns up at Belmont Park hoping to see War Emblem complete the Triple Crown, but goes home disappointed as War Emblem stumbles out of the gate, and 70–1 long shot Sarava wins the race by half a length over Medaglia d'Oro. Sarava is the greatest long-shot winnner in Belmont history.

June 23—Jockey Chris McCarron ends his career, during which he won 7,141 races and more than $264 million, with a victory, riding Came Home in the Affirmed Stakes at Hollywood Park.

July 15—Belmont winner Sarava breaks a foreleg during a workout at Churchill Downs and will miss the rest of the season.

Aug 4—War Emblem wins the $1 million Haskell Invitational at Monmouth Park.

Aug 5—Cigar, who won 16 straight races in 1995 and '96, is inducted into the National Racing Hall of Fame at Saratoga Springs, N.Y.

Aug 24—Medaglia d'Oro, who finished half a length behind winner Sarava at the Belmont, wins the $1 million Travers Stakes at Saratoga.

Aug 25—Came Home wins the $1 million Pacific Classic in Del Mar, Calif.

Sept 11—Kentucky Derby and Preakness winner War Emblem is sold to Shadai Stallion Station of Japan for $17 million. The horse will run in the Breeders's Cup Classic on Oct. 27 and then retire to stud.

Oct 6—Pleasantly Perfect wins the Goodwood Breeders' Cup Handicap at Santa Anita by 3 ¼ lengths over Momentum. The $500,000 race is a tuneup for the $4 million Breeders' Cup Classic three weeks later.

Motor Sports

Nov 1, 2001—After a two-hour meeting among drivers, crew chiefs and car owners in Huntersville, N.C., NASCAR officials decide to make several aerodynamic rule changes, including increasing the angle of the rear spoiler on cars, and removing the upright bend in the spoilers. The restrictor plates on carburetors will remain in place.

Nov 11—Three members of Ricky Rudd's crew and a NASCAR official are hit by Ward Burton's car on pit road during the Homestead 400 in Florida. Rudd crewmember Bobby Burrell is most seriously injured, and is airlifted to a Miami hospital, where he is in serious but stable condition. Bill Elliott wins the race, his first victory since 1994..

Nov 18—With a sixth-place finish at the Atlanta 500 in Hampton, Ga., Jeff Gordon clinches his fourth career Winston Cup season points title. Gordon joins Richard Petty and Dale Earnhardt as the only drivers with more than three season titles.

Nov 26—Kevin Harvick, 25, is named NASCAR rookie of the year after a season in which he won two races and more than $3 million in prize money. Harvick took over the late Dale Earnhardt's car after the season-opening Daytona 500.

Dec 4—The results of online voting by fans and a media panel are in: Jeff Gordon is named 2001 Driver of the Year.

Dec 6—Roger Penske, a CART owner whose drivers have won 11 Indianapolis 500s, announces he is leaving CART for its rival circuit, the Indy Racing League. The move comes at the request of his sponsor, which wants exposure in the IRL-run Indy 500.

Feb 13, 2002—After having his request for an apology from NASCAR denied, seat-belt manufacturer Bill Simpson files an $8.5 million lawsuit against the racing circuit, claiming NASCAR scapegoated him and his firm by announcing it had found one of his lap belts broken in Dale Earnhardt's car following the legendary driver's fatal wreck on Feb. 18, 2001.

Feb 17—Ward Burton wins a wild and unusual Daytona 500. There are several crashes in the race, including a frightening 18-car pileup, and a red flag stops the race on the backstretch for 20 minutes.

March 3—Sterling Marlin, who was penalized at the Daytona 500 for getting out of his car to fix a bent fender, wins the Las Vegas 400 after race officials fail to notify his crew of a 15-second penalty in time to levy it. The win gives Marlin a 75-point lead in the season points standings.

March 3—Michael Schumacher begins his defense of his Formula One title with a victory at the Australian Grand Prix. At the Homestead-Miami Speedway in Florida, another defending champ takes the checkered flag as Sam Hornish Jr. wins the Indy Racing League season opener.

March 10—Continuing to rebound from a poor beginning to the season, which included a last-place finish at the Daytona 500, Tony Stewart wins the Atlanta 500 in Hampton, Ga.

March 24—In the second-closest finish in Indy-car racing history, Sam Hornish Jr. defeats Jacques Lazier by 0.028 seconds at the Indy 400.

March 31—Brothers Michael and Ralf Schumacher finish 1–2 at the Brazilian Grand Prix.

April 7—Larry Dixon blazes to his third NHRA win of the season, taking the Las Vegas Nationals with a top speed of 319.29.

May 12—In a move that draws heavy criticism, Ferrari's Rubens Barrichello follows team orders and cedes first place to his teammate Michael Schumacher at the Austrian Grand Prix, which Schumacher goes on to win.

May 18—NASCAR rookie Ryan Newman wins the $750,000 Winston at Lowe's Motor Speedway in Concord, N.C. He joins Dale Earnhardt Jr. as the only rookies to win the event.

May 26—Attempting to duplicate Tony Stewart's feat of 2001, Robby Gordon races in the Indy 500, finishes eighth, then flies to Concord, N.C., for the Charlotte 600 later that night, finishing 16th in the NASCAR race. Stewart finished ninth and sixth, respectively in the races last year.

May 27—After IRL officials reject a protest by runner-up Paul Tracy, who was penalized for taking the lead on a caution, Helio Castroneves is declared the winner of the Indianapolis 500.

June 16—Clocking 4.619 seconds and streaking at 319.14 mph at the Pontiac Nationals, Top Fuel driver Larry Dixon wins his seventh title in 11 events this season.

June 23—Holding on to the lead he took at the start of the race, Rubens Barrichello wins the European Grand Prix by 0.2 seconds over teammate Michael Schumacher.

July 6—Michael Waltrip wins the Daytona 400 under caution, a ruling that causes fans, who wanted the race stopped and restarted under a green flag, to shower the track with debris.

July 21—Michael Schumacher wins the French Grand Prix to clinch the fifth championship of his F/1 career. Schumacher, who wrapped up the title with six races to go in the season, joins Juan Manuel Fangio of Argentina as the only five-time winners in the 52-year history of F/1.

Aug 11—One week after he is fined and put on probation for punching a photographer, Tony Stewart wins the NASCAR race at Watkins Glen.

Sept 15—Sam Hornish, who beat Al Unser Jr. in the closest finish in Indy-car history the previous week, edges Helio Castroneves by .0096 seconds to win the IRL season points title in the final race of the year.

Sept 29—Jeff Gordon keeps himself in contention for the Winston Cup points title by winning the Kansas 400 by .618 seconds over rookie Ryan Newman.

Oct 2—Sterling Marlin, who stands fifth in the Winston Cup standings, learns he will miss the rest of the season after doctors discover a fractured vertebra in his neck, the result of two hard crashes in the last four races.

Oct 6—Cristiano da Matta wins the Grand Prix of the Americas to clinch the CART season title. It is da Matta's seventh victory of the year.

Oct 13—In only his second NASCAR start, Jamie McMurray, 26, wins the Charlotte 500. Tony Stewart finishes third in the race to increase his season points lead to 97.

Olympics

Nov 27, 2001—U.S. President George W. Bush denies a request by IOC President Jacques Rogge for a cease-fire in the American-led war in Afghanistan during the Winter Olympics, scheduled for Salt Lake City in February 2002.

Dec 4—At Centennial Olympic Park in Atlanta, boxing legend Muhammad Ali lights the first torch for the Olympic Torch Relay that will end in Salt Lake City on Feb. 8.

Dec 20—Jim Shea becomes the first third-generation U.S. Olympian when he qualifies for the Salt Lake City Games with a second place finish in a World Cup skeleton event in Lake Placid, N.Y. Shea follows his grandfather, Jack Shea, who won two speed skating gold medals at the 1932 Games, and his father, Jim Sr., a skier at the 1964 Olympics, into Olympic competition.

Jan 6, 2002—In an Olympic tuneup in Detroit, the U.S. women's ice hockey team whips Canada 7–3 as Katie King scores three goals. The U.S. is 26–0—including 7–0 against Canada—during its pre-Olympic exhibition tour.

Feb 6—Jim Easton of the U.S. is elected a vice president on the IOC's executive board.

Feb 8—The 2002 Winter Games open in Salt Lake City as the 1980 U.S. men's ice hockey team lights the Olympic flame in a ceremony that includes Native American dancers and the American flag that had flown over the World Trade Center.

Feb 10—The Utah Olympic Oval is one of the top stories of the first two days of competition in Salt Lake, as it yields a bumper crop of world records in speed skating. The top two finishers in the men's 5,000, the Netherlands' Jochem Uytdehaage and Derek Parra of the U.S., both break the previous world record, and Germany's Claudia Pechstein breaks the world record in the women's 3,000 meters winning the gold ahead of three other women who also break the old record. Parra is the first Mexican American to medal at a Winter Games.

Feb 10—Austria's Fritz Strobl wins the men's downhill skiing gold medal. His countryman Stephan Eberharter wins the bronze, while Norway's Kjetil Andre Aamodt takes the silver.

Feb 11—Controversy hits the 2002 Winter Games as Yelena Berezhnaya and Anton Sikharulidze of Russia win the pairs figure skating gold medal over Jamie Salé and David Pelletier of Canada, despite most observers' belief that the pair from Canada clearly outskated the Russians .

Feb 11—German luger Georg Hackl's attempt to become the first Winter Olympian to win four consecutive gold medals falls short when Armin Zoeggler of Italy upsets him to take the men's singles gold medal.

Feb 11—Ross Powers, Danny Kass, and J.J. Thomas finish 1-2-3 in the men's snowboarding halfpipe to complete the first U.S. Winter Olympics medal sweep since 1956.

Feb 12—Casey FitzRandolph of the U.S. wins the men's 500 meter speed skating event, while his countryman Kip Carpenter finishes third.

Feb 12—Carole Montillet becomes France's first woman downhill Olympic champion, edging Isolde Kostner of Italy for the gold medal. Picabo Street of the U.S. finishes 16th, then announces her retirement from the sport. Street won a silver medal in the downhill in the 1994 Games and gold in the Super G in '98.

Feb 13—Norway's Kjetil Andre Aamodt wins the men's combined for his sixth Olympic medal, an Alpine skiing record. Bode Miller of the U.S. wins the silver medal after nearly falling.in his downhill run then staging an astonishing slalom run. Benjamin Raich of Austria wins the.bronze medal.

Feb 13—Germany sweeps the women's singles luge event as Sylke Otto wins the gold medal, finishing 0.321 seconds ahead of Barbara Niedernhuber and 0.401 ahead of Silke Kraushaar.

Feb 14—Catriona Le May Doan of Canada repeats as women's 500-meter speed skating champ, topping Germany's Monique Garbrecht-Enfeldt and Sabine Voelker.

Feb 16—Leading the 1,000-meter short track speed skating event in the final turn, Apolo Anton Ohno is knocked down and crashes into the boards. He suffers a cut on his thigh from his skate blade that requires six stitches, but scrambles across the finish line in time to win the silver medal.

Feb 17—With a world-record time of 1:13.83, Chris Witty of the U.S. wins the 1,000-meter speed skating event. Her countrywoman and training partner Jennifer Rodriguez finishes third.

Feb 17—In the wake of the pairs figure skating judging controversy of Feb. 11, Olympic officials decide to award another gold medal for the event to Canada's Jamie Salé and David Pelletier. In an auxiliary medals ceremony, Salé and Pelletier share the top step of the podium with Russia's Berezhnaya and Sikharulidze.

Feb 18—The U.S. men's hockey team, which trailed 1–0 after 20 seconds of the first period, whips Belarus 8–1 in its final preliminary-round game to finish 2-0-1 and clinch the top spot in its group heading into the quarterfinals.

Feb 18—Canada rallies to tie the Czech Republic 3–3 in men's hockey and book passage to the quarterfinals as the No. 3 seed in its group, behind the Czech team and Sweden.

Feb 19—Vonetta Flowers of the U.S. becomes the first black athlete in Olympic history to win a gold medal in the Winter Games when she teams with Jill Bakken to win the women's two-person Bobsled. In speed skating, the U.S.'s Derek Parra sets a world record (1:43.95) while winning the gold medal in the 1,500 meters.

Feb 20—Seventy years after his grandfather, Jack Shea, won two Olympic gold medals in speed skating, Jim Shea Jr., the first third-generation Olympian, wins a gold medal in skeleton.

Feb 20—Belarus pulls off one of the biggest upsets in Olympic hockey history, stunning gold-medal favorite Sweden 4–3 in the quarterfinals.

Feb 21—Russia and South Korea threaten to leave the Games after a series of decisions go

Public outcry led to Salé (left) and Pelletier being named co-gold medalists in the Salt Lake City pairs competition.

PETER READ MILLER

against their athletes. The South Koreans gripe that speed skater Kim Dong-sung was improperly disqualified from a 1,500-meter short-track speed skating race on Feb. 20, while the Russians are upset with the officiating in their 1–0 *victory* over the Czech Republic in the men's hockey quarterfinals, and that Nordic skier Larissa Lazutina's prerace drug test came back positive.

Feb 21—After going 0–8 against the Americans in pre-Olympics exhibitions, Canada wins when it matters, defeating the U.S. 3–2 to win the women's hockey gold medal.

Feb 21—In fourth place after the short program, 16-year-old Sarah Hughes of the U.S. skates a nearly flawless free program and wins the women's figure skating gold medal.

Feb 22—Janica Kostelic of Croatia becomes the first Alpine skier to win four medals at a single Olympics, taking the gold medal in the giant slalom. She already has medals in the combined (gold) slalom (gold) and super G (silver).

Feb 24—More controversy roils the Salt Lake Games as three cross-country skiers have performances nullified because of positive tests for darbepoetin, a substance similar to erythropoetin (EPO), which boosts oxygen-storing red blood cells. Former German Olympian Johann Muehlegg, who is now competing for Spain, loses the 50k

classical gold medal; Russia's Larisa Lazutina is stripped of the 30k classical gold medal; and Olga Danilova of Russia is disqualified from her eighth place finish in the 30k. Since the positives come from so-called out-of-competition tests, which cannot be applied retroactively, the athletes will keep medals they won earlier in the Games.

Feb 24—In the final event of the Salt Lake City Olympics, Canada, which began the men's hockey tournament with a 5–2 loss to Sweden, rebounds to end its 50-year gold-medal drought in the sport, knocking off the U.S. 5–2 in a spirited final. Joe Sakic and Jarome Iginla each score twice for Canada.

May 24—USOC President Sandy Baldwin resigns amid revelations of inaccuracies on her résumé, including a false claim that she has a Ph.D. in English from Arizona State. She is replaced on Aug 15 by Marty Mankamyer, a 68-year-old realtor and grandmother of nine.

Aug 6—Uzbek-born Alimzhan Tokhtakhounov, a reputed mobster who is alleged to have tried to rig the figure skating pairs and dance competitions at the Salt Lake City Olympics, refuses voluntary extradition from Italy to the U.S., ensuring that a time-consuming series of legal maneuvers will have to be enacted before the investigation can proceed.

Pro Basketball

Oct 30, 2001—The NBA season kicks off with an extra jolt of excitement as Michael Jordan returns to the league after a three-year retirement, the second of his career. He joins the Washington Wizards, of whom he was part owner until deciding to return as a player, and scores 19 points in a 93–91 loss to the New York Knicks at Madison Square Garden.

Nov 5—Scoring seven of his 32 points in the final 1:52, Seattle SuperSonics guard Gary Payton leads his team to a 113–111 double-overtime road victory over the Orlando Magic.

Nov 28—Michael Jordan and Allen Iverson put on a show in Philadelphia as the visiting Wizards down the 76ers 94–87. Iverson scores a season-high 40 points for Philadelphia and Jordan leads Washington with 30.

Dec 10—In the wake of coach Jeff Van Gundy's unexpected resignation, the Knicks (11–9) tab Don Chaney, an assistant coach in New York for seven years, to lead the team for the rest of the season

Dec 18—The Miami Heat scores the fourth-lowest single-game point total in NBA history, losing 95–56 to the Utah Jazz in Miami.

Dec 19—Orlando forward Grant Hill has surgery on his left ankle and will miss the rest of the year. It is the third operation on the ankle in 20 months.

Dec 24—Chicago Bulls coach Tim Floyd resigns after slightly more than three seasons in charge of the team. He was 49–190 in that span.

Dec 25—Former NBA coach P.J. Carlesimo and New York's Latrell Sprewell speak for the first time since their notorious altercation in 1997. They meet in Madison Square Garden after the Knicks 102–94 win over the Toronto Raptors, shake hands and exchange Christmas greetings.

Dec 26—Denver Nuggets coach Dan Issel offers his resignation in the wake of ethnically-charged remarks he made to a fan on Dec. 12.

Dec 29—Rebounding from a six-point outing in his previous game, Washington's Michael Jordan, 38, becomes the oldest player in NBA history to score at least 50 points in a game, pouring in 51 against Charlotte in the Wizards' 107–90 win. Two nights later, Jordan scores 45 as the Wizards beat New Jersey 98–76.

Jan 7, 2002—The NBA fines Dallas Mavericks owner Mark Cuban $500,000 for his remarks about the officiating in Dallas's 105–103 loss to San Antonio on Jan. 5. The amount of the fine is a league record.

Jan 14—Shaquille O'Neal is fined $15,000 and suspended for three games after he throws two punches at Chicago center Brad Miller following

JOHN W. MC DONOUGH

Jordan provided a jolt for the NBA with his return, but didn't make it through the year.

Miller's and Charles Oakley's hard fouls against him in their game on Jan. 12. Miller and Oakley are also fined and suspended, Oakley for two games, Miller for one.

Jan 15—Sinking 21 of 42 field goal attempts and all 14 of his free throws, Philadelphia's Allen Iverson explodes for 58 points, the most in an NBA game in nearly two years, to lead the 76ers to 112–106 win over Houston.

Feb 3—The Eastern Conference–leading Nets fire a shot across the bow of the Western Conference with a 117–83 rout of the Sacramento Kings, who have the best record in the league.

Feb 10—Shrugging off the boos by the fans from his hometown of Philadelphia, Lakers guard Kobe Bryant scores 31 points to lead the West to a 135–120 win in the All-Star Game. He is named MVP of the game at the First Union Center.

Feb 13—Minnesota Timberwolves guard Terrell Brandon has surgery to repair a cartilage fracture on the surface of his left femur. He will miss the remainder of the year.

Feb 19—The Pacers and the Bulls make a seven-player trade that sends Indiana guards Jalen Rose and Travis Best and rookie Norm Richardson to Chicago in return for center Brad Miller, swingman Ron Artest and guards Ron Mercer and Kevin Ollie.

Feb 21—Dallas trades forward Juwan Howard and guards Tim Hardaway and Donnell Harvey to Denver in exchange for center Raef LaFrentz, guards Nick Van Exel and Avery Johnson and swingman Tariq Abdul-Wahad.

March 3—The NBA suspends the Lakers' Kobe Bryant and Indiana's Reggie Miller for two games each after they scuffle following the final buzzer in Los Angeles's 96–84 win on March 1.

March 24—In a matchup of teams with the top two records in the league, the Lakers nip the Kings 97–96 in Sacramento as Kobe Bryant scores eight of Los Angeles's final 10 points. In Detroit, Ben Wallace pulls down a season-high 28 rebounds in the Pistons' 109–101 victory over Boston.

April 3—On the heels of a career-low two-point performance against the Lakers, Michael Jordan announces that he will sit out the rest of the season to allow his knee, which underwent arthroscopic surgery on Feb. 27, to heal properly.

April 4—University of Tennessee women's coach Pat Summitt signs on as a consultant to the WNBA's Washington Mystics. She will continue her job in Knoxville as well.

April 9—In what turns out to be his final game at Madison Square Garden, future Hall of Fame center Patrick Ewing, who spent 15 years with the Knicks, gets a standing ovation when he is introduced as a starter in the Orlando lineup. Ewing wins the opening tip, and the Magic goes on to win, 108–97.

April 17—The Pacers, Bucks and Raptors tip off their regular-season finales tied in the standings for the last two playoff spots, and Indiana and Toronto advance as the Pacers whip the 76ers 103–80, Milwaukee loses 123–89 to Detroit and the Raptors, completing one of the most dramatic turnarounds in NBA history, crush the Cleveland Cavaliers 103–85. Toronto lost 17 of 18 games after the All-Star break, including 13 in a row, then flipped the script to win 12 of its last 14—after star guard Vince Carter went down with a season-ending knee injury.

April 24—Receiving 117 of a possible 126 votes, Memphis Grizzlies center Pau Gasol is named NBA Rookie of the Year. Gasol, a native of Spain, is the first European to win the award; he averaged 17.6 points and 8.9 rebounds a game in 2001–02.

April 28—The Lakers complete a three-game sweep of the Portland Trail Blazers in their first-round series as forward Robert Horry hits a three-pointer with 2.1 seconds left in the game to give his team a 92–91 victory. In Minnesota, the Mavericks sweep the Timberwolves out of the playoffs with a 115–102 win, while in Philadelphia,

Sixers guard Allen Iverson scores 42 points to lead his team to a 108–103 victory over Boston and stave off first-round elimination.

April 30—Former Lakers star guard, GM and consultant Jerry West is introduced as the new president of the Memphis Grizzlies.

April 30—The Charlotte Hornets, who will relocate to New Orleans after the season, eliminate Orlando from the playoffs with a 102–85 rout in Game 4 of their first-round playoff series.

May 2—The New Jersey Nets, the top seed in the Eastern Conference with a 52–30 record, must go the distance, and then some, to eliminate No. 8 seed Indiana from the first round of the playoffs, taking Game 5 120–109 in double overtime. In Detroit, the Pistons eliminate Toronto with an 85–82 Game 5 win, and the following day in Boston, the Celtics dispatch Philadelphia with a 120–87 win in Game 5 of their first-round series.

May 7—Detroit coach Rick Carlisle is named NBA Coach of the Year, joining Pistons forwards Ben Wallace (defensive player of the year) and Corliss Wiliamson (sixth man) as postseason honorees.

May 9—Tim Duncan of the Spurs is named MVP of the 2001–02 season, sparking controversy in New Jersey and Los Angeles, where fans, players and coaches alike think their stars, Jason Kidd and Shaquille O'Neal, respectively, were more deserving of the award.

May 15—All four conference semifinal series end in five games as the Kings close out Dallas four games to one with a 114–101 victory on May 13; Boston eliminates Detroit by the same margin with a 90–81 win on May 14, the same day that the Lakers knock San Antonio out of the playoffs for the second straight year, winning Game 5 93–87; and New Jersey completes the NBA's final four, winning its series 4–1 with a 103–95 home defeat of Charlotte as Jason Kidd produces a triple-double.

May 28—Mike Bibby drains a 22-foot jump shot with 8.2 seconds remaining to lift Sacramento to a 92–91 victory over the Lakers and push Los Angeles to the brink of elimination, down 3–2 in the Western Conference finals.

May 31—The New Jersey Nets advance to the NBA Finals for the first time in their 26-year league history as Jason Kidd produces his third triple-double of the conference finals (15 points, 13 rebounds, 13 assists) to lead his team to a 96–88 victory in Game 6. Kidd joins Oscar Robertson (1963) and Wilt Chamberlain ('67) as the only players ever to produce three triple-doubles in a best-of-seven series.

May 31—The Lakers beat the Kings 106–102 in Game 6 to even the Western Conference finals series at three games apiece, but many fans and observers cry foul as Los Angeles takes 27 foul shots in the fourth quarter to Sacramento's nine. The disparity moves consumer advocate and 2000 presidential candidate Ralph Nader to fire off a letter to NBA commissioner David Stern, insinuating that the officials felt pressure to produce a revenue-increasing Game 7.

June 2—With a 112–106 overtime victory over Sacramento in Game 7 of the Western Conference finals, the Lakers advance to the NBA Finals for the third straight season.

June 5—Despite allowing a 23-point lead to be cut to three in the fourth quarter, the Lakers defeat the Nets 99–94 in Game 1 of the NBA Finals.

June 5—Former Los Angeles great Magic Johnson and late Nets star Drazen Petrovic lead a class of five individuals and one team, the Harlem Globetrotters, into the Basketball Hall of Fame. The other electees are 76ers coach Larry Brown, University of Arizona coach Lute Olsen and North Carolina State women's coach Kay Yow.

June 12—The Lakers win the NBA title for the third consecutive year, downing New Jersey 113–107 in Game 4 to complete a sweep of the Finals. Shaquille O'Neal scores 34 points and grabs 10 rebounds in the clincher and is named MVP of the finals for the third year in a row. Los Angeles coach Phil Jackson ties Celtics legend Red Auerbach for the most NBA titles (9) and surpasses Pat Riley to top the alltime coaches' playoff victories list with 156.

June 26—Yao Ming, a 7'5" center from China, is the No. 1 pick of the NBA draft, going to the Houston Rockets. Former Duke guard Jay Williams (known as Jason in college) goes second, to Chicago, while his former Blue Devils teammate Mike Dunleavy is the No. 3 selection, taken by the Golden State Warriors.

July 2—The Utah Starzz's 7'2", 223-pound center, Margo Dydek, is suspended by WNBA officials for one game for elbowing her counterpart on the Cleveland Rocker's, the 6'4", 193-pound Ann Wauters, during Utah's 79–62 victory on June 30.

July 16—Lisa Leslie wins the third WNBA All-Star Game MVP award of her career after she scores 18 points and grabs 14 rebounds to lead the West to a 81–76 win over the East in Washington, D.C.

July 22—The Sonics trade forward Vin Baker and guard Shammond Williams to the Celtics in exchange for guards Kenny Anderson and Joseph Forte and center Vitaly Potapenko.

July 29—The NBA's board of governors votes to use instant replay as an officiating tool in the 2002–03 season.

Aug 6—Dikembe Mutombo moves up I-95 from Philadelphia to New Jersey as the Sixers trade him to the Nets in return for forward Keith Van Horn and center Todd MacCulloch. Eight days later the Nets sign free-agent forward Rodney Rogers.

Aug 31—Los Angeles edges the New York Liberty 69–66 in Game 2 to repeat as WNBA champion. The Sparks' Lisa Leslie wins the series MVP award for the second year in a row.

Sept 4—At the World basketball Championships in Indianapolis, Argentina stuns the U.S. 87–80, handing the Americans professionals their first loss in international competition.

Sept 8—Yugoslavia defeats Argentina 84–77 in overtime to win the World Basketball Championships in Indianapolis. Both finalists, as well as Spain defeated the U.S., which finished sixth in the tournament.

Sept 11—Detroit sends All-Star guard Jerry Stackhouse, forward Brian Cardinal and center Ratko Varda to the Wizards in exchange for guards Richard Hamilton and Hubert Davis and forward Bobby Simmons.

Sept 16—Former Knicks center Patrick Ewing, an 11-time All-Star announces his retirement after 18 seasons in the NBA.

Sept 25—The U.S. edges Russia 79–74 to win the gold medal at the Women's World Basketball Championship in Nanjing, China.

Sept 26—Michael Jordan, 39, announces that he will return to play for the Wizards in 2002–03.

Oct 13—The Knicks, who are already without Latrell Sprewell (broken finger), learn that their prize offseason signing, All-Star forward Antonio McDyess, will miss most, if not all, of the season with a fractured kneecap suffered in a preseason game on Oct. 12.

Oct 28, 2001—The NFL's only unbeaten team, the St. Louis Rams, lose their first game of the year as the New Orleans Saints (4–2) intercept quarterback Kurt Warner four times, score 25 points in the third quarter and beat the Rams (6–1) 34–31 in St. Louis.

Nov 4—Scoring two touchdowns in the final 28 seconds of regulation time—the second one on a 34-yard "Hail Mary" pass as the clock runs out—the Chicago Bears force overtime against the Cleveland Browns and then win the game 27–21 on safety Mike Brown's interception return for a touchdown. It is the second straight week that the Bears have won a game in overtime on an interception return for a TD by Brown.

Nov 11—Marshall Faulk, back in action after a four week layoff due to a bruised knee, rushes for 183 yards in the first half of the Rams' 48–14 pasting of Carolina in St. Louis. Faulk sits out the second half to rest his injury.

Nov 12—Two weeks after returning to the lineup following a six-week layoff for surgery on his right knee, Denver Broncos running back Terrell Davis undergoes surgery to repair torn lateral meniscus cartilage in his left knee. He suffered the latest injury in Denver's 26–16 win over the San Diego Chargers on Nov. 11.

Nov 22—The NFL's annual Thanksgiving Day competitors, the Cowboys and the Lions, both stage furious fourth-quarter comebacks in their Turkey Day games, but fall short of victory. The Lions (0–10) recover an onside kick in the waning seconds of the game and score a touchdown but lose 29–27 to visiting Green Bay when their two-point conversion attempt fails. Playing at home, the Cowboys (2–8) score 21 points in the fourth quarter but lose 26–24 to Denver.

Nov 25—The Washington Redskins become the first team in NFL history to win five games in a row after losing its first five games of the season, pulling back to .500 with a 13–3 victory over the Philadelphia Eagles. In Foxboro, Mass., the New England Patriots, who started the season at 0–2, run their record to 6–5 with a 34–17 win over New Orleans. Quarterback Tom Brady, who took over for New England after Drew Bledsoe was injured in Week 2, is named the starting quarterback for the rest of the season.

Nov 25—Marcus Crandell passes for 309 yards and two touchdowns to lead the Calgary Stampeders to a 27-19 win over the Winnipeg Blue Bombers in the 89th Grey Cup. It is Calgary's second CFL championship in four years with.

Dec 16—The Bears and the Oakland Raiders are the first teams to clinch playoff spots as Chicago rolls over the Buccaneers 27–3 to hit double-digits in victories (10–3) for the first time since 1991, and the Raiders beat the Chargers 13–6 to clinch the AFC West for the second year in a row. In Cleveland, an ugly scene develops after an instant-replay call goes against the Browns in the final minute of play, negating a first down at the Jacksonville Jaguars nine-yard-line. Fans throw plastic beer bottles and garbage onto the field and several players and officials are showered with beer and cups of ice. The uproar causes a 30-minute delay in Jacksonville's 15–10 victory.

Dec 16—The Lions (1–12) get their first win of the year, defeating the Minnesota Vikings 27–24 at home.

Dec 23—The Rams outscore Carolina 38–32 in Charlotte, N.C., to become the sixth team since 1970 to go unbeaten on the road (8–0) and run their record to 12–2. In Pittsburgh, the Steelers (12–2 for the first time since 1978) clinch a bye in the first round of the AFC playoffs

Dec 30—With a nerve-wracking 24–21 win over the Giants, Philadelphia wins the NFC East title for the first time since 1988. After David Akers kicks a 35-yard field goal to put the Eagles up by three with seven seconds left, the Giants execute one play from scrimmage: a short pass over the middle to running back Tiki Barber, who laterals to receiver Rod Dixon, who follows a phalanx of blockers down the sideline as time expires, getting all the way to the Eagles' four-yard line before being shoved out of bounds.

Jan 4, 2002—Vikings coach Dennis Green tenders his resignation after leading Minnesota to a 5–10 record.

Jan 6—Emmitt Smith of the Cowboys becomes the first running back to top 1,000 yards in 11 straight seasons, running for 77 yards in Dallas's 15–10 loss to Detroit to finish the season with 1,021 rushing yards. In Oakland, John Hall kicks a 53-yard field goal with 59 seconds on the clock to lift the Jets to a 24–22 win over the Raiders and a berth in the playoffs. At Giants Stadium, the Packers beat the Giants 34–25 as New York's Michael Strahan breaks the single-season sack record (22½) in dubious fashion. Green Bay quarterback Brett Favre surprises his offensive line by rolling out, then obligingly falls to the turf in front of the Strahan.

Jan 6—The Patriots (11–5) win their sixth game in a row, routing Carolina 38–6 to clinch the AFC East title.

Jan 7—The Panthers (1–15) fire coach George Seifert after a season in which Carolina became the first NFL team to lose 15 games in a row.

Jan 9—Rams quarterback Kurt Warner, who passed for 4,830 yards and 36 touchdowns, is named MVP of the 2001–02 season.

Jan 13—Wild-card weekend yields two close games and two yawners as the Packers get by San Francisco 25–15 in Green Bay, he Raiders hold off the Jets 38–24 in Oakland, the Ravens rout the Dolphins 20–3 in Miami, and the Eagles soar past Tampa Bay 31–9 in Philadelphia.

Jan 14—Former University of Florida coach Steve Spurrier signs a five-year, $25 million contract to coach the Redskins, making him the highest-paid coach in the NFL. In Tampa Bay, the Buccaneers dismiss coach Tony Dungy after the team's first-round exit from the playoffs.

Jan 20—The divisional playoff games feature a controversial outcome in the snow in Foxboro, Mass. and three clear-cut results elsewhere as the Steelers stomp the Ravens 27–10 in Pittsburgh, the Rams paste the Packers 45–17 in St. Louis, the Eagles upend the Bears 33–19 in Chicago and the Patriots get past Oakland 16–13 at home thanks to a replay ruling that reverses what looked like a fumble by

quarterback Tom Brady with 1:47 remaining in the game.

Jan 27—St. Louis advances to the Super Bowl for the second time in three years with a 29–24 win over Philadelphia in the NFC Championship Game, while in Pittsburgh, the Patriots stun the Steelers 24–17 in the AFC title game as Drew Bledsoe returns to the lineup after 126 days on the sidelines, replacing the injured Tom Brady. Bledsoe throws a touchdown pass in the victory.

Feb 3—In the first Super Bowl played in February (the NFL schedule was interrupted for one week due to the Sept 11 terrrorist attacks), the Patriots win their first title as Adam Vinatieri kicks a 48-yard field goal as time expires to give his team a 20–17 victory over the 14-point favorite Rams. Tom Brady completes 16 of 27 passes for 145 yards and a touchdown and is named MVP of the game.

Feb 3—Former Buffalo Bills quarterback Jim Kelly, who guided his team to four Super Bowls (all losses), leads a class of five into the Pro Football Hall of Fame. The others: former Steelers wide receiver John Stallworth, ex-Raider tight end Dave Casper, former Bears defensive lineman Dan Hampton, and former Rams and Redskins coach George Allen.

Spurrier left Florida for a five-year deal to coach the NFL's Washington Redskins.

JOHN IOCONO

BILL FRAKES

Quarterback Carr and the Texans lost five straight games after an opening win over Dallas.

league's other broadcast partners, Fox and CBS.

April 20—The Houston Texans, an expansion team set to join the league in 2002–03, take Fresno State quarterback David Carr with the first selection of the NFL draft. Picking second, Carolina takes North Carolina defensive end Julius Peppers, and Detroit selects Oregon QB Joey Harrington with the third pick.

April 21—New England trades quarterback Drew Bledsoe to Buffalo in return for a first-round draft choice in 2003.

April 31—Yet another team benefits from Baltimore's ongoing efforts to get under the NFL salary cap as former Ravens safety Rod Woodson, a 10-time Pro Bowler, signs a six-year $8.5 million deal with Oakland.

May 21—The Vikings announce that their eight-time Pro Bowl receiver Cris Carter has retired.

June 4—The steady stream of proven NFL veterans finding themselves without a job because of their teams' salary-cap problems thickens as the Falcons release running back Jamal Anderson, the Packers cut receiver Antonio Freeman and Jacksonville releases receiver Keenan McCardell and linebacker Hardy Nickerson. McCardell later signs with Tampa Bay, while Nickerson latches on with Green Bay and Freeman joins the Eagles.

June 28—In a story seemingly ripped from the pages of the satirical newspaper *The Onion*, Jacksonville Jaguars kicker Jaret Holmes and punter Chris Hanson tell reporters that they were badly burned in a fondue spill at Hanson's home earlier in the month. Hanson suffered first- and second-degree burns on both hands and his right ankle.

July 23—The day after Carolina agrees to terms with defensive end Julius Peppers, the second pick of the 2002 NFL draft, the Lions sign No. 3 pick quarterback Joey Harrington to a six-year, $36 million contract.

Aug 1—Baltimore signs Pro Bowl linebacker Ray Lewis to a five-year, $50 million contract extension.

Aug 19—Citing doctors advice regarding his numerous leg injuries since 1999, Denver running back Terrell Davis, who is one of four players to top 2,000 yards rushing in a season, announces his retirement after seven seasons.

Feb 9—Rich Gannon throws two touchdown passes and becomes the first two-time MVP of the Pro Bowl as he leads the AFC to a 38–30 win over the NFC in Honolulu.

Feb 18—The Buccaneers hire John Gruden away from the Raiders to be their new head coach. Tampa Bay sends four high draft picks and $8 million to Oakland in exchange for Gruden's services.

Feb 19—The Ravens inform their eight-time Pro Bowl tight end, Shannon Sharpe, that they must release him as part of the team's effort to get under the NFL salary cap. Baltimore, which won the Super Bowl in 2001, has seen Tony Siragusa, Jamie Sharper and Jermaine Lewis depart since then.

Feb 25—Tampa Bay guard Randall McDaniel, who set a league record by starting in 12 consecutive Pro Bowls, announces his retirement after 14 NFL seasons.

Feb 25—To get under the NFL salary cap of $71.8 million, the Atlanta Falcons cut 14-year veteran quarterback Chris Chandler, receiver Terrance Mathis and free safety Ronnie Bradford. The move makes second year QB Michael Vick the Falcons' starter for 2002–03.

March 4—Elvis Grbac, who made the Pro Bowl as a member of the Chiefs in 2000, announces his retirement at the age of 31.

March 18—Commissioner Paul Tagliabue announces that the NFL's 2002 schedule may allow for some late-season Sunday games to be switched to ABC's *Monday Night Football*. The announcement comes as a surprise to the

Sept 2—Defensive end Michael Strahan signs a seven-year, $46 million deal to remain with the Giants.

Sept 5—The 2002–03 NFL season kicks off with an unprecedented Thursday-night opener, in which visiting San Francisco squeaks by the Giants 16–13.

Sept 8— The league's new team, the Texans, win their first game, topping their in-state rivals, the Cowboys, 19–10, in Houston. Five teams— Kansas City, Chicago, Tennessee, Green Bay and the Jets—rally from double-digit deficits to win their openers, and in Cleveland, the Chiefs beat the Browns after Cleveland linebacker Dwayne Rudd, thinking the game is over, flings his helmet downfield and is penalized for unsportsmanlike conduct. The officials move the ball half the distance to the goal line, setting up a 30-yard field goal by Morten Anderson that gives Kansas City a 40–39 victory.

Sept 9—The Patriots open their defense of the NFL title with a 30–14 rout of Pittsburgh in Foxboro, Mass.

Sept 11—Falcons cornerback Ray Buchanan and Bears safety Damon Moore are suspended for four games each for violating the NFL's substance-abuse policy. While Moore's failed drug test is not publicized, Buchanan admits he has tested positive for steroids but insists he took them by mistake.

Sept 29—Seattle Seahawks running back Shaun Alexander sets an NFL record with five touchdowns in the first half of his team's 48–28 victory over Minnesota.

Sept 30—Baltimore's Chris McAlister completes the longest play in NFL history when he returns a missed field goal 108 yards for a score during the Ravens' 34–23 win over Denver.

Oct 6—The defending NFC champion Rams, who lost quarterback Kurt Warner to a broken finger the previous week (he is to miss two months with the injury), go to 0–5 after a 37–13 loss to San Francisco. It is the Rams' worst start since 1963.

Oct 20—Nailbiters dominate the schedule as six games come down to the final two minutes and four go to overtime. Arizona, Detroit, Denver and San Diego all win in OT. The Chargers beat division rival Oakland 27–21 to improve to 6–1, tops in the NFL along with Green Bay, which dismantles Washington 30–9 at Lambeau Field.

Soccer

Nov 11, 2001—In Mexico City, the home team defeats Honduras 3–0 to clinch the final World Cup berth from the CONCACAF region and complete its recovery from a 1-3-1 start in the final round of qualifying.

Nov 25—Uruguay secures the 32nd and final berth for the 2002 World Cup finals in Japan and Korea, defeating Australia 3–0 in Montevideo.

Nov 27—Bayern Munich wins the Intercontinental Cup in Tokyo, defeating Boca Juniors 1–0 on a goal by Samuel Kuffour.

Dec 1—The World Cup draw unfolds in Busan, South Korea, and the U.S. learns it will be grouped with Poland, co-hosts South Korea and European power Portugal. England and Argentina head up the tournament's toughest group, which also includes Nigeria and Sweden. The defending champions, France, will kick off the tournament against former French colony Senegal.

Dec 9—The U.S. plays its final game of 2001, losing 1–0 to South Korea, whom it will face in its second game of the World Cup, before 42,000 fans on the resort island of Jeju.

Dec 12—Earnie Stewart, who led the U.S. national team in scoring in 2001, is named Player of the Year.

Jan 19, 2002—Nineteen-year-old DaMarcus Beasley scores three minutes into stoppage time to give the U.S. a 2–1 victory over South Korea in the Gold Cup opener for both teams at the Rose Bowl.

Feb 2—The U.S. wins the Gold Cup with a 2–0 win over Costa Rica in Pasadena, Calif. It is the first Gold Cup title for the U.S. since 1991.

Feb 13—The U.S. controls the first half of an exhibition game against Italy in Catania, Italy, but loses 1–0 after a goal by Alessandro Del Piero in the 62nd minute.

March 2—In the U.S. starting lineup for the first time in nearly a year following a severe knee injury, Clint Mathis picks up where he left off, scoring two goals in a 4–0 victory over Honduras in Seattle. Nineteen-year-old Landon Donovan scores the other two U.S. goals.

March 23—Major League Soccer kicks off its seventh season as the defending champion San Jose Earthquakes shut out the Dallas Burn 2–0 at the Cotton Bowl; the MetroStars rally from a 1–0 deficit to beat the New England Revolution 2–1 at Giants Stadium; the visiting Chicago Fire blanks the Columbus Crew 2–0; the Los Angeles Galaxy gets two goals from new signing Carlos Ruiz of Guatemala to beat D.C. United 2–1 in overtime at the Rose Bowl; and the host Kansas City Wizards tie the Colorado Rapids 1–1.

March 27—Germany overpowers the U.S. 4–2 in an exhibiton in Rostock. A bright spot for the Yanks is Clint Mathis, who scores two goals.

Captain America: U.S. skipper Claudio Reyna led his team to the World Cup quarterfinals.

April 17—The U.S. falls 2–1 to Ireland in a waterlogged exhibition in Dublin. Eddie Pope scores for the Yanks.

April 22—U.S. national team coach Bruce Arena names his 23-man roster for the 2002 World Cup in Japan and South Korea. There are two mild surprises as 19-year-old midfielder DaMarcus Beasley and Pablo Mastroeni, a midfielder who didn't appear in a single qualifier for the U.S., both make the team.

May 12—In an exhibition against Uruguay at RFK stadium, DaMarcus Beasley has a breakout game, scoring the winning goal in a 2–1 U.S. win. The victory is a costly one for the U.S., however, as midfield stalwart Chris Armas tears his ACL in the first half and will miss the World Cup.

May 14—Tab Ramos of the MetroStars, the first player signed by MLS and arguably the best American player of all time, announces that this season will be his last.

May 16—The U.S. whips Jamaica 5–0 in an exhibition game at Giants Stadium but once again suffers injuries to key players as defender Greg Vanney, who was named to the roster to replace the injured Chris Armas, leaves the game in the 45th minute with a knee injury; goalkeeper Kasey Keller exits after bruising his knee in a collision in the 51st minute; and Clint Mathis, who scores the second goal of the game, leaves with an injured toe in the 63rd minute.

May 19—The U.S. loses 2–0 to the Netherlands in Foxboro, Mass. in its final World Cup tuneup.

May 27—France's star midfielder, Zinedine Zidane, injures his thigh in Les Bleus 3–2 exhibition victory over South Korea and will miss the World Cup opener against Senegal, and probably France's second Cup game as well.

May 31—The 2002 World Cup kicks off with a shocker as the defending champion France loses 1–0 to Senegal, a former French colony. Papa Bouba Diop scores the goal in the 30th minute.

June 3—The tournament co-hosts begin play and each earns its first point in a World Cup as Japan holds on for a 2–2 tie against Belgium and South Korea blanks Poland 2–0.

June 5—Robbie Keane scores a last-minute goal to lift Ireland into a 1–1 tie with Germany and keep alive its hopes of advancing.

June 5—Scoring three goals in the first 36 minutes of its World Cup opener, the U.S. holds on for a stunning 3–2 upset of Portugal, a team many picked as a favorite to win the tournament.

June 6—Continuing to labor in the absence of playmaker Zinedine Zidane, defending World Cup champion France ties Uruguay 0–0 in

TONY GUTIERREZ/AP

Busan. In Daegu, upstart Senegal picks up another point, tying Denmark 1–1.

June 7—The highly anticipated match between England and Argentina, who played one of the best games of the '98 World Cup, is a dour affair compared to its famous predecessor. England wins 1–0 on a penalty kick by David Beckham, who was memorably red-carded in the '98 match. Beckham sends his shot almost straight down the middle, where it hits the net because keeper Pablo Cavallero dives the wrong way. The result gives England, which tied Sweden in its opener, four points in the "Group of Death." Sweden, which defeats Nigeria 2–1 on this day, is tied with England atop the group. Argentina has three points from its opening win over Nigeria, which is without a point.

June 8—Brazil routs China 4–0 as each of its top stars, Rivaldo, Ronaldo and Ronaldinho, scores a goal. In Ibaraki, Croatia upsets Italy 2–1 to keep its tournament hopes alive.

June 10—In Daegu, in front of a stadium packed with red-clad fans who chant and sing for the home team the entire game, the U.S. ties co-host South Korea 1–1. Clint Mathis scores in the 24th minute, and Ahn Jung Hwan ties it in the 78th.

June 11—After a 2–0 loss to Denmark in Incheon, France exits the World Cup without scoring a goal in three games. In Yokohama, Ireland whips Saudi Arabia 3–0 to clinch a berth in the second round. In Shizuoka, Germany defeats Cameroon 2–0 to advance as well.

June 13—Alessandro Del Piero scores with five minutes left to salvage a 1–1 tie for Italy against

Mexico and send the Azzurri into the second round. In Suwon, Brazil and Costa Rica play the tournament's most wide-open game, which ends with Brazil on top 5–2. Costa Rica, which goes 1-1-1 in group play, is eliminated on goal difference.

June 14—The U.S. stumbles against Poland, giving up two goals in the first five minutes and losing 3–1, but still advances thanks to South Korea's dicey 1–0 win over Portugal, which has two players sent off and narrowly misses three golden scoring chances in the waning minutes.

June 14—Both co-hosts not only advance to the second round but also win their groups as Japan defeats Tunisia 2–0 to complement South Korea's group-clinching win over Portugal.

June 16—Four of the World Cup quarterfinalists are set as Germany gets by Paraguay 1–0, England routs Denmark 3–0, Senegal defeats Sweden 2–1 in extra time, and Spain beats Ireland on penalties after a 1–1 draw.

June 17—The U.S. beats Mexico 2–0 on goals by Brian McBride and Landon Donovan and advances to the quarterfinals of the World Cup. It is the best World Cup showing by the U.S. since 1930. The Americans will face Germany in the next round. In Kobe, Brazil beats Belgium 2–0 to advance to the quarterfinals.

June 18—The last two quarterfinalists are set as Turkey upends Japan 1–0 in Miyagi, and South Korea edges Italy 2–1 in extra time after several questionable calls by the referee and a couple of missed chances by Italy.

June 21—The U.S. outplays three-time World Cup champion Germany, but gives up a goal to Michael Ballack in the 39th minute. The lead stands up despite the U.S.'s furious pressure in the second half, which features a moment of controversy as a shot by Gregg Berhalter of the U.S. appears not only to cross the goal line, but also to be handled by German defender Torsten Frings. Referee Hugh Dallas makes no call, and Germany advances to the semis with a 1–0 victory.

June 21—England takes a 1–0 lead in its quarterfinal match against Brazil but gives up a goal in first-half injury time and another in the 50th minute on a horrendous misplay by goalkeeper David Seaman. In the 57th minute, Brazil's Ronaldinho, who set up the first goal and scored the second, is red-carded. Despite having a man advantage for the final 33 minutes, England doesn't put a single shot on goal and loses 2–1.

June 22—South Korea defeats Spain on penalties after a 0–0 draw to advance to the semifinals. In the first period of extra time, Spain scores, but the referee rules that the ball went over the byline before being put in the net, and disallows the goal. Replays show that the ball never went out. In Osaka, Turkey defeats Senegal 1–0 to reach the semifinals.

June 26—Both World Cup semifinals end 1–0 as Germany edges South Korea on a goal by Michael Ballack, who picks up his second yellow card of the knockout round and will have to miss the final. Germany will face Brazil, whose Ronaldo scores in the 49th minute to defeat Turkey.

June 30—Before the World Cup began, Brazil's Ronaldo promised that he would score a goal in every game, and he keeps his word all the way through to the final, scoring two second-half goals in Yokohama to lead Brazil to a 2–0 win over Germany. Ronaldo tops all scorers in the tournament with eight goals and moves into a tie for third place on the career World Cup scoring list with none other than Pelé. It is an unprecedented fifth World Cup title for Brazil.

July 21—The U.S. women's team routs Norway 4–0 in Blaine, Minn.

Aug 3—The seventh MLS All-Star Game pits a lineup of league all-stars against the U.S. national team at RFK Stadium. D.C.'s Marco Etcheverry is MVP of the game as the MLS team wins 3–2.

Aug 24—The Carolina Courage wins the second WUSA championship, defeating the Washington Power 3–2 in the final in Atlanta. Birgit Prinz of Germany scores a goal and sets up another and is named MVP of the game.

Sept 21—Needing just one point from their last three games, the MetroStars lose all three, ending with a 3–0 defeat at New England, and miss the playoffs.

Sept 28—The defending champion Earthquakes are eliminated from the MLS playoffs as Columbus defeats them 2–1 to take their first-round series.

Oct 2—Brian Kamler and MLS goals leader Taylor Twellman score as New England defeats Chicago 2–0 to clinch their first-round series and advance to the MLS semifinals, where they'll meet Columbus. At the Rose Bowl, Los Angeles eliminates Kansas City with a 5–2 victory, and at the Cotton Bowl, the Rapids tie Dallas 1–1, then win the series-deciding minigame 1–0 to advance.

Oct 9—The Galaxy advances to the MLS Cup for the third time in four years, nipping Colorado 1–0 on Carlos Ruiz's record seventh goal of the playoffs.

Oct 12—Needing only a tie to advance to the MLS Cup for the first time in its history, the Revolution jumps out to a 2–0 lead on Columbus then holds on for a 2–2 draw. With one of the best fan bases but worst track records in the league, New England finally rewards its faithful with a shot at a title.

Oct 20—In front of an MLS-Cup record 61,316 fans at Foxboro's Gillette Stadium, regular-season MVP Carlos Ruiz scores in the 23rd minute of extra time to give the Los Angeles Galaxy a 1–0 victory over New England and their first MLS title after four trips to the championship game.

Oct 26, 2001—With her husband, Andre Agassi, standing by, seven-time Wimbledon champ Steffi Graf gives birth to Jaden Gil Agassi at Valley Hospital in Las Vegas.

Nov 4—Lindsay Davenport loses to Serena Williams in a walkover in the final of the season-ending Sanex WTA Tour Championships in Munich, but in reaching the final, Davenport, who won the Tour's previous two tournaments, clinches the No. 1 ranking for 2001.

Nov 18—Lleyton Hewitt wins the Masters Cup with a 6–3, 6–3, 6–4 victory over Sebastien Grosjean in the final. The triumph gives him the year-end No. 1 world ranking.

Dec 2—France defeats Australia 3–2 to win the Davis Cup in Melbourne

Jan 13, 2002—Hours before the Australian Open, the year's first major, is to begin, Serena Williams and two-time defending champion Andre Agassi withdraw with an ankle and a wrist injury, respectively.

Jan 26—Jennifer Capriati wins the Australian Open, rallying from an 0–4 deficit in the second set of the final to defeat Martina Hingis 4–6, 7–6 (9–7), 6–2.

Jan 27—Sixteenth-seeded Thomas Johansson of Sweden wins the men's Australian Open title, defeating Russia's Marat Safin 3–6, 6–4, 6–4, 7–6 (7–4) in the final, which lasts nearly three hours.

Feb 3—Martina Hingis has been in the final of all three tournaments played this season, and she wins her second, beating Monica Seles 7–6 (8–6), 4–6, 6–3 in the final of the Pan Pacific Open.

Feb 24—In only the 11th all-American ATP final since 1997, Andy Roddick tops James Blake to win the Kroger St. Jude tournament in Memphis.

Feb 25—Venus Williams becomes the first African-American in tennis history to top either the ATP or WTA rankings, when she takes the No. 1 spot in the WTA rankings.

March 10—Andre Agassi defeats Juan Balcells of Spain 6–2, 7–6 (7–2) to win the Franklin Templeton Classic in Scottsdale, Ariz.,

Serena Williams beat her sister Venus in the finals of three Grand Slam events in 2002.

for his 50th professional title. He is the eighth player in tennis history to reach 50 titles.

March 30—Serena Williams wins her first title of 2002, defeating top seed Jennifer Capriati in the final of the Nasdaq-100 Open in Miami.

March 30—Andre Agassi wins the Nasdaq-100 Open for the fifth time with a 6–3,6–3,3–6, 6–4 triumph over Switzerland's Roger Federer. Agassi's wife, Steffi Graf, also won five Nasdaq-100 Opens.

April 14—Claiming her fourth title of the year, Venus Williams rallies to defeat Justine Henin 2–6, 7–5, 7–6 (7–5) in the final of the Bausch & Lomb Championships on Amelia Island, Fla.

April 14—After a heated dispute over practice rules, captain Billie Jean King dismisses Jennifer Capriati from the U.S. Fed Cup team.

May 12—Nineteen-year-old Justine Henin of Belgium knocks off Serena Williams 6–2, 1–6, (7–6), 7–5 to win the German Open. In Rome, Andre Agassi takes the Italian Open with a 6–3, 6–3, 6–0 rout of Germany's Tommy Haas.

June 8—Venus and Serena Williams meet in the French Open final, marking the first time siblings have reached the Roland Garros final and held the No. 1 and No. 2 rankings in the world. Serena wins the match 7–5, 6–3.

June 9—With a 6–1, 6–0, 4–6, 6–3 triumph over countryman Juan Carlos Ferrero, Albert Costa of Spain wins the men's French Open singles title.

July 6—Meeting her sister Venus again in a Grand Slam final, Serena Williams again prevails in straight sets, winning at Wimbledon 7–6 (7–4), 6–3. The following day the sisters team up to win the women's doubles title.

July 9—Twenty-year-old Lleyton Hewitt of Australia wins Wimbledon, trouncing Argentina's David Nalbandian 6–1, 6–3, 6–2 in the final.

Aug 4—Venus Williams wins the Acura Classic at Carlsbad, Calif., for the third year in a row.

Aug 7—Without a victory since the 2000 Wimbledon, a 32-tournament span, Pete Sampras continues to struggle as he is ousted from the Tennis Masters Series Cincinnati by Australia's Wayne Arthurs, who wins 4–6, 6–3, 7–6 (7–4).

Aug 12—After undergoing ankle surgery in May, former

MANNY MILLAN

world No. 1 Martina Hingis returns to the WTA Tour, knocking off Spains's Magui Serna 6–4, 6–3 at the Rogers Cup in Montreal.

Sept 3—Smashing 27 aces, Pete Sampras defeats Tommy Haas 7–5, 6–4, 6–7 (7–5), 7–5 to advance to a quarterfinal match with Andy Roddick at the U.S. Open.

Sept 7—Andre Agassi upends defending U.S. Open champion and world No. 1 Lleyton Hewitt 6–4, 7–6, 6–7, 6–2 to advance to the final of the U.S. Open, where he will meet his longtime rival Pete Sampras, who defeats Sjeng Schalken 7–6, 7–6, 6–2 in the other semifinal.

Sept 7—For the third time this season, the Williams sisters meet in the final of a Grand Slam, and also for the third time, Serena wins. The younger sister establishes herself as the best player in the women's game with a 6–4, 6–3 triumph.

Sept 8—Completing a remarkable turnaround from what had been a lackluster and winless season for him, 31-year-old Pete Sampras wins

the U.S. Open with a 6–3, 6–4, 5–7, 6–4 victory over Andre Agassi in the final. It is Sampras's fifth U.S. Open championship and his 14th Grand Slam singles title.

Sept 29—Serena Williams wins her sixth title in seven tournaments, taking the Sparkassen Cup in Leipzig, Germany with a 6–3, 6–2 victory over Anastasia Mskina of Russia in the final. After the tournament, Williams, the world No. 1 who has not lost a match in four and a half months, says she's going on vacation.

Oct 13—Kim Clijsters of Belgium wins her eighth career title at the Porsche Grand Prix in Filderstadt, Germany, rallying from a set down in the final to beat Slovakia's Daniela Hantuchova 4–6, 6–3, 6–4.

Oct 18—Andre Agassi silences the home crowd with a 6–3, 6–2 dismissal of Spain's Juan Carlos Ferrero in the quarterfinals of the Tennis Masters Series Madrid. Two days later, Agassi, ranked No. 2 in the world, wins the tournament when Jiri Novak pulls out of the final with a groin injury. Agassi's victory cuts world No. 1 Lleyton Hewitt's lead in the rankings to 43 points with three events remaining.

Other Sports

Oct 31, 2001—French World Cup skier Regine Cavagnoud, 31, the 2000 super-G champion, dies two days after crashing into a coach from the German team on the Pitztal glacier in Austria.

Oct 31—The U.S. men's and women's gymnastics teams redeem their poor performances at the 2000 Sydney Olympics with a fine showing at the world championships in Ghent, Belgium. The men win the silver medal—their highest finish ever—and the women take the bronze. It is the first time both teams have finished in the top three at a world championships.

Nov 3—Ethiopia's Tesfaye Jifar wins the New York City marathon in a course-record time of 2:07:43. Margaret Okayo of Kenya wins the women's race in 2:24:21.

Nov 11—Walter Ray Williams Jr. wins the 34th PBA title of his career, routing rookie Mike Machuga 247–194 in the final of the Greater Cincinnati Classic. The win ties Williams with Mark Roth for second on the PBA's alltime victory list.

Nov 14—Leading a class of four into the National Track & Field Hall of Fame is nine-time Olympic gold medalist Carl Lewis. Boston and New York marathon champ Alberto Salazar, and four-time Olympians Henry Marsh and Larry Myricks are also inducted.

Nov 22—The World Cup event at Copper Mountain, Colo., begins with a tribute to fallen French skier Regine Cavagnoud, and ends with France's Laure Pequegnot winning the women's slalom title.

Nov 25—Croatia's Ivica Kostelic stuns the field in Aspen, Colo., by winning the men's slalom. Kostelic's previous best World Cup finish 21st.

Dec 9—The men's U.S. Open Bowling championships get their first foreign winner as Finland's Mike Koivuniemi defeats Patrick Healey 247–182 in the final, earning $100,000. In the Women's U.S. Open, Kim Terrell beats Wendy Macpherson 234–220 in the final to claim the record $55,000 winner's check.

Dec 9—Wrestler Rulon Gardner, a gold medalist at the 2000 Olympics, wins the heavyweight gold at the world Greco-Roman championships in Patras, Greece. In Franconia, N.H., Bode Miller becomes the first U.S. male skier to win a World Cup giant slalom since Phil Mahre in 1983.

Dec 15—Cody Ohl wins his first all-around title at the National Finals Rodeo in Las Vegas.

Jan 15, 2002—NCAA president Cedric Dempsey announces that he will retire on Dec. 31 2002. In October, Indiana University president Myles Brand is named to succeed him.

Jan 23—One day after he set world records in the 50- and 200-meter breaststrokes at the short-course World Cup meet in Stockholm, U.S. swimmer Ed Moses wins the 100-meter backstroke in 57.47 for his third world record in two days.

Feb 6—U.S. distance runner Tom Johnson beats top endurance horse Al Baraaq in an 80-mile race in Abu Dhabi, United Arab Emirates, covering the distance in 5 hours 45 minutes to defeat his equine counterpart by 10 seconds.

Feb 10—Russia's Svetlana Feofanova sets her third women's pole vault world record in a week clearing 15' 6¼" in Ghent, Belgium.

March 9—Louisiana State wins its ninth Division I women's indoor track title, while the Tennessee men win their first.

March 10—U.S. skiers Shannon Bahrke and Ann Battelle finish 1–2 in the moguls at a freestyle World Cup event in Iyama, Japan.

March 13—Martin Buser wins the Iditarod sled dog race completing the course in 8 days, 22 hours 46 minutes and two seconds.

March 23—With a 12–4 decision over Jon Trenge of Lehigh, Iowa State wrestler Cael Sanderson wins his fourth national title and his unprecedented 159th straight victory. Sanderson completes his college career without a loss.

March 24—Brown wins its second consecutive NCAA Division I women's ice hockey title, edging Minnesota-Duluth in the final.

April 6—Minnesota wins its first NCAA men's ice hockey championship since 1979, defeating Maine 4–3 in overtime.

April 14—Khalid Kannouchi, who became a U.S. citizen in 2000, wins the London Marathon in 2:05:38, shaving four seconds off the world record and holding off furious challenges from Kenya's Paul Tergat and Ethiopia's Haile Gebrselassie. Great Britain's Paula Radcliffe wins the women's race in 2:18:56.

April 15—Kenya's Rodgers Rop wins a tight Boston Marathon, clocking 2:09:02, to finish three seconds ahead of countryman Christopher Cheboiboch. Margaret Okayo sets a course record (2:20:43) while winning the women's race.

May 6—Parker Bohn III is named PBA player of the year for the second time in his career.

May 19—Princeton wins the NCAA women's lacrosse championship, downing Georgetown 12–7 in the final in Baltimore.

May 27—Syracuse wins its second NCAA lacrosse title in three years, edging Princeton 13-12 in front of 19,706 fans at Rutgers University.

June 18—Runner Alan Webb, who set the national high school mile record (3:53.43) in 2001, announces that he will leave the University of Michigan and turn pro.

June 22—Texas defeats South Carolina 12–6 to win the College World Series in Omaha, Neb.

July 25—Figure skating judge Marie-Reine Le Gougne, who was at the center of the pairs skating controversy at the Salt Lake City Olympics, drops her appeal of the three-year suspension imposed on her by the International Skating Union in May.

July 28—Lance Armstrong wins the Tour de France for the fourth consecutive year, finishing the 21-stage race 7:17 ahead of runner-up Joseba Beloki of Spain.

Aug 4—Nineteen-year-old Ian Thorpe of Australia wins his sixth gold medal of the Commonwealth Games in Manchester, England, anchoring the winning 4x100-meter medley relay team.

Aug 13—Natalie Coughlin becomes the first woman to break the one-minute barrier in the 100-meter backstroke, clocking 59.58 at the U.S. championships in Fort Lauderdale.

Aug 25—Louisville beats Sendai, Japan, 1–0 to win the Little League World Series in Williamsport, Pa. Louisville pitcher Aaron Alvey fires a three-hitter with 11 strikeouts and hits the game-winning home run in the first inning.

Aug 29—U.S. swimmers dominate the Pan Pacific championships in Yokohama, Japan, winning 21 gold medals. Australia wins 11 golds.

Sept 14—Tim Montgomery sets a world record in the 100-meter dash, clocking 9.78 in Paris to break Maurice Greene's three-year-old record by .01 seconds.

Sept 15—Italy defeats the U.S. 18–25, 25–18, 25–16, 22–25, 15–11 to win the Women's Volleyball World Championships in Berlin.

Oct 15—In only her second marathon, Great Britain's Paula Radcliffe breaks the women's world record in the event, clocking 2:17:18 to win in Chicago. Khalid Khannouchi wins the men's race in 2:05:56.

Radcliffe broke the marathon world record in her second attempt at the distance.

Baseball

JOHN IACONO

The World Series
champion
Anaheim Angels

Heaven Sent

Riding a string of divinely guided comebacks, the Angels won the first World Series in team history

BY MARK BECHTEL

THE 2002 postseason was all about monkeys—the rally monkey that became the mascot of the never-say-die Angels, and the symbolic simian living on the back of Barry Bonds, the Giants slugger who entered the playoffs desperate to rid himself of his reputation as a chronic October flop.

Not only was Bonds the active player with the most games played without winning a World Series, but his postseason statistical shortcomings were well-documented. In 27 playoff games before 2002, he had just one home run and six RBIs. But following a season in which his home run production dropped from 73 in 2001 to 46, the 38-year-old kicked things into overdrive in the playoffs. Bonds hit three homers in the Giants' five-game Division Series win over the Braves, and added one more—and six RBIs—in San Francisco's four-games-to-one NLCS win over the Cardinals. More incredibly, Bonds did all of that despite rarely seeing a decent pitch to hit. In the first two rounds of the playoffs, he walked 14 times—six of them intentional passes.

So while Giants fans spent much of their postseason waving rubber chickens at the opposition, Anaheim fans were waving stuffed monkeys. The practice dates back to June of 2000, when the Angels were trailing the Giants, of all teams. Anaheim's scoreboard operator showed a clip of Abbie, a capuchin monkey wearing an Angels jersey, on the video screen to get the crowd fired up, and the Halos responded by coming back to beat San Francisco closer Robb Nen in the ninth. With that, a tradition was born.

The monkey's finest moment came in Game 6 of the World Series—after Anaheim had dispatched the world champion Yankees (with three rally monkey–inspired comebacks) and the upstart Twins to reach its first Fall Classic. Facing elimination, and trailing 5–0 in the seventh, the Angels bats appeared dead. Their first 22 hitters had produced only two hits: an infield single and a Texas leaguer. But eight of the next 10 Anaheim hitters reached base. Scott Spiezio hit a three-run homer in the seventh to cut the lead to 5–3, and a three-run rally in the eighth—with the go-ahead run coming from

a Troy Glaus double off of Nen, the monkey's original victim—won it for the Angels. That set up the decisive Game 7, which belonged to Anaheim's 24-year-old righthander John Lackey, who allowed one run in five innings and became the first rookie in 93 years to win the seventh game of a World Series. Garret Anderson got the game winning hit in the 4–1 win with a bases-clearing double in the third inning.

As for Bonds, while he remained ringless, he did exorcise his personal playoff demons, setting a postseason record with eight home runs and producing ridiculously gaudy numbers in the World Series—a .471 average, a 1.294 slugging percentage and a .700 on-base percentage.

It was fitting that two wild-card teams dominated the postseason, because the regular season was full of surprising teams as well. Sure, the Yankees won 103 games, but that league-leading win total was matched by a surprising squad—the Oakland A's, who lost their best player, Jason Giambi, in free agency to the Bombers during the off-season. They also lost leadoff man Johnny

Glaus, the Series MVP, hit .385 with three doubles, three home runs and eight RBIs.

Damon, who signed with the Red Sox. Their departures didn't kill Oakland's chances, but for a while it looked like they might.

The A's got off to a horrible start, and a three-game sweep by the Blue Jays in mid-May dropped Oakland to 19-24, 10 games behind first-place Seattle. The team that earned a reputation for having one of baseball's loosest—yet most cohesive—clubhouses was going sour off the field, too. On May 19, after an 11-0 loss to Toronto in the final game of the trip, manager Art Howe must have expected a subdued flight back to the West Coast. Instead, outfielder Jeremy Giambi put on a what a local paper quoted a team source as calling a "drunken, obnoxious" performance.

That was the last straw. GM Billy Beane began a housecleaning the next day that sent second baseman Frank Menechino, first baseman Carlos Peña and reliever Jeff Tam to Triple A Sacramento, and Giambi to the Philadelphia Phillies in return for journeyman outfielder John Mabry. The moves were shocking. Giambi was a popular player in the midst of the best year of his career. Menechino, a decent player, was the unofficial clubhouse leader, and the highly touted Peña had been acquired from the Rangers in the offseason to be Jason Giambi's replacement. (Frustrated by Peña's .240 average in Sacramento and his refusal to make adjustments at the plate, the A's exiled him to Detroit in early July.)

"People were starting to place too much of an emphasis on how great the clubhouse atmosphere was and not enough on playing soundly," said Beane. "And that's what we started to become known as—a fun team. Well, that's great. But if you're a fun team that loses, it defeats the purpose. We felt some changes were needed." The moves—and the subsequent acquisitions of quiet veterans like second baseman Ray Durham and reliever Ricardo Rincon—paid dividends. The working environment was more professional. In the words of third baseman Eric Chavez, "It's still a great, enjoyable clubhouse but not as insane."

The A's immediately elevated their play, and in mid-August they reached truly rarefied air. Starting on the 13th, Oakland won an American League–record 20 straight games, with the first 11 of those victories going to their starting pitchers, who established themselves as the league's best rotation. Great things had been expected of Oakland's top three of Tim Hudson, Barry Zito and Mark Mulder, but things were going so well that the team's fourth starter, Cory Lidle, threw 32⅔ consecutive scoreless innings in one stretch.

On offense, shortstop Miguel Tejada improved dramatically, going a long way toward making up for the loss of Giambi. "He used to be erratic, but no more," said Mariners manager Lou Piniella. "He hits for average, he hits for power, he drives in runs, and he's an athletic kid. He's got a great future."

Yet when Oakland's record streak was finally snapped, by the Twins, the A's were only three games ahead of the Angels, who ran off a 10-game winning streak of their own. Anaheim's success in 2002 was every bit as surprising as Oakland's. The two teams had much in common: they had the AL's top two pitching staffs, each anchored by a twentysomething lefthander (the A's 24-year-old Zito, the Angels' 28-year-old Jarrod Washburn), as well as breakout MVP candidates (Tejada and Anaheim leftfielder Garret Anderson). When the season ended, the Angels had the best batting average and second-best ERA in the AL and the wild-card berth for their first playoff appearance since 1986.

They were joined in the postseason by another team that had endured a lengthy postseason absence, the Twins. After surprising their AL Central foes with a spirited run in 2001, then being threatened with contraction as the 2002 season dawned, the Twins ran away with their division despite losing pitcher Joe Mays for much of the year with an arm injury and seeing their two other aces, Brad Radke and Eric Milton, have off years. But no one in the Central even challenged them. The White Sox were too inconsistent, and the Indians, who had won the division every year since its inception, dismantled their team in the name of fiscal responsibility.

The Tribe initially planned on restocking its depleted farm system while still trying to win the division. They shipped second baseman Robert Alomar, a future Hall of Famer in the prime of his career, to the Mets in the offseason for outfielder Matt Lawton and prospects. The loss of Alomar, coupled with the team's decision not to re-sign free agent Juan Gonzalez, left them with an offense that was mediocre at best. By June it became apparent that Cleveland wasn't going to contend. "It's a very difficult thing to do, transition and contend," said GM Mark Shapiro. "We couldn't. We have openly admitted that we're rebuilding."

And with that, they shipped their young ace, Bartolo Colon, to the Expos, another team that survived a proposed contraction to contend for a postseason spot. The move was hard to swallow, both for the fans who were responsible for Jacobs Field being sold out for the better part of five straight sea-

The dramatically improved Tejada made up for Giambi's departure from Oakland.

sons, and the Indians players. "Bartolo was our man," reliever Paul Shuey said. "But the reality is that we're going through a rebuilding stage and it's a tough pill to swallow."

Within a month Shuey was gone, too, sent to the Dodgers. The Tribe also dealt Chuck Finley to the Cardinals, who also acquired third baseman Scott Rolen from the Phillies. The new pickups helped deliver the NL Central pennant to St. Louis. Joining the Cardinals in the postseason were the Braves, who continued to rule the NL East, as well as the defending champion Arizona Diamondbacks, who rode the arms of Curt Schilling and Randy Johnson to the West division title.

The Diamondbacks two big guns spent the season dueling for the Cy Young award. Schilling looked like the early favorite, and at one point his season stats listed 21 wins and 20 walks. But he struggled down the stretch, allowing Johnson, who went 24–5, to stake a claim for his fourth consecutive Cy Young. The Big Unit added a split-finger fastball to his already formidable repertoire of a fastball in the high-90s and a devilish slider. "I think this year has been better than last year," Arizona manager Bob Brenly said. "I think the experiences he went through last year made him a better pitcher, and he realizes now, I believe, that he's got other ways to get hitters out. If you have to face him, that's a terrifying thought."

The Giants finished 2½ games behind the

D'backs to claim the NL wild-card, holding off the Dodgers down the stretch. On the flip side of this season of surprises, the Giants—or anyone else, for that matter—didn't have to worry about the Mets, playoff contenders in recent years who had retooled their team with World Series hopes in mind. The Mets were never in the race. The first indication that something was rotten in Flushing came in April, when shortstop Rey Ordoñez made eight errors, or twice as many as he made during the entire 1999 season. The final indication came in September when Ordoñez blasted the fans. "The fans here are too stupid," he said. "You have to play perfect every game. You can't make an error. You can't go 0 for 4. Are we like machines?" The Mets machine ground to a halt in last place in the NL East, with a 75–86 record.

While Ordoñez and his teammates showed their all-too-human sides, some players went superhuman in 2002. Seattle's Mike Cameron and LA's Shawn Green each homered four times in a game in May. Shortstop Alfonso Soriano of the Yankees and outfielder Vladimir Guerrero of the Expos each came within one homer of joining the 40–40 club. Alex Rodriguez, in the second year of a 10-year, $252 million deal with Texas, hit 57 homers, the most ever for

CHUCK SOLOMON

A leadoff man, Soriano drove in 102 runs, hit .300 and came within one homer of joining the exclusive 40-40 club.

a shortstop. And Bonds became the fourth player to top 600 career home runs, finishing the season with 613. The 38-year-old also became the oldest first-time batting champ, leading the NL with a .370 average, and he set major league records for walks (198) and on-base percentage (.582).

For all its pleasant surprises and stunning performances, the season wasn't without its dubious moments. The two most significant of these involved the Milwaukee Brewers, the team formerly owned by commissioner Bud Selig. Milwaukee hosted the All-Star game in July, and Selig was forced to call the game after 11 innings with the score tied at 7–7 after both managers had exhausted their pitching staffs. The decision was the right one—how would he have explained it to a GM if he had to send a pitcher back to a team with an arm injury suffered in the increasingly meaningless exhibition that is the All-Star game?—but it was a public relations nightmare, as fans booed, shouted for

refunds and were shown in newspapers coast to coast the next morning giving the emphatic thumbs-down signal to the decision. "My heart was breaking because this is the last thing in the world I wanted to have happen," Selig said. "The more I talked to [the managers], I realized I didn't have what I consider a reasonable alternative. I didn't want to turn the game into a farce by having [Brewers shortstop] Jose Hernandez come into pitch, maybe have a 12-run inning and besmirch every All-Star record."

The season's other low moment also involved Hernandez, a free-swinger who looked like a safe bet to break Bobby Bonds's single-season record of 189 strikeouts. But when he got to 188 manager Jerry Royster stopped playing him, even though he was one of Milwaukee's best hitters, and Hernandez did not object. "I don't think I can get criticized for not breaking the record, [which] people wanted to see," Hernandez said. "I am not going to show them."

The World Series, which was otherwise compelling, featured another lowlight. That came when a credit card company tapped fans to vote for the 10 greatest moments in the history of the game. The results of this vote, which were announced in a ceremony prior to Game 4 in San Francisco, were skewed, to put it mildly. Absent were Bobby Thomson's epochal home run off Ralph Branca in 1951, Carlton Fisk's famous foul-pole-flirting homer against the Reds in 1975, and Joe Carter's walk-off World Series winner in 1993, to name just a few.

Selig presided over this farce as well, but despite the fact that the season's three most dubious episodes involved the team he once owned, or his misguided leadership, Selig did have one very positive moment in 2002. With the threat of yet another labor stoppage looming over the sport, baseball's owners and players reached an agreement on a new collective bargaining agreement hours before the strike deadline in September. The labor peace kept the postseason from being cancelled for the second time in eight years, which paved the way for some memorable monkey business.

Final Standings

National League
EASTERN DIVISION

Team	Won	Lost	Pct	GB	Home	Away
Atlanta	101	59	.631	—	52–28	49–31
Montreal	83	79	.512	19	49–32	34–47
Philadelphia	80	81	.497	21½	40–40	40–41
Florida	79	83	.488	23	46–35	33–48
New York	75	86	.466	26½	38–43	37–43

CENTRAL DIVISION

Team	Won	Lost	Pct	GB	Home	Away
St. Louis	97	65	.599	—	52–29	45–36
Houston	84	78	.519	13	47–34	37–44
Cincinnati	78	84	.481	19	38–43	40–41
Pittsburgh	72	89	.447	24½	38–42	34–47
Chicago	67	95	.414	30	36–45	31–50
Milwaukee	56	106	.346	41	31–50	25–56

WESTERN DIVISION

Team	Won	Lost	Pct	GB	Home	Away
Arizona	98	64	.605	—	55–26	43–38
†San Francisco	95	66	.590	2½	50–31	45–35
Los Angeles	92	70	.568	6	46–35	46–35
Colorado	73	89	.451	25	47–34	26–55
San Diego	66	96	.407	32	41–40	25–56

†Wild-card team.

American League
EASTERN DIVISION

Team	Won	Lost	Pct	GB	Home	Away
New York	103	58	.640	—	52–28	51–30
Boston	93	69	.574	10½	42–39	51–30
Toronto	78	84	.481	25½	42–39	36–45
Baltimore	67	95	.414	36½	34–47	33–48
Tampa Bay	55	106	.342	48	30–51	25–55

CENTRAL DIVISION

Team	Won	Lost	Pct	GB	Home	Away
Minnesota	94	67	.584	—	54–27	40–40
Chicago	81	81	.500	13.5	47–34	34–47
Cleveland	74	88	.457	20.5	39–42	35–46
Kansas City	62	100	.383	32.5	37–44	25–56
Detroit	55	106	.342	39	33–47	22–59

WESTERN DIVISION

Team	Won	Lost	Pct	GB	Home	Away
Oakland	103	59	.636	—	54–27	49–32
†Anaheim	99	63	.611	4	54–27	45–36
Seattle	93	69	.574	10	48–33	45–36
Texas	72	90	.444	31	42–39	30–51

2002 Playoffs

National League Division Playoffs

Oct 1 ....St. Louis 12 at Arizona 2
Oct 3 ....St. Louis 2 at Arizona 1

Oct 5 ....Arizona 3 at St. Louis 6

(St. Louis won series 3–0)

Oct 2 ....San Francisco 8 at Atlanta 5
Oct 3 ....San Francisco 3 at Atlanta 7
Oct 5 ....Atlanta 10 at San Francisco 2

Oct 6 ....Atlanta 3 at San Francisco 8
Oct 7 ....San Francisco 3 at Atlanta 1

(San Francisco won series 3–2)

National League Championship Series

Oct 9 ....San Francisco 9 at St. Louis 6
Oct 10 ....San Francisco 4 at St. Louis 1
Oct 12 ....St. Louis 5 at San Francisco 4

Oct 13 ....St. Louis 3 at San Francisco 4
Oct 14 ....St. Louis 1 at San Francisco 2

(San Francisco won series 4–1)

GAME 1

											R	H	E
San Francisco	1	4	1	0	1	2	0	0	0		**9**	**11**	**0**
St. Louis	0	1	0	0	2	2	0	1	0		**6**	**11**	**0**

W—Rueter. **L**—Morris. **SV**—Nen.
LOB—SF 6, StL 8. **2B**—StL: Marrero, Edmonds.
3B—SF: Bonds. **HR**—SF: Lofton, Bell, Santiago; StL: Pujols, Cairo, Drew. **S**—SF: Aurilia; StL: Morris. **SB**—SF: Lofton. **CS**—StL: Robinson. **HBP**—StL: Renteria.
GIDP—SF: Santiago; StL: Renteria. **T**—3:31. **A**—52,175.

Recap: Barry Bonds' two-run triple highlighted a four-run second inning as San Francisco jumped on St. Louis's ace, Matt Morris, early. The Giants hammered Morris for seven runs and 10 hits in 4 ⅓ innings. Bonds contributed to a big night by the middle of the San Francisco order, going 1-for-2 with three walks, two runs scored and two RBIs. Jeff Kent, Bonds and Benito Santiago combined for six hits, six RBIs and four runs scored.

GAME 2

											R	H	E
San Francisco	1	0	0	0	2	0	0	0	1		**4**	**7**	**0**
St. Louis	0	0	0	0	0	0	0	1	0		**1**	**6**	**0**

W—Schmidt. **L**—Williams. **SV**—Nen.
LOB—SF 7, StL 5. **2B**—StL: Edmonds. **3B**—SF: Snow. **HR**—SF: Aurilia 2; StL: Perez. **S**—SF: Schmidt, Martinez; StL: Williams. **T**—3:17. **A**—52,195.

Recap: Jason Schmidt carried a shutout into the eighth inning and Rich Aurilia homered twice as San Francisco swept the first two games in St. Louis. Schmidt allowed only four hits and a walk while whiffing eight Cardinals in eight-plus innings. Aurilia's two-run shot in the fifth gave him 11 RBIs for the postseason, tying the record for most runs driven in by a shortstop in the playoffs.

National League Championship Series (Cont.)

GAME 3

St. Louis	0	0 2	1 1 1	0 0 0	**5**	**6**	**1**
San Francisco	0	1 0	0 3 0	0 0 0	**4**	**10**	**0**

W—Finley. **L**—Witasick. **SV**—Isringhausen.
E—StL: Renteria. **LOB**—StL 5, SF 11. **2B**—StL: Pujols, Vina; SF: Aurilia. **HR**—StL: Matheny, Edmonds, Marrero; SF: Bonds. **S**—SF: Aurilia, Dunston, Ortiz. **SF**: StL: Renteria; SF: Aurilia. **GIDP**—SF: Snow. **T**—3:32. **A**—42,177.

Recap: After a solo homer by Eli Marrero snapped a sixth-inning tie, St. Louis got a fine effort from its bullpen to get back into the series. Dave Veres, Steve Kline, Rick White and Jason Isringhausen shut down the Giants in the final four innings to preserve the 5–4 win. Barry Bonds was a factor again, hitting a three-run homer in the fifth inning that erased a 4–1 deficit. He also walked three times but popped up with the bases loaded and two outs in the second.

GAME 4

St. Louis	2 0 0	0 0 0	0 0 1	**3**	**12**	**0**
San Francisco	0 0 0	0 0 2	0 2 x	**4**	**4**	**1**

W—Worrell. **L**—White. **SV**—Nen.
E—SF: Aurilia. **LOB**—StL 11, SF 5. **2B**—StL: Vina, Matheny; SF: Snow. **HR**—SF: Santiago. **S**—StL: Renteria, Benes; SF: Hernandez. **GIDP**—StL: Drew, Vina. **SB**—StL: Martinez. **T**—3:26. **A**—42,676.

GAME 4 (Cont.)

Recap: After an intentional walk to Barry Bonds with two outs in the eighth inning, Benito Santiago, who would be named MVP of the series, rose to the challenge and hit a two-run homer that lifted San Francisco to a 4–3 win. Robb Nen escaped danger in the top of the ninth to nail down his third save of the LCS. After Jim Edmonds singled in a run, Nen struck out Albert Pujols and J.D. Drew with the tying run on third to end the threat.

GAME 5

St. Louis	0 0 0	0 0 0	1 0 0	**1**	**9**	**0**
San Francisco	0 0 0	0 0 0	0 1 1	**2**	**7**	**0**

W—Worrell. **L**—Morris.
LOB—StL 10, SF 9. **2B**—StL: Matheny; SF: Bell. **S**—StL: Morris; SF: Aurilia. **SF**—StL: Vina; SF: Bonds. **GIDP**—SF: Kent. **HBP**—SF: Lofton, Aurilia, Kent. **T**—3:01. **A**—42,673.

Recap: Kenny Lofton hit an RBI single with two outs in the ninth inning, sending San Francisco to the World Series for the first time since 1989. Barry Bonds, who has underperformed in recent postseasons, did his part by hitting a game-tying sacrifice fly in the eighth off Matt Morris. Morris got the first two outs in the ninth, but after two singles, he was lifted in favor of Steve Kline. Lofton connected on Kline's first offering.

American League Division Playoffs

Oct 1 ....Minnesota 7 at Oakland 5
Oct 2 ....Minnesota 1 at Oakland 9
Oct 4 ....Oakland 6 at Minnesota 3
Oct 5 ....Oakland 2 at Minnesota 11
Oct 6 ....Minnesota 5 at Oakland 4

(Minnesota won series 3–2)

Oct 1 ....Anaheim 5 at New York 8
Oct 2 ....Anaheim 8 at New York 6
Oct 4 ....New York 6 at Anaheim 9
Oct 5 ....New York 5 at Anaheim 9

(Anaheim won series 3–1)

American League Championship Series

Oct 8 ....Anaheim 1 at Minnesota 2
Oct 9 ....Anaheim 6 at Minnesota 3
Oct 11 ....Minnesota 1 at Anaheim 2
Oct 12 ....Minnesota 1 at Anaheim 7
Oct 13 ....Minnesota 5 at Anaheim 13

(Anaheim won series 4–1)

GAME 1

Anaheim	0 0 1	0 0 0	0 0 0	**1**	**4**	**0**
Minnesota	0 1 0	0 1 0	0 0 x	**2**	**5**	**1**

W—Mays. **L**—Appier. **SV**—Guardado.
E—Minn: Guzman. **LOB**—Ana 4, Minn 7. **2B**—Minn: Hunter, Koskie. **Sac**—Minn: Hunter. **SF**—Minn: Pierzynski. **HBP**—Minn: Guzman. **GIDP**—Ana: Salmon. **T**—2:58. **A**—55,562.

Recap: Joe Mays limited Anaheim to four singles in eight innings, and 55,000 fans cheered the Twins to a 2–1 Game 1 victory. Minnesota improved to 13–2 alltime in the Metrodome during the postseason. The Twins took the lead in the second when Torii Hunter doubled, advanced on a wild pitch and came home on A.J. Pierzynski's sacrifice fly. After Anaheim tied the score on an unearned run in the third, Corey Koskie scored Luis Rivas with a double in the fifth to put Minnesota back on top for good.

GAME 2

Anaheim	1 3 0	0 0 2	0 0 0	**6**	**10**	**0**
Minnesota	0 0 0	0 0 3	0 0 0	**3**	**11**	**1**

W—Ortiz. **L**—Reed. **SV**—Percival.
E—Minn: Pierzynski. **LOB**—Ana 6, Minn 7. **2B**—Ana: Fullmer, Spiezio; Minn: Guzman, Hunter. **3B**—Ana: Glaus. **HR**—Ana: Erstad, Fullmer. **GIDP**—Minn: Hunter, Rivas. **CS**—Ana: Spiezio. **WP**—Minn: Santana. **T**—3:13. **A**—55,990.

Recap: Anaheim jumped out to a six-run lead and escaped the Metrodome with a 1–1 split after the first two games of ALCS. The Angels scored three runs in the second when Minnesota bungled a rundown play and catcher A.J. Pierzynski couldn't hold onto the ball on a play at the plate. Minnesota crept back into the game with three runs in the sixth, only to see Anaheim closer Troy Percival extinguish the threat in the ninth.

American League Championship Series *(Cont.)*

GAME 3

Minnesota	0	0	0	0	0	0	1	0	0	**1**	**6**	**0**
Anaheim	0	1	0	0	0	0	1	x		**2**	**7**	**2**

W—Rodriguez. **L**—Romero. **SV**—Percival.
E—Ana: Eckstein, Gil. **LOB**—Minn 7, Ana 9. **2B**—Minn: Jones; Ana: Anderson, Glaus. **S**—Ana: Gil. **SB**—Minn: Mohr. **WP**—Minn: Santana. **T**—3:13. **A**—44,234.

Recap: Troy Glaus hit a solo homer in the bottom of the eighth inning to give Anaheim a 2–1 victory. Jarrod Washburn and Eric Milton locked up in a duel as the Angels took a 1–0 lead to the seventh. Anaheim's Washburn left after that inning, having allowed one run and six hits while striking out seven and walking none. Milton was almost as good, yielding a run and five hits with two walks and four strikeouts in six innings. With the help of two superb catches in the outfield, Troy Percival fired a perfect ninth for his second straight save and fourth of the playoffs.

GAME 4

Minnesota	0	0	0	0	0	0	0	0	1	**1**	**6**	**2**
Anaheim	0	0	0	0	0	0	2	5	x	**7**	**10**	**0**

W—Lackey. **L**—Radke.
E—Minn: Pierzynski, Santana. **LOB**—Minn 4, Ana 5. **2B**—Minn: Mientkiewicz, Koskie; Ana: Spiezio, Fullmer. **3B**—Ana: Molina. **S**—Ana: Kennedy. **HBP**—Ana: Molina. **SB**—Ana: Erstad. **CS**—Minn: Pierzynski. **T**—2:49. **A**—44,830.

GAME 4 *(Cont.)*

Recap: Troy Glaus delivered a key late-inning hit for the second straight night, singling in the go-ahead run in the seventh inning, as Anaheim pulled away for a 7–1 victory. The Angels broke open the game with five runs in the eighth, but the cushion proved unnecessary as rookie John Lackey went seven innings limiting the Twins to three hits, and striking out seven without issuing a single walk.

GAME 5

Minnesota	1	1	0	0	0	0	3	0	0	**5**	**9**	**0**
Anaheim	0	0	1	0	2	0	10	0	x	**13**	**18**	**0**

W—Rodriguez. **L**—Santana.
LOB—Minn 3, Ana 5. **2B**—Minn: Ortiz, Mohr. **HR**—Kennedy 3, Spiezio. **S**—Minn: Guzman. **GIDP**—Minn: Rivas, Hunter; Ana: Fullmer. **HBP**—Ana: Eckstein. **CS**—Ana: Anderson. **WP**—Minn: Romero; Ana: Appier, Donnelly, Rodriguez. **T**—3:30. **A**—44,835.

Recap: Adam Kennedy tied a playoff record with three home runs, including a go-ahead three-run shot in a 10-run seventh inning, as Anaheim advanced to their first World Series. After Minnesota rallied for three runs in the top of the seventh to take a 5–3 lead, the Angels blitzed the Twins' bullpen in the bottom of the inning. Kennedy, who was only 1 for 10 in the first four games, went 4 for 4 with five RBI and was named MVP of the series.

Composite Box Scores

National League Championship Series

SAN FRANCISCO

BATTING	AB	R	H	HR	RBI	Avg
Dunston	2	0	1	0	0	.500
Bell	17	4	7	1	4	.412
Aurilia	15	4	5	2	5	.333
Santiago	20	2	6	2	6	.300
Bonds	11	5	3	1	6	.273
Kent	19	3	5	0	2	.263
Snow	20	1	5	0	2	.250
Lofton	21	4	5	1	2	.238
Sanders	16	0	1	0	0	.063
Feliz	1	0	0	0	0	.000
Goodwin	3	0	0	0	0	.000
Martinez	1	0	0	0	1	.000
Shinjo	1	0	0	0	0	.000
Pitchers	11	0	1	0	0	.091
Totals	158	23	39	7	23	.247

PITCHING	G	IP	H	BB	SO	ERA
Eyre	4	1⅔	2	0	0	0.00
Fultz	1	⅓	0	0	0	0.00
Schmidt (1–0)	1	7⅔	4	1	8	1.17
Rodriguez	4	4⅔	3	2	2	1.93
Worrell (2–0)	4	4⅓	2	0	3	2.08
Nen (3 SV)	3	3⅓	3	1	4	2.70
Hernandez	1	6⅓	9	1	0	2.84
Rueter (1–0)	2	11	15	2	3	4.09
Ortiz	1	4⅔	5	3	3	7.71
Witasick (0–1)	1	1	1	0	0	9.00
Totals	5	45	44	10	23	3.20

ST. LOUIS

BATTING	AB	R	H	HR	RBI	Avg
Edmonds	20	2	8	1	4	.400
Cairo	13	2	5	1	2	.385
Drew	13	1	5	1	1	.385
Matheny	19	2	6	1	1	.316
Pujols	19	2	5	1	2	.263
Vina	23	2	6	0	2	.261
Perez	4	1	1	1	1	.250
Marrero	16	1	3	1	1	.188
Renteria	19	0	3	0	1	.158
Martinez	14	1	2	0	1	.143
DiFelice	1	0	0	0	0	.000
Robinson	2	1	0	0	0	.000
Pitchers	8	1	0	0	0	.125
Totals	171	16	44	7	16	.257

PITCHING	G	IP	H	BB	SO	ERA
Fassero	1	⅔	0	0	1	0.00
Kline	4	2⅓	2	0	1	0.00
Veres	2	3⅔	2	1	5	0.00
Benes	1	5⅓	2	4	5	3.38
Is'hausen (1 SV)	2	2	1	3	3	4.50
White (0–1)	3	4	2	2	5	4.50
Williams (0–1)	1	6	6	1	7	4.50
Morris (0–2)	2	13	16	6	6	6.23
Finley (1–0)	1	5	7	3	1	7.20
Crudale	1	1⅔	1	1	2	10.80
Totals	5	43⅔	39	21	36	4.74

American League Championship Series

ANAHEIM

BATTING	AB	R	H	HR	RBI	Avg
Figgins 1	2	1	0	0	1.000
Erstad..............22	4	8	1	2	.364
Kennedy...........14	5	5	5	3	5	.357
Spiezio 17	5	6	1	5	.353
Fullmer 12	2	4	1	4	.333
Glaus...............19	4	6	1	2	.316
Eckstein..........21	1	6	0	2	.286
Anderson..........20	3	5	1	3	.250
Wooten 8	1	2	0	1	.250
B. Molina 14	0	3	0	2	.214
Salmon 14	0	3	0	0	.214
Ochoa 4	2	0	0	0	.000
Gil.....................2	0	0	0	0	.000
Palmeiro 2	0	0	0	0	.000
J. Molina............1	0	0	0	0	.000
Totals.............171	29	49	8	26	.287

PITCHING	G	IP	H	BB	SO	ERA
Lackey (1–0) 1	7	3	0	7	0.00
Rodriguez (2–0) 4	4⅓	2	2	7	0.00
Percival (2 SV)...3	3⅓	0	0	3	0.00
Schoeneweis.....1	⅔	0	0	0	0.00
Washburn..........1	7	6	0	7	1.29
Weber...............3	2⅔	3	0	3	3.38
Appier (0–1) 2	10⅓	10	4	3	3.48
Ortiz (1–0) 1	5⅓	10	1	3	5.06
Donnelly 3	3⅓	3	0	5	8.10
Totals.................5	44	37	7	38	2.45

MINNESOTA

BATTING	AB	R	H	HR	RBI	Avg
Mohr 12	3	5	0	0	.417
LeCroy...............3	0	1	0	0	.333
Ortiz 16	0	5	0	2	.313
Koskie 18	3	5	0	2	.278
Mientkiewicz....18	1	5	0	2	.278
Pierzynski 16	1	4	0	2	.250
Rivas 12	1	3	0	0	.250
Cuddyer 5	0	1	0	0	.200
Guzman 18	1	3	0	0	.167
Hunter 18	2	3	0	0	.167
Jones 20	0	2	0	2	.100
Kielty 3	0	0	0	1	.000
Prince 1	0	0	0	0	.000
Totals.............160	12	37	0	11	.231

PITCHING	G	IP	H	BB	SO	ERA
Guardado (1 SV) 1	1	0	1	2	0.00
Lohse 1	1	0	0	1	0.00
Milton.................1	6	5	2	4	1.50
Mays (1–0) 2	13⅓	12	0	3	2.03
Radke (0–1).......1	6⅔	5	1	4	2.70
Wells.................2	1	2	0	2	9.00
Reed (0–1) 1	5⅓	8	0	0	10.13
Santana (0–1)....4	3⅓	4	0	4	10.80
Hawkins............4	1⅓	4	1	1	20.25
Romero (0–1) 4	2	4	2	3	22.50
Jackson 3	1	5	2	2	27.00
Totals.................5	42	49	9	26	5.57

2002 World Series

Oct 19 ....San Francisco 4 at Anaheim 3	Oct 24 ....Anaheim 4 at San Francisco 16
Oct 20 ....San Francisco 10 at Anaheim 11	Oct 26 ....San Francisco 5 at Anaheim 6
Oct 22 ....Anaheim 10 at San Francisco 4	Oct 27 ....San Francisco 1 at Anaheim 4
Oct 23 ....Anaheim 3 at San Francisco 4	

(Anaheim won series 4–3)

GAME 1

```
San Francisco 0  2  0  0  0  2  0  0  0   4  6  0
Anaheim       0  1  0  0  0  2  0  0/0  3  9  0
```

W—Schmidt. **L**—Washburn. **SV**—Nen.
LOB—SF 5, Ana 8. **2B**—Ana: Kennedy, Spiezio.
HR—SF: Bonds, Sanders, Snow; Ana: Glaus 2.
Sac—SF: Lofton. **SB**—Ana: Fullmer. **T**—3:44. **A**—44,603.

Recap: The game's first three hits were home runs, including a 418-foot drive by Barry Bonds in his first World Series at-bat, and the San Francisco bullpen shut down all of the Angels except Troy Glaus en route to a 4–3 victory in Game 1. Bolstered by 3⅓ innings of hitless relief and a sparkling defensive play from first baseman J.T. Snow, the Giants handed the Angels their first home loss of the postseason.

GAME 2

```
San Francisco 0  4  1  0  4  0  0  0  1  10 12  1
Anaheim       5  2  0  0  1  1  0  2  x  11 16  1
```

W—Rodriguez. **L**—Rodriguez. **SV**—Percival.
E—SF: Lofton; Ana: Anderson. **LOB**—SF 4, Ana 5.
2B—SF: Aurilia; Ana: Erstad 2, Glaus. **HR**—SF: Sanders, Bell, Kent, Bonds; Ana: Salmon 2. **SF**—Ana: Spiezio. **GIDP**—Ana: Molina. **SB**—SF: Sanders; Ana:

GAME 2 *(Cont.)*

Spiezio, Fullmer. **PB**—SF: Santiago. **T**—3:57. **A**—44,584.

Recap: Anaheim squandered a 5–0 lead and needed two Tim Salmon home runs to pull out an 11–10 victory and even the Series at one win apiece. Anaheim's 20-year-old Francisco Rodriguez became the youngest pitcher to earn a WS victory, throwing three perfect innings of relief. Salmon went 4 for 4 with a walk, driving in four runs and scoring three.

GAME 3

```
Anaheim       0  0  4  4  0  1  0  1  0  10 16  0
San Francisco 1  0  0  0  3  0  0  0  0  4  6  2
```

W—Ortiz. **L**—Hernandez.
E—SF: Bell, Santiago. **LOB**—Ana 15, SF 7. **2B**—Ana: Kennedy, Erstad, Salmon. **3B**—Ana: Spiezio. **HR**—SF: Aurilia, Bonds. **S**—SF: Hernandez. **GIDP**—SF: Bell; Ana: Spiezio. **SB**—SF: Lofton; Ana: Salmon, Erstad. **HBP**—Ana: Kennedy. **T**—3:37. **A**—42,707.

Recap: The Angels became the first team in Series history to bat around in consecutive innings, unleashing a torrent of hits, walks and steals to take an 8-1 lead by the fourth inning. Barry Bonds set a postseason record with his seventh home run.

GAME 4

Anaheim	0	1	2	0	0	0	0	0	**3**	**10**	**1**
San Francisco	0	0	0	0	3	0	0	1	x	**4**	**12**	**1**

W—Worrell. **L**—Rodriguez. **SV**—Nen.
E—Ana: Salmon; SF: Bell. **LOB**—Ana 5, SF 8. **2B**—SF: Aurilia. **HR**—Ana: Glaus. **SF**—Ana: Eckstein; SF: Kent. **GIDP**—Ana: Glaus, Molina, Fullmer; SF: Santiago 2. **SB**—SF: Goodwin. **CS**—SF: Bell. **PB**—Ana: Molina. **T**—3:02. **A**—42,703.

Recap: David Bell lined a tiebreaking single off rookie sensation Francisco Rodriguez in the eighth inning and the Giants came back from a 3–0 deficit to even the Series. Kenny Lofton had three hits, including a bunt single that extended a fifth-inning rally.

GAME 5

Anaheim	0	0	0	0	3	1	0	0	0	**4**	**10**	**2**
San Francisco	3	3	0	0	0	2	4	4	x	**16**	**16**	**0**

W—Zerbe. **L**—Washburn.
E—Ana: Erstad, Glaus. **LOB**—Ana 9, SF 8. **2B**—Ana: Palmeiro, Glaus, Gil; SF: Bonds 2, Kent. **3B**—SF: Lofton. **HR**—SF: Kent 2, Aurilia. **S**—SF: Schmidt, Shinjo. **SF**—Ana: Erstad; SF: Santiago, Sanders. **SB**—Ana: Eckstein. **T**—3:53. **A**—42,713.

Recap: San Francisco jumped all over Angels' ace Jarrod Washburn, and Jeff Kent sealed it with a pair of two-run homers. The Giants tied a Series record with their 12th home run, and the total of 17 by both teams equaled another record.

GAME 6

San Francisco	0	0	0	0	3	1	0	0	**5**	**8**	**1**
Anaheim	0	0	0	0	0	0	3	3	x	**6**	**10**	**1**

W—Donnelly. **L**—Worrell. **SV**—Percival.
E—SF: Bonds; Ana: B Molina. **LOB**—SF 6, Ana 6. **2B**—SF: Lofton; Ana: Glaus. **HR**—SF: Dunston, Bonds; Ana: Spiezio, Erstad. **S**—Ana: J Molina. **GIDP**—SF: Santiago; Ana: Anderson. **SB**—SF: Lofton 2. **WP**—Ana: Rodriguez. **T**—3:48. **A**—44,506.

Recap: World Series MVP Troy Glaus lined a two-run double after a key misplay by Barry Bonds in the eighth, capping a wild rally that forced a Game 7. After spotting the Giants a 5–0 lead, the Angels got a homer from Scott Spiezio in the seventh to make it 5-3. A solo shot by Darin Erstad started the rally in the eighth.

GAME 7

San Francisco	0	1	0	0	0	0	0	0	0	**1**	**6**	**0**
Anaheim	0	1	3	0	0	0	0	0	x	**4**	**5**	**0**

W—Lackey. **L**—Hernandez. **SV**—Percival.
LOB—SF 9, Ana 6. **2B**—SF: Snow; Ana: Molina 2, Anderson. **3B**—Ana: Erstad. **SF**—SF: Sanders. **HBP**—Ana: Salmon. **T**—3:16. **A**—44,598.

Recap: Pitching on three days' rest, John Lackey became only the second rookie to win Game 7 of the World Series, and the Angels became the eighth straight home team to win that decisive game of the Series. Garret Anderson delivered the big hit, sending a line drive into the rightfield corner that scored three runners. Anaheim and San Francisco combined for a record 85 runs and 21 homers in the Series.

2002 World Series Composite Box Score

ANAHEIM

BATTING	AB	R	H	HR	RBI	Avg
Gil	5	1	4	0	0	.800
Wooten	2	0	1	0	0	.500
Glaus	26	7	10	3	8	.385
Salmon	26	7	9	2	5	.346
Eckstein	29	6	9	0	3	.310
Erstad	30	6	9	1	3	.300
B. Molina	21	2	6	0	2	.286
Anderson	32	3	9	0	6	.281
Kennedy	25	1	7	0	2	.280
Fullmer	15	3	4	0	1	.267
Spiezio	23	3	6	1	8	.261
Palmiero	4	1	1	0	0	.250
Ochoa	1	0	0	0	0	.000
J. Molina	0	0	0	0	0	—
Figgins	0	1	0	0	0	—
Pitchers	6	0	1	0	0	.167
Totals	245	41	76	7	38	.310

PITCHING	G	IP	H	BB	SO	ERA
Donnelly (1–0)	5	7⅓	1	4	6	0.00
Schoeneweis	2	2	1	1	2	0.00
Rodriguez (1–1)	4	8⅔	6	1	13	2.08
Percival (3 SV)	3	3	2	1	3	3.00
Lackey (1–0)	3	12⅓	15	5	7	4.38
Shields	1	1⅔	5	0	1	5.40
Ortiz (1–0)	1	5	4	3	3	7.20
Washburn (0–2)	2	9⅔	12	7	6	9.31
Appier	2	6⅓	9	5	4	11.37
Weber	4	4⅔	10	2	5	13.50
Totals	7	61	66	30	50	5.75

SAN FRANCISCO

BATTING	AB	R	H	HR	RBI	Avg
Bonds	17	8	8	4	6	.471
Snow	27	6	11	1	4	.407
Bell	23	4	7	1	4	.304
Lofton	31	7	9	0	2	.290
Kent	29	6	8	3	7	.276
Aurilia	32	5	8	2	5	.250
Sanders	21	3	5	2	6	.238
Santiago	26	2	6	0	5	.231
Dunston	9	1	2	1	3	.222
Shinjo	6	1	1	0	0	.167
Feliz	5	0	0	0	0	.000
Goodwin	4	0	0	0	0	.000
Martinez	2	0	0	0	0	.000
Pitchers	3	1	1	0	0	.333
Totals	235	44	66	14	42	.281

PITCHING	G	IP	H	BB	SO	ERA
Eyre	3	3	5	1	2	0.00
Nen (2 SV)	3	3	2	1	3	0.00
Rueter	2	10	10	1	5	2.70
Zerbe (1–0)	3	6	6	0	0	3.00
Worrell (1–1)	6	5⅔	4	1	4	3.18
Fultz	2	4⅔	4	1	0	3.86
Rodriguez (0–1)	6	5⅔	4	1	3	4.76
Schmidt (1–0)	2	10⅓	16	4	14	5.23
Ortiz	2	8	13	2	2	10.12
Hernandez (0–2)	2	5⅔	9	9	4	14.29
Witasick	2	⅓	3	2	1	54.00
Totals	7	60	76	23	38	5.55

National League Batting

BATTING AVERAGE

Barry Bonds, SF	.370
Larry Walker, Col	.338
Vladimir Guerrero, Mtl	.336
Todd Helton, Col	.329
Chipper Jones, Atl	.327
Jose Vidro, Mtl	.315
Albert Pujols, StL	.314
Jeff Kent, SF	.313
Jim Edmonds, StL	.311
Edgardo Alfonzo, NY	.308

HITS

Vladimir Guerrero, Mtl	206
Jeff Kent, SF	195
Jose Vidro, Mtl	190
Luis Castillo, Fla	185
Albert Pujols, StL	185
Todd Walker, Cin	183
Todd Helton, Col	182
Chipper Jones, Atl	179
Bobby Abreu, Phil	176
Rafael Furcal, Atl	175

DOUBLES

Bobby Abreu, Phil	50
Mike Lowell, Fla	44
Orlando Cabrera, Mtl	43
Jose Vidro, Mtl	43
Todd Walker, Cin	42
Jeff Kent, SF	42

TRIPLES

Jimmy Rollins, Phil	10
Kenny Lofton, SF	9
Quinton McCracken, Ariz	8
Rafael Furcal, Atl	8
Brad Wilkerson, Mtl	8
Scott Rolen, StL	8

HOME RUNS

Sammy Sosa, Chi	49
Barry Bonds, SF	46
Lance Berkman, Hou	42
Shawn Green, LA	42
Vladimir Guerrero, Mtl	39
Brian Giles, Pitt	38
Pat Burrell, Phil	37
Jeff Kent, SF	37
Andruw Jones, Atl	35
Albert Pujols, StL	34

RUNS SCORED

Sammy Sosa, Chi	122
Albert Pujols, StL	118
Barry Bonds, SF	117
Shawn Green, LA	110
Todd Helton, Col	107
Lance Berkman, Hou	106
Vladimir Guerrero, Mtl	106
Junior Spivey, Ariz	103
Jose Vidro, Mtl	103
Bobby Abreu, Phil	102
Jeff Kent, SF	102

TOTAL BASES

Vladimir Guerrero, Mtl	364
Jeff Kent, SF	352
Lance Berkman, Hou	334
Albert Pujols, StL	331
Sammy Sosa, Chi	330

STOLEN BASES

Luis Castillo, Fla	48
Juan Pierre, Col	47
Dave Roberts, LA	45
Vladimir Guerrero, Mtl	40
Alex Sanchez, Mil	37

RUNS BATTED IN

Lance Berkman, Hou	128
Albert Pujols, StL	127
Pat Burrell, Phil	116
Shawn Green, LA	114
Vladimir Guerrero, Mtl	111
Barry Bonds, SF	110
Scott Rolen, StL	110
Todd Helton, Col	109
Sammy Sosa, Chi	108
Jeff Kent, SF	108

SLUGGING PERCENTAGE

Barry Bonds, SF	.799
Brian Giles, Pitt	.622
Larry Walker, Col	.602
Sammy Sosa, Chi	.594
Vladimir Guerrero, Mtl	.593

ON-BASE PERCENTAGE

Barry Bonds, SF	.582
Brian Giles, Pitt	.450
Chipper Jones, Atl	.435
Todd Helton, Col	.429
Larry Walker, Col	.421

BASES ON BALLS

Barry Bonds, SF	198
Brian Giles, Pitt	135
Adam Dunn, Cin	128
Chipper Jones, Atl	107
Lance Berkman, Hou	107

National League Pitching

EARNED RUN AVERAGE

Randy Johnson, Ariz	2.32
Greg Maddux, Atl	2.62
Tom Glavine, Atl	2.96
Odalis Perez, LA	3.00
Roy Oswalt, Hou	3.01
Elmer Dessens, Cin	3.03
Toma Ohka, Mtl	3.18
Randy Wolf, Phil	3.20
Kirk Rueter, SF	3.23
Curt Schilling, Ariz	3.23

SAVES

John Smoltz, Atl	55
Eric Gagne, LA	52
Mike Williams, Pitt	46
Jose Mesa, Phil	45
Robb Nen, SF	43
Jose Jimenez, Col	41
Trevor Hoffman, SD	38
Byung-Hyun Kim, Ariz	36
Billy Wagner, Hou	35
Armando Benitez, NY	33

WINS

Randy Johnson, Ariz	24
Curt Schilling, Ariz	23
Roy Oswalt, Hou	19
Tom Glavine, Atl	18
Kevin Millwood, Atl	18
Matt Morris, StL	17
Jason Jennings, Col	16
Greg Maddux, Atl	16
Hideo Nomo, LA	16
Three tied with 15.	

GAMES PITCHED

Paul Quantrill, LA	86
Octavio Dotel, Hou	83
Tim Worrell, SF	80
Todd Jones, Col	79
Three tied with 78.	

INNINGS PITCHED

Randy Johnson, Ariz	260
Curt Schilling, Ariz	259⅓
Roy Oswalt, Hou	233
Javier Vazquez, Mtl	230⅓
Tom Glavine, Atl	224⅔

STRIKEOUTS

Randy Johnson, Ariz	334
Curt Schilling, Ariz	316
Kerry Wood, Chi	217
Matt Clement, Chi	215
Roy Oswalt, Hou	208
A.J. Burnett, Fla	203
Jason Schmidt, SF	196
Hideo Nomo, LA	193
Javier Vazquez, Mtl	179
Kevin Millwood, Atl	178

COMPLETE GAMES

Randy Johnson, Ariz	8
A.J Burnett, Fla	7
Livan Hernandez, SF	5
Curt Schilling, Ariz	5
Five tied with 4.	

SHUTOUTS

A.J Burnett, Fla	5
Randy Johnson, Ariz	4
Livan Hernandez, SF	3
Six tied with 2.	

American League Batting

BATTING AVERAGE

Manny Ramirez, Bos	.349
Mike Sweeney, KC	.340
Bernie Williams, NY	.333
Ichiro Suzuki, Sea	.321
Magglio Ordonez, Chi	.320
Jason Giambi, NY	.314
Adam Kennedy, Ana	.312
Nomar Garciaparra, Bos	.310
Miguel Tejada, Oak	.308
Garret Anderson, Ana	.306

HITS

Alfonso Soriano, NY	209
Ichiro Suzuki, Sea	208
Bernie Williams, NY	204
Miguel Tejada, Oak	204
Nomar Garciaparra, Bos	197
Garret Anderson, Ana	195
Derek Jeter, NY	191
Magglio Ordonez, Chi	189
Alex Rodriguez, Tex	187
Shea Hillenbrand, Bos	186

DOUBLES

Garret Anderson, Ana	56
Nomar Garciaparra, Bos	56
Alfonso Soriano, NY	51
Magglio Ordonez, Chi	47
Carlos Beltran, KC	44

TRIPLES

Johnny Damon, Bos	11
Randy Winn, TB	9
Mike Young, Tex	8
Ichiro Suzuki, Sea	8
Carlos Beltran, KC	7

HOME RUNS

Alex Rodriguez, Tex	57
Jim Thome, Clev	52
Rafael Palmeiro, Tex	43
Jason Giambi, NY	41
Alfonso Soriano, NY	39
Magglio Ordonez, Chi	38
Miguel Tejada, Oak	34
Eric Chavez, Oak	34
Manny Ramirez, Bos	33
Carlos Delgado, Tor	33

RUNS SCORED

Alfonso Soriano, NY	128
Alex Rodriguez, Tex	125
Derek Jeter, NY	124
Jason Giambi, NY	120
Johnny Damon, Bos	118
Magglio Ordonez, Chi	116
Ray Durham, Oak	114
Carlos Beltran, KC	114
Ichiro Suzuki, Sea	111
Miguel Tejada, Oak	108

TOTAL BASES

Alex Rodriguez, Tex	389
Alfonso Soriano, NY	381
Magglio Ordonez, Chi	352
Garret Anderson, Ana	344
Miguel Tejada, Oak	336

STOLEN BASES

Alfonso Soriano, NY	41
Carlos Beltran, KC	35
Derek Jeter, NY	32
Johnny Damon, Bos	31
Mike Cameron, Sea	31
Ichiro Suzuki, Sea	31

RUNS BATTED IN

Alex Rodriguez, Tex	142
Magglio Ordonez, Chi	135
Miguel Tejada, Oak	131
Garret Anderson, Ana	123
Jason Giambi, NY	122
Nomar Garciaparra, Bos	120
Jim Thome, Clev	118
Troy Glaus, Ana	111
Eric Chavez, Oak	109
Carlos Delgado, Tor	108

SLUGGING PERCENTAGE

Jim Thome, Clev	.677
Manny Ramirez, Bos	.647
Alex Rodriguez, Tex	.623
Jason Giambi, NY	.598
Magglio Ordonez, Chi	.597

ON-BASE PERCENTAGE

Manny Ramirez, Bos	.450
Jim Thome, Clev	.445
Jason Giambi, NY	.435
Mike Sweeney, KC	.417
Bernie Williams, NY	.415

BASES ON BALLS

Jim Thome, Clev	122
Jason Giambi, NY	109
Rafael Palmeiro, Tex	104
Carlos Delgado, Tor	102
John Olerud, Sea	98

American League Pitching

EARNED RUN AVERAGE

Pedro Martinez, Bos	2.26
Derek Lowe, Bos	2.58
Barry Zito, Oak	2.75
Tim Wakefield, Bos	2.81
Roy Halladay, Tor	2.93
Tim Hudson, Oak	2.98
Jarrod Washburn, Ana	3.15
Joel Pineiro, Sea	3.24
Jamie Moyer, Sea	3.32
Mark Mulder, Oak	3.47

SAVES

Eddie Guardado, Minn	45
Billy Koch, Oak	44
Troy Percival, Ana	40
Ugueth Urbina, Bos	40
Kelvim Escobar, Tor	38
Kazuhiro Sasaki, Sea	37
Juan Acevedo, Det	28
Mariana Rivera, NY	28
Roberto Hernandez, KC	26
Jorge Julio, Balt	25

WINS

Barry Zito, Oak	23
Derek Lowe, Bos	21
Pedro Martinez, Bos	20
David Wells, NY	19
Roy Halladay, Tor	19
Mark Mulder, Oak	19
Mark Buehrle, Chi	19
Mike Mussina, NY	18
Jarrod Washburn, Ana	18
Paul Byrd, KC	17

GAMES PITCHED

Billy Koch, Oak	84
JC Romero, Minn	81
Mike Stanton, NY	79
Steve Karsay, NY	78
Kelvim Escobar, Tor	76

SHUTOUTS

Jeff Weaver, NY	3
Seven tied with 2.	

STRIKEOUTS

Pedro Martinez, Bos	239
Roger Clemens, NY	192
Mike Mussina, NY	182
Barry Zito, Oak	182
Freddy Garcia, Sea	181
Roy Halladay, Tor	168
Ramon Ortiz, Ana	162
Mark Mulder, Oak	159
Tim Hudson, Oak	152
C.C. Sabathia, Clev	149

INNINGS PITCHED

Roy Halladay, Tor	239⅓
Mark Buehrle, Chi	239
Tim Hudson, Oak	238⅓
Jamie Moyer, Sea	230⅔
Barry Zito, Oak	229⅓

COMPLETE GAMES

Paul Byrd, KC	7
Mark Buehrle, Chi	5
Joe Kenneddy, TB	5
Five tied with 4.	

2002 Team Statistics

National League

TEAM BATTING	G	AB	R	H	2B	3B	HR	RBI	TB	BB	SO	SB	OBP	SLG	BA
Colorado	162	5512	778	1508	283	41	152	726	2329	497	1043	103	.337	.423	.274
St. Louis	162	5505	787	1475	285	26	175	758	2337	542	927	86	.338	.425	.268
Arizona	162	5508	819	1471	283	41	165	783	2331	643	1016	92	.346	.423	.267
San Francisco	162	5497	783	1465	300	35	198	751	2429	616	961	74	.344	.442	.267
Los Angeles	162	5619	722	1477	291	30	155	700	2293	430	961	96	.319	.408	.263
Houston	162	5503	749	1441	291	32	167	719	2297	589	1120	71	.338	.417	.262
Florida	162	5496	699	1433	280	32	146	653	2215	595	1130	177	.337	.403	.261
Montreal	162	5553	744	1447	304	36	162	699	2309	583	1118	119	.334	.416	.261
Atlanta	161	5495	708	1428	280	25	164	669	2250	558	1028	76	.331	.409	.260
Philadelphia	161	5523	710	1428	325	41	165	676	2330	640	1095	104	.339	.422	.259
New York	161	5496	690	1409	238	22	160	650	2171	486	1044	87	.322	.395	.256
Cincinnati	162	5470	709	1386	297	21	169	678	2232	583	1188	116	.330	.408	.253
Milwaukee	162	5415	627	1369	269	29	139	597	2113	500	1125	94	.320	.390	.253
San Diego	162	5515	662	1393	243	29	136	627	2102	547	1062	71	.321	.381	.253
Chicago	162	5496	706	1351	259	29	200	676	2268	585	1269	63	.321	.413	.246
Pittsburgh	161	5330	641	1300	263	20	142	610	2029	537	1109	86	.319	.381	.244

TEAM PITCHING	W	L	ERA	CG	Sho	SV	Inn	H	R	ER	BB	SO
Atlanta	101	59	3.13	3	15	57	1467⅓	1302	565	511	554	1058
San Francisco	95	66	3.54	10	13	43	1437⅓	1349	616	566	523	992
Los Angeles	92	70	3.69	4	15	56	1457⅔	1311	643	598	555	1132
St. Louis	97	65	3.70	4	9	42	1446⅓	1355	648	595	547	1009
New York	75	86	3.89	9	10	36	1442⅔	1408	703	624	543	1107
Arizona	98	64	3.92	14	10	40	1446⅔	1361	674	630	421	1303
Montreal	83	79	3.97	9	3	39	1453	1475	718	641	508	1088
Houston	84	78	4.00	2	11	43	1445	1423	695	643	546	1219
Philadelphia	80	81	4.17	5	9	47	1449⅔	1381	724	671	570	1075
Pittsburgh	72	89	4.23	2	7	47	1412⅔	1447	730	664	572	920
Cincinnati	78	84	4.27	2	8	42	1453⅔	1502	774	690	550	980
Chicago	67	95	4.29	11	9	23	1441⅓	1373	759	687	606	1333
Florida	79	83	4.36	11	12	36	1456⅓	1449	763	706	631	1104
San Diego	66	96	4.62	5	10	40	1436⅓	1522	815	738	582	1108
Milwaukee	56	106	4.72	7	4	32	1432⅓	1468	821	751	666	1026
Colorado	73	89	5.20	1	8	43	1426⅔	1554	898	825	582	920

American League

TEAM BATTING	G	AB	R	H	2B	3B	HR	RBI	TB	BB	SO	SB	OBP	SLG	BA
Anaheim	162	5678	851	1603	333	32	152	811	2456	462	805	117	.341	.433	.282
Boston	162	5640	859	1560	348	33	177	810	2505	545	944	80	.345	.444	.277
New York	161	5601	897	1540	314	12	223	857	2547	640	1171	100	.354	.455	.275
Seattle	162	5569	814	1531	285	31	152	771	2334	629	1003	137	.350	.419	.275
Minnesota	161	5582	768	1518	348	36	167	731	2439	472	1089	79	.332	.437	.272
Chicago	162	5847	927	1578	309	31	226	867	2627	604	1011	95	.341	.449	.270
Texas	162	5618	843	1510	304	27	230	806	2558	554	1055	62	.338	.455	.269
Oakland	162	5558	800	1450	279	28	205	772	2400	609	1008	46	.339	.432	.261
Toronto	162	5581	813	1457	305	38	187	771	2399	522	1142	71	.327	.430	.261
Kansas City	162	5535	737	1415	285	42	140	695	2204	524	921	140	.323	.398	.256
Tampa Bay	161	5605	673	1419	297	35	133	641	2185	456	1115	102	.314	.390	.253
Cleveland	162	5423	739	1349	255	26	192	706	2232	542	1000	52	.321	.412	.249
Detroit	161	5406	575	1340	265	37	124	546	2051	363	1035	65	.300	.379	.248
Baltimore	162	5491	667	1353	311	27	165	636	2213	452	993	110	.309	.403	.246

TEAM PITCHING	W	L	ERA	CG	Sho	SV	Inn	H	R	ER	BB	SO
Oakland	103	59	3.68	9	19	48	1452	1391	654	593	474	1021
Anaheim	99	63	3.69	7	14	54	1452⅔	1345	644	595	509	999
Boston	93	69	3.75	5	17	51	1446	1339	665	603	430	1157
New York	103	58	3.87	9	11	53	1452	1441	697	625	403	1135
Seattle	93	69	4.07	8	12	43	1445⅓	1422	699	654	441	1063
Minnesota	94	67	4.12	8	9	47	1444⅔	1454	712	662	439	1026
Baltimore	67	95	4.46	8	3	31	1450⅔	1491	773	719	549	967
Chicago	81	81	4.55	7	7	35	1423	1422	798	720	528	945
Toronto	78	84	4.80	6	6	41	1438⅓	1504	828	767	590	991
Cleveland	74	88	4.91	9	4	34	1424⅔	1508	837	777	603	1058
Detroit	55	106	4.92	11	7	33	1414	1593	864	773	463	794
Texas	72	90	5.15	4	4	33	1439⅔	1528	882	824	669	1030
Kansas City	62	100	5.21	11	6	30	1441	1587	891	834	572	909
Tampa Bay	55	106	5.29	12	3	25	1440⅓	1567	918	846	620	925

Arizona Diamondbacks

BATTING	G	AB	R	H	2B	3B	HR	RBI	TB	BB	SO	SB	OBP	SLG	BA
Greg Colbrunn	72	171	30	57	16	2	10	27	107	13	19	0	.378	.626	.333
Danny Bautista	40	154	22	50	5	2	6	23	77	11	21	4	.367	.500	.325
Quinton McCracken	123	348	60	108	27	8	3	40	160	32	67	5	.368	.460	.310
Junior Spivey	143	538	103	162	34	6	16	78	256	65	100	11	.389	.476	.301
Luis Gonzalez	148	524	90	151	19	3	28	103	260	97	76	9	.400	.496	.288
Steve Finley	150	505	82	145	24	4	25	89	252	65	73	16	.370	.499	.287
Craig Counsell	112	436	63	123	22	1	2	51	153	45	52	7	.348	.351	.282
Tony Womack	153	590	90	160	23	5	5	57	208	46	80	29	.325	.353	.271
Erubial Durazo	76	222	46	58	12	2	16	48	122	49	60	0	.395	.550	.261
Matt Williams	60	215	29	56	7	2	12	40	103	21	41	3	.324	.479	.260
Mark Grace	124	298	43	75	19	0	7	48	115	46	30	2	.351	.386	.252
Damian Miller	101	297	40	74	22	0	11	42	129	38	88	0	.340	.434	.249
Dave Dellucci	97	229	34	56	11	2	7	29	92	28	55	2	.326	.402	.245
Rod Barajas	70	154	12	36	10	0	3	23	55	10	25	1	.288	.357	.234

PITCHING	W–L	ERA	G	GS	CG	SV	INN	H	R	ER	BB	SO
Byung-Hyun Kim	8–3	2.04	72	0	0	36	84	64	20	19	26	92
Randy Johnson	24–5	2.32	35	35	8	0	260	197	78	67	71	334
Curt Schilling	23–7	3.23	36	35	5	0	259.1	218	95	93	33	316
Mike Koplove	6–1	3.36	55	0	0	0	61.2	47	24	23	23	46
Mike Fetters	3–3	4.09	65	0	0	0	55	53	31	25	37	53
Miguel Batista	8–9	4.29	36	29	1	0	184.2	172	99	88	70	112
Mike Myers	4–3	4.38	69	0	0	4	37	39	18	18	17	31
Rick Helling	10–12	4.51	30	30	0	0	175.2	180	94	88	48	120
Brian Anderson	6–11	4.79	35	24	0	0	156	174	86	83	32	81
Mike Morgan	1–1	5.29	29	0	0	0	34	41	22	20	9	13

Atlanta Braves

BATTING	G	AB	R	H	2B	3B	HR	RBI	TB	BB	SO	SB	OBP	SLG	BA
Chipper Jones	158	548	90	179	35	1	26	100	294	107	89	8	.435	.536	.327
Matt Franco	81	205	25	65	15	4	6	30	106	27	31	1	.395	.517	.317
Gary Sheffield	135	492	82	151	26	0	25	84	252	72	53	12	.404	.512	.307
Mark DeRosa	72	212	24	63	9	2	5	23	91	12	24	2	.339	.429	.297
Julio Franco	125	338	51	96	13	1	6	30	129	39	75	5	.357	.382	.284
Rafael Furcal	154	636	95	175	31	8	8	47	246	43	114	27	.323	.387	.275
Darren Bragg	109	212	34	57	15	2	3	15	85	24	52	5	.347	.401	.269
Andruw Jones	154	560	91	148	34	0	35	94	287	83	135	8	.366	.513	.264
Wes Helms	85	210	20	51	16	0	6	22	85	11	57	1	.283	.405	.243
Javy Lopez	109	347	31	81	15	0	11	52	129	26	63	0	.299	.372	.233
Vinny Castilla	143	543	56	126	23	2	12	61	189	22	69	4	.268	.348	.232
Keith Lockhart	128	296	34	64	13	3	5	32	98	27	50	0	.282	.331	.216

PITCHING	W–L	ERA	G	GS	CG	SV	INN	H	R	ER	BB	SO
Chris Hammond	7–2	0.95	63	0	0	0	76	53	15	8	31	63
Darren Holmes	2–2	1.81	55	0	0	1	54.2	41	12	11	12	47
Mike Remlinger	7–3	1.99	73	0	0	0	68	48	17	15	28	69
Greg Maddux	16–6	2.62	34	34	0	0	199.1	194	67	58	45	118
Tom Glavine	18–11	2.96	36	36	2	0	224.2	210	85	74	78	127
Kerry Ligtenberg	3–4	2.97	52	0	0	0	66.2	52	23	22	33	51
Kevin Millwood	18–8	3.24	35	34	1	0	217	186	83	78	65	178
John Smoltz	3–2	3.25	75	0	0	55	80.1	59	30	29	24	85
Damian Moss	12–6	3.42	33	29	0	0	179	140	80	68	89	111
Albie Lopez	1–4	4.37	30	4	0	0	55.2	66	29	27	18	39
Jason Marquis	8–9	5.04	22	22	0	0	114.1	127	66	64	49	84

Chicago Cubs

BATTING	G	AB	R	H	2B	3B	HR	RBI	TB	BB	SO	SB	OBP	SLG	BA
Sammy Sosa	150	556	122	160	19	2	49	108	330	103	144	2	.399	.594	.288
Moises Alou	132	484	50	133	23	1	15	61	203	47	61	8	.337	.419	.275
Fred McGriff	146	523	67	143	27	2	30	103	264	63	99	1	.353	.505	.273
Mark Bellhorn	146	445	86	115	24	4	27	56	228	76	144	7	.374	.512	.258
Bobby Hill	59	190	26	48	7	2	4	20	71	17	42	6	.327	.374	.253
Corey Patterson	153	592	71	150	30	5	14	54	232	19	142	18	.284	.392	.253
Alex Gonzalez	142	513	58	127	27	5	18	61	218	46	136	5	.312	.425	.248
Chris Stynes	98	195	25	47	9	1	5	26	73	21	29	1	.314	.374	.241
Joe Girardi	90	234	19	53	10	1	1	13	68	16	35	1	.275	.291	.226
Roosevelt Brown	111	204	14	43	12	0	3	23	64	23	50	2	.299	.314	.211
Todd Hundley	92	266	32	56	8	0	16	35	112	32	80	0	.301	.421	.211
Chad Hermansen	100	237	25	49	14	1	8	18	89	22	82	7	.276	.376	.207

Chicago Cubs *(Cont.)*

PITCHING	W–L	ERA	G	GS	CG	SV	INN	H	R	ER	BB	SO
Joe Borowski	4–4	2.73	73	0	0	2	95.2	84	31	29	29	97
Mark Prior	6–6	3.32	19	19	1	0	116.2	98	45	43	38	147
Matt Clement	12–11	3.60	32	32	3	0	205	162	84	82	85	215
Kerry Wood	12–11	3.66	33	33	4	0	213.2	169	92	87	97	217
Carlos Zambrano	4–8	3.66	32	16	0	0	108.1	94	53	44	63	93
Jon Lieber	6–8	3.70	21	21	3	0	141	153	64	58	12	87
Juan Cruz	3–11	3.98	45	9	0	1	97.1	84	56	43	59	81
Antonio Alfonseca	2–5	4.00	66	0	0	19	74.1	73	34	33	36	61
Jason Bere	1–10	5.67	16	16	0	0	85.2	98	63	54	28	65

Cincinnati Reds

BATTING	G	AB	R	H	2B	3B	HR	RBI	TB	BB	SO	SB	OBP	SLG	BA
Austin Kearns	107	372	66	117	24	3	13	56	186	54	81	6	.407	.500	.315
Todd Walker	155	612	79	183	42	3	11	64	264	50	81	8	.353	.431	.299
Ken Griffey	70	197	17	52	8	0	8	23	84	28	39	1	.358	.426	.264
Sean Casey	120	425	56	111	25	0	6	42	154	43	47	2	.334	.362	.261
Corky Miller	39	114	9	29	10	0	3	15	48	9	20	1	.328	.421	.254
Reggie Taylor	135	287	41	73	15	4	9	38	123	14	79	11	.291	.429	.254
Adam Dunn	158	535	84	133	28	2	26	71	243	128	170	19	.400	.454	.249
Jason LaRue	113	353	42	88	17	1	12	52	143	27	117	1	.324	.405	.249
Barry Larkin	145	507	72	124	37	2	7	47	186	44	57	13	.305	.367	.245
Russell Branyan	84	217	34	53	9	1	16	39	112	34	86	3	.349	.516	.244
Aaron Boone	162	606	83	146	38	2	26	87	266	56	111	32	.314	.439	.241
Jose Guillen	85	240	25	57	7	0	8	31	88	14	43	4	.287	.367	.238

PITCHING	W–L	ERA	G	GS	CG	SV	INN	H	R	ER	BB	SO
Scott Williamson	3–4	2.92	63	0	0	8	74	46	27	24	36	84
Gabe White	6–1	2.98	62	0	0	0	54.1	49	19	18	10	41
Elmer Dessens	7–8	3.03	30	30	0	0	178	173	70	60	49	93
Danny Graves	7–3	3.19	68	4	0	32	98.2	99	37	35	25	58
Chris Reitsma	6–12	3.64	32	21	1	0	138.1	144	73	56	45	84
Jimmy Haynes	15–10	4.12	34	34	0	0	196.2	210	97	90	81	126
Shawn Estes	5–12	5.10	29	29	1	0	160.2	171	94	91	83	109
Jose Rijo	5–4	5.14	31	9	0	0	77	89	48	44	20	38
Joey Hamilton	4–10	5.27	39	17	0	1	124.2	136	78	73	50	85
Ryan Dempster	10–13	5.38	33	33	4	0	209	228	127	125	93	153
Bruce Chen	2–5	5.56	55	6	0	0	77.2	85	53	48	43	80
Scott Sullivan	6–5	6.06	71	0	0	1	78.2	93	60	53	31	78

Colorado Rockies

BATTING	G	AB	R	H	2B	3B	HR	RBI	TB	BB	SO	SB	OBP	SLG	BA
Larry Walker	136	477	95	161	40	4	26	104	287	65	73	6	.421	.602	.338
Todd Helton	156	553	107	182	39	4	30	109	319	99	91	5	.429	.577	.329
Gabe Kapler	40	119	12	37	4	3	2	17	53	8	23	6	.359	.445	.311
Jay Payton	134	445	69	135	20	7	16	59	217	29	54	7	.351	.488	.303
Juan Pierre	152	592	90	170	20	5	1	35	203	31	52	47	.332	.343	.287
Todd Zeile	144	506	61	138	23	0	18	87	215	66	92	1	.353	.425	.273
Sandy Alomar	38	116	8	31	4	0	0	12	35	4	19	0	.292	.302	.267
Gary Bennett	90	291	26	77	10	2	4	26	103	15	45	1	.314	.354	.265
Brent Butler	113	344	55	89	18	4	9	42	142	10	40	2	.287	.413	.259
Junior Ortiz	65	192	22	48	7	1	1	12	60	16	30	2	.315	.313	.250
Juan Uribe	155	566	69	136	25	7	6	49	193	34	120	9	.286	.341	.240
Terry Shumpert	106	234	30	55	12	1	6	21	87	21	41	4	.304	.372	.235
Greg Norton	113	168	19	37	8	1	7	37	68	24	52	2	.314	.405	.220
Benny Agbayani	48	117	10	24	5	0	4	19	41	10	35	1	.266	.350	.205

PITCHING	W–L	ERA	G	GS	CG	SV	INN	H	R	ER	BB	SO
Jose Jimenez	2–10	3.56	74	0	0	41	73.1	76	34	29	11	47
Denny Stark	11–4	4.00	32	20	0	0	128.1	108	69	57	64	64
Justin Speier	5–1	4.33	63	0	0	1	62.1	51	31	30	19	47
Jason Jennings	16–8	4.52	32	32	0	0	185.1	201	102	93	70	127
Todd Jones	1–4	4.70	79	0	0	1	82.1	84	43	43	28	73
Denny Neagle	8–11	5.26	35	28	1	0	164.1	170	101	96	63	111
Shawn Chacon	5–11	5.73	21	21	0	0	119.1	122	84	76	60	67
Sean Lowe	5–3	5.79	51	1	0	0	79.1	101	58	51	41	64
Kent Mercker	3–1	6.14	58	0	0	0	44	55	33	30	22	37
Mike Hampton	7–15	6.15	30	30	0	0	178.2	228	135	122	91	74

Florida Marlins

BATTING	G	AB	R	H	2B	3B	HR	RBI	TB	BB	SO	SB	OBP	SLG	BA
Kevin Millar	126	438	58	134	41	0	16	57	223	40	74	0	.366	.509	.306
Luis Castillo	146	606	86	185	18	5	2	39	219	55	76	48	.364	.361	.305
Mike Redmond	89	256	19	78	15	0	2	28	99	21	34	0	.372	.387	.305
Mike Lowell	160	597	88	165	44	0	24	92	281	65	92	4	.346	.471	.276
Juan Encarnacion	152	584	77	158	22	5	24	85	262	46	113	21	.324	.449	.271
Derrek Lee	162	581	95	157	35	7	27	86	287	98	164	19	.378	.494	.270
Eric Owens	131	385	44	104	15	5	4	37	141	31	33	26	.324	.366	.270
Andy Fox	133	435	55	109	14	5	4	41	145	49	94	31	.338	.333	.251
Preston Wilson	141	510	80	124	22	2	23	65	219	58	140	20	.329	.429	.243
Ramon Castro	54	101	11	24	4	0	6	18	46	14	24	0	.322	.455	.238
Alex Gonzalez	42	151	15	34	7	1	2	18	49	12	32	3	.296	.325	.225
Charles Johnson	83	244	18	53	19	0	6	36	90	31	61	0	.301	.369	.217

PITCHING	W–L	ERA	G	GS	CG	SV	INN	H	R	ER	BB	SO
Vladimir Nunez	4–5	2.74	52	3	0	0	92	79	33	28	30	64
Braden Looper	2–5	3.14	78	0	0	13	86	73	31	30	28	55
A.J. Burnett	12–9	3.30	31	29	7	0	204.1	153	84	75	90	203
Vladimir Nunez	6–5	3.41	77	0	0	20	97.2	80	38	37	37	73
Josh Beckett	6–7	4.10	23	21	0	0	107.2	93	56	49	44	113
Michael Tejera	8–8	4.45	47	18	0	1	139.2	144	71	69	60	95
Kevin Olsen	0–5	4.53	17	8	0	0	55.2	57	31	28	31	38
Brad Penny	8–7	4.66	24	24	1	0	129.1	148	76	67	50	93
Carl Pavano	6–10	5.16	37	22	0	0	136	174	88	78	45	92
Graeme Lloyd	4–5	5.21	66	0	0	5	57	67	34	33	19	37
Julian Tavarez	10–12	5.39	29	27	0	0	153.2	188	100	92	15	74

Houston Astros

BATTING	G	AB	R	H	2B	3B	HR	RBI	TB	BB	SO	SB	OBP	SLG	BA
Mark Loretta	107	283	33	86	18	0	4	27	116	32	37	1	.381	.410	.304
Jose Vizcaino	125	406	53	123	19	2	5	37	161	24	40	3	.342	.397	.303
Lance Berkman	158	578	106	169	35	2	42	128	334	107	118	8	.405	.578	.292
Jeff Bagwell	158	571	94	166	33	2	31	98	296	101	130	7	.401	.518	.291
Orlando Merced	123	251	35	72	13	3	6	30	109	26	50	4	.350	.434	.287
Geoff Blum	130	368	45	104	20	4	10	52	162	49	70	2	.367	.440	.283
Daryl Ward	136	453	41	125	31	0	12	72	192	33	82	1	.324	.424	.276
Brian L. Hunter	98	201	32	54	16	3	3	20	85	16	39	5	.329	.423	.269
Julio Lugo	88	322	45	84	15	1	8	3	125	28	74	9	.322	.388	.261
Brad Ausmus	130	447	57	115	19	3	6	50	158	38	71	2	.322	.353	.257
Craig Biggio	145	577	96	146	36	3	15	58	233	50	111	16	.330	.404	.253
Richard Hidalgo	114	388	54	91	17	4	15	48	161	43	85	6	.319	.415	.235
Gregg Zaun	76	185	18	41	7	1	3	24	59	12	36	1	.275	.319	.222

PITCHING	W–L	ERA	G	GS	CG	SV	INN	H	R	ER	BB	SO
Octavio Dotel	6–4	1.85	83	0	0	6	97.1	58	21	20	27	118
Billy Wagner	4–2	2.52	70	0	0	35	75	51	21	21	22	88
Roy Oswalt	19–9	3.01	35	34	0	0	233	215	86	78	62	208
Wade Miller	15–4	3.28	26	26	1	0	164.2	151	63	60	62	144
Peter Munro	5–5	3.57	19	4	0	0	80.2	89	37	32	23	45
Ricky Stone	3–3	3.61	78	0	0	1	77.1	78	36	31	34	63
Carlos Hernandez	7–5	4.38	23	21	0	0	111.0	112	56	54	61	93
Nelson Cruz	2–6	4.48	43	5	0	0	78.1	90	44	39	29	61
Shane Reynolds	3–6	4.86	13	13	0	0	74	80	43	40	26	47
Dave Mlicki	4–10	5.34	22	16	0	0	86	101	57	51	34	57
Tim Redding	3–6	5.40	18	14	0	0	73.1	78	49	44	35	63
Kirk Saarloos	6–7	6.01	17	17	1	0	85.1	100	59	57	27	54

Los Angeles Dodgers

BATTING	G	AB	R	H	2B	3B	HR	RBI	TB	BB	SO	SB	OBP	SLG	BA
Tyler Houston	76	255	25	77	15	2	7	33	117	14	41	1	.347	.459	.302
Dave Hansen	96	120	15	35	6	0	2	17	47	14	22	1	.363	.392	.292
Alex Cora	115	258	37	75	14	4	5	28	112	26	3	7	.371	.434	.291
Shawn Green	158	582	110	166	31	1	42	114	325	93	112	8	.385	.558	.285
Brian Jordan	128	471	65	134	27	3	18	80	221	34	86	2	.338	.469	.285
Paul Lo Duca	149	580	74	163	38	1	10	64	233	34	31	3	.330	.402	.281
Marquis Grissom	111	343	57	95	21	4	17	60	175	22	68	5	.32	.510	.277
Dave Roberts	127	422	63	117	14	7	3	34	154	48	51	45	.353	.365	.277
Mark Grudzielanek	150	536	56	145	23	0	9	50	195	22	89	4	.301	.364	.271
Eric Karros	142	524	52	142	26	1	13	73	209	37	74	0	.323	.399	.271
Adrian Beltre	159	587	70	151	26	5	21	75	250	37	96	7	.303	.426	.257
Cesar Izturis	135	439	43	102	24	2	1	31	133	14	39	7	.253	.303	.232

Los Angeles Dodgers *(Cont.)*

PITCHING	W–L	ERA	G	GS	CG	SV	INN	H	R	ER	BB	SO
Eric Gagne	4–1	1.97	77	0	0	52	82.1	55	18	18	16	114
Paul Quantrill	5–4	2.70	86	0	0	1	76.2	80	27	23	25	53
Odalis Perez	15–10	3.00	32	32	4	0	222.1	182	76	74	38	155
Giovanni Carrara	6–3	3.28	63	1	0	1	90.2	83	34	33	32	56
Hideo Nomo	16–6	3.39	34	34	0	0	220.1	189	92	83	101	193
Omar Daal	11–9	3.90	39	23	0	0	161.1	142	73	70	54	105
Andy Ashby	9–13	3.91	30	30	0	0	181.2	179	85	79	65	107
Guillermo Mota	1–3	4.15	43	0	0	0	60.2	45	30	28	27	49
Kazuhisa Ishii	14–10	4.27	28	28	0	0	154	137	82	73	106	143
Kevin Brown	3–4	4.81	17	10	0	0	63.2	68	36	34	23	58

Milwaukee Brewers

BATTING	G	AB	R	H	2B	3B	HR	RBI	TB	BB	SO	SB	OBP	SLG	BA
Lenny Harris	122	197	23	60	8	2	3	17	81	14	17	4	.355	.411	.305
Alex Sanchez	112	394	55	114	10	7	1	33	141	31	62	37	.343	.358	.289
Jose Hernandez	152	525	72	151	24	2	24	73	251	52	188	3	.356	.478	.288
Eric Young	138	496	57	139	29	3	3	28	183	39	38	31	.338	.369	.280
Richie Sexson	157	570	86	159	37	2	29	102	287	70	136	0	.363	.504	.279
Robert Machado	73	211	19	55	14	1	3	22	80	17	41	0	.316	.379	.261
Jeff Hammonds	128	448	47	115	26	5	9	41	178	52	86	4	.332	.397	.257
Alex Ochoa	85	215	32	55	9	0	6	21	82	32	30	8	.357	.381	.256
Ryan Thompson	62	137	16	34	9	2	8	24	71	7	38	1	.295	.518	.248
Matt Stairs	107	270	41	66	15	0	16	41	129	36	50	2	.349	.478	.244
Geoff Jenkins	67	243	35	59	17	1	10	29	108	22	60	1	.320	.444	.243
Paul Bako	87	234	24	55	8	1	4	20	77	20	46	0	.295	.329	.235
Ron Belliard	104	289	30	61	13	0	3	26	83	18	46	2	.257	.287	.211

PITCHING	W–L	ERA	G	GS	CG	SV	INN	H	R	ER	BB	SO
Luis Vizcaino	5–3	2.99	76	0	0	5	81.1	55	27	27	30	79
Ray King	3–2	3.05	76	0	0	0	65	61	24	22	24	50
Valerio De Los Santos	2–3	3.12	51	0	0	0	57.2	42	21	20	2	38
Mike DeJean	1–5	3.12	68	0	0	27	75	66	28	26	39	65
Ben Sheets	11–16	4.15	34	34	1	0	216.2	237	105	100	70	170
Glendon Rusch	10–16	4.70	34	34	4	0	210.2	227	118	110	76	140
Nick Neugebauer	1–7	4.72	12	12	0	0	55.1	56	33	29	44	47
Nelson Figueroa	1–7	5.03	30	11	0	0	93	96	59	52	37	51
Ruben Quevedo	6–11	5.76	26	25	1	0	139	159	100	89	68	93
Jose Cabrera	6–10	6.79	50	11	0	0	103.1	131	84	78	36	61

Montreal Expos

BATTING	G	AB	R	H	2B	3B	HR	RBI	TB	BB	SO	SB	OBP	SLG	BA
Vladimir Guerrero	161	614	106	206	37	2	39	111	364	84	70	40	.417	.593	.336
Jose Vidro	152	604	103	190	43	3	19	96	296	60	70	2	.378	.490	.315
Endy Chavez	36	125	20	37	8	5	1	9	58	5	16	3	.321	.464	.296
Troy O'Leary	97	273	27	78	12	2	3	37	103	34	47	1	.371	.377	.286
Cliff Floyd	99	349	56	96	22	0	21	61	181	61	78	11	.394	.519	.275
Brian Schneider	73	207	21	57	19	2	5	29	95	21	41	1	.339	.459	.275
Wil Cordero	66	143	21	39	9	0	6	29	66	17	26	2	.349	.462	.273
Brad Wilkerson	153	507	92	135	28	8	20	59	238	81	161	7	.370	.469	.266
Michael Barrett	117	376	41	99	20	1	12	49	157	40	65	6	.332	.418	.263
Orlando Cabrera	153	563	64	148	43	1	7	56	214	48	53	25	.321	.380	.263
Andres Galarraga	104	292	30	76	12	0	9	40	115	30	81	2	.344	.394	.260
Chris Truby	35	105	12	27	5	2	2	7	42	5	27	1	.297	.400	.257
Jose Macias	90	231	33	59	17	1	7	33	99	13	44	5	.294	.429	.255
Fernando Tatis	114	381	43	87	18	1	15	55	152	35	90	2	.303	.399	.228
Lee Stevens	63	205	28	39	6	1	10	31	77	39	57	1	.318	.376	.190
Peter Bergeron	31	123	24	23	3	2	0	7	30	22	44	10	.310	.244	.187

PITCHING	W–L	ERA	G	GS	CG	SV	INN	H	R	ER	BB	SO
Joey Eischen	6–1	1.34	59	0	0	2	53.2	43	11	8	18	51
Scott Stewart	4–2	3.09	67	0	0	17	64	49	29	22	22	67
Toma Ohka	13–8	3.18	32	31	2	0	192.2	194	83	68	45	118
Bartolo Colon	10–4	3.31	17	17	4	0	117	11	48	43	39	74
Javier Vazquez	10–13	3.91	34	34	2	0	230.1	243	111	100	49	179
Matt Herges	2–5	4.04	62	0	0	6	64.2	80	33	29	26	50
T.J. Tucker	6–3	4.11	57	0	0	4	61.1	69	32	28	31	42
Masato Yoshii	4–9	4.11	31	20	1	0	131.1	143	66	60	32	74
Jim Brower	3–2	4.37	52	0	0	0	80.1	77	40	39	32	57
Tony Armas	12–12	4.44	29	9	0	0	164.1	149	8	81	78	131
Britt Reames	1–4	5.03	42	6	0	0	68	70	4	38	38	76

New York Mets

BATTING	G	AB	R	H	2B	3B	HR	RBI	TB	BB	SO	SB	OBP	SLG	BA
Edgardo Alfonzo	135	490	78	151	26	0	16	56	225	62	55	6	.391	.459	.308
Ty Wigginton	46	116	18	35	8	0	6	18	61	8	19	2	.354	.526	.302
Timo Perez	136	444	52	131	27	6	8	47	194	23	36	10	.331	.437	.295
Mike Piazza	135	478	69	134	23	2	33	98	260	57	82	0	.359	.544	.280
Roberto Alomar	149	590	73	157	24	4	11	53	222	57	83	16	.331	.376	.266
Roger Cedeno	149	511	65	133	19	2	7	41	177	42	92	25	.318	.346	.260
Raul Gonzalez	40	104	13	27	3	0	3	12	39	6	22	4	.297	.375	.260
Mo Vaughn	139	487	67	126	18	0	26	72	222	59	145	0	.349	.456	.259
Rey Ordonez	144	460	53	117	25	2	1	42	149	24	46	2	.292	.324	.254
Vance Wilson	74	163	19	40	7	0	5	26	62	5	32	0	.301	.380	.245
John Valentin	114	208	18	50	15	0	3	30	74	22	37	0	.339	.356	.240
Jeromy Burnitz	154	479	65	103	15	0	19	54	175	58	135	10	.311	.365	.215
Joe McEwing	105	196	22	39	8	1	3	26	58	9	50	4	.242	.296	.199

PITCHING	W–L	ERA	G	GS	CG	SV	INN	H	R	ER	BB	SO
Steve Reed	2–5	2.01	64	0	0	1	67	56	15	15	14	50
Armando Benitez	1–0	2.27	62	0	0	33	67.1	46	20	17	25	79
David Weathers	6–3	2.91	71	0	0	0	77.1	69	30	25	36	61
Steve Trachsel	11–11	3.37	30	30	1	0	173.2	170	80	65	69	105
Al Leiter	13–13	3.48	33	33	2	0	204.1	194	99	79	69	172
Scott Strickland	6–9	3.54	69	0	0	2	68.2	61	29	27	33	69
Mike Bacsik	3–2	4.37	11	9	1	0	55.2	63	29	27	19	30
John Thomson	9–14	4.71	30	30	0	0	181.2	201	116	95	44	107
Jason Middlebrook	2–3	4.73	15	5	0	0	51.1	44	27	27	22	42
Pedro Astacio	12–11	4.79	31	31	3	0	191.2	192	106	102	63	152
Jeff D'Amico	6–10	4.94	29	22	1	0	145.2	152	84	80	37	101

Philadelphia Phillies

BATTING	G	AB	R	H	2B	3B	HR	RBI	TB	BB	SO	SB	OBP	SLG	BA
Todd Pratt	39	106	14	33	11	0	3	16	53	24	28	2	.449	.500	.311
Bobby Abreu	157	572	102	176	50	6	20	85	298	104	117	31	.413	.521	.308
Placido Polanco	147	548	75	158	32	2	9	49	221	26	41	5	.330	.403	.288
Pat Burrell	157	586	96	165	39	2	37	116	319	89	153	1	.376	.544	.282
Mike Lieberthal	130	476	46	133	29	2	15	52	211	38	58	0	.349	.443	.279
Jason Michaels	81	105	16	28	10	3	2	11	50	13	33	1	.347	.476	.267
Travis Lee	153	536	55	142	26	2	13	70	211	54	104	5	.331	.394	.265
Marlon Anderson	145	539	64	139	30	6	8	48	205	42	71	5	.315	.380	.258
Tomas Perez	92	212	22	53	13	1	5	20	83	21	40	1	.319	.392	.250
Jimmy Rollins	154	637	82	156	33	10	11	60	242	54	103	31	.306	.380	.245
Jeremy Giambi	82	156	32	38	10	0	12	28	84	52	54	0	.435	.538	.244
Ricky Ledee	96	203	33	46	13	1	8	23	85	35	50	1	.342	.419	.227

PITCHING	W–L	ERA	G	GS	CG	SV	INN	H	R	ER	BB	SO
Jose Mesa	4–6	2.97	74	0	0	45	75.2	65	26	25	39	64
Mike Timlin	4–6	2.98	72	1	0	0	96.2	75	35	32	14	50
Randy Wolf	11–9	3.20	31	31	3	0	210.2	172	77	75	63	172
Carlos Silva	5–0	3.21	68	0	0	1	84	88	34	30	22	41
Vicente Padilla	14–11	3.28	32	32	1	0	206	198	83	75	53	128
Joe Roa	4–4	4.04	14	11	0	0	71.1	78	33	32	13	35
Brett Myers	4–5	4.25	12	12	1	0	72	73	38	34	29	34
Terry Adams	7–9	4.35	46	19	0	0	136.2	132	76	66	58	96
Dave Coggin	2–5	4.68	38	7	0	0	77	65	42	40	51	64
Rheal Cormier	5–6	5.25	54	0	0	0	60	61	38	35	32	49
Brandon Duckworth	8–9	5.41	30	29	0	0	163	167	103	98	69	167
Robert Person	4–5	5.44	16	16	0	0	87.2	79	58	53	51	61

Pittsburgh Pirates

BATTING	G	AB	R	H	2B	3B	HR	RBI	TB	BB	SO	SB	OBP	SLG	BA
Brian Giles	153	497	95	148	37	5	38	103	309	135	74	15	.450	.622	.298
Jason Kendall	145	545	59	154	25	3	3	44	194	49	29	15	.350	.356	.283
Pokey Reese	119	421	46	111	25	0	4	50	148	41	81	12	.330	.352	.264
Armando Rios	76	208	20	55	11	0	1	24	69	16	39	1	.319	.332	.264
Craig Wilson	131	368	48	97	16	1	16	57	163	32	116	2	.355	.443	.264
Jack Wilson	147	527	77	133	22	4	4	47	175	37	74	5	.306	.332	.252
Kevin Young	146	468	60	115	26	1	6	51	191	50	101	4	.322	.408	.246
Aramis Ramirez	142	522	51	122	26	0	18	71	202	29	95	2	.279	.387	.234
Abraham Nunez	112	253	28	59	14	1	2	15	81	27	44	3	.311	.320	.233
Adam Hyzdu	59	155	24	36	6	0	11	34	75	21	44	0	.324	.484	.232
Adrian Brown	91	208	20	45	10	2	1	21	62	19	34	10	.284	.298	.216
Keith Osik	55	100	6	16	3	0	2	11	25	6	25	0	.211	.250	.160
Mike Benjamin	108	120	7	18	2	1	0	3	22	7	31	0	.202	.183	.150

PITCHING	W–L	ERA	G	GS	CG	SV	INN	H	R	ER	BB	SO
Scott Sauerbeck	5–4	2.30	78	0	0	0	62.2	50	18	16	27	70
Mike Williams	2–6	2.93	59	0	0	46	61.1	54	24	20	21	43
Mike Lincoln	2–4	3.11	55	0	0	0	72.1	80	28	25	27	50
Brian Boehringer	4–4	3.39	70	0	0	1	79.2	65	30	30	33	65
Kip Wells	12–14	3.58	33	33	1	0	198.1	197	92	79	71	134
Brian Meadows	1–6	3.88	11	11	0	0	62.2	62	29	27	14	31
Josh Fogg	12–12	4.35	33	33	0	0	194.1	199	102	94	69	113
Joe Beimel	2–5	4.64	53	8	0	0	85.1	88	49	44	45	53
Kris Benson	9–6	4.70	25	25	0	0	130.1	152	76	68	50	79
Jimmy Anderson	8–13	5.44	28	25	1	0	140.2	167	91	85	63	47
Ron Villone	4–6	5.81	45	7	0	0	93	95	63	60	34	55

St. Louis Cardinals

BATTING	G	AB	R	H	2B	3B	HR	RBI	TB	BB	SO	SB	OBP	SLG	BA
Albert Pujols	157	590	118	185	40	2	34	127	331	72	69	2	.394	.561	.314
Jim Edmonds	144	476	96	148	31	2	28	83	267	86	134	4	.420	.561	.311
Edgar Renteria	152	544	77	166	36	2	11	83	239	49	57	22	.364	.439	.305
Fernando Vina	150	622	75	168	29	5	1	54	210	44	36	17	.333	.338	.270
Scott Rolen	155	580	89	154	29	8	31	110	292	72	102	8	.357	.503	.266
Eli Marrero	131	397	63	104	19	1	18	66	179	40	72	14	.327	.451	.262
Tino Martinez	150	511	63	134	25	1	21	75	224	58	71	3	.337	.438	.262
Kerry Robinson	124	181	27	47	7	4	1	15	65	11	29	7	.301	.359	.260
J.D. Drew	135	424	61	107	19	1	18	56	182	57	104	8	.34	.429	.252
Miguel Cairo	108	184	28	46	9	2	2	23	65	13	36	1	.307	.353	.250
Mike Matheny	110	315	31	77	12	1	3	35	100	32	49	1	.313	.317	.244
Mike DiFelice	70	174	17	40	11	0	4	19	63	17	42	0	.297	.362	.230
Eduardo Perez	96	154	22	31	9	0	10	26	70	17	36	0	.290	.455	.201

PITCHING	W–L	ERA	G	GS	CG	SV	INN	H	R	ER	BB	SO
Jason Isringhausen	3–2	2.48	60	0	0	32	65.1	46	22	18	18	68
Woody Williams	9–4	2.53	17	17	1	0	103.1	84	30	29	25	76
Andy Benes	5–4	2.78	18	17	1	0	97	80	39	30	51	64
Steve Kline	2–1	3.39	66	0	0	6	58.1	54	23	22	21	41
Matt Morris	17–9	3.42	32	32	1	0	210.1	210	86	80	64	171
Dave Veres	5–8	3.48	71	0	0	4	82.2	67	34	32	39	68
Darryl Kile	5–4	3.72	14	14	0	0	84.2	82	36	35	28	50
Chuck Finley	7–4	3.80	14	14	1	0	85.1	69	41	36	30	83
Jason Simontacchi	11–5	4.02	24	24	0	0	143.1	134	68	64	54	72
Luther Hackman	5–4	4.11	43	6	0	0	81	90	42	37	39	46
Rick White	5–7	4.31	61	0	0	0	62.2	62	33	30	21	41
Jamey Wright	7–13	5.29	23	22	1	0	129.1	130	80	76	75	77
Jeff Fassero	8–6	5.35	73	0	0	0	69	81	43	41	27	56

San Diego Padres

BATTING	G	AB	R	H	2B	3B	HR	RBI	TB	BB	SO	SB	OBP	SLG	BA
Ryan Klesko	146	540	90	162	39	1	29	95	290	76	86	6	.388	.537	.300
Mark Kotsay	153	578	82	169	27	7	17	61	261	59	89	11	.359	.452	.292
Phil Nevin	107	407	53	116	16	0	12	57	168	38	87	4	.344	.413	.285
Gene Kingsale	89	216	27	60	10	3	2	28	82	20	47	9	.346	.380	.278
Ramon Vazquez	128	423	50	116	21	5	2	32	153	45	79	7	.344	.362	.274
Sean Burroughs	63	192	18	52	5	1	1	11	62	12	30	2	.317	.323	.271
Deivi Cruz	151	514	49	135	28	2	7	47	188	22	58	2	.294	.366	.263
Ron Gant	102	309	58	81	14	1	18	59	151	36	59	4	.338	.489	.262
Bubba Trammell	133	403	54	98	16	1	17	56	167	53	71	1	.333	.414	.243
D'Angelo Jimenez	87	321	39	77	11	4	3	33	105	34	63	4	.311	.327	.240
Julius Matos	76	185	19	44	3	0	2	19	53	9	33	1	.279	.286	.238
Ray Lankford	81	205	20	46	7	1	6	26	73	30	61	2	.326	.356	.224
Wiki Gonzalez	56	164	16	36	8	1	1	20	49	27	24	0	.330	.299	.220
Tom Lampkin	104	281	32	61	10	1	10	37	103	38	59	4	.313	.367	.217
Trenidad Hubbard	89	129	16	27	5	0	1	7	35	14	28	9	.285	.271	.209

PITCHING	W–L	ERA	G	GS	CG	SV	INN	H	R	ER	BB	SO
Trevor Hoffman	2–5	2.73	61	0	0	38	59.1	52	20	18	18	69
Oliver Perez	4–5	3.50	16	15	0	0	90	71	37	35	48	94
Brian Lawrence	12–12	3.69	35	31	2	0	210	230	97	86	52	149
Brett Tomko	10–10	4.49	32	32	3	0	204.1	212	107	102	60	126
Jake Peavy	6–7	4.52	17	17	0	0	97.2	106	54	49	33	90
Jeremy Fikac	4–7	5.48	65	0	0	0	69	74	50	42	34	66
Bobby J. Jones	7–8	5.50	19	18	0	0	108	134	68	66	21	60
Brian Tollberg	1–5	6.13	12	11	0	0	61.2	88	47	42	19	33
Dennis Tankersley	1–4	8.06	17	9	0	0	51.1	59	46	46	40	39

San Francisco Giants

BATTING	G	AB	R	H	2B	3B	HR	RBI	TB	BB	SO	SB	OBP	SLG	BA
Barry Bonds	143	403	117	149	31	2	46	110	322	198	47	9	.582	.799	.370
Jeff Kent	152	623	102	195	42	2	37	108	352	52	101	5	.368	.565	.313
Benito Santiago	126	478	56	133	24	5	16	74	215	27	73	4	.315	.450	.278
Ramon E. Martinez	72	181	26	49	10	2	4	25	75	14	26	2	.335	.414	.271
Kenny Lofton	46	180	30	48	10	3	3	9	73	23	22	7	.353	.406	.267
Bill Mueller	111	366	51	96	19	4	7	38	144	52	42	0	.350	.393	.262
David Bell	154	552	82	144	29	2	20	73	237	54	80	1	.333	.429	.261
Tom Goodwin	78	154	23	40	5	2	1	17	52	14	25	16	.321	.338	.260
Rich Aurilia	133	538	76	138	35	2	15	61	222	37	90	1	.305	.413	.257
Pedro Feliz	67	146	14	37	4	1	2	13	49	6	27	0	.281	.336	.253
Reggie Sanders	140	505	75	126	23	6	23	85	230	47	121	18	.324	.455	.250
J.T. Snow	143	422	47	104	26	2	6	53	152	59	90	0	.344	.360	.246
Tsuyoshi Shinjo	118	362	42	86	15	3	9	37	134	24	46	5	.294	.370	.238
Damon Minor	83	173	21	41	6	0	10	24	77	24	34	0	.333	.445	.237
Shawon Dunston	72	147	7	34	5	0	1	9	42	3	33	1	.250	.286	.231

PITCHING	W–L	ERA	G	GS	CG	SV	INN	H	R	ER	BB	SO
Robb Nen	6–2	2.20	68	0	0	43	73.2	64	19	18	20	81
Tim Worrell	8–2	2.25	80	0	0	0	72	55	21	18	30	55
Jay Witasick	1–0	2.37	44	0	0	0	68.1	58	19	18	21	54
Chad Zerbe	2–0	3.04	50	0	0	0	56.1	52	22	19	21	26
Kirk Rueter	14–8	3.23	33	33	0	0	203.2	204	83	73	54	76
Jason Schmidt	13–8	3.45	29	29	2	0	185.1	148	78	71	73	196
Russ Ortiz	14–10	3.61	33	33	2	0	214.1	191	89	86	94	137
Felix Rodriguez	8–6	4.17	71	0	0	0	69	53	33	32	29	58
Livan Hernandez	12–16	4.38	33	33	5	0	216	233	113	105	71	134
Ryan Jensen	13–8	4.51	32	30	1	0	171.2	183	93	86	66	105

American League Team-by-Team Statistical Leaders

Anaheim Angels

BATTING	G	AB	R	H	2B	3B	HR	RBI	TB	BB	SO	SB	OBP	SLG	BA
Adam Kennedy	144	474	65	148	32	6	7	52	213	19	80	17	.345	.449	.312
Garret Anderson	158	638	93	195	56	3	29	123	344	30	80	6	.332	.539	.306
Orlando Palmeiro	110	263	35	79	12	1	0	31	93	30	22	7	.368	.354	.300
David Eckstein	152	608	107	178	22	6	8	63	236	45	44	21	.363	.388	.293
Shawn Wooten	49	113	13	33	8	0	3	19	50	7	24	2	.336	.442	.292
Brad Fullmer	129	429	75	124	35	6	19	59	228	31	44	10	.356	.531	.289
Tim Salmon	38	483	84	138	37	1	22	88	243	71	102	6	.380	.503	.286
Benji Gil	61	130	11	37	8	1	3	20	56	5	33	2	.307	.431	.285
Scott Spiezio	153	491	80	140	34	2	12	82	214	67	52	6	.371	.436	.285
Darin Erstad	150	625	99	177	28	4	10	73	243	27	67	23	.313	.389	.283
Troy Glaus	156	569	99	142	24	1	30	111	258	88	144	10	.352	.453	.250
Ben Molina	122	428	34	105	18	0	5	47	138	15	34	0	.274	.322	.245

PITCHING	W–L	ERA	G	GS	CG	SV	INN	H	R	ER	BB	SO
Troy Percival	4–1	1.92	58	0	0	40	56⅓	38	12	12	25	68
Brendan Donnelly	1–1	2.17	46	0	0	1	49⅔	32	13	12	19	54
Scot Shields	5–3	2.20	29	1	0	0	49	31	13	12	21	30
Ben Weber	7–2	2.54	63	0	0	7	78	70	25	22	22	43
Jarrod Washburn	18–6	3.15	32	32	1	0	206	183	75	72	59	139
Lou Pote	0–2	3.22	31	0	0	0	50⅓	33	20	18	26	32
John Lackey	9–4	3.66	18	18	1	0	108⅓	113	52	44	33	69
Ramon Ortiz	15–9	3.77	32	32	4	0	217⅓	188	97	91	68	162
Kevin Appier	14–12	3.92	32	32	0	0	188⅓	191	89	82	64	132
Al Levine	4–4	4.24	52	0	0	5	63⅔	61	35	30	34	40
Scott Schoeneweis	9–8	4.88	54	15	0	1	118	119	68	64	49	65
Aaron Sele	8–9	4.89	26	26	1	0	160	190	92	87	49	82

Baltimore Orioles

BATTING	G	AB	R	H	2B	3B	HR	RBI	TB	BB	SO	SB	OBP	SLG	BA
Gary Matthews Jr.	109	344	54	95	25	3	7	38	147	43	69	15	.355	.427	.276
Jeff Conine	116	451	44	123	26	4	15	63	202	25	66	8	.307	.448	.273
Jerry Hairston	122	426	55	114	25	3	5	32	160	34	55	21	.329	.376	.268
Chris Singleton	136	466	67	122	30	6	9	50	191	21	83	20	.296	.410	.262
Marty Cordova	131	458	55	116	25	2	18	64	199	47	111	1	.325	.434	.253
Jay Gibbons	136	490	71	121	29	1	28	69	236	45	66	1	.311	.482	.247
Tony Batista	161	615	90	150	36	1	31	87	281	50	107	5	.309	.457	.244
Melvin Mora	149	557	86	130	30	4	19	64	225	70	108	16	.338	.404	.233
Mike Bordick	117	367	37	85	19	3	8	36	134	35	63	7	.302	.365	.232
Geronimo Gil	125	422	33	98	19	0	12	45	153	21	88	2	.270	.363	.232
Chris Richard	50	155	15	36	11	0	4	21	59	12	30	0	.292	.381	.232
Brook Fordyce	56	130	7	30	8	0	1	8	41	9	19	1	.301	.315	.231
Brian Roberts	37	128	18	29	6	0	1	11	38	15	21	9	.308	.297	.227

PITCHING	W–L	ERA	G	GS	CG	SV	INN	H	R	ER	BB	SO
Buddy Groom	3–2	1.60	70	0	0	2	62	44	11	11	12	48
Jorge Julio	5–6	1.99	67	0	0	25	68	55	22	15	27	55
Willis Roberts	5–4	3.36	66	0	0	1	75	79	34	28	32	51
Rodrigo Lopez	15–9	3.57	33	28	1	0	196⅔	172	83	78	62	136
Rick Bauer	6–7	3.98	56	1	0	1	83⅔	84	41	37	36	45
Sidney Ponson	7–9	4.09	28	28	3	0	176	172	84	80	63	120
Jason Johnson	5–14	4.59	22	22	1	0	131⅓	141	68	67	41	97
B.J. Ryan	2–1	4.68	67	0	0	1	57⅔	51	31	30	33	56
Travis Driskill	8–8	4.95	29	19	0	0	132⅔	150	78	73	48	78
Scott Erickson	5–12	5.55	29	28	3	0	160⅔	192	109	99	68	74
Calvin Maduro	2–5	5.56	12	10	0	0	56⅔	64	37	35	22	29
John Stephens	2–5	6.09	12	11	0	0	65	68	44	44	22	56

American League Team-by-Team Statistical Leaders *(Cont.)*

Boston Red Sox

BATTING	G	AB	R	H	2B	3B	HR	RBI	TB	BB	SO	SB	OBP	SLG	BA
Manny Ramirez	120	436	84	152	31	0	33	107	282	73	85	0	.450	.647	.349
Cliff Floyd	47	171	30	54	21	0	7	18	96	15	28	4	.374	.561	.316
Nomar Garciaparra	156	635	101	197	56	5	24	120	335	41	63	5	.352	.528	.310
Shea Hillenbrand	156	634	94	186	43	4	18	83	291	25	95	4	.330	.459	.293
Carlos Baerga	73	182	17	52	11	0	2	19	69	7	20	6	.316	.379	.286
Johnny Damon	154	623	118	178	34	11	14	63	276	65	70	31	.356	.443	.286
Rey Sanchez	107	357	46	102	12	3	1	38	123	17	31	2	.318	.345	.286
Brian Daubach	137	444	62	118	24	2	20	78	206	51	126	2	.348	.464	.266
Jason Varitek	132	467	58	124	27	1	10	61	183	41	95	4	.332	.392	.266
Trot Nixon	152	532	81	136	36	3	24	94	250	65	109	4	.338	.470	.256
Lou Merloni	84	194	28	48	12	2	4	18	76	20	35	1	.332	.392	.247
Doug Mirabelli	57	151	17	34	7	0	7	25	62	17	33	0	.312	.411	.225
Ricky Henderson	72	179	40	40	6	1	5	16	63	38	47	8	.369	.352	.223
Tony Clark	90	275	25	57	12	1	3	29	80	21	57	0	.265	.291	.207

PITCHING	W–L	ERA	G	GS	CG	SV	INN	H	R	ER	BB	SO
Pedro Martinez	20–4	2.26	30	30	2	0	199⅓	144	62	50	40	239
Derek Lowe	21–8	2.58	32	32	1	0	219⅔	166	65	63	48	127
Tim Wakefield	11–5	2.81	45	15	0	3	163⅓	121	57	51	51	134
Ugueth Urbina	1–6	3.00	61	0	0	40	60	44	21	20	20	71
Casey Fossum	5–4	3.46	43	12	0	1	106⅔	113	56	41	30	101
Bob Howry	3–5	4.19	67	0	0	0	68⅔	67	37	32	21	45
John Burkett	13–8	4.53	29	29	1	0	173	199	93	87	50	124
Darren Oliver	4–5	4.66	14	9	1	0	58	70	30	30	27	32
Rolando Arrojo	4–3	4.98	29	8	0	1	81⅓	83	47	45	27	51
Frank Castillo	6–15	5.07	36	23	0	1	163⅓	174	101	92	58	112

Chicago White Sox

BATTING	G	AB	R	H	2B	3B	HR	RBI	TB	BB	SO	SB	OBP	SLG	BA
Magglio Ordonez	153	590	116	189	47	1	38	135	352	53	77	7	.381	.597	.320
Paúl Konerko	151	570	81	173	30	0	27	104	284	44	72	0	.359	.498	.304
Sandy Alomar	51	167	21	48	10	1	7	25	81	5	14	0	.309	.485	.287
D'Angelo Jimenez	27	108	22	31	4	3	1	11	44	16	10	2	.384	.407	.287
Joe Crede	53	200	28	57	10	0	12	35	103	8	40	0	.311	.515	.285
Carlos Lee	140	492	82	130	26	2	26	80	238	75	73	1	.359	.484	.264
Tony Graffanino	70	229	35	60	12	4	6	31	98	22	38	2	.329	.428	.262
Kenny Lofton	93	352	68	91	20	6	8	42	147	49	51	22	.348	.418	.259
Aaron Rowand	126	302	41	78	16	2	7	29	119	12	54	0	.298	.394	.258
Frank Thomas	148	523	77	132	29	1	28	92	247	88	115	3	.361	.472	.252
Royce Clayton	112	342	51	86	14	2	7	35	125	20	67	5	.295	.365	.251
Jose Valentin	135	474	70	118	26	4	25	75	227	43	99	3	.311	.479	.249
Willie Harris	49	163	14	38	4	0	2	12	48	9	21	8	.270	.294	.233
Jeff Liefer	76	204	28	47	8	0	7	26	76	19	60	0	.295	.373	.230
Mark Johnson	86	263	31	55	8	1	4	18	77	30	52	0	.297	.293	.209

PITCHING	W–L	ERA	G	GS	CG	SV	INN	H	R	ER	BB	SO
Damaso Marte	1–1	2.83	68	0	0	10	60⅓	44	19	19	18	72
Keith Foulke	2–4	2.90	65	0	0	11	77⅔	65	26	25	13	58
Mark Buehrle	19–12	3.58	34	34	5	0	239	236	102	95	61	134
Antonio Osuna	8–2	3.86	59	0	0	11	67⅔	64	32	29	28	66
Rocky Biddle	3–4	4.06	44	7	0	1	77⅔	7	42	35	39	64
Matt Ginter	1–0	4.47	33	0	0	1	54⅓	59	34	27	21	37
Jon Garland	12–12	4.58	33	33	1	0	192⅔	188	109	98	83	112
Danny Wright	14–12	5.18	33	33	1	0	196⅓	200	124	113	71	136
Gary Glover	7–8	5.20	41	22	0	1	138⅓	136	86	80	52	70
Todd Ritchie	5–15	6.06	26	23	0	0	133⅔	176	104	90	52	77

Cleveland Indians

BATTING	G	AB	R	H	2B	3B	HR	RBI	TB	BB	SO	SB	OBP	SLG	BA
Jim Thome	147	480	101	146	19	2	52	118	325	122	139	1	.445	.677	.304
Ellis Burks	138	518	92	156	28	0	32	91	280	44	108	2	.362	.541	.301
Karim Garcia	53	202	30	60	8	0	16	52	116	6	41	0	.314	.574	.297
Ricky Gutierrez	94	353	38	97	13	0	4	38	122	20	48	0	.325	.346	.275
Omar Vizquel	151	582	85	160	31	5	14	72	243	56	64	18	.341	.418	.275
John McDonald	93	264	35	66	11	3	1	12	86	10	50	3	.288	.326	.250
Milton Bradley	98	325	48	81	18	3	9	38	132	32	58	6	.317	.406	.249
Matt Lawton	114	416	71	98	19	2	15	57	166	59	34	8	.342	.399	.236
Lee Stevens	53	153	22	34	7	1	5	26	58	15	32	0	.285	.379	.222
Travis Fryman	118	397	42	86	14	3	11	55	139	40	82	0	.292	.350	.217
Chris Magruder	87	258	34	56	15	1	6	29	91	15	55	2	.261	.353	.217
Bill Selby	65	159	15	34	7	2	6	21	63	15	27	0	.278	.396	.214
Einar Diaz	102	320	34	66	19	0	2	16	91	17	27	0	.258	.284	.206
Russell Branyan	50	161	16	33	4	0	8	17	61	17	65	1	.278	.379	.205

PITCHING	W–L	ERA	G	GS	CG	SV	INN	H	R	ER	BB	SO
Bartolo Colon	10–4	2.55	16	16	4	0	116⅓	104	37	33	31	75
C.C. Sabathia	13–11	4.37	33	33	2	0	210	198	109	102	88	149
Danys Baez	10–11	4.41	39	26	1	6	165⅓	160	84	81	82	130
Chuck Finley	4–11	4.44	18	18	1	0	105⅓	114	56	52	48	91
Bob Wickman	1–3	4.46	36	0	0	20	34⅓	42	22	17	10	36
Terry Mulholland	3–2	4.60	16	3	0	0	47	56	27	24	14	21
Mark Wohlers	3–4	4.79	64	0	0	7	71⅓	71	41	38	26	46
Dave Burba	5–5	5.20	35	21	1	0	145⅓	155	91	84	57	95
David Riske	2–2	5.26	51	0	0	1	51⅓	49	32	30	35	65
Ryan Drese	10–9	6.55	26	26	1	0	137⅓	176	104	100	62	102

Detroit Tigers

BATTING	G	AB	R	H	2B	3B	HR	RBI	TB	BB	SO	SB	OBP	SLG	BA
Randall Simon	130	482	51	145	17	1	19	82	221	13	30	0	.320	.459	.301
Dmitri Young	54	201	25	57	14	0	7	27	92	12	39	2	.329	.458	.284
Bobby Higginson	119	444	50	125	24	3	10	63	185	41	45	12	.345	.417	.282
Wendall Magee	97	347	34	94	19	1	6	35	133	10	64	2	.289	.383	.271
Robert Fick	148	556	66	150	36	2	17	63	241	46	90	0	.331	.433	.270
Damian Jackson	81	245	31	63	20	1	1	25	88	21	36	12	.320	.359	.257
Ramon Santiago	65	222	33	54	5	5	4	20	81	13	48	8	.306	.365	.243
Carlos Pena	115	397	43	96	17	4	19	52	178	41	111	2	.316	.448	.242
George Lombard	72	241	34	58	11	3	5	13	90	20	78	13	.300	.373	.241
Shane Halter	122	410	46	98	22	6	10	39	162	39	92	0	.309	.395	.239
Mike Rivera	39	132	11	30	8	1	1	11	43	4	35	0	.254	.326	.227
Damian Easley	85	304	29	68	14	1	8	30	108	27	43	1	.307	.355	.224
Brandon Inge	95	321	27	65	15	3	7	24	107	24	101	1	.266	.333	.202
Chris Truby	89	277	23	55	13	2	2	15	78	5	71	1	.215	.282	.199
Craig Paquette	72	252	20	49	14	1	4	20	77	10	53	1	.223	.306	.194

PITCHING	W–L	ERA	G	GS	CG	SV	INN	H	R	ER	BB	SO
Juan Acevedo	1–5	2.65	65	0	0	28	74⅔	68	33	22	23	43
Julio Santana	3–5	2.84	38	0	0	0	57	49	19	18	28	38
Mark Redman	8–15	4.21	30	30	3	0	203	211	107	95	51	109
Mike Maroth	6–10	4.48	21	21	0	0	128⅔	136	68	64	36	58
Brian Powell	1–5	4.84	13	9	0	0	57⅔	64	34	31	21	30
Nate Cornejo	1–5	5.04	9	9	1	0	50	63	33	28	18	23
Steve Sparks	8–16	5.52	32	30	3	0	189	238	134	116	67	98
Jeff Farnsworth	2–3	5.79	44	0	0	0	70	100	47	45	29	28
Adam Bernero	4–7	6.20	28	11	0	0	101⅔	128	74	70	31	69
Jose Lima	4–6	7.77	20	12	0	0	68⅓	86	60	59	21	33

Kansas City Royals

BATTING	G	AB	R	H	2B	3B	HR	RBI	TB	BB	SO	SB	OBP	SLG	BA
Mike Sweeney	126	471	81	160	31	1	24	86	265	61	46	9	.417	.563	.340
Raul Ibanez	137	497	70	146	37	6	24	103	267	40	76	5	.346	.537	.294
Joe Randa	151	549	63	155	36	5	11	80	234	46	69	2	.341	.426	.282
Carlos Beltran	162	637	114	174	44	7	29	105	319	71	135	35	.346	.501	.273
A.J. Hinch	72	197	25	49	7	1	7	27	79	18	35	3	.321	.401	.249
Michael Tucker	144	475	65	118	27	6	12	56	193	56	105	23	.330	.406	.248
Carlos Febles	119	351	44	86	16	4	4	26	122	41	63	16	.336	.348	.245
Brent Mayne	101	326	35	77	8	2	4	30	101	34	54	4	.309	.310	.236
Neifi Perez	145	554	65	131	20	4	3	37	168	20	53	8	.260	.303	.236
Aaron Guiel	70	240	30	56	13	0	4	38	81	19	61	1	.296	.338	.233
Luis Alicea	94	237	28	54	8	2	1	23	69	32	34	2	.322	.291	.228
Chuck Knoblauch	80	300	41	63	9	0	6	22	90	28	32	19	.284	.300	.210
Brandon Berger	51	134	16	27	5	1	6	17	52	8	32	1	.255	.388	.201

PITCHING	W–L	ERA	G	GS	CG	SV	INN	H	R	ER	BB	SO
Paul Byrd	17–11	3.90	33	33	7	0	228⅓	224	111	99	38	129
Jason Grimsley	4–7	3.91	70	0	0	1	71⅓	64	32	31	37	59
Cory Bailey	3–4	4.11	37	0	0	1	46	53	24	21	31	24
Roberto Hernandez	1–3	4.33	53	0	0	26	52	62	29	25	12	39
Runelvys Hernandez	4–4	4.36	12	12	0	0	74½	79	36	36	22	45
Jeremy Affeldt	3–4	4.64	34	7	0	0	77⅔	85	41	40	37	67
Miguel Asencio	4–7	5.11	31	21	0	0	123⅓	136	73	70	64	58
Dan Reichert	3–5	5.32	30	6	0	0	66	77	48	39	25	36
Jeff Suppan	9–16	5.32	33	33	3	0	208	229	134	123	68	109
Darrell May	4–10	5.35	30	21	1	0	131⅓	144	83	78	50	95
Shawn Sedlacek	3–5	6.72	16	14	0	0	84½	99	64	63	36	52
Blake Stein	0–4	7.91	27	2	0	1	46⅔	59	41	41	27	42

Minnesota Twins

BATTING	G	AB	R	H	2B	3B	HR	RBI	TB	BB	SO	SB	OBP	SLG	BA
Jacque Jones	149	577	96	173	37	2	27	85	295	37	129	6	.341	.511	.300
A.J. Pierzynski	130	440	54	132	31	6	6	49	193	13	61	1	.334	.439	.300
Bobby Kielty	112	289	49	84	14	3	12	46	140	52	66	4	.405	.484	.291
Torii Hunter	148	561	89	162	37	4	29	94	294	35	118	23	.334	.524	.289
Cristian Guzman	148	623	80	170	31	6	9	59	240	17	79	12	.292	.385	.273
David Ortiz	125	412	52	112	32	1	20	75	206	43	87	1	.339	.500	.272
Dustan Mohr	120	383	55	103	23	2	12	45	166	31	86	6	.325	.433	.269
Corey Koskie	140	490	71	131	37	3	15	69	219	72	127	10	.368	.447	.267
Doug Mientkiewicz	143	467	60	122	29	1	10	64	183	74	69	1	.365	.392	.261
Matt LeCroy	63	181	19	47	11	1	7	27	81	13	38	0	.306	.448	.260
Luis Rivas	93	316	46	81	23	4	4	35	124	19	51	9	.305	.392	.256
Brian Buchanan	44	135	19	34	5	1	5	15	56	6	33	2	.294	.415	.252
Denny Hocking	102	260	28	65	13	0	2	25	84	24	44	0	.310	.323	.250

PITCHING	W–L	ERA	G	GS	CG	SV	INN	H	R	ER	BB	SO
J.C. Romero	9–2	1.89	81	0	0	1	81	62	17	17	36	76
LaTroy Hawkins	6–0	2.13	65	0	0	0	80⅓	63	23	19	15	63
Eddie Guardado	1–3	2.93	68	0	0	45	67⅔	53	22	22	18	70
Johan Santana	8–6	2.99	27	14	0	1	108⅓	84	41	36	49	137
Tony Fiore	10–3	3.16	48	2	0	0	91	74	32	32	43	55
Mike Jackson	2–3	3.27	58	0	0	0	55	59	20	20	13	29
Rick Reed	15–7	3.78	33	32	2	0	188	192	89	79	26	121
Kyle Lohse	13–8	4.23	32	31	1	0	180⅔	181	92	85	70	124
Matt Kinney	2–7	4.64	14	12	0	0	66	78	39	34	33	45
Brad Radke	9–5	4.72	21	21	2	0	118⅓	124	64	62	20	62
Eric Milton	13–9	4.84	29	29	2	0	171	173	96	92	30	121
Joe Mays	4–8	5.38	17	17	1	0	95⅓	113	60	57	25	38

New York Yankees

BATTING	G	AB	R	H	2B	3B	HR	RBI	TB	BB	SO	SB	OBP	SLG	BA
Bernie Williams	154	612	102	204	37	2	19	102	302	83	97	8	.415	.493	.333
Jason Giambi	155	560	120	176	34	1	41	122	335	109	112	2	.435	.598	.314
Alfonso Soriano	156	696	128	209	51	2	39	102	381	23	157	41	.332	.547	.300
Derek Jeter	157	644	124	191	26	0	18	75	271	73	114	32	.373	.421	.297
Jorge Posada	143	511	79	137	40	1	20	99	239	81	143	1	.370	.468	.268
Juan Rivera	28	83	9	22	5	0	1	6	30	6	10	1	.311	.361	.265
Ron Coomer	55	148	14	39	7	0	3	17	55	6	23	0	.290	.372	.264
John Vander Wal	84	219	30	57	17	1	6	20	94	23	58	1	.327	.429	.260
Shane Spencer	94	288	32	71	15	2	6	34	108	31	62	0	.324	.375	.247
Robin Ventura	141	465	68	115	17	0	27	93	213	90	101	3	.368	.458	.247
Nick Johnson	129	378	56	92	15	0	15	58	152	48	98	1	.347	.402	.243
Rondell White	126	455	59	109	21	0	14	62	172	25	86	1	.288	.378	.240
Raul Mondesi	146	569	90	132	34	1	26	88	246	59	103	15	.308	.432	.232
Enrique Wilson	60	105	17	19	2	2	2	11	31	8	22	1	.239	.295	.181

PITCHING	W–L	ERA	G	GS	CG	SV	INN	H	R	ER	BB	SO
Mariano Rivera	1–4	2.74	45	0	0	28	46	35	16	14	11	41
Mike Stanton	7–1	3.00	79	0	0	6	78	73	29	26	28	44
Steve Karsay	6–4	3.26	78	0	0	12	88⅓	87	33	32	30	65
Andy Pettitte	13–5	3.27	22	22	3	0	134¾	144	58	49	32	97
Ramiro Mendoza	8–4	3.44	62	0	0	4	91⅔	102	43	35	16	61
Jeff Weaver	11–11	3.52	32	25	3	2	199⅔	193	88	78	48	132
Orlando Hernandez	8–5	3.64	24	22	0	1	146	131	63	59	36	113
David Wells	19–7	3.75	31	31	2	0	206⅓	210	100	86	45	137
Mike Mussina	18–10	4.05	33	33	2	0	215⅔	208	103	97	48	182
Roger Clemens	13–6	4.35	29	29	0	0	180	172	94	87	63	192

Oakland Athletics

BATTING	G	AB	R	H	2B	3B	HR	RBI	TB	BB	SO	SB	OBP	SLG	BA
Miguel Tejada	162	662	108	204	30	0	34	131	336	38	84	7	.354	.508	.308
Ray Durham	150	564	114	163	34	6	15	70	254	73	93	26	.374	.450	.289
Scott Hatteberg	136	492	58	138	22	4	15	61	213	68	56	0	.374	.433	.280
Olmedo Saenz	68	156	15	43	10	1	6	18	73	13	31	1	.354	.468	.276
Eric Chavez	153	585	87	161	31	3	34	109	300	65	119	4	.348	.513	.275
John Mabry	89	193	27	53	13	1	11	40	101	14	37	1	.322	.523	.275
Jeremy Giambi	42	157	26	43	7	0	8	17	74	27	40	0	.390	.471	.274
Mark Ellis	98	345	58	94	16	4	6	35	136	44	54	4	.359	.394	.272
David Justice	118	398	54	106	18	3	11	49	163	70	66	4	.376	.410	.266
Jermaine Dye	131	488	74	123	27	1	24	86	224	52	108	2	.333	.459	.252
Terrence Long	162	587	71	141	32	4	16	67	229	48	96	3	.298	.390	.240
Adam Piatt	55	137	18	32	8	0	5	18	55	12	33	2	.303	.401	.234
Ramon Hernandez	136	403	51	94	20	0	7	42	135	43	64	0	.313	.335	.233
Randy Velarde	56	133	22	30	8	0	2	8	44	15	32	3	.325	.331	.226
Greg Myers	65	144	15	32	5	0	6	21	55	26	36	0	.341	.382	.222

PITCHING	W–L	ERA	G	GS	CG	SV	INN	H	R	ER	BB	SO
Barry Zito	23–5	2.75	35	35	1	0	229⅓	182	79	70	78	182
Tim Hudson	15–9	2.98	34	34	4	0	238⅓	237	87	79	62	152
Chad Bradford	4–2	3.11	75	0	0	2	75⅓	73	29	26	14	56
Billy Koch	11–4	3.27	84	0	0	44	93⅔	73	38	34	46	93
Mark Mulder	19–7	3.47	30	30	2	0	207¼	182	88	80	55	159
Ted Lilly	5–7	3.69	22	16	2	0	100	80	43	41	31	77
Cory Lidle	8–10	3.89	31	30	2	0	192	191	90	83	39	111
Ricardo Rincon	1–4	4.18	71	0	0	1	56	47	28	26	11	49
Jim Mecir	6–4	4.26	61	0	0	1	67¾	68	36	32	29	53
Aaron Harang	5–4	4.83	16	15	0	0	78⅓	78	44	42	45	64

Seattle Mariners

BATTING	G	AB	R	H	2B	3B	HR	RBI	TB	BB	SO	SB	OBP	SLG	BA
Ichiro Suzuki	157	647	111	208	27	8	8	51	275	68	62	31	.388	.425	.321
John Olerud	154	553	85	166	39	0	22	102	271	98	66	0	.403	.490	.300
Dan Wilson	115	359	35	106	16	1	6	44	142	18	81	1	.326	.396	.295
Bret Boone	155	608	88	169	34	3	24	107	281	53	102	12	.339	.462	.278
Edgar Martinez	97	328	42	91	23	0	15	59	159	67	69	1	.403	.485	.277
Mark McLemore	104	337	54	91	17	2	7	41	133	61	63	18	.380	.395	.270
Ruben Sierra	122	419	47	113	23	0	13	60	175	31	66	4	.319	.418	.270
Desi Relaford	112	329	55	88	13	2	6	43	123	33	51	10	.339	.374	.267
Carlos Guillen	134	475	73	124	24	6	9	56	187	46	91	4	.326	.394	.261
Ben Davis	80	228	24	59	10	1	7	43	92	18	58	1	.313	.404	.259
Jeff Cirillo	146	485	51	121	20	0	6	54	159	31	67	8	.301	.328	.249
Mike Cameron	158	545	84	130	26	5	25	80	241	79	176	31	.340	.442	.239
Jose Offerman	101	284	48	66	12	1	5	31	95	37	38	9	.320	.335	.232

PITCHING	W–L	ERA	G	GS	CG	SV	INN	H	R	ER	BB	SO
Arthur Rhodes	10–4	2.33	66	0	0	2	69⅔	45	18	18	13	81
Kazuhiro Sasaki	4–5	2.52	61	0	0	37	60⅔	44	24	17	20	73
Shigetoshi Hasegawa	8–3	3.20	53	0	0	1	70½	60	26	25	30	39
Joel Pineiro	14–7	3.24	37	28	2	0	194½	189	75	70	54	136
Jamie Moyer	13–8	3.32	34	34	4	0	230⅔	198	89	85	50	147
John Halama	6–5	3.56	31	10	0	0	101	112	45	40	33	70
Jeff Nelson	3–2	3.94	41	0	0	2	45⅔	36	20	20	27	55
Ryan Franklin	7–5	4.02	41	12	0	0	118⅔	117	62	53	22	65
Ismael Valdes	8–12	4.18	31	31	1	0	196	194	94	91	47	102
Freddy Garcia	16–7	4.39	34	34	1	0	223⅔	227	110	109	63	181
James Baldwin	7–10	5.28	30	23	0	0	150	179	95	88	49	88
Doug Creek	3–2	5.82	52	0	0	0	55⅔	57	37	36	35	56

Tampa Bay Devil Rays

BATTING	G	AB	R	H	2B	3B	HR	RBI	TB	BB	SO	SB	OBP	SLG	BA
Aubrey Huff	113	454	67	142	25	0	23	59	236	37	55	4	.364	.520	.313
Randy Winn	152	607	87	181	39	9	14	75	280	55	109	27	.360	.461	.298
Chris Gomez	130	461	51	122	31	3	10	46	189	21	58	1	.305	.410	.265
John Flaherty	76	281	27	73	20	0	4	33	105	15	50	2	.296	.374	.260
Carl Crawford	63	259	23	67	11	6	2	30	96	9	41	9	.290	.371	.259
Toby Hall	85	330	37	85	19	1	6	42	124	17	27	0	.293	.376	.258
Jason Conti	78	222	26	57	15	2	3	21	85	18	55	4	.315	.383	.257
Steve Cox	148	560	65	142	30	1	16	72	222	60	116	5	.330	.396	.254
Ben Grieve	136	482	62	121	30	0	19	64	208	69	121	8	.353	.432	.251
Andy Sheets	41	149	18	37	4	0	4	22	53	12	41	2	.301	.356	.248
Brent Abernathy	117	463	46	112	18	4	2	40	144	25	46	10	.288	.311	.242
Jared Sandberg	102	358	55	82	21	1	18	54	159	39	139	3	.305	.444	.229
Felix Escalona	59	157	17	34	8	2	0	9	46	3	44	7	.262	.293	.217
Jason Tyner	44	168	17	36	2	1	0	9	40	7	19	7	.249	.238	.214
Greg Vaughn	69	251	28	41	10	2	8	29	79	41	82	3	.286	.315	.163

PITCHING	W–L	ERA	G	GS	CG	SV	INN	H	R	ER	BB	SO
Esteban Yan	7–8	4.30	55	0	0	19	69	70	35	33	29	53
Joe Kennedy	8–11	4.53	30	30	5	0	196⅔	204	114	99	55	109
Paul Wilson	6–12	4.83	30	30	1	0	193⅔	219	113	104	67	111
Tanyon Sturtze	4–18	5.18	33	33	4	0	224	271	141	129	89	137
Wilson Alvarez	2–3	5.28	23	10	0	1	75	80	47	44	36	56
Travis Harper	5–9	5.46	37	7	0	1	85⅔	101	54	52	27	60
Jorge Sosa	2–7	5.53	31	14	0	0	99½	88	63	61	54	48
Victor Zambrano	8–8	5.53	42	11	0	1	114.0	120	77	70	68	73
Ryan Rupe	5–10	5.60	15	15	2	0	90	83	60	56	25	67
Steve Kent	0–2	5.65	34	0	0	1	57⅓	67	41	36	38	41

American League Team-by-Team Statistical Leaders *(Cont.)*

Texas Rangers

BATTING	G	AB	R	H	2B	3B	HR	RBI	TB	BB	SO	SB	OBP	SLG	BA
Ivan Rodriguez	108	408	67	128	32	2	19	60	221	25	71	5	.353	.542	.314
Alex Rodriguez	162	624	125	187	27	2	57	142	389	87	122	9	.392	.623	.300
Rusty Greer	51	199	24	59	9	2	1	17	75	19	17	1	.356	.377	.296
Mike Lamb	115	314	54	89	13	0	9	33	129	33	48	0	.354	.411	.283
Juan Gonzalez	70	277	38	78	21	1	8	35	125	17	56	2	.324	.451	.282
Herbert Perry	132	450	64	124	24	1	22	77	216	34	66	4	.333	.480	.276
Rafael Palmeiro	155	546	99	149	34	0	43	105	312	104	94	2	.391	.571	.273
Frank Catalanotto	68	212	42	57	16	6	3	23	94	25	27	9	.364	.443	.269
Carl Everett	105	374	47	100	16	0	16	62	164	33	77	2	.333	.439	.267
Mike Young	156	573	77	150	26	8	9	62	219	41	112	6	.308	.382	.262
Gabe Kapler	72	196	25	51	12	1	0	17	65	8	30	5	.285	.332	.260
Kevin Mench	110	366	52	95	20	2	15	60	164	31	83	1	.327	.448	.260
Bill Haselman	69	179	16	44	7	0	3	18	60	11	25	0	.297	.335	.246
Hank Blalock	49	147	16	31	8	0	3	17	48	20	43	0	.306	.327	.211
Ruben Rivera	69	158	17	33	4	0	4	14	49	17	45	4	.302	.310	.209

PITCHING	W–L	ERA	G	GS	CG	SV	INN	H	R	ER	BB	SO
Francisco Cordero	2–0	1.79	39	0	0	10	45⅓	33	12	9	13	41
Jay Powell	3–2	3.44	51	0	0	0	49⅔	50	28	19	24	35
Kenny Rogers	13–8	3.84	33	33	2	0	210⅔	212	101	90	70	107
Doug Davis	3–5	4.98	10	10	1	0	59⅔	67	36	33	22	28
Joaquin Benoit	4–5	5.31	17	13	0	1	84⅔	91	51	50	58	59
Todd Van Poppel	3–2	5.45	50	0	0	1	72⅔	80	44	44	29	85
Hideki Irabu	3–8	5.74	38	2	0	16	47	51	30	30	16	30
Chan Ho Park	9–8	5.75	25	25	0	0	145⅔	154	95	9	78	121
Rob Bell	4–3	6.22	17	15	0	0	94	113	69	65	35	70
Aaron Myette	2–5	10.06	15	12	0	0	48⅓	64	57	54	41	48

Toronto Blue Jays

BATTING	G	AB	R	H	2B	3B	HR	RBI	TB	BB	SO	SB	OBP	SLG	BA
Josh Phelps	74	265	41	82	20	1	15	58	149	19	82	0	.362	.562	.309
Shannon Stewart	141	577	103	175	38	6	10	45	255	54	60	14	.371	.442	.303
Eric Hinske	151	566	99	158	38	2	24	84	272	77	138	13	.365	.481	.279
Carlos Delgado	143	505	103	140	34	2	33	108	277	102	126	1	.406	.549	.277
Orlando Hudson	54	192	20	53	10	5	4	23	85	11	27	0	.319	.443	.276
Chris Woodward	90	312	48	86	13	4	13	45	146	26	72	3	.330	.468	.276
Vernon Wells	159	608	87	167	34	4	23	100	278	27	85	9	.305	.457	.275
Dave Berg	109	374	42	101	26	2	4	39	143	26	57	0	.322	.382	.270
Tom Wilson	96	265	33	68	10	0	8	37	102	28	79	0	.334	.385	.257
Jose Cruz	124	466	64	114	26	5	18	70	204	51	106	7	.317	.438	.245
Kevin Huckaby	88	273	29	67	6	1	3	22	84	9	44	0	.270	.308	.245
Felipe Lopez	85	282	35	64	15	3	8	34	109	23	90	5	.287	.387	.227
Darrin Fletcher	45	127	8	28	6	0	3	22	43	4	13	0	.239	.339	.220
Joe Lawrence	55	150	16	27	4	0	2	15	37	16	38	2	.262	.247	.180

PITCHING	W–L	ERA	G	GS	CG	SV	INN	H	R	ER	BB	SO
Roy Halladay	19–7	2.93	34	34	2	0	239⅓	223	93	78	62	168
Felix Heredia	1–2	3.61	53	0	0	0	52⅓	51	29	21	26	31
Cliff Politte	1–3	3.61	55	0	0	1	57⅓	38	23	23	19	57
Kelvim Escobar	5–7	4.27	76	0	0	38	78	75	39	37	44	85
Pete Walker	10–5	4.33	37	20	0	1	139⅓	143	72	67	51	80
Corey Thurman	2–3	4.37	43	1	0	0	68	65	34	33	45	56
Scott Eyre	2–4	4.97	49	3	0	0	63.	69	37	35	29	51
Chris Carpenter	4–5	5.28	13	13	1	0	73⅓	89	45	43	27	45
Justin Miller	9–5	5.54	25	18	0	0	102⅓	103	70	63	66	68
Esteban Loaiza	9–10	5.71	25	25	3	0	151⅓	192	102	96	38	87
Scott Cassidy	1–4	5.73	58	0	0	0	66	52	42	42	32	48
Steve Parris	5–5	5.97	14	14	0	0	75⅓	96	50	50	35	48
Brandon Lyon	1–4	6.53	15	10	0	0	62	78	47	45	19	30
Luke Prokopec	2–9	6.78	22	12	0	0	71⅔	90	57	54	25	41

The World Series

Results

1903	Boston (A) 5, Pittsburgh (N) 3
1904	No series
1905	New York (N) 4, Philadelphia (A) 1
1906	Chicago (A) 4, Chicago (N) 2
1907	Chicago (N) 4, Detroit (A) 0; 1 tie
1908	Chicago (N) 4, Detroit (A) 1
1909	Pittsburgh (N) 4, Detroit (A) 3
1910	Philadelphia (A) 4, Chicago (N) 1
1911	Philadelphia (A) 4, New York (N) 2
1912	Boston (A) 4, New York (N) 3; 1 tie
1913	Philadelphia (A) 4, New York (N) 1
1914	Boston (N) 4, Philadelphia (A) 0
1915	Boston (A) 4, Philadelphia (N) 1
1916	Boston (A) 4, Brooklyn (N) 1
1917	Chicago (A) 4, New York (N) 2
1918	Boston (A) 4, Chicago (N) 2
1919	Cincinnati (N) 5, Chicago (A) 3
1920	Cleveland (A) 5, Brooklyn (N) 2
1921	New York (N) 5, New York (A) 3
1922	New York (N) 4, New York (A) 0; 1 tie
1923	New York (A) 4, New York (N) 2
1924	Washington (A) 4, New York (N) 3
1925	Pittsburgh (N) 4, Washington (A) 3
1926	St. Louis (N) 4, New York (A) 3
1927	New York (A) 4, Pittsburgh (N) 0
1928	New York (A) 4, St. Louis (N) 0
1929	Philadelphia (A) 4, Chicago (N) 1
1930	Philadelphia (A) 4, St. Louis (N) 2
1931	St. Louis (N) 4, Philadelphia (A) 3
1932	New York (A) 4, Chicago (N) 0
1933	New York (N) 4, Washington (A) 1
1934	St. Louis (N) 4, Detroit (A) 3
1935	Detroit (A) 4, Chicago (N) 2
1936	New York (A) 4, New York (N) 2
1937	New York (A) 4, New York (N) 1
1938	New York (A) 4, Chicago (N) 0
1939	New York (A) 4, Cincinnati (N) 0
1940	Cincinnati (N) 4, Detroit (A) 3
1941	New York (A) 4, Brooklyn (N) 1
1942	St. Louis (N) 4, New York (A) 1
1943	New York (A) 4, St. Louis (N) 1
1944	St. Louis (N) 4, St. Louis (A) 2
1945	Detroit (A) 4, Chicago (N) 3
1946	St. Louis (N) 4, Boston (A) 3
1947	New York (A) 4, Brooklyn (N) 3
1948	Cleveland (A) 4, Boston (N) 2
1949	New York (A) 4, Brooklyn (N) 1
1950	New York (A) 4, Philadelphia (N) 0
1951	New York (A) 4, New York (N) 2
1952	New York (A) 4, Brooklyn (N) 3
1953	New York (A) 4, Brooklyn (N) 2
1954	New York (N) 4, Cleveland (A) 0
1955	Brooklyn (N) 4, New York (A) 3
1956	New York (A) 4, Brooklyn (N) 3
1957	Milwaukee (N) 4, New York (A) 3
1958	New York (A) 4, Milwaukee (N) 3
1959	Los Angeles (N) 4, Chicago (A) 2
1960	Pittsburgh (N) 4, New York (A) 3
1961	New York (A) 4, Cincinnati (N) 1
1962	New York (A) 4, San Francisco (N) 3
1963	Los Angeles (N) 4, New York (A) 0
1964	St. Louis (N) 4, New York (A) 3
1965	Los Angeles (N) 4, Minnesota (A) 3
1966	Baltimore (A) 4, Los Angeles (N) 0
1967	St. Louis (N) 4, Boston (A) 3
1968	Detroit (A) 4, St. Louis (N) 3
1969	New York (N) 4, Baltimore (A) 1
1970	Baltimore (A) 4, Cincinnati (N) 1
1971	Pittsburgh (N) 4, Baltimore (A) 3
1972	Oakland (A) 4, Cincinnati (N) 3
1973	Oakland (A) 4, New York (N) 3
1974	Oakland (A) 4, Los Angeles (N) 1
1975	Cincinnati (N) 4, Boston (A) 3
1976	Cincinnati (N) 4, New York (A) 0
1977	New York (A) 4, Los Angeles (N) 2
1978	New York (A) 4, Los Angeles (N) 2
1979	Pittsburgh (N) 4, Baltimore (A) 3
1980	Philadelphia (N) 4, Kansas City (A) 2
1981	Los Angeles (N) 4, New York (A) 2
1982	St. Louis (N) 4, Milwaukee (A) 3
1983	Baltimore (A) 4, Philadelphia (N) 1
1984	Detroit (A) 4, San Diego (N) 1
1985	Kansas City (A) 4, St. Louis (N) 3
1986	New York (N) 4, Boston (A) 3
1987	Minnesota (A) 4, St. Louis (N) 3
1988	Los Angeles (N) 4, Oakland (A) 1
1989	Oakland (A) 4, San Francisco (N) 0
1990	Cincinnati (N) 4, Oakland (A) 0
1991	Minnesota (A) 4, Atlanta (N) 3
1992	Toronto (A) 4, Atlanta (N) 2
1993	Toronto (A) 4, Philadelphia (N) 2
1994	Series canceled due to players' strike.
1995	Atlanta (N) 4, Cleveland (A) 2
1996	New York (A) 4, Atlanta (N) 2
1997	Florida (N) 4, Cleveland (A) 3
1998	New York (A) 4, San Diego (N) 0
1999	New York (A) 4, Atlanta (N) 0
2000	New York (A) 4 , New York (N) 1
2001	Arizona (N) 4, New York (A) 3
2002	Anaheim (A) 4, San Francisco (N) 3

Most Valuable Players

1955	Johnny Podres, Bklyn
1956	Don Larsen, NY (A)
1957	Lew Burdette, Mil
1958	Bob Turley, NY (A)
1959	Larry Sherry, LA
1960	Bobby Richardson, NY (A)
1961	Whitey Ford, NY (A)
1962	Ralph Terry, NY (A)
1963	Sandy Koufax, LA
1964	Bob Gibson, StL
1965	Sandy Koufax, LA
1966	Frank Robinson, Balt
1967	Bob Gibson, StL
1968	Mickey Lolich, Det
1969	Donn Clendenon, NY (N)
1970	Brooks Robinson, Balt
1971	Roberto Clemente, Pitt
1972	Gene Tenace, Oak
1973	Reggie Jackson, Oak
1974	Rollie Fingers, Oak
1975	Pete Rose, Cin
1976	Johnny Bench, Cin
1977	Reggie Jackson, NY (A)
1978	Bucky Dent, NY (A)
1979	Willie Stargell, Pitt
1980	Mike Schmidt, Phil
1981	Ron Cey, LA; Steve Yeager, LA; Pedro Guerrero, LA
1982	Darrell Porter, StL
1983	Rick Dempsey, Balt
1984	Alan Trammell, Det
1985	Bret Saberhagen, KC
1986	Ray Knight, NY (N)
1987	Frank Viola, Minn
1988	Orel Hershiser, LA
1989	Dave Stewart, Oak
1990	Jose Rijo, Cin
1991	Jack Morris, Minn
1992	Pat Borders, Tor
1993	Paul Molitor, Tor
1994	Series canceled due to strike.
1995	Tom Glavine, Atl
1996	John Wetteland, NY (A)
1997	Livan Hernandez, Fla
1998	Scott Brosius, NY (A)
1999	Mariano Rivera, NY (A)
2000	Derek Jeter, NY (A)
2001	Randy Johnson, Ariz; Curt Schilling, Ariz
2002	Troy Glaus, Ana

Career Batting Leaders (Minimum 40 at bats)

GAMES

Yogi Berra	75
Mickey Mantle	65
Elston Howard	54
Hank Bauer	53
Gil McDougald	53
Phil Rizzuto	52
Joe DiMaggio	51
Frankie Frisch	50
Pee Wee Reese	44
Roger Maris	41
Babe Ruth	41

AT BATS

Yogi Berra	259
Mickey Mantle	230
Joe DiMaggio	199
Frankie Frisch	197
Gil McDougald	190
Hank Bauer	188
Phil Rizzuto	183
Elston Howard	171
Pee Wee Reese	169
Roger Maris	152

HITS

Yogi Berra	71
Mickey Mantle	59
Frankie Frisch	58
Joe DiMaggio	54
Pee Wee Reese	46
Hank Bauer	46
Phil Rizzuto	45
Gil McDougald	45
Lou Gehrig	43
Eddie Collins	42
Babe Ruth	42
Elston Howard	42

BATTING AVERAGE

Bobby Brown	.439
Paul Molitor	.418
Pepper Martin	.418
Hal McRae	.400
Lou Brock	.391
Marquis Grissom	.390
Thurman Munson	.373
George Brett	.373
Pat Borders	.372
Hank Aaron	.364

HOME RUNS

Mickey Mantle	18
Babe Ruth	15
Yogi Berra	12
Duke Snider	11
Reggie Jackson	10
Lou Gehrig	10
Frank Robinson	8
Bill Skowron	8
Joe DiMaggio	8
Goose Goslin	7
Hank Bauer	7
Gil McDougald	7

RUNS BATTED IN

Mickey Mantle	40
Yogi Berra	39
Lou Gehrig	35
Babe Ruth	33
Joe DiMaggio	30
Bill Skowron	29
Duke Snider	26
Reggie Jackson	24
Bill Dickey	24
Hank Bauer	24
Gil McDougald	24

RUNS

Mickey Mantle	42
Yogi Berra	41
Babe Ruth	37
Lou Gehrig	30
Joe DiMaggio	27
Roger Maris	26
Elston Howard	25
Gil McDougald	23
Jackie Robinson	22
Derek Jeter	22

STOLEN BASES

Lou Brock	14
Eddie Collins	14
Frank Chance	10
Davey Lopes	10
Phil Rizzuto	10
Honus Wagner	9
Frankie Frisch	9
Johnny Evers	8
Kenny Lofton	8
Roberto Alomar	7
Joe Tinker	7
Pepper Martin	7
Joe Morgan	7
Rickey Henderson	7

Career Batting Leaders (Cont.)

TOTAL BASES

Mickey Mantle	123
Yogi Berra	117
Babe Ruth	96
Lou Gehrig	87
Joe DiMaggio	84
Duke Snider	79
Hank Bauer	75
Reggie Jackson	74
Frankie Frisch	74
Gil McDougald	72

SLUGGING AVERAGE

Reggie Jackson	.755
Babe Ruth	.744
Lou Gehrig	.731
Bobby Brown	.707
Lenny Dykstra	.700
Al Simmons	.658
Lou Brock	.655
Pepper Martin	.636
Paul Molitor	.636
Joe Harris	.625

STRIKEOUTS

Mickey Mantle	54
Elston Howard	37
Duke Snider	33
Babe Ruth	30
David Justice	30
Gil McDougald	29
Bill Skowron	26
Derek Jeter	26
Hank Bauer	25
Reggie Jackson	24
Bob Meusel	24
Bernie Williams	24

Career Pitching Leaders

GAMES

Whitey Ford	22
Mike Stanton	19
Mariano Rivera	18
Rollie Fingers	16
Allie Reynolds	15
Bob Turley	15
Clay Carroll	14
Clem Labine	13
Mark Wohlers	13
Jeff Nelson	13

LOSSES

Whitey Ford	8
Eddie Plank	5
Schoolboy Rowe	5
Joe Bush	5
Rube Marquard	5
Christy Mathewson	5

COMPLETE GAMES

Christy Mathewson	10
Chief Bender	9
Bob Gibson	8
Red Ruffing	7
Whitey Ford	7
George Mullin	6
Eddie Plank	6
Art Nehf	6
Waite Hoyt	6

INNINGS PITCHED

Whitey Ford	146
Christy Mathewson	101⅔
Red Ruffing	85⅔
Chief Bender	85
Waite Hoyt	83⅔
Bob Gibson	81
Art Nehf	79
Allie Reynolds	77
Jim Palmer	65
Catfish Hunter	63

SAVES

Mariano Rivera	8
Rollie Fingers	6
Allie Reynolds	4
Johnny Murphy	4
John Wetteland	4
Robb Nen	4

STRIKEOUTS

Whitey Ford	94
Bob Gibson	92
Allie Reynolds	62
Sandy Koufax	61
Red Ruffing	61
Chief Bender	59
George Earnshaw	56
John Smoltz	52
Waite Hoyt	49
Christy Mathewson	48

*EARNED RUN AVERAGE

Jack Billingham	0.35
Harry Brecheen	0.83
Babe Ruth	0.87
Sherry Smith	0.89
Sandy Koufax	0.95
Hippo Vaughn	1.00
Monte Pearson	1.01
Christy Mathewson	1.06
Babe Adams	1.29
Eddie Plank	1.32

WINS

Whitey Ford	10
Bob Gibson	7
Red Ruffing	7
Allie Reynolds	7
Lefty Gomez	6
Chief Bender	6
Waite Hoyt	6
Jack Coombs	5
Three Finger Brown	5
Herb Pennock	5
Christy Mathewson	5
Vic Raschi	5
Catfish Hunter	5

SHUTOUTS

Christy Mathewson	4
Three Finger Brown	3
Whitey Ford	3
Bill Hallahan	2
Lew Burdette	2
Bill Dinneen	2
Sandy Koufax	2
Allie Reynolds	2
Art Nehf	2
Bob Gibson	2

BASES ON BALLS

Whitey Ford	34
Allie Reynolds	32
Art Nehf	32
Jim Palmer	31
Bob Turley	29
Paul Derringer	27
Red Ruffing	27
Don Gullett	26
Burleigh Grimes	26
Vic Raschi	25

*Minimum 25 innings pitched.

Alltime Team Rankings (by championships)

Team	W	L	Appearances	Pct.	Most Recent	Last Championship
New York Yankees	26	12	38	.684	2001	2000
Phil/KC/Oakland Athletics	9	5	14	.643	1990	1989
St. Louis Cardinals	9	6	15	.600	1987	1982
Brooklyn/LA Dodgers	6	12	18	.333	1988	1988
Pittsburgh Pirates	5	2	7	.714	1979	1979
Cincinnati Reds	5	4	9	.556	1990	1990
Boston Red Sox	5	4	9	.556	1986	1918
New York/San Francisco Giants	5	12	17	.294	2002	1954
Detroit Tigers	4	5	9	.444	1984	1984
Washington/Minnesota Twins	3	3	6	.500	1991	1991
St. Louis/Baltimore Orioles	3	4	7	.429	1983	1983
Boston/Milwaukee/Atlanta Braves	3	6	9	.333	1999	1995
Toronto Blue Jays	2	0	2	1.000	1993	1993
New York Mets	2	2	4	.500	2000	1986
Chicago White Sox	2	2	4	.500	1959	1917
Cleveland Indians	2	3	5	.400	1997	1948
Chicago Cubs	2	8	10	.200	1945	1908
Anaheim Angels	1	0	1	1.000	2002	2002
Arizona Diamondbacks	1	0	1	1.000	2001	2001
Florida Marlins	1	0	1	1.000	1997	1997
Kansas City Royals	1	1	2	.500	1985	1985
Philadelphia Phillies	1	4	5	.200	1993	1980
Seattle/Milwaukee Brewers	0	1	1	.000	1982	—
San Diego Padres	0	2	2	.000	1998	—

League Championship Series

National League

1969	New York (E) 3, Atlanta (W) 0
1970	Cincinnati (W) 3, Pittsburgh (E) 0
1971	Pittsburgh (E) 3, San Francisco (W) 1
1972	Cincinnati (W) 3, Pittsburgh (E) 2
1973	New York (E) 3, Cincinnati (W) 2
1974	Los Angeles (W) 3, Pittsburgh (E) 1
1975	Cincinnati (W) 3, Pittsburgh (E) 0
1976	Cincinnati (W) 3, Philadelphia (E) 0
1977	Los Angeles (W) 3, Philadelphia (E) 1
1978	Los Angeles (W) 3, Philadelphia (E) 1
1979	Pittsburgh (E) 3, Cincinnati (W) 0
1980	Philadelphia (E) 3, Houston (W) 2
1981	Los Angeles (W) 3, Montreal (E) 2
1982	St. Louis (E) 3, Atlanta (W) 0
1983	Philadelphia (E) 3, Los Angeles (W) 1
1984	San Diego (W) 3, Chicago (E) 2
1985	St. Louis (E) 4, Los Angeles (W) 2
1986	New York (E) 4, Houston (W) 2
1987	St. Louis (E) 4, San Francisco (W) 3
1988	Los Angeles (W) 4, New York (E) 3
1989	San Francisco (W) 4, Chicago (E) 1
1990	Cincinnati (W) 4, Pittsburgh (E) 2
1991	Atlanta (W) 4, Pittsburgh (E) 3
1992	Atlanta (W) 4, Pitsburgh (E) 3
1993	Philadelphia (E) 4, Atlanta (W) 2
1994	Playoffs canceled due to players' strike.
1995	Atlanta (E) 4, Cincinnati (C) 0
1996	Atlanta (E) 4, St. Louis (C) 3
1997	Florida (wc) 4, Atlanta (E) 2
1998	San Diego (W) 4, Atlanta (E) 2
1999	Atlanta (E) 4, New York (wc) 2
2000	New York (wc) 4, St. Louis (C) 1
2001	Arizona (W) 4, Atlanta (E) 1
2002	San Francisco (wc) 4, St. Louis (C) 1

American League

1969	Baltimore (E) 3, Minnesota (W) 0
1970	Baltimore (E) 3, Minnesota (W) 0
1971	Baltimore (E) 3, Oakland (W) 0
1972	Oakland (W) 3, Detroit (E) 2
1973	Oakland (W) 3, Baltimore (E) 2
1974	Oakland (W) 3, Baltimore (E) 1
1975	Boston (E) 3, Oakland (W) 0
1976	New York (E) 3, Kansas City (W) 2
1977	New York (E) 3, Kansas City (W) 2
1978	New York (E) 3, Kansas City (W) 1
1979	Baltimore (E) 3, California (W) 1
1980	Kansas City (W) 3, New York (E) 0
1981	New York (E) 3, Oakland (W) 0
1982	Milwaukee (E) 3, California (W) 2
1983	Baltimore (E) 3, Chicago (W) 1
1984	Detroit (E) 3, Kansas City (W) 0
1985	Kansas City (W) 4, Toronto (E) 3
1986	Boston (E) 4, California (W) 3
1987	Minnesota (W) 4, Detroit (E) 1
1988	Oakland (W) 4, Boston (E) 0
1989	Oakland (W) 4, Toronto (E) 1
1990	Oakland (W) 4, Boston (E) 0
1991	Minnesota (W) 4, Toronto (E) 1
1992	Toronto (E) 4, Oakland (W) 2
1993	Toronto (E) 4, Chicago (W) 2
1994	Playoffs canceled due to players' strike.
1995	Cleveland (C) 4, Seattle (W) 2
1996	New York (E) 4, Baltimore (wc) 1
1997	Cleveland (C) 4, Baltimore (E) 2
1998	New York (E) 4, Cleveland (C) 2
1999	New York (E) 4, Boston (wc) 1
2000	New York (E) 4, Seattle (wc) 2
2001	New York (wc) 4, Seattle (W) 1
2002	Anaheim (wc) 4, Minnesota (C) 1

NLCS Most Valuable Player

1977.......Dusty Baker, LA	1986.......Mike Scott, Hou	1995........Mike Devereaux, Atl
1978........Steve Garvey, LA	1987.......Jeffrey Leonard, SF	1996........Javier Lopez, Atl
1979........Willie Stargell, Pitt	1988........Orel Hershiser, LA	1997........Livan Hernandez, Fla
1980........Manny Trillo, Phil	1989........Will Clark, SF	1998........Sterling Hitchcock, SD
1981........Burt Hooton, LA	1990........R. Myers/R. Dibble, Cin	1999........Eddie Perez, Atl
1982........Darrell Porter, StL	1991........Steve Avery, Atl	2000........Mike Hampton, NY
1983........Gary Matthews, Phil	1992........John Smoltz, Atl	2001........Craig Counsell, Ariz
1984........Steve Garvey, SD	1993........Curt Schilling, Phil	2002........Benito Santiago, SF
1985........Ozzie Smith, StL	1994........Playoffs canceled	

ALCS Most Valuable Player

1980........Frank White, KC	1988........Dennis Eckersley, Oak	1996........Bernie Williams, NY
1981........Graig Nettles, NY	1989........Rickey Henderson, Oak	1997........Marquis Grissom, Clev
1982........Fred Lynn, Calif	1990........Dave Stewart, Oak	1998........David Wells, NY
1983........Mike Boddicker, Balt	1991........Kirby Puckett, Minn	1999........Orlando Hernandez, NY
1984........Kirk Gibson, Det	1992........Roberto Alomar, Tor	2000........David Justice, NY
1985........George Brett, KC	1993........Dave Stewart, Tor	2001........Andy Pettitte, NY
1986........Marty Barrett, Bos	1994........Playoffs canceled	2002........Adam Kennedy, Ana
1987........Gary Gaetti, Minn	1995........Orel Hershiser, Clev	

Divisional Playoffs

National League

1995	Atlanta (E) 3, Colorado (wc) 1
	Cincinnati (C) 3, Los Angeles (W) 0
1996	St. Louis (C) 3, San Diego (W) 0
	Atlanta (E) 3, Los Angeles (wc) 0
1997	Atlanta (E) 3, Houston (C) 0
	Florida (wc) 3, San Francisco (W) 0
1998	San Diego (W) 3, Houston (C) 1
	Atlanta (E) 3, Chicago (wc) 0
1999	Atlanta (E) 3, Houston (C) 1
	New York (wc) 3, Arizona (W) 1
2000	St. Louis (C) 3, Atlanta (E) 0
	New York (wc) 3, San Francisco (W) 1
2001	Atlanta (E) 3, Houston (C) 0
	Arizona (W) 3, St. Louis (wc) 2
2002	St. Louis (C) 3, Arizona (W) 0
	San Francisco (wc) 3, Atlanta (E) 2

American League

1995	Cleveland (C) 3, Boston (E) 0
	Seattle (W) 3, New York (wc) 2
1996	Baltimore (wc) 3, Cleveland (C) 1
	New York (E) 3, Texas (W) 1
1997	Baltimore (E) 3, Seattle (W) 1
	Cleveland (C) 3, New York (wc) 2
1998	New York (E) 3, Texas (W) 0
	Cleveland (C) 3, Boston (wc) 1
1999	New York (E) 3, Texas (W) 1
	Boston (wc) 3, Cleveland (C) 2
2000	New York (E) 3, Oakland (W) 2
	Seattle (wc) 3, Chicago (C) 0
2001	Seattle (W) 3, Cleveland (wc) 2
	New York (E) 3, Oakland (wc) 2
2002	Minnesota (C) 3, Oakland (W) 2
	Anaheim (wc) 3, New York (E) 1

The All-Star Game

Results

Date	Winner	Score	Site	Date	Winner	Score	Site
7-6-33	American	4–2	Comiskey Park, Chi	7-14-53	National	5–1	Crosley Field, Cin
7-10-34	American	9–7	Polo Grounds, NY	7-13-54	American	11–9	Municipal Stadium, Clev
7-8-35	American	4–1	Municipal Stadium, Clev	7-12-55	National	6–5	County Stadium, Mil
7-7-36	National	4–3	Braves Field, Bos	7-10-56	National	7–3	Griffith Stadium, Wash
7-7-37	American	8–3	Griffith Stadium, Wash	7-9-57	American	6–5	Busch Stadium, StL
7-6-38	National	4–1	Crosley Field, Cin	7-8-58	American	4–3	Memorial Stadium, Balt
7-11-39	American	3–1	Yankee Stadium, NY	7-7-59	National	5–4	Forbes Field, Pitt
7-10-40	National	4–0	Sportsman's Park, StL	8-3-59	American	5–3	Memorial Coliseum, LA
7-8-41	American	7–5	Briggs Stadium, Det	7-11-60	National	5–3	Municipal Stadium, KC
7-6-42	American	3–1	Polo Grounds, NY	7-13-60	National	6–0	Yankee Stadium, NY
7-13-43	American	5–3	Shibe Park, Phil	7-11-61	National	5–4	Candlestick Park, SF
7-11-44	National	7–1	Forbes Field, Pitt	7-31-61	Tie*	1–1	Fenway Park, Bos
1945 ....No game due to wartime travel restrictions.				7-10-62	National	3–1	D.C. Stadium, Wash
7-9-46	American	12–0	Fenway Park, Bos	7-30-62	American	9–4	Wrigley Field, Chi
7-8-47	American	2–1	Wrigley Field, Chi	7-9-63	National	5–3	Municipal Stadium, Clev
7-13-48	American	5–2	Sportsman's Park, StL	7-7-64	National	7–4	Shea Stadium, NY
7-12-49	American	11–7	Ebbets Field, Bklyn	7-13-65	National	6–5	Metropolitan Stadium, Minn
7-11-50	National	4–3	Comiskey Park, Chi				
7-10-51	National	8–3	Briggs Stadium, Det	7-12-66	National	2–1	Busch Stadium, StL
7-8-52	National	3–2	Shibe Park, Phil	7-11-67	National	2–1	Anaheim Stadium, Cal
				7-9-68	National	1–0	Astrodome, Hou

*Game called because of rain after nine innings.

Results *(Cont.)*

Date	Winner	Score	Site
7-23-69....National	9–3	R.F.K. Memorial Stadium, Wash
7-14-70....National	5–4	Riverfront Stadium, Cin
7-13-71....American	6–4	Tiger Stadium, Det
7-25-72....National	4–3	Atlanta Stadium, Atl
7-24-73....National	7–1	Royals Stadium, KC
7-23-74....National	7–2	Three Rivers Stadium, Pitt
7-15-75....National	6–3	County Stadium, Mil
7-13-76....National	7–1	Veterans Stadium, Phil
7-19-77....National	7–5	Yankee Stadium, NY
7-11-78....National	7–3	Jack Murphy Stadium, SD
7-17-79....National	7–6	Kingdome, Sea
7-8-80.....National	4–2	Dodger Stadium, LA
8-9-81 ....National	5–4	Municipal Stadium, Clev
7-13-82....National	4–1	Olympic Stadium, Mtl
7-6-83 ....American	13–3	Comiskey Park, Chi
7-10-84....National	3–1	Candlestick Park, SF
7-16-85 ...National	6–1	Metrodome, Minn

Date	Winner	Score	Site
7-15-86 ...American	3–2	Astrodome, Hou
7-14-87 ...National	2–0	Oakland Coliseum, Oak
7-12-88 ...American	2–1	Riverfront Stadium, Cin
7-11-89 ...American	5–3	Anaheim Stadium, Cal
7-10-90 ...American	2–0	Wrigley Field, Chi
7-9-91 .....American	4–2	SkyDome, Tor
7-14-92 ...American	13–6	Jack Murphy Stadium, SD
7-13-93 ...American	9–3	Camden Yards, Balt
7-12-94 ...National	8–7	Three Rivers Stadium, Pitt
7-11-95....National	3–2	The Ballpark in Arlington, Tex
7-9-96......National	6–0	Veterans Stadium, Phil
7-8-97......American	3–1	Jacobs Field, Clev
7-7-98......American	13–8	Coors Field, Col
7-13-99....American	4–1	Fenway Park, Bos
7-11-00....American	6–3	Turner Field, Atl
7-10-01 ...American	4–1	Safeco Field, Sea
7-9-02 .....Tie (11 inn)	7–7	Miller Park, Milwaukee

Most Valuable Players

1962...Maury Wills, LA	NL	
Leon Wagner, LA	AL	
1963...Willie Mays, SF	NL	
1964...Johnny Callison, Phil	NL	
1965...Juan Marichal, SF	NL	
1966...Brooks Robinson, Balt	AL	
1967...Tony Perez, Cin	NL	
1968...Willie Mays, SF	NL	
1969...Willie McCovey, SF	NL	
1970...Carl Yastrzemski, Bos	AL	
1971...Frank Robinson, Balt	AL	
1972...Joe Morgan, Cin	NL	
1973...Bobby Bonds, SF	NL	
1974...Steve Garvey, LA	NL	
1975...Bill Madlock, Chi	NL	
Jon Matlack, NY	NL	
1976...George Foster, Cin	NL	
1977...Don Sutton, LA	NL	
1978...Steve Garvey, LA	NL	
1979...Dave Parker, Pitt	NL	
1980...Ken Griffey, Cin	NL	
1981...Gary Carter, Mtl	NL	
1982...Dave Concepcion, Cin	NL	
1983...Fred Lynn, Calif	AL	
1984...Gary Carter, Mtl	NL	
1985...LaMarr Hoyt, SD	NL	
1986...Roger Clemens, Bos	AL	
1987...Tim Raines, Mtl	NL	
1988...Terry Steinbach, Oak	AL	
1989...Bo Jackson, KC	AL	
1990...Julio Franco, Tex	AL	
1991...Cal Ripken Jr., Balt	AL	
1992...Ken Griffey Jr., Sea	AL	
1993...Kirby Puckett, Minn	AL	
1994...Fred McGriff, Atl	NL	
1995...Jeff Conine, Fla	NL	
1996...Mike Piazza, LA	NL	
1997...Sandy Alomar, Clev	AL	
1998...Roberto Alomar, Balt	AL	
1999...Pedro Martinez, Bos	AL	
2000...Derek Jeter, NY	AL	
2001...Cal Ripken Jr., Balt	AL	
2002...Not selected		

The Regular Season

Most Valuable Players
NATIONAL LEAGUE

Year	Name and Team	Position	Noteworthy
1911 ....Wildfire Schulte, Chi	Outfield	21 HR†, 121 RBI†, .300
1912 ....*Larry Doyle, NY	Second base	10 HR, 90 RBI, .330
1913 ....Jake Daubert, Bklyn	First base	52 RBI, .350†
1914 ....*Johnny Evers, Bos	Second base	FA .976†, .279
1915–23 ....No selection		
1924 ....Dazzy Vance, Bklyn	Pitcher	28†–6, 2.16 ERA†, 262 K†
1925 ....Rogers Hornsby, StL	Second base, Manager	39 HR†, 143 RBI†, .403†
1926 ....*Bob O'Farrell, StL	Catcher	7 HR, 68 RBI, .293
1927 ....*Paul Waner, Pitt	Outfield	237 hits†, 131 RBI†, .380†
1928 ....*Jim Bottomley, StL	First base	31 HR†, 136 RBI†, .325
1929 ....*Rogers Hornsby, Chi	Second base	39 HR, 149 RBI, 156 runs†, .380
1930 ....No selection		
1931 ....*Frankie Frisch, StL	Second base	4 HR, 82 RBI, 28 SB†, .311
1932 ....Chuck Klein, Phil	Outfield	38 HR†, 137 RBI, 226 hits†, .348
1933 ....*Carl Hubbell, NY	Pitcher	23†–12, 1.66 ERA†, 10 SO†
1934 ....*Dizzy Dean, StL	Pitcher	30†–7, 2.66 ERA, 195 K†
1935 ....*Gabby Hartnett, Chi	Catcher	13 HR, 91 RBI, .344
1936 ....*Carl Hubbell, NY	Pitcher	26†–6, 2.31 ERA†
1937 ....Joe Medwick, StL	Outfield	31 HR†, 154 RBI†, 111 runs†, .374†
1938 ....Ernie Lombardi, Cin	Catcher	19 HR, 95 RBI, .342†
1939 ....*Bucky Walters, Cin	Pitcher	27†–11, 2.29 ERA†, 137 K‡
1940 ....*Frank McCormick, Cin	First base	19 HR, 127 RBI, 191 hits†, .309
1941 ....*Dolph Camilli, Bklyn	First base	34 HR†, 120 RBI†, .285

*Played for pennant or, after 1968, division winner. †Led league. ‡Tied for league lead.

Most Valuable Players *(Cont.)*

NATIONAL LEAGUE *(Cont.)*

Year	Name and Team	Position	Noteworthy
1942	*Mort Cooper, StL	Pitcher	22†–7, 1.78 ERA†, 10 SO†
1943	*Stan Musial, StL	Outfield	13 HR, 81 RBI, 220 hits†, .357†
1944	*Marty Marion, StL	Shortstop	FA .972†, 63 RBI
1945	*Phil Cavarretta, Chi	First base	6 HR, 97 RBI, .355†
1946	*Stan Musial, StL	First base, Outfield	103 RBI, 124 runs†, 228 hits†, .365†
1947	Bob Elliott, Bos	Third base	22 HR, 113 RBI, .317
1948	Stan Musial, StL	Outfield	39 HR, 131 RBI†, .376†
1949	*Jackie Robinson, Bklyn	Second base	16 HR, 124 RBI, 37 SB†, .342†
1950	*Jim Konstanty, Phil	Pitcher	16–7, 22 saves†, 2.66 ERA
1951	Roy Campanella, Bklyn	Catcher	33 HR, 108 RBI, .325
1952	Hank Sauer, Chi	Outfield	37 HR‡, 121 RBI†, .270
1953	*Roy Campanella, Bklyn	Catcher	41 HR, 142 RBI†, .312
1954	*Willie Mays, NY	Outfield	41 HR, 110 RBI, 13 3B†, .345†
1955	*Roy Campanella, Bklyn	Catcher	32 HR, 107 RBI, .318
1956	*Don Newcombe, Bklyn	Pitcher	27†–7, 3.06 ERA
1957	*Hank Aaron, Mil	Outfield	44 HR†, 132 RBI†, .322
1958	Ernie Banks, Chi	Shortstop	47 HR†, 129 RBI†, .313
1959	Ernie Banks, Chi	Shortstop	45 HR, 143 RBI†, .304
1960	*Dick Groat, Pitt	Shortstop	2 HR, 50 RBI, .325†
1961	*Frank Robinson, Cin	Outfield	37 HR, 124 RBI, .323
1962	Maury Wills, LA	Shortstop	104 SB†, 208 hits, .299, GG
1963	*Sandy Koufax, LA	Pitcher	25‡–5, 1.88 ERA†, 306 K†
1964	*Ken Boyer, StL	Third Base	24 HR, 119 RBI†, .295
1965	Willie Mays, SF	Outfield	52 HR†, 112 RBI, .317, GG
1966	Roberto Clemente, Pitt	Outfield	29 HR, 119 RBI, 202 hits, .317, GG
1967	*Orlando Cepeda, StL	First base	25 HR, 111 RBI†, .325
1968	*Bob Gibson, StL	Pitcher	22–9, 1.12 ERA†, 268 K†, 13 SO†, GG
1969	Willie McCovey, SF	First base	45 HR†, 126 RBI†, .320
1970	*Johnny Bench, Cin	Catcher	45 HR†, 148 RBI†, .293, GG
1971	Joe Torre, StL	Third base	24 HR, 137 RBI†, .363†
1972	*Johnny Bench, Cin	Catcher	40 HR†, 125 RBI†, .270, GG
1973	*Pete Rose, Cin	Outfield	5 HR, 64 RBI, .338†, 230 hits†
1974	*Steve Garvey, LA	First base	21 HR, 111 RBI, 200 hits, .312, GG
1975	*Joe Morgan, Cin	Second base	17 HR, 94 RBI, 67 SB, .327, GG
1976	*Joe Morgan, Cin	Second base	27 HR, 111 RBI, 60 SB, .320, GG
1977	George Foster, Cin	Outfield	52 HR†, 149 RBI†, .320
1978	Dave Parker, Pitt	Outfield	30 HR, 117 RBI, .334†, GG
1979	Keith Hernandez, StL	First base	11 HR, 105 RBI, 210 hits, .344†, GG
	*Willie Stargell, Pitt	First base	32 HR, 82 RBI, .281
1980	*Mike Schmidt, Phil	Third base	48 HR†, 121 RBI†, .286, GG
1981	Mike Schmidt, Phil	Third base	31 HR†, 91 RBI†, 78 runs†, .316, GG
1982	*Dale Murphy, Atl	Outfield	36 HR, 109 RBI‡, .281, GG
1983	Dale Murphy, Atl	Outfield	36 HR, 121 RBI†, .302, GG
1984	*Ryne Sandberg, Chi	Second base	19 HR, 84 RBI, 114 runs†, .314, GG
1985	*Willie McGee, StL	Outfield	10 HR, 82 RBI, 18 3B†, .353†, GG
1986	Mike Schmidt, Phil	Third base	37 HR†, 119 RBI†, .290, GG
1987	Andre Dawson, Chi	Outfield	49 HR†, 137 RBI†, .287, GG
1988	*Kirk Gibson, LA	Outfield	25 HR, 76 RBI, 106 runs, .290
1989	*Kevin Mitchell, SF	Outfield	47 HR†, 125 RBI†, .291
1990	*Barry Bonds, Pitt	Outfield	33 HR, 114 RBI, .301
1991	*Terry Pendleton, Atl	Third base	23 HR, 86 RBI, .319†
1992	Barry Bonds, Pitt	Outfield	34 HR, 103 RBI, .311
1993	Barry Bonds, SF	Outfield	46 HR†, 123 RBI†, .336
1994	Jeff Bagwell, Hou	First base	39 HR, 116 RBI†, .368
1995	*Barry Larkin, Cin	Shortstop	15 HR, 66 RBI, 51 SB, .319
1996	*Ken Caminiti, SD	Third base	40 HR, 130 RBI, .326
1997	Larry Walker, Col	Outfield	49 HR†, 130 RBI, .452 OBA†, .366, GG
1998	Sammy Sosa, Chi	Outfield	66 HR, 158 RBI†, 134 runs†, 416 TB†, .308
1999	*Chipper Jones, Atl	Third Base	45 HR, 110 RBI, 116 runs, .319
2000	*Jeff Kent, SF	Second Base	33 HR, 125 RBI, 114 runs, .334
2001	Barry Bonds, SF	Outfield	73 HR†, 137 RBI, 177 BB†, .328, .863 SLG†

*Played for pennant or, after 1968, division winner. †Led league. ‡Tied for league lead.

Most Valuable Players *(Cont.)*

AMERICAN LEAGUE

Year	Name and Team	Position	Noteworthy
1911	Ty Cobb, Det	Outfield	8 HR, 144 RBI†, 24 3B†, .420†
1912	*Tris Speaker, Bos	Outfield	10 HR‡, 98 RBI, 53 2B†, .383
1913	Walter Johnson, Wash	Pitcher	36†–7, 1.09 ERA†, 11 SO†, 243 K†
1914	*Eddie Collins, Phil	Second base	2 HR, 85 RBI, 122 runs†, .344
1915–21	No selection		
1922	George Sisler, StL	First base	8 HR, 105 RBI, 246 hits†, .420†
1923	*Babe Ruth, NY	Outfield	41 HR†, 131 RBI†, .393
1924	*Walter Johnson, Wash	Pitcher	23†–7, 2.72 ERA†, 158 K†
1925	*Roger Peckinpaugh, Wash	Shortstop	4 HR, 64 RBI, .294
1926	George Burns, Clev	First base	114 RBI, 216 hits‡, 64 2B†, .358
1927	*Lou Gehrig, NY	First base	47 HR, 175 RBI†, 52 2B†, .373
1928	Mickey Cochrane, Phil	Catcher	10 HR, 57 RBI, .293
1929	No selection		
1930	No selection		
1931	*Lefty Grove, Phil	Pitcher	31†–4, 2.06 ERA†, 175 K†
1932	Jimmie Foxx, Phil	First base	58 HR†, 169 RBI†, 151 runs†, .364
1933	Jimmie Foxx, Phil	First base	48 HR†, 163 RBI†, .356†
1934	*Mickey Cochrane, Det	Catcher	2 HR, 76 RBI, .320
1935	*Hank Greenberg, Det	First base	36 HR‡, 170 RBI†, 203 hits, .328
1936	*Lou Gehrig, NY	First base	49 HR†, 152 RBI, 167 runs†, .354
1937	Charlie Gehringer, Det	Second base	14 HR, 96 RBI, 133 runs, .371†
1938	Jimmie Foxx, Bos	First base	50 HR, 175 RBI†, .349†
1939	*Joe DiMaggio, NY	Outfield	30 HR, 126 RBI, .381†
1940	*Hank Greenberg, Det	Outfield	41 HR†, 150 RBI†, 50 2B†, .340
1941	*Joe DiMaggio, NY	Outfield	30 HR, 125 RBI†, .357
1942	*Joe Gordon, NY	Second base	18 HR, 103 RBI, .322
1943	*Spud Chandler, NY	Pitcher	20†–4, 1.64 ERA†, 5 SO‡
1944	Hal Newhouser, Det	Pitcher	29†–9, 2.22 ERA†, 187 K†
1945	*Hal Newhouser, Det	Pitcher	25†–9, 1.81 ERA†, 8 SO†, 212 K†
1946	*Ted Williams, Bos	Outfield	38 HR, 123 RBI, 142 runs†, .342
1947	*Joe DiMaggio, NY	Outfield	20 HR, 97 RBI, .315
1948	*Lou Boudreau, Clev	Shortstop	18 HR, 106 RBI, .355
1949	Ted Williams, Bos	Outfield	43 HR†, 159 RBI‡, 150 runs†, .343
1950	*Phil Rizzuto, NY	Shortstop	125 runs, 200 hits, .324
1951	*Yogi Berra, NY	Catcher	27 HR, 88 RBI, .294
1952	Bobby Shantz, Phil	Pitcher	24†–7, 2.48 ERA
1953	Al Rosen, Clev	Third base	43 HR†, 145 RBI†, 115 runs†, .336
1954	Yogi Berra, NY	Catcher	22 HR, 125 RBI, .307
1955	*Yogi Berra, NY	Catcher	27 HR, 108 RBI, .272
1956	*Mickey Mantle, NY	Outfield	52 HR†, 130 RBI†, 132 runs†, .353†
1957	*Mickey Mantle, NY	Outfield	34 HR, 94 RBI, 121 runs†, .365
1958	Jackie Jensen, Bos	Outfield	35 HR, 122 RBI†, .286
1959	*Nellie Fox, Chi	Second base	2 HR, 70 RBI, .306, GG
1960	*Roger Maris, NY	Outfield	39 HR, 112 RBI†, .283, GG
1961	*Roger Maris, NY	Outfield	61 HR†, 142 RBI†, .269
1962	*Mickey Mantle, NY	Outfield	30 HR, 89 RBI, .321, GG
1963	*Elston Howard, NY	Catcher	28 HR, 85 RBI, .287, GG
1964	Brooks Robinson, Balt	Third base	28 HR, 118 RBI†, .317, GG
1965	*Zoilo Versalles, Minn	Shortstop	126 runs†, 45 2B‡, 12 3B‡, GG
1966	*Frank Robinson, Balt	Outfield	49 HR†, 122 RBI†, 122 runs†, .316†
1967	*Carl Yastrzemski, Bos	Outfield	44 HR†, 121 RBI†, 112 runs†, .326†, GG
1968	*Denny McLain, Det	Pitcher	31†–6, 1.96 ERA, 280 K
1969	*Harmon Killebrew, Minn	Third base, First base	49 HR†, 140 RBI†, .276
1970	*Boog Powell, Balt	First base	35 HR, 114 RBI, .297
1971	*Vida Blue, Oak	Pitcher	24–8, 1.82 ERA†, 8 SO†, 301 K
1972	Dick Allen, Chi	First base	37 HR†, 113 RBI†, .308
1973	*Reggie Jackson, Oak	Outfield	32 HR†, 117 RBI†, 99 runs†, .293
1974	Jeff Burroughs, Tex	Outfield	25 HR, 118 RBI†, .301
1975	*Fred Lynn, Bos	Outfield	21 HR, 105 RBI, 103 runs†, .331, GG
1976	*Thurman Munson, NY	Catcher	17 HR, 105 RBI, .302
1977	Rod Carew, Minn	First base	100 RBI, 128 runs†, 239 hits†, .388†
1978	Jim Rice, Bos	Outfield, DH	46 HR†, 139 RBI†, 213 hits†, .315
1979	*Don Baylor, Calif	Outfield, DH	36 HR, 139 RBI†, 120 runs†, .296
1980	*George Brett, KC	Third base	24 HR, 118 RBI, .390†

Most Valuable Players (Cont.)
AMERICAN LEAGUE (Cont.)

Year	Name and Team	Position	Noteworthy
1981	*Rollie Fingers, Mil	Pitcher	6–3, 28 saves†, 1.04 ERA
1982	*Robin Yount, Mil	Shortstop	29 HR, 114 RBI, 210 hits†, .331, GG
1983	*Cal Ripken Jr., Balt	Shortstop	27 HR, 102 RBI, 121 runs†, 211 hits†, .318
1984	*Willie Hernandez, Det	Pitcher	9–3, 32 saves, 1.92 ERA
1985	Don Mattingly, NY	First base	35 HR, 145 RBI†, 48 2B†, .324, GG
1986	*Roger Clemens, Bos	Pitcher	24†–4, 2.48 ERA†, 238 K
1987	George Bell, Tor	Outfield	47 HR, 134 RBI†, .308
1988	*Jose Canseco, Oak	Outfield	42 HR†, 124 RBI†, 40 SB, .307
1989	Robin Yount, Mil	Outfield	21 HR, 103 RBI, 101 runs, .318
1990	*Rickey Henderson, Oak	Outfield	28 HR, 119 runs†, 65 SB†, .325
1991	Cal Ripken Jr., Balt	Shortstop	34 HR, 114 RBI, .323
1992	Dennis Eckersley, Oak	Pitcher	7–1, 1.91 ERA, 51 saves
1993	Frank Thomas, Chi	First base	41 HR, 128 RBI, .317
1994	Frank Thomas, Chi	First base	38 HR, 101 RBI, .353
1995	*Mo Vaughn, Bos	First base	39 HR, 126 RBI, .300
1996	*Juan Gonzalez, Tex	Outfield	47 HR, 144 RBI, .314
1997	*Ken Griffey Jr., Sea	Outfield	56 HR†, 125 runs†, 393 TB†, 147 RBI†, .304
1998	*Juan Gonzalez, Tex	Outfield	45 HR, 157 RBI†, 50 2B†, .318
1999	*Ivan Rodriguez, Tex	Catcher	35 HR, 113 RBI, 116 runs, .332, GG
2000	*Jason Giambi, Oak	First Base	43 HR, 137 RBI, .333
2001	*Ichiro Suzuki, Sea	Outfield	.350†, 242 H†, 127 R, 56 SB†

*Played for pennant or, after 1968, division winner. †Led league. ‡Tied for league lead.

Notes: 2B=doubles; 3B=triples; FA=fielding average; GG=won Gold Glove, award begun in 1957; K=strikeouts; SO=shutouts; SB=stolen bases; TB=total bases.

Rookies of the Year

NATIONAL LEAGUE

1947*	Jackie Robinson, Bklyn (1B)
1948*	Alvin Dark, Bos (SS)
1949	Don Newcombe, Bklyn (P)
1950	Sam Jethroe, Bos (OF)
1951	Willie Mays, NY (OF)
1952	Joe Black, Bklyn (P)
1953	Junior Gilliam, Bklyn (2B)
1954	Wally Moon, StL (OF)
1955	Bill Virdon, StL (OF)
1956	Frank Robinson, Cin (OF)
1957	Jack Sanford, Phil (P)
1958	Orlando Cepeda, SF (1B)
1959	Willie McCovey, SF (1B)
1960	Frank Howard, LA (OF)
1961	Billy Williams, Chi (OF)
1962	Ken Hubbs, Chi (2B)
1963	Pete Rose, Cin (2B)
1964	Dick Allen, Phil (3B)
1965	Jim Lefebvre, LA (2B)
1966	Tommy Helms, Cin (2B)
1967	Tom Seaver, NY (P)
1968	Johnny Bench, Cin (C)
1969	Ted Sizemore, LA (2B)
1970	Carl Morton, Mtl(P)
1971	Earl Williams, Atl (C)
1972	Jon Matlack, NY (P)
1973	Gary Matthews, SF (OF)
1974	Bake McBride, StL (OF)
1975	John Montefusco, SF (P)
1976	Pat Zachry, Cin (P)
	Butch Metzger, SD (P)
1977	Andre Dawson, Mtl (OF)
1978	Bob Horner, Atl (3B)
1979	Rick Sutcliffe, LA (P)
1980	Steve Howe, LA (P)
1981	Fernando Valenzuela, LA (P)
1982	Steve Sax, LA (2B)

AMERICAN LEAGUE

1949	Roy Sievers, StL (OF)
1950	Walt Dropo, Bos (1B)
1951	Gil McDougald, NY (3B)
1952	Harry Byrd, Phil (P)
1953	Harvey Kuenn, Det (SS)
1954	Bob Grim, NY (P)
1955	Herb Score, Clev (P)
1956	Luis Aparicio, Chi (SS)
1957	Tony Kubek, NY (OF, SS)
1958	Albie Pearson, Wash (OF)
1959	Bob Allison, Wash (OF)
1960	Ron Hansen, Balt (SS)
1961	Don Schwall, Bos (P)
1962	Tom Tresh, NY (SS)
1963	Gary Peters, Chi (P)
1964	Tony Oliva, Minn (OF)
1965	Curt Blefary, Balt (OF)
1966	Tommie Agee, Chi (OF)
1967	Rod Carew, Minn (2B)
1968	Stan Bahnsen, NY (P)
1969	Lou Piniella, KC (OF)
1970	Thurman Munson, NY (C)
1971	Chris Chambliss, Clev (1B)
1972	Carlton Fisk, Bos (C)
1973	Al Bumbry, Balt (OF)
1974	Mike Hargrove, Tex (1B)
1975	Fred Lynn, Bos (OF)
1976	Mark Fidrych, Det (P)
1977	Eddie Murray, Balt (DH)
1978	Lou Whitaker, Det (2B)
1979	Alfredo Griffin, Tor (SS)
	John Castino, Minn (3B)
1980	Joe Charboneau, Clev (OF)
1981	Dave Righetti, NY (P)
1982	Cal Ripken Jr., Balt (SS)
1983	Ron Kittle, Chi (OF)
1984	Alvin Davis, Sea (1B)

*Just one selection for both leagues.

Rookies of the Year (Cont.)

NATIONAL LEAGUE (Cont.)

1983 ....Darryl Strawberry, NY (OF)
1984 ....Dwight Gooden, NY (P)
1985 ....Vince Coleman, StL (OF)
1986 ....Todd Worrell, StL (P)
1987 ....Benito Santiago, SD (C)
1988 ....Chris Sabo, Cin (3B)
1989 ....Jerome Walton, Chi (OF)
1990 ....Dave Justice, Atl (OF)
1991 ....Jeff Bagwell, Hou (3B)
1992 ....Eric Karros, LA (1B)
1993 ....Mike Piazza, LA (C)
1994 ....Raul Mondesi, LA (OF)
1995 ....Hideo Nomo, LA (P)
1996 ....Todd Hollandsworth, LA (OF)
1997 ....Scott Rolen, Phil (3B)
1998 ....Kerry Wood, Chi (P)
1999 ....Scott Williamson, Cin (P)
2000 ....Rafael Furcal, Atl (SS)
2001 ....Albert Pujols, StL (OF)

AMERICAN LEAGUE (Cont.)

1985 ....Ozzie Guillen, Chi (SS)
1986 ....Jose Canseco, Oak (OF)
1987 ....Mark McGwire, Oak (1B)
1988 ....Walt Weiss, Oak (SS)
1989 ....Gregg Olson, Balt (P)
1990 ....Sandy Alomar Jr, Clev (C)
1991 ....Chuck Knoblauch, Minn (2B)
1992 ....Pat Listach, Mil (SS)
1993 ....Tim Salmon, Calif (OF)
1994 ....Bob Hamelin, KC (DH)
1995 ....Marty Cordova, Minn (OF)
1996 ....Derek Jeter, NY (SS)
1997 ....Nomar Garciaparra, Bos (SS)
1998 ....Ben Grieve, Oak (OF)
1999 ....Carlos Beltran, KC (OF)
2000 ....Kazuhiro Sasaki, Sea (P)
2001 ....Ichiro Suzuki, Sea (OF)

Cy Young Award

Year		W–L	Sv	ERA	Year		W–L	Sv	ERA
1956	*Don Newcombe, Bklyn (NL)	27–7	0	3.06	1962	Don Drysdale, LA (NL)	25–9	1	2.83
1957	Warren Spahn, Mil (NL)	21–11	3	2.69	1963	*Sandy Koufax, LA (NL)	25–5	0	1.88
1958	Bob Turley, NY (AL)	21–7	1	2.97	1964	Dean Chance, LA (AL)	20–9	4	1.65
1959	Early Wynn, Chi (AL)	22–10	0	3.17	1965	Sandy Koufax, LA (NL)	26–8	2	2.04
1960	Vernon Law, Pitt (NL)	20–9	0	3.08	1966	Sandy Koufax, LA (NL)	27–9	0	1.73
1961	Whitey Ford, NY (AL)	25–4	0	3.21					

NATIONAL LEAGUE

Year		W–L	Sv	ERA
1967	Mike McCormick, SF	22–10	0	2.85
1968	*Bob Gibson, StL	22–9	0	1.12
1969	Tom Seaver, NY	25–7	0	2.21
1970	Bob Gibson, StL	23–7	0	3.12
1971	Ferguson Jenkins, Chi	24–13	0	2.77
1972	Steve Carlton, Phil	27–10	0	1.97
1973	Tom Seaver, NY	19–10	0	2.08
1974	Mike Marshall, LA	15–12	21	2.42
1975	Tom Seaver, NY	22–9	0	2.38
1976	Randy Jones, SD	22–14	0	2.74
1977	Steve Carlton, Phil	23–10	0	2.64
1978	Gaylord Perry, SD	21–6	0	2.72
1979	Bruce Sutter, Chi	6–6	37	2.23
1980	Steve Carlton, Phil	24–9	0	2.34
1981	Fernando Valenzuela, LA	13–7	0	2.48
1982	Steve Carlton, Phil	23–11	0	3.10
1983	John Denny, Phil	19–6	0	2.37
1984	†Rick Sutcliffe, Chi	16–1	0	2.69
1985	Dwight Gooden, NY	24–4	0	1.53
1986	Mike Scott, Hou	18–10	0	2.22
1987	Steve Bedrosian, Phil	5–3	40	2.83
1988	Orel Hershiser, LA	23–8	1	2.26
1989	Mark Davis, SD	4–3	44	1.85
1990	Doug Drabek, Pitt	22–6	0	2.76
1991	Tom Glavine, Atl	20–11	0	2.55
1992	Greg Maddux, Chi	20–11	0	2.18
1993	Greg Maddux, Atl	20–10	0	2.36
1994	Greg Maddux, Atl	16–6	0	1.56
1995	Greg Maddux, Atl	19–2	0	1.63
1996	John Smoltz, Atl	24–8	0	2.94
1997	Pedro Martinez, Mtl	17–8	0	1.90
1998	Tom Glavine, Atl	20–6	0	2.47
1999	Randy Johnson, Ariz	17–9	0	2.48
2000	Randy Johnson, Ariz	19–7	0	2.64
2001	Randy Johnson, Ariz	21–6	0	2.49

AMERICAN LEAGUE

Year		W–L	Sv	ERA
1967	Jim Lonborg, Bos	22–9	0	3.16
1968	*Denny McLain, Det	31–6	0	1.96
1969	Denny McLain, Det	24–9	0	2.80
	Mike Cuellar, Balt	23–11	0	2.38
1970	Jim Perry, Minn	24–12	0	3.03
1971	*Vida Blue, Oak	24–8	0	1.82
1972	Gaylord Perry, Clev	24–16	1	1.92
1973	Jim Palmer, Balt	22–9	1	2.40
1974	Catfish Hunter, Oak	25–12	0	2.49
1975	Jim Palmer, Balt	23–11	1	2.09
1976	Jim Palmer, Balt	22–13	0	2.51
1977	Sparky Lyle, NY	13–5	26	2.17
1978	Ron Guidry, NY	25–3	0	1.74
1979	Mike Flanagan, Balt	23–9	0	3.08
1980	Steve Stone, Balt	25–7	0	3.23
1981	*Rollie Fingers, Mil	6–3	28	1.04
1982	Pete Vuckovich, Mil	18–6	0	3.34
1983	LaMarr Hoyt, Chi	24–10	0	3.66
1984	*Willie Hernandez, Det	9–3	32	1.92
1985	Bret Saberhagen, KC	20–6	0	2.87
1986	*Roger Clemens, Bos	24–4	0	2.48
1987	Roger Clemens, Bos	20–9	0	2.97
1988	Frank Viola, Minn	24–7	0	2.64
1989	Bret Saberhagen, KC	23–6	0	2.16
1990	Bob Welch, Oak	27–6	0	2.95
1991	Roger Clemens, Bos	18–10	0	2.62
1992	*Dennis Eckersley, Oak	7–1	51	1.91
1993	Jack McDowell, Chi	22–10	0	3.37
1994	David Cone, KC	16–4	0	2.94
1995	Randy Johnson, Sea	18–2	0	2.48
1996	Pat Hentgen, Tor	20–10	0	3.22
1997	Roger Clemens, Tor	21–7	0	2.05
1998	Roger Clemens, Tor	20–6	0	2.65
1999	Pedro Martinez, Bos	23–4	0	1.55
2000	Pedro Martinez, Bos	18–6	0	1.74
2001	Roger Clemens, NY	20–3	0	3.51

*Won the MVP and Cy Young awards in the same season.
†NL games only. Sutcliffe pitched 15 games with Cleveland before being traded to the Cubs.

Career Individual Batting

GAMES

Pete Rose	3562
Carl Yastrzemski	3308
Hank Aaron	3298
*Rickey Henderson	3051
Ty Cobb	3034
Stan Musial	3026
Eddie Murray	3026
Cal Ripken Jr.	3001
Willie Mays	2992
Dave Winfield	2973
Rusty Staub	2951
Brooks Robinson	2896
Robin Yount	2856
Al Kaline	2834
Harold Baines	2830
Eddie Collins	2826
Reggie Jackson	2820
Frank Robinson	2808
Honus Wagner	2792
Tris Speaker	2789

HITS

Pete Rose	4256
Ty Cobb	4189
Hank Aaron	3771
Stan Musial	3630
Tris Speaker	3515
Carl Yastrzemski	3419
Cap Anson	3418
Honus Wagner	3415
Paul Molitor	3319
Eddie Collins	3313
Willie Mays	3283
Eddie Murray	3255
Nap Lajoie	3251
Cal Ripken Jr.	3184
George Brett	3154
Paul Waner	3152
Robin Yount	3142
Tony Gwynn	3141
Dave Winfield	3110
Rod Carew	3053

DOUBLES

Tris Speaker	793
Pete Rose	746
Stan Musial	725
Ty Cobb	724
George Brett	665
Nap Lajoie	657
Carl Yastrzemski	646
Honus Wagner	640
Hank Aaron	624
Paul Molitor	605
Paul Waner	604
Cal Ripken Jr.	603
Robin Yount	583
Cap Anson	581
Wade Boggs	578
Charlie Gehringer	574
Eddie Murray	560
Tony Gwynn	543
Harry Heilmann	542
Rogers Hornsby	541

AT BATS

Pete Rose	14053
Hank Aaron	12364
Carl Yastrzemski	11988
Cal Ripken Jr.	11551
Ty Cobb	11429
Eddie Murray	11336
Robin Yount	11008
Dave Winfield	11003
Stan Musial	10972
*Rickey Henderson	10889
Willie Mays	10881
Paul Molitor	10835
Brooks Robinson	10654
Honus Wagner	10427
George Brett	10349
Lou Brock	10332
Cap Anson	10278
Luis Aparicio	10230
Tris Speaker	10208
Al Kaline	10116

BATTING AVERAGE (5,000 AB)

Ty Cobb	.367
Rogers Hornsby	.358
Ed Delahanty	.346
Tris Speaker	.345
Ted Williams	.344
Billy Hamilton	.344
Dan Brouthers	.342
Jesse Burkett	.342
Babe Ruth	.342
Harry Heilmann	.342
Willie Keeler	.341
Bill Terry	.341
George Sisler	.340
Lou Gehrig	.340
Jesse Burkett	.338
Tony Gwynn	.338
Nap Lajoie	.338
Al Simmons	.334
Paul Waner	.333
Eddie Collins	.333

TRIPLES

Sam Crawford	312
Ty Cobb	297
Honus Wagner	252
Jake Beckley	244
Roger Connor	233
Tris Speaker	223
Fred Clarke	223
Dan Brouthers	206
Joe Kelley	194
Paul Waner	190
Bid McPhee	189
Eddie Collins	187
Ed Delahanty	185
Sam Rice	184
Jesse Burkett	182
Edd Roush	182
Ed Konetchy	182
Buck Ewing	178
Rabbit Maranville	177
Stan Musial	177

HOME RUNS

Hank Aaron	755
Babe Ruth	714
Willie Mays	660
*Barry Bonds	613
Frank Robinson	586
Mark McGwire	583
Harmon Killebrew	573
Reggie Jackson	563
Mike Schmidt	548
Mickey Mantle	536
Jimmie Foxx	534
Ted Williams	521
Willie McCovey	521
Eddie Mathews	512
Ernie Banks	512
Mel Ott	511
Eddie Murray	504
*Sammy Sosa	499
Lou Gehrig	493
*Rafael Palmeiro	490

RUNS

*Rickey Henderson	2288
Ty Cobb	2245
Babe Ruth	2174
Hank Aaron	2174
Pete Rose	2165
Willie Mays	2062
Cap Anson	1996
Stan Musial	1949
Lou Gehrig	1888
Tris Speaker	1881
Mel Ott	1859
*Barry Bonds	1830
Frank Robinson	1829
Eddie Collins	1820
Carl Yastrzemski	1816
Ted Williams	1798
Paul Molitor	1782
Charlie Gehringer	1774
Jimmie Foxx	1751
Honus Wagner	1740

BASES ON BALLS

*Rickey Henderson	2179
Babe Ruth	2062
Ted Williams	2019
*Barry Bonds	1922
Joe Morgan	1865
Carl Yastrzemski	1845
Mickey Mantle	1735
Mel Ott	1708
Eddie Yost	1614
Darrell Evans	1605
Stan Musial	1599
Pete Rose	1566
Harmon Killebrew	1559
Lou Gehrig	1508
Mike Schmidt	1507
Eddie Collins	1503
Willie Mays	1463
Jimmie Foxx	1452
Eddie Mathews	1444
Frank Robinson	1420

* Active in 2002.

Career Individual Batting (Cont.)

RUNS BATTED IN	STOLEN BASES	TOTAL BASES
Hank Aaron.......................2297	*Rickey Henderson...........1403	Hank Aaron.......................6856
Babe Ruth.........................2213	Lou Brock 938	Stan Musial 6134
Cap Anson........................2076	Billy Hamilton....................912	Willie Mays.......................6066
Lou Gehrig........................1995	Ty Cobb.............................892	Ty Cobb............................5854
Stan Musial 1951	*Tim Raines........................808	Babe Ruth.........................5793
Ty Cobb............................1937	Vince Coleman 752	Pete Rose.........................5752
Jimmie Foxx......................1922	Eddie Collins......................744	Carl Yastrzemski...............5539
Eddie Murray 1917	Arlie Latham.......................739	Eddie Murray 5397
Willie Mays.......................1903	Max Carey 738	Frank Robinson.................5373
Mel Ott 1860	Honus Wagner...................722	Dave Winfield....................5221
Carl Yastrzemski...............1844	Joe Morgan........................689	Cal Ripken Jr. 5168
Ted Williams 1839	Willie Wilson......................668	Tris Speaker.....................5101
Dave Winfield....................1833	Tom Brown.........................657	Lou Gehrig........................5060
Al Simmons.......................1827	Bert Campaneris.................649	George Brett 5044
Frank Robinson.................1812	Otis Nixon 620	Mel Ott 5041
Honus Wagner...................1732	George Davis......................616	*Barry Bonds 4961
Reggie Jackson.................1702	Dummy Hoy 594	Jimmie Foxx......................4956
Cal Ripken Jr. 1695	Maury Wills 586	Ted Williams 4884
Tony Perez........................1652	George Van Haltren............583	Honus Wagner...................4862
*Barry Bonds.....................1652	Ozzie Smith 580	Paul Molitor.......................4854

SLUGGING AVERAGE (5,000 AB)	ON-BASE PERCENTAGE (5,000 AB)	STRIKEOUTS
Babe Ruth.........................690	Ted Williams 482	Reggie Jackson.................2597
Ted Williams 634	Babe Ruth..........................474	Jose Canseco....................1942
Lou Gehrig........................632	Billy Hamilton.....................455	*Andres Galarraga.............1939
Jimmie Foxx......................609	Lou Gehrig.........................447	Willie Stargell....................1936
Hank Greenberg................605	Rogers Hornsby..................434	Mike Schmidt 1883
*Barry Bonds.....................595	Ty Cobb.............................433	Tony Perez........................1867
Mark McGwire 588	*Frank Thomas 432	*Sammy Sosa 1832
Joe DiMaggio 579	Jimmie Foxx.......................428	Dave Kingman...................1816
Rogers Hornsby.................577	Tris Speaker.......................428	*Fred McGriff 1797
*Mike Piazza 575	*Barry Bonds 428	Bobby Bonds.....................1757
*Larry Walker.....................574	*Edgar Martinez..................424	Dale Murphy 1748
*Frank Thomas...................568	Eddie Collins......................424	Lou Brock 1730
Albert Belle 564	Dan Brouthers....................423	Mickey Mantle....................1710
*Juan Gonzalez 563	Mickey Mantle....................421	Harmon Killebrew 1699
*Ken Griffey Jr. 562	Mickey Cochrane................419	Chili Davis.........................1698
Johnny Mize......................562	Stan Musial 417	Dwight Evans.....................1697
Stan Musial 559	Cupid Childs......................416	Dave Winfield.....................1686
Willie Mays.......................557	Jesse Burkett.....................415	*Rickey Henderson............1678
Mickey Mantle....................557	Wade Boggs.......................415	Gary Gaetti 1602
Hank Aaron.......................555	*Jeff Bagwell......................414	Mark McGwire 1596

The 30–30 Club (30 HR, 30 SB in single season)

Year		HR	SB	Year		HR	SB
1922	Kenny Williams, StL	39	37	1992	Barry Bonds, Pitt	34	39
1956	Willie Mays, NYG	36	40	1993	Sammy Sosa, ChiC	33	36
1957	Willie Mays, NYG	35	38	1995	Barry Bonds, SF	33	31
1963	Hank Aaron, Mil	44	31	1995	Sammy Sosa, ChiC	36	34
1969	Bobby Bonds, SF	32	45	1996	Barry Bonds, SF	42	40
1970	Tommy Harper, Mil	31	38	1996	Ellis Burks, Col	40	32
1973	Bobby Bonds, SF	39	43	1996	Barry Larkin, Cin	33	36
1975	Bobby Bonds, NYY	32	30	1996	Dante Bichette, Col	31	31
1977	Bobby Bonds, Cal	37	41	1997	Larry Walker, Col	49	33
1978	Bobby Bonds, Chi/Tex	31	43	1997	Jeff Bagwell, Hou	43	31
1983	Dale Murphy, Atl	36	30	1997	Raul Mondesi, LA	30	32
1987	Joe Carter, Clev	32	31	1997	Barry Bonds, SF	40	37
1987	Eric Davis, Cin	37	50	1998	Alex Rodriguez, Sea	42	46
1987	Darryl Strawberry, NYM	39	36	1998	Shawn Green, Tor	35	35
1987	Howard Johnson, NYM	36	32	1999	Jeff Bagwell, Hou	42	30
1988	Jose Canseco, Oak	42	40	1999	Raul Mondesi, LA	33	36
1989	Howard Johnson, NYM	36	41	2000	Preston Wilson, Fla	31	36
1990	Ron Gant, Atl	32	33	2001	Vladimir Guerrero, Mtl	34	37
1990	Barry Bonds, Pitt	33	52	2001	Jose Cruz Jr., Tor	34	32
1991	Ron Gant, Atl	32	34	2001	Bobby Abreu, Phil	31	36
1991	Howard Johnson, NYM	38	30	2002	Alfonso Soriano	39	41
				2002	Vladimir Guerrero	39	40

*Active in 2002.

Career Individual Pitching

GAMES

*Jesse Orosco	1187
Dennis Eckersley	1071
Hoyt Wilhelm	1070
Kent Tekulve	1050
*Dan Plesac	1046
Lee Smith	1022
Goose Gossage	1002
*John Franco	998
Lindy McDaniel	987
*Mike Jackson	960
Rollie Fingers	944
Gene Garber	931
Cy Young	906
Sparky Lyle	899
Jim Kaat	898
Paul Assenmacher	884
Jeff Reardon	880
Don McMahon	874
Phil Niekro	864
Charlie Hough	858

LOSSES

Cy Young	316
Pud Galvin	308
Nolan Ryan	292
Walter Johnson	279
Phil Niekro	274
Gaylord Perry	265
Don Sutton	256
Jack Powell	254
Eppa Rixey	251
Bert Blyleven	250
Bobby Mathews	248
Robin Roberts	245
Warren Spahn	245
Steve Carlton	244
Early Wynn	244
Jim Kaat	237
Frank Tanana	236
Gus Weyhing	232
Tommy John	231
Bob Friend	230
Ted Lyons	230

EARNED RUN AVERAGE (2,000 IP)

Ed Walsh	1.82
Addie Joss	1.89
Al Spalding	2.04
Three Finger Brown	2.06
John Ward	2.10
Christy Mathewson	2.13
Tommy Bond	2.14
Rube Waddell	2.16
Walter Johnson	2.17
Ed Reulbach	2.28
Will White	2.28
Eddie Plank	2.35
Larry Corcoran	2.36
Eddie Cicotte	2.38
Candy Cummings	2.39
Doc White	2.39
Nap Rucker	2.42
George Bradley	2.43
Jim McCormick	2.43
Chief Bender	2.46

INNINGS PITCHED

Cy Young	7356⅔
Pud Galvin	5941⅓
Walter Johnson	5914⅔
Phil Niekro	5404⅓
Nolan Ryan	5386
Gaylord Perry	5350⅓
Don Sutton	5282⅔
Warren Spahn	5243⅔
Steve Carlton	5217⅓
Grover Alexander	5190
Kid Nichols	5056⅓
Tim Keefe	5047⅓
Bert Blyleven	4970
Bobby Mathews	4956
Mickey Welch	4802
Tom Seaver	4782⅔
Christy Mathewson	4780⅔
Tommy John	4710⅓
Robin Roberts	4688⅔
Early Wynn	4564

WINNING PERCENTAGE**

Al Spalding	.796
Spud Chandler	.717
*Pedro Martinez	.707
Whitey Ford	.690
Dave Foutz	.690
Bob Caruthers	.688
Don Gullett	.686
Lefty Grove	.680
*Randy Johnson	.679
Joe Wood	.671
Vic Raschi	.667
Larry Corcoran	.665
Christy Mathewson	.665
Sam Leever	.660
*Roger Clemens	.660
Sal Maglie	.658
Dick McBride	.656
Sandy Koufax	.655
Johnny Allen	.654
Ron Guidry	.651

SHUTOUTS

Walter Johnson	110
Grover Alexander	90
Christy Mathewson	79
Cy Young	76
Eddie Plank	69
Warren Spahn	63
Nolan Ryan	61
Tom Seaver	61
Bert Blyleven	60
Don Sutton	58
Pud Galvin	57
Ed Walsh	57
Bob Gibson	56
Three Finger Brown	55
Steve Carlton	55
Jim Palmer	53
Gaylord Perry	53
Juan Marichal	52
Rube Waddell	50
Vic Willis	50

WINS

Cy Young	511
Walter Johnson	417
Grover Alexander	373
Christy Mathewson	373
Pud Galvin	365
Warren Spahn	363
Kid Nichols	361
Tim Keefe	342
Steve Carlton	329
John Clarkson	328
Eddie Plank	326
Nolan Ryan	324
Don Sutton	324
Phil Niekro	318
Gaylord Perry	314
Tom Seaver	311
Charley Radbourn	309
Mickey Welch	307
Lefty Grove	300
Early Wynn	300

SAVES

Lee Smith	478
*John Franco	422
Dennis Eckersley	390
Jeff Reardon	367
*Trevor Hoffman	352
Randy Myers	347
Rollie Fingers	341
John Wetteland	330
*Roberto Hernandez	320
Rick Aguilera	318
*Robb Nen	314
Tom Henke	311
Goose Gossage	310
Jeff Montgomery	304
Doug Jones	303
Bruce Sutter	300
Rod Beck	266
Todd Worrell	256
Dave Righetti	252
*Troy Percival	250

COMPLETE GAMES

Cy Young	749
Pud Galvin	639
Tim Keefe	554
Walter Johnson	531
Kid Nichols	531
Mickey Welch	525
Bobby Mathews	525
Charley Radbourn	489
John Clarkson	485
Tony Mullane	468
Jim McCormick	466
Gus Weyhing	448
Grover Alexander	437
Christy Mathewson	434
Jack Powell	422
Eddie Plank	410
Will White	394
Amos Rusie	392
Vic Willis	388
Tommy Bond	386

* Active in 2002.   ** Minumum 100 victories.

Career Individual Pitching *(Cont.)*

STRIKEOUTS		BASES ON BALLS	
Nolan Ryan	5714	Nolan Ryan	2795
Steve Carlton	4136	Steve Carlton	1833
*Roger Clemens	3909	Phil Niekro	1809
*Randy Johnson	3746	Early Wynn	1775
Bert Blyleven	3701	Bob Feller	1764
Tom Seaver	3640	Bobo Newsom	1732
Don Sutton	3574	Amos Rusie	1704
Gaylord Perry	3534	Charlie Hough	1665
Walter Johnson	3509	Gus Weyhing	1566
Phil Niekro	3342	Red Ruffing	1541
Ferguson Jenkins	3192	Bump Hadley	1442
Bob Gibson	3117	Warren Spahn	1434
Jim Bunning	2855	Earl Whitehill	1431
Mickey Lolich	2832	Tony Mullane	1408
Cy Young	2803	Sad Sam Jones	1396
Frank Tanana	2773	Jack Morris	1390
David Cone	2655	Tom Seaver	1390
*Greg Maddux	2641	Gaylord Perry	1379
*Chuck Finley	2610	Bobby Witt	1375
Warren Spahn	2583	Mike Torrez	1371

Alltime Winningest Managers

CAREER

	W	L	Pct	Yrs		W	L	Pct	Yrs
Connie Mack	3755	3967	.486	53	Bill McKechnie	1904	1737	.523	25
John McGraw	2810	1987	.586	33	*Bobby Cox	1864	1449	.563	21
Sparky Anderson	2238	1855	.547	26	*Joe Torre	1635	1474	.526	21
Bucky Harris	2168	2228	.493	29	Ralph Houk	1627	1539	.514	20
Joe McCarthy	2155	1346	.616	24	Fred Clarke	1609	1189	.575	19
Walter Alston	2063	1634	.558	23	Dick Williams	1592	1474	.519	21
Leo Durocher	2015	1717	.540	24	Tommy Lasorda	1589	1434	.526	20
*Tony LaRussa	1957	1744	.529	24	Earl Weaver	1506	1080	.582	17
Casey Stengel	1942	1868	.510	25	Clark Griffith	1491	1367	.522	20
Gene Mauch	1907	2044	.483	26	Miller Huggins	1431	1149	.555	17

REGULAR SEASON

	W	L	Pct	Yrs		W	L	Pct	Yrs
Connie Mack	3731	3948	.486	53	Bill McKechnie	1896	1723	.524	25
John McGraw	2784	1959	.587	33	*Bobby Cox	1805	1404	.562	21
Sparky Anderson	2194	1834	.545	26	Ralph Houk	1619	1531	.514	20
Bucky Harris	2157	2218	.493	29	Fred Clarke	1602	1181	.576	19
Joe McCarthy	2125	1333	.615	24	*Joe Torre	1579	1448	.522	21
Walter Alston	2040	1613	.558	23	Dick Williams	1571	1451	.520	21
Leo Durocher	2008	1709	.540	24	Tommy Lasorda	1558	1404	.526	20
*Tony LaRussa	1924	1712	.529	24	Clark Griffith	1491	1367	.522	20
Casey Stengel	1905	1842	.508	25	Earl Weaver	1480	1060	.583	17
Gene Mauch	1902	2037	.483	26	Miller Huggins	1413	1134	.555	17

WORLD SERIES

	W	L	T	Pct	App	WS		W	L	T	Pct	App	WS
Casey Stengel	37	26	0	.587	10	7	Bucky Harris	11	10	0	.524	3	2
Joe McCarthy	30	13	0	.698	9	7	Billy Southworth	11	11	0	.500	4	2
John McGraw	26	28	2	.482	9	2	Earl Weaver	11	13	0	.458	4	1
Connie Mack	24	19	0	.558	8	5	*Bobby Cox	11	18	0	.379	5	1
Walter Alston	20	20	0	.500	7	4	Whitey Herzog	10	11	0	.476	3	1
*Joe Torre	19	7	0	.731	5	4	Bill Carrigan	8	2	0	.800	2	2
Miller Huggins	18	15	1	.544	6	3	Cito Gaston	8	4	0	.667	2	2
Sparky Anderson	16	12	0	.571	5	3	Danny Murtaugh	8	6	0	.571	2	2
Tommy Lasorda	12	11	0	.522	4	2	*Tom Kelly	8	6	0	.571	2	2
Dick Williams	12	14	0	.462	4	2	Ralph Houk	8	8	0	.500	3	2
Frank Chance	11	9	1	.548	4	2	Bill McKechnie	8	14	0	.364	4	2

*Active in 2002.

Individual Batting (Single Season)

HITS

George Sisler, 1920.............257
Lefty O'Doul, 1929...............254
Bill Terry, 1930......................254
Al Simmons, 1925.................253
Rogers Hornsby, 1922.......250
Chuck Klein, 1930 250
Ty Cobb, 1911 248
George Sisler, 1922.............246
Ichiro Suzuki, 2001 242
Heinie Manush, 1928...........241
Babe Herman, 1930 241

BATTING AVERAGE

Hugh Duffy, 1894............... .440
Tip O'Neill, 1887 .... .435
Ross Barnes, 1876 .... .429
Nap Lajoie, 1901 .... .426
Willie Keeler, 1897.............. .424
Rogers Hornsby, 1924....... .424
George Sisler, 1922........... .420
Ty Cobb, 1911 .... .420
Fred Dunlap, 1884.............. .412
Ed Delahanty, 1899 .... .410

DOUBLES

Earl Webb, 1931 67
George Burns, 1926 64
Joe Medwick, 1936...............64
Hank Greenberg, 1934..........63
Paul Waner, 1932 62
Charlie Gehringer, 1936........60
Tris Speaker, 1923................59
Chuck Klein, 1930 59
Todd Helton, 2000 59
Billy Herman, 1936 57
Billy Herman, 1935 57
Carlos Delgado, 2000...........57

TOTAL BASES

Babe Ruth, 1921...................457
Rogers Hornsby, 1922.........450
Lou Gehrig, 1927..................447
Chuck Klein, 1930 445
Jimmie Foxx, 1932...............438
Stan Musial, 1948 429
Sammy Sosa, 2001..............425
Hack Wilson, 1930...............423
Chuck Klein, 1932...............420
Luis Gonzalez, 2001...........419
Lou Gehrig, 1930.................419

TRIPLES

Chief Wilson, 1912.................36
Dave Orr, 1886 31
Heinie Reitz, 1894.................31
Perry Werden, 1893...............29
Harry Davis, 1897 28
George Davis, 1893................27
Sam Thompson, 1894............27
Jimmy Williams, 1899............27
John Reilly, 1890 26
George Treadway, 1894........26
Joe Jackson, 1912.................26
Sam Crawford, 1914..............26
Kiki Cuyler, 1925....................26

HOME RUNS

Barry Bonds, 2001.................73
Mark McGwire, 1998 70
Sammy Sosa, 1998................66
Mark McGwire, 1999..............65
Sammy Sosa, 2001................64
Sammy Sosa, 1999................63
Roger Maris, 1961 61
Babe Ruth, 1927....................60
Babe Ruth, 1921....................59
Jimmie Foxx, 1932.................58
Hank Greenberg, 1938..........58
Mark McGwire, 1997 58

RUNS BATTED IN

Hack Wilson, 1930...............190
Lou Gehrig, 1931..................184
Hank Greenberg, 1937........183
Lou Gehrig, 1927..................175
Jimmie Foxx, 1938...............175
Lou Gehrig, 1930..................174
Babe Ruth, 1921...................171
Chuck Klein, 1930 170
Hank Greenberg, 1935..........170
Jimmie Foxx, 1932...............169

STRIKEOUTS

Bobby Bonds, 1970..............189
Jose Hernandez, 2002 188
Bobby Bonds, 1969.............187
Preston Wilson, 2000...........187
Rob Deer, 1987 186
Jose Hernandez, 2001 185
Jim Thome, 2001..................185
Pete Incaviglia, 1986...........185
Cecil Fielder, 1990...............182
Mo Vaughn, 2000 181

RUNS

Billy Hamilton, 1894.............192
Tom Brown, 1891..................177
Babe Ruth, 1921...................177
Tip O'Neill, 1887 167
Lou Gehrig, 1936..................167
Billy Hamilton, 1895.............166
Willie Keeler, 1894...............165
Joe Kelley, 1894 165
Arlie Latham, 1887...............163
Babe Ruth, 1928...................163
Lou Gehrig, 1931..................163

STOLEN BASES

Hugh Nicol, 1887.................138
Rickey Henderson, 1982 130
Arlie Latham, 1887...............129
Lou Brock, 1974 118
Charlie Comiskey, 1887.......117
John Ward, 1887..................111
Billy Hamilton, 1889.............111
Billy Hamilton, 1891.............111
Vince Coleman, 1985 110
Arlie Latham, 1888...............109
Vince Coleman, 1987 109

BASES ON BALLS

Barry Bonds, 2002...............198
Barry Bonds, 2001...............177
Babe Ruth, 1923...................170
Ted Williams, 1947...............162
Ted Williams, 1949 162
Mark McGwire, 1998 162
Ted Williams, 1946...............156
Eddie Yost, 1956 151
Eddie Joost, 1949................149
Jeff Bagwell, 1999 149

SLUGGING AVERAGE

Barry Bonds, 2001............. .863
Babe Ruth, 1920.................. .847
Babe Ruth, 1921.................. .846
Barry Bonds, 2002............... .799
Babe Ruth, 1927.................. .772
Lou Gehrig, 1927................. .765
Babe Ruth, 1923.................. .764
Rogers Hornsby, 1925........ .756
Mark McGwire, 1998 .... .752
Jeff Bagwell, 1994 .... .750

Individual Pitching (Single Season)

GAMES

Mike Marshall, 1974.............106
Kent Tekulve, 1979................94
Mike Marshall, 1973..............92
Kent Tekulve, 1978................91
Wayne Granger, 1969 :.........90
Mike Marshall, 1979..............90
Kent Tekulve, 1987................90
Steve Kline, 2001...................89
Mark Eichhorn, 1987..............89
Wilbur Wood, 1968................88
Mike Myers, 1997 88

GAMES STARTED

Will White, 1879 75
Jim Galvin, 1883.....................75
Jim McCormick, 1880..............75
Charley Radbourn, 1884 73
Guy Hecker, 1884...................73
Jim Galvin, 1884.....................72
John Clarkson, 1889...............72
Bill Hutchison, 1892...............71
John Clarkson, 1885...............70
Matt Kilroy, 1887....................69

INNINGS PITCHED

Will White, 1878 ....680.0
Charley Radbourn, 1884....678.2
Guy Hecker, 1884.............670.2
Jim McCormick, 1880.........657.2
Jim Galvin, 1883................656.1
Jim Galvin, 1884................636.1
Charley Radbourn, 1883....632.1
Bill Hutchison, 1892..........627.0
John Clarkson, 1885..........623.0
Jim Devlin, 1876 ....622.0

WINS

Charley Radbourn, 1884 59
John Clarkson, 1885..............53
Guy Hecker, 1884...................52
John Clarkson, 1889...............49
Charley Radbourn, 1883 48
Charlie Buffinton, 1884 48
Al Spalding, 1876 47
John Ward, 1879 47
Jim Galvin, 1883....................46
Jim Galvin, 1884....................46
Matt Kilroy, 1887....................46

LOSSES

John Coleman, 1883..............48
Will White, 1880 42
Larry McKeon, 1884 41
George Bradley, 1879 40
Jim McCormick, 1879.............40
Henry Porter, 1888.................37
Kid Carsey, 1891 37
George Cobb, 1892................37
Stump Weidman, 1886 36
Bill Hutchison, 1892...............36

WINNING PERCENTAGE

Roy Face, 1959.................. .947
Johnny Allen, 1937 .... .938
Greg Maddux, 1995 .... .905
Randy Johnson, 1995........ .900
Ron Guidry, 1978............... .893
Freddie Fitzsimmons, 1940.. .889
Lefty Grove, 1931 .... .886
Bob Stanley, 1978 .... .882
Preacher Roe, 1951........... .880
Fred Goldsmith, 1880 .... .875
Tom Seaver, 1981.............. .875

SAVES

Bobby Thigpen, 1990...........57
John Smoltz, 2002 55
Randy Myers, 1993...............53
Trevor Hoffman, 1998...........53
Eric Gagne, 2002.................52
Dennis Eckersley, 1992........51
Rod Beck, 1998....................51
Mariano Rivera, 2001............50
Dennis Eckersley, 1990........48
Rod Beck, 1993....................48
Jeff Shaw, 1998 48

EARNED RUN AVERAGE

Tim Keefe, 1880.................0.86
Dutch Leonard, 1914..........0.96
Three Finger Brown, 1906...1.04
Bob Gibson, 1968...............1.12
Christy Mathewson, 1909...1.14
Walter Johnson, 1913.........1.14
Jack Pfiester, 1907 ....1.15
Addie Joss, 1908................1.16
Carl Lundgren, 1907...........1.17
Denny Driscoll, 1882 ....1.21

SHUTOUTS

George Bradley, 1876 16
Grover Alexander, 1916 16
Jack Coombs, 1910...............13
Bob Gibson, 1968.................13
Jim Galvin, 1884 12
Ed Morris, 1886 12
Grover Alexander, 1915 12
Tommy Bond, 1879 11
Charley Radbourn, 1884 11
Dave Foutz, 1886...................11
Christy Mathewson, 1908 11
Ed Walsh, 1908.....................11
Walter Johnson, 1913 :..........11
Sandy Koufax, 1963 11
Dean Chance, 1964...............11

COMPLETE GAMES

Will White, 1879 75
Charley Radbourn, 1884 73
Jim McCormick, 1880..............72
Jim Galvin, 1883.....................72
Guy Hecker, 1884...................72
Jim Galvin, 1884.....................71
Tim Keefe, 1883.....................68
John Clarkson, 1885...............68
John Clarkson, 1889...............68
Bill Hutchison, 1892...............67

STRIKEOUTS

Matt Kilroy, 1886...................513
Toad Ramsey, 1886...:..........499
Hugh Daily, 1884 483
Dupee Shaw, 1884 451
Charley Radbourn, 1884 441
Charlie Buffinton, 1884 417
Guy Hecker, 1884.................385
Nolan Ryan, 1973 383
Sandy Koufax, 1965 382
Bill Sweeney, 1884 374

BASES ON BALLS

Amos Rusie, 1890.................289
Mark Baldwin, 1889..............274
Amos Rusie, 1892.................267
Amos Rusie, 1891.................262
Mark Baldwin, 1890..............249
Jack Stivetts, 1891................232
Mark Baldwin, 1891..............227
Phil Knell, 1891 226
Bob Barr, 1890 219
Amos Rusie 1893.................218

Manager of the Year

NATIONAL LEAGUE	AMERICAN LEAGUE
1983 ....Tommy Lasorda, LA	1983 ....Tony La Russa, Chi
1984 ....Jim Frey, Chi	1984 ....Sparky Anderson, Det
1985 ....Whitey Herzog, StL	1985 ....Bobby Cox, Tor
1986 ....Hal Lanier, Hou	1986 ....John McNamara, Bos
1987 ....Buck Rodgers, Mtl	1987 ....Sparky Anderson, Det
1988 ....Tommy Lasorda, LA	1988 ....Tony La Russa, Oak
1989 ....Don Zimmer, Chi	1989 ....Frank Robinson, Balt
1990 ....Jim Leyland, Pitt	1990 ....Jeff Torborg, Chi
1991 ....Bobby Cox, Atl	1991 ....Tom Kelly, Minn
1992 ....Jim Leyland, Pitt	1992 ....Tony La Russa, Oak
1993 ....Dusty Baker, SF	1993 ....Gene Lamont, Chi
1994 ....Felipe Alou, Mtl	1994 ....Buck Showalter, NY
1995 ....Don Baylor, Col	1995 ....Lou Piniella, Sea
1996 ....Bruce Bochy, SD	1996 ....Joe Torre, NY/Johnny Oates, Tex
1997 ....Dusty Baker, SF	1997 ....Davey Johnson, Balt
1998 ....Larry Dierker, Hou	1998 ....Joe Torre, NY
1999 ....Jack McKeon, Cin	1999 ....Jimy Williams, Bos
2000 ....Dusty Baker, SF	2000 ....Jerry Manuel, Chi
2001 ....Larry Bowa, Phil	2001 ....Lou Piniella, Sea

Individual Batting (Single Game)

MOST RUNS

7 ....Guy Hecker, Lou   Aug 15, 1886

MOST HITS

7 ....Wilbert Robinson, Balt   June 10, 1892
       Rennie Stennett, Pitt   Sept 16, 1975

MOST HOME RUNS

4 ....Bobby Lowe, Bos (N)   May 30, 1894
       Ed Delahanty, Phil   July 13, 1896
       Lou Gehrig, NY (A)   June 3, 1932
       Gil Hodges, Bklyn   Aug 31, 1950
       Joe Adcock, Mil (N)   July 31, 1954
       Rocky Colavito, Clev   June 10, 1959
       Willie Mays, SF   April 30, 1961
       Bob Horner, Atl   July 6, 1986
       Mark Whiten, StL   Sept 7, 1993
       Mike Cameron, Sea   May 2, 2002
       Shawn Green, LA   May 23, 2002

MOST GRAND SLAMS

2 ..:....Tony Lazzeri, NY (A)   May 24, 1936
       Jim Tabor, Bos (A)   July 4, 1939
       Rudy York, Bos (A)   July 27, 1946
       Jim Gentile, Balt   May 9, 1961
       Tony Cloninger, Atl   July 3, 1966
       Jim Northrup, Det   June 24, 1968
       Frank Robinson, Balt   June 26, 1970
       Robin Ventura, Chi (A)   Sept 4, 1995
       Chris Hoiles, Balt   Aug 14, 1998
       Fernando Tatis, StL   Apr 23, 1999
       N. Garciaparra, Bos   May 10, 1999

MOST RBIs

12 .....Jim Bottomley, StL   Sept 16, 1924
       Mark Whiten, StL   Sept 7, 1993

Individual Batting (Single Inning)

MOST RUNS

3 ....Tommy Burns, Chi (N)   Sept 6, 1883, 7th inning
       Ned Williamson, Chi (N) Sept 6, 1883, 7th inning
       Sammy White, Bos (A)   June 18, 1953, 7th inning

MOST RBIs

8.......Fernando Tatis, StL   Apr 23, 1999, 3rd inning

MOST HITS

3 ....Tommy Burns, Chi (N)   Sept 6, 1883, 7th inning
       Fred Pfeiffer, Chi (N)   Sept 6, 1883, 7th inning
       Ned Williamson, Chi (N) Sept 6, 1883, 7th inning
       Gene Stephens, Bos (A)   June 18, 1953, 7th inning

Note: All single-game hitting records for a nine-inning game.

Individual Pitching (Single Game)

MOST INNINGS PITCHED

26	Leon Cadore, Bklyn	May 1, 1920, tie 1–1
	Joe Oeschger, Bos (N)	May 1, 1920, tie 1–1

MOST RUNS ALLOWED

24 .....Al Travers, Det   May 18, 1912

MOST HITS ALLOWED

36 .....Jack Wadsworth, Lou   Aug 17, 1894

MOST STRIKEOUTS

20	Roger Clemens, Bos	April 29, 1986
20	Roger Clemens, Bos	Sept 18, 1996
20	Kerry Wood, Chi (N)	May 6, 1998
20	Randy Johnson, Ariz	May 8, 2001

MOST WALKS ALLOWED

16	Bill George, NY (N)	May 30, 1887
	George Van Haltren, Chi (N)	June 27, 1887
	Henry Gruber, Clev	Apr 19, 1890
	Bruno Haas, Phil (A)	June 2, 1915

MOST WILD PITCHES

6	J.R. Richard, Hou	April 10, 1979
	Phil Niekro, Atl	Aug 14, 1979
	Bill Gullickson, Mtl	April 10, 1982

Individual Pitching (Single Inning)

MOST RUNS ALLOWED

13 .....Lefty O'Doul, Bos (A)   July 7, 1923

MOST WALKS ALLOWED

8 ....Dolly Gray, Wash   Aug 28, 1909

MOST WILD PITCHES

4	Walter Johnson, Wash	Sept 21, 1914
	Phil Niekro, Atl	Aug 14, 1979

Miscellaneous

LONGEST GAME, BY INNINGS

26 .....Brooklyn 1, Boston 1   May 1, 1920

LONGEST NINE-INNING GAME, BY TIME

4:27 ..Los Angeles 11, San Francisco 10 Oct 5, 2001

Baseball Hall of Fame

Players

	Position	Career	Selected		Position	Career	Selected
Hank Aaron	OF	1954–76	1982	Orlando Cepeda	1B	1958–74	1999
Grover Alexander	P	1911–30	1938	Frank Chance	1B	1898–1914	1946
Cap Anson	1B	1876–97	1939	Oscar Charleston*	OF		1976
Luis Aparicio	SS	1956–73	1984	Jack Chesbro	P	1899–1909	1946
Luke Appling	SS	1930–50	1964	Fred Clarke	OF	1894–1915	1945
Richie Ashburn	OF	1948–62	1995	John Clarkson	P	1882–94	1963
Earl Averill	OF	1929–41	1975	Roberto Clemente	OF	1955–72	1973
Frank Baker	3B	1908–22	1955	Ty Cobb	OF	1905–28	1936
Dave Bancroft	SS	1915–30	1971	Mickey Cochrane	C	1925–37	1947
Ernie Banks	SS-1B	1953–71	1977	Eddie Collins	2B	1906–30	1939
Jake Beckley	1B	1888–1907	1971	Jimmy Collins	3B	1895–1908	1945
Cool Papa Bell*	OF		1974	Earle Combs	OF	1924–35	1970
Johnny Bench	C	1967–83	1989	Roger Connor	1B	1880–97	1976
Chief Bender	P	1903–25	1953	Stan Coveleski	P	1912–28	1969
Yogi Berra	C	1946–65	1972	Sam Crawford	OF	1899–1917	1957
Jim Bottomley	1B	1922–37	1974	Joe Cronin	SS	1926–45	1956
Lou Boudreau	SS	1938–52	1970	Candy Cummings	P	1872–77	1939
Roger Bresnahan	C	1897–1915	1945	Kiki Cuyler	OF	1921–38	1968
George Brett	3B	1973–93	1999	Ray Dandridge*	3B		1987
Lou Brock	OF	1961–79	1985	George Davis	SS	1890–1909	1998
Dan Brouthers	1B	1879–1904	1945	Leon Day*	P		1995
Three Finger Brown	P	1903–16	1949	Dizzy Dean	P	1930–47	1953
Jim Bunning	P	1955–71	1996	Ed Delahanty	OF	1888–1903	1945
Jesse Burkett	OF	1890–1905	1946	Bill Dickey	C	1928–46	1954
Roy Campanella	C	1948–57	1969	Martin Dihigo*	P-OF		1977
Rod Carew	1B-2B	1967–85	1991	Joe DiMaggio	OF	1936–51	1955
Max Carey	OF	1910–29	1961	Larry Doby	OF	1947–59	1998
Steve Carlton	P	1965–88	1994	Bobby Doerr	2B	1937–51	1986

Note: Career dates indicate first and last appearances in the majors.
*Elected on the basis of his career in the Negro leagues.

Players (Cont.)

	Position	Career	Selected
Don Drysdale	P	1956–69	1984
Hugh Duffy	OF	1888–1906	1945
Johnny Evers	2B	1902–29	1939
Buck Ewing	C	1880–97	1946
Red Faber	P	1914–33	1964
Bob Feller	P	1936–56	1962
Rick Ferrell	C	1929–47	1984
Rollie Fingers	P	1968–85	1992
Carlton Fisk	C	1969–93	2000
Elmer Flick	OF	1898–1910	1963
Whitey Ford	P	1950–67	1974
Bill Foster*	P		1996
Nellie Fox	2B	1947–65	1997
Jimmie Foxx	1B	1925–45	1951
Frankie Frisch	2B	1919–37	1947
Pud Galvin	P	1879–92	1965
Lou Gehrig	1B	1923–39	1939
Charlie Gehringer	2B	1924–42	1949
Bob Gibson	P	1959–75	1981
Josh Gibson*	C		1972
Lefty Gomez	P	1930–43	1972
Goose Goslin	OF	1921–38	1968
Hank Greenberg	1B	1930–47	1956
Burleigh Grimes	P	1916–34	1964
Lefty Grove	P	1925–41	1947
Chick Hafey	OF	1924–37	1971
Jesse Haines	P	1918–37	1970
Billy Hamilton	OF	1888–1901	1961
Gabby Hartnett	C	1922–41	1955
Harry Heilmann	OF	1914–32	1952
Billy Herman	2B	1931–47	1975
Harry Hooper	OF	1909–25	1971
Rogers Hornsby	2B	1915–37	1942
Waite Hoyt	P	1918–38	1969
Carl Hubbell	P	1928–43	1947
Catfish Hunter	P	1965–79	1987
Monte Irvin*	OF	1949–56	1973
Reggie Jackson	OF	1967–87	1993
Travis Jackson	SS	1922–36	1982
Ferguson Jenkins	P	1965–83	1991
Hugh Jennings	SS	1891–1918	1945
Judy Johnson*	3B		1975
Walter Johnson	P	1907–27	1936
Addie Joss	P	1902–10	1978
Al Kaline	OF	1953–74	1980
Tim Keefe	P	1880–93	1964
Willie Keeler	OF	1892–1910	1939
George Kell	3B	1943–57	1983
Joe Kelley	OF	1891–1908	1971
George Kelly	1B	1915–32	1973
King Kelly	C	1878–93	1945
Harmon Killebrew	1B-3B	1954–75	1984
Ralph Kiner	OF	1946–55	1975
Chuck Klein	OF	1928–44	1980
Sandy Koufax	P	1955–66	1972
Nap Lajoie	2B	1896–1916	1937
Tony Lazzeri	2B	1926–39	1991
Bob Lemon	P	1941–58	1976
Buck Leonard*	1B		1977
Fred Lindstrom	3B	1924–36	1976
Pop Lloyd*	SS-1B		1977
Ernie Lombardi	C	1931–47	1986
Ted Lyons	P	1923–46	1955
Mickey Mantle	OF	1951–68	1974
Heinie Manush	OF	1923–39	1964
Rabbit Maranville	SS-2B	1912–35	1954
Juan Marichal	P	1960–75	1983
Rube Marquard	P	1908–25	1971
Eddie Mathews	3B	1952–68	1978
Christy Mathewson	P	1900–16	1936
Willie Mays	OF	1951–73	1979
Bill Mazeroski	2B	1956–72	2001
Tommy McCarthy	OF	1884–96	1946
Willie McCovey	1B	1959–80	1986
Joe McGinnity	P	1899–1908	1946
Bid McPhee	2B	1882–99	2000
Joe Medwick	OF	1932–48	1968
Johnny Mize	1B	1936–53	1981
Joe Morgan	2B	1963–84	1990
Stan Musial	OF-1B	1941–63	1969
Hal Newhouser	P	1939–55	1992
Kid Nichols	P	1890–1906	1949
Phil Niekro	P	1964–87	1997
Jim O'Rourke	OF	1876–1904	1945
Mel Ott	OF	1926–47	1951
Satchel Paige*	P	1948–65	1971
Jim Palmer	P	1965–84	1990
Herb Pennock	P	1912–34	1948
Tony Perez	1B	1964–86	2000
Gaylord Perry	P	1962–83	1991
Eddie Plank	P	1901–17	1946
Kirby Puckett	OF	1984–95	2001
Charley Radbourn	P	1880–91	1939
Pee Wee Reese	SS	1940–58	1984
Sam Rice	OF	1915–35	1963
Eppa Rixey	P	1912–33	1963
Phil Rizzuto	SS	1941–56	1994
Robin Roberts	P	1948–66	1976
Brooks Robinson	3B	1955–77	1983
Frank Robinson	OF	1956–76	1982
Jackie Robinson	2B	1947–56	1962
Joe (Bullet) Rogan*	P		1998
Edd Roush	OF	1913–31	1962
Red Ruffing	P	1924–47	1967
Amos Rusie	P	1889–1901	1977
Babe Ruth	OF	1914–35	1936
Nolan Ryan	P	1966–93	1999
Ray Schalk	C	1912–29	1955
Mike Schmidt	3B	1972–89	1995
Red Schoendienst	2B	1945–63	1989
Tom Seaver	P	1967–86	1992
Joe Sewell	SS	1920–33	1977
Al Simmons	OF	1924–44	1953
George Sisler	1B	1915–30	1939
Enos Slaughter	OF	1938–59	1985
Hilton Smith*	P		2001
Ozzie Smith	SS	1978–96	2002
Duke Snider	OF	1947–64	1980
Warren Spahn	P	1942–65	1973
Al Spalding	P	1871–78	1939
Tris Speaker	OF	1907–28	1937
Willie Stargell	OF-1B	1962–82	1988
Turkey Stearns*	CF		2000
Don Sutton	P	1966–88	1998
Bill Terry	1B	1923–36	1954
Sam Thompson	OF	1885–1906	1974
Joe Tinker	SS	1902–16	1946
Pie Traynor	3B	1920–37	1948
Dazzy Vance	P	1915–35	1955
Arky Vaughan	SS	1932–48	1985
Rube Waddell	P	1897–1910	1946
Honus Wagner	SS	1897–1917	1936
Bobby Wallace	SS	1894–1918	1953
Ed Walsh	P	1904–17	1946

*Elected on the basis of his career in the Negro leagues.

Players *(Cont.)*

	Position	Career	Selected
Lloyd Waner	OF	1927–45	1967
Paul Waner	OF	1926–45	1952
John Ward	2B-P	1878–94	1964
Mickey Welch	P	1880–92	1973
Willie Wells*	SS	1924–49	1997
Zach Wheat	OF	1909–27	1959
Hoyt Wilhelm	P	1952–72	1985
Billy Williams	OF	1959–76	1987
Ted Williams	OF	1939–60	1966
Vic Willis	P	1898–1910	1995
Hack Wilson	OF	1923–34	1979
Dave Winfield	OF	1973–95	2001
Early Wynn	P	1939–63	1972
Carl Yastrzemski	OF	1961–83	1989
Cy Young	P	1890–1911	1937
Ross Youngs	OF	1917–26	1972
Robin Yount	SS	1974–93	1999

Pioneers/Executives *(Cont.)*

	Selected
Happy Chandler (commissioner)	1982
Charles Comiskey (manager-executive)	1939
Rube Foster (player-manager-executive)	1981
Ford Frick (commissioner-executive)	1970
Warren Giles (executive)	1979
Will Harridge (executive)	1972
William Hulbert (executive)	1995
Ban Johnson (executive)	1937
Kenesaw M. Landis (commissioner)	1944
Larry MacPhail (executive)	1978
Lee MacPhail Jr. (executive)	1998
Branch Rickey (manager-executive)	1967
Al Spalding (player-executive)	1939
Bill Veeck (owner)	1991
George Weiss (executive)	1971
George Wright (player-manager)	1937
Harry Wright (player-manager-executive)	1953
Tom Yawkey (executive)	1980

Umpires

	Selected
Al Barlick	1989
Nestor Chylak	1999
Jocko Conlan	1974
Tom Connolly	1953
Billy Evans	1973
Cal Hubbard	1976
Bill Klem	1953
Bill McGowan	1992

Managers

	Managed	Selected
Walt Alston	1954–76	1983
Sparky Anderson	1970–94	2000
Leo Durocher	1939–73	1994
Clark Griffith	1901–20	1946
Bucky Harris	1924–56	1975
Ned Hanlon	1899–1907	1996
Miller Huggins	1913–29	1964
Tommy Lasorda	1977–96	1997
Al Lopez	1951–69	1977
Connie Mack	1894–1950	1937
Joe McCarthy	1926–50	1957
John McGraw	1899–1932	1937
Bill McKechnie	1915–46	1962
Wilbert Robinson	1902–31	1945
Frank Selee	1890–1905	1999
Casey Stengel	1934–65	1966
Earl Weaver	1968–82, 85–86	1996

Pioneers/Executives

	Selected
Ed Barrow (manager-executive)	1953
Morgan Bulkeley (executive)	1937
Alexander Cartwright (executive)	1938
Henry Chadwick (writer-executive)	1938

*Elected on the basis of his career in the Negro leagues.

Notable Achievements

No-Hit Games, Nine Innings or More

NATIONAL LEAGUE

Date	Pitcher and Game
1876......July 15	George Bradley, StL vs Hart 2–0
1880......June 12	John Richmond, Wor vs Clev 1–0 (perfect game)
June 17	Monte Ward, Prov vs Buff 5–0 (perfect game)
Aug 19	Larry Corcoran, Chi vs Bos 6–0
Aug 20	Pud Galvin, Buff vs Wor 1–0
1882......Sept 20	Larry Corcoran, Chi vs Wor 5–0
Sept 22	Tim Lovett, Bklyn vs NY 4–0
1883......July 25	Hoss Radbourn, Prov vs Clev 8–0
Sept 13	Hugh Daily, Clev vs Phil 1–0
1884......June 27	Larry Corcoran, Chi vs Prov 6–0
Aug 4	Pud Galvin, Buff vs Det 18–0
1885......July 27	John Clarkson, Chi vs Prov 4–0
Aug 29	Charles Ferguson, Phil vs Prov 1–0
1891......July 31	Amos Rusie, NY vs Bklyn 6–0
June 22	Tom Lovett, Bklyn vs NY 4–0
1892......Aug 6	Jack Stivetts, Bos vs Bklyn 11–0
Aug 22	Alex Sanders, Lou vs Balt 6–2

Date	Pitcher and Game
1892......Oct 15	Bumpus Jones, Cin vs Pitt 7–1 (first major league game)
1893.....Aug 16	Bill Hawke, Balt vs Wash 5–0
1897.....Sept 18	Cy Young, Clev vs Cin 6–0
1898.....Apr 22	Ted Breitenstein, Cin vs Pitt 11–0
Apr 22	Jim Hughes, Balt vs Bos 8–0
July 8	Frank Donahue, Phil vs Bos 5–0
Aug 21	Walter Thornton, Chi vs Bklyn 2–0
1899.....May 25	Deacon Phillippe, Lou vs NY 7–0
Aug 7	Vic Willis, Bos vs Wash 7–1
1900.....July 12	Noodles Hahn, Cin vs Phil 4–0
1901.....July 15	Christy Mathewson, NY vs StL 5–0
1903.....Sept 18	Chick Fraser, Phil vs Chi 10–0
1904.....June 11	Bob Wicker, Chi at NY 1–0 (hit in 10th; won in 12th)
1905.....June 13	Christy Mathewson, NY vs Chi 1–0
1906.....May 1	John Lush, Phil vs Bklyn 6–0
July 20	Mal Eason, Bklyn vs StL 2–0

No-Hit Games, Nine Innings or More (Cont.)
NATIONAL LEAGUE (Cont.)

Date		Pitcher and Game	Date		Pitcher and Game
1906	Aug 1	Harry McIntire, Bklyn vs Pitt 0–1 (hit in 11th; lost in 13th)	1965	Sept 9	Sandy Koufax, LA vs Chi 1–0 (perfect game)
1907	May 8	Frank Pfeffer, Bos vs Cin 6–0	1967	June 18	Don Wilson, Hou vs Atl 2–0
	Sept 20	Nick Maddox, Pitt vs Bklyn 2–1	1968	July 29	George Culver, Cin vs Phil 6–1
1908	July 4	George Wiltse, NY vs Phil 1–0 (10 innings)		Sept 17	Gaylord Perry, SF vs StL 1–0
	Sept 5	Nap Rucker, Bklyn vs Bos 6–0		Sept 18	Ray Washburn, StL vs SF 2–0
1909	Apr 15	Leon Ames, NY vs Bklyn 0–3 (hit in 10th; lost in 13th)	1969	Apr 17	Bill Stoneman, Mtl vs Phil 7–0
				Apr 30	Jim Maloney, Cin vs Hou 10–0
1912	Sept 6	Jeff Tesreau, NY vs Phil 3–0		May 1	Don Wilson, Hou vs Cin 4–0
1914	Sept 9	George Davis, Bos vs Phil 7–0		Aug 19	Ken Holtzman, Chi vs Atl 3–0
1915	Apr 15	Rube Marquard, NY vs Bklyn 2–0		Sept 20	Bob Moose, Pitt vs NY 4–0
	Aug 31	Jimmy Lavender, Chi vs NY 2–0	1970	June 12	Dock Ellis, Pitt vs SD 2–0
1916	June 16	Tom Hughes, Bos vs Pitt 2–0		July 20	Bill Singer, LA vs Phil 5–0
1917	May 2	Jim Vaughn, Chi vs Cin 0–1 (hit in 10th; lost in 10th)	1971	June 3	Ken Holtzman, Chi vs Cin 1–0
				June 23	Rick Wise, Phil vs Cin 4–0
	May 2	Fred Toney, Cin vs Chi 1–0 (10 innings)		Aug 14	Bob Gibson, StL vs Pitt 11–0
			1972	Apr 16	Burt Hooton, Chi vs Phil 4–0
1919	May 11	Hod Eller, Cin vs StL 6–0		Sept 2	Milt Pappas, Chi vs SD 8–0
1922	May 7	Jesse Barnes, NY vs Phil 6–0		Oct 2	Bill Stoneman, Mtl vs NY 7–0
1924	July 17	Jesse Haines, StL vs Bos 5–0	1973	Aug 5	Phil Niekro, Atl vs SD 9–0
1925	Sept 13	Dazzy Vance, Bklyn vs Phil 10–1	1975	Aug 24	Ed Halicki, SF vs NY 6–0
1929	May 8	Carl Hubbell, NY vs Pitt 11–0	1976	July 9	Larry Dierker, Hou vs Mtl 6–0
1934	Sept 21	Paul Dean, StL vs Bklyn 3–0		Aug 9	John Candelaria, Pitt vs LA 2–0
1938	June 11	Johnny Vander Meer, Cin vs Bos 3–0		Sept 29	John Montefusco, SF vs Atl 9–0
	June 15	Johnny Vander Meer, Cin vs Bklyn 6–0	1978	Apr 16	Bob Forsch, StL vs Phil 5–0
				June 16	Tom Seaver, Cin vs StL 4–0
1940	Apr 30	Tex Carleton, Bklyn vs Cin, 3–0	1979	Apr 7	Ken Forsch, Hou vs Atl 6–0
1941	Aug 30	Lon Warneke, StL vs Cin 2–0	1980	June 27	Jerry Reuss, LA vs SF 8–0
1944	Apr 27	Jim Tobin, Bos vs Bklyn 2–0	1981	May 10	Charlie Lea, Mtl vs SF 4–0
	May 15	Clyde Shoun, Cin vs Bos 1–0		Sept 26	Nolan Ryan, Hou vs LA 5–0
1946	Apr 23	Ed Head, Bklyn vs Bos 5–0	1983	Sept 26	Bob Forsch, StL vs Mtl 3–0
1947	June 18	Ewell Blackwell, Cin vs Bos 6–0	1986	Sept 25	Mike Scott, Hou vs SF 2–0
1948	Sept 9	Rex Barney, Bklyn vs NY 2–0	1988	Sept 16	Tom Browning, Cin vs LA 1–0 (perfect game)
1950	Aug 11	Vern Bickford, Bos vs Bklyn 7–0			
1951	May 6	Cliff Chambers, Pitt vs Bos 3–0	1990	June 29	Fernando Valenzuela, LA vs StL 6–0
1952	June 19	Carl Erskine, Bklyn vs Chi 5–0			
1954	June 12	Jim Wilson, Mil vs Phil 2–0	1990	Aug 15	Terry Mulholland, Phil vs SF 6–0
1955	May 12	Sam Jones, Chi vs Pitt 4–0	1991	May 23	Tommy Greene, Phil vs Mtl 2–0
1956	May 12	Carl Erskine, Bklyn vs NY 3–0		July 26	Mark Gardner, Mtl vs LA 0–1 (hit in 10th, lost in 10th)
	Sept 25	Sal Maglie, Bklyn vs Phil 5–0		July 28	Dennis Martinez, Mtl vs LA 2–0 (perfect game)
1959	May 26	Harvey Haddix, Pitt vs Mil 0–1 (hit in 13th; lost in 13th)		Sept 11	Kent Mercker (6), Mark Wohlers (2), and Alejandro Pena (1), Atl vs SD 1–0
1960	May 15	Don Cardwell, Chi vs StL 4–0			
	Aug 18	Lew Burdette, Mil vs Phil 1–0	1992	Aug 17	Kevin Gross, LA vs SF 2–0
	Sept 16	Warren Spahn, Mil vs Phil 4–0	1993	Sept 8	Darryl Kile, Hou vs NY 7–1
1961	Apr 28	Warren Spahn, Mil vs SF 1–0	1994	Apr 8	Kent Mercker, Atl vs LA 6–0
1962	June 30	Sandy Koufax, LA vs NY 5–0	1995	June 3	Pedro Martinez, Mtl vs SD 1–0 (perfect through nine, hit in 10th)
1963	May 11	Sandy Koufax, LA vs SF 8–0			
	May 17	Don Nottebart, Hou vs Phil 4–1		July 14	Ramon Martinez, LA vs Fla 7–0
	June 15	Juan Marichal, SF vs Hou 1–0	1996	May 11	Al Leiter, Fla vs Col 11–0
1964	Apr 23	Ken Johnson, Hou vs Cin 0–1		Sept 17	Hideo Nomo, LA vs Col 9–0
	June 4	Sandy Koufax, LA vs Phil 3–0	1997	June 10	Kevin Brown, Fla vs SF 9–0
	June 21	Jim Bunning, Phil vs NY 6–0 (perfect game)		July 12	Francisco Cordova (9) and Ricardo Rincon (1), Pitt vs Col 3–0
1965	June 14	Jim Maloney, Cin vs NY 0–1 (hit in 11th; lost in 11th)	1999	June 25	Jose Jimenez, StL vs Ariz 1–0
	Aug 19	Jim Maloney, Cin vs Chi 1–0 (10 innings)	2001	May 12	A.J. Burnett, Fla vs SD 3–0
				Sept 3	Bud Smith, StL vs SD 4–0

Note: Includes the games struck from the official record book on Sept. 4, 1991, when baseball's committee on statistical accuracy voted to define no-hitters as games of nine innings or more that end with a team getting no hits.

No-Hit Games, Nine Innings or More *(Cont.)*

AMERICAN LEAGUE

Date	Pitcher and Game
1901......May 9	Earl Moore, Clev vs Chi 2–4 (hit in 10th; lost in 10th)
1902......Sept 20	Jimmy Callahan, Chi vs Det 3–0
1904......May 5	Cy Young, Bos vs Phil 3–0 (perfect game)
Aug 17	Jesse Tannehill, Bos vs Chi 6–0
1905......July 22	Weldon Henley, Phil vs StL 6–0
Sept 6	Frank Smith, Chi vs Det 15–0
Sept 27	Bill Dinneen, Bos vs Chi 2–0
1908......June 30	Cy Young, Bos vs NY 8–0
Sept 18	Bob Rhoades, Clev vs Bos 2–1
Sept 20	Frank Smith, Chi vs Phil 1–0
1908......Oct 2	Addie Joss, Clev vs Chi 1–0 (perfect game)
1910......Apr 20	Addie Joss, Clev vs Chi 1–0
May 12	Chief Bender, Phil vs Clev 4–0
Aug 30	Tom Hughes, NY vs Clev 0–5 (hit in 10th; lost in 11th)
1911......July 29	Joe Wood, Bos vs StL 5–0
Aug 27	Ed Walsh, Chi vs Bos 5–0
1912......July 4	George Mullin, Det vs StL 7–0
Aug 30	Earl Hamilton, StL vs Det 5–1
1914......May 14	Jim Scott, Chi vs Wash 0–1 (hit in 10th; lost in 10th)
May 31	Joe Benz, Chi vs Clev 6–1
1916......June 21	George Foster, Bos vs NY 2–0
Aug 26	Joe Bush, Phil vs Clev 5–0
Aug 30	Dutch Leonard, Bos vs StL 4–0
1917......Apr 14	Ed Cicotte, Chi vs StL 11–0
Apr 24	George Mogridge, NY vs Bos 2–1
May 5	Ernie Koob, StL vs Chi 1–0
May 6	Bob Groom, StL vs Chi 3–0
June 23	Ernie Shore, Bos vs Wash 4–0 (perfect game)
1918......June 3	Dutch Leonard, Bos vs Det 5–0
1919......Sept 10	Ray Caldwell, Clev vs NY 3–0
1920......July 1	Walter Johnson, Wash vs Bos 1–0
1922......Apr 30	Charlie Robertson, Chi vs Det 2–0 (perfect game)
1923......Sept 4	Sam Jones, NY vs Phil 2–0
Sept 7	Howard Ehmke, Bos vs Phil 4–0
1926......Aug 21	Ted Lyons, Chi vs Bos 6–0
1931......Apr 29	Wes Ferrell, Clev vs StL 9–0
Aug 8	Bob Burke, Wash vs Bos 5–0
1934......Sept 18	Bobo Newsom, StL vs Bos 1–2 (hit in 10th; lost in 10th)
1935......Aug 31	Vern Kennedy, Chi vs Clev 5–0
1937......June 1	Bill Dietrich, Chi vs StL 8–0
1938......Aug 27	Mtle Pearson, NY vs Clev 13–0
1940......Apr 16	Bob Feller, Clev vs Chi 1–0 (opening day)
1945......Sept 9	Dick Fowler, Phil vs StL 1–0
1946......Apr 30	Bob Feller, Clev vs NY 1–0
1947......July 10	Don Black, Clev vs Phil 3–0
Sep 3	Bill McCahan, Phil vs Wash 3–0
1948......June 30	Bob Lemon, Clev vs Det 2–0
1951......July 1	Bob Feller, Clev vs Det 2–1
July 12	Allie Reynolds, NY vs Clev 1–0
Sept 28	Allie Reynolds, NY vs Bos 8–0
1952......May 15	Virgil Trucks, Det vs Wash 1–0
Aug 25	Virgil Trucks, Det vs NY 1–0
1953......May 6	Bobo Holloman, StL vs Phil 6–0 (first major league start)
1956......July 14	Mel Parnell, Bos vs Chi 4–0

Date	Pitcher and Game
1966......Oct 8	Don Larsen, NY (A) vs Bklyn (N) 2–0 (World Series) (perfect game)
1957......Aug 20	Bob Keegan, Chi vs Wash 6–0
1958......July 20	Jim Bunning, Det vs Bos 3–0
Sept 20	Hoyt Wilhelm, Balt vs NY 1–0
1962......May 5	Bo Belinsky, LA vs Balt 2–0
June 26	Earl Wilson, Bos vs LA 2–0
Aug 1	Bill Monbouquette, Bos vs Chi 1–0
Aug 26	Jack Kralick, Minn vs KC 1–0
1965......Sept 16	Dave Morehead, Bos vs Clev 2–0
1966......June 10	Sonny Siebert, Clev vs Wash 2–0
1967......Apr 30	Steve Barber (8⅔) and Stu Miller (⅓), Balt vs Det 1–2
Aug 25	Dean Chance, Minn vs Clev 2–1
Sept 10	Joel Horlen, Chi vs Det 6–0
1968......Apr 27	Tom Phoebus, Balt vs Bos 6–0
May 8	Catfish Hunter, Oak vs Minn 4–0 (perfect game)
1969......Aug 13	Jim Palmer, Balt vs Oak 8–0
1970......July 3	Clyde Wright, Cal vs Oak 4–0
Sept 21	Vida Blue, Oak vs Minn 6–0
1973......Apr 27	Steve Busby, KC vs Det 3–0
May 15	Nolan Ryan, Cal vs KC 3–0
July 15	Nolan Ryan, Cal vs Det 6–0
July 30	Jim Bibby, Tex vs Oak 6–0
1974......June 19	Steve Busby, KC vs Mil 2–0
July 19	Dick Bosman, Clev vs Oak 4–0
Sept 28	Nolan Ryan, Cal vs Minn 4–0
1975......June 1	Nolan Ryan, Cal vs Balt 1–0
Sept 28	Vida Blue (5), Glenn Abbott and Paul Lindblad (1), Rollie Fingers (2), Oak vs Cal 5–0
1976......July 28	John Odom (5) and Francisco Barrios (4), Chi vs Oak 2–1
1977......May 14	Jim Colborn, KC vs Tex 6–0
May 30	Dennis Eckersley, Clev vs Cal 1–0
Sept 22	Bert Blyleven, Tex vs Cal 6–0
1981......May 15	Len Barker, Clev vs Tor 3–0 (perfect game)
1983......July 4	Dave Righetti, NY vs Bos 4–0
Sept 29	Mike Warren, Oak vs Chi 3–0
1984......Apr 7	Jack Morris, Det vs Chi 4–0
Sept 30	Mike Witt, Cal vs Tex 1–0 (perfect game)
1986......Sept 19	Joe Cowley, Chi vs Cal 7–1
1987......Apr 15	Juan Nieves, Mil vs Balt 7–0
1990......Apr 11	Mark Langston (7), Mike Witt (2), Cal vs Sea 1–0
June 2	Randy Johnson, Sea vs Det 2–0
June 11	Nolan Ryan, Tex vs Oak 5–0
June 29	Dave Stewart, Oak vs Tor 5–0
1990......July 1	Andy Hawkins, NY vs Chi 0–4 (pitched eight of nine-innning game)
Sept 2	Dave Stieb, Tor vs Clev 3–0
1991......May 1	Nolan Ryan, Tex vs Tor 3–0
July 13	Bob Milacki (6), Mike Flanagan (1), Mark Williamson (1), and Gregg Olson (1), Balt vs Oak 2–0
Aug 11	Wilson Alvarez, Chi vs Balt 7–0
Aug 26	Bret Saberhagen, KC vs Chi 7–0
1993......Apr 22	Chris Bosio, Sea vs Bos 7–0
Sept 4	Jim Abbott, NY vs Clev 4–0

Notable Achievements (Cont.)

No-Hit Games, Nine Innings or More (Cont.)

AMERICAN LEAGUE (Cont.)

Date	Pitcher and Game	Date	Pitcher and Game
1994......Apr 27	Scott Erickson, Minn vs Mil 6–0	1999......July 18	David Cone, NY vs Mtl 6–0
July 28	Kenny Rogers, Texas vs Cal 4–0		(perfect game)
	(perfect game)	Sept 11	Eric Milton, Minn vs Ana 7–0
1996......May 14	Dwight Gooden, NY vs Sea 2–0	2001......Apr 4	Hideo Nomo, Bos vs Balt 3–0
1998......May 17	David Wells, NY vs Minn 4–0	2002......Apr 27	Derek Lowe, Bos vs TB 10–0
	(perfect game)		

Longest Hitting Streaks

NATIONAL LEAGUE

Player and Team	Year	G
Willie Keeler, Balt	1897	44
Pete Rose, Cin	1978	44
Bill Dahlen, Chi	1894	42
Tommy Holmes, Bos	1945	37
Billy Hamilton, Phil	1894	36
Luis Castillo, Fla	2002	35
Fred Clarke, Lou	1895	35
Benito Santiago, SD	1987	34
George Davis, NY	1893	33
Rogers Hornsby, StL	1922	32

AMERICAN LEAGUE

Player and Team	Year	G
Joe DiMaggio, NY	1941	56
George Sisler, StL	1922	41
Ty Cobb, Det	1911	40
Paul Molitor, Mil	1987	39
Ty Cobb, Det	1917	35
Ty Cobb, Det	1912	34
George Sisler, StL	1925	34
John Stone, Det	1930	34
George McQuinn, StL	1938	34
Dom DiMaggio, Bos	1949	34

Triple Crown Hitters

NATIONAL LEAGUE

Player and Team	Year	HR	RBI	BA
Paul Hines, Prov	1878	4	50	.358
Hugh Duffy, Bos	1894	18	145	.438
Heinie Zimmerman*, Chi	1912	14	103	.372
Rogers Hornsby, StL	1922	42	152	.401
	1925	39	143	.403
Chuck Klein, Phil	1933	28	120	.368
Joe Medwick, StL	1937	31	154	.374

*Zimmerman ranked first in RBIs as calculated by Ernie Lanigan, but only third as calculated by Information Concepts Inc.

AMERICAN LEAGUE

Player and Team	Year	HR	RBI	BA
Nap Lajoie, Phil	1901	14	125	.422
Ty Cobb, Det	1909	9	115	.377
Jimmie Foxx, Phil	1933	48	163	.356
Lou Gehrig, NY	1934	49	165	.363
Ted Williams, Bos	1942	36	137	.356
	1947	32	114	.343
Mickey Mantle, NY	1956	52	130	.353
Frank Robinson, Balt	1966	49	122	.316
Carl Yastrzemski, Bos	1967	44	121	.326

THEY SAID IT

Tim Raines, Marlins outfielder, on being a 42-year-old major leaguer: "I'm only 32 in the Dominican Republic."

Triple Crown Pitchers

NATIONAL LEAGUE						AMERICAN LEAGUE				
Player and Team	Year	W	L	SO	ERA	Player and Team	Year	W	L	SO	ERA
Tommy Bond, Bos	1877	40	17	170	2.11	Cy Young, Bos	1901	33	10	158	1.62
Hoss Radbourn, Prov.	1884	60	12	441	1.38	Rube Waddell, Phil	1905	26	11	287	1.48
Tim Keefe, NY	1888	35	12	333	1.74	Walter Johnson, Wash	1913	36	7	303	1.09
John Clarkson, Bos	1889	49	19	284	2.73		1918	23	13	162	1.27
Amos Rusie, NY	1894	36	13	195	2.78		1924	23	7	158	2.72
Christy Mathewson, NY	1905	31	8	206	1.27	Lefty Grove, Phil	1930	28	5	209	2.54
	1908	37	11	259	1.43		1931	31	4	175	2.06
Grover Alexander, Phil.	1915	31	10	241	1.22	Lefty Gomez, NY	1934	26	5	158	2.33
	1916	33	12	167	1.55		1937	21	11	194	2.33
	1917	30	13	201	1.86	Hal Newhouser, Det	1945	25	9	212	1.81
Hippo Vaughn, Chi	1918	22	10	148	1.74	Roger Clemens, Tor	1997	21	7	292	2.05
Grover Alexander, Chi	1920	27	14	173	1.91		1998	20	6	271	2.64
Dazzy Vance, Bklyn	1924	28	6	262	2.16	Pedro Martinez, Bos	1999	23	4	313	2.07
Bucky Walters, Cin	1939	27	11	137	2.29						
Sandy Koufax, LA	1963	25	5	306	1.88						
	1965	26	8	382	2.04						
	1966	27	9	317	1.73						
Steve Carlton, Phil.	1972	27	10	310	1.97						
Dwight Gooden, NY	1985	24	4	268	1.53						
Randy Johnson, Ariz	2002	24	5	334	2.32						

Consecutive Games Played, 500 or More Games

Cal Ripken Jr.	2,632	Frank McCormick	652
Lou Gehrig	2,130	Sandy Alomar Sr.	648
Everett Scott	1,307	Eddie Brown	618
Steve Garvey	1,207	Roy McMillan	585
Billy Williams	1,117	George Pinckney	577
Joe Sewell	1,103	Steve Brodie	574
Stan Musial	895	Aaron Ward	565
Eddie Yost	829	Candy LaChance	540
Gus Suhr	822	Buck Freeman	535
Nellie Fox	798	Fred Luderus	533
Pete Rose	745	Clyde Milan	511
Dale Murphy	740	Charlie Gehringer	511
Richie Ashburn	730	Vada Pinson	508
Ernie Banks	717	Tony Cuccinello	504
Pete Rose	678	Charlie Gehringer	504
Earl Averill	673	Omar Moreno	503

Unassisted Triple Plays

Player and Team	Date	Pos	Opp	Opp Batter
Neal Ball, Clev	7-19-09	SS	Bos	Amby McConnell
Bill Wambsganss, Clev	10-10-20	2B	Bklyn	Clarence Mitchell
George Burns, Bos	9-14-23	1B	Clev	Frank Brower
Ernie Padgett, Bos	10-6-23	SS	Phil	Walter Holke
Glenn Wright, Pitt	5-7-25	SS	StL	Jim Bottomley
Jimmy Cooney, Chi	5-30-27	SS	Pitt	Paul Waner
Johnny Neun, Det	5-31-27	1B	Clev	Homer Summa
Ron Hansen, Wash	7-30-68	SS	Clev	Joe Azcue
Mickey Morandini, Phil	9-20-92	2B	Pitt	Jeff King
John Valentin, Bos	7-15-94	SS	Minn	Marc Newfield
Randy Velarde, Oak	5-29-00	2B	NYY	Shane Spencer

Pennant Winners

Year	Team	Manager	W	L	Pct	GA
1900	Brooklyn	Ned Hanlon	82	54	.603	4½
1901	Pittsburgh	Fred Clarke	90	49	.647	7½
1902	Pittsburgh	Fred Clarke	103	36	.741	27½
1903	Pittsburgh	Fred Clarke	91	49	.650	6½
1904	New York	John McGraw	106	47	.693	13
1905	New York	John McGraw	105	48	.686	9
1906	Chicago	Frank Chance	116	36	.763	20
1907	Chicago	Frank Chance	107	45	.704	17
1908	Chicago	Frank Chance	99	55	.643	1
1909	Pittsburgh	Fred Clarke	110	42	.724	6½
1910	Chicago	Frank Chance	104	50	.675	13
1911	New York	John McGraw	99	54	.647	7½
1912	New York	John McGraw	103	48	.682	10
1913	New York	John McGraw	101	51	.664	12½
1914	Boston	George Stallings	94	59	.614	10½
1915	Philadelphia	Pat Moran	90	62	.592	7
1916	Brooklyn	Wilbert Robinson	94	60	.610	2½
1917	New York	John McGraw	98	56	.636	10
1918	Chicago	Fred Mitchell	84	45	.651	10½
1919	Cincinnati	Pat Moran	96	44	.686	9
1920	Brooklyn	Wilbert Robinson	93	61	.604	7
1921	New York	John McGraw	94	59	.614	4
1922	New York	John McGraw	93	61	.604	7
1923	New York	John McGraw	95	58	.621	4½
1924	New York	John McGraw	93	60	.608	1½
1925	Pittsburgh	Bill McKechnie	95	58	.621	8½
1926	St. Louis	Rogers Hornsby	89	65	.578	2
1927	Pittsburgh	Donie Bush	94	60	.610	1½
1928	St. Louis	Bill McKechnie	95	59	.617	2
1929	Chicago	Joe McCarthy	98	54	.645	10½
1930	St. Louis	Gabby Street	92	62	.597	2
1931	St. Louis	Gabby Street	101	53	.656	13
1932	Chicago	Charlie Grimm	90	64	.584	4
1933	New York	Bill Terry	91	61	.599	5
1934	St. Louis	Frankie Frisch	95	58	.621	2
1935	Chicago	Charlie Grimm	100	54	.649	4
1936	New York	Bill Terry	92	62	.597	5
1937	New York	Bill Terry	95	57	.625	3
1938	Chicago	Gabby Hartnett	89	63	.586	2
1939	Cincinnati	Bill McKechnie	97	57	.630	4½
1940	Cincinnati	Bill McKechnie	100	53	.654	12
1941	Brooklyn	Leo Durocher	100	54	.649	2½
1942	St. Louis	Billy Southworth	106	48	.688	2
1943	St. Louis	Billy Southworth	105	49	.682	18
1944	St. Louis	Billy Southworth	105	49	.682	14½
1945	Chicago	Charlie Grimm	98	56	.636	3
1946	St. Louis*	Eddie Dyer	98	58	.628	2
1947	Brooklyn	Burt Shotton	94	60	.610	5
1948	Boston	Billy Southworth	91	62	.595	6½
1949	Brooklyn	Burt Shotton	97	57	.630	1
1950	Philadelphia	Eddie Sawyer	91	63	.591	2
1951	New York†	Leo Durocher	98	59	.624	1
1952	Brooklyn	Chuck Dressen	96	57	.627	4½
1953	Brooklyn	Chuck Dressen	105	49	.682	13
1954	New York	Leo Durocher	97	57	.630	5
1955	Brooklyn	Walt Alston	98	55	.641	13½
1956	Brooklyn	Walt Alston	93	61	.604	1
1957	Milwaukee	Fred Haney	95	59	.617	8
1958	Milwaukee	Fred Haney	92	62	.597	8
1959	Los Angeles‡	Walt Alston	88	68	.564	2
1960	Pittsburgh	Danny Murtaugh	95	59	.617	7
1961	Cincinnati	Fred Hutchinson	93	61	.604	4
1962	San Francisco#	Al Dark	103	62	.624	1
1963	Los Angeles	Walt Alston	99	63	.611	6
1964	St. Louis	Johnny Keane	93	69	.574	1

Pennant Winners (Cont.)

Year	Team	Manager	W	L	Pct	GA
1965	Los Angeles	Walt Alston	97	65	.599	2
1966	Los Angeles	Walt Alston	95	67	.586	1½
1967	St. Louis	Red Schoendienst	101	60	.627	10½
1968	St. Louis	Red Schoendienst	97	65	.599	9
1969	New York (E)††	Gil Hodges	100	62	.617	8
1970	Cincinnati (W)††	Sparky Anderson	102	60	.630	14½
1971	Pittsburgh (E)††	Danny Murtaugh	97	65	.599	7
1972	Cincinnati (W)††	Sparky Anderson	95	59	.617	10½
1973	New York (E)††	Yogi Berra	82	79	.509	1½
1974	Los Angeles (W)††	Walt Alston	102	60	.630	4
1975	Cincinnati (W)††	Sparky Anderson	108	54	.667	20
1976	Cincinnati (W)††	Sparky Anderson	102	60	.630	10
1977	Los Angeles (W)††	Tommy Lasorda	98	64	.605	10
1978	Los Angeles (W)††	Tommy Lasorda	95	67	.586	2½
1979	Pittsburgh (E)††	Chuck Tanner	98	64	.605	2
1980	Philadelphia (E)††	Dallas Green	91	71	.562	1
1981	Los Angeles (W)††	Tommy Lasorda	63	47	.573	**
1982	St. Louis (E)††	Whitey Herzog	92	70	.568	3
1983	Philadelphia (E)††	Pat Corrales/ Paul Owens	90	72	.556	6
1984	San Diego (W)††	Dick Williams	92	70	.568	12
1985	St. Louis (E)††	Whitey Herzog	101	61	.623	3
1986	New York (E)††	Dave Johnson	108	54	.667	21½
1987	St. Louis (E)††	Whitey Herzog	95	67	.586	3
1988	Los Angeles (W)††	Tommy Lasorda	94	67	.584	7
1989	San Francisco (W)††	Roger Craig	92	70	.568	3
1990	Cincinnati (W)††	Lou Piniella	91	71	.562	5
1991	Atlanta (W)††	Bobby Cox	94	68	.580	1
1992	Atlanta (W)††	Bobby Cox	98	64	.605	8
1993	Philadelphia (E)††	Jim Fregosi	97	65	.599	3
1994	Season ended Aug. 11 due to players' strike.					
1995	Atlanta (E)††	Bobby Cox	90	54	.625	21
1996	Atlanta (E)††	Bobby Cox	96	66	.593	8
1997	Florida (wc)††	Jim Leyland	92	70	.568	-9
1998	San Diego (W)††	Bruce Bochy	98	64	.605	9½
1999	Atlanta Braves (E)††	Bobby Cox	103	59	.636	6½
2000	New York Mets (wc)††	Bobby Valentine	94	68	.580	-6½
2001	Arizona (W)††	Bob Brenly	92	70	.568	2
2002	San Francisco (wc)††	Dusty Baker	95	66	.590	-2½

*Defeated Brooklyn, two games to none, in playoff for pennant. †Defeated Brooklyn, two games to one, in playoff for pennant. ‡Defeated Milwaukee, two games to none, in playoff for pennant. #Defeated Los Angeles, two games to one, in playoff for pennant. ††Won Championship Series. **First half 36–21; second half 27–26, in season split by strike; defeated Houston in playoff for Western Division title.

THEY SAID IT

George W. Bush, U.S. President, upon meeting Diamondbacks general manager Joe Garagiola Jr.: "I'm always suspicious of guys who've got a famous father."

Leading Batsmen

Year	Player and Team	BA	Year	Player and Team	BA
1900	Honus Wagner, Pitt	.381	1952	Stan Musial, StL	.336
1901	Jesse Burkett, StL	.382	1953	Carl Furillo, Bklyn	.344
1902	Ginger Beaumtl, Pitt	.357	1954	Willie Mays, NY	.345
1903	Honus Wagner, Pitt	.355	1955	Richie Ashburn, Phil	.338
1904	Honus Wagner, Pitt	.349	1956	Hank Aaron, Mil	.328
1905	Cy Seymour, Cin	.377	1957	Stan Musial, StL	.351
1906	Honus Wagner, Pitt	.339	1958	Richie Ashburn, Phil	.350
1907	Honus Wagner, Pitt	.350	1959	Hank Aaron, Mil	.355
1908	Honus Wagner, Pitt	.354	1960	Dick Groat, Pitt	.325
1909	Honus Wagner, Pitt	.339	1961	Roberto Clemente, Pitt	.351
1910	Sherry Magee, Phil	.331	1962	Tommy Davis, LA	.346
1911	Honus Wagner, Pitt	.334	1963	Tommy Davis, LA	.326
1912	Heinie Zimmerman, Chi	.372	1964	Roberto Clemente, Pitt	.339
1913	Jake Daubert, Bklyn	.350	1965	Roberto Clemente, Pitt	.329
1914	Jake Daubert, Bklyn	.329	1966	Matty Alou, Pitt	.342
1915	Larry Doyle, NY	.320	1967	Roberto Clemente, Pitt	.357
1916	Hal Chase, Cin	.339	1968	Pete Rose, Cin	.335
1917	Edd Roush, Cin	.341	1969	Pete Rose, Cin	.348
1918	Zach Wheat, Bklyn	.335	1970	Rico Carty, Atl	.366
1919	Edd Roush, Cin	.321	1971	Joe Torre, StL	.363
1920	Rogers Hornsby, StL	.370	1972	Billy Williams, Chi	.333
1921	Rogers Hornsby, StL	.397	1973	Pete Rose, Cin	.338
1922	Rogers Hornsby, StL	.401	1974	Ralph Garr, Atl	.353
1923	Rogers Hornsby, StL	.384	1975	Bill Madlock, Chi	.354
1924	Rogers Hornsby, StL	.424	1976	Bill Madlock, Chi	.339
1925	Rogers Hornsby, StL	.403	1977	Dave Parker, Pitt	.338
1926	Bubbles Hargrave, Cin	.353	1978	Dave Parker, Pitt	.334
1927	Paul Waner, Pitt	.380	1979	Keith Hernandez, StL	.344
1928	Rogers Hornsby, Bos	.387	1980	Bill Buckner, Chi	.324
1929	Lefty O'Doul, Phil	.398	1981	Bill Madlock, Pitt	.341
1930	Bill Terry, NY	.401	1982	Al Oliver, Mtl	.331
1931	Chick Hafey, StL	.349	1983	Bill Madlock, Pitt	.323
1932	Lefty O'Doul, Bklyn	.368	1984	Tony Gwynn, SD	.351
1933	Chuck Klein, Phil	.368	1985	Willie McGee, StL	.353
1934	Paul Waner, Pitt	.362	1986	Tim Raines, Mtl	.334
1935	Arky Vaughan, Pitt	.385	1987	Tony Gwynn, SD	.370
1936	Paul Waner, Pitt	.373	1988	Tony Gwynn, SD	.313
1937	Joe Medwick, StL	.374	1989	Tony Gwynn, SD	.336
1938	Ernie Lombardi, Cin	.342	1990	Willie McGee, StL	.335
1939	Johnny Mize, StL	.349	1991	Terry Pendleton, Atl	.319
1940	Debs Garms, Pitt	.355	1992	Gary Sheffield, SD	.330
1941	Pete Reiser, Bklyn	.343	1993	Andres Galarraga, Col	.370
1942	Ernie Lombardi, Bos	.330	1994	Tony Gwynn, SD	.394
1943	Stan Musial, StL	.357	1995	Tony Gwynn, SD	.368
1944	Dixie Walker, Bklyn	.357	1996	Tony Gwynn, SD	.353
1945	Phil Cavarretta, Chi	.355	1997	Tony Gwynn, SD	.372
1946	Stan Musial, StL	.365	1998	Larry Walker, Col	.363
1947	Harry Walker, StL-Phil	.363	1999	Larry Walker, Col	.379
1948	Stan Musial, StL	.376	2000	Todd Helton, Col	.372
1949	Jackie Robinson, Bklyn	.342	2001	Larry Walker, Col	.350
1950	Stan Musial, StL	.346	2002	Barry Bonds, SF	.370
1951	Stan Musial, StL	.355			

Leaders in Runs Scored

Year	Player and Team	Runs	Year	Player and Team	Runs
1900	Roy Thomas, Phil	131	1952	Stan Musial, StL	105
1901	Jesse Burkett, StL	139		Solly Hemus, StL	105
1902	Honus Wagner, Pitt	105	1953	Duke Snider, Bklyn	132
1903	Ginger Beaumont, Pitt	137	1954	Stan Musial, StL	120
1904	George Browne, NY	99		Duke Snider, Bklyn	120
1905	Mike Donlin, NY	124	1955	Duke Snider, Bklyn	126
1906	Honus Wagner, Pitt	103	1956	Frank Robinson, Cin	122
	Frank Chance, Chi	103	1957	Hank Aaron, Mil	118
1907	Spike Shannon, NY	104	1958	Willie Mays, SF	121
1908	Fred Tenney, NY	101	1959	Vada Pinson, Cin	131
1909	Tommy Leach, Pitt	126	1960	Bill Bruton, Mil	112
1910	Sherry Magee, Phil	110	1961	Willie Mays, SF	129
1911	Jimmy Sheckard, Chi	121	1962	Frank Robinson, Cin	134
1912	Bob Bescher, Cin	120	1963	Hank Aaron, Mil	121
1913	Tommy Leach, Chi	99	1964	Dick Allen, Phil	125
	Max Carey, Pitt	99	1965	Tommy Harper, Cin	126
1914	George Burns, NY	100	1966	Felipe Alou, Atl	122
1915	Gavvy Cravath, Phil	89	1967	Hank Aaron, Atl	113
1916	George Burns, NY	105		Lou Brock, StL	113
1917	George Burns, NY	103	1968	Glenn Beckert, Chi	98
1918	Heinie Groh, Cin	88	1969	Bobby Bonds, SF	120
1919	George Burns, NY	86		Pete Rose, Cin	120
1920	George Burns, NY	115	1970	Billy Williams, Chi	137
1921	Rogers Hornsby, StL	131	1971	Lou Brock, StL	126
1922	Rogers Hornsby, StL	141	1972	Joe Morgan, Cin	122
1923	Ross Youngs, NY	121	1973	Bobby Bonds, SF	131
1924	Frankie Frisch, NY	121	1974	Pete Rose, Cin	110
	Rogers Hornsby, StL	121	1975	Pete Rose, Cin	112
1925	Kiki Cuyler, Pitt	144	1976	Pete Rose, Cin	130
1926	Kiki Cuyler, Pitt	113	1977	George Foster, Cin	124
1927	Lloyd Waner, Pitt	133	1978	Ivan DeJesus, Chi	104
	Rogers Hornsby, NY	133	1979	Keith Hernandez, StL	116
1928	Paul Waner, Pitt	142	1980	Keith Hernandez, StL	111
1929	Rogers Hornsby, Chi	156	1981	Mike Schmidt, Phil	78
1930	Chuck Klein, Phil	158	1982	Lonnie Smith, StL	120
1931	Bill Terry, NY	121	1983	Tim Raines, Mtl	133
	Chuck Klein, Phil	121	1984	Ryne Sandberg, Chi	114
1932	Chuck Klein, Phil	152	1985	Dale Murphy, Atl	118
1933	Pepper Martin, StL	122	1986	Von Hayes, Phil	107
1934	Paul Waner, Pitt	122		Tony Gwynn, SD	107
1935	Augie Galan, Chi	133	1987	Tim Raines, Mtl	123
1936	Arky Vaughan, Pitt	122	1988	Brett Butler, SF	109
1937	Joe Medwick, StL	111	1989	Howard Johnson, NY	104
1938	Mel Ott, NY	116		Will Clark, SF	104
1939	Billy Werber, Cin	115		Ryne Sandberg, Chi	104
1940	Arky Vaughan, Pitt	113	1990	Ryne Sandberg, Chi	116
1941	Pete Reiser, Bklyn	117	1991	Brett Butler, LA	112
1942	Mel Ott, NY	118	1992	Barry Bonds, Pitt	109
1943	Arky Vaughan, Bklyn	112	1993	Lenny Dykstra, Phil	143
1944	Bill Nicholson, Chi	116	1994	Jeff Bagwell, Hou	104
1945	Eddie Stanky, Bklyn	128	1995	Craig Biggio, Hou	123
1946	Stan Musial, StL	124	1996	Ellis Burks, Col	142
1947	Johnny Mize, NY	137	1997	Craig Biggio, Hou	146
1948	Stan Musial, StL	135	1998	Sammy Sosa, Chi	134
1949	Pee Wee Reese, Bklyn	132	1999	Jeff Bagwell, Hou	143
1950	Earl Torgeson, Bos	120	2000	Jeff Bagwell, Hou	152
1951	Stan Musial, StL	124	2001	Sammy Sosa, Chi	146
	Ralph Kiner, Pitt	124	2002	Sammy Sosa, Chi	122

Leaders in Hits

Year	Player and Team	Hits	Year	Player and Team	Hits
1900	Willie Keeler, Bklyn	208	1954	Don Mueller, NY	212
1901	Jesse Burkett, StL	228	1955	Ted Kluszewski, Cin	192
1902	Ginger Beaumont, Pitt	194	1956	Hank Aaron, Mil	200
1903	Ginger Beaumont, Pitt	209	1957	Red Schoendienst, NY-Mil	200
1904	Ginger Beaumont, Pitt	185	1958	Richie Ashburn, Phil	215
1905	Cy Seymour, Cin	219	1959	Hank Aaron, Mil	223
1906	Harry Steinfeldt, Chi	176	1960	Willie Mays, SF	190
1907	Ginger Beaumont, Bos	187	1961	Vada Pinson, Cin	208
1908	Honus Wagner, Pitt	201	1962	Tommy Davis, LA	230
1909	Larry Doyle, NY	172	1963	Vada Pinson, Cin	204
1910	Honus Wagner, Pitt	178	1964	Roberto Clemente, Pitt	211
	Bobby Byrne, Pitt	178		Curt Flood, StL	211
1911	Doc Miller, Bos	192	1965	Pete Rose, Cin	209
1912	Heinie Zimmerman, Chi	207	1966	Felipe Alou, Atl	218
1913	Gavvy Cravath, Phil	179	1967	Roberto Clemente, Pitt	209
1914	Sherry Magee, Phil	171	1968	Felipe Alou, Atl	210
1915	Larry Doyle, NY	189		Pete Rose, Cin	210
1916	Hal Chase, Cin	184	1969	Matty Alou, Pitt	231
1917	Heinie Groh, Cin	182	1970	Pete Rose, Cin	205
1918	Charlie Hollocher, Chi	161		Billy Williams, Chi	205
1919	Ivy Olson, Bklyn	164	1971	Joe Torre, StL	230
1920	Rogers Hornsby, StL	218	1972	Pete Rose, Cin	198
1921	Rogers Hornsby, StL	235	1973	Pete Rose, Cin	230
1922	Rogers Hornsby, StL	250	1974	Ralph Garr, Atl	214
1923	Frankie Frisch, NY	223	1975	Dave Cash, Phil	213
1924	Rogers Hornsby, StL	227	1976	Pete Rose, Cin	215
1925	Jim Bottomley, StL	227	1977	Dave Parker, Pitt	215
1926	Eddie Brown, Bos	201	1978	Steve Garvey, LA	202
1927	Paul Waner, Pitt	237	1979	Garry Templeton, StL	211
1928	Freddy Lindstrom, NY	231	1980	Steve Garvey, LA	200
1929	Lefty O'Doul, Phil	254	1981	Pete Rose, Phil	140
1930	Bill Terry, NY	254	1982	Al Oliver, Mtl	204
1931	Lloyd Waner, Pitt	214	1983	Jose Cruz, Hou	189
1932	Chuck Klein, Phil	226		Andre Dawson, Mtl	189
1933	Chuck Klein, Phil	223	1984	Tony Gwynn, SD	213
1934	Paul Waner, Pitt	217	1985	Willie McGee, StL	216
1935	Billy Herman, Chi	227	1986	Tony Gwynn, SD	211
1936	Joe Medwick, StL	223	1987	Tony Gwynn, SD	218
1937	Joe Medwick, StL	237	1988	Andres Galarraga, Mtl	184
1938	Frank McCormick, Cin	209	1989	Tony Gwynn, SD	203
1939	Frank McCormick, Cin	209	1990	Brett Butler, SF	192
1940	Stan Hack, Chi	191		Lenny Dykstra, Phil	192
	Frank McCormick, Cin	191	1991	Terry Pendleton, Atl	187
1941	Stan Hack, Chi	186	1992	Terry Pendleton, Atl	199
1942	Enos Slaughter, StL	188		Andy Van Slyke, Pitt	199
1943	Stan Musial, StL	220	1993	Lenny Dykstra, Phil	194
1944	Stan Musial, StL	197	1994	Tony Gwynn, SD	165
	Phil Cavarretta, Chi	197	1995	Dante Bichette, Col	197
1945	Tommy Holmes, Bos	224		Tony Gwynn, SD	197
1946	Stan Musial, StL	228	1996	Lance Johnson, NY	227
1947	Tommy Holmes, Bos	191	1997	Tony Gwynn, SD	220
1948	Stan Musial, StL	230	1998	Dante Bichette, Col	219
1949	Stan Musial, StL	207	1999	Luis Gonzalez, Ariz	206
1950	Duke Snider, Bklyn	199	2000	Todd Helton, Col	216
1951	Richie Ashburn, Phil	221	2001	Rich Aurilia, SF	206
1952	Stan Musial, StL	194	2002	Vladimir Guerrero	206
1953	Richie Ashburn, Phil	205			

Home Run Leaders

Year	Player and Team	HR	Year	Player and Team	HR
1900	Herman Long, Bos	12	1949	Ralph Kiner, Pitt	54
1901	Sam Crawford, Cin	16	1950	Ralph Kiner, Pitt	47
1902	Tommy Leach, Pitt	6	1951	Ralph Kiner, Pitt	42
1903	Jimmy Sheckard, Bklyn	9	1952	Ralph Kiner, Pitt	37
1904	Harry Lumley, Bklyn	9		Hank Sauer, Chi	37
1905	Fred Odwell, Cin	9	1953	Eddie Mathews, Mil	47
1906	Tim Jordan, Bklyn	12	1954	Ted Kluszewski, Cin	49
1907	Dave Brain, Bos	10	1955	Willie Mays, NY	51
1908	Tim Jordan, Bklyn	12	1956	Duke Snider, Bklyn	43
1909	Red Murray, NY	7	1957	Hank Aaron, Mil	44
1910	Fred Beck, Bos	10	1958	Ernie Banks, Chi	47
	Wildfire Schulte, Chi	10	1959	Eddie Mathews, Mil	46
1911	Wildfire Schulte, Chi	21	1960	Ernie Banks, Chi	41
1912	Heinie Zimmerman, Chi	14	1961	Orlando Cepeda, SF	46
1913	Gavvy Cravath, Phil	19	1962	Willie Mays, SF	49
1914	Gavvy Cravath, Phil	19	1963	Hank Aaron, Mil	44
1915	Gavvy Cravath, Phil	24		Willie McCovey, SF	44
1916	Dave Robertson, NY	12	1964	Willie Mays, SF	47
	Cy Williams, Chi	12	1965	Willie Mays, SF	52
1917	Dave Robertson, NY	12	1966	Hank Aaron, Atl	44
	Gavvy Cravath, Phil	12	1967	Hank Aaron, Atl	39
1918	Gavvy Cravath, Phil	8	1968	Willie McCovey, SF	36
1919	Gavvy Cravath, Phil	12	1969	Willie McCovey, SF	45
1920	Cy Williams, Phil	15	1970	Johnny Bench, Cin	45
1921	George Kelly, NY	23	1971	Willie Stargell, Pitt	48
1922	Rogers Hornsby, StL	42	1972	Johnny Bench, Cin	40
1923	Cy Williams, Phil	41	1973	Willie Stargell, Pitt	44
1924	Jack Fournier, Bklyn	27	1974	Mike Schmidt, Phil	36
1925	Rogers Hornsby, StL	39	1975	Mike Schmidt, Phil	38
1926	Hack Wilson, Chi	21	1976	Mike Schmidt, Phil	38
1927	Hack Wilson, Chi	30	1977	George Foster, Cin	52
	Cy Williams, Phil	30	1978	George Foster, Cin	40
1928	Hack Wilson, Chi	31	1979	Dave Kingman, Chi	48
	Jim Bottomley, StL	31	1980	Mike Schmidt, Phil	48
1929	Chuck Klein, Phil	43	1981	Mike Schmidt, Phil	31
1930	Hack Wilson, Chi	56	1982	Dave Kingman, NY	37
1931	Chuck Klein, Phil	31	1983	Mike Schmidt, Phil	40
1932	Chuck Klein, Phil	38	1984	Dale Murphy, Atl	36
	Mel Ott, NY	38		Mike Schmidt, Phil	36
1933	Chuck Klein, Phil	28	1985	Dale Murphy, Atl	37
1934	Ripper Collins, StL	35	1986	Mike Schmidt, Phil	37
	Mel Ott, NY	35	1987	Andre Dawson, Chi	49
1935	Wally Berger, Bos	34	1988	Darryl Strawberry, NY	39
1936	Mel Ott, NY	33	1989	Kevin Mitchell, SF	47
1937	Mel Ott, NY	31	1990	Ryne Sandberg, Chi	40
	Joe Medwick, StL	31	1991	Howard Johnson, NY	38
1938	Mel Ott, NY	36	1992	Fred McGriff, SD	35
1939	Johnny Mize, StL	28	1993	Barry Bonds, SF	46
1940	Johnny Mize, StL	43	1994	Matt Williams, SF	43
1941	Dolph Camilli, Bklyn	34	1995	Dante Bichette, Col	40
1942	Mel Ott, NY	30	1996	Andres Galarraga, Col	47
1943	Bill Nicholson, Chi	29	1997	Larry Walker, Col	49
1944	Bill Nicholson, Chi	33	1998	Mark McGwire, StL	70
1945	Tommy Holmes, Bos	28	1999	Mark McGwire, StL	65
1946	Ralph Kiner, Pitt	23	2000	Sammy Sosa, Chi	50
1947	Ralph Kiner, Pitt	51	2001	Barry Bonds, SF	73
	Johnny Mize, NY	51	2002	Sammy Sosa, Chi	49
1948	Ralph Kiner, Pitt	40			
	Johnny Mize, NY	40			

Runs Batted In Leaders

Year	Player and Team	RBI	Year	Player and Team	RBI
1900	Elmer Flick, Phil	110	1952	Hank Sauer, Chi	121
1901	Honus Wagner, Pitt	126	1953	Roy Campanella, Bklyn	142
1902	Honus Wagner, Pitt	91	1954	Ted Kluszewski, Cin	141
1903	Sam Mertes, NY	104	1955	Duke Snider, Bklyn	136
1904	Bill Dahlen, NY	80	1956	Stan Musial, StL	109
1905	Cy Seymour, Cin	121	1957	Hank Aaron, Mil	132
1906	Jim Nealon, Pitt	83	1958	Ernie Banks, Chi	129
	Harry Steinfeldt, Chi	83	1959	Ernie Banks, Chi	143
1907	Sherry Magee, Phil	85	1960	Hank Aaron, Mil	126
1908	Honus Wagner, Pitt	109	1961	Orlando Cepeda, SF	142
1909	Honus Wagner, Pitt	100	1962	Tommy Davis, LA	153
1910	Sherry Magee, Phil	123	1963	Hank Aaron, Mil	130
1911	Wildfire Schulte, Chi	121	1964	Ken Boyer, StL	119
1912	Heinie Zimmerman, Chi	103	1965	Deron Johnson, Cin	130
1913	Gavvy Cravath, Phil	128	1966	Hank Aaron, Atl	127
1914	Sherry Magee, Phil	103	1967	Orlando Cepeda, StL	111
1915	Gavvy Cravath, Phil	115	1968	Willie McCovey, SF	105
1916	Heinie Zimmerman, Chi-NY	83	1969	Willie McCovey, SF	126
1917	Heinie Zimmerman, NY	102	1970	Johnny Bench, Cin	148
1918	Sherry Magee, Phil	76	1971	Joe Torre, StL	137
1919	Hi Myers, Bklyn	73	1972	Johnny Bench, Cin	125
1920	George Kelly, NY	94	1973	Willie Stargell, Pitt	119
	Rogers Hornsby, StL	94	1974	Johnny Bench, Cin	129
1921	Rogers Hornsby, StL	126	1975	Greg Luzinski, Phil	120
1922	Rogers Hornsby, StL	152	1976	George Foster, Cin	121
1923	Irish Meusel, NY	125	1977	George Foster, Cin	149
1924	George Kelly, NY	136	1978	George Foster, Cin	120
1925	Rogers Hornsby, StL	143	1979	Dave Winfield, SD	118
1926	Jim Bottomley, StL	120	1980	Mike Schmidt, Phil	121
1927	Paul Waner, Pitt	131	1981	Mike Schmidt, Phil	91
1928	Jim Bottomley, StL	136	1982	Dale Murphy, Atl	109
1929	Hack Wilson, Chi	159		Al Oliver, Mtl	109
1930	Hack Wilson, Chi	190	1983	Dale Murphy, Atl	121
1931	Chuck Klein, Phil	121	1984	Gary Carter, Mtl	106
1932	Don Hurst, Phil	143		Mike Schmidt, Phil	106
1933	Chuck Klein, Phil	120	1985	Dave Parker, Cin	125
1934	Mel Ott, NY	135	1986	Mike Schmidt, Phil	119
1935	Wally Berger, Bos	130	1987	Andre Dawson, Chi	137
1936	Joe Medwick, StL	138	1988	Will Clark, SF	109
1937	Joe Medwick, StL	154	1989	Kevin Mitchell, SF	125
1938	Joe Medwick, StL	122	1990	Matt Williams, SF	122
1939	Frank McCormick, Cin	128	1991	Howard Johnson, NY	117
1940	Johnny Mize, StL	137	1992	Darren Daulton, Phil	109
1941	Dolph Camilli, Bklyn	120	1993	Barry Bonds, SF	123
1942	Johnny Mize, NY	110	1994	Jeff Bagwell, Hou	116
1943	Bill Nicholson, Chi	128	1995	Dante Bichette, Col	128
1944	Bill Nicholson, Chi	122	1996	Andres Galarraga, Col	150
1945	Dixie Walker, Bklyn	124	1997	Andres Galarraga, Col	140
1946	Enos Slaughter, StL	130	1998	Sammy Sosa, Chi	158
1947	Johnny Mize, NY	138	1999	Mark McGwire, StL	147
1948	Stan Musial, StL	131	2000	Todd Helton, Col	147
1949	Ralph Kiner, Pitt	127	2001	Sammy Sosa, Chi	160
1950	Del Ennis, Phil	126	2002	Lance Berkman, Hou	128
1951	Monte Irvin, NY	121			

Leading Base Stealers

Year	Player and Team	SB	Year	Player and Team	SB
1900	George Van Haltren, NY	45	1950	Sam Jethroe, Bos	35
	Patsy Donovan, StL	45	1951	Sam Jethroe, Bos	35
1901	Honus Wagner, Pitt	48	1952	Pee Wee Reese, Bklyn	30
1902	Honus Wagner, Pitt	43	1953	Bill Bruton, Mil	26
1903	Jimmy Sheckard, Bklyn	67	1954	Bill Bruton, Mil	34
	Frank Chance, Chi	67	1955	Bill Bruton, Mil	35
1904	Honus Wagner, Pitt	53	1956	Willie Mays, NY	40
1905	Billy Maloney, Chi	59	1957	Willie Mays, NY	38
	Art Devlin, NY	59	1958	Willie Mays, SF	31
1906	Frank Chance, Chi	57	1959	Willie Mays, SF	27
1907	Honus Wagner, Pitt	61	1960	Maury Wills, LA	50
1908	Honus Wagner, Pitt	53	1961	Maury Wills, LA	35
1909	Bob Bescher, Cin	54	1962	Maury Wills, LA	104
1910	Bob Bescher, Cin	70	1963	Maury Wills, LA	40
1911	Bob Bescher, Cin	80	1964	Maury Wills, LA	53
1912	Bob Bescher, Cin	67	1965	Maury Wills, LA	94
1913	Max Carey, Pitt	61	1966	Lou Brock, StL	74
1914	George Burns, NY	62	1967	Lou Brock, StL	52
1915	Max Carey, Pitt	36	1968	Lou Brock, StL	62
1916	Max Carey, Pitt	63	1969	Lou Brock, StL	53
1917	Max Carey, Pitt	46	1970	Bobby Tolan, Cin	57
1918	Max Carey, Pitt	58	1971	Lou Brock, StL	64
1919	George Burns, NY	40	1972	Lou Brock, StL	63
1920	Max Carey, Pitt	52	1973	Lou Brock, StL	70
1921	Frankie Frisch, NY	49	1974	Lou Brock, StL	118
1922	Max Carey, Pitt	51	1975	Davey Lopes, LA	77
1923	Max Carey, Pitt	51	1976	Davey Lopes, LA	63
1924	Max Carey, Pitt	49	1977	Frank Taveras, Pitt	70
1925	Max Carey, Pitt	46	1978	Omar Moreno, Pitt	71
1926	Kiki Cuyler, Pitt	35	1979	Omar Moreno, Pitt	77
1927	Frankie Frisch, StL	48	1980	Ron LeFlore, Mtl	97
1928	Kiki Cuyler, Chi	37	1981	Tim Raines, Mtl	71
1929	Kiki Cuyler, Chi	43	1982	Tim Raines, Mtl	78
1930	Kiki Cuyler, Chi	37	1983	Tim Raines, Mtl	90
1931	Frankie Frisch, StL	28	1984	Tim Raines, Mtl	75
1932	Chuck Klein, Phil	20	1985	Vince Coleman, StL	110
1933	Pepper Martin, StL	26	1986	Vince Coleman, StL	107
1934	Pepper Martin, StL	23	1987	Vince Coleman, StL	109
1935	Augie Galan, Chi	22	1988	Vince Coleman, StL	81
1936	Pepper Martin, StL	23	1989	Vince Coleman, StL	65
1937	Augie Galan, Chi	23	1990	Vince Coleman, StL	77
1938	Stan Hack, Chi	16	1991	Marquis Grissom, Mtl	76
1939	Stan Hack, Chi	17	1992	Marquis Grissom, Mtl	78
	Lee Handley, Pitt	17	1993	Chuck Carr, Fla	58
1940	Lonny Frey, Cin	22	1994	Craig Biggio, Hou	39
1941	Danny Murtaugh, Phil	18	1995	Quilvio Veras, Fla	56
1942	Pete Reiser, Bklyn	20	1996	Eric Young, Col	53
1943	Arky Vaughan, Bklyn	20	1997	Tony Womack, Pitt	60
1944	Johnny Barrett, Pitt	28	1998	Tony Womack, Pitt	58
1945	Red Schoendienst, StL	26	1999	Tony Womack, Ariz	72
1946	Pete Reiser, Bklyn	34	2000	Luis Castillo, Fla	62
1947	Jackie Robinson, Bklyn	29	2001	Juan Pierre, Col	46
1948	Richie Ashburn, Phil	32	2002	Luis Castillo, Fla	48
1949	Jackie Robinson, Bklyn	37			

Leading Pitchers—Winning Percentage

Year	Pitcher and Team	W	L	Pct	Year	Pitcher and Team	W	L	Pct
1900	Jesse Tannehill, Pitt	20	6	.769	1952	Hoyt Wilhelm, NY	15	3	.833
1901	Jack Chesbro, Pitt	21	10	.677	1953	Carl Erskine, Bklyn	20	6	.769
1902	Jack Chesbro, Pitt	28	6	.824	1954	Johnny Antonelli, NY	21	7	.750
1903	Sam Leever, Pitt	25	7	.781	1955	Don Newcombe, Bklyn	20	5	.800
1904	Joe McGinnity, NY	35	8	.814	1956	Don Newcombe, Bklyn	27	7	.794
1905	Sam Leever, Pitt	20	5	.800	1957	Bob Buhl, Mil	18	7	.720
1906	Ed Reulbach, Chi	19	4	.826	1958	Warren Spahn, Mil	22	11	.667
1907	Ed Reulbach, Chi	17	4	.810		Lew Burdette, Mil	20	10	.667
1908	Ed Reulbach, Chi	24	7	.774	1959	Roy Face, Pitt	18	1	.947
1909	Christy Mathewson, NY	25	6	.806	1960	Ernie Broglio, StL	21	9	.700
	Howie Camnitz, Pitt	25	6	.806	1961	Johnny Podres, LA	18	5	.783
1910	King Cole, Chi	20	4	.833	1962	Bob Purkey, Cin	23	5	.821
1911	Rube Marquard, NY	24	7	.774	1963	Ron Perranoski, LA	16	3	.842
1912	Claude Hendrix, Pitt	24	9	.727	1964	Sandy Koufax, LA	19	5	.792
1913	Bert Humphries, Chi	16	4	.800	1965	Sandy Koufax, LA	26	8	.765
1914	Bill James, Bos	26	7	.788	1966	Juan Marichal, SF	25	6	.806
1915	Grover Alexander, Phil	31	10	.756	1967	Dick Hughes, StL	16	6	.727
1916	Tom Hughes, Bos	16	3	.842	1968	Steve Blass, Pitt	18	6	.750
1917	Ferdie Schupp, NY	21	7	.750	1969	Tom Seaver, NY	25	7	.781
1918	Claude Hendrix, Chi	19	7	.731	1970	Bob Gibson, StL	23	7	.767
1919	Dutch Ruether, Cin	19	6	.760	1971	Don Gullett, Cin	16	6	.727
1920	Burleigh Grimes, Bklyn	23	11	.676	1972	Gary Nolan, Cin	15	5	.750
1921	Bill Doak, StL	15	6	.714	1973	Tommy John, LA	16	7	.696
1922	Pete Donohue, Cin	18	9	.667	1974	Andy Messersmith, LA	20	6	.769
1923	Dolf Luque, Cin	27	8	.771	1975	Don Gullett, Cin	15	4	.789
1924	Emil Yde, Pitt	16	3	.842	1976	Steve Carlton, Phil	20	7	.741
1925	Bill Sherdel, StL	15	6	.714	1977	John Candelaria, Pitt	20	5	.800
1926	Ray Kremer, Pitt	20	6	.769	1978	Gaylord Perry, SD	21	6	.778
1927	Larry Benton, Bos-NY	17	7	.708	1979	Tom Seaver, Cin	16	6	.727
1928	Larry Benton, NY	25	9	.735	1980	Jim Bibby, Pitt	19	6	.760
1929	Charlie Root, Chi	19	6	.760	1981*	Tom Seaver, Cin	14	2	.875
1930	Freddie Fitzsimmons, NY	19	7	.731	1982	Phil Niekro, Atl	17	4	.810
1931	Paul Derringer, StL	18	8	.692	1983	John Denny, Phil	19	6	.760
1932	Lon Warneke, Chi	22	6	.786	1984	Rick Sutcliffe, Chi	16	1	.941
1933	Ben Cantwell, Bos	20	10	.667	1985	Orel Hershiser, LA	19	3	.864
1934	Dizzy Dean, StL	30	7	.811	1986	Bob Ojeda, NY	18	5	.783
1935	Bill Lee, Chi	20	6	.769	1987	Dwight Gooden, NY	15	7	.682
1936	Carl Hubbell, NY	26	6	.813	1988	David Cone, NY	20	3	.870
1937	Carl Hubbell, NY	22	8	.733	1989	Mike Bielecki, Chi	18	7	.720
1938	Bill Lee, Chi	22	9	.710	1990	Doug Drabeck, Pitt	22	6	.786
1939	Paul Derringer, Cin	25	7	.781	1991	John Smiley, Pitt	20	8	.714
1940	Freddie Fitzsimmons, Bklyn	16	2	.889		Jose Rijo, Cin	15	6	.714
1941	Elmer Riddle, Cin	19	4	.826	1992	Bob Tewksbury, StL	16	5	.762
1942	Larry French, Bklyn	15	4	.789	1993	Tom Glavine, Atl	22	6	.786
1943	Mort Cooper, StL	21	8	.724	1994	Ken Hill, Mtl	16	5	.762
1944	Ted Wilks, StL	17	4	.810	1995	Greg Maddux, Atl	19	2	.905
1945	Harry Brecheen, StL	15	4	.789	1996	John Smoltz, Atl	24	8	.750
1946	Murray Dickson, StL	15	6	.714	1997	Denny Neagle, Atl	20	5	.800
1947	Larry Jansen, NY	21	5	.808	1998	John Smoltz, Atl	17	3	.850
1948	Harry Brecheen, StL	20	7	.741	1999	Mike Hampton, Hou	22	4	.846
1949	Preacher Roe, Bklyn	15	6	.714	2000	Randy Johnson, Ariz	19	7	.730
1950	Sal Maglie, NY	18	4	.818	2001	Curt Schilling, Ariz	22	6	.786
1951	Preacher Roe, Bklyn	22	3	.880	2002	Randy Johnson, Ariz	24	5	.828

*1981 percentages based on 10 or more victories. Note: Percentages based on 15 or more victories in all other years.

Leading Pitchers—Earned Run Average

Year	Player and Team	ERA	Year	Player and Team	ERA
1900	Rube Waddell, Pitt	2.37	1952	Hoyt Wilhelm, NY	2.43
1901	Jesse Tannehill, Pitt	2.18	1953	Warren Spahn, Mil	2.10
1902	Jack Taylor, Chi	1.33	1954	Johnny Antonelli, NY	2.29
1903	Sam Leever, Pitt	2.06	1955	Bob Friend, Pitt	2.84
1904	Joe McGinnity, NY	1.61	1956	Lew Burdette, Mil	2.71
1905	Christy Mathewson, NY	1.27	1957	Johnny Podres, Bklyn	2.66
1906	Three Finger Brown, Chi	1.04	1958	Stu Miller, SF	2.47
1907	Jack Pfiester, Chi	1.15	1959	Sam Jones, SF	2.82
1908	Christy Mathewson, NY	1.43	1960	Mike McCormick, SF	2.70
1909	Christy Mathewson, NY	1.14	1961	Warren Spahn, Mil	3.01
1910	George McQuillan, Phil	1.60	1962	Sandy Koufax, LA	2.54
1911	Christy Mathewson, NY	1.99	1963	Sandy Koufax, LA	1.88
1912	Jeff Tesreau, NY	1.96	1964	Sandy Koufax, LA	1.74
1913	Christy Mathewson, NY	2.06	1965	Sandy Koufax, LA	2.04
1914	Bill Doak, StL	1.72	1966	Sandy Koufax, LA	1.73
1915	Grover Alexander, Phil	1.22	1967	Phil Niekro, Atl	1.87
1916	Grover Alexander, Phil	1.55	1968	Bob Gibson, StL	1.12
1917	Grover Alexander, Phil	1.83	1969	Juan Marichal, SF	2.10
1918	Hippo Vaughn, Chi	1.74	1970	Tom Seaver, NY	2.81
1919	Grover Alexander, Chi	1.72	1971	Tom Seaver, NY	1.76
1920	Grover Alexander, Chi	1.91	1972	Steve Carlton, Phil	1.98
1921	Bill Doak, StL	2.58	1973	Tom Seaver, NY	2.08
1922	Rosy Ryan, NY	3.00	1974	Buzz Capra, Atl	2.28
1923	Dolf Luque, Cin	1.93	1975	Randy Jones, SD	2.24
1924	Dazzy Vance, Bklyn	2.16	1976	John Denny, StL	2.52
1925	Dolf Luque, Cin	2.63	1977	John Candelaria, Pitt	2.34
1926	Ray Kremer, Pitt	2.61	1978	Craig Swan, NY	2.43
1927	Ray Kremer, Pitt	2.47	1979	J.R. Richard, Hou	2.71
1928	Dazzy Vance, Bklyn	2.09	1980	Don Sutton, LA	2.21
1929	Bill Walker, NY	3.08	1981	Nolan Ryan, Hou	1.69
1930	Dazzy Vance, Bklyn	2.61	1982	Steve Rogers, Mtl	2.40
1931	Bill Walker, NY	2.26	1983	Atlee Hammaker, SF	2.25
1932	Lon Warneke, Chi	2.37	1984	Alejandro Pena, LA	2.48
1933	Carl Hubbell, NY	1.66	1985	Dwight Gooden, NY	1.53
1934	Carl Hubbell, NY	2.30	1986	Mike Scott, Hou	2.22
1935	Cy Blanton, Pitt	2.59	1987	Nolan Ryan, Hou	2.76
1936	Carl Hubbell, NY	2.31	1988	Joe Magrane, StL	2.18
1937	Jim Turner, Bos	2.38	1989	Scott Garrelts, SF	2.28
1938	Bill Lee, Chi	2.66	1990	Danny Darwin, Hou	2.21
1939	Bucky Walters, Cin	2.29	1991	Dennis Martinez, Mtl	2.39
1940	Bucky Walters, Cin	2.48	1992	Bill Swift, SF	2.08
1941	Elmer Riddle, Cin	2.24	1993	Greg Maddux, Atl	2.36
1942	Mort Cooper, StL	1.77	1994	Greg Maddux, Atl	1.56
1943	Howie Pollet, StL	1.75	1995	Greg Maddux, Atl	1.63
1944	Ed Heusser, Cin	2.38	1996	Kevin Brown, Fla	1.89
1945	Hank Borowy, Chi	2.14	1997	Pedro Martinez, Mtl	1.90
1946	Howie Pollet, StL	2.10	1998	Greg Maddux, Atl	1.98
1947	Warren Spahn, Bos	2.33	1999	Randy Johnson, Ariz	2.48
1948	Harry Brecheen, StL	2.24	2000	Kevin Brown, LA	2.58
1949	Dave Koslo, NY	2.50	2001	Randy Johnson, Ariz	2.49
1950	Jim Hearn, StL-NY	2.49	2002	Randy Johnson, Ariz	2.32
1951	Chet Nichols, Bos	2.88			

Note: Based on 10 complete games through 1950, then 154 innings until National League expanded in 1962, when it became 162 innings. In strike-shortened 1981, one inning per game required.

Leading Pitchers—Strikeouts

Year	Player and Team	SO	Year	Player and Team	SO
1900	Rube Waddell, Pitt	133	1952	Warren Spahn, Bos	183
1901	Noodles Hahn, Cin	233	1953	Robin Roberts, Phil	198
1902	Vic Willis, Bos	226	1954	Robin Roberts, Phil	185
1903	Christy Mathewson, NY	267	1955	Sam Jones, Chi	198
1904	Christy Mathewson, NY	212	1956	Sam Jones, Chi	176
1905	Christy Mathewson, NY	206	1957	Jack Sanford, Phil	188
1906	Fred Beebe, Chi-StL	171	1958	Sam Jones, StL	225
1907	Christy Mathewson, NY	178	1959	Don Drysdale, LA	242
1908	Christy Mathewson, NY	259	1960	Don Drysdale, LA	246
1909	Orval Overall, Chi	205	1961	Sandy Koufax, LA	269
1910	Christy Mathewson, NY	190	1962	Don Drysdale, LA	232
1911	Rube Marquard, NY	237	1963	Sandy Koufax, LA	306
1912	Grover Alexander, Phil	195	1964	Bob Veale, Pitt	250
1913	Tom Seaton, Phil	168	1965	Sandy Koufax, LA	382
1914	Grover Alexander, Phil	214	1966	Sandy Koufax, LA	317
1915	Grover Alexander, Phil	241	1967	Jim Bunning, Phil	253
1916	Grover Alexander, Phil	167	1968	Bob Gibson, StL	268
1917	Grover Alexander, Phil	200	1969	Ferguson Jenkins, Chi	273
1918	Hippo Vaughn, Chi	148	1970	Tom Seaver, NY	283
1919	Hippo Vaughn, Chi	141	1971	Tom Seaver, NY	289
1920	Grover Alexander, Chi	173	1972	Steve Carlton, Phil	310
1921	Burleigh Grimes, Bklyn	136	1973	Tom Seaver, NY	251
1922	Dazzy Vance, Bklyn	134	1974	Steve Carlton, Phil	240
1923	Dazzy Vance, Bklyn	197	1975	Tom Seaver, NY	243
1924	Dazzy Vance, Bklyn	262	1976	Tom Seaver, NY	235
1925	Dazzy Vance, Bklyn	221	1977	Phil Niekro, Atl	262
1926	Dazzy Vance, Bklyn	140	1978	J.R. Richard, Hou	303
1927	Dazzy Vance, Bklyn	184	1979	J.R. Richard, Hou	313
1928	Dazzy Vance, Bklyn	200	1980	Steve Carlton, Phil	286
1929	Pat Malone, Chi	166	1981	Fernando Valenzuela, LA	180
1930	Bill Hallahan, StL	177	1982	Steve Carlton, Phil	286
1931	Bill Hallahan, StL	159	1983	Steve Carlton, Phil	275
1932	Dizzy Dean, StL	191	1984	Dwight Gooden, NY	276
1933	Dizzy Dean, StL	199	1985	Dwight Gooden, NY	268
1934	Dizzy Dean, StL	195	1986	Mike Scott, Hou	306
1935	Dizzy Dean, StL	182	1987	Nolan Ryan, Hou	270
1936	Van Lingle Mungo, Bklyn	238	1988	Nolan Ryan, Hou	228
1937	Carl Hubbell, NY	159	1989	Jose DeLeon, StL	201
1938	Clay Bryant, Chi	135	1990	David Cone, NY	233
1939	Claude Passeau, Phil-Chi	137	1991	David Cone, NY	241
	Bucky Walters, Cin	137	1992	John Smoltz, Atl	215
1940	Kirby Higbe, Phil	137	1993	Jose Rijo, Cin	227
1941	Johnny Vander Meer, Cin	202	1994	Andy Benes, SD	189
1942	Johnny Vander Meer, Cin	186	1995	Hideo Nomo, LA	236
1943	Johnny Vander Meer, Cin	174	1996	John Smoltz, Atl	276
1944	Bill Voiselle, NY	161	1997	Curt Schilling, Phil	319
1945	Preacher Roe, Pitt	148	1998	Curt Schilling, Phil	300
1946	Johnny Schmitz, Chi	135	1999	Randy Johnson, Ariz	364
1947	Ewell Blackwell, Cin	193	2000	Randy Johnson, Ariz	347
1948	Harry Brecheen, StL	149	2001	Randy Johnson, Ariz	372
1949	Warren Spahn, Bos	151	2002	Randy Johnson, Ariz	334
1950	Warren Spahn, Bos	191			
1951	Warren Spahn, Bos	164			
	Don Newcombe, Bklyn	164			

Leading Pitchers—Saves

Year	Player and Team	SV	Year	Player and Team	SV
1947	Hugh Casey, Bklyn	18	1975	Al Hrabosky, StL	22
1948	Harry Gumpert, Cin	17		Rawly Eastwick, Cin	22
1949	Ted Wilks, StL	9	1976	Rawly Eastwick, Cin	26
1950	Jim Konstanty, Phil	22	1977	Rollie Fingers, SD	35
1951	Ted Wilks, StL, Pitt	13	1978	Rollie Fingers, SD	37
1952	Al Brazle, StL	16	1979	Bruce Sutter, Chi	37
1953	Al Brazle, StL	18	1980	Bruce Sutter, Chi	28
1954	Jim Hughes, Bklyn	24	1981	Bruce Sutter, StL	25
1955	Jack Meyer, Phil	16	1982	Bruce Sutter, StL	36
1956	Clem Labine, Bklyn	19	1983	Lee Smith, Chi	29
1957	Clem Labine, Bklyn	17	1984	Bruce Sutter, StL	45
1958	Roy Face, Pitt	20	1985	Jeff Reardon, Mtl	41
1959	Lindy McDaniel, StL	15	1986	Todd Worrell, StL	36
	Don McMahon, Mil	15	1987	Steve Bedrosian, Phil	40
1960	Lindy McDaniel, StL	26	1988	John Franco, Cin	39
1961	Stu Miller, SF	17	1989	Mark Davis, SD	44
	Roy Face, Pitt	17	1990	John Franco, NY	33
1962	Roy Face, Pitt	28	1991	Lee Smith, StL	47
1963	Lindy McDaniel, Chi	22	1992	Lee Smith, StL	42
1964	Hal Woodeshick, Hou	23	1993	Randy Myers, Chi	53
1965	Ted Abernathy, Chi	31	1994	John Franco, NY	30
1966	Phil Regan, LA	21	1995	Randy Myers, Chi	38
1967	Ted Abernathy, Cin	28	1996	Jeff Brantley, Cin	44
1968	Phil Regan, Chi, LA	25		Todd Worrell, LA	44
1969	Fred Gladding, Hou	29	1997	Jeff Shaw, Cin	42
1970	Wayne Granger, Cin	35	1998	Trevor Hoffman, SD	53
1971	Dave Giusti, Pitt	30	1999	Ugueth Urbina, Mtl	41
1972	Clay Carroll, Cin	37	2000	Antonio Alfonseca, Fla	45
1973	Mike Marshall, Mtl	13	2001	Robb Nen, SF	45
1974	Mike Marshall, LA	21	2002	John Smoltz, Atl	55

A Dopey Policy

Major League Baseball and the players' association made sure to pat themselves on the back for including a steroid-testing program in the labor agreement they announced on Aug. 30, 2002. Yeah. And Communist Russia once boasted of holding free elections. If there is anything in baseball easier to beat than the Tampa Bay Devil Rays, it's the steroid-testing plan. "It's not a drug test. It's an IQ test," said Gary Wadler, a New York University School of Medicine professor and a member of the World Anti-Doping Agency research committee. "You would have to flunk an IQ test to flunk it."

The testing program is the laughingstock of drug experts. The American Swimming Coaches Association is so outraged at the policy that it is seeking to have players' union head Donald Fehr removed from the United States Olympic Committee, calling his position on the board of directors "anathema to the USOC antidoping efforts" and saying that he "continues to give the USA an international black eye." Fehr declined to comment.

Baseball's plan amounts to nothing more than a public relations attempt to quell fan distrust after an SI investigation into rampant use of steroids and other performance-enhancing drugs in baseball. Said Wadler, "They're trying to escape the bullet by coming out with a sound bite."

One veteran player who was close to the negotiations admitted that the owners "came to us and basically said, 'Come up with some-

thing to make this [image problem] go away.'

"Let's face it," the player went on, "they like all the home runs. This policy is a small step forward, but it's not going to change a whole lot."

Unlike the IOC and NFL, baseball will not conduct off-season testing, giving players the green light to juice up for four months before competition. Testing next year will be conducted for survey purposes only. Half the players will be tested in spring training and half in the regular season. Most of the steroids used by players leave the body a couple of weeks after use. "You get off the stuff right before spring training, and then your only risk is which batch of players you're in," the veteran player said. "Then, once you take your test, you're home free [to use again]."

If more than 5% of next year's tests return positive, all players will then be subject to random testing for each of the next two years. If fewer than 5% of the tests are positive, only survey testing will remain in place....

Mets catcher Vance Wilson, the team's assistant player representative, said even one unannounced test "is going to deter people from using—definitely." More likely, it will simply force them to work their steroid cycles around the test. And next spring, when the usual passel of players reports to camp having added 20 pounds of bulk over the winter, you'll have every right to raise an eyebrow when they credit their weight room dedication for the increased strength.

— Tom Verducci

Pennant Winners

Year	Team	Manager	W	L	Pct	GA
1901	Chicago	Clark Griffith	83	53	.610	4
1902	Philadelphia	Connie Mack	83	53	.610	5
1903	Boston	Jimmy Collins	91	47	.659	14½
1904	Boston	Jimmy Collins	95	59	.617	1½
1905	Philadelphia	Connie Mack	92	56	.622	2
1906	Chicago	Fielder Jones	93	58	.616	3
1907	Detroit	Hughie Jennings	92	58	.613	1½
1908	Detroit	Hughie Jennings	90	63	.588	½
1909	Detroit	Hughie Jennings	98	54	.645	3½
1910	Philadelphia	Connie Mack	102	48	.680	14½
1911	Philadelphia	Connie Mack	101	50	.669	13½
1912	Boston	Jake Stahl	105	47	.691	14
1913	Philadelphia	Connie Mack	96	57	.627	6½
1914	Philadelphia	Connie Mack	99	53	.651	8½
1915	Boston	Bill Carrigan	101	50	.669	2½
1916	Boston	Bill Carrigan	91	63	.591	2
1917	Chicago	Pants Rowland	100	54	.649	9
1918	Boston	Ed Barrow	75	51	.595	2½
1919	Chicago	Kid Gleason	88	52	.629	3½
1920	Cleveland	Tris Speaker	98	56	.636	2
1921	New York	Miller Huggins	98	55	.641	4½
1922	New York	Miller Huggins	94	60	.610	1
1923	New York	Miller Huggins	98	54	.645	16
1924	Washington	Bucky Harris	92	62	.597	2
1925	Washington	Bucky Harris	96	55	.636	8½
1926	New York	Miller Huggins	91	63	.591	3
1927	New York	Miller Huggins	110	44	.714	19
1928	New York	Miller Huggins	101	53	.656	2½
1929	Philadelphia	Connie Mack	104	46	.693	18
1930	Philadelphia	Connie Mack	102	52	.662	8
1931	Philadelphia	Connie Mack	107	45	.704	13½
1932	New York	Joe McCarthy	107	47	.695	13
1933	Washington	Joe Cronin	99	53	.651	7
1934	Detroit	Mickey Cochrane	101	53	.656	7
1935	Detroit	Mickey Cochrane	93	58	.616	3
1936	New York	Joe McCarthy	102	51	.667	19½
1937	New York	Joe McCarthy	102	52	.662	13
1938	New York	Joe McCarthy	99	53	.651	9½
1939	New York	Joe McCarthy	106	45	.702	17
1940	Detroit	Del Baker	90	64	.584	1
1941	New York	Joe McCarthy	101	53	.656	17
1942	New York	Joe McCarthy	103	51	.669	9
1943	New York	Joe McCarthy	98	56	.636	13½
1944	St. Louis	Luke Sewell	89	65	.578	1
1945	Detroit	Steve O'Neill	88	65	.575	1½
1946	Boston	Joe Cronin	104	50	.675	12
1947	New York	Bucky Harris	97	57	.630	12
1948	Cleveland†	Lou Boudreau	97	58	.626	1
1949	New York	Casey Stengel	97	57	.630	1
1950	New York	Casey Stengel	98	56	.636	3
1951	New York	Casey Stengel	98	56	.636	5
1952	New York	Casey Stengel	95	59	.617	2
1953	New York	Casey Stengel	99	52	.656	8½
1954	Cleveland	Al Lopez	111	43	.721	8
1955	New York	Casey Stengel	96	58	.623	3
1956	New York	Casey Stengel	97	57	.630	9
1957	New York	Casey Stengel	98	56	.636	8
1958	New York	Casey Stengel	92	62	.597	10
1959	Chicago	Al Lopez	94	60	.610	5
1960	New York	Casey Stengel	97	57	.630	8
1961	New York	Ralph Houk	109	53	.673	8
1962	New York	Ralph Houk	96	66	.593	5
1963	New York	Ralph Houk	104	57	.646	10½
1964	New York	Yogi Berra	99	63	.611	1
1965	Minnesota	Sam Mele	102	60	.630	7
1966	Baltimore	Hank Bauer	97	63	.606	9

Pennant Winners (Cont.)

Year	Team	Manager	W	L	Pct	GA
1967	Boston	Dick Williams	92	70	.568	1
1968	Detroit	Mayo Smith	103	59	.636	12
1969	Baltimore (E)‡	Earl Weaver	109	53	.673	19
1970	Baltimore (E)‡	Earl Weaver	108	54	.667	15
1971	Baltimore (E)‡	Earl Weaver	101	57	.639	12
1972	Oakland (W)‡	Dick Williams	93	62	.600	5½
1973	Oakland (W)‡	Dick Williams	94	68	.580	6
1974	Oakland (W)‡	Al Dark	90	72	.556	5
1975	Boston (E)‡	Darrell Johnson	95	65	.594	4½
1976	New York (E)‡	Billy Martin	97	62	.610	10½
1977	New York (E)‡	Billy Martin	100	62	.617	2½
1978	New York (E)†‡	Billy Martin, Bob Lemon	100	63	.613	1
1979	Baltimore (E)‡	Earl Weaver	102	57	.642	8
1980	Kansas City (W)‡	Jim Frey	97	65	.599	14
1981	New York (E)‡	Gene Michael, Bob Lemon	59	48	.551	#
1982	Milwaukee (E)‡	Buck Rodgers, Harvey Kuenn	95	67	.586	1
1983	Baltimore (E)‡	Joe Altobelli	98	64	.605	6
1984	Detroit (E)‡	Sparky Anderson	104	58	.642	15
1985	Kansas City (W)‡	Dick Howser	91	71	.562	1
1986	Boston (E)‡	John McNamara	95	66	.590	5½
1987	Minnesota (W)‡	Tom Kelly	85	77	.525	2
1988	Oakland (W)‡	Tony La Russa	104	58	.642	13
1989	Oakland (W)‡	Tony La Russa	99	63	.611	7
1990	Oakland (W)‡	Tony La Russa	103	59	.636	9
1991	Minnesota (W)‡	Tom Kelly	95	67	.586	8
1992	Toronto‡	Cito Gaston	96	66	.593	4
1993	Toronto‡	Cito Gaston	95	67	.586	7
1994	Season ended Aug. 11 due to players' strike.					
1995	Cleveland (C)‡	Mike Hargrove	100	44	.694	30
1996	New York (E)‡	Joe Torre	92	70	.568	4
1997	Cleveland (C)‡	Mike Hargrove	86	75	.534	6
1998	New York (E)‡	Joe Torre	114	48	.704	22
1999	New York (E)‡	Joe Torre	98	64	.605	4
2000	New York (E)‡	Joe Torre	87	74	.540	2½
2001	New York (E)‡	Joe Torre	95	65	.594	13½
2002	Anaheim (wc)‡	Mike Scioscia	99	63	.611	-4

†Defeated Boston in one-game playoff. ‡Won championship series.
#First half 34–22; second half 25–26, in season split by strike; defeated Milwaukee in playoff for Eastern Divison title.

Leading Batsmen

Year	Player and Team	BA	Year	Player and Team	BA
1901	Nap Lajoie, Phil	.422	1922	George Sisler, StL	.420
1902	Ed Delahanty, Wash	.376	1923	Harry Heilmann, Det	.403
1903	Nap Lajoie, Clev	.355	1924	Babe Ruth, NY	.378
1904	Nap Lajoie, Clev	.381	1925	Harry Heilmann, Det	.393
1905	Elmer Flick, Clev	.306	1926	Heinie Manush, Det	.378
1906	George Stone, StL	.358	1927	Harry Heilmann, Det	.398
1907	Ty Cobb, Det	.350	1928	Goose Goslin, Wash	.379
1908	Ty Cobb, Det	.324	1929	Lew Fonseca, Clev	.369
1909	Ty Cobb, Det	.377	1930	Al Simmons, Phil	.381
1910	Nap Lajoie, Clev*	.383	1931	Al Simmons, Phil	.390
1911	Ty Cobb, Det	.420	1932	Dale Alexander, Det-Bos	.367
1912	Ty Cobb, Det	.410	1933	Jimmie Foxx, Phil	.356
1913	Ty Cobb, Det	.390	1934	Lou Gehrig, NY	.363
1914	Ty Cobb, Det	.368	1935	Buddy Myer, Wash	.349
1915	Ty Cobb, Det	.369	1936	Luke Appling, Chi	.388
1916	Tris Speaker, Clev	.386	1937	Charlie Gehringer, Det	.371
1917	Ty Cobb, Det	.383	1938	Jimmie Foxx, Bos	.349
1918	Ty Cobb, Det	.382	1939	Joe DiMaggio, NY	.381
1919	Ty Cobb, Det	.384	1940	Joe DiMaggio, NY	.352
1920	George Sisler, StL	.407	1941	Ted Williams, Bos	.406
1921	Harry Heilmann, Det	.394	1942	Ted Williams, Bos	.356

*League president Ban Johnson declared Ty Cobb batting champion with a .385 average, beating Lajoie's .384. However, subsequent research has led to the revision of Lajoie's average to .383 and Cobb's to .382.

Leading Batsmen (Cont.)

Year	Player and Team	BA	Year	Player and Team	BA
1943	Luke Appling, Chi	.328	1973	Rod Carew, Minn	.350
1944	Lou Boudreau, Clev	.327	1974	Rod Carew, Minn	.364
1945	Snuffy Stirnweiss, NY	.309	1975	Rod Carew, Minn	.359
1946	Mickey Vernon, Wash	.353	1976	George Brett, KC	.333
1947	Ted Williams, Bos	.343	1977	Rod Carew, Minn	.388
1948	Ted Williams, Bos	.369	1978	Rod Carew, Minn	.333
1949	George Kell, Det	.343	1979	Fred Lynn, Bos	.333
1950	Billy Goodman, Bos	.354	1980	George Brett, KC	.390
1951	Ferris Fain, Phil	.344	1981	Carney Lansford, Bos	.336
1952	Ferris Fain, Phil	.327	1982	Willie Wilson, KC	.332
1953	Mickey Vernon, Wash	.337	1983	Wade Boggs, Bos	.361
1954	Bobby Avila, Clev	.341	1984	Don Mattingly, NY	.343
1955	Al Kaline, Det	.340	1985	Wade Boggs, Bos	.368
1956	Mickey Mantle, NY	.353	1986	Wade Boggs, Bos	.357
1957	Ted Williams, Bos	.388	1987	Wade Boggs, Bos	.363
1958	Ted Williams, Bos	.328	1988	Wade Boggs, Bos	.366
1959	Harvey Kuenn, Det	.353	1989	Kirby Puckett, Minn	.339
1960	Pete Runnels, Bos	.320	1990	George Brett, KC	.329
1961	Norm Cash, Det	.361	1991	Julio Franco, Tex	.341
1962	Pete Runnels, Bos	.326	1992	Edgar Martinez, Sea	.343
1963	Carl Yastrzemski, Bos	.321	1993	John Olerud, Tor	.363
1964	Tony Oliva, Minn	.323	1994	Paul O'Neill, NY	.359
1965	Tony Oliva, Minn	.321	1995	Edgar Martinez, Sea	.356
1966	Frank Robinson, Balt	.316	1996	Alex Rodriguez, Sea	.358
1967	Carl Yastrzemski, Bos	.326	1997	Frank Thomas, Chi	.347
1968	Carl Yastrzemski, Bos	.301	1998	Bernie Williams, NY	.339
1969	Rod Carew, Minn	.332	1999	Nomar Garciaparra, Bos	.357
1970	Alex Johnson, Cal	.329	2000	Nomar Garciaparra, Bos	.372
1971	Tony Oliva, Minn	.337	2001	Ichiro Suzuki, Sea	.350
1972	Rod Carew, Minn	.318	2002	Manny Ramirez, Bos	.349

Leaders in Runs Scored

Year	Player and Team	Runs	Year	Player and Team	Runs
1901	Nap Lajoie, Phil	145	1935	Lou Gehrig, NY	125
1902	Dave Fultz, Phil	110	1936	Lou Gehrig, NY	167
1903	Patsy Dougherty, Bos	108	1937	Joe DiMaggio, NY	151
1904	Patsy Dougherty, Bos-NY	113	1938	Hank Greenberg, Det	144
1905	Harry Davis, Phil	92	1939	Red Rolfe, NY	139
1906	Elmer Flick, Clev	98	1940	Ted Williams, Bos	134
1907	Sam Crawford, Det	102	1941	Ted Williams, Bos	135
1908	Matty McIntyre, Det	105	1942	Ted Williams, Bos	141
1909	Ty Cobb, Det	116	1943	George Case, Wash	102
1910	Ty Cobb, Det	106	1944	Snuffy Stirnweiss, NY	125
1911	Ty Cobb, Det	147	1945	Snuffy Stirnweiss, NY	107
1912	Eddie Collins, Phil	137	1946	Ted Williams, Bos	142
1913	Eddie Collins, Phil	125	1947	Ted Williams, Bos	125
1914	Eddie Collins, Phil	122	1948	Tommy Henrich, NY	138
1915	Ty Cobb, Det	144	1949	Ted Williams, Bos	150
1916	Ty Cobb, Det	113	1950	Dom DiMaggio, Bos	131
1917	Donie Bush, Det	112	1951	Dom DiMaggio, Bos	113
1918	Ray Chapman, Clev	84	1952	Larry Doby, Clev	104
1919	Babe Ruth, Bos	103	1953	Al Rosen, Clev	115
1920	Babe Ruth, NY	158	1954	Mickey Mantle, NY	129
1921	Babe Ruth, NY	177	1955	Al Smith, Clev	123
1922	George Sisler, StL	134	1956	Mickey Mantle, NY	132
1923	Babe Ruth, NY	151	1957	Mickey Mantle, NY	121
1924	Babe Ruth, NY	143	1958	Mickey Mantle, NY	127
1925	Johnny Mostil, Chi	135	1959	Eddie Yost, Det	115
1926	Babe Ruth, NY	139	1960	Mickey Mantle, NY	119
1927	Babe Ruth, NY	158	1961	Mickey Mantle, NY	132
1928	Babe Ruth, NY	163		Roger Maris, NY	132
1929	Charlie Gehringer, Det	131	1962	Albie Pearson, LA	115
1930	Al Simmons, Phil	152	1963	Bob Allison, Minn	99
1931	Lou Gehrig, NY	163	1964	Tony Oliva, Minn	109
1932	Jimmie Foxx, Phil	151	1965	Zoilo Versalles, Minn	126
1933	Lou Gehrig, NY	138	1966	Frank Robinson, Balt	122
1934	Charlie Gehringer, Det	134	1967	Carl Yastrzemski, Bos	112

Leaders in Runs Scored *(Cont.)*

Year	Player and Team	Runs
1968	Dick McAuliffe, Det	95
1969	Reggie Jackson, Oak	123
1970	Carl Yastrzemski, Bos	125
1971	Don Buford, Balt	99
1972	Bobby Murcer, NY	102
1973	Reggie Jackson, Oak	99
1974	Carl Yastrzemski, Bos	93
1975	Fred Lynn, Bos	103
1976	Roy White, NY	104
1977	Rod Carew, Minn	128
1978	Ron LeFlore, Det	126
1979	Don Baylor, Cal	120
1980	Willie Wilson, KC	133
1981	Rickey Henderson, Oak	89
1982	Paul Molitor, Mil	136
1983	Cal Ripken, Balt	121
1984	Dwight Evans, Bos	121
1985	Rickey Henderson, NY	146
1986	Rickey Henderson, NY	130
1987	Paul Molitor, Mil	114
1988	Wade Boggs, Bos	128
1989	Rickey Henderson, NY-Oak	113
	Wade Boggs, Bos	113
1990	Rickey Henderson, Oak	119
1991	Paul Molitor, Mil	133
1992	Tony Phillips, Det	114
1993	Rafael Palmeiro, Tex	124
1994	Frank Thomas, Chi	106
1995	Albert Belle, Clev	121
	Edgar Martinez, Sea	121
1996	Alex Rodriguez, Sea	141
1997	Ken Griffey Jr., Sea	125
1998	Derek Jeter, NY	127
1999	Roberto Alomar, Clev	138
2000	Johnny Damon, KC	136
2001	Alex Rodriguez, Tex	133
2002	Sammy Sosa, Chi	122

Leaders in Hits

Year	Player and Team	Hits
1901	Nap Lajoie, Phil	229
1902	Piano Legs Hickman, Bos-Clev	194
1903	Patsy Dougherty, Bos	195
1904	Nap Lajoie, Clev	211
1905	George Stone, StL	187
1906	Nap Lajoie, Clev	214
1907	Ty Cobb, Det	212
1908	Ty Cobb, Det	188
1909	Ty Cobb, Det	216
1910	Nap Lajoie, Clev	227
1911	Ty Cobb, Det	248
1912	Ty Cobb, Det	227
1913	Joe Jackson, Clev	197
1914	Tris Speaker, Bos	193
1915	Ty Cobb, Det	208
1916	Tris Speaker, Clev	211
1917	Ty Cobb, Det	225
1918	George Burns, Phil	178
1919	Ty Cobb, Det	191
	Bobby Veach, Det	191
1920	George Sisler, StL	257
1921	Harry Heilmann, Det	237
1922	George Sisler, StL	246
1923	Charlie Jamieson, Clev	222
1924	Sam Rice, Wash	216
1925	Al Simmons, Phil	253
1926	George Burns, Clev	216
	Sam Rice, Wash	216
1927	Earle Combs, NY	231
1928	Heinie Manush, StL	241
1929	Dale Alexander, Det	215
	Charlie Gehringer, Det	215
1930	Johnny Hodapp, Clev	225
1931	Lou Gehrig, NY	211
1932	Al Simmons, Phil	216
1933	Heinie Manush, Wash	221
1934	Charlie Gehringer, Det	214
1935	Joe Vosmik, Clev	216
1936	Earl Averill, Clev	232
1937	Beau Bell, StL	218
1938	Joe Vosmik, Bos	201
1939	Red Rolfe, NY	213
1940	Rip Radcliff, StL	200
	Barney McCosky, Det	200
	Doc Cramer, Bos	200
1941	Cecil Travis, Wash	218
1942	Johnny Pesky, Bos	205
1943	Dick Wakefield, Det	200
1944	Snuffy Stirnweiss, NY	205
1945	Snuffy Stirnweiss, NY	195
1946	Johnny Pesky, Bos	208
1947	Johnny Pesky, Bos	207
1948	Bob Dillinger, StL	207
1949	Dale Mitchell, Clev	203
1950	George Kell, Det	218
1951	George Kell, Det	191
1952	Nellie Fox, Chi	192
1953	Harvey Kuenn, Det	209
1954	Nellie Fox, Chi	201
	Harvey Kuenn, Det	201
1955	Al Kaline, Det	200
1956	Harvey Kuenn, Det	196
1957	Nellie Fox, Chi	196
1958	Nellie Fox, Chi	187
1959	Harvey Kuenn, Det	198
1960	Minnie Minoso, Chi	184
1961	Norm Cash, Det	193
1962	Bobby Richardson, NY	209
1963	Carl Yastrzemski, Bos	183
1964	Tony Oliva, Minn	217
1965	Tony Oliva, Minn	185
1966	Tony Oliva, Minn	191
1967	Carl Yastrzemski, Bos	189
1968	Bert Campaneris, Oak	177
1969	Tony Oliva, Minn	197
1970	Tony Oliva, Minn	204
1971	Cesar Tovar, Minn	204
1972	Joe Rudi, Oak	181
1973	Rod Carew, Minn	203
1974	Rod Carew, Minn	218
1975	George Brett, KC	195
1976	George Brett, KC	215
1977	Rod Carew, Minn	239
1978	Jim Rice, Bos	213
1979	George Brett, KC	212
1980	Willie Wilson, KC	230
1981	Rickey Henderson, Oak	135
1982	Robin Yount, Mil	210
1983	Cal Ripken Jr., Balt	211
1984	Don Mattingly, NY	207
1985	Wade Boggs, Bos	240
1986	Don Mattingly, NY	238
1987	Kirby Puckett, Minn	207
	Kevin Seitzer, KC	207

Leaders in Hits *(Cont.)*

Year	Player and Team	Hits	Year	Player and Team	Hits
1988	Kirby Puckett, Minn	234	1996	Paul Molitor, Minn	225
1989	Kirby Puckett, Minn	215	1997	Nomar Garciaparra, Bos	209
1990	Rafael Palmeiro, Tex	191	1998	Alex Rodriguez, Sea	213
1991	Paul Molitor, Mil	216	1999	Derek Jeter, NY	219
1992	Kirby Puckett, Minn	210	2000	Darin Erstad, Ana	240
1993	Paul Molitor, Tor	211	2001	Ichiro Suzuki, Sea	242
1994	Kenny Lofton, Clev	160	2002	Alfonso Soriano, NY	209
1995	Lance Johnson, Chi	186			

Home Run Leaders

Year	Player and Team	HR	Year	Player and Team	HR
1901	Nap Lajoie, Phil	13	1955	Mickey Mantle, NY	37
1902	Socks Seybold, Phil	16	1956	Mickey Mantle, NY	52
1903	Buck Freeman, Bos	13	1957	Roy Sievers, Wash	42
1904	Harry Davis, Phil	10	1958	Mickey Mantle, NY	42
1905	Harry Davis, Phil	8	1959	Rocky Colavito, Clev	42
1906	Harry Davis, Phil	12		Harmon Killebrew, Wash	42
1907	Harry Davis, Phil	8	1960	Mickey Mantle, NY	40
1908	Sam Crawford, Det	7	1961	Roger Maris, NY	61
1909	Ty Cobb, Det	9	1962	Harmon Killebrew, Minn	48
1910	Jake Stahl, Bos	10	1963	Harmon Killebrew, Minn	45
1911	Frank Baker, Phil	9	1964	Harmon Killebrew, Minn	49
1912	Frank Baker, Phil	10	1965	Tony Conigliaro, Bos	32
	Tris Speaker, Bos	10	1966	Frank Robinson, Balt	49
1913	Frank Baker, Phil	13	1967	Harmon Killebrew, Minn	44
1914	Frank Baker, Phil	9		Carl Yastrzemski, Bos	44
1915	Braggo Roth, Chi-Clev	7	1968	Frank Howard, Wash	44
1916	Wally Pipp, NY	12	1969	Harmon Killebrew, Minn	49
1917	Wally Pipp, NY	9	1970	Frank Howard, Wash	44
1918	Babe Ruth, Bos	11	1971	Bill Melton, Chi	33
	Tilly Walker, Phil	11	1972	Dick Allen, Chi	37
1919	Babe Ruth, Bos	29	1973	Reggie Jackson, Oak	32
1920	Babe Ruth, NY	54	1974	Dick Allen, Chi	32
1921	Babe Ruth, NY	59	1975	Reggie Jackson, Oak	36
1922	Ken Williams, StL	39		George Scott, Mil	36
1923	Babe Ruth, NY	41	1976	Graig Nettles, NY	32
1924	Babe Ruth, NY	46	1977	Jim Rice, Bos	39
1925	Bob Meusel, NY	33	1978	Jim Rice, Bos	46
1926	Babe Ruth, NY	47	1979	Gorman Thomas, Mil	45
1927	Babe Ruth, NY	60	1980	Reggie Jackson, NY	41
1928	Babe Ruth, NY	54		Ben Oglivie, Mil	41
1929	Babe Ruth, NY	46	1981	Tony Armas, Oak	22
1930	Babe Ruth, NY	49	1981	Dwight Evans, Bos	22
1931	Babe Ruth, NY	46		Bobby Grich, Cal	22
	Lou Gehrig, NY	46		Eddie Murray, Balt	22
1932	Jimmie Foxx, Phil	58	1982	Reggie Jackson, Cal	39
1933	Jimmie Foxx, Phil	48		Gorman Thomas, Mil	39
1934	Lou Gehrig, NY	49	1983	Jim Rice, Bos	39
1935	Jimmie Foxx, Phil	36	1984	Tony Armas, Bos	43
	Hank Greenberg, Det	36	1985	Darrell Evans, Det	40
1936	Lou Gehrig, NY	49	1986	Jesse Barfield, Tor	40
1937	Joe DiMaggio, NY	46	1987	Mark McGwire, Oak	49
1938	Hank Greenberg, Det	58	1988	Jose Canseco, Oak	42
1939	Jimmie Foxx, Bos	35	1989	Fred McGriff, Tor	36
1940	Hank Greenberg, Det	41	1990	Cecil Fielder, Det	51
1941	Ted Williams, Bos	37	1991	Jose Canseco, Oak	44
1942	Ted Williams, Bos	36		Cecil Fielder, Det	44
1943	Rudy York, Det	34	1992	Juan Gonzalez, Tex	43
1944	Nick Etten, NY	22	1993	Juan Gonzalez, Tex	46
1945	Vern Stephens, StL	24	1994	Ken Griffey Jr., Sea	40
1946	Hank Greenberg, Det	44	1995	Albert Belle, Clev	50
1947	Ted Williams, Bos	32	1996	Mark McGwire, Oak	52
1948	Joe DiMaggio, NY	39	1997	Ken Griffey Jr., Sea	56
1949	Ted Williams, Bos	43	1998	Ken Griffey Jr., Sea	56
1950	Al Rosen, Clev	37	1999	Ken Griffey Jr., Sea	48
1951	Gus Zernial, Chi-Phil	33	2000	Troy Glaus, Ana	47
1952	Larry Doby, Clev	32	2001	Alex Rodriguez, Tex	52
1953	Al Rosen, Clev	43	2002	Alex Rodriguez, Tex	57
1954	Larry Doby, Clev	32			

Runs Batted In Leaders

Year	Player and Team	RBI	Year	Player and Team	RBI
1907	Ty Cobb, Det	116	1955	Ray Boone, Det	116
1908	Ty Cobb, Det	108		Jackie Jensen, Bos	116
1909	Ty Cobb, Det	107	1956	Mickey Mantle, NY	130
1910	Sam Crawford, Det	120	1957	Roy Sievers, Wash	114
1911	Ty Cobb, Det	144	1958	Jackie Jensen, Bos	122
1912	Frank Baker, Phil	133	1959	Jackie Jensen, Bos	112
1913	Frank Baker, Phil	126	1960	Roger Maris, NY	112
1914	Sam Crawford, Det	104	1961	Roger Maris, NY	142
1915	Sam Crawford, Det	112	1962	Harmon Killebrew, Minn	126
	Bobby Veach, Det	112	1963	Dick Stuart, Bos	118
1916	Del Pratt, StL	103	1964	Brooks Robinson, Balt	118
1917	Bobby Veach, Det	103	1965	Rocky Colavito, Clev	108
1918	Bobby Veach, Det	78	1966	Frank Robinson, Balt	122
1919	Babe Ruth, Bos	114	1967	Carl Yastrzemski, Bos	121
1920	Babe Ruth, NY	137	1968	Ken Harrelson, Bos	109
1921	Babe Ruth, NY	171	1969	Harmon Killebrew, Minn	140
1922	Ken Williams, StL	155	1970	Frank Howard, Wash	126
1923	Babe Ruth, NY	131	1971	Harmon Killebrew, Minn	119
1924	Goose Goslin, Wash	129	1972	Dick Allen, Chi	113
1925	Bob Meusel, NY	138	1973	Reggie Jackson, Oak	117
1926	Babe Ruth, NY	145	1974	Jeff Burroughs, Tex	118
1927	Lou Gehrig, NY	175	1975	George Scott, Mil	109
1928	Babe Ruth, NY	142	1976	Lee May, Balt	109
	Lou Gehrig, NY	142	1977	Larry Hisle, Minn	119
1929	Al Simmons, Phil	157	1978	Jim Rice, Bos	139
1930	Lou Gehrig, NY	174	1979	Don Baylor, Cal	139
1931	Lou Gehrig, NY	184	1980	Cecil Cooper, Mil	122
1932	Jimmie Foxx, Phil	169	1981	Eddie Murray, Balt	78
1933	Jimmie Foxx, Phil	163	1982	Hal McRae, KC	133
1934	Lou Gehrig, NY	165	1983	Cecil Cooper, Mil	126
1935	Hank Greenberg, Det	170		Jim Rice, Bos	126
1936	Hal Trosky, Clev	162	1984	Tony Armas, Bos	123
1937	Hank Greenberg, Det	183	1985	Don Mattingly, NY	145
1938	Jimmie Foxx, Bos	175	1986	Joe Carter, Clev	121
1939	Ted Williams, Bos	145	1987	George Bell, Tor	134
1940	Hank Greenberg, Det	150	1988	Jose Canseco, Oak	124
1941	Joe DiMaggio, NY	125	1989	Ruben Sierra, Tex	119
1942	Ted Williams, Bos	137	1990	Cecil Fielder, Det	132
1943	Rudy York, Det	118	1991	Cecil Fielder, Det	133
1944	Vern Stephens, StL	109	1992	Cecil Fielder, Det	124
1945	Nick Etten, NY	111	1993	Albert Belle, Clev	129
1946	Hank Greenberg, Det	127	1994	Kirby Puckett, Minn	112
1947	Ted Williams, Bos	114	1995	Albert Belle, Clev	126
1948	Joe DiMaggio, NY	155		Mo Vaughn, Bos	126
1949	Ted Williams, Bos	159	1996	Albert Belle, Clev	148
	Vern Stephens, Bos	159	1997	Ken Griffey Jr., Sea	147
1950	Walt Dropo, Bos	144	1998	Juan Gonzales, Tex	157
	Vern Stephens, Bos	144	1999	Manny Ramirez, Clev	165
1951	Gus Zernial, Chi-Phil	129	2000	Edgar Martinez, Sea	145
1952	Al Rosen, Clev	105	2001	Bret Boone, Sea	141
1953	Al Rosen, Clev	145	2002	Alex Rodriguez, Tex	142
1954	Larry Doby, Clev	126			

Note: Runs Batted In not compiled before 1907; officially adopted in 1920.

Leading Base Stealers

Year	Player and Team	SB	Year	Player and Team	SB
1901	Frank Isbell, Chi	48	1911	Ty Cobb, Det	83
1902	Topsy Hartsel, Phil	54	1912	Clyde Milan, Wash	88
1903	Harry Bay, Clev	46	1913	Clyde Milan, Wash	75
1904	Elmer Flick, Clev	42	1914	Fritz Maisel, NY	74
	Harry Bay, Clev	42	1915	Ty Cobb, Det	96
1905	Danny Hoffman, Phil	46	1916	Ty Cobb, Det	68
1906	Elmer Flick, Clev	39	1917	Ty Cobb, Det	55
	John Anderson, Wash	39	1918	George Sisler, StL	45
1907	Ty Cobb, Det	49	1919	Eddie Collins, Chi	33
1908	Patsy Dougherty, Chi	47	1920	Sam Rice, Wash	63
1909	Ty Cobb, Det	76	1921	George Sisler, StL	35
1910	Eddie Collins, Phil	81	1922	George Sisler, StL	51

Leading Base Stealers (Cont.)

Year	Player and Team	SB	Year	Player and Team	SB
1923	Eddie Collins, Chi	49	1963	Luis Aparicio, Balt	40
1924	Eddie Collins, Chi	42	1964	Luis Aparicio, Balt	57
1925	John Mostil, Chi	43	1965	Bert Campaneris, KC	51
1926	John Mostil, Chi	35	1966	Bert Campaneris, KC	52
1927	George Sisler, StL	27	1967	Bert Campaneris, KC	55
1928	Buddy Myer, Bos	30	1968	Bert Campaneris, Oak	62
1929	Charlie Gehringer, Det	27	1969	Tommy Harper, Sea	73
1930	Marty McManus, Det	23	1970	Bert Campaneris, Oak	42
1931	Ben Chapman, NY	61	1971	Amos Otis, KC	52
1932	Ben Chapman, NY	38	1972	Bert Campaneris, Oak	52
1933	Ben Chapman, NY	27	1973	Tommy Harper, Bos	54
1934	Bill Werber, Bos	40	1974	Bill North, Oak	54
1935	Bill Werber, Bos	29	1975	Mickey Rivers, Cal	70
1936	Lyn Lary, StL	37	1976	Bill North, Oak	75
1937	Bill Werber, Phil	35	1977	Freddie Patek, KC	53
	Ben Chapman, Wash-Bos	35	1978	Ron LeFlore, Det	68
1938	Frank Crosetti, NY	27	1979	Willie Wilson, KC	83
1939	George Case, Wash	51	1980	Rickey Henderson, Oak	100
1940	George Case, Wash	35	1981	Rickey Henderson, Oak	56
1941	George Case, Wash	33	1982	Rickey Henderson, Oak	130
1942	George Case, Wash	44	1983	Rickey Henderson, Oak	108
1943	George Case, Wash	61	1984	Rickey Henderson, Oak	66
1944	Snuffy Stirnweiss, NY	55	1985	Rickey Henderson, NY	80
1945	Snuffy Stirnweiss, NY	33	1986	Rickey Henderson, NY	87
1946	George Case, Clev	28	1987	Harold Reynolds, Sea	60
1947	Bob Dillinger, StL	34	1988	Rickey Henderson, NY	93
1948	Bob Dillinger, StL	28	1989	Rickey Henderson, NY-Oak	77
1949	Bob Dillinger, StL	20	1990	Rickey Henderson, Oak	65
1950	Dom DiMaggio, Bos	15	1991	Rickey Henderson, Oak	58
1951	Minnie Minoso, Clev-Chi	31	1992	Kenny Lofton, Clev	66
1952	Minnie Minoso, Chi	22	1993	Kenny Lofton, Clev	70
1953	Minnie Minoso, Chi	25	1994	Kenny Lofton, Clev	60
1954	Jackie Jensen, Bos	22	1995	Kenny Lofton, Clev	54
1955	Jim Rivera, Chi	25	1996	Kenny Lofton, Clev	75
1956	Luis Aparicio, Chi	21	1997	Brian Hunter, Det	74
1957	Luis Aparicio, Chi	28	1998	Rickey Henderson, Oak	66
1958	Luis Aparicio, Chi	29	1999	Brian Hunter, Sea	44
1959	Luis Aparicio, Chi	56	2000	Johnny Damon, KC	46
1960	Luis Aparicio, Chi	51	2001	Ichiro Suzuki, Sea	56
1961	Luis Aparicio, Chi	53	2002	Alfonso Soriano, NY	41
1962	Luis Aparicio, Chi	31			

Leading Pitchers—Winning Percentage

Year	Pitcher and Team	W	L	Pct	Year	Pitcher and Team	W	L	Pct
1901	Clark Griffith, Chi	24	7	.774	1924	Walter Johnson, Wash	23	7	.767
1902	Bill Bernhard, Phil-Clev	18	5	.783	1925	Stan Coveleski, Wash	20	5	.800
1903	Earl Moore, Clev	22	7	.759	1926	George Uhle, Clev	27	11	.711
1904	Jack Chesbro, NY	41	12	.774	1927	Waite Hoyt, NY	22	7	.759
1905	Jess Tannehill, Bos	22	9	.710	1928	General Crowder, StL	21	5	.808
1906	Eddie Plank, Phil	19	6	.760	1929	Lefty Grove, Phil	20	6	.769
1907	Wild Bill Donovan, Det	25	4	.862	1930	Lefty Grove, Phil	28	5	.848
1908	Ed Walsh, Chi	40	15	.727	1931	Lefty Grove, Phil	31	4	.886
1909	George Mullin, Det	29	8	.784	1932	Johnny Allen, NY	17	4	.810
1910	Chief Bender, Phil	23	5	.821	1933	Lefty Grove, Phil	24	8	.750
1911	Chief Bender, Phil	17	5	.773	1934	Lefty Gomez, NY	26	5	.839
1912	Smoky Joe Wood, Bos	34	5	.872	1935	Eldon Auker, Det	18	7	.720
1913	Walter Johnson, Wash	36	7	.837	1936	Monte Pearson, NY	19	7	.731
1914	Chief Bender, Phil	17	3	.850	1937	Johnny Allen, Clev	15	1	.938
1915	Smoky Joe Wood, Bos	15	5	.750	1938	Red Ruffing, NY	21	7	.750
1916	Eddie Cicotte, Chi	15	7	.682	1939	Lefty Grove, Bos	15	4	.789
1917	Reb Russell, Chi	15	5	.750	1940	Schoolboy Rowe, Det	16	3	.842
1918	Sad Sam Jones, Bos	16	5	.762	1941	Lefty Gomez, NY	15	5	.750
1919	Eddie Cicotte, Chi	29	7	.806	1942	Ernie Bonham, NY	21	5	.808
1920	Jim Bagby, Clev	31	12	.721	1943	Spud Chandler, NY	20	4	.833
1921	Carl Mays, NY	27	9	.750	1944	Tex Hughson, Bos	18	5	.783
1922	Joe Bush, NY	26	7	.788	1945	Hal Newhouser, Det	25	9	.735
1923	Herb Pennock, NY	19	6	.760	1946	Boo Ferriss, Bos	25	6	.806

Leading Pitchers—Winning Percentage (Cont.)

Year	Pitcher and Team	W	L	Pct	Year	Pitcher and Team	W	L	Pct
1947	Allie Reynolds, NY	19	8	.704	1975	Mike Torrez, Balt	20	9	.690
1948	Jack Kramer, Bos	18	5	.783	1976	Bill Campbell, Minn	17	5	.773
1949	Ellis Kinder, Bos	23	6	.793	1977	Paul Splittorff, KC	16	6	.727
1950	Vic Raschi, NY	21	8	.724	1978	Ron Guidry, NY	25	3	.893
1951	Bob Feller, Clev	22	8	.733	1979	Mike Caldwell, Mil	16	6	.727
1952	Bobby Shantz, Phil	24	7	.774	1980	Steve Stone, Balt	25	7	.781
1953	Ed Lopat, NY	16	4	.800	1981*	Pete Vuckovich, Mil	14	4	.778
1954	Sandy Consuegra, Chi	16	3	.842	1982	Pete Vuckovich, Mil	18	6	.750
1955	Tommy Byrne, NY	16	5	.762		Jim Palmer, Balt	15	5	.750
1956	Whitey Ford, NY	19	6	.760	1983	Richard Dotson, Chi	22	7	.759
1957	Dick Donovan, Chi	16	6	.727	1984	Doyle Alexander, Tor	17	6	.739
	Tom Sturdivant, NY	16	6	.727	1985	Ron Guidry, NY	22	6	.786
1958	Bob Turley, NY	21	7	.750	1986	Roger Clemens, Bos	24	4	.857
1959	Bob Shaw, Chi	18	6	.750	1987	Roger Clemens, Bos	20	9	.690
1960	Jim Perry, Clev	18	10	.643	1988	Frank Viola, Minn	24	7	.774
1961	Whitey Ford, NY	25	4	.862	1989	Bret Saberhagen, KC	23	6	.793
1962	Ray Herbert, Chi	20	9	.690	1990	Bob Welch, Oak	27	6	.818
1963	Whitey Ford, NY	24	7	.774	1991	Scott Erickson, Minn	20	8	.714
1964	Wally Bunker, Balt	19	5	.792	1992	Mike Mussina, Balt	18	5	.783
1965	Mudcat Grant, Minn	21	7	.750	1993	Jimmy Key, NY	18	6	.750
1966	Sonny Siebert, Clev	16	8	.667	1994	Jimmy Key, NY	17	4	.810
1967	Joel Horlen, Chi	19	7	.731	1995	Randy Johnson, Sea	18	2	.900
1968	Denny McLain, Det	31	6	.838	1996	Charles Nagy, Clev	17	5	.773
1969	Jim Palmer, Balt	16	4	.800	1997	Randy Johnson, Sea	20	4	.833
1970	Mike Cuellar, Balt	24	8	.750	1998	David Wells, NY	18	4	.818
1971	Dave McNally, Balt	21	5	.808	1999	Pedro Martinez, Bos	23	4	.852
1972	Catfish Hunter, Oak	21	7	.750	2000	Tim Hudson, Oak	20	6	.769
1973	Catfish Hunter, Oak	21	5	.808	2001	Roger Clemens, NY	20	3	.870
1974	Mike Cuellar, Balt	22	10	.688	2002	Pedro Martinez, Bos	20	4	.833

*1981 percentages based on 10 or more victories. Note: Percentages based on 15 or more victories in all other years.

Leading Pitchers—Earned Run Average

Year	Player and Team	ERA	Year	Player and Team	ERA
1913	Walter Johnson, Wash	1.14	1945	Hal Newhouser, Det	1.81
1914	Dutch Leonard, Bos	1.01	1946	Hal Newhouser, Det	1.94
1915	Smoky Joe Wood, Bos	1.49	1947	Spud Chandler, NY	2.46
1916	Babe Ruth, Bos	1.75	1948	Gene Bearden, Clev	2.43
1917	Eddie Cicotte, Chi	1.53	1949	Mel Parnell, Bos	2.78
1918	Walter Johnson, Wash	1.27	1950	Early Wynn, Clev	3.20
1919	Walter Johnson, Wash	1.49	1951	Saul Rogovin, Det-Chi	2.78
1920	Bob Shawkey, NY	2.46	1952	Allie Reynolds, NY	2.07
1921	Red Faber, Chi	2.47	1953	Ed Lopat, NY	2.43
1922	Red Faber, Chi	2.80	1954	Mike Garcia, Clev	2.64
1923	Stan Coveleski, Clev	2.76	1955	Billy Pierce, Chi	1.97
1924	Walter Johnson, Wash	2.72	1956	Whitey Ford, NY	2.47
1925	Stan Coveleski, Wash	2.84	1957	Bobby Shantz, NY	2.45
1926	Lefty Grove, Phil	2.51	1958	Whitey Ford, NY	2.01
1927	Wilcy Moore, NY#	2.28	1959	Hoyt Wilhelm, Balt	2.19
1928	Garland Braxton, Wash	2.52	1960	Frank Baumann, Chi	2.68
1929	Lefty Grove, Phil	2.81	1961	Dick Donovan, Wash	2.40
1930	Lefty Grove, Phil	2.54	1962	Hank Aguirre, Det	2.21
1931	Lefty Grove, Phil	2.06	1963	Gary Peters, Chi	2.33
1932	Lefty Grove, Phil	2.84	1964	Dean Chance, LA	1.65
1933	Monte Pearson, Clev	2.33	1965	Sam McDowell, Clev	2.18
1934	Lefty Gomez, NY	2.33	1966	Gary Peters, Chi	1.98
1935	Lefty Grove, Bos	2.70	1967	Joe Horlen, Chi	2.06
1936	Lefty Grove, Bos	2.81	1968	Luis Tiant, Clev	1.60
1937	Lefty Gomez, NY	2.33	1969	Dick Bosman, Wash	2.19
1938	Lefty Grove, Bos	3.07	1970	Diego Segui, Oak	2.56
1939	Lefty Grove, Bos	2.54	1971	Vida Blue, Oak	1.82
1940	Bob Feller, Clev†	2.62	1972	Luis Tiant, Bos	1.91
1941	Thornton Lee, Chi	2.37	1973	Jim Palmer, Balt	2.40
1942	Ted Lyons, Chi	2.10	1974	Catfish Hunter, Oak	2.49
1943	Spud Chandler, NY	1.64	1975	Jim Palmer, Balt	2.09
1944	Dizzy Trout, Det	2.12	1976	Mark Fidrych, Det	2.34

Leading Pitchers—Earned Run Average (Cont.)

Year	Player and Team	ERA	Year	Player and Team	ERA
1977	Frank Tanana, Cal	2.54	1990	Roger Clemens, Bos	1.93
1978	Ron Guidry, NY	1.74	1991	Roger Clemens, Bos	2.62
1979	Ron Guidry, NY	2.78	1992	Roger Clemens, Bos	2.41
1980	Rudy May, NY	2.47	1993	Kevin Appier, KC	2.56
1981	Steve McCatty, Oak	2.32	1994	Steve Ontiveros, Oak	2.65
1982	Rick Sutcliffe, Clev	2.96	1995	Randy Johnson, Sea	2.48
1983	Rick Honeycutt, Tex	2.42	1996	Juan Guzman, Tor	2.93
1984	Mike Boddicker, Balt	2.79	1997	Roger Clemens, Tor	2.05
1985	Dave Stieb, Tor	2.48	1998	Roger Clemens, Tor	2.64
1986	Roger Clemens, Bos	2.48	1999	Pedro Martinez, Bos	2.07
1987	Jimmy Key, Tor	2.76	2000	Pedro Martinez, Bos	1.74
1988	Allan Anderson, Minn	2.45	2001	Freddy Garcia, Sea	3.05
1989	Bret Saberhagen, KC	2.16	2002	Pedro Martinez, Bos	2.26

Note: Based on 10 complete games through 1950, then 154 innings until the American League expanded in 1961, when it became 162 innings. In strike-shortened 1981, one inning per game required. Earned runs not tabulated in American League prior to 1913.

#Wilcy Moore pitched only six complete games—he started 12—in 1927 but was recognized as leader because of 213 innings pitched. †Ernie Bonham, New York, had 1.91 ERA and 10 complete games in 1940 but appeared in only 12 games and 99 innings, and Bob Feller was recognized as leader.

Leading Pitchers—Strikeouts

Year	Player and Team	SO	Year	Player and Team	SO
1901	Cy Young, Bos	159	1945	Hal Newhouser, Det	212
1902	Rube Waddell, Phil	210	1946	Bob Feller, Clev	348
1903	Rube Waddell, Phil	301	1947	Bob Feller, Clev	196
1904	Rube Waddell, Phil	349	1948	Bob Feller, Clev	164
1905	Rube Waddell, Phil	286	1949	Virgil Trucks, Det	153
1906	Rube Waddell, Phil	203	1950	Bob Lemon, Clev	170
1907	Rube Waddell, Phil	226	1951	Vic Raschi, NY	164
1908	Ed Walsh, Chi	269	1952	Allie Reynolds, NY	160
1909	Frank Smith, Chi	177	1953	Billy Pierce, Chi	186
1910	Walter Johnson, Wash	313	1954	Bob Turley, Balt	185
1911	Ed Walsh, Chi	255	1955	Herb Score, Clev	245
1912	Walter Johnson, Wash	303	1956	Herb Score, Clev	263
1913	Walter Johnson, Wash	243	1957	Early Wynn, Clev	184
1914	Walter Johnson, Wash	225	1958	Early Wynn, Chi	179
1915	Walter Johnson, Wash	203	1959	Jim Bunning, Det	201
1916	Walter Johnson, Wash	228	1960	Jim Bunning, Det	201
1917	Walter Johnson, Wash	188	1961	Camilo Pascual, Minn	221
1918	Walter Johnson, Wash	162	1962	Camilo Pascual, Minn	206
1919	Walter Johnson, Wash	147	1963	Camilo Pascual, Minn	202
1920	Stan Coveleski, Clev	133	1964	Al Downing, NY	217
1921	Walter Johnson, Wash	143	1965	Sam McDowell, Clev	325
1922	Urban Shocker, StL	149	1966	Sam McDowell, Clev	225
1923	Walter Johnson, Wash	130	1967	Jim Lonborg, Bos	246
1924	Walter Johnson, Wash	158	1968	Sam McDowell, Clev	283
1925	Lefty Grove, Phil	116	1969	Sam McDowell, Clev	279
1926	Lefty Grove, Phil	194	1970	Sam McDowell, Clev	304
1927	Lefty Grove, Phil	174	1971	Mickey Lolich, Det	308
1928	Lefty Grove, Phil	183	1972	Nolan Ryan, Cal	329
1929	Lefty Grove, Phil	170	1973	Nolan Ryan, Cal	383
1930	Lefty Grove, Phil	209	1974	Nolan Ryan, Cal	367
1931	Lefty Grove, Phil	175	1975	Frank Tanana, Cal	269
1932	Red Ruffing, NY	190	1976	Nolan Ryan, Cal	327
1933	Lefty Gomez, NY	163	1977	Nolan Ryan, Cal	341
1934	Lefty Gomez, NY	158	1978	Nolan Ryan, Cal	260
1935	Tommy Bridges, Det	163	1979	Nolan Ryan, Cal	223
1936	Tommy Bridges, Det	175	1980	Len Barker, Clev	187
1937	Lefty Gomez, NY	194	1981	Len Barker, Clev	127
1938	Bob Feller, Clev	240	1982	Floyd Bannister, Sea	209
1939	Bob Feller, Clev	246	1983	Jack Morris, Det	232
1940	Bob Feller, Clev	261	1984	Mark Langston, Sea	204
1941	Bob Feller, Clev	260	1985	Bert Blyleven, Clev-Minn	206
1942	Bobo Newsom, Wash		1986	Mark Langston, Sea	245
	Tex Hughson, Bos	113	1987	Mark Langston, Sea	262
1943	Allie Reynolds, Clev	151	1988	Roger Clemens, Bos	291
1944	Hal Newhouser, Det	187	1989	Nolan Ryan, Tex	301

Leading Pitchers—Strikeouts (Cont.)

Year	Player and Team	SO	Year	Player and Team	SO
1990	Nolan Ryan, Tex	232	1997	Roger Clemens, Tor	292
1991	Roger Clemens, Bos	241	1998	Roger Clemens, Tor	271
1992	Randy Johnson, Sea	241	1999	Pedro Martinez, Bos	313
1993	Randy Johnson, Sea	308	2000	Pedro Martinez, Bos	284
1994	Randy Johnson, Sea	204	2001	Hideo Nomo, Bos	220
1995	Randy Johnson, Sea	294	2002	Pedro Martinez, Bos	239
1996	Roger Clemens, Bos	257			

Leading Pitchers—Saves

Year	Player and Team	SV	Year	Player and Team	SV
1947	Joe Page, NY	17	1975	Goose Gossage, Chi	26
1948	Russ Christopher, Clev	17	1976	Sparky Lyle, NY	23
1949	Joe Page, NY	29	1977	Bill Campbell, Bos	31
1950	Mickey Harris, Wash	15	1978	Goose Gossage, NY	27
1951	Ellis Kinder, Bos	14	1979	Mike Marshall, Minn	32
1952	Harry Dorish, Chi	11	1980	Dan Quisenberry, KC	33
1953	Ellis Kinder, Bos	27	1981	Rollie Fingers, Mil	28
1954	Johnny Sain, NY	22	1982	Dan Quisenberry, KC	35
1955	Ray Narleski, Clev	19	1983	Dan Quisenberry, KC	35
1956	George Zuverink, Bal	16	1984	Dan Quisenberry, KC	44
1957	Bob Grim, NY	19	1985	Dan Quisenberry, KC	37
1958	Ryne Duren, NY	20	1986	Dave Righetti, NY	46
1959	Turk Lown, Chi	15	1987	Tom, Henke, Tor	34
1960	Mike Fornieles, Bos	14	1988	Dennis Eckersley, Oak	45
	Johnny Klippstein, Clev	14	1989	Jeff Russell, Tex	38
1961	Luis Arroyo, NY	29	1990	Bobby Thigpen, Chi	57
1962	Dick Radatz, Bos	24	1991	Bryan Harvey, Cal	46
1963	Stu Miller, Bal	27	1992	Dennis Eckersley, Oak	51
1964	Dick Radatz, Bos	29	1993	Jeff Montgomery, KC	45
1965	Ron Kline, Wash	29		Duane Ward, Tor	45
1966	Jack Aker, KC	32	1994	Lee Smith, Bal	33
1967	Minnie Rojas, Cal	27	1995	Jose Mesa, Clev	46
1968	Al Worthington, Minn	18	1996	John Wetteland, NY	43
1969	Ron Perranoski, Minn	31	1997	Randy Myers, Balt	45
1970	Ron Perranoski, Minn	34	1998	Tom Gordon, Bos	46
1971	Ken Sanders, Mil	31	1999	Mariano Rivera, NY	45
1972	Sparky Lyle, NY	35	2000	Todd Jones, Det	42
1973	John Hiller, Det	38	2001	Mariano Rivera, NY	50
1974	Terry Forster, Chi	24	2002	Eddie Guardado, Minn	45

The Commissioners of Baseball

Kenesaw Mountain Landis ....Elected Nov. 12, 1920. Served until his death on Nov. 25, 1944.
Happy Chandler ....Elected April 24, 1945. Served until July 15, 1951.
Ford Frick ....Elected Sept. 20, 1951. Served until Nov. 16, 1965.
William Eckert ....Elected Nov. 17, 1965. Served until Dec. 20, 1968.
Bowie Kuhn ....Elected Feb. 8, 1969. Served until Sept. 30, 1984.
Peter Ueberroth ....Elected March 3, 1984. Took office Oct. 1, 1984. Served through March 31, 1989.
A. Bartlett Giamatti ....Elected Sept. 8, 1988. Took office April 1, 1989. Served until his death on Sept. 1, 1989.
Francis Vincent Jr. ....Appointed Acting Commissioner Sept. 2, 1989. Elected Commissioner Sept. 13, 1989. Served through Sept. 7, 1992.
Allan H. (Bud) Selig ....Elected chairman of the executive council and given the powers of interim commissioner on Sept. 9, 1992. Unanimously elected Commissioner July 9, 1998.

Pro Football

Tom Brady of the
Super Bowl champion
Patriots

Brady's Bunch

Led by unheralded second-year quarterback Tom Brady, New England scored a stunning Super Bowl upset

BY HANK HERSCH

NO ONE KNEW what to expect of Tom Brady. A fourth-string quarterback in 2000, he took over in the second game of the 2001 season, after New England Patriots starter Drew Bledsoe went down with a chest injury. Though he had been a lowly sixth-round draft choice in 2000, the 24-year-old Brady had a swagger about him that belied his boyish looks, which included a dime-sized dimple in his chin. He stood 6' 4" and weighed 220 pounds, and when he started dishing out advice on route adjustments during training camp as if he were a seasoned veteran, Patriots wide receiver David Patten recalls thinking, If he's this confident as a backup, I can only imagine how he'd be running the show.

No one knew what to expect from Tom Brady. The St. Louis Rams had tied New England at 17–all, and with 1:21 remaining in Super Bowl XXXVI, Brady had the ball on his own 17-yard line with no timeouts left. Analyst John Madden told the millions watching on television that the Patriots should simply run out the clock and try to win in overtime—too much ground to cover, too little time to do it in, too much risk involved. Coach Bill Belichick thought about doing that, too. Then he thought about Brady. "With a quarterback like Tom, going for a win is not that dangerous," Belichick said, "because he's not going to make a mistake."

Brady, a second-year man out of Michigan, proved that Belichick's belief in him was well-founded. He completed five passes and took New England 53 yards in 74 seconds to put the Patriots in position to win the game with a 48-yard field goal. Out trotted Adam Vinatieri to split the uprights as time expired. Despite being outgained by 160 yards, the Patriots had won, 20–17, and seized the first Super Bowl in franchise history. Along with Vinatieri, they had the cooler-than-dry-ice Brady to thank. For his preternatural poise on the final drive, Brady was named MVP of the game. "You're looking at a team that had some guts," Rams defensive end Chidi Ahanotu said. "Brady never flinched, and they've got one hell of a gutsy coach."

The Patriots' ascendancy from AFC East doormat to conference champion may have been the most stunning turnaround of 2001, but it was by no means the only one. But then, such volatility hardly seemed surprising in light of the season's start: The terrorist attacks of Sept. 11 that leveled the World Trade Center occurred two days after the Sunday openers. Commissioner Paul Tagliabue weighed conflicting opinions from the league's owners on whether to let the Week 2 games proceed, some arguing that postponing the games would signal a victory for the terrorists, others that it would give the nation needed time to grieve.

On Sept. 13, the player reps voted 17–11 to call them off. "It's one thing to see it on TV," said New York Giants cornerback Jason Sehorn. "It's another thing, every day, to look from our practice field and see the towers gone. And it's another thing to even consider playing while they're still pulling people out of the rubble." The following day Tagliabue announced that he would reschedule the games for the end of the season. Three minutes after releasing his decision, the NFL's offices in midtown Manhattan were evacuated because of a bomb threat at a building across the street.

Although at first it seemed that the postponement might force the league to cancel the wild-card round of the playoffs, the National Auto Dealers Association, who had planned a convention in New Orleans for the first weekend of February, consented to give up that date so that the Super Bowl could move back a week and still take place in the Superdome.

AMY SANCETTA/AP

Vinatieri sealed the first championship in Patriots history with a 48-yard kick as time expired.

One team that quickly made it clear that it would be booking no postseason dates was the Carolina Panthers. After a Week 1 win over the Minnesota Vikings, they lost a league-record 15 straight, drawing a franchise-low 21,070 fans for their season finale at Ericsson Stadium. After that ignominious end George Seifert, whose .755 winning percentage over eight years with the San Francisco 49ers had been the highest in NFL history, became one of the six coaches who lost their jobs in 2001. (One of those men, former Tampa Bay coach Tony Dungy, quickly found a new head coaching position with the Indianapolis Colts.)

JONATHAN DANIEL/ALLSPORT

Brown capped two wildly improbable, back-to-back comeback victories for Chicago by returning interceptions for touchdowns.

Before the season began, a similar fate seemed likely for Dick Jauron of the Chicago Bears, who received tepid support from the team's new general manager, Jerry Angelo. But then the Bears did something they hadn't done in Jauron's two previous seasons: They found ways to win. In back-to-back victories over the San Francisco 49ers and the Cleveland Browns, the Bears overcame two-touchdown deficits in the fourth quarter, then won in overtime on interception returns by free safety Mike Brown.

Those two improbable wins should have been sign enough that Chicago was for real, but still, few fans believed in these new Monsters of the Midway. With middle linebacker Brian Urlacher anchoring the NFL's eighth-ranked defense and Anthony Thomas rushing for 1,183 yards to win the Offensive Rookie of the Year award, Chicago shocked the league by going 13–3. They had won only 11 games during the previous two seasons. Though the Bears lost to the Philadelphia Eagles 33–19 in the second round of the playoffs, Jauron was named Coach of the Year. "He's the type of leader you want to play for," said linebacker Rosevelt Colvin. "In three years here I've only seen him really yell at a guy one time." Said quarterback Jim Miller of his coach, "Like Tom Landry, the guy does not waver. And we've taken on his personality."

Much like the Bears, the Pittsburgh Steelers rocketed to a 13–3 record after a string of mediocre seasons. Crucial to their resurgence was a sack-happy linebacking corps buoyed by the Defensive Rookie of the Year, Kendrell Bell, and a rejuvenated Kordell Stewart at quarterback. After leading Pittsburgh to the AFC title game in 1997, his first season as a starter, Stewart had gone through a pair of offensive coordinators, endured a humiliating switch to wide receiver, seen his career passing rating plummet to an abysmal 68.4 and developed bitter feelings toward head coach Bill Cowher.

At a team meeting before the 1999 season Stewart even felt compelled to deny rumors that he was gay, launching into graphic descriptions of his favorite heterosexual acts. "At one point," Stewart recalls, "I said, 'You'd better not leave your girlfriends around me, because I'm out to prove a point.'"

After clearing the air with Cowher during an emotional three-hour phone call in the off-season, Stewart regained his form as a game-breaker. In a new home (Heinz Field) with a new offensive coordinator (Mike Mularkey) and using a recharged pair of starting receivers (Hines Ward and Plaxico Burress, each of whom surpassed 1,000 yards), Stewart completed a career-best 60.2% of his passes for 3,109 yards. His run ended in the AFC Championship Game, when visiting New England intercepted him on each of Pittsburgh's last two possessions to preserve a 24–17 victory.

A week earlier Pittsburgh's defense had helped end the reign of the defending Super Bowl champion, Baltimore, com-

pletely bottling the Ravens' attack in a 27–10 victory. Before the game, Steelers defensive coordinator Tim Lewis told his troops they would have to stuff the run and force Elvis Grbac to win with his arm. "Good quarterback, good pocket presence," Lewis said, "but when you get to him make sure you brush him. He doesn't like to be hit."

Despite Trent Dilfer's 11–1 record as a starter in 2000, Baltimore coach Brian Billick had opted to let Dilfer walk over the summer and sign Grbac. While Dilfer went 4–0 and had a 92.0 rating for the Seattle Seahawks, Grbac threw 18 interceptions against 15 touchdowns for the Ravens and ranked 28th among quarterbacks. Rattled by the pressure in Pittsburgh, Grbac threw a pair of first-half interceptions. He would retire from football during the offseason. "You could see it in his eyes—he freaked out," said Steelers safety Lee Flowers. "By the end he was dropping three steps and ducking."

The New York Giants, Super Bowl XXXV's other entry, failed to even make the playoffs, finishing 7–9. Their lone mark of distinction belonged to end Michael Strahan, the Defensive Player of the Year, who made 22½ sacks to break Mark Gastineau's 17-year-old record of 22. In a five-game spurt the 6' 5", 275-pound Strahan racked up 12½ sacks, and after dropping Eagles quarterback Donovan McNabb 3½ times in Week 16, he entered the final game of the season needing one sack for the record.

He got it in the waning minutes of the Giants' 35–24 loss to Green Bay, when Packers quarterback Brett Favre took the snap from center, rolled out and then fell in the face of Strahan's charge. The play had all the appearances of a gift from Favre to Strahan: The Packer linemen thought it was a running play and thus did not pass-block,

allowing Strahan easy passage into the backfield, and Favre ran right at the Giants defensive end before curling up at his feet to give up the record-breaking "sack." Observers questioned why Green Bay would be passing in that situation instead of running to milk the clock, and the Green Bay offensive line, when questioned about the play, referred reporters to Favre, who coyly denied giftwrapping the record for his friend. Pundits and fans alike cried foul.

After their divisional playoff game against New England, the Oakland Raiders were crying foul as well—only at an infinitely louder volume. With 1:43 remaining they had held a 13–10 lead over the Patriots on the snow-covered field in Foxboro Stadium. Oakland cornerback Charles Woodson, a teammate of Brady's at Michigan, blitzed the young Patriots quarterback and knocked the ball loose as Brady appeared to fake a throw and start to tuck the ball in to run. The Raiders recovered the football, and New England's six-game winning streak seemed to be at an end.

That is, until Brady watched the replay—which was being reviewed by referee Walt Coleman—on the stadium's jumbo video screen. "We're getting the ball back!" Brady screamed at Patriots offensive coor-

HEINZ KLUETMEIER

D in '01. "It's not even close," said coach Mike Martz, comparing his team to the Rams' Supe XXXIV champs. "We've got so much speed on defense that we didn't have two years ago. We're cresting, and I've never been around a team more confident."

After dispatching the Eagles 29–24 in the NFC title game, St. Louis came to New Orleans a two-touchdown favorite. In a 24–17 win over the Patriots in Week 10, Belichick had blitzed Warner repeatedly and without success. This time he emphasized coverage, having cornerbacks Ty Law and Otis Smith press, mixing in zones and hoping to force Warner to hold the ball. The Rams fumbled once and Warner threw two interceptions, one of which Ty Law returned 49 yards for a touchdown.

St. Louis offense didn't find its rhythm until the fourth quarter, by which time New England had built a 17–3 lead. Fatigue began to set in on the Patriots' D. "Tired, man," Law said. "Actually drained. On the ropes." Warner engineered a pair of touchdown drives, capping the second one with a pass to wideout Ricky Proehl, who made a nifty cutback along the sidelines and plunged into the end zone for a 26-yard score that tied the game with 1:37 to play.

dinator Charlie Weis. "What play do you want to run?"

According to Rule 3, Section 21, Article 2 of the NFL rulebook, a passer who has begun to bring the ball forward can't be deemed to have fumbled if he hasn't tucked the ball into his body. Coleman's ruling gave New England new life, and Brady did not squander the second chance. He moved the Patriots 14 more yards to the Oakland 28-yard line. Seven yards behind that snowbound line of scrimmage, as yet more snow swirled in the wind, Vinatieri nailed a game-tying 45-yard field goal. Brady then completed eight more passes in a row to set up Vinatieri's winning 23-yarder in overtime. "We didn't lose this game," said Oakland linebacker William Thomas, "it was taken from us." Paraphrasing Lefty Gomez, Patriots guard Mike Compton said, "Sometimes luck is better than skill."

The Patriots would need both luck and skill, in equally heaping portions it seemed, in the Superdome against St. Louis, whose lethal offense was known as The Greatest Show on Turf. In quarterback Kurt Warner the Rams had the NFL's Most Valuable Player; in running back Marshall Faulk, the league's Offensive Player of the Year. More important, new defensive coordinator Lovie Smith and seven new starters on defense had transformed a unit that ranked last in points allowed in 2000 into the sixth-ranked

That set the stage for Vinatieri's kick, which instantly became the most famous in the history of the Super Bowl, eclipsing Jim O'Brien's last-second game-winner for the Baltimore Colts against Dallas in Super Bowl V, and Scott Norwood's famous miss for Buffalo in Super Bowl XXV against the Giants. And it was all made possible by a kid who had thrown all of three NFL passes before the 2001 season began. Said Brady, "Only you know what you're capable of."

2001 NFL Final Standings

American Football Conference

EASTERN DIVISION

	W	L	T	Pct	Pts	OP
New England	11	5	0	.688	371	272
†Miami	11	5	0	.688	344	290
†NY Jets	10	6	0	.625	308	295
Indianapolis	6	10	0	.375	413	486
Buffalo	3	13	0	.188	265	420

CENTRAL DIVISION

	W	L	T	Pct	Pts	OP
Pittsburgh	13	3	0	.812	352	212
†Baltimore	10	6	0	.625	303	265
Cleveland	7	9	0	.438	285	319
Tennessee	7	9	0	.438	336	388
Jacksonville	6	10	0	.375	294	286
Cincinnati	6	10	0	.375	226	309

WESTERN DIVISION

	W	L	T	Pct	Pts	OP
Oakland	10	6	0	.625	399	327
Seattle	9	7	0	.562	301	324
Denver	8	8	0	.500	340	339
Kansas City	6	10	0	.375	320	344
San Diego	5	11	0	.312	332	321

† Wild-card team.

National Football Conference

EASTERN DIVISION

	W	L	T	Pct	Pts	OP
Philadelphia	11	5	0	.688	343	208
Washington	8	8	0	.500	256	303
NY Giants	7	9	0	.438	294	321
Arizona	7	9	0	.438	295	343
Dallas	5	11	0	.312	246	338

CENTRAL DIVISION

	W	L	T	Pct	Pts	OP
Chicago	13	3	0	.812	338	203
†Green Bay	12	4	0	.750	390	266
†Tampa Bay	9	7	0	.562	324	280
Minnesota	5	11	0	.312	290	390
Detroit	2	14	0	.125	270	424

WESTERN DIVISION

	W	L	T	Pct	Pts	OP
St. Louis	14	2	0	.875	503	273
†San Francisco	12	4	0	.750	409	282
New Orleans	7	9	0	.438	333	409
Atlanta	7	9	0	.438	291	377
Carolina	1	15	0	.062	253	410

2001–02 NFL Playoffs

AFC FIRST ROUND	AFC DIVISIONAL PLAYOFF	AFC CHAMPIONSHIP	NFC CHAMPIONSHIP	NFC DIVISIONAL PLAYOFF	NFC FIRST ROUND

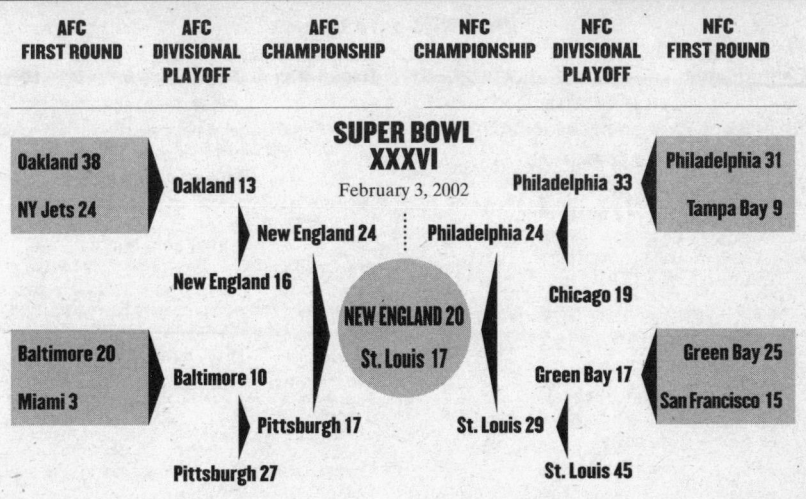

Oakland 38 / NY Jets 24 — Oakland 13 — New England 24 — New England 16

SUPER BOWL XXXVI
February 3, 2002

NEW ENGLAND 20 / St. Louis 17

Philadelphia 33 — Philadelphia 24 — Chicago 19 — Philadelphia 31 / Tampa Bay 9

Baltimore 20 / Miami 3 — Baltimore 10 — Pittsburgh 17 — Pittsburgh 27

Green Bay 17 — St. Louis 29 — St. Louis 45 — Green Bay 25 / San Francisco 15

NFL Playoff Box Scores

AFC Wild-card Games

NY Jets...................0	3	7	14—24
Oakland..................6	10	0	22—38

FIRST QUARTER

Oakland: FG Janikowski 21, 8:26. Drive: 74 yards, 12 plays.
Oakland: FG Janikowski 41, 0:44. Drive: 43 yards, 7 plays.

SECOND QUARTER

NY Jets: FG Hall 45, 12:45. Drive: 21 yards, 6 plays.
Oakland: FG Janikowski 45, 6:45. Drive: 43 yards, 10 plays.
Oakland: Brown 2 pass from Gannon (Janikowski kick), 0:22. Drive: 66 yards, 7 plays.

THIRD QUARTER

NY Jets: Chrebet 17 pass from Testaverde (Hall kick), 11:36. Drive: 72 yards, 8 plays.

FOURTH QUARTER

Oakland: Crockett 2 run (Garner run for two-point conversion), 14:57. Drive: 55 yards, 4 plays.
NY Jets: Anderson 3 pass from Testaverde (Hall kick), 10:18. Drive: 64 yards, 10 plays.
Oakland: Rice 21 pass from Gannon (Janikowski kick), 1:52. Drive: 68 yards, 7 plays.
NY Jets: Chrebet 4 pass from Testaverde (Hall kick), 1:52. Drive: 75 yards, 9 plays.
Oakland: Garner 80 run (Janikowski kick), 1:27. Drive: 79 yards, 3 plays.

A: 61,503; T: 2:56.

Baltimore 0	7	7	6— 20
Miami 3	0	0	0— 3

FIRST QUARTER

Miami: FG Mare 33, 12:46. Drive: 9 yards, 4 plays.

SECOND QUARTER

Baltimore: Allen 4 run (Stover kick), 13:34. Drive: 90 yards, 17 plays.

THIRD QUARTER

Baltimore: Taylor 4 pass from Grbac (Stover kick), 5:42. Drive: 99 yards, 11 plays.

FOURTH QUARTER

Baltimore: FG Stover 35, 11:05. Drive: 20 yards, 6 plays.
Baltimore: FG Stover 40, 2:01. Drive: 50 yards, 11 plays.

A: 72,251; T: 2:51.

NFC Wild-card Games

Tampa Bay.............3	6	0	0— 9
Philadelphia...........3	14	7	7—31

FIRST QUARTER

Tampa Bay: FG Gramatica 36, 10:48. Drive: 21 yards, 7 plays.
Philadelphia: FG Akers 26, 6:18. Drive: 58 yards, 7 plays.

SECOND QUARTER

Philadelphia: Lewis 16 pass from McNabb (Akers kick), 12:17. Drive: 73 yards, 5 plays.
Tampa Bay: FG Gramatica 32, 6:13. Drive: 65 yards, 10 plays.
Philadelphia: Staley 23 pass from McNabb (Akers kick), 1:11. Drive: 31 yards, 6 plays.
Tampa Bay: FG Gramatica 27, 0:00. Drive: 53 yards, 5 plays.

THIRD QUARTER

Philadelphia: Buckhalter 25 run (Akers kick), 2:30. Drive: 60 yards, 6 plays.

FOURTH QUARTER

Philadelphia: Moore 59 interception return (Akers kick), 2:08.

A: 65,847; T: 2:59.

San Francisco........0	7	0	8—15
Green Bay 6	0	9	10—25

FIRST QUARTER

Green Bay: Freeman 5 pass from Favre (kick failed), 4:02. Drive: 40 yards, 7 plays.

SECOND QUARTER

San Francisco: Hearst 2 run (Cortez kick), 0:11. Drive: 86 yards, 15 plays.

THIRD QUARTER

Green Bay: FG Longwell 26, 8:52. Drive: 72 yards, 12 plays.
Green Bay: Franks 19 pass from Favre (two-point conversion failed), 3:26. Drive: 81 yards, 4 plays.

FOURTH QUARTER

San Francisco: Streets 14 pass from Garcia (Streets pass from Garcia for two-point conversion), 12:00. Drive: 61 yards, 6 plays.
Green Bay: FG Longwell 45, 7:02. Drive 49 yards, 10 plays.
Green Bay: Green 9 run (Longwell kick), 1:55. Drive: 93 yards, 8 plays.

A: 59,825; T: 2:49.

AFC Divisional Games

Baltimore 0	3	7	0—10
Pittsburgh 10	10	0	7—27

FIRST QUARTER

Pittsburgh: FG Brown 21, 9:07. Drive: 40 yards, 7 plays.
Pittsburgh: Zereoue 1 run (Brown kick), 3:49. Drive: 51 yards, 7 plays.

SECOND QUARTER

Pittsburgh: Zereoue 1 run (Brown kick), 5:43. Drive: 43 yards, 6 plays.
Pittsburgh: FG Brown 46, 3:46. Drive: 6 yards, 4 plays.
Baltimore: FG Stover 26, 0:51. Drive: 57 yards, 11 plays.

THIRD QUARTER

Baltimore: Lewis 88 punt return (Stover kick), 7:18.

FOURTH QUARTER

Pittsburgh: Burress 32 pass from Stewart (Brown kick), 14:11. Drive: 83 yards, 12 plays.

A: 63,976; T: 3:10.

Oakland 0	7	6	0	0—13
New England 0	0	3	10	3—16

SECOND QUARTER

Oakland: Jett 13 pass from Gannon (Janikowski kick), 12:14. Drive: 50 yards, 8 plays.

THIRD QUARTER

New England: FG Vinatieri 23, 8:39. Drive: 62 yards, 12 plays.
Oakland: FG Janikowski 38, 4:14. Drive: 43 yards, 10 plays.
Oakland: FG Janikowski 45, 1:41. Drive 24 yards, 7 plays.

FOURTH QUARTER

New England: Brady 6 run (Vinatieri kick), 7:52. Drive: 67 yards, 10 plays.
New England: FG Vinatieri 45, 0:27. Drive: 26 yards, 8 plays.

OVERTIME

New England: FG Vinatieri 23, 6:31. Drive: 61 yards, 15 plays.

A: 60,292; T: 3:32.

NFC Divisional Games

Philadelphia 6	7	7	13—33
Chicago 0	7	7	5—19

FIRST QUARTER

Philadelphia: FG Akers 34, 9:04. Drive: 61 yards, 12 plays.
Philadelphia: FG Akers 23, 3:22. Drive: 63 yards, 9 plays.

SECOND QUARTER

Chicago: Merritt 47 run (Edinger kick), 5:29. Drive: 62 yards, 1 play.
Philadelphia: Martin 13 pass from McNabb (Akers kick), 0:14. Drive: 69 yards, 11 plays.

THIRD QUARTER

Chicago: Azumah 39 interception return (Edinger kick), 12:25.
Philadelphia: Staley 6 pass from McNabb (Akers kick), 5:55. Drive: 36 yards, 5 plays.

FOURTH QUARTER

Chicago: FG Edinger 38, 14:16. Drive: 44 yards, 11 plays.
Philadelphia: FG Akers 40, 8:48. Drive:45 yards, 11 plays.
Philadelphia: FG Akers 46, 6:28. Drive: 7 yards, 4 plays.
Philadelphia: McNabb 5 run (Akers kick), 3:21. Drive: 20 yards, 3 plays.
Chicago: Safety, Landeta, 0:00.

A: 66,944; T: 2:58.

Green Bay 7	3	0	7—17
St. Louis 7	17	14	7—45

FIRST QUARTER

St. Louis: Williams 29 interception run (Wilkins kick), 9:11.
Green Bay: Freeman 22 pass from Favre (Longwell kick). 2:35. Drive: 65 yards, 5 plays.

SECOND QUARTER

St. Louis: Holt 4 pass from Warner (Wilkins kick), 14:58. Drive: 66 yards, 5 plays.
St. Louis: Hodgins 4 pass from Warner (Wilkins kick), 12:36. Drive: 4 yards, 2 plays.
Green Bay: FG Longwell 28, 4:18. Drive: 40 yards, 9 plays.
St. Louis: FG Wilkins 27, 0:21. Drive: 61 yards, 8 plays.

THIRD QUARTER

St. Louis: Faulk 7 run (Wilkins kick), 9:44. Drive: 69 yards, 4 plays.
St. Louis: Polley 34 interception return (Wilkins kick), 8:12.

FOURTH QUARTER

St. Louis: Williams 32 interception return (Wilkins kick), 7:50.
Green Bay: Freeman 8 pass from Favre (Longwell kick), 5:46. Drive: 55 yards, 5 plays.

A: 66,338; T: 3:05.

NFL Playoff Box Scores (Cont.)

AFC Championship

New England	7	7	3	24
Pittsburgh	0	3	14	17

FIRST QUARTER
New England: Brown, 55 punt return (Vinatieri kick), 3:42.

SECOND QUARTER
Pittsburgh: FG Brown 30, 13:33. Drive: 65 yards, 10 plays.
New England: Patten 11 pass from Bledsoe (Vinatieri kick), 0:58. Drive: 70 yards, 7 plays.

THIRD QUARTER
New England: Harris, 49 yard blocked FG return (Vinatieri kick), 8:51. Drive: 52 yards, 8 plays.
Pittsburgh: Bettis, 1 run (Brown kick), 5:11. Drive: 79 yards, 8 plays.
Pittsburgh: Zereoue 11 run (Brown kick), 1:29. Drive: 32 yards, 5 plays.

FOURTH QUARTER
New England: FG Vinatieri 44, 11:12. Drive: 45 yards, 5 plays.

A: 64,704; T: 3:46.

NFC Championship

Philadelphia	3	14	0	7—24
St. Louis	10	3	9	7—29

FIRST QUARTER
St. Louis: Bruce 5 pass from Warner (Wilkins kick), 12:00. Drive: 21 yards, 5 plays.
Philadelphia: FG Akers 46, 5:44. Drive: 49 yards, 11 plays.
St. Louis: FG Wilkins 27, 1:06. Drive: 49 yards, 9 plays.

SECOND QUARTER
Philadelphia: Staley 1 run (Akers kick), 6:56. Drive: 57 yards, 5 plays.
St. Louis: FG Wilkins 39, 3:52. Drive: 45 yards, 7 plays.
Philadelphia: Pinkston 12 pass from McNabb (Akers kick), 0:46. Drive: 59 yards, 9 plays.

THIRD QUARTER
St. Louis: FG Wilkins 41, 8:01. Drive: 59 yards, 10 plays.
St. Louis: Faulk 1 run (two-point conversion failed), 1:18. Drive: 71 yards, 10 plays.

FOURTH QUARTER
St. Louis: Faulk 1 run (Wilkins kick), 6:55. Drive: 56 yards, 7 plays.
Philadelphia: McNabb 3 run (Akers kick), 2:56. Drive: 48 yards, 9 plays.

A: 66,502; T: 3:09.

Super Bowl Box Score

St. Louis	3	0	0	14—17
New England	0	14	3	3—20

FIRST QUARTER
St. Louis: FG Wilkins 50, 11:50. Drive 48 yards, 10 plays. Key plays: Warner 8 pass to Holt to St. Louis 28; Warner 11 pass to Bruce on 3rd-and-4 to St. Louis 47; Warner 14 pass to M Faulk to New England 39. **St. Louis 3–0.**

SECOND QUARTER
New England: Law 47 interception return (Vinatieri kick), 6:11.**New England 7–3.**
New England: Patten 8 pass from Brady (Vinatieri kick), 14:29. Drive: 40 yards, 5 plays. Key plays: Buckley 15 return of Proehl fumble to St. Louis 40; Brady 16 pass to Brown to St. Louis 24; Brady 8 pass to Wiggins to St. Louis 16; K Faulk 8 run on 3rd-and-2 to St. Louis 8. **New England 14–3.**

THIRD QUARTER
New England: FG Vinatieri 37, 13:42. Drive: 14 yards, 5 plays. Key plays: Smith 30 int return to St. Louis 33; Brady 11 pass to Brown. **New England 17–3.**

FOURTH QUARTER
St. Louis: Warner 2 run (Wilkins kick), 5:29. Drive 77 yards, 12 plays. Key plays: Warner 14 pass to Hakim on 3rd-and-5 to New England 43; def. holding on New England on 4th-and-goal from Patriots' 3. **New England 17–10.**
St. Louis: Proehl 26 pass from Warner (Wilkins kick), 13:30. Drive: 55 yards, 3 plays. Key plays: Warner 18 pass to Hakim to New England 37; Warner 11 pass to Murphy to New England 26. **New England 17, St. Louis 17.**
New England: FG Vinatieri 48, 15:00. Drive: 53 yards, 9 plays. Key plays: Brady 11 pass to Redmond to New England 41; Brady 23 pass to Brown to St. Louis 36. **New England 20–17.**

Team Statistics

	St. Louis	New England
FIRST DOWNS	26	15
Rushing	7	6
Passing	16	8
Penalty	3	1
THIRD DOWN EFF.	5–13	2–11
FOURTH DOWN EFF	0–0	0–0
TOTAL NET YARDS	427	267
Total plays	69	54
Avg gain	6.2	4.9
NET YARDS RUSHING	90	133
Rushes	22	25
Avg per rush	4.1	5.3
NET YARDS PASSING	337	134
Completed–Att.	28–44	16–27
Yards per pass	7.2	4.6
Sacked–yards lost	3–28	2–11
Had intercepted	2	0
PUNTS–Avg.	4–39.8	8–43.1
TOTAL RETURN YARDS	88	181
Punt returns	3–6	1–4
Kickoff returns	4–82	4–100
Interceptions	0–0	2–77
PENALTIES–Yds.	6–39	5–31
FUMBLES–Lost	2–1	0–0
TIME OF POSSESSION	33:30	26:30

Passing

ST. LOUIS

	Comp	Att	Yds	Int	TD
Warner	28	44	365	2	1

NEW ENGLAND

	Comp	Att	Yds	Int	TD
Brady	16	27	145	0	1
Faulk	0	0	0	0	0

Rushing

ST. LOUIS

	No.	Yds	Lg	TD
Faulk	17	76	15	0
Warner	3	6	5	1
Hakim	1	5	5	0
Hodgins	1	3	3	0

NEW ENGLAND

	No.	Yds	Lg	TD
Smith	18	92	17	0
Patten	1	22	22	0
Faulk	2	15	8	0
Edwards	2	5	3	0
Brady	1	3	3	0
Redmond	1	-4	-4	0

Receiving

ST. LOUIS

	No.	Yds	Lg	TD
Hakim	5	90	29	0
Bruce	5	56	22	0
Holt	5	49	18	0
Faulk	4	54	22	0
Proehl	3	71	30	1
Robinson	2	18	12	0
Conwell	2	8	9	0
Murphy	1	11	11	0
Hodgins	1	8	8	0

NEW ENGLAND

	No.	Yds	Lg	TD
Brown	6	89	23	0
Redmond	3	24	11	0
Wiggins	2	14	8	0
Edwards	2	7	5	0
Patten	1	8	8	1
Smith	1	4	4	0
Faulk	1	-1	-1	0

Defense

ST. LOUIS

	Tck	Ast	Int	Sack
Polley	6	2	0	0
Archuleta	4	3	0	0
Fletcher	4	2	0	0
Wistrom	5	0	0	1
Little	4	1	0	1
Herring	3	2	0	0
Williams	3	2	0	0
Young	3	1	0	0
Zgonina	3	1	0	0
Ahanotu	2	2	0	0
Bly	3	0	0	0
McCleon	2	0	0	0
Davis	0	2	0	0
Jackson	0	1	0	0

NEW ENGLAND

	Tck	Ast	Int	Sack
Law	7	1	1	0
Milloy	6	1	0	0
Jones	5	1	0	0
Phifer	5	0	0	0
Pleasant	5	0	0	0
Bruschi	4	0	0	0
Smith	4	0	1	1
McGinest	3	1	0	1
Hamilton	2	2	0	0
Vrabel	2	2	0	0
Buckley	2	1	0	1
Seymour	2	1	0	0
Harris	2	0	0	0
Cox	1	1	0	0
Mitchell	0	1	0	0

2001 Associated Press All-Pro Team

OFFENSE

David Boston, Arizona	Wide Receiver
Terrell Owens, San Francisco	Wide Receiver
Tony Gonzalez, Kansas City	Tight End
Walter Jones, Seattle	Tackle
Orlando Pace, St. Louis	Tackle
Larry Allen, Dallas	Guard
Alan Faneca, Pittsburgh	Guard
Kevin Mawae, NY Jets	Center
Kurt Warner, St. Louis	Quarterback
Marshall Faulk, St. Louis	Running Back
Priest Holmes, Kansas City	Running Back

DEFENSE

John Abraham, NY Jets	Defensive End
Michael Strahan, NY Giants	Defensive End
Warren Sapp, Tampa Bay	Tackle
Ted Washington, Chicago	Tackle
Jason Gildon, Pittsburgh	Outside Linebacker
Jamir Miller, Cleaveland	Outside Linebacker
Ray Lewis, Baltimore	Inside Linebacker
Brian Urlacher, Chicago	Inside Linebacker
Ronde Barber, Tampa Bay	Cornerback
Aeneas Williams, St. Louis	Cornerback
Mike Brown, Chicago	Saftey
Brian Dawkins, Philadelphia	Saftey

SPECIALISTS

David Akers, Philadelphia	Kicker
Todd Sauerbrun, Carolina	Punter
Steve Smith, Carolina	Kick Returner

2001 AFC Team-by-Team Results

BALTIMORE RAVENS (10–6)

17	CHICAGO	6
10	at Cincinnati	21
20	at Denver	13
26	TENNESSEE	7
23	Green Bay	31
14	at Cleveland	24
18	JACKSONVILLE	17
13	at Pittsburgh	10
16	at Tennessee	10
17	CLEVELAND	27
24	at Jacksonville	21
39	INDIANAPOLIS	27
21	PITTSBURGH	26
16	CINCINNATI	0
10	at Tampa Bay	22
19	MINNESOTA	3
303		265

BUFFALO BILLS (3–13)

6	NEW ORLEANS	24
26	at Indianapolis	42
3	PITTSBURGH	20
36	NY JETS	42
13	at Jacksonville	10
24	at San Diego	27
14	INDIANAPOLIS	30
11	at New England	21
20	SEATTLE	23
27	MIAMI	34
0	at San Francisco	35
25	CAROLINA	24
9	NEW ENGLAND	12
30	at Atlanta	33
14	at NY Jets	9
7	at Miami	34
265		420

CINCINNATI BENGALS (6–10)

23	NEW ENGLAND	17
21	BALTIMORE	10
14	at San Diego	28
7	at Pittsburgh	16
24	CLEVELAND	14
0	CHICAGO	24
31	at Detroit	27
10	at Jacksonville	14
7	TENNESSEE	20
0	at Cleveland	18
13	TAMPA BAY	16
10	JACKSONVILLE	14
14	at NY Jets	15
0	at Baltimore	16
26	PITTSBURGH	23
23	at Tennessee	21
226		309

CLEVELAND BROWNS (7–9)

6	SEATTLE	9
24	DETROIT	14
23	at Jacksonville	14
20	SAN DIEGO	16
14	at Cincinnati	24
24	BALTIMORE	14
21	at Chicago	27
12	PITTSBURGH	15
27	at Baltimore	17
18	CINCINNATI	0
15	TENNESSEE	31
16	at New England	27
10	JACKSONVILLE	15
7	at Green Bay	30
41	at Tennessee	38
7	at Pittsburgh	28
285		319

DENVER BRONCOS (8–8)

31	NY GIANTS	20
38	at Arizona	17
13	BALTIMORE	20
20	KANSAS CITY	6
21	at Seattle	34
10	at San Diego	27
31	NEW ENGLAND	10
28	at Oakland	38
26	SAN DIEGO	16
10	WASHINGTON	17
26	at Dallas	24
10	at Miami	21
20	SEATTLE	7
23	at Kansas City	26
23	OAKLAND	17
10	at Indianapolis	29
340		**339**

INDIANAPOLIS COLTS (6–10)

45	at NY Jets	24
42	BUFFALO	26
13	at New England	44
18	OAKLAND	23
17	NEW ENGLAND	38
35	at Kansas City	28
30	at Buffalo	14
24	MIAMI	27
21	at New Orleans	40
21	SAN FRANCISCO	40
27	at Baltimore	39
6	at Miami	41
41	ATLANTA	27
28	NY JETS	29
17	at St. Louis	42
29	DENVER	10
413		**486**

JACKSONVILLE JAGUARS (6–10)

21	PITTSBURGH	3
13	TENNESSEE	6
14	CLEVELAND	23
15	at Seattle	24
10	BUFFALO	13
17	at Baltimore	18
24	at Tennessee	28
30	CINCINNATI	13
7	at Pittsburgh	20
21	BALTIMORE	24
21	GREEN BAY	28
14	at Cincinnati	10
15	at Cleveland	10
33	at Minnesota	3
26	KANSAS CITY	30
13	at Chicago	33
294		**286**

KANSAS CITY CHIEFS (6–10)

24	OAKLAND	27
3	NY GIANTS	13
45	at Washington	13
6	at Denver	20
17	PITTSBURGH	20
16	at Arizona	24
28	INDIANAPOLIS	35
25	at San Diego	20
7	at NY Jets	27
19	SEATTLE	7
10	PHILADELPHIA	23
26	at Oakland	28
26	DENVER	23
20	SAN DIEGO	17
30	at Jacksonville	26
18	at Seattle	21
320		**344**

MIAMI DOLPHINS (11–5)

31	at Tennessee	23
18	OAKLAND	15
10	at St. Louis	42
30	NEW ENGLAND	10
17	at NY Jets	21
24	at Seattle	20
23	CAROLINA	6
27	at Indianapolis	24
0	NY JETS	24
34	at Buffalo	27
21	DENVER	10
41	INDIANAPOLIS	6
0	at San Francisco	21
13	at New England	20
21	ATLANTA	14
34	BUFFALO	7
344		**290**

NEW ENGLAND PATRIOTS (11–5)

17	at Cincinnati	23
3	NY JETS	10
44	INDIANAPOLIS	13
10	at Miami	30
29	SAN DIEGO	26
38	at Indianapolis	17
20	at Denver	31
24	at Atlanta	10
21	BUFFALO	11
17	ST. LOUIS	24
34	NEW ORLEANS	17
17	at NY Jets	16
27	CLEVELAND	16
12	at Buffalo	9
20	MIAMI	13
38	at Carolina	6
371		**272**

NEW YORK JETS (10–6)

24	INDIANAPOLIS	45
10	at New England	3
17	SAN FRANCISCO	19
42	at Buffalo	36
21	MIAMI	17
14	ST. LOUIS	34
13	at Carolina	12
16	at New Orleans	9
27	KANSAS CITY	7
24	at Miami	0
16	NEW ENGLAND	17
7	at Pittsburgh	18
15	CINCINNATI	14
29	at Indianapolis	28
9	BUFFALO	14
24	at Oakland	22
308		**295**

OAKLAND RAIDERS (10–6)

27	at Kansas City	24
15	at Miami	18
38	SEATTLE	14
28	DALLAS	21
23	at Indianapolis	18
20	at Philadelphia	10
38	DENVER	28
27	at Seattle	34
34	SAN DIEGO	24
28	at NY Giants	10
31	ARIZONA	34
28	KANSAS CITY	26
13	at San Diego	6
10	TENNESSEE	13
17	at Denver	23
22	NY JETS	24
399		**327**

PITTSBURGH STEELERS (13–3)

3	at Jacksonville	21
20	at Buffalo	3
16	CINCINNATI	7
20	at Kansas City	17
17	at Tampa Bay	10
34	TENNESSEE	7
10	BALTIMORE	13
15	at Cleveland	12
20	JACKSONVILLE	7
34	at Tennessee	24
21	MINNESOTA	16
18	NY JETS	7
26	at Baltimore	21
47	DETROIT	14
23	at Cincinnati	26
28	CLEVELAND	7
352		**212**

SAN DIEGO CHARGERS (5–11)

30	WASHINGTON	3
32	at Dallas	21
28	CINCINNATI	14
16	at Cleveland	20
26	at New England	29
27	DENVER	10
27	BUFFALO	24
20	KANSAS CITY	25
16	at Denver	26
24	at Oakland	34
17	ARIZONA	20
10	at Seattle	13
14	at Philadelphia	24
6	OAKLAND	13
17	at Kansas City	20
22	SEATTLE	25
332		321

SEATTLE SEAHAWKS (9–7)

9	at Cleveland	6
3	PHILADELPHIA	27
14	at Oakland	38
24	JACKSONVILLE	15
34	DENVER	21
20	MIAMI	24
14	at Washington	27
34	OAKLAND	27
23	at Buffalo	20
7	at Kansas City	19
13	SAN DIEGO	10
7	at Denver	20
29	DALLAS	3
24	at NY Giants	27
25	at San Diego	22
21	KANSAS CITY	18
301		324

TENNESSEE TITANS (7–9)

23	MIAMI	31
6	at Jacksonville	13
7	at Baltimore	26
31	TAMPA BAY	28
27	at Detroit	24
7	at Pittsburgh	34
28	JACKSONVILLE	24
10	BALTIMORE	16
20	at Cincinnati	7
24	PITTSBURGH	34
31	at Cleveland	15
24	at Minnesota	42
26	GREEN BAY	20
13	at Oakland	10
38	CLEVELAND	41
21	CINCINNATI	23
336		388

2001 NFC Team-by-Team Results

ARIZONA CARDINALS (7–9)

17	DENVER	38
14	ATLANTA	34
21	at Philadelphia	20
13	at Chicago	20
24	KANSAS CITY	16
3	at Dallas	17
7	PHILADELPHIA	21
10	NY GIANTS	17
45	DETROIT	38
20	at San Diego	17
34	at Oakland	31
10	WASHINGTON	20
13	at NY Giants	17
17	DALLAS	10
30	at Carolina	7
17	at Washington	20
295		343

ATLANTA FALCONS (7–9)

13	at San Francisco	16
24	CAROLINA	16
34	at Arizona	14
3	CHICAGO	31
31	SAN FRANCISCO	37
20	at New Orleans	13
10	NEW ENGLAND	24
20	DALLAS	13
23	at Green Bay	20
10	at Carolina	7
6	ST. LOUIS	35
10	NEW ORLEANS	28
27	at Indianapolis	41
33	BUFFALO	30
14	at Miami	21
13	at St. Louis	31
291		377

CAROLINA PANTHERS (1–15)

24	at Minnesota	13
16	at Atlanta	24
7	GREEN BAY	28
14	at San Francisco	24
25	NEW ORLEANS	27
14	at Washington	17
12	NY JETS	13
6	at Miami	23
14	at St. Louis	48
22	SAN FRANCISCO	25
7	ATLANTA	10
23	at New Orleans	27
24	at Buffalo	25
32	ST. LOUIS	38
7	ARIZONA	30
6	NEW ENGLAND	38
253		410

CHICAGO BEARS (13–3)

6	at Baltimore	17
17	MINNESOTA	10
31	at Atlanta	3
20	ARIZONA	13
24	at Cincinnati	0
37	SAN FRANCISCO	31
27	CLEVELAND	21
12	GREEN BAY	20
27	at Tampa Bay	24
13	at Minnesota	6
13	DETROIT	10
7	at Green Bay	17
27	TAMPA BAY	3
20	at Washington	15
24	at Detroit	0
33	JACKSONVILLE	13
338		203

DALLAS COWBOYS (5–11)

6	TAMPA BAY	10
21	SAN DIEGO	32
18	at Philadelphia	40
21	at Oakland	28
9	WASHINGTON	7
17	ARIZONA	3
24	at NY Giants	27
13	at Atlanta	20
3	PHILADELPHIA	36
24	DENVER	26
20	at Washington	14
20	NY GIANTS	13
3	at Seattle	29
10	at Arizona	17
27	SAN FRANCISCO	21
10	at Detroit	15
246		338

DETROIT LIONS (2–14)

6	at Green Bay	28
14	at Cleveland	24
0	ST. LOUIS	35
26	at Minnesota	31
24	TENNESSEE	27
27	CINCINNATI	31
13	at San Francisco	31
17	TAMPA BAY	20
38	at Arizona	45
27	GREEN BAY	29
10	at Chicago	13
12	at Tampa Bay	15
27	MINNESOTA	24
14	at Pittsburgh	47
0	CHICAGO	24
15	DALLAS	10
270		424

GREEN BAY PACKERS (12–4)

28	DETROIT	6
37	WASHINGTON	0
28	at Carolina	7
10	at Tampa Bay	14
31	BALTIMORE	23
13	at Minnesota	35
21	TAMPA BAY	20
20	at Chicago	12
20	Atlanta	23
29	at Detroit	27
28	at Jacksonville	21
17	CHICAGO	7
20	at Tennessee	26
30	CLEVELAND	7
24	MINNESOTA	13
34	at NY Giants	25
390		**266**

MINNESOTA VIKINGS (5–11)

13	CAROLINA	24
10	at Chicago	17
20	TAMPA BAY	16
15	at New Orleans	28
31	DETROIT	26
35	GREEN BAY	13
14	at Tampa Bay	41
17	at Philadelphia	48
28	NY GIANTS	16
6	CHICAGO	13
16	at Pittsburgh	21
42	TENNESSEE	24
24	at Detroit	27
3	JACKSONVILLE	33
13	at Green Bay	24
3	at Baltimore	19
290		**390**

NEW ORLEANS SAINTS (7–9)

24	at Buffalo	6
13	at NY Giants	21
28	MINNESOTA	15
27	at Carolina	25
13	ATLANTA	20
34	at St. Louis	31
9	NY JETS	16
27	at San Francisco	28
34	INDIANAPOLIS	20
17	at New England	34
27	CAROLINA	23
28	at Atlanta	10
21	ST. LOUIS	34
21	at Tampa Bay	48
10	WASHINGTON	40
0	SAN FRANCISCO	38
333		**409**

NEW YORK GIANTS (7–9)

20	at Denver	31
13	at Kansas City	3
21	NEW ORLEANS	13
23	WASHINGTON	9
14	at St. Louis	15
9	PHILADELPHIA	10
21	at Washington	35
27	DALLAS	24
17	at Arizona	10
16	at Minnesota	28
10	OAKLAND	28
13	at Dallas	20
17	ARIZONA	13
27	SEATTLE	24
21	at Philadelphia	24
25	GREEN BAY	34
294		**321**

PHILADELPHIA EAGLES (11–5)

17	ST. LOUIS	20
27	at Seattle	3
40	DALLAS	18
20	ARIZONA	21
10	at NY Giants	9
10	OAKLAND	20
21	at Arizona	7
48	MINNESOTA	17
36	at Dallas	3
3	WASHINGTON	13
23	at Kansas City	10
24	SAN DIEGO	14
20	at Washington	6
3	at San Francisco	13
24	NY GIANTS	21
17	at Tampa Bay	13
343		**208**

ST. LOUIS RAMS (14–2)

20	at Philadelphia	17
30	at San Francisco	26
42	MIAMI	10
35	at Detroit	0
15	NY GIANTS	14
34	at NY Jets	14
31	NEW ORLEANS	34
48	CAROLINA	14
24	at New England	17
17	TAMPA BAY	24
35	at Atlanta	6
27	SAN FRANCISCO	14
34	at New Orleans	21
38	at Carolina	32
42	INDIANAPOLIS	17
31	ATLANTA	13
503		**273**

SAN FRANCISCO 49ERS (12–4)

16	ATLANTA	13
26	ST. LOUIS	30
19	at NY Jets	17
24	CAROLINA	14
37	at Atlanta	31
31	at Chicago	37
21	DETROIT	13
28	NEW ORLEANS	27
25	at Carolina	22
40	at Indianapolis	21
35	BUFFALO	0
14	at St. Louis	27
21	MIAMI	0
13	PHILADELPHIA	3
21	at Dallas	27
38	at New Orleans	0
409		**282**

TAMPA BAY BUCCANEERS (9–7)

10	at Dallas	6
16	at Minnesota	20
14	GREEN BAY	10
28	at Tennessee	31
10	PITTSBURGH	17
41	MINNESOTA	14
20	at Green Bay	21
20	at Detroit	17
24	CHICAGO	27
24	at St. Louis	17
16	at Cincinnati	13
15	DETROIT	12
3	at Chicago	27
48	NEW ORLEANS	21
22	BALTIMORE	10
13	PHILADELPHIA	17
324		**280**

WASHINGTON REDSKINS (8–8)

3	at San Diego	30
0	at Green Bay	37
13	KANSAS CITY	45
9	at NY Giants	23
7	at Dallas	9
17	CAROLINA	14
35	NY GIANTS	21
27	SEATTLE	14
17	at Denver	10
13	at Philadelphia	3
14	DALLAS	20
20	at Arizona	10
6	PHILADELPHIA	20
15	CHICAGO	20
40	at New Orleans	10
20	ARIZONA	17
256		**303**

American Football Conference
Scoring

TOUCHDOWNS	TD	Rush	Rec	Ret	Pts	KICKING	PAT	FG	Lg	Pts
Alexander, Sea	16	14	2	0	96	Vanderjagt, Ind	41/42	28/34	52	125
Harrison, Ind	15	0	15	0	90	Elam, Den	31/31	31/36	50	124
Smith, NE	13	12	1	0	78	Brown, Pitt	34/37	30/44	55	124
Dillon, Cin	13	10	3	0	78	Vinatieri, NE	41/42	24/30	54	113
Smith, Den	11	0	11	1	68	Janikowski, Oak	42/42	23/28	52	111
Mason, Tenn	10	0	9	1	62	Peterson, KC	27/28	27/35	51	108
Brown, Oak	10	0	9	0	60	Hall, NYJ	32/32	24/31	53	104
Martin, NYJ	10	10	0	0	60	Stover, Balt	24/24	26/31	49	102
Holmes, KC	10	8	2	0	60	Mare, Mia	39/40	19/21	46	96
Mack, Jax	10	9	1	0	60	Dawson, Clev	29/30	22/25	48	95
Tomlinson, SD	10	10	0	0	60					
Rhodes, Ind	10	9	0	0	60					

Passing

	Att	Comp	Pct Comp	Yds	Avg Gain	TD	Pct TD	Int	Pct Int	Lg	Rating Pts
Gannon, Oak	549	361	65.8	3828	6.97	27	4.9	9	1.6	49	95.5
McNair, Tenn	431	264	61.3	3350	7.77	21	4.9	12	2.8	t71	90.2
Brady, NE	413	264	63.9	2843	6.88	18	4.4	12	2.9	t91	86.5
Manning, Ind	547	343	62.7	4131	7.55	26	4.8	23	4.2	t86	84.1
Brunell, Jax	473	289	61.1	3309	7.00	19	4.0	13	2.7	44	84.1
Stewart, Pitt	442	266	60.2	3109	7.03	14	3.2	11	2.5	t90	81.7
Fiedler, Mia	450	273	60.7	3290	7.31	20	4.4	19	4.2	t74	80.3
Griese, Den	451	275	61.0	2827	6.27	23	5.1	19	4.2	t65	78.5
Van Pelt, Buff	307	178	58.0	2056	6.70	12	3.9	11	3.6	t80	76.4
Testaverde, NYJ	441	260	59.0	2752	6.24	15	3.4	7	3.2	t40	75.3

Pass Receiving

RECEPTIONS	No.	Yds	Avg	Lg	TD	YARDS	Yds	No.	Avg	Lg	TD
R. Smith, Den	113	1343	11.9	t65	11	Harrison, Ind	1524	109	14.0	68	15
J. Smith, Jax	112	1373	12.3	t35	8	J. Smith, Jax	1373	112	12.3	35	8
Harrison, Ind	109	1524	14.0	68	15	R. Smith, Den	1343	113	11.9	65	11
Tr. Brown, NE	101	1199	11.9	t60	5	Tr. Brown, NE	1199	101	11.9	60	5
Ward, Pitt	94	1003	10.7	34	4	Ti. Brown, Oak	1165	91	12.8	46	9
McCardell, Jax	93	1110	11.9	45	6	Rice, Oak	1139	83	13.7	40	9
Ti. Brown, Oak	91	1165	12.8	t46	9	Mason, Tenn	1128	73	15.5	71	9
Johnson, Clev	84	1097	13.1	t55	9	Conway, SD	1125	71	15.8	72	6
Rice, Oak	83	1139	13.7	t40	9	McCardell, Jax	1110	93	11.9	45	6
Centers, Buff	80	620	7.8	26	2	Johnson, Clev	1097	84	13.1	55	9

Rushing

	Att	Yds	Avg	Lg	TD
Holmes, KC	327	1555	4.8	41	8
Martin, NYJ	333	1513	4.5	47	10
Alexander, Sea	309	1318	4.3	t88	14
Dillon, Cin	340	1315	3.9	t96	10
Tomlinson, SD	339	1236	3.6	54	10
Smith, NE	287	1157	4.0	44	12
Rhodes, Ind	233	1104	4.7	t77	9
Bettis, Pitt	225	1072	4.8	48	4
Smith, Mia	313	968	3.1	25	6
George, Tenn	315	939	3.0	27	5

Total Yards from Scrimmage

	Total	Rush	Rec
Holmes, KC	2169	1555	614
Martin, NYJ	1823	1495	328
Alexander, Sea	1661	1318	343
Tomlinson, SD	1603	1236	367
Dillon, Cin	1543	1315	228
Harrison, Ind	1527	3	1524
Garner, Oak	1417	839	578
J. Smith, Jax	1370	-3	1373
R. Smith, Den	1370	27	1343
A. Smith, NE	1349	1157	192

Interceptions

	No.	Yds	Lg	TD
Henry, Clev	10	177	t97	1
O'Neal, Den	9	115	42	0
McNeil, SD	8	55	33	0

Six tied with five.

Sacks

Boulware, Balt	15.0
Miller, Clev	13.0
Abraham, NYJ	13.0
Wiley, SD	13.0
Gildon, Pitt	12.0

American Football Conference (Cont.)

Punting

	No.	Yds	Avg	Net Avg	TB	In 20	Lg	Blk	Ret	Ret Yds
Lechler, Oak	73	3375	46.2	39.4	12	23	65	1	34	502
Rouen, Den	81	3668	45.3	38.9	8	25	64	1	48	517
Smith, Ind	68	3023	44.5	37.3	12	12	65	0	35	486
Feagles, Sea	85	3730	43.9	38.4	7	26	68	1	43	462
Hanson, Jax	82	3577	43.6	40.0	12	24	59	0	38	295

Punt Returns

	No.	Yds	Avg	Lg	TD
Brown, NE	29	413	14.2	t85	2
O'Neal, Den	31	405	13.1	t86	1
J. Lewis, Bal	39	496	12.7	62	0
Ogden, Mia	32	377	11.8	48	0
Dwight, SD	24	271	11.3	t84	1

Kickoff Returns

	No.	Yds	Avg	Lg	TD
Jenkins, SD	58	1541	26.6	t93	2
J. Lewis, Balt	41	1011	24.7	76	0
Cole, Den	48	1127	23.5	52	0
Kirby, Oak	46	1066	23.2	t90	1
Edwards, Pitt	20	462	23.1	81	0

National Football Conference

Scoring

TOUCHDOWNS	TD	Rush	Rec	Ret	Pts
Faulk, StL	21	12	9	0	128
Owens, SF	16	0	16	0	96
Alstott, TB	11	10	1	0	70
Green, GB	11	9	2	0	66
Moss, Minn	10	0	10	0	60
Franks, GB	9	0	9	0	54
Schroeder, GB	9	0	9	0	54
Horn, NO	9	0	9	0	54
Boston, Ariz	8	0	8	0	48
Booker, Chi	8	0	8	0	48

KICKING	PAT	FG	Lg	Pts
Wilkins, StL	58/58	23/29	54	127
Akers, Phil	37/38	26/31	50	115
Feely, Atl	28/28	29/37	55	115
Carney, NO	32/32	27/31	50	113
Edinger, Chi	34/34	26/21	48	112
Longwell, GB	44/45	20/31	54	104
Cortez, SF	47/47	18/25	52	101
Conway, Wash	22/22	26/33	55	100
Andersen, NYG	29/30	23/28	51	98
Gramatica, TB	28/28	23/29	49	97

Passing

	Att	Comp	Pct Comp	Yds	Avg Gain	TD	Pct TD	Int	Pct Int	Lg	Rating Pts
Warner, StL	546	375	68.7	4830	8.85	36	6.6	22	4.0	t65	101.4
Garcia, SF	504	316	62.7	3538	7.02	32	6.3	12	2.4	t61	94.8
Favre, GB	510	314	61.6	3921	7.69	32	6.3	15	2.9	t67	94.1
McNabb, Phil	493	285	57.8	3233	6.56	25	5.1	12	2.4	t64	84.3
Chandler, Atl	365	223	61.1	2847	7.80	16	4.4	14	3.8	t94	84.1
Culpepper, Minn	366	235	64.2	2612	7.14	14	3.8	13	3.6	t57	83.3
Plummer, Ariz	525	304	57.9	3653	6.96	18	3.4	14	2.7	t68	79.6
Johnson, TB	559	340	60.8	3406	6.09	13	2.3	11	2.0	47	77.7
Collins, Phil	568	327	57.6	3764	6.63	19	3.3	16	2.8	76	77.1
Batch, Det	341	198	58.1	2392	7.01	12	3.5	12	3.5	76	76.8

Pass Receiving

RECEPTIONS	No.	Yds	Avg	Lg	TD
Johnson, TB	106	1266	11.9	47	1
Booker, Chi	100	1071	10.7	t66	8
Boston, Ariz	98	1598	16.3	t61	8
Owens, SF	93	1412	15.2	t60	16
Horn, NO	83	1265	15.2	56	9
Faulk, StL	83	765	9.2	t65	9
Holt, StL	81	1363	16.8	51	7
Jackson, NO	81	1046	12.9	63	5
Moss, Minn	80	1224	15.3	t73	10
Morton, Det	77	1154	15.0	76	4

YARDS	Yds	No.	Avg	Lg	TD
Boston, Ariz	1598	98	16.3	t61	8
Owens, SF	1412	93	15.2	t60	16
Holt, StL	1363	81	16.8	51	7
Johnson, TB	1266	106	11.9	47	1
Horn, NO	1265	83	15.2	56	9
Moss, Minn	1224	80	15.3	t73	10
Morton, Det	1154	77	15.0	76	4
Bruce, StL	1106	64	17.3	t51	6
Booker, Chi	1071	100	10.7	t66	8
Toomer, NYG	1054	72	14.6	t60	5

National Football Conference (Cont.)

Rushing

	Att	Yds	Avg	Lg	TD
Davis, Was	356	1432	4.0	32	5
Green, GB	304	1387	4.6	83	9
Faulk, StL	260	1382	5.3	71	12
Williams, NO	313	1245	4.0	46	6
Hearst, SF	252	1206	4.8	43	4
Thomas,Chi	278	1183	4.3	46	7
Smith, Dall	261	1021	3.9	44	3
Barber, NYG	166	865	5.2	36	4
Pittman, Ariz	241	846	3.5	42	5
Smith, Atl	237	760	3.2	586	5

Total Yards from Scrimmage

	Total	Rush	Rec
Faulk, StL	2147	1382	765
Green, GB	1981	1385	596
Williams, NO	1934	1245	511
Boston, Ariz	1633	35	1598
Davis, Wash	1624	1419	205
Hearst, SF	1553	1206	347
Barber, NYG	1433	865	577
Owens, SF	1433	21	1412
Holt, StL	1363	0	1363
Thomas, Chi	1361	1183	178

Interceptions

	No.	Yds	Lg	TD
Barber, TB	10	86	36	1
Lassiter, Ariz	9	80	25	0
Evans, Car	8	126	49	1
Plummer, SF	7	45	24	0
Bronson, SF	7	165	97	2

Four tied with six.

Sacks

Strahan, NYG	22.5
Little, StL	14.5
Clemons, NO	13.5
Gbaja-Biamila, GB	13.5
Kerney, Atl	12.0

Punting

	No.	Yds	Avg	Net Avg	TB	In 20	Lg	Blk	Ret	Ret Yds
Sauerbrun, Car	93	4419	47.5	38.9	17	35	73	0	42	425
Berger, Minn	47	2046	43.5	32.9	10	10	67	0	25	302
Landeta, Phil	97	4221	43.5	36.4	10	26	64	0	56	488
Jett, Det	58	2512	43.3	35.5	6	16	62	0	30	332
Williams, NYG	91	3905	42.9	35.4	8	25	90	0	43	521

Punt Returns

	No.	Yds	Avg	Lg	TD
Gordon, Atl	31	437	14.1	74	0
Swinton, Dall	31	414	13.4	t65	1
Metcalf, Was	33	412	12.5	t89	1
Mitchell, Phil	39	467	12.0	54	0
Jackson, Ariz	40	461	11.5	55	0

Kickoff Returns

	No.	Yds	Avg	Lg	TD
Smith, Car	56	1431	25.6	t99	2
Howard, Det	57	1446	25.4	91	0
Mitchell, Phil	41	1025	25.0	t94	1
Vaughn, Atl	61	1491	24.4	t96	1
McAllister, NO	45	1091	24.2	63	0

2001 NFL Team Leaders

AFC Total Offense

	Total Yds	Yds Rush	Yds Pass	Time of Poss	Pts/ Game
Indianapolis	5955	1966	3989	30:32	25.8
Pittsburgh	5887	2774	3113	34:10	22.0
Kansas City	5673	2008	3665	29:07	20.0
Oakland	5361	1654	3707	30:56	24.9
Tennessee	5352	1794	3558	31:29	21.0
San Diego	5200	1695	3505	30:15	20.8
Buffalo	5137	1686	3451	29:00	16.6
Baltimore	5124	1810	3314	29:39	18.9
New England	4882	1793	3089	30:48	23.2
Jacksonville	4840	1600	3240	28:01	18.4
Miami	4821	1664	3157	30:04	21.5
Denver	4817	1877	2940	31:23	21.3
Cincinnati	4800	1712	3088	29:16	14.1
NY Jets	4795	2054	2741	29:13	19.3
Seattle	4772	1936	2836	29:51	18.8
Cleveland	4152	1351	2801	28:16	17.8

AFC Total Defense

	Opp Total Yds	Opp Yds Rush	Opp Yds Pass	PA/ Game
Pittsburgh	4137	1195	2942	13.3
Baltimore	4446	1411	3035	16.6
Miami	4608	1779	2829	18.1
Denver	4774	1492	3282	21.2
Cincinnati	4832	1675	3157	19.3
San Diego	4904	1504	3400	20.1
Jacksonville	5070	1611	3459	17.9
Oakland	5071	1988	3083	20.4
NY Jets	5153	2154	2999	19.3
Seattle	5206	1721	3485	20.3
Buffalo	5292	2133	3159	26.3
Cleveland	5297	2208	3089	19.9
Kansas City	5304	2140	3164	21.5
New England	5352	1855	3497	17.0
Tennessee	5515	1431	4084	24.3
Indianapolis	5715	2115	3600	30.4

NFC Total Offense

	Total Yds	Yds Rush	Yds Pass	Time of Poss	Pts/Game
St. Louis	6690	2027	4663	31:45	31.4
San Francisco	5689	2244	3445	31:49	25.6
Green Bay	5463	1693	3770	29:32	24.4
NY Giants	5335	1777	3558	29:43	18.4
New Orleans	5226	1712	3514	29:24	20.8
Minnesota	5185	1609	3576	29:11	18.1
Atlanta	5070	1762	3308	31:18	18.2
Detroit	4994	1398	3596	28:34	16.9
Philadelphia	4923	1778	3145	28:39	21.4
Arizona	4898	1449	3449	27:45	18.4
Tampa Bay	4694	1371	3323	31:40	20.3
Chicago	4694	1742	2952	30:35	21.1
Washington	4435	1948	2487	30:15	16.0
Dallas	4402	2184	2218	30:13	15.4
Carolina	4402	2184	2218	30:13	15.4

NFC Total Defense

	Opp Total Yds	Opp Yds Rush	Opp Yds Pass	PA/Game
St. Louis	4471	1374	3097	17.1
Dallas	4599	1710	2889	21.1
Tampa Bay	4653	1702	2951	17.5
Philadelphia	4701	1837	2864	13.0
Washington	4846	1869	2977	18.9
Green Bay	4937	1769	3168	16.6
San Francisco	4954	1571	3383	17.6
NY Giants	4975	1545	3430	20.1
Chicago	4978	1313	3665	12.7
New Orleans	5070	1715	3355	25.6
Detroit	5521	1993	3528	26.5
Minnesota	5666	2299	3367	24.4
Arizona	5685	2087	3598	21.4
Atlanta	5845	1943	3902	18.2
Carolina	5943	2301	3642	15.8

Takeaways/Giveaways

American Football Conference

	Takeaways			Giveaways			Net Diff
	Int	Fum	Total	Int	Fum	Total	
NY Jets	20	19	39	14	22	21	18
Denver	22	15	37	19	24	27	10
Cleveland	33	8	41	21	24	33	8
New England	22	13	35	15	29	28	7
Pittsburgh	16	12	28	12	28	21	7
Seattle	14	13	27	12	24	21	6
San Diego	19	12	31	18	26	29	2
Oakland	17	7	24	9	27	25	-1
Jacksonville	12	12	24	14	29	27	-3
Tennessee	13	11	24	17	18	24	-4
Kansas City	13	13	26	24	19	33	-7
Baltimore	16	12	28	20	31	36	-8
Cincinnati	13	15	28	26	28	37	-9
Miami	17	11	28	19	26	38	-10
Indianapolis	15	10	25	23	20	38	-13
Buffalo	11	8	19	20	26	33	-14

National Football Conference

	Takeaways			Giveaways			Net Diff
	Int	Fum	Total	Int	Fum	Total	
Tampa Bay	28	11	39	12	20	22	17
San Francisco	24	10	34	12	19	19	15
Chicago	20	17	37	16	21	24	13
Green Bay	20	19	39	15	28	27	12
Philadelphia	14	19	33	14	20	24	9
Washington	23	11	34	13	33	28	6
Atlanta	18	12	30	17	27	28	2
Carolina	24	11	35	22	33	35	0
NY Giants	15	13	28	16	41	29	-1
Arizona	17	6	23	14	26	27	-4
New Orleans	15	15	30	22	35	35	-5
Dallas	9	16	25	20	25	34	-9
St. Louis	21	13	34	22	38	44	-10
Detroit	16	6	22	24	24	38	-16
Minnesota	8	9	17	23	35	39	-22

Conference Rankings

American Football Conference

	Offense			Defense		
	Total	Rush	Pass	Total	Rush	Pass
Baltimore	8	7	7	2	2	4
Buffalo	7	12	6	11	13	28
Cincinnati	13	10	12	5	7	7
Cleveland	16	16	15	12	16	6
Denver	12	6	13	4	4	10
Indianapolis	1	4	1	16	12	15
Jacksonville	10	15	8	7	6	12
Kansas City	3	3	3	13	14	9
Miami	11	13	9	3	9	1
New England	9	9	11	14	10	14
NY Jets	14	2	16	9	15	3
Oakland	4	14	2	8	11	5
Pittsburgh	2	1	10	1	1	2
San Diego	6	11	5	6	5	11
Seattle	15	5	14	10	8	13
Tennessee	5	8	4	15	3	16

National Football Conference

	Offense			Defense		
	Total	Rush	Pass	Total	Rush	Pass
Arizona	10	10	7	13	13	12
Atlanta	7	7	10	14	11	15
Carolina	15	14	13	15	15	13
Chicago	11	8	12	9	1	14
Dallas	14	2	15	2	6	2
Detroit	8	13	3	11	12	11
Green Bay	3	10	2	6	8	6
Minnesota	6	11	4	12	14	8
New Orleans	5	9	6	10	7	7
NY Giants	4	6	5	8	3	10
Philadelphia	9	5	11	4	9	1
St. Louis	1	3	1	1	2	5
San Francisco	2	1	8	7	4	9
Tampa Bay	11	15	9	3	5	3
Washington	13	4	14	5	10	4

Baltimore Ravens

SCORING	Rush	TD Rec	Ret	PAT	FG	S	Pts
Stover	0	0	0	25/25	30/35	0	115
Ismail	0	7	0	1	0	0	44
Brookins	5	0	0	0	0	0	30

RUSHING	No.	Yds	Avg	Lg	TD
Allen	168	658	3.9	26	3
Brookins	151	551	3.6	25	5
Williams	65	291	4.5	55	0

PASSING	Att	Comp	Pct Comp	Yds	Avg Gain	TD	Int	Rating Pts
Grbac	467	265	56.7	3033	6.49	15	18	71.1
C'ningham	89	54	60.7	573	6.44	3	2	81.3

RECEIVING	No.	Yds	Avg	Lg	TD
Ismail	74	1059	14.3	77	7
Sharpe	73	811	11.1	37	2
Taylor	42	560	13.3	63	3
Stokley	24	344	14.3	46	2
Williams	23	210	9.1	45	0

INTERCEPTIONS: Starks, 4

PUNTING	No.	Yds	Avg	Net Avg	TB	In 20	Lg	Blk
Richard'n	85	3307	38.9	33.6	10	29	65	0

SACKS: Boulware, 15

Buffalo Bills

SCORING	Rush	TD Rec	Ret	PAT	FG	S	Pts
Arians	0	0	0	16/17	12/21	0	52
Price	0	7	0	0	0	0	42
Moulds	0	5	0	0	0	0	32
Graham	0	0	0	7/7	6/8	0	25

RUSHING	No.	Yds	Avg	Lg	TD
Henry	213	729	3.4	25	4
Bryson	80	341	4.3	68	2

PASSING	Att	Comp	Pct Comp	Yds	Avg Gain	TD	Int	Rating Pts
Van Pelt	307	178	58.0	2056	6.70	12	11	76.4
Johnson	216	134	62.0	1465	6.78	5	2	76.3

RECEIVING	No.	Yds	Avg	Lg	TD
Moulds	67	904	13.5	80	5
Price	55	895	16.3	70	7
Centers	80	620	7.8	26	2
Riemersma	53	590	11.1	36	3

INTERCEPTIONS: Clements, 3

PUNTING	No.	Yds	Avg	Net Avg	TB	In 20	Lg	Blk
Moorman	80	3264	40.8	33.8	7	16	66	0

SACKS: Schobel, 6.5

Cincinnati Bengals

SCORING	Rush	TD Rec	Ret	PAT	FG	S	Pts
Dillon	10	3	0	0	0	0	78
Rackers	0	0	0	23/24	17/28	0	74
Dugans	0	2	0	1	0	0	14
Scott	0	2	0	0	0	0	12

RUSHING	No.	Yds	Avg	Lg	TD
Dillon	340	1315	3.9	96	10
Bennett	50	232	4.6	36	0
Kitna	27	73	2.7	20	1
Keaton	15	20	9.6	21	0

PASSING	Att	Comp	Pct Comp	Yds	Avg Gain	TD	Int	Rating Pts
Kitna	581	313	53.9	3216	5.54	12	22	61.1
Smith	8	5	62.5	37	4.63	0	0	73.4

RECEIVING	No.	Yds	Avg	Lg	TD
Scott	57	819	14.4	49	2
Warrick	70	667	9.5	33	1
Johnson	28	329	11.8	28	1
Dugans	28	251	9.0	31	2

INTERCEPTIONS: Hawkins and Kaesviharn, 3

PUNTING	No.	Yds	Avg	Net Avg	TB	In 20	Lg	Blk
Harris	84	3368	40.1	33.9	6	21	57	0

SACKS: Wilson, 9

Cleveland Browns

SCORING	Rush	TD Rec	Ret	PAT	FG	S	Pts
Dawson	0	0	0	29/30	22/25	0	95
Johnson	0	9	0	0	0	0	54
White	5	1	0	1	0	0	38

RUSHING	No.	Yds	Avg	Lg	TD
Jackson	195	554	2.8	22	2
White	126	443	3.5	51	5

PASSING	Att	Comp	Pct Comp	Yds	Avg Gain	TD	Int	Rating Pts
Couch	454	272	59.9	3040	6.70	17	21	73.1
Holcomb	12	7	58.3	114	9.50	1	0	118.1

RECEIVING	No.	Yds	Avg	Lg	TD
Johnson	84	1097	13.1	55	9
Morgan	30	432	14.4	78	2
White	44	418	9.5	45	1
Dawson	22	281	12.8	44	1
Northcutt	18	211	11.7	26	0

INTERCEPTIONS: Henry, 10

PUNTING	No.	Yds	Avg	Net Avg	TB	In 20	Lg	Blk
Gardocki	99	4247	42.9	34.6	9	25	69	0

SACKS: Miller, 13

Denver Broncos

SCORING		TD					
	Rush	Rec	Ret	PAT	FG	S	Pts
Elam	0	0	0	31/31	31/36	0	124
R. Smith	0	11	0	0	0	0	68
Clark	0	6	0	0	0	0	36
Anderson	4	0	0	1	0	0	26
Carswell	0	4	0	1	0	0	26

RUSHING	No.	Yds	Avg	Lg	TD
Davis	167	701	4.2	57	0
Anderson	175	678	3.9	62	4

PASSING	Att	Comp	Pct Comp	Yds	Avg Gain	TD	Int	Rating Pts
Griese	451	275	61.0	2837	6.29	23	19	78.5
Frerotte	48	30	62.5	308	6.42	3	0	101.7

RECEIVING	No.	Yds	Avg	Lg	TD
R. Smith	113	1343	11.9	65	11
Clark	51	566	11.1	39	6
Carswell	34	299	8.8	25	4
Kennison	15	169	11.3	36	1
Cole	9	128	14.2	21	0
Hape	11	99	9.0	23	0

INTERCEPTIONS: O'Neal, 9

PUNTING	No.	Yds	Avg	Net Avg	TB	In 20	Lg	Blk
Rouen	81	3669	45.3	36.5	8	25	64	0

SACKS: Pryce and Romanowski, 7

Indianapolis Colts

SCORING		TD					
	Rush	Rec	Ret	PAT	FG	S	Pts
Vanderjagt	0	0	0	41/42	28/34	0	125
Harrison	0	15	0	0	0	0	90
Rhodes	9	0	1	0	0	0	60
Pollard	0	8	0	0	0	0	48

RUSHING	No.	Yds	Avg	Lg	TD
Rhodes	233	1104	4.7	77	9
James	151	662	4.4	29	3

PASSING	Att	Comp	Pct Comp	Yds	Avg Gain	TD	Int	Rating Pts
Manning	547	343	62.7	4131	7.55	26	23	84.1

RECEIVING	No.	Yds	Avg	Lg	TD
Harrison	109	1524	14.0	68	15
Pollard	47	739	15.7	86	8
Wayne	27	345	12.8	43	0
Dilger	34	343	10.7	44	1

INTERCEPTIONS: Burris and Macklin, 3

PUNTING	No.	Yds	Avg	Net Avg	TB	In 20	Lg	Blk
Smith	68	3026	44.5	33.8	12	12	65	0

SACKS: Bratzke, 8.5

Jacksonville Jaguars

SCORING		TD					
	Rush	Rec	Ret	PAT	FG	S	Pts
Hollis	0	0	0	29/31	18/28	0	83
Mack	9	1	0	0	0	0	60
Smith	0	8	0	0	0	0	48
McCardell	0	6	0	1	0	0	38

RUSHING	No.	Yds	Avg	Lg	TD
Mack	213	877	4.1	54	9
Joseph	68	294	4.3	27	0
Brunell	39	224	5.7	38	1

PASSING	Att	Comp	Pct Comp	Yds	Avg Gain	TD	Int	Rating Pts
Brunell	473	289	61.1	3309	7.00	19	13	84.1
Quinn	61	31	52.5	361	5.92	1	1	69.1

RECEIVING	No.	Yds	Avg	Lg	TD
Smith	112	1373	12.3	35	8
McCardell	93	1110	11.9	45	6
Brady	36	386	10.7	20	2
Dawkins	20	234	11.7	28	0
Joseph	18	183	10.2	29	2

INTERCEPTIONS: Stewart and Beasley, 3

PUNTING	No.	Yds	Avg	Net Avg	TB	In 20	Lg	Blk
Hanson	82	3575	43.6	37.1	12	24	59	0

SACKS: Walker, 7.5

Kansas City Chiefs

SCORING		TD					
	Rush	Rec	Ret	PAT	FG	S	Pts
Peterson	0	0	0	27/28	27/35	0	108
Holmes	8	2	0	0	0	0	60
Richardson	7	0	0	0	0	0	42
Gonzalez	0	6	0	1	0	0	38

RUSHING	No.	Yds	Avg	Lg	TD
Holmes	327	1555	4.8	41	8
Richardson	66	191	2.9	19	7
Green	35	158	4.5	16	0

PASSING	Att	Comp	Pct Comp	Yds	Avg Gain	TD	Int	Rating Pts
Green	523	296	56.6	3783	7.23	17	24	71.1

RECEIVING	No.	Yds	Avg	Lg	TD
Gonzalez	73	917	12.6	36	6
Holmes	62	614	9.9	67	2
Minnis	33	511	15.5	56	1
Alexander	27	470	17.4	46	3
Kennison	16	322	20.1	65	0

INTERCEPTIONS: Warfield, 4

PUNTING	No.	Yds	Avg	Net Avg	TB	In 20	Lg	Blk
Stryzinski	73	2978	40.8	35.6	5	27	76	0
Peterson	2	61	30.5	25.0	0	0	34	0

SACKS: Hicks, 3.5

Miami Dolphins

SCORING	Rush	Rec	Ret	PAT	FG	S	Pts
Mare	0	0	0	39/40	19/21	0	96
Smith	6	2	0	0	0	0	48
Chambers	0	7	0	0	0	0	42
Fiedler	4	0	0	0	0	0	24

RUSHING	No.	Yds	Avg	Lg	TD
Smith	313	968	3.1	25	6
Fiedler	73	321	4.4	26	4
Minor	59	281	4.8	56	2

PASSING	Att	Comp	Pct Comp	Yds	Avg Gain	TD	Int	Rating Pts
Fiedler	450	273	60.7	3290	7.15	20	19	80.3
Lucas	3	2	66.7	45	15.00	0	0	109.7

RECEIVING	No.	Yds	Avg	Lg	TD
McKnight	55	684	12.4	74	3
Gadsden	55	674	12.3	61	3
Chambers	48	883	18.4	74	7
Smith	30	234	7.8	65	2
Minor	29	263	9.1	29	1

INTERCEPTIONS: Marion, 5

PUNTING	No.	Yds	Avg	Net Avg	TB	In 20	Lg	Blk
Mare	81	3321	41.0	37.6	7	28	77	0

SACKS: Taylor, 8.5

New England Patriots

SCORING	Rush	Rec	Ret	PAT	FG	S	Pts
Vinatieri	0	0	0	41/42	24/30	0	113
Smith	12	1	0	0	0	0	78
Brown	0	5	2	0	0	0	42
Patten	1	4	0	0	0	0	30

RUSHING	No.	Yds	Avg	Lg	TD
Smith	287	1157	4.0	44	12
Faulk	41	169	4.1	24	1
Edwards	51	141	2.8	14	1
Redmond	35	119	3.4	16	0

PASSING	Att	Comp	Pct Comp	Yds	Avg Gain	TD	Int	Rating Pts
Brady	413	264	63.9	2843	6.88	18	12	86.5
Bledsoe	66	40	60.6	400	6.06	2	2	75.3

RECEIVING	No.	Yds	Avg	Lg	TD
Brown	101	1199	11.9	60	5
Patten	51	749	14.7	91	4
Faulk	30	189	6.3	28	1
Edwards	25	166	6.6	17	2

INTERCEPTIONS: Smith, 5

PUNTING	No.	Yds	Avg	Net Avg	TB	In 20	Lg	Blk
Walter	81	1964	40.1	38.1	2	24	58	0
Johnson	24	1045	43.5	38.3	3	3	76	0

SACKS: Hamilton, 7.0

New York Jets

SCORING	Rush	Rec	Ret	PAT	FG	S	Pts
Hall	0	0	0	32/32	24/31	0	104
Martin	10	0	0	0	0	0	60
Coles	0	7	0	0	0	0	42
Becht	0	5	0	0	0	0	30

RUSHING	No.	Yds	Avg	Lg	TD
Martin	333	1513	4.5	47	10
Jordan	39	292	7.5	46	1
Coles	10	108	10.8	20	0
Anderson	26	102	3.9	12	0
Testaverde	31	25	0.8	12	0

PASSING	Att	Comp	Pct Comp	Yds	Avg Gain	TD	Int	Rating Pts
Testaverde	441	260	59.0	2752	6.24	15	14	75.3
Pennington	20	10	50.0	92	4.60	1	0	79.6

RECEIVING	No.	Yds	Avg	Lg	TD
Coles	59	868	14.7	40	7
Chrebet	56	750	13.4	36	1
Martin	53	252	6.0	27	0
Anderson	40	203	6.3	22	2
Becht	36	321	8.9	24	5

INTERCEPTIONS: Glenn, 5

PUNTING	No.	Yds	Avg	Net Avg	TB	In 20	Lg	Blk
Tupa	67	2573	38.4	32.0	5	21	59	0

SACKS: Abraham, 13

Oakland Raiders

SCORING	Rush	Rec	Ret	PAT	FG	S	Pts
Janikowski	0	0	0	42/42	23/28	0	111
Brown	0	9	1	0	0	0	60
Rice	0	9	0	0	0	0	54
Crockett	6	0	0	0	0	0	36
Wheatley	5	1	0	0	0	0	36

RUSHING	No.	Yds	Avg	Lg	TD
Garner	211	839	4.0	38	1
Wheatley	88	276	3.1	22	5
Gannon	63	231	3.7	17	2
Crockett	57	145	2.5	10	6

PASSING	Att	Comp	Pct Comp	Yds	Avg Gain	TD	Int	Rating Pts
Gannon	549	361	65.8	3828	6.97	27	9	95.5
Tuiasosopa	4	3	75.0	34	8.50	0	0	100.0

RECEIVING	No.	Yds	Avg	Lg	TD
Brown	91	1165	12.8	46	9
Rice	83	1139	13.7	40	9
Garner	72	578	8.0	27	2
Williams	33	298	9.0	49	3

INTERCEPTIONS: James, 5

PUNTING	No.	Yds	Avg	Net Avg	TB	In 20	Lg	Blk
Lechler	73	3373	46.2	35.6	12	23	65	0

SACKS: Upshaw, 7

Pittsburgh Steelers

SCORING	Rush	TD Rec	Ret	PAT	FG	S	Pts
Brown	0	0	0	34/37	30/44	0	124
Burress	0	6	0	0	0	0	36
Stewart	5	0	0	0	0	0	30
Fuamatu-Ma'afala	3	1	0	0	0	0	24
Ward	0	4	0	0	0	0	24
Bettis	4	0	0	0	0	0	24

RUSHING	No.	Yds	Avg	Lg	TD
Bettis	225	1072	4.8	48	4
Stewart	96	537	5.6	48	5
Fuamatu-Ma'afala	120	453	3.8	46	3
Zereoue	85	441	5.2	32	1

PASSING	Att	Comp	Pct Comp	Yds	Avg Gain	TD	Int	Rating Pts
Stewart	442	266	60.2	3109	7.03	14	11	81.7
Maddox	9	7	77.8	154	17.11	1	1	116.2

RECEIVING	No.	Yds	Avg	Lg	TD
Ward	94	1003	10.7	34	4
Burress	66	1008	15.3	43	6
Shaw	24	409	17.0	90	2

INTERCEPTIONS: Scott, 5

PUNTING	No.	Yds	Avg	Net Avg	TB	In 20	Lg	Blk
Miller	59	2508	42.5	34.9	5	23	64	0
Brown	3	106	35.3	27.3	0	0	46	0

SACKS: Gildon, 12

Seattle Seahawks

SCORING	Rush	TD Rec	Ret	PAT	FG	S	Pts
Alexander	14	2	0	0	0	0	96
Lindell	0	0	0	33/33	20/32	0	93
Jackson	0	8	0	0	0	0	48

RUSHING	No.	Yds	Avg	Lg	TD
Alexander	309	1318	4.3	88	14
Hasselbeck	40	141	3.5	17	0

PASSING	Att	Comp	Pct Comp	Yds	Avg Gain	TD	Int	Rating Pts
Hasselbeck	321	176	54.8	2023	6.30	7	8	70.9
Dilfer	122	73	59.8	1014	8.31	7	4	92.0

RECEIVING	No.	Yds	Avg	Lg	TD
Jackson	70	1081	15.4	64	8
Alexander	44	343	7.8	28	2
Robinson	39	536	13.7	42	1
Engram	29	400	13.8	31	0

INTERCEPTIONS: W. Williams, 4

PUNTING	No.	Yds	Avg	Net Avg	TB	In 20	Lg	Blk
Feagles	85	3732	43.9	36.4	7	26	68	0

SACKS: Randle, 11

San Diego Chargers

SCORING	Rush	TD Rec	Ret	PAT	FG	S	Pts
Richey	0	0	0	26/26	21/32	0	89
Tomlinson	10	0	0	0	0	0	60
Conway	7	6	0	0	0	0	42
Christie	0	0	0	6/6	9/11	0	33
Graham	5	5	0	0	0	0	30

RUSHING	No.	Yds	Avg	Lg	TD
Tomlinson	339	1236	3.6	54	10
Flutie	53	192	3.6	16	1
Conway	7	116	16.6	67	1
Fletcher	29	107	3.7	16	0

PASSING	Att	Comp	Pct Comp	Yds	Avg Gain	TD	Int	Rating Pts
Flutie	521	294	56.4	3463	6.65	15	18	72.0
Brees	27	15	55.6	221	8.19	1	0	94.8

RECEIVING	No.	Yds	Avg	Lg	TD
Conway	71	1125	15.8	72	6
Tomlinson	59	367	6.2	27	0
Graham	52	811	15.6	61	5
Jones	35	388	11.1	34	4

INTERCEPTIONS: McNeil, 8

PUNTING	No.	Yds	Avg	Net Avg	TB	In 20	Lg	Blk
Bennett	78	3307	42.4	36.9	4	25	62	0

SACKS: Wiley, 13

Tennessee Titans

SCORING	Rush	TD Rec	Ret	PAT	FG	S	Pts
Nedney	0	0	0	34/35	20/28	0	94
Mason	0	9	1	0	0	0	62
Dyson	0	7	0	1	0	0	44
George	5	0	0	0	0	0	30
McNair	5	0	0	0	0	0	30
Wycheck	0	4	0	0	0	0	24

RUSHING	No.	Yds	Avg	Lg	TD
George	315	939	3.0	27	5
McNair	75	414	5.5	24	5
Hicks	56	341	6.1	51	1

PASSING	Att	Comp	Pct Comp	Yds	Avg Gain	TD	Int	Rating Pts
McNair	431	264	61.3	3350	7.77	21	12	90.2
O'Donnell	76	42	55.3	496	6.53	2	2	73.1

RECEIVING	No.	Yds	Avg	Lg	TD
Mason	73	1128	15.5	71	9
Wycheck	60	672	11.2	30	4
Dyson	54	825	15.3	68	7
George	33	279	7.5	25	0

INTERCEPTIONS: Rolle and Dyson, 3

PUNTING	No.	Yds	Avg	Net Avg	TB	In 20	Lg	Blk
Hentrich	85	3570	42.0	37.0	8	28	70	0

SACKS: Kearse, 10

Arizona Cardinals

SCORING	Rush	Rec	Ret	PAT	FG	S	Pts
			TD				
Gramatica 0	0	0		25/25	16/20	0	73
Boston 0	8	0	0	0	0	0	48
Jones 5	0	0	0	0	0	0	30
Pittman 5	0	0	0	0	0	0	30

RUSHING	No.	Yds	Avg	Lg	TD
Pittman 241	846	3.5	42	5
Jones.........................112	380	3.4	21	5
Plummer 35	163	4.7	21	0

PASSING	Att	Comp	Pct Comp	Yds	Avg Gain	TD	Int	Rating Pts
Plummer......525	304	57.9	3653	6.96	18	14	79.6
Sanders 1	0	0	0	0.00	0	0	39.6

RECEIVING	No.	Yds	Avg	Lg	TD
Boston 98	1598	16.3	61	8
Pittman 42	264	6.3	27	0
Sanders 41	618	15.1	68	2
Jenkins 32	518	16.2	53	3

INTERCEPTIONS: Lassiter, 9

PUNTING	No.	Yds	Avg	Net Avg	TB	In 20	Lg	Blk
Player 67	2781	41.5	33.8	7	17	58	0
Stanley 19	751	39.5	34.2	1	4	54	0
Gramatica ..1	41	41.0	19.0	0	0	41	0

SACKS: Fredrickson, 4

Carolina Panthers

SCORING	Rush	Rec	Ret	PAT	FG	S	Pts
			TD				
Kasay 0	0	0	22/23	23/28	0	91
Weinke 6	0	0	0	0	0	36
Walls 0	5	0	0	0	0	30

RUSHING	No.	Yds	Avg	Lg	TD
Huntley 165	665	4.0	25	2
Biakabutuka 53	230	4.3	27	1
Goings.......................66	197	3.0	16	0
Weinke.......................37	128	3.5	23	6

PASSING	Att	Comp	Pct Comp	Yds	Avg Gain	TD	Int	Rating Pts
Weinke........540	293	54.3	2931	5.43	11	19	62.0
Lytle 30	17	56.7	133	4.43	1	3	39.3
Craig...............8	4	50.0	34	4.25	0	0	61.5

RECEIVING	No.	Yds	Avg	Lg	TD
Hayes 52	597	11.5	48	2
Muhammad 50	585	11.7	43	1
Walls.........................43	452	10.5	25	5
Byrd..........................37	492	13.3	42	1

INTERCEPTIONS: Evans, 8

PUNTING	No.	Yds	Avg	Net Avg	TB	In 20	Lg	Blk
Sauerbrun 93	4418	47.5	38.9	17	35	73	0

SACKS: Rucker, 9

Atlanta Falcons

SCORING	Rush	Rec	Ret	PAT	FG	S	Pts
			TD				
Feely 0	0	0	28/28	29/37	0	115
Smith 5	1	0	0	0	0	36
Christian................2	2	0	0	0	0	24

RUSHING	No.	Yds	Avg	Lg	TD
Smith 237	760	3.2	58	5
Vick..............................31	289	9.3	35	1
Christian 44	284	6.5	53	2
Anderson....................55	190	3.5	14	1
Thomas.......................37	126	3.4	21	0

PASSING	Att	Comp	Pct Comp	Yds	Avg Gain	TD	Int	Rating Pts
Chandler.....365	223	61.1	2847	7.80	16	14	84.1
Vick.............113	50	44.2	785	6.95	2	3	62.7
Mohr................2	2	100.0	40	20.00	0	0	118.8
Johnson 5	3	60.0	23	4.60	1	0	110.8

RECEIVING	No.	Yds	Avg	Lg	TD
Mathis.......................51	564	11.1	34	2
Christian 45	392	8.7	42	2
Martin 37	548	14.8	63	3
Jefferson 37	539	14.6	48	2

INTERCEPTIONS: Ambrose and Buchanan, 5

PUNTING	No.	Yds	Avg	Net Avg	TB	In 20	Lg	Blk
Mohr..........69	2677	38.8	36.1	3	25	55	0

SACKS: Kerney, 12

Chicago Bears

SCORING	Rush	Rec	Ret	PAT	FG	S	Pts
			TD				
Edinger 0	0	0	34/34	26/31	0	112
Booker..................0	8	0	0	0	0	48
Thomas 7	0	0	1	0	0	44
Terrell...................0	4	0	0	0	0	24
Johnson 4	0	0	0	0	0	24

RUSHING	No.	Yds	Avg	Lg	TD
Thomas.......................278	1183	4.3	46	7
Allen 135	469	3.5	19	1
Johnson 20	99	5.0	34	4

PASSING	Att	Comp	Pct Comp	Yds	Avg Gain	TD	Int	Rating Pts
Miller 395	228	57.7	2299	5.82	13	10	74.9
Matthews ..129	84	65.1	694	5.30	5	6	72.3

RECEIVING	No.	Yds	Avg	Lg	TD
Booker.....................100	1071	10.7	66	8
White 45	428	9.5	32	0
Terrell 34	415	12.2	62	4
Allen 30	203	6.8	34	1

INTERCEPTIONS: Brown, 5

PUNTING	No.	Yds	Avg	Net Avg	TB	In 20	Lg	Blk
Maynard 87	3706	42.6	37.0	8	36	60	0
Edinger.......1	34	34.0	34.0	0	1	34	0

SACKS: Colvin, 10.5

Dallas Cowboys

SCORING	TD Rush	Rec	Ret	PAT	FG	S	Pts
Seder	1	0	0	12/12	11/17	0	51
Hilbert	0	0	0	12/12	11/16	0	45
Galloway	0	3	0	0	0	0	18
Smith	3	0	0	0	0	0	18

RUSHING	No.	Yds	Avg	Lg	TD
Smith	261	1021	3.9	44	3
Hambrick	113	579	5.1	80	2
Wiley	34	247	7.3	58	0
Carter	45	150	3.3	17	1

PASSING	Att	Comp	Pct Comp	Yds	Avg Gain	TD	Int	Rating Pts
Carter	176	90	51.1	1072	6.09	5	7	63.0
Wright	98	48	49.0	529	5.40	5	5	61.1
Leaf	88	45	51.1	494	5.61	1	3	57.7
Stoerner	49	26	53.1	314	6.41	3	5	53.8

RECEIVING	No.	Yds	Avg	Lg	TD
Ismail	53	834	15.7	80	2
Galloway	52	699	13.4	47	3

INTERCEPTIONS: Woodson, 3

PUNTING	No.	Yds	Avg	Net Avg	TB	In 20	Lg	Blk
Knorr	78	3136	40.2	31.1	6	25	57	0

SACKS: Ellis, 6

Detroit Lions

SCORING	TD Rush	Rec	Ret	PAT	FG	S	Pts
Hanson	0	0	0	23/23	21/30	0	86
Sloan	0	7	0	0	0	0	42
Warren	3	1	0	1	0	0	26
Morton	0	4	0	0	0	0	24

RUSHING	No.	Yds	Avg	Lg	TD
J. Stewart	143	685	4.8	38	1
Warren	61	191	3.1	34	3
Schlesinger	47	154	3.3	26	3
McMahon	27	145	5.4	22	1

PASSING	Att	Comp	Pct Comp	Yds	Avg Gain	TD	Int	Rating Pts
Batch	341	198	58.1	2392	7.01	12	12	76.8
Detmer	151	92	60.9	906	6.00	3	10	56.9
McMahon	115	53	46.1	671	5.83	3	1	69.9

RECEIVING	No.	Yds	Avg	Lg	TD
Morton	77	1154	15.0	76	4
Schlesinger	60	466	7.8	38	0
Warren	40	336	8.4	36	1
Sloan	37	409	11.1	36	7

INTERCEPTIONS: Lyght, 4

PUNTING	No.	Yds	Avg	Net Avg	TB	In 20	Lg	Blk
Jett	58	2511	43.3	35.5	6	16	62	0
Araguz	17	712	41.9	34.0	4	6	55	0

SACKS: Porcher, 11

Green Bay Packers

SCORING	TD Rush	Rec	Ret	PAT	FG	S	Pts
Longwell	0	0	0	44/45	20/31	0	104
Green	9	2	0	0	0	0	66
Franks	0	9	0	0	0	0	54
Schroeder	0	9	0	0	0	0	54
Freeman	0	6	0	1	0	0	38

RUSHING	No.	Yds	Avg	Lg	TD
Green	304	1387	4.6	83	9
Levens	44	165	3.8	40	0

PASSING	Att	Comp	Pct Comp	Yds	Avg Gain	TD	Int	Rating Pts
Favre	510	314	61.6	3921	7.69	32	15	94.1

RECEIVING	No.	Yds	Avg	Lg	TD
Green	62	594	9.6	42	2
Schroeder	53	918	17.3	67	9
Freeman	52	818	15.7	63	6
Franks	36	322	8.9	31	9
Bradford	31	526	17.0	56	2

INTERCEPTIONS: Sharper, 6

PUNTING	No.	Yds	Avg	Net Avg	TB	In 20	Lg	Blk
Bidwell	82	3485	42.5	36.5	10	21	68	0

SACKS: Gbaha-Biamila, 13.5

Minnesota Vikings

SCORING	TD Rush	Rec	Ret	PAT	FG	S	Pts
Anderson	0	0	0	29/30	15/18	0	74
Moss	0	10	0	0	0	0	60
Carter	0	6	0	0	0	0	36
Culpepper	5	0	0	2	0	0	34

RUSHING	No.	Yds	Avg	Lg	TD
Bennett	172	682	4.0	31	2
Culpepper	71	416	5.9	34	5
Chapman	63	195	3.1	19	0

PASSING	Att	Comp	Pct Comp	Yds	Avg Gain	TD	Int	Rating Pts
Culpepper	366	235	64.2	2612	7.14	14	13	83.3
Bouman	89	51	57.3	795	8.93	8	4	98.3
Wynn	98	48	49.0	418	4.27	1	6	38.6

RECEIVING	No.	Yds	Avg	Lg	TD
Moss	82	1233	15.0	73	10
Carter	73	871	11.9	52	6
Chamberlain	57	666	11.7	47	3

INTERCEPTIONS: Griffith and Kelly, 2

PUNTING	No.	Yds	Avg	Net Avg	TB	In 20	Lg	Blk
Berger	47	2045	43.5	32.9	10	10	67	0

SACKS: Hovan, 6

New Orleans Saints

SCORING	Rush	TD Rec	Ret	PAT	FG	S	Pts
Carney 0	0	0	32/32	27/31	0	113
Horn 0	9	0	0	0	0	54
Williams................6	1	0	0	0	0	42
Jackson.................0	5	0	1	0	0	32
Cleeland...............0	4	0	0	*0	0	24

RUSHING	No.	Yds	Avg	Lg	TD
R. Williams..............313	1245	4.0	46	6
Brooks 80	358	4.5	26	1
McAllister..................16	91	5.7	54	1

PASSING	Att	Comp	Pct Comp	Yds	Avg Gain	TD	Int	Rating Pts
Brooks.........558	312	55.9	3832	6.87	26	22	76.4

RECEIVING	No.	Yds	Avg	Lg	TD
Horn 83	1265	15.2	56	9
Jackson.....................81	1046	12.9	63	5
R. Williams................60	511	8.5	42	1

INTERCEPTIONS: Knight, 6

PUNTING	No.	Yds	Avg	Net Avg	TB	In 20	Lg	Blk
Gowin..........76	3177	41.8	35.8	7	24	62	0

SACKS: Clemons, 13.5

New York Giants

SCORING	Rush	TD Rec	Ret	PAT	FG	S	Pts
Andersen 0	0	0	29/30	23/28	0	98
Dayne...................7	0	0	1	0	0	44
Hillard..................0	6	0	0	0	0	36
Toomer..................0	5	0	0	0	0	30
Barber 4	0	0	1	0	0	26

RUSHING	No.	Yds	Avg	Lg	TD
Barber 166	865	5.2	36	4
Dayne 180	690	3.8	61	7

PASSING	Att	Comp	Pct Comp	Yds	Avg Gain	TD	Int	Rating Pts
Collins 568	327	57.6	3764	6.63	19	16	77.1

RECEIVING	No.	Yds	Avg	Lg	TD
Toomer 72	1054	14.6	60	5
Barber 72	577	8.0	44	0
Hilliard 52	659	12.7	38	6
Jurevicius 51	706	13.8	46	3

INTERCEPTIONS: Allen, 4

PUNTING	No.	Yds	Avg	Net Avg	TB	In 20	Lg	Blk
Williams....91	3904	42.9	35.4	8	25	90	0
Pochman 5	146	29.2	24.8	0	3	39	0

SACKS: Strahan, 22.5

Philadelphia Eagles

SCORING	Rush	TD Rec	Ret	PAT	FG	S	Pts
Akers...................0	0	0	37/38	26/31	0	115
Thrash 0	8	0	0	0	0	48
Lewis....................0	6	0	0	0	0	36
Pinkston 0	4	2	0	0	0	24
Staley 2	2	0	0	0	0	24

RUSHING	No.	Yds	Avg	Lg	TD
Staley..........................166	604	3.6	44	2
Buckhalter 129	586	4.5	48	2
McNabb 82	482	5.9	33	2

PASSING	Att	Comp	Pct Comp	Yds	Avg Gain	TD	Int	Rating Pts
McNabb......493	285	57.8	3233	6.56	25	12	84.3
Feeley...........14	10	71.4	143	10.21	2	1	114.0
Detmer..........14	5	35.7	51	3.64	0	1	17.3

RECEIVING	No.	Yds	Avg	Lg	TD
Thrash 63	833	13.2	64	8
Staley 63	626	9.9	46	2
Pinkston....................42	586	14.0	62	4
Lewis 41	422	10.3	33	6

INTERCEPTIONS: Vincent, 3

PUNTING	No.	Yds	Avg	Net Avg	TB	In 20	Lg	Blk
Landeta....97	4220	43.5	36.4	10	26	64	0

SACKS: H. Douglas, 9.5

St. Louis Rams

SCORING	Rush	TD Rec	Ret	PAT	FG	S	Pts
Faulk 12	9	0	0	0	0	128
Wilkins..................0	0	0	58/58	23/29	0	127
Holt......................0	7	0	0	0	0	42
Bruce 0	6	0	0	0	0	36
Canidate 5	0	1	0	0	0	36
Proehl..................0	5	0	1	0	0	32
Conwell 1	4	0	0	0	0	30

RUSHING	No.	Yds	Avg	Lg	TD
Faulk...........................260	1382	5.3	71	12
Canidate....................78	441	5.7	45	6

PASSING	Att	Comp	Pct Comp	Yds	Avg Gain	TD	Int	Rating Pts
Warner 546	375	68.7	4830	8.85	36	22	101.4

RECEIVING	No.	Yds	Avg	Lg	TD
Faulk..........................82	765	9.2	65	9
Holt............................81	1363	16.8	51	7
Bruce.........................64	1106	17.3	51	6

INTERCEPTIONS: Bly, 6

PUNTING	No.	Yds	Avg	Net Avg	TB	In 20	Lg	Blk
Baker........43	1810	42.1	34.9	7	9	58	0

SACKS: Little, 14.5

San Francisco 49ers

SCORING	Rush	Rec	Ret	PAT	FG	S	Pts
Cortez	0	0	0	47/47	18/25	0	101
Owens	0	16	0	0	0	0	96
Stokes	0	7	0	0	0	0	42
Hearst	4	1	0	0	0	0	30
Barlow	4	1	0	0	0	0	30
Garcia	5	0	0	0	0	0	30

RUSHING	No.	Yds	Avg	Lg	TD
Hearst	252	1206	4.8	43	4
Barlow	125	512	4.1	25	4
Garcia	72	254	3.5	25	5

PASSING	Att	Comp	Pct Comp	Yds	Avg Gain	TD	Int	Rating Pts
Garcia	504	316	62.7	3538	7.02	32	12	94.8
Rattay	2	2	100.0	21	10.50	0	0	110.4

RECEIVING	No.	Yds	Avg	Lg	TD
Owens	93	1412	15.2	60	16
Stokes	54	585	10.8	47	7
Johnson	40	362	9.1	24	3
Hearst	41	347	8.5	60	1

INTERCEPTIONS: Bronson and Plummer, 7

PUNTING	No.	Yds	Avg	Net Avg	TB	In 20	Lg	Blk
Baker	69	2815	40.8	35.4	4	21	64	0

SACKS: Carter, 6.5

Washington Redskins

SCORING	Rush	Rec	Ret	PAT	FG	S	Pts
Conway	0	0	0	22/22	26/33	0	100
Davis	5	0	0	1	0	0	32
Gardner	0	4	0	0	0	0	24
Westbrook	0	4	0	0	0	0	24

RUSHING	No.	Yds	Avg	Lg	TD
Davis	356	1432	4.0	32	5
Gardner	1	16	16.0	16	0

PASSING	Att	Comp	Pct Comp	Yds	Avg Gain	TD	Int	Rating Pts
Banks	370	198	53.5	2386	6.45	10	10	71.3
George	42	23	54.8	168	4.00	0	3	34.6
Graham	19	13	68.4	131	6.89	2	0	122.9
Lockett	1	1	100.0	31	31.00	1	0	158.3

RECEIVING	No.	Yds	Avg	Lg	TD
Westbrook	57	664	11.7	76	4
Gardner	46	741	16.1	85	4
Lockett	22	293	13.3	34	0
Davis	28	205	7.3	29	0

INTERCEPTIONS: Smoot, 5

PUNTING	No.	Yds	Avg	Net Avg	TB	In 20	Lg	Blk
Barker	90	3744	41.6	34.8	9	27	59	0
Conway	1	28	28.0	28.0	0	1	28	0

SACKS: Smith, 5

Tampa Bay Buccaneers

SCORING	Rush	Rec	Ret	PAT	FG	S	Pts
Gramatica	0	0	0	28/28	23/29	0	97
Alstott	10	1	0	2	0	0	70
Dunn	3	3	0	0	0	0	36
Moore	0	4	0	1	0	0	24

RUSHING	No.	Yds	Avg	Lg	TD
Alstott	165	680	4.1	39	10
Dunn	158	447	2.8	21	3
Johnson	39	120	3.1	21	3

PASSING	Att	Comp	Pct Comp	Yds	Avg Gain	TD	Int	Rating Pts
Johnson	559	340	60.8	3406	6.09	13	11	77.7
King	31	21	67.7	210	6.77	0	1	73.3

RECEIVING	No.	Yds	Avg	Lg	TD
Johnson	106	1266	11.9	47	1
Dunn	68	557	8.2	31	3
Green	36	402	11.2	35	1

INTERCEPTIONS: Barber, 10

PUNTING	No.	Yds	Avg	Net Avg	TB	In 20	Lg	Blk
Royals	83	3378	40.7	34.2	8	26	61	0

SACKS: Rice, 11

First two rounds of the 67th annual NFL Draft held April 20–21 in New York City.

First Round

Team	Selection	Position
1. ....Houston	David Carr, Fresno St	QB
2. ....Carolina	Julius Peppers, N Carolina	DE
3. ....Detroit	Joey Harrington, Oregon	QB
4. ....Buffalo	Mike Williams, Texas	OT
5. ....San Diego	Quentin Jammer, Texas	CB
6. ....Kansas City (from Dallas)	Ryan Sims, North Carolina	DT
7. ....Minnesota	Bryant McKinnie, Miami	OT
8. ....Dallas (from KC)	Roy Williams, Oklahoma	SS
9. ....Jacksonville	John Henderson, Tennessee	DT
10. ......Cincinnati	Levi Jones, Arizona St	OT
11. ......Indianapolis	Dwight Freeney, Syracuse	DE
12. ......Arizona	Wendell Bryant, Wisconsin	WR
13. ......New Orleans	Donte Stallworth, Tennessee	WR
14. ......NY Giants (from Tenn)	Jeremy Shockey, Miami (FL)	TE
15. ......Tennessee (from NYG)	Albert Haynesworth, Tennessee	DT
16. ......Cleveland	William Green, Boston College	RB
17. ......Oakland (from Atl)	Philip Buchanon, Miami (FL)	CB
18. ......Atlanta (from Wash via Oak)	T.J. Duckett, Michigan St	RB
19. ......Denver	Ashley Lelie, Hawaii	WR
20. ......Green Bay (from Sea)	Jayon Walker, Florida St	WR
21. ......New England (from TB via Oak and Wash)	Daniel Graham, Colorado	TE
22. ......NY Jets	Bryan Thomas, Alabama-Birmingham	DE
23. ......Oakland	Napoleon Harris, Northwestern	OLB
24. ......Baltimore	Edward Reed, Miami (FL)	FS
25. ......New Orleans (from Mia)	Charles Grant, Georgia	DE
26. ......Philadelphia	Lito Sheppard, Florida	CB
27. ......San Francisco	Mike Rumph, Miami (FL)	CB
28. ......Seattle (from GB)	Jerramy Stevens, Washington	TE
29. ......Chicago	Marc Colombo, Boston College	OT
30. ......Pittsburgh	Kendall Simmons, Auburn	OT
31. ......St. Louis	Robert Thomas, UCLA	OLB
32. ......Washington (from NE)	Patrick Ramsey, Tulane	QB

Second Round

Team	Selection	Position
33. ......Houston	Jabar Gaffney, Florida	WR
34. ......Carolina	De'Shaun Foster, UCLA	RB
35. ......Detroit	Kalimba Edwards, S Carolina	WR
36. ......Buffalo	Josh Reed, Louisiana St	WR
37. ......Dallas	Andre Gurode, Colorado	G
38. ......Minnesota	Raonall Smith, Wahington State	OLB
39. ......San Diego	Toniu Fonoti, Nebraska	G
40. ......Jacksonville	Mike Pearson, Florida	OT
41. ......Cincinnati	Lamont Thompson, Washington St	FS
42. ......Indianapolis	Larry Tripplett, Washington	DT
43. ......Kansas City	Eddie Freeman, Alabama-Birmingham	DT
44. ......New Orleans	LeCharles Bentley, Ohio St	C
45. ......Tennessee	Clevan (Tank) Williams, Stanford	FS
46. ......NY Giants	Tim Carter, Auburn	WR
47. ......Cleveland	Andre Davis, Virginia Tech	WR
48. ......San Diego (from Atlanta)	Reche Caldwell, Florida	WR
49. ......Arizona	Levar Fisher, N Carolina St	OLB
50. ......Houston (Supp Selection)	Chester Pitts, San Diego St	OT
51. ......Denver	Clinton Portis, Miami (FL)	RB
52. ......Baltimore (from Wash)	Anthony Weaver, Notre Dame	DT
53. ......Oakland (from TB)	Langston Walker, California	OT
54. ......Seattle	Maurice Morris, Oregon	RB
55. ......Oakland	Doug Jolley, Brigham Young	TE
56. ......Washington (from Bal)	Ladell Bets, Iowa	RB
57. ......NY Jets	Jon McGraw, Kansas St	FS
58. .....Philadelphia	Michael Lewis, Colorado	SS
59. ......Philadelphia (from Mia)	Sheldon Brown, S Carolina	CB
60. ......Seattle (from GB)	Anton Palepoi, Nevada–Las Vegas	DE
61. .....Buffalo (from SF)	Ryan Denney, Brigham Young	DE
62. ......Pittsburgh	Antwaan Randle El, Indiana	WR
63. ......Dallas (from Chi)	Antonio Bryant, Pittsburgh	WR
64. ....St. Louis	Travis Fisher, Central Florida	CB
65. ....New England	Anthony (Deion) Branch, Louisville	WR

2002 NFL Europe

Final Standings

	W	L	T	Pct	Pts	OP
Rhein*	7	3	0	.700	166	156
Berlin*	6	4	0	.600	231	188
Frankfurt	6	4	0	.600	189	174
Scotland	5	5	0	.500	197	172
Amsterdam	4	6	0	.400	218	202
Barcelona	2	8	0	.200	202	311

*Clinched World Bowl 2002 berth.

2002 World Bowl

June 22, 2002, in Dusseldorf, Germany

Berlin Thunder	13	7	3	3—26
Rhein Fire	0	0	7	13—20

FIRST QUARTER

Berlin: FG Boyd 47, 11:32.
Berlin: Looker 41 pass from Husak (Kruse kick), 5:01.
Berlin: FG Krse 27, 0:59.

SECOND QUARTER

Berlin: Looker 15 pass from Husak (Kruse kick), 1:56.

THIRD QUARTER

Rhein: Taylor 6 run (Witzcak kick), 4:39.
Berlin: FG Boyd 45, 0:26.

FOURTH QUARTER

Rhein: Cloman 2 pass from Martin (pass failed), 10:40.
Berlin: FG Boyd 38, 8:00.
Rhein: Martin 1 run (Burgsmuller kick), 0:20.

NFL Europe Individual Leaders

PASSING

	Att	Comp	Pct Comp	Yds	Avg Gain	TD	Pct TD	Int	Pct Int	Lg	Rating Pts
White, Barcelona	171	96	56.1	1165	6.81	13	7.6	5	2.9	69	90.4
Daft, Amsterdam	301	178	59.1	1981	6.58	15	5.0	9	3.0	59	83.0
Husak, Berlin	356	208	58.4	2386	6.70	14	3.9	14	3.9	66	75.4
Hamilton, Frankfurt	193	99	51.3	1301	6.74	8	4.1	8	4.1	68	69.5
Martin, Rhein	203	101	49.8	1017	5.01	5	2.5	6	3.0	35	60.3

RECEIVING

RECEPTIONS	No.	Yds	Avg	Lg	TD
Looker, Berlin	54	661	12.2	t55	5
Knight, Amsterdam	40	546	13.7	51	5
White, Berlin	38	370	9.7	t41	0
Pitts, Barcelona	36	393	10.9	t40	5
Flowers, Barcelona	34	508	14.9	t61	6
Collins, Amsterdam	34	280	8.2	t31	2

YARDS	Yds	No.	Avg	Lg	T
Looker, Berlin	661	54	12.2	t55	5
Knight, Amsterdam	546	40	13.7	51	5
Flowers, Barcelona	508	34	14.9	t61	6
Redmond, Frank	493	32	15.4	39	0
Hambrick, Ams	407	28	14.5	52	3

RUSHING

	Att	Yds	Avg	Lg	TD
Goodman, Bar	206	877	4.3	t36	6
Alexander, Frank	152	831	5.5	t36	6
Robertson, Rhein	151	792	5.2	t90	8
Cooper, Ams	155	751	4.8	t77	8
White, Ber	113	525	4.6	62	6

Other Statistical Leaders

Points (TDs)	Cooper, Amsterdam	60
Points (Kicking)	Kimrin, Frankfurt	57
Yards from Scrimmage	Alexander, Frankfurt	1094
Interceptions	Cooper, Rhein	5
Sacks	Warner, Barcelona	6.0
Punting Avg	Bayes, Amsterdam	37.6
	Lindstrom, Frankfurt	37.6
Punt Return Avg	Moses, Scotland	11.2
Kickoff Return Avg	Rooths, Scotland	28.6

THEY SAID IT

Gerard Warren, the Browns' second-year defensive tackle, on whether he feels like a seasoned NFL veteran: "Maybe not a seasoned vet, but a marinating one."

2001 Canadian Football League

EASTERN DIVISION

	W	L	T	Pts	Pct	PF	PA
†Winnipeg	14	4	0	28	.778	509	383
*Hamilton	11	7	0	22	.611	440	419
*Montreal	9	9	0	18	.500	453	419
Toronto	7	11	0	15	.389	432	455

WESTERN DIVISION

	W	L	T	Pts	Pct	PF	PA
†Edmonton	9	9	0	19	.500	439	463
*Calgary	8	10	0	17	.444	478	476
*British Columbia	8	10	0	16	.444	417	445
Saskatchewan	6	12	0	12	.333	308	416

†Clinched division title.

*Clinched playoff berth

Regular Season Statistical Leaders

Points (TDs)	Pringle, Montreal	102
Points (Kicking)	Fleming, Edmonton	183
Rushing Yards	Jenkins, Toronto	1484
Passing Yards	Jones, Winnipeg	4545
Receiving Yards	Vaughn, Edmonton	1497
Receptions	Vaughn, Edmonton	98

2001 Playoff Results

DIVISION SEMIFINALS

East: Montreal 12, HAMILTON 24
West: British Columbia 19, CALGARY 28

DIVISION FINALS

East: Hamilton 13, WINNIPEG 27
West: Calgary 34, EDMONTON 16

Home team in caps.

2001 Grey Cup Championship

Nov. 25, 2001, at Montreal, Quebec

Winnipeg Bluebombers	4	0	8	7—19
Calgary Stampeders	0	17	0	10—27

A: 65,255.

History Book

**Nov. 27, 1966: A grudge fuels the highest-scoring game in NFL history.
Redskins 72, Giants 41**

When the Giants dealt Pro Bowl linebacker Sam Huff to the Redskins in 1964, Huff vowed to get even with New York coach Allie Sherman, whom he blamed for trading him from the team he loved. "I took an oath: I will never quit this game until I get Allie Sherman fired," Huff recalled in late November 2001. Huff got sky-high before games against New York, and on this day he felt a rout coming on against a team that would finish 1-12-1. "Otto," he said he told coach Otto Graham before the game, "show no mercy." Never since has an NFL game produced 100 points. With the Redskins leading 69–41, Huff screamed for a timeout from the sideline with seven seconds left. "Field goal team!" Huff yelled. The unit ran onto the field before Graham knew what was happening, and Charlie Gogolak kicked a 29-yard field goal. Two years later, after his fifth straight nonwinning season, Sherman was fired.

The Super Bowl

Results

	Date	Winner (Share)	Loser (Share)	Score	Site (Attendance)
I	1-15-67	Green Bay ($15,000)	Kansas City ($7,500)	35–10	Los Angeles (61,946)
II	1-14-68	Green Bay ($15,000)	Oakland ($7,500)	33–14	Miami (75,546)
III	1-12-69	NY Jets ($15,000)	Baltimore ($7,500)	16–7	Miami (75,389)
IV	1-11-70	Kansas City ($15,000)	Minnesota ($7,500)	23–7	New Orleans (80,562)
V	1-17-71	Baltimore ($15,000)	Dallas ($7,500)	16–13	Miami (79,204)
VI	1-16-72	Dallas ($15,000)	Miami ($7,500)	24–3	New Orleans (81,023)
VII	1-14-73	Miami ($15,000)	Washington ($7,500)	14–7	Los Angeles (90,182)
VIII	1-13-74	Miami ($15,000)	Minnesota ($7,500)	24–7	Houston (71,882)
IX	1-12-75	Pittsburgh ($15,000)	Minnesota ($7,500)	16–6	New Orleans (80,997)
X	1-18-76	Pittsburgh ($15,000)	Dallas ($7,500)	21–17	Miami (80,187)
XI	1-9-77	Oakland ($15,000)	Minnesota ($7,500)	32–14	Pasadena (103,438)
XII	1-15-78	Dallas ($18,000)	Denver ($9,000)	27–10	New Orleans (75,583)
XIII	1-21-79	Pittsburgh ($18,000)	Dallas ($9,000)	35–31	Miami (79,484)
XIV	1-20-80	Pittsburgh ($18,000)	Los Angeles ($9,000)	31–19	Pasadena (103,985)
XV	1-25-81	Oakland ($18,000)	Philadelphia ($9,000)	27–10	New Orleans (76,135)
XVI	1-24-82	San Francisco ($18,000)	Cincinnati ($9,000)	26–21	Pontiac, MI (81,270)
XVII	1-30-83	Washington ($36,000)	Miami ($18,000)	27–17	Pasadena (103,667)
XVIII	1-22-84	LA Raiders ($36,000)	Washington ($18,000)	38–9	Tampa (72,920)
XIX	1-20-85	San Francisco ($36,000)	Miami ($18,000)	38–16	Stanford (84,059)
XX	1-26-86	Chicago ($36,000)	New England ($18,000)	46–10	New Orleans (73,818)
XXI	1-25-87	NY Giants ($36,000)	Denver ($18,000)	39–20	Pasadena (101,063)
XXII	1-31-88	Washington ($36,000)	Denver ($18,000)	42–10	San Diego (73,302)
XXIII	1-22-89	San Francisco ($36,000)	Cincinnati ($18,000)	20–16	Miami (75,129)
XXIV	1-28-90	San Francisco ($36,000)	Denver ($18,000)	55–10	New Orleans (72,919)
XXV	1-27-91	NY Giants ($36,000)	Buffalo ($18,000)	20–19	Tampa (73,813)
XXVI	1-26-92	Washington ($36,000)	Buffalo ($18,000)	37–24	Minneapolis (63,130)
XXVII	1-31-93	Dallas ($36,000)	Buffalo ($18,000)	52–17	Pasadena (98,374)
XXVIII	1-30-94	Dallas ($38,000)	Buffalo ($23,500)	30–13	Atlanta (72,817)
XXIX	1-29-95	San Francisco ($42,000)	San Diego ($26,000)	49–26	Miami (74,107)
XXX	1-28-96	Dallas ($42,000)	Pittsburgh ($27,000)	27–17	Tempe, AZ (76,347)
XXXI	1-26-97	Green Bay ($48,000)	New England ($29,000)	35–21	New Orleans (72,301)
XXXII	1-25-98	Denver ($48,000)	Green Bay ($27,500)	31–24	San Diego (68,912)
XXXIII	1-31-99	Denver ($53,000)	Atlanta ($32,500)	34–19	Miami (74,803)
XXXIV	1-30-00	St. Louis ($58,000)	Tennessee ($33,000)	23–16	Atlanta (72,625)
XXXV	1-28-01	Baltimore ($58,000)	NY Giants ($34,500)	34–7	Tampa (71,921)
XXXVI	2-3-02	New England ($63,000)	St. Louis ($34,500)	20–17	New Orleans (72,922)

Most Valuable Players

Super Bowl	Player/Team	Position	Super Bowl	Player/Team	Position
I	Bart Starr, GB	QB	XIX	Joe Montana, SF	QB
II	Bart Starr, GB	QB	XX	Richard Dent, Chi	DE
III	Joe Namath, NYJ	QB	XXI	Phil Simms, NYG	QB
IV	Len Dawson, KC	QB	XXII	Doug Williams, Wash	QB
V	Chuck Howley, Dall	LB	XXIII	Jerry Rice, SF	WR
VI	Roger Staubach, Dall	QB	XXIV	Joe Montana, SF	QB
VII	Jake Scott, Mia	S	XXV	Ottis Anderson, NYG	RB
VIII	Larry Csonka, Mia	RB	XXVI	Mark Rypien, Wash	QB
IX	Franco Harris, Pitt	RB	XXVII	Troy Aikman, Dall	QB
X	Lynn Swann, Pitt	WR	XXVIII	Emmitt Smith, Dall	RB
XI	Fred Biletnikoff, Oak	WR	XXIX	Steve Young, SF	QB
XII	Randy White, Dall	DT	XXX	Larry Brown, Dall	DB
	Harvey Martin, Dall	DE	XXXI	Desmond Howard, GB	KR
XIII	Terry Bradshaw, Pitt	QB	XXXII	Terrell Davis, Den	RB
XIV	Terry Bradshaw, Pitt	QB	XXXIII	John Elway, Den	QB
XV	Jim Plunkett, Oak	QB	XXXIV	Kurt Warner, StL	QB
XVI	Joe Montana, SF	QB	XXXV	Ray Lewis, Balt	LB
XVII	John Riggins, Wash	RB	XXXVI	Tom Brady, NE	QB
XVIII	Marcus Allen, Rai	RB			

Composite Standings

	W	L	Pct	Pts	Opp Pts
San Francisco 49ers	5	0	1.000	188	89
Baltimore Ravens	1	0	1.000	34	7
Chicago Bears	1	0	1.000	46	10
New York Jets	1	0	1.000	16	7
Pittsburgh Steelers	4	1	.800	120	100
Green Bay Packers	3	1	.750	127	76
Oakland/LA Raiders	3	1	.750	111	66
New York Giants	2	1	.667	66	73
Dallas Cowboys	5	3	.625	221	132
Washington Redskins	3	2	.600	122	103
Baltimore Colts	1	1	.500	23	29
Kansas City Chiefs	1	1	.500	33	42
Miami Dolphins	2	3	.400	74	103
Denver Broncos	2	4	.333	115	206
Los Angeles/St. Louis Rams	1	2	.333	59	67
New England Patriots	1	2	.333	51	98
Philadelphia Eagles	0	1	.000	10	27
San Diego Chargers	0	1	.000	26	49
Atlanta Falcons	0	1	.000	19	34
Tennesse Titans	0	1	.000	16	23
Cincinnati Bengals	0	2	.000	37	46
Buffalo Bills	0	4	.000	73	139
Minnesota Vikings	0	4	.000	34	95

Career Leaders

Passing

	GP	Att	Comp	Pct Comp	Yds	Avg Gain	TD	Pct TD	Int	Pct Int	Lg	Rating Pts
Joe Montana, SF	4	122	83	68.0	1142	9.36	11	9.0	0	0.0	44	127.8
Jim Plunkett, Rai	2	46	29	63.0	433	9.41	4	8.7	0	0.0	t80	122.8
Terry Bradshaw, Pitt	4	84	49	58.3	932	11.10	9	10.7	4	4.8	t75	112.8
Troy Aikman, Dall	3	80	56	70.0	689	8.61	5	6.3	1	1.3	t56	111.9
Bart Starr, GB	2	47	29	61.7	452	9.62	3	6.4	1	2.1	t62	106.0
Kurt Warner, StL	2	89	52	58.4	779	8.75	3	3.4	1	1.1	t73	93.8
Brett Favre, GB	2	69	39	56.5	502	7.28	5	7.2	1	1.4	t81	97.7
Roger Staubach, Dall	4	98	61	62.2	734	7.49	8	8.2	4	4.1	t45	95.4
Len Dawson, KC	2	44	28	63.6	353	8.02	2	4.5	2	4.5	t46	84.8
Bob Griese, Mia	3	41	26	63.4	295	7.20	1	2.4	2	4.9	t28	72.7

Note: Minimum 40 attempts.

Rushing

	GP	Yds	Att	Avg	Lg	TD
Franco Harris, Pitt	4	354	101	3.5	25	4
Larry Csonka, Mia	3	297	57	5.2	9	2
Emmitt Smith, Dall	3	289	70	4.1	38	5
Terrell Davis, Den	2	259	75	4.1	15	3
John Riggins, Wash	2	230	64	3.6	43	2
Timmy Smith, Wash	1	204	22	9.3	58	2
Thurman Thomas, Buff	4	204	52	3.9	31	4
Roger Craig, SF	3	198	52	3.8	18	2
Marcus Allen, Rai	1	191	20	9.6	t74	2
Tony Dorsett, Dall	2	162	31	5.2	29	1

Receiving

	GP	No.	Yds	Avg	Lg	TD
Jerry Rice, SF	3	28	512	18.3	t44	7
Andre Reed, Buff	4	27	323	11.9	40	0
Roger Craig, SF	3	20	212	10.6	40	2
Thurman Thomas, Buff	4	20	144	7.2	24	0
Jay Novacek, Dall	3	17	178	10.5	23	2
Lynn Swann, Pitt	4	16	364	22.8	t64	3
Michael Irvin, Dall	3	16	256	16.0	25	2
Chuck Foreman, Minn	3	15	139	9.3	26	0
Cliff Branch, Rai	3	14	181	12.9	50	3
Preston Pearson, Balt-Pitt-Dall	5	12	105	8.8	14	0
Don Beebe, Buff-GB	5	12	171	14.3	43	2
Kenneth Davis, Buff	4	12	72	6.0	19	0
Antonio Freeman, GB	2	12	231	19.3	t81	3
Torry Holt, StL	2	12	158	13.2	32	1

Single-Game Leaders

Scoring

	Pts
Roger Craig: XIX, San Francisco vs Miami (1 R, 2 P)	18
Jerry Rice: XXIV, San Francisco vs Denver (3 P); XXIX, SF vs San Diego (3 P)	18
Ricky Watters: XXIX, San Francisco vs San Diego (1 R, 2 P)	18
Terrell Davis: XXXII, Denver vs Green Bay (3 R)	18

Rushing Yards

	Yds
Timmy Smith: XXII, Washington vs Denver	204
Marcus Allen: XVIII, LA Raiders vs Washington	191
John Riggins: XVII, Washington vs Miami	166
Franco Harris: IX, Pittsburgh vs Minnesota	158
Terrell Davis: XXXII, Denver vs Green Bay	157
Larry Csonka: VIII, Miami vs Minnesota	145
Clarence Davis: XI, Oakland vs Minnesota	137
Thurman Thomas: XXV, Buffalo vs NY Giants	135
Emmitt Smith: XXVIII, Dallas vs Buffalo	132
Matt Snell: III, New York Jets vs Baltimore Colts	121

Receptions

	No.
Dan Ross: XVI, Cincinnati vs San Francisco	11
Jerry Rice: XXIII, San Francisco vs Cincinnati	11
Tony Nathan: XIX, Miami vs San Francisco	10
Jerry Rice: XXIX, San Francisco vs San Diego	10
Andre Hastings: XXX, Pittsburgh vs Dallas	10
Ricky Sanders: XXII, Washington vs Denver	9
Antonio Freeman: XXXII, Green Bay vs Denver	9

Six tied with eight.

Touchdown Passes

	No.
Steve Young: XXIX, San Francisco vs San Diego	6
Joe Montana: XXIV, San Francisco vs Denver	5
Terry Bradshaw: XIII, Pittsburgh vs Dallas	4
Doug Williams: XXII, Washington vs Denver	4
Troy Aikman: XXVII, Dallas vs Buffalo	4

Five tied with three.

Passing Yards

	Yds
Kurt Warner: XXXIV, St. Louis vs Tennessee	414
Kurt Warner: XXXVI, St. Louis vs New England	365
Joe Montana: XXIII, San Francisco vs Cincinnati	357
Doug Williams: XXII, Washington vs Denver	340
John Elway: XXXIII, Denver vs Atlanta	336
Joe Montana: XIX, San Francisco vs Miami	331
Steve Young: XXIX, San Francisco vs San Diego	325
Terry Bradshaw: XIII, Pittsburgh vs Dallas	318
Dan Marino: XIX, Miami vs San Francisco	318
Terry Bradshaw: XIV, Pittsburgh vs LA Rams	309

Receiving Yards

	Yds
Jerry Rice: XXIII, San Francisco vs Cincinnati	215
Ricky Sanders: XXII, Washington vs Denver	193
Isaac Bruce: XXXIV, St. Louis vs Tennessee	162
Lynn Swann: X, Pittsburgh vs Dallas	161
Andre Reed: XXVII, Buffalo vs Dallas	152
Rod Smith: XXXIII, Denver vs Atlanta	152
Jerry Rice: XXIX, San Francisco vs San Diego	149
Jerry Rice: XXIV, San Francisco vs Denver	148
Max McGee: I, Green Bay vs Kansas City	138

NFL Playoff History

1933

NFL championship	Chicago Bears 23, NY Giants 21

1934

NFL championship	NY Giants 30, Chicago Bears 13

1935

NFL championship	Detroit 26, NY Giants 7

1936

NFL championship	Green Bay 21, Boston 6

1937

NFL championship	Washington 28, Chicago Bears 21

1938

NFL championship	NY Giants 23, Green Bay 17

1939

NFL championship	Green Bay 27, NY Giants 0

1940

NFL championship	Chicago Bears 73, Washington 0

1941

W. div. playoff	Chicago Bears 33, Green Bay 14
NFL championship	Chicago Bears 37, NY Giants 9

1942

NFL championship	Washington 14, Chicago Bears 6

1943

E. div. playoff	Washington 28, NY Giants 0
NFL championship	Chicago Bears 41, Washington 21

1944

NFL championship	Green Bay 14, NY Giants 7

1945

NFL championship	Cleveland 15, Washington 14

1946

NFL championship	Chicago Bears 24, NY Giants 14

1947

E. div. playoff	Philadelphia 21, Pittsburgh 0
NFL championship	Chi Cardinals 28, Philadelphia 21

1948

NFL championship	Philadelphia 7, Chi Cardinals 0

1949

NFL championship	Philadelphia 14, Los Angeles 0

1950

Am. Conf. playoff	Cleveland 8, NY Giants 3
Nat. Conf. playoff	Los Angeles 24, Chicago Bears 14
NFL championship	Cleveland 30, Los Angeles 28

1951

NFL championship	Los Angeles 24, Cleveland 17

1952

Nat. Conf. playoff	Detroit 31, Los Angeles 21
NFL championship	Detroit 17, Cleveland 7

1953

NFL championship	Detroit 17, Cleveland 16

1954

NFL championship	Cleveland 56, Detroit 10

1955

NFL championship	Cleveland 38, Los Angeles 14

1956

NFL championship	NY Giants 47, Chicago Bears 7

1957

W. Conf. playoff	Detroit 31, San Francisco 27
NFL championship	Detroit 59, Cleveland 14

1958

E. Conf. playoff	NY Giants 10, Cleveland 0
NFL championship	Baltimore 23, NY Giants 17

1959

NFL championship	Baltimore 31, NY Giants 16

1960

NFL championship	Philadelphia 17, Green Bay 13
AFL championship	Houston 24, LA Chargers 16

1961

NFL championship	Green Bay 37, NY Giants 0
AFL championship	Houston 10, San Diego 3

1962

NFL championship	Green Bay 16, NY Giants 7
AFL championship	Dallas Texans 20, Houston 17

1963

NFL championship	Chicago 14, NY Giants 10
AFL E. div. playoff	Boston 26, Buffalo 8
AFL championship	San Diego 51, Boston 10

1964

NFL championship	Cleveland 27, Baltimore 0
AFL championship	Buffalo 20, San Diego 7

1965

NFL W. Conf. playoff	Green Bay 13, Baltimore 10
NFL championship	Green Bay 23, Cleveland 12
AFL championship	Buffalo 23, San Diego 0

1966

NFL championship	Green Bay 34, Dallas 27
AFL championship	Kansas City 31, Buffalo 7

1967

NFL E. Conf. championship	Dallas 52, Cleveland 14
NFL W. Conf. championship	Green Bay 28, Los Angeles 7
NFL championship	Green Bay 21, Dallas 17
AFL championship	Oakland 40, Houston 7

1968

NFL E. Conf. championship	Cleveland 31, Dallas 20
NFL W. Conf. championship	Baltimore 24, Minnesota 14
NFL championship	Baltimore 34, Cleveland 0

1968 *(Cont.)*

AFL W. div. playoff	Oakland 41, Kansas City 6
AFL championship	NY Jets 27, Oakland 23

1969

NFL E. Conf. championship	Cleveland 38, Dallas 14
NFL W. Conf. championship	Minnesota 23, Los Angeles 20
NFL championship	Minnesota 27, Cleveland 7
AFL div. playoffs	Kansas City 13, NY Jets 6
	Oakland 56, Houston 7
AFL championship	Kansas City 17, Oakland 7

1970

AFC div. playoffs	Baltimore 17, Cincinnati 0
	Oakland 21, Miami 14
AFC championship	Baltimore 27, Oakland 17
NFC div. playoffs	Dallas 5, Detroit 0
	San Francisco 17, Minnesota 14
NFC championship	Dallas 17, San Francisco 10

1971

AFC div. playoffs	Miami 27, Kansas City 24
	Baltimore 20, Cleveland 3
AFC championship	Miami 21, Baltimore 0
NFC div. playoffs	Dallas 20, Minnesota 12
	San Francisco 24, Washington 20
NFC championship	Dallas 14, San Francisco 3

1972

AFC div. playoffs	Pittsburgh 13, Oakland 7
	Miami 20, Cleveland 14
AFC championship	Miami 21, Pittsburgh 17
NFC div. playoffs	Dallas 30, San Francisco 28
	Washington 16, Green Bay 3
NFC championship	Washington 26, Dallas 3

1973

AFC div. playoffs	Oakland 33, Pittsburgh 14
	Miami 34, Cincinnati 16
AFC championship	Miami 27, Oakland 10
NFC div. playoffs	Minnesota 27, Washington 20
	Dallas 27, Los Angeles 16
NFC championship	Minnesota 27, Dallas 10

1974

AFC div. playoffs	Oakland 28, Miami 26
	Pittsburgh 32, Buffalo 14
AFC championship	Pittsburgh 24, Oakland 13
NFC div. playoffs	Minnesota 30, St Louis 14
	Los Angeles 19, Washington 10
NFC championship	Minnesota 14, Los Angeles 10

1975

AFC div. playoffs	Pittsburgh 28, Baltimore 10
	Oakland 31, Cincinnati 28
AFC championship	Pittsburgh 16, Oakland 10
NFC div. playoffs	Los Angeles 35, St Louis 23
	Dallas 17, Minnesota 14
NFC championship	Dallas 37, Los Angeles 7

1976

AFC div. playoffs	Oakland 24, New England 21
	Pittsburgh 40, Baltimore 14
AFC championship	Oakland 24, Pittsburgh 7
NFC div. playoffs	Minnesota 35, Washington 20
	Los Angeles 14, Dallas 12
NFC championship	Minnesota 24, Los Angeles 13

NFL Playoff History *(Cont.)*

1977

AFC div. playoffs	Denver 34, Pittsburgh 21
	Oakland 37, Baltimore 31
AFC championship	Denver 20, Oakland 17
NFC div. playoffs	Dallas 37, Chicago 7
	Minnesota 14, Los Angeles 7
NFC championship	Dallas 23, Minnesota 6

1978

AFC 1st-rd. playoff	Houston 17, Miami 9
AFC div. playoffs	Houston 31, New England 14
	Pittsburgh 33, Denver 10
AFC championship	Pittsburgh 34, Houston 5
NFC 1st-rd. playoff	Atlanta 14, Philadelphia 13
NFC div. playoffs	Dallas 27, Atlanta 20
	Los Angeles 34, Minnesota 10
NFC championship	Dallas 28, Los Angeles 0

1979

AFC 1st-rd. playoff	Houston 13, Denver 7
AFC div. playoffs	Houston 17, San Diego 14
	Pittsburgh 34, Miami 14
AFC championship	Pittsburgh 27, Houston 13
NFC 1st-rd. playoff	Philadelphia 27, Chicago 17
NFC div. playoffs	Tampa Bay 24, Philadelphia 17
	Los Angeles 21, Dallas 19
NFC championship	Los Angeles 9, Tampa Bay 0

1980

AFC 1st-rd. playoff	Oakland 27, Houston 7
AFC div. playoffs	San Diego 20, Buffalo 14
	Oakland 14, Cleveland 12
AFC championship	Oakland 34, San Diego 27
NFC 1st-rd. playoff	Dallas 34, Los Angeles 13
NFC div. playoffs	Philadelphia 31, Minnesota 16
	Dallas 30, Atlanta 27
NFC championship	Philadelphia 20, Dallas 7

1981

AFC 1st-rd. playoff	Buffalo 31, NY Jets 27
AFC div. playoffs	San Diego 41, Miami 38
	Cincinnati 28, Buffalo 21
AFC championship	Cincinnati 27, San Diego 7
NFC 1st-rd. playoff	NY Giants 27, Philadelphia 21
NFC div. playoffs	Dallas 38, Tampa Bay 0
	San Francisco 38, NY Giants 24
NFC championship	San Francisco 28, Dallas 27

1982

AFC 1st-rd. playoffs	Miami 28, New England 13
	LA Raiders 27, Cleveland 10
	NY Jets 44, Cincinnati 17
	San Diego 31, Pittsburgh 28
AFC div. playoffs	NY Jets 17, LA Raiders 14
	Miami 34, San Diego 13
AFC championship	Miami 14, NY Jets 0
NFC 1st-rd. playoffs	Washington 31, Detroit 7
	Green Bay 41, St Louis 16
	Minnesota 30, Atlanta 24
	Dallas 30, Tampa Bay 17
NFC div. playoffs	Washington 21, Minnesota 7
	Dallas 37, Green Bay 26
NFC championship	Washington 31, Dallas 17

1983

AFC 1st-rd. playoff	Seattle 31, Denver 7
AFC div. playoffs	Seattle 27, Miami 20
	LA Raiders 38, Pittsburgh 10
AFC championship	LA Raiders 30, Seattle 14
NFC 1st-rd. playoff	LA Rams 24, Dallas 17

1983 *(Cont.)*

NFC div. playoffs	San Francisco 24, Detroit 23
	Washington 51, LA Rams 7
NFC championship	Washington 24, San Francisco 21

1984

AFC 1st-rd. playoff	Seattle 13, LA Raiders 7
AFC div. playoffs	Miami 31, Seattle 10
	Pittsburgh 24, Denver 17
AFC championship	Miami 45, Pittsburgh 28
NFC 1st-rd. playoff	NY Giants 16, LA Rams 13
NFC div. playoffs	San Francisco 21, NY Giants 10
	Chicago 23, Washington 19
NFC championship	San Francisco 23, Chicago 0

1985

AFC 1st-rd. playoff	New England 26, NY Jets 14
AFC div. playoffs	Miami 24, Cleveland 21
	New England 27, LA Raiders 20
AFC championship	New England 31, Miami 14
NFC 1st-rd. playoff	NY Giants 17, San Francisco 3
NFC div. playoffs	LA Rams 20, Dallas 0
	Chicago 21, NY Giants 0
NFC championship	Chicago 24, LA Rams 0

1986

AFC 1st-rd. playoff	NY Jets 35, Kansas City 15
AFC div. playoffs	Cleveland 23, NY Jets 20
	Denver 22, New England 17
AFC championship	Denver 23, Cleveland 20
NFC 1st-rd. playoff	Washington 19, LA Rams 7
NFC div playoffs	Washington 27, Chicago 13
	NY Giants 49, San Francisco 3
NFC championship	NY Giants 17, Washington 0

1987

AFC 1st-rd. playoff	Houston 23, Seattle 20
AFC div. playoffs	Cleveland 38, Indianapolis 21
	Denver 34, Houston 10
AFC championship	Denver 38, Cleveland 33
NFC 1st-rd. playoff	Minnesota 44, New Orleans 10
NFC div playoffs	Minnesota 36, San Francisco 24
	Washington 21, Chicago 17
NFC championship	Washington 17, Minnesota 10

1988

AFC 1st-rd. playoff	Houston 24, Cleveland 23
AFC div. playoffs	Cincinnati 21, Seattle 13
	Buffalo 17, Houston 10
AFC championship	Cincinnati 21, Buffalo 10
NFC 1st-rd. playoff	Minnesota 28, LA Rams 17
NFC div. playoffs	Chicago 20, Philadelphia 12
	San Francisco 34, Minnesota 9
NFC championship	San Francisco 28, Chicago 3

1989

AFC 1st-rd. playoff	Pittsburgh 26, Houston 23
AFC div. playoffs	Cleveland 34, Buffalo 30
	Denver 24, Pittsburgh 23
AFC championship	Denver 37, Cleveland 21
NFC 1st-rd. playoff	LA Rams 21, Philadelphia 7
NFC div. playoffs	LA Rams 19, NY Giants 13
	San Francisco 41, Minnesota 13
NFC championship	San Francisco 30, LA Rams 3

1990

AFC 1st-rd. playoffs	Miami 17, Kansas City 16
	Cincinnati 41, Houston 14
AFC div. playoffs	Buffalo 44, Miami 34
	LA Raiders 20, Cincinnati 10
AFC championship	Buffalo 51, LA Raiders 3
NFC 1st-rd. playoffs	Chicago 16, New Orleans 6

1990 (Cont.)

NFC 1st-rd. playoffs	Washington 20, Philadelphia 6
NFC div. playoffs	NY Giants 31, Chicago 3
	San Francisco 28, Washington 10
NFC championship	NY Giants 15, San Francisco 13

1991

AFC 1st-rd. playoffs	Houston 17, NY Jets 10
	Kansas City 10, LA Raiders 6
AFC div. playoffs	Denver 26, Houston 24
	Buffalo 37, Kansas City 14
AFC championship	Buffalo 10, Denver 7
NFC 1st-rd. playoffs	Atlanta 27, New Orleans 20
	Dallas 17, Chicago 13
NFC div. playoffs	Washington 24, Atlanta 7
	Detroit 38, Dallas 6
NFC championship	Washington 41, Detroit 10

1992

AFC 1st-rd. playoffs	San Diego 17, Kansas City 0
	Buffalo 41, Houston 38 (OT)
AFC div. playoffs	Buffalo 24, Pittsburgh 3
	Miami 31, San Diego 0
AFC championship	Buffalo 29, Miami 10
NFC 1st-rd. playoffs	Washington 24, Minnesota 7
	Philadelphia 36, New Orleans 20
NFC div. playoffs	San Francisco 20, Washington 13
	Dallas 34, Philadelphia 10
NFC championship	Dallas 30, San Francisco 20

1993

AFC 1st-rd. playoffs	LA Raiders 42, Denver 24
	Kansas City 27, Pittsburgh 24 (OT)
AFC div. playoffs	Buffalo 29, LA Raiders 23
	Kansas City 28, Houston 20
AFC championship	Buffalo 30, Kansas City 13
NFC 1st-rd. playoffs	NY Giants 17, Minnesota 10
	Green Bay 28, Detroit 24
NFC div. playoffs	San Francisco 44, NY Giants 3
	Dallas 27, Green Bay 17
NFC championship	Dallas 38, San Francisco 21

1994

AFC 1st-rd. playoffs	Miami 27, Kansas City 17
	Cleveland 20, New England 13
AFC div. playoffs	San Diego 22, Miami 21
	Pittsburgh 29, Cleveland 9
AFC championship	San Diego 17, Pittsburgh 13
NFC 1st-rd. playoffs	Green Bay 16, Detroit 12
	Chicago 35, Minnesota 18
NFC div. playoffs	Dallas 35, Green Bay 9
	San Francisco 44, Chicago 15
NFC championship	San Francisco 38, Dallas 28

1995

AFC 1st-rd. playoffs	Buffalo 37, Miami 22
	Indianapolis 35, San Diego 20
AFC div. playoffs	Pittsburgh 40, Buffalo 21
	Indianapolis 10, Kansas City 7
AFC championship	Pittsburgh 20, Indianapolis 16
NFC 1st-rd. playoffs	Philadelphia 58, Detroit 37
	Green Bay 37, Atlanta 20
NFC div. playoffs	Dallas 30, Philadelphia 11
	Green Bay 27, San Francisco 17
NFC championship	Dallas 38, Green Bay 27

1996

AFC 1st-rd. playoffs	Jacksonville 30, Buffalo 27
	Pittsburgh 42, Indianapolis 14
AFC div. playoffs	Jacksonville 30, Denver 27
	New England 28, Pittsburgh 3
AFC championship	New England 20, Jacksonville 6

1996 (Cont.)

NFC 1st-rd. playoffs	Dallas 40, Minnesota 15
	San Francisco 14, Philadelphia 0
NFC div. playoffs	Green Bay 35, San Francisco 14
	Carolina 26, Dallas 17
NFC championship	Green Bay 30, Carolina 13

1997

AFC 1st-rd. playoffs	Denver 42, Jacksonville 17
	New England 17, Miami 3
AFC div. playoffs	Denver 14, Kansas City 0
	Pittsburgh 7, New England 6
AFC championship	Denver 24, Pittsburgh 21
NFC 1st-rd. playoffs	Minnesota 23, NY Giants 22
	Tampa Bay 20, Detroit 10
NFC div. playoffs	Green Bay 21, Tampa Bay 7
	San Francisco 38, Minnesota 22
NFC championship	Green Bay 23, San Francisco 10

1998

AFC 1st-rd. playoffs	Miami 24, Buffalo 17
	Jacksonville 25, New England 10
AFC div. playoffs	Denver 38, Miami 3
	NY Jets 34, Jacksonville 24
AFC championship	Denver 23, NY Jets 10
NFC 1st-rd. playoffs	Arizona 20, Dallas 7
	San Francisco 30, Green Bay 27
NFC div. playoffs	Atlanta 20, San Francisco 18
	Minnesota 41, Arizona 21
NFC championship	Atlanta 30, Minnesota 27 (ot)

1999

AFC 1st-rd. playoffs	Tennessee 22, Buffalo 16
	Miami 20, Seattle 17
AFC div. playoffs	Jacksonville 62, Miami 7
	Tennessee 19, Indianapolis 16
AFC championship	Tennessee 33, Jacksonville 14
NFC 1st-rd. playoffs	Washington 27, Detroit 13
	Minnesota 27, Dallas 10
NFC div. playoffs	Tampa Bay 14, Washington 13
	St Louis 49, Minnesota 37
NFC championship	St Louis 11, Tampa Bay 6

2000

AFC 1st-rd. playoffs	Baltimore 21, Denver 3
	Miami 23, Indianapolis 17 (ot)
AFC div. playoffs	Baltimore 24, Tennessee 10
	Oakland 27, Miami 0
AFC championship	Baltimore 16, Oakland 3
NFC 1st-rd. playoffs	New Orleans 31, St. Louis 28
	Philadelphia 21, Tampa Bay 3
NFC div. playoffs	NY Giants 20, Philadelphia 10
	Minnesota 34, New Orleans 16
NFC championship	NY Giants 41, Minnesota 0

2001

AFC 1st-rd. playoffs	Oakland 38, NY Jets 24
	Baltimore 20, Miami 3
AFC div. playoffs	New England 16, Oakland 13(ot)
	Pittsburgh 27, Baltimore 10
AFC championship	New England 24, Pittsburgh 17
NFC 1st-rd. playoffs	Philadelphia 31, Tampa Bay 9
	Green Bay 25, San Francisco 15
NFC div. playoffs	Philadelphia 33, Chicago 19
	St. Louis 45, Green Bay 17
NFC championship	St. Louis 29, Philadelphia 24

Career Leaders

Scoring

	Yrs	TD	FG	PAT	Pts
†Gary Anderson	20	0	476	705	2,133
†Morten Andersen	20	0	464	644	2,036
George Blanda	26	9	335	943	2,002
Norm Johnson	18	0	366	638	1,736
Nick Lowery	18	0	383	562	1,711
Jan Stenerud	19	0	373	580	1,699
Eddie Murray	19	0	352	539	1,595
Al Del Greco	17	0	347	543	1,584
Pat Leahy	18	0	304	558	1,470
Jim Turner	16	1	304	521	1,439
Matt Bahr	17	0	300	522	1,422
Mark Moseley	16	0	300	482	1,382
Jim Bakken	17	0	282	534	1,380
Fred Cox	15	0	282	519	1,365
Lou Groza	17	1	234	641	1,349
Jim Breech	14	0	243	517	1,246
Pete Stoyanovich	12	0	272	420	1,236
Chris Bahr	14	0	241	490	1,213
Kevin Butler	13	0	265	426	1,208
†Steve Christie	12	0	281	364	1,207

Rushing

	Yrs	Att	Yds	Avg	Lg	TD
Walter Payton	13	3,838	16,726	4.4	76	110
†Emmitt Smith	12	3,798	16,187	4.3	75	145
Barry Sanders	10	3,062	15,269	5.0	85	99
Eric Dickerson	11	2,996	13,259	4.4	85	90
Tony Dorsett	12	2,936	12,739	4.3	99	77
Jim Brown	9	2,359	12,312	5.2	80	106
Marcus Allen	16	3,022	12,243	4.1	61	123
Franco Harris	13	2,949	12,120	4.1	75	91
Thurman Thomas	13	2,877	12,074	4.2	80	66
John Riggins	14	2,916	11,352	3.9	66	104
O.J. Simpson	11	2,404	11,236	4.7	94	61
†Jerome Bettis	9	2,686	10,876	4.1	71	53
†Ricky Watters	9	2,550	10,325	4.1	57	77
Ottis Anderson	14	2,562	10,273	4.0	76	81
Marshall Faulk	8	2,155	9,442	4.4	71	79
Earl Campbell	8	2,187	9,407	4.3	81	74
Curtis Martin	7	2,343	9,267	4.0	70	64
†Terry Allen	10	2,152	8,614	4.0	55	73
Jim Taylor	10	1,941	8,597	4.4	84	83
Joe Perry	14	1,737	8,378	4.8	78	53

Touchdowns

	Yrs	Rush	Rec	Ret	Total TD
†Jerry Rice	17	10	185	1	196
†Emmitt Smith	12	148	11	0	159
Marcus Allen	16	123	21	1	145
†Cris Carter	15	0	129	1	130
Jim Brown	9	106	20	0	126
Walter Payton	13	110	15	0	125
John Riggins	14	104	12	0	116
Lenny Moore	12	63	48	2	113
†Marshall Faulk	8	79	31	0	110
Barry Sanders	10	99	10	0	109

	Yrs	Rush	Rec	Ret	Total TD
Don Hutson	11	3	99	3	105
Steve Largent	14	1	100	0	101
Franco Harris	13	91	9	0	100
†Tim Brown	14	1	95	3	99
Eric Dickerson	11	90	6	0	96
Jim Taylor	10	83	10	0	93
Tony Dorsett	12	77	13	1	91
Bobby Mitchell	11	18	65	8	91
†Ricky Watters	10	78	13	0	91

Two tied with 90.

Combined Yards Gained

	Yrs	Total	Rush	Rec	Int Ret	Punt Ret	Kickoff Ret	Fum Ret
Walter Payton	13	21,803	16,726	4,538	0	0	539	0
†Jerry Rice	17	21,017	625	20,386	0	0	6	0
†Brian Mitchell	12	20,265	1,947	2,298	0	3,811	10,710	7
†Emmitt Smith	12	19,110	16,187	2,923	0	0	0	0
Barry Sanders	10	18,308	15,269	2,921	0	0	118	0
Herschel Walker	12	18,168	8,225	4,859	0	0	5,084	0
†Tim Brown	14	17,863	171	13,237	0	3,217	1,235	3
Marcus Allen	16	17,648	12,243	5,411	0	0	0	-6
Eric Metcalf	11	16,727	2,385	5,553	0	3,042	5,747	0
Thurman Thomas	13	16,532	12,074	4,458	0	0	0	0
Tony Dorsett	12	16,326	12,739	3,554	0	0	0	33
Henry Ellard	16	15,718	50	13,777	0	1,527	364	0
Irving Fryar	17	15,594	242	12,785	0	2055	505	7
Jim Brown	9	15,459	12,312	2,499	0	0	648	0
Eric Dickerson	11	15,411	13,259	2,137	0	0	0	15
James Brooks	12	14,910	7,962	3,621	0	565	2,762	0
†Marshall Faulk	8	14,889	9,442	5,447	0	0	0	0
Franco Harris	13	14,622	12,120	2,287	0	0	233	-18
†Ricky Watters	9	14,499	10,325	4,141	0	0	0	33
O.J. Simpson	11	14,368	11,236	2,142	0	0	990	0

† Active in 2001.

Career Leaders (Cont.)

Passing

PASSING EFFICIENCY*

	Yrs	Att	Comp	Pct Comp	Yds	Avg Gain	TD	Pct TD	Int	Pct Int	Rating Pts
Steve Young	15	4,149	2,667	64.3	33,124	7.98	232	5.6	107	2.6	96.8
Joe Montana	15	5,391	3,409	63.2	40,551	7.52	273	5.1	139	2.6	92.3
†Brett Favre	11	5,422	3,311	60.8	38,627	7.10	287	5.3	172	3.2	86.8
Dan Marino	17	8,358	4,967	59.4	61,361	7.34	420	5.0	252	3.0	86.4
†Peyton Manning	4	2,226	1,357	61.0	16,418	7.36	111	5.0	81	3.6	85.1
†Mark Brunell	8	3,145	1,897	60.3	22,521	7.16	125	4.0	79	2.5	85.0
Jim Kelly	11	4,779	2,874	60.1	35,467	7.42	237	5.0	175	3.7	84.4
Roger Staubach	11	2,958	1,685	57.0	22,700	7.67	153	5.2	109	3.7	83.4
†Rich Gannon	13	3,295	1,949	59.2	22,256	6.76	145	4.4	88	2.7	83.1
†Brad Johnson	8	2,379	1,465	61.6	16,379	6.89	92	3.9	68	2.9	83.1
Neil Lomax	8	3,153	1,817	57.6	22,771	7.22	136	4.3	90	2.9	82.7
Sonny Jurgensen	18	4,262	2,433	57.1	32,224	7.56	255	6.0	189	4.4	82.6
Len Dawson	19	3,741	2,136	57.1	28,711	7.67	239	6.4	183	4.9	82.6
†Neil O'Donnell	12	3,167	1,844	58.2	21,434	6.77	118	3.7	67	2.1	82.4
Troy Aikman	12	4,715	2,898	61.5	32,942	6.99	171	3.6	141	3.0	82.0
Ken Anderson	16	4,475	2,654	59.3	32,838	7.34	197	4.4	160	3.6	81.9
Bernie Kosar	12	3,365	1,994	59.3	23,301	6.92	124	3.7	87	2.6	81.8
Danny White	13	2,950	1,761	59.7	21,959	7.44	155	5.3	132	4.5	81.7
Dave Krieg	19	5,311	3,105	58.5	38,147	7.18	261	4.9	199	3.7	81.5
†Randall Cunningham	16	4,289	2,429	56.6	29,979	6.99	207	4.8	134	3.1	81.5

*1,500 or more attempts. The passer ratings are based on performance standards established for completion percentage, interception percentage, touchdown percentage and average gain. Passers are allocated points according to how their marks compare with those standards.

YARDS

	Yrs	Att	Comp	Pct Comp	Yds			Yrs	Att	Comp	Pct Comp	Yds
Dan Marino	17	8,358	4,967	59.4	61,361		Boomer Esiason	14	5,205	2,969	57.0	37,920
John Elway	16	7,250	4,123	56.9	51,475		Jim Kelly	11	4,779	2,874	60.1	35,467
Warren Moon	17	6,823	3,988	58.5	49,325		Jim Everett	12	4,923	2,841	57.7	34,837
Fran Tarkenton	18	6,467	3,686	57.0	47,003		Jim Hart	19	5,076	2,593	51.1	34,665
Dan Fouts	15	5,604	3,297	58.8	43,040		Steve DeBerg	17	4,746	2,924	61.6	34,241
Joe Montana	15	5,391	3,409	63.2	40,551		John Hadl	16	4,687	2,363	50.4	33,503
Johnny Unitas	18	5,186	2,830	54.6	40,239		Phil Simms	14	4,647	2,576	55.4	33,462
†Vinny Testaverde	15	5,649	3,157	55.9	39,059		Steve Young	15	4,149	2,667	64.3	33,124
†Brett Favre	11	5,422	3,311	60.8	38,627		Troy Aikman	12	4,715	2,898	61.5	32,942
Dave Krieg	19	5,311	3,105	58.5	38,147		Ken Anderson	16	4,475	2,654	59.3	32,838

TOUCHDOWNS

	No.		No.		No.
Dan Marino	420	Boomer Esiason	247	Jim Hart	209
Fran Tarkenton	342	John Hadl	244	†Randall Cunningham	207
John Elway	300	†Vinny Testaverde	241	Jim Everett	203
Warren Moon	291	Len Dawson	239	Phil Simms	199
Johnny Unitas	290	Jim Kelly	237	Ken Anderson	197
†Brett Favre	287	George Blanda	236	Joe Ferguson	196
Joe Montana	273	Steve Young	232	Bobby Layne	196
Dave Krieg	261	John Brodie	214	Norm Snead	196
Sonny Jurgensen	255	Terry Bradshaw	212	Steve DeBerg	196
Dan Fouts	254	Y.A. Tittle	212	Ken Stabler	194

† Active in 2001.

Career Leaders *(Cont.)*
Receiving
RECEPTIONS

	Yrs	No.	Yds	Avg	Lg	TD		Yrs	No.	Yds	Avg	Lg	TD
†Jerry Rice	17	1,364	20,386	15.0	96	185	Michael Irvin	12	750	11,904	15.9	87	65
†Cris Carter	15	1,093	13,833	12.7	80	129	Charlie Joiner	18	750	12,146	16.2	87	65
Andre Reed	16	951	13,198	13.9	83	87	Andre Rison	12	743	10,205	13.7	80	84
Art Monk	16	940	12,721	13.5	79	68	Gary Clark	11	699	10,856	15.5	84	65
†Tim Brown	14	937	13,237	14.1	80	95	†Shannon Sharpe	12	692	8,604	12.4	68	51
Irving Fryar	17	851	12,785	15.0	80	84	†Herman Moore	11	670	9,174	13.7	93	62
Steve Largent	14	819	13,089	16.0	74	100	†Terance Mathis	12	666	8,591	12.9	81	61
Henry Ellard	16	814	13,777	16.9	81	65	Ozzie Newsome	13	662	7,980	12.1	74	47
†Larry Centers	12	765	6,303	8.2	54	27	Charley Taylor	13	649	9,110	14.0	88	79
James Lofton	16	764	14,004	18.3	80	75	Drew Hill	14	634	9,831	15.5	81	60

YARDS

†Jerry Rice	20,386	Art Monk	12,721	Harold Jackson	10,372
James Lofton	14,004	Charlie Joiner	12,146	Lance Alworth	10,266
Henry Ellard	13,777	†Tim Brown	13,237	Andre Rison	10,205
Andre Reed	13,198	Michael Irvin	11,904	Drew Hill	9,831
Steve Largent	13,089	Don Maynard	11,834	†Rob Moore	9,368
†Cris Carter	13,833	Gary Clark	10,856	Raymond Berry	9,275
Irving Fryar	12,785	Stanley Morgan	10,716		

Sacks

Reggie White	198.0	Chris Doleman	150.5
†Bruce Smith	186.0	Richard Dent	137.5
Kevin Greene	160.0		

Note: Officially compiled since 1982.

Interceptions

	Yrs	No.	Yds	Avg	Lg	TD
Paul Krause	16	81	1185	14.6	81	3
Emlen Tunnell	14	79	1282	16.2	55	4
Dick (Night Train) Lane	14	68	1207	17.8	80	5
Ken Riley	15	65	596	9.2	66	5
Ronnie Lott	14	63	730	11.6	83	5

Punting

	Yrs	No.	Yds	Avg	Lg	Blk
Sammy Baugh	16	338	15,245	45.1	85	9
Tommy Davis	11	511	22,833	44.7	82	2
†Darren Bennett	7	602	26,800	44.5	66	1
Yale Lary	11	503	22,279	44.3	74	4
†Tom Rouen	9	612	26,907	44.0	76	5

Note: 250 or more punts.

Punt Returns

	Yrs	No.	Yds	Avg	Lg	TD
George McAfee	8	112	1431	12.8	74	2
Jack Christiansen	8	85	1084	12.8	89	8
†Darrien Gordon	7	250	3163	12.7	94	6
Claude Gibson	5	110	1381	12.6	85	3
†Desmond Howard	10	235	2847	12.1	95	8
†Jermaine Lewis	6	231	2730	11.8	62	6

Note: 75 or more returns.

Kickoff Returns

	Yrs	No.	Yds	Avg	Lg	TD
Gale Sayers	7	91	2781	30.6	103	6
Lynn Chandnois	7	92	2720	29.6	93	3
Abe Woodson	9	193	5538	28.7	105	5
Claude (Buddy) Young	6	90	2514	27.9	104	2
Travis Williams	5	102	2801	27.5	105	6

Note: 75 or more returns.

† Active in 2001.

Single-Season Leaders

Scoring

POINTS

	Year	TD	PAT	FG	Pts
Paul Hornung, GB	1960	15	41	15	176
Gary Anderson, Minn	1998	0	59	35	164
Mark Moseley, Wash	1983	0	62	33	161
Marshall Faulk, StL	2000	26	0	0	156
Gino Cappelletti, Bos	1964	7	38	25	155
Emmitt Smith, Dall	1995	25	0	0	150
Chip Lohmiller, Wash	1991	0	56	31	149
Gino Cappelletti, Bos	1961	8	48	17	147
Paul Hornung, GB	1961	10	41	15	146
Jim Turner, NYJ	1968	0	43	34	145
John Kasay, Car	1996	0	34	37	145
Mike Vanderjagt,	1999	0	34	38	145
John Riggins, Wash	1983	24	0	0	144
Kevin Butler, Chi	1985	0	51	31	144
Olindo Mare, Mia	1999	0	27	39	144

Note: Cappelletti's 1964 total includes a two-point conversion.

TOUCHDOWNS

	Year	Rush	Rec	Ret	Total
Marshall Faulk, StL	2000	18	8	0	26
Emmitt Smith, Dall	1995	25	0	0	25
John Riggins, Wash	1983	24	0	0	24
O.J. Simpson, Buff	1975	16	7	0	23
Jerry Rice, SF	1987	1	22	0	23
Terrell Davis, Den	1998	21	2	0	23
Gale Sayers, Chi	1965	14	6	2	22
Emmitt Smith, Dall	1994	21	1	0	22

FIELD GOALS

	Year	Att	No.
Olindo Mare, Mia	1999	46	39
John Kasay, Car	1996	45	37
Cary Blanchard, Ind	1996	40	36
Al Del Greco, Tenn	1998	39	36
Gary Anderson, Minn	1998	35	35
Jeff Jaeger, LA Raiders	1993	44	35
Ali Haji-Sheikh, NYG	1983	42	35
Matt Stover, Balt	2000	39	35

Six tied with 34.

Rushing

YARDS GAINED

	Year	Att	Yds	Avg
Eric Dickerson, LA Rams	1984	379	2105	5.6
Barry Sanders, Det	1997	335	2053	6.1
Terrell Davis, Den	1998	392	2008	5.1
O.J. Simpson, Buff	1973	332	2003	6.0
Earl Campbell, Hou	1980	373	1934	5.2
Jim Brown, Clev	1963	291	1883	6.4
Barry Sanders, Det	1994	331	1883	5.7
Walter Payton, Chi	1977	339	1852	5.5
Jamal Anderson, Atl	1998	410	1846	4.5
Eric Dickerson, LA Rams	1986	404	1821	4.5
O.J. Simpson, Buff	1975	329	1817	5.5
Eric Dickerson, LA Rams	1983	390	1808	4.6

AVERAGE GAIN

	Year	Avg
Beattie Feathers, Chi	1934	8.44
Randall Cunningham, Phil	1990	7.98
Bobby Douglass, Chi	1972	6.87

Minimum 100 attempts.

TOUCHDOWNS

	Year	No.
Emmitt Smith, Dall	1995	25
John Riggins, Wash	1983	24
Emmitt Smith, Dall	1994	21
Joe Morris, NYG	1985	21
Terry Allen, Wash	1996	21
Terrell Davis, Den	1998	21

Passing

YARDS GAINED

	Year	Att	Comp	Pct	Yds
Dan Marino, Mia	1984	564	362	64.2	5084
Kurt Warner, StL	2001	546	375	68.7	4830
Dan Fouts, SD	1981	609	360	59.1	4802
Dan Marino, Mia	1986	623	378	60.7	4746
Dan Fouts, SD	1980	589	348	59.1	4715
Warren Moon, Hou	1991	655	404	61.7	4690
Warren Moon, Hou	1990	584	362	62.0	4689
Neil Lomax, StL Cards	1984	560	345	61.6	4614
Drew Bledsoe, NE	1994	691	400	57.9	4555
Lynn Dickey, GB	1983	484	289	59.7	4458

PASSER RATING

	Year	Rat.
Steve Young, SF	1994	112.8
Joe Montana, SF	1989	112.4
Milt Plum, Clev	1960	110.4
Sammy Baugh, Wash	1945	109.9
Kurt Warner, Rams	1999	109.2

TOUCHDOWNS

	Year	No.
Dan Marino, Mia	1984	48
Dan Marino, Mia	1986	44
Kurt Warner, StL	1999	41
Brett Favre, GB	1995	38

Four tied with 36.

Single-Season Leaders (Cont.)
Receiving

RECEPTIONS

	Year	No.	Yds
Herman Moore, Det	1995	123	1686
Cris Carter, Minn	1994	122	1256
Jerry Rice, SF	1995	122	1848
Cris Carter, Minn	1995	122	1371
Isaac Bruce, Rams	1995	119	1781
Jimmy Smith, Jax	1999	116	1636
Marvin Harrison, Ind	1999	115	1663
Rod Smith, Den	2001	113	1343
Sterling Sharpe, GB	1993	112	1274
Jerry Rice, SF	1994	112	1499
Jimmy Smith, Jax	2001	112	1373

YARDS GAINED

	Year	Yds
Jerry Rice, SF	1995	1848
Isaac Bruce, Rams	1995	1781
Charley Hennigan, Hou	1961	1746
Herman Moore, Det	1995	1686
Marvin Harrison, Ind	1999	1663

TOUCHDOWNS

	Year	No.
Jerry Rice, SF	1987	22
Mark Clayton, Mia	1984	18
Sterling Sharpe, GB	1994	18

Six tied with 17.

All-Purpose Yards

	Year	Run	Rec	Ret	Total
Lionel James, SD	1985	516	1027	992	2535
Terry Metcalf, StL Cards	1975	816	378	1268	2462
Mack Herron, NE	1974	824	474	1146	2444
Gale Sayers, Chi	1966	1231	447	762	2440
Marshall Faulk, Rams	1999	1381	1048	0	2429
Timmy Brown, Phil	1963	841	487	1100	2428
Barry Sanders, Det	1997	2053	305	0	2358
Tim Brown, Rai	1988	50	725	1542	2317
Marcus Allen, Rai	1985	1759	555	–6	2308
Timmy Brown, Phil	1962	545	849	912	2306
Edgerrin James, Ind	2000	1709	594	0	2303
Gale Sayers, Chi	1965	867	507	898	2272

Punting

	Year	No.	Yds	Avg
Sammy Baugh, Wash	1940	35	1799	51.4
Yale Lary, Det	1963	35	1713	48.9
Sammy Baugh, Wash	1941	30	1462	48.7
Yale Lary, Det	1961	52	2516	48.4
Sammy Baugh, Wash	1942	37	1783	48.2

Sacks

	Year	No.
Michael Strahan, NYG	2001	22.5
Mark Gastineau, NYJ	1984	22
Reggie White, Phil	1987	21
Chris Doleman, Minn	1989	21
Lawrence Taylor, NYG	1986	20.5

Interceptions

	Year	No.
Dick (Night Train) Lane, Rams	1952	14
Dan Sandifer, Wash	1948	13
Spec Sanders, NY Yanks	1950	13
Lester Hayes, Oak	1980	13

Nine tied with 12.

Kickoff Returns

	Year	Avg
Travis Williams, GB	1967	41.1
Gale Sayers, Chi	1967	37.7
Ollie Matson, Chi Cards	1958	35.5
Jim Duncan, Balt Colts	1970	35.4
Lynn Chandnois, Pitt	1952	35.2

Punt Returns

	Year	Avg
Herb Rich, Balt Colts	1950	23.0
Jack Christiansen, Det	1952	21.5
Dick Christy, NY Titans	1961	21.3
Bob Hayes, Dall	1968	20.8

Single-Game Leaders
Scoring

POINTS

	Date	Pts
Ernie Nevers, Chi Cards vs Chi	11-28-29	40
Dub Jones, Clev vs Chi	11-25-51	36
Gale Sayers, Chi vs SF	12-12-65	36
Paul Hornung, GB vs Balt Colts	10-8-61	33

On Thanksgiving Day, 1929, Nevers scored all the Cardinals' points on six rushing TDs and four PATs. The Cards defeated Red Grange and the Bears, 40–6. Jones and Sayers each rushed for four touchdowns and scored two more on returns in their teams' victories. Hornung scored four touchdowns and kicked 6 PATs and a field goal in a 45-7 win over the Colts.

FIELD GOALS

	Date	No.
Jim Bakken, StL Cards vs Pitt	9-24-67	7
Rich Karlis, Minn vs Rams	11-5-89	7
Chris Boniol, Dall vs GB	11-18-96	7

Fourteen players tied with 6 FGs each.

Bakken was 7 for 9, Karlis and Boniol 7 for 7.

Single-Game Leaders *(Cont.)*

Scoring *(Cont.)*

TOUCHDOWNS

	Date	No.
Ernie Nevers, Chi Cards vs Chi	11-28-29	6
Dub Jones, Clev vs Chi	11-25-51	6
Gale Sayers, Chi vs SF	12-12-65	6
Bob Shaw, Chi Cards vs Balt Colts	10-2-50	5
Jim Brown, Clev vs Balt Colts	11-1-59	5
Abner Haynes, Dall Texans vs Oak	11-26-61	5
Billy Cannon, Hou vs NY Titans	12-10-61	5
Cookie Gilchrist, Buff vs NYJ	12-8-63	5
Paul Hornung, GB vs Balt Colts	12-12-65	5
Kellen Winslow, SD vs Oak	11-22-81	5
Jerry Rice, SF vs Atl	10-14-90	5
James Stewart, Jax vs Phil	10-12-97	5

Rushing

YARDS GAINED

	Date	Yds
Corey Dillon, Cin vs Den	10-22-00	278
Walter Payton, Chi vs Minn	11-20-77	275
O.J. Simpson, Buff vs Det	11-25-76	273
Shaun Alexander, Sea vs Oak	11-11-01	266
Mike Anderson, Den vs NO	12-3-00	251

CARRIES

	Date	No.
Jamie Morris, Wash vs Cin	12-17-88	45
Butch Woolfolk, NYG vs Phil	11-20-83	43
James Wilder, TB vs GB	9-30-84	43
James Wilder, TB vs Pitt	10-30-83	42
Terrell Davis, Den vs Buff.	10-26-97	42

TOUCHDOWNS

	Date	No.
Ernie Nevers, Chi Cards vs Chi	11-28-29	6
Jim Brown, Clev vs Balt Colts	11-1-59	5
Cookie Gilchrist, Buff vs NYJ	12-8-63	5
James Stewart, Jax vs Phil	10-12-97	5

Passing

YARDS GAINED

	Date	Yds
N. Van Brocklin, Rams vs NY Yanks	9-28-51	554
Warren Moon, Hou vs KC	12-16-90	527
Boomer Esiason, Ariz vs Wash	11-10-96	522
Dan Marino, Mia vs NYJ	10-23-88	521
Phil Simms, NYG vs Cin	10-13-85	513

TOUCHDOWNS

	Date	No.
Sid Luckman, Chi vs NYG	11-14-43	7
Adrian Burk, Phil vs Wash	10-17-54	7
George Blanda, Hou vs NY Titans	11-19-61	7
Y. A. Tittle, NYG vs Wash	10-28-62	7
Joe Kapp, Minn vs Balt Colts	9-28-69	7

COMPLETIONS

	Date	No.
Drew Bledsoe, NE vs Minn	11-13-94	45
Richard Todd, NYJ vs SF	9-21-80	42
Vinny Testaverde, NYJ vs Sea	12-6-98	42
Warren Moon, Hou vs Dall	11-10-91	41
Ken Anderson, Cin vs SD	12-20-82	40
Phil Simms, NYG vs Cin	10-13-85	40
Brad Johnson, TB vs Chi	11-18-01	40

Receiving

YARDS GAINED

	Date	Yds
Flipper Anderson, Rams vs NO	11-26-89	336
Stephone Paige, KC vs SD	12-22-85	309
Jim Benton, Clev vs Det	11-22-45	303
Cloyce Box, Det vs Balt Colts	12-3-50	302
Jimmy Smith, Jax vs Balt Ravens	9-10-00	291

RECEPTIONS

	Date	No.
Terrell Owens, SF vs Chi	12-17-00	20
Tom Fears, Rams vs GB	12-3-50	18
Clark Gaines, NYJ vs SF	9-21-80	17
Sonny Randle, StL Cards vs NYG	11-4-62	16
Jerry Rice, SF vs Rams	11-20-94	16
Keenan McCardell, Jax vs Rams	10-20-96	16

Five tied with 15.

Single-Game Leaders *(Cont.)*

Receiving *(Cont.)*

TOUCHDOWNS

	Date	No.
Bob Shaw, Chi Cards vs Balt Colts	10-2-50	5
Kellen Winslow, SD vs Oak	11-22-81	5
Jerry Rice, SF vs Atl	10-14-90	5

All-Purpose Yards

	Date	Yds
Glyn Milburn, Den vs Sea	12-10-95	404
Billy Cannon, Hou vs NY Titans	12-10-61	373
Tyrone Hughes, NO vs LA Rams	10-23-94	347
Lionel James, SD vs LA Rai	11-10-85	345
Timmy Brown, Phil vs StL Cards	12-16-62	341

Longest Plays

RUSHING	Opponent	Year	Yds
Tony Dorsett, Dall	Minn	1983	99
Andy Uram, GB	Chi Cards	1939	97
Bob Gage, Pitt	Chi	1949	97
Jim Spavital, Balt Colts	GB	1950	96
Bob Hoernschemeyer, Det	NY Yanks	1950	96
Garrison Hearst, SF	NYJ	1998	96
Corey Dillon, Cin	Det	2001	96

PASSING	Opponent	Year	Yds
Frank Filchock to Andy Farkas, Wash	Pitt	1939	99
George Izo to Bobby Mitchell, Wash	Clev	1963	99
Karl Sweetan to Pat Studstill, Det	Balt Colts	1966	99
Sonny Jurgensen to Gerry Allen, Wash	Chi	1968	99
Jim Plunkett to Cliff Branch, LA Rai	Wash	1983	99
Ron Jaworski to Mike Quick, Phil	Atl	1985	99
Stan Humphries to Tony Martin, SD	Sea	1994	99
Brett Favre to Robert Brooks, GB	Chi	1995	99

FIELD GOALS	Opponent	Year	Yds
Tom Dempsey, NO	Det	1970	63
Jason Elam, Den	Jax	1998	63
Steve Cox, Clev	Cin	1984	60
Morten Andersen, NO	Chi	1991	60

PUNTS	Opponent	Year	Yds
Steve O'Neal, NYJ	Den	1969	98
Joe Lintzenich, Chi	NYG	1931	94
Shawn McCarthy, NE	Buff	1991	93
Randall Cunningham, Phil	NYG	1989	91

INTERCEPTION RETURNS	Opponent	Year	Yds
Vencie Glenn, SD	Den	1987	103
Louis Oliver, Mia	Buff	1992	103

Six players tied at 102.

KICKOFF RETURNS	Opponent	Year	Yds
Al Carmichael, GB	Chi	1956	106
Noland Smith, KC	Den	1967	106
Roy Green, StL Cards	Dall	1979	106

PUNT RETURNS	Opponent	Year	Yds
Robert Bailey, LA Rams	NO	1994	103
Gil LeFebvre, Cin	Brooklyn	1933	98
Charlie West, Minn	Wash	1968	98
Dennis Morgan, Dall	StL Cards	1974	98
Terance Mathis, NYJ	Dall	1990	98

Film Review: Song Sung Blue

There are only two occasions when it's acceptable for a grown man to cry: while listening to Lou Gehrig's farewell speech and while watching Brian's Song, the 1971 tearjerker about Bears halfback Gale Sayers and his doomed teammate Brian Piccolo. In late 2001 ABC aired a remake of Brian's Song, starring Sean Maher as Piccolo and Mekhi Phifer as Sayers. We asked World Toughman heavyweight champ Hardbody Harrison, 35, for his thoughts on the film.

The remake is much more touching than the original because you see more of Piccolo's life while he's suffering from cancer. Piccolo had a lot of love for his wife and kids—the original didn't show that. It made you think he was just another football-playing jock. You also see the friendship between Piccolo and Sayers develop, really bridging the color gap. Sayers initially came off as arrogant, but he was just shy and din't know how to express himself. As for Piccolo, they finally gave him a personality in this movie. Now he's someone you can relate to.

As far as crying goes, it's definitely a tearjerker, but no, I didn't cry. The men who'll cry at this movie will be men who haven't been through it. They'll say, "Man, this guy is catching it hard. This disease is spreading, and he's got a family. He's making money but not enough. Can this happen to me?" Me, I've been in both of these guys shoes. Like Sayers, I'm a minority and I've had to take less money because of my color. Like Piccolo, I've been second-string. I've also gone through tough times—I've had two brothers stabbed. Those things took away all my tears.

Rushing

Year	Player, Team	Att	Yards	Avg	TD	Year	Player, Team	Att	Yards	Avg	TD
1932	Cliff Battles, Bos	148	576	3.9	3	1971	Floyd Little, Den, AFC	284	1133	4.0	6
1933	Jim Musick, Bos	173	809	4.7	5		John Brockington,				
1934	Beattie Feathers,						GB, NFC	216	1105	5.1	4
	Chi	101	1004	9.9	8	1972	O.J. Simpson, Buff, AFC	292	1251	4.3	6
1935	Doug Russell,						Larry Brown, Wash, NFC	285	1216	4.3	8
	Chi Cards	140	499	3.6	0	1973	O.J. Simpson, Buff, AFC	332	2003	6.0	12
1936	Alphonse Leemans, NY	206	830	4.0	2		John Brockington,				
1937	Cliff Battles, Wash	216	874	4.0	5		GB, NFC	265	1144	4.3	3
1938	Byron White, Pitt	152	567	3.7	4	1974	Otis Armstrong,				
1939	Bill Osmanski,						Den, AFC	263	1407	5.3	9
	Chi	121	699	5.8	7		Lawrence McCutcheon,				
1940	Byron White, Det	146	514	3.5	5		LA, NFC	236	1109	4.7	3
1941	Clarence Manders,					1975	O.J. Simpson, Buff, AFC	329	1817	5.5	16
	Bklyn	111	486	4.4	5		Jim Otis, StL, NFC	269	1076	4.0	5
1942	Bill Dudley, Pitt	162	696	4.3	5	1976	O.J. Simpson, Buff, AFC	290	1503	5.2	8
1943	Bill Paschal, NY	147	572	3.9	10		Walter Payton, Chi, NFC	311	1390	4.5	13
1944	Bill Paschal, NY	196	737	3.8	9	1977	Walter Payton, Chi, NFC	339	1852	5.5	14
1945	Steve Van Buren, Phil	143	832	5.8	15		Mark van Eeghen,				
1946	Bill Dudley, Pitt	146	604	4.1	3		Oak, AFC	324	1273	3.9	7
1947	Steve Van Buren, Phil	217	1008	4.6	13	1978	Earl Campbell, Hou, AFC	302	1450	4.8	13
1948	Steve Van Buren, Phil	201	945	4.7	10		Walter Payton, Chi, NFC	333	1395	4.2	11
1949	Steve Van Buren, Phil	263	1146	4.4	11	1979	Earl Campbell, Hou, AFC	368	1697	4.6	19
1950	Marion Motley, Clev	140	810	5.8	3		Walter Payton, Chi, NFC	369	1610	4.4	14
1951	Eddie Price, NY	271	971	3.6	7	1980	Earl Campbell, Hou, AFC	373	1934	5.2	13
1952	Dan Towler, LA	156	894	5.7	10		Walter Payton, Chi, NFC	317	1460	4.6	6
1953	Joe Perry, SF	192	1018	5.3	10	1981	George Rogers,				
1954	Joe Perry, SF	173	1049	6.1	8		NO, NFC	378	1674	4.4	13
1955	Alan Ameche, Balt	213	961	4.5	9		Earl Campbell, Hou, AFC	361	1376	3.8	10
1956	Rick Casares,					1982	Freeman McNeil,				
	Chi	234	1126	4.8	12		NY Jets, AFC	151	786	5.2	6
1957	Jim Brown, Clev	202	942	4.7	9		Tony Dorsett, Dall, NFC	177	745	4.2	5
1958	Jim Brown, Clev	257	1527	5.9	17	1983	Eric Dickerson,				
1959	Jim Brown, Clev	290	1329	4.6	14		LA Rams, NFC	390	1808	4.6	18
1960	Jim Brown, Clev, NFL	215	1257	5.8	9		Curt Warner, Sea, AFC	335	1449	4.3	13
	Abner Haynes,					1984	Eric Dickerson,				
	Dall Texans, AFL	156	875	5.6	9		LA Rams, NFC	379	2105	5.6	14
1961	Jim Brown, Clev, NFL	305	1408	4.6	8		Earnest Jackson,				
	Billy Cannon, Hou, AFL	200	948	4.7	6		SD, AFC	296	1179	4.0	8
1962	Jim Taylor, GB, NFL	272	1474	5.4	19	1985	Marcus Allen,				
	Cookie Gilchrist,						LA Raiders, AFC	380	1759	4.6	11
	Buff, AFL	214	1096	5.1	13		Gerald Riggs, Atl, NFC	397	1719	4.3	10
1963	Jim Brown, Clev, NFL	291	1863	6.4	12	1986	Eric Dickerson,				
	Clem Daniels, Oak, AFL	215	1099	5.1	3		LA Rams, NFC	404	1821	4.5	11
1964	Jim Brown, Clev, NFL	280	1446	5.2	7		Curt Warner, Sea, AFC	319	1481	4.6	13
	Cookie Gilchrist,					1987	Charles White,				
	Buff, AFL	230	981	4.3	6		LA Rams, NFC	324	1374	4.2	11
1965	Jim Brown, Clev, NFL	289	1544	5.3	17		Eric Dickerson, Ind, AFC	223	1011	4.5	5
	Paul Lowe, SD, AFL	222	1121	5.0	7	1988	Eric Dickerson, Ind, AFC	388	1659	4.3	14
1966	Jim Nance, Bos, AFL	299	1458	4.9	11		Herschel Walker,				
	Gale Sayers, Chi, NFL	229	1231	5.4	8		Dall, NFC	361	1514	4.2	5
1967	Jim Nance, Bos, AFL	269	1216	4.5	7	1989	Christian Okoye, KC, AFC	370	1480	4.0	12
	Leroy Kelly, Clev, NFL	235	1205	5.1	11		Barry Sanders, Det, NFC	280	1470	5.3	14
1968	Leroy Kelly, Clev, NFL	248	1239	5.0	16	1990	Barry Sanders, Det, NFC	255	1304	5.1	13
	Paul Robinson, Cin, AFL	238	1023	4.3	8		Thurman Thomas,				
1969	Gale Sayers, Chi, NFL	236	1032	4.4	8		Buff, AFC	271	1297	4.8	11
	Dickie Post, SD, AFL	182	873	4.8	6	1991	Emmitt Smith, Dall, NFC	365	1563	4.3	12
1970	Larry Brown, Wash, NFC	237	1125	4.7	5		Thurman Thomas,				
	Floyd Little, Den, AFC	209	901	4.3	3		Buff, AFC	288	1407	4.9	7
						1992	Emmitt Smith, Dall, NFC	373	1713	4.6	18
							Barry Foster, Pitt, AFC	390	1690	4.3	11

Rushing (Cont.)

Year	Player, Team	Att	Yards	Avg	TD
1993	Emmitt Smith, Dall, NFC	283	1486	5.3	9
	Thurman Thomas, Buff, AFC	355	1315	3.7	6
1994	Barry Sanders, Det, NFC	331	1883	5.7	7
	Chris Warren, Sea, AFC	333	1545	4.6	9
1995	Emmitt Smith, Dall, NFC	377	1773	4.7	25
	Curtis Martin, NE, AFC	368	1487	4.0	14
1996	Barry Sanders, Det, NFC	307	1553	5.1	11
	Terrell Davis, Den, AFC	345	1538	4.5	13
1997	Barry Sanders, Det, NFC	335	2053	6.1	11
	Terrell Davis, Den, AFC	369	1730	4.7	15

Year	Player, Team	Att	Yards	Avg	TD
1998	Terrell Davis, Den, AFC	392	2008	5.1	21
	Jamal Anderson, Atl, NFC	410	1846	4.5	14
1999	Edgerrin James, Ind, AFC	369	1553	4.2	13
	Stephen Davis, Wash, NFC	290	1405	4.8	17
2000	Edgerrin James, Ind, AFC	387	1709	4.4	13
	Robert Smith, Minn, NFC	295	1521	5.2	7
2001	Priest Holmes, Kan, AFC	327	1555	4.8	8
	Stephen Davis, Wash, NFC	356	1432	4.0	5

Passing*

Year	Player, Team	Att	Comp	Yards	TD	Int
1932	Arnie Herber, GB	101	37	639	9	9
1933	Harry Newman, NY	136	53	973	11	17
1934	Arnie Herber, GB	115	42	799	8	12
1935	Ed Danowski, NY	113	57	794	10	9
1936	Arnie Herber, GB	173	77	1239	11	13
1937	Sammy Baugh, Wash	171	81	1127	8	14
1938	Ed Danowski, NY	129	70	848	7	8
1939	Parker Hall, Clev	208	106	1227	9	13
1940	Sammy Baugh, Wash	177	111	1367	12	10
1941	Cecil Isbell, GB	206	117	1479	15	11
1942	Cecil Isbell, GB	268	146	2021	24	14
1943	Sammy Baugh, Wash	239	133	1754	23	19
1944	Frank Filchock, Wash	147	84	1139	13	9
1945	Sammy Baugh, Wash	182	128	1669	11	4
	Sid Luckman, Chi	217	117	1725	14	10
1946	Bob Waterfield, LA	251	127	1747	18	17
1947	Sammy Baugh, Wash	354	210	2938	25	15
1948	Tommy Thompson, Phil	246	141	1965	25	11
1949	Sammy Baugh, Wash	255	145	1903	18	14
1950	Norm Van Brocklin, LA	233	127	2061	18	14
1951	Bob Waterfield, LA	176	88	1566	13	10
1952	Norm Van Brocklin, LA	205	113	1736	14	17
1953	Otto Graham, Clev	258	167	2722	11	9
1954	Norm Van Brocklin, LA	260	139	2637	13	21
1955	Otto Graham, Clev	185	98	1721	15	8
1956	Ed Brown, Chi	168	96	1667	11	12
1957	Tommy O'Connell, Clev	110	63	1229	9	8
1958	Eddie LeBaron, Wash	145	79	1365	11	10
1959	Charlie Conerly, NY	194	113	1706	14	4
1960	Milt Plum, Clev, NFL	250	151	2297	21	5
	Jack Kemp, LA, AFL	406	211	3018	20	25
1961	George Blanda, Hou, AFL	362	187	3330	36	22
	Milt Plum, Clev, NFL	302	177	2416	18	10
1962	Len Dawson, Dall, AFL	310	189	2759	29	17
	Bart Starr, GB, NFL	285	178	2438	12	9
1963	Y.A. Tittle, NY, NFL	367	221	3145	36	14
	Tobin Rote, SD, AFL	286	170	2510	20	17
1964	Len Dawson, KC, AFL	354	199	2879	30	18
	Bart Starr, GB, NFL	272	163	2144	15	4
1965	Rudy Bukich, Chi, NFL	312	176	2641	20	9
	John Hadl, SD, AFL	348	174	2798	20	21
1966	Bart Starr, GB, NFL	251	156	2257	14	3
	Len Dawson, KC, AFL	284	159	2527	26	10
1967	Sonny Jurgensen, Wash, NFL	508	288	3747	31	16
	Daryle Lamonica, Oakland, AFL	425	220	3228	30	20

Year	Player, Team	Att	Comp	Yards	TD	Int
1968	Len Dawson, KC, AFL	224	131	2109	17	9
	Earl Morrall, Balt, NFL	317	182	2909	26	17
1969	Sonny Jurgensen, Wash, NFL	442	274	3102	22	15
	Greg Cook, Cin, AFL	197	106	1854	15	11
1970	John Brodie, SF, NFC	378	223	2941	24	10
	Daryle Lamonica, Oak, AFC	356	179	2516	22	15
1971	Roger Staubach, Dall, NFC	211	126	1882	15	4
	Bob Griese, Mia, AFC	263	145	2089	19	9
1972	Norm Snead, NY, NFC	325	196	2307	17	12
	Earl Morrall, Mia, AFC	150	83	1360	11	7
1973	Roger Staubach, Dall, NFC	286	179	2428	23	15
	Ken Stabler, Oak, AFC	260	163	1997	14	10
1974	Ken Anderson, Cin, AFC	328	213	2667	18	10
	Sonny Jurgensen, Wash, NFC	167	107	1185	11	5
1975	Ken Anderson, Cin, AFC	377	228	3169	21	11
	Fran Tarkenton, Minn, NFC	425	273	2994	25	13
1976	Ken Stabler, Oak, AFC	291	194	2737	27	17
	James Harris, LA, NFC	158	91	1460	8	6
1977	Bob Griese, Mia, AFC	307	180	2252	22	13
	Roger Staubach, Dall, NFC	361	210	2620	18	9
1978	Roger Staubach, Dall, NFC	413	231	3190	25	16
	Terry Bradshaw, Pitt, AFC	368	207	2915	28	20
1979	Roger Staubach, Dall, NFC	461	267	3586	27	11
	Dan Fouts, SD, AFC	530	332	4082	24	24
1980	Brian Sipe, Clev, AFC	554	337	4132	30	14
	Ron Jaworski, Phi, NFC	451	257	3529	27	12
1981	Ken Anderson, Cin, AFC	479	300	3754	29	10
	Joe Montana, SF, NFC	488	311	3565	19	12
1982	Ken Anderson, Cin, AFC	309	218	2495	12	9
	Joe Theismann, Wash, NFC	252	161	2033	13	9
1983	Steve Bartkowski, Atl, NFC	432	274	3167	22	5
	Dan Marino, Mia AFC	296	173	2210	20	6
1984	Dan Marino, Mia, AFC	564	362	5084	48	17
	Joe Montana, SF, NFC	432	279	3630	28	10
1985	Ken O'Brien, NY, AFC	488	297	3888	25	8
	Joe Montana, SF, NFC	494	303	3653	27	13

Passing (Cont.)

Year	Player, Team	Att	Comp	Yards	TD	Int
1986	Tommy Kramer, Minn, NFC	372	208	3000	24	10
	Dan Marino, Mia, AFC	623	378	4746	44	23
1987	Joe Montana, SF, NFC	398	266	3054	31	13
	Bernie Kosar, Clev, AFC	389	241	3033	22	9
1988	Boomer Esiason, Cin, AFC	388	223	3572	28	14
	Wade Wilson, Minn, NFC	332	204	2746	15	9
1989	Joe Montana, SF, NFC	386	271	3521	26	8
	Boomer Esiason, Cin, AFC	455	258	3525	28	11
1990	Jim Kelly, Buffalo, AFC	346	219	2829	24	9
	Phil Simms, NY, NFC	311	184	2284	15	4
1991	Steve Young, SF, NFC	279	180	2517	17	8
	Jim Kelly, Buff, AFC	474	304	3844	33	17
1992	Steve Young, SF, NFC	402	268	3465	25	7
	Warren Moon, Hou, AFC	346	224	2521	18	12
1993	Steve Young, SF, NFC	462	314	4023	29	16
	John Elway, Den, AFC	551	348	4030	25	10
1994	Steve Young, SF, NFC	461	324	3969	35	10
	Dan Marino, Mia, AFC	615	385	4453	30	17
1995	Brett Favre, GB, NFC	570	359	4413	38	13
	Jeff Blake, Cin, AFC	567	326	3822	28	17
1996	Vinny Testaverde, Balt, AFC	549	325	4177	33	19
	Brett Favre, GB, NFC	543	325	3899	39	13
1997	Steve Young, SF, NFC	356	241	3029	19	6
	Mark Brunell, Jax, AFC	435	264	3281	18	7
1998	Randall Cunningham, Minn, NFC	425	259	3704	34	10
	Vinny Testaverde, NYJ, AFC	421	259	3256	29	7
1999	Kurt Warner, StL, NFC	499	325	4353	41	13
	Peyton Manning, Ind, AFC	533	331	4135	26	15
2000	Trent Green, StL, NFC	240	145	2063	16	5
	Brian Griese, Den, AFC	336	216	2688	19	4
2001	Kurt Warner, StL, NFC	546	375	4830	36	22
	Rich Gannon, Oak, AFC	549	361	3828	27	9

*Since 1973, the annual passing leaders have been determined by a passer rating system that compares individual performances to a fixed performance standard.

Pass Receiving*

Year	Player, Team	No.	Yds	Avg	TD
1932	Ray Flaherty, NY	21	350	16.7	3
1933	John Kelly, Brooklyn	22	246	11.2	3
1934	Joe Carter, Phil	16	238	14.9	4
	Morris Badgro, NY	16	206	12.9	1
1935	Tod Goodwin, NY	26	432	16.6	4
1936	Don Hutson, GB	34	536	15.8	8
1937	Don Hutson, GB	41	552	13.5	7
1938	Gaynell Tinsley, Chi Cards	41	516	12.6	1
1939	Don Hutson, GB	34	846	24.9	6
1940	Don Looney, Phil	58	707	12.2	4
1941	Don Hutson, GB	58	738	12.7	10
1942	Don Hutson, GB	74	1211	16.4	17
1943	Don Hutson, GB	47	776	16.5	11
1944	Don Hutson, GB	58	866	14.9	9
1945	Don Hutson, GB	47	834	17.7	9
1946	Jim Benton, LA	63	981	15.6	6
1947	Jim Keane, Chi	64	910	14.2	10
1948	Tom Fears, LA	51	698	13.7	4
1949	Tom Fears, LA	77	1013	13.2	9
1950	Tom Fears, LA	84	1116	13.3	7
1951	Elroy Hirsch, LA	66	1495	22.7	17
1952	Mac Speedie, Clev	62	911	14.7	5
1953	Pete Pihos, Phil	63	1049	16.7	10
1954	Pete Pihos, Phil	60	872	14.5	10
	Billy Wilson, SF	60	830	13.8	5
1955	Pete Pihos, Phil	62	864	13.9	7
1956	Billy Wilson, SF	60	889	14.8	5
1957	Billy Wilson, SF	52	757	14.6	6
1958	Raymond Berry, Balt	56	794	14.2	9
	Pete Retzlaff, Phil	56	766	13.7	2
1959	Raymond Berry, Balt	66	959	14.5	14
1960	Lionel Taylor, Den, AFL	92	1235	13.4	12
	Raymond Berry, Balt, NFL	74	1298	17.5	10
1961	Lionel Taylor, Den, AFL	100	1176	11.8	4
	Jim Phillips, LA, NFL	78	1092	14.0	5
1962	Lionel Taylor, Den, AFL	77	908	11.8	4
	Bobby Mitchell, Wash, NFL	72	1384	19.2	11
1963	Lionel Taylor, Den, AFL	78	1101	14.1	10
	Bobby Joe Conrad, St. Louis, NFL	73	967	13.2	10
1964	Charley Hennigan, Houston, AFL	101	1546	15.3	8
	Johnny Morris, Chi, NFL	93	1200	12.9	10
1965	Lionel Taylor, Den, AFL	85	1131	13.3	6
	Dave Parks, SF, NFL	80	1344	16.8	12
1966	Lance Alworth, SD, AFL	73	1383	18.9	13
	Charley Taylor, Wash, NFL	72	1119	15.5	12
1967	George Sauer, NY, AFL	75	1189	15.9	6
	Charley Taylor, Wash, NFL	70	990	14.1	9
1968	Clifton McNeil, SF, NFL	71	994	14.0	7
	Lance Alworth, SD, AFL	68	1312	19.3	10
1969	Dan Abramowicz, NO, NFL	73	1015	13.9	7
	Lance Alworth, SD, AFL	64	1003	15.7	4
1970	Dick Gordon, Chi, NFC	71	1026	14.5	13
	Marlin Briscoe, Buff, AFC	57	1036	18.2	8
1971	Fred Biletnikoff, Oak, AFC	61	929	15.2	9
	Bob Tucker, NY, NFC	59	791	13.4	4
1972	Harold Jackson, Phil, NFC	62	1048	16.9	4
	Fred Biletnikoff, Oak, AFC	58	802	13.8	7
1973	Harold Carmichael, Phil, NFC	67	1116	16.7	9
	Fred Willis, Hou, AFC	57	371	6.5	1
1974	Lydell Mitchell, Balt, AFC	72	544	7.6	2
	Charles Young, Phil, NFC	63	696	11.0	3

*Most catches.

Pass Receiving (Cont.)

Year	Player, Team	No.	Yds	Avg	TD
1975	Chuck Foreman, Minn, NFC	73	691	9.5	9
	Reggie Rucker, Clev, AFC	60	770	12.8	3
	Lydell Mitchell, Balt, AFC	60	544	9.1	4
1976	MacArthur Lane, KC, AFC	66	686	10.4	1
	Drew Pearson, Dall, NFC	58	806	13.9	6
1977	Lydell Mitchell, Balt, AFC	71	620	8.7	4
	Ahmad Rashad, Minn, NFC	51	681	13.4	2
1978	Rickey Young, Minn, NFC	88	704	8.0	5
	Steve Largent, Sea, AFC	71	1168	16.5	8
1979	Joe Washington, Balt, AFC	82	750	9.1	3
	Ahmad Rashad, Minn, NFC	80	1156	14.5	9
1980	Kellen Winslow, SD, AFC	89	1290	14.5	9
	Earl Cooper, SF, NFC	83	567	6.8	4
1981	Kellen Winslow, SD, AFC	88	1075	12.2	10
	Dwight Clark, SF, NFC	85	1105	13.0	4
1982	Dwight Clark, SF, NFC	60	913	15.2	5
	Kellen Winslow, SD, AFC	54	721	13.4	6
1983	Todd Christensen, LA, AFC	92	1247	13.6	12
	Roy Green, StL, NFC	78	1227	15.7	14
	Charlie Brown, Wash, NFC	78	1225	15.7	8
	Earnest Gray, NY, NFC	78	1139	14.6	5
1984	Art Monk, Wash, NFC	106	1372	12.9	7
	Ozzie Newsome, Clev, AFC	89	1001	11.2	5
1985	Roger Craig, SF, NFC	92	1016	11.0	6
	Lionel James, SD, AFC	86	1027	11.9	6
1986	Todd Christensen, LA Rai, AFC	95	1153	12.1	8
	Jerry Rice, SF, NFC	86	1570	18.3	15
1987	J.T. Smith, StL Card, NFC	91	1117	12.3	8
	Al Toon, NY, AFC	68	976	14.4	5
1988	Al Toon, NY, AFC	93	1067	11.5	5
	Henry Ellard, LA Rams, NFC	86	1414	16.4	10
1989	Sterling Sharpe, GB, NFC	90	1423	15.8	12
	Andre Reed, Buff, AFC	88	1312	14.9	9
1990	Jerry Rice, SF, NFC	100	1502	15.0	13
	Haywood Jeffires, Hou, AFC	74	1048	14.2	8
	Drew Hill, Hou, AFC	74	1019	13.8	5
1991	Haywood Jeffires, Hou, AFC	100	1181	11.8	7
	Michael Irvin, Dall, NFC	93	1523	16.4	8
1992	Sterling Sharpe, GB, NFC	108	1461	13.5	13
	Haywood Jeffires, Hou, AFC	90	913	10.1	9
1993	Sterling Sharpe, GB, NFC	112	1274	11.4	11
	Reggie Langhorne, Ind, AFC	85	1038	12.2	3
1994	Cris Carter, Minn, NFC	122	1256	10.3	7
	Ben Coates, NE, AFC	96	1174	12.2	7
1995	Herman Moore, Det, NFC	123	1686	13.7	14
	Carl Pickens, Cin, AFC	99	1234	12.5	17
1996	Jerry Rice, SF, NFC	108	1254	11.6	8
	Carl Pickens, Cin, AFC	100	1180	11.8	12
1997	Herman Moore, Det, NFC	104	1293	12.4	8
	Tim Brown, Oak, AFC	104	1408	13.5	5
1998	Frank Sanders, Ariz, NFC	89	1145	12.9	3
	O.J. McDuffie, Mia, AFC	90	1050	11.7	7
1999	Mushin Muhammad, Car, NFC	96	1253	13.1	8
	Jimmy Smith, Jax, AFC	116	1636	14.1	6
2000	Mushin Muhammad, Car, NFC	102	1183	11.6	6
	Marvin Harrison, Ind, AFC	102	1413	13.9	14
2001	Rod Smith, Den, AFC	113	1343	11.9	11
	Keyshawn Johnson, TB, NFC	106	1266	11.9	1

THEY SAID IT

Tony Siragusa, rotund recently retired Ravens tackle, placing his dinner order at Emeril Lagasse's restaurant in New Orlean: "Keep it coming until I puke. Then hit me again."

Scoring

Year	Player, Team	TD	FG	PAT	TP
1932	Earl Clark, Portsmouth	6	3	10	55
1933	Ken Strong, NY	6	5	13	64
	Glenn Presnell, Ports	6	6	10	64
1934	Jack Manders, Chi	3	10	31	79
1935	Earl Clark, Det	6	1	16	55
1936	Earl Clark, Det	7	4	19	73
1937	Jack Manders, Chi	5	18	15	69
1938	Clarke Hinkle, GB	7	3	7	58
1939	Andy Farkas, Wash	11	0	2	68
1940	Don Hutson, GB	7	0	15	57
1941	Don Hutson, GB	12	1	20	95
1942	Don Hutson, GB	17	1	33	138
1943	Don Hutson, GB	12	3	36	117
1944	Don Hutson, GB	9	0	31	85
1945	Steve Van Buren, Phil	18	0	2	110
1946	Ted Fritsch, GB	10	9	13	100
1947	Pat Harder, Chicago Cards	7	7	39	102
1948	Pat Harder, Chicago Cards	6	7	53	110
1949	Pat Harder, Chicago Cards	8	3	45	102
	Gene Roberts, NY	17	0	0	102
1950	Doak Walker, Det	11	8	38	128
1951	Elroy Hirsch, LA	17	0	0	102
1952	Gordy Soltau, SF	7	6	34	94
1953	Gordy Soltau, SF	6	10	48	114
1954	Bobby Walston, Phil	11	4	36	114
1955	Doak Walker, Det	7	9	27	96
1956	Bobby Layne, Det	5	12	33	99
1957	Sam Baker, Wash	1	14	29	77
	Lou Groza, Clev	0	15	32	77
1958	Jim Brown, Clev	18	0	0	108
1959	Paul Hornung, GB	7	7	31	94
1960	Paul Hornung, GB, NFL	15	15	41	176
	Gene Mingo, Den, AFL	6	18	33	123
1961	Gino Cappelletti, Bos, AFL	8	17	48	147
	Paul Hornung, GB, NFL	10	15	41	146
1962	Gene Mingo, Den, AFL	4	27	32	137
	Jim Taylor, GB, NFL	19	0	0	114
1963	Gino Cappelletti, Bos, AFL	2	22	35	113
	Don Chandler, NY, NFL	0	18	52	106
1964	Gino Cappelletti, Bos, AFL	7	25	36	155
	Lenny Moore, Balt, NFL	20	0	0	120
1965	Gale Sayers, Chi, NFL	22	0	0	132
	Gino Cappelletti, Bos, AFL	9	17	27	132
1966	Gino Cappelletti, Bos, AFL	6	16	35	119
	Bruce Gossett, LA, NFL	0	28	29	113
1967	Jim Bakken, StL, NFL	0	27	36	117
	George Blanda, Oak, AFL	0	20	56	116
1968	Jim Turner, NY, AFL	0	34	43	145
	Leroy Kelly, Clev, NFL	20	0	0	120
1969	Jim Turner, NY, AFL	0	32	33	129
	Fred Cox, Minn, NFL	0	26	43	121
1970	Fred Cox, Minn, NFC	0	30	35	125
	Jan Stenerud, KC, AFC	0	30	26	116
1971	Garo Yepremian, Mia, AFC	0	28	33	117
	Curt Knight, Wash, NFC	0	29	27	114
1972	Chester Marcol, GB, NFC	0	33	29	128
	Bobby Howfield, NY AFC	0	27	40	121
1973	David Ray, LA, NFC	0	30	40	130
	Roy Gerela, Pitt, AFC	0	29	36	123
1974	Chester Marcol, GB, NFC	0	25	19	94
	Roy Gerela, Pitt, AFC	0	20	33	93
1975	O.J. Simpson, Buff, AFC	23	0	0	138
	Chuck Foreman, Minn, NFC	22	0	0	132
1976	Toni Linhart, Balt, AFC	0	20	49	109
	Mark Moseley, Wash, NFC	0	22	31	97
1977	Errol Mann, Oak, AFC	0	20	39	99
	Walter Payton, Chi, NFC	16	0	0	96
1978	Frank Corral, LA, NFC	0	29	31	118
	Pat Leahy, NY, AFC	0	22	41	107
1979	John Smith, NE, AFC	0	23	46	115
	Mark Moseley, Wash, NFC	0	25	39	114
1980	John Smith, NE, AFC	0	26	51	129
	Ed Murray, Det, NFC	0	27	35	116
1981	Ed Murray, Det, NFC	0	25	46	121
	Rafael Septien, Dall, NFC	0	27	40	121
	Jim Breech, Cin, AFC	0	22	49	115
	Nick Lowery, KC, AFC	0	26	37	115
1982	Marcus Allen, LA, AFC	14	0	0	84
	Wendell Tyler, LA, NFC	13	0	0	78
1983	Mark Moseley, Wash, NFC	0	33	62	161
	Gary Anderson, Pitt, AFC	0	27	38	119
1984	Ray Wersching, SF, NFC	0	25	56	131
	Gary Anderson, Pitt, AFC	0	24	45	117
1985	Kevin Butler, Chi, NFC	0	31	51	144
	Gary Anderson, Pitt, AFC	0	33	40	139
1986	Tony Franklin, NE, AFC	0	32	44	140
	Kevin Butler, Chi, NFC	0	28	36	120
1987	Jerry Rice, SF, NFC	23	0	0	138
	Jim Breech, Cin, AFC	0	24	25	97
1988	Scott Norwood, Buff, AFC	0	32	33	129
	Mike Cofer, SF, NFC	0	27	40	121
1989	Mike Cofer, SF, NFC	0	29	49	136
	David Treadwell, Den, AFC	0	27	39	120
1990	Nick Lowery, KC, AFC	0	34	37	139
	Chip Lohmiller, Wash, NFC	0	30	41	131
1991	Chip Lohmiller, Wash, NFC	0	31	56	149
	Pete Stoyanovich, Mia, AFC	0	31	28	121
1992	Pete Stoyanovich, Mia, AFC	0	30	34	124
	Morten Anderson, NO, NFC	0	29	33	120
	Chip Lohmiller, Wash, NFC	0	30	30	120
1993	Jeff Jaeger, Rai, AFC	0	35	27	132
	Jason Hanson, Det, NFC	0	34	28	130
1994	John Carney, SD, AFC	0	34	33	135
	Fuad Reveiz, Minn, NFC	0	34	30	132
	Emmitt Smith, Dall, NFC	22	0	0	132
1995	Emmitt Smith, Dall, NFC	25	0	0	150
	Norm Johnson, Pitt, AFC	0	34	39	141
1996	John Kasay, Car, NFC	0	37	34	145
	Cary Blanchard, Ind, AFC	0	36	27	135
1997	Richie Cunningham, Dall, NFC	0	34	24	126
	Mike Hollis, Jax, AFC	0	41	31	134
1998	Gary Anderson, Minn, NFC	0	35	59	164
	Steve Christie, Buff, AFC	0	33	41	140
1999	Jeff Wilkins, StL, NFC	0	20	28	124
	Mike Vanderjagt, Ind, AFC	0	34	38	145
2000	Marshall Faulk, StL, NFC	26	0	0	156
	Matt Stover, Balt, AFC	0	35	30	135
2001	Marshall Faulk, StL, NFC	21	0	2	128
	Mike Vanderjagt, Ind, AFC	0	28	41	125

Pro Bowl Alltime Results

Date	Result	Date	Result	Date	Result
1-15-39	NY Giants 13, Pro All-Stars 10	1-13-63	NFL East 30, West 20	1-29-79	NFC 13, AFC 7
1-14-40	Green Bay 16, NFL All-Stars 7	1-12-64	NFL West 31, East 17	1-27-80	NFC 37, AFC 27
12-29-40	Chi Bears 28, NFL All-Stars 14	1-19-64	AFL West 27, East 24	2-1-81	NFC 21, AFC 7
1-4-42	Chi Bears 35, NFL All-Stars 24	1-10-65	NFL West 34, East 14	1-31-82	AFC 16, NFC 13
12-27-42	NFL All-Stars 17, Washington 14	1-16-65	AFL West 38, East 14	2-6-83	NFC 20, AFC 19
1-14-51	A. Conf. 28, N. Conf. 27	1-15-66	AFL All-Stars 30, Buffalo 19	1-29-84	NFC 45, AFC 3
1-12-52	N. Conf. 30, A. Conf. 13	1-15-66	NFL East 36, West 7	1-27-85	AFC 22, NFC 14
1-10-53	N. Conf. 27, A. Conf. 7	1-21-67	AFL East 30, West 23	2-2-86	NFC 28, AFC 24
1-17-54	East 20, West 9	1-22-67	NFL East 20, West 10	2-1-87	AFC 10, NFC 6
1-16-55	West 26, East 19	1-21-68	AFL East 25, West 24	2-7-88	AFC 15, NFC 6
1-15-56	East 31, West 30	1-21-68	NFL West 38, East 20	1-29-89	NFC 34, AFC 3
1-13-57	West 19, East 10	1-19-69	AFL West 38, East 25	2-4-90	NFC 27, AFC 21
1-12-58	West 26, East 7	1-19-69	NFL West 10, East 7	2-3-91	AFC 23, NFC 21
1-11-59	East 28, West 21	1-17-70	AFL West 26, East 3	2-2-92	NFC 21, AFC 15
1-17-60	West 38, East 21	1-18-70	NFL West 16, East 13	2-7-93	AFC 23, NFC 20
1-15-61	West 35, East 31	1-24-71	NFC 27, AFC 6	2-6-94	NFC 17, AFC 3
1-7-62	AFL West 47, East 27	1-23-72	AFC 26, NFC 13	2-5-95	AFC 41, NFC 13
1-14-62	NFL West 31, East 30	1-21-73	AFC 33, NFC 28	2-4-96	NFC 20, AFC 13
1-13-63	AFL West 21, East 14	1-20-74	AFC 15, NFC 13	2-2-97	AFC 26, NFC 23
		1-20-75	NFC 17, AFC 10	2-1-98	AFC 29, NFC 24
		1-26-76	NFC 23, AFC 20	2-7-99	AFC 23, NFC 10
		1-17-77	AFC 24, NFC 14	2-6-00	NFC 51, AFC 31
		1-23-78	NFC 14, AFC 13	2-4-01	AFC 38, NFC 17
				2-9-02	AFC 38, NFC 30

Chicago All-Star Game* Results

Date	Result (Attendance)	Date	Result (Attendance)
8-31-34	Chi Bears 0, All-Stars 0 (79,432)	8-10-56	Cleveland 26, All-Stars 0 (75,000)
8-29-35	Chi Bears 5, All-Stars 0 (77,450)	8-9-57	NY Giants 22, All-Stars 12 (75,000)
9-3-36	All-Stars 7, Detroit 7 (76,000)	8-15-58	All-Stars 35, Detroit 19 (70,000)
9-1-37	All-Stars 6, Green Bay 0 (84,560)	8-14-59	Baltimore 29, All-Stars 0 (70,000)
8-31-38	All-Stars 28, Washington 16 (74,250)	8-12-60	Baltimore 32, All-Stars 7 (70,000)
8-30-39	NY Giants 9, All-Stars 0 (81,456)	8-4-61	Philadelphia 28, All-Stars 14 (66,000)
8-29-40	Green Bay 45, All-Stars 28 (84,567)	8-3-62	Green Bay 42, All-Stars 20 (65,000)
8-28-41	Chi Bears 37, All-Stars 13 (98,203)	8-2-63	All-Stars 20, Green Bay 17 (65,000)
8-28-42	Chi Bears 21, All-Stars 0 (101,100)	8-7-64	Chicago 28, All-Stars 17 (65,000)
8-25-43	All-Stars 27, Washington 7 (48,471)	8-6-65	Cleveland 24, All-Stars 16 (68,000)
8-30-44	Chi Bears 24, All-Stars 21 (48,769)	8-5-66	Green Bay 38, All-Stars 0 (72,000)
8-30-45	Green Bay 19, All-Stars 7 (92,753)	8-4-67	Green Bay 27, All-Stars 0 (70,934)
8-23-46	All-Stars 16, Los Angeles 0 (97,380)	8-2-68	Green Bay 34, All-Stars 17 (69,917)
8-22-47	All-Stars 16, Chi Bears 0 (105,840)	8-1-69	NY Jets 26, All-Stars 24 (74,208)
8-20-48	Chi Cardinals 28, All-Stars 0 (101,220)	7-31-70	Kansas City 24, All-Stars 3 (69,940)
8-12-49	Philadelphia 38, All-Stars 0 (93,780)	7-30-71	Baltimore 24, All-Stars 17 (52,289)
8-11-50	All-Stars 17, Philadelphia 7 (88,885)	7-28-72	Dallas 20, All-Stars 7 (54,162)
8-17-51	Cleveland 33, All-Stars 0 (92,180)	7-27-73	Miami 14, All-Stars 3 (54,103)
8-15-52	Los Angeles 10, All-Stars 7 (88,316)	1974	No game
8-14-53	Detroit 24, All-Stars 10 (93,818)	8-1-75	Pittsburgh 21, All-Stars 14 (54,103)
8-13-54	Detroit 31, All-Stars 6 (93,470)	7-23-76	Pittsburgh 24, All-Stars 0 (52,895)
8-12-55	All-Stars 30, Cleveland 27 (75,000)		

*Discontinued.

History Book: Nov. 28, 1948

A remarkable road trip anchors a perfect season: Cleveland coach Paul Brown wanted a perfect season in the All-America Football Conference pretty badly because no NFL or AAFC team had finished with an unblemished record. However, the 10–0 Browns would have to navigate one tough road trip: Nov. 21 at the two-time Eastern Division champ New York Yankees; Nov. 25 at the Los Angeles Dons; and Nov. 28 at the San Francisco 49ers, their bitter rivals. Cleveland won by 13 in New York and 17 in Los Angeles, but star passer Otto Graham wrenched a knee in L.A. and was limping against the Niners. "The 49ers coach told his guys, 'Don't hit Graham below the knee. We want to beat them with Graham so they won't have any excuses,'" Browns center Frank Gatski recalled. Graham rallied Cleveland from a 21–10 deficit with three touchdown passes. The Browns, 14–0 in the regular season, routed the Buffalo Bills 49–7 in the AAFC title game.

Alltime Winningest NFL Coaches

Most Career Wins

Coach	Yrs	Teams	Regular Season				Career			
			W	L	T	Pct	W	L	T	Pct
Don Shula	33	Colts, Dolphins	328	156	6	.676	347	173	6	.665
George Halas	40	Bears	318	148	31	.671	324	151	31	.671
Tom Landry	29	Cowboys	250	162	6	.605	270	178	6	.601
Curly Lambeau	33	Packers, Cardinals, Redskins	226	132	22	.624	229	134	22	.623
Chuck Noll	23	Steelers	193	148	1	.566	209	156	1	.572
Chuck Knox	22	Rams, Bills, Seahawks	186	147	1	.558	193	158	1	.550
†Dan Reeves	20	Broncos, Giants, Falcons	178	149	1	.544	188	157	1	.545
Paul Brown	21	Browns, Bengals	166	100	6	.621	170	108	6	.609
Bud Grant	18	Vikings	158	96	5	.620	168	108	5	.607
†M. Schottenheimer	15	Browns, Chiefs, Redskins	153	93	1	.622	158	104	1	.603
Marv Levy	17	Chiefs, Bills	143	112	0	.561	154	120	0	.562
Steve Owen	23	Giants	151	100	17	.595	153	108	17	.581
Bill Parcells	15	Giants, Patriots, Jets	138	100	1	.579	149	106	1	.582
Joe Gibbs	12	Redskins	124	60	0	.674	140	65	0	.683
Hank Stram	17	Chiefs, Saints	131	97	10	.571	136	100	10	.573
Weeb Ewbank	20	Colts, Jets	130	129	7	.502	134	130	7	.507
Mike Ditka	14	Bears, Saints	121	95	0	.560	127	101	0	.557
†Jim Mora	15	Saints, Colts	125	106	0	.541	125	112	0	.527
†George Seifert	10	49ers, Panthers	114	62	0	.648	124	67	0	.649
Sid Gillman	18	Rams, Chargers, Oilers	122	99	7	.550	123	104	7	.541

†Active in 2001.

Top Winning Percentages

	W	L	T	Pct		W	L	T	Pct
Vince Lombardi	105	35	6	.740	Don Shula	347	173	6	.665
John Madden	112	39	7	.731	†George Seifert	124	67	0	.649
Joe Gibbs	140	65	0	.683	Curly Lambeau	229	134	22	.623
George Allen	118	54	5	.681	Bill Walsh	102	63	1	.617
George Halas	324	151	31	.671	†Mike Holmgren	108	67	0	.617

Note: Minimum 100 victories.

†Active in 2001.

Alltime Number-One Draft Choices

Year	Team	Selection	Position
1936	Philadelphia	Jay Berwanger, Chicago	HB
1937	Philadelphia	Sam Francis, Nebraska	FB
1938	Cleveland	Corbett Davis, Indiana	FB
1939	Chicago Cardinals	Ki Aldrich, Texas Christian	C
1940	Chicago Cardinals	George Cafego, Tennessee	HB
1941	Chicago Bears	Tom Harmon, Michigan	HB
1942	Pittsburgh	Bill Dudley, Virginia	HB
1943	Detroit	Frank Sinkwich, Georgia	HB
1944	Boston	Angelo Bertelli, Notre Dame	QB
1945	Chicago Cardinals	Charley Trippi, Georgia	HB
1946	Boston	Frank Dancewicz, Notre Dame	QB
1947	Chicago Bears	Bob Fenimore, Oklahoma A&M	HB
1948	Washington	Harry Gilmer, Alabama	QB
1949	Philadelphia	Chuck Bednarik, Pennsylvania	C
1950	Detroit	Leon Hart, Notre Dame	E
1951	New York Giants	Kyle Rote, Southern Methodist	HB
1952	Los Angeles	Bill Wade, Vanderbilt	QB
1953	San Francisco	Harry Babcock, Georgia	E
1954	Cleveland	Bobby Garrett, Stanford	QB
1955	Baltimore	George Shaw, Oregon	QB
1956	Pittsburgh	Gary Glick, Colorado A&M	DB
1957	Green Bay	Paul Hornung, Notre Dame	HB
1958	Chicago Cardinals	King Hill, Rice	QB
1959	Green Bay	Randy Duncan, Iowa	QB
1960	Los Angeles	Billy Cannon, Louisiana St	RB

Year	Team	Selection	Position
1961	Minnesota	Tommy Mason, Tulane	RB
	Buffalo (AFL)	Ken Rice, Auburn	G
1962	Washington	Ernie Davis, Syracuse	RB
	Oakland (AFL)	Roman Gabriel, N Carolina St	QB
1963	LA Rams	Terry Baker, Oregon St	QB
	Kansas City (AFL)	Buck Buchanan, Grambling	DT
1964	San Francisco	Dave Parks, Texas Tech	E
	Boston (AFL)	Jack Concannon, Boston College	QB
1965	NY Giants	Tucker Frederickson, Auburn	RB
	Houston (AFL)	Lawrence Elkins, Baylor	E
1966	Atlanta	Tommy Nobis, Texas	LB
	Miami (AFL)	Jim Grabowski, Illinois	RB
1967	Baltimore	Bubba Smith, Michigan St	DT
1968	Minnesota	Ron Yary, Southern California	T
1969	Buffalo (AFL)	O.J. Simpson, Southern California	RB
1970	Pittsburgh	Terry Bradshaw, Louisiana Tech	QB
1971	New England	Jim Plunkett, Stanford	QB
1972	Buffalo	Walt Patulski, Notre Dame	DE
1973	Houston	John Matuszak, Tampa	DE
1974	Dallas	Ed Jones, Tennessee St	DE
1975	Atlanta	Steve Bartkowski, California	QB
1976	Tampa Bay	Lee Roy Selmon, Oklahoma	DE
1977	Tampa Bay	Ricky Bell, Southern California	RB
1978	Houston	Earl Campbell, Texas	RB
1979	Buffalo	Tom Cousineau, Ohio St	LB
1980	Detroit	Billy Sims, Oklahoma	RB
1981	New Orleans	George Rogers, South Carolina	RB
1982	New England	Kenneth Sims, Texas	DT
1983	Baltimore	John Elway, Stanford	QB
1984	New England	Irving Fryar, Nebraska	WR
1985	Buffalo	Bruce Smith, Virginia Tech	DE
1986	Tampa Bay	Bo Jackson, Auburn	RB
1987	Tampa Bay	Vinny Testaverde, Miami (FL)	QB
1988	Atlanta	Aundray Bruce, Auburn	LB
1989	Dallas	Troy Aikman, UCLA	QB
1990	Indianapolis	Jeff George, Illinois	QB
1991	Dallas	Russell Maryland, Miami (FL)	DT
1992	Indianapolis	Steve Emtman, Washington	DT
1993	New England	Drew Bledsoe, Washington St	QB
1994	Cincinnati	Dan Wilkinson, Ohio St	DT
1995	Cincinnati	Ki-Jana Carter, Penn St	RB
1996	New York Jets	Keyshawn Johnson, Southern California	WR
1997	St Louis	Orlando Pace, Ohio St	OT
1998	Indianapolis	Peyton Manning, Tennessee	QB
1999	Cleveland	Tim Couch, Kentucky	QB
2000	Cleveland	Courtney Brown, Penn St	DE
2001	Atlanta	Michael Vick, Virginia Tech	QB
2002	Houston	David Carr, Fresno St	QB

From 1947 through 1958, the first selection in the draft was a bonus pick, awarded to the winner of a random draw. That club, in turn, forfeited its last-round draft choice. The winner of the bonus choice was eliminated from future draws. The system was abolished after 1958, by which time all clubs had received a bonus choice.

Members of the Pro Football Hall of Fame

Herb Adderley
George Allen
Lance Alworth
Doug Atkins
Morris (Red) Badgro
Lem Barney
Cliff Battles
Sammy Baugh
Chuck Bednarik
Bert Bell
Bobby Bell
Raymond Berry
Charles W. Bidwill Sr.

Fred Biletnikoff
George Blanda
Mel Blount
Terry Bradshaw
Jim Brown
Paul Brown
Roosevelt Brown
Willie Brown
Buck Buchanan
Nick Buoniconti
Dick Butkus
Earl Campbell
Tony Canadeo

Joe Carr
Dave Casper
Guy Chamberlin
Jack Christiansen
Earl (Dutch) Clark
George Connor
Jimmy Conzelman
Lou Creekmur
Larry Csonka
Al Davis
Willie Davis
Len Dawson
Eric Dickerson

Dan Dierdorf
Mike Ditka
Art Donovan
Tony Dorsett
John (Paddy) Driscoll
Bill Dudley
Albert Glen (Turk) Edwards
Weeb Ewbank
Tom Fears
Jim Finks
Ray Flaherty
Len Ford
Dan Fortmann
Dan Fouts
Frank Gatski
Bill George
Joe Gibbs
Frank Gifford
Sid Gillman
Otto Graham
Harold (Red) Grange
Bud Grant
Joe Greene
Forrest Gregg
Bob Griese
Lou Groza
Joe Guyon
George Halas
Jack Ham
Dan Hampton
John Hannah
Franco Harris
Mike Haynes
Ed Healey
Mel Hein
Ted Hendricks
Wilbur (Pete) Henry
Arnie Herber
Bill Hewitt
Clarke Hinkle
Elroy (Crazylegs) Hirsch
Paul Hornung
Ken Houston
Cal Hubbard
Sam Huff
Lamar Hunt
Don Hutson
Jimmy Johnson
John Henry Johnson
Charlie Joiner
David (Deacon) Jones
Stan Jones
Henry Jordan
Sonny Jurgensen
Jim Kelly
Leroy Kelly
Walt Kiesling
Frank (Bruiser) Kinard
Paul Krause

Earl (Curly) Lambeau
Jack Lambert
Tom Landry
Dick (Night Train) Lane
Jim Langer
Willie Lanier
Steve Largent
Yale Lary
Dante Lavelli
Bobby Layne
Alphonse (Tuffy) Leemans
Marv Levy
Bob Lilly
Larry Little
Vince Lombardi
Howie Long
Ronnie Lott
Sid Luckman
William Roy (Link) Lyman
Tom Mack
John Mackey
Tim Mara
Wellington Mara
Gino Marchetti
George Preston Marshall
Ollie Matson
Don Maynard
George McAfee
Mike McCormack
Tommy McDonald
Hugh McElhenny
Johnny (Blood) McNally
Mike Michalske
Wayne Millner
Bobby Mitchell
Ron Mix
Joe Montana
Lenny Moore
Marion Motley
Mike Munchak
Anthony Munoz
George Musso
Bronko Nagurski
Joe Namath
Earle (Greasy) Neale
Ernie Nevers
Ozzie Newsome
Ray Nitschke
Chuck Noll
Leo Nomellini
Merlin Olsen
Jim Otto
Steve Owen
Alan Page
Clarence (Ace) Parker
Jim Parker
Walter Payton
Joe Perry
Pete Pihos

Hugh (Shorty) Ray
Dan Reeves
Mel Renfro
John Riggins
Jim Ringo
Andy Robustelli
Art Rooney
Dan Rooney
Pete Rozelle
Bob St. Clair
Gale Sayers
Joe Schmidt
Tex Schramm
Lee Roy Selmon
Billy Shaw
Art Shell
Don Shula
O.J. Simpson
Mike Singletary
Jackie Slater
Jackie Smith
John Stallworth
Bart Starr
Roger Staubach
Ernie Stautner
Jan Stenerud
Dwight Stephenson
Ken Strong
Joe Stydahar
Lynn Swann
Fran Tarkenton
Charley Taylor
Jim Taylor
Lawrence Taylor
Jim Thorpe
Y.A. Tittle
George Trafton
Charley Trippi
Emlen Tunnell
Clyde (Bulldog) Turner
Johnny Unitas
Gene Upshaw
Norm Van Brocklin
Steve Van Buren
Doak Walker
Bill Walsh
Paul Warfield
Bob Waterfield
Mike Webster
Arnie Weinmeister
Randy White
Dave Wilcox
Bill Willis
Larry Wilson
Kellen Winslow
Alex Wojciechowicz
Willie Wood
Ron Yary
Jack Youngblood

Canadian Football League Grey Cup

Year	Results	Site	Attendance
1909	U of Toronto 26, Parkdale 6	Toronto	3,807
1910	U of Toronto 16, Hamilton Tigers 7	Hamilton	12,000
1911	U of Toronto 14, Toronto 7	Toronto	13,687
1912	Hamilton Alerts 11, Toronto 4	Hamilton	5,337
1913	Hamilton Tigers 44, Parkdale 2	Hamilton	2,100
1914	Toronto 14, U of Toronto 2	Toronto	10,500
1915	Hamilton Tigers 13, Toronto RAA 7	Toronto	2,808
1916–19	No game	—	—
1920	U of Toronto 16, Toronto 3	Toronto	10,088
1921	Toronto 23, Edmonton 0	Toronto	9,558
1922	Queen's U 13, Edmonton 1	Kingston	4,700
1923	Queen's U 54, Regina 0	Toronto	8,629
1924	Queen's U 11, Balmy Beach 3	Toronto	5,978
1925	Ottawa Senators 24, Winnipeg 1	Ottawa	6,900
1926	Ottawa Senators 10, Toronto U 7	Toronto	8,276
1927	Balmy Beach 9, Hamilton Tigers 6	Toronto	13,676
1928	Hamilton Tigers 30, Regina 0	Hamilton	4,767
1929	Hamilton Tigers 14, Regina 3	Hamilton	1,906
1930	Balmy Beach 11, Regina 6	Toronto	3,914
1931	Montreal AAA 22, Regina 0	Montreal	5,112
1932	Hamilton Tigers 25, Regina 6	Hamilton	4,806
1933	Toronto 4, Sarnia 3	Sarnia	2,751
1934	Sarnia 20, Regina 12	Toronto	8,900
1935	Winnipeg 18, Hamilton Tigers 12	Hamilton	6,405
1936	Sarnia 26, Ottawa RR 20	Toronto	5,883
1937	Toronto 4, Winnipeg 3	Toronto	11,522
1938	Toronto 30, Winnipeg 7	Toronto	18,778
1939	Winnipeg 8, Ottawa 7	Ottawa	11,738
1940	Ottawa 12, Balmy Beach 5	Ottawa	1,700
1940	Ottawa 8, Balmy Beach 2	Toronto	4,998
1941	Winnipeg 18, Ottawa 16	Toronto	19,065
1942	Toronto RCAF 8, Winnipeg RCAF 5	Toronto	12,455
1943	Hamilton F Wild 23, Winnipeg RCAF 14	Toronto	16,423
1944	Montreal St H-D Navy 7, Hamilton F Wild 6	Hamilton	3,871
1945	Toronto 35, Winnipeg 0	Toronto	18,660
1946	Toronto 28, Winnipeg 6	Toronto	18,960
1947	Toronto 10, Winnipeg 9	Toronto	18,885
1948	Calgary 12, Ottawa 7	Toronto	20,013
1949	Montreal Als 28, Calgary 15	Toronto	20,087
1950	Toronto 13, Winnipeg 0	Toronto	27,101
1951	Ottawa 21, Saskatchewan 14	Toronto	27,341
1952	Toronto 21, Edmonton 11	Toronto	27,391
1953	Hamilton Ticats 12, Winnipeg 6	Toronto	27,313
1954	Edmonton 26, Montreal 25	Toronto	27,321
1955	Edmonton 34, Montreal 19	Vancouver	39,417
1956	Edmonton 50, Montreal 27	Toronto	27,425
1957	Hamilton 32, Winnipeg 7	Toronto	27,051
1958	Winnipeg 35, Hamilton 28	Vancouver	36,567
1959	Winnipeg 21, Hamilton 7	Toronto	33,133
1960	Ottawa 16, Edmonton 6	Vancouver	38,102
1961	Winnipeg 21, Hamilton 14	Toronto	32,651
1962	Winnipeg 28, Hamilton 27	Toronto	32,655
1963	Hamilton 21, British Columbia 10	Vancouver	36,545
1964	British Columbia 34, Hamilton 24	Toronto	32,655
1965	Hamilton 22, Winnipeg 16	Toronto	32,655
1966	Saskatchewan 29, Ottawa 14	Vancouver	36,553
1967	Hamilton 24, Saskatchewan 1	Ottawa	31,358
1968	Ottawa 24, Calgary 21	Toronto	32,655
1969	Ottawa 29, Saskatchewan 11	Montreal	33,172
1970	Montreal 23, Calgary 10	Toronto	32,669
1971	Calgary 14, Toronto 11	Vancouver	34,484
1972	Hamilton 13, Saskatchewan 10	Hamilton	33,993
1973	Ottawa 22, Edmonton 18	Toronto	36,653
1974	Montreal 20, Edmonton 7	Vancouver	34,450
1975	Edmonton 9, Montreal 8	Calgary	32,454

Canadian Football League Grey Cup *(Cont.)*

Year	Results	Site	Attendance
1976	Ottawa 23, Saskatchewan 20	Toronto	53,467
1977	Montreal 41, Edmonton 6	Montreal	68,318
1978	Edmonton 20, Montreal 13	Toronto	54,695
1979	Edmonton 17, Montreal 9	Montreal	65,113
1980	Edmonton 48, Hamilton 10	Toronto	54,661
1981	Edmonton 26, Ottawa 23	Montreal	52,478
1982	Edmonton 32, Toronto 16	Toronto	54,741
1983	Toronto 18, British Columbia 17	Vancouver	59,345
1984	Winnipeg 47, Hamilton 17	Edmonton	60,081
1985	British Columbia 37, Hamilton 24	Montreal	56,723
1986	Hamilton 39, Edmonton 15	Vancouver	59,621
1987	Edmonton 38, Toronto 36	Vancouver	59,478
1988	Winnipeg 22, British Columbia 21	Ottawa	50,604
1989	Saskatchewan 43, Hamilton 40	Toronto	54,088
1990	Winnipeg 50, Edmonton 11	Vancouver	46,968
1991	Toronto 36, Calgary 21	Winnipeg	51,985
1992	Calgary 24, Winnipeg 10	Toronto	45,863
1993	Edmonton 33, Winnipeg 23	Calgary	50,035
1994	British Columbia 26, Baltimore 23	Vancouver	55,097
1995	Baltimore 37, Calgary 20	Regina, Saskatchewan	52,564
1996	Toronto 43, Edmonton 37	Hamilton, Ontario	38,595
1997	Toronto 47, Saskatchewan 23	Edmonton	60,431
1998	Calgary 26, Hamilton 24	Winnipeg	34,157
1999	Hamilton 32, Calgary 21	Vancouver	45,118
2000	British Columbia 28, Montreal 26	Calgary	43,822
2001	Calgary 27, Winnipeg 19	Montreal	65,255

In 1909, Earl Grey, the Governor-General of Canada, donated a trophy for the Rugby Football Championship of Canada. The trophy, which subsequently became known as the Grey Cup, was originally open only to teams registered with the Canada Rugby Union. Since 1954, it has been awarded to the winner of the Canadian Football League's championship game.

AMERICAN FOOTBALL LEAGUE I

Year	Champion	Record
1926	Philadelphia Quakers	7-2

AMERICAN FOOTBALL LEAGUE II

Year	Champion	Record
1936	Boston Shamrocks	8-3
1937	LA Bulldogs	8-0

AMERICAN FOOTBALL LEAGUE III

Year	Champion	Record
1940	Columbus Bullies	8-1-1
1941	Columbus Bullies	5-1-2

ALL-AMERICAN FOOTBALL CONFERENCE

Year	Championship Game
1946	Cleveland 14, NY Yankees 9
1947	Cleveland 14, NY Yankees 3
1948	Cleveland 49, Buffalo 7
1949	Cleveland 21, San Francisco 7

WORLD FOOTBALL LEAGUE

Year	World Bowl Championship
1974	Birmingham 22, Florida 21
1975	Disbanded midseason

UNITED STATES FOOTBALL LEAGUE

Year	Championship Game
1983	Michigan 24, Philadelphia 22
1984	Philadelphia 23, Arizona 3
1985	Baltimore 28, Oakland 24

NFL EUROPE

Year	Champion	Record
1991	London	9-1-0
1992	Sacramento	8-2-0
1995	Frankfurt	6-4-0
1996	Scotland	7-3-0
1997	Barcelona	5-5-0
1998	Rhein	7-3-0
1999	Frankfurt	6-4-0
2000	Rhein	7-3-0
2001	Berlin	6-4-0
2002	Berlin	6-4-0

Known as World League of American Football until 1998.

Ken Dorsey of
national champion
Miami

College
Football

Miami Nice

Ditching the trash-talking ways of previous Hurricanes teams, Miami gave the BCS an unbeaten and undisputed champion

BY B.J. SCHECTER

LET THE RECORD show that for the fourth consecutive year the best team won the national championship. There is not a shred of doubt about those results, but there was plenty of carping, passionate debate and outrage-in-waiting leading up to them. The much maligned, four-year-old Bowl Championship Series, which rates teams in an effort to guarantee that the best two play for the national title, has been retooled each offseason to compensate for its flaws. Much has been said about the near-comic complexity, distortions and injustices of the BCS system, but this much is true: Tennessee (champions of the 1998 season), Florida State (1999), Oklahoma (2000) and Miami (2001) were undeniably, the best teams in the country during their respective championship seasons.

That's the good news. The bad news is that the carpers, complainers and passionate debaters had a point, and that the greatest strength of the BCS, especially during the past two seasons, seems to have been good fortune. The system has been vindicated by the right team prevailing at the right time. Miami proved its might this year with an impressive 37–14 stomping of Nebraska in the Rose Bowl. No one could argue with the 12–0 Hurricanes being crowned national champs. Nor could anyone complain about Oklahoma's national title following the 2000 season, when the Sooners capped a perfect season with a 13–2 victory over Florida State in the Orange Bowl.

But what would have happened if Florida State had upset the orange cart with a victory over Oklahoma in 2000, or if Nebraska had pruned Miami this season? A split vote, that's what, and the entire convoluted BCS system would have been undermined. Its sole purpose, after all, is to produce a clear-cut national champion.

But no system, short of one involving playoffs, can guarantee a controversy-free result every year. It's against all odds that the BCS has a perfect 4–0 record and seemingly only a matter of time before it produces a genuine season-ending controversy.

Running back Clinton Portis sparked Miami's 27-point second-quarter burst with a 39-yard touchdown run.

JOHN BIEVER

Before the Rose Bowl, bashers of the system from coast to coast wondered how Nebraska (11–1), which was coming off an embarrassing 62–36 loss to Colorado and didn't even win its own conference, could be a more worthy national title contender than, say, Pac-10 champion Oregon (10–1).

But the Hurricanes stormed the Rose Bowl and swept away all debate, proving they were in a class by themselves. Miami raced to a 34–0 halftime lead and held on to win its fifth national title, completing an impressive comeback from NCAA purgatory. When Butch Davis took over the Miami program in 1995, the Hurricanes were a mess. The team was filled with bad seeds who had frequent brushes with the law, and the NCAA had recently stripped the Hurricanes of 31 scholarships for rules violations. It took more than six years, but when Davis left Miami for the NFL's Cleveland Browns after the 2000 season, the Hurricanes were national contenders again.

Davis booted the thugs off the team, changed Miami's recruiting philosophy and banned the woofing, showboating antics that Miami had become famous for. When Davis left, the players lobbied for soft-spoken offensive coordinator Larry Coker to get the job. "By hiring coach Coker we know we can keep this thing going," said junior quarterback Ken Dorsey during Miami's search for a new coach. "There's no feeling-out process or a new set of rules. He's comfortable with us, we're comfortable with him."

"When he was named coach there was no doubt we were going to win the national championship," said senior safety Ed Reed.

Coker didn't change much from the Davis regime, and the Hurricanes didn't miss a beat. Possessed of blazing team speed, Miami bottled up opponents on defense and blew past them on offense. Some wondered whether Coker would crack under the immense pressure that comes with being Miami's football coach. Those concerns were misplaced, to say the least, as Coker relied on the stoicism instilled in him during his more than 25 years as an assistant and strode the sidelines with quiet confidence. Some of his understated persona even rubbed off on the Hurricanes, who were, dare we say, humble—an adjective that almost certainly has never been applied to them in the past.

To illustrate how far Miami has come since the trash-talking days of the late '80s and early '90s, one need look no further than their game against Temple on Nov. 3. In the first half, Owls defensive lineman Dan

Harrington and the Ducks had a legitimate gripe with the Bowl Championship Series.

Klecko got in the face of Hurricanes tackle Martin Bibla after a running play during which Klecko felt he was held. Fellow Hurricanes offensive lineman Joaquin Gonzalez quickly interceded. "He was ready to fight," says Gonzalez of Klecko. "I put my arm around him and said, 'Dude, you have the most beautiful eyes I've ever seen.' He had no clue what to do."

Miami players were just as resourceful when it came to winning close games. Late in their Nov. 10 meeting with Boston College in Chestnut Hill, the Hurricanes led 12–7 but were giving up chunks of yardage to the Eagles as time wound down. A 21-yard pass from Boston College quarterback Brian St. Pierre to receiver Dedric Dewalt brought BC to the Miami nine-yard line with one minute remaining. On the next play, Hurricanes cornerback Mike Rumph deflected a St. Pierre pass into the arms of defensive tackle Matt Walters, who started rumbling upfield with the ball. As Walters was about to be tackled, safety Ed Reed ripped the ball out of his hands and raced 80 yards for a touchdown, giving Miami an 18–7 victory. Reed figured in the Hurricanes' other tight win—a 26–24 defeat of 13th-ranked Virginia Tech on Dec. 1—making an interception late in the game to preserve the victory.

When they hit their stride, the Hurricanes were all but unstoppable. Led by a quarterback who looked like a displaced member of the tennis team, Miami could be utterly dominating. California native Ken Dorsey, a rail-thin 6' 5", 200-pound junior, had long dreamed about playing in the Rose Bowl. Problem was, most of the top-flight programs that caught a glimpse of his gangly frame decided not to take a chance on him. California didn't want him; Michigan passed. Miami rolled the dice on Dorsey and discovered that the heart of an unusually fiery competitor burned within his lean exterior.

Dorsey never forgot his only loss in two seasons as a starter—a 34–29 defeat at Washington in 2000—and used it as motivation. It worked. With the Rose Bowl win

PETER READ MILLER

over Nebraska, Dorsey improved his record as a starter to 26–1. He picked apart the Cornhuskers secondary with precision passing, throwing for a career-high 362 yards and three touchdowns, and was named the game's co-MVP.

On the other side of the ball, Miami's defense blunted Nebraska's normally razor-sharp option offense. Even though he rushed for 114 yards, Eric Crouch, the Cornhuskers' Heisman Trophy–winning quarterback, wasn't much of a factor. More often than not, the option play left him, well, limited options. "Even if they did get outside," said Miami sophomore linebacker D.J. Williams, "we felt we had the speed to run them down." Williams did just that, stripping Crouch of the football in the first quarter for the first of two turnovers by the Nebraska quarterback.

Among the swarming Miami defense, Williams stood out in the first half, and sophomore linebacker Jonathan Vilma starred in the second. He had eight tackles, including two bone-crushing hits that drew roars from the crowd. Not that Vilma or his teammates would gloat. These Hurricanes knew that actions speak louder than words. "We have a lot of quiet, easygoing guys like me who leave it all on the field," said Vilma. "People talk at us and we listen and say, 'That's nice. Now look at the scoreboard.'"

Fans watching the scoreboards during the last two weeks of the college football season had to wonder if they were hallucinating. After Nebraska was walloped by Colorado, it looked like the Cornhuskers would need a minor miracle to get back into the national title race. They got a succession of them, as contenders began to fall one by one. First, Oklahoma was upset by Oklahoma State on Nov. 24. It was the Sooners' second loss of the season, effectively ending the defending champs chances of repeating. Then Florida took its second loss of the year, a 34–32 defeat at home to Tennessee on Dec. 1.

The following weekend, Colorado edged Texas 39–37 in the Big 12 championship game, opening the BCS door for 10–1 Tennessee. On Dec. 8, the day Tennessee faced LSU for the SEC title in Atlanta, Nebraska's Crouch won the Heisman by a narrow margin over Florida quarterback Rex Grossman. Crouch's day got even better, for in Atlanta, Matt Mauck, a little-used backup quarterback from Santa Claus, Ind., gave Crouch and Nebraska an early Christmas present, leading the Tigers to a 31–20 upset of Tennessee.

The series of improbable results nearly short-circuited the BCS computers, not to mention the wiring of Oregon coach Mike Bellotti, whose 10–1 Ducks felt snubbed by the system. Bellotti didn't mince words, "I liken the BCS to a bad disease," he said, "like a cancer." The Ducks would prove that as a motivating force, righteous indignation has few equals. With a chip teetering on its collective shoulder, Oregon traveled to Tempe, Ariz., for a Fiesta Bowl showdown against Colorado.

At the beginning of the season, Oregon had been the darling of the college football nation. Something of a new kid on the block, Oregon embarked on a huge public relations campaign during the summer to promote quarterback Joey Harrington as a Heisman Trophy candidate. Alumni and boosters paid $250,000 to rent a 100-foot billboard in New York City that set Harrington's mug towering across the street from Madison Square Garden. Ducks supporters rented smaller billboards all up and down the West Coast. Initially, Oregon took a lot of heat for spending so much money on publicity, but it accomplished its goal of drawing attention to the team, which had the talent to back up the hype: SPORTS ILLUSTRATED picked Oregon as its preseaon No. 2, and the Ducks lived up to the ranking with six straight wins to start the season.

A 49–42 loss to Stanford on Oct. 20 dented the Ducks' national championship hopes, but they stayed the course and won the rest of their games to take the Pac-10 title. With a win over Colorado in the Fiesta Bowl, Oregon could put itself in a position to claim a piece of the national title. Harrington didn't miss his opportunity. In front of a national television audience, he completed passes from all over the field to seven receivers, leading Oregon to a 38–16 win. "Not only was it the biggest win, but it was on the biggest stage, and we did it in one of the most emphatic manners," said Harrington, who threw for 350 yards and four touchdowns. "We made a statement today, 38 unanswered points, and shot down the hottest team in the country."

One of the hottest teams early in the season was unheralded Fresno State. Unranked in the preseason, Fresno vaulted into the Top 10 with wins over three quality opponents to start the year. The Bulldogs opened the season with a head-turning 24–22 victory at Colorado and then showed the win was no fluke by knocking off Oregon State 44–24 at home the following week. (Oregon State was SI's preseason No. 1.) On Sept. 8, the Bulldogs pulled off their most impressive win, rallying from a 20–10 halftime deficit at Wisconsin to shock the Badgers 32–20. After the victory over Wisconsin, Bulldogs players and coaches played it cool, their muted celebration suggesting that they'd expected to win. Instead of whooping and hollering, Fresno State players held their

index fingers to their lips and said, "Shhh! Fresno State football—it's a secret."

It wouldn't be a secret for long. With strong-armed quarterback David Carr, a variety of players ignored by bigger programs and gutsy coach Pat Hill, the Bulldogs threatened to crash the BCS party. (Fresno State plays in the Western Athletic Conference, which doesn't have an automatic bid to one of the four BCS games.) But Fresno's star dropped precipitously with consecutive losses to Boise State and Hawaii in October. Brigham Young, which won its first 12 games, also caused a stir by threatening to take the NCAA to court if it were left out of the BCS. The Cougars wisely scrapped that idea after they were blown out by Hawaii in their season finale.

In a year that will be forever remembered for catastrophe, tragedy struck college football before practices officially started. During a routine conditioning drill on Aug. 3, Northwestern defensive back Rashidi Wheeler collapsed and died of an acute bronchial asthma attack. The nation, of course, would endure horrific losses the following month as hijacked planes hit New York City, Washington, D.C., and western Pennsylvania. In addition to raising security concerns and causing many schools to institute no-fly zones over their stadiums, the Sept. 11 attacks created widespread debate over whether or not games should be played on Sept. 15. In the end, every conference in the country postponed that weekend's slate of games.

The bowl season and its aftermath brought a couple of high-profile coaching changes. Notre Dame fired coach Bob Davie, who had gone 35–25 during five seasons in South Bend. The school hired former Georgia Tech coach George O'Leary to replace Davie, but forced him to resign five days later after a New Hampshire newspaper revealed that O'Leary had lied on his résumé for more than 20 years. Notre Dame quickly papered over this p.r. disaster by hiring former Stanford coach Tyrone Willingham, who had run a spotless program in Palo Alto. Willingham would be the first African-American to lead the most storied college football program in the country, following the likes of Knute Rockne and Ara Parseghian.

Florida coach Steve Spurrier shocked the college football world by unexpectedly resigning after 12 seasons. He later signed a five-year deal to coach the NFL's Washington Redskins. The Gators tried to sign big-name coaches Bob Stoops (Oklahoma) and Mike Shanahan (Denver Broncos) before finally settling on New Orleans Saints defensive coordinator Ron Zook.

In a year when infinitely larger issues occupied our attention, it was almost refreshing to see fans and coaches getting riled up about the BCS at season's end. It was left to Miami to cut through the static with a clear reminder of a perennial college

Final Polls

Associated Press

	Record	Pts	Head Coach	SI Preseason Rank
1. Miami (FL) (72)	12–0	1,800	Larry Coker	3
2. Oregon	11–1	1,726	Mike Belotti	2
3. Florida	10–2	1,611	Steve Spurrier	7
4. Tennessee	11–2	1,581	Phillip Fulmer	9
5. Texas	11–2	1,374	Mack Brown	4
6. Oklahoma	11–2	1,373	Bob Stoops	5
7. Louisiana St	10–3	1,350	Nick Saban	13
8. Nebraska	11–2	1,348	Frank Solich	8
9. Colorado	10–3	1,335	Gary Barnett	27
10. Washington St	10–2	1,074	Mike Price	79
11. Maryland	10–2	1,065	Ralph Friedgen	63
12. Illinois	10–2	1,045	Ron Turner	49
13. S Carolina	9–3	975	Lou Holtz	19
14. Syracuse	10–3	856	Paul Pasqualoni	41
15. Florida St	8–4	686	Bobby Bowden	6
16. Stanford	9–3	673	Tyrone Willingham	42
17. Louisville	11–2	621	John Smith	34
18. Virginia Tech	8–4	437	Frank Beamer	10
19. Washington	8–4	414	Rick Neuheisel	16
20. Michigan	8–4	325	Lloyd Carr	14
21. Boston College	8–4	318	Tom O'Brien	46
22. Georgia	8–4	277	Mark Richt	26
23. Toledo	10–2	237	Tom Amstutz	55
24. Georgia Tech	8–5	178	George O'Leary	11
25. Brigham Young	12–2	144	Gary Crowton	38

Note: As voted by a panel of 72 sportswriters and broadcasters following bowl games (1st-place votes in parentheses).

USA Today/ESPN

	Pts	Prev Rank		Pts	Prev Rank
1. Miami (FL) (60)	1,500	1	14. Syracuse	736	18
2. Oregon	1,434	2	15. Florida St	556	24
3. Florida	1,351	5	16. Louisville	524	22
4. Tennessee	1,284	8	17. Stanford	502	11
5. Texas	1,207	9	18. Virginia Tech	394	16
6. Oklahoma	1,141	10	19. Washington	369	20
7. Nebraska	1,101	4	20. Michigan	363	15
8. Louisiana St	1,099	12	21. Marshall	223	25
9. Colorado	1,031	3	22. Toledo	188	NR
10. Maryland	885	6	23. Boston College	174	NR
11. Washington St	879	13	24. Brigham Young	172	17
12. Illinois	846	7	25. Georgia	163	19
13. S Carolina	837	14			

Note: As voted by a panel of 60 Division I-A head coaches; 25 points for 1st, 24 for 2nd, etc. (1st-place votes in parentheses).

Bowls and Playoffs

NCAA Division I-A Bowl Results

Date	Bowl	Result	Payout/Team ($)	Attendance
12-18-01	New Orleans	Colorado State 45, N Texas 20	750,000	27,004
12-19-01	GMAC	Marshall 64, E Carolina 61	750,000	40,139
12-20-01	Tangerine	Pittsburgh 34, North Carolina St 19	750,000	28,562
12-25-01	Las Vegas	Utah 10, Southern California 6	800,000	30,894
12-27-01	Seattle	Georgia Tech 24, Stanford 14	750,000	30,144
12-27-01	Independence	Alabama 14, Iowa State 13	1 million	45,627
12-28-01	galleryfurniture.com	Texas A&M 28, Texas Christian 9	750,000	53,480
12-28-01	Music City	Boston College 20, Georgia 16	750,000	46,125
12-28-01	Holiday	Texas 47, Washington 43	2 million	60,548

NCAA Division I-A Bowl Results *(Cont.)*

Date	Bowl	Result	Payout/Team ($)	Attendance
12-29-01	Motor City	Toledo 23, Cincinnati 16	750,000	44,164
12-29-01	Alamo	Iowa 16, Texas Tech 13	1.2 million	65,232
12-29-01	Insight.com	Syracuse 26, Kansas St 3	750,000	40,028
12-31-01	Sun	Washington St 33, Purdue 27	1 million	47,812
12-31-01	Humanitarian	Clemson 49, Louisiana Tech 24	750,000	23,472
12-31-01	Silicon Valley Classic	Michigan St 44, Fresno St 35	750,000	30,456
12-31-01	Liberty	Louisville 28, Brigham Young 10	1.3 million	58,968
12-31-01	Peach	N Carolina 16, Auburn 10	1.8 million	71,827
1-1-02	Cotton	Oklahoma 10, Arkansas 3	2 million	72,955
1-1-02	Outback	S Carolina 31, Ohio St 28	2.2 million	66,249
1-1-02	Gator	Florida St 30, Virginia Tech 17	1.4 million	72,202
1-1-02	Florida Citrus	Tennessee 45, Michigan 17	4.25 million	59,693
1-1-02	Fiesta	Oregon 38, Colorado 16	11-13 million	74,118
1-1-02	Sugar	Louisiana St 47, Illinois 34	11-13 million	77,688
1-2-02	Orange	Florida 56, Maryland 23	11-13 million	73,640
1-3-02	Rose	Miami 37, Nebraska 14	11-13 million	93,781

NCAA Division I-AA Championship Boxscore

Furman	0	0	6	— 6
Montana	0	10	0	3 —13

SECOND QUARTER

M: Humphery 2 run (Snyder kick), 6:27
M: FG Snyder 35, 0:53

FOURTH QUARTER

M: FG Snyder 30, 6:12
F: Thomas 54 pass from Napier, 0:00

	Furman	Montana
First downs	14	16
Rushed–yards	39–121	43–173
Passing yards	172	124
Sacked–yards lost	2–4	2–14
Return yards	7	106
Passes	10-26-2	18-28-0
Punts	7–38.7	6–40.7
Fumbles-lost	1–1	0-0
Penalties-yards	5–22	5–28
Time of possession	28:09	31:51

Att: 12,698.

Small College Championship Summaries

NCAA DIVISION II

First round: N Dakota 42, Winona St 28; Pittsburg St 20, NE–Omaha 7; Tarleton St 28, Chadron St 24; UC–Davis 37, TX A&M–Kingsville 32; Valdosta St 40, Fort Valley St 24; Catawba 35, Central Arkansas 34; Grand Valley St 42, Bloomsburg 14; Saginaw Valley St 33, Indiana (PA) 32.

Quarterfinals: N Dakota 38, Pittsburg St 0; UC–Davis 42, Tarleton St 25; Catawba 37, Valdosta St 34; Grand Valley St 33, Saginaw Valley St 30.

Semifinals: N Dakota 14, UC–Davis 2; Grand Valley St 34, Catawba 16.

Championship: 12-8-01 Florence, AL

Grand Valley St	3	0	0	14—17
N Dakota	7	0	0	7—14

NCAA DIVISION III

First round: Augustana (IL) 54, Defiance (OH) 14; Thomas More (KY) 34, MacMurray (IL) 30; Ithaca 35, Montclair St 23; Rowan (NJ) 40, Brockport (NY) 17; Western Connecticut St 8, Westfield St (MA) 7; Washington & Jefferson (PA) 24, Western Maryland 21; Widener (PA) 56, Christopher Newport (VA) 7; Wittenberg (OH) 38, Hardin–Simmons TX 35 (ot); WI–Stevens Point 37, Bethel (MN) 27; St. John's, (MN) 27, St. Norbert (WI) 20; Trinity (TX) 30, Mary Hardin–Baylor (TX) 6; Pacific Lutheran (WA) 27, Whitworth (WA) 26 (ot).

NCAA DIVISION III *(Cont.)*

Second Round: Mount Union 32, Augustana 7; Wittenberg 41, Thomas More 0; Ithaca 27, RPI 10; Rowan 43, Western Connecticut St 14; Bridgewater 41, Trinity 37, Widener 46, Washington & Jefferson 30; Pacific Lutheran 27, Central (IA) 21; St. John's 9, WI–Stevens Point 7.

Quarterfinals: Rowan 48, Ithaca 0; Bridgewater 57, Widener 32; Mount Union 49, Wittenberg 21; St. John's 31, Pacific Lutheran 6.

Semifinals: Mount Union 35, St. John's 14; Bridgewater 29, Rowan 24.

Championship: 12-15-01 Salem, VA

Bridgewater	7	6	0	14—27
Mount Union	7	16	7	0—30

NAIA CHAMPIONSHIP

12-15-01 Hardin County, TN

Georgetown (KY)	7	21	14	7—49
Sioux Falls (SD)	7	6	7	7—27

Awards

Heisman Memorial Trophy

Player, School	Class	Pos	1st	2nd	3rd	Total
Eric Crouch, Nebraska	Sr	QB	162	98	88	770
Rex Grossman, Florida	So	QB	137	105	87	708
Ken Dorsey, Miami (FL)	Jr	QB	109	122	67	638
Joey Harrington, Oregon	Sr	QB	54	68	66	364
David Carr, Fresno St	Sr	QB	34	60	58	280
Antwaan Randle El, Indiana	Sr	QB	46	39	51	267
Roy Williams, Oklahoma	Jr	DB	13	36	35	146
Bryant McKinnie, Miami (FL)	Sr	OL	26	12	14	116
Dwight Freeney, Syracuse	Sr	DL	2	6	24	42
Julius Peppers, N Carolina	Jr	DL	2	10	15	41

Note: Former Heisman winners and the media vote, with ballots allowing for three names (3 points for 1st, 2 for 2nd, 1 for 3rd).

Other Awards

Maxwell Award ....Ken Dorsey, Miami (FL), QB
Sporting News Player of the Year ....Eric Crouch, Nebraska, QB
Walter Camp Player of the Year ....Eric Crouch, Nebraska, QB
Chuck Bednarik Award (Defense) ....Julius Peppers, N Carolina, DL
Vince Lombardi/Rotary Award (Lineman)...Julius Peppers, N Carolina, DL
Outland Trophy (Interior lineman) ....Bryant McKinnie, Miami (FL), OL
Davey O'Brien Award (QB) ....Eric Crouch, Nebraska, QB
Unitas Golden Arm Award (Senior QB).....David Carr, Fresno St, QB
Doak Walker Award (RB) ....Luke Staley, Brigham Young, RB
Biletnikoff Award (WR) ....Josh Reed, Louisiana St, WR
Butkus Award (Linebacker) ....Rocky Calmus, Oklahoma, LB
Jim Thorpe Award (Defensive back)..........Roy Williams, Oklahoma, DB
Walter Payton Award (Div I-AA Player) ......Brian Westbrook, Villanova, RB
Harlon Hill Trophy (Div II Player) ....Dusty Bonner, Valdosta St, QB
Gagliardi Trophy (Div III Player) ....Scott Hvistendahl, Augsburg, WR

Coaches' Awards

Walter Camp Award ....Ralph Friedgen, Maryland
Eddie Robinson Award ....Ralph Friedgen, Maryland
Bobby Dodd Award ....Ralph Friedgen, Maryland
Bear Bryant Award ....Larry Coker, Miami (FL)

AFCA COACHES OF THE YEAR

Division I-A ....Ralph Friedgen, Maryland; Larry Coker, Miami (FL)
Division I-AA ....Bobby Johnson, Furman
Division II ....Dale Lennon, N Dakota
Division III ....Larry Kehres, Mount Union

Football Writers Association of America All-America Team

OFFENSE

QB........Antwaan Randle El, Indiana, Sr
RB........Travis Stephens, Tennessee, Sr
RB........Luke Staley, Brigham Young, Jr
WR ......Josh Reed, Louisiana St, Jr
WR .....Jabar Gaffney, Florida, So
TE ....Daniel Graham, Colorado, Sr
C ....LeCharles Bentley, Ohio St, Sr
OL........Toniu Fonoti, Nebraska, Jr
OL........Joaquin Gonzalez, Miami (FL), Sr
OL........Bryant McKinnie, Miami (FL), Sr
OL........Mike Pearson, Florida, Jr
K ....Seth Marler, Tulane, Jr
KR........Luke Powell, Stanford, Jr

DEFENSE

DL ....Alex Brown, Florida, Sr
DL ....Dwight Freeney, Syracuse, Sr
DL ....John Henderson, Tennessee, Sr
DL ....Julius Peppers, N Carolina, Jr
LB ....Rocky Calmus, Oklahoma, Sr
LB ........E.J. Henderson, Maryland, Jr
LB ....Robert Thomas, UCLA, Sr
DB........Quentin Jammer, Texas, Sr
DB........Troy Polamalu, Southern California, Jr
DB........Edward Reed, Miami (FL), Sr
DB........Roy Williams, Oklahoma, Jr
P ....Dave Zastudil, Ohio, Sr

Division I-A

ATLANTIC COAST CONFERENCE

	Conference		Full Season		
	W	L	W	L	Pct
Maryland	7	1	10	2	.833
Florida St	6	2	8	4	.667
N Carolina	5	3	8	5	.615
Georgia Tech	4	4	8	5	.615
N Carolina St	4	4	7	5	.583
Clemson	4	4	7	5	.583
Wake Forest	3	5	6	5	.545
Virginia	3	5	5	7	.417
Duke	0	8	0	11	.000

BIG EAST CONFERENCE

	Conference		Full Season		
	W	L	W	L	Pct
Miami (FL)	7	0	12	0	1.000
Syracuse	6	1	10	3	.769
Virginia Tech	4	3	8	4	.667
Boston College	4	3	8	4	.667
Pittsburgh	4	3	7	5	.583
Temple	2	5	4	7	.364
W Virginia	1	6	3	8	.273
Rutgers	0	7	2	9	.182

BIG TEN CONFERENCE

	Conference		Full Season		
	W	L	W	L	Pct
Illinois	7	1	10	2	.833
Michigan	6	2	8	4	.667
Ohio St	5	3	7	5	.583
Purdue	4	4	6	6	.500
Iowa	4	4	7	5	.583
Penn St	4	4	5	6	.455
Indiana	4	4	5	6	.455
Michigan St	3	5	7	5	.583
Wisconsin	3	5	5	7	.417
Minnesota	2	6	4	7	.363
Northwestern	2	6	4	7	.363

BIG 12 CONFERENCE

	Conference		Full Season		
NORTH	W	L	W	L	Pct
*Colorado	7	1	10	3	.769
Nebraska	7	1	11	2	.846
Iowa St	4	4	7	5	.583
Kansas St	3	5	6	6	.500
Missouri	3	5	4	7	.364
Kansas	1	7	3	8	.273
SOUTH					
*Texas	7	1	11	2	.846
Oklahoma	6	2	11	2	.846
Texas A&M	4	4	8	4	.667
Texas Tech	4	4	7	5	.583
Oklahoma St	2	6	4	7	.364
Baylor	0	8	3	8	.273

*Full season record includes Big 12 Championship Game in which Colorado defeated Texas 39–37, on Dec. 1.

Division I-A *(Cont.)*

CONFERENCE USA

	Conference		Full Season		
	W	L	W	L	Pct
Louisville	6	1	11	2	.846
Cincinnati	5	2	6	5	.545
AL–Birmingham	5	2	6	5	.545
E Carolina	5	2	6	6	.500
Texas Christian	4	3	6	6	.500
Southern Miss	4	3	6	5	.545
Memphis	3	4	5	6	.455
Army	2	5	3	8	.273
Tulane	1	6	3	9	.250
Houston	0	7	0	11	.000

MID-AMERICAN ATHLETIC CONFERENCE

	Conference		Full Season		
EAST	W	L	W	L	Pct
*Marshall	8	0	11	2	.846
Miami (OH)	6	2	7	5	.583
Bowling Green	5	3	8	3	.727
Kent St	5	3	6	5	.545
Akron	4	4	4	7	.364
Buffalo	1	7	3	8	.273
Ohio University	1	7	1	10	.091
WEST					
*Toledo	5	2	10	2	.833
Northern Illinois	4	3	6	5	.545
Ball St	4	3	5	6	.455
Western Michigan	4	4	5	6	.455
Central Michigan	2	6	3	8	.273
Eastern Michigan	1	6	2	9	.182

*Full season record includes MAC Championship Game in which Toledo defeated Marshall 41–36, on Nov. 30.

MOUNTAIN WEST CONFERENCE

	Conference		Full Season		
	W	L	W	L	Pct
Brigham Young	7	0	12	2	.857
Colorado St	5	2	7	5	.583
Utah	4	3	8	4	.667
New Mexico	4	3	6	5	.545
Air Force	3	4	6	6	.500
Nevada–Las Vegas	3	4	4	7	.364
San Diego St	2	5	3	8	.273
Wyoming	0	7	2	9	.182

PACIFIC 10 CONFERENCE

	Conference		Full Season		
	W	L	W	L	Pct
Oregon	7	1	11	1	.917
Washington St	6	2	10	2	.833
Stanford	6	2	9	3	.750
Washington	6	2	8	4	.667
Southern California	5	3	6	6	.500
UCLA	4	4	7	4	.636
Oregon St	3	5	5	6	.455
Arizona	2	6	5	6	.455
Arizona St	1	7	4	7	.364
California	0	8	1	10	.091

Division I-A (Cont.)

SOUTHEASTERN CONFERENCE

EAST	Conference		Full Season		
	W	L	W	L	Pct
*Tennessee	7	1	11	2	.846
Florida	6	2	10	2	.833
S Carolina	5	3	9	3	.750
Georgia	5	3	8	4	.667
Kentucky	1	7	2	9	.182
Vanderbilt	0	8	2	9	.182
WEST					
*Louisiana St	5	3	10	3	.769
Auburn	5	3	7	5	.583
Alabama	4	4	7	5	.583
Arkansas	4	4	7	5	.583
Ole Miss	4	4	7	4	.636
Mississippi St	2	6	3	8	.273

*Full season record includes SEC Championship Game in which Louisiana St defeated Tennessee 31–20, on Dec. 8.

SUN BELT CONFERENCE

	Conference		Full Season		
	W	L	W	L	Pct
N Texas	5	1	5	7	.417
Middle Tennessee	5	1	8	3	.727
New Mexico St	4	2	5	7	.417
Louisiana-Lafayette	2	4	3	8	.273
Louisiana-Monroe	2	4	2	9	.182
Arkansas St	2	4	2	9	.182
Idaho	1	5	1	10	.091

WESTERN ATHLETIC CONFERENCE

	Conference		Full Season		
	W	L	W	L	Pct
Louisiana Tech	7	1	7	5	.583
Fresno St	6	2	11	3	.786
Boise St	6	2	8	4	.667
Hawaii	5	3	9	3	.750
Rice	5	3	8	4	.667
Southern Methodist	4	4	4	7	.364
Nevada	3	5	3	8	.273
San Jose St	3	5	3	9	.250
Texas–El Paso	1	7	2	9	.182
Tulsa	0	8	1	10	.091

INDEPENDENTS

	Full Season		
	W	L	Pct
S Florida	8	3	.727
Troy St	7	4	.636
Central Florida	6	5	.545
Notre Dame	5	6	.455
Utah St	4	7	.364
Connecticut	2	9	.182
Navy	0	10	.000

Division I-AA

ATLANTIC 10 CONFERENCE

	Conference		Full Season		
	W	L	W	L	Pct
Hofstra	7	2	9	3	.750
William & Mary	7	2	8	4	.667
Maine	7	2	9	3	.750
Villanova	7	2	8	3	.727
Rhode Island	6	3	8	3	.727
Delaware	4	5	4	6	.400
Northeastern	4	5	5	6	.455
Massachusetts	3	6	3	8	.273
Richmond	3	6	3	8	.273
New Hampshire	2	7	4	7	.364
James Madison	0	9	2	9	.182

BIG SKY CONFERENCE

	Conference		Full Season		
	W	L	W	L	Pct
Montana	7	0	15	1	.938
Northern Arizona	5	2	8	4	.667
Portland St	5	2	7	4	.636
Montana St	4	3	5	6	.455
Eastern Washington	3	4	7	4	.636
Weber St	2	5	3	8	.273
Idaho St	1	6	4	7	.364
Sacramento St	1	6	2	9	.182

GATEWAY COLLEGIATE ATHLETIC CONFERENCE

	Conference		Full Season		
	W	L	W	L	Pct
Northern Iowa	6	1	11	2	.846
Youngstown St	5	2	8	3	.727
Western Kentucky	5	2	8	4	.667
Western Illinois	4	3	5	5	.500
SW Missouri St	3	4	6	5	.545
Indiana State	2	5	3	8	.273
Illinois St	2	5	2	9	.182
Southern Illinois	1	6	1	10	.091

IVY LEAGUE

	Conference		Full Season		
	W	L	W	L	Pct
Harvard	7	0	9	0	1.000
Pennsylvania	6	1	8	1	.889
Brown	5	2	6	3	.667
Princeton	3	4	3	6	.333
Columbia	3	4	3	7	.300
Cornell	2	5	2	7	.222
Yale	1	6	3	6	.333
Dartmouth	1	6	1	8	.111

METRO ATLANTIC ATHLETIC CONFERENCE

	Conference		Full Season		
	W	L	W	L	Pct
Duquesne	6	0	8	2	.800
St. Peter's	6	1	10	1	.909
Fairfield	5	2	5	5	.500
Iona	3	3	4	5	.444
La Salle	2	4	5	4	.556
Marist	2	4	3	6	.333
Siena	1	6	1	8	.111
Canisius	1	6	1	9	.100

Division I-AA *(Cont.)*

MID-EASTERN ATHLETIC CONFERENCE

	Conference		Full Season		
	W	L	W	L	Pct
Florida A&M	7	1	7	4	.636
Hampton	6	2	7	4	.636
N Carolina A&T	5	3	8	3	.727
Bethune–Cookman	5	3	6	4	.600
S Carolina St	5	3	6	5	.545
Norfolk St	3	5	5	6	.455
Delaware St	3	5	5	6	.455
Morgan St	1	7	2	9	.182
Howard	1	7	2	9	.182

NORTHEAST CONFERENCE

	Conference		Full Season		
	W	L	W	L	Pct
Sacred Heart	8	0	11	0	1.000
Robert Morris	6	1	6	3	.667
Monmouth	5	2	7	3	.700
Albany	5	2	7	3	.700
Wagner	3	5	3	6	.333
Stony Brook	3	5	3	6	.333
Central Connecticut St	2	5	2	7	.222
St. John's	1	6	1	9	.100
St. Francis (PA)	0	7	0	10	.000

OHIO VALLEY CONFERENCE

	Conference		Full Season		
	W	L	W	L	Pct
Eastern Illinois	6	0	9	2	.818
Eastern Kentucky	5	1	8	2	.800
Tennessee Tech	4	2	7	3	.700
Tennessee St	3	3	8	3	.727
Murray St	2	4	4	6	.400
SE Missouri St	2	5	4	7	.364
Tennessee–Martin	0	6	1	10	.091

PATRIOT LEAGUE

	Conference		Full Season		
	W	L	W	L	Pct
Lehigh	7	0	11	1	.917
Colgate	5	1	7	3	.700
Fordham	5	2	7	4	.636
Bucknell	4	3	6	4	.600
Holy Cross	3	4	4	6	.400
Towson	2	5	3	7	.300
Lafayette	1	6	2	8	.200
Georgetown	0	6	3	7	.300

PIONEER CONFERENCE

	Conference		Full Season		
NORTH	W	L	W	L	Pct
*Dayton	4	0	10	1	.909
Butler	2	2	5	5	.500
San Diego	2	2	6	3	.667
Drake	1	3	5	5	.500
Valparaiso	1	3	3	8	.273
SOUTH					
*Jacksonville	3	0	6	5	.545
Morehead St	2	1	6	5	.545
Davidson	1	2	5	4	.556
Austin Peay	0	3	3	7	.300

*Full season record includes Pioneer Conference Championship in which Dayton def. Jacksonville 46–14, on Nov. 17.

Division I-AA *(Cont.)*

SOUTHERN CONFERENCE

	Conference		Full Season		
	W	L	W	L	Pct
Georgia Southern	7	1	12	2	.857
Furman	7	1	12	3	.800
Appalachian St	6	2	9	4	.692
Western Carolina	5	3	7	4	.637
E Tennessee St	4	4	6	5	.545
Wofford	3	5	4	7	.364
The Citadel	2	6	3	7	.300
Chattanooga	1	7	3	8	.273
Virginia Military	1	7	1	10	.091

SOUTHLAND CONFERENCE

	Conference		Full Season		
	W	L	W	L	Pct
Sam Houston St	5	1	10	3	.769
McNeese St	5	1	8	4	.667
Northwestern St	4	2	8	4	.667
Stephen F. Austin	4	2	6	5	.545
Jacksonville St	2	4	5	6	.455
Nicholls St	1	5	3	8	.273
SW Texas St	0	6	4	7	.364

SOUTHWESTERN ATHLETIC CONFERENCE

	Conference		Full Season		
EASTERN	W	L	W	L	Pct
*Alabama St	6	1	8	4	.667
Jackson St	5	2	7	4	.636
Alcorn St	5	2	6	5	.545
Alabama A&M	3	4	4	7	.364
Mississippi Valley St	0	7	0	11	.000
WESTERN					
*Grambling	6	1	10	1	.909
Southern	5	2	7	4	.636
Prairie View A&M	2	5	3	7	.300
Texas Southern	2	5	3	7	.300
Arkansas–Pine Bluff	1	6	4	7	.364

*Full season record includes SWAC Championship Game in which Grambling defeated Alabama St 38–31, on Dec. 1.

INDEPENDENTS

	Full Season		
	W	L	Pct
Davidson	10	0	1.000
Gardner-Webb	6	4	.600
St. Mary's (CA)	6	5	.545
Cal Poly	6	5	.545
Samford	5	5	.500
Charleston Southern	5	6	.455
Morris Brown	5	6	.455
Florida Atlantic	4	6	.400
Cal St–Northridge	3	7	.300
Liberty	3	8	.273
Savannah St	2	7	.222
Southern Utah	2	9	.182
Elon	2	9	.182

Division I-A

SCORING

	Class	GP	TD	XP	FG	Pts	Pts/Game
Luke Staley, Brigham Young	Jr	11	28	0	0	170	15.45
Dwone Hicks, Middle Tennessee St	Jr	11	24	0	0	148	13.45
Chester Taylor, Toledo	Jr	11	23	0	0	138	12.55
Todd Sievers, Miami (FL)	Jr	11	0	56	21	119	10.82
Levron Williams, Indiana	Sr	11	19	0	0	114	10.36
Jeff Chandler, Florida	Sr	10	0	46	19	103	10.30
William Green, Boston College	Jr	10	17	0	0	102	10.20
Leonard Henry, E Carolina	Sr	11	18	0	0	108	9.82
Ricky Williams, Texas Tech	Sr	11	18	0	0	108	9.82
Eric Crouch, Nebraska	Sr	12	19	0	0	116	9.67

FIELD GOALS

	Class	GP	FGA	FG	Pct	FG/Game
Todd Sievers, Miami (FL)	Jr	11	26	21	.808	1.91
Jeff Chandler, Florida	Sr	10	22	19	.864	1.90
Travis Dorsch, Purdue	Sr	11	25	20	.800	1.82
Jarvis Wallum, Wyoming	Jr	11	23	20	.870	1.82
Steve Azar, Northern Illiniois	So	11	26	20	.769	1.82

TOTAL OFFENSE

			Rushing		Passing		Total Offense		
	Class	GP	Car	Net	Att	Yds	Yds	Yds/Play	Yds/Game
Rex Grossman, Florida	So	11	34	8	395	3896	3904	9.10	354.9
Byron Leftwich, Marshall	Jr	12	64	92	470	4132	4224	7.91	352.0
David Carr, Fresno St	Sr	13	88	97	476	4299	4396	7.79	338.2
Nick Rolovich, Hawaii	Sr	10	49	4	405	3361	3365	7.41	336.5
Luke McCown, Louisiana Tech	So	11	87	144	470	3337	3481	6.25	316.5
Kliff Kingsbury, Texas Tech	Jr	11	66	-48	528	3502	3454	5.81	314.0
Brandon Doman, BYU	Sr	13	142	456	408	3542	3998	7.27	307.5
Woodrow Dantzler, Clemson	Sr	11	206	1004	311	2360	3364	6.51	305.8
Zak Kustok, Northwestern	Sr	11	175	580	404	2692	3272	5.65	297.5
Ryan Dinwiddie, Boise St	So	11	71	97	322	3043	3140	7.99	285.5

RUSHING

	Class	GP	Car	Yds	TD	Avg	Yds/Game
Chance Kretschmer, Nevada	Fr	11	302	1732	15	5.74	157.45
William Green, Boston College	Jr	10	265	1559	15	5.88	155.90
Luke Staley, Brigham Young	Jr	11	196	1582	24	8.07	143.82
Larry Ned, San Diego St	Sr	11	311	1549	15	4.98	140.82
Anthony Davis, Wisconsin	Fr	11	291	1466	11	5.04	133.27
Leonard Henry, E Carolina	Sr	11	184	1432	16	7.78	130.18
Chester Taylor, Toledo	Jr	11	268	1430	20	5.34	130.00
Levron Williams, Indiana	Sr	11	212	1401	17	6.61	127.36
Dameon Hunter, Utah	Sr	11	257	1396	9	5.43	126.91
Marcus Merriweather, Ball St	Sr	10	268	1244	12	4.64	124.40

PASSING EFFICIENCY

	Class	GP	Att	Comp	Pct Comp	Yds	Yds/Att	TD	Int	Rating Pts
Rex Grossman, Florida	So	11	395	259	65.57	3896	9.86	34	12	170.8
David Carr, Fresno St	Sr	13	476	308	64.71	4299	9.03	42	7	166.7
Wes Counts, Middle Tennessee St	Sr	11	259	188	72.59	2327	8.98	17	4	166.6
Ryan Dinwiddie, Boise St	So	11	322	201	62.42	3043	9.45	29	11	164.7
Byron Leftwich, Marshall	Jr	12	470	315	67.02	4132	8.79	38	7	164.6
Jeff Smoker, Michigan St	So	10	230	144	62.61	2203	9.58	18	7	162.8
Brandon Doman, BYU	Sr	13	408	261	63.97	3542	8.68	33	8	159.7
Chris Rix, Florida St	Fr	11	286	165	57.69	2734	9.56	24	13	156.6
Jeff Krohn, Arizona St	So	10	213	115	53.99	1942	9.12	19	7	153.4
Nick Rolovich, Hawaii	Sr	10	405	233	57.53	3361	8.30	34	9	150.5

Note: Minimum 15 attempts per game.

Division I-A *(Cont.)*

RECEPTIONS PER GAME

	Class	GP	No.	Yds	TD	R/Game
Kevin Curtis, Utah St	Jr	11	100	1531	10	9.09
Ricky Williams, Texas Tech	Sr	11	92	617	4	8.36
Josh Reed, Lousiana St	Jr	12	94	1740	7	7.83
Darius Watts, Marshall	So	12	91	1417	18	7.58
Don Shoals, Tulsa	Sr	10	75	908	4	7.50

RECEIVING YARDS PER GAME

	Class	GP	No.	Yds	TD	Yds/Game
Josh Reed, Louisiana St	Jr	12	94	1740	7	145.00
Ashley Lelie, Hawaii	Jr	12	84	1713	19	142.75
Kevin Curtis, Utah St	Jr	11	100	1531	10	139.18
Lee Evans, Wisconsin	Jr	12	75	1545	9	128.75
Edell Shepherd, San Jose St	Sr	12	83	1500	14	125.00

ALL-PURPOSE RUNNERS

	Class	GP	Rush	Rec	PR	KOR	Yds	Yds/Game
Levron Williams, Indiana	Sr	11	1401	289	0	511	2201	200.09
Bernard Berrian, Fresno St	Jr	13	101	1270	552	668	2591	199.31
Mewelde Moore, Tulane	So	12	1421	756	0	82	2259	188.25
Luke Staley, Brigham Young	Jr	11	1582	334	0	102	2018	183.45
Emmett White, Utah St	Sr	11	1361	408	125	120	2014	183.09

INTERCEPTIONS

	Class	GP	No.	Int/Game
Edward Reed, Miami (FL)	Sr	11	9	.82
Lamont Thompson, WSU	Sr	11	8	.73
Derek Ross, Ohio St	Sr	11	7	.64
Kevin Thomas, UNLV	Sr	11	7	.64
Nathan Vasher, Texas	So	12	7	.58

PUNTING

	Class	No.	Avg
Travis Dorsch, Purdue	Sr	49	48.37
Dave Zastudil, Ohio	Sr	50	45.60
Andy Groom, Ohio St	Sr	44	45.02
Steve Mullins, Utah St	Jr	50	44.82
John Skaggs, Navy	So	48	44.81

Note: Minimum of 3.6 per game.

PUNT RETURNS

	Class	No.	Yds	TD	Avg
Roman Hollowell, Colorado	Sr	29	522	2	18.00
Luke Powell, Stanford	Jr	19	304	0	16.00
DeAndrew Rubin, S Florida	Jr	26	406	1	15.62
Ronnie Hamilton, Duke	Sr	20	311	1	15.55
Dexter Wynn, Colorado St	So	14	214	0	15.29

Note: Minimum 1.2 per game.

KICKOFF RETURNS

	Class	No.	Yds	TD	Avg
Chris Massey, Oklahoma St	Jr	15	522	1	34.80
Chad Owens, Hawaii	Fr	24	807	2	33.63
Derrick Hamilton, Clemson	Fr	15	476	1	31.73
Tom Pace, Arizona St	Sr	17	537	1	31.59
Corey Parchman, Ball St	Sr	15	465	2	31.00

Note: Minimum of 1.2 per game.

Division I-A Team Single-Game Highs

RUSHING AND PASSING

Rushing and passing plays: 73—Brian Lindgren, Idaho, Oct 1 (vs Middle Tennessee St).
Rushing and passing yards: 657—Brian Lindgren, Idaho, Oct 1 (vs Middle Tennessee St).
Rushing plays: 47—Larry Ned, San Diego St, Nov 17 (vs Wyoming).
Net rushing yards: 327—Chance Kretschmer, Nevada, Nov 24 (vs Texas-El Paso).
Passes attempted: 71—Brian Lindgren, Idaho, Oct 1 (vs Middle Tennessee St).
Passes completed: 49—Brian Lindgren, Idaho, Oct 1 (vs Middle Tennessee St).
Passing yards: 637—Brian Lindgren, Idaho, Oct 1 (vs Middle Tennessee St).

RECEIVING AND RETURNS

Passes caught: 19—Josh Reed, Louisiana St, Nov 3 (vs Alabama).
Receiving yards: 326—Nate Burleson, Nevada, Nov 10 (vs San Jose St).
Punt return yards: 186—Keenan Howry, Oregon, Oct 20 (vs Stanford).
Kickoff return yards: 249—Chad Owens, Hawaii, Dec 8 (vs Brigham Young).

Division I-AA

SCORING

	Class	GP	TD	XP	FG	Pts	Pts/Game
Brian Westbrook, Villanova	Sr	11	29	0	0	176	16.00
Jesse Chatman, Eastern Washington	Sr	11	28	0	0	172	15.64
J.R. Taylor, Eastern Illinois	Jr	10	20	0	0	120	12.00
P.J. Mays, Youngstown St	Jr	11	22	0	0	132	12.00
Stephan Lewis, New Hampshire	Jr	11	19	0	0	120	10.91

FIELD GOALS

	Class	GP	FGA	FG	Pct	FG/Game
Brian Morgan, Grambling	Fr	11	25	18	.720	1.64
Shane Andrus, Murray St	So	10	22	15	.682	1.50
Taylor Northrop, Princeton	Sr	9	18	13	.722	1.44
Troy Griggs, Eastern Washington	Sr	11	20	14	.700	1.27
Javier Garcia, Idaho St.	Sr	11	18	14	.778	1.27
MacKenzie Hoambrecker, No. Iowa	Jr	11	19	14	.737	1.27
Ryan Rossner, Stephen F. Austin	So	11	26	14	.538	1.27

TOTAL OFFENSE

			Rushing		Passing		Total Offense		
	Class	GP	Car	Net	Att	Yds	Yds	Yds/Play	Yds/Game
Marcus Brady, Cal St—N'ridge	Sr	10	104	277	428	3355	3632	6.83	363.2
Robert Kent, Jackson St	So	11	131	170	453	3615	3785	6.48	344.1
Rocky Butler, Hofstra	Sr	11	115	453	335	3311	3764	8.36	342.2
Darnell Kennedy, Alabama St	Sr	12	97	511	347	3158	3669	8.26	305.8
Josh McCown, Sam Houston St	Sr	11	90	354	341	2884	3238	7.51	294.4

RUSHING

	Class	GP	Car	Yds	Avg	TD	Yds/Game
Jesse Chatman, Eastern Washington	Sr	11	285	2096	7.35	24	190.55
L.J. McKanas, Northeastern	Sr	11	342	1756	5.13	14	159.64
Brian Westbrook, Villanova	Sr	11	249	1603	6.44	22	145.73
Kris Ryan, Pennsylvania	Sr	9	267	1304	4.88	15	144.89
Ryan Fuqua, Portland St	Fr	11	210	1586	7.55	15	144.18

PASSING EFFICIENCY

	Class	GP	Att	Comp	Pct Comp	Yds	Yds/Att	TD	Int	Rating Pts
Tony Romo, Eastern Illinois	Jr	10	207	138	66.67	2068	9.99	21	6	178.3
Rocky Butler, Hofstra	Sr	11	335	206	61.49	3311	9.88	30	4	171.7
Brant Hall, Lehigh	Sr	8	176	106	60.23	1684	9.57	16	3	167.2
Neil Rose, Harvard	Sr	8	198	127	64.14	1830	9.24	15	5	161.7
Darnell Kennedy, Alabama St	Sr	12	347	202	58.21	3158	9.10	33	12	159.1

Note: Minimum 15 attempts per game.

RECEPTIONS PER GAME

	Class	GP	No.	Yds	TD	R/G
Drew Amerson, CS–N'ridge	Jr	10	97	1244	5	9.70
Chas Gessner, Brown	Jr	9	83	1182	12	9.22
Carl Morris, Harvard	Jr	9	71	943	12	7.89
Billy Brown, Yale	Sr	9	71	946	6	7.89
T.C. Taylor, Jackson St	Sr	11	84	1234	11	7.64

RECEIVING YARDS PER GAME

	Class	GP	No.	Yds	TD	Yds/G
Chas Gessner, Brown	Jr	9	83	1182	12	131.3
Drew Amerson, CS–N'ridge	Jr	10	97	1244	5	124.4
Josh Snyder, Lehigh	Sr	10	74	1241	12	124.1
J. Cooper, Sam Houston St	Sr	11	78	1301	17	118.3
R. Musinski, William & Mary	So	11	54	1242	11	112.91

INTERCEPTIONS

	Class	GP	No.	Yds	TD	Int/G
Jon Ambrose, St. Peter's	Jr	11	11	222	2	1.00
Mark Kasmer, Dayton	Jr	10	9	212	3	.90
Leigh Bodden, Duquesne	Jr	10	9	51	1	.90
Jamar Williams, Morgan St	Jr	11	8	-4	1	.73
Tony Tiller, E Tenn St	So	11	7	102	0	.64
Terrence Arnold, Southern	Sr	11	7	50	0	.64
Chuck Wesley, URI	Sr	11	7	138	1	.64
Art Smith, Northeastern	Jr	11	7	143	1	.64
LeVar Greene, Youngstown St	Sr	11	7	73	1	.64

PUNTING

	Class	No.	Avg
Eddie Johnson, Idaho St	Jr	49	46.33
Aaron Wall, Arkansas-Pine Bluff	Jr	78	43.62
Mark Gould, Northern Arizona	So	44	43.39
Mark Spencer, Montana	Jr	51	43.16
Alex Ware, Dartmouth	Jr	39	42.92

Division I-AA (Cont)

ALL-PURPOSE RUNNERS

	Class	GP	Rush	Rec	PR	KOR	Yds	Yds/Game
Brian Westbrook, Villanova	Sr	11	1603	658	122	440	2823	256.64
Jesse Chatman, Eastern Washington	Sr	11	2096	424	0	0	2520	229.09
Stephan Lewis, New Hampshire	Jr	11	1390	527	0	471	2388	217.09
Johnnie Gray, Weber St	Sr	11	1571	446	0	369	2386	216.91
Curtis Cooper, SE Missouri St	Sr	11	1198	319	215	395	2127	193.36

Division II

SCORING

	Class	GP	TD	XP	FG	Pts	Pts/Game
David Kircus, Grand Valley St	Jr	10	28	0	0	168	16.80
Ian Smart, C.W. Post	Jr	12	33	0	0	198	16.50
Eddie Acosta, Bemidji St	Jr	11	25	1	0	152	13.82
Wesley Cates Jr., Calif. (PA)	Sr	10	22	2	0	136	13.60
Milan Smado, Southeastern Oklahoma	Sr	10	17	0	10	132	13.20

FIELD GOALS

	Class	GP	FGA	FG	Pct	FG/Game
Cameron Peterka, N Dakota	Sr	11	29	20	69.0	1.82
Matt Pifer, Ashland	Sr	10	23	16	69.6	1.60
Matt Gross, Catawba	Sr	10	21	14	66.7	1.40
Eddie Ibarra, NW Missouri St	Sr	11	21	15	71.4	1.36
Austin Lepper, Truman	Jr	11	18	14	77.8	1.27
Wes Wilson, W Georgia	Sr	11	19	14	73.7	1.27

TOTAL OFFENSE

	Class	GP	Yds	Yds/Game
Curt Anes, Grand Valley St	Jr	10	3621	362.10
Todd Cunningham, Presbyterian	Sr	11	3959	359.91
Bryan Harman, Fairmont St	Sr	9	3021	335.67
J.T. O'Sullivan, UC–Davis	Sr	10	3167	316.70
Nate Jackson, Colorado Mines	Jr	11	3328	302.55

RUSHING

	Class	GP	Car	Yds	TD	Yds/Game
Ian Smart, C.W. Post	Jr	12	308	2536	33	211.33
Wesley Cates Jr., California (PA)	Sr	10	277	1673	21	167.30
Josh Ranek, South Dakota St	Sr	11	312	1804	18	164.00
Bobby Wilson, Tuskegee	Sr	11	250	1771	21	161.00
Orlando Wiley, Fort Valley St	Sr	9	268	1401	16	155.67

PASSING EFFICIENCY

	Class	GP	Att	Comp	Pct Comp	Yds	TD	Int	Rating Pts
Curt Anes, Grand Valley St	Jr	10	271	189	69.7	3086	48	3	221.63
Dusty Bonner, Valdosta St	Sr	11	319	231	72.4	3214	43	8	196.51
Brian Stallworth, Central Arkansas	Sr	11	272	177	65.1	2544	27	7	171.25
Geoff Martinson, Bemidji St	Jr	11	295	185	62.7	2798	26	9	165.37
Cedric Jackson, Midwestern St	Jr	9	145	86	59.3	1265	15	1	165.35

Note: Minimum 15 attempts per game.

RECEPTIONS PER GAME

	Class	GP	No.	Yds	TD	Rec/G
Jamal Allen, Fort Lewis	Jr	11	106	1086	7	9.64
Kory Wright, Concord	So	10	87	1087	4	8.70
D.J. Humphries, Presbyterian	Sr	11	95	1340	14	8.64
Chris Barnes, E Central	Sr	10	86	930	6	8.60
Clarence Coleman, Ferris St	Sr	11	94	1346	12	8.55

RECEIVING YARDS PER GAME

	Class	GP	No.	Yds	TD	Yds/G
Pierre Brown, Wayne St	Jr	10	66	1492	17	149.2
D. D. Carter, Central OK	So	11	76	1469	8	133.6
D. Kircus, Grand Valley St	Jr	10	62	1301	28	130.1
C. Coleman, Ferris St	Sr	11	94	1346	12	122.4
D.J. Humphries, Presbyterian	Sr	11	95	1340	14	121.8
J. Rector, NW MO St	Fr	9	61	1081	9	120.1

Division II *(Cont.)*

INTERCEPTIONS

	Class	GP	No.	Yds	Int/ Game
Gregg Albano, Bentley	Jr	12	12	156	1.0
Joey Flora, Indiana (PA)	Sr	8	8	75	1.0
Ralph Hunter, Virginia Union	Sr	10	10	25	1.0
Jason Patterson, Central WA	Sr	11	11	86	1.0
Todd Geter, Newberry	So	11	10	54	0.9

PUNTING

	Class	No.	Avg
Adam Hostetter, East Stroudsburg	Sr	54	44.4
Brad Raphelt, Abilene Christian	Sr	56	44.1
Jason Langland, S Dakota St	Jr	46	43.6
Ryan Wettstein, Northern Michigan	So	57	42.5
Joe Smith, Central Washington	Fr	68	42.3

Note: Minimum 3.6 per game.

Division III

SCORING

	Class	GP	TD	XP	FG	Pts	Pts/Game
Chuck Moore, Mount Union	Sr	10	24	0	0	144	14.40
Jason Augustynowicz, St. Norbert	Sr	9	21	0	0	126	14.00
Steve Ballinger, MacMurray	Jr	10	23	1	0	140	14.00
Shearrod Duncan, Ursinus	Sr	10	23	1	0	140	14.00
Scott Lipford, Rowan	Sr	9	19	0	0	114	12.67

FIELD GOALS

	Class	GP	FGA	FG	Pct	FG/Game
George Merrill, Albright	Sr	10	26	16	61.5	1.60
Carlos Martinez, Buena Vista	Sr	10	19	14	73.7	1.40
Drew McMaster, Howard Payne	Jr	10	15	14	98.2	1.40
Andrew Beals, Millikin	Fr	10	21	13	61.9	1.30
Andy Beniciwicz, Western Conn. St.	Jr	7	9	9	100.0	1.29

TOTAL OFFENSE

	Class	GP	Yds	Yds/Game
Steve Slowke, Alma	Jr	10	3630	363.00
Chris Czernek, Cal Lutheran	Sr	9	3040	337.78
Tom Stetzer, WI-Platteville	So	10	3284	328.40
Jason Visconti, Wesley	Sr	9	2950	327.78
Jake Knott, Wabash	Jr	10	3224	322.40

RUSHING

	Class	GP	Car	Yds	TD	Yds/Game
Shearrod Duncan, Ursinus	Sr	10	306	1747	19	174.70
Ryan Gocong, Claremont-Mudd-Scripps	Jr	8	252	1202	11	150.25
Shawn Lyman, Westfield St	Sr	10	294	1452	14	145.20
Jake Barkley, St. Thomas (MN)	Jr	9	249	1294	9	143.78
Jason Augustynowicz, St. Norbert	Sr	9	217	1275	14	141.67

PASSING EFFICIENCY

	Class	GP	Att	Comp	Pct Comp	Yds	TD	Int	Rating Pts
Dustin Proctor, Hardin–Simmons	Jr	9	178	116	65.2	2194	28	3	217.24
Roy Hampton, Trinity (TX)	Sr	9	251	168	66.9	2465	33	7	187.24
Rob Adamson, Mount Union	Jr	10	216	137	63.4	2252	20	6	176.00
Mike Warker, Widener	Jr	10	272	157	57.7	2751	32	8	175.62
Jason Lutz, Bridgewater (VA)	Sr	9	140	82	58.6	1440	15	6	171.76

Note: Minimum 15 attempts per game.

Division III (Cont.)

RECEPTIONS PER GAME

	Class	GP	No.	Yds	TD	Rec/Game
Nate Jackson, Menlo	Sr	10	105	1520	17	10.50
Brandy Spoerl, Carroll (WI)	Sr	9	83	1196	11	9.22
T.J. Thayer, Kalamazoo	Jr	9	81	956	3	9.00
John Stephens, DePauw	Jr	10	88	991	6	8.80
Greg Siebers, WI–Platteville	So	10	85	568	1	8.50

RECEIVING YARDS PER GAME

	Class	GP	No.	Yds	TD	Yds/Game
Nate Jackson, Menlo	Sr	10	105	1520	17	152.00
Todd Fry, Washington & Jefferson	Jr	10	77	1362	13	136.20
Brandy Spoerl, Carroll (WI)	Sr	9	83	1196	11	132.89
Danny Noyes, Colby	Sr	8	65	977	4	122.13
Darryl Deshields, Greenville	Jr	9	66	1092	12	121.33

INTERCEPTIONS

	Class	GP	No.	Yds	Int/G
Kip Daniels, Aurora	Sr	9	9	76	1.0
Dino Rossi, Chapman	Sr	9	9	117	1.0
Brian Britt, Centre	Sr	10	9	56	0.9
Kennard Davis, Thiel	Fr	10	9	220	0.9
Kevin McGovern, NE Wesleyan	Sr	10	9	2	0.9

PUNTING

	Class	No.	Avg
Scott Verhalen, E Texas Baptist	So	56	43.7
Randy Byington, McMurry	Fr	61	41.1
Doug Loomis, Maryville (TN)	Jr	66	40.9
Shaun Gehres, Rhodes	Sr	65	40.9
Carlos Martinez, Buena Vista	Sr	54	40.8

Note: Minimum 3.6 per game.

2001 NCAA Division I-A Team Leaders

Offense

SCORING

	GP	Pts	Avg
Florida	10	482	48.20
Brigham Young	13	608	46.77
Hawaii	11	483	43.91
Miami (FL)	11	475	43.18
Marshall	11	448	40.73
Fresno St	13	525	40.38
Texas	12	470	39.17
Nebraska	12	449	37.42
Middle Tennessee St	11	408	37.09
Stanford	11	408	37.09

RUSHING

	GP	Car	Yds	Avg	TD	Yds/Game
Nebraska	12	672	3776	5.6	47	314.7
Rice	12	751	3378	4.5	30	281.5
Air Force	12	677	3279	4.8	36	273.3
Indiana	10	541	2964	5.5	33	269.5
Kansas St	11	606	2835	4.7	34	257.7
Ohio	11	567	2641	4.7	20	240.1
Middle Tennessee St	11	471	2615	5.6	32	237.7
Colorado	12	575	2742	4.8	27	228.5
Alabama	10	472	2490	5.3	19	226.4
Wake Forest	11	609	2438	4.0	27	221.6

TOTAL OFFENSE

	GP	Plays	Yds	Avg	TD*	Yds/Game
Brigham Young	13	991	7057	7.12	82	542.85
Florida	10	788	5803	7.36	61	527.55
Marshall	11	880	6060	6.89	61	505.00
Fresno St	13	983	6464	6.58	65	497.23
Middle Tennessee St	11	781	5296	6.78	56	481.45
Idaho	10	872	5113	5.86	42	464.82
Hawaii	11	855	5552	6.49	61	462.67
Miami (FL)	11	762	5003	6.57	59	454.82
Nevada	10	871	4993	5.73	35	453.91
Stanford	11	840	4967	5.91	54	451.55

*Defensive and special teams TDs not included.

Offense *(Cont.)*

PASSING

	GP	Att	Comp	Yds	Pct Comp	Yds/Att	TD	Int	Yds/Game
Florida	10	464	299	4457	64.4	9.61	43	13	405.2
Hawaii	11	570	327	4576	57.4	8.03	41	16	381.3
Marshall	11	477	319	4201	66.9	8.81	40	7	350.1
Idaho	10	497	309	3826	62.2	7.70	28	15	347.8
Texas Tech	10	569	390	3710	68.5	6.52	27	11	337.3
Fresno St	13	483	311	4336	64.4	8.98	42	8	333.5
Brigham Young	13	486	315	4225	64.8	8.69	39	9	325.0
Louisiana Tech	11	482	283	3443	58.7	7.14	30	14	313.0
Central Florida	11	407	230	3391	56.5	8.33	21	12	308.3
Washington St	11	393	214	3310	54.5	8.42	30	12	300.9

Single-Game Highs

Points Scored: 80—W Virginia, Nov 3 (vs Rutgers).
Net Rushing Yards: 641—Nebraska, Oct 13 (vs Baylor).
Passing Yards: 637—Idaho, Oct 6 (vs Middle Tennessee St).
Rushing and Passing Yards: 849—San Jose St, Nov 10 (vs Nevada).
Fewest Rushing and Passing Yards Allowed: 57—Louisiana-Lafayette, Sept 1 (vs Nicholls St).

Defense

SCORING

	GP	Pts	Avg
Miami (FL)	11	103	9.4
Virginia Tech	11	147	13.4
Texas	12	164	13.7
Oklahoma	12	166	13.8
Florida	10	155	14.1
Nebraska	12	189	15.8
Kansas St	11	179	16.3
Southern Miss	10	186	16.9
Michigan	10	192	17.5
Louisville	11	213	17.8

TOTAL DEFENSE

	GP	Plays	Yds	Avg	Yds/Game
Texas	12	754	2834	3.76	236.17
Virginia Tech	11	725	2617	3.61	237.91
Kansas St	11	684	2886	4.22	262.36
Oklahoma	12	813	3154	3.88	262.83
AL-Birmingham	11	719	2925	4.07	265.91
Miami (FL)	11	758	2980	3.93	270.91
Pittsburgh	11	786	3131	3.98	284.64
Nebraska	12	813	3446	4.24	287.17
Florida	10	712	3192	4.48	290.18
Texas A&M	11	798	3234	4.05	294.00

RUSHING

	GP	Car	Yds	Avg	TD	Yds/Game
AL-Birmingham	11	333	630	1.9	6	57.3
Virginia Tech	11	371	788	2.1	7	71.6
Tennessee	11	384	1024	2.7	8	85.3
Bowling Green	11	372	949	2.6	5	86.3
New Mexico	11	383	961	2.5	9	87.4
Texas	12	385	1074	2.8	13	89.5
Oklahoma	12	430	1079	2.5	5	89.9
Michigan	10	391	996	2.6	9	90.5
Maryland	11	387	997	2.6	5	90.6
Texas Christian	10	376	1032	2.7	12	93.8

TURNOVER MARGIN

	Turnovers Gained			Turnovers Lost			Margin/
	GP	Fum	Int	Total	Fum	Int	Total	Game
Miami (FL)	11	18	27	45	10	9	19	2.36
Fresno St	13	13	23	36	5	8	13	1.77
Bowling Green	11	17	18	35	5	13	18	1.55
Maryland	11	10	24	34	9	9	18	1.45
Oregon	11	7	18	25	6	5	11	1.27
Southern Cal	11	14	19	33	7	12	19	1.27
Syracuse	12	17	13	30	7	8	15	1.25
Iowa St	11	8	18	26	2	12	14	1.09
Purdue	11	18	18	36	11	13	24	1.09
Ohio St	11	10	19	29	8	10	18	1.00
Wash St	11	13	22	35	12	12	24	1.00

PASSING EFFICIENCY

	GP	Att	Comp	Yds	Pct Comp	Yds/Att	TD	Pct TD	Int	Pct Int	Rating Pts
Miami (FL)	11	290	129	44.48	1520	5.24	5	1.72	27	9.31	75.60
Nebraska	12	395	171	43.29	2043	5.17	8	2.03	19	4.81	83.81
Virginia Tech	11	354	161	45.48	1829	5.17	8	2.26	19	5.37	85.62
Texas	12	369	187	50.68	1760	4.77	6	1.63	15	4.07	88.00
Oklahoma	12	383	177	46.21	2075	5.42	9	2.35	20	5.22	89.02
Kansas St	11	320	152	47.50	1825	5.70	11	3.44	18	5.63	95.50
N Carolina	12	403	203	50.37	2166	5.37	9	2.23	8	1.99	98.95
W Virginia	11	251	122	48.61	1504	5.99	7	2.79	11	4.38	99.37
Texas A&M	11	369	206	55.83	1987	5.38	7	1.90	14	3.79	99.70
Boston College	11	313	154	49.20	1911	6.11	11	3.51	18	5.75	100.58

National Champions

Year	Champion	Record	Bowl Game	Head Coach
1883	Yale	8-0-0	No bowl	Ray Tompkins (Captain)
1884	Yale	9-0-0	No bowl	Eugene L. Richards (Captain)
1885	Princeton	9-0-0	No bowl	Charles DeCamp (Captain)
1886	Yale	9-0-1	No bowl	Robert N. Corwin (Captain)
1887	Yale	9-0-0	No bowl	Harry W. Beecher (Captain)
1888	Yale	13-0-0	No bowl	Walter Camp
1889	Princeton	10-0-0	No bowl	Edgar Poe (Captain)
1890	Harvard	11-0-0	No bowl	George A. Stewart/George C. Adams
1891	Yale	13-0-0	No bowl	Walter Camp
1892	Yale	13-0-0	No bowl	Walter Camp
1893	Princeton	11-0-0	No bowl	Tom Trenchard (Captain)
1894	Yale	16-0-0	No bowl	William C. Rhodes
1895	Pennsylvania	14-0-0	No bowl	George Woodruff
1896	Princeton	10-0-1	No bowl	Garrett Cochran
1897	Pennsylvania	15-0-0	No bowl	George Woodruff
1898	Harvard	11-0-0	No bowl	W. Cameron Forbes
1899	Harvard	10-0-1	No bowl	Benjamin H. Dibblee
1900	Yale	12-0-0	No bowl	Malcolm McBride
1901	Michigan	11-0-0	Won Rose	Fielding Yost
1902	Michigan	11-0-0	Won Rose	Fielding Yost
1903	Princeton	11-0-0	No bowl	Art Hillebrand
1904	Pennsylvania	12-0-0	No bowl	Carl Williams
1905	Chicago	11-0-0	No bowl	Amos Alonzo Stagg
1906	Princeton	9-0-1	No bowl	Bill Roper
1907	Yale	9-0-1	No bowl	Bill Knox
1908	Pennsylvania	11-0-1	No bowl	Sol Metzger
1909	Yale	10-0-0	No bowl	Howard Jones
1910	Harvard	8-0-1	No bowl	Percy Houghton
1911	Princeton	8-0-2	No bowl	Bill Roper
1912	Harvard	9-0-0	No bowl	Percy Houghton
1913	Harvard	9-0-0	No bowl	Percy Houghton
1914	Army	9-0-0	No bowl	Charley Daly
1915	Cornell	9-0-0	No bowl	Al Sharpe
1916	Pittsburgh	8-0-0	No bowl	Pop Warner
1917	Georgia Tech	9-0-0	No bowl	John Heisman
1918	Pittsburgh	4-1-0	No bowl	Pop Warner
1919	Harvard	9-0-1	Won Rose	Bob Fisher
1920	California	9-0-0	Won Rose	Andy Smith
1921	Cornell	8-0-0	No bowl	Gil Dobie
1922	Cornell	8-0-0	No bowl	Gil Dobie
1923	Illinois	8-0-0	No bowl	Bob Zuppke
1924	Notre Dame	10-0-0	Won Rose	Knute Rockne
1925	Alabama (H)	10-0-0	Won Rose	Wallace Wade
	Dartmouth (D)	8-0-0	No bowl	Jesse Hawley
1926	Alabama (H)	9-0-1	Tied Rose	Wallace Wade
	Stanford (D)(H)	10-0-1	Tied Rose	Pop Warner
1927	Illinois	7-0-1	No bowl	Bob Zuppke
1928	Georgia Tech (H)	10-0-0	Won Rose	Bill Alexander
	Southern Cal (D)	9-0-1	No bowl	Howard Jones
1929	Notre Dame	9-0-0	No bowl	Knute Rockne
1930	Notre Dame	10-0-0	No bowl	Knute Rockne
1931	Southern Cal	10-1-0	Won Rose	Howard Jones
1932	Southern Cal (H)	10-0-0	Won Rose	Howard Jones
	Michigan (D)	8-0-0	No bowl	Harry Kipke
1933	Michigan	7-0-1	No bowl	Harry Kipke
1934	Minnesota	8-0-0	No bowl	Bernie Bierman
1935	Minnesota (H)	8-0-0	No bowl	Bernie Bierman
	Southern Methodist (D)	12-1-0	Lost Rose	Matty Bell
1936	Minnesota	7-1-0	No bowl	Bernie Bierman
1937	Pittsburgh	9-0-1	No bowl	Jock Sutherland
1938	Texas Christian (AP)	11-0-0	Won Sugar	Dutch Meyer
	Notre Dame (D)	8-1-0	No bowl	Elmer Layden
1939	Southern Cal (D)	8-0-2	Won Rose	Howard Jones
	Texas A&M (AP)	11-0-0	Won Sugar	Homer Norton
1940	Minnesota	8-0-0	No bowl	Bernie Bierman
1941	Minnesota	8-0-0	No bowl	Bernie Bierman
1942	Ohio St	9-1-0	No bowl	Paul Brown

Year	Champion	Record	Bowl Game	Head Coach
1943	Notre Dame	9-1-0	No bowl	Frank Leahy
1944	Army	9-0-0	No bowl	Red Blaik
1945	Army	9-0-0	No bowl	Red Blaik
1946	Notre Dame	8-0-1	No bowl	Frank Leahy
1947	Notre Dame	9-0-0	No bowl	Frank Leahy
	Michigan*	10-0-0	Won Rose	Fritz Crisler
1948	Michigan	9-0-0	No bowl	Bennie Oosterbaan
1949	Notre Dame	10-0-0	No bowl	Frank Leahy
1950	Oklahoma	10-1-0	Lost Sugar	Bud Wilkinson
1951	Tennessee	10-1-0	Lost Sugar	Bob Neyland
1952	Michigan St	9-0-0	No bowl	Biggie Munn
1953	Maryland	10-1-0	Lost Orange	Jim Tatum
1954	Ohio St	10-0-0	Won Rose	Woody Hayes
	UCLA (UPI)	9-0-0	No bowl	Red Sanders
1955	Oklahoma	11-0-0	Won Orange	Bud Wilkinson
1956	Oklahoma	10-0-0	No bowl	Bud Wilkinson
1957	Auburn	10-0-0	No bowl	Shug Jordan
	Ohio St (UPI)	9-1-0	Won Rose	Woody Hayes
1958	Louisiana St	11-0-0	Won Sugar	Paul Dietzel
1959	Syracuse	11-0-0	Won Cotton	Ben Schwartzwalder
1960	Minnesota	8-2-0	Lost Rose	Murray Warmath
1961	Alabama	11-0-0	Won Sugar	Bear Bryant
1962	Southern Cal	11-0-0	Won Rose	John McKay
1963	Texas	11-0-0	Won Cotton	Darrell Royal
1964	Alabama	10-1-0	Lost Orange	Bear Bryant
1965	Alabama	9-1-1	Won Orange	Bear Bryant
	Michigan St (UPI)	10-1-0	Lost Rose	Duffy Daugherty
1966	Notre Dame	9-0-1	No bowl	Ara Parseghian
1967	Southern Cal	10-1-0	Won Rose	John McKay
1968	Ohio St	10-0-0	Won Rose	Woody Hayes
1969	Texas	11-0-0	Won Cotton	Darrell Royal
1970	Nebraska	11-0-1	Won Orange	Bob Devaney
	Texas (UPI)	10-1-0	Lost Cotton	Darrell Royal
1971	Nebraska	13-0-0	Won Orange	Bob Devaney
1972	Southern Cal	12-0-0	Won Rose	John McKay
1973	Notre Dame	11-0-0	Won Sugar	Ara Parseghian
	Alabama (UPI)	11-1-0	Lost Sugar	Bear Bryant
1974	Oklahoma	11-0-0	No bowl	Barry Switzer
	Southern Cal (UPI)	10-1-1	Won Rose	John McKay
1975	Oklahoma	11-1-0	Won Orange	Barry Switzer
1976	Pittsburgh	12-0-0	Won Sugar	Johnny Majors
1977	Notre Dame	11-1-0	Won Cotton	Dan Devine
1978	Alabama	11-1-0	Won Sugar	Bear Bryant
	Southern Cal (UPI)	12-1-0	Won Rose	John Robinson
1979	Alabama	12-0-0	Won Sugar	Bear Bryant
1980	Georgia	12-0-0	Won Sugar	Vince Dooley
1981	Clemson	12-0-0	Won Orange	Danny Ford
1982	Penn St	11-1-0	Won Sugar	Joe Paterno
1983	Miami (FL)	11-1-0	Won Orange	Howard Schnellenberger
1984	Brigham Young	13-0-0	Won Holiday	LaVell Edwards
1985	Oklahoma	11-1-0	Won Orange	Barry Switzer
1986	Penn St	12-0-0	Won Fiesta	Joe Paterno
1987	Miami (FL)	12-0-0	Won Orange	Jimmy Johnson
1988	Notre Dame	12-0-0	Won Fiesta	Lou Holtz
1989	Miami (FL)	11-1-0	Won Sugar	Dennis Erickson
1990	Colorado	11-1-1	Won Orange	Bill McCartney
	Georgia Tech (UPI)	11-0-1	Won Citrus	Bobby Ross
1991	Miami (FL)	12-0-0	Won Orange	Dennis Erickson
	Washington (CNN)	12-0-0	Won Rose	Don James
1992	Alabama	13-0-0	Won Sugar	Gene Stallings
1993	Florida St	12-1-0	Won Orange	Bobby Bowden
1994	Nebraska	13-0-0	Won Orange	Tom Osborne
1995	Nebraska	12-0-0	Won Fiesta	Tom Osborne
†1996	Florida	12–1	Won Sugar	Steve Spurrier
1997	Michigan	12–0	Won Rose	Lloyd Carr
	Nebraska (ESPN)	13–0	Won Orange	Tom Osborne
1998	Tennessee	13–0	Won Fiesta	Phillip Fulmer

Year	Champion	Record	Bowl Game	Head Coach
1999	Florida St	12–0	Won Sugar	Bobby Bowden
2000	Oklahoma	13–0	Won Orange	Bob Stoops
2001	Miami (FL)	12–0	Won Rose	Larry Coker

*The AP, which had voted Notre Dame No. 1, took a second vote, giving the national title to Michigan after its 49–0 win over Southern Cal in the Rose Bowl.   Note: Selectors: Helms Athletic Foundation (H) 1883–1935, The Dickinson System (D) 1924–40, The Associated Press (AP) 1936–present, United Press International (UPI) 1958–90, *USA Today*/CNN (CNN) 1991–96, and *USA Today*/ESPN (ESPN) 1997–present. †In 1996 the NCAA introduced overtime to break ties.

Results of Major Bowl Games

Rose Bowl

Date	Result
1-1-02	Michigan 49, Stanford 0
1-1-16	Washington St 14, Brown 0
1-1-17	Oregon 14, Pennsylvania 0
1-1-18	Mare Island 19, Camp Lewis 7
1-1-19	Great Lakes 17, Mare Island 0
1-1-20	Harvard 7, Oregon 6
1-1-21	California 28, Ohio St 0
1-2-22	Washington & Jefferson 0, California 0
1-1-23	Southern Cal 14, Penn St 3
1-1-24	Navy 14, Washington 14
1-1-25	Notre Dame 27, Stanford 10
1-1-26	Alabama 20, Washington 19
1-1-27	Alabama 7, Stanford 7
1-2-28	Stanford 7, Pittsburgh 6
1-1-29	Georgia Tech 8, California 7
1-1-30	Southern Cal 47, Pittsburgh 14
1-1-31	Alabama 24, Washington St 0
1-1-32	Southern Cal 21, Tulane 12
1-2-33	Southern Cal 35, Pittsburgh 0
1-1-34	Columbia 7, Stanford 0
1-1-35	Alabama 29, Stanford 13
1-1-36	Stanford 7, Southern Methodist 0
1-1-37	Pittsburgh 21, Washington 0
1-1-38	California 13, Alabama 0
1-2-39	Southern Cal 7, Duke 3
1-1-40	Southern Cal 14, Tennessee 0
1-1-41	Stanford 21, Nebraska 13
1-1-42	Oregon St 20, Duke 16
1-1-43	Georgia 9, UCLA 0
1-1-44	Southern Cal 29, Washington 0
1-1-45	Southern Cal 25, Tennessee 0
1-1-46	Alabama 34, Southern Cal 14
1-1-47	Illinois 45, UCLA 14
1-1-48	Michigan 49, Southern Cal 0
1-1-49	Northwestern 20, California 14
1-2-50	Ohio St 17, California 14
1-1-51	Michigan 14, California 6
1-1-52	Illinois 40, Stanford 7
1-1-53	Southern Cal 7, Wisconsin 0
1-1-54	Michigan St 28, UCLA 20
1-1-55	Ohio St 20, Southern Cal 7
1-2-56	Michigan St 17, UCLA 14
1-1-57	Iowa 35, Oregon St 19
1-1-58	Ohio St 10, Oregon 7
1-1-59	Iowa 38, California 12
1-1-60	Washington 44, Wisconsin 8
1-2-61	Washington 17, Minnesota 7
1-1-62	Minnesota 21, UCLA 3
1-1-63	Southern Cal 42, Wisconsin 37
1-1-64	Illinois 17, Washington 7
1-1-65	Michigan 34, Oregon St 7
1-1-66	UCLA 14, Michigan St 12
1-2-67	Purdue 14, Southern Cal 13
1-1-68	Southern Cal 14, Indiana 3
1-1-69	Ohio St 27, Southern Cal 16
1-1-70	Southern Cal 10, Michigan 3
1-1-71	Stanford 27, Ohio St 17
1-1-72	Stanford 13, Michigan 12
1-1-73	Southern Cal 42, Ohio St 17
1-1-74	Ohio St 42, Southern Cal 21
1-1-75	Southern Cal 18, Ohio St 17
1-1-76	UCLA 23, Ohio St 10
1-1-77	Southern Cal 14, Michigan 6
1-2-78	Washington 27, Michigan 20
1-1-79	Southern Cal 17, Michigan 10
1-1-80	Southern Cal 17, Ohio St 16
1-1-81	Michigan 23, Washington 6
1-1-82	Washington 28, Iowa 0
1-1-83	UCLA 24, Michigan 14
1-2-84	UCLA 45, Illinois 9
1-1-85	Southern Cal 20, Ohio St 17
1-1-86	UCLA 45, Iowa 28
1-1-87	Arizona St 22, Michigan 15
1-1-88	Michigan St 20, Southern Cal 17
1-2-89	Michigan 22, Southern Cal 14
1-1-90	Southern Cal 17, Michigan 10
1-1-91	Washington 46, Iowa 34
1-1-92	Washington 34, Michigan 14
1-1-93	Michigan 38, Washington 31
1-1-94	Wisconsin 21, UCLA 16
1-2-95	Penn St 38, Oregon 20
1-1-96	Southern Cal 41, Northwestern 32
1-1-97	Ohio St 20, Arizona St 17
1-1-98	Michigan 21, Washington St 16
1-1-99	Wisconsin 38, UCLA 31
1-1-00	Wisconsin 17, Stanford 9
1-1-01	Washington 34, Purdue 24
1-3-02	Miami 37, Nebraska 14

City: Pasadena. Stadium: Rose Bowl, capacity 96,576.

Playing Sites: Tournament Park (1902, 1916–22), Rose Bowl (1923–41, since 1943), Duke Stadium, Durham, NC (1942).

Orange Bowl

Date	Result
1-1-35	Bucknell 26, Miami (FL) 0
1-1-36	Catholic 20, Mississippi 19
1-1-37	Duquesne 13, Mississippi St 12
1-1-38	Auburn 6, Michigan St 0

Note: The Fiesta, Orange, Rose and Sugar Bowls constitute the Bowl Alliance, formed in 1995. The Alliance holds eight berths: one each for the champions of the ACC, Big 10, Big 12, Big East, Pac 10 and SEC, and two at-large, reserved for any Division I-A team with at least nine wins and ranked in the top 12 of the BCS rankings. Of the eight teams, the two highest-ranked go to the Fiesta Bowl in 2003, and the Sugar Bowl in 2004. Once these four BCS matches have been set conferences may place the remaining qualified teams in the other bowls. Teams that have won at least six games against Division I-A teams qualify.

Orange Bowl *(Cont.)*

1-2-39 ....Tennessee 17, Oklahoma 0
1-1-40 ....Georgia Tech 21, Missouri 7
1-1-41 ....Mississippi St 14, Georgetown 7
1-1-42 ....Georgia 40, Texas Christian 26
1-1-43 ....Alabama 37, Boston College 21
1-1-44 ....Louisiana St 19, Texas A&M 14
1-1-45 ....Tulsa 26, Georgia Tech 12
1-1-46 ....Miami (FL) 13, Holy Cross 6
1-1-47 ....Rice 8, Tennessee 0
1-1-48 ....Georgia Tech 20, Kansas 14
1-1-49 ....Texas 41, Georgia 28
1-2-50 ....Santa Clara 21, Kentucky 13
1-1-51 ....Clemson 15, Miami (FL) 14
1-1-52 ....Georgia Tech 17, Baylor 14
1-1-53 ....Alabama 61, Syracuse 6
1-1-54 ....Oklahoma 7, Maryland 0
1-1-55 ....Duke 34, Nebraska 7
1-2-56 ....Oklahoma 20, Maryland 6
1-1-57 ....Colorado 27, Clemson 21
1-1-58 ....Oklahoma 48, Duke 21
1-1-59 ....Oklahoma 21, Syracuse 6
1-1-60 ....Georgia 14, Missouri 0
1-2-61 ....Missouri 21, Navy 14
1-1-62 ....Louisiana St 25, Colorado 7
1-1-63 ....Alabama 17, Oklahoma 0
1-1-64 ....Nebraska 13, Auburn 7
1-1-65 ....Texas 21, Alabama 17
1-1-66 ....Alabama 39, Nebraska 28
1-2-67 ....Florida 27, Georgia Tech 12
1-1-68 ....Oklahoma 26, Tennessee 24
1-1-69 ....Penn St 15, Kansas 14
1-1-70 ....Penn St 10, Missouri 3
1-1-71 ....Nebraska 17, Louisiana St 12
1-1-72 ....Nebraska 38, Alabama 6
1-1-73 ....Nebraska 40, Notre Dame 6
1-1-74 ....Penn St 16, Louisiana St 9
1-1-75 ....Notre Dame 13, Alabama 11
1-1-76 ....Oklahoma 14, Michigan 6
1-1-77 ....Ohio St 27, Colorado 10
1-2-78 ....Arkansas 31, Oklahoma 6
1-1-79 ....Oklahoma 31, Nebraska 24
1-1-80 ....Oklahoma 24, Florida St 7
1-1-81 ....Oklahoma 18, Florida St 17
1-1-82 ....Clemson 22, Nebraska 15
1-1-83 ....Nebraska 21, Louisiana St 20
1-2-84 ....Miami (FL) 31, Nebraska 30
1-1-85 ....Washington 28, Oklahoma 17
1-1-86 ....Oklahoma 25, Penn St 10
1-1-87 ....Oklahoma 42, Arkansas 8
1-1-88 ....Miami (FL) 20, Oklahoma 14
1-2-89 ....Miami (FL) 23, Nebraska 3
1-1-90 ....Notre Dame 21, Colorado 6
1-1-91 ....Colorado 10, Notre Dame 9
1-1-92 ....Miami (FL) 22, Nebraska 0
1-1-93 ....Florida St 27, Nebraska 14
1-1-94 ....Florida St 18, Nebraska 16
1-1-95 ....Nebraska 24, Miami (FL) 17
1-1-96 ....Florida St 31, Notre Dame 26
12-31-96 ....Nebraska 41, Virginia Tech 21
1-2-98 ....Nebraska 42, Tennessee 17
1-2-99 ....Florida 31, Syracuse 10
1-1-00 ....Michigan 35, Alabama 34 (ot)
1-3-01 ....Oklahoma 13, Florida St 2
1-2-02 ....Florida 56, Maryland 23

City: Miami. Stadium: Pro Player Stadium, capacity 75,192.
Playing Sites: Orange Bowl (1935–96), Pro Player Stadium
(since 1996).

Sugar Bowl

1-1-35 ....Tulane 20, Temple 14
1-1-36 ....Texas Christian 3, Louisiana St 2
1-1-37 ....Santa Clara 21, Louisiana St 14
1-1-38 ....Santa Clara 6, Louisiana St 0
1-2-39 ....Texas Christian 15, Carnegie Tech 7
1-1-40 ....Texas A&M 14, Tulane 13
1-1-41 ....Boston Col 19, Tennessee 13
1-1-42 ....Fordham 2, Missouri 0
1-1-43 ....Tennessee 14, Tulsa 7
1-1-44 ....Georgia Tech 20, Tulsa 18
1-1-45 ....Duke 29, Alabama 26
1-1-46 ....Oklahoma St 33, St. Mary's (CA) 13
1-1-47 ....Georgia 20, N Carolina 10
1-1-48 ....Texas 27, Alabama 7
1-1-49 ....Oklahoma 14, N Carolina 6
1-2-50 ....Oklahoma 35, Louisiana St 0
1-1-51 ....Kentucky 13, Oklahoma 7
1-1-52 ....Maryland 28, Tennessee 13
1-1-53 ....Georgia Tech 24, Mississippi 7
1-1-54 ....Georgia Tech 42, W Virginia 19
1-1-55 ....Navy 21, Mississippi 0
1-2-56 ....Georgia Tech 7, Pittsburgh 0
1-1-57 ....Baylor 13, Tennessee 7
1-1-58 ....Mississippi 39, Texas 7
1-1-59 ....Louisiana St 7, Clemson 0
1-1-60 ....Mississippi 21, Louisiana St 0
1-2-61 ....Mississippi 14, Rice 6
1-1-62 ....Alabama 10, Arkansas 3
1-1-63 ....Mississippi 17, Arkansas 13
1-1-64 ....Alabama 12, Mississippi 7
1-1-65 ....Louisiana St 13, Syracuse 10
1-1-66 ....Missouri 20, Florida 18
1-2-67 ....Alabama 34, Nebraska 7
1-1-68 ....Louisiana St 20, Wyoming 13
1-1-69 ....Arkansas 16, Georgia 2
1-1-70 ....Mississippi 27, Arkansas 22
1-1-71 ....Tennessee 34, Air Force 13
1-1-72 ....Oklahoma 40, Auburn 22
12-31-72 ....Oklahoma 14, Penn St 0
12-31-73 ....Notre Dame 24, Alabama 23
12-31-74 ....Nebraska 13, Florida 10
12-31-75 ....Alabama 13, Penn St 6
1-1-77 ....Pittsburgh 27, Georgia 3
1-2-78 ....Alabama 35, Ohio St 6
1-1-79 ....Alabama 14, Penn St 7
1-1-80 ....Alabama 24, Arkansas 9
1-1-81 ....Georgia 17, Notre Dame 10
1-1-82 ....Pittsburgh 24, Georgia 20
1-1-83 ....Penn St 27, Georgia 23
1-2-84 ....Auburn 9, Michigan 7
1-1-85 ....Nebraska 28, Louisiana St 10
1-1-86 ....Tennessee 35, Miami (FL) 7
1-1-87 ....Nebraska 30, Louisiana St 15
1-1-88 ....Syracuse 16, Auburn 16
1-2-89 ....Florida St 13, Auburn 7
1-1-90 ....Miami (FL) 33, Alabama 25
1-1-91 ....Tennessee 23, Virginia 22
1-1-92 ....Notre Dame 39, Florida 28
1-1-93 ....Alabama 34, Miami (FL) 13
1-1-94 ....Florida 41, West Virginia 7
1-2-95 ....Florida St 23, Florida 17
12-31-95 ....Virginia Tech 28, Texas 10
1-2-97 ....Florida 52, Florida St 20
1-1-98 ....Florida St 31, Ohio St 14
1-1-99 ....Ohio St 24, Texas A&M 14
1-4-00 ....Florida St 46, Virginia Tech 29

Sugar Bowl *(Cont.)*

1-2-01 ....Miami (FL) 37, Florida 20
1-1-02 ....Louisiana St 47, Illinois 34
City: New Orleans. Stadium: Louisiana Superdome, capacity 76,791.
Playing Sites: Tulane Stadium (1935–74), Louisiana Superdome (since 1975).

Cotton Bowl

1-1-37 ....Texas Christian 16, Marquette 6
1-1-38 ....Rice 28, Colorado 14
1-2-39 ....St. Mary's (CA) 20, Texas Tech 13
1-1-40 ....Clemson 6, Boston Col 3
1-1-41 ....Texas A&M 13, Fordham 12
1-1-42 ....Alabama 29, Texas A&M 21
1-1-43 ....Texas 14, Georgia Tech 7
1-1-44 ....Texas 7, Randolph Field 7
1-1-45 ....Oklahoma St 34, Texas Christian 0
1-1-46 ....Texas 40, Missouri 27
1-1-47 ....Arkansas 0, Louisiana St 0
1-1-48 ....Southern Methodist 13, Penn St 13
1-1-49 ....Southern Methodist 21, Oregon 13
1-2-50 ....Rice 27, N Carolina 13
1-1-51 ....Tennessee 20, Texas 14
1-1-52 ....Kentucky 20, Texas Christian 7
1-1-53 ....Texas 16, Tennessee 0
1-1-54 ....Rice 28, Alabama 6
1-1-55 ....Georgia Tech 14, Arkansas 6
1-2-56 ....Mississippi 14, Texas Christian 13
1-1-57 ....Texas Christian 28, Syracuse 27
1-1-58 ....Navy 20, Rice 7
1-1-59 ....Texas Christian 0, Air Force 0
1-1-60 ....Syracuse 23, Texas 14
1-2-61 ....Duke 7, Arkansas 6
1-1-62 ....Texas 12, Mississippi 7
1-1-63 ....Louisiana St 13, Texas 0
1-1-64 ....Texas 28, Navy 6
1-1-65 ....Arkansas 10, Nebraska 7
1-1-66 ....Louisiana St 14, Arkansas 7
12-31-66 ....Georgia 7, Southern Methodist 9
1-1-68 ....Texas A&M 20, Alabama 16
1-1-69 ....Texas 36, Tennessee 13
1-1-70 ....Texas 21, Notre Dame 17
1-1-71 ....Notre Dame 24, Texas 11
1-1-72 ....Penn St 30, Texas 6
1-1-73 ....Texas 17, Alabama 13
1-1-74 ....Nebraska 19, Texas 3
1-1-75 ....Penn St 41, Baylor 20
1-1-76 ....Arkansas 31, Georgia 10
1-1-77 ....Houston 30, Maryland 21
1-2-78 ....Notre Dame 38, Texas 10
1-1-79 ....Notre Dame 35, Houston 34
1-1-80 ....Houston 17, Nebraska 14
1-1-81 ....Alabama 30, Baylor 2
1-1-82 ....Texas 14, Alabama 12
1-1-83 ....SMU 7, Pittsburgh 3
1-2-84 ....Georgia 10, Texas 9
1-1-85 ....Boston Col 45, Houston 28
1-1-86 ....Texas A&M 36, Auburn 16
1-1-87 ....Ohio St 28, Texas A&M 12
1-1-88 ....Texas A&M 35, Notre Dame 10
1-2-89 ....UCLA 17, Arkansas 3
1-1-90 ....Tennessee 31, Arkansas 27
1-1-91 ....Miami (FL) 46, Texas 3
1-1-92 ....Florida St 10, Texas A&M 2
1-1-93 ....Notre Dame 28, Texas A&M 3
1-1-94 ....Notre Dame 24, Texas A&M 21
1-2-95 ....Southern Cal 55, Texas Tech 14

Cotton Bowl *(Cont.)*

1-1-96 ....Colorado 38, Oregon 6
1-1-97 ....Brigham Young 19, Kansas St 15
1-1-98 ....UCLA 29, Texas A&M 23
1-1-99 ....Texas 38, Mississippi St 11
1-1-00 ....Arkansas 27, Texas 6
1-1-01 ....Kansas St 35, Tennessee 21
1-1-02 ....Oklahoma 10, Arkansas 3
City: Dallas. Stadium: Cotton Bowl, capacity 68,252.

Sun Bowl

1-1-36 ....Hardin-Simmons 14, New Mexico St 14
1-1-37 ....Hardin-Simmons 34, UTEP 6
1-1-38 ....W Virginia 7, Texas Tech 6
1-2-39 ....Utah 26, New Mexico 0
1-1-40 ....Catholic 0, Arizona St 0
1-1-41 ....Case Reserve 26, Arizona St 13
1-1-42 ....Tulsa 6, Texas Tech 0
1-1-43 ....2nd Air Force 13, Hardin-Simmons 7
1-1-44 ....Southwestern (TX) 7, New Mexico 0
1-1-45 ....Southwestern (TX) 35, New Mexico 0
1-1-46 ....New Mexico 34, Denver 24
1-1-47 ....Cincinnati 18, Virginia Tech 6
1-1-48 ....Miami (OH) 13, Texas Tech 12
1-1-49 ....W Virginia 21, UTEP 12
1-2-50 ....UTEP 33, Georgetown 20
1-1-51 ....W Texas St 14, Cincinnati 13
1-1-52 ....Texas Tech 25, Pacific 14
1-1-53 ....Pacific 26, Southern Miss 7
1-1-54 ....UTEP 37, Southern Miss 14
1-1-55 ....UTEP 47, Florida St 20
1-2-56 ....Wyoming 21, Texas Tech 14
1-1-57 ....George Washington 13, UTEP 0
1-1-58 ....Louisville 34, Drake 20
12-31-58 ....Wyoming 14, Hardin-Simmons 6
12-31-59 ....New Mexico St 28, N Texas 8
12-31-60 ....New Mexico St 20, Utah St 13
12-30-61 ....Villanova 17, Wichita St 9
12-31-62 ....W Texas St 15, Ohio 14
12-31-63 ....Oregon 21, Southern Methodist 14
12-26-64 ....Georgia 7, Texas Tech 0
12-31-65 ....UTEP 13, Texas Christian 12
12-24-66 ....Wyoming 28, Florida St 20
12-30-67 ....UTEP 14, Mississippi 7
12-28-68 ....Auburn 34, Arizona 10
12-20-69 ....Nebraska 45, Georgia 6
12-19-70 ....Georgia Tech 17, Texas Tech 9
12-18-71 ....Louisiana St 33, Iowa St 15
12-30-72 ....N Carolina 32, Texas Tech 28
12-29-73 ....Missouri 34, Auburn 17
12-28-74 ....Mississippi St 26, N Carolina 24
12-26-75 ....Pittsburgh 33, Kansas 19
1-2-77 ....Texas A&M 37, Florida 14
12-31-77 ....Stanford 24, Louisiana St 14
12-23-78 ....Texas 42, Maryland 0
12-22-79 ....Washington 14, Texas 7
12-27-80 ....Nebraska 31, Mississippi St 17
12-26-81 ....Oklahoma 40, Houston 14
12-25-82 ....N Carolina 26, Texas 10
12-24-83 ....Alabama 28, Southern Methodist 7
12-22-84 ....Maryland 28, Tennessee 27
12-28-85 ....Georgia 13, Arizona 13
12-25-86 ....Alabama 28, Washington 6
12-25-87 ....Oklahoma St 35, W Virginia 33
12-24-88 ....Alabama 29, Army 28
12-30-89 ....Pittsburgh 31, Texas A&M 28
12-31-90 ....Michigan St 17, Southern Cal 16
12-31-91 ....UCLA 6, Illinois 3

Sun Bowl *(Cont.)*

12-31-92.........Baylor 20, Arizona 15
12-24-93.........Oklahoma 41, Texas Tech 10
12-30-94.........Texas 35, N Carolina 31
12-29-95.........Iowa 38, Washington 18
12-31-96.........Stanford 38, Michigan St 0
12-31-97.........Arizona St 17, Iowa 7
12-31-98.........Texas Christian 28, Southern Cal 19
12-31-99.........Oregon 24, Minnesota 20
12-29-00.........Wisconsin 21, UCLA 20
12-31-01.........Washington St 33, Purdue 27

City: El Paso. Stadium: Sun Bowl, capacity 51,270.

Name Changes: Sun Bowl (1936–86; 94–), John Hancock Sun Bowl (1987–88), John Hancock Bowl (1989–93).

Playing Sites: Kidd Field (1936–62), Sun Bowl (since 1963).

Gator Bowl

1-1-46 ....Wake Forest 26, S Carolina 14
1-1-47 ....Oklahoma 34, N Carolina St 13
1-1-48 ....Maryland 20, Georgia 20
1-1-49 ....Clemson 24, Missouri 23
1-2-50 ....Maryland 20, Missouri 7
1-1-51 ....Wyoming 20, Washington & Lee 7
1-1-52 ....Miami (FL) 14, Clemson 0
1-1-53 ....Florida 14, Tulsa 13
1-1-54 ....Texas Tech 35, Auburn 13
12-31-54 ....Auburn 33, Baylor 13
12-31-55 ....Vanderbilt 25, Auburn 13
12-29-56 ....Georgia Tech 21, Pittsburgh 14
12-28-57 ....Tennessee 3, Texas A&M 0
12-27-58 ....Mississippi 7, Florida 3
1-2-60 ....Arkansas 14, Georgia Tech 7
12-31-60 ....Florida 13, Baylor 12
12-30-61 ....Penn St 30, Georgia Tech 15
12-29-62 ....Florida 17, Penn St 7
12-28-63 ....N Carolina 35, Air Force 0
1-2-65 ....Florida St 36, Oklahoma 19
12-31-65 ....Georgia Tech 31, Texas Tech 21
12-31-66 ....Tennessee 18, Syracuse 12
12-30-67 ....Penn St 17, Florida St 17
12-28-68 ....Missouri 35, Alabama 10
12-27-69 ....Florida 14, Tennessee 13
1-2-71 ....Auburn 35, Mississippi 28
12-31-71 ....Georgia 7, N Carolina 3
12-30-72 ....Auburn 24, Colorado 3
12-29-73 ....Texas Tech 28, Tennessee 19
12-30-74 ....Auburn 27, Texas 3
12-29-75 ....Maryland 13, Florida 0
12-27-76 ....Notre Dame 20, Penn St 9
12-30-77 ....Pittsburgh 34, Clemson 3
12-29-78 ....Clemson 17, Ohio St 15
12-28-79 ....N Carolina 17, Michigan 15
12-29-80 ....Pittsburgh 37, S Carolina 9
12-28-81 ....N Carolina 31, Arkansas 27
12-30-82 ....Florida St 31, W Virginia 12
12-30-83 ....Florida 14, Iowa 6
12-28-84 ....Oklahoma St 21, S Carolina 14
12-30-85 ....Florida St 34, Oklahoma St 23
12-27-86 ....Clemson 27, Stanford 21
12-31-87 ....Louisiana St 30, S Carolina 13
1-1-89 ....Georgia 34, Michigan St 27
12-30-89 ....Clemson 27, W Virginia 7
1-1-91 ....Michigan 35, Mississippi 3
12-29-91 ....Oklahoma 48, Virginia 14
12-31-92 ....Florida 27, N Carolina St 10
12-31-93 ....Alabama 24, North Carolina 10
12-30-94 ....Tennessee 45, Virginia Tech 23
1-1-96 ....Syracuse 41, Clemson 0
1-1-97 ....N Carolina 20, W Virginia 13
1-1-98 ....N Carolina 42, Viginia Tech 13

Gator Bowl (Cont.)

1-1-99 ....Georgia Tech 35, Notre Dame 28
1-1-00 ....Miami 27, Georgia Tech 13
1-1-01 ....Virginia Tech 41, Clemson 20
1-1-02 ....Florida St 30, Virginia Tech 17

City: Jacksonville, FL. Stadium: Alltel Stadium, capacity 76,976.

Florida Citrus Bowl

1-1-47 ....Catawba 31, Maryville (TN) 6
1-1-48 ....Catawba 7, Marshall 0
1-1-49 ....Murray St 21, Sul Ross St 21
1-2-50 ....St. Vincent 7, Emory & Henry 6
1-1-51 ....Morris Harvey 35, Emory & Henry 14
1-1-52 ....Stetson 35, Arkansas St 20
1-1-53 ....E Texas St 33, Tennessee Tech 0
1-1-54 ....E Texas St 7, Arkansas St 7
1-1-55 ....NE-Omaha 7, Eastern Kentucky 6
1-2-56 ....Juniata 6, Missouri Valley 6
1-1-57 ....W Texas St 20, Southern Miss 13
1-1-58 ....E Texas St 10, Southern Miss 9
12-27-58 ....E Texas St 26, Missouri Valley 7
1-1-60 ....Middle Tennessee St 21, Presbyterian 12
12-30-60 ....Citadel 27, Tennessee Tech 0
12-29-61 ....Lamar 21, Middle Tennessee St 14
12-22-62 ....Houston 49, Miami (OH) 21
12-28-63 ....Western Kentucky 27, Coast Guard 0
12-12-64 ....E Carolina 14, Massachusetts 13
12-11-65 ....E Carolina 31, Maine 0
12-10-66 ....Morgan St 14, W Chester 6
12-16-67 ....TN-Martin 25, W Chester 8
12-27-68 ....Richmond 49, Ohio 42
12-26-69 ....Toledo 56, Davidson 33
12-28-70 ....Toledo 40, William & Mary 12
12-28-71 ....Toledo 28, Richmond 3
12-29-72 ....Tampa 21, Kent St 18
12-22-73 ....Miami (OH) 16, Florida 7
12-21-74 ....Miami (OH) 21, Georgia 10
12-20-75 ....Miami (OH) 20, S Carolina 7
12-18-76 ....Oklahoma St 49, Brigham Young 21
12-23-77 ....Florida St 40, Texas Tech 17
12-23-78 ....N Carolina St 30, Pittsburgh 17
12-22-79 ....Louisiana St 34, Wake Forest 10
12-20-80 ....Florida 35, Maryland 20
12-19-81 ....Missouri 19, Southern Miss 17
12-18-82 ....Auburn 33, Boston Col 26
12-17-83 ....Tennessee 30, Maryland 23
12-22-84 ....Georgia 17, Florida St 17
12-28-85 ....Ohio St 10, Brigham Young 7
1-1-87 ....Auburn 16, Southern Cal 7
1-1-88 ....Clemson 35, Penn St 10
1-2-89 ....Clemson 13, Oklahoma 6
1-1-90 ....Illinois 31, Virginia 21
1-1-91 ....Georgia Tech 45, Nebraska 21
1-1-92 ....California 37, Clemson 13
1-1-93 ....Georgia 21, Ohio State 14
1-1-94 ....Penn State 31, Tennessee 13
1-2-95 ....Alabama 24, Ohio St 17
1-1-96 ....Tennessee 20, Ohio St 14
1-1-97 ....Tennessee 48, Northwestern 28
1-1-98 ....Florida 21, Penn St 6
1-1-99 ....Michigan 45, Arkansas 31
1-1-00 ....Michigan St 37, Florida 34
1-1-01 ....Michigan 31, Auburn 28
1-1-02 ....Tennessee 45, Michigan 17

City: Orlando, FL. Stadium: Florida Citrus Bowl, capacity 70,000.

Name Change: Tangerine Bowl (1947–82).

Playing Sites: Tangerine Bowl (1947–72, 1974–82); Florida Field, Gainesville (1973); Orlando Stadium/Florida Citrus Bowl-Orlando (since 1983).

Liberty Bowl

12-19-59..........Penn St 7, Alabama 0
12-17-60..........Penn St 41, Oregon 12
12-16-61..........Syracuse 15, Miami (FL) 14
12-15-62..........Oregon St 6, Villanova 0
12-21-63..........Mississippi St 16, N Carolina St 12
12-19-64..........Utah 32, W Virginia 6
12-18-65..........Mississippi 13, Auburn 7
12-10-66..........Miami (FL) 14, Virginia Tech 7
12-16-67..........N Carolina St 14, Georgia 7
12-14-68..........Mississippi 34, Virginia Tech 17
12-13-69..........Colorado 47, Alabama 33
12-12-70..........Tulane 17, Colorado 3
12-20-71..........Tennessee 14, Arkansas 13
12-18-72..........Georgia Tech 31, Iowa St 30
12-17-73..........N Carolina St 31, Kansas 18
12-16-74..........Tennessee 7, Maryland 3
12-22-75..........Southern Cal 20, Texas A&M 0
12-20-76..........Alabama 36, UCLA 6
12-19-77..........Nebraska 21, N Carolina 17
12-23-78..........Missouri 20, Louisiana St 15
12-22-79..........Penn St 9, Tulane 6
12-27-80..........Purdue 28, Missouri 25
12-30-81..........Ohio St 31, Navy 28
12-29-82..........Alabama 21, Illinois 15
12-29-83..........Notre Dame 19, Boston Col 18
12-27-84..........Auburn 21, Arkansas 15
12-27-85..........Baylor 21, Louisiana St 7
12-29-86..........Tennessee 21, Minnesota 14
12-29-87..........Georgia 20, Arkansas 17
12-28-88..........Indiana 34, S Carolina 10
12-28-89..........Mississippi 42, Air Force 29
12-27-90..........Air Force 23, Ohio St 11
12-29-91..........Air Force 38, Mississippi St 15
12-31-92..........Mississippi 13, Air Force 0
12-28-93..........Louisville 18, Michigan St 7
12-31-94..........Illinois 30, E Carolina 0
12-30-95..........East Carolina 19, Stanford 13
12-27-96..........Syracuse 30, Houston 17
12-31-97..........Southern Miss 41, Pittsburgh 7
12-31-98..........Tulane 41, Brigham Young 27
12-31-99..........Southern Miss 23, Colorado St 17
12-29-01..........Colorado St 22, Louisville 17
12-31-01..........Louisville 28, Brigham Young 10

City: Memphis (since 1965). Stadium: Liberty Bowl Memorial Stadium, capacity 62,921.

Playing Sites: Philadelphia (Municipal Stadium, 1959–63), Atlantic City (Convention Center, 1964).

Bluebonnet Bowl

12-19-59..........Clemson 23, Texas Christian 7
12-17-60..........Texas 3, Alabama 3
12-16-61..........Kansas 33, Rice 7
12-22-62..........Missouri 14, Georgia Tech 10
12-21-63..........Baylor 14, LSU 7
12-19-64..........Tulsa 14, Mississippi 7
12-18-65..........Tennessee 27, Tulsa 6
12-17-66..........Texas 19, Mississippi 0
12-23-67..........Colorado 31, Miami (FL) 21
12-31-68..........Southern Methodist 28, Oklahoma 27
12-31-69..........Houston 36, Auburn 7
12-31-70..........Alabama 24, Oklahoma 24
12-31-71..........Colorado 29, Houston 17
12-30-72..........Tennessee 24, Louisiana St 17
12-29-73..........Houston 47, Tulane 7
12-23-74..........N Carolina St 31, Houston 31
12-27-75..........Texas 38, Colorado 21
12-31-76..........Nebraska 27, Texas Tech 24
12-31-77..........Southern Cal 47, Texas A&M 28
12-31-78..........Stanford 25, Georgia 22

Bluebonnet Bowl *(Cont.)*

12-31-79..........Purdue 27, Tennessee 22
12-31-80..........N Carolina 16, Texas 7
12-31-81..........Michigan 33, UCLA 14
12-31-82..........Arkansas 28, Florida 24
12-31-83..........Oklahoma St 24, Baylor 14
12-31-84..........W Virginia 31, Texas Christian 14
12-31-85..........Air Force 24, Texas 16
12-31-86..........Baylor 21, Colorado 9
12-31-87..........Texas 32, Pittsburgh 27

City: Houston. Playing sites: Rice Stadium (1959–67; 1985–86), Astrodome (1968–84, 1987).

Name change: Astro-Bluebonnet Bowl (1968–76). Bowl was discontinued after 1987.

Peach Bowl

12-30-68..........Louisiana St 31, Florida St 27
12-30-69..........W Virginia 14, S Carolina 3
12-30-70..........Arizona St 48, N Carolina 26
12-30-71..........Mississippi 41, Georgia Tech 18
12-29-72..........N Carolina St 49, W Virginia 13
12-28-73..........Georgia 17, Maryland 16
12-28-74..........Vanderbilt 6, Texas Tech 6
12-31-75..........W Virginia 13, N Carolina St 10
12-31-76..........Kentucky 21, N Carolina 0
12-31-77..........N Carolina St 24, Iowa St 14
12-25-78..........Purdue 41, Georgia Tech 21
12-31-79..........Baylor 24, Clemson 18
1-2-81.............Miami (FL) 20, Virginia Tech 10
12-31-81..........W Virginia 26, Florida 6
12-31-82..........Iowa 28, Tennessee 22
12-30-83..........Florida St 28, N Carolina 3
12-31-84..........Virginia 27, Purdue 24
12-31-85..........Army 31, Illinois 29
12-31-86..........Virginia Tech 25, N Carolina St 24
1-2-88.............Tennessee 27, Indiana 22
12-31-88..........N Carolina St 28, Iowa 23
12-30-89..........Syracuse 19, Georgia 18
12-29-90..........Auburn 27, Indiana 23
1-1-92.............E Carolina 37, N Carolina St 34
1-2-93.............N Carolina 21, Mississippi St 17
12-31-93..........Clemson 14, Kentucky 13
1-1-95.............N Carolina St 28, Mississippi St 24
12-30-95..........Virginia 34, Georgia 27
12-28-96..........Louisiana St 10, Clemson 7
1-2-98.............Auburn 21, Clemson 17
12-31-98..........Georgia 35, Virginia 33
12-30-99..........Mississippi St 17, Clemson 7
12-29-00..........Louisiana St 28, Georgia Tech 14
12-31-01..........N Carolina 16, Auburn 10

City: Atlanta. Stadium: Georgia Dome, capacity 71,500.
Playing Sites: Grant Field (1968–70), Atlanta–Fulton County Stadium (1971–92), Georgia Dome (since 1993).

Fiesta Bowl

12-27-71..........Arizona St 45, Florida St 38
12-23-72..........Arizona St 49, Missouri 35
12-21-73..........Arizona St 28, Pittsburgh 7
12-28-74..........Oklahoma St 16, Brigham Young 6
12-26-75..........Arizona St 17, Nebraska 14
12-25-76..........Oklahoma 41, Wyoming 7
12-25-77..........Penn St 42, Arizona St 30
12-25-78..........Arkansas 10, UCLA 10
12-25-79..........Pittsburgh 16, Arizona 10
12-26-80..........Penn St 31, Ohio St 19
1-1-82.............Penn St 26, Southern Cal 10
1-1-83.............Arizona St 32, Oklahoma 21
1-2-84.............Ohio St 28, Pittsburgh 23
1-1-85.............UCLA 39, Miami (FL) 37

Fiesta Bowl (Cont.)

1-1-86..............Michigan 27, Nebraska 23
1-2-87..............Penn St 14, Miami (FL) 10
1-1-88..............Florida St 31, Nebraska 28
1-2-89..............Notre Dame 34, W Virginia 21
1-1-90..............Florida St 41, Nebraska 17
1-1-91..............Louisville 34, Alabama 7
1-1-92..............Penn St 42, Tennessee 17
1-1-93..............Syracuse 26, Colorado 22
1-1-94..............Arizona 29, Miami (FL) 0
1-2-95..............Colorado 41, Notre Dame 24
1-2-96..............Nebraska 62, Florida 24
1-1-97..............Penn St 38, Texas 15
12-31-97..........Kansas St 35, Syracuse 18
1-4-99..............Tennessee 23, Florida St 16
1-2-00..............Nebraska 31, Tennessee 21
1-1-01..............Oregon St 41, Notre Dame 9
1-1-02..............Oregon 38, Colorado 16

City: Tempe, AZ. Stadium: Sun Devil Stadium, capacity 73,471.

Independence Bowl

12-13-76..........McNeese St 20, Tulsa 16
12-17-77..........Louisiana Tech 24, Louisville 14
12-16-78..........E Carolina 35, Louisiana Tech 13
12-15-79..........Syracuse 31, McNeese St 7
12-13-80..........Southern Miss 16, McNeese St 14
12-12-81..........Texas A&M 33, Oklahoma St 16
12-11-82..........Wisconsin 14, Kansas St 3
12-10-83..........Air Force 9, Mississippi 3
12-15-84..........Air Force 23, Virginia Tech 7
12-21-85..........Minnesota 20, Clemson 13
12-20-86..........Mississippi 20, Texas Tech 17
12-19-87..........Washington 24, Tulane 12
12-23-88..........Southern Miss 38, UTEP 18
12-16-89..........Oregon 27, Tulsa 24
12-15-90..........Louisiana Tech 34, Maryland 34
12-29-91..........Georgia 24, Arkansas 15
12-31-92..........Wake Forest 39, Oregon 35
12-31-93..........Virginia Tech 45, Indiana 20
12-28-94..........Virginia 20, Texas Christian 10
12-29-95..........Louisiana St 45, Michigan St 26
12-31-96..........Auburn 32, Army 29
12-28-97..........Louisiana St 27, Notre Dame 9
12-31-98..........Mississippi 35, Texas Tech 18
12-31-99..........Mississippi 27, Oklahoma 25
12-31-00..........Mississippi St 43, Texas A&M 41
12-27-01..........Alabama 14, Iowa St 13

City: Shreveport, LA. Stadium: Independence Stadium, capacity 50,459.

All-American Bowl

12-22-77..........Maryland 17, Minnesota 7
12-20-78..........Texas A&M 28, Iowa St 12
12-29-79..........Missouri 24, S Carolina 14
12-27-80..........Arkansas 34, Tulane 15
12-31-81..........Mississippi St 10, Kansas 0
12-31-82..........Air Force 36, Vanderbilt 28
12-22-83..........W Virginia 20, Kentucky 16
12-29-84..........Kentucky 20, Wisconsin 19
12-31-85..........Georgia Tech 17, Michigan St 14
12-31-86..........Florida St 27, Indiana 13
12-22-87..........Virginia 22, Brigham Young 16
12-29-88..........Florida 14, Illinois 10
12-28-89..........Texas Tech 49, Duke 21
12-28-90..........N Carolina St 31, Southern Miss. 27

City: Birmingham, AL. Stadium: Legion Field.
Name Change: Hall of Fame Classic (1977–84). Bowl was discontinued after 1990.

Holiday Bowl

12-22-78..........Navy 23, Brigham Young 16
12-21-79..........Indiana 38, Brigham Young 37
12-19-80..........Brigham Young 46, SMU45
12-18-81..........Brigham Young 38, Washington St 36
12-17-82..........Ohio St 47, Brigham Young 17
12-23-83..........Brigham Young 21, Missouri 17
12-21-84..........Brigham Young 24, Michigan 17
12-22-85..........Arkansas 18, Arizona St 17
12-30-86..........Iowa 39, San Diego St 38
12-30-87..........Iowa 20, Wyoming 19
12-30-88..........Oklahoma St 62, Wyoming 14
12-29-89..........Penn St 50, Brigham Young 39
12-29-90..........Texas A&M 65, Brigham Young 14
12-30-91..........Iowa 13, Brigham Young 13
12-30-92..........Hawaii 27, Illinois 17
12-30-93..........Ohio St 28, Brigham Young 21
12-30-94..........Michigan 24, Colorado St 14
12-29-95..........Kansas St 54, Colorado St 21
12-30-96..........Colorado 33, Washington 21
12-29-97..........Colorado St 35, Missouri 24
12-30-98..........Arizona 23, Nebraska 20
12-29-99..........Kansas St 24, Washington 20
12-29-00..........Oregon 35, Texas 30
12-28-01..........Texas 47, Washington 43

City: San Diego. Stadium: Qualcomm Stadium, capacity 70,000.

Las Vegas Bowl

12-19-81..........Toledo 27, San Jose St 25
12-18-82..........Fresno St 29, Bowling Green 28
12-17-83..........Northern Illinois 20, Cal St–Fullerton 13
12-15-84..........UNLV 30, Toledo 13*
12-14-85..........Fresno St 51, Bowling Green 7
12-13-86..........San Jose St 37, Miami (OH) 7
12-12-87..........Eastern Michigan 30, San Jose St 27
12-10-88..........Fresno St 35, Western Michigan 30
12-9-89..........Fresno St 27, Ball St 6
12-8-90..........San Jose St 48, Central Michigan 24
12-14-91..........Bowling Green 28, Fresno St 21
12-18-92..........Bowling Green 35, Nevada 34
12-17-93..........Utah St 42, Ball St 33
12-15-94..........UNLV 52, Central Michigan 24
12-14-95..........Toledo 40, Nevada 37
12-19-96..........Nevada 18, Ball St 15
12-19-97..........Oregon 41, Air Force 13
12-19-98..........N Carolina 20, San Diego St 13
12-18-99..........Utah 17, Fresno St 16
12-21-00..........UNLV 31, Arkansas 14
12-25-01..........Utah 10, Southern Cal 6

* Toledo won later by forfeit.

City: Las Vegas (since 1992). Stadium: Sam Boyd Silver Bowl Stadium, capacity 40,000.

Name change: California Bowl (1981–91).

Playing sites: Fresno, CA (Bulldog Stadium, 1981–91), Las Vegas.

Aloha Bowl

12-25-82..........Washington 21, Maryland 20
12-26-83..........Penn St 13, Washington 10
12-29-84..........Southern Methodist 27, Notre Dame 20
12-28-85..........Alabama 24, Southern Cal 3
12-27-86..........Arizona 30, N Carolina 21
12-25-87..........UCLA 20, Florida 16
12-25-88..........Washington St 24, Houston 22
12-25-89..........Michigan St 33, Hawaii 13
12-25-90..........Syracuse 28, Arizona 0
12-25-91..........Georgia Tech 18, Stanford 17

Aloha Bowl (Cont.)

12-25-92 ....Kansas 23, Brigham Young 20
12-25-93 ....Colorado 41, Fresno St 30
12-25-94 ....Boston College 12, Kansas St 7
12-25-95 ....Kansas 51, UCLA 30
12-25-96 ....Navy 42, California 38
12-25-97 ....Washington 51, Michigan St 23
12-25-98 ....Colorado 51, Oregon 43
12-25-99 ....Wake Forest 23, Arizona St 3
12-25-00 ....Boston College 31, Arizona St 17

City: Honolulu. Stadium: Aloha Stadium. Bowl was discontinued after 2000.

Freedom Bowl

12-16-84 ....Iowa 55, Texas 17
12-30-85 ....Washington 20, Colorado 17
12-30-86 ....UCLA 31, Brigham Young 10
12-30-87 ....Arizona St 33, Air Force 28
12-29-88 ....Brigham Young 20, Colorado 17
12-30-89 ....Washington 34, Florida 7
12-29-90 ....Colorado St 32, Oregon 31
12-30-91 ....Tulsa 28, San Diego St 17
12-29-92 ....Fresno St 24, Southern Cal 7
12-30-93 ....Southern Cal 28, Utah 21
12-29-94 ....Utah 16, Arizona 13

City: Anaheim. Stadium: Anaheim Stadium. Bowl was discontinued after 1994.

Outback Bowl

12-23-86 ....Boston College 27, Georgia 24
1-2-88 ....Michigan 28, Alabama 24
1-2-89 ....Syracuse 23, Louisiana St 10
1-1-90 ....Auburn 31, Ohio St 14
1-1-91 ....Clemson 30, Illinois 0
1-1-92 ....Syracuse 24, Ohio St 17
1-1-93 ....Tennessee 38, Boston College 23
1-1-94 ....Michigan 42, N Carolina St 7
1-2-95 ....Wisconsin 34, Duke 20
1-1-96 ....Penn St 43, Auburn 14
1-1-97 ....Alabama 17, Michigan 14
1-1-98 ....Georgia 33, Wisconsin 6
1-1-99 ....Penn St 26, Kentucky 14
1-1-00 ....Georgia 28, Purdue 25
1-1-01 ....S Carolina 24, Ohio St 7
1-1-02 ....S Carolina 31, Ohio St 28

City: Tampa. Stadium: Raymond James Stadium, capacity 75,000. Name change: Hall of Fame Bowl (1986–95).

Insight.com Bowl

12-31-89 ....Arizona 17, N Carolina St 10
12-31-90 ....California 17, Wyoming 15
12-31-91 ....Indiana 24, Baylor 0
12-29-92 ....Washington St 31, Utah 28
12-29-93 ....Kansas St 52, Wyoming 17
12-29-94 ....Brigham Young 31, Oklahoma 6
12-27-95 ....Texas Tech 55, Air Force 41
12-27-96 ....Wisconsin 38, Utah 10
12-27-97 ....Arizona 20, New Mexico 14
12-26-98 ....Missouri 34, W Virginia 31
12-31-99 ....Colorado 62, Boston College 28
12-28-00 ....Iowa St 37, Pittsburgh 29
12-29-01 ....Syracuse 26, Kansas St 3

City: Tucson. Stadium: Arizona Stadium, capacity 55,883. Name change: Copper Bowl 1989–97.

Tangerine Bowl

12-28-90 ....Florida St 24, Penn St 17
12-28-91 ....Alabama 30, Colorado 25
1-1-93 ....Stanford 24, Penn St 3
1-1-94 ....Boston College 31, Virginia 13
1-2-95 ....S Carolina 24, W Virginia 21
12-30-95 ....N Carolina 20, Arkansas 10
12-27-96 ....Miami (FL) 31, Virginia 21
12-29-97 ....Georgia Tech 35, W Virginia 30
12-29-98 ....Miami (FL) 46, N Carolina St 23
12-30-99 ....Illinois 62, Virginia 21
12-28-00 ....N Carolina St 38, Minnesota 30
12-20-01 ....Pittsburgh 34, N Carolina St 19

City: Miami. Stadium: Pro Player Stadium, capacity 75,192. Name change: Blockbuster Bowl (1990–93), Carquest Bowl (1994–97), Micron PC Bowl (1998–00).

Alamo Bowl

12-31-93 ....California 37, Iowa 3
12-31-94 ....Washington St 10, Baylor 3
12-28-95 ....Texas A&M 22, Michigan 20
12-29-96 ....Iowa 27, Texas Tech 0
12-30-97 ....Purdue 33, Oklahoma St 20
12-29-98 ....Purdue 37, Kansas St 34
12-28-99 ....Penn St 24, Texas A&M 0
12-30-00 ....Nebraska 66, Northwestern 17
12-29-01 ....Iowa 16, Texas Tech 13

City: San Antonio, TX. Stadium: Alamodome, capacity 67,000.

Top Billingsley

Bowl Championship Series founder Roy Kramer has at his disposal a team of high-powered mathematical minds whose formulas help determine the BCS participants. Among them are an astrophysicist, a rocket scientist, and a prominent medical researcher. There's also Richard Billingsley, who doesn't even have a B.A.: He left Gulf Coast Bible College in Houston after two years. "I don't like math, and I hate computers," says Billingsley, an unmarried 50-year-old personnel consultant and former minister in the United Pentecostal Church.

What he likes is college football. As a teenager in Hugo, Okla., Billingsley was frustrated by the imprecision of the AP and UPI polls, so he devised his own formula for determining the top team—one based mainly on strength of schedule and recent performance while minimizing margin of victory. In 1970 he began circulating his rankings to a network of friends. Billingsley was first published in the NCAA record book in '94 and was tapped for the BCS selection team when it was created in '97. Now the Billingsley Report, updated every Monday, is available on cfrc.com (the initials stand for the College Football Research Center), on which Billingsley explains what he calls the "dynamics" of his system in copious detail.

During the season Billingsley spends Saturday watching football games and devotes the next three days to updating the rankings and preparing for the following weekend. Did he ever dream he would have a hand in deciding the national champion? "I have to say it was a goal," Billingsley says, "but I never imagined that it would come true."

—John O'Keefe

1936

		Record	Coach
1.	Minnesota	7-1-0	Bernie Bierman
2.	Louisiana St	9-0-1	Bernie Moore
3.	Pittsburgh	7-1-1	Jack Sutherland
4.	Alabama	8-0-1	Frank Thomas
5.	Washington	7-1-1	Jimmy Phelan
6.	Santa Clara	7-1-0	Buck Shaw
7.	Northwestern	7-1-0	Pappy Waldorf
8.	Notre Dame	6-2-1	Elmer Layden
9.	Nebraska	7-2-0	Dana X. Bible
10.	Pennsylvania	7-1-0	Harvey Harman
11.	Duke	9-1-0	Wallace Wade
12.	Yale	7-1-0	Ducky Pond
13.	Dartmouth	7-1-1	Red Blaik
14.	Duquesne	7-2-0	John Smith
15.	Fordham	5-1-2	Jim Crowley
16.	Texas Christian	8-2-2	Dutch Meyer
17.	Tennessee	6-2-2	Bob Neyland
18.	Arkansas	7-3-0	Fred Thomsen
19.	Navy	6-3-0	Tom Hamilton
20.	Marquette	7-1-0	Frank Murray

1937

		Record	Coach
1.	Pittsburgh	9-0-1	Jack Sutherland
2.	California	9-0-1	Stub Allison
3.	Fordham	7-0-1	Jim Crowley
4.	Alabama	9-0-0	Frank Thomas
5.	Minnesota	6-2-0	Bernie Bierman
6.	Villanova	8-0-1	Clipper Smith
7.	Dartmouth	7-0-2	Red Blaik
8.	Louisiana St	9-1-0	Bernie Moore
9.	Notre Dame	6-2-1	Elmer Layden
	Santa Clara	8-0-0	Buck Shaw
11.	Nebraska	6-1-2	Biff Jones
12.	Yale	6-1-1	Ducky Pond
13.	Ohio St	6-2-0	Francis Schmidt
14.	Holy Cross	8-0-2	Eddie Anderson
	Arkansas	6-2-2	Fred Thomsen
16.	Texas Christian	4-2-2	Dutch Meyer
17.	Colorado	8-0-0	Bunnie Oakes
18.	Rice	5-3-2	Jimmy Kitts
19.	N Carolina	7-1-1	Ray Wolf
20.	Duke	7-2-1	Wallace Wade

1938

		Record	Coach
1.	Texas Christian	10-0-0	Dutch Meyer
2.	Tennessee	10-0-0	Bob Neyland
3.	Duke	9-0-0	Wallace Wade
4.	Oklahoma	10-0-0	Tom Stidham
5.	#Notre Dame	8-1-0	Elmer Layden
6.	Carnegie Tech	7-1-0	Bill Kern
7.	Southern Cal	8-2-0	Howard Jones
8.	Pittsburgh	8-2-0	Jack Sutherland
9.	Holy Cross	8-1-0	Eddie Anderson
10.	Minnesota	6-2-0	Bernie Bierman
11.	Texas Tech	10-0-0	Pete Cawthon
12.	Cornell	5-1-1	Carl Snavely
13.	Alabama	7-1-1	Frank Thomas
14.	California	10-1-0	Stub Allison
15.	Fordham	6-1-2	Jim Crowley
16.	Michigan	6-1-1	Fritz Crisler
17.	Northwestern	4-2-2	Pappy Waldorf

1938 (Cont.)

		Record	Coach
18.	Villanova	8-0-1	Clipper Smith
19.	Tulane	7-2-1	Red Dawson
20.	Dartmouth	7-2-0	Red Blaik

#Selected No. 1 by the Dickinson System.

1939

		Record	Coach
1.	Texas A&M	10-0-0	Homer Norton
2.	Tennessee	10-0-0	Bob Neyland
3.	#Southern Cal	7-0-2	Howard Jones
4.	Cornell	8-0-0	Carl Snavely
5.	Tulane	8-0-1	Red Dawson
6.	Missouri	8-1-0	Don Faurot
7.	UCLA	6-0-4	Babe Horrell
8.	Duke	8-1-0	Wallace Wade
9.	Iowa	6-1-1	Eddie Anderson
10.	Duquesne	8-0-1	Buff Donelli
11.	Boston College	9-1-0	Frank Leahy
12.	Clemson	8-1-0	Jess Neely
13.	Notre Dame	7-2-0	Elmer Layden
14.	Santa Clara	5-1-3	Buck Shaw
15.	Ohio St	6-2-0	Francis Schmidt
16.	Georgia Tech	7-2-0	Bill Alexander
17.	Fordham	6-2-0	Jim Crowley
18.	Nebraska	7-1-1	Biff Jones
19.	Oklahoma	6-2-1	Tom Stidham
20.	Michigan	6-2-0	Fritz Crisler

#Selected No. 1 by the Dickinson System.

1940

		Record	Coach
1.	Minnesota	8-0-0	Bernie Bierman
2.	Stanford	9-0-0	C. Shaughnessy
3.	Michigan	7-1-0	Fritz Crisler
4.	Tennessee	10-0-0	Bob Neyland
5.	Boston College	10-0-0	Frank Leahy
6.	Texas A&M	8-1-0	Homer Norton
7.	Nebraska	8-1-0	Biff Jones
8.	Northwestern	6-2-0	Pappy Waldorf
9.	Mississippi St	9-0-1	Allyn McKeen
10.	Washington	7-2-0	Jimmy Phelan
11.	Santa Clara	6-1-1	Buck Shaw
12.	Fordham	7-1-0	Jim Crowley
13.	Georgetown	8-1-0	Jack Hagerty
14.	Pennsylvania	6-1-1	George Munger
15.	Cornell	6-2-0	Carl Snavely
16.	SMU	8-1-1	Matty Bell
17.	Hard.-Simmons	9-0-0	Abe Woodson
18.	Duke	7-2-0	Wallace Wade
19.	Lafayette	9-0-0	Hooks Mylin
20.	—		

Only 19 teams selected.

1941

		Record	Coach
1.	Minnesota	8-0-0	Bernie Bierman
2.	Duke	9-0-0	Wallace Wade
3.	Notre Dame	8-0-1	Frank Leahy
4.	Texas	8-1-1	Dana X. Bible
5.	Michigan	6-1-1	Fritz Crisler
6.	Fordham	7-1-0	Jim Crowley
7.	Missouri	8-1-0	Don Faurot
8.	Duquesne	8-0-0	Buff Donelli
9.	Texas A&M	9-1-0	Homer Norton
10.	Navy	7-1-1	Swede Larson
11.	Northwestern	5-3-0	Pappy Waldorf
12.	Oregon St	7-2-0	Lon Stiner
13.	Ohio St	6-1-1	Paul Brown
14.	Georgia	8-1-1	Wally Butts
15.	Pennsylvania	7-1-1	George Munger
16.	Mississippi St	8-1-1	Allyn McKeen
17.	Mississippi	6-2-1	Harry Mehre
18.	Tennessee	8-2-0	John Barnhill
19.	Washington St	6-4-0	Babe Hollingbery
20.	Alabama	8-2-0	Frank Thomas

1942

		Record	Coach
1.	Ohio St	9-1-0	Paul Brown
2.	Georgia	10-1-0	Wally Butts
3.	Wisconsin	8-1-1	H. Stuhldreher
4.	Tulsa	10-0-0	Henry Frnka
5.	Georgia Tech	9-1-0	Bill Alexander
6.	Notre Dame	7-2-2	Frank Leahy
7.	Tennessee	8-1-1	John Barnhill
8.	Boston College	8-1-0	Denny Myers
9.	Michigan	7-3-0	Fritz Crisler
10.	Alabama	7-3-0	Frank Thomas
11.	Texas	8-2-0	Dana X. Bible
12.	Stanford	6-4-0	Marchie Schwartz
13.	UCLA	7-3-0	Babe Horrell
14.	William & Mary	9-1-1	Carl Voyles
15.	Santa Clara	7-2-0	Buck Shaw
16.	Auburn	6-4-1	Jack Meagher
17.	Washington St	6-2-2	Babe Hollingbery
18.	Mississippi St	8-2-0	Allyn McKeen
19.	Minnesota	5-4-0	George Hauser
	Holy Cross	5-4-1	Ank Scanlon
	Penn St	6-1-1	Bob Higgins

1943

		Record	Coach
1.	Notre Dame	9-1-0	Frank Leahy
2.	Iowa Pre-Flight	9-1-0	Don Faurot
3.	Michigan	8-1-0	Fritz Crisler
4.	Navy	8-1-0	Billick Whelchel
5.	Purdue	9-0-0	Elmer Burnham
6.	Great Lakes	10-2-0	Tony Hinkle
7.	Duke	8-1-0	Eddie Cameron
8.	Del Monte P-F	7-1-0	Bill Kern
9.	Northwestern	6-2-0	Pappy Waldorf
10.	March Field	9-1-0	Paul Schissler
11.	Army	7-2-1	Red Blaik
12.	Washington	4-0-0	Ralph Welch
13.	Georgia Tech	7-3-0	Bill Alexander

1943 (Cont.)

		Record	Coach
14.	Texas	7-1-0	Dana X. Bible
15.	Tulsa	6-0-1	Henry Frnka
16.	Dartmouth	6-1-0	Earl Brown
17.	Bainbridge NTS	7-0-0	Joe Maniaci
18.	Colorado College	7-0-0	Hal White
19.	Pacific	7-2-0	Amos A. Stagg
20.	Pennsylvania	6-2-1	George Munger

1944

		Record	Coach
1.	Army	9-0-0	Red Blaik
2.	Ohio St	9-0-0	Carroll Widdoes
3.	Randolph Field	11-0-0	Frank Tritico
4.	Navy	6-3-0	Oscar Hagberg
5.	Bainbridge NTS	9-0-0	Joe Maniaci
6.	Iowa Pre-Flight	10-1-0	Jack Meagher
7.	Southern Cal	7-0-2	Jeff Cravath
8.	Michigan	8-2-0	Fritz Crisler
9.	Notre Dame	8-2-0	Ed McKeever
10.	March Field	7-1-2	Paul Schissler
11.	Duke	5-4-0	Eddie Cameron
12.	Tennessee	8-0-1	John Barnhill
13.	Georgia Tech	8-2-0	Bill Alexander
	Norman P-F	6-0-0	John Gregg
15.	Illinois	5-4-1	Ray Eliot
16.	El Toro Marines	8-1-0	Dick Hanley
17.	Great Lakes	9-2-1	Paul Brown
18.	Fort Pierce	9-0-0	Hamp Pool
19.	St. Mary's P-F	4-4-0	Jules Sikes
20.	2nd Air Force	7-2-1	Bill Reese

1945

		Record	Coach
1.	Army	9-0-0	Red Blaik
2.	Alabama	9-0-0	Frank Thomas
3.	Navy	7-1-1	Oscar Hagberg
4.	Indiana	9-0-1	Bo McMillan
5.	Oklahoma A&M	8-0-0	Jim Lookabaugh
6.	Michigan	7-3-0	Fritz Crisler
7.	St. Mary's (CA)	7-1-0	Jimmy Phelan
8.	Pennsylvania	6-2-0	George Munger
9.	Notre Dame	7-2-1	Hugh Devore
10.	Texas	9-1-0	Dana X. Bible
11.	Southern Cal	7-3-0	Jeff Cravath
12.	Ohio St	7-2-0	Carroll Widdoes
13.	Duke	6-2-0	Eddie Cameron
14.	Tennessee	8-1-0	John Barnhill
15.	Louisiana St	7-2-0	Bernie Moore
16.	Holy Cross	8-1-0	John DeGrosa
17.	Tulsa	8-2-0	Henry Frnka
18.	Georgia	8-2-0	Wally Butts
19.	Wake Forest	4-3-1	Peahead Walker
20.	Columbia	8-1-0	Lou Little

1946

		Record	Coach
1.	Notre Dame	8-0-1	Frank Leahy
2.	Army	9-0-1	Red Blaik
3.	Georgia	10-0-0	Wally Butts
4.	UCLA	10-0-0	B. LaBrucherie

Note: Except where indicated with an asterisk, the polls from 1936 through 1964 were taken before the bowl games and those from 1965 through the present were taken after the bowl games.

1946 *(Cont.)*

		Record	Coach
5.	Illinois	7-2-0	Ray Eliot
6.	Michigan	6-2-1	Fritz Crisler
7.	Tennessee	9-1-0	Bob Neyland
8.	Louisiana St	9-1-0	Bernie Moore
9.	N Carolina	8-1-1	Carl Snavely
10.	Rice	8-2-0	Jess Neely
11.	Georgia Tech	8-2-0	Bobby Dodd
12.	Yale	7-1-1	Howard Odell
13.	Pennsylvania	6-2-0	George Munger
14.	Oklahoma	7-3-0	Jim Tatum
15.	Texas	8-2-0	Dana X. Bible
16.	Arkansas	6-3-1	John Barnhill
17.	Tulsa	9-1-0	J.O. Brothers
18.	N Carolina St	8-2-0	Beattie Feathers
19.	Delaware	9-0-0	Bill Murray
20.	Indiana	6-3-0	Bo McMillan

1947

		Record	Coach
1.	Notre Dame	9-0-0	Frank Leahy
2.	#Michigan	9-0-0	Fritz Crisler
3.	SMU	9-0-1	Matty Bell
4.	Penn St	9-0-0	Bob Higgins
5.	Texas	9-1-0	Blair Cherry
6.	Alabama	8-2-0	Red Drew
7.	Pennsylvania	7-0-1	George Munger
8.	Southern Cal	7-1-1	Jeff Cravath
9.	N Carolina	8-2-0	Carl Snavely
10.	Georgia Tech	9-1-0	Bobby Dodd
11.	Army	5-2-2	Red Blaik
12.	Kansas	8-0-2	George Sauer
13.	Mississippi	8-2-0	Johnny Vaught
14.	William & Mary	9-1-0	Rube McCray
15.	California	9-1-0	Pappy Waldorf
16.	Oklahoma	7-2-1	Bud Wilkinson
17.	N Carolina St	5-3-1	Beattie Feathers
18.	Rice	6-3-1	Jess Neely
19.	Duke	4-3-2	Wallace Wade
20.	Columbia	7-2-0	Lou Little

#The AP, which had voted Notre Dame No. 1 before the bowl games, took a second vote, giving the title to Michigan after its 49–0 win over Southern Cal in the Rose Bowl.

1948

		Record	Coach
1.	Michigan	9-0-0	Bennie Oosterbaan
2.	Notre Dame	9-0-1	Frank Leahy
3.	N Carolina	9-0-1	Carl Snavely
4.	California	10-0-0	Pappy Waldorf
5.	Oklahoma	9-1-0	Bud Wilkinson
6.	Army	8-0-1	Red Blaik
7.	Northwestern	7-2-0	Bob Voigts
8.	Georgia	9-1-0	Wally Butts
9.	Oregon	9-1-0	Jim Aiken
10.	SMU	8-1-1	Matty Bell
11.	Clemson	10-0-0	Frank Howard
12.	Vanderbilt	8-2-1	Red Sanders
13.	Tulane	9-1-0	Henry Frnka
14.	Michigan St	6-2-2	Biggie Munn
15.	Mississippi	8-1-0	Johnny Vaught
16.	Minnesota	7-2-0	Bernie Bierman
17.	William & Mary	6-2-2	Rube McCray
18.	Penn St	7-1-1	Bob Higgins
19.	Cornell	8-1-0	Lefty James
20.	Wake Forest	6-3-0	Peahead Walker

1949

		Record	Coach
1.	Notre Dame	10-0-0	Frank Leahy
2.	Oklahoma	10-0-0	Bud Wilkinson
3.	California	10-0-0	Pappy Waldorf
4.	Army	9-0-0	Red Blaik
5.	Rice	9-1-0	Jess Neely
6.	Ohio St	6-1-2	Wes Fesler
7.	Michigan	6-2-1	Bennie Oosterbaan
8.	Minnesota	7-2-0	Bernie Bierman
9.	Louisiana St	8-2-0	Gaynell Tinsley
10.	Pacific	11-0-0	Larry Siemering
11.	Kentucky	9-2-0	Bear Bryant
12.	Cornell	8-1-0	Lefty James
13.	Villanova	8-1-0	Jim Leonard
14.	Maryland	8-1-0	Jim Tatum
15.	Santa Clara	7-2-1	Len Casanova
16.	N Carolina	7-3-0	Carl Snavely
17.	Tennessee	7-2-1	Bob Neyland
18.	Princeton	6-3-0	Charlie Caldwell
19.	Michigan St	6-3-0	Biggie Munn
20.	Missouri	7-3-0	Don Faurot
	Baylor	8-2-0	Bob Woodruff

1950

		Record	Coach
1.	Oklahoma	10-0-0	Bud Wilkinson
2.	Army	8-1-0	Red Blaik
3.	Texas	9-1-0	Blair Cherry
4.	Tennessee	10-1-0	Bob Neyland
5.	California	9-0-1	Pappy Waldorf
6.	Princeton	9-0-0	Charlie Caldwell
7.	Kentucky	10-1-0	Bear Bryant
8.	Michigan St	8-1-0	Biggie Munn
9.	Michigan	5-3-1	Bennie Oosterbaan
10.	Clemson	8-0-1	Frank Howard
11.	Washington	8-2-0	Howard Odell
12.	Wyoming	9-0-0	Bowden Wyatt
13.	Illinois	7-2-0	Ray Eliot
14.	Ohio St	6-3-0	Wes Fesler
15.	Miami (FL)	9-0-1	Andy Gustafson
16.	Alabama	9-2-0	Red Drew
17.	Nebraska	6-2-1	Bill Glassford
18.	Washington & Lee	8-2-0	George Barclay
19.	Tulsa	9-1-1	J.O. Brothers
20.	Tulane	6-2-1	Henry Frnka

1951

		Record	Coach
1.	Tennessee	10-0-0	Bob Neyland
2.	Michigan St	9-0-0	Biggie Munn
3.	Maryland	9-0-0	Jim Tatum
4.	Illinois	8-0-1	Ray Eliot
5.	Georgia Tech	10-0-1	Bobby Dodd
6.	Princeton	9-0-0	Charlie Caldwell
7.	Stanford	9-1-0	Chuck Taylor
8.	Wisconsin	7-1-1	Ivy Williamson
9.	Baylor	8-1-1	George Sauer
10.	Oklahoma	8-2-0	Bud Wilkinson
11.	Texas Christian	6-4-0	Dutch Meyer
12.	California	8-2-0	Pappy Waldorf
13.	Virginia	8-1-0	Art Guepe
14.	San Francisco	9-0-0	Joe Kuharich
15.	Kentucky	7-4-0	Bear Bryant
16.	Boston University	6-4-0	Buff Donelli
17.	UCLA	5-3-1	Red Sanders
18.	Washington St	7-3-0	Forest Evashevski

1951 *(Cont.)*

		Record	Coach
19.	Holy Cross	8-2-0	Eddie Anderson
20.	Clemson	7-2-0	Frank Howard

1952

		Record	Coach
1.	Michigan St	9-0-0	Biggie Munn
2.	Georgia Tech	11-0-0	Bobby Dodd
3.	Notre Dame	7-2-1	Frank Leahy
4.	Oklahoma	8-1-1	Bud Wilkinson
5.	Southern Cal	9-1-0	Jess Hill
6.	UCLA	8-1-0	Red Sanders
7.	Mississippi	8-0-2	Johnny Vaught
8.	Tennessee	8-1-1	Bob Neyland
9.	Alabama	9-2-0	Red Drew
10.	Texas	8-2-0	Ed Price
11.	Wisconsin	6-2-1	Ivy Williamson
12.	Tulsa	8-1-1	J.O. Brothers
13.	Maryland	7-2-0	Jim Tatum
14.	Syracuse	7-2-0	Ben Schwartzwalder
15.	Florida	7-3-0	Bob Woodruff
16.	Duke	8-2-0	Bill Murray
17.	Ohio St	6-3-0	Woody Hayes
18.	Purdue	4-3-2	Stu Holcomb
19.	Princeton	8-1-0	Charlie Caldwell
20.	Kentucky	5-4-2	Bear Bryant

1953

		Record	Coach
1.	Maryland	10-0-0	Jim Tatum
2.	Notre Dame	9-0-1	Frank Leahy
3.	Michigan St	8-1-0	Biggie Munn
4.	Oklahoma	8-1-1	Bud Wilkinson
5.	UCLA	8-1-0	Red Sanders
6.	Rice	8-2-0	Jess Neely
7.	Illinois	7-1-1	Ray Eliot
8.	Georgia Tech	8-2-1	Bobby Dodd
9.	Iowa	5-3-1	Forest Evashevski
10.	W Virginia	8-1-0	Art Lewis
11.	Texas	7-3-0	Ed Price
12.	Texas Tech	10-1-0	DeWitt Weaver
13.	Alabama	6-2-3	Red Drew
14.	Army	7-1-1	Red Blaik
15.	Wisconsin	6-2-1	Ivy Williamson
16.	Kentucky	7-2-1	Bear Bryant
17.	Auburn	7-2-1	Shug Jordan
18.	Duke	7-2-1	Bill Murray
19.	Stanford	6-3-1	Chuck Taylor
20.	Michigan	6-3-0	Bennie Oosterbaan

1954

		Record	Coach
1.	Ohio St	9-0-0	Woody Hayes
2.	#UCLA	9-0-0	Red Sanders
3.	Oklahoma	10-0-0	Bud Wilkinson
4.	Notre Dame	9-1-0	Terry Brennan
5.	Navy	7-2-0	Eddie Erdelatz
6.	Mississippi	9-1-0	Johnny Vaught
7.	Army	7-2-0	Red Blaik
8.	Maryland	7-2-1	Jim Tatum
9.	Wisconsin	7-2-0	Ivy Williamson
10.	Arkansas	8-2-0	Bowden Wyatt

1954 *(Cont.)*

		Record	Coach
11.	Miami (FL)	8-1-0	Andy Gustafson
12.	W Virginia	8-1-0	Art Lewis
13.	Auburn	7-3-0	Shug Jordan
14.	Duke	7-2-1	Bill Murray
15.	Michigan	6-3-0	Bennie Oosterbaan
16.	Virginia Tech	8-0-1	Frank Moseley
17.	Southern Cal	8-3-0	Jess Hill
18.	Baylor	7-3-0	George Sauer
19.	Rice	7-3-0	Jess Neely
20.	Penn St	7-2-0	Rip Engle

#Selected No. 1 by UP.

1955

		Record	Coach
1.	Oklahoma	10-0-0	Bud Wilkinson
2.	Michigan St	8-1-0	Duffy Daugherty
3.	Maryland	10-0-0	Jim Tatum
4.	UCLA	9-1-0	Red Sanders
5.	Ohio St	7-2-0	Woody Hayes
6.	Texas Christian	9-1-0	Abe Martin
7.	Georgia Tech	8-1-1	Bobby Dodd
8.	Auburn	8-1-1	Shug Jordan
9.	Notre Dame	8-2-0	Terry Brennan
10.	Mississippi	9-1-0	Johnny Vaught
11.	Pittsburgh	7-3-0	John Michelosen
12.	Michigan	7-2-0	Bennie Oosterbaan
13.	Southern Cal	6-4-0	Jess Hill
14.	Miami (FL)	6-3-0	Andy Gustafson
15.	Miami (OH)	9-0-0	Ara Parseghian
16.	Stanford	6-3-1	Chuck Taylor
17.	Texas A&M	7-2-1	Bear Bryant
18.	Navy	6-2-1	Eddie Erdelatz
19.	W Virginia	8-2-0	Art Lewis
20.	Army	6-3-0	Red Blaik

1956

		Record	Coach
1.	Oklahoma	10-0-0	Bud Wilkinson
2.	Tennessee	10-0-0	Bowden Wyatt
3.	Iowa	8-1-0	Forest Evashevski
4.	Georgia Tech.	9-1-0	Bobby Dodd
5.	Texas A&M	9-0-1	Bear Bryant
6.	Miami (FL)	8-1-1	Andy Gustafson
7.	Michigan	7-2-0	Bennie Oosterbaan
8.	Syracuse	7-1-0	Ben Schwartzwalder
9.	Michigan St	7-2-0	Duffy Daugherty
10.	Oregon St	7-2-1	Tommy Prothro
11.	Baylor	8-2-0	Sam Boyd
12.	Minnesota	6-1-2	Murray Warmath
13.	Pittsburgh	7-2-1	John Michelosen
14.	Texas Christian	7-3-0	Abe Martin
15.	Ohio St	6-3-0	Woody Hayes
16.	Navy	6-1-2	Eddie Erdelatz
17.	Geo Washington	7-1-1	Gene Sherman
18.	Southern Cal	8-2-0	Jess Hill
19.	Clemson	7-1-2	Frank Howard
20.	Colorado	7-2-1	Dallas Ward
	Penn St	6-2-1	Rip Engle

1957

		Record	Coach
1.	Auburn	10-0-0	Shug Jordan
2.	#Ohio St	8-1-0	Woody Hayes
3.	Michigan St	8-1-0	Duffy Daugherty
4.	Oklahoma	9-1-0	Bud Wilkinson
5.	Navy	8-1-1	Eddie Erdelatz
6.	Iowa	7-1-1	Forest Evashevski
7.	Mississippi	8-1-1	Johnny Vaught
8.	Rice	7-3-0	Jess Neely
9.	Texas A&M	8-2-0	Bear Bryant
10.	Notre Dame	7-3-0	Terry Brennan
11.	Texas	6-3-1	Darrell Royal
12.	Arizona St	10-0-0	Dan Devine
13.	Tennessee	7-3-0	Bowden Wyatt
14.	Mississippi St	6-2-1	Wade Walker
15.	N Carolina St	7-1-2	Earle Edwards
16.	Duke	6-2-2	Bill Murray
17.	Florida	6-2-1	Bob Woodruff
18.	Army	7-2-0	Red Blaik
19.	Wisconsin	6-3-0	Milt Brunt
20.	VMI	9-0-1	John McKenna

#Selected No. 1 by UP.

1958

		Record	Coach
1.	Louisiana St	10-0-0	Paul Dietzel
2.	Iowa	7-1-1	Forest Evashevski
3.	Army	8-0-1	Red Blaik
4.	Auburn	9-0-1	Shug Jordan
5.	Oklahoma	9-1-0	Bud Wilkinson
6.	Air Force	9-0-1	Ben Martin
7.	Wisconsin	7-1-1	Milt Bruhn
8.	Ohio St	6-1-2	Woody Hayes
9.	Syracuse	8-1-0	Ben Schwartzwalder
10.	Texas Christian	8-2-0	Abe Martin
11.	Mississippi	8-2-0	Johnny Vaught
12.	Clemson	8-2-0	Frank Howard
13.	Purdue	6-1-2	Jack Mollenkopf
14.	Florida	6-3-1	Bob Woodruff
15.	S Carolina	7-3-0	Warren Giese
16.	California	7-3-0	Pete Elliott
17.	Notre Dame	6-4-0	Terry Brennan
18.	SMU	6-4-0	Bill Meek
19.	Oklahoma St	7-3-0	Cliff Speegle
20.	Rutgers	8-1-0	John Stiegman

1959

		Record	Coach
1.	Syracuse	10-0-0	Ben Schwartzwalder
2.	Mississippi	9-1-0	Johnny Vaught
3.	Louisiana St	9-1-0	Paul Dietzel
4.	Texas	9-1-0	Darrell Royal
5.	Georgia	9-1-0	Wally Butts
6.	Wisconsin	7-2-0	Milt Bruhn
7.	Texas Christian	8-2-0	Abe Martin
8.	Washington	9-1-0	Jim Owens
9.	Arkansas	8-2-0	Frank Broyles
10.	Alabama	7-1-2	Bear Bryant
11.	Clemson	8-2-0	Frank Howard

1959 *(Cont.)*

		Record	Coach
12.	Penn St	8-2-0	Rip Engle
13.	Illinois	5-3-1	Ray Eliot
14.	Southern Cal	8-2-0	Don Clark
15.	Oklahoma	7-3-0	Bud Wilkinson
16.	Wyoming	9-1-0	Bob Devaney
17.	Notre Dame	5-5-0	Joe Kuharich
18.	Missouri	6-4-0	Dan Devine
19.	Florida	5-4-1	Bob Woodruff
20.	Pittsburgh	6-4-0	John Michelosen

1960

		Record	Coach
1.	Minnesota	8-1-0	Murray Warmath
2.	Mississippi	9-0-1	Johnny Vaught
3.	Iowa	8-1-0	Forest Evashevski
4.	Navy	9-1-0	Wayne Hardin
5.	Missouri	9-1-0	Dan Devine
6.	Washington	9-1-0	Jim Owens
7.	Arkansas	8-2-0	Frank Broyles
8.	Ohio St	7-2-0	Woody Hayes
9.	Alabama	8-1-1	Bear Bryant
10.	Duke	7-3-0	Bill Murray
11.	Kansas	7-2-1	Jack Mitchell
12.	Baylor	8-2-0	John Bridgers
13.	Auburn	8-2-0	Shug Jordan
14.	Yale	9-0-0	Jordan Oliver
15.	Michigan St	6-2-1	Duffy Daugherty
16.	Penn St	6-3-0	Rip Engle
17.	New Mexico St	10-0-0	Warren Woodson
18.	Florida	8-2-0	Ray Graves
19.	Syracuse	7-2-0	Ben Schwartzwalder
	Purdue	4-4-1	Jack Mollenkopf

1961

		Record	Coach
1.	Alabama	10-0-0	Bear Bryant
2.	Ohio St	8-0-1	Woody Hayes
3.	Texas	9-1-0	Darrell Royal
4.	Louisiana St	9-1-0	Paul Dietzel
5.	Mississippi	9-1-0	Johnny Vaught
6.	Minnesota	7-2-0	Murray Warmath
7.	Colorado	9-1-0	Sonny Grandelius
8.	Michigan St	7-2-0	Duffy Daugherty
9.	Arkansas	8-2-0	Frank Broyles
10.	Utah St	9-0-1	John Ralston
11.	Missouri	7-2-1	Dan Devine
12.	Purdue	6-3-0	Jack Mollenkopf
13.	Georgia Tech	7-3-0	Bobby Dodd
14.	Syracuse	7-3-0	Ben Schwartzwalder
15.	Rutgers	9-0-0	John Bateman
16.	UCLA	7-3-0	Bill Barnes
17.	Rice	7-3-0	Jess Neely
	Penn St	7-3-0	Rip Engle
	Arizona	8-1-1	Jim LaRue
20.	Duke	7-3-0	Bill Murray

1962

		Record	Coach
1.	Southern Cal	10-0-0	John McKay
2.	Wisconsin	8-1-0	Milt Bruhn
3.	Mississippi	9-0-0	Johnny Vaught
4.	Texas	9-0-1	Darrell Royal
5.	Alabama	9-1-0	Bear Bryant
6.	Arkansas	9-1-0	Frank Broyles
7.	Louisiana St	8-1-1	Charlie McClendon
8.	Oklahoma	8-2-0	Bud Wilkinson
9.	Penn St	9-1-0	Rip Engle
10.	Minnesota	6-2-1	Murray Warmath

11–20: UPI

		Record	Coach
11.	Georgia Tech	7-2-1	Bobby Dodd
12.	Missouri	7-1-2	Dan Devine
13.	Ohio St	6-3-0	Woody Hayes
14.	Duke	8-2-0	Bill Murray
	Washington	7-1-2	Jim Owens
16.	Northwestern	7-2-0	Ara Parseghian
	Oregon St	8-2-0	Tommy Prothro
18.	Arizona St	7-2-1	Frank Kush
	Miami (FL)	7-3-0	Andy Gustafson
	Illinois	2-7-0	Pete Elliott

1963

		Record	Coach
1.	Texas	10-0-0	Darrell Royal
2.	Navy	9-1-0	Wayne Hardin
3.	Illinois	7-1-1	Pete Elliott
4.	Pittsburgh	9-1-0	John Michelosen
5.	Auburn	9-1-0	Shug Jordan
6.	Nebraska	9-1-0	Bob Devaney
7.	Mississippi	7-0-2	Johnny Vaught
8.	Alabama	8-2-0	Bear Bryant
9.	Oklahoma	8-2-0	Bud Wilkinson
10.	Michigan St	6-2-1	Duffy Daugherty

11–20: UPI

		Record	Coach
11.	Mississippi St	6-2-2	Paul Davis
12.	Syracuse	8-2-0	Ben Schwartzwalder
13.	Arizona St	8-1-0	Frank Kush
14.	Memphis St	9-0-1	Billy J. Murphy
15.	Washington	6-4-0	Jim Owens
16.	Penn St	7-3-0	Rip Engle
	Southern Cal	7-3-0	John McKay
	Missouri	7-3-0	Dan Devine
19.	N Carolina	8-2-0	Jim Hickey
20.	Baylor	7-3-0	John Bridgers

1964

		Record	Coach
1.	Alabama	10-0-0	Bear Bryant
2.	Arkansas	10-0-0	Frank Broyles
3.	Notre Dame	9-1-0	Ara Parseghian
4.	Michigan	8-1-0	Bump Elliott
5.	Texas	9-1-0	Darrell Royal
6.	Nebraska	9-1-0	Bob Devaney
7.	Louisiana St	7-2-1	Charlie McClendon
8.	Oregon St	8-2-0	Tommy Prothro
9.	Ohio St	7-2-0	Woody Hayes
10.	Southern Cal	7-3-0	John McKay

1964 *(Cont.)*

11–20: UPI

		Record	Coach
11.	Florida St	8-1-1	Bill Peterson
12.	Syracuse	7-3-0	Ben Schwartzwalder
13.	Princeton	9-0-0	Dick Colman
14.	Penn St	6-4-0	Rip Engle
	Utah	8-2-0	Ray Nagel
16.	Illinois	6-3-0	Pete Elliott
	New Mexico	9-2-0	Bill Weeks
18.	Tulsa	8-2-0	Glenn Dobbs
19.	Missouri	6-3-1	Dan Devine
20.	Mississippi	5-4-1	Johnny Vaught
	Michigan St	4-5-1	Duffy Daugherty

1965

		Record	Coach
1.	Alabama	9-1-1	Bear Bryant
2.	#Michigan St	10-1-0	Duffy Daugherty
3.	Arkansas	10-1-0	Frank Broyles
4.	UCLA	8-2-1	Tommy Prothro
5.	Nebraska	10-1-0	Bob Devaney
6.	Missouri	8-2-1	Dan Devine
7.	Tennessee	8-1-2	Doug Dickey
8.	Louisiana St	8-3-0	Charlie McClendon
9.	Notre Dame	7-2-1	Ara Parseghian
10.	Southern Cal	7-2-1	John McKay

11–20: UPI

		Record	Coach
11.	Texas Tech	8-2-0	J.T. King
12.	Ohio St	7-2-0	Woody Hayes
13.	Florida	7-3-0	Ray Graves
14.	Purdue	7-2-1	Jack Mollenkopf
15.	Georgia	6-4-0	Vince Dooley
16.	Tulsa	8-2-0	Glenn Dobbs
17.	Mississippi	6-4-0	Johnny Vaught
18.	Kentucky	6-4-0	Charlie Bradshaw
19.	Syracuse	7-3-0	Ben Schwartzwalder
20.	Colorado	6-2-2	Eddie Crowder

#Selected No. 1 by UPI.

1966*

		Record	Coach
1.	Notre Dame	9-0-1	Ara Parseghian
2.	Michigan St	9-0-1	Duffy Daugherty
3.	Alabama	10-0-0	Bear Bryant
4.	Georgia	9-1-0	Vince Dooley
5.	UCLA	9-1-0	Tommy Prothro
6.	Nebraska	9-1-0	Bob Devaney
7.	Purdue	8-2-0	Jack Mollenkopf
8.	Georgia Tech	9-1-0	Bobby Dodd
9.	Miami (FL)	7-2-1	Charlie Tate
10.	SMU	8-2-0	Hayden Fry

11–20: UPI

		Record	Coach
11.	Florida	8-2-0	Ray Graves
12.	Mississippi	8-2-0	Johnny Vaught
13.	Arkansas	8-2-0	Frank Broyles
14.	Tennessee	7-3-0	Doug Dickey
15.	Wyoming	9-1-0	Lloyd Eaton
16.	Syracuse	8-2-0	Ben Schwartzwalder
17.	Houston	8-2-0	Bill Yeoman
18.	Southern Cal	7-3-0	John McKay
19.	Oregon St	7-3-0	Dee Andros
20.	Virginia Tech	8-1-1	Jerry Claiborne

Note: Except where indicated with an asterisk, the polls from 1936 through 1964 were taken before the bowl games and those from 1965 through the present were taken after the bowl games. Additionally, the AP ranked only ten teams in its polls from 1962–67; positions 11–20 from those years are from the UPI poll.

1967*

		Record	Coach
1.	Southern Cal	9-1-0	John McKay
2.	Tennessee	9-1-0	Doug Dickey
3.	Oklahoma	9-1-0	Chuck Fairbanks
4.	Indiana	9-1-0	John Pont
5.	Notre Dame	8-2-0	Ara Parseghian
6.	Wyoming	10-0-0	Lloyd Eaton
7.	Oregon St	7-2-1	Dee Andros
8.	Alabama	8-1-1	Bear Bryant
9.	Purdue	8-2-0	Jack Mollenkopf
10.	Penn St	8-2-0	Joe Paterno

11–20: UPI†

		Record	Coach
11.	UCLA	7-2-1	Tommy Prothro
12.	Syracuse	8-2-0	Ben Schwartzwalder
13.	Colorado	8-2-0	Eddie Crowder
14.	Minnesota	8-2-0	Murray Warmath
15.	Florida St	7-2-1	Bill Peterson
16.	Miami (FL)	7-3-0	Charlie Tate
17.	N Carolina St	8-2-0	Earle Edwards
18.	Georgia	7-3-0	Vince Dooley
19.	Houston	9-2-0	Bill Yeoman
20.	Arizona St	8-2-0	Frank Kush

†UPI ranked Penn St 11th and did not rank Alabama, which was on probation.

1968

		Record	Coach
1.	Ohio St	10-0-0	Woody Hayes
2.	Penn St	11-0-0	Joe Paterno
3.	Texas	9-1-1	Darrell Royal
4.	Southern Cal	9-1-1	John McKay
5.	Notre Dame	7-2-1	Ara Parseghian
6.	Arkansas	10-1-0	Frank Broyles
7.	Kansas	9-2-0	Pepper Rodgers
8.	Georgia	8-1-2	Vince Dooley
9.	Missouri	8-3-0	Dan Devine
10.	Purdue	8-2-0	Jack Mollenkopf
11.	Oklahoma	7-4-0	Chuck Fairbanks
12.	Michigan	8-2-0	Bump Elliott
13.	Tennessee	8-2-1	Doug Dickey
14.	SMU	8-3-0	Hayden Fry
15.	Oregon St	7-3-0	Dee Andros
16.	Auburn	7-4-0	Shug Jordan
17.	Alabama	8-3-0	Bear Bryant
18.	Houston	6-2-2	Bill Yeoman
19.	Louisiana St	8-3-0	Charlie McClendon
20.	Ohio	10-1-0	Bill Hess

1969

		Record	Coach
1.	Texas	11-0-0	Darrell Royal
2.	Penn St	11-0-0	Joe Paterno
3.	Southern Cal	10-0-1	John McKay
4.	Ohio St	8-1-0	Woody Hayes
5.	Notre Dame	8-2-1	Ara Parseghian
6.	Missouri	9-2-0	Dan Devine
7.	Arkansas	9-2-0	Frank Broyles
8.	Mississippi	8-3-0	Johnny Vaught
9.	Michigan	8-3-0	Bo Schembechler
10.	Louisiana St	9-1-0	Charlie McClendon

1969 (Cont.)

		Record	Coach
11.	Nebraska	9-2-0	Bob Devaney
12.	Houston	9-2-0	Bill Yeoman
13.	UCLA	8-1-1	Tommy Prothro
14.	Florida	9-1-1	Ray Graves
15.	Tennessee	9-2-0	Doug Dickey
16.	Colorado	8-3-0	Eddie Crowder
17.	W Virginia	10-0-1	Jim Carlen
18.	Purdue	8-2-0	Jack Mollenkopf
19.	Stanford	7-2-1	John Ralston
20.	Auburn	8-3-0	Shug Jordan

1970

		Record	Coach
1.	Nebraska	11-0-1	Bob Devaney
2.	Notre Dame	10-1-0	Ara Parseghian
3.	#Texas	10-1-0	Darrell Royal
4.	Tennessee	11-0-1	Bill Battle
5.	Ohio St	9-1-0	Woody Hayes
6.	Arizona St	11-0-0	Frank Kush
7.	Louisiana St	9-3-0	Charlie McClendon
8.	Stanford	9-3-0	John Ralston
9.	Michigan	9-1-0	Bo Schembechler
10.	Auburn	9-2-0	Shug Jordan
11.	Arkansas	9-2-0	Frank Broyles
12.	Toledo	12-0-0	Frank Lauterbur
13.	Georgia Tech	9-3-0	Bud Carson
14.	Dartmouth	9-0-0	Bob Blackman
15.	Southern Cal	6-4-1	John McKay
16.	Air Force	9-3-0	Ben Martin
17.	Tulane	8-4-0	Jim Pittman
18.	Penn St	7-3-0	Joe Paterno
19.	Houston	8-3-0	Bill Yeoman
20.	Oklahoma	7-4-1	Chuck Fairbanks
	Mississippi	7-4-0	Johnny Vaught

#Selected No. 1 by UPI.

1971

		Record	Coach
1.	Nebraska	13-0-0	Bob Devaney
2.	Oklahoma	11-1-0	Chuck Fairbanks
3.	Colorado	10-2-0	Eddie Crowder
4.	Alabama	11-1-0	Bear Bryant
5.	Penn St	11-1-0	Joe Paterno
6.	Michigan	11-1-0	Bo Schembechler
7.	Georgia	11-1-0	Vince Dooley
8.	Arizona St	11-1-0	Frank Kush
9.	Tennessee	10-2-0	Bill Battle
10.	Stanford	9-3-0	John Ralston
11.	Louisiana St	9-3-0	Charlie McClendon
12.	Auburn	9-2-0	Shug Jordan
13.	Notre Dame	8-2-0	Ara Parseghian
14.	Toledo	12-0-0	John Murphy
15.	Mississippi	10-2-0	Billy Kinard
16.	Arkansas	8-3-1	Frank Broyles
17.	Houston	9-3-0	Bill Yeoman
18.	Texas	8-3-0	Darrell Royal
19.	Washington	8-3-0	Jim Owens
20.	Southern Cal	6-4-1	John McKay

1972

		Record	Coach
1.	Southern Cal	12-0-0	John McKay
2.	Oklahoma	11-1-0	Chuck Fairbanks
3.	Texas	10-1-0	Darrell Royal
4.	Nebraska	9-2-1	Bob Devaney
5.	Auburn	10-1-0	Shug Jordan
6.	Michigan	10-1-0	Bo Schembechler
7.	Alabama	10-2-0	Bear Bryant
8.	Tennessee	10-2-0	Bill Battle
9.	Ohio St	9-2-0	Woody Hayes
10.	Penn St	10-2-0	Joe Paterno
11.	Louisiana St	9-2-1	Charlie McClendon
12.	N Carolina	11-1-0	Bill Dooley
13.	Arizona St	10-2-0	Frank Kush
14.	Notre Dame	8-3-0	Ara Parseghian
15.	UCLA	8-3-0	Pepper Rodgers
16.	Colorado	8-4-0	Eddie Crowder
17.	N Carolina St	8-3-1	Lou Holtz
18.	Louisville	9-1-0	Lee Corso
19.	Washington St	7-4-0	Jim Sweeney
20.	Georgia Tech	7-4-1	Bill Fulcher

1973

		Record	Coach
1.	Notre Dame	11-0-0	Ara Parseghian
2.	Ohio St	10-0-1	Woody Hayes
3.	Oklahoma	10-0-1	Barry Switzer
4.	#Alabama	11-1-0	Bear Bryant
5.	Penn St	12-0-0	Joe Paterno
6.	Michigan	10-0-1	Bo Schembechler
7.	Nebraska	9-2-1	Tom Osborne
8.	Southern Cal	9-2-1	John McKay
9.	Arizona St	11-1-0	Frank Kush
	Houston	11-1-0	Bill Yeoman
11.	Texas Tech	11-1-0	Jim Carlen
12.	UCLA	9-2-0	Pepper Rodgers
13.	Louisiana St	9-3-0	Charlie McClendon
14.	Texas	8-3-0	Darrell Royal
15.	Miami (OH)	11-0-0	Bill Mallory
16.	N Carolina St	9-3-0	Lou Holtz
17.	Missouri	8-4-0	Al Onofrio
18.	Kansas	7-4-1	Don Fambrough
19.	Tennessee	8-4-0	Bill Battle
20.	Maryland	8-4-0	Jerry Claiborne
	Tulane	9-3-0	Bennie Ellender

#Selected No. 1 by UPI.

1974

		Record	Coach
1.	Oklahoma	11-0-0	Barry Switzer
2.	#Southern Cal	10-1-1	John McKay
3.	Michigan	10-1-0	Bo Schembechler
4.	Ohio St	10-2-0	Woody Hayes
5.	Alabama	11-1-0	Bear Bryant
6.	Notre Dame	10-2-0	Ara Parseghian
7.	Penn St	10-2-0	Joe Paterno
8.	Auburn	10-2-0	Shug Jordan
9.	Nebraska	9-3-0	Tom Osborne
10.	Miami (OH)	10-0-1	Dick Crum
11.	N Carolina St	9-2-1	Lou Holtz
12.	Michigan St	7-3-1	Denny Stolz

1974 *(Cont.)*

		Record	Coach
13.	Maryland	8-4-0	Jerry Claiborne
14.	Baylor	8-4-0	Grant Teaff
15.	Florida	8-4-0	Doug Dickey
16.	Texas A&M	8-3-0	Emory Ballard
17.	Mississippi St	9-3-0	Bob Tyler
	Texas	8-4-0	Darrell Royal
19.	Houston	8-3-1	Bill Yeoman
20.	Tennessee	7-3-2	Bill Battle

#Selected No. 1 by UPI.

1975

		Record	Coach
1.	Oklahoma	11-1-0	Barry Switzer
2.	Arizona St	12-0-0	Frank Kush
3.	Alabama	11-1-0	Bear Bryant
4.	Ohio St	11-1-0	Woody Hayes
5.	UCLA	9-2-1	Dick Vermeil
6.	Texas	10-2-0	Darrell Royal
7.	Arkansas	10-2-0	Frank Broyles
8.	Michigan	8-2-2	Bo Schembechler
9.	Nebraska	10-2-0	Tom Osborne
10.	Penn St	9-3-0	Joe Paterno
11.	Texas A&M	10-2-0	Emory Bellard
12.	Miami (OH)	11-1-0	Dick Crum
13.	Maryland	9-2-1	Jerry Claiborne
14.	California	8-3-0	Mike White
15.	Pittsburgh	8-4-0	Johnny Majors
16.	Colorado	9-3-0	Bill Mallory
17.	Southern Cal	8-4-0	John McKay
18.	Arizona	9-2-0	Jim Young
19.	Georgia	9-3-0	Vince Dooley
20.	W Virginia	9-3-0	Bobby Bowden

1976

		Record	Coach
1.	Pittsburgh	12-0-0	Johnny Majors
2.	Southern Cal	11-1-0	John Robinson
3.	Michigan	10-2-0	Bo Schembechler
4.	Houston	10-2-0	Bill Yeoman
5.	Oklahoma	9-2-1	Barry Switzer
6.	Ohio St	9-2-1	Woody Hayes
7.	Texas A&M	10-2-0	Emory Bellard
8.	Maryland	11-1-0	Jerry Claiborne
9.	Nebraska	9-3-1	Tom Osborne
10.	Georgia	10-2-0	Vince Dooley
11.	Alabama	9-3-0	Bear Bryant
12.	Notre Dame	9-3-0	Dan Devine
13.	Texas Tech	10-2-0	Steve Sloan
14.	Oklahoma St	9-3-0	Jim Stanley
15.	UCLA	9-2-1	Terry Donahue
16.	Colorado	8-4-0	Bill Mallory
17.	Rutgers	11-0-0	Frank Burns
18.	Kentucky	9-3-0	Fran Curci
19.	Iowa St	8-3-0	Earle Bruce
20.	Mississippi St	9-2-0	Bob Tyler

1977

		Record	Coach
1.	Notre Dame	11-1-0	Dan Devine
2.	Alabama	11-1-0	Bear Bryant
3.	Arkansas	11-1-0	Lou Holtz
4.	Texas	11-1-0	Fred Akers
5.	Penn St	11-1-0	Joe Paterno
6.	Kentucky	10-1-0	Fran Curci
7.	Oklahoma	10-2-0	Barry Switzer
8.	Pittsburgh	9-2-1	Jackie Sherrill
9.	Michigan	10-2-0	Bo Schembechler
10.	Washington	10-2-0	Don James
11.	Ohio St	9-3-0	Woody Hayes
12.	Nebraska	9-3-0	Tom Osborne
13.	Southern Cal	8-4-0	John Robinson
14.	Florida St	10-2-0	Bobby Bowden
15.	Stanford	9-3-0	Bill Walsh
16.	San Diego St	10-1-0	Claude Gilbert
17.	N Carolina	8-3-1	Bill Dooley
18.	Arizona St	9-3-0	Frank Kush
19.	Clemson	8-3-1	Charley Pell
20.	Brigham Young	9-2-0	LaVell Edwards

1978

		Record	Coach
1.	Alabama	11-1-0	Bear Bryant
2.	#Southern Cal	12-1-0	John Robinson
3.	Oklahoma	11-1-0	Barry Switzer
4.	Penn St	11-1-0	Joe Paterno
5.	Michigan	10-2-0	Bo Schembechler
6.	Clemson	11-1-0	Charley Pell
7.	Notre Dame	9-3-0	Dan Devine
8.	Nebraska	9-3-0	Tom Osborne
9.	Texas	9-3-0	Fred Akers
10.	Houston	9-3-0	Bill Yeoman
11.	Arkansas	9-2-1	Lou Holtz
12.	Michigan St	8-3-0	Darryl Rogers
13.	Purdue	9-2-1	Jim Young
14.	UCLA	8-3-1	Terry Donahue
15.	Missouri	8-4-0	Warren Powers
16.	Georgia	9-2-1	Vince Dooley
17.	Stanford	8-4-0	Bill Walsh
18.	N Carolina St	9-3-0	Bo Rein
19.	Texas A&M	8-4-0	Emory Bellard (4–2) Tom Wilson (4–2)
20.	Maryland	9-3-0	Jerry Claiborne

#Selected No. 1 by UPI.

1979

		Record	Coach
1.	Alabama	12-0-0	Bear Bryant
2.	Southern Cal	11-0-1	John Robinson
3.	Oklahoma	11-1-0	Barry Switzer
4.	Ohio St	11-1-0	Earle Bruce
5.	Houston	11-1-0	Bill Yeoman
6.	Florida St	11-1-0	Bobby Bowden
7.	Pittsburgh	11-1-0	Jackie Sherrill
8.	Arkansas	10-2-0	Lou Holtz
9.	Nebraska	10-2-0	Tom Osborne
10.	Purdue	10-2-0	Jim Young
11.	Washington	10-1-0	Don James
12.	Texas	9-3-0	Fred Akers
13.	Brigham Young	11-1-0	LaVell Edwards
14.	Baylor	8-4-0	Grant Teaff
15.	N Carolina	8-3-1	Dick Crum
16.	Auburn	8-3-0	Doug Barfield
17.	Temple	10-2-0	Wayne Hardin

1979 *(Cont.)*

		Record	Coach
18.	Michigan	8-4-0	Bo Schembechler
19.	Indiana	8-4-0	Lee Corso
20.	Penn St	8-4-0	Joe Paterno

1980

		Record	Coach
1.	Georgia	12-0-0	Vince Dooley
2.	Pittsburgh	11-1-0	Jackie Sherrill
3.	Oklahoma	10-2-0	Barry Switzer
4.	Michigan	10-2-0	Bo Schembechler
5.	Florida St	10-2-0	Bobby Bowden
6.	Alabama	10-2-0	Bear Bryant
7.	Nebraska	10-2-0	Tom Osborne
8.	Penn St	10-2-0	Joe Paterno
9.	Notre Dame	9-2-1	Dan Devine
10.	N Carolina	11-1-0	Dick Crum
11.	Southern Cal	8-2-1	John Robinson
12.	Brigham Young	12-1-0	LaVell Edwards
13.	UCLA	9-2-0	Terry Donahue
14.	Baylor	10-2-0	Grant Teaff
15.	Ohio St	9-3-0	Earle Bruce
16.	Washington	9-3-0	Don James
17.	Purdue	9-3-0	Jim Young
18.	Miami (FL)	9-3-0	H. Schnellenberger
19.	Mississippi St	9-3-0	Emory Bellard
20.	SMU	8-4-0	Ron Meyer

1981

		Record	Coach
1.	Clemson	12-0-0	Danny Ford
2.	Texas	10-1-0	Fred Akers
3.	Penn St	10-2-0	Joe Paterno
4.	Pittsburgh	11-1-0	Jackie Sherrill
5.	SMU	10-1-0	Ron Meyer
6.	Georgia	10-2-0	Vince Dooley
7.	Alabama	9-2-1	Bear Bryant
8.	Miami (FL)	9-2-0	H. Schnellenberger
9.	N Carolina	10-2-0	Dick Crum
10.	Washington	10-2-0	Don James
11.	Nebraska	9-3-0	Tom Osborne
12.	Michigan	9-3-0	Bo Schembechler
13.	Brigham Young	11-2-0	LaVell Edwards
14.	Southern Cal	9-3-0	John Robinson
15.	Ohio St	9-3-0	Earle Bruce
16.	Arizona St	9-2-0	Darryl Rogers
17.	W Virginia	9-3-0	Don Nehlen
18.	Iowa	8-4-0	Hayden Fry
19.	Missouri	8-4-0	Warren Powers
20.	Oklahoma	7-4-1	Barry Switzer

1982

		Record	Coach
1.	Penn St	11-1-0	Joe Paterno
2.	SMU	11-0-1	Bobby Collins
3.	Nebraska	12-1-0	Tom Osborne
4.	Georgia	11-1-0	Vince Dooley
5.	UCLA	10-1-1	Terry Donahue
6.	Arizona St	10-2-0	Darryl Rogers
7.	Washington	10-2-0	Don James
8.	Clemson	9-1-1	Danny Ford
9.	Arkansas	9-2-1	Lou Holtz
10.	Pittsburgh	9-3-0	Foge Fazio
11.	Louisiana St	8-3-1	Jerry Stovall
12.	Ohio St	9-3-0	Earle Bruce

1982 *(Cont.)*

	Record	Coach
13. Florida St	9-3-0	Bobby Bowden
14. Auburn	9-3-0	Pat Dye
15. Southern Cal	8-3-0	John Robinson
16. Oklahoma	8-4-0	Barry Switzer
17. Texas	9-3-0	Fred Akers
18. N Carolina	8-4-0	Dick Crum
19. W Virginia	9-3-0	Don Nehlen
20. Maryland	8-4-0	Bobby Ross

1983

	Record	Coach
1. Miami (FL)	11-1-0	H. Schnellenberger
2. Nebraska	12-1-0	Tom Osborne
3. Auburn	11-1-0	Pat Dye
4. Georgia	10-1-1	Vince Dooley
5. Texas	11-1-0	Fred Akers
6. Florida	9-2-1	Charlie Pell
7. Brigham Young	11-1-0	LaVell Edwards
8. Michigan	9-3-0	Bo Schembechler
9. Ohio St	9-3-0	Earle Bruce
10. Illinois	10-2-0	Mike White
11. Clemson	9-1-1	Danny Ford
12. SMU	10-2-0	Bobby Collins
13. Air Force	10-2-0	Ken Hatfield
14. Iowa	9-3-0	Hayden Fry
15. Alabama	8-4-0	Ray Perkins
16. W Virginia	9-3-0	Don Nehlen
17. UCLA	7-4-1	Terry Donahue
18. Pittsburgh	8-3-1	Foge Fazio
19. Boston College	9-3-0	Jack Bicknell
20. E Carolina	8-3-0	Ed Emory

1984

	Record	Coach
1. Brigham Young	13-0-0	LaVell Edwards
2. Washington	11-1-0	Don James
3. Florida	9-1-1	Chas Pell (0-1-1) Galen Hall (9-0)
4. Nebraska	10-2-0	Tom Osborne
5. Boston College	10-2-0	Jack Bicknell
6. Oklahoma	9-2-1	Barry Switzer
7. Oklahoma St	10-2-0	Pat Jones
8. SMU	10-2-0	Bobby Collins
9. UCLA	9-3-0	Terry Donahue
10. Southern Cal	10-3-0	Ted Tollner
11. S Carolina	10-2-0	Joe Morrison
12. Maryland	9-3-0	Bobby Ross
13. Ohio St	9-3-0	Earle Bruce
14. Auburn	9-4-0	Pat Dye
15. Louisiana St	8-3-1	Bill Arnsparger
16. Iowa	8-4-1	Hayden Fry
17. Florida St	7-3-2	Bobby Bowden
18. Miami (FL)	8-5-0	Jimmy Johnson
19. Kentucky	9-3-0	Jerry Claiborne
20. Virginia	8-2-2	George Welsh

1985

	Record	Coach
1. Oklahoma	11-1-0	Barry Switzer
2. Michigan	10-1-1	Bo Schembechler
3. Penn St	11-1-0	Joe Paterno
4. Tennessee	9-1-2	Johnny Majors
5. Florida	9-1-1	Galen Hall
6. Texas A&M	10-2-0	Jackie Sherrill
7. UCLA	9-2-1	Terry Donahue
8. Air Force	12-1-0	Fisher DeBerry

1985 *(Cont.)*

	Record	Coach
9. Miami (FL)	10-2-0	Jimmy Johnson
10. Iowa	10-2-0	Hayden Fry
11. Nebraska	9-3-0	Tom Osborne
12. Arkansas	10-2-0	Ken Hatfield
13. Alabama	9-2-1	Ray Perkins
14. Ohio St	9-3-0	Earle Bruce
15. Florida St	9-3-0	Bobby Bowden
16. Brigham Young	11-3-0	LaVell Edwards
17. Baylor	9-3-0	Grant Teaff
18. Maryland	9-3-0	Bobby Ross
19. Georgia Tech	9-2-1	Bill Curry
20. Louisiana St	9-2-1	Bill Arnsparger

1986

	Record	Coach
1. Penn St	12-0-0	Joe Paterno
2. Miami (FL)	11-1-0	Jimmy Johnson
3. Oklahoma	11-1-0	Barry Switzer
4. Arizona St	10-1-1	John Cooper
5. Nebraska	10-2-0	Tom Osborne
6. Auburn	10-2-0	Pat Dye
7. Ohio St	10-3-0	Earle Bruce
8. Michigan	11-2-0	Bo Schembechler
9. Alabama	10-3-0	Ray Perkins
10. Louisiana St	9-3-0	Bill Arnsparger
11. Arizona	9-3-0	Larry Smith
12. Baylor	9-3-0	Grant Teaff
13. Texas A&M	9-3-0	Jackie Sherrill
14. UCLA	8-3-1	Terry Donahue
15. Arkansas	9-3-0	Ken Hatfield
16. Iowa	9-3-0	Hayden Fry
17. Clemson	8-2-2	Danny Ford
18. Washington	8-3-1	Don James
19. Boston College	9-3-0	Jack Bicknell
20. Virginia Tech	9-2-1	Bill Dooley

1987

	Record	Coach
1. Miami (FL)	12-0-0	Jimmy Johnson
2. Florida St	11-1-0	Bobby Bowden
3. Oklahoma	11-1-0	Barry Switzer
4. Syracuse	11-0-1	Dick MacPherson
5. Louisiana St	10-1-1	Mike Archer
6. Nebraska	10-2-0	Tom Osborne
7. Auburn	9-1-2	Pat Dye
8. Michigan St	9-2-1	George Perles
9. UCLA	10-2-0	Terry Donahue
10. Texas A&M	10-2-0	Jackie Sherrill
11. Oklahoma St	10-2-0	Pat Jones
12. Clemson	10-2-0	Danny Ford
13. Georgia	9-3-0	Vince Dooley
14. Tennessee	10-2-1	Johnny Majors
15. S Carolina	8-4-0	Joe Morrison
16. Iowa	10-3-0	Hayden Fry
17. Notre Dame	8-4-0	Lou Holtz
18. Southern Cal	8-4-0	Larry Smith
19. Michigan	8-4-0	Bo Schembechler
20. Arizona St	7-4-1	John Cooper

1988

		Record	Coach
1.	Notre Dame	12-0-0	Lou Holtz
2.	Miami (FL)	11-1-0	Jimmy Johnson
3.	Florida St	11-1-0	Bobby Bowden
4.	Michigan	9-2-1	Bo Schembechler
5.	W Virginia	11-1-0	Don Nehlen
6.	UCLA	10-2-0	Terry Donahue
7.	Southern Cal	10-2-0	Larry Smith
8.	Auburn	10-2-0	Pat Dye
9.	Clemson	10-2-0	Danny Ford
10.	Nebraska	11-2-0	Tom Osborne
11.	Oklahoma St	10-2-0	Pat Jones
12.	Arkansas	10-2-0	Ken Hatfield
13.	Syracuse	10-2-0	Dick MacPherson
14.	Oklahoma	9-3-0	Barry Switzer
15.	Georgia	9-3-0	Vince Dooley
16.	Washington St	9-3-0	Dennis Erickson
17.	Alabama	9-3-0	Bill Curry
18.	Houston	9-3-0	Jack Pardee
19.	Louisiana St	8-4-0	Mike Archer
20.	Indiana	8-3-1	Bill Mallory

†1989

		Record	Coach
1.	Miami (FL)	11-1-0	Dennis Erickson
2.	Notre Dame	12-1-0	Lou Holtz
3.	Florida St	10-2-0	Bobby Bowden
4.	Colorado	11-1-0	Bill McCartney
5.	Tennessee	11-1-0	Johnny Majors
6.	Auburn	10-2-0	Pat Dye
7.	Michigan	10-2-0	Bo Schembechler
8.	Southern Cal	9-2-1	Larry Smith
9.	Alabama	10-2-0	Bill Curry
10.	Illinois	10-2-0	John Mackovic
11.	Nebraska	10-2-0	Tom Osborne
12.	Clemson	10-2-0	Danny Ford
13.	Arkansas	10-2-0	Ken Hatfield
14.	Houston	9-2-0	Jack Pardee
15.	Penn St	8-3-1	Joe Paterno
16.	Michigan St	8-4-0	George Perles
17.	Pittsburgh	8-3-1	Mike Gottfried
18.	Virginia	10-3-0	George Welsh
19.	Texas Tech	9-3-0	Spike Dykes
20.	Texas A&M	8-4-0	R.C. Slocum
21.	W Virginia	8-3-1	Don Nehlen
22.	Brigham Young	10-3-0	LaVell Edwards
23.	Washington	8-4-0	Don James
24.	Ohio St	8-4-0	John Cooper
25.	Arizona	8-4-0	Dick Tomey

1990

		Record	Coach
1.	Colorado	11-1-1	Bill McCartney
2.	#Georgia Tech	11-0-1	Bobby Ross
3.	Miami (FL)	10-2-0	Dennis Erickson
4.	Florida St	10-2-0	Bobby Bowden
5.	Washington	10-2-0	Don James
6.	Notre Dame	9-3-0	Lou Holtz
7.	Michigan	9-3-0	Gary Moeller
8.	Tennessee	9-2-2	Johnny Majors
9.	Clemson	10-2-0	Ken Hatfield
10.	Houston	10-1-0	John Jenkins
11.	Penn St	9-3-0	Joe Paterno
12.	Texas	10-2-0	David McWilliams

1990 *(Cont.)*

		Record	Coach
13.	Florida	9-2-0	Steve Spurrier
14.	Louisville	10-1-1	H. Schnellenberger
15.	Texas A&M	9-3-1	R.C. Slocum
16.	Michigan St	8-3-1	George Perles
17.	Oklahoma	8-3-0	Gary Gibbs
18.	Iowa	8-4-0	Hayden Fry
19.	Auburn	8-3-1	Pat Dye
20.	Southern Cal	8-4-1	Larry Smith
21.	Mississippi	9-3-0	Billy Brewer
22.	Brigham Young	10-3-0	LaVell Edwards
23.	Virginia	8-4-0	George Welsh
24.	Nebraska	9-3-0	Tom Osborne
25.	Illinois	8-4-0	John Mackovic

#Selected No. 1 by UPI.

1991

		Record	Coach
1.	Miami (FL)	12-0-0	Dennis Erickson
2.	#Washington	12-0-0	Don James
3.	Penn St	11-2-0	Joe Paterno
4.	Florida St	11-2-0	Bobby Bowden
5.	Alabama	11-1-0	Gene Stallings
6.	Michigan	10-2-0	Gary Moeller
7.	Florida	10-2-0	Steve Spurrier
8.	California	10-2-0	Bruce Snyder
9.	E Carolina	11-1-0	Bill Lewis
10.	Iowa	10-1-1	Hayden Fry
11.	Syracuse	10-2-0	Paul Pasqualoni
12.	Texas A&M	10-2-0	R.C. Slocum
13.	Notre Dame	10-3-0	Lou Holtz
14.	Tennessee	9-3-0	Johnny Majors
15.	Nebraska	9-2-1	Tom Osborne
16.	Oklahoma	9-3-0	Gary Gibbs
17.	Georgia	9-3-0	Ray Goff
18.	Clemson	9-2-1	Ken Hatfield
19.	UCLA	9-3-0	Terry Donahue
20.	Colorado	8-3-1	Bill McCartney
21.	Tulsa	10-2-0	David Rader
22.	Stanford	8-4-0	Dennis Green
23.	Brigham Young	8-3-2	LaVell Edwards
24.	N Carolina St	9-3-0	Dick Sheridan
25.	Air Force	10-3-0	Fisher DeBerry

#Selected No. 1 by *USA Today*/ CNN.

1992

		Record	Coach
1.	Alabama	13-0-0	Gene Stallings
2.	Florida St	11-1-0	Bobby Bowden
3.	Miami	11-1-0	Dennis Erickson
4.	Notre Dame	10-1-1	Lou Holtz
5.	Michigan	9-0-3	Gary Moeller
6.	Syracuse	10-2-0	Paul Pasqualoni
7.	Texas A&M	12-1-0	R.C. Slocum
8.	Georgia	10-2-0	Ray Goff
9.	Stanford	10-3-0	Bill Walsh
10.	Florida	9-4-0	Steve Spurrier
11.	Washington	9-3-0	Don James
12.	Tennessee	9-3-0	Johnny Majors
13.	Colorado	9-2-1	Bill McCartney
14.	Nebraska	9-3-0	Tom Osborne
15.	Washington St	9-3-0	Mike Price
16.	Mississippi	9-3-0	Billy Brewer
17.	N Carolina St	9-3-1	Dick Sheridan
18.	Ohio St	8-3-1	John Cooper
19.	N Carolina	9-3-0	Mack Brown
20.	Hawaii	11-2-0	Bob Wagner

1992 *(Cont.)*

	Record	Coach
21. Boston College	8-3-1	Tom Coughlin
22. Kansas	8-4-0	Glen Mason
23. Mississippi St	7-5-0	Jackie Sherrill
24. Fresno St	9-4-0	Jim Sweeney
25. Wake Forest	8-4-0	Bill Dooley

1993

	Record	Coach
1. Florida St	12-1-0	Bobby Bowden
2. Notre Dame	11-1-0	Lou Holtz
3. Nebraska	11-1-0	Tom Osborne
4. Auburn	11-0-0	Terry Bowden
5. Florida	11-2-0	Steve Spurrier
6. Wisconsin	10-1-1	Barry Alvarez
7. W Virginia	11-1-0	Don Nehlen
8. Penn St	10-2-0	Joe Paterno
9. Texas A&M	10-2-0	R.C. Slocum
10. Arizona	10-2-0	Dick Tomey
11. Ohio St	10-1-1	John Cooper
12. Tennessee	9-2-1	Phil Fulmer
13. Boston College	9-3-0	Tom Coughlin
14. Alabama	9-3-1	Gene Stallings
15. Miami	9-3-0	Dennis Erickson
16. Colorado	8-3-1	Bill McCartney
17. Oklahoma	9-3-0	Gary Gibbs
18. UCLA	8-4-0	Terry Donahue
19. N Carolina	10-3-0	Mack Brown
20. Kansas St	9-2-1	Bill Snyder
21. Michigan	8-4-0	Gary Moeller
22. Virginia Tech	9-3-0	Frank Beamer
23. Clemson	9-3-0	Ken Hatfield
24. Louisville	9-3-0	H. Schnellenberger
25. California	9-4-0	Keith Gilbertson

1994

	Record	Coach
1. Nebraska	13-0-0	Tom Osborne
2. Penn St	12-0-0	Joe Paterno
3. Colorado	11-1-0	Bill McCartney
4. Florida St	10-1-1	Bobby Bowden
5. Alabama	12-1-0	Gene Stallings
6. Miami (FL)	10-2-0	Dennis Erickson
7. Florida	10-2-1	Steve Spurrier
8. Texas A&M	10-0-1	R.C. Slocum
9. Auburn	9-1-1	Terry Bowden
10. Utah	10-2-0	Ron McBride
11. Oregon	9-4-0	Rich Brooks
12. Michigan	8-4-0	Gary Moeller
13. Southern Cal	8-3-1	John Robinson
14. Ohio St	9-4-0	John Cooper
15. Virginia	9-3-0	George Welsh
16. Colorado St	10-2-0	Sonny Lubick
17. N Carolina St	9-3-0	Mike O'Cain
18. Brigham Young	10-3-0	LaVell Edwards
19. Kansas St	9-3-0	Bill Snyder
20. Arizona	8-4-0	Dick Tomey
21. Washington St	8-4-0	Mike Price
22. Tennessee	8-4-0	Phillip Fulmer
23. Boston College	7-4-1	Dan Henning
24. Mississippi St	8-4-0	Jackie Sherrill
25. Texas	8-4-0	John Mackovic

1995

	Record	Coach
1. Nebraska	12-0-0	Tom Osborne
2. Florida	12-1-0	Steve Spurrier
3. Tennessee	11-1-0	Phillip Fulmer
4. Florida St	10-2-0	Bobby Bowden
5. Colorado	10-2-0	Rick Neuheisel
6. Ohio St	11-2-0	John Cooper
7. Kansas St	10-2-0	Bill Snyder
8. Northwestern	10-2-0	Gary Barnett
9. Kansas	10-2-0	Glen Mason
10. Virginia Tech	10-2-0	Frank Beamer
11. Notre Dame	9-3-0	Lou Holtz
12. Southern Cal	9-2-1	John Robinson
13. Penn St	9-3-0	Joe Paterno
14. Texas	10-2-1	John Mackovic
15. Texas A&M	9-3-0	S.C. Slocum
16. Virginia	9-4-0	George Welsh
17. Michigan	9-4-0	Lloyd Carr
18. Oregon	9-3-0	Mike Bellotti
19. Syracuse	9-3-0	Paul Pasqualoni
20. Miami (FL)	8-3-0	Butch Davis
21. Alabama	8-3-0	Gene Stallings
22. Auburn	8-4-0	Terry Bowden
23. Texas Tech	9-3-0	Spike Dykes
24. Toledo	11-0-1	Gary Pinkel
25. Iowa	8-4-0	Hayden Fry

1996

	Record*	Coach
1. Florida	12–1	Steve Spurrier
2. Ohio St	11–1	John Cooper
3. Florida St	11–1	Bobby Bowden
4. Arizona St	11–1	Bruce Snyder
5. Brigham Young	14–1	LaVell Edwards
6. Nebraska	11–2	Tom Osborne
7. Penn St	11–2	Joe Paterno
8. Colorado	10–2	Rick Neuheisel
9. Tennessee	10–2	Phillip Fulmer
10. N Carolina	10–2	Mack Brown
11. Alabama	10–3	Gene Stallings
12. Louisiana St	10–2	Gerry DiNardo
13. Virginia Tech	10–2	Frank Beamer
14. Miami (FL)	9–3	Butch Davis
15. Northwestern	9–3	Gary Barnett
16. Washington	9–3	Jim Lambright
17. Kansas St	9–3	Bill Snyder
18. Iowa	9–3	Hayden Fry
19. Notre Dame	8–3	Lou Holtz
20. Michigan	8–4	Lloyd Carr
21. Syracuse	9–3	Paul Pasqualoni
22. Wyoming	10–2	Joe Tiller
23. Texas	8–5	John Mackovic
24. Auburn	8–4	Terry Bowden
25. Army	10–2	Bob Sutton

1997

	Record	Coach
1. Michigan	12–0	Lloyd Carr
2. Nebraska	13–0	Tom Osborne
3. Florida St	11–1	Bobby Bowden
4. Florida	10–2	Steve Spurrier
5. UCLA	10–2	Bob Toledo
6. N Carolina	11–1	Mack Brown
7. Tennessee	11–2	Phillip Fulmer
8. Kansas St	11–1	Bill Snyder

†In 1989 the AP expanded its final poll to 25 teams.
*In 1996 the NCAA introduced overtime to break ties.

1997 (Cont.)

		Record	Coach
9.	Washington St	10–2	Mike Price
10.	Georgia	10–2	Jim Donnan
11.	Auburn	10–3	Terry Bowden
12.	Ohio St	10–3	John Cooper
13.	Louisiana St	9–3	Gerry DiNardo
14.	Arizona St	8–3	Bruce Snyder
15.	Purdue	9–3	Joe Tiller
16.	Penn St	9–3	Joe Paterno
17.	Colorado St	11–2	Sonny Lubick
18.	Washington	8–4	Jim Lambright
19.	Southern Mississippi	9–3	Jeff Bower
20.	Texas A&M	9–4	R. C. Slocum
21.	Syracuse	9–4	Paul Pasqualoni
22.	Mississippi	8–4	Tommy Tuberville
23.	Missouri	7–5	Larry Smith
24.	Oklahoma St	8–4	Bob Simmons
25.	Georgia Tech	7–5	George O'Leary

1998

		Record	Coach
1.	Tennessee	13–0	Phillip Fulmer
2.	Ohio St	11–1	John Cooper
3.	Florida St	11–2	Bobby Bowden
4.	Arizona	12–1	Dick Tomey
5.	Florida	10–2	Steve Spurrier
6.	Wisconsin	11–1	Barry Alvarez
7.	Tulane	12–0	Tommy Bowden
8.	UCLA	10–2	Bob Toledo
9.	Georgia Tech	10–2	George O'Leary
10.	Kansas St	11–2	Bill Snyder
11.	Texas A&M	11–3	R.C. Slocum
12.	Michigan	10–3	Lloyd Carr
13.	Air Force	12–1	Fisher DeBerry
14.	Georgia	9–3	Jim Donnan
15.	Texas	9–3	Mack Brown
16.	Arkansas	9–3	Houston Nutt
17.	Penn St	9–3	Joe Paterno
18.	Virginia	9–3	George Welsh
19.	Nebraska	9–4	Frank Solich
20.	Miami (FL)	9–3	Butch Davis
21.	Missouri	8–4	Larry Smith
22.	Notre Dame	9–3	Bob Davie
23.	Virginia Tech	9–3	Frank Beamer
24.	Purdue	9–4	Joe Tiller
25.	Syracuse	8–4	Paul Pasqualoni

1999

		Record	Coach
1.	Florida St	12–0	Bobby Bowden
2.	Virginia Tech	11–1	Frank Beamer
3.	Nebraska	12–1	Frank Solich
4.	Wisconsin	10–2	Barry Alvarez
5.	Michigan	10–2	Lloyd Carr
6.	Kansas St	11–1	Bill Snyder
7.	Michigan St	10–2	Nick Saban
8.	Alabama	10–3	Mike DuBose
9.	Tennessee	9–3	Phillip Fulmer
10.	Marshall	13–0	Bob Pruett
11.	Penn St	10–3	Joe Paterno
12.	Florida	9–4	Steve Spurrier
13.	Mississippi St	10–2	Jackie Sherrill
14.	Southern Miss	9–3	Jeff Bower
15.	Miami (FL)	9–4	Butch Davis
16.	Georgia	8–4	Jim Donnan
17.	Arkansas	8–4	Houston Nutt

1999 (Cont.)

		Record	Coach
18.	Minnesota	8–4	Glen Mason
19.	Oregon	9–3	Mike Bellotti
20.	Georgia Tech	8–4	Goerge O'Leary
21.	Texas	9–5	Mack Brown
22.	Mississippi	8–4	David Cutcliffe
23.	Texas A&M	8–4	R.C. Slocum
24.	Illinois	8–4	Ron Turner
25.	Purdue	7–5	Joe Tiller

2000

		Record	Coach
1.	Oklahoma	13–0	Bob Stoops
2.	Miami (FL)	11–1	Butch Davis
3.	Washington	11–1	Rick Neuheisel
4.	Oregon St	11–1	Dennis Erickson
5.	Florida St	11–2	Bobby Bowden
6.	Virginia Tech	11–1	Frank Beamer
7.	Oregon	10–2	Mike Belotti
8.	Nebraska	10–2	Frank Solich
9.	Kansas St	11–3	Bill Snyder
10.	Florida	10–3	Steve Spurrier
11.	Michigan	9–3	Lloyd Carr
12.	Texas	9–3	Mack Brown
13.	Purdue	8–4	Joe Tiller
14.	Colorado St	10–2	Sonny Lubick
15.	Notre Dame	9–3	Bob Davie
16.	Clemson	9–3	Tommy Bowden
17.	Georgia Tech	9–3	George O'Leary
18.	Auburn	9–4	Tommy Tuberville
19.	S Carolina	8–4	Lou Holtz
20.	Georgia	8–4	Jim Donnan
21.	Texas Christian	10–2	Dennis Franchione
22.	Louisiana State	8–4	Nick Saban
23.	Wisconsin	9–4	Barry Alvarez
24.	Mississippi St	8–4	Jackie Sherrill
25.	Iowa St	9–3	Dan McCarney

2001

		Record	Coach
1.	Miami (FL)	12–0	Larry Coker
2.	Oregon	11–1	Mike Belotti
3.	Florida	10–2	Steve Spurrier
4.	Tennessee	11–2	Phillip Fulmer
5.	Texas	11–2	Mack Brown
6.	Oklahoma	11–2	Bob Stoops
7.	Louisiana St	10–3	Nick Saban
8.	Nebraska	11–2	Frank Solich
9.	Colorado	10–3	Gary Barnett
10.	Washington St	10–2	Mike Price
11.	Maryland	10–2	Ralph Friedgen
12.	Illinois	10–2	Ron Turner
13.	S Carolina	9–3	Lou Holtz
14.	Syracuse	10–3	Paul Pasqualoni
15.	Florida St	8–4	Bobby Bowden
16.	Stanford	9–3	Tyrone Willingham
17.	Louisville	11–2	John Smith
18.	Virginia Tech	8–4	Frank Beamer
19.	Washington	8–4	Rick Neuheisel
20.	Michigan	8–4	Lloyd Carr
21.	Boston College	8–4	Tom O'Brien
22.	Georgia	8–4	Mark Richt
23.	Toledo	10–2	Tom Amstutz
24.	Georgia Tech	8–5	George O'Leary
25.	Brigham Young	12–2	Gary Crowton

Division I-AA

Year	Winner	Runner-Up	Score
1978	Florida A&M	Massachusetts	35–28
1979	Eastern Kentucky	Lehigh	30–7
1980	Boise St	Eastern Kentucky	31–29
1981	Idaho St	Eastern Kentucky	34–23
1982	Eastern Kentucky	Delaware	17–14
1983	Southern Illinois	Western Carolina	43–7
1984	Montana St	Louisiana Tech	19–6
1985	Georgia Southern	Furman	44–42
1986	Georgia Southern	Arkansas St	48–21
1987	NE Louisiana	Marshall	43–42
1988	Furman	Georgia Southern	17–12
1989	Georgia Southern	Stephen F. Austin St	37–34
1990	Georgia Southern	NV-Reno	36–13
1991	Youngstown St	Marshall	25–17
1992	Marshall	Youngstown St	31–28
1993	Youngstown St	Marshall	17–5
1994	Youngstown St	Boise St	28–14
1995	Montana	Marshall	22–20
1996	Marshall	Montana	49–29
1997	Youngstown St	McNesse St	10–9
1998	Massachusetts	Georgia Southern	55–43
1999	Georgia Southern	Youngstown St	59–24
2000	Georgia Southern	Montana	27–25
2001	Montana	Furman	13–6

Division II

Year	Winner	Runner-Up	Score
1973	Louisiana Tech	Western Kentucky	34–0
1974	Central Michigan	Delaware	54–14
1975	Northern Michigan	Western Kentucky	16–14
1976	Montana St	Akron	24–13
1977	Lehigh	Jacksonville St	33–0
1978	Eastern Illinois	Delaware	10–9
1979	Delaware	Youngstown St	38–21
1980	Cal Poly SLO	Eastern Illinois	21–13
1981	SW Texas St	N Dakota St	42–13
1982	SW Texas St	UC–Davis	34–9
1983	N Dakota St	Central St (OH)	41–21
1984	Troy St	N Dakota St	18–17
1985	N Dakota St	N Alabama	35–7
1986	N Dakota St	S Dakota	27–7
1987	Troy St	Portland St	31–17
1988	N Dakota St	Portland St	35–21
1989	Mississippi College	Jacksonville St	3–0
1990	N Dakota St	Indiana (PA)	51–11
1991	Pittsburg St	Jacksonville St	23–6
1992	Jacksonville St	Pittsburg St	17–13
1993	N Alabama	Indiana (PA)	41–34
1994	N Alabama	Texas A&M–Kingsville	16–10
1995	N Alabama	Pittsburg St	27–7
1996	Northern Colorado	Carson-Newman	23–14
1997	Northern Colorado	New Haven	51–0
1998	NW Missouri St	Carson-Newman	24–6
1999	NW Missouri St	Carson-Newman	58–52 (OT)
2000	Delta St	Bloomsburg	63–34
2001	Grand Valley St	N Dakota	17–14

Division III

1973	Wittenberg	Juniata	41–0
1974	Central (IA)	Ithaca	10–8
1975	Wittenberg	Ithaca	28–0
1976	St. John's (MN)	Towson St	31–28
1977	Widener	Wabash	39–36
1978	Baldwin-Wallace	Wittenberg	24–10
1979	Ithaca	Wittenberg	14–10
1980	Dayton	Ithaca	63–0
1981	Widener	Dayton	17–10
1982	W Georgia	Augustana (IL)	14–0
1983	Augustana (IL)	Union (NY)	21–17

Division III *(Cont.)*

Year	Winner	Runner-Up	Score
1984	Augustana (IL)	Central (IA)	21–12
1985	Augustana (IL)	Ithaca	20–7
1986	Augustana (IL)	Salisbury St	31–3
1987	Wagner	Dayton	19–3
1988	Ithaca	Central (IA)	39–24
1989	Dayton	Union (NY)	17–7
1990	Allegheny	Lycoming	21–14 (OT)
1991	Ithaca	Dayton	34–20
1992	WI-LaCrosse	Washington & Jefferson	16–12
1993	Mount Union	Rowan	34–24
1994	Albion	Washington & Jefferson	38–15
1995	WI-LaCrosse	Rowan	36–7
1996	Mount Union	Rowan	56–24
1997	Mount Union	Lycoming	61–12
1998	Mount Union	Rowan	44–24
1999	Pacific Lutheran	Rowan	42–13
2000	Mount Union	St. John's	10–7
2001	Mount Union	Bridgewater	30–27

NAIA Divisional Championships

Division I

Year	Winner	Runner-Up	Score
1956	St. Joseph's (IN)/ Montana St		0–0
1957	Pittsburg St (KS)	Hillsdale (MI)	27–26
1958	NE Oklahoma	Northern Arizona	19–13
1959	Texas A&I	Lenoir-Rhyne (NC)	20–7
1960	Lenoir-Rhyne (NC)	Humboldt St (CA)	15–14
1961	Pittsburg St (KS)	Linfield (OR)	12–7
1962	Central St (OK)	Lenoir-Rhyne (NC)	28–13
1963	St. John's (MN)	Prairie View (TX)	33–27
1964	Concordia-Moorhead/ Sam Houston		7–7
1965	St. John's (MN)	Linfield (OR)	33–0
1966	Waynesburg (PA)	WI-Whitewater	42–21
1967	Fairmont St (WV)	Eastern Washington	28–21
1968	Troy St (MI)	Texas A&I	43–35
1969	Texas A&I	Concordia-Moorhead (MN)	32–7
1970	Texas A&I	Wofford (SC)	48–7
1971	Livingston (AL)	Arkansas Tech	14–12
1972	E Texas St	Carson-Newman (TN)	21–18
1973	Abilene Christian	Elon (NC)	42–14
1974	Texas A&I	Henderson St (AR)	34–23
1975	Texas A&I	Salem (WV)	37–0
1976	Texas A&I	Central Arkansas	26–0
1977	Abilene Christian	SW Oklahoma	24–7
1978	Angelo St (TX)	Elon (NC)	34–14
1979	Texas A&I	Central St (OK)	20–14
1980	Elon (NC)	NE Oklahoma	17–10
1981	Elon (NC)	Pittsburg St	3–0
1982	Central St (OK)	Mesa (CO)	14–11
1983	Carson-Newman (TN)	Mesa (CO)	36–28
1984	Carson-Newman (TN)/Central Arkansas		19–19
1985	Central Arkansas/ Hillsdale (MI)		10–10
1986	Carson-Newman (TN)	Cameron (OK)	17–0
1987	Cameron (OK)	Carson-Newman (TN)	30–2
1988	Carson-Newman (TN)	Adams St (CO)	56–21
1989	Carson-Newman (TN)	Emporia St (KS)	34–20
1990	Central St (OH)	Mesa St (CO)	38–16
1991	Central Arkansas	Central St (OH)	19–16
1992	Central St (OH)	Gardner-Webb (NC)	19–16
1993	E Central (OK)	Glenville St (WV)	49–35
1994	Northeastern St (OK)	Arkansas–Pine Bluff	13–12
1995	Central St (OH)	Northeastern St (OK)	37–7
1996	SW Oklahoma St	Montana Tech	33–31
1997	Findlay (OH)	Willamette (OR)	14–7
1998	Azusa Pacific	Olivet Nazarene	17–14
1999	Northwestern Oklahoma St	Georgetown (KY)	34–26
2000	Georgetown (KY)	Northwestern Oklahoma St	20–0
2001	Georgetown (KY)	Sioux Falls	49–27

Division II

Year	Winner	Runner-Up	Score
1970	Westminster (PA)	Anderson (IN)	21–16
1971	California Lutheran	Westminster (PA)	30–14
1972	Missouri Southern	Northwestern (IA)	21–14
1973	Northwestern (IA)	Glenville St (WV)	10–3
1974	Texas Lutheran	Missouri Valley	42–0
1975	Texas Lutheran	California Lutheran	34–8
1976	Westminster (PA)	Redlands (CA)	20–13
1977	Westminster (PA)	California Lutheran	17–9
1978	Concordia-Moorhead (MN)	Findlay (OH)	7–0
1979	Findlay (OH)	Northwestern (IA)	51–6
1980	Pacific Lutheran	Wilmington (OH)	38–10
1981	Austin Coll./ Conc.-Moorhead (MN)		24–24
1982	Linfield (OR)	William Jewell (MO)	33–15
1983	Northwestern (IA)	Pacific Lutheran	25–21
1984	Linfield (OR)	Northwestern (IA)	33–22
1985	WI-La Crosse	Pacific Lutheran	24–7
1986	Linfield (OR)	Baker (KS)	17–0
1987	Pacific Lutheran	WI-Stevens Point*	16–16
1988	Westminster (PA)	WI-La Crosse	21–14
1989	Westminster (PA)	WI-La Crosse	51–30
1990	Peru St (NE)	Westminster (PA)	17–7
1991	Georgetown (KY)	Pacific Lutheran	28–20
1992	Findlay (OH)	Linfield (OR)	26–13
1993	Pacific Lutheran (WA)	Westminster (PA)	50–20
1994	Westminster (PA)	Pacific Lutheran	27–7
1995	Findlay (OH)/ Central Washington		21–21
1996	Sioux Falls (SD)	Western Washington	47–25

*Forfeited 1987 season due to use of an ineligible player.   †In 1997 the NAIA consolidated its two divisions into one.

Awards

Heisman Memorial Trophy

Awarded to the best college player by the Downtown Athletic Club of New York City. The trophy is named after John W. Heisman, who coached Georgia Tech to the national championship in 1917 and later served as DAC athletic director.

Year	Winner, College, Position	Winner's Season Statistics	Runner-Up, College
1935	Jay Berwanger, Chicago, HB	Rush: 119 Yds: 577 TD: 6	Monk Meyer, Army
1936	Larry Kelley, Yale, E	Rec: 17 Yds: 372 TD: 6	Sam Francis, Nebraska
1937	Clint Frank, Yale, HB	Rush: 157 Yds: 667 TD: 11	Byron White, Colorado
1938	†Davey O'Brien, Texas Christian, QB	Att/Comp: 194/110 Yds: 1733 TD: 19	Marshall Goldberg, Pittsburgh
1939	Nile Kinnick, Iowa, HB	Rush: 106 Yds: 374 TD: 5	Tom Harmon, Michigan
1940	Tom Harmon, Michigan, HB	Rush: 191 Yds: 852 TD: 16	John Kimbrough, Texas A&M
1941	†Bruce Smith, Minnesota, HB	Rush: 98 Yds: 480 TD: 6	Angelo Bertelli, Notre Dame
1942	Frank Sinkwich, Georgia, HB	Att/Comp: 166/84 Yds: 1392 TD: 10	Paul Governali, Columbia
1943	Angelo Bertelli, Notre Dame, QB	Att/Comp: 36/25 Yds: 511 TD: 10	Bob Odell, Pennsylvania
1944	Les Horvath, Ohio State, QB	Rush: 163 Yds: 924 TD: 12	Glenn Davis, Army
1945	*†Doc Blanchard, Army, FB	Rush: 101 Yds: 718 TD: 13	Glenn Davis, Army
1946	Glenn Davis, Army, HB	Rush: 123 Yds: 712 TD: 7	Charley Trippi, Georgia
1947	†John Lujack, Notre Dame, QB	Att/Comp: 109/61 Yds: 777 TD: 9	Bob Chappius, Michigan
1948	*Doak Walker, Southern Methodist, HB	Rush: 108 Yds: 532 TD: 8	Charlie Justice, N Carolina
1949	†Leon Hart, Notre Dame, E	Rec: 19 Yds: 257 TD: 5	Charlie Justice, N Carolina
1950	*Vic Janowicz, Ohio St, HB	Att/Comp: 77/32 Yds: 561 TD: 12	Kyle Rote, Southern Methodist
1951	Dick Kazmaier, Princeton, HB	Rush: 149 Yds: 861 TD: 9	Hank Lauricella, Tennessee
1952	Billy Vessels, Oklahoma, HB	Rush: 167 Yds: 1072 TD: 17	Jack Scarbath, Maryland
1953	John Lattner, Notre Dame, HB	Rush: 134 Yds: 651 TD: 6	Paul Giel, Minnesota
1954	Alan Ameche, Wisconsin, FB	Rush: 146 Yds: 641 TD: 9	Kurt Burris, Oklahoma
1955	Howard Cassady, Ohio St, HB	Rush: 161 Yds: 958 TD: 15	Jim Swink, Texas Christian
1956	Paul Hornung, Notre Dame, QB	Att/Comp: 111/59 Yds: 917 TD: 3	Johnny Majors, Tennessee
1957	John David Crow, Texas A&M, HB	Rush: 129 Yds: 562 TD: 10	Alex Karras, Iowa
1958	Pete Dawkins, Army, HB	Rush: 78 Yds: 428 TD: 6	Randy Duncan, Iowa

Heisman Memorial Trophy (Cont.)

Year	Winner, College, Position	Winner's Season Statistics	Runner-Up, College
1959	Billy Cannon, Louisiana St, HB	Rush: 139 Yds: 598 TD: 6	Rich Lucas, Penn St
1960	Joe Bellino, Navy, HB	Rush: 168 Yds: 834 TD: 18	Tom Brown, Minnesota
1961	Ernie Davis, Syracuse, HB	Rush: 150 Yds: 823 TD: 15	Bob Ferguson, Ohio St
1962	Terry Baker, Oregon St, QB	Att/Comp: 203/112 Yds: 1738 TD: 15	Jerry Stovall, Louisiana St
1963	*Roger Staubach, Navy, QB	Att/Comp: 161/107 Yds: 1474 TD: 7	Billy Lothridge, Georgia Tech
1964	John Huarte, Notre Dame, QB	Att/Comp: 205/114 Yds: 2062 TD: 16	Jerry Rhome, Tulsa
1965	Mike Garrett, Southern Cal, HB	Rush: 267 Yds: 1440 TD: 16	Howard Twilley, Tulsa
1966	Steve Spurrier, Florida, QB	Att/Comp: 291/179 Yds: 2012 TD: 16	Bob Griese, Purdue
1967	Gary Beban, UCLA, QB	Att/Comp: 156/87 Yds: 1359 TD: 8	O.J. Simpson, Southern Cal
1968	O.J. Simpson, Southern Cal, HB	Rush: 383 Yds: 1880 TD: 23	Leroy Keyes, Purdue
1969	Steve Owens, Oklahoma, FB	Rush: 358 Yds: 1523 TD: 23	Mike Phipps, Purdue
1970	Jim Plunkett, Stanford, QB	Att/Comp: 358/191 Yds: 2715 TD: 18	Joe Theismann, Notre Dame
1971	Pat Sullivan, Auburn, QB	Att/Comp: 281/162 Yds: 2012 TD: 20	Ed Marinaro, Cornell
1972	Johnny Rodgers, Nebraska, FL	Rec: 55 Yds: 942 TD: 17	Greg Pruitt, Oklahoma
1973	John Cappelletti, Penn St, HB	Rush: 286 Yds: 1522 TD: 17	John Hicks, Ohio St
1974	*Archie Griffin, Ohio St, HB	Rush: 256 Yds: 1695 TD: 12	Anthony Davis, Southern Cal
1975	Archie Griffin, Ohio St, HB	Rush: 262 Yds: 1450 TD: 4	Chuck Muncie, California
1976	†Tony Dorsett, Pittsburgh, HB	Rush: 370 Yds: 2150 TD: 23	Ricky Bell, Southern Cal
1977	Earl Campbell, Texas, FB	Rush: 267 Yds: 1744 TD: 19	Terry Miller, Oklahoma St
1978	*Billy Sims, Oklahoma, HB	Rush: 231 Yds: 1762 TD: 20	Chuck Fusina, Penn St
1979	Charles White, Southern Cal, HB	Rush: 332 Yds: 1803 TD: 19	Billy Sims, Oklahoma
1980	George Rogers, S Carolina, HB	Rush: 324 Yds: 1894 TD: 14	Hugh Green, Pittsburgh
1981	Marcus Allen, Southern Cal, HB	Rush: 433 Yds: 2427 TD: 23	Herschel Walker, Georgia
1982	*Herschel Walker, Georgia, HB	Rush: 335 Yds: 1752 TD: 17	John Elway, Stanford
1983	Mike Rozier, Nebraska, HB	Rush: 275 Yds: 2148 TD: 29	Steve Young, Brigham Young
1984	Doug Flutie, Boston College, QB	Att/Comp: 396/233 Yds: 3454 TD: 27	Keith Byars, Ohio St
1985	Bo Jackson, Auburn, HB	Rush: 278 Yds: 1786 TD: 17	Chuck Long, Iowa
1986	Vinny Testaverde, Miami (FL), QB	Att/Comp: 276/175 Yds: 2557 TD: 26	Paul Palmer, Temple
1987	Tim Brown, Notre Dame, WR	Rec: 39 Yds: 846 TD: 7	Don McPherson, Syracuse
1988	*Barry Sanders, Oklahoma St, RB	Rush: 344 Yds: 2628 TD: 39	Rodney Peete, Southern Cal
1989	*Andre Ware, Houston, QB	Att/Comp: 578/365 Yds: 4699 TD: 46	Anthony Thompson, Indiana
1990	*Ty Detmer, Brigham Young, QB	Att/Comp: 562/361 Yds: 5188 TD: 41	Raghib Ismail, Notre Dame
1991	*Desmond Howard, Michigan, WR	Rec: 61 Yds: 950 TD: 23	Casey Weldon, Florida St
1992	Gino Torretta, Miami (FL), QB	Att/Comp: 402/228 Yds: 3060 TD: 19	Marshall Faulk, San Diego St
1993	†Charlie Ward, Florida St, QB	Att/Comp: 380/264 Yds: 3032 TD: 27	Heath Shuler, Tennessee
1994	Rashaan Salaam, Colorado, RB	Rush: 298 Yds: 2055 TD: 24	Ki-Jana Carter, Penn St
1995	Eddie George, Ohio State, RB	Rush: 303 Yds: 1826 TD: 23	Tommie Frazier, Nebraska
1996	†Danny Wuerffel, Florida, QB	Att/Comp: 360/207 Yds: 3625 TD: 39	Troy Davis, Iowa St
1997	†Charles Woodson, Michigan, CB/ WR	7 interceptions; Rec: 11 Yds: 231 TD: 4	Peyton Manning, Tennessee
1998	Ricky Williams, Texas, RB	Rush: 361 Yds: 2124 TD: 28	Michael Bishop, Kansas St
1999	Ron Dayne, Wisconsin, RB	Rush: 303 Yds: 1834 TD: 19	Joe Hamilton, Georgia Tech
2000	Chris Weinke, Florida St, QB	Att/Comp: 431/266 Yds: 4167 TD: 33	Josh Heupel, Oklahoma
2001	Eric Crouch, Nebraska, QB	Att/Comp: 189/105 Yds: 1510 TD: 7; Rush: 1115 Yds, 18 TD	Rex Grossman, Florida

*Juniors (all others seniors). †Winners who played for national championship teams the same year.

Note: Former Heisman winners and national media cast votes, with ballots allowing for three names (3 points for first, 2 for second and 1 for third).

Maxwell Award

Given to the nation's outstanding college football player by the Maxwell Football Club of Philadelphia.

Year	Player, College, Position	Year	Player, College, Position
1937	Clint Frank, Yale, HB	1970	Jim Plunkett, Stanford, QB
1938	Davey O'Brien, Texas Christian, QB	1971	Ed Marinaro, Cornell, RB
1939	Nile Kinnick, Iowa, HB	1972	Brad Van Pelt, Michigan St, DB
1940	Tom Harmon, Michigan, HB	1973	John Cappelletti, Penn St, RB
1941	Bill Dudley, Virginia, HB	1974	Steve Joachim, Temple, QB
1942	Paul Governali, Columbia, QB	1975	Archie Griffin, Ohio St, RB
1943	Bob Odell, Pennsylvania, HB	1976	Tony Dorsett, Pittsburgh, RB
1944	Glenn Davis, Army, HB	1977	Ross Browner, Notre Dame, DE
1945	Doc Blanchard, Army, FB	1978	Chuck Fusina, Penn St, QB
1946	Charley Trippi, Georgia, HB	1979	Charles White, Southern Cal, RB
1947	Doak Walker, Southern Meth, HB	1980	Hugh Green, Pittsburgh, DE
1948	Chuck Bednarik, Pennsylvania, C	1981	Marcus Allen, Southern Cal, RB
1949	Leon Hart, Notre Dame, E	1982	Herschel Walker, Georgia, RB
1950	Reds Bagnell, Pennsylvania, HB	1983	Mike Rozier, Nebraska, RB
1951	Dick Kazmaier, Princeton, HB	1984	Doug Flutie, Boston College, QB
1952	John Lattner, Notre Dame, HB	1985	Chuck Long, Iowa, QB
1953	John Lattner, Notre Dame, HB	1986	Vinny Testaverde, Miami (FL), QB
1954	Ron Beagle, Navy, E	1987	Don McPherson, Syracuse, QB
1955	Howard Cassady, Ohio St, HB	1988	Barry Sanders, Oklahoma St, RB
1956	Tommy McDonald, Oklahoma, HB	1989	Anthony Thompson, Indiana, RB
1957	Bob Reifsnyder, Navy, T	1990	Ty Detmer, Brigham Young, QB
1958	Pete Dawkins, Army, HB	1991	Desmond Howard, Michigan, WR
1959	Rich Lucas, Penn St, QB	1992	Gino Torretta, Miami (FL), QB
1960	Joe Bellino, Navy, HB	1993	Charlie Ward, Florida St, QB
1961	Bob Ferguson, Ohio St, FB	1994	Kerry Collins, Penn St, QB
1962	Terry Baker, Oregon St, QB	1995	Eddie George, Ohio St, RB
1963	Roger Staubach, Navy, QB	1996	Danny Wuerffel, Florida, QB
1964	Glenn Ressler, Penn St, C	1997	Peyton Manning, Tennessee, QB
1965	Tommy Nobis, Texas, LB	1998	Ricky Williams, Texas, RB
1966	Jim Lynch, Notre Dame, LB	1999	Ron Dayne, Wisconsin, RB
1967	Gary Beban, UCLA, QB	2000	Drew Brees, Purdue, QB
1968	O.J. Simpson, Southern Cal, RB	2001	Ken Dorsey, Miami (FL), QB
1969	Mike Reid, Penn St, DT		

Davey O'Brien National Quarterback Award

Given to the top quarterback in the nation by the Davey O'Brien Educational and Charitable Trust of Fort Worth. Named for Texas Christian Hall of Fame quarterback Davey O'Brien (1936–38).

Year	Player, College	Year	Player, College
1981	Jim McMahon, Brigham Young	1992	Gino Torretta, Miami (FL)
1982	Todd Blackledge, Penn St	1993	Charlie Ward, Florida St
1983	Steve Young, Brigham Young	1994	Kerry Collins, Penn St
1984	Doug Flutie, Boston College	1995	Danny Wuerffel, Florida
1985	Chuck Long, Iowa	1996	Danny Wuerffel, Florida
1986	Vinny Testaverde, Miami (FL)	1997	Peyton Manning, Tennessee
1987	Don McPherson, Syracuse	1998	Michael Bishop, Kansas St
1988	Troy Aikman, UCLA	1999	Joe Hamilton, Georgia Tech
1989	Andre Ware, Houston	2000	Chris Weinke, Florida St
1990	Ty Detmer, Brigham Young	2001	Eric Crouch, Nebraska
1991	Ty Detmer, Brigham Young		

Note: Originally honored the outstanding football player in the Southwest as follows: 1977—Earl Campbell, Texas, RB; 1978—Billy Sims, Oklahoma, RB; 1979—Mike Singletary, Baylor, LB; 1980—Mike Singletary, Baylor, LB.

Vince Lombardi/Rotary Award

Given to the outstanding college lineman of the year, the award is sponsored by the Rotary Club of Houston.

Year	Player, College, Position	Year	Player, College, Position
1970	Jim Stillwagon, Ohio St, MG	1984	Tony Degrate, Texas, DT
1971	Walt Patulski, Notre Dame, DE	1985	Tony Casillas, Oklahoma, NG
1972	Rich Glover, Nebraska, MG	1986	Cornelius Bennett, Alabama, LB
1973	John Hicks, Ohio St, OT	1987	Chris Spielman, Ohio St, LB
1974	Randy White, Maryland, DT	1988	Tracy Rocker, Auburn, DT
1975	Lee Roy Selmon, Oklahoma, DT	1989	Percy Snow, Michigan St, LB
1976	Wilson Whitley, Houston, DT	1990	Chris Zorich, Notre Dame, NG
1977	Ross Browner, Notre Dame, DE	1991	Steve Emtman, Washington, DT
1978	Bruce Clark, Penn St, DT	1992	Marvin Jones, Florida St, LB
1979	Brad Budde, Southern Cal, G	1993	Aaron Taylor, Notre Dame, OT
1980	Hugh Green, Pittsburgh, DE	1994	Warren Sapp, Miami (FL), DT
1981	Kenneth Sims, Texas, DT	1995	Orlando Pace, Ohio St, OT
1982	Dave Rimington, Nebraska, C	1996	Orlando Pace, Ohio St, OT
1983	Dean Steinkuhler, Nebraska, G	1997	Grant Wistrom, Nebraska, DE

Lombardi Trophy (Cont.)

Year	Player, College, Position	Year	Player, College, Position
1998	Dat Nguyen, Texas A&M, LB	2000	Jamal Reynolds, Florida St, DE
1999	Corey Moore, Virginia Tech, DE	2001	Julius Peppers, N Carolina, DE

Outland Trophy

Given to the outstanding interior lineman, selected by the Football Writers Association of America.

Year	Player, College, Position	Year	Player, College, Position
1946	George Connor, Notre Dame, T	1974	Randy White, Maryland, DE
1947	Joe Steffy, Army, G	1975	Lee Roy Selmon, Oklahoma, DT
1948	Bill Fischer, Notre Dame, G	1976	Ross Browner, Notre Dame, DE
1949	Ed Bagdon, Michigan St, G	1977	Brad Shearer, Texas, DT
1950	Bob Gain, Kentucky, T	1978	Greg Roberts, Oklahoma, G
1951	Jim Weatherall, Oklahoma, T	1979	Jim Ritcher, N Carolina St, C
1952	Dick Modzelewski, Maryland, T	1980	Mark May, Pittsburgh, OT
1953	J.D. Roberts, Oklahoma, G	1981	Dave Rimington, Nebraska, C
1954	Bill Brooks, Arkansas, G	1982	Dave Rimington, Nebraska, C
1955	Calvin Jones, Iowa, G	1983	Dean Steinkuhler, Nebraska, G
1956	Jim Parker, Ohio St, G	1984	Bruce Smith, Virginia Tech, DT
1957	Alex Karras, Iowa, T	1985	Mike Ruth, Boston College, NG
1958	Zeke Smith, Auburn, G	1986	Jason Buck, Brigham Young, DT
1959	Mike McGee, Duke, T	1987	Chad Hennings, Air Force, DT
1960	Tom Brown, Minnesota, G	1988	Tracy Rocker, Auburn, DT
1961	Merlin Olsen, Utah St, T	1989	Mohammed Elewonibi, Brigham Young, G
1962	Bobby Bell, Minnesota, T	1990	Russell Maryland, Miami (FL), DT
1963	Scott Appleton, Texas, T	1991	Steve Emtman, Washington, DT
1964	Steve DeLong, Tennessee, T	1992	Will Shields, Nebraska, G
1965	Tommy Nobis, Texas, G	1993	Rob Waldrop, Arizona, NG
1966	Loyd Phillips, Arkansas, T	1994	Zach Wiegert, Nebraska, G
1967	Ron Yary, Southern Cal, T	1995	Jonathan Ogden, UCLA, OT
1968	Bill Stanfill, Georgia, T	1996	Orlando Pace, Ohio St, OT
1969	Mike Reid, Penn St, DT	1997	Aaron Taylor, Nebraska, G
1970	Jim Stillwagon, Ohio St, MG	1998	Kris Farris, UCLA, OL
1971	Larry Jacobson, Nebraska, DT	1999	Chris Samuels, Alabama, OL
1972	Rich Glover, Nebraska, MG	2000	John Henderson, Tennessee, DT
1973	John Hicks, Ohio St, OT	2001	Bryant McKinnie, Miami (FL), OT

Butkus Award

Given to the top collegiate linebacker, the award was established by the Downtown Athletic Club of Orlando and named for college Hall of Famer Dick Butkus of Illinois.

Year	Player, College	Year	Player, College
1985	Brian Bosworth, Oklahoma	1994	Dana Howard, Illinois
1986	Brian Bosworth, Oklahoma	1995	Kevin Hardy, Illinois
1987	Paul McGowan, Florida St	1996	Matt Russell, Colorado
1988	Derrick Thomas, Alabama	1997	Andy Katzenmoyer, Ohio St
1989	Percy Snow, Michigan St	1998	Chris Claiborne, Southern Cal
1990	Alfred Williams, Colorado	1999	LaVar Arrington, Penn St
1991	Erick Anderson, Michigan	2000	Dan Morgan, Miami (FL)
1992	Marvin Jones, Florida St	2001	Rocky Calmus, Oklahoma
1993	Trev Alberts, Nebraska		

Jim Thorpe Award

Given to the best defensive back of the year, the award is presented by the Jim Thorpe Athletic Club of Oklahoma City.

Year	Player, College	Year	Player, College
1986	Thomas Everett, Baylor	1994	Chris Hudson, Colorado
1987	Bennie Blades, Miami (FL)	1995	Greg Myers, Colorado St
	Rickey Dixon, Oklahoma	1996	Lawrence Wright, Florida
1988	Deion Sanders, Florida St	1997	Charles Woodson, Michigan
1989	Mark Carrier, Southern Cal	1998	Antoine Winfield, Ohio St
1990	Darryl Lewis, Arizona	1999	Tyrone Carter, Minnesota
1991	Terrell Buckley, Florida St	2000	Jamar Fletcher, Wisconsin
1992	Deon Figures, Colorado	2001	Roy Williams, Oklahoma
1993	Antonio Langham, Alabama		

Awards (Cont.)

Walter Payton Player of the Year Award

Given to the top Division I-AA player as voted by Division I-AA sports information directors. Sponsored by Sports Network.

Year	Player, College, Position	Year	Player, College, Position
1987	Kenny Gamble, Colgate, RB	1995	Dave Dickenson, Montana, QB
1988	Dave Meggett, Towson St, RB	1996	Archie Amerson, Northern Arizona, RB
1989	John Friesz, Idaho, QB	1997	Brian Finneran, Villanova, WR
1990	Walter Dean, Grambling, RB	1998	Jerry Azumah, New Hampshire, RB
1991	Jamie Martin, Weber St, QB	1999	Adrian Peterson, Georgia Southern, RB
1992	Michael Payton, Marshall, QB	2000	Louis Ivory, Furman, RB
1993	Doug Nussmeier, Idaho, QB	2001	Brian Westbrook, Villanova, RB
1994	Steve McNair, Alcorn St, QB		

NCAA Division I-A Individual Records

Career

SCORING

Most Points Scored: 468—Travis Prentice, Miami (OH), 1996–99

Most Points Scored per Game: 12.1—Marshall Faulk, San Diego St, 1991–93

Most Touchdowns Scored: 78—Travis Prentice, Miami (OH), 1996–99

Most Touchdowns Scored per Game: 2.0—Marshall Faulk, San Diego St, 1991–93

Most Touchdowns Scored, Rushing: 73—Travis Prentice, Miami (OH), 1996–99

Most Touchdowns Scored, Passing: 121—Ty Detmer, Brigham Young, 1988–91

Most Touchdowns Scored, Receiving: 50—Troy Edwards, Louisiana Tech, 1996–98

Most Touchdowns Scored, Interception Returns: 5—Ken Thomas, San Jose St, 1979–82; Jackie Walker, Tennessee, 1969–71; Deltha O'Neal, California, 1996–99

Most Touchdowns Scored, Punt Returns: 7—Johnny Rodgers, Nebraska, 1970–72; Jack Mitchell, Oklahoma, 1946–48; David Allen, Kansas St, 1997–99

Most Touchdowns Scored, Kickoff Returns: 6—Anthony Davis, Southern Cal, 1972–74

TOTAL OFFENSE

Most Plays: 1,917—Antwaan Randle El, Indiana, 1998–01

Most Plays per Game: 48.5—Doug Gaynor, Long Beach St, 1984–85

Most Yards Gained: 14,665—Ty Detmer, Brigham Young, 1988–91 (15,031 passing, -366 rushing)

Most Yards Gained per Game: 382.4—Tim Rattay, Louisiana Tech, 1997–99

Most 300+ Yard Games: 33—Ty Detmer, Brigham Young, 1988–91

RUSHING

Most Rushes: 1,215—Steve Bartalo, Colorado St, 1983–86 (4813 yds)

Most Rushes per Game: 34.0—Ed Marinaro, Cornell, 1969–71

Most Yards Gained: 6,397—Ron Dayne, Wisconsin, 1996–99

Most Yards Gained per Game: 174.6—Ed Marinaro, Cornell, 1969–71

Most 100+ Yard Games: 33—Tony Dorsett, Pittsburgh, 1973–76; Archie Griffin, Ohio St, 1972–75

Most 200+ Yard Games: 11—Marcus Allen, Southern Cal, 1978–81; Ricky Williams, Texas, 1995–98; Ron Dayne, Wisconsin, 1996–99

PASSING

Highest Passing Efficiency Rating: 163.6—Danny Wuerffel, Florida, 1993–96 (1,170 attempts, 708 completions, 42 interceptions, 10,875 yards, 114 touchdown passes)

Most Passes Attempted: 1,679—Chris Redman, Louisville, 1996–99

Most Passes Attempted per Game: 47.0—Tim Rattay, Louisiana Tech, 1997–99

Most Passes Completed: 1,031—Chris Redman, Louisville, 1996–99

Most Passes Completed per Game: 30.8—Tim Rattay, Louisiana Tech, 1997–99

*Highest Completion Percentage: 67.1—Tim Couch, Kentucky, 1996–98

Most Yards Gained: 15,031—Ty Detmer, Brigham Young, 1988–91

Most Yards Gained per Game: 386.2—Tim Rattay, Louisiana Tech, 1997–99

*Minimum 1,000 attempts.

RECEIVING

Most Passes Caught: 300—Arnold Jackson, Louisville, 1997–00

Most Passes Caught per Game: 10.5—Emmanuel Hazard, Houston, 1989–90

Most Yards Gained: 5,005—Trevor Insley, Nevada, 1996–99

Most Yards Gained per Game: 140.9—Alex Van Dyke, Nevada, 1994–95

Highest Average Gain per Reception: 25.7—Wesley Walker, California, 1973–75

Career (Cont.)

ALL-PURPOSE RUNNING

Most Plays: 1,347—Steve Bartalo, Colorado St, 1983-86 (1,215 rushes, 132 receptions)
Most Yards Gained: 7,206—Ricky Williams, Texas, 1995–98 (6,279 rushing, 927 receiving)
Most Yards Gained per Game: 237.8—Ryan Benjamin, Pacific, 1990–92
Highest Average Gain per Play: 17.4—Anthony Carter, Michigan, 1979–82

INTERCEPTIONS

Most Passes Intercepted: 29—Al Brosky, Illinois, 1950–52
Most Passes Intercepted per Game: 1.1—Al Brosky, Illinois, 1950–52
Most Yards on Interception Returns: 501—Terrell Buckley, Florida St, 1989–91
Highest Average Gain per Interception: 26.5—Tom Pridemore, W Virginia, 1975–77

SPECIAL TEAMS

Highest Punt Return Average: 23.6—Jack Mitchell, Oklahoma, 1946–48
Highest Kickoff Return Average: 36.2—Forrest Hall, San Francisco, 1946–47
Highest Average Yards per Punt: 46.3—Todd Sauerbrun, W Virginia, 1991–94

Single Season

SCORING

Most Points Scored: 234—Barry Sanders, Oklahoma St, 1988
Most Points Scored per Game: 21.3—Barry Sanders, Oklahoma St, 1988
Most Touchdowns Scored: 39—Barry Sanders, Oklahoma St, 1988
Most Touchdowns Scored, Rushing: 37—Barry Sanders, Oklahoma St, 1988
Most Touchdowns Scored, Passing: 54—David Klingler, Houston, 1990
Most Touchdowns Scored, Receiving: 27—Troy Edwards, Louisiana Tech, 1998
Most Touchdowns Scored, Interception Returns: 4—Deltha O'Neal, California, 1999
Most Touchdowns Scored, Punt Returns: 4—Santana Moss, Miami (FL), 2000; David Allen, Kansas St, 1998; Quinton Spotwood, Syracuse, 1997; Tinker Keck, Cincinnati, 1997; James Henry, Southern Miss, 1987; Golden Richards, Brigham Young, 1971; Cliff Branch, Colorado, 1971
Most Touchdowns Scored, Kickoff Returns: 3—Leland McElroy, Texas A&M, 1993; Terance Mathis, New Mexico, 1989; Willie Gault, Tennessee, 1980; Anthony Davis, Southern Cal, 1974; Stan Brown, Purdue, 1970; Forrest Hall, San Francisco, 1946

TOTAL OFFENSE

Most Plays: 704—David Klingler, Houston, 1990
Most Yards Gained: 5,221—David Klingler, Houston, 1990
Most Yards Gained per Game: 474.6—David Klingler, Houston, 1990
Most 300+ Yard Games: 12—Ty Detmer, Brigham Young, 1990

RUSHING

Most Rushes: 403—Marcus Allen, Southern Cal, 1981
Most Rushes per Game: 39.6—Ed Marinaro, Cornell, 1971
Most Yards Gained: 2,628—Barry Sanders, Oklahoma St, 1988
Most Yards Gained per Game: 238.9—Barry Sanders, Oklahoma St, 1988
Most 100+ Yard Games: 11—By 14 players, most recently Ahman Green, Nebraska, 1997

PASSING

Highest Passing Efficiency Rating: 183.3—Shaun King, Tulane, 1998 (328 attempts, 223 completions, 6 interceptions, 3,232 yards, 36 TD passes)
Most Passes Attempted: 643—David Klingler, Houston, 1990
Most Passes Attempted per Game: 58.5—David Klingler, Houston, 1990
Most Passes Completed: 400—Tim Couch, Kentucky, 1998
Most Passes Completed per Game: 36.4—Tim Couch, Kentucky, 1998
Highest Completion Percentage: 73.6—Daunte Culpepper, Central Florida, 1998
Most Yards Gained: (12 games) 5,188—Ty Detmer, Brigham Young, 1990; (11 games) 5,140—David Klingler, Houston, 1990
Most Yards Gained per Game: 467.3—David Klingler, Houston, 1990

RECEIVING

Most Passes Caught: 142—Emmanuel Hazard, Houston, 1989
Most Passes Caught per Game: 13.4—Howard Twilley, Tulsa, 1965
Most Yards Gained: 2,060—Trevor Insley, Nevada, 1999
Most Yards Gained per Game: 187.3—Trevor Insley, Nevada, 1999
Highest Average Gain per Reception: 27.9—Elmo Wright, Houston, 1968 (min. 30 receptions)

ALL-PURPOSE RUNNING

Most Plays: 432—Marcus Allen, Southern Cal, 1981
Most Yards Gained: 3,250—Barry Sanders, Oklahoma St, 1988
Most Yards Gained per Game: 295.5—Barry Sanders, Oklahoma St, 1988
Highest Average Gain per Play: 18.5—Henry Bailey, UNLV, 1992

Single Season *(Cont.)*

INTERCEPTIONS

Most Passes Intercepted: 14 — Al Worley, Washington, 1968
Most Yards on Interception Returns: 302 — Charles Phillips, Southern Cal, 1974
Highest Average Gain per Interception: 50.6 — Norm Thompson, Utah, 1969

SPECIAL TEAMS

Highest Punt Return Average: 25.9 — Bill Blackstock, Tennessee, 1951
Highest Kickoff Return Average: 40.1 — Paul Allen, Brigham Young, 1961
Highest Average Yards per Punt: 50.3 — Chad Kessler, Louisiana St, 1997

Single Game

SCORING

Most Points Scored: 48—Howard Griffith, Illinois, 1990 (vs Southern Illinois)
Most Field Goals: 7—Dale Klein, Nebraska, 1985 (vs Missouri); Mike Prindle, Western Michigan, 1984 (vs Marshall)
Most Extra Points (Kick): 13—Derek Mahoney, Fresno St, 1991 (vs New Mexico); Terry Leiweke, Houston, 1968 (vs Tulsa)
Most Extra Points (2-Pts): 6—Jim Pilot, New Mexico St, 1961 (vs Hardin-Simmons)

TOTAL OFFENSE

Most Yards Gained: 732—David Klingler, Houston, 1990 (vs Arizona St)

RUSHING

Most Yards Gained: 406—LaDainian Tomlinson, Texas Christian, 1999 (vs UTEP)
Most Touchdowns Rushed: 8—Howard Griffith, Illinois, 1990 (vs Southern Illinois)

PASSING

Most Passes Completed: 55—Rusty LaRue, Wake Forest, 1995 (vs Duke); Drew Brees, Purdue, 1998 (vs Wisconsin)
Most Yards Gained: 716—David Klingler, Houston, 1990 (vs Arizona St)
Most Touchdown Passes: 11—David Klingler, Houston, 1990 [vs Eastern Washington (I-AA)]

RECEIVING

Most Passes Caught: 23—Randy Gatewood, UNLV, 1994 (vs Idaho)
Most Yards Gained: 405—Troy Edwards, Louisiana Tech, 1998 (vs Nebraska)
Most Touchdown Catches: 6—Tim Delaney, San Diego St, 1969 (vs New Mexico St)

NCAA Division I-AA Individual Records

Career

SCORING

Most Points Scored: 544—Brian Westbrook, Villanova, 1998-01
Most Touchdowns Scored: 89—Brian Westbrook, Villanova, 1998-01
Most Touchdowns Scored, Rushing: 84—Adrian Peterson, Georgia Southern, 1998–01
Most Touchdowns Scored, Passing: 139—Willie Totten, Mississippi Valley, 1982–85
Most Touchdowns Scored, Receiving: 50—Jerry Rice, Mississippi Valley, 1981–84

RUSHING

Most Rushes: 1,124—Charles Roberts, Cal St–Sacramento, 1997–00
Most Rushes per Game: 38.2—Arnold Mickens, Butler, 1994–95
Most Yards Gained: 6,559—Adrian Peterson, Georgia Southern, 1998–01
Most Yards Gained per Game: 190.7—Arnold Mickens, Butler, 1994–95

PASSING

Highest Passing Efficiency Rating: 170.8—Shawn Knight, William & Mary, 1991–94
Most Passes Attempted: 1,680—Marcus Brady, Cal St—Northridge, 1998-01; Steve McNair, Alcorn St, 1991–94
Most Passes Completed: 1,039—Marcus Brady, Cal St—Northridge, 1998-01
Most Passes Completed per Game: 26.5—Chris Sanders, Chattanooga, 1999–00
Highest Completion Percentage: 67.3—Dave Dickenson, Montana, 1992–95
Most Yards Gained: 14,496—Steve McNair, Alcorn St, 1991–94
Most Yards Gained per Game: 350.0—Neil Lomax, Portland St, 1978–80

RECEIVING

Most Passes Caught: 317—Jacquay Nunnally, Florida A&M, 1997–00
Most Yards Gained: 4,693—Jerry Rice, Mississippi Valley, 1981–84
Most Yards Gained per Game: 116.9—Derrick Ingram, Alabama–Birmingham, 1993–94
Highest Average Gain per Reception: 24.3—John Taylor, Delaware St, 1982–85

Single Season

SCORING

Most Points Scored: 176—Brian Westbrook, Villanova, 2001
Most Touchdowns Scored: 29—Adrian Peterson, Georgia Southern, 1999; Brian Westbrook, Villanova, 2001
Most Touchdowns Scored, Rushing: 28—Adrian Peterson, Georgia Southern, 1999
Most Touchdowns Scored, Passing: 56—Willie Totten, Mississippi Valley, 1984
Most Touchdowns Scored, Receiving: 27—Jerry Rice, Mississippi Valley, 1984

RUSHING

Most Rushes: 409—Arnold Mickens, Butler, 1994
Most Rushes per Game: 40.9—Arnold Mickens, Butler, 1994
Most Yards Gained: 2,260—Charles Roberts, Cal St–Sacramento, 1998
Most Yards Gained per Game: 225.5—Arnold Mickens, Butler, 1994

PASSING

Highest Passing Efficiency Rating: 204.6—Shawn Knight, William & Mary, 1993
Most Passes Attempted: 577—Joe Lee, Towson, 1999
Most Passes Completed: 324—Willie Totten, Mississippi Valley, 1984
Most Passes Completed per Game: 32.4—Willie Totten, Mississippi Valley, 1984
Highest Completion Percentage: 70.6—Giovanni Carmazzi, Hofstra, 1997
Most Yards Gained: 4,863—Steve McNair, Alcorn St, 1994
Most Yards Gained per Game: 455.7—Willie Totten, Mississippi Valley, 1984

RECEIVING

Most Passes Caught: 120—Stephen Campbell, Brown, 2000
Most Yards Gained: 1,712—Eddie Conti, Delaware, 1998
Most Yards Gained per Game: 168.2—Jerry Rice, Mississippi Valley, 1984
Highest Average Gain per Reception: 28.9—Mikhael Ricks, Stephen F. Austin, 1997; (min. 35 receptions)

Single Game

SCORING

Most Points Scored: 42—Jesse Burton, McNeese St, 1998 (vs Southern Utah); Archie Amerson, Northern Arizona, 1996 (vs Weber St)
Most Field Goals: 8—Goran Lingmerth, Northern Arizona, 1986 (vs Idaho)

RUSHING

Most Yards Gained: 437—Maurice Hicks, N Carolina A&T, 2001 (vs Morgan St)
Most Touchdowns Rushed: 7—Archie Amerson, Northern Arizona, 1996 (vs Weber St)

PASSING

Most Passes Completed: 48—Clayton Millis, Cal St–Northridge, 1995 (vs St. Mary's [CA])
Most Yards Gained: 624—Jamie Martin, Weber St, 1991 (vs Idaho St)
Most Touchdown Passes: 9—Willie Totten, Mississippi Valley, 1984 (vs Kentucky St)

RECEIVING

Most Passes Caught: 24—Jerry Rice, Mississippi Valley, 1983 (vs Southern–BR)
Most Yards Gained: 376—Kassim Osgood, Cal Poly, 2000 (vs Northern Iowa)
Most Touchdown Catches: 6—Cos DeMatteo, Chattanooga, 2000 (vs Mississippi Valley)

NCAA Division II Individual Records

Career

SCORING

Most Points Scored: 544—Brian Shay, Emporia St, 1995–98
Most Touchdowns Scored: 88—Brian Shay, Emporia St, 1995–98
Most Touchdowns Scored, Rushing: 81—Brian Shay, Emporia St, 1995–98
Most Touchdowns Scored, Passing: 116—Chris Hatcher, Valdosta St, 1991–94
Most Touchdowns Scored, Receiving: 49—Bruce Cerone, Yankton/Emporia St, 1965–69

RUSHING

Most Rushes: 1,131—Josh Ranek, S Dakota St, 1997–01
Most Rushes per Game: 29.8—Bernie Peeters, Luther, 1968–71
Most Yards Gained: 6,958—Brian Shay, Emporia St, 1995–98
Most Yards Gained per Game: 183.4—Anthony Gray, Western NM, 1997–98

Career (Cont.)

PASSING

Highest Passing Efficiency Rating: 190.8—Dusty Bonner, Valdosta St, 2000–01
Most Passes Attempted: 1,719—Bob McLaughlin, Lock Haven, 1992–95
Most Passes Completed: 1,001—Chris Hatcher, Valdosta St, 1991–94
Most Passes Completed per Game: 25.7—Chris Hatcher, Valdosta St, 1991–94
Highest Completion Percentage: 72.7—Dusty Bonner, Valdosta St, 2000–01
Most Yards Gained: 11,213—Justin Coleman, Nebraska–Kearney, 1997–00
Most Yards Gained per Game: 323.7—Dusty Bonner, Valdosta St, 2000–01

RECEIVING

Most Passes Caught: 323—Clarence Coleman, Ferris St, 1998–01
Most Yards Gained: 4,983—Clarence Coleman, Ferris St, 1998–01
Most Yards Gained per Game: 160.8—Chris George, Glenville St, 1993–94
Highest Average Gain per Reception: 22.8—Tyrone Johnson, Western St (CO), 1990–93

Single Season

SCORING

Most Points Scored: 206—Kavin Gailliard, American International, 1999
Most Touchdowns Scored: 34—Kavin Gailliard, American International, 1999
Most Touchdowns Scored, Rushing: 33—Ian Smart, C.W. Post, 2001
Most Touchdowns Scored, Passing: 54—Dusty Bonner, Valdosta St, 2000
Most Touchdowns Scored, Receiving: 28—David Kircus, Grand Valley St, 2001

RUSHING

Most Rushes: 385—Joe Gough, Wayne St (MI), 1994
Most Rushes per Game: 38.6—Mark Perkins, Hobart, 1968
Most Yards Gained: 2,653—Kavin Gailliard, American International, 1999
Most Yards Gained per Game: 222.0—Anthony Gray, Western New Mexico, 1997

PASSING

Highest Passing Efficiency Rating: 221.63—Curt Anes, Grand Valley St, 2001
Most Passes Attempted: 544—Lance Funderburk, Valdosta St, 1995
Most Passes Completed: 356—Lance Funderburk, Valdosta St, 1995
Most Passes Completed per Game: 32.4—Lance Funderburk, Valdosta St, 1995
Highest Completion Percentage: 74.7—Chris Hatcher, Valdosta St, 1994
Most Yards Gained: 4,189—Wilkie Perez, Glenville St, 1997
Most Yards Gained per Game: 393.4—Grady Benton, W Texas A&M, 1994

RECEIVING

Most Passes Caught: 119—Brad Bailey, W Texas A&M, 1994
Most Yards Gained: 1,876—Chris George, Glenville St, 1993
Most Yards Gained per Game: 187.6—Chris George, Glenville St, 1993
Highest Average Gain per Reception: 32.5—Tyrone Johnson, Western St, 1991 (min. 30 receptions)

Single Game

SCORING

Most Points Scored: 48—Paul Zaeske, N Park, 1968 (vs N Central); Junior Wolf, Panhandle St, 1958 (vs St. Mary [KS])
Most Field Goals: 6—Steve Huff, Central Missouri St, 1985 (vs SE Missouri St)

RUSHING

Most Yards Gained: 405—Alvon Brown, Kentucky St, 2000 (vs Kentucky Wesleyan)
Most Touchdowns Rushed: 8—Junior Wolf, Panhandle St, 1958 (vs St. Mary [KS])

PASSING

Most Passes Completed: 56—Jarrod DeGeorgia, Wayne St (NE),1996 (vs Drake)
Most Yards Gained: 642—Wilkie Perez, Glenville St, 1997, (vs Concord)
Most Touchdowns Passed: 10—Bruce Swanson, N Park, 1968 (vs N Central)

RECEIVING

Most Passes Caught: 23—Chris George, Glenville St, 1994 (vs WV Wesleyan); Barry Wagner, Alabama A&M, 1989 (vs Clark Atlanta)
Most Yards Gained: 401—Kevin Ingram, W Chester, 1998 (vs Clarion)
Most Touchdown Catches: 8—Paul Zaeske, N Park, 1968 (vs N Central)

NCAA Division III Individual Records

Career

SCORING

Most Points Scored: 562—R.J. Bowers, Grove City, 1997–00
Most Touchdowns Scored: 92—R.J. Bowers, Grove City, 1997–00
Most Touchdowns Scored, Rushing: 91—R.J. Bowers, Grove City, 1997–00
Most Touchdowns Scored, Passing: 148—Justin Peery, Westminster (MO), 1996–99
Most Touchdowns Scored, Receiving: 75—Scott Pingel, Westminster (MO), 1996–99

RUSHING

Most Rushes: 1,190—Steve Tardif, Maine Maritime, 1996–99
Most Rushes per Game: 32.7—Chris Sizemore, Bridgewater (VA), 1972–74
Most Yards Gained: 7,353—R.J. Bowers, Grove City, 1997–00
Most Yards Gained per Game: 183.8—R.J. Bowers, Grove City, 1997–00

PASSING

Highest Passing Efficiency Rating: 194.2—Bill Borchert, Mount Union, 1994–97
Most Passes Attempted: 1,696—Kirk Baumgartner, WI-Stevens Point, 1986–89
Most Passes Completed: 1,012—Justin Peery, Westminster (MO), 1996–99
Most Passes Completed per Game: 25.9—Justin Peery, Westminster (MO), 1996–99
Highest Completion Percentage: 67.0—Gary Smeck, Mount Union, 1997–00
Most Yards Gained: 13,262—Justin Peery, Westminster (MO), 1996–99
Most Yards Gained per Game: 340.1—Justin Peery, Westminster (MO), 1996–99

RECEIVING

Most Passes Caught: 436—Scott Pingel, Westminster (MO), 1996–99
Most Yards Gained: 6,108—Scott Pingel, Westminster (MO), 1996–99
Most Yards Gained per Game: 156.6—Scott Pingel, Westminster (MO), 1996–99
Highest Average Gain per Reception: 22.9—Kirk Aikens, Hartwick, 1995–98

Single Season

SCORING

Most Points Scored: 206—R. J. Bowers, Grove City, 1998
Most Points Scored per Game: 20.8—James Regan, Pomona-Pitzer, 1997
Most Touchdowns Scored: 34—R. J. Bowers, Grove City, 1998
Most Touchdowns Scored, Rushing: 34—R. J. Bowers, Grove City, 1998
Most Touchdowns Scored, Passing: 54—Justin Peery, Westminster (MO), 1999
Most Touchdowns Scored, Receiving: 26—Scott Pingel, Westminster (MO), 1998

RUSHING

Most Rushes: 380—Mike Birosak, Dickinson, 1989
Most Rushes per Game: 38.0—Mike Birosak, Dickinson, 1989
Most Yards Gained: 2,385—Dante Brown, Marietta, 1996

PASSING

Highest Passing Efficiency Rating: 225.0—Mike Simpson, Eureka, 1994
Most Passes Attempted: 527—Kirk Baumgartner, WI-Stevens Point, 1988
Most Passes Completed: 329—Justin Peery, Westminster (MO), 1999
Most Passes Completed per Game: 32.9—Justin Peery, Westminster (MO), 1999
Highest Completion Percentage: 72.9—Jim Ballard, Mount Union, 1993
Most Yards Gained: 4,501—Justin Peery, Westminster (MO), 1998
Most Yards Gained per Game: 450.1—Justin Peery, Westminster (MO), 1998

RECEIVING

Most Passes Caught: 136—Scott Pingel, Westminster (MO), 1999
Most Yards Gained: 2,157—Scott Pingel, Westminster, (MO), 1998
Most Yards Gained per Game: 215.7—Scott Pingel, Westminster, (MO), 1998
Highest Average Gain per Reception: 26.9—Marty Redlawsk, Concordia (IL), 1985

Single Game

SCORING

Most Field Goals: 6—Jim Hever, Rhodes, 1984 (vs Millsaps)

PASSING

Most Passes Completed: 50—Justin Peery, Westminster (MO), 1998 (vs MacMurray); Tim Lynch, Hofstra, 1991 (vs Fordham)
Most Yards Gained: 731—Zamir Amin, Menlo, 2000 (vs California Lutheran)
Most Touchdown Passes: 9—Joe Zarlinga, Ohio Northern, 1998 (vs Capital)

RUSHING

Most Yards Gained: 441—Dante Brown, Marietta, 1996 (vs Baldwin-Wallace)
Most Touchdowns Rushed: 8—Carey Bender, Coe, 1994 (vs Beloit)

RECEIVING

Most Passes Caught: 23—Sean Munroe, Mass-Boston, 1992 (vs Mass-Maritime)
Most Yards Gained: 397—Matt Eisenberg, Juniata, 1999 (vs Widener)
Most Touchdown Catches: 7—Matt Perceval, Wesleyan (CT), 1998 (vs Middlebury)

Career

Scoring

POINTS (KICKERS)

	Years	Pts
Roman Anderson, Houston	1988–91	423
Carlos Huerta, Miami (FL)	1988–91	397
Jason Elam, Hawaii	1988–92	395
Derek Schmidt, Florida St	1984–87	393
Kris Brown, Nebraska	1995–98	388

POINTS (NON-KICKERS)

	Years	Pts
Travis Prentice, Miami (OH)	1996–99	468
Ricky Williams, Texas	1995–98	452
Anthony Thompson, Indiana	1986–89	394
Ron Dayne, Wisconsin	1996–99	378
Marshall Faulk, San Diego St	1991–93	376

POINTS PER GAME (NON-KICKERS)

	Years	Pts/Game
Marshall Faulk, San Diego St	1991–93	12.1
Ed Marinaro, Cornell	1969–71	11.8
Bill Burnett, Arkansas	1968–70	11.3
Steve Owens, Oklahoma	1967–69	11.2
Eddie Talboom, Wyoming	1948–50	10.8

Total Offense

YARDS GAINED

	Years	Yds
Ty Detmer, Brigham Young	1988–91	14,665
Tim Rattay, Louisiana Tech	1997–99	12,618
Chris Redman, Louisville	1996–99	12,129
Drew Brees, Purdue	1997–00	11,815
David Neill, Nevada	1998–01	11,664

YARDS PER GAME

	Years	Yds/Game
Tim Rattay, Louisiana Tech	1997–99	382.4
Chris Vargas, Nevada	1992–93	320.9
Ty Detmer, Brigham Young	1988–91	318.8
Daunte Culpepper, Central Florida	1996–98	313.5
Mike Perez, San Jose St	1986–87	309.1

Rushing

YARDS GAINED

	Years	Yds
Ron Dayne, Wisconsin	1996–99	6,397
Ricky Williams, Texas	1995–98	6,279
Tony Dorsett, Pittsburgh	1973–76	6,082
Charles White, Southern Cal	1976–79	5,598
Travis Prentice, Miami (OH)	1996–99	5,596

YARDS PER GAME

	Years	Yds/Game
Ed Marinaro, Cornell	1969–71	174.6
O.J. Simpson, Southern Cal	1967–68	164.4
Herschel Walker, Georgia	1980–82	159.4
LeShon Johnson, Northern Illinois	1992–93	150.6
Ron Dayne, Wisconsin	1996–99	148.8

TOUCHDOWNS RUSHING

	Years	TD
Travis Prentice, Miami (OH)	1996–99	73
Ricky Williams, Texas	1995–98	72
Anthony Thompson, Indiana	1986–89	64
Ron Dayne, Wisconsin	1996–99	63
Eric Crouch, Nebraska	1998–01	59

Passing

PASSING EFFICIENCY

	Years	Rating
Danny Wuerffel, Florida	1993–96	163.6
Ty Detmer, Brigham Young	1988–91	162.7
Steve Sarkisian, Brigham Young	1995–96	162.0
Billy Blanton, San Diego St	1993–96	157.1
Jim McMahon, Brigham Young	1977–78, 80–81	156.9

Note: Minimum 500 completions.

YARDS GAINED

	Years	Yds
Ty Detmer, Brigham Young	1988–91	15,031
Tim Rattay, Louisiana Tech	1997–99	12,746
Chris Redman, Louisville	1996–99	12,541
Todd Santos, San Diego St	1984–87	11,425
Tim Lester, Western Michigan	1997–99	11,299

COMPLETIONS

	Years	Comp
Chris Redman, Louisville	1996–99	1,031
Tim Rattay, Louisiana Tech	1997–99	1,015
Ty Detmer, Brigham Young	1988–91	958
Drew Brees, Purdue	1997–00	942
Todd Santos, San Diego St	1984–87	910

TOUCHDOWNS PASSING

	Years	TD
Ty Detmer, Brigham Young	1988–91	121
Tim Rattay, Louisiana Tech	1997–99	115
Danny Wuerffel, Florida	1993–96	114
Chad Pennington, Marshall	1997–99	100
David Klingler, Houston	1988–91	91

Receiving

CATCHES

	Years	No.
Arnold Jackson, Louisville	1997–00	300
Trevor Insley, Nevada	1996–99	298
Geoff Noisy, Nevada	1995–98	295
Troy Edwards, Louisiana Tech	1996–98	280
Aaron Turner, Pacific	1989–92	266

CATCHES PER GAME

	Years	No./Game
Emmanuel Hazard, Houston	1989–90	10.5
Alex Van Dyke, Nevada	1994–95	10.3
Howard Twilley, Tulsa	1963–65	10.0
Jason Phillips, Houston	1987–88	9.4
Troy Edwards, Louisiana Tech	1996–98	8.2

YARDS GAINED

	Years	Yds
Trevor Insley, Nevada	1996–99	5,005
Marcus Harris, Wyoming	1993–96	4,518
Ryan Yarborough, Wyoming	1990–93	4,357
Troy Edwards, Louisiana Tech	1996–98	4,352
Aaron Turner, Pacific	1989–92	4,345

TOUCHDOWN CATCHES

	Years	TD
Troy Edwards, Louisiana Tech	1996–98	50
Aaron Turner, Pacific	1989–92	43
Ryan Yarborough, Wyoming	1990–93	42
Marcus Harris, Wyoming	1993–96	38
Clarkston Hines, Duke	1986–89	38

Career *(Cont.)*

All-Purpose Running

YARDS GAINED	Years	Yds
Ricky Williams, Texas	1996–98	7,206
Napoleon McCallum, Navy	1981–85	7,172
Darrin Nelson, Stanford	1977–78, 80–81	6,885
Kevin Faulk, Louisiana St	1995–98	6,833
Ron Dayne, Wisconsin	1996–99	6,701

YARDS PER GAME	Years	Yds/Game
Ryan Benjamin, Pacific	1990–92	237.8
Sheldon Canley, San Jose St	1988–90	205.8
Howard Stevens, Louisville	1971–72	193.7
O.J. Simpson, Southern Cal	1967–68	192.9
Alex Van Dyke, Nevada	1994–95	188.5

Interceptions

PLAYER/SCHOOL	Years	Int
Al Brosky, Illinois	1950–52	29
John Provost, Holy Cross	1972–74	27
Martin Bayless, Bowling Green	1980–83	27
Tom Curtis, Michigan	1967–69	25
Tony Thurman, Boston Col	1981–84	25
Tracy Saul, Texas Tech	1989–92	25

Punting Average

PLAYER/SCHOOL	Years	Avg
Todd Sauerbrun, W Virginia	1991–94	46.3
Reggie Roby, Iowa	1979–82	45.6
Greg Montgomery, Michigan St	1985–87	45.4
Tom Tupa, Ohio St	1984–87	45.2
Barry Helton, Colorado	1984–87	44.9

Note: At least 150 punts.

Punt Return Average

PLAYER/SCHOOL	Years	Avg
Jack Mitchell, Oklahoma	1946–48	23.6
Gene Gibson, Cincinnati	1949–50	20.5
Eddie Macon, Pacific	1949–51	18.9
Jackie Robinson, UCLA	1939–40	18.8
Bobby Dillon, Texas	1949–51	17.7

Note: At least 30 returns.

Kickoff Return Average

PLAYER/SCHOOL	Years	Avg
Anthony Davis, Southern Cal	1972–74	35.1
Eric Booth, Southern Miss	1994–97	32.4
Overton Curtis, Utah St	1957–58	31.0
Fred Montgomery, New Mexico St	1991–92	30.5
Altie Taylor, Utah St	1966–68	29.3

Note: At least 30 returns.

YET ANOTHER SIGN OF THE APOCALYPSE

During its game with visiting Wofford, Clemson ordered its marching band and cheerleaders to remain silent during breaks in the action so that TV commercials could be played on the Memorial Stadium video screen.

Single Season

Scoring

POINTS	Year	Pts
Barry Sanders, Oklahoma St	1988	234
Troy Edwards, Louisiana Tech	1998	188
Mike Rozier, Nebraska	1983	174
Lydell Mitchell, Penn St	1971	174
Luke Staley, Brigham Young	2001	170

FIELD GOALS	Year	FG
John Lee, UCLA	1984	29
Paul Woodside, W Virginia	1982	28
Luis Zendejas, Arizona St	1983	28
Fuad Reveiz, Tennessee	1982	27
Sebastian Janikowski, Florida St	1998	27

Four tied with 25.

All-Purpose Running

YARDS GAINED	Year	Yds
Barry Sanders, Oklahoma St	1988	3,250
Troy Edwards, Louisiana Tech	1998	2,794
Ryan Benjamin, Pacific	1991	2,995
Mike Pringle, Fullerton St	1989	2,690
Paul Palmer, Temple	1986	2,633

All-Purpose Running *(Cont.)*

YARDS PER GAME	Year	Yds/Game
Barry Sanders, Oklahoma St	1988	295.5
Ryan Benjamin, Pacific	1991	249.6
Byron (Whizzer) White, Colorado	1937	246.3
Mike Pringle, Fullerton St	1989	244.6
Paul Palmer, Temple	1986	239.4

Total Offense

YARDS GAINED	Year	Yds
David Klingler, Houston	1990	5,221
Ty Detmer, Brigham Young	1990	5,022
Tim Rattay, Louisiana Tech	1998	4,840
Andre Ware, Houston	1989	4,661
Jim McMahon, Brigham Young	1980	4,627

YARDS PER GAME	Year	Yds/Game
David Klingler, Houston	1990	474.6
Andre Ware, Houston	1989	423.7
Ty Detmer, Brigham Young	1990	418.5
Tim Rattay, Louisiana Tech	1998	403.3
Mike Maxwell, Nevada	1995	402.6

Single Season *(Cont.)*

Rushing

YARDS GAINED

	Year	Yds
Barry Sanders, Oklahoma St.	1988	2,628
Marcus Allen, Southern Cal	1981	2,342
Troy Davis, Iowa St.	1996	2,185
LaDainian Tomlinson, Texas Christian	2000	2,158
Mike Rozier, Nebraska	1983	2,148

YARDS PER GAME

	Year	Yds/Game
Barry Sanders, Oklahoma St.	1988	238.9
Marcus Allen, Southern Cal	1981	212.9
Ed Marinaro, Cornell	1971	209.0
Troy Davis, Iowa St.	1996	198.6
LaDainian Tomlinson, Texas Christian	2000	196.2

TOUCHDOWNS RUSHING

	Year	TD
Barry Sanders, Oklahoma St.	1988	37
Mike Rozier, Nebraska	1983	29
Ricky Williams, Texas	1998	27
Lee Suggs, Virginia Tech	2000	27
Five tied with 24.		

Passing

PASSING EFFICIENCY

	Year	Rating
Shaun King, Tulane	1998	183.3
Michael Vick, Virginia Tech	1999	180.4
Danny Wuerffel, Florida	1995	178.4
Jim McMahon, Brigham Young	1980	176.9
Ty Detmer, Brigham Young	1989	175.6

YARDS GAINED

	Year	Yds
Ty Detmer, Brigham Young	1990	5,188
David Klingler, Houston	1990	5,140
Tim Rattay, Louisiana Tech	1998	4,943
Andre Ware, Houston	1989	4,699
Jim McMahon, Brigham Young	1980	4,571

COMPLETIONS

	Year	Att	Comp
Tim Couch, Kentucky	1998	553	400
Tim Rattay, Louisiana Tech	1998	559	380
David Klingler, Houston	1990	643	374
Andre Ware, Houston	1989	578	365
Tim Couch, Kentucky	1997	547	363

Passing *(Cont.)*

TOUCHDOWNS PASSING

	Year	TD
David Klingler, Houston	1990	54
Jim McMahon, Brigham Young	1980	47
Andre Ware, Houston	1989	46
Tim Rattay, Louisiana Tech	1998	46
David Carr, Fresno St.	2001	42

Receiving

CATCHES

	Year	GP	No.
Emmanuel Hazard, Houston	1989	11	142
Troy Edwards, Louisiana Tech	1998	12	140
Howard Twilley, Tulsa	1965	10	134
Trevor Insley, Nevada	1999	11	134
Alex Van Dyke, Nevada	1995	11	129

CATCHES PER GAME

	Year	No.	No./Game
Howard Twilley, Tulsa	1965	134	13.4
Emmanuel Hazard, Houston	1989	142	12.9
Trevor Insley, Nevada	1999	134	12.2
Troy Edwards, Louisiana Tech	1998	140	11.7
Alex Van Dyke, Nevada	1995	129	11.7

YARDS GAINED

	Year	Yds
Trevor Insley, Nevada	1999	2,060
Troy Edwards, Louisiana Tech	1998	1,996
Alex Van Dyke, Nevada	1995	1,854
Howard Twilley, Tulsa	1965	1,779
Josh Reed, Louisiana St.	2001	1,740

TOUCHDOWN CATCHES

	Year	TD
Troy Edwards, Louisiana Tech	1998	27
Randy Moss, Marshall	1997	25
Emmanuel Hazard, Houston	1989	22
Desmond Howard, Michigan	1991	19
Ashley Lelie, Hawaii	2001	19

Single Game

Scoring

POINTS

	Opponent	Year	Pts
Howard Griffith, Illinois	Southern Illinois	1990	48
Marshall Faulk, San Diego St.	Pacific	1991	44
Jim Brown, Syracuse	Colgate	1956	43
Showboat Boykin, Mississippi	Mississippi St	1951	42
Fred Wendt, UTEP*	New Mexico St	1948	42

*UTEP was Texas Mines in 1948.

FIELD GOALS

	Opponent	Year	FG
Dale Klein, Nebraska	Missouri	1985	7
Mike Prindle, Western Michigan	Marshall	1984	7

Note: 13 tied with 6.
Klein's distances were 32-22-43-44-29-43-43. Prindle's distances were 32-44-42-23-48-41-27.

Single Game (Cont.)

Total Offense

YARDS GAINED	Opponent	Year	Yds
David Klingler, Houston	Arizona St	1990	732
Matt Vogler, TCU	Houston	1990	696
Brian Lindgren, Idaho	Middle Tenn St	2001	657
David Klingler, Houston	Texas Christian	1990	625
Scott Mitchell, Utah	Air Force	1988	625

Passing

YARDS GAINED	Opponent	Year	Yds
David Klingler, Houston	Arizona St	1990	716
Matt Vogler, TCU	Houston	1990	690
Brian Lindgren, Idaho	Middle Tenn St	2001	637
Scott Mitchell, Utah	Air Force	1988	631
Jeremy Leach, New Mexico	Utah	1989	622

COMPLETIONS	Opponent	Year	Comp
Drew Brees, Purdue	Wisconsin	1998	55
Rusty LaRue, Wake Forest	Duke	1995	55
Rusty LaRue, Wake Forest	NC St	1995	50
Brian Lindgren, Idaho	Middle Tenn St	2001	49
David Klingler, Houston	SMU	1990	48

TOUCHDOWNS PASSING	Opponent	Year	TD
David Klingler, Houston	E Wash	1990	11

Note: Klingler's TD passes were 5-48-29-7-3-7-40-10-7-8-51.

Rushing

YARDS GAINED	Opponent	Year	Yds
LaDainian Tomlinson, Texas Christian	UTEP	1999	406
Tony Sands, Kansas	Missouri	1991	396
Marshall Faulk, San Diego St	Pacific	1991	386
Troy Davis, Iowa St	Missouri	1996	378
Anthony Thompson, Indiana	Wisconsin	1989	377

TOUCHDOWNS RUSHING	Opponent	Year	TD
Howard Griffith, Illinois	Southern Illinois	1990	8

Note: Griffith's TD runs were 5-51-7-41-5-18-5-3.

Receiving

CATCHES	Opponent	Year	No.
Randy Gatewood, UNLV	Idaho	1994	23
Jay Miller, Brigham Young	New Mexico	1973	22
Troy Edwards, La. Tech	Nebraska	1998	21
Chris Daniels, Purdue	Michigan St	1999	21
Rick Eber, Tulsa	Idaho St	1967	20
Kenny Christian, Eastern Michigan	Temple	2000	20

YARDS GAINED	Opponent	Year	Yds
Troy Edwards, Louisiana Tech	Nebraska	1998	405
Randy Gatewood, UNLV	Idaho	1994	363
Chuck Hughes, UTEP*	N Texas St	1965	349
Nate Burleson, Nevada	San Jose St	2001	326
Rick Eber, Tulsa	Idaho St	1967	322

*UTEP was Texas Western in 1965.

TOUCHDOWN CATCHES	Opponent	Year	TD
Tim Delaney, San Diego St	New Mex. St	1969	6

Note: Delaney's TD catches were 2-22-34-31-30-9.

Longest Plays (since 1941)

PASSING	Opponent	Year	Yds
Fred Owens to Jack Ford, Portland	St. Mary's (CA)	1947	99
Bo Burris to Warren McVea, Houston	Washington St	1966	99
Colin Clapton to Eddie Jenkins, Holy Cross	Boston U	1970	99
Terry Peel to Robert Ford, Houston	Syracuse	1970	99
Terry Peel to Robert Ford, Houston	San Diego St	1972	99
Cris Collinsworth to Derrick Gaffney, Florida	Rice	1977	99
Scott Ankrom to James Maness, Texas Christian	Rice	1984	99
Gino Toretta to Horace Copeland, Miami (FL)	Arkansas	1991	99
John Paci to Thomas Lewis, Indiana	Penn St	1993	99
Troy DeGar to Wes Caswell, Tulsa	Oklahoma	1996	99
Drew Brees to Vinny Sutherland, Purdue	Northwestern	1999	99
Dan Urban to Justin McCariens, Northern Illinois	Ball St	2000	99
Jason Johnson to Brandon Marshall, Arizona	Idaho	2001	99

RUSHING	Opponent	Year	Yd
Gale Sayers, Kansas	Nebraska	1963	99
Max Anderson, Arizona St	Wyoming	1967	99
Ralph Thompson, W Texas St	Wichita St	1970	99
Kelsey Finch, Tennessee	Florida	1977	99
Eric Vann, Kansas	Oklahoma	1997	99

FIELD GOALS	Opponent	Year	Yds
Steve Little, Arkansas	Texas	1977	67
Russell Erxleben, Texas	Rice	1977	67
Joe Williams, Wichita St	Southern IL	1978	67
Martin Gramatica, Kansas St	Northern IL	1998	65
Tony Franklin, Texas A&M	Baylor	1976	65

PUNTS	Opponent	Year	Yds
Pat Brady, Nevada*	Loyola (CA)	1950	99
George O'Brien, Wisconsin	Iowa	1952	96
John Hadl, Kansas	Oklahoma	1959	94
Carl Knox, Texas Christian	Oklahoma St	1947	94
Preston Johnson, SMU	Pittsburgh	1940	94

*Nevada was Nevada-Reno in 1950.

DIVISION I-A WINNINGEST TEAMS
Alltime Winning Percentage

	Yrs	W	L	T	Pct	GP	Bowl Record
Notre Dame	113	781	247	42	.750	1,070	13-11-0
Michigan	123	813	266	36	.745	1,115	16-16-0
Alabama	107	744	281	43	.717	1,068	29-19-3
Nebraska	112	764	301	40	.710	1,105	20-20-0
Oklahoma	107	713	280	53	.707	1,046	21-12-1
Texas	109	755	304	33	.707	1,092	19-20-2
Ohio St	112	731	292	53	.704	1,076	14-19-0
Tennessee	105	718	294	52	.699	1,064	23-19-0
Penn St	115	744	318	41	.693	1,103	23-11-2
Southern Cal	109	684	294	54	.689	1,032	25-15-0
Florida St	55	400	189	17	.674	606	18-10-2
Boise St	34	259	133	2	.660	394	2-0-0
Washington	112	625	341	50	.640	1,016	14-13-1
Miami (OH)	113	604	337	44	.636	985	5-2-0
Georgia	108	649	366	54	.632	1,069	19-15-3
Miami (FL)	75	484	282	19	.629	785	15-11-0
Louisiana St	108	628	363	47	.628	1,038	16-16-1
Arizona St	89	494	297	24	.621	815	10-7-1
Central Michigan	101	515	309	36	.620	860	0-2-0
Auburn	109	617	370	47	.619	1,034	14-12-2
Army	112	621	382	51	.613	1,054	2-2-0
Florida	95	574	349	40	.617	963	13-15-0
Colorado	112	621	379	36	.617	1,036	11-13-0
Texas A&M	107	617	390	48	.608	1,055	13-14-0
Syracuse	112	648	414	49	.605	1,111	12-8-1

Note: Includes bowl games.

Alltime Victories

Michigan	813	Georgia	649	N Carolina	608
Notre Dame	781	Syracuse	648	Miami (OH)	604
Nebraska	764	Louisiana St	628	Pittsburgh	603
Texas	755	Washington	625	Arkansas	601
Penn St	744	Army	621	Minnesota	591
Alabama	744	Colorado	621	Virginia Tech	587
Ohio St	731	Auburn	617	Navy	579
Tennessee	718	Texas A&M	617	Clemson	578
Oklahoma	713	Georgia Tech	609	Florida	574
Southern Cal	684	W Virginia	606	Michigan St	568

NUMBER ONE VS NUMBER TWO

The No. 1 and No. 2 teams, according to the Associated Press Poll, have met 33 times, including 13 bowl games, since the poll's inception in 1936. The No. 1 teams have a 20-11-2 record in these matchups. Notre Dame (4-3-2) has played in nine of the games.

Date	Results	Stadium
10-9-43	No. 1 Notre Dame 35, No. 2 Michigan 12	Michigan (Ann Arbor)
11-20-43	No. 1 Notre Dame 14, No. 2 Iowa Pre-Flight 13	Notre Dame (South Bend)
12-2-44	No. 1 Army 23, No. 2 Navy 7	Municipal (Baltimore)
11-10-45	No. 1 Army 48, No. 2 Notre Dame 0	Yankee (New York)
12-1-45	No. 1 Army 32, No. 2 Navy 13	Municipal (Philadelphia)
11-9-46	No. 1 Army 0, No. 2 Notre Dame 0	Yankee (New York)
1-1-63	No. 1 Southern Cal 42, No. 2 Wisconsin 37 (Rose Bowl)	Rose Bowl (Pasadena)
10-12-63	No. 2 Texas 28, No. 1 Oklahoma 7	Cotton Bowl (Dallas)
1-1-64	No. 1 Texas 28, No. 2 Navy 6 (Cotton Bowl)	Cotton Bowl (Dallas)
11-19-66	No. 1 Notre Dame 10, No. 2 Michigan St 10	Spartan (E Lansing)
9-28-68	No. 1 Purdue 37, No. 2 Notre Dame 22	Notre Dame (South Bend)
1-1-69	No. 1 Ohio St 27, No. 2 Southern Cal 16 (Rose Bowl)	Rose Bowl (Pasadena)
12-6-69	No. 1 Texas 15, No. 2 Arkansas 14	Razorback (Fayetteville)
11-25-71	No. 1 Nebraska 35, No. 2 Oklahoma 31	Owen Field (Norman)
1-1-72	No. 1 Nebraska 38, No. 2 Alabama 6 (Orange Bowl)	Orange Bowl (Miami)
1-1-79	No. 2 Alabama 14, No. 1 Penn St 7 (Sugar Bowl)	Sugar Bowl (New Orleans)
9-26-81	No. 1 Southern Cal 28, No. 2 Oklahoma 24	Coliseum (Los Angeles)
1-1-83	No. 2 Penn St 27, No. 1 Georgia 23 (Sugar Bowl)	Sugar Bowl (New Orleans)

NUMBER ONE VS NUMBER TWO *(Cont.)*

Date	Results	Stadium
10-19-85	No. 1 Iowa 12, No. 2 Michigan 10	Kinnick (Iowa City)
9-27-86	No. 2 Miami (FL) 28, No. 1 Oklahoma 16	Orange Bowl (Miami)
1-2-87	No. 2 Penn St 14, No. 1 Miami (FL) 10 (Fiesta Bowl)	Sun Devil (Tempe)
11-21-87	No. 2 Oklahoma 17, No. 1 Nebraska 7	Memorial (Lincoln)
1-1-88	No. 2 Miami (FL) 20, No. 1 Oklahoma 14 (Orange Bowl)	Orange Bowl (Miami)
11-26-88	No. 1 Notre Dame 27, No. 2 Southern Cal 10	Coliseum (Los Angeles)
9-16-89	No. 1 Notre Dame 24, No. 2 Michigan 19	Michigan (Ann Arbor)
11-16-91	No. 2 Miami (FL) 17, No. 1 Florida St 16	Campbell (Tallahassee)
1-1-93	No. 2 Alabama 34, No. 1 Miami (FL) 13 (Sugar Bowl)	Superdome (New Orleans)
11-13-93	No. 2 Notre Dame 31, No. 1 Florida St 24	Notre Dame (South Bend)
1-1-94	No. 1 Florida St 18, No. 2 Nebraska 16 (Orange Bowl)	Orange Bowl (Miami)
1-2-96	No. 1 Nebraska 62, No. 2 Florida 24 (Fiesta Bowl)	Sun Devil (Tempe)
11-30-96	No. 2 Florida St 24, No. 1 Florida 21	Campbell (Tallahassee)
1-4-99	No. 1 Tennessee 23, No. 2 Florida St 16 (Fiesta Bowl)	Sun Devil (Tempe)
1-4-00	No. 1 Florida St 46, No. 2 Virginia Tech 29 (Sugar Bowl)	Superdome (New Orleans)

LONGEST DIVISION I-A WINNING STREAKS

Wins	Team	Yrs	Ended by	Score
47	Oklahoma	1953–57	Notre Dame	7–0
39	Washington	1908–14	Oregon St	0–0
37	Yale	1890–93	Princeton	6–0
37	Yale	1887–89	Princeton	10–0
35	Toledo	1969–71	Tampa	21–0
34	Pennsylvania	1894–96	Lafayette	6–4
31	Oklahoma	1948–50	Kentucky	13–7
31	Pittsburgh	1914–18	Cleveland Naval Reserve	10–9
31	Pennsylvania	1896–98	Harvard	10–0
30	Texas	1968–70	Notre Dame	24–11

LONGEST DIVISION I-A UNBEATEN STREAKS

No.	W	T	Team	Yrs	Ended by	Score
63	59	4	Washington	1907–17	California	27–0
56	55	1	Michigan	1901–05	Chicago	2–0
50	46	4	California	1920–25	Olympic Club	15–0
48	47	1	Oklahoma	1953–57	Notre Dame	7–0
48	47	1	Yale	1885–89	Princeton	10–0
47	42	5	Yale	1879–85	Princeton	6–5
44	42	2	Yale	1894–96	Princeton	24–6
42	39	3	Yale	1904–08	Harvard	4–0
39	37	2	Notre Dame	1946–50	Purdue	28–14
37	36	1	Oklahoma	1972–75	Kansas	23–3
37	37	0	Yale	1890–93	Princeton	6–0
35	35	0	Toledo	1969–71	Tampa	21–0
35	34	1	Minnesota	1903–05	Wisconsin	16–12
34	33	1	Nebraska	1912–16	Kansas	7–3
34	34	0	Pennsylvania	1894–96	Lafayette	6–4
34	32	2	Princeton	1884–87	Harvard	12–0
34	29	5	Princeton	1877–82	Harvard	1–0
33	30	3	Tennessee	1926–30	Alabama	18–6
33	31	2	Georgia Tech	1914–18	Pittsburgh	32–0
33	30	3	Harvard	1911–15	Cornell	10–0
32	31	1	Nebraska	1969–71	UCLA	20–17
32	30	2	Army	1944–47	Columbia	21–20
32	31	1	Harvard	1898–1900	Yale	28–0
31	30	1	Penn St	1967–70	Colorado	41–13
31	30	1	San Diego St	1967–70	Long Beach St	27–11
31	29	2	Georgia Tech	1950–53	Notre Dame	27–14
31	31	0	Oklahoma	1948–50	Kentucky	13–7
31	31	0	Pittsburgh	1914–18	Cleveland Naval	10–9
31	31	0	Pennsylvania	1896–98	Harvard	10–0

Note: Includes bowl games.

LONGEST DIVISION I-A LOSING STREAKS

Losses		Seasons	Ended Against	Score
34	Northwestern	1979–82	Northern Illinois	31–6
28	Virginia	1958–61	William & Mary	21–6
28	Kansas St	1945–48	Arkansas St	37–6
27	New Mexico St	1988–90	Cal St–Fullerton	43–9
27	Eastern Michigan	1980–82	Kent St	9–7

MOST-PLAYED DIVISION I-A RIVALRIES

GP	Opponents (Series Leader Listed First)	Record	First Game	GP	Opponents (Series Leader Listed First)	Record	First Game
111	Minnesota-Wisconsin	58-45-8	1890	102	Army–Navy	49-46-7	1890
110	Missouri-Kansas	51-50-9	1891	101	Utah–Utah St	69-28-4	1892
108	Nebraska-Kansas	84-21-3	1892	99	Clemson–S Carolina	59-36-4	1896
108	Texas–Texas A&M	69-34-5	1894	99	Kansas–Kansas St	61-33-5	1902
106	Miami (OH)–Cincinnati	56-43-7	1888	98	N Carolina–Wake Forest	65-31-2	1888
106	N Carolina–Virginia	56-46-4	1892	98	Michigan–Ohio St	56-36-6	1897
105	Auburn-Georgia	51-46-8	1892	98	Mississippi–Miss St	55-37-6	1901
105	Oregon–Oregon St	53-42-10	1894	97	Oklahoma-Kansas	64-27-6	1903
104	Purdue-Indiana	63-35-6	1891	97	Tennessee-Kentucky	65-23-9	1893
104	Stanford-California	54-39-11	1892	96	Penn St–Pittsburgh	50-42-4	1893
103	Baylor–Texas Christian*	49-47-7	1899	96	Georgia–Georgia Tech	53-38-5	1893

*Have not met since 1996.

NCAA Coaches' Records

ALLTIME WINNINGEST DIVISION I-A COACHES

Coach (Alma Mater)	Colleges Coached	Yrs	W	L	T	Pct
Knute Rockne (Notre Dame '14)†	Notre Dame 1918–30	13	105	12	5	.881
Frank W. Leahy (Notre Dame '31)†	Boston Col 1939–40; Notre Dame 1941–43, 1946–53	13	107	13	9	.864
George W. Woodruff (Yale 1889)†	Pennsylvania 1892–01; Illinois 1903; Carlisle 1905	12	142	25	2	.846
Barry Switzer (Arkansas '60)	Oklahoma 1973–88	16	157	29	4	.837
Tom Osborne (Hastings '59)†	Nebraska 1973–98	25	255	49	3	.836
Percy D. Haughton (Harvard 1899)†	Cornell 1899–1900; Harvard 1908–16; Columbia 1923–24	13	96	17	6	.832
Bob Neyland (Army '16)†	Tennessee 1926–34, 1936–40, 1946–52	21	173	31	12	.829
Fielding Yost (W Virginia 1895)†	Ohio Wesleyan 1897; Nebraska 1898; Kansas 1899; Stanford 1900; Michigan 1901–23, 1925–26	29	196	36	12	.828
*Phillip Fulmer (Tennessee '71)	Tennessee 1992–	10	95	20	0	.826
Bud Wilkinson (Minnesota '37)†	Oklahoma 1947–63	17	145	29	4	.826
Jock Sutherland (Pittsburgh '18)†	Lafayette 1919–23; Pittsburgh 1924–38	20	144	28	14	.812
Bob Devaney (Alma, MI '39)†	Wyoming 1957–61; Nebraska 1962–72	16	136	30	7	.806
Frank W. Thomas (Notre Dame '23)†	Tenn.-Chattanooga 1925–28; Alabama 1931–42, 1944–46	19	141	33	9	.795
Henry L. Williams (Yale 1891)†	Army 1891; Minnesota 1900–21	23	141	34	12	.786
Gil Dobie (Minnesota '02)†	N Dakota St 1906–07; Washington 1908-16; Navy 1917–19; Cornell 1920–35; Boston College 1936–38	33	180	45	15	.781
Bear Bryant (Alabama '36)†	Maryland 1945, Kentucky 1946–53, Texas A&M 1954–57, Alabama 1958–82	38	323	85	17	.780

*Active in 2001. †Hall of Fame member.

Note: Minimum 10 years as head coach at Division I institutions; record at four-year colleges only; bowl games included; ties computed as half won, half lost.

ALLTIME WINNINGEST DIVISION I-A COACHES (Cont.)

By Victories

	Yrs	W	L	T	Pct		Yrs	W	L	T	Pct
*Joe Paterno	36	327	96	3	.771	*Lou Holtz	30	233	113	7	.670
Paul (Bear) Bryant	38	323	85	17	.780	Hayden Fry	37	232	178	10	.564
*Bobby Bowden	36	323	91	4	.778	Jess Neely	40	207	176	19	.539
Glenn (Pop) Warner	44	319	106	32	.733	Warren Woodson	31	203	95	14	.673
Amos Alonzo Stagg	57	314	199	35	.605	Don Nehlen	30	202	128	8	.609
LaVell Edwards	29	257	100	3	.718	Vince Dooley	25	201	77	10	.715
Tom Osborne	25	255	49	3	.836	Eddie Anderson	39	201	128	15	.606
Woody Hayes	33	238	72	10	.759	*Active in 2001.					
Bo Schembechler	27	234	65	8	.775						

Most Bowl Victories

	W	L	T		W	L	T
*Joe Paterno	20	9	1	Barry Switzer	8	5	0
*Bobby Bowden	18	6	1	*Jackie Sherrill	8	6	0
Paul (Bear) Bryant	15	12	2	Darrell Royal	8	7	1
Jim Wacker	13	2	0	Vince Dooley	8	10	2
*Lou Holtz	12	8	2	Pat Dye	7	2	1
Tom Osborne	12	13	0	Bob Devaney	7	3	0
Don James	10	5	0	Dan Devine	7	3	0
John Vaught	10	8	0	Earle Bruce	7	5	0
Bobby Dodd	9	4	0	Charlie McClendon	7	6	0
Johnny Majors	9	7	0	Hayden Fry	7	9	1
*John Robinson	8	1	0	LaVell Edwards	7	14	1
Terry Donahue	8	4	1	*Active in 2001.			

WINNINGEST ACTIVE DIVISION I-A COACHES

By Percentage

Coach, College	Yrs	W	L	T	Pct#	Bowls W	L	T
Bob Pruett, Marshall	6	69	11	0	.863	4	1	0
Phillip Fulmer, Tennessee	10	95	20	0	.826	6	4	0
Bobby Bowden, Florida St	36	323	91	4	.778	18	6	1
Joe Paterno, Penn St	36	327	96	3	.771	20	9	1
Lloyd Carr, Michigan	7	66	20	0	.767	4	3	0
R. C. Slocum, Texas A&M	13	117	41	2	.738	3	8	0
Dennis Erickson, Oregon St	16	136	51	1	.722	5	4	0
Rick Neuheisel, Washington	7	59	24	0	.711	4	2	0
Tommy Bowden, Clemson	5	40	18	0	.690	1	2	0
Paul Pasqualoni, Syracuse	16	125	56	1	.690	6	2	0

#Bowl games included in overall record.   Ties computed as half win, half loss..

Note: Minimum five years as Division I-A head coach; record at four-year colleges only.

YET ANOTHER SIGN OF THE APOCALYPSE

An interactive poll in the midst of ESPN's bowl coverage asked viewers, "From which bowl sponsor would you most like a gift certificate."

WINNINGEST ACTIVE DIVISION I-A COACHES (Cont.)
By Victories

Joe Paterno, Penn St	327	Frank Beamer, Virginia Tech	149
Bobby Bowden, Florida St	323	Dennis Franchione, Alabama	145
Lou Holtz, S Carolina	233	Fisher DeBerry, Air Force	141
Jackie Sherrill, Mississippi St	175	Dennis Erickson, Oregon St	136
Ken Hatfield, Rice	155	Paul Pasqualoni, Syracuse	125

WINNINGEST ACTIVE DIVISION I-AA COACHES
By Percentage

Coach, College	Yrs	W	L	T	Pct*
Mike Kelly, Dayton	21	195	40	1	.828
Al Bagnoli, Pennsylvania	20	154	50	0	.755
Greg Gattuso, Duquesne	9	71	24	0	.747
Pete Richardson, Southern	14	120	41	1	.744
Joe Walton, Robert Morris	8	58	21	1	.731
Joe Gardi, Hofstra	12	99	36	2	.730
Roy Kidd, Eastern Kentucky	38	307	119	8	.717
Billy Joe, Florida A&M	28	221	89	4	.710
Joe Taylor, Hampton	19	146	59	4 *	.708
Walt Hameline, Wagner	21	150	67	2	.690

*Playoff games included.

Note: Minimum five years as a Division I-A and/or Division I-AA head coach; record at four-year colleges only.

By Victories

Roy Kidd, Eastern Kentucky	307	Al Bagnoli, Pennsylvania	154
Billy Joe, Florida A&M	221	Walt Hameline, Wagner	150
Ron Randleman, Sam Houston St	201	Jimmye Laycock, William & Mary	148
Mike Kelly, Dayton	195	Joe Taylor, Hampton	146
Bill Hayes, N Carolina A&T	191	Bob Ricca, St. John's (NY)	146

WINNINGEST ACTIVE DIVISION II COACHES
By Percentage

Coach, College	Yrs	W	L	T	Pct*
Chuck Broyles, Pittsburg St (KS)	12	123	23	2	.838
Ken Sparks, Carson-Newman	22	211	51	2	.803
John Luckhardt, California (PA)	17	137	37	2	.784
Bob Babich, N Dakota St	5	44	14	0	.759
Bob Biggs, UC–Davis	9	81	27	1	.748
Dale Lennon, N Dakota	5	43	15	0	.741
Danny Hale, Bloomsburg	14	113	42	1	.728
Brian Kelly, Grand Valley St	11	90	34	2	.722
Peter Yetten, Bentley	14	98	39	1	.714
Frank Cignetti, Indiana (PA)	20	165	67	1	.710

*Ties computed as half win, half loss. Playoff games included.

Note: Minimum five years as a college head coach; record at four-year colleges only.

By Victories

Ken Sparks, Carson-Newman	211	Gary Howard, Central Oklahoma	155
Willard Bailey, Virginia Union	199	John Luckhardt, California (PA)	137
Bud Elliott, Eastern New Mexico	185	Jerry Vandergriff, Angelo St	136
Frank Cignetti, Indiana (PA)	165	Mel Tjeersdma, NW Missouri St	135
Dennis Douds, E Stroudsburg	162	Monte Cater, Shepherd	130

WINNINGEST ACTIVE DIVISION III
By Percentage

Coach, College	Yrs	W	L	T	Pct*
Larry Kehres, Mount Union	16	178	17	3	.907
Joe Fincham, Wittenberg	6	63	7	0	.900
Rich Kacmarynski, Central (IA)	5	49	8	0	.860
Dick Farley, Williams	15	101	16	3	.854
Rick Willis, Wartburg	5	43	8	0	.843
Chris Creighton, Wabash	5	40	9	0	.816
Bill Zwaan, Widener	5	45	13	0	.776
E. J. Mills, Amherst	5	31	9	0	.775
John Gagliardi, St. John's (MN)	53	388	112	11	.770
Frosty Westering, Pacific Lutheran	37	294	89	7	.763

*Ties computed as half won, half lost. Playoff games included.

Note: Minimum five years as a college head coach; record at four-year colleges only.

By Victories

John Gagliardi, St John's (MN)	388	Tom Gilburg, Franklin & Marshall	156
Frosty Westering, Pacific Lutheran	294	Eric Hamilton, College of New Jersey	153
Frank Girardi, Lycoming	226	Lou Wacker, Emory & Henry	151
Peter Mazzaferro, Bridgewater (MA)	193	Wayne Perry, Hanover	140
Larry Kehres, Mount Union	178	Rick Giancola, Montclair St	134

NAIA Coaches' Records

WINNINGEST ACTIVE NAIA COACHES
By Percentage

Coach, College	Yrs	W	L	T	Pct*
Ted Kessinger, Bethany (KS)	26	208	50	1	.805
Hank Biesiot, Dickinson St (ND)	27	182	66	1	.733
Carl Poelker, McKendree (IL)	20	129	58	1	.689
Bob Young, Sioux Falls (SD)	20	137	66	3	.672
Geno DeMarco, Geneva (PA)	6	41	21	0	.661
Larry Wilcox, Benedictine (KS)	23	159	82	0	.660
Orv Otten, Northwestern (IA)	7	48	26	0	.649
Vic Wallace, Lambuth (TN)	20	139	75	4	.647
Todd Sturdy, St. Ambrose (IA)	7	44	26	0	.629
John Frangoulis, Baker (KS)	6	38	25	0	.603

*Playoff games included.

Note: Minimum five years as a collegiate head coach and includes record against four-year institutions only.

By Victories

Ted Kessinger, Bethany (KS)	208	Bob Young, Sioux Falls (SD)	137
Hank Biesiot, Dickinson St (ND)	182	Carl Poelker, McKendree (IL)	129
Larry Wilcox, Benedictine (KS)	159	Jim Dennison, Walsh (OH)	127
Kevin Donley, St. Francis (IN)	144	Fran Schwenk, Doane (NE)	103
Vic Wallace, Lambuth (TN)	139	Bob Green, Montana Tech	91

Pro Basketball

Shaquille O'Neal
of the NBA champion
Los Angeles Lakers

Hollywood Franchise

The Lakers produced a third installment of their championship drama, and the number of sequels to come is up to their leading men

BY MARK BEECH

DETRACTORS—particularly those living in the Sacramento area—might protest that luck has propelled the Los Angeles Lakers to three straight NBA championships. But while good fortune has certainly played a part, the Lakers owe their ascent to something deeper than mere luck. Consider that almost everyone who mattered on the team's roster at the end of the 2001–02 season had started somewhere else and looked to Los Angeles for a measure of redemption. Shaquille O'Neal was unhappy in Orlando, and even floundered at first in L.A., before finding a mentor-motivator in coach Phil Jackson. The Charlotte Hornets drafted Kobe Bryant in 1996 but shipped him off almost immediately, unwilling to gamble on a high school swingman. Jackson, the guiding hand in the Chicago Bulls' six championships, was eager to start anew on the Left Coast, and even more eager to prove he could win without No. 23 in his lineup. Rick Fox? He played six fruitless seasons for the Boston Celtics before finding a niche in L.A. Forward

Robert Horry? He won NBA titles with Houston in 1994 and '95, but had just finished an unsatisfying season in Phoenix before joining the Lakers. Samaki Walker? He toured Texas with Dallas and San Antonio, but neither the Mavericks nor the Spurs loved him. Backup guard Brian Shaw, who, at 36, contributed on-court composure and off-court leadership to the Lakers? He played for six teams before finding a home in the Jackson system.

On June 12, with a 113–107 victory over the New Jersey Nets in Game 4 of the NBA Finals, the Lakers became the seventh team to sweep a Finals and joined Michael Jordan's Bulls, Bill Russell's Celtics and George Mikan's Lakers as the only teams to win three straight championships. They treated the Nets like so much sawdust on the floor—irritating, but easily collected, bagged and discarded. "We played good enough to beat 99 percent of the teams in the NBA in these four games," said New Jersey rookie Richard Jefferson after the decisive game. "They're a tough team to go against."

Bryant averaged 25.5 points and 5.5 assists a game.

Tough, indeed. By the time Los Angeles reached the Finals, it had already survived a regular season that saw O'Neal miss 15 games with toe, wrist and ankle ailments, not to mention the rise of several formidable challengers in the Western Conference. Its 58–24 regular season record was due in part to the performance of a solid supporting cast, including forwards Fox and Horry, guard Derek Fisher, swingman Devean George and the ageless Shaw. Most important, though, was the continued development of Bryant, who had perhaps his finest all-around season, making a genuine effort to involve his teammates in the Laker offense, especially when O'Neal was on the bench. Kobe's scoring dipped slightly (to 25.2 points a game, from 28.5 last season), but his assists rose (to a career high 5.5 a game). Fox summed it up by saying that Bryant was willing "to open up to a group of guys who were going to be there when he wasn't at his best and who could make his game easier."

The Lakers rolled through the first two rounds of the playoffs, dispatching Portland in three games and San Antonio in five, before running into the Sacramento Kings in a conference final that was clearly about more than basketball. The Kings had gone 61–21 and finished three games ahead of Los Angeles in the Pacific Divison. This was the third playoff meeting between the teams in three years and the second to go the dis-

tance. For Sacramento, it was personal, and the Kings injected the series with emotion, producing seven games full of posturing, woofing and flopping, not to mention a sparkling array of rallies and runs. "They pushed us to the limits," Jackson said after Game 7. Kings coach Rick Adelman saw it otherwise. "You want to say they're a better team?" he said. "You say it, but I'm not."

After winning one of two in Sacramento, Los Angeles returned home and lost Game 3, 103–90. In Game 4, the Lakers trailed by 24 points in the second quarter but clawed their way back, setting the stage for Robert Horry, who drained a walk-off three-pointer

MANNY MILLAN

I've needed to, I've hit them," Shaq said. Then, referring to the Kings, he added, "They felt it was their time. It wasn't."

That was an interesting choice of words, considering the Kings'—and thousands of fans'—complaints that the officiating in Game 6 grossly favored the Lakers, who shot 27 free throws in the fourth quarter of that game, getting 16 of their final 18 points from the line. The critics charged that league officials and NBC much preferred a Lakers-Nets Finals to a Kings-Nets matchup.

The controversy eventually blew over, and L.A. swamped the Nets in the Finals. Now all they are pursuing is history. No NBA team has won more than three straight championships since Red Auerbach's Boston Celtics took eight in a row from 1958–59 through '65–66. How many in a row can the Lakers win? Four? Five? Ten? It seems entirely up to Shaq and Kobe—and Jackson.

to give the Lakers a breathtaking 100–99 victory. The win evened the series at two games apiece and devastated the Kings.

O'Neal, for his part, played brilliantly in the series, averaging 30 points a game despite being frustrated by the theatrics of Sacramento center Vlade Divac, who crumpled at the slightest touch from the 7' 1", 345-pound L.A. center. And the best part of Shaq's performance was his free-throw shooting, a well-known weakness in his game. O'Neal drained 11 of 15 free throws in Game 7 (and 24 of 32 in the final two games, both won by the Lakers), while Sacramento clanged away from the line to the tune of 16 for 30. "Over the last couple of years when

It would be unfortunate, though, if L.A.'s budding dynasty blinded anyone to the rebirth of professional basketball in the Garden State. Led by point-guard-supreme Jason Kidd, the New Jersey Nets' road to the Finals was paved with a mixture of grit and destiny. One year after finishing with the sixth-worst record in the league (26–56), the Nets took the No. 1 seed in the Eastern Conference with a 52–30 record, and Kidd was a strong candidate for the regular-season MVP award, which ultimately went to San Antonio's Tim Duncan. Kidd's numbers weren't particularly eye-catching (he averaged 14.7 points, 7.3 rebounds and 9.9 assists for the season), but no player—with the possible exception of Jordan, but more on that later—made a greater impact on his team this season than Kidd.

Acquired in an off-season trade with the Phoenix Suns, he turned the Nets around with his unselfish play at both ends of the floor and lifted them to their first division title since they joined the NBA in 1976. Kidd ranked second in the league in assists and third in steals (2.13 per game); he hit dozens of clutch shots, and he finished second on the team in rebounding. "He's one of my favorite players," said former Phoenix Suns coach Danny Ainge. "You look at Jason's fundamentals, they're not great. You look at his shooting, it's not great. The guy just finds ways to win, defensively and offensively. And his greatest asset to an organization, other than his will to win, is that all the players love playing with him."

While Kidd sailed East to save basketball in New Jersey, a former MVP returned to resuscitate the game in the nation's capital. In late October, Jordan stepped out of the Washington Wizards owner's box and onto the court again at the age of 38. Citing his love of the game, he divested himself of his 5% to 10% stake in one of the NBA's most dreadful teams and took a hands-on approach to turning them around. "Nobody in his right mind should doubt him," said the Dallas Mavericks' All-Star swingman, Michael Finley, who frequently guarded His Airness in summer pickup games in Chicago. "He may not be able to do all the things physically he used to, but he'll still be one of the best players in the league."

By most standards, save, quite possibly, his own exacting ones, Jordan's comeback was a success, even though he missed 13 games with a knee injury that eventually caused him to sit down for the season in early April. To be sure, it was not vintage-era Jordan: Those creaky knees had slowed his first step, and he scored field goals almost exclusively on midrange jumpers and his patented fadeaway. Still, relying more than ever on craft and guile, Jordan averaged 22.9 points, 5.7 rebounds

and 5.2 assists. Most impressively, he helped the Wizards go from 19 wins in 2000–01 to 37 in 2001–02, and turned them into a bona fide playoff contender in the Eastern Conference. "People had their doubts," said Wizards coach Doug Collins, "but I knew that if Michael was going to do this, he thought he still could play pretty damn well."

Jordan deserved MVP consideration not only for his play, but also for the impact he made on the league's bottom line. No other player generated more revenue for the NBA and its 29 teams in 2001–02 than the incomparable No. 23. Thanks to him, leaguewide attendance rose. With Jordan on the roster, the Wizards had the biggest jump in average attendance (from 15,577 in 2000–01 to 20,674 in 2001–02), with a total of 375,715 more paying customers than the previous year. Yet, the NBA's overall attendance only increased by 225,184 fans, which meant that Washington pushed it over the top. Jordan also made a tangible impact on television ratings, which were up a reported 3% on NBC, and as high as 9% on the Turner cable network. In January, the league signed a new six-year TV deal with ABC, ESPN and AOL Time Warner worth approximately $4.6 billion. "We don't give [the MVP] out on the basis of finances," NBA deputy commissioner Russ Granik joked. "But I think it's fair to say Michael had a very positive impact for us."

In addition to increased attendance, the league also saw a rise in scoring, from 91.7 points per game to 95.4. This was partly due to the introduction of new rules that sought to reverse a trend toward boring isolation play. For the first time in NBA history, teams were no longer required to play man-to-man at all times. Free to play any defense they liked—just like in college basketball—defenses ignored players who couldn't score and swarmed those who could. The change forced even the NBA's most predictable team to change its M.O. The Jazz's bread-and-butter pick-and-roll game with John Stockton and Karl Malone became harder to execute because Malone could be double-

JOHN W. MCDONOUGH

teamed before he got the ball. Teams that could run the transition game effectively, like Sacramento and the Dallas Mavericks, succeeded and played some of the most entertaining basketball in recent memory.

Dallas had more weapons than a Schwarzenegger movie. The Mavs had four players (Nick Van Exel, Michael Finley, Steve Nash and Dirk Nowitzki) who scored more than 17 points a game, and one more, Raef LaFrentz, who averaged 13.5. In Nash, Van Exel and Avery Johnson, Dallas had three worthy starters at point guard. The Mavericks also dressed five 7-footers, give or take an inch, in LaFrentz, Nowitzki, Evan Eschmeyer, Zhizhi Wang and Shawn Bradley. Coach Don Nelson could start a lineup (Nowitzki, Van Exel, Nash, LaFrentz and Finley) that buried a total of 594 threes. Dallas finished second to San Antonio in the Midwest Division, going 57–25 and leaving a trail of gaping jaws in its wake. "It is impossible to have too many good offensive players," said Avery Johnson. "The key is for those players to understand there are going to be nights when their individual numbers will be down. Do we have that here? I absolutely guarantee it."

The Mavs' playoff run ground to a halt against Sacramento, the NBA's other practitioner of rocket-fueled roundball. Led by Chris Webber, the Kings finished with the league's best record and showcased many of the qualities—shooting, teamwork, a willingness to fast-break—that make basketball such an appealing game. While they will continue to find a stern test in the Lakers, the Kings do possess the ingredients of a championship team. Peja Stojakovic was an All-Star complement to Chris Webber at forward, and their potential Kobe-stopper, Doug Christie, had a strong season. Much of the Kings' success was attributable to the arrival of point guard Mike Bibby in a draft-night trade for Jason Williams and swingman Nick Anderson. Bibby got everyone involved in the offense (a league-high seven Kings averaged in double figures) and scored 13.7 points a game himself.

Unfortunately for Sacramento, the division rivals from downstate ruled the NBA roost for another year and may do so for the forseeable future. Unless something happens to Shaq or Kobe, the road to the championship should run through LA-LA Land for some time to come.

FOR THE RECORD · 2001-02

NBA Final Standings

Eastern Conference

ATLANTIC DIVISION

Team	W	L	Pct	GB
New Jersey	52	30	.634	—
Boston	49	33	.598	3
Orlando	44	38	.537	8
Philadelphia	43	39	.524	9
Washington	37	45	.451	15
Miami	36	46	.439	16
New York	30	52	.366	22

CENTRAL DIVISION

Team	W	L	Pct	GB
Detroit	50	32	.610	—
Charlotte	44	38	.537	6
Toronto	42	40	.512	8
Indiana	42	40	.512	8
Milwaukee	41	41	.500	9
Atlanta	33	49	.402	17
Cleveland	29	53	.354	21
Chicago	21	61	.256	29

Western Conference

MIDWEST DIVISION

Team	W	L	Pct	GB
San Antonio	58	24	.707	—
Dallas	57	25	.695	1
Minnesota	50	32	.610	8
Utah	44	38	.537	14
Houston	28	54	.341	30
Denver	27	55	.329	31
Memphis	23	59	.280	35

PACIFIC DIVISION

Team	W	L	Pct	GB
Sacramento	61	21	.744	—
LA Lakers	58	24	.707	3
Portland	49	33	.598	12
Seattle	45	37	.549	16
LA Clippers	39	43	.476	22
Phoenix	36	46	.439	25
Golden State	21	61	.256	40

2002 NBA Playoffs

2002 NBA Playoff Results

Eastern Conference First Round

April 20	Indiana	89	at New Jersey	83
April 22	Indiana	79	at New Jersey	95
April 26	New Jersey	85	at Indiana	84
April 30	New Jersey	74	at Indiana	97
May 2	Indiana	109	at New Jersey	120

New Jersey won series 3–2.

April 20	Orlando	79	at Charlotte	80
April 23	Orlando	111	at Charlotte	103
April 27	Charlotte	110	at Orlando	100
April 30	Charlotte	102	at Orlando	85

Charlotte won series 3–1.

April 21	Toronto	63	at Detroit	85
April 24	Toronto	91	at Detroit	96
April 27	Detroit	84	at Toronto	94
April 29	Detroit	83	at Toronto	89
May 2	Toronto	82	at Detroit	85

Detroit won series 3–2.

April 21	Philadelphia	82	at Boston	92
April 25	Philadelphia	85	at Boston	93
April 28	Boston	103	at Philadelphia	108
May 1	Boston	81	at Philadelphia	83
May 3	Philadelphia	87	at Boston	120

Boston won series 3–2.

Western Conference First Round

April 20	Seattle	89	at San Antonio	110
April 22	Seattle	98	at San Antonio	90
April 27	San Antonio	102	at Seattle	75
May 1	San Antonio	79	at Seattle	91
May 3	Seattle	78	at San Antonio	101

San Antonio won series 3–2.

April 20	Utah	86	at Sacramento	89
April 23	Utah	93	at Sacramento	86
April 28	Sacramento	90	at Utah	87
April 29	Sacramento	91	at Utah	86

Sacramento won series 3–1.

April 21	Portland	87	at LA Lakers	95
April 26	Portland	96	at LA Lakers	103
April 28	LA Lakers	92	at Portland	91

LA Lakers won series 3–0.

April 21	Minnesota	94	at Dallas	101
April 24	Minnesota	110	at Dallas	122
April 28	Dallas	115	at Minnesota	102

Dallas won series 3–0.

Eastern Conference Semifinals

May 5	Charlotte	93	at New Jersey	99
May 7	Charlotte	88	at New Jersey	102
May 9	New Jersey	97	at Charlotte	115
May 12	New Jersey	89	at Charlotte	79
May 15	Charlotte	95	at New Jersey	103

New Jersey won series 4–1.

May 5	Boston	84	at Detroit	96
May 8	Boston	85	at Detroit	77
May 10	Detroit	64	at Boston	66
May 12	Detroit	79	at Boston	90
May 14	Boston	90	at Detroit	81

Boston won series 4–1.

Western Conference Semifinals

May 4	Dallas	91	at Sacramento	108
May 6	Dallas	110	at Sacramento	102
May 9	Sacramento	125	at Dallas	119
May 11	Sacramento	115	at Dallas	113
May 13	Dallas	101	at Sacramento	114

Sacramento won series 4–1.

May 5	San Antonio	80	at LA Lakers	86
May 7	San Antonio	88	at LA Lakers	85
May 10	LA Lakers	99	at San Antonio	89
May 12	LA Lakers	87	at San Antonio	85
May 14	San Antonio	87	at LA Lakers	93

LA Lakers won series 4–1.

Eastern Conference Finals

May 19	Boston	97	at New Jersey	104
May 21	Boston	93	at New Jersey	86
May 25	New Jersey	90	at Boston	94
May 27	New Jersey	94	at Boston	92
June 1	Boston	92	at New Jersey	103
May 31	New Jersey	96	at Boston	88

New Jersey won series 4–2.

Western Conference Finals

May 18	LA Lakers	106	at Sacramento	99
May 20	LA Lakers	90	at Sacramento	96
May 24	Sacramento	103	at LA Lakers	90
May 26	Sacramento	99	at LA Lakers	100
May 28	LA Lakers	91	at Sacramento	92
May 31	Sacramento	102	at LA Lakers	106
June 2	LA Lakers	112	at Sacramento	106

LA Lakers won series 4–3.

Finals

June 5	New Jersey	94	at LA Lakers	99
June 7	New Jersey	83	at LA Lakers	106
June 9	LA Lakers	106	at New Jersey	103
June 12	LA Lakers	113	at New Jersey	107

LA Lakers won series 4–0.

*Overtime game.

NBA Finals Composite Box Score

NEW JERSEY NETS

Player	GP	Field Goals FGM	Pct	3-Pt FG FGM	Pct	Free Throws FTM	Pct	Rebounds Off	Total	A	Stl	TO	BS	Ppg	Hi
Martin	4	35	46.7	1	20.0	17	65.4	8	26	10	6	14	4	22.0	35
Kidd	4	35	43.8	6	30.0	7	63.6	12	29	39	9	12	3	20.8	30
Kittles	4	19	45.2	5	31.3	7	70.0	4	8	10	6	3	2	12.5	23
Van Horn	4	17	38.6	5	41.7	3	75.0	7	23	9	2	5	1	10.5	14
Harris	4	11	34.4	1	20.0	8	80.0	5	11	8	4	0	0	7.8	22
MacCulloch	4	14	50.0	0	—	2	50.0	12	20	2	3	5	4	7.5	10
Jefferson	4	11	52.4	0	—	5	45.5	2	18	5	4	3	0	6.8	10
Collins	4	5	50.0	0	—	7	87.5	5	10	1	1	3	2	4.3	6
Williams	4	6	37.5	0	—	2	100.0	4	9	1	3	0	2	3.5	4
Johnson	4	2	33.3	0	—	1	50.0	1	2	1	0	0	0	1.3	4
Marshall	2	0	—	0	—	0	—	0	0	0	0	0	0	0.0	0
Scalabrine	1	0	—	0	—	0	—	0	0	0	0	0	0	0.0	0
Totals	**4**	**155**	**43.7**	**18**	**30.5**	**59**	**67.0**	**60**	**156**	**86**	**38**	**45**	**18**	**96.8**	**107**

LOS ANGELES LAKERS

Player	GP	Field Goals FGM	Pct	3-Pt FG FGM	Pct	Free Throws FTM	Pct	Rebounds Off	Total	A	Stl	TO	BS	Ppg	Hi
O'Neal	4	50	59.5	0	—	45	66.2	13	49	15	2	14	11	36.3	40
Bryant	4	36	51.4	6	54.5	29	80.6	3	23	21	6	15	3	26.8	36
Fisher	4	17	51.5	8	66.7	9	64.3	2	14	15	1	7	0	12.8	13
Fox	4	12	52.2	5	45.5	10	83.3	6	25	14	6	11	2	9.8	14
Horry	4	11	45.8	5	45.5	5	83.3	6	29	17	11	6	7	8.0	12
George	4	10	43.5	3	60.0	3	100.0	5	19	0	1	2	2	6.5	11
Shaw	4	6	28.6	2	22.2	0	0.0	3	7	10	1	2	2	3.5	6
Richmond	1	1	100.0	0	—	0	0.0	0	0	0	0	0	0	2.0	2
Medvedenko	2	1	100.0	0	—	0	0.0	1	1	0	0	0	0	1.0	2
Walker	4	1	25.0	0	—	2	100.0	3	8	0	0	3	1	1.0	2
Hunter	3	1	20.0	0	0.0	0	0.0	1	1	0	0	0	0	0.7	2
Madsen	1	0	0.00	0	—	0	0.0	0	0	0	0	0	0	0.0	0
Totals	**4**	**146**	**50.5**	**29**	**47.5**	**103**	**73.0**	**43**	**176**	**92**	**28**	**60**	**28**	**106.0**	**108**

NBA Finals Box Scores

Game 1

NEW JERSEY 94

NJ	Min	FG M-A	FT M-A	Reb O-T	A	PF	S	TO	TP
Kidd	43	11-26	0-1	6-10	10	1	3	1	23
Kittles	25	3-7	2-2	0-0	1	1	0	1	9
Martin	37	7-22	6-9	3-6	2	3	0	3	21
Van Horn	35	5-14	0-0	2-6	1	6	0	4	12
MacCulloch	25	5-9	0-0	6-8	0	3	2	2	10
Harris	25	1-5	3-4	1-3	2	3	0	0	5
Jefferson	22	2-4	0-2	0-6	1	3	1	0	4
Williams	15	2-5	0-0	1-4	1	4	3	0	4
Collins	8	1-1	3-4	2-2	1	5	0	0	5
Johnson	5	0-1	0-0	0-0	0	0	0	0	1
Totals	240	37-94	15-26	21-45	19	29	9	11	94

Percentages: FG—.394, FT—.577. 3-pt goals: 5-16, .313 (Kidd 1-3, Kittles 1-2, Martin 1-3, Van Horn 2-6, Harris 0-2). Team rebounds: 15. Blocked shots: 4 (Kittles, Martin, MacCulloch, Williams).

LA LAKERS 99

LA LAKERS	Min	FG M-A	FT M-A	Reb O-T	A	PF	S	TO	TP
Bryant	43	6-16	10-11	1-3	6	2	1	4	22
Fisher	36	4-7	4-4	0-1	2	1	1	2	13
Horry	41	2-6	1-2	1-8	4	2	3	0	5
Fox	39	5-8	4-6	5-8	3	5	2	2	14
O'Neal	40	12-22	12-21	2-16	1	2	1	5	36
Shaw	11	0-2	0-0	2-2	5	2	0	0	0
George	11	1-5	1-1	1-3	0	2	0	1	3
Walker	8	1-2	0-0	3-7	0	1	0	2	2
Hunter	6	1-3	0-0	1-1	0	2	0	0	2
Medvedenko	5	1-1	0-0	1-1	0	1	0	0	2
Totals	240	33-72	32-45	17-50	21	20	8	16	99

Percentages: FG—.458, FT—.711. 3-pt goals: 1-10, .100 (Bryant 0-2, Fisher 1-2, Horry 0-2, Fox 0-1, Shaw 0-1, George 0-1, Hunter 0-1). Team rebounds: 10. Blocked shots: 8 (O'Neal 4, Horry 2, Shaw, Walker).

A: 18,997. Officials: Crawford, Garretson, Niles.

Game 2

NEW JERSEY 83

NJ	Min	FG M–A	FT M–A	Reb O–T	A	PF	S	TO	TP
Kidd	39	6–17	2–3	4–9	7	3	2	5	17
Kittles	29	9–19	2–4	1–3	3	4	2	1	23
Martin	35	2–8	2–4	2–5	2	5	3	4	6
Van Horn	24	3–9	3–4	4–8	1	2	2	0	9
MacCulloch	15	1–3	0–0	2–5	0	4	1	1	2
Jefferson	32	3–6	4–8	2–5	3	2	0	1	10
Collins	21	2–2	2–2	0–1	0	4	0	1	6
Harris	18	0–9	2–2	2–2	2	1	1	0	2
Williams	15	2–7	0–0	2–3	0	2	0	0	4
Johnson	1	2–5	0–0	1–2	0	0	0	0	0
Marshall	1	0–1	0–0	0–0	0	0	0	0	0
Scalabrine	1	0–0	0–0	0–0	0	0	0	0	0
Totals	240	30–86	17–27	20–43	16	27	11	13	83

Percentages: FG—.349, FT—.630. 3-pt goals: 6–22, .273 (Kidd 3–8, Kittles 3–9, Martin 0–1, Van Horn 0–1, Harris 0–2, Marshall 0–1). Team rebounds:11. Blocked shots: 5 (Kidd 1, Kittles 1, MacCulloch 1, Collins 1, Williams 1).

LA LAKERS 106

LA LAKERS	Min	FG M–A	FT M–A	Reb O–T	A	PF	S	TO	TP
Bryant	42	9–15	3–4	1–8	3	2	2	4	24
Fisher	29	4–9	2–4	2–5	3	5	0	2	12
Horry	43	4–9	0–0	4–10	4	2	3	2	9
Fox	36	3–6	2–2	1–8	6	5	1	2	10
O'Neal	41	14–23	12–14	3–12	8	2	0	4	40
Shaw	22	2–6	0–0	0–2	2	2	0	1	5
George	17	3–7	0–0	1–2	0	1	0	0	6
Walker	5	0–1	0–0	0–0	0	2	0	0	0
Hunter	3	0–2	0–0	0–0	0	0	0	0	0
Madsen	2	0–0	0–0	0–0	0	0	0	0	0
Totals	240	39–78	19–24	12–47	26	21	6	16	106

Percentages: FG—.500, FT—.792. 3-pt goals: 9–16, .563 (Bryant 3–3, Fisher 2–3, Horry 1–3, Fox 2–4, Shaw 1–2, Hunter 0–1). Team rebounds: 9. Blocked shots: 7 (Bryant 1, Horry 3, Fox 1, O'Neal 1, Shaw 1).

A: 18,997. Officials: Javie, Salvatore, Vaden.

Game 3

NEW JERSEY 103

NJ	Min	FG M–A	FT M–A	Reb O–T	A	PF	S	TO	TP
Kidd	43	13–23	3–5	1–5	10	3	3	2	30
Kittles	29	3–6	1–2	1–3	3	1	3	0	7
Martin	43	11–17	4–6	1–4	4	3	2	5	26
Van Horn	31	6–14	0–0	0–5	3	5	0	0	14
MacCulloch	14	4–8	2–2	0–1	0	3	0	2	10
Collins	27	0–4	2–2	2–3	0	4	0	2	2
Jefferson	22	4–5	0–0	0–3	0	1	2	2	8
Harris	19	1–5	0–	0–3	2	1	3	0	2
Williams	7	1–1	2–2	0–0	6	0	0	4	4
Johnson	5	0–0	0–0	0–0	0	0	0	0	0
Totals	240	43–83	14–19	14–42	22	27	13	13	103

Percentages: FG—.518, FT—.737. 3-pt goals: 3–12, .250 (Kidd 1–5, Van Horn 2–4, Kittles 0–2, Martin 0–1). Team rebounds:9. Blocked shots: 5 (Martin 2, Kidd 1, Van Horn 1, MacCulloch 1).

LA LAKERS 106

LA LAKERS	Min	FG M–A	FT M–A	Reb O–T	A	PF	S	TO	TP
Bryant	46	14–23	7–10	1–6	4	3	1	6	36
Fisher	31	4–7	2–4	0–3	6	3	0	3	13
Fox	37	2–6	2–2	0–4	2	2	1	3	7
Horry	31	2–4	0–0	0–7	3	5	3	3	6
O'Neal	42	12–19	11–17	5–11	2	1	0	2	35
George	24	2–4	2–2	1–8	0	3	1	1	6
Shaw	17	1–4	0–0	0–1	0	0	1	1	3
Walker	6	0–1	0–0	0–0	0	1	0	0	0
Medvedenko	4	0–0	0–0	0–0	0	2	0	0	0
Hunter	2	0–0	0–0	0–0	0	0	0	0	0
Totals	240	37–68	24–35	7–40	17	22	7	19	106

Percentages: FG—.544, FT—.686. 3-pt goals: 8–16, .500 (Bryant 1–3, Fisher 3–3, Fox 1–3, Horry 2–3, Shaw 1–4). Team rebounds: 11. Blocked shots: 10 (O'Neal 4, Bryant 2, George 2, Fox 1, Horry 1).

A: 19,215. Officials: Bavetta, Crawford, Delaney.

Game 4

LA LAKERS 113

LA LAKERS	Min	FG M–A	FT M–A	Reb O–T	A	PF	S	TO	TP
Bryant	44	7–16	9–11	0–6	8	4	2	1	25
Fisher	36	5–10	1–2	0–5	4	1	0	0	13
Horry	44	3–5	4–4	1–6	4	2	1	1	12
Fox	32	2–3	2–2	0–5	3	2	2	4	8
O'Neal	43	12–20	10–16	3–10	4	2	1	3	34
George	20	4–7	0–0	2–6	0	1	0	1	11
Shaw	15	3–9	0–0	1–2	3	0	0	0	6
Walker	5	0–0	2–2	0–1	0	1	0	0	2
Richmond	1	1–1	0–0	0–0	0	0	0	0	2
Totals	240	37–71	28–37	7–39	28	15	7	9	113

Percentages: FG—.521, FT—.757. 3-pt goals: 11–19, .579 (Bryant 2–3, Fisher 2–4, Horry 2–3, Fox 2–3, George 3–4, Shaw 0–2). Team rebounds: 5. Blocked shots: 3 (O'Neal 2, Horry).

NEW JERSEY 107

NJ	Min	FG M–A	FT M–A	Reb O–T	A	PF	S	TO	TP
Kidd	43	5–14	2–2	1–5	12	1	1	4	13
Kittles	23	4–10	2–2	2–2	3	1	1	1	11
Martin	43	15–28	5–7	2–11	2	4	1	2	35
Van Horn	31	3–7	0–0	1–4	4	2	0	1	7
MacCulloch	20	4–8	0–0	4–6	2	4	0	0	8
Harris	29	9–13	3–4	2–3	2	1	0	0	22
Jefferson	21	2–6	1–1	0–4	1	1	1	0	5
Collins	19	2–3	0–0	1–4	0	6	1	0	4
Williams	9	1–3	0–0	1–2	0	2	0	0	2
Marshall	1	0–0	0–0	0–0	0	0	0	0	0
Johnson	1	0–0	0–0	0–0	0	0	0	0	0
Totals	240	45–92	13–16	14–41	27	22	5	8	107

Percentages: FG—.489, FT—.813. 3-pt goals: 4–9, .444 (Kidd 1–4, Kittles 1–3, Van Horn 1–1, Harris 1–1). Team rebounds: 8. Blocked shots: 4 (Kidd, Martin, MacCulloch, Collins).

A: 19,296. Officials: Bernhardt, Fryer, Rush.

NBA Awards

All-NBA Teams

FIRST TEAM	SECOND TEAM	THIRD TEAM
G Kobe Bryant, LA Lakers	Gary Payton, Seattle	Paul Pierce, Boston
G Jason Kidd, New Jersey	Allen Iverson, Philadelphia	Steve Nash, Dallas
C Shaquille O'Neal, LA Lakers	Kevin Garnett, Minnesota	Dikembe Mutombo, Philadelphia
F/G Tracy McGrady, Orlando	Dirk Nowitzki, Dallas	Ben Wallace, Detroit
F Tim Duncan, San Antonio	Chris Webber, Sacramento	Jermaine O'Neal, Indiana

NBA All-Defensive Teams

FIRST TEAM	SECOND TEAM
G Gary Payton, Seattle	Kobe Bryant, LA Lakers
G Jason Kidd, New Jersey	Doug Christie, Sacramento
F/C Ben Wallace, Detroit	Dikembe Mutombo, Philadelphia
F Tim Duncan, San Antonio	Bruce Bowen, San Antonio
F Kevin Garnett, Minnesota	Clifford Robinson, Detroit

All-Rookie Teams
(Chosen Without Regard to Position)

FIRST TEAM	SECOND TEAM
Pau Gasol, Memphis	Jamaal Tinsley, Indiana
Shane Battier, Memphis	Richard Jefferson, New Jersey
Jason Richardson, Golden State	Eddie Griffin, Houston
Tony Parker, San Antonio	Zeljko Revraca, Detroit
Andrei Kirilenko, Utah	Vladimir Radmanovic, Seattle
	Joe Johnson, Phoenix

THEY SAID IT

*Popeye Jones, Wizards forward, on
what he learned while teammate
Michael Jordan sat out for
three weeks with a knee injury:
"I found out I had fewer relatives
on the road."*

NBA Individual Leaders

Scoring

	GP	Pts	Avg
Allen Iverson, Phil	60	1883	31.4
Shaquille O'Neal, LA Lakers	67	1822	27.2
Paul Pierce, Bos	82	2144	26.1
Tracy McGrady, Orl	76	1948	25.6
Tim Duncan, SA	82	2089	25.5
Kobe Bryant, LA Lakers	80	2019	25.2
Dirk Nowitzki, Dal	76	1779	23.4
Karl Malone, Utah	80	1788	22.4
Antoine Walker, Bos	81	1794	22.1
Gary Payton, Mil	82	1815	22.1

Rebounds

	GP	Reb	Avg
Ben Wallace, Det	80	1039	13.0
Tim Duncan, SA	82	1042	12.7
Kevin Garnett, Minn	81	981	12.1
Danny Fortson, GS	77	899	11.7
Elton Brand, LA Clippers	80	925	11.6
Dikembe Mutombo, Phil	80	863	10.8
Jermaine O'Neal, Ind	72	757	10.5
Dirk Nowitzki, Dal	76	755	9.9
Shawn Marion, Phoe	81	803	9.9
P.J. Brown, Char	80	786	9.8

Assists

	GP	Assists	Avg
Andre Miller, Clev	81	882	10.9
Jason Kidd, NJ	82	808	9.9
Gary Payton, Sea	82	737	9.0
Baron Davis, Char	82	698	8.5
John Stockton, Utah	82	674	8.2
Stephon Marbury, Phoe	82	666	8.1
Jamaal Tinsley, Ind	80	647	8.1
Jason Williams, Mem	65	519	8.0
Steve Nash, Dal	82	634	7.7
Mark Jackson, NY	82	605	7.4

Field-Goal Percentage

	FGA	FGM	Pct
Shaquille O'Neal, LA Lakers	1229	712	.579
Elton Brand, LA Clippers	1010	532	.527
Donyell Marshall, Utah	661	343	.519
Pau Gasol, Mem	1064	551	.518
John Stockton, Utah	775	401	.517
Alonzo Mourning, Mia	866	447	.516
Ruben Patterson, Port	619	319	.515
Corliss Williamson, Det	806	411	.510
Tim Duncan, SA	1504	764	.508
Brent Barry, Sea	790	401	.508
Wally Szczerbiak, Minn	1200	609	.508

Free-Throw Percentage

	FTA	FTM	Pct
Reggie Miller, Ind	325	296	.911
Richard Hamilton, Wash	337	300	.890
Darrell Armstrong, Orl	205	182	.888
Damon Stoudamire, Port	196	174	.888
Steve Nash, Dall	293	260	.887
Chauncey Billups, Minn	234	207	.885
Chris Whitney, Wash	175	154	.880
Steve Smith, SA	181	159	.878
Predrag Stojakovic, Sac	323	283	.876
Troy Hudson, Orl	201	176	.876
Jamal Mashburn, Char	241	211	.876

Three-Point Field-Goal Percentage

	FGA	FGM	Pct
Steve Smith, SA	246	116	.472
Jon Barry, Det	258	121	.469
Eric Piatkowski, LA Clippers	238	111	.466
Wally Szczerbiak, Minn	191	87	.455
Steve Nash, Dal	343	156	.455
Hubert Davis, Wash	126	57	.452
Tyronn Lue, Wash	141	63	.447
Michael Redd, Mil	198	88	.444
Wesley Person, Clev	322	143	.444
Ray Allen, Mil	528	229	.434

Steals

	GP	Steals	Avg
Allen Iverson, Phil	60	168	2.80
Ron Artest, Ind	55	141	2.56
Jason Kidd, NJ	82	175	2.13
Baron Davis, Char	82	172	2.10
Doug Christie, Sac	81	160	1.98
Darrell Armstrong, Orl	82	157	1.91
Karl Malone, Utah	80	152	1.90
Paul Pierce, Bos	82	154	1.88
Kenny Anderson, Bos	76	141	1.86
John Stockton, Utah	82	152	1.85
Jason Terry, Atl	78	144	1.85

Blocked Shots

	GP	BS	Avg
Ben Wallace, Det	80	278	3.48
Raef LaFrentz, Dal	78	213	2.73
Alonzo Mourning, Mia	75	186	2.48
Tim Duncan, SA	82	203	2.48
Dikembe Mutombo, Phil	80	190	2.38
Jermaine O'Neal, Ind	72	166	2.31
Erick Dampier, GS	73	167	2.29
Adonal Foyle, GS	79	168	2.13
Pau Gasol, Mem	82	169	2.06
Shaquille O'Neal, LA Lakers	67	137	2.04
Elton Brand, LA Clippers	80	163	2.04

Offense

Team	Field Goals FGM	Pct	3-Pt Field Goals FGM	Pct	Free Throws FTM	Pct	Rebounds Off	Total	A	Stl	Scoring Avg
Dallas	3200	46.2	621	37.8	1608	80.6	918	3486	1811	581	105.2
Sacramento	3267	46.7	426	36.7	1618	75.1	1013	3715	1958	741	104.6
LA Lakers	3150	46.1	510	35.4	1494	69.9	1022	3629	1882	625	101.3
Orlando	3087	44.8	620	37.3	1446	75.4	942	3382	1804	524	100.5
Minnesota	3175	46.1	396	37.8	1399	79.8	1059	3621	1993	665	99.3
Seattle	3131	46.9	489	37.8	1263	75.5	968	3301	1926	698	97.7
Golden State	2998	46.2	320	32.2	1693	72.2	1332	3827	1706	650	97.7
Milwaukee	3041	46.2	593	37.5	1321	74.8	841	3398	1847	596	97.5
Indiana	2935	44.6	405	33.9	1663	77.2	930	3498	1884	658	96.8
San Antonio	2913	45.8	438	36.2	1668	74.2	907	3473	1643	625	96.7
Portland	3004	45.0	466	35.4	1451	76.3	1085	3529	1926	702	96.6
Boston	2852	42.4	699	35.9	1498	76.4	891	3461	1722	793	96.4
New Jersey	3042	44.6	403	33.8	1402	73.5	1039	3554	1990	716	96.3
Utah	2869	45.0	280	33.3	1853	76.3	1109	3458	1999	749	96.0
LA Clippers	2970	44.5	408	35.6	1498	73.9	1083	2474	1714	510	95.7
Cleveland	2948	44.8	387	37.7	1529	77.2	968	3451	1891	572	95.3
Phoenix	3097	44.7	358	32.7	1250	76.7	1072	3502	1838	668	95.1
Detroit	2845	45.2	567	37.6	1478	75.6	810	3176	1765	648	94.3
Atlanta	2901	43.9	423	35.4	1486	76.5	955	3400	1656	667	94.0
Charlotte	2893	44.0	346	34.8	1568	74.5	1059	3564	1759	653	93.9
Washington	2938	44.1	305	38.8	1428	76.5	1055	3448	1715	570	92.8
Houston	2837	42.8	496	33.5	1402	74.1	1025	3436	1482	537	92.3
Denver	2915	42.4	423	32.9	1306	74.4	1117	3427	1817	613	92.2
New York	2817	43.2	474	35.3	1406	78.7	876	3334	1720	558	91.6
Toronto	2919	43.4	387	34.9	1717	73.9	1114	3450	1779	688	91.4
Philadelphia	2804	43.6	214	29.9	2104	77.9	1092	3626	1638	705	91.0
Memphis	2851	43.6	336	30.7	1883	70.8	984	3397	1785	646	89.9
Chicago	2811	43.3	300	34.6	1958	72.2	924	3283	1817	633	89.5
Miami	2801	43.9	312	34.7	1708	72.4	902	3446	1664	547	87.2

Defense (Opponent's Statistics)

Team	Field Goals FGM	Pct	3-Pt Field Goals 3FGM	Pct	Free Throws FTM	Pct	Rebounds Off	Total	Stl	Scoring Avg	Diff
Miami	2666	42.5	379	34.2	1565	73.6	894	3378	620	88.7	-1.5
Philadelphia	2771	42.6	438	33.1	1350	75.1	981	3329	654	89.4	+1.6
San Antonio	2883	42.6	374	33.8	1283	77.7	1003	3432	635	90.5	+6.2
Toronto	2820	44.1	377	34.6	1513	75.2	995	3431	628	91.8	-0.4
New Jersey	2858	42.9	409	34.8	1423	75.3	999	3416	669	92.0	+4.2
Detroit	2926	44.7	359	36.2	1349	75.5	991	3502	651	92.2	+2.1
New Orleans	2850	43.2	433	37.5	1488	76.8	963	3362	625	92.9	+1.0
Portland	2951	45.3	466	36.3	1312	74.1	890	3218	612	93.7	+3.0
Boston	2872	42.4	399	31.7	1577	76.1	954	3761	623	94.1	+7.1
LA Lakers	2797	42.5	514	34.0	1612	77.1	1016	3542	587	94.1	+2.2
Washington	2953	4.2	422	35.4	1396	75.5	960	3336	573	94.2	-1.4
Seattle	2966	44.9	472	34.4	1362	73.9	1091	3417	568	94.7	+3.0
Utah	2777	44.7	465	38.3	1779	77.1	927	3131	748	95.1	+0.9
New York	2924	44.5	443	35.3	1550	75.7	959	3499	686	95.6	-4.0
Phoenix	2957	44.4	433	35.8	1511	75.1	1030	3523	685	95.8	-0.7
Minnesota	2962	44.5	492	37.2	1452	74.2	912	3238	542	96.0	+3.4
LA Clippers	3074	44.8	407	35.5	1329	74.5	1064	3443	612	96.1	-0.5
Indiana	2977	43.8	418	34.8	1544	74.9	1048	3562	618	96.5	+0.3
Sacramento	3128	44.0	386	33.7	1312	74.4	1065	3682	633	97.0	+7.6
Houston	3191	46.4	370	36.0	1221	75.2	1045	3552	576	97.2	-4.9
Memphis	3119	45.7	398	35.8	1346	75.3	1135	3695	781	97.3	-7.4
Milwaukee	3016	44.1	493	35.8	1489	75.7	1050	3488	599	97.7	-0.2
Denver	3027	46.5	421	35.8	1560	74.6	995	3524	671	98.0	-8.5
Chicago	3005	45.9	424	36.1	1602	74.7	944	3497	681	98.0	-5.8
Atlanta	3065	45.9	472	35.5	1456	74.4	1004	3527	705	98.3	-4.2
Cleveland	3053	45.7	473	39.4	1506	74.8	928	3310	602	98.6	-3.3
Orlando	3116	45.6	409	35.2	1470	73.7	1086	3719	659	98.9	+1.6
Dallas	3094	45.2	452	35.0	1640	75.1	1065	3665	589	101.0	+4.3
Golden State	3213	45.9	404	34.8	1622	76.3	1100	3550	706	103.1	-5.4

Atlanta Hawks

Player	GP	Min	Field Goals		3-Pt FG		Free Throws		Rebounds		A	Stl	TO	BS	Avg
			FGM	Pct	FGA	FGM	FTM	Pct	Off	Total					
Abdur-Rahim	77	2980	598	46.1	70	21	419	80.1	198	696	239	98	250	81	21.2
Terry	78	2967	524	43.0	444	172	284	83.5	40	270	444	144	181	13	19.3
Kukoc	59	1494	211	41.9	171	53	109	71.2	43	218	210	48	113	17	9.9
Mohammed	82	2168	329	46.1	1	0	137	61.7	242	651	33	63	118	61	9.7
Glover	55	1156	192	42.1	91	30	78	75.7	36	169	84	45	76	14	8.9
Johnson	72	1727	214	39.6	247	89	85	81.0	59	247	81	62	102	56	8.4
Newble	42	1273	131	49.8	7	1	75	85.2	80	222	45	38	49	20	8.0
Davis	28	774	70	35.4	85	29	16	88.9	19	74	68	27	52	5	6.6
Vaughn	82	1856	206	47.0	54	24	104	82.5	18	168	349	65	112	2	6.6
Henderson	26	422	59	50.9	1	1	24	53.3	31	97	11	11	21	15	5.5
Mottola	82	1371	169	44.0	13	1	57	75.0	81	268	50	20	70	19	4.8
Strickland	46	654	91	44.6	4	1	25	56.8	41	131	20	19	28	17	4.5
Bowdler	52	585	61	35.1	5	1	39	83.0	38	110	11	18	11	15	3.1
Smith	14	100	10	38.5	0	0	11	64.7	10	31	3	5	3	1	2.2
Hawks	**82**	**19780**	**2901**	**43.9**	**1194**	**423**	**1486**	**76.5**	**955**	**3400**	**1656**	**667**	**1275**	**350**	**94.0**
Opponents	**82**	**19780**	**3065**	**45.9**	**1329**	**472**	**1456**	**74.4**	**1004**	**3527**	**1856**	**705**	**1239**	**509**	**98.3**

Boston Celtics

Player	GP	Min	Field Goals		3-Pt FG		Free Throws		Rebounds		A	Stl	TO	BS	Avg
			FGM	Pct	FGA	FGM	FTM	Pct	Off	Total					
Pierce	82	3302	707	44.2	520	210	520	80.9	81	566	261	154	241	86	26.1
Walker	81	3406	666	39.4	645	222	240	74.1	150	714	407	122	251	38	22.1
Rogers	27	626	107	48.2	95	39	35	70.0	34	107	40	16	42	12	10.7
Anderson	76	2430	312	43.6	33	9	98	74.2	57	275	403	141	119	10	9.6
Strickland	79	1643	190	38.9	247	95	131	84.5	22	213	184	56	94	1	7.7
Dek	22	570	60	34.9	67	20	22	73.3	20	79	51	22	19	6	7.4
Battie	74	1819	211	54.1	2	0	88	67.7	184	481	35	60	219	51	6.9
Williams	74	1747	144	37.4	86	24	160	73.1	58	221	109	77	95	8	6.4
Johnson	48	1003	130	43.9	88	24	20	76.9	40	139	74	33	28	9	6.3
Potapenko	79	1343	137	45.5	0	0	89	74.2	167	347	30	37	63	18	4.6
McCarty	56	718	80	44.4	99	39	13	68.4	32	128	41	18	22	7	3.8
Palacio	41	518	52	38.5	34	12	36	70.6	8	50	54	21	24	3	3.7
K. Brown	29	245	23	32.9	27	5	12	60.0	11	50	15	18	7	7	2.2
Blount	44	415	32	42.1	0	0	30	81.1	26	85	10	16	23	19	2.1
Celtics	**82**	**19830**	**2852**	**42.4**	**1946**	**699**	**1498**	**76.4**	**891**	**3461**	**1722**	**793**	**1113**	**292**	**96.4**
Opponents	**82**	**19830**	**2797**	**42.5**	**1511**	**514**	**1612**	**77.1**	**954**	**3761**	**1802**	**623**	**1335**	**476**	**94.1**

Charlotte Hornets

Player	GP	Min	Field Goals		3-Pt FG		Free Throws		Rebounds		A	Stl	TO	BS	Avg
			FGM	Pct	FGA	FGM	FTM	Pct	Off	Total					
Mashburn	40	1601	303	40.7	112	41	211	87.6	31	242	171	45	110	6	21.5
Davis	82	3318	559	41.7	478	170	196	58.0	93	349	698	172	246	47	18.1
Wesley	67	2487	364	40.0	256	85	138	73.4	44	143	236	74	119	15	14.2
Campbell	77	2156	384	48.4	2	0	306	79.7	133	530	102	60	138	137	13.9
Nailon	79	1912	369	48.3	2	1	112	74.7	103	291	94	59	96	17	10.8
Magloire	82	1549	228	55.1	1	0	243	73.0	153	461	31	27	118	86	8.5
Brown	80	2563	250	47.4	0	0	169	85.8	273	786	107	59	86	78	8.4
Augmon	77	1319	140	42.7	3	0	77	76.2	59	225	103	56	54	12	4.6
Lynch	45	893	73	36.9	6	1	25	62.5	70	186	54	40	41	14	3.8
Traylor	61	678	87	42.6	1	1	53	63.1	67	187	37	24	45	37	3.7
Bullard	31	350	39	33.9	57	16	11	91.7	10	47	16	2	12	2	3.4
Drew	61	774	78	42.9	73	31	23	79.3	14	72	101	32	33	2	3.4
Haston	15	77	11	28.2	3	0	4	50.0	5	20	5	0	3	1	1.7
Moiso	15	76	8	40.0	0	0	0	0.0	4	25	4	3	8	2	1.1
Hornets	**82**	**19755**	**2893**	**44.0**	**994**	**346**	**1568**	**74.5**	**1059**	**3564**	**1759**	**663**	**1150**	**456**	**93.9**
Opponents	**82**	**19755**	**2850**	**43.2**	**1156**	**433**	**1488**	**76.8**	**963**	**3362**	**1639**	**625**	**1140**	**422**	**92.9**

Chicago Bulls

Player	GP	Min	FGM	Pct	FGA	FGM	FTM	Pct	Off	Total	A	Stl	TO	BS	Avg
			Field Goals		3-Pt FG		Free Throws		Rebounds						
Rose	30	1216	276	47.0	100	37	125	83.9	14	124	158	33	96	16	23.8
Mercer	40	1503	286	39.9	57	17	84	77.8	44	155	118	30	79	10	16.8
Artest	27	823	152	43.3	91	36	81	62.8	40	131	77	75	69	23	15.6
Miller	48	1391	208	46.0	4	2	190	75.1	176	401	101	52	74	29	12.7
Fizer	76	1963	371	43.8	41	7	189	66.8	128	299	120	49	131	24	12.3
Best	30	793	112	44.1	25	8	47	92.2	10	81	149	32	40	1	9.3
Crawford	23	481	89	47.6	58	26	10	76.9	5	34	55	18	32	5	9.3
Robinson	29	653	112	45.3	5	2	36	75.0	24	78	37	23	36	11	9.0
Hassell	78	2237	267	42.5	165	60	87	76.3	65	255	172	55	101	44	8.7
Anthony	36	961	113	39.4	90	29	47	67.1	16	88	203	49	58	4	8.4
Curry	72	1150	189	50.1	0	0	105	65.6	111	272	25	16	69	53	6.7
Chandler	71	1389	151	49.7	0	0	134	60.4	113	343	54	28	99	93	6.1
Ollie	52	1146	97	38.3	2	1	109	83.8	18	128	193	36	80	1	5.8
Guyton	45	607	88	36.1	123	46	22	81.5	12	44	81	10	37	7	5.4
Hoiberg	79	1408	121	41.6	92	24	79	84.0	18	210	136	61	32	5	4.4
Oakley	57	1383	97	39.9	6	1	21	75.0	72	343	114	49	87	11	3.8
Bagaric	50	638	72	40.4	1	0	41	58.6	55	162	23	17	46	24	3.7
Bulls	**82**	**19805**	**2811**	**43.3**	**868**	**300**	**1413**	**72.2**	**924**	**3283**	**1817**	**633**	**1252**	**361**	**89.5**
Opponents	**82**	**19805**	**3027**	**46.5**	**1177**	**421**	**1560**	**74.6**	**944**	**3497**	**2066**	**681**	**1178**	**399**	**98.0**

Cleveland Cavaliers

Player	GP	Min	FGM	Pct	FGA	FGM	FTM	Pct	Off	Total	A	Stl	TO	BS	Avg
			Field Goals		3-Pt FG		Free Throws		Rebounds						
Murray	71	2312	430	43.6	238	101	215	81.7	81	372	157	70	141	43	16.6
Miller	81	3023	474	45.4	87	22	365	81.7	108	379	882	126	245	34	16.5
Person	78	2793	467	49.5	322	143	99	79.8	50	294	173	77	74	37	15.1
Davis	82	1954	376	48.1	35	11	196	79.0	63	243	178	69	148	23	11.7
Ilgauskas	62	1329	241	42.5	5	0	208	75.4	136	334	70	17	94	84	11.1
Jones	81	2142	287	44.8	168	52	45	66.2	125	490	116	75	79	46	8.3
Hill	26	810	71	39.0	1	0	67	65.0	79	274	23	17	48	13	8.0
Mihm	74	1659	221	42.0	7	3	124	69.3	133	392	24	18	97	89	7.7
Langdon	44	477	70	39.8	74	27	42	91.3	13	55	60	13	40	5	4.8
Doleac	42	705	78	41.7	0	0	38	82.6	47	168	25	15	37	11	4.6
Stith	50	665	70	37.2	68	24	44	84.6	20	85	24	29	30	6	4.2
Skinner	65	1107	88	54.3	0	0	48	60.8	93	281	17	24	42	61	3.4
Coles	47	693	56	38.4	20	4	33	89.2	12	55	107	13	31	4	3.2
Trepagnier	12	77	7	30.4	1	0	4	57.1	3	12	12	8	11	4	1.5
Diop	18	109	12	41.4	0	0	1	20.0	5	17	5	1	12	10	1.4
Cavs	**82**	**19855**	**2948**	**44.8**	**1026**	**387**	**1529**	**77.2**	**968**	**3483**	**1891**	**572**	**1196**	**470**	**95.3**
Opponents	**82**	**19855**	**3053**	**45.7**	**1200**	**473**	**1506**	**74.8**	**928**	**3310**	**1989**	**602**	**1063**	**459**	**98.6**

Dallas Mavericks

Player	GP	Min	FGM	Pct	FGA	FGM	FTM	Pct	Off	Total	A	Stl	TO	BS	Avg
			Field Goals		3-Pt FG		Free Throws		Rebounds						
Nowitzki	76	2891	600	47.7	350	139	440	85.3	120	755	186	83	145	77	23.4
Finley	69	2754	569	46.3	224	76	210	83.7	90	360	230	65	117	25	20.6
Nash	82	2837	525	48.3	343	156	260	88.7	50	254	634	53	229	4	17.9
Van Exel	37	1257	129	41.1	98	34	65	84.4	9	85	113	14	35	4	13.2
Howard	53	1659	270	46.2	1	0	144	75.4	138	390	93	28	78	30	12.9
LeFrentz	27	787	114	43.7	95	29	35	76.1	59	200	29	24	34	60	10.8
Hardaway	54	1276	179	36.2	279	95	65	83.3	13	97	201	40	73	8	9.6
Griffin	58	1383	179	49.9	54	16	41	83.7	68	229	106	75	42	12	7.2
Najera	62	1357	150	50.0	2	0	100	67.6	149	342	38	56	40	30	6.5
Buckner	44	885	104	52.5	16	5	40	69.0	67	173	48	31	27	19	5.8
Wang	55	600	109	44.0	116	48	42	73.7	19	111	22	11	25	18	5.6
Newman	47	724	67	45.3	57	22	42	72.4	9	49	14	29	21	4	4.2
Bradley	53	757	78	47.9	1	0	59	92.2	53	123	176	20	64	28	4.1
Manning	41	552	71	47.7	7	1	22	66.7	25	108	30	21	25	21	4.0
Johnson	17	152	21	42.9	0	0	12	70.6	0	5	28	5	9	1	3.2
Harvey	18	162	14	53.8	0	0	10	45.5	12	46	5	4	8	5	2.1
Eschmeyer	31	299	21	42.0	0	0	20	60.6	35	98	9	10	16	9	2.0
Mavericks	**82**	**19880**	**3200**	**46.2**	**1645**	**621**	**1608**	**80.6**	**918**	**3486**	**1811**	**581**	**992**	**392**	**105.2**
Opponents	**82**	**19880**	**3094**	**45.2**	**1293**	**452**	**1640**	**75.1**	**1065**	**3665**	**1865**	**589**	**1155**	**377**	**101.0**

Denver Nuggets

Player	GP	Min	Field Goals		3-Pt FG		Free Throws		Rebounds		A	Stl	TO	BS	Avg
			FGM	Pct	FGA	FGM	FTM	Pct	Off	Total					
Van Exel	45	1739	372	40.8	252	85	136	78.2	19	169	365	30	116	7	21.4
Howard	28	976	192	45.7	1	0	117	77.0	85	222	76	18	74	17	17.9
LaFrentz	51	1668	307	46.6	173	75	70	66.7	117	379	60	31	60	153	14.9
Lenard	71	1665	315	41.0	240	89	94	78.3	38	183	130	59	91	25	11.5
McDyess	10	236	43	57.3	0	0	27	81.8	18	55	18	10	20	8	11.3
Posey	73	2238	277	37.6	237	67	161	79.3	109	429	180	114	127	39	10.7
Hardaway	14	325	47	37.3	75	28	12	63.2	1	27	77	17	38	2	9.6
Johnson	51	1200	186	48.6	5	0	109	74.7	14	64	258	35	67	8	9.4
McCloud	69	1830	206	35.8	222	60	132	81.0	67	251	204	58	144	19	8.8
Harvey	29	679	94	49.2	0	0	44	64.7	68	181	32	17	25	19	8.0
Cheaney	68	1631	224	48.1	4	0	46	68.7	57	240	110	34	70	21	7.3
Abdul-Wahad	20	417	55	37.9	2	1	24	75.0	39	78	22	18	24	9	6.8
Hamilton	54	848	103	42.0	0	0	118	65.2	110	253	14	21	60	18	6.0
Satterfield	36	560	73	36.7	27	7	36	78.3	17	52	108	31	53	1	5.3
Bateer	27	408	53	40.2	12	4	29	78.4	32	96	22	10	32	5	5.1
Williams	41	737	86	39.6	2	0	30	73.2	82	209	13	17	35	33	4.9
Bowen	75	1686	147	47.9	12	1	69	75.0	134	299	52	75	41	41	4.9
Arroyo	20	275	36	43.9	2	0	9	75.0	9	28	49	5	11	1	4.1
Scott	21	252	37	49.3	0	0	8	40.0	53	103	8	3	15	6	3.9
Andersen	24	262	25	33.8	4	0	22	78.6	38	76	7	7	13	28	3.0
Nuggets	**82**	**19805**	**2915**	**42.4**	**1285**	**423**	**1306**	**74.4**	**1117**	**3427**	**1817**	**613**	**1205**	**462**	**92.2**
Opponents	**82**	**19805**	**3005**	**45.9**	**1173**	**424**	**1602**	**74.7**	**995**	**3524**	**1968**	**671**	**1173**	**560**	**98.0**

Detroit Pistons

Player	GP	Min	Field Goals		3-Pt FG		Free Throws		Rebounds		A	Stl	TO	BS	Avg
			FGM	Pct	FGA	FGM	FTM	Pct	Off	Total					
Stackhouse	76	2685	524	39.7	300	86	495	85.8	77	315	403	77	266	37	21.4
Robinson	80	2855	454	42.5	304	115	143	69.4	79	386	202	89	151	95	14.6
Williamson	78	1701	411	51.0	5	1	240	80.5	117	319	94	49	137	26	13.6
Atkins	79	2285	368	46.6	336	138	83	69.2	31	127	263	72	128	11	12.1
Barry	82	1985	255	48.9	258	121	108	93.1	42	234	274	94	111	20	9.0
B. Wallace	80	2921	255	53.1	3	0	99	42.3	318	1039	115	138	70	278	7.6
Rebraca	74	1179	189	50.5	0	0	135	77.1	84	290	38	28	84	73	6.9
Barros	29	582	74	38.5	71	24	21	77.8	1	57	78	14	33	2	6.7
Jones	67	1083	114	40.1	186	69	43	72.9	13	103	140	23	61	1	5.1
Curry	82	1912	125	45.3	26	7	72	79.1	15	168	127	47	60	10	4.0
White	16	129	21	35.0	9	2	12	85.7	2	18	12	9	14	2	3.5
Alexander	15	97	18	35.3	2	0	4	50.0	7	29	6	0	5	1	2.7
Moore	30	217	29	47.5	2	1	20	76.9	22	53	11	7	14	9	2.6
Pistons	**82**	**19680**	**2845**	**46.2**	**1509**	**567**	**1478**	**75.6**	**810**	**3176**	**1765**	**648**	**1193**	**565**	**94.3**
Opponents	**82**	**19680**	**2926**	**44.7**	**993**	**359**	**1349**	**75.5**	**991**	**3502**	**1638**	**651**	**1273**	**335**	**92.2**

Golden State Warriors

Player	GP	Min	Field Goals		3-Pt FG		Free Throws		Rebounds		A	Stl	TO	BS	Avg
			FGM	Pct	FGA	FGM	FTM	Pct	Off	Total					
Jamison	82	3033	614	44.7	210	68	323	73.4	211	556	161	70	161	45	19.7
Richardson	80	2629	464	42.6	246	82	141	67.1	124	340	236	106	160	31	14.4
Hughes	73	2049	343	42.3	93	18	191	73.7	83	245	316	113	171	23	12.3
Fortson	77	2216	309	42.8	4	1	245	79.5	290	899	127	44	160	17	11.2
Arenas	47	1155	174	45.3	113	39	124	77.5	41	132	174	69	97	11	10.9
Sura	78	1780	250	42.4	133	42	236	72.0	89	256	275	88	133	17	10.0
Dampier	73	1740	209	43.5	0	0	136	64.5	167	387	87	17	156	167	7.6
Mills	66	1237	178	41.7	127	48	85	79.4	51	190	72	31	56	13	7.4
Murphy	82	1448	178	42.1	9	3	121	77.6	99	322	70	36	84	21	5.9
Jackson	17	169	22	33.8	0	0	40	83.3	17	43	7	5	12	3	4.9
Foyle	79	1485	171	44.4	0	0	37	39.8	150	384	41	36	76	168	4.8
Blaylock	35	599	50	34.2	42	15	4	50.0	8	52	114	24	37	4	3.4
Oliver	20	139	17	37.0	13	2	6	66.7	0	8	21	3	11	0	2.1
Warriors	**82**	**19780**	**2998**	**42.9**	**994**	**320**	**1693**	**72.2**	**1334**	**3827**	**1706**	**650**	**1378**	**523**	**97.7**
Opponents	**82**	**19780**	**3213**	**45.9**	**1162**	**404**	**1622**	**76.3**	**1100**	**3550**	**2002**	**706**	**1176**	**512**	**103.1**

Houston Rockets

| Player | GP | Min | Field Goals | | 3-Pt FG | | Free Throws | | Rebounds | | A | Stl | TO | BS | Avg |
			FGM	Pct	FGA	FGM	FTM	Pct	Off	Total					
Mobley	74	3116	595	43.8	377	149	267	85.0	63	300	187	109	180	37	21.7
Francis	57	2343	420	41.7	210	68	326	77.3	102	401	362	71	221	25	21.6
Thomas	72	2484	396	47.8	16	0	223	66.4	158	516	137	85	143	66	14.1
Williams	48	1117	166	41.9	183	78	40	78.4	37	162	69	18	53	10	9.4
Griffin	73	1896	244	36.6	273	90	64	74.4	117	416	53	17	47	134	8.8
Rice	20	606	65	38.9	64	18	24	80.0	5	47	31	12	24	3	8.6
Norris	82	2249	251	39.8	134	36	127	75.1	73	246	403	81	156	4	8.1
Cato	75	1917	190	58.3	1	0	113	58.2	176	525	29	40	53	95	6.6
Wills	52	865	125	44.0	1	0	65	74.7	105	299	14	25	41	23	6.1
Torres	65	1075	135	39.6	126	37	82	78.1	47	122	40	25	49	9	6.0
Collier	25	365	41	43.2	1	0	24	75.0	31	82	9	6	13	4	4.2
Morris	68	1110	111	38.4	78	15	18	64.3	77	211	64	21	45	27	3.8
Brown	40	403	49	42.6	12	4	21	75.0	12	42	70	19	40	3	3.1
Langhi	34	434	49	39.2	4	1	8	72.7	22	67	14	8	9	5	3.1
Rockets	**82**	**19980**	**2837**	**42.8**	**1480**	**496**	**1402**	**74.1**	**1025**	**3436**	**1482**	**537**	**1156**	**445**	**92.3**
Opponents	**82**	**19980**	**3191**	**46.4**	**1028**	**370**	**1221**	**75.2**	**1045**	**3552**	**1838**	**576**	**988**	**415**	**97.9**

Indiana Pacers

| Player | GP | Min | Field Goals | | 3-Pt FG | | Free Throws | | Rebounds | | A | Stl | TO | BS | Avg |
			FGM	Pct	FGA	FGM	FTM	Pct	Off	Total					
O'Neal	72	2707	543	47.9	14	1	284	68.8	188	757	118	45	174	166	19.0
Rose	53	1937	387	44.4	146	52	156	83.9	29	220	197	45	105	29	18.5
R. Miller	79	2889	414	45.3	443	180	296	91.1	23	219	253	88	120	10	16.5
B. Miller	28	872	158	56.2	3	1	107	82.3	76	220	51	24	41	12	15.1
Harrington	44	1313	230	47.5	3	.1	115	79.9	96	276	54	41	78	21	13.1
Artest	28	819	117	41.1	79	17	55	73.3	33	140	50	66	49	16	10.9
Tinsley	80	2442	289	38.0	175	42	131	70.4	78	298	647	138	270	40	9.4
Bender	78	1647	198	43.0	125	45	140	77.3	64	244	62	19	96	49	7.4
Best	44	954	116	43.9	34	13	57	87.7	10	70	175	57	59	6	6.9
Croshere	76	1286	185	41.3	145	49	97	85.1	74	294	77	26	67	29	6.8
Foster	82	1786	177	44.9	15	2	111	61.0	206	556	70	71	79	38	5.7
Ollie	29	577	40	40.0	0	0	78	80.4	7	56	98	26	26	1	5.4
Mercer	13	213	25	37.3	5	1	11	100.0	6	23	10	2	9	3	4.8
Rogers	22	168	24	55.8	6	1	10	52.6	14	38	3	5	5	6	2.7
Brezec	22	160	14	48.3	0	0	15	60.0	16	28	6	0	6	7	2.0
Sundov	22	88	16	40.0	1	0	0	0.0	7	21	3	3	4	3	1.5
Pacers	**82**	**19905**	**2935**	**44.6**	**1195**	**405**	**1663**	**77.2**	**930**	**3498**	**1884**	**658**	**1249**	**436**	**96.8**
Opponents	**82**	**19905**	**2977**	**43.8**	**1200**	**418**	**1544**	**74.9**	**1048**	**3562**	**1771**	**618**	**1173**	**466**	**96.5**

Los Angeles Clippers

| Player | GP | Min | Field Goals | | 3-Pt FG | | Free Throws | | Rebounds | | A | Stl | TO | BS | Avg |
			FGM	Pct	FGA	FGM	FTM	Pct	Off	Total					
Brand	80	3020	532	52.7	0	0	389	74.2	396	925	191	80	173	163	18.2
McInnis	81	3030	463	41.3	234	75	183	83.6	45	213	500	63	147	6	14.6
Richardson	81	2152	400	43.2	349	133	143	76.5	113	334	128	21	102	21	13.3
Odom	29	999	151	41.9	84	16	61	65.6	31	176	171	23	97	36	13.1
Maggette	63	1615	235	44.4	139	46	201	80.1	54	231	112	41	116	19	11.4
Olowokandi	80	2568	384	43.3	0	0	117	62.2	164	711	90	55	175	145	11.1
Miles	82	2227	309	48.1	19	3	158	62.0	109	344	453	71	160	103	9.5
Piatkowski	71	1718	207	43.9	238	111	101	89.4	43	184	112	41	64	12	8.8
Dooling	14	155	22	38.6	14	4	10	83.3	0	3	12	4	10	3	4.1
Boykins	68	761	110	40.0	42	13	47	77.0	27	54	145	20	44	2	4.1
Fowkes	22	343	25	39.1	0	0	24	77.4	32	64	17	11	13	1	3.4
Rooks	61	728	81	41.8	0	0	21	72.4	32	124	25	12	20	21	3.0
Jamison	25	176	22	51.2	0	0	10	66.7	24	39	6	5	6	1	2.2
Overton	18	130	14	31.8	27	7	4	57.1	1	12	13	3	12	1	2.2
Ekezie	29	152	13	33.3	0	0	28	70.0	12	34	3	2	10	6	1.9
Clippers	**82**	**19805**	**2970**	**44.5**	**1147**	**408**	**1498**	**73.9**	**1083**	**3557**	**1714**	**510**	**1214**	**540**	**95.7**
Opponents	**82**	**19805**	**3074**	**44.8**	**1145**	**407**	**1329**	**74.5**	**1064**	**3443**	**1859**	**612**	**1055**	**439**	**96.1**

Los Angeles Lakers

Player	GP	Min	FGM	Pct	FGA	FGM	FTM	Pct	Off	Total	A	Stl	TO	BS	Avg
O'Neal	67	2422	712	57.9	1	0	398	55.5	235	715	200	41	171	137	27.2
Bryant	80	3063	749	46.9	132	33	488	82.9	112	441	438	118	223	35	25.2
Fisher	70	1974	274	41.1	349	144	94	84.7	15	146	181	66	62	9	11.2
Fox	82	2289	255	42.1	208	65	70	82.4	90	389	283	67	132	21	7.9
George	82	1759	215	41.1	178	66	85	67.5	78	303	111	71	66	42	7.1
Horry	81	2140	183	39.8	203	76	108	78.3	130	479	232	77	88	89	6.8
Walker	69	1655	187	51.2	0	0	86	66.7	129	481	64	28	53	88	6.7
Hunter	82	1616	187	38.2	208	79	20	50.0	18	121	129	66	55	19	5.8
Medvedenko	71	729	145	47.7	4	0	41	66.1	85	158	43	29	42	11	4.7
Richmond	64	709	100	40.5	62	18	42	95.5	14	94	57	18	40	6	4.1
Shaw	58	631	61	35.3	88	29	18	69.2	19	112	89	25	32	3	2.9
Madsen	59	650	66	45.2	2	0	35	64.8	89	162	44	16	22	13	2.8
McCoy	21	104	12	57.1	0	0	2	25.0	8	25	7	0	8	5	1.2
Lakers	82	19780	3150	46.1	1439	510	1494	69.9	1022	3629	1882	625	1040	478	101.3
Opponents	82	19780	2872	42.4	1259	399	1577	76.1	1016	3542	1643	587	1148	354	94.1

Memphis Grizzlies

Player	GP	Min	FGM	Pct	FGA	FGM	FTM	Pct	Off	Total	A	Stl	TO	BS	Avg
Gasol	82	3007	551	51.8	5	1	338	70.9	238	730	223	41	224	169	17.6
Williams	65	2236	376	38.2	430	127	80	79.2	22	195	519	111	214	7	14.8
Battier	78	3097	412	42.9	276	103	198	70.0	180	418	216	121	155	81	14.4
Wright	43	1251	223	45.9	2	0	70	56.9	130	405	44	30	72	23	12.0
Swift	68	1805	293	48.0	3	0	217	71.1	161	430	50	53	122	113	11.8
Buford	63	1769	258	43.5	70	17	58	72.5	52	272	71	42	63	12	9.4
Knight	53	1151	141	42.2	8	2	87	75.7	11	109	302	79	111	7	7.0
Long	66	1868	164	42.6	17	3	86	69.9	31	231	136	63	103	12	6.3
Massenburg	73	1247	159	45.6	1	1	84	71.8	100	324	26	30	65	31	5.5
Solomon	62	872	113	34.1	162	46	49	67.1	12	68	92	35	7	62	5.2
Gill	23	384	39	42.4	22	7	31	79.5	7	28	49	11	3	34	5.0
Fotsis	28	320	42	40.4	23	7	17	85.0	25	62	10	9	21	11	3.9
Grizzlies	82	19780	2851	43.6	1096	336	1334	70.8	984	3397	1785	646	1344	488	89.9
Opponents	82	19780	3119	45.7	1112	398	1346	75.3	1135	3695	1961	781	1207	457	97.3

Miami Heat

Player	GP	Min	FGM	Pct	FGA	FGM	FTM	Pct	Off	Total	A	Stl	TO	BS	Avg
Jones	81	3156	517	43.2	382	149	297	83.7	61	378	262	117	148	77	18.3
Mourning	75	2455	447	51.6	3	1	283	65.7	182	632	87	27	182	186	15.7
Jackson	55	1825	238	44.2	81	38	75	86.2	54	290	140	42	106	14	10.7
Strickland	76	2294	316	44.3	26	8	154	76.6	49	232	463	82	159	11	10.4
Grant	72	2256	286	46.9	2	0	101	84.9	168	575	137	48	122	31	9.3
House	64	1230	209	39.9	157	54	42	85.7	17	110	123	43	80	5	8.0
Ellis	66	1684	189	41.8	124	38	53	63.1	107	287	56	30	73	37	7.1
Gatling	54	809	131	44.7	8	1	82	70.1	71	206	25	17	58	11	6.4
Gill	65	1410	162	38.4	44	6	42	67.7	29	184	100	44	55	8	5.7
Marks	21	319	38	43.2	0	0	20	58.8	19	75	8	5	19	10	4.6
Carter	46	1050	89	34.2	19	1	19	52.8	19	117	214	50	72	3	4.3
Allen	12	161	22	43.1	1	0	8	80.0	15	38	5	3	2	8	4.3
Stepania	67	884	117	47.0	2	1	50	48.1	100	270	16	24	52	44	4.3
Mack	12	159	14	28.6	28	7	5	71.4	2	14	4	5	7	1	3.3
James	15	119	15	34.9	21	8	4	57.1	2	14	19	6	13	1	2.8
Heat	82	19930	2801	43.9	899	312	1236	72.4	902	3446	1664	547	1217	448	87.2
Opponents	82	19930	2666	42.5	1109	379	1565	73.6	894	3378	1461	620	1134	353	88.7

Milwaukee Bucks

Player	GP	Min	Field Goals FGM	Pct	3-Pt FG FGA	FGM	Free Throws FTM	Pct	Rebounds Off	Total	A	Stl	TO	BS	Avg
Allen	69	2525	530	46.2	528	229	214	87.3	81	312	271	88	159	18	21.8
Robinson	66	2346	536	46.7	178	58	236	83.7	70	406	168	97	174	41	20.7
Cassell	74	2605	554	46.3	204	71	282	86.0	54	312	493	90	177	12	19.7
Thomas	74	1987	316	42.0	291	95	142	79.3	64	300	105	65	127	32	11.7
Redd	67	1417	294	48.3	198	88	91	79.1	77	224	91	42	57	7	11.4
Mason	82	3143	316	50.5	1	1	154	69.7	124	646	346	57	130	22	9.6
Anthony	24	553	70	37.2	73	19	13	61.9	6	44	79	28	36	1	7.2
Caffey	23	283	36	50.0	1	0	27	62.8	24	50	12	4	19	5	4.3
Ham	70	1208	120	56.9	7	1	62	50.4	91	202	73	25	83	37	4.3
Alston	50	600	66	34.6	71	27	18	62.1	10	72	143	32	40	2	3.5
Przybilla	71	1128	76	53.5	1	0	38	42.2	78	283	21	20	43	118	2.7
Johnson	81	1660	89	46.1	1	0	30	45.5	142	466	27	37	52	82	2.6
Pope	45	426	36	39.6	25	4	11	52.4	20	73	17	11	15	11	1.9
Bucks	**82**	**19905**	**3041**	**46.2**	**1583**	**593**	**1321**	**74.8**	**841**	**3398**	**1847**	**596**	**1157**	**388**	**97.5**
Opponents	**82**	**19905**	**3016**	**44.1**	**1377**	**493**	**1489**	**75.7**	**1050**	**3488**	**1883**	**599**	**1054**	**361**	**97.7**

Minnesota Timberwolves

Player	GP	Min	Field Goals FGM	Pct	3-Pt FG FGA	FGM	Free Throws FTM	Pct	Rebounds Off	Total	A	Stl	TO	BS	Avg
K. Garnett	81	3175	659	47.0	116	37	359	80.1	243	981	422	96	229	126	21.2
Szczerbiak	82	3117	609	50.8	191	87	226	83.1	120	391	257	66	181	21	18.7
Billups	82	2355	348	42.3	315	124	207	88.5	35	226	450	66	138	17	12.5
Brandon	32	962	155	42.5	23	4	83	98.8	17	93	264	52	43	6	12.4
Smith	72	1922	297	51.1	3	2	171	83.0	152	453	82	39	86	59	10.7
Peeler	82	2060	288	42.1	283	111	50	86.2	37	206	177	61	76	11	9.0
Nesterovic	82	2218	324	49.3	1	0	39	54.9	200	534	75	45	94	109	8.4
Trent	64	1140	193	50.7	2	0	92	63.9	104	270	60	21	58	27	7.5
Jackson	22	326	38	38.4	1	0	26	81.3	31	85	7	6	18	3	4.6
Pack	16	252	25	36.8	4	1	11	73.3	7	23	49	13	20	0	3.9
Mitchell	74	726	98	43.2	35	10	38	77.6	18	80	45	12	26	4	3.3
Lopez	67	581	59	37.8	33	14	37	67.3	29	80	39	18	36	1	2.5
Avery	28	258	26	28.9	35	6	13	68.4	4	24	36	7	19	0	2.5
Woods	60	516	33	34.4	2	0	44	73.3	46	122	22	17	36	34	1.8
D. Garrett	29	152	14	35.0	0	0	0	0.0	13	47	4	5	7	9	1.0
T'wolves	**82**	**19805**	**3175**	**46.1**	**1047**	**396**	**1399**	**79.8**	**1059**	**3621**	**1993**	**524**	**1097**	**427**	**99.3**
Opponents	**82**	**19805**	**2962**	**44.5**	**1321**	**492**	**1452**	**74.2**	**912**	**3238**	**1855**	**542**	**1097**	**407**	**96.0**

New Jersey Nets

Player	GP	Min	Field Goals FGM	Pct	3-Pt FG FGA	FGM	Free Throws FTM	Pct	Rebounds Off	Total	A	Stl	TO	BS	Avg
Martin	73	2504	445	46.3	67	15	181	67.8	113	388	192	90	172	121	14.9
Van Horn	81	2465	471	43.3	293	101	156	80.0	137	609	164	63	146	42	14.8
Kidd	82	3056	445	39.1	364	117	201	81.4	130	595	808	175	286	20	14.7
Kittles	82	2601	438	46.6	242	98	128	74.4	68	275	216	130	109	31	13.4
McCulloch	62	1502	247	52.1	0	0	110	67.1	157	378	78	24	66	89	9.7
Jefferson	79	1917	270	45.7	56	13	189	71.3	85	293	140	64	107	48	9.4
Harris	74	1553	249	46.4	118	44	133	84.2	49	207	116	53	61	6	9.1
Williams	82	1546	231	52.6	2	0	130	69.9	115	339	77	29	79	76	7.2
Collins	77	1407	117	42.1	2	1	115	70.1	132	301	81	29	72	47	4.5
Dial	25	249	30	31.9	7	0	13	72.2	12	45	31	8	13	4	2.9
Johnson	34	366	37	41.1	12	4	16	64.0	10	29	48	31	20	1	2.8
Scalabrine	28	290	23	34.3	10	3	11	73.3	12	51	21	9	24	2	2.1
Armstrong	35	196	27	31.8	17	5	5	50.0	10	16	8	7	8	1	1.8
Marshall	20	118	29	27.6	4	2	12	66.7	8	21	5	3	2	0	1.5
Nets	**82**	**19830**	**3042**	**44.6**	**1194**	**403**	**1402**	**73.5**	**1039**	**3554**	**1990**	**716**	**1189**	**490**	**96.2**
Opponents	**82**	**19830**	**2958**	**42.9**	**1175**	**409**	**1423**	**75.3**	**999**	**3416**	**1563**	**669**	**1317**	**439**	**92.0**

New York Knicks

Player	GP	Min	Field Goals		3-Pt FG		Free Throws		Rebounds		A	Stl	TO	BS	Avg
			FGM	Pct	FGA	FGM	FTM	Pct	Off	Total					
Houston	77	2914	568	43.7	346	136	295	87.0	37	252	190	54	170	10	20.4
Sprewell	81	3326	573	40.4	403	145	284	82.1	59	298	314	94	223	14	19.4
Thomas	82	2771	463	49.4	6	1	216	81.5	214	747	87	71	153	79	13.9
Camby	29	1007	130	44.8	1	0	62	62.6	89	322	33	34	42	50	11.1
Weatherspoon	56	1728	189	41.8	0	0	116	79.5	149	460	60	37	47	48	8.8
Jackson	82	2367	260	43.9	195	79	87	79.1	56	309	605	74	150	1	8.4
Harrington	77	1563	237	52.7	2	0	122	70.9	125	349	37	30	95	36	7.7
Ward	63	1058	113	37.3	164	53	47	81.0	15	127	203	68	75	14	5.2
Anderson	82	1596	149	39.9	141	39	74	69.2	57	249	76	48	97	15	5.0
Eisley	39	609	59	33.7	58	14	39	79.6	9	49	100	24	53	2	4.4
Postell	23	179	28	33.3	26	6	31	75.6	2	16	5	6	11	0	4.0
Knight	49	429	41	36.3	0	0	16	76.2	48	104	8	11	27	10	2.0
Spencer	32	248	6	23.1	0	0	17	51.5	16	50	3	7	12	8	0.9
Knicks	82	19805	2817	43.2	1344	474	1406	78.7	876	3334	1720	558	1192	288	91.6
Opponents	82	19805	2924	44.5	1256	443	1550	75.7	959	3499	1762	686	1103	385	95.6

Orlando Magic

Player	GP	Min	Field Goals		3-Pt FG		Free Throws		Rebounds		A	Stl	TO	BS	Avg
			FGM	Pct	FGA	FGM	FTM	Pct	Off	Total					
McGrady	76	2912	15	45.1	283	103	415	74.8	150	597	400	119	189	73	25.6
Hill	14	512	83	42.6	2	0	69	86.3	29	125	64	8	37	4	16.8
Miller	63	2123	351	43.8	303	116	138	76.2	49	273	198	47	108	23	15.2
Armstrong	82	2730	347	41.9	398	139	182	88.8	83	319	453	157	175	10	12.4
Hudson	81	1854	354	43.4	187	66	176	87.6	30	145	255	57	163	6	11.7
Garrity	80	2406	327	42.6	396	169	61	83.6	77	338	99	61	68	28	11.1
Grant	76	2210	264	51.3	0	0	80	72.1	159	481	104	57	51	49	8.0
Williams	68	1284	198	54.7	4	0	88	65.7	80	235	96	49	86	17	7.1
Ewing	65	901	148	44.4	1	0	94	70.1	60	263	35	22	65	45	6.0
Hunter	53	516	67	45.6	0	0	55	58.5	40	97	5	5	16	43	3.6
Outlaw	10	160	13	61.9	0	0	8	44.4	15	29	5	9	11	9	3.4
Reid	68	714	90	47.4	0	0	44	64.7	65	176	27	20	54	44	3.3
DeClercq	61	633	67	45.0	0	0	28	56.0	74	163	22	23	34	24	2.7
Buechler	60	630	42	37.5	54	19	2	50.0	27	108	29	20	14	8	1.8
Magic	82	19830	3087	44.8	1660	620	1446	75.4	942	3382	1804	665	1119	384	100.5
Opponents	82	19830	3116	45.6	1161	409	1470	73.7	1086	3719	1930	659	1292	384	98.9

Philadelphia 76ers

Player	GP	Min	Field Goals		3-Pt FG		Free Throws		Rebounds		A	Stl	TO	BS	Avg
			FGM	Pct	FGA	FGM	FTM	Pct	Off	Total					
Iverson	60	2622	665	39.8	268	78	475	81.2	44	269	331	168	237	13	31.4
Coleman	58	2080	331	45.0	83	28	185	81.5	167	509	98	42	119	51	15.1
McKie	48	1471	220	44.9	128	51	96	78.7	26	192	179	56	93	14	12.2
Snow	61	2225	276	44.2	27	3	183	80.6	33	215	400	95	138	9	12.1
Harping	81	2541	386	46.1	69	21	165	74.3	203	573	107	70	127	5	11.8
Mutombo	80	2907	321	50.1	0	0	278	76.4	254	863	83	29	156	190	11.5
Claxton	67	1528	181	40.0	33	4	114	83.8	46	160	198	95	95	6	7.2
Blount	72	1426	115	45.8	1	0	29	64.4	149	368	44	49	52	26	3.6
Bell	74	890	103	42.9	44	12	36	75.0	31	111	71	21	48	4	3.4
Cummings	58	501	78	41.7	46	12	24	75.0	14	52	60	18	36	5	3.3
McKey	41	784	52	42.6	12	5	10	71.4	48	127	45	41	22	4	2.9
Dalembert	34	177	22	44.0	0	0	7	38.9	25	68	5	6	14	13	1.5
Brown	17	67	8	38.1	1	0	7	87.5	2	4	2	1	9	1	1.4
Jones	23	126	8	40.0	0	0	10	50.0	13	36	3	3	11	9	1.1
Ruffin	15	169	7	26.9	0	0	2	25.0	23	51	5	5	11	8	1.1
76ers	82	19730	2804	43.6	715	214	1639	77.9	1092	3626	1638	705	1256	363	91.0
Opponents	82	19730	2771	42.6	1322	438	1350	75.1	981	3329	1768	654	1208	458	89.4

Phoenix Suns

Player	GP	Min	Field Goals		3-Pt FG		Free Throws		Rebounds		A	Stl	TO	BS	Avg
			FGM	Pct	FGA	FGM	FTM	Pct	Off	Total					
Marbury	82	3187	625	44.2	248	71	353	78.1	75	266	666	77	284	13	20.4
Marion	81	3109	654	46.9	122	48	191	84.5	211	803	162	149	144	86	19.1
Rogers	50	1254	249	46.6	140	23	82	82.8	95	241	72	50	66	17	12.6
Hardaway	80	2462	389	41.8	83	49	158	81.0	98	350	324	122	189	32	12.0
Dek	41	877	166	39.9	147	47	56	83.6	38	124	81	31	40	4	10.6
Johnson	29	913	121	42.0	42	14	21	77.8	35	118	105	26	43	11	9.6
Tsakalidis	67	1582	190	47.5	1	0	111	69.8	130	374	23	23	78	69	7.3
Gugliotta	44	1129	127	42.2	9	3	28	75.7	59	221	77	39	61	30	6.5
Voskuhl	59	900	107	55.4	0	0	82	75.2	103	250	18	11	48	23	5.0
Wallace	46	490	93	43.5	13	5	40	87.0	27	85	29	11	29	9	5.0
Outlaw	73	1768	153	55.0	2	1	35	41.7	132	335	122	61	85	83	4.7
Majerle	65	1180	99	34.3	235	79	23	59.0	28	176	90	48	35	15	4.6
Crispin	15	129	23	41.1	35	15	8	100.0	2	10	24	2	9	0	4.6
Ford	53	452	61	51.7	0	0	42	73.7	32	107	7	6	32	7	3.1
Palacio	28	272	30	38.0	7	1	18	78.3	3	23	29	9	16	1	2.8
Suns	**82**	**19830**	**3097**	**44.7**	**1096**	**358**	**1250**	**76.7**	**1072**	**3502**	**1838**	**668**	**1205**	**401**	**95.1**
Opponents	**82**	**19830**	**2957**	**44.4**	**1208**	**433**	**1511**	**75.1**	**1030**	**3523**	**1821**	**685**	**1265**	**475**	**95.8**

Portland Trail Blazers

Player	GP	Min	Field Goals		3-Pt FG		Free Throws		Rebounds		A	Stl	TO	BS	Avg
			FGM	Pct	FGA	FGM	FTM	Pct	Off	Total					
Wallace	79	2963	603	46.9	317	114	201	73.4	136	645	152	101	131	101	19.3
Wells	74	2348	487	46.9	172	66	215	74.1	121	444	204	113	191	25	17.0
Stoudamire	75	2796	369	40.2	295	104	174	88.8	78	292	490	67	149	7	13.5
Patterson	75	1765	319	51.5	36	9	192	70.1	155	298	107	79	114	37	11.2
Anderson	70	1860	247	40.4	228	85	178	85.6	47	189	216	68	87	8	10.8
Pippen	62	1996	246	41.1	177	54	113	77.4	77	321	363	101	171	35	10.6
Davis	78	2447	296	51.0	0	0	150	70.8	262	688	96	62	62	83	9.5
Kemp	75	1232	175	43.0	4	0	104	79.4	90	288	52	43	81	33	6.1
Kerr	65	775	102	47.0	66	26	39	97.5	6	60	63	13	24	1	4.1
Barkley	19	228	24	35.3	7	1	9	90.0	5	18	34	17	12	1	3.1
Randolph	41	238	48	44.9	0	0	18	66.7	31	69	13	7	15	4	2.8
Brunson	59	520	45	39.8	11	6	29	70.7	23	68	114	25	47	2	2.1
B'je-Boumtje	33	245	13	40.6	0	0	13	52.0	21	55	4	3	14	16	1.2
Dudley	43	90	10	40.0	3	1	8	53.3	6	14	5	0	5	1	1.1
Trail Blazers	**82**	**19830**	**3004**	**45.0**	**1318**	**466**	**1451**	**76.3**	**1085**	**3529**	**1926**	**702**	**1172**	**368**	**96.6**
Opponents	**82**	**19830**	**2951**	**45.3**	**1285**	**466**	**1312**	**74.1**	**890**	**3218**	**1945**	**612**	**1208**	**410**	**93.7**

Sacramento Kings

Player	GP	Min	Field Goals		3-Pt FG		Free Throws		Rebounds		A	Stl	TO	BS	Avg
			FGM	Pct	FGA	FGM	FTM	Pct	Off	Total					
Webber	54	2071	532	49.5	19	5	253	74.9	150	546	258	90	158	76	24.5
Stojakovic	71	2649	547	48.4	310	129	283	87.6	72	373	175	81	140	14	21.2
Bibby	80	2659	446	45.3	138	51	155	80.3	37	222	403	87	134	15	13.7
Christie	81	2798	338	46.0	256	90	206	85.1	74	300	340	160	164	25	12.0
Divac	80	2420	338	47.2	13	3	209	61.5	205	671	297	79	158	94	11.1
Jackson	81	1750	334	44.3	219	79	149	81.0	82	251	164	73	99	11	11.1
Turkoglu	80	1970	290	42.2	171	63	167	72.6	63	363	163	57	81	31	10.1
Pollard	80	1881	197	55.0	0	0	115	69.3	188	565	53	70	68	76	6.4
Funderburke	56	722	115	46.9	3	0	34	60.7	76	198	32	11	33	18	4.7
Wallace	54	430	75	42.9	7	0	23	50.0	49	89	27	19	22	6	3.2
Cleaves	32	153	30	44.1	8	2	8	88.9	1	8	25	7	27	0	2.2
Price	20	89	9	33.3	15	4	9	69.2	4	8	9	3	10	1	1.6
Kings	**82**	**19755**	**3267**	**46.7**	**1160**	**426**	**1618**	**75.1**	**1013**	**3715**	**1958**	**741**	**1128**	**375**	**104.6**
Opponents	**82**	**19755**	**3128**	**44.0**	**1145**	**386**	**1312**	**74.4**	**1065**	**3682**	**1839**	**633**	**1246**	**387**	**97.0**

San Antonio Spurs

Player	GP	Min	FGM	Pct	FGA	FGM	FTM	Pct	Off	Total	A	Stl	TO	BS	Avg
Duncan	82	3329	764	50.8	10	1	560	79.9	268	1042	307	61	263	203	25.5
Robinson	78	2303	341	50.7	0	0	269	68.1	191	647	94	86	104	140	12.2
S. Smith	77	2211	310	45.5	246	116	159	87.8	45	193	151	54	108	15	11.6
Rose	82	1725	293	46.3	12	1	185	72.0	172	492	61	70	140	42	9.4
Daniels	82	2175	269	44.0	196	57	158	75.2	23	176	228	48	70	12	9.2
Parker	77	2267	268	41.9	189	61	108	67.5	33	197	334	89	151	7	9.2
C. Smith	60	1141	182	42.5	131	35	42	64.6	34	133	80	52	59	44	7.4
Bowen	59	1699	155	38.9	148	56	46	47.9	42	162	88	62	66	25	7.0
Porter	72	1294	136	42.4	142	59	68	81.9	12	164	205	45	85	16	5.5
Ferry	50	799	76	42.9	99	43	34	94.4	15	75	90	48	22	9	4.6
Jackson	23	227	34	37.4	36	9	12	70.6	3	23	26	11	23	3	3.9
McCaskill	27	153	20	40.8	0	0	12	46.2	16	36	4	6	14	10	1.9
Bryant	30	206	55	45.5	0	0	6	75.0	25	44	10	7	6	2	1.9
Parks	42	234	83	36.1	0	0	3	37.5	24	58	10	7	14	8	1.5
Spurs	**82**	**19855**	**2913**	**45.8**	**1211**	**438**	**1668**	**74.2**	**907**	**3473**	**1643**	**625**	**1180**	**625**	**96.7**
Opponents	**82**	**19855**	**2883**	**42.6**	**1108**	**374**	**1283**	**77.7**	**1003**	**3432**	**1543**	**635**	**1192**	**635**	**90.5**

Seattle SuperSonics

Player	GP	Min	FGM	Pct	FGA	FGM	FTM	Pct	Off	Total	A	Stl	TO	BS	Avg
Payton	82	3301	737	46.7	236	74	267	79.7	80	396	737	131	209	26	22.1
Lewis	71	2585	455	46.8	316	123	162	81.0.	139	498	123	104	97	40	16.8
Barry	81	3040	401	50.8	387	164	198	84.6	58	441	426	147	165	37	14.4
Baker	55	1710	315	48.5	8	1	143	63.3	168	350	72	22	127	36	14.1
Mason	75	2420	357	46.4	59	16	201	84.8	92	351	104	67	104	27	12.4
Drobnjak	64	1174	191	46.1	2	0	55	75.3	75	219	51	20	51	31	6.8
Radmanovic	61	1230	146	41.2	157	66	49	68.1	45	230	81	56	72	24	6.7
Sesay	9	142	22	50.0	0	0	14	70.0	7	20	8	3	2	2	6.4
Booth	15	279	35	42.7	0	0	23	95.8	20	54	16	6	16	13	6.2
James	56	949	134	49.1	0	0	30	50.0	89	232	24	25	74	86	5.3
Long	63	989	120	49.2	0	0	45	52.9	107	251	41	22	63	28	4.5
Williams	50	603	81	42.0	75	28	31	79.5	16	63	83	21	35	2	4.4
Watson	64	964	96	45.3	44	16	23	63.9	31	83	125	60	51	5	3.6
Livingston	13	176	15	27.8	8	1	10	90.9	9	25	26	9	2	2	3.2
Harvey	5	47	4	33.3	0	0	1	50.0	5	9	5	1	3	3	1.8
Ovedeii	36	221	22	53.7	0	0	11	61.1	27	79	4	4	14	2	1.5
SuperSonics	**82**	**19830**	**3131**	**46.9**	**1292**	**489**	**1263**	**75.5**	**968**	**3301**	**1926**	**698**	**1124**	**364**	**97.7**
Opponents	**82**	**19830**	**2966**	**44.9**	**1374**	**472**	**1362**	**73.9**	**1091**	**3417**	**1832**	**568**	**1254**	**400**	**94.7**

Toronto Raptors

Player	GP	Min	FGM	Pct	FGA	FGM	FTM	Pct	Off	Total	A	Stl	TO	BS	Avg
Carter	60	2385	559	42.8	313	121	245	79.8	138	313	239	94	154	43	24.7
Davis	77	2978	410	42.6	1	0	293	81.8	254	740	155	54	159	83	14.5
Peterson	63	1988	336	43.8	231	84	127	75.1	91	223	153	73	86	11	14.0
A. Williams	82	2927	403	41.5	193	62	103	73.6	58	281	468	135	150	26	11.8
Clark	81	2185	380	49.0	5	0	155	67.4	182	603	88	58	140	122	11.3
J. Williams	68	1641	190	49.0	0	0	138	67.6	165	386	75	78	68	11	7.6
Olajuwon	61	1378	194	46.4	2	0	47	56.0	98	366	66	74	98	90	7.1
Curry	56	886	141	40.6	131	45	33	89.2	23	81	61	22	41	6	6.4
Murray	40	473	85	41.1	104	40	17	81.0	18	53	19	11	25	8	5.7
Childs	69	1576	97	32.8	120	33	58	81.7	18	154	351	56	123	5	4.1
Montross	49	655	53	40.2	1	0	10	32.3	36	140	16	12	25	23	2.4
Jackson	24	280	20	47.6	2	1	16	66.7	3	27	57	9	14	1	2.4
Arroyo	17	96	13	44.8	0	0	4	66.7	3	12	21	6	12	0	1.8
Bradley	26	118	13	52.0	2	0	4	50.0	7	24	3	0	6	6	1.2
Raptors	**82**	**19755**	**2919**	**43.4**	**1109**	**387**	**1269**	**73.9**	**1114**	**3450**	**1779**	**688**	**1174**	**454**	**91.4**
Opponents	**82**	**19755**	**2820**	**44.1**	**1089**	**377**	**1513**	**75.2**	**995**	**3431**	**1629**	**628**	**1250**	**393**	**91.8**

Utah Jazz

Player	GP	Min	FGM	Pct	FGA	FGM	FTM	Pct	Off	Total	A	Stl	TO	BS	Avg
			Field Goals		3-Pt FG		Free Throws		Rebounds						
Malone.............80	80	3040	635	45.4	25	9	509	79.7	142	686	341	152	263	59	22.4
Marshall...........58	58	1750	343	51.9	42	13	160	70.8	158	443	101	50	124	67	14.8
Stockton 82	82	2566	401	51.7	78	25	275	85.7	59	263	674	152	208	24	13.4
Kirilenko...........82	82	2151	285	45.0	100	25	285	76.8	149	402	94	116	108	156	10.7
Russell.............66	66	1998	222	38.0	226	77	115	82.1	79	295	136	64	110	19	9.6
Crotty...............41	41	802	98	47.1	69	31	57	86.4	16	75	141	19	51	1	6.9
Padgett.............75	75	1295	188	47.6	113	49	75	73.5	111	285	82	43	69	13	6.7
Collins..............70	70	1440	158	46.1	1	0	134	74.0	138	296	58	29	56	22	6.4
LaRue...............33	33	542	73	39.5	50	17	30	85.7	11	49	71	17	43	7	5.8
Stevenson........67	67	1134	143	38.5	25	2	37	69.8	44	131	116	29	68	24	4.9
Starks 66	66	929	114	36.8	95	29	33	80.5	15	68	70	33	52	0	4.4
Lewis 36	36	490	64	44.8	18	3	13	65.0	10	43	36	23	32	9	4.0
Ostertag 74	74	1107	91	45.3	0	0	63	48.5	125	313	50	15	51	109	3.3
Amaechi 54	54	586	54	32.5	0	0	67	63.8	52	109	29	7	55	10	3.2
Jazz..................82	82	19830	2869	45.0	842	280	1853	76.3	1109	3458	1999	749	1353	523	96.0
Opponents......82	82	19830	2777	44.7	1215	465	1779	77.1	927	3131	1585	748	1371	548	95.1

Washington Wizards

Player	GP	Min	FGM	Pct	FGA	FGM	FTM	Pct	Off	Total	A	Stl	TO	BS	Avg
			Field Goals		3-Pt FG		Free Throws		Rebounds						
Jordan...............60	60	2093	551	41.6	53	10	263	79.0	50	339	310	85	162	26	22.9
Hamilton 63	63	2203	472	43.5	42	16	300	89.0	73	216	171	38	132	14	20.0
Whitney............82	82	2171	274	41.8	323	131	154	88.0	11	152	314	72	85	6	10.2
Alexander........51	51	1325	223	47.0	18	5	98	81.0	43	148	86	35	60	7	9.8
Lue 71	71	1458	222	42.7	141	63	48	76.2	14	122	246	49	96	0	7.8
Davis 51	51	1231	146	44.8	126	57	16	76.2	7	77	107	28	44	58	7.2
Laettner...........57	57	1441	168	46.4	10	2	66	86.8	74	301	151	60	85	25	7.1
Jones...............79	79	1920	222	43.7	11	4	106	81.5	233	578	127	50	88	19	7.0
Nesby...............70	70	1498	183	43.5	47	13	64	68.8	105	318	91	61	49	22	6.3
White 71	71	1346	150	53.8	0	0	83	53.9	159	444	17	25	65	75	5.4
Haywood 62	62	1266	109	49.3	0	0	97	60.6	143	322	29	21	50	91	5.1
Brown 57	57	817	94	38.7	1	0	70	70.7	63	198	43	16	43	26	4.5
Thomas............47	47	618	81	53.6	0	0	41	55.4	55	181	6	17	26	35	4.3
Wizards...........82	82	19730	2938	44.1	786	305	1428	76.5	1055	3448	1715	570	1068	354	92.8
Opponents......82	82	19730	2953	45.2	1191	422	1396	75.5	960	3336	1818	573	1095	414	94.2

2002 NBA Draft

The 2002 NBA Draft was held on June 26 in New York City.

First Round

1. Yao Ming, Houston
2. Jay Williams, Chicago
3. Mike Dunleavy, Golden State
4. Drew Gooden, Memphis
5. Nikoloz Tkitishvili, Denver
6. Dajuan Wagner, Cleveland
7. Maybyner Hilario, New York (to Denver)
8. Chris Wilcox, LA Clippers (from Atlanta)
9. Amare Stoudemire, Phoenix
10. Caron Butler, Miami
11. Jared Jeffries, Washington
12. Melvin Ely, LA Clippers
13. Marcus Haislip, Milwaukee
14. Fred Jones, Indiana
15. Bostjan Nachbar, Houston (from Toronto)
16. Jiri Welsch, Philadelphia
17. Juan Dixon, Washington (from New Orleans)
18. Curtis Borchardt, Orlando (to Utah)
19. Ryan Humphrey, Utah (to Orlando)
20. Kareem Rush, Toronto (to LA Lakers; from Seattle via New York)
21. Qyntel Woods, Portland
22. Casey Jacobsen, Phoenix (from Boston)
23. Tayshaun Prince, Detroit
24. Nenad Krstic, New Jersey
25. Frank Williams, Denver (from Dallas)
26. John Salmons, San Antonio
27. Chris Jefferies, LA Lakers (to Toronto)
28. Dan Dickau, Sacramento

Second Round

30. Steve Logan, Golden State
31. Roger Mason Jr., Chicago
32. Robert Archibald, Memphis
33. Vincent Yarbrough, Denver
34. Dan Gadzuric, Milwaukee (from Houston)
35. Carlos Boozer, Cleveland
36. Milos Vujanic, New York
37. David Andersen, Atlanta
38. Tito Maddox, Houston
39. Rod Grizzard, Washington (from Phoenix via Denver)
40. Juan Carlos Navarro, Wash
41. Mario Kasun, LA Clippers
42. Ronald Murray, Milwaukee
43. Jason Jennings, Portland (from Toronto via Chicago)
44. Lonny Baxter, Chicago (from Indiana)
45. Sam Clancy, Philadelphia
46. Matt Barnes, Memphis (to Cleveland; from Orlando)
47. Jamal Sampson, Utah (to Orlando)
48. Chris Owens, Milwaukee (to Memphis; from New Orleans)
49. Peter Fehse, Seattle
50. Darius Songaila, Boston
51. Federico Kammerichs, Por
52. Marcus Taylor, Minnesota
53. Rasual Butler, Miami
54. Tamar Slay, New Jersey
55. Mladen Sekularac, Dallas
56. Luis Scola, San Antonio (from LA Lakers)
57. Randy Holcomb, SA (to Philadelphia)
58. Corsley Edwards, Sac

Women's National Basketball Association

Final Standings

EASTERN CONFERENCE

Team	W	L	Pct	GB
†New York	18	14	.563	—
*Charlotte	18	14	.563	—
*Washington	17	15	.531	1
*Indiana	16	16	.500	2
Orlando	16	16	.500	2
Miami	15	17	.469	3
Cleveland	10	22	.313	8
Detroit	9	23	.281	9

WESTERN CONFERENCE

Team	W	L	Pct	GB
†Los Angeles	25	7	.781	—
*Houston	24	8	.750	1
*Utah	20	12	.625	5
*Seattle	17	15	.531	8
Portland	16	16	.500	9
Sacramento	14	18	.438	11
Phoenix	11	21	.344	14
Minnesota	10	22	.313	15

†Clinched conference title. *Clinched playoff berth.

2002 Playoffs

FIRST ROUND

EASTERN CONFERENCE

| Aug 15 | Charlotte | 62 | at Washington | 74 |
| Aug 17 | Washington | 62 | at Charlotte | 59 |

Washington won series 2–0.

Aug 16	New York	55	at Indiana	73
Aug 18	Indiana	65	at New York	84
Aug 20	Indiana	60	at New York	75

New York won series 2–1.

WESTERN CONFERENCE

| Aug 15 | Los Angeles | 78 | at Seattle | 61 |
| Aug 17 | Seattle | 59 | at Los Angeles | 69 |

Los Angeles won series 2–0.

Aug 16	Houston	59	at Utah	66
Aug 18	Utah	77	at Houston	83†
Aug 20	Utah	75	at Houston	72

Utah won series 2–1.

EASTERN CONFERENCE FINALS

Aug 22	New York	74	at Washington	79
Aug 24	Washington	79	at New York	96
Aug 25	Washington	57	at New York	64

New York won series 2–1.

WESTERN CONFERENCE FINALS

| Aug 22 | Los Angeles | 75 | at Utah | 67 |
| Aug 24 | Utah | 77 | at Los Angeles | 103 |

Los Angeles won series 2–0.

WNBA FINALS

| Aug 29 | Los Angeles | 71 | at New York | 63 |
| Aug 31 | New York | 66 | at Los Angeles | 69 |

Los Angeles won series 2–0.

†Double overtime.

WHO IS ... Margo Dydek

Why they call her Large Marge Dydek, at 7' 2", is the tallest player in WNBA history by four inches. In her fifth season playing center for the Utah Starzz she was leading the league in blocks (3.71) per game, flagrant fouls (three) and suspensions (two) through mid-August 2002. She also spearheaded the Starzz into a first-round matchup against the Los Angeles Sparks.

Why she calls herself a good girl Is it her fault that she looms large in the low post, she wonders. This year the WNBA has been cracking down on fouls, and each of Dydek's flagrants (and suspensions) has come, she insists, as a result of her elbows being face-level with most players in the league. "It's not intentional," she said. "Most times, I don't even see the othe player coming." The suspensions haven't spoiled her best all-around season: In addition to her blocks Dydek, 28, was averaging 13.2 points a game and was third in the WNBA in rebounding (9.1)

Tall story Her father is 6' 7", her mother is 6' 3", and Margo has an 85-inch wingspan....A native of Warsaw, she played six seasons of pro ball in Europe before jumping to the WNBA, and she still plays in the old country during the off-season....She once dunked in a game in Madrid but says she's still waiting for the right opportunity to do it in the U.S.

NBA Champions

Season	Winner	Series	Runner-Up	Winning Coach	Finals MVP
1946–47	Philadelphia	4–1	Chicago	Eddie Gottlieb	—
1947–48	Baltimore	4–2	Philadelphia	Buddy Jeannette	—
1948–49	Minneapolis	4–2	Washington	John Kundla	—
1949–50	Minneapolis	4–2	Syracuse	John Kundla	—
1950–51	Rochester	4–3	New York	Les Harrison	—
1951–52	Minneapolis	4–3	New York	John Kundla	—
1952–53	Minneapolis	4–1	New York	John Kundla	—
1953–54	Minneapolis	4–3	Syracuse	John Kundla	—
1954–55	Syracuse	4–3	Ft Wayne	Al Cervi	—
1955–56	Philadelphia	4–1	Ft Wayne	George Senesky	—
1956–57	Boston	4–3	St Louis	Red Auerbach	—
1957–58	St Louis	4–2	Boston	Alex Hannum	—
1958–59	Boston	4–0	Minneapolis	Red Auerbach	—
1959–60	Boston	4–3	St Louis	Red Auerbach	—
1960–61	Boston	4–1	St Louis	Red Auerbach	—
1961–62	Boston	4–3	LA Lakers	Red Auerbach	—
1962–63	Boston	4–2	LA Lakers	Red Auerbach	—
1963–64	Boston	4–1	San Francisco	Red Auerbach	—
1964–65	Boston	4–1	LA Lakers	Red Auerbach	—
1965–66	Boston	4–3	LA Lakers	Red Auerbach	—
1966–67	Philadelphia	4–2	San Francisco	Alex Hannum	—
1967–68	Boston	4–2	LA Lakers	Bill Russell	—
1968–69	Boston	4–3	LA Lakers	Bill Russell	Jerry West, LA
1969–70	New York	4–3	LA Lakers	Red Holzman	Willis Reed, NY
1970–71	Milwaukee	4–0	Baltimore	Larry Costello	Kareem Abdul-Jabbar, Mil
1971–72	LA Lakers	4–1	New York	Bill Sharman	Wilt Chamberlain, LA
1972–73	New York	4–1	LA Lakers	Red Holzman	Willis Reed, NY
1973–74	Boston	4–3	Milwaukee	Tommy Heinsohn	John Havlicek, Bos
1974–75	Golden State	4–0	Washington	Al Attles	Rick Barry, GS
1975–76	Boston	4–2	Phoenix	Tommy Heinsohn	JoJo White, Bos
1976–77	Portland	4–2	Philadelphia	Jack Ramsay	Bill Walton, Port
1977–78	Washington	4–3	Seattle	Dick Motta	Wes Unseld, Wash
1978–79	Seattle	4–1	Washington	Lenny Wilkens	Dennis Johnson, Sea
1979–80	LA Lakers	4–2	Philadelphia	Paul Westhead	Magic Johnson, LA
1980–81	Boston	4–2	Houston	Bill Fitch	Cedric Maxwell, Bos
1981–82	LA Lakers	4–2	Philadelphia	Pat Riley	Magic Johnson, LA
1982–83	Philadelphia	4–0	LA Lakers	Billy Cunningham	Moses Malone, Phil
1983–84	Boston	4–3	LA Lakers	K.C. Jones	Larry Bird, Bos
1984–85	LA Lakers	4–2	Boston	Pat Riley	Kareem Abdul-Jabbar, LA
1985–86	Boston	4–2	Houston	K.C. Jones	Larry Bird, Bos
1986–87	LA Lakers	4–2	Boston	Pat Riley	Magic Johnson, LA
1987–88	LA Lakers	4–3	Detroit	Pat Riley	James Worthy, LA
1988–89	Detroit	4–0	LA Lakers	Chuck Daly	Joe Dumars, Det
1989–90	Detroit	4–1	Portland	Chuck Daly	Isiah Thomas, Det
1990–91	Chicago	4–1	LA Lakers	Phil Jackson	Michael Jordan, Chi
1991–92	Chicago	4–2	Portland	Phil Jackson	Michael Jordan, Chi
1992–93	Chicago	4–2	Phoenix	Phil Jackson	Michael Jordan, Chi
1993–94	Houston	4–3	New York	Rudy Tomjanovich	Hakeem Olajuwon, Hou
1994–95	Houston	4–0	Orlando	Rudy Tomjanovich	Hakeem Olajuwon, Hou
1995–96	Chicago	4–2	Seattle	Phil Jackson	Michael Jordan, Chi
1996–97	Chicago	4–2	Utah	Phil Jackson	Michael Jordan, Chi
1997–98	Chicago	4–2	Utah	Phil Jackson	Michael Jordan, Chi
1998–99	San Antonio	4–1	New York	Gregg Popovich	Tim Duncan, SA
1999–00	LA Lakers	4–2	Indiana	Phil Jackson	Shaquille O'Neal, LA
2000–01	LA Lakers	4–1	Philadelphia	Phil Jackson	Shaquille O'Neal, LA
2001–02	LA Lakers	4–0	New Jersey	Phil Jackson	Shaquille O'Neal, LA

Most Valuable Player: Maurice Podoloff Trophy

Season	Player, Team	GP	Field Goals		3-Pt FG		Free Throws		Rebounds		A	Stl	BS	Avg
			FGM	Pct	FGM	Pct	FTM	Pct	Off	Total				
1955–56	Bob Pettit, StL	72	646	42.9	–	–	557	73.6	–	1,164	189	–	–	25.7
1956–57	Bob Cousy, Bos	64	478	37.8	–	–	363	82.1	–	309	478	–	–	20.6
1957–58	Bill Russell, Bos	69	456	44.2	–	–	230	51.9	–	1,564	202	–	–	16.6
1958–59	Bob Pettit, StL	72	719	43.8	–	–	667	75.9	–	1,182	221	–	–	29.2
1959–60	Wilt Chamberlain, Phil	72	1,065	46.1	–	–	577	58.2	–	1,941	168	–	–	37.6
1960–61	Bill Russell, Bos	78	532	42.6	–	–	258	55.0	–	1,868	264	–	–	16.9
1961–62	Bill Russell, Bos	76	575	45.7	–	–	286	59.5	–	1,891	341	–	–	18.9
1962–63	Bill Russell, Bos	78	511	43.2	–	–	287	55.5	–	1,843	348	–	–	16.8
1963–64	Oscar Robertson, Cin	79	840	48.3	–	–	800	85.3	–	783	868	–	–	31.4
1964–65	Bill Russell, Bos	78	429	43.8	–	–	244	57.3	–	1,878	410	–	–	14.1
1965–66	Wilt Chamberlain, Phil	79	1,074	54.0	–	–	501	51.3	–	1,943	414	–	–	33.5
1966–67	Wilt Chamberlain, Phil	81	785	68.3	–	–	386	44.1	–	1,957	630	–	–	24.1
1967–68	Wilt Chamberlain, Phil	82	819	59.5	–	–	354	38.0	–	1,952	702	–	–	24.3
1968–69	Wes Unseld, Balt	82	427	47.6	–	–	277	60.5	–	1,491	213	–	–	13.8
1969–70	Willis Reed, NY	81	702	50.7	–	–	351	75.6	–	1,126	161	–	–	21.7
1970–71	Kareem Abdul-Jabbar, Mil	82	1,063	57.7	–	–	470	69.0	–	1,311	272	–	–	31.7
1971–72	Kareem Abdul-Jabbar, Mil	81	1,159	57.4	–	–	504	68.9	–	1,346	370	–	–	34.8
1972–73	Dave Cowens, Bos	82	740	45.2	–	–	204	77.9	–	1,329	333	–	–	20.5
1973–74	Kareem Abdul-Jabbar, Mil	81	948	53.9	–	–	295	70.2	287	1,178	386	112	283	27.0
1974–75	Bob McAdoo, Buff	82	1,095	51.2	–	–	641	80.5	307	1,155	179	92	174	34.5
1975–76	Kareem Abdul-Jabbar, LA	82	914	52.9	–	–	447	70.3	272	1,383	413	119	338	37.7
1976–77	Kareem Abdul-Jabbar, LA	82	888	57.9	–	–	376	70.1	266	1,090	319	101	261	26.2
1977–78	Bill Walton, Port	58	460	52.2	–	–	177	72.0	118	766	291	60	146	18.9
1978–79	Moses Malone, Hou	82	716	54.0	–	–	599	73.9	587	1,444	147	79	119	24.8
1979–80	Kareem Abdul-Jabbar, LA	82	835	60.4	0	00.0	364	76.5	190	886	371	81	280	24.8
1980–81	Julius Erving, Phil	82	794	52.1	4	22.2	422	78.7	244	657	364	173	147	24.6
1981–82	Moses Malone, Hou	81	945	51.9	0	00.0	630	76.2	558	1,188	142	76	125	31.1
1982–83	Moses Malone, Phil	78	654	50.1	0	00.0	600	76.1	445	1,194	101	89	157	24.5
1983–84	Larry Bird, Bos	79	758	49.2	18	24.7	374	88.8	181	796	520	144	69	24.2
1984–85	Larry Bird, Bos	80	918	52.2	56	42.7	403	88.2	164	842	531	129	98	28.7
1985–86	Larry Bird, Bos	82	796	49.6	82	42.3	441	89.6	190	805	557	166	51	25.8
1986–87	Magic Johnson, LA Lakers	80	683	52.2	8	20.5	535	84.8	122	504	977	138	36	23.9
1987–88	Michael Jordan, Chi	82	1,069	53.5	7	13.2	723	84.1	139	449	485	259	131	35.0
1988–89	Magic Johnson, LA Lakers	77	579	50.9	59	31.4	513	91.1	111	607	988	138	22	22.5
1989–90	Magic Johnson, LA Lakers	79	546	48.0	106	38.4	567	89.0	128	522	907	132	34	22.3
1990–91	Michael Jordan, Chi	82	990	53.9	29	31.2	571	85.1	118	492	453	223	83	31.5
1991–92	Michael Jordan, Chi	80	943	51.9	27	27.0	491	83.2	91	511	489	182	75	30.1
1992–93	Charles Barkley, Phoe	76	716	52.0	67	30.5	445	76.5	237	928	385	119	74	25.6
1993–94	Hakeem Olajuwon, Hou	80	894	52.8	8	42.1	388	71.6	229	955	287	128	297	27.3
1994–95	David Robinson, SA	81	788	53.0	6	30.0	656	77.4	234	877	364	136	262	27.6
1995–96	Michael Jordan, Chi	82	916	49.5	111	42.7	548	83.4	148	543	352	180	42	30.4
1996–97	Karl Malone, Utah	82	864	55.0	0	00.0	521	75.5	193	809	368	113	48	27.4
1997–98	Michael Jordan, Chi	82	881	46.5	30	23.8	565	78.4	130	475	283	141	45	28.7
1998–99	Karl Malone, Utah	49	393	49.3	0	00.0	378	78.8	107	463	201	62	28	23.8
1999–00	Shaquille O'Neal, LA Lakers	79	956	57.4	0	00.0	432	52.4	336	1078	299	36	239	29.7
2000–01	Allen Iverson, Phil	71	762	42.0	98	32.0	585	81.4	50	273	325	78	20	31.1
2001–02	Tim Duncan, SA	82	764	50.8	1	10.0	560	79.9	268	1042	307	61	203	25.5

Coach of the Year: Arnold (Red) Auerbach Trophy

1962–63...Harry Gallatin, StL	1976–77...Tom Nissalke, Hou	1989–90...Pat Riley, LA Lakers
1963–64...Alex Hannum, SF	1977–78...Hubie Brown, Atl	1990–91...Don Chaney, Hou
1964–65...Red Auerbach, Bos	1978–79...Cotton Fitzsimmons, KC	1991–92...Don Nelson, GS
1965–66...Dolph Schayes, Phil	1979–80...Bill Fitch, Bos	1992–93...Pat Riley, NY
1966–67...Johnny Kerr, Chi	1980–81...Jack McKinney, Ind	1993–94...Lenny Wilkens, Atl
1967–68...Richie Guerin, StL	1981–82...Gene Shue, Wash	1994–95...Del Harris, LA Lakers
1968–69...Gene Shue, Balt	1982–83...Don Nelson, Mil	1995–96...Phil Jackson, Chi
1969–70...Red Holzman, NY	1983–84...Frank Layden, Utah	1996–97...Pat Riley, Mia
1970–71...Dick Motta, Chi	1984–85...Don Nelson, Mil	1997–98...Larry Bird, Ind
1971–72...Bill Sharman, LA	1985–86...Mike Fratello, Atl	1998–99...Mike Dunleavy, Port
1972–73...Tom Heinsohn, Bos	1986–87...Mike Schuler, Port	1999–00...Glenn (Doc) Rivers, Orl
1973–74...Ray Scott, Det	1987–88...Doug Moe, Den	2000–01...Larry Brown, Phil
1974–75...Phil Johnson, KC-Oma	1988–89.....Cotton Fitzsimmons, Phoe	2001–02...Rick Carlisle, Det
1975–76...Bill Fitch, Clev		

Note: Award named after Auerbach in 1986.

Rookie of the Year: Eddie Gottlieb Trophy

1952–53...Don Meineke, FW
1953–54...Ray Felix, Balt
1954–55...Bob Pettit, Mil
1955–56...Maurice Stokes, Roch
1956–57...Tom Heinsohn, Bos
1957–58...Woody Sauldsberry, Phil
1958–59...Elgin Baylor, Minn
1959–60...Wilt Chamberlain, Phil
1960–61...Oscar Robertson, Cin
1961–62...Walt Bellamy, Chi
1962–63...Terry Dischinger, Chi
1963–64...Jerry Lucas, Cin
1964–65...Willis Reed, NY
1965–66...Rick Barry, SF
1966–67...Dave Bing, Det
1967–68...Earl Monroe, Balt
1968–69...Wes Unseld, Balt
1969–70...K. Abdul-Jabbar, Mil

1970–71...Dave Cowens, Bos
          Geoff Petrie, Port
1971–72...Sidney Wicks, Port
1972–73...Bob McAdoo, Buff
1973–74...Ernie DiGregorio, Buff
1974–75...Keith Wilkes, GS
1975–76...Alvan Adams, Phoe
1976–77...Adrian Dantley, Buff
1977–78...Walter Davis, Phoe
1978–79...Phil Ford, KC
1979–80...Larry Bird, Bos
1980–81...Darrell Griffith, Utah
1981–82...Buck Williams, NJ
1982–83...Terry Cummings, SD
1983–84...Ralph Sampson, Hou
1984–85...Michael Jordan, Chi
1985–86...Patrick Ewing, NY
1986–87...Chuck Person, Ind

1987–88...Mark Jackson, NY
1988–89...Mitch Richmond, GS
1989–90...David Robinson, SA
1990–91...Derrick Coleman, NJ
1991–92...Larry Johnson, Char
1992–93...Shaquille O'Neal, Orl
1993–94...Chris Webber, GS
1994–95...J. Kidd, Dall/G. Hill, Det
1995–96...Damon Stoudamire, Tor
1996–97...Allen Iverson, Phil
1997–98...Tim Duncan, SA
1998–99...Vince Carter, Tor
1999–00..Steve Francis, Hou
          Elton Brand, Chi
2000–01..Mike Miller, Orl
2001–02..Pau Gasol, Mem

Defensive Player of the Year

1982–83...Sidney Moncrief, Mil
1983–84...Sidney Moncrief, Mil
1984–85...Mark Eaton, Utah
1985–86...Alvin Robertson, SA
1986–87...Michael Cooper, Lakers
1987–88...Michael Jordan, Chi
1988–89...Mark Eaton, Utah

1989–90...Dennis Rodman, Det
1990–91...Dennis Rodman, Det
1991–92...David Robinson, SA
1992–93...Hakeem Olajuwon, Hou
1993–94...Hakeem Olajuwon, Hou
1994–95...Dikembe Mutombo, Den
1995–96...Gary Payton, Sea

1996–97...Dikembe Mutombo, Den
1997–98...Dikembe Mutombo, Atl
1998–99...Alonzo Mourning, Mia
1999–00...Alonzo Mourning, Mia
2000–01...Dikembe Mutombo, Phil
2001–02...Ben Wallace, Det

Sixth Man Award

1982–83...Bobby Jones, Phil
1983–84...Kevin McHale, Bos
1984–85...Kevin McHale, Bos
1985–86...Bill Walton, Bos
1986–87...Ricky Pierce, Mil
1987–88...Roy Tarpley, Dall
1988–89...Eddie Johnson, Phoe

1989–90...Ricky Pierce, Mil
1990–91...Detlef Schrempf, Ind
1991–92...Detlef Schrempf, Ind
1992–93...Cliff Robinson, Port
1993–94...Dell Curry, Char
1994–95...Anthony Mason, NY
1995–96...Tony Kukoc, Chi

1996–97...John Starks, NY
1997–98...Danny Manning, Phoe
1998–99...Darrell Armstrong, Orl
1999–00...Rodney Rogers, Phoe
2000–01...Aaron McKie, Phil
2001–02...Corliss Williamson, Det

J. Walter Kennedy Citizenship Award

1974–75...Wes Unseld, Wash
1975–76...Slick Watts, Sea
1976–77...Dave Bing, Wash
1977–78...Bob Lanier, Det
1978–79...Calvin Murphy, Hou
1979–80...Austin Carr, Clev
1980–81...Mike Glenn, NY
1981–82...Kent Benson, Det
1982–83...Julius Erving, Phil
1983–84...Frank Layden, Utah

1984–85...Dan Issel, Den
1985–86...Michael Cooper, Lakers
          Rory Sparrow, NY
1986–87...Isiah Thomas, Det
1987–88...Alex English, Den
1988–89...Thurl Bailey, Utah
1989–90...Glenn Rivers, Atl
1990–91...Kevin Johnson, Phoe
1991–92...Magic Johnson, Lakers
1992–93...Terry Porter, Port

1993–94...Joe Dumars, Det
1994–95...Joe O'Toole, Atl
1995–96...Chris Dudley, Port
1996–97...P.J. Brown, Mia
1997–98...Steve Smith, Atl
1998–99...Brian Grant, Port
1999–00...Vlade Divac, Sac
2000–01...Dikembe Mutombo, Phil
2001–02...Alonzo Mourning, Mia

Most Improved Player

1985–86...Alvin Robertson, SA
1986–87...Dale Ellis, Sea
1987–88...Kevin Duckworth, Port
1988–89...Kevin Johnson, Phoe
1989–90...Rony Seikaly, Mia
1990–91...Scott Skiles, Orl

1991–92...Pervis Ellison, Wash
1992–93...Chris Jackson, Den
1993–94...Don MacLean, Wash
1994–95...Dana Barros, Phil
1995–96...Gheorghe Muresan, Wash
1996–97...Isaac Austin, Mia

1997–98...Alan Henderson, Atl
1998–99...Darrell Armstrong, Orl
1999–00...Jalen Rose, Ind
2000–01...Tracy McGrady, Orl
2001–02...Jermaine O'Neal, Ind

Executive of the Year

1972–73...Joe Axelson, KC-Oma
1973–74...Eddie Donovan, Buff
1974–75...Dick Vertlieb, GS
1975–76...Jerry Colangelo, Phoe
1976–77...Ray Patterson, Hou
1977–78...Angelo Drossos, SA
1978–79...Bob Ferry, Wash
1979–80...Red Auerbach, Bos
1980–81...Jerry Colangelo, Phoe
1981–82...Bob Ferry, Wash

1982–83...Zollie Volchok, Sea
1983–84...Frank Layden, Utah
1984–85...Vince Boryla, Den
1985–86...Stan Kasten, Atl
1986–87...Stan Kasten, Atl
1987–88...Jerry Krause, Chi
1988–89...Jerry Colangelo, Phoe
1989–90...Bob Bass, SA
1990–91...Bucky Buckwalter, Port
1991–92...Wayne Embry, Clev

1992–93...Jerry Colangelo, Phoe
1993–94...Bob Whitsitt, Sea
1994–95...Jerry West, LA Lakers
1995–96...Jerry Krause, Chi
1996–97...Bob Bass, Char
1997–98...Wayne Embry, Clev
1998–99...Geoff Petrie, Sac
1999–00...John Gabriel, Orl
2000–01...Geoff Petrie, Sac
2001–02...Rod Thorn, NJ

Sponsored by *The Sporting News.*

NBA Alltime Individual Leaders

Scoring

MOST POINTS, CAREER

	Pts	Avg
Kareem Abdul-Jabbar	38,387	24.6
Karl Malone	34,707	25.7
Wilt Chamberlain	31,419	30.1
Michael Jordan	30,652	31.0
Moses Malone	27,409	20.6
Elvin Hayes	27,313	21.0
Hakeem Olajuwon	26,946	21.8
Oscar Robertson	26,710	25.7
Dominique Wilkins	26,669	24.8
John Havlicek	26,395	20.8

MOST POINTS, SEASON

Wilt Chamberlain, Phil	4,029	1961–62
Wilt Chamberlain, SF	3,586	1962–63
Michael Jordan, Chi	3,041	1986–87
Wilt Chamberlain, Phil	3,033	1960–61
Wilt Chamberlain, SF	2,948	1963–64
Michael Jordan, Chi	2,868	1987–88
Bob McAdoo, Buff	2,831	1974–75
Rick Barry, SF	2,775	1966–67
Michael Jordan, Chi	2,753	1989–90
Elgin Baylor, LA	2,719	1962–63

HIGHEST SCORING AVERAGE, CAREER

Michael Jordan	31.0	990 games
Wilt Chamberlain	30.1	1,045 games
Shaquille O'Neal	27.6	675 games
Elgin Baylor	27.4	846 games
Jerry West	27.0	932 games
Allen Iverson	26.9	405 games
Bob Pettit	26.4	792 games
George Gervin	26.2	791 games
Karl Malone	25.7	1,353 games
Oscar Robertson	25.7	1,040 games

Note: Minimum 400 games.

HIGHEST SCORING AVERAGE, SEASON

Wilt Chamberlain, Phil	50.4	1961–62
Wilt Chamberlain, SF	44.8	1962–63
Wilt Chamberlain, Phil	38.4	1960–61
Wilt Chamberlain, Phil	37.6	1959–60
Michael Jordan, Chi	37.1	1986–87
Wilt Chamberlain, SF	36.9	1963–64
Rick Barry, SF	35.6	1966–67
Michael Jordan, Chi	35.0	1987–88
Elgin Baylor, LA	34.8	1960–61

Note: Minimum 70 games.

MOST POINTS, GAME

	Player, Team	Opp	Date
100	Wilt Chamberlain, Phil	NY	3/2/62
78	Wilt Chamberlain, Phil	LA	12/8/61
73	Wilt Chamberlain, Phil	Chi	1/13/62
73	Wilt Chamberlain, SF	NY	11/16/62
73	David Thompson, Den	Det	4/9/78
72	Wilt Chamberlain, SF	LA	11/3/62
71	David Robinson, SA	LAC	4/24/94
71	Elgin Baylor, LA	NY	11/15/60
70	Wilt Chamberlain, SF	Syr	3/10/63
69	Michael Jordan, Chi	Clev	3/28/90

Field-Goal Percentage

Highest FG Percentage, Career: .599—Artis Gilmore
Highest FG Percentage, Season: .727—Wilt
  Chamberlain, LA Lakers, 1972–73 (426/586)

Free Throws

HIGHEST FREE-THROW PERCENTAGE, CAREER

Mark Price	.904
Rick Barry	.900
Calvin Murphy	.892
Scott Skiles	.889
Larry Bird	.886

Note: Minimum 1200 free throws made.

HIGHEST FREE-THROW PERCENTAGE, SEASON

Calvin Murphy, Hou	.958	1980–81
Mahmoud Abdul-Rauf, Den	.956	1993–94
Jeff Hornacek, Utah	.950	1999–00
Mark Price, Clev	.948	1992–93
Mark Price, Clev	.947	1991–92

MOST FREE THROWS MADE, CAREER

	No.	Yrs	Pct
Karl Malone	9,145	17	.741
Moses Malone	8,531	19	.769
Oscar Robertson	7,694	14	.838
Jerry West	7,160	14	.814
Michael Jordan	7,061	14	.836

Three-Point Field Goals

Most Three-Point Field-Goals, Career: 2,217—Reggie
  Miller
Highest Three-Point Field-Goal Percentage, Career:
  .459—Steve Kerr
Most Three-Point Field Goals, Season: 267—Dennis
  Scott, Orl, 1995–96
Highest Three-Point Field-Goal Percentage, Season:
  .524—Steve Kerr, Chi, 1994–95
Most Three-Point Field Goals, Game: 11—Dennis
  Scott, Orlando vs Atlanta, 4/18/96

Note: First year of shot: 1979–80.

Steals

Most Steals, Career: 3,128—John Stockton
Most Steals, Season: 301—Alvin Robertson, San
  Antonio, 1985–86
Most Steals, Game: 11—Kendall Gill, New Jersey vs
  Miami, 4/3/99; Larry Kenon, San Antonio
  vs Kansas City, 12/26/76

Rebounds

MOST REBOUNDS, CAREER

	No.	Yrs	Avg
Wilt Chamberlain	23,924	14	22.9
Bill Russell	21,620	13	22.5
Kareem Abdul-Jabbar	17,440	20	11.4
Elvin Hayes	16,279	16	12.5
Moses Malone	16,212	19	12.2
Robert Parish	14,715	21	9.1
Nate Thurmond	14,464	14	15.0
Walt Bellamy	14,241	14	13.7
Karl Malone	13,973	17	10.3
Wes Unseld	13,769	13	14.0

Rebounds (Cont.)
MOST REBOUNDS, SEASON

Wilt Chamberlain, Phil	2,149	1960–61
Wilt Chamberlain, Phil	2,052	1961–62
Wilt Chamberlain, Phil	1,957	1966–67
Wilt Chamberlain, Phil	1,952	1967–68
Wilt Chamberlain, SF	1,946	1962–63
Wilt Chamberlain, Phil	1,943	1965–66
Wilt Chamberlain, Phil	1,941	1959–60
Bill Russell, Bos	1,930	1963–64
Bill Russell, Bos	1,878	1964–65
Bill Russell, Bos	1,868	1960–61

MOST REBOUNDS, GAME

	Player, Team	Opp	Date
55	Wilt Chamberlain, Phil	Bos	11/24/60
51	Bill Russell, Bos	Syr	2/5/60
49	Bill Russell, Bos	Phil	11/16/57
49	Bill Russell, Bos	Det	3/11/65
45	Wilt Chamberlain, Phil	Syr	2/6/60
45	Wilt Chamberlain, Phil	LA	1/21/61

Assists
MOST ASSISTS, CAREER

John Stockton	15,177
Magic Johnson	10,141
Oscar Robertson	9,887
Mark Jackson	9,840
Isiah Thomas	9,061

Assists (Cont.)
MOST ASSISTS, SEASON

John Stockton, Utah	1,164	1990–91
John Stockton, Utah	1,134	1989–90
John Stockton, Utah	1,128	1987–88
John Stockton, Utah	1,126	1991–92
Isiah Thomas, Det	1,123	1984–85

MOST ASSISTS, GAME: 30—Scott Skiles, Orlando vs Denver, 12/30/90

Blocked Shots
MOST BLOCKED SHOTS, CAREER

Hakeem Olajuwon	3,830
Kareem Abdul-Jabbar	3,189
Mark Eaton	3,064
Patrick Ewing	2,894
David Robinson	2,843

MOST BLOCKED SHOTS, SEASON

Mark Eaton, Utah	456	1984–85
Manute Bol, Wash	397	1985–86
Elmore Smith, LA	393	1973–74

MOST BLOCKED SHOTS, GAME: 17—Elmore Smith, LA Lakers vs Portland, 10/28/73

NBA Alltime Playoff Leaders

Scoring
MOST POINTS, CAREER

	Pts	Yrs	Avg
Michael Jordan	5,987	13	33.4
Kareem Abdul-Jabbar	5,762	18	24.3
Jerry West	4,457	13	29.1
Karl Malone	4,421	17	26.5
Larry Bird	3,897	12	23.8
John Havlicek	3,776	13	22.0
Hakeem Olajuwon	3,755	15	25.9
Magic Johnson	3,701	13	19.5
Elgin Baylor	3,623	12	27.0
Scottie Pippen	3,619	15	17.7

*HIGHEST SCORING AVERAGE, CAREER

	Avg	Games
Michael Jordan	33.4	179
Allen Iverson	30.3	45
Jerry West	29.1	153
Shaquille O'Neal	28.2	124
Elgin Baylor	27.0	134
George Gervin	27.0	59
Karl Malone	26.5	167
Hakeem Olajuwon	25.9	145
Bob Pettit	25.5	88
Dominique Wilkins	25.4	55

*Minimum of 25 games.

Scoring (Cont.)
MOST POINTS, GAME

	Player, Team	Opp	Date
†63	Michael Jordan, Chi	Bos	4/20/86
61	Elgin Baylor, LA	Bos	4/14/62
56	Wilt Chamberlain, Phil	Syr	3/22/62
56	Michael Jordan, Chi	Mia	4/29/92
56	Charles Barkley, Phoe	GS	5/4/94
55	Rick Barry, SF	Phil	4/18/67
55	Michael Jordan, Chi	Clev	5/1/88
55	Michael Jordan, Chi	Phoe	4/16/95
55	Michael Jordan, Chi	Wash	4/27/97

†Double overtime game.

Rebounds
MOST REBOUNDS, CAREER

	No.	Yrs	Avg
Bill Russell	4,104	13	24.9
Wilt Chamberlain	3,913	13	24.5
Kareem Abdul-Jabbar	2,481	18	10.5
Karl Malone	1,843	17	11.1
Wes Unseld	1,777	12	14.9

MOST REBOUNDS, GAME

	Player, Team	Opp	Date
41	Wilt Chamberlain, Phil	Bos	4/5/67
40	Bill Russell, Bos	Phil	3/23/58
40	Bill Russell, Bos	StL	3/29/60
*40	Bill Russell, Bos	LA	4/18/62

Three tied at 39.

*Overtime game.

Assists

MOST ASSISTS, CAREER

	No.	Games
Magic Johnson	2,346	190
John Stockton	1,813	177
Larry Bird	1,062	164
Scottie Pippen	1,035	204
Michael Jordan	1,022	179

MOST ASSISTS, GAME

Player, Team	Opp	Date
24 .... Magic Johnson, LAL	Pho	5/15/84
24 .... John Stockton, Utah	LAL	5/17/88
23 .... Magic Johnson, LAL	Port	5/3/85
22 .... Doc Rivers, Atl	Bos	5/16/88
Four tied at 21.		

Games played

Kareem Abdul-Jabbar	237
Scottie Pippen	204
Danny Ainge	193
Magic Johnson	190
Robert Parish	184

Appearances

Kareem Abdul-Jabbar	18
John Stockton	18
Karl Malone	17
Robert Parish	16
Dolph Schayes	15
Clyde Drexler	15
Tree Rollins	15
Jerome Kersey	15
Hakeem Olajuwon	15

NBA Season Leaders

Scoring

Season	Player	Total		Season	Player	Avg
1946–47	Joe Fulks, Phil	1389		1974–75	Bob McAdoo, Buff	34.5
1947–48	Max Zaslofsky, Chi	1007		1975–76	Bob McAdoo, Buff	31.1
1948–49	George Mikan, Minn	1698		1976–77	Pete Maravich, NO	31.1
1949–50	George Mikan, Minn	1865		1977–78	George Gervin, SA	27.2
1950–51	Paul Arizin, Phil	1932		1978–79	George Gervin, SA	29.6
1951–52	Paul Arizin, Phil	1674		1979–80	George Gervin, SA	33.1
1952–53	Neil Johnston, Phil	1564		1980–81	Adrian Dantley, Utah	30.7
1953–54	Neil Johnston, Phil	1759		1981–82	George Gervin, SA	32.3
1954–55	Neil Johnston, Phil	1631		1982–83	Alex English, Den	28.4
1955–56	Bob Pettit, StL	1849		1983–84	Adrian Dantley, Utah	30.6
1956–57	Paul Arizin, Phil	1817		1984–85	Bernard King, NY	32.9
1957–58	George Yardley, Det	2001		1985–86	Dominique Wilkins, Atl	30.3
1958–59	Bob Pettit, StL	2105		1986–87	Michael Jordan, Chi	37.1
1959–60	Wilt Chamberlain, Phil	2707		1987–88	Michael Jordan, Chi	35.0
1960–61	Wilt Chamberlain, Phil	3033		1988–89	Michael Jordan, Chi	32.5
1961–62	Wilt Chamberlain, Phil	4029		1989–90	Michael Jordan, Chi	33.6
1962–63	Wilt Chamberlain, SF	3586		1990–91	Michael Jordan, Chi	31.5
1963–64	Wilt Chamberlain, SF	2948		1991–92	Michael Jordan, Chi	30.1
1964–65	Wilt Chamberlain, SF-Phil	2534		1992–93	Michael Jordan, Chi	32.6
1965–66	Wilt Chamberlain, Phil	2649		1993–94	David Robinson, SA	29.8
1966–67	Rick Barry, SF	2775		1994–95	Shaquille O'Neal, Orl	29.3
1967–68	Dave Bing, Det	2142		1995–96	Michael Jordan, Chi	30.4
1968–69	Elvin Hayes, SD	2327		1996–97	Michael Jordan, Chi	29.6
1969–70	Jerry West, LA	*31.2		1997–98	Michael Jordan, Chi	28.7
1970–71	Kareem Abdul-Jabbar, Mil	31.7		1998–99	Allen Iverson, Phil	26.8
1971–72	Kareem Abdul-Jabbar, Mil	34.8		1999–00	Shaquille O'Neal, LA Lakers	29.7
1972–73	Nate Archibald, KC-Oma	34.0		2000–01	Allen Iverson, Phil	31.1
1973–74	Bob McAdoo, Buff	30.6		2001–02	Allen Iverson, Phil	31.4

*Based on per game average since 1969–70.

Rebounding

Season	Player	Total		Season	Player	Total
1950–51	Dolph Schayes, Syr	1080		1961–62	Wilt Chamberlain, Phil	2052
1951–52	Larry Foust, FW	880		1962–63	Wilt Chamberlain, SF	1946
	Mel Hutchins, Mil	880		1963–64	Bill Russell, Bos	1930
1952–53	George Mikan, Minn	1007		1964–65	Bill Russell, Bos	1878
1953–54	Harry Gallatin, NY	1098		1965–66	Wilt Chamberlain, Phil	1943
1954–55	Neil Johnston, Phil	1085		1966–67	Wilt Chamberlain, Phil	1957
1955–56	Bob Pettit, StL	1164		1967–68	Wilt Chamberlain, Phil	1952
1956–57	Maurice Stokes, Roch	1256		1968–69	Wilt Chamberlain, LA	1712
1957–58	Bill Russell, Bos	1564		1969–70	Elvin Hayes, SD	*16.9
1958–59	Bill Russell, Bos	1612		1970–71	Wilt Chamberlain, LA	18.2
1959–60	Wilt Chamberlain, Phil	1941		1971–72	Wilt Chamberlain, LA	19.2
1960–61	Wilt Chamberlain, Phil	2149		1972–73	Wilt Chamberlain, LA	18.6
				1973–74	Elvin Hayes, Capital	18.1

Rebounding (Cont.)

1974–75	Wes Unseld, Wash	14.8	1988–89	Hakeem Olajuwon, Hou	13.5
1975–76	Kareem Abdul-Jabbar, LA	16.9	1989–90	Hakeem Olajuwon, Hou	14.0
1976–77	Bill Walton, Port	14.4	1990–91	David Robinson, SA	13.0
1977–78	Len Robinson, NO	15.7	1991–92	Dennis Rodman, Det	18.7
1978–79	Moses Malone, Hou	17.6	1992–93	Dennis Rodman, Det	18.3
1979–80	Swen Nater, SD	15.0	1993–94	Dennis Rodman, SA	17.3
1980–81	Moses Malone, Hou	14.8	1994–95	Dennis Rodman, SA	16.8
1981–82	Moses Malone, Hou	14.7	1995–96	Dennis Rodman, Chi	14.9
1982–83	Moses Malone, Phil	15.3	1996–97	Dennis Rodman, Chi	16.1
1983–84	Moses Malone, Phil	13.4	1997–98	Dennis Rodman, Chi	15.0
1984–85	Moses Malone, Phil	13.1	1998–99	Chris Webber, Sac	13.0
1985–86	Bill Laimbeer, Det	13.1	1999–00	Dikembe Mutombo, Atl	14.1
1986–87	Charles Barkley, Phil	14.6	2000–01	Dikembe Mutombo, Atl	13.5
1987–88	Michael Cage, LA Clippers	13.0	2001–02	Ben Wallace, Det	13.0

*Based on per game average since 1969–70.

Assists

1946–47	Ernie Calverly, Prov	202	1974–75	Kevin Porter, Wash	8.0
1947–48	Howie Dallmar, Phil	120	1975–76	Don Watts, Sea	8.1
1948–49	Bob Davies, Roch	321	1976–77	Don Buse, Ind	8.5
1949–50	Dick McGuire, NY	386	1977–78	Kevin Porter, NJ-Det	10.2
1950–51	Andy Phillip, Phil	414	1978–79	Kevin Porter, Det	13.4
1951–52	Andy Phillip, Phil	539	1979–80	Micheal Richardson, NY	10.1
1952–53	Bob Cousy, Bos	547	1980–81	Kevin Porter, Wash	9.1
1953–54	Bob Cousy, Bos	578	1981–82	Johnny Moore, SA	9.6
1954–55	Bob Cousy, Bos	557	1982–83	Magic Johnson, LA	10.5
1955–56	Bob Cousy, Bos	642	1983–84	Magic Johnson, LA	13.1
1956–57	Bob Cousy, Bos	478	1984–85	Isiah Thomas, Det	13.9
1957–58	Bob Cousy, Bos	463	1985–86	Magic Johnson, LA Lakers	12.6
1958–59	Bob Cousy, Bos	557	1986–87	Magic Johnson, LA Lakers	12.2
1959–60	Bob Cousy, Bos	715	1987–88	John Stockton, Utah	13.8
1960–61	Oscar Robertson, Cin	690	1988–89	John Stockton, Utah	13.6
1961–62	Oscar Robertson, Cin	899	1989–90	John Stockton, Utah	14.5
1962–63	Guy Rodgers, SF	825	1990–91	John Stockton, Utah	14.2
1963–64	Oscar Robertson, Cin	868	1991–92	John Stockton, Utah	13.7
1964–65	Oscar Robertson, Cin	861	1992–93	John Stockton, Utah	12.0
1965–66	Oscar Robertson, Cin	847	1993–94	John Stockton, Utah	12.6
1966–67	Guy Rodgers, Chi	908	1994–95	John Stockton, Utah	12.3
1967–68	Wilt Chamberlain, Phil	702	1995–96	John Stockton, Utah	11.2
1968–69	Oscar Robertson, Cin	772	1996–97	Mark Jackson, Ind	11.4
1969–70	Len Wilkens, Sea	*9.1	1997–98	Rod Strickland, Wash	10.1
1970–71	Norm Van Lier, Cin	10.1	1998–99	Jason Kidd, Phoe	10.8
1971–72	Jerry West, LA	9.7	1999–00	Jason Kidd, Phoe	10.1
1972–73	Nate Archibald, KC-Oma	11.4	2000–01	Jason Kidd, Phoe	9.8
1973–74	Ernie DiGregorio, Buff	8.2	2001–02	Andre Miller, Clev	10.9

*Based on per game average since 1969–70.

Field-Goal Percentage

1946–47	Bob Feerick, Wash	40.1	1966–67	Wilt Chamberlain, Phil	68.3
1947–48	Bob Feerick, Wash	34.0	1967–68	Wilt Chamberlain, Phil	59.5
1948–49	Arnie Risen, Roch	42.3	1968–69	Wilt Chamberlain, LA	58.3
1949–50	Alex Groza, Ind	47.8	1969–70	Johnny Green, Cin	55.9
1950–51	Alex Groza, Ind	47.0	1970–71	Johnny Green, Cin	58.7
1951–52	Paul Arizin, Phil	44.8	1971–72	Wilt Chamberlain, LA	64.9
1952–53	Neil Johnston, Phil	45.2	1972–73	Wilt Chamberlain, LA	72.7
1953–54	Ed Macauley, Bos	48.6	1973–74	Bob McAdoo, Buff	54.7
1954–55	Larry Foust, FW	48.7	1974–75	Don Nelson, Bos	53.9
1955–56	Neil Johnston, Phil	45.7	1975–76	Wes Unseld, Wash	56.1
1956–57	Neil Johnston, Phil	44.7	1976–77	Kareem Abdul-Jabbar, LA	57.9
1957–58	Jack Twyman, Cin	45.2	1977–78	Bobby Jones, Den	57.8
1958–59	Ken Sears, NY	49.0	1978–79	Cedric Maxwell, Bos	58.4
1959–60	Ken Sears, NY	47.7	1979–80	Cedric Maxwell, Bos	60.9
1960–61	Wilt Chamberlain, Phil	50.9	1980–81	Artis Gilmore, Chi	67.0
1961–62	Walt Bellamy, Chi	51.9	1981–82	Artis Gilmore, Chi	65.2
1962–63	Wilt Chamberlain, SF	52.8	1982–83	Artis Gilmore, SA	62.6
1963–64	Jerry Lucas, Cin	52.7	1983–84	Artis Gilmore, SA	63.1
1964–65	Wilt Chamberlain, SF-Phil	51.0	1984–85	James Donaldson, LA Clippers	63.7
1965–66	Wilt Chamberlain, Phil	54.0	1985–86	Steve Johnson, SA	63.2

Field-Goal Percentage (Cont.)

1986–87	Kevin McHale, Bos	60.4	1994–95 ..... Chris Gatling, GS	63.3
1987–88	Kevin McHale, Bos	60.4	1995–96 ..... Gheorghe Muresan, Wash	58.4
1988–89	Dennis Rodman, Det	59.5	1996–97 ..... Gheorghe Muresan, Wash	60.4
1989–90	Mark West, Phoe	62.5	1997–98 ..... Shaquille O'Neal, LA Lakers	58.4
1990–91	Buck Williams, Port	60.2	1998–99 ..... Shaquille O'Neal, LA Lakers	57.6
1991–92	Buck Williams, Port	60.4	1999–00 ..... Shaquille O'Neal, LA Lakers	57.4
1992–93	Cedric Ceballos, Phoe	57.6	2000–01 ..... Shaquille O'Neal, LA Lakers	57.2
1993–94	Shaquille O'Neal, Orl	59.9	2001–02 ..... Shaquille O'Neal, LA Lakers	57.9

Free-Throw Percentage

1946–47	Fred Scolari, Wash	81.1	1974–75 ..... Rick Barry, GS	90.4
1947–48	Bob Feerick, Wash	78.8	1975–76 ..... Rick Barry, GS	92.3
1948–49	Bob Feerick, Wash	85.9	1976–77 ..... Ernie DiGregorio, Buff	94.5
1949–50	Max Zaslofsky, Chi	84.3	1977–78 ..... Rick Barry, GS	92.4
1950–51	Joe Fulks, Phil	85.5	1978–79 ..... Rick Barry, Hou	94.7
1951–52	Bob Wanzer, Roch	90.4	1979–80 ..... Rick Barry, Hou	93.5
1952–53	Bill Sharman, Bos	85.0	1980–81 ..... Calvin Murphy, Hou	95.8
1953–54	Bill Sharman, Bos	84.4	1981–82 ..... Kyle Macy, Phoe	89.9
1954–55	Bill Sharman, Bos	89.7	1982–83 ..... Calvin Murphy, Hou	92.0
1955–56	Bill Sharman, Bos	86.7	1983–84 ..... Larry Bird, Bos	88.8
1956–57	Bill Sharman, Bos	90.5	1984–85 ..... Kyle Macy, Phoe	90.7
1957–58	Dolph Schayes, Syr	90.4	1985–86 ..... Larry Bird, Bos	89.6
1958–59	Bill Sharman, Bos	93.2	1986–87 ..... Larry Bird, Bos	91.0
1959–60	Dolph Schayes, Syr	89.2	1987–88 ..... Jack Sikma, Mil	92.2
1960–61	Bill Sharman, Bos	92.1	1988–89 ..... Magic Johnson, LA Lakers	91.1
1961–62	Dolph Schayes, Syr	89.6	1989–90 ..... Larry Bird, Bos	93.0
1962–63	Larry Costello, Syr	88.1	1990–91 ..... Reggie Miller, Ind	91.8
1963–64	Oscar Robertson, Cin	85.3	1991–92 ..... Mark Price, Clev	94.7
1964–65	Larry Costello, Phil	87.7	1992–93 ..... Mark Price, Clev	94.8
1965–66	Larry Siegfried, Bos	88.1	1993–94 ..... Mahmoud Abdul-Rauf, Den	95.6
1966–67	Adrian Smith, Cin	90.3	1994–95 ..... Spud Webb, Sac	93.4
1967–68	Oscar Robertson, Cin	87.3	1995–96 ..... Mahmoud Abdul-Rauf, Den	93.0
1968–69	Larry Siegfried, Bos	86.4	1996–97 ..... Mark Price, GS	90.6
1969–70	Flynn Robinson, Mil	89.8	1997–98 ..... Chris Mullin, Ind	93.9
1970–71	Chet Walker, Chi	85.9	1998–99 ..... Reggie Miller, Ind	91.5
1971–72	Jack Marin, Balt	89.4	1999–00 ..... Jeff Hornacek, Utah	95.0
1972–73	Rick Barry, GS	90.2	2000–01 ..... Reggie Miller, Ind	92.8
1973–74	Ernie DiGregorio, Buff	90.2	2001–02 ..... Reggie Miller, Ind	91.1

Three-Point Field-Goal Percentage

1979–80	Fred Brown, Sea	44.3	1991–92 ..... Dana Barros, Sea	44.6
1980–81	Brian Taylor, SD	38.3	1992–93 ..... B.J. Armstrong, Chi	45.3
1981–82	Campy Russell, NY	43.9	1993–94 ..... Tracy Murray, Por	45.9
1982–83	Mike Dunleavy, SA	34.5	1994–95 ..... Steve Kerr, Chi	52.4
1983–84	Darrell Griffith, Utah	36.1	1995–96 ..... Tim Legler, Wash	52.2
1984–85	Byron Scott, LA Lakers	43.3	1996–97 ..... Kevin Gamble, Sac	48.2
1985–86	Craig Hodges, Mil	45.1	1997–98 ..... Dale Ellis, Sea	46.0
1986–87	Kiki Vandeweghe, Por	48.1	1998–99 ..... Dell Curry, Char	47.6
1987–88	Craig Hodges, Mil-Phoe	49.1	1999–00 ..... Hubert Davis, Dall	49.1
1988–89	Jon Sundvold, Mia	52.2	2000–01 ..... Brent Barry, Sea	47.6
1989–90	Steve Kerr, Clev	50.7	2001–02 ..... Steve Smith, SA	47.2
1990–91	Jim Les, Sac	46.1		

Steals

1973–74	Larry Steele, Por	2.68	1988–89 ..... John Stockton, Utah	3.21
1974–75	Rick Barry, GS	2.85	1989–90 ..... Michael Jordan, Chi	2.77
1975–76	Don Watts, Sea	3.18	1990–91 ..... Alvin Robertson, Mil	3.04
1976–77	Don Buse, Ind	3.47	1991–92 ..... John Stockton, Utah	2.98
1977–78	Ron Lee, Phoe	2.74	1992–93 ..... Michael Jordan, Chi	2.83
1978–79	M.L. Carr, Det	2.46	1993–94 ..... Nate McMillan, Sea	2.96
1979–80	Micheal Richardson, NY	3.23	1994–95 ..... Scottie Pippen, Chi	2.94
1980–81	Magic Johnson, LA	3.43	1995–96 ..... Gary Payton, Sea	2.85
1981–82	Magic Johnson, LA	2.67	1996–97 ..... Mookie Blaylock, Atl	2.72
1982–83	Micheal Richardson, GS-NJ	2.84	1997–98 ..... Mookie Blaylock, Atl	2.61
1983–84	Rickey Green, Utah	2.65	1998–99 ..... Kendall Gill, NJ	2.68
1984–85	Micheal Richardson, NJ	2.96	1999–00 ..... Eddie Jones, Char	2.67
1985–86	Alvin Robertson, SA	3.67	2000–01 ..... Allen Iverson, Phil	2.51
1986–87	Alvin Robertson, SA	3.21	2001–02 ..... Allen Iverson, Phil	2.80
1987–88	Michael Jordan, Chi	3.16		

Blocked Shots

1973–74	Elmore Smith, LA	4.85	
1974–75	Kareem Abdul-Jabbar, Mil	3.26	
1975–76	Kareem Abdul-Jabbar, LA	4.12	
1976–77	Bill Walton, Port	3.25	
1977–78	George Johnson, NJ	3.38	
1978–79	Kareem Abdul-Jabbar, LA	3.95	
1979–80	Kareem Abdul-Jabbar, LA	3.41	
1980–81	George Johnson, SA	3.39	
1981–82	George Johnson, SA	3.12	
1982–83	Wayne Rollins, Atl	4.29	
1983–84	Mark Eaton, Utah	4.28	
1984–85	Mark Eaton, Utah	5.56	
1985–86	Manute Bol, Wash	4.96	
1986–87	Mark Eaton, Utah	4.06	
1987–88	Mark Eaton, Utah	3.71	
1988–89	Manute Bol, GS	4.31	
1989–90	Hakeem Olajuwon, Hou	4.59	
1990–91	Hakeem Olajuwon, Hou	3.95	
1991–92	David Robinson, SA	4.49	
1992–93	Hakeem Olajuwon, Hou	4.17	
1993–94	Dikembe Mutombo, Den	4.10	
1994–95	Dikembe Mutombo, Den	3.91	
1995–96	Dikembe Mutombo, Den	4.49	
1996–97	Shawn Bradley, NJ	3.40	
1997–98	Marcus Camby, Tor	3.65	
1998–99	Alonzo Mourning, Mia	3.91	
1999–00	Alonzo Mourning, Mia	3.72	
2000–01	Theo Ratliff, Phil/Atl	3.74	
2001–02	Ben Wallace, Det	3.48	

NBA All-Star Game Results

Year	Result	Site	Winning Coach	Most Valuable Player
1951	East 111, West 94	Boston	Joe Lapchick	Ed Macauley, Bos
1952	East 108, West 91	Boston	Al Cervi	Paul Arizin, Phil
1953	West 79, East 75	Ft Wayne	John Kundla	George Mikan, Minn
1954	East 98, West 93 (OT)	New York	Joe Lapchick	Bob Cousy, Bos
1955	East 100, West 91	New York	Al Cervi	Bill Sharman, Bos
1956	West 108, East 94	Rochester	Charley Eckman	Bob Pettit, StL
1957	East 109, West 97	Boston	Red Auerbach	Bob Cousy, Bos
1958	East 130, West 118	St Louis	Red Auerbach	Bob Pettit, StL
1959	West 124, East 108	Detroit	Ed Macauley	B. Pettit, StL/ E. Baylor, Minn
1960	East 125, West 115	Philadelphia	Red Auerbach	Wilt Chamberlain, Phil
1961	West 153, East 131	Syracuse	Paul Seymour	Oscar Robertson, Cin
1962	West 150, East 130	St Louis	Fred Schaus	Bob Pettit, StL
1963	East 115, West 108	Los Angeles	Red Auerbach	Bill Russell, Bos
1964	East 111, West 107	Boston	Red Auerbach	Oscar Robertson, Cin
1965	East 124, West 123	St Louis	Red Auerbach	Jerry Lucas, Cin
1966	East 137, West 94	Cincinnati	Red Auerbach	Adrian Smith, Cin
1967	West 135, East 120	San Francisco	Fred Schaus	Rick Barry, SF
1968	East 144, West 124	New York	Alex Hannum	Hal Greer, Phil
1969	East 123, West 112	Baltimore	Gene Shue	Oscar Robertson, Cin
1970	East 142, West 135	Philadelphia	Red Holzman	Willis Reed, NY
1971	West 108, East 107	San Diego	Larry Costello	Lenny Wilkens, Sea
1972	West 112, East 110	Los Angeles	Bill Sharman	Jerry West, LA
1973	East 104, West 84	Chicago	Tom Heinsohn	Dave Cowens, Bos
1974	West 134, East 123	Seattle	Larry Costello	Bob Lanier, Det
1975	East 108, West 102	Phoenix	K.C. Jones	Walt Frazier, NY
1976	East 123, West 109	Philadelphia	Tom Heinsohn	Dave Bing, Wash
1977	West 125, East 124	Milwaukee	Larry Brown	Julius Erving, Phil
1978	East 133, West 125	Atlanta	Billy Cunningham	Randy Smith, Buff
1979	West 134, East 129	Detroit	Lenny Wilkens	David Thompson, Den
1980	East 144, West 135 (OT)	Washington	Billy Cunningham	George Gervin, SA
1981	East 123, West 120	Cleveland	Billy Cunningham	Nate Archibald, Bos
1982	East 120, West 118	New Jersey	Bill Fitch	Larry Bird, Bos
1983	East 132, West 123	Los Angeles	Billy Cunningham	Julius Erving, Phil
1984	East 154, West 145 (OT)	Denver	K.C. Jones	Isiah Thomas, Det
1985	West 140, East 129	Indiana	Pat Riley	Ralph Sampson, Hou
1986	East 139, West 132	Dallas	K.C. Jones	Isiah Thomas, Det
1987	West 154, East 149 (OT)	Seattle	Pat Riley	Tom Chambers, Sea
1988	East 138, West 133	Chicago	Mike Fratello	Michael Jordan, Chi
1989	West 143, East 134	Houston	Pat Riley	Karl Malone, Utah
1990	East 130, West 113	Miami	Chuck Daly	Magic Johnson, LA Lakers
1991	East 116, West 114	Charlotte	Chris Ford	Charles Barkley, Phil
1992	West 153, East 113	Orlando	Don Nelson	Magic Johnson, LA Lakers
1993	West 135, East 132	Salt Lake City	Paul Westphal	K. Malone/ J. Stockton ,Utah
1994	East 127, West 118	Minneapolis	Lenny Wilkens	Scottie Pippen, Chi
1995	West 139, East 112	Phoenix	Paul Westphal	Mitch Richmond, Sac
1996	East 129, West 118	San Antonio	Phil Jackson	Michael Jordan, Chi
1997	East 132, West 120	Cleveland	Doug Collins	Glen Rice, Char
1998	East 135, West 114	New York	Larry Bird	Michael Jordan, Chi
1999	Cancelled due to lockout.			
2000	West 137, East 126	Oakland	Phil Jackson	O'Neal, Lakers/T. Duncan, SA
2001	East 111, West 110	Washington	Larry Brown	Allen Iverson, Phil
2002	West 135, East 120	Philadelphia	Don Nelson	Kobe Bryant, LA Lakers

Contributors

Senda Abbott (1984)
Forest C. (Phog) Allen (1959)
Clair F. Bee (1967)
Danny Biasone (2000)
Walter A. Brown (1965)
John W. Bunn (1964)
Bob Douglas (1971)
Al Duer (1981)
Wayne Embry (1999)
Clifford Fagan (1983)
Harry A. Fisher (1973)
Larry Fleisher (1991)
Edward Gottlieb (1971)
Luther H. Gulick (1959)
Lester Harrison (1979)
Ferenc Hepp (1980)

Edward J. Hickox (1959)
Paul D. (Tony) Hinkle (1965)
Ned Irish (1964)
R. William Jones (1964)
J. Walter Kennedy (1980)
Emil S. Liston (1974)
John B. McLendon (1978)
Bill Mokray (1965)
Ralph Morgan (1959)
Frank Morgenweck (1962)
James Naismith (1959)
Peter F. Newell (1978)
C.M. Newton (2000)
John J. O'Brien (1961)
Larry O'Brien (1991)
Harold G. Olsen (1959)

Maurice Podoloff (1973)
H. V. Porter (1960)
William A. Reid (1963)
Elmer Ripley (1972)
Lynn W. St. John (1962)
Abe Saperstein (1970)
Arthur A. Schabinger (1961)
Amos Alonzo Stagg (1959)
Boris Stankovic (1991)
Edward Steitz (1983)
Chuck Taylor (1968)
Oswald Tower (1959)
Arthur L. Trester (1961)
Clifford Wells (1971)
Lou Wilke (1982)
Fred Zollner (1999)

Players

Kareem Abdul-Jabbar (1995)
Nate (Tiny) Archibald (1991)
Paul J. Arizin (1977)
Thomas B. Barlow (1980)
Rick Barry (1987)
Elgin Baylor (1976)
John Beckman (1972)
Walt Bellamy (1993)
Sergei Belov (1992)
Dave Bing (1990)
Larry Bird (1998)
Carol Blazejowski (1994)
Bennie Borgmann (1961)
Bill Bradley (1982)
Joseph Brennan (1974)
Al Cervi (1984)
Wilt Chamberlain (1978)
Charles (Tarzan) Cooper (1976)
Kresimir Cosic (1996)
Bob Cousy (1970)
Dave Cowens (1991)
Joan Crawford (1997)
Billy Cunningham (1986)
Denise Curry (1997)
Bob Davies (1969)
Forrest S. DeBernardi (1961)
Dave DeBusschere (1982)
H.G. (Dutch) Dehnert (1968)
Anne Donovan (1995)
Paul Endacott (1971)
Alex English (1997)
Julius Erving (1993)
Harold (Bud) Foster (1964)
Walter (Clyde) Frazier (1987)
Max (Marty) Friedman (1971)
Joe Fulks (1977)
Lauren (Laddie) Gale (1976)
Harry (the Horse) Gallatin (1991)
William Gates (1989)
George Gervin (1996)
Tom Gola (1975)

Gail Goodrich (1996)
Hal Greer (1981)
Robert (Ace) Gruenig (1963)
Clifford O. Hagan (1977)
Victor Hanson (1960)
John Havlicek (1983)
Connie Hawkins (1992)
Elvin Hayes (1990)
Marques Haynes (1998)
Tom Heinsohn (1986)
Nat Holman (1964)
Robert J. Houbregs (1987)
Bailey Howell (1997)
Chuck Hyatt (1959)
Dan Issel (1993)
Harry (Buddy) Jeannette (1994)
Earvin (Magic) Johnson (2002)
William C. Johnson (1976)
D. Neil Johnston (1990)
K.C. Jones (1989)
Sam Jones (1983)
Edward (Moose) Krause (1975)
Bob Kurland (1961)
Bob Lanier (1992)
Joe Lapchick (1966)
Nancy Lieberman-Cline (1996)
Clyde Lovellette (1988)
Jerry Lucas (1979)
Angelo (Hank) Luisetti (1959)
C. Edward Macauley (1960)
Moses Malone (2001)
Peter P. Maravich (1987)
Slater Martin (1981)
Bob McAdoo (2000)
Branch McCracken (1960)
Jack McCracken (1962)
Bobby McDermott (1988)
Dick McGuire (1993)
Kevin McHale (1999)
Ann Meyers (1993)
George L. Mikan (1959)

Vern Mikkelsen (1995)
Cheryl Miller (1995)
Earl Monroe (1990)
Calvin Murphy (1993)
Charles (Stretch) Murphy (1960)
H. O. (Pat) Page (1962)
Drazen Petrovic (2002)
Bob Pettit (1970)
Andy Phillip (1961)
Jim Pollard (1977)
Frank Ramsey (1981)
Willis Reed (1981)
Arnie Risen (1998)
Oscar Robertson (1979)
John S. Roosma (1961)
Bill Russell (1974)
John (Honey) Russell (1964)
Adolph Schayes (1972)
Ernest J. Schmidt (1973)
John J. Schommer (1959)
Barney Sedran (1962)
Uljana Semjonova (1993)
Bill Sharman (1975)
Christian Steinmetz (1961)
Lusia Harris Stewart (1992)
Isiah Thomas (2000)
David Thompson (1996)
John A. (Cat) Thompson (1962)
Nate Thurmond (1984)
Jack Twyman (1982)
Wes Unseld (1988)
Robert (Fuzzy) Vandivier (1974)
Edward A. Wachter (1961)
Bill Walton (1993)
Robert F. Wanzer (1987)
Jerry West (1979)
Nera White (1992)
Lenny Wilkens (1989)
John R. Wooden (1960)
George (Bird) Yardley (1996)

Coaches

Harold Anderson (1984)
Red Auerbach (1968)
Sam Barry (1978)
Ernest A. Blood (1960)
Larry Brown (2002)
Howard G. Cann (1967)
H. Clifford Carlson (1959)
Note: Year of election in parentheses.

Lou Carnesecca (1992)
Ben Carnevale (1969)
Pete Carril (1997)
Everett Case (1981)
John Chaney (2001)
Jody Conradt (1998)

Denny Crum (1994)
Chuck Daly (1994)
Everett S. Dean (1966)
Antonio Diaz-Miguel (1997)
Edgar A. Diddle (1971)
Bruce Drake (1972)

Coaches *(Cont.)*

Clarence Gaines (1981)
Jack Gardner (1983)
Amory T. (Slats) Gill (1967)
Aleksandr Gomelsky (1995)
Alex Hannum (1998)
Marv Harshman (1984)
Don Haskins (1997)
Edgar S. Hickey (1978)
Howard A. Hobson (1965)
Red Holzman (1986)
Hank Iba (1968)
Alvin F. (Doggie) Julian (1967)
Frank W. Keaney (1960)
George E. Keogan (1961)
Bob Knight (1991)
Mike Krzyzewski (2001)

John Kundla (1995)
Ward L. Lambert (1960)
Harry Litwack (1975)
Kenneth D. Loeffler (1964)
A.C. (Dutch) Lonborg (1972)
Arad A. McCutchan (1980)
Al McGuire (1992)
Frank McGuire (1976)
Walter E. Meanwell (1959)
Raymond J. Meyer (1978)
Ralph Miller (1988)
Billie Moore (1999)
Aleksandar Nikolic (1998)
Lute Olson (2002
Jack Ramsay (1992)
Cesare Rubini (1994)

Adolph F. Rupp (1968)
Leonard D. Sachs (1961)
Everett F. Shelton (1979)
Dean Smith (1982)
Pat Summitt (2000)
Fred R. Taylor (1985)
Bertha Teague (1984)
John Thompson (1999)
Margaret Wade (1984)
Stanley H. Watts (1985)
Lenny Wilkens (1998)
John R. Wooden (1972)
Morgan Wooten (2000)
Phil Woolpert (1992)
Kay Yow (2002)

Referees

James E. Enright (1978)
George T. Hepbron (1960)
George Hoyt (1961)
Matthew P. Kennedy (1959)
Lloyd Leith (1982)
Zigmund J. Mihalik (1985)

John P. Nucatola (1977)
Ernest C. Quigley (1961)
J. Dallas Shirley (1979)
Earl Strom (1995)
David Tobey (1961)
David H. Walsh (1961)

Teams

Buffalo Germans (1961)
First Team (1959)
Harlem Globetrotters (2002)
Original Celtics (1959)
Renaissance (1963)

ABA Champions

Year	Champion	Series	Runner-up	Winning Coach
1968	Pittsburgh Pipers	4–3	New Orleans Bucs	Vince Cazetta
1969	Oakland Oaks	4–1	Indiana Pacers	Alex Hannum
1970	Indiana Pacers	4–2	Los Angeles Stars	Bob Leonard
1971	Utah Stars	4–3	Kentucky Colonels	Bill Sharman
1972	Indiana Pacers	4–2	New York Nets	Bob Leonard
1973	Indiana Pacers	4–3	Kentucky Colonels	Bob Leonard
1974	New York Nets	4–1	Utah Stars	Kevin Loughery
1975	Kentucky Colonels	4–1	Indiana Pacers	Hubie Brown
1976	New York Nets	4–2	Denver Nuggets	Kevin Loughery

ABA Postseason Awards

Most Valuable Player

1967–68 .... Connie Hawkins, Pitt
1968–69 .... Mel Daniels, Ind
1969–70 .... Spencer Haywood, Den
1970–71 .... Mel Daniels, Ind
1971–72 .... Artis Gilmore, Ken
1972–73 .... Billy Cunningham, Car
1973–74 .... Julius Erving, NY
1974–75 .... Julius Erving, NY
                 George McGinnis, Ind
1975–76 .... Julius Erving, NY

Rookie of the Year

1967–68 .... Mel Daniels, Minn
1968–69 .... Warren Armstrong, Oak
1969–70 .... Spencer Haywood, Den
1970–71 .... Charlie Scott, Vir
                 Dan Issel, Ken
1971–72 .... Artis Gilmore, Ken
1972–73 .... Brian Taylor, NY
1973–74 .... Swen Nater, SA
1974–75 .... Marvin Barnes, StL
1975–76 .... David Thompson, Den

Coach of the Year

1967–68 .... Vince Cazetta, Pitt
1968–69 .... Alex Hannum, Oak
1969–70 .... Bill Sharman, LA
                 Joe Belmont, Den
1970–71 .... Al Bianchi, Vir
1971–72 .... Tom Nissalke, Dall
1972–73 .... Larry Brown, Car
1973–74 .... Babe McCarthy, Ken
                 Joe Mullaney, Utah
1974–75 .... Larry Brown, Den
1975–76 .... Larry Brown, Den

ABA Season Leaders

Scoring

		GP	Pts	Avg
1967–68	Connie Hawkins, Pitt	70	1875	26.8
1968–69	Rick Barry, Oak	35	1190	34.0
1969–70	Spencer Haywood, Den	84	2519	30.0
1970–71	Dan Issel, Ken	83	2480	29.4
1971–72	Charlie Scott, Vir	73	2524	34.6
1972–73	Julius Erving, Vir	71	2268	31.9
1973–74	Julius Erving, NY	84	2299	27.4
1974–75	George McGinnis, Ind	79	2353	29.8
1975–76	Julius Erving, NY	84	2462	29.3

Assists

1967–68	Larry Brown, NO	6.5
1968–69	Larry Brown, Oak	7.1
1969–70	Larry Brown, Wash	7.1
1970–71	Bill Melchionni, NY	8.3
1971–72	Bill Melchionni, NY	8.4
1972–73	Bill Melchionni, NY	7.5
1973–74	Al Smith, Den	8.2
1974–75	Mack Calvin, Den	7.7
1975–76	Don Buse, Ind	8.2

Rebounds

1967–68	Mel Daniels, Minn	15.6
1968–69	Mel Daniels, Ind	16.5
1969–70	Spencer Haywood, Den	19.5
1970–71	Mel Daniels, Ind	18.0
1971–72	Artis Gilmore, Ken	17.8
1972–73	Artis Gilmore, Ken	17.5
1973–74	Artis Gilmore, Ken	18.3
1974–75	Swen Nater, SA	16.4
1975–76	Artis Gilmore, Ken	15.5

Steals

1973–74	Ted McClain, Car	2.98
1974–75	Brian Taylor, NY	2.80
1975–76	Don Buse, Ind	4.12

Blocked Shots

1973–74	Caldwell Jones, SD	4.00
1974–75	Caldwell Jones, SD	3.24
1975–76	Billy Paultz, SA	3.05

World Championship of Basketball

Year	Winner	Runner-Up	Score	Site
1950	Argentina	United States	†	Rio de Janeiro
1954	United States	Brazil	†	Rio de Janeiro
1959	Brazil	United States	†	Santiago, Chile
1963	Brazil	Yugoslavia	†	Rio de Janeiro
1967	Soviet Union	Yugoslavia	†	Montevideo, Uruguay
1970	Yugoslavia	Brazil	†	Ljubljana, Yugoslavia
1974	Soviet Union	Yugoslavia	†	San Juan
1978	Yugoslavia	Soviet Union	82–81 (OT)	Manila
1982	Soviet Union	United States	95–94	Cali, Colombia
1986	United States	Soviet Union	87–85	Madrid
1990	Yugoslavia	Soviet Union	92–75	Buenos Aires
1994*	United States	Russia	137–91	Toronto
1998	Yugoslavia	Russia	64–62	Athens
2002	Yugoslavia	Argentina	84–77 (OT)	Indianapolis

*U.S. professionals began competing in 1994. In 1998, a labor dispute resulted in a boycott of the World Championship by NBA stars; the U.S. roster was filled by members of the CBA and European professional leagues and college players.
†Result determined by overall record in final round of competition.

THEY SAID IT

George Karl, coach of the U.S. team at the 2002 World Basketball Championship, after the Americans' sixth-place finish: "Is the money and greed of the NBA having an effect on our competitive nature? Yeah."

College Basketball

Juan Dixon of
national champion
Maryland

Over the Hump

Maryland defeated its longtime nemesis, Duke, won the ACC title and then made a stirring run to its first national championship

BY B.J. SCHECTER

WHEN THE final buzzer sounded and he got the first taste of what he had accomplished—the astoundingly improbable, if not unimaginable—Maryland's senior shooting guard Juan Dixon looked up toward the heavens and thrust his hands in the air. He was so overcome by emotion and joy that basketball suddenly became secondary. Dixon recalled his parents, who were addicted to heroin and both died of AIDS before he turned 18. He looked back on his long, uphill battle to become a college basketball star. Then he embraced Terrapins coach Gary Williams.

Dixon had shined on the college game's biggest stage, carrying the University of Maryland to the first basketball national title in school history and helping Williams win the championship he had dedicated his life to pursuing. It fit that Dixon should share this moment with Williams—both men are fighters who have overcome difficulties in their personal lives, and both men have turned to basketball as a lifelong source of shelter from those difficulties. The Maryland program's ascension was full of similar struggles. Though the Terps went to the Final Four in 2001 and were considered among the nation's elite programs, they couldn't shake their image as the little brother to Duke in the Atlantic Coast Conference. Twice during the 2000–01 season, Maryland outplayed Duke only to suffer second-half meltdowns, including blowing a 22-point lead in the Final Four. After a 21-point loss to the Blue Devils at Cameron Indoor Stadium on Jan. 17, 2002, most observers decided that Maryland couldn't be considered a title contender until it beat Duke.

Williams tried to downplay the psychological hurdle that Duke presented to his team, and he demanded that his players keep striving. And strive the Terps did; they improved with each game, as senior forward Lonny Baxter and sophomore forward Chris Wilcox became an indomitable tandem inside, and Dixon and point guard Steve Blake established themselves as perhaps the best backcourt in the nation. When Duke came to Cole Field House one month after that catastrophic first meeting, well, Maryland may have started the same

While Blake (rear) held the ball at the final buzzer, Tahj Holden, Dixon and Baxter celebrated the Terps victory.

players that took the court back in January, but the Terps were a different team. And they proved it, dominating from start to finish and exorcising some demons—and Devils—with a convincing 87–73 victory. After the game, Williams was quick to downplay the accomplishment. "We didn't win anything today," he said. "All we proved is that we can beat Duke."

Of course, by beating Duke, the defending national champions, the Terps sent a message to the college basketball nation that they could beat anyone. Further, since Maryland had lost five of its previous six games against Duke, the message also hit home: one mental block removed, psychological chains unshackled.

The Terrapins were ready to play with abandon, and though they fell to North Carolina State in the semifinals of the ACC tournament, the Terps still received the No. 1 seed in the East. They cruised past Siena, Wisconsin and Kentucky in short order, before being tested in the regional final against Connecticut. The Huskies gave Maryland everything it could handle, but like it had done all season, Maryland rolled with the punches and found a way to deliver a knockout counterpunch.

Despite outstanding efforts from Baxter (29 points) and Dixon (27), Maryland couldn't shake UConn until the final minute. The game featured 22 ties and 23 lead changes, and Huskies sophomore forward Caron Butler produced one of the best individual performances of the NCAAs, scoring 32 points and grabbing seven rebounds. Leading 83–80 with 25 seconds remaining, Maryland called a timeout. Williams designed a play to get the ball to Dixon or Baxter. Surprisingly, Blake, who had not made a field goal all night, interrupted his coach and said he wanted the ball. Williams obliged. Blake calmly nailed a three-pointer. Ballgame. "Blake's a clutch player," said Dixon. "He came through at the right time."

Maryland almost always came through at the right time in 2001–02, though sometimes the Terps needed some prodding. After Kansas took a 13–2 lead in the opening minutes of the national semifinal, Williams called a timeout and let his team have it. "If we're gonna lose this game, we're gonna lose it fighting," he screamed. "We aren't gonna be punks!" Dixon took his coach's words to heart, scoring 10 consecutive points as the Terps regained control.

Later, after Kansas had staged a rally of its own, cutting the Terps' 20-point lead to five, Dixon badly missed a three-pointer. It appeared as though a Maryland meltdown of old was at hand. But instead of throwing a fit as he normally might have done in that situation, Williams looked at Dixon and said, "Take the next one!" Sure enough, after a defensive stop, Dixon came down the floor and hit a baseline runner to help seal the Terps' 97–88 victory. "A lot of guys can score 20 points, but then they run and hide during the last few minutes," said Williams. "Juan hits every big shot for us."

Dixon hit plenty of big shots in the championship game, including two doozies in the second half. When Indiana erased a 12-point Maryland lead to tie the score at 42–42, Dixon pointed to his brother, Phil, in the stands and said, "It's all right, it's all right. I got it." But Indiana forward Jared Jeffries quickly gave the Hoosiers their first lead of the game. Then Dixon took over. He sank a three-pointer to put the Terps back in the lead, then he hit a preposterous fadeaway jumper with Indiana guard Dane Fife draped all over him. That sparked a 22–5 run and allowed Maryland to coast the rest of the way to a 64–52 victory. "I wasn't nervous at all," said Dixon. "I've been through tougher situations in my life. I knew we were going to win."

Williams's fighting, winning mentality rubbed off on his players. Whether it was Dixon, who developed himself from a wispy 6' 1", 150-pound guard at Baltimore's Calvert Hall High into a star for the Terps, or Byron Mouton, who accepted his backup role and consistently made hustle plays, the Terps reflected the iron will and unflagging spirit of their coach. Williams built a program with unheralded players, and Maryland became the first team to win a national title without a single McDonald's All-America since the honor was created in 1978.

"The longer you coach the more you realize you don't have to have the best talent," Williams said. "You can beat teams that might be a little more talented than you if you're willing to work harder. Plus it's more fun. You're not dealing with a bunch of guys who are upset that they're still in college when they're juniors."

In Kansas, a pair of juniors were the main reason the Jayhawks finished 33–4 and entered the NCAA tournament as a bona fide favorite. With agile All-Americas Drew Gooden and Nick Collison at the forward positions, and a pair of guards who could push the tempo, the Jayhawks were a high-powered outfit. As usual, college hoop wags made much of coach Roy Williams's previous tournament failures, but Kansas ignored the scrutiny and fulfilled its role as a tournament heavy, obliterating Holy Cross and Stanford before edging a tough Illinois team to reach the regional final against Oregon. That one wasn't even close, as Gooden and Collison each produced double-doubles and Kansas romped 104–86. The Jayhawks' run would end in the Final Four against Maryland, but Williams and his charges had gone a long way toward erasing the Jayhawks' bitter memories of tournaments past.

The surprise team of the Final Four was Indiana, which featured a star (Jared Jeffries), an embattled second-year coach (Mike Davis) and a bunch of sweet-shooting, scrappy role players who could have come out of the movie *Hoosiers*. Before rolling into Atlanta, Indiana pulled off the tournament's biggest upset, knocking off Duke 74–73 in the South regional semifinal. Jeffries scored 24 points against the Blue Devils, but more importantly he influenced almost every offensive play for IU. "Our guards are not quick enough to drive past people," said Davis. "I needed to create something where they could catch and shoot. Jared is unselfish, he's a great passer, and he knows where people are supposed to be on the floor."

Before the game, Davis showed his team

In his second year as coach, Davis took the Hoosiers to the national title game.

a tape that featured footage of North Carolina State's 1983 upset of Houston in the NCAA championship game, Villanova's stunner over Georgetown to win the 1985 title and Buster Douglas's shocking knockout of Mike Tyson in 1990. The ploy worked, and after knocking off Oklahoma with a gutsy effort in the Final Four, Davis's team did what Bob Knight's couldn't do during his last 13 years at Indiana—they made it to the NCAA championship game.

In the women's game, one thing was clear before the season began: The road to the national championship would pass through Connecticut. After falling to Notre Dame in the 2001 Final Four, the Huskies were determined to make amends, and they started four seniors who were widely considered to be the best single class in women's basketball history. And boy did they deliver: UConn not only won but also dominated all 39 games it played. The Huskies outscored opponents by an average of 35.4 points, allowed an NCAA-lowest 51.6 points per game and outrebounded the opposition by 15.5 boards per game.

Connecticut was so overpowering in its 79–56 rout of Tennessee in the national semifinal that Vols coach Pat Summitt went into the Huskies locker room after the game and addressed the team. "I know this is out of character," she said, "but I have to tell you, though I hated to be on the receiving end of it, you played a great game. You are a great team." If you know Pat Summitt, then you know what kind of a tribute that was.

With superb talent and athleticism, and one of the best starting fives ever, not to mention a team unity that most coaches could only dream of, Geno Auriemma had it all. In point guard Sue Bird he had the best player in the nation and an unselfish leader whom he practically had to beg to take shots at times; in junior Diana Taurasi he had the best shooter in the country; and in Swain

ED REINKE/AP PHOTO

Cash, Asjha Jones and Tamika Williams he had the best frontcourt in the nation.

"One of the beauties of this group is that individually they've gotten tremendous accolades, but it's their collective spirit and will that makes them stand out," said Auriemma. "As good as they are, they look to each other to get better. These four seniors have done so many great things that I would have felt absolutely horrible if I'd sent them out without something like this."

From the start of the season it was evident that Connecticut was in a different league from most of its competition. The Huskies were mildly tested twice during the regular season: once in a January meeting with Tennessee in Knoxville, during which Connecticut trailed by six points in the first half but rallied for an 86–72 win; and once during a nine-point win over Virginia Tech in a Big East game. In the

NCAA tournament, the Huskies didn't just cruise through the early rounds, they coasted—downhill. They won their first five tournament games by an average of 29.8 points. They beat Iowa by 38; they dispatched archrival Tennessee, in the national semifinals, mind you, by 23 points.

But then came the championship game in San Antonio. There, the Huskies met their biggest challenge against an Oklahoma team that was talented, confident and unintimidated by the Huskies' impressive track record. The Sooners had lost to Connecticut by 14 in Hartford in December, but given what UConn did to most of its opponents, that could be considered a squeaker. Oklahoma took heart from the defeat. With a three-guard lineup of All-America Stacey Dales, LaNeishea Caufield and Rosalind Ross, the Sooners presented some matchup problems for the Huskies, and their defensive game plan was to pressure the Connecticut guards all night. The strategy worked, as Bird and Taurasi were 0 for 9 from three-point range—it was the only game all season that UConn was held without a three-pointer—but Oklahoma didn't have an answer for the Huskies' frontcourt players. Connecticut dominated the paint, scoring 44 points from the inside and outrebounding Oklahoma 44–25. After the Sooners cut a 16-point lead to six, Taurasi helped seal the deal by scoring and drawing a fifth foul on Dales with 1:31 remaining. "That was, without question, the most difficult game we had to play," Auriemma said. "Oklahoma was unbelievably good."

That compliment might have been a stretch, but not if it were applied to UConn's four seniors. Expected to win every time they stepped on the floor during their four years together, they delivered almost every night. Roommates and best friends, Bird, Cash, Jones and Williams were intensely competitive, whether it was playing a game of cards, cooking dinner or winning a game or drill

DAMIAN STROHMEYER

in practice. When it came to dorm-room card games, these Huskies were not above bending—or even breaking—the rules. "Sue's definitely the biggest cheater and the biggest competitor and the biggest sore loser," said Taurasi. "That's why our team was so good. We take on her personality in everything we do."

That personality put winning before any individual goal. Bird would rather set up a teammate for a shot than take one herself. Bird would rather that her team win than that she collect any individual awards, and she felt uneasy when she received nearly every player-of-the-year award in the days leading up to the championship game. "When you have teammates who are just as talented as you are," Bird said, "it's kind of weird to get all the attention."

Bird and her teammates deserved all the attention they received. With two national titles in four years and a perfect 39–0 record to cap off their college careers, these Huskies will go down as one of the greatest quartets in college basketball history.

NCAA Championship Game Box Score

Maryland 64

MARYLAND	Min	FG M–A	FT M–A	Reb O–T	A	PF	TP
Mouton	27	1–5	2–2	2–4	1	2	4
Wilcox	24	4–8	2–4	2–7	0	3	10
Baxter	32	6–15	3–8	2–14	0	1	15
Dixon	38	6–9	4–4	1–5	3	1	18
Blake	33	2–6	2–2	0–6	3	2	6
Nicholas	22	1–2	5–6	1–3	0	0	7
Randle	4	1–1	0–0	0–0	0	1	2
Holden	20	0–2	2–2	1–3	4	3	2
Totals	200	21–48	20–28	9–42	11	13	64

Percentages: FG—.438, FT—.714. 3-pt goals: 2–9, .222 (Dixon 2–4, Blake 0–3, Nicholas 0–1, Holden 0–1). Team rebounds: 0. Blocked shots: 6 (Baxter 3, Holden, Mouton, Wilcox). Turnovers: 16 (Dixon 7, Blake 4, Baxter, Holden, Mouton, Nicholas, Wilcox). Steals: 12 (Dixon 5, Blake 2, Mouton 2, Baxter, Nicholas, Wilcox).

Halftime: Maryland 31, Indiana 25. A: 53,406.

Indiana 52

INDIANA	Min	FG M–A	FT M–A	Reb O–T	A	PF	TP
Jeffries	32	4–11	0–1	1–7	3	4	8
Hornsby	35	5–12	0–1	2–5	0	4	14
Odle	18	0–4	0–3	1–4	1	2	0
Coverdale	32	3–11	0–0	0–4	2	2	8
Fife	36	4–9	0–0	2–5	1	3	11
Moye	7	1–1	0–0	0–0	0	1	2
Leach	2	0–0	0–0	0–0	0	0	0
Perry	10	1–3	0–0	0–1	0	1	3
Newton	28	2–7	2–2	3–5	2	3	6
Totals	200	20–58	2–7	9–31	9	20	52

Percentages: FG—.345, FT—.286. 3-pt goals: 10–23, .435 (Jeffries 0–1, Hornsby 4–8, Coverdale 2–7, Fife 3–6, Perry 1–1). Team rebounds: 0. Blocked shots: 3 (Jeffries, Leach, Newton). Turnovers: 16 (Coverdale 4, Jeffries 4, Fife 2, Moye 2, Hornsby, Newton, Odle, Perry). Steals: 10 (Coverdale 2, Fife 2, Hornsby 2, Jeffries, Moye, Newton, Odle).

Officials: Dick Cartmell, Jim Burr, Tony Greene.

Final AP Top 25

Poll taken before NCAA Tournament.

1. Duke (58)	29–3	
2. Kansas (10)	29–3	
3. Oklahoma (2)	27–4	
4. Maryland (1)	26–4	
5. Cincinnati	30–3	
6. Gonzaga	29–3	
7. Arizona	22–9	
8. Alabama	26–7	
9. Pittsburgh	27–5	
10. Connecticut	24–6	
11. Oregon	23–8	
12. Marquette	26–6	
13. Illinois	24–8	
14. Ohio St	23–7	
15. Florida	22–8	
16. Kentucky	20–9	
17. Mississippi St	26–7	
18. Southern California	22–9	
19. Western Kentucky	28–3	
20. Oklahoma St	23–8	
21. Miami	24–7	
22. Xavier	25–5	
23. Georgia	21–9	
24. Stanford	19–9	
25. Hawaii	27–5	

National Invitation Tournament Scores

Opening round: Ball St 98, S Florida 92; St. Joseph's 73, George Mason 64; Montana St 77, Utah St 69; Richmond 74, Wagner 67, OT; Dayton 80, Detroit 69; Vanderbilt 59, Houston 50; Louisiana Tech 83, Louisiana–Lafayette 63; Tennessee Tech 64, Georgia State 62.

First round: Louisville 66, Princeton 65; Nevada–Las Vegas 96, Arizona St 91; Syracuse 76, St. Bonaventure 66; S Carolina 74, Virginia 67; Minnesota 96, New Mexico 62; Louisiana St 63, Iowa 61; Temple 81, Fresno St 75; Butler 81, Bowling Green 69; Villanova 84, Manhattan 69; Yale 67, Rutgers 65; Memphis 82, N Carolina–Greensboro 62; Brigham Young 78, California–Irvine 55; Ball St 76, St. Joseph's 54; Tennessee Tech 68, Dayton 59; Louisiana Tech 83, Vanderbilt 68; Richmond 63, Montana State 48.

Second round: Syracuse 66, Butler 65, OT; Richmond 67, Minnesota 66; Temple 65, Louisville 62; Tennessee Tech 80, Yale 61; Villanova 67, Louisiana Tech 64; Ball St 75, Louisiana St 65; S Carolina 75, Nevada–Las Vegas 65; Memphis 80, Brigham Young 69.

Third round: Syracuse 62, Richmond 46; S Carolina 82, Ball St 47; Temple 63, Villanova 57; Memphis 79, Tennesee Tech 73

Semifinals: S Carolina 66, Syracuse 59; Memphis 78, Temple 77

Consolation Game: Temple 65, Syracuse 54

Championship Game: Memphis 72, S Carolina 62

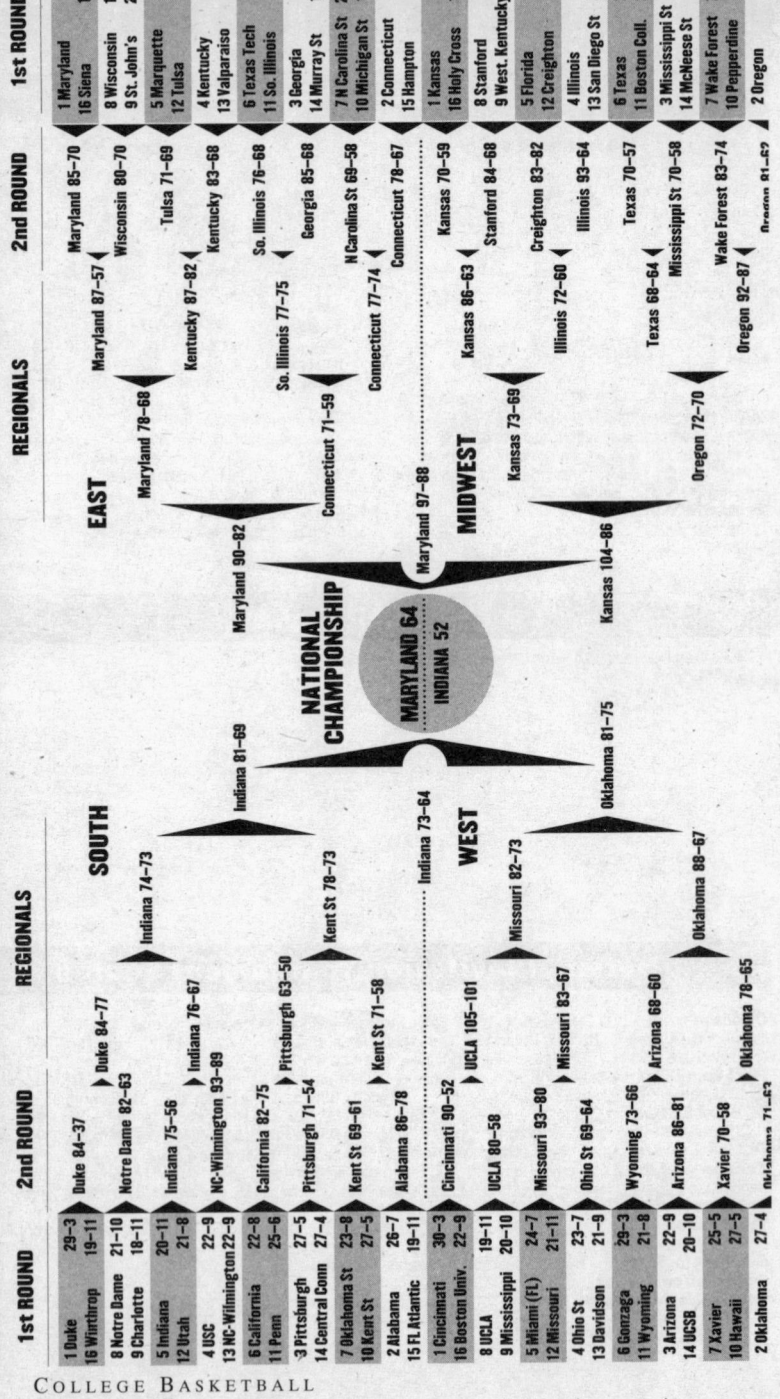

America East

	Conference			All Games		
	W	L	Pct	W	L	Pct
†Boston University	13	3	.813	22	10	.688
Vermont	13	3	.813	21	8	.724
Hartford	10	6	.625	14	18	.438
New Hampshire	8	8	.500	11	17	.393
Maine	7	9	.438	12	18	.400
Binghamton	6	10	.375	9	19	.321
Albany	5	11	.313	8	20	.286
Northeastern	5	11	.313	7	21	.250
Stony Brook	5	11	.313	6	22	.214

Atlantic Coast

	Conference			All Games		
	W	L	Pct	W	L	Pct
Maryland	15	1	.938	32	4	.889
†Duke	13	3	.813	31	4	.886
N Carolina St	9	7	.563	23	11	.676
Wake Forest	9	7	.563	21	13	.618
Virginia	7	9	.438	17	12	.586
Georgia Tech	7	9	.438	15	16	.484
Clemson	4	12	.250	13	17	.433
Florida St	4	12	.250	12	17	.414
N Carolina	4	12	.250	8	20	.286

Atlantic Sun

	Conference			All Games		
	W	L	Pct	W	L	Pct
Georgia St	14	6	.700	20	11	.645
Troy State	14	6	.700	18	10	.643
†Florida Atlantic	13	7	.650	19	12	.613
Jacksonville	12	8	.600	18	12	.600
Central Florida	12	8	.600	17	12	.586
Samford	12	8	.600	15	14	.517
Jacksonville St	8	12	.400	13	16	.448
Belmont	8	12	.400	11	17	.393
Stetson	7	13	.350	10	16	.385
Campbell	6	14	.300	7	19	.269
Mercer	4	16	.200	6	23	.207

Atlantic 10

	Conference			All Games		
	W	L	Pct	W	L	Pct
EAST						
St. Joseph's	12	4	.750	19	12	.613
Temple	12	4	.750	19	15	.559
St. Bonaventure	8	8	.500	17	13	.567
Massachusetts	6	10	.375	13	16	.448
Fordham	4	12	.250	8	20	.286
Rhode Island	4	12	.250	8	20	.286
WEST						
†Xavier	14	2	.875	26	6	.813
Richmond	11	5	.688	22	14	.611
Dayton	10	6	.625	21	11	.656
LaSalle	6	10	.375	15	17	.468
George Washington	5	11	.313	12	16	.429
Duquesne	4	12	.250	9	19	.321

Big East

	Conference			All Games		
EAST	W	L	Pct	W	L	Pct
†Connecticut	13	3	.813	27	7	.794
Miami (FL)	10	6	.625	24	8	.750
St. John's	9	7	.563	20	12	.625
Boston College	8	8	.500	20	12	.625
Villanova	7	9	.438	19	13	.594
Providence	6	10	.375	15	16	.484
Virginia Tech	10	18	.357	4	12	.250
WEST						
Pittsburgh	13	3	.813	29	6	.829
Notre Dame	10	6	.625	22	11	.667
Syracuse	9	7	.563	23	13	.639
Georgetown	9	7	.563	19	11	.633
Rutgers	8	8	.500	18	13	.581
Seton Hall	5	11	.313	12	18	.400
W Virginia	1	15	.063	8	20	.286

Big Sky

	Conference			All Games		
	W	L	Pct	W	L	Pct
Montana St	12	2	.857	20	10	.667
Eastern Washington	10	4	.714	17	13	.567
Weber St	8	6	.571	18	11	.621
†Montana	7	7	.500	16	15	.516
Northern Arizona	7	7	.500	14	14	.500
Portland St	6	8	.429	12	16	.429
Idaho St	3	11	.214	10	17	.370
Cal St–Sacramento	3	11	.214	9	19	.321

Big South

	Conference			All Games		
	W	L	Pct	W	L	Pct
†Winthrop	10	4	.714	19	12	.613
N Carolina–Asheville	10	4	.714	13	15	.464
Radford	9	5	.643	15	16	.484
Charleston Southern	8	6	.571	12	17	.414
Elon	7	7	.500	13	16	.448
High Point	5	9	.357	11	19	.367
Coastal Carolina	5	9	.357	8	20	.286
Liberty	2	12	.143	5	25	.167

Big 10

	Conference			All Games		
	W	L	Pct	W	L	Pct
Illinois	11	5	.688	26	9	.743
Indiana	11	5	.688	25	12	.676
†Ohio St	11	5	.688	24	8	.750
Wisconsin	11	5	.688	19	13	.594
Michigan St	10	6	.625	19	12	.613
Minnesota	9	7	.563	18	13	.581
Northwestern	7	9	.438	16	13	.552
Iowa	5	11	.313	19	16	.543
Purdue	5	11	.313	13	18	.419
Michigan	5	11	.313	11	18	.379
Penn St	3	13	.188	7	21	.250

† Conference tourney winner.
Note: Standings based on regular-season conference play only; overall records include all tournament play.

Big 12

	Conference			All Games		
	W	L	Pct	W	L	Pct
Kansas	16	0	1.000	33	4	.892
†Oklahoma	13	3	.813	31	5	.861
Oklahoma St	10	6	.625	23	9	.719
Texas Tech	10	6	.625	23	9	.719
Texas	10	6	.625	22	12	.647
Missouri	9	7	.563	24	12	.667
Nebraska	6	10	.375	13	15	.464
Kansas St	6	10	.375	13	16	.448
Colorado	5	11	.313	15	14	.517
Baylor	4	12	.250	14	16	.467
Iowa St	4	12	.250	12	19	.387
Texas A&M	3	13	.188	9	22	.290

Big West

	Conference			All Games		
	W	L	Pct	W	L	Pct
Utah St	13	5	.722	23	8	.742
Cal-Irvine	13	5	.722	21	11	.656
Pacific	11	7	.611	20	10	.667
†Santa Barbara	11	7	.611	20	11	.645
Cal St–Northridge	11	7	.611	12	16	.429
Cal Poly	9	9	.500	15	12	.556
Long Beach St	9	9	.500	13	17	.433
Idaho	6	12	.333	9	19	.321
UC–Riverside	5	13	.278	8	18	.308
Cal St–Fullerton	2	16	.111	5	22	.185

Colonial

	Conference			All Games		
	W	L	Pct	W	L	Pct
†NC–Wilmington	14	4	.778	23	10	.697
George Mason	13	5	.722	19	10	.655
VA Commonwealth	11	7	.611	21	11	.656
Drexel	11	7	.611	14	14	.500
Delaware	9	9	.500	14	16	.467
Old Dominion	7	11	.389	13	16	.448
Towson	7	11	.389	11	18	.379
William & Mary	7	11	.389	10	19	.345
James Madison	6	12	.333	14	15	.483
Hofstra	5	13	.278	12	20	.375

Conference USA

	Conference			All Games		
AMERICAN	W	L	Pct	W	L	Pct
†Cincinnati	14	2	.875	31	4	.886
Marquette	13	3	.813	26	7	.788
Charlotte	11	5	.688	18	12	.600
St. Louis	9	7	.563	15	16	.484
Louisville	8	8	.500	19	13	.594
E Carolina	5	11	.313	12	18	.400
DePaul	2	14	.125	9	19	.321
NATIONAL						
Memphis	12	4	.750	27	9	.750
Houston	9	7	.563	18	15	.545
S Florida	8	8	.500	19	13	.594
Texas Christian	6	10	.375	16	15	.516
AL–Birmingham	6	10	.375	13	17	.433
Tulane	5	11	.313	14	15	.483
Southern Miss	4	12	.250	10	17	.370

Horizon League

	Conference			All Games		
	W	L	Pct	W	L	Pct
Butler	12	4	.750	26	6	.813
Detroit	11	5	.688	18	13	.581
WI–Milwaukee	11	5	.688	16	13	.552
Wright St	9	7	.563	17	11	.607
Loyola (IL)	9	7	.563	17	13	.567
†Illinois–Chicago	8	8	.500	20	14	.588
Cleveland St	6	10	.375	12	16	.429
WI–Green Bay	4	12	.250	9	21	.300
Youngstown St	2	14	.125	5	23	.179

Ivy League

	Conference			All Games		
	W	L	Pct	W	L	Pct
Pennsylvania	11	3	.786	25	7	.781
Yale	11	3	.786	21	11	.656
Princeton	11	3	.786	16	12	.571
Brown	8	6	.571	17	10	.630
Harvard	7	7	.500	14	12	.538
Columbia	4	10	.286	11	17	.393
Dartmouth	2	12	.143	9	18	.333
Cornell	2	12	.143	5	22	.185

Metro Atlantic

	Conference			All Games		
	W	L	Pct	W	L	Pct
Marist	13	5	.722	19	9	.679
Rider	13	5	.722	17	11	.607
Manhattan	12	6	.667	20	9	.690
Niagara	12	6	.667	18	14	.563
Iona	10	8	.556	13	17	.433
†Siena	9	9	.500	17	19	.472
Fairfield	9	9	.500	12	17	.414
Canisius	5	13	.278	10	20	.333
Loyola (MD)	4	14	.222	5	23	.179
St. Peter's	3	15	.167	4	24	.143

Mid-American

	Conference			All Games		
EAST	W	L	Pct	W	L	Pct
†Kent St	17	1	.944	30	6	.833
Bowling Green	12	6	.667	24	9	.727
Ohio	11	7	.611	17	11	.607
Miami (OH)	9	9	.500	13	18	.419
Marshall	8	10	.444	15	15	.500
Buffalo	7	11	.389	12	18	.400
Akron	5	13	.278	10	21	.323
WEST						
Ball St	12	6	.667	23	12	.657
Toledo	11	7	.611	16	14	.533
Western Michigan	10	8	.556	17	13	.567
Northern Illinois	8	10	.444	12	16	.429
Central Michigan	5	13	.278	9	19	.321
Eastern Michigan	2	16	.111	6	24	.200

Mid-Continent

	Conference			All Games		
	W	L	Pct	W	L	Pct
†Valparaiso	12	2	.857	25	8	.758
Oakland	10	4	.714	17	13	.567
Oral Roberts	10	4	.714	16	14	.533
Southern Utah	8	6	.571	11	16	.407
MO–Kansas City	7	7	.500	18	11	.621
Indiana–Purdue	6	8	.429	15	15	.500
Western Illinois	3	11	.214	12	16	.429
Chicago St	0	14	.000	2	26	.071

Mid-Eastern Athletic

	Conference			All Games		
	W	L	Pct	W	L	Pct
†Hampton	17	1	.944	26	7	.788
Delaware St	12	6	.667	16	13	.552
S Carolina St	11	7	.611	15	16	.484
Howard	11	7	.611	18	13	.581
N Carolina A&T	10	8	.556	11	17	.393
Norfolk St	9	9	.500	10	19	.345
Florida A&M	9	9	.500	9	19	.321
Bethune Cookman	8	10	.444	12	17	.414
MD–Eastern Shore	7	11	.389	11	18	.379
Coppin St	3	15	.167	6	25	.194
Morgan St	2	16	.111	3	25	.107

Missouri Valley

	Conference			All Games		
	W	L	Pct	W	L	Pct
Southern Illinois	14	4	.778	28	8	.778
†Creighton	14	4	.778	23	9	.719
Illinois St	12	6	.667	17	14	.548
SW Missouri St	11	7	.611	17	15	.531
Wichita St	9	9	.500	15	15	.500
Drake	9	9	.500	14	15	.483
Northern Iowa	8	10	.444	14	15	.483
Bradley	5	13	.278	9	20	.310
Evansville	4	14	.222	7	21	.250
Indiana State	4	14	.222	6	22	.214

Mountain West

	Conference			All Games		
	W	L	Pct	W	L	Pct
Wyoming	11	3	.786	22	9	.710
Utah	10	4	.714	21	9	.700
Nevada–Las Vegas	9	5	.643	21	11	.656
San Diego St	7	7	.500	21	12	.636
Brigham Young	7	7	.500	18	12	.600
New Mexico	6	8	.429	16	14	.533
Colorado St	3	11	.214	12	18	.400
Air Force	3	11	.214	9	19	.321

Northeast

	Conference			All Games		
	W	L	Pct	W	L	Pct
†Central CT St	19	1	.950	27	5	.844
MD–Baltimore	15	5	.750	20	9	.690
Wagner	15	5	.750	19	10	.655
Monmouth	14	6	.700	18	12	.600
St. Francis (NY)	13	7	.650	18	11	.621
Robert Morris	11	9	.550	12	18	.400
Quinnipiac	10	10	.500	14	16	.467
Sacred Heart	7	13	.350	8	20	.286
St. Francis (PA)	5	15	.250	6	21	.222
LIU–Brooklyn	5	15	.250	5	22	.185
Fairleigh Dickinson	4	16	.200	4	25	.138
Mt. St. Mary's	2	18	.100	3	24	.111

Ohio Valley

	Conference			All Games		
	W	L	Pct	W	L	Pct
Tennessee Tech	15	1	.938	27	7	.794
Morehead St	11	5	.688	18	11	.621
Murray St	10	6	.625	19	13	.594
Austin Peay	8	8	.500	14	18	.438
Tennessee–Martin	7	9	.438	15	14	.517
Eastern Illinois	7	9	.438	15	16	.484
Tennessee St	7	9	.438	11	17	.393
SE Missouri St	4	12	.250	6	22	.214
Eastern Kentucky	3	13	.188	7	20	.259

Pac 10

	Conference			All Games		
	W	L	Pct	W	L	Pct
Oregon	14	4	.778	26	9	.743
California	12	6	.667	24	10	.706
†Arizona	12	6	.667	23	9	.719
Southern California	12	6	.667	22	10	.688
Stanford	12	6	.667	20	10	.667
UCLA	11	7	.611	21	12	.636
Arizona St	7	11	.389	14	15	.483
Washington	5	13	.278	11	18	.379
Oregon St	4	14	.222	12	17	.414
Washington St	1	17	.056	6	21	.222

Patriot League

	Conference			All Games		
EAST	W	L	Pct	W	L	Pct
American	10	4	.714	18	12	.600
†Holy Cross	9	5	.643	18	15	.545
Colgate	8	6	.571	17	11	.607
Lafayette	8	6	.571	15	14	.517
Bucknell	8	6	.571	13	16	.448
Army	6	8	.429	12	16	.429
Navy	5	9	.357	10	20	.333
Lehigh	2	12	.143	5	23	.179

†Conference tourney winner.

Southeastern

EAST	Conference			All Games		
	W	L	Pct	W	L	Pct
Florida	10	6	.625	22	9	.710
Georgia	10	6	.625	22	10	.688
Kentucky	10	6	.625	22	10	.688
Tennessee	7	9	.438	15	16	.484
S Carolina	6	10	.375	22	15	.595
Vanderbilt	6	10	.375	17	15	.531
WEST						
Alabama	12	4	.750	27	8	.771
†Mississippi St	10	6	.625	27	8	.771
Mississippi	9	7	.563	20	11	.645
Louisiana St	6	10	.375	19	15	.559
Arkansas	6	10	.375	14	15	.483
Auburn	4	12	.250	12	16	.429

Southern

NORTH	Conference			All Games		
	W	L	Pct	W	L	Pct
†Davidson	11	5	.688	21	10	.677
NC–Greensboro	11	5	.688	20	11	.645
E Tennessee St	11	5	.688	18	10	.643
Western Carolina	6	10	.375	12	16	.429
Appalachian St	5	11	.313	10	18	.357
Virginia Military	5	11	.313	10	18	.357
WEST						
Charleston	9	7	.563	21	9	.700
Georgia Southern	9	7	.563	16	12	.571
TN–Chattanooga	9	7	.563	16	14	.533
The Citadel	8	8	.500	17	12	.586
Furman	7	9	.438	17	14	.548
Wofford	5	11	.313	11	18	.379

Southland

	Conference			All Games		
	W	L	Pct	W	L	Pct
†McNeese St	17	3	.850	21	9	.700
Louisiana-Monroe	15	5	.750	20	12	.625
Texas–San Antonio	13	7	.650	19	10	.655
Lamar	11	9	.550	15	14	.517
Stephen F. Austin	10	10	.500	13	15	.464
SW Texas St	10	10	.500	12	16	.429
Texas–Arlington	9	11	.450	12	15	.444
Sam Houston St	9	11	.450	14	14	.500
Northwestern St	9	11	.450	13	18	.419
SE Louisiana	6	14	.300	7	20	.259
Nicholls St	1	19	.050	2	25	.074

Southwestern Athletic

	Conference			All Games		
	W	L	Pct	W	L	Pct
†Alcorn St	16	2	.889	20	10	.667
Alabama A&M	12	6	.667	19	10	.655
Alabama St	12	6	.667	19	13	.594
Texas Southern	10	8	.556	11	17	.393
Mississippi Valley St	9	9	.500	12	17	.414
Prairie View	8	10	.444	10	20	.333
Jackson St	8	10	.444	9	19	.321
Grambling	7	11	.389	9	19	.321
Southern	6	12	.333	7	20	.259
Arkansas–Pine Bluff	2	16	.111	2	26	.071

Sun Belt

EAST	Conference			All Games		
	W	L	Pct	W	L	Pct
†Western Kentucky	13	1	.929	28	4	.875
AR–Little Rock	8	6	.571	18	11	.621
Middle Tennessee St	6	8	.429	14	15	.483
Arkansas State	5	9	.357	15	16	.484
Florida International	4	10	.286	10	20	.333
WEST						
Louisiana-Lafayette	11	4	.733	20	11	.645
New Mexico St	11	4	.733	20	12	.625
New Orleans	9	6	.600	15	14	.517
N Texas	8	7	.533	15	14	.517
Denver	3	12	.200	8	20	.286
S Alabama	2	13	.133	7	21	.250

West Coast

	Conference			All Games		
	W	L	Pct	W	L	Pct
†Gonzaga	13	1	.879	29	4	.929
Pepperdine	13	1	.879	22	9	.710
San Francisco	8	6	.571	13	15	.464
Santa Clara	8	6	.571	13	15	.464
San Diego	7	7	.500	16	13	.552
St. Mary's (CA)	3	11	.214	9	20	.310
Loyola Marymount	2	12	.143	9	20	.310
Portland	2	12	.143	6	24	.200

Western Athletic

	Conference			All Games		
	W	L	Pct	W	L	Pct
†Hawaii	15	3	.833	27	6	.818
Tulsa	15	3	.833	27	7	.794
Louisiana Tech	14	4	.778	22	10	.688
Southern Methodist	10	8	.556	15	14	.517
Fresno St	9	9	.500	19	15	.559
Nevada	9	9	.500	17	13	.567
Boise St	6	12	.333	13	17	.433
Rice	5	13	.278	10	19	.345
San Jose St	4	14	.222	10	22	.313
Texas–El Paso	3	15	.167	10	22	.313

Independents

	All Games		
	W	L	Pct
Gardner Webb	19	8	.704
TX–Pan American	20	10	.667
Centenary	14	13	.519
Birmingham Southern	13	14	.481
TX A&M–Corpus Christi	12	15	.444
Lipscomb	6	21	.222
Morris Brown	4	25	.138
Savannah St	2	26	.071

†Conference tourney winner.

Scoring

	Class	GP	FG	3FG	FT	Pts	Avg
Jason Conley, Virginia Military	Fr	28	285	79	171	820	29.3
Henry Domercant, Eastern Illinois	Jr	31	262	104	189	817	26.4
Mire Chatman, TX–Pan American	Sr	29	265	65	165	760	26.2
Ernest Bremer, St. Bonaventure	Sr	30	231	88	188	738	24.6
Melvin Ely, Fresno St.	Sr	28	246	0	161	653	23.3
Lynn Greer, Temple	Sr	31	226	95	172	719	23.2
Nick Stapleton, Austin Peay	Sr	32	270	72	130	742	23.2
Keith McLeod, Bowling Green	Sr	33	224	89	218	755	22.9
Chris Davis, N Texas	Jr	29	217	46	173	653	22.5
Ricky Minard, Morehead St	So	29	227	65	127	646	22.3
Kevin Martin, Western Carolina	Fr	28	196	73	154	619	22.1
Steve Logan, Cincinnati	Sr	35	246	86	192	770	22.0
Damon Hancock, Southern Methodist	Sr	26	183	48	158	572	22.0
Casey Jacobsen, Stanford	Jr	30	205	64	184	658	21.9
Michael Watson, MO–Kansas City	So	29	221	92	101	635	21.9
David Bailey, Loyola (IL)	Jr	30	224	54	149	651	21.7
Troy Bell, Boston College	Jr	32	207	65	212	691	21.6
Richard Toussaint, Bethune-Cookman	Jr	29	197	2	229	625	21.6
Jason Williams, Duke	Jr	35	249	108	140	746	21.3
Leon Rodgers, Northern Illinois	Sr	28	195	33	173	596	21.3
Dajuan Wagner, Memphis	Fr	36	265	66	166	762	21.2
Antawn Dobie, Long Island	Sr	26	188	48	126	550	21.2
Chris Monroe, George Washington	Jr	28	167	55	203	592	21.1
Jermaine Hall, Wagner	Jr	29	240	4	126	610	21.0
Reece Gaines, Louisville	Jr	32	209	91	164	673	21.0

FIELD-GOAL PERCENTAGE

	Class	GP	FG	FGA	Pct
Adam Mark, Belmont	So	26	150	212	70.8
Carlos Boozer, Duke	Jr	35	230	346	66.5
David Harrison, Colorado	Fr	27	139	218	63.8
Rolan Roberts, Southern Ilinois	Sr	29	155	260	60.4
Jermaine Hall, Wagner	Jr	29	240	400	60.0
Chris Sockwell, St. Francis (NY)	Jr	29	155	260	59.6
Len Matela, Bowling Green	Sr	33	192	323	59.4
Justin Rowe, Maine	Jr	30	158	266	59.4
James Moore, New Mexico St	So	32	184	310	59.4
Nick Collison, Kansas	Jr	37	245	414	59.2

Note: Minimum 5 made per game.

FREE-THROW PERCENTAGE

	Class	GP	FT	FTA	Pct
Cary Cochran, Nebraska	Sr	28	71	77	92.2
Gary Buchanan, Villanova	Jr	32	112	123	91.1
Cain Doliboa, Wright St.	Sr	28	80	88	90.9
Salim Stoudamire, Arizona	Fr	34	103	114	90.4
Jake Sullivan, Iowa St	So	28	117	130	90.0
Jobey Thomas, Charlotte	Sr	30	98	109	89.9
Juan Dixon, Maryland	Sr	36	141	157	89.8
Chris Spatola, Army	Sr	28	113	126	89.7
Eric Channing, New Mexico St	Sr	31	93	104	89.4
Travis Cantrell, Citadel	Sr	29	92	103	89.3

Note: Minimum 2.5 made per game.

REBOUNDS

	Class	GP	Reb	Avg
Jeremy Bishop, Quinnipiac	Jr	29	347	12.0
Bruce Jenkins, N Carolina A&T	Sr	28	329	11.8
Curtis Borchardt, Stanford	Jr	29	332	11.4
Drew Gooden, Kansas	Jr	37	423	11.4
Corey Jackson, Nevada	Sr	29	323	11.1
Reggie Evans, Iowa	Sr	34	378	11.1
Trevor Gaines, Vermont	Sr	29	320	11.0
Theron-Smith, Ball St	Jr	35	381	10.9
Ryan Humphrey, Notre Dame	Sr	31	337	10.9
Stephane Pelle, Colorado	Jr	29	314	10.8

ASSISTS

	Class	GP	A	Avg
T.J. Ford, Texas	Fr	33	273	8.3
Steve Blake, Maryland	Jr	36	286	7.9
Edward Scott, Clemson	Jr	30	238	7.9
Sean Kennedy, Marist	Sr	28	222	7.9
Chris Thomas, Notre Dame	Fr	33	252	7.6
Matt Montague, Brigham Young	Sr	30	217	7.2
Brandin Knight, Pittsburgh	Jr	35	251	7.2
Mychal Covington, Oakland	Sr	28	198	7.1
Reggie Kohn, S Florida	Jr	32	220	6.9
Aaron Miles, Kansas	Fr	37	252	6.8

*Includes games played in tournaments.

THREE-POINT FIELD-GOAL PERCENTAGE

	Class	GP	FG	FGA	Pct
Dante Swanson, Tulsa	Jr	33	73	149	49.0
Cain Doliboa, Wright St.	Sr	28	104	217	47.9
Jake Sullivan, Iowa St	So	28	60	127	47.2
Jeff Boschee, Kansas	Sr	37	110	237	46.4
Ray Abellard, Central Florida	Jr	29	80	173	46.2
Cameron Crisp, Tennessee Tech	So	34	72	156	46.2
John Hamilton, Weber St	So	29	76	165	46.1
Eric Channing, New Mexico St	Sr	31	81	176	46.0
Jordan Kardos, IL-Chicago	Sr	34	69	150	46.0
Dan Dickau, Gonzaga	Sr	32	117	256	45.7

Note: Minimum 1.5 made per game.

THREE-POINT FIELD GOALS MADE PER GAME

	Class	GP	FG	Avg
Cain Doliboa, Wright St	Sr	28	104	3.7
Jobey Thomas, Charlotte	Sr	30	110	3.7
Dan Dickau, Gonzaga	Sr	32	117	3.7
Wes Burtner, Belmont	Sr	28	100	3.6
Jason Morgan, St. Francis (NY)	Sr	28	100	3.6
Sharif Chambliss, Penn St	So	28	99	3.5
Travis Cantrell, Citadel	Sr	29	102	3.5
Bryan Buchanan, IUPUI	Jr	25	84	3.4
Henry Domercant, Eastern Illinois	Jr	31	104	3.4
Nick Zachery, Arkansas–Little Rock	So	28	93	3.3

BLOCKED SHOTS

	Class	GP	BS	Avg
Wojciech Myrda, LA-Monroe	Sr	32	172	5.4
D'or Fischer, Northwestern St	So	30	133	4.4
Emeka Okafor, Connecticut	Fr	34	138	4.1
Justin Rowe, Maine	Jr	30	121	4.0
Deng Gai, Fairfield	Fr	29	115	4.0
Nick Billings, Binghamton	Fr	21	80	3.8
Moussa Badiane, E Carolina	Fr	24	87	3.6
Jason Jennings, Arkansas St	Sr	30	101	3.4
Kendrick Moore, Oral Roberts	Jr	31	103	3.3
Robert Battle, Drexel	Jr	28	91	3.3

STEALS

	Class	GP	S	Avg
Desmond Cambridge, Alabama A&M	Sr	29	160	5.5
John Linehan, Providence	Sr	31	139	4.5
Mire Chatman, Texas–Pan American	Sr	29	105	3.6
Marques Green, St. Bonaventure	So	30	102	3.4
Marcus Hatten, St. John's (NY)	Jr	32	105	3.3
Carlos Morban, Florida International	Fr	29	87	3.0
Jason Conley, Virginia Military	Fr	28	82	2.9
James Thues, Syracuse	So	36	101	2.8
Markus Carr, Cal St–Northridge	Sr	28	78	2.8
Kevin Braswell, Georgetown	Sr	30	81	2.7

Single-Game Highs

POINTS

50 ....Desmond Cambridge, Alabama A&M, Feb 25 (vs TX Southern)
49 ....Casey Jacobsen, Stanford, Jan 31 (vs Arizona St)
47 ....Lynn Greer, Temple, Dec 3 (vs Wisconsin)

REBOUNDS

27 ....Andre Brown, DePaul, Feb 6 (vs Texas Christian)
27 ....Amien Hicks, Morris Brown, Jan 14 (vs Clark Atlanta)
26 ....Jamal Brown, Texas Christian, Dec 23 (vs N Texas)

ASSISTS

17 ....Brad Boyd, LA–Lafayette, Jan 24 (vs N Texas)
17.............Sean Peterson, Georgia Southern, Jan 21 (vs Western Carolina)
17 ....Imari Sawyer, DePaul, Nov 25 (vs Youngstown St)

THREE-POINT FIELD GOALS

14 ....Ronald Blackshear, Marshall, Mar 1 (vs Akron)
12 ....Clarence Gilbert, Missouri, Feb 23 (vs Colorado)
11 .............T.J. Sorrentine, Vermont, Jan 17 (vs Northeastern)

STEALS

12 ....Jehiel Lewis, Navy, Jan 12 (vs Bucknell)
11 ....Travis Demanby, Fresno St, Feb 10 (vs Oklahoma St)
11 ....John Linehan, Providence, Jan 22 (vs Rutgers)
11 ....Drew Schifino, W Virginia, Dec 1 (vs Arkansas–Monticello)
11 ....Chris Thomas, Notre Dame, Nov 16 (vs New Hampshire)

BLOCKED SHOTS

13.............Wojciech Myrda, Louisiana-Monroe, Jan 17 (vs TX–San Antonio)
12 ....D'or Fischer, Northwestern St, Nov 21 (vs Siena)
11 ....Wojciech Myrda, Louisiana-Monroe, Feb 16 (vs Nicholls St)

NCAA Men's Division I Team Leaders

SCORING OFFENSE

	GP	W	L	Pts	Avg
Kansas	37	33	4	3365	90.9
Duke	35	31	4	3112	88.9
Oregon	35	26	9	2994	85.5
Texas Christian	31	16	15	2645	85.3
Maryland	36	32	4	3060	85.0
Arizona	34	24	10	2793	82.1
Wake Forest	34	21	13	2789	82.0
E Tennessee St	28	18	10	2281	81.5
Wagner	29	19	10	2362	81.4
Pepperdine	31	22	9	2519	81.3

SCORING DEFENSE

	GP	W	L	Pts	Avg
Columbia	28	11	17	1596	57.0
Princeton	28	16	12	1606	57.4
Butler	32	26	6	1849	57.8
Utah St	31	23	8	1800	58.1
Northwestern	29	16	13	1715	59.1
Holy Cross	33	18	15	1968	59.6
Samford	29	15	14	1748	60.3
Cincinnati	35	31	4	2115	60.4
Marquette	33	26	7	2004	60.7
Charleston	30	21	9	1824	60.8

SCORING MARGIN

	Off	Def	Mar
Duke	88.9	69.2	19.7
Cincinnati	78.2	60.4	17.8
Kansas	90.9	74.7	16.2
Gonzaga	81.1	66.6	14.5
Maryland	85.0	70.9	14.1
Florida	80.5	66.6	13.9
Oklahoma	78.0	64.6	13.3
Western Kentucky	77.8	64.7	13.2
Oregon	85.5	72.5	13.0
Butler	70.3	57.8	12.6

FIELD-GOAL PERCENTAGE

	FG	FGA	Pct
Kansas	1259	2487	50.6
Duke	1093	2209	49.5
Bowling Green	834	1709	48.8
Oregon	1014	2082	48.7
Ohio St	825	1702	48.5
Ohio	741	1531	48.4
Morehead St	796	1647	48.3
Connecticut	972	2012	48.3
Maryland	1083	2248	48.2
Hampton	933	1940	48.1

FIELD-GOAL PERCENTAGE DEFENSE

	FG	FGA	Pct
Virginia Commonwealth	767	2052	37.4
Cincinnati	761	2035	37.4
Charleston	663	1762	37.6
Davidson	692	1822	38.0
Connecticut	830	2182	38.0
Santa Barbara	623	1625	38.3
Gonzaga	773	2006	38.5
Boston	687	1760	39.0
Villanova	739	1883	39.2
Louisiana–Lafayette	709	1803	39.3

FREE-THROW PERCENTAGE

	FT	FTA	Pct
Morehead St	485	619	78.4
Loyola Marymount	466	600	77.7
Illinois St	427	551	77.5
Miami (FL)	523	678	77.1
Michigan St	442	573	77.1
Oregon	662	861	76.9
Oklahoma	549	716	76.7
SE Missouri St	428	560	76.4
Brigham Young	523	688	76.0
Missouri–Kansas City	361	475	76.0

THREE-POINT FIELD GOALS MADE PER GAME

	GP	FG	Avg
St. Bonaventure	30	314	10.5
Dartmouth	27	263	9.7
Nebraska	28	267	9.5
Belmont	28	264	9.4
Troy St	28	258	9.2
Baylor	30	273	9.1
Missouri	36	326	9.1
Mississippi Valley St	29	258	8.9
WI–Milwaukee	29	257	8.9
Ball St	35	310	8.9

REBOUNDING MARGIN

	GP	REB	Opp REB	Margin/G
Gonzaga	33	1370	1076	+8.9
Louisiana Tech	32	1310	1030	8.8
Kansas	37	1638	1315	8.7
Stanford	30	1254	998	8.5
Dayton	32	1278	1014	8.3
Michigan St	31	1163	919	7.9
Wyoming	31	1245	1005	7.7
Tennessee Tech	34	1309	1064	7.2
Central Connecticut St	32	1247	1024	7.0
Virginia Tech	28	1115	926	6.8

2002 NCAA Basketball Women's Division I Tournament

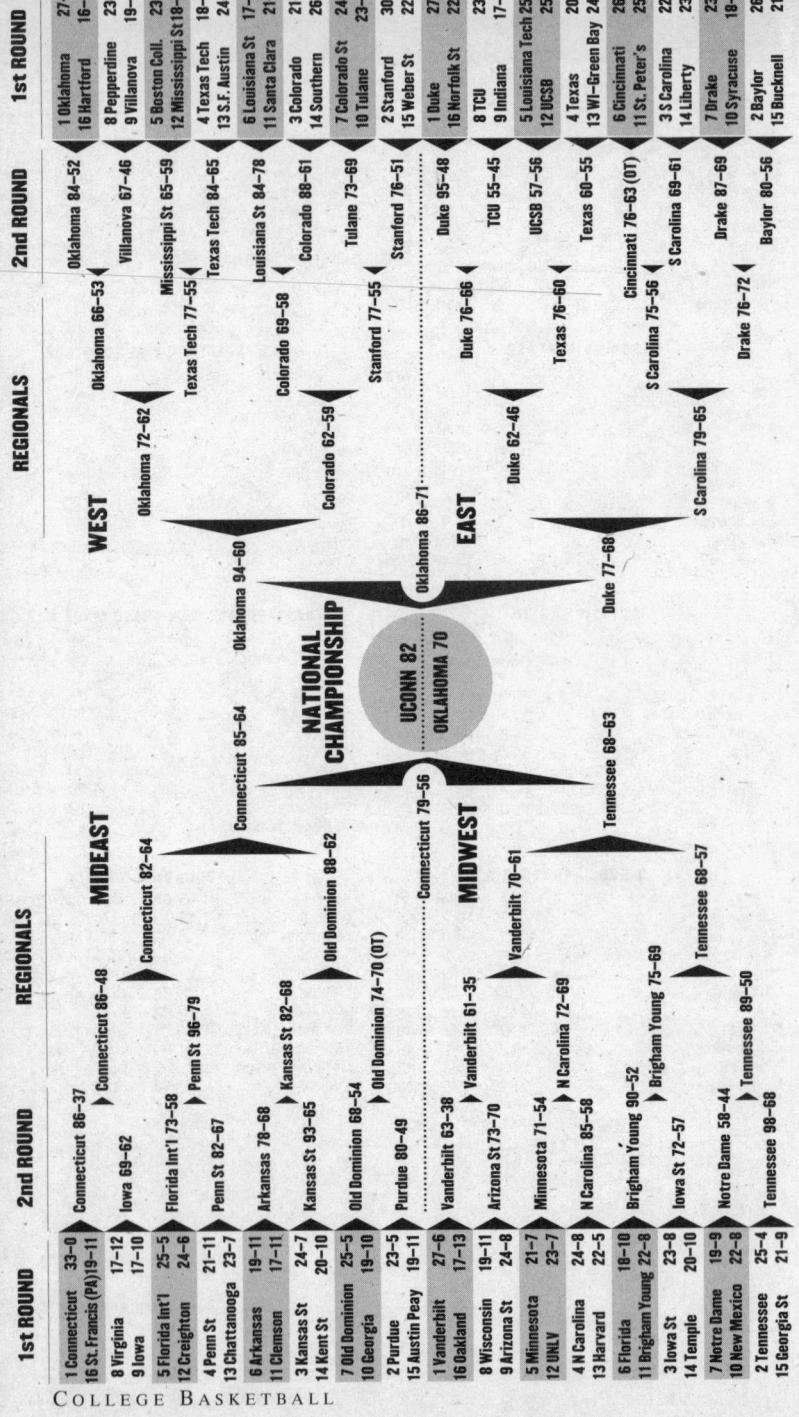

Connecticut 82

Connecticut	Min	FG M-A	FT M-A	Reb O-T	A	PF	TP
Cash	39	5–9	10–12	6–13	4	2	20
Williams	36	6–7	0–0	5–9	2	2	12
Jones	30	9–14	1–2	1–9	0	4	19
Taurasi	39	5–16	3–3	1–3	4	3	13
Bird	36	3–9	8–8	0–3	4	3	14
Battle	4	1–1	0–0	0–0	0	1	2
Moore	11	1–1	0–0	0–1	0	0	2
Conlon	5	0–0	0–0	0–2	1	1	0
Totals	200	30–57	22–25	13–40	15	16	82

Percentages: FG—.526, FT—.880. 3-pt goals: 0–9, .000 (Taurasi 0–6, Bird 0–3). Team rebounds: 4. Blocked shots: 8 (Jones 5, Cash, Moore, Williams). Turnovers: 21 (Cash 6, Jones 5, Bird 4, Taurasi 2, Williams 2, Battle, Conlon). Steals: 7 (Cash 2, Taurasi 2, Bird, Williams, Jones).

Oklahoma 70

Oklahoma	Min	FG M-A	FT M-A	Reb O-T	A	PF	TP
Hill	32	3–10	1–2	3–8	4	4	9
Ross	35	6–13	1–2	3–4	1	1	17
Talbert	26	2–6	2–2	2–4	0	2	6
Caufield	40	3–10	8–9	1–3	4	3	14
Dales	34	7–15	2–3	0–3	1	5	18
Jackson	28	3–8	0–2	0–0	2	1	6
Selmon	5	0–0	0–0	0–0	0	1	0
Totals	200	24–62	14–20	9–22	12	17	70

Percentages: FG—.387, FT—.700. 3-pt goals: 8–20, .400 (Hill 2–3, Ross 4–10, Caufield 0–1, Dales 2–4, Jackson 0–2). Team rebounds: 3. Blocked shots: 2 (Dales, Talbert). Turnovers: 15 (Caufield 4, Dales 3, Jackson 3, Hill 2, Ross 2, Talbert). Steals: 12 (Caufield 4, Talbert 3, Hill 2, Jackson 2, Ross).

Halftime: Connecticut 42, Oklahoma 30.
A: 29,619. Officials: Barlow, Yarbrough, Mattingly.

NCAA Women's Division I Individual Leaders

SCORING

Player and Team	Class	GP	TFG	3FG	FT	Pts	Avg
Kelly Mazzante, Penn St	So	35	313	102	144	872	24.9
LaToya Thomas, Mississippi St	Jr	31	286	1	190	763	24.6
Janet Holt, Tennessee Tech	Sr	30	255	21	183	714	23.8
Susan Moran, St. Joseph's	Sr	32	264	8	208	744	23.3
Chandi Jones, Houston	So	34	277	47	165	766	22.5
Lenae Williams, DePaul	Sr	29	231	93	98	653	22.5
Molly Creamer, Bucknell	Jr	31	233	63	166	695	22.4
Lindsay Whalen, Minnesota	So	30	245	30	147	667	22.2
Brooke Armistead, Austin Peay	Jr	31	234	41	178	687	22.2
Jacklyn Winfield, Southern	Sr	31	218	84	146	666	21.5
Nikki Reddick, Coastal Carolina	So	29	195	64	167	621	21.4
Jenny Nett, Wofford	Sr	29	213	51	136	613	21.1
Katharine Hanks, Dartmouth	Jr	25	198	3	118	517	20.7
Chantelle Anderson, Vanderbilt	Jr	37	295	5	170	765	20.7
Shameka Jackson, Alabama St	Jr	29	219	20	141	599	20.7.

YET ANOTHER SIGN OF THE APOCALYPSE

The father of a 15-year-old who was cut from the varsity basketball team at Logan High in Union City, Calif., is suing the school district for $1.5 million because he says his son's chances of earning NBA riches have been damaged.

FIELD-GOAL PERCENTAGE

Player and Team	Class	GP	FG	FGA	Pct
Angie Welle, Iowa St	Sr	33	244	369	66.1
Chantelle Anderson, Vanderbilt	Jr	37	295	456	64.7
Teana McKiver, Tulane	Jr	35	235	377	62.3
Thea Herring, Troy St	So	28	171	275	62.2
Jocelyn Penn, S Carolina	Jr	32	218	351	62.1
Kate Kreager, Xavier	So	31	183	297	61.6
Iveta Marcauskaite, Illinois	So	29	206	337	61.1
Gerlonda Hardin, Austin Peay	So	31	192	315	61.0
Courtney Coleman, Ohio St	Jr	28	180	296	60.8
Liene Jansone, Siena	So	23	135	223	60.5

Note: Minimum 5 made per game.

REBOUNDS

Player and Team	Class	GP	Reb	Avg
Mandi Carver, Idaho St	Sr	27	336	12.4
Jermisha Dosty, St. Mary's (CA)	Sr	29	344	11.9
Rosalee Mason, Manhattan	So	29	344	11.9
Vanessa Hayden, Florida	So	29	343	11.8
Jennifer Butler, Massachusetts	Jr	30	353	11.8
Andrea Gardner, Howard	Sr	28	325	11.6
Cheryl Moody, Florida International	Sr	33	378	11.5
Natasha Thomas, AL–Birmingham	So	28	319	11.4
Angela Buckner, Wichita St	So	24	272	11.3
Sheena Johnson, Texas–Arlington	So	24	271	11.3

FREE-THROW PERCENTAGE

Player and Team	Class	GP	FT	FTA	Pct
Sue Bird, Connecticut	Sr	39	98	104	94.2
Kandi Brown, Morehead St	So	29	74	79	93.7
Jennifer Mitchell, Loyola (MD)	Jr	29	90	98	91.8
Carey Sauer, San Francisco	So	30	90	98	91.8
Sarah Judd, Oakland	Sr	31	125	137	91.2
Shaquala Williams, Oregon	Jr	35	108	119	90.8
Brooke Armistead, Austin Peay	Jr	31	178	198	89.9
Courtney Davidson, Navy	So	27	122	136	89.7
Laurie Koehn, Kansas St	Fr	34	94	105	89.5
Stephanie Schmitz, Drake	Sr	33	102	114	89.5
Amy White, Stetson	Sr	29	85	95	89.5

Note: Minimum 2.5 made per game.

ASSISTS

Player and Team	Class	GP	A	Avg
La'Terrica Dobin, Northwestern St	Jr	29	250	8.6
Sara Nord, Louisville	So	30	235	7.8
Temeka Johnson, Louisiana St	So	24	179	7.5
Michele Koclanes, Richmond	Sr	30	221	7.4
Becki Ashbaugh, Santa Clara	Sr	31	227	7.3
Erica Vicente, SW Missouri St	Sr	29	208	7.2
Krisey Sanders, Chicago St	Jr	29	197	6.8
Jess Strom, Penn St	Fr	35	235	6.7
Jayme Chikos, Elon	Jr	27	181	6.7
Shiri Sharon, Duquesne	So	28	184	6.6

THREE-POINT FIELD-GOAL PERCENTAGE

Player and Team	Class	GP	FG	FGA	Pct
Lindsay Herbert, Utah	Sr	27	70	145	48.3
Sara Boyer, WI–Green Bay	Jr	31	64	134	47.8
Kristin Rethman, Kansas St	Sr	34	69	145	47.6
Jenia Dimitrova, New Mexico St	Jr	28	62	131	47.3
Kerri Nakamoto, San Diego	Jr	28	64	139	46.0
Courtney Risinger, Toledo	Sr	28	76	169	45.0
Caroline Gruening, Santa Clara	Sr	31	75	167	44.9
Diana Taurasi, Connecticut	So	39	92	209	44.0
Tracy Gahan, Iowa St	Sr	33	72	164	43.9
Velicity Burkhalter, Southeastern Louisiana	So	28	58	133	43.6

Note: Minimum 1.5 made per game.

BLOCKED SHOTS

Player and Team	Class	GP	BS	Avg
Vanessa Hayden, Florida	So	29	126	4.3
Sonja Brown, Southern Miss	Jr	28	101	3.6
Sarah Richey, LA–Lafayette	Jr	28	86	3.1
Amanda Barksdale, Notre Dame	Jr	26	78	3.0
Jordan Adams, New Mexico	Jr	31	92	3.0
Ayanna Brown, Fairfield	So	29	84	2.9
Ugo Oha, George Washington	So	30	86	2.9
Sandora Irvin, Texas Christian	Fr	31	85	2.7
Jamie Smith, DePaul	Jr	29	79	2.7
Ieva Kublina, Virginia Tech	So	32	86	2.7

NCAA Men's Division II Individual Leaders

SCORING

Player and Team	Class	GP	TFG	3FG	FT	Pts	Avg
Angel Figueroa, Dowling	So	25	216	79	143	654	26.2
Clint Keown, S Carolina–Aiken	Sr	28	222	84	163	691	24.7
John Flynn, Grand Valley St	Sr	28	237	34	165	673	24.0
Ronald Murray, Shaw	Sr	33	256	45	220	777	23.5
Leon Smith, Bluefield St	Fr	25	190	88	108	576	23.0
Curtis Small, Southampton	Sr	29	231	97	109	668	23.0
Lavar Griffin, Virginia St	Sr	26	222	78	71	593	22.8
Malik Moore, American International	Sr	29	223	74	141	661	22.8
Justin Leith, Merrimack	So	25	247	14	61	569	22.8
Austin Nichols, Humboldt St	So	29	194	37	216	641	22.1

NCAA Men's Division II Individual Leaders (Cont.)

REBOUNDS

Player and Team	Class	GP	Reb	Avg
Danny Jones, Tarleton St	Jr	33	416	12.6
Dominique Liverpool, Glenville St.	So	28	346	12.4
Fred Hooks, Humboldt St.	So	29	342	11.8
Jamar Thompkins, WV Wesleyan	Sr	29	333	11.5
John Laramore, Texas Lutheran	Sr	25	287	11.5
Dennis Mims, Indiana (PA)	Sr	31	349	11.3
Ramzee Stanton, W Chester	Jr	27	297	11.0
Dwight Windom, Lincoln Memorial	Jr	27	291	10.8
Jim Reeves, Philadelphia	Sr	28	299	10.7
Craig Griffin, Merrimack	Jr	26	277	10.7

ASSISTS

Player and Team	Class	GP	A	Avg
Pat Delany, St. Anselm	Sr	30	234	7.8
Eddin Santiago, MO Southern St.	Sr	28	214	7.6
Ross Hodge, TX A&M–Commerce	Jr	29	213	7.3
Ryan Stock, Southwest Baptist	Jr	27	188	7.0
Josh Mueller, S Dakota	Fr	27	180	6.7
Yuta Tabuse, BYU–Hawaii	Jr	29	187	6.4
Lorinza Harrington, Wingate	Sr	32	204	6.4
Mark White, Humboldt St	So	29	181	6.2
Ronald Murray, Shaw	Sr	33	205	6.2
Matt Fryer, St. Rose	Sr	30	186	6.2

FIELD-GOAL PERCENTAGE

Player and Team	Class	GP	FG	FGA	Pct
Brett Barnard, Le Moyne	So	27	141	211	66.8
Steve Bynes, Shaw	Sr	33	197	296	66.6
Raymond Strachan, Columbia Union	Jr	26	164	248	66.1
Kantonio Davis, Montevallo	Sr	27	140	213	65.7
Matt Jones, S Dakota St	Fr	30	161	247	65.2
Jon Sheppard, Northeastern St	Jr	30	174	268	64.9
Chris Ellis, Mesa St	Sr	27	142	225	63.1
David Siebrands, NC–Pembroke	Jr	27	164	264	62.1
Byron Johnson, Belmont Abbey	Sr	30	201	327	61.5
Ramzee Stanton, W Chester	Jr	27	204	333	61.3

Note: Minimum 5 made per game.

FREE-THROW PERCENTAGE

Player and Team	Class	GP	FT	FTA	Pct
Curtis Small, Southampton	Sr	29	109	116	94.0
Steve Serwatka, Clarion	Sr	26	66	72	91.7
Sean Nolen, Northern Colorado	So	27	85	93	91.4
Reggie Moore, Wheeling Jesuit	Jr	28	118	130	90.8
Todd Manuel, St. Anselm	Sr	30	174	193	90.2
Ryan Bucci, C.W. Post	Sr	28	114	127	89.8
Eddin Santiago, MO Southern St.	Sr	28	141	158	89.2
Nick Johnson, Seattle Pacific	Sr	29	90	101	89.1
Matt Miller, Drury	Sr	25	97	109	89.0
Mike Palm, Western Washington	Jr	27	121	136	89.0

Note: Minimum 2.5 made per game.

NCAA Women's Division II Individual Leaders

SCORING

Player and Team	Class	GP	TFG	3FG	FT	Pts	Avg
Heather Garay, Cal St–Bakersfield	Jr	29	265	0	183	713	24.6
Lauri McIntosh, Cal Poly Pomona	Sr	30	261	9	161	692	23.1
Becky Moen, N Dakota	Jr	29	223	70	141	657	22.7
Ginnell Curtis, N Carolina–Pembroke	Sr	26	220	30	115	585	22.5
Denise Shelton, Mars Hill	Sr	31	219	52	205	695	22.4
Diane Dittburner, Cal St–Bakersfield	Jr	29	186	100	159	631	21.8
Marisa DellAngelo, Northern Michigan	Sr	28	210	82	101	603	21.5
Elizabeth Biedrycki, Wingate	Sr	25	185	0	165	535	21.4
Mandy Koupal, S Dakota	So	28	212	20	152	596	21.3
Amba Kongolo, NC Central	Sr	26	214	2	118	548	21.1

REBOUNDS

Player and Team	Class	GP	Reb	Avg
Erica Harris, Montevallo	Sr	26	336	12.9
Elizabeth Biedrycki, Wingate	Sr	25	321	12.8
Georgia Gordon, New York Tech	Jr	25	314	12.6
Mary Harrison, Molloy	Sr	27	337	12.5
Lucresia West, Florida Southern	Fr	23	275	12.0
Stacy Knapp, Merrimack	Sr	28	332	11.9
Rhona McKenzie, American Int'l	Sr	32	374	11.7
Amanda Young, St. Rose	Jr	26	297	11.4
Cherese Hinckson, Dowling	Sr	29	328	11.3
Heather Garay, Cal St–Bakersfield	Jr	29	326	11.2

ASSISTS

Player and Team	Class	GP	A	Avg
Kelly West, W Liberty St	So	31	265	8.5
Jen Gwin, Gannon	Sr	27	209	7.7
Latisha Martin, Wayne St (MI)	Sr	27	192	7.1
Jamie McDonald, Shaw	Sr	28	185	6.6
Carliss Holland, MO Western St	Jr	30	186	6.2
Dena Mcmullen, NW Missouri St	Sr	26	159	6.1
Melanie Wagner, AK–Fairbanks	Sr	27	162	6.0
Liz Leonard, Bentley	Jr	29	172	5.9
Jacquie Negrelli, Indiana (PA)	Sr	26	154	5.9
Holly Armstrong, Cal St–Bakersfield	So	27	158	5.9

FIELD-GOAL PERCENTAGE

Player and Team	Class	GP	FGA	FG	Pct
Melanie Carter, Abilene Christian	So	24	165	243	67.9
Elizabeth Biedrycki, Wingate	Sr	25	185	287	64.5
Jackie Mason, Ashland	So	27	164	259	63.3
Martha Brinker, St. Mary's (TX)	So	29	181	288	62.8
Sammy Kromm, WI–Parkside	Fr	25	147	234	62.8
M. Cottrell, Northern Kentucky	Sr	27	184	297	62.0
Stormy Griffith, E Central	So	25	175	283	61.8
Krissy Hatfield, Lander	Jr	24	128	209	61.2
Felicia Hallums, Limestone	Sr	24	209	345	60.6
Catreia Renee Shaw, Clayton St	Jr	28	164	274	59.9

Note: Minimum 5 made per game.

FREE-THROW PERCENTAGE

Player and Team	Class	GP	FTA	FT	Pct
Molly Knobbe, Central MO St	Sr	30	132	144	91.7
Toni Leopard, Presbyterian	Sr	30	138	153	90.2
Marisa DellAngelo, Northern Michigan	Sr	28	101	113	89.4
Julie Szabo, SC–Aiken	Jr	28	101	114	88.6
J. Rzeszut, MO Southern St	Jr	27	84	95	88.4
Beth Swift, NE–Kearney	Sr	30	101	115	87.8
Nickie Randall, Bellarmine	Jr	28	72	82	87.8
Misty Wilson, Tarleton St	Sr	25	132	152	86.8
Lindsay Baker, Pitt-Johnstown	Sr	27	99	114	86.8
Ali Sprague, Emporia St	Sr	28	79	91	86.8
S. Wardman, Slippery Rock	Sr	27	79	91	86.8

Note: Minimum 2.5 made per game.

NCAA Men's Division III Individual Leaders

SCORING

Player and Team	Class	GP	TFG	3FG	FT	Pts	Avg
Patrick Glover, Johnson St	Jr	24	237	28	147	649	27.0
Steve Wood, Grinnell	So	24	222	52	150	646	26.9
Keith Schubert, Bethany (WV)	Sr	29	260	55	184	759	26.2
Colin Tabb, Trinity (CT)	Sr	25	191	66	171	619	24.8
K.B. Debord, Concordia–Austin	Sr	24	222	37	110	591	24.6
Willie Chandler, Misericordia	Jr	29	234	65	168	701	24.2
Kyle Williford, Bridgewater (VA)	Sr	26	231	46	119	627	24.1
Brandon Jones, St. Mary's (MD)	Sr	26	224	63	101	612	23.5
Jeff Gibbs, Otterbein	Sr	32	281	0	190	752	23.5
Tim Dworak, WI–Oshkosh	Jr	30	247	16	194	704	23.5

REBOUNDS

Player and Team	Class	GP	Reb	Avg
Jeff Gibbs, Otterbein	Sr	32	523	16.3
Pat Reardon, MA Liberal Arts	Jr	23	302	13.1
Jed Johnson, Maine Maritime	Jr	23	285	12.4
Joe Corbett, Hobart	Jr	24	293	12.2
Jared Hite, Rensselaer	So	23	276	12.0
Darren Pugh, Lebanon Valley	Jr	27	315	11.7
Dan Luciano, Ursinus	Jr	24	261	10.9
Jonathan Bird, Cal Tech	Jr	22	230	10.5
Eddie Washetas, Maranatha Baptist	So	27	282	10.4
Luis Melo, Mt. St. Mary (NY)	Sr	27	278	10.3

ASSISTS

Player and Team	Class	GP	A	Avg
Tennyson Whitted, Ramapo	Jr	29	319	11.0
Trevelle Boyd, E Texas Baptist	Jr	24	169	7.0
Rocky Parise, Elizabethtown	Sr	32	217	6.8
Danny Kanamori, MIT	Fr	25	169	6.8
Tim Gaspar, UMass-Dartmouth	Jr	29	196	6.8
Steve Kohl, Ripon	Sr	26	175	6.7
Ryan Keating, St. John's (MN)	Sr	21	137	6.5
Richard Jackson, Mount Union	Sr	27	176	6.5
Michael Crotty, Williams	So	28	180	6.4
Mike Howland, DePauw	Sr	28	180	6.4

FIELD-GOAL PERCENTAGE

Player and Team	Class	GP	FG	FGA	Pct
Omar Warthen, Neumann	Jr	27	135	202	66.8
Jeff Gibbs, Otterbein	Sr	32	281	421	66.7
John Thomas, Fontbonne	Jr	24	158	237	66.7
Pat Fitzsimons, Amherst	Jr	29	160	241	66.4
Tim Dworak, WI–Oshkosh	Jr	30	247	381	64.8
Kevin Matthews, Western CT St	Sr	24	187	289	64.7
Jonathon Jarrett, Sewanee	Jr	23	133	206	64.6
Kanem Johnson, Wesleyan (CT)	So	25	185	287	64.5
Edmund Johnson, WI–River Falls	Sr	25	126	198	63.6
Darryl Munroe, Hunter	Sr	26	177	279	63.4

Note: Minimum 5 made per game.

FREE-THROW PERCENTAGE

Player and Team	Class	GP	FT	FTA	Pct
Jason Luisi, Suffolk	Sr	28	87	94	92.6
Shawn McCormick, Baldwin-Wallace	Sr	26	74	80	92.5
Kyle Vogt, Lakeland	Sr	26	71	78	91.0
Kevin Broene, Calvin	So	27	81	89	91.0
Mike Moler, Muskingum	Sr	26	90	99	90.9
Steve Kohl, Ripon	Sr	26	102	113	90.3
Robby Pridgen, Roanoke	Jr	27	125	139	89.9
Scott Beebe, Gordon	Jr	27	71	79	89.9
Joe Witherspoon, Gordon	Jr	27	106	118	89.8
Steve Vega, Clarkson	Sr	25	136	152	89.5

Note: Minimum 2.5 made per game.

NCAA Women's Division III Individual Leaders

SCORING

Player and Team	Class	GP	TFG	3FG	FT	Pts	Avg
E'Lisa Ladson, Wesleyan (GA)	So	25	222	93	113	650	26.0
Angel Hall, Anderson (IN)	So	28	211	117	118	657	23.5
Jill Dewane, Lakeland	Sr	29	261	22	123	667	23.0
Heather Francouer, Oglethorpe	Jr	25	197	9	160	563	22.5
Rachael Poland, Heidelberg	Sr	26	215	9	143	582	22.4
Lauren Cargill, CCNY	Jr	27	200	77	112	589	21.8
Misty Carneal, NC Wesleyan	Sr	25	204	2	121	531	21.2
Heidi Burkhart, Rockford	Sr	25	171	24	154	520	20.8
Tiffany Corey, Johnson St	Sr	25	211	3	91	516	20.6
Doris Zimmerman, Wilson	Jr	25	211	5	86	513	20.5

REBOUNDS

Player and Team	Class	GP	Reb	Avg
Keisha Toms, Medgar Evers	Jr	23	357	15.5
Keisha Cook, Staten Island	Jr	21	318	15.1
Tiffany Stewart, Cedar Crest	Sr	25	369	14.8
Tiffany Corey, Johnson St	Sr	25	361	14.4
Janice Coppolino, Framingham St	Jr	25	357	14.3
Tenielle Hill, Elms	Jr	27	379	14.0
Doris Zimmerman, Wilson	Jr	25	331	13.2
Joy Silver, Rutgers–Camden	Jr	27	350	13.0
Kristine O'Coin, Nichols	Jr	24	307	12.8
Amy Abernathy, Franklin & Marshall	So	27	343	12.7

FIELD-GOAL PERCENTAGE

Player and Team	Class	GP	FG	FGA	Pct
Alicia Davis, Loras	So	26	222	306	72.5
Jacclyn Rock, Staten Island	So	28	168	264	63.6
Jessica Dunlap, Millsaps	So	25	181	286	63.3
Kasey Bostow, Concordia–M'head	Jr	25	158	254	62.2
Kathy Darling, Johns Hopkins	Jr	27	173	285	60.7
Shevon Gibbons, Norwich	Fr	26	195	322	60.6
Danielle Fitzpatrick, Brandeis	So	21	107	177	60.5
Jill Dewane, Lakeland	Sr	29	261	433	60.3
Kelly Etzel, Gust. Adolphus	Jr	27	144	239	60.3
Rachel Zimet, WPI	Sr	27	142	236	60.2

Note: Minimum 5 made per game.

ASSISTS

Player and Team	Class	GP	A	Avg
M. Pearson, Concordia–M'head	Fr	25	172	6.9
Sera' Godfrey, Pine Manor	Sr	26	175	6.7
Diana Esterkamp, Otterbein	So	26	172	6.6
Cristina Morales, New Jersey City	So	25	153	6.1
Kira Peterson, Coast Guard	Fr	27	161	6.0
Nicki Mueller, Loras	Jr	26	155	6.0
Rachel Bard, Maine–Farmington	Sr	27	160	5.9
A. Poppleton, Notre Dame (MD)	Jr	27	159	5.9
B. Dannelly, Washington & Lee	Fr	26	152	5.8
Shawndra McDonald, Washington & Jefferson	So	25	145	5.8

FREE-THROW PERCENTAGE

Player and Team	Class	GP	FT	FTA	Pct
Kerry Deshefy, Wheaton (MA)	Sr	24	67	74	90.5
Amie Kretzing, Messiah	Jr	27	86	97	88.7
Jill Dewane, Lakeland	Sr	29	123	139	88.5
Kristi Royer, Bowdoin	Jr	28	74	84	88.1
Heidi Burkhart, Rockford	Sr	25	154	176	87.5
Kat Dunikoski, Austin	Sr	23	61	70	87.1
Katie Walsh, John Carroll	Jr	27	117	135	86.7
Amy Barlow, Centre	So	24	97	112	86.6
Missy Pederson, St. Thomas (MN)	Sr	26	114	132	86.4
Tanasha Ellis, E Texas Baptist	Jr	25	101	117	86.3

Note: Minimum 2.5 made per game.

Multimedia: Fair to Middlin'

They used to be called Cinderella teams, but after the recent stellar NCAA tournament performances of such schools as Butler, Gonzaga and Utah State, the fairy-tale moniker seems condescending. Now emerging basketball minipowers have their own classification: mid-major. Over the last three years the website Collegeinsider.com has made a niche for itself by tracking these teams with its Mid-Major Top 25.

Each Sunday evening, Collegeinsider posts its rankings, which are derived from a poll of 30 Division I coaches and the judgements of the site's five-person editorial team. To be eligible a school must rest outside the realm of the 10 so-called major conferences. If you'd followed the rankings last season, you might not have been shocked when Midwestern Collegiate power Butler—which finished the regular season unranked in the AP poll but second in the Mid-Major Top 25—waxed the ACC's Wake Forest 79–63 in the NCAA tournament's first round. The site also chose a preseason Mid-Major All-America team, headed by Gonzaga (West Coast) senior point guard Dan Dickau.

Collegeinsider editor-in-chief Joe Dwyer, a former music producer, watches as many as 15 games a day by means of satellite dish and videotape at his office in Norwood, Mass. He has given the site a lighter side: In the Fashionable Four, it selects the game's best-dressed coach (last year's winner: Bruiser Flint, then at UMass, now at Drexel). Collegeinsider even posts coaches' Recipes for Success. For Thanksgiving, the dish was fried turkey with Louisiana hot sauce from Auburn's Cliff Ellis.

—John O'Keefe

NCAA Men's Division I Championship Results

NCAA Final Four Results

Year	Winner	Score	Runner-up	Third Place	Fourth Place	Winning Coach
1939	Oregon	46–33	Ohio St	*Oklahoma	*Villanova	Howard Hobson
1940	Indiana	60–42	Kansas	*Duquesne	*Southern Cal	Branch McCracken
1941	Wisconsin	39–34	Washington St	*Pittsburgh	*Arkansas	Harold Foster
1942	Stanford	53–38	Dartmouth	*Colorado	*Kentucky	Everett Dean
1943	Wyoming	46–34	Georgetown	*Texas	*DePaul	Everett Shelton
1944	Utah	42–40 (OT)	Dartmouth	*Iowa St	*Ohio St	Vadal Peterson
1945	Oklahoma St	49–45	NYU	*Arkansas	*Ohio St	Hank Iba
1946	Oklahoma St	43–40	N Carolina	Ohio St	California	Hank Iba
1947	Holy Cross	58–47	Oklahoma	Texas	CCNY	Alvin Julian
1948	Kentucky	58–42	Baylor	Holy Cross	Kansas St	Adolph Rupp
1949	Kentucky	46–36	Oklahoma St	Illinois	Oregon St	Adolph Rupp
1950	CCNY	71–68	Bradley	N Carolina St	Baylor	Nat Holman
1951	Kentucky	68–58	Kansas St	Illinois	Oklahoma St	Adolph Rupp
1952	Kansas	80–63	St. John's (NY)	Illinois	Santa Clara	Forrest Allen
1953	Indiana	69–68	Kansas	Washington	Louisiana St	Branch McCracken
1954	La Salle	92–76	Bradley	Penn St	Southern Cal	Kenneth Loeffler
1955	San Francisco	77–63	La Salle	Colorado	Iowa	Phil Woolpert
1956	San Francisco	83–71	Iowa	Temple	Southern Meth	Phil Woolpert
1957	N Carolina	54–53 (3OT)	Kansas	San Francisco	Michigan St	Frank McGuire
1958	Kentucky	84–72	Seattle	Temple	Kansas St	Adolph Rupp
1959	California	71–70	W Virginia	Cincinnati	Louisville	Pete Newell
1960	Ohio St	75–55	California	Cincinnati	NYU	Fred Taylor
1961	Cincinnati	70–65 (OT)	Ohio St	Vacated‡	Utah	Edwin Jucker
1962	Cincinnati	71–59	Ohio St	Wake Forest	UCLA	Edwin Jucker
1963	Loyola (IL)	60–58 (OT)	Cincinnati	Duke	Oregon St	George Ireland
1964	UCLA	98–83	Duke	Michigan	Kansas St	John Wooden
1965	UCLA	91–80	Michigan	Princeton	Wichita St	John Wooden
1966	UTEP	72–65	Kentucky	Duke	Utah	Don Haskins
1967	UCLA	79–64	Dayton	Houston	N Carolina	John Wooden
1968	UCLA	78–55	N Carolina	Ohio St	Houston	John Wooden
1969	UCLA	92–72	Purdue	Drake	N Carolina	John Wooden
1970	UCLA	80–69	Jacksonville	New Mexico St	St. Bonaventure	John Wooden
1971	UCLA	68–62	Vacated‡	Vacated‡	Kansas	John Wooden
1972	UCLA	81–76	Florida St	N Carolina	Louisville	John Wooden
1973	UCLA	87–66	Memphis St	Indiana	Providence	John Wooden
1974	N Carolina St	76–64	Marquette	UCLA	Kansas	Norm Sloan
1975	UCLA	92–85	Kentucky	Louisville	Syracuse	John Wooden
1976	Indiana	86–68	Michigan	UCLA	Rutgers	Bob Knight
1977	Marquette	67–59	N Carolina	UNLV	NC-Charlotte	Al McGuire
1978	Kentucky	94–88	Duke	Arkansas	Notre Dame	Joe Hall
1979	Michigan St	75–64	Indiana St	DePaul	Penn	Jud Heathcote
1980	Louisville	59–54	Vacated‡	Purdue	Iowa	Denny Crum
1981	Indiana	63–50	N Carolina	Virginia	Louisiana St	Bob Knight
1982	N Carolina	63–62	Georgetown	*Houston	*Louisville	Dean Smith
1983	N Carolina St	54–52	Houston	*Georgia	*Louisville	Jim Valvano
1984	Georgetown	84–75	Houston	*Kentucky	*Virginia	John Thompson
1985	Villanova	66–64	Georgetown	St. John's (NY)	Vacated‡	Rollie Massimino
1986	Louisville	72–69	Duke	*Kansas	*Louisiana St	Denny Crum
1987	Indiana	74–73	Syracuse	*UNLV	*Providence	Bob Knight
1988	Kansas	83–79	Oklahoma	*Arizona	*Duke	Larry Brown
1989	Michigan	80–79 (OT)	Seton Hall	*Duke	*Illinois	Steve Fisher
1990	UNLV	103–73	Duke	*Arkansas	*Georgia Tech	Jerry Tarkanian
1991	Duke	72–65	Kansas	*UNLV	*N Carolina	Mike Krzyzewski
1992	Duke	71–51	Michigan	*Cincinnati	*Indiana	Mike Krzyzewski
1993	N Carolina	77–71	Michigan	*Kansas	*Kentucky	Dean Smith
1994	Arkansas	76–72	Duke	*Arizona	*Florida	Nolan Richardson
1995	UCLA	89–78	Arkansas	*N Carolina	*Oklahoma St	Jim Harrick
1996	Kentucky	76–67	Syracuse	Vacated‡	Mississippi St	Rick Pitino
1997	Arizona	84–79 (OT)	Kentucky	*Minnesota	*N Carolina	Lute Olson
1998	Kentucky	78–69	Utah	*Stanford	*N Carolina	Tubby Smith
1999	Connecticut	77–74	Duke	*Michigan St	*Ohio St	Jim Calhoun
2000	Michigan St	89–76	Florida	*Wisconsin	*N Carolina	Tom Izzo
2001	Duke	82–72	Arizona	*Maryland	*Michigan St	Mike Krzyzewski
2002	Maryland	64–52	Indiana	*Kansas	*Oklahoma	Gary Williams

*Tied for third place. ‡Student-athletes representing St. Joseph's (PA) in 1961, Villanova in 1971, Western Kentucky in 1971, UCLA in 1980, Memphis State in 1985 and Massachusetts in 1996 were declared ineligible subsequent to the tournament. Under NCAA rules, the teams' and ineligible student-athletes' records were deleted, and the teams' places in the standings were vacated.

NCAA Final Four MVPs

Year	Winner, School	GP	Field Goals		3-Pt FG		Free Throws		Reb	A	Stl	BS	Avg
			FGM	Pct	FGA	FGM	FTM	Pct					
1939	....None selected												
1940	....Marv Huffman, Indiana	2	7	—	—	—	4	—	—	—	—	—	9.0
1941	....John Kotz, Wisconsin	2	8	—	—	—	6	—	—	—	—	—	11.0
1942	....Howard Dallmar, Stanford	2	8	—	—	—	4	66.7	—	—	—	—	10.0
1943	....Ken Sailors, Wyoming	2	10	—	—	—	8	72.7	—	—	—	—	14.0
1944	....Arnie Ferrin, Utah	2	11	—	—	—	6	—	—	—	—	—	14.0
1945	....Bob Kurland, Oklahoma St	2	16	—	—	—	5	—	—	—	—	—	18.5
1946	....Bob Kurland, Oklahoma St	2	21	—	—	—	10	66.7	—	—	—	—	26.0
1947	....George Kaftan, Holy Cross	2	18	—	—	—	12	70.6	—	—	—	—	24.0
1948	....Alex Groza, Kentucky	2	16	—	—	—	5	—	—	—	—	—	18.5
1949	....Alex Groza, Kentucky	2	19	—	—	—	14	—	—	—	—	—	26.0
1950	....Irwin Dambrot, CCNY	2	12	42.9	—	—	4	50.0	—	—	—	—	14.0
1951	....None selected												
1952	....Clyde Lovellette, Kansas	2	24	—	—	—	18	—	—	—	—	—	33.0
1953	....*B.H. Horn, Kansas	2	17	—	—	—	17	—	—	—	—	—	25.5
1954	....Tom Gola, La Salle	2	12	—	—	—	14	—	—	—	—	—	19.0
1955	....Bill Russell, San Francisco	2	19	—	—	—	9	—	—	—	—	—	23.5
1956	....*Hal Lear, Temple	2	32	—	—	—	16	—	—	—	—	—	40.0
1957	....*Wilt Chamberlain, Kansas	2	18	51.4	—	—	19	70.4	25	—	—	—	32.5
1958	....*Elgin Baylor, Seattle	2	18	34.0	—	—	12	75.0	41	—	—	—	24.0
1959	....*Jerry West, West Virginia	2	22	66.7	—	—	22	68.8	25	—	—	—	33.0
1960	....Jerry Lucas, Ohio State	2	16	66.7	—	—	3	100.0	23	—	—	—	17.5
1961	....*Jerry Lucas, Ohio State	2	20	71.4	—	—	16	94.1	25	—	—	—	28.0
1962	....Paul Hogue, Cincinnati	2	23	63.9	—	—	12	63.2	38	—	—	—	29.0
1963	....Art Heyman, Duke	2	18	41.0	—	—	15	68.2	19	—	—	—	25.5
1964	....Walt Hazzard, UCLA	2	11	55.0	—	—	8	66.7	10	—	—	—	15.0
1965	....*Bill Bradley, Princeton	2	34	63.0	—	—	19	95.0	24	—	—	—	43.5
1966	....*Jerry Chambers, Utah	2	25	53.2	—	—	20	83.3	35	—	—	—	35.0
1967	....Lew Alcindor, UCLA	2	14	60.9	—	—	11	45.8	38	—	—	—	19.5
1968	....Lew Alcindor, UCLA	2	22	62.9	—	—	9	90.0	34	—	—	—	26.5
1969	....Lew Alcindor, UCLA	2	23	67.7	—	—	16	64.0	41	—	—	—	31.0
1970	....Sidney Wicks, UCLA	2	15	71.4	—	—	9	60.0	34	—	—	—	19.5
1971	....*†Howard Porter, Villanova	2	20	48.8	—	—	7	77.8	24	—	—	—	23.5
1972	....Bill Walton, UCLA	2	20	69.0	—	—	17	73.9	41	—	—	—	28.5
1973	....Bill Walton, UCLA	2	28	82.4	—	—	2	40.0	30	—	—	—	29.0
1974	....David Thompson, NC State	2	19	51.4	—	—	11	78.6	17	—	—	—	24.5
1975	....Richard Washington, UCLA	2	23	54.8	—	—	8	72.7	20	—	—	—	27.0
1976	....Kent Benson, Indiana	2	17	50.0	—	—	7	63.6	18	—	—	—	20.5
1977	....Butch Lee, Marquette	2	11	34.4	—	—	8	100.0	6	2	1	1	15.0
1978	....Jack Givens, Kentucky	2	28	65.1	—	—	8	66.7	17	4	1	3	32.0
1979	....Earvin Johnson, Michigan St	2	17	68.0	—	—	19	86.4	17	3	0	2	26.5
1980	....Darrell Griffith, Louisville	2	23	62.2	—	—	11	68.8	7	15	0	2	28.5
1981	....Isiah Thomas, Indiana	2	14	56.0	—	—	9	81.8	4	9	3	4	18.5
1982	....James Worthy, N Carolina	2	20	74.1	—	—	2	28.6	8	9	0	4	21.0
1983	....*Akeem Olajuwon, Houston	2	16	55.2	—	—	9	64.3	40	3	2	5	20.5
1984	....Patrick Ewing, Georgetown	2	8	57.1	—	—	2	100.0	18	1	1	15	9.0
1985	....Ed Pinckney, Villanova	2	8	57.1	—	—	12	75.0	15	6	3	0	14.0
1986	....Pervis Ellison, Louisville	2	15	60.0	—	—	6	75.0	24	2	3	1	18.0
1987	....Keith Smart, Indiana	2	14	63.6	1	0	7	77.8	7	7	0	2	17.5
1988	....Danny Manning, Kansas	2	25	55.6	1	0	6	66.7	17	4	8	9	28.0
1989	....Glen Rice, Michigan	2	24	49.0	16	7	4	100.0	16	1	0	3	29.5
1990	....Anderson Hunt, UNLV	2	19	61.3	16	9	2	50.0	4	9	1	1	24.5
1991	....Christian Laettner, Duke	2	12	54.5	1	1	21	91.3	17	2	1	2	23.0
1992	....Bobby Hurley, Duke	2	10	41.7	12	7	8	80.0	3	11	0	3	17.5
1993	....Donald Williams, N Carolina	2	15	65.2	14	10	10	100.0	4	2	2	0	25.0
1994	....Corliss Williamson, Arkansas	2	21	50.0	0	0	10	71.4	21	8	4	3	26.0
1995	....Ed O'Bannon, UCLA	2	16	45.7	8	3	10	76.9	25	3	7	1	22.5
1996	....Tony Delk, Kentucky	2	15	41.7	16	8	6	54.6	9	2	3	2	22.0
1997	....Miles Simon, Arizona	2	17	45.9	10	3	17	77.3	8	6	0	1	27.0
1998	....Jeff Sheppard, Kentucky	2	16	55.2	10	4	7	77.8	10	7	4	0	21.5
1999	....Richard Hamilton, Connecticut	2	20	51.3	7	3	8	72.7	12	4	2	1	25.5
2000	....Mateen Cleaves, Michigan St	2	8	44.4	4	3	10	83.3	6	5	2	0	14.5
2001	....Shane Battier, Duke	2	13	50.0	12	5	12	70.6	19	8	2	6	21.5
2002	....Juan Dixon, Maryland	2	16	59.3	15	7	12	80.0	8	5	7	0	25.5

*Not a member of the championship-winning team.   †Record later vacated.

Best NCAA Tournament Single-Game Scoring Performances

Player and Team	Year	Round	FG	3FG	FT	TP
Austin Carr, Notre Dame vs Ohio	1970	1st	25	—	11	61
Bill Bradley, Princeton vs Wichita St	1965	C*	22	—	14	58
Oscar Robertson, Cincinnati vs Arkansas	1958	C	21	—	14	56
Austin Carr, Notre Dame vs Kentucky	1970	2nd	22	—	8	52
Austin Carr, Notre Dame vs Texas Christian	1971	1st	20	—	12	52
David Robinson, Navy vs Michigan	1987	1st	22	0	6	50
Elvin Hayes, Houston vs Loyola (IL)	1968	1st	20	—	9	49
Hal Lear, Temple vs SMU	1956	C*	17	—	14	48
Austin Carr, Notre Dame vs Houston	1971	C	17	—	13	47
Dave Corzine, DePaul vs Louisville	1978	2nd	18	—	10	46

C=regional third place; C*=third-place game.

NIT Championship Results

Year	Winner	Score	Runner-up	Year	Winner	Score	Runner-up
1938	Temple	60–36	Colorado	1971	N Carolina	84–66	Georgia Tech
1939	Long Island U	44–32	Loyola (IL)	1972	Maryland	100–69	Niagara
1940	Colorado	51–40	Duquesne	1973	Virginia Tech	92–91 (OT)	Notre Dame
1941	Long Island U	56–42	Ohio U	1974	Purdue	97–81	Utah
1942	W Virginia	47–45	W Kentucky	1975	Princeton	80–69	Providence
1943	St. John's (NY)	48–27	Toledo	1976	Kentucky	71–67	NC-Charlotte
1944	St. John's (NY)	47–39	DePaul	1977	St. Bonaventure	94–91	Houston
1945	DePaul	71–54	Bowling Green	1978	Texas	101–93	N Carolina St
1946	Kentucky	46–45	Rhode Island	1979	Indiana	53–52	Purdue
1947	Utah	49–45	Kentucky	1980	Virginia	58–55	Minnesota
1948	St. Louis	65–52	NYU	1981	Tulsa	86–84 (OT)	Syracuse
1949	San Francisco	48–47	Loyola (IL)	1982	Bradley	67–58	Purdue
1950	CCNY	69–61	Bradley	1983	Fresno St	69–60	DePaul
1951	BYU	62–43	Dayton	1984	Michigan	83–63	Notre Dame
1952	La Salle	75–64	Dayton	1985	UCLA	65–62	Indiana
1953	Seton Hall	58–46	St. John's (NY)	1986	Ohio St	73–63	Wyoming
1954	Holy Cross	71–62	Duquesne	1987	Southern Miss	84–80	La Salle
1955	Duquesne	70–58	Dayton	1988	Connecticut	72–67	Ohio St
1956	Louisville	93–80	Dayton	1989	St. John's (NY)	73–65	St. Louis
1957	Bradley	84–83	Memphis St	1990	Vanderbilt	74–72	St. Louis
1958	Xavier (OH)	78–74 (OT)	Dayton	1991	Stanford	78–72	Oklahoma
1959	St. John's (NY)	76–71 (OT)	Bradley	1992	Virginia	81–76	Notre Dame
1960	Bradley	88–72	Providence	1993	Minnesota	62–61	Georgetown
1961	Providence	62–59	St. Louis	1994	Villanova	80–73	Vanderbilt
1962	Dayton	73–67	St. John's (NY)	1995	Virginia Tech	65–64 (OT)	Marquette
1963	Providence	81–66	Canisius	1996	Nebraska	60–56	St. Joseph's
1964	Bradley	86–54	New Mexico	1997	Michigan	82–73	Florida St
1965	St. John's (NY)	55–51	Villanova	1998	Minnesota	79–72	Penn St
1966	BYU	97–84	NYU	1999	California	61–60	Clemson
1967	Southern Illinois	71–56	Marquette	2000	Wake Forest	71–61	Notre Dame
1968	Dayton	61–48	Kansas	2001	Tulsa	79–60	Alabama
1969	Temple	89–76	Boston College	2002	Memphis	72–62	S Carolina
1970	Marquette	65–53	St. John's (NY)				

NCAA Men's Division I Season Leaders

Scoring Average

Year	Player and Team	Ht	Class	GP	FG	3FG	FT	Pts	Avg
1948	Murray Wier, Iowa	5-9	Sr	19	152	—	95	399	21.0
1949	Tony Lavelli, Yale	6-3	Sr	30	228	—	215	671	22.4
1950	Paul Arizin, Villanova	6-3	Sr	29	260	—	215	735	25.3
1951	Bill Mlkvy, Temple	6-4	Sr	25	303	—	125	731	29.2
1952	Clyde Lovellette, Kansas	6-9	Sr	28	315	—	165	795	28.4
1953	Frank Selvy, Furman	6-3	Jr	25	272	—	194	738	29.5
1954	Frank Selvy, Furman	6-3	Sr	29	427	—	355	1209	41.7
1955	Darrell Floyd, Furman	6-1	Jr	25	344	—	209	897	35.9
1956	Darrell Floyd, Furman	6-1	Sr	28	339	—	268	946	33.8
1957	Grady Wallace, S Carolina	6-4	Sr	29	336	—	234	906	31.2
1958	Oscar Robertson, Cincinnati	6-5	So	28	352	—	280	984	35.1
1959	Oscar Robertson, Cincinnati	6-5	Jr	30	331	—	316	978	32.6
1960	Oscar Robertson, Cincinnati	6-5	Sr	30	369	—	273	1011	33.7
1961	Frank Burgess, Gonzaga	6-1	Sr	26	304	—	234	842	32.4
1962	Billy McGill, Utah	6-9	Sr	26	394	—	221	1009	38.8
1963	Nick Werkman, Seton Hall	6-3	Jr	22	221	—	208	650	29.5
1964	Howard Komives, Bowling Green	6-1	Sr	23	292	—	260	844	36.7

Scoring Average (Cont.)

ear	Player and Team	Ht	Class	GP	FG	3FG	FT	Pts	Avg
1965	Rick Barry, Miami (FL)	6-7	Sr	26	340	—	293	973	37.4
1966	Dave Schellhase, Purdue	6-4	Sr	24	284	—	213	781	32.5
1967	Jim Walker, Providence	6-3	Sr	28	323	—	205	851	30.4
1968	Pete Maravich, Louisiana St	6-5	So	26	432	—	274	1138	43.8
1969	Pete Maravich, Louisiana St	6-5	Jr	26	433	—	282	1148	44.2
1970	Pete Maravich, Louisiana St	6-5	Sr	31	522	—	337	1381	44.5
1971	Johnny Neumann, Mississippi	6-6	So	23	366	—	191	923	40.1
1972	Dwight Lamar, Southwestern Louisiana	6-1	Jr	29	429	—	196	1054	36.3
1973	William Averitt, Pepperdine	6-1	Sr	25	352	—	144	848	33.9
1974	Larry Fogle, Canisius	6-5	So	25	326	—	183	835	33.4
1975	Bob McCurdy, Richmond	6-7	Sr	26	321	—	213	855	32.9
1976	Marshall Rodgers, TX-Pan American	6-2	Sr	25	361	—	197	919	36.8
1977	Freeman Williams, Portland St	6-4	Jr	26	417	—	176	1010	38.8
1978	Freeman Williams, Portland St	6-4	Sr	27	410	—	149	969	35.9
1979	Lawrence Butler, Idaho St	6-3	Sr	27	310	—	192	812	30.1
1980	Tony Murphy, Southern-BR	6-3	Sr	29	377	—	178	932	32.1
1981	Zam Fredrick, S Carolina	6-2	Sr	27	300	—	181	781	28.9
1982	Harry Kelly, Texas Southern	6-7	Jr	29	336	—	190	862	29.7
1983	Harry Kelly, Texas Southern	6-7	Sr	29	333	—	169	835	28.8
1984	Joe Jakubick, Akron	6-5	Sr	27	304	—	206	814	30.1
1985	Xavier McDaniel, Wichita St	6-8	Sr	31	351	—	142	844	27.2
1986	Terrance Bailey, Wagner	6-2	Jr	29	321	—	212	854	29.4
1987	Kevin Houston, Army	5-11	Sr	29	311	63	268	953	32.9
1988	Hersey Hawkins, Bradley	6-3	Sr	31	377	87	284	1125	36.3
1989	Hank Gathers, Loyola Marymount	6-7	Jr	31	419	0	177	1015	32.7
1990	Bo Kimble, Loyola Marymount	6-5	Sr	32	404	92	231	1131	35.3
1991	Kevin Bradshaw, U.S. Int'l	6-6	Sr	28	358	60	278	1054	37.6
1992	Brett Roberts, Morehead St	6-8	Sr	29	278	66	193	815	28.1
1993	Greg Guy, TX-Pan American	6-1	Jr	19	189	67	111	556	29.3
1994	Glenn Robinson, Purdue	6-8	Jr	34	368	79	215	1030	30.3
1995	Kurt Thomas, Texas Christian	6-9	Sr	27	288	3	202	781	28.9
1996	Kevin Granger, Texas Southern	6-3	Sr	24	194	30	230	648	27.0
1997	Charles Jones, LIU-Brooklyn	6-3	Jr	30	338	109	118	903	30.1
1998	Charles Jones, LIU-Brooklyn	6-3	Sr	30	326	116	101	869	29.0
1999	Alvin Young, Niagara	6-3	Sr	29	253	65	157	728	25.1
2000	Courtney Alexander, Fresno St	6-6	Sr	27	252	58	107	669	24.8
2001	Ronnie McCollum, Centenary	6-4	Sr	27	244	85	214	787	29.1
2002	Jason Conley, Virginia Military	6-5	Fr	28	285	79	171	820	29.3

Rebounds

Year	Player and Team	Ht	Class	GP	Reb	Avg
1951	Ernie Beck, Pennsylvania	6-4	So	27	556	20.6
1952	Bill Hannon, Army	6-3	So	17	355	20.9
1953	Ed Conlin, Fordham	6-5	So	26	612	23.5
1954	Art Quimby, Connecticut	6-5	Jr	26	588	22.6
1955	Charlie Slack, Marshall	6-5	Jr	21	538	25.6
1956	Joe Holup, George Washington	6-6	Sr	26	604	†.256
1957	Elgin Baylor, Seattle	6-6	Jr	25	508	†.235
1958	Alex Ellis, Niagara	6-5	Sr	25	536	†.262
1959	Leroy Wright, Pacific	6-8	Jr	26	652	†.238
1960	Leroy Wright, Pacific	6-8	Sr	17	380	†.234
1961	Jerry Lucas, Ohio St	6-8	Jr	27	470	†.198
1962	Jerry Lucas, Ohio St	6-8	Sr	28	499	†.211
1963	Paul Silas, Creighton	6-7	Sr	27	557	20.6
1964	Bob Pelkington, Xavier (OH)	6-7	Sr	26	567	21.8
1965	Toby Kimball, Connecticut	6-8	Sr	23	483	21.0
1966	Jim Ware, Oklahoma City	6-8	Sr	29	607	20.9
1967	Dick Cunningham, Murray St	6-10	Jr	22	479	21.8
1968	Neal Walk, Florida	6-10	Jr	25	494	19.8
1969	Spencer Haywood, Detroit	6-8	So	22	472	21.5
1970	Artis Gilmore, Jacksonville	7-2	Jr	28	621	22.2
1971	Artis Gilmore, Jacksonville	7-2	Sr	26	603	23.2
1972	Kermit Washington, American	6-8	Jr	23	455	19.8
1973	Kermit Washington, American	6-8	Sr	22	439	20.0
1974	Marvin Barnes, Providence	6-9	Sr	32	597	18.7
1975	John Irving, Hofstra	6-9	So	21	323	15.4
1976	Sam Pellom, Buffalo	6-8	So	26	420	16.2
1977	Glenn Mosley, Seton Hall	6-8	Sr	29	473	16.3
1978	Ken Williams, N Texas St	6-7	Sr	28	411	14.7
1979	Monti Davis, Tennessee St	6-7	Jr	26	421	16.2
1980	Larry Smith, Alcorn St	6-8	Sr	26	392	15.1
1981	Darryl Watson, Miss Valley	6-7	Sr	27	379	14.0

Rebounds (Cont.)

Year	Player and Team	Ht	Class	GP	Reb	Avg
1982	LaSalle Thompson, Texas	6-10	Jr	27	365	13.5
1983	Xavier McDaniel, Wichita St	6-7	So	28	403	14.4
1984	Akeem Olajuwon, Houston	7-0	Jr	37	500	13.5
1985	Xavier McDaniel, Wichita St	6-8	Sr	31	460	14.8
1986	David Robinson, Navy	6-11	Jr	35	455	13.0
1987	Jerome Lane, Pittsburgh	6-6	So	33	444	13.5
1988	Kenny Miller, Loyola (IL)	6-9	Fr	29	395	13.6
1989	Hank Gathers, Loyola (CA)	6-7	Jr	31	426	13.7
1990	Anthony Bonner, St. Louis	6-8	Sr	33	456	13.8
1991	Shaquille O'Neal, Louisiana St	7-1	So	28	411	14.7
1992	Popeye Jones, Murray St	6-8	Sr	30	431	14.4
1993	Warren Kidd, Middle Tenn St	6-9	Sr	26	386	14.8
1994	Jerome Lambert, Baylor	6-8	Jr	24	355	14.8
1995	Kurt Thomas, Texas Christian	6-9	Sr	27	393	14.6
1996	Marcus Mann, Mississippi Valley	6-8	Sr	29	394	13.6
1997	Tim Duncan, Wake Forest	6-11	Sr	31	457	14.7
1998	Ryan Perryman, Dayton	6-7	Sr	33	412	12.5
1999	Ian McGinnis, Dartmouth	6-8	So	26	317	12.2
2000	Darren Phillips, Fairfield	6-7	Sr	29	405	14.0
2001	Chris Marcus, Western Kentucky	7-1	Jr	31	374	12.1
2002	Jeremy Bishop, Quinnipiac	6-6	Jr	29	347	12.0

†From 1956–1962, title was based on highest individual recoveries out of total by both teams in all games.

Assists

Year	Player and Team	Class	GP	A	Avg
1984	Craig Lathen, IL-Chicago	Jr	29	274	9.45
1985	Rob Weingard, Hofstra	Sr	24	228	9.50
1986	Mark Jackson, St. John's (NY)	Jr	36	328	9.11
1987	Avery Johnson, Southern-BR	Jr	31	333	10.74
1988	Avery Johnson, Southern-BR	Sr	30	399	13.30
1989	Glenn Williams, Holy Cross	Sr	28	278	9.93
1990	Todd Lehmann, Drexel	Sr	28	260	9.29
1991	Chris Corchiani, N Carolina St	Sr	31	299	9.65
1992	Van Usher, Tennessee Tech	Sr	29	254	8.76
1993	Sam Crawford, New Mex St	Sr	34	310	9.12
1994	Jason Kidd, California	So	30	272	9.06
1995	Nelson Haggerty, Baylor	Sr	28	284	10.10
1996	Raimonds Miglinieks, UC-Irvine	Sr	27	230	8.52
1997	Kenny Mitchell, Dartmouth	Sr	26	203	7.81
1998	Ahlon Lewis, Arizona St	Sr	32	294	9.19
1999	Doug Gottlieb, Oklahoma St	Jr	34	299	8.79
2000	Mark Dickel, UNLV	Sr	31	280	9.03
2001	Markus Carr, Cal St–Northridge	Jr	32	286	8.94
2002	T.J. Ford, Texas	Fr	33	273	8.27

Blocked Shots

Year	Player and Team	Class	GP	BS	Avg
1986	David Robinson, Navy	Jr	35	207	5.91
1987	David Robinson, Navy	Sr	32	144	4.50
1988	Rodney Blake, St. Joseph's (PA)	Sr	29	116	4.00
1989	Alonzo Mourning, Georgetown	Fr	34	169	4.97
1990	Kenny Green, Rhode Island	Sr	26	124	4.77
1991	Shawn Bradley, Brigham Young	Fr	34	177	5.21
1992	Shaquille O'Neal, Louisiana St	Jr	30	157	5.23
1993	Theo Ratliff, Wyoming	Jr	28	124	4.43
1994	Grady Livingston, Howard	Jr	26	115	4.42
1995	Keith Closs, Central Conn St	Fr	26	139	5.35
1996	Keith Closs, Central Conn St	So	28	178	6.36
1997	Adonal Foyle, Colgate	Jr	28	180	6.43
1998	Jerome James, Florida A&M	Sr	27	125	4.63
1999	Tarvis Williams, Hampton	Jr	27	135	5.00
2000	Ken Johnson, Ohio St	Sr	30	161	5.37
2001	Tarvis Williams, Hampton	Sr	32	147	4.59
2002	Wojciech Myrda, LA-Monroe	Sr	32	172	5.38

Steals

Year	Player and Team	Class	GP	S	Avg
1986	Darron Brittman, Chicago St	Sr	28	139	4.96
1987	Tony Fairley, Charleston Sou	Sr	28	114	4.07
1988	Aldwin Ware, Florida A&M	Sr	29	142	4.90
1989	Kenny Robertson, Cleveland St	Jr	28	111	3.96
1990	Ronn McMahon, E Washington	Sr	29	130	4.48
1991	Van Usher, Tennessee Tech	Jr	28	104	3.71

Steals (Cont.)

Year	Player and Team	Class	GP	S	Avg
1992	Victor Snipes, NE Illinois	So	25	86	3.44
1993	Jason Kidd, California	Fr	29	110	3.80
1994	Shawn Griggs, SW Louisiana	Sr	30	120	4.00
1995	Roderick Anderson, Texas	Sr	30	101	3.37
1996	Pointer Williams, McNeese St	Sr	27	118	4.37
1997	Joel Hoover, MD-Eastern Shore	Fr	28	90	3.21
1998	Bonzi Wells, Ball St	Sr	29	103	3.55
1999	Shawnta Rogers, George Wash	Sr	29	103	3.55
2000	Carl Williams, Liberty	Sr	28	107	3.82
2001	Greedy Daniels, Texas Christian	Jr	25	108	4.32
2002	Desmond Cambridge, AL A&M	Sr	29	160	5.52

Single Game Records

SCORING HIGHS VS NON-DIVISION I OPPONENT

Pts	Player and Team vs Opponent	Date
72	Kevin Bradshaw, U.S. Int'l vs Loyola Marymount	1-5-91
69	Pete Maravich, Louisiana St vs Alabama	2-7-70
68	Calvin Murphy, Niagara vs Syracuse	12-7-68
66	Jay Handlan, Washington & Lee vs Furman	2-17-51
66	Pete Maravich, Louisiana St vs Tulane	2-10-69
66	Anthony Roberts, Oral Roberts vs N Carolina A&T	2-19-77
65	Anthony Roberts, Oral Roberts vs Oregon	3-9-77
65	Scott Haffner, Evansville vs Dayton	2-18-89
64	Pete Maravich, Louisiana St vs Kentucky	2-21-70
63	Johnny Neumann, Mississippi vs Louisiana St	1-30-71
63	Hersey Hawkins, Bradley vs Detroit	2-22-88

SCORING HIGHS VS NON-DIVISION I OPPONENT

Pts	Player and Team vs Opponent	Date
100	Frank Selvy, Furman vs Newberry	2-13-54
85	Paul Arizin, Villanova vs Philadelphia NAMC	2-12-49
81	Freeman Williams, Portland St vs Rocky Mountain	2-3-78
73	Bill Mlkvy, Temple vs Wilkes	3-3-51
71	Freeman Williams, Portland St vs Southern Oregon	2-9-77

REBOUNDING HIGHS BEFORE 1973

Reb	Player and Team vs Opponent	Date
51	Bill Chambers, William & Mary vs Virginia	2-14-53
43	Charlie Slack, Marshall vs Morris Harvey	1-12-54
42	Tom Heinsohn, Holy Cross vs Boston College	3-1-55
40	Art Quimby, Connecticut vs Boston U	1-11-55
39	Maurice Stokes, St. Francis (PA) vs John Carroll	1-28-55
39	Dave DeBusschere, Detroit vs Central Michigan	1-30-60
39	Keith Swagerty, Pacific vs UC-Santa Barbara	3-5-65

REBOUNDING HIGHS SINCE 1973*

Reb	Player and Team vs Opponent	Date
35	Larry Abney, Fresno St vs Southern Methodist	2-17-00
34	David Vaughn, Oral Roberts vs Brandeis	1-8-73
32	Jervaughn Scales, Southern-BR vs Grambling	2-7-94
32	Durand Macklin, Louisiana St vs Tulane	11-26-76
31	Jim Bradley, Northern Illinois vs WI-Milwaukee	2-19-73
31	Calvin Natt, NE Louisiana vs Georgia Southern	12-29-76

ASSISTS

A	Player and Team vs Opponent	Date
22	Tony Fairley, Baptist vs Armstrong St	2-9-87
22	Avery Johnson, Southern-BR vs Texas Southern	1-25-88
22	Sherman Douglas, Syracuse vs Providence	1-28-89
21	Mark Wade, UNLV vs Navy	12-29-86
21	Kelvin Scarborough, New Mexico vs Hawaii	2-13-87
21	Anthony Manuel, Bradley vs UC-Irvine	12-19-87
21	Avery Johnson, Southern-BR vs Alabama St	1-16-88

Single Game Records (Cont.)

STEALS

S	Player and Team vs Opponent	Date
13	Mookie Blaylock, Oklahoma vs Centenary	12-12-87
13	Mookie Blaylock, Oklahoma vs Loyola Marymount	12-17-88
12	Kenny Robertson, Cleveland St vs Wagner	12-3-88
12	Terry Evans, Oklahoma vs Florida A&M	1-27-93
12	Richard Duncan, Middle Tenn St vs Eastern Kentucky	2-20-99
12	Greedy Daniels, Texas Christian vs AR–Pine Bluff	12-30-00
12	Jehiel Lewis, Navy vs Bucknell	1-12-02

BLOCKED SHOTS

BS	Player and Team vs Opponent	Date
14	David Robinson, Navy vs NC–Wilmington	1-4-86
14	Shawn Bradley, Brigham Young vs Eastern Kentucky	12-7-90
14	Roy Rogers, Alabama vs Georgia	2-10-96
14	Loren Woods, Arizona vs Oregon	2-3-00
13	Kevin Roberson, Vermont vs New Hampshire	1-9-92
13	Jim McIlvaine, Marquette vs Northeastern (IL)	12-9-92
13	Keith Closs, Central Conn. St vs St. Francis (PA)	12-21-94
13	D'or Fischer, Northwestern St vs SW Texas St	1-22-01
13	Wojciech Myrda, LA–Monroe vs Texas–San Antonio	1-17-02

Single Season Records

POINTS

Player and Team	Year	GP	FG	3FG	FT	Pts
Pete Maravich, Louisiana St	1970	31	522	—	337	1381
Elvin Hayes, Houston	1968	33	519	—	176	1214
Frank Selvy, Furman	1954	29	427	—	355	1209
Pete Maravich, Louisiana St	1969	26	433	—	282	1148
Pete Maravich, Louisiana St	1968	26	432	—	274	1138
Bo Kimble, Loyola Marymount	1990	32	404	92	231	1131
Hersey Hawkins, Bradley	1988	31	377	87	284	1125
Austin Carr, Notre Dame	1970	29	444	—	218	1106
Austin Carr, Notre Dame	1971	29	430	—	241	1101
Otis Birdsong, Houston	1977	36	452	—	186	1090

SCORING AVERAGE

Player and Team	Year	GP	FG	3FG	FT	Pts
Pete Maravich, Louisiana St	1970	31	522	337	1381	44.5
Pete Maravich, Louisiana St	1969	26	433	282	1148	44.2
Pete Maravich, Louisiana St	1968	26	432	274	1138	43.8
Frank Selvy, Furman	1954	29	427	355	1209	41.7
Johnny Neumann, Mississippi	1971	23	366	191	923	40.1
Freeman Williams, Portland St	1977	26	417	176	1010	38.8
Billy McGill, Utah	1962	26	394	221	1009	38.8
Calvin Murphy, Niagara	1968	24	337	242	916	38.2
Austin Carr, Notre Dame	1970	29	444	218	1106	38.1
Austin Carr, Notre Dame	1971	29	430	241	1101	38.0

REBOUNDS

Player and Team	Year	GP	Reb	Player and Team	Year	GP	Reb
Walt Dukes, Seton Hall	1953	33	734	Artis Gilmore, Jacksonville	1970	28	621
Leroy Wright, Pacific	1959	26	652	Tom Gola, La Salle	1955	31	618
Tom Gola, La Salle	1954	30	652	Ed Conlin, Fordham	1953	26	612
Charlie Tyra, Louisville	1956	29	645	Art Quimby, Connecticut	1955	25	611
Paul Silas, Creighton	1964	29	631	Bill Russell, San Francisco	1956	29	609
Elvin Hayes, Houston	1968	33	624	Jim Ware, Oklahoma City	1966	29	607

REBOUND AVERAGE BEFORE 1973

Player and Team	Year	GP	Reb	Avg
Charlie Slack, Marshall	1955	21	538	25.6
Leroy Wright, Pacific	1959	26	652	25.1
Art Quimby, Connecticut	1955	25	611	24.4
Charlie Slack, Marshall	1956	22	520	23.6
Ed Conlin, Fordham	1953	26	612	23.5

REBOUND AVERAGE SINCE 1973*

Player and Team	Year	GP	Reb	Avg
Kermit Washington, American	1973	22	439	20.0
Marvin Barnes, Providence	1973	30	571	19.0
Marvin Barnes, Providence	1974	32	597	18.7
Pete Padgett, NV-Reno	1973	26	462	17.8
Jim Bradley, Northern Illinois	1973	24	426	17.8

*Freshmen became eligible for varsity play in 1973.

Single Season Records (Cont.)

ASSISTS

Player and Team	Year	GP	A	Player and Team	Year	GP	A
Mark Wade, UNLV	1987	38	406	Sherman Douglas, Syracuse	1989	38	326
Avery Johnson, Southern-BR	1988	30	399	Sam Crawford, New Mex. St	1993	34	310
Anthony Manuel, Bradley	1988	31	373	Greg Anthony, UNLV	1991	35	310
Avery Johnson, Southern-BR	1987	31	333	Reid Gettys, Houston	1984	37	309
Mark Jackson, St. John's (NY)	1986	32	328	Carl Golston, Loyola (IL)	1985	33	305

ASSIST AVERAGE

Player and Team	Year	GP	A	Avg	Player and Team	Year	GP	A	Avg
Avery Johnson, Southern-BR	1988	30	399	13.3	Chris Corchiani, N Carolina St	1991	31	299	9.6
Anthony Manuel, Bradley	1988	31	373	12.0	Tony Fairley, Charleston So.*	1987	28	270	9.6
Avery Johnson, Southern-BR	1987	31	333	10.7	Tyrone Bogues, Wake Forest	1987	29	276	9.5
Mark Wade, UNLV	1987	38	406	10.7	Ron Weingard, Hofstra	1985	24	228	9.5
Nelson Haggerty, Baylor	1995	28	284	10.1	Craig Neal, Georgia Tech	1988	32	303	9.5
Glenn Williams, Holy Cross	1989	28	278	9.9	*Formerly Baptist.				

FIELD-GOAL PERCENTAGE

Player and Team	Year	GP	FG	FGA	Pct
Steve Johnson, Oregon St	1981	28	235	315	74.6
Dwayne Davis, Florida	1989	33	179	248	72.2
Keith Walker, Utica	1985	27	154	216	71.3
Steve Johnson, Oregon St	1980	30	211	297	71.0
Adam Mark, Belmont	2002	26	150	212	70.8
Oliver Miller, Arkansas	1991	38	254	361	70.4
Alan Williams, Princeton	1987	25	163	232	70.3
Mark McNamara, California	1982	27	231	329	70.2
Warren Kidd, Middle Tennessee St	1991	30	173	247	70.0
Pete Freeman, Akron	1991	28	175	250	70.0

Based on qualifiers for annual championship.

FREE-THROW PERCENTAGE

Player and Team	Year	GP	FT	FTA	Pct
Craig Collins, Penn St	1985	27	94	98	95.9
Rod Foster, UCLA	1982	27	95	100	95.0
Clay McKnight, Pacific	2000	24	74	78	94.9
Danny Basile, Marist	1994	27	84	89	94.4
Carlos Gibson, Marshall	1978	28	84	89	94.4
Jim Barton, Dartmouth	1986	26	65	69	94.2
Gary Buchanan, Villanova	2001	31	97	103	94.2
Jack Moore, Nebraska	1982	27	123	131	93.9
Dandrea Evans, Troy St	1994	27	72	77	93.5
Rob Robbins, New Mexico	1990	34	101	108	93.5

Based on qualifiers for annual championship.

THREE-POINT FIELD-GOAL PERCENTAGE

Player and Team	Year	GP	3FG	3FGA	Pct
Glenn Tropf, Holy Cross	1988	29	52	82	63.4
Sean Wightman, Western Michigan	1992	30	48	76	63.2
Keith Jennings, E Tennessee St	1991	33	84	142	59.2
Dave Calloway, Monmouth (NJ)	1989	28	48	82	58.5
Steve Kerr, Arizona	1988	38	114	199	57.3
Reginald Jones, Prairie View	1987	28	64	112	57.1
Jim Cantamessa, Siena	1998	29	66	117	56.4
Joel Tribelhorn, Colorado St	1989	33	76	135	56.3
Mike Joseph, Bucknell	1988	28	65	116	56.0
Brian Jackson, Evansville	1995	27	53	95	55.8
Amory Sanders, SE Missouri St	2001	24	53	95	55.8

Based on qualifiers for annual championship.

Single Season Records *(Cont.)*

STEALS

Player and Team	Year	GP	S
Desmond Cambridge, Alabama A&M	2002	29	160
Mookie Blaylock, Oklahoma	1988	39	150
Aldwin Ware, Florida A&M	1988	29	142
Darron Brittman, Chicago St	1986	28	139
John Linehan, Providence	2002	31	139

BLOCKED SHOTS

Player and Team	Year	GP	BS
David Robinson, Navy	1986	35	207
Adonal Foyle, Colgate	1997	28	180
Keith Closs, Central Conn St	1996	28	178
Shawn Bradley, BYU	1991	34	177
Wojiech Myrda, LA–Monroe	2002	32	172

STEAL AVERAGE

Player and Team	Year	GP	S	Avg
D. Cambridge, Alabama A&M	2002	29	160	5.52
Darron Brittman, Chicago St	1986	28	139	4.96
Aldwin Ware, Florida A&M	1988	29	142	4.90
John Linehan, Providence	2002	31	139	4.48
Ronn McMahon, E Washington	1990	29	130	4.48

BLOCKED-SHOT AVERAGE

Player and Team	Year	GP	BS	Avg
Adonal Foyle, Colgate	1997	28	180	6.43
Keith Closs, Central Conn St	1996	28	178	6.36
David Robinson, Navy	1986	35	207	5.91
Adonal Foyle, Colgate	1996	29	165	5.69
Wojiech Myrda, LA-Monroe	2002	32	172	5.37

Career Records

POINTS

Player and Team	Ht	Final Year	GP	FG	3FG*	FT	Pts
Pete Maravich, Louisiana St	6-5	1970	83	1387	—	893	3667
Freeman Williams, Portland St	6-4	1978	106	1369	—	511	3249
Lionel Simmons, La Salle	6-7	1990	131	1244	56	673	3217
Alphonso Ford, Mississippi Valley	6-2	1993	109	1121	333	590	3165
Harry Kelly, Texas Southern	6-7	1983	110	1234	—	598	3066
Hersey Hawkins, Bradley	6-3	1988	125	1100	118	690	3008
Oscar Robertson, Cincinnati	6-5	1960	88	1052	—	869	2973
Danny Manning, Kansas	6-10	1988	147	1216	10	509	2951
Alfredrick Hughes, Loyola (IL)	6-5	1985	120	1226	—	462	2914
Elvin Hayes, Houston	6-8	1968	93	1215	—	454	2884
Larry Bird, Indiana St	6-9	1979	94	1154	—	542	2850
Otis Birdsong, Houston	6-4	1977	116	1176	—	480	2832
Kevin Bradshaw, Bethune-Cookman, U.S. Int'l	6-6	1991	111	1027	132	618	2804
Allan Houston, Tennessee	6-6	1993	128	902	346	651	2801
Hank Gathers, Southern Cal, Loyola Marymount	6-7	1990	117	1127	0	469	2723
Reggie Lewis, Northeastern	6-7	1987	122	1043	30 (1)	592	2708
Daren Queenan, Lehigh	6-5	1988	118	1024	29	626	2703
Byron Larkin, Xavier (OH)	6-3	1988	121	1022	51	601	2696
David Robinson, Navy	7-1	1987	127	1032	1	604	2669
Wayman Tisdale, Oklahoma	6-9	1985	104	1077	—	507	2661

*Listed is the number of three-pointers scored since it became the national rule in 1987; the number in the parentheses is number scored prior to 1987—these counted as three points in the game but counted as two-pointers in the national rankings. The three-pointers in the parentheses are not included in total points.

SCORING AVERAGE

Player and Team	Final Year	GP	FG	FT	Pts	Avg
Pete Maravich, Louisiana St	1968	83	1387	893	3667	44.2
Austin Carr, Notre Dame	1971	74	1017	526	2560	34.6
Oscar Robertson, Cincinnati	1960	88	1052	869	2973	33.8
Calvin Murphy, Niagara	1970	77	947	654	2548	33.1
Dwight Lamar, Southwestern Louisiana	1973	57	768	326	1862	32.7
Frank Selvy, Furman	1954	78	922	694	2538	32.5
Rick Mount, Purdue	1970	72	910	503	2323	32.3
Darrell Floyd, Furman	1956	71	868	545	2281	32.1
Nick Werkman, Seton Hall	1964	71	812	649	2273	32.0
Willie Humes, Idaho St	1971	48	565	380	1510	31.5
William Averitt, Pepperdine	1973	49	615	311	1541	31.4
Elgin Baylor, Coll. of Idaho, Seattle	1958	80	956	588	2500	31.3
Elvin Hayes, Houston	1968	93	1215	454	2884	31.0
Freeman Williams, Portland St	1978	106	1369	511	3249	30.7
Larry Bird, Indiana St	1979	94	1154	542	2850	30.3

Career Records (Cont.)

REBOUNDS BEFORE 1973

Player and Team	Final Year	GP	Reb
Tom Gola, La Salle	1955	118	2201
Joe Holup, George Washington	1956	104	2030
Charlie Slack, Marshall	1956	88	1916
Ed Conlin, Fordham	1955	102	1884
Dickie Hemric, Wake Forest	1955	104	1802

REBOUNDS SINCE 1973*

Player and Team	Final Year	GP	Reb
Tim Duncan, Wake Forest	1997	128	1570
Derrick Coleman, Syracuse	1990	143	1537
Malik Rose, Drexel	1996	120	1514
Ralph Sampson, Virginia	1983	132	1511
Pete Padgett, NV-Reno	1976	104	1464

ASSISTS

Player and Team	Final Year	GP	A
Bobby Hurley, Duke	1993	140	1076
Chris Corchiani, N Carolina St	1991	124	1038
Ed Cota, N Carolina	2000	138	1030
Keith Jennings, E Tennessee St	1991	127	983
Sherman Douglas, Syracuse	1989	138	960

FIELD-GOAL PERCENTAGE

Player and Team	Final Year	FG	FGA	Pct
Steve Johnson, Oregon St	1981	828	1222	67.8
Michael Bradley, Kentucky/Villanova	2001	441	651	67.7
Murray Brown, Florida St	1980	566	847	66.8
Lee Campbell, SW Missouri St	1990	411	618	66.5
Warren Kidd, Middle Tennessee St	1993	496	747	66.4

Note: Minimum 400 field goals and 4 FG made per game.

FREE-THROW PERCENTAGE

Player and Team	Final Year	FT	FTA	Pct
Greg Starrick, Kentucky; Southern Illinois	1972	341	375	90.9
Jack Moore, Nebraska	1982	446	495	90.1
Steve Henson, Kansas St	1990	361	401	90.0
Steve Alford, Indiana	1987	535	596	89.8
Bob Lloyd, Rutgers	1967	543	605	89.8

Note: Minimum 300 free throws made.

*Freshmen became eligible for varsity play in 1973.

THEY SAID IT

Rick Pitino, Louisville basketball coach, on forward Joseph N'Sima, who was 11 for 26 from the foul line in January: "I'm a coach who's a big believer in execution. And when I watch him shoot free throws, I want to execute him."

Career Records (Cont.)

THREE-POINT FIELD GOALS MADE

Player and Team	Final Year	GP	3FG
Curtis Staples, Virginia	1998	122	413
Keith Veney, Lamar; Marshall	1997	111	409
Doug Day, Radford	1993	117	401
Ronnie Schmitz, MO–Kansas City	1993	112	378
Mark Alberts, Akron	1993	103	375

THREE-POINT FIELD-GOAL PERCENTAGE

Player and Team	Final Year	3FG	3FGA	Pct
Tony Bennett, WI–Green Bay	1992	290	584	49.7
David Olson, Eastern Illinois	1992	262	562	46.6
Ross Land, Northern Arizona	2000	308	664	46.4
Dan Dickau, Washington/Gonzaga	2002	215	465	46.2
Sean Jackson, Ohio/Princeton	1992	243	528	46.0

Note: Minimum 200 3-point field goals and 2.0 3FG/G.

STEALS

Player and Team	Final Year	GP	S
John Linehan, Providence	2002	122	385
Eric Murdock, Providence	1991	117	376
Pepe Sanchez, Temple	2000	116	365
Cookie Belcher, Nebraska	2001	131	353
Kevin Braswell, Georgetown	2002	128	349

BLOCKED SHOTS

Player and Team	Final Year	GP	BS
Wojciech Myrda, Louisiana-Monroe	2002	115	535
Adonal Foyle, Colgate	1997	87	492
Tim Duncan, Wake Forest	1997	128	481
Alonzo Mourning, Georgetown	1992	120	453
Tarvis Williams, Hampton	2001	114	452

NCAA Men's Division I Team Leaders

Division I Team Alltime Wins

Team	First Year	Yrs	W	L	T
Kentucky	1903	99	1817	568	1
N Carolina	1911	92	1789	650	0
Kansas	1899	104	1771	745	0
Duke	1906	97	1680	768	0
St. John's (NY)	1908	95	1641	750	0
Temple	1895	106	1590	858	0
Syracuse	1901	101	1572	732	0
Pennsylvania	1897	102	1533	870	2
Indiana	1901	102	1519	812	0
UCLA	1920	83	1510	653	0
Notre Dame	1898	97	1505	828	1
Oregon St	1902	101	1504	1052	0
Utah	1909	94	1467	767	0
Princeton	1901	102	1459	885	0
Washington	1896	100	1434	963	0
Purdue	1897	104	1434	838	0

Note: Minimum of 25 years in Division I.

Division I Alltime Winning Percentage

Team	First Year	Yrs	W	L	T	Pct
Kentucky	1903	99	1817	568	1	.762
N Carolina	1911	92	1789	650	0	.733
UNLV	1959	44	904	352	0	.720
Kansas	1899	104	1771	745	0	.704
UCLA	1920	83	1510	653	0	.698
St. John's (NY)	1908	95	1641	750	0	.686
Duke	1906	97	1680	768	0	.686
Syracuse	1901	101	1572	732	0	.682
Western Kentucky	1915	83	1442	714	0	.669
Utah	1909	94	1467	767	0	.657
Arkansas	1924	79	1368	723	0	.654
Indiana	1901	102	1519	812	0	.652
Temple	1895	106	1590	858	0	.650
Louisville	1912	88	1406	771	0	.646
Notre Dame	1898	97	1505	828	1	.645

Note: Minimum of 25 years in Division I.

NCAA Men's Division I Winning Streaks

Longest—Full Season

Team	Games	Years	Ended by
UCLA	88	1971–74	Notre Dame (71–70)
San Francisco	60	1955–57	Illinois (62–33)
UCLA	47	1966–68	Houston (71–69)
UNLV	45	1990–91	Duke (79–77)
Texas	44	1913–17	Rice (24–18)
Seton Hall	43	1939–41	LIU-Brooklyn (49–26)
LIU-Brooklyn	43	1935–37	Stanford (45–31)
UCLA	41	1968–69	Southern Cal (46–44)
Marquette	39	1970–71	Ohio St (60–59)
Cincinnati	37	1962–63	Wichita St (65–64)
N Carolina	37	1957–58	W Virginia (75–64)

Longest—Regular Season

Team	Games	Years	Ended by
UCLA	76	1971–74	Notre Dame (71–70)
Indiana	57	1975–77	Toledo (59–57)
Marquette	56	1970–72	Detroit (70–49)
Kentucky	54	1952–55	Georgia Tech (59–58)
San Francisco	51	1955–57	Illinois (62–33)
Pennsylvania	48	1970–72	Temple (57–52)
Ohio State	47	1960–62	Wisconsin (86–67)
Texas	44	1913–17	Rice (24–18)
UCLA	43	1966–68	Houston (71–69)
LIU-Brooklyn	43	1935–37	Stanford (45–31)
Seton Hall	42	1939–41	LIU-Brooklyn (49–26)

Longest—Home Court

Team	Games	Years
Kentucky	129	1943–55
St. Bonaventure	99	1948–61
UCLA	98	1970–76
Cincinnati	86	1957–64
Marquette	81	1967–73
Arizona	81	1945–51

Team	Games	Years
Lamar	80	1978–84
Long Beach St	75	1968–74
UNLV	72	1974–78
Arizona	71	1987–92
Cincinnati	68	1972–78
Western Kentucky	67	1949–55

NCAA Men's Division I Winningest Coaches

Active Coaches

WINS

Coach and Team	W
James Phelan, Mt. St. Mary's (MD)	819
Bob Knight, Texas Tech	787
Lefty Driesell, Georgia St	782
Lou Henson, New Mexico St	742
Eddie Sutton, Oklahoma St	702
John Chaney, Temple	675
Lute Olson, Arizona	662
Mike Krzyzewski, Duke	637
Jim Calhoun, Connecticut	624
Jim Boeheim, Syracuse	623

Note: Minimum 5 years as a Division I head coach; includes record at 4-year colleges only.

WINNING PERCENTAGE

Coach and Team	Yrs	W	L	Pct
Roy Williams, Kansas	14	388	93	.807
Bob Huggins, Cincinnati	21	500	172	.744
Rick Majerus, Utah	18	382	134	.740
Jim Boeheim, Syracuse	26	623	221	.738
Mike Krzyzewski, Duke	27	637	227	.737
Lute Olson, Arizona	29	662	236	.737
Rick Pitino, Louisville	16	371	137	.730
John Chaney, Temple	30	675	253	.727
Bob Knight, Texas Tech	36	787	298	.725
Tom Izzo, Michigan St	7	167	65	.720

Note: Minimum 5 years as a Division I head coach; includes record at 4-year colleges only.

Alltime Winningest Men's Division I Coaches

	W
Dean Smith (N Carolina)	879
Adolph Rupp (Kentucky)	876
Jim Phelan (Mt. St. Mary's)	819
Bob Knight (Army, Indiana, Texas Tech)	787
Lefty Driesell (Davidson, Maryland, James Madison, Georgia St)	782
Jerry Tarkanian (Long Beach St, UNLV, Fresno St)	778
Hank Iba (NW Missouri St, Colorado, Oklahoma St)	767
Ed Diddle (Western Kentucky)	759
Phog Allen (Baker, Kansas, Haskell, Central Missouri St, Kansas)	746
Lou Henson (Hardin-Simmons, New Mexico St, Illinois)	742
Norm Stewart (Northern Iowa, Missouri)	731
Ray Meyer (DePaul)	724
Don Haskins (UTEP)	719
Eddie Sutton (Creighton, Arkansas, Kentucky, Oklahoma St)	702
Denny Crum (Louisville)	675
John Chaney (Cheyney St, Temple)	675

Note: Minimum 10 head coaching seasons in Division I.

Alltime Winningest Men's Division I Coaches *(Cont.)*
WINNING PERCENTAGE

Coach (Team, Years)	Yrs	W	L	Pct
Clair Bee (Rider 29–31, LIU-Brooklyn 32–45, 46–51)	21	412	87	.826
Adolph Rupp (Kentucky 31–72)	41	876	190	.822
Roy Williams (Kansas 89–)	14	388	93	.807
John Wooden (Indiana St 47–48, UCLA 49–75)	29	664	162	.804
John Kresse (Charleston 80–02)	23	560	143	.797
Jerry Tarkanian (Long Beach St 69–73, UNLV 74–92, Fresno St 95–02)	31	778	202	.794
Dean Smith (N Carolina 62–97)	36	879	254	.776
Harry Fisher (Columbia 07–16, Army 22–23, 25)	13	147	44	.770
Frank Keaney (Rhode Island 21–48)	27	387	117	.768
George Keogan (St. Louis 16, Allegheny 19, Valparaiso 20–21, Notre Dame 24–43)	24	385	117	.767
Jack Ramsay (St. Joseph's [PA] 56–66)	11	231	71	.765
Vic Bubas (Duke 60–69)	10	213	67	.761
Charles (Chick) Davies (Duquesne 25–43, 47–48)	21	314	106	.748
Ray Mears (Wittenberg 57–62, Tennessee 63–77)	21	399	135	.747
Bob Huggins (Walsh 81–83, Akron 85–89, Cincinnati 90–)	21	500	172	.744
Rick Majerus (Marquette 84–86, Ball St 88–89, Utah 90–)	18	382	134	.740
Al McGuire (Belmont Abbey 58–64, Marquette 65–77)	20	405	143	.739
Everett Case (N Carolina St 47–64)	18	376	133	.739
Phog Allen (Baker 06–08, Kansas 08–09, Haskell 09, Cent MO St 13–19, Kansas 20–56)	48	746	264	.739
Jim Boeheim (Syracuse 77–)	26	623	221	.738

Note: Minimum 10 head coaching seasons in Division I.

NCAA Women's Division I Championship Results

Year	Winner	Score	Runner-up	Winning Coach
1982	Louisiana Tech	76–62	Cheyney	Sonja Hogg
1983	Southern Cal	69–67	Louisiana Tech	Linda Sharp
1984	Southern Cal	72–61	Tennessee	Linda Sharp
1985	Old Dominion	70–65	Georgia	Marianne Stanley
1986	Texas	97–81	Southern Cal	Jody Conradt
1987	Tennessee	67–44	Louisiana Tech	Pat Summitt
1988	Louisiana Tech	56–54	Auburn	Leon Barmore
1989	Tennessee	76–60	Auburn	Pat Summitt
1990	Stanford	88–81	Auburn	Tara VanDerveer
1991	Tennessee	70–67 (OT)	Virginia	Pat Summitt
1992	Stanford	78–62	Western Kentucky	Tara VanDerveer
1993	Texas Tech	84–82	Ohio State	Marsha Sharp
1994	N Carolina	60–59	Louisiana Tech	Sylvia Hatchell
1995	Connecticut	70–64	Tennessee	Geno Auriemma
1996	Tennessee	83–65	Georgia	Pat Summitt
1997	Tennessee	68–59	Old Dominion	Pat Summitt
1998	Tennessee	93–75	Louisiana Tech	Pat Summitt
1999	Purdue	62–45	Duke	Carolyn Peck
2000	Connecticut	71–52	Tennessee	Geno Auriemma
2001	Notre Dame	68–66	Purdue	Muffet McGraw
2002	Connecticut	82–70	Oklahoma	Geno Auriemma

NCAA Women's Division I Alltime Individual Leaders

Single-Game Records
SCORING HIGHS

Pts	Player and Team vs Opponent	Year
60	Cindy Brown, Long Beach St vs San Jose St	1987
58	Kim Perrot, SW Louisiana vs SE Louisiana	1990
58	Lorri Bauman, Drake vs SW Missouri St	1984
56	Jackie Stiles, SW Missouri St vs Evansville	2000
55	Patricia Hoskins, Mississippi Valley vs Southern-BR	1989
55	Patricia Hoskins, Mississippi Valley vs Alabama St	1989
54	Anjinea Hopson, Grambling vs Jackson St	1994
54	Mary Lowry, Baylor vs Texas	1994
54	Wanda Ford, Drake vs SW Missouri St	1986

Three tied with 53.

Single-Game Records (Cont.)

REBOUNDS

Reb	Player and Team vs Opponent	Year
40	Deborah Temple, Delta St vs AL-Birmingham	1983
37	Rosina Pearson, Bethune-Cookman vs Florida Memorial	1985
33	Maureen Formico, Pepperdine vs Loyola (CA)	1985
31	Darlene Beale, Howard vs S Carolina St	1987
30	Cindy Bonforte, Wagner vs Queens (NY)	1983
30	Kayone Hankins, New Orleans vs. Nicholls St	1994
30	Wanda Ford, Drake vs Eastern Illinois	1985
29	Gail Norris, Alabama St vs Texas Southern	1992
29	Joy Kellogg, Oklahoma City vs Oklahoma Christian	1984
29	Joy Kellogg, Oklahoma City vs UTEP	1984

ASSISTS

A	Player and Team vs Opponent	Year
23	Michelle Burden, Kent St vs Ball St	1991
22	Shawn Monday, Tennessee Tech vs Morehead St	1988
22	Veronica Pettry, Loyola (IL) vs Detroit	1989
22	Tine Freil, Pacific vs Wichita St	1991
21	Tine Freil, Pacific vs Fresno St	1992
21	Amy Bauer, Wisconsin vs Detroit	1989
21	Neacole Hall, Alabama St vs Southern-BR	1989

Five tied with 20.

Single Season Records

POINTS

Player and Team	Year	GP	FG	3FG	FT	Pts
Jackie Stiles, SW Missouri St	2001	35	365	65	267	1062
Cindy Brown, Long Beach St	1987	35	362	—	250	974
Genia Miller, Cal St-Fullerton	1991	33	376	0	217	969
Sheryl Swoopes, Texas Tech	1993	34	356	32	211	955
Andrea Congreaves, Mercer	1992	28	353	77	142	925
Wanda Ford, Drake	1986	30	390	—	139	919
Chamique Holdsclaw, Tennessee	1998	39	370	9	166	915
Barbara Kennedy, Clemson	1982	31	392	—	124	908
Patricia Hoskins, Mississippi Valley	1989	27	345	13	205	908
LaTaunya Pollard, Long Beach St	1983	31	376	—	155	907

SEASON SCORING AVERAGE

Player and Team	Year	GP	FG	3FG	FT	Pts	Avg
Patricia Hoskins, Mississippi Valley	1989	27	345	13	205	908	33.6
Andrea Congreaves, Mercer	1992	28	353	77	142	925	33.0
Deborah Temple, Delta St	1984	28	373	—	127	873	31.2
Andrea Congreaves, Mercer	1993	26	302	51	150	805	31.0
Wanda Ford, Drake	1986	30	390	—	139	919	30.6
Anucha Browne, Northwestern	1985	28	341	—	173	855	30.5
LeChandra LeDay, Grambling	1988	28	334	36	146	850	30.4
Jackie Stiles, SW Missouri St	2001	35	365	65	267	1062	30.3
Kim Perrot, Southwestern Louisiana	1990	28	308	95	128	839	30.0
Tina Hutchinson, San Diego St	1984	30	383	—	132	898	29.9
Jan Jensen, Drake	1991	30	358	6	166	888	29.6
Genia Miller, Cal St-Fullerton	1991	33	376	0	217	969	29.4
Barbara Kennedy, Clemson	1982	31	392	—	124	908	29.3
LaTaunya Pollard, Long Beach St	1983	31	376	—	155	907	29.3
Lisa McMullen, Alabama St	1991	28	285	126	119	815	29.1

Single Season Records *(Cont.)*

Player and Team	Year	GP	Reb	Player and Team	Year	GP	Reb
Wanda Ford, Drake	1985	30	534	Rosina Pearson, Beth.-Cookman	1985	26	480
Wanda Ford, Drake	1986	30	506	Patricia Hoskins, Miss Valley	1987	28	476
Anne Donovan, Old Dominion	1983	35	504	Cheryl Miller, Southern Cal	1985	30	474
Darlene Jones, Miss Valley	1983	31	487	Darlene Beale, Howard	1987	29	459
Melanie Simpson, Okla. City	1982	37	481	Olivia Bradley, W Virginia	1985	30	458

REBOUND AVERAGE

Player and Team	Year	GP	Reb	Avg
Rosina Pearson, Bethune-Cookman	1985	26	480	18.5
Wanda Ford, Drake	1985	30	534	17.8
Katie Beck, E Tennessee St	1988	25	441	17.6
DeShawne Blocker, E Tennessee St	1994	26	450	17.3
Patricia Hoskins, Mississippi Valley	1987	28	476	17.0
Wanda Ford, Drake	1986	30	506	16.9
Patricia Hoskins, Mississippi Valley	1989	27	440	16.3
Joy Kellogg, Oklahoma City	1984	23	373	16.2
Deborah Mitchell, Mississippi Coll.	1983	28	447	16.0
Cheryl Miller, Southern California	1985	30	474	15.8

FIELD-GOAL PERCENTAGE

Player and Team	Year	GP	FG	FGA	Pct
Myndee Larsen, Southern Utah	1998	28	249	344	72.4
Chantelle Anderson, Vanderbilt	2001	34	292	404	72.3
Deneka Knowles, Southeastern La.	1996	26	199	276	72.1
Barbara Farris, Tulane	1998	27	151	210	71.9
Renay Adams, Tennessee Tech	1991	30	185	258	71.7
Regina Days, Georgia Southern	1986	27	234	332	70.5
Kim Wood, WI-Green Bay	1994	27	188	271	69.4
Kelly Lyons, Old Dominion	1990	31	308	444	69.4
Alisha Hill, Howard	1995	28	194	281	69.0
Ruth Riley, Notre Dame	1999	31	198	290	68.3

Based on qualifiers for annual championship.

FREE-THROW PERCENTAGE

Player and Team	Year	GP	FT	FTA	Pct
Ginny Doyle, Richmond	1992	29	96	101	95.0
Sue Bird, Connecticut	2002	39	98	104	94.2
Paula Corder-King, SE Missouri St	1999	28	111	118	94.1
Linda Cyborski, Delaware	1991	29	74	79	93.7
Kandi Brown, Morehead St	2002	29	74	79	93.7
Paula Corder-King, SE Missouri St	2000	27	69	74	93.2
Jennifer Howard, N Carolina St	1994	27	118	127	92.9
Keely Feeman, Cincinnati	1986	30	76	82	92.7
Amy Slowikowski, Kent St	1989	27	112	121	92.6
Lea Ann Parsley, Marshall	1990	28	96	104	92.3

Based on qualifiers for annual championship.

Career Records

POINTS

Player and Team	Yrs	GP	Pts
Jackie Stiles, SW Missouri St	1997–01	129	3393
Patricia Hoskins, Mississippi Valley	1985–89	110	3122
Lorri Bauman, Drake	1981–84	120	3115
Chamique Holdsclaw, Tennessee	1995–99	148	3025
Cheryl Miller, Southern Cal	1983–86	128	3018
Cindy Blodgett, Maine	1994–98	118	3005
Valorie Whiteside, Appalachian St	1984–88	116	2944
Joyce Walker, Louisiana St	1981–84	117	2906
Sandra Hodge, New Orleans	1981–84	107	2860
Andrea Congreaves, Mercer	1989–93	108	2796

SCORING AVERAGE

Player and Team	Yrs	GP	FG	3FG	FT	Pts	Avg
Patricia Hoskins, Mississippi Valley	1985–89	110	1196	24	706	3122	28.4
Sandra Hodge, New Orleans	1981–84	107	1194	—	472	2860	26.7
Jackie Stiles, SW Missouri St	1997–01	129	1160	221	852	3393	26.3
Lorri Bauman, Drake	1981–84	120	1104	—	907	3115	26.0
Andrea Congreaves, Mercer	1989–93	108	1107	153	429	2796	25.9
Cindy Blodgett, Maine	1994–98	118	1055	219	676	3005	25.5
Valorie Whiteside, Appalachian St	1984–88	116	1153	0	638	2944	25.4
Joyce Walker, Louisiana St	1981–84	117	1259	—	388	2906	24.8
Tarcha Hollis, Grambling	1988–91	85	904	3	247	2058	24.2
Korie Hlede, Duquesne	1994–98	109	1045	162	379	2631	24.1

NCAA Men's Division II Championship Results

Year	Winner	Score	Runner-up	Third Place	Fourth Place
1957	Wheaton (IL)	89–65	Kentucky Wesleyan	Mount St Mary's (MD)	Cal St-Los Angeles
1958	S Dakota	75–53	St. Michael's	Evansville	Wheaton (IL)
1959	Evansville	83–67	SW Missouri St	N Carolina A&T	Cal St-Los Angeles
1960	Evansville	90–69	Chapman	Kentucky Wesleyan	Cornell College
1961	Wittenberg	42–38	SE Missouri St	S Dakota St	Mount St Mary's (MD)
1962	Mount St Mary's (MD)	58–57 (OT)	Cal St-Sacramento	Southern Illinois	Nebraska Wesleyan
1963	S Dakota St	44–42	Wittenberg	Oglethorpe	Southern Illinois
1964	Evansville	72–59	Akron	N Carolina A&T	Northern Iowa
1965	Evansville	85–82 (OT)	Southern Illinois	N Dakota	St Michael's
1966	Kentucky Wesleyan	54–51	Southern Illinois	Akron	N Dakota
1967	Winston-Salem	77–74	SW Missouri St	Kentucky Wesleyan	Illinois St
1968	Kentucky Wesleyan	63–52	Indiana St	Trinity (TX)	Ashland
1969	Kentucky Wesleyan	75–71	SW Missouri St	†Vacated	Ashland
1970	Philadelphia Textile	76–65	Tennessee St	UC-Riverside	Buffalo St
1971	Evansville	97–82	Old Dominion	†Vacated	Kentucky Wesleyan
1972	Roanoke	84–72	Akron	Tennessee St	Eastern Mich
1973	Kentucky Wesleyan	78–76 (OT)	Tennessee St	Assumption	Brockport St
1974	Morgan St	67–52	SW Missouri St	Assumption	New Orleans
1975	Old Dominion	76–74	New Orleans	Assumption	TN-Chattanooga
1976	Puget Sound	83–74	TN-Chattanooga	Eastern Illinois	Old Dominion
1977	TN-Chattanooga	71–62	Randolph-Macon	N Alabama	Sacred Heart
1978	Cheyney	47–40	WI-Green Bay	Eastern Illinois	Central Florida
1979	N Alabama	64–50	WI-Green Bay	Cheyney	Bridgeport
1980	Virginia Union	80–74	New York Tech	Florida Southern	N Alabama
1981	Florida Southern	73–68	Mount St Mary's (MD)	Cal Poly-SLO	WI-Green Bay
1982	District of Columbia	73–63	Florida Southern	Kentucky Wesleyan	Cal St-Bakersfield
1983	Wright St	92–73	District of Columbia	*Cal St-Bakersfield	*Morningside
1984	Central Missouri St	81–77	St. Augustine's	*Kentucky Wesleyan	*N Alabama
1985	Jacksonville St	74–73	S Dakota St	*Kentucky Wesleyan	*Mount St. Mary's (MD)
1986	Sacred Heart	93–87	SE Missouri St	*Cheyney	*Florida Southern
1987	Kentucky Wesleyan	92–74	Gannon	*Delta St	*Eastern Montana
1988	Lowell	75–72	AK-Anchorage	Florida Southern	Troy St
1989	N Carolina Central	73–46	SE Missouri St	UC-Riverside	Jacksonville St
1990	Kentucky Wesleyan	93–79	Cal St-Bakersfield	N Dakota	Morehouse
1991	N Alabama	79–72	Bridgeport (CT)	*Cal St-Bakersfield	*Virginia Union

*Indicates tied for third. †Student-athletes representing American International in 1969 and Southwestern Louisiana in 1971 were declared ineligible subsequent to the tournament. Under NCAA rules, the teams' and ineligible student-athletes' records were deleted, and the teams' places in the final standings were vacated.

Year	Winner	Score	Runner-up	Third Place	Fourth Place
1992	Virginia Union	100–75	Bridgeport (CT)	*Cal St-Bakersfield	*California (PA)
1993	Cal St-Bakersfield	85–72	Troy St (AL)	*New Hampshire Coll	*Wayne St (MI)
1994	Cal St-Bakersfield	92–86	Southern Indiana	*New Hampshire Coll	*Washburn
1995	Southern Indiana	71–63	UC–Riverside	*Norfolk St	*Indiana (PA)
1996	Fort Hays St	70–63	Northern Kentucky	*California (PA)	*Virginia Union
1997	Cal St-Bakersfield	57–56	Northern Kentucky	*Lynn	*Salem-Teikyo
1998	UC-Davis	83–77	Kentucky Wesleyan	*St. Rose	*Virginia Union
1999	Kentucky Wesleyan	75–60	Metropolitan St	*Truman St	*Florida Southern
2000	Metropolitan St	97–79	Kentucky Wesleyan	*Missouri Southern	*Seattle Pacific
2001	Kentucky Wesleyan	72–63	Washburn	*Western Washington	*Tampa
2002	Metropolitan St	80–72	Kentucky Wesleyan	*Shaw	*Indiana (PA)

NCAA Men's Division II Alltime Individual Leaders

SINGLE-GAME SCORING HIGHS

Pts	Player and Team vs Opponent	Date
113	Bevo Francis, Rio Grande vs Hillsdale	1954
84	Bevo Francis, Rio Grande vs Alliance	1954
82	Bevo Francis, Rio Grande vs Bluffton	1954
80	Paul Crissman, Southern Cal Col vs Pacific Christian	1966
77	William English, Winston-Salem vs Fayetteville St	1968

Single Season Records

SCORING AVERAGE

Player and Team	Year	GP	FG	FT	Pts	Avg
Bevo Francis, Rio Grande	1954	27	444	367	1255	46.5
Earl Glass, Mississippi Industrial	1963	19	322	171	815	42.9
Earl Monroe, Winston-Salem	1967	32	509	311	1329	41.5
John Rinka, Kenyon	1970	23	354	234	942	41.0
Willie Shaw, Lane	1964	18	303	121	727	40.4

REBOUND AVERAGE

Player and Team	Year	GP	Reb	Avg
Tom Hart, Middlebury	1956	21	620	29.5
Tom Hart, Middlebury	1955	22	649	29.5
Frank Stronczek, American Int'l	1966	26	717	27.6
R.C. Owens, College of Idaho	1954	25	677	27.1
Maurice Stokes, St Francis (PA)	1954	26	689	26.5

ASSISTS

Player and Team	Year	GP	A
Steve Ray, Bridgeport	1989	32	400
Steve Ray, Bridgeport	1990	33	385
Tony Smith, Pfeiffer	1992	35	349
Jim Ferrer, Bentley	1989	31	309
Rob Paternostro, New Hamp. Coll.	1995	33	309

ASSIST AVERAGE

Player and Team	Year	GP	A	Avg
Steve Ray, Bridgeport	1989	32	400	12.5
Steve Ray, Bridgeport	1990	33	385	11.7
Demetri Beekman, Assumption	1993	23	264	11.5
Ernest Jenkins, NM Highlands	1995	27	291	10.8
Brian Gregory, Oakland	1989	28	300	10.7

FIELD-GOAL PERCENTAGE

Player and Team	Year	Pct
Todd Linder, Tampa	1987	75.2
Maurice Stafford, N Alabama	1984	75.0
Matthew Cornegay, Tuskegee	1982	74.8
Brian Moten, W Georgia	1992	73.4
Ed Phillips, Alabama A&M	1968	73.3

FREE-THROW PERCENTAGE

Player and Team	Year	Pct
Paul Cluxton, Northern Kentucky	1997	100.0
Tomas Rimkus, Pace	1997	95.6
C.J. Cowgill, Chaminade	2001	95.0
Billy Newton, Morgan St	1976	94.4
Kent Andrews, McNeese St	1968	94.4

Career Records

POINTS

Player and Team	Yrs	Pts
Travis Grant, Kentucky St	1969–72	4045
Bob Hopkins, Grambling	1953–56	3759
Tony Smith, Pfeiffer	1989–92	3350
Earnest Lee, Clark Atlanta	1984–87	3298
Joe Miller, Alderson-Broaddus	1954–57	3294

Career Records (Cont.)

CAREER SCORING AVERAGE

Player and Team	Yrs	GP	Pts	Avg
Travis Grant, Kentucky St	1969–72	121	4045	33.4
John Rinka, Kenyon	1967–70	99	3251	32.8
Florindo Vieira, Quinnipiac	1954–57	69	2263	32.8
Willie Shaw, Lane	1961–64	76	2379	31.3
Mike Davis, Virginia Union	1966–69	89	2758	31.0

REBOUND AVERAGE

Player and Team	Yrs	GP	Reb	Avg
Tom Hart, Middlebury	1953, 55–56	63	1738	27.6
Maurice Stokes, St. Francis (PA)	1953–55	72	1812	25.2
Frank Stronczek, American Int'l	1965–67	62	1549	25.0
Bill Thieben, Hofstra	1954–56	76	1837	24.2
Hank Brown, Lowell Tech	1965–67	49	1129	23.0

ASSISTS

Player and Team	Yrs	A
Demetri Beekman, Assumption	1990–93	1044
Adam Kaufman, Edinboro	1998–01	936
Rob Paternostro, New Hamp. Coll.	1992–95	919
Gallagher Driscoll, St. Rose	1989–92	878
Tony Smith, Pfeiffer	1989–92	828

ASSIST AVERAGE

Player and Team	Yrs	GP	A	Avg
Steve Ray, Bridgeport	1989–90	65	785	12.1
Demetri Beekman, Assumption	1990–93	119	1044	8.8
Ernest Jenkins, NM Highlands	1992–95	84	699	8.3
Adam Kaufman, Edinboro	1998–01	116	936	8.1
Mark Benson, Texas A&I	1989–91	86	674	7.8

Note: Minimum 550 Assists.

FIELD-GOAL PERCENTAGE

Player and Team	Yrs	Pct
Todd Linder, Tampa	1984–87	70.8
Tom Schurfranz, Bellarmine	1989–92	70.2
Chad Scott, California (PA)	1991–94	70.0
Ed Phillips, Alabama, A&M	1968–71	68.9
Ulysses Hackett, SC-Spartanburg	1990–92	67.9

Note: Minimum 400 FGM.

FREE-THROW PERCENTAGE

Player and Team	Yrs	Pct
Paul Cluxton, Northern Kentucky	1994–97	93.5
Kent Andrews, McNeese St	1967–69	91.6
Jon Hagen, Mankato St	1963–65	90.0
Dave Reynolds, Davis & Elkins	1986–89	89.3
Michael Shue, Lock Haven	1994–97	88.5

Note: Minimum 250 FTM.

NCAA Men's Division III Championship Results

Year	Winner	Score	Runner-up	Third Place	Fourth Place
1975	LeMoyne-Owen	57–54	Glassboro St	Augustana (IL)	Brockport St
1976	Scranton	60–57	Wittenberg	Augustana (IL)	Plattsburgh St
1977	Wittenberg	79–66	Oneonta St	Scranton	Hamline
1978	North Park	69–57	Widener	Albion	Stony Brook
1979	North Park	66–62	Potsdam St	Franklin & Marshall	Centre
1980	North Park	83–76	Upsala	Wittenberg	Longwood
1981	Potsdam St	67–65 (OT)	Augustana (IL)	Ursinus	Otterbein
1982	Wabash	83–62	Potsdam St	Brooklyn	Cal St-Stanislaus
1983	Scranton	64–63	Wittenberg	Roanoke	WI–Whitewater
1984	WI–Whitewater	103–86	Clark (MA)	DePauw	Upsala
1985	North Park	72–71	Potsdam St	Nebraska Wesleyan	Widener
1986	Potsdam St	76–73	LeMoyne-Owen	Nebraska Wesleyan	Jersey City St
1987	North Park	106–100	Clark (MA)	Wittenberg	Stockton St
1988	Ohio Wesleyan	92–70	Scranton	Nebraska Wesleyan	Hartwick
1989	WI–Whitewater	94–86	Trenton St	Southern Maine	Centre
1990	Rochester	43–42	DePauw	Washington (MD)	Calvin
1991	WI–Platteville	81–74	Franklin & Marshall	Otterbein	Ramapo (NJ)
1992	Calvin	62–49	Rochester	WI–Platteville	Jersey City St
1993	Ohio Northern	71–68	Augustana	Mass–Dartmouth	Rowan
1994	Lebanon Valley Coll	66–59 (OT)	New York University	Wittenberg	St Thomas (MN)
1995	WI–Platteville	69–55	Manchester	Rowan	Trinity (CT)
1996	Rowan	100–93	Hope (MI)	Illinois Wesleyan	Franklin & Marshall
1997	Illinois Wesleyan	89–86	Nebraska Wesleyan	Williams	Alvernia
1998	WI–Platteville	69–56	Hope (MI)	Williams	Wilkes
1999	WI–Platteville	76–75 (2 OT)	Hampden-Sydney	William Paterson	Connecticut Coll.
2000	Calvin	79–74	WI–Eau Claire	Salem St	Franklin & Marshall
2001	Catholic	76–62	William Paterson	*Illinois Wesleyan	*Ohio Northern
2002	Otterbein	102–83	Elizabethtown	Carthage	Rochester

SINGLE-GAME SCORING HIGHS

Pts	Player and Team vs Opponent	Year
77	Jeff Clement, Grinnell vs Illinois College	1998
69	Steve Diekmann, Grinnell vs Simpson	1995
63	Joe DeRoche, Thomas vs St. Joseph's (ME)	1988
62	Shannon Lilly, Bishop vs Southwest Assembly of God	1983
61	Steve Honderd, Calvin vs Kalamazoo	1993
61	Dana Wilson, Husson vs Ricker	1974
61	Joshua Metzger, Wisconsin Lutheran vs Grinnell	2000

Single Season Records

SCORING AVERAGE

Player and Team	Year	GP	FG	FT	Pts	Avg
Steve Diekmann, Grinnell	1995	20	223	162	745	37.3
Rickey Sutton, Lyndon St	1976	14	207	93	507	36.2
Shannon Lilly, Bishop	1983	26	345	218	908	34.9
Dana Wilson, Husson	1974	20	288	122	698	34.9
Rickey Sutton, Lyndon St	1977	16	223	112	558	34.9

REBOUND AVERAGE

Player and Team	Year	GP	Reb	Avg
Joe Manley, Bowie St	1976	29	579	20.0
Fred Petty, New Hampshire College	1974	22	436	19.8
Larry Williams, Pratt	1977	24	457	19.0
Charles Greer, Thomas	1977	17	318	18.7
Larry Parker, Plattsburgh St	1975	23	430	18.7

ASSISTS

Player and Team	Year	GP	A
Robert James, Kean	1989	29	391
Tennyson Whitted, Ramapo	2002	29	319
Ricky Spicer, WI-Whitewater	1989	31	295
Joe Marcotte, New Jersey Tech	1995	30	292
Andre Bolton, Chris. Newport	1996	30	289

ASSIST AVERAGE

Player and Team	Year	GP	A	Avg
Robert James, Kean	1989	29	391	13.5
Albert Kirchner, Mt. St. Vincent	1990	24	267	11.1
Tennyson Whitted, Ramapo	2002	29	319	11.0
Ron Torgalski, Hamilton	1989	26	275	10.6
Louis Adams, Rust	1989	22	227	10.3

FIELD-GOAL PERCENTAGE

Player and Team	Year	Pct
Travis Weiss, St. John's (MN)	1994	76.6
Pete Metzelaars, Wabash	1982	75.3
Tony Rychlec, Mass. Maritime	1981	74.9
Tony Rychlec, Mass. Maritime	1982	73.1
Russ Newnan, Menlo	1991	73.0

FREE-THROW PERCENTAGE

Player and Team	Year	Pct
Korey Coon, IL Wesleyan	2000	96.3
Chanse Young, Manchester	1998	95.6
Andy Enfield, Johns Hopkins	1991	95.3
Chris Carideo, Widener	1992	95.2
Yudi Teichman, Yeshiva	1989	95.2

Career Records

POINTS

Player and Team	Yrs	Pts
Andre Foreman, Salisbury St	1989–92	2940
Lamont Strothers, Chris. Newport	1988–91	2709
Matt Hancock, Colby	1987–90	2678
Scott Fitch, Geneseo St	1990–94	2634
Greg Grant, Trenton St	1987–89	2611

CAREER SCORING AVERAGE

Player and Team	Yrs	GP	Avg
Dwain Govan, Bishop	1974–75	55	32.8
Dave Russell, Shepherd	1974–75	60	30.6
Rickey Sutton, Lyndon St	1976–79	80	29.7
John Atkins, Knoxville	1976–78	70	28.7
Steve Petnik, Windham	1974–77	76	27.6

REBOUND AVERAGE

Player and Team	Yrs	GP	Reb	Avg
Larry Parker, Plattsburgh St	1975–78	85	1482	17.4
Charles Greer, Thomas	1975–77	58	926	16.0
Willie Parr, LeMoyne-Owen	1974–76	76	1182	15.6
Michael Smith, Hamilton	1989–92	107	1632	15.2
Dave Kufeld, Yeshiva	1977–80	81	1222	15.1

ASSIST AVERAGE

Player and Team	Yrs	Avg
Phil Dixon, Shenandoah	1993–96	8.6
Steve Artis, Chris. Newport	1990–93	8.1
David Genovese, Mt. St. Vincent	1992–95	7.5
Kevin Root, Eureka	1989–91	7.1
Dennis Jacobi, Bowdoin	1989–92	7.1

The Stanley Cup champion Detroit Red Wings

Hockey

Scott Free

Detroit coach Scotty Bowman said goodbye to the pressures of coaching in the NHL, but not before he won a ninth Stanley Cup

BY B.J. SCHECTER

SCOTTY BOWMAN had a secret. Several months before the start of the playoffs, the 68-year-old coach of the Detroit Red Wings had decided that, after 30 years as an NHL head coach, he was going to retire at the end of the season. But he hardly told anyone—not his players, not his loyal assistants, not even Detroit general manager Ken Holland, who had assembled a glittering collection of talent to play for Bowman. No one could blame Bowman for wanting to step aside after all those years and all of his accomplishments, but he didn't tell anyone associated with the team about his plans because he didn't want to ratchet up the already considerable pressure on his team.

From the moment the playoffs started, Detroit was expected to win back the Cup, which would be their third title in six years. After all, the Red Wings had the second-highest payroll in the NHL, one of the most talented and experienced teams, one of the league's elite goalies and the best group of scorers. Watching his team drop the first two games to Vancouver in the first round, get

pushed to the limit in a seven-game series with the defending champion Avalanche in the conference finals, and lose the opener of the finals in overtime must have been torture for Bowman, especially considering his plans for after the season.

As it happened, Bowman began his permanent off-season in style. The title was his ninth, an NHL record that breaks the mark held by Bowman's mentor, Toe Blake, who, like Bowman, went out on top. On the morning of Game 5, hours before his Red Wings closed out their series with the upstart Carolina Hurricanes, Bowman confided in his longtime friend, Canadian broadcaster Harry Neale, that he was done. "So what now?" Neale said. "Consultant," said Bowman without missing a beat. "Now I can go to the games and I don't have to win them."

With the off-season acquisitions Detroit made, Bowman had no such luxury in 2001–02. The team from the Motor City was retooled and souped up for one purpose, to win a championship. The Red Wings

acquired goalie Dominik Hasek and forwards Brett Hull and Luc Robitaille to complement veterans Brendan Shanahan, Chris Chelios, Sergei Fedorov, Igor Larionov, Nicklas Lidstrom and Steve Yzerman. With Hasek backstopping an SUV-tough defense and Hull and Robitaille adding fuel injection to the offense, the Wings didn't disappoint, jumping out to a 22-3-1-1 start. They finished the regular season with a whopping 116 points, 15 points more than the team with the second-best record (Boston). Bowman knew he was coaching a special team, and as a season that was both gratifying and trying neared its end, he started telling people about his retirement plans.

As the final seconds ticked away in Detroit's Cup-clinching 3–1 victory over pesky Carolina, Bowman let the news leak. It spread down the Red Wings' bench like a gasoline fire. When the final whistle blew, Bowman put on his skates and made his way

Conn Smythe winner Lidstrom (above left) took only one penalty in 23 playoff games.

to center ice, where Yzerman handed him the Cup. Bowman spun around the rink, showing off the fabled trophy to the screaming fans at Joe Louis Arena as confetti rained down. After his victory lap, Bowman skated over to Holland at center ice. The two men embraced, and Bowman told his boss that his career was over.

For the second year in a row, an NHL legend was able to cap his career with a Stanley Cup; Ray Bourque did it the previous year with Colorado. But Bowman's happy ending was nearly ruined by the Canucks in the first round. Vancouver put a mighty scare into the Red Wings with victories in the first two games of their series. Before the playoffs began, one national magazine, somewhat hyperbolically, had dubbed the Red Wings the best team ever, and early in their opening-round series it was

Francis (10) scored the winner in Game 1, beating Hasek in the first minute of OT.

clear the Red Wings had spent too much time reading their press clippings.

But to the keen hockey observer, Vancouver's two victories weren't all that surprising. Detroit had stumbled down the stretch, going winless in its final seven regular-season games, while the Canucks had been the hottest team in the second half of the season, having gone an NHL-best 28-9-3-3 since Christmas. Regardless of the teams' recent form, an 0–2 hole was not something the fans in Hockeytown, USA, were willing to stand for, and as the Red Wings skated off the ice following their lethargic 5–2 loss in Game 2, they were booed loudly. Hasek had played like a shadow of himself, and all signs pointed to an early vacation for him and his teammates. But Yzerman, the Detroit captain, refused to panic. "Before the series is over, you're going to say [Hasek] played fantastic," he said following Game 2. "I'm not concerned about our goaltending. He's fantastic, and will prove it."

Detroit fans know that Yzerman makes a habit of being right, and this instance was no exception: The Red Wings quickly righted the ship and took four straight from Vancouver to win the series. And Hasek was indeed fantastic in those four victories. The dominant team of the regular season had returned to form, and it had little trouble with St. Louis in the next round, dispatching the Blues in five games.

That set up an epic Western Conference finals series against the Avalanche. What has lately developed into the greatest rivalry in hockey added another chapter to its legend. The series was a knock-down, drag-out affair that stretched for 14 days and spotlighted the very best the game has to offer. It pitted the two best goalies in the world against each other, and featured no fewer than 13 future Hall of Famers. There was also the matter of a deep-seated animosity between the two franchises.

And it could hardly have been any closer. Three of the seven games went into overtime and four were decided by one goal. In 321 minutes played in the first five games, there were only three minutes in which a team led by two goals or more. "It's been good hockey," Yzerman said midway through the series. "It's easy to get ready to play when everybody is playing at this high level. I can't recall a series being this close."

Before his players took the ice for Game 7, Bowman told them to savor the experience. "No matter what happens," he said, "it will be memorable." The Red Wings made sure they could both savor the experience and look back on the memory with fondness for the rest of their lives, as they scored on four of their first eight shots and rolled to a surprisingly easy 7–0 victory. Just like that, all the tension rushed out of the series like air from a balloon. The Wings would advance to the Stanley Cup Finals.

Their opponents in the Finals were the surprise team of the playoffs, the Carolina Hurricanes. While Detroit was trading punches with Colorado, the Hurricanes, née the Hartford Whalers, were carving out an impressive story of their own. Relocated to Raleigh, N.C., in 1997, the Hurricanes had to be persistent to build a fan base in the heart of ACC basketball and NASCAR country, but they eventually succeeded. They won the NHL's Southeast division after their second season in Raleigh and made the playoffs again in 2001. Early this season, though, Carolina gave no indication that it could contend for a championship. In December, the Hurricanes were reeling, and the team lost four straight games by a combined score of 19–7. As Carolina prepared to meet the Florida Panthers on Dec. 8, the word was that coach Paul Maurice's job was in jeopardy. But the Hurricanes won that day and, with three victories in their next four games, saved Maurice's job.

Using its combination of seasoned veterans and budding young stars, Carolina hit its stride and cruised to another division title, then dispatched the defending Eastern Conference champions, the Devils, in six games in the first round of the playoffs. The Hurricanes won six of nine road games and six of seven overtime games in the playoffs, steaming through Montreal and Toronto without ever being forced to a Game 7. "This is not just a team that's going to be good for a short stand," said center Rod Brind'Amour, one of Carolina's elder statesmen. "We've got a chance to always be good."

But they weren't given much of a chance to beat the mighty Red Wings in the Finals. Not that the Hurricanes were intimidated by Detroit and its spoils from the free-agency market, far from it: Carolina took the opening game of the series, 3–2 in overtime on a goal by 39-year-old center Ron Francis. Some fans started to think, Hey, maybe Carolina— but the Red Wings and their superior talent quickly snuffed out such thoughts. Detroit bounced back to take the second game 3–1, and after they won Game 3, the third-longest game in Stanley Cup history, a 3–2 triple-overtime thriller, the Red Wings went on to win the series in five games.

There was great joy in Hockeytown, but for some it was bittersweet, as Bowman, and then a few days later Hasek, announced their retirements. But the Red Wings—call them the New York Yankees of Hockey—immediately locked up former Toronto goalie Curtis Joseph, the top free agent netminder on the market.

A few other teams tried to emulate the Red Wings' free-spending style, but with considerably less success. The Stars, Flyers and Rangers all spent big in the off-season and all three failed miserably. The Stars and Rangers didn't even make the playoffs. But for all of those teams' failures, no single off-season pickup was a bigger flop than the Washington Capitals' acquisition of flashy winger Jaromir Jagr, late of the Pittsburgh Penguins. For their $88 million (over eight years), the Capitals got 31 goals and 48 assists from Jagr—a good year for most players, but substandard for the great Jagr. He never seemed to get in sync with his new teammates, and the Capitals missed the playoffs, going 36-33-11-2.

There were two impressive comebacks in 2001–02. One involved Montreal captain Saku Koivu, who prepared for the season

Iginla (12) starred for both Calgary and Canada.

though, he was simply the best player in the league. In 20 games, he led all players with 27 playoff points (9 goals, 18 assists) prompting many scribes to consider voting for him as playoff MVP even through the Avalanche didn't make it to the Finals. "It's really amazing what he was able to do," said Avalanche captain Joe Sakic. "What else is there to say, he's a world class player."

Another world-class player emerged in Calgary in the person of 24-year-old forward Jarome Iginla. Iginla led the NHL in scoring with 52 goals and carried himself with poise and class as the NHL's first black star forward (with apologies to Tony McKegney), a role that Iginla openly embraced. At 6' 1" and 200 pounds, Iginla has size, speed, a solid shot and a savvy all-around game. "I'm trying to train more like a track athlete," he said. "Forty-meter sprints on a track, powerlifting instead of strength lifting. My strength coach is an ex-decathlete." Iginla was a key contributor to the Canadian Olympic team that defeated the U.S. 5–2 for the gold medal in Salt Lake City. Flames fans—and NHL fans—could count on him to be a star for years to come.

much like he had in many other years, by lifting weights, skating regularly and trying to improve his conditioning. But a few days before training camp, Koivu was diagnosed with abdominal cancer. He went through eight cycles of chemotherapy in five months and, astoundingly, returned to the ice for the final three regular-season games.

Koivu contributed to the eighth-seeded Canadiens' upset of the top-seeded Bruins in the first round of the playoffs. "It's been an overwhelming year," he said. "In the beginning, when I heard the word cancer, I didn't know what to expect. For the first time, hockey didn't play a role in my life. As I got better, I started to miss hockey again ... to dream about it."

The other comeback story concerned Avalanche star Peter Forsberg, who fought a series of injuries, including a ruptured spleen and numerous ankle problems that required surgeries. He missed the entire regular season. When he returned for the playoffs,

Joining Iginla on the youth brigade were Atlanta Thrashers rookies Dany Heatley (26 goals, 41 assists) and Ilya Kovalchuk (29 goals, 22 assists), two wingers who were by far the top two rookies in the league. But for now, the Iginlas and the Kovalchuks of the league would have to wait. It was the veteran Red Wings' year, and with more money to spend, a stockpile of talent and a tradition of success, there could be more championships in store for Hockeytown.

NHL Final Standings

Eastern Conference

NORTHEAST DIVISION

	GP	W	L	T	RT	GF	GA	Pts
Boston	82	43	24	6	9	236	201	101
Toronto	82	43	25	10	4	249	207	100
Ottawa	82	39	27	9	7	243	208	94
Montreal	82	36	31	12	3	207	209	87
Buffalo	82	35	35	11	1	213	200	82

ATLANTIC DIVISION

	GP	W	L	T	RT	GF	GA	Pts
Philadelphia	82	42	27	10	3	234	192	97
NY Islanders	82	42	28	8	4	239	220	96
New Jersey	82	41	28	9	4	205	187	95
NY Rangers	82	36	38	4	4	227	258	80
Pittsburgh	82	28	41	8	5	198	249	69

SOUTHEAST DIVISION

	GP	W	L	T	RT	GF	GA	Pts
Carolina	82	35	26	16	5	217	217	91
Washington	82	36	33	11	2	228	240	85
Tampa Bay	82	27	40	11	4	178	219	69
Florida	82	22	44	10	6	180	250	60
Atlanta	82	19	47	11	5	187	288	54

Western Conference

CENTRAL DIVISION

	GP	W	L	T	RT	GF	GA	Pts
Detroit	82	51	17	10	4	251	187	116
St. Louis	82	43	27	8	4	227	188	98
Chicago	82	41	27	13	1	216	207	96
Nashville	82	28	41	13	0	196	230	69
Columbus	82	22	47	8	5	164	255	57

PACIFIC DIVISION

	GP	W	L	T	RT	GF	GA	Pts
San Jose	82	44	27	8	3	248	199	99
Los Angeles	82	40	27	11	4	214	190	95
Phoenix	82	40	27	9	6	228	210	95
Dallas	82	36	28	13	5	215	213	90
Anaheim	82	29	42	8	3	175	198	69

NORTHWEST DIVISION

	GP	W	L	T	RT	GF	GA	Pts
Colorado	82	45	28	8	1	212	169	99
Vancouver	82	42	30	7	3	254	211	94
Edmonton	82	38	28	12	4	205	182	92
Calgary	82	32	35	12	3	201	220	79
Minnesota	82	26	35	12	9	195	238	73

RT=regulation ties—games lost in overtime; worth 1 pt.

2002 Stanley Cup Playoffs

EASTERN CONFERENCE

QUARTERFINALS SEMIFINALS CONFERENCE FINAL

WESTERN CONFERENCE

CONFERENCE FINAL SEMIFINALS QUARTERFINALS

STANLEY CUP

Eastern Conference bracket:
- Boston
- Montreal
- Montreal (4-2)
- Carolina (4-2)
- Carolina
- New Jersey
- Carolina (4-2)
- Carolina (4-2)
- Philadelphia
- Ottawa
- Ottawa (4-1)
- Toronto (4-3)
- Toronto
- NY Islanders
- Toronto (4-3)

Detroit (4-1)

Western Conference bracket:
- Detroit (4-2)
- Detroit
- Vancouver
- Detroit (4-1)
- St. Louis (4-1)
- St. Louis
- Chicago
- Detroit (4-3)
- Colorado (4-3)
- Colorado
- Los Angeles
- Colorado (4-3)
- San Jose (4-1)
- San Jose
- Phoenix

Stanley Cup Playoff Results

Conference Quarterfinals

EASTERN CONFERENCE

April 18	Montreal 5	at Boston 2	April 27	Montreal 2 at Boston 1
April 21	Montreal 4	at Boston 6	April 29	Boston 1 at Montreal 2
April 23	Boston 3	at Montreal 5		Montreal won series 4-2.
April 25	Boston 5	at Montreal 2		

Conference Quarterfinals *(Cont.)*

EASTERN CONFERENCE *(Cont.)*

April 17	Ottawa	0	at Philadelphia	1*	April 18	NY Islanders	1	at Toronto	3
April 20	Ottawa	3	at Philadelphia	0	April 20	NY Islanders	0	at Toronto	2
April 22	Philadelphia	0	at Ottawa	3	April 23	Toronto	1	at NY Islanders	6
April 24	Philadelphia	0	at Ottawa	3	April 24	Toronto	3	at NY Islanders	4
April 26	Ottawa	2	at Philadelphia	1*	April 26	NY Islanders	3	at Toronto	6

Ottawa won series 4–1.

April 28 ....Toronto 3 at NY Islanders 5
April 30 ....NY Islanders 2 at Toronto 4

Toronto won series 4–3.

April 17	New Jersey	1	at Carolina	2
April 19	New Jersey	1	at Carolina	2*
April 21	Carolina	0	at New Jersey	4
April 23	Carolina	1	at New Jersey	3

April 24.........New Jersey 2 at Carolina 3*
April 27.........Carolina 1 at New Jersey 0

Carolina won series 4–2.

WESTERN CONFERENCE

April 17 ....Vancouver 4 at Detroit 3*
April 19 ....Vancouver 5 at Detroit 2
April 21.......Detroit 3 at Vancouver 1
April 23.......Detroit 4 at Vancouver 2
April 25.......Vancouver 0 at Detroit 4
April 27.......Detroit 6 at Vancouver 4

Detroit won series 4–2.

April 18 ....Los Angeles 3 at Colorado 4
April 20 ....Los Angeles 3 at Colorado 5
April 22 ....Colorado 1 at Los Angeles 3
April 23 ....Colorado 1 at Los Angeles 4
April 25 ....Los Angeles 1 at Colorado 0*
April 27 ....Colorado 1 at Los Angeles 3
April 29 ....Los Angeles 0 at Colorado 4

Colorado won series 4–3.

April 17 ....Phoenix 1 at San Jose 2
April 20 ....Phoenix 3 at San Jose 1
April 22 ....San Jose 4 at Phoenix 1
April 24 ....San Jose 2 at Phoenix 1
April 26 ....Phoenix 1 at San Jose 4

San Jose won series 4–1.

April 18 ....Chicago 2 at St. Louis 1
April 20 ....Chicago 0 at St. Louis 2
April 22 ....St. Louis 4 at Chicago 0
April 23 ....St. Louis 1 at Chicago 0
April 25 ....Chicago 3 at St. Louis 5

St. Louis won series 4–1.

Conference Semifinals

EASTERN CONFERENCE

May 3 ....Montreal 0 at Carolina 2
May 5 ....Montreal 4 at Carolina 1
May 7 ....Carolina 1 at Montreal 2*
May 9 ....Carolina 4 at Montreal 3*
May 12 ....Montreal 1 at Carolina 5
May 13 ....Carolina 8 at Montreal 2

Carolina won series 4–2.

May 2 ....Ottawa 5 at Toronto 0
May 4 ....Ottawa 2 at Toronto 3†
May 6 ....Toronto 2 at Ottawa 3
May 8 ....Toronto 2 at Ottawa 1
May 10 ....Ottawa 4 at Toronto 2
May 12 ....Toronto 4 at Ottawa 3
May 14 ....Ottawa 0 at Toronto 3

Toronto won series 4–3.

WESTERN CONFERENCE

May 2 ....St. Louis 0 at Detroit 2
May 4 ....St. Louis 2 at Detroit 3.
May 7 ....Detroit 1 at St. Louis 6
May 9 ....Detroit 4 at St. Louis 3
May 11 ....St. Louis 0 at Detroit 4

Detroit won series 4–1.

May 1 ....San Jose 6 at Colorado 3
May 4 ....San Jose 2 at Colorado 8
May 6 ....Colorado 4 at San Jose 6
May 8 ....Colorado 4 at San Jose 1
May 11 ....San Jose 5 at Colorado 3
May 13 ....Colorado 2 at San Jose 1*
May 15 ....San Jose 0 at Colorado 1

Colorado won series 4–3.

Eastern Finals

May 16 ....Toronto 2 at Carolina 1
May 19 ....Toronto 1 at Carolina 2*
May 21 ....Carolina 2 at Toronto 1*
May 23 ....Carolina 3 at Toronto 0
May 25 ....Toronto 1 at Carolina 0
May 28 ....Carolina 2 at Toronto 1*

Carolina won series 4–2.

Western Finals

May 18 ....Colorado 3 at Detroit 5
May 20 ....Colorado 4 at Detroit 3*
May 22 ....Detroit 2 at Colorado 1*
May 25 ....Detroit 2 at Colorado 3
May 27 ....Colorado 2 at Detroit 1*
May 29 ....Detroit 2 at Colorado 0
May 31 ....Colorado 0 at Detroit 7

Detroit won series 4–3.

Stanley Cup Finals

June 4 ....Carolina 3 at Detroit 2*
June 6 ....Carolina 1 at Detroit 3
June 8 ....Detroit 3 at Carolina 2†

June 10 ....Detroit 3 at Carolina 0
June 13 ....Carolina 1 at Detroit 3

Detroit won series 4–1.

*Overtime game. †Triple overtime game.

Game 1

Carolina	0	2	0	1	—3
Detroit	1	1	0	0	—2

FIRST PERIOD
Scoring: 1,Detroit, Fedorov 5 (pp) (Yzerman), 15:21. Penalties: Hedican, Car (high sticking) 8:03; Robitaille, Det (tripping), 10:28; Hill, Car (tripping) 11:15; Wesley, Car (interference), 15:03.

SECOND PERIOD
Scoring: 2, Carolina, Hill 4 (pp) (Kapanen, Francis), 3:30. 3, Detroit, Maltby 2 (McCarty), 10:39. 4, Carolina, O'Neill 6 (Ward) 19:10. Penalties: bench, Car (too many men; served by Cole), 0:34; Larionov, Det (high sticking), 2:07; Draper, Det (hooking), 2:44. Svoboda, Car (high sticking), 4:28. Wallin, Car (roughing), 7:41; Dandenault, Det (tripping), 12:12.

THIRD PERIOD
Scoring: None. Penalties: Devereaux, Det (holding stick), 5:49; Larionov, Det (high sticking), 12:17; Cole, Car (hooking), 18:19.

OVERTIME
Scoring: 5, Carolina, Francis 6 (O'Neill, Kapanen), 0:58.

Shots on goal: Carolina—7-13-5-1—26. Detroit—8-12-5-0—25. Power-play opportunities: Car 1 of 6, Det 1 of 7. Goalies: Car, Irbe (25 shots, 23 saves); Det, Hasek (26 shots, 23 saves). A: 20,058.

Referees: McCreary, Walkom. Linesmen: Lazarowich, Murphy.

Game 2

Carolina	1	0	0	—1
Detroit	1	0	2	—3

FIRST PERIOD
Scoring: 1, Detroit, Maltby 3 (sh) (Draper), 6:33. 2, Carolina, Brind'Amour 4, (sh) (unassisted), 14:47. 3. Penalties: Draper, Det (boarding), 1:25; Duchesne, Det (holding), 5:21; Hill, Car (slashing), 6:33; Svoboda, Car (roughing), 14:03; Hill, Car (holding), 16:23.

SECOND PERIOD
Scoring: None. Penalties: Battaglia, Car (holding), 1:05; Duchesne, Det (tripping), 3:55; bench, Det (too many men; served by Devereaux), 7:23; Gelinas, Car (interference), 10:10; Ward, Car (holding), 18:03.

THIRD PERIOD
Scoring: 3, Detroit, Lidstrom 5 (pp) (Fedorov, Yzerman), 14:52. 4, Detroit, Draper 2 (Lidstrom, Olausson), 15:05. Penalties: Fischer, Det (high sticking), 9:38; Gelinas, Car (slashing), 14:00; Fisher, Det (slashing), 17:15; Battaglia, Car (charging), 17:45; Brind'Amour, Car (roughing), 19:33; Cole, Car (roughing), 19:33; McCarty, Det (roughing), 19:33; Chelios, Det (roughing), 19:33; Maltby, Det (roughing), 19:33; Hull, Det (tripping), 19:41.

Shots on goal: Car—7-4-6—17. Det—9-8-13—30. Power-play opportunities: Car 0-of-8; Det 1-of-8. Goalies: Car, Irbe (30 shots, 27 saves); Det, Hasek (17 shots, 16 saves). A: 20,058.

Referees: Koharski, Devorski. Linesmen: Lazarowich, Morin.

Game 3

Detroit	0	1	1	0	0	1	—3
Carolina	1	0	1	0	0	0	—2

FIRST PERIOD
Scoring:1, Carolina, Vasicek 3 (Gelinas, Wesley), 14:49. Penalties: Brind'Amour, Car (holding stick), 1:45; Hedican, Car (boarding), 3:32; O'Neill, Car (boarding), 11:34; Lidstrom Det (tripping), 12:30; Devereaux, Det (slashing), 19:15.

SECOND PERIOD
Scoring: 2, Detroit, Larionov 3 (Hull), 5:33. Penalties: Maltby, Det (unsportsmanlike. conduct.), 5:13; Ward (unsportsmanlike conduct), 5:13; Chelios, Det (int.), 8:12; Fedorov, Det (holding), 19:44; Hill, Car (holding), 19:44.

THIRD PERIOD
Scoring: 3, Carolina, O'Neill 7 (Francis), 7:34. 4, Detroit, Hull 9 (Lidstrom, Fedorov), 18:46. Penalties: Shanahan, Det (roughing), 5:25; Vasicek, Car (roughing), 5:25; Duchesne, Det (holding), 9:58; Shanahan, Det (roughing), 19:01; Hill, Car (roughing), 19:01.

FIRST OVERTIME
Scoring: None. Penalties: Duchesne, Det (roughing), 18:23; Svoboda, Car (roughing), 18:23.

SECOND OVERTIME
Scoring: None. Penalties: Cole, Car (holding stick), 8:35; Olausson, Det (holding), 13:25.

THIRD OVERTIME
Scoring: 5, Detroit, Larionov 4 (Holmstrom, Duchesne), 14:47. Penalties: None.

Shots on goal: Det—6-7-16-11-6-7—53. Car—8-6-7-5-8-9—43. Power-play opportunities: Det 0-of-4; Car 0-of-5. Goalies: Det, Hasek (43 shots, 41 saves); Car, Irbe (53 shots, 50 saves). A: 18,982.

Referees: McCreary, Walkom. Linesmen: Murphy, Schachte.

Game 4

Detroit	0	1	2—3
Carolina	0	0	0—0

FIRST PERIOD

Scoring: None. Penalties: Wesley, Car (hooking), 2:05; Cole, Car (goalie interference), 16:54; Fedorov, Det (high sticking), 16:54.

SECOND PERIOD

Scoring: 1, Detroit, Hull 10 (Devereaux, Olausson), 6:32. Penalties: Robitaille, Det (high sticking), 9:06; Duchesne, Det (holding stick), 14:34.

THIRD PERIOD

Scoring: 2, Detroit, Larionov 5 (Fischer, Robitaille), 3:43. 3, Detroit, Shanahan 6 (Fedorov, Chelios), 14:43. Penalties: Hill, Car (boarding), 8:34.

Shots on goal: Det—10-6-11—27. Car—6-7-4—17. Power-play opportunities: Det 0-of-2; Car 0-of-2. Goalies: Det, Hasek (17 shots, 17 saves); Car, Irbe (27 shots, 24 saves). A: 18,986.

Referees: Koharski, Devorski. Linesmen: Schachte, Morin.

Game 5

Carolina	0	1	0—1
Detroit	0	2	1—3

FIRST PERIOD

Scoring: None. Penalties: bench, Car (too many men; served by Vasicek), 12:09.

SECOND PERIOD

Scoring: 1, Detroit, Holmstrom 8 (Larionov, Chelios), 4:07. 2, Detroit, Shanahan 7 (pp) (Fedorov, Yzerman), 14:04. 3, Carolina, O'Neill (pp) (Hill, Wesley), 18:50. Penalties: Slegr, Det (holding), 6:00; Svobodo, Car (roughing), 13:34; Cole, Car (roughing), 16:15; Chelios Det (hooking), 16:53.

THIRD PERIOD

Scoring: 4, Detroit, Shanahan 8 (empty net) (Yzerman), 19:15. Penalties: Fedorov, Det (cross-checking), 5:23; Vasicek, Car (interference), 8:12.

Shots on goal: Car—5-7-5—17; Det—12-8-7—27. Power-play opportunities: Car 1-of-3; Det 1-of-4. Goalies: Car, Irbe (26 shots, 24 saves); Det, Hasek (17 shots, 16 saves). A: 20,058.

Referees: McCreary, Walkom. Linesmen: Lazarowich, Murphy.

Individual Playoff Leaders

Scoring

POINTS

Player and Team	GP	G	A	Pts	+/–	PM
Peter Forsberg, Col	20	9	18	27	8	20
Steve Yzerman, Det	23	6	17	23	4	10
Joe Sakic, Col	21	9	10	19	-2	4
Brendan Shanahan, Det	23	8	11	19	5	20
Gary Roberts, Tor	19	7	12	19	6	56
Sergei Fedorov, Det	23	5	14	19	4	20
Brett Hull, Det	23	10	8	18	1	4
Ron Francis, Car	23	6	10	16	-2	6
Nicklas Lidstrom, Det	23	5	11	16	6	2
Alyn McCauley, Tor	20	5	10	15	3	4
Bates Battaglia, Car	23	5	9	14	2	14
Chris Chelios, Det	23	1	13	14	15	44

Player and Team	GP	G	A	Pts	+/–	PM
Jeff O'Neill, Car	22	8	5	13	2	27
Daniel Alfredsson, Ott	12	7	6	13	6	4
Alex Tanguay, Col	19	5	8	13	-8	0
Greg de Vries, Col	21	4	9	13	1	2
Steve Reinprecht, Col	21	7	5	12	7	8
Rob Blake, Col	20	6	6	12	-1	16
Chris Drury, Col	21	5	7	12	4	10
Rod Brind'Amour, Car	23	4	8	12	-3	16

Five tied with 11.

Good Sports: Jeff Odgers

Forward Jeff Odgers is the Thrashers' designated brawler, and he has a ready explanation for how a tough guy can be a teddy bear around children. "A lot of the scrapping has to do with caring about your teammates, standing up for them," says Odgers, who's logged more than 2,000 penalty minutes in his 11-season, four-team NHL career. "That's not much different from caring about kids."

Since arriving in Atlanta before the 2000–01 season, Odgers has volunteered regularly with Special Olympics Georgia, conducting hockey clinics, serving as a spokesperson and filming public-service announcements. For four months he's coached a Special Olympics floor hockey team of 15 sixth- to ninth-graders. Even when a broken ankle kept him off the ice for 10 weeks, he ran weekly drills. He also secured the Thrashers' practice rink for an afternoon with his club, which won the gold medal at the state Special Olympics indoor games in January 2002. "I enjoyed seeing the same faces every week," Odgers says. "You could see their self-confidence growing." Says Georgia Milton-Sheats, executive director of Special Olympics Georgia, "Jeff is very competitive, but he's also very kind and open-minded. Sometimes people don't know how to react to those with intellectual disabilities; they tend to look at their disability. Jeff looks for their ability."

About the only person Odgers hasn't impressed is himself. "The people who do the real work are the full-time volunteers," he says. "I can come in and make an impact, but the real heroes do it every day."

—Daniel G. Habib

GOALS

Player and Team	GP	G
Brett Hull, Det	23	10
Peter Forsberg, Col	20	9
Joe Sakic, Col	21	9
Four tied with 8.		

GAME-WINNING GOALS

Player and Team	GP	GW
Jeff O'Neill, Car	22	2
Erik Cole, Car	23	2

POWER PLAY GOALS

Player and Team	GP	PP
Joe Sakic, Col	21	4
Scott Mellanby, StL	10	4
Steve Yzerman, Det	23	4
Ron Francis, Car	23	4
Sean Hill, Car	23	4

SHORT-HANDED GOALS

Player and Team	GP	SH
Brett Hull, Det	23	2
Kirk Maltby, Det	23	2

ASSISTS

Player and Team	GP	A
Peter Forsberg, Col	20	18
Steve Yzerman, Det	23	17
Sergei Fedorov, Det	23	14
Chris Chelios, Det	23	13
Gary Roberts, Tor	19	12

PLUS/MINUS

Player and Team	GP	+/-
Chris Chelios, Det	23	15
Darius Kasparaitis, Col	21	10
Peter Forsberg, Col	20	8
Benoit Brunet, Ott	12	8

Goaltending (Minimum 420 minutes)

GOALS AGAINST AVERAGE

Player and Team	GP	Mins	GA	Avg
Patrick Lalime, Ott	12	674	18	1.60
Arturs Irbe, Car	18	1079	30	1.67
Brent Johnson, StL	10	591	18	1.83
Dominik Hasek, Det	23	1454	45	1.86
Curtis Joseph, Tor	20	1151	48	2.50

SAVE PERCENTAGE

Player and Team	GP	Mins	GA	SA	Pct	W	L
Patrick Lalime, Ott	12	674	18	332	.946	7	5
Arturs Irbe, Car	18	1079	30	480	.938	10	8
Brent Johnson, StL	10	591	18	252	.929	5	5
Dominik Hasek, Det	23	1454	45	562	.920	16	7
Jose Theodore, Mtl	12	683	34	413	.918	6	6

NHL Awards

Award	Player and Team
Hart Trophy (MVP)	Jose Theodore, Mtl
Calder Trophy (top rookie)	Dany Heatley, Atl
Vezina Trophy (top goaltender)	Jose Theodore, Mtl
Norris Trophy (top defenseman)	Nicklas Lidstrom, Det
Lady Byng Trophy (for gentlemanly play)	Ron Francis, Car
Adams Award (top coach)	Bob Francis, Phoe

Award	Player and Team
Selke Trophy (top defensive forward)	Michael Peca, NYI
Jennings Trophy (goaltender on club allowing fewest goals)	Patrick Roy, Col
Conn Smythe Trophy (playoff MVP)	Nicklas Lidstrom, Det

Individual Regular Season Leaders

Scoring

POINTS

Player and Team	GP	G	A	Pts	+/-	PM
Jarome Iginla, Cal	82	52	44	96	27	77
Markus Naslund, Van	81	40	50	90	22	50
Todd Bertuzzi, Van	72	36	49	85	21	110
Mats Sundin, Tor	82	41	39	80	6	94
Jaromir Jagr, Wash	69	31	48	79	0	30
Joe Sakic, Col	82	26	53	79	12	18
Pavol Demitra, StL	82	35	43	78	14	46
Ron Francis, Car	80	27	50	77	4	18
Mike Modano, Dall	78	34	43	77	14	38
Alexei Kovalev, Pitt	67	32	44	76	2	80

Player and Team	GP	G	A	Pts	+/-	PM
Craig Conroy, Cal	81	27	48	75	24	32
Brendan Shanahan, Det	80	37	38	75	23	118
Keith Tkachuk, StL	73	38	37	75	21	117
Alexei Yashin, NYI	78	32	43	75	-3	25
Jason Allison, LA	73	19	55	74	2	68
Eric Lindros, NYR	72	37	36	73	19	138
Miroslav Satan, Buff	82	37	36	73	14	33
Daniel Alfredsson, Ott	78	37	34	71	3	45
Four tied with 70.						

GOALS

Player and Team	GP	G
Jarome Iginla, Cal	82	52
Bill Guerin, Bos	78	41
Mats Sundin, Tor	82	41
Markus Naslund, Van	81	40
Peter Bondra, Wash	77	39

GAME-WINNING GOALS

Player and Team	GP	GW
Pavol Demitra, StL	82	10
Mats Sundin, Tor	82	9
Five tied with eight.		

ASSISTS

Player and Team	GP	A
Adam Oates, Phil	80	64
Jason Allison, LA	73	55
Joe Sakic, Col	82	53
Four tied with 50.		

POWER PLAY GOALS

Player and Team	GP	PP
Peter Bondra, Wash	77	17
Jarome Iginla, Cal	82	16
Zigmund Palffy, LA	63	15
Miroslav Satan, Buff	82	15
Alexei Yashin, NYI	78	15

SHORT-HANDED GOALS

Player and Team	GP	SHG
Brian Rolston, Bos	82	9
Michale Peca, NYI	80	6
Miroslav Satan, Buff	82	5
Shawn Bates, NYI	71	4
Stacy Roest, Minn	58	4

PLUS/MINUS

Player and Team	GP	+/-
Chris Chelios, Det	79	40
Jeremy Roenick, Phil	75	32
Simon Gagne, Phil	79	31
Zdeno Chara, Ott	75	30
Michael Nylander, Chi	82	28

Goaltending
(Minimum 25 games)

GOALS AGAINST AVERAGE

Player and Team	GP	Mins	GA	Avg
Patrick Roy, Col 63		3773	122	1.94
Roman Cechmanek, Phil...46		2601	89	2.05
Marty Turco, Dall.............32		1518	53	2.09
Jose Theodore, Mtl...........67		3856	136	2.12
J.-S. Giguere, Ana 53		3129	111	2.13

SAVE PERCENTAGE

Player and Team	GP	GA	SA	Pct	W	L	T
Jose Theodore, Mtl...67	136	1971	.932	30	24	10
Patrick Roy, Col 63	122	1629	.925	32	23	8
R. Cechmanek, Phil ...46	89	1131	.921	24	13	6

Four tied with .920.

WINS

Player and Team	GP	Mins	W	L	T
Dominik Hasek, Det 65	3814	41	15	8
Martin Brodeur, NJ 73	4346	38	26	9
Evgeni Nabokov, SJ 67	3786	37	24	5
Byron Dafoe, Bos 64	3830	35	26	3
Brent Johnson, StL................58	3491	34	20	4

SHUTOUTS

Player and Team	GP	Mins	SO	W	L	T
Patrick Roy, Col...............63	3773	9	32	23	8
Jose Theodore, Mtl 67	3856	7	30	24	10
Evgeni Nabokov, SJ 67	3786	7	37	24	5
Nikolai Khabibulin, TB....70	3891	7	24	32	10
Dan Cloutier, Van 62	3506	7	31	22	5
Patrick Lalime, Ott.........61	3516	7	27	24	8

NHL Team-by-Team Statistical Leaders

Anaheim Mighty Ducks
SCORING

Player	GP	G	A	Pts	+/-	PM
Paul Kariya, L................82	32	25	57	-15	28
Matt Cullen, C 79	18	30	48	-1	24
Mike LeClerc, L................82	20	24	44	-12	107
Jeff Friesen, L 81	17	26	43	-1	44
Oleg Tverdovsky, D.......73	6	26	32	0	31
*Andy McDonald, C 53	7	21	28	2	10
German Titov, L...........66	13	14	27	4	36
Jason York, D...............74	5	20	25	-11	60
Steve Rucchin, C 38	7	16	23	-3	6
Samuel Pahlsson, C......80	6	14	20	-16	26
Patric Kjellberg, R.......77	8	11	19	-12	16
Dan Bylsma, R 77	8	9	17	5	28
Keith Carney, D...........60	5	9	14	14	30
Pavel Trnka, D.......71	2	11	13	-5	66
Ruslan Salei, D...........82	4	7	11	-10	97
Marc Chouinard, C 45	4	5	9	2	10
Denny Lambert, L 73	2	5	7	1	213
Sergei Krivokrasov, R...26	2	3	5	-2	36
Vitaly Vishnevski, D.......74	0	3	3	-10	60
Niclas Havelid, D 52	1	2	3	-13	40
Kevin Sawyer, L 57	1	1	2	-4	221

GOALTENDING

Player	GP	Mins	Avg	W	L	T	SO
J.-S. Giguere..........53	3126	2.13	20	25	6	4
Steve Shields........33	1777	2.67	9	20	2	0
Team total 82	4976	2.39	29	45	8	5

*Rookie.

Atlanta Thrashers
SCORING

Player	GP	G	A	Pts	+/-	PM
*Dany Heatley, R...........82	26	41	67	-19	56
*Ilya Kovalchuk, R.........65	29	22	51	-19	28
Tony Hrkac, C................80	18	26	44	-12	12
Lubos Bartecko, R........71	13	14	27	-15	30
Frantisek Kaberle, D 61	5	20	25	-11	24
Yannick Tremblay, D......66	9	15	24	-15	47
Patrik Stefan, L..............59	7	16	23	-4	22
Pascal Rheaume, C 61	11	11	22	-4	29
Tomi Kallio, R 60	8	14	22	-8	12
*Daniel Tjarnqvist, D 75	2	16	18	-22	14
Per Svartvadet, C...........78	3	12	15	-12	24
Andy Sutton, D...............43	2	8	10	-4	81
*Brian Pothier, D............33	3	6	9	-19	22
Jeff Odgers, R...............46	4	4	8	-3	135
Todd Reirden, D.............65	3	5	8	-25	82
Andreas Karlsson, L 42	1	7	8	-8	20
Chris Tamer, D 78	3	3	6	-11	111
Jeff Cowan, L................57	5	1	6	-14	90
*Brad Tapper, R 20	2	4	6	-3	43
*Jean-Pierre Vigier, R....15	4	1	5	-5	4
David Harlock, D............19	0	1	1	-2	18

GOALTENDING

Player	GP	Mins	Avg	W	L	T	SO
Milan Hnilicka.......60	3367	3.19	13	33	10	3
Frederick Cassivi....6	307	3.32	2	3	0	0
Pasi Nurminen........9	465	3.61	2	5	0	0
Damian Rhodes....15	769	3.67	2	10	1	0
Team total 82	4994	3.46	19	52	11	3

Boston Bruins

SCORING

Player	GP	G	A	Pts	+/–	PM
Glen Murray, R	82	41	30	71	31	40
Sergei Samsonov, L	74	29	41	70	21	27
Joe Thornton, C	66	22	46	68	7	127
Bill Guerin, R	78	41	25	66	-1	91
Brian Rolston, C	82	31	31	62	11	30
Jozef Stumpel, C	81	8	50	58	22	18
Martin Lapointe, R	68	17	23	40	12	101
Marty McInnis, R	79	11	17	28	-15	33
Rob Zamuner, L	66	12	13	25	6	24
Sean O'Donnell, D	80	3	22	25	27	89
P.J. Axlesson, L	78	7	17	24	6	16
Hal Gill, D	79	4	18	22	16	77
Don Sweeney, D	81	3	15	18	22	35
*Nicholas Boynton, D	80	4	14	18	18	107
Mike Knuble, R	54	8	6	14	9	42
Sean Brown, D	73	6	5	11	7	174
Kyle McLaren, D	38	0	8	8	-4	19
Jamie Rivers, D	66	4	2	6	3	49
Jeff Norton, D	32	0	5	5	-5	10
Dennis Bonvie, R	23	1	2	3	3	84
P.J. Stock, C	58	0	3	3	-2	122
Jonathan Girard, D	20	0	3	3	0	9
Jarno Kultanen, D	38	0	3	3	-1	33

GOALTENDING

Player	GP	Mins	Avg	W	L	T	SO
Byron Dafoe	64	3826	2.21	35	26	3	4
John Grahame	19	1078	2.77	8	7	2	0
Team total	82	4993	2.42	43	33	6	6

Buffalo Sabres

SCORING

Player	GP	G	A	Pts	+/–	PM
Miroslav Satan, R	82	37	36	73	14	33
Stu Barnes, R	68	17	31	48	6	26
Tim Connolly, C	82	10	35	45	4	34
J.P. Dumont, R	76	23	21	44	-10	42
Maxim Afinogenov, R	81	21	19	40	-9	69
Chris Gratton, C	82	15	24	39	0	75
Curtis Brown, C	82	20	17	37	-4	32
Alexei Zhitnik, D	82	1	33	34	-1	80
Jason Woolley, D	59	8	20	28	-6	34
Vaclav Varada, R	76	7	16	23	-7	82
Vyacheslav Kozlov, L	38	9	13	22	0	16
Taylor Pyatt, L	48	10	10	20	4	35
Erik Rasmussen, C	69	8	11	19	-1	34
James Patrick, D	56	5	8	13	3	16
Jay McKee, D	81	2	11	13	18	43
Dmitri Kalinin, D	58	2	11	13	-6	26
Rhett Warrener, D	65	5	5	10	15	113
Richard Smehlik, D	60	3	6	9	-9	22
Bob Corkum, C	75	3	5	8	-32	20
Denis Hamel, R	61	2	6	8	-1	28
Brian Campbell, D	29	3	3	6	0	12
Rob Ray, R	71	2	3	5	-3	200
Eric Boulton, L	35	2	3	5	-1	129
*Ales Kotalik, R	13	1	3	4	-1	2

GOALTENDING

Player	GP	Mins	Avg	W	L	T	SO
Martin Biron	72	4084	2.22	31	28	10	4
Mika Noronen	10	518	2.66	4	3	1	0
Bob Essensa	9	350	2.91	0	5	0	0
Team total	82	4986	2.41	35	36	11	4

Calgary Flames

SCORING

Player	GP	G	A	Pts	+/–	PM
Jarome Iginla, R	82	52	44	96	27	77
Craig Conroy, C	81	27	48	75	24	32
Dean McAmmond, C	73	21	30	51	2	60
Derek Morris, D	61	4	30	34	-4	88
Marc Savard, C	56	14	19	33	-18	48
Toni Lydman, D	79	6	22	28	-8	52
Igor Kravchuk, D	78	4	22	26	3	19
Rob Niedermayer, C	57	6	14	20	-15	49
Clarke Wilm, C	66	4	14	18	-1	61
Scott Nichol, C	60	8	9	17	-9	107
Chris Clark, R	64	10	7	17	-12	79
Jamie Wright, L	44	4	12	16	6	20
Dave Lowry, L	62	7	6	13	-20	51
Denis Gauthier, D	66	5	8	13	9	91
*Steve Begin, C	51	7	5	12	-3	79

SCORING (CONT.)

Player	GP	G	A	Pts	+/–	PM*
Ronald Petrovicky, L	77	7	5	12	0	85
Blake Sloan, R	67	2	9	11	-17	50
Robyn Regehr, D	77	2	6	8	-24	93
Bob Boughner, D	79	2	4	6	9	170
Jeff Shantz, C	40	3	3	6	-3	23
Craig Berube, L	66	3	1	4	-2	164
Petr Buzek, D	41	1	3	4	0	27

GOALTENDING

Player	GP	Mins	Avg	W	L	T	SO
Roman Turek	69	4081	2.53	30	28	11	5
Mike Vernon	18	825	2.76	2	9	1	1
Team total	82	4990	2.65	32	38	12	7

*Rookie.

Carolina Hurricanes

SCORING

Player	GP	G	A	Pts	+/-	PM
Ron Francis, C	80	27	50	77	4	18
Sami Kapanen, R	77	27	42	69	9	23
Jeff O'Neill, C	76	31	33	64	-5	63
Rod Brind'Amour, C	81	23	32	55	3	40
Bates Battaglia, L	82	21	25	46	-6	44
*Erik Cole, L	81	16	24	40	-10	35
Sean Hill, D	72	7	26	33	0	89
Josef Vasicek, C	78	14	17	31	-7	53
Martin Gelinas, L	72	13	16	29	-1	30
Marek Malik, D	82	4	19	23	8	88
Glen Wesley, D	77	5	13	18	-8	56
Kevyn Adams, C	77	6	11	17	-5	43
Bret Hedican, D	57	5	11	16	-1	22
David Tanabe, D	78	1	15	16	-13	35
Aaron Ward, D	79	3	11	14	0	74
Jeff Daniels, L	65	4	1	5	-6	12
*Jaroslav Svoboda, L	10	2	2	4	0	4
Darren Langdon, L	58	2	1	3	2	106
Niclas Wallin, D	52	1	2	3	1	36
*Craig MacDonald, C	12	1	1	2	-1	0
Tommy Westlund, L	40	0	2	2	-8	6

GOALTENDING

Player	GP	Mins	Avg	W	L	T	SO
Arturs Irbe	51	2974	2.54	20	19	11	3
Kevin Weekes	21	119	2.72	5	9	0	2
Team total	82	5021	2.59	35	31	16	5

Chicago Blackhawks

SCORING

Player	GP	G	A	Pts	+/-	PM
Eric Daze, L	82	38	32	70	17	36
Alexei Zhamnov, C	77	22	45	67	8	67
Tony Amonte, R	82	27	39	66	11	67
Michael Nylander, C	82	15	46	61	28	50
Steve Sullivan, R	78	21	39	60	23	67
Kyle Calder, L	81	17	36	53	8	47
Phil Housley, D	80	15	24	39	-3	34
Igor Korolev, C	82	9	20	29	-5	20
*Mark Bell, L	80	12	16	28	-6	124
Tom Fitzgerald, R	78	8	12	20	-7	39
Jon Klemm, D	82	4	16	20	-3	42
Lyle Odelein, D	77	2	16	18	-28	93
Boris Mironov, D	64	4	14	18	-15	68
Steve Thomas, L	34	11	4	15	0	17
Alex Karpovtsev, D	65	1	9	10	10	40
Joe Reekie, D	55	2	6	8	-5	69
Steve Poapst, D	56	1	7	8	6	30
Peter White, C	48	3	3	6	-8	10
Mike Peluso, L	37	4	2	6	-3	19
Bob Probert, L	61	1	3	4	-9	176
*Tyler Arnason, C	21	3	1	4	-3	4
Chris McAlpine, D	40	0	3	3	8	36

GOALTENDING

Player	GP	Mins	Avg	W	L	T	SO
Steve Passmore	23	1142	2.26	8	5	4	0
Jocelyn Thibault	67	3837	2.49	33	23	9	6
Team total	82	4996	2.49	41	28	13	6

Colorado Avalanche

SCORING

Player	GP	G	A	Pts	+/-	PM
Joe Sakic, C	82	26	53	79	12	18
Rob Blake, D	75	16	40	56	16	58
Alex Tanguay, L	70	13	35	48	8	36
Chris Drury, C	82	21	25	46	1	38
Steven Reinprecht, C	67	19	27	46	14	18
Milan Hejduk, R	62	21	23	44	0	24
Martin Skoula, D	82	10	21	31	-3	42
*Radim Vrbata, R	52	18	12	30	7	14
Adam Foote, D	55	5	22	27	7	55
Greg De Vries, D	82	8	12	20	18	57
Mike Keane, L	78	6	11	17	-4	38
Stephane Yelle, C	73	5	12	17	1	48
Eric Messier, L	74	5	10	15	-5	26
Darius Kasparaitis, D	80	2	12	14	0	142
*Brian Willsie, R	56	7	7	14	4	14
Pascal Trepanier, D	74	4	9	13	4	59
Dan Hinote, R	58	6	6	12	8	39
*Brad Larsen, L	50	2	7	9	4	47
Scott Parker, R	63	1	4	5	0	154
*Riku Hall, C	22	2	3	5	1	14

GOALTENDING

Player	GP	Mins	Avg	W	L	T	SO
David Aebischer	21	1184	1.88	13	6	0	2
Patrick Roy	63	3773	1.94	32	23	8	9
Team total	82	4979	2.04	45	29	8	11

Columbus Blue Jackets

SCORING

Player	GP	G	A	Pts	+/-	PM
Ray Whitney, L	67	21	40	61	-22	12
Mike Sillinger, C	80	20	23	43	-35	54
Espen Knutsen, C	77	11	31	42	-28	47
Grant Marshall, R	81	15	18	33	-20	86
Deron Quint, D	75	7	18	25	-34	26
Tyler Wright, C	77	13	11	24	-40	100
Jaroslav Spacek, D	74	5	13	18	-4	53
Geoff Sanderson, L	42	11	5	16	-15	12
Serge Aubin, C	71	8	8	16	-20	32
*Rostislav Klesla, D	75	8	8	16	-6	74
Robert Kron, D	59	4	11	15	-14	4
Brett Harkins, L	25	2	12	14	-5	8
Kevin Dineen, R	59	5	8	13	-6	62
Mattias Timander, D	78	4	7	11	-34	44
J.L. Grand-Pierre, D	81	2	6	8	-28	90
Radim Bicanek, D	60	1	5	6	-15	34
*Jody Shelley, L	52	3	3	6	1	206
Chris Nielsen, R	23	2	3	5	-3	4
Sean Pronger, L	26	3	1	4	-4	4

GOALTENDING

Player	GP	Mins	Avg	W	L	T	S
Ron Tugnutt	44	2501	2.85	12	27	3	2
Jean Labbe	3	117	3.08	1	1	0	0
Marc Dennis	42	2335	3.11	9	24	5	1
Team total	82	4979	3.07	22	52	8	3

* Rookie.

Dallas Stars

SCORING

Player	GP	G	A	Pts	+/–	PM
Mike Modano, C	78	34	43	77	14	38
Jere Lehtinen, R	73	25	24	49	27	14
Pierre Turgeon, C	66	15	32	47	-4	16
Jason Arnott, C	73	25	20	45	2	65
Sergei Zubov, D	80	12	32	44	-4	22
Brenden Morrow, L	72	17	18	35	12	109
Darryl Sydor, D	78	4	29	33	3	50
Kirk Muller, L	78	10	20	30	-12	28
Derian Hatcher, D	80	4	21	25	12	87
Richard Matvichuk, D	82	9	12	21	11	52
Pat Verbeek, R	64	7	13	20	-4	72
Randy McKay, R	69	7	11	18	4	72
Scott Pellerin, L	68	4	10	14	-11	41
Manny Malhotra, C	72	8	6	14	-4	47
Rob DiMaio, R	61	6	6	12	-2	25
Brent Gilchrist, L	45	3	6	9	-9	14
Brad Lukowich, D	66	1	6	7	-1	40
John MacLean, R	20	3	3	6	-1	17
Jonathan Sim, C	26	3	0	3	-3	10
Dave Manson, D	47	0	2	2	2	33
Jim Montgomery, R	8	0	2	2	-1	0

GOALTENDING

Player	GP	Mins	Avg	W	L	T	SO
Marty Turco	31	1518	2.09	15	6	2	2
Ed Belfour	60	3467	2.65	21	27	11	1
Team total	82	5008	2.55	36	33	13	3

Detroit Red Wings

SCORING

Player	GP	G	A	Pts	+/–	PM
Brendan Shanahan, L	80	37	38	75	23	118
Sergei Federov, C	81	31	37	68	20	36
Brett Hull, R	82	30	33	63	18	35
Nicklas Lidstrom, D	78	9	50	59	13	20
Luc Robitaille, L	81	30	20	50	-2	38
Steve Yzerman, C	52	13	35	48	11	18
Igor Larionov, C	70	11	32	43	-5	50
Chris Chelios, D	79	6	33	39	40	126
*Pavel Datsyuk, C	70	11	24	35	4	4
Kris Draper, R	82	15	15	30	26	56
Tomas Holstrom, L	69	8	18	26	-12	58
Boyd Devereaux, C	79	9	16	25	9	24
Kirk Maltby, L	82	9	15	24	15	40
Mathieu Dandenault, D	81	8	12	20	-5	44
Steve Duchesne, D	64	3	15	18	3	28
Fredrik Olausson, D	47	2	13	15	9	22
Darren McCarty, R	62	5	7	12	2	98
Jiri Fischer, D	80	2	8	10	17	67
*Jason Williams, C	25	8	2	10	2	4
Jiri Slegr, D	46	3	6	9	-20	59
*Sean Avery, C	36	2	2	4	1	68
*Maxim Kuznetsov, D	39	1	2	3	0	40

GOALTENDING

Player	GP	Mins	Avg	W	L	T	SO
Dominik Hasek	65	3872	2.17	41	15	8	5
Manny Legace	20	1117	2.42	10	6	2	1
Team total	82	5008	2.24	51	21	10	7

Edmonton Oilers

SCORING

Player	GP	G	A	Pts	+/–	PM
Mike York, L	81	20	41	61	7	16
Anson Carter, R	82	28	32	60	3	25
Mike Comrie, C	82	33	27	60	16	45
Ryan Smyth, L	61	15	35	50	7	48
Janne Niinimaa, D	81	5	39	44	13	80
Jochen Hecht, L	82	16	24	40	4	60
Todd Marchant, C	82	12	22	34	7	41
Daniel Cleary, R	65	10	19	29	-1	51
Mike Grier, R	82	8	17	25	1	32
Eric Brewer, D	81	7	18	25	-5	45
Shawn Horcoff, C	61	8	14	22	3	18
Georges Laraque, R	80	5	14	19	6	157
Jason Smith, D	74	5	13	18	14	103
Ethan Moreau, L	80	11	5	16	4	81
Josh Green, L	61	10	5	15	9	52
Marty Reasoner, C	52	6	5	11	0	41
Steve Staios, D	73	5	10	10	10	108
Domenic Pittis, C	22	0	6	6	-2	8
Scott Ferguson, D	50	3	2	5	11	75
*Brian Swanson, L	8	1	1	2	-1	0
*Jason Chimera, L	3	1	0	1	-3	0

GOALTENDING

Player	GP	Mins	Avg	W	L	T	SO
Ty Conklin	4	147	1.62	2	0	0	0
Jussi Markkanen	14	784	1.84	6	4	2	2
Tommy Salo	69	4034	2.22	30	28	10	6
Team total	82	4996	2.19	38	32	12	8

* Rookie.

Florida Panthers

SCORING

Player	GP	G	A	Pts	+/–	PM
Sandis Ozolinsh, D	83	14	38	52	-7	58
*Kristian Huselius, R	79	23	22	45	-4	14
Marcus Nilson, L	81	14	19	33	-14	55
Jason Wiemer, C	70	11	20	31	-4	178
Robert Svehla, D	82	7	22	29	-19	87
Olli Jokinen, C	80	9	20	29	-16	98
Ivan Novoseltsev, R	70	13	16	29	-10	44
*Niklas Hagman, R	78	10	18	28	-6	8
Viktor Kozlov, C	50	9	18	27	-16	20
Valeri Bure, R	31	8	10	18	-3	12
Brad Ference, D	80	2	15	17	-13	254
*Pierre Dagenais, L	42	10	4	14	-10	8
Byron Ritchie, C	35	5	6	11	-2	36
Igor Ulanov, D	53	0	10	10	-7	64
Peter Worrell, L	79	4	5	9	-15	354
Paul Laus, D	45	4	3	7	1	157
Lance Ward, D	68	1	4	5	-20	131
Ryan Johnson, C	29	1	3	4	-5	10
*Eric Beaudoin, L	8	1	3	4	-2	4
Denis Shvidki, R	8	1	2	3	-4	2
Lance Pitlick, D	35	1	1	2	-14	12

GOALTENDING

Player	GP	Mins	Avg	W	L	T	SO
Roberto Longo	58	3030	2.77	16	33	4	4
Wade Flaherty	4	245	2.94	2	1	1	0
Trevor Kidd	33	1683	3.21	4	16	5	1
Team total	82	4987	3.01	22	50	10	5

Los Angeles Kings

SCORING

Player	GP	G	A	Pts	+/–	PM
Jason Allison, C	73	19	55	74	2	68
Adam Deadmarsh, L	76	29	33	62	8	71
Zigmund Palffy, R	63	32	27	59	5	26
Cliff Ronning, L	81	19	35	54	0	32
Jaroslav Modry, D	80	4	38	42	-4	65
Bryan Smolinski, C	80	13	25	38	7	56
Steve Heinze, R	73	15	16	31	-15	46
Mathieu Schneider, D	55	7	23	30	3	68
Philippe Boucher, D	80	7	23	30	0	94
Craig Johnson, L	72	13	14	27	14	24
Eric Belanger, C	53	8	16	24	2	21
Ian Lapierriere, C	81	8	14	22	5	125
Lubomir Visnovsky, D	72	4	17	21	-5	14
Mikko Eloranta, L	77	9	9	18	-1	56
Aaron Miller, D	74	5	12	17	14	54
Brad Chartrand, R	46	7	9	16	5	40
Kelly Buchberger, R	74	6	7	13	-13	105
Mattias Norstrom, D	79	2	9	11	-2	38
Nelson Emerson, R	41	5	2	7	-8	25
*Jaroslav Bednar, C	22	4	2	6	-4	8
Andreas Lilja, D	26	1	4	5	3	22

GOALTENDING

Player	GP	Mins	Avg	W	L	T	SO
Jamie Storr	19	886	1.90	9	4	3	2
Felix Potvin	71	4071	2.31	31	27	8	6
Team total	82	4989	2.29	40	31	11	8

Minnesota Wild

SCORING

Player	GP	G	A	Pts	+/–	PM
Andrew Brunette, L	81	21	48	69	-4	18
Marian Gaborik, R	78	30	37	67	0	34
Jim Dowd, C	82	13	30	43	-14	54
Sergei Zholtok, C	73	19	20	39	-10	28
Antti Laaksonen, L	82	16	17	33	-5	22
Wes Walz, C	64	10	20	30	0	43
*Pascal Dupuis, L	76	15	12	27	-10	16
Richard Park, C	63	10	15	25	-1	10
Hnat Domenichelli, L	67	9	16	25	-23	44
Darby Hendrickson, C	68	9	15	24	-22	50
Filip Kuba, D	62	5	19	24	-6	32
Lubomir Sekeras, D	69	4	20	24	-7	38
Stacy Roest, R	58	10	11	21	-3	8
Aaron Gavey, C	71	6	11	17	-21	38
Willie Mitchell, D	68	3	10	13	-16	68
Jason Marshall, D	80	5	6	11	-8	148
Nick Schultz, D	52	4	6	10	0	14
Ladislav Benysek, D	74	1	7	8	-12	28
Brad Brown, D	51	0	4	4	-11	123
Matt Johnson, L	60	4	0	4	-13	183
Sylvain Blouin, R	43	0	2	2	-11	130

GOALTENDING

Player	GP	Mins	Avg	W	L	T	SO
Dwayne Roloson	45	2506	2.68	14	20	7	5
Manny Fernandez	44	2462	3.05	12	24	5	1
Team total	82	5004	2.85	26	44	12	6

Montreal Canadiens

SCORING

Player	GP	G	A	Pts	+/–	PM
Yannic Perreault, C	82	27	29	56	-3	40
Richard Zednik, R	82	22	22	44	-3	59
Doug Gilmour, C	70	10	31	41	-7	48
Oleg Petrov, R	75	24	17	41	-4	12
Joe Juneau, C	70	8	28	36	-3	10
Patrice Brisebois, D	71	4	29	33	9	25
Andreas Dackell, R	79	15	18	33	-3	24
Sergei Berezin, L	70	11	15	26	2	8
Craig Rivet, D	82	8	17	25	1	76
Andrei Markov, D	56	5	19	24	-1	24
Chad Kilger, L	75	8	15	23	-7	27
Shaun Van Allen, C	73	8	13	21	0	26
Jan Bulis, C	53	9	10	19	-2	8
Donald Audette, R	33	5	13	18	3	20
Mike Ribeiro, C	43	8	10	18	-11	12
Stephane Quintal, D	75	6	10	16	-7	87
Bill Lindsay, L	76	5	10	15	-11	140
Karl Dykhuis, D	80	5	7	12	16	32
Stephane Robidas, D	56	1	10	11	-25	14
Arron Asham, C	35	5	4	9	7	55
Gino Odjick, L	36	4	4	8	3	104

GOALTENDING

Player	GP	Mins	Avg	W	L	T	SO
Jose Theodore	67	3864	2.11	30	24	10	7
Jeff Hackett	15	717	3.18	5	5	2	0
Stephane Fiset	2	109	3.85	0	1	0	0
Mathieu Garon	5	261	4.37	1	4	0	0
Team total	82	4989	2.51	36	34	12	7

Nashville Predators
SCORING

Player	GP	G	A	Pts	+/-	PM
Greg Johnson, C	82	18	26	44	-14	38
Kimmo Timonen, D	82	13	29	42	2	28
Denis Arkhipov, C	82	20	22	42	-18	16
Scott Hartnell, L	75	14	27	41	5	111
Andy Delmore, D	73	16	22	38	-13	22
Vladimir Orszagh, R	79	15	21	36	-15	56
*Martin Erat, L	80	9	24	33	-11	32
David Legwand, C	63	11	19	30	1	54
Vitali Yachmenev, L	75	11	16	27	-16	14
Petr Tenkrat, R	67	8	16	24	-10	34
Karlis Skrastins, D	82	4	13	17	-12	36
Greg Classen, C	55	5	6	11	1	30
*Andy Berenzweig, D	26	3	7	10	-3	14
Scott Walker, R	28	4	5	9	-13	18
Jukka Hentunen, R	38	4	5	9	-9	4
Bill Houlder, D	82	0	8	8	-1	40
Steve Dubinsky, C	29	6	2	8	-1	14
Mark Eaton, D	58	3	5	8	-12	24
Reid Simpson, L	51	6	1	7	-1	132
*Nathan Perrott, R	22	1	2	3	-1	74

GOALTENDING

Player	GP	Mins	Avg	W	L	T	SO
Mike Dunham	58	3316	2.61	23	24	9	3
Tomas Vokoun	29	1471	2.69	5	14	4	2
Jan Lasak	3	177	4.41	0	3	0	0
Team total	82	4995	2.76	28	41	13	5

New Jersey Devils
SCORING

Player	GP	G	A	Pts	+/-	PM
Patrik Elias, L	75	29	32	61	4	36
Joe Nieuwendyk, C	81	25	33	58	0	22
Bobby Holik, C	81	25	29	54	7	97
Petr Sykora, R	73	21	27	48	12	44
Scott Gomez, R	76	10	38	48	-4	36
Brian Rafalski, D	76	7	40	47	15	18
Sergei Brylin, C	76	16	28	44	21	10
Scott Niedermayer, D	76	11	22	33	12	30
Jamie Langenbrunner, R	82	13	19	32	-9	77
Stephane Richer, R	68	14	14	28	-9	14
John Madden, C	82	15	8	23	6	25
Valeri Kamensky, L	54	7	14	21	1	20
Scott Stevens, D	82	1	16	17	15	44
Jay Pandolfo, L	65	4	10	14	12	15
*Brian Gionta, R	33	4	7	11	10	8
Sergei Nemchinov, L	68	5	5	10	-9	10
Christian Berglund, C	15	2	7	9	-3	8
*Andreas Salomonsson, L	39	4	5	9	-12	22
Jim McKenzie, L	67	3	5	8	0	123
Ken Danyeko, D	67	0	6	6	2	60
Colin White, D	73	2	3	5	6	133

GOALTENDING

Player	GP	Mins	Avg	W	L	T	SO
J. Vanbiesbrouck	5	300	2.00	2	3	0	0
Martin Brodeur	73	4347	2.15	38	26	9	4
J.-F Damphousse	6	294	2.45	1	3	0	0
Team total	82	4988	2.25	41	32	9	4

New York Islanders
SCORING

Player	GP	G	A	Pts	+/-	PM
Alexei Yashin, C	78	32	43	75	-3	25
Michael Peca, R	80	25	35	60	19	62
Mark Parrish, R	78	30	30	60	10	32
Shawn Bates, L	71	17	35	52	18	30
Mariusz Czerkawski, R	82	22	29	51	-8	48
Brad Isbister, L	79	17	21	38	1	113
Oleg Kvasha, L	71	13	25	38	-4	80
Roman Hamrlik, D	70	11	26	37	-7	78
Adrian Aucoin, D	81	12	22	34	23	62
Kenny Jonsson, D	76	10	22	32	15	26
Dave Scatchard, L	80	12	15	27	-4	111
Kip Miller, L	37	7	17	24	2	6
Claude Lapointe, C	80	9	12	21	-9	60
Dick Tarnstrom, D	62	3	16	19	-12	38
Jason Blake, C	82	8	10	18	-11	36
Mats Lindgren, L	59	3	12	15	0	16
Darren Van Impe, D	67	3	8	11	12	59
Eric Cairns, D	74	2	5	7	-2	176
Marko Kiprusoff, D	27	0	6	6	0	4
Steve Webb, R	60	2	4	6	0	104
*Radek Martinek, D	23	1	4	5	5	16
Ken Sutton, D	21	0	2	2	-5	8

GOALTENDING

Player	GP	Mins	Avg	W	L	T	SO
Chris Osgood	66	3742	2.50	32	25	6	4
Garth Snow	25	1216	2.71	10	7	2	2
Team total	82	4987	2.65	42	32	8	6

New York Rangers
SCORING

Player	GP	G	A	Pts	+/-	PM
Eric Lindros, C	72	37	36	73	19	138
Pavel Bure, R	68	34	35	69	-5	62
Theoren Fleury, L	82	24	39	63	0	216
Brian Leetch, D	82	10	45	55	14	28
Petr Nedved, C	78	21	25	46	-8	36
Martin Rucinsky, L	75	11	27	38	8	42
Radek Dvorak, R	65	17	20	37	-20	14
Vladimir Malakhov, D	81	6	22	28	-10	83
Rem Murray, C	80	8	19	27	-4	18
Tom Poti, D	66	2	23	25	-10	44
Andreas Johansson, L	70	14	10	24	6	46
Mark Messier, C	41	7	16	23	-1	32
Sandy McCarthy, R	82	10	13	23	-8	171
Bryan Berard, D	82	2	21	23	-1	60
Matthew Barnaby, R	77	8	13	21	-10	214
*Mikael Samuelsson, R	58	6	10	16	10	23
Dave Karpa, D	75	1	10	11	-9	131
Sylvain Lefebvre, D	41	0	5	5	-3	23
Michal Grosek, L	15	3	2	5	-3	12

GOALTENDING

Player	GP	Mins	Avg	W	L	T	SO
Mike Richter	55	3195	2.95	24	26	4	2
Daniel Blackburn	31	1737	3.28	12	16	0	0
Team total	82	4963	3.12	36	42	4	2

* Rookie.

Ottawa Senators

SCORING

Player	GP	G	A	Pts	+/–	PM
Daniel Alfredsson, R.....78		37	34	71	3	45
Radek Bonk, C.............82		25	45	70	3	52
Marian Hossa, R 80		31	35	66	11	50
Todd White, C 81		20	30	50	12	24
Martin Havlat, R 72		22	28	50	-7	66
Shawn McEachern, L....80		15	31	46	9	52
Magnus Arvedson, L....74		12	27	39	27	35
Wade Redden, D 79		9	25	34	22	48
Mike Fisher, C 58		15	9	24	8	55
Benoit Brunet, L.........61		9	14	23	-3	12
Zdeno Chara, D 75		10	13	23	30	156
Chris Phillips, D...........63		6	16	22	5	29
Sami Salo, D 66		4	14	18	1	14
Karel Rachunek, D.......51		3	15	18	7	24
*Chris Neil, R.............72		10	7	17	5	231
Juha Ylonen, C...........80		4	11	15	-11	10
Chris Herperger, L 72		4	9	13	4	43
Curtis Leschyshyn, D....79		1	9	10	-5	44
Richard Persson, D......34		2	7	9	3	42
Bill Muckalt, R 70		0	8	8	-3	46
Jody Hull, R.................24		2	2	4	0	6
Shane Hnidy, D 33		1	1	2	-10	57

GOALTENDING

Player	GP	Mins	Avg	W	L	T	SO
Patrick Lalime......61		3582	2.48	27	24	8	7
Jani Hurme...........25		1308	2.48	12	9	1	3
Martin Prusek 1		62	2.90	0	1	0	0
Team total.............82		4991	2.50	39	34	9	10

Philadelphia Flyers

SCORING

Player	GP	G	A	Pts	+/–	PM
Adam Oates, C 80		14	64	78	-4	28
Jeremy Roenick, C.......75		21	46	67	32	74
Simon Gagne, L............79		33	33	66	31	32
Mark Recchi, R 80		22	42	64	5	46
John LeClair, L............82		25	26	51	5	30
Keith Primeau, C...........75		19	29	48	-3	128
Kim Johnsson, D..........82		11	30	41	12	42
Justin Williams, R.........75		17	23	40	11	32
Donald Brashear, L.......81		9	23	32	-8	199
Jiri Dopita, C 52		11	16	27	9	8
Marty Murray, C 74		12	15	27	10	10
Ruslan Fedotenko, L.....78		17	9	26	15	43
Eric Desjardins, D..........65		6	19	25	-1	24
Eric Weinrich, D............80		4	20	24	27	26
Daniel McGillis, D 75		5	14	19	17	46
Chris Therien, D...........77		4	10	14	16	30
Paul Ranheim, L...........79		5	4	9	5	36
Luke Richardson, D 72		1	8	9	18	102
Todd Fedoruk, L............55		3	4	7	-2	141
Billy Tibbetts, R............42		1	6	7	-16	178
Chris McAllister, D 42		0	5	5	-7	113
Rick Tocchet, R...........14		0	2	2	-2	28

GOALTENDING

Player	GP	Mins	Avg	W	L	T	SO
R. Cechmanek......46		2603	2.05	24	13	6	4
Brian Boucher 41		2294	2.41	18	16	4	2
Neil Little.................1		60	4.00	0	1	0	0
Team total.............82		4986	2.31	42	30	10	7

Phoenix Coyotes

SCORING

Player	GP	G	A	Pts	+/–	PM
Daymond Langkow, C .:80		27	35	62	18	36
Daniel Briere, C.............78		32	28	60	6	52
Shane Doan, R..............81		20	29	49	11	61
Teppo Numminen, D......76		13	35	48	13	20
Michal Handzus, C 79		15	30	45	-8	34
Ladislav Nagy, L 74		23	19	42	6	50
Claude Lemieux, R.........82		16	25	41	-5	70
Brian Savage, L 77		20	21	41	-13	38
Danny Markov, D 72		6	30	36	-7	67
Mike Johnson, R...........57		5	22	27	14	28
Paul Mara, D 75		7	17	24	-6	58
Brad May, L..................72		10	12	22	11	95
*Krystofer Kolanos 57		11	11	22	6	48
Landon Wilson, R 47		7	12	19	4	46
Radoslav Suchy, D........81		4	13	17	25	10
Todd Simpson, D...........67		2	13	15	20	152
Ossi Vaananen, D............76		2	12	14	6	74

Player	GP	G	A	Pts	+/–	PM
Andrei Nazarov, L 77		6	5	11	5	215
Drake Berehowsky, D...57		2	6	8	0	60
Denis Pederson, C........48		2	6	8	-4	51
*Branko Radivojevic, R.18		4	2	6	1	4
Mike Sullivan, C 42		1	2	3	-3	16
*Darcy Hordichuk, L 34		1	1	2	-5	141

GOALTENDING

Player	GP	Mins	Avg	W	L	T	SO
Sean Burke...........60		3586	2.29	33	21	6	5
Robert Esche 22		1144	2.72	6	10	2	1
Patrick Desrochers...5		243	3.70	1	2	1	0
Team total.............82		4993	2.52	40	33	9	6

* Rookie.

Pittsburgh Penguins
SCORING

Player	GP	G	A	Pts	+/–	PM
Alexei Kovalev, R	67	32	44	76	2	80
Jan Hrdina, C	79	24	33	57	-7	50
Robert Lang, C	62	18	32	50	9	16
Alexei Morozov, R	72	20	29	49	-7	16
Randy Robitaille, C	58	14	23	37	-23	33
Mario Lemieux, C	24	6	25	31	0	14
Michal Rozsival, D	79	9	20	29	-6	47
Ville Nieminen, L	66	11	16	27	-1	38
*Kris Beech, C	79	10	15	25	-25	45
*Toby Petersen, C	79	8	10	18	-15	4
Dan LaCoutre, L	82	6	11	17	-19	71
Milan Kraft, C	68	8	8	16	-9	16
Shean Donovan, R	61	8	7	15	-21	44
Jeff Toms, L	52	9	5	14	-9	14
Janne Laukkanen, D	47	6	7	13	-18	28
Andrew Ference, D	75	4	7	11	-12	73
Ian Moran, R	64	2	8	10	-11	54
Wayne Primeau, C	33	3	7	10	-1	18
Martin Straka, C	13	5	4	9	3	0
Kent Manderville, C	38	3	5	8	3	12
Jamie Pushor, D	76	0	8	8	-13	84
Hans Jonsson, D	53	2	5	7	-12	22
Kevin Stevens, L	32	1	4	5	-9	25
John Jakopin, D	19	0	4	4	2	42
*Josef Melichar, D	60	0	3	3	-1	68
*Tom Kostopoulos, R	11	1	2	3	-1	9
Mike Wilson, D	21	1	1	2	-12	17
Kryzysztof Oliwa, L	57	0	2	2	-5	150

GOALTENDING

Player	GP	Mins	Avg	W	L	T	SO
Johan Hedberg	66	3876	2.75	25	34	7	6
J.-S. Aubin	21	1094	3.56	3	12	1	0
Team total	82	4994	2.99	28	46	8	6

St. Louis Blues
SCORING

Player	GP	G	A	Pts	+/–	PM
Pavol Demitra, C	82	35	43	78	13	46
Keith Tkachuk, L	73	38	37	75	21	117
Doug Weight, C	61	15	34	49	20	40
Chris Pronger, D	78	7	40	47	23	120
Al MacInnis, D	71	11	35	46	3	52
Cory Stillman, L	80	23	22	45	8	36
Scott Mellanby, R	64	15	26	41	-5	93
Scott Young, R	67	19	22	41	11	26
Ray Ferraro, C	76	14	23	37	-30	74
Dallas Drake, R	80	11	15	26	8	87
Alexander Khavanov, D	81	3	21	24	9	55
Shjon Podein, L	64	8	10	18	2	41
Mike Eastwood, C	71	7	10	17	-2	41
Jamal Mayers, R	77	9	8	17	9	99
Tyson Nash, L	64	6	7	13	2	100
Bryce Salvador, D	66	5	7	12	3	78
*Sergei Varlamov, L	52	5	7	12	4	26
Daniel Corso, C	41	4	7	11	3	6
*Mike Van Ryn, D	48	2	8	10	10	18
Jeff Finley, D	78	0	6	6	12	30
Reed Low, R	58	0	5	5	-3	160
Marc Bergevin, D	30	0	3	3	6	2
Richard Pilon, D	8	0	2	2	-1	9
Eric Boguniecki, C	8	0	1	1	-2	4
Christian LaFlamme, D	8	0	1	1	3	4

GOALTENDING

Player	GP	Mins	Avg	W	L	T	SO
Brent Johnson	58	3491	2.18	34	20	4	5
Fred Brathwaite	25	1446	2.24	9	11	4	2
Team total	82	4990	2.26	43	31	8	7

San Jose Sharks
SCORING

Player	GP	G	A	Pts	+/–	PM
Owen Nolan, R	75	23	43	66	7	93
Vincent Damphousse, C	82	20	38	58	8	60
Teemu Selanne, R	82	29	25	54	-11	40
Mike Ricci, C	79	19	34	53	9	44
Patrick Marleau, C	79	21	23	44	9	40
Scott Thornton, L	77	26	16	42	11	116
Marco Sturm, L	77	21	20	41	23	32
Niklas Sundstrom, R	73	9	30	39	7	50
Gary Suter, D	82	6	27	33	13	57
Adam Graves, L	81	17	14	31	11	51
Brad Stuart, D	82	6	23	29	13	39
Bryan Marchment, D	72	2	20	22	22	178
Todd Harvey, R	69	9	13	22	16	73
*Matt Bradley, R	54	9	13	22	22	43
Marcus Ragnarsson, D	70	5	15	20	4	44
*Jeff Jillson, D	48	5	13	18	2	29
Mark Rathje, D	52	5	12	17	23	48
Scott Hannan, D	75	2	12	14	10	57
Stephane Matteau, L	55	7	4	11	4	15
Alexander Korolyuk, R	32	3	7	10	2	14
Mark Smith, C	49	3	3	6	-1	72
Shawn Heins, D	17	0	2	2	1	24
Steve Bancroft, D	5	0	1	1	-2	2

GOALTENDING

Player	GP	Mins	Avg	W	L	T	SO
Evgeni Nabakov	67	3901	2.29	37	24	5	7
Miikka Kirprusoff	20	1040	2.49	7	6	3	2
Team total	82	4973	2.40	44	30	8	9

Tampa Bay Lightning

SCORING

Player	GP	G	A	Pts	+/-	PM
Brad Richards, C	82	20	42	62	-18	13
Vaclav Prospal, C	81	18	37	55	-11	38
Dave Andreychuk, L	82	21	17	38	-12	109
Vincent Lecavalier, C	76	20	17	37	-18	61
Martin St. Louis, R	53	16	19	35	4	20
Pavel Kubina, D	82	11	23	34	-22	106
Ben Clymer, R	81	14	20	34	-10	36
Fredrik Modin, L	54	14	17	31	0	27
Dan Boyle, D	66	8	18	26	-16	39
Zdeno Ciger, L	56	12	13	25	-15	26
Shane Willis, R	80	11	13	24	-8	30
Andre Roy, L	65	7	9	16	-2	211
*Jimmie Olvestad, L	74	3	11	14	3	24
Jassen Cullimore, D	78	4	9	13	-1	58
Sheldon Keefe, R	39	6	7	13	-11	16
Cory Sarich, D	72	0	11	11	-4	105
Tim Taylor, C	48	4	4	8	-2	25
Stan Neckar, D	77	1	7	8	-18	24
*Nikita Alexeev, R	44	4	4	8	-9	8
*Martin Cibak, C	26	1	5	6	-6	8
Chris Dingman, L	44	0	5	5	-10	103
Grant Ledyard, D	53	1	3	4	-5	12
Brian Holzinger, C	23	1	2	3	-4	4
Nolan Pratt, D	46	0	3	3	-4	51
Gordie Dwyer, L	26	0	2	2	-4	60

GOALTENDING

Player	GP	Mins	Avg	W	L	T	SO
Nikolai Khabibulin	70	3895	2.36	24	32	10	7
Dieter Kochan	5	236	4.05	0	3	1	0
Team total	82	4997	2.63	27	44	11	9

Toronto Maple Leafs

SCORING

Player	GP	G	A	Pts	+/-	PM
Mats Sundin, C	82	41	39	80	6	94
Darcy Tucker, C	77	24	35	59	24	92
Alexander Mogilny, R	66	24	33	57	1	8
Mikael Renberg, R	71	14	38	52	11	36
Robert Reichel, C	78	20	31	51	7	26
Gary Roberts, L	69	21	27	48	-4	63
Jonas Hoglund, R	82	13	34	47	11	26
Bryan McCabe, D	82	17	26	43	16	129
Tomas Kaberle, D	69	10	29	39	5	2
Travis Green, C	82	11	23	34	13	61
Shayne Corson, L	74	12	21	33	11	120
Tie Domi, R	74	9	10	19	3	157
Dimitri Yushkevich, D	55	6	13	19	14	26
Alyn McCauley, C	82	6	10	16	10	18
Garry Valk, R	63	5	10	15	2	28
Jyrki Lumme, D	66	4	9	13	8	22
Cory Cross, D	50	3	9	12	11	54
Aki Berg, D	81	1	10	11	14	46
Paul Healy, R	21	3	7	10	7	2
Wade Belak, D	63	1	3	4	2	142
*Karel Pilar, D	23	1	3	4	3	8
Anders Eriksson, D	34	0	2	2	-1	12
Jeff Farkas, C	6	0	2	2	1	4
Nik Antropov, C	11	1	1	2	-1	4

GOALTENDING

Player	GP	Mins	Avg	W	L	T	SO
Curtis Joseph	68	3064	2.23	29	17	5	4
Tom Barrasso	38	218	2.62	15	14	5	2
Corey Schwab	30	1645	2.73	12	10	5	1
Team Total	82	4986	2.49	43	29	10	5

Vancouver Canucks

SCORING

Player	GP	G	A	Pts	+/-	PM
Markus Naslund, L	81	40	50	90	22	50
Todd Bertuzzi, L	72	36	49	85	21	110
Brendan Morrison, C	82	23	44	67	18	26
Andrew Cassels, C	53	11	39	50	5	22
Ed Jovanovski, D	82	17	31	48	-7	101
Trevor Linden, C	80	13	24	37	-5	71
Mattias Ohlund, D	81	10	26	36	16	56
Henrik Sedin, C	82	16	20	36	9	36
Matt Cooke, C	82	13	20	33	4	111
Daniel Sedin, L	79	9	23	32	1	32
Jan Hlavac, L	77	16	15	31	9	18
Brent Sopel, D	66	8	17	25	21	44
Trevor Letowski, C	75	9	16	25	4	19
Trent Klatt, R	34	8	7	15	9	10
Scott Lachance, D	81	1	10	11	15	50
Bryan Helmer, D	40	5	5	10	0	53
Artem Chubarov, C	51	5	5	10	-3	10
Todd Warriner, L	32	2	7	9	1	20
Jarkko Ruutu, L	49	2	7	9	-1	74
Justin Kurtz, R	27	3	5	8	-4	14
Harold Druken, C	27	4	4	8	-1	6

GOALTENDING

Player	GP	Mins	Avg	W	L	T	SO
Peter Skudra	23	1165	2.42	10	8	2	1
Dan Cloutier	62	3501	2.43	31	22	5	7
Martin Brochu	6	216	4.17	0	3	0	0
Team total	82	4978	2.54	42	33	7	8

* Rookie.

Washington Capitals

SCORING

Player	GP	G	A	Pts	+/-	PM
Jaromir Jagr, R	69	31	48	79	0	30
Peter Bondra, R	77	39	31	70	-2	80
Sergei Gonchar, D	76	26	33	59	-1	58
Ulf Dahlen, L	69	23	29	52	-5	8
Dainius Zubrus, R	71	17	26	43	5	38
Andrei Nikolishin, C	80	13	23	36	-1	40
Chris Simon, L	82	14	17	31	-8	137
Dmitri Khristich, R	61	9	12	21	2	12
Jeff Halpern, C	48	5	14	19	-9	29
Glen Metropolit, C	35	1	16	17	1	6
Ken Klee, D	68	8	8	16	4	38
Benoit Hogue, L	58	7	8	15	-5	37
Sylvain Cote, D	70	3	11	14	-15	20
Frantisek Kucera, D	56	1	13	14	7	12
Steve Konowalchuk, L	28	2	12	14	-2	23
Brendan Witt, D	68	3	7	10	-1	78
Matt Pettinger, L	61	7	3	10	-8	44
Colin Forbes, C	38	5	3	8	-2	15
Joe Sacco, R	65	0	7	7	-13	51
Rob Zettler, D	49	1	4	5	3	56
Ivan Ciernik, L	29	1	3	4	0	6

GOALTENDING

Player	GP	Mins	Avg	W	L	T	SO
S. Charpentie	2	122	2.46	1	1	0	0
Olaf Kolzig	71	4131	2.79	31	29	8	6
Craig Billington	17	710	3.04	4	5	3	0
Team total	82	4987	2.89	36	35	11	6

2002 NHL Draft

First Round

The opening round of the 2002 NHL draft was held on June 22 in Toronto, Ont.

Team	Selection	Position	Team	Selection	Position
1.....Columbus	Rick Nash	L	16...Ottawa	Jakub Klepis	C
2.....Atlanta	Kari Lehtonen	G	17...Washington	Boyd Gordon	R
3.....Florida	Jay Bouwmeester	D	18...Los Angeles	Denis Grebeshkov	D
4.....Philadelphia	Joni Pitkanen	D	19...Phoenix	Jakub Koreis	C
5.....Pittsburgh	Ryan Whitney	D	20...Buffalo	Dan Paille	L
6.....Nashville	Scottie Upshall	R	21...Chicago	Anton Babchuk	D
7.....Anaheim	Joffrey Lupul	C	22...NY Islanders	Sean Bergenheim	L
8.....Minnesota	Pierre-Marc Bouchard	C	23...Phoenix	Ben Eager	L
9.....Florida	Petr Taticek	C	24...Toronto	Alexander Steen	C
10...Calgary	Eric Nystrom	L	25...Carolina	Cam Ward	G
11...Buffalo	Keith Ballard	D	26...Dallas	Martin Vagner	D
12...Washington	Steve Eminger	D	27...San Jose	Mike Morris	R
13...Washington	Alexander Syemin	L	28...Colorado	Jonas Johansson	R
14...Montreal	Christopher Higgins	C	29...Boston	Hannu Toivonen	G
15...Edmonton	Jesse Niinimaki	C	30...Atlanta	Jim Slater	C

FOR THE RECORD · Year by Year

The Stanley Cup

Awarded annually to the team that wins the NHL's best-of-seven final-round playoffs. The Stanley Cup is the oldest trophy competed for by professional athletes in North America. It was donated in 1893 by Frederick Arthur, Lord Stanley of Preston.

Results

1892–93.....Montreal A.A.A.	1900–01.....Winnipeg Victorias	1907–08.....Montreal Wanderers
1893–94.....Montreal A.A.A.	1901–02.....Winnipeg Victorias (Jan)	1908–09.....Ottawa Senators
1894–95.....Montreal Victorias	1901–02.....Montreal A.A.A. (Mar)	1909–10.....Montreal Wanderers
1895–96.....Winnipeg Victorias (Feb)	1902–03.....Montreal A.A.A. (Feb)	1910–11.....Ottawa Senators
1895–96.....Montreal Victorias (Dec)	1902–03.....Ottawa Silver Seven (Mar)	1911–12.....Quebec Bulldogs
1896–97.....Montreal Victorias	1903–04.....Ottawa Silver Seven	1912–13.....Quebec Bulldogs
1897–98.....Montreal Victorias	1904–05.....Ottawa Silver Seven	1913–14.....Toronto Blueshirts
1898–99.....Montreal Victorias (Feb)	1905–06.....Ottawa Silver Seven (Feb)	1914–15.....Vancouver Millionaires
1898–99.....Montreal Shamrocks (Mar)	1905–06.....Montreal Wanderers (Mar)	1915–16.....Montreal Canadiens
1899–1900...Montreal Shamrocks	1906–07.....Kenora Thistles (Jan)	1916–17.....Seattle Metropolitans
	1906–07.....Montreal Wanderers (Mar)	

NHL WINNERS AND FINALISTS

Season	Champion	Finalist	GP in Final
1917–18	Toronto Arenas	Vancouver Millionaires	5
1918–19	No decision*	No decision*	5
1919–20	Ottawa Senators	Seattle Metropolitans	5
1920–21	Ottawa Senators	Vancouver Millionaires	5
1921–22	Toronto St. Pats	Vancouver Millionaires	5
1922–23	Ottawa Senators	Vancouver Maroons, Edmonton Eskimos	2, 4
1923–24	Montreal Canadiens	Vancouver Maroons, Calgary Tigers	2, 2
1924–25	Victoria Cougars	Montreal Canadiens	4
1925–26	Montreal Maroons	Victoria Cougars	4
1926–27	Ottawa Senators	Boston Bruins	4
1927–28	New York Rangers	Montreal Maroons	5
1928–29	Boston Bruins	New York Rangers	2
1929–30	Montreal Canadiens	Boston Bruins	2
1930–31	Montreal Canadiens	Chicago Blackhawks	5
1931–32	Toronto Maple Leafs	New York Rangers	3
1932–33	New York Rangers	Toronto Maple Leafs	4
1933–34	Chicago Blackhawks	Detroit Red Wings	4
1934–35	Montreal Maroons	Toronto Maple Leafs	3

NHL WINNERS AND FINALISTS *(CONT.)*

Season	Champion	Finalist	GP in Final
1935–36	Detroit Red Wings	Toronto Maple Leafs	4
1936–37	Detroit Red Wings	New York Rangers	5
1937–38	Chicago Blackhawks	Toronto Maple Leafs	4
1938–39	Boston Bruins	Toronto Maple Leafs	5
1939–40	New York Rangers	Toronto Maple Leafs	6
1940–41	Boston Bruins	Detroit Red Wings	4
1941–42	Toronto Maple Leafs	Detroit Red Wings	7
1942–43	Detroit Red Wings	Boston Bruins	4
1943–44	Montreal Canadiens	Chicago Blackhawks	4
1944–45	Toronto Maple Leafs	Detroit Red Wings	7
1945–46	Montreal Canadiens	Boston Bruins	5
1946–47	Toronto Maple Leafs	Montreal Canadiens	6
1947–48	Toronto Maple Leafs	Detroit Red Wings	4
1948–49	Toronto Maple Leafs	Detroit Red Wings	4
1949–50	Detroit Red Wings	New York Rangers	7
1950–51	Toronto Maple Leafs	Montreal Canadiens	5
1951–52	Detroit Red Wings	Montreal Canadiens	4
1952–53	Montreal Canadiens	Boston Bruins	5
1953–54	Detroit Red Wings	Montreal Canadiens	7
1954–55	Detroit Red Wings	Montreal Canadiens	7
1955–56	Montreal Canadiens	Detroit Red Wings	5
1956–57	Montreal Canadiens	Boston Bruins	5
1957–58	Montreal Canadiens	Boston Bruins	6
1958–59	Montreal Canadiens	Toronto Maple Leafs	5
1959–60	Montreal Canadiens	Toronto Maple Leafs	4
1960–61	Chicago Blackhawks	Detroit Red Wings	6
1961–62	Toronto Maple Leafs	Chicago Blackhawks	6
1962–63	Toronto Maple Leafs	Detroit Red Wings	5
1963–64	Toronto Maple Leafs	Detroit Red Wings	7
1964–65	Montreal Canadiens	Chicago Blackhawks	7
1965–66	Montreal Canadiens	Detroit Red Wings	6
1966–67	Toronto Maple Leafs	Montreal Canadiens	6
1967–68	Montreal Canadiens	St. Louis Blues	4
1968–69	Montreal Canadiens	St. Louis Blues	4
1969–70	Boston Bruins	St. Louis Blues	4
1970–71	Montreal Canadiens	Chicago Blackhawks	7
1971–72	Boston Bruins	New York Rangers	6
1972–73	Montreal Canadiens	Chicago Blackhawks	6
1973–74	Philadelphia Flyers	Boston Bruins	6
1974–75	Philadelphia Flyers	Buffalo Sabres	6
1975–76	Montreal Canadiens	Philadelphia Flyers	4
1976–77	Montreal Canadiens	Boston Bruins	4
1977–78	Montreal Canadiens	Boston Bruins	6
1978–79	Montreal Canadiens	New York Rangers	5
1979–80	New York Islanders	Philadelphia Flyers	6
1980–81	New York Islanders	Minnesota North Stars	5
1981–82	New York Islanders	Vancouver Canucks	4
1982–83	New York Islanders	Edmonton Oilers	4
1983–84	Edmonton Oilers	New York Islanders	5
1984–85	Edmonton Oilers	Philadelphia Flyers	5
1985–86	Montreal Canadiens	Calgary Flames	6
1986–87	Edmonton Oilers	Philadelphia Flyers	7
1987–88	Edmonton Oilers	Boston Bruins	4
1988–89	Calgary Flames	Montreal Canadiens	6
1989–90	Edmonton Oilers	Boston Bruins	5
1990–91	Pittsburgh Penguins	Minnesota North Stars	6
1991–92	Pittsburgh Penguins	Chicago Blackhawks	4
1992–93	Montreal Canadiens	Los Angeles Kings	5
1993–94	New York Rangers	Vancouver Canucks	7
1994–95	New Jersey Devils	Detroit Red Wings	4
1995–96	Colorado Avalanche	Florida Panthers	4
1996–97	Detroit Red Wings	Philadelphia Flyers	4
1997–98	Detroit Red Wings	Washington Capitals	4
1998–99	Dallas Stars	Buffalo Sabres	6

NHL WINNERS AND FINALISTS *(CONT.)*

Season	Champion	Finalist	GP in Final
1999–00	New Jersey Devils	Dallas Stars	6
2000–01	Colorado Avalanche	New Jersey Devils	7
2001–02	Detroit Red Wings	Carolina Hurricanes	5

*In 1919 the Montreal Canadiens traveled to meet Seattle, the PCHL champions. After 5 games had been played—the teams were tied at 2 wins and 1 tie—the series was called off by the local Department of Health because of the influenza epidemic and the death of Canadiens defenseman Joe Hall from influenza.

Conn Smythe Trophy

Awarded to the Most Valuable Player of the Stanley Cup playoffs, as selected by the Professional Hockey Writers Association. The trophy is named after the former coach, general manager, president and owner of the Toronto Maple Leafs.

1965	Jean Beliveau, Mtl	1984	Mark Messier, Edm
1966	Roger Crozier, Det	1985	Wayne Gretzky, Edm
1967	Dave Keon, Tor	1986	Patrick Roy, Mtl
1968	Glenn Hall, StL	1987	Ron Hextall, Phil
1969	Serge Savard, Mtl	1988	Wayne Gretzky, Edm
1970	Bobby Orr, Bos	1989	Al MacInnis, Cgy
1971	Ken Dryden, Mtl	1990	Bill Ranford, Edm
1972	Bobby Orr, Bos	1991	Mario Lemieux, Pitt
1973	Yvan Cournoyer, Mtl	1992	Mario Lemieux, Pitt
1974	Bernie Parent, Phil	1993	Patrick Roy, Mtl
1975	Bernie Parent, Phil	1994	Brian Leetch, NYR
1976	Reggie Leach, Phil	1995	Claude Lemieux, NJ
1977	Guy Lafleur, Mtl	1996	Joe Sakic, Col
1978	Larry Robinson, Mtl	1997	Mike Vernon, Det
1979	Bob Gainey, Mtl	1998	Steve Yzerman, Det
1980	Bryan Trottier, NYI	1999	Joe Nieuwendyk, Dall
1981	Butch Goring, NYI	2000	Scott Stevens, NJ
1982	Mike Bossy, NYI	2001	Patrick Roy, Col
1983	Bill Smith, NYI	2002	Nicklas Lidstrom, Det

Alltime Stanley Cup Playoff Leaders

Points

	Yrs	GP	G	A	Pts		Yrs	GP	G	A	Pts
Wayne Gretzky, four teams	16	208	122	260	382	*Steve Yzerman, Det	17	177	67	108	175
*Mark Messier, Edm, NYR	17	236	109	186	295	*Mario Lemieux, Pitt	8	107	76	96	172
Jari Kurri, four teams	15	200	106	127	233	Denis Savard, Chi	14	185	56	108	164
Glenn Anderson, four teams	15	225	93	121	214	Mike Bossy, NYI	10	129	85	75	160
Paul Coffey, six teams	16	198	59	137	196	Gordie Howe, Det, Hart	20	157	68	92	160
*Brett Hull, Cal, StL, Dall, Det	17	186	100	84	184	Bobby Smith, Minn, Mtl	13	184	64	96	160
Bryan Trottier, NYI, Pitt	17	221	71	113	184	Sergei Fedorov, Det	12	158	49	111	160
Ray Bourque, Bos, Col	21	214	41	139	180	*Al MacInnis, Cgy, StL	18	174	39	120	159
*Doug Gilmour, seven teams	17	182	60	128	188	*Claude Lemieux, four teams	16	226	80	77	157
Jean Beliveau, Mtl	17	162	79	97	176						
Denis Savard, Chi, Mtl	16	169	66	109	175						

*Active in 2001–02.

Goals

	Yrs	GP	G
Wayne Gretzky, four teams	17	208	122
*Mark Messier, Edm, NYR	17	236	109
Jari Kurri, five teams	15	200	106
*Brett Hull, Cgy, StL, Dall, Det	17	186	100
Glenn Anderson, four teams	15	225	93
Mike Bossy, NYI	10	129	85
Maurice Richard, Mtl	15	133	82
*Claude Lemieux, Mtl, NJ, Col	16	226	80
Jean Beliveau, Mtl	17	162	79
*Mario Lemieux, Pitt	8	107	76

*Active in 2001–02.

Assists

	Yrs	GP	A
Wayne Gretzky, four teams	17	208	260
*Mark Messier, Edm, NYR	17	236	186
Ray Bourque, Bos, Col	21	214	139
Paul Coffey, six teams	16	198	137
*Doug Gilmour, five teams	17	182	128
Jari Kurri, five teams	15	196	127
Glenn Anderson, four teams	15	225	121
*Al MacInnis, Cgy, StL	18	174	120
Larry Robinson, Mtl, LA	20	227	116
Larry Murphy, six teams	20	215	115
Bryan Trottier, NYI, Pitt	17	221	113

*Active in 2001–02.

Alltime Stanley Cup Playoff Goaltending Leaders

WINS	W	L	Pct	SHUTOUTS	GP	W	SO
*Patrick Roy, Mtl, Col	148	90	.622	*Patrick Roy, Mtl, Col	238	148	22
Grant Fuhr, five teams	92	50	.648	Clint Benedict, Ott, Mtl M.	48	25	15
Billy Smith, LA, NYI	88	36	.710	*Curtis Joseph, StL, Edm, Tor	118	58	15
Ken Dryden, Mtl	80	32	.714	Jacques Plante, five teams	112	71	14
*Ed Belfour, Chi, SJ, Dall	79	57	.581	Turk Broda, Tor	101	58	13
*Mike Vernon, four teams	77	56	.579	*Martin Brodeur, NJ	115	67	13
Jacques Plante, five teams	71	37	.657	Terry Sawchuk, Det, LA	106	54	12
Andy Moog, four teams	68	57	.544	Dominik Hasek, Buff, Det	97	53	12
*Martin Brodeur, NJ	67	48	.583	**GOALS AGAINST AVG**			**Avg**
*Tom Barrasso, four teams	61	54	.530	*Martin Brodeur, NJ			1.88
				George Hainsworth, Mtl, Tor			1.93
*Active in 2001–02.				Turk Broda, Tor			1.98
				*Dominik Hasek, Edm, Tor, Buff			2.03
				*Ed Belfour, Chi, Dall			2.14

Note: At least 50 games played.
*Active in 2001–02.

Alltime Stanley Cup Playoff Wins

TEAM	W	L	Pct	TEAM	W	L	Pct
Montreal	387	255	.603	Buffalo	99	110	.474
Detroit	251	226	.526	New Jersey†	90	74	.549
Toronto	242	258	.484	Calgary*	69	87	.442
Boston	238	256	.482	Washington	67	81	.453
Chicago	188	218	.463	Los Angeles	65	101	.392
NY Rangers	183	195	.484	Vancouver	56	78	.418
Philadelphia	161	147	.523	Carolina§	35	49	.417
St. Louis	134	157	.461	San Jose	29	38	.433
Edmonton	133	86	.607	Phoenix††	28	63	.308
NY Islanders	131	94	.582	Ottawa	17	27	.386
Dallas#	130	127	.506	Florida	13	18	.419
Colorado**	113	93	.549	Anaheim	4	11	.267
Pittsburgh	109	99	.524	Tampa Bay	2	4	.333

*Atlanta Flames 1972–80. †Colorado Rockies 1976–82. #Minnesota North Stars 1967–93. **Quebec Nordiques 1979–95. ††Winnipeg Jets 1979–96. §Hartford Whalers 1979–97. Note: Teams ranked by playoff victories.

Stanley Cup Playoff Coaching Records

				Series			Games				
Coach	Team	Yrs	Series	W	L	Games	W	L	T	Cups	Pct
Glen Sather	Edm	10	27	21	6	*126	89	37	0	4	.706
Toe Blake	Mtl	13	23	18	5	119	82	37	0	8	.689
†Scott Bowman	Five teams	28	68	49	19	353	223	130	0	9	.632
Hap Day	Tor	9	14	10	4	80	49	31	0	5	.613
Jacques Lemaire	Mtl, NJ	6	15	10	5	83	49	34	0	1	.590
Al Arbour	StL, NYI	16	42	30	12	209	123	86	0	4	.589
†Ken Hitchcock	Dall	5	14	10	4	80	47	33	0	1	.588
Mike Keenan	five teams	11	28	18	10	160	91	69	0	1	.569
Fred Shero	Phil, NYR	8	21	15	6	108	61	47	0	2	.565
Bob Hartley	Col	4	13	10	3	80	49	31	0	1	.613

*Does not include suspended game, May 24, 1988. †Active in 2001–02.
Note: Coaches ranked by winning percentage. Minimum: 65 games.

The 10 Longest Overtime Games

Date	Result	OT	Scorer	Series	Series Winner
3-24-36	Det 1 vs Mtl M 0	116:30	Mud Bruneteau	SF	Det
4-3-33	Tor 1 vs Bos 0	104:46	Ken Doraty	SF	Tor
5-4-00	Phil 2 vs Pitt 1	92:01	Keith Primeau	CSF	Phil
4-24-96	Pitt 3 vs Wash 2	79:15	Petr Nedved	CQF	Pitt
3-23-43	Tor 3 vs Det 2	70:18	Jack McLean	SF	Det
3-28-30	Mtl 2 vs NYR 1	68:52	Gus Rivers	SF	Mtl
4-18-87	NYI 3 vs Wash 2	68:47	Pat LaFontaine	DSF	NYI
4-27-94	Buff 1 vs NJ 0	65:43	Dave Hannan	CQF	NJ
3-27-51	Mtl 3 vs Det 2	61:09	Maurice Richard	SF	Mtl
3-27-38	NYA 3 vs NYR 2	60:40	Lorne Carr	QF	NYA

Hart Memorial Trophy

Awarded annually "to the player adjudged to be the most valuable to his team." The original trophy was donated by Dr. David A. Hart, father of Cecil Hart, former manager-coach of the Montreal Canadiens. In the 1980s Wayne Gretzky won the award nine times.

Year	Winner	Key Statistics	Runner-Up
1924	Frank Nighbor, Ott	10 goals, 3 assists in 20 games	Sprague Cleghorn, Mtl
1925	Billy Burch, Ham	20 goals, 4 assists in 27 games	Howie Morenz, Mtl
1926	Nels Stewart, Mtl M	42 points in 36 games	Sprague Cleghorn, Mtl
1927	Herb Gardiner, Mtl	12 points in 44 games as defenseman	Bill Cook, NYR
1928	Howie Morenz, Mtl	33 goals, 18 assists	Roy Worters, Pitt
1929	Roy Worters, NYA	1.21 goals against, 13 shutouts	Ace Bailey, Tor
1930	Nels Stewart, Mtl M	39 goals, 16 assists	Lionel Hitchman, Bos
1931	Howie Morenz, Mtl	28 goals, 23 assists	Eddie Shore, Bos
1932	Howie Morenz, Mtl	24 goals, 25 assists	Ching Johnson, NYR
1933	Eddie Shore, Bos	27 assists in 48 games as defenseman	Bill Cook, NYR
1934	Aurel Joliat, Mtl	27 points	Lionel Conacher, Chi
1935	Eddie Shore, Bos	26 assists in 48 games as defenseman	Charlie Conacher, Tor
1936	Eddie Shore, Bos	16 assists in 46 games as defenseman	Hooley Smith, Mtl M
1937	Babe Siebert, Mtl	28 points	Lionel Conacher, Mtl M
1938	Eddie Shore, Bos	17 points in 47 games as defenseman	Paul Thompson, Chi
1939	Toe Blake, Mtl	led NHL in points (47)	Syl Apps, Tor
1940	Ebbie Goodfellow, Det	28 points	Syl Apps, Tor
1941	Bill Cowley, Bos	led NHL in assists (45) and points (62)	Dit Clapper, Bos
1942	Tom Anderson, Bos	41 points	Syl Apps, Tor
1943	Bill Cowley, Bos	led NHL in assists (45)	Doug Bentley, Chi
1944	Babe Pratt, Tor	57 points in 50 games	Bill Cowley, Bos
1945	Elmer Lach, Mtl	led NHL in assists (54) and points (80)	Maurice Richard, Mtl
1946	Max Bentley, Chi	61 points in 47 games	Gaye Stewart, Tor
1947	Maurice Richard, Mtl	led NHL in goals (45); 26 assists	Milt Schmidt, Bos
1948	Buddy O'Connor, NYR	60 points in 60 games	Frank Brimsek, Bos
1949	Sid Abel, Det	28 goals, 26 assists	Bill Durnan, Mtl
1950	Charlie Rayner, NYR	6 shutouts	Ted Kennedy, Tor
1951	Milt Schmidt, Bos	61 points in 62 games	Maurice Richard, Mtl
1952	Gordie Howe, Det	led NHL in goals (47) and points (86)	Elmer Lach, Mtl
1953	Gordie Howe, Det	led NHL in goals (49) and points (95)	Al Rollins, Chi
1954	Al Rollins, Chi	5 shutouts	Red Kelly, Det
1955	Ted Kennedy, Tor	52 points	Harry Lumley, Tor
1956	Jean Beliveau, Mtl	led NHL in goals (47) and points (88)	Tod Sloan, Tor
1957	Gordie Howe, Det	led NHL in goals (44) and points (89)	Jean Beliveau, Mtl
1959	Andy Bathgate, NYR	74 points in 70 games	Gordie Howe, Det
1960	Gordie Howe, Det	45 assists, 73 points	Bobby Hull, Chi
1961	Bernie Geoffrion, Mtl	50 goals, 95 points	Johnny Bower, Tor
1962	Jacques Plante, Mtl	42 wins, 2.37 goals against avg.	Doug Harvey, NYR
1963	Gordie Howe, Det	47 assists, 73 points	Stan Mikita, Chi
1964	Jean Beliveau, Mtl	50 assists, 78 points	Bobby Hull, Chi
1965	Bobby Hull, Chi	39 goals, 32 assists	Norm Ullman, Det
1966	Bobby Hull, Chi	led NHL in goals (54) and points (97)	Jean Beliveau, Mtl
1967	Stan Mikita, Chi	led NHL in assists (62) and points (97)	Ed Giacomin, NYR
1968	Stan Mikita, Chi	40 goals, 47 assists	Jean Beliveau, Mtl
1969	Phil Esposito, Bos	led NHL in assists (77) and points (126)	Jean Beliveau, Mtl
1970	Bobby Orr, Bos	led NHL in assists (87) and points (120)	Tony Esposito, Chi
1971	Bobby Orr, Bos	102 assists, 139 points	Tony Esposito, Chi
1972	Bobby Orr, Bos	80 assists, 117 points	Ken Dryden, Mtl
1973	Bobby Clarke, Phil	67 assists, 104 points	Phil Esposito, Bos
1974	Phil Esposito, Bos	led NHL in goals (68) and points (145)	Bernie Parent, Phil
1975	Bobby Clarke, Phil	89 assists, 116 points	Rogatien Vachon, LA
1976	Bobby Clarke, Phil	89 assists, 119 points	Denis Potvin, NYI
1977	Guy Lafleur, Mtl	led NHL in assists (80) and points (136)	Bobby Clarke, Phil
1978	Guy Lafleur, Mtl	led NHL in goals (60) and points (132)	Bryan Trottier, NYI
1979	Bryan Trottier, NYI	led NHL in assists (87) and points (134)	Guy Lafleur, Mtl
1980	Wayne Gretzky, Edm	51 goals, 86 assists	Marcel Dionne, LA
1981	Wayne Gretzky, Edm	led NHL in assists (109) and points (164)	Mike Liut, StL
1982	Wayne Gretzky, Edm	NHL-record 92 goals and 212 points	Bryan Trottier, NYI
1983	Wayne Gretzky, Edm	led NHL in goals (71) and points (196)	Pete Peeters, Bos
1984	Wayne Gretzky, Edm	led NHL in goals (87) and points (205)	Rod Langway, Wash
1985	Wayne Gretzky, Edm	led NHL in goals (73) and points (208)	Dale Hawerchuk, Winn
1986	Wayne Gretzky, Edm	NHL-record 163 assists and 215 points	Mario Lemieux, Pitt

Hart Memorial Trophy (Cont.)

Year	Winner	Key Statistics	Runner-Up
1987	Wayne Gretzky, Edm	led NHL in assists (121) and points (183)	Ray Bourque, Bos
1988	Mario Lemieux, Pitt	led NHL in goals (70) and points (168)	Grant Fuhr, Edm
1989	Wayne Gretzky, LA	114 assists, 168 points	Mario Lemieux, Pitt
1990	Mark Messier, Edm	84 assists, 129 points	Ray Bourque, Bos
1991	Brett Hull, StL	led NHL in goals (86); 131 points	Wayne Gretzky, LA
1992	Mark Messier, NYR	72 assists, 107 points	Patrick Roy, Mtl
1993	Mario Lemieux, Pitt	69 goals, 91 assists in 60 games	Doug Gilmour, Tor
1994	Sergei Fedorov, Det	56 goals, 64 assists	Dominik Hasek, Buff
1995	Eric Lindros, Phil	29 goals, 41 assists in 46 games	Jaromir Jagr, Pitt
1996	Mario Lemieux, Pitt	led NHL in goals (69) and points (161)	Mark Messier, NYR
1997	Dominik Hasek, Buff	5 shutouts, 2.27 goals against avg.	Paul Kariya, Ana
1998	Dominik Hasek, Buff	13 shutouts, 2.09 goals against avg.	Jaromir Jagr, Pitt
1999	Jaromir Jagr, Pitt	44 goals, 127 points	Alexei Yashin, Ott
2000	Chris Pronger, StL	62 points, +52 plus/minus rating	Jaromir Jagr, Pitt
2001	Joe Sakic, Col	118 points, +45 plus/minus rating	Mario Lemieux, Pitt
2002	Jose Theodore, Mtl	2.11 goals against avg./7 shutouts	Jarome Iginla, Cal

Art Ross Trophy

Awarded annually "to the player who leads the league in scoring points at the end of the regular season." The trophy was presented to the NHL in 1947 by Arthur Howie Ross, former manager-coach of the Boston Bruins. The tie-breakers, in order, are as follows: (1) player with most goals, (2) player with fewer games played, (3) player scoring first goal of the season. Bobby Orr is the only defenseman in NHL history to win this trophy, and he won it twice (1970 and 1975).

Year	Winner	Pts	Year	Winner	Pts
1919	Newsy Lalonde, Mtl	44	1957	Gordie Howe, Det	89
1920	Joe Malone, Que	30	1958	Dickie Moore, Mtl	84
1921	Newsy Lalonde, Mtl	48	1959	Dickie Moore, Mtl	96
1922	Punch Broadbent, Ott	41	1960	Bobby Hull, Chi	81
1923	Babe Dye, Tor	46	1961	Bernie Geoffrion, Mtl	95
1924	Cy Denneny, Ott	37	1962	Bobby Hull, Chi	84
1925	Babe Dye, Tor	23	1963	Gordie Howe, Det	86
1926	Nels Stewart, Mtl M	44	1964	Stan Mikita, Chi	89
1927	Bill Cook, NYR	42	1965	Stan Mikita, Chi	87
1928	Howie Morenz, Mtl	37	1966	Bobby Hull, Chi	97
1929	Ace Bailey, Tor	51	1967	Stan Mikita, Chi	97
1930	Cooney Weiland, Bos	32	1968	Stan Mikita, Chi	87
1931	Howie Morenz, Mtl	73	1969	Phil Esposito, Bos	126
1932	Harvey Jackson, Tor	51	1970	Bobby Orr, Bos	120
1933	Bill Cook, NYR	53	1971	Phil Esposito, Bos	152
1934	Charlie Conacher, Tor	50	1972	Phil Esposito, Bos	133
1935	Charlie Conacher, Tor	57	1973	Phil Esposito, Bos	130
1936	Sweeney Schriner, NYA	45	1974	Phil Esposito, Bos	145
1937	Sweeney Schriner, NYA	46	1975	Bobby Orr, Bos	135
1938	Gordie Drillon, Tor	52	1976	Guy Lafleur, Mtl	125
1939	Toe Blake, Mtl	47	1977	Guy Lafleur, Mtl	136
1940	Milt Schmidt, Bos	52	1978	Guy Lafleur, Mtl	132
1941	Bill Cowley, Bos	62	1979	Bryan Trottier, NYI	134
1942	Bryan Hextall, NYR	56	1980	Marcel Dionne, LA	137
1943	Doug Bentley, Chi	73	1981	Wayne Gretzky, Edm	164
1944	Herb Cain, Bos	82	1982	Wayne Gretzky, Edm	212
1945	Elmer Lach, Mtl	80	1983	Wayne Gretzky, Edm	196
1946	Max Bentley, Chi	61	1984	Wayne Gretzky, Edm	205
1947	*Max Bentley, Chi	72	1985	Wayne Gretzky, Edm	208
1948	Elmer Lach, Mtl	61	1986	Wayne Gretzky, Edm	215
1949	Roy Conacher, Chi	68	1987	Wayne Gretzky, Edm	183
1950	Ted Lindsay, Det	78	1988	Mario Lemieux, Pitt	168
1951	Gordie Howe, Det	86	1989	Mario Lemieux, Pitt	199
1952	Gordie Howe, Det	86	1990	Wayne Gretzky, LA	142
1953	Gordie Howe, Det	95	1991	Wayne Gretzky, LA	163
1954	Gordie Howe, Det	81	1992	Mario Lemieux, Pitt	131
1955	Bernie Geoffrion, Mtl	75	1993	Mario Lemieux, Pitt	160
1956	Jean Beliveau, Mtl	88	1994	Wayne Gretzky, LA	130
			1995	Jaromir Jagr, Pitt	70

Art Ross Trophy *(Cont.)*

1996	Mario Lemieux, Pitt	161	2000	Jaromir Jagr, Pitt	96
1997	Mario Lemieux, Pitt	122	2001	Jaromir Jagr, Pitt	121
1998	Jaromir Jagr, Pitt	102	2002	Jarome Iginla, Cal	96
1999	Jaromir Jagr, Pitt	127			

Note: Listing includes scoring leaders prior to inception of Art Ross Trophy in 1947–48.

Lady Byng Memorial Trophy

Awarded annually "to the player adjudged to have exhibited the best type of sportsmanship and gentlemanly conduct combined with a high standard of playing ability." Lady Byng, who first presented the trophy in 1925, was the wife of Canada's Governor-General. She donated a second trophy in 1936 after the first was given permanently to Frank Boucher of the New York Rangers, who won it seven times in eight seasons. Stan Mikita, one of the league's most penalized players during his early years in the NHL, won the trophy twice late in his career (1967 and 1968).

1925..........Frank Nighbor, Ott	1952.........Sid Smith, Tor	1979..........Bob MacMillan, Atl
1926..........Frank Nighbor, Ott	1953..........Red Kelly, Det	1980..........Wayne Gretzky, Edm
1927..........Billy Burch, NYA	1954..........Red Kelly, Det	1981..........Rick Kehoe, Pitt
1928..........Frank Boucher, NYR	1955..........Sid Smith, Tor	1982..........Rick Middleton, Bos
1929..........Frank Boucher, NYR	1956..........Earl Reibel, Det	1983..........Mike Bossy, NYI
1930..........Frank Boucher, NYR	1957..........Andy Hebenton, NYR	1984..........Mike Bossy, NYI
1931..........Frank Boucher, NYR	1958..........Camille Henry, NYR	1985..........Jari Kurri, Edm
1932..........Joe Primeau, Tor	1959..........Alex Delvecchio, Det	1986..........Mike Bossy, NYI
1933..........Frank Boucher, NYR	1960..........Don McKenney, Bos	1987..........Joe Mullen, Cgy
1934..........Frank Boucher, NYR	1961..........Red Kelly, Tor	1988..........Mats Naslund, Mtl
1935..........Frank Boucher, NYR	1962..........Dave Keon, Tor	1989..........Joe Mullen, Cgy
1936..........Doc Romnes, Chi	1963..........Dave Keon, Tor	1990..........Brett Hull, StL
1937..........Marty Barry, Det	1964..........Ken Wharram, Chi	1991..........Wayne Gretzky, LA
1938..........Gordie Drillon, Tor	1965..........Bobby Hull, Cbi	1992..........Wayne Gretzky, LA
1939..........Clint Smith, NYR	1966..........Alex Delvecchio, Det	1993..........Pierre Turgeon, NYI
1940..........Bobby Bauer, Bos	1967..........Stan Mikita, Chi	1994..........Wayne Gretzky, LA
1941..........Bobby Bauer, Bos	1968..........Stan Mikita, Chi	1995..........Ron Francis, Pitt
1942..........Syl Apps, Tor	1969..........Alex Delvecchio, Det	1996..........Paul Kariya, Ana
1943..........Max Bentley, Chi	1970..........Phil Goyette, StL	1997..........Paul Kariya, Ana
1944..........Clint Smith, Chi	1971..........John Bucyk, Bos	1998..........Ron Francis, Pitt
1945..........Billy Mosienko, Chi	1972..........Jean Ratelle, NYR	1999..........Wayne Gretzky, NYR
1946..........Toe Blake, Mtl	1973..........Gilbert Perreault, Buff	2000..........Pavol Demitra, StL
1947..........Bobby Bauer, Bos	1974..........John Bucyk, Bos	2001..........Joe Sakic, Col
1948..........Buddy O'Connor, NYR	1975..........Marcel Dionne, Det	2002..........Ron Francis, Car
1949..........Bill Quackenbush, Det	1976..........Jean Ratelle, NYR-Bos	
1950..........Edgar Laprade, NYR	1977..........Marcel Dionne, LA	
1951..........Red Kelly, Det	1978..........Butch Goring, LA	

James Norris Memorial Trophy

Awarded annually "to the defense player who demonstrates throughout the season the greatest all-around ability in the position." James Norris was the former owner-president of the Detroit Red Wings. Bobby Orr holds the record for most consecutive times winning the award (eight, 1968–1975).

1954.......Red Kelly, Det	1971.......Bobby Orr, Bos	1988.......Ray Bourque, Bos
1955.......Doug Harvey, Mtl	1972.......Bobby Orr, Bos	1989.......Chris Chelios, Mtl
1956.......Doug Harvey, Mtl	1973.......Bobby Orr, Bos	1990.......Ray Bourque, Bos
1957.......Doug Harvey, Mtl	1974.......Bobby Orr, Bos	1991.......Ray Bourque, Bos
1958.......Doug Harvey, Mtl	1975.......Bobby Orr, Bos	1992.......Brian Leetch, NYR
1959.......Tom Johnson, Mtl	1976.......Denis Potvin, NYI	1993.......Chris Chelios, Chi
1960.......Doug Harvey, Mtl	1977.......Larry Robinson, Mtl	1994.......Ray Bourque, Bos
1961.......Doug Harvey, Mtl	1978.......Denis Potvin, NYI	1995.......Paul Coffey, Det
1962.......Doug Harvey, NYR	1979.......Denis Potvin, NYI	1996.......Chris Chelios, Chi
1963.......Pierre Pilote, Chi	1980.......Larry Robinson, Mtl	1997.......Brian Leetch, NYR
1964.......Pierre Pilote, Chi	1981.......Randy Carlyle, Pitt	1998.......Rob Blake, LA
1965.......Pierre Pilote, Chi	1982.......Doug Wilson, Chi	1999.......Al MacInnis, StL
1966.......Jacques Laperriere, Mtl	1983.......Rod Langway, Wash	2000.......Chris Pronger, StL
1967.......Harry Howell, NYR	1984.......Rod Langway, Wash	2001.......Nicklas Lidstrom, Det
1968.......Bobby Orr, Bos	1985.......Paul Coffey, Edm	2002.......Nicklas Lidstrom, Det
1969.......Bobby Orr, Bos	1986.......Paul Coffey, Edm	
1970.......Bobby Orr, Bos	1987.......Ray Bourque, Bos	

Calder Memorial Trophy

Awarded annually "to the player selected as the most proficient in his first year of competition in the National Hockey League." Frank Calder was a former NHL president. Sergei Makarov, who won the award in 1989–90, was the oldest recipient of the trophy, at 31. Players are no longer eligible for the award if they are 26 or older as of September 15th of the season in question.

1933 ....Carl Voss, Det	1957 ....Larry Regan, Bos	1981 ....Peter Stastny, Que
1934 ....Russ Blinko, Mtl M	1958 ....Frank Mahovlich, Tor	1982 ....Dale Hawerchuk, Winn
1935 ....Dave Schriner, NYA	1959 ....Ralph Backstrom, Mtl	1983 ....Steve Larmer, Chi
1936 ....Mike Karakas, Chi	1960 ....Bill Hay, Chi	1984 ....Tom Barrasso, Buff
1937 .....Syl Apps, Tor	1961 ....Dave Keon, Tor	1985 ....Mario Lemieux, Pitt
1938 ....Cully Dahlstrom, Chi	1962 ....Bobby Rousseau, Mtl	1986 ....Gary Suter, Cgy
1939 ....Frank Brimsek, Bos	1963 ....Kent Douglas, Tor	1987 ....Luc Robitaille, LA
1940 ....Kilby MacDonald, NYR	1964 ....Jacques Laperriere, Mtl	1988 ....Joe Nieuwendyk, Cgy
1941 ....Johnny Quilty, Mtl	1965 ....Roger Crozier, Det	1989 ....Brian Leetch, NYR
1942 ....Grant Warwick, NYR	1966 ....Brit Selby, Tor	1990 ....Sergei Makarov, Cgy
1943 ....Gaye Stewart, Tor	1967 ....Bobby Orr, Bos	1991 ....Ed Belfour, Chi
1944 ....Gus Bodnar, Tor	1968 ....Derek Sanderson, Bos	1992 ....Pavel Bure, Van
1945 ....Frank McCool, Tor	1969 ....Danny Grant, Minn	1993 ....Teemu Selanne, Winn
1946 ....Edgar Laprade, NYR	1970 ....Tony Esposito, Chi	1994 ....Martin Brodeur, NJ
1947 ....Howie Meeker, Tor	1971 ....Gilbert Perreault, Buff	1995 ....Peter Forsberg, Que
1948 ....Jim McFadden, Det	1972 ....Ken Dryden, Mtl	1996 ....Daniel Alfredsson, Ott
1949 ....Pentti Lund, NYR	1973 ....Steve Vickers, NYR	1997 ....Bryan Berard, NYI
1950 ....Jack Gelineau, Bos	1974 ....Denis Potvin, NYI	1998 ....Sergei Samsonov, Bos
1951 ....Terry Sawchuk, Det	1975 ....Eric Vail, Atl	1999 ....Chris Drury, Col
1952 ....Bernie Geoffrion, Mtl	1976 ....Bryan Trottier, NYI	2000 ....Scott Gomez, NJ
1953 ....Gump Worsley, NYR	1977 ....Willi Plett, Atl	2001 ....Evgeni Nabakov, SJ
1954 ....Camille Henry, NYR	1978 ....Mike Bossy, NYI	2002 ....Dany Heatley, Atl
1955 ....Ed Litzenberger, Chi	1979 ....Bobby Smith, Minn	
1956 ....Glenn Hall, Det	1980 ....Ray Bourque, Bos	

Vezina Trophy

Awarded annually "to the goalkeeper adjudged to be the best at his position." The trophy is named after Georges Vezina, an outstanding goalie for the Montreal Canadiens who collapsed during a game on November 28, 1925, and died four months later of tuberculosis. The general managers of the NHL teams vote on the award.

1927 ....George Hainsworth, Mtl	1958 ....Jacques Plante, Mtl	1980 ....Bob Sauve, Buff
1928 ....George Hainsworth, Mtl	1959 ....Jacques Plante, Mtl	Don Edwards, Buff
1929 ....George Hainsworth, Mtl	1960 ....Jacques Plante, Mtl	1981 ....Richard Sevigny, Mtl
1930 ....Tiny Thompson, Bos	1961 ....Johnny Bower, Tor	Denis Herron, Mtl
1931 ....Roy Worters, NYA	1962 ....Jacques Plante, Mtl	Michel Larocque, Mtl
1932 ....Charlie Gardiner, Chi	1963 ....Glenn Hall, Chi	1982 ....Billy Smith, NYI
1933 ....Tiny Thompson, Bos	1964 ....Charlie Hodge, Mtl	1983 ....Pete Peeters, Bos
1934 ....Charlie Gardiner, Chi	1965 ....Terry Sawchuk, Tor	1984 ....Tom Barrasso, Buff
1935 ....Lorne Chabot, Chi	Johnny Bower, Tor	1985 ....Pelle Lindbergh, Phil
1936 ....Tiny Thompson, Bos	1966 ....Gump Worsley, Mtl	1986 ....John Vanbiesbrouck, NYR
1937 ....Normie Smith, Det	Charlie Hodge, Mtl	
1938 ....Tiny Thompson, Bos	1967 ....Glenn Hall, Chi	1987 ....Ron Hextall, Phil
1939 ....Frank Brimsek, Bos	Rogie Vachon, Mtl	1988 ....Grant Fuhr, Edm
1940 ....Dave Kerr, NYR	1969 ....Jacques Plante, StL	1989 ....Patrick Roy, Mtl
1941 ....Turk Broda, Tor	Glenn Hall, StL	1990 ....Patrick Roy, Mtl
1942 ....Frank Brimsek, Bos	1970 ....Tony Esposito, Chi	1991 ....Ed Belfour, Chi
1943 ....Johnny Mowers, Det	1971 ....Ed Giacomin, NYR	1992 ....Patrick Roy, Mtl
1944 ....Bill Durnan, Mtl	Gilles Villemure, NYR	1993 ....Ed Belfour, Chi
1945 ....Bill Durnan, Mtl	1972 ....Tony Esposito, Chi	1994 ....Dominik Hasek, Buff
1946 ....Bill Durnan, Mtl	Gary Smith, Chi	1995 ....Dominik Hasek, Buff
1947 ....Bill Durnan, Mtl	1973 ....Ken Dryden, Mtl	1996 ....Jim Carey, Wash
1948 ....Turk Broda, Tor	1974 ....Bernie Parent, Phil	1997 ....Dominik Hasek, Buff
1949 ....Bill Durnan, Mtl	Tony Esposito, Chi	1998 ....Dominik Hasek, Buff
1950 ....Bill Durnan, Mtl	1975 ....Bernie Parent, Phil	1999 ....Dominik Hasek, Buff
1951 ....Al Rollins, Tor	1976 ....Ken Dryden, Mtl	2000 ....Olaf Kolzig, Wash
1952 ....Terry Sawchuk, Det	1977 ....Ken Dryden, Mtl	2001 ....Dominik Hasek, Buff
1953 ....Terry Sawchuk, Det	Michel Larocque, Mtl	2002 ....Jose Theodore, Mtl
1954 ....Harry Lumley, Tor	1978 ....Ken Dryden, Mtl	
1955 ....Terry Sawchuk, Det	Michel Larocque, Mtl	
1956 ....Jacques Plante, Mtl	1979 ....Ken Dryden, Mtl	
1957 ....Jacques Plante, Mtl	Michel Larocque, Mtl	

Selke Trophy

Awarded annually "to the forward who best excels in the defensive aspects of the game." The trophy is named after Frank J. Selke, the architect of the Montreal Canadians dynasty that won five consecutive Stanley Cups in the late '50s. The winner is selected by a vote of the Professional Hockey Writers Association.

1978........Bob Gainey, Mtl	1987........Dave Poulin, Phil	1996........Sergei Fedorov, Det
1979........Bob Gainey, Mtl	1988........Guy Carbonneau, Mtl	1997........Michael Peca, Buff
1980........Bob Gainey, Mtl	1989........Guy Carbonneau, Mtl	1998........Jere Lehtinen, Dall
1981........Bob Gainey, Mtl	1990........Rick Meagher, StL	1999........Jere Lehtinen, Dall
1982........Steve Kasper, Bos	1991........Dirk Graham, Chi	2000........Steve Yzerman, Det
1983........Bobby Clarke, Phil	1992........Guy Carbonneau, Mtl	2001........John Madden, NJ
1984........Doug Jarvis, Wash	1993........Doug Gilmour, Tor	2002........Michael Peca, NYI
1985........Craig Ramsay, Buff	1994........Sergei Fedorov, Det	
1986........Troy Murray, Chi	1995........Ron Francis, Pitt	

Adams Award

Awarded annually "to the NHL coach adjudged to have contributed the most to his team's success." The trophy is named in honor of Jack Adams, longtime coach and general manager of the Detroit Red Wings. The winner is selected by a vote of the National Hockey League Broadcasters' Association.

1974.....Fred Shero, Phil	1984.....Bryan Murray, Wash	1994.....Jacques Lemaire, NJ
1975.....Bob Pulford, LA	1985.....Mike Keenan, Phil	1995.....Marc Crawford, Que
1976.....Don Cherry, Bos	1986.....Glen Sather, Edm	1996.....Scotty Bowman, Det
1977.....Scott Bowman, Mtl	1987.....Jacques Demers, Det	1997.....Ted Nolan, Buff
1978.....Bobby Kromm, Det	1988.....Jacques Demers, Det	1998.....Pat Burns, Bos
1979.....Al Arbour, NYI	1989.....Pat Burns, Mtl	1999.....Jacques Martin, Ott
1980.....Pat Quinn, Phil	1990....:.Bob Murdoch, Winn	2000.....Joel Quenneville, StL
1981.....Red Berenson, StL	1991.....Brian Sutter, StL	2001.....Bill Barber, Phil
1982.....Tom Watt, Winn	1992.....Pat Quinn, Van	2002.....Bob Francis, Phoe
1983.....Orval Tessier, Chi	1993.....Pat Burns, Tor	

Wild Cherry

He's been called the Canadian Cosell (and a lot worse), but no broadcaster in his country is more popular than the jingoistic Don Cherry, the star of *Coach's Corner* on CBC's *Hockey Night in Canada*, which airs on Saturday's.

SI: Which of the following nicknames fits you best: Prime Minister of Saturday Night, the Last Real Canadian or National Embarrassment?
Cherry: I'll take the second one.

SI: *Monday Night Football* is perpetually searching for a colorful analyst. Any interest?
Cherry: I don't want to broadcast a game in which the players wear visors and run out of bounds.

SI: Would you rather call a beautiful goal by a Swede or a great fight between Canadian boys?
Cherry: Need you ask? Nothing like two good guys having a go.

SI: You consider yourself a sex symbol. Who's the sexier Canadian: you or Celine Dion?
Cherry: Who does she play for?

SI: You're famous for your keen fashion sense. Do you have a favorite ensemble?
Cherry: My lime-green suit is a beauty, and when I wear it with a pink tie, look out! When I go into certain bars, all the guys want to hold my hand and buy me a drink.

SI: Years ago Pavel Bure responded to one of your criticisms of him by saying, "Do you comment on the clowns at the circus?" Isn't that unfair to hardworking clowns?
Cherry: Pavel and I have kissed and made up. I guess he saw me in my lime green suit.

SI: Speaking of kissing, you kissed a player—Doug Gilmour—on the air. Isn't that European behavior?
Cherry: It is, but it wasn't a French kiss.

SI: Do you regret calling Swedish players "chicken Swedes"?
Cherry: I've never called a Swede a chicken because I have nothing against chickens.

SI: What kind of hockey player would your CBC partner Ron MacLean be?
Cherry: A chicken swede.

—Richard Deitsch

Alltime Point Leaders

	Player	Yrs	GP	G	A	Pts	Pts/game
1.	Wayne Gretzky, Edm, LA, StL, NYR	20	1487	894	1963	2857	1.921
2.	Gordie Howe, Det, Hart	26	1767	801	1049	1850	1.047
3.	*Mark Messier, Edm, NYR, Van	23	1602	658	1146	1804	1.126
4.	Marcel Dionne, Det, LA, NYR	18	1348	731	1040	1771	1.314
5.	*Ron Francis, Hart, Pitt, Car	21	1569	514	1187	1701	1.084
6.	*Steve Yzerman, Det	19	1362	658	1004	1662	1.220
7.	*Mario Lemieux, Pitt	14	812	654	947	1601	1.972
8.	Phil Esposito, Chi, Bos, NYR	18	1282	717	873	1590	1.240
9.	Ray Bourque, Bos, Col	22	1612	410	1169	1579	.980
10.	Paul Coffey, eight teams	21	1409	396	1135	1531	1.087
11.	Stan Mikita, Chi	22	1394	541	926	1467	1.052
12.	Bryan Trottier, NYI, Pitt	18	1279	524	901	1425	1.114
13.	Dale Hawerchuk, Winn, Buff, StL, Phil	16	1188	518	891	1409	1.186
14.	Jari Kurri, Edm, LA, NYR, Ana, Col	17	1251	601	797	1397	1.118
15.	Doug Gilmour, StL, Cgy, Tor, NJ, Chi, Buff, Mtl	19	1412	439	945	1384	.980

*Active in 2001–02.

Alltime Goal-Scoring Leaders

	Player	Yrs	GP	G	G/game
1.	Wayne Gretzky, Edm, LA, StL, NYR	20	1487	894	.601
2.	Gordie Howe, Det, Hart	26	1767	801	.453
3.	Marcel Dionne, Det, LA, NYR	18	1348	731	.542
4.	Phil Esposito, Chi, Bos, NYR	18	1282	717	.559
5.	Mike Gartner, Wash, Minn, NYR, Tor, Phoe	19	1432	708	.494
6.	*Mark Messier, Edm, NYR, Van	23	1602	658	.411
7.	*Brett Hull, Cal, StL, Dall, Det	17	1101	679	.617
8.	*Mario Lemieux, Pitt	14	812	654	.805
9.	*Steve Yzerman, Det	19	1362	658	.483
10.	*Luc Robitaille, LA, Pitt, NYR, Det	16	1205	620	.515

*Active in 2001–02.

Alltime Assist Leaders

	Player	Yrs	GP	A	A/game
1.	Wayne Gretzky, Edm, LA, StL, NYR	20	1487	1963	1.320
2.	Ray Bourque, Bos, Col	22	1612	1169	.725
3.	*Ron Francis, Hart, Pitt, Car	21	1569	1187	.757
4.	Paul Coffey, eight teams	21	1409	1135	.806
5.	*Mark Messier, Edm, NYR, Van	23	1602	1146	.715
6.	Gordie Howe, Det, Hart	26	1767	1049	.594
7.	Marcel Dionne, Det, LA, NYR	18	1348	1040	.771
8.	*Adam Oates, Det, StL, Bos, Wash	17	1210	1027	.849
9.	*Steve Yzerman, Det	19	1362	1004	.737
10.	*Mario Lemieux, Pitt	14	812	947	1.166

*Active player in 2001–02.

YET ANOTHER SIGN OF THE APOCALYPSE

In early 2002, the Western Hockey League's Kelowna Rockets assigned bodyguards to protect their mascot, Rocky Raccoon, because he had been assaulted by two fans during a game against the Kamloops Blazers.

Alltime Penalty Minutes Leaders

Player		Yrs	GP	PIM	Min/game
1.	Dave Williams, Tor, Van, Det, LA, Hart	14	962	3966	4.12
2.	Dale Hunter, Que, Wash, Col	19	1407	3565	2.53
3.	Marty McSorley, Pitt, Edm, LA, NYR, SJ, Bos	17	961	3381	3.52
4.	*Bob Probert, Det, Chi	16	935	3300	3.53
5.	Tim Hunter, Cgy, Que, Van, SJ	16	815	3146	3.86
6.	*Rob Ray, Buff	13	848	3097	3.65
7.	*Craig Berube, Phil, Tor, Cgy, Wash	16	999	3049	3.05
8.	Chris Nilan, Mtl, NYR, Bos	13	688	3043	4.42
9.	*Tie Domi, Tor, NYR, Winn	13	784	3027	3.86
10.	*Rick Tocchet, Phil, Pitt, LA, Bos, Wash, Phoe	18	1144	2974	2.60

*Active in 2001–02.

Goaltending Records

ALLTIME WIN LEADERS

Goaltender	W	L	T	Pct
*Patrick Roy, Mtl, Col	516	300	118	.616
Terry Sawchuk, five teams	447	330	173	.562
Jacques Plante, five teams	434	246	147	.614
Tony Esposito, Mtl, Chi	423	306	152	.566
Glenn Hall, Det, Chi, StL	407	327	163	.545
Grant Fuhr, six teams	403	295	114	.567
*Mike Vernon, Cgy, Det, SJ, Fla	385	273	92	.575
Andy Moog, Edm, Bos, Dall, Mtl	372	209	88	.622
*John Vanbiesbrouck, five teams	374	346	119	.517
Tom Barrasso, Buff, Pitt, Ott, Tor	368	273	86	.565

*Active in 2001–02.

ACTIVE GOALTENDING LEADERS

Goaltender	W	L	T	Pct
Martin Brodeur, NJ	324	168	85	.635
Chris Osgood, Det	253	135	52	.634
Patrick Roy, Mtl, Col	516	300	118	.616
Dominik Hasek, Chi, Buff, Det	288	189	80	.589
Ed Belfour, Chi, SJ, Dall	364	242	100	.586
Mike Vernon, Cgy, Det, SJ, Fla	385	273	92	.575
Tom Barrasso, Buff, Pitt, Ott, Tor	368	273	86	.565
Curtis Joseph, StL, Edm, Tor	346	260	81	.563
Mike Richter, NYR	296	252	72	.535
Olaf Kolzig, Wash	182	160	48	.528

Note: Ranked by winning percentage; minimum 250 games played. All players active in 2001–02.

ALLTIME SHUTOUT LEADERS

Goaltender	Team	Yrs	GP	SO
Terry Sawchuk	Det, Bos, Tor, LA, NYR	21	971	103
George Hainsworth	Mtl, Tor	11	465	94
Glenn Hall	Det, Chi, StL	18	906	84
Jacques Plante	Mtl, NYR, StL, Tor, Bos	18	837	82
Tiny Thompson	Bos, Det	12	553	81
Alex Connell	Ott, Det, NYA, Mtl M	12	417	81
Tony Esposito	Mtl, Chi	16	886	76
Lorne Chabot	NYR, Tor, Mtl, Chi, Mtl M, NYA	11	411	73
Harry Lumley	Det, NYR, Chi, Tor, Bos	16	804	71
Roy Worters	Pitt Pir, NYA, *Mtl	12	484	66

*Played 1 game for Canadiens in 1929–30, not a shutout.

ALLTIME GOALS AGAINST AVERAGE LEADERS (PRE-1950)

Goaltender	Team	Yrs	GP	GA	GAA
George Hainsworth	Mtl, Tor	11	465	937	1.91
Alex Connell	Ott, Det, NYA, Mtl M	12	417	830	1.91
Chuck Gardiner	Chi	7	316	664	2.02
Lorne Chabot	NYR, Tor, Mtl, Chi, Mtl M, NYA	11	411	861	2.04
Tiny Thompson	Bos, Det	12	553	1183	2.08

ALLTIME GOALS AGAINST AVERAGE LEADERS (POST-1950)

Goaltender	Team	Yrs	GP	GA	GAA
*Martin Brodeur	NJ	10	592	1272	2.21
*Dominik Hasek	Chi, Buff, Det	12	581	1254	2.23
Ken Dryden	Mtl	8	397	870	2.24
Jacques Plante	Mtl, NYR, StL, Tor, Bos	18	837	1965	2.38
*Chris Osgood	Det, NYI	9	455	1056	2.42

*Active in 2001–02.

Note: Minimum 250 games played. Goals against average equals goals against per 60 minutes played.

Coaching Records

Coach	Team	Seasons	W	L	T	Pct
*Scott Bowman	five teams	1967–87, 91–	1244	583	314	.654
Toe Blake	Mtl	1955–68	500	255	159	.634
Glen Sather	Edm	1979–89, 93–94	464	268	110	.616
Fred Shero	Phil, NYR	1971–81	390	225	119	.612
Emile Francis	NYR, StL	1965–77, 81–83	388	273	117	.574
Billy Reay	Tor, Chi	1957–59, 63–77	542	385	175	.571
Al Arbour	StL, NYI	1970–94	781	577	248	.564
Bryan Murray	Wash, Det, Fla	1981–98	484	368	123	.559
*Pat Burns	Mtl, Tor, Bos	1988–	412	314	129	.557
*Pat Quinn	Phil, LA, Van, Tor	1978–	527	408	137	.556

Note: Minimum 600 regular-season games. Ranked by percentage.

The Lying Game

The gamesmanship of the NHL playoffs began even before the games, when Islanders center Alexei Yashin was held out of New York's final four regular-season matches, and several practices, with what the team called an "injured groin"—a catchall phrase that in hockey parlance might translate to "broken toe" or "wrenched neck." "If a team says it's a guy's foot, it's probably his shoulder," says Red Wings forward Kris Draper of the NHL's widely accepted practice of dissembling about the disabled.

Perhaps Yashin, who struggled in New York's first two postseason games against the Maple Leafs, really did have a groin ache. ("I'm not allowed to say," he says.) Perhaps Leafs center Robert Reichel really did miss a game with a "leg injury." Perhaps Devils center Joe Nieuwendyk really did have a "stomach virus" when he sat out the opener against the Hurricanes. There's no way to know. The league's official injury list features more misdirection than a David Copperfield show. At week's end the Avalanche's Milan Hejduk was out "indefinitely" with an "abdominal strain." Avalanche coach Bob Hartley kept telling the media, "As soon as we know anything, you'll be the first to know," which invariably broke everyone up.

The motive behind the mendacity is clear: Teams don't want opponents to know where their players are most vulnerable. "I won't necessarily try to injure a guy if I know where he's hurt," said the Canadiens' fang-toothed forward Doug Gilmour last Friday. Then he paused, and he chuckled. "But will I give him an extra shot where it hurts? Sure."

When the Stars were playing the Avalanche in the 1999 playoffs, Dallas intelligence revealed that Colorado's Peter Forsberg had a bum left shoulder. "We knew he had it, so we gave him that extra little bump," says Mike Keane, then a Stars forward. Forsberg had surgery after the series.

The NHL's policy requires teams to announce the "approximate nature" of the injury, but it also has a loophole that you could drive a Zamboni through. If a team fears that revealing an injury might endanger a player, it may "provide a more general overview of the player's status."

"Teams can basically say whatever they want," says NHL spokesman Frank Brown. "They just have to say something."

How different things are in pro football, the other major sport in which an injured body part might be legally attacked. The NFL makes teams file two comprehensive injury reports a week, hits insubordinate clubs with fines of up to $25,000 and does it in the name of what spokesman Greg Aiello calls "maintaining the integrity of the game." Integrity means making sure all the high rollers know what's up. "[Disclosing injuries] eliminates opportunity for someone to benefit from inside information, as it might relate to gambling activities," Aiello says.

The NHL, which attracts little betting action, preaches no such honesty. Sometimes, though, people get their lies crossed. In last year's postseason, Red Wings coach Scotty Bowman declared that Steve Yzerman was nursing a sore leg, only to have Yzerman tell reporters, "I have a broken finger." After the playoffs Yzerman revealed he'd also had a fractured right fibula.

Whatever the facts about this year's injuries, the truth won't prevail until after the playoffs. In the meantime we can only hope for slips such as the one in 1990, when Islanders center Brent Sutter missed practice during a series against the Rangers. Sutter had been bashed to the ice several times in the previous game, but when reporters asked what ailed him, he fell silent and excused himself to huddle with the team trainer. Moments later he returned. "I have a cold," he announced.

—Kostya Kennedy

Single-Season Records

Goals

Player	Season	GP	G	Player	Season	GP	G
Wayne Gretzky, Edm	1981–82	80	92	Wayne Gretzky, Edm	1982–83	80	71
Wayne Gretzky, Edm	1983–84	74	87	Brett Hull, StL	1991–92	73	70
Brett Hull, StL	1990–91	78	86	Mario Lemieux, Pitt	1987–88	77	70
Mario Lemieux, Pitt	1988–89	76	85	Bernie Nicholls, LA	1988–89	79	70
Alexander Mogilny, Buff	1992–93	77	76	Mario Lemieux, Pitt	1992–93	60	69
Phil Esposito, Bos	1970–71	78	76	Mario Lemieux, Pitt	1995–96	70	69
Teemu Selanne, Winn	1992–93	84	76	Mike Bossy, NYI	1978–79	80	69
Wayne Gretzky, Edm	1984–85	80	73	Phil Esposito, Bos	1973–74	78	68
Brett Hull, StL	1989–90	80	72	Jari Kurri, Edm	1985–86	78	68
Jari Kurri, Edm	1984–85	73	71	Mike Bossy, NYI	1980–81	79	68

Assists

Player	Season	GP	A	Player	Season	GP	A
Wayne Gretzky, Edm	1985–86	80	163	Wayne Gretzky, LA	1989–90	73	102
Wayne Gretzky, Edm	1984–85	80	135	Bobby Orr, Bos	1970–71	78	102
Wayne Gretzky, Edm	1982–83	80	125	Mario Lemieux, Pitt	1987–88	77	98
Wayne Gretzky, LA	1990–91	78	122	Adam Oates, Bos	1992–93	84	97
Wayne Gretzky, Edm	1986–87	79	121	Doug Gilmour, Tor	1992–93	83	95
Wayne Gretzky, Edm	1981–82	80	120	Pat LaFontaine, Buff	1992–93	84	95
Wayne Gretzky, Edm	1983–84	74	118	Mario Lemieux, Pitt	1985–86	79	93
Mario Lemieux, Pitt	1988–89	76	114	Peter Stastny, Que	1981–82	80	93
Wayne Gretzky, LA	1988–89	78	114	Wayne Gretzky, LA	1993–94	81	92
Wayne Gretzky, Edm	1987–88	64	109	Mario Lemieux, Pitt	1995–96	70	92
Wayne Gretzky, Edm	1980–81	80	109	Ron Francis, Pitt	1995–96	77	92

Points

Player	Season	G	A	Pts	Player	Season	G	A	Pts
Wayne Gretzky, Edm	1985–86	52	163	215	Wayne Gretzky, LA	1990–91	41	122	163
Wayne Gretzky, Edm	1981–82	92	120	212	Mario Lemieux, Pitt	1995–96	69	92	161
Wayne Gretzky, Edm	1984–85	73	135	208	Mario Lemieux, Pitt	1992–93	69	91	160
Wayne Gretzky, Edm	1983–84	87	118	205	Steve Yzerman, Det	1988–89	65	90	155
Mario Lemieux, Pitt	1988–89	85	114	199	Phil Esposito, Bos	1970–71	76	76	152
Wayne Gretzky, Edm	1982–83	71	125	196	Bernie Nicholls, LA	1988–89	70	80	150
Wayne Gretzky, Edm	1986–87	62	121	183	Wayne Gretzky, Edm	1987–88	40	109	149
Mario Lemieux, Pitt	1987–88	70	98	168	Pat LaFontaine, Buff	1992–93	53	95	148
Wayne Gretzky, LA	1988–89	54	114	168	Mike Bossy, NYI	1981–82	64	83	147
Wayne Gretzky, Edm	1980–81	55	109	164	Phil Esposito, Bos	1973–74	68	77	145

Points per Game

Player	Season	GP	Pts	Avg	Player	Season	GP	Pts	Avg
Wayne Gretzky, Edm	1983–84	74	205	2.77	Mario Lemieux, Pitt	1987–88	77	168	2.18
Wayne Gretzky, Edm	1985–86	80	215	2.69	Wayne Gretzky, LA	1988–89	78	168	2.15
Mario Lemieux, Pitt	1992–93	60	160	2.67	Wayne Gretzky, LA	1990–91	78	163	2.09
Wayne Gretzky, Edm	1981–82	80	212	2.65	Mario Lemieux, Pitt	1989–90	59	123	2.08
Mario Lemieux, Pitt	1988–89	76	199	2.62	Wayne Gretzky, Edm	1980–81	80	164	2.05
Wayne Gretzky, Edm	1984–85	80	208	2.60	Mario Lemieux, Pitt	1991–92	64	131	2.05
Wayne Gretzky, Edm	1982–83	80	196	2.45	Bill Cowley, Bos	1943–44	36	71	1.97
Wayne Gretzky, Edm	1987–88	64	149	2.33	Phil Esposito, Bos	1970–71	78	152	1.95
Wayne Gretzky, Edm	1986–87	79	183	2.32	Wayne Gretzky, LA	1989–90	73	142	1.95
Mario Lemieux, Pitt	1995–96	70	161	2.30	Steve Yzerman, Det	1988–89	80	155	1.94

Note: Minimum 50 points in one season.

Goals per Game

Player	Season	GP	G	Avg
Joe Malone, Mtl	1917–18	20	44	2.20
Cy Denneny, Ott	1917–18	22	36	1.64
Newsy Lalonde, Mtl	1917–18	14	23	1.64
Joe Malone, Que	1919–20	24	39	1.63
Newsy Lalonde, Mtl	1919–20	23	36	1.57
Joe Malone, Ham	1920–21	20	30	1.50
Babe Dye, Ham-Tor	1920–21	24	35	1.46
Cy Denneny, Ott	1920–21	24	34	1.42
Reg Noble, Tor	1917–18	20	28	1.40
Newsy Lalonde, Mtl	1920–21	24	33	1.38

Note: Minimum 20 goals in one season.

Assists per Game

Player	Season	GP	A	Avg
Wayne Gretzky, Edm	1985–86	80	163	2.04
Wayne Gretzky, Edm	1987–88	64	109	1.70
Wayne Gretzky, Edm	1984–85	80	135	1.69
Wayne Gretzky, Edm	1983–84	74	118	1.59
Wayne Gretzky, Edm	1982–83	80	125	1.56
Wayne Gretzky, LA	1990–91	78	122	1.56
Wayne Gretzky, Edm	1986–87	79	121	1.53
Mario Lemieux, Pitt	1992–93	60	91	1.52
Wayne Gretzky, Edm	1981–82	80	120	1.50
Mario Lemieux, Pitt	1988–89	76	114	1.50

Note: Minimum 35 assists in one season.

Shutout Leaders

	Season	SO	Length of Schedule		Season	SO	Length of Schedule
George Hainsworth, Mtl	1928–29	22	44	Harry Holmes, Det	1927–28	11	44
Alex Connell, Ott	1925–26	15	36	Clint Benedict, Mtl M	1928–29	11	44
Alex Connell, Ott	1927–28	15	44	Joe Miller, Pitt Pirates	1928–29	11	44
Hal Winkler, Bos	1927–28	15	44	Tiny Thompson, Bos	1932–33	11	48
Tony Esposito, Chi	1969–70	15	76	Terry Sawchuk, Det	1950–51	11	70
George Hainsworth, Mtl	1926–27	14	44	Dominik Hasek, Buff	2000–01	11	82
Clint Benedict, Mtl M	1926–27	13	44	Lorne Chabot, NYR	1926–27	10	44
Alex Connell, Ott	1926–27	13	44	Roy Worters, Pitt Pirates	1927–28	10	44
George Hainsworth, Mtl	1927–28	13	44	Clarence Dolson, Det	1928–29	10	44
John Roach, NYR	1928–29	13	44	John Roach, Det	1932–33	10	48
Roy Worters, NYA	1928–29	13	44	Chuck Gardiner, Chi	1933–34	10	48
Harry Lumley, Tor	1953–54	13	70	Tiny Thompson, Bos	1935–36	10	48
Dominik Hasek, Buff	1997–98	13	82	Frank Brimsek, Bos	1938–39	10	48
Tiny Thompson, Bos	1928–29	12	44	Bill Durnan, Mtl	1948–49	10	60
Lorne Chabot, Tor	1928–29	12	44	Gerry McNeil, Mtl	1952–53	10	70
Chuck Gardiner, Chi	1930–31	12	44	Harry Lumley, Tor	1952–53	10	70
Terry Sawchuk, Det	1951–52	12	70	Tony Esposito, Chi	1973–74	10	78
Terry Sawchuk, Det	1953–54	12	70	Ken Dryden, Mtl	1976–77	10	80
Terry Sawchuk, Det	1954–55	12	70	Martin Brodeur, NJ	1996–97	10	82
Glenn Hall, Det	1955–56	12	70	Martin Brodeur, NJ	1997–98	10	82
Bernie Parent, Phil	1973–74	12	78	Roman Cechmanek, Phil	2000–01	10	82
Bernie Parent, Phil	1974–75	12	80	Byron Dafoe, Bos	1998–99	10	82
Lorne Chabot, NYR	1927–28	11	44				

Wins

	Season	Record
Bernie Parent, Phil	1973–74	47-13-12
Bernie Parent, Phil	1974–75	44-14-9
Terry Sawchuk, Det	1950–51	44-13-13
Terry Sawchuk, Det	1951–52	44-14-12
Tom Barasso, Pitt	1992–93	43-14-5
Ed Belfour, Chi	1990–91	43-19-7
Martin Brodeur, NJ	1997–98	43-17-8
Martin Brodeur, NJ	1999–00	43-20-8
Jacques Plante, Mtl	1955–56	42-12-10
Jacques Plante, Mtl	1961–62	42-14-14
Ken Dryden, Mtl	1975–76	42-10-8
Mike Richter, NYR	1993–94	42-12-6
Roman Turek, StL	1999–00	42-15-9
Martin Brodeur, NJ	2000–01	42-17-11

Goals Against Average

(PRE-1950)

	Season	GP	GAA
George Hainsworth, Mtl	1928–29	44	0.92
George Hainsworth, Mtl	1927–28	44	1.05
Alex Connell, Ott	1925–26	36	1.12
Tiny Thompson, Bos	1928–29	44	1.18
Roy Worters, NYA	1928–29	38	1.21

(POST-1950)

	Season	GP	GAA
Tony Esposito, Chi	1971–72	48	1.7698
Al Rollins, Tor	1950–51	40	1.7744
Ron Tugnutt, Ott	1998–99	43	1.7943
Harry Lumley, Tor	1953–54	69	1.8551
Jacques Plante, Mtl	1955–56	64	1.8594
Dominik Hasek, Buff	1998–99	64	1.8706
Martin Brodeur, NJ	1996–97	67	1.8759
Ed Belfour, Dall	1997–98	61	1.8766

Single-Game Records

Goals

	Date	G
Joe Malone, Que vs Tor	1-31-20	7
Newsy Lalonde, Mtl vs Tor	1-10-20	6
Joe Malone, Que vs Ott	3-10-20	6
Corb Denneny, Tor vs Ham	1-26-21	6
Cy Denneny, Ott vs Ham	3-7-21	6
Syd Howe, Det vs NYR	2-3-44	6
Red Berenson, StL vs Phil	11-7-68	6
Darryl Sittler, Tor vs Bos	2-7-76	6

Assists

	Date	A
Billy Taylor, Det vs Chi	3-16-47	7
Wayne Gretzky, Edm vs Wash	2-15-80	7
Wayne Gretzky, Edm vs Chi	12-11-85	7
Wayne Gretzky, Edm vs Que	2-14-86	7

Note: 24 tied with 6.

Points

	Date	G	A	Pts
Darryl Sittler, Tor vs Bos	2-7-76	6	4	10
Maurice Richard, Mtl vs Det	12-28-44	5	3	8
Bert Olmstead, Mtl vs Chi	1-9-54	4	4	8
Tom Bladon, Phil vs Clev	12-11-77	4	4	8
Bryan Trottier, NYI vs NYR	12-23-78	5	3	8
Peter Stastny, Que vs Wash	2-22-81	4	4	8
Anton Stastny, Que vs Wash	2-22-81	3	5	8
Wayne Gretzky, Edm vs NJ	11-19-83	3	5	8
Wayne Gretzky, Edm vs Minn	1-4-84	4	4	8
Paul Coffey, Edm vs Det	3-14-86	2	6	8
Mario Lemieux, Pitt vs StL	10-15-88	2	6	8
Bernie Nicholls, LA vs Tor	12-1-88	2	6	8
Mario Lemieux, Pitt vs NJ	12-31-88	5	3	8

NHL Season Leaders

Points

Season	Player and Club	Pts	Season	Player and Club	Pts
1917–18	Joe Malone, Mtl	44	1956–57	Gordie Howe, Det	89
1918–19	Newsy Lalonde, Mtl	30	1957–58	Dickie Moore, Mtl	84
1919–20	Joe Malone, Que	48	1958–59	Dickie Moore, Mtl	96
1920–21	Newsy Lalonde, Mtl	41	1959–60	Bobby Hull, Chi	81
1921–22	Punch Broadbent, Ott	46	1960–61	Bernie Geoffrion, Mtl	95
1922–23	Babe Dye, Tor	37	1961–62	Andy Bathgate, NY	84
1923–24	Cy Denneny, Ott	23		Bobby Hull, Chi	84
1924–25	Babe Dye, Tor	44	1962–63	Gordie Howe, Det	86
1925–26	Nels Stewart, Mtl M	42	1963–64	Stan Mikita, Chi	89
1926–27	Bill Cook, NY	37	1964–65	Stan Mikita, Chi	87
1927–28	Howie Morenz, Mtl	51	1965–66	Bobby Hull, Chi	97
1928–29	Ace Bailey, Tor	32	1966–67	Stan Mikita, Chi	97
1929–30	Cooney Weiland, Bos	73	1967–68	Stan Mikita, Chi	87
1930–31	Howie Morenz, Mtl	51	1968–69	Phil Esposito, Bos	126
1931–32	Harvey Jackson, Tor	53	1969–70	Bobby Orr, Bos	120
1932–33	Bill Cook, NY	50	1970–71	Phil Esposito, Bos	152
1933–34	Charlie Conacher, Tor	52	1971–72	Phil Esposito, Bos	133
1934–35	Charlie Conacher, Tor	57	1972–73	Phil Esposito, Bos	130
1935–36	Sweeney Schriner, NYA	45	1973–74	Phil Esposito, Bos	145
1936–37	Sweeney Schriner, NYA	46	1974–75	Bobby Orr, Bos	135
1937–38	Gord Drillon, Tor	52	1975–76	Guy Lafleur, Mtl	125
1938–39	Hector Blake, Mtl	47	1976–77	Guy Lafleur, Mtl	136
1939–40	Milt Schmidt, Bos	52	1977–78	Guy Lafleur, Mtl	132
1940–41	Bill Cowley, Bos	62	1978–79	Bryan Trottier, NYI	134
1941–42	Bryan Hextall, NY	54	1979–80	Marcel Dionne, LA	137
1942–43	Doug Bentley, Chi	73		Wayne Gretzky, Edm	137
1943–44	Herb Cain, Bos	82	1980–81	Wayne Gretzky, Edm	164
1944–45	Elmer Lach, Mtl	80	1981–82	Wayne Gretzky, Edm	212
1945–46	Max Bentley, Chi	61	1982–83	Wayne Gretzky, Edm	196
1946–47	Max Bentley, Chi	72	1983–84	Wayne Gretzky, Edm	205
1947–48	Elmer Lach, Mtl	61	1984–85	Wayne Gretzky, Edm	208
1948–49	Roy Conacher, Chi	68	1985–86	Wayne Gretzky, Edm	215
1949–50	Ted Lindsay, Det	78	1986–87	Wayne Gretzky, Edm	183
1950–51	Gordie Howe, Det	86	1987–88	Mario Lemieux, Pitt	168
1951–52	Gordie Howe, Det	86	1988–89	Mario Lemieux, Pitt	199
1952–53	Gordie Howe, Det	95	1989–90	Wayne Gretzky, LA	142
1953–54	Gordie Howe, Det	81	1990–91	Wayne Gretzky, LA	163
1954–55	Bernie Geoffrion, Mtl	75	1991–92	Mario Lemieux, Pitt	131
1955–56	Jean Beliveau, Mtl	88	1992–93	Mario Lemieux, Pitt	160

Points (Cont.)

Season	Player and Club	Pts	Season	Player and Club	Pts
1993–94	Wayne Gretzky, LA	130	1998–99	Jaromir Jagr, Pitt	127
1994–95	Jaromir Jagr, Pitt	70	1999–00	Jaromir Jagr, Pitt	96
1995–96	Mario Lemieux, Pitt	161	2000–01	Jaromir Jagr, Pitt	121
1996–97	Mario Lemieux, Pitt	122	2001–02	Jarome Iginla, Cal	96
1997–98	Jaromir Jagr, Pitt	102			

Goals

Season	Player and Club	G	Season	Player and Club	G
1917–18	Joe Malone, Mtl	44	1959–60	Bobby Hull, Chi	39
1918–19	Odie Cleghorn, Mtl	23		Bronco Horvath, Bos	39
1919–20	Joe Malone, Que	39	1960–61	Bernie Geoffrion, Mtl	50
1920–21	Babe Dye, Ham-Tor	35	1961–62	Bobby Hull, Chi	50
1921–22	Punch Broadbent, Ott	32	1962–63	Gordie Howe, Det	38
1922–23	Babe Dye, Tor	26	1963–64	Bobby Hull, Chi	43
1923–24	Cy Denneny, Ott	22	1964–65	Norm Ullman, Det	42
1924–25	Babe Dye, Tor	38	1965–66	Bobby Hull, Chi	54
1925–26	Nels Stewart, Mtl	34	1966–67	Bobby Hull, Chi	52
1926–27	Bill Cook, NY	33	1967–68	Bobby Hull, Chi	44
1927–28	Howie Morenz, Mtl	33	1968–69	Bobby Hull, Chi	58
1928–29	Ace Bailey, Tor	22	1969–70	Phil Esposito, Bos	43
1929–30	Cooney Weiland, Bos	43	1970–71	Phil Esposito, Bos	76
1930–31	Bill Cook, NY	30	1971–72	Phil Esposito, Bos	66
1931–32	Charlie Conacher, Tor	34	1972–73	Phil Esposito, Bos	55
	Bill Cook, NY	34	1973–74	Phil Esposito, Bos	68
1932–33	Bill Cook, NY	28	1974–75	Phil Esposito, Bos	61
1933–34	Charlie Conacher, Tor	32	1975–76	Guy Lafleur, Mtl	56
1934–35	Charlie Conacher, Tor	36	1976–77	Steve Shutt, Mtl	60
1935–36	Charlie Conacher, Tor	23	1977–78	Guy Lafleur, Mtl	60
	Bill Thoms, Tor	23	1978–79	Mike Bossy, NYI	69
1936–37	Larry Aurie, Det	23	1979–80	Charlie Simmer, LA	56
	Nels Stewart, Bos-NYA	23		Blaine Stoughton, Hart	56
1937–38	Gord Drill, Tor	26	1980–81	Mike Bossy, NYI	68
1938–39	Roy Conacher, Bos	26	1981–82	Wayne Gretzky, Edm	92
1939–40	Bryan Hextall, NY	24	1982–83	Wayne Gretzky, Edm	71
1940–41	Bryan Hextall, NY	26	1983–84	Wayne Gretzky, Edm	87
1941–42	Lynn Patrick, NY	32	1984–85	Wayne Gretzky, Edm	73
1942–43	Doug Bentley, Chi	43	1985–86	Jari Kurri, Edm	68
1943–44	Doug Bentley, Chi	38	1986–87	Wayne Gretzky, Edm	62
1944–45	Maurice Richard, Mtl	50	1987–88	Mario Lemieux, Pitt	70
1945–46	Gaye Stewart, Tor	37	1988–89	Mario Lemieux, Pitt	85
1946–47	Maurice Richard, Mtl	50	1989–90	Brett Hull, StL	72
1947–48	Ted Lindsay, Det	33	1990–91	Brett Hull, StL	78
1948–49	Sid Abel, Det	28	1991–92	Brett Hull, StL	70
1949–50	Maurice Richard, Mtl	43	1992–93	Alexander Mogilny, Buff	76
1950–51	Gordie Howe, Det	43		Teemu Selanne, Winn	76
1951–52	Gordie Howe, Det	47	1993–94	Pavel Bure, Van	60
1952–53	Gordie Howe, Det	49	1994–95	Peter Bondra, Wash	34
1953–54	Maurice Richard, Mtl	37	1995–96	Mario Lemieux, Pitt	69
1954–55	Bernie Geoffrion, Mtl	38	1996–97	Keith Tkachuk, Phoe	52
	Maurice Richard, Mtl	38	1997–98	Teemu Selanne, Ana	52
1955–56	Jean Beliveau, Mtl	47		Peter Bondra, Wash	52
1957–58	Dickie Moore, Mtl	36	1998–99	Teemu Selanne, Ana	47
1956–57	Gordie Howe, Det	44	1999–00	Pavel Bure, Fla	58
1958–59	Jean Beliveau, Mtl	45	2000–01	Pavel Bure, Fla	59
			2001–02	Jarome Iginla, Cal	52

Assists

Season	Player and Club	A	Season	Player and Club	A
1917–18	statistic not kept		1962–63	Henri Richard, Mtl	50
1918–19	Newsy Lalonde, Mtl	9	1963–64	Andy Bathgate, NY-Tor	58
1919–20	Corbett Denneny, Tor	12	1964–65	Stan Mikita, Chi	59
1920–21	Louis Berlinquette, Mtl	9	1965–66	Stan Mikita, Chi	48
1921–22	Punch Broadbench, Ott	14		Bobby Rousseau, Mtl	48
1922–23	Babe Dye, Tor	11		Jean Beliveau, Mtl	48
1923–24	Billy Boucher, Mtl	6	1966–67	Stan Mikita, Chi	62
1924–25	Cy Denneny, Ott	15	1967–68	Phil Esposito, Bos	49
1925–26	Cy Denneny, Ott	12	1968–69	Phil Esposito, Bos	77
1926–27	Dick Irvin, Chi	18	1969–70	Bobby Orr, Bos	87
1927–28	Howie Morenz, Mtl	18	1970–71	Bobby Orr, Bos	102
1928–29	Frank Boucher, NY	16	1971–72	Bobby Orr, Bos	80
1929–30	Frank Boucher, NY	36	1972–73	Phil Esposito, Bos	75
1930–31	Joe Primeau, Tor	36	1973–74	Bobby Orr, Bos	89
1931–32	Joe Primeau, Tor	37	1974–75	Bobby Clarke, Phil	89
1932–33	Frank Boucher, NY	28		Bobby Orr, Bos	89
1933–34	Joe Primeau, Tor	32	1975–76	Bobby Clarke, Phil	89
1934–35	Art Chapman, NYA	28	1976–77	Guy Lafleur, Mtl	80
1935–36	Art Chapman, NYA	28	1977–78	Bryan Trottier, NYI	77
1936–37	Syl Apps, Tor	29	1978–79	Bryan Trottier, NYI	87
1937–38	Syl Apps, Tor	29	1979–80	Wayne Gretzky, Edm	86
1938–39	Bill Cowley, Bos	34	1980–81	Wayne Gretzky, Edm	109
1939–40	Milt Schmidt, Bos	30	1981–82	Wayne Gretzky, Edm	120
1940–41	Bill Cowley, Bos	45	1982–83	Wayne Gretzky, Edm	125
1941–42	Phil Watson, NY	37	1983–84	Wayne Gretzky, Edm	118
1942–43	Bill Cowley, Bos	45	1984–85	Wayne Gretzky, Edm	135
1943–44	Clint Smith, Chi	49	1985–86	Wayne Gretzky, Edm	163
1944–45	Elmer Lach, Mtl	54	1986–87	Wayne Gretzky, Edm	121
1945–46	Elmer Lach, Mtl	34	1987–88	Wayne Gretzky, Edm	109
1946–47	Billy Taylor, Det	46	1988–89	Wayne Gretzky, LA	114
1947–48	Doug Bentley, Chi	37		Mario Lemieux, Pitt	114
1948–49	Doug Bentley, Chi	43	1989–90	Wayne Gretzky, LA	102
1949–50	Ted Lindsay, Det	55	1990–91	Wayne Gretzky, LA	122
1950–51	Gordie Howe, Det	43	1991–92	Wayne Gretzky, LA	90
	Ted Kennedy, Tor	43	1992–93	Adam Oates, Bos	97
1951–52	Elmer Lach, Mtl	50	1993–94	Wayne Gretzky, LA	92
1952–53	Gordie Howe, Det	46	1994–95	Ron Francis, Pitt	48
1953–54	Gordie Howe, Det	48	1995–96	Mario Lemieux, Pitt	92
1954–55	Bert Olmstead, Mtl	48		Ron Francis, Pitt	92
1955–56	Bert Olmstead, Mtl	56	1996–97	Mario Lemieux, Pitt	72
1956–57	Ted Lindsay, Det	55	1997–98	Jaromir Jagr, Pitt	67
1957–58	Henri Richard, Mtl	52		Wayne Gretzky, NYR	67
1958–59	Dickie Moore, Mtl	55	1998–99	Jaromir Jagr, Pitt	83
1959–60	Bobby Hull, Chi	42	1999–00	Mark Recchi, Phil	63
1960–61	Jean Beliveau, Mtl	58	2000–01	Jaromir Jagr, Pitt	69
1961–62	Andy Bathgate, NY	56		Adam Oates, Wash	69
			2001–02	Adam Oates, Wash	57

Iron Man of the Islanders

During a family vacation in Montego Bay, Jamaica, over the 2002 Olympic break, Islanders defenseman Adrian Aucoin couldn't help being pegged as a puckhead. "I broke my nose in our last game [a 1–0 win at Philadelphia on Feb. 12], and I had two black eyes," Aucoin says with a laugh. "People kept asking me, 'Are you a hockey player?' I guess I was hard to miss."

The 28-year-old Aucoin's high-profile of late has had more to do with his on-ice ubiquity than with that injury. In his eighth NHL season he has become New York's iron man, averaging 28:34 of ice time per game through March 3, 2002, third in the league behind the Blues' Chris Pronger (29:01) and the Red Wings' Nicklas Lidstrom (28:50). Aucoin, who had 11 goals and 16 assists, has been at his best on special teams. He has excellent defensive range, and he has been a vocal mainstay of New York's fifth-ranked penalty-killing unit, calling out directions to teammates before face-offs and on the backcheck. With his booming shot, he has also thrived at the point on the Islanders' top power-play unit.

Lately, Aucoin had been even more effective and hard-working—10 goals and five assists in his last 17 games, while averaging 33:24 of ice time. "The jump from 24 to 25 minutes a night is tough, but once you're up around 30 as a regular occurrence, it's easier," he says. "Being on the ice half of every game, your play becomes much more instinctive."

Goals Against Average

Season	Goaltender and Club	GP	Min	GA	SO	Avg
1917–18	Georges Vezina, Mtl	21	1282	84	1	3.93
1918–19	Clint Benedict, Ott	18	1113	53	2	2.86
1919–20	Clint Benedict, Ott	24	1444	64	5	2.66
1920–21	Clint Benedict, Ott	24	1457	75	2	3.09
1921–22	Clint Benedict, Ott	24	1508	84	2	3.34
1922–23	Clint Benedict, Ott	24	1478	54	4	2.19
1923–24	Georges.Vezina, Mtl	24	1459	48	3	1.97
1924–25	Georges Vezina, Mtl	30	1860	56	5	1.81
1925–26	Alex Connell, Ott	36	2251	42	15	1.12
1926–27	Clint Benedict, Mtl M	43	2748	65	13	1.42
1927–28	George Hainsworth, Mtl	44	2730	48	13	1.05
1928–29	George Hainsworth, Mtl	44	2800	43	22	0.92
1929–30	Tiny Thompson, Bos	44	2680	98	3	2.19
1930–31	Roy Worters, NYA	44	2760	74	8	1.61
1931–32	Chuck Gardiner, Chi	48	2989	92	4	1.85
1932–33	Tiny Thompson, Bos	48	3000	88	11	1.76
1933–34	Wilf Cude, Det-Mtl	30	1920	47	5	1.47
1934–35	Lorne Chabot, Chi	48	2940	88	8	1.80
1935–36	Tiny Thompson, Bos	48	2930	82	10	1.68
1936–37	Normie Smith, Det	48	2980	102	6	2.05
1937–38	Tiny Thompson, Bos	48	2970	89	7	1.80
1938–39	Frank Brimsek, Bos	43	2610	68	10	1.56
1939–40	Dave Kerr, NYR	48	3000	77	8	1.54
1940–41	Turk Broda, Tor	48	2970	99	5	2.00
1941–42	Frank Brimsek, Bos	47	2930	115	3	2.35
1942–43	Johnny Mowers, Det	50	3010	124	6	2.47
1943–44	Bill Durnan, Mtl	50	3000	109	2	2.18
1944–45	Bill Durnan, Mtl	50	3000	121	1	2.42
1945–46	Bill Durnan, Mtl	40	2400	104	4	2.60
1946–47	Bill Durnan, Mtl	60	3600	138	4	2.30
1947–48	Turk Broda, Tor	60	3600	143	5	2.38
1948–49	Bill.Durnan, Mtl	60	3600	126	10	2.10
1949–50	Bill Durnan, Mtl	64	3840	141	8	2.20
1950–51	Al Rollins, Tor	40	2367	70	5	1.77
1951–52	Terry Sawchuk, Det	70	4200	133	12	1.90
1952–53	Terry Sawchuk, Det	63	3780	120	9	1.90
1953–54	Harry Lumley, Tor	69	4140	128	13	1.86
1954–55	Harry Lumley, Tor	69	4140	134	8	1.94
	Terry Sawchuk, Det	68	4060	132	12	1.94
1955–56	Jacques Plante, Mtl	64	3840	119	7	1.86
1956–57	Jacques Plante, Mtl	61	3660	123	9	2.02
1957–58	Jacques Plante, Mtl	57	3386	119	9	2.11
1958–59	Jacques Plante, Mtl	67	4000	144	9	2.16
1959–60	Jacques Plante, Mtl	69	4140	175	3	2.54
1960–61	Johnny Bower, Tor	58	3480	145	2	2.50
1961–62	Jacques Plante, Mtl	70	4200	166	4	2.37
1962–63	Jacques Plante, Mtl	56	3320	138	5	2.49
1963–64	Johnny Bower, Tor	51	3009	106	5	2.11
1964–65	Johnny Bower, Tor	34	2040	81	3	2.38
1965–66	Johnny Bower, Tor	35	1998	75	3	2.25
1966–67	Glenn Hall, Chi	32	1664	66	2	2.38
1967–68	Gump Worsley, Mtl	40	2213	73	6	1.98
1968–69	Jacques Plante, StL	37	2139	70	5	1.96
1969–70	Ernie Wakely, StL	30	1651	58	4	2.11
1970–71	Jacques Plante, Tor	40	2329	73	4	1.88
1971–72	Tony Esposito, Chi	48	2780	82	9	1.77
1972–73	Ken Dryden, Mtl	54	3165	119	6	2.26
1973–74	Bernie Parent, Phil	73	4314	136	12	1.89
1974–75	Bernie Parent, Phil	68	4041	137	12	2.03
1975–76	Ken Dryden, Mtl	62	3580	121	8	2.03
1976–77	Michael Larocque, Mtl	26	1525	53	4	2.09
1977–78	Ken Dryden, Mtl	52	3071	105	5	2.05
1978–79	Ken Dryden, Mtl	47	2814	108	5	2.30
1979–80	Bob Sauve, Buff	32	1880	74	4	2.36
1980–81	Richard Sevigny, Mtl	33	1777	71	2	2.40
1981–82	Denis Herron, Mtl	27	1547	68	3	2.64

Goals Against Average *(Cont.)*

Season	Goaltender and Club	GP	Min	GA	SO	Avg
1982–83	Pete Peeters, Bos	62	3611	142	8	2.36
1983–84	Pat Riggin, Wash	41	2299	102	4	2.66
1984–85	Tom Barrasso, Buff	54	3248	144	5	2.66
1985–86	Bob Froese, Phil	51	2728	116	5	2.55
1986–87	Brian Hayward, Mtl	37	2178	102	1	2.81
1987–88	Pete Peeters, Wash	35	1896	88	2	2.78
1988–89	Patrick Roy, Mtl	48	2744	113	4	2.47
1989–90	Patrick Roy, Mtl	54	3173	134	3	2.53
	Mike Liut, Hart-Wash	37	2161	91	4	2.53
1990–91	Ed Belfour, Chi	74	4127	170	4	2.47
1991–92	Patrick Roy, Mtl	67	3935	155	5	2.36
1992–93	*Felix Potvin, Tor	48	2781	116	2	2.50
1993–94	Dominik Hasek, Buff	58	3358	109	7	1.95
1994–95	Dominik Hasek, Buff	41	2416	85	5	2.11
1995–96	Ron Hextall, Phil	53	3102	112	4	2.17
	Chris Osgood, Det	50	2933	106	5	2.17
1996–97	Martin Brodeur, NJ	67	3838	120	10	1.88
1997–98	Ed Belfour, Dall	61	3581	112	9	1.88
1998–99	Ron Tugnutt, Ott	43	2508	75	3	1.79
1999–00	Brian Boucher, Phil	35	2038	65	4	1.91
2000–01	Marty Turco, Dall	26	1266	40	3	1.90
2001–02	Patrick Roy, Col	63	3774	122	9	1.94

*Rookie.

Penalty Minutes

Season	Player and Club	GP	PIM	Season	Player and Club	GP	PIM
1918–19	Joe Hall, Mtl	17	85	1960–61	Pierre Pilote, Chi	70	165
1919–20	Cully Wilson, Tor	23	79	1961–62	Lou Fontinato, Mtl	54	167
1920–21	Bert Corbeau, Mtl	24	86	1962–63	Howie Young, Det	64	273
1921–22	Sprague Cleghorn, Mtl	24	63	1963–64	Vic Hadfield, NYR	69	151
1922–23	Billy Boucher, Mtl	24	52	1964–65	Carl Brewer, Tor	70	177
1923–24	Bert Corbeau, Tor	24	55	1965–66	Reggie Fleming, Bos-NYR	69	166
1924–25	Billy Boucher, Mtl	30	92	1966–67	John Ferguson, Mtl	67	177
1925–26	Bert Corbeau, Tor	36	121	1967–68	Barclay Plager, StL	49	153
1926–27	Nels Stewart, Mtl M	44	133	1968–69	Forbes Kennedy, Phil-Tor	77	219
1927–28	Eddie Shore, Bos	44	165	1969–70	Keith Magnuson, Chi	76	213
1928–29	Red Dutton, Mtl M	44	139	1970–71	Keith Magnuson, Chi	76	291
1929–30	Joe Lamb, Ott	44	119	1971–72	Brian Watson, Pitt	75	212
1930–31	Harvey Rockburn, Det	42	118	1972–73	Dave Schultz, Phil	76	259
1931–32	Red Dutton, NYA	47	107	1973–74	Dave Schultz, Phil	73	348
1932–33	Red Horner, Tor	48	144	1974–75	Dave Schultz, Phil	76	472
1933–34	Red Horner, Tor	42	126	1975–76	Steve Durbano, Pitt-KC	69	370
1934–35	Red Horner, Tor	46	125	1976–77	Dave Williams, Tor	77	338
1935–36	Red Horner, Tor	43	167	1977–78	Dave Schultz, LA-Pitt	74	405
1936–37	Red Horner, Tor	48	124	1978–79	Dave Williams, Tor	77	298
1937–38	Red Horner, Tor	47	82	1979–80	Jimmy Mann, Winn	72	287
1938–39	Red Horner, Tor	48	85	1980–81	Dave Williams, Van	77	343
1939–40	Red Horner, Tor	30	87	1981–82	Paul Baxter, Pitt	76	409
1940–41	Jimmy Orlando, Det	48	99	1982–83	Randy Holt, Wash	70	275
1941–42	Jimmy Orlando, Det	48	81	1983–84	Chris Nilan, Mtl	76	338
1942–43	Jimmy Orlando, Det	40	89	1984–85	Chris Nilan, Mtl	77	358
1943–44	Mike McMahon, Mtl	42	98	1985–86	Joey Kocur, Det	59	377
1944–45	Pat Egan, Bos	48	86	1986–87	Tim Hunter, Cgy	73	361
1945–46	Jack Stewart, Det	47	73	1987–88	Bob Probert, Det	74	398
1946–47	Gus Mortson, Tor	60	133	1988–89	Tim Hunter, Cgy	75	375
1947–48	Bill Barilko, Tor	57	147	1989–90	Basil McRae, Minn	66	351
1948–49	Bill Ezinicki, Tor	52	145	1990–91	Bob Ray, Buff	66	350
1949–50	Bill Ezinicki, Tor	67	144	1991–92	Mike Peluso, Chi	63	408*
1950–51	Gus Mortson, Tor	60	142	1992–93	Marty McSorley, LA	81	399
1951–52	Gus Kyle, Bos	69	127	1993–94	Tie Domi, Winn	81	347
1952–53	Maurice Richard, Mtl	70	112	1994–95	Enrico Ciccone, TB	41	225
1953–54	Gus Mortson, Chi	68	132	1995–96	Matthew Barnaby, Buff	73	335
1954–55	Fern Flaman, Bos	70	150	1996–97	Gino Odjick, Van	70	371
1955–56	Lou Fontinato, NYR	70	202	1997–98	Donald Brashear, Van	77	372
1956–57	Gus Mortson, Chi	70	147	1998–99	Rob Ray, Buff	76	261
1957–58	Lou Fontinato, NYR	70	152	1999–00	Denny Lambert, Atl	73	219
1958–59	Ted Lindsay, Chi	70	184	2000–01	Matthew Barnaby, TB	76	265
1959–60	Carl Brewer, Tor	67	150	2001–02	Peter Worrell, Fla	79	354

NHL All-Star Game

First played in 1947, this game was scheduled before the start of the regular season and used to match the defending Stanley Cup Champions against a squad made up of the league All-stars from other teams. In 1966 the games were moved to mid-season, although there was no game that year. The format changed to a conference versus conference showdown in 1969.

Results

Year	Site	Score	MVP	Attendance
1947	Toronto	All-Stars 4, Toronto 3	None named	14,169
1948	Chicago	All-Stars 3, Toronto 1	None named	12,794
1949	Toronto	All-Stars 3, Toronto 1	None named	13,541
1950	Detroit	Detroit 7, All-Stars 1	None named	9,166
1951	Toronto	1st team 2, 2nd team 2	None named	11,469
1952	Detroit	1st team 1, 2nd team 1	None named	10,680
1953	Montreal	All-Stars 3, Montreal 1	None named	14,153
1954	Detroit	All-Stars 2, Detroit 2	None named	10,689
1955	Detroit	Detroit 3, All-Stars 1	None named	10,111
1956	Montreal	All-Stars 1, Montreal 1	None named	13,095
1957	Montreal	All-Stars 5, Montreal 3	None named	13,003
1958	Montreal	Montreal 6, All-Stars 3	None named	13,989
1959	Montreal	Montreal 6, All-Stars 1	None named	13,818
1960	Montreal	All-Stars 2, Montreal 1	None named	13,949
1961	Chicago	All-Stars 3, Chicago 1	None named	14,534
1962	Toronto	Toronto 4, All-Stars 1	Eddie Shack, Tor	14,236
1963	Toronto	All-Stars 3, Toronto 3	Frank Mahovlich, Tor	14,034
1964	Toronto	All-Stars 3, Toronto 2	Jean Beliveau, Mtl	14,232
1965	Montreal	All-Stars 5, Montreal 2	Gordie Howe, Det	13,529
1967	Montreal	Montreal 3, All-Stars 0	Henri Richard, Mtl	14,284
1968	Toronto	Toronto 4, All-Stars 3	Bruce Gamble, Tor	15,753
1969	Montreal	East 3, West 3	Frank Mahovlich, Det	16,260
1970	St Louis	East 4, West 1	Bobby Hull, Chi	16,587
1971	Boston	West 2, East 1	Bobby Hull, Chi	14,790
1972	Minnesota	East 3, West 2	Bobby Orr, Bos	15,423
1973	NY Rangers	East 5, West 4	Greg Polis, Pitt	16,986
1974	Chicago	West 6, East 4	Garry Unger, StL	16,426
1975	Montreal	Wales 7, Campbell 1	Syl Apps Jr, Pitt	16,080
1976	Philadelphia	Wales 7, Campbell 5	Pete Mahovlich, Mtl	16,436
1977	Vancouver	Wales 4, Campbell 3	Rick Martin, Buff	15,607
1978	Buffalo	Wales 3, Campbell 2 (OT)	Billy Smith, NYI	16,433
1980	Detroit	Wales 6, Campbell 3	Reg Leach, Phil	21,002
1981	Los Angeles	Campbell 4, Wales 1	Mike Liut, StL	15,761
1982	Washington	Wales 4, Campbell 2	Mike Bossy, NYI	18,130
1983	NY Islanders	Campbell 9, Wales 3	Wayne Gretzky, Edm	15,230
1984	NJ Devils	Wales 7, Campbell 6	Don Maloney, NYR	18,939
1985	Calgary	Wales 6, Campbell 4	Mario Lemieux, Pitt	16,825
1986	Hartford	Wales 4, Campbell 3 (OT)	Grant Fuhr, Edm	15,100
1988	St Louis	Wales 6, Campbell 5 (OT)	Mario Lemieux, Pitt	17,878
1989	Edmonton	Campbell 9, Wales 5	Wayne Gretzky, LA	17,503
1990	Pittsburgh	Wales 12, Campbell 7	Mario Lemieux, Pitt	16,236
1991	Chicago	Campbell 11, Wales 5	Vince Damphousse, Tor	18,472
1992	Philadelphia	Campbell 10, Wales 6	Brett Hull, StL	17,380
1993	Montreal	Wales 16, Campbell 6	Mike Gartner, NYR	17,137
1994	NY Rangers	East 9, West 8	Mike Richter, NYR	18,200
1996	Boston	East 5, West 4	Ray Bourque, Bos	17,565
1997	San Jose	East 11, West 7	Mark Recchi, Mtl	17,565
1998	Vancouver	N America 8, World 7	Teemu Selanne, Ana (World)	18,422
1999	Tampa Bay	N America 8, World 6	Wayne Gretzky, NYR (N America)	19,758
2000	Toronto	World 9, N America 4	Pavel Bure, Fla (World)	19,300
2001	Denver	N America 14, World 12	Bill Guerin, Bos (N America)	18,646
2002	Los Angeles	World 8, N America 5	Eric Daze, Chi (N America)	18,118

Note: The Challenge Cup, a series between the NHL All-Stars and the Soviet Union, was played instead of the All-Star Game in 1979. Eight years later, Rendez-Vous '87, a two-game series matching the Soviet Union and the NHL All-Stars, replaced the All-Star Game. The 1995 NHL All-Star game was cancelled due to a labor dispute. The 1998 NHL All-Star game, billed as a preview to the 1998 Winter Olympics in Nagano, Japan, matched North American–born All-Stars and All-Stars born elsewhere.

Hockey Hall of Fame

Located in Toronto, the Hockey Hall of Fame was officially opened on August 26, 1961. The current chairman is William C. Hay. There are, at present, 306 members of the Hockey Hall of Fame—209 players, 84 "builders," and 14 on-ice officials. (One member, Alan Eagleson, resigned from the Hall 3-25-98.) To be eligible, player and referee/linesman candidates should have been out of the game for three years, but the Hall's Board of Directors can make exceptions.

Players

Sid Abel (1969)
Jack Adams (1959)
Charles (Syl) Apps (1961)
George Armstrong (1975)
Irvine (Ace) Bailey (1975)
Donald H. (Dan) Bain (1945)
Hobey Baker (1945)
Bill Barber (1990)
Marty Barry (1965)
Andy Bathgate (1978)
Bobby Bauer (1996)
Jean Beliveau (1972)
Clint Benedict (1965)
Douglas Bentley (1964)
Max Bentley (1966)
Hector (Toe) Blake (1966)
Leo Boivin (1986)
Dickie Boon (1952)
Mike Bossy (1991)
Emile (Butch) Bouchard (1966)
Frank Boucher (1958)
George (Buck) Boucher (1960)
Johnny Bower (1976)
Russell Bowie (1945)
Frank Brimsek (1966)
Harry L. (Punch) Broadbent
  (1962)
Walter (Turk) Broda (1967)
John Bucyk (1981)
Billy Burch (1974)
Harry Cameron (1962)
Gerry Cheevers (1985)
Francis (King) Clancy (1958)
Aubrey (Dit) Clapper (1947)
Bobby Clarke (1987)
Sprague Cleghorn (1958)
Neil Colville (1967)
Charlie Conacher (1961)
Lionel Conacher (1994)
Roy Conacher (1998)
Alex Connell (1958)
Bill Cook (1952)
Fred (Bun) Cook (1995)
Arthur Coulter (1974)
Yvan Cournoyer (1982)
Bill Cowley (1968)
Samuel (Rusty) Crawford (1962)
Jack Darragh (1962)
Allan M. (Scotty) Davidson
  (1950)
Clarence (Hap) Day (1961)
Alex Delvecchio (1977)
Cy Denneny (1959)
Marcel Dionne (1992)
Gordie Drillon (1975)
Charles Drinkwater (1950)
Ken Dryden (1983)

Woody Dumart (1992)
Thomas Dunderdale (1974)
Bill Durnan (1964)
Mervyn A. (Red) Dutton (1958)
Cecil (Babe) Dye (1970)
Phil Esposito (1984)
Tony Esposito (1988)
Arthur F. Farrell (1965)
Bernie Federko (2002)
Viacheslav Fetisov (2001)
Ferdinand (Fern) Flaman (1990)
Frank Foyston (1958)
Frank Frederickson (1958)
Bill Gadsby (1970)
Bob Gainey (1992)
Chuck Gardiner (1945)
Herb Gardiner (1958)
Jimmy Gardner (1962)
Mike Gartner (2001)
Bernie (Boom Boom) Geoffrion
  (1972)
Eddie Gerard (1945)
Ed Giacomin (1987)
Rod Gilbert (1982)
Clark Gilles (2002)
Hamilton (Billy) Gilmour (1962)
Frank (Moose) Goheen (1952)
Ebenezer R. (Ebbie)
  Goodfellow (1963)
Michel Goulet (1998)
Mike Grant (1950)
Wilfred (Shorty) Green (1962)
Wayne Gretzky (1999)
Si Griffis (1950)
George Hainsworth (1961)
Glenn Hall (1975)
Joe Hall (1961)
Doug Harvey (1973)
Dale Hawerchuk (2001)
George Hay (1958)
William (Riley) Hern (1962)
Bryan Hextall (1969)
Harry (Hap) Holmes (1972)
Tom Hooper (1962)
George (Red) Horner (1965)
Miles (Tim) Horton (1977)
Gordie Howe (1972)
Syd Howe (1965)
Harry Howell (1979)
Bobby Hull (1983)
John (Bouse) Hutton (1962)
Harry M. Hyland (1962)
James (Dick) Irvin (1958)
Harvey (Busher) Jackson
  (1971)
Ernest (Moose) Johnson (1952)
Ivan (Ching) Johnson (1958)

Tom Johnson (1970)
Aurel Joliat (1947)
Gordon (Duke) Keats (1958)
Leonard (Red) Kelly (1969)
Ted (Teeder) Kennedy (1966)
Dave Keon (1986)
Jari Kurri (2001)
Elmer Lach (1966)
Guy Lafleur (1988)
Edouard (Newsy) Lalonde (1950)
Rod Langway (2002)
Jacques Laperriere (1987)
Guy LaPointe (1993)
Edgar Laprade (1993)
Reed Larson (1996)
Jean (Jack) Laviolette (1962)
Hugh Lehman (1958)
Jacques Lemaire (1984)
Mario Lemieux (1997)
Percy LeSueur (1961)
Herbert A. Lewis (1989)
Ted Lindsay (1966)
Harry Lumley (1980)
Lanny McDonald (1992)
Frank McGee (1945)
Billy McGimsie (1962)
George McNamara (1958)
Duncan (Mickey) MacKay (1952)
Frank Mahovlich (1981)
Joe Malone (1950)
Sylvio Mantha (1960)
Jack Marshall (1965)
Fred G. (Steamer) Maxwell
  (1962)
Stan Mikita (1983)
Dicky Moore (1974)
Patrick (Paddy) Moran (1958)
Howie Morenz (1945)
Billy Mosienko (1965)
Joe Mullen (2000)
Frank Nighbor (1947)
Reg Noble (1962)
Herbert (Buddy) O'Connor (1988)
Harry Oliver (1967)
Bert Olmstead (1985)
Bobby Orr (1979)
Bernie Parent (1984)
Brad Park (1988)
Lester Patrick (1947)
Lynn Patrick (1980)
Gilbert Perreault (1990)
Tommy Phillips (1945)
Pierre Pilote (1975)
Didier (Pit) Pitre (1962)
Jacques Plante (1978)
Denis Potvin (1991)
Walter (Babe) Pratt (1966)

Players *(Cont.)*

Joe Primeau (1963)
Marcel Pronovost (1978)
Bob Pulford (1991)
Harvey Pulford (1945)
Hubert (Bill) Quackenbush (1976)
Frank Rankin (1961)
Jean Ratelle (1985)
Claude (Chuck) Rayner (1973)
Kenneth Reardon (1966)
Henri Richard (1979)
Maurice (Rocket) Richard (1961)
George Richardson (1950)
Gordon Roberts (1971)
Larry Robinson (1995)
Art Ross (1945)
Blair Russel (1965)
Ernest Russell (1965)
Jack Ruttan (1962)
Borje Salming (1996)
Denis Savard (2000)
Serge Savard (1986)
Terry Sawchuk (1971)
Fred Scanlan (1965)
Milt Schmidt (1961)
Dave (Sweeney) Schriner (1962)
Earl Seibert (1963)
Oliver Seibert (1961)
Eddie Shore (1947)
Steve Shutt (1993)
Albert C. (Babe) Siebert (1964)
Harold (Bullet Joe) Simpson (1962)
Daryl Sittler (1989)
Alfred E. Smith (1962)
Billy Smith (1993)
Clint Smith (1991)
Reginald (Hooley) Smith (1972)
Thomas Smith (1973)
Allan Stanley (1981)
Russell (Barney) Stanley (1962)
Peter Stastny (1998)
John (Black Jack) Stewart (1964)
Nels Stewart (1962)
Bruce Stuart (1961)
Hod Stuart (1945)
Frederic (Cyclone) (O.B.E.)
    Taylor (1947)
Cecil R. (Tiny) Thompson
    (1959)
Vladislav Tretiak (1989)
Harry J. Trihey (1950)
Bryan Trottier (1997)
Norm Ullman (1982)
Georges Vezina (1945)
Jack Walker (1960)
Marty Walsh (1962)
Harry Watson (1994)
Harry E. Watson (1962)
Ralph (Cooney) Weiland (1971)
Harry Westwick (1962)
Fred Whitcroft (1962)

Players *(Cont.)*

Gordon (Phat) Wilson (1962)
Lorne (Gump) Worsley (1980)
Roy Worters (1969)

Builders

Charles Adams (1960)
Weston W. Adams (1972)
Thomas (Frank) Ahearn (1962)
John (Bunny) Ahearne (1977)
Montagu Allan (C.V.O.) (1945)
Keith Allen (1992)
Al Arbour (1996)
Harold Ballard (1977)
David Bauer (1989)
John Bickell (1978)
Scott Bowman (1991)
George V. Brown (1961)
Walter A. Brown (1962)
Frank Buckland (1975)
Walter L. Bush (2000)
Jack Butterfield (1980)
Frank Calder (1947)
Angus D. Campbell (1964)
Clarence Campbell (1966)
Joe Cattarinich (1977)
Bob Cole (1996)
Joseph (Leo) Dandurand (1963)
Francis Dilio (1964)
George S. Dudley (1958)
James A. Dunn (1968)
Robert Alan Eagleson (1989–98*)
Sergio Gambucci (1996)
Emile Francis (1982)
Jack Gibson (1976)
Tommy Gorman (1963)
Frank Griffiths (1993)
William Hanley (1986)
Charles Hay (1974)
James C. Hendy (1968)
Foster Hewitt (1965)
William Hewitt (1947)
Fred J. Hume (1962)
George (Punch) Imlach (1984)
Tommy Ivan (1974)
William M. Jennings (1975)
Bob Johnson (1992)
Gordon W. Juckes (1979)
John Kilpatrick (1960)
Seymour Knox III (1993)
George Leader (1969)
Robert LeBel (1970)
Thomas F. Lockhart (1965)
Paul Loicq (1961)
Frederic McLaughlin (1963)
John Mariucci (1985)
Frank Mathers (1992)
John (Jake) Milford (1984)
Hartland Molson (1973)
Scotty Morrison (1999)

Builders *(Cont.)*

Mngr. Athol (Pere) Murray (1998)
Roger Neilson (2002)
Francis Nelson (1947)
Bruce A. Norris (1969)
James Norris, Sr. (1958)
James D. Norris (1962)
William M. Northey (1947)
John O'Brien (1962)
Brian O'Neill (1994)
Fred Page (1993)
Craig Patrick (1996)
Frank Patrick (1958)
Allan W. Pickard (1958)
Rudy Pilous (1985)
Norman (Bud) Poile (1990)
Samuel Pollock (1978)
Donat Raymond (1958)
John Robertson (1947)
Claude C. Robinson (1947)
Philip D. Ross (1976)
Gunther Sabetzki (1995)
Glen Sather (1997)
Frank J. Selke (1960)
Harry Sinden (1983)
Frank D. Smith (1962)
Conn Smythe (1958)
Edward M. Snider (1988)
Lord Stanley of Preston
    (G.C.B.) (1945)
James T. Sutherland (1947)
Anatoli V. Tarasov (1974)
Bill Torrey (1995)
Lloyd Turner (1958)
William Tutt (1978)
Carl Potter Voss (1974)
Fred C. Waghorn (1961)
Arthur Wirtz (1971)
Bill Wirtz (1976)
John A. Ziegler, Jr. (1987)

Referees/Linesmen

Neil Armstrong (1991)
John Ashley (1981)
William L. Chadwick (1964)
John D'Amico (1993)
Chaucer Elliott (1961)
George Hayes (1988)
Robert W. Hewitson (1963)
Fred J. (Mickey) Ion (1961)
Matt Pavelich (1987)
Mike Rodden (1962)
J. Cooper Smeaton (1961)
Roy (Red) Storey (1967)
Frank Udvari (1973)
Andy van Hellemond (1999)

Note: Year of election to the Hall of Fame is in parentheses after the member's name.
*Eagleson resigned from Hall March 25, 1998.

Tennis

CHUCK SOLOMON

Wimbledon, French
and U.S. Open champ
Serena Williams

Loud and Clear

While Serena Williams left no doubt as to who rules the women's tour, Pete Sampras sent an unmistakable message of his own

BY B.J. SCHECTER

IS ONCE bushy head of hair was balding, and his serve had lost a considerable amount of pace. Fatigue had cost him matches and caused him to contemplate retirement. And a murmur from a chorus of critics, rising in volume as the U.S. Open got under way, was telling him that he was done.

Swimming against this current of negativism, Pete Sampras made his way to Flushing, the spawning ground of four of his record 13 Grand Slam singles titles, and the place where his legend was born in 1990, when, at 19, he knocked off Ivan Lendl, John McEnroe and Andre Agassi to became the youngest men's champion in U.S. Open history. Just when he—and the men's game—needed it most, the 31-year-old Sampras produced a stunning return to form that culminated in a 6–3, 6–4, 5–7, 6–4 victory over his oldest rival, Agassi, for his fifth Open title and 14th Grand Slam. Should he so choose, Sampras's 2002 U.S. Open run would provide the perfect coda to his superb career.

For more than a year, Sampras had heard the rumblings that he should hang it up. Sampras hadn't won a Grand Slam final since his 2000 Wimbledon title, and before this year's Open, he hadn't won a title of any kind in 2002. And the rumblings were not limited to the fans and tennis wags. After Sampras beat Greg Rusedski in five sets six days before the final, Rusedski said, "You're used to seeing Pete Sampras, 13-time Grand Slam champion. It's not the same player."

Of course, where Rusedski found the chutzpah to make those remarks after being *beaten* by Sampras is anybody's guess, but criticism and self-doubt had gotten the best of Sampras during 2002. Following a loss to George Bastl in the second round of Wimbledon, Sampras seriously considered retirement, but his wife, Bridgette Wilson, couldn't see her husband go out like that. "Don't believe this crap that people are saying," she told him. "Stop on your own terms. Just promise me that." Sampras did. "When she said that, it gave me some life," he said. "I was like,

Sampras improved with each match at the Open, eventually seizing his fifth title at Flushing and record 14th Slam.

screw these people. Just believe."

Though he played better and better in each match at the Open, few observers believed that Sampras could actually win the tournament. A step slower than he was in his prime, he could no longer rely on his talent alone. Instead, Sampras used his mind, his determination, and his heart. It was a strange thing to see the formerly cool—even bland—Sampras unabashedly letting his emotions show. And a funny thing happened: He won over a lot of fans who rooted against him when he was methodically winning all those championships.

Sampras also remembered his promise to Wilson, and he wasn't about to let her down. As he sat in the locker room preparing to face Agassi in the final, Sampras opened his bag and read a note from his pregnant wife. "I'm so proud of you," the note read. "Go out there and enjoy today, and enjoy yourself, attack from the first point on. Continue to do what you've been doing, playing your game.... Stay strong. Find your zone. This is your house."

No one could affirm the validity of that last statement better than the 32-year-old Agassi. As a 20-year-old, he had faced Sampras in that 1990 Open Final in which Sampras won his first Slam. But the long-time rivals couldn't be more different: Agassi has always emphasized flair and lived a very public life; Sampras has an all-business personality and guards his privacy. As a result, fans usually embraced Agassi while claiming Sampras was boring.

Though Agassi and Sampras have never been good friends, they have an abiding mutual respect. After he dispatched top-seeded and defending champion Lleyton Hewitt in one semifinal, Agassi was asked if he had heard the roar of the crowd. He responded by saying, "Wait till tomorrow."

Agassi's tout was on the money. The lat-est—and possibly final—Sampras-Agassi showdown was indeed a classic. Sampras played as if he'd regained that step he'd appeared all season to have lost. Serving and volleying like the greatest player who ever lived and hitting screaming winners, Sampras played as if he were 19 again. The 23,157 fans at Arthur Ashe Stadium watched in awe and seemed to appreciate the moment. For a struggling men's game and two players refusing to accept retirement, it was exactly what the doctor ordered.

When it was over, Sampras threw his arms in the air and then put a hand on his head in disbelief. Then he did something even more remarkable. He approached the net, hugged Agassi and said, "You're the best I ever played." The players walked off the court and Sampras climbed into the stands to find Wilson. "I love you," he whispered into her ear. "Thank you. You kept me together."

Serena and Venus Williams almost single-handedly kept the WTA tour together by taking the women's game to another level. The Williams sisters used 2002 to establish beyond any reasonable doubt that they are the top two players on the women's tour. As for which sister is No. 1 and which No. 2, well, there is little doubt about that, either. In a fitting conclusion to the year, Serena beat her older sister 6–4, 6–3, to take her third major of the year—she defeated her sister in the final of each of them—and solidify her grip on the No. 1 spot. The year's first Slam, the Australian Open, was the only major Serena didn't win—she was forced to withdraw from the tournament with a severely sprained ankle.

The only legitimate criticism of the Williams sisters' games arises when they play one another. For some reason, and particularly in Grand Slam finals, their matches against each other had been ugly, error-plagued affairs. But in 2002, even that gripe dissolved: The three All-Williams Grand Slam finals yielded exciting tennis, with the Wimbledon decider taking the prize as the most competitive match the two sisters have played against one another. In addition to being worth watching, those matches demonstrated that the 20-year-old Serena has become noticeably better than Venus, 22. Serena currently stands alone at the top of the women's tennis world. "It's not that I thought I could win all three [Grand Slams]," said Serena after the Open final. "I just said, 'I'm tired of losing. I'm not going to lose anymore.' Life was passing me by."

Injuries to top players on the men's and women's side caused many fans to pass by the Australian Open, back in January, without taking note. A depleted men's field cleared the way for Thomas Johansson of Sweden to win the title. On the women's side, with Serena Williams and Lindsay Davenport on the shelf with injuries, and Venus Williams seemingly disinterested, the draw didn't get exciting until the finals, where Martina Hingis met Jennifer Capriati.

For Hingis, the Australian provided a measure of redemption. Considered the No. 1 player in the world in the mid-'90s,

Hingis hadn't won a slam since the '99 Australian. Her confidence waning, Hingis put together a terrific run in Melbourne and appeared to be on her way to the title. With Hingis ahead 6–4, 4–0 in the final, a television camera was wheeled to courtside for the trophy presentation. This incensed Capriati, spurring her to hold off four match points en route to a 4–6, 7–6, 6–2 victory. "Even though the score showed I was far behind," Carpaiti said. "I felt I was right there in the match."

Hingis never recovered, and ended up missing several months, including the French Open and Wimbledon, with an ankle injury. Capriati would have a meltdown of her own. In the spring, she was dismissed from the U.S. Federation Cup team after she violated team rules by practicing with her own coach. After her dismissal, she unleashed a profanity-laced diatribe at team captain Billie Jean King. The incident soured the remainder of Capriati's season.

Before the U.S. Open, sour would have been one of the nicer words used to describe the men's tour. With three different champions in the first three Slams, the men's game had a lot of parity, but little pizzazz. After Spain's Albert Costa beat countryman Juan Carlos Ferrero in the French Open final, the men had eight different winners in the last eight Slams. Hewitt, the No. 1-ranked player, put on a stunning display to win Wimbledon, but his arrogance and immaturity prevented him, for the moment, from being seen as anything but a talented enfant terrible.

It wasn't until the U.S. Open final that the men's season acquired some luster. "This title might have meant more than any of them," Sampras said after his victory. "I take pride in having the whole package—the talent, the heart and the mind—and if there was a year I needed that heart and mind and support, it was this year. There were moments I felt empty. To get through that, to come back and beat all these young guys and beat Andre in the final, is a fitting way to end it."

We couldn't agree more, Pete.

2002 Grand Slam Champions

Australian Open
Men's Singles

	Winner	Runner-up	Score
Quarterfinals	Thomas Johansson (16)..........Jonas Bjorkman		6–0, 2–6, 6–3, 6–4
	Marat Safin (9)........................Wayne Ferreira		5–2, retired
	Tommy Haas (7)......................Marcelo Rios		7–6 (7–2), 6–4, 6–7 (2–7), 7–6 (7–5)
	Jiri Novak (26) ....Stefan Koubek		6–2, 6–3, 6–2,
Semifinals	Thomas Johansson ....Jiri Novak		7–6 (7–5), 0–6, 4–6, 6–3, 6–4
	Marat Safin ....Tommy Haas		6–7 (5–7), 7–6 (7–4), 3–6, 6–0, 6–2
Final	Thomas Johansson ....Marat Safin		3–6, 6–4, 6–4, 7–6 (7–4)

Women's Singles

	Winner	Runner-up	Score
Quarterfinals	Jennifer Capriati (1) ....Amelie Mauresmo (7)		6–2, 6–2
	Martina Hingis (3)....................Adriana Serra-Zanetti		6–2, 6–3
	Kim Clijsters (4)......................Justine Henin (6)		6–2, 6–3
	Monica Seles (8) ....Venus Williams (2)		6–7 (4–7), 6–2, 6–3
Semifinals	Jennifer Capriati......................Kim Clijsters		7–5, 3–6, 6–1
	Martina Hingis ....Monica Seles		4–6, 6–1, 6–4
Final	Jennifer Capriati......................Martina Hingis		4–6, 7–6 (9–7), 6–2

Doubles

	Winner	Runner-up	Score
Men's Final	Mark Knowles/ Daniel Nestor (9)....................Michael Llodra/ Fabrice Santoro		7–6 (7–4), 6–3
Women's Final	Martina Hingis/ Anna Kournikova (8) ....Daniela Hantuchova/ Arantxa Sanchez-Vicario (13)		6–2, 6–7 (4–7), 6–1
Mixed Final	Kevin Ullyett/ Daniela Hantuchova................Guston Etlis/ Paola Suarez		6–3, 6–2

French Open
Men's Singles

	Winner	Runner-up	Score
Quarterfinals	Albert Costa (20).....................Guillermo Canas (15)		7–5, 6–3, 6–7 (3–7), 6–4, 6–0
	Juan Carlos Ferrero (11).........Andre Agassi (4)		6–3, 5–7, 7–5, 6–3
	Alex Corretja (18) ....Andrei Pavel (22)		7–6 (7–5), 7–5, 7–5
	Marat Safin (2).........................Sebastien Grosjean (10)		6–3, 6–2, 6–2
Semifinals	Albert Costa ....Alex Corretja		6–3, 6–4, 3–6, 6–3
	Juan Carlos Ferrero ....Marat Safin		6–3, 6–2, 6–4
Final	Albert Costa ....Juan Carlos Ferrero		6–1, 6–0, 4–6, 6–3

Women's Singles

	Winner	Runner-up	Score
Quarterfinals	Serena Williams (3) ....Mary Pierce		6–1, 6–1
	Venus Williams (2)..................Monica Seles (6)		6–4, 6–3
	Jennifer Capriati (1) ....Jelena Dokic (7)		6–4, 4–6, 6–1
	Clarisa Fernandez..................Paola Suarez		2–6, 7–6 (7–5), 6–1
Semifinals	Serena Williams......................Jennifer Capriati		3–6, 7–6 (7–2), 6–2
	Venus Williams........................Clarisa Fernandez		6–1, 6–4
Final	Serena Williams......................Venus Williams		7–5, 6–3

Note: Seedings in parentheses.

French Open *(Cont.)*

Doubles

	Winner	Runner-Up	Score
Men's Final	Paul Haarhuis/ Yevgeny Kafelnikov	Mark Knowles/ Daniel Nestor (2)	7–5, 6–4
Women's Final	Virginia Ruano Pascual/ Paola Suarez (2)	Lisa Raymond/ Rennae Stubbs (1)	6–4, 6–2
Mixed Final	Cara Black/ Wayne Black (5)	Elena Bovina/ Mark Knowles	6–3, 6–3

Wimbledon

Men's Singles

	Winner	Runner-Up	Score
Quarterfinals	Lleyton Hewitt (1)	Sjeng Schalken (18)	6–2, 6–2, 6–7 (5–7), 1–6, 7–5
	Daniel Nalbandian (28)	Nicolas Lapentti (22)	6–4, 6–4, 4–6, 4–6, 6–4
	Tim Henman (4)	Andre Sa	6–3, 5–7, 6–4, 6–3
	Xavier Malisse (27)	Richard Krajicek	6–1, 4–6, 6–2, 3–6, 9–7
Semifinals	Lleyton Hewitt	Tim Henman	7–5, 6–1, 7–5
	David Nalbandian	Xavier Malisse	7–6 (7–2), 6–4, 1–6, 2–6, 6–2
Final	Lleyton Hewitt	David Nalbandian	6–1, 6–3, 6–2

Women's Singles

	Winner	Runner-Up	Score
Quarterfinals	Serena Williams (2)	Daniela Hantuchova (11)	6–3, 6–2
	Venus Williams (1)	Elena Likhovtseva	6–2, 6–0
	Amelie Mauresmo (9)	Jennifer Capriati (3)	6–3, 6–2
	Justine Henin (6)	Monica Seles (4)	7–5, 7–6 (7–4)
Semifinals	Serena Williams	Amelie Mauresmo	6–2, 6–1
	Venus Williams	Justine Henin	6–3, 6–2
Final	Serena Williams	Venus Williams	7–6 (7–4), 6–3

Doubles

	Winner	Runner-Up	Score
Men's Final	Jonas Bjorkman/ Todd Woodbridge (5)	Mark Knowles/ Daniel Nestor (2)	6–1, 6–2, 6–7 (7–9), 7–5
Women's Final	Serena Williams/ Venus Williams (3)	Virginia Ruano Pascual/ Paola Suarez (2)	6–2, 7–5
Mixed Final	Mahesh Bhupathi/ Elena Likhovtseva (3)	Kevin Ullyett/ Daniela Hantuchova (4)	6–2, 1–6, 6–1

U.S. Open

Men's Singles

	Winner	Runner-Up	Score
Quarterfinals	Lleyton Hewitt (1)	Y. El Aynaoui (20)	6–1, 7–6 (8–6), 4–6, 6–2
	Andre Agassi (6)	Max Mirnyi (32)	6–7 (5–7), 6–3, 7–5, 6–3
	Pete Sampras (17)	Andy Roddick (11)	6–3, 6–2, 6–4
	Sjeng Schalken (24)	Fernando Gonzalez (28)	6–7 (5–7), 6–3, 6–3 6–7 (5–7), 7–6 (7–2)
Semifinals	Andre Agassi	Lleyton Hewitt	6–4, 7–6, 6–7, 6–2
	Pete Sampras	Sjeng Schalken	7–6, 7–6, 6–2
Final	Pete Sampras	Andre Agassi	6–3, 6–4, 5–7, 6–4

Note: Seedings in parentheses.

U.S. Open *(Cont.)*

Women's Singles

	Winner	Runner-Up	Score
Quarterfinals	Serena Williams (1)	Daniela Hantuchova (11)	6–2, 6–2
	Lindsay Davenport (4)	Elena Bovina	3–6, 6–0, 6–2
	Amelie Mauresmo (10)	Jennifer Capriati (3)	4–6, 7–6 (7–5), 6–3
	Venus Williams (2)	Monica Seles (6)	6–2, 6–3
Semifinals	Serena Williams	Lindsay Davenport	6–3, 7–5
	Venus Williams	Amelie Mauresmo	6–3, 5–7, 6–4
Final	Serena Williams	Venus Williams	6–4, 6–3

Doubles

	Winner	Runner-Up	Score
Men's Final	M. Bhupathi/	Jiri Novak/	6–3, 3–6, 6–4
	Max Mirnyi (3)	Radek Stepanek (11)	
Women's Final	V. Ruano Pascual/	Elena Dementieva/	6–2, 6–1
	Paola Suarez (2)	Janette Husarova (6)	
Mixed Final	Lisa Raymond/	Katarina Srebotnik/	7–6 (11–9), 7–6 (7–1)
	Mike Bryan (2)	Bob Bryan	

Major Tournament Results

Men's Tour (late 2001)

Date	Tournament	Site	Winner	Runner-Up	Score
Oct 8–14	CA Trophy Tournament	Vienna	Tommy Haas	Guillermo Canas	6–2, 7–6 (8–6), 6–4
Oct 8–14	Lyon Grand Prix	Lyon, France	Ivan Ljubicic	Y. El Aynaoui	6–3, 6–2
Oct 22–28	Swiss Indoors	Basel, Switzerland	Tim Henman	Roger Federer	6–3, 6–4, 6–2
Oct 22–28	St. Petersburg Open	St. Petersburg, Russia	Marat Safin	Rainer Schuettler	3–6, 6–3, 6–3
Oct 22–28	Stockholm Open	Stockholm	S. Schalken	J. Nieminen	3–6, 6–3, 6–3, 4–6, 6–3
Oct 29–Nov 4	Paris Masters	Paris	S. Grosjean	Y. Kafelnikov	7–6 (7–3), 6–1, 6–7 (5–7), 6–4
Nov 12–18	Tennis Masters Cup	Sydney	Lleyton Hewitt	S. Grosjean	6–3, 6–3, 6–4

Men's Tour (Through September 8, 2002)

Date	Tournament	Site	Winner	Runner-Up	Score
Dec 31–Jan 6	Qatar Open	Doha, Qatar	Y. El Aynaoui	F. Mantilla	4–6, 6–2, 6–2
Jan 14–27	Australian Open	Melbourne	T. Johansson	Marat Safin	3–6, 6–4, 6–4, 7–6 (7–4)
Feb 11–17	Marseille Open	Marseille, France	Thomas Enqvist	Nicolas Escude	6–7 (4–7), 6–3, 6–1
Feb 18–24	ABN/Amro Tournament	Rotterdam, Amsterdam	Nicolas Escude	Tim Henman	3–6, 7–6 (9–7), 6–4
Feb 18–24	Kroger St. Jude	Memphis	Andy Roddick	James Blake	6–4, 3–6, 7–5
Feb 25–Mar 3	Dubai Open	Dubai, UAE	Fabrice Santoro	Y. El Aynaoui	6–4, 3–6, 6–3
Mar 11–17	Pacific Life Open	Indian Wells, California	Lleyton Hewitt	Tim Henman	6–1, 6–2
Mar 18–31	NASDAQ 100 Open	Miami	Andre Agassi	Roger Federer	6–3, 6–3, 3–6, 6–4
Apr 8–14	Estoril Open	Estoril, Portugal	David Nalbandian	J. Nieminen	6–4, 7–6 (7–5)
Apr 15–21	Monte Carlo Open	Monte Carlo	J. C. Ferrero	Carlos Moya	7–5, 6–3, 6–4
Apr 29–May 5	BMW Open	Munich	Y. El Aynaoui	R. Schuettler	6–4, 6–4
May 6–12	Italian Open	Rome	Andre Agassi	Tommy Haas	6–3, 6–3, 6–0

Men's Tour (Through September 8, 2002) (Cont.)

Date	Tournament	Site	Winner	Runner-Up	Score
May14–19	German Open	Hamburg	Roger Federer	Marat Safin	6–1, 6–3, 6–4
May 27–Jun 9	French Open	Paris	Albert Costa	Juan Carlos Ferrero	6–1, 6–0, 4–6, 6–3
June 9–16	Gerry Weber Open	Halle, Germany	Y. Kafelnikov	Nicholas Kiefer	2–6, 6–4, 6–4
June 17–23	Ordina Open	'S-Hertogenbosch Netherlands	Sjeng Schalken	Arnaud Clement	3–6, 6–3, 6–2
June 24–July 7	Wimbledon	Wimbledon	Lleyton Hewitt	D. Nalbandian	6–1, 6–3, 6–2
July 8–14	Swiss Open	Gstaad, Switzerland	Alex Corretja	Gaston Gaudio	6–3, 7–6 (7–3), 7–6 (7–3)
July 15–21	Mercedes Cup	Stuttgart, Germany	Mikhail Youzhny	Guillermo Canas	6–3, 3–6, 3–6, 6–4, 6–4
July 22–28	Generali Open	Kitzbuhel, Austria	Alex Corretja	Juan Carlos Ferrero	6–4, 6–1, 6–3
Jul 29–Aug 4	Canadian Open	Toronto	G. Canas	Andy Roddick	6–4, 7–5
Aug 5–11	Tennis Masters Series	Cincinnati	Carlos Moya	Lleyton Hewitt	7–5, 7–6 (7–5)
Aug 12–18	RCA Championships	Indianapolis	Greg Rusedski	Felix Mantilla	6–7 (6–8), 6–4, 6–4
Aug 12–18	Legg Mason Classic	Wash., D.C.	James Blake	P. Srichaphan	1–6, 7–6 (7–5), 6–4
Aug 26–Sept 8	U.S. Open	New York City	Pete Sampras	Andre Agassi	6–3, 6–4, 5–7, 6–4

Women's Tour (Late 2001)

Date	Tournament	Site	Winner	Runner-Up	Score
Sept 24–30	Sparkassen Cup	Leipzig, Germany	Kim Clijsters	M. Maleeva	6–1, 6-1
Oct 1–7	Ladies Kremlin Cup	Moscow	Jelena Dokic	E. Likhovtseva	6–3, 6–3
Oct 1–7	Japan Open	Tokyo	Monica Seles	T. Tanasugarn	6–3, 6–2
Oct 15–21	Swisscom Challenge	Zurich	L. Davenport	Jelena Dokic	6–3, 6–1
Oct 22–28	Generali Ladies Open	Linz, Aust.	L. Davenport	Jelena Dokic	6–4, 6–1

Women's Tour (Through September 8, 2002)

Date	Tournament	Site	Winner	Runner-Up	Score
Jan 7–13	Adidas International	Sydney	Martina Hingis	M. Shaughnessy	6–2, 6–3
Jan 14–27	Australian Open	Melbourne	Jennfier Capriati	Martina Hingis	4–6, 7–6 (9–7), 6–2
Jan 28–Feb 3	Pan Pacific Open	Tokyo	Martina Hingis	Monica Seles	7–6 (8–6), 4–6, 6–3
Feb 5–11	Open Gaz de France	Paris	A. Mauresmo	Anke Huber	7–6 (7–2), 6–1
Feb 11–17	Qatar Open	Doha, Qatar	Monica Seles	T. Tanasugam	7–6 (8–6), 6–3
Mar 4–17	Pacific Life Open	Indian Wells, California	Daniela Hantuchova	Martina Hingis	6–3, 6–4
Mar 18–31	NASDAQ-100 Open	Miami	Serena Williams	Jennifer Capriati	7–5, 7–6 (7–4)
Apr 8–14	Bausch & Lomb Championships	Amelia Island, Florida	Venus Williams	Justine Henin	2–6, 7–5, 7–6 (7–5)
Apr 15–21	Family Circle Cup	Charleston, S Carolina	Iva Majoli	Patty Schnyder	7–6 (7–5), 6–4
Apr 29–May 5	Betty Barclay Cup	Hamburg	Kim Clijsters	Venus Williams	1–6, 6–3, 6–4
May 9–12	German Open	Berlin	Justine Henin	Serena Williams	6–2, 1–6, 7–6 (7–5)
May 13–19	Italian Open	Rome	Serena Williams	Justine Henin	7–6 (8–6), 6–4
May 20–26	Int'l de Strasbourg	Strasbourg, France	Silvia Farena Elia	Jelena Dokic	6–4, 3–6, 6–3
May 27–Jun 9	French Open	Paris	Serena Williams	Venus Williams	7–5, 6–3
June 17–23	Britannic Asset Championships	Eastbourne, England	Chanda Rubin	A. Myskina	6–1, 6–3
Jun 24–July 7	Wimbledon	Wimbledon	Serena Williams	Venus Williams	7–6 (7–4), 6–3
July 22–28	Bank of the West	Stanford	Venus Williams	Kim Clijsters	6–3, 6–3
July 29–Aug 4	Acura Classic	San Diego	Venus Williams	Jelena Dokic	6–2, 6–2
Aug 5–11	JP Morgan Chase Open	Los Angeles	Chanda Rubin	L. Davenport	5–7, 7–6 (7–5), 6–3
Aug 12–18	AT&T Canada Cup	Montreal	A. Mauresmo	Jennifer Capriati	6–4, 6–1
Aug 19–25	Pilot Pen Int'l	New Haven,CT	Venus Williams	L. Davenport	7–5, 6–0
Aug 26–Sept 8	U.S. Open	New York City	Serena Williams	Venus Williams	6–4, 6–3

Men

Rank	Player	Tournament Wins	Match Record	Earnings ($)
1.	Lleyton Hewitt	6	79–17	3,770,618
2.	Gustavo Kuerten	6	60–18	2,441,004
3.	Andre Agassi	4	45–15	2,091,766
4.	Yevgeny Kafelnikov	2	69–28	2,263,889
5.	Juan Carlos Ferrero	4	57–21	1,864,671
6.	Sebastien Grosjean	1	51–24	1,918,584
7.	Patrick Rafter	1	47–18	1,670,592
8.	Tommy Haas	4	57–21	1,404,640
9.	Tim Henman	2	51–20	918,699
10.	Pete Sampras	0	35–16	994,331
11.	Marat Safin	2	45–27	1,122,702
12.	Roger Federer	1	49–21	865,425
13.	Goran Ivanisevic	1	29–22	1,215,040
14.	Guillermo Canas	1	45–21	606,341
15.	Alex Corretja	1	34–20	806,152
16.	Andy Roddick	3	42–16	746,504
17.	Arnaud Clement	0	37–28	773,999
18.	Thomas Johansson	2	46–25	702,792
19.	Carlos Moya	1	35–24	562,862
20.	Albert Portas	1	32–28	821,804

Note: Compiled by the ATP Tour, as of Dec. 18, 2001.
Note: Prize money reflects both singles and doubles.

Women

Rank	Player	Tournament Wins	Match Record	Earnings ($)
1.	Lindsay Davenport	7	62–9	2,102,242
2.	Jennifer Capriati	3	56–14	2,268,624
3.	Venus Williams	6	46–5	2,662,610
4.	Martina Hingis	3	60–15	1,765,116
5.	Kim Clijsters	3	54–18	1,335,659
6.	Serena Williams	3	38–7	2,136,263
8.	Jelena Dokic	3	53–23	1,169,716
9.	Amelie Mauresmo	4	42–11	867,702
10.	Monica Seles	4	40–10	627,211
11.	Sandrine Testud	1	53–27	815,601
12.	Meghann Shaughnessy	0	45–24	593,776
13.	Nathalie Tauziat	1	34–21	925,785
14.	Silvia Farina Elia	1	45–27	471,426
15.	Elena Dementieva	0	33–21	567,964
16.	Magdalena Maleeva	1	35–24	481,784
17.	Arantxa Sanchez Vicario	2	34–21	725,342
18.	Anke Huber	0	35–20	516,522
19.	Amanda Coetzer	1	32–21	560,857
20.	Iroda Tulyaganova	2	31–24	285,740

Note: Compiled by the WTA, as of Nov. 20, 2001.
Note: Prize money reflects singles play only.

THEY SAID IT

Jennifer Capriati, the tennis star, when asked if she wanted to say something to President Bush about the importance of changing the Title IX legislation: "I have no idea what Title IX is. Sorry."

2001 Davis Cup World Group Final

France def. Australia 3–2, Nov. 30–Dec. 2, 2001 in Melbourne, Australia
    Nicolas Escude (FRA) def. Lleyton Hewitt (AUS), 4–6, 6–3, 3–6, 6–3, 6–4
    Patrick Rafter (AUS) def. Sebastien Grosjean (FRA), 6–3, 7–6, 7–5
    Fabrice Santoro and Cedric Pioline (FRA) def. Lleyton Hewitt and Patrick Rafter (AUS)
    2–6, 6–3, 7–6 (7–5), 6–1
    Lleyton Hewitt (AUS) def. Sebastien Grosjean (FRA) 6–3, 6–2, 6–3
    Nicolas Escude (FRA) def. Wayne Arthurs (AUS) 7–6 (7–3), 6–7 (5–7), 6–3, 6–3

2002 Davis Cup World Group Tournament

FIRST ROUND

Sweden def. Great Britain, 3–2
Russia def. Switzerland, 3–2
Spain def. Morocco, 3–2
Croatia def. Germany, 4–1
France def. Netherlands, 3–1
Czech Republic def. Brazil, 4–1
Argentina def. Australia, 5–0
United States def. Slovakia, 5–0

QUARTERFINAL ROUND

France def. Czech Republic, 3–2
United States def. Spain, 3–1
Russia def. Sweden, 4–1
Argentina def. Croatia, 3–2

SEMIFINALS

Russia def. Argentina 3–2
    Marat Safin (Rus) def. Juan Ignacio Chela
    (Arg), 6–7 (1–7), 7–5, 7–5, 6–1
    Yevgeny Kafelnikov (Rus) def. Gaston Gaudio (Arg)
    3–6, 7–5, 6–3, 2–6, 8–6
    Arnold and Nalbandain (Arg) def. Kafelnikov and
    Safin (Rus) 6–4, 6–4, 5–7, 3–6, 19–17
    Marat Safin (Rus) def. David Nalbandian (Arg)
    7–6 (7–3), 6–7 (5–7), 6–0, 6–3
    Juan Ignacio Chela (Arg) def. Mikhail Youzhny
    (Rus) 7–6 (7–5), 6–7 (3–7), 6–4

France def. United States, 3–2
    Arnaud Clement (Fra) def. Andy Roddick (U.S.),
    4–6, 7–6 (8–6), 7–6 (7–5), 6–1
    Sebastien Grosjean (Fra) def. James Blake (U.S.),
    6–4, 6–1, 6–7 (7–9), 7–5
    Blake and Martin (U.S.) def. Llodra and Santoro (Fra)
    2–6, 7–6 (7–2), 2–6, 6–4, 6–4
    Sebastien Grosjean (Fra) def. Andy Roddick (U.S.)
    6–4, 3–6, 6–3, 6–4
    James Blake (U.S.) def Arnaud Clement (Fra)
    6–4, 6–3

FINAL: Russia versus France to be held Nov. 29–Dec. 1, 2002, in Paris.

2002 Federation Cup World Group Tournament

FIRST ROUND

Austria def. United States, 3–2
Croatia def. Czech Rep., 3–2
Spain def. Hungary, 4–1
Germany def. Russia, 3–2
Slovakia def. Switzerland, 3–2
France def. Argentina, 3–2
Italy def. Sweden, 5–0
Belgium def. Australia, 3–1

QUARTERFINALS

Austria def. Croatia, 4–1
Spain def. Germany, 5–0
Slovakia def. France, 4–1
Italy def. Belgium, 4–1

Note: Semifinals and Finals to be held Oct. 28–Nov. 3, 2002, in Maspalomas, Canary Islands.

Grand Slam Tournaments

MEN

Australian Championships

Year	Winner	Finalist	Score
1905	Rodney Heath	A. H. Curtis	4–6, 6–3, 6–4, 6–4
1906	Tony Wilding	H. A. Parker	6–0, 6–4, 6–4
1907	Horace M. Rice	H. A. Parker	6–3, 6–4, 6–4
1908	Fred Alexander	A. W. Dunlop	3–6, 3–6, 6–0, 6–2, 6–3
1909	Tony Wilding	E. F. Parker	6–1, 7–5, 6–2
1910	Rodney Heath	Horace M. Rice	6–4, 6–3, 6–2
1911	Norman Brookes	Horace M. Rice	6–1, 6–2, 6–3
1912	J. Cecil Parke	A. E. Beamish	3–6, 6–3, 1–6, 6–1, 7–5
1913	E. F. Parker	H. A. Parker	2–6, 6–1, 6–2, 6–3
1914	Pat O'Hara Wood	G. L. Patterson	6–4, 6–3, 5–7, 6–1
1915	Francis G. Lowe	Horace M. Rice	4–6, 6–1, 6–1, 6–4
1916–18	No tournament		
1919	A. R. F. Kingscote	E. O. Pockley	6–4, 6–0, 6–3
1920	Pat O'Hara Wood	Ron Thomas	6–3, 4–6, 6–8, 6–1, 6–3
1921	Rhys H. Gemmell	A. Hedeman	7–5, 6–1, 6–4
1922	Pat O'Hara Wood	Gerald Patterson	6–0, 3–6, 3–6, 6–3, 6–2
1923	Pat O'Hara Wood	C. B. St John	6–1, 6–1, 6–3
1924	James Anderson	R. E. Schlesinger	6–3, 6–4, 3–6, 5–7, 6–3
1925	James Anderson	Gerald Patterson	11–9, 2–6, 6–2, 6–3
1926	John Hawkes	J. Willard	6–1, 6–3, 6–1
1927	Gerald Patterson	John Hawkes	3–6, 6–4, 3–6, 18–16, 6–3
1928	Jean Borotra	R. O. Cummings	6–4, 6–1, 4–6, 5–7, 6–3
1929	John C. Gregory	R. E. Schlesinger	6–2, 6–2, 5–7, 7–5
1930	Gar Moon	Harry C. Hopman	6–3, 6–1, 6–3
1931	Jack Crawford	Harry C. Hopman	6–4, 6–2, 2–6, 6–1
1932	Jack Crawford	Harry C. Hopman	4–6, 6–3, 3–6, 6–3, 6–1
1933	Jack Crawford	Keith Gledhill	2–6, 7–5, 6–3, 6–2
1934	Fred Perry	Jack Crawford	6–3, 7–5, 6–1
1935	Jack Crawford	Fred Perry	2–6, 6–4, 6–4, 6–4
1936	Adrian Quist	Jack Crawford	6–2, 6–3, 4–6, 3–6, 9–7
1937	Vivian B. McGrath	John Bromwich	6–3, 1–6, 6–0, 2–6, 6–1
1938	Don Budge	John Bromwich	6–4, 6–2, 6–1
1939	John Bromwich	Adrian Quist	6–4, 6–1, 6–3
1940	Adrian Quist	Jack Crawford	6–3, 6–1, 6–2
1941–45	No tournament		
1946	John Bromwich	Dinny Pails	5–7, 6–3, 7–5, 3–6, 6–2
1947	Dinny Pails	John Bromwich	4–6, 6–4, 3–6, 7–5, 8–6
1948	Adrian Quist	John Bromwich	6–4, 3–6, 6–3, 2–6, 6–3
1949	Frank Sedgman	Ken McGregor	6–3, 6–3, 6–2
1950	Frank Sedgman	Ken McGregor	6–3, 6–4, 4–6, 6–1
1951	Richard Savitt	Ken McGregor	6–3, 2–6, 6–3, 6–1
1952	Ken McGregor	Frank Sedgman	7–5, 12–10, 2–6, 6–2
1953	Ken Rosewall	Mervyn Rose	6–0, 6–3, 6–4
1954	Mervyn Rose	Rex Hartwig	6–2, 0–6, 6–4, 6–2
1955	Ken Rosewall	Lew Hoad	9–7, 6–4, 6–4
1956	Lew Hoad	Ken Rosewall	6–4, 3–6, 6–4, 7–5
1957	Ashley Cooper	Neale Fraser	6–3, 9–11, 6–4, 6–2
1958	Ashley Cooper	Mal Anderson	7–5, 6–3, 6–4
1959	Alex Olmedo	Neale Fraser	6–1, 6–2, 3–6, 6–3
1960	Rod Laver	Neale Fraser	5–7, 3–6, 6–3, 8–6, 8–6
1961	Roy Emerson	Rod Laver	1–6, 6–3, 7–5, 6–4
1962	Rod Laver	Roy Emerson	8–6, 0–6, 6–4, 6–4
1963	Roy Emerson	Ken Fletcher	6–3, 6–3, 6–1
1964	Roy Emerson	Fred Stolle	6–3, 6–4, 6–2
1965	Roy Emerson	Fred Stolle	7–9, 2–6, 6–4, 7–5, 6–1
1966	Roy Emerson	Arthur Ashe	6–4, 6–8, 6–2, 6–3
1967	Roy Emerson	Arthur Ashe	6–4, 6–1, 6–1
1968	Bill Bowrey	Juan Gisbert	7–5, 2–6, 9–7, 6–4
1969*	Rod Laver	Andres Gimeno	6–3, 6–4, 7–5

*Became Open (amateur and professional) in 1969.

MEN *(Cont.)*

Australian Championships *(Cont.)*

Year	Winner	Finalist	Score
1970	Arthur Ashe	Dick Crealy	6–4, 9–7, 6–2
1971	Ken Rosewall	Arthur Ashe	6–1, 7–5, 6–3
1972	Ken Rosewall	Mal Anderson	7–6, 6–3, 7–5
1973	John Newcombe	Onny Parun	6–3, 6–7, 7–5, 6–1
1974	Jimmy Connors	Phil Dent	7–6, 6–4, 4–6, 6–3
1975	John Newcombe	Jimmy Connors	7–5, 3–6, 6–4, 7–5
1976	Mark Edmondson	John Newcombe	6–7, 6–3, 7–6, 6–1
1977 (Jan)	Roscoe Tanner	Guillermo Vilas	6–3, 6–3, 6–3
1977 (Dec)	Vitas Gerulaitis	John Lloyd	6–3, 7–6, 5–7, 3–6, 6–2
1978	Guillermo Vilas	John Marks	6–4, 6–4, 3–6, 6–3
1979	Guillermo Vilas	John Sadri	7–6, 6–3, 6–2
1980	Brian Teacher	Kim Warwick	7–5, 7–6, 6–3
1981	Johan Kriek	Steve Denton	6–2, 7–6, 6–7, 6–4
1982	Johan Kriek	Steve Denton	6–3, 6–3, 6–2
1983	Mats Wilander	Ivan Lendl	6–1, 6–4, 6–4
1984	Mats Wilander	Kevin Curren	6–7, 6–4, 7–6, 6–2
1985 (Dec)	Stefan Edberg	Mats Wilander	6–4, 6–3, 6–3
1987 (Jan)	Stefan Edberg	Pat Cash	6–3, 6–4, 3–6, 5–7, 6–3
1988	Mats Wilander	Pat Cash	6–3, 6–7, 3–6, 6–1, 8–6
1989	Ivan Lendl	Miloslav Mecir	6–2, 6–2, 6–2
1990	Ivan Lendl	Stefan Edberg	4–6, 7–6, 5-2, ret.
1991	Boris Becker	Ivan Lendl	1–6, 6–4, 6–4, 6–4
1992	Jim Courier	Stefan Edberg	6–3, 3–6, 6–4, 6–2
1993	Jim Courier	Stefan Edberg	6–2, 6–1, 2–6, 7–5
1994	Pete Sampras	Todd Martin	7–6, 6–4, 6–4
1995	Andre Agassi	Pete Sampras	4–6, 6–1, 7–6, 6–4
1996	Boris Becker	Michael Chang	6–2, 6–4, 2–6, 6–2
1997	Pete Sampras	Carlos Moya	6–2, 6–3, 6–3
1998	Petr Korda	Marcelo Ríos	6–2, 6–2, 6–2
1999	Yevgeny Kafelnikov	Thomas Enqvist	4–6, 6–0, 6–3, 7–6
2000	Andre Agassi	Yevgeny Kafelnikov	3–6, 6–3, 6–2, 6–4
2001	Andre Agassi	Arnaud Clement	6–4, 6–2, 6–2
2002	Thomas Johansson	Marat Safin	3–6, 6–4, 6–4, 7–6 (7–4)

French Championships

Year	Winner	Finalist	Score
1925†	Rene Lacoste	Jean Borotra	7–5, 6–1, 6–4
1926	Henri Cochet	Rene Lacoste	6–2, 6–4, 6–3
1927	Rene Lacoste	Bill Tilden	6–4, 4–6, 5–7, 6–3, 11–9
1928	Henri Cochet	Rene Lacoste	5–7, 6–3, 6–1, 6–3
1929	Rene Lacoste	Jean Borotra	6–3, 2–6, 6–0, 2–6, 8–6
1930	Henri Cochet	Bill Tilden	3–6, 8–6, 6–3, 6–1
1931	Jean Borotra	Claude Boussus	2–6, 6–4, 7–5, 6–4
1932	Henri Cochet	Giorgio de Stefani	6–0, 6–4, 4–6, 6–3
1933	Jack Crawford	Henri Cochet	8–6, 6–1, 6–3
1934	Gottfried von Cramm	Jack Crawford	6–4, 7–9, 3–6, 7–5, 6–3
1935	Fred Perry	Gottfried von Cramm	6–3, 3–6, 6–1, 6–3
1936	Gottfried von Cramm	Fred Perry	6–0, 2–6, 6–2, 2–6, 6–0
1937	Henner Henkel	Henry Austin	6–1, 6–4, 6–3
1938	Don Budge	Roderick Menzel	6–3, 6–2, 6–4
1939	Don McNeill	Bobby Riggs	7–5, 6–0, 6–3
1940	No tournament		
1941‡	Bernard Destremau	n/a	n/a
1942‡	Bernard Destremau	n/a	n/a
1943‡	Yvon Petra	n/a	n/a
1944‡	Yvon Petra	n/a	n/a
1945‡	Yvon Petra	Bernard Destremau	7–5, 6–4, 6–2
1946	Marcel Bernard	Jaroslav Drobny	3–6, 2–6, 6–1, 6–4, 6–3
1947	Joseph Asboth	Eric Sturgess	8–6, 7–5, 6–4
1948	Frank Parker	Jaroslav Drobny	6–4, 7–5, 5–7, 8–6
1949	Frank Parker	Budge Patty	6–3, 1–6, 6–1, 6–4
1950	Budge Patty	Jaroslav Drobny	6–1, 6–2, 3–6, 5–7, 7–5
1951	Jaroslav Drobny	Eric Sturgess	6–3, 6–3, 6–3
1952	Jaroslav Drobny	Frank Sedgman	6–2, 6–0, 3–6, 6–4

MEN *(Cont.)*
French Championships *(Cont.)*

Year	Winner	Finalist	Score
1953	Ken Rosewall	Vic Seixas	6–3, 6–4, 1–6, 6–2
1954	Tony Trabert	Arthur Larsen	6–4, 7–5, 6–1
1955	Tony Trabert	Sven Davidson	2–6, 6–1, 6–4, 6–2
1956	Lew Hoad	Sven Davidson	6–4, 8–6, 6–3
1957	Sven Davidson	Herbie Flam	6–3, 6–4, 6–4
1958	Mervyn Rose	Luis Ayala	6–3, 6–4, 6–4
1959	Nicola Pietrangeli	Ian Vermaak	3–6, 6–3, 6–4, 6–1
1960	Nicola Pietrangeli	Luis Ayala	3–6, 6–3, 6–4, 4–6, 6–3
1961	Manuel Santana	Nicola Pietrangeli	4–6, 6–1, 3–6, 6–0, 6–2
1962	Rod Laver	Roy Emerson	3–6, 2–6, 6–3, 9–7, 6–2
1963	Roy Emerson	Pierre Darmon	3–6, 6–1, 6–4, 6–4
1964	Manuel Santana	Nicola Pietrangeli	6–3, 6–1, 4–6, 7–5
1965	Fred Stolle	Tony Roche	3–6, 6–0, 6–2, 6–3
1966	Tony Roche	Istvan Gulyas	6–1, 6–4, 7–5
1967	Roy Emerson	Tony Roche	6–1, 6–4, 2–6, 6–2
1968*	Ken Rosewall	Rod Laver	6–3, 6–1, 2–6, 6–2
1969	Rod Laver	Ken Rosewall	6–4, 6–3, 6–4
1970	Jan Kodes	Zeljko Franulovic	6–2, 6–4, 6–0
1971	Jan Kodes	Ilie Nastase	8–6, 6–2, 2–6, 7–5
1972	Andres Gimeno	Patrick Proisy	4–6, 6–3, 6–1, 6–1
1973	Ilie Nastase	Nikki Pilic	6–3, 6–3, 6–0
1974	Bjorn Borg	Manuel Orantes	6–7, 6–0, 6–1, 6–1
1975	Bjorn Borg	Guillermo Vilas	6–2, 6–3, 6–4
1976	Adriano Panatta	Harold Solomon	6–1, 6–4, 4–6, 7–6
1977	Guillermo Vilas	Brian Gottfried	6–0, 6–3, 6–0
1978	Bjorn Borg	Guillermo Vilas	6–1, 6–1, 6–3
1979	Bjorn Borg	Victor Pecci	6–3, 6–1, 6–7, 6–4
1980	Bjorn Borg	Vitas Gerulaitis	6–4, 6–1, 6–2
1981	Bjorn Borg	Ivan Lendl	6–1, 4–6, 6–2, 3–6, 6–1
1982	Mats Wilander	Guillermo Vilas	1–6, 7–6, 6–0, 6–4
1983	Yannick Noah	Mats Wilander	6–2, 7–5, 7–6
1984	Ivan Lendl	John McEnroe	3–6, 2–6, 6–4, 7–5, 7–5
1985	Mats Wilander	Ivan Lendl	3–6, 6–4, 6–2, 6–2
1986	Ivan Lendl	Mikael Pernfors	6–3, 6–2, 6–4
1987	Ivan Lendl	Mats Wilander	7–5, 6–2, 3–6, 7–6
1988	Mats Wilander	Henri Leconte	7–5, 6–2, 6–1
1989	Michael Chang	Stefan Edberg	6–1, 3–6, 4–6, 6–4, 6–2
1990	Andres Gomez	Andre Agassi	6–3, 2–6, 6–4, 6–4
1991	Jim Courier	Andre Agassi	3–6, 6–4, 2–6, 6–1, 6–4
1992	Jim Courier	Petr Korda	7–5, 6–2, 6–1
1993	Sergi Bruguera	Jim Courier	6–4, 2–6, 6–2, 3–6, 6–3
1994	Sergi Bruguera	Alberto Berasategui	6–3, 7–5, 2–6, 6–1
1995	Thomas Muster	Michael Chang	7–5, 6–2, 6–4
1996	Yevgeny Kafelnikov	Michael Stich	7–6, 7–5, 7–6
1997	Gustavo Kuerten	Sergi Bruguera	6–3, 6–4, 6–2
1998	Carlos Moya	Alex Corretja	6–3, 7–5, 6–3
1999	Andre Agassi	Andrei Medvedev	1–6, 2–6, 6–4, 6–3, 6–4
2000	Gustavo Kuerten	Magnus Norman	6–2, 6–3, 2–6, 7–6
2001	Gustavo Kuerten	Alex Corretja	6–7, 7–5, 6–2, 6–0
2002	Albert Costa	Juan Carlos Ferrero	6–1, 6–0, 4–6, 6–3

*Became Open (amateur and professional) in 1968 but closed to contract professionals in 1972.

†1925 was the first year that entries were accepted from all countries.

Wimbledon Championships

Year	Winner	Finalist	Score
1877	Spencer W. Gore	William C. Marshall	6–1, 6–2, 6–4
1878	P. Frank Hadow	Spencer W. Gore	7–5, 6–1, 9–7
1879	John T. Hartley	V. St Leger Gould	6–2, 6–4, 6–2
1880	John T. Hartley	Herbert F. Lawford	6–0, 6–2, 6–2, 6–3
1881	William Renshaw	John T. Hartley	6–0, 6–2, 6–1
1882	William Renshaw	Ernest Renshaw	6–1, 2–6, 4–6, 6–2, 6–2
1883	William Renshaw	Ernest Renshaw	2–6, 6–3, 6–3, 4–6, 6–3

MEN (Cont.)

Wimbledon Championship (Cont.)

Year	Winner	Finalist	Score
1884	William Renshaw	Herbert F. Lawford	6–0, 6–4, 9–7
1885	William Renshaw	Herbert F. Lawford	7–5, 6–2, 4–6, 7–5
1886	William Renshaw	Herbert F. Lawford	6–0, 5–7, 6–3, 6–4
1887	Herbert F. Lawford	Ernest Renshaw	1–6, 6–3, 3–6, 6–4, 6–4
1888	Ernest Renshaw	Herbert F. Lawford	6–3, 7–5, 6–0
1889	William Renshaw	Ernest Renshaw	6–4, 6–1, 3–6, 6–0
1890	William J. Hamilton	William Renshaw	6–8, 6–2, 3–6, 6–1, 6–1
1891	Wilfred Baddeley	Joshua Pim	6–4, 1–6, 7–5, 6–0
1892	Wilfred Baddeley	Joshua Pim	4–6, 6–3, 6–3, 6–2
1893	Joshua Pim	Wilfred Baddeley	3–6, 6–1, 6–3, 6–2
1894	Joshua Pim	Wilfred Baddeley	10–8, 6–2, 8–6
1895	Wilfred Baddeley	Wilberforce V. Eaves	4–6, 2–6, 8–6, 6–2, 6–3
1896	Harold S. Mahoney	Wilfred Baddeley	6–2, 6–8, 5–7, 8–6, 6–3
1897	Reggie F. Doherty	Harold S. Mahoney	6–4, 6–4, 6–3
1898	Reggie F. Doherty	H. Laurie Doherty	6–3, 6–3, 2–6, 5–7, 6–1
1899	Reggie F. Doherty	Arthur W. Gore	1–6, 4–6, 6–2, 6–3, 6–3
1900	Reggie F. Doherty	Sidney H. Smith	6–8, 6–3, 6–1, 6–2
1901	Arthur W. Gore	Reggie F. Doherty	4–6, 7–5, 6–4, 6–4
1902	H. Laurie Doherty	Arthur W. Gore	6–4, 6–3, 3–6, 6–0
1903	H. Laurie Doherty	Frank L. Riseley	7–5, 6–3, 6–0
1904	H. Laurie Doherty	Frank L. Riseley	6–1, 7–5, 8–6
1905	H. Laurie Doherty	Norman E. Brookes	8–6, 6–2, 6–4
1906	H. Laurie Doherty	Frank L. Riseley	6–4, 4–6, 6–2, 6–3
1907	Norman E. Brookes	Arthur W. Gore	6–4, 6–2, 6–2
1908	Arthur W. Gore	H. Roper Barrett	6–3, 6–2, 4–6, 3–6, 6–4
1909	Arthur W. Gore	M. J. G. Ritchie	6–8, 1–6, 6–2, 6–2, 6–2
1910	Anthony F. Wilding	Arthur W. Gore	6–4, 7–5, 4–6, 6–2
1911	Anthony F. Wilding	H. Roper Barrett	6–4, 4–6, 2–6, 6–2 ret
1912	Anthony F. Wilding	Arthur W. Gore	6–4, 6–4, 4–6, 6–4
1913	Anthony F. Wilding	Maurice E. McLoughlin	8–6, 6–3, 10–8
1914	Norman E. Brookes	Anthony F. Wilding	6–4, 6–4, 7–5
1915–18	No tournament		
1919	Gerald L. Patterson	Norman E. Brookes	6–3, 7–5, 6–2
1920	Bill Tilden	Gerald L. Patterson	2–6, 6–3, 6–2, 6–4
1921	Bill Tilden	Brian I. C. Norton	4–6, 2–6, 6–1, 6–0, 7–5
1922	Gerald L. Patterson	Randolph Lycett	6–3, 6–4, 6–2
1923	Bill Johnston	Francis T. Hunter	6–0, 6–3, 6–1
1924	Jean Borotra	Rene Lacoste	6–1, 3–6, 6–1, 3–6, 6–4
1925	Rene Lacoste	Jean Borotra	6–3, 6–3, 4–6, 8–6
1926	Jean Borotra	Howard Kinsey	8–6, 6–1, 6–3
1927	Henri Cochet	Jean Borotra	4–6, 4–6, 6–3, 6–4, 7–5
1928	Rene Lacoste	Henri Cochet	6–1, 4–6, 6–4, 6–2
1929	Henri Cochet	Jean Borotra	6–4, 6–3, 6–4
1930	Bill Tilden	Wilmer Allison	6–3, 9–7, 6–4
1931	Sidney B. Wood Jr	Francis X. Shields	walkover
1932	Ellsworth Vines	Henry Austin	6–4, 6–2, 6–0
1933	Jack Crawford	Ellsworth Vines	4–6, 11–9, 6–2, 2–6, 6–4
1934	Fred Perry	Jack Crawford	6–3, 6–0, 7–5
1935	Fred Perry	Gottfried von Cramm	6–2, 6–4, 6–4
1936	Fred Perry	Gottfried von Cramm	6–1, 6–1, 6–0
1937	Don Budge	Gottfried von Cramm	6–3, 6–4, 6–2
1938	Don Budge	Henry Austin	6–1, 6–0, 6–3
1939	Bobby Riggs	Elwood Cooke	2–6, 8–6, 3–6, 6–3, 6–2
1940–45	No tournament		
1946	Yvon Petra	Geoff E. Brown	6–2, 6–4, 7–9, 5–7, 6–4
1947	Jack Kramer	Tom P. Brown	6–1, 6–3, 6–2
1948	Bob Falkenburg	John Bromwich	7–5, 0–6, 6–2, 3–6, 7–5
1949	Ted Schroeder	Jaroslav Drobny	3–6, 6–0, 6–3, 4–6, 6–4
1950	Budge Patty	Frank Sedgman	6–1, 8–10, 6–2, 6–3
1951	Dick Savitt	Ken McGregor	6–4, 6–4, 6–4
1952	Frank Sedgman	Jaroslav Drobny	4–6, 6–3, 6–2, 6–3
1953	Vic Seixas	Kurt Nielsen	9–7, 6–3, 6–4
1954	Jaroslav Drobny	Ken Rosewall	13–11, 4–6, 6–2, 9–7
1955	Tony Trabert	Kurt Nielsen	6–3, 7–5, 6–1

MEN *(Cont.)*

Wimbledon Championships *(Cont.)*

Year	Winner	Finalist	Score
1956	Lew Hoad	Ken Rosewall	6–2, 4–6, 7–5, 6–4
1957	Lew Hoad	Ashley Cooper	6–2, 6–1, 6–2
1958	Ashley Cooper	Neale Fraser	3–6, 6–3, 6–4, 13–11
1959	Alex Olmedo	Rod Laver	6–4, 6–3, 6–4
1960	Neale Fraser	Rod Laver	6–4, 3–6, 9–7, 7–5
1961	Rod Laver	Chuck McKinley	6–3, 6–1, 6–4
1962	Rod Laver	Martin Mulligan	6–2, 6–2, 6–1
1963	Chuck McKinley	Fred Stolle	9–7, 6–1, 6–4
1964	Roy Emerson	Fred Stolle	6–4, 12–10, 4–6, 6–3
1965	Roy Emerson	Fred Stolle	6–2, 6–4, 6–4
1966	Manuel Santana	Dennis Ralston	6–4, 11–9, 6–4
1967	John Newcombe	Wilhelm Bungert	6–3, 6–1, 6–1
1968*	Rod Laver	Tony Roche	6–3, 6–4, 6–2
1969	Rod Laver	John Newcombe	6–4, 5–7, 6–4, 6–4
1970	John Newcombe	Ken Rosewall	5–7, 6–3, 6–2, 3–6, 6–1
1971	John Newcombe	Stan Smith	6–3, 5–7, 2–6, 6–4, 6–4
1972	Stan Smith	Ilie Nastase	4–6, 6–3, 6–3, 4–6, 7–5
1973	Jan Kodes	Alex Metreveli	6–1, 9–8, 6–3
1974	Jimmy Connors	Ken Rosewall	6–1, 6–1, 6–4
1975	Arthur Ashe	Jimmy Connors	6–1, 6–1, 5–7, 6–4
1976	Bjorn Borg	Ilie Nastase	6–4, 6–2, 9–7
1977	Bjorn Borg	Jimmy Connors	3–6, 6–2, 6–1, 5–7, 6–4
1978	Bjorn Borg	Jimmy Connors	6–2, 6–2, 6–3
1979	Bjorn Borg	Roscoe Tanner	6–7, 6–1, 3–6, 6–3, 6–4
1980	Bjorn Borg	John McEnroe	1–6, 7–5, 6–3, 6–7, 8–6
1981	John McEnroe	Bjorn Borg	4–6, 7–6, 7–6, 6–4
1982	Jimmy Connors	John McEnroe	3–6, 6–3, 6–7, 7–6, 6–4
1983	John McEnroe	Chris Lewis	6–2, 6–2, 6–2
1984	John McEnroe	Jimmy Connors	6–1, 6–1, 6–2
1985	Boris Becker	Kevin Curren	6–3, 6–7, 7–6, 6–4
1986	Boris Becker	Ivan Lendl	6–4, 6–3, 7–5
1987	Pat Cash	Ivan Lendl	7–6, 6–2, 7–5
1988	Stefan Edberg	Boris Becker	4–6, 7–6, 6–4, 6–2
1989	Boris Becker	Stefan Edberg	6–0, 7–6, 6–4
1990	Stefan Edberg	Boris Becker	6–2, 6–2, 3–6, 3–6, 6–4
1991	Michael Stich	Boris Becker	6–4, 7–6, 6–4
1992	Andre Agassi	Goran Ivanisevic	6–7, 6–4, 6–4, 1–6, 6–4
1993	Pete Sampras	Jim Courier	7–6, 7–6, 3–6, 6–3
1994	Pete Sampras	Goran Ivanisevic	7–6, 7–6, 6–0
1995	Pete Sampras	Boris Becker	6–7, 6–2, 6–4, 6–2
1996	Richard Krajicek	MaliVai Washington	6–3, 6–4, 6–3
1997	Pete Sampras	Cedric Pioline	6–4, 6–2, 6–4
1998	Pete Sampras	Goran Ivanisevic	6–7, 7–6, 6–4, 3–6, 6–2
1999	Pete Sampras	Andre Agassi	6–3, 6–4, 7–5
2000	Pete Sampras	Patrick Rafter	6–7, 7–6, 6–4, 6–2
2001	Goran Ivanisevic	Patrick Rafter	6–3, 3–6, 6–3, 2–6, 9–7
2002	Lleyton Hewitt	David Nalbandian	6–1, 6–3, 6–2

*Became Open (amateur and professional) in 1968 but closed to contract professionals in 1972

Note: Prior to 1922 the tournament was run on a challenge-round system. The previous year's winner "stood out"of an All Comers event, which produced a challenger to play him for the title.

United States Championships

Year	Winner	Finalist	Score
1881	Richard D. Sears	W.E. Glyn	6–0, 6–3, 6–2
1882	Richard D. Sears	C.M. Clark	6–1, 6–4, 6–0
1883	Richard D. Sears	James Dwight	6–2, 6–0, 9–7
1884	Richard D. Sears	H.A. Taylor	6–0, 1–6, 6–0, 6–2
1885	Richard D. Sears	G.M. Brinley	6–3, 4–6, 6–0, 6–3
1886	Richard D. Sears	R.L. Beeckman	4–6, 6–1, 6–3, 6–4
1887	Richard D. Sears	H.W. Slocum Jr	6–1, 6–3, 6–2
1888‡	H. W. Slocum Jr	H.A. Taylor	6–4, 6–1, 6–0
1889	H. W. Slocum Jr	Q.A. Shaw	6–3, 6–1, 4–6, 6–2
1890	Oliver S. Campbell	H.W. Slocum Jr	6–2, 4–6, 6–3, 6–1
1891	Oliver S. Campbell	Clarence Hobart	2–6, 7–5, 7–9, 6–1, 6–2
1892	Oliver S. Campbell	Frederick H. Hovey	7–5, 3–6, 6–3, 7–5

MEN *(Cont.)*

United States Championships *(Cont.)*

Year	Winner	Finalist	Score
1893‡	Robert D. Wrenn	Frederick H. Hovey	6–4, 3–6, 6–4, 6–4
1894	Robert D. Wrenn	M.F. Goodbody	6–8, 6–1, 6–4, 6–4
1895	Frederick H. Hovey	Robert D. Wrenn	6–3, 6–2, 6–4
1896	Robert D. Wrenn	Frederick H. Hovey	7–5, 3–6, 6–0, 1–6, 6–1
1897	Robert D. Wrenn	Wilberforce V. Eaves	4–6, 8–6, 6–3, 2–6, 6–2
1898‡	Malcolm D. Whitman	Dwight F. Davis	3–6, 6–2, 6–2, 6–1
1899	Malcolm D. Whitman	J. Parmly Paret	6–1, 6–2, 3–6, 7–5
1900	Malcolm D. Whitman	William A. Larned	6–4, 1–6, 6–2, 6–2
1901‡	William A. Larned	Beals C. Wright	6–2, 6–8, 6–4, 6–4
1902	William A. Larned	Reggie F. Doherty	4–6, 6–2, 6–4, 8–6
1903	H. Laurie Doherty	William A. Larned	6–0, 6–3, 10–8
1904‡	Holcombe Ward	William J. Clothier	10–8, 6–4, 9–7
1905	Beals C. Wright	Holcombe Ward	6–2, 6–1, 11–9
1906	William J. Clothier	Beals C. Wright	6–3, 6–0, 6–4
1907‡	William A. Larned	Robert LeRoy	6–2, 6–2, 6–4
1908	William A. Larned	Beals C. Wright	6–1, 6–2, 8–6
1909	William A. Larned	William J. Clothier	6–1, 6–2, 5–7, 1–6, 6–1
1910	William A. Larned	Thomas C. Bundy	6–1, 5–7, 6–0, 6–8, 6–1
1911	William A. Larned	Maurice E. McLoughlin	6–4, 6–4, 6–2
1912†	Maurice E. McLoughlin	Bill Johnson	3–6, 2–6, 6–2, 6–4, 6–2
1913	Maurice E. McLoughlin	Richard N. Williams	6–4, 5–7, 6–3, 6–1
1914	Richard N. Williams	Maurice E. McLoughlin	6–3, 8–6, 10–8
1915	Bill Johnston	Maurice E. McLoughlin	1–6, 6–0, 7–5, 10–8
1916	Richard N. Williams	Bill Johnston	4–6, 6–4, 0–6, 6–2, 6–4
1917#	R.L. Murray	N. W. Niles	5–7, 8–6, 6–3, 6–3
1918	R.L. Murray	Bill Tilden	6–3, 6–1, 7–5
1919	Bill Johnston	Bill Tilden	6–4, 6–4, 6–3
1920	Bill Tilden	Bill Johnston	6–1, 1–6, 7–5, 5–7, 6–3
1921	Bill Tilden	Wallace F. Johnson	6–1, 6–3, 6–1
1922	Bill Tilden	Bill Johnston	4–6, 3–6, 6–2, 6–3, 6–4
1923	Bill Tilden	Bill Johnston	6–4, 6–1, 6–4
1924	Bill Tilden	Bill Johnston	6–1, 9–7, 6–2
1925	Bill Tilden	Bill Johnston	4–6, 11–9, 6–3, 4–6, 6–3
1926	Rene Lacoste	Jean Borotra	6–4, 6–0, 6–4
1927	Rene Lacoste	Bill Tilden	11–9, 6–3, 11–9
1928	Henri Cochet	Francis T. Hunter	4–6, 6–4, 3–6, 7–5, 6–3
1929	Bill Tilden	Francis T. Hunter	3–6, 6–3, 4–6, 6–2, 6–4
1930	John H. Doeg	Francis X. Shields	10–8, 1–6, 6–4, 16–14
1931	Ellsworth Vines	George M. Lott Jr	7–9, 6–3, 9–7, 7–5
1932	Ellsworth Vines	Henri Cochet	6–4, 6–4, 6–4
1933	Fred Perry	Jack Crawford	6–3, 11–13, 4–6, 6–0, 6–1
1934	Fred Perry	Wilmer L. Allison	6–4, 6–3, 1–6, 8–6
1935	Wilmer L. Allison	Sidney B. Wood Jr	6–2, 6–2, 6–3
1936	Fred Perry	Don Budge	2–6, 6–2, 8–6, 1–6, 10–8
1937	Don Budge	Gottfried von Cramm	6–1, 7–9, 6–1, 3–6, 6–1
1938	Don Budge	Gene Mako	6–3, 6–8, 6–2, 6–1
1939	Bobby Riggs	Welby Van Horn	6–4, 6–2, 6–4
1940	Don McNeill	Bobby Riggs	4–6, 6–8, 6–3, 6–3, 7–5
1941	Bobby Riggs	Francis Kovacs II	5–7, 6–1, 6–3, 6–3
1942	Ted Schroeder	Frank Parker	8–6, 7–5, 3–6, 4–6, 6–2
1943	Joseph R. Hunt	Jack Kramer	6–3, 6–8, 10–8, 6–0
1944	Frank Parker	William F. Talbert	6–4, 3–6, 6–3, 6–3
1945	Frank Parker	William F. Talbert	14–12, 6–1, 6–2
1946	Jack Kramer	Tom P. Brown	9–7, 6–3, 6–0
1947	Jack Kramer	Frank Parker	4–6, 2–6, 6–1, 6–0, 6–3
1948	Pancho Gonzales	Eric W. Sturgess	6–2, 6–3, 14–12
1949	Pancho Gonzales	Ted Schroeder	16–18, 2–6, 6–1, 6–2, 6–4
1950	Arthur Larsen	Herbie Flam	6–3, 4–6, 5–7, 6–4, 6–3
1951	Frank Sedgman	Vic Seixas	6–4, 6–1, 6–1
1952	Frank Sedgman	Gardnar Mulloy	6–1, 6–2, 6–3
1953	Tony Trabert	Vic Seixas	6–3, 6–2, 6–3
1954	Vic Seixas	Rex Hartwig	3–6, 6–2, 6–4, 6–4
1955	Tony Trabert	Ken Rosewall	9–7, 6–3, 6–3

MEN (Cont.)
United States Championships (Cont.)

Year	Winner	Finalist	Score
1956	Ken Rosewall	Lew Hoad	4–6, 6–2, 6–3, 6–3
1957	Mal Anderson	Ashley J. Cooper	10–8, 7–5, 6–4
1958	Ashley J. Cooper	Mal Anderson	6–2, 3–6, 4–6, 10–8, 8–6
1959	Neale Fraser	Alex Olmedo	6–3, 5–7, 6–2, 6–4
1960	Neale Fraser	Rod Laver	6–4, 6–4, 9–7
1961	Roy Emerson	Rod Laver	7–5, 6–3, 6–2
1962	Rod Laver	Roy Emerson	6–2, 6–4, 5–7, 6–4
1963	Rafael Osuna	Frank Froehling III	7–5, 6–4, 6–2
1964	Roy Emerson	Fred Stolle	6–4, 6–2, 6–4
1965	Manuel Santana	Cliff Drysdale	6–2, 7–9, 7–5, 6–1
1966	Fred Stolle	John Newcombe	4–6, 12–10, 6–3, 6–4
1967	John Newcombe	Clark Graebner	6–4, 6–4, 8–6
1968*	Arthur Ashe	Tom Okker	14–12, 5–7, 6–3, 3–6, 6–3
1968**	Arthur Ashe	Bob Lutz	4–6, 6–3, 8–10, 6–0, 6–4
1969	Rod Laver	Tony Roche	7–9, 6–1, 6–3, 6–2
1969**	Stan Smith	Bob Lutz	9–7, 6–3, 6–1
1970	Ken Rosewall	Tony Roche	2–6, 6–4, 7–6, 6–3
1971	Stan Smith	Jan Kodes	3–6, 6–3, 6–2, 7–6
1972	Ilie Nastase	Arthur Ashe	3–6, 6–3, 6–7, 6–4, 6–3
1973	John Newcombe	Jan Kodes	6–4, 1–6, 4–6, 6–2, 6–3
1974	Jimmy Connors	Ken Rosewall	6–1, 6–0, 6–1
1975	Manuel Orantes	Jimmy Connors	6–4, 6–3, 6–3
1976	Jimmy Connors	Bjorn Borg	6–4, 3–6, 7–6, 6–4
1977	Guillermo Vilas	Jimmy Connors	2–6, 6–3, 7–6, 6–0
1978	Jimmy Connors	Bjorn Borg	6–4, 6–2, 6–2
1979	John McEnroe	Vitas Gerulaitis	7–5, 6–3, 6–3
1980	John McEnroe	Bjorn Borg	7–6, 6–1, 6–7, 5–7, 6–4
1981	John McEnroe	Bjorn Borg	4–6, 6–2, 6–4, 6–3
1982	Jimmy Connors	Ivan Lendl	6–3, 6–2, 4–6, 6–4
1983	Jimmy Connors	Ivan Lendl	6–3, 6–7, 7–5, 6–0
1984	John McEnroe	Ivan Lendl	6–3, 6–4, 6–1
1985	Ivan Lendl	John McEnroe	7–6, 6–3, 6–4
1986	Ivan Lendl	Miloslav Mecir	6–4, 6–2, 6–0
1987	Ivan Lendl	Mats Wilander	6–7, 6–0, 7–6, 6–4
1988	Mats Wilander	Ivan Lendl	6–4, 4–6, 6–3, 5–7, 6–4
1989	Boris Becker	Ivan Lendl	7–6, 1–6, 6–3, 7–6
1990	Pete Sampras	Andre Agassi	6–4, 6–3, 6–2
1991	Stefan Edberg	Jim Courier	6–2, 6–4, 6–0
1992	Stefan Edberg	Pete Sampras	3–6, 6–4, 7–6, 6–2
1993	Pete Sampras	Cedric Pioline	6–4, 6–4, 6–3
1994	Andre Agassi	Michael Stich	6–1, 7–6, 7–5
1995	Pete Sampras	Andre Agassi	6–4, 6–3, 4–6, 7–5
1996	Pete Sampras	Michael Chang	6–1, 6–4, 7–6
1997	Patrick Rafter	Greg Rusedski	6–3, 6–2, 4–6, 7–5
1998	Patrick Rafter	Mark Philippoussis	6–3, 3–6, 6–2, 6–0
1999	Andre Agassi	Todd Martin	6–4, 6–7, 6–7, 6–3, 6–2
2000	Marat Safin	Pete Sampras	6–4, 6–3, 6–3
2001	Lleyton Hewitt	Pete Sampras	7–6, 6–1, 6–1
2002	Pete Sampras	Andre Agassi	6–3, 6–4, 5–7, 6–4

‡No challenge round played.*Became Open (amateur and professional) in 1968.†Challenge round abolished; #National Patriotic Tournament.**Amateur event held.

WOMEN
Australian Championships

Year	Winner	Finalist	Score
1922	Margaret Molesworth	Esna Boyd	6–3, 10–8
1923	Margaret Molesworth	Esna Boyd	6–1, 7–5
1924	Sylvia Lance	Esna Boyd	6–3, 3–6, 6–4
1925	Daphne Akhurst	Esna Boyd	1–6, 8–6, 6–4
1926	Daphne Akhurst	Esna Boyd	6–1, 6–3
1927	Esna Boyd	Sylvia Harper	5–7, 6–1, 6–2
1928	Daphne Akhurst	Esna Boyd	7–5, 6–2
1929	Daphne Akhurst	Louise Bickerton	6–1, 5–7, 6–2

WOMEN (Cont.)
Australian Championships (Cont.)

Year	Winner	Finalist	Score
1930	Daphne Akhurst	Sylvia Harper	10–8, 2–6, 7–5
1931	Coral Buttsworth	Margorie Crawford	1–6, 6–3, 6–4
1932	Coral Buttsworth	Kathrine Le Messurier	9–7, 6–4
1933	Joan Hartigan	Coral Buttsworth	6–4, 6–3
1934	Joan Hartigan	Margaret Molesworth	6–1, 6–4
1935	Dorothy Round	Nancye Wynne Bolton	1–6, 6–1, 6–3
1936	Joan Hartigan	Nancye Wynne Bolton	6–4, 6–4
1937	Nancye Wynne Bolton	Emily Westacott	6–3, 5–7, 6–4
1938	Dorothy Bundy	D. Stevenson	6–3, 6–2
1939	Emily Westacott	Nell Hopman	6–1, 6–2
1940	Nancye Wynne Bolton	Thelma Coyne	5–7, 6–4, 6–0
1941–45	No tournament		
1946	Nancye Wynne Bolton	Joyce Fitch	6–4, 6–4
1947	Nancye Wynne Bolton	Nell Hopman	6–3, 6–2
1948	Nancye Wynne Bolton	Marie Toomey	6–3, 6–1
1949	Doris Hart	Nancye Wynne Bolton	6–3, 6–4
1950	Louise Brough	Doris Hart	6–4, 3–6, 6–4
1951	Nancye Wynne Bolton	Thelma Long	6–1, 7–5
1952	Thelma Long	H. Angwin	6–2, 6–3
1953	Maureen Connolly	Julia Sampson	6–3, 6–2
1954	Thelma Long	J. Staley	6–3, 6–4
1955	Beryl Penrose	Thelma Long	6–4, 6–3
1956	Mary Carter	Thelma Long	3–6, 6–2, 9–7
1957	Shirley Fry	Althea Gibson	6–3, 6–4
1958	Angela Mortimer	Lorraine Coghlan	6–3, 6–4
1959	Mary Carter-Reitano	Renee Schuurman	6–2, 6–3
1960	Margaret Smith	Jan Lehane	7–5, 6–2
1961	Margaret Smith	Jan Lehane	6–1, 6–4
1962	Margaret Smith	Jan Lehane	6–0, 6–2
1963	Margaret Smith	Jan Lehane	6–2, 6–2
1964	Margaret Smith	Lesley Turner	6–3, 6–2
1965	Margaret Smith	Maria Bueno	5–7, 6–4, 5–2 ret.
1966	Margaret Smith	Nancy Richey	Default
1967	Nancy Richey	Lesley Turner	6–1, 6–4
1968	Billie Jean King	Margaret Smith	6–1, 6–2
1969*	Margaret Smith Court	Billie Jean King	6–4, 6–1
1970	Margaret Smith Court	Kerry Melville Reid	6–3, 6–1
1971	Margaret Smith Court	Evonne Goolagong	2–6, 7–6, 7–5
1972	Virginia Wade	Evonne Goolagong	6–4, 6–4
1973	Margaret Smith Court	Evonne Goolagong	6–4, 7–5
1974	Evonne Goolagong	Chris Evert	7–6, 4–6, 6–0
1975	Evonne Goolagong	Martina Navratilova	6–3, 6–2
1976	Evonne Goolagong Cawley	Renata Tomanova	6–2, 6–2
1977 (Jan)	Kerry Melville Reid	Dianne Balestrat	7–5, 6–2
1977 (Dec)	Evonne Goolagong Cawley	Helen Gourlay	6–3, 6–0
1978	Chris O'Neil	Betsy Nagelsen	6–3, 7–6
1979	Barbara Jordan	Sharon Walsh	6–3, 6–3
1980	Hana Mandlikova	Wendy Turnbull	6–0, 7–5
1981	Martina Navratilova	Chris Evert Lloyd	6–7, 6–4, 7–5
1982	Chris Evert Lloyd	Martina Navratilova	6–3, 2–6, 6–3
1983	Martina Navratilova	Kathy Jordan	6–2, 7–6
1984	Chris Evert Lloyd	Helena Sukova	6–7, 6–1, 6–3
1985 (Dec)	Martina Navratilova	Chris Evert Lloyd	6–2, 4–6, 6–2
1987 (Jan)	Hana Mandlikova	Martina Navratilova	7–5, 7–6
1988	Steffi Graf	Chris Evert	6–1, 7–6
1989	Steffi Graf	Helena Sukova	6–4, 6–4
1990	Steffi Graf	Mary Joe Fernandez	6–3, 6–4
1991	Monica Seles	Jana Novotna	5–7, 6–3, 6–1
1992	Monica Seles	Mary Joe Fernandez	6–2, 6–3
1993	Monica Seles	Steffi Graf	4–6, 6–3, 6–2
1994	Steffi Graf	Arantxa Sánchez Vicario	6–0, 6–2
1995	Mary Pierce	Arantxa Sánchez Vicario	6–3, 6–2
1996	Monica Seles	Anke Huber	6–4, 6–1
1997	Martina Hingis	Mary Pierce	6–2, 6–2
1998	Martina Hingis	Conchita Martinez	6–3, 6–3
1999	Martina Hingis	Amelie Mauresmo	6–2, 6–3

WOMEN (Cont.)

Australian Championships (Cont.)

Year	Winner	Finalist	Score
2000	Lindsay Davenport	Martina Hingis	6–1, 7–5
2001	Jennifer Capriati	Martina Hingis	6–4, 6–3
2002	Jennifer Capriati	Martina Hingis	4–6, 7–6 (9–7), 6–2

*Became Open (amateur and professional) in 1969.

French Championships

Year	Winner	Finalist	Score
1925†	Suzanne Lenglen	Kathleen McKane	6–1, 6–2
1926	Suzanne Lenglen	Mary K. Browne	6–1, 6–0
1927	Kea Bouman	Irene Peacock	6–2, 6–4
1928	Helen Wills	Eileen Bennett	6–1, 6–2
1929	Helen Wills	Simone Mathieu	6–3, 6–4
1930	Helen Wills Moody	Helen Jacobs	6–2, 6–1
1931	Cilly Aussem	Betty Nuthall	8–6, 6–1
1932	Helen Wills Moody	Simone Mathieu	7–5, 6–1
1933	Margaret Scriven	Simone Mathieu	6–2, 4–6, 6–4
1934	Margaret Scriven	Helen Jacobs	7–5, 4–6, 6–1
1935	Hilde Sperling	Simone Mathieu	6–2, 6–1
1936	Hilde Sperling	Simone Mathieu	6–3, 6–4
1937	Hilde Sperling	Simone Mathieu	6–2, 6–4
1938	Simone Mathieu	Nelly Landry	6–0, 6–3
1939	Simone Mathieu	Jadwiga Jedrzejowska	6–3, 8–6
1940–45	No tournament		
1946	Margaret Osborne	Pauline Betz	1–6, 8–6, 7–5
1947	Patricia Todd	Doris Hart	6–3, 3–6, 6–4
1948	Nelly Landry	Shirley Fry	6–2, 0–6, 6–0
1949	Margaret Osborne duPont	Nelly Adamson	7–5, 6–2
1950	Doris Hart	Patricia Todd	6–4, 4–6, 6–2
1951	Shirley Fry	Doris Hart	6–3, 3–6, 6–3
1952	Doris Hart	Shirley Fry	6–4, 6–4
1953	Maureen Connolly	Doris Hart	6–2, 6–4
1954	Maureen Connolly	Ginette Bucaille	6–4, 6–1
1955	Angela Mortimer	Dorothy Knode	2–6, 7–5, 10–8
1956	Althea Gibson	Angela Mortimer	6–0, 12–10
1957	Shirley Bloomer	Dorothy Knode	6–1, 6–3
1958	Zsuzsi Kormoczi	Shirley Bloomer	6–4, 1–6, 6–2
1959	Christine Truman	Zsuzsi Kormoczi	6–4, 7–5
1960	Darlene Hard	Yola Ramirez	6–3, 6–4
1961	Ann Haydon	Yola Ramirez	6–2, 6–1
1962	Margaret Smith	Lesley Turner	6–3, 3–6, 7–5
1963	Lesley Turner	Ann Haydon Jones	2–6, 6–3, 7–5
1964	Margaret Smith	Maria Bueno	5–7, 6–1, 6–2
1965	Lesley Turner	Margaret Smith	6–3, 6–4
1966	Ann Jones	Nancy Richey	6–3, 6–1
1967	Francoise Durr	Lesley Turner	4–6, 6–3, 6–4
1968*	Nancy Richey	Ann Jones	5–7, 6–4, 6–1
1969	Margaret Smith Court	Ann Jones	6–1, 4–6, 6–3
1970	Margaret Smith Court	Helga Niessen	6–2, 6–4
1971	Evonne Goolagong	Helen Gourlay	6–3, 7–5
1972	Billie Jean King	Evonne Goolagong	6–3, 6–3
1973	Margaret Smith Court	Chris Evert	6–7, 7–6, 6–4
1974	Chris Evert	Olga Morozova	6–1, 6–2
1975	Chris Evert	Martina Navratilova	2–6, 6–2, 6–1
1976	Sue Barker	Renata Tomanova	6–2, 0–6, 6–2
1977	Mima Jausovec	Florenza Mihai	6–2, 6–7, 6–1
1978	Virginia Ruzici	Mima Jausovec	6–2, 6–2
1979	Chris Evert Lloyd	Wendy Turnbull	6–2, 6–0
1980	Chris Evert Lloyd	Virginia Ruzici	6–0, 6–3
1981	Hana Mandlikova	Sylvia Hanika	6–2, 6–4
1982	Martina Navratilova	Andrea Jaeger	7–6, 6–1
1983	Chris Evert Lloyd	Mima Jausovec	6–1, 6–2
1984	Martina Navratilova	Chris Evert Lloyd	6–3, 6–1
1985	Chris Evert Lloyd	Martina Navratilova	6–3, 6–7, 7–5

WOMEN *(Cont.)*
French Championships *(Cont.)*

Year	Winner	Finalist	Score
1986	Chris Evert Lloyd	Martina Navratilova	2–6, 6–3, 6–3
1987	Steffi Graf	Martina Navratilova	6–4, 4–6, 8–6
1988	Steffi Graf	Natalia Zvereva	6–0, 6–0
1989	Arantxa Sánchez Vicario	Steffi Graf	7–6, 3–6, 7–5
1990	Monica Seles	Steffi Graf	7–6, 6–4
1991	Monica Seles	Arantxa Sánchez Vicario	6–3, 6–4
1992	Monica Seles	Steffi Graf	6–2, 3–6, 10–8
1993	Steffi Graf	Mary Joe Fernández	4–6, 6–2, 6–4
1994	Arantxa Sánchez Vicario	Mary Pierce	6–4, 6–4
1995	Steffi Graf	Arantxa Sánchez Vicario	7–5, 4–6, 6–0
1996	Steffi Graf	Arantxa Sánchez Vicario	6–3, 6–7 (4–7), 10–8
1997	Iva Majoli	Martina Hingis	6–4, 6–2
1998	Arantxa Sánchez Vicario	Monica Seles	7–6 (7–5), 0–6, 6–2
1999	Steffi Graf	Martina Hingis	4–6, 7–5, 6–2
2000	Mary Pierce	Conchita Martinez	6–2, 7–5
2001	Jennifer Capriati	Kim Clijsters	1–6, 6–4, 12–10
2002	Serena Williams	Venus Williams	7–5, 6–3

†1925 was the first year that entries were accepted from all countries.

Wimbledon Championships

Year	Winner	Finalist	Score
1884	Maud Watson	Lilian Watson	6–8, 6–3, 6–3
1885	Maud Watson	Blanche Bingley	6–1, 7–5
1886	Blanche Bingley	Maud Watson	6–3, 6–3
1887	Charlotte Dod	Blanche Bingley	6–2, 6–0
1888	Charlotte Dod	Blanche Bingley Hillyard	6–3, 6–3
1889	Blanche Bingley Hillyard	n/a	n/a
1890	Lena Rice	n/a	n/a
1891	Charlotte Dod	n/a	n/a
1892	Charlotte Dod	Blanche Bingley Hillyard	6–1, 6–1
1893	Charlotte Dod	Blanche Bingley Hillyard	6–8, 6–1, 6–4
1894	Blanche Bingley Hillyard	n/a	n/a
1895	Charlotte Cooper	n/a	
1896	Charlotte Cooper	Mrs. W. H. Pickering	6–2, 6–3
1897	Blanche Bingley Hillyard	Charlotte Cooper	5–7, 7–5, 6–2
1898	Charlotte Cooper	n/a	n/a
1899	Blanche Bingley Hillyard	Charlotte Cooper	6–2, 6–3
1900	Blanche Bingley Hillyard	Charlotte Cooper	4–6, 6–4, 6–4
1901	Charlotte Cooper Sterry	Blanche Bingley Hillyard	6–2, 6–2
1902	Muriel Robb	Charlotte Cooper Sterry	7–5, 6–1
1903	Dorothea Douglass	n/a	n/a
1904	Dorothea Douglass	Charlotte Cooper Sterry	6–0, 6–3
1905	May Sutton	Dorothea Douglass	6–3, 6–4
1906	Dorothea Douglass	May Sutton	6–3, 9–7
1907	May Sutton	Dorothea Douglass Lambert Chambers	6–1, 6–4
1908	Charlotte Cooper Sterry	n/a	n/a
1909	Dora Boothby	n/a	n/a
1910	Dorothea Douglass Lambert Chambers	Dora Boothby	6–2, 6–2
1911	Dorothea Douglass Lambert Chambers	Dora Boothby	6–0, 6–0
1912	Ethel Larcombe	n/a	n/a
1913	Dorothea Douglass Lambert Chambers		
1914	Dorothea Douglass Lambert Chambers	Ethel Larcombe	7–5, 6–4
1915–18	No tournament		
1919	Suzanne Lenglen	Dorothea Douglass Lambert Chambers	10–8, 4–6, 9–7
1920	Suzanne Lenglen	Dorothea Douglass Lambert Chambers	6–3, 6–0

WOMEN *(Cont.)*
Wimbledon Championships *(Cont.)*

Year	Winner	Finalist	Score
1921	Suzanne Lenglen	Elizabeth Ryan	6–2, 6–0
1922	Suzanne Lenglen	Molla Mallory	6–2, 6–0
1923	Suzanne Lenglen	Kathleen McKane	6–2, 6–2
1924	Kathleen McKane	Helen Wills	4–6, 6–4, 6–2
1925	Suzanne Lenglen	Joan Fry	6–2, 6–0
1926	Kathleen McKane Godfree	Lili de Alvarez	6–2, 4–6, 6–3
1927	Helen Wills	Lili de Alvarez	6–2, 6–4
1928	Helen Wills	Lili de Alvarez	6–2, 6–3
1929	Helen Wills	Helen Jacobs	6–1, 6–2
1930	Helen Wills Moody	Elizabeth Ryan	6–2, 6–2
1931	Cilly Aussem	Hilde Kranwinkel	7–5, 7–5
1932	Helen Wills Moody	Helen Jacobs	6–3, 6–1
1933	Helen Wills Moody	Dorothy Round	6–4, 6–8, 6–3
1934	Dorothy Round	Helen Jacobs	6–2, 5–7, 6–3
1935	Helen Wills Moody	Helen Jacobs	6–3, 3–6, 7–5
1936	Helen Jacobs	Hilde Kranwinkel Sperling	6–2, 4–6, 7–5
1937	Dorothy Round	Jadwiga Jedrzejowska	6–2, 2–6, 7–5
1938	Helen Wills Moody	Helen Jacobs	6–4, 6–0
1939	Alice Marble	Kay Stammers	6–2, 6–0
1940–45	No tournament		
1946	Pauline Betz	Louise Brough	6–2, 6–4
1947	Margaret Osborne	Doris Hart	6–2, 6–4
1948	Louise Brough	Doris Hart	6–3, 8–6
1949	Louise Brough	Margaret Osborne duPont	10–8, 1–6, 10–8
1950	Louise Brough	Margaret Osborne duPont	6–1, 3–6, 6–1
1951	Doris Hart	Shirley Fry	6–1, 6–0
1952	Maureen Connolly	Louise Brough	6–4, 6–3
1953	Maureen Connolly	Doris Hart	8–6, 7–5
1954	Maureen Connolly	Louise Brough	6–2, 7–5
1955	Louise Brough	Beverly Fleitz	7–5, 8–6
1956	Shirley Fry	Angela Buxton	6–3, 6–1
1957	Althea Gibson	Darlene Hard	6–3, 6–2
1958	Althea Gibson	Angela Mortimer	8–6, 6–2
1959	Maria Bueno	Darlene Hard	6–4, 6–3
1960	Maria Bueno	Sandra Reynolds	8–6, 6–0
1961	Angela Mortimer	Christine Truman	4–6, 6–4, 7–5
1962	Karen Hantze Susman	Vera Sukova	6–4, 6–4
1963	Margaret Smith	Billie Jean Moffitt	6–3, 6–4
1964	Maria Bueno	Margaret Smith	6–4, 7–9, 6–3
1965	Margaret Smith	Maria Bueno	6–4, 7–5
1966	Billie Jean King	Maria Bueno	6–3, 3–6, 6–1
1967	Billie Jean King	Ann Haydon Jones	6–3, 6–4
1968*	Billie Jean King	Judy Tegart	9–7, 7–5
1969	Ann Haydon Jones	Billie Jean King	3–6, 6–3, 6–2
1970	Margaret Smith Court	Billie Jean King	14–12, 11–9
1971	Evonne Goolagong	Margaret Smith Court	6–4, 6–1
1972	Billie Jean King	Evonne Goolagong	6–3, 6–3
1973	Billie Jean King	Chris Evert	6–0, 7–5
1974	Chris Evert	Olga Morozova	6–0, 6–4
1975	Billie Jean King	Evonne Goolagong Cawley	6–0, 6–1
1976	Chris Evert	Evonne Goolagong Cawley	6–3, 4–6, 8–6
1977	Virginia Wade	Betty Stove	4–6, 6–3, 6–1
1978	Martina Navratilova	Chris Evert	2–6, 6–4, 7–5
1979	Martina Navratilova	Chris Evert Lloyd	6–4, 6–4
1980	Evonne Goolagong Cawley	Chris Evert Lloyd	6–1, 7–6
1981	Chris Evert Lloyd	Hana Mandlikova	6–2, 6–2
1982	Martina Navratilova	Chris Evert Lloyd	6–1, 3–6, 6–2
1983	Martina Navratilova	Andrea Jaeger	6–0, 6–3
1984	Martina Navratilova	Chris Evert Lloyd	7–6, 6–2
1985	Martina Navratilova	Chris Evert Lloyd	4–6, 6–3, 6–2
1986	Martina Navratilova	Hana Mandlikova	7–6, 6–3
1987	Martina Navratilova	Steffi Graf	7–5, 6–3
1988	Steffi Graf	Martina Navratilova	5–7, 6–2, 6–1

WOMEN *(Cont.)*

Wimbledon Championships *(Cont.)*

Year	Winner	Finalist	Score
1989	Steffi Graf	Martina Navratilova	6–2, 6–7, 6–1
1990	Martina Navratilova	Zina Garrison	6–4, 6–1
1991	Steffi Graf	Gabriela Sabatini	6–4, 3–6, 8–6
1992	Steffi Graf	Monica Seles	6–2, 6–1
1993	Steffi Graf	Jana Novotna	7–6, 1–6, 6–4
1994	Conchita Martinez	Martina Navratilova	6–4, 3–6, 6–3
1995	Steffi Graf	Arantxa Sánchez Vicario	4–6, 6–1, 7–5
1996	Steffi Graf	Arantxa Sánchez Vicario	6–3, 7–5
1997	Martina Hingis	Jana Novotna	2–6, 6–3, 6–3
1998	Jana Novotna	Nathalie Tauziat	6–4, 7–6
1999	Lindsay Davenport	Steffi Graf	6–4, 7–5
2000	Venus Williams	Lindsay Davenport	6–3, 7–6
2001	Venus Williams	Justine Henin	6–1, 3–6, 6–0
2002	Serena Williams	Venus Williams	7–6 (7–4), 6–3

*Became Open (amateur and professional) in 1968 but closed to contract professionals in 1972.

Note: Prior to 1922 the tournament was run on a challenge-round system. The previous year's winner "stood out" of an All-Comers event, which produced a challenger to play her for the title.

United States Championships

Year	Winner	Finalist	Score
1887	Ellen Hansell	Laura Knight	6–1, 6–0
1888	Bertha L. Townsend	Ellen Hansell	6–3, 6–5
1889	Bertha L. Townsend	Louise Voorhes	7–5, 6–2
1890	Ellen C. Roosevelt	Bertha L. Townsend	6–2, 6–2
1891	Mabel Cahill	Ellen C. Roosevelt	6–4, 6–1, 4–6, 6–3
1892	Mabel Cahill	Elisabeth Moore	5–7, 6–3, 6–4, 4–6, 6–2
1893	Aline Terry	Alice Schultze	6–1, 6–3
1894	Helen Hellwig	Aline Terry	7–5, 3–6, 6–0, 3–6, 6–3
1895	Juliette Atkinson	Helen Hellwig	6–4, 6–2, 6–1
1896	Elisabeth Moore	Juliette Atkinson	6–4, 4–6, 6–2, 6–2
1897	Juliette Atkinson	Elisabeth Moore	6–3, 6–3, 4–6, 3–6, 6–3
1898	Juliette Atkinson	Marion Jones	6–3, 5–7, 6–4, 2–6, 7–5
1899	Marion Jones	Maud Banks	6–1, 6–1, 7–5
1900	Myrtle McAteer	Edith Parker	6–2, 6–2, 6–0
1901	Elisabeth Moore	Myrtle McAteer	6–4, 3–6, 7–5, 2–6, 6–2
1902**	Marion Jones	Elisabeth Moore	6–1, 1–0, ret.
1903	Elisabeth Moore	Marion Jones	7–5, 8–6
1904	May Sutton	Elisabeth Moore	6–1, 6–2
1905	Elisabeth Moore	Helen Homans	6–4, 5–7, 6–1
1906	Helen Homans	Maud Barger–Wallach	6–4, 6–3
1907	Evelyn Sears	Carrie Neely	6–3, 6–2
1908	Maud Barger–Wallach	Evelyn Sears	6–3, 1–6, 6–3
1909	Hazel Hotchkiss	Maud Barger–Wallach	6–0, 6–1
1910	Hazel Hotchkiss	Louise Hammond	6–4, 6–2
1911	Hazel Hotchkiss	Florence Sutton	8–10, 6–1, 9–7
1912†	Mary K. Browne	Eleanora Sears	6–4, 6–2
1913	Mary K. Browne	Dorothy Green	6–2, 7–5
1914	Mary K. Browne	Marie Wagner	6–2, 1–6, 6–1
1915	Molla Bjurstedt	Hazel Hotchkiss Wightman	4–6, 6–2, 6–0
1916	Molla Bjurstedt	Louise Hammond Raymond	6–0, 6–1
1917‡	Molla Bjurstedt	Marion Vanderhoef	4–6, 6–0, 6–2
1918	Molla Bjurstedt	Eleanor Goss	6–4, 6–3
1919	Hazel Hotchkiss Wightman	Marion Zinderstein	6–1, 6–2
1920	Molla Bjurstedt Mallory	Marion Zinderstein	6–3, 6–1
1921	Molla Bjurstedt Mallory	Mary K. Browne	4–6, 6–4, 6–2
1922	Molla Bjurstedt Mallory	Helen Wills	6–3, 6–1
1923	Helen Wills	Molla Bjurstedt Mallory	6–2, 6–1
1924	Helen Wills	Molla Bjurstedt Mallory	6–1, 6–3
1925	Helen Wills	Kathleen McKane	3–6, 6–0, 6–2
1926	Molla Bjurstedt Mallory	Elizabeth Ryan	4–6, 6–4, 9–7
1927	Helen Wills	Betty Nuthall	6–1, 6–4
1928	Helen Wills	Helen Jacobs	6–2, 6–1
1929	Helen Wills	Phoebe Holcroft Watson	6–4, 6–2
1930	Betty Nuthall	Anna McCune Harper	6–1, 6–4
1931	Helen Wills Moody	Eileen Whitingstall	6–4, 6–1
1932	Helen Jacobs	Carolin Babcock	6–2, 6–2
1933	Helen Jacobs	Helen Wills Moody	8–6, 3–6, 3–0, ret.

WOMEN (Cont.)

United States Championships (Cont.)

Year	Winner	Finalist	Score
1934	Helen Jacobs	Sarah Palfrey	6–1, 6–4
1935	Helen Jacobs	Sarah Palfrey Fabyan	6–2, 6–4
1936	Alice Marble	Helen Jacobs	4–6, 6–3, 6–2
1937	Anita Lizane	Jadwiga Jedrzejowska	6–4, 6–2
1938	Alice Marble	Nancye Wynne	6–0, 6–3
1939	Alice Marble	Helen Jacobs	6–0, 8–10, 6–4
1940	Alice Marble	Helen Jacobs	6–2, 6–3
1941	Sarah Palfrey Cooke	Pauline Betz	7–5, 6–2
1942	Pauline Betz	Louise Brough	4–6, 6–1, 6–4
1943	Pauline Betz	Louise Brough	6–3, 5–7, 6–3
1944	Pauline Betz	Margaret Osborne	6–3, 8–6
1945	Sarah Palfrey Cooke	Pauline Betz	3–6, 8–6, 6–4
1946	Pauline Betz	Patricia Canning	11–9, 6–3
1947	Louise Brough	Margaret Osborne	8–6, 4–6, 6–1
1948	Margaret Osborne duPont	Louise Brough	4–6, 6–4, 15–13
1949	Margaret Osborne duPont	Doris Hart	6–4, 6–1
1950	Margaret Osborne duPont	Doris Hart	6–4, 6–3
1951	Maureen Connolly	Shirley Fry	6–3, 1–6, 6–4
1952	Maureen Connolly	Doris Hart	6–3, 7–5
1953	Maureen Connolly	Doris Hart	6–2, 6–4
1954	Doris Hart	Louise Brough	6–8, 6–1, 8–6
1955	Doris Hart	Patricia Ward	6–4, 6–2
1956	Shirley Fry	Althea Gibson	6–3, 6–4
1957	Althea Gibson	Louise Brough	6–3, 6–2
1958	Althea Gibson	Darlene Hard	3–6, 6–1, 6–2
1959	Maria Bueno	Christine Truman	6–1, 6–4
1960	Darlene Hard	Maria Bueno	6–4, 10–12, 6–4
1961	Darlene Hard	Ann Haydon	6–3, 6–4
1962	Margaret Smith	Darlene Hard	9–7, 6–4
1963	Maria Bueno	Margaret Smith	7–5, 6–4
1964	Maria Bueno	Carole Graebner	6–1, 6–0
1965	Margaret Smith	Billie Jean Moffitt	8–6, 7–5
1966	Maria Bueno	Nancy Richey	6–3, 6–1
1967	Billie Jean King	Ann Haydon Jones	11–9, 6–4
1968*	Virginia Wade	Billie Jean King	6–4, 6–4
1968#	Margaret Smith Court	Maria Bueno	6–2, 6–2
1969	Margaret Smith Court	Nancy Richey	6–2, 6–2
1969#	Margaret Smith Court	Virginia Wade	4–6, 6–3, 6–0
1970	Margaret Smith Court	Rosie Casals	6–2, 2–6, 6–1
1971	Billie Jean King	Rosie Casals	6–4, 7–6
1972	Billie Jean King	Kerry Melville	6–3, 7–5
1973	Margaret Smith Court	Evonne Goolagong	7–6, 5–7, 6–2
1974	Billie Jean King	Evonne Goolagong	3–6, 6–3, 7–5
1975	Chris Evert	Evonne Goolagong Cawley	5–7, 6–4, 6–2
1976	Chris Evert	Evonne Goolagong Cawley	6–3, 6–0
1977	Chris Evert	Wendy Turnbull	7–6, 6–2
1978	Chris Evert	Pam Shriver	7–6, 6–4
1979	Tracy Austin	Chris Evert Lloyd	6–4, 6–3
1980	Chris Evert Lloyd	Hana Mandlikova	5–7, 6–1, 6–1
1981	Tracy Austin	Martina Navratilova	1–6, 7–6, 7–6
1982	Chris Evert Lloyd	Hana Mandlikova	6–3, 6–1
1983	Martina Navratilova	Chris Evert Lloyd	6–1, 6–3
1984	Martina Navratilova	Chris Evert Lloyd	4–6, 6–4, 6–4
1985	Hana Mandlikova	Martina Navratilova	7–6, 1–6, 7–6
1986	Martina Navratilova	Helena Sukova	6–3, 6–2
1987	Martina Navratilova	Steffi Graf	7–6, 6–1
1988	Steffi Graf	Gabriela Sabatini	6–3, 3–6, 6–1
1989	Steffi Graf	Martina Navratilova	3–6, 6–4, 6–2
1990	Gabriela Sabatini	Steffi Graf	6–2, 7–6
1991	Monica Seles	Martina Navratilova	7–6, 6–1
1992	Monica Seles	Arantxa Sánchez Vicario	6–3, 6–2
1993	Steffi Graf	Helena Sukova	6–3, 6–3
1994	Arantxa Sánchez Vicario	Steffi Graf	1–6, 7–6, 6–4
1995	Steffi Graf	Monica Seles	7–6, 0–6, 6–3
1996	Steffi Graf	Monica Seles	7–5, 7–4
1997	Martina Hingis	Venus Williams	6–0, 6–4
1998	Lindsay Davenport	Martina Hingis	6–3, 7–5
1999	Serena Williams	Martina Hingis	6–3, 7–6
2000	Venus Williams	Lindsay Davenport	6–4, 7–5

WOMEN *(Cont.)*
United States Championships *(Cont.)*

Year	Winner	Finalist	Score
2001	Venus Williams	Serena Williams	6–2, 6–4
2002	Serena Williams	Venus Williams	6-4, 6–3

**Five-set final abolished; †Challenge round abolished. *Became Open (amateur and professional) in 1968.
‡National Patriotic Tournament; #Amateur event held.

Grand Slams

Singles

Don Budge, 1938
Maureen Connolly, 1953
Rod Laver, 1962, 1969
Margaret Smith Court, 1970
Steffi Graf, 1988

Doubles

Frank Sedgman and Ken McGregor, 1951
Martina Navratilova and Pam Shriver, 1984
Maria Bueno and two partners: Christine Truman
(Australian), Darlene Hard (French, Wimbledon
and U.S. Championships), 1960
Martina Hingis and two partners: Mirjana Lucic
(Australian), Jana Novotna (French, Wimbledon
and U.S. Championships), 1998

Mixed Doubles

Margaret Smith and Ken Fletcher, 1963
Owen Davidson and two partners: Lesley Turner
(Australian), Billie Jean King (French, Wimbledon
and U.S. Championships), 1967

Alltime Grand Slam Champions
MEN

Player	Aus. S-D-M	French S-D-M	Wim. S-D-M	U.S. S-D-M	Total
Roy Emerson	6-3-0	2-6-0	2-3-0	2-4-0	28
John Newcombe	2-5-0	0-3-0	3-6-0	2-3-1	25
Frank Sedgman	2-2-2	0-2-2	1-3-2	2-2-2	22
Bill Tilden	†	0-0-1	3-1-0	7-5-4	21
Rod Laver	3-4-0	2-1-1	4-1-2	2-0-0	20
John Bromwich	2-8-1	0-0-0	0-2-2	0-3-1	19
Jean Borotra	1-1-1	1-5-2	2-3-1	0-0-1	18
Fred Stolle	0-3-1	1-2-0	0-2-3	1-3-2	18
Ken Rosewall	4-3-0	2-2-0	0-2-0	2-2-1	18
Neale Fraser	0-3-1	0-3-0	1-2-0	2-3-3	18
Adrian Quist	3-10-0	0-1-0	0-2-0	0-1-0	17
John McEnroe	0-0-0	0-0-1	3-4-0	4-5-0	17
Jack Crawford	4-4-3	1-1-1	1-1-1	0-0-0	17
*Mark Woodforde	0-2-2	0-1-1	0-6-1	0-3-1	17

†Did not compete.

WOMEN

Player	Aus. S-D-M	French S-D-M	Wim. S-D-M	U.S. S-D-M	Total
Margaret Smith Court	11-8-2	5-4-4	3-2-5	5-5-8	62
Martina Navratilova	3-8-0	2-7-2	9-7-3	4-9-2	56
Billie Jean King	1-0-1	1-1-2	6-10-4	4-5-4	39
Doris Hart	1-1-2	2-5-3	1-4-5	2-4-5	35
Helen Wills Moody	†	4-2-0	8-3-1	7-4-2	31
Louise Brough	1-1-0	0-3-0	4-5-4	1-8-3	30**
Margaret Osborne duPont	†	2-3-0	1-5-1	3-8-6	29**
Elizabeth Ryan	†	0-4-0	0-12-7	0-1-2	26
Steffi Graf	4-0-0	6-0-0	7-1-0	5-0-0	23
Pam Shriver	0-7-0	0-4-1	0-5-0	0-5-0	22
Chris Evert	2-0-0	7-2-0	3-1-0	6-0-0	21
Darlene Hard	†	1-3-2	0-4-3	2-6-0	21
Suzanne Lenglen	†	2-2-2#	6-6-3	0-0-0	21
Nancye Wynne Bolton	6-10-4	0-0-0	0-0-0	0-0-0	20
Maria Bueno	†	0-1-1	3-5-0	4-4-0	19
Thelma Coyne Long	2-12-4	0-0-1	0-0-0	0-0-0	19

*Active player. †Did not compete. #Suzanne Lenglen also won four singles titles at the French Championships before 1925, when competition was first opened to entries from all nations.**From 1940–45, with competition in the U.S. Championships thinned due to wartime constraints, Louise Brough Clapp also won four doubles titles (1942–45) and one mixed doubles title (1942); and Margaret Osborne duPont won five doubles titles (1941–45) and three mixed doubles titles (1943–45).

Alltime Grand Slam Singles Champions

MEN

Player	Aus.	French	Wim.	U.S.	Total
*Pete Sampras	2	0	7	5	14
Roy Emerson	6	2	2	2	12
Bjorn Borg	0	6	5	0	11
Rod Laver	3	2	4	2	11
Bill Tilden	†	0	3	7	10
Jimmy Connors	1	0	2	5	8
Ivan Lendl	2	3	0	3	8
Fred Perry	1	1	3	3	8
Ken Rosewall	4	2	0	2	8
Henri Cochet	†	4	2	1	7
Rene Lacoste	†	3	2	2	7
Bill Larned	†	†	0	7	7
John McEnroe	0	0	3	4	7
John Newcombe	2	0	3	2	7
Willie Renshaw	†	†	7	†	7
Dick Sears	†	†	0	7	7
*Andre Agassi	3	1	1	2	7

*Active player. †Did not compete.

WOMEN

Player	Aus.	French	Wim.	U.S.	Total
Margaret Smith Court	11	5	3	5	24
Steffi Graf	4	6	7	5	22
Helen Wills Moody	†	4	8	7	19
Chris Evert	2	7	3	6	18
Martina Navratilova	3	2	9	4	18
Billie Jean King	1	1	6	4	12
Maureen Connolly	1	2	3	3	9
*Monica Seles	4	3	0	2	9
Suzanne Lenglen	†	2#	6	0	8
Molla Bjurstedt Mallory	†	†	0	8	8
Maria Bueno	0	0	3	4	7
Evonne Goolagong	4	1	2	0	7
Dorothea D.L. Chambers	†	†	7	0	7
Nancye Wynne Bolton	6	0	0	0	6
Louise Brough	1	0	4	1	6
Margaret Osborne duPont	†	2	1	3	6
Doris Hart	1	2	1	2	6
Blanche Bingley Hillyard	†	†	6	†	6

*Active player. †Did not compete.

#Suzanne Lenglen also won four singles titles at the French Championships before 1925, when competition was first opened to entries from all nations.

Davis Cup

the 1898 U.S. Championships. A Davis Cup meeting between two countries is known as a tie and is a three-day event consisting of two singles matches, followed by one doubles match and then two more singles matches. The United States boasts the greatest number of wins (31), followed by Australia (20).

Year	Winner	Finalist	Site	Score
1900	United States	Great Britain	Boston	3–0
1901	No tournament			
1902	United States	Great Britain	New York	3–2
1903	Great Britain	United States	Boston	4–1
1904	Great Britain	Belgium	Wimbledon	5–0
1905	Great Britain	United States	Wimbledon	5–0
1906	Great Britain	United States	Wimbledon	5–0
1907	Australasia	Great Britain	Wimbledon	3–2
1908	Australasia	United States	Melbourne	3–2
1909	Australasia	United States	Sydney	5–0
1910	No tournament			
1911	Australasia	United States	Christchurch, NZ	5–0
1912	Great Britain	Australasia	Melbourne	3–2
1913	United States	Great Britain	Wimbledon	3–2
1914	Australasia	United States	New York	3–2
1915–18	No tournament			
1919	Australasia	Great Britain	Sydney	4–1
1920	United States	Australasia	Auckland, NZ	5–0
1921	United States	Japan	New York	5–0
1922	United States	Australasia	New York	4–1
1923	United States	Australasia	New York	4–1
1924	United States	Australia	Philadelphia	5–0
1925	United States	France	Philadelphia	5–0
1926	United States	France	Philadelphia	4–1
1927	France	United States	Philadelphia	3–2
1928	France	United States	Paris	4–1
1929	France	United States	Paris	3–2
1930	France	United States	Paris	4–1
1931	France	Great Britain	Paris	3–2
1932	France	United States	Paris	3–2
1933	Great Britain	France	Paris	3–2
1934	Great Britain	United States	Wimbledon	4–1
1935	Great Britain	United States	Wimbledon	5–0
1936	Great Britain	Australia	Wimbledon	3–2
1937	United States	Great Britain	Wimbledon	4–1
1938	United States	Australia	Philadelphia	3–2
1939	Australia	United States	Philadelphia	3–2
1940–45	No tournament			
1946	United States	Australia	Melbourne	5–0
1947	United States	Australia	New York	4–1
1948	United States	Australia	New York	5–0
1949	United States	Australia	New York	4–1
1950	Australia	United States	New York	4–1
1951	Australia	United States	Sydney	3–2
1952	Australia	United States	Adelaide	4–1
1953	Australia	United States	Melbourne	3–2
1954	United States	Australia	Sydney	3–2
1955	Australia	United States	New York	5–0
1956	Australia	United States	Adelaide	5–0
1957	Australia	United States	Melbourne	3–2
1958	United States	Australia	Brisbane	3–2
1959	Australia	United States	New York	3–2
1960	Australia	Italy	Sydney	4–1
1961	Australia	Italy	Melbourne	5–0
1962	Australia	Mexico	Brisbane	5–0
1963	United States	Australia	Adelaide	3–2
1964	Australia	United States	Cleveland	3–2
1965	Australia	Spain	Sydney	4–1
1966	Australia	India	Melbourne	4–1
1967	Australia	Spain	Brisbane	4–1
1968	United States	Australia	Adelaide	4–1
1969	United States	Romania	Cleveland	5–0
1970	United States	W Germany	Cleveland	5–0
1971	United States	Romania	Charlotte, NC	3–2
1972	United States	Romania	Bucharest	3–2

Davis Cup (Cont.)

Year	Winner	Finalist	Site	Score
1973	Australia	United States	Cleveland	5–0
1974	South Africa	India	*	walkover
1975	Sweden	Czechoslovakia	Stockholm	3–2
1976	Italy	Chile	Santiago	4–1
1977	Australia	Italy	Sydney	3–1
1978	United States	Great Britain	Palm Springs	4–1
1979	United States	Italy	San Francisco	5–0
1980	Czechoslovakia	Italy	Prague	4–1
1981	United States	Argentina	Cincinnati	3–1
1982	United States	France	Grenoble, France	4–1
1983	Australia	Sweden	Melbourne	3–2
1984	Sweden	United States	Göteborg, Sweden	4–1
1985	Sweden	W Germany	Munich	3–2
1986	Australia	Sweden	Melbourne	3–2
1987	Sweden	India	Göteborg, Sweden	5–0
1988	West Germany	Sweden	Göteborg, Sweden	4–1
1989	West Germany	Sweden	Stuttgart	3–2
1990	United States	Australia	St. Petersburg	3–2
1991	France	United States	Lyon	3–1
1992	United States	Switzerland	Fort Worth, TX	3–1
1993	Germany	Australia	Dusseldorf	4–1
1994	Sweden	Russia	Moscow	4–1
1995	United States	Russia	Moscow	3–2
1996	France	Sweden	Malmö, Sweden	3–2
1997	Sweden	United States	Göteborg, Sweden	5–0
1998	Sweden	Italy	Milan	4–1
1999	Australia	France	Nice, France	3–2
2000	Spain	Australia	Barcelona	3–1
2001	France	Australia	Melbourne	3–2

*India refused to play the final in protest over South Africa's governmental policy of apartheid.
Note: Prior to 1972 the challenge-round system was in effect, with the previous year's winner "standing out" of the competition until the finals. A straight 16-nation tournament has been held since 1981.

Federation Cup

The Federation Cup was started in 1963 by the International Lawn Tennis Federation (now the ITF). Until 1991 all entrants gathered at one site at one time for a tournament that was concluded within one week. Since 1995 the Fed Cup, as it is now called, has been contested in three rounds by a World Group of eight nations. A meeting between two countries now consists of five matches: four singles and one doubles. The United States has the most wins (15), followed by Australia (7).

Year	Winner	Finalist	Site	Score
1963	United States	Australia	London	2–1
1964	Australia	United States	Philadelphia	2–1
1965	Australia	United States	Melbourne	2–1
1966	United States	W Germany	Turin	3–0
1967	United States	Great Britain	W Berlin	2–0
1968	Australia	Netherlands	Paris	3–0
1969	United States	Australia	Athens	2–1
1970	Australia	Great Britain	Freiburg	3–0
1971	Australia	Great Britain	Perth	3–0
1972	South Africa	Great Britain	Johannesburg	2–1
1973	Australia	South Africa	Bad Homburg	3–0
1974	Australia	United States	Naples	2–1
1975	Czechoslovakia	Australia	Aix-en-Provence	3–0
1976	United States	Australia	Philadelphia	2–1
1977	United States	Australia	Eastbourne, G.B.	2–1
1978	United States	Australia	Melbourne	2–1
1979	United States	Australia	Madrid	3–0
1980	United States	Australia	W Berlin	3–0
1981	United States	Great Britain	Nagoya	3–0
1982	United States	W Germany	Santa Clara, CA	3–0
1983	Czechoslovakia	W Germany	Zurich	2–1
1984	Czechoslovakia	Australia	Sao Paulo	2–1
1985	Czechoslovakia	United States	Tokyo	2–1
1986	United States	Czechoslovakia	Prague	3–0
1987	W Germany	United States	Vancouver	2–1

Federation Cup *(Cont.)*

Year	Winner	Finalist	Site	Score
1988	Czechoslovakia	USSR	Melbourne	2–1
1989	United States	Spain	Tokyo	3–0
1990	United States	USSR	Atlanta	2–1
1991	Spain	United States	Nottingham	2–1
1992	Germany	Spain	Frankfurt	2–1
1993	Spain	Australia	Frankfurt	3–0
1994	Spain	United States	Frankfurt	3–0
1995	Spain	United States	Valencia, Spain	3–2
1996	United States	Spain	Atlantic City	5–0
1997	France	Netherlands	Hertogenbosch, Neth.	4–1
1998	Spain	Switzerland	Geneva	3–2
1999	United States	Russia	Palo Alto, California	4–1
2000	United States	Spain	Las Vegas, Nevada	5–0
2001	Belgium	Russia	Barcelona	2–1

Rankings

ATP Computer Year-End Top 10

MEN

1973
1. Ilie Nastase
2. John Newcombe
3. Jimmy Connors
4. Tom Okker
5. Stan Smith
6. Ken Rosewall
7. Manuel Orantes
8. Rod Laver
9. Jan Kodes
10. Arthur Ashe

1974
1. Jimmy Connors
2. John Newcombe
3. Bjorn Borg
4. Rod Laver
5. Guillermo Vilas
6. Tom Okker
7. Arthur Ashe
8. Ken Rosewall
9. Stan Smith
10. Ilie Nastase

1975
1. Jimmy Connors
2. Guillermo Vilas
3. Bjorn Borg
4. Arthur Ashe
5. Manuel Orantes
6. Ken Rosewall
7. Ilie Nastase
8. John Alexander
9. Roscoe Tanner
10. Rod Laver

1976
1. Jimmy Connors
2. Bjorn Borg
3. Ilie Nastase
4. Manuel Orantes
5. Raul Ramirez
6. Guillermo Vilas
7. Adriano Panatta
8. Harold Solomon
9. Eddie Dibbs
10. Brian Gottfried

1977
1. Jimmy Connors
2. Guillermo Vilas
3. Bjorn Borg
4. Vitas Gerulaitis
5. Brian Gottfried
6. Eddie Dibbs
7. Manuel Orantes
8. Raul Ramirez
9. Ilie Nastase
10. Dick Stockton

1978
1. Jimmy Connors
2. Bjorn Borg
3. Guillermo Vilas
4. John McEnroe
5. Vitas Gerulaitis
6. Eddie Dibbs
7. Brian Gottfried
8. Raul Ramirez
9. Harold Solomon
10. Corrado Barazzutti

1979
1. Bjorn Borg
2. Jimmy Connors
3. John McEnroe
4. Vitas Gerulaitis
5. Roscoe Tanner
6. Guillermo Vilas
7. Arthur Ashe
8. Harold Solomon
9. Jose Higueras
10. Eddie Dibbs

1980
1. Bjorn Borg
2. John McEnroe
3. Jimmy Connors
4. Gene Mayer
5. Guillermo Vilas
6. Ivan Lendl
7. Harold Solomon
8. Jose–Luis Clerc
9. Vitas Gerulaitis
10. Eliot Teltscher

1981
1. John McEnroe
2. Ivan Lendl
3. Jimmy Connors
4. Bjorn Borg
5. Jose–Luis Clerc
6. Guillermo Vilas
7. Gene Mayer
8. Eliot Teltscher
9. Vitas Gerulaitis
10. Peter McNamara

ATP Computer Year-End Top 10
MEN (CONT.)

1982
1 ....John McEnroe
2 ....Jimmy Connors
3 ....Ivan Lendl
4 ...Guillermo Vilas
5 ...Vitas Gerulaitis
6 ....Jose–Luis Clerc
7 ...Mats Wilander
8 ...Gene Mayer
9 ....Yannick Noah
10 ..Peter McNamara

1983
1 ....John McEnroe
2 ....Ivan Lendl
3 ....Jimmy Connors
4 ....Mats Wilander
5 ...Yannick Noah
6 ...Jimmy Arias
7 ....Jose Higueras
8 ....Jose–Luis Clerc
9 ....Kevin Curren
10 ..Gene Mayer

1984
1 ....John McEnroe
2 ....Jimmy Connors
3 ....Ivan Lendl
4 ....Mats Wilander
5 ...Andres Gomez
6 ....Anders Jarryd
7 ....Henrik Sundstrom
8 ...Pat Cash
9 ....Eliot Teltscher
10 ..Yannick Noah

1985
1 ....Ivan Lendl
2 ....John McEnroe
3 ....Mats Wilander
4 ....Jimmy Connors
5 ....Stefan Edberg
6 ....Boris Becker
7 ....Yannick Noah
8 ....Anders Jarryd
9 ....Miloslav Mecir
10 ..Kevin Curren

1986
1 ....Ivan Lendl
2 ....Boris Becker
3 ....Mats Wilander
4 ....Yannick Noah
5 ....Stefan Edberg
6 ....Henri Leconte
7 ....Joakim Nystrom
8 ...Jimmy Connors
9 ....Miloslav Mecir
10 ..Andres Gomez

1987
1 ....Ivan Lendl
2 ....Stefan Edberg
3 ....Mats Wilander
4 ....Jimmy Connors
5 ....Boris Becker
6 ....Miloslav Mecir
7 ...Pat Cash
8 ....Yannick Noah
9 ....Tim Mayotte
10 ..John McEnroe

1988
1 ....Mats Wilander
2 ....Ivan Lendl
3 ....Andre Agassi
4 ....Boris Becker
5 ....Stefan Edberg
6 ....Kent Carlsson
7 ....Jimmy Connors
8 ...Jakob Hlasek
9 ....Henri Leconte
10 ..Tim Mayotte

1989
1 ....Ivan Lendl
2 ....Boris Becker
3 ....Stefan Edberg
4 ....John McEnroe
5 ....Michael Chang
6 ....Brad Gilbert
7 ....Andre Agassi
8 ....Aaron Krickstein
9 ....Alberto Mancini
10 ..Jay Berger

1990
1 ....Stefan Edberg
2 ....Boris Becker
3 ....Ivan Lendl
4 ....Andre Agassi
5 ....Pete Sampras
6 ....Andres Gomez
7 ....Thomas Muster
8 ....Emilio Sanchez
9 ....Goran Ivanisevic
10 ..Brad Gilbert

1991
1 ....Stefan Edberg
2 ....Jim Courier
3 ....Boris Becker
4 ....Michael Stich
5 ....Ivan Lendl
6 ....Pete Sampras
7 ....Guy Forget
8 ....Karel Novacek
9 ....Petr Korda
10 ..Andre Agassi

1992
1 ....Jim Courier
2 ....Stefan Edberg
3 ....Pete Sampras
4 ....Goran Ivanisevic
5 ....Boris Becker
6 ....Michael Chang
7 ....Petr Korda
8 ....Ivan Lendl
9 ....Andre Agassi
10 ...Richard Krajicek

1993
1 ....Pete Sampras
2 ....Michael Stich
3 ....Jim Courier
4 ....Sergi Bruguera
5 ....Stefan Edberg
6 ....Andrei Medvedev
7 ....Goran Ivanisevic
8 ....Michael Chang
9 ....Thomas Muster
10 ..Cedric Pioline

1994
1 ....Pete Sampras
2 ....Andre Agassi
3 ....Boris Becker
4 ....Sergi Bruguera
5 ....Goran Ivanisevic
6 ....Michael Chang
7 ....Stefan Edberg
8 ....Alberto Berasategui
9 ....Michael Stich
10 ...Todd Martin

1995
1 ....Pete Sampras
2 ....Andre Agassi
3 ....Thomas Muster
4 ....Boris Becker
5 ....Michael Chang
6 ....Yevgeny Kafelnikov
7 ....Thomas Enqvist
8 ....Jim Courier
9 ....Wayne Ferreira
10 ...Goran Ivanisevic

1996
1 ....Pete Sampras
2 ....Michael Chang
3 ....Yevgeny Kafelnikov
4 ....Goran Ivanisevic
5 ....Thomas Muster
6 ....Boris Becker
7 ....Richard Krajicek
8 ....Andre Agassi
9 ....Thomas Enqvist
10 ...Wayne Ferreira

ATP Computer Year-End Top 10
MEN (CONT.)

1997
1 ....Pete Sampras
2 ....Patrick Rafter
3 ...Michael Chang
4 ....Jonas Bjorkman
5 ....Yevgeny Kafelnikov
6 ....Greg Rusedski
7 ....Carlos Moya
8 ....Sergei Bruguera
9 ....Thomas Muster
10...Marcelo Ríos

1998
1 ....Pete Sampras
2 ....Marcelo Rios
3 ....Alex Corretja
4 ....Patrick Rafter
5 ....Carlos Moya
6 ....Andre Agassi
7 ....Tim Henman
8 ....Karol Kucera
9 ...Greg Rusedski
10...Richard Krajicek

1999
1 ....Andre Agassi
2 ....Yevgeny Kafelnikov
3 ....Pete Sampras
4 ....Thomas Enqvist
5 ....Gustavo Kuerten
6 ....Nicolas Kiefer
7 ....Todd Martin
8 ....Nicolas Lapentti
9 ....Marcelo Rios
10 ..Richard Krajicek

2000
1 ....Gustavo Kuerten
2 ....Marat Safin
3 ....Pete Sampras
4 ....Magnus Norman
5 ....Yevgeny Kafelnikov
6 ....Andre Agassi
7 ....Lleyton Hewitt
8 ....Alex Corretja
9 ....Thomas Enqvist
10 ..Tim Henman

2001
1 ....Lleyton Hewitt
2 ....Gustavo Kuerten
3 ....Andre Agassi
4 ....Yevgeny Kafelnikov
5 ....Juan Carlos Ferrero
6 ....Sebastien Grosjean
7 ....Patrick Rafter
8 ....Tommy Haas
9 ....Tim Henman
10 ..Pete Sampras

WTA Computer Year-End Top 10
WOMEN

1973
1 ....Margaret Smith Court
2 ....Billie Jean King
3 ....Evonne Goolagong
4 ....Chris Evert
5 ....Rosie Casals
6 ....Virginia Wade
7 ....Kerry Reid
8 ....Nancy Gunter
9 ....Julie Heldman
10...Helga Masthoff

1974
1 ....Billie Jean King
2 ....Evonne Goolagong
3 ....Chris Evert
4 ....Virginia Wade
5 ....Julie Heldman
6 ....Rosie Casals
7 ....Kerry Reid
8 ....Olga Morozova
9 ....Lesley Hunt
10...Francoise Durr

1975
1 ....Chris Evert
2 ....Billie Jean King
3 ....Evonne Goolagong Cawley
4 ....Martina Navratilova
5 ....Virginia Wade
6 ....Margaret Smith Court
7 ....Olga Morozova
8 ....Nancy Gunter
9 ....Francoise Durr
10...Rosie Casals

1976
1 ....Chris Evert
2 ....Evonne Goolagong Cawley
3 ....Virginia Wade
4 ....Martina Navratilova
5 ....Sue Barker
6 ....Betty Stove
7 ....Dianne Balestrat
8 ....Mima Jausovec
9 ....Rosie Casals
10...Francoise Durr

1977
1 ....Chris Evert
2 ....Billie Jean King
3 ....Martina Navratilova
4 ....Virginia Wade
5 ....Sue Barker
6 ....Rosie Casals
7 ....Betty Stove
8 ....Dianne Balestrat
9 ....Wendy Turnbull
10...Kerry Reid

1978
1 ....Martina Navratilova
2 ....Chris Evert
3 ....Evonne Goolagong Cawley
4 ....Virginia Wade
5 ....Billie Jean King
6 ....Tracy Austin
7 ....Wendy Turnbull
8 ....Kerry Reid
9 ....Betty Stove
10...Dianne Balestrat

1979
1 ....Martina Navratilova
2 ....Chris Evert Lloyd
3 ....Tracy Austin
4 ....Evonne Goolagong Cawley
5 ....Billie Jean King
6 ....Dianne Balestrat
7 ....Wendy Turnbull
8 ....Virginia Wade
9 ....Kerry Reid
10...Sue Barker

1980
1 ....Chris Evert Lloyd
2 ....Tracy Austin
3 ....Martina Navratilova
4 ....Hana Mandlikova
5 ....Evonne Goolagong Cawley
6 ....Billie Jean King
7 ....Andrea Jaeger
8 ....Wendy Turnbull
9 ....Pam Shriver
10...Greer Stevens

1981
1 ....Chris Evert Lloyd
2 ....Tracy Austin
3 ....Martina Navratilova
4 ....Andrea Jaeger
5 ....Hana Mandlikova
6 ....Sylvia Hanika
7 ....Pam Shriver
8 ....Wendy Turnbull
9 ....Bettina Bunge
10...Barbara Potter

1982
1 ....Martina Navratilova
2 ....Chris Evert Lloyd
3 ....Andrea Jaeger
4 ....Tracy Austin
5 ....Wendy Turnbull
6 ....Pam Shriver
7 ....Hana Mandlikova
8 ....Barbara Potter
9 ....Bettina Bunge
10...Sylvia Hanika

1983
1 ....Martina Navratilova
2 ....Chris Evert Lloyd
3 ....Andrea Jaeger
4 ....Pam Shriver
5 ....Sylvia Hanika
6 ....Jo Durie
7...Bettina Bunge
8 ....Wendy Turnbull
9 ....Tracy Austin
10...Zina Garrison

1984
1 ....Martina Navratilova
2 ....Chris Evert Lloyd
3 ....Hana Mandlikova
4 ....Pam Shriver
5 ....Wendy Turnbull
6 ....Manuela Maleeva
7 ....Helena Sukova
8 ....Claudia Kohde-Kilsch
9 ...Zina Garrison
10...Kathy Jordan

WTA Computer Year-End Top 10 (Cont.)
WOMEN (CONT.)

1985
1 ....Martina Navratilova
2 ....Chris Evert Lloyd
3 ....Hana Mandlikova
4 ....Pam Shriver
5 ....Claudia Kohde-
    Kilsch
6 ....Steffi Graf
7 ....Manuela Maleeva
8 ....Zina Garrison
9 ....Helena Sukova
10...Bonnie Gadusek

1986
1 ....Martina Navratilova
2 ....Chris Evert Lloyd
3 ....Pam Shriver
4 ....Hana Mandlikova
5 ....Helena Sukova
6 ....Pam Shriver
7 ....Claudia Kohde-
    Kilsch
8 ....Manuela Maleeva
9 ....Kathy Rinaldi
10...Gabriela Sabatini

1987
1 ....Steffi Graf
2 ....Martina Navratilova
3 ....Chris Evert
4 ....Pam Shriver
5 ....Hana Mandlikova
6 ....Gabriela Sabatini
7 ....Helena Sukova
8 ....Manuela Maleeva
9 ....Zina Garrison
10...Claudia Kohde-
    Kilsch

1988
1 ....Steffi Graf
2 ....Martina Navratilova
3 ....Chris Evert
4 ....Gabriela Sabatini
5 ....Pam Shriver
6 ....Manuela Maleeva-
    Fragniere
7 ....Natalia Zvereva
8 ....Helena Sukova
9 ....Zina Garrison
10...Barbara Potter

1989
1 ....Steffi Graf
2 ....Martina Navratilova
3 ....Gabriela Sabatini
4 ....Zina Garrison
5 ....A.S. Vicario
6 ....Monica Seles
7 ....Conchita Martinez
8 ....Helena Sukova
9 ....Manuela Maleeva-
    Fragniere
10...Chris Evert*

1990
1 ....Steffi Graf
2 ....Monica Seles
3 ....Martina Navratilova
4 ....Mary Joe Fernandez
5 ....Gabriela Sabatini
6 ....Katerina Maleeva
7 ....A.S. Vicario
8 ....Jennifer Capriati
9 ....M. Maleeva-Fragniere
10...Zina Garrison

1991
1 ....Monica Seles
2 ....Steffi Graf
3 ....Gabriela Sabatini
4 ....Martina Navratilova
5 ....Arantxa Sánchez
    Vicario
6 ....Jennifer Capriati
7 ....Jana Novotna
8 ....Mary Joe Fernandez
9 ....Conchita Martinez
10...M. Maleeva-Fragniere

1992
1 ....Monica Seles
2 ....Steffi Graf
3 ....Gabriela Sabatini
4 ....Arantxa Sánchez
    Vicario
5 ....Martina Navratilova
6 ....Mary Joe Fernandez
7 ....Jennifer Capriati
8 ....Conchita Martinez
9 ....M. Maleeva-Fragniere
10 ..Jana Novotna

1993
1 ....Steffi Graf
2 ....Arantxa Sánchez
    Vicario
3 ....Martina Navratilova
4 ....Conchita Martinez
5 ....Gabriela Sabatini
6 ....Jana Novotna
7 ....Mary Joe Fernandez
8 ....Monica Seles
9 ....Jennifer Capriati
10 ..Anke Huber

1994
1 ....Steffi Graf
2 ....Arantxa Sánchez
    Vicario
3 ....Conchita Martinez
4 ....Jana Novotna
5 ....Mary Pierce
6 ....Lindsay Davenport
7 ....Gabriela Sabatini
8 ....Martina Navratilova
9 ....Kimiko Date
10 ..Natasha Zvereva

1995
1 ....Steffi Graf (co-No. 1)
1 ....Monica Seles
    (co-No. 1)
2 ....Conchita Martinez
3 ....A. S.Vicario
4 ....Kimiko Date
5 ....Mary Pierce
6 ....Magdalena Maleeva
7 ....Gabriela Sabatini
8 ....Mary Joe Fernandez
9 ....Iva Majoli
10 ..Anke Huber

1996
1 ....Steffi Graf
2 ....Monica Seles
3 ....Jana Novotna
4 ....Lindsay Davenport
5 ....Martina Hingis
6 ....Stephanie de Ville
7 ....Tamarine
    Tanasugarn
8 ....Anke Huber
9 ....Conchita Martinez
10 ..Julie Halard-
    Decugis

1997
1 ....Martina Hingis
2 ....Jana Novotna
3 ....Lindsay Davenport
4 ....Amanda Coetzer
5 ....Monica Seles
6 ....Iva Majoli
7 ....Mary Pierce
8 ....Irina Spirlea
9 ....Arantxa Sánchez
    Vicario
10...Mary Joe Fernandez

1998
1 ....Lindsay Davenport
2 ....Martina Hingis
3 ....Jana Novotna
4 ....A.S. Vicario
5 ....Venus Williams
6 ....Monica Seles
7 ....Mary Pierce
8 ....Conchita Martinez
9 ....Steffi Graf
10...Nathalie Tauziat

1999
1 ....Martina Hingis
2 ....Lindsay Davenport
3 ....Venus Williams
4 ....Serena Williams
5 ....Mary Pierce
6 ....Monica Seles
7 ....Nathalie Tauziat
8 ....Barbara Schett
9 ....J. Halard-Decugis
10 ..Amelie Mauresmo

2000
1 ....Martina Hingis
2 ....Lindsay Davenport
3 ....Venus Williams
4 ....Monica Seles
5 ....Conchita Martinez
6 ....Serena Williams
7 ....Mary Pierce
8 ....Anna Kournikova
9 ....Arantxa
    Sánchez Vicario
10 ..Nathalie Tauziat

2001
1 ....Lindsay Davenport
2 ....Jennifer Capriati
3 ....Venus Williams
4 ....Martina Hingis
5 ....Kim Clijsters
6 ....Serena Williams
7 ....Justine Henin
8 ....Jelena Dokic
9 ....Amelie Mauresmo
10 ..Monica Seles

*When Chris Evert announced her retirement at the 1989 United States Open, she was ranked fourth in the world. That was her last official series tournament.

Prize Money

Top 25 Men's Career Prize Money Leaders

Note: From arrival of Open tennis in 1968 through October 7, 2002.

	Earnings ($)
Pete Sampras	43,280,489
Andre Agassi	25,111,976
Boris Becker	25,080,956
Yevgeny Kafelnikov	22,334,975
Ivan Lendl	21,262,417
Stefan Edberg	20,630,941
Goran Ivanisevic	19,748,638
Michael Chang	19,067,357
Jim Courier	14,033,132
Gustavo Kuerten	13,337,349
Michael Stich	12,590,152
John McEnroe	12,539,622
Thomas Muster	12,224,410
Sergi Bruguera	11,632,199
Patrick Rafter	11,103,311
Petr Korda	10,448,450
Richard Krajicek	9,977,484
Alex Corretja	9,778,739
Thomas Enqvist	9,771,370
Marcelo Rios	9,327,981
Wayne Ferreira	9,227,992
Jonas Bjorkman	9,032,385
Jimmy Connors	8,641,040
Todd Woodbridge	8,634,649
Lleyton Hewitt	8,373,684

Top 25 Women's Career Prize Money Leaders

Note: From arrival of Open tennis in 1968 through October 1, 2002.

	Earnings ($)
Steffi Graf	21,895,277
Martina Navratilova	20,527,874
Martina Hingis	17,923,100
Arantxa Sánchez Vicario	16,847,432
Lindsay Davenport	14,419,603
Monica Seles	14,375,832
Venus Williams	11,363,098
Jana Novotna	11,249,134
Conchita Martinez	10,055,570
Serena Williams	9,382,150
Chris Evert	8,896,195
Gabriela Sabatini	8,785,850
Natasha Zvereva	7,784,503
Nathalie Tauziat	6,645,660
Mary Pierce	6,451,861
Helena Sukova	6,391,245
Jennifer Capriati	6,157,303
Pam Shriver	5,460,566
Mary Joe Fernandez	5,258,471
Amanda Coetzer	5,123,341
Anke Huber	4,768,292
Gigi Fernandez	4,681,906
Zina Garrison Jackson	4,590,816
Lisa Raymond	4,420,048
Iva Majoli	4,226,363

Big Return

In May 2001, the Detroit-born Corina Morariu learned she had leukemia. In early August 2002, she returned to the WTA tour. As she prepared for the U.S. Open, Morariu, 24, spoke to SI.

Recently I received a wild card to pay sinles at the Open. I could draw Venus Williams or Jennifer Capriati—it doesn't matter. I'm approaching this the way I approached my first singles match back, at the J.P. Morgan Chase tournament earlier in August. It was so incredible to be back! I couldn't be devastated even when I lost in the first round. This is a long process and a long journey.

There were symptoms months before I was even diagnosed in May 2001. I felt lethargic, and I had difficulty concentrating but I was in great shape and had been ranked Number 1 in doubles. So I told myself I was just tired from working out. Soon, though, I was getting nosebleeds five, six times a night and waking up with bruises all over. When my doctor told me I had leukemia, I finally went to the hospital. I was so sick I couldn't get out of bed to go to the bathroom, and they started chemotherapy immediately.

When I left the hospital a month later, the cancer was in remission. But because of infections I had to go back for three more stays. When I finally stepped back onto the court in January, I'd tire after five minutes. By April I could practice two hours a day, but it wasn't until June that I was putting in close to the work I once did.

At the Open I'll play doubles with Kimberly Po-Messerli. Tennis is now a new battle. I'm unranked, and I'm just getting back into it. I take chemo pills each day. There are frustrating moments out there, but I have the perspective of knowing where I was this time last year. There are worse things in life than losing tennis matches.

Men's Career Leaders—Singles Titles Won

The top tournament-winning men from the institution of Open tennis in 1968 through Sept. 30, 2002.

	W		W
Jimmy Connors	109	Thomas Muster	44
Ivan Lendl	94	Stefan Edberg	41
John McEnroe	77	Stan Smith	39
Pete Sampras	64	Michael Chang	34
Bjorn Borg	62	Arthur Ashe	33
Guillermo Vilas	62	Mats Wilander	33
Ilie Nastase	57	John Newcombe	32
Andre Agassi	53	Manuel Orantes	32
Boris Becker	49	Ken Rosewall	32
Rod Laver	47	Tom Okker	31

Women's Career Leaders—Singles Titles Won

The top tournament-winning women from the institution of Open tennis in 1968 through Sept. 30, 2002.

	W		W
Martina Navratilova	167	Lindsay Davenport	36
Chris Evert	157	Tracy Austin	29
Steffi Graf	108	Arantxa Sánchez Vicario	29
Evonne Goolagong Cawley	88	Hana Mandlikova	27
Margaret Smith Court	79	Gabriela Sabatini	27
Billie Jean King	67	Venus Williams	27
Virginia Wade	55	Nancy Richey	25
Monica Seles	53	Jana Novotna	24
Martina Hingis	40	Kerry Melville Reid	22
Conchita Martinez	32		

Two tied with 21.

Annual ATP/WTA Champions

Men—ATP Tour World Championship

Year	Player	Year	Player
1970	Stan Smith	1986 (Dec)	Ivan Lendl
1971	Ilie Nastase	1987	Ivan Lendl
1972	Ilie Nastase	1988	Boris Becker
1973	Ilie Nastase	1989	Stefan Edberg
1974	Guillermo Vilas	1990	Andre Agassi
1975	Ilie Nastase	1991	Pete Sampras
1976	Manuel Orantes	1992	Boris Becker
1977	Not held	1993	Michael Stich
1978	Jimmy Connors	1994	Pete Sampras
1979	John McEnroe	1995	Boris Becker
1980	Bjorn Borg	1996	Pete Sampras
1981	Bjorn Borg	1997	Pete Sampras
1982	Ivan Lendl	1998	Alex Corretja
1983	Ivan Lendl	1999	Pete Sampras
1984	John McEnroe	2000	Gustavo Kuerten
1985	John McEnroe	2001	Lleyton Hewitt
1986 (Jan)	Ivan Lendl		

Note: Event held twice in 1986. *Since 1984 the final has been best-of-five sets.

Women—WTA Tour Championship

Year	Player	Year	Player
1972	Chris Evert	1987	Steffi Graf
1973	Chris Evert	1988	Gabriela Sabatini
1974	Evonne Goolagong	1989	Steffi Graf
1975	Chris Evert	1990	Monica Seles
1976	Evonne Goolagong Cawley	1991	Monica Seles
1977	Chris Evert	1992	Monica Seles
1978	Martina Navratilova	1993	Steffi Graf
1979	Martina Navratilova	1994	Gabriela Sabatini
1980	Tracy Austin	1995	Steffi Graf
1981	Martina Navratilova	1996	Steffi Graf
1982	Sylvia Hanika	1997	Jana Novotna
1983	Martina Navratilova	1998	Martina Hingis
1984*	Martina Navratilova	1999	Lindsay Davenport
1985	Martina Navratilova	2000	Martina Hingis
1986 (Mar)	Martina Navratilova	2001	Serena Williams
1986 (Nov)	Martina Navratilova		

YET ANOTHER SIGN OF THE APOCALYPSE

Damir Dokic, tennis player Jelena Dokic's father, whose pattern of drunken and abusive behavior has led to his being banned from numerous events, is the pitchman in a series of ads for automaker and event sponsor Kia to be aired Down Under during the Australian Open.

Pauline Betz Addie (1965)
George T. Adee (1964)
Fred B. Alexander (1961)
Wilmer L. Allison (1963)
Manuel Alonso (1977)
Malcolm Anderson (2000)
Arthur Ashe (1985)
Juliette Atkinson (1974)
H.W. Bunny Austin (1997)
Tracy Austin (1992)
Lawrence A. Baker Sr. (1975)
Maud Barger–Wallach (1958)
Angela Mortimer Barrett (1993)
Karl Behr (1969)
Bjorn Borg (1987)
Jean Borotra (1976)
Lesley Turner Bowrey (1997)
Maureen Connolly Brinker(1968)
John Bromwich (1984)
Norman Everard Brookes (1977)
Mary K. Browne (1957)
Jacques Brugnon (1976)
J. Donald Budge (1964)
Maria E. Bueno (1978)
May Sutton Bundy (1956)
Mabel E. Cahill (1976)
Rosie Casals (1996)
Oliver S. Campbell (1955)
Malcolm Chace (1961)
Dorothea Douglass
    Chambers (1981)
Philippe Chatrier (1992)
Louise Brough Clapp (1967)
Clarence Clark (1983)
Joseph S. Clark (1955)
William J. Clothier (1956)
Henri Cochet (1976)
Arthur W. (Bud) Collins Jr. (1994)
Jimmy Connors (1998)
Ashley Cooper (1991)
Margaret Smith Court (1979)
Gottfried von Cramm (1977)
Jack Crawford (1979)
Joseph F. Cullman III (1990)
Allison Danzig (1968)
Sarah Palfrey Danzig (1963)
Herman David (1998)
Dwight F. Davis (1956)
Charlotte Dod (1983)
John H. Doeg (1962)
Lawrence Doherty (1980)
Reginald Doherty (1980)
Jaroslav Drobny (1983)
Margaret Osborne duPont
    (1967)

James Dwight (1955)
Roy Emerson (1982)
Pierre Etchebaster (1978)
Chris Evert (1995)
Robert Falkenburg (1974)
Neale Fraser (1984)
Shirley Fry-Irvin (1970)
Charles S. Garland (1969)
Althea Gibson (1971)
Kathleen McKane Godfree
    (1978)
Richard A. Gonzales (1968)
Evonne Goolagong Cawley
    (1988)
Bryan M. Grant Jr. (1972)
David Gray (1985)
Clarence Griffin (1970)
King Gustaf V of Sweden
    (1980)
Harold H. Hackett (1961)
Ellen Forde Hansell (1965)
Darlene R. Hard (1973)
Doris J. Hart (1969)
Gladys M. Heldman (1979)
W.E. (Slew) Hester Jr. (1981)
Bob Hewitt (1992)
Lew Hoad (1980)
Harry Hopman (1978)
Fred Hovey (1974)
Joseph R. Hunt (1966)
Lamar Hunt (1993)
Francis T. Hunter (1961)
Helen Hull Jacobs (1962)
William Johnston (1958)
Ann Haydon Jones (1985)
Perry Jones (1970)
Robert Kelleher (2000)
Billie Jean King (1987)
Jan Kodes (1990)
John A. Kramer (1968)
Rene Lacoste (1976)
Al Laney (1979)
William A. Larned (1956)
Arthur D. Larsen (1969)
Rod G. Laver (1981)
Ivan Lendl (2001)
Suzanne Lenglen (1978)
Dorothy Round Little (1986)
George M. Lott Jr. (1964)
Gene Mako (1973)
Molla Bjurstedt Mallory (1958)
Hana Mandlikova (1994)
Alice Marble (1964)
Alastair B. Martin (1973)
Dan Maskell (1996)

William McChesney Martin (1982)
John McEnroe (1999)
Ken McGregor (1999)
Chuck McKinley (1986)
Maurice McLoughlin (1957)
Frew McMillan (1992)
W. Donald McNeill (1965)
Elisabeth H. Moore (1971)
Gardnar Mulloy (1972)
R. Lindley Murray (1958)
Julian S. Myrick (1963)
Ilie Nastase (1991)
Martina Navratilova (2000)
John D. Newcombe (1986)
Arthur C. Nielsen Sr (1971)
Alex Olmedo (1987)
Rafael Osuna (1979)
Mary Ewing Outerbridge (1981)
Frank A. Parker (1966)
Gerald Patterson (1989)
Budge Patty (1977)
Theodore R. Pell (1966)
Fred Perry (1975)
Tom Pettitt (1982)
Nicola Pietrangeli (1986)
Adrian Quist (1984)
Dennis Ralston (1987)
Ernest Renshaw (1983)
William Renshaw (1983)
Vincent Richards (1961)
Bobby Riggs (1967)
Helen Wills Moody Roark
    (1959)
Anthony D. Roche (1986)
Ellen C. Roosevelt (1975)
Mervyn Rose (2001)
Ken Rosewall (1980)
Elizabeth Ryan (1972)
Manuel Santana (1984)
Richard Savitt (1976)
Frederick R. Schroeder (1966)
Eleonora Sears (1968)
Richard D. Sears (1955)
Frank Sedgman (1979)
Pancho Segura (1984)
Vic Seixas Jr. (1971)
Francis X. Shields (1964)
Betty Nuthall Shoemaker (1977)
Pam Shriver (2002)
Henry W. Slocum Jr. (1955)
Stan Smith (1987)
Fred Stolle (1985)
William F. Talbert (1967)
Bill Tilden (1959)
Lance Tingay (1982)

Ted Tinling (1986)
Bertha Townsend Toulmin
  (1974)
Tony Trabert (1970)
James H. Van Alen (1965)
John Van Ryn (1963)
Guillermo Vilas (1991)
Ellsworth Vines (1962)
Virginia Wade (1989)
Marie Wagner (1969)

Holcombe Ward (1956)
Watson Washburn (1965)
Malcolm D. Whitman (1955)
Hazel Hotchkiss Wightman
  (1957)
Mats Wilander (2002)
Anthony Wilding (1978)
Richard Norris Williams II
  (1957)

Major Walter Clopton Wingfield
  (1997)
Sidney B. Wood (1964)
Robert D. Wrenn (1955)
Beals C. Wright (1956)

Note: Years in parentheses are dates of induction.

Court Drama

Almost from the moment Lisa Bonder, splashed onto the pro tennis circuit in 1982 as a 16-year-old, she made headlines. In '83 she beat Chris Evert Lloyd in the semis of a tournament in Tokyo, leading Evert to gush, "She's lethal from the baseline." A year later Bonder finishded No. 16 in the world (the highest year-end ranking of her career), and she soon developed a cult following in Japan, where she modeled clothes and drew adoring fans. "She was very good at a young age," said Carling Bassett-Seguso, another tennis starlet of that era. "She was also a dominant personality who was always out for an angle."

That became clear after Bonder, 36, filed suit in January 2002 in L.A. Superior Court seeking $324,000 a month in child support from her ex-husband, billionaire financier Kirk Kerkorian. The $3.8-million-a-year request, a California record for a child-support case, was made on behalf of the couple's three-year-old daughter, Kira, and was abcked up with a list of monthly expenses that included $1,500 to care for indoor plants and $14,000 for parties and play dates. On January 18, 2002, Kerkorian, 84, whose net worth has been estimated at $6.4 billion, fired back with a breach-of-contract suit, saying Bonder had breached confiden-tiality papers she'd signed at the time of their 1999 divorce.

The couple signed a lot of papers that year. Even by standards of the rich and famous, theirs was a dismal contract: They agreed beforehand to divorce after one month. Bonder's court papers say they married to confer "dignity and respect" on their relationship and on Kira, who was five months old at the time. Bonder also agreed never to seek spousal support. "The purpose of child support is not to pay for the life of the mother," said Dan Jaffe, a divorce lawyer in L.A. "There's no cap on child support in California, but I can't see this going into the stratosphere suggested in Bonder's demands. There's nothing in the law that says a child must live on a 10-acre estate just because the father does."

Bonder wouldn't comment on the case, but whatever the outcome, she was playing for far higher stakes in the courtroom than she did on the courts. Though she made close to $500,000 before retiring in 1989, that sum didn't fulfill her aspirations. "As far as long-term goals," she told New Jersey's The Record in '86, "I want to become financially secure so that when I leave the sport I won't have to depend on anyone else."

Golf

TIM CLARY/AFP

**Masters and U.S.
Open champ
Tiger Woods**

Slam, Interrupted

Tiger Woods's quest to win all four majors in one year ended in a driving rainstorm at Muirfield

BY MARK BEECH

IT WAS THE year of the Grand Slam that wasn't, when Tiger Woods—who would never admit it—set out to capture a prize he felt he had already earned. He had won the 2001 Masters to complete a historic sweep begun the year before, with his victories in the U.S. and British Opens and the PGA Championship. But because he didn't win all four titles in the same calendar year, his feat wasn't unanimously accepted as a Grand Slam, a fact he seemed resigned to, if not especially thrilled with. "I've won four majors in a row before," he said. "It'd be great to do it in one year, 'cause it'd be different."

The 26-year old Woods began his quest at Augusta National in April, methodically winning his third Masters title, and seventh major championship, with a 12-under 276. As he wore down the rest of the field nothing seemed to bother him, not the rain, not the world-class competition and certainly not a course that seemed to have been redesigned to take away some of Woods's edge: Nine of the 18 tee boxes had been moved back, and

new trees had been planted where previously there had been none. "You want to Tiger-proof a course?" Earl Woods said after his son's victory. "Move the tee box to the ladies' tee. Eliminate the rough completely. Cut the greens to 8 or 9 [on the stimpmeter]. And I'll guarantee you Tiger won't win. But this course plays right into his hands."

It certainly did on Saturday, when he arose at 4:30 a.m. to finish Friday's round, which had been interrupted by a rain delay. He began his early morning trailing Vijay Singh by six shots, but after running through 26 holes in eight under par, he went back to bed that evening tied for the lead at 11 under with Retief Goosen. On Sunday, he put everyone away, besting Goosen by three strokes.

"For years, talk of a Grand Slam has been laughable, ridiculed," said Brad Faxon. "Now it's something you've got to think about. Tiger has won four majors in a row and the first one this year. Nothing is out of his reach. Nobody's been able to handle the pressure like this guy. I'm a believer: He's

Balanced Beem: The unsung Texan held off Woods at the PGA.

better than anybody who's ever played the game."

Woods won more converts in June, when he defeated Phil Mickelson—who now officially owns the dubious distinction of being the best player never to have won a major—by three strokes at the U.S. Open. The victory gave Tiger seven of the previous 11 major championships. Playing before a loud, brazen crowd at New York's Bethpage State Park, Woods led wire-to-wire, with hardly a hint of drama. He was the only player to finish the tournament under par. "The guys chasing him don't have experience winning majors," said Jack Nicklaus. "Tiger's dominating. That makes a big difference."

The dominance came to a crashing halt for Woods in the third round of the British Open in July, when whipping winds and ugly weather made him seem human, if only for a short while. He began that Saturday only two strokes off the lead, but he teed off at the same time as an enormous black cloud gathered over Muirfield. With it came 30-mph winds, a 40° windchill and a driving rain. "I was just hoping to get in alive," said Ian Garbutt of England. Woods spent the day mired in high rough and bunkers, and shot a 42 through the first nine. When he birdied 17, he doffed his cap and took a bow. He finished with an 81, his worst round as a professional. Even a final-round 65 helped him finish no better than 28th place. "I tried all the way around," he said after Saturday's round. "I don't bag it. I tried on each and every shot, and that's the best I *could* have shot. I tried. And unfortunately, it wasn't meant to be."

Woods' collapse left the door open for Ernie Els of South Africa, who managed to wobble through it. Up a stroke after 15 on Sunday, he was down a stroke after an ago-nizing double bogey on 16, and then he finished birdie, par to force a four-way playoff with Australia's Steve Elkington and Stuart Appleby and Thomas Levet of France. Els has won two majors, both U.S. Opens, but the last had come five years ago. After his shaky finish in regulation, he recovered to win the fifth hole of the sudden-death playoff and earn the claret jug. "I still play like a man with a lot of talent who can win," he said. "But I also play pretty poorly now and then."

At Muirfield, Woods was beaten by the weather and an established champion, but at the PGA Championship in Chaska, Minn., he was beaten by Rich Beem in a thriller. A formerly anonymous tour pro from El Paso, Texas, Beem did what nobody else had ever done: He beat Woods in a major championship by a shot. Tiger started the final round trailing the leader, Justin Leonard, by five strokes. Beem, who was playing with Leonard on Sunday, was three shots off the lead. Ten holes into the final round, Beem stood at 8-under, a stroke ahead of Woods

TODD BIGELOW/AURORA

was that the early matches featured European stars Colin Montgomerie, Bernhard Langer and Padraig Harrington schooling the U.S. team's second string of Scott Hoch, Hal Sutton and Mark Calcavecchia, respectively. All of those matches were decided before the 15th hole. By the time Woods and Davis Love III were in the middle of their rounds, the Europeans had a lead they would never surrender. "Any superstar wants to take the last shot," Strange tried to explain. Woods offered his own understated assessment. "It was frustrating."

Consistency was the theme of this year's LPGA Tour. The major championships went to Annika Sorenstam (Nabisco), Se Ri Pak (LPGA), Juli Inkster (U.S. Open) and Karrie Webb (British Open). That foursome has combined to win 16 of the last 19 majors, with Sorenstam taking two, Inkster and Pak winning four each, and Webb seizing a whopping six. As for the rest of the tour, Sorenstam dominated it unequivocally. She became the first woman to have back-to-back seasons of eight or more victories since Nancy Lopez in 1978 and '79, and she added a third-place finish at the LPGA and a second-place finish at the U.S. Open to her long list of accomplishments—though she did miss a cut, at the British Open, for the first time in 74 tournaments.

Surprisingly, it was Sorenstam's failure to win a match that sent the U.S. to victory in the Solheim Cup, held at Interlachen Country Club in Edina, Minn., in September. On the final day of the event, with the Americans trailing by two points after two days of pairs competitions, Wendy Ward drew a singles match against Sorenstam. Ward played her Swedish rival to an 18-hole standoff, keying a 8½–3½ singles rout of the Europeans, and a 15½-12½ U.S. victory. "I knew it was going to be a tough match," said Ward, a rookie at the Solheim Cup. "But I wasn't that nervous. I knew Annika could be beaten."

It's just that, like Woods, she isn't beaten very often.

and two up on Leonard. After Beem eagled the 11th hole, it was a two-man fight to the finish, and, against type, Tiger blinked first. He parred 12, but bogeyed 13 and 14. Beem was in command.

Woods did not go quietly, though, stringing together birdies on 15, 16, 17 and 18. It was vintage stuff, and when he stopped in the scorer's trailer, he was the low man in at nine under par. Beem still held a two-stroke lead, and calmly played his way home, finishing with a harmless bogey on 18. "Maybe for Tiger this gets old," he said. "But I'm going to soak in this forever."

Golf's next big show came at the Ryder Cup in Sutton Coldfield, England, where the U.S. surrendered the trophy to an inspired team from Europe. The loss was especially frustrating for the Americans because their team had entered the final day of match-play at the Belfry tied with Europe at 8–8. U.S. captain Curtis Strange had back-loaded his lineup, putting his best golfers last. Europe's captain, Sam Torrance, had done the opposite with his roster, placing his best golfers first. The result

Men's Majors

The Masters
Augusta National GC (par 72; 7,270 yds); Augusta, GA, April 11–14

Player	Score	Earnings ($)
Tiger Woods	70-69-66-71—276	1,008,000
Retief Goosen	69-67-69-74—279	604,800
Phil Mickelson	69-72-68-71—280	380,800
Jose Maria Olazabal	70-69-71-71—281	268,800
Ernie Els	70-67-72-73—282	212,800
Padraig Harrington	69-70-72-71—282	212,800
Vijay Singh	70-65-72-76—283	187,600
Sergio Garcia	68-71-70-75—284	173,600
Angel Cabrera	68-71-73-73—285	151,200
Miguel Angel Jiminez	70-71-74-70—285	151,200
Adam Scott	71-72-72-70—285	151,200
Chris DiMarco	70-71-72-73—286	123,200
Brad Faxon	71-75-69-71—286	123,200
Thomas Bjorn	74-67-70-76—287	98,000
Nick Faldo	75-67-73-72—287	98,000
Davis Love III	67-75-74-71—287	98,000
Shigeki Maruyama	75-72-73-67—287	98,000
Colin Montgomerie	75-71-70-71—287	98,000
Paul McGinley	72-74-71-71—288	81,200
Darren Clarke	70-74-73-72—289	65,240
Jerry Kelly	72-74-71-72—289	65,240
Justin Leonard	70-75-74-70—289	65,240
Nick Price	70-76-70-73—289	65,240

U.S. Open
Bethpage State Park, Black Course (par 70; 7,214 yds); Farmingdale, NY, June 13–16

Player	Score	Earnings ($)
Tiger Woods	67-68-70-72—277	1,000,000
Phil Mickelson	70-73-67-70—280	585,000
Jeff Maggert	69-73-68-72—282	362,356
Sergio Garcia	68-74-67-74—283	252,546
Nick Faldo	70-76-66-73—285	182,882
Scott Hoch	71-75-70-69—285	182,882
Billy Mayfair	69-74-68-74—285	182,882
Tom Byrum	72-72-70-72—286	138,669
Padraig Harrington	70-68-73-75—286	138,669
Nick Price	72-75-69-70—286	138,669
Peter Lonard	73-74-73-67—287	119,357
Robert Allenby	74-70-67-77—288	102,338
Justin Leonard	73-71-68-76—288	102,338
Jay Haas	73-73-70-72—288	102,338
Dudley Hart	69-76-70-73—288	102,338
Shigeki Maruyama	76-67-73-73—289	86,372
Steve Stricker	72-77-69-71—289	86,372
Luke Donald	76-72-70-72—290	68,995
Steve Flesch	72-72-75-71—290	68,995
Charles Howell III	71-74-70-75—290	68,995
Thomas Levet	71-77-70-72—290	68,995
Mark O'Meara	76-70-69-75—290	68,995
Craig Stadler	74-72-70-74—290	68,995

British Open
Muirfield Golf Links (par 71; 7,034 yds); Ailsa, Scotland, July 18–21

Player	Score	Earnings ($)
Ernie Els*	70-66-72-70—278	1,106,140
Stuart Appleby	73-70-70-65—278	452,990
Steve Elkington	73-70-70-65—278	452,990
Thomas Levet	72-66-74-66—278	452,990
Gary Evans	72-68-74-65—279	221,228
Padraig Harrington	69-67-76-67—279	221,228
Shigeki Maruyama	68-68-75-68—279	221,228
Thomas Bjorn	68-70-73-69—280	122,465
Sergio Garcia	71-69-71-69—280	122,465
Retief Goosen	71-68-74-67—280	122,465
Soren Hansen	68-69-73-70—280	122,465
Scott Hoch	74-69-71-66—280	122,465
Peter O'Malley	72-68-75-65—280	122,465
Justin Leonard	71-72-68-70—281	78,614
Peter Lonard	72-72-68-69—281	78,614
Davis Love III	71-72-71-67—281	78,614
Nick Price	68-70-75-68—281	78,614
Bob Estes	71-70-73-68—282	64,788
Scott McCarron	71-68-72-71—282	64,788
Greg Norman	71-72-71-68—282	64,788
Duffy Waldorf	67-69-77-69—282	64,788

*Won on first sudden-death hole after four-hole playoff left him tied with Thomas Levet.

PGA Championship
Hazeltine National GC (par 72; 7,360 yds); Chaska, MN, August 15–18

Player	Score	Earnings ($)
Rich Beem	72-66-72-68—278	990,000
Tiger Woods	71-69-72-67—279	594,000
Chris Riley	71-70-72-70—283	374,000
Fred Funk	68-70-73-73—284	235,000
Justin Leonard	72-66-69-77—284	235,000
Rocco Mediate	72-73-70-70—285	185,000
Mark Calcavecchia	70-68-74-74—286	172,000
Vijay Singh	71-74-74-68—287	159,000
Jim Furyk	68-73-76-71—288	149,000
Robert Allenby	76-66-77-70—289	110,714
Stewart Cink	74-74-72-69—289	110,714
Jose Coceres	72-71-72-74—289	110,714
Pierre Fulke	72-68-78-71—289	110,714
Sergio Garcia	75-73-73-68—289	110,714
Ricardo Gonzalez	74-73-71-71—289	110,714
Steve Lowery	71-71-73-74—289	110,714
Stuart Appleby	73-74-74-69—290	72,000
Steve Flesch	72-74-73-71—290	72,000
Padraig Harrington	71-73-74-72—290	72,000
Charles Howell III	72-69-80-69—290	72,000
Peter Lonard	69-73-75-73—290	72,000

Late 2001 PGA Tour Events

Tournament	Final Round	Winner	Score/ Under Par	Earnings ($)
National Car Rental Classic	Oct 21	Jose Coceres	265/–23	666,000
The Buick Challenge	Oct 28	Chris DiMarco	267/–21	612,000
The Tour Championship	Nov 4	Mike Weir	270/–14	900,000
Southern Farm Bureau Classic	Nov 4	Cameron Beckman	269/–19	432,000
Franklin Templeton Shootout	Nov 11	Brad Faxon/Scott McCarron	183/–33	225,000 each
EMC World Cup	Nov 18	Ernie Els/Retief Goosen	264/–24	500,000 each
The Skins Game	Nov 25	Greg Norman	18 skins	1,000,000
Hyundai Team Matches	Dec 9	Mark Calcavecchia/Fred Couples	1-up	100,000 each
Williams World Challenge	Dec 16	Tiger Woods	273/–15	1,000,000

2002 PGA Tour Events

Tournament	Final Round	Winner	Score/ Under Par	Earnings ($)
Mercedes Championships	Jan 6	Sergio Garcia*	274/–18	720,000
Sony Open in Hawaii	Jan 13	Jerry Kelly	266/–14	720,000
Bob Hope Chrysler Classic	Jan 20	Phil Mickelson*	330/–30	720,000
Phoenix Open	Jan 27	Chris DiMarco	267/–17	720,000
AT&T Pebble Beach National Pro-Am	Feb 3	Matt Gogel	274/–14	720,000
Buick Invitational	Feb 10	Jose Maria Olazabal	275/–13	648,000
Nissan Open	Feb 17	Len Mattiace	269/–15	666,000
WGC: Accenture Match Play Champ.	Feb 24	Kevin Sutherland	1-up	1,000,000
Touchstone Energy Tucson Open	Feb 24	Ian Leggett	268/–20	540,000
Genuity Championship	Mar 3	Ernie Els	271/–17	846,000
Honda Classic	Mar 10	Matt Kuchar	269/–19	630,000
Bay Hill Invitational	Mar 17	Tiger Woods	275/–13	720,000
The Players Championship	Mar 24	Craig Perks	280/–18	1,080,000
Shell Houston Open	Mar 31	Vijay Singh	266/–22	720,000
BellSouth Classic	Apr 7	Retief Goosen	272/–16	684,000
The Masters	Apr 14	Tiger Woods	276/–12	1,008,000
Worldcom Classic	Apr 21	Justin Leonard	270/–14	720,000
Greater Greensboro Chrysler Classic	Apr 28	Rocco Mediate	272/–16	684,000
Compaq Classic	May 5	K.J. Choi	271/–17	810,000
Verizon Byron Nelson Classic	May 12	Shigeki Maruyama	266/–14	864,000
The MasterCard Colonial	May 19	Nick Price	267/–13	774,000
The Memorial	May 26	Jim Furyk	274/–14	810,000
Kemper Insurance Open	June 2	Bob Estes	273/–11	648,000
Buick Classic	June 9	Chris Smith	272/–12	630,000
U.S. Open	June 16	Tiger Woods	277/–3	1,000,000
Canon Greater Hartford Open	June 23	Phil Mickelson	266/–14	720,000
FedEx St. Jude Classic	June 30	Len Mattiace	266/–18	684,000
Advil Western Open	July 7	Jerry Kelly	269/–19	720,000
Greater Milwaukee Open	July 14	Jeff Sluman	261/–23	558,000
British Open	July 21	Ernie Els*	278/–6	1,106,140
B.C. Open	July 21	Spike McRoy	269/–19	378,000
John Deere Classic	July 28	J.P. Hayes	262/–22	540,000
The International	Aug 4	Rich Beem	+44‡	810,000
Buick Open	Aug 11	Tiger Woods	271/–17	594,000
PGA Championship	Aug 18	Rich Beem	278/–10	990,000
WGC: NEC Invitational	Aug 25	Craig Perry	268/–16	1,000,000
Reno-Tahoe Open	Aug 25	Chris Riley*	271/–17	540,000
Air Canada Championship	Sept 1	Gene Sauers	269/–15	630,000
Bell Canadian Open	Sept 8	John Rollins*	272/–16	720,000
SEI Pennsylvania Classic	Sept 15	Dan Forsman	270/–14	594,000
WGC: American Express Champ.	Sept 22	Tiger Woods	263/–25	1,000,000
Tampa Bay Classic	Sept 22	K.J. Choi	267/–17	468,000
Valero Texas Open	Sept 29	Loren Roberts	261/–19	630,000
Michelob Championship	Oct 6	Charles Howell III	270/–14	666,000
Invensys Classic	Oct 13	Phil Tataurangi	330/–29	900,000

* Won playoff. ‡ Revised Stableford scoring.

Kraft Nabisco Championship
Mission Hills CC; Rancho Mirage, CA
(par 72; 6,520 yds) March 28–31

layer	Score	Earnings ($)
Annika Sorenstam	70-71-71-68—280	225,000
Liselotte Neumann	69-70-73-69—281	136,987
Christie Kerr	74-70-70-68—282	88,125
Rosie Jones	72-69-72-69—282	88,125
Akiko Fukushima	73-76-68-66—283	56,220
Carin Koch	73-73-71-66—283	56,220
Karrie Webb	75-70-67-72—284	42,375
Lorena Ochoa	75-69-71-70—285	amateur
Grace Park	75-73-70-68—286	31,050
Se Ri Pak	74-71-71-70—286	31,050
Leta Lindley	72-72-72-70—286	31,050
Lorie Kane	73-72-70-71—286	31,050
Becky Iverson	71-74-68-73—286	31,050
Heather Bowie	75-71-72-69—287	21,900
Kris Tschetter	74-69-73-71—287	21,900
Beth Daniel	71-70-75-71—287	21,900
Vicki Goetze-Ackerman	74-73-68-72—287	21,900
Dorothy Delasin	72-73-69-73—287	21,900
Juli Inkster	73-76-71-68—288	18,222
Mhairi McKay	73-72-73-70—288	18,225

U.S. Women's Open
Prairie Dunes CC; Hutchinson, KA (par 70; 6,267 yds [Th, Fr]; 6,293 [Sa, Su]) July 4–7

Player	Score	Earnings ($)
Juli Inkster	67-72-71-66—276	535,000
Annika Sorenstam	70-69-69-70—278	315,000
Shani Waugh	67-73-71-72—283	202,568
Raquel Carriedo	75-71-72-66—284	141,219
Se Ri Pak	74-75-68-68—285	114,370
Mhairi McKay	70-75-71-70—286	101,421
Jennifer Rosales	73-72-74-68—287	78,016
Kelli Kuehne	70-76-72-69—287	78,016
Beth Daniel	71-76-71-69—287	78,016
Laura Diaz	67-72-77-71—287	78,016
Janice Moodie	71-72-71-73—287	78,016
Kelly Robbins	71-74-74-69—288	54,201
Joanne Morley	78-68-73-69—288	54,201
Rachel Teske	75-71-72-70—288	54,201
Stephanie Keever	72-71-73-72—288	54,201
Lynnette Brooky	73-73-69-73—288	54,201
Jill McGill	71-70-69-78—288	54,201
Grace Park	71-77-71-70—289	40,738
Donna Andrews	74-74-70-71—289	40,738
Beth Bauer	74-72-71-72—289	40,738
Lorie Kane	69-77-69-74—289	40,738

McDonald's LPGA Championship
DuPont CC; Wilmington, DE
(par 71; 6,408 yds) June 6–9

Player	Score	Earnings ($)
Se Ri Pak	71-70-68-70—279	225,000
Beth Daniel	67-70-68-77—282	136,987
Annika Sorenstam	70-76-73-65—284	99,375
Juli Inkster	69-75-70-71—285	69,375
Karrie Webb	68-71-72-74—285	69,375
Carin Koch	68-73-73-72—286	46,500
Michele Redman	74-69-70-73—286	46,500
Catriona Matthew	74-73-75-70—288	37,125
Kristi Albers	74-73-73-70—290	30,625
Michelle McGann	71-72-72-75—290	30,625
Meg Mallon	73-72-76-70—291	24,650
Karen Weiss	70-74-75-72—291	24,650
Kim Saiki	71-71-69-80—291	24,650
Kelli Kuehne	71-75-74-72—292	19,650
Rachel Teske	72-71-77-72—292	19,650
Natalie Gulbis	72-72-75-73—292	19,650
Grace Park	72-73-73-74—292	19,650
Akiko Fukushima	71-71-76-74—292	19,650
Barb Mucha	70-73-75-75—293	16,950
Laura Diaz	73-71-71-78—293	16,950

Weetabix Women's British Open
Turnberry GC; Ayrshire, Scotland
(par 72; 6,407 yds) August 8–11

Player	Score	Earnings ($)
Karrie Webb	66-71-70-66—273	236,383
Michelle Ellis	69-70-68-68—275	129,629
Paula Marti	69-68-69-69—275	129,629
Jeong Jang	73-69-66-69—277	64,528
Catrin Nilsmark	70-69-69-69—277	64,528
Candie Kung	65-71-71-70—277	64,528
Jennifer Rosales	69-70-65-73—277	64,528
Meg Mallon	69-71-68-70—278	38,380
Beth Bauer	70-67-70-71—278	38,380
Carin Koch	68-68-68-74—278	38,380
Sophie Gustafson	69-73-69-68—279	30,120
Se Ri Pak	67-72-69-71—279	30,120
Angela Stanford	69-70-69-72—280	25,290
Pat Hurst	69-70-69-72—280	25,290
Natalie Gulbis	69-70-67-74—280	25,290
Beth Daniel	73-68-68-74—283	21,884
Tina Barrett	67-70-70-76—283	21,884
Fiona Pike	72-73-67-72—284	18,453
Jean Bartholomew	71-72-72-69—284	18,453
Marine Monnet	71-70-70-73—284	18,453
Jane Geddes	71-69-70-74—284	18,453
Wendy Doolan	70-69-71-74—284	18,453
Rachel Teske	67-74-68-75—284	18,453

Late 2001 LPGA Tour Events

Tournament	Final Round	Winner	Score/ Under Par	Earnings ($)
Cisco World Ladies Match Play	Oct 28	Annika Sorenstam	1-up	144,000
Mizuno Classic	Nov 4	Annika Sorenstam	203/–13	162,000
Tyco/ADT Championship	Nov 18	Karrie Webb	279/–9	215,000
Hyundai Team Matches	Dec 9	Lorie Kane/Janice Moodie	5&4	100,000 each

2002 LPGA Tour Events

Tournament	Final Round	Winner	Score/ Under Par	Earnings ($)
Takefuji Classic	Mar 2	Annika Sorenstam*	196/–14	135,000
Ping Banner Health	Mar 17	Rachel Teske*	281/–7	150,000
Welch's/Circle K Championship	Mar 24	Laura Diaz	270/–18	120,000
Nabisco Championship	Mar 31	Annika Sorenstam	280/–8	225,000
The Office Depot	Apr 7	Se Ri Pak	209/–7	150,000
Longs Drugs Challenge	Apr 21	Cristie Kerr	280/–8	135,000
Chick-fil-A Charity Championship	May 5	Juli Inkster	132/–12	187,500
Aerus Electrolux USA Championship	May 12	Annika Sorenstam	271/–17	120,000
Corning Classic	May 26	Laura Diaz	274/–14	150,000
Kellog-Keebler Classic	June 2	Annika Sorenstam	195/–21	180,000
McDonald's LPGA Championship	June 9	Se Ri Pak	279/–5	225,000
Evian Masters	June 15	Annika Sorenstam	269/–19	315,000
Wegmans Rochester LPGA	June 23	Karrie Webb	276/–12	180,000
ShopRite LPGA Classic	June 30	Annika Sorenstam	201/–12	180,000
U.S. Women's Open	July 7	Juli Inkster	276/–4	535,000
Jamie Farr Kroger Classic	July 14	Rachel Teske	202/–14	150,000
Giant Eagle LPGA Classic	July 21	Mi Hyun Kim	270/–14	150,000
Sybase Big Apple Classic	July 28	Gloria Park*	270/–14	142,500
Wendy's Championship for Children	Aug 4	Mi Hyun kim	208/–8	150,000
Women's British Open	Aug 11	Karrie Webb	273/–15	236,383
Bank of Montreal Can. Wom. Open	Aug 18	Meg Mallon	284/–4	180,000
First Union Betsy King Classic	Aug 25	Se Ri Pak	267/–21	180,000
State Farm Classic	Sep 1	Patricia Meunier-Lebouc	270/–18	165,000
Williams Championship	Sep 8	Annika Sorenstam	199/–11	150,000
Safeway Classic	Sep 15	Annika Sorenstam	199/–17	150,000
Samsung World Championship	Oct 6	Annika Sorenstam	266/–22	162,000
Mobile Tournament of Championships	Oct 13	Se Ri Pak	268/–20	122,000

* Won sudden-death playoff.

Burning Question: Do Masters champions get to keep their green jackets?

Only for a year. When the winner returns to the course to defend his title, he is expected to return the green blazer to Augusta National, where it stays for good. The jacket is available to the champion whenever he visits but is not to leave the premises—the garments are even cleaned on the grounds. Multiple winners receive the same jacket with each victory. (That's why Tiger Woods asked for extra-roomy measurements when he won as a 21-year-old in 1997, figuring he would be slipping on the same blazer in future ceremonies as an older man.) This mirrors the policy for Augusta National members, who have been wearing some form of the green jacket since Masters founder Clifford Roberts purchased the first batch in bulk from Brooks Uniform Company of New York in 1937. "It's just a tradition that has evolved," says Masters publicist Glenn Greenspan of the coat's travel restrictions. "The champions guard the tradition as much as anyone."

With a few exceptions. The late Henry Picard, who won the tournament in 1938, for years had his jacket proudly hanging in his closet at home in Charleston, S.C. Gary Player also took his jacket home, to South Africa, after he won his first Masters title in 1961. When Roberts called Player to remind him of the jacket's no-travel tradition, Player told Roberts he'd have to come to South Africa and fetch the jacket himself. As a concession Player agreed not to ever wear the jacket, and he never has—not even to dinner in his own house.

Late 2001 Senior Tour Events

Tournament	Final Round	Winner	Score/ Under Par	Earnings ($)
SBC Championship	Oct 21	Larry Nelson	199/–17	210,000
Senior TOUR Championship	Oct 28	Bob Gilder	277/–11	440,000
Senior Slam	Nov 11	Allen Doyle	134/–10	300,000
Office Depot Father-Son Challenge	Dec 2	Raymond/Robert Floyd	124/–20	100,000 each
Hyundai Team Matches	Dec 9	Allen Doyle/Dana Quigley	1-up	100,000 each

2002 Senior Tour Events

Tournament	Final Round	Winner	Score/ Under Par	Earnings ($)
MasterCard Championship	Jan 20	Tom Kite	199/–17	258,000
Senior Skins Game	Jan 26	Hale Irwin	11 skins	450,000
Royal Caribbean Classic#	Feb 3	John Jacobs	133/–11	217,500
ACE Group Classic	Feb 10	Hale Irwin	200/–16	225,000
Verizon Classic	Feb 17	Doug Tewell	203/–10	225,000
Audi Senior Classic	Feb 24	Bruce Lietzke	208/–8	255,000
SBC Senior Classic	Mar 3	Tom Kite*	212/–4	210,000
Toshiba Senior Classic	Mar 10	Hale Irwin	196/–17	225,000
Siebel Classic	Mar 17	Dana Quigley	212/–4	210,000
Emerald Coast Classic#	Mar 31	Dave Eichelberger	130/–10	217,500
Liberty Mutual Legends of Golf	April 7	Doug Tewell	205/–11	308,000
Countrywide Tradition	April 28	Jim Thorpe*	277/–11	300,000
Bruno's Memorial Classic	May 5	Sammy Rachels*	201/–15	210,000
TD Waterhouse Championship#	May 12	Bruce Litzke	133/–11	240,000
Instinct Classic	May 19	Isao Aoki	201/–15	225,000
Farmers Charity	May 26	Jay Sigel	203/–13	225,000
NFL Golf Classic	June 2	James Mason	207/–9	195,000
Senior PGA Championship	June 9	Fuzzy Zoeller	278/–2	360,000
BellSouth Senior Classic at Opryland	June 16	Gil Morgan	202/–14	240,000
Greater Baltimore Classic	June 23	J.C. Snead	203/–13	217,500
U.S. Senior Open	June 30	Don Pooley*	274/–10	450,000
AT&T Canada Senior Open	July 7	Tom Jenkins	195/–18	240,000
Ford Senior Players Championship	July 14	Stewart Ginn	274/–14	375,000
SBC Senior Open	July 21	Bob Gilder*	204/–12	217,500
FleetBoston Classic	July 28	Bob Gilder*	203/–13	225,000
Lightpath Long Island Classic	Aug 4	Hubert Green*	199/–14	255,000
3M Championship	Aug 11	Hale Irwin	204/–12	262,500
Uniting Fore Care Classic	Aug 25	Morris Hatalsky	42‡	225,000
Allianz Championship	Sep 1	Bob Gilder	200/–13	277,500
Kroger Senior Classic	Sep 8	Bob Gilder*	200/–16	225,000
RJR Championship	Sep 15	Bruce Fleisher	191/–19	240,000
SAS Championship	Sep 22	Bruce Lietzke	202/–14	255,000
Turtle Bay Championship	Oct 6	Hale Irwin*	208/–8	225,000
Napa Championship	Oct 13	Tom Kite	204/–12	195,000

*Won playoff. #Shortened due to rain. ‡ Revised Stableford scoring.

THEY SAID IT

Sergio Garcia, Spanish golfer recalling the reaction that Arnold Palmer got from the gallery at the 2002 Masters: "Listening to the ovation they gave him on the first tee, I was getting—what do you call it?—chicken pox."

U.S. Amateur Results

Tournament	Final Round	Winner	Score	Runner-Up
Women's Amateur Public Links	June 23	Annie Thurman	6 & 5	Hwanhee Lee
Men's Amateur Public Links	July 20	Ryan Moore	10 & 9	Lee Williamson
Girls' Junior Amateur	July 27	In-Bee Park	4 & 3	J. Tangtiphaiboontana
Boys' Junior Amateur	July 27	Charlie Beljan	20 holes	Zac Reynolds
Women's Amateur	Aug 17	Becky Lucidi	3 & 2	Brandi Jackson
Men's Amateur	Aug 25	Ricky Barnes	2 & 1	Hunter Mahan
Men's Mid-Amateur	Sep 26	George Zahringer	3 & 2	Jerry Courville
Women's Mid-Amateur	Sep 26	Kathy Hartwiger	2-up	Ellen Port
Senior Men	Oct 3	Greg Reynolds	4 & 3	Mark Bemowski
Senior Women	Oct 10	Carol Semple Thompson	3 & 1	Barbara Berkmeyer

International Results

Tournament	Final Round	Winner	Score	Runner-Up
Curtis Cup	Aug 4	United States	11–7	GB/Ireland
Solheim Cup	Sep 22	United States	15½–12½	GB/Ireland
Ryder Cup	Sep 29	Europe	15½–12½	United States

PGA Tour Final 2001 Money Leaders

Name	Events	Best Finish	Scoring Average*	Money ($)
Tiger Woods	19	1 (5)	68.81	5,687,777
Phil Mickelson	23	1 (2)	69.21	4,403,883
David Toms	28	1 (3)	69.97	3,791,595
Vijay Singh	26	2 (2)	69.21	3,440,829
Davis Love III	20	1 (1)	69.06	3,169,463
Sergio Garcia	18	1 (2)	69.13	2,898,635
Scott Hoch	24	1 (2)	69.85	2,875,319
David Duval	20	1 (1)	69.73	2,801,760
Bob Estes	26	1 (2)	69.73	2,795,477
Scott Verplank	26	1 (1)	69.88	2,783,401

*Adjusted for average score of field in each tournament entered.

LPGA Tour Final 2001 Money Leaders

Name	Events	Best Finish	Scoring Average	Money ($)
Annika Sorenstam	26	1 (8)	69.42	2,105,868
Se Ri Pak	21	1 (5)	69.69	1,623,009
Karrie Webb	22	1 (3)	70.16	1,535,404
Lorie Kane	27	1 (1)	70.59	947,489
Maria Hjorth	29	2 (4)	71.46	848,195
Rosie Jones	23	1 (2)	70.51	785,010
Dottie Pepper	23	2 (2)	70.63	776,482
Mi Hyun Kim	29	2 (3)	70.49	762,363
Laura Diaz	27	2 (4)	70.88	751,466
Catriona Matthew	29	1 (1)	71.41	747,970

Senior Tour Final 2001 Money Leaders

Name	Events	Best Finish	Scoring Average	Money ($)
Allen Doyle	34	1 (2)	69.41	2,553,582
Bruce Fleisher	31	1 (3)	69.52	2,411,543
Hale Irwin	26	1 (3)	69.29	2,147,422
Larry Nelson	28	1 (5)	69.91	2,109,936
Gil Morgan	24	1 (2)	68.83	1,885,871
Jim Thorpe	35	1 (2)	70.15	1,827,223
Doug Tewell	28	1 (1)	69.94	1,721,339
Bob Gilder	30	1 (2)	70.37	1,684,986
Dana Quigley	37	1 (1)	70.43	1,537,931
Tom Kite	35	1 (1)	69.80	1,398,802

Burning Question: Why aren't there more lefties in pro golf?

Lefties abound in most sports and some of the greatest athletes (Babe Ruth, Bill Russell, Martina Navratilova, Steve Young) were port-siders. Yet there's a distinct dextralism in golf. The PGA Tour has only six lefties, the LPGA one. Bob Charles, the 1963 British Open champion, is the only left-hander to have won a major.

Blame a market bias for the lack of links lefties. Most sports don't require specialized equipment for left-handers—a basketball can be dribbled with either hand—but south-paw golfers need left-handers' clubs, which until recently were hard to find. "It was as if we were from a different planet," says Kevin Compare, a left-handed instructor at the PGA Learning Center in Port St. Lucie, Fla. "If someone had eight sets of clubs in his shop, none were left-handed." That's why natural lefties like Ben Hogan, Byron Nelson and Johnny Miller took up the sport from the right side.

Lately, however, the emergence of south-paw swingers like Phil Mickelson and Mike Weir has led equipment makers to increase production of left-handed gear. Also important is the precedent set by these stars. As Greg Chalmers, a Tour pro who plays lefty, says, "If I were a left-handed kid today and someone suggested I switch to righty, I'd say, 'Hey, playing lefty works for Phil Mickelson. It could work for me.'"

THEY SAID IT

Lee Trevino, 62-year-old golfer, on his curent play: "If I grew tomatoes, they'd come up sliced."

Men's Golf

THE MAJOR TOURNAMENTS

The Masters

Year	Winner	Score	Runner-Up
1934	Horton Smith	284	Craig Wood
1935	Gene Sarazen* (144)	282	Craig Wood (149)
	(only 36-hole playoff)		
1936	Horton Smith	285	Harry Cooper
1937	Byron Nelson	283	Ralph Guldahl
1938	Henry Picard	285	Ralph Guldahl
			Harry Cooper
1939	Ralph Guldahl	279	Sam Snead
1940	Jimmy Demaret	280	Lloyd Mangrum
1941	Craig Wood	280	Byron Nelson
1942	Byron Nelson* (69)	280	Ben Hogan (70)
1943–45	No tournament		
1946	Herman Keiser	282	Ben Hogan
1947	Jimmy Demaret	281	Byron Nelson
			Frank Stranahan
1948	Claude Harmon	279	Cary Middlecoff
1949	Sam Snead	282	Johnny Bulla
			Lloyd Mangrum
1950	Jimmy Demaret	283	Jim Ferrier
1951	Ben Hogan	280	Skee Riegel
1952	Sam Snead	286	Jack Burke Jr..
1953	Ben Hogan	274	Ed Oliver Jr.
1954	Sam Snead* (70)	289	Ben Hogan (71)
1955	Cary Middlecoff	279	Ben Hogan
1956	Jack Burke Jr.	289	Ken Venturi
1957	Doug Ford	282	Sam Snead
1958	Arnold Palmer	284	Doug Ford
			Fred Hawkins
1959	Art Wall Jr.	284	Cary Middlecoff
1960	Arnold Palmer	282	Ken Venturi
1961	Gary Player	280	Charles R. Coe
			Arnold Palmer
1962	Arnold Palmer* (68)	280	Gary Player (71)
			D. Finsterwald (77)
1963	Jack Nicklaus	286	Tony Lema
1964	Arnold Palmer	276	Dave Marr
			Jack Nicklaus
1965	Jack Nicklaus	271	Arnold Palmer
			Gary Player
1966	Jack Nicklaus* (70)	288	Tommy Jacobs (72)
			Gay Brewer Jr. (78)
1967	Gay Brewer Jr.	280	Bobby Nichols
1968	Bob Goalby	277	Roberto DeVicenzo
1969	George Archer	281	Billy Casper
			George Knudson
			Tom Weiskopf
1970	Billy Casper* (69)	279	Gene Littler (74)

Year	Winner	Score	Runner-Up
1971	Charles Coody	279	Johnny Miller
			Jack Nicklaus
1972	Jack Nicklaus	286	Bruce Crampton
			Bobby Mitchell
			Tom Weiskopf
1973	Tommy Aaron	283	J.C. Snead
1974	Gary Player	278	Tom Weiskopf
			Dave Stockton
1975	Jack Nicklaus	276	Johnny Miller
			Tom Weiskopf
1976	Ray Floyd	271	Ben Crenshaw
1977	Tom Watson	276	Jack Nicklaus
1978	Gary Player	277	Hubert Green
			Rod Funseth
			Tom Watson
1979	Fuzzy Zoeller* (4–3)†	280	Ed Sneed (4–4)
			Tom Watson (4–4)
1980	Seve Ballesteros	275	Gibby Gilbert
			Jack Newton
1981	Tom Watson	280	Johnny Miller
			Jack Nicklaus
1982	Craig Stadler* (4)	284	Dan Pohl (5)
1983	Seve Ballesteros	280	Ben Crenshaw
			Tom Kite
1984	Ben Crenshaw	277	Tom Watson
1985	Bernhard Langer	282	Curtis Strange
			Seve Ballesteros
			Ray Floyd
1986	Jack Nicklaus	279	Greg Norman
			Tom Kite
1987	Larry Mize* (4–3)	285	Seve Ballesteros (5)
			Greg Norman (4–4)
1988	Sandy Lyle	281	Mark Calcavecchia
1989	Nick Faldo* (5–3)	283	Scott Hoch (5–4)
1990	Nick Faldo* (4–4)	278	Ray Floyd (4–x)
1991	Ian Woosnam	277	José María Olazábal
1992	Fred Couples	275	Ray Floyd
1993	Bernhard Langer	277	Chip Beck
1994	José María Olazábal	279	Tom Lehman
1995	Ben Crenshaw	274	Davis Love III
1996	Nick Faldo	276	Greg Norman
1997	Tiger Woods	270	Tom Kite
1998	Mark O'Meara	279	David Duval
			Fred Couples
1999	José María Olazábal	280	Davis Love III
2000	Vijay Singh	278	Ernie Els
2001	Tiger Woods	272	David Duval
2002	Tiger Woods	276	Retief Goosen

*Winner in playoff. Playoff scores are in parentheses. †Playoff cut from 18 holes to sudden death.
Note: Played at Augusta National Golf Club, Augusta, GA.

United States Open Championship

Year	Winner	Score	Runner-Up	Site
1895	Horace Rawlins	†173	Willie Dunn	Newport GC, Newport, RI
1896	James Foulis	†152	Horace Rawlins	Shinnecock Hills GC, Southampton, NY
1897	Joe Lloyd	†162	Willie Anderson	Chicago GC, Wheaton, IL
1898	Fred Herd	328	Alex Smith	Myopia Hunt Club, Hamilton, MA
1899	Willie Smith	315	George Low	Baltimore CC, Baltimore
			Val Fitzjohn	
			W.H. Way	
1900	Harry Vardon	313	John H. Taylor	Chicago GC, Wheaton, IL
1901	Willie Anderson* (85)	331	Alex Smith (86)	Myopia Hunt Club, Hamilton, MA
1902	Laurie Auchterlonie	307	Stewart Gardner	Garden City GC, Garden City, NY
1903	Willie Anderson* (82)	307	David Brown (84)	Baltusrol GC, Springfield, NJ
1904	Willie Anderson	303	Gil Nicholls	Glen View Club, Golf, IL
1905	Willie Anderson	314	Alex Smith	Myopia Hunt Club, Hamilton, MA
1906	Alex Smith	295	Willie Smith	Onwentsia Club, Lake Forest, IL
1907	Alex Ross	302	Gil Nicholls	Philadelphia Cricket Club, Chestnut Hill, PA
1908	Fred McLeod* (77)	322	Willie Smith (83)	Myopia Hunt Club, Hamilton, MA
1909	George Sargent	290	Tom McNamara	Englewood GC, Englewood, NJ
1910	Alex Smith* (71)	298	John McDermott (75)	Philadelphia Cricket Club, Chestnut Hill, PA
			Macdonald Smith (77)	
1911	John McDermott* (80)	307	Mike Brady (82)	Chicago GC, Wheaton, IL
			George Simpson (85)	
1912	John McDermott	294	Tom McNamara	CC of Buffalo, Buffalo
1913	Francis Ouimet* (72)	304	Harry Vardon (77)	The Country Club, Brookline, MA
			Edward Ray (78)	
1914	Walter Hagen	290	Chick Evans	Midlothian CC, Blue Island, IL
1915	Jerry Travers	297	Tom McNamara	Baltusrol GC, Springfield, NJ
1916	Chick Evans	286	Jock Hutchison	Minikahda Club, Minneapolis
1917–18	No tournament			
1919	Walter Hagen* (77)	301	Mike Brady (78)	Brae Burn CC, West Newton, MA
1920	Edward Ray	295	Harry Vardon	Inverness CC, Toledo
			Jack Burke	
			Leo Diegel	
			Jock Hutchison	
1921	Jim Barnes	289	Walter Hagen	Columbia CC, Chevy Chase, MD
			Fred McLeod	
1922	Gene Sarazen	288	John L. Black	Skokie CC, Glencoe, IL
			Bobby Jones	
1923	Bobby Jones* (76)	296	Bobby Cruickshank (78)	Inwood CC, Inwood, NY
1924	Cyril Walker	297	Bobby Jones	Oakland Hills CC, Birmingham, MI
1925	W. MacFarlane* (75–72)	291	Bobby Jones (75–73)	Worcester CC, Worcester, MA
1926	Bobby Jones	293	Joe Turnesa	Scioto CC, Columbus, OH
1927	Tommy Armour* (76)	301	Harry Cooper (79)	Oakmont CC, Oakmont, PA
1928	Johnny Farrell* (143)	294	Bobby Jones (144)	Olympia Fields CC, Matteson, IL
1929	Bobby Jones* (141)	294	Al Espinosa (164)	Winged Foot GC, Mamaroneck, NY
1930	Bobby Jones	287	Macdonald Smith	Interlachen CC, Hopkins, MN
1931	Billy Burke* (149–148)	292	George Von Elm	Inverness Club, Toledo
			(149–149)	
1932	Gene Sarazen	286	Phil Perkins	Fresh Meadows CC, Flushing, NY
			Bobby Cruickshank	
1933	Johnny Goodman	287	Ralph Guldahl	North Shore CC, Glenview, IL
1934	Olin Dutra	293	Gene Sarazen	Merion Cricket Club, Ardmore, PA
1935	Sam Parks Jr.	299	Jimmy Thompson	Oakmont CC, Oakmont, PA
1936	Tony Manero	282	Harry Cooper	Baltusrol GC (Upper Course), Springfield, NJ
1937	Ralph Guldahl	281	Sam Snead	Oakland Hills CC, Birmingham, MI
1938	Ralph Guldahl	284	Dick Metz	Cherry Hills CC, Denver
1939	Byron Nelson* (68–70)	284	Craig Wood (68–73)	Philadelphia CC, Philadelphia
			Denny Shute (76)	
1940	Lawson Little* (70)	287	Gene Sarazen (73)	Canterbury GC, Cleveland
1941	Craig Wood	284	Denny Shute	Colonial Club, Fort Worth
1942–45	No tournament			
1946	Lloyd Mangrum* (72–72)	284	Vic Ghezzi (72–73)	Canterbury GC, Cleveland
			Byron Nelson (72–73)	

United States Open Championship *(Cont.)*

Year	Winner	Score	Runner-Up	Site
1947	Lew Worsham* (69)	282	Sam Snead (70)	St. Louis CC, Clayton, MO
1948	Ben Hogan	276	Jimmy Demaret	Riviera CC, Los Angeles
1949	Cary Middlecoff	286	Sam Snead Clayton Heafner	Medinah CC, Medinah, IL
1950	Ben Hogan* (69)	287	Lloyd Mangrum (73) George Fazio (75)	Merion GC, Ardmore, PA
1951	Ben Hogan	287	Clayton Heafner	Oakland Hills CC, Birmingham, MI
1952	Julius Boros	281	Ed Oliver	Northwood CC, Dallas
1953	Ben Hogan	283	Sam Snead	Oakmont CC, Oakmont, PA
1954	Ed Furgol	284	Gene Littler	Baltusrol GC (Lower Course), Springfield, NJ
1955	Jack Fleck* (69)	287	Ben Hogan (72)	Olympic Club (Lake Course), San Francisco
1956	Cary Middlecoff	281	Ben Hogan Julius Boros	Oak Hill CC, Rochester, NY
1957	Dick Mayer* (72)	282	Cary Middlecoff (79)	Inverness Club, Toledo
1958	Tommy Bolt	283	Gary Player	Southern Hills CC, Tulsa
1959	Billy Casper	282	Bob Rosburg	Winged Foot GC, Mamaroneck, NY
1960	Arnold Palmer	280	Jack Nicklaus	Cherry Hills CC, Denver
1961	Gene Littler	281	Bob Goalby Doug Sanders	Oakland Hills CC, Birmingham, MI
1962	Jack Nicklaus* (71)	283	Arnold Palmer (74)	Oakmont CC, Oakmont, PA
1963	Julius Boros* (70)	293	Jacky Cupit (73) Arnold Palmer (76)	The Country Club, Brookline, MA
1964	Ken Venturi	278	Tommy Jacobs	Congressional CC, Bethesda, MD
1965	Gary Player* (71)	282	Kel Nagle (74)	Bellerive CC, St. Louis
1966	Billy Casper* (69)	278	Arnold Palmer (73)	Olympic Club (Lake Course), San Francisco
1967	Jack Nicklaus	275	Arnold Palmer	Baltusrol GC (Lower Course), Springfield, NJ
1968	Lee Trevino	275	Jack Nicklaus	Oak Hill CC, Rochester, NY
1969	Orville Moody	281	Deane Beman Al Geiberger Bob Rosburg	Champions GC (Cypress Creek Course), Houston
1970	Tony Jacklin	281	Dave Hill	Hazeltine GC, Chaska, MN
1971	Lee Trevino* (68)	280	Jack Nicklaus (71)	Merion GC (East Course), Ardmore, PA
1972	Jack Nicklaus	290	Bruce Crampton	Pebble Beach GL, Pebble Beach, CA
1973	Johnny Miller	279	John Schlee	Oakmont CC, Oakmont, PA
1974	Hale Irwin	287	Forrest Fezler	Winged Foot GC, Mamaroneck, NY
1975	Lou Graham* (71)	287	John Mahaffey (73)	Medinah CC, Medinah, IL
1976	Jerry Pate	277	Tom Weiskopf Al Geiberger	Atlanta Athletic Club, Duluth, GA
1977	Hubert Green	278	Lou Graham	Southern Hills CC, Tulsa
1978	Andy North	285	Dave Stockton J.C. Snead	Cherry Hills CC, Denver
1979	Hale Irwin	284	Gary Player Jerry Pate	Inverness Club, Toledo
1980	Jack Nicklaus	272	Isao Aoki	Baltusrol GC (Lower Course), Springfield, NJ
1981	David Graham	273	George Burns Bill Rogers	Merion GC, Ardmore, PA
1982	Tom Watson	282	Jack Nicklaus	Pebble Beach GL, Pebble Beach, CA
1983	Larry Nelson	280	Tom Watson	Oakmont CC, Oakmont, PA
1984	Fuzzy Zoeller* (67)	276	Greg Norman (75)	Winged Foot GC, Mamaroneck, NY
1985	Andy North	279	Dave Barr T.C. Chen Denis Watson	Oakland Hills CC, Birmingham, MI
1986	Ray Floyd	279	Lanny Wadkins Chip Beck	Shinnecock Hills GC, Southampton, NY
1987	Scott Simpson	277	Tom Watson	Olympic Club (Lake Course), San Francisco
1988	Curtis Strange* (71)	278	Nick Faldo (75)	The Country Club, Brookline, MA
1989	Curtis Strange	278	Chip Beck Mark McCumber Ian Woosnam	Oak Hill CC, Rochester, NY
1990	Hale Irwin* (74) (3)	280	Mike Donald (74) (4)	Medinah CC, Medinah, IL
1991	Payne Stewart* (75)	282	Scott Simpson (77)	Hazeltine GC, Chaska, MN
1992	Tom Kite	285	Jeff Sluman	Pebble Beach GL, Pebble Beach, CA
1993	Lee Janzen	272	Payne Stewart	Baltusrol GC, Springfield, NJ
1994	Ernie Els*	279	Loren Roberts Colin Montgomerie	Oakmont CC, Oakmont, PA

United States Open Championship *(Cont.)*

Year	Winner	Score	Runner-Up	Site
1995	Corey Pavin	280	Greg Norman	Shinnecock Hills GC, Southampton, NY
1996	Steve Jones	278	Davis Love III	Oakland Hills CC, Birmingham, MI
			Tom Lehman	
1997	Ernie Els	276	Colin Montgomerie	Congressional CC, Bethesda, MD
1998	Lee Janzen	280	Payne Stewart	The Olympic Club, San Francisco
1999	Payne Stewart	279	Phil Mickelson	Pinehurst Resort and CC, Pinehurst, NC
2000	Tiger Woods	272	Miguel Angel Jiménez	Pebble Beach GL, Pebble Beach, CA
			Ernie Els	
2001	Retief Goosen* (70)	276	Mark Brooks (72)	Southern Hills CC, Tulsa
2002	Tiger Woods	277	Phil Mickelson	Bethpage Black Course, Bethpage, NY

*Winner in playoff. Playoff scores are in parentheses. The 1990 playoff went to one hole of sudden death after an 18-hole playoff. In the 1994 playoff, Montgomerie was eliminated after 18 playoff holes, and Els beat Roberts on the 20th.
†Before 1898, 36 holes. From 1898 on, 72 holes.

British Open

Year	Winner	Score	Runner-Up	Site
1860†	Willie Park	174	Tom Morris Sr.	Prestwick, Scotland
1861‡	Tom Morris Sr.	163	Willie Park	Prestwick, Scotland
1862	Tom Morris Sr.	163	Willie Park	Prestwick, Scotland
1863	Willie Park	168	Tom Morris Sr.	Prestwick, Scotland
1864	Tom Morris, Sr.	160	Andrew Strath	Prestwick, Scotland
1865	Andrew Strath	162	Willie Park	Prestwick, Scotland
1866	Willie Park	169	David Park	Prestwick, Scotland
1867	Tom Morris Sr.	170	Willie Park	Prestwick, Scotland
1868	Tom Morris Jr.	154	Tom Morris Sr.	Prestwick, Scotland
1869	Tom Morris Jr.	157	Tom Morris Sr.	Prestwick, Scotland
1870	Tom Morris Jr.	149	David Strath	Prestwick, Scotland
			Bob Kirk	
1871	No tournament			
1872	Tom Morris Jr.	166	David Strath	Prestwick, Scotland
1873	Tom Kidd	179	Jamie Anderson	St. Andrews, Scotland
1874	Mungo Park	159	No record	Musselburgh, Scotland
1875	Willie Park	166	Bob Martin	Prestwick, Scotland
1876	Bob Martin#	176	David Strath	St. Andrews, Scotland
1877	Jamie Anderson	160	Bob Pringle	Musselburgh, Scotland
1878	Jamie Anderson	157	Robert Kirk	Prestwick, Scotland
1879	Jamie Anderson	169	Andrew Kirkaldy	St. Andrews, Scotland
			James Allan	
1880	Robert Ferguson	162	No record	Musselburgh, Scotland
1881	Robert Ferguson	170	Jamie Anderson	Prestwick, Scotland
1882	Robert Ferguson	171	Willie Fernie	St. Andrews, Scotland
1883	Willie Fernie*	159	Robert Ferguson	Musselburgh, Scotland
1884	Jack Simpson	160	Douglas Rolland	Prestwick, Scotland
			Willie Fernie	
1885	Bob Martin	171	Archie Simpson	St. Andrews, Scotland
1886	David Brown	157	Willie Campbell	Musselburgh, Scotland
1887	Willie Park Jr.	161	Bob Martin	Prestwick, Scotland
1888	Jack Burns	171	Bernard Sayers	St. Andrews, Scotland
			David Anderson	
1889	Willie Park Jr.* (158)	155	Andrew Kirkaldy (163)	Musselburgh, Scotland
1890	John Ball	164	Willie Fernie	Prestwick, Scotland
1891	Hugh Kirkaldy	166	Andrew Kirkaldy	St. Andrews, Scotland
			Willie Fernie	
1892	Harold Hilton	**305	John Ball	Muirfield, Scotland
			Hugh Kirkaldy	
1893	William Auchterlonie	322	John E. Laidlay	Prestwick, Scotland
1894	John H. Taylor	326	Douglas Rolland	Royal St. George's, England
1895	John H. Taylor	322	Alexander Herd	St. Andrews, Scotland
1896	Harry Vardon* (157)	316	John H. Taylor (161)	Muirfield, Scotland
1897	Harold Hilton	314	James Braid	Hoylake, England
1898	Harry Vardon	307	Willie Park Jr.	Prestwick, Scotland
1899	Harry Vardon	310	Jack White	Royal St. George's, England
1900	John H. Taylor	309	Harry Vardon	St. Andrews, Scotland
1901	James Braid	309	Harry Vardon	Muirfield, Scotland
1902	Alexander Herd	307	Harry Vardon	Hoylake, England

British Open *(Cont.)*

Year	Winner	Score	Runner-Up	Site
1903	Harry Vardon	300	Tom Vardon	Prestwick, Scotland
1904	Jack White	296	John H. Taylor	Royal St. George's, England
1905	James Braid	318	John H. Taylor	St. Andrews, Scotland
			Rolland Jones	
1906	James Braid	300	John H. Taylor	Muirfield, Scotland
1907	Arnaud Massy	312	John H. Taylor	Hoylake, England
1908	James Braid	291	Tom Ball	Prestwick, Scotland
1909	John H. Taylor	295	James Braid	Deal, England
			Tom Ball	
1910	James Braid	299	Alexander Herd	St. Andrews, Scotland
1911	Harry Vardon	303	Arnaud Massy	Royal St. George's, England
1912	Ted Ray	295	Harry Vardon	Muirfield, Scotland
1913	John H. Taylor	304	Ted Ray	Hoylake, England
1914	Harry Vardon	306	John H. Taylor	Prestwick, Scotland
1915–19	No tournament			
1920	George Duncan	303	Alexander Herd	Deal, England
1921	Jock Hutchison* (150)	296	Roger Wethered (159)	St. Andrews, Scotland
1922	Walter Hagen	300	George Duncan	Royal St. George's, England
			Jim Barnes	
1923	Arthur G. Havers	295	Walter Hagen	Troon, Scotland
1924	Walter Hagen	301	Ernest Whitcombe	Hoylake, England
1925	Jim Barnes	300	Archie Compston	Prestwick, Scotland
			Ted Ray	
1926	Bobby Jones	291	Al Watrous	Royal Lytham & St. Annes, England
1927	Bobby Jones	285	Aubrey Boomer	St. Andrews, Scotland
1928	Walter Hagen	292	Gene Sarazen	Royal St. George's, England
1929	Walter Hagen	292	Johnny Farrell	Muirfield, Scotland
1930	Bobby Jones	291	Macdonald Smith	Hoylake, England
			Leo Diegel	
1931	Tommy Armour	296	Jose Jurado	Carnoustie, Scotland
1932	Gene Sarazen	283	Macdonald Smith	Prince's, England
1933	Denny Shute* (149)	292	Craig Wood (154)	St. Andrews, Scotland
1934	Henry Cotton	283	Sidney F. Brews	Royal St. George's, England
1935	Alfred Perry	283	Alfred Padgham	Muirfield, Scotland
1936	Alfred Padgham	287	James Adams	Hoylake, England
1937	Henry Cotton	290	Reginald A. Whitcombe	Carnoustie, Scotland
1938	Reginald A. Whitcombe	295	James Adams	Royal St. George's, England
1939	Richard Burton	290	Johnny Bulla	St. Andrews, Scotland
1940–45	No tournament			
1946	Sam Snead	290	Bobby Locke	St. Andrews, Scotland
			Johnny Bulla	
1947	Fred Daly	293	Reginald W. Horne	Hoylake, England
			Frank Stranahan	
1948	Henry Cotton	294	Fred Daly	Muirfield, Scotland
1949	Bobby Locke* (135)	283	Harry Bradshaw (147)	Royal St. George's, England
1950	Bobby Locke	279	Roberto DeVicenzo	Troon, Scotland
1951	Max Faulkner	285	Tony Cerda	Portrush, Ireland
1952	Bobby Locke	287	Peter Thomson	Royal Lytham & St. Annes, England
1953	Ben Hogan	282	Frank Stranahan	Carnoustie, Scotland
			Dai Rees	
			Peter Thomson	
			Tony Cerda	
1954	Peter Thomson	283	Sidney S. Scott	Royal Birkdale, England
			Dai Rees	
			Bobby Locke	
1955	Peter Thomson	281	John Fallon	St. Andrews, Scotland
1956	Peter Thomson	286	Flory Van Donck	Hoylake, England
1957	Bobby Locke	279	Peter Thomson	St. Andrews, Scotland
1958	Peter Thomson* (139)	278	Dave Thomas (143)	Royal Lytham & St. Annes, England
1959	Gary Player	284	Fred Bullock	Muirfield, Scotland
			Flory Van Donck	
1960	Kel Nagle	278	Arnold Palmer	St. Andrews, Scotland
1961	Arnold Palmer	284	Dai Rees	Royal Birkdale, England
1962	Arnold Palmer	276	Kel Nagle	Troon, Scotland

British Open (Cont.)

Year	Winner	Score	Runner-Up	Site
1963	Bob Charles* (140)	277	Phil Rodgers (148)	Royal Lytham & St. Annes, England
1964	Tony Lema	279	Jack Nicklaus	St. Andrews, Scotland
1965	Peter Thomson	285	Brian Huggett	Southport, England
			Christy O'Connor	
1966	Jack Nicklaus	282	Doug Sanders	Muirfield, Scotland
			Dave Thomas	
1967	Robert DeVicenzo	278	Jack Nicklaus	Hoylake, England
1968	Gary Player	289	Jack Nicklaus	Carnoustie, Scotland
			Bob Charles	
1969	Tony Jacklin	280	Bob Charles	Royal Lytham & St. Annes, England
1970	Jack Nicklaus* (72)	283	Doug Sanders (73)	St. Andrews, Scotland
1971	Lee Trevino	278	Lu Liang Huan	Royal Birkdale, England
1972	Lee Trevino	278	Jack Nicklaus	Muirfield, Scotland
1973	Tom Weiskopf	276	Johnny Miller	Troon, Scotland
1974	Gary Player	282	Peter Oosterhuis	Royal Lytham & St. Annes, England
1975	Tom Watson* (71)	279	Jack Newton (72)	Carnoustie, Scotland
1976	Johnny Miller	279	Jack Nicklaus	Royal Birkdale, England
			Seve Ballesteros	
1977	Tom Watson	268	Jack Nicklaus	Turnberry, Scotland
1978	Jack Nicklaus	281	Ben Crenshaw	St. Andrews, Scotland
			Tom Kite	
			Ray Floyd	
			Simon Owen	
1979	Seve Ballesteros	283	Ben Crenshaw	Royal Lytham & St. Annes, England
			Jack Nicklaus	
1980	Tom Watson	271	Lee Trevino	Muirfield, Scotland
1981	Bill Rogers	276	Bernhard Langer	Royal St. George's, England
1982	Tom Watson	284	Nick Price	Troon, Scotland
			Peter Oosterhuis	
1983	Tom Watson	275	Andy Bean	Royal Birkdale, England
1984	Seve Ballesteros	276	Tom Watson	St. Andrews, Scotland
			Bernhard Langer	
1985	Sandy Lyle	282	Payne Stewart	Royal St. George's, England
1986	Greg Norman	280	Gordon Brand	Turnberry, Scotland
1987	Nick Faldo	279	Paul Azinger	Muirfield, Scotland
			Rodger Davis	
1988	Seve Ballesteros	273	Nick Price	Royal Lytham & St. Annes, England
1989††	Mark Calcavecchia* (4-3-3-3)	275	Wayne Grady (4-4-4-4)	Troon, Scotland
			Greg Norman (3-3-4-x)	
1990	Nick Faldo	270	Payne Stewart	St. Andrews, Scotland
			Mark McNulty	
1991	Ian Baker-Finch	272	Mike Harwood	Royal Birkdale, England
1992	Nick Faldo	272	John Cook	Muirfield, Scotland
1993	Greg Norman	267	Nick Faldo	Royal St. George's, England
1994	Nick Price	268	Jesper Parnevik	Turnberry, Scotland
1995	John Daly* (4-3-4-4)	282	C. Rocca (5-4-7-3)	St. Andrews, Scotland
1996	Tom Lehman	271	Mark McCumber	Royal Lytham & St. Annes, England
			Ernie Els	
1997	Justin Leonard	272	Jesper Parnevik	Troon, Scotland
			Darren Clarke	
1998	Mark O'Meara* (4-4-5-4)	280	Brian Watts (5-4-5-5)	Southport, England
1999	Paul Lawrie* (5-4-3-3)	290	Jean Van de Velde (6-4-3-5)	Carnoustie GC, Carnoustie,
			Justin Leonard (5-4-4-5)	Scotland
2000	Tiger Woods	269	Thomas Bjorn	St. Andrews, Scotland
			Ernie Els	
2001	David Duval	274	Niclas Fasth	Royal Lytham & St. Annes, England
2002	Ernie Els*	278	Stuart Appleby	Muirfield, Scotland

*Winner in playoff. Playoff scores are in parentheses. †The first event was open only to professional golfers.
‡The second annual open was open to amateurs and pros. #Tied, but refused playoff.
**Championship extended from 36 to 72 holes. ††Playoff cut from 18 holes to 4 holes.

PGA Championship

Year	Winner	Score	Runner-Up	Site
1916	Jim Barnes	1 up	Jock Hutchison	Siwanoy CC, Bronxville, NY
1917–18	No tournament			
1919	Jim Barnes	6 & 5	Fred McLeod	Engineers CC, Roslyn, NY
1920	Jock Hutchison	1 up	J. Douglas Edgar	Flossmoor CC, Flossmoor, IL
1921	Walter Hagen	3 & 2	Jim Barnes	Inwood CC, Far Rockaway, NY
1922	Gene Sarazen	4 & 3	Emmet French	Oakmont CC, Oakmont, PA
1923	Gene Sarazen	1 up 38 holes	Walter Hagen	Pelham CC, Pelham, NY
1924	Walter Hagen	2 up	Jim Barnes	French Lick CC, French Lick, IN
1925	Walter Hagen	6 & 5	William Mehlhorn	Olympia Fields CC, Olympia Fields, IL
1926	Walter Hagen	5 & 3	Leo Diegel	Salisbury GC, Westbury, NY
1927	Walter Hagen	1 up	Joe Turnesa	Cedar Crest CC, Dallas
1928	Leo Diegel	6 & 5	Al Espinosa	Five Farms CC, Baltimore
1929	Leo Diegel	6 & 4	Johnny Farrell	Hillcrest CC, Los Angeles
1930	Tommy Armour	1 up	Gene Sarazen	Fresh Meadow CC, Flushing, NY
1931	Tom Creavy	2 & 1	Denny Shute	Wannamoisett CC, Rumford, RI
1932	Olin Dutra	4 & 3	Frank Walsh	Keller GC, St. Paul
1933	Gene Sarazen	5 & 4	Willie Goggin	Blue Mound CC, Milwaukee
1934	Paul Runyan	1 up	Craig Wood	Park CC, Williamsville, NY
1935	Johnny Revolta	5 & 4 38 holes	Tommy Armour	Twin Hills CC, Oklahoma City
1936	Denny Shute	3 & 2	Jimmy Thomson	Pinehurst CC, Pinehurst, NC
1937	Denny Shute	1 up 37 holes	Harold McSpaden	Pittsburgh FC, Aspinwall, PA
1938	Paul Runyan	8 & 7	Sam Snead	Shawnee CC, Shawnee-on-Delaware, PA
1939	Henry Picard	1 up 37 holes	Byron Nelson	Pomonok CC, Flushing, NY
1940	Byron Nelson	1 up	Sam Snead	Hershey CC, Hershey, PA
1941	Vic Ghezzi	1 up 38 holes	Byron Nelson	Cherry Hills CC, Denver
1942	Sam Snead	2 & 1	Jim Turnesa	Seaview CC, Atlantic City
1943	No tournament			
1944	Bob Hamilton	1 up	Byron Nelson	Manito G & CC, Spokane, WA
1945	Byron Nelson	4 & 3	Sam Byrd	Morraine CC, Dayton
1946	Ben Hogan	6 & 4	Ed Oliver	Portland GC, Portland, OR
1947	Jim Ferrier	2 & 1	Chick Harbert	Plum Hollow CC, Detroit
1948	Ben Hogan	7 & 6	Mike Turnesa	Norwood Hills CC, St. Louis
1949	Sam Snead	3 & 2	Johnny Palmer	Hermitage CC, Richmond
1950	Chandler Harper	4 & 3	Henry Williams Jr.	Scioto CC, Columbus, OH
1951	Sam Snead	7 & 6	Walter Burkemo	Oakmont CC, Oakmont, PA
1952	Jim Turnesa	1 up	Chick Harbert	Big Spring CC, Louisville
1953	Walter Burkemo	2 & 1	Felice Torza	Birmingham CC, Birmingham, MI
1954	Chick Harbert	4 & 3	Walter Burkemo	Keller GC, St. Paul
1955	Doug Ford	4 & 3	Cary Middlecoff	Meadowbrook CC, Detroit
1956	Jack Burke	3 & 2	Ted Kroll	Blue Hill CC, Boston
1957	Lionel Hebert	2 & 1	Dow Finsterwald	Miami Valley CC, Dayton
1958	Dow Finsterwald	276	Billy Casper	Llanerch CC, Havertown, PA
1959	Bob Rosburg	277	Jerry Barber Doug Sanders	Minneapolis GC, St. Louis Park, MN
1960	Jay Hebert	281	Jim Ferrier	Firestone CC, Akron
1961	Jerry Barber* (67)	277	Don January (68)	Olympia Fields CC, Olympia Fields, IL
1962	Gary Player	278	Bob Goalby	Aronimink GC, Newton Square, PA
1963	Jack Nicklaus	279	Dave Ragan Jr.	Dallas Athletic Club, Dallas
1964	Bobby Nichols	271	Jack Nicklaus Arnold Palmer	Columbus CC, Columbus, OH
1965	Dave Marr	280	Billy Casper Jack Nicklaus	Laurel Valley CC, Ligonier, PA
1966	Al Geiberger	280	Dudley Wysong	Firestone CC, Akron
1967	Don January* (69)	281	Don Massengale (71)	Columbine CC, Littleton, CO
1968	Julius Boros	281	Bob Charles Arnold Palmer	Pecan Valley CC, San Antonio
1969	Ray Floyd	276	Gary Player	NCR CC, Dayton
1970	Dave Stockton	279	Arnold Palmer Bob Murphy	Southern Hills CC, Tulsa

PGA Championship (Cont.)

Year	Winner	Score	Runner-Up	Site
1971	Jack Nicklaus	281	Billy Casper	PGA Nat'l GC, Palm Beach Gardens, FL
1972	Gary Player	281	Tommy Aaron	Oakland Hills CC, Birmingham, MI
			Jim Jamieson	
1973	Jack Nicklaus	277	Bruce Crampton	Canterbury GC, Cleveland
1974	Lee Trevino	276	Jack Nicklaus	Tanglewood GC, Winston-Salem, NC
1975	Jack Nicklaus	276	Bruce Crampton	Firestone CC, Akron
1976	Dave Stockton	281	Ray Floyd	Congressional CC, Bethesda, MD
			Don January	
1977†	Lanny Wadkins* (4-4-4)	282	Gene Littler (4-4-5)	Pebble Beach GL, Pebble Beach, CA
1978	John Mahaffey* (4–3)	276	Jerry Pate (4–4)	Oakmont CC, Oakmont, PA
			Tom Watson (4–5)	
1979	David Graham* (4-4-2)	272	Ben Crenshaw (4-4-4)	Oakland Hills CC, Birmingham, MI
1980	Jack Nicklaus	274	Andy Bean	Oak Hill CC, Rochester, NY
1981	Larry Nelson	273	Fuzzy Zoeller	Atlanta Athletic Club, Duluth, GA
1982	Raymond Floyd	272	Lanny Wadkins	Southern Hills CC, Tulsa
1983	Hal Sutton	274	Jack Nicklaus	Riviera CC, Pacific Palisades, CA
1984	Lee Trevino	273	Gary Player	Shoal Creek, Birmingham, AL
			Lanny Wadkins	
1985	Hubert Green	278	Lee Trevino	Cherry Hills CC, Denver
1986	Bob Tway	276	Greg Norman	Inverness CC, Toledo
1987	Larry Nelson* (4)	287	Lanny Wadkins (5)	PGA Natl GC, Palm Beach Gardens, FL
1988	Jeff Sluman	272	Paul Azinger	Oak Tree GC, Edmond, OK
1989	Payne Stewart	276	Mike Reid	Kemper Lakes GC, Hawthorn Woods, IL
1990	Wayne Grady	282	Fred Couples	Shoal Creek, Birmingham, AL
1991	John Daly	276	Bruce Lietzke	Crooked Stick GC, Carmel, IN
1992	Nick Price	278	Jim Gallagher Jr.	Bellerive CC, St. Louis
1993	Paul Azinger* (4–4)	272	Greg Norman (4–5)	Inverness CC, Toledo
1994	Nick Price	269	Corey Pavin	Southern Hills CC, Tulsa
1995	Steve Elkington* (3)	267	Colin Montgomerie (4)	Riviera CC, Pacific Palisades, CA
1996	Mark Brooks* (3)	277	Kenny Perry (x)	Valhalla GC, Louisville
1997	Davis Love III	269	Justin Leonard	Winged Foot GC, Mamaroneck, NY
1998	Vijay Singh	271	Steve Stricker	Sahalee CC, Redmond, WA
1999	Tiger Woods	277	Sergio Garcia	Medinah CC, Medinah, IL
2000	Tiger Woods* (3-4-5)	270	Bob May (4-4-x)	Valhalla GC, Louisville
2001	David Toms	265	Phil Mickelson	Atlanta AC, Duluth, GA
2002	Rich Beem	278	Tiger Woods	Hazeltine National GC, Shaska, MN

*Winner in playoff. Playoff scores are in parentheses. †Playoff changed from 18 holes to sudden death.

Alltime Major Championship Winners

	Masters	U.S. Open	British Open	PGA Champ.	U.S. Amateur	British Amateur	Total
†Jack Nicklaus	6	4	3	5	2	0	20
Bobby Jones	0	4	3	0	5	1	13
Walter Hagen	0	2	4	5	0	0	11
*Tiger Woods	3	2	1	2	3	0	11
Ben Hogan	2	4	1	2	0	0	9
†Gary Player	3	1	3	2	0	0	9
John Ball	0	0	1	0	0	8	9
†Arnold Palmer	4	1	2	0	1	0	8
†Tom Watson	2	1	5	0	0	0	8
Harold Hilton	0	0	2	0	1	4	7
Gene Sarazen	1	2	1	3	0	0	7
Sam Snead	3	0	1	3	0	0	7
Harry Vardon	0	1	6	0	0	0	7

*Active PGA player. †Active Senior PGA player.

Alltime Multiple Professional Major Winners

MASTERS		U.S. OPEN (Cont.)		BRITISH OPEN (Cont.)		PGA CHAMPIONSHIP	
Jack Nicklaus	6	Hale Irwin	3	Peter Thomson	5	Walter Hagen	5
Arnold Palmer	4	Julius Boros	2	Tom Watson	5	Jack Nicklaus	5
Jimmy Demaret	3	Billy Casper	2	Walter Hagen	4	Gene Sarazen	3
Nick Faldo	3	Ernie Els	2	Bobby Locke	4	Sam Snead	3
Gary Player	3	Ralph Guldahl	2	Tom Morris Sr.	4	Jim Barnes	2
Sam Snead	3	Walter Hagen	2	Tom Morris Jr.	4	Leo Diegel	2
Tiger Woods	3	Lee Janzen	2	Willie Park	4	Raymond Floyd	2
Seve Ballesteros	2	John McDermott	2	Jamie Anderson	3	Ben Hogan	2
Ben Crenshaw	2	Cary Middlecoff	2	Seve Ballesteros	3	Byron Nelson	2
Ben Hogan	2	Andy North	2	Henry Cotton	3	Larry Nelson	2
Bernhard Langer	2	Gene Sarazen	2	Nick Faldo	3	Gary Player	2
Byron Nelson	2	Alex Smith	2	Robert Ferguson	3	Paul Runyan	2
José María Olazábal	2	Payne Stewart	2	Bobby Jones	3	Denny Shute	2
Horton Smith	2	Curtis Strange	2	Jack Nicklaus	3	Dave Stockton	2
Tom Watson	2	Lee Trevino	2	Gary Player	3	Lee Trevino	2
		Tiger Woods	2	Harold Hilton	2	Tiger Woods	2
				Bob Martin	2		
U.S. OPEN				Greg Norman	2		
		BRITISH OPEN		Arnold Palmer	2		
Willie Anderson	4			Willie Park Jr.	2		
Ben Hogan	4	Harry Vardon	6	Lee Trevino	2		
Bobby Jones	4	James Braid	5				
Jack Nicklaus	4	J.H. Taylor	5				

THE PGA TOUR

Most Career Wins

	Wins		Wins		Wins
Sam Snead	81	Billy Casper	51	Tom Watson	34
Jack Nicklaus	70	Walter Hagen	40	Tiger Woods	34
Ben Hogan	63	Cary Middlecoff	40	Horton Smith	32
Arnold Palmer	60	Gene Sarazen	38	Harry Cooper	31
Byron Nelson	52	Lloyd Mangrum	36	Jimmy Demaret	31

Season Money Leaders

		Earnings ($)			Earnings ($)			Earnings ($)
1934	Paul Runyan	6,767.00	1957	Dick Mayer	65,835.00	1980	Tom Watson	530,808.33
1935	Johnny Revolta	9,543.00	1958	Arnold Palmer	42,607.50	1981	Tom Kite	375,698.84
1936	Horton Smith	7,682.00	1959	Art Wall	53,167.60	1982	Craig Stadler	446,462.00
1937	Harry Cooper	14,138.69	1960	Arnold Palmer	75,262.85	1983	Hal Sutton	426,668.00
1938	Sam Snead	19,534.49	1961	Gary Player	64,540.45	1984	Tom Watson	476,260.00
1939	Henry Picard	10,303.00	1962	Arnold Palmer	81,448.33	1985	Curtis Strange	542,321.00
1940	Ben Hogan	10,655.00	1963	Arnold Palmer	128,230.00	1986	Greg Norman	653,296.00
1941	Ben Hogan	18,358.00	1964	Jack Nicklaus	113,284.50	1987	Curtis Strange	925,941.00
1942	Ben Hogan	13,143.00	1965	Jack Nicklaus	140,752.14	1988	Curtis Strange	1,147,644.00
1943	No statistics compiled		1966	Billy Casper	121,944.92	1989	Tom Kite	1,395,278.00
1944	Byron Nelson*	37,967.69	1967	Jack Nicklaus	188,998.08	1990	Greg Norman	1,165,477.00
1945	Byron Nelson*	63,335.66	1968	Billy Casper	205,168.67	1991	Corey Pavin	979,430.00
1946	Ben Hogan	42,556.16	1969	Frank Beard	164,707.11	1992	Fred Couples	1,344,188.00
1947	Jimmy Demaret	27,936.83	1970	Lee Trevino	157,037.63	1993	Nick Price	1,478,557.00
1948	Ben Hogan	32,112.00	1971	Jack Nicklaus	244,490.50	1994	Nick Price	1,499,927.00
1949	Sam Snead	31,593.83	1972	Jack Nicklaus	320,542.26	1995	Greg Norman	1,654,959.00
1950	Sam Snead	35,758.83	1973	Jack Nicklaus	308,362.10	1996	Tom Lehman	1,780,159.00
1951	Lloyd Mangrum	26,088.83	1974	Johnny Miller	353,021.59	1997	Tiger Woods	2,066,833.00
1952	Julius Boros	37,032.97	1975	Jack Nicklaus	298,149.17	1998	David Duval	2,591,031.00
1953	Lew Worsham	34,002.00	1976	Jack Nicklaus	266,438.57	1999	Tiger Woods	6,616,585.00
1954	Bob Toski	65,819.81	1977	Tom Watson	310,653.16	2000	Tiger Woods	9,188,321.00
1955	Julius Boros	63,121.55	1978	Tom Watson	362,428.93	2001	Tiger Woods	5,687,777.00
1956	Ted Kroll	72,835.83	1979	Tom Watson	462,636.00			

* War bonds. Note: Total money listed from 1968 through 1974. Official money listed from 1975 on.

Career Money Leaders*

		Earnings ($)			Earnings ($)			Earnings ($)
1.	Tiger Woods	32,687,252	18.	Paul Azinger	12,457,891	35.	Jesper Parnevik	9,276,274
2.	Phil Mickelson	21,708,369	19.	David Toms	12,010,092	36.	Jay Haas	9,142,948
3.	Davis Love III	19,763,069	20.	Payne Stewart	11,737,008	37.	Rocco Mediate	9,128,731
4.	Vijay Singh	17,367,325	21.	Loren Roberts	11,696,028	38.	Billy Mayfair	9,116,366
5.	Nick Price	16,557,337	22.	Brad Faxon	11,499,393	39.	Craig Stadler	9,008,663
6.	David Duval	16,142,421	23.	John Cook	10,996,271	40.	Scott Verplank	8,948,275
7.	Scott Hoch	15,929,575	24.	Tom Kite	10,920,309	41.	Steve Lowery	8,306,643
8.	Ernie Els	15,197,329	25.	Fred Funk	10,658,762	42.	Kirk Triplett	8,173,029
9.	M. Calcavecchia	14,573,517	26.	John Huston	10,413,649	43.	Billy Andrade	8,051,218
10.	Hal Sutton	14,198,473	27.	Bob Estes	10,284,355	44.	David Frost	8,001,237
11.	Greg Norman	13,812,130	28.	Lee Janzen	10,071,209	45.	Mike Weir	7,926,298
12.	Jim Furyk	13,737,902	29.	Jeff Maggert	9,988,185	46.	Mark Brooks	7,843,778
13.	Justin Leonard	13,561,234	30.	Corey Pavin	9,898,182	47.	Chris DiMarco	7,722,304
14.	Fred Couples	13,327,971	31.	Steve Elkington	9,864,808	48.	Stewart Cink	7,714,216
15.	Tom Lehman	12,949,405	32.	Tom Watson	9,773,761	49.	Steve Pate	7,613,719
16.	Mark O'Meara	12,755,331	33.	Bob Tway	9,526,842	50.	Curtis Strange	7,592,144
17.	Jeff Sluman	12,717,753	34.	Kenny Perry	9,335,192			

*Through 10/13/02.

Year by Year Statistical Leaders

SCORING AVERAGE

1980	Lee Trevino	69.73
1981	Tom Kite	69.80
1982	Tom Kite	70.21
1983	Raymond Floyd	70.61
1984	Calvin Peete	70.56
1985	Don Pooley	70.36
1986	Scott Hoch	70.08
1987	David Frost	70.09
1988	Greg Norman	69.38
1989	Payne Stewart	69.485†
1990	Greg Norman	69.10
1991	Fred Couples	69.59
1992	Fred Couples	69.38
1993	Greg Norman	68.90
1994	Greg Norman	68.81
1995	Greg Norman	69.06
1996	Tom Lehman	69.32
1997	Nick Price	68.98
1998	David Duval	69.13
1999	Tiger Woods	68.43
2000	Tiger Woods	67.79
2001	Tiger Woods	68.81

Note: Scoring average per round, with adjustments made at each round for the field's course scoring average.

DRIVING DISTANCE

		Yds
1980	Dan Pohl	274.3
1981	Dan Pohl	280.1
1982	Bill Calfee	275.3
1983	John McComish	277.4
1984	Bill Glasson	276.5
1985	Andy Bean	278.2
1986	Davis Love III	285.7
1987	John McComish	283.9
1988	Steve Thomas	284.6
1989	Ed Humenik	280.9
1990	Tom Purtzer	279.6
1991	John Daly	288.9

DRIVING DISTANCE *(Cont.)*

1992	John Daly	283.4
1993	John Daly	288.9
1994	Davis Love III	283.8
1995	John Daly	289.0
1996	John Daly	288.8
1997	John Daly	302.0
1998	John Daly	299.4
1999	John Daly	305.6
2000	John Adams	301.4
2001	John Daly	306.7

Note: Average computed by charting distance of two tee shots on a predetermined par-four or par-five hole (one on front nine, one on back nine).

DRIVING ACCURACY

1980	Mike Reid	79.5
1981	Calvin Peete	81.9
1982	Calvin Peete	84.6
1983	Calvin Peete	81.3
1984	Calvin Peete	77.5
1985	Calvin Peete	80.6
1986	Calvin Peete	81.7
1987	Calvin Peete	83.0
1988	Calvin Peete	82.5
1989	Calvin Peete	82.6
1990	Calvin Peete	83.7
1991	Hale Irwin	78.3
1992	Doug Tewell	82.3
1993	Doug Tewell	82.5
1994	David Edwards	81.6
1995	Fred Funk	81.3
1996	Fred Funk	78.7
1997	Allen Doyle	80.8
1998	Bruce Fleisher	81.4
1999	Fred Funk	80.2
2000	Fred Funk	79.7
2001	Joe Durant	81.1

Note: Percentage of fairways hit on number of par-four and par-five holes played; par-three holes excluded.

GREENS IN REGULATION

1980	Jack Nicklaus	72.1
1981	Calvin Peete	73.1
1982	Calvin Peete	72.4
1983	Calvin Peete	71.4
1984	Andy Bean	72.1
1985	John Mahaffey	71.9
1986	John Mahaffey	72.0
1987	Gil Morgan	73.3
1988	John Adams	73.9
1989	Bruce Lietzke	72.6
1990	Doug Tewell	70.9
1991	Bruce Lietzke	73.3
1992	Tim Simpson	74.0
1993	Fuzzy Zoeller	73.6
1994	Bill Glasson	73.0
1995	Lenny Clements	72.3
1996	Fred Couples	71.8
	Mark O'Meara	71.8
1997	Tom Lehman	72.7
1998	Hal Sutton	71.3
1999	Tiger Woods	71.4
2000	Tiger Woods	75.2
2001	Tom Lehman	74.5

Note: Average of greens reached in regulation out of total holes played; hole is considered hit in regulation if any part of the ball rests on the putting surface in two shots less than the hole's par—a par-5 hit in two shots is one green in regulation.

PUTTING

1980	Jerry Pate	28.81
1981	Alan Tapie	28.70
1982	Ben Crenshaw	28.65
1983	Morris Hatalsky	27.96
1984	Gary McCord	28.57
1985	Craig Stadler	28.627†
1986	Greg Norman	1.736
1987	Ben Crenshaw	1.743
1988	Don Pooley	1.729
1989	Steve Jones	1.734

† Number had to be carried to extra decimal place to determine winner.

Year by Year Statistical Leaders (Cont.)

PUTTING (Cont.)

1990	Larry Rinker	1.7467†	1994	Loren Roberts	1.737	
1991	Jay Don Blake	1.7326†	1995	Jim Furyk	1.708	
1992	Mark O'Meara	1.731	1996	Brad Faxon	1.709	
1993	David Frost	1.739	1997	Don Pooley	1.718	

1998	Rick Fehr	1.722
1999	Brad Faxon	1.723
2000	Brad Faxon	1.704
2001	David Frost	1.708

Note: Average number of putts taken on greens reached in regulation; prior to 1986, based on average number of putts per 18 holes.

SAND SAVES

1980	Bob Eastwood	65.4	1988	Greg Powers	63.5	1996	Gary Rusnak	64.0
1981	Tom Watson	60.1	1989	Mike Sullivan	66.0	1997	Bob Estes	70.3
1982	Isao Aoki	60.2	1990	Paul Azinger	67.2	1998	Keith Fergus	71.0
1983	Isao Aoki	62.3	1991	Ben Crenshaw	64.9	1999	Jeff Sluman	67.3
1984	Peter Oosterhuis	64.7	1992	Mitch Adcock	66.9	2000	Fred Couples	67.0
1985	Tom Purtzer	60.8	1993	Ken Green	64.4	2001	Franklin Langham	68.9
1986	Paul Azinger	63.8	1994	Corey Pavin	65.4			
1987	Paul Azinger	63.2	1995	Billy Mayfair	68.6			

Note: Percentage of up-and-down efforts from greenside sand traps only—fairway bunkers excluded.

PAR BREAKERS

1980	Tom Watson	.213	1984	Craig Stadler	.220	1988	Ken Green	.236
1981	Bruce Lietzke	.225	1985	Craig Stadler	.218	1989	Greg Norman	.224
1982	Tom Kite	.2154†	1986	Greg Norman	.248	1990	Greg Norman	.219
1983	Tom Watson	.211	1987	Mark Calcavecchia	.221			

Note: Average based on total birdies and eagles scored out of total holes played. Discontinued as an official category after 1990.

EAGLES

1980	Dave Eichelberger	16	1987	Phil Blackmar	20	1994	Davis Love III	18
1981	Bruce Lietzke	12	1988	Ken Green	21	1995	Kelly Gibson	16
1982	Tom Weiskopf	10	1989	Lon Hinkle	14	1996	Tom Watson	97.2
	J.C. Snead	10		Duffy Waldorf	14	1997	Tiger Woods	104.1
	Andy Bean	10	1990	Paul Azinger	14	1998	Davis Love III	83.3
1983	Chip Beck	15	1991	Andy Bean	15	1999	Vijay Singh	104.8
1984	Gary Hallberg	15	1992	Dan Forsman	18	2000	Tiger Woods	72.0
1985	Larry Rinker	14	1993	Davis Love III	15	2001	Phil Mickelson	73.8
1986	Joey Sindelar	16						

Note: Total of eagles scored 1980–1995. Since 1996 winner determined by number of holes played per eagle.

BIRDIES

1980	Andy Bean	388	1988	Dan Forsman	465	1996	Fred Couples	4.20
1981	Vance Heafner	388	1989	Ted Schulz	415	1997	Tiger Woods	4.25
1982	Andy Bean	392	1990	Mike Donald	401	1998	David Duval	4.29
1983	Hal Sutton	399	1991	Scott Hoch	446	1999	Tiger Woods	4.46
1984	Mark O'Meara	419	1992	Jeff Sluman	417	2000	Tiger Woods	4.92
1985	Joey Sindelar	411	1993	John Huston	426	2001	Phil Mickelson	4.49
1986	Joey Sindelar	415	1994	Brad Bryant	397			
1987	Dan Forsman	409	1995	Steve Lowery	410			

Note: Total of birdies scored 1980–95. Since 1996, winner determined by average number of birdies per round.

ALL-AROUND

1987	Dan Pohl	170	1992	Fred Couples	256	1997	Bill Glasson	282
1988	Payne Stewart	170	1993	Gil Morgan	252	1998	John Huston	151
1989	Paul Azinger	250	1994	Bob Estes	227	1999	Tiger Woods	120
1990	Paul Azinger	162	1995	Justin Leonard	323	2000	Tiger Woods	113
1991	Scott Hoch	283	1996	Fred Couples	214	2001	Phil Mickelson	174

Note: Sum of the places of standing from the other statistical categories; the player with the number closest to zero leads.

† Number had to be carried to extra decimal place to determine winner.

PGA Player of the Year Award

1948 ....Ben Hogan	1966 ....Billy Casper	1984 ....Tom Watson
1949 ....Sam Snead	1967 ....Jack Nicklaus	1985 ....Lanny Wadkins
1950 ....Ben Hogan	1968 ....Not awarded	1986 ....Bob Tway
1951 ....Ben Hogan	1969 ....Orville Moody	1987 ....Paul Azinger
1952 ....Julius Boros	1970 ....Billy Casper	1988 ....Curtis Strange
1953 ....Ben Hogan	1971 ....Lee Trevino	1989 ....Tom Kite
1954 ....Ed Furgol	1972 ....Jack Nicklaus	1990 ....Wayne Levi
1955 ....Doug Ford	1973 ....Jack Nicklaus	1991 ....Fred Couples
1956 ....Jack Burke	1974 ....Johnny Miller	1992 ....Fred Couples
1957 ....Dick Mayer	1975 ....Jack Nicklaus	1993 ....Nick Price
1958 ....Dow,Finsterwald	1976 ....Jack Nicklaus	1994 ....Nick Price
1959 ....Art Wall	1977 ....Tom Watson	1995 ....Greg Norman
1960 ....Arnold Palmer	1978 ....Tom Watson	1996 ....Tom Lehman
1961 ....Jerry Barber	1979 ....Tom Watson	1997 ....Tiger Woods
1962 ....Arnold Palmer	1980 ....Tom Watson	1998 ....David Duval
1963 ....Julius Boros	1981 ....Bill Rogers	1999 ....Tiger Woods
1964 ....Ken Venturi	1982 ....Tom Watson	2000 ....Tiger Woods
1965 ....Dave Marr	1983 ....Hal Sutton	2001 ....Tiger Woods

Vardon Trophy: Scoring Average

Year	Winner	Avg	Year	Winner	Avg	Year	Winner	Avg
1937	Harry Cooper	*500	1961	Arnold Palmer	69.85	1981	Tom Kite	69.80
1938	Sam Snead	520	1962	Arnold Palmer	70.27	1982	Tom Kite	70.21
1939	Byron Nelson	473	1963	Billy Casper	70.58	1983	Raymond Floyd	70.61
1940	Ben Hogan	423	1964	Arnold Palmer	70.01	1984	Calvin Peete	70.56
1941	Ben Hogan	494	1965	Billy Casper	70.85	1985	Don Pooley	70.36
1942–46	No award		1966	Billy Casper	70.27	1986	Scott Hoch	70.08
1947	Jimmy Demaret	69.90	1967	Arnold Palmer	70.18	1987	Don Pohl	70.25
1948	Ben Hogan	69.30	1968	Billy Casper	69.82	1988	Chip Beck	69.46
1949	Sam Snead	69.37	1969	Dave Hill	70.34	1989	Greg Norman	69.49
1950	Sam Snead	69.23	1970	Lee Trevino	70.64	1990	Greg Norman	69.10
1951	Lloyd Mangrum	70.05	1971	Lee Trevino	70.27	1991	Fred Couples	69.59
1952	Jack Burke	70.54	1972	Lee Trevino	70.89	1992	Fred Couples	69.38
1953	Lloyd Mangrum	70.22	1973	Bruce Crampton	70.57	1993	Nick Price	69.11
1954	E.J. Harrison	70.41	1974	Lee Trevino	70.53	1994	Greg Norman	68.81
1955	Sam Snead	69.86	1975	Bruce Crampton	70.51	1995	Steve Elkington	69.62
1956	Cary Middlecoff	70.35	1976	Don January	70.56	1996	Tom Lehman	69.32
1957	Dow Finsterwald	70.30	1977	Tom Watson	70.32	1997	Nick Price	68.98
1958	Bob Rosburg	70.11	1978	Tom Watson	70.16	1998	David Duval	69.13
1959	Art Wall	70.35	1979	Tom Watson	70.27	1999	Tiger Woods	68.43
1960	Billy Casper	69.95	1980	Lee Trevino	69.73	2000	Tiger Woods	67.79
						2001	Tiger Woods	68.81

*Point system used, 1937–41.

Note: As of 1988, based on minimum of 60 rounds per year. Adjusted for average score of field in tournaments entered.

Alltime PGA Tour Records*

Scoring

90 HOLES

324—(65-61-67-66-65) by Joe Durant, at four courses, La Quinta, CA, to win the 2001 Bob Hope Classic (36 under par).

72 HOLES

256—(65-60-64-67) by Mark Calcavecchia, at the TPC at Scottsdale, Scottsdale, AZ, to win the 2001 Phoenix Open (28 under par).

54 HOLES, OPENING ROUNDS

189—(64-62-63) by John Cook, at the TPC at Southwind, Memphis, en route to winning the 1996 St. Jude Classic.

54 HOLES, OPENING ROUNDS (Cont.)

189—(65-60-64) Mark Calcavecchia, at the TPC at Scottsdale, Scottsdale, AZ, en route to winning the 2001 Phoenix Open.

54 HOLES, CONSECUTIVE ROUNDS

189—(63-63-63) by Chandler Harper in the last three rounds to win the 1954 Texas Open at Brackenridge Park GC, San Antonio.

189—(64-62-63) by John Cook, at the TPC at Southwind, Memphis, in the first three rounds en route to winning the 1996 St. Jude Classic.

189—(65-60-64) Mark Calcavecchia, at the TPC at Scottsdale, Scottsdale, AZ, in the first three rounds en route to winning the 2001 Phoenix Open.

Alltime PGA Tour Records (Cont.)*

Scoring (Cont.)

36 HOLES, OPENING ROUNDS

125—(64–61) by Tiger Woods, in the 2000 World Golf Championships/ NEC Invitational, which he won, at Firestone CC, Akron.

125—(65–60) by Mark Calcavecchia, in the 2001 Phoenix Open, which he won, at TPC at Scottsdale, Scottsdale, AZ.

36 HOLES, CONSECUTIVE ROUNDS

125—(64–61) by Gay Brewer, in the middle rounds of the 1967 Pensacola Open, which he won, at Pensacola CC, Pensacola, FL.

125—(63–62) by Ron Streck, in the last two rounds to win the 1978 Texas Open at Oak Hills CC, San Antonio.

125—(62–63) by Blaine McCallister, in the middle two rounds of the 1988 Hardee's Golf Classic, which he won at Oakwood CC, Coal Valley, IL.

125—(62–63) by John Cook, in the middle two rounds of the 1996 St. Jude Classic, which he won at the TPC at Southwind, Memphis.

125—(62–63) by John Cook, in the fourth and fifth rounds in winning the 1997 Bob Hope Chrysler Classic at Indian Wells CC, Indian Hills, CA.

125—(64–61) by Tiger Woods, in the first two rounds of the 2000 World Golf Championship/ NEC Invitational, which he won, at Firestone CC, Akron.

125—(65–60) by Mark Calcavecchia, in the first two rounds of the 2001 Phoenix Open, which he won, at TPC at Scottsdale, Scottsdale, AZ.

18 HOLES

59—by Al Geiberger, at Colonial Country Club, Memphis, in second round in winning the 1977 Memphis Classic.

59—by Chip Beck, at Sunrise Golf Club, Las Vegas, in third round of the 1991 Las Vegas Invitational.

59—by David Duval, on the Palmer Course at PGA West, La Quinta, CA, in the fifth round of the 1999 Bob Hope Chrysler Classic.

9 HOLES

27—by Mike Souchak, at Brackenridge Park GC, San Antonio, on par-35 second nine of first round in the 1955 Texas Open.

27—by Andy North, at En-Joie GC, Endicott, NY, on par-34 second nine of first round in the 1975 BC Open.

27—by Billy Mayfair, at Warwick Hills, Grand Blanc, MI, on par-36 back nine of fourth round, 2001 Buick Open.

MOST CONSECUTIVE ROUNDS UNDER 70

19—Byron Nelson in 1945.

MOST BIRDIES IN A ROW

8—Bob Goalby, at Pasadena GC, St. Petersburg, FL, during fourth round in winning the 1961 St Petersburg Open.

8—Fuzzy Zoeller, at Oakwood CC, Coal Valley, IL, during first round of 1976 Quad Cities Open.

8—Dewey Arnette, at Warwick Hills GC, Grand Blanc, MI, during first round of the 1987 Buick Open.

8—Edward Fryatt, at the Blue Course of the Doral Resort and Spa, Miami, during second round of the 2000 Doral-Ryder Open.

MOST BIRDIES IN A ROW TO WIN

5—Jack Nicklaus, to win 1978 Jackie Gleason Inverrary Classic (last 5 holes).

Wins

MOST CONSECUTIVE YEARS WINNING AT LEAST ONE TOURNAMENT

17—Jack Nicklaus, 1962–78.

17—Arnold Palmer, 1955–71.

16—Billy Casper, 1956–71.

MOST CONSECUTIVE WINS

11—Byron Nelson, from Miami Four Ball, March 8–11, 1945, through Canadian Open, August 2–4, 1945.

MOST WINS IN A SINGLE EVENT

8—Sam Snead, Greater Greensboro Open, 1938, 1946, 1949, 1950, 1955, 1956, 1960, and 1965.

MOST CONSECUTIVE WINS IN A SINGLE EVENT

4—Walter Hagen, PGA Championships, 1924–27.

4—Gene Sarazen, Miami Open, 1926, (schedule change) 1928–30.

MOST WINS IN A CALENDAR YEAR

18—Byron Nelson, 1945

MOST YEARS BETWEEN WINS

15 yrs, 5 mos—Butch Baird, 1961–76.

MOST YEARS FROM FIRST WIN TO LAST

28 yrs, 11 mos, 20 days—Raymond Floyd, 1963–92.

YOUNGEST WINNERS

19 yrs, 10 mos—John McDermott, 1911 U.S. Open.

OLDEST WINNER

52 yrs, 10 mos—Sam Snead, 1965 Greater Greensboro Open.

WIDEST WINNING MARGIN: STROKES

16—Bobby Locke, 1948 Chicago Victory National Championship.

Putting

FEWEST PUTTS, ONE ROUND

18—Andy North, at Kingsmill GC, in second round of 1990 Anheuser Busch Golf Classic.

18—Kenny Knox, at Harbour Town GL, in first round of 1989 MCI Heritage Classic.

18—Mike McGee, at Colonial CC, in first round of 1987 Federal Express St. Jude Classic.

18—Sam Trahan, at Whitemarsh Valley CC, in final round of 1979 IVB Philadelphia Golf Classic.

18—Jim McGovern, at TPC at Southwind, in second round of 1992 Federal Express St. Jude Classic.

FEWEST PUTTS, FOUR ROUNDS

93—Kenny Knox, in 1989 MCI Heritage Classic at Harbour Town GL.

*Through 10/22/01.

THE MAJOR TOURNAMENTS

LPGA Championship

Year	Winner	Score	Runner-Up	Site
1955	Beverly Hanson† (4 & 3)	220	Louise Suggs	Orchard Ridge CC, Ft Wayne, IN
1956	Marlene Hagge*	291	Patty Berg	Forest Lake CC, Detroit
1957	Louise Suggs	285	Wiffi Smith	Churchill Valley CC, Pittsburgh
1958	Mickey Wright	288	Fay Crocker	Churchill Valley CC, Pittsburgh
1959	Betsy Rawls	288	Patty Berg	Sheraton Hotel CC, French Lick, IN
1960	Mickey Wright	292	Louise Suggs	Sheraton Hotel CC, French Lick, IN
1961	Mickey Wright	287	Louise Suggs	Stardust CC, Las Vegas
1962	Judy Kimball	282	Shirley Spork	Stardust CC, Las Vegas
1963	Mickey Wright	294	Mary Lena Faulk Mary Mills Louise Suggs	Stardust CC, Las Vegas
1964	Mary Mills	278	Mickey Wright	Stardust CC, Las Vegas
1965	Sandra Haynie	279	Clifford A. Creed	Stardust CC, Las Vegas
1966	Gloria Ehret	282	Mickey Wright	Stardust CC, Las Vegas
1967	Kathy Whitworth	284	Shirley Englehorn	Pleasant Valley CC, Sutton, MA
1968	Sandra Post* (68)	294	Kathy Whitworth (75)	Pleasant Valley CC, Sutton, MA
1969	Betsy Rawls	293	Susie Berning Carol Mann	Concord GC, Kiameshia Lake, NY
1970	Shirley Englehorn* (74)	285	Kathy Whitworth (78)	Pleasant Valley CC, Sutton, MA
1971	Kathy Whitworth	288	Kathy Ahern	Pleasant Valley CC, Sutton, MA
1972	Kathy Ahern	293	Jane Blalock	Pleasant Valley CC, Sutton, MA
1973	Mary Mills	288	Betty Burfeindt	Pleasant Valley CC, Sutton, MA
1974	Sandra Haynie	288	JoAnne Carner	Pleasant Valley CC, Sutton, MA
1975	Kathy Whitworth	288	Sandra Haynie	Pine Ridge GC, Baltimore
1976	Betty Burfeindt	287	Judy Rankin	Pine Ridge GC, Baltimore
1977	Chako Higuchi	279	Pat Bradley Sandra Post Judy Rankin	Bay Tree Golf Plantation, N Myrtle Beach, SC
1978	Nancy Lopez	275	Amy Alcott	Jack Nicklaus GC, Kings Island, OH
1979	Donna Caponi	279	Jerilyn Britz	Jack Nicklaus GC, Kings Island, OH
1980	Sally Little	285	Jane Blalock	Jack Nicklaus GC, Kings Island, OH
1981	Donna Caponi	280	Jerilyn Britz Pat Meyers	Jack Nicklaus GC, Kings Island, OH
1982	Jan Stephenson	279	JoAnne Carner	Jack Nicklaus GC, Kings Island, OH
1983	Patty Sheehan	279	Sandra Haynie	Jack Nicklaus GC, Kings Island, OH
1984	Patty Sheehan	272	Beth Daniel Pat Bradley	Jack Nicklaus GC, Kings Island, OH
1985	Nancy Lopez	273	Alice Miller	Jack Nicklaus GC, Kings Island, OH
1986	Pat Bradley	277	Patty Sheehan	Jack Nicklaus GC, Kings Island, OH
1987	Jane Geddes	275	Betsy King	Jack Nicklaus GC, Kings Island, OH
1988	Sherri Turner	281	Amy Alcott	Jack Nicklaus GC, Kings Island, OH
1989	Nancy Lopez	274	Ayako Okamoto	Jack Nicklaus GC, Kings Island, OH
1990	Beth Daniel	280	Rosie Jones	Bethesda CC, Bethesda, MD
1991	Meg Mallon	274	Pat Bradley Ayako Okamoto	Bethesda CC, Bethesda, MD
1992	Betsy King	267	Karen Noble	Bethesda CC, Bethesda, MD
1993	Patty Sheehan	275	Lauri Merten	Bethesda CC, Bethesda, MD
1994	Laura Davies	279	Alice Ritzman	DuPont CC, Wilmington, DE
1995	Kelly Robbins	274	Laura Davies	DuPont CC, Wilmington, DE
1996	Laura Davies	213†	Julie Piers	DuPont CC, Wilmington, DE
1997	Chris Johnson*	281	Leta Lindley	DuPont CC, Wilmington, DE
1998	Se Ri Pak	273	Donna Andrews	DuPont CC, Wilmington, DE
1999	Juli Inkster	268	Liselotte Neumann	DuPont CC, Wilmington, DE
2000	Juli Inkster*	281	Stefania Croce	DuPont CC, Wilmington, DE
2001	Karrie Webb	270	Laura Diaz	DuPont CC, Wilmington, DE
2002	Se Ri Pak	279	Beth Daniel	DuPont CC, Wilmington, DE

*Won in playoff. Playoff scores are in parentheses. 1956 and 1997 were sudden death; 1968 and 1970 were 18-hole playoffs. †Won match-play final. #Shortened due to rain.

U.S. Women's Open

Year	Winner	Score	Runner-Up	Site
1946	Patty Berg	5 & 4	Betty Jameson	Spokane CC, Spokane, WA
1947	Betty Jameson	295	Sally Sessions	Starmount Forest CC, Greensboro, NC
			Polly Riley	
1948	Babe Zaharias	300	Betty Hicks	Atlantic City CC, Northfield, NJ
1949	Louise Suggs	291	Babe Zaharias	Prince George's G & CC, Landover, MD
1950	Babe Zaharias	291	Betsy Rawls	Rolling Hills CC, Wichita, KS
1951	Betsy Rawls	293	Louise Suggs	Druid Hills GC, Atlanta
1952	Louise Suggs	284	Marlene Bauer	Bala GC, Philadelphia
			Betty Jameson	
1953	Betsy Rawls* (71)	302	Jackie Pung (77)	CC of Rochester, Rochester, NY
1954	Babe Zaharias	291	Betty Hicks	Salem CC, Peabody, MA
1955	Fay Crocker	299	Mary Lena Faulk	Wichita CC, Wichita, KS
			Louise Suggs	
1956	Kathy Cornelius* (75)	302	Barbara McIntire (82)	Northland CC, Duluth, MN
1957	Betsy Rawls	299	Patty Berg	Winged Foot GC, Mamaroneck, NY
1958	Mickey Wright	290	Louise Suggs	Forest Lake CC, Detroit
1959	Mickey Wright	287	Louise Suggs	Churchill Valley CC, Pittsburgh
1960	Betsy Rawls	292	Joyce Ziske	Worcester CC, Worcester, MA
1961	Mickey Wright	293	Betsy Rawls	Baltusrol GC (Lower Course), Springfield, NJ
1962	Murle Breer	301	Jo Ann Prentice	Dunes GC, Myrtle Beach, SC
			Ruth Jessen	
1963	Mary Mills	289	Sandra Haynie	Kenwood CC, Cincinnati
			Louise Suggs	
1964	Mickey Wright* (70)	290	Ruth Jessen (72)	San Diego CC, Chula Vista, CA
1965	Carol Mann	290	Kathy Cornelius	Atlantic City CC, Northfield, NJ
1966	Sandra Spuzich	297	Carol Mann	Hazeltine Natl GC, Chaska, MN
1967	Catherine LaCoste	294	Susie Berning	Hot Springs GC (Cascades Course),
			Beth Stone	Hot Springs, VA
1968	Susie Berning	289	Mickey Wright	Moslem Springs GC, Fleetwood, PA
1969	Donna Caponi	294	Peggy Wilson	Scenic Hills CC, Pensacola, FL
1970	Donna Caponi	287	Sandra Haynie	Muskogee CC, Muskogee, OK
			Sandra Spuzich	
1971	JoAnne Carner	288	Kathy Whitworth	Kahkwa CC, Erie, PA
1972	Susie Berning	299	Kathy Ahern	Winged Foot GC, Mamaroneck, NY
			Pam Barnett	
			Judy Rankin	
1973	Susie Berning	290	Gloria Ehret	CC of Rochester, Rochester, NY
			Shelley Hamlin	
1974	Sandra Haynie	295	Carol Mann	La Grange CC, La Grange, IL
			Beth Stone	
1975	Sandra Palmer	295	JoAnne Carner	Atlantic City CC, Northfield, NJ
			Sandra Post	
			Nancy Lopez	
1976	JoAnne Carner* (76)	292	Sandra Palmer (78)	Rolling Green CC, Springfield, PA
1977	Hollis Stacy	292	Nancy Lopez	Hazeltine Natl GC, Chaska, MN
1978	Hollis Stacy	289	JoAnne Carner	CC of Indianapolis, Indianapolis
			Sally Little	
1979	Jerilyn Britz	284	Debbie Massey	Brooklawn CC, Fairfield, CT
			Sandra Palmer	
1980	Amy Alcott	280	Hollis Stacy	Richland CC, Nashville
1981	Pat Bradley	279	Beth Daniel	La Grange CC, La Grange, IL
1982	Janet Anderson	283	Beth Daniel	Del Paso CC, Sacramento
			Sandra Haynie	
			Donna White	
			JoAnne Carner	
1983	Jan Stephenson	290	JoAnne Carner	Cedar Ridge CC, Tulsa
			Patty Sheehan	
1984	Hollis Stacy	290	Rosie Jones	Salem CC, Peabody, MA
1985	Kathy Baker	280	Judy Dickinson	Baltusrol GC (Upper Course), Springfield, NJ
1986	Jane Geddes* (71)	287	Sally Little (73)	NCR GC, Dayton
1987	Laura Davies* (71)	285	Ayako Okamoto (73)	Plainfield CC, Plainfield, NJ
			JoAnne Carner (74)	
1988	Liselotte Neumann	277	Patty Sheehan	Baltimore CC, Baltimore
1989	Betsy King	278	Nancy Lopez	Indianwood G & CC, Lake Orion, MI
1990	Betsy King	284	Patty Sheehan	Atlanta Athletic Club, Duluth, GA
1991	Meg Mallon	283	Pat Bradley	Colonial Club, Fort Worth

U.S. Women's Open *(Cont.)*

Year	Winner	Score	Runner-Up	Site
1992	Patty Sheehan* (72)	280	Juli Inkster	Oakmont CC, Oakmont, PA
1993	Lauri Merten	280	Donna Andrew Helen Alfredsson	Crooked Stick, Carmel, IN
1994	Patty Sheehan	277	Tammie Green	Indianwood G & CC, Lake Orion, MI
1995	Annika Sorenstam	278	Meg Mallon	The Broadmoor GC, Colorado Springs, CO
1996	Annika Sorenstam	272	Kris Tschetter	Pine Needles GC, Southern Pines, NC
1997	Alison Nicholas	274	Nancy Lopez	Pumpkin Ridge CC, North Plains, OR
1998	Se Ri Pak†	290	Jenny Chuasiriporn	Blackwolf Run Golf Resort, Kohler, WI
1999	Juli Inkster	272	Sherri Turner	Old Waverly GC, West Point, MS
2000	Karrie Webb	282	Cristie Kerr Meg Mallon	Merit GC, Libertyville, IL
2001	Karrie Webb	273	Se Ri Pak	Pine Needles GC, Southern Pines, NC
2002	Juli Inkster	276	Annika Sorenstam	Prairie Dunes CC, Hutchinson, KS

* Winner in playoff; 18-hole playoff scores are in parentheses. † Winner on second hole of sudden death after 18-hole playoff ended in a tie.

Nabisco Championship

Year	Winner	Score	Runner-Up	Year	Winner	Score	Runner-Up
1972	Jane Blalock	213	Carol Mann Judy Rankin	1988	Amy Alcott	274	Colleen Walker
1973	Mickey Wright	284	Joyce Kazmierski	1989	Juli Inkster	279	Tammie Green JoAnne Carner
1974	Jo Ann Prentice*	289	Jane Blalock Sandra Haynie	1990	Betsy King	283	Kathy Postlewait Shirley Furlong
1975	Sandra Palmer	283	Kathy McMullen	1991	Amy Alcott	273	Dottie Mochrie
1976	Judy Rankin	285	Betty Burfeindt	1992	Dottie Mochrie*	279	Juli Inkster
1977	Kathy Whitworth	289	JoAnne Carner Sally Little	1993	Helen Alfredsson	284	Amy Benz Tina Barrett
1978	Sandra Post*	283	Penny Pulz				Betsy King
1979	Sandra Post	276	Nancy Lopez	1994	Donna Andrews	276	Laura Davies
1980	Donna Caponi	275	Amy Alcott	1995	Nanci Bowen	285	Susie Redman
1981	Nancy Lopez	277	Carolyn Hill	1996	Patti Sheehan	281	Kelly Robbins
1982	Sally Little	278	Hollis Stacy Sandra Haynie				Meg Mallon Annika Sörenstam
1983	Amy Alcott	282	Beth Daniel Kathy Whitworth	1997	Betsy King	276	Kris Tschetter
				1998	Pat Hurst	281	Helen Dobson
1984	Juli Inkster*	280	Pat Bradley	1999	Dottie Pepper	269	Meg Mallon
1985	Alice Miller	275	Jan Stephenson	2000	Karrie Webb	274	Dottie Pepper
1986	Pat Bradley	280	Val Skinner	2001	Annika Sorenstam	281	five players
1987	Betsy King*	283	Patty Sheehan	2002	Annika Sorenstam	280	Liselotte Neumann

*Winner in sudden-death playoff. Note: Designated fourth major in 1983; played at Mission Hills CC, Rancho Mirage, CA.

du Maurier Classic

Year	Winner	Score	Runner-Up	Site
1973	Jocelyne Bourassa*	214	Sandra Haynie Judy Rankin	Montreal GC, Montreal
1974	Carole Jo Callison	208	JoAnne Carner	Candiac GC, Montreal
1975	JoAnne Carner*	214	Carol Mann	St. George's CC, Toronto
1976	Donna Caponi*	212	Judy Rankin	Cedar Brae G & CC, Toronto
1977	Judy Rankin	214	Pat Meyers Sandra Palmer	Lachute G & CC, Montreal
1978	JoAnne Carner	278	Hollis Stacy	St. George's CC, Toronto
1979	Amy Alcott	285	Nancy Lopez	Richelieu Valley CC, Montreal
1980	Pat Bradley	277	JoAnne Carner	St. George's CC, Toronto
1981	Jan Stephenson	278	Nancy Lopez Pat Bradley	Summerlea CC, Dorion, Quebec
1982	Sandra Haynie	280	Beth Daniel	St. George's CC, Toronto
1983	Hollis Stacy	277	JoAnne Carner Alice Miller	Beaconsfield GC, Montreal
1984	Juli Inkster	279	Ayako Okamoto	St. George's G & CC, Toronto
1985	Pat Bradley	278	Jane Geddes	Beaconsfield CC, Montreal
1986	Pat Bradley*	276	Ayako Okamoto	Board of Trade CC, Toronto
1987	Jody Rosenthal	272	Ayako Okamoto	Islesmere GC, Laval, Quebec
1988	Sally Little	279	Laura Davies	Vancouver GC, Coquitlam, British Columbia
1989	Tammie Green	279	Pat Bradley Betsy King	Beaconsfield GC, Montreal

du Maurier Classic (Cont.)

Year	Winner	Score	Runner-Up	Site
1990	Cathy Johnston	276	Patty Sheehan	Westmount G & CC, Kitchener, Ontario
1991	Nancy Scranton	279	Debbie Massey	Vancouver GC, Coquitlam, British Columbia
1992	Sherri Steinhauer	277	Judy Dickinson	St. Charles CC, Winnipeg, Manitoba
1993	Brandie Burton	277	Betsy King	London Hunt and CC, London, Ontario
1994	Martha Nause	279	Michelle McGann	Ottawa Hunt and GC, Ottawa, Ont.
1995	Jenny Lidback	280	Liselotte Neumann	Beaconsfield GC, Pointe-Claire, Quebec
1996	Laura Davies	277	Nancy Lopez Karrie Webb	Edmonton CC, Edmonton, Alberta
1997	Colleen Walker	278	Liselotte Neumann	Glen Abbey GC, Oakville, Ontario
1998	Brandie Burton	270	Annika Sorenstam	Essex G & CC, Windsor, Ontario
1999	Karrie Webb	277	Laura Davies	Priddis Greens G & CC, Calgary, Alberta
2000	Meg Mallon	282	Rosie Jones	Royal Ottawa GC, Aylmer, Quebec

*Winner in sudden-death playoff. Note: Designated third major in 1979; discontinued in 2001.

Women's British Open

Year	Winner	Score	Runner-Up	Site
2001	Se Ri Pak	277	Mi Hyun Kim	Sunningdale GC, Berkshire, England
2002	Karrie Webb	273	Michelle Ellis Paula Marti	Turnberry GC, Ailsa, Scotland

Note: Designated fourth major in 2001.

Alltime Major Championship Winners

	LPGA	U.S. Open	Dinah Shore	‡du Maurier	#Titleholders	†Western	U.S. Am	British Am	Total
Patty Berg	0	1	0	0	7	7	1	0	16
Mickey Wright	4	4	0	0	2	3	0	0	13
Louise Suggs	1	2	0	0	4	4	1	1	13
Babe Zaharias	0	3	0	0	3	4	1	1	12
*Juli Inkster	2	2	2	1	0	0	3	0	10
Betsy Rawls	2	4	0	0	0	2	0	0	8
*JoAnne Carner	0	2	0	0	0	0	5	0	7
Kathy Whitworth	3	0	0	0	2	1	0	0	6
Pat Bradley	1	1	1	3	0	0	0	0	6
*Patty Sheehan	3	2	1	0	0	0	0	0	6
Glenna Vare	0	0	0	0	0	0	6	0	6
*Betsy King	1	2	3	0	0	0	0	0	6

*Active LPGA player.
#Major from 1937–1972. †Major from 1937–1967. ‡Major from 1979–2000.

Alltime Multiple Professional Major Winners

LPGA

Mickey Wright	4
Nancy Lopez	3
Patty Sheehan	3
Kathy Whitworth	3
Donna Caponi	2
Sandra Haynie	2
Mary Mills	2
Betsy Rawls	2
Laura Davies	2
Juli Inkster	2
Se Ri Pak	2

U.S. OPEN

Betsy Rawls	4
Mickey Wright	4
Susie Maxwell Berning	3

U.S. OPEN (Cont.)

Hollis Stacy	3
Babe Zaharias	3
JoAnne Carner	2
Donna Caponi	2
Betsy King	2
Patty Sheehan	2
Louise Suggs	2
Annika Sorenstam	2
Karrie Webb	2
Juli Inkster	2

NABISCO/DINAH SHORE

Amy Alcott	3
Betsy King	3
Juli Inkster	2
Annika Sorenstam	2

DU MAURIER

Pat Bradley	3
Brandie Burton	2
JoAnne Carner	2

TITLEHOLDERS

Patty Berg	7
Louise Suggs	4
Babe Zaharias	3
Dorothy Kirby	2
Marilynn Smith	2
Kathy Whitworth	2
Mickey Wright	2

WESTERN OPEN

Patty Berg	7
Louise Suggs	4
Babe Zaharias	4
Mickey Wright	3
June Beebe	2
Opal Hill	2
Betty Jameson	2
Betsy Rawls	2

THE LPGA TOUR

Most Career Wins†

	Wins		Wins		Wins
Kathy Whitworth	88	Sandra Haynie	42	Pat Bradley	31
Mickey Wright	82	Babe Zaharias	41	*Amy Alcott	29
Patty Berg	60	*Annika Sorenstam	40	*Juli Inkster	28
Louise Suggs	58	Carol Mann	38	*Karrie Webb	28
Betsy Rawls	55	*Patty Sheehan	35	Jane Blalock	27
Nancy Lopez	48	*Betsy King	34	Judy Rankin	26
*JoAnne Carner	43	*Beth Daniel	32		

*Active player.

Season Money Leaders

		Earnings ($)			Earnings ($)			Earnings ($)
1950	Babe Zaharias	14,800	1968	Kathy Whitworth	48,379	1986	Pat Bradley	492,021
1951	Babe Zaharias	15,087	1969	Carol Mann	49,152	1987	Ayako Okamoto	466,034
1952	Betsy Rawls	14,505	1970	Kathy Whitworth	30,235	1988	Sherri Turner	350,851
1953	Louise Suggs	19,816	1971	Kathy Whitworth	41,181	1989	Betsy King	654,132
1954	Patty Berg	16,011	1972	Kathy Whitworth	65,063	1990	Beth Daniel	863,578
1955	Patty Berg	16,492	1973	Kathy Whitworth	82,864	1991	Pat Bradley	763,118
1956	Marlene Hagge	20,235	1974	JoAnne Carner	87,094	1992	Dottie Mochrie	693,335
1957	Patty Berg	16,272	1975	Sandra Palmer	76,374	1993	Betsy King	595,992
1958	Beverly Hanson	12,639	1976	Judy Rankin	150,734	1994	Laura Davies	687,201
1959	Betsy Rawls	26,774	1977	Judy Rankin	122,890	1995	Annika Sorenstam	666,533
1960	Louise Suggs	16,892	1978	Nancy Lopez	189,814	1996	Karrie Webb	1,002,000
1961	Mickey Wright	22,236	1979	Nancy Lopez	197,489	1997	Annika Sorenstam	1,236,789
1962	Mickey Wright	21,641	1980	Beth Daniel	231,000	1998	Annika Sorenstam	1,092,748
1963	Mickey Wright	31,269	1981	Beth Daniel	206,998	1999	Karrie Webb	1,591,959
1964	Mickey Wright	29,800	1982	JoAnne Carner	310,400	2000	Karrie Webb	1,876,853
1965	Kathy Whitworth	28,658	1983	JoAnne Carner	291,404	2001	Annika Sorenstam	2,105,868
1966	Kathy Whitworth	33,517	1984	Betsy King	266,771			
1967	Kathy Whitworth	32,937	1985	Nancy Lopez	416,472			

Career Money Leaders†

		Earnings ($)			Earnings ($)			Earnings ($)
1.	Annika Sorenstam	10,715,371	11.	Se Ri Pak	5,377,999	21.	Chris Johnson	3,476,055
2.	Karrie Webb	8,599,059	12.	Patty Sheehan	5,507,155	22.	Amy Alcott	3,408,074
3.	Juli Inkster	7,652,836	13.	Nancy Lopez	5,320,876	23.	Donna Andrews	3,229,072
4.	Betsy King	7,350,162	14.	Kelly Robbins	4,915,210	24.	Michelle McGann	3,215,138
5.	Beth Daniel	6,904,694	15.	Liselotte Neumann	4,472,836	25.	D. Ammaccapane	3,185,537
6.	Dottie Pepper	6,658,613	16.	Lorie Kane	4,098,697	26.	Mi Hyun Kim	3,161,765
7.	Meg Mallon	6,371,804	17.	Sherri Steinhauer	3,918,666	27.	Jan Stephenson	3,019,075
8.	Rosie Jones	6,286,416	18.	Jane Geddes	3,787,058	28.	Michele Redman	2,971,372
9.	Laura Davies	6,027,610	19.	Tammie Green	3,711,455	29.	JoAnne Carner	2,961,986
10.	Pat Bradley	5,743,605	20.	Brandie Burton	3,594,946	30.	Dawn Coe-Jones	2,883,321

LPGA Player of the Year

1966	Kathy Whitworth	1978	Nancy Lopez	1990	Beth Daniel
1967	Kathy Whitworth	1979	Nancy Lopez	1991	Pat Bradley
1968	Kathy Whitworth	1980	Beth Daniel	1992	Dottie Mochrie
1969	Kathy Whitworth	1981	JoAnne Carner	1993	Betsy King
1970	Sandra Haynie	1982	JoAnne Carner	1994	Beth Daniel
1971	Kathy Whitworth	1983	Patty Sheehan	1995	Annika Sorenstam
1972	Kathy Whitworth	1984	Betsy King	1996	Laura Davies
1973	Kathy Whitworth	1985	Nancy Lopez	1997	Annika Sorenstam
1974	JoAnne Carner	1986	Pat Bradley	1998	Annika Sorenstam
1975	Sandra Palmer	1987	Ayako Okamoto	1999	Karrie Webb
1976	Judy Rankin	1988	Nancy Lopez	2000	Karrie Webb
1977	Judy Rankin	1989	Betsy King	2001	Annika Sorenstam

†Through 10/13/02.

Vare Trophy: Best Scoring Average

Year	Player	Avg	Year	Player	Avg	Year	Player	Avg
1953	Patty Berg	75.00	1969	Kathy Whitworth	72.38	1985	Nancy Lopez	70.73
1954	Babe Zaharias	75.48	1970	Kathy Whitworth	72.26	1986	Pat Bradley	71.10
1955	Patty Berg	74.47	1971	Kathy Whitworth	72.88	1987	Betsy King	71.14
1956	Patty Berg	74.57	1972	Kathy Whitworth	72.38	1988	Colleen Walker	71.26
1957	Louise Suggs	74.64	1973	Judy Rankin	73.08	1989	Beth Daniel	70.38
1958	Beverly Hanson	74.92	1974	JoAnne Carner	72.87	1990	Beth Daniel	70.54
1959	Betsy Rawls	74.03	1975	JoAnne Carner	72.40	1991	Pat Bradley	70.76
1960	Mickey Wright	73.25	1976	Judy Rankin	72.25	1992	Dottie Mochrie	70.80
1961	Mickey Wright	73.55	1977	Judy Rankin	72.16	1993	Nancy Lopez	70.83
1962	Mickey Wright	73.67	1978	Nancy Lopez	71.76	1994	Beth Daniel	70.90
1963	Mickey Wright	72.81	1979	Nancy Lopez	71.20	1995	Annika Sorenstam	71.00
1964	Mickey Wright	72.46	1980	Amy Alcott	71.51	1996	Annika Sorenstam	70.47
1965	Kathy Whitworth	72.61	1981	JoAnne Carner	71.75	1997	Karrie Webb	70.00
1966	Kathy Whitworth	72.60	1982	JoAnne Carner	71.49	1998	Annika Sorenstam	69.99
1967	Kathy Whitworth	72.74	1983	JoAnne Carner	71.41	1999	Karrie Webb	69.43
1968	Carol Mann	72.04	1984	Patty Sheehan	71.40	2000	Karrie Webb	70.05
						2001	Annika Sorenstam	69.42

Alltime LPGA Tour Records†

Scoring

72 HOLES

261—(71-61-63-66) by Se Ri Pak to win at the Highland Meadows CC, Sylvania, OH, in the 1998 Jamie Farr Kroger Classic (23 under par).

261—(65-59-69-68) by Annika Sorenstam to win at the Moon Valley CC, Phoenix, in the 2001 Standard Register PING (27 under par).

54 HOLES

193—(66-61-66) by Karrie Webb to lead at the Walnut Hills CC, East Lansing, MI, in the 2000 Oldsmobile Classic (23 under par).

193—(65-59-69) by Annika Sorenstam to lead at the Moon Valley CC, Phoenix, in the 2001 Standard Register PING (23 under par).

36 HOLES

124—(65-59) by Annika Sorenstam to lead at the Moon Valley CC, Phoenix, in the 2001 Standard Register PING (20 under par).

18 HOLES

59—by Annika Sorenstam at the Moon Valley CC, Phoenix, in the second round in winning the 2001 Standard Register PING (13 under par).

9 HOLES

28—by Mary Beth Zimmerman at Rail GC, 1984 Rail Charity Golf Classic, Springfield, IL (par 36). Zimmerman shot 64.

28—by Pat Bradley at Green Gables CC, Denver, 1984 Columbia Savings Classic (par 35). Bradley shot 65.

28—by Muffin Spencer-Devlin at Knollwood CC, Elmsford, NY, in winning the 1985 MasterCard International Pro-Am (par 35). Spencer-Devlin shot 64.

†Through 10/13/02.

Scoring (Cont.)

9 HOLES (Cont.)

28—by Peggy Kirsch at Squaw Creek CC, Vienna, OH, in the 1991 Phar-Mor (par 35).

28—by Renee Heiken at Highland Meadows CC, Sylvania, OH, in the 1996 Jamie Farr Kroger Classic (par 34).

28—by Annika Sorenstam at the Moon Valley CC, Phoenix, in the 2001 Standard Register PING (par 36).

28—by Danielle Ammaccapane at Highland Meadows CC, Sylvania, OH, in the 2002 Jamie Farr Kroger Classic (par 34)

MOST CONSECUTIVE ROUNDS UNDER 70

9—Beth Daniel, in 1990.

MOST BIRDIES IN A ROW

9—Beth Daniel at Onion Creek Club in Austin, in the second round of the 1999 Philips Invitational. Daniel shot 62 (8 under par).

Wins

MOST CONSECUTIVE WINS IN SCHEDULED EVENTS

4—Mickey Wright, in 1962.

4—Mickey Wright, in 1963.

4—Kathy Whitworth, in 1969.

4—Annika Sorenstam in 2001.

MOST CONSECUTIVE WINS IN ENTERED TOURNAMENTS

5—Nancy Lopez, in 1978.

MOST WINS IN A CALENDAR YEAR

13—Mickey Wright, in 1963.

WIDEST WINNING MARGIN, STROKES

14—Louise Suggs, 1949 U.S. Women's Open.

14—Cindy Mackey, 1986 MasterCard Int'l Pro-Am.

U.S. Senior Open

Year	Winner	Score	Runner-Up	Site
1980	Roberto DeVicenzo	285	William C. Campbell	Winged Foot GC, Mamaroneck, NY
1981	Arnold Palmer* (70)	289	Bob Stone (74)	Oakland Hills CC, Birmingham, MI
			Billy Casper (77)	
1982	Miller Barber	282	Gene Littler	Portland GC, Portland, OR
			Dan Sikes, Jr.	
1983	Billy Casper* (75) (3)	288	Rod Funseth (75) (4)	Hazeltine GC, Chaska, MN
1984	Miller Barber	286	Arnold Palmer	Oak Hill CC, Rochester, NY
1985	Miller Barber	285	Roberto DeVicenzo	Edgewood Tahoe GC, Stateline, NV
1986	Dale Douglass	279	Gary Player	Scioto CC, Columbus, OH
1987	Gary Player	270	Doug Sanders	Brooklawn CC, Fairfield, CT
1988	Gary Player* (68)	288	Bob Charles (70)	Medinah CC, Medinah, IL
1989	Orville Moody	279	Frank Beard	Laurel Valley GC, Ligonier, PA
1990	Lee Trevino	275	Jack Nicklaus	Ridgewood CC, Paramus, NJ
1991	Jack Nicklaus (65)	282	Chi Chi Rodriguez (69)	Oakland Hills CC, Birmingham, MI
1992	Larry Laoretti	275	Jim Colbert	Saucon Valley CC, Bethlehem, PA
1993	Jack Nicklaus	278	Tom Weiskopf	Cherry Hills CC, Englewood, CO
1994	Simon Hobday	274	Jim Albus	Pinehurst Resort & CC, Pinehurst, NC
1995	Tom Weiskopf	275	Jack Nicklaus	Congressional CC, Bethesda, MD
1996	Dave Stockton	277	Hale Irwin	Canterbury GC, Beachwood, OH
1997	Graham Marsh	280	Hale Irwin	Olympia Fields CC, Olympia Fields, IL
1998	Hale Irwin	285	Vicente Fernandez	Riviera CC, Pacific Palisades, CA
1999	Dave Eichelberger	281	Ed Dougherty	Des Moines G & CC, Des Moines, IA
2000	Hale Irwin	267	Bruce Fleisher	Saucon Valley CC, Bethlehem, PA
2001	Bruce Fleisher	280	Isao Aoki	Salem CC, Peabody, MA
			Gil Morgan	
2002	Don Pooley*	274	Tom Watson	Caves Valley GC, Owings Mill, MD

*Winner in playoff. Playoff scores are in parentheses. The 1983 playoff went to one hole of sudden death after an 18-hole playoff.

SENIOR TOUR

Season Money Leaders

		Earnings ($)			Earnings ($)			Earnings ($)
1980	Don January	44,100	1988	Bob Charles	533,929	1996	Jim Colbert	1,627,890
1981	Miller Barber	83,136	1989	Bob Charles	725,887	1997	Hale Irwin	2,449,420
1982	Miller Barber	106,890	1990	Lee Trevino	1,190,518	1998	Hale Irwin	2,861,945
1983	Don January	237,571	1991	Mike Hill	1,065,657	1999	Bruce Fleisher	2,515,705
1984	Don January	328,597	1992	Lee Trevino	1,027,002	2000	Larry Nelson	2,708,005
1985	Peter Thomson	386,724	1993	Dave Stockton	1,175,944	2001	Allen Doyle	2,553,582
1986	Bruce Crampton	454,299	1994	Dave Stockton	1,402,519			
1987	Chi Chi Rodriguez	509,145	1995	Jim Colbert	1,444,386			

Career Money Leaders†

		Earnings ($)			Earnings ($)			Earnings ($)
1.	Hale Irwin	16,750,916	11.	Iaso Aoki	8,211,784	21.	Chi Chi Rodriguez	6,625,370
2.	Jim Colbert	10,840,374	12.	Jim Dent	8,199,548	22.	Bruce Summerhays	6,491,245
3.	Gil Morgan	10,768,993	13.	Mike Hill	7,707,818	23.	Tom Wargo	6,456,090
4.	Dave Stockton	9,719,719	14.	Dana Quigley	7,520,446	24.	John Jacobs	6,118,826
5.	Lee Trevino	9,615,172	15.	Allen Doyle	7,395,141	25.	Jim Albus	5,858,053
6.	Larry Nelson	9,115,261	16.	Jay Sigel	7,235,054	26.	Jim Thorpe	5,772,357
7.	Bruce Fleisher	9,111,671	17.	Graham Marsh	6,775,794	27.	John Bland	5,745,844
8.	Bob Charles	8,760,346	18.	Dale Douglass	6,734,462	28.	Gary Player	5,731,489
9.	Ray Floyd	8,424,384	19.	J.C. Snead	6,730,931	29.	Vicente Fernandez	5,478,070
10.	George Archer	8,274,896	20.	Bob Murphy	6,634,979	30.	Al Geiberger	5,282,995

Most Career Wins†

	Wins		Wins
Hale Irwin	36	Bruce Crampton	20
Lee Trevino	29	Jim Colbert	20
Miller Barber	24	Gary Player	19
Bob Charles	23	George Archer	19
Don January	22	Mike Hill	18
Chi Chi Rodriguez	22	Larry Nelson	16
Gil Morgan	21	Bruce Fleisher	15

†Through 10/13/02.

MAJOR MEN'S AMATEUR CHAMPIONSHIPS

U.S. Amateur

Year	Winner	Score	Runner-Up	Site
1895	Charles B. Macdonald	12 & 11	Charles E. Sands	Newport GC, Newport, RI
1896	H.J. Whigham	8 & 7	J.G Thorp	Shinnecock Hills GC, Southampton, NY
1897	H.J. Whigham	8 & 6	W. Rossiter Betts	Chicago GC, Wheaton, IL
1898	Findlay S. Douglas	5 & 3	Walter B. Smith	Morris County GC, Morristown, NJ
1899	H.M. Harriman	3 & 2	Findlay S. Douglas	Onwentsia Club, Lake Forest, IL
1900	Walter Travis	2 up	Findlay S. Douglas	Garden City GC, Garden City, NY
1901	Walter Travis	5 & 4	Walter E. Egan	CC of Atlantic City, NJ
1902	Louis N. James	4 & 2	Eben M. Byers	Glen View Club, Golf, IL
1903	Walter Travis	5 & 4	Eben M. Byers	Nassau CC, Glen Cove, NY
1904	H. Chandler Egan	8 & 6	Fred Herreshoff	Baltusrol GC, Springfield, NJ
1905	H. Chandler Egan	6 & 5	D.E. Sawyer	Chicago GC, Wheaton, IL
1906	Eben M. Byers	2 up	George S. Lyon	Englewood GC, Englewood, NJ
1907	Jerry Travers	6 & 5	Archibald Graham	Euclid Club, Cleveland, OH
1908	Jerry Travers	8 & 7	Max H. Behr	Garden City GC, Garden City, NY
1909	Robert A. Gardner	4 & 3	H. Chandler Egan	Chicago GC, Wheaton, IL
1910	William C. Fownes Jr.	4 & 3	Warren K. Wood	The Country Club, Brookline, MA
1911	Harold Hilton	1 up	Fred Herreshoff	The Apawamis Club, Rye, NY
1912	Jerry Travers	7 & 6	Charles Evans Jr.	Chicago GC, Wheaton, IL
1913	Jerry Travers	5 & 4	John G. Anderson	Garden City GC, Garden City, NY
1914	Francis Ouimet	6 & 5	Jerry Travers	Ekwanok CC, Manchester, VT
1915	Robert A. Gardner	5 & 4	John G. Anderson	CC of Detroit, Grosse Pt. Farms, MI
1916	Chick Evans	4 & 3	Robert A. Gardner	Merion Cricket Club, Haverford, PA
1917–18	No tournament			
1919	S. Davidson Herron	5 & 4	Bobby Jones	Oakmont CC, Oakmont, PA
1920	Chick Evans	7 & 6	Francis Ouimet	Engineers' CC, Roslyn, NY
1921	Jesse P. Guilford	7 & 6	Robert A. Gardner	St. Louis CC, Clayton, MO
1922	Jess W. Sweetser	3 & 2	Chick Evans	The Country Club, Brookline, MA
1923	Max R. Marston	1 up	Jess W. Sweetser	Flossmoor CC, Flossmoor, IL
1924	Bobby Jones	9 & 8	George Von Elm	Merion Cricket Club, Ardmore, PA
1925	Bobby Jones	8 & 7	Watts Gunn	Oakmont CC, Oakmont, PA
1926	George Von Elm	2 & 1	Bobby Jones	Baltusrol GC, Springfield, NJ
1927	Bobby Jones	8 & 7	Chick Evans	Minikahda Club, Minneapolis
1928	Bobby Jones	10 & 9	T. Phillip Perkins	Brae Burn CC, West Newton, MA
1929	Harrison R. Johnston	4 & 3	Dr. O.F. Willing	Del Monte G & CC, Pebble Beach, CA
1930	Bobby Jones	8 & 7	Eugene V. Homans	Merion Cricket Club, Ardmore, PA
1931	Francis Ouimet	6 & 5	Jack Westland	Beverly CC, Chicago, IL
1932	C. Ross Somerville	2 & 1	John Goodman	Baltimore CC, Timonium, MD
1933	George T. Dunlap Jr.	6 & 5	Max R. Marston	Kenwood CC, Cincinnati, OH
1934	Lawson Little	8 & 7	David Goldman	The Country Club, Brookline, MA
1935	Lawson Little	4 & 2	Walter Emery	The Country Club, Cleveland, OH
1936	John W. Fischer	1 up	Jack McLean	Garden City GC, Garden City, NY
1937	John Goodman	2 up	Raymond E. Billows	Alderwood CC, Portland, OR
1938	William P. Turnesa	8 & 7	B. Patrick Abbott	Oakmont CC, Oakmont, PA
1939	Marvin H. Ward	7 & 5	Raymond E. Billows	North Shore CC, Glenview, IL
1940	Richard D. Chapman	11 & 9	W. McCullough Jr.	Winged Foot GC, Mamaroneck, NY
1941	Marvin H. Ward	4 & 3	B. Patrick Abbott	Omaha Field Club, Omaha, NE
1942–45	No tournament			
1946	Ted Bishop	1 up	Smiley L. Quick	Baltusrol GC, Springfield, NJ
1947	Skee Riegel	2 & 1	John W. Dawson	Del Monte G & CC, Pebble Beach, CA
1948	William P. Turnesa	2 & 1	Raymond E. Billows	Memphis CC, Memphis, TN
1949	Charles R. Coe	11 & 10	Rufus King	Oak Hill CC, Rochester, NY
1950	Sam Urzetta	1 up	Frank Stranahan	Minneapolis GC, Minneapolis, MN
1951	Billy Maxwell	4 & 3	Joseph F. Gagliardi	Saucon Valley CC, Bethlehem, PA
1952	Jack Westland	3 & 2	Al Mengert	Seattle GC, Seattle, WA
1953	Gene Littler	1 up	Dale Morey	Oklahoma City G & CC, Oklahoma City
1954	Arnold Palmer	1 up	Robert Sweeny	CC of Detroit, Grosse Pt. Farms, MI
1955	E. Harvie Ward Jr.	9 & 8	William Hyndman III	CC of Virginia, Richmond, VA
1956	E. Harvie Ward Jr.	5 & 4	Charles Kocsis	Knollwood Club, Lake Forest, IL
1957	Hillman Robbins Jr.	5 & 4	Dr. Frank M. Taylor	The Country Club, Brookline, MA
1958	Charles R. Coe	5 & 4	Tommy Aaron	Olympic Club, San Francisco, CA
1959	Jack Nicklaus	1 up	Charles R. Coe	Broadmoor GC, Colorado Springs, CO
1960	Deane Beman	6 & 4	Robert W. Gardner	St. Louis CC, Clayton, MO
1961	Jack Nicklaus	8 & 6	H. Dudley Wysong	Pebble Beach GL, Pebble Beach, CA

U.S. Amateur (Cont.)

Year	Winner	Score	Runner-Up	Site
1962	Labron E. Harris Jr.	1 up	Downing Gray	Pinehurst CC, Pinehurst, NC
1963	Deane Beman	2 & 1	Richard H. Sikes	Wakonda Club, Des Moines, IA
1964	William C. Campbell	1 up	Edgar M. Tutwiler	Canterbury GC, Cleveland, OH
1965	Robert J. Murphy Jr.	291	Robert B. Dickson	Southern Hills, CC, Tulsa
1966	Gary Cowan	285–75	Deane Beman	Merion GC, Ardmore, PA
1967	Robert B. Dickson	285	Marvin Giles III	Broadmoor GC, Colorado Springs
1968	Bruce Fleisher	284	Marvin Giles III	Scioto CC, Columbus, OH
1969	Steven N. Melnyk	286	Marvin Giles III	Oakmont CC, Oakmont, PA
1970	Lanny Wadkins	279	Tom Kite	Waverley CC, Portland, OR
1971	Gary Cowan	280	Eddie Pearce	Wilmington CC, Wilmington DE
1972	Marvin Giles III	285	two tied	Charlotte CC, Charlotte, NC
1973	Craig Stadler	6 & 5	David Strawn	Inverness Club, Toledo
1974	Jerry Pate	2 & 1	John P. Grace	Ridgewood CC, Ridgewood, NJ
1975	Fred Ridley	2 up	Keith Fergus	CC of Virginia, Richmond
1976	Bill Sander	8 & 6	C. Parker Moore Jr.	Bel Air CC, Los Angeles
1977	John Fought	9 & 8	Doug Fischesser	Aronimink GC, Newton Square, PA
1978	John Cook	5 & 4	Scott Hoch	Plainfield CC, Plainfield, NJ
1979	Mark O'Meara	8 & 7	John Cook	Canterbury GC, Cleveland
1980	Hal Sutton	9 & 8	Bob Lewis	CC of North Carolina, Pinehurst, NC
1981	Nathaniel Crosby	1 up	Brian Lindley	Olympic Club, San Francisco
1982	Jay Sigel	8 & 7	David Tolley	The Country Club, Brookline, MA
1983	Jay Sigel	8 & 7	Chris Perry	North Shore CC, Glenview, IL
1984	Scott Verplank	4 & 3	Sam Randolph	Oak Tree GC, Edmond, OK
1985	Sam Randolph	1 up	Peter Persons	Montclair GC, West Orange, NJ
1986	Buddy Alexander	5 & 3	Chris Kite	Shoal Creek, Shoal Creek, AL
1987	Bill Mayfair	4 & 3	Eric Rebmann	Jupiter Hills Club, Jupiter, FL
1988	Eric Meeks	7 & 6	Danny Yates	Va. Hot Springs G & CC, VA
1989	Chris Patton	3 & 1	Danny Green	Merion GC, Ardmore, PA
1990	Phil Mickelson	5 & 4	Manny Zerman	Cherry Hills CC, Englewood, CO
1991	Mitch Voges	7 & 6	Manny Zerman	The Honors Course, Ooltewah, TN
1992	Justin Leonard	8 & 7	Tom Scherrer	Muirfield Village GC, Dublin, OH
1993	John Harris	5 & 3	Danny Ellis	Champions GC, Houston
1994	Tiger Woods	2 up	Trip Kuehne	TPC-Sawgrass, Ponte Vedre, FL
1995	Tiger Woods	2 up	Buddy Marucci	Newport Country Club, Newport, RI
1996	Tiger Woods	38 holes	Steve Scott	Pumpkin Ridge GC, Cornelius, OR
1997	Matthew Kuchar	2 & 1	Joel Kribel	Cog Hill G & CC, Lemont, IL
1998	Hank Kuehne	2 & 1	Tom McKnight	Oak Hill CC, Rochester, NY
1999	David Gossett	9 & 8	Sung Yoon Kim	Pebble Beach GL, Pebble Beach, CA
2000	Jeff Quinney	39 holes	James Driscoll	Baltusrol GC, Upper Springfield, NJ
2001	Bubba Dickerson	1 up	Robert Hamilton	East Lake GC, Atlanta
2002	Ricky Barnes	2 & 1	Hunter Mahan	Oakland Hills CC, Bloomfield Hills, MI

Note: All stroke play from 1965 to 1972.

U.S. Junior Amateur

1948...Dean Lind	1962...Jim Wiechers	1976...Madden Hatcher III	1990...Mathew Todd
1949...Gay Brewer	1963...Gregg McHatton	1977...Willie Wood Jr.	1991...Tiger Woods
1950...Mason Rudolph	1964...Johnny Miller	1978...Don Hurter	1992...Tiger Woods
1951...Tommy Jacobs	1965...James Masserio	1979...Jack Larkin	1993...Tiger Woods
1952...Don Bisplinghoff	1966...Gary Sanders	1980...Eric Johnson	1994...Terry Noe
1953...Rex Baxter	1967...John Crooks	1981...Scott Erickson	1995...D. Scott Hailes
1954...Foster Bradley	1968...Eddie Pearce	1982...Rich Marik	1996...Shane McMenamy
1955...William Dunn	1969...Aly Trompas	1983...Tim Straub	1997...Jason Allred
1956...Harlan Stevenson	1970...Gary Koch	1984...Doug Martin	1998...James Oh
1957...Larry Beck	1971...Mike Brannan	1985...Charles Rymer	1999...Hunter Mahan
1958...Buddy Baker	1972...Bob Byman	1986...Brian Montgomery	2000...Matthew Rosenfeld
1959...Larry Lee	1973...Jack Renner	1987...Brett Quigley	2001...Henry Liaw
1960...Bill Tindall	1974...David Nevatt	1988...Jason Widener	2002...Charlie Beljan
1961...Charles McDowell	1975...Brett Mullin	1989...David Duval	

Mid-Amateur Championship

1981...Jim Holtgrieve	1987...Jay Sigel	1993...Jeff Thomas	1999...Danny Green
1982...William Hoffer	1988...David Eger	1994...Tim Jackson	2000...Greg Puga
1983...Jay Sigel	1989...James Taylor	1995...Jerry Courville Jr.	2001...Tim Jackson
1984...Mike Podolak	1990...Jim Stuart	1996...John Miller	2002...George Zahringer
1985...Jay Sigel	1991...Jim Stuart	1997...Ken Bakst	
1986...Bill Loeffler	1992...Danny Yates	1998...John Miller	

British Amateur

887 ....H. G. Hutchinson	1927 ....Dr. W. Tweddell	1968 ....M. Bonallack
1888 ....John Ball	1928 .............T.P. Perkins	1969 ....M. Bonallack
1889 .............J.E. Laidlay	1929 .............C.J.H. Tolley	1970 ....M. Bonallack
1890 ....John Ball	1930 ....Robert T. Jones Jr	1971 ....Steve Melnyk
1891 .............J.E. Laidlay	1931 ....E. Martin Smith	1972 ....Trevor Homer
1892 ....John Ball	1932 ....J. DeForest	1973 ....R. Siderowf
1893 ....Peter Anderson	1933 ....M. Scott	1974 ....Trevor Homer
1894 ....John Ball	1934 ....W. Lawson Little	1975 ....M. Giles
1895 .............L.M.B. Melville	1935 ....W. Lawson Little	1976 ....R. Siderowf
1896 .............F.G. Tait	1936 ....H. Thomson	1977 ....P. McEvoy
1897 .............A.J.T. Allan	1937 ....R. Sweeney Jr	1978 ....P. McEvoy
1898 .............F.G. Tait	1938 .............C.R. Yates	1979 ....J. Sigel
1899 ....John Ball	1939 .............A.T. Kyle	1980 ....D. Evans
1900 .............H.H. Hilton	1940–45 ....not held	1981 ....P. Ploujoux
1901 .............H.H. Hilton	1946 ....J. Bruen	1982 ....M. Thompson
1902 ....C. Hutchings	1947 ....Willie D. Turnesa	1983 ....A. Parkin
1903 ....R. Maxwell	1948 ....Frank R. Stranahan	1984 .............J.M. Olazabal
1904 .............W.J. Travis	1949 .............S.M. McReady	1985 ....G. McGimpsey
1905 .............A.G. Barry	1950 ....Frank R. Stranahan	1986 ....D. Curry
1906 ....James Robb	1951 ....Richard D. Chapman	1987 ....P. Mayo
1907 ....John Ball	1952 .............E.H. Ward	1988 ....C. Hardin
1908 .............E.A. Lassen	1953 .............J.B. Carr	1989 ....S. Dodd
1909 ....R. Maxwell	1954 .............D.W. Bachli	1990 ....R. Muntz
1910 ....John Ball	1955 .............J.W. Conrad	1991 ....G. Wolstenholme
1911 .............H.H. Hilton	1956 .............J.C. Beharrel	1992 ....S. Dundas
1912 ....John Ball	1957 ....R. Reid Jack	1993 ....I. Pyman
1913 .............H.H. Hilton	1958 .............J.B. Carr	1994 ....L. James
1914 .............J.L.C. Jenkins	1959 ....Deane Beman	1995 ....G. Sherry
1915–19 ....not held	1960 .............J.B. Carr	1996 ....W. Bladon
1920 .............C.J.H. Tolley	1961 ....M. Bonallack	1997 ....C. Watson
1921 .............W.I. Hunter	1962 ....R. Davies	1998 ....Sergio Garcia
1922 .............E.W.E. Holderness	1963 ....M. Lunt	1999 ....Graeme Storm
1923 .............R.H. Wethered	1964 ....C. Clark	2000 ....Mikko Ilonen
1924 .............E.W.E. Holderness	1965 ....M. Bonallack	2001 ....Michael Hoey
1925 ....R. Harris	1966 .............C.R. Cole	2002 ....Alejandro Larrazabal
1926 ....Jess Sweetser	1967 ....R. Dickson	

Amateur Public Links

1922 ....Edmund R. Held	1951 ....Dave Stanley	1978 ....Dean Prince
1923 ....Richard J. Walsh	1952 ....Omer L. Bogan	1979 ....Dennis Walsh
1924 ....Joseph Coble	1953 ....Ted Richards Jr	1980 ....Jodie Mudd
1925 ....Raymond J. McAuliffe	1954 ....Gene Andrews	1981 ....Jodie Mudd
	1955 ....Sam D. Kocsis	1982 ....Billy Tuten
1926 ....Lester Bolstad	1956 ....James H. Buxbaum	1983 ....Billy Tuten
1927 ....Carl F. Kauffmann	1957 ....Don Essig III	1984 ....Bill Malley
1928 ....Carl F. Kauffmann	1958 ....Daniel D. Sikes Jr	1985 ....Jim Sorenson
1929 ....Carl F. Kauffmann	1959 ....William A. Wright	1986 ....Bill Mayfair
1930 ....Robert E. Wingate	1960 ....Verne Callison	1987 ....Kevin Johnson
1931 ....Charles Ferrera	1961 ....Richard H. Sikes	1988 ....Ralph Howe III
1932 .............R.L. Miller	1962 ....Richard H. Sikes	1989 ....Tim Hobby
1933 ....Charles Ferrera	1963 ....Robert Lunn	1990 ....Michael Combs
1934 ....David A. Mitchell	1964 ....William McDonald	1991 ....David Berganio Jr
1935 ....Frank Strafaci	1965 ....Arne Dokka	1992 ....Warren Schulte
1936 ....B. Patrick Abbott	1966 ....Lamont Kaser	1993 ....David Berganio Jr
1937 ....Bruce N. McCormick	1967 ....Verne Callison	1994 ....Guy Yamamoto
1938 ....Al Leach	1968 ....Gene Towry	1995 ....Chris Wollmann
1939 ....Andrew Szwedko	1969 ....John M. Jackson Jr	1996 ....Tim Hogarth
1940 ....Robert C. Clark	1970 ....Robert Risch	1997 ....Tim Clark
1941 ....William M. Welch Jr	1971 ....Fred Haney	1998 ....Trevor Immelman
1942–45 ....not held	1972 ....Bob Allard	1999 ....Hunter Haas
1946 ....Smiley L. Quick	1973 ....Stan Stopa	2000 .............D.J. Trahan
1947 ....Wilfred Crossley	1974 ....Charles Barenaba	2001 ....Chez Reavie
1948 ....Michael R. Ferentz	1975 ....Randy Barenaba	2002 ....Ryan Moore
1949 ....Kenneth J. Towns	1976 ....Eddie Mudd	
1950 ....Stanley Bielat	1977 ....Jerry Vidovic	

U.S. Senior Golf

1955 ....J. Wood Platt	1971 ....Tom Draper	1987 ....John Richardson
1956 ....Frederick J. Wright	1972 ....Lewis W. Oehmig	1988 ....Clarence Moore
1957 ....J. Clark Espie	1973 ....William Hyndman III	1989 ....Bo Williams
1958 ....Thomas C. Robbins	1974 ....Dale Morey	1990 ....Jackie Cummings
1959 ....J. Clark Espie	1975 ....William F. Colm	1991 ....Bill Bosshard
1960 ....Michael Cestone	1976 ....Lewis W. Oehmig	1992 ....Clarence Moore
1961 ....Dexter H. Daniels	1977 ....Dale Morey	1993 ....Joe Ungvary
1962 ....Merrill L. Carlsmith	1978 ..........K.K. Compton	1994 ....O. Gordon Brewer
1963 ....Merrill L. Carlsmith	1979 ....William C. Campbell	1995 ....James Stahl Jr.
1964 ....William D. Higgins	1980 ....William C. Campbell	1996 ....O. Gordon Brewer
1965 ....Robert B. Kiersky	1981 ....Ed Updegraff	1997 ....Cliff Cunningham
1966 ....Dexter H. Daniels	1982 ....Alton Duhon	1998 ....Bill Shean Jr.
1967 ....Ray Palmer	1983 ....William Hyndman III	1999 ....Bill Ploeger
1968 ....Curtis Person Sr.	1984 ....Bob Rawlins	2000 ....Bill Shean Jr.
1969 ....Curtis Person Sr.	1985 ....Lewis W. Oehmig	2001 ....Kemp Richardson
1970 ....Gene Andrews	1986 ....Bo Williams	2002 ....Greg Reynolds

Note: Event is for amateur golfers at least 55 years of age.

MAJOR WOMEN'S AMATEUR CHAMPIONSHIPS

U.S. Women's Amateur

Year	Winner	Score	Runner-Up	Site
1895 ....Mrs. Charles S. Brown		132	Nellie Sargent	Meadow Brook Club, Hempstead, NY
1896 ....Beatrix Hoyt		2 & 1	Mrs. Arthur Turnure	Morris Couty GC, Morristown, NJ
1897 ....Beatrix Hoyt		5 & 4	Nellie Sargent	Essex County Club, Manchester, MA
1898 ....Beatrix Hoyt		5 &3	Maude Wetmore	Ardsley Club, Ardsley-on-Hudson, NY
1899 ....Ruth Underhill		2 & 1	Margaret Fox	Philadelphia CC, Philadelphia, PA
1900 ....Frances C. Griscom		6 & 5	Margaret Curtis	Shinnecock Hills GC, Shinnecock Hills, NY
1901 ....Genevieve Hecker		5 & 3	Lucy Herron	Baltusrol GC, Springfield, NJ
1902 ....Genevieve Hecker		4 & 3	Louisa A. Wells	The Country Club, Brookline, MA
1903 ....Bessie Anthony		7 & 6	J. Anna Carpenter	Chicago GC, Wheaton, IL
1904 ....Georgianna M. Bishop		5 & 3	Mrs. E.F. Sanford	Merion Cricket Club, Haverford, PA
1905 ....Pauline Mackay		1 up	Margaret Curtis	Morris County GC, Convent, NJ
1906 ....Harriot S. Curtis		2 & 1	Mary B. Adams	Brae Burn CC, West Newton, MA
1907 ....Margaret Curtis		7 & 6	Harriot S. Curtis	Midlothian CC, Blue Island, IL
1908 ....Katherine C. Harley		6 & 5	Mrs. T.H. Polhemus	Chevy Chase Club, Chevy Chase, MD
1909 ....Dorothy I. Campbell		3 & 2	Nonna Barlow	Merion Cricket Club, Haverford, PA
1910 ....Dorothy I. Campbell		2 & 1	Mrs. G.M. Martin	Homewood CC, Flossmoor, IL
1911 ....Margaret Curtis		5 & 3	Lillian B. Hyde	Baltusrol GC, Springfield, NJ
1912 ....Margaret Curtis		3 & 2	Nonna Barlow	Essex County Club, Manchester, MA
1913 ....Gladys Ravenscroft		2 up	Marion Hollins	Wilmington CC, Wilmington, DE
1914 ....Katherine Harley		1 up	Elaine V. Rosenthal	Nassau CC, Glen Cove, NY
1915 ....Florence Vanderbeck		3 & 2	Margaret Gavin	Onwentsia Club, Lake Forest, IL
1916 ....Alexa Stirling		2 & 1	Mildred Caverly	Belmont Springs CC, Waverley, MA
1917–18 .....No tournament				
1919 ....Alexa Stirling		6 & 5	Margaret Gavin	Shawnee CC, Shawnee-on-Delaware, PA
1920 ....Alexa Stirling		5 & 4	Dorothy Campbell	Mayfield CC, Cleveland
1921 ....Marion Hollins		5 & 4	Alexa Stirling	Hollywood GC, Deal, NJ
1922 ....Glenna Collett		5 & 4	Margaret Gavin	Greenbriar GC, White Sulphur Springs, WV
1923 ....Edith Cummings		3 & 2	Alexa Stirling	Westchester-Biltmore CC, Rye, NY
1924 ....Dorothy Campbell		7 & 6	Mary K. Browne	Rhode Island CC, Nyatt, RI
1925 ....Glenna Collett		9 & 8	Alexa Stirling	St. Louis CC, Clayton, MO
1926 ....Helen Stetson		3 & 1	Elizabeth Goss	Merion Cricket Club, Ardmore, PA
1927 ....Miiriam Burns Horn		5 & 4	Maureen Orcutt	Cherry Valley Club, Garden City, NY
1928 ....Glenna Collett		13 & 12	Virginia Van Wie	Va. Hot Springs G & TC, Hot Springs, VA
1929 ....Glenna Collett		4 & 3	Leona Pressler	Oakland Hills CC, Birmingham, MI
1930 ....Glenna Collett		6 & 5	Virginia Van Wie	Los Angeles CC, Beverly Hills, CA
1931 ....Helen Hicks		2 & 1	Glenna Collet Vare	CC of Buffalo, Williamsville, NY
1932 ....Virginia Van Wie		10 & 8	Glenna Collet Vare	Salem CC, Peabody, MA
1933 ....Virginia Van Wie		4 & 3	Helen Hicks	Exmoor CC, Highland Park, IL
1934 ....Virginia Van Wie		2 & 1	Dorothy Traung	Whitemarsh Valley CC, Chestnut Hill, PA
1935 ....Glenna Collett Vare		3 & 2	Patty Berg	Interlachen CC, Hopkins, MN
1936 ....Pamela Barton		4 & 3	Maureen Orcutt	Canoe Brook CC, Summit, NJ
1937 ....Estelle Lawson		7 & 6	Patty Berg	Memphis CC, Memphis, TN
1938 ....Patty Berg		6 & 5	Estelle Lawson	Westmoreland CC, Wilmette, IL

U.S. Women's Amateur (Cont.)

Year	Winner	Score	Runner-Up	Site
1939	Betty Jameson	3 & 2	Dorothy Kirby	Wee Burn Club, Darien, CT
1940	Betty Jameson	6 & 5	Jane S. Cothran	Del Monte G & CC, Pebble Beach, CA
1941	Elizabeth Hicks	5 & 3	Helen Sigel	The Country Club, Brookline, MA
1942–45	No tournament			
1946	Babe Zaharias	11 & 9	Clara Sherman	Southern Hills CC, Tulsa
1947	Louise Suggs	2 up	Dorothy Kirby	Franklin Hills CC, Franklin, MI
1948	Grace S. Lenczyk	4 & 3	Helen Sigel	Del Monte G & CC, Pebble Beach, CA
1949	Dorothy Porter	3 & 2	Dorothy Kielty	Merion GC, Ardmore, PA
1950	Beverly Hanson	6 & 4	Mae Murray	Atlanta AC, Atlanta
1951	Dorothy Kirby	2 & 1	Claire Doran	Town & CC, St. Paul
1952	Jacqueline Pung	2 & 1	Shirley McFedters	Waverley CC, Portland, OR
1953	Mary Lena Faulk	3 & 2	Polly Riley	Rhode Island CC, West Barrington, RI
1954	Barbara Romack	4 & 2	Mickey Wright	Allegheny CC, Sewickley, PA
1955	Patricia A. Lesser	7 & 6	Jane Nelson	Myers Park CC, Charlotte
1956	Marlene Stewart	2 & 1	JoAnne Gunderson	Meridian Hills CC, Indianapolis
1957	JoAnne Gunderson	8 & 6	Ann Casey Johnstone	Del Paso CC, SacramentoA
1958	Anne Quast	3 & 2	Barbara Romack	Wee Burn CC, Darien, CT
1959	Barbara McIntire	4 & 3	Joanne Goodwin	Congressional CC, Washington, D.C.
1960	JoAnne Gunderson	6 & 5	Jean Ashley	Tulsa CC, Tulsa
1961	Anne Quast Decker	14 & 13	Phyllis Preuss	Tacoma G & CC, Tacoma, WA
1962	JoAnne Gunderson	9 & 8	Anne Baker	CC of Rochester, Rochester, NY
1963	Anne Quast Decker	2 & 1	Peggy Conley	Taconic CC, Williamstown, MA
1964	Barbara McIntire	3 & 2	JoAnne Gunderson	Prairie Dunes CC, Hutchinson, KS
1965	Jean Ashley	5 & 4	Anne Quast Decker	Lakewood CC, Denver
1966	JoAnne Gunderson	1 up	Marlene Stewart Streit	Sewickley Heights GC, Sewickley, PA
1967	Mary Lou Dill	5 & 4	Jean Ashley	Annandale GC, Pasadena
1968	JoAnne Gunderson Carner	5 & 4	Anne Quast Decker	Birmingham CC, Birmingham, MI
1969	Catherine Lacoste	3 & 2	Shelley Hamling	Las Colinas CC, Irving, TX
1970	Martha Wilkinson	3 & 2	Cynthia Hall	Wee Burn CC, Darien, CT
1971	Laura Baugh	1 up	Beth Barry	Atlanta CC, Atlanta
1972	Mary Budke	5 & 4	Cynthia Hill	St. Louis CC, St. Louis
1973	Carol Semple	1 up	Anne Quast Decker	Montclair GC, Montclair, NJ
1974	Cynthia Hill	5 & 4	Carol Semple	Broadmoor GC, Seattle
1975	Beth Daniel	3 & 2	Donna Horton	Brae Burn CC, West Newton, MA
1976	Donna Horton	2 & 1	Marianne Bretton	Del Paso CC, Sacramento
1977	Beth Daniel	3 & 1	Cathy Sherk	Cincinnati CC, Cincinnati
1978	Cathy Sherk	4 & 3	Judith Oliver	Sunnybrook GC, Plymouth Meeting, PA
1979	Carolyn Hill	7 & 6	Patty Sheehan	Memphis CC, Memphis
1980	Juli Inkster	2 up	Patti Rizzo	Prairie Dunes CC, Hutchinson, KS
1981	Juli Inkster	1 up	Lindy Goggin	Waverley CC, Portland, OR
1982	Juli Inkster	4 & 3	Cathy Hanlon	Broadmoor GC, Colorado Springs, CO
1983	Joanne Pacillo	2 & 1	Sally Quinlan	Canoe Brook CC, Summit, NJ
1984	Deb Richard	1 up	Kimberly Williams	Broadmoor GC, Seattle
1985	Michiko Hattori	5 & 4	Cheryl Stacy	Fox Chapel CC, Pittsburgh
1986	Kay Cockerill	9 & 7	Kathleen McCarthy	Pasatiempo GC, Santa Cruz, CA
1987	Kay Cockerill	3 & 2	Tracy Kerdyk	Rhode Island CC, Barrington, RI
1988	Pearl Sinn	6 & 5	Karen Noble	Minikahda Club, Minneapolis
1989	Vicki Goetze	4 & 3	Brandie Burton	Pinehurst CC (No. 2), Pinehurst, NC
1990	Pat Hurst	37 holes	Stephanie Davis	Canoe Brook CC, Summit, NJ
1991	Amy Fruhwirth	5 & 4	Heidi Voorhees	Prairie Dunes CC, Hutchinson, KN
1992	Vicki Goetz	1 up	Annika Sorensteam	Kemper Lakes GC, Hawthorne Hills, IL
1993	Jill McGill	1 up	Sarah Ingram	San Diego CC, Chula Vista, CA
1994	Wendy Ward	2 & 1	Jill McGill	The Homestead, Hot Springs, WV
1995	Kelli Kuehne	4 & 3	Anne-Marie Knight	The Country Club, Brookline, MA
1996	Kelli Kuehne	2 & 1	Marisa Baena	Firethorn GC, Lincoln, NE
1997	Silvia Cavalleri	5 & 4	Robin Burke	Brae Burn CC, West Newton, MA
1998	Grace Park	7 & 6	Jenny Chuasiriporn	Barton Hills CC, Ann Arbor, MI
1999	Dorothy Delasin	4 & 3	Jimin Kang	Biltmore Forest CC, Asheville, NC
2000	Marcy Newton	8 & 7	Laura Myerscough	Waverley CC, Portland, OR
2001	Meredith Duncan	37 holes	Nicole Perrot	Flint Hills GC, Wichita, KA
2002	Becky Lucidi	3 & 2	Brandi Jackson	Sleepy Hollow CC, Scarborough, NY

U.S. Girls' Junior Amateur

1949 ....Marlene Bauer	1968 ....Peggy Harmon	1987 ....Michelle McGann
1950 ....Patricia Lesser	1969 ....Hollis Stacy	1988 ....Jamille Jose
1951 ....Arlene Brooks	1970 ....Hollis Stacy	1989 ....Brandie Burton
1952 ....Mickey Wright	1971 ....Hollis Stacy	1990 ....Sandrine Mendiburu
1953 ....Millie Meyerson	1972 ....Nancy Lopez	1991 ....Emilee Klein
1954 ....Margaret Smith	1973 ....Amy Alcott	1992 ....Jamie Koizumi
1955 ....Carole Jo Kabler	1974 ....Nancy Lopez	1993 ....Kellee Booth
1956 ....JoAnne Gunderson	1975 ....Dayna Benson	1962 ....Maureen Orcutt
1957 ....Judy Eller	1976 ....Pilar Dorado	1963 ....Sis Choate
1958 ....Judy Eller	1977 ....Althea Tome	1994 ....Kelli Kuehne
1959 ....Judy Rand	1978 ....Lori Castillo	1995 ....Marcy Newton
1960 ....Carol Sorenson	1979 ....Penny Hammel	1996 ....Dorothy Delasin
1961 ....Mary Lowell	1980 ....Laurie Rinker	1997 ....Beth Bauer
1962 ....Mary Lou Daniel	1981 ....Kay Cornelius	1998 ....Leigh Anne Hardin
1963 ....Janis Ferraris	1982 ....Heather Farr	1999 ....Aree Wongluekiet
1964 ....Peggy Conley	1983 ....Kim Saiki	2000 ....Lisa Ferrero
1965 ....Gail Sykes	1984 ....Cathy Mockett	2001 ....Nicole Perrot
1966 ....Claudia Mayhew	1985 ....Dana Lofland	2002 ....In-Bee Park
1967 ....Elizabeth Story	1986 ....Pat Hurst	

Women's British Amateur

1893 ....Lady Margaret Scott	1929 ....Miss J. Wethered	1966 ....E. Chadwick
1894 ....Lady Margaret Scott	1930 ....Miss D. Fishwick	1967 ....E. Chadwick
1895 ....Lady Margaret Scott	1931 ....Miss E. Wilson	1968 ....B. Varangot
1896 ....Miss Pascoe	1932 ....Miss E. Wilson	1975 ....C. Lacoste
1897 ....Miss E.C. Orr	1933 ....Miss E. Wilson	1976 ....D. Oxley
1898 ....Miss L. Thomson	1934 ....Mrs. A.M. Holm	1977 ....A. Uzielli
1899 ....Miss M. Hezlet	1935 ....Miss W. Morgan	1978 ....E. Kennedy
1900 ....Miss Adair	1936 ....Miss P. Barton	1979 ....M. Madill
1901 ....Miss Graham	1937 ....Miss J. Anderson	1980 ....A. Quast
1902 ....Miss M. Hezlet	1938 ....Mrs. A.M. Holm	1981 .............I.C. Robertson
1903 ....Miss Adair	1939 ....Miss P. Barton	1982 ....K. Douglas
1904 ....Miss L. Dod	1940–45 ....not held	1983 ....J. Thornhill
1905 ....Miss B. Thompson	1946 .............G.W. Hetherington	1984 ....J. Rosenthal
1906 ....Mrs. Kennon	1947 ....B. Zaharias	1985 ....L. Beman
1907 ....Miss M. Hezlet	1948 ....L. Suggs	1986 ....M. McGuire
1908 ....Miss M. Titterton	1949 ....F. Stephens	1987 ....J. Collingham
1909 ....Miss D. Campbell	1950 ....Vicomtesse de Saint	1988 ....J. Furby
1910 ....Miss Grant Suttie	Sauveur	1989 ....H. Dobson
1911 ....Miss D. Campbell	1951 .............P.J. MacCann	1990 ....J. Hall
1912 ....Miss G. Ravenscroft	1952 ....M. Paterson	1991 ....V. Michaud
1913 ....Miss M. Dodd	1953 ....M. Stewart	1992 ....P. Pedersen
1914 ....Miss C. Leitch	1954 ....F. Stephens	1993 ....Catriona Lambert
1915–19 ....not held	1955 ....J. Valentine	1994 ....Emma Duggleby
1920 ....Miss C. Leitch	1956 ....M. Smith	1995 ....Julie Hall
1921 ....Miss C. Leitch	1957 ....P. Garvey	1996 ....Kelli Kuehne
1922 ....Miss J. Wethered	1958 ....J. Valentine	1997 ....Alison Rose
1923 ....Miss D. Chambers	1959 ....E. Price	1998 ....K. Rostron
1924 ....Miss J. Wethered	1960 ....B. McIntyre	1999 ....Marine Monnet
1925 ....Miss J. Wethered	1961 ....M. Spearman	2000 ....Rebecca Hudson
1926 ....Miss C. Leitch	1962 ....M. Spearman	2001 ....Rebecca Hudson
1927 ....Miss Thion de la	1963 ....B. Varangot	2002 ....Rebecca Hudson
Chaume	1964 ....C. Sorensen	
1928 ....Miss N. Le Blan	1965 ....B. Varangot	

Women's Amateur Public Links

1977 ....Kelly Fuiks	1986 ....Cindy Schreyer	1996 ....Heather Graff
1978 ....Kelly Fuiks	1987 ....Tracy Kerdyk	1997 ....Jo Jo Robertson
1979 ....Lori Castillo	1988 ....Pearl Sinn	1998 ....Amy Spooner
1980 ....Lori Castillo	1989 ....Pearl Sinn	1999 ....Jody Niemann
1981 ....Mary Enright	1990 ....Cathy Mockett	2000 ....Catherine Cartwright
1982 ....Nancy Taylor	1991 ....Tracy Hanson	2001 ....Candie Kung
1983 ....Kelli Antolock	1992 ....Amy Fruhwirth	2002 ....Annie Thurman
1984 ....Heather Farr	1993 ....Connie Masterson	
1985 ....Danielle	1994 ....Jill McGill	
Ammaccapane	1995 ....Jo Jo Robertson	

U.S. Senior Women's Amateur

Year	Winner	Year	Winner	Year	Winner
1964	Loma Smith	1977	Dorothy Porter	1990	Anne Sander
1965	Loma Smith	1978	Alice Dye	1991	Phyllis Preuss
1966	Maureen Orcutt	1979	Alice Dye	1992	Rosemary Thompson
1967	Marge Mason	1980	Dorothy Porter	1993	Anne Sander
1968	Carolyn Cudone	1981	Dorothy Porter	1994	Marlene Streit
1969	Carolyn Cudone	1982	Edean Ihlanfeldt	1995	Jean Smith
1970	Carolyn Cudone	1983	Dorothy Porter	1996	Gayle Borthwick
1971	Carolyn Cudone	1984	Constance Guthrie	1997	Nancy Fitzgerald
1972	Carolyn Cudone	1985	Marlene Streit	1998	Gayle Borthwick
1973	Gwen Hibbs	1986	Connie Guthrie	1999	C. Semple Thompson
1974	Justine Cushing	1987	Anne Sander	2000	C. Semple Thompson
1975	Alberta Bower	1988	Lois Hodge	2001	C. Semple Thompson
1976	Cecile H. Maclaurin	1989	Anne Sander	2002	C. Semple Thompson

Women's Mid-Amateur Championship

Year	Winner	Year	Winner	Year	Winner
1987	Cindy Scholefield	1993	Sarah Ingram	1999	Alissa Herron
1988	Martha Lang	1994	Sarah Ingram	2000	Ellen Port
1989	Robin Weiss	1995	Ellen Port	2001	Laura Shanahan
1990	C. Semple Thompson	1996	Ellen Port	2002	Kathy Hartwiger
1991	Sarah LeBrun Ingram	1997	C. Semple Thompson		
1992	M. Mamey-McInerney	1998	Virginia Derby Grimes		

International Golf

Ryder Cup Matches

Year	Results	Site
1927	United States 9½, Great Britain 2½	Worcester CC, Worcester, MA
1929	Great Britain 7, United States 5	Moortown GC, Leeds, England
1931	United States 9, Great Britain 3	Scioto CC, Columbus, OH
1933	Great Britain 6½, United States 5½	Southport and Ainsdale Courses, Southport, England
1935	United States 9, Great Britain 3	Ridgewood CC, Ridgewood, NJ
1937	United States 8, Great Britain 4	Southport and Ainsdale Courses, Southport, England
1939–1945	No tournament	
1947	United States 11, Great Britain 1	Portland GC, Portland, OR
1949	United States 7, Great Britain 5	Ganton GC, Scarborough, England
1951	United States 9½, Great Britain 2½	Pinehurst CC, Pinehurst, NC
1953	United States 6½, Great Britain 5½	Wentworth Club, Surrey, England
1955	United States 8, Great Britain 4	Thunderbird Ranch & CC, Palm Springs, CA
1957	Great Britain 7½, United States 4½	Lindrick GC, Yorkshire, England
1959	United States 8½, Great Britain 3½	Eldorado CC, Palm Desert, CA
1961	United States 14½, Great Britain 9½	Royal Lytham & St. Annes GC, St Anne's-on-the-Sea, England
1963	United States 23, Great Britain 9	East Lake CC, Atlanta
1965	United States 19½, Great Britain 12½	Royal Birkdale GC, Southport, England
1967	United States 23½, Great Britain 8½	Champions GC, Houston
1969	United States 16, Great Britain 16	Royal Birkdale GC, Southport, England
1971	United States 18½, Great Britain 13½	Old Warson CC, St. Louis
1973	United States 19, Great Britain 13	Hon Co of Edinburgh Golfers, Muirfield, Scotland
1975	United States 21, Great Britain 11	Laurel Valley GC, Ligonier, PA
1977	United States 12½, Great Britain 7½	Royal Lytham & St. Annes GC, St. Annes-on-the-Sea, England
1979	United States 17, Europe 11	Greenbrier, White Sulphur Springs, WV
1981	United States 18½, Europe 9½	Walton Heath GC, Surrey, England
1983	United States 14½, Europe 13½	PGA National GC, Palm Beach Gardens, FL
1985	Europe 16½, United States 11½	Belfry GC, Sutton Coldfield, England
1987	Europe 15, United States 13	Muirfield GC, Dublin, OH
1989	Europe 14, United States 14	Belfry GC, Sutton Coldfield, England
1991	United States 14½, Europe 13½	Ocean Course, Kiawah Island, SC
1993	United States 15, Europe 13	Belfry GC, Sutton Coldfield, England
1995	Europe 14½, United States 13½	Oak Hill CC, Rochester, NY
1997	Europe 14½, United States 13½	Valderrama GC, Sotogrande, Spain
1999	United States 14½, Europe 13½	The Country Club, Brookline, MA
2002	Europe 15½, Unites States 12½	Belfry GC, Sutton Coldfield, England

Team matches held every odd year between U.S. professionals and those of Great Britain/Europe. Team members selected on basis of finishes in PGA and European tour events. Match in 2001 canceled due to 9/11 terrorist attacks.

Walker Cup Matches

Year	Results	Site
1922	United States 8, Great Britain 4	Nat'l Golf Links of America, Southampton, NY
1923	United States 6, Great Britain 5	St. Andrews, Scotland
1924	United States 9, Great Britain 3	Garden City GC, Garden City, NY
1926	United States 6, Great Britain 5	St. Andrews, Scotland
1928	United States 11, Great Britain 1	Chicago GC, Wheaton, IL
1930	United States 10, Great Britain 2	Royal St. George GC, Sandwich, England
1932	United States 8, Great Britain 1	The Country Club, Brookline, MA
1934	United States 9, Great Britain 2	St. Andrews, Scotland
1936	United States 9, Great Britain 0	Pine Valley GC, Clementon, NJ
1938	Great Britain 7, United States 4	St. Andrews, Scotland
1940–46	No tournament	
1947	United States 8, Great Britain 4	St. Andrews, Scotland
1949	United States 10, Great Britain 2	Winged Foot GC, Mamaroneck, NY
1951	United States 6, Great Britain 3	Birkdale GC, Southport, England
1953	United States 9, Great Britain 3	The Kittansett Club, Marion, MA
1955	United States 10, Great Britain 2	St. Andrews, Scotland
1957	United States 8, Great Britain 3	Minikahda Club, Minneapolis
1959	United States 9, Great Britain 3	Muirfield, Scotland
1961	United States 11, Great Britain 1	Seattle GC, Seattle
1963	United States 12, Great Britain 8	Ailsa Course, Turnberry, Scotland
1965	Great Britain 11, United States 11	Baltimore CC, Five Farms, Baltimore, MD
1967	United States 13, Great Britain 7	Royal St. George's GC, Sandwich, England
1969	United States 10, Great Britain 8	Milwaukee CC, Milwaukee, WI
1971	Great Britain 13, United States 11	St. Andrews, Scotland
1973	United States 14, Great Britain 10	The Country Club, Brookline, MA
1975	United States 15½, Great Britain 8½	St. Andrews, Scotland
1977	United States 16, Great Britain 8	Shinnecock Hills GC, Southampton, NY
1979	United States 15½, Great Britain 8½	Muirfield, Scotland
1981	United States 15, Great Britain 9	Cypress Point Club, Pebble Beach, CA
1983	United States 13½, Great Britain 10½	Royal Liverpool GC, Hoylake, England
1985	United States 13, Great Britain 11	Pine Valley GC, Pine Valley, NJ
1987	United States 16½, Great Britain 7½	Sunningdale GC, Berkshire, England
1989	Great Britain 12½, United States 11½	Peachtree Golf Club, Atlanta
1991	United States 14, Great Britain 10	Portmarnock GC, Dublin, Ireland
1993	United States 19, Great Britain 5	Interlachen CC, Edina, MN
1995	Great Britain/Ireland 14, United States 10	Royal Porthcawl, Porthcawl, Wales
1997	United States 18, Great Britain/Ireland 6	Quaker Ridge GC, Scarsdale, NY
1999	Great Britain/Ireland 15, United States 9	Nairn GC, Nairn, Scotland
2001	Great Britain/Ireland 15, United States 9	Ocean Forest GC, Sea Island, GA

Men's amateur team competition every other year between United States and Great Britain/Ireland. U.S. team members selected by USGA.

Solheim Cup Matches

Year	Results	Site
1990	United States 11½, Europe 4½	Lake Nona GC, Orlando, FL
1992	Europe 11½, United States 6½	Dalmahoy Hotel GC, Edinburgh
1994	United States 13, Europe 7	The Greenbriar, White Sulpher Springs, WV
1996	United States 17, Europe 11	Marriot St Pierre Hotel & CC, Chepstow, Wales
1998	United States 16, Europe 12	Muirfield Village GC; Dublin, OH
2000	Europe 14½, United States, 11½	Loch Lomond GC, Luss, Scotand
2002	United States 15½, Europe 12½	Interlachen CC, Minneapolis, MN

Team matches held every other year between U.S. professionals and those of Europe. Team members selected on basis of finishes in LPGA and European tour events.

Curtis Cup Matches

Year	Results	Site
1932	United States 5½, British Isles 3½	Wentworth GC, Wentworth, England
1934	United States 6½, British Isles 2½	Chevy Chase Club, Chevy Chase, MD
1936	United States 4½, British Isles 4½	King's Course, Gleneagles, Scotland
1938	United States 5½, British Isles 3½	Essex CC, Manchester, MA
1940–46	No tournament	
1948	United States 6½, British Isles 2½	Birkdale GC, Southport, England
1950	United States 7½, British Isles 1½	CC of Buffalo, Williamsville, NY
1952	British Isles 5, United States 4	Muirfield, Scotland
1954	United States 6, British Isles 3	Merion GC, Ardmore, PA
1956	British Isles 5, United States 4	Prince's GC, Sandwich Bay, England

Curtis Cup Matches (Cont.)

Year	Results	Site
1958	British Isles 4½, United States 4½	Brae Burn CC, West Newton, Mass.
1960	United States 6½, British Isles 2½	Lindrick GC, Worksop, England
1962	United States 8, British Isles 1	Broadmoor CG, Colorado Springs,CO
1964	United States 10½, British Isles 7½	Royal Porthcawl GC, Porthcawl, South Wales
1966	United States 13, British Isles 5	Va. Hot Springs G & TC, Hot Springs, VA
1968	United States 10½, British Isles 7½	Royal County Down GC, Newcastle, N. Ire.
1970	United States 11½, British Isles 6½	Brae Burn CC, West Newton, MA
1972	United States 10, British Isles 8	Western Gailes, Ayrshire, Scotland
1974	United States 13, British Isles 5	San Francisco GC, San Francisco
1976	United States 11½, British Isles 6½	Royal Lytham & St. Annes GC, England
1978	United States 12, British Isles 6	Apawamis Club, Rye, NY
1980	United States 13, British Isles 5	St. Pierre G & CC, Chepstow, Wales
1982	United States 14½, British Isles 3½	Denver CC, Denver
1984	United States 9½, British Isles 8½	Muirfield, Scotland
1986	British Isles 13, United States 5	Prairie Dunes CC, Hutchinson, KS
1988	British Isles 11, United States 7	Royal St. George's GC, Sandwich, England
1990	United States 14, British Isles 4	Somerset Hills CC, Bernardsville, NJ
1992	Great Britain/Ireland 10, United States 8	Royal Liverpool GC, Hoylake, England
1994	Great Britain/Ireland 9, United States 9	The Honors Course, Ooltewah, TN
1996	Great Britain/Ireland 11½, United States 6½	Killarney Golf & Fishing Club, Killarney, Ireland
1998	United States 10, Great Britain/Ireland 8	The Minikahda Club, Minneapolis
2000	United States 10, Great Britain/Ireland 8	Ganton GC, North Yorkshire, England
2002	United States 11, Great Britain/Ireland 7	Fox Chapel GC, Pittsburgh, PA

Women's amateur team competition every other year between the United States and Great Britain/Ireland. U.S. team members selected by USGA.

Where the Boys Are

For many golf fans, watching the Masters on TV is like dreaming in green. In April 2003 it will only be better. Instead of four minutes of commercials per hour, there will be no ads at all. The first major of the year will still be on CBS, just as it has been since 1956. It will just seem like PBS. Or heaven.

There is nothing serene, however, about what's going on behind the sponsor-free Masters, though matters started out genteelly enough in June 2002. That's when Hootie Johnson, chairman of the Augusta National Golf Club, received a brief, polite letter from Martha Burk, head of the National Council of Women's Organizations. Burk asked Johnson to "review your policies and practices . . . and open your membership to women now, so that this is not an issue when the tournament is staged next year."

Women seem to have a powerful effect on the 71-year-old retired South Carolina banker who runs Augusta National. Burk's measured request got Hootie all hot and haughty. Perhaps it brought him back to the highly annoying year of 1990, when public pressure forced the club to admit its first black member. In his mind it also raised the possibility of boycotts of the tournament's sponsors and picketers at his gates. Johnson went public, issuing a statement saying that change at his club will not come "at the point of a bayonet." On August 30, 2002, he cut loose the three sponsors of the Masters broadcast—Coca-Cola, Citigroup and IBM— rather than force them to face the wrath of the feminists whom he intends to fight till. . . .

Wait a minute: How does Hootie think this is going to turn out, anyway? On his side he has the dwindling herd of club folk, who like to point out that they have the legal right to exclude anyone they want. The viewing public may tune in the tournament, but not because they actively support Hootie's position. They just want to see one of the finest tournaments in golf, famous golfers and all those lovely azaleas.

Arrayed against Johnson are Burk, her millions of constituents and, despite the lack of animosity, CBS. A network spokesman told SI, "CBS will broadcast the Masters next April" and declined further comment. Even though Augusta will pay millions that the sponsors were set to shell out, Johnson is putting the network in an embarrassing position. Rest assured, CBS will not go on indefinitely presenting a two-day 7½-hour infomercial for the Good Ol' Boy Way.

Hootie could also come under pressure from his own influential pals—for example, Warren Buffett, a board member of Coca-Cola, and Sandy Weill, chairman of Citigroup, are Augusta members. These men are not the type to sit quietly by while Hootie turns a golfer's paradise into a hotbed of controversy. The view from here is that this problem won't last much longer; it's too easy to solve. Simply let that first woman slip on a green jacket. It won't be a great moment in fashion, but it will be a fine day for golf.

Boxing

AL BELLO/GETTY IMAGES

Lennox Lewis decks
Mike Tyson for the
WBC heavywight title

Memphis Mismatch

Lennox Lewis retained his title and dropped the final curtain on Mike Tyson's career with a pounding in Tennessee

BY MARK BEECH

WHEN IT WAS over, boxing fans across the country had to be shaking their heads and asking, What did we expect? They'd allowed themselves to be blinded by the promotional blitz and fished in once again by the counterfeit mystique of Mike Tyson. Maybe this time, the thinking went, the original Iron Mike would show up. But Tyson's formerly fearsome persona had been laid bare, exposed as a relic, supported by nothing more than the hurricane of pre-fight hoopla. The buildup to the $100 million heavyweight title bout between Tyson and Lennox Lewis in June 2002 was just an act, a facade. It was almost sad to realize that the one-time baddest man on the planet was nothing more than a paper tiger, completely and undeniably washed up. Tyson lay on his back in the eighth round, eyes closed, face bloodied. The fight, like his career, was over.

The jig was up, and fans knew they'd been had. For all of his searing performances in the 1980s, Tyson hadn't produced a respectable bout since he decked Razor Ruddock in 1991. He'd long been substituting erratic behavior for athletic accomplishment—the latest installment had been his bizarre pre-fight tussle with Lewis in January, during which Tyson allegedly bit the champion on the leg. Yet Iron Mike's aura somehow remained powerful, despite his public meltdowns. That was a testament to his brief but electrifying prime, during which his fights were often measured in seconds, instead of minutes or rounds.

But at 35, with those days way behind him, Tyson was good for nothing more than nostalgia. Against Lewis, a genuine heavyweight champion, Tyson would need more than hype and bygone glory. He began well, bobbing and charging Lewis and generally giving the Englishman a hard time in the first round. But Lewis overcame this initial difficulty, and began nailing Tyson with jab after jab. The rhythm of this potent weapon thoroughly bamboozled Tyson, keeping him off balance and unsure when to dodge a blow or launch one of his own. As a result, he appeared almost paralyzed

Barrera (right) and Morales produced a bout that nearly rivaled their epic 2000 fight.

in the ring, while Lewis's shots invariably found their mark.

The bout, which could have ended even earlier, was held in Memphis after Las Vegas refused to sanction it in the wake of Tyson's outburst in January. Shaking off the dubious distinction of having been beaten to the high moral ground by Las Vegas, Memphis went all out, gussying itself up in impressive fashion for the occasion. Little did it know the big night would yield a fight so completely one-sided that it not only forced fans to reassess Lewis's talents, it also made them grudgingly admire Tyson's toughness. By the third round his right eye was bleeding. Shortly after that, his left. Then his nose. And the Lewis jab kept snapping.

Yet Tyson lasted until the eighth round. He absorbed round after round of punishment until Lewis caught him with a left

uppercut, causing him to sag halfway to the canvas. A minute later, Lewis whistled a right into Tyson's jaw, and that was it.

What will become of Iron Mike now? As he told a TV reporter in his dressing room afterward, "I have nowhere to go." For his part, Lewis, 36, asserted that the performance "cements my legacy." He had never been much beloved or respected outside of Great Britain, but this victory won him some converts. Critics will rightly point out that a man of Lewis's size (6' 5", 249 pounds) and power might have been more dominant, but history will probably place him just below the first rank of heavyweights. That is, Lewis is no Muhammad Ali or Joe Louis, but he may take a rightful place alongside Larry Holmes or Ken Norton.

But after dropping Tyson, Lewis protested, "What more can you ask me to do?" Well, for starters, not lose to Oliver McCall, or Hasim Rahman. Lewis is undoubtedly the premier heavyweight of his generation, but those losses—even though both were avenged—bar him from historical greatness.

That category may or may not be open to welterweight Vernon Forrest, but by defeating Shane Mosley twice in 2002 and improving his record to 35–0, he made sure that he wouldn't fall through the cracks of boxing history. In the two weeks leading up to their July bout, Mosley kept up a steady stream of trash talk, razzing Forrest for everything from his boxing skills to his intelligence, to his wardrobe. Forrest had little to say in reply. "The action," he said, "will answer a lot of questions."

It did. While the fight at Conseco Fieldhouse in Indianapolis featured far too much clutching and grabbing, along with an excess of wild flailing, Forrest brought some measure of order to the proceedings. He used his lethal right hand to keep the smaller, quicker Mosley at bay. Forrest never knocked Mosley down, or even got him in real trouble, as he had during their first fight in January. He just tapped out a steady rhythm—bing, bing, bing—with his right against Mosley's face, and won a unanimous decision.

Until his back-to-back victories over Mosley, Forrest, 31, had been something of an also-ran, a regular on undercards but always fighting well away from television cameras and big purses. It didn't help that Forrest has a textbook style that eschews flashiness altogether. With a rangy body in the Tommy Hearns mold, and a hammer-of-Thor right hand, Forrest nonetheless fights with workmanlike precision. "If you want a lot of blood and knockdowns, you might not like me," he said. "If you want to see someone who knows the sport and knows what he's doing, I'm your man."

Two men who know what they're doing when it comes to providing visceral thrills for fight fans are featherweights Marco Antonio Barrera and Erik Morales, whose epic bout in 2000 was named Fight of the Year by *Ring* magazine. Their June rematch in Las Vegas may not have equaled that 2000 fight, but it was easily one of the best fights of 2002. And like their earlier meeting, it ended with a controversial decision, this time in Barrera's favor.

The pace of their first bout was maniacal—Morales threw 868 punches, or 72 a round, en route to his victory. In the dramatic, seesaw rematch this year, the two men launched 600 punches apiece—or a mere 50 per round. You could have built a credible rationale behind almost any decision following this fight. Morales took the initiative through the first six rounds, bringing the fight to Barrera. Then Barrera forced the action, swelling the defending WBC champion's right eye and bloodying the bridge of his nose with repeated shots.

The first bit of controversy came in the seventh round. Morales caught Barrera with a body blow, sending him down to one hand. Plenty of folks would have scored the sequence a knockdown in Morales's favor. Referee Jay Nady ruled it a slip. The three-point swing at stake in Nady's ruling would have given Morales the victory.

"A slip," said Barrera afterward.

"A legitimate drop," said Morales, who was so peeved by the final decision that he left the ring after it was announced. He quickly returned, but said, "I thought I did enough" to win the bout.

Barrera, who had similar gripes after their first fight, pointed to his unmarked visage as his best evidence of victory. "Most important," he explained, "I'm going to celebrate with a clean face."

And despite Tyson's vulgar display in Vegas in January, boxing escaped 2002 with more or less of a clean face, too. The capper, and one of the biggest fights of the year, was Oscar De La Hoya's 11th-round destruction of Fernando Vargas in September. Lately dismissed as a pretty boy whose interest in the fight game had been replaced by fluffier pursuits, such as singing (the CD he released in 2000 earned a Grammy nomination), De La Hoya won a huge measure of redemption with his gritty performance in Las Vegas. Mixing it up more than is usual for him, De La Hoya staggered Vargas in the 10th, and dropped him in the 11th to claim the WBC and WBA junior middleweight titles.

FOR THE RECORD·2001–2002

Current Champions

Division	Weight Limit	WBA Champion	WBC Champion	IBF Champion
Heavyweight	None	John Ruiz	Lennox Lewis	vacant
Cruiserweight	190	Jean-Marc Mormeck	vacant	Vassiliy Jirov
Light Heavyweight	175	Bruno Girard	Roy Jones	Roy Jones
Super Middleweight	168	Byron Mitchell	Eric Lucas	Sven Ottke
Middleweight	160	William Joppy	Bernard Hopkins	Bernard Hopkins
Junior Middleweight	154	Oscar De La Hoya	Oscar De La Hoya	Ronald Wright
Welterweight	147	Ricardo Mayorga	Vernon Forrest	Michele Piccirillo
Junior Welterweight	140	Diobelys Hurtado	Kostya Tszyu	Kostya Tszyu
Lightweight	135	Leonard Dorin	Floyd Mayweather	Paul Spadafora
Junior Lightweight	130	Yodsanan Nanthachai	S. Singmanassak	vacant
Featherweight	126	Derrick Gainer	vacant	Johnny Tapia
Junior Featherweight	122	Osamu Sato	Willie Jorrin	Manny Pacquiao
Bantamweight	118	Johnny Bredahl	Veerapol Sahaprom	Tim Austin
Junior Bantamweight	115	Alexander Munoz	Masanori Tokuyama	Felix Machado
Flyweight	112	Eric Morel	Pongsaklek Wonjongkam	Irene Pacheco
Junior Flyweight	108	Rosendo Alvarez	Jorge Arce	Ricardo Lopez
Strawweight	105	Noel Arambulent	Jose Aguirre	Miguel Barrera

Note: WBC=World Boxing Council; WBA=World Boxing Association; IBF=International Boxing Federation. Champions as of Sept. 16, 2002

Championship and Major Fights of 2001 and 2002

Abbreviations: WBC=World Boxing Council; WBA= World Boxing Association; IBF=International Boxing Federation; KO=knockout; TKO=technical knockout; UD=unanimous decision; SD=split decision; DQ=disqualification; MD=majority decision; TD=technical decision.

Heavyweight

Date	Winner	Loser	Result	Title	Site
Nov 17	Lennox Lewis	Hasim Rahman	KO 4	WBC/IBF	Las Vegas
Dec 15	John Ruiz	Evander Holyfield	Draw	WBA	Mashantucket, CT
June 8	Lennox Lewis	Mike Tyson	KO 8	WBC/IBF	Memphis
July 27	John Ruiz	Kirk Johnson	DQ 10	WBA	Las Vegas

Cruiserweight

Date	Winner	Loser	Result	Title	Site
Nov 3	Juan Carlos Gomez	Pietro Aurino	TKO 6	WBC	Lubeck, Germany
Feb 1	Vassiliy Jirov	Jorge Castro	UD	IBF	Phoenix
Feb 23	Jean-Marc Mormeck	Virgil Hill	TKO 9	WBA	Marseille
Aug 10	Jean-Marc Mormeck	Dale Brown	TKO 8	WBA	Marseille

Light Heavyweight

Date	Winner	Loser	Result	Title	Site
Dec 22	Bruno Girard	Robert Koon	TKO 11	WBA	Orleans, France
Feb 2	Roy Jones	Glenn Kelly	KO 7	WBC/WBA/IBF	Miami
May 23	Bruno Girard	Thomas Hansvoll	UD	WBA	Levallois, France
July 13	Bruno Girard	Lou Del Valle	SD	WBA	Palavas-les-Flots, Fr.
Sept 7	Roy Jones	Clinton Woods	TKO 6	WBC/WBA/IBF	Portland, OR

Super Middleweight

Date	Winner	Loser	Result	Title	Site
Nov 30	Eric Lucas	Dingaan Thobela	TKO 8	WBC	Montreal
Dec 1	Sven Ottke	Anthony Mundine	KO 10	IBF	Dortmund, Germany
Mar 1	Eric Lucas	Vinnie Pazienza	UD	WBC	Mashantucket, CT
Mar 16	Sven Ottke	Rick Thornberry	UD	IBF	Magdeburg, Germany
June 1	Sven Ottke	Thomas Tate	UD	IBF	Nuremberg, Germany
July 27	Byron Mitchell	Julio Cesar Green	TKO 4	WBA	Las Vegas
Aug 24	Sven Ottke	Joe Gatti	KO 9	IBF	Leipzig, Germany

Middleweight

Date	Winner	Loser	Result	Title	Site
Nov 17	William Joppy	Howard Eastman	MD	WBA	Las Vegas
Feb 2	Bernard Hopkins	Carl Daniels	TKO 10	WBC/WBA/IBF	Reading, PA

Junior Middleweight (Super Welterweight)

Date	Winner	Loser	Result	Title	Site
Oct 12	Ronald Wright	Robert Frazier	UD	IBF	Indio, CA
Feb 2	Ronald Wright	Jason Papillion	TKO 5	IBF	Miami
July 13	Javier Castillejo	Roman Karmazin	UD	interim WBC	Parla, Spain
Aug 10	Santiago Samaniego	Mamadou Thiam	TKO 12	interim WBA	Marseille
Sept 7	Ronald Wright	Bronco McKart	DQ 8	IBF	Portland, OR
Sept 13	Oscar De La Hoya	Fernando Vargas	TKO 11	WBC/WBA	Las Vegas

Welterweight

Date	Winner	Loser	Result	Title	Site
Jan 26	Vernon Forrest	Shane Mosley	UD	WBC	New York City
Mar 30	Ricardo Mayorga	Andrew Lewis	TKO 5	WBA	Reading, PA
Apr 13	Michele Piccirillo	Cory Spinks	UD	IBF	Campione d'Italia, Italy
July 20	Vernon Forrest	Shane Mosley	UD	WBC	Indianapolis

Junior Welterweight (Super Lightweight)

Date	Winner	Loser	Result	Title	Site
Nov 3	Kostya Tszyu	Zab Judah	TKO 2	IBF/WBA/WBC	Las Vegas
Feb 2	Randall Bailey	Demetrio Ceballos	KO 3	WBA	Reading, PA
May 11	Diobelys Hurtado	Randall Bailey	KO 7	WBA	San Juan, PR
May 18	Kostya Tszyu	Ben Tackie	UD	IBF/WBA/WBC	Las Vegas

Lightweight

Date	Winner	Loser	Result	Title	Site
Oct 8	Raul Balbi	Julien Lorcy	MD	WBA	Paris
Jan 5	Leonard Dorin	Raul Balbi	SD	WBA	San Antonio
Mar 9	Paul Spadafora	Angel Manfredy	UD	IBF	Pittsburgh
Apr 20	Floyd Mayweather	Jose Luis Castillo	UD	WBC	Las Vegas
May 31	Leonard Dorin	Raul Balbi	UD	WBA	Bucharest

Junior Lightweight (Super Featherweight)

Date	Winner	Loser	Result	Title	Site
Sept 29	Joel Casamayor	Joe Morales	TKO 8	WBA	Miami
Nov 10	Floyd Mayweather	Jesus Chavez	TKO 9	WBC	San Francisco
Jan 12	Acelino Freitas	Joel Casamayor	UD	WBA	Las Vegas
Apr 13	Yodsanan Nanthachai	Lakva Sim	UD	WBA	Nakhon Ratchasima, Thai.
Aug 3	Acelino Freitas	Daniel Attah	UD	WBA	Phoenix
Aug 18	Steve Forbes	David Santos	SD	IBF	Temacula, CA
Aug 24	S. Singmanassak	Kengo Nagashima	KO 2	WBC	Tokyo

Featherweight

Date	Winner	Loser	Result	Title	Site
Nov 16	Manuel Medina	Frankie Toledo	TKO 6	IBF	Las Vegas
Apr 27	Johnny Tapia	Manuel Medina	MD	IBF	New York City
June 22	Marco Antonio Barrera	Erik Morales	UD	WBC	Las Vegas
Aug 24	Derrick Gainer	Daniel Seda	Tech draw 2	WBA	Carolina, PR

Junior Featherweight (Super Bantamweight)

Date	Winner	Loser	Result	Title	Site
Nov 10	Manny Pacquiao	Agapito Sanchez	Tech Draw 6	IBF	San Francisco
Nov 17	Yober Ortega	José Rojas	KO 4	WBA	Las Vegas
Feb 5	Willie Jorrin	Osamu Sato	Maj Draw	WBC	Tokyo
Feb 21	Y. Sithyodthong	Yober Ortega	UD	WBA	Dankoonthod, Thai.
May 17	Oscar Larios	Israel Vazquez	TKO 12	interim WBC	Sacramento, CA
May 18	Osamu Sato	Y. Sithyodthong	KO 8	WBA	Saitama, Japan
June 8	Manny Pacquiao	Jorge Julio	TKO 2	IBF	Memphis
Aug 24	Oscar Larios	Manabu Fukushima	TKO 8	interim WBC	Tokyo

Bantamweight

Date	Winner	Loser	Result	Title	Site
Oct 14	Eidy Moya	Adan Vargas	KO 11	WBA	McAllen, TX
Dec 15	Tim Austin	Ratanachai Voraphin	UD	IBF	Mashantucket, CT
Jan 11	Veerapol Sahaprom	Sergio Perez	UD	WBC	Thanyaburi, Thailand
Apr 19	Johnny Bredahl	Eidy Moya	KO 9	WBA	Copenhagen
May 1	Veerapol Sahaprom	Julio Coronel	UD	WBC	Nonthaburi, Thailand
July 27	Tim Austin	Adan Vargas	TKO 10	IBF	Las Vegas

Junior Bantamweight (Super Flyweight)

Date	Winner	Loser	Result	Title	Site
Sept 24	Masamori Tokuyama	Gerry Penalosa	UD	WBC	Yokohama
Mar 9	Alexander Munoz	Celes Kobayashi	TKO 8	WBA	Tokyo
Mar 23	Masamori Tokuyama	Kazuhiro Ryuko	TKO 9	WBC	Yokohama
Mar 30	Felix Machado	Martin Castillo	TD	IBF	Reading, PA
July 31	Alexander Munoz	Eiji Kojima	KO 2	WBA	Osaka
Aug 26	Masamori Tokuyama	Erik Lopez	TKO 6	WBC	Saitama, Japan

Flyweight

Date	Winner	Loser	Result	Title	Site
Oct 26	P. Wonjongkam	Alex Baba	TD 8	WBC	Hat Yai, Thailand
Nov 9	Irene Pacheco	Mike Trejo	TKO 4	IBF	San Antonio
Dec 6	P. Wonjongkam	Luis Lazarte	TKO 2	WBC	Pattaya, Thailand
Apr 19	P. Wonkongjam	Daisuke Naito	KO 1	WBC	Khonkaen, Thailand

Junior Flyweight

Date	Winner	Loser	Result	Title	Site
Sept 29	Roberto Leyva	Miguel Barrera	Tech Draw 3	IBF	Ensenada, Mexico
Oct 20	Jorge Arce	Juanito Rubillar	UD	interim WBC	Tijuana, Mexico
Jan 19	Rosendo Alvarez	Phichit Chor Siriwat	TKO 12	WBA	Miami
Feb 23	Choi Yo-Sam	Shingo Yamaguchi	TKO 10	WBC	Chiba, Japan
July 6	Jorge Arce	Choi Yo-Sam	TKO 6	WBC	Seoul

Strawweight (Mini Flyweight)

Date	Winner	Loser	Result	Title	Site
Nov 11	Jose Antonio Aguirre	Yasuo Tokimitsu	TKO 3	WBC	Okayama, Japan
Jan 29	Keitaro Hoshino	Joma Gamboa	UD	WBA	Yokohama
July 29	Noel Arambulet	Keitaro Hoshino	MD	WBA	Yokohama
Aug 9	Miguel Barrera	Roberto Leyva	UD	IBF	Las Vegas

FOR THE RECORD · Year by Year

World Champions

Sanctioning bodies: the National Boxing Association (NBA), the New York State Athletic Commission (NY), the World Boxing Association (WBA), the World Boxing Council (WBC), and the International Boxing Federation (IBF).

Heavyweights
(Weight: Unlimited)

Champion	Reign	Champion	Reign	Champion	Reign
John L. Sullivan*	1885–92	Joe Frazier* NY	1968–70	Evander Holyfield*	1990–92
James J. Corbett*	1892–97	Jimmy Ellis WBA	1968–70	Lennox Lewis WBC	1993–95
Bob Fitzsimmons*	1897–99	Joe Frazier*	1970–73	Riddick Bowe*	1992–93
James J. Jeffries*	1899–05†	George Foreman*	1973–74	Evander Holyfield*	1993–94
Marvin Hart*	1905–06	Muhammad Ali*	1974–78	Michael Moorer*	1994
Tommy Burns*	1906–08	Leon Spinks*	1978	George Foreman*	1994–95
Jack Johnson*	1908–15	Ken Norton WBC	1978	Oliver McCall WBC	1995
Jess Willard*	1915–19	Larry Holmes WBC	1978–80	Frank Bruno WBC	1995–96
Jack Dempsey*	1919–26	Muhammad Ali*	1978–79†	Bruce Seldon WBA	1995–96
Gene Tunney*	1926–28†	John Tate WBA	1979–80	Mike Tyson WBA	1996
Max Schmeling*	1930–32	Mike Weaver WBA	1980–82	Michael Moorer IBF	1996–97
Jack Sharkey*	1932–33	Larry Holmes*	1980–85	Shannon Briggs*	1997–98
Primo Carnera*	1933–34	Michael Dokes WBA	1982–83	Lennox Lewis* WBC	1997–01
Max Baer*	1934–35	Gerrie Coetzee WBA	1983–84	E. Holyfield WBA, IBF	1996–99
James J. Braddock*	1935–37	Tim Witherspoon WBC	1984	Lennox Lewis	1999–01
Joe Louis*	1937–49†	Pinklon Thomas WBC	1984–86	E. Holyfield WBA	2000–01
Ezzard Charles*	1949–51	Greg Page WBA	1984–85	John Ruiz WBA	2001–
Jersey Joe Walcott*	1951–52	Michael Spinks*	1985–87	Hasim Rahman*	
Rocky Marciano*	1952–56†	Tim Witherspoon WBA	1986	WBC, IBF	2001
Floyd Patterson*	1956–59	Trevor Berbick WBC	1986	Lennox Lewis*	
Ingemar Johansson*	1959–60	Mike Tyson WBC	1986–87	WBC, IBF	2001–
Floyd Patterson*	1960–62	James Smith WBA	1986–87		
Sonny Liston*	1962–64	Tony Tucker IBF	1987		
Muhammad Ali*	1964–70†	Mike Tyson*	1987–90		
Ernie Terrell WBA	1965–67	Buster Douglas*	1990		

Cruiserweights
(Weight Limit: 190 pounds)

Champion	Reign	Champion	Reign	Champion	Reign
Marvin Camel* WBC	1980	Ricky Parkey IBF	1986–87	Alfred Cole IBF	1992–96
Carlos De Leon* WBC	1980–82	E. Holyfield* WBA, IBF	1987–88	Orlin Norris WBA	1993–95
Ossie Ocasio WBA	1982–84	Evander Holyfield*	1988†	Nate Miller WBA	1995–97
S.T. Gordon* WBC	1982–83	Toufik Belbouli WBA	1989	M. Dominguez* WBC	1996–98
Carlos De Leon* WBC	1983–85	Robert Daniels WBA	1989–91	A. Washington IBF	1996–97
Marvin Camel IBF	1983–84	Carlos De Leon* WBC	1989–90	Uriah Grant IBF	1997
Lee Roy Murphy IBF	1984–86	Glenn McCrory IBF	1989–90	Imamu Mayfield IBF	1997–98
Piet Crous WBA	1984–85	Jeff Lampkin IBF	1990	Fabrice Tiozzo WBA	1997–00
Alfonso Ratliff* WBC	1985	M. Duran* WBC	1990–91	J.C. Gomez* WBC	1998–02†
Dwight Braxton WBA	1985–86	Bobby Czyz WBC	1991–92†	Arthur Williams IBF	1998–99
Bernard Benton* WBC	1985–86	Anaclet Wamba* WBC	1991–95†	Vassiliy Jirov* IBF	1999–
Carlos De Leon* WBC	1986–88	James Pritchard IBF	1991	Virgil Hill WBA	2000–02
Evander Holyfield* WBA	1986–88	James Warring IBF	1991–92	J.M. Mormeck WBA	2002–

*Lineal champion.
†Champion relinquished title to retire or switch weight classes, or had title stripped by boxing organization.

ANOTHER SIGN OF
THE APOCALYPSE

Pete Rose has been elected to the Summit County (Ohio) Boxing Hall of Fame.

Light Heavyweights
(Weight Limit: 175 pounds)

Champion	Reign	Champion	Reign	Champion	Reign
Jack Root*	1903	Harold Johnson NBA	1961	Leslie Stewart WBA	1987
George Gardner*	1903	Harold Johnson*	1962–63	Virgil Hill* WBA	1987–91
Bob Fitzsimmons*	1903–05	Willie Pastrano*	1963–65	Pr Charles Williams IBF	1987–93
Jack O'Brien*	1905–12†	Jose Torres*	1965–66	Thomas Hearns WBC	1987†
Jack Dillon*	1914–16	Dick Tiger*	1966–68	Donny Lalonde WBC	1987–88
Battling Levinsky*	1916–20	Bob Foster*	1968–74†	Sugar Ray Leonard WBC	1988
Georges Carpentier*	1920–22	Vicente Rondon WBA	1971–72	Dennis Andries WBC	1989
Battling Siki*	1922–23	John Conteh WBC	1974–77	Jeff Harding WBC	1989–90
Mike McTigue*	1923–25	Victor Galindez* WBA	1974–78	Dennis Andries WBC	1990–91
Paul Berlenbach*	1925–26	Miguel A. Cuello WBC	1977–78	Thomas Hearns* WBA	1991–92
Jack Delaney*	1926–27†	Mate Parlov WBC	1978	Jeff Harding WBC	1991–94
Jimmy Slattery NBA	1927	Mike Rossman* WBA	1978–79	Iran Barkley* WBA	1992
Tommy Loughran*	1927–29†	Victor Galindez* WBA	1979	Virgil Hill* WBA	1992–97
Maxie Rosenbloom*	1930–34	Marvin Johnson* WBC	1978–79	Henry Maske IBF	1993–96
George Nichols NBA	1932	M.S. Muhammad* WBC	1979–81	Mike McCallum WBC	1994–95
Bob Godwin NBA	1933	Marvin Johnson WBA	1979–80	Fabrice Tiozzo WBC	1995–96
Bob Olin*	1934–35	E.M. Muhammad* WBA	1980–81	D. Michalczewski* IBF	1997†
John Henry Lewis*	1935–38†	Michael Spinks* WBA	1981–83	Roy Jones Jr. WBC, WBA	1997–
Melio Bettina	1939	Dwight Qawi WBC	1981–83	William Guthrie IBF	1997–98
Billy Conn*	1939–40†	Michael Spinks*	1983–85†	Reggie Johnson IBF	1998–99
Anton Christoforidis	1941	J. B. Williamson WBC	1985–86	Roy Jones Jr.	1999–
Gus Lesnevich*	1941–48	Slobodan Kacar IBF	1985–86	Bruno Girard WBA	2001–
Freddie Mills*	1948–50	Marvin Johnson* WBA	1986–87		
Joey Maxim*	1950–52	Dennis Andries WBC	1986–87		
Archie Moore*	1952–62†	Bobby Czyz IBF	1986–87		

Super Middleweights
(Weight Limit: 168 pounds)

Champion	Reign	Champion	Reign	Champion	Reign
Murray Sutherland* IBF	1984	Darrin Van Horn IBF	1991–92	Charles Brewer IBF	1997–98
Chong-Pal Park* IBF	1984–87	Iran Barkley IBF	1992	Thulane Malinga WBC	1997–98
Chong-Pal Park* WBA	1987–88	Nigel Benn WBC	1992–96	Richie Woodhall WBC	1998–99
G. Rocchigiani IBF	1988–89	James Toney IBF	1992–94	Sven Ottke IBF	1998–
F. Obelmejias* WBA	1988–89	Michael Nunn* WBA	1992–94	Byron Mitchell* WBA	1999–00
Sugar Ray Leonard WBC	1988–90†	Steve Little* WBA	1994	Markus Beyer WBC	1999–00
In-Chul Baek* WBA	1989–90	Frank Liles* WBA	1994–99	Bruno Girard* WBA	2000–01†
Lindell Holmes IBF	1990–91	Roy Jones Jr. IBF	1994–96	Glenn Catley WBC	2000–01
Chris Tiozzo* WBA	1990–91	Thulane Malinga WBC	1996	Eric Lucas WBC	2000–
Mauro Galvano WBC	1990–92	V. Nardiello WBC	1996	Byron Mitchell WBA	2000–
Victor Cordova* WBA	1991	Robin Reid WBC	1996–97		

*Lineal champion. †Champion retired or relinquished title.

Lost Classics: Superman vs. Muhammad Ali

Long before Howard Stern, Muhammad Ali was the original King of All Media. The subject of feature films, hit singles, TV specials and trading cards, Ali was ubiquitous in the pop-cultural landscape of the 1970s—his likeness even appeared on a brand of shoe polish. For my money, though, the thing that truly immortalized the champ was a comic book: *Superman vs. Muhammad Ali*.

Published as a special oversized edition by DC Comics in 1978, this logic-defying yarn occasioned one of the comic industry's first so-called event issues. To a nine-year-old weaned on tales of Caped Crusaders and Men of Steel, the appearance of the Greatest in the medium of cosmically endowed heroes cemented his larger-than-life status. I memorized every detail of the issue, down to the wraparound cover that featured Superman going toe-to-toe with Ali while numerous '70s celebs (Sonny Bono, Jimmy Carter, Raquel Welch, etc.) watched from ringside.

The story was classic comic-book hyperbole. An alien race demands that Earth come up with a champion to represent humanity in a blood match that'll determine the fate of the planet. Superman and Ali both want to be the hero, so they square off. For the record, Ali wins handily—once Superman's powers are nullified by the effects of red sunlight. Naturally, the two heroes band together in the end to save the day.

Shortly before the comic's release, Ali lost his crown to Leon Spinks. Not that it mattered to me. After all, how serious could that setback be for a fighter who could whup Superman?

—Tom Russo

Middleweights
(Weight Limit: 160 pounds)

Champion	Reign
Jack Dempsey*	1884–91
Bob Fitzsimmons*	1891–97†
Kid McCoy	1897–98
Tommy Ryan*	1898–07†
Stanley Ketchel*	1908
Billy Papke*	1908
Stanley Ketchel*	1908–10†
Frank Klaus*	1913
George Chip*	1913–14
Al McCoy*	1914–17
Mike O'Dowd*	1917–20
Johnny Wilson*	1920–23
Harry Greb*	1923–26
Tiger Flowers*	1926
Mickey Walker*	1926–31†
Gorilla Jones*	1931–32
Marcel Thil*	1932–37
Fred Apostoli*	1937–39
Al Hostak NBA	1938
Solly Krieger NBA	1938–39
Al Hostak NBA	1939–40
Ceferino Garcia*	1939–40
Ken Overlin*	1940–41
Tony Zale NBA	1940–41
Billy Soose*	1941
Tony Zale*	1941–47
Rocky Graziano*	1947–48
Tony Zale*	1948
Marcel Cerdan*	1948–49

Champion	Reign
Jake La Motta*	1949–51
Sugar Ray Robinson*	1951
Randy Turpin*	1951
Sugar Ray Robinson*	1951–52†
Bobo Olson*	1953–55
Sugar Ray Robinson*	1955–57
Gene Fullmer*	1957
Sugar Ray Robinson*	1957
Carmen Basilio*	1957–58
Sugar Ray Robinson*	1958–60
Gene Fullmer NBA	1959–62
Paul Pender*	1960–61
Terry Downes*	1961–62
Paul Pender*	1962–63†
Dick Tiger WBA	1962–63
Dick Tiger*	1963
Joey Giardello*	1963–65
Dick Tiger*	1965–66
Emile Griffith*	1966–67
Nino Benvenuti*	1967
Emile Griffith*	1967–68
Nino Benvenuti*	1968–70
Carlos Monzon*	1970–77†
Rodrigo Valdez WBC	1974–76
Rodrigo Valdez*	1977–78
Hugo Corro*	1978–79
Vito Antuofermo*	1979–80
Alan Minter*	1980
Marvin Hagler*	1980–87

Champion	Reign
Sugar Ray Leonard*	1987†
Frank Tate IBF	1987–88
Sumbu Kalambay WBA	1987–89
Thomas Hearns* WBC	1987–88
Iran Barkley*	1988–89
Michael Nunn IBF	1988–91
Roberto Duran* WBC	1989–90†
Michael Nunn*	1991
Mike McCallum WBA	1989–91
Julian Jackson WBC	1990–93
James Toney* IBF	1991–93†
Reggie Johnson WBA	1992–94
Roy Jones Jr.* IBF	1993–95†
G. McClellan WBC	1993–95†
Jorge Castro WBA	1994–95
Shinji Takehara WBA	1995–96
Jullian Jackson WBC	1995
Quincy Taylor WBC	1995–96
Bernard Hopkins* IBF	1994–
Keith Holmes WBC	1996–98
William Joppy WBA	1996–97
J.C. Green WBA	1997
William Joppy WBA	1998–01
Hassine Cherifi WBC	1998–99
Keith Holmes WBC	1999–00
Felix Trinidad WBA	2001
Bernard Hopkins*	2001–
William Joppy WBA	2001

Junior Middleweights
(Weight Limit: 154 pounds)

Champion	Reign
Emile Griffith (EBU)	1962–63
Dennis Moyer*	1962–63
Ralph Dupas*	1963
Sandro Mazzinghi*	1963–65
Nino Benvenuti*	1965–66
Ki-Soo Kim*	1966–68
Sandro Mazzinghi*	1968
Freddie Little*	1969–70
Carmelo Bossi*	1970–71
Koichi Wajima*	1971–74
Oscar Albarado*	1974–75
Koichi Wajima*	1975
Miguel de Oliveira WBC	1975–76
Jae-Do Yuh*	1975–76
Elisha Obed WBC	1975–76
Koichi Wajima*	1976
Jose Duran*	1976
Eckhard Dagge WBC	1976–77
Miguel Angel Castellini*	1976–77
Eddie Gazo*	1977–78
Rocky Mattioli WBC	1977–79
Masashi Kudo*	1978–79
Maurice Hope WBC	1979–81
Ayub Kalule*	1979–81
Wilfred Benitez WBC	1981–82

Champion	Reign
Sugar Ray Leonard*	1981–82†
Tadashi Mihara WBA	1981–82
Davey Moore WBA	1982–83
Thomas Hearns* WBC	1982–84
Roberto Duran WBA	1983–84
Mark Medal IBF	1984
Thomas Hearns*	1984–86†
Mike McCallum* WBA	1984–87†
Carlos Santos IBF	1984–86
Buster Drayton IBF	1986–87
Duane Thomas WBC	1986–87
Matthew Hilton IBF	1987–88
Lupe Aquino WBC	1987
Gianfranco Rosi WBC	1987–88
Julian Jackson WBA	1987–90
Donald Curry WBC	1988–89
Robert Hines IBF	1988–89
Darrin Van Horn IBF	1989
Rene Jacquot WBC	1989
John Mugabi* WBC	1989–90
Gianfranco Rosi IBF	1989–94
Terry Norris* WBC	1990–93
Gilbert Dele WBA	1991
Vinny Pazienza WBA	1991–92

Champion	Reign
Julio C. Vasquez WBA	1992–95
Simon Brown* WBC	1993–94
Terry Norris* WBC	1994
Luis Santana* WBC	1995–95
Vincent Pettway IBF	1994–95
Paul Vaden IBF	1995
Carl Daniels WBA	1995
Terry Norris* WBC	1995–97
Terry Norris* IBF	1995–96†
L. Boudouani WBA	1996–99
Raul Marquez IBF	1997
Keith Mullings* WBC	1997–99
Yori Boy Campas IBF	1997–98
Fernando Vargas IBF	1998–00
F. Javier Castillejo* WBC	1999–01
David Reid WBA	1999–00
Felix Trinidad WBA	2000–01
Felix Trinidad WBA, IBF	2001†
Oscar De La Hoya*	
WBC	2001–
Fernando Vargas WBA	2001–02
Ronald Wright IBF	2001–
Oscar De La Hoya*	
WBC/WBA	2002–

*Lineal champion.
†Champion relinquished title to retire or switch weight classes, or had title stripped by boxing organization.

Welterweights
(Weight Limit: 147 pounds)

Champion	Reign	Champion	Reign	Champion	Reign
Paddy Duffy*	1888–90†	Jimmy McLarnin*	1934–35	Thomas Hearns WBA	1980–81
Mysterious Billy Smith*	1892–94	Barney Ross*	1935–38	Sugar Ray Leonard*	1980–82†
Tommy Ryan*	1894–98†	Henry Armstrong*	1938–40	Donald Curry* WBA	1983–85
Mysterious Billy Smith*	1898–1900	Fritzie Zivic*	1940–41	Milton McCrory WBC	1983–85
Rube Ferns*	1900	Red Cochrane*	1941–46	Donald Curry*	1985–86
Matty Matthews*	1900–01	Marty Servo*	1946	Lloyd Honeyghan*	1986–87
Rube Ferns*	1901	Sugar Ray Robinson*	1946–51†	Jorge Vaca* WBC	1987–88
Joe Walcott*	1901–04	Johnny Bratton	1951	Lloyd Honeyghan* WBC	1988–89
The Dixie Kid*	1904–05†	Kid Gavilan*	1951–54	Mark Breland WBA	1987
Honey Mellody*	1906–07	Johnny Saxton*	1954–55	Marlon Starling WBA	1987–88
Mike Sullivan*	1907–08†	Tony DeMarco*	1955	Tomas Molinares WBA	1988–89
Jimmy Gardner*	1908†	Carmen Basilio*	1955–56	Simon Brown IBF	1988–91
Jimmy Clabby*	1910–1††	Johnny Saxton*	1956	Mark Breland WBA	1989–90
Waldemar Holberg*	1914	Carmen Basilio*	1956–57†	Marlon Starling* WBC	1989–90
Tom McCormick*	1914	Virgil Akins*	1958	Aaron Davis WBA	1990–91
Matt Wells*	1914–15	Don Jordan*	1958–60	Maurice Blocker* WBC	1990–91
Mike Glover*	1915	Kid Paret*	1960–61	Meldrick Taylor WBA	1991–92
Jack Britton*	1915	Emile Griffith*	1961	Simon Brown* WBC	1991
Ted "Kid" Lewis*	1915–16	Kid Paret*	1961–62	Buddy McGirt* WBC	1991–93
Jack Britton*	1916–17	Emile Griffith*	1962–63	Felix Trinidad IBF	1993–00
Ted "Kid" Lewis*	1917–19	Luis Rodriguez*	1963	Pernell Whitaker* WBC	1993–97
Jack Britton*	1919–22	Emile Griffith*	1963–66†	Crisanto Espana WBA	1992–94
Mickey Walker*	1922–26	Curtis Cokes*	1966–69	Ike Quartey WBA	1994–97†
Pete Latzo*	1926–27	Jose Napoles*	1969–70	Oscar De La Hoya* WBC	1997–99
Joe Dundee*	1927–29	Billy Backus*	1970–71	James Page WBA	1998–01
Jackie Fields*	1929–30	Jose Napoles*	1971–75	Felix Trinidad* IBF, WBA	1999–00†
Young Jack Thompson*	1930	Hedgemon Lewis NY	1972–73	Shane Mosley* WBC	2000–02
Tommy Freeman*	1930–31	Angel Espada WBA	1975–76	Andrew Lewis WBA	2001–02
Young Jack Thompson*	1931	John H. Stracey*	1975–76	Vernon Forrest IBF	2001
Lou Brouillard*	1931–32	Carlos Palomino*	1976–79	Vernon Forrest* WBC	2001–
Jackie Fields*	1932–33	Pipino Cuevas WBA	1976–80	Ricardo Mayorga WBA	2002–
Young Corbett III*	1933	Wilfredo Benitez*	1979	Michele Piccirillo IBF	2002–
Jimmy McLarnin*	1933–34	Sugar Ray Leonard*	1979–80		
Barney Ross*	1934	Roberto Duran*	1980		

Junior Welterweights
(Weight Limit: 140 pounds)

Champion	Reign	Champion	Reign	Champion	Reign
Pinkey Mitchell*	1922–25	Wilfred Benitez*	1976–79†	Julio César Chávez* IBF	1990–91
Red Herring	1925	M. Velasquez WBC	1976	Loreto Garza WBA	1990–91
Mushy Callahan*	1926–30	S. Muangsurin WBC	1976–78	Juan Coggi WBA	1991
Jack (Kid) Berg*	1930–31	A. Cervantes WBA	1977–80	Edwin Rosario WBA	1991–92
Tony Canzoneri*	1931–32	Sang-Hyun Kim WBC	1978–80	Rafael Pineda IBF	1991–92
Johnny Jadick*	1932–33	Saoul Mamby WBC	1980–82	Akinobu Hiranaka WBA	1992
Sammy Fuller	1932–33	Aaron Pryor* WBA	1980–83	Pernell Whitaker IBF	1992–93†
Battling Shaw*	1933	Leroy Haley WBC	1982–83	Charles Murray IBF	1993–94
Tony Canzoneri*	1933	Aaron Pryor* IBF	1983–85†	Jake Rodriguez IBF	1994–95
Barney Ross*	1933–35†	Bruce Curry WBC	1983–84	Juan Coggi WBA	1993–94
Tippy Larkin*	1946	Johnny Bumphus WBA	1984	Frankie Randall* WBC	1994
Carlos Ortiz*	1959–60	Bill Costello WBC	1984–85	Frankie Randall WBA	1994–96
Duilio Loi*	1960–62	Gene Hatcher WBA	1984–85	Juan Coggi WBA	1996
Eddie Perkins*	1962	Ubaldo Sacco WBA	1985–86	Julio César Chávez* WBC	1994–96
Duilio Loi*	1962–63†	Lonnie Smith* WBC	1985–86	Kostya Tszyu IBF	1995–97
Roberto Cruz WBA	1963	Patrizio Oliva WBA	1986–87	Frankie Randall WBA	1996–97
Eddie Perkins*	1963–65	Gary Hinton IBF	1986	Oscar De La Hoya* WBC	1996–97†
Carlos Hernandez*	1965–66	Rene Arredondo* WBC	1986	Khalid Rahilou WBA	1997–98
Sandro Lopopolo*	1966–67	Tsuyoshi Hamada WBC	1986–87	Vincent Phillips* IBF	1997–99
Paul Fujii*	1967–68	Joe Louis Manley IBF	1986–87	Sharmba Mitchell WBA	1998–01
Nicolino Loche*	1968–72	Terry Marsh IBF	1987	Kostya Tszyu WBC	1998–
Pedro Adigue WBC	1968–70	Juan Coggi WBA	1987–90	Terronn Millett* IBF	1999–00
Bruno Arcari WBC	1970–74	Rene Arredondo WBC	1987	Zab Judah* IBF	2000–01
Alfonso Frazer*	1972	R. Mayweather* WBC	1987–89	Kostya Tszyu*	
Antonio Cervantes*	1972–76	James McGirt IBF	1988	WBA/WBC	2001–
Perico Fernandez WBC	1974–75	Meldrick Taylor IBF	1988–90	Kostya Tszyu*	2001–
S. Muangsurin WBC	1975–76	Julio César Chávez* WBC	1989–94		

Lightweights
(Weight Limit: 135 pounds)

Champion	Reign
Jack McAuliffe*	1886–94†
Kid Lavigne*	1896–99
Frank Erne*	1899–1902
Joe Gans*	1902–04
Jimmy Britt*	1904–05
Battling Nelson*	1905–06
Joe Gans*	1906–08
Battling Nelson*	1908–10
Ad Wolgast*	1910–12
Willie Ritchie*	1912–14
Freddie Welsh*	1915–17
Benny Leonard*	1917–25†
Jimmy Goodrich*	1925
Rocky Kansas*	1925–26
Sammy Mandell*	1926–30
Al Singer*	1930
Tony Canzoneri*	1930–33
Barney Ross*	1933–35†
Tony Canzoneri*	1935–36
Lou Ambers*	1936–38
Henry Armstrong*	1938–39
Lou Ambers*	1939–40
Sammy Angott NBA	1940–41
Lew Jenkins*	1940–41
Sammy Angott*	1941–42†
Beau Jack* NY	1942–43
Bob Montgomery* NY	1943
Sammy Angott NBA	1943–44
Beau Jack* NY	1943–44
Bob Montgomery* NY	1944–47
Juan Zurita NBA	1944–45
Ike Williams*	1947–51
James Carter*	1951–52
Lauro Salas*	1952
James Carter*	1952–54
Paddy DeMarco*	1954

Champion	Reign
James Carter*	1954–55
Wallace Smith*	1955–56
Joe Brown*	1956–62
Carlos Ortiz*	1962–65
Ismael Laguna*	1965
Carlos Ortiz*	1965–68
Carlos Teo Cruz*	1968–69
Mando Ramos*	1969–70
Ismael Laguna*	1970
Ken Buchanan*	1970–72
Roberto Duran*	1972–79†
Chango Carmona WBC	1972
Rodolfo Gonzalez WBC	1972–74
Ishimatsu Suzuki WBC	1974–76
Estaban DeJesus WBC	1976–78
Jim Watt WBC*	1979–81
Ernesto Espana WBA	1979–80
Hilmer Kenty WBA	1980–81
Sean O'Grady WBA	1981
Claude Noel WBA	1981
Alexis Arguello* WBC	1981–82†
Arturo Frias WBA	1981–82
Ray Mancini* WBA	1982–84
Alexis Arguello	1982–83
Edwin Rosario WBC	1983–84
Choo Choo Brown IBF	1984
L. Bramble* WBA	1984–86
Jose Luis Ramirez WBC	1984–85
Harry Arroyo IBF	1984–85
Jimmy Paul IBF	1985–86
Hector Camacho WBC	1985–86
Greg Haugen IBF	1986–87
Edwin Rosario* WBA	1986–87
Julio César Chávez* WBA	1987–88
Jose Luis Ramirez WBC	1987–88
Julio César Chávez*	1988–89†

Champion	Reign
Vinny Pazienza IBF	1987–88
Greg Haugen IBF	1988–89
P. Whitaker* WBC, IBF	1989–90
Edwin Rosario WBA	1989–90
Juan Nazario WBA	1990
P. Whitaker* WBA, WBC	1990–92†
Pernell Whitaker* IBF	1991–92†
Julio César Chávez IBF	1990–91
Edwin Rosario WBA	1991–92
Julio César Chávez WBC	1990–92
Miguel Gonzalez WBC	1992–95
Joey Gamache WBA	1992–93
Dingaan Thobela WBA	1993
Fred Pendleton* IBF	1993–94
Orzubek Nazarov WBA	1993–98
Rafael Ruelas* IBF	1994–95
Oscar De La Hoya* IBF	1995†
Phillip Holiday IBF	1995–97
Jean B. Mendy* WBC	1996–97
Steve Johnston* WBC	1997–98
Shane Mosley IBF	1997–99†
Jean B. Mendy WBA	1998–99
Cesar Bazan* WBC	1998–99
Steve Johnston* WBC	1999–00
Julien Lorcy WBA	1999
Stefano Zoff WBA	1999
Paul Spadafora IBF	1999–
Gilbert Serrano WBA	1999–00
T. Hatakeyama WBA	2000–01
Jose Luis Castillo* WBC	2000–02
Julien Lorcy WBA	2001
Raul Balbi WBA	2001
F. Mayweather* WBC	2002–
Leonard Dorin WBA	2002–

Junior Lightweights
(Weight Limit: 130 pounds)

Champion	Reign
Johnny Dundee*	1921–23
Jack Bernstein*	1923
Johnny Dundee*	1923–24
Steve (Kid) Sullivan*	1924–25
Mike Ballerino*	1925
Tod Morgan*	1925–29
Benny Bass*	1929–31
Kid Chocolate*	1931–33
Frankie Klick*	1933–34†
Sandy Saddler*	1949–50†
Harold Gomes*	1959–60
Gabriel (Flash) Elorde*	1960–67
Yoshiaki Numata*	1967
Hiroshi Kobayashi*	1967–71
Rene Barrientos WBC	1969–70
Yoshiaki Numata WBC	1970–71
Alfredo Marcano*	1971–72
R. Arredondo WBC	1971–74
Ben Villaflor*	1972–73
Kuniaki Shibata*	1973
Ben Villaflor*	1973–76
Kuniaki Shibata WBC	1974–75
Alfredo Escalera WBC	1975–78
Samuel Serrano*	1976–80

Champion	Reign
Alexis Arguello WBC	1978–80
Yasutsune Uehara*	1980–81
Rafael Limon WBC	1980–81
C. Boza-Edwards WBC	1981
Samuel Serrano*	1981–83
R. Navarrete WBC	1981–82
Rafael Limon WBC	1982
Bobby Chacon WBC	1982–83
Roger Mayweather*	1983–84
Hector Camacho WBC	1983–84
Rocky Lockridge*	1984–85
Hwan-Kil Yuh IBF	1984–85
Julio César Chávez WBC	1984–87
Lester Ellis IBF	1985
Wilfredo Gomez*	1985–86
Barry Michael IBF	1985–87
Alfredo Layne* WBA	1986
Brian Mitchell* WBA	1986–91†
Rocky Lockridge IBF	1987–88
Azumah Nelson* WBC	1988–94
Tony Lopez IBF	1988–89
Juan Molina IBF	1989–90
Tony Lopez IBF	1990–91
Joey Gamache WBA	1991

Champion	Reign
Brian Mitchell IBF	1991
Genaro Hernandez WBA	1991–95
James Leija* WBC	1994
Juan Molina IBF	1991–95
Gabriel Ruelas* WBC	1994–95
Eddie Hopson IBF	1995
Tracy Patterson IBF	1995
Azumah Nelson* WBC	1995–97
Choi Yong-Soo WBA	1995–98
Arturo Gatti IBF	1995–98†
Genaro Hernandez* WBC	1997–98
Roberto Garcia IBF	1998–99
Floyd Mayweather* WBC	1998–01†
T. Hatakeyama WBA	1998–99
Lakva Sim WBA	1999
Diego Corrales IBF	1999–01
Jong Kwon Baek WBA	1999–00
Joel Casamayor WBA	2000–02
Steve Forbes IBF	2000–02†
Acelino Freitas* WBA	2002–
Y. Nantchachai WBA	2002–
S. Singmanassak WBC	2002–

Featherweights
(Weight Limit: 126 pounds)

Champion	Reign
Torpedo Billy Murphy*	1890
Young Griffo*	1890–92†
George Dixon*	1892–97
Solly Smith*	1897–98
Dave Sullivan*	1898
George Dixon*	1898–1900
Terry McGovern*	1900–01
Young Corbett II*	1901–03†
Abe Attell*	1903–04
Tommy Sullivan*	1904–05†
Abe Attell*	1906–12
Johnny Kilbane*	1912–23
Eugene Criqui*	1923
Johnny Dundee*	1923–24†
"Kid" Kaplan*	1925–26†
Tony Canzoneri*	1927–28
Andre Routis*	1928–29
Battling Battalino*	1929–32†
Tommy Paul NBA	1932–33
Kid Chocolate NY	1932–33†
Freddie Miller NBA	1933–36
Mike Beloise NY	1936–37
Petey Sarron NBA	1936–37
Maurice Holtzer	1937–38
Henry Armstrong*	1937–38†
Joey Archibald* NY	1938–39
Leo Rodak NBA	1938–39
Joey Archibald	1939–40
Petey Scalzo NBA	1940–41
Harry Jeffra*	1940–41
Joey Archibald*	1941
Richie Lamos NBA	1941
Chalky Wright*	1941–42
Jackie Wilson NBA	1941–43
Willie Pep*	1942–48
Jackie Callura NBA	1943
Phil Terranova NBA	1943–44

Champion	Reign
Sal Bartolo NBA	1944–46
Sandy Saddler*	1948–49
Willie Pep*	1949–50
Sandy Saddler*	1950–57†
Kid Bassey*	1957–59
Davey Moore*	1959–63
Sugar Ramos*	1963–64
Vicente Saldivar*	1964–67†
Paul Rojas WBA	1968
Jose Legra WBC	1968–69
Shozo Saijyo WBA	1968–71
J. Famechon* WBC	1969–70
Vicente Saldivar* WBC	1970
Kuniaki Shibata* WBC	1970–72
Antonio Gomez WBA	1971–72
C. Sanchez* WBC	1972
Ernesto Marcel WBA	1972–74
Jose Legra* WBC	1972–73
Eder Jofre* WBC	1973–74†
Ruben Olivares WBA	1974
Bobby Chacon WBC	1974–75
Alexis Arguello* WBA	1974–76†
Ruben Olivares WBA	1975
Poison Kotey WBC	1975–76
Danny Lopez* WBC	1976–80
Rafael Ortega WBA	1977
Cecilio Lastra WBA	1977–78
Eusebio Pedroza* WBA	1978–85
S. Sanchez* WBC	1980–82†
Juan LaPorte WBC	1982–84
Wilfredo Gomez WBC	1984
Min-Keun Oh IBF	1984–85
Azumah Nelson WBC	1984–88
Barry McGuigan* WBA	1985–86
Ki Young Chung IBF	1985–86
Steve Cruz* WBA	1986–87
Antonio Rivera IBF	1986–88

Champion	Reign
A. Esparragoza* WBA	1987–91
Calvin Grove IBF	1988
Jorge Paez IBF	1988–91
Jeff Fenech WBC	1988–90†
Marcos Villasana WBC	1990–91
Paul Hodkinson WBC	1991–93
Troy Dorsey IBF	1991
Manuel Medina IBF	1991–93
Yung Kyun Park* WBA	1991–93
Gregorio Vargas WBC	1993
Tom Johnson IBF	1993–97†
Eloy Rojas* WBA	1993–96
Kevin Kelley WBC	1993–95
A. Gonzalez WBC	1995
Manuel Medina WBC	1995–95
Luisito Espinosa WBC	1995–99
Wilfredo Vazquez* WBA	1996–98
Hector Lizarraga IBF	1997–98
Naseem Hamed* WBA	1998†
Naseem Hamed*	1998–01
Freddy Norwood WBA	1998
Manuel Medina IBF	1998–99
Antonio Cermeno WBA	1998–99
Cesar Soto WBC	1999
Freddy Norwood WBA	1999–00
Naseem Hamed* WBC	1999†
Paul Ingle IBF	1999–00
Guty Espadas WBC	2000–01
Erik Morales WBC	2000–02
Derrick Gainer WBA	2000–
Mbulelo Botile IBF	2001
Frankie Toledo IBF	2001
Manuel Medina IBF	2001–02
Marco A. Barrera*	2001–
Johnny Tapia IBF	2002–
Marco A. Barrera* WBC	2002†

Junior Featherweights
(Weight Limit: 122 pounds)

Champion	Reign
Jack (Kid) Wolfe*	1922–23
Carl Duane*	1923–24
Rigoberto Riasco* WBC	1976
R. Kobayashi* WBC	1976
Dong-Kyun Yum* WBC	1976–77
Wilfredo Gomez* WBC	1977–83†
Soo-Hwan Hong WBA	1977–78
Ricardo Cardona WBA	1978–80
Leo Randolph WBA	1980
Sergio Palma WBA	1980–82
Leonardo Cruz WBA	1982–84
Jaime Garza* WBC	1983
Bobby Berna IBF	1983–84
Loris Stecca WBA	1984
Seung-Il Suh IBF	1984–85
Victor Callejas WBA	1984–86
Juan Meza* WBC	1984–85
Ji-Won Kim IBF	1985–86

Champion	Reign
Lupe Pintor* WBC	1985–86
S. Payakaroon* WBC	1986–87
Seung-Hoon Lee IBF	1987–88
Louie Espinoza WBA	1987
Jeff Fenech* WBC	1987†
Julio Gervacio WBA	1987–88
Daniel Zaragoza* WBC	1988–90
Jose Sanabria IBF	1988–89
B. Pinango WBA	1988
J.J. Estrada WBA	1988–89
Fabrice Benichou IBF	1989–90
Jesus Salud WBA	1989–90
Welcome Ncita IBF	1990–92
Paul Banke* WBC	1990
Luis Mendoza WBA	1990–91
Raul Perez WBA	1992
Pedro Decima* WBC	1990–91
K. Hatanaka* WBC	1991

Champion	Reign
Daniel Zaragoza* WBC	1991–92
Thiery Jacob* WBC	1992
Tracy Patterson* WBC	1992–94
Kennedy McKinney IBF	1993–94
Wilfredo Vasquez WBA	1992–95
Vuyani Bungu IBF	1994–99†
H. Acero* Sanchez WBC	1994–95
Antonio Cermeno WBA	1995–98†
Daniel Zaragoza* WBC	1995–97
Erik Morales* WBC	1997–00†
Enrique Sanchez WBA	1998
Nestor Garza WBA	1998–00
Benedict Ledwaba IBF	1999–01
Clarence Adams WBA	2000–01†
Willie Jorrin WBC	2000–
Manny Pacquiao IBF	2001–
Yober Ortega WBA	2001–02
Y. Sithyodthong WBA	2002
Osamu Sato WBA	2002–

*Lineal champion.

†Champion relinquished title to retire or switch weight classes, or had title stripped by boxing organization.

Bantamweights
(Weight Limit: 118 pounds)

Champion	Reign	Champion	Reign	Champion	Reign
Spider Kelly	1887	Sixto Escobar*	1938–39†	Daniel Zaragoza WBC	1985
Hughey Boyle	1887–88	Georgie Pace NBA	1939–40	Miguel Lora WBC	1985–88
Spider Kelly	1889	Lou Salica*	1940–42	Gaby Canizales*	1986
Chappie Moran	1889–90	Manuel Ortiz*	1942–47	Bernardo Pinango*	1986–87†
George Dixon	1890–91	Harold Dade*	1947	W. Vasquez WBA	1987–88
Pedlar Palmer	1895–99	Manuel Ortiz*	1947–50	Kevin Seabrooks* IBF	1987–88
Terry McGovern*	1899–00†	Vic Toweel*	1950–52	Kaokor Galaxy WBA	1988
Harry Harris	1901	Jimmy Carruthers*	1952–54†	Moon Sung-Kil WBA	1988–89
Harry Forbes*	1901–03	Robert Cohen*	1954–56	Kaokor Galaxy WBA	1989
Frankie Neil*	1903–04	Paul Macias NBA	1955–57	Raul Perez WBC	1988–91
Joe Bowker*	1904–05†	Mario D'Agata*	1956–57	O. Canizales* IBF	1988–95†
Jimmy Walsh*	1905–06†	Alphonse Halimi*	1957–59	Luisito Espinosa WBA	1989–91
Owen Moran	1907–08	Joe Becerra*	1959–60†	Israel Contreras WBA	1991–92
Monte Attell	1909–10	Eder Jofre*	1961–65	Eddie Cook WBA	1992–93
Frankie Conley	1910–11	Fighting Harada*	1965–68	Greg Richardson WBC	1991
Johnny Coulon*	1910–14	Lionel Rose*	1968–69	J. Tatsuyoshi, WBC	1991–92
Kid Williams*	1914–17	Ruben Olivares*	1969–70	Victor Rabanales WBC	1992–93
Kewpie Ertle	1915	Chucho Castillo*	1970–71	Jung-Il Byun WBC	1993
Pete Herman*	1917–20	Ruben Olivares*	1971–72	Jorge Julio WBA	1993
Joe Lynch*	1920–21	Rafael Herrera*	1972	Yasuei Yakushiji WBC	1993–95
Pete Herman*	1921	Enrique Pinder*	1972–73	Junior Jones WBA	1994
Johnny Buff*	1921–22	Romeo Anaya*	1973	John M. Johnson WBA	1994
Joe Lynch*	1922–24	Arnold Taylor*	1973–74	D. Chuvatana WBA	1994–95
Abe Goldstein*	1924	Rafael Herrera WBC	1973–74	V. Sahaprom* WBA	1995–96
Cannonball Martin*	1924–25	Soo-Hwan Hong*	1974–75	W. McCullough WBC	1995–96
Phil Rosenberg*	1925–27†	Rodolfo Martinez WBC	1974–76	Harold Mestre IBF	1995
Bud Taylor NBA	1927–28	Alfonso Zamora*	1975–77	Mbulelo Botile IBF	1995–97
Bushy Graham NY	1928–29	Carlos Zarate* WBC	1976–79	Nana Konadu* WBA	1996–98
Panama Al Brown*	1929–35	Jorge Lujan	1977–80	S. Singmanassak WBC	1996–97
Sixto Escobar NBA	1934–35	Lupe Pintor* WBC	1979–83†	Tim Austin IBF	1997–
Baltazar Sangchilli*	1935–36	Julian Solis	1980	J.Tatsuyoshi WBC	1997–98
Lou Salica NBA	1935	Jeff Chandler*	1980–84	Johnny Tapia* WBA	1998–99
Sixto Escobar NBA	1935–36	Albert Davila WBC	1983–85	V. Sahaprom* WBC	1998–
Tony Marino*	1936	Richard Sandoval*	1984–86	Paulie Ayala* WBA	1999–01†
Sixto Escobar*	1936–37	Satoshi Shingaki IBF	1984–85	Eidy Moya WBA	2001–02
Harry Jeffra*	1937–38	Jeff Fenech IBF	1985	Johnny Bredahl WBA	2002–

Junior Bantamweights
(Weight Limit: 115 pounds)

Champion	Reign	Champion	Reign	Champion	Reign
Rafael Orono* WBC	1980–81	Sugar Rojas* WBC	1987–88	Harold Grey IBF	1996
Chul-Ho Kim* WBC	1981–82	Ellyas Pical IBF	1987–89	Danny Romero IBF	1996–97
Gustavo Ballas WBA	1981	Gilberto Roman* WBC	1988–89	Gerry Penalosa* WBC	1997–98
Rafael Pedroza WBA	1981–82	Juan Polo Perez IBF	1989–90	Johnny Tapia IBF	1997–99†
Jiro Watanabe WBA	1982–84	Nana Konadu* WBC	1989–90	Satoshi Iida WBA	1997–98
Rafael Orono* WBC	1982–83	Sung-Kil Moon* WBC	1990–93	In-Joo Cho* WBC	1998–00
Payao Poontarat* WBC	1983–84	Robert Quiroga IBF	1990–93	Jesus Rojas WBA	1998–99
Joo-Do Chun IBF	1983–85	Julio Borboa IBF	1993–94	Mark Johnson IBF	1999–00
Jiro Watanabe*	1984–86	Katsuya Onizuka WBA	1993–94	Hideki Todaka WBA	1999–00
Kaosai Galaxy WBA	1984	Lee Hyung-Chul WBA	1994–95	Felix Machado IBF	2000–
Ellyas Pica IBF	1985–86	Jose Luis Bueno* WBC	1993–94	M. Tokuyama* WBC	2000–
Cesar Polanco IBF	1986	H. Kawashima* WBC	1994–97	Leo Gamez WBA	2000–01
Gilberto Roman* WBC	1986–87	Harold Grey IBF	1994–95	Celes Kobayashi WBA	2001–02
Ellyas Pical IBF	1986	Alimi Goitia WBA	1995–96	Alexander Munoz WBA	2002–
Santos Laciar* WBC	1987	Yokthai Sith-Oar WBA	1996–97		
Tae-Il Chang IBF	1987	Carlos Salazar IBF	1995–96		

*Lineal champion.
†Champion relinquished title to retire or switch weight classes, or had title stripped by boxing organization.

Flyweights
(Weight Limit: 112 pounds)

Champion	Reign	Champion	Reign	Champion	Reign
Sid Smith*	1913	B. Villacampo WBA	1969–70	Hilario Zapate WBA	1985–87
Bill Ladbury*	1913–14	Chartchai Chionoi*	1970	Chong-Kwan Chung IBF	1985–86
Percy Jones*	1914†	B. Chartvanchai WBA	1970	Bi-Won Chung IBF	1986
Joe Symonds*	1914–16	Masao Ohba WBA	1970–73	Hi-Sup Shin IBF	1986–87
Jimmy Wilde*	1916–23	Erbito Salavarria*	1970–73†	Dodie Penalosa IBF	1987
Pancho Villa*	1923–25†	B. Gonzalez WBA	1972	Fidel Bassa WBA	1987–89
Fidel La Barba*	1925–27†	V. Borkorsor WBC	1972–73†	Choi-Chang Ho IBF	1987–88
Frenchy Belanger* NBA	1927–28	Venice Borkorsor*	1973†	Rolando Bohol IBF	1988
Izzy Schwartz NY	1927–29	Chartchai Chionoi WBA	1973–74	Yong-Kang Kim* WBC	1988–89
Frankie Genaro* NBA	1928–29	B. Gonzalez* WBA	1973–74	Duke McKenzie IBF	1988–89
Spider Pladner* NBA	1929	Shoji Oguma* WBC	1974–75	Sot Chitalada* WBC	1989–91
Frankie Genaro* NBA	1929–31	S. Hanagata WBA	1974–75	Dave McAuley IBF	1989–92
Midget Wolgast NY	1930–35	Miguel Canto* WBC	1975–79	Jesus Rojas WBA	1989–90
Young Perez* NBA	1931–32	Erbito Salavarria WBA	1975–76	Yul-Woo Lee WBA	1990
Jackie Brown* NBA	1932–35	Alfonso Lopez WBA	1976	L. Tamakuma WBA	1990–91
Benny Lynch*	1935–38†	G. Espadas WBA	1976–78	M. Kittikasem* WBC	1991–92
Small Montana NY	1935–37	B. Gonzalez WBA	1978–79	Yuri Arbachakov* WBC	1992–97
Peter Kane*	1938–43	Chan-Hee Park* WBC	1979–80	Yong Kang Kim WBA	1991–92
Little Dado NY	1938–40	Luis Ibarra WBA	1979–80	Rodolfo Blanco IBF	1992–93
Jackie Paterson*	1943–48	Tae-Shik Kim WBA	1980	P. Sithbangprachan IBF	1993–95
Rinty Monaghan*	1948–50†	Shoji Oguma* WBC	1980–81	David Griman WBA	1992–94
Terry Allen*	1950	Peter Mathebula WBA	1980–81	S.S. Ploenchit WBA	1994–96
Dado Marino*	1950–52	Santos Laciar WBA	1981	Francisco Tejedor IBF	1995
Yoshio Shirai*	1952–54	Antonio Avelar* WBC	1981–82	Danny Romero IBF	1995–96
Pascual Perez*	1954–60	Luis Ibarra WBA	1981	Mark Johnson IBF	1996–99†
Pone Kingpetch*	1960–62	Juan Herrera WBA	1981–82	Jose Bonilla WBA	1996–98
Masahiko Harada*	1962–63	P. Cardona* WBC	1982	Chatchai Sasakul* WBC	1997–98
Pone Kingpetch*	1963	Santos Laciar WBA	1982–85	Hugo Soto WBA	1998–99
Hiroyuki Ebihara*	1963–64	Freddie Castillo* WBC	1982	Manny Pacquiao* WBC	1998–99
Pone Kingpetch*	1964–65	E. Mercedes* WBC	1982–83	Leo Gamez WBA	1999
Salvatore Burrini*	1965–66	Charlie Magri* WBC	1983	Irene Pacheco IBF	1999–
H. Accavallo WBA	1966–68	Frank Cedeno* WBC	1983–84	S. Pisnurachan WBA	1999–00
Walter McGowan*	1966	Soon-Chun Kwon IBF	1983–85	M. Sinsurat* WBC	1999–00
Chartchai Chionoi*	1966–69	Koji Kobayashi* WBC	1984	Malcolm Tunacao* WBC	2000–01
Efren Torres*	1969–70	Gabriel Bernal* WBC	1984	Eric Morel WBA	2000–
Hiroyuki Ebihara WBA	1969	Sot Chitalada* WBC	1984–88	P. Wonjongkam* WBC	2001–

Tattoo You

Even by boxing's standards, it was an eye-catching publicity stunt. For his pay-per-view title bout against middleweight champion Felix Trinidad in September 2001, Bernard Hopkins wore a temporary tattoo featuring the URL GoldenPalace.com across his back. The online casino paid Hopkins $100,000 for the ad, which the casino says has more than paid off in increased hits on its website. For his part Hopkins says, "I'd put tattoos on my forehead if they paid me."

Clearly, the final frontier for sports marketers—the human body—is now open for business. Since its experiment with Hopkins, GoldenPalace.com has tattooed more than two dozen boxers with its name. Last spring the Lincoln (Neb.) Lightning, an Arena Football 2 team, put tattoo logos on the midriffs of its cheerleaders. Fans are also fair game: In November the Class A Daytona Cubs announced a promotion in which any fan who got the team's logo permanently tattooed on his body would receive a lifetime pass to home games. Also, several unnamed players on the women's tennis tour have reportedly said they'd be willing to wear a tattooed endorsement for $1.5 million.

Predictably, tattoo ads have critics. In February the Nevada Athletic Commission banned the practice, calling it "demeaning to the sport" and distracting to judges. GoldenPalace.com challenged the commission, and last week a Nevada District Court ruled in favor of the casino, saying the ban violated a right to free speech. The issue has bubbled over in the NBA as well. Last year, when the Blazers' Rasheed Wallace considered a deal to wear a temporary tattoo ad, the NBA quickly asserted that players are prohibited from wearing ads anywhere but on their shoes. Wallace turned down the ad, not because of the NBA but because, as his agent, Bill Strickland, put it, it would have "detracted from the integrity of his current body art."...

"Now that we have a legal precedent, we're going to push the issue even more," says Hopkins's agent, Joe Lear, who's also negotiating tattoo deals for tennis players, golfers and racehorse owners. "For example, the side of the horse's neck is a prime spot."

—Albert Chen

Junior Flyweights
(Weight Limit: 108 pounds)

Champion	Reign
Franco Udella WBC	1975
Jaime Rios WBA	1975–76
Luis Estaba* WBC	1975–78
Juan Guzman WBA	1976
Yoko Gushiken WBA	1976–81
Freddy Castillo* WBC	1978
Sor Vorasingh* WBC	1978
Sung-Jun Kim* WBC	1978–80
Shigeo Nakajima* WBC	1980
Hilario Zapata* WBC	1980–82
Pedro Flores WBA	1981
Hwan-Jin Kim WBA	1981
Katsuo Tokashiki WBA	1981–83
Amado Urzua* WBC	1982
Tadashi Tomori* WBC	1982
Hilario Zapata* WBC	1982–83
Jung-Koo Chang* WBC	1983–88†

Champion	Reign
Lupe Madera WBA	1983–84
Dodie Penalosa IBF	1983–86
Francisco Quiroz WBA	1984–85
Joey Olivo WBA	1985
Myung-Woo Yuh* WBA	1985–91
Jum-Hwan Choi IBF	1986–88
Tacy Macalos IBF	1988–89
German Torres WBC	1988–89
Yul-Woo Lee WBC	1989
M. Kittikasem IBF	1989–90
H. Gonzalez WBC	1989–90
Michael Carbajal IBF	1990–94
R. Pascua WBC	1990
M. C. Castro WBC	1991
H. Gonzalez WBC	1991–93
Hirokia Ioka* WBA	1991–92
Myung-Woo Yuh* WBA	1993†

Champion	Reign
Michael Carbajal* WBC	1993–94
Leo Gamez WBA	1993–95
H. Gonzalez* WBC, IBF	1994–95
Choi Hi-Yong WBA	1995–96
S. Sor Jaturong WBC, IBF	1995–96
Carlos Murillo WBA	1996
Keiji Yamaguchi WBA	1996
Michael Carbajal IBF	1996–97
Saman Jaturong* WBC	1995–99
Phichitchor Siriwat WBA	1996–00
Mauricio Pastrana IBF	1997–98†
Will Grigsby IBF	1998–99
Ricardo Lopez IBF	1999–
Yo-Sam Choi* WBC	1999–02
Beibis Mendoza WBA	2000–01
Rosendo Alvarez WBA	2001–
Jorge Arce* WBC	2002–

Strawweights
(Weight Limit: 105 pounds)

Champion	Reign
Kyung-Yun Lee* IBF	1987
Hiroki Ioka* WBC	1987–88
Leo Gamez WBA	1988–89
S. Sithnaruepol IBF	1988–89
N. Kiatwanchai* WBC	1988–89
Bong-Jun Kim WBA	1989–91
Nico Thomas IBF	1989
Eric Chavez IBF	1989–90
Jum-Hwan Choi* WBC	1989–90
Hideyuki Ohashi* WBC	1990
F. Lookmingkwan IBF	1990–92

Champion	Reign
Ricardo Lopez* WBC	1990–98†
Hi-Yong Choi WBA	1991–92
Manny Melchor IBF	1992
Hideyuki Ohashi WBA	1992–93
R.S. Voraphin IBF	1992–96
Chana Porpaoin WBA	1993–95
Rosendo Alvarez WBA	1995–98
R. Sor Vorapin IBF	1996–97
Zolani Petelo* IBF	1997–00†
W. Chor Charoen WBC	1998–00
R. Lopez* WBA, WBC	1998–99†

Champion	Reign
Songkram Popaoin WBA	1999
Noel Arambulet WBA	1999–00
Jose Aguirre* WBC	2000–
Joma Gamboa WBA	2000
Keitaro Hoshino WBA	2000–01
Chana Porpaoin WBA	2001
Roberto Leyva IBF	2001–02
Yutaka Niida WBA	2001†
Miguel Barrera IBF	2002–
Noel Arambulet WBA	2002–

*Lineal champion.
†Champion relinquished title to retire or switch weight classes, or had title stripped by boxing organization.

Alltime Career Leaders

Total Bouts

ame	Years Active	Bouts	Name	Years Active	Bouts
Len Wickwar	1928–47	463	Maxie Rosenbloom	1923–39	299
Jack Britton	1905–30	350	Harry Greb	1913–26	298
Johnny Dundee	1910–32	333	Young Stribling	1921–33	286
Billy Bird	1920–48	318	Battling Levinsky	1910–29	282
George Marsden	1928–46	311	Ted (Kid) Lewis	1909–29	279

Note: Based on records in *The Ring Record Book* and *Boxing Encyclopedia.*

Most Knockouts

Name	Years Active	KOs	Name	Years Active	KOs
Archie Moore	1936–63	130	Sandy Saddler	1944–56	103
Young Stribling	1921–33	126	Sam Langford	1902–26	102
Billy Bird	1920–48	125	Henry Armstrong	1931–45	100
George Odwell	1930–45	114	Jimmy Wilde	1911–23	98
Sugar Ray Robinson	1940–65	110	Len Wickwar	1928–47	93

Note: Based on records in *The Ring Record Book* and *Boxing Encyclopedia.*

The Madness of King Mike

We don't know what to do with Mike Tyson. For every person who wants to ban him from boxing, there's another willing to shell out pay-per-view dollars to see him fight. The reaction is ritual: A world grows smug when he's slapped for a temper tantrum and is exiled from Nevada, as he was in January 2002, and then wonders mightily where his bout with Lennox Lewis will be held, if not Las Vegas. After 10 years of this—proper revulsion followed by a powerball clamor—we have to wonder exactly who is bipolar here.

Tyson's appeal, generated at first by an earnest malevolence, hasn't been damaged as he has devolved into an unhinged and oddly juvenile monster. He rapes, he bites, he delivers increasingly frightening monologues. The regression of personality, the loss of self-control, is becoming a reverse Alzheimer's: He now crawls on the floor like an infant and bites the leg of his playmate and then rants and cries.

Yet this ongoing breakdown gives us little pause. Poor Nevada, backed into a corner by its past sanctions of Tyson, couldn't have licensed him for the Lewis fight, even had it wanted to. Tyson's latest behavior was far too reminiscent of the ear-chomping that cost him his tag in the first place. Few other states or countries feel obliged to adopt similar restrictions. In fact, the bidding has already begun. The man from the California Athletic Commission was saying just the other night what the local spending generated by an event like this—$100 million, minimum—would mean to out-of-work chambermaids.

Aren't we dainty, to encourage the fight on grounds of economic impact. The bout has absolutely no athletic importance. Tyson, once the most prominent boxer of this generation, has long since squandered his significance in a decadelong debacle of disappointing escapades and defeats. In any case, he's 35 and of suspect resolve. Lewis, himself 36, participates only for the plunder suddenly available to him at retirement. (He has already had his tetanus shot.)

No, it's not about the chambermaids. As with every other Tyson event, in which he becomes our proxy for perversity, we only want to see where his madness can take us, to explore (secondhand, of course) man's psychotic underside. Will this fight be made? Of course. This is the reality programming of the new millennium, psychological pornography, in which our thrills grow more and more sleazy. And all it costs is $49.95.

—Richard Hoffer

World Heavyweight Championship Fights

Date	Winner	Wgt	Loser	Wgt	Result	Site
Sept 7, 1892	James J. Corbett*	178	John L. Sullivan	212	KO 21	New Orleans
Jan 25, 1894	James J. Corbett*	184	Charley Mitchell	158	KO 3	Jacksonville
Mar 17, 1897	Bob Fitzsimmons*	167	James J. Corbett	183	KO 14	Carson City, NV
June 9, 1899	James J. Jeffries*	206	Bob Fitzsimmons	167	KO 11	Coney Island, NY
Nov 3, 1899	James J. Jeffries*	215	Tom Sharkey	183	Ref 25	Coney Island, NY
Apr 6, 1900	James J. Jeffries*	n/a	Jack Finnegan	n/a	KO 1	Detroit
May 11, 1900	James J. Jeffries*	218	James J. Corbett	188	KO 23	Coney Island, NY
Nov 15, 1901	James J. Jeffries*	211	Gus Ruhlin	194	TKO 6	San Francisco
July 25, 1902	James J. Jeffries*	219	Bob Fitzsimmons	172	KO 8	San Francisco
Aug 14, 1903	James J. Jeffries*	220	James J. Corbett	190	KO 10	San Francisco
Aug 25, 1904	James J. Jeffries*	219	Jack Munroe	186	TKO 2	San Francisco
July 3, 1905	Marvin Hart*	190	Jack Root	171	KO 12	Reno
Feb 23, 1906	Tommy Burns*	180	Marvin Hart	188	Ref 20	Los Angeles
Oct 2, 1906	Tommy Burns*	n/a	Jim Flynn	n/a	KO 15	Los Angeles
Nov 28, 1906	Tommy Burns*	172	Jack O'Brien	163½	Draw 20	Los Angeles
May 8, 1907	Tommy Burns*	180	Jack O'Brien	167	Ref 20	Los Angeles
Jul 4, 1907	Tommy Burns*	181	Bill Squires	180	KO 1	Colma, CA
Dec 2, 1907	Tommy Burns*	177	Gunner Moir	204	KO 10	London
Feb 10, 1908	Tommy Burns*	n/a	Jack Palmer	n/a	KO 4	London
Mar 17, 1908	Tommy Burns*	n/a	Jem Roche	n/a	KO 1	Dublin
Apr 18, 1908	Tommy Burns*	n/a	Jewey Smith	n/a	KO 5	Paris
June 13, 1908	Tommy Burns*	184	Bill Squires	183	KO 8	Paris
Aug 24, 1908	Tommy Burns*	181	Bill Squires	184	KO 13	Sydney
Sept 2, 1908	Tommy Burns*	183	Bill Lang	187	KO 6	Melbourne
Dec 26, 1908	Jack Johnson*	192	Tommy Burns	168	TKO 14	Sydney
Mar 10, 1909	Jack Johnson*	n/a	Victor McLaglen	n/a	ND 6	Vancouver
May 19, 1909	Jack Johnson*	205	Jack O'Brien	161	ND 6	Philadelphia
June 30, 1909	Jack Johnson*	207	Tony Ross	214	ND 6	Pittsburgh
Sept 9, 1909	Jack Johnson*	209	Al Kaufman	191	ND 10	San Francisco
Oct 16, 1909	Jack Johnson*	205½	Stanley Ketchel	170¼	KO 12	Colma, CA
July 4, 1910	Jack Johnson*	208	James J. Jeffries	227	KO 15	Reno
July 4, 1912	Jack Johnson*	195½	Jim Flynn	175	TKO 9	Las Vegas
Dec 19, 1913	Jack Johnson*	n/a	Jim Johnson	n/a	Draw 10	Paris
June 27, 1914	Jack Johnson*	221	Frank Moran	203	Ref 20	Paris
Apr 5, 1915	Jess Willard*	230	Jack Johnson	205½	KO 26	Havana
Mar 25, 1916	Jess Willard*	225	Frank Moran	203	ND 10	New York City
July 4, 1919	Jack Dempsey*	187	Jess Willard	245	TKO 4	Toledo, OH
Sept 6, 1920	Jack Dempsey*	185	Billy Miske	187	KO 3	Benton Harbor, MI
Dec 14, 1920	Jack Dempsey*	188¼	Bill Brennan	197	KO 12	New York City
July 2, 1921	Jack Dempsey*	188	Georges Carpentier	172	KO 4	Jersey City
July 4, 1923	Jack Dempsey*	188	Tommy Givvons	175½	Ref 15	Shelby, MT
Sept 14, 1923	Jack Dempsey*	192½	Luis Firpo	216½	KO 2	New York City
Sept 23, 1926	Gene Tunney*	189½	Jack Dempsey	190	UD 10	Philadelphia
Sept 22, 1927	Gene Tunney*	189½	Jack Dempsey	192½	UD 10	Chicago
July 26, 1928	Gene Tunney*	192	Tom Heeney	203½	TKO 11	New York City
June 12, 1930	Max Schmeling*	188	Jack Sharkey	197	DQ 4	New York City
July 3, 1931	Max Schmeling*	189	Young Stribling	186½	TKO 15	Cleveland
June 21, 1932	Jack Sharkey*	205	Max Schmeling	188	Split 15	Long Island City
June 29, 1933	Primo Carnera*	260½	Jack Sharkey	201	KO 6	Long Island City
Oct 22, 1933	Primo Carnera*	259½	Paulino Uzcudun	229¼	UD 15	Rome
Mar 1, 1934	Primo Carnera*	270	Tommy Loughran	184	UD 15	Miami
June 14, 1934	Max Baer*	209½	Primo Carnera	263¼	TKO 11	Long Island City
June 13, 1935	James J. Braddock*	193¾	Max Baer	209½	UD 15	Long Island City
June 22, 1937	Joe Louis*	197¼	James J. Braddock	197	KO 8	Chicago
Aug 30, 1937	Joe Louis*	197	Tommy Farr	204¼	UD 15	New York City
Feb 23, 1938	Joe Louis*	200	Nathan Mann	193½	KO 3	New York City
Apr 1, 1938	Joe Louis*	202½	Harry Thomas	196	KO 5	Chicago
June 22, 1938	Joe Louis*	198¼	Max Schmeling	193	KO 1	New York City
Jan 25, 1939	Joe Louis*	200¼	John Henry Lewis	180¾	KO 1	New York City
Apr 17, 1939	Joe Louis*	201¼	Jack Roper	204¾	KO 1	Los Angeles
June 28, 1939	Joe Louis*	200¾	Tony Galento	233¾	TKO 4	New York City
Sept 20, 1939	Joe Louis*	200	Bob Pastor	183	KO 11	Detroit
Feb 9, 1940	Joe Louis*	203	Arturo Godoy	202	Split 15	New York City
Mar 29, 1940	Joe Louis*	201½	Johnny Paychek	187½	KO 2	New York City
June 20, 1940	Joe Louis*	199	Arturo Godoy	201¼	TKO 8	New York City
Dec 16, 1940	Joe Louis*	202¼	Al McCoy	180¾	TKO 6	Boston
Jan 31, 1941	Joe Louis*	202½	Red Burman	188	KO 5	New York City

Date	Winner	Wgt	Loser	Wgt	Result	Site
Feb 17, 1941	Joe Louis*	203½	Gus Dorazio	193½	KO 2	Philadelphia
Mar 21, 1941	Joe Louis*	202	Abe Simon	254½	TKO 13	Detroit
Apr 8, 1941	Joe Louis*	203½	Tony Musto	199½	TKO 9	St Louis
May 23, 1941	Joe Louis*	201½	Buddy Baer	237½	DQ 7	Washington, D.C.
June 18, 1941	Joe Louis*	199½	Billy Conn	174	KO 13	New York City
Sept 29, 1941	Joe Louis*	202¼	Lou Nova	202½	TKO 6	New York City
Jan 9, 1942	Joe Louis*	206¾	Buddy Baer	250	KO 1	New York City
Mar 27, 1942	Joe Louis*	207½	Abe Simon	255½	KO 6	New York City
June 9, 1946	Joe Louis*	207	Billy Conn	187	KO 8	New York City
Sept 18, 1946	Joe Louis*	211	Tami Mauriello	198½	KO 1	New York City
Dec 5, 1947	Joe Louis*	211½	Jersey Joe Walcott	194½	Split 15	New York City
June 25, 1948	Joe Louis*	213½	Jersey Joe Walcott	194¾	KO 11	New York City
June 22, 1949	Ezzard Charles*	181¾	Jersey Joe Walcott	195½	UD 15	Chicago
Aug 10, 1949	Ezzard Charles*	180	Gus Lesnevich	182	TKO 8	New York City
Oct 14, 1949	Ezzard Charles*	182	Pat Valentino	188½	KO 8	San Francisco
Aug 15, 1950	Ezzard Charles*	183¼	Freddie Beshore	184½	TKO 14	Buffalo
Sept 27, 1950	Ezzard Charles*	184½	Joe Louis	218	UD 15	New York City
Dec 5, 1950	Ezzard Charles*	185	Nick Barone	178½	KO 11	Cincinnati
Jan 12, 1951	Ezzard Charles*	185	Lee Oma	193	TKO 10	New York City
Mar 7, 1951	Ezzard Charles*	186	Jersey Joe Walcott	193	UD 15	Detroit
May 30, 1951	Ezzard Charles*	182	Joey Maxim	181½	UD 15	Chicago
July 18, 1951	Jersey Joe Walcott*	194	Ezzard Charles	182	KO 7	Pittsburgh
June 5, 1952	Jersey Joe Walcott*	196	Ezzard Charles	191½	UD 15	Philadelphia
Sept 23, 1952	Rocky Marciano*	184	Jersey Joe Walcott	196	KO 13	Philadelphia
May 15, 1953	Rocky Marciano*	184½	Jersey Joe Walcott	197¾	KO 1	Chicago
Sept 24, 1953	Rocky Marciano*	185	Roland LaStarza	184¾	TKO 11	New York City
June 17, 1954	Rocky Marciano*	187½	Ezzard Charles	185½	UD 15	New York City
Sept 17, 1954	Rocky Marciano*	187	Ezzard Charles	192½	KO 8	New York City
May 16, 1955	Rocky Marciano*	189	Don Cockell	205	TKO 9	San Francisco
Sept 21, 1955	Rocky Marciano*	188¼	Archie Moore	188	KO 9	New York City
Nov 30, 1956	Floyd Patterson*	182¼	Archie Moore	187¾	KO 5	Chicago
July 29, 1957	Floyd Patterson*	184	Tommy Jackson	192½	TKO 10	New York City
Aug 22, 1957	Floyd Patterson*	187¼	Pete Rademacher	202	KO 6	Seattle
Aug 18, 1958	Floyd Patterson*	184½	Roy Harris	194	TKO 13	Los Angeles
May 1, 1959	Floyd Patterson*	182½	Brian London	206	KO 11	Indianapolis
June 26, 1959	Ingemar Johansson*	196	Floyd Patterson	182	TKO 3	New York City
June 20, 1960	Floyd Patterson*	190	Ingemar Johansson	194¾	KO 5	New York City
Mar 13, 1961	Floyd Patterson*	194¾	Ingemar Johansson	206½	KO 6	Miami Beach
Dec 4, 1961	Floyd Patterson*	188½	Tom McNeeley	197	KO 4	Toronto
Sept 25, 1962	Sonny Liston*	214	Floyd Patterson	189	KO 1	Chicago
July 22, 1963	Sonny Liston*	215	Floyd Patterson	194½	KO 1	Las Vegas
Feb 25, 1964	Cassius Clay*	210½	Sonny Liston	218	TKO 7	Miami Beach
Mar 5, 1965	Ernie Terrell	199	Eddie Machen	192	UD 15	Chicago
May 25, 1965	Muhammad Ali*	206	Sonny Liston	215¼	KO 1	Lewiston, ME
Nov 1, 1965	Ernie Terrell	206	George Chuvalo	209	UD 15	Toronto
Nov 22, 1965	Muhammad Ali*	210	Floyd Patterson	196¾	TKO 12	Las Vegas
Mar 29, 1966	Muhammad Ali*	214½	George Chuvalo	216	UD 15	Toronto
May 21, 1966	Muhammad Ali*	201½	Henry Cooper	188	TKO 6	London
June 28, 1966	Ernie Terrell	209½	Doug Jones	187½	UD 15	Houston
Aug 6, 1966	Muhammad Ali*	209½	Brian London	201½	KO 3	London
Sept 10, 1966	Muhammad Ali*	203½	Karl Mildenberger	194¼	TKO 12	Frankfurt
Nov 14, 1966	Muhammad Ali*	212¾	Cleveland Williams	210½	TKO 3	Houston
Feb 6, 1967	Muhammad Ali*	212¼	Ernie Terrell	212½	UD 15	Houston
Mar 22, 1967	Muhammad Ali*	211½	Zora Folley	202½	KO 7	New York City
Mar 4, 1968	Joe Frazier	204½	Buster Mathis	243½	TKO 11	New York City
Apr 27, 1968	Jimmy Ellis	197	Jerry Quarry	195	Maj 15	Oakland
June 24, 1968	Joe Frazier NY	203½	Manuel Ramos	208	TKO 2	New York City
Aug 14, 1968	Jimmy Ellis	198	Floyd Patterson	188	Ref 15	Stockholm
Dec 10, 1968	Joe Frazier NY	203	Oscar Bonavena	207	UD 15	Philadelphia
Apr 22, 1969	Joe Frazier NY	204½	Dave Zyglewicz	190½	KO 1	Houston
June 23, 1969	Joe Frazier NY	203½	Jerry Quarry	198½	TKO 8	New York City
Feb 16, 1970	Joe Frazier NY	205	Jimmy Ellis	201	TKO 5	New York City
Nov 18, 1970	Joe Frazier	209	Bob Foster	188	KO 2	Detroit
Mar 8, 1971	Joe Frazier*	205½	Muhammad Ali	215	UD 15	New York City
Jan 15, 1972	Joe Frazier*	215½	Terry Daniels	195	TKO 4	New Orleans
May 26, 1972	Joe Frazier*	217½	Ron Stander	218	TKO 5	Omaha
Jan 22, 1973	George Foreman*	217½	Joe Frazier	214	TKO 2	Kingston, Jam.

World Heavyweight Championship Fights (Cont.)

Date	Winner	Wgt	Loser	Wgt	Result	Site
Sept 1, 1973	George Foreman*	219½	Jose Roman	196½	KO 1	Tokyo
Mar 26, 1974	George Foreman*	224¼	Ken Norton	212¼	TKO 2	Caracas
Oct 30, 1974	Muhammad Ali*	216½	George Foreman	220	KO 8	Kinshasa, Zaire
Mar 24, 1975	Muhammad Ali*	223½	Chuck Wepner	225	TKO 15	Cleveland
May 16, 1975	Muhammad Ali*	224½	Ron Lyle	219	TKO 11	Las Vegas
July 1, 1975	Muhammad Ali*	224½	Joe Bugner	230	UD 15	Kuala Lumpur, Malay.
Oct 1, 1975	Muhammad Ali*	224½	Joe Frazier	215	TKO 15	Manila
Feb 20, 1976	Muhammad Ali*	226	Jean Pierre Coopman	206	KO 5	San Juan
Apr 30, 1976	Muhammad Ali*	230	Jimmy Young	209	UD 15	Landover, MD
May 24, 1976	Muhammad Ali*	230	Richard Dunn	206½	TKO 5	Munich
Sept 28, 1976	Muhammad Ali*	221	Ken Norton	217½	UD 15	New York City
May 16, 1977	Muhammad Ali*	221¼	Alfredo Evangelista	209¼	UD 15	Landover, MD
Sept 29, 1977	Muhammad Ali*	225	Earnie Shavers	211¼	UD 15	New York City
Feb 15, 1978	Leon Spinks*	197¼	Muhammad Ali	224¼	Split 15	Las Vegas
June 9, 1978	Larry Holmes	209	Ken Norton	220	Split 15	Las Vegas
Sept 15, 1978	Muhammad Ali*	221	Leon Spinks	201	UD 15	New Orleans
Nov 10, 1978	Larry Holmes*	214	Alfredo Evangelista	208¼	KO 7	Las Vegas
Mar 23, 1979	Larry Holmes*	214	Osvaldo Ocasio	207	TKO 7	Las Vegas
June 22, 1979	Larry Holmes*	215	Mike Weaver	202	TKO 12	New York City
Sept 28, 1979	Larry Holmes*	210	Earnie Shavers	211	TKO 11	Las Vegas
Oct 20, 1979	John Tate	240	Gerrie Coetzee	222	UD 15	Pretoria
Feb 3, 1980	Larry Holmes *	213½	Lorenzo Zanon	215	TKO 6	Las Vegas
Mar 31, 1980	Mike Weaver	232	John Tate	232	KO 15	Knoxville
Mar 31, 1980	Larry Holmes*	211	Leroy Jones	254½	TKO 8	Las Vegas
July 7, 1980	Larry Holmes*	214¼	Scott LeDoux	226	TKO 7	Minneapolis
Oct 2, 1980	Larry Holmes*	211¼	Muhammad Ali	217½	TKO 11	Las Vegas
Oct 25, 1980	Mike Weaver	210	Gerrie Coetzee	226½	KO 13	Sun City, S.A.
Apr 11, 1981	Larry Holmes*	215	Trevor Berbick	215½	UD 15	Las Vegas
June 12, 1981	Larry Holmes*	212¼	Leon Spinks	200¼	TKO 3	Detroit
Oct 3, 1981	Mike Weaver	215	James Quick Tillis	209	UD 15	Rosemont, IL
Nov 6, 1981	Larry Holmes*	213¼	Renaldo Snipes	215¾	TKO 11	Pittsburgh
June 11, 1982	Larry Holmes*	212½	Gerry Cooney	225½	TKO 13	Las Vegas
Nov 26, 1982	Larry Holmes*	217½	Tex Cobb	234¼	UD 15	Houston
Dec 10, 1982	Michael Dokes	216	Mike Weaver	209¾	TKO 1	Las Vegas
Mar 27, 1983	Larry Holmes*	221	Lucien Rodriguez	209	UD 12	Scranton, PA
May 20, 1983	Michael Dokes	223	Mike Weaver	218½	Draw 15	Las Vegas
May 20, 1983	Larry Holmes*	213	Tim Witherspoon	219½	Split 12	Las Vegas
Sept 10, 1983	Larry Holmes*	223	Scott Frank	211¼	TKO 5	Atlantic City
Sept 23, 1983	Gerrie Coetzee	215	Michael Dokes	217	KO 10	Richfield, OH
Nov 25, 1983	Larry Holmes*	219	Marvis Frazier	200	TKO 1	Las Vegas
Mar 9, 1984	Tim Witherspoon	220¼	Greg Page	239½	Maj 12	Las Vegas
Aug 31, 1984	Pinklon Thomas	216	Tim Witherspoon	217	Maj 12	Las Vegas
Nov 9, 1984	Larry Holmes* IBF	221½	James Smith	227	TKO 12	Las Vegas
Dec 1, 1984	Greg Page	236½	Gerrie Coetzee	218	KO 8	Sun City, S.A.
Mar 15, 1985	Larry Holmes*	223½	David Bey	233¼	TKO 10	Las Vegas
Apr 29, 1985	Tony Tubbs	229	Greg Page	239½	UD 15	Buffalo
May 20, 1985	Larry Holmes*	224¼	Carl Williams	215	UD 15	Las Vegas
June 15, 1985	Pinklon Thomas	220¼	Mike Weaver	221¼	KO 8	Las Vegas
Sept 21, 1985	Michael Spinks*	200	Larry Holmes	221½	UD 15	Las Vegas
Jan 17, 1986	Tim Witherspoon	227	Tony Tubbs	229	Maj 15	Atlanta
Mar 22, 1986	Trevor Berbick	218½	Pinklon Thomas	222¾	UD 15	Las Vegas
Apr 19, 1986	Michael Spinks*	205	Larry Holmes	223	Split 15	Las Vegas
July 19, 1986	Tim Witherspoon	234¾	Frank Bruno	228	TKO 11	Wembley, Eng.
Sept 6, 1986	Michael Spinks*	201	Steffen Tangstad	214¾	TKO 4	Las Vegas
Nov 22, 1986	Mike Tyson	221¼	Trevor Berbick	218½	TKO 2	Las Vegas
Dec 12, 1986	James Smith	228½	Tim Witherspoon	233½	TKO 1	New York City
Mar 7, 1987	Mike Tyson	219	James Smith	233	UD 12	Las Vegas
May 30, 1987	Mike Tyson	218¾	Pinklon Thomas	217¾	TKO 6	Las Vegas
May 30, 1987	Tony Tucker	222¼	Buster Douglas	227¼	TKO 10	Las Vegas
June 15, 1987	Michael Spinks*	208¾	Gerry Cooney	238	TKO 5	Atlantic City
Aug 1, 1987	Mike Tyson	221	Tony Tucker	221	UD 12	Las Vegas
Oct 16, 1987	Mike Tyson	216	Tyrell Biggs	228¾	TKO 7	Atlantic City
Jan 22, 1988	Mike Tyson	215¾	Larry Holmes	225¾	TKO 4	Atlantic City
Mar 20, 1988	Mike Tyson	216¼	Tony Tubbs	238¼	KO 2	Tokyo
June 27, 1988	Mike Tyson*	218¼	Michael Spinks	212¼	KO 1	Atlantic City
Feb 25, 1989	Mike Tyson*	218	Frank Bruno	228	TKO 5	Las Vegas
July 21, 1989	Mike Tyson*	219¼	Carl Williams	218	TKO 1	Atlantic City

Date	Winner	Wgt	Loser	Wgt	Result	Site
Feb 10, 1990	Buster Douglas*	231½	Mike Tyson	220½	KO 10	Tokyo
Oct 25, 1990	Evander Holyfield*	208	Buster Douglas	246	KO 3	Las Vegas
Apr 19, 1991	Evander Holyfield*	212	George Foreman	257	UD 12	Atlantic City
Nov 23, 1991	Evander Holyfield*	210	Bert Cooper	215	TKO 7	Atlanta
June 19, 1992	Evander Holyfield*	210	Larry Holmes	233	UD 12	Las Vegas
Nov 13, 1992	Riddick Bowe*	235	Evander Holyfield	205	UD 12	Las Vegas
Feb 6, 1993	Riddick Bowe*	243	Michael Dokes	244	KO 1	New York City
May 8, 1993	Lennox Lewis	235	Tony Tucker	235	UD 12	Las Vegas
May 22, 1993	Riddick Bowe*	244	Jesse Ferguson	224	KO 2	Washington, D.C.
Oct 2, 1993	Lennox Lewis	229	Frank Bruno	233	KO 7	London
Nov 6, 1993	Evander Holyfield*	217	Riddick Bowe	246	Split 12	Las Vegas
Apr 22, 1994	Michael Moorer*	214	Evander Holyfield	214	Split 12	Las Vegas
May 6, 1994	Lennox Lewis	235	Phil Jackson	218	TKO 8	Atlantic City
Nov 6, 1994	George Foreman*	250	Michael Moorer	222	KO 10	Las Vegas
Mar 11, 1995	Riddick Bowe	241	Herbie Hide	214	KO 6	Las Vegas
Apr 8, 1995	Oliver McCall	231	Larry Holmes	236	UD 12	Las Vegas
Apr 8, 1995	Bruce Seldon	236	Tony Tucker	243	TKO 7	Las Vegas
Apr 22, 1995	George Foreman*	256	Axel Schulz	221	Split 12	Las Vegas
Jun 17, 1995	Riddick Bowe	243	Jorge Luis Gonzalez	237	KO 6	Las Vegas
Aug 19, 1995	Bruce Seldon	234	Joe Hipp	233	TKO 10	Las Vegas
Sept 2, 1995	Frank Bruno	247¾	Oliver McCall	234¾	UD 12	London
Dec 9, 1995	Frans Botha	237	Axel Schulz	223	Split 12	Stuttgart
Mar 16, 1996	Mike Tyson	220	Frank Bruno	247	TKO 3	Las Vegas
June 22, 1996	Michael Moorer	222¼	Axel Schulz	222¾	Split 12	Dortmund, Ger.
Sept 7, 1996	Mike Tyson	219	Bruce Seldon	229	TKO 1	Las Vegas
Nov 3, 1996	George Foreman	253	Crawford Grimsley		UD 12	Tokyo
Nov 9, 1996	Evander Holyfied	215	Mike Tyson	222	TKO 11	Las Vegas
Feb 7, 1997	Lennox Lewis	251	Oliver McCall	237	TKO 5	Las Vegas
Apr 26, 1997	George Foreman	253	Lou Savarese		Split 12	Atlantic City
June 28, 1997	Evander Holyfield	218	Mike Tyson	218	DQ 4	Las Vegas
Oct 4, 1997	Lennox Lewis	244	Andrew Golota	244	TKO 1	Atlantic City
Nov 8, 1997	Evander Holyfield	214	Michael Moorer	223	TKO 8	Las Vegas
Nov 22, 1997	Shannon Briggs*		George Foreman		MD 12	Atlantic City
Mar 28, 1998	Lennox Lewis*	243	Shannon Briggs	228	TKO 5	Atlantic City
Mar 13, 1999	Evander Holyfield	215	Lennox Lewis*	246	Draw 12	New York City
Nov 13, 1999	Lennox Lewis*	242	Evander Holyfield	217	UD 12	Las Vegas
Apr 29, 2000	Lennox Lewis*	247	Michael Grant	250	KO 2	New York
July 15, 2000	Lennox Lewis*	250	Frans Botha	236	TKO 2	London
Aug 12, 2000	Evander Holyfield	221	John Ruiz	224	UD 12	Las Vegas
Nov 11, 2000	Lennox Lewis*	249	David Tua	245	UD 12	Las Vegas
Mar 3, 2001	John Ruiz	227	Evander Holyfield	217	UD 12	Las Vegas
Apr 22, 2001	Hasim Rahman*	238	Lennox Lewis	253½	KO 5	Brakpan, S Africa
Nov 17, 2001	Lennox Lewis*	246½	Hasim Rahman	236	KO 4	Las Vegas
Dec 15, 2001	John Ruiz	232	Evander Holyfield	219	Draw 12	Mashantucket, CT
June 8, 2002	Lennox Lewis*	249¼	Mike Tyson	234½	KO 8	Memphis, TN
July 27, 2002	John Ruiz	233	Kirk Johnson	238	DQ 10	Las Vegas

*Lineal champion. KO=knockout; TKO=technical knockout; UD=unanimous decision; Split=split decision; Ref=referee's decision; MD=majority decision; DQ=disqualification; ND=no decision.

YET ANOTHER SIGN OF THE APOCALYPSE

Former heavyweight champion Larry Holmes, 52, agreed to—and won—a 10-round bout against onetime Toughman champ and novelty act Butterbean.

Year	Fighter	Year	Fighter	Year	Fighter
1928	Gene Tunney	1935	Barney Ross	1940	Billy Conn
1929	Tommy Loughran	1936	Joe Louis	1941	Joe Louis
1930	Max Schmeling	1937	Henry Armstrong	1942	Ray Robinson
1932	Jack Sharkey	1938	Joe Louis	1943	Fred Apostoli
1934	T. Canzoneri/B. Ross	1939	Joe Louis	1944	Beau Jack

Note: No award in 1933; no fight of the year named until 1945

Year	Fighter	Fight	Winner	Site
1945	Willie Pep	Rocky Graziano–Freddie Cochrane	Rocky Graziano	New York City
1946	Tony Zale	Tony Zale–Rocky Graziano	Tony Zale	New York City
1947	Gus Lesnevich	Rocky Graziano–Tony Zale	Rocky Graziano	Chicago
1948	Ike Williams	Marcel Cerdan–Tony Zale	Marcel Cerdan	Jersey City
1949	Ezzard Charles	Willie Pep–Sandy Saddler	Willie Pep	New York City
1950	Ezzard Charles	Jake LaMotta–Laurent Dauthuille	Jake LaMotta	Detroit
1951	Ray Robinson	Jersey Joe Walcott–Ezzard Charles	Jersey Joe Walcott	Pittsburgh
1952	Rocky Marciano	Rocky Marciano–Jersey Joe Walcott	Rocky Marciano	Philadelphia
1953	Carl Olson	Rocky Marciano–Roland LaStarza	Rocky Marciano	New York City
1954	Rocky Marciano	Rocky Marciano–Ezzard Charles	Rocky Marciano	New York City
1955	Rocky Marciano	Carmen Basilio–Tony DeMarco	Carmen Basilio	Boston
1956	Floyd Patterson	Carmen Basilio–Johnny Saxton	Carmen Basilio	Syracuse
1957	Carmen Basilio	Carmen Basilio–Ray Robinson	Carmen Basilio	New York City
1958	Ingemar Johansson	Ray Robinson–Carmen Basilio	Ray Robinson	Chicago
1959	Ingemar Johansson	Gene Fullmer–Carmen Basilio	Gene Fullmer	San Francisco
1960	Floyd Patterson	Floyd Patterson–Ingemar Johansson	Floyd Patterson	New York City
1961	Joe Brown	Joe Brown–Dave Charnley	Joe Brown	London
1962	Dick Tiger	Joey Giardello–Henry Hank	Joey Giardello	Philadelphia
1963	Cassius Clay	Cassius Clay–Doug Jones	Cassius Clay	New York City
1964	Emile Griffith	Cassius Clay–Sonny Liston	Cassius Clay	Miami Beach
1965	Dick Tiger	Floyd Patterson–George Chuvalo	Floyd Patterson	New York City
1966	No award	Jose Torres–Eddie Cotton	Jose Torres	Las Vegas
1967	Joe Frazier	Nino Benvenuti–Emile Griffith	Nino Benvenuti	New York City
1968	Nino Benvenuti	Dick Tiger–Frank DePaula	Dick Tiger	New York City
1969	Jose Napoles	Joe Frazier–Jerry Quarry	Joe Frazier	New York City
1970	Joe Frazier	Carlos Monzon–Nino Benvenuti	Carlos Monzon	Rome
1971	Joe Frazier	Joe Frazier–Muhammad Ali	Joe Frazier	New York City
1972	Muhammad Ali Carlos Monzon	Bob Foster–Chris Finnegan	Bob Foster	London
1973	George Foreman	George Foreman–Joe Frazier	George Foreman	Kingston, Jam.
1974	Muhammad Ali	Muhammad Ali–George Foreman	Muhammad Ali	Kinshasa, Zaire
1975	Muhammad Ali	Muhammad Ali–Joe Frazier	Muhammad Ali	Manila
1976	George Foreman	George Foreman–Ron Lyle	George Foreman	Las Vegas
1977	Carlos Zarate	Joe Young–George Foreman	Joe Young	San Juan
1978	Muhammad Ali	Leon Spinks–Muhammad Ali	Leon Spinks	Las Vegas
1979	Ray Leonard	Danny Lopez–Mike Ayala	Danny Lopez	San Antonio
1980	Thomas Hearns	Saad Muhammad–Yaqui Lopez	Saad Muhammad	McAfee, NJ
1981	Ray Leonard Salvador Sanchez	Ray Leonard–Tommy Hearns	Ray Leonard	Las Vegas
1982	Larry Holmes	Bobby Chacon–Rafael Limon	Bobby Chacon	Sacramento
1983	Marvin Hagler	Bobby Chacon–Cornelius Boza-Edwards	Bobby Chacon	Las Vegas
1984	Thomas Hearns	Jose Luis Ramirez–Edwin Rosario	Jose Luis Ramirez	San Juan
1985	Donald Curry Marvin Hagler	Marvin Hagler–Tommy Hearns	Marvin Hagler	Las Vegas
1986	Mike Tyson	Stevie Cruz–Barry McGuigan	Stevie Cruz	Las Vegas
1987	Evander Holyfield	Ray Leonard–Marvin Hagler	Ray Leonard	Las Vegas
1988	Mike Tyson	Tony Lopez–Rocky Lockridge	Tony Lopez	Inglewood, CA
1989	Pernell Whitaker	Roberto Duran–Iran Barkley	Roberto Duran	Atlantic City
1990	Julio César Chávez	Julio César Chávez–Meldrick Taylor	Julio César Chávez	Las Vegas
1991	James Toney	Robert Quiroga–Kid Akeem Anifowoshe	Robert Quiroga	San Antonio
1992	Riddick Bowe	Riddick Bowe–Evander Holyfield	Riddick Bowe	Las Vegas
1993	Michael Carbajal	Michael Carbajal–Humberto Gonzalez	Michael Carbajal	Las Vegas
1994	Roy Jones	Jorge Castro–John David Jackson	Jorge Castro	Monterrey, Mex.
1995	Oscar De La Hoya	Saman Sor Jaturong–Chiquita Gonzalez	Saman Sor Jaturong	Inglewood, CA
1996	Evander Holyfield	Evander Holyfield–Mike Tyson	Evander Holyfield	Las Vegas
1997	Evander Holyfield	Arturo Gatti–Gabriel Ruelas	Arturo Gatti	Atlantic City
1998	Floyd Mayweather	Ivan Robinson–Arturo Gatti	Ivan Robinson	Atlantic City
1999	Paulie Ayala	Paulie Ayala–Johnny Tapia	Paulie Ayala	Las Vegas
2000	Felix Trinidad	Erik Morales–Marco Antonio Barrera	Erik Morales	Las Vegas
2001	Bernard Hopkins	Mickey Ward–Emanuel Burton	Mickey Ward	Las Vegas

U.S. Olympic Gold Medalists

LIGHT FLYWEIGHT

1984 .... Paul Gonzales

FLYWEIGHT

1904 .... George Finnegan
1920 .... Frank Di Gennara
1024 .... Fidel LaBarba
1952 .... Nathan Brooks
1976 .... Leo Randolph
1984 .... Steve McCrory

BANTAMWEIGHT

1904 .... Oliver Kirk
1988 .... Kennedy McKinney

FEATHERWEIGHT

1904 .... Oliver Kirk
1924 .... John Fields
1984 .... Meldrick Taylor

LIGHTWEIGHT

1904 .... Harry Spanger
1920 .... Samuel Mosberg
1968 .... Ronald W. Harris
1976 .... Howard Davis
1984 .... Pernell Whitaker
1992 .... Oscar De La Hoya

LIGHT WELTERWEIGHT

1952 .... Charles Adkins
1972 .... Ray Seales
1976 .... Ray Leonard
1984 .... Jerry Page

WELTERWEIGHT

1904 .... Albert Young
1932 .... Edward Flynn
1984 .... Mark Breland

LIGHT MIDDLEWEIGHT

1960 .... Wilbert McClure
1984 .... Frank Tate
1996 .... David Reid

MIDDLEWEIGHT

1904 .... Charles Mayer
1932 .... Carmen Bath
1952 .... Floyd Patterson
1960 .... Edward Crook
1976 .... Michael Spinks

LIGHT HEAVYWEIGHT

1920 .... Eddie Eagan
1952 .... Norvel Lee
1956 .... James Boyd
1960 .... Cassius Clay
1976 .... Leon Spinks
1988 .... Andrew Maynard

HEAVYWEIGHT

1984 .... Henry Tillman
1988 .... Ray Mercer

SUPER HEAVYWEIGHT

1904 .... Samuel Berger
1952 .... H. Edward Sanders
1956 .... T. Peter Rademacher
1964 .... Joe Frazier
1968 .... George Foreman
1984 .... Tyrell Biggs

Philadelphia Phenom

When it comes to Jewish boxers, the undisputed champ was Benny Leonard, who from 1917 to '23 lorded over the lightweight division. The now defunct New York City paper *The Jewish Daily Bulletin* proposed that Leonard was greater even than Einstein because he was not only known by millions but understood by them as well. Anthony Thompson is a Jewish boxer known by thousands and just beginning to be understood by the rest of us.

Over the past two years Thompson, a fast, flexible Philadelphia welterweight, was the most decorated amateur in North America. In 2000 he finished first in the national Golden Gloves and national Police Athletic League tournaments, and that year and the next he won the U.S. championships. In 2001 he also received silver medals at the world championships in Belfast and the Goodwill Games in Brisbane, Australia, getting outpointed in each final by a seasoned Cuban.

Unable to get by on the U.S. Olympic Committee's $600 monthly stipend, Thompson signed with promoter Cedric Kushner in February. "I could have made the 2004 Olympic team," he says, "but the fun was gone in the amateurs." On March 17 Thompson made his pro debut as a super welterweight, dispatching Elvesto Mills in a third-round TKO.

The legendary Leonard wore a Jewish star on his boxing trunks and refused to fight on religious holidays. Thompson wears a Star of David around his neck and won't box on the Sabbath unless "it's a major, major tournament." Like Abraham, he's willing to make sacrifices.

Thompson, 20, is a Hebrew Israelite, a black Judaic sect that believes its members are descended from one of the 12 Biblical tribes of Israel. Taught to read and speak Hebrew by his father, Kezz, a housing developer who until recently ran a kosher soul-food deli in North Philly, Anthony adheres strictly to the law of the Torah. After graduating from Benjamin Franklin High in 1999 with a 3.7 average, he took accounting during his one semester in college (naturally, this nice Jewish boy went to Temple) before dropping out to be a boxer. "The kid shows great discipline and humility," says middleweight champ Bernard Hopkins, a fellow Philadelphian. "For a guy who's the big topic in the neighborhood, he carries his own bags and doesn't have a big entourage. Religion must keep him focused."

Thompson, who's a slender 5'11", has one of those opaque faces that seldom divulge anything. "I like Solomon because he was smooth," says Thompson, who draws fistic inspiration from feisty Old Testament figures. He admires Judah Maccabbee: "Judah's attitude was, Fight till you die, and fall out later." He reveres King David: "Look what he did to Goliath. Size didn't matter—he just kept his faith and fought."

Thompson bore up as stoically as Job under the loss of two daughters to a genetic disorder. Ya-kira and Ya-sheva were born with Zellweger syndrome, a rare and incurable disease that affects the liver, kidneys and brain. ... "My girlfriend [and the children's mother], Tanisha, took it very hard," says Thompson. "I had to set an example. When Tanisha saw my strength, she had no choice but to follow."

Still, Ya-sheva's death was such a crushing blow that Anthony considered skipping the PAL tournament two months later in New Orleans. He wound up going and was named the event's outstanding boxer. "Anthony punches not for show but to take an opponent apart, which is rare for a boxer so young," says trainer Emanuel Steward. "He throws short; powerful shots that hurt. As good as he was as an amateur, he'll be even better as a professional." ...

—Franz Lidz

Lineal Heavyweight Champions

Champion	Reign	Age*	Career	W-L-D (KO)	Successful Defenses
John L. Sullivan	1885–92	26	1878–92	38-1-3 (33)	0
James J. Corbett	1892–97	26	1884–03	11-4-2 (7)	1
Bob Fitzsimmons	1897–99	33	1880–16	74-8-3 (67)	0
James J. Jeffries†	1899–05	24	1896–10	18-1-2 (15)	7
Marvin Hart	1905–06	28	1899–10	28-7-4 (19)	0
Tommy Burns	1906–08	24	1900–20	46-5-8 (37)	11
Jack Johnson	1908–15	30	1894–28	77-13-14 (48)	9
Jess Willard	1915–19	33	1911–23	23-6-1 (20)	1
Jack Dempsey	1919–26	24	1914–27	60-6-8 (50)	5
Gene Tunney†	1926–28	29	1915–28	61-1-1 (45)	2
Max Schmeling	1930–32	24	1924–48	56-10-4 (39)	1
Jack Sharkey	1932–33	29	1924–36	38-13-3 (14)	0
Primo Carnera	1933–34	26	1928–37	88-14-0 (69)	2
Max Baer	1934–35	25	1929–41	72-12-0 (53)	0
James J. Braddock	1935–37	29	1926–38	51-26-7 (26)	0
Joe Louis†	1937–49	23	1934–51	68-3-0 (54)	25
Ezzard Charles	1949–51	27	1940–59	96-25-1 (59)	8
Jersey Joe Walcott	1951–52	37	1930–53	53-18-1 (33)	1
Rocky Marciano†	1952–56	29	1947–56	49-0-0 (43)	6
Floyd Patterson	1956–59	21	1952–72	55-8-1 (40)	4
Ingemar Johansson	1959–60	26	1952–63	26-2-0 (17)	0
Floyd Patterson	1960–62	25	1952–72	55-8-1 (40)	2
Sonny Liston	1962–64	30	1953–70	50-4-0 (39)	1
Muhammad Ali	1964–71	22	1960–81	56-5-0 (37)	9
Joe Frazier	1971–73	27	1965–81	32-4-1 (27)	2
George Foreman	1973–74	24	1969–97	76-5-0 (68)	2
Muhammad Ali	1974–78	32	1960–81	56-5-0 (37)	10
Leon Spinks	1978	24	1977–95	26-17-3 (14)	0
Muhammad Ali†	1978–79	36	1960–81	56-5-0 (37)	0
Larry Holmes	1980–85	29	1973–	69-6-0 (44)	20
Michael Spinks	1985–88	29	1977–88	32-1-0 (21)	3
Mike Tyson	1988–90	21	1985–	49-4-0 (43)	2
Buster Douglas	1990	29	1981–99	38-6-1 (25)	0
Evander Holyfield	1990–92	28	1984–	38-5-2 (26)	3
Riddick Bowe	1992–93	25	1989–96	40-1-0 (32)	2
Evander Holyfield	1993–94	31	1984–	38-5-2 (26)	0
Michael Moorer	1994	26	1988–97	39-2-0 (31)	0
George Foreman	1994–97	45	1969–97	76-5-0 (68)	3
Shannon Briggs	1997–98	25	1992–00	32-3-1 (25)	0
Lennox Lewis	1998–01	32	1989–	40-2-1 (31)	5
Hasim Rahman	2001	28	1994–	35-4-0 (29)	0
Lennox Lewis	2001–	36	1989–	40-2-1 (31)	1

*Age when boxer won world championship.
† Boxer retired or relinquished world title.

Horse Racing

Kentucky Derby and Preakness winner War Emblem

Knocking on the Door

Bob Baffert has won eight Triple Crown races since '97, but has yet to sweep them in one year

BY MARK BEECH

DESPITE THE best efforts of trainer Bob Baffert, the most important legacy in horse racing came to an end in 2002. Ever since Sir Barton became the first colt to win the Kentucky Derby, Preakness and Belmont in 1919, there has always been a living Triple Crown champion. But no horse has accomplished the fabled sweep since the late Affirmed did it in 1978, and with the death of '77 Triple Crown winner Seattle Slew on May 7, the Sport of Kings was left without a reigning monarch.

Baffert has come agonizingly close in recent years, missing the Crown in the Belmont twice—by three quarters of a length with Silver Charm in 1997, and by a nose with Real Quiet in '98. He nearly won it again in 2002, with an unheralded colt whom he had never seen until a month before the Derby. But once again, his quest fell short at Belmont Park.

Three days before Seattle Slew's death, Baffert had won the 128th running of the Derby with his new colt, who bore a striking resemblance to Slew in both appearance and style. War Emblem, a jet black son of the stallion Our Emblem, used his overpow-

ering speed to go wire to wire in the Run for the Roses. Just before the Derby, Baffert had paid a special visit to the 28-year-old Slew at Hill 'n' Dale Farm, outside Lexington, Ky., where the aged champion was living out his final days tortured by arthritis. "It felt almost like a sacred visit," Baffert said. "Like meeting Muhammad Ali, or what it will be like someday to meet Michael Jordan." After War Emblem's victory in Kentucky, Baffert mused, "Maybe there's a reason for the way things happen."

Baffert's remark would gain credence as War Emblem made a run for the Triple Crown that seemed to carry with it a whisper of destiny. As late as a month before the Derby, the trainer had been without a legitimate three-year old contender, having watched several of his more prized colts succumb to injury or mediocrity. Just three weeks before the first Saturday in May, however, the trainer linked up with Saudi Prince Ahmed bin Salman after the prince spent $900,000 for War Emblem, who had won the Illinois Derby on April 6, getting loose on the lead and crushing Repent, a Derby favorite at the time. War Emblem was owned by 84-year-old Chicago steel

Baffert (left) and Prince Ahmed were as surprised as anyone by their Derby win.

executive Russel Reineman, who needed money to support his struggling business. "My steel company is losing money," he said. "My horse business has lost money for the last two years. It's never easy to sell a horse, but in life you sometimes make tough decisions for economic reasons."

Despite War Emblem's impressive performance in Illinois, Derby handicappers kissed him off at odds of 20–1, dismissing the speedy colt as a front-runner who would crack under the strain of trying to hold off 17 challengers for 1¼ miles. Baffert, the thinking went, was clearly desperate to try to win America's greatest race with a horse he bought off the scrap heap. They underestimated War Emblem, and the colt made them pay. With Victor Espinoza up, War Emblem took the lead immediately, and was allowed to hold it through relaxed fractions of 23⅕ and 47 seconds. The slow pace compromised the race's closers, and War Emblem opened up in the stretch, cruising under the wire in front by four lengths.

Every trainer who showed up in Baltimore two weeks later vowed that the 1³⁄₁₆-mile Preakness would be different. Never

again, they said, would War Emblem be allowed to set such an easy pace for himself. Even Baffert was worried. War Emblem was naturally fast enough that he could get to the front out of the gate without sprinting, but his trainer worried about the colt's ability to relax if he was challenged early. "If we're not in front, I don't know what will happen," he said just one hour before the race. When long shot Menacing Dennis got the jump on War Emblem at the start and went to the lead, Espinoza was forced to wrap up on the colt to control his speed. As War Emblem ran into the first turn, Baffert turned to his fiancée, Jill Moss, and said, "He's not rating, we're screwed." But no sooner had Baffert uttered those words than War Emblem settled. With Ezpinoza maintaining a solid hold on him, the colt followed crisp fractions of 22.87, 46.10 and 1:10.60, then began to surge as he headed into the final turn. War Emblem took the lead and bounded for the wire, with Espinoza hitting the colt once to repel a mid-stretch challenge from Proud Citizen and his jockey, Mike Smith. "Once I got to him and saw him dig back in, I knew it was over," said Smith. And it was: War Emblem held off 45–1 long shot Magic Weisner by three quarters of a length and captured the sec-

BILL FRAKES

Going off at 70–1, Sarava was longest-priced winner in Belmont history.

ond leg of the Triple Crown. It was a gutsy victory, and it confirmed War Emblem's talent to the world. "Can you believe he kept running?" shouted Prince Ahmed after the race.

For the prince, War Emblem's triumphs were especially sweet. In 2001, he joined the Triple Crown fray as the owner of the scintillating Point Given. Though the giant red colt earned Horse of the Year honors and won five straight Grade I stakes, including the Preakness and Belmont, he had flopped as the 2–1 favorite in the Kentucky Derby, finishing fifth. With War Emblem, Prince Ahmed laughed his way through the spring, marveling at how effortlessly everything seemed to be going for him. "Other years I raised horses to win the Kentucky Derby," he said after the Derby. "This is different. This is the easy way." Sadly, the Preakness was the last time Prince Ahmed saw War Emblem run live. In July, at the age of 43, he died of a heart attack in his home in Saudi Arabia.

Family obligations kept the prince in Riyadh when War Emblem tried to complete his sweep of the Triple Crown in the 1 ½-mile Belmont, and it was just as well. War Emblem's flirtation with history ended with striking suddenness. The roar of the record crowd of 103,222 turned quickly to a gasp when the starting gates banged open and the colt nearly fell to his knees, effectively ending his race before it began. "No strategy with this horse," Baffert had said the morning of the Belmont. "Get in the gate, break and go. Break, break, break."

With War Emblem hamstrung by his start, the Belmont was a wide open affair, taken, appropriately enough, by the longest-priced winner in Belmont history. Sarava, a rangy bay who went off at 70–1, outdueled Medaglia d'Oro by a half-length in a courageous stretch drive. The victory provided a measure of redemption for Sarava's trainer, Ken McPeek, who had guided Derby favorite Harlan's Holiday to a disappointing seventh-place finish at Churchill Downs. "Sometimes you've got to throw a horse in there to see what he can do," McPeek said after the race.

Baffert has now won eight Triple Crown races since 1997 without completing the sweep. With no Triple Crown horse since Affirmed in 1978, the record 25-year gap between Triple Crown winners Citation (1948) and Secretariat (1973) will be matched when the series begins again next spring. "They run these races every year," said Baffert. "We'll be here again."

There's little doubt about that. By the end of the summer, Baffert's talented stable of two-year-olds was already making a name for itself, with nine legitimate talents on its roster. They include Bull Market, Chief Planner, Friendly Mike, Icecoldbeeratreds, Kafwain, Martinblestme, Truckle Feature, Vindication and Spensive. All of Baffert's up-and-comers got their careers off to great starts. In the Del Mar Futurity, a race he has won every year since 1996, Baffert entered five colts, and took the first four spots. The winner was Icecoldbeeratreds, followed by Kafwain, Chief Planner and Friendly Mike. Still, Vindication may prove to be the most talented of them all. He won his third race in three starts in September 2002, taking the Kentucky Cup Juvenile at Turfway Park. Sired by Seattle Slew, he cost $2.15 million as a yearling. "When you spend that much, you're buying pedigree," Baffert said.

After his run with War Emblem, he should know that you can get a Derby winner for a lot cheaper.

THOROUGHBRED RACING

The Triple Crown

128th Kentucky Derby

May 4, 2002. Grade I, 3-year-olds; 9th race, Churchill Downs, Louisville. All 126 lbs. Distance: 1¼ miles. Stakes value: $2,175,000; Winner: $1,875,000; Second: $170,000; Third: $85,000; Fourth: $45,000. Track: Fast. Off: 6:12 p.m. Winner: War Emblem (B. c, Our Emblem out of Sweetest Lady by Lord At War); Times: 0:23.25, 0:47.04, 1:11.75, 1:36.70, 2:01.13. Won: Driving. Breeder: Charles Nuckols Jr & Sons.

Horse	Finish-PP	Margin	Jockey/Owner
War Emblem	1–5	4	Victor Espinoza/The Thoroughbred Corporation
Proud Citizen	2–12	¾	Mike Smith/R. Baker & W. Mack & D. Cornstein
Perfect Drift	3–3	3¼	Eddie Delahoussaye/Stonecrest Farm
Medaglia d'Oro	4–9	1½	Laffit Pincay Jr./Edmund A. Gann
Request for Parole	5–7	¾	Robby Albarado/Jeri & Sam Knighton
Came Home	6–14	2	Chris McCarron/John Toffan & Trudy McCaffery
Harlan's Holiday	7–13	¾	Edgar Prado/Starlight Stables
Johannesburg	8–1	nose	Gary Stevens/Michael Tabor
Essence of Dubai	9–8	1	David Flores/Godolphin Racing, Inc.
Saarland	10–15	2½	John Velazquez/Cynthia Phipps
Blue Burner	11–18	½	Pat Day/Kinsman Stable
Castle Gandolfo	12–11	4¼	Jerry Bailey/Mrs. John Magnier
Easy Grades	13–17	neck	Jorge Chavez/Desperado Stables
Private Emblem	14–10	4½	Donnie Meche/James Cassels & Bob Zollers
Lusty Latin	15–4	2¼	Glenn Corbett/Joey & Wendy Platz
It'sallinthechase	16–16	2¾	Eddie Martin Jr./Darwin Olson
Ocean Sound	17–6	2¼	Alex Solis/KM Stable
Wild Horses	18–2	—	Rene Douglas/Peachtree Stable

127th Preakness Stakes

May 18, 2002. Grade I, 3-year-olds; 12th race, Pimlico Race Course, Baltimore. All 126 lbs. Distance: 1³⁄₁₆ miles; Stakes value: $1,000,000; Winner: $650,000; Second: $200,000; Third: $100,000; Fourth: $50,000. Track: Fast. Off: 6:12 p.m. Winner: War Emblem (B. c, Our Emblem out of Sweetest Lady by Lord At War); Times: 0:22.87, 0:46.10, 1:10.60, 1:36.22, 1:56.36. Won: Driving. Breeder: Charles Nuckols Jr & Sons.

Horse	Finish-PP	Margin	Jockey/Owner
War Emblem	1–8	¾	Victor Espinoza/The Thoroughbred Corporation
Magic Weisner	2–2	¾	Richard Migliore/Nancy H. Alberts
Proud Citizen	3–12	1½	Mike Smith/R. Baker & W. Mack & D. Cornstein
Harlan's Holiday	4–6	neck	Edgar Prado/Starlight Stable
Easyfromthegitgo	5–7	7	Donnie Meche/James Cassels & Bob Zollars
USS Tinosa	6–1	6½	Kent Desormeaux/Peter Abruzzo & Barry Thiriot
Crimson Hero	7–4	½	Chris McCarron/Tracy Farmer
Medaglia d'Oro	8–5	¾	Jerry Bailey/Edmund A. Gann
Straight Gin	9–3	3	Robby Albarado/Marylou Whitney Stable
Menacing Dennis	10–11	6¾	Mario Pino/Jmj Racing Stables
Table Limit	11–9	head	Gary Stevens/Overbrook Farm
Booklet	12–10	½	Pat Day/John C. Oxley
Equality	13–13	—	Ramon Dominguez/Pin Oak Stable

134th Belmont Stakes

June 8, 2002. Grade I, 3-year-olds; 10th race, Belmont Park, Elmont, NY. All 126 lbs. Distance: 1½ miles. Stakes purse: $1,000,000; Winner: $600,000; Second: $200,000; Third: $110,000; Fourth: $60,000; Fifth: $30,000 Track: Fast. Off: 6:15 p.m. Winner: Sarava (B. c, Wild Again out of Rhythm of Life by Deputy Minister); Times: 0:24.11, 48.09, 1:12.38, 1:37.01, 2:03.50, 2:29.71. Won: Driving. Breeder: Timber Bay Farm.

Horse	Finish-PP	Margin	Jockey/Owner
Sarava	1–11	½	Edgar Prado/New Phoenix Stable & Mrs. Susan Roy
Medaglia d'Oro	2–7	9½	Kent Desormeaux/Edmund Gann
Sunday Break	3–5	1	Gary Stevens/Koji Maeda
Magic Weisner	4–10	1¼	Richard Migliore/Nancy H. Alberts
Proud Citizen	5–8	1¼	Mike Smith/R. Baker & W. Mack & D. Cornstein
Essence of Dubai	6–4	4¼	Jerry Bailey/Godolphin Racing, Inc.
Like a Hero	7–2	1¾	Pat Day/Columbine Stable
War Emblem	8–9	30¾	Victor Espinoza/The Thoroughbred Corporation
Wiseman's Ferry	9–3	1	Jorge Chavez/Lee Sacks, Morton Fink, Swifty Farms
Perfect Drift	10–6	24¾	Eddie Delahoussaye/William A. Reed & Mary Reed
Artax Too	11–1	—	Jose Santos/Paraneck Stable

Major Stakes Races

Late 2001

Date	Race	Track	Distance	Winner	Jockey/Trainer	Purse ($)
Sept 9	Atto Mile Stakes	Woodbine	1 mile	Numerous Times	Paul Husbands/ S. Attard	1,000,000
Sept 22	Kentucky Cup Classic Handicap	Turfway Park	1 1/8 miles	Guided Tour	Lonnie Melancon/ N. O'Callaghan	400,000
Sept 22	Vosburg Stakes	Belmont Park	7 furlongs	Left Bank	John Velazquez/ T. Pletcher	300,000
Sept 28	Meadowlands Cup Handicap	Meadowlands	1 1/8 miles	Gander	John Velazquez/ J. Terranova	500,000
Sept 29	Turf Classic Invitational	Belmont Park	1 1/2 miles	Timboroa	Edgar Prado/ Robert Frankel	750,000
Sept 29	Flower Bowl Invitational Handicap	Belmont Park	1 1/4 miles	Lailani	Jerry Bailey/ E. Dunlop	750,000
Sept 30	Super Derby	Louisiana Downs	1 1/4 miles	Outofthebox	L. Meche/ B. Flint	500,000
Sept 30	Yellow Ribbon Stakes	Santa Anita Park	1 1/4 miles	Janet	David Flores/ D. Vienna	500,000
Oct 6	Winstar Galaxy Stakes	Keeneland	1 3/16 miles	Spook Express	Mike Smith/ T. Skiffington	563,500
Oct 6	The Jockey Club Gold Cup	Belmont Park	1 1/4 miles	Aptitude	Jerry Bailey/ Robert Frankel	1,000,000
Oct 6	Beldame Stakes	Belmont Park	1 1/8 miles	Exogenous	Javier Castellano/ Fred Schulhofer	750,000
Oct 6	Champagne Stakes	Belmont Park	1 1/16 miles	Officer	Victor Espinoza/ Bob Baffert	500,000
Oct 6	Frizette Stakes	Belmont Park	1 1/16 miles	You	Edgar Prado/ Robert Frankel	500,000
Oct 6	Lane's End Breeders Futurity	Keeneland	1 1/16 miles	Siphonic	Chris McCarron/ D. Hofmans	454,400
Oct 6	Alcibiades Stakes	Keeneland	1 1/16 miles	Take Charge Lady	A. D'Amico K. McPeek	452,800
Oct 7	Keeneland Turf Mile	Keeneland	1 mile	Hap	Jerry Bailey William Mott	558,500
Oct 7	Spinster Stakes	Keeneland	1 1/8 miles	Miss Linda	Richard Migliore/ J. Kimmel	562,000
Oct 7	Goodwood Breeders Cup Handicap	Santa Anita	1 1/8 miles	Freedom Crest	Kent Desormeaux/ R. Baltas	488,000
Oct 13	Queen Elizabeth II Challenge Cup	Keeneland	1 1/8 miles	Affluent	Eddie Delahoussaye/ R. McAnally	500,000
Oct 27	Breeders' Cup Classic	Belmont Park	1 1/4 miles	Tiznow	Chris McCarron/ J. Robbins	4,000,000
Oct 27	Breeders' Cup Turf	Belmont Park	1 1/2 miles	Fantastic Light	Frankie Dettori/ S. bin-Suroor	2,140,000
Oct 27	Breeders' Cup Sprint	Belmont Park	6 furlongs	Squirtle Squirt	Jerry Bailey/ Robert Frankel	916,000
Oct 27	Breeders' Cup Mile	Belmont Park	1 mile	Val Royal	Jose Valdivia/ J. Canani	1,140,000
Oct 27	Breeders' Cup Juvenile Fillies	Belmont Park	1 1/16 miles	Tempera	David Flores/ E. Harty	1,000,000
Oct 27	Breeders' Cup Distaff	Belmont Park	1 1/8 miles	Unbridled Elaine	Pat Day/ D. Stewart	2,360,000
Oct 27	Breeders' Cup Juvenile	Belmont Park	1 1/16 miles	J'annesburg	Mike Kinane/ A. O'Brien	1,000,000
Oct 27	Breeders' Cup Filly Filly & Mare Turf	Belmont Park	1 1/4 miles	Banks Hill	O. Pesller A. Fabre	1,390,000
Nov 23	Clark Handicap	Churchill Downs	1 1/8 miles	Ubiquity	Craig Perret William Mott	454,000
Nov 24	Cigar Mile Handicap	Aqueduct	1 mile	Cigar	John Velazquez/ T. Pletcher	350,000
Nov 24	Citation Handicap	Hollywood Park	1 1/16 miles	Good Journey	Chris McCarron/ W. Dollase	500,000
Nov 25	Matriarch Stakes	Hollywood Park	1 1/8 miles	Starine	John Velazquez/ Robert Frankel	500,000
Nov 25	Hollywood Derby	Hollywood Park	1 1/8 miles	Denon	Chris McCarron/ Robert Frankel	500,000
Dec 15	Hollywood Futurity	Hollywood Park	1 1/16 miles	Siphonic	Jerry Bailey/ D. Hofmans	456,750

2002 (Through September 7)

Date	Race	Track	Distance	Winner	Jockey/Trainer	Purse ($)
Jan 13	San Fernando B.C. Stakes	Santa Anita	1 1/16 miles	Western Pride	Garrett Gomez/ J. Chapman	214,200
Jan 26	Santa Monica Handicap	Santa Anita	7 furlongs	Kalookan Queen	Alex Solis/ B. Headley	200,000
Feb 2	Strub Stakes	Santa Anita	1 1/8 miles	Mizzen Mast	Kent Desormeaux/ Robert Frankel	400,000
Feb 9	Donn Handicap	Gulfstream Park	1 1/8 miles	Mongoose	Edgar Prado/ J. Bond	500,000
Mar 2	Santa Anita Handicap	Santa Anita Park	1 1/4 miles	Milwaukee Brew	Kent Desormeaux/ R. Frankel	1,000,000
Mar 3	New Orleans Handicap	Fair Grounds	1 1/8 miles	Parade Leader	Cory Laneri/ N. Howard	500,000
Mar 9	Fair Grounds Oaks	Fair Grounds	1 1/16 miles	Take Charge Lady	Tony D'Amico/ K. McPeek	350,000
Mar 10	Santa Margarita Handicap	Santa Anita Park	1 1/8 miles	Azeri	Mike Smith/ L. de Seroux	300,000
Mar 10	Louisiana Derby	Fair Grounds	1 1/16 miles	Repent	Jerry Bailey/ K. McPeek	750,000
Mar 16	Florida Derby	Gulfstream Park	1 1/8 miles	Harlan's Holiday	Edgar Prado/ K. McPeek	1,000,000
Mar 23	Dubai World Cup	Nad Al Sheba	1 1/4 miles	Street Cry	Jerry Bailey/ S. bin Suroor	6,000,000
Mar 23	Dubai Golden Shaeen	Nad Al Sheba	6 furlongs	Caller One	Gary Stevens/ J. Chapman	2,000,000
Mar 23	Dubai UAE Derby	Nad Al Sheba	1 1/4 miles	Essence of Dubai	Frankie Dettori/ S. bin Suroor	2,000,000
Mar 23	Spiral Stakes	Turfway Park	1 1/8 miles	Perfect Drift	Eddie Delahoussaye/ M. Johnson	500,000
Mar 24	Explosive Bid Handicap	Fair Grounds	1 1/8 miles	Sarafan	Corey Nakatani/ Neil Drysdale	700,000
Apr 7	Santa Anita Derby	Santa Anita Park	1 1/8 miles	Came Home	Chris McCarron/ P. Gonzalez	750,000
Apr 7	Oaklawn Handicap	Oaklawn Park	1 1/8 miles	Kudos	Eddie Delahoussaye/ R. Mandella	500,000
Apr 7	Ashland Stakes	Keeneland	1 1/16 miles	Take Charge Lady	Tony D'Amico/ K. McPeek	557,750
Apr 7	Illinois Derby	Sportsman's Park	1 1/8 miles	War Emblem	L.J. Sterling Jr./ F. Springer	500,000
Apr 7	Apple Blossom Handicap	Oaklawn Park	1 1/16 miles	Azeri	Mike Smith/ L. de Seroux	500,000
Apr 13	Arkansas Derby	Oaklawn Park	1 1/8 miles	Pivate Emblem	Don Meche/ S. Asmussen	500,000
Apr 13	Bluegrass Stakes	Keeneland	1 1/8 miles	Harlan's Holiday	Edgar Prado/ K. McPeek	750,000
Apr 13	Wood Memorial Stakes	Aqueduct	1 1/8 miles	Buddha	Pat Day/ J. Bond	750,000
Apr 13	Carter Handicap	Aqueduct	7 furlongs	Affirmed Success	Richard Migliore/ R. Schosberg	350,000
May 3	Kentucky Oaks	Churchill Downs	1 1/8 miles	Farda Amiga	Chris McCarron/ P. Lobo	562,100
May 4	Kentucky Derby	Churchill Downs	1 1/4 miles	War Emblem	Victor Espinoza/ Bob Baffert	1,000,000
May 11	Lone Star Derby	Lone Star Park	1 1/8 miles	Wiseman's Ferry	Jorge Chavez/ N. O'Callaghan	500,000
May 18	Preakness Stakes	Pimlico	1 3/16 miles	War Emblem	Victor Espinoza/ Bob Baffert	1,000,000
May 27	Metropolitan Handicap	Belmont Park	1 mile	Swept Overboard	Jorge Chavez/ C. Dollase	750,000
May 27	Gamely Breeders' Cup Handicap	Hollywood Park	1 1/8 miles	Astra	Kent Desormeaux/ L. de Seroux	474,000
May 27	Shoemaker Breeders' Cup Mile	Hollywood Park	1 mile	Lady's Din	Pat Valenzuela/ J. Canani	408,000
June 1	Massachusetts Handicap	Suffolk Downs	1 1/8 miles	Macho Uno	Gary Stevens/ J. Orseno	500,000
June 8	Belmont Stakes	Belmont Park	1 1/2 miles	Sarava	Edgar Prado/ K. McPeek	1,000,000

2002 (Through September 7) (Cont.)

Date	Race	Track	Distance	Winner	Jockey/Trainer	Purse ($)
June 15	Stephen Foster Handicap	Churchill Downs	1⅛ miles	Street Cry	Jerry Bailey/ S. bin Suroor	833,250
June 23	Queen's Plate Stakes	Woodbine	1¼ miles	T.J.'s Lucky Moon	S. Bahen/ V. Armata	1,000,000
July 1	Hollywood Gold Cup	Hollywood Park	1¼ miles	Aptitude	Laffit Pincay/ Robert Frankel	750,000
July 6	Suburban Handicap	Belmont Park	1¼ miles	Essence of Dubai	John Velazquez/ S. bin Suroor	500,000
July 21	Delaware Handicap	Delaware Park	1¼ miles	Summer Colony	John Velazquez/ M. Hennig	601,200
Aug 3	Whitney Handicap	Saratoga	1⅛ miles	Left Bank	John Velazquez/ T. Pletcher	750,000
Aug 4	Jim Dandy Stakes	Saratoga	1⅛ miles	Medaglia d'Oro	Jerry Bailey/ Robert Frankel	500,000
Aug 4	Haskell Invitational	Monmouth Park	1⅛ miles	War Emblem	Victor Espinoza/ Bob Baffert	1,000,000
Aug 17	Arlington Million	Arlington	1¼ miles	Beat Hollow	Jerry Bailey/ Robert Frankel	1,000,000
Aug 17	Alabama Stakes	Saratoga	1¼ miles	Farda Amiga	Pat Day/ P. Lobo	750,000
Aug 24	Travers Stakes	Saratoga	1¼ miles	Medaglia d'Oro	Jerry Bailey/ Robert Frankel	1,000,000
Aug 25	Pacific Classic	Del Mar	1¼ miles	Came Home	Mike Smith/ P. Gonzalez	1,000,000
Sept 2	Pennsylvania Derby	Philadelphia Park	1⅛ miles	Harlan's Holiday	Edgar Prado/ T. Pletcher	500,000
Sept 7	Woodward Stakes	Belmont Park	1⅛ miles	Lido Palace	Jorge Chavez/ Robert Frankel	500,000
Sept 7	Man O' War Stakes	Belmont Park	1⅜ miles	With Anticipation	Pat Day/ J. Sheppard	500,000

2001 Statistical Leaders

Horses

Horse	Starts	1st	2nd	3rd	Purses ($)	Horse	Starts	1st	2nd	3rd	Purses ($)
Captain Steve	6	2	1	1	4,201,200	Albert the Great	9	3	4	1	1,740,000
Point Given	7	6	0	0	3,350,000	Monarchos	7	4	1	1	1,711,600
Tiznow	6	3	1	2	2,981,880	Unbridled Elaine	8	4	1	1	1,663,175
Fantastic Light	3	2	1	0	2,896,615	Sakhee	2	1	1	0	1,640,000
Jungle Pocket	1	1	0	0	2,036,423	Include	9	5	1	2	1,435,400

Jockeys

Jockey	Mounts	1st	2nd	3rd	Purses ($)	Win Pct	$ Pct*
Jerry Bailey	912	227	194	137	22,597,720	.25	.61
John R. Velazquez	1411	305	220	166	15,073,790	.22	.49
Pat Day	1197	249	208	187	14,497,879	.21	.54
Edgar Prado	1569	259	255	211	14,133,395	.17	.46
Jorge Chavez	1344	247	172	165	13,856,699	.18	.43
Chris McCarron	607	123	100	92	12,933,932	.20	.52
Gary Stevens	535	99	91	82	12,000,331	.19	.51
Alex Solis	1200	222	178	196	11,531,521	.19	.50
Robby Albarado	1401	272	210	165	10,631,669	.19	.46
Ramon Dominguez	1864	431	368	278	10,514,207	.23	.58

*Percentage in the Money (1st, 2nd, and 3rd).

Trainers

Trainer	Starts	1st	2nd	3rd	Purses ($)	Win Pct	$ Pct*
Bob Baffert	660	138	100	95	16,354,996	.21	.50
Robert Frankel	392	101	68	57	14,727,446	.26	.58
William Mott	744	152	132	109	9,418,657	.20	.53
Steven Asmussen	1459	294	245	212	8,068,409	.20	.51
Scott Lake	1566	407	298	215	7,817,856	.26	.59
Todd Pletcher	583	128	106	55	7,731,203	.22	.50
D. Wayne Lukas	646	96	82	90	5,947,971	.15	.41
Saeed bin Suroor	43	8	9	2	5,751,828	.19	.44
Christophe Clement	356	75	60	48	5,557,669	.21	.51
Jerry Hollendorfer	1133	263	167	191	5,497,046	.23	.55

*Percentage in the Money (1st, 2nd, and 3rd).

Owners

Owner	Starts	1st	2nd	3rd	Purses ($)
Richard Englander	2041	405	337	271	9,783,472
The Thoroughbred Corporation	367	66	58	48	8,000,763
Juddmonte Farms, Inc.	138	41	28	15	6,926,015
Godolphin, Inc.	53	13	10	3	6,627,172
Stronach Stable	770	127	98	112	6,537,681
Michael Pegram	123	22	18	21	5,034,588
Gary Tanaka	179	28	18	23	4,413,658
Sam-Son Farms	218	39	31	39	4,055,490
John Franks	1018	118	130	139	3,605,752
John Oxley	92	23	14	18	3,164,339

HARNESS RACING

Major Stakes Races

Late 2001

Date	Race	Location	Winner	Driver/Trainer	Purse ($)
Oct 19	BC Two-year-old Colt Trot	Woodbine	Duke of York	Paul MacDonnell/ John Bax	812,292
Oct 19	BC Two-year-old Filly Pace	Woodbine	Cam Swifty	James Meittinis/ Donald Swick	781,050
Oct 19	BC Two-year-old Colt Pace	Woodbine	Western Shooter	John Campbell/ Robert McIntosh	968,502
Oct 19	BC Two-year-old Filly Trot	Woodbine	Cameron Hall	Michel Lachance/ Robert Stewart	789,050
Oct 19	BC Three-year-old Colt Trot	Woodbine	Liberty Balance	Randall Waples/ Patrick Hunt	906,018
Oct 19	BC Three-year-old Filly Trot	Woodbine	Syrinx Hanover	John Campbell/ Christopher Marino	624,840
Oct 19	BC Three-year-old Filly Pace	Woodbine	Bunny Lake	John Stark Jr./ John Stark Jr.	812,292
Oct 19	BC Three-year-old Colt Pace	Woodbine	Real Desire	John Campbell/ Blair Burgess	781,050
Nov 24	Three Diamonds Filly Pace	Meadowlands	Worldly Beauty	Luc Ouellette/ Pat Lachance	350,000
Nov 24	Governor's Cup Colt Pace	Meadowlands	Western Shooter	John Campbell/ Robert McIntosh	500,000

2002 (Through September 19)

Date	Race	Location	Winner	Driver/Trainer	Purse ($)
June 1	New Jersey Classic	Meadowlands	McArdle	Cat Manzi Chris Ryder	500,000
June 22	North America Cup	Woodbine	Red River Hanover	Luc Ouellette/ Bill Robinson	945,000
July 6	William Haughton Memorial	Meadowlands	Four Starzzz Shark	Jim Morrill Jr./ Edward Hart	650,000

Major Stakes Races (Cont.)

2002 (Through September 19) (Cont.)

Date	Race	Location	Winner	Driver/Trainer	Purse ($)
July 13	Meadowlands Pace	Meadowlands	Mach Three	John Campbell/ Monty Gelrod	1,000,000
July 27	BC Three and up Open Trot	Meadowlands	Fool's Gold	Jack Moiseyev/ Jim Doherty	1,000,000
July 27	BC Three and up Mare Pace	Meadowlands	Molly Can Do It	Jack Moiseyev/ Linda Toscano	350,000
July 27	BC Three and up Open Pace	Meadowlands	Real Desire	John Campell/ Blair Burgess	500,000
Aug 2	Peter Haughton Memorial	Meadowlands	CC's Chuckie T	David Miller/ David Columbo	460,000
Aug 3	Woodrow Wilson	Meadowlands	Allamerican Native	George Brennan Mark Capone	650,000
Aug 3	Sweetheart Pace	Meadowlands	Must See	George Brennan/ Gregory Sudol	460,000
Aug 3	Hambletonian	Meadowlands	Chip Chip Hooray	Eric Ledford/ Chuck Sylvester	1,000,000
Aug 3	Hambletonian Oaks	Meadowlands	Windylane Hanover	Ron Pierce/ Brett Bittle	500,000
Aug 3	Nat Ray	Meadowlands	Victory Tilly	Stig Johansson/ Stig Johansson	500,000
Sept 19	Little Brown Jug	Delaware, OH	Million Dollar Cam	Luc Ouellette/ Bill Robinson	618,625

Major Races

The Hambletonian

Raced at The Meadowlands, East Rutherford, NJ, on August 3, 2002.

Horse	Driver	PP	¼	½	¾	Stretch-Margin	Finish-Margin
Chip Chip Hooray	Eric Ledford	2	4	4	4<	2–nose	1–neck
Like A Prayer	Ron Pierce	10	6<	6	6<	5–2h	2–neck
Duke of York	Paul MacDonnell	3	5	5	5<	3–1h	3–3
Malabar Maple	Luc Ouellette	4	7	7	7<	7–3h	4–3h
Taurus Dream	Mickey McNichol	9	1	1	1	1–nose	5–6h
Likely Lad	Berndt Lindstedt	7	3	3	3	4–2	6–8
ENS Snapshot	Cat Manzi	8	2<	2<	2<	6–3h	7–9
Really Suspicious	John Duke Sugg	5	9<	8	8	8–6	8–9t
Chipmate	Jimmy Takter	6	10<	9x	X9	9–dis	9–dis
Andover Hall	John Campbell	1x	X8x	X10x	10	X10x–dis	DNF

Times: 0:28.1, 0:55.2, 1:23.2, 1:53.3.

The Little Brown Jug

Raced at the Delaware County Fairgrounds, in Delaware, OH, on September 19, 2002.

Horse	Driver	PP	¼	½	¾	Stretch–Margin	Finish–Margin
Million Dollar Cam	Luc Ouellette	1	1	1	1	1–1q	1–1
Life Is A Cabaret	George Brennan	6	7	7<	4<	2–1q	2–1
Western Resolve	Ron Pierce	9	4	4<	5	4–2t	3–2
Art Major	Michel Lachance	5	5	5	6<	5–3q	4–2
Allamerican Ingot	David Miller	2	3	3	3	3–1t	5–2h
Three Olives	Dave Palone	4	6	6	8<	6–4h	6–3q
Fancy Schmansy	Brett Miller	8	9	9	9	7–6h	7–5h
Camystic	Randy Waples	7	8	8	7	8–7	8–5t
Mach Three	John Campbell	3	2<	2<	2<	9–11	9–8t

Time: 0:25.4, 0:53.1, 1:21.3, 1:50.2.

2001 Leading Moneywinners by Age, Sex and Gait

Division	Horse	Starts	1st	2nd	3rd	Earnings ($)
2-Year-Old Pacing Colts	Mach Three	9	7	2	0	954,708
2-Year-Old Pacing Fillies	Worldly Beauty	7	6	0	0	660,410
3-Year-Old Pacing Colts	Bettor's Delight	16	9	5	0	1,776,800
3-Year-Old Pacing Fillies	Bunny Lake	21	19	2	0	1,146,219
Aged Pacing Horses	Gallo Blue Chip	19	10	4	1	1,123,940
Aged Pacing Mares	Eternal Camnation	17	7	5	0	763,315
2-Year-Old Trotting Colts	Duke of York	12	5	2	1	671,142
2-Year-Old Trotting Fillies	Cameron Hall	7	6	0	0	639,426
3-Year-Old Trotting Colts	SJ's Caviar	20	15	1	0	1,198,490
3-Year-Old Trotting Fillies	Syrinx Hanover	12	12	0	0	1,018,629
Aged Trotting Horses	Varenne*	14	13	1	0	1,822,675
Aged Trotting Mares	Earl Of My Dreams	24	8	7	2	315,700

* Statistics include foreign start information.

Drivers

Driver	Earnings ($)	Driver	Earnings ($)
John Campbell	14,184,863	Chris Christoforou	9,570,998
Michel Lachance	10,696,993	Mario Baillargeon	7,460,680
Randall Waples	10,636,348	Mike Saftic	6,120,014
David Miller	10,551,102	Sylvain Filion	5,830,873
Luc Ouellette	10,006,054	Eric Ledford	5,417,365

YET ANOTHER SIGN OF THE APOCALYPSE

An Italian woman went to court to change her baby's name after her husband secretly named him Varenne Giampaolo to honor Italy's top trotting horse (Varenne) and its driver (Giampaolo Minnucci).

FOR THE RECORD · Year by Year

THOROUGHBRED RACING

Kentucky Derby

Run at Churchill Downs, Louisville, KY, on the first Saturday in May.

Year	Winner (Margin)	Jockey	Second	Third	Time
1875	Aristides (1)	Oliver Lewis	Volcano	Verdigris	2:37¾
1876	Vagrant (2)	Bobby Swim	Creedmoor	Harry Hill	2:38¼
1877	Baden-Baden (2)	William Walker	Leonard	King William	2:38
1878	Day Star (2)	Jimmie Carter	Himyar	Leveler	2:37¼
1879	Lord Murphy (1)	Charlie Shauer	Falsetto	Strathmore	2:37
1880	Fonso (1)	George Lewis	Kimball	Bancroft	2:37½
1881	Hindoo (4)	Jimmy McLaughin	Lelex	Alfambra	2:40
1882	Apollo (½)	Babe Hurd	Runnymede	Bengal	2:40¼
1883	Leonatus (3)	Billy Donohue	Drake Carter	Lord Raglan	2:43
1884	Buchanan (2)	Isaac Murphy	Loftin	Audrain	2:40¼
1885	Joe Cotton (Neck)	Erskine Henderson	Bersan	Ten Booker	2:37¼
1886	Ben Ali (½)	Paul Duffy	Blue Wing	Free Knight	2:36½
1887	Montrose (2)	Isaac Lewis	Jim Gore	Jacobin	2:39¼
1888	MacBeth II (1)	George Covington	Gallifet	White	2:38¼
1889	Spokane (Nose)	Thomas Kiley	Proctor Knott	Once Again	2:34½
1890	Riley (2)	Isaac Murphy	Bill Letcher	Robespierre	2:45
1891	Kingman (1)	Isaac Murphy	Balgowan	High Tariff	2:52¼
1892	Azra (Nose)	Alonzo Clayton	Huron	Phil Dwyer	2:41½
1893	Lookout (5)	Eddie Kunze	Plutus	Boundless	2:39¼
1894	Chant (2)	Frank Goodale	Pearl Song	Sigurd	2:41
1895	Halma (3)	Soup Perkins	Basso	Laureate	2:37½
1896	Ben Brush (Nose)	Willie Simms	Ben Eder	Semper Ego	2:07¼
1897	Typhoon II (Head)	Buttons Garner	Ornament	Dr. Catlett	2:12½
1898	Plaudit (Neck)	Willie Simms	Lieber Karl	Isabey	2:09
1899	Manuel (2)	Fred Taral	Corsini	Mazo	2:12
1900	Lieut. Gibson (4)	Jimmy Boland	Florizar	Thrive	2:06¼
1901	His Eminence (2)	Jimmy Winkfield	Sannazarro	Driscoll	2:07¾
1902	Alan-a-Dale (Nose)	Jimmy Winkfield	Inventor	The Rival	2:08¾
1903	Judge Himes (¾)	Hal Booker	Early	Bourbon	2:09
1904	Elwood (½)	Frankie Prior	Ed Tierney	Brancas	2:08½
1905	Agile (3)	Jack Martin	Ram's Horn	Layson	2:10¾
1906	Sir Huon (2)	Roscoe Troxler	Lady Navarre	James Reddick	2:08⅕
1907	Pink Star (2)	Andy Minder	Zal	Ovelando	2:12⅗
1908	Stone Street (1)	Arthur Pickens	Sir Cleges	Dunvegan	2:15⅕
1909	Wintergreen (4)	Vincent Powers	Miami	Dr. Barkley	2:08⅕
1910	Donau (½)	Fred Herbert	Joe Morris	Fighting Bob	2:06⅖
1911	Meridian (¾)	George Archibald	Governor Gray	Colston	2:05
1912	Worth (Neck)	Carroll H. Schilling	Duval	Flamma	2:09⅖
1913	Donerail (½)	Roscoe Goose	Ten Point	Gowell	2:04⅘
1914	Old Rosebud (8)	John McCabe	Hodge	Bronzewing	2:03⅖
1915	Regret (2)	Joe Notter	Pebbles	Sharpshooter	2:05⅖
1916	George Smith (Neck)	Johnny Loftus	Star Hawk	Franklin	2:04
1917	Omar Khayyam (2)	Charles Borel	Ticket	Midway	2:04⅗
1918	Exterminator (1)	William Knapp	Escoba	Viva America	2:10⅘
1919	Sir Barton (5)	Johnny Loftus	Billy Kelly	Under Fire	2:09⅘
1920	Paul Jones (Head)	Ted Rice	Upset	On Watch	2:09
1921	Behave Yourself (Head)	Charles Thompson	Black Servant	Prudery	2:04⅕
1922	Morvich (½)	Albert Johnson	Bet Mosie	John Finn	2:04⅗
1923	Zev (1½)	Earl Sande	Martingale	Vigil	2:05⅖
1924	Black Gold (½)	John Mooney	Chilhowee	Beau Butler	2:05⅕
1925	Flying Ebony (1½)	Earl Sande	Captain Hal	Son of John	2:07⅗
1926	Bubbling Over (5)	Albert Johnson	Bagenbaggage	Rock Man	2:03⅗
1927	Whiskery (Head)	Linus McAtee	Osmond	Jock	2:06
1928	Reigh Count (3)	Chick Lang	Misstep	Toro	2:10⅖
1929	Clyde Van Dusen (2)	Linus McAtee	Naishapur	Panchio	2:10⅘
1930	Gallant Fox (2)	Earl Sande	Gallant Knight	Ned O.	2:07⅗
1931	Twenty Grand (4)	Charles Kurtsinger	Sweep All	Mate	2:01⅘
1932	Burgoo King (5)	Eugene James	Economic	Stepenfetchit	2:05⅕
1933	Brokers Tip (Nose)	Don Meade	Head Play	Charley O.	2:06⅘
1934	Cavalcade (2½)	Mack Garner	Discovery	Agrarian	2:04
1935	Omaha (1½)	Willie Saunders	Roman Soldier	Whiskolo	2:05
1936	Bold Venture (Head)	Ira Hanford	Brevity	Indian Broom	2:03⅗

Kentucky Derby (Cont.)

Year	Winner (Margin)	Jockey	Second	Third	Time
1937	War Admiral (1¾)	Charles Kurtsinger	Pompoon	Reaping Reward	2:03⅕
1938	Lawrin (1)	Eddie Arcaro	Dauber	Can't Wait	2:04⅘
1939	Johnstown (8)	James Stout	Challedon	Heather Broom	2:03⅗
1940	Gallahadion (1½)	Carroll Bierman	Bimelech	Dit	2:05
1941	Whirlaway (8)	Eddie Arcaro	Staretor	Market Wise	2:01⅖
1942	Shut Out (2½)	Wayne Wright	Alsab	Valdina Orphan	2:04⅖
1943	Count Fleet (3)	John Longden	Blue Swords	Slide Rule	2:04
1944	Pensive (4½)	Conn McCreary	Broadcloth	Stir Up	2:04⅕
1945	Hoop Jr. (6)	Eddie Arcaro	Pot o' Luck	Darby Dieppe	2:07
1946	Assault (8)	Warren Mehrtens	Spy Song	Hampden	2:06⅗
1947	Jet Pilot (Head)	Eric Guerin	Phalanx	Faultless	2:06⅘
1948	Citation (3½)	Eddie Arcaro	Coaltown	My Request	2:05⅖
1949	Ponder (3)	Steve Brooks	Capot	Palestinian	2:04⅕
1950	Middleground (1¼)	William Boland	Hill Prince	Mr. Trouble	2:01⅗
1951	Count Turf (4)	Conn McCreary	Royal Mustang	Ruhe	2:02⅗
1952	Hill Gail (2)	Eddie Arcaro	Sub Fleet	Blue Man	2:01⅗
1953	Dark Star (Head)	Hank Moreno	Native Dancer	Invigorator	2:02
1954	Determine (1½)	Ray York	Hasty Road	Hasseyampa	2:03
1955	Swaps (1½)	Bill Shoemaker	Nashua	Summer Tan	2:01⅘
1956	Needles (¾)	Dave Erb	Fabius	Come On Red	2:03⅖
1957	Iron Liege (Nose)	Bill Hartack	Gallant Man	Round Table	2:02⅕
1958	Tim Tam (½)	Ismael Valenzuela	Lincoln Road	Noureddin	2:05
1959	Tomy Lee (Nose)	Bill Shoemaker	Sword Dancer	First Landing	2:02⅕
1960	Venetian Way (3½)	Bill Hartack	Bally Ache	Victoria Park	2:02⅖
1961	Carry Back (¾)	John Sellers	Crozier	Bass Clef	2:04
1962	Decidedly (2¼)	Bill Hartack	Roman Line	Ridan	2:00⅖
1963	Chateaugay (1¼)	Braulio Baeza	Never Bend	Candy Spots	2:01⅘
1964	Northern Dancer (Neck)	Bill Hartack	Hill Rise	The Scoundrel	2:00
1965	Lucky Debonair (Neck)	Bill Shoemaker	Dapper Dan	Tom Rolfe	2:01⅕
1966	Kauai King (½)	Don Brumfield	Advocator	Blue Skyer	2:02
1967	Proud Clarion (1)	Bobby Ussery	Barbs Delight	Damascus	2:00⅗
1968	Forward Pass (Disq.)	Ismael Valenzuela	Francie's Hat	T.V. Commercial	2:02⅕
1969	Majestic Prince (Neck)	Bill Hartack	Arts and Letters	Dike	2:01⅘
1970	Dust Commander (5)	Mike Manganello	My Dad George	High Echelon	2:03⅖
1971	Canonero II (3¾)	Gustavo Avila	Jim French	Bold Reason	2:03⅕
1972	Riva Ridge (3¼)	Ron Turcotte	No Le Hace	Hold Your Peace	2:01⅘
1973	Secretariat (2½)	Ron Turcotte	Sham	Our Native	1:59⅖
1974	Cannonade (2¼)	Angel Cordero Jr.	Hudson County	Agitate	2:04
1975	Foolish Pleasure (1¾)	Jacinto Vasquez	Avatar	Diabolo	2:02
1976	Bold Forbes (1)	Angel Cordero Jr.	Honest Pleasure	Elocutionist	2:01⅗
1977	Seattle Slew (1¾)	Jean Cruguet	Run Dusty Run	Sanhedrin	2:02⅕
1978	Affirmed (1¼)	Steve Cauthen	Alydar	Believe It	2:01⅕
1979	Spectacular Bid (2¾)	Ronald J. Franklin	General Assembly	Golden Act	2:02⅖
1980	Genuine Risk (1)	Jacinto Vasquez	Rumbo	Jaklin Klugman	2:02
1981	Pleasant Colony (¾)	Jorge Velasquez	Woodchopper	Partez	2:02
1982	Gato Del Sol (2½)	Eddie Delahoussaye	Laser Light	Reinvested	2:02⅕
1983	Sunny's Halo (2)	Eddie Delahoussaye	Desert Wine	Caveat	2:02⅕
1984	Swale (3¼)	Laffit Pincay Jr.	Coax Me Chad	At the Threshold	2:02⅖
1985	Spend A Buck (5)	Angel Cordero Jr.	Stephan's Odyssey	Chief's Crown	2:00⅕
1986	Ferdinand (2¼)	Bill Shoemaker	Bold Arrangement	Broad Brush	2:02⅘
1987	Alysheba (¾)	Chris McCarron	Bet Twice	Avies Copy	2:03⅗
1988	Winning Colors (Neck)	Gary Stevens	Forty Niner	Risen Star	2:02⅕
1989	Sunday Silence (2½)	Pat Valenzuela	Easy Goer	Awe Inspiring	2:05
1990	Unbridled (3½)	Craig Perret	Summer Squall	Pleasant Tap	2:02
1991	Strike the Gold (1¾)	Chris Antley	Best Pal	Mane Minister	2:03
1992	Lil E. Tee (1)	Pat Day	Casual Lies	Dance Floor	2:03
1993	Sea Hero (2½)	Jerry Bailey	Prairie Bayou	Wild Gale	2:02⅖
1994	Go for Gin (2½)	Chris McCarron	Strodes Creek	Blumin Affair	2:03⅗
1995	Thunder Gulch (2¼)	Gary Stevens	Tejano Run	Timber Country	2:01⅕
1996	Grindstone (Nose)	Jerry Bailey	Cavonnier	Prince of Thieves	2:01
1997	Silver Charm (Head)	Gary Stevens	Captain Bodgit	Free House	2:02⅖
1998	Real Quiet (½)	Kent Desormeaux	Victory Gallop	Indian Charlie	2:02⅒
1999	Charismatic (Neck)	Chris Antley	Menifee	Cat Thief	2:03⅕
2000	Fusaichi Pegasus (1½)	Kent Desormeaux	Aptitude	Impeachment	2:01.12
2001	Monarchos (4 ¾)	Jorge Chavez	Invisible Ink	Congaree	1:59.97
2002	War Emblem (4)	Victor Espinoza	Proud Citizen	Perfect Drift	2:01.13

Note: Distance: 1½ miles (1875–95), 1¼ miles (1896–present).

Preakness

Run at Pimlico Race Course, Baltimore, Md., two weeks after the Kentucky Derby.

Year	Winner (Margin)	Jockey	Second	Third	Time
1873	Survivor (10)	G. Barbee	John Boulger	Artist	2:43
1874	Culpepper (¾)	W. Donohue	King Amadeus	Scratch	2:56½
1875	Tom Ochiltree (2)	L. Hughes	Viator	Bay Final	2:43½
1876	Shirley (4)	G. Barbee	Rappahannock	Algerine	2:44¾
1877	Cloverbrook (4)	C. Holloway	Bombast	Lucifer	2:45½
1878	Duke of Magenta (6)	C. Holloway	Bayard	Albert	2:41¾
1879	Harold (3)	L. Hughes	Jericho	Rochester	2:40½
1880	Grenada (¾)	L. Hughes	Oden	Emily F.	2:40½
1881	Saunterer (½)	T. Costello	Compensation	Baltic	2:40½
1882	Vanguard (Neck)	T. Costello	Heck	Col Watson	2:44½
1883*	Jacobus (4)	G. Barbee	Parnell		2:42½
1884*	Knight of Ellerslie (2)	S. Fisher	Welcher		2:39½
1885	Tecumseh (2)	Jim McLaughlin	Wickham	John C.	2:49
1886	The Bard (3)	S. Fisher	Eurus	Elkwood	2:45
1887	Dunboyne (1)	W. Donohue	Mahoney	Raymond	2:39½
1888	Refund (3)	F. Littlefield	Judge Murray	Glendale	2:49
1889*	Buddhist (8)	W. Anderson	Japhet	*	2:17½
1890*	Montague (3)	W. Martin	Philosophy	Barrister	2:36¾
1894	Assignee (3)	Fred Taral	Potentate	Ed Kearney	1:49¼
1895	Belmar (1)	Fred Taral	April Fool	Sue Kittie	1:50½
1896	Margrave (1)	H. Griffin	Hamilton II	Intermission	1:51
1897	Paul Kauvar (1½)	C. Thorpe	Elkins	On Deck	1:51¼
1898	Sly Fox (2)	C. W. Simms	The Huguenot	Nuto	1:49⅗
1899	Half Time (1)	R. Clawson	Filigrane	Lackland	1:47
1900	Hindus (Head)	H. Spencer	Sarmation	Ten Candles	1:48⅖
1901	The Parader (2)	F. Landry	Sadie S.	Dr. Barlow	1:47⅕
1902	Old England (Nose)	L. Jackson	Major Daingerfield	Namtor	1:45⅘
1903	Flocarline (½)	W. Gannon	Mackey Dwyer	Rightful	1:44⅘
1904	Bryn Mawr (1)	E. Hildebrand	Wotan	Dolly Spanker	1:44⅕
1905	Cairngorm (Head)	W. Davis	Kiamesha	Coy Maid	1:45⅘
1906	Whimsical (4)	Walter Miller	Content	Larabie	1:45
1907	Don Enrique (1)	G. Mountain	Ethon	Zambesi	1:45⅖
1908	Royal Tourist (4)	E. Dugan	Live Wire	Robert Cooper	1:46⅖
1909	Effendi (1)	Willie Doyle	Fashion Plate	Hilltop	1:39⅘
1910	Layminster (½)	R. Estep	Dalhousie	Sager	1:40⅗
1911	Watervale (1)	E. Dugan	Zeus	The Nigger	1:51
1912	Colonel Holloway (5)	C. Turner	Bwana Tumbo	Tipsand	1:56⅗
1913	Buskin (Neck)	J. Butwell	Kleburne	Barnegat	1:53⅖
1914	Holiday (¾)	A. Schuttinger	Brave Cunarder	Defendum	1:53⅘
1915	Rhine Maiden (1½)	Douglas Hoffman	Half Rock	Runes	1:58
1916	Damrosch (1½)	Linus McAtee	Greenwood	Achievement	1:54⅘
1917	Kalitan (2)	E. Haynes	Al M. Dick	Kentucky Boy	1:54⅖
1918*	War Cloud (¾)	Johnny Loftus	Sunny Slope	Lanius	1:53⅗
1918*	Jack Hare, Jr (2)	C. Peak	The Porter	Kate Bright	1:53⅖
1919	Sir Barton (4)	Johnny Loftus	Eternal	Sweep On	1:53
1920	Man o' War (1½)	Clarence Kummer	Upset	Wildair	1:51⅗
1921	Broomspun (¾)	F. Coltiletti	Polly Ann	Jeg	1:54⅕
1922	Pillory (Head)	L. Morris	Hea	June Grass	1:51⅗
1923	Vigil (1¼)	B. Marinelli	General Thatcher	Rialto	1:53⅗
1924	Nellie Morse (1½)	J. Merimee	Transmute	Mad Play	1:57⅕
1925	Coventry (4)	Clarence Kummer	Backbone	Almadel	1:59
1926	Display (Head)	J. Maiben	Blondin	Mars	1:59⅘
1927	Bostonian (½)	A. Abel	Sir Harry	Whiskery	2:01⅗
1928	Victorian (Nose)	Sonny Workman	Toro	Solace	2:00⅕
1929	Dr. Freeland (1)	Louis Schaefer	Minotaur	African	2:01⅗
1930	Gallant Fox (¾)	Earl Sande	Crack Brigade	Snowflake	2:00⅗
1931	Mate (1½)	G. Ellis	Twenty Grand	Ladder	1:59
1932	Burgoo King (Head)	E. James	Tick On	Boatswain	1:59⅘
1933	Head Play (4)	Charles Kurtsinger	Ladysman	Utopian	2:02
1934	High Quest (Nose)	R. Jones	Cavalcade	Discovery	1:58⅕
1935	Omaha (6)	Willie Saunders	Firethorn	Psychic Bid	1:58⅖
1936	Bold Venture (Nose)	George Woolf	Granville	Jean Bart	1:59
1937	War Admiral (Head)	Charles Kurtsinger	Pompoon	Flying Scot	1:58⅖
1938	Dauber (7)	M. Peters	Cravat	Menow	1:59⅘
1939	Challedon (1¼)	George Seabo	Gilded Knight	Volitant	1:59⅘
1940	Bimelech (3)	F. A. Smith	Mioland	Gallahadion	1:58⅗

Preakness (Cont.)

Year	Winner (Margin)	Jockey	Second	Third	Time
1941	Whirlaway (5½)	Eddie Arcaro	King Cole	Our Boots	1:58⅘
1942	Alsab (1)	B. James	Requested Sun Again	(dead heat for second)	1:57
1943	Count Fleet (8)	Johnny Longden	Blue Swords	Vincentive	1:57⅖
1944	Pensive (¾)	Conn McCreary	Platter	Stir Up	1:59⅕
1945	Polynesian (2½)	W. D. Wright	Hoop Jr.	Darby Dieppe	1:58⅘
1946	Assault (Neck)	Warren Mehrtens	Lord Boswell	Hampden	2:01⅖
1947	Faultless (1¼)	Doug Dodson	On Trust	Phalanx	1:59
1948	Citation (5½)	Eddie Arcaro	Vulcan's Forge	Boyard	2:02⅖
1949	Capot (Head)	Ted Atkinson	Palestinian	Noble Impulse	1:56
1950	Hill Prince (5)	Eddie Arcaro	Middleground	Dooley	1:59⅕
1951	Bold (7)	Eddie Arcaro	Counterpoint	Alerted	1:56⅖
1952	Blue Man (3½)	Conn McCreary	Jampol	One Count	1:57⅖
1953	Native Dancer (Neck)	Eric Guerin	Jamie K.	Royal Bay Gem	1:57⅘
1954	Hasty Road (Neck)	Johnny Adams	Correlation	Hasseyampa	1:57⅖
1955	Nashua (1)	Eddie Arcaro	Saratoga	Traffic Judge	1:54⅗
1956	Fabius (¾)	Bill Hartack	Needles	No Regrets	1:58⅖
1957	Bold Ruler (2)	Eddie Arcaro	Iron Liege	Inside Tract	1:56⅕
1958	Tim Tam (1½)	I. Valenzuela	Lincoln Road	Gone Fishin'	1:57⅕
1959	Royal Orbit (4)	William Harmatz	Sword Dancer	Dunce	1:57
1960	Bally Ache (4)	Bobby Ussery	Victoria Park	Celtic Ash	1:57⅗
1961	Carry Back (¾)	Johnny Sellers	Globemaster	Crozier	1:57⅗
1962	Greek Money (Nose)	John Rotz	Ridan	Roman Line	1:56⅕
1963	Candy Spots (3½)	Bill Shoemaker	Chateaugay	Never Bend	1:56⅕
1964	Northern Dancer (2¼)	Bill Hartack	The Scoundrel	Hill Rise	1:56⅘
1965	Tom Rolfe (Neck)	Ron Turcotte	Dapper Dan	Hail to All	1:56⅕
1966	Kauai King (1¾)	Don Brumfield	Stupendous	Amberoid	1:55⅖
1967	Damascus (2¼)	Bill Shoemaker	In Reality	Proud Clarion	1:55⅕
1968	Forward Pass (6)	I. Valenzuela	Out of the Way	Nodouble	1:56⅘
1969	Majestic Prince (Head)	Bill Hartack	Arts and Letters	Jay Ray	1:55⅗
1970	Personality (Neck)	Eddie Belmonte	My Dad George	Silent Screen	1:56⅕
1971	Canonero II (1½)	Gustavo Avila	Eastern Fleet	Jim French	1:54
1972	Bee Bee Bee (1¼)	Eldon Nelson	No Le Hace	Key to the Mint	1:55⅗
1973	Secretariat (2½)	Ron Turcotte	Sham	Our Native	1:54⅖
1974	Little Current (7)	Miguel Rivera	Neapolitan Way	Cannonade	1:54⅗
1975	Master Derby (1)	Darrel McHargue	Foolish Pleasure	Diabolo	1:56⅖
1976	Elocutionist (3)	John Lively	Play the Red	Bold Forbes	1:55
1977	Seattle Slew (1½)	Jean Cruguet	Iron Constitution	Run Dusty Run	1:54⅖
1978	Affirmed (Neck)	Steve Cauthen	Alydar	Believe It	1:54⅖
1979	Spectacular Bid (5½)	Ron Franklin	Golden Act	Screen King	1:54⅕
1980	Codex (4¾)	Angel Cordero Jr.	Genuine Risk	Colonel Moran	1:54⅕
1981	Pleasant Colony (1)	Jorge Velasquez	Bold Ego	Paristo	1:54⅗
1982	Aloma's Ruler (½)	Jack Kaenel	Linkage	Cut Away	1:55⅖
1983	Deputed Testamony (2¾)	Donald Miller Jr.	Desert Wine	High Honors	1:55⅖
1984	Gate Dancer (1½)	Angel Cordero Jr.	Play On	Fight Over	1:53⅗
1985	Tank's Prospect (Head)	Pat Day	Chief's Crown	Eternal Prince	1:53⅖
1986	Snow Chief (4)	Alex Solis	Ferdinand	Broad Brush	1:54⅘
1987	Alysheba (½)	Chris McCarron	Bet Twice	Cryptoclearance	1:55⅘
1988	Risen Star (1¼)	E. Delahoussaye	Brian's Time	Winning Colors	1:56⅕
1989	Sunday Silence (Nose)	Pat Valenzuela	Easy Goer	Rock Point	1:53⅘
1990	Summer Squall (2¼)	Pat Day	Unbridled	Mister Frisky	1:53⅗
1991	Hansel (Head)	Jerry Bailey	Corporate Report	Mane Minister	1:54
1992	Pine Bluff (¾)	Chris McCarron	Alydeed	Casual Lies	1:55⅗
1993	Prairie Bayou (½)	Mike Smith	Cherokee Run	El Bakan	1:56⅗
1994	Tabasco Cat (¾)	Pat Day	Go For Gin	Concern	1:56⅖
1995	Timber Country (½)	Pat Day	Oliver's Twist	Thunder Gulch	1:54⅖
1996	Louis Quatorze (3¼)	Pat Day	Skip Away	Editor's Note	1:53⅖
1997	Silver Charm (Head)	Gary Stevens	Free House	Captain Bodgit	1:54⅖
1998	Real Quiet (2¼)	Kent Desormeaux	Victory Gallop	Classic Cat	1:54⅗
1999	Charismatic (1½)	Chris Antley	Menifee	Badge	1:55⅕
2000	Red Bullet (3¾)	Jerry Bailey	Fusaichi Pegasus	Impeachment	1:56.04
2001	Point Given (2¼)	Gary Stevens	A P Valentine	Congaree	1:55.51
2002	War Emblem (¾)	Victor Espinoza	Magic Weisner	Proud Citizen	1:56.36

*Preakness was a two-horse race in 1883, '84 and '89. It was not run 1891–1893; and in 1918, it was run in two divisions.

Note: Distance: 1½ miles (1873–88), 1¼ miles (1889), 1½ miles (1890), 1 1/16 miles (1894–1900), 1 mile and 70 yards (1901–1907), 1 1/16 miles (1908), 1 mile (1909–10), 1⅛ miles (1911–24), 1 3/16 miles (1925–present).

Belmont

Run at Belmont Park, Elmont, NY, three weeks after the Preakness Stakes. Held previously at two locations in the Bronx (NY): Jerome Park (1867–1889) and Morris Park (1890–1904).

Year	Winner (Margin)	Jockey	Second	Third	Time
1867	Ruthless (Head)	J. Gilpatrick	De Courcy	Rivoli	3:05
1868	General Duke (2)	R. Swim	Northumberland	Fannie Ludlow	3:02
1869	Fenian (Unknown)	C. Miller	Glenelg	Invercauld	3:04¼
1870	Kingfisher (½)	E. Brown	Foster	Midday	2:59½
1871	Harry Bassett (3)	W. Miller	Stockwood	By-the-Sea	2:56
1872	Joe Daniels (¾)	James Rowe	Meteor	Shylock	2:58¼
1873	Springbok (4)	James Rowe	Count d'Orsay	Strachino	3:01¾
1874	Saxon (Neck)	G. Barbee	Grinstead	Aaron Pennington	2:39½
1875	Calvin (2)	R. Swim	Aristides	Milner	2:40¼
1876	Algerine (Head)	W. Donahue	Fiddlestick	Barricade	2:40½
1877	Cloverbrook (1)	C. Holloway	Loiterer	Baden-Baden	2:46
1878	Duke of Magenta (2)	L. Hughes	Bramble	Sparta	2:43½
1879	Spendthrift (5)	S. Evans	Monitor	Jericho	2:42¾
1880	Grenada (½)	L. Hughes	Ferncliffe	Turenne	2:47
1881	Saunterer (Neck)	T. Costello	Eole	Baltic	2:47
1882	Forester (5)	James McLaughlin	Babcock	Wyoming	2:43
1883	George Kinney (2)	James McLaughlin	Trombone	Renegade	2:42½
1884	Panique (½)	James McLaughlin	Knight of Ellerslie	Himalaya	2:42
1885	Tyrant (3½)	Paul Duffy	St. Augustine	Tecumseh	2:43
1886	Inspector B (1)	James McLaughlin	The Bard	Linden	2:41
1887*	Hanover (28-32)	James McLaughlin	Oneko		2:43½
1888*	Sir Dixon (12)	James McLaughlin	Prince Royal		2:40¼
1889	Eric (Head)	W. Hayward	Diable	Zephyrus	2:47
1890	Burlington (1)	S. Barnes	Devotee	Padishah	2:07¾
1891	Foxford (Neck)	E. Garrison	Montana	Laurestan	2:08¾
1892*	Patron (Unknown)	W. Hayward	Shellbark		2:17
1893	Comanche (Head)	Willie Simms	Dr. Rice	Rainbow	1:53¼
1894	Henry of Navarre (2-4)	Willie Simms	Prig	Assignee	1:56½
1895	Belmar (Head)	Fred Taral	Counter Tenor	Nanki Pooh	2:11½
1896	Hastings (Neck)	H. Griffin	Handspring	Hamilton II	2:24½
1897	Scottish Chieftain (1)	J. Scherrer	On Deck	Octagon	2:23¼
1898	Bowling Brook (8)	P. Littlefield	Previous	Hamburg	2:32
1899	Jean Bereaud (Head)	R. R. Clawson	Half Time	Glengar	2:23
1900	Ildrim (Head)	N. Turner	Petrucio	Missionary	2:21½
1901	Commando (½)	H. Spencer	The Parader	All Green	2:21
1902	Masterman (2)	John Bullmann	Ranald	King Hanover	2:22½
1903	Africander (2)	John Bullmann	Whorler	Red Knight	2:23⅕
1904	Delhi (3½)	George Odom	Graziallo	Rapid Water	2:06⅗
1905	Tanya (1/2)	E. Hildebrand	Blandy	Hot Shot	2:08
1906	Burgomaster (4)	L. Lyne	The Quail	Accountant	2:20
1907	Peter Pan (1)	G. Mountain	Superman	Frank Gill	Unknown
1908	Colin (Head)	Joe Notter	Fair Play	King James	Unknown
1909	Joe Madden (8)	E. Dugan	Wise Mason	Donald MacDonald	2:21⅗
1910*	Sweep (6)	J. Butwell	Duke of Ormonde		2:22
1913	Prince Eugene (½)	Roscoe Troxler	Rock View	Flying Fairy	2:18
1914	Luke McLuke (8)	M. Buxton	Gainer	Charlestonian	2:20
1915	The Finn (4)	G. Byrne	Half Rock	Pebbles	2:18⅖
1916	Friar Rock (3)	E. Haynes	Spur	Churchill	2:22
1917	Hourless (10)	J. Butwell	Skeptic	Wonderful	2:17⅘
1918	Johren (2)	Frank Robinson	War Cloud	Cum Sah	2:20⅖
1919	Sir Barton (5)	Johnny Loftus	Sweep On	Natural Bridge	2:17⅖
1920*	Man o' War (20)	Clarence Kummer	Donnacona		2:14⅕
1921	Grey Lag (3)	Earl Sande	Sporting Blood	Leonardo II	2:16⅘
1922	Pillory (2)	C. H. Miller	Snob II	Hea	2:18⅘
1923	Zev (1½)	Earl Sande	Chickvale	Rialto	2:19
1924	Mad Play (2)	Earl Sande	Mr. Mutt	Modest	2:18⅘
1925	American Flag (8)	Albert Johnson	Dangerous	Swope	2:16⅘
1926	Crusader (1)	Albert Johnson	Espino	Haste	2:32⅕
1927	Chance Shot (1½)	Earl Sande	Bois de Rose	Flambino	2:32⅖
1928	Vito (3)	Clarence Kummer	Genie	Diavolo	2:33⅕
1929	Blue Larkspur (¾)	Mack Garner	African	Jack High	2:32⅘
1930	Gallant Fox (3)	Earl Sande	Whichone	Questionnaire	2:31⅗

Belmont (Cont.)

Year	Winner (Margin)	Jockey	Second	Third	Time
1931	Twenty Grand (10)	Charles Kurtsinger	Sun Meadow	Jamestown	2:29⅗
1932	Faireno (1½)	T. Malley	Osculator	Flag Pole	2:32⅘
1933	Hurryoff (1½)	Mack Garner	Nimbus	Union	2:32⅗
1934	Peace Chance (6)	W. D. Wright	High Quest	Good Goods	2:29⅕
1935	Omaha (1½)	Willie Saunders	Firethorn	Rosemont	2:30⅗
1936	Granville (Nose)	James Stout	Mr. Bones	Hollyrood	2:30
1937	War Admiral (3)	Charles Kurtsinger	Sceneshifter	Vamoose	2:28⅗
1938	Pasteurized (Neck)	James Stout	Dauber	Cravat	2:29⅖
1939	Johnstown (5)	James Stout	Belay	Gilded Knight	2:29⅗
1940	Bimelech (¾)	F. A. Smith	Your Chance	Andy K	2:29⅗
1941	Whirlaway (2½)	Eddie Arcaro	Robert Morris	Yankee Chance	2:31
1942	Shut Out (2)	Eddie Arcaro	Alsab	Lochinvar	2:29⅕
1943	Count Fleet (25)	Johnny Longden	Fairy Manhurst	Deseronto	2:28⅕
1944	Bounding Home (½)	G. L. Smith	Pensive	Bull Dandy	2:32⅕
1945	Pavot (5)	Eddie Arcaro	Wildlife	Jeep	2:30⅕
1946	Assault (3)	Warren Mehrtens	Natchez	Cable	2:30⅘
1947	Phalanx (5)	R. Donoso	Tide Rips	Tailspin	2:29⅖
1948	Citation (8)	Eddie Arcaro	Better Self	Escadru	2:28⅕
1949	Capot (½)	Ted Atkinson	Ponder	Palestinian	2:30⅕
1950	Middleground (1)	William Boland	Lights Up	Mr. Trouble	2:28⅗
1951	Counterpoint (4)	D. Gorman	Battlefield	Battle Morn	2:29
1952	One Count (2½)	Eddie Arcaro	Blue Man	Armageddon	2:30⅕
1953	Native Dancer (Neck)	Eric Guerin	Jamie K.	Royal Bay Gem	2:38⅗
1954	High Gun (Neck)	Eric Guerin	Fisherman	Limelight	2:30⅘
1955	Nashua (9)	Eddie Arcaro	Blazing Count	Portersville	2:29
1956	Needles (Neck)	David Erb	Career Boy	Fabius	2:29⅘
1957	Gallant Man (8)	Bill Shoemaker	Inside Tract	Bold Ruler	2:26⅗
1958	Cavan (6)	Pete Anderson	Tim Tam	Flamingo	2:30⅕
1959	Sword Dancer (¾)	Bill Shoemaker	Bagdad	Royal Orbit	2:28⅖
1960	Celtic Ash (5½)	Bill Hartack	Venetian Way	Disperse	2:29⅗
1961	Sherluck (2¼)	Braulio Baeza	Globemaster	Guadalcanal	2:29⅕
1962	Jaipur (Nose)	Bill Shoemaker	Admiral's Voyage	Crimson Satan	2:28⅘
1963	Chateaugay (2½)	Braulio Baeza	Candy Spots	Choker	2:30⅕
1964	Quadrangle (2)	Manuel Ycaza	Roman Brother	Northern Dancer	2:28⅖
1965	Hail to All (Neck)	John Sellers	Tom Rolfe	First Family	2:28⅖
1966	Amberold (2½)	William Boland	Buffle	Advocator	2:29⅗
1967	Damascus (2½)	Bill Shoemaker	Cool Reception	Gentleman James	2:28⅘
1968	Stage Door Johnny (1¼)	Hellodoro Gustines	Forward Pass	Call Me Prince	2:27⅕
1969	Arts and Letters (5½)	Braulio Baeza	Majestic Prince	Dike	2:28⅘
1970	High Echelon (¾)	John L. Rotz	Needles N Pins	Naskra	2:34
1971	Pass Catcher (¾)	Walter Blum	Jim French	Bold Reason	2:30⅖
1972	Riva Ridge (7)	Ron Turcotte	Ruritania	Cloudy Dawn	2:28
1973	Secretariat (31)	Ron Turcotte	Twice a Prince	My Gallant	2:24
1974	Little Current (7)	Miguel A. Rivera	Jolly Johu	Cannonade	2:29⅕
1975	Avatar (Neck)	Bill Shoemaker	Foolish Pleasure	Master Derby	2:28⅕
1976	Bold Forbes (Neck)	Angel Cordero Jr.	McKenzie Bridge	Great Contractor	2:29
1977	Seattle Slew (4)	Jean Cruguet	Run Dusty Run	Sanhedrin	2:29⅗
1978	Affirmed (Head)	Steve Cauthen	Alydar	Darby Creek Road	2:26⅘
1979	Coastal (3¼)	Ruben Hernandez	Golden Act	Spectacular Bid	2:28⅗
1980	Temperence Hill (2)	Eddie Maple	Genuine Risk	Rockhill Native	2:29⅘
1981	Summing (Neck)	George Martens	Highland Blade	Pleasant Colony	2:29
1982	Conquistador Cielo (14½)	Laffit Pincay, Jr.	Gato Del Sol	Illuminate	2:28⅕
1983	Caveat (3½)	Laffit Pincay Jr.	Slew o'Gold	Barberstown	2:27⅘
1984	Swale (4)	Laffit Pincay Jr.	Pine Circle	Morning Bob	2:27⅕
1985	Creme Fraiche (½)	Eddie Maple	Stephan's Odyssey	Chief's Crown	2:27
1986	Danzig Connection (1¼)	Chris McCarron	Johns Treasure	Ferdinand	2:29⅘
1987	Bet Twice (14)	Craig Perret	Cryptoclearance	Gulch	2:28⅕
1988	Risen Star (14¾)	Eddie Delahoussaye	Kingpost	Brian's Time	2:26⅖
1989	Easy Goer (8)	Pat Day	Sunday Silence	Le Voyageur	2:26
1990	Go and Go (8¼)	Michael Kinane	Thirty Six Red	Baron de Vaux	2:27⅕
1991	Hansel (Head)	Jerry Bailey	Strike the Gold	Mane Minister	2:28
1992	A.P. Indy (¾)	Eddie Delahoussaye	My Memoirs	Pine Bluff	2:26

Belmont (Cont.)

Year	Winner (Margin)	Jockey	Second	Third	Time
1993	Colonial Affair (2¼)	Julie Krone	Kissin Kris	Wild Gale	2:29⅘
1994	Tabasco Cat (2)	Pat Day	Go For Gin	Strodes Creek	2:26⅘
1995	Thunder Gulch (2)	Gary Stevens	Star Standard	Citadeed	2:32
1996	Editor's Note (1)	Rene Douglas	Skip Away	My Flag	2:28⅘
1997	Touch Gold (¾)	Chris McCarron	Silver Charm	Free House	2:28⅘
1998	Victory Gallop (Nose)	Gary Stevens	Real Quiet	Thomas Jo	2:28⅘
1999	Lemon Drop Kid (Head)	Jose Santos	Vision and Verse	Charismatic	2:27⅘
2000	Commendable (1½)	Pat Day	Aptitude	Unshaded	2:31.19
2001	Point Given (12¼)	Gary Stevens	A P Valentine	Monarchos	2:26.56
2002	Sarava (½)	Edgar Prado	Medaglia d'Oro	Sunday Break	2:29.71

*Belmont was a two-horse race in 1887, '88, '92, 1910 and '20; and was not held in 1911–1912.
Note: Distance: 1 mile 5 furlongs (1867–89), 1¼ miles (1890–1905), 1⅜ miles (1906–25), 1½ miles (1926–present).

Triple Crown Winners

Year	Horse	Jockey	Owner	Trainer
1919	Sir Barton	John Loftus	J. K. L. Ross	H. G. Bedwell
1930	Gallant Fox	Earle Sande	Belair Stud	James Fitzsimmons
1935	Omaha	William Saunders	Belair Stud	James Fitzsimmons
1937	War Admiral	Charles Kurtsinger	Samuel D. Riddle	George Conway
1941	Whirlaway	Eddie Arcaro	Calumet Farm	Ben Jones
1943	Count Fleet	John Longden	Mrs J. D. Hertz	Don Cameron
1946	Assault	Warren Mehrtens	King Ranch	Max Hirsch
1948	Citation	Eddie Arcaro	Calumet Farm	Jimmy Jones
1973	Secretariat	Ron Turcotte	Meadow Stable	Lucien Laurin
1977	Seattle Slew	Jean Cruguet	Karen L. Taylor	William H. Turner Jr.
1978	Affirmed	Steve Cauthen	Harbor View Farm	Laz Barrera

One Well-Paid Groom

Bob Baffert isn't hard to pick out of a crowd, and as he arrived at his box at Monmouth Park in August, shortly before his superstar colt, War Emblem, romped to victory in the 2002 Haskell Invitational, many of the 45,212 fans turned and cheered. When the trainer and his bride of 24 hours, Jill Moss, raised their hands jointly in acknowledgement—just call them the Juan and Evita of the horsey set—the cheers rose to a powerful roar. "He's a star, and the horse is a star," said George Zoffinger, the president of the New Jersey Sports & Exposition Authority. "Anybody who doesn't think we did the right thing by bringing this horse here is nuts."

Zoffinger was referring to the controversy that erupted over the news that the NJSEA was paying Baffert a $50,000 appearance fee to bring War Emblem to the Haskell. Appearance fees are almost unheard of in racing, though Baffert claims they are offered to him regularly. This large sum is a testimony not only to the prestige of War Emblem, the 2002 Kentucky Derby and Preakness winner, but also to Baffert's celebrity power. "I've turned down a lot of deals where I didn't go because the horse wasn't right," said Baffert. "Nobody works harder to promote racing than me, and if somebody wants to pay me for it, I'm going to take it." (He did, however, donate half his fee to the Thoroughbred Retirement Foundation in the name of War Emblem's owner, Prince Ahmed bin Salman, who died on July 22, 2002.)

A little extra dough, and War Emblem's wire-to-wire, 3½-length victory, is nothing unusual for Hollywood Bob, whose horses had won 80 races and more than $7 million in 2002: that wasn't even the best day of the weekend for him. Twenty-four hours earlier, at the Hotel Del Coronado outside San Diego, Baffert and Moss were married before more than 250 guests as well as a handful of paparazzi. "When was the last time a trainer's marriage was covered in the papers?" wondered one veteran turf writer. Is Baffert a star without his horses? Of course not, but that hardly mattered to Zoffinger. "Look at this," he said, gesturing to the second-largest crowd in the track's 132-year history. "Having him here is good for the sport, and it's good for us."

—Mark Beech

Horse of the Year

Year	Horse	Owner	Trainer	Breeder
1936	Granville	Belair Stud	James Fitzsimmons	Belair Stud
1937	War Admiral	Samuel D. Riddle	George Conway	Mrs. Samuel D. Riddle
1938	Seabiscuit	Charles S. Howard	Tom Smith	Wheatley Stable
1939	Challedon	William L. Brann	Louis J. Schaefer	Branncastle Farm
1940	Challedon	William L. Brann	Louis J. Schaefer	Branncastle Farm
1941	Whirlaway	Calumet Farm	Ben Jones	Calumet Farm
1942	Whirlaway	Calumet Farm	Ben Jones	Calumet Farm
1943	Count Fleet	Mrs. John D. Hertz	Don Cameron	Mrs. John D. Hertz
1944	Twilight Tear	Calumet Farm	Ben Jones	Calumet Farm
1945	Busher	Louis B. Mayer	George Odom	Idle Hour Stock Farm
1946	Assault	King Ranch	Max Hirsch	King Ranch
1947	Armed	Calumet Farm	Jimmy Jones	Calumet Farm
1948	Citation	Calumet Farm	Jimmy Jones	Calumet Farm
1949	Capot	Greentree Stable	John M. Gaver Sr.	Greentree Stable
1950	Hill Prince	C.T. Chenery	Casey Hayes	C.T. Chenery
1951	Counterpoint	C.V. Whitney	Syl Veitch	C.V. Whitney
1952	One Count	Mrs. W. M. Jeffords	O. White	W M. Jeffords
1953	Tom Fool	Greentree Stable	John M. Gaver Sr.	D.A. Headley
1954	Native Dancer	A.G. Vanderbilt	Bill Winfrey	A.G. Vanderbilt
1955	Nashua	Belair Stud	James Fitzsimmons	Belair Stud
1956	Swaps	Ellsworth-Galbreath	Mesh Tenney	R. Ellsworth
1957	Bold Ruler	Wheatley Stable	James Fitzsimmons	Wheatley Stable
1958	Round Table	Kerr Stables	Willy Molter	Claiborne Farm
1959	Sword Dancer	Brookmeade Stable	Elliott Burch	Brookmeade Stable
1960	Kelso	Bohemia Stable	C. Hanford	Mrs. R.C. duPont
1961	Kelso	Bohemia Stable	C. Hanford	Mrs. R.C. duPont
1962	Kelso	Bohemia Stable	C. Hanford	Mrs. R.C. duPont
1963	Kelso	Bohemia Stable	C. Hanford	Mrs. R.C. duPont
1964	Kelso	Bohemia Stable	C. Hanford	Mrs. R.C. duPont
1965	Roman Brother	Harbor View Stable	Burley Parke	Ocala Stud
1966	Buckpasser	Ogden Phipps	Eddie Neloy	Ogden Phipps
1967	Damascus	Mrs. E. W. Bancroft	Frank Y. Whiteley Jr.	Mrs. E. W. Bancroft
1968	Dr. Fager	Tartan Stable	John A. Nerud	Tartan Farms
1969	Arts and Letters	Rokeby Stable	Elliott Burch	Paul Mellon
1970	Fort Marcy	Rokeby Stable	Elliott Burch	Paul Mellon
1971	Ack Ack	E.E. Fogelson	Charlie Whittingham	H.F. Guggenheim
1972	Secretariat	Meadow Stable	Lucien Laurin	Meadow Stud
1973	Secretariat	Meadow Stable	Lucien Laurin	Meadow Stud
1974	Forego	Lazy F Ranch	Sherrill W. Ward	Lazy F Ranch
1975	Forego	Lazy F Ranch	Sherrill W. Ward	Lazy F Ranch
1976	Forego	Lazy F Ranch	Frank Y. Whiteley Jr.	Lazy F Ranch
1977	Seattle Slew	Karen L. Taylor	Billy Turner Jr.	B.S. Castleman
1978	Affirmed	Harbor View Farm	Laz Barrera	Harbor View Farm
1979	Affirmed	Harbor View Farm	Laz Barrera	Harbor View Farm
1980	Spectacular Bid	Hawksworth Farm	Bud Delp	Mmes. Gilmore and Jason
1981	John Henry	Dotsam Stable	Ron McAnally and Lefty Nickerson	Golden Chance Farm
1982	Conquistador Cielo	H. de Kwiatkowski	Woody Stephens	L.E. Landoli
1983	All Along	Daniel Wildenstein	P.L. Biancone	Dayton
1984	John Henry	Dotsam Stable	Ron McAnally	Golden Chance Farm
1985	Spend a Buck	Hunter Farm	Cam Gambolati	Irish Hill & R.W. Harper
1986	Lady's Secret	Mr. & Mrs. Eugene Klein	D. Wayne Lukas	R.H. Spreen
1987	Ferdinand	Mrs. H.B. Keck	Charlie Whittingham	H.B. Keck
1988	Alysheba	D. & P. Scharbauer	Jack Van Berg	Preston Madden
1989	Sunday Silence	Gaillard, Hancock, & Whittingham	Charlie Whittingham	Oak Cliff Thoroughbreds
1990	Criminal Type	Calumet Farm	D. Wayne Lukas	Calumet Farm
1991	Black Tie Affair	Jeffrey Sullivan	Ernie Poulos	Stephen D. Peskoff
1992	A.P. Indy	Tomonori Tsurumaki	Neil Drysdale	W.S. Farish & W.S. Kilroy
1993	Kotashaan	La Presle Farm	Richard Mandella	La Presle Farm
1994	Holy Bull	Jimmy Croll	Jimmy Croll	Pelican Stable
1995	Cigar	Allen E. Paulson	William Mott	Allen E. Paulson
1996	Cigar	Allen E. Paulson	William Mott	Allen E. Paulson

Horse of the Year (Cont.)

Year	Horse	Owner	Trainer	Breeder
1997	Favorite Trick	Joseph LaCombe	William Mott	Mr. & Mrs. M.L. Wood
1998	Skip Away	Carolyn Hine	Hubert Hine	Anna Marie Barnhart
1999	Charismatic	Robert & Beverly Lewis	D. Wayne Lukas	William Farish/Partners
2000	Tiznow	Michael Cooper and Cecilia Straub-Rubens	Jay M. Robbins	Cecilia Straub-Rubens
2001	Point Given	The Thoroughbred Corp.	Bob Baffert	The Thoroughbred Corp.

Note: From 1936 to 1970, the *Daily Racing Form* annually selected a "Horse of the Year." In 1971 the *Daily Racing Form*,

Eclipse Award Winners

2-YEAR-OLD COLT

1971	Riva Ridge
1972	Secretariat
1973	Protagonist
1974	Foolish Pleasure
1975	Honest Pleasure
1976	Seattle Slew
1977	Affirmed
1978	Spectacular Bid
1979	Rockhill Native
1980	Lord Avie
1981	Deputy Minister
1982	Roving Boy
1983	Devil's Bag
1984	Chief's Crown
1985	Tasso
1986	Capote
1987	Forty Niner
1988	Easy Goer
1989	Rhythm
1990	Fly So Free
1991	Arazi
1992	Gilded Time
1993	Dehere
1994	Timber Country
1995	Maria's Mon
1996	Boston Harbor
1997	Favorite Trick
1998	Answer Lively
1999	Anees
2000	Macho Uno
2001	Johannesburg

2-YEAR-OLD FILLY

1971	Numbered Account
1972	La Prevoyante
1973	Talking Picture
1974	Ruffian
1975	Dearly Precious
1976	Sensational
1977	Lakeville Miss
1978	Candy Eclair, It's in the Air
1979	Smart Angle
1980	Heavenly Cause
1981	Before Dawn
1982	Landaluce
1983	Althea
1984	Outstandingly
1985	Family Style
1986	Brave Raj
1987	Epitome
1988	Open Mind
1989	Go for Wand
1990	Meadow Star
1991	Pleasant Stage
1992	Eliza
1993	Phone Chatter
1994	Flanders
1995	Golden Attraction
1996	Storm Song
1997	Countess Diana
1998	Silverbulletday
1999	Chilukki
2000	Caressing
2001	Tempera

3-YEAR-OLD COLT

1971	Canonero II
1972	Key to the Mint
1973	Secretariat
1974	Little Currant
1975	Wajima
1976	Bold Forbes
1977	Seattle Slew
1978	Affirmed
1979	Spectacular Bid
1980	Temperence Hill
1981	Pleasant Colony
1982	Conquistador Cielo
1983	Slew o' Gold
1984	Swale
1985	Spend A Buck
1986	Snow Chief
1987	Alysheba
1988	Risen Star
1989	Sunday Silence
1990	Unbridled
1991	Hansel
1992	A.P. Indy
1993	Prairie Bayou
1994	Holy Bull
1995	Thunder Gulch
1996	Skip Away
1997	Silver Charm
1998	Real Quiet
1999	Charismatic
2000	Tiznow
2001	Point Given

CHAMPION TURF HORSE

1971	Run the Gantlet (3)
1972	Cougar II (6)
1973	Secretariat (3)
1974	Dahlia (4)
1975	Snow Knight (4)
1976	Youth (3)
1977	Johnny D (3)
1978	Mac Diarmida (3)

CHAMPION MALE TURF HORSE

1979	Bowl Game (5)
1980	John Henry (5)
1981	John Henry (6)
1982	Perrault (5)
1983	John Henry (8)
1984	John Henry (9)
1985	Cozzene (4)
1986	Manila (3)
1987	Theatrical (5)
1988	Sunshine Forever (3)
1989	Steinlen (6)
1990	Itsallgreektome (3)

CHAMPION MALE TURF HORSE (Cont.)

1991	Tight Spot (4)
1992	Sky Classic (5)
1993	Kotashaan (5)
1994	Paradise Creek (5)
1995	Northern Spur (4)
1996	Singspiel (4)
1997	Chief Bearhart (4)
1998	Buck's Boy (5)
1999	Daylami (5)
2000	Kalanisi (4)
2001	Fantastic Light (5)

CHAMPION FEMALE TURF HORSE

1979	Trillion (5)
1980	Just a Game II (4)
1981	De La Rose (3)
1982	April Run (4)
1983	All Along (4)
1984	Royal Heroine (4)
1985	Pebbles (4)
1986	Estrapade (6)

CHAMPION FEMALE TURF HORSE (Cont.)

1987	Miesque (3)
1988	Miesque (4)
1989	Brown Bess (7)
1990	Laugh and Be Merry (5)
1991	Miss Alleged (4)
1992	Flawlessly (4)
1993	Flawlessly (5)
1994	Hatoof (5)
1995	Possibly Perfect (5)
1996	Wandesta (5)
1997	Ryafan (3)
1998	Fiji (4)
1999	Soaring Softly (4)
2000	Perfect Sting (4)
2001	Banks Hill (3)

Eclipse Award Winners (Cont.)

3-YEAR-OLD FILLY

1971 ....Turkish Trousers
1972 ....Susan's Girl
1973 ....Desert Vixen
1974 ....Chris Evert
1975 ....Ruffian
1976 ....Revidere
1977 ....Our Mims
1978 ....Tempest Queen
1979 ....Davona Dale
1980 ....Genuine Risk
1981 ....Wayward Lass
1982 ....Christmas Past
1983 ....Heartlight No. One
1984 ....Life's Magic
1985 ....Mom's Command
1986 ....Tiffany Lass
1987 ....Sacahuista
1988 ....Winning Colors
1989 ....Open Mind
1990 ....Go for Wand
1991 ....Dance Smartly
1992 ....Saratoga Dew
1993 ....Hollywood Wildcat
1994 ....Heavenly Prize
1995 ....Serena's Song
1996 ....Yank's Music
1997 ....Ajina
1998 ....Banshee Breeze
1999 ....Silverbulletday
2000 ....Surfside
2001 ....Xtra Heat

OLDER COLT, HORSE OR GELDING

1971 ....Ack Ack (5)
1972 ....Autobiography (4)
1973 ....Riva Ridge (4)
1974 ....Forego (4)
1975 ....Forego (5)
1976 ....Forego (6)
1977 ....Forego (7)
1978 ....Seattle Slew (4)
1979 ....Affirmed (4)
1980 ....Spectacular Bid (4)
1981 ....John Henry (6)
1982 ....Lemhi Gold (4)
1983 ....Bates Motel (4)
1984 ....Slew o'Gold (4)
1985 ....Vanlandingham (4)
1986 ....Turkoman (4)
1987 ....Ferdinand (4)
1988 ....Alysheba (4)
1989 ....Blushing John (4)
1990 ....Criminal Type (5)
1991 ....Black Tie Affair (5)
1992 ....Pleasant Tap (5)
1993 ....Bertrando (4)
1994 ....The Wicked North (5)
1995 ....Cigar (5)
1996 ....Cigar (6)
1997 ....Skip Away (4)
1998 ....Skip Away (5)
1999 ....Victory Gallop (4)
2000 ....Lemon Drop Kid (4)
2001 ....Tiznow (4)

OLDER FILLY OR MARE

1971 ....Shuvee (5)
1972 ....Typecast (6)
1973 ....Susan's Girl (4)
1974 ....Desert Vixen (4)
1975 ....Susan's Girl (6)
1976 ....Proud Delta (4)
1977 ....Cascapedia (4)
1978 ....Late Bloomer (4)
1979 ....Waya (5)
1980 ....Glorious Song (4)
1981 ....Relaxing (5)
1982 ....Track Robbery (6)
1983 ....Ambassador of Luck (4)
1984 ....Princess Rooney (4)
1985 ....Life's Magic (4)
1986 ....Lady's Secret (4)
1987 ....North Sider (5)
1988 ....Personal Ensign (4)
1989 ....Bayakoa (5)
1990 ....Bayakoa (6)
1991 ....Queena (5)
1992 ....Paseana (5)
1993 ....Paseana (6)
1994 ....Sky Beauty (4)
1995 ....Inside Information (4)
1996 ....Jewel Princess (4)
1997 ....Hidden Lake (4)
1998 ....Escena (5)
1999 ....Beautiful Pleasure (4)
2000 ....Riboletta (6)
2001 ....Gourmet Girl (6)

STEEPLECHASE OR HURDLE HORSE

1971 .....Shadow Brook (7)
1972 .....Soothsayer (5)
1973 .....Athenian Idol (5)
1974 .....Gran Kan (8)
1975 .....Life's Illusion (4)
1976 .....Straight & True (6)
1977 .....Cafe Prince (7)
1978 .....Cafe Prince (8)
1979 .....Martie's Anger (4)
1980 .....Zaccio (4)
1981 .....Zaccio (5)
1982 .....Zaccio (6)
1983 .....Flatterer (4)
1984 .....Flatterer (5)
1985 .....Flatterer (6)
1986 .....Flatterer (7)
1987 .....Inlander (6)
1988 .....Jimmy Lorenzo (6)
1989 .....Highland Bud (4)
1990 .....Morley Street (7)
1991 .....Morley Street (8)
1992 .....Lonesome Glory (4)
1993 .....Lonesome Glory (5)
1994 .....Warm Spell (6)
1995 .....Lonesome Glory (7)
1996 .....Corregio (5)
1997 .....Lonesome Glory (9)
1998 .....Flat Top (5)
1999 .....Lonesome Glory (11)
2000 .....All Gong (6)
2001 .....Pompeyo (7)

SPRINTER

1971 .....Ack Ack (5)
1972 .....Chou Croute (4)
1973 .....Shecky Greene (3)
1974 .....Forego (4)
1975 .....Gallant Bob (3)
1976 .....My Juliet (4)
1977 .....What a Summer (4)
1978 .....Dr. Patches (4)
       J.O. Tobin (4)
1979 .....Star de Naskra (4)
1980 .....Plugged Nickel (3)
1981 .....Guilty Conscience (5)
1982 .....Gold Beauty (3)
1983 .....Chinook Pass (4)
1984 .....Eillo (4)
1985 .....Precisionist (4)
1986 .....Smile (4)
1987 .....Groovy (4)
1988 .....Gulch (4)
1989 .....Safely Kept (3)
1990 .....Housebuster (3)
1991 .....Housebuster (4)
1992 .....Rubiano (5)
1993 .....Cardmania (7)
1994 .....Cherokee Run (4)
1995 .....Not Surprising (5)
1996 .....Lit de Justice (6)
1997 .....Smoke Glacken (3)
1998 .....Reraise (3)
1999 .....Artax (4)
2000 .....Kone Gold (6)
2001 .....Squirtle Squirt (3)

OUTSTANDING OWNER

1971 .....Mr. & Mrs. E. E. Fogleson
1974 .....Dan Lasater
1975 .....Dan Lasater
1976 .....Dan Lasater
1977 .....Maxwell Gluck
1978 .....Harbor View Farm
1979 .....Harbor View Farm
1980 .....Mr. & Mrs. Bertram
1981 .....Dotsam Stable
1982 .....Viola Sommer
1983 .....John Franks
1984 .....John Franks
1985 .....Mr. & Mrs. Eugene Klein
1986 .....Mr. & Mrs. Eugene Klein
1987 .....Mr. & Mrs. Eugene Klein
1988 .....Ogden Phipps
1989 .....Ogden Phipps
1990 .....Frances Genter
1991 .....Sam-Son Farm
1992 .....Juddmonte Farms
1993 .....John Franks
1994 .....John Franks
1995 .....Allen E. Paulson
1996 .....Allen E. Paulson
1997 .....Carolyn Hine
1998 .....Frank Stronach
1999 .....Frank Stronach
2000 .....Frank Stronach
2001 .....Richard Englander

Note: Number in parentheses is horse's age.

Eclipse Award Winners (Cont.)

OUTSTANDING TRAINER	OUTSTANDING JOCKEY	OUTSTANDING APPRENTICE JOCKEY
1971.....Charlie Whittingham	1971.....Laffit Pincay Jr.	1971.....Gene St. Leon
1972.....Lucien Laurin	1972.....Braulio Baeza	1972.....Thomas Wallis
1973.....H. Allen Jerkens	1973.....Laffit Pincay Jr	1973.....Steve Valdez
1974.....Sherrill Ward	1974.....Laffit Pincay Jr	1974.....Chris McCarron
1975.....Steve DiMauro	1975.....Braulio Baeza	1975.....Jimmy Edwards
1976.....Lazaro Barrera	1976.....Sandy Hawley	1976.....George Martens
1977.....Lazaro Barrera	1977.....Steve Cauthen	1977.....Steve Cauthen
1978.....Lazaro Barrera	1978.....Darrel McHargue	1978.....Ron Franklin
1979.....Lazaro Barrera	1979.....Laffit Pincay Jr.	1979.....Cash Asmussen
1980.....Bud Delp	1980.....Chris McCarron	1980.....Frank Lovato Jr.
1981.....Ron McAnally	1981.....Bill Shoemaker	1981.....Richard Migliore
1982.....Charlie Whittingham	1982.....Angel Cordero Jr	1982.....Alberto Delgado
1983.....Woody Stephens	1983.....Angel Cordero Jr	1983.....Declan Murphy
1984.....Jack Van Berg	1984.....Pat Day	1984.....Wesley Ward
1985.....D. Wayne Lukas	1985.....Laffit Pincay Jr	1985.....Art Madrid Jr.
1986.....D. Wayne Lukas	1986.....Pat Day	1986.....Allen Stacy
1987.....D. Wayne Lukas	1987.....Pat Day	1987.....Kent Desormeaux
1988.....Claude R. McGaughey III	1988.....Jose Santos	1988.....Steve Capanas
1989.....Charlie Whittingham	1989.....Kent Desormeaux	1989.....Michael Luzzi
1990.....Carl Nafzger	1990.....Craig Perret	1990.....Mark Johnston
1991.....Ron McAnally	1991.....Pat Day	1991.....Mickey Walls
1992.....Ron McAnally	1992.....Kent Desormeaux	1992.....Jesus A. Bracho
1993.....Bobby Frankel	1993.....Mike Smith	1993.....Juan Umana
1994.....D. Wayne Lukas	1994.....Mike Smith	1994.....Dale Beckner
1995.....William Mott	1995.....Jerry Bailey	1995.....Ramon Perez
1996.....William Mott	1996.....Jerry Bailey	1996.....Neil Pozansky
1997.....Bob Baffert	1997.....Jerry Bailey	1997.....Phil Teator
1998.....Bob Baffert	1998.....Gary Stevens	Roberto Rosado
1999.....Bob Baffert	1999.....Jorge Chavez	1998.....Shaun Bridgmohan
2000.....Robert Frankel	2000.....Jerry Bailey	1999.....Ariel Smith
2001.....Robert Frankel	2001.....Jerry Bailey	2000.....Tyler Baze
		2001.....Jeremy Rose

Russian Bare

For two centuries the world has been clamoring for a tale about a naked Russian woman and an amorous horse that doesn't involve Catherine the Great. Well, thanks to WTA star Anastasia Myskina, we've finally got one. The 21-year-old appeared in the October 2002 issue of *GQ* lying atop a very happy-looking horse name Norman and wearing nothing but herskina. As *GQ*'s heavy-breathing editor's letter described it, Norman was a little too excited about the Muscovite's climbing aboard: the shoot couldn't commence until he calmed down.

Eclipse Award Winners (Cont.)

OUTSTANDING BREEDER

1974.....John W. Galbreath
1975.....Fred W. Hooper
1976.....Nelson Bunker Hunt
1977.....Edward Plunket Taylor
1978.....Harbor View Farm
1979.....Claiborne Farm
1980.....Mrs. Henry D. Paxson
1981.....Golden Chance Farm
1982.....Fred W. Hooper
1983.....Edward Plunket Taylor
1984.....Claiborne Farm
1985.....Nelson Bunker Hunt
1986.....Paul Mellon
1987.....Nelson Bunker Hunt
1988.....Ogden Phipps
1989.....North Ridge Farm
1990.....Calumet Farm
1991.....John and Betty Mabee
1992.....William S. Farish III
1993.....Allen Paulson
1994.....William T. Young

OUTSTANDING BREEDER (Cont.)

1995.....Juddmonte Farms
1996.....Fansworth Farms
1997.....Golden Eagle Farm
1998.....John and Betty Mabee
1999.....William Farish/Partners
2000.....Frank Stronach/Adena Springs
2001.....Juddmonte Farms

AWARD OF MERIT

1976.....Jack J. Dreyfus
1977.....Steve Cauthen
1978.....Ogden Phipps
1979.....Frank E. Kilroe
1980.....John D. Schapiro
1981.....Bill Shoemaker
1984.....John Gaines
1985.....Keene Daingerfield
1986.....Herman Cohen
1987.....J. B. Faulconer
1988.....John Forsythe
1989.....Michael P. Sandler

AWARD OF MERIT (Cont.)

1991.....Fred W. Hooper
1994.....Alfred G. Vanderbilt
1996.....Allen E. Paulson

SPECIAL AWARD

1971.....Robert J. Kleberg
1974.....Charles Hatton
1976.....Bill Shoemaker
1980.....John T. Landry
       Pierre E. Bellocq (Peb)
1984.....C. V. Whitney
1985.....Arlington Park
1987.....Anheuser-Busch
1988.....Edward J. DeBartolo Sr.
1989.....Richard Duchossois
1994.....John Longden
       Edward Arcaro
1998.....Oak Tree Racing Association

Note: Special Award and Award of Merit, for long-term and/or outstanding service to the industry, not presented annually.

Horse Racing Books

In real life Seabiscuit had no prominent offspring. In the publishing world, however, Seabiscuit, Laura Hillenbrand's surprise bestseller about the charismatic thoroughbred who captured a nation's imagination during the Depression, has sired a slew of horse racing books. At least half a dozen works about horses were due in 2002, including: Jim Squires's Horse of a Different Color, about how the author trained the lightly regarded Monarchos into a Kentucky Derby winnner; Nan Mooney's My Racing Heart, a memoir based on the writer's relationship with her grandmother, a passionate horse fan; and Jason Lebin's From the Desert to the Derby, a detailed look at the thoroughbred racing empire of Sheikh Mohammed bin Rashid al Maktoum, the crown prince of Dubai.

Like Seabiscuit, these books focus on the colorful people who populate the sport. "Readers are looking for larger-than-life characters who show both the glamour and the underbelly of the horse racing world," says Leigh Habber, an executive editor at Hyperion and the editor of Elizabeth Mitchell's Three Strides Before the Wire: The Dark and Beautiful World of Horse Racing. Credit Hillenbrand for also proving that as a central character, a horse can have as much gravity as a human protagonist. "Horse racing had seemed like such an untouchable, intimidating sport," said Harper Collins's Kelli Martin, who edited Mooney's Heart. "But like Hillenbrand, these authors are treating horses like personal subjects. All these stories are really raw and really personal."

Breeders' Cup

Location: Hollywood Park 1984, '87, '97; Aqueduct Racetrack 1985; Santa Anita Park 1986, '93; Churchill Downs 1988, '91, '98,'00; Gulfstream Park (FL) 1989, '92, '99; Belmont Park 1990, '95, '01; Woodbine (Toronto) 1996.

Juveniles

Year	Winner (Margin)	Jockey	Second	Third	Time
1984	Chief's Crown (¾)	Don MacBeth	Tank's Prospect	Spend a Buck	1:36⅕
1985	Tasso (Nose)	Laffit Pincay Jr.	Storm Cat	Scat Dancer	1:36⅕
1986	Capote (1¼)	Laffit Pincay Jr.	Qualify	Alysheba	1:43⅘
1987	Success Express (1¾)	Jose Santos	Regal Classic	Tejano	1:35⅕
1988	Is It True (1¼)	Laffit Pincay Jr.	Easy Goer	Tagel	1:46⅗
1989	Rhythm (2)	Craig Perret	Grand Canyon	Slavic	1:43⅗
1990	Fly So Free (3)	Jose Santos	Take Me Out	Lost Mountain	1:43⅖
1991	Arazi (4¾)	Pat Valenzuela	Bertrando	Snappy Landing	1:44⅗
1992	Gilded Time (¾)	Chris McCarron	It'sali'lknownfact	River Special	1:43⅖
1993	Brocco (5)	Gary Stevens	Blumin Affair	Tabasco Cat	1:42⅘
1994	Timber Country (½)	Pat Day	Eltish	Tejano Run	1:44⅖
1995	Unbridled's Song (Neck)	Mike Smith	Hennessy	Editor's Note	1:41⅗
1996	Boston Harbor (Neck)	Jerry Bailey	Acceptable	Ordway	1:43⅖
1997	Favorite Trick (5½)	Pat Day	Dawson's Legacy	Nationalore	1:41⅗
1998	Answer Lively (Head)	Jerry Bailey	Aly's Alley	Cat Thief	1:44
1999	Anees (2½)	Gary Stevens	Chief Seattle	High Yield	1:42.29
2000	Macho Uno (Nose)	Jerry Bailey	Point Given	Street Cry	1:42.05
2001	Johannesburg (1¼)	Michael Kinane	Repent	Siphonic	1:42.27

Note: One mile (1984–85, '87), 1$\frac{1}{16}$ miles (1986 and since 1988).

Juvenile Fillies

Year	Winner (Margin)	Jockey	Second	Third	Time
1984	Outstandingly*	Walter Guerra	Dusty Heart	Fine Spirit	1:37⅘
1985	Twilight Ridge (1)	Jorge Velasquez	Family Style	Steal a Kiss	1:35⅘
1986	Brave Raj (5½)	Pat Valenzuela	Tappiano	Saros Brig	1:43⅕
1987	Epitome (Nose)	Pat Day	Jeanne Jones	Dream Team	1:36⅖
1988	Open Mind (1¾)	Angel Cordero Jr.	Darby Shuffle	Lea Lucinda	1:46⅗
1989	Go for Wand (2¾)	Randy Romero	Sweet Roberta	Stella Madrid	1:44⅕
1990	Meadow Star (5)	Jose Santos	Private Treasure	Dance Smartly	1:44
1991	Pleasant Stage (Neck)	Eddie Delahoussaye	La Spia	Cadillac Women	1:46⅖
1992	Eliza (1½)	Pat Valenzuela	Educated Risk	Boots 'n Jackie	1:42⅘
1993	Phone Chatter (Head)	Laffit Pincay	Sardula	Heavenly Prize	1:43
1994	Flanders (Head)	Pat Day	Serena's Song	Stormy Blues	1:45⅕
1995	My Flag (½)	Jerry Bailey	Cara Rafaela	Golden Attraction	1:42⅖
1996	Storm Song (4½)	Craig Perret	Love That Jazz	Critical Factor	1:43⅗
1997	Countess Diana (8½)	Shane Sellers	Career Collection	Primaly	1:42⅕
1998	Silverbulletday (½)	Gary Stevens	Excellent Meeting	Three Ring	1:43⅗
1999	Cash Run (1¼)	Jerry Bailey	Chilukki	Surfside	1:43.31
2000	Caressing (½)	John Velazquez	Platinum Tiara	Shes a Devil Due	1:42.72
2001	Tempera (1½)	David Flores	Imperial Gesture	Bella Bellucci	1:41.49

*In 1984, winner Fran's Valentine was disqualified for interference in the stretch and placed 10th.
Note: One mile (1984–85, '87), 1$\frac{1}{16}$ miles (1986 and since 1988).

Sprint

Year	Winner (Margin)	Jockey	Second	Third	Time
1984	Eillo (Nose)	Craig Perret	Commemorate	Fighting Fit	1:10⅕
1985	Precisionist (¾)	Chris McCarron	Smile	Mt. Livermore	1:08⅖
1986	Smile (1¼)	Jacinto Vasquez	Pine Tree Lane	Bedside Promise	1:08⅖
1987	Very Subtle (4)	Pat Valenzuela	Groovy	Exclusive Enough	1:08⅘
1988	Gulch (¾)	Angel Cordero Jr	Play the King	Afleet	1:10⅖
1989	Dancing Spree (Neck)	Angel Cordero Jr	Safely Kept	Dispersal	1:09
1990	Safely Kept (Neck)	Craig Perret	Dayjur	Black Tie Affair	1:09⅗
1991	Sheikh Albadou (Neck)	Pat Eddery	Pleasant Tap	Robyn Dancer	1:09⅕
1992	Thirty Slews (Neck)	Eddie Delahoussaye	Meafara	Rubiano	1:08⅕
1993	Cardmania (Neck)	Eddie Delahoussaye	Meafara	Gilded Time	1:08⅗
1994	Cherokee Run (Head)	Mike Smith	Soviet Problem	Cardmania	1:09⅖
1995	Desert Stormer (Neck)	Kent Desormeaux	Mr. Greeley	Lit de Justice	1:09
1996	Lit de Justice (1¼)	Corey Nakatani	Paying Dues	Honour and Glory	1:08⅗
1997	Elmhurst (½)	Corey Nakatani	Hesabull	Bet on Sunshine	1:08
1998	Reraise (2)	Corey Nakatani	Grand Slam	Kona Gold	1:09
1999	Artax (½)	Jorge Chavez	Kona Gold	Big Jag	1:07.89
2000	Kona Gold (½)	Alex Solis	Honest Lady	Bet on Sunshine	1:07.77
2001	Squirtle Squirt (½)	Jerry Bailey	Xtra Heat	Caller One	1:08.41

Note: Six furlongs (since 1984).

Breeders' Cup (Cont.)

Mile

Year	Winner (Margin)	Jockey	Second	Third	Time
1984	Royal Heroine (1½)	Fernando Toro	Star Choice	Cozzene	1:32⅗
1985	Cozzene (2¼)	Walter Guerra	Al Mamoon*	Shadeed	1:35
1986	Last Tycoon (Head)	Yves St-Martin	Palace Music	Fred Astaire	1:35⅕
1987	Miesque (3½)	Freddie Head	Show Dancer	Sonic Lady	1:32⅘
1988	Miesque (4)	Freddie Head	Steinlen	Simply Majestic	1:38⅗
1989	Steinlen (¾)	Jose Santos	Sabona	Most Welcome	1:37⅕
1990	Royal Academy (Neck)	Lester Piggott	Itsallgreektome	Priolo	1:35⅕
1991	Opening Verse (2¼)	Pat Valenzuela	Val de Bois	Star of Cozzene	1:37⅖
1992	Lure (3)	Mike Smith	Paradise Creek	Brief Truce	1:32⅘
1993	Lure (2¼)	Mike Smith	Ski Paradise	Fourstars Allstar	1:33⅖
1994	Barathea (Head)	Frankie Dettori	Johann Quatz	Unfinished Symph	1:34⅖
1995	Ridgewood Pearl (2)	John Murtagh	Fastness	Sayyedati	1:43⅗
1996	Da Hoss (1½)	Gary Stevens	Spinning World	Same Old Wish	1:35⅘
1997	Spinning World (2)	Cash Asmussen	Geri	Decorated Hero	1:32⅘
1998	Da Hoss (Head)	John Velazquez	Hawksley Hill	Labeeb	1:35⅕
1999	Silic (Neck)	Corey Nakatani	Tuzla	Docksider	1:34.26
2000	War Chant (Neck)	Gary Stevens	North East Bound	Dansili	1:34.67
2001	Val Royal (1¾)	Jose Valdivia	Forbidden Apple	Bach	1:32.05

*2nd place finisher Palace Music was disqualified for interference and placed 9th.

Distaff

Year	Winner (Margin)	Jockey	Second	Third	Time
1984	Princess Rooney (7)	Eddie Delahoussaye	Life's Magic	Adored	2:02⅖
1985	Life's Magic (6¼)	Angel Cordero Jr.	Lady's Secret	Dontstop Themusic	2:02
1986	Lady's Secret (2½)	Pat Day	Fran's Valentine	Outstandingly	2:01⅕
1987	Sacahuista (2¼)	Randy Romero	Clabber Girl	Oueee Bebe	2:02⅘
1988	Personal Ensign (Nose)	Randy Romero	Winning Colors	Goodbye Halo	1:52
1989	Bayakoa (1½)	Laffit Pincay Jr.	Gorgeous	Open Mind	1:47⅖
1990	Bayakoa (6¾)	Laffit Pincay Jr.	Colonial Waters	Valay Maid	1:49⅕
1991	Dance Smarty (½)	Pat Day	Versailles Treaty	Brought to Mind	1:50⅘
1992	Paseana (4)	Chris McCarron	Versailles Treaty	Magical Maiden	1:48
1993	Hollywood Wildcat (Nose)	Eddie Delahoussaye	Paseana	Re Toss	1:48⅕
1994	One Dreamer (Neck)	Gary Stevens	Heavenly Prize	Miss Dominique	1:50⅗
1995	Inside Information (13½)	Mike Smith	Heavenly Prize	Lakeway	1:46
1996	Jewel Princess (1½)	Corey Nakatani	Serena's Song	Different	1:48⅖
1997	Ajina (2)	Mike Smith	Sharp Cat	Escena	1:47⅕
1998	Escena (Nose)	Gary Stevens	Banshee Breeze	Keeper Hill	1:49⅘
1999	Beautiful Pleasure (¾)	Jorge Chavez	Banshee Breeze	Heritage of Gold	1:47.56
2000	Spain (1½)	Victor Espinoza	Surfside	Heritage of Gold	1:47.66
2001	Unbridled Elaine (head)	Pat Day	Spain	Too Item Limit	1:49.21

Note: 1¼ miles (1984–87), 1⅛ miles (since 1988).

Turf

Year	Winner (Margin)	Jockey	Second	Third	Time
1984	Lashkari (Neck)	Yves St. Martin	All Along	Raami	2:25⅕
1985	Pebbles (Neck)	Pat Eddery	Strawberry Rd II	Mourjane	2:27
1986	Manila (Neck)	Jose Santos	Theatrical	Estrapade	2:25⅖
1987	Theatrical (½)	Pat Day	Trempolino	Village Star II	2:24⅖
1988	Great Communicator (½)	Ray Sibille	Sunshine Forever	Indian Skimmer	2:35⅕
1989	Prized (Head)	Eddie Delahoussaye	Sierra Roberta	Star Lift	2:28
1990	In the Wings (½)	Gary Stevens	With Approval	El Senor	2:29⅗
1991	Miss Alleged (2)	Eric Legrix	Itsallgreektome	Quest for Fame	2:30⅘
1992	Fraise (Nose)	Pat Valenzuela	Sky Classic	Quest For Fame	2:24
1993	Kotashaan (½)	Kent Desormeaux	Bien Bien	Luazar	2:25
1994	Tikkanen (1½)	Mike Smith	Hatoof	Paradise Creek	2:26⅖
1995	Northern Spur (Neck)	Chris McCarron	Freedom Cry	Carnegie	2:42
1996	Pilsudski (1¼)	Walter Swinburn	Singspiel	Swain	2:30⅕
1997	Chief Bearhart (¾)	Jose Santos	Borgia	Flag Down	2:23⅘
1998	Buck's Boy (1¼)	Shane Sellers	Yagli	Dushyantor	2:28⅗
1999	Daylami (2½)	Frankie Dettori	Royal Anthem	Buck's Boy	2:24.73
2000	Kalanisi (½)	John Murtagh	Quiet Resolve	John's Call	2:26.96
2001	Fantastic Light (¾)	Frankie Dettori	Milan	Timboroa	2:24.36

Note: 1½ miles.

Breeders' Cup *(Cont.)*

Classic

Year	Winner (Margin)	Jockey	Second	Third	Time
1984	Wild Again (Head)	Pat Day	Slew o' Gold*	Gate Dancer	2:03⅖
1985	Proud Truth (Head)	Jorge Velasquez	Gate Dancer	Turkoman	2:00⅘
1986	Skywalker (1¼)	Laffit Pincay Jr.	Turkoman	Precisionist	2:00⅖
1987	Ferdinand (Nose)	Bill Shoemaker	Alysheba	Judge Angelucci	2:01⅖
1988	Alysheba (Nose)	Chris McCarron	Seeking the Gold	Waquoit	2:04⅘
1989	Sunday Silence (½)	Chris McCarron	Easy Goer	Blushing John	2:00⅕
1990	Unbridled (1)	Pat Day	Ibn Bey	Thirty Six Red	2:02⅕
1991	Black Tie Affair (1¼)	Jerry Bailey	Twilight Agenda	Unbridled	2:02⅘
1992	A.P. Indy (2)	Eddie Delahoussaye	Pleasant Tap	Jolypha	2:00⅕
1993	Arcangues (2)	Jerry Bailey	Bertrando	Kissin Kris	2:00⅘
1994	Concern (Neck)	Jerry Bailey	Tabasco Cat	Dramatic Gold	2:02⅖
1995	Cigar (2½)	Jerry Bailey	L'Carriere	Unaccounted For	1:59⅖
1996	Alphabet Soup (Nose)	Chris McCarron	Louis Quatorze	Cigar	2:01
1997	Skip Away (6)	Mike Smith	Deputy Commander	Dowty	1:59⅕
1998	Awesome Again (¾)	Pat Day	Silver Charm	Swain	2:02
1999	Cat Thief (1¼)	Pat Day	Budroyale	Golden Missile	1:59.52
2000	Tiznow (Neck)	Chris McCarron	Giant's Causeway	Captain Steve	2:00.75
2001	Tiznow (Nose)	Chris McCarron	Sakhee	Albert the Great	2:00.62

*2nd place finisher Gate Dancer was disqualified for interference and placed 3rd.

Note: 1¼ miles.

England's Triple Crown Winners

England's Triple Crown consists of the Two Thousand Guineas, held at Newmarket; the Epsom Derby, held at Epsom Downs; and the St. Leger Stakes, held at Doncaster.

Year	Horse	Owner
1853	West Australian	Mr. Bowes
1865	Gladiateur	F. DeLagrange
1866	Lord Lyon	R. Sutton
1886	*Ormonde	Duke of Westminster
1891	Common	†F. Johnstone
1893	Isinglass	H. McCalmont
1897	Galtee More	J. Gubbins
1899	Flying Fox	Duke of Westminster
1900	Diamond Jubilee	Prince of Wales
1903	*Rock Sand	J. Miller
1915	Pommern	S. Joel
1917	Gay Crusader	Mr. Fairie
1918	Gainsborough	Lady James Douglas
1935	*Bahram	Aga Khan
1970	‡Nijinsky II	C. W. Engelhard

*Imported into United States. †Raced in name of Lord Alington in Two Thousand Guineas. ‡Canadian-bred.

THEY SAID IT

D. Wayne Lukas, trainer of Kentucky Derby runner-up Proud Citizen, on Bob Baffert's Derby and Preakness winner War Emblem: "Never in my life has a horse been given to me, ready-made, just sitting on a win like that."

Annual Leaders

Horse—Money Won

Year	Horse	Age	Starts	1st	2nd	3rd	Winnings ($)
1919	Sir Barton	3	13	8	3	2	88,250
1920	Man o' War	3	11	11	0	0	166,140
1921	Morvich	2	11	11	0	0	115,234
1922	Pillory	3	7	4	1	1	95,654
1923	Zev	3	14	12	1	0	272,008
1924	Sarzen	3	12	8	1	1	95,640
1925	Pompey	2	10	7	2	0	121,630
1926	Crusader	3	15	9	4	0	166,033
1927	Anita Peabody	2	7	6	0	1	111,905
1928	High Strung	2	6	5	0	0	153,590
1929	Blue Larkspur	3	6	4	1	0	153,450
1930	Gallant Fox	3	10	9	1	0	308,275
1931	Gallant Flight	2	7	7	0	0	219,000
1932	Gusto	3	16	4	3	2	145,940
1933	Singing Wood	2	9	3	2	2	88,050
1934	Cavalcade	3	7	6	1	0	111,235
1935	Omaha	3	9	6	1	2	142,255
1936	Granville	3	11	7	3	0	110,295
1937	Seabiscuit	4	15	11	2	2	168,580
1938	Stagehand	3	15	8	2	3	189,710
1939	Challedon	3	15	9	2	3	184,535
1940	Bimelech	3	7	4	2	1	110,005
1941	Whirlaway	3	20	13	5	2	272,386
1942	Shut Out	3	12	8	2	0	238,872
1943	Count Fleet	3	6	6	0	0	174,055
1944	Pavot	2	8	8	0	0	179,040
1945	Busher	3	13	10	2	1	273,735
1946	Assault	3	15	8	2	3	424,195
1947	Armed	6	17	11	4	1	376,325
1948	Citation	3	20	19	1	0	709,470
1949	Ponder	3	21	9	5	2	321,825
1950	Noor	5	12	7	4	1	346,940
1951	Counterpoint	3	15	7	2	1	250,525
1952	Crafty Admiral	4	16	9	4	1	277,225
1953	Native Dancer	3	10	9	1	0	513,425
1954	Determine	3	15	10	3	2	328,700
1955	Nashua	3	12	10	1	1	752,550
1956	Needles	3	8	4	2	0	440,850
1957	Round Table	3	22	15	1	3	600,383
1958	Round Table	4	20	14	4	0	662,780
1959	Sword Dancer	3	13	8	4	0	537,004
1960	Bally Ache	3	15	10	3	1	445,045
1961	Carry Back	3	16	9	1	3	565,349
1962	Never Bend	2	10	7	1	2	402,969
1963	Candy Spots	3	12	7	2	1	604,481
1964	Gun Bow	4	16	8	4	2	580,100
1965	Buckpasser	2	11	9	1	0	568,096
1966	Buckpasser	3	14	13	1	0	669,078
1967	Damascus	3	16	12	3	1	817,941
1968	Forward Pass	3	13	7	2	0	546,674
1969	Arts and Letters	3	14	8	5	1	555,604
1970	Personality	3	18	8	2	1	444,049
1971	Riva Ridge	2	9	7	0	0	503,263
1972	Droll Role	4	19	7	3	4	471,633
1973	Secretariat	3	12	9	2	1	860,404
1974	Chris Evert	3	8	5	1	2	551,063
1975	Foolish Pleasure	3	11	5	4	1	716,278
1976	Forego	6	8	6	1	1	401,701
1977	Seattle Slew	3	7	6	0	1	641,370
1978	Affirmed	3	11	8	2	0	901,541
1979	Spectacular Bid	3	12	10	1	1	1,279,334
1980	Temperence Hill	3	17	8	3	1	1,130,452
1981	John Henry	6	10	8	0	0	1,798,030
1982	Perrault	5	8	4	1	2	1,197,400
1983	All Along	4	7	4	1	1	2,138,963

Horse—Money Won (Cont.)

Year	Horse	Age	Starts	1st	2nd	3rd	Winnings ($)
1984	Slew o'Gold	4	6	5	1	0	2,627,944
1985	Spend A Buck	3	7	5	1	1	3,552,704
1986	Snow Chief	3	9	6	1	1	1,875,200
1987	Alysheba	3	10	3	3	1	2,511,156
1988	Alysheba	4	9	7	1	0	3,808,600
1989	Sunday Silence	3	9	7	2	0	4,578,454
1990	Unbridled	3	11	4	3	2	3,718,149
1991	Dance Smartly	3	8	8	0	0	2,876,821
1992	A.P. Indy	3	7	5	0	1	2,622,560
1993	Kotashaan	3	10	6	3	0	2,619,014
1994	Paradise Creek	5	11	8	2	1	2,610,187
1995	Cigar	5	10	10	0	0	4,819,800
1996	Cigar	6	8	5	2	1	4,910,000
1997	Skip Away	4	11	4	5	2	4,089,000
1998	Silver Charm	4	9	6	2	0	4,696,506
1999	Almutawakel	4	4	1	1	1	3,290,000
2000	Dubai Millennium	4	1	1	0	0	3,600,000
2001	Captain Steve	4	6	2	1	1	4,201,200

Trainer—Money Won

Year	Trainer	Wins	Winnings ($)	Year	Trainer	Wins	Winnings ($)
1908	James Rowe, Sr.	50	284,335	1956	Willie Molter	142	1,227,402
1909	Sam Hildreth	73	123,942	1957	Jimmy Jones	70	1,150,910
1910	Sam Hildreth	84	148,010	1958	Willie Molter	69	1,116,544
1911	Sam Hildreth	67	49,418	1959	Willie Molter	71	847,290
1912	John F. Schorr	63	58,110	1960	Hirsch Jacobs	97	748,349
1913	James Rowe, Sr.	18	45,936	1961	Jimmy Jones	62	759,856
1914	R. C. Benson	45	59,315	1962	Mesh Tenney	58	1,099,474
1915	James Rowe, Sr.	19	75,596	1963	Mesh Tenney	40	860,703
1916	Sam Hildreth	39	70,950	1964	Bill Winfrey	61	1,350,534
1917	Sam Hildreth	23	61,698	1965	Hirsch Jacobs	91	1,331,628
1918	H. Guy Bedwell	53	80,296	1966	Eddie Neloy	93	2,456,250
1919	H. Guy Bedwell	63	208,728	1967	Eddie Neloy	72	1,776,089
1920	L. Feustal	22	186,087	1968	Eddie Neloy	52	1,233,101
1921	Sam Hildreth	85	262,768	1969	Elliott Burch	26	1,067,936
1922	Sam Hildreth	74	247,014	1970	Charlie Whittingham	82	1,302,354
1923	Sam Hildreth	75	392,124	1971	Charlie Whittingham	77	1,737,115
1924	Sam Hildreth	77	255,608	1972	Charlie Whittingham	79	1,734,020
1925	G. R. Tompkins	30	199,245	1973	Charlie Whittingham	85	1,865,385
1926	Scott P. Harlan	21	205,681	1974	Pancho Martin	166	2,408,419
1927	W. H. Bringloe	63	216,563	1975	Charlie Whittingham	93	2,437,244
1928	John F. Schorr	65	258,425	1976	Jack Van Berg	496	2,976,196
1929	James Rowe, Jr.	25	314,881	1977	Laz Barrera	127	2,715,848
1930	Sunny Jim Fitzsimmons	47	397,355	1978	Laz Barrera	100	3,307,164
1931	Big Jim Healey	33	297,300	1979	Laz Barrera	98	3,608,517
1932	Sunny Jim Fitzsimmons	68	266,650	1980	Laz Barrera	99	2,969,151
1933	Humming Bob Smith	53	135,720	1981	Charlie Whittingham	74	3,993,300
1934	Humming Bob Smith	43	249,938	1982	Charlie Whittingham	63	4,587,457
1935	Bud Stotler	87	303,005	1983	D. Wayne Lukas	78	4,267,261
1936	Sunny Jim Fitzsimmons	42	193,415	1984	D. Wayne Lukas	131	5,835,921
1937	Robert McGarvey	46	209,925	1985	D. Wayne Lukas	218	11,155,188
1938	Earl Sande	15	226,495	1986	D. Wayne Lukas	259	12,345,180
1939	Sunny Jim Fitzsimmons	45	266,205	1987	D. Wayne Lukas	343	17,502,110
1940	Silent Tom Smith	14	269,200	1988	D. Wayne Lukas	318	17,842,358
1941	Plain Ben Jones	70	475,318	1989	D. Wayne Lukas	305	16,103,998
1942	John M. Gaver Sr.	48	406,547	1990	D. Wayne Lukas	267	14,508,871
1943	Plain Ben Jones	73	267,915	1991	D. Wayne Lukas	289	15,942,223
1944	Plain Ben Jones	60	601,660	1992	D. Wayne Lukas	230	9,806,436
1945	Silent Tom Smith	52	510,655	1993	Robert Frankel	79	8,883,252
1946	Hirsch Jacobs	99	560,077	1994	D. Wayne Lukas	147	9,247,457
1947	Jimmy Jones	85	1,334,805	1995	D. Wayne Lukas	194	12,842,865
1948	Jimmy Jones	81	1,118,670	1996	D. Wayne Lukas	192	15,966,344
1949	Jimmy Jones	76	978,587	1997	D. Wayne Lukas	175	10,338,957
1950	Preston Burch	96	637,754	1998	Bob Baffert	139	15,000,870
1951	John M. Gaver Sr.	42	616,392	1999	Bob Baffert	169	16,934,607
1952	Plain Ben Jones	29	662,137	2000	Bob Baffert	146	11,831,605
1953	Harry Trotsek	54	1,028,873	2001	Bob Baffert	138	16,354,996
1954	Willie Molter	136	1,107,860				
1955	Sunny Jim Fitzsimmons	66	1,270,055				

Jockey—Money Won

Year	Jockey	Mts	1st	2nd	3rd	Pct	Winnings ($)
1919	John Loftus	177	65	36	24	.37	252,707
1920	Clarence Kummer	353	87	79	48	.25	292,376
1921	Earl Sande	340	112	69	59	.33	263,043
1922	Albert Johnson	297	43	57	40	.14	345,054
1923	Earl Sande	430	122	89	79	.28	569,394
1924	Ivan Parke	844	205	175	121	.24	290,395
1925	Laverne Fator	315	81	54	44	.26	305,775
1926	Laverne Fator	511	143	90	86	.28	361,435
1927	Earl Sande	179	49	33	19	.27	277,877
1928	Pony McAtee	235	55	43	25	.23	301,295
1929	Mack Garner	274	57	39	33	.21	314,975
1930	Sonny Workman	571	152	88	79	.27	420,438
1931	Charles Kurtsinger	519	93	82	79	.18	392,095
1932	Sonny Workman	378	87	48	55	.23	385,070
1933	Robert Jones	471	63	57	70	.13	226,285
1934	Wayne D. Wright	919	174	154	114	.19	287,185
1935	Silvio Coucci	749	141	125	103	.19	319,760
1936	Wayne D. Wright	670	100	102	73	.15	264,000
1937	Charles Kurtsinger	765	120	94	106	.16	384,202
1938	Nick Wall	658	97	94	82	.15	385,161
1939	Basil James	904	191	165	105	.21	353,333
1940	Eddie Arcaro	783	132	143	112	.17	343,661
1941	Don Meade	1,164	210	185	158	.18	398,627
1942	Eddie Arcaro	687	123	97	89	.18	481,949
1943	John Longden	871	173	140	121	.20	573,276
1944	Ted Atkinson	1,539	287	231	213	.19	899,101
1945	John Longden	778	180	112	100	.23	981,977
1946	Ted Atkinson	1,377	233	213	173	.17	1,036,825
1947	Douglas Dodson	646	141	100	75	.22	1,429,949
1948	Eddie Arcaro	726	188	108	98	.26	1,686,230
1949	Steve Brooks	906	209	172	110	.23	1,316,817
1950	Eddie Arcaro	888	195	153	144	.22	1,410,160
1951	Bill Shoemaker	1,161	257	197	161	.22	1,329,890
1952	Eddie Arcaro	807	188	122	109	.23	1,859,591
1953	Bill Shoemaker	1,683	485	302	210	.29	1,784,187
1954	Bill Shoemaker	1,251	380	221	142	.30	1,876,760
1955	Eddie Arcaro	820	158	126	108	.19	1,864,796
1956	Bill Hartack	1,387	347	252	184	.25	2,343,955
1957	Bill Hartack	1,238	341	208	178	.28	3,060,501
1958	Bill Shoemaker	1,133	300	185	137	.26	2,961,693
1959	Bill Shoemaker	1,285	347	230	159	.27	2,843,133
1960	Bill Shoemaker	1,227	274	196	158	.22	2,123,961
1961	Bill Shoemaker	1,256	304	186	175	.24	2,690,819
1962	Bill Shoemaker	1,126	311	156	128	.28	2,916,844
1963	Bill Shoemaker	1,203	271	193	137	.22	2,526,925
1964	Bill Shoemaker	1,056	246	147	133	.23	2,649,553
1965	Braulio Baeza	1,245	270	200	201	.22	2,582,702
1966	Braulio Baeza	1,341	298	222	190	.22	2,951,022
1967	Braulio Baeza	1,064	256	184	127	.24	3,088,888
1968	Braulio Baeza	1,089	201	184	145	.18	2,835,108
1969	Jorge Velasquez	1,442	258	230	204	.18	2,542,315
1970	Laffit Pincay Jr.	1,328	269	208	187	.20	2,626,526
1971	Laffit Pincay Jr.	1,627	380	288	214	.23	3,784,377
1972	Laffit Pincay Jr.	1,388	289	215	205	.21	3,225,827
1973	Laffit Pincay Jr.	1,444	350	254	209	.24	4,093,492
1974	Laffit Pincay Jr.	1,278	341	227	180	.27	4,251,060
1975	Braulio Baeza	1,190	196	208	180	.16	3,674,398
1976	Angel Cordero Jr.	1,534	274	273	235	.18	4,709,500
1977	Steve Cauthen	2,075	487	345	304	.23	6,151,750
1978	Darrel McHargue	1,762	375	294	263	.21	6,188,353
1979	Laffit Pincay Jr.	1,708	420	302	261	.25	8,183,535
1980	Chris McCarron	1,964	405	318	282	.20	7,666,100
1981	Chris McCarron	1,494	326	251	207	.22	8,397,604
1982	Angel Cordero Jr.	1,838	397	338	227	.22	9,702,520
1983	Angel Cordero Jr.	1,792	362	296	237	.20	10,116,807
1984	Chris McCarron	1,565	356	276	218	.23	12,038,213
1985	Laffit Pincay Jr.	1,409	289	246	183	.21	13,415,049
1986	Jose Santos	1,636	329	237	222	.20	11,329,297
1987	Jose Santos	1,639	305	268	208	.19	12,407,355

Jockey—Money Won (Cont.)

Year	Jockey	Mts	1st	2nd	3rd	Pct	Winnings ($)
1988	Jose Santos	1,867	370	287	265	.20	14,877,298
1989	Jose Santos	1,459	285	238	220	.20	13,847,003
1990	Gary Stevens	1,504	283	245	202	.19	13,881,198
1991	Chris McCarron	1,440	265	228	206	.18	14,441,083
1992	Kent Desormeaux	1,568	361	260	208	.23	14,193,006
1993	Mike Smith	1,510	343	235	214	.23	14,008,148
1994	Mike Smith	1,484	317	250	196	.21	15,979,820
1995	Jerry Bailey	1,265	287	193	144	.23	16,308,230
1996	Jerry Bailey	1,187	298	189	165	.25	19,465,376
1997	Jerry Bailey	1,143	272	186	178	.26	18,260,553
1998	Gary Stevens	869	178	145	122	.20	19,358,840
1999	Pat Day	1,265	254	209	209	.20	18,092,845
2000	Pat Day	1,219	267	206	186	.22	17,479,838
2001	Jerry Bailey	912	227	194	137	.25	22,597,720

Jockey—Races Won

Year	Jockey	Mts	1st	2nd	3rd	Pct
1895	J. Perkins	762	192	177	129	.25
1896	J. Scherrer	1,093	271	227	172	.24
1897	H. Martin	803	173	152	116	.21
1898	T. Burns	973	277	213	149	.28
1899	T. Burns	1,064	273	173	266	.26
1900	C. Mitchell	874	195	140	139	.23
1901	W. O'Connor	1,047	253	221	192	.24
1902	J. Ranch	1,069	276	205	181	.26
1903	G.C. Fuller	918	229	152	122	.25
1904	E. Hildebrand	1,169	297	230	171	.25
1905	D. Nicol	861	221	143	136	.26
1906	W. Miller	1,384	388	300	199	.28
1907	W. Miller	1,194	334	226	170	.28
1908	V. Powers	1,260	324	204	185	.26
1909	V. Powers	704	173	121	114	.25
1910	G. Garner	947	200	188	153	.20
1911	T. Koerner	813	162	133	112	.20
1912	P. Hill	967	168	141	129	.17
1913	M. Buxton	887	146	131	136	.16
1914	J. McTaggart	787	157	132	106	.20
1915	M. Garner	775	151	118	90	.19
1916	F. Robinson	791	178	131	124	.23
1917	W. Crump	803	151	140	101	.19
1918	F. Robinson	864	185	140	108	.21
1919	C. Robinson	896	190	140	126	.21
1920	J. Butwell	721	152	129	139	.21
1921	C. Lang	696	135	110	105	.19
1922	M. Fator	859	188	153	116	.22
1923	I. Parke	718	173	105	95	.24
1924	I. Parke	844	205	175	121	.24
1925	A. Mortensen	987	187	145	138	.19
1926	R. Jones	1,172	190	163	152	.16
1927	L. Hardy	1,130	207	192	151	.18
1928	J. Inzelone	1,052	155	152	135	.15
1929	M. Knight	871	149	132	133	.17
1930	H.R. Riley	861	177	145	123	.21
1931	H. Roble	1,174	173	173	155	.15
1932	J. Gilbert	1,050	212	144	160	.20
1933	J. Westrope	1,224	301	235	166	.25
1934	M. Peters	1,045	221	179	147	.21
1935	C. Stevenson	1,099	206	169	146	.19
1936	B. James	1,106	245	195	161	.22
1937	J. Adams	1,265	260	186	177	.21
1938	J. Longden	1,150	236	168	171	.21
1939	D. Meade	1,284	255	221	180	.20
1940	E. Dew	1,377	287	201	180	.21
1941	D. Meade	1,164	210	185	158	.18
1942	J. Adams	1,120	245	185	150	.22
1943	J. Adams	1,069	228	159	171	.21

Jockey—Races Won (Cont.)

Year	Jockey	Mts	1st	2nd	3rd	Pct
1944	T. Atkinson	1,539	287	231	213	.19
1945	J.D. Jessop	1,085	290	182	168	.27
1946	T. Atkinson	1,377	233	213	173	.17
1947	J. Longden	1,327	316	250	195	.24
1948	J. Longden	1,197	319	233	161	.27
1949	G. Glisson	1,347	270	217	181	.20
1950	W. Shoemaker	1,640	388	266	230	.24
1951	C. Burr	1,319	310	232	192	.24
1952	A. DeSpirito	1,482	390	247	212	.26
1953	W. Shoemaker	1,683	485	302	210	.29
1954	W. Shoemaker	1,251	380	221	142	.30
1955	W. Hartack	1,702	417	298	215	.25
1956	W. Hartack	1,387	347	252	184	.25
1957	W. Hartack	1,238	341	208	178	.28
1958	W. Shoemaker	1,133	300	185	137	.26
1959	W. Shoemaker	1,285	347	230	159	.27
1960	W. Hartack	1,402	307	247	190	.22
1961	J. Sellers	1,394	328	212	227	.24
1962	R. Ferraro	1,755	352	252	226	.20
1963	W. Blum	1,704	360	286	215	.21
1964	W. Blum	1,577	324	274	170	.21
1965	J. Davidson	1,582	319	228	190	.20
1966	A. Gomez	996	318	173	142	.32
1967	J. Velasquez	1,939	438	315	270	.23
1968	A. Cordero Jr.	1,662	345	278	219	.21
1969	L. Snyder	1,645	352	290	243	.21
1970	S. Hawley	1,908	452	313	265	.24
1971	L Pincay Jr.	1,627	380	288	214	.23
1972	S. Hawley	1,381	367	269	200	.27
1973	S. Hawley	1,925	515	336	292	.27
1974	C.J. McCarron	2,199	546	392	297	.25
1975	C.J. McCarron	2,194	458	389	305	.21
1976	S. Hawley	1,637	413	245	201	.25
1977	S. Cauthen	2,075	487	345	304	.23
1978	E. Delahoussaye	1,666	384	285	238	.23
1979	D. Gall	2,146	479	396	326	.22
1980	C.J. McCarron	1,964	405	318	282	.20
1981	D. Gall	1,917	376	305	297	.20
1982	Pat Day	1,870	399	326	255	.21
1983	Pat Day	1,725	454	321	251	.26
1984	Pat Day	1,694	399	296	259	.24
1985	C.W. Antley	2,335	469	371	288	.20
1986	Pat Day	1,417	429	246	202	.30
1987	Kent Desormeaux	2,207	450	370	294	.28
1988	Kent Desormeaux	1,897	474	295	276	.25
1989	Kent Desormeaux	2,312	598	385	309	.25
1990	Pat Day	1,421	364	265	222	.26
1991	Pat Day	1,405	430	256	213	.31
1992	Russell Baze	1,691	433	296	237	.25
1993	Russell Baze	1,579	410	297	225	.26
1994	Russell Baze	1,588	415	301	266	.26
1995	Russell Baze	1,531	445	310	232	.29
1996	Russell Baze	1,482	415	297	200	.28
1997	Edgar S. Prado	2,037	533	384	308	.26
1998	Edgar S. Prado	1,969	470	377	285	.23
1999	Edgar S. Prado	1,902	402	307	276	.21
2000	Ramon Dominguez	1,586	361	293	238	.23
2001	Ramon Dominguez	1,864	431	368	278	.23

Leading Jockeys—Career Records

Jockey	Years Riding	Mts	1st	2nd	3rd	Win Pct	Winnings ($)
Laffit Pincay Jr.	38	47,933	9,421	7,703	6,569	.197	232,475,000
Bill Shoemaker (1990)	42	40,350	8,833	6,136	4,987	.219	123,375,524
Pat Day	30	38,052	8,314	6,462	5,407	.219	267,399,772
Russell Baze	29	37,112	7,932	6,197	5,289	.214	115,827,055
Dave Gall (1999)	41	41,775	7,396	6,525	6,131	.177	24,547,584
Chris McCarron (2002)	28	34,244	7,141	5,670	4,673	.209	264,351,679
Angel Cordero (1992)	31	38,656	7,057	6,136	5,359	.183	164,561,227
Jorge Velasquez (1998)	35	40,852	6,795	6,178	5,755	.166	125,544,379
Sandy Hawley (1998)	31	31,455	6,449	4,825	4,159	.205	88,681,292
Eddie Delahoussaye	32	39,213	6,384	5,676	5,585	.163	195,881,170
Larry Snyder (1994)	35	35,681	6,388	5,030	3,440	.179	47,207,289
Carl Gambardella (1994)	39	39,018	6,349	5,953	5,353	.163	29,389,041
Earlie Fires	38	42,928	6,207	5,291	5,111	.145	78,972,130
John Longden (1966)	40	32,413	6,032	4,914	4,273	.186	24,665,800
Jerry Bailey	29	28,599	5,324	4,150	3,614	.186	235,587,248
Jacinto Vasquez (1998)	38	37,337	5,228	4,714	4,510	.140	82,754,115
Ron Ardoin	30	32,118	5,206	4,305	3,772	.162	58,536,697
Mario Pino	23	31,390	5,005	4,577	4,287	.160	75,950,451
Rodolfo Baez (1999)	26	28,609	4,875	4,291	4,103	.170	30,474,225
Eddie Arcaro (1961)	31	24,092	4,779	3,807	3,302	.198	30,039,543
Rick Wilson	31	23,804	4,775	4,104	3,335	.201	73,335,913
Gary Stevens	28	26,471	4,682	4,201	3,805	.177	205,667,099
Edgar Prado	19	24,036	4,631	3,910	3,399	.193	106,875,114
Don Brumfield (1989)	37	33,223	4,573	4,076	3,758	.138	43,567,861
Anthony Black	26	30,139	4,515	3,913	3,856	.150	47,929,971

Note: Records go through September 18, 2002, and include available statistics for races ridden in foreign countries. Figures in parentheses after jockey's name indicate last year in which he rode.

Leading jockeys courtesy of *National Thoroughbred Racing Association*.

THEY SAID IT

Bob Baffert, trainer of Kentucky Derby and Preakness winner War Emblem, on visiting 1977 Triple Crown winner Seattle Slew: "It felt almost like a sacred visit, like meeting Muhammad Ali, or what it will be like someday to meet Michael Jordan."

HORSES

Ack Ack (1986, 1966)
Affectionately (1989, 1960)
Affirmed (1980, 1975)
All Along (1990, 1979)
Alsab (1976, 1939)
Alydar (1989, 1975)
Alysheba (1993, 1984)
American Eclipse (1970, 1814)
A.P. Indy (2000, 1989)
Armed (1963, 1941)
Artful (1956, 1902)
Arts and Letters (1994, 1966)
Assault (1964, 1943)
Battleship (1969, 1927)
Bayakoa (1998, 1984)
Bed o' Roses (1976, 1947)
Beldame (1956, 1901)
Ben Brush (1955, 1893)
Bewitch (1977, 1945)
Bimelech (1990, 1937)
Black Gold (1989, 1921)
Black Helen (1991, 1932)
Blue Larkspur (1957, 1926)
Bold 'n Determined (1997, 1977)
Bold Ruler (1973, 1954)
Bon Nouvel (1976, 1960)
Boston (1955, 1833)
Broomstick (1956, 1901)
Buckpasser (1970, 1963)
Busher (1964, 1942)
Bushranger (1967, 1930)
Cafe Prince (1985, 1970)
Carry Back (1975, 1958)
Cavalcade (1993, 1931)
Challedon (1977, 1936)
Chris Evert (1988, 1971)
Cicada (1967, 1959)
Cigar (2002, 1990)
Citation (1959, 1945)
Coaltown (1983, 1945)
Colin (1956, 1905)
Commando (1956, 1898)
Count Fleet (1961, 1940)
Crusader (1995, 1923)
Dahlia (1981, 1970)
Damascus (1974, 1964)
Dark Mirage (1974, 1965)
Davona Dale (1985, 1976)
Desert Vixen (1979, 1970)
Devil Diver (1980, 1939)
Discovery (1969, 1931)
Domino (1955, 1891)
Dr. Fager (1971, 1964)
Easy Goer (1997, 1986)
Eight Thirty (1994, 1936)
Elkridge (1966, 1938)

Emperor of Norfolk (1988, 1885)
Equipoise (1957, 1928)
Exceller (1999, 1973)
Exterminator (1957, 1915)
Fairmount (1985, 1921)
Fair Play (1956, 1905)
Fashion (1980, 1837)
Firenze (1981, 1884)
Flatterer (1994, 1979)
Foolish Pleasure (1995, 1972)
Forego (1979, 1970)
Fort Marcy (1998, 1964)
Gallant Bloom (1977, 1966)
Gallant Fox (1957, 1927)
Gallant Man (1987, 1954)
Gallorette (1962, 1942)
Gamely (1980, 1964)
Genuine Risk (1986, 1977)
Go For Wand (1996, 1987)
Good and Plenty (1956, 1900)
Grandville (1997, 1933)
Grey Lag (1957, 1918)
Gun Bow (1999, 1960)
Hamburg (1986, 1895)
Hanover (1955, 1884)
Henry of Navarre (1985, 1891)
Hill Prince (1991, 1947)
Hindoo (1955, 1878)
Holy Bull (2001, 1991)
Imp (1965, 1894)
Jay Trump (1971, 1957)
John Henry (1990, 1975)
Johnstown (1992, 1936)
Jolly Roger (1965, 1922)
Kelso (1967, 1957)
Kentucky (1983, 1861)
Kingston (1955, 1884)
Lady's Secret (1992, 1982)
La Prevoyante (1995, 1970)
L'Escargot (1977, 1963)
Lexington (1955, 1850)
Longfellow (1971, 1867)
Luke Blackburn (1956, 1877)
Majestic Prince (1988, 1966)
Man o' War (1957, 1917)
Maskette (2001, 1908)
Miesque (1999, 1984)
Miss Woodford (1967, 1880)
Myrtlewood (1979, 1932)
Nashua (1965, 1952)
Native Dancer (1963, 1950)
Native Diver (1978, 1959)
Needles (2000, 1953)
Neji (1966, 1950)
Noor (2002, 1945)
Northern Dancer (1976, 1961)

Oedipus (1978, 1946)
Old Rosebud (1968, 1911)
Omaha (1965, 1932)
Pan Zareta (1972, 1910)
Parole (1984, 1873)
Paseana (2001, 1987)
Personal Ensign (1993, 1984)
Peter Pan (1956, 1904)
Princess Doreen (1982, 1921)
Princess Rooney (1991, 1980)
Real Delight (1987, 1949)
Regret (1957, 1912)
Reigh Count (1978, 1923)
Riva Ridge (1998, 1969)
Roamer (1981, 1911)
Roseben (1956, 1901)
Round Table (1972, 1954)
Ruffian (1976, 1972)
Ruthless (1975, 1864)
Salvator (1955, 1886)
Sarazen (1957, 1921)
Seabiscuit (1958, 1933)
Searching (1978, 1952)
Seattle Slew (1981, 1974)
Secretariat (1974, 1970)
Serena's Song (2002, 1992)
Shuvee (1975, 1966)
Silver Spoon (1978, 1956)
Sir Archy (1955, 1805)
Sir Barton (1957, 1916)
Slew o' Gold (1992, 1980)
Spectacular Bid (1982, 1976)
Stymie (1975, 1941)
Sun Beau (1996, 1925)
Sunday Silence (1996, 1986)
Susan's Girl (1976, 1969)
Swaps (1966, 1952)
Sword Dancer (1977, 1956)
Sysonby (1956, 1902)
Ta Wee (1994, 1967)
Ten Broeck (1982, 1872)
Tim Tam (1985, 1955)
Tom Fool (1960, 1949)
Top Flight (1966, 1929)
Tosmah (1984, 1961)
Twenty Grand (1957, 1928)
Twilight Tear (1963, 1941)
Two Lea (1982, 1946)
War Admiral (1958, 1934)
Whirlaway (1959, 1938)
Whisk Broom II (1979, 1907)
Winning Colors (2000, 1985)
Zaccio (1990, 1976)
Zev (1983, 1920)

Note: Years of election and foaling in parentheses.

HARNESS RACING

Hambletonian

Year	Winner	Driver	Year	Winner	Driver
1926	Guy McKinney	Nat Ray	1965	Egyptian Candor	Del Cameron
1927	Iosola's Worthy	Marvin Childs	1966	Kerry Way	Frank Ervin
1928	Spenser	W. H. Leese	1967	Speedy Streak	Del Cameron
1929	Walter Dear	Walter Cox	1968	Nevele Pride	Stanley Dancer
1930	Hanover's Bertha	Tom Berry	1969	Lindy's Pride	H. Beissinger
1931	Calumet Butler	R. D. McMahon	1970	Timothy T.	J. Simpson Jr.
1932	The Marchioness	William Caton	1971	Speedy Crown	H. Beissinger
1933	Mary Reynolds	Ben White	1972	Super Bowl	Stanley Dancer
1934	Lord Jim	Doc Parshall	1973	Flirth	Ralph Baldwin
1935	Greyhound	Sep Palin	1974	Christopher T.	Bill Haughton
1936	Rosalind	Ben White	1975	Bonefish	Stanley Dancer
1937	Shirley Hanover	Henry Thomas	1976	Steve Lobell	Bill Haughton
1938	McLin Hanover	Henry Thomas	1977	Green Speed	Bill Haughton
1939	Peter Astra	Doc Parshall	1978	Speedy Somolli	H. Beissinger
1940	Spencer Scott	Fred Egan	1979	Legend Hanover	George Sholty
1941	Bill Gallon	Lee Smith	1980	Burgomeister	Bill Haughton
1942	The Ambassador	Ben White	1981	Shiaway St. Pat	Ray Remmen
1943	Volo Song	Ben White	1982	Speed Bowl	Tom Haughton
1944	Yankee Maid	Henry Thomas	1983	Duenna	Stanley Dancer
1945	Titan Hanover	H. Pownall Sr.	1984	Historic Freight	Ben Webster
1946	Chestertown	Thomas Berry	1985	Prakas	Bill O'Donnell
1947	Hoot Mon	Sep Palin	1986	Nuclear Kosmos	Ulf Thoresen
1948	Demon Hanover	Harrison Hoyt	1987	Mack Lobell	John Campbell
1949	Miss Tilly	Fred Egan	1988	Armbro Goal	John Campbell
1950	Lusty Song	Del Miller	1989	Park Ave. Joe/Probe*	R. Waples/B. Fahy
1951	Mainliner	Guy Crippen	1990	Harmonious	John Campbell
1952	Sharp Note	Bion Shively	1991	Giant Victory	Jack Moiseyev
1953	Helicopter	Harry Harvey	1992	Alf Palema	Mickey McNichol
1954	Newport Dream	Del Cameron	1993	American Winner	Ron Pierce
1955	Scott Frost	Joe O'Brien	1994	Victory Dream	Michel Lachance
1956	The Intruder	Ned Bower	1995	Tagliabue	John Campbell
1957	Hickory Smoke	J. Simpson Sr.	1996	Continentalvictory	Michel Lachance
1958	Emily's Pride	Flave Nipe	1997	Malabar Man	Mal Burroughs
1959	Diller Hanover	Frank Ervin	1998	Muscles Yankee	John Campbell
1960	Blaze Hanover	Joe O'Brien	1999	Self Possessed	Michel Lachance
1961	Harlan Dean	James Arthur	2000	Yankee Paco	T.J. Ritchie
1962	A. C.'s Viking	Sanders Russell	2001	Scarlet Knight	Stefan Melander
1963	Speedy Scot	Ralph Baldwin	2002	Chip Chip Hooray	Eric Ledford
1964	Ayres	J. Simpson Sr.			

*Park Avenue Joe and Probe dead-heated for win. Park Avenue finished first in the summary 2-1-1 to Probe's 1-9-1 finish.
Note: Run at 1 mile since 1947.

Little Brown Jug

Year	Winner	Driver	Year	Winner	Driver
1946	Ensign Hanover	Wayne Smart	1975	Seatrain	Ben Webster
1947	Forbes Chief	Del Cameron	1976	Keystone Ore	Stanley Dancer
1948	Knight Dream	Frank Safford	1977	Governor Skipper	John Chapman
1949	Good Time	Frank Ervin	1978	Happy Escort	William Popfinger
1950	Dudley Hanover	Del Miller	1979	Hot Hitter	Herve Filion
1951	Tar Heel	Del Cameron	1980	Niatross	Clint Galbraith
1952	Meadow Rice	Wayne Smart	1981	Fan Hanover	Glen Garnsey
1953	Keystoner	Frank Ervin	1982	Merger	John Campbell
1954	Adios Harry	Morris MacDonald	1983	Ralph Hanover	Ron Waples
1955	Quick Chief	Bill Haughton	1984	Colt Fortysix	Chris Boring
1956	Noble Adios	John Simpson Sr.	1985	Nihilator	Bill O'Donnell
1957	Torpid	John Simpso Sr.	1986	Barberry Spur	Bill O'Donnell
1958	Shadow Wave	Joe O'Brien	1987	Jaguar Spur	Dick Stillings
1959	Adios Butler	Clint Hodgins	1988	B. J. Scoot	Michel Lachance
1960	Bullet Hanover	John Simpson Sr.	1989	Goalie Jeff	Michel Lachance
1961	Henry T. Adios	Stanley Dancer	1990	Beach Towel	Ray Remmen
1962	Lehigh Hanover	Stanley Dancer	1991	Precious Bunny	Jack Moiseye
1963	Overtrick	John Patterson	1992	Fake Left	Ron Waples
1964	Vicar Hanover	Bill Haughton	1993	Life Sign	John Campbell
1965	Bret Hanover	Frank Ervin	1994	Magical Mike	Michel Lachance
1966	Romeo Hanover	George Sholty	1995	Nick's Fantasy	John Campbell
1967	Best of All	James Hackett	1996	Armbro Operative	Jack Moiseyev
1968	Rum Customer	Bill Haughton	1997	Western Dreamer	Michel Lachance
1969	Laverne Hanover	Bill Haughton	1998	Shady Character	Ron Pierce
1970	Most Happy Fella	Stanley Dancer	1999	Blissful Hall	Ron Pierce
1971	Nansemond	Herve Filion	2000	Astreos	Chris Christoforou
1972	Strike Out	Keith Waples	2001	Bettor's Delight	Michel Lachance
1973	Melvin's Woe	Joe O'Brien	2002	Million Dollar Cam	Luc Ouellette
1974	Armbro Omaha	Bill Haughton			

Handicapping Honeys

Some people know their studs. The annual media handicapping championship, sponsored by the *Daily Racing Form* and the National Thoroughbred Racing Association, is typically contested by savvy racing journalists and veteran bettors. In January 2002, four five-member teams competed at Las Vegas's MGM Grand for the $10,000 first prize (which went to charity). The winners: Team Penthouse, led by December 2001 Pet of the Month Cheyenne Silver and September 1999 Pet Alexa Lauren. The models, who were invited as a publicity stunt, had no betting experience but nonetheless beat a field of noted horseplayers that included *Daily Racing Form* chairman and publisher Steven Crist. "When the other players first saw me, this blonde girl with big boobs, they were like, 'Are you going to pick the horseys all by yourself?' " recalled Lauren, 27, who won $175.60 in the 30-race event, the fifth-highest individual total. "Then we won, and they were asking me seriously how I did it." The extent of the Pets' preparation was to read *The Female Fan Guide to Thoroughbred Racing* on the plane ride to the contest. "I didn't know much about the event," said Silver, 23, "but anything to do with horses is fun for me."

Breeders' Crown

1984

Div	Winner	Driver
2PC	Dragon's Lair	Jeff Mallet
2PF	Amneris	John Campbell
3PC	Troublemaker	Bill O'Donnell
3PF	Naughty But Nice	Tommy Haughton
2TC	Workaholic	Berndt Lindstedt
2TF	Conifer	George Sholty
3TC	Baltic Speed	Jan Nordin
3TF	Fancy Crown	Bill O'Donnell

1985

Div	Winner	Driver
2PC	Robust Hanover	John Campbell
2PF	Caressable	Herve Filion
3PC	Nihilator	Bill O'Donnell
3PF	Stienam	Buddy Gilmour
2TC	Express Ride	John Campbell
2TF	JEF's Spice	Mickey McNichol
3TC	Prakas	John Campbell
3TF	Armbro Devona	Bill O'Donnell
AP	Division Street	Michel Lachance
AT	Sandy Bowl	John Campbell

1986

Div	Winner	Driver
2PC	Sunset Warrior	Bill Gale
2PF	Halcyon	Ray Remmen
3PC	Masquerade	Richard Silverman
3PF	Glow Softly	Ron Waples
2TC	Mack Lobell	John Campbell
2TF	Super Flora	Ron Waples
3TC	Sugarcane Hanover	Ron Waples
3TF	JEF's Spice	Bill O'Donnell
APM	Samshu Bluegrass	Michel Lachance
ATM	Grades Singing	Herve Filion
APH	Forrest Skipper	Lucien Fontaine
ATH	Nearly Perfect	Mickey McNichol

1987

Div	Winner	Driver
2PC	Camtastic	Bill O'Donnell
2PF	Leah Almahurst	Bill Fahy
3PC	Call For Rain	Clint Galbraith
3PF	Pacific	Tom Harmer
2TC	Defiant One	Howard Beissinger
2TF	Nan's Catch	Berndt Lindstedt
3TC	Mack Lobell	John Campbell
3TF	Armbro Fling	George Sholty
APM	Follow My Star	John Campbell
ATM	Grades Singing	Olle Goop
APH	Armbro Emerson	Walter Whelan
ATH	Sugarcane Hanover	Ron Waples

1988

Div	Winner	Driver
2PC	Kentucky Spur	Dick Stillings
2PF	Central Park West	John Campbell
3PC	Camtastic	Bill O'Donnell
3PF	Sweet Reflection	Bill O'Donnell
2TC	Valley Victory	Bill O'Donnell
2TF	Peace Corps	John Campbell
3TC	Firm Tribute	Mark O'Mara
3TF	Nalda Hanover	Mickey McNichol
APM	Anniecrombie	Dave Magee
ATM	Armbro Flori	Larry Walker
APH	Call For Rain	Clint Galbraith
ATH	Mack Lobell	John Campbell

1989

Div	Winner	Driver
2PC	Till We Meet Again	Mickey McNichol
2PF	Town Pro	Doug Brown
3PC	Goalie Jeff	Michel Lachance
3PF	Cheery Hello	John Campbell
2TC	Royal Troubador	Carl Allen
2TF	Delphi's Lobell	Ron Waples
3TC	Esquire Spur	Dick Stillings
3TF	Pace Corps	John Campbell
APM	Armbro Feather	John Kopas
ATM	Grades Singing	Olle Goop
APH	Matt's Scooter	Michel Lachance
ATH	Delray Lobell	John Campbell

1990

Div	Winner	Driver
2PC	Artsplace	John Campbell
2PF	Miss Easy	John Campbell
3PC	Beach Towel	Ray Remmen
3PF	Town Pro	Doug Brown
2TC	Crysta's Best	Dick Richardson Jr.
2TF	Jean Bi	Jan Nordin
3TC	Embassy Lobell	Michel Lachance
3TF	Me Maggie	Berndt Lindstedt
APM	Caesar's Jackpot	Bill Fahy
ATM	Peace Corps	Stig Johansson
APH	Bay's Fella	Paul MacDonell
ATH	No Sex Please	Ron Waples

Note: 2=Two-year-old; T=Trotter; C=Colt; 3=Three-year-old; P=Pacer; F=Filly; A=Aged; H=Horse; M=Mare.

Breeders' Crown (Cont.)

1991

Div	Winner	Driver
2PC	Digger Almahurst	Doug Brown
2PF	Hazleton Kay	John Campbell
3PC	Three Wizzards	Bill Gale
3PF	Miss Easy	John Campbell
2TC	King Conch	Bill Gale
2TF	Armbro Keepsake	John Campbell
3TC	Giant Victory	Ron Pierce
3TF	Twelve Speed	Ron Waples
APM	Delinquent Account	Bill O'Donnell
ATM	Me Maggie	Berndt Lindstedt
APH	Camluck	Michel Lachance
ATH	Billyjojimbob	Paul MacDonell

1992

Div	Winner	Driver
2PC	Village Jiffy	Ron Waples
2PF	Immortality	John Campbell
3PC	Kingsbridge	Roger Mayotte
3PF	So Fresh	John Campbell
2TC	Giant Chill	John Patterson Jr.
2TF	Winky's Goal	Cat Manzi
3TC	Baltic Striker	Michel Lachance
3TF	Imperfection	Michel Lachance
APM	Shady Daisy	Ron Pierce
ATM	Peace Corps	Torbjorn Jansson
APH	Artsplace	John Campbell
ATH	No Sex Please	Ron Waples

1993

Div	Winner	Driver
2PC	Expensive Scooter	Jack Moiseyev
2PF	Electric Scooter	Mike Lachance
3PC	Life Sign	John Campbell
3PF	Immortality	John Campbell
2TC	Westgate Crown	John Campbell
2TF	Gleam	Jimmy Takter
3TC	Pine Chip	John Campbell
3TF	Expressway Hanover	Per Henriksen
APM	Swing Back	Kelly Sheppard
ATM	Lifetime Dream	Paul MacDonell
APH	Staying Together	Bill O'Donnell
ATH	Earl	Chris Christoforou Jr.

1994

Div	Winner	Driver
2PC	Jenna's Beach Boy	Bill Fahy
2PF	Yankee Cashmere	Peter Wrenn
3PC	Magical Mike	Michel Lachance
3PF	Hardie Hanover	Tim Twaddle
2TC	Eager Seelster	Teddy Jacobs
2TF	Lookout Victory	John Patterson
3TC	Incredible Abe	Italo Tamborrino
3TF	Imageofa Clear Day	Bill O'Donnell
APM	Shady Daisy	Michel Lachance
ATM	Armbro Keepsake	Stig Johansson
APH	Village Jiffy	Paul MacDonell
ATH	Pine Chip	John Campbell

1995

Div	Winner	Driver
2PC	John Street North	Jack Moiseyev
2PF	Paige Nicole Q	John Campbell
3PC	Jenna's Beach Boy	Bill Fahy
3PF	Headline Hanover	Doug Brown
2TC	Armbro Officer	Steve Condren
2TF	Continentalvictory	Michel Lachance
3TC	Abundance	Bill O'Donnell
3TF	Lookout Victory	Sonny Patterson
APM	Ellamony	Mike Saftic
ATM	CR Kay Suzie	Rod Allen
APH	That'll Be Me	Roger Mayotte
ATH	Panifesto	Luc Ouellette

1996

Div	Winner	Driver
2PC	His Mattjesty	Doug Brown
2PF	Before Sunrise	Steve Condren
3PC	Armbro Operative	Michel Lachance
3PF	Mystical Maddy	Michel Lachance
2TC	Malabar Man	Mal Burroughs
2TF	Armbro Prowess	Jimmy Takter
3TC	Running Sea	Wally Hennessey
3TF	Personal Banner	Peter Wrenn
APM	She's A Great Lady	John Campbell
APH	Jenna's Beach Boy	Bill Fahy
AT	CR Kay Suzie	Rod Allen

1997

Div	Winner	Driver
2PC	Artiscape	Michel Lachance
2PF	Take Flight	Luc Ouellette
3PC	Village Jasper	Paul McDonnell
3PF	Stienam's Place	Jack Moiseyev
2TC	Catch As Catch Can	Wally Hennessey
2TF	My Dolly	Wally Hennessey
3TC	Malabar Man	Malvern Burroughs
3TF	No Nonsense Woman	Jim Doherty
APM	Jay's Table	John Campbell
APH	Red Bow Tie	Luc Ouellette
AT	Moni Maker	Wally Hennessey

1998

Div	Winner	Driver
2PC	Badlands Hanover	Ron Pierce
2PF	Juliet's Fate	George Brennan
3PC	Artiscape	Michel Lachance
3PF	Galleria	George Brennan
2TC	CR Commando	Carl Allen
2TF	Musical Victory	Luc Ouellette
3TC	Muscles Yankee	John Campbell
3TF	Lassie's Goal	Mark O'Mara
APM	Shore By Five	Daniel Dube
APH	Red Bow Tie	Luc Ouellette
AT	Supergrit	Ron Pierce

Breeders' Crown (Cont.)

1999

Div	Winner	Driver
2PC	Tyberwood	Richard Silverman
2PF	Eternal Camnation	Eric Ledford
3PC	Grinfromeartoear	Chris Christoforou
3PF	Odies Fame	David Wall
2TC	Master Lavec	Daniel Daley
2TF	Dream of Joy	James Meittinis
3TC	CR Renegade	Rodney Allen
3TF	Oolong	Ronald Pierce
APM	Shore By Five	Daniel Dube
APH	Red Bow Tie	Luc Ouellette
AT	Supergrit	Ronald Pierce

2000

Div	Winner	Driver
2PC	Bettor's Delight	Michel Lachance
2PF	Lady MacBeach	Luc Ouellette
3PC	Gallo Blue Chip	Daniel Dube
3PF	Popcorn Penny	Ryan Anderson
2TC	Banker Hall	Trevor Ritchie
2TF	Syrinx Hanover	Trevor Ritchie
3TC	Fast Photo	Michel Lachance
3TF	Aviano	Trevor Ritchie
APM	Ron's Girl	Michel Lachance
APH	Western Ideal	Michel Lachance
AT	Magician	David Miller

2001

Div	Winner	Driver
2PC	Western Shooter	John Campbell
2PF	Cam Swifty	Jim Meittinis
3PC	Real Desire	John Campbell
3PF	Bunny Lake	John Stark Jr.
2TC	Duke Of York	Paul MacDonnell
2TF	Cameron Hall	Michel Lachance
3TC	Liberty Balance	Randall Waples
3TF	Syrinx Hanover	John Campbell
APM	Eternal Camnation	Eric Ledford
APH	Goliath Bayama	Sylvain Filion
AT	Varenne	G. Minnucci

Note: 2=Two-year-old; T=Trotter; C=Colt; 3=Three-year-old; P=Pacer; F=Filly; A=Aged; H=Horse; M=Mare.

Triple Crown Winners

Trotting

Trotting's Triple Crown consists of the Hambletonian (first run in 1926), the Kentucky Futurity (first run in 1893) and the Yonkers Trot (known as the Yonkers Futurity when it began in 1955).

Year	Horse	Owner	Breeder	Trainer & Driver
1955	Scott Frost	S.A. Camp Farms	Est of W.N. Reynolds	Joe O'Brien
1963	Speedy Scot	Castleton Farms	Castleton Farms	Ralph Baldwin
1964	Ayres	Charlotte Sheppard	Charlotte Sheppard	John Simpson Sr
1968	Nevele Pride	Nevele Acres & Lou Resnick	Mr & Mrs E.C. Quin	Stanley Dancer
1969	Lindy's Pride	Lindy Farm	Hanover Shoe Farms	Howard Beissinger
1972	Super Bowl	Rachel Dancer & Rose Hild Breeding Farm	Stoner Creek Stud	Stanley Dancer

Pacing

Pacing's Triple Crown consists of the Cane Pace (called the Cane Futurity when it began in 1955), the Little Brown Jug (first run in 1946) and the Messenger Stakes (first run in 1956).

Year	Horse	Owner	Breeder	Trainer/Driver
1959	Adios Butler	Paige West & Angelo Pellillo	R.C. Carpenter	Paige West/Clint Hodgins
1965	Bret Hanover	Richard Downing	Hanover Shoe Farms	Frank Ervin
1966	Romeo Hanover	Lucky Star Stables & Morton Finder	Hanover Shoe Farms	Jerry Silverman/ William Meyer (Cane) & George Sholty (Jug & Messenger)
1968	Rum Customer	Kennilworth Farms & L. C. Mancuso	Mr. & Mrs. R.C. Larkin	Bill Haughton
1970	Most Happy Fella	Egyptian Acres Stable	Stoner Creek Stud	Stanley Dancer
1980	Niatross	Niagara Acres, C. Galbraith & Niatross Stables	Niagara Acres	Clint Galbraith
1983	Ralph Hanover	Waples Stable, Pointsetta Stable, Grant's Direct Stable & P. J. Baugh	Hanover Shoe Farms	Stew Firlotte/Ron Waples
1997	Western Dreamer	Daniel and Matthew Daly and Patrick Daly Jr.	Kentuckiana Farms	Bill Robinson/Michel Lachance
1999	Blissful Hall	Daniel Plouffe	Walnut Hall Limited	Ben Wallace/Ron Pierce

Horse of the Year

Year	Horse	Gait	Owner
1947	Victory Song	T	Castleton Farm
1948	Rodney	T	R.H. Johnston
1949	Good Time	P	William Cane
1950	Proximity	T	Ralph and Gordon Verhurst
1951	Pronto Don	T	Hayes Fair Acres Stable
1952	Good Time	P	William Cane
1953	Hi Lo's Forbes	P	Mr. and Mrs. Earl Wagner
1954	Stenographer	T	Max Hempt
1955	Scott Frost	T	S.A. Camp Farms
1956	Scott Frost	T	S.A. Camp Farms
1957	Torpid	P	Sherwood Farm
1958	Emily's Pride	T	Walnut Hall and Castleton Farms
1959	Bye Bye Byrd	P	Mr. and Mrs. Rex Larkin
1960	Adios Butler	P	Adios Butler Syndicate
1961	Adios Butler	P	Adios Butler Syndicate
1962	Su Mac Lad	T	I.W. Berkemeyer
1963	Speedy Scot	T	Castleton Farm
1964	Bret Hanover	P	Richard Downing
1965	Bret Hanover	P	Richard Downing
1966	Bret Hanover	P	Richard Downing
1967	Nevele Pride	T	Nevele Acres
1968	Nevele Pride	T	Nevele Acres, Louis Resnick
1969	Nevele Pride	T	Nevele Acres, Louis Resnick
1970	Fresh Yankee	T	Duncan MacDonald
1971	Albatross	P	Albatross Stable
1972	Albatross	P	Amicable Stable
1973	Sir Dalrae	P	A La Carte Racing Stable
1974	Delmonica Hanover	T	Delvin Miller, W. Arnold Hanger
1975	Savoir	T	Allwood Stable
1976	Keystone Ore	P	Mr. and Mrs. Stanley Dancer, Rose Hild Farms, Robert Jones
1977	Green Speed	T	Beverly Lloyds
1978	Abercrombie	P	Shirley Mitchell, L. Keith Bulen
1979	Niatross	P	Niagara Acres, Clint Galbraith
1980	Niatross	P	Niatross Syndicate, Niagara Acres, Clint Galbraith
1981	Fan Hanover	P	Dr. J. Glen Brown
1982	Cam Fella	P	Norm Clements, Norm Faulkner
1983	Cam Fella	P	JEF's Standardbred, Norm Clements, Norm Faulkner
1984	Fancy Crown	T	Fancy Crown Stable
1985	Nihilator	P	Wall Street-Nihilator Syndicate
1986	Forrest	P	Forrest L. Bartlett
1987	Mack Lobell	T	One More Time Stable and Fair Wind Farm
1988	Mack Lobell	T	John Erik Magnusson
1989	Matt's Scooter	P	Gordon and Illa Rumpel, Charles Jurasvinski
1990	Beach Towel	P	Uptown Stables
1991	Precious Bunny	P	R. Peter Heffering
1992	Artsplace	P	George Segal
1993	Staying Together	P	Robert Hamather
1994	Cam's Card Shark	P	Jeffrey S. Snyder
1995	CR Kay Suzie	T	Carl & Rod Allen Stable, Inc.
1996	Continentalvictory	T	Continentalvictory Stables
1997	Malabar Man	T	Malvern Burroughs
1998	Moni Maker	T	Moni Maker Stable
1999	Moni Maker	T	Moni Maker Stable
2000	Gallo Blue Chip	P	Dan Gernatt Farms
2001	Bunny Lake	P	W. Springtime Racing Stable

Driver of the Year

Year	Driver	Year	Driver	Year	Driver
1968	Stanley Dancer	1979	Ron Waples	1991	Walter Case Jr.
1969	Herve Filion	1980	Ron Waples	1992	Walter Case Jr.
1970	Herve Filion	1981	Herve Filion	1993	Jack Moiseyev
1971	Herve Filion	1982	Bill O'Donnell	1994	Dave Magee
1972	Herve Filion	1983	John Campbell	1995	Luc Ouellette
1973	Herve Filion	1984	Bill O'Donnell	1996	Tony Morgan
1974	Herve Filion	1985	Michel Lachance		Luc Ouellette
1975	Joe O'Brien	1986	Michel Lachance	1997	Tony Morgan
1976	Herve Filion	1987	Michel Lachance	1998	Walter Case Jr.
1977	Donald Dancer	1988	John Campbell	1999	Dave Palone
1978	Carmine Abbatiello	1989	Herve Filion	2000	Dave Palone
	Herve Filion	1990	John Campbell	2001	Stephane Bouchard

Note: Balloting is conducted by the U.S Trotting Association for the U.S. Harness Writers Association.

Leading Drivers—Money Won

Year	Driver	Winnings ($)	Year	Driver	Winnings ($)
1946	Thomas Berry	121,933	1974	Herve Filion	3,474,315
1947	H.C. Fitzpatrick	133,675	1975	Carmine Abbatiello	2,275,093
1948	Ralph Baldwin	153,222	1976	Herve Filion	2,278,634
1949	Clint Hodgins	184,108	1977	Herve Filion	2,551,058
1950	Del Miller	306,813	1978	Carmine Abbatiello	3,344,457
1951	John Simpson Sr.	333,316	1979	John Campbell	3,308,984
1952	Bill Haughton	311,728	1980	John Campbell	3,732,306
1953	Bill Haughton	374,527	1981	Bill O'Donnell	4,065,608
1954	Bill Haughton	415,577	1982	Bill O'Donnell	5,755,067
1955	Bill Haughton	599,455	1983	John Campbell	6,104,082
1956	Bill Haughton	572,945	1984	Bill O'Donnell	9,059,184
1957	Bill Haughton	586,950	1985	Bill O'Donnell	10,207,372
1958	Bill Haughton	816,659	1986	John Campbell	9,515,055
1959	Bill Haughton	771,435	1987	John Campbell	10,186,495
1960	Del Miller	567,282	1988	John Campbell	11,148,565
1961	Stanley Dancer	674,723	1989	John Campbell	9,738,450
1962	Stanley Dancer	760,343	1990	John Campbell	11,620,878
1963	Bill Haughton	790,086	1991	Jack Moiseyev	9,568,468
1964	Stanley Dancer	1,051,538	1992	John Campbell	8,202,108
1965	Bill Haughton	889,943	1993	John Campbell	9,926,482
1966	Stanley Dancer	1,218,403	1994	John Campbell	9,834,139
1967	Bill Haughton	1,305,773	1995	John Campbell	9,469,797
1968	Bill Haughton	1,654,463	1996	Michel Lachance	8,408,231
1969	Del Insko	1,635,463	1997	Michel Lachance	9,215,388
1970	Herve Filion	1,647,837	1998	John Campbell	10,768,771
1971	Herve Filion	1,915,945	1999	Luc Ouellette	10,841,495
1972	Herve Filion	2,473,265	2000	John Campbell	11,160,462
1973	Herve Filion	2,233,303	2001	John Campbell	14,184,863

Four Questions for Track Announcer Tom Durkin

SI: If you drank a couple of mint juleps before the Derby, would viewers know?

Durkin: By past performances I would say yes.

SI: Who's the better Triple Crown winner: Seattle Slew or Frank Robinson?

Durkin: Slew. He only had one chance. Frank Robinson had his entire career to do it.

SI: Who's the more annoying horse owner: George Steinbrenner of Rick Pitino?

Durkin: George Steinbrenner. He fired me once. [The Boss canned Durkin two decades ago while Durkin was calling races at Tampa Bay Downs, which was owned by Steinbrenner.]

SI: Could you handle the call of a three-horse race among She Sells Seashells, Flat Fleet Feet and Shiningcityshoes?

Durkin: Yes, if I had six mint juleps.

—Richard Deitsch

Motor Sports

2002 IRL champion
Sam Hornish (4)

Down to the Wire

Two of the tightest seasons in memory, the 2002 NASCAR and IRL points races, weren't decided until the final weeks

BY MARK BECHTEL

THE FOUR NASCAR season points races that preceded the 2002 edition were rather dull affairs. The lead never changed hands late in those seasons, and in each year the championship was wrapped up before the final race. But all of that changed in 2002, a season in which NASCAR fans, as well as those of the Indy Racing League, feasted on tight races and wild finishes.

The Daytona 500 set the tone. Late in the race, leader Jeff Gordon was doing all he could to block his pursuers. That blocking led to a little paint swapping, which in turn set up one of the most bizarre finishes—and certainly the least dramatic race-winning pass—Daytona has seen. With six laps left, Sterling Marlin tried to sneak under Gordon. The defending series champ dropped down to block Marlin and their cars touched, sending Gordon spinning through the infield grass. As Gordon fought to regain control of his car, Marlin and Ward Burton, who was running third, flew around the track. They assumed the race would end under the ensu-

ing yellow flag, so whoever got to the start/finish line first would be the winner. Marlin beat Burton by inches, but rather than let the race end under caution, NASCAR decided to throw the red flag and have the cars stop on the backstretch until the track was cleaned up.

That meant the race would be decided by real racing, which raised a problem for Marlin. When he bumped Gordon he dented his right front fender, causing it to rub against the tire. Racing with the car in that condition would be impossible, so Marlin hopped out of his car to fix it. "I saw [Dale] Earnhardt do it at Richmond one time in '87," Marlin said. "He got out and cleaned off his windshield, so I thought it was okay. I don't guess it was."

Alas, it wasn't. By straightening out the fender he violated a NASCAR rule prohibiting any work from being done on a car under a red flag. Marlin was sent to the tail end of the lead lap on the restart and the lead was Burton's by default. (Marlin took a lot of heat for the move, but he had no choice. The car needed to be fixed, and had

AP PHOTO/STEVE HELBER

heck of a jump on the field, is the 40 car," Jimmy Makar, crew chief for 2000 Winston Cup champ Bobby Labonte, said of Marlin's Dodge prior to the season's fourth race, in Atlanta. "That's the guy we're going to be chasing most of the year, if Sterling and his crew don't shoot themselves in the foot."

Notice Makar didn't say "all year." Marlin hung onto the lead throughout the summer, but that was due to the inconsistency of the rest of the field more than anything else. The overwhelming preseason favorite was Gordon, but he was mired in a winless streak worse than any he had endured since his rookie year. His wife filed for divorce in the spring, which amateur shrinks everywhere blamed for his on-track woes.

But if anything, Gordon seems to focus even more when faced with difficult situations. "There's no doubt something like that affects you," said Gordon of his divorce. "How could it not? But I've had a lot of things that have been distractions throughout the years that have tried to take my mind off driving the race car, and I've won races and won championships."

In the summer of 2001, Gordon spent a lot of time assembling the deal that put Jimmie Johnson into a car owned by Gordon and sponsored by Lowe's—while at the same time making a mockery of the championship race, which he wrapped up with two events left. "I know when I'm in the race car whether or not I'm getting the most out of the race car, whether or not I'm doing my job well," says Gordon. "And I feel like I've done my job about as well as I know how this year."

Indeed, Gordon stayed near the top despite his prolonged drought. He finally got off the schneid in August at Bristol, and won the following race, in Darlington, as well, cutting significantly into Marlin's lead. But it wasn't Gordon who finally caught Marlin. It was Mark Martin, who, like Gordon, lurked

he pulled into the pits for the repair, he would have ended up as the last car on the lead lap anyway.)

Burton, who was caught up in a nasty wreck at Daytona in 2001, drove a patient race and did his best to keep his nose clean—which was no easy feat on a day in which only 30 cars were running at the finish. "We try to be smart," Burton said. "We try to drive everybody the way we want to be driven. At the same time, just like [crew chief] Tommy [Baldwin] always says, we try to drive it like we stole it."

Marlin's fortunes would change for the better in the ensuing weeks. At the next race he lost a chance to catch leader Matt Kenseth when NASCAR decided to let the Rockingham 400 end under the caution flag that came out with five laps left, but still finished second. He finally took the checkered flag the following week in Las Vegas, a win that put him atop the Winston Cup standings and established him as the man to beat. "The car I think you're going to see near the top of the standings continuously, and he's got a near the top of the standings without winning too frequently. (His first win of the season didn't come until Memorial Day weekend in Charlotte.) Martin took over the points lead with a 16th place finish in New Hampshire in September, but his lead was a narrow one. In addition to Marlin, who was hot on Martin's heels, Gordon, Tony Stewart, Rusty Wallace and Johnson, a rookie who showed an amazing consistency, were all well within range. It was one of the closest points races in NASCAR history.

But it wasn't as close as the IRL title chase. Sam Hornish went to the final race of the season needing to finish ahead of Helio Castroneves to win his second consecutive championship, which he did—by .0096 of a second, or about nine inches. "Definitely, I gave my blood," Castroneves said. "The only thing I didn't try was get out of my car and try to push, which I don't think would help."

"This shows you how competitive it has been all year and Sam drove a terrific race," said Roger Penske, Castroneves' team owner. "What a way to finish, fighting like that for the last 25 laps. I'm proud to be a member of the IRL, and it was a great way to end it." Penske's presence in the IRL was one of the year's top stories. He was a founder of CART, the IRL's open-wheel rival and archenemy. But his primary sponsor, Marlboro, wanted a presence at the Indianapolis 500, which necessitated switching series.

The Indy 500 turned out to be just as strange as the Daytona 500. On the penultimate lap Paul Tracy blew by the leader, Castroneves, in Turn 3. As Tracy pulled alongside the 27-year-old Brazilian; Castroneves noticed a flashing yellow light on his steering wheel, which he assumed meant he was out of gas. Most of the field had stopped for gas 25 laps earlier, but Castroneves gambled that he could make it the rest of the way, which prompted Tracy to radio to his crew, "He ain't gonna make it!" And it looked like he wouldn't. "I was so tense," said Castroneves. "I thought I was running out of fuel. And then the guys on the radio were yelling, 'Yellow! Yellow!' I was shocked."

A split second—if that—before Tracy got around Castroneves, Laurent Roden and Buddy Lazier wrecked in Turn 2. That brought out a caution, which activated the flashing yellow light on Castroneves' steering wheel and negated Tracy's pass. (Unlike in NASCAR, Indy cars don't race back to the start/finish line. According to the IRL rulebook, "Racing ceases immediately upon display of the yellow flag and/or yellow light.")

Tracy contended that he had gotten by Castroneves before the yellow flag came out, but it was Castroneves celebrating at the conclusion of the race. He jumped on the trackside fence in his signature Spiderman celebration, then hung around the garage until the result became official.

That happened a good five-and-a-half hours later. Castroneves celebrated by scaling the eight-foot fence that borders the garage. Since he was out of uniform and in street clothes, it was more Peter Parker than Spiderman. But Tracy made one last appeal, which was dismissed the following day, allowing Castroneves a third celebration. This time he was packing his clothes in the townhouse where he was staying, so there was no fence for him to climb.

Almost every big name from CART showed up at the Brickyard, except for Cristiano da Matta of Brazil, who made up for his absence at the famous event by running away with the CART series points race. Thanks to a four-race winning streak in the middle of the summer, the colorful da Matta—he wears cycling socks, often with cartoon characters on them, everywhere he goes—held a comfortable lead in the standings for most of the year.

As dominant as da Matta was, he had nothing on Michael Schumacher, who wrapped up the Formula One title with six races left in the season. But such dominance was the exception, not the rule, in 2002, a year that featured racing so exciting that even the runners-up were thrilled. "I wanted to win the championship, but [Hornish] was the best," said Castroneves. "It's great to finish a season like that. I tried really hard, but there is always next year."

And racing fans can't wait.

Indy Racing League

Indianapolis 500

Results of the 86th running of the Indianapolis 500 and fifth race of the 2002 Indy Racing League season. Held Sunday, May 26, 2002, at the 2.5-mile Indianapolis Motor Speedway in Indianapolis.

Distance, 500 miles; starters, 33; time of race, 3 hours, 10.8714 seconds; average speed, 166.499 mph; margin of victory, 0.0376 seconds; caution flags, five for 35 laps; lead changes, 19 among nine drivers.

TOP 10 FINISHERS

Pos.	Driver (start pos.)	Chassis-Engine	Qual. Speed	Laps	Status
1	Helio Castroneves (13)	Dallara-Chevrolet	229.052	200	running
2	Paul Tracy (29)	Dallara-Chevrolet	228.006	200	running
3	Felipe Giaffone (4)	G Force-Chevrolet	230.326	200	running
4	Alex Barron (26)	Dallara-Chevrolet	228.580	200	running
5	Eddie Cheever Jr (6)	Dallara-Infiniti	229.786	200	running
6	Richie Hearn (22)	Dallara-Chevrolet	227.233	200	running
7	Michael Andretti (25)	Dallara-Chevrolet	228.713	200	running
8	Robby Gordon (11)	Dallara-Chevrolet	229.127	200	running
9	Jeff Ward (15)	G Force-Chevrolet	228.557	200	running
10	Gil de Ferran (14)	Dallara-Chevrolet	228.671	200	running

2002 Indy Racing League Results

Date	Race	Winner (start pos.)	Chassis-Engine	Avg Speed
Mar 2	Grand Prix of Miami	Sam Hornish Jr. (1)	Dallara-Chevrolet	140.325
Mar 17	Copper World 200	Helio Castroneves (1)	Dallara-Chevrolet	116.504
Mar 24	Yamaha 400	Sam Hornish Jr (4)	Dallara-Chevrolet	179.345
Apr 21	Firestone 225*	Scott Sharp (11)	Dallara-Chevrolet	93.789
May 26	Indianapolis 500	Helio Castroneves (13)	Dallara-Chevrolet	166.499
June 8	Boomtown 500	Jeff Ward (7)	G Force-Chevrolet	164.984
June 16	Radisson 225	Gil de Ferran (1)	Dallara-Chevrolet	121.465
June 29	Richmond SunTrust 250*	Sam Hornish Jr. (3)	Dallara-Chevrolet	99.124
July 7	Ameristar Casino 200*	Airton Dare (6)	Dallara-Chevrolet	178.527
July 20	Firestone 200*	Alex Barron (5)	Dallara-Chevrolet	127.997
July 28	Michigan 400	Tomas Scheckter (1)	Dallara-Infiniti	179.044
Aug 11	Belterra Casino 300	Felipe Giaffone (3)	G Force-Chevrolet	149.024
Aug 25	Gateway 250	Gil de Ferran (1)	Dallara-Chevrolet	143.711
Sept 8	Delphi 300	Sam Hornish Jr. (1)	Dallara-Chevrolet	146.391
Sept 15	Chevy 500	Sam Hornish Jr. (3)	Dallara-Chevrolet	163.981

Note: Distances are in miles unless followed by K (kilometers) or * (laps).

2001 Final Championship Standings

Driver	Starts	Highest Finish	Pts
Sam Hornish Jr	13	1	503
Buddy Lazier	13	1	398
Scott Sharp	13	1	355
Billy Boat	13	2	313
Eliseo Salazar	13	2	308
Felipe Giaffone	13	2	304
Al Unser Jr	13	1	287
Eddie Cheever Jr	13	1	261
Buzz Calkins	13	3	242
Airton Dare	13	5	239

2002 CART Championship Series Results (through September 14)

Date	Event	Winner (start pos.)	Car	Avg Speed
Mar 10	Monterrey Grand Prix	Cristiano da Matta (5)	Lola-Toyota	90.372
Apr 14	Grand Prix of Long Beach	Michael Andretti (15)	Reynard-Honda	86.935
Apr 26	Bridgestone Potenza 500	Bruno Junqueira (1)	Lola-Toyota	155.447
June 2	Miller LIte 250	Paul Tracy (2)	Lola-Honda	130.028
June 9	Grand Prix of Monterey	Cristiano da Matta (1)	Lola-Toyota	101.164
June 16	G.I. Joe's 200	Cristiano da Matta (1)	Lola-Toyota	105.381
June 30	Grand Prix of Chicago	Cristiano da Matta (3)	Lola-Toyota	121.524
July 7	Molson Indy Toronto	Cristiano da Matta (1)	Lola-Toyota	93.361
July 14	Grand Prix of Cleveland	Patrick Carpentier (2)	Reynard-Ford	120.998
July 28	Molson Indy Vancouver	Dario Franchitti (3)	Lola-Honda	78.525
Aug 11	Grand Prix of Mid Ohio	Patrick Carpentier (1)	Reynard-Ford	106.680
Aug 18	Grand Prix Road America	Cristiano da Matta (2)	Lola-Toyota	124.856
Aug 25	Molson Indy Montreal	Dario Franchitti (2)	Lola-Honda	108.648
Sept 1	Grand Prix of Denver	Bruno Junqueira (1)	Lola-Toyota	90.349
Sept 14	Rockingham 500	Dario Franchetti (27)	Honda-Lola	157.682

2001 Championship Standings

Driver	Starts	Wins	Pts
Gil de Ferran	20	2	199
Kenny Brack	20	4	163
Michael Andretti	20	1	147
Helio Castroneves	20	3	141
Cristiano da Matta	20	3	140
Max Papis	20	2	107
Dario Franchitti	20	1	105
Scott Dixon	20	1	98
Tony Kanaan	19	0	93
Patrick Carpentier	20	1	91

National Association for Stock Car Auto Racing

Daytona 500

Results of the 44th Daytona 500, the opening round of the 2002 Winston Cup series. Held Sunday, February 17, 2002, at the 2.5-mile high-banked Daytona International Speedway.

Distance, 500 miles; starters, 43; time of race, 3:29:50; average speed, 142.971 mph; margin of victory, 0.193 seconds; caution flags, nine for 38 laps; lead changes, 20 among 12 drivers.

TOP 10 FINISHERS

Pos.	Driver (start pos.)	Car	Laps	Winnings ($)
1	Ward Burton (19)	Dodge	200	1,409,017
2	Elliott Sadler (41)	Ford	200	957,037
3	Geoffrey Bodine (35)	Ford	200	644,187
4	Kurt Busch (15)	Ford	200	499,462
5	Michael Waltrip (4)	Chevrolet	200	409,159
6	Mark Martin (39)	Ford	200	300,995
7	Ryan Newman (23)	Ford	200	246,587
8	Sterling Marlin (13)	Dodge	200	248,779
9	Jeff Gordon (3)	Chevrolet	200	289,674
10	Johnny Benson (38)	Pontiac	200	198,612

Late 2001 Winston Cup Series Results

Date	Track/Distance	Winner (start pos.)	Car	Avg Speed	Winnings ($)
Oct 7	Charlotte 500	Sterling Marlin (13)	Dodge	139.006	196,360
Oct 15	Martinsville 500*	Ricky Craven (6)	Ford	75.75	130,475
Oct 21	Talladega 500	Dale Earnhardt Jr (6)	Chevrolet	185.24	165,773
Oct 28	Phoenix 500 K	Jeff Burton (3)	Ford	102.613	213,491
Nov 4	North Carolina 400	Joe Nemechek (13)	Chevrolet	128.941	157,535
Nov 11	Homestead 400	Bill Elliott (1)	Dodge	117.449	319,273
Nov 18	Atlanta 500	Bobby Labonte (39)	Pontiac	151.756	233,227
Nov 23	New Hampshire 300	Robby Gordon (31)	Chevrolet	103.594	203,924

2002 Winston Cup Series Results (through September 29)

Date	Track/Distance	Winner (start pos.)	Car	Avg Speed	Winnings ($)
Feb 17	Daytona 500	Ward Burton (19)	Dodge	142.971	1,409,017
Feb 24	North Carolina 400	Matt Kenseth (25)	Ford	115.478	157,400
Mar 3	Las Vegas 400	Sterling Marlin (24)	Dodge	136.754	412,842
Mar 10	Atlanta 500	Tony Stewart (9)	Pontiac	148.443	174,978
Mar 17	Darlington 400	Sterling Marlin (11)	Dodge	126.07	190,642
Mar 24	Bristol 500*	Kurt Busch (27)	Ford	82.281	143,840
Apr 8	Texas 500	Matt Kenseth (31)	Ford	142.453	418,275
Apr 14	Martinsville 500*	Bobby Labonte (15)	Pontiac	73.951	168,078
Apr 21	Talladega 499	Dale Earnhardt Jr (4)	Chevrolet	159.022	184,830
Apr 28	California 500	Jimmie Johnson (4)	Chevrolet	150.088	176,750
May 5	Richmond 400*	Tony Stewart (3)	Pontiac	86.824	185,653
May 26	Charlotte 600	Mark Martin (25)	Ford	137.729	280,033
June 2	Dover Downs 400	Jimmie Johnson (10)	Chevrolet	117.551	152,400
June 9	Pocono 500	Dale Jarrett (13)	Ford	143.426	206,298
June 16	Michigan 400	Matt Kenseth (20)	Ford	154.822	154,100
June 23	California 350 K	Ricky Rudd (7)	Ford	81.007	184,992
July 6	Daytona 400	Michael Waltrip (7)	Chevrolet	135.952	172,975
July 14	Chicago 400	Kevin Harvick (32)	Chevrolet	136.832	200,028
July 21	New Hampshire 300*	Ward Burton (31)	Dodge	92.342	231,850
July 28	Pennsylvania 500	Bill Elliott (1)	Dodge	125.809	193,401
Aug 4	Brickyard 400	Bill Elliott (2)	Dodge	125.033	449,056
Aug 11	Watkins Glen 90*	Tony Stewart (3)	Pontiac	82.208	165,303
Aug 18	Michigan 400	Dale Jarrett (8)	Ford	140.556	179,530
Aug 25	Bristol 500*	Jeff Gordon (1)	Chevrolet	77.097	245,543
Sept 1	Southern 500	Jeff Gordon (3)	Chevrolet	118.617	212,183
Sept 7	Richmond 400*	Matt Kenseth (25)	Ford	94.787	163,595
Sept 15	New Hampshire 300*	Ryan Newman (1)	Ford	105.081	202,550
Sept 22	Dover Downs 400	Jimmie Johnson (19)	Chevrolet	120.805	152,735
Sept 29	Kansas 400	Jeff Gordon (10)	Chevrolet	119.394	217,928

Note: Distances are in miles unless followed by K (kilometers) or * (laps).

2001 Winston Cup Final Standings

Driver	Pts	Starts	Wins	Top 5	Top 10
Jeff Gordon	5,112	36	6	18	24
Tony Stewart	4,763	36	3	15	22
Sterling Marlin	4,741	36	2	12	20
Ricky Rudd	4,706	36	2	14	22
Dale Jarrett	4,612	36	4	12	19
Bobby Labonte	4,561	36	2	9	20
Rusty Wallace	4,481	36	1	8	14
Dale Earnhardt Jr.	4,460	36	3	9	15
Kevin Harvick	4,406	35	2	6	16
Jeff Burton	4,394	36	2	8	16

2001 Winston Cup Driver Winnings

Driver	Winnings ($)
Jeff Gordon	6,649,076
Dale Earnhardt Jr	5,384,627
Dale Jarrett	4,608,366
Rusty Wallace	4,272,406
Bobby Labonte	4,139,851
Ricky Rudd	3,976,203
Jeff Burton	3,866,333
Kevin Harvick	3,716,633
Tony Stewart	3,493,043
Mark Martin	3,487,719

Formula One Grand Prix Racing

2002 Formula One Results (through September 29)

Date	Grand Prix	Winner	Car	Time
Mar 3	Australia	Michael Schumacher	Ferrari	1:35:36.792
Mar 17	Malaysia	Ralf Schumacher	Williams-BMW	1:34:12.912
Mar 31	Brazil	Michael Schumacher	Ferrari	1:31:43.663
Apr 14	San Marino	Michael Schumacher	Ferrari	1:29:10.789
Apr 28	Spain	Michael Schumacher	Ferrari	1:30:29.981
May 12	Austria	Michael Schumacher	Ferrari	1:33:51.562
May 26	Monaco	David Coulthard	McLaren-Mercedes	1:45:39.055
June 9	Canada	Michael Schumacher	Ferrari	1:33:36.111
June 23	Europe	Rubens Barrichello	Ferrari	1:35:07.426
July 7	Great Britain	Michael Schumacher	Ferrari	1:31:45.015
July 21	France	Michael Schumacher	Ferrari	1:32:09.837
July 28	Germany	Michael Schumacher	Ferrari	1:27:52.078
Aug 18	Hungary	Rubens Barrichello	Ferrari	1:41:49.001
Sept 1	Belgium	Michael Schumacher	Ferrari	1:21:20.634
Sept 15	Italy	Rubens Barrichello	Ferrari	1:16:19.982
Sept 29	United States	Rubens Barrichello	Ferrari	1:31:07.934

2001 World Championship Final Standings

Drivers compete in Grand Prix races for the title of World Driving Champion. Below are the top 10 drivers from the 2001 season. Points are awarded for places 1–6 as follows: 10-6-4-3-2-1.

Driver, Country	Starts	Wins	Car	Pts
Michael Schumacher, Germany	17	9	Ferrari	123
David Coulthard, Scotland	17	2	McLaren-Mercedes	65
Rubens Barrichello, Brazil	17	0	Ferrari	56
Ralf Schumacher, Germany	17	3	Williams-BMW	49
Mika Hakkinen, Finland	17	2	McLaren-Mercedes	37
Juan Montoya, Colombia	17	1	Willaims-BMW	31
Jacques Villeneuve, Canada	17	0	BAR-Honda	12
Nick Heidfeld, Germany	17	0	Sauber-Petronas	12
Jarno Trulli, Italy	17	0	Jordan-Honda	12
Kimi Raikkonen, Finland	17	0	Sauber-Petronas	9

Professional Sports Car Racing, Inc.

The 24 Hours of Daytona

Held at the Daytona International Speedway on February 2–3, 2002, the 24 Hours of Daytona serves as the opening round of Grand American Road Racing Association's season.

Place	Drivers	Car (Class)	Distance
1	Didier Theys, Fredy Lienhard, Max Papis, Mauro Baldi	Dallara-Judd (SRP)	716 laps (106.143 mph)
2	Guy Smith, Jim Matthews, Scott Shart, Robby Gordon	R&S-Elan (SRP)	710
3	Anthony Lazzaro, Bill Rand, Terry Borcheller, Ralf Kelleners	Lola-Nissan (SRPII)	695
4	Andy Wallace, Hurley Haywood, Sascha Maassen, Lucas Luhr	Lola-Porsche (SRP)	681
5	Paul Gentilozzi, Brian Simo, Scott Pruett, Michael Lauer	Jaguar (GTS)	675

2002 American Le Mans Series—Prototype Class (through September 22)

Date	Race	Winners	Car
Mar 16	12 Hours at Sebring	R. Capello, J. Herbert, C. Pescatori	Audi R8
May 19	Grand Prix of Sonoma	David Brabham, Jan Magnussen	Panoz LMP-1
June 30	ALMS at Mid-Ohio	Frank Biela, Emanuele Pirro	Audi R8
July 7	Road America 500	Tom Kristensen, Rinaldo Capello	Audi R8
July 21	National Grand Prix	David Brabham, Jan Magnussen	Panoz LMP-1
Aug 3	Grand Prix de Trois-Rivières	Tom Kristensen, Rinaldo Capello	Audi R8
Aug 18	Grand Prix of Mosport	Tom Kristensen, Rinaldo Capello	Audi R8
Sept 22	Monterey Championships	Frank Biela, Emanuele Pirro	Audi R8

2002 American Le Mans Series—GTS Class (through September 22)

Date	Race	Winners	Car
Mar 16	12 Hours at Sebring	Ron Fellows, Johnny O'Connell, Oliver Gavin	Corvette C5-R
May 19	Grand Prix of Sonoma	Ron Fellows, Johnny O'Connell	Corvette C5-R
June 30	ALMS at Mid-Ohio	Ron Fellows, Johnny O'Connell	Corvette C5-R
July 7	Road America 500	Kelly Collins, Andy Pilgrim	Corvette C5-R
July 21	National Grand Prix	Ron Fellows, Johnny O'Connell	Corvette C5-R
Aug 3	Grand Prix de Trois-Rivières	Kelly Collins, Andy Pilgrim	Corvette C5-R
Aug 18	Grand Prix of Mosport	Ron Fellows, Johnny O'Connell	Corvette C5-R
Sept 22	Monterey Championships	Tomas Enge, Peter Kox	Ferrari 550

2002 American Le Mans Series—GT Class (through September 22)

Date	Race	Winners	Car
Mar 16	12 Hours at Sebring	Lucas Luhr, Sascha Maassen	Porsche 911 GT3
May 19	Grand Prix of Sonoma	Lucas Luhr, Sascha Maassen	Porsche 911 GT3
June 30	ALMS at Mid-Ohio	Kevin Buckler, B.J. Zacharias	Porsche 911 GT3
July 7	Road America 500	Timo Bernhard, Jorg Bergmeister	Porsche 911 GT3
July 21	National Grand Prix	Lucas Luhr, Sascha Maassen	Porsche 911 GT3
Aug 3	Grand Prix de Trois-Rivières	Lucas Luhr, Sascha Maassen	Porsche 911 GT3
Aug 18	Grand Prix of Mosport	Kevin Buckler, Brian Cunningham	Porsche 911 GT3
Sept 22	Monterey Championships	Lucas Luhr, Sascha Maassen	Porsche 911 GT3

2001 American Le Mans Series Championship Final Standings

PROTOTYPE CLASS	Pts	GTS CLASS	Pts	GT CLASS	Pts
Emanuele Pirro	202	Terry Borcheller	187	Jörg Müller	191
Frank Biela	198	Franz Konrad	184	J.J. Lehto	186
Rinaldo Capello	175	Ron Fellows	171	Sascha Maassen	177
Tom Kristensen	161	Johnny O'Connell	170	Lucas Luhr	176
Jan Magnussen	159	Andy Pilgrim	153	Boris Said	169
Andy Wallace	153	Kelly Collins	153	Dirk Müller	164
David Brabham	145	Tom Weikardt	123	Frederik Ekblom	159
Johnny Herbert	113	Shane Lewis	87	Hans Stuck	158
Stefan Johannsson	89	Oliver Gavin	74	Randy Pobst	148
Christophe Tinseau	83	Jeff Altenburg	60	Christian Menzel	148

24 Hours of Le Mans

Held at Le Mans, France, on June 15–16, 2002, the 24 Hours of Le Mans is the most prestigious international event in endurance racing.

Place	Drivers	Car	Laps
1..............	Frank Biela, Tom Kristensen, Emanuele Pirro	Audi R8	375 (3,171.0 mi)
2..............	Rinaldo Capello, Johnny Herbert, Christian Pescatori	Audi R8	374
3..............	Michael Krumm, Philipp Peter, Marco Werner	Audi R8	372
4..............	Andy Wallace, Butch Leitzinger, Eric van de Poele	Bentley EXP Speed 8	362
5..............	Olivier Beretta, Pedro Lamy, Erik Comas	Dallara-Judd	359
6..............	Stéphane Sarrazin, Franck Montangny, Nicolas Minassian	Dallara-Judd	359
7..............	Seiji Ara, Yannick Dalmas, Hiroki Katoh	Audi R8	358
8..............	Jan Lammers, Val Hillebrand, Tom Coronel	Dome-Judd	351
9..............	Wayne Taylor, Massimiliano Angelelli, Christophe Tinseau	Cadillac Northstar LMP	345
10...........	J. C. Boullion, Frank Lagorce, Sebastien Bourdais	Courage-Peugeot	343

National Hot Rod Association

2002 Results (through September 29)
TOP FUEL

Date	Race, Site	Winner	Time	Speed
Feb 7–10	Winternationals, Pomona, CA	Larry Dixon	4.535	324.75
Feb 21–24	Kragen Nationals, Phoenix	Tony Schumacher	4.946	299.40
Mar 14–17	Mac Tools Gatornationals, Gainesville, FL	Larry Dixon	4.629	319.75
Apr 4–7	Las Vegas Nationals	Larry Dixon	4.639	319.29
Apr 11–14	O'Reilly Spring Nationals, Baytown, TX	Kenny Bernstein	4.695	319.37
Apr 26–28	Thunder Valley Nationals, Bristol, TN	Larry Dixon	4.644	317.87
May 2–5	Southern Nationals, Commerce, GA	Larry Dixon	4.637	318.09
May 16–19	Matco Supernationals, Englishtown, NJ	Kenny Bernstein	4.600	321.96
May 23–26	O'Reilly Summer Nationals, Topeka, KS	Darrell Russell	4.638	314.90
May 30–June 2...	Chicagoland Dodge Nationals, Joliet, IL	Larry Dixon	4.580	319.37
June 13–16	Pontiac Nationals, Columbus, OH	Larry Dixon	4.619	319.14
June 27–30	Sears Craftsman Nationals, St. Louis, MO	Kenny Bernstein	5.056	293.22
July 18–21	Mile High Nationals, Denver	Darrell Russell	4.898	295.53
July 26–28	Northwest Nationals, Kent, WA	Darrell Russell	4.657	308.00
Aug 2–4	Fram Autolite Nationals, Sonoma, CA	Doug Herbert	4.727	308.85
Aug 15–18	Rugged Liner Nationals, Brainerd, MN	Kenny Bernstein	4.830	303.16
Aug 28–Sept 2...	U.S. Nationals, Clermont, IN	Tony Schumacher	4.663	315.93
Sept 12–15	Lucas Oil Nationals, Mohnton, PA	Doug Kalitta	4.560	320.51
Sept 19–22	Mid-South Nationals, Millington, TN	Larry Dixon	4.600	318.69
Sept 26–29	Nationals, Joliet, IL	Doug Kalitta	4.594	323.27

FUNNY CAR

Date	Race, Site	Winner	Time	Speed
Feb 7–10	Winternationals, Pomona, CA	John Force	6.260	219.76
Feb 21–24	Kragen Nationals, Phoenix	Del Worsham	4.940	312.86
Mar 14–17	Mac Tools Gatornationals, Gainesville, FL	Tony Pedgregon	5.090	281.25
Apr 4–7	Las Vegas Nationals	Gary Densham	5.409	205.13

2002 Results (through September 29) *(Cont.)*

FUNNY CAR *(CONT.)*

Date	Race, Site	Winner	Time	Speed
Apr 11–14	O'Reilly Spring Nationals, Baytown, TX	John Force	4.991	310.20
Apr 26–28	Thunder Valley Nationals, Bristol, TN	Whit Bazemore	4.936	310.27
May 2–5	Southern Nationals, Commerce, GA	Whit Bazemore	4.963	310.41
May 16–19	Matco Supernationals, Englishtown, NJ	Gary Densham	5.046	316.38
May 23–26	O'Reilly Summer Nationals, Topeka, KS	Tony Pedregon	4.910	320.58
May 30–June 2	Chicagoland Dodge Nationals, Joliet, IL	Del Worsham	4.878	312.21
June 13–16	Pontiac Nationals, Columbus, OH	Ron Capps	6.027	235.60
June 27–30	Sears Craftsman Nationals, St. Louis, MO	John Force	8.837	87.98
July 18–21	Mile High Nationals, Denver	Del Worsham	5.160	293.15
July 26–28	Northwest Nationals, Kent, WA	Tony Pedregon	5.049	293.22
Aug 2–4	Fram Autolite Nationals, Sonoma, CA	John Force	4.953	303.09
Aug 15–18	Rugged Liner Nationals, Brainerd, MN	John Force	5.405	216.62
Aug 28–Sept 2	U.S. Nationals, Clermont, IN	John Force	5.028	280.02
Sept 12–15	Lucas Oil Nationals, Mohnton, PA	Tony Pedregon	4.829	318.62
Sept 19–22	Mid-South Nationals, Millington, TN	Tony Pedregon	4.909	325.12
Sept 26–29	Nationals, Joliet, IL	Tony Pedregon	4.924	310.84

PRO STOCK

Date	Race, Site	Winner	Time	Speed
Feb 7–10	Winternationals, Pomona, CA	George Marnell	6.880	200.89
Feb 21–24	Kragen Nationals, Phoenix	Bruce Allen	6.904	199.02
Mar 14–17	Mac Tools Gatornationals, Gainesville, FL	Darrell Alderman	6.927	200.77
Apr 4–7	Las Vegas Nationals	Ron Krisher	7.016	197.83
Apr 11–14	O'Reilly Spring Nationals, Baytown, TX	Mike Edwards	6.892	199.70
Apr 26–28	Thunder Valley Nationals, Bristol, TN	Warren Johnson	6.986	198.41
May 2–5	Southern Nationals, Commerce, GA	Allen Johnson	6.907	200.92
May 16–19	Matco Supernationals, Englishtown, NJ	Greg Anderson	6.808	201.91
May 23–26	O'Reilly Summer Nationals, Topeka, KS	Troy Coughlin	6.924	198.44
May 30–June 2	Chicagoland Dodge Nationals, Joliet, IL	Bruce Allen	6.888	199.55
June 13–16	Pontiac Nationals, Columbus, OH	Greg Anderson	6.924	199.05
June 27–30	Sears Craftsman Nationals, St. Louis, MO	Greg Anderson	6.938	199.46
July 18–21	Mile High Nationals, Denver	Mike Edwards	7.339	188.41
July 26–28	Northwest Nationals, Kent, WA	Jeg Coughlin	6.864	200.14
Aug 2–4	Fram Autolite Nationals, Sonoma, CA	Larry Morgan	6.845	201.58
Aug 15–18	Rugged Liner Nationals, Brainerd, MN	Jeg Coughlin	6.918	199.11
Aug 28–Sept 2	U.S. Nationals, Clermont, IN	Jeg Coughlin	6.953	199.08
Sept 12–15	Lucas Oil Nationals, Mohnton, PA	Jim Yates	6.870	199.67
Sept 19–22	Mid-South Nationals, Millington, TN	Jeg Coughlin	6.849	200.80
Sept 26–29	Nationals, Joliet, IL	Jeg Coughlin	6.875	200.89

2001 Standings

TOP FUEL

Driver	Wins	Pts
Kenny Bernstein	8	2102
Larry Dixon Jr	6	2007
Doug Kalitta	3	1598
Mike Dunn	2	1594
Gary Scelzi	3	1581
Darrell Russell	1	1505
Doug Herbert	1	1206
Tony Schumacher	0	1153
David Grubnic	0	843
Rhonda Hartman-Smith	0	822

FUNNY CAR

Driver	Wins	Pts
John Force	6	2000
Whit Bazemore	3	1748
Del Worsham	4	1490
Ron Capps	3	1451
Tony Pedregon	3	1406
Bruce Sarver	1	1283
Frank Pedregon	1	1149
Gary Densham	2	1147
Deak Skuza	0	1128
Tommy Johnson Jr.	1	1127

PRO STOCK

Driver	Wins	Pts
Warren Johnson	6	1538
Jim Yates	1	1459
Bruce Allen	2	1383
Mike Edwards	1	1321
Jeg Coughlin Jr	4	1256
Mark Pawuk	1	1221
Mark Osborne	1	1212
Ron Krisher	1	1182
Kurt Johnson	1	1170
Brad Jeter	0	1062

Indianapolis 500

First held in 1911, the Indianapolis 500—200 laps of the 2.5-mile Indianapolis Motor Speedway Track (called the Brickyard in honor of its original pavement)—grew to become the most famous auto race in the world. Though the Memorial Day weekend event lost participants and prestige in the mid-1990s due to feuding in the world of U.S. open-wheel racing, it annually attracts crowds of over 100,000.

Year	Winner (start pos.)	Chassis-Engine	Avg Speed	Pole Winner	Speed
1911	Ray Harroun (28)	Marmon-Marmon	74.590	Lewis Strang	First entered
1912	Joe Dawson (7)	National-National	78.720	Gil Anderson	First entered
1913	Jules Goux (7)	Peugeot-Peugeot	75.930	Caleb Bragg	Drew pole
1914	Rene Thomas (15)	Delage-Delage	82.470	Jean Chassagne	Drew pole
1915	Ralph DePalma (2)	Mercedes-Mercedes	89.840	Howard Wilcox	98.90
1916	Dario Resta (4)	Peugeot-Peugeot	84.000	John Aitken	96.69
1917–18	No race				
1919	Howard Wilcox (2)	Peugeot-Peugeot	88.050	Rene Thomas	104.78
1920	Gaston Chevrolet (6)	Frontenac-Frontenac	88.620	Ralph DePalma	99.15
1921	Tommy Milton (20)	Frontenac-Frontenac	89.620	Ralph DePalma	100.75
1922	Jimmy Murphy (1)	Duesenberg-Miller	94.480	Jimmy Murphy	100.50
1923	Tommy Milton (1)	Miller-Miller	90.950	Tommy Milton	108.17
1924	L.L. Corum Joe Boyer (21)	Duesenberg-Duesenberg	98.230	Jimmy Murphy	108.037
1925	Peter DePaolo (2)	Duesenberg-Duesenberg	101.130	Leon Duray	113.196
1926	Frank Lockhart (20)	Miller-Miller	95.904	Earl Cooper	111.735
1927	George Souders (22)	Duesenberg-Duesenberg	97.545	Frank Lockhart	120.100
1928	Louis Meyer (13)	Miller-Miller	99.482	Leon Duray	122.391
1929	Ray Keech (6)	Miller-Miller	97.585	Cliff Woodbury	120.599
1930	Billy Arnold (1)	Summers-Miller	100.448	Billy Arnold	113.268
1931	Louis Schneider (13)	Stevens-Miller	96.629	Russ Snowberger	112.796
1932	Fred Frame (27)	Wetteroth-Miller	104.144	Lou Moore	117.363
1933	Louis Meyer (6)	Miller-Miller	104.162	Bill Cummings	118.524
1934	Bill Cummings (10)	Miller-Miller	104.863	Kelly Petillo	119.329
1935	Kelly Petillo (22)	Wetteroth-Offy	106.240	Rex Mays	120.736
1936	Louis Meyer (28)	Stevens-Miller	109.069	Rex Mays	119.664
1937	Wilbur Shaw (2)	Shaw-Offy	113.580	Bill Cummings	123.343
1938	Floyd Roberts (1)	Wetteroth-Miller	117.200	Floyd Roberts	125.681
1939	Wilbur Shaw (3)	Maserati-Maserati	115.035	Jimmy Snyder	130.138
1940	Wilbur Shaw (2)	Maserati-Maserati	114.277	Rex Mays	127.850
1941	Floyd Davis Mauri Rose (17)	Wetteroth-Offy	115.117	Mauri Rose	128.691
1942–45	No race				
1946	George Robson (15)	Adams-Sparks	114.820	Cliff Bergere	126.471
1947	Mauri Rose (3)	Deidt-Offy	116.338	Ted Horn	126.564
1948	Mauri Rose (3)	Deidt-Offy	119.814	Rex Mays	130.577
1949	Bill Holland (4)	Deidt-Offy	121.327	Duke Nalon	132.939
1950	Johnnie Parsons (5)	Kurtis-Offy	124.002	Walt Faulkner	134.343
1951	Lee Wallard (2)	Kurtis-Offy	126.244	Duke Nalon	136.498
1952	Troy Ruttman (7)	Kuzma-Offy	128.922	Fred Agabashian	138.010
1953	Bill Vukovich (1)	KK500A-Offy	128.740	Bill Vukovich	138.392
1954	Bill Vukovich (19)	KK500A-Offy	130.840	Jack McGrath	141.033
1955	Bob Sweikert (14)	KK500C-Offy	128.209	Jerry Hoyt	140.045
1956	Pat Flaherty (1)	Watson-Offy	128.490	Pat Flaherty	145.596
1957	Sam Hanks (13)	Salih-Offy	135.601	Pat O'Connor	143.948
1958	Jim Bryan (7)	Salih-Offy	133.791	Dick Rathmann	145.974
1959	Rodger Ward (6)	Watson-Offy	135.857	Johnny Thomson	145.908
1960	Jim Rathmann (2)	Watson-Offy	138.767	Eddie Sachs	146.592
1961	A.J. Foyt (7)	Trevis-Offy	139.130	Eddie Sachs	147.481
1962	Rodger Ward (2)	Watson-Offy	140.293	Parnelli Jones	150.370
1963	Parnelli Jones (1)	Watson-Offy	143.137	Parnelli Jones	151.153
1964	A.J. Foyt (5)	Watson-Offy	147.350	Jim Clark	158.828
1965	Jim Clark (2)	Lotus-Ford	150.686	A.J. Foyt	161.233
1966	Graham Hill (15)	Lola-Ford	144.317	Mario Andretti	165.899
1967	A.J. Foyt (4)	Coyote-Ford	151.207	Mario Andretti	168.982
1968	Bobby Unser (3)	Eagle-Offy	152.882	Joe Leonard	171.559
1969	Mario Andretti (2)	Hawk-Ford	156.867	A.J. Foyt	170.568
1970	Al Unser (1)	PJ Colt-Ford	155.749	Al Unser	170.221
1971	Al Unser (5)	PJ Colt-Ford	157.735	Peter Revson	178.696
1972	Mark Donohue (3)	McLaren-Offy	162.962	Bobby Unser	195.940
1973	Gordon Johncock (11)	Eagle-Offy	159.036	Johnny Rutherford	198.413
1974	Johnny Rutherford (25)	McLaren-Offy	158.589	A.J. Foyt	191.632

Year	Winner (start pos.)	Chassis-Engine	Avg speed	Pole Winner	Speed
1975	Bobby Unser (3)	Racers Eagle-Offy	149.213	A.J. Foyt	193.976
1976	Johnny Rutherford (1)	McLaren-Offy	148.725	Johnny Rutherford	188.957
1977	A.J. Foyt (4)	Coyote-Ford	161.331	Tom Sneva	198.884
1978	Al Unser (5)	Lola-Cosworth	161.361	Tom Sneva	202.156
1979	Rick Mears (1)	Penske-Cosworth	158.899	Rick Mears	193.736
1980	Johnny Rutherford (1)	Chaparral-Cosworth	142.862	Johnny Rutherford	192.256
1981	Bobby Unser (1)	Penske-Cosworth	139.084	Bobby Unser	200.546
1982	Gordon Johncock (5)	Wildcat-Cosworth	162.026	Rick Mears	207.004
1983	Tom Sneva (4)	March-Cosworth	162.117	Teo Fabi	207.395
1984	Rick Mears (3)	March-Cosworth	163.612	Tom Sneva	210.029
1985	Danny Sullivan (8)	March-Cosworth	152.982	Pancho Carter	212.583
1986	Bobby Rahal (4)	March-Cosworth	170.722	Rick Mears	216.828
1987	Al Unser (20)	March-Cosworth	162.175	Mario Andretti	215.390
1988	Rick Mears (1)	Penske-Chevrolet	144.809	Rick Mears	219.198
1989	Emerson Fittipaldi (3)	Penske-Chevrolet	167.581	Rick Mears	223.885
1990	Arie Luyendyk (3)	Lola-Chevrolet	185.981*	Emerson Fittipaldi	225.301
1991	Rick Mears (1)	Penske-Chevrolet	176.457	Rick Mears	224.113
1992	Al Unser Jr (12)	Galmer-Chevrolet	134.477	Roberto Guerrero	232.482
1993	Emerson Fittipaldi (9)	Penske-Chevrolet	157.207	Arie Luyendyk	223.967
1994	Al Unser Jr (1)	Penske-Mercedes	160.872	Al Unser Jr	228.011
1995	Jacques Villeneuve (5)	Reynard-Ford	153.616	Scott Brayton	231.616
1996	Buddy Lazier (5)	Reynard-Ford	147.956	Tony Stewart	233.100†
1997	Arie Luyendyk (1)	G Force-Oldsmobile	145.827	Arie Luyendyk	231.468
1998	Eddie Cheever (17)	Dallara-Oldsmobile	145.155	Billy Boat	223.503
1999	Kenny Brack (8)	Dallara-Oldsmobile	153.176	Arie Luyendyk	225.179
2000	Juan Montoya (2)	G Force-Oldsmobile	167.607	Greg Ray	223.471
2001	Helio Castroneves (11)	Dallara-Oldsmobile	153.601	Scott Sharp	226.037
2002	Helio Castroneves (13)	Dallara-Chevrolet	166.499	Bruno Junqueira	231.342

Indianapolis 500 Rookie of the Year Award

*Track record, winning speed.
†Track record, qualifying speed.

1952	Art Cross
1953	Jimmy Daywalt
1954	Larry Crockett
1955	Al Herman
1956	Bob Veith
1957	Don Edmunds
1958	George Amick
1959	Bobby Grim
1960	Jim Hurtubise
1961	Parnelli Jones*
	Bobby Marshman
1962	Jimmy McElreath
1963	Jim Clark*
1964	Johnny White
1965	Mario Andretti*
1966	Jackie Stewart
1967	Denis Hulme
1968	Billy Vukovich

*Future winner of Indy 500.

1969	Mark Donohue*
1970	Donnie Allison
1971	Denny Zimmerman
1972	Mike Hiss
1973	Graham McRae
1974	Pancho Carter
1975	Bill Puterbaugh
1976	Vern Schuppan
1977	Jerry Sneva
1978	Rick Mears*
	Larry Rice
1979	Howdy Holmes
1980	Tim Richmond
1981	Josele Garza
1982	Jim Hickman
1983	Teo Fabi
1984	Michael Andretti
	Roberto Guerrero
1985	Arie Luyendyk*

1986	Randy Lanier
1987	Fabrizio Barbazza
1988	Billy Vukovich III
1989	Bernard Jourdain
	Scott Pruett
1990	Eddie Cheever*
1991	Jeff Andretti
1992	Lyn St. James
1993	Nigel Mansell
1994	Jacques Villeneuve*
1995	Gil de Ferran
1996	Tony Stewart
1997	Jeff Ward
1998	Steve Knapp
1999	Robby McGehee
2000	Juan Montoya*
2001	Helio Castroneves*
2002	Alex Barron
	Tomas Scheckter

Championship Auto Racing Teams

CART Championship Series Champions

From 1909 to 1955, this championship was awarded by the American Automobile Association (AAA), and from 1956 to 1979 by the United States Auto Club (USAC). Since 1979, Championship Auto Racing Teams (CART) has conducted the championship. Known as PPG CART World Series until 1998.

1909 ....George Robertson	1940 ....Rex Mays	1974 ....Bobby Unser
1910 ....Ray Harroun	1941 ....Rex Mays	1975 ............A.J. Foyt
1911 ....Ralph Mulford	1942–45 ....No racing	1976 ....Gordon Johncock
1912 ....Ralph DePalma	1946 ....Ted Horn	1977 ....Tom Sneva
1913 ....Earl Cooper	1947 ....Ted Horn	1978 ....Tom Sneva
1914 ....Ralph DePalma	1948 ....Ted Horn	1979 ............A.J. Foyt
1915 ....Earl Cooper	1949 ....Johnnie Parsons	1979 ....Rick Mears
1916 ....Dario Resta	1950 ....Henry Banks	1980 ....Johnny Rutherford
1917 ....Earl Cooper	1951 ....Tony Bettenhausen	1981 ....Rick Mears
1918 ....Ralph Mulford	1952 ....Chuck Stevenson	1982 ....Rick Mears
1919 ....Howard Wilcox	1953 ....Sam Hanks	1983 ....Al Unser
1920 ....Tommy Milton	1954 ....Jimmy Bryan	1984 ....Mario Andretti
1921 ....Tommy Milton	1955 ....Bob Sweikert	1985 ....Al Unser
1922 ....Jimmy Murphy	1956 ....Jimmy Bryan	1986 ....Bobby Rahal
1923 ....Eddie Hearne	1957 ....Jimmy Bryan	1987 ....Bobby Rahal
1924 ....Jimmy Murphy	1958 ....Tony Bettenhausen	1988 ....Danny Sullivan
1925 ....Peter DePaolo	1959 ....Rodger Ward	1989 ....Emerson Fittipaldi
1926 ....Harry Hartz	1960 ............A.J. Foyt	1990 ....Al Unser Jr.
1927 ....Peter DePaolo	1961 ............A.J. Foyt	1991 ....Michael Andretti
1928 ....Louis Meyer	1962 ....Rodger Ward	1992 ....Bobby Rahal
1929 ....Louis Meyer	1963 ............A.J. Foyt	1993 ....Nigel Mansell
1930 ....Billy Arnold	1964 ............A.J. Foyt	1994 ....Al Unser Jr.
1931 ....Louis Schneider	1965 ....Mario Andretti	1995 ....Jacques Villeneuve
1932 ....Bob Carey	1966 ....Mario Andretti	1996 ....Jimmy Vasser
1933 ....Louis Meyer	1967 ............A.J. Foyt	1997 ....Alex Zanardi
1934 ....Bill Cummings	1968 ....Bobby Unser	1998 ....Alex Zanardi
1935 ....Kelly Petillo	1969 ....Mario Andretti	1999 ....Juan Montoya
1936 ....Mauri Rose	1970 ....Al Unser	2000 ....Gil de Ferran
1937 ....Wilbur Shaw	1971 ....Joe Leonard	2001 ....Gil de Ferran
1938 ....Floyd Roberts	1972 ....Joe Leonard	
1939 ....Wilbur Shaw	1973 ....Roger McCluskey	

Alltime CART Leaders

WINS	WINNINGS ($)	POLE POSITIONS
A.J. Foyt 67	Al Unser Jr 18,828,406	Mario Andretti 67
Mario Andretti 52	*Michael Andretti 17,709,369	A.J. Foyt 53
*Michael Andretti 41	Bobby Rahal 16,344,008	Bobby Unser 49
Al Unser 39	Emerson Fittipaldi 14,293,625	Rick Mears 40
Bobby Unser.........................35	Mario Andretti 11,552,154	*Michael Andretti 32
Al Unser Jr 31	Rick Mears 11,050,807	Al Unser 27
Rick Mears 29	*Jimmy Vasser 10,125,494	Johnny Rutherford 23
Johnny Rutherford 27	Danny Sullivan 8,884,126	Gordon Johncock 20
Rodger Ward 26	*Paul Tracy................8,331,520	Rex Mays 19
Gordon Johncock 25	Arie Luyendyk 7,732,188	Danny Sullivan 19
Bobby Rahal 24	*Gil de Ferran............7,390,703	Bobby Rahal 18
Ralph DePalma......................24	Raul Boesel................6,971,887	Emerson Fittipaldi 17
Tommy Milton........................23	Al Unser 6,740,843	Tony Bettenhausen 14
Tony Bettenhausen 22	*Adrian Fernandez....6,305,265	Juan Montoya 14
Emerson Fittipaldi 22	Alex Zanardi..............5,893,750	*Gil de Ferran........................14
Earl Cooper...........................20	Scott Pruett 5,440,144	Don Branson 14
Jimmy Bryan 19	A.J. Foyt 5,357,589	Tom Sneva 14
Jimmy Murphy 19	Teo Fabi 5,045,881	*Paul Tracy............................13
*Paul Tracy............................18	*Christian Fittipaldi 4,991,668	Parnelli Jones........................12
Danny Sullivan 17	Scott Brayton 4,807,274	Rodger Ward 11
Ralph Mulford 17		Danny Ongais.........................11

*Active driver. Note: Leaders through 2001 CART season.

Stock Car Racing's Major Events

In 1985, Winston began offering a $1 million bonus to any driver to win three of the top four NASCAR events in the same season. A fifth event, the Brickyard 400 (in Indianapolis) was added in 1994. As of 1998 the Winston million was awarded to any driver who won three of the five events. The other four races are the richest (Daytona 500), the fastest (Talladega 500), the longest (Charlotte 600) and the oldest (Southern 500 at Darlington). Only five drivers, Lee Roy Yarbrough (1969), David Pearson (1976), Bill Elliott (1985), Dale jarrett (1996) and Jeff Gordon (1997, '98) have scored the three-track hat trick.

Daytona 500

Year	Winner	Car	Avg Speed	Pole Winner	Speed
1959	Lee Petty	Oldsmobile	135.520	Cotton Owens	143.198
1960	Junior Johnson	Chevrolet	124.740	Fireball Roberts	151.556
1961	Marvin Panch	Pontiac	149.601	Fireball Roberts	155.709
1962	Fireball Roberts	Pontiac	152.529	Fireball Roberts	156.995
1963	Tiny Lund	Ford	151.566	Johnny Rutherford	165.183
1964	Richard Petty	Plymouth	154.345	Paul Goldsmith	174.910
1965	Fred Lorenzen	Ford	141.539	Darel Dieringer	171.151
1966	Richard Petty	Plymouth	160.627	Richard Petty	175.165
1967	Mario Andretti	Ford	149.926	Curtis Turner	180.831
1968	Cale Yarborough	Mercury	143.251	Cale Yarborough	189.222
1969	Lee Roy Yarbrough	Ford	157.950	David Pearson	190.029
1970	Pete Hamilton	Plymouth	149.601	Cale Yarborough	194.015
1971	Richard Petty	Plymouth	144.462	A.J. Foyt	182.744
1972	A.J. Foyt	Mercury	161.550	Bobby Isaac	186.632
1973	Richard Petty	Dodge	157.205	Buddy Baker	185.662
1974	Richard Petty	Dodge	140.894	David Pearson	185.017
1975	Benny Parsons	Chevrolet	153.649	Donnie Allison	185.827
1976	David Pearson	Mercury	152.181	A.J. Foyt	185.943
1977	Cale Yarborough	Chevrolet	153.218	Donnie Allison	188.048
1978	Bobby Allison	Ford	159.730	Cale Yarborough	187.536
1979	Richard Petty	Oldsmobile	143.977	Buddy Baker	196.049
1980	Buddy Baker	Oldsmobile	177.602*	A.J. Foyt	195.020
1981	Richard Petty	Buick	169.651	Bobby Allison	194.624
1982	Bobby Allison	Buick	153.991	Benny Parsons	196.317
1983	Cale Yarborough	Pontiac	155.979	Ricky Rudd	198.864
1984	Cale Yarborough	Chevrolet	150.994	Cale Yarborough	201.848
1985	Bill Elliott	Ford	172.265	Bill Elliott	205.114
1986	Geoff Bodine	Chevrolet	148.124	Bill Elliott	205.039
1987	Bill Elliott	Ford	176.263	Bill Elliott	210.364†
1988	Bobby Allison	Buick	137.531	Ken Schrader	193.823
1989	Darrell Waltrip	Chevrolet	148.466	Ken Schrader	196.996
1990	Derrike Cope	Chevrolet	165.761	Ken Schrader	196.515
1991	Ernie Irvan	Chevrolet	148.148	Davey Allison	195.955
1992	Davey Allison	Ford	160.256	Sterling Marlin	192.213
1993	Dale Jarrett	Chevrolet	154.972	Kyle Petty	189.426
1994	Sterling Marlin	Chevrolet	156.931	Loy Allen Jr	190.158
1995	Sterling Marlin	Chevrolet	141.710	Dale Jarrett	193.498
1996	Dale Jarrett	Ford	154.308	Dale Earnhardt	189.510
1997	Jeff Gordon	Chevrolet	148.295	Mike Skinner	189.813
1998	Dale Earnhardt	Chevrolet	172.712	Bobby Labonte	192.415
1999	Jeff Gordon	Chevrolet	161.551	Jeff Gordon	195.067
2000	Dale Jarrett	Ford	155.669	Dale Jarrett	191.091
2001	Michael Waltrip	Chevrolet	161.783	Bill Elliott	183.570
2002	Ward Burton	Dodge	142.971	Jimmie Johnson	185.831

*Track record, winning speed. †Track record, qualifying speed. Note: The Daytona 500, held annually in February, now opens the NASCAR season with 200 laps around the high-banked Daytona International Speedway.

Charlotte 600

Year	Winner	Car	Avg Speed	Pole Winner
1960	Joe Lee Johnson	Chevrolet	107.752	Joe Lee Johnson
1961	David Pearson	Pontiac	111.634	Richard Petty
1962	Nelson Stacy	Ford	125.552	Fireball Roberts
1963	Fred Lorenzen	Ford	132.418	Junior Johnson
1964	Jim Paschal	Plymouth	125.772	Junior Johnson
1965	Fred Lorenzen	Ford	121.772	Fred Lorenzon
1966	Marvin Panch	Plymouth	135.042	Paul Goldsmith
1967	Jim Paschal	Plymouth	135.832	Cale Yarborough
1968	Buddy Baker	Dodge	104.207	Donnie Allison
1969	Lee Roy Yarbrough	Mercury	134.631	Donnie Allison
1970	Donnie Allison	Ford	129.680	Bobby Isaac
1971	Bobby Allison	Mercury	140.442	Charlie Glotzbach
1972	Buddy Baker	Dodge	142.255	Bobby Allison
1973	Buddy Baker	Dodge	134.890	Buddy Baker
1974	David Pearson	Mercury	135.720	David Pearson
1975	Richard Petty	Dodge	145.327	David Pearsón
1976	David Pearson	Mercury	137.352	David Pearson
1977	Richard Petty	Dodge	137.636	David Pearson
1978	Darrell Waltrip	Chevrolet	138.355	David Pearson
1979	Darrell Waltrip	Chevrolet	136.674	Neil Bonnet
1980	Benny Parsons	Chevrolet	119.265	Cale Yarborough
1981	Bobby Allison	Buick	129.326	Neil Bonnett
1982	Neil Bonnett	Ford	130.508	David Pearson
1983	Neil Bonnett	Chevrolet	140.406	Buddy Baker
1984	Bobby Allison	Buick	129.233	Harry Gant
1985	Darrell Waltrip	Chevrolet	141.807	Bill Elliott
1986	Dale Earnhardt	Chevrolet	140.406	Geoff Bodine
1987	Kyle Petty	Ford	131.483	Bill Elliott
1988	Darrell Waltrip	Chevrolet	124.460	Davey Allison
1989	Darrell Waltrip	Chevrolet	144.077	Alan Kulwicki
1990	Rusty Wallace	Pontiac	137.650	Ken Schrader
1991	Davey Allison	Ford	138.951	Mark Martin
1992	Dale Earnhardt	Chevrolet	132.980	Bill Elliott
1993	Dale Earnhardt	Chevrolet	145.504	Ken Schrader
1994	Jeff Gordon	Chevrolet	139.445	Jeff Gordon
1995	Bobby Labonte	Chevrolet	151.952	Jeff Gordon
1996	Dale Jarrett	Ford	147.581	Jeff Gordon
1997	Jeff Gordon	Chevrolet	136.745	Jeff Gordon
1998	Jeff Gordon	Chevrolet	136.424	Jeff Gordon
1999	Jeff Burton	Ford	151.367	Bobby Labonte
2000	Matt Kenseth	Ford	142.640	Dale Earnhardt Jr
2001	Jeff Burton	Ford	138.107	Ryan Newman
2002	Mark Martin	Ford	137.729	Jimmie Johnson

Note: Held at the 1.5-mile high-banked Lowe's Motor Speedway in Charlotte on Memorial Day weekend.

Brickyard 400

Year	Winner	Car	Avg Speed	Pole Winner	Speed
1994	Jeff Gordon	Chevrolet	131.977	Rick Mast	172.414
1995	Dale Earnhardt	Chevrolet	155.206	Jeff Gordon	172.536
1996	Dale Jarrett	Ford	139.508	Jeff Gordon	176.419
1997	Ricky Rudd	Ford	130.814	Ernie Irvan	177.736
1998	Jeff Gordon	Chevrolet	126.772	Ernie Irvan	179.394
1999	Dale Jarrett	Ford	148.194	Jeff Gordon	179.612
2000	Bobby Labonte	Pontiac	155.912	Ricky Rudd	181.068
2001	Jeff Gordon	Chevrolet	130.790	Jimmy Spencer	179.666
2002	Bill Elliott	Dodge	125.033	Tony Stewart	182.960

Talladega 500

Year	Winner	Car	Avg Speed	Pole Winner	Speed
1970	Pete Hamilton	Plymouth	152.321	Bobby Isaac	199.658
1971	Donnie Allison	Mercury	147.419	Donnie Allison	185.869
1972	David Pearson	Mercury	134.400	Bobby Isaac	192.428
1973	David Pearson	Mercury	131.956	Buddy Baker	193.435
1974	David Pearson	Mercury	130.220	David Pearson	186.086
1975	Buddy Baker	Ford	144.94	Buddy Baker	189.947
1976	Buddy Baker	Ford	169.887	Dave Marcis	189.197
1977	Darrell Waltrip	Chevrolet	164.887	A.J. Foyt	192.424
1978	Cale Yarborough	Oldsmobile	155.699	Cale Yarborough	191.904
1979	Bobby Allison	Ford	154.770	Darrell Waltrip	195.644
1980	Buddy Baker	Oldsmobile	170.481	David Pearson	197.704
1981	Bobby Allison	Buick	149.376	Bobby Allison	195.864
1982	Darrell Waltrip	Buick	156.697	Benny Parsons	200.176
1983	Richard Petty	Pontiac	135.936	Cale Yarborough	202.650
1984	Cale Yarborough	Chevrolet	172.988	Cale Yarborough	202.692
1985	Bill Elliott	Ford	186.288	Bill Elliott	209.398
1986	Bobby Allison	Buick	157.698	Bill Elliott	212.229
1987	Davey Allison	Ford	154.228	Bill Elliott	221.809
1988	Phil Parsons	Oldsmobile	156.547	Davey Allison	198.969
1989	Davey Allison	Ford	155.869	Mark Martin	193.061
1990	Dale Earnhardt	Chevrolet	159.571	Bill Elliott	199.388
1991	Harry Gant	Oldsmobile	165.620	Ernie Irvan	195.186
1992	Davey Allison	Ford	167.609	Ernie Irvan	192.831
1993	Ernie Irvan	Chevrolet	155.412	Dale Earnhardt	192.355
1994	Dale Earnhardt	Chevrolet	157.478	Ernie Irvan	193.298
1995	Mark Martin	Ford	178.902	Terry Labonte	196.532
1996	Sterling Marlin	Chevrolet	149.999	Ernie Irvan	192.855
1997	Mark Martin	Ford	188.354	John Andretti	193.627
1998	Dale Jarrett	Ford	159.318	Ken Schrader	196.153
1999	Dale Earnhardt	Chevrolet	166.632	Joe Nemechek	198.331
2000	Dale Earnhardt	Chevrolet	165.681	Joe Nemechek	190.279
2001	Dale Earnhardt Jr	Chevrolet	164.185	Stacy Compton	185.240

Note: Formerly the Winston 500, held at the 2.66-mile Talladega Superspeedway.

The Schumacher Formula

In 12 Formula One races through Aug. 4 of the 2002 season, 32-year-old Michael Schumacher had nine wins, two seconds and a third. He clinched his fifth championship with six races remaining. Here are five reasons for his astounding success.

1. His Teutonic Aura. With his steely gaze and air of invincibility the German driver looks indomitable. Behind the wheel he is fearless and seems to possess superhuman reflexes and instincts.

2. His risk-taking. After winning F/1 titles in 1994 and '95 for Bennetton, he gave up a shot at three in a row to join what was then a struggling Ferrari team. Five years later, he was back on top.

3. Ferrari's bankroll. Formula One cars have more gizmos and goodies that Austin Powers's Shaguar, and no other team has the resources or personnel to match Ferrari. In 2001 the car manufacturer sank an estimated $302 million into its F/1 operation—some $15 million more than McLaren, the next-highest-spending team.

4. The front-runner's edge. You're more likely to see a lead change in a funeral procession than at an F/1 race. Schumacher started on the pole in four of his nine victories in 2002, and qualified no worse than fourth.

5. His loyal understudy. The driver with the best chance of beating him is Rubens Barrichello—his teammate. However, Schumacher is the star at Ferrari, so Barrichello's job is to do whatever he can to get the German the title. That might mean pulling over on the final straightaway after dominating the entire race (as he did during Schumacher's victory at the Austrian Grand Prix in May 2002).

Southern 500

Year	Winner	Car	Avg Speed	Pole Winner
1950	Johnny Mantz	Plymouth	76.260	Wally Campbell
1951	Herb Thomas	Hudson	76.900	Marshall Teague
1952	Fonty Flock	Oldsmobile	74.510	Dick Rathman
1953	Buck Baker	Oldsmobile	92.780	Fonty Flock
1954	Herb Thomas	Hudson	94.930	Buck Baker
1955	Herb Thomas	Chevrolet	92.281	Tim Flock
1956	Curtis Turner	Ford	95.067	Buck Baker
1957	Speedy Thompson	Chevrolet	100.100	Paul Goldsmith
1958	Fireball Roberts	Chevrolet	102.590	Fireball Roberts
1959	Jim Reed	Chevrolet	111.836	Fireball Roberts
1960	Buck Baker	Pontiac	105.901	Cotton Owens
1961	Nelson Stacy	Ford	117.880	Fireball Roberts
1962	Larry Frank	Ford	117.965	Fireball Roberts
1963	Fireball Roberts	Ford	129.784	Fireball Roberts
1964	Buck Baker	Dodge	117.757	Richard Petty
1965	Ned Jarrett	Ford	115.924	Junior Johnson
1966	Darel Dieringer	Mercury	114.830	Lee Yarborough
1967	Richard Petty	Plymouth	131.933	David Pearson
1968	Cale Yarborough	Mercury	126.132	Charlie Glotzbach
1969	Lee Roy Yarbrough	Ford	105.612	Cale Yarborough
1970	Buddy Baker	Dodge	128.817	David Pearson
1971	Bobby Allison	Mercury	131.398	Bobby Allison
1972	Bobby Allison	Chevrolet	128.124	David Pearson
1973	Cale Yarborough	Chevrolet	134.033	David Pearson
1974	Cale Yarborough	Chevrolet	111.075	Richard Petty
1975	Bobby Allison	Matador	116.825	David Pearson
1976	David Pearson	Mercury	120.534	David Pearson
1977	David Pearson	Mercury	106.797	Darrell Waltrip
1978	Cale Yarborough	Oldsmobile	116.828	David Pearson
1979	David Pearson	Chevrolet	126.259	Bobby Allison
1980	Terry Labonte	Chevrolet	115.210	Darrell Waltrip
1981	Neil Bonnett	Ford	126.410	Harry Gant
1982	Cale Yarborough	Buick	126.703	David Pearson
1983	Bobby Allison	Buick	123.343	Neil Bonnett
1984	Harry Gant	Chevrolet	128.270	Harry Gant
1985	Bill Elliott	Ford	121.254	Bill Elliott
1986	Tim Richmond	Chevrolet	121.068	Tim Richmond
1987	Dale Earnhardt	Chevrolet	115.520	Davey Allison
1988	Bill Elliott	Ford	128.297	Bill Elliott
1989	Dale Earnhardt	Chevrolet	135.462	Alan Kulwicki
1990	Dale Earnhardt	Chevrolet	123.141	Dale Earnhardt
1991	Harry Gant	Oldsmobile	133.508	Davey Allison
1992	Darrell Waltrip	Chevrolet	129.114	Sterling Marlin
1993	Mark Martin	Ford	137.932	Ken Schrader
1994	Bill Elliott	Ford	127.915	Geoff Bodine
1995	Jeff Gordon	Chevrolet	121.231	John Andretti
1996	Jeff Gordon	Chevrolet	135.757	Dale Jarrett
1997	Jeff Gordon	Chevrolet	121.149	Bobby Labonte
1998	Jeff Gordon	Chevrolet	139.031	Dale Jarrett
1999	Jeff Burton	Ford	100.816	Kenny Irwin
2000	Bobby Labonte	Pontiac	108.275	Jeremy Mayfield
2001	Ward Burton	Dodge	122.773	Kurt Busch
2002	Jeff Gordon	Chevrolet	118.617	Sterling Marlin

Note: Held at the 1.366-mile Darlington (S.C.) Raceway on Labor Day weekend.

Winston Cup NASCAR Champions

Year	Driver	Car	Wins	Poles	Winnings ($)
1949	Red Byron	Oldsmobile	2	1	5,800
1950	Bill Rexford	Oldsmobile	1	0	6,175
1951	Herb Thomas	Hudson	7	4	18,200
1952	Tim Flock	Hudson	8	4	20,210
1953	Herb Thomas	Hudson	11	10	27,300
1954	Lee Petty	Dodge	7	3	26,706
1955	Tim Flock	Chrysler	18	19	33,750
1956	Buck Baker	Chrysler	14	12	29,790
1957	Buck Baker	Chevrolet	10	5	24,712
1958	Lee Petty	Oldsmobile	7	4	20,600
1959	Lee Petty	Plymouth	10	2	45,570
1960	Rex White	Chevrolet	6	3	45,260
1961	Ned Jarrett	Chevrolet	1	4	27,285
1962	Joe Weatherly	Pontiac	9	6	56,110
1963	Joe Weatherly	Mercury	3	6	58,110
1964	Richard Petty	Plymouth	9	8	98,810
1965	Ned Jarrett	Ford	13	9	77,966
1966	David Pearson	Dodge	14	7	59,205
1967	Richard Petty	Plymouth	27	18	130,275
1968	David Pearson	Ford	16	12	118,824
1969	David Pearson	Ford	11	14	183,700
1970	Bobby Isaac	Dodge	11	13	121,470
1971	Richard Petty	Plymouth	21	9	309,225
1972	Richard Petty	Plymouth	8	3	227,015
1973	Benny Parsons	Chevrolet	1	0	114,345
1974	Richard Petty	Dodge	10	7	299,175
1975	Richard Petty	Dodge	13	3	378,865
1976	Cale Yarborough	Chevrolet	9	2	387,173
1977	Cale Yarborough	Chevrolet	9	3	477,499
1978	Cale Yarborough	Oldsmobile	10	8	530,751
1979	Richard Petty	Chevrolet	5	1	531,292
1980	Dale Earnhardt	Chevrolet	5	0	588,926
1981	Darrell Waltrip	Buick	12	11	693,342
1982	Darrell Waltrip	Buick	12	7	873,118
1983	Bobby Allison	Buick	6	0	828,355
1984	Terry Labonte	Chevrolet	2	2	713,010
1985	Darrell Waltrip	Chevrolet	3	4	1,318,735
1986	Dale Earnhardt	Chevrolet	5	1	1,783,880
1987	Dale Earnhardt	Chevrolet	11	1	2,099,243
1988	Bill Elliott	Ford	6	6	1,574,639
1989	Rusty Wallace	Pontiac	6	4	2,247,950
1990	Dale Earnhardt	Chevrolet	9	4	3,083,056
1991	Dale Earnhardt	Chevrolet	4	0	2,396,685
1992	Alan Kulwicki	Ford	2	6	2,322,561
1993	Dale Earnhardt	Chevrolet	6	2	3,353,789
1994	Dale Earnhardt	Chevrolet	4	2	3,400,733
1995	Jeff Gordon	Chevrolet	7	9	4,347,343
1996	Terry Labonte	Chevrolet	2	4	4,030,648
1997	Jeff Gordon	Chevrolet	10	1	4,201,227
1998	Jeff Gordon	Chevrolet	13	7	6,175,867
1999	Dale Jarrett	Ford	4	0	3,608,829
2000	Bobby Labonte	Pontiac	4	2	4,041,750
2001	Jeff Gordon	Chevrolet	6	8	6,649,076

Alltime NASCAR Leaders

WINS		WINNINGS ($)		POLE POSITIONS	
Richard Petty	200	Dale Earnhardt	41,742,384	Richard Petty	126
David Pearson	105	*Jeff Gordon	40,495,851	David Pearson	113
Bobby Allison	84	*Dale Jarrett	31,635,528	Cale Yarborough	70
Darrell Waltrip	84	*Rusty Wallace	28,303,048	Darrell Waltrip	59
Cale Yarborough	83	*Mark Martin	28,081,772	Bobby Allison	57
Dale Earnhardt	76	*Bill Elliott	26,161,396	Bobby Isaac	51
*Jeff Gordon	58	*Terry Labonte	25,818,522	*Bill Elliott	50
Lee Petty	54	*Bobby Labonte	24,241,873	Junior Johnson	47
*Rusty Wallace	54	*Ricky Rudd	22,843,456	Buck Baker	44
Ned Jarrett	50	*Jeff Burton	21,526,436	*Mark Martin	41
Junior Johnson	50	Darrell Waltrip	19,416,618	Buddy Baker	40
Herb Thomas	48	*Sterling Marlin	17,822,962	*Jeff Gordon	39
Buck Baker	46	*Ken Schrader	17,458,675	Tim Flock	39
*Bill Elliott	40	*Geoff Bodine	14,794,719	Herb Thomas	39
Tim Flock	40	*Michael Waltrip	14,196,171	*Geoff Bodine	37

*Active drivers. Note: NASCAR leaders through 2001 NASCAR season.

Formula One Grand Prix Racing

World Driving Champions

Year	Winner	Car	Year	Winner	Car
1950	Guiseppe Farina, Italy	Alfa Romeo	1974	Emerson Fittipaldi, Brazil	McLaren-Ford
1951	Juan-Manuel Fangio, Argentina	Alfa Romeo	1975	Niki Lauda, Austria	Ferrari
1952	Alberto Ascari, Italy	Ferrari	1976	James Hunt, Grt Britain	McLaren-Ford
1953	Alberto Ascari, Italy	Ferrari	1977	Niki Lauda, Austria	Ferrari
1954	Juan-Manuel Fangio, Argentina	Maserati-Mercedes	1978	Mario Andretti, U.S.	Lotus-Ford
1955	Juan-Manuel Fangio, Argentina	Mercedes	1979	Jody Scheckter, S Africa	Ferrari
1956	Juan-Manuel Fangio, Argentina	Ferrari	1980	Alan Jones, Australia	Williams-Ford
1957	Juan-Manuel Fangio, Argentina	Maserati	1981	Nelson Piquet, Brazil	Brabham-Ford
			1982	Keke Rosberg, Finland	Williams-Ford
1958	Mike Hawthorn, Grt Britain	Ferrari	1983	Nelson Piquet, Brazil	Brabham-BMW
1959	Jack Brabham, Australia	Cooper-Climax	1984	Niki Lauda, Austria	McLaren-Porsche
1960	Jack Brabham, Australia	Cooper-Climax	1985	Alain Prost, France	McLaren-Porsche
1961	Phil Hill, U.S.	Ferrari	1986	Alain Prost, France	McLaren-Porsche
1962	Graham Hill, Grt Britain	BRM	1987	Nelson Piquet, Brazil	Williams-Honda
1963	Jim Clark, Scotland	Lotus-Climax	1988	Ayrton Senna, Brazil	McLaren-Honda
1964	John Surtees, Grt Britain	Ferrari	1989	Alain Prost, France	McLaren-Honda
1965	Jim Clark, Scotland	Lotus-Climax	1990	Ayrton Senna, Brazil	McLaren-Honda
1966	Jack Brabham, Australia	Brabham-Repco	1991	Ayrton Senna, Brazil	McLaren-Honda
1967	Denny Hulme, New Zealand	Brabham-Repco	1992	Nigel Mansell, Grt Britain	Williams-Renault
			1993	Alain Prost, France	Williams-Renault
1968	Graham Hill, Grt Britain	Lotus-Ford	1994	Michael Schumacher, Ger	Benetton-Ford
1969	Jackie Stewart, Scotland	Matra-Ford	1995	Michael Schumacher, Ger	Benetton-Renault
1970	Jochen Rindt, Austria*	Lotus-Ford	1996	Damon Hill, Grt Britain	Williams-Renault
1971	Jackie Stewart, Scotland	Tyrell-Ford	1997	Jacques Villeneuve, Can	Williams-Renault
1972	Emerson Fittipaldi, Brazil	Lotus-Ford	1998	Mika Hakkinen, Finland	McLaren-Mercedes
1973	Jackie Stewart, Scotland	Tyrell-Ford	1999	Mika Hakkinen, Finland	McLaren-Mercedes
			2000	Michael Schumacher, Ger	Ferrari
			2001	Michael Schumacher, Ger	Ferrari
			2002	Michael Schumacher, Ger	Ferrari

*The championship was awarded posthumously, after Rindt was killed during practice for the Italian Grand Prix.

Alltime Grand Prix Winners

Driver	Wins	Driver	Wins
*Michael Schumacher, Germany	52	Jim Clark, Great Britain	25
Alain Prost, France	51	Niki Lauda, Austria	25
Ayrton Senna, Brazil	41	Juan Manuel Fangio, Argentina	24
Nigel Mansell, Great Britain	31	Nelson Piquet, Brazil	23
Jackie Stewart, Great Britain	27	Damon Hill, Great Britain	22

*Active driver. Note: Grand Prix winners through 2001 season.

Alltime Grand Prix Pole Winners

Driver	Poles	Driver	Poles
Ayrton Senna, Brazil	65	Juan Manuel Fangio, Argentina	29
*Michael Schumacher, Germany	42	Mika Hakkinen, Finland	26
Alain Prost, France	33	Niki Lauda, Austria	24
Jim Clark, Great Britain	33	Nelson Piquet, Brazil	24
Nigel Mansell, Great Britain	32	Damon Hill, Great Britain	20

*Active driver. Note: Pole winners through 2001 season.

Professional Sports Car Racing, Inc.

The 24 Hours of Daytona

Year	Winner	Car	Avg Speed	Distance
1962	Dan Gurney	Lotus 19-Class SP11	104.101 mph	3 hrs (312.42 mi)
1963	Pedro Rodriguez	Ferrari-Class 12	102.074 mph	3 hrs (308.61 mi)
1964	Pedro Rodriguez/Phil Hill	Ferrari 250 LM	98.230 mph	2,000 km
1965	Ken Miles/Lloyd Ruby	Ford	99.944 mph	2,000 km
1966	Ken Miles/Lloyd Ruby	Ford Mark II	108.020 mph	24 hrs (2,570.63 mi)
1967	Lorenzo Bandini/Chris Amon	Ferrari 330 P4	105.688 mph	24 hrs (2,537.46 mi)
1968	Vic Elford/Jochen Neerpasch	Porsche 907	106.697 mph	24 hrs (2,565.69 mi)
1969	Mark Donohue/Chuck Parsons	Chevy Lola	99.268 mph	24 hrs (2,383.75 mi)
1970	Pedro Rodriguez/Leo Kinnunen	Porsche 917	114.866 mph	24 hrs (2,758.44 mi)
1971	Pedro Rodriguez/Jackie Oliver	Porsche 917K	109.203 mph	24 hrs (2,621.28 mi)
1972*	Mario Andretti/Jacky Ickx	Ferrari 312/P	122.573 mph	6 hrs (738.24 mi)
1973	Peter Gregg/Hurley Haywood	Porsche Carrera	106.225 mph	24 hrs (2,552.7 mi)
1974	(No race)			
1975	Peter Gregg/Hurley Haywood	Porsche Carrera	108.531 mph	24 hrs (2,606.04 mi)
1976†	Peter Gregg/Brian Redman/ John Fitzpatrick	BMW CSL	104.040 mph	24 hrs (2,092.8 mi)
1977	John Graves/Hurley Haywood/ Dave Helmick	Porsche Carrera	108.801 mph	24 hrs (2,615 mi)
1978	Rolf Stommelen/ Antoine Hezemans/Peter Gregg	Porsche Turbo	108.743 mph	24 hrs (2,611.2 mi)
1979	Ted Field/Danny Ongais/ Hurley Haywood	Porsche Turbo	109.249 mph	24 hrs (2,626.56 mi)
1980	Volkert Meri/Rolf Stommelen/ Reinhold Joest	Porsche Turbo	114.303 mph	24 hrs
1981	Bob Garretson/Bobby Rahal/ Brian Redman	Porsche Turbo	113.153 mph	24 hrs
1982	John Paul Jr/John Paul Sr/ Rolf Stommelen	Porsche Turbo	114.794 mph	24 hrs
1983	Preston Henn/Bob Wollek/ Claude Ballot-Lena/A.J. Foyt	Porsche Turbo	98.781 mph	24 hrs
1984	Sarel van der Merwe/ Graham Duxbury/Tony Martin	Porsche March	103.119 mph	24 hrs (2,476.8 mi)
1985	A.J. Foyt/Bob Wollek/ Al Unser/Thierry Boutsen	Porsche 962	104.162 mph	24 hrs (2,502.68 mi)
1986†	Al Holbert/Derek Bell/Al Unser Jr.	Porsche 962	105.484 mph	24 hrs (2,534.72 mi)
1987	Chip Robinson/Derek Bell/ Al Holbert/Al Unser Jr.	Porsche 962	111.599 mph	24 hrs (2,680.68 mi)

The 24 Hours of Daytona *(Cont.)*

Year	Winner	Car	Avg Speed	Distance
1988	Martin Brundle/John Nielsen/ Raul Boesel	Jaguar XJR-9	107.943 mph	24 hrs (2,591.68 mi)
1989	John Andretti/Derek Bell/ Bob Wollek	Porsche 962	92.009 mph	24 hrs (2,210.76 mi)
1990	Davy Jones/ Jan Lammers/ Andy Wallace	Jaguar XJR-12	112.857 mph	24 hrs (2,709.16 mi)
1991	Hurley Haywood/ John Winter/ Frank Jelinski/ Henri Pescarolo/ Bob Wollek	Porsche 962C	106.633 mph	24 hrs (2,559.64 mi)
1992	Massahiro Hasemi/ Kazuoyshi Hoshino/ Toshio Suzuki/ Anders Olofsson	Nissan R91CP	112.987 mph	24 hrs (2,712.72 mi)
1993	P.J. Jones/Mark Dismore/ Rocky Moran	Toyota Eagle MK III	103.537 mph	24 hrs (2,484.88 mi)
1994	Paul Gentilozzi/ Scott Pruett/ Butch Leitzinger/ Steve Millen	Nissan 300 ZX	104.80 mph	24 hrs (2,693.67 mi)
1995	Jurgen Lassig/ Christophe Buochut/ Giovanni Lavaggi/ Marco Werner	Porsche Spyder K8	102.28 mph	690 laps (2,456.4 mi)
1996	Wayne Taylor/ Scott Sharp/ Jim Pace	Oldsmobile Mark III	103.32 mph	697 laps (2,481.32 mi)
1997	Elliot Forbes-Robinson/ John Schneider/Rob Dyson/ John Paul Jr/Butch Leitzinger/ James Weaver/Andy Wallace	Ford R & S MK III	102.292 mph	690 laps (2,456.4 mi)
1998	Arie Luyendyk/Didier Theys/ Mauro Baldi	Ferrari 333 SP	105.565 mph	711 laps (2,531.16 mi)
1999	Elliott Forbes-Robinson/ Butch Leitzinger/ Andy Wallace	Ford R & S MK III	104.9 mph	708 laps (2,520.48 mi)
2000	Olivier Beretta/Karl Wendlinger/ Dominique Dupuy	Dodge Viper	107.207 mph	723 laps (2,573,88 m)
2001	Ron Fellows/Chris Kneifel/Franck Freon/Johnny O'Connell	Corvette	97.293 mph	656 laps (2,335.360 mi)
2002	Didier Theys/Fredy Lienhard/ Max Papis/Mauro Baldi	Dallara-Judd (SRP)	106.143 mph	716 laps (2,548.96 mi)

*Race shortened due to fuel crisis. †Course lengthened from 3.81 miles to 3.84 miles.

World SportsCar Champions*

Year	Winner	Car	Year	Winner	Car
1978	Peter Gregg	Porsche 935	1989	Geoff Brabham	Nissan GTP
1979	Peter Gregg	Porsche 935	1990	Geoff Brabham	Nissan GTP
1980	John Fitzpatrick	Porsche 935	1991	Geoff Brabham	Nissan NPT
1981	Brian Redman	Chevy Lola	1992	Juan Fangio II	Toyota EGL MKIII
1982	John Paul Jr	Chevy Lola	1993	Juan Fangio II	Toyota EGL MKIII
1983	Al Holbert	Chevy March	1994	Wayne Taylor	Mazda Kudzu
1984	Randy Lanier	Chevy March	1995	Fermin Velez	Ferrari 333 SP
1985	Al Holbert	Porsche 962	1996	Wayne Taylor	Mazda Kudzu
1986	Al Holbert	Porsche 962	1997	Butch Leitzinger	Ford R&S MKIII
1987	Chip Robinson	Porsche 962	1998	Butch Leitzinger	Ford R&S MKIII
1988	Geoff Brabham	Nissan GTP			

Year	Prototype	GTS	GT
1999	Elliott Forbes-Robinson	Olivier Beretta	Cort Wagner
2000	Allan McNish	Olivier Beretta	Sascha Maassen
2001	Emanuele Pirro	Terry Borcheller	Jörg Müller

*1978–93 champions raced in the GT series, which in 1994 was replaced by the World SportsCar series. Beginning in 1999, racing was reclassified according to the American Le Mans Series. The Series is comprised of two different types of race cars divided into two categories and five separate classes. The Prototype category features open-cockpit prototype World Sports Cars (WSC) and Le Mans Prototypes (LMP), as well as Grand Touring Prototype (GTP) class cars. The Grand Touring category features the Grand Touring S (GTS) class cars, formerly known as GT2, and Grand Touring (GT) cars, formerly known as GT3. Both classes feature purpose-built race cars with an emphasis on spectator car identification.

Alltime SportsCar Leaders

PROTOTYPE WINS (WSC/GTP ERA: 1994–2002)

James Weaver	14
Butch Leitzinger	13
Rinaldo Capello	9
Wayne Taylor	8
Gianpiero Moretti	7
Frank Biela	6
J.J. Lehto	6
Allan McNish	6
Emanuele Pirro	6
David Brabham	5
John Paul Jr	5
Fermin Velez	5
Eric van de Poele	5
Andy Wallace	5

Note: Leaders through September 22, 2002.

GTS AND GT WINS (IMSA GT: 1971–1993)

Al Holbert	49
Peter Gregg	41
Hurley Haywood	31
Geoff Brabham	26
Parker Johnstone	25
Jim Downing	23
Irv Hoerr	23
Jack Baldwin	22
Don Devendorf	22
Bob Earl	22
Tommy Riggins	22

24 Hours of Le Mans

Year	Winning Drivers	Car
1923	André Lagache/René Léonard	Chenard & Walker
1924	John Duff/Francis Clement	Bentley
1925	Gérard de Courcelles/André Rossignol	La Lorraine
1926	Robert Bloch/André Rossignol	La Lorraine
1927	J. Dudley Benjafield/Sammy Davis	Bentley
1928	Woolf Barnato/Bernard Rubin	Bentley
1929	Woolf Barnato/Sir Henry Birkin	Bentley Speed 6
1930	Woolf Barnato/Glen Kidston	Bentley Speed 6
1931	Earl Howe/Sir Henry Birkin	Alfa Romeo 8C-2300 sc
1932	Raymond Sommer/Luigi Chinetti	Alfa Romeo 8C-2300 sc
1933	Raymond Sommer/Tazio Nuvolari	Alfa Romeo 8C-2300 sc
1934	Luigi Chinetti/Philippe Etancelin	Alfa Romeo 8C-2300 sc
1935	John Hindmarsh/Louis Fontés	Lagonda M45R
1936	Race cancelled	
1937	Jean-Pierre Wimille/Robert Benoist	Bugatti 57G sc
1938	Eugene Chaboud/Jean Tremoulet	Delahaye 135M
1939	Jean-Pierre Wimille/Pierre Veyron	Bugatti 57G sc
1940–48	Races cancelled	
1949	Luigi Chinetti/Lord Selsdon	Ferrari 166MM
1950	Louis Rosier/Jean-Louis Rosier	Talbot-Lago
1951	Peter Walker/Peter Whitehead	Jaguar C
1952	Hermann Lang/Fritz Reiss	Mercedes-Benz 300 SL
1953	Tony Rolt/Duncan Hamilton	Jaguar C
1954	Froilan Gonzales/Maurice Trintignant	Ferrari 375
1955	Mike Hawthorn/Ivor Bueb	Jaguar D
1956	Ron Flockhart/Ninian Sanderson	Jaguar D
1957	Ron Flockhart/Ivor Bueb	Jaguar D
1958	Olivier Gendebien/Phil Hill	Ferrari 250 TR58
1959	Carroll Shelby/Roy Salvadori	Aston Martin DBR1
1960	Olivier Gendebien/Paul Frère	Ferrari 250 TR59/60
1961	Olivier Gendebien/Phil Hill	Ferrari 250 TR61
1962	Olivier Gendebien/Phil Hill	Ferrari 250P
1963	Lodovico Scarfiotti/Lorenzo Bandini	Ferrari 250P
1964	Jean Guichel/Nino Vaccarella	Ferrari 275P
1965	Jochen Rindt/Masten Gregory	Ferrari 250LM
1966	Chris Amon/Bruce McLaren	Ford Mk2
1967	Dan Gurney/A.J. Foyt	Ford Mk4
1968	Pedro Rodriguez/Lucien Bianchi	Ford GT40
1969	Jacky Ickx/Jackie Oliver	Ford GT40
1970	Hans Herrmann/Richard Attwood	Porsche 917
1971	Helmut Marko/Gijs van Lennep	Porsche 917
1972	Henri Pescarolo/Graham Hill	Matra-Simca MS670
1973	Henri Pescarolo/Gérard Larrousse	Matra-Simca MS670B

Year	Winning Drivers	Car
1974	Henri Pescarolo/Gérard Larrousse	Matra-Simca MS670B
1975	Jacky Ickx/Derek Bell	Mirage-Ford MB
1976	Jacky Ickx/Gijs van Lennep	Porsche 936
1977	Jacky Ickx/Jurgen Barth/Hurley Haywood	Porsche 936
1978	Jean-Pierre Jaussaud/Didier Pironi	Renault-Alpine A442
1979	Klaus Ludwig/Bill Whittington/Don Whittington	Porsche 935
1980	Jean-Pierre Jaussaud/Jean Rondeau	Rondeau-Ford M379B
1981	Jacky Ickx/Derek Bell	Porsche 936-81
1982	Jacky Ickx/Derek Bell	Porsche 956
1983	Vern Schuppan/Hurley Haywood/Al Holbert	Porsche 956-83
1984	Klaus Ludwig/Henri Pescarolo	Porsche 956B
1985	Klaus Ludwig/Paolo Barilla/John Winter	Porsche 956B
1986	Derek Bell/Hans-Joachim Stuck/Al Holbert	Porsche 962C
1987	Derek Bell/Hans-Joachim Stuck/Al Holbert	Porsche 962C
1988	Jan Lammers/Johnny Dumfries/Andy Wallace	Jaguar XJR9LM
1989	Jochen Mass/Manuel Reuter/Stanley Dickens	Sauber-Mercedes C9-88
1990	John Nielsen/Price Cobb/Martin Brundle	TWR Jaguar XJR-12
1991	Volker Weidler/Johnny Herbert/Bertrand Gachof	Mazda 787B
1992	Derek Warwick/Yannick Dalmas/Mark Blundell	Peugeot 905B
1993	Geoff Brabham/Christophe Bouchut/Eric Helary	Peugeot 905
1994	Yannick Dalmas/Hurley Haywood/Mauro Baldi	Porsche 962
1995	Yannick Dalmas/J.J. Lehto/Masanori Sekiya	McLaren BMW
1996	Manuel Reuter/Davy Jones/Alexander Wurz	TWR Porsche
1997	Michele Alboreto/Stefan Johansson/Tom Kristensen	TWR Porsche
1998	Allan McNish/Laurent Aiello/Stephane Ortelli	Porsche GT One
1999	Yannick Dalmas/Joachim Winkelhock/Pierluigi Martini	BMW V12 LMR
2000	Frank Biela/Tom Kristensen/Emanuele Pirro	Audi R8
2001	Frank Biela/Tom Kristensen/Emanuele Pirro	Audi R8
2002	Frank Biela/Tom Kristensen/Emanuele Pirro	Audi R8

Tribute

The death of TLC singer Lisa (Left Eye) Lopes struck a nerve in the sports world. Lopes, who was killed in a car crash in Honduras on April 25, 2002, was an on-again, off-again girlfriend of former NFL receiver Andre Rison. (During the summer of 2001 Rison announced that he and Lopes were to be married but it never happened.) Rison refused to talk about Lopes's death. Also shaken was Dale Earnhardt Jr. The NASCAR star, who says he's been a fan of TLC since his teen years, became incensed when he heard that autopsy photos of of Lopes's body were available on the Internet. Since 2001 Earnhardt and his family have been involved in a legal battle to keep similar pictures of Dal Earnhardt Sr. private. "Circulating pictures of [Lopes's] body on the Internet is just plain wrong," said Junior. "I know exactly what her family is going through. At the April 2002 Richmond 400, the members of Earnhardt's pit crew paid tribute to Lopes by wearing black stripes under their left eyes, and a black stripe was taped under the left headlight of Earnhardt's car.

Drag Racing: Milestone Performances

Top Fuel

ELAPSED TIME

Time (Sec.)	Driver	Date	Site
9.00	Jack Chrisman	Feb 18, 1961	Pomona, CA
8.97	Jack Chrisman	May 20, 1961	Empona, VA
7.96	Bobby Vodnick	May 16, 1964	Bayview, MD
6.97	Don Johnson	May 7, 1967	Carlsbad, CA
5.97	Mike Snively	Nov 17, 1972	Ontario, CA
5.78	Don Garlits	Nov 18, 1973	Ontario, CA
5.698	Gary Beck	Oct 10, 1975	Ontario, CA
5.573	Gary Beck	Oct 18, 1981	Irvine, CA
5.484	Gary Beck	Sept 6, 1982	Clermont, IN
5.391	Gary Beck	Oct 1, 1983	Fremont, CA
5.280	Darrell Gwynn	Sept 25, 1986	Ennis, TX
5.176	Darrell Gwynn	April 4, 1987	Ennis, TX
5.090	Joe Amato	Oct 1, 1987	Ennis, TX
4.990	Eddie Hill	April 9, 1988	Ennis, TX
4.881	Gary Ormsby	Sept 28, 1990	Topeka, KS
4.799	Cory McClenathan	Sept 19, 1992	Mohnton, PA
4.762	Cory McClenathan	Oct 3, 1993	Topeka, KS
4.690	Michael Brotherton	May 20, 1994	Englishtown, NJ
4.595	Joe Amato	July 5,1996	Topeka, KS
4.539	Joe Amato	Mar 21, 1998	Baytown, TX
4.525	Gary Scelzi	Oct 23, 1998	Ennis, TX
4.503	Mike Dunn	Feb 5, 1999	Pomona, CA
4.486	Larry Dixon	Apr 9, 1999	Houston
4.480	Gary Scelzi	Oct 31, 1999	Houston
4.477	Kenny Bernstein	June 2, 2001	Joliet, IL

SPEED

MPH	Driver	Date	Site
180.36	Connie Kalitta	Sept 3, 1962	Indianapolis
190.26	Don Garlits	Sept 21, 1963	East Haddam, CT
201.34	Don Garlits	Aug 1, 1964	Great Meadows, NJ
211.26	Donny Milani	May 15, 1965	Sacramento, CA
223.32	Don Cook	Apr 24, 1965	Fremont, CA
230.17	James Warren	Apr 10, 1967	Fresno, CA
243.24	Don Garlits	Mar 18, 1973	Gainesville, FL
250.69	Don Garlits	Oct 11, 1975	Ontario, CA
260.11	Joe Amato	Mar 18, 1984	Gainesville, FL
272.56	Don Garlits	Mar 23, 1986	Gainesville, FL
282.13	Joe Amato	Sept 5, 1987	Clermont, IN
291.54	Connie Kalitta	Feb 11, 1989	Pomona, CA
301.70	Kenny Bernstein	Mar 20, 1992	Gainesville, FL
311.86	Kenny Bernstein	Oct 30, 1994	Pomona, CA
319.82	Joe Amato	Mar 21, 1998	Baytown, TX
323.50	Joe Amato	May 17, 1998	Englishtown, NJ
326.44	Gary Scelzi	Nov 2, 1998	Houston
326.91	Tony Schumacher	Oct 22, 1999	Dallas
330.55	Mike Dunn	June 2, 2001	Joliet, IL
332.18	Kenny Bernstein	Oct. 7, 2001	Richardson, TX

YET ANOTHER SIGN OF THE APOCALYPSE

As a result of a sponsorship deal with the National Pork Board, the Nov. 17, 2001, ARCA stock car race at Atlanta Motor Speedway was the Pork the Other White Meat 400.

Funny Car

ELAPSED TIME

Time (sec.)	Driver	Date	Site
6.92	Leroy Goldstein	Sept 3, 1970	Clermont, IN
5.987	Don Prudhomme	Oct 12, 1975	Ontario, CA
5.868	Raymond Beadle	July 16, 1981	Englishtown, NJ
5.799	Tom Anderson	Sept 3, 1982	Clermont, IN
5.637	Don Prudhomme	Sept 4, 1982	Clermont, IN
5.588	Rick Johnson	Feb 3, 1985	Pomona, CA
5.425	Kenny Bernstein	Sept 26, 1986	Ennis, TX
5.397	Kenny Bernstein	April 5, 1987	Ennis, TX
5.255	Ed McCulloch	April 17, 1988	Ennis, TX
5.193	Don Prudhomme	Mar 2, 1989	Baytown, TX
5.077	Cruz Pedregon	Sept 20, 1992	Mohnton, PA
4.987	Chuck Etcholis	Oct 2, 1993	Topeka, KS
4.819	Cruz Pedregon	Mar 21, 1998	Baytown, TX
4.807	Cruz Pedregon	Nov 1, 1998	Houston
4.788	John Force	Apr 11, 1999	Houston
4.763	John Force	June 2, 2001	Joliet, IL
4.750	William Bazemore	Sept 28, 2001	Joliet, IL
4.731	John Force	Oct. 7, 2001	Yorba Linda, CA

SPEED

MPH	Driver	Date	Site
200.44	Gene Snow	Aug, 1968	Houston
250.00	Don Prudhomme	May 23, 1982	Baton Rouge
260.11	Kenny Bernstein	Mar 18, 1984	Gainesville, FL
271.41	Kenny Bernstein	Aug 30, 1986	Indianapolis
280.72	Mike Dunn	Oct 2, 1987	Ennis, TX
290.13	Jim White	Oct 11, 1991	Ennis, TX
291.82	Jim White	Oct 25, 1991	Pomona, CA
300.40	Jim Epler	Oct 3, 1993	Topeka, KS
303.64	John Force	Sept 2, 1995	Indianapolis
308.74	John Force	Sept 28, 1997	Topeka, KS
317.46	John Force	Mar 21, 1998	Baytown, TX
323.89	John Force	May 17, 1998	Englishtown, NJ
324.05	John Force	Mar 19, 1999	Gainesville, FL
325.45	William Bazemore	Sept 28, 2001	Joliet, IL
326.87	Gary Densham	Feb. 9, 2002	Bellflower, CA

Pro Stock

ELAPSED TIME

Time (sec.)	Driver	Date	Site
7.778	Lee Shepherd	Mar 12, 1982	Gainesville, FL
7.655	Lee Shepherd	Oct 1, 1982	Fremont, CA
7.557	Bob Glidden	Feb 2, 1985	Pomona, CA
7.497	Bob Glidden	Sep 13, 1985	Maple Grove, PA
7.377	Bob Glidden	Aug 28, 1986	Clermont, IN
7.294	Frank Sanchez	Oct 7, 1988	Baytown, TX
7.184	Darrell Alderman	Oct 12, 1990	Ennis, TX
7.099	Scott Geoffrion	Sept 19, 1992	Mohnton, PA
6.988	Kurt Johnson	May 20, 1994	Englishtown, NJ
6.873	Warren Johnson	Mar 14, 1998	Gainesville, FL
6.867	Warren Johnson	Oct 23, 1998	Ennis, TX
6.866	Warren Johnson	Mar 19, 1999	Gainesville, FL
6.843	Warren Johnson	Apr 30, 1999	Dinwiddie, VA
6.840	Kurt Johnson	May 1, 1999	Dinwiddie, VA
6.822	Warren Johnson	Oct 23, 1999	Dallas
6.801	Kurt Johnson	Sept 29, 2001	Joliet, IL
6.750	Jeg Coughlin	Oct. 7, 2001	Delaware, OH

Pro Stock *(Cont.)*
SPEED

MPH	Driver	Date	Site
181.08	Warren Johnson	Oct 1, 1982	Fremont, CA
190.07	Warren Johnson	Aug 29, 1986	Clermont, IN
191.32	Bob Glidden	Sept 4, 1987	Clermont, IN
192.18	Warren Johnson	Oct 13, 1990	Ennis, TX
193.21	Bob Glidden	July 28, 1991	Sonoma, CA
194.51	Warren Johnson	July 31, 1992	Sonoma, CA
195.99	Warren Johnson	May 21, 1993	Englishtown, NJ
196.24	Warren Johnson	Mar 19, 1993	Gainesville, FL
197.15	Warren Johnson	Apr 23, 1994	Commerce, GA
199.15	Warren Johnson	Mar 10, 1995	Baytown, TX
201.20	Warren Johnson	Mar 14, 1998	Gainesville, FL
201.34	Warren Johnson	Oct 23, 1998	Ennis, TX
201.37	Warren Johnson	Mar 19, 1999	Gainesville, FL
202.24	Warren Johnson	Apr 30,1999	Dinwiddie, VA
202.33	Warren Johnson	Oct 23, 1999	Dallas
202.36	Warren Johnson	Oct 31, 1999	Houston
202.70	Kurt Johnson	Sept 29, 2001	Joliet, IL
204.35	Mark Osborne	Oct. 6, 2001	Abdingdon, VA

Alltime Drag Racing Leaders

NHRA CAREER WINS

*John Force	98
*Warren Johnson	87
Bob Glidden	85
*Kenny Bernstein	60
Joe Amato	52
Don Prudhomme	49
David Schultz	45
Don Garlits	35
John Myers	33
*Matt Hines	28

BEST WON-LOST RECORD (WINNING PCT.)

*Matt Hines	211–52 (.802)
John Myers	268–69 (.795)
*Angelle Savoie	175–53 (.768)
*John Force	748–247 (.752)
*Bob Panella Jr	116–40 (.744)
*Jeg Coughlin	173–60 (.742)
*Warren Johnson	756–287 (.725)
*Gary Scelzi	221–85 (.722)
*Randy Daniels	86–40 (.683)
*Antron Brown	91–44 (.674)

*Active driver. Note: Leaders through 2001 season.

Japanese Driver in Winston Cup?

In 1996, when NASCAR ran the first of three exhibition races in Japan, owner Travis Carter was looking for someone to drive his Camel-sponsored car. He picked the perfect guy: Hideo Fukuyama is as popular in Japan as Richard Petty is in the U.S., and he bears, by his own admission, a striking resemblance to Joe Camel. Against a field full of Winston Cup regulars, such as Jeff Gordon and Rusty Wallace, Fukuyama ran in the top 10 until he wrecked late.

Fukuyama made a lasting impression on Carter. Sources told SI that the owner will put Fukuyama, 47, behind the wheel of a Winston Cup car at Dover on Sept. 22, 2002, and in two subsequent races, likely at Martinsville and Rockingham. A sports car driver who won his class at the last two 24 Hours of Le Mans races, Fukuyama tested the Dover oval—dubbed the Monster Mile—on Aug. 27, 2002. "I want to forget about it," said a laughing Fukuyama. Still, the three-race deal could turn into a full-time ride in 2003.

—Mark Bechtel

Bowling

PWBA Bowler of the
Year Carolyn
Dorin-Ballard.

PWBA

Jersey Gems

The Garden State produced Carolyn Dorin-Ballard and Parker Bohn III, the PWBA and PBA players of the year

BY HANK HERSCH

SEPARATED BY 80 miles and innumerable obscure communities, Jackson and Linden have little readily in common besides their plenitude of soccer moms and shared New Jersey addresses. Jackson (pop. 42,816) is in the southern end of the state, 30 miles outside Philadelphia, and is home to a Six Flags Great Adventure theme park. Linden (pop. 39,394) is in the northern part, 20 miles outside New York City and has no major attractions to speak of. But in 2002 those two Garden State towns shared a rather large impact on the bowling world: They produced the male and female players of the year.

Growing up in Jackson proved to be an advantage for Parker Bohn III, who learned from fellow New Jersey natives Dave Davis, Johnny Petraglia and Mark Roth, PBA Hall of Famers all. In 2001–02, Bohn led the tour in victories (five), earnings ($245,200), average (221.54), championship round appearances (nine), match play appearances (24) and cashes (27).

Named the PBA's player of the year in 1999, he became only the ninth bowler to earn a bookend trophy when he received 83% of the vote among his fellow bowlers. "Winning for a second time is more special because it proves the first wasn't a fluke," said the 38-year-old Bohn, who has failed to earn more than $100,000 in a season only once since 1989. "There are players of the year every season, but very few have won it more than once. That puts me in an elite category."

The five victories in '01–02 raised Bohn's career total to 29, fourth alltime and second among lefthanders to Earl Anthony's 41. "What separates champions from the rest is the ability to shrug off bad shots and bad weeks, and at the same time know how to take it to the finish lines once you've figured out the lanes," Bohn has said. "It takes a great mental outlook."

Nowhere was championship form more necessary than at the 2001 American Bowling Congress Masters in Reno, Nev. In search of the first major of his 17-year

career, Bohn faced his friend, rival and fellow southpaw Jason Couch in the title match. "It's no secret that Jason and I are great friends—and great competitors," Bohn said. "We really have a unique understanding and relationship." While Couch began with a double, followed by single-pin spares in frames three and four, Bohn started spare, spare, strike, spare. Each struck the next four frames before Bohn ran his string to five. Couch, too, found the pocket in the ninth, but left a solid nine-pin. "I couldn't have thrown the ball better," he said. "It was a perfect shot."

Needing a nine-count spare and a strike to close out the match, Bohn struck on his first ball in the 10th to seal the win, 248–237. "I've been knocking on the door of the Masters for a long time now," he said. "And to tell you the truth I've been sick of being the bridesmaid in majors."

Carolyn Dorin-Ballard knows how Bohn feels: For four straight years she was runner-up in the player of the year voting. "The first two years I'm like, 'O.K., just bad luck,'" she told the Belleville (IL) *News-Democrat*. "But by the third or fourth year I think I said to myself, 'I don't know if I'm not doing something right or what.'" There were no such doubts in 2001. Not only did she win a record-tying seven titles, matching Patty Costello's total in 1976—one of

Player of the year Bohn won five titles in 2001–02, including his first major.

11 marks Dorin-Ballard equaled or surpassed—but she also led the PWBA in earnings ($135,045) and average (214.73). Of her unanimous selection as the tour's top performer, she said, "I guess perseverance paid off."

Growing up in Linden, Dorin-Ballard started bowling at age six. Her father, George, was her first coach and sponsor, and her younger sister, Cathy, would also turn pro. (Carolyn later married 12-time PBA champ Del Ballard Jr. and moved to North Richland Hills, Texas.) Her metronomic consistency reflects her comfort on the lanes: The 37-year-old Dorin-Ballard cashed in all 23 tournaments in 2001, running her streak to 70, and has not finished below 15th in two years. "I'm not a big, strong power player," she says, "but I know what I can and cannot do with my game, so I am versatile."

Dorin-Ballard's season culminated in a nomination for the ESPY Award for bowling. Though Pete Weber received the honor, Dorin-Ballard did attend a party at the Playboy mansion, where she watched boxing matches by the backyard pool. "I weigh 123 pounds, and I was the fat girl," she says. "But it was a great experience. I got a picture with Hugh Hefner."

The Majors

MEN

2001 U.S. Open

	Games	Total	Earnings ($)
Mika Koivuniemi	1	247	100,000
Patrick Healey Jr.	2	461	50,000
Walter Ray Williams Jr.	2	432	25,000
Mike DeVaney	1	189	15,000

Playoff Results: Williams def. DeVaney, 223–189; Healey def. Williams, 279–209; Koivuniemi def. Healey, 247–182.

Held at the Fountain Bowl in Fountain Valley, CA, Dec 2–9, 2001

2002 ABC Masters
CHAMPIONSHIP ROUND

Bowler	Games	Total	Earnings ($)
Brett Wolfe	1	269	100,000
Dennis Horan Jr.	3	618	50,000
Ricky Ward	1	224	25,000
Steve Jaros	1	190	15,000

Playoff Results: Horan def. Jaros, 216–190; Horan def. Ward, 230–224; Wolfe def. Horan, 269–172.

Held at National Bowling Stadium in Reno, NV, Jan 15–20, 2002.

2002 PBA World Championship
CHAMPIONSHIP ROUND

Bowler	Games	Total	Earnings ($)
Doug Kent	2	417	120,000
Lonnie Waliczek	2	362	50,000
Rick Steelsmith	1	194	20,000
Brian Voss	1	200	20,000

Playoff Results: Waliczek def. Voss, 202–200; Kent def. Steelsmith, 202–194; Kent def. Waliczek, 215–160.

Held at Southwyck Lanes, Toledo, OH, Feb 24–Mar 3, 2002.

WOMEN

2001 Brunswick Women's World Open
CHAMPIONSHIP ROUND

Bowler	Games	Total	Earnings ($)
Carolyn Dorin-Ballard	2	497	15,000
Michelle Feldman	1	258	7,500
Lisa Bishop	2	478	5,000
Liz Johnson	1	209	4,300
Kelly Kulick	1	164	3,700

Playoff Results: Bishop def. Johnson and Kulick, 268–209–164; Dorin-Ballard def. Bishop, 217–210; Dorin-Ballard def. Feldman, 280–258.

Held at the Suncoast Bowling Center, Las Vegas, Nov 5–10, 2001.

2001 U.S. Open
CHAMPIONSHIP ROUND

Bowler	Games	Total	Earnings ($)
Kim Terrell	3	708	55,000
Wendy Macpherson	1	220	30,000
Leanne Barrette	1	207	22,000
Liz Johnson	1	212	17,000
Kelly Kulick	1	238	13,000

Playoff Results: Terrell def. Kulick and Johnson, 244–238–212; Terrell def. Barrette, 228–207; Terrell def. Macpherson, 234–220.

Held at the Riverside Resort, Laughlin, NV, Dec 2–9, 2001.

2002 WIBC Queens
CHAMPIONSHIP ROUND

Bowler	Games	Total	Earnings ($)
Kim Terrell	1	227	18,000
Kim Adler	3	717	12,000
Kari Schwager	1	205	7,550
Kirsten Penny	1	201	6,560
Cara Honeychurch	1	190	4,440

Playoff Results: Adler def. Penny and Honeychurch, 278–201–190; Adler def. Schwager 225–205; Terrell def. Adler, 227–214.

Held at AMF Bowlero Lanes, Wauwatosa, WI, May 5–10, 2002.

2002 Miller High Life National Players Championship
CHAMPIONSHIP ROUND

Bowler	Games	Total	Earnings ($)
Marianne DiRupo	3	689	13,000
Leanne Barrette	1	158	7,000
Michelle Feldman	1	191	4,600
Kelly Kulick	1	152	4,200
Tammy Turner	1	190	3,700

Playoff Results: DiRupo def. Turner and Kulick, 266–190–152; DiRupo def. Feldman, 243–191; DiRupo def. Barrette 180–158.

Held at Funquest Lanes, Collierville, TN, July 21–25, 2002.

PBA Tour Results

Men
2001–02 Tour

Date	Event	Winner	Earnings ($)	Runner-Up
Jan 9–14, 2001 ....National Bowling Stadium		Parker Bohn III	30,000	J. Yajima
	National/Senior Doubles	Rohn Morton		M. Koivuniemi
Jan 16–21	...........Silicon Valley Open	Mike Aulby	19,000	Jason Couch
Jan 21–25	...........Orleans Casino Open	Ryan Shafer	25,000	Jeff Lizzi
Jan 26–Feb 4	........PBA National Championship	Walter Ray Williams Jr.	25,000	Jeff Lizzi
Feb 7–11	...............Parker Bohn III Empire State Open	Parker Bohn III	20,000	Chris Barnes
Feb 13–18	...........Tar Heel Open	Ricky Ward	20,000	Jason Couch
Feb 20–24	...........The Villages PBA Open	Jason Couch	25,000	Chris Barnes
Mar 1–4	.................Battle at Little Creek	Steve Wilson	20,000	Jason Couch
June 11–16	..........ABC Masters	Parker Bohn III	40,000	Jason Couch
Sept 20–25	..........Peoria Open	Kurt Pilon	40,000	Paul Koehler
Sept 27–Oct 2	...Greater Nashville Open	Chris Barnes	40,000	Mike Scroggins
Oct 4–9	.............:...Miller High Life Open	Dave Arnold	40,000	Roger Bowker
Oct 11–16	...........Great Lakes Classic	Pete Weber	40,000	Parker Bohn III
Oct 18–23	...........Greater Detroit Open	Patrick Allen	40,000	Robert Smith
Oct 25–30	...........Johnny Petraglia Open	Danny Wiseman	40,000	Steve Jaros
Nov 6–11	.............Greater Cincinnati Open	Walter Ray Williams, Jr.	40,000	Mike Machuga
Nov 13–18	............Long Island Open	Tommy Delutz, Jr.	40,000	Chris Barnes
Nov 21–25	...........Greater Louisville Open	Pete Weber	40,000	Michael Haugen, Jr.
Dec 2–9	................U.S. Open	Mika Koivuniemi	100,000	Patrick Healey, Jr.
Jan 1–6	................Earl Anthony Memorial Classic	Parker Bohn III	40,000	Patrick Healey, Jr.
Jan 8–13, 2002	....Medford Open	Ricky Ward	40,000	Ryan Shafer
Jan 15–20	...........ABC Masters	Brett Wolfe	100,000	Dennis Horan, Jr.
Jan 19–24	...........Orleans Casino Open	Brian Voss	40,000	Ricky Ward
Jan 29–Feb 3	........Dallas Open	Ritchie Allen	40,000	Rick Steelsmith
Feb 5–9	................Columbia 300 Tar Heel Open	Pete Weber	40,000	Roger Bowker
Feb 13–17	...........Empire State Open	Robert Smith	40,000	Jason Couch
Feb 20–24	...........Flagship Open	Steve Wilson	40,000	Jason Queen
Feb 24–Mar 3	......PBA World Championship	Doug Kent	120,000	Lonnie Waliczek
Mar 13–17	...........Battle at Little Creek	Parker Bohn III	40,000	Patrick Healey, Jr.

2001–2002 Senior Tour

Date	Event	Winner	Earnings ($)	Runner-Up
Sept 23–27	...............Senior Tar Heel Open	Bob Chamberlain	8,000	Guppy Troup
Oct 13–18	...............Senior National Championship	Dale Eagle	12,000	Gene Stus
Oct 23–26	...............Senior Hammond Open	Bob Glass	8,000	Charlie Tapp
Apr 26–30	...............Senior Chillicothe Open	Steve Neff	8,000	Bob Glass
May 4–7	...................Senior Pennsylvania Open	Bob Chamberlain	8,000	Bob Glass
May 11–14	.............Senior Greater Detroit Open	Dave Davis	8,000	Norb Wetzel
May 27–31	...............ABC Senior Masters	Pete Couture	20,000	Darrell Storkson
June 2–7	..................Suncoast Senior World Championship	Mark Roth	20,000	Mel Wolf
June 10–12	...............Senior Northern California Classic	Gene Stus	8,000	Bob Chamberlain
June 16–19	.............Senior Epicenter Classic	Ron Winger	8,000	John Shreve, Sr.
June 23–26	.............Senior Northwest Classic	John Bennett	8,000	Bob Glass
Aug 18–21	...............Senior Lake County Open	Dave Soutar	8,000	Mark Roth
Aug 24–28	...............Senior Jackson Open	Pete Couture	8,000	Vince Mazzanti

†PWBA Tour Results

2001 Fall Tour

Date	Event	Winner	Earnings ($)	Runner-Up
Sept 24–27	Jacksonville Open	Carolyn Dorin-Ballard	9,000	Leanne Barrette
Sept 30–Oct 4	N Myrtle Beach Classic	Cara Honeychurch	9,000	Wendy Macpherson
Oct 8–11	Columbia 300 Open	Wendy Macpherson	11,000	Leanne Barrette
Oct 14–18	Three Rivers Open	Michelle Feldman	9,000	Tammy Turner
Oct 21–24	Hammer Players Championship	Liz Johnson	13,000	Michelle Feldman
Oct 28–Nov 1	Las Cruces New Mexico Open	Dede Davidson	9,000	Carolyn Dorin-Ballard
Nov 4–10	Brunswick Women's World Open	Carolyn Dorin-Ballard	15,000	Michelle Feldman
Dec 1–9	U.S. Open	Kim Terrell	55,000	Wendy Macpherson

2002 Tour

Date	Event	Winner	Earnings ($)	Runner-Up
May 5–10	WIBC Queens	Kim Terrell	18,000	Kim Adler
May 12–16	St. Clair Shores Classic	Michelle Feldman	10,000	Kim Adler
May 19–23	St. Clair Classic	Kim Adler	10,500	Cara Honeychurch
May 26–June 2	PWBA Collegiate/Pro Doubles	Melissa Brownie	5,000	April Ellis
		Kendra Gaines		Michelle Feldman
June 5–9	Greater Terre Haute Open	Brenda Norman	10,500	Tiffany Stanbrough
June 12–16	Greater Harrisburg Open	Cara Honeychurch	10,500	Kim Terrell
June 19–23	Empire State Cassic	Leanne Barrette	10,000	Wendy Macpherson
June 26–30	Greater Syracuse Classic	Leanne Barrette	10,000	Kendra Gaines
July 13–19	Dallas Open	Carolyn Dorin-Ballard	10,000	Tiffany Stanbrough
July 21–25	National Players Championships	Marianne DiRupo	13,000	Leanne Barrette
July 28–Aug 1	Louisville Open	Michelle Feldman	10,000	Kim Terrell

†Known as LBPT until 1998.

Tour Leaders

PBA: 2001–2002

MONEY LEADERS

Name (Titles)	Tournaments	Earnings ($)
Parker Bohn III (5)	30	245,200
Doug Kent (1)	29	185,010
Pete Weber (3)	26	170,125
Walter Ray Williams Jr. (2)	30	164,450
Mika Koivuniemi (1)	27	158,550

AVERAGE

Name		Average
Parker Bohn III	829	221.54
Jason Couch	753	220.93
Chris Barnes	729	219.03
Pete Weber	645	217.99
Ryan Shafer	750	217.83

Seniors 2002

MONEY LEADERS

Name	Tournaments	Earnings ($)
Mark Roth (1)	7	34,375
Pete Couture (2)	10	32,725
Robert Glass (0)	10	27,780
Bob Chamberlain (1)	10	25,575
Gene Stus (1)	10	25,200

AVERAGE

Name	Games	Average
Robert Glass	302	221.56
Ron Winger	298	219.86
Gene Stus	322	219.62
Steve Neff	278	219.37
Dale Eagle	280	218.40

PWBA: 2001

MONEY LEADERS

Name (Titles)	Tournaments	Earnings ($)
Carolyn Dorin-Ballard (7)	23	135,045
Kim Terrell (1)	22	96,500
Wendy Macpherson (1)	23	92,940
Cara Honeychurch (4)	23	92,565
Michelle Feldman (2)	23	90,285

AVERAGE

Name	Games	Average
Carolyn Dorin-Ballard	985	214.73
Liz Johnson	795	212.41
Cara Honeychurch	929	212.36
Wendy Macpherson	946	212.36
Leanne Barrette	926	210.42

Men's Majors

BPAA United States Open

Year	Winner	Score	Runner-Up	Site
1942	John Crimmins	265.09–262.33	Joe Norris	Chicago
1943	Connie Schwoegler	not available	Frank Benkovic	Chicago
1944	Ned Day	315.21–298.21	Paul Krumske	Chicago
1945	Buddy Bomar	304.46–296.16	Joe Wilman	Chicago
1946	Joe Wilman	310.27–305.37	Therman Gibson	Chicago
1947	Andy Varipapa	314.16–308.04	Allie Brandt	Chicago
1948	Andy Varipapa	309.23–309.06	Joe Wilman	Chicago
1949	Connie Schwoegler	312.31–307.27	Andy Varipapa	Chicago
1950	Junie McMahon	318.37–307.17	Ralph Smith	Chicago
1951	Dick Hoover	305.29–304.07	Lee Jouglard	Chicago
1952	Junie McMahon	309.29–305.41	Bill Lillard	Chicago
1953	Don Carter	304.17–297.36	Ed Lubanski	Chicago
1954	Don Carter	308.02–307.25	Bill Lillard	Chicago
1955	Steve Nagy	307.17–303.34	Ed Lubanski	Chicago
1956	Bill Lillard	304.30–304.22	Joe Wilman	Chicago
1957	Don Carter	308.49–305.45	Dick Weber	Chicago
1958	Don Carter	311.03–308.09	Buzz Fazio	Minneapolis
1959	Billy Welu	311.48–310.26	Ray Bluth	Buffalo
1960	Harry Smith	312.24–308.12	Bob Chase	Omaha
1961	Bill Tucker	318.49–309.11	Dick Weber	San Bernardino, CA
1962	Dick Weber	299.34–297.38	Roy Lown	Miami Beach
1963	Dick Weber	642–591	Billy Welu	Kansas City, MO
1964	Bob Strampe	714–616	Tommy Tuttle	Dallas
1965	Dick Weber	608–586	Jim St. John	Philadelphia
1966	Dick Weber	684–681	Nelson Burton Jr.	Lansing, MI
1967	Les Schissler	613–610	Pete Tountas	St. Ann, MO
1968	Jim Stefanich	12,401–12,104	Billy Hardwick	Garden City, NY
1969	Billy Hardwick	12,585–11,463	Dick Weber	Miami
1970	Bobby Cooper	12,936–12,307	Billy Hardwick	Northbrook, IL
1971	Mike Limongello	397 (2 games)	Teata Semiz	St. Paul, MN
1972	Don Johnson	233 (1 game)	George Pappas	New York City
1973	Mike McGrath	712 (3 games)	Earl Anthony	New York City
1974	Larry Laub	749 (3 games)	Dave Davis	New York City
1975	Steve Neff	279 (1 game)	Paul Colwell	Grand Prairie, TX
1976	Paul Moser	226 (1 game)	Jim Frazier	Grand Prairie, TX
1977	Johnny Petraglia	279 (1 game)	Bill Spigner	Greensboro, NC
1978	Nelson Burton Jr.	873 (4 games)	Jeff Mattingly	Greensboro, NC
1979	Joe Berardi	445 (2 games)	Earl Anthony	Windsor Locks, CT
1980	Steve Martin	930 (4 games)	Earl Anthony	Windsor Locks, CT
1981	Marshall Holman	684 (3 games)	Mark Roth	Houston
1982	Dave Husted	1011 (4 games)	Gil Sliker	Houston
1983	Gary Dickinson	214 (1 game)	Steve Neff	Oak Lawn, IL
1984	Mark Roth	244 (1 game)	Guppy Troup	Oak Hill, IL
1985	Marshall Holman	233 (1 game)	Wayne Webb	Venice, FL
1986	Steve Cook	467 (2 games)	Frank Ellenburg	Venice, FL
1987	Del Ballard Jr.	525 (2 games)	Pete Weber	Tacoma, WA
1988	Pete Weber	929 (4 games)	Marshall Holman	Atlantic City
1989	Mike Aulby	429 (2 games)	Jim Pencak	Edmond, OK
1990	Ron Palombi Jr.	269 (1 game)	Amleto Monacelli	Indianapolis
1991	Pete Weber	956 (4 games)	Mark Thayer	Indianapolis
1992	Robert Lawrence	667 (3 games)	Scott Devers	Canandaigua, NY
1993	Del Ballard Jr.	505 (2 games)	Walter Ray Williams Jr.	Canandaigua, NY
1994	Justin Hromek	267 (1 game)	Parker Bohn III	Troy, MI
1995	Dave Husted	266 (1 game)	Paul Koehler	Troy, MI
1996	Dave Husted	730 (3 games)	George Brooks	Indianapolis
1997	No event—tournament rescheduled to April, beginning in 1998.			
1998	Walter Ray Williams Jr.	466 (2 games)	Tim Criss	Fairfield, CT
1999	Bob Learn Jr.	231 (1 game)	Jason Couch	Uncasville, CT
2000	Robert Smith	202 (1 game)	Norm Duke	Phoenix
2001	Mika Koivuniemi	247 (1 game)	Patrick Healey, Jr	Fountain Valley, CA

Note: From 1942 to 1970, the tournament was called the BPAA All-Star. Peterson scoring was used from 1942 through 1962. Under this system, the winner of an individual match game gets one point, plus one point for each 50 pins knocked down. From 1963 through 1967, a three-game championship was held between the two top qualifiers. From 1968 through 1970 total pinfall determined the winner. From 1971 to the present, five qualifiers compete for the championship.

Touring Players Championship

Year	Winner	Score	Runner-Up	Site
1996	Mike Aulby	268 (1 game)	Parker Bohn III	Harmarville, PA
1997	Steve Hoskins	932 (4 games)	Danny Wiseman	Harmarville, PA
1998	Dennis Horan	481 (2 games)	Parker Bohn III	Akron, OH
1999	Steve Hoskins	503 (2 games)	Parker Bohn III	Akron, OH
2000	Dennis Horan	924 (4 games)	Pete Weber	Akron, OH
2001	Not held			

PBA World Championship

Year	Winner	Score	Runner-Up	Site
1960	Don Carter	6512 (30 games)	Ronnie Gaudern	Memphis
1961	Dave Soutar	5792 (27 games)	Morrie Oppenheim	Cleveland
1962	Carmen Salvino	5369 (25 games)	Don Carter	Philadelphia
1963	Billy Hardwick	13,541 (61 games)	Ray Bluth	Long Island, NY
1964	Bob Strampe	13,979 (61 games)	Ray Bluth	Long Island, NY
1965	Dave Davis	13,895 (61 games)	Jerry McCoy	Detroit
1966	Wayne Zahn	14,006 (61 games)	Nelson Burton Jr.	Long Island, NY
1967	Dave Davis	421 (2 games)	Pete Tountas	New York City
1968	Wayne Zahn	14,182 (60 games)	Nelson Burton Jr.	New York City
1969	Mike McGrath	13,670 (60 games)	Bill Allen	Garden City, NY
1970	Mike McGrath	660 (3 games)	Dave Davis	Garden City, NY
1971	Mike Limongello	911 (4 games)	Dave Davis	Paramus, NJ
1972	Johnny Guenther	12,986 (56 games)	Dick Ritger	Rochester, NY
1973	Earl Anthony	212 (1 game)	Sam Flanagan	Oklahoma City
1974	Earl Anthony	218 (1 game)	Mark Roth	Downey, CA
1975	Earl Anthony	245 (1 game)	Jim Frazier	Downey, CA
1976	Paul Colwell	191 (1 game)	Dave Davis	Seattle
1977	Tommy Hudson	206 (1 game)	Jay Robinson	Seattle
1978	Warren Nelson	453 (2 games)	Joseph Groskind	Reno
1979	Mike Aulby	727 (3 games)	Earl Anthony	Las Vegas
1980	Johnny Petraglia	235 (1 game)	Gary Dickinson	Sterling Heights, MI
1981	Earl Anthony	242 (1 game)	Ernie Schlegel	Toledo, OH
1982	Earl Anthony	233 (1 game)	Charlie Tapp	Toledo, OH
1983	Earl Anthony	210 (1 game)	Mike Durbin	Toledo, OH
1984	Bob Chamberlain	961 (4 games)	Dan Eberl	Toledo, OH
1985	Mike Aulby	476 (2 games)	Steve Cook	Toledo, OH
1986	Tom Crites	190 (1 game)	Mike Aulby	Toledo, OH
1987	Randy Pedersen	759 (3 games)	Amleto Monacelli	Toledo, OH
1988	Brian Voss	246 (1 game)	Todd Thompson	Toledo, OH
1989	Pete Weber	221 (1 game)	Dave Ferraro	Toledo, OH
1990	Jim Pencak	900 (4 games)	Chris Warren	Toledo, OH
1991	Mike Miller	450 (2 games)	Norm Duke	Toledo, OH
1992	Eric Forkel	833 (4 games)	Bob Vespi	Toledo, OH
1993	Ron Palombi Jr.	237 (1 game)	Eugene McCune	Toledo, OH
1994	David Traber	196 (1 game)	Dale Traber	Toledo, OH
1995	Scott Alexander	246 (1 game)	Wayne Webb	Toledo, OH
1996	Butch Soper	442 (2 games)	Walter Ray Williams Jr.	Toledo, OH
1997	Rick Steelsmith	888 (4 games)	Brian Voss	Toledo, OH
1998	Pete Weber	277 (1 game)	David Ozio	Toledo, OH
1999	Tim Criss	238 (1 game)	Dave Arnold	Toledo, OH
2000	Norm Duke	492 (2 games)	Jason Couch	Toledo, OH
2001	Walter Ray Williams Jr.	258 (1 game)	Jeff Lizzi	Toledo, OH
2002	Doug Kent	417 (2 games)	Lonnie Waliczek	Toledo, OH

Note: Totals from 1963–66, 1968–69 and 1972 include bonus pins.

Tournament of Champions

Year	Winner	Score		Runner-Up	Site
1965	Billy Hardwick	484	(2 games)	Dick Weber	Akron, OH
1966	Wayne Zahn	595	(3 games)	Dick Weber	Akron, OH
1967	Jim Stefanich	227	(1 game)	Don Johnson	Akron, OH
1968	Dave Davis	213	(1 game)	Don Johnson	Akron, OH
1969	Jim Godman	266	(1 game)	Jim Stefanich	Akron, OH
1970	Don Johnson	299	(1 game)	Dick Ritger	Akron, OH
1971	Johnny Petraglia	245	(1 game)	Don Johnson	Akron, OH
1972	Mike Durbin	775	(3 games)	Tim Harahan	Akron, OH
1973	Jim Godman	451	(2 games)	Barry Asher	Akron, OH
1974	Earl Anthony	679	(3 games)	Johnny Petraglia	Akron, OH
1975	Dave Davis	448	(2 games)	Barry Asher	Akron, OH
1976	Marshall Holman	441	(2 games)	Billy Hardwick	Akron, OH
1977	Mike Berlin	434	(2 games)	Mike Durbin	Akron, OH
1978	Earl Anthony	237	(1 game)	Teata Semiz	Akron, OH
1979	George Pappas	224	(1 game)	Dick Ritger	Akron, OH
1980	Wayne Webb	750	(3 games)	Gary Dickinson	Akron, OH
1981	Steve Cook	287	(1 game)	Pete Couture	Akron, OH
1982	Mike Durbin	448	(2 games)	Steve Cook	Akron, OH
1983	Joe Berardi	865	(4 games)	Henry Gonzalez	Akron, OH
1984	Mike Durbin	950	(4 games)	Mike Aulby	Akron, OH
1985	Mark Williams	616	(3 games)	Bob Handley	Akron, OH
1986	Marshall Holman	233	(1 game)	Mark Baker	Akron, OH
1986	Marshall Holman	233	(1 game)	Mark Baker	Akron, OH
1987	Pete Weber	928	(4 games)	Jim Murtishaw	Akron, OH
1988	Mark Williams	237	(1 game)	Tony Westlake	Fairlawn, OH
1989	Del Ballard Jr.	490	(2 games)	Walter Ray Williams Jr.	Fairlawn, OH
1990	Dave Ferraro	226	(1 game)	Tony Westlake	Fairlawn, OH
1991	David Ozio	476	(2 games)	Amleto Monacelli	Fairlawn, OH
1992	Marc McDowell	471	(2 games)	Don Genalo	Fairlawn, OH
1993	George Branham III	227	(1 game)	Parker Bohn III	Fairlawn, OH
1994	Norm Duke	422	(2 games)	Eric Forkel	Fairlawn, OH
1995	Mike Aulby	502	(2 games)	Bob Spaulding	Lake Zurich, IL
1996	Dave D'Entremont	971	(4 games)	Dave Arnold	Lake Zurich, IL
1997	John Gant	446	(2 games)	Mike Aulby	Reno
1998	Bryan Goebel	245	(1 game)	Steve Hoskins	Overland Park, KS
1999	Jason Couch	427	(2 games)	Chris Barnes	Overland Park, KS
2000	Jason Couch	198	(1 game)	Ryan Shafer	Lake Zurich, IL
2001	Not held				

Spare Us, Please

During the 2002 Winter Olympics, Jerry Koenig, president of the International Bowling Federation, strode into the lobby of Salt Lake City's downtown Hilton wearing a bright yellow sweater and fresh off an interview with a Toledo radio station. "There are a lot of bowlers in Toledo," he said, beaming. "They want to know when we're getting in."

The IBF has been petitioning to get bowling into the Summer Games since 1979, when the IOC recognized the organization as a governing body. This is the fourth straight Games at which Koenig has been trying to persuade IOC members to give new meaning to the term Olympic pins. "The best strategy is to go to where the IOC meetings are and ride up and down in the elevators until you catch somebody," he says.

Koenig, 62, has what you might call a bowler's frame—big, rounded shoulders, beer-barrel torso, meaty limbs. He carries around a folder full of statistics that show bowling's huge popularity in Asia and the fact that nearly half of the globe's 150 million keglers are women. At the Nagano Games, Koenig rolled a few games with then IOC president Juan Antonio Samaranch. "I probably shouldn't say this," Koenig says, lowering his voice, "but Mr. Samaranch only bowls about a 120."

Koenig, a lawyer who broke into the bowling racket as a pin boy in the 1950s, hoped that the IOC would vote on bowling's status in late 2002. While the glutted summer schedule—not to mention the two-toned shoes—hurts bowling's chances, Koenig is convinced that the Olympics have room to spare. "It's a grueling sport," says Koenig. "I'd like to see these athletes try to bowl 48 games in three days like we do at nationals. Bowling is a test of wills. It comes down to whoever can pull it out of his gut at the end."

—Kostya Kennedy

ABC Masters Tournament

Year	Winner	Scoring Avg	Runner-Up	Site
1951	Lee Jouglard	201.8	Joe Wilman	St. Paul, MN
1952	Willard Taylor	200.32	Andy Varipapa	Milwaukee
1953	Rudy Habetler	200.13	Ed Brosius	Chicago
1954	Eugene Elkins	205.19	W. Taylor	Seattle
1955	Buzz Fazio	204.13	Joe Kristof	Ft. Wayne, IN
1956	Dick Hoover	209.9	Ray Bluth	Rochester, NY
1957	Dick Hoover	216.39	Bill Lillard	Ft. Worth, TX
1958	Tom Hennessy	209.15	Lou Frantz	Syracuse, NY
1959	Ray Bluth	214.26	Billy Golembiewski	St. Louis
1960	Billy Golembiewski	206.13	Steve Nagy	Toledo, OH
1961	Don Carter	211.18	Dick Hoover	Detroit
1962	Billy Golembiewski	223.12	Ron Winger	Des Moines, IA
1963	Harry Smith	219.3	Bobby Meadows	Buffalo
1964	Billy Welu	227	Harry Smith	Oakland, CA
1965	Billy Welu	202.12	Don Ellis	St. Paul, MN
1966	Bob Strampe	219.80	Al Thompson	Rochester, NY
1967	Lou Scalia	216.9	Bill Johnson	Miami Beach
1968	Pete Tountas	220.15	Buzz Fazio	Cincinnati
1969	Jim Chestney	223.2	Barry Asher	Madison, WI
1970	Don Glover	215.10	Bob Strampe	Knoxville, TN
1971	Jim Godman	229.8	Don Johnson	Detroit
1972	Bill Beach	220.27	Jim Godman	Long Beach, CA
1973	Dave Soutar	218.61	Dick Ritger	Syracuse, NY
1974	Paul Colwell	234.17	Steve Neff	Indianapolis
1975	Eddie Ressler	213.51	Sam Flanagan	Dayton, OH
1976	Nelson Burton Jr.	220.79	Steve Carson	Oklahoma City
1977	Earl Anthony	218.21	Jim Godman	Reno
1978	Frank Ellenburg	200.61	Earl Anthony	St. Louis
1979	Doug Myers	202.9	Bill Spigner	Tampa
1980	Neil Burton	206.69	Mark Roth	Louisville
1981	Randy Lightfoot	218.3	Skip Tucker	Memphis
1982	Joe Berardi	207.12	Ted Hannahs	Baltimore
1983	Mike Lastowski	212.65	Pete Weber	Niagara Falls
1984	Earl Anthony	212.5	Gil Sliker	Reno
1985	Steve Wunderlich	210.4	Tommy Kress	Tulsa
1986	Mark Fahy	206.5	Del Ballard Jr.	Las Vegas
1987	Rick Steelsmith	210.7	Brad Snell	Niagara Falls
1988	Del Ballard Jr.	219.1	Keith Smith	Jacksonville
1989	Mike Aulby	218.5	Mike Edwards	Wichita
1990	Chris Warren	231.6	David Ozio	Reno
1991	Doug Kent	226.8	George Branham III	Toledo, OH
1992	Ken Johnson	230.0	Dave D'Entremont	Corpus Christi, TX
1993	Norm Duke	245.68	Patrick Allen	Tulsa
1994	Steve Fehr	213.09	Steve Anderson	Greenacres, FL
1995	Mike Aulby	230.7	Mark Williams	Reno
1996	Ernie Schlegel	221.2	Mike Aulby	Salt Lake City
1997	Jason Queen	225.5	Eric Forkel	Huntsville, AL
1998	Mike Aulby	224.0	Parker Bohn III	Reno
1999	Brian Boghosian	246.0	Parker Bohn III	Syracuse, NY
2000	Mika Koivuniemi	241.0	Pete Weber	Albuquerque
2001	Parker Bohn III	224.0	Jason Couch	Reno
2002	Brett Wolfe	222.3	Dennis Horan, Jr.	Reno

BPAA United States Open

Year	Winner	Score	Runner-Up	Site
1949	Marion Ladewig	113.26–104.26	Catherine Burling	Chicago
1950	Marion Ladewig	151.46–146.06	Stephanie Balogh	Chicago
1951	Marion Ladewig	159.17–148.03	Sylvia Wene	Chicago
1952	Marion Ladewig	154.39–142.05	Shirley Garms	Chicago
1953	Not held			
1954	Marion Ladewig	148.29–143.01	Sylvia Wene	Chicago
1955	Sylvia Wene	142.30–141.11	Sylvia Fanta	Chicago
1955	Anita Cantaline	144.40–144.13	Doris Porter	Chicago
1956	Marion Ladewig	150.16–145.41	Marge Merrick	Chicago
1957	Not held			
1958	Merle Matthews	145.09–143.14	Marion Ladewig	Minneapolis
1959	Marion Ladewig	149.33–143.00	Donna Zimmerman	Buffalo
1960	Sylvia Wene	144.14–143.26	Marion Ladewig	Omaha
1961	Phyllis Notaro	144.13–143.12	Hope Riccilli	San Bernardino, CA
1962	Shirley Garms	138.44–135.49	Joy Abel	Miami Beach
1963	Marion Ladewig	586–578	Bobbie Shaler	Kansas City, MO
1964	LaVerne Carter	683–609	Evelyn Teal	Dallas
1965	Ann Slattery	597–550	Sandy Hooper	Philadelphia
1966	Joy Abel	593–538	Bette Rockwell	Lansing, MI
1967	Gloria Bouvia	578–516	Shirley Garms	St. Ann, MO
1968	Dotty Fothergill	9,000–8,187	Doris Coburn	Garden City, NY
1969	Dotty Fothergill	8,284–8,258	Kayoka Suda	Miami
1970	Mary Baker	8,730–8,465	Judy Cook	Northbrook, IL
1971	Paula Carter	5,660–5,650	June Llewellyn	Kansas City, MO
1972	Lorrie Nichols	5,272–5,189	Mary Baker	Denver
1973	Millie Martorella	5,553–5,294	Patty Costello	Garden City, NY
1974	Patty Costello	219–216	Betty Morris	Irving, TX
1975	Paula Carter	6,500–6,352	Lorrie Nichols	Toledo, OH
1976	Patty Costello	11,341–11,281	Betty Morris	Tulsa
1977	Betty Morris	10,511–10,358	Virginia Norton	Milwaukee
1978	Donna Adamek	236–202	Vesma Grinfelds	Miami
1979	Diana Silva	11,775–11,718	Bev Ortner	Phoenix
1980	Pat Costello	223–199	Shinobu Saitoh	Rockford, IL
1981	Donna Adamek	201–190	Nikki Gianulias	Rockford, IL
1982	Shinobu Saitoh	12,184–12,028	Robin Romeo	Hendersonville, TN
1983	Dana Miller-Mackie	247–200	Aleta Sill	St. Louis
1984	Karen Ellingsworth	236–217	Lorrie Nichols	St. Louis
1985	Pat Mercatani	214–178	Nikki Gianulias	Topeka, KS
1986	Wendy Macpherson	265–179	Lisa Wagner	Topeka, KS
1987	Carol Norman	206–179	Cindy Coburn	Mentor, OH
1988	Lisa Wagner	226–218	Lorrie Nichols	Winston-Salem, NC
1989	Robin Romeo	187–163	Michelle Mullen	Addison, IL
1990	Dana Miller-Mackie	190–189	Tish Johnson	Dearborn Heights, MI
1991	Anne Marie Duggan	196–185	Leanne Barrette	Fountain Valley, CA
1992	Tish Johnson	216–213	Aleta Sill	Fountain Valley, CA
1993	Dede Davidson	213–194	Dana Miller-Mackie	Garland, TX
1994	Aleta Sill	229–170	Anne Marie Duggan	Wichita
1995	Cheryl Daniels	235–180	Tish Johnson	Blaine, MN
1996	Liz Johnson	265–236	Marianne DiRupo	Indianapolis
1997	No event—tournament rescheduled to April, beginning in 1998.			
1998	Aleta Sill	276–151	Tammy Turner	Milford, CT
1999	Kim Adler	213–195	Lynda Barnes	Uncasville, CT
2000	Tennelle Grijalva	239–155	Kelly Kulick	Phoenix
2001	Kim Terrell	234–220	Wendy Macpherson	Laughlin, NV

Note: From 1942 to 1970, tournament was called the BPAA All-Star. Peterson scoring used from 1949 to '62. Under this system, the winner of an individual match game gets one point, plus one point for each 50 pins. From 1963 to '67, a three-game championship was held between the two top qualifiers. From 1968 to '73, 1975 to '77, 1979 and 1982, total pinfall determined the winner. In the other years, five qualifiers competed in a playoff for the championship, with the final listed above.

AMF Gold Cup *(Discontinued)*

Year	Winner	Score	Runner-Up	Site
1997	Aleta Sill	221–179	C. Gianotti-Block	Richmond, VA
1998	Dana Miller-Mackie	278–170	Dede Davidson	Richmond, VA
1999	Dana Miller-Mackie	236–222	Cara Honeychurch	Richmond, VA

WIBC Queens

ear	Winner	Score	Runner-Up	Site
1961	Janet Harman	794–776	Eula Touchette	Fort Wayne, IN
1962	Dorothy Wilkinson	799–794	Marion Ladewig	Phoenix
1963	Irene Monterosso	852–803	Georgette DeRosa	Memphis
1964	D. D. Jacobson	740–682	Shirley Garms	Minneapolis
1965	Betty Kuczynski	772–739	LaVerne Carter	Portland, OR
1966	Judy Lee	771–742	Nancy Peterson	New Orleans
1967	Millie Ignizio	840–809	Phyllis Massey	Rochester, NY
1968	Phyllis Massey	884–853	Marian Spencer	San Antonio
1969	Ann Feigel	832–765	Millie Ignizio	San Diego
1970	Millie Ignizio	807–797	Joan Holm	Tulsa
1971	Millie Ignizio	809–778	Katherine Brown	Atlanta
1972	Dotty Fothergill	890–841	Maureen Harris	Kansas City, MO
1973	Dotty Fothergill	804–791	Judy Soutar	Las Vegas
1974	Judy Soutar	939–705	Betty Morris	Houston
1975	Cindy Powell	758–674	Patty Costello	Indianapolis
1976	Pam Buckner	214–178	Shirley Sjostrom	Denver
1977	Dana Stewart	175–167	Vesma Grinfelds	Milwaukee
1978	Loa Boxberger	197–176	Cora Fiebig	Miami
1979	Donna Adamek	216–181	Shinobu Saitoh	Tucson
1980	Donna Adamek	213–165	Cheryl Robinson	Seattle
1981	Katsuko Sugimoto	166–158	Virginia Norton	Baltimore
1982	Katsuko Sugimoto	160–137	Nikki Gianulias	St. Louis
1983	Aleta Sill	214–188	Dana Miller-Mackie	Las Vegas
1984	Kazue Inahashi	248–222	Aleta Sill	Niagara Falls
1985	Aleta Sill	279–192	Linda Graham	Toledo, OH
1986	Cora Fiebig	223–177	Barbara Thorberg	Orange County, CA
1987	Cathy Almeida	850–817	Lorrie Nichols	Hartford, CT
1988	Wendy Macpherson	213–199	Leanne Barrette	Reno/Carson City, NV
1989	Carol Gianotti	207–177	Sandra Jo Shiery	Bismarck-Mandan, ND
1990	Patty Ann	207–173	Vesma Grinfelds	Tampa
1991	Dede Davidson	231–159	Jeanne Maiden	Cedar Rapids, IA
1992	Cindy Coburn-Carroll	184–170	Dana Miller-Mackie	Lansing, MI
1993	Jan Schmidt	201–163	Pat Costello	Baton Rouge, LA
1994	Anne Marie Duggan	224–177	Wendy Macpherson-Papanos	Salt Lake City
1995	Sandra Postma	226–187	Carolyn Dorin	Tucson
1996	Lisa Wagner	231–226	Tammy Turner	Buffalo
1997	S.J. Shiery-Odom	209–185	Audry Allen	Reno
1998	Lynda Norry	213–157	Karen Stroud	Davenport, IA
1999	Leanne Barrette	256–174	Dede Davidson	Indianapolis
2000	Wendy Macpherson	227–202	Marianne DiRupo	Reno
2001	Carolyn Dorin-Ballard	213–197	Kelly Kulick	Ft. Lauderdale, FL
2002	Kim Terrell	227–214	Kim Adler	Wauwatosa, WI

Sam's Town Invitational (Discontinued)

Year	Winner	Score	Runner-Up	Site
1984	Aleta Sill	238 (1 game)	Cheryl Daniels	Las Vegas
1985	Patty Costello	236 (1 game)	Robin Romeo	Las Vegas
1986	Aleta Sill	238 (1 game)	Dina Wheeler	Las Vegas
1987	Debbie Bennett	880 (4 games)	Lorrie Nichols	Las Vegas
1988	Donna Adamek	634 (3 games)	Robin Romeo	Las Vegas
1989	Tish Johnson	210 (1 game)	Dede Davidson	Las Vegas
1990	Wendy Macpherson	900 (4 games)	Jeanne Maiden	Las Vegas
1991	Lorrie Nichols	469 (2 games)	Dana Miller-Mackie	Las Vegas
1992	Tish Johnson	279 (1 game)	Robin Romeo	Las Vegas
1993	Robin Romeo	194 (1 game)	Tammy Turner	Las Vegas
1994	Tish Johnson	178 (1 game)	Carol Gianotti	Las Vegas
1995	Michelle Mullen	202 (1 game)	Cheryl Daniels	Las Vegas
1996	C. Gianotti-Block	892 (4 games)	Leanne Barrette	Las Vegas
1997	Kim Adler	953 (4 games)	Wendy Macpherson	Las Vegas
1998	Julie Gardner	961 (4 games)	Dede Davidson	Las Vegas
1999	Wendy Macpherson	209 (1 game)	Marianne DiRupo	Las Vegas
2000	Dede Davidson	183 (1 game)	Tiffany Stanbrough	Las Vegas

PWBA Championships (Discontinued)

1960...Marion Ladewig	1966...Joy Abel	1972...Patty Costello	1978...Toni Gillard
1961...Shirley Garms	1967...Betty Mivalez	1973...Betty Morris	1979...Cindy Coburn
1962...Stephanie Balogh	1968...Dotty Fothergill	1974...Pat Costello	1980...Donna Adamek
1963...Janet Harman	1969...Dotty Fothergill	1975...Pam Buckner	
1964...Betty Kuczynski	1970...Bobbe North	1976...Patty Costello	
1965...Helen Duval	1971...Patty Costello	1977...Vesma Grinfelds	

Cool Alley Cats

It's a Tuesday night at the Brunswick Zone Carolier Lanes in North Brunswick, N.J., and Danny Wiseman is most definitely in the hizzz-ouse. "He's exotic, he's different, he's off the wall!"

ESPN bowling announcer Jim Kelly tells the audience. "He likes fast cars, he likes fast women.... He likes to strike fast, and he's dangerous. You ready? Let's get it on!"

At this the crowd on hand for the Pro Bowlers Association Johnny Petraglia Open goes crazy. Wiseman, a vision of tenpin recklessness with his blond-tipped mullet, barbed-wire tattoo and soul patch, soaks in the cheers. He steps to the lane in his yellow-and-orange flame-motif jersey, and the fans go quiet. Four steps later Wiseman releases the ball, and instantly the crowd is alive again, cheering with Wheel of Fortune fervor. When, an hour later, Wiseman takes home the $40,000 first prize, he's serenaded with chants of "Danny! Danny! Danny!"

Welcome to the new, hip, hyped world of bowling as envisioned by ESPN, which in May signed a three-year contract to continue telecasting PBA events this fall. The network, which will show 20 tournaments between September and March, is aspiring to pump life into a sport long stereotyped as a cigarette-and-potbelly pursuit of middle America: Players are meeting with media trainers;

ESPN is running humorous ads; and, even though few bowlers are anywhere near as flamboyant as the 34-year-old Wiseman, top players are being heavily promoted.

The first seven shows rolled a solid spare in the Nielsens. Appearing sometimes on Tuesday nights and other times on Sunday afternoons, they averaged a 0.8 rating, a 14% increase from ESPN's numbers last season, when telecasts were less regularly scheduled. Bowling was attracting a larger viewership than either MLS (0.3) or the NHL (0.6) did in their most recent full regular seasons.

ESPN has enhanced the telecasts with a traveling set; graphics that provide ball speed, revolution and accuracy information; and prerecorded bowling tips, such as one on converting "extreme splits." The polished Kelly, late of ESPN's Senior PGA Tour telecasts, teams with analyst Randy Pedersen, a 12-time winner on the PBA tour who's still rough but adds enthusiasm and expertise. "We're trying to blend in all the new stuff and at the same time build characters," says Pedersen. "It's our job to create heroes and villains. We don't care if you like a guy or hate him, as long as he makes you watch."

The same strategy worked for the WWF. Can a Stone Cold Walter Ray Williams Jr. be far behind?

—Chris Ballard

Men's Awards

BWAA Bowler of the Year

1942	Johnny Crimmins	1972	Don Johnson
1943	Ned Day	1973	Don McCune
1944	Ned Day	1974	Earl Anthony
1945	Buddy Bomar	1975	Earl Anthony
1946	Joe Wilman	1976	Earl Anthony
1947	Buddy Bomar	1977	Mark Roth
1948	Andy Varipapa	1978	Mark Roth
1949	Connie Schwoegler	1979	Mark Roth
1950	Junie McMahon	1980	Wayne Webb
1951	Lee Jouglard	1981	Earl Anthony
1952	Steve Nagy	1982	Earl Anthony
1953	Don Carter	1983	Earl Anthony
1954	Don Carter	1984	Mark Roth
1955	Steve Nagy	1985	Mike Aulby
1956	Bill Lillard	1986	Walter Ray Williams Jr.
1957	Don Carter	1987	Marshall Holman
1958	Don Carter	1988	Brian Voss
1959	Ed Lubanski	1989	Mike Aulby
1960	Don Carter		Amleto Monacelli*
1961	Dick Weber	1990	Amleto Monacelli
1962	Don Carter	1991	David Ozio
1963	Dick Weber	1992	Dave Ferraro
	Billy Hardwick*	1993	Walter Ray Williams Jr.
1964	Billy Hardwick	1994	Norm Duke
	Bob Strampe*	1995	Mike Aulby
1965	Dick Weber	1996	Walter Ray Williams Jr.
1966	Wayne Zahn	1997	Walter Ray Williams Jr.
1967	Dave Davis	1998	Walter Ray Williams Jr.
1968	Jim Stefanich	1999	Parker Bohn III
1969	Billy Hardwick	2000	Norm Duke
1970	Nelson Burton Jr.	2001	Parker Bohn III
1971	Don Johnson		

PBA Bowler of the Year. The PBA began selecting a player of the year in 1963. Its selection has been the same as the BWAA's in all but three years.

Women's Awards

BWAA Bowler of the Year

1948	Val Mikiel	1975	Judy Soutar
1949	Val Mikiel	1976	Patty Costello
1950	Marion Ladewig	1977	Betty Morris
1951	Marion Ladewig	1978	Donna Adamek
1952	Marion Ladewig	1979	Donna Adamek
1953	Marion Ladewig	1980	Donna Adamek
1954	Marion Ladewig	1981	Donna Adamek
1955	Marion Ladewig	1982	Nikki Gianulias
1956	Sylvia Martin	1983	Lisa Wagner
1957	Anita Cantaline	1984	Aleta Sill
1958	Marion Ladewig	1985	Aleta Sill/Patty Costello*
1959	Marion Ladewig	1986	Lisa Wagner/Jeanne Madden*
1960	Sylvia Martin	1987	Betty Morris
1961	Shirley Garms	1988	Lisa Wagner
1962	Shirley Garms	1989	Robin Romeo
1963	Marion Ladewig	1990	Tish Johnson/Leanne Barrette*
1964	LaVerne Carter	1991	Leanne Barrette
1965	Betty Kuczynski	1992	Tish Johnson
1966	Joy Abel	1993	Lisa Wagner
1967	Millie Martorella	1994	Anne Marie Duggan
1968	Dotty Fothergill	1995	Tish Johnson
1969	Dotty Fothergill	1996	Wendy Macpherson
1970	Mary Baker	1997	Wendy Macpherson
1971	Paula Sperber Carter	1998	Carol Gianotti-Block
1972	Patty Costello	1999	Wendy Macpherson
1973	Judy Soutar	2000	Wendy Macpherson
1974	Betty Morris	2001	Carolyn Dorin-Ballard

*PWBA Bowler of the Year. The PWBA began selecting a player of the year in 1983. Its selection has been the same as the BWAA's in all but three years.

Career Leaders

Earnings

MEN

Walter Ray Williams Jr.	$2,708,881
Pete Weber	$2,405,387
Parker Bohn III	$2,197,658
Mike Aulby	$2,060,410
Brian Voss	$1,881,153

WOMEN

Wendy Macpherson	$1,167,035
Aleta Sill	$1,071,194
Tish Johnson	$1,036,000
Leanne Barrette	$978,918
Anne Marie Duggan	$924,686

Titles

MEN

Earl Anthony	41
Mark Roth	34
Walter Ray Williams Jr.	34
Parker Bohn III	29
Pete Weber	28

WOMEN

Lisa Wagner	32
Aleta Sill	31
Patty Costello	25
Leanne Barrette	25
Tish Johnson	24

Note: Leaders through Sept 2, 2002

Skirt Chasers

The New York-based company Pacific Pools has found a novel way to advertise; courtesy of PWBA bowler Kim Adler. In September 2002, the swimming pool–design and service firm won an online auction for advertising space on Adler's skirt. The 1991 PWBA Rookie of the Year, Adler earned $14,389.89 for her entrepreneurial ingenuity—or nearly $4,000 more than she earned for winning the St. Clair Classic on May 23, 2002. "I put in less work than I did to win the tournament," said Adler of the auction, for which bidding started at $4,000. A variety of companies battled to place their logo on the side of Adler's skirt that will face television cameras during the 2002–03 season. The agreement lasts for one year. "I just hope it opens up doors for other athletes trying to find sponsors," said Adler.

Brian McBride
of the
United States

Soccer

Here to Stay

A banner season suggested that the anti-soccer dinosaurs, not the game, are headed for extinction in the U.S.

BY HANK HERSCH

THE CORNER kick bent into the penalty box, and 6'1" U.S. defender Gregg Berhalter leapt to meet it. He drove the ball hard and down to the right of jut-jawed German goalkeeper Oliver Kahn, who lunged to parry the shot, only to have it skitter toward the right post, where Torsten Frings stood sentinel. As bodies lunged and cries went up, the ball bounded toward the goalmouth. On it hung the Americans' chances of an upset even more stunning than their very presence in this match, a quarterfinal of the 2002 World Cup.

The Yanks had stormed into the quarters in Ulsan, South Korea, on the bionic goalkeeping of Brad Friedel, the midfield stewardship of captain Claudio Reyna and the relentless aggression of 20-year-old attackers Landon Donovan and DaMarcus Beasley, who combined lethally with stalwart target man Brian McBride. After finishing dead last at World Cup '98 in France, they opened 2002 with a signal of their new resolve, a seismic 3–2 win in Suwon, South Korea, over European power Portugal, the U.S.'s most impressive victory in 50 years. AMERICA E ARRIVATO! (AMERICA HAS ARRIVED!) screamed Italy's *Gazzetta dello Sport*. "We had better win this year," said an Italian TV commentator, "because after this everyone will have to move aside for the USA."

And on the USA came, advancing into the second round with a tough 1–1 tie against co-host South Korea and despite a 3–1 loss to Poland. Defending champion France and pretournament favorite Argentina were headed home, but the U.S. was moving on to face archrival Mexico, a team that, some recent U.S. victories notwithstanding, had consistently prevailed over the Americans in their meetings that mattered most. Boldly, U.S. coach Bruce Arena deployed three men on his back line (instead of four) for the first time in 32 games and inserted a quartet of new starters. "Change can be good," Arena said, and it was: Each of the newbies excelled in a tactically brilliant 2–0 triumph that ensured the U.S. of its best World Cup finish since 1930.

Twellman scored 23 goals in his first MLS season.

DAVID BERGMAN

"It's incredible," said Reyna, whose electrifying 40-yard run had set up Brian McBride for the first goal against Mexico. "We used to play in front of 10,000 people, and now we're in the quarterfinals."

Four years earlier in France, Germany had manhandled Reyna and the Yanks in a 2–0 first-round win. This American side, however, had a bit of the Brooklyn-born Arena's swagger. The U.S. never wavered against the Germans, despite falling behind 1–0 on midfielder Michael Ballack's header, and despite a medley of brilliant saves by Kahn. "The Americans almost pulled us to the ground," said the impossibly Teutonic keeper. "It was amazing what fitness and power they had."

And there was that moment, five minutes into the second half, when the U.S. seemed on the verge of tying the game on Berhalter's deflected header. The ball came off the outstretched Kahn's glove and clearly struck Frings on the left arm. Not only that, it appeared to have crossed the goal line as well. As the Americans screamed for a hand ball, Kahn pounced to smother the threat. Scottish referee Hugh Dallas made no call, ruling that Frings did not move his arm, so the ball played *him* and not the other way around—a non-action that spared Frings a red card and denied the U.S. a potentially momentum-grabbing penalty kick. No less an authority than Pelé disputed the non-call. "[Frings] was moving," the Brazilian legend said. "If he was standing still at the goal line like Jesus Christ, then it is different."

That Dallas's decision and others by referees during the 2002 World Cup would generate a groundswell for instituting instant replay as an officiating device did not matter. The Americans lost to Germany 1–0 in the quarters and headed home, but not before having earned the respect of the soccer world and the attention of their fellow citizens. (Despite a predawn kickoff in much of the U.S., 3.8 million households tuned into the Germany match, ESPN's largest soccer audience ever.) Indeed, the 2002 World Cup reordered soccer's hiearchy to some degree. While France, Argentina and Italy went home early, South Korea, Turkey, Senegal and the U.S. played on. "The satisfying thing is knowing that we could have gone a little further," Friedel said. "It's frustrating, but it's satisfying as well."

Germany went on to beat South Korea by the same 1–0 score and reach the final. There, Kahn ran out of magic and Brazilian star Ronaldo made up for his disappearing act in France four years earlier. Only 21, the incendiary striker had suffered a still-undefined attack before the '98 final—"a brainstorm," the European media called it—and then sleepwalked through a 3–0 loss to host France. A pair of knee injuries followed for Ronaldo; between Nov. 21, 1999, and Sept. 21, 2000, he played only seven minutes of competitive soccer.

But he arrived for Korea/Japan a fit and healthy 25-year-old, ready to reclaim the title of World's Best Player. So ready, in fact, that he promised to score in every game, a promise he kept. He looked dangerous, and a bit ridiculous: to keep his vow on the forefront of his mind, literally, he kept a goal-shaped patch of hair at the front of his otherwise shorn skull. Whatever works; he scored eight goals in Brazil's seven games—the highest output for a single player in a World Cup since Gerd Muller in 1970—to run his career World Cup total to 12, tied for third on the alltime list with the great Pelé. "The nightmare is over," he pronounced before the 2002 final, a statement that proved true for everyone but the hardworking Germans. Ronaldo struck in the 67th minute, pouncing on the rebound of a shot by Rivaldo—one of the few rebounds Kahn gave up all tournament—and burying it for a 1–0 lead. The second goal was prettier, and again involved Ronaldo's equally brilliant teammate, Rivaldo. After making a run down the right wing, Kleberson sent a pass into the middle toward Rivaldo, who gave the appearance of playing the ball, drawing a defender, only to dummy it brilliantly to a wide-open Ronaldo, who placed it perfectly inside the right post, leaving Kahn no chance at all. Brazil won 2–0 for its unprecedented fifth World Cup.

That the tournament took place in June, in the middle of MLS's seventh season, would have seemed disruptive and untimely for the league. It turned out to be the opposite. Donovan & Co. returned as conquering heroes, giving MLS much-needed buzz and propelling it to its finest season since its inaugural one. Attendance rose for the second straight season—though television exposure during the playoffs was dismal—and in addition to the World Cuppers, several creative young American players emerged, including high-scoring striker Taylor Twellman, 22, of the New England Revolution and rookie of the year Kyle Martino of the Columbus Crew.

What's more, Philip Anschutz, the owner of six MLS teams, broke ground on the Los Angeles Galaxy's 27,000-seat, $130 million soccer stadium, which is scheduled to open in June 2003. "Mr. Anschutz will spend $20 million a year for the next 300 years if that's what it is going to take," said Anschutz Entertainment Group president Tim Leiweke. "However, we predict that next season the Galaxy will make a profit."

It won't hurt the bottom line that the new National Training Center will house the MLS champions. The Galaxy had come up short three times in title matches, twice in New England, the site of MLS Cup 2002. To make matters more dire, L.A. was taking on the Revolution, which was not only hot (it closed the regular season with six straight wins before ousting the Chicago Fire and the Crew in the playoffs) but also at home (a record crowd of 61,316 turned up at the new Gillette Stadium).

But in the 113th minute of a scrappy, scoreless game, 22-year-old Carlos Ruiz finished off a Galaxy counterattack with a left-footed one-timer past diving Revs keeper Adin Brown to bring Los Angeles its first title. A Guatemalan striker nicknamed El Pescadito (Little Fish), Ruiz thus capped a brilliant season in which he scored a league-leading 24 goals and won the league's MVP award.

As the U.S. women prepared to defend their World Cup title in China in 2003, national team striker Danielle Fotopolous scored one goal and set up another to help the Carolina Courage defeat the Washington Freedom 3–2 in the WUSA title game, the Founders Cup, in Atlanta. While attendance was down 14% in WUSA's second season, league executives remained optimistic about their prospects.

After all, it was that kind of banner year for soccer in the U.S., one which an Italian headline writer might have heralded thusly: FUTBOL E ARRIVATO!

World Cup 2002

Group Standings

GROUP A

Country	GP	W	L	T	GF	GA	Pts
*Denmark	3	2	0	1	5	2	7
*Senegal	3	1	0	2	5	4	5
Uruguay	3	0	1	2	4	5	2
France	3	0	2	1	0	3	1

GROUP B

Country	GP	W	L	T	GF	GA	Pts
*Spain	3	3	0	0	9	4	9
*Paraguay	3	1	1	1	6	6	4
S Africa	3	1	1	1	5	5	4
Slovenia	3	0	3	0	2	7	0

GROUP C

Country	GP	W	L	T	GF	GA	Pts
*Brazil	3	3	0	0	11	3	9
*Turkey	3	1	1	1	5	3	4
Costa Rica	3	1	1	1	5	6	4
China	3	0	3	0	0	9	0

GROUP D

Country	GP	W	L	T	GF	GA	Pts
*S Korea	3	2	0	1	4	1	7
*United States	3	1	1	1	5	6	4
Portugal	3	1	2	0	6	4	3
Poland	3	1	2	0	3	7	3

GROUP E

Country	GP	W	L	T	GF	GA	Pts
*Germany	3	2	0	1	11	1	7
*Ireland	3	1	0	2	5	2	5
Cameroon	3	1	1	1	2	3	4
Saudi Arabia	3	0	3	0	0	12	0

GROUP F

Country	GP	W	L	T	GF	GA	Pts
*Sweden	3	1	0	2	4	3	5
*England	3	1	0	2	2	1	5
Argentina	3	1	1	1	2	2	4
Nigeria	3	0	2	1	1	3	1

GROUP G

Country	GP	W	L	T	GF	GA	Pts
*Mexico	3	2	0	1	4	2	7
*Italy	3	1	1	1	4	3	4
Croatia	3	1	2	0	2	3	3
Ecuador	3	1	2	0	2	4	3

GROUP H

Country	GP	W	L	T	GF	GA	Pts
*Japan	3	2	0	1	5	2	7
*Belgium	3	1	0	2	6	5	5
Russia	3	1	2	0	4	4	3
Tunisia	3	0	2	1	1	5	1

*Advanced to second round.

Note: In group play, teams are awarded three points for a victory, one for a tie. The top two in each group advance to the Round of 16.

Group Play Scores

GROUP A

Senegal 1, France 0
Denmark, 2, Uruguay 1
France 0, Uruguay 0
Denmark 1, Senegal 1
Denmark 2, France 0
Senegal 3, Uruguay 3

GROUP B

Paraguay 2, S Africa 2
Spain 3, Slovenia 1
Spain 3, Paraguay 1
S Africa 1, Slovenia 0
Spain 3, S Africa 2
Paraguay 3, Slovenia 1

GROUP C

Brazil 2, Turkey 1
Costa Rica 2, China 0
Brazil 4, China 0
Costa Rica 1, Turkey 1
Brazil 5, Costa Rica 2
Turkey 3, China 0

GROUP D

S Korea 2, Poland 0
U.S. 3, Portugal 2
U.S. 1, S Korea 1
Portugal 4, Poland 0
S Korea 1, Portugal 0
Poland 3, U.S. 1

GROUP E

Ireland 1, Cameroon 1
Germany 8, S. Arabia 0
Germany 1, Ireland 1
Cameroon 1, S. Arabia 0
Germany 2, Cameroon 0
Ireland 3, Saudi Arabia 0

GROUP F

Sweden 1, England 1
Argentina 1, Nigeria 0
Sweden 2, Nigeria 1
England 1, Argentina 0
Sweden 1, Argentina 1
Nigeria 0, England 0

GROUP G

Mexico 1, Croatia 0
Italy 2, Ecuador 0
Croatia 2, Italy 1
Mexico 2, Ecuador 1
Mexico 1, Italy 1
Ecuador 1, Croatia 0

GROUP H

Japan 2, Belgium 2
Russia 2, Tunisia 0
Japan 1, Russia 0
Tunisia 1, Belgium 1
Japan 2, Tunisia 0
Belgium 3, Russia 2

WORLD CUP FINAL

England

Denmark

England (3-0)

Brazil (2-1)

Brazil

Belgium

Brazil (2-0)

Brazil (1-0)

Brazil (2-0)

Sweden

Senegal

Senegal (2-1) ot

Turkey (1-0) ot

Japan

Turkey

Turkey (1-0)

Germany (1-0)

Germany (1-0)

Germany (1-0)

United States (2-0)

Spain (1-1)*

S Korea (0-0)*

S Korea (2-1) ot

Germany

Paraguay

Mexico

United States

Spain

Ireland

S Korea

Italy

* Winner advanced on penalty kicks

Major League Soccer

2002 Final Standings

EASTERN CONFERENCE

Team	GP	W	L	T	Pts	GF	GA
†New England	28	12	14	2	38	49	49
*Columbus	28	11	12	5	38	44	43
*Chicago	28	11	13	4	37	43	38
MetroStars	28	11	15	2	35	41	47
D.C. United	28	9	14	5	32	31	40

WESTERN CONFERENCE

Team	GP	W	L	T	Pts	GF	GA
†Los Angeles	28	16	9	3	51	44	33
*San Jose	28	14	11	3	45	45	35
*Dallas	28	12	9	7	43	44	43
*Colorado	28	13	11	4	43	43	48
*Kansas City	28	9	10	9	36	37	45

Note: Three points for a win. One point for a tie. †Conference champion. *Qualified for playoffs

SCORING LEADERS

Player, Team	GP	G	A	Pts
Taylor Twellman, NE	28	23	6	52
Carlos Ruiz, Los Angeles	26	24	1	49
Jeff Cunningham, Columbus	27	16	5	37
Ante Razov, Chicago	25	14	8	36
Ariel Graziani, San Jose	28	14	5	33

ASSISTS LEADERS

Player, Team	GP	A
Steve Ralston, New England	27	19
Carlos Valderrama, Colorado	27	16
Andy Williams, NE/MetroStars	24	15
Cobi Jones, Los Angeles	19	13

Four tied with 10.

GOALS LEADERS

Player, Team	GP	G
Carlos Ruiz, Los Angeles	26	24
Taylor Twellman, NE	28	23
Jeff Cunningham, Columbus	27	16
Ante Razov, Chicago	25	14
Ariel Graziani, San Jose	28	14
Jason Kreis, Dallas	27	13

GOALS-AGAINST-AVERAGE LEADERS

Player, Team	GAA
Kevin Hartman, Los Angeles	1.09
Jon Busch, Columbus	1.09
Joe Cannon, San Jose	1.10
Zach Thornton, Chicago	1.23
Adin Brown, New England	1.23

2002 PLAYOFFS

Los Angeles

Kansas City

Los Angeles (6-3)

Los Angeles (6-0)

Dallas

Colorado

Colorado* (4-4)

Los Angeles 1-0 (ot)

New England (5-2)

New England (6-3)

Columbus (6-0)

New England

Chicago

San Jose

Columbus

*Won tiebreaking minigame. Note: Except for the final, which was a single game, scores in parentheses are points earned (three for a win, one for a tie) in a three-game series, the winner being the first team to accumulate five points.

MLS Cup 2002

Los Angeles 0		0	0	1	—1
New England........................0		0	0	0	—0

Goal: Ruiz (Marshall, Albright) 113.

New England—Brown, Llamosa (Pierce, 92), Franchino, Kante, Heaps, Cullen, Kamler (Griffiths, 90), Hernandez, Ralston, Twellman, Harris (Pineda Chacon).

Los Angeles—Hartman, Lalas, Califf, Marshall, Hendrickson, Victorine, Cienfuegos (Vagenas 61), Elliott, Jones, Moreno (Albright, 67), Ruiz.

Att: 61,316.

A-League

2002 Final Standings

EASTERN CONFERENCE

Northeast Division	GP	W	L	T	Pts	Southeast Division	GP	W	L	T	Pts
Rochester	28	17	8	3	72	Charleston	28	19	3	6	89
Montreal	28	16	9	3	72	Richmond	28	13	9	6	65
Toronto	28	10	13	5	48	Atlanta	28	13	13	2	62
Pittsburgh	28	8	15	5	41	Charlotte	28	10	14	4	50
						Hampton Rds	28	6	19	3	29

WESTERN CONFERENCE

Pacific Division	GP	W	L	T	Pts	Central Division	GP	W	L	T	Pts
Seattle	28	23	4	1	107	Milwaukee	28	16	7	5	75
Portland	28	13	12	3	63	Minnesota	28	14	9	5	70
Vancouver	28	11	12	5	54	Cincinnati	28	8	20	0	35
El Paso	28	10	11	7	54	Indiana	28	6	18	4	29
Calgary	28	4	21	3	22						

2002 Playoffs

FIRST ROUND	QUARTERFINALS	SEMIFINALS
Montreal 1*, Charlotte 1	Rochester 1, Montreal 0	Richmond 1*, Rochester1
Vancouver 2, Portland 0	Richmond 4, Charleston 3	Milwaukee 2, Vancouver 1
Richmond 3, Atlanta 2	Milwaukee 2, Minnesota 1	
Minnesota 3, El Paso 2	Vancouver 8, Seattle 2	

*Advanced on penalties. Note: Scores from first round, quarterfinals and semifinals are two-game aggregates.

A-LEAGUE CHAMPIONSHIP*

Milwaukee 2, Richmond 1 (2ot).

*One game.

U.S. Open Cup

2002 Results

QUARTERFINALS

Kansas City (MLS) 2, Milwaukee (A-League) 0

Columbus (MLS) 2, MetroStars (MLS) 1

Dallas (MLS) 1, Colorado (MLS) 0 (2 ot)

Los Angeles (MLS) 1, San Jose (MLS) 0 (ot)

*Advanced on penalties. Note:MLS: Major League Soccer (1st division); A-League (2nd division).

SEMIFINALS

Columbus 3, Kansas City 2 (2ot)

Los Angeles 4, Dallas 1

2002 LAMAR HUNT U.S. OPEN CUP FINAL, OCTOBER 24, COLUMBUS, OH

Columbus vs. Los Angeles

Women's United Soccer Association

2002 Final Standings

Team	GP	W	L	T	Pts	GF	GA	Diff.	Home	Road
Carolina	21	12	5	4	40	40	30	10	6-3-1	7-2-2
Philadelphia	21	11	4	6	39	36	22	14	7-1-3	4-3-3
Washington	21	11	5	5	38	40	29	11	6-2-3	5-3-2
Atlanta	21	11	9	1	34	34	29	5	6-3-1	5-6-0
San Jose	21	8	8	5	29	34	30	4	7-3-1	1-5-4
Boston	21	6	8	7	25	36	35	1	5-0-5	1-8-2
San Diego	21	5	11	5	20	28	42	-14	3-4-3	2-7-2
New York	21	3	17	1	10	31	62	-31	1-10-1	2-7-1

Note: Top four teams made the playoffs; Carolina and Philadelphia clinched semifinal home game.

2002 PLAYOFFS

SEMIFINALS

Washington 1, Philadelphia 0
Carolina 2, Atlanta 1 (ot)

2002 FOUNDERS CUP, AUGUST 24, ATLANTA

Carolina 3, Washington 2

International Club Competition

Intercontinental Cup

Competition between winners of European Cup and Libertadores Cup.

TOKYO: NOVEMBER 27, 2001

Bayern Munich (Ger) 0   0   1—1
Boca Juniors (Arg) 0   0   0—0

Goal: Kuffour 109.

Att: 50,091.

Bayern Munich: Kahn, Sagnol, R. Kovac, Kuffour, Lizarazu, N. Kovac, (Jancker, 76), Hargreaves (Sforza, 76), Fink, Sergio, Pizarro (Thiam, 118), Ellber.

Boca Juniors: Cordoba, Martinez (Calvo, 17; Carreño, 111), Schiavi, Burdisso, Rodriguez, Sena, Traverso, Villareal (Pinto, 99), Riquelme, Delgado, Schelotto.

UEFA Cup

Competition between teams other than league champions and cup-winners from UEFA.

ROTTERDAM, NETHERLANDS: MAY 8, 2002

Feyenoord (Neth) 2   1—3
Borussia Dortmund (Ger) ...0   2—2

Goals:
Feyenoord: van Hooijdonk 33 (pen.), 40, Tomasson 50.
Dortmund: Amoroso 47 (pen.), Koller 58.

Att: 61,400.

Feyenoord: Zoetebier, Gyan, Rzasa, Bosvelt, Kalou (Elmander, 76), van Wonderen, van Hooijdonk, Tomasson, Ono (de Haan, 85), Paauwe, van Persie (Leonardo, 63).

Dortmund: Lehmann, Woerns, Evanilson, Kohler, Reuter, Koller, Rosicky, Ewerthon (Addo, 61), Dede, Ricken (Heinrich, 70), Amoroso.

European Cup

League champions of the countries belonging to UEFA (Union of European Football Associations).

GLASGOW: MAY 153, 2002

Real Madrid (Spain) 2   0—2
Bayer Leverkusen (Ger) ...1   0—1

Goals: Real Madrid, Raul 9, Zidane 45.
Bayer Leverkusen, Lucio 14.

Att: 52,000.

Real Madrid: Cesar (Casillas, 68), Salgado, Hierro, Helguera, Carlos, Solari, Makelele (Conceicao, 73), Zidane, Figo (McManaman, 61), Raul, Morientes.

Bayer Leverkusen: Butt, Placente, Sebescen (Kirsten, 65), Lucio (Babic, 90), Zivkovic, Schneider, Ramelow, Ballack, Basturk, Neuville, Brdaric (Berbatov, 39).

Libertadores Cup

Competition between champion clubs and runners-up of 10 South American National Associations.

(2ND LEG) SAO PAULO, BRAZIL: JULY 31, 2002

Olimpia* (Paraguay) 0   2—2
Sao Caetano (Brazil) 1   0—1

Goals: Sao Caetao, Ailton 32. Olimpia, Cordoba 49, Baez 58.

* Two-game aggregate: 2–2; Olimpia won 4–2 on penalties.

Att: 59,000.

Olimpia: Tavarelli, Isasi, Zelaya, Caceres, da Silva, Quintana, Enciso, Orteman, Cordoba (Caballero, 74), Benitez (Lopez, 66), Baez (Franco, 82).

Sao Caetano: Luiz, Russo, Daniel, Dininho, Cardoso, Senna, Ailton (Wagner, 79), Adaozinho, Robert (Serginho, 64), Anailson (Marlon, 90), Somalia.

2001–2002 Club Champions—Europe

Country	League Champion	League Scoring Leader, Club	Cup Winner
Albania	Dinamo Tirane	n/a	SK Tirana
Andorra	FC Encamp Diloansa	n/a	FC Lusitanos
Armenia	Pyunik Yerevan*	Arman Karamyan, Pyunik Yerevan*	Mika Ashtarak*
Austria	Tirol Innsbruck	Brunmayr, Grazer AK	Grazer AK
Azerbaijan	FK Samkir	Kaman Karimov, Kapaz	final was
		Dmitriy Kudinov, Qarabag	abandoned
Belarus	Belshyna Babruisk*	Sergey Davydov, Nyoman-Belcard	Belshyna Babruisk
Belgium	KRC Genk	n/a	Club Brugge KV
Bosnia	Zeljeznicar	n/a	Zeljeznicar
Bulgaria	Levski Sofia	n/a	Levski Sofia
Croatia	Dinamo Zagreb	Ivica Olic, Zagreb	Dinamo Zagreb
Cyprus	A.P.O.E.L.	n/a	Anorthosis
Czech Republic	FC Slovan Liberec	n/a	SK Slavia Prague
Denmark	Brøndby	n/a	FC Copenhagen
England	Arsenal	Thierry Henry, Arsenal	Arsenal
Estonia	FC Flora Tallinn*	Maksim Gruznov, JK Trans Narva*	JK Trans Narva*
Faroe Islands	HB Tórshavn*	H. Petersen, GI Gøta*	B 36 Tórshavn*
Finland	United Tampere*	Paulus Roiha, HJK Helsinki*	Atlantis Helsinki*
France	Olympique Lyonnais	Djibril Cisse, Auxerre	FC Lorient
		Pauleta, Bordeaux	
Georgia	Torpedo Kutaisi	Suliko Davitashvili, Lokomotivi/Merani	Lokomitivi Tbilisi
Germany	Borussia Dortmund	Marcio Amoroso, Borussia Dortmund	Schalke 04
		Martin Max, 1860 Munich	
Greece	Olympiakos	Alexandris, Olympiakos	AEK Athens
Hungary	Zalaegerszegi	n/a	Ujpesti Budapest
Iceland	KR Reykjavik	Grétar Hjartarson, Grindavik	FH Hafnafjör
Ireland	Shelbourne	Glen Crowe, Bohemians	Dundalk
Israel	Maccabi Haifa	Cobi Refua, Maccabi Petah-Tikva	Maccabi Tel-Aviv
Italy	Juventus	David Trezeguet, Juventus	Parma
		Dario Hubner, Piacenza	
Kazakhstan	Zhenis Astana*	Arsen Tlekhugov, Zhenis Astana	Zhenis Astana
Latvia	Skonto Riga*	Mihails Miholaps, Skonto Riga*	Skonto Riga*
Lithuania	FBK Kaunas*	Remigijus Polius, FBK Kaunus*	Atlantas Klaipeda*
Luxembourg	F'91 Dudelange	Cicchirillo, F'91 Dudelange	Beggen
Macedonia	Vardar Skopje	n/a	Pobeda Prilep
Malta	Hibernians FC	Danilo Doncic, Sliema Wanderers	Birkirkara
Moldova	Serif Tiraspol	Ruslan Barburos, Serif Tiraspol	Serif Terispol
Netherlands	Ajax Amsterdam	n/tktkt	Ajax Amsterdam
Northern Ireland	Portadown	'n/a	Linfield
Norway	Rosenborg*	n/a	Viking FK*
Poland	Legia Warsaw	n/a	Amica Wronki
Portugal	Sporting Lisbon	n/a	Sporting Lisbon
Romania	Dinamo Bucharest	n/a	Rapid Bucharest
Russia	Spartak Moscow*	Dmitriy Vyaz'mikin, Torpedo Moscow*	Lokomotiv Moscow*
San Marino	Domagnano	n/a	Domagnano
Scotland	Glasgow Celtic	Henrik Larsson, Glasgow Celtic	Glasgow Rangers
Slovakia	MSK Zilina	n/a	Koba Senec
Slovenia	Maribor Lasko	n/a	HIT Nova Gorica
Spain	Valencia	Diego Tristan, Deportivo Coruña	Deportivo Coruña
Sweden	Hammarby*	Stefan Selakovic, Halmstad	Elfsborg IS
Switzerland	FC Basel	Richard Nuñez, Grasshopper	FC Basel
Turkey	Galatasaray	Ilhan Mansiz, Besiktas	Cocaelispor
Ukraine	Shakhtar Donetsk	Serhi Shyshenko, Metalurh Donetsk	Shakhtar Donetsk
Wales	Barry Town	M. Lloyd-Williams, Bangor City	Barry Town
Yugoslavia	Partizan Belgrade	Zoran Djuraskovic, FK Mladost Lucani	CZ Belgrade

Note: Results are from 2002 unless followed by *.

The World Cup

Results

Year	Champion	Score	Runner-Up	Winning Coach
1930	Uruguay	4–2	Argentina	Alberto Supicci
1934	Italy	2–1	Czechoslovakia	Vittorio Pozzo
1938	Italy	4–2	Hungary	Vittorio Pozzo
1950	Uruguay	2–1	Brazil	Juan Lopez
1954	W Germany	3–2	Hungary	Sepp Herberger
1958	Brazil	5–2	Sweden	Vicente Feola
1962	Brazil	3–1	Czechoslovakia	Aymore Moreira
1966	England	4–2	W Germany	Alf Ramsey
1970	Brazil	4–1	Italy	Mario Zagalo
1974	W Germany	2–1	Netherlands	Helmut Schoen
1978	Argentina	3–1	Netherlands	César Menotti
1982	Italy	3–1	W Germany	Enzo Bearzot
1986	Argentina	3–2	W Germany	Carlos Bilardo
1990	W Germany	1–0	Argentina	Franz Beckenbauer
1994	Brazil	0–0 (3–2)	Italy	Carlos Alberto Parreira
1998	France	3–0	Brazil	Aime Jacquet
2002	Brazil	2–0	Germany	Luis Felipe Scolari

Alltime World Cup Participation

Of the 69 nations that have taken part in the World Cup Finals, only Brazil has competed in each of the 17 tournaments held to date. West Germany or an undivided Germany (1934, '38, '94 and '98) has played in 15 World Cups. Ranked by victories.

Nation	Matches	W	T	L	Goals For	Goals Against
Brazil	87	60	14	13	191	82
*Germany	85	50	18	17	176	106
Italy	70	39	17	14	110	67
Argentina	60	30	11	19	102	77
England	50	22	15	13	68	45
France	44	21	7	16	86	61
Spain	45	19	12	14	71	53
Yugoslavia	37	17	6	14	60	46
†Russia	37	17	6	14	64	44
Uruguay	40	15	10	15	65	57
Hungary	32	15	3	14	87	57
Netherlands	31	14	9	8	55	34
Poland	28	14	5	9	42	36
Sweden	41	14	9	18	67	65
Austria	29	12	4	13	42	48
Czechoslovakia	30	11	5	14	44	45
Belgium	36	10	9	17	46	63
Mexico	41	10	11	20	43	79
Romania	21	8	5	8	30	32
Chile	25	7	6	12	31	40
Portugal	12	7	0	5	25	16
Denmark	13	7	2	4	24	18
Switzerland	22	6	3	13	33	51
United States	22	6	2	14	25	45
Paraguay	19	5	7	7	25	34
Turkey	10	5	1	4	20	17
Croatia	9	5	0	4	11	7
Scotland	23	4	7	12	25	41
Peru	15	4	3	8	19	31
Cameroon	17	4	7	6	16	28
Nigeria	11	4	1	6	14	16
Bulgaria	25	3	8	14	22	49
S Korea	21	3	6	12	19	49
Colombia	13	3	2	8	14	23
Northern Ireland	13	3	5	5	13	23
Costa Rica	7	3	1	3	9	12
Wales	5	2	6	1	10	7
Morocco	10	2	4	4	10	13
Senegal	5	2	2	1	7	6
Norway	8	2	3	3	7	8
Saudi Arabia	10	2	1	7	7	25
Algeria	6	2	1	3	6	10
Japan	7	2	1	4	6	7
E Germany	6	2	2	2	5	5
S Africa	6	1	3	2	8	11
N Korea	4	1	1	2	5	9
Tunisia	9	1	3	5	5	11
Cuba	3	1	1	1	5	12
Republic of Ireland	13	1	5	3	4	7
Iran	6	1	1	4	4	12
Jamaica	3	1	0	2	3	9
Ecuador	3	1	0	2	2	4
Israel	3	1	0	2	1	3
Egypt	4	0	2	2	3	6
Honduras	3	0	2	1	2	3
Kuwait	3	0	1	2	2	6
Slovenia	3	0	0	3	2	7
United Arab Emirates	3	0	0	3	2	11
New Zealand	3	0	0	3	2	12
Haiti	3	0	0	3	2	14
Iraq	3	0	0	3	1	4
Bolivia	6	0	1	5	1	20
El Salvador	6	0	0	6	1	22
Australia	3	0	1	2	0	5
Dutch East Indies	1	0	0	1	0	6
Canada	3	0	0	3	0	5
Zaire	3	0	0	3	0	14
Greece	3	0	0	3	0	8
China	3	0	0	3	0	9

*Includes West Germany 1950–90. †Includes USSR 1930–1990.
Note: Matches decided by penalty kicks are shown as drawn games.

World Cup Final Box Scores

URUGUAY 1930

```
Uruguay ........... 1    3 —— 4
Argentina ......... 2    0 —— 2
```

FIRST HALF

Scoring: 1, Uruguay, Dorado (12); 2, Argentina, Peucelle (20); 3, Argentina, Stabile (37).

SECOND HALF

Scoring: 4, Uruguay, Cea (57); 5, Uruguay, Iriarte (68); 6, Uruguay, Castro (89).

Argentina: Botosso, Della Toree, Paternoster, J. Evaristo, Monti, Suarez, Peucelle, Varallo, Stabile, Ferreira, M. Evaristo.

Uruguay: Ballesteros, Nasazzi, Mascheroni, Andrade, Fernandez, Gestido, Dorado, Scarone, Castro, Cea, Iriarte.

Referee: Langenus (Belgium).

FRANCE 1938

```
Italy ................. 3    1 —— 4
Hungary ........... 1    1 —— 2
```

FIRST HALF

Scoring: 1, Italy, Colaussi (5); 2, Hungary, Titkos (7); 3, Italy, Piola (16); 4, Italy, Piola (35).

SECOND HALF

Scoring: 5, Hungary, Sarosi (70); 6, Italy, Colaussi (82).

Italy: Olivieri, Foni, Rava, Serantoni, Andreolo, Locatelli, Biavati, Meazza, Piola, Ferrari, Colaussi.

Hungary: Szabo, Polger, Biro, Szalay, Szucs, Lazar, Sas, Vincze, Sarosi, Zsengeller, Titkos.

Referee: Capdeville (France).

SWITZERLAND 1954

```
W Germany ...... 2    1 —— 3
Hungary ........... 2    0 —— 2
```

FIRST HALF

Scoring: 1, Hungary, Puskas (6); 2, Hungary, Czibor (8); 3, W Germ., Morlock (10); 4, W Germ., Rahn (18).

SECOND HALF

Scoring: 5, W Germany, Rahn (84).

W Germany: Turek, Posipal, Kohlmeyer, Eckel, Liebrich, Mai, Rahn, Morlock, O.Walter, F. Walter, Schaefer.

Hungary: Grosics, Buzansky, Lantos, Bozsik, Lorant, Zakarias, Czibor, Kocsis, Hidegkuti, Puskas, Toth.

Referee: Ling (England).

ITALY 1934

```
Italy ................. 0    1    1 —— 2
Czechoslovakia .... 0    1    0 —— 1
```

SECOND HALF

Scoring: 1, Czech., Puc (70); 2, Italy, Orsi (80).

OVERTIME

Scoring: 3, Italy, Schiavio (95).

Italy: Combi, Monzeglio, Allemandi, Ferraris Monti, Monti, Bertolini, Guaita, Meazza, Schiavio, Ferrari, Orsi.

Czechoslovakia: Planicka, Zenisek, Ctyroky, Kostalek, Cambal, Cambal, Krcil, Junek, Svoboda, Sobotka, Nejedly, Puc.

Referee: Eklind (Sweden).

BRAZIL 1950

```
Uruguay ........... 0    2 —— 2
Brazil ................ 0    1 —— 1
```

SECOND HALF

Scoring: 1, Brazil, Friaca (47); 2, Uruguay, Schiaffino (66); 3, Uruguay, Ghiggia (79).

Uruguay: Maspoli, Gonzales, Tejera, Gambretta, Varela, Andrade, Ghiggia, Perez, Miguez, Schiffiano, Moran.

Brazil: Barbosa, Augusto, Juvenal, Bauer, Banilo, Bigode, Friaca, Zizinho, Ademir, Jair, Chico.

Referee: Reader (England).

SWEDEN 1958

```
Brazil ................ 2    3 —— 5
Sweden ............. 2    1 —— 2
```

FIRST HALF

Scoring:1, Sweden, Liedholm (3); 2, Brazil, Vava (9); 3, Brazil, Vava (32).

SECOND HALF

Scoring: 4, Brazil, Pelé (55); 5, Brazil, Zagalo (68); 6, Sweden Simonsson (80); 7, Brazil, Pelé (90).

Brazil: Glymar, D. Santos, N. Santos, Zito, Bellini, Orlando, Garrincha, Didi, Vava, Pelé, Zagalo.

Sweden: Svensson, Bergmark, Axbom, Boerjesson, Gustavsson, Parling, Hamrin, Gren, Simonsson, Liedholm, Skoglund.

Referee: Guigue (France).

CHILE 1962

```
Brazil ........................... 1    2 —— 3
Czechoslovakia ........... 1    0 —— 1
```

FIRST HALF

Scoring: 1, Czech., Masopust (15); 2, Brazil, Amarildo (17).

SECOND HALF

Scoring: 3, Brazil, Zito (68); 4, Brazil, Vava (77).

Brazil: Glymar, D. Santos, N. Santos, Zito, Mauro, Zozimo, Garrincha, Didi, Vava, Amarildo, Zagalo.

Czechoslovakia: Schroiff, Tichy, Novak, Pluskal, Popluhar, Masopust, Pospichal, Scherer, Kvasnak, Kadraba, Jelinek.

Referee: Latychev (USSR).

World Cup Final Box Scores (Cont.)

ENGLAND 1966

| England | 1 | 1 | 2 —4 |
| W Germany | 1 | 1 | 0 —2 |

FIRST HALF

Scoring: 1, W Germany, Haller (12); 2, England, Hurst (18).

SECOND HALF

Scoring: 3, England, Peters (78); 4, W. Germany, Weber (90).

OVERTIME

Scoring: 5, England, Hurst (101); 6, England, Hurst (120).

England: Banks, Cohen, Wilson, Stiles, J. Charlton, Moore, Ball, Hurst, Hunt, R. Charlton, Peters.

W Germany: Tilkowski, Hottges, Schmellinger, Beckenbauer, Schulz, Weber, Held, Haller, Seeler, Overath, Emmerich.

Referee: Dienst (Switzerland).

W GERMANY 1974

| W Germany | 2 | 0 —2 |
| Netherlands | 1 | 0 —1 |

FIRST HALF

Scoring: 1, Netherlands, Neeskens, PK (1); 2, W Germany, Breitner, PK (26); 3, W Germany, Müller (44).

W Germany: Maier, Vogts, Beckenbauer, Schwarzenbeck, Breitner, Hoeness, Bonhof, Overath, Grabowski, Müller, Holzenbein.

Netherlands: Jongbloed, Suurbier, Rijsbergen (de Jong), Haan, Krol, Jansen, Neeskens, van Hanagem, Cruyff, Rensenbrink (van der Kerkhof).

Referee: Taylor (England).

ITALY 1982

| Italy | 0 | 3 —3 |
| W Germany | 0 | 1 —1 |

SECOND HALF

Scoring: 1, Italy, Rossi (57); 2, Italy, Tardelli (68); 3, Italy, Altobelli (81); 4, W Germany, Breitner (83).

Italy: Zoff, Bergomi, Scirea, Collovati, Cabrini, Oriali, Gentile, Tardelli, Conti, Rossi, Graziani (Altobelli, Causio).

W Germany: Schumacher, Kaltz, Stielike, K. Foerster, B. Foerster, Dremmler (Hrubesch); Breitner, Briegel, Rummenigge (Müller), Fishcher (Littbarski).

Referee: Coelho (Brazil).

MEXICO 1986 (Cont.)

Argentina: Pumpido, Brown, Cuciuffo, Ruggeri, Olarticoecha, Bastista, Giusti, Burruchaga (Trobbiani 90), Enrique, Maradona, Valdona.

W Germany: Schumacher, Jakobs, Forster, Eder, Brehme, Matthaus, Berthold, Magath (Hoeness 62), Briegel, Rummenigge, Allofs (Voller 46).

Referee: Filho (Brazil).

MEXICO 1970

| Brazil | 1 | 3 —4 |
| Italy | 1 | 0 —1 |

FIRST HALF

Scoring: 1, Brazil, Pelé (18); 2, Italy, Boninsegna (32).

SECOND HALF

Scoring: 3, Brazil, Gerson (65); 4, Brazil, Jairzinho (70); 5, Brazil, Alberto (86).

Brazil: Feliz, Alberto, Brito, Wilson, Piazza, Everaldo, Clodoaldo, Gerson, Jairzinho, Tostao, Pelé, Rivelino.

Italy: Albertosi, Burgnich, Cera, Rosato, Facchetti, Bertini (Juliano), Mazzola, De Sisti, Domenghini, Boninsegna (Rivera), Riva.

Referee: Glockner (E Germany).

ARGENTINA 1978

| Argentina | 1 | 0 | 2 —3 |
| Netherlands | 0 | 1 | 0 —1 |

FIRST HALF

Scoring: 1, Argentina, Kempes (38).

SECOND HALF

Scoring: 2, Netherlands, Nanninga (81).

OVERTIME

Scoring: 3, Arg., Kempes (104); 4, Arg., Bertoni (114).

Argentina: Fillol, Olguin, Galvan, Passarella, Tarantini, Ardiles (Larrosa), Gallego, Kempes, Bertoni, Luque, Ortiz (Houseman).

Netherlands: Jongbloed, Jansen (Suurbier), Krol, Brandts, Poortvliet, Neeskens, Haan, W. van der Kerkhoff, R. van der Kerkhoff, Rep (Nanninga), Rensenbrink.

Referee: Gonella (Italy).

MEXICO 1986

| Argentina | 1 | 2 —3 |
| W Germany | 0 | 2 —2 |

FIRST HALF

Scoring: 1, Argentina, Brown (22).

SECOND HALF

Scoring: 2, Arg., Valdano (55); 3, W Germ., Rummenigge (73); 4, W Germ., Voller (81); 5, Arg., Burruchaga (83).

ITALY 1990

| W Germany | 0 | 1 —1 |
| Argentina | 0 | 0 —0 |

SECOND HALF

Scoring: 1, W Germany, Brehme, PK (84).

W Germany: Illgner, Brehme, Kohler, Augenthaler, Buchwald, Berthold (Reuter), Littbarski, Haessler, Mattaeus, Voeller, Klinsmann.

Argentina: Goychoechea, Lorenzo, Serrizuela, Sensini, Ruggeri (Monzon), Simon, Basualdo, Burruchag (Calderon), Maradona, Troglio, Dezottir.

Referee: Coelho (Brazil).

World Cup Final Box Scores (Cont.)

UNITED STATES 1994			
Italy...............0	0	0—0	
Brazil 0	0	0—0	

Scoring: None. Shootout goals: Italy—2: Albertini, Evani; Brazil—3: Romario, Branco, Dunga.

Italy: Pagliuca, Benarrivo, Maldini, Baresi, Mussi (Apolloni 35), Albertini, D. Baggio (Evani 95), Berti, Donadoni, Baggio, Massaro.

Brazil: Taffarel, Jorginho (Cafu 21), Branco, Aldair, Santos, Silva, Dunga, Zinho (Viola 106), Mazinho, Bebeto, Romario.

Referee: Puhl (Hungary).

FRANCE 1998		
Brazil 0	0—0	
France 2	1—3	

FIRST HALF

Scoring: 1, France, Zidane (27); 2, France, Zidane (45).

SECOND HALF

Scoring: 3, France, Petit (90).

Brazil: Taffarel, Cafu, Aldair, Baiano, Carlos, Sampaio (Edmundo 74), Dunga, Rivaldo, Leonardo, (Denilson 46), Bebeto, Ronaldo.

France: Barthez, Lizarazu, Desailly, Thuram, Leboeuf, Djorkaeff (Vieira 75) Deschamps, Zidane, Petit, Karembeu (Boghossian 57), Guivarc'h (Dugarry 66).

Referee: Belqola (Morocco).

KOREA/JAPAN 2002		
Brazil.........................0	2 —2	
Germany 0	0 —0	

SECOND HALF

Scoring: 1, Brazil, Ronaldo (67); 2, Brazil, Ronaldo (79).

Brazil: Marcos, Cafu, Lucio, Roque Junior, Edmilson, Carlos, Silva, Ronaldo (Denilson, 90), Rivaldo, Ronaldinho (Juninho, 85), Kleberson.

Germany: Kahn, Linke, Ramelow, Neuville, Hamann, Klose (Bierhoff, 74), Jeremies (Asamoah, 77), Bode (Ziege, 84), Schneider, Metzelder, Frings.

Referee: Collina (Italy).

Alltime Leaders

GOALS

Player, Nation	Tournaments	Goals	Player, Nation	Tournaments	Goals
Gerd Müller, W Germany	1970, '74	14	Gary Lineker, England	1986, '90	10
Just Fontaine, France	1958	13	Ademir, Brazil	1950	9
Pelé, Brazil	1958, '62, '66, '70	12	Eusebio, Portugal	1966	9
Ronaldo, Brazil	1998, 2002	12	Jairzinho, Brazil	1970, '74	9
Sandor Kocsis, Hungary	1954	11	Paolo Rossi, Italy	1982, '86	9
Teofilo Cubillas, Peru	1970, '78	10	K.H. Rummenigge, W Ger	1978, '82, '86	9
Gregorz Lato, Poland	1974, '78, '82	10	Uwe Seeler, W Germany	1958, '62, '66, '70	9
Helmut Rahn, W Germany	1954, '58	10	Vava, Brazil	1958, '62	9

LEADING SCORER, CUP BY CUP

Year	Player, Nation	Goals	Year	Player, Nation	Goals
1930	Guillermo Stabile, Argentina	8	1966	Eusebio Ferreira, Portugal	9
1934	Oldrich Nejedly, Czechoslovakia	5	1970	Gerd Müller, W Germany	10
1938	Leonidas da Silva, Brazil	8	1974	Gregorz Lato, Poland	7
1950	Ademir de Menezes, Brazil	9	1978	Mario Kempes, Argentina	6
1954	Sandor Kocsis, Hungary	11	1982	Paolo Rossi, Italy	6
1958	Just Fontaine, France	13	1986	Gary Lineker, England	6
1962	Florian Albert, Hungary	4	1990	Salvatore Schillaci, Italy	6
	Valentin Ivanov, USSR		1994	Hristo Stoichkov, Bulgaria	6
	Garrincha, Brazil; Vava, Brazil			Oleg Salenko, Russia	
	Drazan Jerkovic, Yugoslavia		1998	Davor Suker, Croatia	6
	Leonel Sanchez, Chile		2002	Ronaldo, Brazil	8

Most Goals, Individual, One Game

Goals	Player, Nation	Score	Date
5	Oleg Salenko, Russia	Russia–Cameroon, 6–1	6-28-94
4	Leonidas, Brazil	Brazil–Poland, 6–5	6-5-38
4	Ernest Willimowski, Poland	Brazil–Poland, 6–5	6-5-38
4	Gustav Wetterström, Sweden	Sweden–Cuba, 8–0	6-12-38
4	Juan Alberto Schiaffino, Uruguay	Uruguay–Bolivia, 8–0	7-2-50
4	Ademir, Brazil	Brazil–Sweden, 7–1	7-9-50
4	Sandor Kocsis, Hungary	Hungary–W Germany, 8–3	6-20-54
4	Just Fontaine, France	France–W Germany, 6–3	6-28-58
4	Eusebio, Portugal	Portugal–N Korea, 5–3	7-23-66
4	Emilio Butragueño, Spain	Spain–Denmark, 5–1	6-18-86

Note: 31 players have scored 32 World Cup hat tricks. Gerd Müller of West Germany is the only man to have two World Cup hat tricks, both in 1970. The last hat tricks were 6-1-02, Miroslav Klose (Ger) vs. Saudi Arabia; 6-21-98, Gabriel Batistuta (Arg) vs. Jamaica; 6-23-90, Tomas Skuhravy (Czech) vs. Costa Rica; and 6-17-90, Michel (Spain) vs. S Korea.

Attendance and Goal Scoring, Year by Year

Year	Site	No. of Games	Goals	Goals/Game	Attendance	Avg Att
1930	Uruguay	18	70	3.89	434,500	24,139
1934	Italy	17	70	4.12	395,000	23,235
1938	France	18	84	4.67	483,000	26,833
1950	Brazil	22	88	4.00	1,337,000	60,773
1954	Switzerland	26	140	5.38	943,000	36,269
1958	Sweden	35	126	3.60	868,000	24,800
1962	Chile	32	89	2.78	776,000	24,250
1966	England	32	89	2.78	1,614,677	50,459
1970	Mexico	32	95	2.97	1,673,975	52,312
1974	W Germany	38	97	2.55	1,774,022	46,685
1978	Argentina	38	102	2.68	1,610,215	42,374
1982	Spain	52	146	2.80	1,856,277	35,698
1986	Mexico	52	132	2.54	2,441,731	46,956
1990	Italy	52	115	2.21	2,514,443	48,354
1994	United States	52	140	2.69	3,567,415	68,604
1998	France	64	171	2.67	2,775,400	43,366
2002	Korea/Japan	64	161	2.52	2,705,216	42,269
Totals		580	1,754	3.02	25,064,655	43,215

The United States in the World Cup

URUGUAY 1930: FINAL COMPETITION

Date	Opponent	Result	Scoring
7-13-30	Belgium	3–0 W	U.S.: McGhee 2, Patenaude
7-17-30	Paraguay	3–0 W	U.S.: Patenaude 2, Florie
7-26-30	Argentina	1–6 L	Arg.: Monti 2, Scopelli 2, Stabile 2 U.S.: Brown.

ITALY 1934: FINAL COMPETITION

Date	Opponent	Result	Scoring
5-27-34	Italy	1–7 L	U.S.: Donelli Italy: Schiavio 3, Orsi 2, Meazza, Ferrari

BRAZIL 1950: FINAL COMPETITION

Date	Opponent	Result	Scoring
6-25-50	Spain	1–3 L	U.S.: Pariani Spain: Igoa, Basora, Zarra
6-29-50	England	1–0 W	U.S.: Gaetjens.
7-2-50	Chile	2–5 L	U.S.: Wallace, Maca Chile: Robledo, Cremaschi 3, Prieto

ITALY 1990: FINAL COMPETITION

Date	Opponent	Result	Scoring
6-10-90	Czechoslovakia	1–5 L	U.S.: Caligiuri Czech.: Skuhravy 2, Hasek, Bilek, Luhovy
6-14-90	Italy	0–1 L	Italy: Giannini
6-19-90	Austria	1–2 L	U.S.: Murray Austria: Rodax, Ogris

UNITED STATES 1994: FINAL COMPETITION

Date	Opponent	Result	Scoring
6-18-94	Switzerland	1–1 T	U.S.: Wynalda Switz.: Bregy
6-22-94	Colombia	2–1 W	U.S.: Escobar (own goal), Stewart Colombia: Valencia
6-26-94	Romania	1–0 L	Romania: Petrescu
7-4-94	Brazil	1–0 L	Brazil: Bebeto

FRANCE 1998: FINAL COMPETITION

Date	Opponent	Result	Scoring
6-15-98	Germany	2–0 L	Germany: Möller, Klinsmann
6-21-98	Iran	2–1 L	U.S.: McBride Iran: Estili, Mahdavikia
6-25-98	Yugoslavia	1–0 L	Yugoslavia: Komljenovic

KOREA/JAPAN 2002: FINAL COMPETITION

Date	Opponent	Result	Scoring
6-5-02	Portugal	3–2 W	U.S.: O'Brien, Costa (own goal), McBride Portugal: Beto, Agoos (own goal)
6-10-02	S Korea	1–1 T	U.S.: Mathis S Korea: Ahn
6-14-02	Poland	3–1 L	Poland: Olisadebe, Kryszalowicz, Zewlakow U.S.: Donovan
6-17-02	Mexico	2–0 W	U.S.: McBride, Donovan
6-21-02	Germany	1–0 L	Germany: Ballack

International Competition

European Championship

Official name: the European Football Championship. Held every four years since 1960.

Year	Champion	Score	Runner-up	Year	Champion	Score	Runner-up
1960	USSR	2–1	Yugoslavia	1980	W Germany	2–1	Belgium
1964	Spain	2–1	USSR	1984	France	2–0	Spain
1968	Italy	2–0	Yugoslavia	1988	Holland	2–0	USSR
1972	W Germany	3–0	USSR	1992	Denmark	2–0	Germany
1976	Czechoslovakia*	2–2	W Germany	1996	Germany†	2–1	Czech Republic
				2000	France†	2–1	Italy

*Won on penalty kicks. †Won in sudden-death overtime.

Under-20 World Championship

Year	Host	Champion	Runner-Up
1977	Tunisia	USSR	Mexico
1979	Japan	Argentina	USSR
1981	Australia	W Germany	Qatar
1983	Mexico	Brazil	Argentina
1985	USSR	Brazil	Spain
1987	Chile	Yugoslavia	W Germany
1989	Saudi Arabia	Portugal	Nigeria
1991	Portugal	Portugal	Brazil
1993	Australia	Brazil	Ghana
1995	Qatar	Argentina	Brazil
1997	Malaysia	Argentina	Uruguay
1999	Nigeria	Spain	Japan
2001	Argentina	Argentina	Ghana

Under-17 World Championship

Year	Champion
1985	Nigeria
1987	USSR
1989	Saudi Arabia
1991	Ghana

Under-17 *(Cont.)*

Year	Champion
1993	Nigeria
1995	Ghana
1997	Brazil
1999	Brazil
2001	France

Pan American Games

Year	Champion
1951	Argentina
1955	Argentina
1959	Argentina
1963	Brazil
1967	Mexico
1971	Argentina
1975	Brazil/Mexico (tie)
1979	Brazil
1983	Uruguay
1987	Brazil
1991	United States
1995	Argentina
1999	Mexico

South American Championship (Copa America)

Year	Champion	Host	Year	Champion	Host
1916	Uruguay	Argentina	1953	Paraguay	Peru
1917	Uruguay	Uruguay	1955	Argentina	Chile
1919	Brazil	Brazil	1956	Uruguay	Uruguay
1920	Uruguay	Chile	1957	Argentina	Peru
1921	Argentina	Argentina	1958	Argentina	Argentina
1922	Brazil	Brazil	1959	Uruguay	Ecuador
1923	Uruguay	Uruguay	1963	Bolivia	Bolivia
1924	Uruguay	Uruguay	1967	Uruguay	Uruguay
1925	Argentina	Argentina	1975	Peru	Various sites
1926	Uruguay	Chile	1979	Paraguay	Various sites
1927	Argentina	Peru	1983	Uruguay	Various sites
1929	Argentina	Argentina	1987	Uruguay	Argentina
1935	Uruguay	Peru	1989	Brazil	Brazil
1937	Argentina	Argentina	1990	Brazil	Argentina
1939	Peru	Peru	1991	Argentina	Chile
1941	Argentina	Chile	1993	Argentina	Ecuador
1942	Uruguay	Uruguay	1995	Uruguay	Uruguay
1945	Argentina	Chile	1997	Brazil	Bolivia
1946	Argentina	Argentina	1999	Brazil	Paraguay
1947	Argentina	Ecuador	2001	Colombia	Colombia
1949	Brazil	Brazil			

Awards

European Footballer of the Year

Year	Player	Club	Year	Player	Club
1956	Stanley Matthews	Blackpool	1975	Oleg Blokhin	Dynamo Kiev
1957	Alfredo Di Stefano	Real Madrid	1976	Franz Beckenbauer	Bayern Munich
1958	Raymond Kopa	Real Madrid	1977	Allan Simonsen	Borussia M'gladbach
1959	Alfredo Di Stefano	Real Madrid	1978	Kevin Keegan	SV Hamburg
1960	Luis Suarez	Barcelona	1979	Kevin Keegan	SV Hamburg
1961	Omar Sivori	Juventus	1980	Karl-Heinz Rummenigge	Bayern Munich
1962	Josef Masopust	Dukla Prague	1981	Karl-Heinz Rummenigge	Bayern Munich
1963	Lev Yashin	Moscow Dynamo	1982	Paolo Rossi	Juventus
1964	Denis Law	Manchester United	1983	Michel Platini	Juventus
1965	Eusebio	Benfica	1984	Michel Platini	Juventus
1966	Bobby Charlton	Manchester United	1985	Michel Platini	Juventus
1967	Florian Albert	Ferencvaros	1986	Igor Belanov	Dynamo Kiev
1968	George Best	Manchester United	1987	Ruud Gullit	AC Milan
1969	Gianni Rivera	AC Milan	1988	Marco Van Basten	AC Milan
1970	Gerd Mueller	Bayern Munich	1989	Marco Van Basten	AC Milan
1971	Johan Cruyff	Ajax	1990	Lothar Matthaeus	Inter Milan
1972	Franz Beckenbauer	Bayern Munich	1991	Jean-Pierre Papin	Olympique Marseille
1973	Johan Cruyff	Barcelona	1992	Marco Van Basten	AC Milan
1974	Johan Cruyff	Barcelona	1993	Roberto Baggio	Juventus

European Footballer of the Year (Cont.)

Year	Player	Club	Year	Player	Club
1994	Hristo Stoichkov	Barcelona	1998	Zinedine Zidane	Juventus
1995	George Weah	AC Milan	1999	Rivaldo	Barcelona
1996	Matthias Sammer	Borussia Dortmund	2000	Luis Figo	Real Madrid
1997	Ronaldo	Inter Milan	2001	Michael Owen	Liverpool

African Footballer of the Year

Year	Player	Club	Year	Player	Club
1970	Salif Keita	St. Etienne	1986	Badou Ezaki	Real Mallorca
1971	Ibrahim Sunday	Asante Kotoko	1987	Rabah Madjer	FC Porto
1972	Chérif Soueymane	Hafia	1988	Kalusha Bwalya	Cercle Bruges
1973	Tshimen Bwanga	TP Mazembe	1989	George Weah	Monaco
1974	Paul Moukila	CARA Brazzaville	1990	Roger Milla	St. Denis
1975	Ahmed Faras	Mohammedia	1991	Abedi Pele Ayew	Marseille
1976	Roger Milla	Canon Yaounde	1992	Abedi Pele Ayew	Marseille
1977	Tarak Dhiab	Esperance	1993	Rashidi Yekini	FC Zurich
1978	Karim Abdul Razak	Asante Kotoko	1994	George Weah	Paris St. Germain
1979	Thomas Nkono	Canon Yaounde	1995	George Weah	AC Milan
1980	Jean Manga Onguene	Canon Yaounde	1996	Nwankwo Kanu	Inter Milan
1981	Lakhdar Belloumi	GCR Mascara	1997	Victor Ikpeba	Monaco
1982	Thomas Nkono	Espanol	1998	Mustapha Hadji	Deportivo Coruna
1983	Mahmoud Al-Khatib	Al Ahli	1999	Nwankwo Kanu	Arsenal
1984	Theophile Abega	Toulouse	2000	Patrick Mboma	Parma
1985	Mohamed Timoumi	Royal Armed Forces	2001	El Hadji Diouf	Lens

South American Player of the Year

Year	Player	Club	Year	Player	Club
1971	Tostao	Cruzeiro	1987	Carlos Valderrama	Deportivo Cali
1972	Teofilo Cubillas	Alianza Lima	1988	Ruben Paz	Racing Buenos Aires
1973	Pelé	Santos	1989	Bebeto	Vasco da Gama
1974	Elias Figueroa	Internacional	1990	Raul Amarilla	Olimpia
1975	Elias Figueroa	Internacional	1991	Oscar Ruggeri	Velez Sarsfield
1976	Elias Figueroa	Internacional	1992	Rai	São Paulo
1977	Zico	Flamengo	1993	Carlos Valderrama	Junior Barranquilla
1978	Mario Kempes	Valencia	1994	Cafu	São Paulo
1979	Diego Maradona	Argentinos Juniors	1995	Enzo Francescoli	River Plate
1980	Diego Maradona	Boca Juniors	1996	Jose-Luis Chilavert	Velez Sarsfield
1981	Zico	Flamengo	1997	Marcelo Salas	River Plate
1982	Zico	Flamengo	1998	Martin Palermo	Boca Juniors
1983	Socrates	Corinthians	1999	Javier Saviola	River Plate
1984	Enzo Francescoli	River Plate	2000	Romario	Vasco da Gama
1985	Julio Cesar Romero	Fluminense	2001	Juan Riquelme	Boca Juniors
1986	Antonio Alzamendi	River Plate			

International Club Competition

Intercontinental Cup

Competition between winners of European Cup and Libertadores Cup.

1960...Real Madrid, Spain	1974...Atletico de Madrid, Spain	1988...Nacional, Uruguay
1961...Penarol, Uruguay	1975...No tournament	1989...Milan, Italy
1962...Santos, Brazil	1976...Bayern Munich	1990...Milan, Italy
1963...Santos, Brazil	1977...Boca Juniors, Argentina	1991...Red Star Belgrade, Yugos.
1964...Inter, Italy	1978...No tournament	1992...São Paulo, Brazil
1965...Inter, Italy	1979...Olimpia, Paraguay	1993...São Paulo, Brazil
1966...Penarol, Uruguay	1980...Nacional, Uruguay	1994...Velez Sarsfield, Argentina
1967...Racing Club, Argentina	1981...Flamengo, Brazil	1995...Ajax Amsterdam, Netherlands
1968...Estudiantes, Argentina	1982...Penarol, Uruguay	1996...Juventus, Italy
1969...Milan, Italy	1983...Gremio, Brazil	1997...Borussia Dortmund, Ger.
1970...Feyenoord, Netherlands	1984...Independiente, Argentina	1998...Real Madrid, Spain
1971...Nacional, Uruguay	1985...Juventus, Italy	1999...Manchester United, England
1972...Ajax Amsterdam, Netherlands	1986...River Plate, Argentina	2000...Boca Juniors, Argentina
1973...Independiente, Argentina	1987...Porto, Portugal	2001...Bayern Munich, Germany

Note: Until 1968 a best-of-three-games format decided the winner. After that a two-game/total-goal format was used until Toyota became the sponsor in 1980, moved the game to Tokyo and switched the format to a one-game championship. The European Cup runner-up substituted for the winner in 1971, 1973, 1974, and 1979.

European Cup

1956...Real Madrid, Spain
1957...Real Madrid, Spain
1958...Real Madrid, Spain
1959...Real Madrid, Spain
1960...Real Madrid, Spain
1961...Benfica, Portugal
1962...Benfica, Portugal
1963...AC Milan, Italy
1964...Inter-Milan, Italy
1965...Inter-Milan, Italy
1966...Real Madrid, Spain
1967...Celtic, Scotland
1968...Manchester United, England
1969...AC Milan, Italy
1970...Feyenoord, Netherlands
1971...Ajax Amsterdam, Netherlands
1972...Ajax Amsterdam, Netherlands

1973...Ajax Amsterdam, Netherlands
1974...Bayern Munich, W Germany
1975...Bayern Munich, W Germany
1976...Bayern Munich, W Germany
1977...Liverpool, England
1978...Liverpool, England
1979...Nottingham Forest, England
1980...Nottingham Forest, England
1981...Liverpool, England
1982...Aston Villa, England
1983...SV Hamburg, W Germany
1984...Liverpool, England
1985...Juventus, Italy

1986...Steaua Bucharest, Romania
1987...Porto, Portugal
1988...PSV Eindhoven, Netherlands
1989...AC Milan, Italy
1990...AC Milan, Italy
1991...Red Star Belgrade, Yugoslav.
1992...Barcelona, Spain
1993...Olympique Marseille, France
1994...AC Milan, Italy
1995...Ajax Amsterdam, Netherlands
1996...Juventus, Italy
1997...Borussia Dortmund, Ger.
1998...Real Madrid, Spain
1999...Manchester United, England
2000...Real Madrid, Spain
2001...Bayern Munich, Germany
2002...Real Madrid, Spain

Note: On four occasions the European Cup winner has refused to play in the Intercontinental Cup and has been replaced by the runner-up: Panathinaikos (Greece) in 1971, Juventus (Italy) in 1973, Atletico Madrid (Spain) in 1974, and Malmo (Sweden) in 1979.

Libertadores Cup

Competition between champion clubs and runners-up of 10 South American National Associations.

1960...Penarol, Uruguay
1961...Penarol, Uruguay
1962...Santos, Brazil
1963...Santos, Brazil
1964...Independiente, Argentina
1965...Independiente, Argentina
1966...Penarol, Uruguay
1967...Racing Club, Argentina
1968...Estudiantes, Argentina
1969...Estudiantes, Argentina
1970...Estudiantes, Argentina
1971...Nacional, Uruguay
1972...Independiente, Argentina
1973...Independiente, Argentina
1974...Independiente, Argentina

1975...Independiente, Argentina
1976...Cruzeiro, Brazil
1977...Boca Juniors, Argentina
1978...Boca Juniors, Argentina
1979...Olimpia, Paraguay
1980...Nacional, Uruguay
1981...Flamengo, Brazil
1982...Penarol, Uruguay
1983...Gremio, Brazil
1984...Independiente, Argentina
1985...Argentinos Juniors, Arg
1986...River Plate, Argentina
1987...Penarol, Uruguay
1988...Nacional, Uruguay
1989...Atletico Nacional, Colombia

1990...Olimpia, Paraguay
1991...Colo Colo, Chile
1992...São Paulo, Brazil
1993...São Paulo, Brazil
1994...Velez Sarsfield, Argentina
1995...Gremio, Brazil
1996...River Plate, Argentina
1997...Cruzeiro, Brazil
1998...Vasco da Gama, Brazil
1999...Palmeiras, Brazil
2000...Boca Juniors, Argentina
2001...Boca Juniors, Argentina
2002...Olimpia, Paraguay

UEFA Cup

1958...Barcelona, Spain
1959...No tournament
1960...Barcelona, Spain
1961...AS Roma, Italy
1962...Valencia, Spain
1963...Valencia, Spain
1964...Real Zaragoza, Spain
1965...Ferencvaros, Hungary
1966...Barcelona, Spain
1967...Dynamo Zagreb, Yugoslav.
1968...Leeds United, England
1969...Newcastle United, England
1970...Arsenal, England
1971...Leeds United, England
1972...Tottenham Hotspur, England
1973...Liverpool, England
1974...Feyenoord, Netherlands

1975...Borussia Monchengladbach, W Germany
1976...Liverpool, England
1977...Juventus, Italy
1978...PSV Eindhoven, Netherl.
1979...Borussia Monchengladbach, W Germany
1980...Eintracht Frankfurt, W Germany
1981...Ipswich Town, England
1982...IFK Gothenburg, Sweden
1983...Anderlecht, Belgium
1984...Tottenham Hotspur, England
1985...Real Madrid, Spain
1986...Real Madrid, Spain
1987...IFK Gothenburg, Sweden
1988...Bayer Leverkusen,

W Germany
1989...Naples, Italy
1990...Juventus, Italy
1991...Inter-Milan, Italy
1992...Torino, Italy
1993...Juventus, Italy
1994...Internazionale, Italy
1995...Parma, Italy
1996...Bayern Munich, Germany
1997...Schalke 04, Germany
1998...Inter Milan, Italy
1999...Parma, Italy
2000...Galatasaray, Turkey
2001...Liverpool, England
2002...Feyenoord, Netherlands

European Cup-Winners' Cup

1961...AC Fiorentina, Italy	1974...Magdeburg, E Germany	1988...Mechelen, Belgium
1962...Atletico Madrid, Spain	1975...Dynamo Kiev, USSR	1989...Barcelona, Spain
1963...Tottenham Hotspur, England	1976...Anderlecht, Belgium	1990...Sampdoria, Italy
1964...Sporting Lisbon, Portugal	1977...SV Hamburg, W Germ.	1991 ...Manchester United, England
1965...West Ham United, England	1978...Anderlecht, Belgium	1992...Werder Bremen, Germany
1966...Borussia Dortmund, W Germany	1979...Barcelona, Spain	1993...Parma, Italy
1967...Bayern Munich, W Germ.	1980...Valencia, Spain	1994...Arsenal, England
1968...AC Milan, Italy	1981...Dynamo Tbilisi, USSR	1995...Real Zaragoza, Spain
1969...Slovan Bratislava, Czech.	1982...Barcelona, Spain	1996...Paris St. Germain, France
1970...Manchester City, England	1983...Aberdeen, Scotland	1997...Barcelona, Spain
1971...Chelsea, England	1984...Juventus, Italy	1998...Chelsea, England
1972...Glasgow Rangers, Scotland	1985...Everton, England	1999...Lazio, Italy
1973...AC Milan, Italy	1986...Dynamo Kiev, USSR	
	1987...Ajax Amsterdam, Neth.	

Note: the Cup-Winners Cup was discontinued after 1999.

Major League Soccer

MLS Cup Results

Year	Champion	Score	Runner-up	Regular Season MVP
1996	D.C. United	3–2 (ot)	Los Angeles	Carlos Valderrama, TB
1997	D.C. United	2–1	Colorado	Preki, Kansas City
1998	Chicago	2–0	D.C. United	Marco Etcheverry, D.C.
1999	D.C. United	2–0	Los Angeles	Jason Kreis, Dallas
2000	Kansas City	1–0	Chicago	Tony Meola, Kansas City
2001	San Jose	2–1 (ot)	Los Angeles	Alex Pineda Chacon, Mia
2002	Los Angeles	1–0 (ot)	New England	Carlos Ruiz, Los Angeles

A-League

Year	Champion	Score	Runner-Up	Regular Season MVP
1991	San Francisco	1–3, 2–0 (1–0 on PKs)	Albany	Jean Harbor, Maryland
1992	Colorado	1–0	Tampa Bay	Taifour Diane, Colorado
1993	Colorado	3–1 (OT)	Los Angeles	Taifour Diane, Colorado
1994	Montreal	1–0	Colorado	Paulinho, Los Angeles
1995	Seattle	1–2 (SO), 3–0, 2–1 (SO)	Atlanta	Peter Hattrup, Seattle
1996	Seattle	2–0	Rochester	Wolde Harris, Colorado
1997	Milwaukee	2–1 (SO)	Carolina	Doug Miller, Rochester
1998	Rochester	3–1	Minnesota	Mark Baena, Seattle
1999	Minnesota	2–1	Rochester	John Swallen, Minnesota
2000	Rochester	3–1	Minnesota	Vitalis Takawira, Mil
2001	Rochester	2–0	Vancouver	Paul Conway, Charleston
2002	Milwaukee	2–1 (2ot)	Richmond	Leighton O'Brien, Seattle

Woman's United Soccer Association

Founders Cup Results

Year	Champion	Score	Runner-up	Regular Season MVP
2001	Bay Area	3–3 (4–2 PKs)	Atlanta	Tiffeny Milbrett, New York
2002	Carolina	3–2	Washington	Marinette Pichon, Philadelphia

Open to all amateur and professional teams in the United States, the annual U.S. Open Cup is the oldest cup competition in the country and among the oldest in the world. The tournament is a single-elimination event running concurrent to the MLS season. The winner advances to the CONCACAF Cup, a tournament of the top club teams from North and Central America and the Caribbean.

Year	Champion
1914	Brooklyn Field Club (NYC)
1915	Bethlehem Steel FC (PA)
1916	Bethlehem Steel FC (PA)
1917	Fall River Rovers (MA)
1918	Bethlehem Steel FC (PA)
1919	Bethlehem Steel FC (PA)
1920	Ben Miller FC (St. Louis)
1921	Robbins Dry Dock FC (Brooklyn)
1922	Scullin Steel FC (St. Louis)
1923	Paterson FC (NJ)
1924	Fall River FC (MA)
1925	Shawsheen FC (Andover, MA)
1926	Bethlehem Steel FC (PA)
1927	Fall River FC (MA)
1928	New York National FC (NYC)
1929	Hakoah All Star SC (NYC)
1930	Fall River FC (MA)
1931	Fall River FC (MA)
1932	New Bedford FC (MA)
1933	Stix, Baer and Fuller FC (St. Louis)
1934	Stix, Baer and Fuller FC (St. Louis)
1935	Central Breweries FC (Chicago)
1936	German-Americans (Philadelphia)
1937	New York American FC (NYC)
1938	Sparta A and BA (Chicago)
1939	St. Mary's Celtic SC (Brooklyn)
1940	—
1941	Pawtucket FC (RI)
1942	Gallatin SC (PA)
1943	Brooklyn Hispano SC (NYC)
1944	Brooklyn Hispano SC (NYC)
1945	Brookhattan FC (NYC)
1946	Chicago Viking FC (IL)
1947	Ponta Delgada SC (Fall River, MA)
1948	Simpkins-Ford SC (St. Louis)
1949	Morgan SC (PA)
1950	Simpkins-Ford SC (St. Louis)
1951	German Hungarian SC (NYC)
1952	Harmarville SC (PA)
1953	Falcons SC (Chicago)
1954	New York Americans (NYC)
1955	Eintracht Sport Club (NYC)
1956	Harmarville SC (PA)
1957	Kutis SC (St. Louis)
1958	Los Angeles Kickers (CA)
1959	McIlvaine Canvasbacks (Los Angeles)

Year	Champion
1960	Ukrainian Nationals (Philadelphia)
1961	Ukrainian Nationals (Philadelphia)
1962	New York Hungaria (NYC)
1963	Ukrainian Nationals (Philadelphia)
1964	Los Angeles Kickers (CA)
1965	New York Hungaria (NYC)
1966	Ukrainian Nationals (Philadelphia)
1967	Greek American AA (NYC)
1968	Greek American AA (NYC)
1969	Greek American AA (NYC)
1970	Elizabeth SC (Union, NJ)
1971	Hota SC (NYC)
1972	Elizabeth SC (Union, NJ)
1973	Maccabee SC (Los Angeles)
1974	Greek American AA (NYC)
1975	Maccabee SC (Los Angeles)
1976	San Francisco AC (CA)
1977	Maccabee SC (Los Angeles)
1978	Maccabee SC (Los Angeles)
1979	Brooklyn Dodgers SC (NYC)
1980	NY Pancyprian-Freedoms (NYC)
1981	Maccabee SC (Los Angeles)
1982	NY Pancyprian-Freedoms (NYC)
1983	NY Pancyprian-Freedoms (NYC)
1984	AO Krete (NYC)
1985	Greek American AC (San Francisco)
1986	Kutis SC (St. Louis)
1987	Club Espana (Washington, D.C.)
1988	Busch SC (St. Louis)
1989	HRC Kickers (St. Petersburg, FL)
1990	AAC Eagles (Chicago)
1991	Brooklyn Italians SC (East NY)
1992	San Jose Oaks (CA)
1993	Club Deportivo Mexico (San Francisco)
1994	Greek American AC (San Francisco)
1995	Richmond Kickers (VA)
1996	D.C. United (MLS)
1997	Dallas Burn (MLS)
1998	Chicago Fire (MLS)
1999	Rochester Rhinos (A-League)
2000	Chicago Fire (MLS)
2001	Los Angeles Galaxy (MLS)

North American Soccer League

Formed in 1968 by the merger of the National Professional Soccer League and the USA League, both of which had begun operations a year earlier. The NPSL's lone champion was the Oakland Clippers. The USA League, which brought entire teams in from Europe, was won in 1967 by the L.A. Wolves, who were the English League's Wolverhampton Wanderers.

Year	Champion	Score	Runner-Up	Regular Season MVP
1968	Atlanta	0–0, 3–0	San Diego	John Kowalik, Chi
1969	Kansas City	No game	Atlanta	Cirilio Fernandez, KC
1970	Rochester	3–0,1–3	Washington	Carlos Metidieri, Roch
1971	Dallas	1–2, 4–1, 2–0	Atlanta	Carlos Metidieri, Roch
1972	New York	2–1	St. Louis	Randy Horton, NY
1973	Philadelphia	2–0	Dallas	Warren Archibald, Mia
1974	Los Angeles	4–3*	Miami	Peter Silvester, Balt
1975	Tampa Bay	2–0	Portland	Steve David, Mia
1976	Toronto	3–0	Minnesota	Pelé, NY
1977	New York	2–1	Seattle	Franz Beckenbauer, NY
1978	New York	3–1	Tampa Bay	Mike Flanagan, NE
1979	Vancouver	2–1	Tampa Bay	Johan Cruyff, LA
1980	New York	3–0	Ft. Lauderdale	Roger Davies, Sea
1981	Chicago	1–0*	New York	Giorgio Chinaglia, NY
1982	New York	1–0	Seattle	Peter Ward, Sea
1983	Tulsa	2–0	Toronto	Roberto Cabanas, NY
1984	Chicago	2–1, 3–2	Toronto	Steve Zungul, SJ

*Shootout.

Championship Format: 1968 and 1970: Two games/total goals. 1971 and 1984: Best-of-three series. 1972–1983: One-game championship. Title in 1969 went to the regular-season champion.

Statistical Leaders

SCORING

Year	Player/Team	Pts	Year	Player/Team	Pts
1968	John Kowalik, Chi	69	1977	Steven David, LA	58
1969	Kaiser Motaung, Atl	36	1978	Giorgio Chinaglia, NY	79
1970	Kirk Apostolidis, Dall	35	1979	Oscar Fabbiani, Tampa Bay	58
1971	Carlos Metidieri, Roch	46	1980	Giorgio Chinaglia, NY	77
1972	Randy Horton, NY	22	1981	Giorgio Chinaglia, NY	74
1973	Kyle Rote, Dall	30	1982	Giorgio Chinaglia, NY	55
1974	Paul Child, San Jose	36	1983	Roberto Cabanas, NY	66
1975	Steven David, Miami	52	1984	Slavisa Zungul, Golden Bay	50
1976	Giorgio Chinaglia, NY	49			

YET ANOTHER SIGN OF THE APOCALYPSE

H'Angus, the monkey mascot of England's Hartlepool soccer club, has been elected mayor of Hartlepool.

NCAA Sports

**Huston Street of
NCAA champion Texas**

Hither and Yon

The champions in men's soccer, ice hockey and baseball found their star players in unexpected places

BY HANK HERSCH

ACROSS AN ocean, beyond a border or right in the backyard: There's no telling where a college team will unearth the player who will return it to glory. In the NCAA championships of 2001–02, heroes came from far and near to end the title droughts of three schools sprinkled around the country.

MEN'S SOCCER

Only 10 minutes into the final against favored Indiana, North Carolina senior defender Danny Jackson absorbed a shot to the noggin. "That knocked the sense out of me for a little while," he said after the match. Two nights earlier, Jackson had been barely conscious for the last five minutes of the Tar Heels' 136-minute, quadruple-overtime, 3–2 win over Stanford after he took an inadvertent elbow to the head. A willingness to get stuck in, as his fellow Englishmen might say, is in Jackson's nature. And he's not afraid to play hurt, either. As Carolina coach Elmar Bolowich puts it, the only way to keep Jackson off the pitch is "to chop a leg off of him."

A level—if occasionally battered—head is also characteristic of Jackson. He was 16, and a high school graduate, when he began living at the youth academy of Leeds United, his hometown team, in 1996. For two years he played nonstop from July to May, taking one day of college-level classes a week to break up a routine that included little more than training, golf, shopping and TV. Interested in a more advanced education, Jackson remembered hearing about college athletic scholarships in the U.S. from some expatriates on a trip to the States with Leeds in '97. He sent out a few letters to schools, and when Bolowich made him an offer, he packed off for Chapel Hill.

Jackson adapted quickly; Bolowich named him captain in the spring semester of his freshman year. "He's the smartest player I've ever played with," says senior goalkeeper Mike Ueltschey. "There's not a better player in the country at timing his tackles. He's good with both feet, he has a pinpoint long ball and he's fast. He doesn't look fast, but when does he ever get beat?"

Jackson (4) buried a penalty kick in the 75th minute to seal UNC's win over Indiana in the NCAA Final.

In Indiana, Jackson & Co. faced the team that had eliminated them in the quarterfinals in 2000, a five-time champion that had conceded only six goals over 22 matches in 2001. North Carolina, on the other hand, had never won a title, but had watched with envy while its women's program had racked up 16 in 19 seasons. The men's Final Four took place in Columbus, Ohio, in cold and gray December—conditions perfectly suited to an Englishman. "I love it," said Jackson upon his arrival. "I love this kind of weather."

It showed in the title match. Despite his initial grogginess, Jackson anchored a defense that repeatedly repelled the Hoosiers, particularly as Indiana tried to equalize late in the first half. Ryan Kniepper, a 6' 3" junior striker, had staked North Carolina to a 1–0 lead in the 12th minute, beating defender John Swann and goalkeeper Colin Rogers to a long cross and heading the ball in from six yards out. Jackson sealed the win in the 75th minute, blasting a penalty kick past Rogers's fingertips.

The 2–0 victory came just five days after Jackson's final exam. He had completed his degree in political science a semester early to return to the goal he had set aside in England: a pro soccer career. Only this time, he would pursue it in the States. "The experience I've had with soccer in America has only been positive," Jackson said. "I've had a fantastic time." The former Leeds United product signed with Major League Soccer and was allocated to the Colorado Rapids.

MEN'S ICE HOCKEY

For 13 years, Minnesota had never seen fit to go outside its borders to recruit a hockey player. That changed in 2000, when second-year coach Don Lucia—a native Minnesotan, true, but as a Notre Dame grad the first non-Gopher to lead the team in three decades—pursued left wing Grant Potulny. The move wasn't much of a reach; Potulny is from Grand Forks, N.D., all of 50 yards on the far side of the Red River that separates the two states. Still, his alien status was an issue at first, though he soon gained acceptance in his new state (leading the nation in power play goals as a freshman didn't hurt).

The Gophers' closed-shop policy had worked wonders from 1971 through '81, when they reached six NCAA championship games and won three. But despite a fanatical fan base willing to pay the highest ticket prices in college hockey ($26) to pack a 10,000-seat arena, Minnesota had failed to win a title since 1979, as it faced increasing competition from four other state schools as well as the junior leagues of North America and the U.S. development program. "I've made it clear that Minnesota will always be our base, but I envision four or five kids being from the outside," Lucia says. "To be competitive we have to recruit elsewhere."

The Gophers were certainly competitive in 2001–02, reaching the NCAA semifinals, for which they didn't have to travel far: St. Paul's Xcel Energy Center hosted this year's Frozen Four, as the event is clumsily nick-named. Potulny scored a pair of power-play goals in a 3–2 semifinal win over Michigan, but his start was less auspicious in the final against third-seeded Maine. Potulny was in the penalty box for the Black Bears' first goal, and he deflected a shot into his own team's net for Maine's second goal. "I'm thinking, This was the biggest nightmare that ever happened to me," Potulny said. "I was responsible for two Maine goals. I had to do something to bail myself out."

He got some help from wing Matt Koalska and the nation's leading scorer, John Pohl. With Minnesota down 3–2 with 52.4 seconds left in regulation, its goalie on the bench in favor of a sixth attacker, Koalska scored the tying goal. With 4:02 left in overtime, Koalska drew a tripping call to give his team a man advantage. One minute later, Pohl blasted a shot at Maine goalie Matt Yeats and Potulny was there to poke the rebound home, sending the Frozen Four–record crowd of 19,324 into a frenzy. The only non-Minnesotan on the Gophers' 20-man roster was named the tournament's Most Outstanding Player. "I've got that M tattooed on my chest," Potulny said. "I'm a Golden Gopher for the rest of my life."

The loss was a bitter one for the Black Bears, who were wearing green shamrock-shaped patches on their jerseys in memory of their former coach Shawn Walsh, who died of cancer before the season started.

BASEBALL

Texas freshman pitcher Huston Street grew up in Austin and attended his first Long-horns football game when he was six. He went to Texas Memorial Stadium with his father, and lingered for three hours after-ward because of his father. James Street had quarterbacked Texas to the 1969 national championship, and autograph seekers rou-tinely attacked him like piranhas. A decade later, Huston did not hesitate to enroll at Texas. "I've never thought of it as pressure, having a dad who did so well," he says. "He's my best friend, my role model, my advisor. It'd be an honor just to be mentioned in the same breath."

James Street was also a two-time All-America in baseball at Texas. He threw two no-hitters in his college career. Although Huston was an all-state free safety at West-lake High, he chose to play baseball with the Longhorns. Texas coach Augie Garrido used the 6-foot, 179-pound righthander out of the bullpen to start the season, but when Street's low-90s fastball flattened out, he began to get hit—hard.

During February and March, pitching coach Frank Anderson dropped Street's three-quarters delivery slightly lower to get more movement. Using his new release point, Street went 23 innings without giving up a run, and a closer was born. He would finish the season with a 4–1 record, a 0.96 ERA and 14 saves, the second-highest total in school history.

Street carried that scoreless streak to the College World Series in Omaha, where he quickly established himself as a man to be feared in a tight game. The night before his underdog club was to face the Longhorns for the championship, South Carolina coach Ray Tanner said, "You know they have Hus-ton Street waiting. That's not comforting."

When Street entered in the eighth inning, the Gamecocks had cut Texas's six-run lead to 8–4, and had two runners on base with one out. Following a walk and a bobble on a potential double-play ball, it was 8–6. With the game on the line, Street sneaked a 3-2 curveball past South Carolina slugger Yaron Peters. James Street's son closed out the ninth and delivered the Longhorns their first title in 19 years, 12–6.

The save was Street's record fourth in the CWS, and he was named the tournament's Most Outsanding Player. "My dad has always told me that I've got to be Huston," he said. "I've got to make my own mark."

NCAA Team Champions

Fall 2001
Cross-Country
MEN

	Champion	Runner-Up
Division I:	Colorado	Stanford
Division II:	Western St (CO)	Abilene Christian
Division III:	WI-LaCrosse	Calvin

WOMEN

	Champion	Runner-Up
Division I:	Brigham Young	N Carolina St
Division II:	Western St (CO)	Adams St
Division III:	Middlebury	Williams

Field Hockey
WOMEN

	Champion	Runner-Up
Division I:	Michigan	Maryland
Division II	Bentley	E Stroudsburg
Division III:	Cortland St	Messiah

Football
MEN

	Champion	Runner-Up
Division I-AA:	Montana	Furman
Division II:	Grand Valley St	N Dakota
Division III:	Mount Union	Bridgewater

Soccer
MEN

	Champion	Runner-Up
Division I:	N Carolina	Indiana
Division II:	Tampa	Cal St–Dominguez Hills
Division III:	Richard Stockton	Redlands

WOMEN

	Champion	Runner-Up
Division I:	Santa Clara	N Carolina
Division II:	UC–San Diego	Christian Brothers
Division III:	Ohio Wesleyan	Amherst

Volleyball
WOMEN

	Champion	Runner-Up
Division I:	Stanford	Long Beach St
Division II:	Barry	S Dakota St
Division III:	LaVerne	WI-Whitewater

Water Polo
MEN

Champion	Runner-Up
Stanford	UCLA

Winter 2001–2002

Basketball

MEN

	Champion	Runner-Up
Division I:	Maryland	Indiana
Division II:	Metropolitan St	Kentucky Wesleyan
Division III:	Otterbein	Elizabethtown

WOMEN

	Champion	Runner-Up
Division I:	Connecticut	Oklahoma
Division II:	Cal Poly–Pomona	SE Oklahoma
Division III:	WI-Stevens	St. Lawrence

Fencing

Champion	Runner-Up
Penn St	St. John's (NY)

Gymnastics

MEN

Champion	Runner-Up
Oklahoma	Ohio St

WOMEN

Alabama	Georgia

Ice Hockey

MEN

	Champion	Runner-Up
Division I:	Minnesota	Maine
Division III:	WI-Superior	Norwich

WOMEN

MN-Duluth	Brown

Rifle

Champion	Runner-Up
AK-Fairbanks	Kentucky

Skiing

Champion	Runner-Up
Denver	Colorado

Swimming and Diving

MEN

	Champion	Runner-Up
Division I:	Texas	Stanford
Division II:	Cal St-Bakersfield	N Dakota
Division III:	Kenyon	Johns Hopkins

WOMEN

Division I:	Auburn	Georgia
Division II:	Truman St	Drury
Division III:	Kenyon	Denison

Wrestling

MEN

	Champion	Runner-Up
Division I:	Minnesota	Iowa St
Division II:	Central Oklahoma	N Dakota St
Division III:	Augsburg	Buena Vista

Winter 2001–2002 (Cont.)
Indoor Track and Field
MEN

	Champion	Runner-Up
Division I:	Tennessee	Alabama
Division II:	Abilene Christian	St. Augustine's/Western St
Division III:	WI–La Crosse	Lincoln

WOMEN

	Champion	Runner-Up
Division I:	Louisiana	UCLA
Division II:	N Dakota St	St. Augustine's
Division III:	Wheaton (MA)	WI-Oshkosh

Spring 2002

Baseball

	Champion	Runner-Up
Division I:	Texas	S Carolina
Division II:	Columbus St	Chico St
Division III:	Eastern Connecticut	Marietta

Golf
MEN

	Champion	Runner-Up
Division I:	Minnesota	Georgia Tech
Division II:	Rollins (FL)	Cal St–Stanislaus
Division III:	Guilford	Greensboro

WOMEN

	Champion	Runner-Up
Division I:	Duke	Auburn/Texas
Division II:	Florida Southern	Barry
Division III	Methodist	Mary-Hardin Baylor

Lacrosse
MEN

	Champion	Runner-Up
Division I:	Syracuse	Princeton
Division II:	Limestone	New York Tech
Division III:	Middlebury	Gettysburg

WOMEN

	Champion	Runner-Up
Division I:	Princeton	Georgetown
Division II	W Chester	Stonehill
Division III:	Middlebury	College of New Jersey

Rowing
WOMEN

	Champion	Runner-Up
Division I:	Brown	Washington
Division II	UC-Davis	Western Washington
Division III:	Williams	Colby

Softball

	Champion	Runner-Up
Division I:	California	Arizona
Division II:	St. Mary's	Grand Valley St
Division III:	Ithaca	Lake Forest

Tennis
MEN

	Champion	Runner-Up
Division I:	Southern Cal	Georgia
Division II:	Brigham Young	Drury
Division III:	Williams	Emory

Spring 2002 (Cont.)
Tennis (Cont.)
WOMEN

	Champion	Runner-Up
Division I:	Stanford	Florida
Division II:	BYU–Hawaii	Armstrong Atlantic St
Division III:	Williams	Emory

Outdoor Track and Field
MEN

	Champion	Runner-Up
Division I:	Louisiana	Tennessee
Division II:	Abilene Christian	St. Augustine's
Division III:	WI–La Crosse	Calvin

WOMEN

	Champion	Runner-Up
Division I:	S Carolina	UCLA
Division II:	St. Augustine's	N Dakota St
Division III:	Wheaton (MA)	McMurry

Volleyball
MEN

Champion	Runner-Up
Hawaii	Pepperdine

NCAA Division I Individual Champions

Fall 2001
Cross Country
MEN

Champion	Runner-Up
Boaz Cheboiywo, Eastern Mich.	Jorge Torres, Colorado

WOMEN

Champion	Runner-Up
Tara Chaplin, Arizona	Renee Metivier, Georgia Tech

Winter 2001–2002
Fencing
MEN

	Champion	Runner-Up
Sabre	Ivan Lee, St. John's (NY)	Jakub Krochmalski, Wayne St
Foil	Nontapat Panchan, Penn St	Jonathan Tiomkin, St. John's (NY)
Épée	Arpád Horváth, St. John's (NY)	Soren Thompson, Princeton

WOMEN

	Champion	Runner-Up
Sabre	Sada Jacobson, Yale	Louise Bond-Williams, Ohio St
Foil	Alicja Kryczalo, Notre Dame	Andrea Ament, Notre Dame
Épée	Kerry Watton, Notre Dame	Stephanie Eim, Penn St

Gymnastics
MEN

	Champion	Runner-Up
All-around	Raj Bhavsar, Ohio St	Zhang JinJing, California
Vault	Dan Gill, Stanford	Jock Stevens, Oklahoma
Parallel bars	Cody Moore, California	Everette Bierker, Oklahoma
Horizontal bar	Daniel Diaz-Loung, Michigan	Quinn Rowell, Oklahoma
Floor exercise	Clay Stother, Minnesota	Kevin Adderly, Ohio St
Pommel horse	Clay Stother, Minnesota	Cody Moore, California
Rings	Marshall Erwin, Stanford	Kevin Tan, Penn St

Winter 2001–2002 (Cont.)

Gymnastics (Cont.)

WOMEN

	Champion	Runner-Up
All-around	Jamie Dantzscher, UCLA	Andree' Pickens, Alabama
Balance beam	Elise Ray, Michigan	Jeana Rice, Alabama
Uneven bars	Andree Pickens, Alabama	Doni Thompson, UCLA
Floor exercise	Jamie Dantzscher, UCLA	Nicole Arnstad, Louisiana St
Vault	Jamie Dantzscher, UCLA	Marline Stevens, Georgia

Skiing

MEN

	Champion	Runner-Up
Slalom	Roger Brown, Dartmouth	Pierre Olsson, Utah
Giant slalom	Tommi Virret, Nevada	Pierre Olsson, Utah
10-kilometer classic	Ola Berger, Denver	Pietro Broggini, Denver
20-kilometer free	Ola Berger, Denver	Eric Strabel, Alaska

WOMEN

	Champion	Runner-Up
Slalom	Marte Dolva, New Mexico	Mia Cullman, Colorado
Giant slalom	Aurore deMaulmont, Alaska	April Mancuso, Utah
5-kilometer classic	Mari Storeng, Colorado	Katerina Hanusova, Nevada
15-kilometer free	Katerina Hanusova, Nevada	Aubrey Smith, Northern Michigan

Wrestling

	Champion	Runner-Up
125 lb	Stephen Abas, Fresno St	Luke Eustice, Iowa
133 lb	Johnny Thompson, Oklahoma St	Ryan Lewis, Minnesota
141 lb	Aaron Holker, Iowa St	Eric Larkin, Arizona St
149 lb	Jared Lawrence, Minnesota	Jed Frayer, Oklahoma
157 lb	Luke Becker, Minnesota	Brian Snyder, Nebraska
165 lb	Joe Heskett, Iowa St	Matt Lackey, Illinois
174 lb	Greg Jones, W Virginia	Greg Parker, Princeton
184 lb	Rob Rohn, Lehigh	Josh Lambrecht, Oklahoma
197 lb	Cael Sanderson, Iowa St	Jon Trenge, Lehigh
HWT	Tommy Rowlands, Ohio St	Steve Mocco, Iowa

Swimming and Diving

MEN

	Champion	Time	Runner-Up	Time
50-yd freestyle	Roland Schoeman, Arizona	19.08	Anthony Ervin, California	19.10
100-yd freestyle	Anthony Ervin, California	41.62*#	Duje Draganja, California	42.22
200-yd freestyle	Adam Sioui, Florida	1:34.67	Dan Ketchum, Michigan	1:34.76
500-yd freestyle	Klete Keller, Southern Cal	4:12.83	Erik Vendt, Southern Cal	4:13.99
1650-yd freestyle	Erik Vendt, Southern Cal	14:37.48	John Cole, Harvard	14:39.71
100-yd backstroke	Peter Marshall, Stanford	45.91	Alex Lim, California	46.05
200-yd backstroke	Markus Rogan, Stanford	1:41.14	Peter Marshall, Stanford	1:41.85
100-yd breaststroke	Brendan Hansen, Texas	52.47	Patrick Calhoun, Auburn	52.72
200-yd breaststroke	Brendan Hansen, Texas	1:52.88*#	Michael Bruce, Stanford	1:54.81
100-yd butterfly	Ian Crocker, Texas	45.96	Nate Dusing, Texas	46.22
200-yd butterfly	Ioan Gherghel, Alabama	1:42.68	Jeff Lee, Southern Cal	1:44.17
200-yd IM	Markus Rogan, Stanford	1:44.03	Dan Trupin, Stanford	1:44.08
400-yd IM	Erik Vendt, Southern Cal	3:40.65	Robert Margalis, Georiga	3:41.42

	Champion	Pts	Runner-Up	Pts
1-meter diving	Troy Dumais, Texas	390.35	Clayton Moss, Kentucky	379.90
3-meter diving	Troy Dumais, Texas	664.70	Omar Ojeda, Arizona	635.95
Platform	Imre Lengeyel, Miami (FL)	620.25	Justin Dumais, Texas	577.15

*NCAA record. #American record.

Winter 2001–2002 *(Cont.)*

Swimming and Diving *(Cont.)*

WOMEN

	Champion	Time	Runner-Up	Time
50-yd freestyle	Maritza Correia, Georgia	21.69*#	Mandy Mularz, Rice	22.17
100-yd freestyle	Maritza Correia, Georgia	47.56	Stefanie Williams, Georgia	48.37
200-yd freestyle	Sarah Tolar, Arizona	1:44.66	Stefanie Williams, Georgia	1:44.88
500-yd freestyle	Flavia Rigamonti, SMU	4:40.13	Jessica Foschi, Stanford	4:41.10
1650-yd freestyle	Flavia Rigamonti, SMU	15:52.28	Janelle Atkinson, Florida	16:01.01
100-yd backstroke	Natalie Coughlin, California	49.97*#	Susan Woessner, Indiana	53.23
200-yd backstroke	Natalie Coughlin, California	1:49.52*#	Alenka Kezjar, SMU	1:54.18
100-yd breaststroke	Tara Kirk, Stanford	59.03	Maggie Bowen, Auburn	59.94
200-yd breaststroke	Tara Kirk, Stanford	2:07.36	Agnes Kovacs, Arizona St	2:07.64
100-yd butterfly	Natalie Coughlin, California	50.01*#	Shelly Ripple, Stanford	51.50
200-yd butterfly	Shelly Ripple, Stanford	1:53.23	Georgina Lee, SMU	1:54.92
200-yd IM	Maggie Bowen, Auburn	1:53.91*#	Shelly Ripple, Stanford	1:55.58
400-yd IM	Maggie Bowen, Auburn	4:04.69	Alenka Kezjar, SMU	4:06.70

	Champion	Pts	Runner-Up	Pts
1-meter diving	Blythe Hartley, Southern Cal	350.85	Yulia Pakhalina, Houston	320.40
3-meter diving	Yulia Pakhalina, Houston	625.05	Sarah Reiling, Indiana	581.90
Platform	Blythe Hartley, Southern Cal	460.3	Meghan Zack, Texas A&M	435.90

*NCAA record.   #American record.

Indoor Track and Field

MEN

	Champion	Time/Mark	Runner-Up	Time/Mark
60-meter dash	Justin Gatlin, Tennessee	6.59	Leonard Scott, Tennessee	6.61
60-meter hurdles	Ron Bramlett, Alabama	7.59	Chris Pinnock, Texas A&M	7.60
200-meter dash	Justin Gatlin, Tennessee	20.63	Marquis Davis, Mississippi St	20.76
400-meter dash	Alleyne Francique, Louisiana St	45.58	Pete Coley, Louisiana St	45.62
800-meter run	Otukile Lekote, S Carolina	1:46.88	Mark Sylvester, Tennessee	1:47.41
Mile run	Christian Goy, Illinois St	4:00.06	David Kimani, Alabama	4:00.33
3,000-meter run	Adrian Blincoe, Villanova	8:01.76	Balazs Csillag, Northern Iowa	8:01.93
5,000-meter run	Alistair Cragg, Arkansas	13:49.80	Jorge Torres, Colorado	13:50.35
High jump	Tora Harris, Princeton	7 ft 5 in	Adam Shunk, N Carolina	7 ft 3¾ in
Pole vault	Jeff Hansen, BYU	17 ft 11¾ in	Paul Terek, Michigan St	17 ft 11¾ in
Long jump	Miguel Pate, Alabama	27 ft 4½ in	Walter Davis, Louisiana St	26 ft 9 in
Triple jump	Walter Davis, Louisiana St	56 ft6½ in	Miguel Pate, Alabama	54 ft 2½ in
Shot put	Carl Meyerscough, Nebraska	69 ft 9 in	Joachim Olsen, Idaho	69 ft 6¾ in
35-pound wt throw	Scott Russell, Kansas	80 ft 11¼ in*	Thomas Freeman, Manhattan	76 ft 1in

WOMEN

	Champion	Time/Mark	Runner-Up	Time/Mark
60-meter dash	Angela Williams, Southern Cal	7.13	Tahesia Harrigan, Minnesota	7.22
60-meter hurdles	Perdita Felicien, Illinois	7.90	Danielle Carruthers, Indiana	7.92
200-meter dash	Munsa Lee, Louisiana St	22.82	Rachelle Boone, Indiana	22.99
400-meter dash	Allison Beckford, Rice	52.16	Demetria Washington, S Carolina	52.41
800-meter run	Marian Burnett, Louisiana St	2:05.33	Kristina Bratton, Florida	2:05.49
Mile run	Heather Sagan, Liberty	4:38.52	Lena Nilsson, UCLA	4:38.88
3,000-meter run	Lauren Fleshman, Stanford	9:07.45	Lisa Aguilera, Arizona	9:09.67
5,000-meter run	Siri Alfheim, Oklahoma St	16:12.28	Melissa Gulli, Texas A&M	16:13.75
High jump	Darnesha Griffith, UCLA	6 ft ¾ in	Whitney Evans, Washington St	6 ft
Pole vault	Amy Linnen, Arizona	14 ft 10¼ in*	Tracy O'Hara, UCLA	13 ft 11¼ in
Long jump	Elva Goulbourne, Auburn	21 ft 11 in	Angel Heath, Arkansas	20 ft 8 in
Triple jump	Nicole Toney, Louisiana St	45 ft¼ in	Shelley-Ann Gallimore, Auburn	44 ft 9 in
Shot put	Cleopatra Borel, UMBC	57 ft 5 in	Austra Skujyte, Kansas St	55 ft 9 in
20-pound wt throw	Candice Scott, Florida	75 ft 7½ in	Jamine Moton, Clemson	73 ft 10 in

*NCAA record.

Rifle

	Champion	Pts	Runner-Up	Pts
Smallbore	Matthew Emmons, AK-Fairbanks	1190*	Hannah Kerr, Xavier	1179
Air rifle	Ryan Tanoue, Nevada	392	Matthew Emmons, AK-Fairbanks	392

*NCAA record.

NCAA Division I Individual Champions *(Cont.)*

Spring 2002

Golf

MEN

Champion	Score	Runner-Up	Score
Troy Matteson, Georgia Tech	276	Adam Rubinson, Texas Christian	277

WOMEN

Champion	Score	Runner-Up	Score
Virada Nirapathpongporn, Duke	279	Lorena Ochoa, Arizona/Danielle Downey, Auburn/Summer Sirmons, Georgia/ Lindsey Wright, Pepperdine	285

Outdoor Track and Field

MEN

	Champion	Mark	Runner-Up	Mark
100-meter dash	Justin Gatlin, Tennessee	10.22	Dwight Thomas, Clemson	10.29
200-meter dash	Justin Gatlin, Tennessee	20.18	Dwight Thomas, Clemson	20.60
400-meter dash	Gary Kikaya, Tennessee	44.53	Ricky Harris, Florida	44.93
800-meter run	Otukile Lekote, S Carolina	1:45.17	Sam Burley, Pennsylvania	1:45.39
1,500-meter run	Donald Sage, Stanford	3:42.65	Chris Mulvaney, Arkansas	3:43.02
5,000-meter run	David Kimani, Alabama	13:59.30	Jorge Torres, Colorado	13:59.88
10,000-meter run	Boaz Cheboiywo, E Michigan	28:32.10	Ryan Shay, Notre Dame	29:02.92
110-meter hurdles	Ron Bramlett, Alabama	13.49	Todd Matthews, Clemson	13.53
400-meter hurdles	Rickey Harris, Florida	48.16	Bennie Brazell, Louisiana St	48.80
3,000-m steeple	Daniel Lincoln, Arkansas	8:22.34	Scott Slattery, Colorado	8:26.51
High jump	Tora Harris, Princeton	7 ft 4½ in	David Jaworski, Southern Cal	7 ft 4½ in
Pole vault	Brian Hunter, Texas	18 ft 8¼ in	Brad Walker, Washington	18 ft 2½ in
Long jump	Walter Davis, Louisiana St	26 ft 6¼ in	Randy Lewis, Wichita St	26 ft 1¾ in
Triple jump	Walter Davis, Louisiana St	56 ft 10¼ in	Aarik Wilson, Indiana	54 ft 8¾ in
Shot put	Janus Robberts, SMU	70 ft 10½ in	Carl Myerscough, Nebraska	62 ft 9½ in
Discus throw	Scott Moser, UCLA	198ft 3 in	Mark Hoxmeier, Boise St	198 ft 1 in
Hammer throw	Andras Haklits, Georgia	253 ft 8 in	Libor Charfreitag, SMU	252 ft 7 in
Javelin throw	Scott Russell, Kansas	262 ft 0 in	Nathan Junius, Texas	244 ft 9 in
Decathlon	Claston Bernard, Louisiana St	8094 pts	Paul Terek, Michigan St	8041 pts

WOMEN

	Champion	Mark	Runner-Up	Mark
100-meter dash	Angela Williams, Southern Cal	11.29	Natasha Mayers, Southern Cal	11.30
200-meter dash	Natasha Mayers, Southern Cal	22.93	Aleen Bailey, S Carolina	23.12
400-meter dash	Allison Beckford, Rice	50.83	Melisa Barber, S Carolina	50.87
800-meter run	Alice Schmidt, N Carolina	2:04.73	Lauren Simmons, Princeton	2:05.08
1,500-meter run	Lena Nilsson, UCLA	4:12.60	Heather Sagan, Liberty	4:14.71
5,000-meter run	Lauren Fleshman, Stanford	15:53.91	Siri Alfheim, Oklahoma St	16:00.47
10,000-meter run	Kristin Price, N Carolina St	34:26.63	Tara Quinn, S Florida	34:33.85
100-meter hurdles	Perdita Felicien, Illinois	12.91	Lolo Jones, Louisiana St	13.02
400-meter hurdles	Leshinda Demus, S Carolina	54.85	Tiffany Ross, S Carolina	55.22
3,000-m steeple	Michaela Manova, Brigham Young	9:45.94	Ida Nilsson, N Arizona	9:49.94
High jump	Darnesha Griffith, UCLA	6 ft 0 in	Whitney Evans, Washington St	5ft10½ in
Pole vault	Tracy O'Hara, UCLA	13 ft 5¼ in	Andrea Wildrick, Liberty	13 ft 5¼ in
Long jump	Elva Goulbourne, Auburn	22 ft 4½ in	Tiffany Greer, Arizona St	21 ft 3¼ in
Triple jump	Ineta Radovica, Wichita St	43 ft 10 in	Tatyana Obukhova, Southern Cal	43 ft 5¼ in
Shot put	Jessica Cosby, UCLA	57 ft ¼ in	Ashely Dorsey, Texas-Arlington	54 ft 11¼ in
Discus throw	Becky Breisch, Nebraska	181 ft 11 in	Stephanie Brown, Cal Poly	177 ft 6 in
Hammer throw	Jamine Moton, Clemson	222 ft 6 in	Melissa Price, Nebraska	212 ft 9 in
Javelin throw	Serene Ross, Purdue	195 ft 8 in	Inga Stasiulionyte, Southern Cal	177 ft
Heptathlon	Austra Skujyte, Kansas St	6061 pts	Ellannee Richardson, Wash St	5709 pts

Tennis

MEN

	Champion	Score	Runner-Up
Singles	Matias Boeker, Georgia	7–5, 6–0	Jesse Witten, Kentucky
Doubles	Andrew Colombo & Mark Kovacs, Auburn	6–2, 3–6, 6–2	Scott Lipsky & David Martin, Stanford

WOMEN

	Champion	Score	Runner-Up
Singles	Bea Bielik, Wake Forest	6–2, 6–0	Lauren Kalvaria, Stanford
Doubles	Gabriela Lastra & Lauren Kalvaria, Stanford	6–2, 6–3	Meghan Bradley & Lauren Fisher, UCLA

CHAMPIONSHIP RESULTS

Baseball

DIVISION I

Year	Champion	Coach	Score	Runner-Up	Most Outstanding Player
1947	California*	Clint Evans	8–7	Yale	No award
1948	Southern Cal	Sam Barry	9–2	Yale	No award
1949	Texas*	Bibb Falk	10–3	Wake Forest	Charles Teague, Wake Forest, 2B
1950	Texas	Bibb Falk	3–0	Washington St	Ray VanCleef, Rutgers, CF
1951	Oklahoma*	Jack Baer	3–2	Tennessee	Sidney Hatfield, Tennessee, P-1B
1952	Holy Cross	Jack Barry	8–4	Missouri	James O'Neill, Holy Cross, P
1953	Michigan	Ray Fisher	7–5	Texas	J.L. Smith, Texas, P
1954	Missouri	John (Hi) Simmons	4–1	Rollins	Tom Yewcic, Michigan St, C
1955	Wake Forest	Taylor Sanford	7–6	Western Michigan	Tom Borland, Oklahoma St, P
1956	Minnesota	Dick Siebert	12–1	Arizona	Jerry Thomas, Minnesota, P
1957	California*	George Wolfman	1–0	Penn St	Cal Emery, Penn St, P-1B
1958	Southern Cal	Rod Dedeaux	8–7†	Missouri	Bill Thom, Southern Cal, P
1959	Oklahoma St	Toby Greene	5–3	Arizona	Jim Dobson, Oklahoma St, 3B
1960	Minnesota	Dick Siebert	2–1‡	Southern Cal	John Erickson, Minnesota, 2B
1961	Southern Cal*	Rod Dedeaux	1–0	Oklahoma St	Littleton Fowler, Oklahoma St, P
1962	Michigan	Don Lund	5–4	Santa Clara	Bob Garibaldi, Santa Clara, P
1963	Southern Cal	Rod Dedeaux	5–2	Arizona	Bud Hollowell, Southern Cal, C
1964	Minnesota	Dick Siebert	5–1	Missouri	Joe Ferris, Maine, P
1965	Arizona St	Bobby Winkles	2–1#	Ohio St	Sal Bando, Arizona St, 3B
1966	Ohio St	Marty Karow	8–2	Oklahoma St	Steve Arlin, Ohio St, P
1967	Arizona St	Bobby Winkles	11–2	Houston	Ron Davini, Arizona St, C
1968	Southern Cal*	Rod Dedeaux	4–3	Southern Illinois	Bill Seinsoth, Southern Cal, 1B
1969	Arizona St	Bobby Winkles	10–1	Tulsa	John Dolinsek, Arizona St, LF
1970	Southern Cal	Rod Dedeaux	2–1	Florida St	Gene Ammann, Florida St, P
1971	Southern Cal	Rod Dedeaux	7–2	Southern Illinois	Jerry Tabb, Tulsa, 1B
1972	Southern Cal	Rod Dedeaux	1–0	Arizona St	Russ McQueen, Southern Cal, P
1973	Southern Cal*	Rod Dedeaux	4–3	Arizona St	Dave Winfield, Minnesota, P-OF
1974	Southern Cal	Rod Dedeaux	7–3	Miami (FL)	George Milke, Southern Cal, P
1975	Texas	Cliff Gustafson	5–1	S Carolina	Mickey Reichenbach, Texas, 1B
1976	Arizona	Jerry Kindall	7–1	Eastern Michigan	Steve Powers, Arizona, P-DH
1977	Arizona St	Jim Brock	2–1	S Carolina	Bob Horner, Arizona St, 3B
1978	Southern Cal*	Rod Dedeaux	10–3	Arizona St	Rod Boxberger, Southern Cal, P
1979	Cal St–Fullerton	Augie Garrido	2–1	Arkansas	Tony Hudson, Cal St–Fullerton, P
1980	Arizona	Jerry Kindall	5–3	Hawaii	Terry Francona, Arizona, LF
1981	Arizona St	Jim Brock	7–4	Oklahoma St	Stan Holmes, Arizona St, LF
1982	Miami (FL)*	Ron Fraser	9–3	Wichita St	Dan Smith, Miami (FL), P
1983	Texas*	Cliff Gustafson	4–3	Alabama	Calvin Schiraldi, Texas, P
1984	Cal St–Fullerton	Augie Garrido	3–1	Texas	John Fishel, Cal St–Fullerton, LF
1985	Miami (FL)	Ron Fraser	10–6	Texas	Greg Ellena, Miami (FL), DH
1986	Arizona	Jerry Kindall	10–2	Florida St	Mike Senne, Arizona, LF
1987	Stanford	Mark Marquess	9–5	Oklahoma St	Paul Carey, Stanford, RF
1988	Stanford	Mark Marquess	9–4	Arizona St	Lee Plemel, Stanford, P
1989	Wichita St	Gene Stephenson	5–3	Texas	Greg Brummett, Wichita St, P
1990	Georgia	Steve Webber	2–1	Oklahoma St	Mike Rebhan, Georgia, P
1991	Louisiana St	Skip Bertman	6–3	Wichita St	Gary Hymel, Louisiana St, C
1992	Pepperdine	Andy Lopez	3–2	Cal St–Fullerton	Phil Nevin, Cal St–Fullerton, 3B
1993	Louisiana St	Skip Bertman	8–0	Wichita St	Todd Walker, Louisiana St, 2B
1994	Oklahoma	Larry Cochell	13–5	Georgia Tech	Chip Glass, Oklahoma, CF
1995	Cal St–Fullerton*	Augie Garrido	11–5	Southern Cal	Mark Kotsay, Cal St–Fullerton, CF-P
1996	Louisiana St*	Skip Bertman	9–8	Miami (FL)	Pat Burrell, Miami (FL), 3B
1997	Louisiana St*	Skip Bertman	13–6	Alabama	Brandon Larson, Louisiana St, SS
1998	Southern Cal	Mike Gillespie	21–14	Arizona St	Wes Rachels, Southern Cal, 2B
1999	Miami (FL)	Jim Morris	6–5	Florida St	Marshall McDougall, FSU 3B/2B
2000	Louisiana St*	Skip Bertman	6–5	Stanford	Trey Hodges, Louisiana St, P
2001	Miami (FL)*	Jim Morris	12–1	Stanford	Charlton Jimerson, Miami (FL), OF
2002	Texas	Augie Garrido	12–6	S Carolina	Huston Street, Texas, P

*Undefeated teams in College World Series play. †12 innings. ‡10 innings. #15 innings.

DIVISION II

Year	Champion	Year	Champion	Year	Champion
1968	Chapman*	1971	Florida Southern	1974	UC–Irvine
1969	Illinois St*	1972	Florida Southern	1975	Florida Southern
1970	Cal St–Northridge	1973	UC–Irvine*	1976	Cal Poly–Pomona

DIVISION II (Cont.)

Year	Champion	Year	Champion	Year	Champion
1977	UC–Riverside	1987	Troy St*	1997	Cal St–Chico*
1978	Florida Southern	1988	Florida Southern*	1998	Tampa*
1979	Valdosta St	1989	Cal Poly–SLO	1999	Cal St–Chico
1980	Cal Poly–Pomona*	1990	Jacksonville St	2000	SE Oklahoma St
1981	Florida Southern*	1991	Jacksonville St	2001	St. Mary's (TX)
1982	UC–Riverside*	1992	Tampa*	2002	Columbus St
1983	Cal Poly–Pomona*	1993	Tampa		
1984	Cal St–Northridge	1994	Central Missouri St		
1985	Florida Southern*	1995	Florida Southern*		
1986	Troy St	1996	Kennesaw St*		

DIVISION III

Year	Champion	Year	Champion	Year	Champion
1976	Cal St–Stanislaus	1986	Marietta	1996	William Paterson
1977	Cal St–Stanislaus	1987	Montclair St	1997	Southern Maine
1978	Glassboro St	1988	Ithaca	1998	Eastern Connecticut St
1979	Glassboro St	1989	NC Wesleyan	1999	N Carolina Wesleyan
1980	Ithaca	1990	Eastern Connecticut St	2000	Montclair St
1981	Marietta	1991	Southern Maine	2001	St. Thomas (MN)
1982	Eastern Connecticut St	1992	William Paterson	2002	Eastern Connecticut St
1983	Marietta	1993	Montclair St		
1984	Ramapo	1994	WI–Oshkosh		
1985	WI–Oshkosh	1995	La Verne		

*Undefeated teams in final series.

Cross-Country

Men

DIVISION I

Year	Champion	Coach	Pts	Runner-Up	Pts	Individual Champion	Time
1938	Indiana	Earle Hayes	51	Notre Dame	61	Greg Rice, Notre Dame	20:12.9
1939	Michigan St	Lauren Brown	54	Wisconsin	57	Walter Mehl, Wisconsin	20:30.9
1940	Indiana	Earle Hayes	65	Eastern Michigan	68	Gilbert Dodds, Ashland	20:30.2
1941	Rhode Island	Fred Tootell	83	Penn St	110	Fred Wilt, Indiana	20:30.1
1942	Indiana	Earle Hayes	57			Oliver Hunter, Notre Dame	20:18.0
	Penn St	Charles Werner	57				
1943	No meet						
1944	Drake	Bill Easton	25	Notre Dame	64	Fred Feiler, Drake	21:04.2
1945	Drake	Bill Easton	50	Notre Dame	65	Fred Feiler, Drake	21:14.2
1946	Drake	Bill Easton	42	NYU	98	Quentin Brelsford, Ohio Wesleyan	20:22.9
1947	Penn St	Charles Werner	60	Syracuse	72	Jack Milne, N Carolina	20:41.1
1948	Michigan St	Karl Schlademan	41	Wisconsin	69	Robert Black, Rhode Island	19:52.3
1949	Michigan St	Karl Schlademan	59	Syracuse	81	Robert Black, Rhode Island	20:25.7
1950	Penn St	Charles Werner	53	Michigan St	55	Herb Semper Jr, Kansas	20:31.7
1951	Syracuse	Robert Grieve	80	Kansas	118	Herb Semper Jr, Kansas	20:09.5
1952	Michigan St	Karl Schlademan	65	Indiana	68	Charles Capozzoli, Georgetown	19:36.7
1953	Kansas	Bill Easton	70	Indiana	82	Wes Santee, Kansas	19:43.5
1954	Oklahoma St	Ralph Higgins	61	Syracuse	118	Allen Frame, Kansas	19:54.2
1955	Michigan St	Karl Schlademan	46	Kansas	68	Charles Jones, Iowa	19:57.4
1956	Michigan St	Karl Schlademan	28	Kansas	88	Walter McNew, Texas	19:55.7
1957	Notre Dame	Alex Wilson	121	Michigan St	127	Max Truex, Southern Cal	19:12.3
1958	Michigan St	Francis Dittrich	79	Western Michigan	104	Crawford Kennedy, Michigan State	20:07.1
1959	Michigan St	Francis Dittrich	44	Houston	120	Al Lawrence, Houston	20:35.7
1960	Houston	John Morriss	54	Michigan St	80	Al Lawrence, Houston	19:28.2
1961	Oregon St	Sam Bell	68	San Jose St	82	Dale Story, Oregon St	19:46.6
1962	San Jose St	Dean Miller	58	Villanova	69	Tom O'Hara, Loyola (IL)	19:20.3
1963	San Jose St	Dean Miller	53	Oregon	68	Victor Zwolak, Villanova	19:35.0
1964	W Michigan	George Dales	86	Oregon	116	Elmore Banton, Ohio	20:07.5
1965	W Michigan	George Dales	81	Northwestern	114	John Lawson, Kansas	29:24.0
1966	Villanova	James Elliott	79	Kansas St	155	Gerry Lindgren, Washington St	29:01.4
1967	Villanova	James Elliott	91	Air Force	96	Gerry Lindgren, Washington St	30:45.6
1968	Villanova	James Elliott	78	Stanford	100	Michael Ryan, Air Force	29:16.8
1969	UTEP	Wayne Vandenburg	74	Villanova	88	Gerry Lindgren, Wash St	28:59.2

Men (Cont.)
DIVISION I (Cont.)

Year	Champion	Coach	Pts	Runner-Up	Pts	Individual Champion	Time
1970	Villanova	James Elliott	85	Oregon	86	Steve Prefontaine, Oregon	28:00.2
1971	Oregon	Bill Dellinger	83	Washington St	122	Steve Prefontaine, Oregon	29:14.0
1972	Tennessee	Stan Huntsman	134	E Tennessee St	148	Neil Cusack, E Tenn St	28:23.0
1973	Oregon	Bill Dellinger	89	UTEP	157	Steve Prefontaine, Oregon	28:14.0
1974	Oregon	Bill Dellinger	77	Western Kentucky	110	Nick Rose, Western Ky	29:22.0
1975	UTEP	Ted Banks	88	Washington St	92	Craig Virgin, Illinois	28:23.3
1976	UTEP	Ted Banks	62	Oregon	117	Henry Rono, Washington St	28:06.6
1977	Oregon	Bill Dellinger	100	UTEP	105	Henry Rono, Washington St	28:33.5
1978	UTEP	Ted Banks	56	Oregon	72	Alberto Salazar, Oregon	29:29.7
1979	UTEP	Ted Banks	86	Oregon	93	Henry Rono, Washington St	28:19.6
1980	UTEP	Ted Banks	58	Arkansas	152	Suleiman Nyambui, UTEP	29:04.0
1981	UTEP	Ted Banks	17	Providence	109	Mathews Motshwarateu,UTEP	28:45.6
1982	Wisconsin	Dan McClimon	59	Providence	138	Mark Scrutton, Colorado	30:12.6
1983	Vacated			Wisconsin	164	Zakarie Barie, UTEP	29:20.0
1984	Arkansas	John McDonnell	101	Arizona	111	Ed Eyestone, Brigham Young	29:28.8
1985	Wisconsin	Martin Smith	67	Arkansas	104	Timothy Hacker, Wisconsin	29:17.88
1986	Arkansas	John McDonnell	69	Dartmouth	141	Aaron Ramirez, Arizona	30:27.53
1987	Arkansas	John McDonnell	87	Dartmouth	119	Joe Falcon, Arkansas	29:14.97
1988	Wisconsin	Martin Smith	105	Northern Arizona	160	Robert Kennedy, Indiana	29:20.0
1989	Iowa St	Bill Bergan	54	Oregon	72	John Nuttall, Iowa St	29:30.55
1990	Arkansas	John McDonnell	68	Iowa St	96	Jonah Koech, Iowa St	29:05.0
1991	Arkansas	John McDonnell	52	Iowa St	114	Sean Dollman, Western Ky	30:17.1
1992	Arkansas	John McDonnell	46	Wisconsin	87	Bob Kennedy, Indiana	30:15.3
1993	Arkansas	John McDonnell	31	Brigham Young	153	Josephat Kapkory, Wash St	29:32.4
1994	Iowa St	Bill Bergan	65	Colorado	88	Martin Keino, Arizona	30:08.7
1995	Arkansas	John McDonnell	100	Northern Arizona	142	Godfrey Siamusiye, Arkansas	30:09
1996	Stanford	Vin Lananna	46	Arkansas	74	Godfrey Siamusiye, Arkansas	29:49
1997	Stanford	Vin Lananna	53	Arkansas	56	Mebrahtom Keflezighi, UCLA	28:54
1998	Arkansas	John McDonnell	97	Stanford	114	Adam Goucher, Colorado	29:26
1999	Arkansas	John McDonnell	58	Wisconsin	185	David Kimani, S Alabama	30:06.6
2000	Arkansas	John McDonnell	83	Colorado	94	Keith Kelly, Providence	30:14.5
2001	Colorado	Mark Wetmore	90	Stanford	91	Boaz Cheboiywo, E Michigan	28:47

DIVISION II

Year	Champion	Year	Champion	Year	Champion
1958	Northern Illinois	1973	S Dakota St	1988	Edinboro/ Mankato St
1959	S Dakota St	1974	SW Missouri St	1989	S Dakota St
1960	Central St (OH)	1975	UC–Irvine	1990	Edinboro
1961	Southern Illinois	1976	UC–Irvine	1991	MA–Lowell
1962	Central St (OH)	1977	Eastern Illinois	1992	Adams St
1963	Emporia St	1978	Cal Poly–SLO	1993	Adams St
1964	Kentucky St	1979	Cal Poly–SLO	1994	Adams St
1965	San Diego St	1980	Humboldt St	1995	Western St
1966	San Diego St	1981	Millersville	1996	S Dakota St
1967	San Diego St	1982	Eastern Washington	1997	S Dakota
1968	Eastern Illinois	1983	Cal Poly–Pomona	1998	Adams St
1969	Eastern Illinois	1984	SE Missouri St	1999	Western St
1970	Eastern Michigan	1985	S Dakota St	2000	Western St
1971	Cal St–Fullerton	1986	Edinboro	2001	Western St
1972	N Dakota St	1987	Edinboro		

DIVISION III

Year	Champion	Year	Champion	Year	Champion
1973	Ashland	1983	Brandeis	1993	N Central
1974	Mount Union	1984	St. Thomas (MN)	1994	Williams
1975	North Central	1985	Luther	1995	Williams
1976	North Central	1986	St. Thomas (MN)	1996	WI–La Crosse
1977	Occidental	1987	N Central	1997	N Central
1978	N Central	1988	WI–Oshkosh	1998	N Central
1979	N Central	1989	WI–Oshkosh	1999	N Central
1980	Carleton	1990	WI–Oshkosh	2000	Calvin
1981	N Central	1991	Rochester	2001	WI–La Crosse
1982	N Central	1992	N Central		

Women
DIVISION I

Year	Champion	Coach	Pts	Runner-Up	Pts	Individual Champion	Time
1981	Virginia	John Vasvary	36	Oregon	83	Betty Springs, N Carolina St	16:19.0
1982	Virginia	Martin Smith	48	Stanford	91	Lesley Welch, Virginia	16:39.7
1983	Oregon	Tom Heinonen	95	Stanford	98	Betty Springs, N Carolina St	16:30.7
1984	Wisconsin	Peter Tegen	63	Stanford	89	Cathy Branta, Wisconsin	16:15.6
1985	Wisconsin	Peter Tegen	58	Iowa St	98	Suzie Tuffey, N Carolina St	16:22.5
1986	Texas	Terry Crawford	62	Wisconsin	64	Angela Chalmers, N Arizona	16:55.49
1987	Oregon	Tom Heinonen	97	N Carolina St	99	Kimberly Betz, Indiana	16:10.85
1988	Kentucky	Don Weber	75	Oregon	128	Michelle Dekkers, Indiana	16:30.0
1989	Villanova	Marty Stern	99	Kentucky	168	Vicki Huber, Villanova	15:59.86
1990	Villanova	Marty Stern	82	Providence	172	Sonia O'Sullivan, Villanova	16:06.0
1991	Villanova	Marty Stern	85	Arkansas	168	Sonia O'Sullivan, Villanova	16:30.3
1992	Villanova	Marty Stern	123	Arkansas	130	Carole Zajac, Villanova	17:01.9
1993	Villanova	Marty Stern	66	Arkansas	71	Carole Zajac, Villanova	16:40.3
1994	Villanova	John Marshall	75	Michigan	108	Jennifer Rhines, Villanova	16:31.2
1995	Providence	Ray Treacy	88	Colorado	123	Kathy Butler, Wisconsin	16:51
1996	Stanford	Beth Alford-Sullivan	101	Villanova	106	Amy Skieresz, Arizona	17:04
1997	BYU	Patrick Shane	100	Stanford	102	Carrie Tollefson, Villanova	16:58
1998	Villanova	Marcus O'Sullivan	106	BYU	110	Katie McGregor, Michigan	16:47.21
1999	BYU	Patrick Shane	72	Arkansas	125	Erica Palmer, Wisconsin	16:39.50
2000	Colorado	Mark Wetmore	117	Brigham Young	167	Kara Grgas-Wheeler, Colorado	20:30.5
2001	BYU	Patrick Shane	62	N Carolina St	148	Tara Chaplin, Arizona	20:24

DIVISION II

Year	Champion	Year	Champion	Year	Champion
1981	S Dakota St	1988	Cal Poly–SLO	1995	Adams St
1982	Cal Poly–SLO	1989	Cal Poly–SLO	1996	Adams St
1983	Cal Poly–SLO	1990	Cal Poly–SLO	1997	Adams St
1984	Cal Poly–SLO	1991	Cal Poly–SLO	1998	Adams St
1985	Cal Poly–SLO	1992	Adams St	1999	Adams St
1986	Cal Poly–SLO	1993	Adams St	2000	Western St
1987	Cal Poly–SLO	1994	Adams St	2001	Western St

DIVISION III

Year	Champion	Year	Champion	Year	Champion
1981	Central (IA)	1988	WI–Oshkosh	1996	WI–Oshkosh
1982	St. Thomas (MN)	1989	Cortland St	1997	Cortland St
1983	WI–La Crosse	1990	Cortland St	1998	Calvin
1984	St. Thomas (MN)	1991	WI–Oshkosh	1999	Calvin
1985	Franklin & Marshall	1992	Cortland St	2000	Middlebury
1986	St. Thomas (MN)	1993	Cortland St	2001	Middlebury
1987	St. Thomas (MN)/ WI–Oshkosh	1994	Cortland St		
		1995	Cortland St		

Fencing

Men's and Women's Combined
TEAM CHAMPIONS

Year	Champion	Coach	Pts	Runner-Up	Pts
1990	Penn St	Emmanuil Kaidanov	36	Columbia–Barnard	35
1991	Penn St	Emmanuil Kaidanov	4700	Columbia–Barnard	4200
1992	Columbia–Barnard	G. Kolombatovich/A. Kogler	4150	Penn St	3646
1993	Columbia–Barnard	G. Kolombatovich/A. Kogler	4525	Penn St	4500
1994	Notre Dame	Michael DeCicco	4350	Penn St	4075
1995	Penn St	Emmanuil Kaidanov	440	St. John's (NY)	413
1996	Penn St	Emmanuil Kaidanov	1500	Notre Dame	1190
1997	Penn St	Emmanuil Kaidanov	1530	Notre Dame	1470
1998	Penn St	Emmanuil Kaidanov	149	Notre Dame	147
1999	Penn St	Emmanuil Kaidanov	171	Notre Dame	139
2000	Penn St	Emmanuil Kaidanov	175	Notre Dame	171
2001	St. John's (NY)	Yuri Gelman	180	Penn St	172
2002	Penn St	Emmanuil Kaidanov	195	St. John's (NY)	190

Men
TEAM CHAMPIONS

Year	Champion	Coach	Pts	Runner-Up	Pts
1941	Northwestern	Henry Zettleman	28½	Illinois	27
1942	Ohio St	Frank Riebel	34	St. John's (NY)	33½
1943–46	No tournament				

Men (Cont.)
TEAM CHAMPIONS (Cont.)

Year	Champion	Coach	Pts	Runner-Up	Pts
1947	NYU	Martinez Castello	72	Chicago	50½
1948	CCNY	James Montague	30	Navy	28
1949	Army/Rutgers	S. Velarde/D. Cetrulo	63		
1950	Navy	Joseph Fiems	67½	NYU/Rutgers	66½
1951	Columbia	Servando Velarde	69	Pennsylvania	64
1952	Columbia	Servando Velarde	71	NYU	69
1953	Pennsylvania	Lajos Csiszar	94	Navy	86
1954	Columbia	Irving DeKoff	61		
	NYU	Hugo Castello	61		
1955	Columbia	Irving DeKoff	62	Cornell	57
1956	Illinois	Maxwell Garret	90	Columbia	88
1957	NYU	Hugo Castello	65	Columbia	64
1958	Illinois	Maxwell Garret	47	Columbia	43
1959	Navy	Andre Deladrier	72	NYU	65
1960	NYU	Hugo Castello	65	Navy	57
1961	NYU	Hugo Castello	79	Princeton	68
1962	Navy	Andre Deladrier	76	NYU	74
1963	Columbia	Irving DeKoff	55	Navy	50
1964	Princeton	Stan Sieja	81	NYU	79
1965	Columbia	Irving DeKoff	76	NYU	74
1966	NYU	Hugo Castello	5–0	Army	5–2
1967	NYU	Hugo Castello	72	Pennsylvania	64
1968	Columbia	Louis Bankuti	92	NYU	87
1969	Pennsylvania	Lajos Csiszar	54	Harvard	43
1970	NYU	Hugo Castello	71	Columbia	63
1971	NYU/Columbia	Hugo Castello/Louis Bankuti	68		
1972	Detroit	Richard Perry	73	NYU	70
1973	NYU	Hugo Castello	76	Pennsylvania	71
1974	NYU	Hugo Castello	92	Wayne St (MI)	87
1975	Wayne St (MI)	Istvan Danosi	89	Cornell	83
1976	NYU	Herbert Cohen	79	Wayne St (MI)	77
1977	Notre Dame	Michael DeCicco	114*	NYU	114
1978	Notre Dame	Michael DeCicco	121	Pennsylvania	110
1979	Wayne St (MI)	Istvan Danosi	119	Notre Dame	108
1980	Wayne St (MI)	Istvan Danosi	111	Pennsylvania/MIT	106
1981	Pennsylvania	Dave Micahnik	113	Wayne St (MI)	111
1982	Wayne St (MI)	Istvan Danosi	85	Clemson	77
1983	Wayne St (MI)	Aladar Kogler	86	Notre Dame	80
1984	Wayne St (MI)	Gil Pezza	69	Penn St	50
1985	Wayne St (MI)	Gil Pezza	141	Notre Dame	140
1986	Notre Dame	Michael DeCicco	151	Columbia	141
1987	Columbia	George Kolombatovich	86	Pennsylvania	78
1988	Columbia	G. Kolombatovich/A. Kogler	90	Notre Dame	83
1989	Columbia	G. Kolombatovich/A. Kogler	88	Penn St	85

*Tie broken by a fence-off. Note: Beginning in 1990, men's and women's combined teams competed for the national championship.

INDIVIDUAL CHAMPIONS

	Foil	Sabre	Épée
1941	Edward McNamara, Northwestern	William Meyer, Dartmouth	G.H. Boland, Illinois
1942	Byron Kreiger, Wayne St (MI)	Andre Deladrier, St. John's (NY)	Ben Burtt, Ohio St
1943–46	No tournament		
1947	Abraham Balk, NYU	Oscar Parsons, Temple	Abraham Balk, NYU
1948	Albert Axelrod, CCNY	James Day, Navy	William Bryan, Navy
1949	Ralph Tedeschi, Rutgers	Alex Treves, Rutgers	Richard C. Bowman, Army
1950	Robert Nielsen, Columbia	Alex Treves, Rutgers	Thomas Stuart, Navy
1951	Robert Nielsen, Columbia	Chamberless Johnston, Princeton	Daniel Chafetz, Columbia
1952	Harold Goldsmith, CCNY	Frank Zimolzak, Navy	James Wallner, NYU
1953	Ed Nober, Brooklyn	Robert Parmacek, Penn	Jack Tori, Pennsylvania
1954	Robert Goldman, Pennsylvania	Steve Sobel, Columbia	Henry Kolowrat, Princeton
1955	Herman Velasco, Illinois	Barry Pariser, Columbia	Donald Tadrawski, Notre Dame
1956	Ralph DeMarco, Columbia	Gerald Kaufman, Columbia	Kinmont Hoitsma, Princeton
1957	Bruce Davis, Wayne St (MI)	Bernie Balaban, NYU	James Margolis, Columbia
1958	Bruce Davis, Wayne St (MI)	Art Schankin, Illinois	Roland Wommack, Navy
1959	Joe Paletta, Navy	Al Morales, Navy	Roland Wommack, Navy
1960	Gene Glazer, NYU	Mike Desaro, NYU	Gil Eisner, NYU
1961	Herbert Cohen, NYU	Israel Colon, NYU	Jerry Halpern, NYU
1962	Herbert Cohen, NYU	Barton Nisonson, Columbia	Thane Hawkins, Navy

Men (Cont.)

INDIVIDUAL CHAMPIONS (Cont.)

	Foil	Sabre	Épée
1963	Jay Lustig, Columbia	Bela Szentivanyi, Wayne St (MI)	Larry Crum, Navy
1964	Bill Hicks, Princeton	Craig Bell, Illinois	Paul Pesthy, Rutgers
1965	Joe Nalven, Columbia	Howard Goodman, NYU	Paul Pesthy, Rutgers
1966	Al Davis, NYU	Paul Apostol, NYU	Bernhardt Hermann, Iowa
1967	Mike Gaylor, NYU	Todd Makler, Pennsylvania	George Masin, NYU
1968	Gerard Esponda, San Francisco	Todd Makler, Pennsylvania	Don Sieja, Cornell
1969	Anthony Kestler, Columbia	Norman Braslow, Penn	James Wetzler, Pennsylvania
1970	Walter Krause, NYU	Bruce Soriano, Columbia	John Nadas, Case Reserve
1971	Tyrone Simmons, Detroit	Bruce Soriano, Columbia	George Szunyogh, NYU
1972	Tyrone Simmons, Detroit	Bruce Soriano, Columbia	Ernesto Fernandez, Penn
1973	Brooke Makler, Pennsylvania	Peter Westbrock, NYU	Risto Hurme, NYU
1974	Greg Benko, Wayne St (MI)	Steve Danosi, Wayne St (MI)	Risto Hurme, NYU
1975	Greg Benko, Wayne St (MI)	Yuri Rabinovich, Wayne St (MI)	Risto Hurme, NYU
1976	Greg Benko, Wayne St (MI)	Brian Smith, Columbia	Randy Eggleton, Pennsylvania
1977	Pat Gerard, Notre Dame	Mike Sullivan, Notre Dame	Hans Wieselgren, NYU
1978	Ernest Simon, Wayne St (MI)	Mike Sullivan, Notre Dame	Bjorne Vaggo, Notre Dame
1979	Andrew Bonk, Notre Dame	Yuri Rabinovich, Wayne St (MI)	Carlos Songini, Cleveland St
1980	Ernest Simon, Wayne St (MI)	Paul Friedberg, Pennsylvania	Gil Pezza, Wayne St (MI)
1981	Ernest Simon, Wayne St (MI)	Paul Friedberg, Pennsylvania	Gil Pezza, Wayne St (MI)
1982	Alexander Flom, George Mason	Neil Hick, Wayne St (MI)	Peter Schifrin, San Jose St
1983	Demetrios Valsamis, NYU	John Friedberg, N Carolina	Ola Harstrom, Notre Dame
1984	Charles Higgs-Coulthard, Notre Dame	Michael Lofton, Wayne St (MI)	Ettore Bianchi, Wayne St (MI)
1985	Stephan Chauvel, Wayne St (MI)	Michael Lofton, NYU	Ettore Bianchi, Wayne St (MI)
1986	Adam Feldman, Penn St	Michael Lofton, NYU	Chris O'Loughlin, Pennsylvania
1987	William Mindel, Columbia	Michael Lofton, NYU	James O'Neill, Harvard
1988	Marc Kent, Columbia	Robert Cottingham, Columbia	Jon Normile, Columbia
1989	Edward Mufel, Penn St	Peter Cox, Harvard	Jon Normile, Columbia
1990	Nick Bravin, Stanford	David Mandell, Columbia	Jubba Beshin, Notre Dame
1991	Ben Atkins, Columbia	Vitali Nazlimov, Penn St	Marc Oshima, Columbia
1992	Nick Bravin, Stanford	Tom Strzalkowski, Penn St	Harald Bauder, Wayne St
1993	Nick Bravin, Stanford	Tom Strzalkowski, Penn St	Ben Atkins, Columbia
1994	Kwame van Leeuwen, Harvard	Tom Strzalkowski, Penn St	Harald Winkman, Princeton
1995	Sean McClain, Stanford	Paul Palestis, NYU	Mike Gattner, Lawrence
1996	Thorstein Becker, Wayne St (MI)	Maxim Pekarev, Princeton	Jeremy Kahn, Duke
1997	Cliff Bayer, Pennsylvania	Keith Smart, St. John's (NY)	Alden Clarke, Stanford
1998	Ayo Griffin, Yale	Luke LaValle, Notre Dame	George Hentea, St. John's (NY)
1999	Felix Reichling, Stanford	Keeth Smart, St. John's (NY)	Alex Roytblat St. John's (NY)
2000	Felix Reichling, Stanford	Gabor Szelle, Notre Dame	Daniel Landgren, Penn St
2001	William Jed Dupree, Columbia	Ivan Lee, St. John's (NY)	Soren Thompson, Princeton
2002	Nonpatat Parchan, Penn St	Ivan Lee, St. John's (NY)	Arpád Horváth, St. John's (NY)

Women

TEAM CHAMPIONS

Year	Champion	Coach	Rec	Runner-Up	Rec
1982	Wayne St (MI)	Istvan Danosi	7–0	San Jose St	6–1
1983	Penn St	Beth Alphin	5–0	Wayne St (MI)	3–2
1984	Yale	Henry Harutunian	3–0	Penn St	2–1
1985	Yale	Henry Harutunian	3–0	Pennsylvania	2–1
1986	Pennsylvania	David Micahnik	3–0	Notre Dame	2–1
1987	Notre Dame	Yves Auriol	3–0	Temple	2–1
1988	Wayne St (MI)	Gil Pezza	3–0	Notre Dame	2–1
1989	Wayne St (MI)	Gil Pezza	3–0	Columbia-Barnard	2–1

Note: Beginning in 1990, men's and women's combined teams competed for the national championship.

INDIVIDUAL CHAMPIONS

Foil	Foil (Cont.)	Sabre
1982 Joy Ellingson, San Jose St	1993 Olga Kalinovskaya, Penn St	2000 Caroline Purcell, MIT
1983 Jana Angelakis, Penn St	1994 Olga Kalinovskaya, Penn St	2001 Sada Jacobson, Yale
1984 Mary Jane O'Neill, Penn	1995 Olga Kalinovskaya, Penn St	2002 Sada Jacobson, Yale
1985 C. Bilodeaux, Columbia-Barn.	1996 Olga Kalinovskaya, Penn St	**Épée**
1986 M. Sullivan, Notre Dame	1997 Yelena Kalkina, Ohio St	1995 Tina Loven, St. John's (NY)
1987 C. Bilodeaux, Columbia-Barn.	1998 F. Zimmermann, Stanford	1996 N. Dygert, St. John's (NY)
1988 M. Sullivan, Notre Dame	1999 Monique DeBruin, Stanford	1997 Magda Krol, Notre Dame
1989 Yasemin Topcu, Wayne St (MI)	2000 Eva Petschnigg, Princeton	1998 Charlotte Walker, Penn St
1990 Tzu Moy, Columbia-Barn.	2001 Iris Zimmerman, Stanford	1999 F. Zimmermann, Stanford
1991 Heidi Piper, Notre Dame	2002 Alicja Kryczalo, Notre Dame	2000 Jessica Burke, Penn St
1992 Olga Cheryak, Penn St		2001 E. Takács, St. John's (NY)
		2002 Stephanie Eim, Penn St

DIVISION I

Year	Champion	Coach	Score	Runner-Up
1981	Connecticut	Diane Wright	4–1	Massachusetts
1982	Old Dominion	Beth Anders	3–2	Connecticut
1983	Old Dominion	Beth Anders	3–1 (3 OT)	Connecticut
1984	Old Dominion	Beth Anders	5–1	Iowa
1985	Connecticut	Diane Wright	3–2	Old Dominion
1986	Iowa	Judith Davidson	2–1 (2 OT)	New Hampshire
1987	Maryland	Sue Tyler	2–1 (OT)	N Carolina
1988	Old Dominion	Beth Anders	2–1	Iowa
1989	N Carolina	Karen Shelton	2–1 (3 OT)*	Old Dominion
1990	Old Dominion	Beth Anders	5–0	N Carolina
1991	Old Dominion	Beth Anders	2–0	N Carolina
1992	Old Dominion	Beth Anders	4–0	Iowa
1993	Maryland	Missy Meharg	2–1 (3 OT)*	N Carolina
1994	James Madison	Christy Morgan	2–1 (3 OT)*	N Carolina
1995	N Carolina	Karen Shelton-Scroggs	5–1	Maryland
1996	N Carolina	Karen Shelton-Scroggs	3–0	Princeton
1997	N Carolina	Karen Shelton	3–2	Old Dominion
1998	Old Dominion	Beth Anders	3–2	Princeton
1999	Maryland	Missy Meharg	2–1	Michigan
2000	Old Dominion	Beth Anders	3–1	N Carolina
2001	Michigan	Marcia Pankratz	2–0	Maryland

*Penalty strokes.

DIVISION II (Discontinued, then renewed)

Year	Champion	Coach	Score	Runner-Up
1981	Pfeiffer	Ellen Briggs	5–3	Bentley
1982	Lock Haven	Sharon E. Taylor	4–1	Bloomsburg
1983	Bloomsburg	Jan Hutchinson	1–0	Lock Haven
1992	Lock Haven	Sharon E. Taylor	3–1	Bloomsburg
1993	Bloomsburg	Jan Hutchinson	2–1 (2 OT)	Lock Haven
1994	Lock Haven	Sharon E. Taylor	2–1	Bloomsburg
1995	Lock Haven	Sharon E. Taylor	1–0	Bloomsburg
1996	Bloomsburg	Jan Hutchinson	1–0	Lock Haven
1997	Bloomsburg	Jan Hutchinson	2–0	Kutztown
1998	Bloomsburg	Jan Hutchinson	4–3 (OT)	Lock Haven
1999	Bloomsburg	Jan Hutchinson	2–0	Bentley
2000	Lock Haven	Pat Rudy	2–0	Bentley
2001	Bentley	Kell McGowan	4–2	E Stroudsburg

DIVISION III

Year	Champion	Year	Champion	Year	Champion
1981	Trenton St	1988	Trenton St	1995	Trenton St
1982	Ithaca	1989	Lock Haven	1996	College of New Jersey*
1983	Trenton St	1990	Trenton St	1997	William Smith
1984	Bloomsburg	1991	Trenton St	1998	Middelbury
1985	Trenton St	1992	William Smith	1999	College of New Jersey*
1986	Salisbury St	1993	Cortland St	2000	William Smith
1987	Bloomsburg	1994	Cortland St	2001	Cortland St

*Formerly Trenton St.

Golf

Men

DIVISION I

Results, 1897–1938

Year	Champion	Site	Individual Champion
1897	Yale	Ardsley Casino	Louis Bayard Jr, Princeton
1898	Harvard (spring)		John Reid Jr, Yale
1898	Yale (fall)		James Curtis, Harvard
1899	Harvard		Percy Pyne, Princeton
1900	No tournament		
1901	Harvard	Atlantic City	H. Lindsley, Harvard
1902	Yale (spring)	Garden City	Charles Hitchcock Jr, Yale
1902	Harvard (fall)	Morris County	Chandler Egan, Harvard
1903	Harvard	Garden City	F.O. Reinhart, Princeton
1904	Harvard	Myopia	A.L. White, Harvard
1905	Yale	Garden City	Robert Abbott, Yale
1906	Yale	Garden City	W.E. Clow Jr, Yale
1907	Yale	Nassau	Ellis Knowles, Yale
1908	Yale	Brae Burn	H.H. Wilder, Harvard
1909	Yale	Apawamis	Albert Seckel, Princeton

Men (Cont.)
DIVISION I (Cont.)
Results, 1897–1938 (Cont.)

Year	Champion	Site	Individual Champion
1910	Yale	Essex County	Robert Hunter, Yale
1911	Yale	Baltusrol	George Stanley, Yale
1912	Yale	Ekwanok	F.C. Davison, Harvard
1913	Yale	Huntingdon Valley	Nathaniel Wheeler, Yale
1914	Princeton	Garden City	Edward Allis, Harvard
1915	Yale	Greenwich	Francis Blossom, Yale
1916	Princeton	Oakmont	J.W. Hubbell, Harvard
1917–18	No tournament		
1919	Princeton	Merion	A.L. Walker Jr, Columbia
1920	Princeton	Nassau	Jess Sweetster, Yale
1921	Dartmouth	Greenwich	Simpson Dean, Princeton
1922	Princeton	Garden City	Pollack Boyd, Dartmouth
1923	Princeton	Siwanoy	Dexter Cummings, Yale
1924	Yale	Greenwich	Dexter Cummings, Yale
1925	Yale	Montclair	Fred Lamprecht, Tulane
1926	Yale	Merion	Fred Lamprecht, Tulane
1927	Princeton	Garden City	Watts Gunn, Georgia Tech
1928	Princeton	Apawamis	Maurice McCarthy, Georgetown
1929	Princeton	Hollywood	Tom Aycock, Yale
1930	Princeton	Oakmont	G.T. Dunlap Jr, Princeton
1931	Yale	Olympia Fields	G.T. Dunlap Jr, Princeton
1932	Yale	Hot Springs	J.W. Fischer, Michigan
1933	Yale	Buffalo	Walter Emery, Oklahoma
1934	Michigan	Cleveland	Charles Yates, Georgia Tech
1935	Michigan	Congressional	Ed White, Texas
1936	Yale	North Shore	Charles Kocsis, Michigan
1937	Princeton	Oakmont	Fred Haas Jr, Louisiana St
1938	Stanford	Louisville	John Burke, Georgetown

Results, 1939–2002

Year	Champion (Score)	Coach	Runner-Up (Score)	Host or Site	Individual Champion
1939	Stanford (612)	Eddie Twiggs	Northwestern (614) Princeton (614)	Wakonda	Vincent D'Antoni, Tulane
1940	Princeton (601) Louisiana St (601)	Walter Bourne Mike Donahue		Ekwanok	Dixon Brooke, Virginia
1941	Stanford (580)	Eddie Twiggs	Louisiana St (599)	Ohio St	Earl Stewart, Louisiana St
1942	Louisiana St (590) Stanford (590)	Mike Donahue Eddie Twiggs		Notre Dame	Frank Tatum Jr, Stanford
1943	Yale (614)	William Neale Jr	Michigan (618)	Olympia Fields	Wallace Ulrich, Carleton
1944	Notre Dame (311)	George Holderith	Minnesota (312)	Inverness	Louis Lick, Minnesota
1945	Ohio St (602)	Robert Kepler	Northwestern (621)	Ohio St	John Lorms, Ohio St
1946	Stanford (619)	Eddie Twiggs	Michigan (624)	Princeton	George Hamer, Georgia
1947	Louisiana St (606)	T.P. Heard	Duke (614)	Michigan	Dave Barclay, Michigan
1948	San Jose St (579)	Wilbur Hubbard	Louisiana St (588)	Stanford	Bob Harris, San Jose St
1949	N Texas (590)	Fred Cobb	Purdue (600) Texas (600)	Iowa St	Harvie Ward, N Carolina
1950	N Texas (573)	Fred Cobb	Purdue (577)	New Mexico	Fred Wampler, Purdue
1951	N Texas (588)	Fred Cobb	Ohio St (589)	Ohio St	Tom Nieporte, Ohio St
1952	N Texas (587)	Fred Cobb	Michigan (593)	Purdue	Jim Vickers, Oklahoma
1953	Stanford (578)	Charles Finger	N Carolina (580)	Broadmoor	Earl Moeller, Oklahoma St
1954	SMU (572)	Graham Ross	N Texas (573)	Houston Hillman	Robbins, Memphis St
1955	Louisiana St (574)	Mike Barbato	N Texas (583)	Tennessee	Joe Campbell, Purdue
1956	Houston (601)	Dave Williams	N Texas (602) Purdue (602)	Ohio St	Rick Jones, Ohio St
1957	Houston (602)	Dave Williams	Stanford (603)	Broadmoor	Rex Baxter Jr., Houston
1958	Houston (570)	Dave Williams	Oklahoma St (582)	Williams	Phil Rodgers, Houston
1959	Houston (561)	Dave Williams	Purdue (571)	Oregon	Dick Crawford, Houston
1960	Houston (603)	Dave Williams	Purdue (607) Oklahoma St (607)	Broadmoor	Dick Crawford, Houston
1961	Purdue (584)	Sam Voinoff	Arizona St (595)	Lafayette	Jack Nicklaus, Ohio St
1962	Houston (588)	Dave Williams	Oklahoma St (598)	Duke	Kermit Zarley, Houston
1963	Oklahoma St (581)	Labron Harris	Houston (582)	Wichita St	R.H. Sikes, Arkansas
1964	Houston (580)	Dave Williams	Oklahoma St (587)	Broadmoor	Terry Small, San Jose St
1965	Houston (577)	Dave Williams	Cal St–LA (587)	Tennessee	Marty Fleckman, Houston
1966	Houston (582)	Dave Williams	San Jose St (586)	Stanford	Bob Murphy, Florida
1967	Houston (585)	Dave Williams	Florida (588)	Shawnee, PA	Hale Irwin, Colorado

Men (Cont.)
DIVISION I (Cont.)
Results, 1939–2002 (Cont.)

Year	Champion (Score)	Coach	Runner-Up (Score)	Host or Site	Individual Champion
1968	Florida (1154)	Buster Bishop	Houston (1156)	New Mexico St	Grier Jones, Oklahoma St
1969	Houston (1223)	Dave Williams	Wake Forest (1232)	Broadmoor	Bob Clark, Cal St–LA
1970	Houston (1172)	Dave Williams	Wake Forest (1182)	Ohio St	John Mahaffey, Houston
1971	Texas (1144)	George Hannon	Houston (1151)	Arizona	Ben Crenshaw, Texas
1972	Texas (1146)	George Hannon	Houston (1159)	Cape Coral	Ben Crenshaw, Texas
					Tom Kite, Texas
1973	Florida (1149)	Buster Bishop	Oklahoma St (1159)	Oklahoma St	Ben Crenshaw, Texas
1974	Wake Forest (1158)	Jess Haddock	Florida (1160)	San Diego St	Curtis Strange, Wake Forest
1975	Wake Forest (1156)	Jess Haddock	Oklahoma St (1189)	Ohio St	Jay Haas, Wake Forest
1976	Oklahoma St (1166)	Mike Holder	Brigham Young (1173)	New Mexico	Scott Simpson, USC
1977	Houston (1197)	Dave Williams	Oklahoma St (1205)	Colgate	Scott Simpson, USC
1978	Oklahoma St (1140)	Mike Holder	Georgia (1157)	Oregon	David Edwards, Oklahoma St
1979	Ohio St (1189)	James Brown	Oklahoma St (1191)	Wake Forest	Gary Hallberg, Wake Forest
1980	Oklahoma St (1173)	Mike Holder	Brigham Young (1177)	Ohio St	Jay Don Blake, Utah St
1981	BYU (1161)	Karl Tucker	Oral Roberts (1163)	Stanford	Ron Commans, USC
1982	Houston (1141)	Dave Williams	Oklahoma St (1151)	Pinehurst	Billy Ray Brown, Houston
1983	Oklahoma St (1161)	Mike Holder	Texas (1168)	Fresno St	Jim Carter, Arizona St
1984	Houston (1145)	Dave Williams	Oklahoma St (1146)	Houston	John Inman, N Carolina
1985	Houston (1172)	Dave Williams	Oklahoma St (1175)	Florida	Clark Burroughs, Ohio St
1986	Wake Forest (1156)	Jess Haddock	Oklahoma St (1160)	Wake Forest	Scott Verplank, Oklahoma St
1987	Oklahoma St (1160)	Mike Holder	Wake Forest (1176)	Ohio St	Brian Watts, Oklahoma St
1988	UCLA (1176)	Eddie Merrins	UTEP (1179)	Southern Cal	E.J. Pfister, Oklahoma St
			Oklahoma (1179)		
			Oklahoma St (1179)		
1989	Oklahoma (1139)	Gregg Grost	Texas (1158)	Oklahoma	Phil Mickelson, Arizona St
				Oklahoma St	
1990	Arizona St (1155)	Steve Loy	Florida (1157)	Florida	Phil Mickelson, Arizona St
1991	Oklahoma St (1161)	Mike Holder	N Carolina (1168)	San Jose St	Warren Schutte, UNLV
1992	Arizona (1129)	Rick LaRose	Arizona St (1136)	New Mexico	Phil Mickelson, Arizona St
1993	Florida (1145)	Buddy Alexander	Georgia Tech (1146)	Kentucky	Todd Demsey, Arizona St
1994	Stanford (1129)	Wally Goodwin	Texas (1133)	McKinney, TX	Justin Leonard, Texas
1995	Oklahoma St* (1156)	Mike Holder	Stanford (1156)	Ohio St	Chip Spratlin, Auburn
1996	Arizona St (1186)	Randy Lein	UNLV (1189)	Chattanooga	Tiger Woods, Stanford
1997	Pepperdine (1148)	John Geiberger	Wake Forest (1151)	Evanston, IL	Charles Warren, Clemson
1998	UNLV (1118)	Dwaine Knight	Clemson (1121)	Albuquerque	James McLean, Minnesota
1999	Georgia (1180)	Chris Haack	Oklahoma St (1183)	Chaska, MN	Donald Luke, Northwestern
2000	Oklahoma St* (1116)	Mike Holder	Georgia Tech (1116)	Opelika, AL	Charles Howell, Oklahoma St
2001	Florida (1126)	Buddy Alexander	Clemson (1144)	Durham, NC	Nick Gilliam, Florida
2002	Minnesota (1134)	Brad James	Georgia Tech		Ohio St	Troy Matteson, Ga. Tech

*Won sudden death playoff. Notes: Match play, 1897–1964; par-70 tournaments held in 1969, 1973 and 1989; par-71 tournaments held in 1968, 1981 and 1988; all other championships par-72 tournaments. Scores are based on 4 rounds instead of 2 after 1967.

DIVISION II

Year	Champion	Year	Champion	Year	Champion
1963	SW Missouri St	1977	Troy St	1991	Florida Southern
1964	Southern Illinois	1978	Columbus St	1992	Columbus St
1965	Middle Tennessee St	1979	UC–Davis	1993	Abilene Christian
1966	Cal St–Chico	1980	Columbus St	1994	Columbus St
1967	Lamar	1981	Florida Southern	1995	Florida Southern
1968	Lamar	1982	Florida Southern	1996	Florida Southern
1969	Cal St–Northridge	1983	SW Texas St	1997	Columbus St
1970	Rollins	1984	Troy St	1998	Florida Southern
1971	New Orleans	1985	Florida Southern	1999	Florida Southern
1972	New Orleans	1986	Florida Southern	2000	Florida Southern
1973	Cal St–Northridge	1987	Tampa	2001	W Florida
1974	Cal St–Northridge	1988	Tampa	2002	Rollins
1975	UC–Irvine	1989	Columbus St		
1976	Troy St	1990	Florida Southern		

Note: Par-71 tournaments held in 1967, 1970, 1976–78, 1985, 1988 and 2001; par-70 tournament held in 1996; all other championships par-72 tournaments.

Men (Cont.)

DIVISION III

Year	Champion	Year	Champion	Year	Champion
1975	Wooster	1985	Cal St–Stanislaus	1995	Methodist (NC)
1976	Cal St–Stanislaus	1986	Cal St–Stanislaus	1996	Methodist (NC)
1977	Cal St–Stanislaus	1987	Cal St–Stanislaus	1997	Methodist (NC)
1978	Cal St–Stanislaus	1988	Cal St–Stanislaus	1998	Methodist (NC)
1979	Cal St–Stanislaus	1989	Cal St–Stanislaus	1999	Methodist (NC)
1980	Cal St–Stanislaus	1990	Methodist (NC)	2000	Greensboro
1981	Cal St–Stanislaus	1991	Methodist (NC)	2001	WI–Eau Claire
1982	Ramapo	1992	Methodist (NC)	2002	Guilford
1983	Allegheny	1993	UC–San Diego		
1984	Cal St–Stanislaus	1994	Methodist (NC)		

Note: All championships par-72 except for 1986, 1988 and 2001, which were par-71; fourth round of 1975 championships canceled as a result of bad weather; first round of 1988 championships canceled as a result of rain.

Women

DIVISION I

Year	Champion	Coach	Score	Runner-Up	Score	Individual Champion
1982	Tulsa	Dale McNamara	1191	Texas Christian	1227	Kathy Baker, Tulsa
1983	Texas Christian	Fred Warren	1193	Tulsa	1196	Penny Hammel, Miami (FL)
1984	Miami (FL)	Lela Cannon	1214	Arizona St	1221	Cindy Schreyer, Georgia
1985	Florida	Mimi Ryan	1218	Tulsa	1233	Danielle Ammaccapane, Arizona St
1986	Florida	Mimi Ryan	1180	Miami (FL)	1188	Page Dunlap, Florida
1987	San Jose St	Mark Gale	1187	Furman	1188	Caroline Keggi, New Mexico
1988	Tulsa	Dale McNamara	1175	Georgia	1182	Melissa McNamara, Tulsa
				Arizona	1182	
1989	San Jose St	Mark Gale	1208	Tulsa	1209	Pat Hurst, San Jose St
1990	Arizona St	Linda Vollstedt	1206	UCLA	1222	Susan Slaughter, Arizona
1991	UCLA*	Jackie Steinmann	1197	San Jose St	1197	Annika Sorenstam, Arizona
1992	San Jose St	Mark Gale	1171	Arizona	1175	Vicki Goetze, Georgia
1993	Arizona St	Linda Vollstedt	1187	Texas	1189	Charlotta Sorenstam, Texas
1994	Arizona St	Linda Vollstedt	1189	Southern Cal	1205	Emilee Klein, Arizona St
1995	Arizona St	Linda Vollstedt	1155	San Jose St	1181	Kristel Mourgue d'Algue, Arizona St
1996	Arizona*	Rick LaRose	1240	San Jose St	1240	Marisa Baena, Arizona
1997	Arizona St	Linda Vollstedt	1178	San Jose St	1180	Heather Bowie, Texas
1998	Arizona St	Linda Vollstedt	1155	Florida	1173	Jennifer Rosales, USC
1999	Duke	Dan Brooks	895	Arizona St/Georgia	903	Grace Park, Arizona St
2000	Arizona	Todd McCorkle	1175	Stanford	1196	Jenna Daniels, Arizona
2001	Georgia	Todd McCorkle	1176	Duke	1179	Candy Hannemann, Duke
2002	Duke	Dan Brooks	1164	Arizona/Auburn/Texas	1160	Virada Nirapathpongporn, Duke

*Won sudden death playoff. Note: Par-74 tournaments held in 1983 and 1988; par-72 tournament held in 1990, 2000 and 2001; all other championships par-73 tournaments.

DIVISIONS II AND III

Year	Champion	Year	Champion
1996	Methodist (NC)	1998	Methodist (NC)
1997	Lynn	1999	Methodist (NC)

DIVISION II

Year	Champion
2000	Florida Southern
2001	Florida Southern
2002	Florida Southern

DIVISION III

Year	Champion
2000	Methodist (NC)
2001	Methodist (NC)
2002	Methodist (NC)

Gymnastics

Men
TEAM CHAMPIONS

Year	Champion	Coach	Pts	Runner-Up	Pts
1938	Chicago	Dan Hoffer	22	Illinois	18
1939	Illinois	Hartley Price	21	Army	17
1940	Illinois	Hartley Price	20	Navy	17
1941	Illinois	Hartley Price	68.5	Minnesota	52.5
1942	Illinois	Hartley Price	39	Penn St	30
1943–47	No tournament				
1948	Penn St	Gene Wettstone	55	Temple	34.5
1949	Temple	Max Younger	28	Minnesota	18
1950	Illinois	Charley Pond	26	Temple	25
1951	Florida St	Hartley Price	26	Illinois	23.5
				Southern Cal	23.5
1952	Florida St	Hartley Price	89.5	Southern Cal	75
1953	Penn St	Gene Wettstone	91.5	Illinois	68
1954	Penn St	Gene Wettstone	137	Illinois	68
1955	Illinois	Charley Pond	82	Penn St	69
1956	Illinois	Charley Pond	123.5	Penn St	67.5
1957	Penn St	Gene Wettstone	88.5	Illinois	80
1958	Michigan St	George Szypula	79		
	Illinois	Charley Pond	79		
1959	Penn St	Gene Wettstone	152	Illinois	87.5
1960	Penn St	Gene Wettstone	112.5	Southern Cal	65.5
1961	Penn St	Gene Wettstone	88.5	Southern Illinois	80.5
1962	Southern Cal	Jack Beckner	95.5	Southern Illinois	75
1963	Michigan	Newton Loken	129	Southern Illinois	73
1964	Southern Illinois	Bill Meade	84.5	Southern Cal	69.5
1965	Penn St	Gene Wettstone	68.5	Washington	51.5
1966	Southern Illinois	Bill Meade	187.200	California	185.100
1967	Southern Illinois	Bill Meade	189.550	Michigan	187.400
1968	California	Hal Frey	188.250	Southern Illinois	188.150
1969	Iowa	Mike Jacobson	161.175	Penn St	160.450
	Michigan*	Newton Loken		Colorado St	
1970	Michigan	Newton Loken	164.150	Iowa St	164.050
				New Mexico St	
1971	Iowa St	Ed Gagnier	319.075	Southern Illinois	316.650
1972	Southern Illinois	Bill Meade	315.925	Iowa St	312.325
1973	Iowa St	Ed Gagnier	325.150	Penn St	323.025
1974	Iowa St	Ed Gagnier	326.100	Arizona St	322.050
1975	California	Hal Frey	437.325	Louisiana St	433.700
1976	Penn St	Gene Wettstone	432.075	Louisiana St	425.125
1977	Indiana St	Roger Counsil	434.475		
	Oklahoma	Paul Ziert	434.475		
1978	Oklahoma	Paul Ziert	439.350	Arizona St	437.075
1979	Nebraska	Francis Allen	448.275	Oklahoma	446.625
1980	Nebraska	Francis Allen	563.300	Iowa St	557.650
1981	Nebraska	Francis Allen	284.600	Oklahoma	281.950
1982	Nebraska	Francis Allen	285.500	UCLA	281.050
1983	Nebraska	Francis Allen	287.800	UCLA	283.900
1984	UCLA	Art Shurlock	287.300	Penn St	281.250
1985	Ohio St	Michael Willson	285.350	Nebraska	284.550
1986	Arizona St	Don Robinson	283.900	Nebraska	283.600
1987	UCLA	Art Shurlock	285.300	Nebraska	284.750
1988	Nebraska	Francis Allen	288.150	Illinois	287.150
1989	Illinois	Yoshi Hayasaki	283.400	Nebraska	282.300
1990	Nebraska	Francis Allen	287.400	Minnesota	287.300
1991	Oklahoma	Greg Buwick	288.025	Penn St	285.500
1992	Stanford	Sadao Hamada	289.575	Nebraska	288.950
1993	Stanford	Sadao Hamada	276.500	Nebraska	275.500
1994	Nebraska	Francis Allen	288.250	Stanford	285.925
1995	Stanford	Sadao Hamada	232.400	Nebraska	231.525
1996	Ohio St	Peter Kormann	232.150	California	231.775
1997	California	Barry Weiner	233.825	Oklahoma	232.725
1998	Caliornia	Barry Weiner	231.200	Iowa	229.675
1999	Michigan	Kurt Golder	232.550	Ohio St	230.850
2000	Penn St	Randy Jepson	231.975	Michigan	231.850
2001	Ohio St	Miles Avery	218.125	Oklahoma	217.775
2002	Oklahoma	Mark Williams	219.300	Ohio St	218.650

*Trampoline.

Men (Cont.)
INDIVIDUAL CHAMPIONS

ALL-AROUND

1938.....Joe Giallombardo, Illinois
1939.....Joe Giallombardo, Illinois
1940.....Joe Giallombardo, Illinois
       Paul Fina, Illinois
1941.....Courtney Shanken, Chicago
1942.....Newt Loken, Minnesota
1948.....Ray Sorenson, Penn St
1949.....Joe Kotys, Kent
1950.....Joe Kotys, Kent
1951.....Bill Roetzheim, Florida St
1952.....Jack Beckner, Southern Cal
1953.....Jean Cronstedt, Penn St
1954.....Jean Cronstedt, Penn St
1955.....Karl Schwenzfeier, Penn St
1956.....Don Tonry, Illinois
1957.....Armando Vega, Penn St
1958.....Abie Grossfeld, Illinois
1959.....Armandò Vega, Penn St
1960.....Jay Werner, Penn St
1961.....Gregor Weiss, Penn St
1962.....Robert Lynn, Southern Cal
1963.....Gil Larose, Michigan
1964.....Ron Barak, Southern Cal
1965.....Mike Jacobson, Penn St
1966.....Steve Cohen, Penn St
1967.....Steve Cohen, Penn St
1968.....Makoto Sakamoto, USC
1969.....Mauno Nissinen, Wash
1970.....Yoshi Hayasaki, Wash
1971.....Yoshi Hayasaki, Wash
1972.....Steve Hug, Stanford
1973.....Steve Hug, Stanford
       Marshall Avener, Penn St
1974.....Steve Hug, Stanford
1975.....Wayne Young, BYU
1976.....Peter Kormann,.
       Southern Conn St
1977.....Kurt Kirsey, Indiana St
1978.....Bart Conner, Oklahoma
1979.....Kurt Thomas, Indiana St
1980.....Jim Hartung, Nebraska
1981.....Jim Hartung, Nebraska
1982.....Peter Vidmar, UCLA
1983.....Peter Vidmar, UCLA
1984.....Mitch Gaylord, UCLA
1985.....Wes Suter, Nebraska
1986.....Jon Louis, Stanford
1987.....Tom Schlesinger, Nebraska
1988.....Vacated†
1989.....Patrick Kirsey, Nebraska
1990.....Mike Racanelli, Ohio St
1991.....John Roethlisberger, Minn
1992.....John Roethlisberger, Minn
1993.....John Roethlisberger, Minn
1994.....Dennis Harrison, Nebraska
1995.....Richard Grace, Nebraska
1996.....Blaine Wilson, Ohio St
1997.....Blaine Wilson, Ohio St
1998.....Travis Romagnoli, Illinois
1999......Justin Hardabura, Nebraska
2000.....Jamie Natalie, Ohio St
2001.....Jamie Natalie, Ohio St
2002.....Raj Bhavsar, Ohio St

HORIZONTAL BAR

1938.....Bob Sears, Army
1939.....Adam Walters, Temple
1940.....Norm Boardman, Temple
1941.....Newt Loken, Minnesota
1942.....Norm Boardman, Temple
1948.....Joe Calvetti, Illinois
1949.....Bob Stout, Temple
1950.....Joe Kotys, Kent
1951.....Bill Roetzheim, Florida St
1952.....Charles Simms, USC
1953.....Hal Lewis, Navy
1954.....Jean Cronstedt, Penn St
1955.....Carlton Rintz, Michigan St
1956.....Ronnie Amster, Florida St
1957.....Abie Grossfeld, Illinois
1958.....Abie Grossfeld, Illinois
1959.....Stanley Tarshis, Mich St
1960.....Stanley Tarshis, Mich St
1961.....Bruno Klaus, Southern Ill
1962.....Robert Lynn, USC
1963.....Gil Larose, Michigan
1964.....Ron Barak, USC
1965.....Jim Curzi, Michigan St
       Mike Jacobsen, Penn St
1966.....Rusty Rock, Cal St–
       Northridge
1967.....Rich Grigsby, Cal St–
       Northridge
1968.....Makoto Sakamoto, USC
1969.....Bob Manna, New Mexico
1970.....Yoshi Hayasaki, Wash
1971.....Brent Simmons, Iowa St
1972.....Tom Lindner, Souhern Ill
1973.....Jon Aitken, New Mexico
1974.....Rick Banley, Indiana St
1975.....Rich Larsen, Iowa St
1976.....Tom Beach, California
1977.....John Hart, UCLA
1978.....Mel Cooley, Washington
1979.....Kurt Thomas, Indiana St
1980.....Philip Cahoy, Nebraska
1981.....Philip Cahoy, Nebraska
1982.....Peter Vidmar, UCLA
1983.....Scott Johnson, Nebraska
1984.....Charles Lakes, Illinois
1985.....Dan Hayden, Arizona St
       Wes Suter, Nebraska
1986.....Dan Hayden, Arizona St
1987.....David Moriel, UCLA
1988.....Vacated†
1989.....Vacated†
1990.....Chris Waller, UCLA
1991.....Luis Lopez, New Mexico
1992.....Jair Lynch, Stanford
1993.....Steve McCain, UCLA
1994.....Jim Foody, UCLA
1995.....Rick Kieffer, Nebraska
1996.....Carl Imhauser, Temple
1997.....Marshall Nelson,Nebraska
1998.....Todd Bishop, Oklahoma
1999.....Todd Bishop, Oklahoma
2000.....Michael Ashe, California
2001.....Michael Ashe, California
2002.....Daniel Diaz-Luong,
       Michigan

PARALLEL BARS

1938.....Erwin Beyer, Chicago
1939.....Bob Sears, Army
1940.....Bob Hanning, Minnesota
1941.....Caton Cobb, Illinois
1942.....Hal Zimmerman, Penn St
1948.....Ray Sorenson, Penn St
1949.....Joe Kotys, Kent
       Mel Stout, Michigan St
1950.....Joe Kotys, Kent
1951.....Jack Beckner, USC
1952.....Jack Beckner, USC
1953.....Jean Cronstedt, Penn St
1954.....Jean Cronstedt, Penn St
1955.....Carlton Rintz, Michigan St
1956.....Armando Vega, Penn St
1957.....Armando Vega, Penn St
1958.....Tad Muzyczko, Mich St
1959.....Armando Vega, Penn St
1960.....Robert Lynn, Southern Cal
1961.....Fred Tijerina, Southern Ill
       Jeff Cardinalli, Springfield
1962.....Robert Lynn, Southern Cal
1963.....Arno Lascari, Michigan
1964.....Ron Barak, Southern Cal
1965.....Jim Curzi, Michigan St
1966.....Jim Curzi, Michigan St
1967.....Makoto Sakamoto, USC
1968.....Makoto Sakamoto, USC
1969.....Ron Rapper, Michigan
1970.....Ron Rapper, Michigan
1971.....Brent Simmons, Iowa St
       Tom Dunn, Penn St
1972.....Dennis Mazur, Iowa St
1973.....Steve Hug, Stanford
1974.....Steve Hug, Stanford
1975.....Yoichi Tomita,
       Long Beach St
1976.....Gene Whelan, Penn St
1977.....Kurt Thomas, Indiana St
1978.....John Corritore, Michigan
1979.....Kurt Thomas, Indiana St
1980.....Philip Cahoy, Nebraska
1981.....Philip Cahoy, Nebraska
       Peter Vidmar, UCLA
       Jim Hartung, Nebraska
1982.....Jim Hartung, Nebraska
1983.....Scott Johnson, Nebraska
1984.....Tim Daggett, UCLA
1985.....Dan Hayden, Arizona St
       Noah Riskin, Ohio St
       Seth Riskin, Ohio St
1986.....Dan Hayden, Arizona St
1987......Kevin Davis, Nebraska
       Tom Schlesinger, Nebraska
1988.....Kevin Davis, Nebraska
1989.....Vacated†
1990.....Patrick Kirksey, Nebraska
1991.....Scott Keswick, UCLA
       John Roethlisberger, Minn
1992.....Dom Minicucci, Temple
1993.....Jair Lynch, Stanford
1994.....Richard Grace, Nebraska
1995.....Richard Grace, Nebraska
1996.....Jamie Ellis, Stanford
       Blaine Wilson, Ohio St
1997.....Marshall Nelson, Nebraska
1998......Marshall Nelson, Nebraska

Men (Cont.)

INDIVIDUAL CHAMPIONS (Cont.)

PARALLEL BARS (CONT.)
1999.....Justin Toman, Michigan
2000.....Kris Zimmerman, Michigan
 Justin Toman, Michigan
2001.....Raj Bhavsar, Ohio St
2002.....Cody Moore, California

VAULT
1938.....Erwin Beyer, Chicago
1939.....Marv Forman, Illinois
1940.....Earl Shanken, Chicago
1941.....Earl Shanken, Chicago
1942.....Earl Shanken, Chicago
1948.....Jim Peterson, Minnesota
1962.....Bruno Klaus, Southern Ill
1963.....Gil Larose, Michigan
1964.....Sidney Oglesby, Syracuse
1965.....Dan Millman, California
1966.....Frank Schmitz, S Illinois
1967.....Paul Mayer, S Illinois
1968.....Bruce Colter, Cal St–
 Los Angeles
1969.....Dan Bowles, California
 Jack McCarthy, Illinois
1970.....Doug Boger, Arizona
1971.....Pat Mahoney, Cal St–
 Northridge
1972.....Gary Morava, Southern Ill
1973.....John Crosby, S Conn St
1974.....Greg Goodhue, Oklahoma
1975.....Tom Beach, California
1976.....Sam Shaw, Cal St–
 Fullerton
1977.....Steve Wejmar, Wash
1978.....Ron Galimore, Louisiana St
1979.....Leslie Moore, Oklahoma
1980.....Ron Galimore, Iowa St
1981.....Ron Galimore, Iowa St
1982.....Randall Wickstrom, Cal
 Steve Elliott, Nebraska
1983.....Chris Riegel, Nebraska
 Mark Oates, Oklahoma
1984.....Chris Riegel, Nebraska
1985.....Derrick Cornelius,
 Cortland St
1986.....Chad Fox, New Mexico
1987.....Chad Fox, New Mexico
1988.....Chad Fox, New Mexico
1989.....Chad Fox, New Mexico
1990.....Brad Hayashi, UCLA
1991.....Adam Carton, Penn St
1992.....Jason Hebert, Syracuse
1993.....Steve Wiegel, N Mexico
1994.....Steve McCain, UCLA
1995.....Ian Bachrach, Stanford
1996.....Jay Thornton, Iowa
1997.....Blaine Wilson, Ohio St
1998.....Travis Romagnoli, Illinois
1999.....Guard Young, BYU
2000.....Guard Young, BYU
2001.....Daren Lynch, Ohio St
2002.....Dan Gill, Stanford

POMMEL HORSE
1938.....Erwin Beyer, Chicago
1939.....Erwin Beyer, Chicago
1940.....Harry Koehnemann, Illinois
1941.....Caton Cobb, Illinois
1942.....Caton Cobb, Illinois
1948.....Steve Greene, Penn St
1949.....Joe Berenato, Temple
1950.....Gene Rabbitt, Syracuse

POMMEL HORSE (CONT.)
1951.....Joe Kotys, Kent
1952.....Frank Bare, Illinois
1953.....Carlton Rintz, Michigan St
1954.....Robert Lawrence, Penn St
1955.....Carlton Rintz, Michigan St
1956.....James Brown, Cal St–
 Los Angeles
1957.....John Davis, Illinois
1958.....Bill Buck, Iowa
1959.....Art Shurlock, California
1960.....James Fairchild, California
1961.....James Fairchild, California
1962.....Mike Aufrecht, Illinois
1963.....Russ Mills, Yale
1964.....Russ Mills, Yale
1965.....Bob Elsinger, Springfield
1966.....Gary Hoskins, Cal St–
 Los Angeles
1967.....Keith McCanless, Iowa
1968.....Jack Ryan, Colorado
1969.....Keith McCanless, Iowa
1970.....Russ Hoffman, Iowa St
 John Russo, Wisconsin
1971.....Russ Hoffman, Iowa St
1972.....Russ Hoffman, Iowa St
1973.....Ed Slezak, Indiana St
1974.....Ted Marcy, Stanford
1975.....Ted Marcy, Stanford
1976.....Ted Marcy, Stanford
1977.....Chuck Walter, New Mexico
1978.....Mike Burke, Northern Ill
1979.....Mike Burke, Northern Ill
1980.....David Stoldt, Illinois
1981.....Mark Bergman, California
 Steve Jennings, New Mexico
1982.....Peter Vidmar, UCLA
 Steve Jennings, New Mexico
1983.....Doug Kieso, Northern Ill
1984.....Tim Daggett, UCLA
1985.....Tony Pineda, UCLA
1986.....Curtis Holdsworth, UCLA
1987.....Li Xiao Ping, Cal St–
 Fullerton
1988.....Vacated†
 Mark Sohn, Penn St
1989.....Mark Sohn, Penn St
 Chris Waller, UCLA
1990.....Mark Sohn, Penn St
1991.....Mark Sohn, Penn St
1992.....Che Bowers, Nebraska
1993.....John Roethlisberger, Minn
1994.....Jason Bertram, California
1995.....Drew Durbin, Ohio St
1996.....Drew Durbin, Ohio St
1997.....Drew Durbin, Ohio St
1998.....Josh Birckelbaw, California
1999.......Brandon Stefaniak, Penn St
2000.......Brandon Stefaniak, Penn St
 Don Jackson, Iowa
2001 .....Clay Strother, Minnesota
2002 .....Clay Strother, Minnesota

FLOOR EXERCISE
1941.....Lou Fina, Illinois
1953.....Bob Sullivan, Illinois
1954.....Jean Cronstedt, Penn St
1955.....Don Faber, UCLA
1956.....Jamile Ashmore, Florida St
1957.....Norman Marks, Cal St–
 Los Angeles

FLOOR EXERCISE (CONT.)
1958.....Abie Grossfeld, Illinois
1959.....Don Tonry, Illinois
1960.....Ray Hadley, Illinois
1961.....Robert Lynn, Southern Cal
1962.....Robert Lynn, Southern Cal
1963.....Tom Seward, Penn St
 Mike Henderson, Michigan
1964.....Rusty Mitchell, S Illinois
1965.....Frank Schmitz, S Illinois
1966.....Frank Schmitz, S Illinois
1967.....Dave Jacobs, Michigan
1968.....Toby Towson, Michigan St
1969.....Toby Towson, Michigan St
1970.....Tom Proulx, Colorado St
1971.....Stormy Eaton, New Mexico
1972.....Odessa Lovin, Oklahoma
1973.....Odessa Lovin, Oklahoma
1974.....Doug Fitzjarrell, Iowa St
1975.....Kent Brown, Arizona St
1976.....Bob Robbins, Colorado St
1977.......Ron Galimore, Louisiana St
1978.....Curt Austin, Iowa St
1979.....Mike Wilson, Oklahoma
 Bart Conner, Oklahoma
1980.....Steve Elliott, Nebraska
1981.....James Yuhashi, Oregon
1982.....Steve Elliott, Nebraska
1983.....Scott Johnson, Nebraska
 David Branch, Arizona St
 Donnie Hinton, Arizona St
1984.....Kevin Ekburg, Northern Ill
1985.....Wes Suter, Nebraska
1986.....Jerry Burrell, Arizona St
 Brian Ginsberg, UCLA
1987.....Chad Fox, New Mexico
1988.....Chris Wyatt, Temple
1989.....Jody Newman, Arizona St
1990.....Mike Racanelli, Ohio St
1991.....Brad Hayashi, UCLA
1992.....Brian Winkler, Michigan
1993.....Richard Grace, Nebraska
1994.....Mark Booth, Stanford
1995.....Jay Thornton, Iowa
1996.....Ian Bachrach, Stanford
1997.....Jeremy Killen, Oklahoma
1998.....Darin Gerlach, Temple
1999.......Jason Hardabura, Nebraska
2000.....Jamie Natalie, Ohio St
2001.....Clay Strother, Minnesota
2002.....Clay Strother, Minnesota

RINGS
1959.....Armando Vega, Penn St
1960.....Sam Garcia, Southern Cal
1961.....Fred Orlofsky, Southern Ill
1962.....Dale Cooper, Michigan St
1963.....Dale Cooper, Michigan St
1964.....Chris Evans, Arizona St
1965.....Glenn Gailis, Iowa
1966.....Ed Gunny, Michigan St
1967.....Josh Robison, California
1968.....Pat Arnold, Arizona
1969.....Paul Vexler, Penn St
 Ward Maythaler, Iowa St
1970.....Dave Seal, Indiana St
1971.....Charles Ropiequet, S Illinois
1972.....Dave Seal, Indiana St
1973.....Bob Mahorney, Indiana St
1974.....Keith Heaver, Iowa St
1975.....Keith Heaver, Iowa St

Men (Cont.)
INDIVIDUAL CHAMPIONS (Cont.)

RINGS (CONT.)

1976.....Doug Wood, Iowa St
1977.....Doug Wood, Iowa St
1978.....Scott McEldowney, Oregon
1979.....Kirk Mango, Northern Ill
1980.....Jim Hartung, Nebraska
1981.....Jim Hartung, Nebraska
1982.....Jim Hartung, Nebraska
1983.....Alex Schwartz, UCLA
1984.....Tim Daggett, UCLA
1985.....Mark Diab, Iowa St
1986.....Mark Diab, Iowa St
1987.....Paul O'Neill, Hou. Baptist

RINGS (CONT.)

1988.....Paul O'Neill, New Mexico
1989.....Vacated†
     Paul O'Neill, New Mexico
1990.....Wayne Cowden, Penn St
1991.....Adam Carton, Penn St
1992.....Scott Keswick, UCLA
1993.....Chris LaMorte, N Mexico
1994.....Chris LaMorte, N Mexico
1995.....Dave Frank, Temple
1996.....Scott McCall, Will. & Mary
     Blaine Wilson, Ohio St
1997.....Blaine Wilson, Ohio St

RINGS (CONT.)

1998.....Dan Fink, Oklahoma
1999.....Cortney Bramwell, BYU
2000.....Cortney Bramwell, BYU
2001.....Chris Lakeman, Penn St
2002.....Marshall Erwin, Stanford

†Championships won by Miguel Rubio (All Around, 1988; Horizontal Bar, 1988–89) and Alfonso Rodriguez (Pommel Horse, 1988; Rings, 1989; Parallel Bars, 1989) were vacated by action of the NCAA Committee on Infractions.

DIVISION II (Discontinued)

Year	Champion	Coach	Pts	Runner-Up	Pts
1968	Cal St–Northridge	Bill Vincent	179.400	Springfield	178.050
1969	Cal St–Northridge	Bill Vincent	151.800	Southern Connecticut St	145.075
1970	Northwestern Louisiana	Armando Vega	160.250	Southern Connecticut St	159.300
1971	Cal St–Fullerton	Dick Wolfe	158.150	Springfield	156.987
1972	Cal St–Fullerton	Dick Wolfe	160.550	Southern Connecticut St	153.050
1973	Southern Connecticut St	Abe Grossfeld	160.750	Cal St–Northridge	158.700
1974	Cal St–Fullerton	Dick Wolfe	309.800	Southern Connecticut St	309.400
1975	Southern Connecticut St	Abe Grossfeld	411.650	IL–Chicago	398.800
1976	Southern Connecticut St	Abe Grossfeld	419.200	IL–Chicago	388.850
1977	Springfield	Frank Wolcott	395.950	Cal St–Northridge	381.250
1978	IL–Chicago	C. Johnson/A. Gentile	406.850	Cal St–Northridge	400.400
1979	IL–Chicago	Clarence Johnson	418.550	WI–Oshkosh	385.650
1980	WI–Oshkosh	Ken Allen	260.550	Cal St–Chico	256.050
1981	WI–Oshkosh	Ken Allen	209.500	Springfield	201.550
1982	WI–Oshkosh	Ken Allen	216.050	E Stroudsburg	211.200
1983	E Stroudsburg	Bruno Klaus	258.650	WI–Oshkosh	257.850
1984	E Stroudsburg	Bruno Klaus	270.800	Cortland St	246.350

Women
TEAM CHAMPIONS

Year	Champion	Coach	Pts	Runner-Up	Pts
1982	Utah	Greg Marsden	148.60	Cal St–Fullerton	144.10
1983	Utah	Greg Marsden	184.65	Arizona St	183.30
1984	Utah	Greg Marsden	186.05	UCLA	185.55
1985	Utah	Greg Marsden	188.35	Arizona St	186.60
1986	Utah	Greg Marsden	186.95	Arizona St	186.70
1987	Georgia	Suzanne Yoculan	187.90	Utah	187.55
1988	Alabama	Sarah Patterson	190.05	Utah	189.50
1989	Georgia	Suzanne Yoculan	192.65	UCLA	192.60
1990	Utah	Greg Marsden	194.900	Alabama	194.575
1991	Alabama	Sarah Patterson	195.125	Utah	194.375
1992	Utah	Greg Marsden	195.650	Georgia	194.600
1993	Georgia	Suzanne Yoculan	198.000	Alabama	196.825
1994	Utah	Greg Marsden	196.400	Alabama	196.350
1995	Utah	Greg Marsden	196.650	Alabama	196.425
				Michigan	196.425
1996	Alabama	Sarah Patterson	198.025	UCLA	197.475
1997	UCLA	Valorie Kondos	197.150	Arizona St	196.850
1998	Georgia	Suzanne Yoculan	197.725	Florida	196.350
1999	Georgia	Suzanne Yoculan	196.850	Michigan	196.55
2000	UCLA	Valorie Kondos	197.300	Utah	196.875
2001	UCLA	Valorie Kondos	197.575	Georgia	197.400
2002	Alabama	Sarah Patterson	197.575	Georgia	197.25

Women (Cont.)

INDIVIDUAL CHAMPIONS

ALL-AROUND

1982.....Sue Stednitz, Utah
1983.....Megan McCunniff, Utah
1984.....Megan McCunniff-Marsden, Utah
1985.......Penney Hauschild, Alabama
1986.......Penney Hauschild, Alabama
            Jackie Brummer, Arizona St
1987.....Kelly Garrison-Steves, Oklahoma
1988.....Kelly Garrison-Steves, Oklahoma
1989.....Corrinne Wright, Georgia
1990.....Dee Dee Foster, Alabama
1991.....Hope Spivey, Georgia
1992.....Missy Marlowe, Utah
1993.....Jenny Hansen, Kentucky
1994.....Jenny Hansen, Kentucky
1995.....Jenny Hansen, Kentucky
1996.....Meredith Willard, Alabama
1997.....Kim Arnold, Georgia
1998.....Kim Arnold, Georgia
1999.....Theresa Kulikowski, Utah
2000.....Mohini Bhardwaj, UCLA
            Heather Brink, Nebraska
2001 ....Onnis Willis, UCLA
            Elise Ray, Michigan
2002 ....Jamie Dantzscher, UCLA

VAULT

1982.....Elaine Alfano, Utah
1983.....Elaine Alfano, Utah
1984.....Megan Marsden, Utah
1985.....Elaine Alfano, Utah
1986.....Kim Neal, Arizona St
            Pam Loree, Penn St
1987.....Yumi Mordre, Washington
1988.....Jill Andrews, UCLA
1989.....Kim Hamilton, UCLA
1990.....Michele Bryant, Nebraska
1991.....Anna Basaldva, Arizona
1992.....Tammy Marshall, Mass.
            Heather Stepp, Georgia
            Kristen Kenoyer, Utah
1993.....Heather Stepp, Georgia
1994.....Jenny Hansen, Kentucky
1995.....Jenny Hansen, Kentucky
1996.....Leah Brown, Georgia
1997.....Susan Hines, Florida
1998.....Susan Hines, Florida
1999.....Heidi Moneymaker, UCLA
2000.....Heather Brink, Nebraska

VAULT (Cont.)

2001.....Cory Fritzinger, Georgia
2002.....Jamie Dantzscher, UCLA

BALANCE BEAM

1982.....Sue Stednitz, Utah
1983.....Julie Goewey, Cal St–Fullerton
1984.....Heidi Anderson, Oregon St
1985.....Lisa Zeis, Arizona St
1986.....Jackie Brummer, Arizona St
1987.....Yumi Mordre, Washington
1988.....Kelly Garrison-Steves, Oklahoma
1989.....Jill Andrews, UCLA
            Joy Selig, Oregon St
1990.....Joy Selig, Oregon St
1991.....Missy Marlowe, Utah
1992.....Missy Marlowe, Utah
1992   Dana Dobransky, Alabama
1993.....Dana Dobransky, Alabama
1994.....Jenny Hansen, Kentucky
1995.....Jenny Hansen, Kentucky
1996.....Summer Reid, UUtah
1997.....Summer Reid, Utah
            Elizabeth Reid, Arizona St
1998   Larissa Fontaine, Stanford
            Susan Hines, Florida
1999.....Theresa Kulikowski, Utah
2000.....Lena Degteva, UCLA
2001.....Theresa Kulikowski, Utah
2002.....Elise Ray, Michigan

FLOOR EXERCISE

1982.....Mary Ayotte-Law, Oregon St
1983.....Kim Neal, Arizona St
1984.....Maria Anz, Florida
1985.....Lisa Mitzel, Utah
1986.....Lisa Zeis, Arizona St
            P. Hauschild, Alabama
1987.....Kim Hamilton, UCLA
1988.....Kim Hamilton, UCLA
1989.....Corrinne Wright, Georgia
            Kim Hamilton, UCLA
1990.....Joy Selig, Oregon St
1991.....Hope Spivey, Georgia
1992.....Missy Marlowe, Utah

FLOOR EXERCISE (Cont.)

1993.....Heather Stepp, Georgia
            Tammy Marshall, Mass.
            Amy Durham, Oregon St
1994.....Hope Spivey-Sheeley, UGA
1995...:.Jenny Hansen, Kentucky
            Stella Umeh, UCLA
            Leslie Angeles, Georgia
1996.....Heidi Hornbeek, Arizona
            Kim Kelly, Alabama
1997.....Leah Brown, Georgia
1998.....Kim Arnold, Georgia
            Jenni Beathard, Georgia
            Betsy Hamm, Florida
1999.....Marny Oestreng, BGSU
2000.....Suzanne Sears, Georgia
2001.....Mohini Bhardwaj, UCLA
2002.....Jamie Dantzscher, UCLA
            Nicole Arnstad, LSU

UNEVEN BARS

1982.....Lisa Shirk, Pittsburgh
1983.....Jeri Cameron, Arizona St
1984.....Jackie Brummer, Arizona St
1985.....Penney Hauschild, Alabama
1986.....Lucy Wener, Georgia
1987.....Lucy Wener, Georgia
1988.....Kelly Garrison-Steves, Oklahoma
1989.....Lucy Wener, Georgia
1990.....Marie Roethlisberger, Minnesota
1991.....Kelly Macy, Georgia
1992.....Missy Marlowe, Utah
1993.....Agina Simpkins, Georgia
            Beth Wymer, Michigan
1994...,.Sandy Woolsey, Utah
            Beth Wymer, Michigan
            Lori Strong, Georgia
1995.....Beth Wymer, Michigan
1996.....Stephanie Woods, Alabama
1997.....Jenni Beathard, Georgia
1998.....Karin Lichey, Georgia
            Stella Umeh, UCLA
1999.....Angie Leionard, Utah
2000.....Mohini Bhardwaj, UCLA
2001.....Yvonne Tousek, UCLA
2002.....Andree' Pickens, Alabama

Men

DIVISION I

Year	Champion	Coach	Score	Runner-Up	Most Outstanding Player
1948	Michigan	Vic Heyliger	8–4	Dartmouth	Joe Riley, Dartmouth, F
1949	Boston College	John Kelley	4–3	Dartmouth	Dick Desmond, Dartmouth, G
1950	Colorado College	Cheddy Thompson	13–4	Boston University	Ralph Bevins, Boston University, G
1951	Michigan	Vic Heyliger	7–1	Brown	Ed Whiston, Brown, G
1952	Michigan	Vic Heyliger	4–1	Colorado College	Kenneth Kinsley, Colorado Coll, G
1953	Michigan	Vic Heyliger	7–3	Minnesota	John Matchefts, Michigan, F
1954	Rensselaer	Ned Harkness	5–4 (OT)	Minnesota	Abbie Moore, Rensselaer, F
1955	Michigan	Vic Heyliger	5–3	Colorado College	Philip Hilton, Colorado College, D
1956	Michigan	Vic Heyliger	7–5	Michigan Tech	Lorne Howes, Michigan, G
1957	Colorado College	Thomas Bedecki	13–6	Michigan	Bob McCusker, Colorado Coll, F
1958	Denver	Murray Armstrong	6–2	N Dakota	Murray Massier, Denver, F
1959	N Dakota	Bob May	4–3 (OT)	Michigan St	Reg Morelli, N Dakota, F
1960	Denver	Murray Armstrong	5–3	Michigan Tech	Bob Marquis, Boston University, F
1961	Denver	Murray Armstrong	12–2	St. Lawrence	Barry Urbanski, Boston Univ, G
1962	Michigan Tech	John MacInnes	7–1	Clarkson	Louis Angotti, Michigan Tech, F
1963	N Dakota	Barney Thorndycraft	6–5	Denver	Al McLean, N Dakota, F
1964	Michigan	Allen Renfrew	6–3	Denver	Bob Gray, Michigan, G
1965	Michigan Tech	John MacInnes	8–2	Boston College	Gary Milroy, Michigan Tech, F
1966	Michigan St	Amo Bessone	6–1	Clarkson	Gaye Cooley, Michigan St, G
1967	Cornell	Ned Harkness	4–1	Boston University	Walt Stanowski, Cornell, D
1968	Denver	Murray Armstrong	4–0	N Dakota	Gerry Powers, Denver, G
1969	Denver	Murray Armstrong	4–3	Cornell	Keith Magnuson, Denver, D
1970	Cornell	Ned Harkness	6–4	Clarkson	Daniel Lodboa, Cornell, D
1971	Boston University	Jack Kelley	4–2	Minnesota	Dan Brady, Boston University, G
1972	Boston University	Jack Kelley	4–0	Cornell	Tim Regan, Boston University, G
1973	Wisconsin	Bob Johnson	4–2	Vacated	Dean Talafous, Wisconsin, F
1974	Minnesota	Herb Brooks	4–2	Michigan Tech	Brad Shelstad, Minnesota, G
1975	Michigan Tech	John MacInnes	6–1	Minnesota	Jim Warden, Michigan Tech, G
1976	Minnesota	Herb Brooks	6–4	Michigan Tech	Tom Vanelli, Minnesota, F
1977	Wisconsin	Bob Johnson	6–5 (OT)	Michigan	Julian Baretta, Wisconsin, G
1978	Boston University	Jack Parker	5–3	Boston College	Jack O'Callahan, Boston Univ, D
1979	Minnesota	Herb Brooks	4–3	N Dakota	Steve Janaszak, Minnesota, G
1980	N Dakota	John Gasparini	5–2	Northern Michigan	Doug Smail, N Dakota, F
1981	Wisconsin	Bob Johnson	6–3	Minnesota	Marc Behrend, Wisconsin, G
1982	N Dakota	John Gasparini	5–2	Wisconsin	Phil Sykes, N Dakota, F
1983	Wisconsin	Jeff Sauer	6–2	Harvard	Marc Behrend, Wisconsin, G
1984	Bowling Green	Jerry York	5–4 (OT)	MN–Duluth	Gary Kruzich, Bowling Green, G
1985	Rensselaer	Mike Addesa	2–1	Providence	Chris Terreri, Providence, G
1986	Michigan St	Ron Mason	6–5	Harvard	Mike Donnelly, Michigan St, F
1987	N Dakota	John Gasparini	5–3	Michigan St	Tony Hrkac, N Dakota, F
1988	Lake Superior St	Frank Anzalone	4–3 (OT)	St. Lawrence	Bruce Hoffort, Lake Superior St, G
1989	Harvard	Bill Cleary	4–3 (OT)	Minnesota	Ted Donato, Harvard, F
1990	Wisconsin	Jeff Sauer	7–3	Colgate	Chris Tancill, Wisconsin, F
1991	N Michigan	Rick Comley	8–7 (3OT)	Boston University	Scott Beattie, N Michigan, F
1992	Lake Superior St	Jeff Jackson	4–2	Wisconsin	Paul Constantin, Lake Superior St, F
1993	Maine	Shawn Walsh	5–4	Lake Superior St	Jim Montgomery, Maine, F
1994	Lake Superior St	Jeff Jackson	9–1	Boston University	Sean Tallaire, Lake Superior St, F
1995	Boston University	Jack Parker	6–2	Maine	Chris O'Sullivan, Boston Univ, F
1996	Michigan	Red Berenson	3–2 (OT)	Colorado College	Brendan Morrison, Michigan, F
1997	N Dakota	Dean Blais	6–4	Boston University	Matt Henderson, N Dakota, F
1998	Michigan	Red Berenson	3–2 (OT)	Boston Coll	Marty Turco, Michigan, G
1999	Maine	Shawn Walsh	3–2 (OT)	New Hampshire	Alfie Michaud, Maine, G
2000	N Dakota	Dean Blais	4–2	Boston College	Lee Goren, N Dakota, F
2001	Boston College	Jerry York	3–2 (OT)	N Dakota	Chuck Kobasew, Boston College, F
2002	Minnesota	Don Lucia	4–3 (OT)	Maine	Grant Potulny, Minnesota, F

DIVISION II *(Discontinued)*

Year	Champion	Coach	Score	Runner-Up
1978	Merrimack	Thom Lawler	12–2	Lake Forest
1979	Lowell	Bill Riley Jr	6–4	Mankato St
1980	Mankato St	Don Brose	5–2	Elmira
1981	Lowell	Bill Riley Jr	5–4	Plattsburgh St
1982	Lowell	Bill Riley Jr	6–1	Plattsburgh St
1983	RIT	Brian Mason	4–2	Bemidji St
1984	Bemidji St	R.H. (Bob) Peters	14–4*	Merrimack
1993	Bemidji St	R.H. (Bob) Peters	15–6*	Mercyhurst
1994	Bemidji St	R.H. (Bob) Peters	7–6*	AL–Huntsville

DIVISION II *(Cont.)*

Year	Champion	Coach	Score	Runner-Up
1995	Bemidji St	R.H. (Bob) Peters	11–6*	Mercyhurst
1996	AL–Huntsville	Doug Ross	10–1*	Bemidji St
1997	Bemidji St	R.H. (Bob) Peters	7–4*	AL–Huntsville
1998	AL–Huntsville	Doug Ross	11–4*	Bemidji St
1999	St. Michael's (VT)	Lou DiMasi	12–9*	New Hamp. Coll

*Two-game, total-goal series.

DIVISION III

Year	Champion	Coach	Score	Runner-Up
1984	Babson	Bob Riley	8–0	Union (NY)
1985	RIT	Bruce Delventhal	5–1	Bemidji St
1986	Bemidji St	R.H. (Bob) Peters	8–5	Vacated
1987	Vacated			Oswego St
1988	WI–River Falls	Rick Kozuback	7–1, 3–5, 3–0	Elmira
1989	WI–Stevens Point	Mark Mazzoleni	3–3, 3–2	RIT
1990	WI–Stevens Point	Mark Mazzoleni	10–1, 3–6, 1–0	Plattsburgh St
1991	WI–Stevens Point	Mark Mazzoleni	6–2	Mankato St
1992	Plattsburgh St	Bob Emery	7–3	WI–Stevens Point
1993	WI–Stevens Point	Joe Baldarotta	4–3	WI–River Falls
1994	WI–River Falls	Dean Talafous	6–4	WI–Superior
1995	Middlebury	Bill Beaney	1–0	Fredonia St
1996	Middlebury	Bill Beaney	3–2	RIT
1997	Middlebury	Bill Beaney	3–2	WI–Superior
1998	Middlebury	Bill Beaney	2–1	WI–Stevens Point
1999	Middlebury	Bill Beaney	5–0	WI–Superior
2000	Norwich	Michael McShane	2–1	St. Thomas (MN)
2001	Plattsburgh	Bob Emery	6–2	RIT
2002	WI–Superior	Dan Stauber	3–2	Norwich

Women

DIVISION I

Year	Champion	Coach	Score	Runner-Up
2001	Minnesota-Duluth	Shannon Miller	4–2	St. Lawrence
2002	Minnesota-Duluth	Shannon Miller	3–2	Brown

Lacrosse

Men

DIVISION I

Year	Champion	Coach	Score	Runner-Up
1971	Cornell	Richie Moran	12–6	Maryland
1972	Virginia	Glenn Thiel	13–12	Johns Hopkins
1973	Maryland	Bud Beardmore	10–9 (2 OT)	Johns Hopkins
1974	Johns Hopkins	Bob Scott	17–12	Maryland
1975	Maryland	Bud Beardmore	20–13	Navy
1976	Cornell	Richie Moran	16–13 (OT)	Maryland
1977	Cornell	Richie Moran	16–8	Johns Hopkins
1978	Johns Hopkins	Henry Ciccarone	13–8	Cornell
1979	Johns Hopkins	Henry Ciccarone	15–9	Maryland
1980	Johns Hopkins	Henry Ciccarone	9–8 (2 OT)	Virginia
1981	N Carolina	Willie Scroggs	14–13	Johns Hopkins
1982	N Carolina	Willie Scroggs	7–5	Johns Hopkins
1983	Syracuse	Roy Simmons Jr	17–16	Johns Hopkins
1984	Johns Hopkins	Don Zimmerman	13–10	Syracuse
1985	Johns Hopkins	Don Zimmerman	11–4	Syracuse
1986	N Carolina	Willie Scroggs	10–9 (OT)	Virginia
1987	Johns Hopkins	Don Zimmerman	11–10	Cornell
1988	Syracuse	Roy Simmons Jr	13–8	Cornell
1989	Syracuse	Roy Simmons Jr	13–12	Johns Hopkins
1990	Syracuse	Roy Simmons Jr	21–9	Loyola (MD)
1991	N Carolina	Dave Klarmann	18–13	Towson St
1992	Princeton	Bill Tierney	10–9	Syracuse
1993	Syracuse	Roy Simmons Jr	13–12	N Carolina
1994	Princeton	Bill Tierney	9–8 (OT)	Virginia
1995	Syracuse	Roy Simmons Jr	13–9	Maryland
1996	Princeton	Bill Tierney	13–12 (OT)	Virginia
1997	Princeton	Bill Tierney	19–7	Maryland
1998	Princeton	Bill Tierney	15–5	Maryland

Men (Cont.)

DIVISION I (Cont.)

Year	Champion	Coach	Score	Runner-Up
1999	Virginia	Dom Starsia	12–10	Syracuse
2000	Syracuse	John Desko	13–7	Princeton
2001	Princeton	Bill Tierney	10–9 (OT)	Syracuse
2002	Syracuse	John Desko	13–12	Princeton

DIVISION II (Discontinued, then renewed)

Year	Champion	Coach	Score	Runner-Up
1974	Towson St	Carl Runk	18–17 (OT)	Hobart
1975	Cortland St	Chuck Winters	12–11	Hobart
1976	Hobart	Jerry Schmidt	18–9	Adelphi
1977	Hobart	Jerry Schmidt	23–13	Washington (MD)
1978	Roanoke	Paul Griffin	14–13	Hobart
1979	Adelphi	Paul Doherty	17–12	MD–Baltimore County
1980	MD–Baltimore County	Dick Watts	23–14	Adelphi
1981	Adelphi	Paul Doherty	17–14	Loyola (MD)
1993	Adelphi	Kevin Sheehan	11–7	LIU–C.W. Post
1994	Springfield	Keith Bugbee	15–12	New York Tech
1995	Adelphi	Sandy Kapatos	12–10	Springfield
1996	LIU–C.W. Post	Tom Postel	15–10	Adelphi
1997	New York Tech	Jack Kaley	18–11	Adelphi
1998	Adelphi	Sandy Kapatos	18–6	LIU–C.W. Post
1999	Adelphi	Sandy Kapatos	11–8	LIU–C.W. Post
2000	Limestone	Mike Cerino	10–9	LIU–C.W. Post
2001	Adelphi	Sandy Kapatos	14–10	Limestone
2002	Limestone	T.W. Johnson	11–9	New York Tech

DIVISION III

Year	Champion	Coach	Score	Runner-Up
1980	Hobart	Dave Urick	11–8	Cortland St
1981	Hobart	Dave Urick	10–8	Cortland St
1982	Hobart	Dave Urick	9–8 (OT)	Washington (MD)
1983	Hobart	Dave Urick	13–9	Roanoke
1984	Hobart	Dave Urick	12–5	Washington (MD)
1985	Hobart	Dave Urick	15–8	Washington (MD)
1986	Hobart	Dave Urick	13–10	Washington (MD)
1987	Hobart	Dave Urick	9–5	Ohio Wesleyan
1988	Hobart	Dave Urick	18–9	Ohio Wesleyan
1989	Hobart	Dave Urick	11–8	Ohio Wesleyan
1990	Hobart	B.J. O'Hara	18–6	Washington (MD)
1991	Hobart	B.J. O'Hara	12–11	Salisbury St
1992	Nazareth (NY)	Scott Nelson	13–12	Hobart
1993	Hobart	B.J. O'Hara	16–10	Ohio Wesleyan
1994	Salisbury St	Jim Berkman	15–9	Hobart
1995	Salisbury St	Jim Berkman	22–13	Nazareth
1996	Nazareth	Scott Nelson	11–10 (OT)	Washington (MD)
1997	Nazareth	Scott Nelson	15–14 (OT)	Washington (MD)
1998	Washington (MD)	John Haus	16–10	Nazareth
1999	Salisbury St	Jim Berkman	13–6	Middlebury
2000	Middlebury	Erin Quinn	16–12	Salisbury St
2001	Middlebury	Erin Quinn	15–10	Gettysburg
2002	Middlebury	Erin Quinn	14–9	Gettysburg

Women*

DIVISION I

Year	Champion	Coach	Score	Runner-Up
2001	Maryland	Cindy Timchal	14–13 (OT)	Georgetown
2002	Princeton	Chris Sailer	12–7	Georgetown

DIVISION II

Year	Champion	Coach	Score	Runner-Up
2001	LIU–C.W. Post	Karen MacCrate	13–9	W Chester
2002	Westchester	Ginny Martino	11–6	Stonehill

*Divisions I and II competed for a single championship until 2001.

Women (Cont.)
DIVISIONS I AND II

Year	Champion	Coach	Score	Runner-Up
1982	Massachusetts	Pamela Hixon	9–6	Trenton St
1983	Delaware	Janet Smith	10–7	Temple
1984	Temple	Tina Sloan Green	6–4	Maryland
1985	New Hampshire	Marisa Didio	6–5	Maryland
1986	Maryland	Sue Tyler	11–10	Penn St
1987	Penn St	Susan Scheetz	7–6	Temple
1988	Temple	Tina Sloan Green	15–7	Penn St
1989	Penn St	Susan Scheetz	7–6	Harvard
1990	Harvard	Carole Kleinfelder	8–7	Maryland
1991	Virginia	Jane Miller	8–6	Maryland
1992	Maryland	Cindy Timchal	11–10	Harvard
1993	Virginia	Jane Miller	8–6 (OT)	Princeton
1994	Princeton	Chris Sailer	10–7	Virginia
1995	Maryland	Cindy Timchal	13–5	Princeton
1996	Maryland	Cindy Timchal	10–5	Virginia
1997	Maryland	Cindy Timchal	8–7	Loyola (MD)
1998	Maryland	Cindy Timchal	11–5	Virginia
1999	Maryland	Cindy Timchal	16–6	Virginia
2000	Maryland	Cindy Timchal	16–8	Princeton

DIVISION III

Year	Champion	Score	Runner-Up	Year	Champion	Score	Runner-Up
1985	Trenton St	7–4	Ursinus	1995	Trenton St	14–13	William Smith
1986	Ursinus	12–10	Trenton St	1996	Trenton St	15–8	Middlebury
1987	Trenton St	8–7 (OT)	Ursinus	1997	Middlebury	14–9	College of NJ*
1988	Trenton St	14–11	William Smith	1998	Coll of NJ	14–9	Williams
1989	Ursinus	8–6	Trenton St	1999	Middlebury	10–9	Amherst
1990	Ursinus	7–6	St. Lawrence	2000	Coll of NJ	14–8	Williams
1991	Trenton St	7–6	Ursinus	2001	Middlebury	11–10	Amherst
1992	Trenton St	5–3	William Smith	2002	Middlebury	12–6	College of NJ*
1993	Trenton St	10–9	William Smith				
1994	Trenton St	29–11	William Smith				

*Formerly Trenton St

Rifle

Individual Champions

Year	Champion	Coach	Score	Runner-Up	Score	Air Rifle	Smallbore
1980	Tennessee Tech	James Newkirk	6201	W Virginia	6150	Rod Fitz-Randolph, Tennessee Tech	Rod Fitz-Randolph, Tennessee Tech
1981	Tennessee Tech	James Newkirk	6139	W Virginia	6136	John Rost, W Virginia	Kurt Fitz-Randolph, Tennessee Tech
1982	Tennessee Tech	James Newkirk	6138	W Virginia	6136	John Rost, W Virginia	Kurt Fitz-Randolph, Tennessee Tech
1983	W Virginia	Edward Etzel	6166	Tennessee Tech	6148	Ray Slonena, Tennessee Tech	David Johnson, W Virginia
1984	W Virginia	Edward Etzel	6206	E Tennessee St	6142	Pat Spurgin, Murray St	Bob Broughton, W Virginia
1985	Murray St	Elvis Green	6150	W Virginia	6149	Christian Heller, W Virginia	Pat Spurgin, Murray St
1986	W Virginia	Edward Etzel	6229	Murray St	6163	Marianne Wallace, Murray St	Mike Anti, W Virginia
1987	Murray St	Elvis Green	6205	W Virginia	6203	Rob Harbison, TN–Martin	Web Wright, W Virginia
1988	W Virginia	Greg Perrine	6192	Murray St	6183	Deena Wigger, Murray St	Web Wright, W Virginia
1989	W Virginia	Edward Etzel	6234	S Florida	6180	Michelle Scarborough, S Florida	Deb Sinclair, AK–Fairbanks
1990	W Virginia	Marsha Beasley	6205	Navy	6101	Gary Hardy, W Virginia	M. Scarborough, S Florida
1991	W Virginia	Marsha Beasley	6171	AK–Fairbanks	6110	Ann Pfiffner, W Virginia	Soma Dutta, UTEP
1992	W Virginia	Marsha Beasley	6214	AK–Fairbanks	6166	Ann Pfiffner, W Virginia	Tim Manges, W Virginia
1993	W Virginia	Marsha Beasley	6179	AK–Fairbanks	6169	Trevor Gathman, W Virginia	Eric Uptagrafft, W Virginia
1994	AK–Fairbanks	Randy Pitney	6194	W Virginia	6187	Nancy Napolski, Kentucky	Cory Brunetti, AK–Fairbanks

Individual Champions

Year	Champion	Coach	Score	Runner-Up	Score	Air Rifle	Smallbore
1995	...W Virginia	Marsha Beasley	6241	Air Force	6187	Benji Belden, Murray St	Oleg Selezner, AK–Fairbanks
1996	...W Virginia	Marsha Beasley	6179	Air Force	6168	Trevor Gathman, W Virginia	Joe Johnson, Navy
1997	...W Virginia	Marsha Beasley	6223	Kentucky	6175	Marra Hastings, Murray St	Marcos Scrivner, W Virginia
1998	...W Virginia	Marsha Beasley	6214	AK–Fairbanks	6175	Emily Caruso, Norwich	Karen Juzinuk, Xavier
1999	...AK–Fairbanks	Randy Pitney	6276	Navy	6168	Kelly Mansfield, AK–Fairbanks	Kelly Mansfield, AK–Fairbanks
2000	....AK–Fairbanks	Randy Pitney	6285	Xavier	6156	Kelly Mansfield, AK–Fairbanks	Nicole Allaire, Nebraska
2001	..AK–Fairbanks	David Johnson	6283	Kentucky	6175	Matthew Emmons, AK–Fairbanks	Matthew Emmons, AK–Fairbanks
2002	....AK–Fairbanks	Randy Pitney	6241	Kentucky	6209	Ryan Tanoue, Nevada	Matthew Emmons, AK–Fairbanks

Skiing

Year	Champion	Coach	Pts	Runner-Up	Pts	Host or Site
1954	.....Denver	Willy Schaeffler	384.0	Seattle	349.6	NV–Reno
1955	.....Denver	Willy Schaeffler	567.05	Dartmouth	558.935	Norwich
1956	.....Denver	Willy Schaeffler	582.01	Dartmouth	541.77	Winter Park
1957	.....Denver	Willy Schaeffler	577.95	Colorado	545.29	Ogden Snow Basin
1958	.....Dartmouth	Al Merrill	561.2	Denver	550.6	Dartmouth
1959	.....Colorado	Bob Beattie	549.4	Denver	543.6	Winter Park
1960	....Colorado	Bob Beattie	571.4	Denver	568.6	Bridger Bowl
1961	.....Denver	Willy Schaeffler	376.19	Middlebury	366.94	Middlebury
1962	.....Denver	Willy Schaeffler	390.08	Colorado	374.30	Squaw Valley
1963	.....Denver	Willy Schaeffler	384.6	Colorado	381.6	Solitude
1964	.....Denver	Willy Schaeffler	370.2	Dartmouth	368.8	Franconia Notch
1965	.....Denver	Willy Schaeffler	380.5	Utah	378.4	Crystal Mountain
1966	.....Denver	Willy Schaeffler	381.02	Western Colorado	365.92	Crested Butte
1967	.....Denver	Willy Schaeffler	376.7	Wyoming	375.9	Sugarloaf Mountain
1968	....Wyoming	John Cress	383.9	Denver	376.2	Mount Werner
1969	.....Denver	Willy Schaeffler	388.6	Dartmouth	372.0	Mount Werner
1970	.....Denver	Willy Schaeffler	386.6	Dartmouth	378.8	Cannon Mountain
1971	.....Denver	Peder Pytte	394.7	Colorado	373.1	Terry Peak
1972	.....Colorado	Bill Marolt	385.3	Denver	380.1	Winter Park
1973	.....Colorado	Bill Marolt	381.89	Wyoming	377.83	Middlebury
1974	.....Colorado	Bill Marolt	176	Wyoming	162	Jackson Hole
1975	.....Colorado	Bill Marolt	183	Vermont	115	Fort Lewis
1976	.....Colorado	Bill Marolt	112			Bates
	Dartmouth	Jim Page	112			
1977	.....Colorado	Bill Marolt	179	Wyoming	154.5	Winter Park
1978	.....Colorado	Bill Marolt	152.5	Wyoming	121.5	Cannon Mountain
1979	.....Colorado	Tim Hinderman	153	Utah	130	Steamboat Springs
1980	.....Vermont	Chip LaCasse	171	Utah	151	Lake Placid and Stowe
1981	.....Utah	Pat Miller	183	Vermont	172	Park City
1982	.....Colorado	Tim Hinderman	461	Vermont	436.5	Lake Placid
1983	.....Utah	Pat Miller	696	Vermont	650	Bozeman
1984	.....Utah	Pat Miller	750.5	Vermont	684	New Hampshire
1985	.....Wyoming	Tim Ameel	764	Utah	744	Bozeman
1986	.....Utah	Pat Miller	612	Vermont	602	Vermont
1987	.....Utah	Pat Miller	710	Vermont	627	Anchorage
1988	.....Utah	Pat Miller	651	Vermont	614	Middlebury
1989	.....Vermont	Chip LaCasse	672	Utah	668	Jackson Hole
1990	.....Vermont	Chip LaCasse	671	Utah	571	Vermont
1991	.....Colorado	Richard Rokos	713	Vermont	682	Park City, UT
1992	.....Vermont	Chip LaCasse	693.5	New Mexico	642.5	New Hampshire
1993	.....Utah	Pat Miller	783	Vermont	700.5	Steamboat Springs
1994	.....Vermont	Chip LaCasse	688	Utah	667	Sugarloaf, ME
1995	.....Colorado	Richard Rokos	720.5	Utah	711	New Hampshire
1996	.....Utah	Pat Miller	719	Denver	635.5	Montana St
1997	.....Utah	Pat Miller	686	Vermont	646.5	Vermont
1998	.....Colorado	Richard Rokos	654	Utah	651.5	Montana St
1999	.....Colorado	Richard Rokos	650	Denver	636	Bates College
2000	.....Denver	Kurt Smitz	720	Colorado	621	Park City, UT
2001	.....Denver	Kurt Smitz	649	Vermont	605	Middlebury, VT
2002	.....Denver	Kurt Smitz	656	Colorado	612	Anchorage

Men
DIVISION I

Year	Champion	Coach	Score	Runner-Up
1959	St. Louis	Bob Guelker	5–2	Bridgeport
1960	St. Louis	Bob Guelker	3–2	Maryland
1961	West Chester	Mel Lorback	2–0	St. Louis
1962	St. Louis	Bob Guelker	4–3	Maryland
1963	St. Louis	Bob Guelker	3–0	Navy
1964	Navy	F.H. Warner	1–0	Michigan St
1965	St. Louis	Bob Guelker	1–0	Michigan St
1966	San Francisco	Steve Negoesco	5–2	LIU–Brooklyn
1967	Michigan St	Gene Kenney	0–0	Game called due to
	St. Louis	Harry Keough		inclement weather
1968	Maryland	Doyle Royal	2–2 (2 OT)	
	Michigan St	Gene Kenney		
1969	St. Louis	Harry Keough	4–0	San Francisco
1970	St. Louis	Harry Keough	1–0	UCLA
1971	Vacated		3–2	St. Louis
1972	St. Louis	Harry Keough	4–2	UCLA
1973	St. Louis	Harry Keough	2–1 (OT)	UCLA
1974	Howard	Lincoln Phillips	2–1 (4 OT)	St. Louis
1975	San Francisco	Steve Negoesco	4–0	SIU–Edwardsville
1976	San Francisco	Steve Negoesco	1–0	Indiana
1977	Hartwick	Jim Lennox	2–1	San Francisco
1978	Vacated		2–0	Indiana
1979	SIU–Edwardsville	Bob Guelker	3–2	Clemson
1980	San Francisco	Steve Negoesco	4–3 (OT)	Indiana
1981	Connecticut	Joe Morrone	2–1 (OT)	Alabama A&M
1982	Indiana	Jerry Yeagley	2–1 (8 OT)	Duke
1983	Indiana	Jerry Yeagley	1–0 (2 OT)	Columbia
1984	Clemson	I.M. Ibrahim	2–1	Indiana
1985	UCLA	Sigi Schmid	1–0 (8 OT)	American
1986	Duke	John Rennie	1–0	Akron
1987	Clemson	I.M. Ibrahim	2–0	San Diego St
1988	Indiana	Jerry Yeagley	1–0	Howard
1989	Santa Clara	Steve Sampson	1–1 (2 OT)	
	Virginia	Bruce Arena		
1990	UCLA	Sigi Schmid	1–0 (OT)	Rutgers
1991	Virginia	Bruce Arena	0–0*	Santa Clara
1992	Virginia	Bruce Arena	2–0	San Diego
1993	Virginia	Bruce Arena	2–0	S Carolina
1994	Virginia	Bruce Arena	1–0	Indiana
1995	Wisconsin	Jim Launder	2–0	Duke
1996	St. John's (NY)	Dave Masur	4–1	Florida International
1997	UCLA	Sigi Schmid	2–1	Virginia
1998	Indiana	Jerry Yeagley	3–1	Stanford
1999	Indiana	Jerry Yeagley	1–0	Santa Clara
2000	Connecticut	Ray Reid	2–0	Creighton
2001	N Carolina	Elmar Bolowich	2–0	Indiana

*Under a rule passed in 1991, the NCAA determined that when a score is tied after regulation and overtime, and the championship is determined by penalty kicks, the official score will be 0–0.

DIVISION II

Year	Champion	Year	Champion	Year	Champion
1972	SIU–Edwardsville	1982	Florida International	1992	Southern Connecticut St
1973	MO–St. Louis	1983	Seattle Pacific	1993	Seattle Pacific
1974	Adelphi	1984	Florida International	1994	Tampa
1975	Baltimore	1985	Seattle Pacific	1995	Southern Connecticut St
1976	Loyola (MD)	1986	Seattle Pacific	1996	Grand Canyon
1977	Alabama A&M	1987	Southern Connecticut St	1997	Cal St-Bakersfield
1978	Seattle Pacific	1988	Florida Tech	1998	Southern Connecticut St
1979	Alabama A&M	1989	New Hampshire College	1999	Southern Connecticut St
1980	Lock Haven	1990	Southern Connecticut St	2000	Cal St–Dominguez Hills
1981	Tampa	1991	Florida Tech	2001	Tampa

Men (Cont.)

DIVISION III

ear	Champion	Year	Champion	Year	Champion
1974	Brockport St	1984	Wheaton (IL)	1994	Bethany (WV)
1975	Babson	1985	NC–Greensboro	1995	Williams
1976	Brandeis	1986	NC–Greensboro	1996	College of New Jersey
1977	Lock Haven	1987	NC–Greensboro	1997	Wheaton (IL)
1978	Lock Haven	1988	UC–San Diego	1998	Ohio Wesleyan
1979	Babson	1989	Elizabethtown	1999	St. Lawrence
1980	Babson	1990	Glassboro St	2000	Messiah
1981	Glassboro St	1991	UC–San Diego	2001	Richard Stockton
1982	NC–Greensboro	1992	Kean		
1983	NC–Greensboro	1993	UC–San Diego		

Women

DIVISION I

Year	Champion	Coach	Score	Runner-Up
1982	N Carolina	Anson Dorrance	2–0	Central Florida
1983	N Carolina	Anson Dorrance	4–0	George Mason
1984	N Carolina	Anson Dorrance	2–0	Connecticut
1985	George Mason	Hank Leung	2–0	N Carolina
1986	N Carolina	Anson Dorrance	2–0	Colorado College
1987	N Carolina	Anson Dorrance	1–0	Massachusetts
1988	N Carolina	Anson Dorrance	4–1	N Carolina St
1989	N Carolina	Anson Dorrance	2–0	Colorado College
1990	N Carolina	Anson Dorrance	6–0	Connecticut
1991	N Carolina	Anson Dorrance	3–1	Wisconsin
1992	N Carolina	Anson Dorrance	9–1	Duke
1993	N Carolina	Anson Dorrance	6–0	George Mason
1994	N Carolina	Anson Dorrance	5–0	Notre Dame
1995	Notre Dame	Chris Petrucelli	1–0	Portland
1996	N Carolina	Anson Dorrance	1–0	Notre Dame
1997	N Carolina	Anson Dorrance	2–0	Connecticut
1998	Florida	Becky Burleigh	1–0	N Carolina
1999	N Carolina	Anson Dorrance	2–0	Notre Dame
2000	N Carolina	Anson Dorrance	2–1	UCLA
2001	Santa Clara	Jerry Smith	1–0	N Carolina

DIVISION II

Year	Champion
1988	Cal St–Hayward
1989	Barry
1990	Sonoma St
1991	Cal St–Dominguez Hills
1992	Barry
1993	Barry
1994	Franklin Pierce
1995	Franklin Pierce
1996	Franklin Pierce
1997	Franklin Pierce
1998	Lynn
1999	Franklin Pierce
2000	UC–San Diego
2001	UC-San Diego

DIVISION III

Year	Champion
1986	Rochester
1987	Rochester
1988	William Smith
1989	UC–San Diego
1990	Ithaca
1991	Ithaca
1992	Cortland St
1993	Trenton St
1994	Trenton St
1995	UC–San Diego
1996	UC–San Diego
1997	UC–San Diego
1998	Macalester
1999	UC–San Diego
2000	College of New Jersey*
2001	Ohio Wesleyan

*Formerly Trenton St

DIVISION I

Year	Champion	Coach	Score	Runner-Up
1982	UCLA*	Sharron Backus	2–0†	Fresno St
1983	Texas A&M	Bob Brock	2–0‡	Cal St–Fullerton
1984	UCLA	Sharron Backus	1–0#	Texas A&M
1985	UCLA	Sharron Backus	2–1**	Nebraska
1986	Cal St–Fullerton*	Judi Garman	3–0	Texas A&M
1987	Texas A&M	Bob Brock	4–1	UCLA
1988	UCLA	Sharron Backus	3–0	Fresno St
1989	UCLA*	Sharron Backus	1–0	Fresno St
1990	UCLA	Sharron Backus	2–0	Fresno St
1991	Arizona	Mike Candrea	5–1	UCLA
1992	UCLA*	Sharron Backus	2–0	Arizona
1993	Arizona	Mike Candrea	1–0	UCLA
1994	Arizona	Mike Candrea	4–0	Cal St–Northridge
1995	Vacated	—		Arizona
1996	Arizona*	Mike Candrea	6–4	Washington
1997	Arizona	Mike Candrea	10–2***	UCLA
1998	Fresno St	Margie Wright	1–0	Arizona
1999	UCLA	Sue Enquist	3–2	Washington
2000	Oklahoma	Patty Gasso	3–1	UCLA
2001	Arizona*	Mike Candrea	1–0	UCLA
2002	California	Diane Ninemire	6–0	Arizona

*Undefeated teams in final series. †Eight innings. ‡12 innings. #13 innings. **Nine innings. ***Five innings.

DIVISION II

Year	Champion	Year	Champion	Year	Champion
1982	Sam Houston St	1989	Cal St–Bakersfield	1996	Kennesaw St
1983	Cal St–Northridge	1990	Cal St–Bakersfield	1997	California (PA)*
1984	Cal St–Northridge	1991	Augustana (SD)	1998	California (PA)
1985	Cal St–Northridge	1992	Missouri Southern	1999	Humboldt St
1986	SF Austin St	1993	Florida Southern	2000	N Dakota St
1987	Cal St–Northridge	1994	Merrimack	2001	Nebraska–Omaha
1988	Cal St–Bakersfield	1995	Kennesaw St	2002	St. Mary's (IA)

DIVISION III

Year	Champion	Year	Champion	Year	Champion
1982	Sam Houston St	1988	Central (IA)	1995	Chapman
1982	Eastern Connecticut St*	1989	Trenton St*	1996	Trenton St*
1983	Trenton St	1990	Eastern Connecticut St	1997	Simpson (IA)*
1984	Buena Vista*	1991	Central (IA)	1998	WI–Stevens Point
1985	Eastern Connecticut St	1992	Trenton St	1999	Simpson (IA)
1986	Eastern Connecticut St	1993	Central (IA)	2000	St. Mary's
1987	Trenton St*	1994	Trenton St	2001	Muskingum*
				2002	Williams

*Undefeated teams in final series.

Swimming and Diving

Men

DIVISION I

Year	Champion	Coach	Pts	Runner-Up	Pts
1937	Michigan	Matt Mann	75	Ohio St	39
1938	Michigan	Matt Mann	46	Ohio St	45
1939	Michigan	Matt Mann	65	Ohio St	58
1940	Michigan	Matt Mann	45	Yale	42
1941	Michigan	Matt Mann	61	Yale	58
1942	Yale	Robert J.H. Kiphuth	71	Michigan	39
1943	Ohio St	Mike Peppe	81	Michigan	47
1944	Yale	Robert J.H. Kiphuth	39	Michigan	38
1945	Ohio St	Mike Peppe	56	Michigan	48
1946	Ohio St	Mike Peppe	61	Michigan	37
1947	Ohio St	Mike Peppe	66	Michigan	39
1948	Michigan	Matt Mann	44	Ohio St	41
1949	Ohio St	Mike Peppe	49	Iowa	35
1950	Ohio St	Mike Peppe	64	Yale	43
1951	Yale	Robert J.H. Kiphuth	81	Michigan St	60
1952	Ohio St	Mike Peppe	94	Yale	81

Men *(Cont.)*

DIVISION I *(Cont.)*

Year	Champion	Coach	Pts	Runner-Up	Pts
1953	Yale	Robert J.H. Kiphuth	96½	Ohio St	73½
1954	Ohio St	Mike Peppe	94	Michigan	67
1955	Ohio St	Mike Peppe	90	Yale/ Michigan	51
1956	Ohio St	Mike Peppe	68	Yale	54
1957	Michigan	Gus Stager	69	Yale	61
1958	Michigan	Gus Stager	72	Yale	63
1959	Michigan	Gus Stager	137½	Ohio St	44
1960	Southern Cal	Peter Daland	87	Michigan	73
1961	Michigan	Gus Stager	85	Southern Cal	62
1962	Ohio St	Mike Peppe	92	Southern Cal	46
1963	Southern Cal	Peter Daland	81	Yale	77
1964	Southern Cal	Peter Daland	96	Indiana	91
1965	Southern Cal	Peter Daland	285	Indiana	278½
1966	Southern Cal	Peter Daland	302	Indiana	286
1967	Stanford	Jim Gaughran	275	Southern Cal	260
1968	Indiana	James Counsilman	346	Yale	253
1969	Indiana	James Counsilman	427	Southern Cal	306
1970	Indiana	James Counsilman	332	Southern Cal	235
1971	Indiana	James Counsilman	351	Southern Cal	260
1972	Indiana	James Counsilman	390	Southern Cal	371
1973	Indiana	James Counsilman	358	Tennessee	294
1974	Southern Cal	Peter Daland	339	Indiana	338
1975	Southern Cal	Peter Daland	344	Indiana	274
1976	Southern Cal	Peter Daland	398	Tennessee	237
1977	Southern Cal	Peter Daland	385	Alabama	204
1978	Tennessee	Ray Bussard	307	Auburn	185
1979	California	Nort Thornton	287	Southern Cal	227
1980	California	Nort Thornton	234	Texas	220
1981	Texas	Eddie Reese	259	UCLA	189
1982	UCLA	Ron Ballatore	219	Texas	210
1983	Florida	Randy Reese	238	Southern Meth	227
1984	Florida	Randy Reese	287½	Texas	277
1985	Stanford	Skip Kenney	403½	Florida	302
1986	Stanford	Skip Kenney	404	California	335
1987	Stanford	Skip Kenney	374	Southern Cal	296
1988	Texas	Eddie Reese	424	Southern Cal	369½
1989	Texas	Eddie Reese	475	Stanford	396
1990	Texas	Eddie Reese	506	Southern Cal	423
1991	Texas	Eddie Reese	476	Stanford	420
1992	Stanford	Skip Kenney	632	Texas	356
1993	Stanford	Skip Kenney	520½	Michigan	396
1994	Stanford	Skip Kenney	566½	Texas	445
1995	Michigan	Jon Urbanchek	561	Stanford	475
1996	Texas	Eddie Reese	479	Auburn	443½
1997	Auburn	David Marsh	496½	Stanford	340
1998	Stanford	Skip Kenney	594	Auburn	394½
1999	Auburn	David Marsh	467½	Stanford	414½
2000	Texas	Eddie Reese	538	Auburn	385
2001	Texas	Eddie Reese	597½	Stanford	457½
2002	Texas	Eddie Reese	512	Stanford	5011

DIVISION II

Year	Champion	Year	Champion	Year	Champion
1963	SW Missouri St	1977	Cal St–Northridge	1991	Cal St–Bakersfield
1964	Bucknell	1978	Cal St–Northridge	1992	Cal St–Bakersfield
1965	San Diego St	1979	Cal St–Northridge	1993	Cal St–Bakersfield
1966	San Diego St	1980	Oakland (MI)	1994	Oakland (MI)
1967	UC–Santa Barbara	1981	Cal St–Northridge	1995	Oakland (MI)
1968	Long Beach St	1982	Cal St–Northridge	1996	Oakland (MI)
1969	UC–Irvine	1983	Cal St–Northridge	1997	Oakland (MI)
1970	UC–Irvine	1984	Cal St–Northridge	1998	Cal St–Bakersfield
1971	UC–Irvine	1985	Cal St–Northridge	1999	Drury
1972	Eastern Michigan	1986	Cal St–Bakersfield	2000	Cal St–Bakersfield
1973	Cal St–Chico	1987	Cal St–Bakersfield	2001	Cal St–Bakersfield
1974	Cal St–Chico	1988	Cal St–Bakersfield	2002	Cal St–Bakersfield
1975	Cal St–Northridge	1989	Cal St–Bakersfield		
1976	Cal Sf–Chico	1990	Cal St–Bakersfield		

DIVISION III

Year	Champion	Year	Champion	Year	Champion
1975	Cal St–Chico	1985	Kenyon	1995	Kenyon
1976	St. Lawrence	1986	Kenyon	1996	Kenyon
1977	Johns Hopkins	1987	Kenyon	1997	Kenyon
1978	Johns Hopkins	1988	Kenyon	1998	Kenyon
1979	Johns Hopkins	1989	Kenyon	1999	Kenyon
1980	Kenyon	1990	Kenyon	2000	Kenyon
1981	Kenyon	1991	Kenyon	2001	Kenyon
1982	Kenyon	1992	Kenyon	2002	Kenyon
1983	Kenyon	1993	Kenyon		
1984	Kenyon	1994	Kenyon		

Women
DIVISION I

Year	Champion	Coach	Pts	Runner-Up	Pts
1982	Florida	Randy Reese	505	Stanford	383
1983	Stanford	George Haines	418½	Florida	389½
1984	Texas	Richard Quick	392	Stanford	324
1985	Texas	Richard Quick	643	Florida	400
1986	Texas	Richard Quick	633	Florida	586
1987	Texas	Richard Quick	648½	Stanford	631½
1988	Texas	Richard Quick	661	Florida	542½
1989	Stanford	Richard Quick	610½	Texas	547
1990	Texas	Mark Schubert	632	Stanford	622½
1991	Texas	Mark Schubert	746	Stanford	653
1992	Stanford	Richard Quick	735½	Texas	651
1993	Stanford	Richard Quick	649½	Florida	421
1994	Stanford	Richard Quick	512	Texas	421
1995	Stanford	Richard Quick	497½	Michigan	478½
1996	Stanford	Richard Quick	478	SMU	397
1997	Southern Cal	Mark Schubert	406	Stanford	395
1998	Stanford	Richard Quick	422	Arizona	378
1999	Georgia	Jack Bauerle	504½	Stanford	441
2000	Georgia	Jack Bauerle	490½	Arizona	472
2001	Georgia	Jack Bauerle	389	Stanford	387½
2002	Auburn	David Marsh	474	Georgia	386

DIVISION II

Year	Champion	Year	Champion	Year	Champion
1982	Cal St–Northridge	1989	Cal St–Northridge	1996	Air Force
1983	Clarion	1990	Oakland (MI)	1997	Drury
1984	Clarion	1991	Oakland (MI)	1998	Drury
1985	S Florida	1992	Oakland (MI)	1999	Drury
1986	Clarion	1993	Oakland (MI)	2000	Drury
1987	Cal St–Northridge	1994	Oakland (MI)	2001	Truman St
1988	Cal St–Northridge	1995	Air Force	2002	Truman St

DIVISION III

Year	Champion	Year	Champion	Year	Champion
1982	Williams	1989	Kenyon	1996	Kenyon
1983	Williams	1990	Kenyon	1997	Kenyon
1984	Kenyon	1991	Kenyon	1998	Kenyon
1985	Kenyon	1992	Kenyon	1999	Kenyon
1986	Kenyon	1993	Kenyon	2000	Kenyon
1987	Kenyon	1994	Kenyon	2001	Denison
1988	Kenyon	1995	Kenyon	2002	Kenyon

Tennis

Men

INDIVIDUAL CHAMPIONS 1883–1945

Year	Champion	Year	Champion
1883	Joseph Clark, Harvard (spring)	1914	George Church, Princeton
1883	Howard Taylor, Harvard (fall)	1915	Richard Williams II, Harvard
1884	W.P. Knapp, Yale	1916	G. Colket Caner, Harvard
1885	W.P. Knapp, Yale	1917–18	No tournament
1886	G.M. Brinley, Trinity (CT)	1919	Charles Garland, Yale
1887	P.S. Sears, Harvard	1920	Lascelles Banks, Yale
1888	P.S. Sears, Harvard	1921	Philip Neer, Stanford
1889	R.P. Huntington Jr, Yale	1922	Lucien Williams, Yale
1890	Fred Hovey, Harvard	1923	Carl Fischer, Philadelphia Osteo
1891	Fred Hovey, Harvard	1924	Wallace Scott, Washington
1892	William Larned, Cornell	1925	Edward Chandler, California
1893	Malcolm Chace, Brown	1926	Edward Chandler, California
1894	Malcolm Chace, Yale	1927	Wilmer Allison, Texas
1895	Malcolm Chace, Yale	1928	Julius Seligson, Lehigh
1896	Malcolm Whitman, Harvard	1929	Berkeley Bell, Texas
1897	S.G. Thompson, Princeton	1930	Clifford Sutter, Tulane
1898	Leo Ware, Harvard	1931	Keith Gledhill, Stanford
1899	Dwight Davis, Harvard	1932	Clifford Sutter, Tulane
1900	Raymond Little, Princeton	1933	Jack Tidball, UCLA
1901	Fred Alexander, Princeton	1934	Gene Mako, Southern Cal
1902	William Clothier, Harvard	1935	Wilbur Hess, Rice
1903	E.B. Dewhurst, Pennsylvania	1936	Ernest Sutter, Tulane
1904	Robert LeRoy, Columbia	1937	Ernest Sutter, Tulane
1905	E.B. Dewhurst, Pennsylvania	1938	Frank Guernsey, Rice
1906	Robert LeRoy, Columbia	1939	Frank Guernsey, Rice
1907	G. Peabody Gardner Jr, Harvard	1940	Donald McNeil, Kenyon
1908	Nat Niles, Harvard	1941	Joseph Hunt, Navy
1909	Wallace Johnson, Pennsylvania	1942	Frederick Schroeder Jr, Stanford
1910	R.A. Holden Jr, Yale	1943	Pancho Segura, Miami (FL)
1911	E.H. Whitney, Harvard	1944	Pancho Segura, Miami (FL)
1912	George Church, Princeton	1945	Pancho Segura, Miami (FL)
1913	Richard Williams II, Harvard		

DIVISION I

Year	Champion	Coach	Pts	Runner-Up	Pts	Individual Champion
1946	Southern Cal	William Moyle	9	William & Mary	6	Robert Falkenburg, Southern Cal
1947	William & Mary	Sharvey G. Umbeck	10	Rice	4	Gardner Larned, William & Mary
1948	William & Mary	Sharvey G. Umbeck	6	San Francisco	5	Harry Likas, San Francisco
1949	San Francisco	Norman Brooks	7	Rollins/Tulane/ Washington	4	Jack Tuero, Tulane
1950	UCLA	William Ackerman	11	California	5	Herbert Flam, UCLA
				Southern Cal	5	
1951	Southern Cal	Louis Wheeler	9	Cincinnati	7	Tony Trabert, Cincinnati
1952	UCLA	J.D. Morgan	11	California	5	Hugh Stewart, Southern Cal
				Southern Cal	5	
1953	UCLA	J.D. Morgan	11	California	6	Hamilton Richardson, Tulane
1954	UCLA	J.D. Morgan	15	Southern Cal	10	Hamilton Richardson, Tulane
1955	Southern Cal	George Toley	12	Texas	7	Jose Aguero, Tulane
1956	UCLA	J.D. Morgan	15	Southern Cal	14	Alejandro Olmedo, Southern Cal
1957	Michigan	William Murphy	10	Tulane	9	Barry MacKay, Michigan
1958	Southern Cal	George Toley	13	Stanford	9	Alejandro Olmedo, Southern Cal
1959	Notre Dame Tulane	Thomas Fallon Emmet Pare	8 8			Whitney Reed, San Jose St
1960	UCLA	J.D. Morgan	18	Southern Cal	8	Larry Nagler, UCLA
1961	UCLA	J.D. Morgan	17	Southern Cal	16	Allen Fox, UCLA
1962	Southern Cal	George Toley	22	UCLA	12	Rafael Osuna, Southern Cal
1963	Southern Cal	George Toley	27	UCLA	19	Dennis Ralston, Southern Cal
1964	Southern Cal	George Toley	26	UCLA	25	Dennis Ralston, Southern Cal
1965	UCLA	J.D. Morgan	31	Miami (FL)	13	Arthur Ashe, UCLA
1966	Southern Cal	George Toley	27	UCLA	23	Charles Pasarell, UCLA
1967	Southern Cal	George Toley	28	UCLA	23	Bob Lutz, Southern Cal
1968	Southern Cal	George Toley	31	Rice	23	Stan Smith, Southern Cal
1969	Southern Cal	George Toley	35	UCLA	23	Joaquin Loyo-Mayo, Southern Cal
1970	UCLA	Glenn Bassett	26	Trinity (TX) Rice	22 22	Jeff Borowiak, UCLA

Men (Cont.)

DIVISION I (Cont.)

Year	Champion	Coach	Pts	Runner-Up	Pts	Individual Champion
1971 ....UCLA	Glenn Bassett	35	Trinity (TX)	27	Jimmy Connors, UCLA
1972 ....Trinity (TX)	Clarence Mabry	36	Stanford	30	Dick Stockton, Trinity (TX)
1973 ....Stanford	Dick Gould	33	Southern Cal	28	Alex Mayer, Stanford
1974 ....Stanford	Dick Gould	30	Southern Cal	25	John Whitlinger, Stanford
1975 ....UCLA	Glenn Bassett	27	Miami (FL)	20	Bill Martin, UCLA
1976 ....Southern Cal	George Toley	21			Bill Scanlon, Trinity (TX)
UCLA	Glenn Bassett	21			
1977 ....Stanford	Dick Gould		Trinity (TX)		Matt Mitchell, Stanford
1978 ....Stanford	Dick Gould		UCLA		John McEnroe, Stanford
1979 ....UCLA	Glenn Bassett		Trinity (TX)		Kevin Curren, Texas
1980 ....Stanford	Dick Gould		California		Robert Van't Hof, Southern Cal
1981 ....Stanford	Dick Gould		UCLA		Tim Mayotte, Stanford
1982 ....UCLA	Glenn Bassett		Pepperdine		Mike Leach, Michigan
1983 ....Stanford	Dick Gould		SMU		Greg Holmes, Utah
1984 ....UCLA	Glenn Bassett		Stanford		Mikael Pernfors, Georgia
1985 ....Georgia	Dan Magill		UCLA		Mikael Pernfors, Georgia
1986 ....Stanford	Dick Gould		Pepperdine		Dan Goldie, Stanford
1987 ....Georgia	Dan Magill		UCLA		Andrew Burrow, Miami (FL)
1988 ....Stanford	Dick Gould		Louisiana St		Robby Weiss, Pepperdine
1989 ....Stanford	Dick Gould		Georgia		Donni Leaycraft, Louisiana St
1990 ....Stanford	Dick Gould		Tennessee		Steve Bryan, Texas
1991 ....Southern Cal	Dick Leach		Georgia		Jared Palmer, Stanford
1992 ....Stanford	Dick Gould		Notre Dame		Alex O'Brien, Stanford
1993 ....Southern Cal	Dick Leach		Georgia		Chris Woodruff, Tennessee
1994 ....Southern Cal	Dick Leach		Stanford		Mark Merklein, Florida
1995 ....Stanford	Dick Gould		Mississippi		Sargis Sargsian, Arizona St
1996 ....Stanford	Dick Gould		UCLA		Cecil Mamiit, Southern Cal
1997 ....Stanford	Dick Gould		Georgia		Luke Smith, UNLV
1998 ....Stanford	Dick Gould		Georgia		Bob Bryan, Stanford
1999 ....Georgia	Manuel Diaz		UCLA		Jeff Morrison, Florida
2000 ....Stanford	Dick Gould		VA–Commonwealth		Alex Kim, Stanford
2001 ....Georgia	Manuel Diaz		Tennessee		Matias Boeker, Georgia
2002 ....Southern Cal	Dick Leach		Georgia		Matias Boeker, Georgia

Note: Prior to 1977, individual wins counted in the team's total points. In 1977, a dual-match single-elimination team championship was initiated, eliminating the point system.

DIVISION II

Year	Champion	Year	Champion	Year	Champion
1963 ....Cal St–LA		1977 ....UC–Irvine		1991 ....Rollins	
1964 ....Cal St–LA/S Illinois		1978 ....SIU–Edwardsville		1992 ....UC–Davis	
1965 ....Cal St–LA		1979 ....SIU–Edwardsville		1993 ....Lander	
1966 ....Rollins		1980 ....SIU–Edwardsville		1994 ....Lander	
1967 ....Long Beach St		1981 ....SIU–Edwardsville		1995 ....Lander	
1968 ....Fresno St		1982 ....SIU–Edwardsville		1996 ....Lander	
1969 ....Cal St–Northridge		1983 ....SIU–Edwardsville		1997 ....Lander	
1970 ....UC–Irvine		1984 ....SIU–Edwardsville		1998 ....Lander	
1971 ....UC–Irvine		1985 ....Chapman		1999 ....Lander	
1972 ....UC–Irvine/ Rollins		1986 ....Cal Poly–SLO		2000 ....Lander	
1973 ....UC–Irvine		1987 ....Chapman		2001 ....Rollins	
1974 ....San Diego		1988 ....Chapman		2002 ....BYU-Hawaii	
1975 ....UC–Irvine/San Diego		1989 ....Hampton			
1976 ....Hampton		1990 ....Cal Poly–SLO			

DIVISION III

Year	Champion	Year	Champion	Year	Champion
1976 ....Kalamazoo		1985 ....Swarthmore		1995 ....UC–Santa Cruz	
1977 ....Swarthmore		1986 ....Kalamazoo		1996 ....UC–Santa Cruz	
1978 ....Kalamazoo		1987 ....Kalamazoo		1997 ....Washington (MD)	
1979 ....Redlands		1988 ....Washington & Lee		1998 ....UC–Santa Cruz	
1980 ....Gustavus Adolphus		1989 ....UC–Santa Cruz		1999 ....Williams	
1981 ....Claremont-M-S/ Swarthmore		1990 ....Swarthmore		2000 ....Trinity (TX)	
1982 ....Gustavus Adolphus		1991 ....Kalamazoo		2001 ....Williams	
1983 ....Redlands		1992 ....Kalamazoo		2002 ....Williams	
1984 ....Redlands		1993 ....Kalamazoo			
		1994 ....Washington (MD)			

Women
DIVISION I

Year	Champion	Coach	Runner-Up	Individual Champion
1982	Stanford	Frank Brennan	UCLA	Alycia Moulton, Stanford
1983	Southern Cal	Dave Borelli	Trinity (TX)	Beth Herr, Southern Cal
1984	Stanford	Frank Brennan	Southern Cal	Lisa Spain, Georgia
1985	Southern Cal	Dave Borelli	Miami (FL)	Linda Gates, Stanford
1986	Stanford	Frank Brennan	Southern Cal	Patty Fendick, Stanford
1987	Stanford	Frank Brennan	Georgia	Patty Fendick, Stanford
1988	Stanford	Frank Brennan	Florida	Shaun Stafford, Florida
1989	Stanford	Frank Brennan	UCLA	Sandra Birch, Stanford
1990	Stanford	Frank Brennan	Florida	Debbie Graham, Stanford
1991	Stanford	Frank Brennan	UCLA	Sandra Birch, Stanford
1992	Florida	Andy Brandi	Texas	Lisa Raymond, Florida
1993	Texas	Jeff Moore	Stanford	Lisa Raymond, Florida
1994	Georgia	Jeff Wallace	Stanford	Angela Lettiere, Georgia
1995	Texas	Jeff Moore	Florida	Keri Phebus, UCLA
1996	Florida	Andy Brandi	Stanford	Jill Craybas, Florida
1997	Stanford	Frank Brennan	Florida	Lilia Osterloh, Stanford
1998	Florida	Andy Brandi	Duke	Vanessa Webb, Duke
1999	Stanford	Frank Brennan	Florida	Zuzana Lesenarova, UC–SD
2000	Georgia	Jeff Wallace	Stanford	Laura Granville, Stanford
2001	Stanford	Lele Forood	Vanderbilt	Laura Granville, Stanford
2002	Stanford	Lele Forood	Florida	Bea Bielek, Wake Forest

DIVISION II

Year	Champion	Year	Champion	Year	Champion
1982	Cal St–Northridge	1989	SIU–Edwardsville	1996	Armstrong St
1983	TN–Chattanooga	1990	UC–Davis	1997	Lynn
1984	TN–Chattanooga	1991	Cal Poly–Pomona	1998	Lynn
1985	TN–Chattanooga	1992	Cal Poly–Pomona	1999	BYU–Hawaii
1986	SIU–Edwardsville	1993	UC–Davis	2000	BYU–Hawaii
1987	SIU–Edwardsville	1994	N Florida	2001	Lynn
1988	SIU–Edwardsville	1995	Armstrong St	2002	BYU–Hawaii

DIVISION III

Year	Champion	Year	Champion	Year	Champion
1982	Occidental	1989	UC–San Diego	1996	Emory
1983	Principia	1990	Gustavus Adolphus	1997	Kenyon
1984	Davidson	1991	Mary Washington	1998	Kenyon
1985	UC–San Diego	1992	Pomona-Pitzer	1999	Amherst
1986	Trenton St	1993	Kenyon	2000	Trinity (TX)
1987	UC–San Diego	1994	UC–San Diego	2001	Williams
1988	Mary Washington	1995	Kenyon	2002	Williams

Indoor Track and Field

Men
DIVISION I

Year	Champion	Coach	Pts	Runner-Up	Pts
1965	Missouri	Tom Botts	14	Oklahoma St	12
1966	Kansas	Bob Timmons	14	Southern Cal	13
1967	Southern Cal	Vern Wolfe	26	Oklahoma	17
1968	Villanova	Jim Elliott	35	Southern Cal	25
1969	Kansas	Bob Timmons	41½	Villanova	33
1970	Kansas	Bob Timmons	27½	Villanova	26
1971	Villanova	Jim Elliott	22	UTEP	19¼
1972	Southern Cal	Vern Wolfe	19	Bowling Green/ Mich St	18
1973	Manhattan	Fred Dwyer	18	Kansas/Kent St/UTEP	12
1974	UTEP	Ted Banks	19	Colorado	18
1975	UTEP	Ted Banks	36	Kansas	17½
1976	UTEP	Ted Banks	23	Villanova	15
1977	Washington St	John Chaplin	25½	UTEP	25
1978	UTEP	Ted Banks	44	Auburn	38
1979	Villanova	Jim Elliott	52	UTEP	51
1980	UTEP	Ted Banks	76	Villanova	42
1981	UTEP	Ted Banks	76	SMU	51

Men (Cont.)
DIVISION I (Cont.)

Year	Champion	Coach	Pts	Runner-Up	Pts
1982	UTEP	John Wedel	67	Arkansas	30
1983	SMU	Ted McLaughlin	43	Villanova	32
1984	Arkansas	John McDonnell	38	Washington St	28
1985	Arkansas	John McDonnell	70	Tennessee	29
1986	Arkansas	John McDonnell	49	Villanova	22
1987	Arkansas	John McDonnell	39	SMU	31
1988	Arkansas	John McDonnell	34	Illinois	29
1989	Arkansas	John McDonnell	34	Florida	31
1990	Arkansas	John McDonnell	44	Texas A&M	36
1991	Arkansas	John McDonnell	34	Georgetown	27
1992	Arkansas	John McDonnell	53	Clemson	46
1993	Arkansas	John McDonnell	66	Clemson	30
1994	Arkansas	John McDonnell	83	UTEP	45
1995	Arkansas	John McDonnell	59	GMU/Tennessee	26
1996	George Mason	John Cook	39	Nebraska	31½
1997	Arkansas	John McDonnell	59	Auburn	27
1998	Arkansas	John McDonnell	56	Stanford	36½
1999	Arkansas	John McDonnell	65	Stanford	42½
2000	Arkansas	John McDonnell	69½	Stanford	52
2001	Louisiana St	Pat Henry	34	Texas Christian	33
2002	Tennessee	Bill Webb	62½	Louisiana St	44

DIVISION II

Year	Champion	Year	Champion	Year	Champion
1985	SE Missouri St	1991	St. Augustine's	1997	Abilene Christian
1986	Not held	1992	St. Augustine's	1998	Abilene Christian
1987	St. Augustine's	1993	Abilene Christian	1999	Abilene Christian
1988	Abil. Christian/St. August.	1994	Abilene Christian	2000	Abilene Christian
1989	St. Augustine's	1995	St. Augustine's	2001	St. Augustine's
1990	St. Augustine's	1996	Abilene Christian	2002	Abilene Christian

DIVISION III

Year	Champion	Year	Champion	Year	Champion
1985	St. Thomas (MN)	1991	WI–La Crosse	1997	WI–La Crosse
1986	Frostburg St	1992	WI–La Crosse	1998	Lincoln (PA)
1987	WI–La Crosse	1993	WI–La Crosse	1999	Lincoln (PA)
1988	WI–La Crosse	1994	WI–La Crosse	2000	Lincoln (PA)
1989	N Central	1995	Lincoln (PA)	2001	WI–La Crosse
1990	Lincoln (PA)	1996	Lincoln (PA)	2002	WI–La Crosse

Women
DIVISION I

Year	Champion	Coach	Pts	Runner-Up	Pts
1983	Nebraska	Gary Pepin	47	Tennessee	44
1984	Nebraska	Gary Pepin	59	Tennessee	48
1985	Florida St	Gary Winckler	34	Texas	32
1986	Texas	Terry Crawford	31	Southern Cal	26
1987	Louisiana St	Loren Seagrave	49	Tennessee	30
1988	Texas	Terry Crawford	71	Villanova	52
1989	Louisiana St	Pat Henry	61	Villanova	34
1990	Texas	Terry Crawford	50	Wisconsin	26
1991	Louisiana St	Pat Henry	48	Texas	39
1992	Florida	Bev Kearney	50	Stanford	26
1993	Louisiana St	Pat Henry	49	Wisconsin	44
1994	Louisiana St	Pat Henry	48	Alabama	29
1995	Louisiana St	Pat Henry	40	UCLA	37
1996	Louisiana St	Pat Henry	52	Georgia	34
1997	Louisiana St	Pat Henry	49	Texas/Wisconsin	39
1998	Texas	Bev Kearney	60	Louisiana St	30
1999	Texas	Bev Kearney	61	Louisiana St	57
2000	UCLA	Jeanette Bolden	51	S Carolina	41
2001	UCLA	Jeanette Bolden	53½	S Carolina	40
2002	Louisiana St	Pat Henry	57	Florida	35

Women (Cont.)

DIVISION II

Year	Champion	Year	Champion	Year	Champion
1985	St. Augustine's	1991	Abilene Christian	1997	Abilene Christian
1986	Not held	1992	Alabama A&M	1998	Abilene Christian
1987	St. Augustine's	1993	Abilene Christian	1999	Abilene Christian
1988	Abilene Christian	1994	Abilene Christian	2000	Abilene Christian
1989	Abilene Christian	1995	Abilene Christian	2001	St. Augustine's
1990	Abilene Christian	1996	Abilene Christian	2002	N Dakota St

DIVISION III

Year	Champion	Year	Champion	Year	Champion
1985	MA–Boston	1991	Cortland St	1997	Christopher Newport
1986	MA–Boston	1992	Christopher Newport	1998	Christopher Newport
1987	MA–Boston	1993	Lincoln (PA)	1999	Wheaton (MA)
1988	Christopher Newport	1994	WI–Oshkosh	2000	Wheaton (MA)
1989	Christopher Newport	1995	WI–Oshkosh	2001	Wheaton (MA)
1990	Christopher Newport	1996	WI–Oshkosh	2002	Wheaton (MA)

Outdoor Track and Field

Men

DIVISION I

Year	Champion	Coach	Pts	Runner-Up	Pts
1921	Illinois	Harry Gill	20†	Notre Dame	16†
1922	California	Walter Christie	28†	Penn St	19†
1923	Michigan	Stephen Farrell	29†	Mississippi St	16
1924	No meet				
1925	Stanford*	R.L. Templeton	31†		
1926	Southern Cal*	Dean Cromwell	27†		
1927	Illinois*	Harry Gill	35†		
1928	Stanford	R.L. Templeton	72	Ohio St	31
1929	Ohio St	Frank Castleman	50	Washington	42
1930	Southern Cal	Dean Cromwell	55†	Washington	40
1931	Southern Cal	Dean Cromwell	77†	Ohio St	31†
1932	Indiana	Billy Hayes	56	Ohio St	49†
1933	Louisiana St	Bernie Moore	58	Southern Cal	54
1934	Stanford	R.L. Templeton	63	Southern Cal	54†
1935	Southern Cal	Dean Cromwell	74†	Ohio St	40†
1936	Southern Cal	Dean Cromwell	103†	Ohio St	73
1937	Southern Cal	Dean Cromwell	62	Stanford	50
1938	Southern Cal	Dean Cromwell	67†	Stanford	38
1939	Southern Cal	Dean Cromwell	86	Stanford	44†
1940	Southern Cal	Dean Cromwell	47	Stanford	28†
1941	Southern Cal	Dean Cromwell	81†	Indiana	50
1942	Southern Cal	Dean Cromwell	85†	Ohio St	44†
1943	Southern Cal	Dean Cromwell	46	California	39
1944	Illinois	Leo Johnson	79	Notre Dame	43
1945	Navy	E.J. Thomson	62	Illinois	48†
1946	Illinois	Leo Johnson	78	Southern Cal	42†
1947	Illinois	Leo Johnson	59†	Southern Cal	34†
1948	Minnesota	James Kelly	46	Southern Cal	41†
1949	Southern Cal	Jess Hill	55†	UCLA	31
1950	Southern Cal	Jess Hill	49†	Stanford	28
1951	Southern Cal	Jess Mortenson	56	Cornell	40
1952	Southern Cal	Jess Mortenson	66†	San Jose St	24†
1953	Southern Cal	Jess Mortenson	80	Illinois	41
1954	Southern Cal	Jess Mortenson	66†	Illinois	31†
1955	Southern Cal	Jess Mortenson	42	UCLA	34
1956	UCLA	Elvin Drake	55†	Kansas	51
1957	Villanova	James Elliott	47	California	32
1958	Southern Cal	Jess Mortenson	48†	Kansas	40†
1959	Kansas	Bill Easton	73	San Jose St	48
1960	Kansas	Bill Easton	50	Southern Cal	37

Men (Cont.)
DIVISION I (Cont.)

Year	Champion	Coach	Pts	Runner-Up	Pts
1961	Southern Cal	Jess Mortenson	65	Oregon	47
1962	Oregon	William Bowerman	85	Villanova	40†
1963	Southern Cal	Vern Wolfe	61	Stanford	42
1964	Oregon	William Bowerman	70	San Jose St	40
1965	Oregon	William Bowerman	32		
	Southern Cal	Vern Wolfe	32		
1966	UCLA	Jim Bush	81	Brigham Young	33
1967	Southern Cal	Vern Wolfe	86	Oregon	40
1968	Southern Cal	Vern Wolfe	58	Washington St	57
1969	San Jose St	Bud Winter	48	Kansas	45
1970	Brigham Young	Clarence Robison	35		
	Kansas	Bob Timmons	35		
	Oregon	William Bowerman	35		
1971	UCLA	Jim Bush	52	Southern Cal	41
1972	UCLA	Jim Bush	82	Southern Cal	49
1973	UCLA	Jim Bush	56	Oregon	31
1974	Tennessee	Stan Huntsman	60	UCLA	56
1975	UTEP	Ted Banks	55	UCLA	42
1976	Southern Cal	Vern Wolfe	64	UTEP	44
1977	Arizona St	Senon Castillo	64	UTEP	50
1978	UCLA/UTEP	Jim Bush/Ted Banks	50		
1979	UTEP	Ted Banks	64	Villanova	48
1980	UTEP	Ted Banks	69	UCLA	46
1981	UTEP	Ted Banks	70	SMU	57
1982	UTEP	John Wedel	105	Tennessee	94
1983	SMU	Ted McLaughlin	104	Tennessee	102
1984	Oregon	Bill Dellinger	113	Washington St	94½
1985	Arkansas	John McDonnell	61	Washington St	46
1986	SMU	Ted McLaughlin	53	Washington St	52
1987	UCLA	Bob Larsen	81	Texas	28
1988	UCLA	Bob Larsen	82	Texas	41
1989	Louisiana St	Pat Henry	53	Texas A&M	51
1990	Louisiana St	Pat Henry	44	Arkansas	36
1991	Tennessee	Doug Brown	51	Washington St	42
1992	Arkansas	John McDonnell	60	Tennessee	46½
1993	Arkansas	John McDonnell	69	LSU/Ohio St	45
1994	Arkansas	John McDonnell	83	UTEP	45
1995	Arkansas	John McDonnell	61½	UCLA	55
1996	Arkansas	John McDonnell	55	George Mason	40
1997	Arkansas	John McDonnell	55	Texas	42½
1998	Arkansas	John McDonnell	58½	Stanford	51
1999	Arkansas	John McDonnell	59	Stanford	52
2000	Stanford	Vin Lananna	72	Arkansas	59
2001	Tennessee	Bill Webb	50	Texas Christian	49
2002	Louisiana St	Pat Henry	64	Tennessee	57

*Unofficial championship. †Fraction of a point.

DIVISION II

Year	Champion	Year	Champion	Year	Champion
1963	MD–Eastern Shore	1976	UC–Irvine	1990	St. Augustine's
1964	Fresno St	1977	Cal St–Hayward	1991	St. Augustine's
1965	San Diego St	1978	Cal St–LA	1992	St. Augustine's
1966	San Diego St	1979	Cal Poly–SLO	1993	St. Augustine's
1967	Long Beach St	1980	Cal Poly–SLO	1994	St. Augustine's
1968	Cal Poly–SLO	1981	Cal Poly–SLO	1995	St. Augustine's
1969	Cal Poly–SLO	1982	Abilene Christian	1996	Abilene Christian
1970	Cal Poly–SLO	1983	Abilene Christian	1997	Abilene Christian
1971	Kentucky St	1984	Abilene Christian	1998	St. Augustine's
1972	Eastern Michigan	1985	Abilene Christian	1999	Abilene Christian
1973	Norfolk St	1986	Abilene Christian	2000	Abilene Christian
1974	Eastern Illinois	1987	Abilene Christian	2001	St. Augustine's
	Norfolk St	1988	Abilene Christian	2002	Abilene Christian
1975	Cal St–Northridge	1989	St. Augustine's		

Men (Cont.)

DIVISION III

Year	Champion	Year	Champion	Year	Champion
1974	Ashland	1984	Glassboro St	1994	N Central
1975	Southern–N Orleans	1985	Lincoln (PA)	1995	Lincoln (PA)
1976	Southern–N Orleans	1986	Frostburg St	1996	Lincoln (PA)
1977	Southern–N Orleans	1987	Frostburg St	1997	WI–La Crosse
1978	Occidental	1988	WI–La Crosse	1998	N Central
1979	Slippery Rock	1989	N Central	1999	Lincoln (PA)
1980	Glassboro St	1990	Lincoln (PA)	2000	Nebraska Wesleyan
1981	Glassboro St	1991	WI–La Crosse	2001	WI–La Crosse
1982	Glassboro St	1992	WI–La Crosse	2002	WI–La Crosse
1983	Glassboro St	1993	WI–La Crosse		

Women

DIVISION I

Year	Champion	Coach	Pts	Runner-Up	Pts
1982	UCLA	Scott Chisam	153	Tennessee	126
1983	UCLA	Scott Chisam	116½	Florida St	108
1984	Florida St	Gary Winckler	145	Tennessee	124
1985	Oregon	Tom Heinonen	52	Florida St/LSU	46
1986	Texas	Terry Crawford	65	Alabama	55
1987	Louisiana St	Loren Seagrave	62	Alabama	53
1988	Louisiana St	Loren Seagrave	61	UCLA	58
1989	Louisiana St	Pat Henry	86	UCLA	47
1990	Louisiana St	Pat Henry	53	UCLA	46
1991	Louisiana St	Pat Henry	78	Texas	67
1992	Louisiana St	Pat Henry	87	Florida	81
1993	Louisiana St	Pat Henry	93	Wisconsin	44
1994	Louisiana St	Pat Henry	86	Texas	43
1995	Louisiana St	Pat Henry	69	UCLA	58
1996	Louisiana St	Pat Henry	81	Texas	52
1997	Louisiana St	Pat Henry	63	Texas	62
1998	Texas	Bev Kearney	60	UCLA	55
1999	Texas	Bev Kearney	62	UCLA	60
2000	Louisiana St	Pat Henry	59	Southern Cal	56
2001	Southern Cal	Ron Allice	64	UCLA	55
2002	South Carolina	Curtis Frye	82	UCLA	72

DIVISION II

Year	Champion	Year	Champion	Year	Champion
1982	Cal Poly–SLO	1989	Cal Poly–SLO	1996	Abilene Christian
1983	Cal Poly–SLO	1990	Cal Poly–SLO	1997	St. Augustine's
1984	Cal Poly–SLO	1991	Cal Poly–SLO	1998	Abilene Christian
1985	Abilene Christian	1992	Alabama A&M	1999	Abilene Christian
1986	Abilene Christian	1993	Alabama A&M	2000	St. Augustine's
1987	Abilene Christian	1994	Alabama A&M	2001	St. Augustine's
1988	Abilene Christian	1995	Abilene Christian	2002	St. Augustine's

DIVISION III

Year	Champion	Year	Champion	Year	Champion
1982	Central (IA)	1989	Chris. Newport	1996	WI–Oshkosh
1983	WI–La Crosse	1990	WI–Oshkosh	1997	WI–Oshkosh
1984	WI–La Crosse	1991	WI–Oshkosh	1998	Chris. Newport
1985	Cortland State	1992	Chris. Newport	1999	Lincoln (PA)
1986	MA–Boston	1993	Lincoln (PA)	2000	Lincoln (PA)
1987	Chris. Newport	1994	Chris. Newport	2001	Wheaton (MA)
1988	Chris. Newport	1995	WI–Oshkosh	2002	Wheaton (MA)

Volleyball

Men

Year	Champion	Coach	Score	Runner-Up	Most Outstanding Player
1970	UCLA	Al Scates	3–0	Long Beach St	Dane Holtzman, UCLA
1971	UCLA	Al Scates	3–0	UC–Santa Barbara	Kirk Kilgore, UCLA
1972	UCLA	Al Scates	3–2	San Diego St	Tim Bonynge, UC–Santa Barbara Dick Irvin, UCLA
1973	San Diego St	Jack Henn	3–1	Long Beach St	Duncan McFarland, San Diego St

Men (Cont.)

Year	Champion	Coach	Score	Runner-Up	Most Outstanding Player
1974	UCLA	Al Scates	3–2	UC–Santa Barbara	Bob Leonard, UCLA
1975	UCLA	Al Scates	3–1	UC–Santa Barbara	John Bekins, UCLA
1976	UCLA	Al Scates	3–0	Pepperdine	Joe Mika, UCLA
1977	Southern Cal	Ernie Hix	3–1	Ohio St	Celso Kalache, Southern Cal
1978	Pepperdine	Marv Dunphy	3–2	UCLA	Mike Blanchard, Pepperdine
1979	UCLA	Al Scates	3–1	Southern Cal	Sinjin Smith, UCLA
1980	Southern Cal	Ernie Hix	3–1	UCLA	Dusty Dvorak, Southern Cal
1981	UCLA	Al Scates	3–2	Southern Cal	Karch Kiraly, UCLA
1982	UCLA	Al Scates	3–0	Penn St	Karch Kiraly, UCLA
1983	UCLA	Al Scates	3–0	Pepperdine	Ricci Luyties, UCLA
1984	UCLA	Al Scates	3–1	Pepperdine	Ricci Luyties, UCLA
1985	Pepperdine	Marv Dunphy	3–1	Southern Cal	Bob Ctvrtlik, Pepperdine
1986	Pepperdine	Rod Wilde	3–2	Southern Cal	Steve Friedman, Pepperdine
1987	UCLA	Al Scates	3–0	Southern Cal	Ozzie Volstad, UCLA
1988	Southern Cal	Bob Yoder	3–2	UC–Santa Barbara	Jen-Kai Liu, Southern Cal
1989	UCLA	Al Scates	3–1	Stanford	Matt Sonnichsen, UCLA
1990	Southern Cal	Jim McLaughlin	3–1	Long Beach St	Bryan Ivie, Southern Cal
1991	Long Beach St	Ray Ratelle	3–1	Southern Cal	Brent Hilliard, Long Beach St
1992	Pepperdine	Marv Dunphy	3–0	Stanford	Alon Grinberg, Pepperdine
1993	UCLA	Al Scates	3–0	Cal St–Northridge	Mike Sealy/Jeff Nygaard, UCLA
1994	Penn St	Tom Peterson	3–2	UCLA	Ramon Hernandez, Penn St
1995	UCLA	Al Scates	3–0	Penn St	Jeff Nygaard, UCLA
1996	UCLA	Al Scates	3–2	Hawaii	Yuval Katz, Hawaii
1997	Stanford	Ruben Nieves	3–2	UCLA	Mike Lambert, Stanford
1998	UCLA	Al Scates	3–2	Pepperdine	George Roumain, Pepperdine
1999	Brigham Young	Carl McGown	3–0	Long Beach St	Ossie Antonetti, Brigham Young
2000	UCLA	Al Scates	3–0	Ohio St	Brandon Taliaferro, UCLA
2001	Brigham Young	Carl McGown	3–0	UCLA	Mike Wall, Brigham Young
2002	Hawaii	Mike Wilton	3–1	Pepperdine	Costas Theochardis, Hawaii

Women

DIVISION I

Year	Champion	Coach	Score	Runner-Up
1981	Southern Cal	Chuck Erbe	3–2	UCLA
1982	Hawaii	Dave Shoji	3–2	Southern Cal
1983	Hawaii	Dave Shoji	3–0	UCLA
1984	UCLA	Andy Banachowski	3–2	Stanford
1985	Pacific	John Dunning	3–1	Stanford
1986	Pacific	John Dunning	3–0	Nebraska
1987	Hawaii	Dave Shoji	3–1	Stanford
1988	Texas	Mick Haley	3–0	Hawaii
1989	Long Beach St	Brian Gimmillaro	3–0	Nebraska
1990	UCLA	Andy Banachowski	3–0	Pacific
1991	UCLA	Andy Banachowski	3–2	Long Beach St
1992	Stanford	Don Shaw	3–1	UCLA
1993	Long Beach St	Brian Gimmillaro	3–1	Penn St
1994	Stanford	Don Shaw	3–1	UCLA
1995	Nebraska	Terry Pettit	3–1	Texas
1996	Stanford	Don Shaw	3–0	Hawaii
1997	Stanford	Don Shaw	3–2	Penn St
1998	Long Beach St	Brian Gimmillaro	3–2	Penn St
1999	Penn St	Russ Rose	3–0	Stanford
2000	Nebraska	John Cook	3–2	Wisconsin
2001	Stanford	Don Shaw	3–0	Long Beach St

DIVISION II

Year	Champion	Year	Champion	Year	Champion
1981	Cal St–Sacramento	1988	Portland St	1995	Barry
1982	UC–Riverside	1989	Cal St–Bakersfield	1996	Nebraska–Omaha
1983	Cal St–Northridge	1990	West Texas A&M	1997	West Texas A&M
1984	Portland St	1991	West Texas A&M	1998	Hawaii Pacific
1985	Portland St	1992	Portland St	1999	BYU–Hawaii
1986	UC–Riverside	1993	Northern Michigan	2000	Hawaii Pacific
1987	Cal St–Northridge	1994	Northern Michigan	2001	Barry

DIVISION III

Year	Champion	Year	Champion	Year	Champion	Year	Champion
1981	UC–San Diego	1987	UC–San Diego	1992	Washington (MO)	1997	UC–San Diego
1982	La Verne	1988	UC–San Diego	1993	Washington (MO)	1998	Central (IA)
1983	Elmhurst	1989	Washington (MO)	1994	Washington (MO)	1999	Central (IA)
1984	UC–San Diego	1990	UC–San Diego	1995	Washington (MO)	2000	Central (IA)
1985	Elmhurst	1991	Washington (MO)	1996	Washington (MO)	2001	La Verne
1986	UC–San Diego						

Water Polo

Men

Year	Champion	Coach	Score	Runner-Up
1969	UCLA	Bob Horn	5–2	California
1970	UC–Irvine	Ed Newland	7–6 (3 OT)	UCLA
1971	UCLA	Bob Horn	5–3	San Jose St
1972	UCLA	Bob Horn	10–5	UC–Irvine
1973	California	Pete Cutino	8–4	UC–Irvine
1974	California	Pete Cutino	7–6	UC–Irvine
1975	California	Pete Cutino	9–8	UC–Irvine
1976	Stanford	Art Lambert	13–12	UCLA
1977	California	Pete Cutino	8–6	UC–Irvine
1978	Stanford	Dante Dettamanti	7–6 (3 OT)	California
1979	UC–Santa Barbara	Pete Snyder	11–3	UCLA
1980	Stanford	Dante Dettamanti	8–6	California
1981	Stanford	Dante Dettamanti	17–6	Long Beach St
1982	UC–Irvine	Ed Newland	7–4	Stanford
1983	California	Pete Cutino	10–7	Southern Cal
1984	California	Pete Cutino	9–8	Stanford
1985	Stanford	Dante Dettamanti	12–11 (2 OT)	UC–Irvine
1986	Stanford	Dante Dettamanti	9–6	California
1987	California	Pete Cutino	9–8 (OT)	Southern Cal
1988	California	Pete Cutino	14–11	UCLA
1989	UC–Irvine	Ed Newland	9–8	California
1990	California	Steve Heaston	8–7	Stanford
1991	California	Steve Heaston	7–6	UCLA
1992	California	Steve Heaston	12–11	Stanford
1993	Stanford	Dante Dettamanti	11–9	Southern Cal
1994	Stanford	Dante Dettamanti	14–10	Southern Cal
1995	UCLA	Guy Baker	10–8	California
1996	UCLA	Guy Baker	8–7	Southern Cal
1997	Pepperdine	Terry Schroeder	8–7 (OT)	Southern Cal
1998	Southern Cal	John Williams	9–8 (2 OT)	Stanford
1999	UCLA	Guy Baker	6–5	Stanford
2000	UCLA	Guy Baker/Adam Krikorian	11–2	UC–San Diego
2001	Stanford	Dante Dettamanti	8–5	UCLA

Women

Year	Champion	Coach	Score	Runner-Up
2001	UCLA	Adam Krikorian	5–4	Stanford
2002	Stanford	John Tanner	8–4	UCLA

Wrestling

DIVISION I

Year	Champion	Coach	Pts	Runner-Up	Pts	Most Outstanding Wrestler
1928	Oklahoma St*	E.C. Gallagher				
1929	Oklahoma St	E.C. Gallagher	26	Michigan	18	
1930	Oklahoma St*	E.C. Gallagher	27	Illinois	14	
1931	Oklahoma St*	E.C. Gallagher		Michigan		
1932	Indiana*	W.H. Thom		Oklahoma St		Edwin Belshaw, Indiana
1933	OK St*/Iowa St*	E. Gallagher/H. Otopalik				A. Kelley, OK St/P. Johnson, Harv
1934	Oklahoma St	E.C. Gallagher	29	Indiana	19	Ben Bishop, Lehigh
1935	Oklahoma St	E.C. Gallagher	36	Oklahoma	18	Ross Flood, Oklahoma St
1936	Oklahoma	Paul Keen	14	Central St/ OK St	10	Wayne Martin, Oklahoma
1937	Oklahoma St	E.C. Gallagher	31	Oklahoma	13	Stanley Henson, Oklahoma St
1938	Oklahoma St	E.C. Gallagher	19	Illinois	15	Joe McDaniels, Oklahoma St
1939	Oklahoma St	E.C. Gallagher	33	Lehigh	12	Dale Hanson, Minnesota
1940	Oklahoma St	E.C. Gallagher	24	Indiana	14	Don Nichols, Michigan
1941	Oklahoma St	Art Griffith	37	Michigan St	26	Al Whitehurst, Oklahoma St
1942	Oklahoma St	Art Griffith	31	Michigan St	26	David Arndt, Oklahoma St
1946	Oklahoma St	Art Griffith	25	Northern Iowa	24	Gerald Leeman, Northern Iowa
1947	Cornell	Paul Scott	32	Northern Iowa	19	William Koll, Northern Iowa
1948	Oklahoma St	Art Griffith	33	Michigan St	28	William Koll, Northern Iowa
1949	Oklahoma St	Art Griffith	32	Northern Iowa	27	Charles Hetrick, Oklahoma St
1950	Northern Iowa	David McCuskey	30	Purdue	16	Anthony Gizoni, Waynesburg
1951	Oklahoma	Port Robertson	24	Oklahoma St	23	Walter Romanowski, Cornell
1952	Oklahoma	Port Robertson	22	Northern Iowa	21	Tommy Evans, Oklahoma
1953	Penn St	Charles Speidel	21	Oklahoma	15	Frank Bettucci, Cornell
1954	Oklahoma St	Art Griffith	32	Pittsburgh	17	Tommy Evans, Oklahoma
1955	Oklahoma St	Art Griffith	40	Penn St	31	Edward Eichelberger, Lehigh
1956	Oklahoma St	Art Griffith	65	Oklahoma	62	Dan Hodge, Oklahoma
1957	Oklahoma	Port Robertson	73	Pittsburgh	66	Dan Hodge, Oklahoma
1958	Oklahoma St	Myron Roderick	77	Iowa St	62	Dick Delgado, Oklahoma
1959	Oklahoma St	Myron Roderick	73	Iowa St	51	Ron Gray, Iowa St
1960	Oklahoma	Thomas Evans	59	Iowa St	40	Dave Auble, Cornell

DIVISION I (Cont.)

Year	Champion	Coach	Pts	Runner-Up	Pts	Most Outstanding Wrestler
1961	Oklahoma St	Myron Roderick	82	Oklahoma	63	E. Gray Simons, Lock Haven
1962	Oklahoma St	Myron Roderick	82	Oklahoma	45	E. Gray Simons, Lock Haven
1963	Oklahoma	Thomas Evans	48	Iowa St	45	Mickey Martin, Oklahoma
1964	Oklahoma St	Myron Roderick	87	Oklahoma	58	Dean Lahr, Colorado
1965	Iowa St	Harold Nichols	87	Oklahoma St	86	Yojiro Uetake, Oklahoma St
1966	Oklahoma St	Myron Roderick	79	Iowa St	70	Yojiro Uetake, Oklahoma St
1967	Michigan St	Grady Peninger	74	Michigan	63	Rich Sanders, Portland St
1968	Oklahoma St	Myron Roderick	81	Iowa St	78	Dwayne Keller, Oklahoma St
1969	Iowa St	Harold Nichols	104	Oklahoma	69	Dan Gable, Iowa St
1970	Iowa St	Harold Nichols	99	Michigan St	84	Larry Owings, Washington
1971	Oklahoma St	Tommy Chesbro	94	Iowa St	66	Darrell Keller, Oklahoma St
1972	Iowa St	Harold Nichols	103	Michigan St	72½	Wade Schalles, Clarion
1973	Iowa St	Harold Nichols	85	Oregon St	72½	Greg Strobel, Oregon St
1974	Oklahoma	Stan Abel	69½	Michigan	67	Floyd Hitchcock, Bloomsburg
1975	Iowa	Gary Kurdelmeier	102	Oklahoma	77	Mike Frick, Lehigh
1976	Iowa	Gary Kurdelmeier	123½	Iowa St	85¾	Chuch Yagla, Iowa
1977	Iowa St	Harold Nichols	95½	Oklahoma St	88¾	Nick Gallo, Hofstra
1978	Iowa	Dan Gable	94½	Iowa St	94	Mark Churella, Michigan
1979	Iowa	Dan Gable	122½	Iowa St	88	Bruce Kinseth, Iowa
1980	Iowa	Dan Gable	110¾	Oklahoma St	87	Howard Harris, Oregon St
1981	Iowa	Dan Gable	129¾	Oklahoma	100¼	Gene Mills, Syracuse
1982	Iowa	Dan Gable	131¾	Iowa St	111	Mark Schultz, Oklahoma
1983	Iowa	Dan Gable	155	Oklahoma St	102	Mike Sheets, Oklahoma St
1984	Iowa	Dan Gable	123¾	Oklahoma St	98	Jim Zalesky, Iowa
1985	Iowa	Dan Gable	145¼	Oklahoma	98½	Barry Davis, Iowa
1986	Iowa	Dan Gable	158	Oklahoma	84¼	Marty Kistler, Iowa
1987	Iowa St	Jim Gibbons	133	Iowa	108	John Smith, Oklahoma St
1988	Arizona St	Bobby Douglas	93	Iowa	85½	Scott Turner, N Carolina St
1989	Oklahoma St	Joe Seay	91¼	Arizona St	70½	Tim Krieger, Iowa St
1990	Oklahoma St	Joe Seay	117¾	Arizona St	104¾	Chris Barnes, Oklahoma St
1991	Iowa	Dan Gable	157	Oklahoma St	108¾	Jeff Prescott, Penn St
1992	Iowa	Dan Gable	149	Oklahoma St	100½	Tom Brands, Iowa
1993	Iowa	Dan Gable	123¾	Penn St	87½	Terry Steiner, Iowa
1994	Oklahoma St	John Smith	94¾	Iowa	76½	Pat Smith, Oklahoma St
1995	Iowa	Dan Gable	134	Oregon St	77½	T.J. Jaworsky, N Carolina
1996	Iowa	Dan Gable	122½	Iowa St	78½	Les Gutches, Oregon St
1997	Iowa	Dan Gable	170	Oklahoma St	113½	Lincoln McIlravy, Iowa
1998	Iowa	Jim Zalesky	115	Minnesota	102	Joe Williams, Iowa
1999	Iowa	Jim Zalesky	100½	Minnesota	98½	Cael Sanderson, Iowa St
2000	Iowa	Jim Zalesky	116	Iowa St	109½	Cael Sanderson, Iowa St
2001	Minnesota	J Robinson	138½	Iowa	125½	Cael Sanderson, Iowa St
2002	Minnesota	J Robinson	126½	Iowa St	104	Cael Sanderson, Iowa St

*Unofficial champions.

DIVISION II

Year	Champion	Year	Champion	Year	Champion
1963	Western St (CO)	1977	Cal St–Bakersfield	1991	NE–Omaha
1964	Western St (CO)	1978	Northern Iowa	1992	Central Oklahoma
1965	Mankato St	1979	Cal St–Bakersfield	1993	Central Oklahoma
1966	Cal Poly–SLO	1980	Cal St–Bakersfield	1994	Central Oklahoma
1967	Portland St	1981	Cal St–Bakersfield	1995	Central Oklahoma
1968	Cal Poly–SLO	1982	Cal St–Bakersfield	1996	Pittsburgh–Johnstown
1969	Cal Poly–SLO	1983	Cal St–Bakersfield	1997	San Francisco St
1970	Cal Poly–SLO	1984	SIU–Edwardsville	1998	N Dakota St
1971	Cal Poly–SLO	1985	SIU–Edwardsville	1999	Pittsburgh–Johnstown
1972	Cal Poly–SLO	1986	SIU–Edwardsville	2000	N Dakota St
1973	Cal Poly–SLO	1987	Cal St–Bakersfield	2001	N Dakota St
1974	Cal Poly–SLO	1988	N Dakota St	2002	Central Oklahoma
1975	Northern Iowa	1989	Portland St		
1976	Cal St–Bakersfield	1990	Portland St		

DIVISION III

Year	Champion	Year	Champion	Year	Champion
1974	Wilkes	1984	Trenton St	1994	Ithaca
1975	John Carroll	1985	Trenton St	1995	Augsburg
1976	Montclair St	1986	Montclair St	1996	Wartburg
1977	Brockport St	1987	Trenton St	1997	Augsburg
1978	Buffalo	1988	St. Lawrence	1998	Augsburg
1979	Trenton St	1989	Ithaca	1999	Wartburg
1980	Brockport St	1990	Ithaca	2000	Augsburg
1981	Trenton St	1991	Augsburg	2001	Augsburg
1982	Brockport St	1992	Brockport	2002	Augsburg
1983	Brockport St	1993	Augsburg		

INDIVIDUAL CHAMPIONSHIP
RECORDS

Swimming

Men

Event	Time	Record Holder	Date
50-yard freestyle	19.08	Neil Walker, Texas	3-27-97
100-yard freestyle	41.62	Anthony Ervin, California	3-20-02
200-yard freestyle	1:33.03	Matt Biondi, California	4-3-87
500-yard freestyle	4:08.75	Tom Dolan, Michigan	3-23-95
1,650-yard freestyle	14:26.62	Chris Thompson, Michigan	3-24-01
100-yard backstroke	45.25	Neil Walker, Texas	3-28-97
200-yard backstroke	1:40.06	Brian Retterer, Stanford	3-25-95
100-yard breaststroke	52.32	Jeremy Linn, Tennessee	3-28-97
200-yard breaststroke	1:52.88	Brendan Hansen, Texas	3-30-02
100-yard butterfly	45.44	Ian Crocker, Texas	3-29-02
200-yard butterfly	1:41.78	Melvin Stewart, Tennessee	3-30-91
200-yard individual medley	1:42.85	Nate Dusing, Texas	3-22-01
400-yard individual medley	3:38.18	Tom Dolan, Michigan	3-24-95

Women

Event	Time	Record Holder	Date
50-yard freestyle	21.69	Maritza Correia, Georgia	3-21-02
100-yard freestyle	47.56	Maritza Correia, Georgia	3-22-02
200-yard freestyle	1:43.08	Martina Moravcova, Southern Methodist.	3-28-97
500-yard freestyle	4:34.39	Janet Evans, Stanford	3-15-90
1,650-yard freestyle	15:39.14	Janet Evans, Stanford	3-17-90
100-yard backstroke	49.97	Natalie Coughlin, California	3-22-02
200-yard backstroke	1:49.52	Natalie Coughlin, California	3-22-02
100-yard breaststroke	59.05	Kristy Kowal, Georgia	3-20-98
200-yard breaststroke	2:07.36	Tara Kirk, Stanford	3-22-02
100-yard butterfly	50.01	Natalie Coughlin, California	3-22-02
200-yard butterfly	1:53.36	Limin Liu, Nevada	3-20-99
200-yard individual medley	1:53.91	Maggie Bowen, Auburn	3-21-02
400-yard individual medley	4:02.28	Summer Sanders, Stanford	3-20-92

Indoor Track and Field

Men

Event	Mark	Record Holder	Date
55-meter dash	6.00	Lee McRae, Pittsburgh	3-14-86
55-meter hurdles	7.07	Allèn Johnson, N Carolina	3-13-92
200-meter dash	20.26	Shawn Crawford, Clemson	3-10-00
400-meter dash	45.60	Brandon Couts, Baylor	3-10-00
800-meter run	1:45.33	Patrick Nduwimana, Arizona	3-10-01
Mile run	3:55.33	Kevin Sullivan, Michigan	3-11-95
3,000-meter run	7:46.03	Adam Goucher, Colorado	3-14-98
5,000-meter run	13:36.64	Jonah Koech, Iowa St	3-8-91
High jump	7 ft 9¼ in	Hollis Conway, SW Louisiana	3-11-89
Pole vault	19 ft 2¼ in	Jacob Davis, Texas	3-6-99
Long jump	27 ft 10 in	Carl Lewis, Houston	3-13-81
Triple jump	56 ft 9½ in	Keith Connor, Southern Methodist	3-13-81
Shot put	70 ft 1 in	Janus Robberts, Southern Methodist	3-10-01
35-pound weight throw	80 ft 11¼ in	Scott Russell, Kansas	3-9-02

Indoor Track and Field (Cont.)

Women

Event	Mark	Record Holder	Date
55-meter dash	6.56	Gwen Torrence, Georgia	3-14-87
55-meter hurdles	7.39	Tiffany Lott, BYU	3-7-97
200-meter dash	22.83	Peta-Gaye Dowdie, Louisiana St	3-6-99
400-meter dash	51.05	Maicel Malone, Arizona St	3-9-91
800-meter run	2:01.77	Hazel Clark, Florida	3-5-99
Mile run	4:30.63	Suzy Favor, Wisconsin	3-11-89
3,000-meter run	8:54.98	Stephanie Herbst, Wisconsin	3-15-86
5,000-meter run	15:39.75	Amy Skieresz, Arizona	3-7-97
High jump	6 ft 5½ in	Amy Acuff, UCLA	3-11-95
Pole vault	14 ft 10 ¼ in	Amy Linnen, Arizona	3-13-02
Long jump	22 ft 1 in	Daphne Saunders, Louisiana St	3-12-94
Triple jump	46 ft 9 in	Suzette Lee, Louisiana St	3-8-97
Shot put	60 ft 5¼ in	Teri Tunks, Southern Methodist	3-14-98
35-pound weight throw	71 ft 8¾ in	Dawn Ellerbe, S Carolina	3-7-97

Outdoor Track and Field

Men

Event	Mark	Record Holder	Date
100-meter dash	9.92	Ato Bolden, UCLA	6-1-96
200-meter dash	19.87	Lorenzo Daniel, Mississippi St	6-3-88
		John Capel, Florida	6-5-99
400-meter dash	44.00	Quincy Watts, Southern Cal	6-6-92
800-meter run	1:44.70	Mark Everett, Florida	6-1-90
1,500-meter run	3:35.30	Sydney Maree, Villanova	6-6-81
3,000-meter steeplechase	8:12.39	Henry Rono, Washington St	6-1-78
5,000-meter run	13:20.63	Sydney Maree, Villanova	6-2-79
10,000-meter run	28:01.30	Suleiman Nyambui, UTEP	6-1-79
110-meter high hurdles	13.22	Greg Foster, UCLA	6-2-78
400-meter intermediate hurdles	47.85	Kevin Young, UCLA	6-3-88
High jump	7 ft 9¾ in	Hollis Conway, SW Louisiana	6-3-89
Pole vault	19 ft 1 in	Lawrence Johnson, Tennessee	5-29-96
Long jump	28 ft	Erick Walder, Arkansas	6-3-93
Triple jump	57 ft 7¾ in	Keith Connor, Southern Methodist	6-5-82
Shot put	72 ft 2¼ in	John Godina, UCLA	6-3-95
Discus throw	220 ft	Kamy Keshmiri, Nevada	6-5-92
Hammer throw	265 ft 3 in	Balazs Kiss, Southern Cal	5-31-96
Javelin throw (new javelin)	268 ft 7 in	Esko Mikkola, Arizona	6-3-98
Decathlon	8279 pts	Tito Steiner, Brigham Young	6-2/3-81

Women

Event	Mark	Record Holder	Date
100-meter dash	10.78	Dawn Sowell, Louisiana St	6-3-89
200-meter dash	22.04	Dawn Sowell, Louisiana St	6-2-89
400-meter dash	50.18	Pauline Davis, Alabama	6-3-89
800-meter run	1:59.11	Suzy Favor, Wisconsin	6-1-90
1,500-meter run	4:08.26	Suzy Favor, Wisconsin	6-2-90
3,000-meter run	8:47.35	Vicki Huber, Villanova	6-3-88
5,000-meter run	15:37.77	Amy Skieresz, Arizona	6-5-98
10,000-meter run	32:28.57	Sylvia Mosqueda, Cal St–Los Angeles	6-1-88
100-meter hurdles	12.70	Tananjalyn Stanley, Louisiana St	6-3-89
400-meter hurdles	54.54	Ryan Tolbert, Vanderbilt	6-6-97
High jump	6 ft 5 in	Amy Acuff, UCLA	6-3-95
Pole vault	14 ft 5¼ in	Tracy O'Hara, UCLA	6-2-00
Long jump	22 ft 9¼ in	Sheila Echols, Louisiana St	6-5-87
Triple jump	46 ft ¾ in	Sheila Hudson, California	6-2-90
Shot put	61 ft 2¼ in	Tressa Thompson, Nebraska	6-4-98
Discus throw	210 ft 10 in	Seilala Sua, UCLA	6-6-99
Hammer throw	219 ft 4 in	Florence Ezah, Southern Methodist	6-2-01
Javelin throw (new javelin)	197 ft 8 in	Angeliki Tsiolakoudi, Texas–El Paso	6-3-00
Heptathlon	6527 pts	Diane Guthrie-Gresham, George Mason	6-2/3-95

MIKE SEGAR/REUTERS

Olympics

Patriot Games

Opening only five months after the Sept. 11 terrorist attacks, the Salt Lake Games were largely a U.S. showcase

BY MERRELL NODEN

UNTIL THE 2002 Winter Olympics were well under way and medals were being handed out each night under the stars at Medals Plaza in downtown Salt Lake City, it seemed that the only good news that could possibly come out of these Games was what didn't happen. Scheduled to begin on Feb. 9, only five months after the terrorist attacks on New York City and Washington, D.C., the Games looked like an obvious target for terrorists. At these Olympics, everyone agreed beforehand, no news would be good news.

But that was to underestimate the resilience of the Salt Lake City Games and their organizers. Already they had survived the worst political scandal in Olympic history—the bribes-for-votes affair that brought the Games to Utah in the first place—and they survived several controversies during the Olympics themselves, most notably the judging scandal in pairs figure skating that is still being unravelled.

Under the cool leadership of Salt Lake Organizing Committee (SLOC) president Mitt Romney, who went to Congress soon after the attacks to apply, successfully, for an additional $40 million for security, Salt Lake City launched an impressive security effort. Chain link fencing was built around every venue. The surrounding air space was designated a restricted area, while at every venue officials checked bags examined cell phones and pagers to make sure they were what they appeared to be. Men with high powered rifles patrolled rooftops, roared through the surrounding woods on snowmobiles and hung from Black Hawk helicopters.

All of this cost $310 million of the Games' $1.9 billion price tag, but no one doubted it was worth it. If it took 90 minutes to pass through security at the Opening Ceremonies, well, so be it. The most serious breach of security was probably the dustup among revelers at a beer garden on the final Saturday night of the Games, a melee that had to be broken up by police using rubber bullets.

After some wrangling, the U.S. flag that had flown over the World Trade Center was

given a place in the Opening Ceremonies. Eight athletes carried it in, making for a somber interlude in the otherwise upbeat party. To no one's surprise, the task of lighting the Olympic torch fell to the 1980 "Miracle on Ice" U.S. hockey team. President Bush attended the Opening Ceremonies, sitting in the crowd with the U.S. athletes.

And so the Games not only went on five months after the terrorist attacks on the U.S., but they also proved to be, from a competitive standpoint, the most successful Winter Games ever for the host country. U.S. athletes, who previously had never won more than 13 total medals in any single Winter Olympics, won 34, doubling Canada's haul and more than doubling those of Russia (16) and France (11). Only Germay won more medals than the U.S., with 35. Of the 34 U.S. medals, 10 were gold, and even though several came in newfangled events like snowboarding and freestyle skiing, where American dudes and dudettes seem to have a distinct cultural advantage, U.S. athletes also had their best ever performances in sports like bobsledding and speed skating.

"This was definitely an exclamation mark," concluded Derek Parra, the ebullient Mexican American speedskater who transformed himself from an inline skater to a speed skating gold medalist.

Several factors surely contributed to the

Sakic beat Mike Richter to give Canada a 5–2 victory in the gold medal game.

U.S. success. One of course was home-field advantage. The host team always experiences an upwards blip in its medals count. Nor can it have hurt that the IOC, anxious to please American corporate sponsors who essentially bankroll the Games, has recently been including new sports in which Americans have at least as long a tradition as anyone else. The U.S. dominated these newfangled, X Games events. The first U.S. medal, a silver, went to Shannon Bahrke in freestyle moguls skiing, and Bahrke's teammates, Joe Pack and Travis Mayer, won silvers too, in the men's aerials and moguls, respectively. The trio of Ross Powers, Danny Kass and J.J. Thomas swept the men's halfpipe, while Kelly Clark won the women's halfpipe.

But even as these early medalists were celebrating with high fives and cries of "Way to go, dude!" the Games' great scandal was starting to unfold. At the Salt Lake Ice Center, chants of "Six! Six!" greeted the emotional performance of the Canadian pairs team of Jamie Salé and David Pelletier, who skated to "Love Story." In contrast to the Russian pair of Yelena Berezhnaya and Anton Sikharulidze, who had skated earlier and made a few noticeable errors, the Canadians appeared to give a flawless, joyful and emotionally resonant performance. Their choreography was old, but by itself that did not seem enough to cost them the gold medal everyone watching was sure they deserved. So the crowd in the Ice Center and the vast television audience were stunned when the judges' scores came up and gave the gold to the Russians, 5–4.

Block voting and vote swapping are nothing new in figure skating. What gave this scandal legs and a smoking gun of sorts was the bizarre behavior of the French judge, Marie-Reine Le Gougne, who broke down in tears the following day, complaining to no one in particular that "no one knows the pressure we are under." An investigation was launched, and it was decided to award the Canadiens' a second pair of gold medals in a separate ceremony 11 days later. The poor Russians, whom no one accused of wrongdoing, did their best to smile gamely during the auxiliary ceremony, but it was a sour, awkward moment. In the spring, the International Skating Union (ISU) changed its judging rules and suspended both Le Gougne and French federation head Didier Gailhaguet. Then it launched an investigation of further allegations that a Russian mobster may have had a hand in fixing both the pairs and ice dance competition (won by the French team of Marina Anissina and Gwendal Peizerat).

The saddest thing about the whole affair was that it threw a dark cloud over the rest of the Games, diverting attention from some great performances. Like those of Ole Einar Bjoerndalen of Norway, who won all three individual medals in men's biathlon, and helped the Norwegians win the 4 x 7.5K relay, too. Another sweep came from the most unlikely looking of all Olympians, Simon Amman, the Swiss ski jumper who is 20 but looks about 12. In both the 90- and 120-meter events Annan upset Adam Malysz of Poland, the pre-Games favorite who had to be satisfied with a silver and a bronze.

In men's alpine skiing an Austrian won the glamour event, the downhill, though to everyone's surprise he was not Stephan Eberharter, who'd won five of eight World Cup downhills this winter after Hermann Maier injured himself badly in a motorcy-

cle crash last August. It was Fritz Strobl, a 29-year-old policeman from the small town of Hallein who careened fearlessly down Snowbasin's Grizzly course to win his nation's sixth Olympic downhill title but first since 1992. After finishing third in the downhill, Eberharter came back to win the Giant slalom. The star of men's skiing, though, was Kjetil André Aamodt of Norway, who claimed golds in both the combined and the Super-G events, to raise his career total to seven medals, an Olympic record. Bode Miller, the highly-touted U.S. skier, recovered from a near fall in the giant slalom to win the silver medal, then added a second silver, in the combined.

Among the women, 20-year-old Janica Kostelic of Croatia became the first alpine skier to win four medals at a single games, taking gold in the combined, slalom and giant slalom and silver in the super-G. The women's downhill went to Carole Montillet of France.

Great things were expected at the Olympic speed skating oval, where altitude and superb cooling capacity made for some extraordinarily fast ice. U.S. skaters, who'd won no gold medals four years earlier in Nagano, won three here, with the men's 500 going to Casey FitzRandolph, the men's 1,500 to Derek Parra, and the women's 1,000 to Chris Witty. She and Parra both set world records.

Parra became the poster boy for many of the good things about these Games. First, his success was in some ways a culmination of an effort that had begun back in 1988, when the U.S. won just six medals at the Calgary Olympics. Frustrated by that paltry haul, the USOC had created an advisory board headed up by that well-known sore loser, New York Yankees owner George Steinbrenner. Among the board's recommendations were better support for athletes in training and a recruiting effort that extended beyond the usual frozen ponds of Wisconsin and Vermont. These Games—and Parra in particular—were a testament to the success of that program, as athletes who would never have even tried a winter sport won medals.

A 31-year-old former inline skater from

Flowers became the first African American gold medalist in Winter Games history.

San Bernadino, Calif., the 5' 3½" Parra had made the tough decision to give up his original sport for one in which he'd been a clumsy rookie for some time. As the Games approached, Parra also opted to train in Salt Lake City while his wife, Tiffany, and their five-month old daughter, Mia, stayed home in Orlando. Juggling 20 hours a week of work at the flooring department at Home Depot along with training and travel, Parra prepared for Salt Lake City alone.

In his first race, the 5,000, he broke the world record only to see it broken in a later heat by double gold medalist Jochem Uytdehaage of the Netherlands. No matter. It wasn't Parra's best event. He came back to smash the world record in the 1500.

This was an Olympic full of firsts. Parra became the first Mexican American Winter gold medalist, and Jennifer Rodriguez, who won bronze medals in 1,000 and 1,500 speed skating events, became the first Cuban American to medal. And in the new (and somewhat confusingly named) event of Women's Two-Man Bobsled, the U.S. claimed the inaugural gold medal, when a former University of Alabama sprinter named Vonetta Flowers teamed up with driver Jill Bakken. Flowers had been a winter sports athlete for less than two years, taking up the sport when she was given a brochure at the track and field Olympic Trials in 2000. She would have been the first African-American Winter Olympics medalist, period, but she was beaten to that distinction by former American football players Todd Hays and Garrett Hines, who won silver medals in the four-man bobsled.

Expanding the U.S. medal haul was Apolo Anton Ohno, a 19-year-old Japanese American from Seattle who was favored to win several medals in short track speed skating. He overcame the flu and a nasty crash to win one gold (in a collision-marred 1500 that caused South Korea to threaten to boycott the closing ceremonies) and one silver. With his long dark hair flying as he sailed round the tiny track, Ohno seemed to herald a newer, more wide open Winter Olympics, which can only mean more medals for the U.S.

For tradition, though, you needed look no further than Chez Shea, home of the gold medalist in the skeleton, an event returning to the Olympics after a 54-year hiatus. Jack Shea had won two gold medals in speed skating at the 1932 Games, and his son, Jim, had been a Nordic skier in the 1964 Winter Olympics. In Salt Lake City it was Jim Jr.'s turn. In a terrible turn of events, 91-year-old Jack had been killed by a drunk driver in Lake Placid just 28 days before the skeleton competition. After his win, Jim Jr. carried his grandfather's Olympic medal with him to the medal stand.

As the Closing Ceremonies approached, bad news came in the form of positive drug tests and threats by two countries to withdraw. Out-of-competition drug tests on the final Thursday of the Games revealed that the Games' three biggest cross country skiing stars all had suspiciously high levels of oxygen-carrying red blood cells. Johann Muehlegg, a German-born cross country skier competing for Spain, lost the gold medal he'd won in the 50K classical race but kept the golds he'd won in the 30K freestyle and 10K pursuit. Also losing medals to positive drug tests were Russia's Olga Danilova and Larissa Lazutina.

Norway's Aamodt won a record seventh career Olympic medal.

CARL YARBROUGH

The Russians howled in protest, and while they were at it, they threw in their complaints about the 10-day-old pairs skating fiasco and the refereeing in Russia's 1–0 quarterfinal hockey win over the Czech Republic. "If these issues are not resolved, the Russian team will pack its bags and leave for Russia," huffed Minister of Sport Pavel Rozkoz, "and it will lead to the further deterioration of the Olympic movement."

In the end, neither the Russians or the Koreans (whose short-track skater was ruled to have interfered with Ohno in the 1500) left the Olympics, but, still, these Games needed a shot of positive energy. They got one from women's figure skating. The sentimental favorite was Michelle Kwan, who'd won silver four years earlier in Nagano. If Kwan had a shortcoming, it was skating prettily but not particularly athletically. In Salt Lake she seemed tentative, and stumbled several times during her short program. Irina Slutskaya of Russia produced a similarly shaky performance.

Standing fourth after the preliminary round was Sarah Hughes, a 16-year-old high school student from Great Neck, Long Island. Realizing she had nothing to lose, Hughes skated a wonderfully graceful and athletic long program, which left her gasping with radiant surprise as roses rained down from the crowd all around her. She then had to wait as the others skated. A prescient TV producer had sent a handheld camera to monitor her as she watched back in the otherwise empty lockerroom. Her genuine shock and delight at her victory would give these Games a lasting positive image.

The final event of the Olympics was the men's hockey gold medal game, which pitted the U.S. against Canada, after both teams had fought through a scintillating tournament loaded with NHL pros. Incredibly, Canada had not won an Olympic gold medal in its favorite sport since 1952. After Canada finished out of the medals in Nagano, it enlisted none other than Wayne Gretzky as national team manager.

Despite his help, Canada started off badly in Salt Lake City, losing their opening game 5–2 to Sweden. They would rally though, and—perhaps inspired by the Canadian women, who ended a long string of futility against the Americans by upsetting them for the gold medal—the Canadians whipped the U.S. 5–2, in the gold medal game, as Joe Sakic of the Colorado Avalanche scored two goals and assisted on two others. "We're a hockey power in the world, and it was good to reassure everyone that we still have some good, hard-nosed players in Canada," said goalie Martin Brodeur.

Indeed, despite the controversies, there were many winners at these Games. Chief among them was Mitt Romney, whose flawless leadership has earned him consideration for political office, and NBC, which scored an impressive prime-time Nielsen rating of 19.2 for the Games. Amid the spectacle of the closing ceremonies, Romney said, "Olympians, volunteers, spectators, remember these 17 days. We have rocked the world."

So now it's on to Turin, Italy, in four years time. It would be asking a lot to expect another 34 medals, but as the U.S. showed in Salt Lake City, it's never too late to learn some new tricks.

2000 Summer Games

TRACK AND FIELD
Men

100 METERS
1. ...Maurice Green, United States — 9.87
2. ...Ato Boldon, Trinidad and Tobago — 9.99
3. ...Obadele Thomoson, Barbados — 10.04

200 METERS
1. ...Konstadinos Kederis, Greece — 20.09
2. ...Darren Campbell, Great Britain — 20.14
3. ...Ato Boldon, Trinidad and Tobago — 20.20

400 METERS
1. ...Michael Johnson, United States — 43.84
2. ...Alvin Harrison, United States — 44.40
3. ...Gregory Haughton, Jamaica — 44.70

800 METERS
1. ...Nils Schumann, Germany — 1:45.08
2. ...Wilson Kipketer, Denmark — 1:45.14
3. ...Aissa Djabir Said-Guerni, Algeria — 1:45.16

1,500 METERS
1. ...Noah Ngeny, Kenya — 3:32.07 OR
2. ...Hicham El Guerrouj, Morocco — 3:32.32
3. ...Bernard Lagat, Kenya — 3:32.44

5,000 METERS
1. ...Millon Wolde, Ethiopia — 13:35.49
2. ...Ali Saidi-Sief, Algeria — 13:36.20
3. ...Brahim Lahlafi, Morocco — 13:36.47

10,000 METERS
1. ...Haile Gebrselassie, Ethiopia — 27:18.20
2. ...Paul Tergat, Kenya — 27:18.29
3. ...Assefa Mezgebu, Ethiopia — 27:19.75

MARATHON
1. ...Geznghe Abera, Ethiopia — 2:10:11
2. ...Eric Wainaina, Kenya — 2:10:31
3. ...Tesfaye Tola, Ethiopia — 2:11:10

110-METER HURDLES
1. ...Anier Garcia, Cuba — 13.00
2. ...Terrence Trammell, United States — 13.16
3. ...Mark Crear, United States — 13.22

400-METER HURDLES
1. ...Angelo Taylor, United States — 47.50
2. ...Hadi Souan Somalyi, Saudi Arabia — 47.53
3. ...Llewelyn Herbert, South Africa — 47.81

3,000-METER STEEPLECHASE
1. ...Reuben Kosgei, Kenya — 8:21.43
2. ...Wilson Boit Kipketer, Kenya — 8:21.77
3. ...Ali Ezzine, Morocco — 8:22.15

4 X 100-METER RELAY
1. ...United States: (Jon Drummond — 37.61
   Bernard Williams III, Brian Lewis,
   Maurice Greene)
2. ...Brazil — 37.90
3. ...Cuba — 38.04

4 X 400-METER RELAY
1. ...United States: (Alvin Harrison, — 2:56.35
   Antonio Pettigrew, Calvin Harrison,
   Michael Johnson)
2. ...Nigeria — 2:58.68
3. ...Jamaica — 2:58.78

20-KILOMETER WALK
1. ...Robert Korzeniowski, Poland — 1:18:59
2. ...Noe Hernandez, Mexico — 1:19:03
3. ...Vladimir Andreyev, Russia — 1:19:27

50-KILOMETER WALK
1. ...Robert Korzeniowski, Poland — 3:42:22
2. ...Aigars Fadejevs, Latvia — 3:43:40
3. ...Joel Sanchez, Mexico — 3:44:36

HIGH JUMP
1. ...Sergey Kliugin, Russia — 7 ft 8¼ in
2. ...Javier Sotomayor, Cuba — 7 ft 7¼ in
3. ...Abderrahmane Hammad, Algeria — 7 ft 7¼ in

POLE VAULT
1. ...Nick Hysong, United States — 19 ft 4¼ in
2. ...Lawrence Johnson, United States — 19 ft 4¼ in
3. ...Maksim Tarasov, Russia — 19 ft 4¼ in

LONG JUMP
1. ...Ivan Pedroso, Cuba — 28 ft ¾ in
2. ...Jai Taurima, Australia — 27 ft 10¼ in
3. ...Roman Schurenko, Ukraine — 27 ft 3¼ in

TRIPLE JUMP
1. ...Jonathan Edwards, Great Britain — 58 ft 1¼ in
2. ...Yoel Garcia, Cuba — 57 ft 3¾ in
3. ...Denis Kapustin, Russia — 57 ft 3½ in

SHOT PUT
1. ...Arsi Harju, Finland — 69 ft 10¼ in
2. ...Adam Nelson, United States — 69 ft 7 in
3. ...John Godina, United States — 69 ft 6¾ in

DISCUS THROW
1. ...Virgilijus Alekna, Lithuania — 227 ft 4 in
2. ...Lars Riedel, Germany — 224 ft 9 in
3. ...Frantz Kruger, South Africa — 223 ft 8 in

HAMMER THROW
1. ...Szymon Ziolkowski, Poland — 262 ft 6 in
2. ...Nicola Vizzoni, Italy — 261 ft 3 in
3. ...Igor Astapkovich, Belarus — 259 ft 8½ in

JAVELIN
1. ...Jan Zelezny, Czech Republic — 295 ft 9½ in
2. ...Steve Backley, Great Britain — 294 ft 9½ in
3. ...Sergey Makarov, Russia — 290 ft 10½ in

DECATHLON
Pts
1. ...Erki Nool, Estonia — 8641
2. ...Roman Seberle, Czech Republic — 8606
3. ...Chris Huffins, United States — 8595

Note: OR=Olympic record. WR=world record. EOR=equals Olympic record. EWR=equals world record.

TRACK AND FIELD (Cont.)
Women

100 METERS
1. ...Marion Jones, United States 10.75
2. ...Ekaterini Thanou, Greece 11.12
3. ...Tanya Lawrence, Jamaica 11.18

200 METERS
1. ...Marion Jones, United States 21.84
2. ...P. Davis-Thompson, Bahamas 22.27
3. ...Susanthika Jayasinghe, Sri Lanka 22.28

400 METERS
1. ...Cathy Freeman, Australia 49.11
2. ...Lorraine Graham, Jamaica 49.58
3. ...Katharine Merry, Great Britain 49.72

800 METERS
1. ...Maria Mutola, Mozambique 1:56.15
2. ...Stephanie Graf, Austria 1:56.64
3. ...Kelly Holmes, Great Britain 1:56.80

1,500 METERS
1. ...Nouria Merah-Benida, Algeria 4:05.10
2. ...Violeta Szekely, Romania 4:05.15
3. ...Gabriela Szabo, Romania 4:05.27

5,000 METERS
1. ...Gabriela Szabo, Romania 14:40.79 OR
2. ...Sonia O'Sullivan, Ireland 14:41.02
3. ...Gete Wami, Ethiopia 14:42.23

10,000 METERS
1. ...Derartu Tulu, Ethiopia 30:17.49 OR
2. ...Gete Wami, Ethiopia 30:22.48
3. ...Fernanda Ribeiro, Portugal 30:22.88

MARATHON
1. ...Naoko Takahashi, Japan 2:23:14 OR
2. ...Lidia Simon, Romania 2:23:22
3. ...Joyce Chepchumba, Kenya 2:24:45

100-METER HURDLES
1. ...Olga Shishigina, Kazakhstan 12.65
2. ...Glory Alozie, Nigeria 12.68
3. ...Melissa Morrison, United States 12.76

400-METER HURDLES
1. ...Irina Privalova, Russia 53.02
2. ...Deon Hemmings, Jamaica 53.45
3. ...Nouza Bidouane, Morocco 53.57

4 X 100-METER RELAY
1. ...Bahamas (S. Fynes, C. Sturrup, P. Davis-Thompson, D. Ferguson) 41.95
2. ...Jamaica 42.13
3. ...United States 42.20

4 X 400-METER RELAY
1. ...United States (Jearl Miles-Clark, Monique Hennagan, Marion Jones, La Tasha Colander-Richardson) 3:22.62
2. ...Jamaica 3:23.25
3. ...Russia 3:23.46

20-KILOMETER WALK
1. ...Wang Liping, China 1:29.05
2. ...Kiersti Plaetzer, Norway 1:29.33
3. ...Maria Vasco, Spain 1:30.23

HIGH JUMP
1. ...Yelena Yelesina, Russia 6 ft 7 in
2. ...Hestrie Cloete, S Africa 6 ft 7 in
3. ...Kajsa Bergqvist, Sweden 6 ft 7 in

POLE VAULT
1. ...Stacy Dragila, United States 15 ft 1 in OR
2. ...Tatiana Grigorieva, Australia 14 ft 11 in
3. ...Vala Flosadottir, Iceland 14 ft 9 in

LONG JUMP
1. ...Heike Drechsler, Germany 22 ft 11¼ in
2. ...Fiona May, Italy 22 ft 8½ in
3. ...Marion Jones, United States 22 ft 8½ in

TRIPLE JUMP
1. ...Tereza Marinova, Bulgaria 49 ft 10½ in
2. ...Tatyana Lebedeva, Russia 49 ft 2½ in
3. ...Olena Hovorova, Ukraine 49 ft 1 in

SHOT PUT
1. ...Yanina Korolchik, Belarus 67 ft 5½ in
2. ...Laris Peleshenko, Russia 65 ft 4¼ in
3. ...Astrid Kumbernuss, Germany 64 ft 4½ in

DISCUS THROW
1. ...Ellina Zvereva, Belarus 224 ft 5 in
2. ...Anastasia Kelesidou, Greece 215 ft 7 in
3. ...Irina Yatchenko, Belarus 213 ft 11 in

JAVELIN
1. ...Trine Hattestad, Norway 226 ft ½ in OR
2. ...Mirella Maniani-Tzelili, Greece 221 ft 5½ in
3. ...Osleidys Menendez, Cuba 217 ft 1 in

HEPTATHLON — Pts
1. ...Denise Lewis, Great Britain 6584
2. ...Yelena Prokhorova, Russia 6531
3. ...Natalya Sazanovich, Belarus 6527

HAMMER THROW
1. ...Kamila Skolimowska, Russia 233 ft 5 in OR
2. ...Olga Kuzenkova, Russia 228 ft 11 in
3. ...Kirsten Muenchow, Germany 227 ft 3 in

INDIVIDUAL ARCHERY

Men
1. ....Simon Fairweather, Australia
2. ....Victor Wuderle, United States
3. ....Wietse van Alten, Netherlands

Women
1. ....Yun Mi-Jin, S Korea
2. ....Kim Nam-Soon, S Korea
3. ....Kim Soo-Nyuong, S Korea

TEAM ARCHERY

Men
1. ...S Korea
2. ...Italy
3. ...United States

Women
1. ...S Korea
2. ...Ukraine
3. ...Germany

Note: OR=Olympic record. WR=world record. EOR=equals Olympic record. EWR=equals world record.

BADMINTON

Men

SINGLES
1. ...Ji Xinpeng, China
2. ...Henra Wan, Indonesia
3. ...Xia Xuanze, China

DOUBLES
1. ...Tony Gunawan/ Candra Wijaya, Indonesia
2. ...Lee Dong-soo/ Yoo Yong-sung, S Korea
3. ...Ha Tae-kwan/ Kim Dong-moon, S Korea

Women

SINGLES
1. ...Gong Zhichao, China
2. ...Camilla Martin, Denmark
3. ...Ye Zhaoying, China

DOUBLES
1. ....Ge Fei/ Gu Jun, China
2. ...Huang Nanyan/ Yang Wei, China
3. ...Gao Ling/ Qin Yiyuan, China

MIXED DOUBLES
1. ....Zhang Jun/Gao Ling, China
2. ....Tri Kushanjanto/Minarti Timur, Indonesia
3. ....Simon Archer/Joanne Goode, Great Britain

BASEBALL

1. ....United States
2. ....Cuba
3. ....S Korea

BASKETBALL

Men

Final: United States 85, France 75
Lithuania (3rd)
United States: Shareef Abdur-Rahim, Ray Allen, Vin Baker, Vince Carter, Kevin Garnett, Tim Hardaway, Allan Houston, Jason Kidd, Antonio McDyess, Alonzo Mourning, Gary Payton, Steve Smith

Women

Final: United States 76, Australia 54
Brazil (3rd)
United States: Ruthie Bolton-Holifield, Teresa Edwards, Yolanda Griffith, Chamique Holdsclaw, Lisa Leslie, Nikki McCray, Delisha Milton, Katie Smith Dawn Staley, Sheryl Swoopes, Natalie Williams, Kara Wolters

BOXING

LIGHT FLYWEIGHT (106 LB)
1. ....Brahim Asloum, France
2. ....Rafael Lozano Munoz, Spain
3. ....Un Chol Kim, N Korea
3. ....Maikro Romero Esquirol, Cuba

FLYWEIGHT (112 LB)
1. ....Wijan Ponlid, Thailand
2. ....Bulat Jumadilov, Kazakhstan
3. ....Jerome Thomas, France
3. ....Vladimir Sidorenko, Ukraine

BANTAMWEIGHT (119 LB)
1. ....Guillermo Ortiz, Cuba
2. ....Raimkoul Malakhbekov, Russia
3. ....Serguey Daniltchenko, Ukraine
3. ....Clarence Vinson, United States

FEATHERWEIGHT (125 LB)
1. ....Bekzat Sattarkhanov, Kazakhstan
2. ....Ricardo Juarez, United States
3. ....Tahar Tamsamani, Morocco
3. ....Kamil Dzamalutdinov, Russia

LIGHTWEIGHT (132 LB)
1. ....Mario Kindelan, Cuba
2. ....Andriy Kotelnyk, Ukraine
3. ....Cristian Benitez, Mexico
3. ....Alexandr Maletin, Russia

LIGHT WELTERWEIGHT (139 LB)
1. ....Mahamadkadyz Abdullaev, Uzbekistan
2. ....Ricardo Williams, United States
3. ....Diogenes Luna Martinez, Cuba
3. ....Mohamed Allalou, Algeria

WELTERWEIGHT (147 LB)
1. ....Oleg Saitov, Russia
2. ....Sergey Dotsenko, Ukraine
3. ....Vitalii Grusac, Moldova
3. ....Dorel Simion, Romania

LIGHT MIDDLEWEIGHT (156 LB)
1. ....Yermakhan Ibraimov, Kazakhstan
2. ....Marin Simion, Romania
3. ....Pornchai Thongburan, Thailand
3. ....Jermain Taylor, United States

MIDDLEWEIGHT (165 LB)
1. ....Jorge Gutierrez, Cuba
2. ....Gaidarbek Gaidarbekov, Russia
3. ....Vugar Alekperov, Azerbaijan
3. ....Zsolt Erdei, Hungary

LIGHT HEAVYWEIGHT (178 LB)
1. ....Alexander Lebziak, Russia
2. ....Rudolf Kraj, Czech Republic
3. ....Andri Fedtchouk, Ukraine
3. ....Sergei Mikhailov, Uzbekistan

HEAVYWEIGHT (201 LB)
1. ....Félix Sávon, Cuba
2. ....Sultanahmed Ibzagimov, Russia
3. ....Sebastian Kober, Germany
3. ....Vladimir Tchantouria, Georgia

SUPERHEAVYWEIGHT (201+ LB)
1. ....Audley Harrison, Great Britain
2. ....:Mukhtarkhan Dildabkov, Kazakhstan
3. ....Rustam Saidov, Uzbekistan
3. ....Paolo Vidoz, Italy

CANOE/KAYAK

Men

C-1 FLATWATER 500 METERS

1.	Gyorgy Kolonics, Hungary	2:24.813
2.	Maxim Opalev, Russia	2:25.809
3.	Andreas Dittmer, Germany	2:27.591

C-1 FLATWATER 1,000 METERS

1.	Andreas Dittmer, Germany	3:54.379
2.	Ledys Frank Balceiro, Cuba	3:56.071
3.	Steve Giles, Canada	3:56.437

C-2 FLATWATER 500 METERS

1.	F. Novak/ I. Pulai, Hungary	1:51.284
2.	D. Jedraszko/ P. Baraszkiewicz, Poland	1:51.536
3.	F. Popescu/ M. Pricop, Romania	1:54.260

C-2 FLATWATER 1,000 METERS

1.	F. Popescu/ M. Pricop, Romania	3:37.355
2.	I. Rojas/ L. Pereira, Cuba	3:38.753
3.	L. Kober/ S. Utess, Germany	3:41.129

C-1 WHITEWATER SLALOM

		Pts
1.	Tony Estanguet, France	231.87
2.	Michal Martikan, Slovakia	233.76
3.	Juraj Mincik, Slovakia	234.22

C-2 WHITEWATER SLALOM

		Pts
1.	Pavel/ Peter Hochschorner, Slovakia	237.74
2.	K. Kolomanski/ M. Staniszewski, Poland	243.81
3.	M. Jiras/ T. Mader, Czech Republic	249.45

K-1 FLATWATER 500 METERS

1.	Knut Holmann, Norway	1:57.847
2.	Petar Merkov, Bulgaria	1:58.393
3.	Michael Kolganov, Israel	1:59.563

K-1 FLATWATER 1,000 METERS

1.	Knut Holmann, Norway	3:33.260
2.	Petar Merkov, Bulgaria	3:34.640
3.	Tim Brabants, Great Britain	3:35.057

Men (Cont.)

K-2 FLATWATER 500 METERS

1.	Z. Kammerer/ B. Storcz, Hungary	1:47.055
2.	D. Collins/ A. Trim, Australia	1:47.895
3.	R. Rauhe/ T. Wieskoetter, Germany	1:48.771

K-2 FLATWATER 1,000 METERS

1.	B. Bonomi/ A. Rossi, Italy	3:14.461
2.	M. Oscarsson/ H. Nilsson, Sweden	3:16.075
3.	K. Bartfai/ K. Vereb, Hungary	3:16.357

K-4 FLATWATER 1,000 METERS

1.	Hungary	2:55.188
2.	Germany	2:55.704
3.	Poland	2:57.192

K-1 WHITEWATER SLALOM

		Pts
1.	Thomas Schmidt, Germany	217.25
2.	Paul Ratcliffe, Great Britain	223.71
3.	Pierpaolo Ferrazzi, Italy	225.03

Women

K-1 FLATWATER 500 METERS

1.	Josefa Idem Geurrini, Italy	2:13.848
2.	Caroline Brunet, Canada	2:14.646
3.	Katrin Borchert, Australia	2:15.138

K-2 FLATWATER 500 METERS

1.	B. Fischer/ K. Wagner, Germany	1:56.996
2.	K. Kovacs/ S. Szabo, Hungary	1:58.580
3.	A. Pastuszka/ B. Sokoloska, Poland	1:58.784

K-4 FLATWATER 500 METERS

1.	Germany	1:34.532
2.	Hungary	1:34.946
3.	Romania	1:37.010

K-1 WHITEWATER SLALOM

		Pts
1.	Stepanka Hilgertova, Czech Republic	247.04
2.	Brigitte Guibal, France	251.88
3.	Anne-Lise Bardet, France	254.77

CYCLING

Men

ROAD RACE

1.	Jan Ullrich, Germany	5:29:17.001
2.	Alexander Vinokourov, Kazakhstan	5:29:17.002
3.	Andreas Kloeden, Germany	5:29:29.003

INDIVIDUAL TIME TRIAL

1.	Vyachslev Ekimov, Russia	57:40.420
2.	Jan Ullrich, Germany	57:48.333
3.	Lance Armstrong, United States	58:14.267

1KM TIME TRIAL

1.	Jason Queally, Great Britain	101.609
2.	Stefan Nimke, Germany	102.487
3.	Shane Kelly, Australia	102.818

4,000-METER INDIVIDUAL PURSUIT

1.	Robert Bartko, Germany	4:18.515 OR
2.	Jens Lehmann, Germany	4:23.824
3.	Bradley McGee, Australia	4:19.250

4,000-METER TEAM PURSUIT

1.	Germany (Robert Bartko, Guido Fulst, Daniel Becke, Jens Lehmann)	3:59.710WR
2.	Russia	4:04.520
3.	Great Britain	4:01.979

Men (Cont.)

SPRINT

1.	Marty Nothstein, United States	10.874
2.	Florian Rousseau, France	11.066
3.	Jens Fiedler, Germany	10.732

40-KM POINTS RACE

1.	Juan Llaneras, Spain	14
2.	Milton Wynant, Uruguay	18
3.	Alexey Markov, Russia	16

KIERIN

1.	Florian Rousseau, France	11.020
2.	Gary Neiwand, Australia	
3.	Jens Fiedler, Germany	

MADISON

1.	B. Aiken/ S. McGrory, Australia	26
2.	E. DeWilde/ M. Gilmore, Belgium	22
3.	S. Martinello/ M. Villa, Italy	15

OLYMPIC SPRINT

1.	France	44.233
2.	Great Britain	44.680
3.	Australia	45.161

CYCLING (Cont.)

Women

24-KM POINTS RACE
1. ...Antonella Bellutti, Italy — 19
2. ...Leontien Zijlaard, Netherlands — 16
3. ...Olga Slioussareva, Russia — 15

SPRINT
1. ...Felicia Ballanger, France — 12.553
2. ...Oxana Grichina, Russia — 13.112
3. ...Irina Yanovych, Ukraine — 12.310

INDIVIDUAL TIME TRIAL
1. ...Leontien Zijlaard, Netherlands — 42:00.781
2. ...Mari Holden, United States — 42:37.372
3. ...Jeannie Longo-Ciprelli, France — 42:52:547

ROAD RACE
1. ...Leontien Zijlaard, Netherlands — 3:6:31.001
2. ...Hanka Kupfernagel, Germany — 3:6:31.002
3. ...Diana Ziliute, Lithuania — 3:6:31.003

3,000-METER INDIVIDUAL PURSUIT
1. ...Leontien Zijlaard, Netherlands — 3:33:360
2. ...Marion Clignet, France — 3:38:751
3. ...Yvonne McGregor, Great Britain — 3:38:850

500-M TIME TRIAL
1. ...Felicia Ballanger, France — 34.140
2. ...Michelle Ferris, Australia — 34.696
3. ...Jiang Cuihua, China — 34.768

DIVING

Men

SPRINGBOARD
		Pts
1.	...Xiong Ni, China	708.72
2.	...Fernando Platas, Mexico	708.42
3.	...Dmitri Sautin, Russia	703.20

PLATFORM
		Pts
1.	...Tian Liang, China	724.53
2.	...Hu Jia, China	713.55
3.	...Dmitri Sautin, Russia	679.26

Women

SPRINGBOARD
		Pts
1.	...Fu Mingxia, China	609.42
2.	...Guo Jingjing, China	597.81
3.	...Doerte Linder, Germany	574.35

PLATFORM
		Pts
1.	...Laura Wilkinson, United States	543.75
2.	...Li Na, China	542.01
3.	...Anne Montminy, Canada	540.15

EQUESTRIAN

3-DAY TEAM
		Pts
1.	...Australia (Phillip Dutton, Andrew Hoy, Stuart Tinney, Matt Ryan)	146.8
2.	...Great Britain	161.0
3.	...United States	175.8

3-DAY INDIVIDUAL
		Pts
1.	...David O'Connor, United States	34.00
2.	...Andrew Hoy, Australia	39.80
3.	...Mark Todd, New Zealand	42.00

TEAM DRESSAGE
		Pts
1.	...Germany (Isabell Werth, Nadine Capellmann, Ulla Salzgeber, Alexandra Simons de Ridder)	5632
2.	...Netherlands	5579
3.	...United States	5166

INDIVIDUAL DRESSAGE
		Pts
1.	...Anky van Grunsven, Netherlands	239.18
2.	...Isabell Werth, Germany	234.19
3.	...Ulla Salzberger, Germany	230.57

TEAM JUMPING
		Pts
1.	...Germany (Ludger Beerbaum, Lars Nieberg, Marcus Ehning, Otto Becker)	7.00
2.	...Switzerland	8.00
3.	...Brazil	12.00

INDIVIDUAL JUMPING
		Pts
1.	...Jeroen Dubbeldam, Netherlands	4.00
2.	...Albert Voorn, Netherlands	4.00
3.	...Khaled Al Eid, Saudi Arabia	4.00

FENCING

Men

FOIL
1. ...Kim Young Ho, S Korea
2. ...Ralf Bissdorf, Germany
3. ...Dmitri Chevtchenko, Russia

TEAM FOIL
1. ...France
2. ...China
3. ...Italy

SABRE
1. ...Mihai Claudiu Covaliu, Romania
2. ...Mathieu Gourdain, France
3. ...Wiradech Kothny, Germany

TEAM SABRE
1. ...Russia
2. ...France
3. ...Germany

ÉPÉE
1. ...Pavel Kolobkov, Russia
2. ...Hugues Obry, France
3. ...Lee Sang Ki, S Korea

TEAM ÉPÉE
1. ...Italy
2. ...France
3. ...Cuba

FENCING (Cont.)

Women

FOIL

1. ....Valentina Vezzali, Italy
2. ....Rita Koenig, Germany
3. ....Giovanna Trillini, Italy

TEAM FOIL

1. ....Italy
2. ....Poland
3. ....Germany

ÉPÉE

1. ....Timea Nagy, Hungary
2. ....Gianna Habluetzel-Buerki, Switzerland
3. ....Laura Flessel-Colovic, France

TEAM ÉPÉE

1. ....Russia
2. ....Switzerland
3. ....China

FIELD HOCKEY

Men

1. ....Netherlands
2. ....S Korea
3. ....Australia

Women

1. ....Australia
2. ....Argentina
3. ....Netherlands

GYMNASTICS

Men

ALL-AROUND

		Pts
1.	Alexei Nemov, Russia	58.474
2.	Wei Yang, China	58.361
3.	O. Beresh, Ukraine	58.212

HORIZONTAL BAR

		Pts
1.	Alexei Nemov, Russia	9.787
2.	Benjamin Varonian, France	9.787
3.	Joo-hyung Lee, S Korea	9.775

PARALLEL BARS

		Pts
1.	Xiaopeng Li, China	9.825
2.	Joo-hyung Lee, S Korea	9.812
3.	Alexei Nemov, Russia	9.800

VAULT

		Pts
1.	Gervasio Deferr, Spain	9.712
2.	Alexei Bondarenko, Russia	9.587
3.	Leszsk Blanik, Poland	9.475

POMMEL HORSE

		Pts
1.	Marius Urzica, Romania	9.862
2.	Eric Poujade, France	9.825
3.	Alexei Nemov, Russia	9.800

RINGS

		Pts
1.	Szilveszter Csollany, Hungary	9.850
2.	Dimosthenis Tampakos, Kasakhstan	9.762
2.	Iordan Iovtchev, Bulgaria	9.737

FLOOR EXERCISE

		Pts
1.	Igors Vihrovs, Latvia	9.812
2.	Alexei Nemov, Russia	9.800
3.	Iordan Iovtchev, Bulgaria	9.787

TEAM COMBINED EXERCISES

		Pts
1.	China	231.919
2.	Ukraine	230.306
3.	Russia	230.019

Women

ALL-AROUND

		Pts
1.	Simona Amanar, Romania	38.642
2.	Maria Olaru, Romania	38.581
3.	Xuan Li, China	38.418

VAULT

		Pts
1.	Yelena Zamolodtchikova, Russia	9.731
2.	Andreea Raducan, Romania	9.693
3.	Yekaterina Lobazniouk, Russia	9.674

UNEVEN BARS

		Pts
1.	Svetlana Khorkina, Russia	9.862
2.	Ling Jie, China	9.837
2.	Yang Yun, China	9.787

BALANCE BEAM

		Pts
1.	Li Xuan, China	9.825
2.	Yekaterina Lobazniouk, Russia	9.787
3.	Yelena Prodounova, Russia	9.775

FLOOR EXERCISE

		Pts
1.	Yelena Zamolodtchikova, Russia	9.850
2.	Svetlana Khorkina, Russia	9.812
3.	Simona Amanar, Romania	9.712

TEAM COMBINED EXERCISES

		Pts
1.	Romania	154.608
2.	Russia	154.403
3.	China	154.008

RHYTHMIC ALL-AROUND

		Pts
1.	Yulia Barsukova, Russia	39.632
2.	Yulia Raskina, Belarus	39.548
3.	Alina Kabaeva, Russia	39.466

RHYTHMIC TEAM COMBINED EXERCISES

		Pts
1.	Russia	39.500
2.	Belarus	39.500
3.	Greece	39.283

JUDO

Men

EXTRA-LIGHTWEIGHT
1. Tadahiro Nomura, Japan
2. Jung Bu-Kyung, S Korea
3. Manolo Poulot, Cuba
3. Aidyn Smagulov, Kirghyzstan

HALF-LIGHTWEIGHT
1. Huseyin Ozkan, Turkey
2. Larbi Benboudaoud, France
3. Giorgi Vazagashvili, Georgia
3. Girolamo Giovinazzo, Italy

LIGHTWEIGHT
1. Giuseppe Maddaloni, Italy
2. Tiago Camilo, Brazil
3. Anatoly Laryukov, Belarus
3. Vselvolods Zelonijs, Latvia

HALF-MIDDLEWEIGHT
1. Makoto Takimoto, Japan
2. Cho In Chul, S Korea
3. Nuno Delgado, Portugal
3. Aleksei Budolin, Estonia

MIDDLEWEIGHT
1. Mark Huizinga, Netherlands
2. Carlos Honorato, Brazil
3. Frederic Demontfaucon, France
3. Ruslan Mashurenko, Ukraine

HALF-HEAVYWEIGHT
1. Kosei Inoue, Japan
2. Nicolas Gill, Canda
3. Iouri Stepkine, Russial
3. Stéphane Traineau, France

HEAVYWEIGHT
1. David Douillet, France
2. Shinichi Shinohara, Japan
3. Indrek Pertelson, Estonia
3. Tamerlan Tmenov, Russia

Women

EXTRA-LIGHTWEIGHT
1. Ryoko Tamura, Japan
2. Lioubov Brouletova, Russia
3. Anna-Maria Gradante, Germany
3. Ann Simons, Belgium

HALF-LIGHTWEIGHT
1. Legna Verdecia, Cuba
2. Noriko Narazaki, Japan
3. Kye Sun Hi, N Korea
3. Liu Yuxiang, China

LIGHTWEIGHT
1. Isabel Fernández, Spain
2. Driulis González, Cuba
3. Kie Kusakabe, Japan
3. Maria Pekli, Australia

HALF-MIDDLEWEIGHT
1. Severine Vandenhende, France
2. Li Shufang, China
3. Gella Vandecaveye, Belgium
3. Jung Sung Sook, S Korea

MIDDLEWEIGHT
1. Sibelis Veranes, Cuba
2. Kate Howey, Great Britain
3. Cho Min Sun, S Korea
3. Ylenia Scapin, Italy

HALF-HEAVYWEIGHT
1. Lin Tang, China
2. Celine LeBrun, France
3. Simona Marcela Richter, Romania
3. Emanuela Pierantozzi, Italy

HEAVYWEIGHT
1. Hua Yuan, China
2. Daima Mayelis Beltran, Cuba
3. Kim Seon-Young, S Korea
3. Mayumi Yamashita, Japan

MOUNTAIN BIKING

Men
1. Miguel Martinez, France — 2:09:02
2. Filip Meirhaeghe, Belgium — 2:10.05
3. Christoph Sauser, Switzerland — 2:11:21

Women
1. Paola Pezzo, Italy — 1:49:24
2. Barbara Blatter, Switzerland — 1:49.51
3. Margarita Fullana, Spain — 1:49.57

MODERN PENTATHLON

Men
1. Dmitry Svatlovsky, Russia
2. Gabor Balogh, Hungary
3. Pavel Dovgal, Belarus

Women
1. Stephanie Cook, Great Britain
2. Emily deRiel, United States
3. Kate Allenby, Great Britain

ROWING

Men

SINGLE SCULLS
1. Rob Waddell, New Zealand — 6:48.90
2. Xeno Mueller, Switzerland — 6:50.55
3. Marcel Hacker, Germany — 6:50.83

DOUBLE SCULLS
1. I. Cop/L. Spik, Slovenia — 6:16.63
2. F. Beeken/O Tufte, Norway — 6:17.98
3. G. Calabrese/N. Sartori, Italy — 6:20.49

LIGHTWEIGHT DOUBLE SCULLS
1. T. Kucharski/R. Sycz, Poland — 6:21.75
2. E. Liunii/L. Pettinari, Italy — 6:23.57
3. T. Chappelle/P. Touron, France — 6:24.85

QUADRUPLE SCULLS
1. Italy — 5:45.56
2. Netherlands — 5:47.91
3. Germany — 5:48.64

ROWING *(Cont.)*
Men *(Cont.)*

COXLESS PAIR		LIGHTWEIGHT COXLESS FOUR	
1. ...M. Andrieux/ J. Rolland, France	6:32.97	1. ...France	6:01.68
2. ...S. Bea/ T. Murphy, United States	6:33.80	2. ...Australia	6:02.09
3. ...J. Tomkins/ M. Long, Australia	6:34.26	3. ...Denmark	6:03.51

COXLESS FOUR		EIGHT-OARS	
1. ...Great Britain	5:56.24	1. ...Great Britain	5:33.08
2. ...Italy	5:56.62	2. ...Australia	5:33.88
3. ...Australia	5:57.61	3. ...Croatia	5:34.85

Women

SINGLE SCULLS		QUADRUPLE SCULLS	
1. ...Ekaterina Karsten, Belarus	7:28.14	1. ...Germany	6:19.58
2. ...Rumyana Neykova, Bulgaria	7:28.15	2. ...Great Britain	6:21.64
3. ...K. Rutschow-Stomporowski, Germany	7:28.99	3. ...Russia	6:21.65

DOUBLE SCULLS		COXLESS PAIR	
1. ...K. Boron/ J. Thieme, Germany	6:55.44	1. ...G. Damian/D. Ignat, Romania	7:11.00
2. ...P. Van Dishoeck/ E. Van Nes, Netherlands	7:00.36	2. ...R. Taylor/K. Slatter, Australia	7:12.56
3. ...B. Sakickiene/ K. Poplavskaya, Lithuania	7:01.71	3. ..,K. Kraft/M. Ryan, United States	7:13.00

LIGHTWEIGHT DOUBLE SCULLS		EIGHT-OARS	
1. ...C. Burcica/ A. Alupei, Romania	7:02.64	1. ...Romania	6:06.44
2. ...V. Viehoff/ C. Blaserg, Germany	7:02.95	2. ...Netherlands	6:09.39
3. ...C. Collins/ S. Garner, United States	7:06.37	3. ...Canada	6:11.58

SHOOTING
Men

RAPID-FIRE PISTOL	Pts	SMALL-BORE RIFLE, PRONE	Pts
1......Serguei Alifirenko, Russia	687.6	1......Jonas Edman, Swedem	701.3
2......Michel Ansermet, Switzerland	686.1	2......Torben Grimmel, Denmark	700.4
3......Iulian Raicen, Romania	684.6	3......Sergei Martynov, Belarus	700.3

FREE PISTOL	Pts	AIR RIFLE	Pts
1......Tanyu Kiriakov, Bulgaria	666.0	1......Yalin Cai, China	696.4
2......Igor Basinski, Belarus	663.3	2......Artem Khadjibekov, Russia	695.1
3......Martin Tenk, Czech Republic	662.5	3......Evgueni Aleinikov, Russia	693.8

AIR PISTOL	Pts	TRAP	Pts
1......Franck Dumoulin, France	688.9	1......Michael Diamond, Australia	122.0
2......Yifu Wang, China	686.9	2......Ian Peel, Great Britain	118.0
3......Igor Basinsky, Belarus	682.7	3......David Kostelecky, Czech Republic	116.0

RUNNING TARGET	Pts	DOUBLE TRAP	Pts
1......Ling Yang, China	681.1	1......Richard Faulds, Great Britain	187.0
2......Oleg Moldovan, Moldova	681.0	2......Russell Mark, Australia	187.0
3......Zhiyuan Niu, China	677.4	3......Fehaid Al Deehani, Kuwait	186.0

SMALL-BORE RIFLE, THREE-POSITION	Pts	SKEET	Pts
1......Rajmond Debevec, Slovenia	1275.1	1......Mykola Milchen, Ukraine	150.0
2......Juha Hirvi, Finland	1270.5	2......Petr Malek, Czech Republic	148.0
3......Harald Stenvaag, Norway	1268.6	3......James Graves, United States	147.0

Women

SPORT PISTOL	Pts	AIR PISTOL	Pts
1......Maria Grozdeva, Bulgaria	690.3	1......Luna Tao, China	488.2
2......Luna Tao, China	689.8	2......Jasna Sekaric, Yugoslavia	486.5
3......Lolita Evglevskaya, Belarus	686.0	3......Annemarie Forder, Australia	484.0

SHOOTING (Cont.)

Women (Cont.)

SMALL-BORE RIFLE, THREE-POSITION

	Pts
1......Renata Mauer-Rozanska, Poland	684.6
2......Tatiana Goldobina, Russia	680.9
3......Maria Feklistova, Russia	679.9

AIR RIFLE

	Pts
1......Nancy Johnson, United States	497.7
2......Kang Cho-Hyan, S Korea	497.5
3......Jing Gao, China	497.2

DOUBLE TRAP

	Pts
1......Pia Hansen, United States	148.0
2......Deborah Gelisio, Italy	144.0
3......Kimberly Rhode, United States	139.0

TRAP

	Pts
1......Daina Gudzineviciute, Lithuania	93.0
2......Delphine Racinet, France	92.0
3......E Gao, China	90.0

SKEET

	Pts
1......Zemfira Meftakhetdinova, Azerbaijan	98.0
2......Svetlana Demina, Russia	95.0
3......Diana Igaly, Hungary	93.0

SOCCER

Men
1. ....Cameroon
2. ....Spain
3. ....Chile

Women
1. ....Norway
2. ....United States
3. ....Germany

SOFTBALL

1. ....United States
2. ....Japan
3. ....Australia

SWIMMING

Men

50-METER FREESTYLE
1. ...Gary Hall Jr., United States	21.98
1. ...Anthony Ervin, United States	21.98
3. ...Pieter van den Hoogenband, Netherlands	22.03

100-METER FREESTYLE
1. ...Pieter van den Hoogenband, Netherlands	48.30
2. ...Alexander Popov, Russia	48.69
3. ...Gary Hall Jr., United States	48.73

200-METER FREESTYLE
1. ...Pieter van den Hoogenband, Netherlands	1:45.35 EWR
2. ...Ian Thorpe, Australia	1:45.83
3. ...Massimiliano Rosolino, Italy	1:46.65

400-METER FREESTYLE
1. ...Ian Thorpe, Australia	3:40.59 WR
2. ...Massimiliano Rosolino, Italy	3:43.50
3. ...Klete Keller, United States	3:47.00

1,500-METER FREESTYLE
1. ...Grant Hackett, Australia	14:48.33
2. ...Kieren Perkins Australia	14:53.59
3. ...Chris Thompson, United States	14:56.81

100-METER BACKSTROKE
1. ...Lenny Krayzelburg, United States	53.72 OR
2. ...Matthew Welsh, Australia	54.07
3. ...Stev Theloke, Germany	54.82

200-METER BACKSTROKE
1. ...Lenny Krayzelburg, United States	1:56.76 OR
2. ...Aaron Piersol, United States	1:57.35
3. ...Matthew Welsh, Australia	1:59.59

100-METER BREASTSTROKE
1. ...Domenico Fioravanti, Italy	1:00.46 OR
2. ...Ed Moses, United States	1:00.73
3. ...Roman Sloudnov, Russia	1:00.91

200-METER BREASTSTROKE
1. ...Domenico Fioravanti, Italy	2:10.87
2. ...Terence Parkin, S Africa	2:12.50
3. ...Davide Rummolo, Italy	2:12.73

100-METER BUTTERFLY
1. ...Lars Froelander, Sweden	52.00
2. ...Michael Klim, Australia	52.18
3. ...Geoff Huegill, Australia	52.22

200-METER BUTTERFLY
1. ...Tom Malchow, United States	1:55.35 OR
2. ...Denys Sylant'yev, Ukraine	1:55.76
3. ...Justin Norris, Australia	1:56.17

200-METER INDIVIDUAL MEDLEY
1. ...Massimiliano Rosolino, Italy	1:58.98 OR
2. ...Tom Dolan, United States	1:59.77
3. ...Tom Wilkens, United States	2:00.87

400-METER INDIVIDUAL MEDLEY
1. ...Tom Dolan, United States	4:11.76 WR
2. ...Eric Vendt, United States	4:14.23
3. ...Curtis Myden, Canada	4:15.33

4 X 100-METER MEDLEY RELAY
1. ...United States (Lenny Krayzelburg, Ed Moses, Ian Crocker, Gary Hall Jr.)	3:34.84 WR
2. ...Australia	3:35.27
3. ...Germany	3:35.88

4 X 100-METER FREESTYLE RELAY
1. ...Australia (Ian Thorpe, Michael Klim, Ashley Callus, Chris Fydler)	3:13.67 WR
2. ...United States	3:13.86
3. ...Brazil	3:17.40

4 X 200-METER FREESTYLE RELAY
1. ...Australia (Ian Thorpe, Michael Klim, William Kirby, Todd Pearson)	7:07.05 WR
2. ...United States	7:12.64
3. ...Netherlands	7:12.70

Note: OR=Olympic record. WR=world record. EOR=equals Olympic record. EWR=equals world record.

SWIMMING *(Cont.)*
Women

50-METER FREESTYLE
1. ...Inge de Bruijn, Netherlands — 24.32
2. ...Therese Alshammar, Sweden — 24.51
3. ...Dara Torres, United States — 24.63

100-METER FREESTYLE
1. ...Inge de Bruijn, Netherlands — 53.83
2. ...Therese Alshammar, Sweden — 54.33
3. ...Dara Torres, United States — 54.43

200-METER FREESTYLE
1. ...Susie O'Neill, Australia — 1:58.24
2. ...Martina Moravcova, Slovakia — 1:58.32
3. ...Claudia Poll Ahrens, Costa Rica — 1:58.81

400-METER FREESTYLE
1. ...Brooke Bennett, United States — 4:05.80
2. ...Diana Munz, United States — 4:07.07
3. ...Claudia Poll Ahrens, Costa Rica — 4:07.83

800-METER FREESTYLE
1. ...Brooke Bennett, United States — 8:19.67 OR
2. ...Yana Klochkova, Ukraine — 8:22.66
3. ...Kaitlin Sandeno, United States — 8:24.29

100-METER BACKSTROKE
1. ...Diana Iuliana Mocanu, Romania — 1:00.21 OR
2. ...Mai Nakamura, Japan — 1:00.55
3. ...Nina Zhivanevskaya, Spain — 1:00.89

200-METER BACKSTROKE
1. ...Diana Iuliana Mocanu, Romania — 2:08.16
2. ...Roxana Maracineanu, France — 2:10.25
3. ...Miki Nakao, Japan — 2:11.05

100-METER BREASTSTROKE
1. ...Megan Quann, United States — 1:07.05
2. ...Leisel Jones, Australia — 1:07.49
3. ...Penny Heyns, S Africa — 1:07.55

200-METER BREASTSTROKE
1. ...Agnes Kovacs, Hungary — 2:24.35
2. ...Kristy Kowal, United States — 2:24.56
3. ...Amanda Beard, United States — 2:25.35

100-METER BUTTERFLY
1. ...Inge de Bruijn, Netherlands — 56.61 WR
2. ...Martina Moravcova, Slovakia — 57.97
3. ...Dara Torres, United States — 58.20

200-METER BUTTERFLY
1. ...Misty Hyman, United States — 2:05.88 OR
2. ...Susie O'Neill, Australia — 2:06.58
3. ...Petria Thomas, Australia — 2:07.12

200-METER INDIVIDUAL MEDLEY
1. ...Yana Klochkova, Ukraine — 2:10.68 OR
2. ...Beatrice Nicoleta Caslaru, Rom — 2:12.57
3. ...Cristina Teuscher, United States — 2:13.32

400-METER INDIVIDUAL MEDLEY
1. ...Yana Klochkova, Ukraine — 4:33.59 WR
2. ...Yasuko Tajima, Japan — 4:35.90
3. ...Beatrice Nicoleta Caslaru, Romania — 4:37.18

4 X 100-METER MEDLEY RELAY
1. ...United States (BJ Bedford, Megan Quann, Jenny Thompson, Dara Torres) — 3:58.30 WR
2. ...Australia — 4:01.59
3. ...Japan — 4:04.16

4 X 100-METER FREESTYLE RELAY
1. ...United States (Jenny Thompson, Courtney Shealy, Dara Torres, Amy Van Dyken) — 3:36.61 WR
2. ...Netherlands — 3:39.83
3. ...Sweden — 3:40.30

4 X 200-METER FREESTYLE RELAY
1. ...United States (Samantha Arsenault, Diana Munz, Lindsay Benko, Jenny Thompson) — 7:57.80 OR
2. ...Australia — 7:58.52
3. ...Germany — 7:58.64

Note: OR=Olympic record. WR=world record. EOR=equals Olympic record. EWR=equals world record.

SYNCHRONIZED SWIMMING

DUET
1. ...Russia — 99.580
2. ...Japan — 98.650
3. ...France — 97.437

TEAM
1. ...Russia — 99.146
2. ...Japan — 98.860
3. ...Canada — 97.357

SYNCHRONIZED DIVING

Men
3M SPRINGBOARD
	Pts
1. ....Xiang Ni/ Xiao Hailang, China	365.58
2. ....D. Sautin/ A. Dobroskoki, Russia	329.97
3. ....D. Pullan/ R. Newbery, Australia	322.86

10M PLATFORM
	Pts
1. ....I. Loukachine/ D. Sautin, Russia	365.04
2. ....Tian Liang/ Hu Jia, China	358.74
3. ....J.Hempel/ H. Meyer, Germany	338.88

Women
3M SPRINGBOARD
	Pts
1. ....V. Ilina/ I. Pakhalina, Russia	332.64
2. ....Guo Jing Jing/ Fu Mingxia, China	321.60
3. ....G. Sorokina/ O. Zhupina, Ukraine	290.34

10M PLATFORM
	Pts
1. ....Li Na/ Sang Zue, China	345.12
2. ....A. Montminy/ E.Heymanns, Canada	312.02
3............L. Tourky/ R. Gilmore, Australia	301.50

TABLE TENNIS

Men
SINGLES
1. ....Kong Linghui, China
2. ....Jan-Ove Wablner, Sweden
3. ....Liu Guoliang, China

DOUBLES
1. ....Wang Liqin/ Yan Sen, China
2. ....Kong Linghu/ Liu Guoliang, China
3. ....Patrick Chila/ J.P: Gatien, France

Women
SINGLES
1. ....Wang Nan, China
2. ....Li Ju, China
3. ....Chen Jing, Taiwan

DOUBLES
1. ....Li Ju/ Wang Nan, China
2. ....Sun Jin/ Yang Yin, China
3. ....Kim Moo Kyo/ Ji-Hye Ryu, S Korea

TAEKWONDO

Men
FLYWEIGHT
1. ....Michail Mouroutsos, Greece
2. ....Gabriel Esparza, Spain
3. ....Chi-Hsiung Huang, China

FEATHERWEIGHT
1. ....Steven Lopez, United States
2. ....Sin Joon Sik, S Korea
3. ....Hadi Saeibonehkohal, Iran

WELTERWEIGHT
1. ....Angel Valodia Matos Fuentes, Cuba
2. ....Faissal Ebnoutalib, Germany
3. ....Victor Estrada Garibay, Mexico

HEAVYWEIGHT
1. ....Kyong-Hun Kim, S Korea
2. ....Daniel Trenton, Australia
3. ....Pascal Gentil, France

Women
FLYWEIGHT
1. ....Lauren Burns, Australia
2. ....Urbia Melendez Rodriguez, Cuba
3. ....Ju Chi Shu, China

FEATHERWEIGHT
1. ....Jung Jae Eun, S Korea
2. ....Hieu Ngan Tran, Vietnam
3. ....Hamide Bikcin, Turkey

WELTERWEIGHT
1. ....Sun-Hee Lee, S Korea
2. ....Trude Gunderson, Denmark
3. ....Yoriko Okamoto, Japan

HEAVYWEIGHT
1. ....Chen Zhong, China
2. ....Natalia Ivanova, Russia
3. ....Dominique Bosshart, Canada

TEAM HANDBALL

Men
1. ....Russia
2. ....Sweden
3. ....Spain

Women
1. ....Denmark
2. ....Hungary
3. ....Norway

TENNIS

Men
SINGLES
1. ....Yevgeni Kafelnikov, Russia
2. ....Tommy Haas, Germany
3. ....Arnaud Di Pasquale, France

DOUBLES
1. ....Daniel Nestor/ Sebastien Lareau, Canada
2. ....Todd Woodbridge/ Mark Woodforde, Australia
3. ....Alex Corretja/ Albert Costa, Spain

Women
SINGLES
1. ....Venus Williams, United States
2. ....Elena Dementieva, Russia
3. ....Monica Seles, United States

DOUBLES
1. ....V. Williams/ S. Williams, United States
2. ....Kristie Boogert/ Miriam Oremans, Netherlands
3. ....Dominique van Roost/ Els Callens, Belgium

TRAMPOLINE

Men
1. ....Alexandre Mosalenko, Russia 41.70
2. ....Ji Wallace, Australia 39.30
3. ....Mathieu Turgeon, Canada 39.10

Women
1. ....Irina Karavaeva, Russia 38.90
2. ....Oxana Tsyhuleva, Ukraine 37.70
3. ....Karen Cockburn, Canada 37.40

TRIATHLON

Men
1. ....Simon Whitfield, Canada 1:48.24.02
2. ....Stefan Vucovic, Germany 1:48.37.58
3. ....Jan Rehula, Czech Rep. 1:48.46,64

Women
1. ....Brigitte McMahon, Switz. 2:00.40.52.
2. ....Michellie Jones, Australia 2:00.42.55
3. ....Magali Messmer, Switz. 2:01.08.83

VOLLEYBALL

Men
1. ....Yugoslavia
2. ....Russia
3. ....Italy

Women
1. ....Cuba
2. ....Russia
3. ....Brazil

BEACH VOLLEYBALL

Men
1. ....Dain Blanton/ E. Fonoimoana, United States
2. ....Ze Marco Melo/ Ricardo Santos, Brazil
3. ....Joerg Ahmann/ Axel Hager, Germany

Women
1. ....Kerri Pottharst/ Natalie Cook, Australia
2. ....Shelda Bede/ Adriana Behar, Brazil
3. ....Adriana Samuel/ Sandra Pires, Brazil

WATER POLO

Men
1. ....Hungary
2. ....Russia
3. ....Yugoslavia

Women
1. ....Australia
2. ....United States
3. ....Russia

WEIGHTLIFTING

Men

123 POUNDS
1. ....Halil Mutlu, Turkey	671 lb WR
2. ....Wu Wenxiong, China	631 lb
3. ....Zhang Xiangxiang, China	631 lb

137 POUNDS
1. ....Nikolay Pechaliv, Croatia	715 lb OR
2. ....Leonidas Sabanis, Greece	697 lb
3. ....Gennady Oleshchuk, Belarus	697 lb

152 POUNDS
1. ....Galabin Boevski, Bulgaria	785 lb OR
2. ....Georgi Markov, Bulgaria	774 lb
3. ....Sergei Lavrenov, Belarus	680 lb

170 POUNDS
1. ....Zhan Xugang, China	807 lb
2. ....Viktor Mitrou, Greece	807 lb
3. ....Arsen Melikyan, Armenia	803 lb

187 POUNDS
1. ....Pyrros Dimas, Greece	858 lb
2. ....Marc Huster, Germany	858 lb
3. ....George Asanidze, Georgia	858 lb

207 POUNDS
1. ....Akakios Kakiasvilis, Greece	891 lb
2. ....Szymon Kolecki, Poland	891 lb
3. ....Alexei Petrov. Russia	884 lb

231 POUNDS
1. ....Hossein Tavakoli, Iran	935 lb
2. ....Alan Tsagaev, Bulgaria	928 lb
3. ....Said Asaad, Qatar	924 lb

231+ POUNDS
1. ....Hossein Rezazadeh, Iran	1,045 lb WR
2. ....Ronny Weller, Germany	1,025 lb
3. ....Andrei Chermerkin, Russia	1,017 lb

Women

106 POUNDS
1. ....Tara Nott, United States	407 lb
2. ....Raema Rumbewas, Indonesia	407 lb
3. ....Sri Indriyani, Indonesia	400 lb

117 POUNDS
1. ....Yang Xia, China	495 lb WR
2. ....Li Feng ying, Taipei	466 lb
3. ....Winarni Slamet, Indonesia	444 lb

128 POUNDS
1. ....Soraya Mendivil, Mexico	488 lb
2. ....Ri Song Hui, N Korea	484 lb
3. ....Khassaraporn Suta, Thailand	462 lb

139 POUNDS
1. ....Xiaomin Chen, China	532 lb
2. ....Valentina Popova, Russia	517 lb
3. ....Ioanna Chatziioannou, Greece	488 lb

152 POUNDS
1. ....Lin Weining, China	532 lb
2. ....Erzsebet Markus, Hungary	532 lb
3. ....Karnam Malleswari. Indonesia	528 lb

165 POUNDS
1. ....Maria Isabel Urrutia, Colombia	539 lb
2. ....Ruth Ogbeifo, Nigeria	539 lb
3. ....Kuo Yi Hang, Taipei	539 lb

165 + POUNDS
1. ....Ding Meiyuan, China	660 lb WR
2. ....Agata Wrobel, Poland	649 lb OR
3. ....Cheryl Haworth, United States	594 lb

FREESTYLE WRESTLING

119 POUNDS
1. ....Namig Abdullayev, Azerbaijan
2. ....Samuel Henson, United States
3. ....Amiran Karntanov, Greece

127.75 POUNDS
1. ....Alireza Dabir, Iran
2. ....Yevgen Buslovych, Ukraine
3. ....Terry Brands, United States

138.75 POUNDS
1. ....Mourad Oumakhanov, Russia
2. ....Serafim Barzakov, Bulgaria
3. ....Jang Jae Sung, S Korea

152 POUNDS
1. ....Daniel Igali, Canada
2. ....Arsen Gitinov, Russia
3. ....Lincoln McIlvray, United States

167.5 POUNDS
1. ....Alexander Leipold, Germany
2. ....Brandon Slay, United States
3. ....Moon Eui Jae, S Korea

187.25 POUNDS
1. ....Adam Saitiev, Russia
2. ....Yoel Romero, Cuba
3. ....Mogamed Ibragimov, Macedonia

213.75 POUNDS
1. ....Sagid Mourtasaliyev, Russia
2. ....Islam Bairamukov, Kazakhstan
3. ....Eldar Kurtanidze, Georgia

286 POUNDS
1. ....David Moussoulbes, Russia
2. ....Artur Taymazov, Uzbekistan
3. ....Alexis Rodriguez, Cuba

GRECO-ROMAN WRESTLING

119 POUNDS
1. ....Kwon Ho Sim, S Korea
2. ....Lazaro Rivas, Cuba
3. ....Young Gyun Kang, N Korea

127.75 POUNDS
1. ....Armen Nazarian, Bulgaria
2. ....Kim In Sub, S Korea
3. ....Zertian Sheng, China

138.75 POUNDS
1. ....Varteres Samourgachev, Russia
2. ....Juan Luis Maren, Cuba
3. ....Akaki Chachua, Georgia

152 POUNDS
1. ....Filiberto Azcuy, Cuba
2. ....Katsushiko Nagata, Japan
3. ....Alexei Glouchkov, Russia

167.5 POUNDS
1. ....Mourat Kardanov, Russia
2. ....Matt James Lindland, United States
3. ....M. Yli-Hannuksela, Finland

187.25 POUNDS
1. ....Hamza Yerlikaya, Turkey
2. ....Sandor Istvan Bardosi, Hungary
3. ....Mukhran Vakhtangadze, Georgia

213.75 POUNDS
1. ....Mikael Ljundberg, Sweden
2. ....Davyd Saldadze, Ukraine
3. ....Garrett Lowney, United States

286 POUNDS
1. ....Rulon Gardner, United States
2. ....Alexander Karelin, Russia
3. ....Dmitry Debelka, Belarus

YACHTING

MEN'S 470
1. ....Australia
2. ....United States
3. ....Argentina

MEN'S FINN
1. ....Iain Percy, Great Britain
2. ....Luca Devoti, Italy
3. ....Fredrik Loof, Sweden

MEN'S BOARD
1. ....Christoph Sieber, Austria
2. ....Carlos Espinosa, Argentina
3. ....Aaron McIntosh, New Zealand

WOMEN'S 470
1. ....Australia
2. ....United States
3. ....Ukraine

WOMEN'S EUROPE
1. ....Shirley Robertson, Great Britain
2. ....Margriet Matthysse, Netherlands
3. ....Serena Amato, Argentina

WOMEN'S BOARD
1. ....Alessandra Sensini, Italy
2. ....Amelie Lux, Germany
3. ....Barbara Kendall, New Zealand

SOLING
1. ....Denmark
2. ....Germany
3. ....Norway

STAR
1. ....M. Reynolds/M. Liljedahl, United States
2. ....M. Covell/ I. Walker, Great Britain
3. ....T. Grael/ M. Ferreira, Brazil

TORNADO
1. ....H. Steinacher/ R.Hagara, Austria
2. ....J. Forbes/ D. Bundock, Australia
3. ....R. Gaebler/ R. Schwall, Germany

LASER
1. ....Ben Ainslie, Great Britain
2. ....Robert Scheidt, Brazil
3. ....Michael Blackburn, Australia

49ER
1. ....T. Johnson/ J. Jarvi, Finland
2. ....I. Barker/ S. Hicksocks, Great Britain
3. ....J. McKee/ C. McKee, United States

BIATHLON

Men

10 KILOMETERS
1. ...Ole Einar Bjoerndalen, Norway	24:51.3
2. ...Sven Fisher, Germany	25:20.2
3. ...Wolfgang Perner, Austria	25:44.4

20 KILOMETERS
1. ...Ole Einar Bjoerndalen, Norway	51:03.3
2. ...Frank Luck, Germany	51:39.4
3. ...Victor Maigovrov, Russia	51:40.6

4 X 7.5-KILOMETER RELAY
1. ....Norway	1:23:42.3
2. ....Germany	1:24:27.7
3. ....France	1:24:36.6

Women

7.5 KILOMETERS
1. ...Kati Wilhelm, Germany	20:41.4
2. ...Uschi Disl, Germany	20:57.0
3. ...Magdalena Forsberg, Sweden	21:20.4

15 KILOMETERS
1. ...Andrea Henkel, Germany	47:29.1
2. ...Liv Grete Poiree, Norway	47:37.0
3. ...Magdalena Forsberg, Sweden	48:08.3

4 X 7.5-KILOMETER RELAY
1. ....Germany	1:27:55.0
2. ....Norway	1:28:25.6
3. ....Russia	1:29:19.7

BOBSLED

Men

TWO-MAN
1. ...Christoph Langen/ Markus Zimmerman, Germany I	3:10.10
2...Christian Reich/ Steve Anderhub, Switz.I	3:10.20
3...Martin Annen/ Beat Hefti, Switz II	3:10.62

FOUR-MAN
1. ....Germany II	3:07.51
2. ....USA I	3:07.81
3. ....USA II	3:07.86

Women

TWO-PERSON
1. ...Jill Bakken/ Vonetta Flowers, USA II	1:37.76
2. ...Sandra Prokoff/ Ulrike Holzner, Ger. I	1:38.06
3. ...S.L. Erdmann/ N. Herschmann, Ger II	1:38.29

CURLING

Men
1. ....Norway
2. ....Canada
3. ....Switzerland

Women
1. ....Britain
2. ....Switzerland
3. ....Canada

FIGURE SKATING

Men
1. ....Alexei Yagudin, Russia
2. ....Evgeni Plushenko, Russia
3. ....Timothy Goebel, United States

Pairs
1. ...Elena Berezhnaya/ Anton Sikharulidze, Russia
1. ...David Pelletier/ Jamie Sale, Canada
3. ...Hongbo Zhao/ Xue Shen, China

Women
1. ....Sarah Hughes, United States
2. ....Irina Slutskaya, Russia
3. ....Michelle Kwan, United States

Ice Dancing
1. ...Marina Anissina/ Gwendal Peizerat, France
2. ...Irina Lobacheva/ Ilia Averbukh, Russia
3. ...Barbara Fusar Poli/ Maurizio Margaglio, Italy

ICE HOCKEY

Men
1. ....Canada
2. ....USA
3. ....Russia

Women
1. ....Canada
2. ....USA
3. ....Sweden

LUGE

Men

SINGLES
1. ...Armin Zoeggeler, Italy	2:57.941
2. ...Georg Hackl, Germany	2:58.270
3. ...Markus Prock, Austria	2:58.283

DOUBLES
1. ...Alexander Resch/ P.F. Leitner, Ger	1:26.082
2. ...Mark Grimmette/ Brian Martin, U.S.	1:26.216
3. ...Chris Thorpe/ Clay Ives, U.S.	1:26.220

Women

SINGLES
1. ...Sylke Otto, Germany	2:52.464
2. ...Barbara Niedernhuber, Germany	2:52.785
3. ...Silke Kraushaar, Germany	2:52.865

SKELETON

Men
1. ....Jim Shea Jr., United States	1:41.96
2. ....Martin Rettl, Austria	1:42.01
3. ....Gregor Staehli, Switzerland	1:42.15

Women
1. ....Tristan Gale, United States	1:45.11
2. ....Lea Ann Parsley, United States	1:45.21
3. ....Alex Coomber, Great Britain	1:45.37

SPEED SKATING
Men

500 METERS
1. ...Casey FitzRandolph, United States — 1:09.23
2. ...Hiroyasu Shimizu, Japan — 1:09.26
3. ...Kip Carpenter, United States — 1:09.47

1,000 METERS
1. ...Gerard Van Velde, Netherlands — 1:07.18
2. ...Jan Bos, Netherlands — 1:07.53
3. ...Joey Cheek, United States — 1:07.61

1,500 METERS
1. ...Derek Parra, United States — 1:43.95
2. ...Jochem Uytdehaage, Netherlands — 1:44.57
3. ...Adne Sondral, Norway — 1:45.26

5,000 METERS
1. ...Jochem Uytdehaage, Netherlands — 6:14.66
2. ...Derek Parra, United States — 6:17.98
3. ...Jens Boden, Germany — 6:21.73

10,000 METERS
1. ...Jochem Uytdenhaage, Netherlands — 12:58.92 WR
2. ...Gianni Romme, Netherlands — 13:10.03
3. ...Lasse Saetre, Norway — 13:16.92

500 METERS SHORT TRACK
1. ...Marc Gagnon, Canada — 41.802 OR
2. ...Jonathan Guilmette, Canada — 41.994
3. ...Rusty Smith, United States — 42.027

1,000 METERS SHORT TRACK
1. ...Steven Bradbury, Austrialia — 1:29.109
2. ...Apolo Anton Ohno, United States — 1:30.160
3. ...Mathieu Turcotte, Canada — 1:30.563

1,500 METERS SHORT TRACK
1. ...Apolo Anton Ohno, United States — 2:18.541
2. ...Jiajun Li, China — 2:18.731
3. ...Marc Gagnon, Canada — 2:18.806

5,000-METER SHORT TRACK RELAY
1. ...Canada — 6:51.579
2. ...Italy — 6:56.327
3. ...China — 6:59.633

Women

500 METERS
1. ...Catriona LeMay Doan, Canada — 1:14.75
2. ...Monique Garbrecht-Enfeld, Ger — 1:14.94
3. ...Sabine Voelker, Germany — 1:15.19

1,000 METERS
1. ...Chris Witty, United States — 1:13.83
2. ...Sabine Voelker, Germany — 1:13.96
3. ...Jennifer Rodriguez, United States — 1:14.24

1,500 METERS
1. ...Anni Friesinger, Germany — 1:54.02
2. ...Sabine Voelker, Germany — 1:54.94
3. ...Jennifer Rodriguez, United States — 1:55.32

3,000 METERS
1. ...Claudia Pechstein, Germany — 3:57.70
2. ...Renate Groenwold, Netherlands — 3:58.94
3. ...Cindy Klassen, Canada — 3:58.94

5,000 METERS
1. ...Claudia Pechstein, Germany — 6:46.91 WR
2. ...Gretha Smit, Germany — 6:49.22
3. ...Clara Hughes, Canada — 6:53.53

500 METERS SHORT TRACK
1. ...Annie Perreault, Canada — 46.568
2. ...Yang Yang, China — 46.627
3. ...Chun Lee Kyung, S Korea — 46.335

1,000 METERS
1. ...Yang A. Yang, China — 1:36.391
2. ...Gi-Hyun Ko, Korea — 1:36.427
3. ...Yang S. Yang, China — 1:37.008

1,500 METERS
1. ...Gi-Hyan Ko, Korea — 2:31.581
2. ...Eun-Kyung Choi, Korea — 2:31.610
3. ...Evgenia Radanova, Bulgaria — 2:31.723

3,000-METER SHORT TRACK RELAY
1. ...Korea — 4:12.793
2. ...China — 4:13.236
3. ...Canada — 4:15.738

Note: OR=Olympic Record. WR=World Record. EOR=Equals Olympic Record. EWR=Equals World Record. WB=World Best.

ALPINE SKIING

Men

DOWNHILL
1. ...Fritz Strobl, Austria — 1:39.13
2. ...Lasse Kjus, Norway — 1:39.35
3. ...Stephan Eberharter, Austria — 1:39.41

SLALOM
1. ...Jean-Pierre Vidal, France — 1:41.06
2. ...Sebastien Amiez, France — 1:41.82
3. ...Benjamin Raich, Austria — 1:42.41

GIANT SLALOM
1. ...Stephan Eberharter, Austria — 2:23.28
2. ...Bode Miller, United States — 2:24.16
3. ...Lasse Kjus, Norway — 2:24.32

SUPER GIANT SLALOM
1. ...Kjetil Andre Aamodt, Norway — 1:21.58
2. ...Stephan Eberharter, Austria — 1:21.68
3. ...Andreas Schifferer, Austria — 1:21.83

COMBINED
1. ...Kjetil Andre Aamodt, Norway — 3:17.56
2. ...Bode Miller, United States — 3:17.84
3. ...Benjamin Raich, Austria — 3:18.26

Women

DOWNHILL
1. ...Carole Montillet, France — 1:39.56
2. ...Isolde Kostner, Italy — 1:40.01
3. ...Renate Goetschl, Austria — 1:40.39

SLALOM
1. ...Janica Kostelic, Croatia — 1:46.10
2. ...Laure Pequegnot, France — 1:46.17
3. ...Anja Paerson, Sweden — 1:47.09

GIANT SLALOM
1. ...Janica Kostelic, Croatia — 2:30.01
2. ...Anja Paerson, Sweden — 2:31.33
3. ...Sonja Nef, Switzerland — 2:31.67

SUPER GIANT SLALOM
1. ...Daniela Ceccarelli, Italy — 1:13.59
2. ...Janica Kostelic, Croatia — 1:13.64
3. ...Karen Putzer, Italy — 1:13.86

COMBINED
1. ...Janica Kostelic, Croatia — 2:43.28
2. ...Renate Goetschl, Austria — 2:44.77
3. ...Martina Ertl, Germany — 2:45.16

FREESTYLE SKIING

Men

MOGULS	Pts
1. ...Janne Lahtela, Finland	27.97
2. ...Travis Mayer, United States	27.59
3. ...Richard Gay, France	26.91

AERIALS	Pts
1. ...Ales Valenta, Czech Republic	257.02
2. ...Joe Pack, United States	251.64
3. ...Alexei Grichin, Belarus	251.19

Women

MOGULS	Pts
1. ...Kari Traa, Norway	25.94
2. ...Shannon Bahrke, United States	25.06
3. ...Tae Satoya, Japan	24.85

AERIALS	Pts
1. ...Alisa Camplin, Australia	193.47
2. ...Veronica Brenner, Canada	190.02
3. ...Deidra Dionne, Canada	189.26

NORDIC SKIING

Men

1.5 KILOMETERS SPRINT
1. ...Tor Arne Hetland, Norway	2:56.9
2. ...Peter Schlickenrieder, Germany	2:57.0
3. ...Cristian Zorzi, Italy	2:57.2

10 KILOMETERS PURSUIT FREESTYLE
1. ...Johann Muehlegg, Spain	49:20.4
2. ...Frode Estil, Norway	49:48.9
2. ...Thomas Alsgaard, Norway	49:48.9

15 KILOMETERS CLASSICAL
1. ...Andrus Veerpalu, Estonia	37:07.4
2. ...Frode Estil, Norway	37:43.4
3. ...Jaak Mae, Estonia	37:50.8

30 KILOMETERS FREESTYLE
1. ...Johann Muelegg, Spain	1:09:28.9
2. ...Christian Hoffman, Austria	1:11:31.0
3. ...Mikhail Botvinov, Austria	1:11:32.3

50 KILOMETERS CLASSICAL
1. ...Mikhail Ivanov, Russia	2:06:20.8
2. ...Andrus Veerpalu, Estonia	2:06:44.5
3. ...Odd-Bjoern Hjelmeset, Norway	2:08:41.5

4 X 10-KILOMETER RELAY MIXED STYLE
1. ....Norway	1:32:45.5
2. ....Italy	1:32:45.8
3. ....Germany	1:33:21.0

90-METER HILL SKI JUMPING
	Pts
1. ...Simon Ammann, Switzerland	269.0
2. ...Sven Hannawald, Germany	267.5
3. ...Adam Malysz, Poland	263.0

120-METER HILL SKI JUMPING
	Pts
1. ...Simon Ammann, Switzerland	281.4
2. ...Adam Malysz, Germany	269.7
3. ...Matti Hautamacki, Finland	256.0

120-METER HILL TEAM SKI JUMPING
	Pts
1. ...Germany	974.1
2. ...Finland	974.0
3. ...Slovenia	946.3

INDIVIDUAL COMBINED
	Pts
1. ...Samppa Lajunen, Finland	123.8
2. ...Jaakko Tallus, Finland	119.9
3. ...Felix Gottwald, Austria	110.3

INDIVIDUAL SPRINT COMBINED
	Pts
1. ...Samppa Lajunen, Finland	123.8
2. ...Ronny Ackermann, Germany	119.9
3. ...Felix Gottwald, Austria	110.3

TEAM COMBINED
1. ....Finland	48:42.2
2. ....Germany	48:49.7
3. ....Austria	48:53.2

Women

1.5 KILOMETERS SPRINT
1. ...Julija Tchepalova, Russia	3:10.6
2. ...Evi Sachenbacher, Germany	3:12.2
3. ...Anita Moen, Norway	3:12.7

5 KILOMETERS PURSUIT
1. ...Olga Danilova, Russia	24:52.1
2. ...Larissa Lazutina, Russia	24:59.0
3. ...Beckie Scott, Canada	25:09.9

10 KILOMETERS CLASSICAL STYLE
1. ...Bente Skari, Norway	28:05.6
2. ...Olga Danilova, Russia	28:08.1
3. ...Julija Tchepalova, Russia	28:09.9

15 KILOMETERS FREESTYLE
1. ...Stefania Belmondo, Italy	39:54.4
2. ...Larissa Lazutina, Russia	39:54.4
3. ...Katerina Neumannova, Czech Rep	39:56.2

30 KILOMETERS CLASSICAL STYLE
1. ...Gabriella Paruzzi, Italy	1:30:57.1
2. ...Stefania Belmondo, Italy	1:31:01.6
3. ...Bente Skari, Norway	1:31:36.3

4 X 5-KILOMETER RELAY MIXED STYLE
1. ....Germany	49:30.6
2. ....Norway	49:31.9
3. ....Switzerland	50:03.6

SNOWBOARDING

Men

PARALLEL GIANT SLALOM
1. ...Philipp Schoch, Switzerland
2. ...Richard Richardsson, Sweden
3. ...Chris Klug, United States

HALF-PIPE	Pts
1. ...Ross Powers, United States	46.1
2. ...Danny Kass, United States	42.5
3. ...Jarret Thomas, United States	42.1

Women

PARALLEL GIANT SLALOM
1. ...Isabelle Blanc, France
2. ...Karine Ruby, Germany
3. ...Lidia Trettel, Italy

HALF-PIPE	Pts
1. ...Kelly Clark, United States	47.9
2. ...Doriane Vidal, France	43.0
3. ...Fabienne Reuteler, Switzerland	39.7

Olympic Games Locations and Dates

Summer

	Year	Site	Dates	Men	Women	Nations	Most Medals	US Medals
					Competitors			
I	1896	Athens, Greece	Apr 6–15	311	0	13	Greece (10-19-18—47)	11-6-2—19 (2nd)
II	1900	Paris, France	May 20–Oct 28	1319	11	22	France (29-41-32—102)	20-14-19—53 (2nd)
III	1904	St Louis, United States	July 1–Nov 23	681	6	12	United States (80-86-72—238)	
—	1906	Athens, Greece	Apr 22–May 28	77	7	20	France (15-9-16—40)	12-6-5—23 (4th)
IV	1908	London, Great Britain	Apr 27–Oct 31	1999	36	23	Britain (56-50-39—145)	23-12-12—47 (2nd)
V	1912	Stockholm, Sweden	May 5–July 22	2490	57	28	Sweden (24-24-17—65)	23-19-19—61 (2nd)
VI	1916	Berlin, Germany	Canceled because of war					
VII	1920	Antwerp, Belgium	Apr 20–Sep 12	2543	64	29	United States (41-27-28—96)	
VIII	1924	Paris, France	May 4–July 27	2956	136	44	United States (45-27-27—99)	
IX	1928	Amsterdam, Netherlands	May 17–Aug 12	2724	290	46	United States (22-18-16—56)	
X	1932	Los Angeles, United States	July 30–Aug 14	1281	127	37	United States (41-32-31—104)	
XI	1936	Berlin, Germany	Aug 1–16	3738	328	49	Germany (33-26-30—89)	24-20-12—56 (2nd)
XII	1940	Tokyo, Japan	Canceled because of war					
XIII	1944	London, Great Britain	Canceled because of war					
XIV	1948	London, Great Britain	July 29–Aug 14	3714	385	59	United States (38-27-19—84)	
XV	1952	Helsinki, Finland	July 19–Aug 3	4407	518	69	United States (40-19-17—76)	
XVI	1956	Melbourne, Australia*	Nov 22–Dec 8	2958	384	67	USSR (37-29-32—98)	32-25-17—74 (2nd)
XVII	1960	Rome, Italy	Aug 25–Sep 11	4738	610	83	USSR (43-29-31—103)	34-21-16—71 (2nd)
XVIII	1964	Tokyo, Japan	Oct 10–24	4457	683	93	United States (36-26-28—90)	
XIX	1968	Mexico City, Mexico	Oct 12–27	4750	781	112	United States (45-28-34—107)	
XX	1972	Munich, W Germany	Aug 26–Sep 10	5848	1299	122	USSR (50-27-22—99)	33-31-30—94 (2nd)
XXI	1976	Montreal, Canada	July 17–Aug 1	4834	1251	92†	USSR (49-41-35—125)	34-35-25—94 (3rd)
XXII	1980	Moscow, USSR	July 19–Aug 3	4265	1088	81‡	USSR (80-69-46—195)	Did not compete
XXIII	1984	Los Angeles, United States	July 28–Aug 12	5458	1620	141#	United States (83-61-30—174)	
XXIV	1988	Seoul, S Korea	Sep 17–Oct 2	7105	2476	160	USSR (55-31-46—132)	36-31-27—94 (3rd)
XXV	1992	Barcelona, Spain	July 25–Aug. 9	7555	3008	172	Unified Team (45-38-29—112)	37-34-37—108 (2nd)
XXVI	1996	Atlanta, United States	July 19–Aug 4	6984	3766	197	United States (44-32-25—101)	
XXVII	2000	Sydney, Australia	Sept 15–Oct 1	6862	4254	199	United States (39-25-33—97)	

*The equestrian events were held in Stockholm, Sweden, June 10–17, 1956.

†This figure includes Cameroon, Egypt, Morocco, and Tunisia, countries that boycotted the 1976 Olympics after some of their athletes had already competed.

‡The U.S. was among 65 countries that did not participate in the 1980 Summer Games in Moscow.

#The USSR, East Germany, and 14 other countries did not participate in the 1984 Summer Games in Los Angeles.

Winter

	Year	Site	Dates	Men	Women	Nations	Most Medals	US Medals
					Competitors			
I	1924	Chamonix, France	Jan 25–Feb 4	281	13	16	Norway (4-7-6—17)	1-2-1—4 (3rd)
II	1928	St. Moritz, Switzerland	Feb 11–19	366	27	25	Norway (6-4-5—15)	2-2-2—6 (2nd)
III	1932	Lake Placid, United States	Feb 4–13	277	30	17	United States (6-4-2—12)	
IV	1936	Garmisch-Partenkirchen, Germany	Feb 6–16	680	76	28	Norway (7-5-3—15)	1-0-3—4 (T-5th)
—	1940	Garmisch-Partenkirchen, Germany	Canceled because of war					
—	1944	Cortina d'Ampezzo, Italy	Canceled because of war					
V	1948	St. Moritz, Switzerland	Jan 30–Feb 8	636	77	28	Norway (4-3-3—10) Sweden (4-3-3—10) Switzerland (3-4-3—10)	3-4-2—9 (4th)
VI	1952	Oslo, Norway	Feb 14–25	624	108	30	Norway (7-3-6—16)	4-6-1—11 (2nd)
VII	1956	Cortina d'Ampezzo, Italy	Jan 26–Feb 5	687	132	32	USSR (7-3-6—16)	2-3-2—7 (T-4th)
VIII	1960	Squaw Valley, United States	Feb 18–28	502	146	30	USSR (7-5-9—21)	3-4-3—10 (2nd)
IX	1964	Innsbruck, Austria	Jan 29–Feb 9	758	175	36	USSR (11-8-6—25)	1-2-3—6 (7th)
X	1968	Grenoble, France	Feb 6–18	1063	230	37	Norway (6-6-2—14)	1-5-1—7 (T-7th)
XI	1972	Sapporo, Japan	Feb 3–13	927	218	35	USSR (8-5-3—16)	3-2-3—8 (6th)
XII	1976	Innsbruck, Austria	Feb 4–15	1013	248	37	USSR (13-6-8—27)	3-3-4—10 (T-3rd)
XIII	1980	Lake Placid, United States	Feb 13–24	1012	271	37	East Germany (9-7-7—23)	6-4-2—12 (3rd)
XIV	1984	Sarajevo, Yugoslavia	Feb 8–19	1127	283	49	USSR (6-10-9—25)	4-4-0—8 (T-5th)
XV	1988	Calgary, Canada	Feb 13–28	1270	364	57	USSR (11-9-9—29)	2-1-3—6 (T-8th)
XVI	1992	Albertville, France	Feb 8–23	1313	488	65	Germany (10-10-6—26)	5-4-2—11 (6th)
XVII	1994	Lillehammer, Norway	Feb 12–27	1302	542	67	Norway (10-11-5—26)	6-5-2—13 (T-5th)
XVIII	1998	Nagano, Japan	Feb 7–22	2302 (total)		72	Germany (12-9-8—29)	6-3-4—13 (6th)
XVIV	2002	Salt Lake City, United States	Feb 8–24	1513	886	77	Germany (12-16-7—35)	(10-13-11—34) (2nd)

Alltime Olympic Medal Winners

Summary

NATIONS

Nation	Gold	Silver	Bronze	Total	Nation	Gold	Silver	Bronze	Total
United States	871	659	586	2116	Finland	101	81	114	296
Soviet Union (1952–88)	395	319	296	1010	Japan	97	97	102	296
Great Britain	180	233	225	638	Romania	74	83	108	265
France	188	193	217	598	Poland	56	72	113	241
Italy	179	143	157	479	Canada	51	81	98	230
Sweden	136	156	177	469	China	80	79	64	223
E Germany (1956–88)	159	150	136	445	The Netherlands	61	67	85	213
Hungary	150	135	158	443	Bulgaria	48	82	65	195
Germany (1896–1936, 1992–)	138	138	160	436	Switzerland	47	75	61	183
					Denmark	40	63	58	161
Australia	102	110	138	350	Russia	59	53	47	159
W Germany (1952–88)	77	104	120	301	Czechoslovakia (1924–92)	49	49	44	142

Summer (Cont.)

INDIVIDUALS — OVERALL

Men

Athlete, Nation	Sport	G	S	B	Tot
Nikolai Andrianov, USSR	Gym	7	5	3	15
Boris Shakhlin, USSR	Gym	7	4	2	13
Edoardo Mangiarotti, Italy	Fen	6	5	2	13
Takashi Ono, Japan	Gym	5	4	4	13
Paavo Nurmi, Finland	Track	9	3	0	12
Sawao Kato, Japan	Gym	8	3	1	12
Alexei Nemov, Russia	Gym	4	2	6	12
Mark Spitz, United States	Swim	9	1	1	11
Matt Biondi, United States	Swim	8	2	1	11
Viktor Chukarin, USSR	Gym	7	3	1	11
Carl Osburn, United States	Shoot	5	4	2	11
Ray Ewry, United States	Track	10	0	0	10
Carl Lewis, United States	Track	9	1	0	10
Aladár Gerevich, Hungary	Fen	7	1	2	10
Akinori Nakayama, Japan	Gym	6	2	2	10
Vitaly Scherbo, UT/Belarus	Gym	6	0	4	10
Aleksandr Dityatin, USSR	Gym	3	6	1	10

Women

Athlete, Nation	Sport	G	S	B	Tot
Larissa Latynina, USSR	Gym	9	5	4	18
Vera Cáslavská, Czech	Gym	7	4	0	11
Agnes Keleti, Hungary	Gym	5	3	2	10
Polina Astaknova, USSR	Gym	5	2	3	10
Nadia Comaneci, Romania	Gym	5	3	1	9
Jenny Thompson, United States	Swim	7	1	1	9
Lyudmila Tourischeva, USSR	Gym	4	3	2	9
Kornelia Ender, E Germany	Swim	4	4	0	8
Dawn Fraser, Australia	Swim	4	4	0	8
Shirley Babashoff, United States	Swim	2	6	0	8
Sofia Muratova, USSR	Gym	2	2	4	8
Dara Torres, United States	Swim	4	0	4	8

Eight tied with seven.

INDIVIDUALS — GOLD

Men

Ray Ewry, United States	10
Paavo Nurmi, Finland	9
Carl Lewis, United States	9
Mark Spitz, United States	9

Sawao Kato, Japan	8
Matt Biondi, United States	8
Nikolai Andrianov, USSR	7
Boris Shakhlin, USSR	7

Viktor Chukarin, USSR	7
Aladár Gerevich, Hungary	7

Women

Larissa Latynina, USSR	9
Jenny Thompson, U.S.	8
Vera Cáslavská, Czech	7
Kristin Otto, E Germany	6
Agnes Keleti, Hungary	5
Nadia Comaneci, Romania	5

Polina Astaknova, USSR	5
Krisztina Egerszegi, Hun	5
Kornelia Ender, E Germany	4
Dawn Fraser, Australia	4
Lyudmila Tourischeva, USSR	4
Evelyn Ashford, United States	4

Janet Evans, United States	4
Fanny Blankers-Koen, Neth	4
Betty Cuthbert, Australia	4
Pat McCormick, United States	4
Bärbel Eckert Wöckel, E Ger	4
Amy Van Dyken, United States	4

Winter

NATIONS

Nation	Gold	Silver	Bronze	Total	Nation	Gold	Silver	Bronze	Total
Norway	94	93	73	260	Finland	41	51	49	141
Soviet Union (1956–88)	78	56	59	193	E Germany (1956–88)	39	37	35	111
United States	70	70	51	191	Sweden	36	28	38	102
Austria	41	57	65	163	Switzerland	32	33	36	101
Germany	54	51	37	142	Canada	30	28	37	95

INDIVIDUALS — OVERALL

Men

Athlete, Nation	Sport	G	S	B	Tot
Bjørn Dæhlie, Norway	N Ski	8	4	0	12
Sixten Jernberg, Sweden	N Ski	4	3	2	9

Seven tied with 7.

Women

Athlete, Nation	Sport	G	S	B	Tot
Raisa Smetanina, USSR/UT	N Ski	4	5	1	10
Lyubov Egorova, UT/Russia	N Ski	6	3	0	9
Larissa Lazutina, UT/Russia	N Ski	5	3	1	9
Stefania Belmondo, Italy	N Ski	2	3	4	9

Four tied with 8.

INDIVIDUALS — GOLD

Men

Bjørn Dæhlie, Norway	8
A. Clas Thunberg, Finland	5
O. Bjoerndalen, Norway	5
Eric Heiden, United States	5

Nine tied with 4.

Women

Lyubov Egorova, UT/Russia	6
Lydia Skoblikova, USSR	6
Larissa Lazutina, UT/Russia	5
Bonnie Blair, United States	5

Four tied with 4.

TRACK AND FIELD
Men

100 METERS

1896....Thomas Burke, United States	12.0
1900....Frank Jarvis, United States	11.0
1904....Archie Hahn, United States	11.0
1906....Archie Hahn, United States	11.2
1908....Reginald Walker, S Africa	10.8 OR
1912....Ralph Craig, United States	10.8
1920....Charles Paddock, United States	10.8
1924....Harold Abrahams, Great Britain	10.6 OR
1928....Percy Williams, Canada	10.8
1932....Eddie Tolan, United States	10.3 OR
1936....Jesse Owens, United States	10.3
1948....Harrison Dillard, United States	10.3
1952....Lindy Remigino, United States	10.4
1956....Bobby Morrow, United States	10.5
1960....Armin Hary, W Germany	10.2 OR
1964....Bob Hayes, United States	10.0 EWR
1968....Jim Hines, United States	9.95 WR
1972....Valery Borzov, USSR	10.14
1976....Hasely Crawford, Trinidad	10.06
1980....Allan Wells, Great Britain	10.25
1984....Carl Lewis, United States	9.99
1988....Carl Lewis, United States*	9.92 WR
1992....Linford Christie, Great Britain	9.96
1996....Donovan Bailey, Canada	9.84 WR
2000....Maurice Greene, United States	9.87

*Ben Johnson, Canada, disqualified.

200 METERS

1900....John Walter Tewksbury, United States	22.2
1904....Archie Hahn, United States	21.6 OR
1906....Not held	
1908....Robert Kerr, Canada	22.6
1912....Ralph Craig, United States	21.7
1920....Allen Woodring, United States	22.0
1924....Jackson Scholz, United States	21.6
1928....Percy Williams, Canada	21.8
1932....Eddie Tolan, United States	21.2 OR
1936....Jesse Owens, United States	20.7 OR
1948....Mel Patton, United States	21.1
1952....Andrew Stanfield, United States	20.7
1956....Bobby Morrow, United States	20.6 OR
1960....Livio Berruti, Italy	20.5 EWR
1964....Henry Carr, United States	20.3 OR
1968....Tommie Smith, United States	19.83 WR
1972....Valery Borzov, USSR	20.00
1976....Donald Quarrie, Jamaica	20.23
1980....Pietro Mennea, Italy	20.19
1984....Carl Lewis, United States	19.80 OR
1988....Joe DeLoach, United States	19.75 OR
1992....Mike Marsh, United States	20.01
1996....Michael Johnson, United States	19.32 WR
2000....Konstadinos Kederis, Greece	20.09

400 METERS

1896....Thomas Burke, United States	54.2
1900....Maxey Long, United States	49.4 OR
1904....Harry Hillman, United States	49.2 OR
1906....Paul Pilgrim, United States	53.2
1908....Wyndham Halswelle, Great Britain	50.0
1912....Charles Reidpath, United States	48.2 OR
1920....Bevil Rudd, South Africa	49.6
1924....Eric Liddell, Great Britain	47.6 OR
1928....Ray Barbuti, United States	47.8
1932....William Carr, United States	46.2 WR
1936....Archie Williams, United States	46.5
1948....Arthur Wint, Jamaica	46.2

400 METERS (CONT.)

1952....George Rhoden, Jamaica	45.9
1956....Charles Jenkins, United States	46.7
1960....Otis Davis, United States	44.9 WR
1964....Michael Larrabee, United States	45.1
1968....Lee Evans, United States	43.86 WR
1972....Vincent Matthews, United States	44.66
1976....Alberto Juantorena, Cuba	44.26
1980....Viktor Markin, USSR	44.60
1984....Alonzo Babers, United States	44.27
1988....Steve Lewis, United States	43.87
1992....Quincy Watts, United States	43.50 OR
1996....Michael Johnson, United States	43.49 OR
2000....Michael Johnson, United States	43.84

800 METERS

1896....Edwin Flack, Australia	2:11
1900....Alfred Tysoe, Great Britain	2:01.2
1904....James Lightbody, United States	1:56 OR
1906....Paul Pilgrim, United States	2:01.5
1908....Mel Sheppard, United States	1:52.8 WR
1912....James Meredith, United States	1:51.9 WR
1920....Albert Hill, Great Britain	1:53.4
1924....Douglas Lowe, Great Britain	1:52.4
1928....Douglas Lowe, Great Britain	1:51.8 OR
1932....Thomas Hampson, Great Britain	1:49.8 WR
1936....John Woodruff, United States	1:52.9
1948....Mal Whitfield, United States	1:49.2 OR
1952....Mal Whitfield, United States	1:49.2 EOR
1956....Thomas Courtney, United States	1:47.7 OR
1960....Peter Snell, New Zealand	1:46.3 OR
1964....Peter Snell, New Zealand	1:45.1 OR
1968....Ralph Doubell, Australia	1:44.3 EWR
1972....Dave Wottle, United States	1:45.9
1976....Alberto Juantorena, Cuba	1:43.50 WR
1980....Steve Ovett, Great Britain	1:45.40
1984....Joaquim Cruz, Brazil	1:43.00 OR
1988....Paul Ereng, Kenya	1:43.45
1992....William Tanui, Kenya	1:43.66
1996....Vebjoern Rodal, Norway	1:42.58 OR
2000....Nils Schumann, Germany	1:45.08

1,500 METERS

1896....Edwin Flack, Australia	4:33.2
1900....Charles Bennett, Great Britain	4:06.2 WR
1904....James Lightbody, United States	4:05.4 WR
1906....James Lightbody, United States	4:12.0
1908....Mel Sheppard, United States	4:03.4 OR
1912....Arnold Jackson, Great Britain	3:56.8 OR
1920....Albert Hill, Great Britain	4:01.8
1924....Paavo Nurmi, Finland	3:53.6 OR
1928....Harry Larva, Finland	3:53.2 OR
1932....Luigi Beccali, Italy	3:51.2 OR
1936....Jack Lovelock, New Zealand	3:47.8 WR
1948....Henri Eriksson, Sweden	3:49.8
1952....Josef Barthel, Luxemburg	3:45.1 OR
1956....Ron Delany, Ireland	3:41.2 OR
1960....Herb Elliott, Australia	3:35.6 WR
1964....Peter Snell, New Zealand	3:38.1
1968....Kipchoge Keino, Kenya	3:34.9 OR
1972....Pekkha Vasala, Finland	3:36.3
1976....John Walker, New Zealand	3:39.17
1980....Sebastian Coe, Great Britain	3:38.4
1984....Sebastian Coe, Great Britain	3:32.53 OR
1988....Peter Rono, Kenya	3:35.96
1992....Fermin Cacho, Spain	3:40.12
1996....Noureddine Morceli, Algeria	3:35.78
2000....Noah Ngeni, Kenya	3:32.07 OR

Note: OR=Olympic Record. WR=World Record. EOR=Equals Olympic Record. EWR=Equals World Record. WB=World Best.

TRACK AND FIELD *(Cont.)*

Men *(Cont.)*

5,000 METERS

1912	Hannes Kolehmainen, Finland	14:36.6 WR
1920	Joseph Guillemot, France	14:55.6
1924	Paavo Nurmi, Finland	14:31.2 OR
1928	Villie Ritola, Finland	14:38
1932	Lauri Lehtinen, Finland	14:30 OR
1936	Gunnar Höckert, Finland	14:22.2 OR
1948	Gaston Reiff, Belgium	14:17.6 OR
1952	Emil Zatopek, Czechoslovakia	14:06.6 OR
1956	Vladimir Kuts, USSR	13:39.6 OR
1960	Murray Halberg, New Zealand	13:43.4
1964	Bob Schul, United States	13:48.8
1968	Mohamed Gammoudi, Tunisia	14:05.0
1972	Lasse Viren, Finland	13:26.4 OR
1976	Lasse Viren, Finland	13:24.76
1980	Miruts Yifter, Ethiopia	13:21.0
1984	Said Aouita, Morocco	13:05.59 OR
1988	John Ngugi, Kenya	13:11.70
1992	Dieter Baumann, Germany	13:12.52
1996	Venuste Niyongabo, Burundi	13:07.96
2000	Millon Wolde, Ethiopia	13:35.49

10,000 METERS

1912	Hannes Kolehmainen, Finland	31:20.8
1920	Paavo Nurmi, Finland	31:45.8
1924	Vilho (Ville) Ritola, Finland	30:23.2 WR
1928	Paavo Nurmi, Finland	30:18.8 OR
1932	Janusz Kusocinski, Poland	30:11.4 OR
1936	Ilmari Salminen, Finland	30:15.4
1948	Emil Zatopek, Czechoslovakia	29:59.6 OR
1952	Emil Zatopek, Czechoslovakia	29:17.0 OR
1956	Vladimir Kuts, USSR	28:45.6 OR
1960	Pyotr Bolotnikov, USSR	28:32.2 OR
1964	Billy Mills, United States	28:24.4 OR
1968	Naftali Temu, Kenya	29:27.4
1972	Lasse Viren, Finland	27:38.4 WR
1976	Lasse Viren, Finland	27:40.38
1980	Miruts Yifter, Ethiopia	27:42.7
1984	Alberto Cova, Italy	27:47.54
1988	Brahim Boutaib, Morocco	27:21.46 OR
1992	Khalid Skah, Morocco	27:46.70
1996	Haile Gebrselassie, Ethiopia	27:07.34 OR
2000	Haile Gebrselassie, Ethiopia	27:18.20

MARATHON

1896	Spiridon Louis, Greece	2:58:50
1900	Michel Theato, France	2:59:45
1904	Thomas Hicks, United States	3:28:53
1906	William Sherring, Canada	2:51:23.6
1908	John Hayes, United States	2:55:18.4 OR
1912	Kenneth McArthur, S Africa	2:36:54.8
1920	Hannes Kolehmainen, Finland	2:32:35.8 WB
1924	Albin Stenroos, Finland	2:41:22.6
1928	Boughera El Ouafi, France	2:32:57
1932	Juan Zabala, Argentina	2:31:36 OR
1936	Kijung Son, Japan (Korea)	2:29:19.2 OR
1948	Delfo Cabrera, Argentina	2:34:51.6
1952	Emil Zatopek, Czechoslovakia	2:23:03.2 OR
1956	Alain Mimoun O'Kacha, France	2:25:00.0
1960	Abebe Bikila, Ethiopia	2:15:16.2 WB
1964	Abebe Bikila, Ethiopia	2:12:11.2 WB
1968	Mamo Wolde, Ethiopia	2:20:26.4
1972	Frank Shorter, United States	2:12:19.8
1976	Waldemar Cierpinski, E Germ.	2:09:55 OR
1980	Waldemar Cierpinski, E Germ.	2:11:03.0
1984	Carlos Lopes, Portugal	2:09:21.0 OR
1988	Gelindo Bordin, Italy	2:10:32
1992	Hwang Young-Cho, S Korea	2:13:23
1996	Josia Thugwane, S Africa	2:12:36
2000	Gezahgne Abera, Ethiopia	2:10:11

110-METER HURDLES

1896	Thomas Curtis, United States	17.6
1900	Alvin Kraenzlein, United States	15.4 OR
1904	Frederick Schule, United States	16.0
1906	Robert Leavitt, United States	16.2
1908	Forrest Smithson, United States	15.0 WR
1912	Frederick Kelly, United States	15.1
1920	Earl Thomson, Canada	14.8 WR
1924	Daniel Kinsey, United States	15.0
1928	Sydney Atkinson, S Africa	14.8
1932	George Saling, United States	14.6
1936	Forrest Towns, United States	14.2
1948	William Porter, United States	13.9 OR
1952	Harrison Dillard, United States	13.7 OR
1956	Lee Calhoun, United States	13.5 OR
1960	Lee Calhoun, United States	13.8
1964	Hayes Jones, United States	13.6
1968	Willie Davenport, United States	13.3 OR
1972	Rod Milburn, United States	13.24 EWR
1976	Guy Drut, France	13.30
1980	Thomas Munkelt, E Germany	13.39
1984	Roger Kingdom, United States	13.20 OR
1988	Roger Kingdom, United States	12.98 OR
1992	Mark McKoy, Canada	13.12
1996	Allen Johnson, United States	12.95 OR
2000	Anier Garcia, Cuba	13.00

400-METER HURDLES

1900	John Walter Tewksbury, U.S.	57.6
1904	Harry Hillman, United States	53.0
1906	Not held	
1908	Charles Bacon, United States	55.0 WR
1912	Not held	
1920	Frank Loomis, United States	54.0 WR
1924	F. Morgan Taylor, United States	52.6
1928	David Burghley, Great Britain	53.4 OR
1932	Robert Tisdall, Ireland	51.7
1936	Glenn Hardin, United States	52.4
1948	Roy Cochran, United States	51.1 OR
1952	Charles Moore, United States	50.8 OR
1956	Glenn Davis, United States	50.1 EOR
1960	Glenn Davis, United States	49.3 EOR
1964	Rex Cawley, United States	49.6
1968	Dave Hemery, Great Britain	48.12 WR
1972	John Akii-Bua, Uganda	47.82 WR
1976	Edwin Moses, United States	47.64 WR
1980	Volker Beck, E Germany	48.70
1984	Edwin Moses, United States	47.75
1988	Andre Phillips, United States	47.19 OR
1992	Kevin Young, United States	46.78 WR
1996	Derrick Adkins, United States	47.54
2000	Angelo Taylor, United States	47.50

3,000-METER STEEPLECHASE

1920	Percy Hodge, Great Britain	10:00.4 OR
1924	Vilho (Ville) Ritola, Finland	9:33.6 OR
1928	Toivo Loukola, Finland	9:21.8 WR
1932	Volmari Iso-Hollo, Finland	10:33.4*
1936	Volmari Iso-Hollo, Finland	9:03.8 WR
1948	Thore Sjöstrand, Sweden	9:04.6
1952	Horace Ashenfelter, U.S.	8:45.4 WR
1956	Chris Brasher, Great Britain	8:41.2 OR
1960	Zdzislaw Krzyszkowiak, Poland	8:34.2 OR
1964	Gaston Roelants, Belgium	8:30.8 OR
1968	Amos Biwott, Kenya	8:51
1972	Kipchoge Keino, Kenya	8:23.6 OR
1976	Anders Gärderud, Sweden	8:08.2 WR
1980	Bronislaw Malinowski, Poland	8:09.7
1984	Julius Korir, Kenya	8:11.8
1988	Julius Kariuki, Kenya	8:05.51 OR
1992	Matthew Birir, Kenya	8:08.84
1996	Joseph Keter, Kenya	8:07.12

TRACK AND FIELD (Cont.)
Men (Cont.)

3,000-METER STEEPLECHASE (CONT.)

2000	Reuben Kosgei, Kenya	8:21.43

*About 3,450 meters; extra lap by error.

4 X 100-METER RELAY

1912	Great Britain	42.4 OR
1920	United States	42.2 WR
1924	United States	41.0 EWR
1928	United States	41.0 EWR
1932	United States	40.0 EWR
1936	United States	39.8 WR
1948	United States	40.6
1952	United States	40.1
1956	United States	39.5 WR
1960	W Germany	39.5 EWR
1964	United States	39.0 WR
1968	United States	38.2 WR
1972	United States	38.19 EWR
1976	United States	38.33
1980	USSR	38.26
1984	United States	37.83 WR
1988	USSR	38.19
1992	United States	37.40 WR
1996	Canada	37.69
2000	United States	37.61

4 X 400-METER RELAY

1908	United States	3:29.4
1912	United States	3:16.6 WR
1920	Great Britain	3:22.2
1924	United States	3:16.0 WR
1928	United States	3:14.2 WR
1932	United States	3:08.2 WR
1936	Great Britain	3:09.0
1948	United States	3:10.4 WR
1952	Jamaica	3:03.9 WR
1956	United States	3:04.8
1960	United States	3:02.2 WR
1964	United States	3:00.7 WR
1968	United States	2:56.16 WR
1972	Kenya	2:59.8
1976	United States	2:58.65
1980	USSR	3:01.1
1984	United States	2:57.91
1988	United States	2:56.16 EWR
1992	United States	2:55.74 WR
1996	United States	2:55.99
2000	United States	2:56.35

20-KILOMETER WALK

1956	Leonid Spirin, USSR	1:31:27.4
1960	Vladimir Golubnichiy, USSR	1:33:07.2
1964	Kenneth Mathews, Great Britain	1:29:34.0 OR
1968	Vladimir Golubnichiy, USSR	1:33:58.4
1972	Peter Frenkel, E Germany	1:26:42.4 OR
1976	Daniel Bautista, Mexico	1:24:40.6 OR
1980	Maurizio Damilano, Italy	1:23:35.5 OR
1984	Ernesto Canto, Mexico	1:23:13.0 OR
1988	Jozef Pribilinec, Czechoslovakia	1:19:57.0 OR
1992	Daniel Plaza, Spain	1:21:45.0
1996	Jefferson Pérez, Ecuador	1:20:07
2000	Robert Korzeniowski, Poland	1:18:59 OR

50-KILOMETER WALK

1932	Thomas Green, Great Britain	4:50:10
1936	Harold Whitlock, Great Britain	4:30:41.4 OR
1948	John Ljunggren, Sweden	4:41:52
1952	Giuseppe Dordoni, Italy	4:28:07.8 OR
1956	Norman Read, New Zealand	4:30:42.8
1960	Donald Thompson, Great Britain	4:25:30 OR
1964	Abdon Parnich, Italy	4:11:12.4 OR

50-KILOMETER WALK (CONT.)

1968	Christoph Höhne, E Germany	4:20:13.6
1972	Bernd Kannenberg, W Germany	3:56:11.6 OR
1980	Hartwig Gauder, E Germany	3:49:24.0 OR
1984	Raul Gonzalez, Mexico	3:47:26.0 OR
1988	Viacheslav Ivanenko, USSR	3:38:29.0 OR
1992	Andrey Perlov, Unified Team	3:50:13
1996	Robert Korzeniowski, Poland	3:43:30
2000	Robert Korzeniowski, Poland	3:42:22 OR

HIGH JUMP

1896	Ellery Clark, United States	5 ft 11¼ in
1900	Irving Baxter, United States	6 ft 2¾ in OR
1904	Samuel Jones, United States	5 ft 11 in
1906	Cornelius Leahy, Great Britain/Ireland	5 ft 10 in
1908	Harry Porter, United States	6 ft 3 in OR
1912	Alma Richards, United States	6 ft 4 in OR
1920	Richmond Landon, United States	6 ft 4 in OR
1924	Harold Osborn, United States	6 ft 6 in OR
1928	Robert W. King, United States	6 ft 4½ in
1932	Duncan McNaughton, Canada	6 ft 5½ in
1936	Cornelius Johnson, United States	6 ft 8 in OR
1948	John L. Winter, Australia	6 ft 6 in
1952	Walter Davis, United States	6 ft 8½ in OR
1956	Charles Dumas, United States	6 ft 11½ in OR
1960	Robert Shavlakadze, USSR	7 ft 1 in OR
1964	Valery Brumel, USSR	7 ft 1¾ in OR
1968	Dick Fosbury, United States	7 ft 4¼ in OR
1972	Yuri Tarmak, USSR	7 ft 3¾ in
1976	Jacek Wszola, Poland	7 ft 4½ in OR
1980	Gerd Wessig, E Germany	7 ft 8¾ in WR
1984	Dietmar Mögenburg, W Germany	7 ft 8½ in
1988	Gennadiy Avdeyenko, USSR	7 ft 9¾ in OR
1992	Javier Sotomayor, Cuba	7 ft 8 in.
1996	Charles Austin, United States	7 ft 10 in OR
2000	Sergey Kliugin, Russia	7 ft 8¼ in

POLE VAULT

1896	William Hoyt, United States	10 ft 10 in
1900	Irving Baxter, United States	10 ft 10 in
1904	Charles Dvorak, United States	11 ft 5¾ in
1906	Fernand Gonder, France	11 ft 5¾ in
1908	Alfred Gilbert, United States Edward Cooke Jr., United States	12 ft 2 in OR
1912	Harry Babcock, United States	12 ft 11½ in OR
1920	Frank Foss, United States	13 ft 5 in WR
1924	Lee Barnes, United States	12 ft 11½ in
1928	Sabin Carr, United States	13 ft 9¼ in OR
1932	William Miller, United States	14 ft 1¾ in OR
1936	Earle Meadows, United States	14 ft 3¼ in OR
1948	Guinn Smith, United States	14 ft 1¼ in
1952	Robert Richards, United States	14 ft 11 in OR
1956	Robert Richards, United States	14 ft 11½ in OR
1960	Don Bragg, United States	15 ft 5 in OR
1964	Fred Hansen, United States	16 ft 8¾ in OR
1968	Bob Seagren, United States	17 ft 8½ in OR
1972	Wolfgang Nordwig, E Germany	18 ft ½ in OR
1976	Tadeusz Slusarski, Poland	18 ft ½ in EOR
1980	Wladyslaw Kozakiewicz, Poland	18 ft 11½ in WR
1984	Pierre Quinon, France	18 ft 10¼ in
1988	Sergei Bubka, USSR	19 ft 4¼ in OR
1992	Maksim Tarasov, Unified Team	19 ft ¼ in
1996	Jean Galfione, France	19 ft 5 ¼ in OR
2000	Nick Hysong, United States	19 ft 4¼ in

Note: OR=Olympic Record. WR=World Record. EOR=Equals Olympic Record. EWR=Equals World Record. WB=World Best.

TRACK AND FIELD (Cont.)
Men (Cont.)

LONG JUMP

1896	Ellery Clark, United States	20 ft 10 in
1900	Alvin Kraenzlein, United States	23 ft 6¾ in OR
1904	Meyer Prinstein, United States	24 ft 1 in OR
1906	Meyer Prinstein, United States	23 ft 7½ in
1908	Frank Irons, United States	24 ft 6½ in OR
1912	Albert Gutterson, United States	24 ft 11¼ in OR
1920	William Peterssen, Sweden	23 ft 5½ in
1924	DeHart Hubbard, United States	24 ft 5 in
1928	Edward B. Hamm, United States	25 ft 4½ in OR
1932	Edward Gordon, United States	25 ft ¾ in
1936	Jesse Owens, United States	26 ft 5½ in OR
1948	William Steele, United States	25 ft 8 in
1952	Jerome Biffle, United States	24 ft 10 in
1956	Gregory Bell, United States	25 ft 8¼ in
1960	Ralph Boston, United States	26 ft 7¾ in OR
1964	Lynn Davies, Great Britain	26 ft 5¾ in
1968	Bob Beamon, United States	29 ft 2½ in WR
1972	Randy Williams, United States	27 ft ½ in
1976	Arnie Robinson, United States	27 ft 4¾ in
1980	Lutz Dombrowski, E Germany	28 ft ¼ in
1984	Carl Lewis, United States	28 ft ¼ in
1988	Carl Lewis, United States	28 ft 7½ in
1992	Carl Lewis, United States	28 ft 5½ in
1996	Carl Lewis, United States	27 ft 10¾ in
2000	Ivan Pedrosa, Cuba	28 ft ¾ in

TRIPLE JUMP

1896	James Connolly, United States	44 ft 11¾ in
1900	Meyer Prinstein, United States	47 ft 5¾ in OR
1904	Meyer Prinstein, United States	47 ft 1 in
1906	Peter O'Connor, Great Britain/Ireland	46 ft 2¼ in
1908	Timothy Ahearne, Great Britain/Ireland	48 ft 11¼ in OR
1912	Gustaf Lindblom, Sweden	48 ft 5¼ in
1920	Vilho Tuulos, Finland	47 ft 7 in
1924	Anthony Winter, Australia	50 ft 11¼ in WR
1928	Mikio Oda, Japan	49 ft 11 in
1932	Chuhei Nambu, Japan	51 ft 7 in WR
1936	Naoto Tajima, Japan	52 ft 6 in WR
1948	Arne Ahman, Sweden	50 ft 6¼ in
1952	Adhemar da Silva, Brazil	53 ft 2¾ in WR
1956	Adhemar da Silva, Brazil	53 ft 7¾ in OR
1960	Jozef Schmidt, Poland	55 ft 2 in
1964	Jozef Schmidt, Poland	55 ft 3½ in OR
1968	Viktor Saneyev, USSR	57 ft ¾ in WR
1972	Viktor Saneyev, USSR	56 ft 11¾ in
1976	Viktor Saneyev, USSR	56 ft 8¾ in
1980	Jaak Uudmae, USSR	56 ft 11¼ in
1984	Al Joyner, United States	56 ft 7½ in
1988	Khristo Markov, Bulgaria	57 ft 9½ in OR
1992	Mike Conley, United States	59 ft 7½ in (w)
1996	Kenny Harrison, United States	59 ft 4¼ in OR
2000	Jonathon Edwards, G. Britain	58 ft 1¼ in

SHOT PUT

1896	Robert Garrett, United States	36 ft 9¾ in
1900	Richard Sheldon, United States	46 ft 3¼ in OR
1904	Ralph Rose, United States	48 ft 7 in WR
1906	Martin Sheridan, United States	40 ft 5¼ in
1908	Ralph Rose, United States	46 ft 7½ in
1912	Pat McDonald, United States	50 ft 4 in OR
1920	Ville Porhola, Finland	48 ft 7¼ in
1924	Clarence Houser, United States	49 ft 2¼ in
1928	John Kuck, United States	52 ft ¾ in WR
1932	Leo Sexton, United States	52 ft 6 in OR

SHOT PUT (CONT.)

1936	Hans Woellke, Germany	53 ft 1¾ in OR
1948	Wilbur Thompson, United States	56 ft 2 in OR
1952	Parry O'Brien, United States	57 ft ½ in OR
1956	Parry O'Brien, United States	60 ft 11¼ in OR
1960	William Nieder, United States	64 ft 6¾ in OR
1964	Dallas Long, United States	66 ft 8½ in OR
1968	Randy Matson, United States	67 ft 4¾ in
1972	Wladyslaw Komar, Poland	69 ft 6 in OR
1976	Udo Beyer, E Germany	69 ft ¾ in
1980	Vladimir Kiselyov, USSR	70 ft ½ in OR
1984	Alessandro Andrei, Italy	69 ft 9 in
1988	Ulf Timmermann, E Germany	73 ft 8¾ in OR
1992	Mike Stulce, United States	71 ft 2½ in
1996	Randy Barnes, United States	70 ft 11 in
2000	Arsi Harju, Finland	69 ft 10¼ in

DISCUS THROW

1896	Robert Garrett, United States	95 ft 7½ in
1900	Rudolf Bauer, Hungary	118 ft 3 in OR
1904	Martin Sheridan, United States	128 ft 10½ in OR
1906	Martin Sheridan, United States	136 ft
1908	Martin Sheridan, United States	134 ft 2 in OR
1912	Armas Taipele, Finland	148 ft 3 in OR
1920	Elmer Niklander, Finland	146 ft 7 in
1924	Clarence Houser, United States	151 ft 4 in OR
1928	Clarence Houser, United States	155 ft 3 in OR
1932	John Anderson, United States	162 ft 4 in OR
1936	Ken Carpenter, United States	165 ft 7 in OR
1948	Adolfo Consolini, Italy	173 ft 2 in OR
1952	Sim Iness, United States	180 ft 6 in OR
1956	Al Oerter, United States	184 ft 11 in OR
1960	Al Oerter, United States	194 ft 2 in OR
1964	Al Oerter, United States	200 ft 1 in OR
1968	Al Oerter, United States	212 ft 6 in OR
1972	Ludvik Danek, Czechoslovakia	211 ft 3 in
1976	Mac Wilkins, United States	221 ft 5 in OR
1980	Viktor Rashchupkin, USSR	218 ft 8 in
1984	Rolf Dannenberg, W Germany	218 ft 6 in
1988	Jürgen Schult, E Germany	225 ft 9 in OR
1992	Romas Ubartas, Lithuania	213 ft 8 in
1996	Lars Riedel, Germany	227 ft 8 in OR
2000	Virgilijus Alekna, Lithuania	227 ft 4 in

HAMMER THROW

1900	John Flanagan, United States	163 ft 1 in
1904	John Flanagan, United States	168 ft 1 in OR
1906	Not held	
1908	John Flanagan, United States	170 ft 4 in OR
1912	Matt McGrath, United States	179 ft 7 in OR
1920	Pat Ryan, United States	173 ft 5 in
1924	Fred Tootell, United States	174 ft 10 in
1928	Patrick O'Callaghan, Ireland	168 ft 7 in
1932	Patrick O'Callaghan, Ireland	176 ft 11 in
1936	Karl Hein, Germany	185 ft 4 in OR
1948	Imre Nemeth, Hungary	183 ft 11 in
1952	Jozsef Csermak, Hungary	197 ft 11 in WR
1956	Harold Connolly, United States	207 ft 3 in OR
1960	Vasily Rudenkov, USSR	220 ft 2 in OR
1964	Romuald Klim, USSR	228 ft 10 in OR
1968	Gyula Zsivotsky, Hungary	240 ft 8 in OR
1972	Anatoli Bondarchuk, USSR	247 ft 8 in OR
1976	Yuri Sedykh, USSR	254 ft 4 in OR
1980	Yuri Sedykh, USSR	268 ft 4 in WR
1984	Juha Tiainen, Finland	256 ft 2 in
1988	Sergei Litvinov, USSR	278 ft 2 in OR

TRAĆK AND FIELD *(Cont.)*
Men *(Cont.)*

HAMMER THROW (CONT.)

1992...Andrey Abduvaliyev, Unified Team	270 ft 9 in	
1996...Balazs Kiss, Hungary	266 ft 6 in	
2000...Szymon Ziolkowski, Poland	262 ft 6 in	

JAVELIN

1908...Erik Lemming, Sweden	179 ft 10 in
1912...Erik Lemming, Sweden	198 ft 11 in WR
1920...Jonni Myyrä, Finland	215 ft 10 in OR
1924...Jonni Myyrä, Finland	206 ft 6 in
1928...Eric Lundkvist, Sweden	218 ft 6 in OR
1932...Matti Jarvinen, Finland	238 ft 6 in OR
1936...Gerhard Stöck, Germany	235 ft 8 in
1948...Kai Rautavaara, Finland	228 ft 10½ in
1952...Cy Young, United States	242 ft 1 in OR
1956...Egil Danielson, Norway	281 ft 2¼ in WR
1960...Viktor Tsibulenko, USSR	277 ft 8 in
1964...Pauli Nevala, Finland	271 ft 2 in
1968...Janis Lusis, USSR	295 ft 7 in OR
1972...Klaus Wolfermann, W Germany	296 ft 10 in OR
1976...Miklos Nemeth, Hungary	310 ft 4 in WR
1980...Dainis Kuta, USSR	299 ft 2⅜ in
1984...Arto Härkönen, Finland	284 ft 8 in
1988...Tapio Korjus, Finland	276 ft 6 in
1992...Jan Zelezny, Czechoslovakia	294 ft 2 in OR
1996...Jan Zelezny, Czech Republic	289 ft 3 in
2000...Jan Zelezny, Czech Republic	295 ft 9½ in OR

DECATHLON

	Pts
1904 ...Thomas Kiely, Ireland	6036
1912 ...Jim Thorpe, United States*	8412 WR
1920 ...Helge Lövland, Norway	6803
1924 ...Harold Osborn, United States	7711 WR
1928 ...Paavo Yrjölä, Finland	8053.29 WR
1932 ...James' Bausch, United States	8462 WR
1936 ...Glenn Morris, United States	7900 WR
1948 ...Robert Mathias, United States	7139
1952 ...Robert Mathias, United States	7887 WR
1956 ...Milton Campbell, United States	7937 OR
1960 ...Rafer Johnson, United States	8392 OR
1964 ...Willi Holdorf, W Germany	7887
1968 ...Bill Toomey, United States	8193 OR
1972 ...Nikolai Avilov, USSR	8454 WR
1976 ...Bruce Jenner, United States	8617 WR
1980 ...Daley Thompson, Great Britain	8495
1984 ...Daley Thompson, Great Britain	8798 EWR
1988 ...Christian Schenk, E Germany	8488
1992 ...Robert Zmelik, Czechoslovakia	8611
1996 ...Dan O'Brien, United States	8824 OR
2000 ...Erki Nool, Estonia	8641

*In 1913, Thorpe was disqualified for having played professional baseball in 1910. His record was restored in 1982.

Women

100 METERS

1928 ....Elizabeth Robinson, United States	12.2 EWR
1932 ....Stella Walsh, Poland	11.9 EWR
1936 ....Helen Stephens, United States	11.5
1948 ....Francina Blankers-Koen, Netherlands	11.9
1952 ....Marjorie Jackson, Australia	11.5 EWR
1956 ....Betty Cuthbert, Australia	11.5 EWR
1960 ....Wilma Rudolph, United States	11.0
1964 ....Wyomia Tyus, United States	11.4
1968 ....Wyomia Tyus, United States	11.0 WR
1972 ....Renate Stecher, E Germany	11.07
1976 ....Annegret Richter, W Germany	11.08
1980 ....Lyudmila Kondratyeva, USSR	11.06
1984 ....Evelyn Ashford, United States	10.97 OR
1988 ....Florence Griffith Joyner, United States	10.54 WR
1992 ....Gail Devers, United States	10.82
1996 ....Gail Devers, United States	10.94
2000 ....Marion Jones, United States	10.75

200 METERS

1948 ....Francina Blankers-Koen, Netherlands	24.4
1952 ....Marjorie Jackson, Australia	23.7
1956 ....Betty Cuthbert, Australia	23.4 EOR
1960 ....Wilma Rudolph, United States	24.0
1964 ....Edith McGuire, United States	23.0 OR
1968 ....Irena Szewinska, Poland	22.5 WR
1972 ....Renate Stecher, E Germany	22.40 EWR
1976 ....Bärbel Eckert, E Germany	22.37 OR
1980 ....Bärbel Wöckel (Eckert), E Germ.	22.03 OR
1984 ....Valerie Brisco-Hooks, U.S.	21.81 OR

200 METERS *(CONT.)*

1988 ....Florence Griffith Joyner, U.S.	21.34 WR
1992 ....Gwen Torrence, United States	21.81
1996 ....Marie-José Pérec, France	22.12
2000 ....Marion Jones, United States	21.84

400 METERS

1964 ....Betty Cuthbert, Australia	52.0 OR
1968 ....Colette Besson, France	52.0 EOR
1972 ....Monika Zehrt, E Germany	51.08 OR
1976 ....Irena Szewinska, Poland	49.29 WR
1980 ....Marita Koch, E Germany	48.88 OR
1984 ....Valerie Brisco-Hooks, United States	48.83 OR
1988 ....Olga Bryzgina, USSR	48.65 OR
1992 ....Marie-José Pérec, France	48.83
1996 ....Marie-José Pérec, France	48.25 OR
2000 ....Cathy Freeman, Australia	49.11

800 METERS

1928 ....Lina Radke, Germany	2:16.8 WR
1932 ....Not held 1932–1956	
1960 ....Lyudmila Shevtsova, USSR	2:04.3 EWR
1964 ....Ann Packer, Great Britain	2:01.1 OR
1968 ....Madeline Manning, United States	2:00.9 OR
1972 ....Hildegard Falck, W Germany	1:58.55 OR
1976 ....Tatyana Kazankina, USSR	1:54.94 WR
1980 ....Nadezhda Olizarenko, USSR	1:53.42 WR
1984 ....Doina Melinte, Romania	1:57.6
1988 ....Sigrun Wodars, E Germany	1:56.10
1992 ....Ellen Van Langen, Netherlands	1:55.54
1996 ....Svetlana Masterkova, Russia	1:57.73
2000 ....Maria Mutola, Mozambique	1:56.15

Note: OR=Olympic Record. WR=World Record. EOR=Equals Olympic Record. EWR=Equals World Record. WB=World Best.

TRACK AND FIELD (Cont.)

Women (Cont.)

1,500 METERS		
1972	Lyudmila Bragina, USSR	4:01.4 WR
1976	Tatyana Kazankina, USSR	4:05.48
1980	Tatyana Kazankina, USSR	3:56.6 OR
1984	Gabriella Dorio, Italy	4:03.25
1988	Paula Ivan, Romania	3:53.96 OR
1992	Hassiba Boulmerka, Algeria	3:55.30
1996	Svetlana Masterkova, Russia	4:00.83
2000	Nouria Merah-Benida, Algeria	4:05.10

3,000 METERS		
1984	Maricica Puica, Romania	8:35.96 OR
1988	Tatyana Samolenko, USSR	8:26.53 OR
1992	Elena Romanova, Unified Team	8:46.04

5,000 METERS		
1996	Wang Junxia, China	14:57.88
2000	Gabriela Szabo, Romania	14:40.79 OR

10,000 METERS		
1988	Olga Bondarenko, USSR	31:05.21 OR
1992	Derartu Tulu, Ethiopia	31:06.02
1996	Fernanda Ribeiro, Portugal	31:01.63 OR
2000	Derartu Tulu, Ethiopia	30:17.49 OR

MARATHON		
1984	Joan Benoit, United States	2:24:52 OR
1988	Rosa Mota, Portugal	2:25:40
1992	Valentin Yegorova, Unified Team	2:32:41
1996	Fatuma Roba, Ethiopia	2:26:05
2000	Naoko Takahashi, Japan	2:23.14 OR

80-METER HURDLES		
1932	Babe Didrikson, United States	11.7 WR
1936	Trebisonda Valla, Italy	11.7
1948	Francina Blankers-Koen, Netherlands	11.2 OR
1952	Shirley Strickland, Australia	10.9 WR
1956	Shirley Strickland, Australia	10.7 OR
1960	Irina Press, USSR	10.8
1964	Karin Balzer, E Germany	10.5
1968	Maureen Caird, Australia	10.3 OR

100-METER HURDLES		
1972	Annelie Ehrhardt, E Germany	12.59 WR
1976	Johanna Schaller, E Germany	12.77
1980	Vera Komisova, USSR	12.56 OR
1984	Benita Fitzgerald-Brown, United States	12.84
1988	Yordanka Donkova, Bulgaria	12.38 OR
1992	Paraskevi Patoulidou, Greece	12.64
1996	Lyudmila Engqvist, Sweden	12.58
2000	Olga Shishigina, Kazakhstan	12.65

400-METER HURDLES		
1984	Nawal el Moutawakel, Morocco	54.61 OR
1988	Debra Flintoff-King, Australia	53.17 OR
1992	Sally Gunnell, Great Britain	53.23
1996	Deon Hemmings, Jamaica	52.82 OR
2000	Irina Privalova, Russia	53.02

4 X 100-METER RELAY		
1928	Canada	48.4 WR
1932	United States	46.9 WR
1936	United States	46.9
1948	Netherlands	47.5
1952	United States	45.9 WR
1956	Australia	44.5 WR

4 X 100-METER RELAY (CONT.)		
1960	United States	44.5
1964	Poland	43.6
1968	United States	42.8 WR
1972	W Germany	42.81 EWR
1976	E Germany	42.55 OR
1980	E Germany	41.60 WR
1984	United States	41.65
1988	United States	41.98
1992	United States	42.11
1996	United States	41.95
2000	Bahamas	41.95

4 X 400-METER RELAY		
1972	E Germany	3:23 WR
1976	E Germany	3:19.23 WR
1980	USSR	3:20.02
1984	United States	3:18.29 OR
1988	USSR	3:15.18 WR
1992	Unified Team	3:20.20
1996	United States	3:20.91
2000	United States	3:22.62

10-KILOMETER WALK		
1992	Chen Yueling, China	44:32
1996	Elena Nikolayeva, Russia	41:49 OR

20-KILOMETER WALK		
2000	Liping Wang, China	1:29.05

HIGH JUMP		
1928	Ethel Catherwood, Canada	5 ft 2½ in
1932	Jean Shiley, United States	5 ft 5¼ in WR
1936	Ibolya Csak, Hungary	5 ft 3 in
1948	Alice Coachman, United States	5 ft 6 in OR
1952	Esther Brand, South Africa	5 ft 5¾ in
1956	Mildred L. McDaniel, U.S.	5 ft 9¼ in WR
1960	Iolanda Balas, Romania	6 ft ¾ in OR
1964	Iolanda Balas, Romania	6 ft 2¾ in OR
1968	Miloslava Reskova, Czech.	5 ft 11½ in
1972	Ulrike Meyfarth, W. Germany	6 ft 3½ in EWR
1976	Rosemarie Ackermann, E Germ	6 ft 4 in OR
1980	Sara Simeoni, Italy	6 ft 5½ in OR
1984	Ulrike Meyfarth, W. Germany	6 ft 7½ in OR
1988	Louise Ritter, United States	6 ft 8 in OR
1992	Heike Henkel, Germany	6 ft 7½ in
1996	Stefka Kostadinova, Bulgaria	6 ft 8¾ in OR
2000	Yelena Yelesina, Russia	6 ft 7 in

LONG JUMP		
1948	Olga Gyarmati, Hungary	18 ft 8¼ in
1952	Yvette Williams, New Zealand	20 ft 5¾ in OR
1956	Elzbieta Krzeskinska, Poland	20 ft 10 in EWR
1960	Vyera Krepkina, USSR	20 ft 10¾ in OR
1964	Mary Rand, Great Britain	22 ft 2¼ in WR
1968	Viorica Viscopoleanu, Romania	22 ft 4½ in WR
1972	Heidemarie Rosendahl, W Germany	22 ft 3 in
1976	Angela Voigt, E Germany	22 ft ¾ in
1980	Tatyana Kolpakova, USSR	23 ft 2 in OR
1984	Anisoara Stanciu, Romania	22 ft 10 in
1988	Jackie Joyner-Kersee, United States	24 ft 3½ in OR
1992	Heike Drechsler, Germany	23 ft 5¼ in
1996	Chioma Ajunwa, Nigeria	23 ft 4½ in
2000	Heike Drechsler, Germany	22 ft 11¼ in

Note: OR=Olympic Record; WR=World Record; EOR=Equals Olympic Record; EWR=Equals World Record; WB=World Best.

TRACK AND FIELD (Cont.)
Women (Cont.)

TRIPLE JUMP
1996...Inessa Kravets, Ukraine	50 ft 3½ in
2000...Tereza Marinova, Bulgaria	49 ft 10½ in

SHOT PUT
1948...Micheline Ostermeyer, France	45 ft 1½ in
1952...Galina Zybina, USSR	50 ft 1¾ in WR
1956...Tamara Tyshkevich, USSR	54 ft 5 in OR
1960...Tamara Press, USSR	56 ft 10 in OR
1964...Tamara Press, USSR	59 ft 6¼ in OR
1968...Margitta Gummel, E Germany	64 ft 4 in WR
1972...Nadezhda Chizhova, USSR	69 ft WR
1976...Ivanka Hristova, Bulgaria	69 ft 5¼ in OR
1980...Ilona Slupianek, E Germany	73 ft 6¼ in
1984...Claudia Losch, W Germany	67 ft 2¼ in
1988...Natalya Lisovskaya, USSR	72 ft 11¾ in
1992...Svetlana Kriveleva, Unified Team	69 ft 1¼ in
1996...Astrid Kumbernuss, Germany	67 ft 5½ in
2000...Yanina Korolchik, Belarus	67 ft 5½ in

DISCUS THROW
1928...Helena Konopacka, Poland	129 ft 11¾ in WR
1932...Lillian Copeland, United States	133 ft 2 in OR
1936...Gisela Mauermayer, Germany	156 ft 3 in OR
1948...Micheline Ostermeyer, France	137 ft 6 in
1952...Nina Romaschkova, USSR	168 ft 8 in OR
1956...Olga Fikotova, Czechoslovakia	176 ft 1 in OR
1960...Nina Ponomaryeva, USSR	180 ft 9 in OR
1964...Tamara Press, USSR	187 ft 10 in OR
1968...Lia Manoliu, Romania	191 ft 2 in OR
1972...Faina Melnik, USSR	218 ft 7 in OR
1976...Evelin Schlaak, E Germany	226 ft 4 in OR
1980...Evelin Jahl (Schlaak), E Germ.	229 ft 6 in OR
1984...Ria Stalman, Netherlands	214 ft 5 in
1988...Martina Hellmann, E Germany	237 ft 2 in OR
1992...Maritza Martén, Cuba	229 ft 10 in
1996...Ilke Wyludda, Germany	228 ft 6 in
2000...Ellina Zvereva, Belarus	224 ft 5 in

HAMMER THROW
2000...Kamila Skolimowska, Russia	233 ft 5 in OR

JAVELIN THROW
1932...Babe Didrikson, United States	143 ft 4 in OR
1936...Tilly Fleischer, Germany	148 ft 3 in OR
1948...Herma Bauma, Austria	149 ft 6 in
1952...Dana Zatopkova, Czechoslovakia	165 ft 7 in
1956...Inese Jaunzeme, USSR	176 ft 8 in
1960...Elvira Ozolina, USSR	183 ft 8 in OR
1964...Mihaela Penes, Romania	198 ft 7 in
1968...Angela Nemeth, Hungary	198 ft
1972...Ruth Fuchs, E Germany	209 ft 7 in OR
1976...Ruth Fuchs, E Germany	216 ft 4 in OR
1980...Maria Colon, Cuba	224 ft 5 in OR
1984...Tessa Sanderson, Great Britain	228 ft 2 in OR
1988...Petra Felke, E Germany	245 ft OR
1992...Silke Renk, Germany	224 ft 2 in
1996...Heli Rantanen, Finland	222 ft 11 in
2000...Trine Hattestad, Norway	226 ft ½ in OR

PENTATHLON
		Pts
1964 ...Irina Press, USSR	5246 WR
1968 ...Ingrid Becker, W Germany	5098
1972 ...Mary Peters, Great Britain	4801 WR*
1976 ...Siegrun Siegl, E Germany	4745
1980 ...Nadezhda Tkachenko, USSR	5083 WR

HEPTATHLON
		Pts
1984 ...Glynis Nunn, Australia	6390 OR
1988 ...Jackie Joyner-Kersee, U.S.	7291 WR
1992 ...Jackie Joyner-Kersee, U.S.	7044
1996 ...Ghada Shouaa, Syria	6780
2000 ...Denise Lewis, Great Britain	6584

*In 1971, the 100-meter hurdles replaced the 80-meter hurdles, requiring a change in scoring tables.

BASKETBALL
Men

1936
Final: United States 19, Canada 8
United States: Ralph Bishop, Joe Fortenberry, Carl Knowles, Jack Ragland, Carl Shy, William Wheatley, Francis Johnson, Samuel Balter, John Gibbons, Frank Lubin, Arthur Mollner, Donald Piper, Duane Swanson, Willard Schmidt

1948
Final: United States 65, France 21
United States: Cliff Barker, Don Barksdale, Ralph Beard, Lewis Beck, Vince Boryla, Gordon Carpenter, Alex Groza, Wallace Jones, Bob Kurland, Ray Lumpp, Robert Pitts, Jesse Renick, Bob Robinson, Ken Rollins

1952
Final: United States 36, USSR 25
United States: Charles Hoag, Bill Hougland, Melvin Dean Kelley, Bob Kenney, Clyde Lovellette, Marcus Freiberger, Victor Wayne Glasgow, Frank McCabe, Daniel Pippen, Howard Williams, Ronald Bontemps, Bob Kurland, William Lienhard, John Keller

1956
Final: United States 89, USSR 55
United States: Carl Cain, Bill Hougland, K.C. Jones, Bill Russell, James Walsh, William Evans, Burdette Haldorson, Ron Tomsic, Dick Boushka, Gilbert Ford, Bob Jeangerard, Charles Darling

1960
Final: United States 90, Brazil 63
United States: Jay Arnette, Walt Bellamy, Bob Boozer, Terry Dischinger, Jerry Lucas, Oscar Robertson, Adrian Smith, Burdette Haldorson, Darrall Imhoff, Allen Kelley, Lester Lane, Jerry West

1964
Final: United States 73, USSR 59
United States: Jim Barnes, Bill Bradley, Larry Brown, Joe Caldwell, Mel Counts, Richard Davies, Walt Hazzard, Lucius Jackson, John McCaffrey, Jeff Mullins, Jerry Shipp, George Wilson

1968
Final: United States 65, Yugoslavia 50
United States: John Clawson, Ken Spain, Jo-Jo White, Michael Barrett, Spencer Haywood, Charles Scott, William Hosket, Calvin Fowler, Michael Silliman, Glynn Saulters, James King, Donald Dee

1972
Final: USSR 51, United States 50
United States: Kenneth Davis, Doug Collins, Thomas Henderson, Mike Bantom, Bobby Jones, Dwight Jones, James Forbes, James Brewer, Tom Burleson, Tom McMillen, Kevin Joyce, Ed Ratleff

BASKETBALL (Cont.)
Men (Cont.)

1976

Final: United States 95, Yugoslavia 74
United States: Phil Ford, Steve Sheppard, Adrian Dantley, Walter Davis, Quinn Buckner, Ernie Grunfield, Kenny Carr, Scott May, Michel Armstrong, Tom La Garde, Phil Hubbard, Mitch Kupchak

1980

Final: Yugoslavia 86, Italy 77
U.S. participated in boycott.

1984

Final: United States 96, Spain 65
United States: Steve Alford, Leon Wood, Patrick Ewing, Vern Fleming, Alvin Robertson, Michael Jordan, Joe Kleine, Jon Koncak, Wayman Tisdale, Chris Mullin, Sam Perkins, Jeff Turner

1988

Final: USSR 76, Yugoslavia 63
United States (3rd): Mitch Richmond, Charles E. Smith IV, Vernell Coles, Hersey Hawkins, Jeff Grayer, Charles D. Smith, Willie Anderson, Stacey Augmon, Dan Majerle, Danny Manning, J.R. Reid, David Robinson

1992

Final: United States 117, Croatia 85
United States: David Robinson, Christian Laettner, Patrick Ewing, Larry Bird, Scottie Pippen, Michael Jordan, Clyde Drexler, Karl Malone, John Stockton, Chris Mullin, Charles Barkley, Earvin Johnson

1996

Final: United States 95, Yugoslavia 69
United States: Charles Barkley, Anfernee Hardaway, Grant Hill, Karl Malone, Reggie Miller, Hakeem Olajuwon, Shaquille O'Neal, Scottie Pippen, Mitch Richmond, John Stockton, David Robinson, Gary Payton

2000

Final: United States 85, France 75
United States: Shareef Abdur-Rahim, Ray Allen, Vin Baker, Vince Carter, Kevin Garnett, Tim Hardaway, Allan Houston, Jason Kidd, Antonio McDyess, Alonzo Mourning, Gary Payton, Steve Smith

Women

1976

Gold, USSR; Silver, United States*
United States: Cindy Brogdon, Susan Rojcewicz, Ann Meyers, Lusia Harris, Nancy Dunkle, Charlotte Lewis, Nancy Lieberman, Gail Marquis, Patricia Roberts, Mary Anne O'Connor, Patricia Head, Julienne Simpson
*In 1976 the women played a round-robin tournament, with the gold medal going to the team with the best record. The USSR won with a 5–0 record, and the USA, with a 3–2 record, was given the silver by virtue of a 95–79 victory over Bulgaria, which was also 3–2.

1980

Final: USSR 104, Bulgaria 73
U.S. participated in boycott.

1984

Final: United States 85, Korea 55
United States: Teresa Edwards, Lea Henry, Lynette Woodard, Anne Donovan, Cathy Boswell, Cheryl Miller, Janice Lawrence, Cindy Noble, Kim Mulkey, Denise Curry, Pamela McGee, Carol Menken-Schaudt

1988

Final: United States 77, Yugoslavia 70
United States: Teresa Edwards, Mary Ethridge, Cynthia Brown, Anne Donovan, Teresa Weatherspoon, Bridgette Gordon, Victoria Bullett, Andrea Lloyd, Katrina McClain, Jennifer Gillom, Cynthia Cooper, Suzanne McConnell

1992

Final: Unified Team 76, China 66
United States (3rd): Teresa Edwards, Teresa Weatherspoon, Victoria Bullett, Katrina McClain, Cynthia Cooper, Suzanne McConnell, Daedra Charles, Clarissa Davis, Tammy Jackson, Vickie Orr, Carolyn Jones, Medina Dixon

1996

Final: United States 111, Brazil 87
United States: Jennifer Azzi, Ruthie Bolton, Teresa Edwards, Lisa Leslie, Rebecca Lobo, Katrina McClain, Nikki McCray, Carla McGhee, Dawn Staley, Katy Steding, Sheryl Swoopes, Venus Lacey

2000

Final: United States 76, Australia 54
United States: Ruthie Bolton-Holifield, Teresa Edwards, Yolanda Griffith, Chamique Holdsclaw, Lisa Leslie, Nikki McCray, Delisha Milton, Katie Smith, Dawn Staley, Sheryl Swoopes, Natalie Williams, Kara Wolters

BOXING

LIGHT FLYWEIGHT (106 LB)

Year	Champion
1968	Francisco Rodriguez, Venezuela
1972	Gyorgy Gedo, Hungary
1976	Jorge Hernandez, Cuba
1980	Shamil Sabyrov, USSR
1984	Paul Gonzalez, United States

LIGHT FLYWEIGHT (CONT.)

Year	Champion
1988	Ivailo Hristov, Bulgaria
1992	Rogelio Marcelo, Cuba
1996	Daniel Petrov, Bulgaria
2000	Brahim Asloum, France

BOXING *(Cont.)*

FLYWEIGHT (112 LB)
1904 ....George Finnegan, United States
1906–1912......Not held
1920 ....Frank Di Gennara, United States
1924 ....Fidel LaBarba, United States
1928 ....Antal Kocsis, Hungary
1932 ....Istvan Enekes, Hungary
1936 ....Willi Kaiser, Germany
1948 ....Pascual Perez, Argentina
1952 ....Nathan Brooks, United States
1956 ....Terence Spinks, Great Britain
1960 ....Gyula Torok, Hungary
1964 ....Fernando Atzori, Italy
1968 ....Ricardo Delgado, Mexico
1972 ....Georgi Kostadinov, Bulgaria
1976 ....Leo Randolph, United States
1980 ....Peter Lessov, Bulgaria
1984 ....Steve McCrory, United States
1988 ....Kim Kwang Sun, S Korea
1992 ....Su Choi Chol, N Korea
1996 ....Maikro Romero, Cuba
2000 ....Wijan Ponlid, Thailand

BANTAMWEIGHT (119 LB)
1904 ....Oliver Kirk, United States
1906 ....Not held
1908 ....A. Henry Thomas, Great Britain
1912 ....Not held
1920 ....Clarence Walker, S Africa
1924 ....William Smith, S Africa
1928 ....Vittorio Tamagnini, Italy
1932 ....Horace Gwynne, Canada
1936 ....Ulderico Sergo, Italy
1948 ....Tibor Csik, Hungary
1952 ....Pentti Hamalainen, Finland
1956 ....Wolfgang Behrendt, E Germany
1960 ....Oleg Grigoryev, USSR
1964 ....Takao Sakurai, Japan
1968 ....Valery Sokolov, USSR
1972 ....Orlando Martinez, Cuba
1976 ....Yong Jo Gu, N Korea
1980 ....Juan Hernandez, Cuba
1984 ....Maurizio Stecca, Italy
1988 ....Kennedy McKinney, United States
1992 ....Joel Casamayor, Cuba
1996 ....István Kovács, Hungary
2000 ....Guillermo Ortiz, Cuba

FEATHERWEIGHT (125 LB)
1904 ....Oliver Kirk, United States
1906 ....Not held
1908 ....Richard Gunn, Great Britain
1912 ....Not held
1920 ....Paul Fritsch, France
1924 ....John Fields, United States
1928 ....Lambertus van Klaveren, Netherlands
1932 ....Carmelo Robledo, Argentina
1936 ....Oscar Casanovas, Argentina
1948 ....Ernesto Formenti, Italy
1952 ....Jan Zachara, Czechoslovakia
1956 ....Vladimir Safronov, USSR
1960 ....Francesco Musso, Italy
1964 ....Stanislav Stephashkin, USSR
1968 ....Antonio Roldan, Mexico
1972 ....Boris Kousnetsov, USSR
1976 ....Angel Herrera, Cuba
1980 ....Rudi Fink, E Germany
1984 ....Meldrick Taylor, United States
1988 ....Giovanni Parisi, Italy
1992 ....Andreas Tews, Germany
1996 ....Somluck Kamsing, Thailand
2000 ....Bekzat Sattarkhanox, Kazakhstan

LIGHTWEIGHT (132 LB)
1904 ....Harry Spanger, United States
1906 ....Not held
1908 ....Frederick Grace, Great Britain
1912 ....Not held
1920 ....Samuel Mosberg, United States
1924 ....Hans Nielsen, Denmark
1928 ....Carlo Orlandi, Italy
1932 ....Lawrence Stevens, S Africa
1936 ....Imre Harangi, Hungary
1948 ....Gerald Dreyer, S Africa
1952 ....Aureliano Bolognesi, Italy
1956 ....Richard McTaggart, Great Britain
1960 ....Kazimierz Pazdzior, Poland
1964 ....Jozef Grudzien, Poland
1968 ....Ronald Harris, United States
1972 ....Jan Szczepanski, Poland
1976 ....Howard Davis, United States
1980 ....Angel Herrera, Cuba
1984 ....Pernell Whitaker, United States
1988 ....Andreas Zuelow, E Germany
1992 ....Oscar De La Hoya, United States
1996 ....Hocine Soltani, Algeria
2000 ....Mario Kindelan, Cuba

LIGHT WELTERWEIGHT (139 LB)
1952 ....Charles Adkins, United States
1956 ....Vladimir Yengibaryan, USSR
1960 ....Bohumil Nemecek, Czechoslovakia
1964 ....Jerzy Kulej, Poland
1968 ....Jerzy Kulej, Poland
1972 ....Ray Seales, United States
1976 ....Ray Leonard, United States
1980 ....Patrizio Oliva, Italy
1984 ....Jerry Page, United States
1988 ....Viatcheslav Janovski, USSR
1992 ....Hector Vinent, Cuba
1996 ....Hector Vinent, Cuba
2000 ....Mahamadkadyz Abdullaev, Uzbekistan

WELTERWEIGHT (147 LB)
1904 ....Albert Young, United States
1906–1912......Not held
1920 ....Albert Schneider, Canada
1924 ....Jean Delarge, Belgium
1928 ....Edward Morgan, New Zealand
1932 ....Edward Flynn, United States
1936 ....Sten Suvio, Finland
1948 ....Julius Torma, Czechoslovakia
1952 ....Zygmunt Chychla, Poland
1956 ....Nicolae Linca, Romania
1960 ....Giovanni Benvenuti, Italy
1964 ....Marian Kasprzyk, Poland
1968 ....Manfred Wolke, E Germany
1972 ....Emilio Correa, Cuba
1976 ....Jochen Bachfeld, E Germany
1980 ....Andres Aldama, Cuba
1984 ....Mark Breland, United States
1988 ....Robert Wangila, Kenya
1992 ....Michael Carruth, Ireland
1996 ....Oleg Saitov, Russia
2000 ....Oleg Saitov, Russia

LIGHT MIDDLEWEIGHT (156 LB)
1952 ....Laszlo Papp, Hungary
1956 ....Laszlo Papp, Hungary
1960 ....Wilbert McClure, United States
1964 ....Boris Lagutin, USSR
1968 ....Boris Lagutin, USSR
1972 ....Dieter Kottysch, W Germany
1976 ....Jerzy Rybicki, Poland
1980 ....Armando Martinez, Cuba
1984 ....Frank Tate, United States

BOXING *(Cont.)*

LIGHT MIDDLEWEIGHT *(CONT.)*

1988 ....Park Si-Hun, S Korea
1992 ....Juan Lemus, Cuba
1996 ....David Reid, United States
2000 ....Yermakhan Ibraimov, Kazakhstan

MIDDLEWEIGHT (165 LB)

1904 ....Charles Mayer, United States
1908 ....John Douglas, Great Britain
1912 ....Not held
1920 ....Harry Mallin, Great Britain
1924 ....Harry Mallin, Great Britain
1928 ....Piero Toscani, Italy
1932 ....Carmen Barth, United States
1936 ....Jean Despeaux, France
1948 ....Laszlo Papp, Hungary
1952 ....Floyd Patterson, United States
1956 ....Gennady Schatkov, USSR
1960 ....Edward Crook, United States
1964 ....Valery Popenchenko, USSR
1968 ....Christopher Finnegan, Great Britain
1972 ....Vyacheslav Lemechev, USSR
1976 ....Michael Spinks, United States
1980 ....Jose Gomez, Cuba
1984 ....Shin Joon Sup, S Korea
1988 ....Henry Maske, E Germany
1992 ....Ariel Hernandez, Cuba
1996 ....Ariel Hernandez, Cuba
2000 ....Jorge Gutierrez, Cuba

LIGHT HEAVYWEIGHT (178 LB)

1920 ....Edward Eagan, United States
1924 ....Harry Mitchell, Great Britain
1928 ....Victor Avendano, Argentina
1932 ....David Carstens, S Africa
1936 ....Roger Michelot, France
1948 ....George Hunter, S Africa
1952 ....Norvel Lee, United States
1956 ....James Boyd, United States
1960 ....,Cassius Clay, United States
1964 ....Cosimo Pinto, Italy
1968 ....Dan Poznyak, USSR
1972 ....Mate Parlov, Yugoslavia
1976 ....Leon Spinks, United States

LIGHT HEAVYWEIGHT *(CONT.)*

1980 ....Slobodan Kacer, Yugoslavia
1984 ....Anton Josipovic, Yugoslavia
1988 ....Andrew Maynard, United States
1992 ....,Torsten May, Germany
1996 ....Vassili Jirov, Kazakhstan
2000 ....Alexander Lebziak, Russia

HEAVYWEIGHT (OVER 201 LB)

1904 ....Samuel Berger, United States
1906 ....Not held
1908 ....Albert Oldham, Great Britain
1912 ....Not held
1920 ....Ronald Rawson, Great Britain
1924 ....Otto von Porat, Norway
1928 ....Arturo Rodriguez Jurado, Argentina
1932 ....Santiago Lovell, Argentina
1936 ....Herbert Runge, Germany
1948 ....Rafael Inglesias, Argentina
1952 ....H. Edward Sanders, United States
1956 ....T. Peter Rademacher, United States
1960 ....Franco De Piccoli, Italy
1964 ....Joe Frazier, United States
1968 ....George Foreman, United States
1972 ....Teofilo Stevenson, Cuba
1976 ....Teofilo Stevenson, Cuba
1980 ....Teofilo Stevenson, Cuba

HEAVYWEIGHT (201* LB)

1984 ....Henry Tillman, United States
1988 ....Ray Mercer, United States
1992 ....Félix Sávon, Cuba
1996 ....Félix Sávon, Cuba
2000 ....Félix Sávon, Cuba

SUPERHEAVYWEIGHT (UNLIMITED)

1984 ....Tyrell Biggs, United States
1988 ....Lennox Lewis, Canada
1992 ....Roberto Balado, Cuba
1996 ....Vladimir Klitchko, Ukraine
2000 ....Audley Harrison, Great Britain

*Until 1984 the heavyweight division was unlimited. With the addition of the super heavyweight division, a limit of 201 pounds was imposed.

SWIMMING

Men

50-METER FREESTYLE

1904 ....Zoltan Halmay, Hungary (50 yds)	28.0	
1988 ....Matt Biondi, United States	22.14	WR
1992 ....Aleksandr Popov, Unified Team	22.30	
1996 ....Aleksandr Popov, Russia	22.13	
2000 ....Anthony Ervin, United States	21.98	
Gary Hall Jr, United States	21.98	

100-METER FREESTLYE

1896 ....Alfred Hajos, Hungary	1:22.2	OR
1904 ....Zoltan Halmay, Hungary (100 yds)	1:02.8	
1906 ....Charles Daniels, United States	1:13.4	
1908 ....Charles Daniels, United States	1:05.6	WR
1912 ....Duke Kahanamoku, United States	1:03.4	
1920 ....Duke Kahanamoku, United States	1:00.4	WR
1924 ....John Weissmuller, United States	59.0	OR
1928 ....John Weissmuller, United States	58.6	OR
1932 ....Yasuji Miyazaki, Japan	58.2	

100-METER FREESTYLE *(CONT.)*

1936 ....Ferenc Csik, Hungary	57.6	
1948 ....Wally Ris, United States	57.3	OR
1952 ....Clarke Scholes, United States	57.4	
1956 ....Jon Henricks, Australia	55.4	OR
1960 ....John Devitt, Australia	55.2	OR
1964 ....Don Schollander, United States	53.4	OR
1968 ....Mike Wenden, Australia	52.2	WR
1972 ....Mark Spitz, United States	51.22	WR
1976 ....Jim Montgomery, United States	49.99	WR
1980 ....Jörg Woithe, E Germany	50.40	
1984 ....Rowdy Gaines, United States	49.80	OR
1988 ....Matt Biondi, United States	48.63	OR
1992 ....Aleksandr Popov, Unified Team	49.02	
1996 ....Aleksandr Popov, Russia	48.74	
2000 ....P. van den Hoogenband, Neth.	48.30	

Note: OR=Olympic Record. WR=World Record. EOR=Equals Olympic Record. EWR=Equals World Record. WB=World Best.

SWIMMING *(Cont.)*
Men *(Cont.)*

200-METER FREESTYLE

1900	Frederick Lane, Australia	2:25.2 OR
1904	Charles Daniels, United States	2:44.2
1906–1964	Not held	
1968	Michael Wenden, Australia	1:55.2 OR
1972	Mark Spitz, United States	1:52.78 WR
1976	Bruce Furniss, United States	1:50.29 WR
1980	Sergei Kopliakov, USSR	1:49.81 OR
1984	Michael Gross, W Germany	1:47.44 WR
1988	Duncan Armstrong, Australia	1:47.25 WR
1992	Evgueni Sadovyi, Unified Team	1:46.70 OR
1996	Danyon Loader, New Zealand	1:47.63
2000	Pieter van den Hoogenband, Netherlands	1:45.35 EWR

400-METER FREESTYLE

1896	Paul Neumann, Austria (500 yds)	8:12.6
1904	Charles Daniels, U.S. (440 yds)	6:16.2
1906	Otto Scheff, Austria (440 yds)	6:23.8
1908	Henry Taylor, Great Britain	5:36.8
1912	George Hodgson, Canada	5:24.4
1920	Norman Ross, United States	5:26.8
1924	John Weissmuller, United States	5:04.2 OR
1928	Albert Zorilla, Argentina	5:01.6 OR
1932	Buster Crabbe, United States	4:48.4 OR
1936	Jack Medica, United States	4:44.5 OR
1948	William Smith, United States	4:41.0 OR
1952	Jean Boiteux, France	4:30.7 OR
1956	Murray Rose, Australia	4:27.3 OR
1960	Murray Rose, Australia	4:18.3 OR
1964	Don Schollander, United States	4:12.2 WR
1968	Mike Burton, United States	4:09.0 OR
1972	Brad Cooper, Australia	4:00.27 OR
1976	Brian Goodell, United States	3:51.93 WR
1980	Vladimir Salnikov, USSR	3:51.31 OR
1984	George DiCarlo, United States	3:51.23 OR
1988	Uwe Dassler, E Germany	3:46.95 WR
1992	Evgueni Sadovyi, Unified Team	3:45.00 WR
1996	Danyon Loader, New Zealand	3:47.97
2000	Ian Thorpe, Australia	3:40.59 WR

1,500-METER FREESTYLE

1908	Henry Taylor, Great Britain	22:48.4 WR
1912	George Hodgson, Canada	22:00.0 WR
1920	Norman Ross, United States	22:23.2
1924	Andrew Charlton, Australia	20:06.6 WR
1928	Arne Borg, Sweden	19:51.8 OR
1932	Kusuo Kitamura, Japan	19:12.4 OR
1936	Noboru Terada, Japan	19:13.7
1948	James McLane, United States	19:18.5
1952	Ford Konno, United States	18:30.3 OR
1956	Murray Rose, Australia	17:58.9
1960	John Konrads, Australia	17:19.6 OR
1964	Robert Windle, Australia	17:01.7 OR
1968	Mike Burton, United States	16:38.9 OR
1972	Mike Burton, United States	15:52.58 OR
1976	Brian Goodell, United States	15:02.40 WR
1980	Vladimir Salnikov, USSR	14:58.27 WR
1984	Michael O'Brien, United States	15:05.20
1988	Vladimir Salnikov, USSR	15:00.40
1992	Kieren Perkins, Australia	14:43.48 WR
1996	Kieren Perkins, Australia	14:56.40
2000	Grant Hackett, Australia	14:48.33

100-METER BACKSTROKE

1904	Walter Brack, Germany (100 yds)	1:16.8
1908	Arno Bieberstein, Germany	1:24.6 WR
1912	Harry Hebner, United States	1:21.2

100-METER BACKSTROKE *(CONT.)*

1920	Warren Kealoha, United States	1:15.2
1924	Warren Kealoha, United States	1:13.2 OR
1928	George Kojac, United States	1:08.2 WR
1932	Masaji Kiyokawa, Japan	1:08.6
1936	Adolph Kiefer, United States	1:05.9 OR
1948	Allen Stack, United States	1:06.4
1952	Yoshi Oyakawa, United States	1:05.4 OR
1956	David Thiele, Australia	1:02.2 OR
1960	David Thiele, Australia	1:01.9 OR
1964	Not held	
1968	Roland Matthes, E Germany	58.7 OR
1972	Roland Matthes, E Germany	56.58 OR
1976	John Naber, United States	55.49 WR
1980	Bengt Baron, Sweden	56.33
1984	Rick Carey, United States	55.79
1988	Daichi Suzuki, Japan	55.05
1992	Mark Tewksbury, Canada	53.98 WR
1996	Jeff Rouse, United States	54.10
2000	Lenny Krayzelburg, United States	53.72 OR

200-METER BACKSTROKE

1900	Ernst Hoppenberg, Germany	2:47.0
1906–1960	Not held	
1964	Jed Graef, United States	2:10.3 WR
1968	Roland Matthes, E Germany	2:09.6 OR
1972	Roland Matthes, E Germany	2:02.82 EWR
1976	John Naber, United States	1:59.19 WR
1980	Sandor Wladar, Hungary	2:01.93
1984	Rick Carey, United States	2:00.23
1988	Igor Polianski, USSR	1:59.37
1992	Martin Lopez-Zubero, Spain	1:58.47 OR
1996	Brad Bridgewater, United States	1:58.54
2000	Lenny Krayzelburg, United States	1:56.76 OR

100-METER BREASTSTROKE

1968	Don McKenzie, United States	1:07.7 OR
1972	Nobutaka Taguchi, Japan	1:04.94 WR
1976	John Hencken, United States	1:03.11 WR
1980	Duncan Goodhew, Great Britain	1:03.44
1984	Steve Lundquist, United States	1:01.65 WR
1988	Adrian Moorhouse, Great Britain	1:02.04
1992	Nelson Diebel, United States	1:01.50 OR
1996	Fred DeBurghgraeve, Belgium	1:00.65
2000	Domenico Fioravanti, Italy	1:00.46 OR

200-METER BREASTSTROKE

1908	Frederick Holman, Great Britain	3:09.2 WR
1912	Walter Bathe, Germany	3:01.8 OR
1920	Haken Malmroth, Sweden	3:04.4
1924	Robert Skelton, United States	2:56.6
1928	Yoshiyuki Tsuruta, Japan	2:48.8 OR
1932	Yoshiyuki Tsuruta, Japan	2:45.4
1936	Tetsuo Hamuro, Japan	2:41.5 OR
1948	Joseph Verdeur, United States	2:39.3 OR
1952	John Davies, Australia	2:34.4 OR
1956	Masura Furukawa, Japan	2:34.7 OR
1960	William Mulliken, United States	2:37.4
1964	Ian O'Brien, Australia	2:27.8 WR
1968	Felipe Munoz, Mexico	2:28.7
1972	John Hencken, United States	2:21.55 WR
1976	David Wilkie, Great Britain	2:15.11 WR
1980	Robertas Zhulpa, USSR	2:15.85
1984	Victor Davis, Canada	2:13.34 WR
1988	Jozsef Szabo, Hungary	2:13.52
1992	Mike Barrowman, United States	2:10.16 WR
1996	Norbert Rózsa, Hungary	2:12.57
2000	Domenico Fioravanti, Italy	2:10.87

Note: OR=Olympic Record. WR=World Record. EOR=Equals Olympic Record. EWR=Equals World Record. WB=World Best.

SWIMMING (Cont.)

Men (Cont.)

100-METER BUTTERFLY

1968	Doug Russell, United States	55.9 OR
1972	Mark Spitz, United States	54.27 WR
1976	Matt Vogel, United States	54.35
1980	Pär Arvidsson, Sweden	54.92
1984	Michael Gross, W Germany	53.08 WR
1988	Anthony Nesty, Suriname	53.00 OR
1992	Pablo Morales, United States	53.32
1996	Denis Pankratov, Russia	52.27 WR
2000	Lars Froelander, Sweden	52.00

200-METER BUTTERFLY

1956	William Yorzyk, United States	2:19.3 OR
1960	Michael Troy, United States	2:12.8 WR
1964	Kevin Berry, Australia	2:06.6 WR
1968	Carl Robie, United States	2:08.7
1972	Mark Spitz, United States	2:00.70 WR
1976	Mike Bruner, United States	1:59.23 WR
1980	Sergei Fesenko, USSR	1:59.76
1984	Jon Sieben, Australia	1:57.04 WR
1988	Michael Gross, W Germany	1:56.94 OR
1992	Melvin Stewart, United States	1:56.26 OR
1996	Denis Pankratov, Russia	1:56.51
2000	Tom Malchow, United States	1:55.35 OR

200-METER INDIVIDUAL MEDLEY

1968	Charles Hickcox, United States	2:12.0 OR
1972	Gunnar Larsson, Sweden	2:07.17 WR
1984	Alex Baumann, Canada	2:01.42 WR
1988	Tamas Darnyi, Hungary	2:00.17 WR
1992	Tamas Darnyi, Hungary	2:00.76
1996	Attila Czene, Hungary	1:59.91 OR
2000	Massimiliano Rosolino, Italy	1:58.98 OR

400-METER INDIVIDUAL MEDLEY

1964	Richard Roth, United States	4:45.4 WR
1968	Charles Hickcox, United States	4:48.4
1972	Gunnar Larsson, Sweden	4:31.98 OR
1976	Rod Strachan, United States	4:23.68 WR
1980	Aleksandr Sidorenko, USSR	4:22.89 OR
1984	Alex Baumann, Canada	4:17.41 WR
1988	Tamas Darnyi, Hungary	4:14.75 WR
1992	Tamas Darnyi, Hungary	4:14.23 OR
1996	Tom Dolan, United States	4:14.90
2000	Tom Dolan, United States	4:11.76 WR

4 X 100-METER MEDLEY RELAY

1960	United States	4:05.4 WR
1964	United States	3:58.4 WR
1968	United States	3:54.9 WR
1972	United States	3:48.16 WR
1976	United States	3:42.22 WR
1980	Australia	3:45.70
1984	United States	3:39.30 WR
1988	United States	3:36.93 WR
1992	United States	3:36.93 EWR
1996	United States	3:34.84 WR
2000	United States	3:33.73 WR

4 X 100-METER FREESTYLE RELAY

1964	United States	3:32.2 WR
1968	United States	3:31.7 WR
1972	United States	3:26.42 WR
1976–1980	Not held	
1984	United States	3:19.03 WR
1988	United States	3:16.53 WR
1992	United States	3:16.74
1996	United States	3:15.41 OR
2000	Australia	3:13.67 WR

4 X 200-METER FREESTYLE RELAY

1906	Hungary (1,000 m)	16:52.4
1908	Great Britain	10:55.6
1912	Australia/New Zealand	10:11.6 WR
1920	United States	10:04.4 WR
1924	United States	9:53.4 WR
1928	United States	9:36.2 WR
1932	Japan	8:58.4 WR
1936	Japan	8:51.5 WR
1948	United States	8:46.0 WR
1952	United States	8:31.1 OR
1956	Australia	8:23.6 WR
1960	United States	8:10.2 WR
1964	United States	7:52.1 WR
1968	United States	7:52.33
1972	United States	7:35.78 WR
1976	United States	7:23.22 WR
1980	USSR	7:23.50
1984	United States	7:15.69 WR
1988	United States	7:12.51 WR
1992	Unified Team	7:11.95 WR
1996	United States	7:14.84
2000	Australia	7:07.05 WR

Women

50-METER FREESTYLE

1988	Kristin Otto, E Germany	25.49 OR
1992	Yang Wenyi, China	24.79 WR
1996	Amy Van Dyken, United States	24.87
2000	Inge de Bruijn, Netherlands	24.32 WR

100-METER FREESTYLE

1912	Fanny Durack, Australia	1:22.2
1920	Ethelda Bleibtrey, United States	1:13.6 WR
1924	Ethel Lackie, United States	1:12.4
1928	Albina Osipowich, United States	1:11.0 OR
1932	Helene Madison, United States	1:06.8 OR
1936	Hendrika Mastenbroek, Netherlands	1:05.9 OR
1948	Greta Andersen, Denmark	1:06.3
1952	Katalin Szöke, Hungary	1:06.8
1956	Dawn Fraser, Australia	1:02.0 WR
1960	Dawn Fraser, Australia	1:01.2 OR
1964	Dawn Fraser, Australia	59.5 OR

100-METER FREESTYLE (CONT.)

1968	Jan Henne, United States	1:00.0
1972	Sandra Neilson, United States	58.59 OR
1976	Kornelia Ender, E Germany	55.65 WR
1980	Barbara Krause, E Germany	54.79 WR
1984	Carrie Steinseifer, United States	55.92
	Nancy Hogshead, United States	55.92
1988	Kristin Otto, E Germany	54.93
1992	Zhuang Yong, China	54.64 OR
1996	Le Jingyi, China	54.50 OR
2000	Inge de Bruijn, Netherlands	53.83 OR

200-METER FREESTYLE

1968	Debbie Meyer, United States	2:10.5 OR
1972	Shane Gould, Australia	2:03.56 WR
1976	Kornelia Ender, E Germany	1:59.26 WR
1980	Barbara Krause, E Germany	1:58.33 OR
1984	Mary Wayte, United States	1:59.23
1988	Heike Friedrich, E Germany	1:57.65 OR

Note: OR=Olympic Record. WR=World Record. EOR=Equals Olympic Record. EWR=Equals World Record. WB=World Best.

SWIMMING (Cont.)
Women (Cont.)

200-METER FREESTYLE (CONT.)

1992	Nicole Haislett, United States	1:57.90
1996	Claudia Poll, Costa Rica	1:58.16
2000	Susie O'Neill, Australia	1:58.24

400-METER FREESTYLE

1924	Martha Norelius, United States	6:02.2 OR
1928	Martha Norelius, United States	5:42.8 WR
1932	Helene Madison, United States	5:28.5 WR
1936	Hendrika Mastenbroek, Netherlands	5:26.4 OR
1948	Ann Curtis, United States	5:17.8 OR
1952	Valeria Gyenge, Hungary	5:12.1 OR
1956	Lorraine Crapp, Australia	4:54.6 OR
1960	Chris von Saltza, United States	4:50.6 OR
1964	Virginia Duenkel, United States	4:43.3 OR
1968	Debbie Meyer, United States	4:31.8 OR
1972	Shane Gould, Australia	4:19.44 WR
1976	Petra Thümer, E Germany	4:09.89 WR
1980	Ines Diers, E Germany	4:08.76 WR
1984	Tiffany Cohen, United States	4:07.10 OR
1988	Janet Evans, United States	4:03.85 WR
1992	Dagmar Hase, Germany	4:07.18
1996	Michelle Smith, Ireland	4:07.25
2000	Brooke Bennett, United States	4:05.80

800-METER FREESTYLE

1968	Debbie Meyer, United States	9:24.0 OR
1972	Keena Rothhammer, United States	8:53.68 WR
1976	Petra Thümer, E Germany	8:37.14 WR
1980	Michelle Ford, Australia	8:28.90 OR
1984	Tiffany Cohen, United States	8:24.95 OR
1988	Janet Evans, United States	8:20.20 OR
1992	Janet Evans, United States	8:25.52
1996	Brooke Bennett, United States	8:27.89
2000	Brooke Bennett, United States	8:19.67 OR

100-METER BACKSTROKE

1924	Sybil Bauer, United States	1:23.2 OR
1928	Marie Braun, Netherlands	1:22.0
1932	Eleanor Holm, United States	1:19.4
1936	Dina Senff, Netherlands	1:18.9
1948	Karen Harup, Denmark	1:14.4 OR
1952	Joan Harrison, South Africa	1:14.3
1956	Judy Grinhäm, Great Britain	1:12.9 OR
1960	Lynn Burke, United States	1:09.3 OR
1964	Cathy Ferguson, United States	1:07.7 WR
1968	Kaye Hall, United States	1:06.2 WR
1972	Melissa Belote, United States	1:05.78 OR
1976	Ulrike Richter, E Germany	1:01.83 OR
1980	Rica Reinisch, E Germany	1:00.86 WR
1984	Theresa Andrews, United States	1:02.55
1988	Kristin Otto, E Germany	1:00.89
1992	Krisztina Egerszegi, Hungary	1:00.68 OR
1996	Beth Botsford, United States	1:01.19
2000	Diana Iuliana Mocanu, Romania	1:00.21 OR

200-METER BACKSTROKE

1968	Pokey Watson, United States	2:24.8 OR
1972	Melissa Belote, United States	2:19.19 WR
1976	Ulrike Richter, E Germany	2:13.43 OR
1980	Rica Reinisch, E Germany	2:11.77 WR
1984	Jolanda De Rover, Netherlands	2:12.38
1988	Krisztina Egerszegi, Hungary	2:09.29 OR
1992	Krisztina Egerszegi, Hungary	2:07.06 OR
1996	Krisztina Egerszegi, Hungary	2:07.83
2000	Diana Iuliana Mocanu, Romania	2:08.16

100-METER BREASTSTROKE

1968	Djurdjica Bjedov, Yugoslavia	1:15.8 OR
1972	Catherine Carr, United States	1:13.58 WR
1976	Hannelore Anke, E Germany	1:11.16
1980	Ute Geweniger, E Germany	1:10.22
1984	Petra Van Staveren, Netherlands	1:09.88 OR
1988	Tania Dangalakova, Bulgaria	1:07.95 OR
1992	Elena Roudkovskaia, Unified Team	1:08.00
1996	Penelope Heyns, S Africa	1:07.73
2000	Megan Quann, United States	1:07.05

200-METER BREASTSTROKE

1924	Lucy Morton, Great Britain	3:33.2 OR
1928	Hilde Schrader, Germany	3:12.6
1932	Clare Dennis, Australia	3:06.3 OR
1936	Hideko Maehata, Japan	3:03.6
1948	Petronella Van Vliet, Netherlands	2:57.2
1952	Eva Szekely, Hungary	2:51.7 OR
1956	Ursula Happe, W Germany	2:53.1 OR
1960	Anita Lonsbrough, Great Britain	2:49.5 WR
1964	Galina Prozumenshikova, USSR	2:46.4 OR
1968	Sharon Wichman, United States	2:44.4 OR
1972	Beverly Whitfield, Australia	2:41.71 OR
1976	Marina Koshevaia, USSR	2:33.35 WR
1980	Lina Kaciusyte, USSR	2:29.54 OR
1984	Anne Ottenbrite, Canada	2:30.38
1988	Silke Hoerner, E Germany	2:26.71 WR
1992	Kyoko Iwasaki, Japan	2:26.65 OR
1996	Penelope Heyns, S Africa	2:25.41 OR
2000	Agnes Kovacs, Hungary	2:24.35 OR

100-METER BUTTERFLY

1956	Shelley Mann, United States	1:11.0 OR
1960	Carolyn Schuler, United States	1:09.5 OR
1964	Sharon Stouder, United States	1:04.7 WR
1968	Lynn McClements, Australia	1:05.5
1972	Mayumi Aoki, Japan	1:03.34 WR
1976	Kornelia Ender, E Germany	1:00.13 EWR
1980	Caren Metschuck, E Germany	1:00.42
1984	Mary T. Meagher, United States	59.26
1988	Kristin Otto, E Germany	59.00 OR
1992	Qian Hong, China	58.62 OR
1996	Amy Van Dyken, United States	59.13
2000	Inge de Bruijn, Netherlands	56.61 WR

200-METER BUTTERFLY

1968	Ada Kok, Netherlands	2:24.7 OR
1972	Karen Moe, United States	2:15.57 WR
1976	Andrea Pollack, E Germany	2:11.41 OR
1980	Ines Geissler, E Germany	2:10.44 OR
1984	Mary T. Meagher, United States	2:06.90 OR
1988	Kathleen Nord, E Germany	2:09.51
1992	Summer Sanders, United States	2:08.67
1996	Susan O'Neill, Australia	2:07.76
2000	Misty Hyman, United States	2:05.88 OR

200-METER INDIVIDUAL MEDLEY

1968	Claudia Kolb, United States	2:24.7 OR
1972	Shane Gould, Australia	2:23.07 WR
1976–1980	Not held	
1984	Tracy Caulkins, United States	2:12.64 OR
1988	Daniela Hunger, E Germany	2:12.59 OR
1992	Lin Li, China	2:11.65 WR
1996	Michelle Smith, Ireland	2:13.93
2000	Yana Klochkova, Ukraine	2:10.68 OR

Note: OR=Olympic Record. WR=World Record. EOR=Equals Olympic Record. EWR=Equals World Record. WB=World Best.

SWIMMING (Cont.)

Women (Cont.)

400-METER INDIVIDUAL MEDLEY

1964	Donna de Varona, United States	5:18.7 OR
1968	Claudia Kolb, United States	5:08.5 OR
1972	Gail Neall, Australia	5:02.97 WR
1976	Ulrike Tauber, E Germany	4:42.77 WR
1980	Petra Schneider, E Germany	4:36.29 WR
1984	Tracy Caulkins, United States	4:39.24
1988	Janet Evans, United States	4:37.76
1992	Krisztina Egerszegi, Hungary	4:36.54
1996	Michelle Smith, Ireland	4:39.18
2000	Yana Klochkova, Ukraine	4:33.59 WR

4 X 100-METER MEDLEY RELAY

1960	United States	4:41.1 WR
1964	United States	4:33.9 WR
1968	United States	4:28.3 OR
1972	United States	4:20.75 WR
1976	E Germany	4:07.95 WR
1980	E Germany	4:06.67 WR
1984	United States	4:08.34
1988	E Germany	4:03.74 OR
1992	United States	4:02.54 WR
1996	United States	4:02.88
2000	United States	3:58.30 WR

4 X 100-METER FREESTYLE RELAY

1912	Great Britain	5:52.8 WR
1920	United States	5:11.6 WR
1924	United States	4:58.8 WR
1928	United States	4:47.6 WR
1932	United States	4:38.0 WR
1936	Netherlands	4:36.0 OR
1948	United States	4:29.2 OR
1952	Hungary	4:24.4 WR
1956	Australia	4:17.1 WR
1960	United States	4:08.9 WR
1964	United States	4:03.8 WR
1968	United States	4:02.5 OR
1972	United States	3:55.19 WR
1976	United States	3:44.82 WR
1980	E Germany	3:42.71 WR
1984	United States	3:43.43
1988	E Germany	3:40.63 OR
1992	United States	3:39.46 WR
1996	United States	3:39.29 OR
2000	United States	3:36.61 WR

4 X 200-METER FREESTYLE RELAY

1996	United States	7:59.87
2000	United States	7:57.80 OR

DIVING

Men

SPRINGBOARD

		Pts
1908	Albert Zürner, Germany	85.5
1912	Paul Günther, Germany	79.23
1920	Louis Kuehn, United States	675.40
1924	Albert White, United States	97.46
1928	Pete DesJardins, United States	185.04
1932	Michael Galitzen, United States	161.38
1936	Richard Degener, United States	163.57
1948	Bruce Harlan, United States	163.64
1952	David Browning, United States	205.29
1956	Robert Clotworthy, United States	159.56
1960	Gary Tobian, United States	170.00
1964	Kenneth Sitzberger, United States	159.90
1968	Bernie Wrightson, United States	170.15
1972	Vladimir Vasin, USSR	594.09
1976	Phil Boggs, United States	619.05
1980	Aleksandr Portnov, USSR	905.02
1984	Greg Louganis, United States	754.41
1988	Greg Louganis, United States	730.80
1992	Mark Lenzi, United States	676.53
1996	Xiong Ni, China	701.46
2000	Xiong Ni, China	708.72

PLATFORM

		Pts
1904	George Sheldon, United States	12.66
1906	Gottlob Walz, Germany	156.0
1908	Hjalmar Johansson, Sweden	83.75
1912	Erik Adlerz, Sweden	73.94
1920	Clarence Pinkston, United States	100.67
1924	Albert White, United States	97.46
1928	Pete DesJardins, United States	98.74
1932	Harold Smith, United States	124.80
1936	Marshall Wayne, United States	113.58
1948	Sammy Lee, United States	130.05
1952	Sammy Lee, United States	156.28
1956	Joaquin Capilla, Mexico	152.44
1960	Robert Webster, United States	165.56
1964	Robert Webster, United States	148.58
1968	Klaus Dibiasi, Italy	164.18
1972	Klaus Dibiasi, Italy	504.12
1976	Klaus Dibiasi, Italy	600.51
1980	Falk Hoffmann, E Germany	835.65
1984	Greg Louganis, United States	710.91
1988	Greg Louganis, United States	638.61
1992	Sun Shuwei, China	677.31
1996	Dmitri Sautin, Russia	692.34
2000	Tian Liang, China	724.53

Women

SPRINGBOARD

		Pts
1920	Aileen Riggin, United States	539.90
1924	Elizabeth Becker, United States	474.50
1928	Helen Meany, United States	78.62
1932	Georgia Coleman, United States	87.52
1936	Marjorie Gestring, United States	89.27
1948	Victoria Draves, United States	108.74

SPRINGBOARD (CONT.)

		Pts
1952	Patricia McCormick, United States	147.30
1956	Patricia McCormick, United States	142.36
1960	Ingrid Krämer, E Germany	155.81
1964	Ingrid Engel Krämer, E Germany	145.00
1968	Sue Gossick, United States	150.77
1972	Micki King, United States	450.03

DIVING (Cont.)
Women (Cont.)

SPRINGBOARD (CONT.)

		Pts
1976	Jennifer Chandler, United States	506.19
1980	Irina Kalinina, USSR	725.91
1984	Sylvie Bernier, Canada	530.70
1988	Gao Min, China	580.23
1992	Gao Min, China	572.40
1996	Fu Mingxia, China	547.68
2000	Fu Mingxia, China	609.42

PLATFORM

		Pts
1912	Greta Johansson, Sweden	39.90
1920	Stefani Fryland-Clausen, Denmark	34.60
1924	Caroline Smith, United States	33.20
1928	Elizabeth B. Pinkston, United States	31.60
1932	Dorothy Poynton, United States	40.26
1936	Dorothy Poynton Hill, United States	33.93

PLATFORM (CONT.)

		Pts
1948	Victoria Draves, United States	68.87
1952	Patricia McCormick, United States	79.37
1956	Patricia McCormick, United States	84.85
1960	Ingrid Krämer, E Germany	91.28
1964	Lesley Bush, United States	99.80
1968	Milena Duchkova, Czechoslovakia	109.59
1972	Ulrika Knape, Sweden	390.00
1976	Elena Vaytsekhovskaya, USSR	406.59
1980	Martina Jäschke, E Germany	596.25
1984	Zhou Jihong, China	435.51
1988	Xu Yanmei, China	445.20
1992	Mingxia Fu, China	461.43
1996	Mingxia Fu, China	521.58
2000	Laura Wilkinson, United States	543.75

GYMNASTICS
Men

ALL-AROUND

		Pts
1900	Gustave Sandras, France	302
1904	Julius Lenhart, Austria	69.80
1906	Pierre Paysse, France	97
1908	Alberto Braglia, Italy	317.0
1912	Alberto Braglia, Italy	135.0
1920	Giorgio Zampori, Italy	88.35
1924	Leon Stukelj, Yugoslavia	110.340
1928	Georges Miez, Switzerland	247.500
1932	Romeo Neri, Italy	140.625
1936	Alfred Schwarzmann, Germany	113.100
1948	Veikko Huhtanen, Finland	229.70
1952	Viktor Chukarin, USSR	115.70
1956	Viktor Chukarin, USSR	114.25
1960	Boris Shakhlin, USSR	115.95
1964	Yukio Endo, Japan	115.95
1968	Sawao Kato, Japan	115.90
1972	Sawao Kato, Japan	114.65
1976	Nikolai Andrianov, USSR	116.65
1980	Aleksandr Dityatin, USSR	118.65
1984	Koji Gushiken, Japan	118.70
1988	Vladimir Artemov, USSR	119.125
1992	Vitaly Scherbo, Unified Team	59.025
1996	Li Xiaoshuang, China	58.423
2000	Alexei Nemov, Russia	58.474

HORIZONTAL BAR

		Pts
1896	Hermann Weingärtner, Germany	—
1904	Anton Heida, United States	40
1924	Leon Stukelj, Yugoslavia	19.73
1928	Georges Miez, Switzerland	19.17
1932	Dallas Bixler, United States	18.33
1936	Aleksanteri Saarvala, Finland	19.367
1948	Josef Stalder, Switzerland	19.85
1952	Jack Günthard, Switzerland	19.55
1956	Takashi Ono, Japan	19.60
1960	Takashi Ono, Japan	19.60
1964	Boris Shakhlin, USSR	19.625
1968	Akinori Nakayama, Japan	19.55
1972	Mitsuo Tsukahara, Japan	19.725
1976	Mitsuo Tsukahara, Japan	19.675
1980	Stoyan Deltchev, Bulgaria	19.825
1984	Shinji Morisue, Japan	20.00
1988	Vladimir Artemov, USSR	19.90
1992	Trent Dimas, United States	9.875
1996	Andreas Wecker, Germany	9.850
2000	Alexei Nemov, Russia	9.787

PARALLEL BARS

		Pts
1896	Alfred Flatow, Germany	—
1904	George Eyser, United States	44
1924	August Güttinger, Switzerland	21.63
1928	Ladislav Vacha, Czechoslovakia	18.83
1932	Romeo Neri, Italy	18.97
1936	Konrad Frey, Germany	19.067
1948	Michael Reusch, Switzerland	19.75
1952	Hans Eugster, Switzerland	19.65
1956	Viktor Chukarin, USSR	19.20
1960	Boris Shakhlin, USSR	19.40
1964	Yukio Endo, Japan	19.675
1968	Akinori Nakayama, Japan	19.475
1972	Sawao Kato, Japan	19.475
1976	Sawao Kato, Japan	19.675
1980	Aleksandr Tkachyov, USSR	19.775
1984	Bart Conner, United States	19.95
1988	Vladimir Artemov, USSR	19.925
1992	Vitaly Scherbo, Unified Team	9.900
1996	Rustan Sharipov, Ukraine	9.837
2000	Xiaopeng Li, China	9.825

VAULT

		Pts
1896	Karl Schumann, Germany	—
1904	George Eyser, United States	36
1924	Frank Kriz, United States	9.98
1928	Eugen Mack, Switzerland	9.58
1932	Savino Guglielmetti, Italy	18.03
1936	Alfred Schwarzmann, Germany	19.20
1948	Paavo Aaltonen, Finland	19.55
1952	Viktor Chukarin, USSR	19.20
1956	Helmut Bantz, Germany	18.85
1960	Takashi Ono, Japan	19.35
1964	Haruhiro Yamashita, Japan	19.60
1968	Mikhail Voronin, USSR	19.00
1972	Klaus Köste, E Germany	18.85
1976	Nikolai Andrianov, USSR	19.45
1980	Nikolai Andrianov, USSR	19.825
1984	Lou Yun, China	19.95
1988	Lou Yun, China	19.875
1992	Vitaly Scherbo, Unified Team	9.856
1996	Alexei Nemov, Russia	9.787
2000	Gervasio Deferr, Spain	9.712

GYMNASTICS *(Cont.)*
Men *(Cont.)*

POMMEL HORSE

	Pts
1896 .....Louis Zutter, Switzerland	—
1900 .....Not held	
1904 .....Anton Heida, United States	42
1908–1920......Not held	
1924 .....Josef Wilhelm, Switzerland	21.23
1928 .....Hermann Hänggi, Switzerland	19.75
1932 .....Istvan Pelle, Hungary	19.07
1936 .....Konrad Frey, Germany	19.333
1948 .....Paavo Aaltonen, Finland	19.35
1952 .....Viktor Chukarin, USSR	19.50
1956 .....Boris Shakhlin, USSR	19.25
1960 .....Eugen Ekman, Finland	19.375
1964 .....Miroslav Cerar, Yugoslavia	19.525
1968 .....Miroslav Cerar, Yugoslavia	19.325
1972 .....Viktor Klimenko, USSR	19.125
1976 .....Zoltan Magyar, Hungary	19.70
1980 .....Zoltan Magyar, Hungary	19.925
1984 .....Li Ning, China	19.95
1988 .....Dmitri Bilozerchev, USSR	19.95
1992 .....Vitaly Scherbo, Unified Team	9.925
1996 .....Donghua Li, Switzerland	9.875
2000 .....Marius Urzica, Romania	9.862

RINGS

	Pts
1896 .....Ioannis Mitropoulos, Greece	—
1900 .....Not held	
1904 .....Hermann Glass, United States	45
1908–1920......Not held	
1924 .....Francesco Martino, Italy	21.553
1928 .....Leon Stukelj, Yugoslavia	19.25
1932 .....George Gulack, United States	18.97
1936 .....Alois Hudec, Czechoslovakia	19.433
1948 .....Karl Frei, Switzerland	19.80
1952 .....Grant Shaginyan, USSR	19.75
1956 .....Albert Azaryan, USSR	19.35
1960 .....Albert Azaryan, USSR	19.725
1964 .....Takuji Haytta, Japan	19.475
1968 .....Akinori Nakayama, Japan	19.45
1972 .....Akinori Nakayama, Japan	19.35
1976 .....Nikolai Andrianov, USSR	19.65
1980 .....Aleksandr Dityatin, USSR	19.875
1984 .....Koji Gushiken, Japan	19.85
1988 .....Holger Behrendt, E Germany	19.925
1992 .....Vitaly Scherbo, Unified Team	9.937
1996 .....Yuri Chechi, Italy	9.887
2000 .....Szilveszter Csollany, Hungary	9.862

FLOOR EXERCISE

	Pts
1932 .....Istvan Pelle, Hungary	9.60
1936 .....Georges Miez, Switzerland	18.666
1948 .....Ferenc Pataki, Hungary	19.35
1952 .....K. William Thoresson, Sweden	19.25
1956 .....Valentin Muratov, USSR	19.20
1960 .....Nobuyuki Aihara, Japan	19.45
1964 .....Franco Menichelli, Italy	19.45
1968 .....Sawao Kato, Japan	19.475
1972 .....Nikolai Andrianov, USSR	19.175
1976 .....Nikolai Andrianov, USSR	19.45
1980 .....Roland Brückner, E Germany	19.75
1984 .....Li Ning, China	19.925
1988 .....Sergei Kharkov, USSR	19.925
1992 .....Li Xiaoshuang, China	9.925
1996 .....Ioannis Melissanidis, Greece	9.850
2000 .....Igors Vihrovs, Latvia	9.812

TEAM COMBINED EXERCISES

		Pts
1904 ....Turngemeinde Philadelphia		374.43
1906 ....Norway		19.00
1908 ....Sweden		438
1912 ....Italy		265.75
1920 ....Italy		359.855
1924 ....Italy		839.058
1928 ....Switzerland		1718.625
1932 ....Italy		541.850
1936 ....Germany		657.430
1948 ....Finland		1358.30
1952 ....USSR		574.40
1956 ....USSR		568.25
1960 ....Japan		575.20
1964 ....Japan		577.95
1968 ....Japan		575.90
1972 ....Japan		571.25
1976 ....Japan		576.85
1980 ....USSR		598.60
1984 ....United States		591.40
1988 ....USSR		593.35
1992 ....Unified Team		585.45
1996 ....Russia		576.778
2000 ....China		231.919

Women

ALL-AROUND

	Pts
1952 .....Maria Gorokhovskaya, USSR	76.78
1956 .....Larissa Latynina, USSR	74.933
1960 .....Larissa Latynina, USSR	77.031
1964 .....Vera Caslavska, Czechoslovakia	77.564
1968 .....Vera Caslavska, Czechoslovakia	78.25
1972 .....Lyudmila Tousischeva, USSR	77.025
1976 .....Nadia Comaneci, Romania	79.275
1980 .....Yelena Davydova, USSR	79.15
1984 .....Mary Lou Retton, United States	79.175
1988 .....Yelena Shushunova, USSR	79.662
1992 .....Tatiana Gutsu, Unified Team	39.737
1996 .....Lilia Podkopayeva, Ukraine	39.255
2000 .....Simona Amanar, Romania	38.642

VAULT

	Pts
1952 .....Yekaterina Kalinchuk, USSR	19.20
1956 .....Larissa Latynina, USSR	18.833
1960 .....Margarita Nikolayeva, USSR	19.316
1964 .....Vera Caslavska, Czechoslovakia	19.483
1968 .....Vera Caslavska, Czechoslovakia	19.775
1972 .....Karin Janz, E Germany	19.525
1976 .....Nelli Kim, USSR	19.80
1980 .....Natalya Shaposhnikova, USSR	19.725
1984 .....Ecaterina Szabo, Romania	19.875
1988 .....Svetlana Boginskaya, USSR	19.905
1992 .....Henrietta Onodi, Hungary	9.925
Lavinia Milosovici, Romania	9.925
1996 .....Simona Amanar, Romania	9.825
2000 .....Yelena Zamolodtchikova, Russia	9.731

GYMNASTICS *(Cont.)*
Women *(Cont.)*

UNEVEN BARS

		Pts
1952	Margit Korondi, Hungary	19.40
1956	Agnes Keleti, Hungary	18.966
1960	Polina Astakhova, USSR	19.616
1964	Polina Astakhova, USSR	19.332
1968	Vera Caslavska, Czechoslovakia	19.65
1972	Karin Janz, E Germany	19.675
1976	Nadia Comaneci, Romania	20.00
1980	Maxi Gnauck, E Germany	19.875
1984	Ma Yanhong, China	19.95
1988	Daniela Silivas, Romania	20.00
1992	Lu Li, China	10.00
1996	Svetlana Khorkina, Russia	9.850
2000	Svetlana Khorkina, Russia	9.862

BALANCE BEAM

		Pts
1952	Nina Bocharova, USSR	19.22
1956	Agnes Keleti, Hungary	18.80
1960	Eva Bosakova, Czechoslovakia	19.283
1964	Vera Caslavska, Czechoslovakia	19.449
1968	Natalya Kuchinskaya, USSR	19.65
1972	Olga Korbut, USSR	19.40
1976	Nadia Comaneci, Romania	19.95
1980	Nadia Comaneci, Romania	19.80
1984	Simona Pauca, Romania	19.80
1988	Daniela Silivas, Romania	19.924
1992	Tatiana Lisenko, Unified Team	9.975
1996	Shannon Miller, United States	9.862
2000	Xuan Li, China	9.825

FLOOR EXERCISE

		Pts
1952	Agnes Keleti, Hungary	19.36
1956	Agnes Keleti, Hungary	18.733
1960	Larissa Latynina, USSR	19.583
1964	Larissa Latynina, USSR	19.599
1968	Vera Caslavska, Czechoslovakia	19.675
1972	Olga Korbut, USSR	19.575
1976	Nelli Kim, USSR	19.85
1980	Nadia Comaneci, Romania	19.875

FLOOR EXERCISE *(Cont.)*

		Pts
1984	Ecaterina Szabo, Romania	19.975
1988	Daniela Silivas, Romania	19.937
1992	Lavinia Milosovici, Romania	10.00
1996	Lilia Podkopayeva, Ukraine	9.887
2000	Yelena Zamolodtchikova, Russia	9.850

TEAM COMBINED EXERCISES

		Pts
1928	The Netherlands	316.75
1932	Not held	
1936	Germany	506.50
1948	Czechoslovakia	445.45
1952	USSR	527.03
1956	USSR	444.800
1960	USSR	382.320
1964	USSR	280.890
1968	USSR	382.85
1972	USSR	380.50
1976	USSR	466.00
1980	USSR	394.90
1984	Romania	392.02
1988	USSR	395.475
1992	Unified Team	395.666
1996	United States	389.225
2000	Romania	154.608

RHYTHMIC ALL-AROUND

		Pts
1984	Lori Fung, Canada	57.95
1988	Marina Lobach, USSR	60.00
1992	A. Timoshenko, Unified Team	59.037
1996	E. Serebrianskaya, Ukraine	39.683
2000	Yulia Barsukova, Russia	39.632

RHYTHMIC TEAM COMBINED EXERCISES

		Pts
1996	Spain	38.933
2000	Russia	39.500

SOCCER
Men

1900	Great Britain
1904	Canada
1908	Great Britain
1912	Great Britain
1920	Belgium
1924	Uruguay
1928	Uruguay
1936	Italy
1948	Sweden
1952	Hungary
1956	Soviet Union
1960	Yugoslavia
1964	Hungary
1968	Hungary
1972	Poland
1976	E Germany
1980	Czechoslovakia
1984	France
1988	Soviet Union
1992	Spain
1996	Nigeria
2000	Cameroon

Women

1996	United States
2000	Norway

BIATHLON
Men

10 KILOMETERS

1980	Frank Ullrich, E Germany	32:10.69
1984	Eirik Kvalfoss, Norway	30:53.8
1988	Frank-Peter Rötsch, W Germany	25:08.1
1992	Mark Kirchner, Germany	26:02.3
1994	Sergei Tchepikov, Russia	28:07.0
1998	Ole Einar Bjorndalen, Norway	27:16.2
2002	Ole Einar Bjorndalen, Norway	24:51.3

20 KILOMETERS

1960	Klas Lestander, Sweden	1:33:21.6
1964	Vladimir Melyanin, Soviet Union	1:20:26.8
1968	Magnar Solberg, Norway	1:13:45.9
1972	Magnar Solberg, Norway	1:15:55.5
1976	Nikolay Kruglov, Soviet Union	1:14:12.26
1980	Anatoliy Alyabiev, Soviet Union	1:08:16.31
1984	Peter Angerer, W Germany	1:11:52.7
1988	Frank-Peter Rötsch, W Germany	56:33.3

20 KILOMETERS (Cont.)

1992	Evgueni Redkine, Unified Team	57:34.4
1994	Sergei Tarasov, Russia	57:25.3
1998	Halvard Hanevold, Norway	56:16.4
2002	Ole Einar Bjordalen, Norway	51:03.3

4 X 7.5-KILOMETER RELAY

1968	Soviet Union	2:13:02.4
1972	Soviet Union	1:51:44.92
1976	Soviet Union	1:57:55.64
1980	Soviet Union	1:34:03.27
1984	Soviet Union	1:38:51.7
1988	Soviet Union	1:22:30.0
1992	Germany	1:24:43.5
1994	Germany	1:30:22.1
1998	Germany	1:19:43.3
2002	Norway	1:23:42.3

12.5 KILOMETERS PURSUIT

2002	Ole Einar Bjorndalen	1:23:42.3

Women

7.5 KILOMETERS

1992	Antissa Restzova, Unified Team	24:29.2
1994	Myriam Bedard, Canada	26:08.8
1998	Galina Koukleva, Russia	23:08.0
2002	Kati Wilhemn, Germany	20:41.4

10 KILOMETERS PURSUIT

2002	Olga Pyleva, Russia	31:07.7

15 KILOMETERS

1992	Antje Misersky, Germany	51:47.2
1994	Myriam Bedard, Canada	52:06.6
1998	Ekaterina Dofovska, Bulgaria	54:52.0
2002	Andrea Henkel, Germany	47:29.1

3 X 7.5-KILOMETER RELAY

1992	France	1:15:55.6
1994	Russia	1:47:19.5
1998	Germany	1:40:13.6
2002	Germany	1:27:55.0

BOBSLED

4-MAN

1924	Switzerland (Eduard Scherrer)	5:45.54
1928	United States	3:20.50
	(William Fiske) (5-man)	
1932	United States (William Fiske)	7:53.68
1936	Switzerland (Pierre Musy)	5:19.85
1948	United States (Francis Tyler)	5:20.10
1952	Germany (Andreas Ostler)	5:07.84
1956	Switzerland (Franz Kapus)	5:10.44
1960	Not held	
1964	Canada (Victor Emery)	4:14.46
1968	Italy (Eugenio Monti) (2 runs)	2:17.39
1972	Switzerland (Jean Wicki)	4:43.07
1976	E Germany (Meinhard Nehmer)	3:40.43
1980	E Germany (Meinhard Nehmer)	3:59.92
1984	E Germany (Wolfgang Hoppe)	3:20.22
1988	Switzerland (Ekkehard Fasser)	3:47.51
1992	Austria (Ingo Appelt)	3:53.90
1994	Germany (Harold Czudaj)	3:27.78
1998	Germany (Christoph Langen)	2:39.41
2002	Germany (Andre Lange)	3:10.11

Note: Driver in parentheses.

2-MAN

1932	United States (Hubert Stevens)	8:14.74
1936	United States (Ivan Brown)	5:29.29
1948	Switzerland (Felix Endrich)	5:29.20
1952	Germany (Andreas Ostler)	5:24.54
1956	Italy (Lamberto Dalla Costa)	5:30.14
1960	Not held	
1964	Great Britain (Anthony Nash)	4:21.90
1968	Italy (Eugenio Monti)	4:41.54
1972	W Germany	4:57.07
	(Wolfgang Zimmerer)	
1976	E Germany (Meinhard Nehmer)	3:44.42
1980	Switzerland (Erich Schärer)	4:09.36
1984	E Germany (Wolfgang Hoppe)	3:25.56
1988	USSR (Janis Kipours)	3:53.48
1992	Switzerland (Gustav Weder)	4:03.26
1994	Switzerland (Gustav Weder)	3:30.81
1998	Canada (Pierre Lueders)	3:37.24
	Italy (Guenther Huber)	3:37.24
2002	Germany (Martin Langen)	3:10:11

WOMEN
2-PERSON

2002	United States (Jill Bakken)	1:37:76

Note: Driver in parentheses.

CURLING

Men

1998 .....Switzerland, Canada, Norway
2002 .....Norway, Canada, Switzerland
Note: Gold, silver, and bronze medals.

Women

1998 .....Canada, Denmark, Sweden
2002 .....Britain, Switzerland, Canada
Note: Gold, silver, and bronze medals.

ICE HOCKEY

Men

1920* ....Canada, United States, Czechoslovakia
1924 .....Canada, United States, Great Britain
1928 .....Canada, Sweden, Switzerland
1932 .....Canada, United States, Germany
1936 .....Great Britain, Canada, United States
1948 .....Canada, Czechoslovakia, Switzerland
1952 .....Canada, United States, Sweden
1956 .....USSR, United States, Canada
1960 .....United States, Canada, USSR
1964 .....USSR, Sweden, Czechoslovakia
1968 .....USSR, Czechoslovakia, Canada

1972 .....USSR, United States, Czechoslovakia
1976 .....USSR, Czechoslovakia, W Germany
1980 .....United States, USSR, Sweden
1984 .....USSR, Czechoslovakia, Sweden
1988 .....USSR, Finland, Sweden
1992 .....Unified Team, Canada, Czechoslovakia
1994 .....Sweden, Canada, Finland
1998 .....Czech Republic, Russia, Finland
2002 .....Canada, United States, Russia
*Competition held at Summer Games in Antwerp.
Note: Gold, silver, and bronze medals.

Women

1998 .....United States, Canada, Finland
2002 .....Canada, United States, Sweden

Note: Gold, silver, and bronze medals.

LUGE

Men

SINGLES		
1964 .....Thomas Köhler, East Germany	3:26.77
1968 .....Manfred Schmid, Austria	2:52.48
1972 .....Wolfgang Scheidel, W Germany	3:27.58
1976 .....Detlef Guenther, W Germany	3:27.688
1980 .....Bernhard Glass, W Germany	2:54.796
1984 .....Paul Hildgartner, Italy	3:04.258
1988 .....Jens Müller, W Germany	3:05.548
1992 .....Georg Hackl, Germany	3:02.363
1994 .....Georg Hackl, Germany	3:21.571
1998 .....Georg Hackl, Germany	3:18.44
2002 .....Armin Zoeggeler, Italy	2:57.941

DOUBLES		
1964 ....Austria	1:41.62
1968 ....E Germany	1:35.85
1972 ....E Germany	1:28.35
1976 ....E Germany	1:25.604
1980 ....E Germany	1:19.331
1984 ....W Germany	1:23.620
1988 ....E Germany	1:31.940
1992 ....Germany	1:32.053
1994 ....Italy	1:36.720
1998 ....Germany	1:41.105
2002 ....Germany	1:26.082

Women

SINGLES		
1964 .....Ortrun Enderlein, Germany	3:24.67
1968 .....Erica Lechner, Italy	2:28.66
1972 .....Anna-Maria Müller, E Germany	2:59.18
1976 .....Margit Schumann, E Germany	2:50.621
1980 .....Vera Zozulya, USSR	2:36.537

SINGLES (Cont.)		
1984 .....Steffi Martin, E Germany	2:46.570
1988 .....Steffi Walter (Martin) E Germany	3:03.973
1992 .....Doris Neuner, Austria	3:06.696
1994 .....Gerda Weissensteiner, Italy	3:15.517
1998 .....Silke Kraushaar, Germany	3:23.779
2002 .....Sylke Otto, Germany	2:52.464

THEY SAID IT

*Jim Shea Jr., skeleton gold medalist:
"If bobsled is the champagne
of thrills, skeleton is the moonshine
of thrills."*

FIGURE SKATING

Men

1908* ....Ulrich Salchow, Sweden
1920† ....Gillis Grafström, Sweden
1924 ....Gillis Grafström, Sweden
1928 ....Gillis Grafström, Sweden
1932 ....Karl Schäfer, Austria
1936 ....Karl Schäfer, Austria
1948 ....Dick Button, United States
1952 ....Dick Button, United States
1956 ....Hayes Alan Jenkins, United States
1960 ....David Jenkins, United States
1964 ....Manfred Schnelldorfer, W Germany
1968 ....Wolfgang Schwarz, Austria
1972 ....Ondrej Nepela, Czechoslovakia
1976 ....John Curry, Great Britain
1980 ....Robin Cousins, Great Britain
1984 ....Scott Hamilton, United States
1988 ....Brian Boitano, United States
1992 ....Victor Petrenko, Unified Team
1994 ....Alexei Urmanov, Russia
1998 ....Ilia Kulik, Russia
2002 ....Alexei Yagudin, Russia

*Competition held at Summer Games in London.
†Competition held at Summer Games in Antwerp.

Women

1908* ....Madge Syers, Great Britain
1920† ....Magda Julin, Sweden
1924 ....Herma Szabo-Planck, Austria
1928 ....Sonja Henie, Norway
1932 ....Sonja Henie, Norway
1936 ....Sonja Henie, Norway
1948 ....Barbara Ann Scott, Canada
1952 ....Jeanette Altwegg, Great Britain
1956 ....Tenley Albright, United States
1960 ....Carol Heiss, United States
1964 ....Sjoukje Dijkstra, Netherlands
1968 ....Peggy Fleming, United States
1972 ....Beatrix Schuba, Austria
1976 ....Dorothy Hamill, United States
1980 ....Anett Pötzsch, E Germany
1984 ....Katarina Witt, E Germany
1988 ....Katarina Witt, E Germany
1992 ....Kristi Yamaguchi, United States
1994 ....Oksana Baiul, Ukraine
1998 ....Tara Lipinski, United States
2002 ....Sarah Hughes, United States

Mixed

PAIRS

1908* ..Anna Hübler & Heinrich Burger, Germany
1920†..Ludovika & Walter Jakobsson, Finland
1924....Helene Engelmann & Alfred Berger, Austria
1928....Andree Joly & Pierre Brunet, France
1932....Andree Brunet (Joly) & Pierre Brunet, France
1936....Maxi Herber & Ernst Baier, Germany
1948....Micheline Lannoy & Pierre Baugniet, Belgium
1952....Ria Falk and Paul Falk, W Germany
1956....Elisabeth Schwartz & Kurt Oppelt, Austria
1960....Barbara Wagner & Robert Paul, Canada
1964....Lyudmila Beloussova & Oleg Protopopov, USSR
1968....Lyudmila Beloussova & Oleg Protopopov, USSR
1972....Irina Rodnina & Alexei Ulanov, USSR
1976....Irina Rodnina & Aleksandr Zaitzev, USSR
1980....Irina Rodnina & Aleksandr Zaitzev, USSR
1984....Elena Valova & Oleg Vasiliev, USSR
1988....Ekaterina Gordeeva & Sergei Grinkov, USSR
1992....Natalia Michkouteniok & Artour Dmitriev, Unified Team
1994....Ekaterina Gordeeva & Sergei Grinkov, Russia
1998....Oksana Kazakova & Artur Dmitriev, Russia
2002....Elena Berezhnaya & Anton Sikharulidze, Russia/ Jamie Sale & David Pelletier, Canada

DANCE

1976....Lyudmila Pakhomova & Aleksandr Gorshkov, USSR
1980....Natalia Linichuk & Gennadi Karponosov, USSR
1984....Jayne Torvill & Christopher Dean, Great Britain
1988....Natalia Bestemianova & Andrei Bukin, USSR
1992....Marina Klimova & Sergei Ponomarenko, Unified Team
1994....Oksana Grishuk & Evgeny Platov, Russia
1998....Pasha Grishuk & Evgeny Platov, Russia
2002....Marina Anissina & Gwendal Peizeralt, France

*Competition held at Summer Games in London.
†Competition held at Summer Games in Antwerp.

SKELETON

Men

1928 .....Jennison Heaton, United States   3:01.8
1948 .....Nino Bibbia, Italy   5:23.2
2002 .....Jim Shea Jr., United States   1:41.96

Women

2002 .....Tristan Gale, United States   1:45.11

SPEED SKATING

Men

500 METERS

1924	Charles Jewtraw, United States	44.0
1928	Clas Thunberg, Finland	43.4 OR
	Bernt Evensen, Norway	43.4 OR
1932	John Shea, United States	43.4 EOR
1936	Ivar Ballangrud, Norway	43.4 EOR
1948	Finn Helgesen, Norway	43.1 OR
1952	Kenneth Henry, United States	43.2
1956	Yevgeny Grishin, USSR	40.2 EWR
1960	Yevgeny Grishin, USSR	40.2 EWR
1964	Terry McDermott, United States	40.1 OR
1968	Erhard Keller, W Germany	40.3
1972	Erhard Keller, W Germany	39.44 OR
1976	Yevgeny Kulikov, USSR	39.17 OR
1980	Eric Heiden, United States	38.03 OR
1984	Sergei Fokichev, USSR	38.19
1988	Uwe-Jens Mey, E Germany	36.45 WR
1992	Uwe-Jens Mey, E Germany	37.14
1994	Aleksandr Golubev, Russia	36.33
1998	Hiroyasu Shimizu, Japan (second run)	35.59 OR
2002	Casey FitzRandolph, U.S.	1:09.23*

1,000 METERS

1976	Peter Mueller, United States	1:19.32
1980	Eric Heiden, United States	1:15.18 OR
1984	Gaetan Boucher, Canada	1:15.80
1988	Nikolai Gulyaev, USSR	1:13.03 OR
1992	Olaf Zinke, Germany	1:14.85
1994	Dan Jansen, United States	1:12.43 WR
1998	Ids Postma, Netherlands	1:10.64 OR
2002	Gerard van Velde, Netherlands	1:07.18

1,500 METERS

1924	Clas Thunberg, Finland	2:20.8
1928	Clas Thunberg, Finland	2:21.1
1932	John Shea, United States	2:57.5
1936	Charles Mathisen, Norway	2:19.2 OR
1948	Sverre Farstad, Norway	2:17.6 OR
1952	Hjalmar Andersen, Norway	2:20.4
1956	Yevgeny Grishin, USSR	2:08.6 WR
	Yuri Mikhailov, USSR	2:08.6 WR
1960	Roald Aas, Norway	2:10.4
	Yevgeny Grishin, USSR	2:10.4
1964	Ants Anston, USSR	2:10.3
1968	Cornelis Verkerk, Netherlands	2:03.4 OR
1972	Ard Schenk, Netherlands	2:02.96 OR
1976	Jan Egil Storholt, Norway	1:59.38 OR
1980	Eric Heiden, United States	1:55.44 OR

1,500 METERS (Cont.)

1984	Gaetan Boucher, Canada	1:58.36
1988	Andre Hoffmann, E Germany	1:52.06 WR
1992	Johann Olav Koss, Norway	1:54.81
1994	Johann Olav Koss, Norway	1:51.29 WR
1998	Aadne Sondral, Norway	1:47.87 WR
2002	Derek Parra, United States	1:43.95

5,000 METERS

1924	Clas Thunberg, Finland	8:39.0
1928	Ivar Ballangrud, Norway	8:50.5
1932	Irving Jaffee, United States	9:40.8
1936	Ivar Ballangrud, Norway	8:19.6 OR
1948	Reidar Liaklev, Norway	8:29.4
1952	Hjalmar Andersen, Norway	8:10.6 OR
1956	Boris Shilkov, USSR	7:48.7 OR
1960	Viktor Kosichkin, USSR	7:51.3
1964	Knut Johannesen, Norway	7:38.4 OR
1968	Fred Anton Maier, Norway	7:22.4 WR
1972	Ard Schenk, Netherlands	7:23.61
1976	Sten Stensen, Norway	7:24.48
1980	Eric Heiden, United States	7:02.29 OR
1984	Sven Tomas Gustafson, Sweden	7:12.28
1988	Tomas Gustafson, Sweden	6:44.63 WR
1992	Geir Karlstad, Norway	6:59.97
1994	Johann Olav Koss, Norway	6:34.96 WR
1998	Gianni Romme, Netherlands	6:22.20 WR
2002	Jochem Uytdehaage, Net	6:41.66

10,000 METERS

1924	Julius Skutnabb, Finland	18:04.8
1928	Not held, thawing of ice	
1932	Irving Jaffee, United States	19:13.6
1936	Ivar Ballangrud, Norway	17:24.3 OR
1948	Ake Seyffarth, Sweden	17:26.3
1952	Hjalmar Andersen, Norway	16:45.8 OR
1956	Sigvard Ericsson, Sweden	16:35.9 OR
1960	Knut Johannesen, Norway	15:46.6 WR
1964	Jonny Nilsson, Sweden	15:50.1
1968	Johnny Höglin, Sweden	15:23.6 OR
1972	Ard Schenk, Netherlands	15:01.35 OR
1976	Piet Kleine, Netherlands	14:50.59 OR
1980	Eric Heiden, United States	14:28.13 WR
1984	Igor Malkov, USSR	14:39.90
1988	Tomas Gustafson, Sweden	13:48.20 WR
1992	Bart Veldkamp, Netherlands	14:12.12
1994	Johann Olav Koss, Norway	13:30.55 WR
1998	Gianni Romme, Netherlands	13:15.33 WR
2002	Jochem Uytdehaage, Neth	12:58.92 WR

Women

500 METERS

1960	Helga Haase, E Germany	45.9
1964	Lydia Skoblikova, USSR	45.0 OR
1968	Lyudmila Titova, USSR	46.1
1972	Anne Henning, United States	43.33 OR
1976	Sheila Young, United States	42.76 OR
1980	Karin Enke, E Germany	41.78 OR
1984	Christa Rothenburger, E Germany	41.02 OR

500 METERS (Cont.)

1988	Bonnie Blair, United States	39.10 WR
1992	Bonnie Blair, United States	40.33
1994	Bonnie Blair, United States	39.25
1998	Catriona LeMay Doan, Canada (second run)	38.21 OR
2002	Catriona LeMay, Canada	1:14.75*

Note: OR=Olympic Record; WR=World Record; EOR=Equals Olympic Record; EWR=Equals World Record; WB=World Best.

*Combined time.

SPEED SKATING *(Cont.)*

Women *(Cont.)*

1,000 METERS

1960	Klara Guseva, USSR	1:34.1
1964	Lydia Skoblikova, USSR	1:33.2 OR
1968	Carolina Geijssen, Netherlands	1:32.6 OR
1972	Monika Pflug, W Germany	1:31.40 OR
1976	Tatiana Averina, USSR	1:28.43 OR
1980	Natalya Petruseva, USSR	1:24.10 OR
1984	Karin Enke, E Germany	1:21.61 OR
1988	Christa Rothenburger, E Germany	1:17.65 WR
1992	Bonnie Blair, United States	1:21.90
1994	Bonnie Blair, United States	1:18.74
1998	Marianne Timmer, Netherlands	1:16.51 OR
2002	Chris Witty, United States	1:13.83

1,500 METERS

1960	Lydia Skoblikova, USSR	2:25.2 WR
1964	Lydia Skoblikova, USSR	2:22.6 OR
1968	Kaija Mustonen, Finland	2:22.4 OR
1972	Dianne Holum, United States	2:20.85 OR
1976	Galina Stepanskaya, USSR	2:16.58 OR
1980	Anne Borckink, Netherlands	2:10.95 OR
1984	Karin Enke, E Germany	2:03.42 WR
1988	Yvonne van Gennip, Netherlands	2:00.68 OR
1992	Jacqueline Boerner, Germany	2:05.87
1994	Emese Hunyady, Austria	2:02.19
1998	Marianne Timmer, Netherlands	1:57.58 WR

1,500 METERS *(Cont.)*

2002	Anni Friesinger, Germany	1:54.02

3,000 METERS

1960	Lydia Skoblikova, USSR	5:14.3
1964	Lydia Skoblikova, USSR	5:14.9
1968	Johanna Schut, Netherlands	4:56.2 OR
1972	Christina Baas-Kaiser, Netherlands	4:52.14 OR
1976	Tatiana Averina, USSR	4:45.19 OR
1980	Bjorg Eva Jensen, Norway	4:32.13 OR
1984	Andrea Schöne, E Germany	4:24.79 OR
1988	Yvonne van Gennip, Netherlands	4:11.94 WR
1992	Gunda Niemann, Germany	4:19.90
1994	Svetlana Bazhanova, Russia	4:17.43
1998	Gunda Niemann-Stirnemann, Germany	4:07.29 OR
2002	Claudia Pechstein, Germany	3:57.70

5,000 METERS

1988	Yvonne van Gennip, Netherlands	7:14.13 WR
1992	Gunda Niemann, Germany	7:31.57
1994	Claudia Pechstein, Germany	7:14.37
1998	Claudia Pechstein, Germany	6:59.61 WR
2002	Claudia Pechstein, Germany	6:46.91 WR

SHORT TRACK SPEED SKATING

Men

500 METERS

1994	Chae Ji-Hoon, S Korea	43.54
1998	Takafumi Nishitani, Japan	42.862
2002	Marc Gagnon, Canada	41.802 OR

1,000 METERS

1992	Kim Ki-Hoon, S Korea	1:30.76
1994	Kim Ki-Hoon, S Korea	1:34.57
1998	Kim Dong Sung, S Korea	1:32.375
2002	Steve Bradbury, Austrailia	1:29.109

1,500 METERS

2002	Apolo Anton Ohno, United States	2:18.541

5,000-METER RELAY

1992	Korea	7:14.02
1994	Italy	7:11.74
1998	Canada	7:06.075
2002	Canada	6:51.579

Women

500 METERS

1992	Cathy Turner, United States	47.04
1994	Cathy Turner, United States	45.98
1998	Annie Perreault, Canada	46.568
2002	Yang Yang, China	44.187

1,000 METERS

1994	Chun Lee Kyung, S Korea	1:36.87
1998	Chun Lee Kyung, S Korea	1:42.776
2002	Yang A. Yang, China	1:36.391

1,500 METERS

2002	Ko Gi-Hyun, Korea	2:31.581

3,000-METER RELAY

1992	Canada	4:36.62
1994	S Korea	4:26.64
1998	S Korea	4:16.260
2002	S Korea	4:12.793

ALPINE SKIING

Men

DOWNHILL

1948	Henri Oreiller, France	2:55.0
1952	Zeno Colo, Italy	2:30.8
1956	Anton Sailer, Austria	2:52.2
1960	Jean Vuarnet, France	2:06.0
1964	Egon Zimmermann, Austria	2:18.16
1968	Jean-Claude Killy, France	1:59.85
1972	Bernhard Russi, Switzerland	1:51.43
1976	Franz Klammer, Austria	1:45.73
1980	Leonhard Stock, Austria	1:45.50
1984	Bill Johnson, United States	1:45.59
1988	Pirmin Zurbriggen, Switzerland	1:59.63
1992	Patrick Ortlieb, Austria	1:50.37
1994	Tommy Moe, United States	1:45.75
1998	Jean-Luc Crétier, France	1:50.11
2002	Fritz Strobl, Austria	1:39.13

SLALOM

1948	Edi Reinalter, Switzerland	2:10.3
1952	Othmar Schneider, Austria	2:00.0
1956	Anton Sailer, Austria	3:14.7
1960	Ernst Hinterseer, Austria	2:08.9
1964	Josef Stiegler, Austria	2:11.13
1968	Jean-Claude Killy, France	1:39.73
1972	F. Fernandez Ochoa, Spain	1:49.27
1976	Piero Gros, Italy	2:03.29
1980	Ingemar Stenmark, Sweden	1:44.26
1984	Phil Mahre, United States	1:39.41
1988	Alberto Tomba, Italy	1:39.47
1992	Finn Christian Jagge, Norway	1:44.39
1994	Thomas Stangassinger, Austria	2:02.02
1998	Hans-Petter Buraas, Norway	1:49.31
2002	Jean-Pierre Vidal, France	1:41.06

ALPINE SKIING
Men *(Cont.)*

GIANT SLALOM		
1952....Stein Eriksen, Norway	2:25.0	
1956....Anton Sailer, Austria	3:00.1	
1960....Roger Staub, Switzerland	1:48.3	
1964....Francois Bonlieu, France	1:46.71	
1968....Jean-Claude Killy, France	3:29.28	
1972....Gustav Thöni, Italy	3:09.62	
1976....Heini Hemmi, Switzerland	3:26.97	
1980....Ingemar Stenmark, Sweden	2:40.74	
1984....Max Julen, Switzerland	2:41.18	
1988....Alberto Tomba, Italy	2:06.37	
1992....Alberto Tomba, Italy	2:06.98	
1994....Markus Wasmeier, Germany	2:52.46	
1998....Hermann Maier, Austria	2:38.51	
2002....Stephan Eberharter, Austria	2:23.28	

SUPER GIANT SLALOM	
1988....Franck Piccard, France	1:39.66
1992....Kjetil Andre Aamodt, Norway	1:13.04
1994....Markus Wasmeier, Germany	1:32.53
1998....Hermann Maier, Austria	1:34.82
2002....Kjetil Andre Aamodt, Norway	1:21.58

COMBINED*	
1936.....Franz Pfnür, Germany	99.25
1948.....Henri Oreiller, France	3.27
1988.....Hubert Strolz, Austria	36.55
1992.....Josef Polig, Italy	14.58
1994.....Lasse Kjus, Norway	3:17.53
1998.....Mario Reiter, Austria	3:08.06
2002.....Kjetil Andre Aamodt, Norway	3:17.56

Women

DOWNHILL		
1948....Hedy Schlunegger, Switzerland	2:28.3	
1952....Trude Jochum-Beiser, Austria	1:47.1	
1956....Madeleine Berthod, Switzerland	1:40.7	
1960....Heidi Biebl, W Germany	1:37.6	
1964....Christl Haas, Austria	1:55.39	
1968....Olga Pall, Austria	1:40.87	
1972....Marie-Theres Nadig, Switzerland	1:36.68	
1976....Rosi Mittermaier, W Germany	1:46.16	
1980....Annemarie Moser-Pröll, Austria	1:37.52	
1984....Michela Figini, Switzerland	1:13.36	
1988....Marina Kiehl, W Germany	1:25.86	
1992....Kerrin Lee-Gartner, Canada	1:52.55	
1994....Katja Seizinger, Germany	1:35.93	
1998....Katja Seizinger, Germany	1:28.89	
2002....Carole Montillet, France	1:39.56	

SLALOM	
1948....Gretchen Fraser, United States	1:57.2
1952....Andrea Mead Lawrence, United States	2:10.6
1956....Renee Colliard, Switzerland	1:52.3
1960....Anne Heggtveigt, Canada	1:49.6
1964....Christine Goitschel, France	1:29.86
1968....Marielle Goitschel, France	1:25.86
1972....Barbara Cochran, United States	1:31.24
1976....Rosi Mittermaier, W Germany	1:30.54
1980....Hanni Wenzel, Liechtenstein	1:25.09
1984....Paoletta Magoni, Italy	1:36.47
1988....Vreni Schneider, Switzerland	1:36.69
1992....Petra Kronberger, Austria	1:32.68
1994....Vreni Schneider, Switzerland	1:56.01
1998....Hilde Gerg, Germany	1:32.40
2002....Janica Kostelic, Croatia	1:46.10

GIANT SLALOM	
1952....Andrea Mead Lawrence, U.S.	2:06.8
1956....Ossi Reichert, W Germany	1:56.5
1960....Yvonne Rüegg, Switzerland	1:39.9
1964....Marielle Goitschel, France	1:52.24
1968....Nancy Greene, Canada	1:51.97
1972....Marie-Theres Nadig, Switzerland	1:29.90
1976....Kathy Kreiner, Canada	1:29.13
1980....Hanni Wenzel, Liechtenstein (2 runs)	2:41.66
1984....Debbie Armstrong, United States	2:20.98
1988....Vreni Schneider, Switzerland	2:06.49
1992....Pernilla Wiberg, Sweden	2:12.74
1994....Deborah Compagnoni, Italy	2:30.97
1998....Deborah Compagnoni, Italy	2:50.59
2002....Janica Kostelic, Croatia	2:30.01

SUPER GIANT SLALOM	
1988....Sigrid Wolf, Austria	1:19.03
1992....Deborah Compagnoni, Italy	1:21.22
1994....Diann Roffe-Steinrotter, U.S.	1:22.15
1998....Picabo Street, United States	1:18.02
2002....Daniela Ceccarelli, Italy	1:13.59

COMBINED*	
1988....Anita Wachter, Austria	29.25
1992....Petra Kronberger, Austria	2.55
1994....Pernilla Wiberg, Sweden	3:05.16
1998....Katja Seizinger, Germany	2:40.74
2002....Janica Kostelic, Croatia	2:43.28

*Beginning in 1994, scoring was based on time.

FREESTYLE SKIING

Men

MOGULS	Pts
1992....Edgar Grospiron, France	25.81
1994....Jean-Luc Brassard, Canada	27.24
1998....Jonny Moseley, United States	26.93
2002....Janne Lahtela, Finland	27.97

AERIALS	Pts
1994....Andreas Schoenbaechler, Switz.	234.67
1998....Eric Bergoust, United States	255.64
2002....Ales Valenta, Czech Republic	257.02

Women

MOGULS	Pts
1992....Donna Weinbrecht, United States	23.69
1994....Stine Lise Hattestad, Norway	25.97
1998....Tae Satoya, Japan	25.06
2002....Kari Traa, Norway	25.94

AERIALS	Pts
1994....Lina Cherjazova, Uzbekistan	166.84
1998....Nikki Stone, United States	193.00
2002....Alisa Camplin, Australia	193.47

NORDIC SKIING
Men

10 KILOMETERS CLASSICAL STYLE
1992	Vegard Ulvang, Norway	27:36.0
1994	Bjørn Dæhlie, Norway	24:20.1
1998	Bjørn Dæhlie, Norway	27:24.5

15 KILOMETERS CLASSICAL STYLE
1924	Thorlief Haug, Norway	1:14:31.0*
1928	Johan Gröttumsbraaten, Norway	1:37:01.0†
1932	Sven Utterström, Sweden	1:23:07.0‡
1936	Erik-August Larsson, Sweden	1:14:38.0*
1948	Martin Lundström, Sweden	1:13:50.0*
1952	Hallgeir Brenden, Norway	1:01:34.0*
1956	Hallgeir Brenden, Norway	49:39.0
1960	Haakon Brusveen, Norway	51:55.5
1964	Eero Mantyränta, Finland	50:54.1
1968	Harald Grönningen, Norway	47:54.2
1972	Sven-Ake Lundback, Sweden	45:28.24
1976	Nikolay Bajukov, Unified Team	43:58.47
1980	Thomas Wassberg, Sweden	41:57.63
1984	Gunde Swan, Sweden	41:25.6
1988	Michael Deviatyarov, USSR	41:18.9
2002	Andrus Veerpalu, Estonia	37:07.4

*Distance was 18 km. †Distance was 19.7 km.

‡Distance was 18.2 km.

15 KILOMETERS PURSUIT FREESTYLE
1992	Bjørn Dæhlie, Norway	1:05:37.9
1994	Bjørn Dæhlie, Norway	1:00:08.8
1998	Thomas Alsgaard, Norway	1:07:01.7

30 KILOMETERS CLASSICAL STYLE
1956	Veikko Hakulinen, Finland	1:44:06.0
1960	Sixten Jernberg, Sweden	1:51:03.9
1964	Eero Mantyränta, Finland	1:30:50.7
1968	Franco Nones, Italy	1:35:39.2
1972	Viaceslav Vedenine, USSR	1:36:31.2
1976	Sergei Savelyev, USSR	1:30:29.38
1980	Nikolai Simyatov, USSR	1:27:02.80
1984	Nikolai Simyatov, USSR	1:28:56.3
1988	Alexey Prokororov, USSR	1:24:26.3
1992	Vegard Ulvang, Norway	1:22:27.8
1994	Thomas Alsgaard, Norway	1:12:26.4
1998	Mika Myllylae, Finland	1:33:55.8

50 KILOMETERS FREESTYLE
1924	Thorleif Haug, Norway	3:44:32.0
1928	Per Erik Hedlund, Sweden	4:52:03.0
1932	Veli Saarinen, Finland	4:28:00.0
1936	Elis Wiklund, Sweden	3:30:11.0
1948	Nils Karlsson, Sweden	3:47:48.0
1952	Veikko Hakulinen, Finland	3:33:33.0
1956	Sixten Jernberg, Sweden	2:50:27.0
1960	Kalevi Hämäläinen, Finland	2:59:06.3
1964	Sixten Jernberg, Sweden	2:43:52.6
1968	Olle Ellefsaeter, Norway	2:28:45.8
1972	Paal Tyldrum, Norway	2:43:14.75
1976	Ivar Formo, Norway	2:37:30.50
1980	Nikolai Simyatov, USSR	2:27:24.60
1984	Thomas Wassberg, Sweden	2:15:55.8
1988	Gunde Swan, Sweden	2:04:30.9
1992	Bjørn Dæhlie, Norway	2:03:41.5
1994	Vladimir Smirnov, Kazakhstan	2:07:20.3
1998	Bjørn Dæhlie, Norway	2:05:08.2

4 X 10-KILOMETER RELAY MIXED STYLE
1936	Finland	2:41:33.0
1948	Sweden	2:32:80.0
1952	Finland	2:20:16.0

4 X 10-KILOMETER RELAY MIXED STYLE (Cont.)
1956	USSR	2:15:30.0
1960	Finland	2:18:45.6
1964	Sweden	2:18:34.6
1968	Norway	2:08:33.5
1972	USSR	2:04:47.94
1976	Finland	2:07:59.72
1980	USSR	1:57:03.46
1984	Sweden	1:55:06.3
1988	Sweden	1:43:58.6
1992	Norway	1:39:26.0
1994	Italy	1:41:15.0
1998	Norway	1:40:55.7
2002	Norway	1:32:45.5

SKI JUMPING (NORMAL HILL)
		Pts
1964	Veikko Kankkonen, Finland	229.90
1968	Jiri Raska, Czechoslovakia	216.5
1972	Yukio Kasaya, Japan	244.2
1976	Hans-Georg Aschenbach, E Germany	252.0
1980	Toni Innauer, Austria	266.3
1984	Jens Weissflog, E Germany	215.2
1988	Matti Nykänen, Finland	229.1
1992	Ernst Vettori, Austria	222.8
1994	Espen Bredesen, Norway	282.0
1998	Jani Soininen, Finland	234.5
2002	Simon Ammann, Switzerland	269.0

SKI JUMPING (LARGE HILL)
		Pts
1924	Jacob Tullin Thams, Norway	18.960
1928	Alf Andersen, Norway	19.208
1932	Birger Ruud, Norway	228.1
1936	Birger Ruud, Norway	232.0
1948	Petter Hugsted, Norway	228.1
1952	Arnfinn Bergmann, Norway	226.0
1956	Antti Hyvärinen, Finland	227.0
1960	Helmut Recknagel, E Germany	227.2
1964	Toralf Engan, Norway	230.70
1968	Vladimir Beloussov, USSR	231.3
1972	Wojciech Fortuna, Poland	219.9
1976	Karl Schnabl, Austria	234.8
1980	Jouko Tormanen, Finland	271.0
1984	Matti Nykänen, Finland	231.2
1988	Matti Nykänen, Finland	224.0
1992	Toni Nieminen, Finland	239.5
1994	Jens Weissflog, Germany	274.5
1998	Kazuyoshi Funaki, Japan	272.3
2002	Simon Amman, Switzerland	281.4

TEAM SKI JUMPING
		Pts
1988	Finland	634.4
1992	Finland	644.4
1994	Germany	970.1
1998	Japan	933.0
2002	Germany	974.1

NORDIC SKIING *(Cont.)*

Men *(Cont.)*

NORDIC COMBINED	Pts		NORDIC COMBINED *(Cont.)*	Pts
1924....Thorleif Haug, Norway	18.906*		1988....Hippolyt Kempf, Switzerland	432.230
1928....Johan Gröttumsbraaten, Norway	17.833*		1992....Fabrice Guy, France	426.47
1932....Johan Gröttumsbraaten, Norway	446.0		1994....Fred B. Lundberg, Norway	457.970
1936....Oddbjörn Hagen, Norway	430.30		1998....Bjarte Engen Vik, Norway	41:21.1†
1948....Heikki Hasu, Finland	448.80		2002....Samppa Lajunen, Finland	38:18.7
1952....Simon Slattvik, Norway	451.621			
1956....Sverre Stenersen, Norway	455.0		**TEAM NORDIC COMBINED**	
1960....Georg Thoma, W Germany	457.952		1988....W Germany	
1964....Tormod Knutsen, Norway	469.28.		1992....Japan	
1968....Frantz Keller, W Germany	449.04		1994....Japan	
1972....Ulrich Wehling, E Germany	413.34		1998....Norway	
1976....Ulrich Wehling, E Germany	423.39		2002....Finland	
1980....Ulrich Wehling, E Germany	432.20		**SPRINT NORDIC COMBINED**	
1984....Tom Sandberg, Norway	422.595		2002....Samppa Lajunen, Finland	123.8

* Different scoring system; 1924–1952 distance was 18 km; 1952–present, 15 km.

† Times in the cross-country race were not converted into points. According to the Gundersen Method, used since 1988, starting times in the race are staggered in proportion to points earned in the ski jumping segment of the event.

Women

5 KILOMETERS CLASSICAL STYLE			15 KILOMETERS CLASSICAL STYLE	
1964....Klaudia Boyarskikh, USSR	17:50.5		1992....Lyubov Egorova, Unified Team	42:20.8
1968....Toini Gustafsson, Sweden	16:45.2		1994....Manuela Di Centa, Italy	39:44.5
1972....Galina Kulakova, USSR	17:00.50		1998....Olga Danilova, Russia	46:55.04
1976....Helena Takalo, Finland	15:48.69			
1980....Raisa Smetanina, USSR	15:06.92		**20 KILOMETERS FREESTYLE**	
1984....Marja-Liisa Hamalainen, Finland	17:04.0		1984....Marja-Liisa Hamalainen, Finland	1:01:45.0
1988....Marjo Matikainen, Finland	15:04.0		1988....Tamara Tikhonova, USSR	55:53.6
1992....Marjut Lukkarinen, Finland	14:13.8			
1994....Lyubova Egorova, Russia	14:08.8		**30 KILOMETERS FREESTYLE**	
1998....Larissa Lazhutina, Russia	17:37.9		1992....Stefania Belmondo, Italy	1:22:30.1
			1994....Manuela Di Centa, Italy	1:25:41.6
10 KILOMETERS CLASSICAL STYLE			1998....Julija Tchepalova, Russia	1:22:01.5
1952....Lydia Widemen, Finland	41:40.0			
1956....Lyubov Kosyryeva, USSR	38:11.0		**4 X 5-KILOMETER RELAY MIXED STYLE**	
1960....Maria Gusakova, USSR	39:46.6		1956....Finland	1:9:01.0
1964....Klaudia Boyarskikh, USSR	40:24.3		1960....Sweden	1:4:21.4
1968....Toini Gustafsson, Sweden	36:46.5		1964....USSR	59:20.0
1972....Galina Kulakova, USSR	34:17.8		1968....Norway	57:30.0
1976....Raisa Smetanina, USSR	30:13.41		1972....USSR	48:46.15
1980....Barbara Petzold, E Germany	30:31.54		1976....USSR	1:07:49.75
1984....Marja-Lissa Hamalainen, Finland	31:44.2		1980....E Germany	1:02:11.10
1988....Vida Ventsene, USSR	30:08.3		1984....Norway	1:06:49.7
2002....Bante Skari, Norway	28:05.6		1988....USSR	59:51.1
			1992....Unified Team	59:34.8
10 KILOMETERS PURSUIT FREESTYLE			1994....Russia	57:12.5
1992....Lyubov Egorova, Unified Team	40:07.7		1998....Russia	55:13.5
1994....Lyubov Egorova, Russia	41:38.1		2002....Germany	49:30.6
1998....Larissa Lazhutina, Russia	46:06.9			

SNOWBOARDING

Men		Women	
GIANT SLALOM		**GIANT SLALOM**	
1998....Ross Rebagliati, Canada	2:03.96	1998....Karine Ruby, France	2:17.34
PARALLEL GIANT SLALOM		**PARALLEL GIANT SLALOM**	
2002....Philipp Schoch, Switzerland		2002....Isabella Blanc, France	
HALF-PIPE		**HALF-PIPE**	
	Pts		Pts
1998....Gian Simmen, Switzerland	85.2	1998....Nicola Thost, Germany	74.6
2002....Ross Powers, United States	46.1	2002....Kelly Clark, United States	47.9

Track & Field

PARIS 2002

79

C7 DE FRANCE

Tim Montgomery
of the U.S.

Monty Burns

There was one word for Tim Montgomery's blazing world record in the 100: Excellent

BY MERRELL NODEN

WITH NO OLYMPICS or world championships for athletes to point for, 2002 was expected to be, and for the longest time was, a somewhat uneventful year for track and field. We were already two weeks into September when Tim Montgomery abruptly changed that, surprising everyone by breaking his nemesis Maurice Greene's three-year-old world record for 100 meters with a time of 9.78 seconds at the Grand Prix Final in Paris.

After losing several early summer races, Montgomery had used the midseason hiatus during the Commonwealth Games and European Championships to sharpen up. Returning to Europe, he won the Zurich 100 impressively, running 9.97 into a headwind, far ahead of Greene, who wound up fifth. He then ran 9.91 in Brussels. Still, no one, not even he, thought he would run so fast on a relatively cool night in Paris.

For Greene, who from 1997 through 2001 was as dominant as any sprinter in history, it was becoming increasingly clear that this was a year to forget. Claiming fatigue and lack of fitness, he sat out the Grand Prix Final, but was in the stands to see Montgomery break his mark. "When I saw Tim's time," said Greene, "I said, 'Oh man! What was the wind?'" At 2.0 meters per second, it was strong but allowable for record purposes.

Until Montgomery ran his startling time, the only world record set in an Olympic track or field event was the 7:53.17 Brahim Boulami had run in the 3,000 steeplechase at Zurich. Unfortunately, Boulami's time was disallowed a few weeks later when his urine sample came back positive for EPO, the blood boosting drug.

The year had begun with the greatest men's marathon field in history assembling in London on April 14. The field included not only the world record holder, Khalid Khannouchi, but also Haile Gebrselassie, the world record holder in both the 5,000 and the 10,000-meter runs, who was making his long-awaited marathon debut, and Geb's old rival, five-time world cross country champion Paul Tergat. The race's depth was astounding: Poor Stefano Baldini ran 2:07:29—4:52 per mile!—and finished sixth. Leading the pack was Khannouchi, whose 2:05:38 trimmed four seconds off his own world record. Tergat finished second, in 2:05:48, and Gebrselassie third, in 2:06:35.

That was the fastest marathon debut in history, but it might not even have been the best debut of the day, for in the women's race, Paula Radcliffe missed the world record by a mere nine seconds with her first marathon of 2:18:56.

Closer to home, Alan Webb, last year's high school mile sensation, surprised

Former schoolboy hero Webb (622) left Michigan to train as a pro under his old coach.

sistency on the men's side, it was Hicham El Guerrouj, who dominated the 1500 for the sixth straight year. This year the 28-year-old Moroccan broke 3:30 six times, more than anyone else has in an entire career. To appreciate how this elegant runner has revolutionized 1500 times, consider that Steve Cram, Seb Coe and Said Aouita, world record holders all, broke that mark a total of four times between them.

For bravely going where no man has gone before, there was Felix Sanchez, the world champion in the 400 hurdles, who is American-born but who runs for his parents' homeland of the Dominican Republic. A glutton for punishment, Sanchez, 25, chose to run both his specialty and the flat 400 in several meets. In London he pulled off an extraordinary double, winning both, in 48.08 and 45.14.

Against even higher odds than Sanchez's double, the shot put became a spectator favorite in 2002, with the event's little big man, Adam Nelson, turning it into a cross between a strongman contest and a rock concert. The Dartmouth grad, who, at 6-foot, 255 pounds, is small by his event's standards, shocked everyone by tossing 73-10¼ in Portland and then won the nationals with an incredible series topped by a throw of 72-10 ¾. Behind him came John Godina and Kevin Toth.

This was a season that raised intriguing questions—how Webb will fare; whether Krummenacker can build on his promising season; whether anyone will emerge to challenge Marion Jones. But most interesting of all will be watching the rivalry between Montgomery and Greene. We've seen the king toppled and a new one crowned: Will we see that reversed next year?

many by leaving the University of Michigan to return home and train as a professional under his high school coach, Scott Raczko. Webb finished fourth in the 2002 NCAA 1500.

Webb's move did little to change the state of uncertainty that has plagued U.S. middle distance running for some time. In the now decade-long U.S. quest for a middle distance runner capable of challenging the Africans, David Krummenacker, a tall 27-year-old Georgia Tech grad, impressed everyone. He ran 1:43.95 for 800 and 3:31.93 for 1500, making him the only American to break both 1:44 and 3:32 and the first to be world class in both events in a single year since the 70's.

And then there was that handful of utterly consistent superstars who merely did what we expect of them. Marion Jones did not run as fast as she has in previous years, but went undefeated in both the 100 and the 200. And at 35 Gail Devers produced one of her most consistent years in the 100-meter hurdles, topped by a seasonal best of 12.40.

If Jones had a counterpart for perfect con-

USATF Outdoor Championships

Palo Alto, California, June 21–23, 2002

Men

100 METERS

1.	Maurice Greene, adidas	9.88
2.	Tim Montgomery, Nike	9.89
3.	Jon Drummond, Nike	10.04

200 METERS

1.	Ramon Clay, adidas	20.27
2.	Darvis Patton, adidas	20.31
3.	Bernard Williams, Nike	20.37

400 METERS

1.	Alvin Harrison, Nike	44.62
2.	Angelo Taylor, Nike	45.00
3.	Antonio Pettigrew, adidas	45.17

800 METERS

1.	David Krummenacker, adidas	1:47.24
2.	Khadevis Robinson, Nike	1:47.58
3.	Derrick Peterson, adidas	1:48.14

1,500 METERS

1.	Seneca Lassiter, Nike	3:40.90
2.	Bryan Berryhill, adidas	3:40.98
3.	Ibrahim Aden, Nike	3:41.19

5,000 METERS

1.	Alan Culpepper, adidas	13:27.52
2.	Mebrahtom Keflezighi, Nike	13:30.05
3.	Matt Lane, Nike	13:30.58

10,000 METERS

1.	Mebrahtom Keflezighi, Nike	27:41.68
2.	Abdi Abdirahman, Nike	27:42.83
3.	Alan Culpepper, adidas	27:48.09

110-METER HURDLES

1.	Allen Johnson, Nike	13.08
2.	Terrence Trammell, Mizuno	13.17
3.	Larry Wade, Nike	13.18

400-METER HURDLES

1.	James Carter, Nike	48.12
2.	Joey Woody, adidas	48.52
3.	Eric Thomas	48.72

3,000-METER STEEPLECHASE

1.	Anthony Famiglietti, adidas	8:19.07
2.	Steve Slattery	8:23.44
3.	Tim Broe, adidas	8:23.61

HIGH JUMP

1.	Nathan Leeper, Nike	7 ft 7¼ in
2.	Charles Clinger	7 ft 6 in
3.	Matt Hemmingway, COTI	7 ft 6 in

POLE VAULT

1.	Jeff Hartwig, Nike	19 ft 2 in
2.	Timothy Mack, Nike	18 ft 10 in
3.	Nicholas Hysong, Nike	18 ft 10 in

LONG JUMP

1.	Savante Stringfellow, Nike	27 ft 11½ in
2.	Miguel Pate, Nike	27 ft 8¾ in
3.	Dwight Phillips, Nike	27 ft 1 in

TRIPLE JUMP

1.	Walter Davis, Louisiana St	57 ft 8½ in
2.	Tim Rusan, Nike	56 ft 9¼ in
3.	LeVar Anderson,	54 ft 11¼ in

SHOT PUT

1.	Adam Nelson, Nike	72 ft 11 in
2.	John Godina, adidas	71 ft 10¾ in
3.	Kevin Toth, Nike	70 ft 7¾ in

DISCUS

1.	Adam Setliff, Nike	209 ft 1 in
2.	John Godina, adidas	207 ft 3 in
3.	Ian Waltz, Bronco TC	204 ft 3 in

HAMMER THROW

1.	Lance Deal, NYAC	244 f 5 in
2.	John McEwen, Team ZMA	243 ft 4 in
3.	Kevin McMahon, NYAC	237 ft 9 in

JAVELIN

1.	Breaux Greer, adidas	268 ft 4 in
2.	Latrell Frederick	255 ft 7 in
3.	Christopher Clever	248 ft 11 in

DECATHLON

1.	Tom Pappas, Adidas	8398 pts
2.	Bryan Clay, Azusa Pacific	8230
3.	Phil McMullen, Nike	7934

20,000-METER RACE WALK

1.	Tim Seaman, NYAC	1:26:40
2.	Albert Heppner, Army	1:27:56
3.	Kevin Eastler, Air Force	1:28:35

Women

100 METERS

1.	Marion Jones, Nike	11.01
2.	Chryste Gaines, ZMA TC	11.05
3.	Kelli White, Nike	11.22

200 METERS

1.	Marion Jones, Nike	22.35
2.	Kelli White, Nike	22.50
3.	Stephanie Durst, Louisiana St	23.14

400 METERS

1.	Jearl Mile Clark, New Balance	50.91
2.	Michelle Collins, Nike	51.20
3.	Monique Hennagan, adidas	51.34

800 METERS

1.	Nicole Teter, Nike Farm Team	1:58.03
2.	Jennifer Toomey, New Balance	2:02.11
3.	Sasha Spencer, Nike	2:02.34

1,500 METERS

1.	Regina Jacobs, Nike	4:09.57
2.	Suzy Favor Hamilton, Nike	4:11.31
3.	Sarah Schwald, Nike	4:11.40

5,000 METERS

1.	Marla Runyan, Nike	15:07.19
2.	Deena Drossen, Asics	15:13.93
3.	Carrie Tollefson, adidas	15:21.37

10,000 METERS

1.	Jen Rhines, adidas	31:57.38
2.	Milena Glusac, adidas	32:15.09
3.	Katie McGregor, adidas	32:17.49

100-METER HURDLES

1.	Gail Devers, Nike	12.51
2.	Miesha McKelvy, Nike	12.60
3.	Anjanette Kirkland, Nike	12.85

400-METER HURDLES

1.	Sandra Glover, Nike	55.22
2.	Megan Addy	57.28
3.	Brenda Taylor, Harvard	57.62

3,000-METER STEEPLECHASE

1.	Elizabeth Jackson, Nike	9:47.35
2.	Lisa Nye, Nike	9:52.61
3.	Lisa Aguilera, Arizona St	9:59.66

HIGH JUMP

1.	Tisha Waller, Nike	6 ft 5 in
2.	Gwen Wentland	6 ft 4 in
3.	Amy Acuff, Asics TC	6 ft 2¾ in

POLE VAULT

1.	Stacy Dragila, Nike	15 ft 3 in
2.	Mary Sauer, Asics TC	14 ft 7¾ in
3.	Melissa Mueller, Nike	14 ft 5¼ in

LONG JUMP

1.	Briana Glenn, Tucson Elite	21 ft 2½ in
2.	Grace Upshaw	21 ft 1¼ in
3.	Tiffany Greer, Arizona St	20 ft 11¾ in

TRIPLE JUMP

1.	Yuliana Perez, Pima CC	46 ft 7¾ in
2.	Vanitta Kinard	45 ft 4½ in
3.	Teresa Bundy, Florida St	45 ft 3 in

SHOT PUT

1.	Teri Steer, Nike	63 ft 0 in
2.	Seilala Sue, Nike	60 ft 8¾ in
3.	Kristin Heaston, Sacramento TC	57 ft 8½ in

DISCUS

1.	Kris Kuehl	211 ft 5 in
2.	Suzy Powell, Asics TC	205 ft 3 in
3.	Aretha Hill, Nike	204 ft 9 in

HAMMER THROW

1.	Anna Mahon	230 ft 6 in
2.	Dawn Ellerbe, NYAC	220 ft 5 in
3.	Jamie Moton, Clemson	216 ft

JAVELIN

1.	Serene Ross	197 ft
2.	Kim Kreiner	190 ft 1 in
3.	Erica Wheeler	180 ft 4 in

HEPTATHLON

1.	Shelia Burrell, Nike	6299 pts
2.	DeDee Nathan, Indiana Invaders	5995
3.	Kim Schiemenz	5840

20,000-METER RACE WALK

1.	Joanne Dow, adidas	1:34:46
2.	Teresa Vaill	1:34:53
3.	Amber Antonia, Wisconsin-Pa	1:35:59

Edmonton, Canada, August 3–12, 2001

Men

100 METERS

1. ....Maurice Greene, USA — 9.82
2. ....Tim Montgomery, USA — 9.85
3. ....Bernard Williams, USA — 9.94

200 METERS

1. ....Konstadínos Kedéris, Greece — 20.04
2. ....Christopher Williams, Jamaica — 20.20
3. ....Kim Collins, St. Kitts & Nevis — 20.20

400 METERS

1. ....Avard Moncur, Bahamas — 44.64
2. ....Ingo Schultz, Germany — 44.87
3. ....Gregory Haughton, Jamaica — 44.98

800 METERS

1. ....André Bucher, Switzerland — 1:43.70
2. ....Wilfred Bungei, Kenya — 1:44.55
3. ....Pawal Czapiewski, Poland — 1:44.63

1,500 METERS

1. ....Hicham El Guerrouj, Morocco — 3:30.68
2. ....Bernard Lagat, Kenya — 3:31.10
3. ....Driss Maazouzi, France — 3:31.54

5,000 METERS

1. ....Richard Limo, Kenya — 13:00.77
2. ....Ail Saïdi-Sief, Algeria — 13:02.16
3. ....Million Wolde, Ethiopia — 13:03.47

10,000 METERS

1. ....Charles Kamathi, Kenya — 27:53.25
2. ....Assefa Mezgebu, Ethiopia — 27:53.97
3. ....Haile Gebrselassie, Ethiopia — 27:54.41

MARATHON

1. ....Gezahegne Abera, Ethiopia — 2:12:42
2. ....Simon Biwott, Kenya — 2:12.43
3. ....Stefano Baldini, Italy — 2:13:18

3,000-METER STEEPLECHASE

1. ....Reuben Kosgei, Kenya — 8:15.16
2. ....Ali Ezzine, Morocco — 8:16.21
3. ....Bernard Barmasai, Kenya — 8:16.59

110-METER HURDLES

1. ....Allen Johnson, USA — 13.04
2. ....Anier García, Cuba — 13.07
3. ....Dudley Dorival, Haiti — 13.25

400-METER HURDLES

1. ....Felix Sánchez, Dominican Rep. — 47.49
2. ....Fabrizio Mori, Italy — 47.54
3. ....Dai Tamesue, Japan — 47.89

HIGH JUMP

1. ....Martin Buss, Germany — 7 ft 8¾ in
2. ....Vyacheslav Voronin, Russia — 7 ft 7¾ in
2. ....Yaroslav Rybakov, Russia — 7 ft 7¾ in

POLE VAULT

1. ....Dmitri Markov, Australia — 19 ft 10¼ in
2. ....Aleksandr Averbukh, Israel — 19 ft 2¼ in
3. ....Nick Hysong, USA — 19 ft 2¼ in

LONG JUMP

1. ....Iván Pedroso, Cuba — 27 ft 6¾ in
2. ....Savante Stringfellow, USA — 27 ft ½ in
3. ....Carlos Calado, Portugal — 26 ft 11¼ in

TRIPLE JUMP

1. ....Jonathan Edwards, Great Britain — 58 ft 9½ in
2. ....Christian Olsson, Sweden — 57 ft 3¾ in
3. ....Igor Spasovkhodskiy, Russia — 57 ft 2¾ in

SHOT PUT

1. ....John Godina, USA — 71 ft 9 in
2. ....Adam Nelson, USA — 68 ft 9¼ in
3. ....Arsi Harju, Finland — 68 ft 8 in

DISCUS

1. ....Lars Riedel, Germany — 228 ft 9 in
2. ....Virgilijus Alekna, Lithuania — 227 ft 8 in
3. ....Michael Möllenbeck, Ger. — 221 ft 10 in

HAMMER THROW

1. ....Szymon Ziółkowski, Poland — 273 ft 7 in
2. ....Koji Murofuski, Japan — 272 ft
3. ....Ilya Konovalov, Russia — 263 ft 4 in

JAVELIN

1. ....Jan Zelezny, Czech Republic — 304 ft 5 in
2. ....Aki Parviainen, Finland — 299 ft 7 in
3. ....K. Gatssioúdis, Greece — 295 ft 1 in

20-KILOMETER WALK

1. ....Roman Rasskazov, Russia — 1:20:31
2. ....Ilya Markov, Russia — 1:20:33
3. ....Viktor Burayev, Russia — 1:20:36

50-KILOMETER WALK

1. ....Robert Korzeniowski, Poland — 3:42:08
2. ....Jesús Angel García, Spain — 3:43:07
3. ....Edgar Hernandez, Mexico — 3:46:12

4 x 100 RELAY

1. ....United States — 37.96
2. ....South Africa — 38.47
3. ....Trindad and Tobago — 38.58

4 x 400 RELAY

1. ....United States — 2:57.54
2. ....Bahamas — 2:58.19
3. ....Jamaica — 2:58.39

DECATHLON

1. ....Tomás Dvorák, Czech Republic — 8902 pts
2. ....Erki Nool, Estonia — 8815
3. ....Dean Macey, Great Britain — 8603

Women

100 METERS

1. ....Zhanna Pintusevich-Block, Ukraine	10.82
2. ....Marion Jones, USA	10.85
3. ....Ekateríni Thánou, Greece	10.91

200 METERS

1. ....Marion Jones, USA	22.39
2. ....Debbie Ferguson, Bahamas	22.52
3. ....Kelli White, USA	22.56

400 METERS

1. ...;........Amy Mbacke Thiam, Senegal	49.86
2. ....Lorraine Fenton, Jamaica	49.88
3. ....Ana Guevara, Mexico	49.97

800 METERS

1. ....Maria Mutola, Mozambique	1:57.17
2. ....Stephanie Graf, Austria	1:57.20
3. ....Letitia Vriesde, Surinam	1:57.35

1,500 METERS

1. ....Gabriela Szabo, Romania	4:00.57
2. ....Violeta Szekely, Romania	4:01.70
3. ....Natalya Gorelova, Russia	4:02.40

5,000 METERS

1. ....Olga Yegorova, Russia	15:03.39
2. ....Marta Domínguez, Spain	15:06.59
3. ....Ayelech Worku, Ethiopia	15:10.17

10,000 METERS

1. ....Derartu Tulu, Ethiopia	31:48.81
2. ....Berhane Adere, Ethiopia	31:48.85
3. ....Gete Wami, Ethiopia	31:49.98

MARATHON

1. ....Lidia Simon, Romania	2:26:01
2. ....Reiko Tosa, Japan	2:26:06
3. ....Svetlana Zakharova, Russia	2:26:18

100-METER HURDLES

1. ....Anjanette Kirkland, USA	12.42
2. ....Gail Devers, USA	12.54
3. ....Olga Shishigina, Kazakhstan	12.58

400-METER HURDLES

1. ....Nezha Bidouane, Morocco	53.34
2. ....Yuliya Nosova, Russia	54.27
3. ....Daimí Pernía, Cuba	54.51

HIGH JUMP

1. ....Hestrie Cloete, S Africa	6 ft 6¾ in
2. ....Inha Babakova, Ukraine	6 ft 6¾ in
3. ....Kajsa Bergqvist, Sweden	6 ft 5½ in

POLE VAULT

1. ....Stacy Dragila, USA	15 ft 7 in
2. ....Svetlana Feofanova, Russia	15 ft 7 in
3. ....Monika Pyrek, Poland	14 ft 11 in

LONG JUMP

1. ...,........Fiona May, Italy	23 ft ½ in
2. ....Tatyana Kotova, Russia	23 ft
3. ....Niurka Montalvo, Spain	22 ft 7 in

TRIPLE JUMP

1. ....Tatyana Lebedeva, Russia	50 ft ½ in
2. ....Etone F. Mbango, Cameroon	47 ft 10¾ in
3. ....Tereza Marinova, Bulgaria	47 ft 10 in

SHOT PUT

1. ....Yanina Korolchik, Belarus	67 ft 7½ in
2. ....N. Kleinert-Schmitt, Germany	61 ft 10¼ in
3. ....Vita Pavlysh, Ukraine	56 ft 4 in

DISCUS

1. ....Natalya Sadova, Russia	224 ft 11 in
2. ....Ellina Zvereva, Belarus	220 ft 1 in
3. ....Nicoleta Grasu, Romania	217 ft 4 in

HAMMER THROW

1. ....Yipsi Moreno, Cuba	231 ft 9 in
2. ....Olga Kuzenkova, Russia	231 ft 8 in
3. ....Bronwyn Eagles, Australia	225 ft 11 in

JAVELIN

1. ....Osleidys Menéndez, Cuba	228 ft 1 in
2. ....Miréla Manjani-Tzelili, Greece	215 ft 9 in
3. ....Sonia Bisset, Cuba	212 ft 3 in

20-KILOMETER WALK

1. ....Olimpiada Ivanova, Russia	1:27:48
2. ....Valentina Tsybulskaya, Belarus	1:28:49
3. ....Elisabetta Perrone, Italy	1:28:56

4 x 100 RELAY

1. ....United States	41.71
2. ....Germany	42.32
3. ....France	42.39

4 x 400 RELAY

1. ....Jamaica	3:20.65
2. ....Germany	3:21.97
3. ....Russia	3:24.92

HEPTATHLON

1. ....Yelena Prokhorova, Russia	6694 pts
2. ....Natalya Sazanovich, Belarus	6539
3. ....Shelia Burrell, USA	6472

IAAF World Cross-Country Championships

Dublin, Ireland, March 23–24, 2002

MEN (12,000 METERS; 7.5 MILES)

1. ....Bekele Kenenisa, Ethiopia — 34:52
2. ....Yuda John, Tanzania — 34:58
3. ....Talel Wilberforce, Kenya — 35:20

WOMEN (8,000 METERS; 5 MILES)

1. ....Paula Radcliffe, Great Britain — 26:55
2. ....Deena Drossin, United States — 27:04
3. ....Colleen de Reuck, United States — 27:17

Major Marathons

Chicago: October 7, 2001

MEN

1. ....Ben Kimondiu, Kenya — 2:08:52
2. ....Paul Tergat, Kenya — 2:08:56
3. ....Peter Githuka, Kenya — 2:09:00

WOMEN

1. ....Catherine Ndereba, Kenya — 2:18:47
2. ....Elfenesh Alemu, Ethiopia — 2:24:54
3. ....Kerryn McCann, Australia — 2:26:04

New York City: November 3, 2001

MEN

1. ....Tesfaye Jifar, Ethiopia — 2:07:43
2. ....Japhet Kosgei, Kenya — 2:09:19
3. ....Rogers Rop, Kenya — 2:09:51

WOMEN

1. ....Margaret Okayo, Kenya — 2:24:21
2. ....Susan Chepkemei, Kenya — 2:25:12
3. ....Svetlana Zakharova, Russia — 2:25:13

Tokyo: November 11, 2001

WOMEN ONLY

1. ....Derartu Tulu, Ethiopia — 2:25:08
2. ....Irina Timofeyeva, Russia — 2:25:29
3. ....Bruna Genovese, Italy — 2:25:35

Tokyo: February 10, 2002

MEN ONLY

1. ....Eric Wainaina, Kenya — 2:08:43
2. ....Alberto Juzdado, Kenya — 2:08:59
3. ....Julio Rey, Spain — 2:11:14

Rome: March 25, 2002

MEN

1. ....Vincent Kipsos, Kenya — 2:09:30
2. ....Steven Matebo, Kenya — 2:10:39
3. ....Moges Taye, Ethiopia — 2:11:08

WOMEN

1. ....Maria Cocchetti, Italy — 2:33:06
2. ....Gabisse Edato, Ethiopia — 2:33:36
3. ....Sandra Van Den Haesevelde, Belgium — 2:35:30

Paris: April 7, 2002

MEN

1. ....Benoit Zwierzchlewski, France — 2:08:18
2. ....Pavel Loskutov, Estonia — 2:08:53
3. ....Migidio Bourifa, Italy — 2:09:07

WOMEN

1. ....Marleen Renders, Belgium — 2:23:05
2. ....Rie Matsuoka, Japan — 2:24:33
3. ....Esther Kiplagat, Kenya — 2:25:32

Boston: April 15, 2002

MEN

1. ....Rodgers Rop, Kenya — 2:09:02
2. ....Christopher Cheboiboch, Kenya — 2:09:05
3. ....Fred Kiprop, Kenya — 2:09:45

WOMEN

1. ....Margaret Okayo, Kenya — 2:20:43
2. ....Catherine Ndereba, Kenya — 2:21:12
3. ....Elfenesh Alemu, Ethiopia — 2:26:01

Rotterdam: April 21, 2002

MEN

1. ....Simon Biwott, Kenya — 2:08:39
2. ....Kenneth Cheruiyot, Kenya — 2:09:43
3. ....Jose Manuel Martinez, Spain — 2:09:55

WOMEN

1. ....Takami Oniami, Japan — 2:23:43
2. ....Turba Neguse, Ethiopia — 2:10:24
3. ....Junko Akagi, Japan — 2:29:10

London: April 14, 2002

MEN

1. ....Khalid Khannouchi, United States — 2:05:38*
2. ....Paul Tergat, Kenya — 2:05:48
3. ....Haile Gebrselassi, Ethiopia — 2:06:35

WOMEN

1. ....Paula Radcliffe, Great Britain — 2:18:56
2. ....Svetlana Zakharova, Russia — 2:22:31
3. ....Lyudmila Petrova, Russia — 2:22:33

*World Record.

TRACK AND FIELD

World Records

As of October 1, 2002. World outdoor records are recognized by the International Amateur Athletics Federation (IAAF).

Men

Event	Mark	Record Holder	Date	Site
100 meters	9.78	Tim Montgomery, United States	9-14-02	Paris
200 meters	19.32	Michael Johnson, United States	8-1-96	Atlanta
400 meters	43.18	Michael Johnson, United States	8-26-99	Seville
800 meters	1:41.11	Wilson Kipketer, Denmark	8-24-97	Cologne
1,000 meters	2:11.96	Noah Ngeny, Kenya	9-5-99	Rieti, Italy
1,500 meters	3:26.00	Hicham El Guerrouj, Morocco	7-14-98	Rome
Mile	3:43.13	Hicham El Guerrouj, Morocco	7-7-99	Rome
2,000 meters	4:44.79	Hicham El Guerrouj, Morocco	9-7-99	Berlin
3,000 meters	7:20.67	Daniel Komen, Kenya	9-1-96	Rieti, Italy
Steeplechase	7:55.28	Brahim Boulami, Morocco	8-24-01	Brussels
5,000 meters	12:39.36	Haile Gebrselassie, Ethiopia	6-13-98	Helsinki
10,000 meters	26:22.75	Haile Gebrselassie, Ethiopia	6-1-98	Hengelo, Netherlands
20,000 meters	56:55.6	Arturo Barrios, Mexico	3-30-91	La Flâche, France
Hour	21,101 meters	Arturo Barrios, Mexico	3-30-91	La Flâche, France
25,000 meters	1:13:55.8	Toshihiko Seko, Japan	3-22-81	Christchurch, New Zealand
30,000 meters	1:29:18.8	Toshihiko Seko, Japan	3-22-81	Christchurch, New Zealand
Marathon	2:05:38	Khalid Khannouchi, United States	4-14-02	London
110-meter hurdles	12.91	Colin Jackson, Great Britain	8-20-93	Stuttgart, Germany
400-meter hurdles	46.78	Kevin Young, United States	8-6-92	Barcelona
20-kilometer walk	1:17:22	Javier Fernandez, Spain	4-28-02	Turku, Finland
30-kilometer walk	2:01:44.1	Maurizio Damilano, Italy	10-3-92	Cuneo, Italy
50-kilometer walk	3:40:57.9	Thierry Toutain, France	9-29-96	Héricourt, France
4 x 100-meter relay	37.40	United States (Mike Marsh, Leroy Burrell, Dennis Mitchell, Carl Lewis)	8-8-92	Barcelona
		United States (Jon Drummond, Andre Cason, Dennis Mitchell, Leroy Burrell)	8-21-93	Stuttgart, Germany
4 x 200-meter relay	1:18.68	Santa Monica TC (Mike Marsh, Leroy Burrell, Floyd Heard, Carl Lewis)	4-17-94	Walnut, CA
4 x 400-meter relay	2:54.20	United States (Jerome Young, Antonio Pettigrew, Tyree Washington, Michael Johnson)	7-22-98	New York City
4 x 800-meter relay	7:03.89	Great Britain (Peter Elliott, Garry Cook, Steve Cram, Sebastian Coe)	8-30-82	London
4 x 1,500-meter relay	14:38.8	W Germany (Thomas Wessinghage, Harald Hudak, Michael Lederer, Karl Fleschen)	8-17-77	Cologne
High jump	8 ft ½ in	Javier Sotomayor, Cuba	7-27-93	Salamanca, Spain
Pole vault	20 ft 1¾ in	Sergei Bubka, Ukraine	7-31-94	Sestriere, Italy
Long jump	29 ft 4½ in	Mike Powell, United States	8-30-91	Tokyo
Triple jump	60 ft ¼ in	Jonathan Edwards, Great Britain	8-7-95	Göteborg, Sweden
Shot put	75 ft 10¼ in	Randy Barnes, United States	5-20-90	Westwood, CA
Discus throw	243 ft 0 in	Jürgen Schult, E Germany	6-6-86	Neubrandenburg, Germany
Hammer throw	284 ft 7 in	Yuri Syedikh, USSR	8-30-86	Stuttgart, Germany
Javelin throw	323 ft 1 in	Jan Zelezny, Czech Republic	5-25-96	Jena, Germany
Decathlon	9026 pts	Roman Sebrle, Czech Republic	5-27-01	Götzis

Note: The decathlon consists of 10 events: the 100 meters, long jump, shot put, high jump and 400 meters on the first day; the 110-meter hurdles, discus, pole vault, javelin and 1,500 meters on the second.

Women

Event	Mark	Record Holder	Date	Site
100 meters	10.49	Florence Griffith Joyner, United States	7-16-88	Indianapolis
200 meters	21.34	Florence Griffith Joyner, United States	9-29-88	Seoul
400 meters	47.60	Marita Koch, E Germany	10-6-85	Canberra, Australia
800 meters	1:53.28	Jarmila Kratochvílová, Czechoslovakia	7-26-83	Munich
1,000 meters	2:28.98	Svetlana Masterkova, Russia	8-23-96	Brussels
1,500 meters	3:50.46	Qu Yunxia, China	9-11-93	Beijing
Mile	4:12.56	Svetlana Masterkova, Russia	8-14-96	Zurich
2,000 meters	5:25.36	Sonia O'Sullivan, Ireland	7-8-94	Edinburgh
3,000 meters	8:06.11	Wang Junxia, China	9-13-93	Beijing
Steeplechase	9:16.51	Alesya Turova, Belarus	7-27-02	Gdansk
5,000 meters	14:28.09	Jiang Bo, China	10-23-97	Shanghai
10,000 meters	29:31.78	Wang Junxia, China	9-8-93	Beijing
Hour	18,340 meters	Tegla Loroupe, Kenya	8-8-98	Borgholzhausen, Germany
20,000 meters	1:05:26.6	Tegla Loroupe, Kenya	9-3-00	Borgholzhausen, Germany
25,000 meters	1:29:29.2	Karolina Szabó, Hungary	4-22-88	Budapest
30,000 meters	1:47:05.6	Karolina Szabó, Hungary	4-22-88	Budapest
Marathon	2:18:47	Catherine Ndereba, Kenya	10-7-01	Chicago
100-meter hurdles	12.21	Yordanka Donkova, Bulgaria	8-20-88	Stara Zagora, Bulgaria
400-meter hurdles	52.61	Kim Batten, United States	8-11-95	Göteborg, Sweden
5-kilometer walk	20:02.60	Gillian O'Sullivan, Ireland	7-13-02	Dublin
10-kilometer walk	41:56.23	Nadezhda Ryashkina, URS	7-24-90	Seattle
4 x 100-meter relay	41.37	East Germany (Silke Gladisch, Sabine Reiger, Ingrid Auerswald, Marlies Göhr)	10-6-85	Canberra, Australia
4 x 200-meter relay	1:27.46	United States (LaTasha Jenkins, LaTasha Colander-Richardson, Nanceen Perry, Marion Jones)	4-29-00	Philadelphia
4 x 400-meter relay	3:15.17	USSR (Tatyana Ledovskaya, Olga Nazarova, Maria Pinigina, Olga Bryzgina)	10-1-88	Seoul
4 x 800-meter relay	7:50.17	USSR (Nadezhda Olizarenko, Lyubov Gurina, Lyudmila Borisova, Irina Podyalovskaya)	8-5-84	Moscow
High jump	6 ft 10¼ in	Stefka Kostadinova, Bulgaria	8-30-87	Rome
Pole vault	15 ft 9¼ in	Stacy Dragila, United States	6-9-01	Palo Alto, California
Long jump	24 ft 8¼ in	Galina Chistyakova, USSR	6-11-88	Leningrad
Triple jump	50 ft 10¼ in	Inessa Kravets, Ukraine	8-10-95	Göteborg, Sweden
Shot put	74 ft 3 in	Natalya Lisovskaya, USSR	6-7-87	Moscow
Discus throw	252 ft	Gabriele Reinsch, E Germany	7-9-88	Neubrandenburg, Germany
Hammer throw	247 ft 3 in	Mihaela Melinte, Romania	8-29-99	Rüdlingen, Switzerland
Javelin throw	234 ft 8 in	Osleidys Menéndez, Cuba	7-1-01	Réthymno, Greece
Heptathlon	7291 pts	Jackie Joyner-Kersee, United States	9-23/24-88	Seoul

Note: The heptathlon consists of 7 events: the 100-meter hurdles, high jump, shot put and 200 meters on the first day; the long jump, javelin and 800 meters on the second.

As of September 26, 2002. American outdoor records are recognized by USA Track and Field (USATF). WR=world record. EWR=equals world record.

Men

Event	Mark	Record Holder	Date	Site
100 meters	9.78 WR	Tim Montgomery	9-14-02	Paris
200 meters	19.32 WR	Michael Johnson	8-1-96	Atlanta
400 meters	43.18 WR	Michael Johnson	8-26-99	Seville
800 meters	1:42.60	Johnny Gray	8-28-85	Koblenz, Germany
1,000 meters	2:13.9	Rick Wohlhuter	7-30-74	Oslo
1,500 meters	3:29.77	Sydney Maree	8-25-85	Cologne
Mile	3:47.69	Steve Scott	7-7-82	Oslo
2,000 meters	4:52.44	Jim Spivey	9-15-87	Lausanne
3,000 meters	7:30.84	Bob Kennedy	8-8-98	Monte Carlo
Steeplechase	8:09.17	Henry Marsh	8-28-85	Koblenz, Germany
5,000 meters	12:58.21	Bob Kennedy	8-14-96	Zurich
10,000 meters	27:13.98	Mebrahtom Keflezighi	5-4-01	Palo Alto, California
20,000 meters	58:25.0	Bill Rodgers	8-9-77	Boston
Hour	20,547 meters	Bill Rodgers	8-9-77	Boston
25,000 meters	1:14:11.8	Bill Rodgers	2-21-79	Saratoga, CA
30,000 meters	1:31:49	Bill Rodgers	2-21-79	Saratoga, CA
Marathon	2:05:38 WR	Khalid Khannouchi	4-14-02	London
110-meter hurdles	12.92	Roger Kingdom	8-16-89	Zurich
		Allen Johnson	6-23-96	Atlanta
		Allen Johnson	8-23-96	Brussels
400-meter hurdles	46.78 WR	Kevin Young	8-6-92	Barcelona
20-kilometer walk	1:23:40	Tim Seaman	8-14-00	La Jolla, CA
30-kilometer walk	2:14:31	Allen James	10-31-93	Atlanta
50-kilometer walk	3:59:41.1	Herman Nelson	6-9-96	Seattle
4x100-meter relay	37.40 WR	United States (Mike Marsh, Leroy Burrell, Dennis Mitchell, Carl Lewis)	8-8-92	Barcelona
		United States (Jon Drummond, Andre Cason, Dennis Mitchell, Leroy Burrell)	8-21-93	Stuttgart, Germany
4x200-meter relay	1:18.68 WR	Santa Monica Track Club (Mike Marsh, Leroy Burrell, Floyd Heard, Carl Lewis)	4-17-94	Walnut, CA
4x400-meter relay	2:54.20 WR	United States (Jerome Young, Antonio Pettigrew, Tyree Washington, Michael Johnson)	7-22-98	New York City
4x800-meter relay	7:06.5	Santa Monica Track Club (James Robinson, David Mack, Earl Jones, Johnny Gray)	4-26-86	Walnut, CA
4x1,500-meter relay	14:46.3	National Team (Dan Aldredge, Andy Clifford, Todd Harbour, Tom Duits)	6-24-79	Bourges, France
High jump	7 ft 10½ in	Charles Austin	8-17-91	Zurich
Pole vault	19 ft 9¼ in	Jeff Hartwig	6-14-00	Jonesboro, AR
Long jump	29 ft 4½ in WR	Mike Powell	8-30-91	Tokyo
Triple jump	59 ft 4¼ in	Kenny Harrison	7-27-96	Atlanta
Shot put	75 ft 10¼ in WR	Randy Barnes	5-20-90	Westwood, CA
Discus throw	237 ft 4 in	Ben Plucknett	7-7-81	Stockholm
Hammer throw	270 ft 9 in	Lance Deal	9-7-96	Milan
Javelin throw	285 ft 10 in	Tom Pukstys	5-25-97	Jena, Germany
Decathlon	8891 pts	Dan O'Brien	9-4/5-92	Talence, France

Women

Event	Mark	Record Holder	Date	Site
100 meters	10.49 WR	Florence Griffith Joyner	7-16-88	Indianapolis
200 meters	21.34 WR	Florence Griffith Joyner	9-29-88	Seoul
400 meters	48.83	Valerie Brisco-Hooks	8-6-84	Los Angeles
800 meters	1:56.40	Jearl Miles-Clark	8-11-99	Zurich
1,500 meters	3:57.12	Mary Slaney	7-26-83	Stockholm
Mile	4:16.71	Mary Slaney	8-21-85	Zurich
2,000 meters	5:32.7	Mary Slaney	8-3-84	Eugene, OR
3,000 meters	8:25.83	Mary Slaney	9-7-85	Rome
Steeplechase	9:41.94	Elizabeth Jackson	9-4-01	Brisbane
5,000 meters	14:45.38	Regina Jacobs	7-21-00	Sacramento, CA
10,000 meters	30:50.32	Deena Drossin	5-3-02	Palo Alto, CA
Marathon	2:21:21	Joan Samuelson	10-20-85	Chicago
100-meter hurdles	12.33	Gail Devers	7-23-00	Sacramento, CA
400-meter hurdles	52.61 WR	Kim Batten	8-11-95	Göteborg, Sweden
5,000-meter walk	20:56.88	Michelle Rohl	4-27-96	Philadelphia
10,000-meter walk	44:41.87	Michelle Rohl	7-26-94	St. Petersburg
4 x 100-meter relay	41.47	National Team (Chryste Gaines, Marion Jones, Inger Miller, Gail Devers)	8-9-97	Athens
4 x 200-meter relay	1:27.46 WR	USA Blue (LaTasha Jenkins, LaTasha Colander, Nanceen Perry, Marion Jones)	4-29-00	Philadelphia
4 x 400-meter relay	3:15.51	United States (Denean Howard, Diane Dixon, Valerie Brisco, Florence Griffith Joyner)	10-1-88	Seoul
4 x 800-meter relay	8:17.09	Athletics West (Sue Addison, Lee Arbogast, Mary Decker, Chris Mullen)	4-24-83	Walnut, CA
High jump	6 ft 8 in	Louise Ritter	7-9-88	Austin
		Louise Ritter	9-30-88	Seoul
Pole vault	15 ft 9¼ in WR	Stacy Dragila	6-9-01	Palo Alto, CA
Long jump	24 ft 7 in	Jackie Joyner-Kersee	5-22-94	New York City
			7-31-94	Sestriere, Italy
Triple jump	47 ft 3½ in	Sheila Hudson	7-8-96	Stockholm
Shot put	66 ft 2⅛ in	Ramona Pagel	6-25-88	San Diego
Discus throw	227 ft 10 in	Suzy Powell	4-27-02	La Jolla, CA
Hammer throw	236 ft 3 in	Anna Norgren-Mahon	7-28-02	Walnut, CA
Javelin throw	199 ft 1 in	Kim Kreiner	7-26-02	Rheinfeld, Germany
Heptathlon	7291 pts WR	Jackie Joyner-Kersee	9-23/24-88	Seoul

World and American Indoor Records

As of September 26, 2002. American indoor records are recognized by USA Track and Field. World Indoor records are recognized by the International Amateur Athletics Federation (IAAF).

Men

Event	Mark	Record Holder	Date	Site
50 meters	5.56	Donovan Bailey, Canada (W)	2-9-96	Reno
	5.56	Maurice Greene (A)	2-13-99	Los Angeles
55 meters*	5.99	Obadele Thompson, Barbados (W)	2-22-97	Colorado Springs
	6.00	Lee McRae (A)	3-14-86	Oklahoma City
60 meters	6.39	Maurice Greene (W, A)	3-1-98	Madrid
	6.39	Maurice Greene (W, A)	3-3-01	Atlanta
200 meters	19.92	Frankie Fredericks, Namibia (W)	2-18-96	Liévin, France
	20.26	Shawn Crawford (A)	3-11-00	Fayetteville, AR
	20.26	John Capel (A)	3-11-00	Fayetteville, AR
400 meters	44.63	Michael Johnson (W, A)	3-4-95	Atlanta
800 meters	1:42.67	Wilson Kipketer, Denmark (W)	3-9-97	Paris
	1:45.00	Johnny Gray (A)	3-8-92	Sindelfingen, Germany
1,000 meters	2:14.96	Wilson Kipketer, Denmark (W)	2-20-00	Birmingham, England
	2:17.85	David Krummenacker (A)	1-27-02	Boston

Men (Cont.)

Event	Mark	Record Holder	Date	Site
1,500 meters	3:31.18	Hicham El Guerrouj, Morocco (W)	2-02-97	Stuttgart, Germany
	3:38.12	Jeff Atkinson (A)	3-5-89	Budapest
Mile	3:48.45	Hicham El Guerrouj, Morocco (W)	2-12-97	Ghent, Belgium
	3:51.8	Steve Scott (A)	2-20-81	San Diego
3,000 meters	7:24.90	Daniel Komen, Kenya (W)	2-6-98	Budapest
	7:39.23	Tim Broe (A)	1-27-02	Boston
5,000 meters	12:50.38	Haile Gebrselassie, Ethiopia (W)	2-14-99	Birmingham, England
	13:20.55	Doug Padilla (A)	2-12-82	New York City
50-meter hurdles	6.25	Mark McKoy, Canada (W)	3-5-86	Kobe, Japan
	6.35	Greg Foster (A)	1-27-85	Rosemont, Illinois
55-meter hurdles*	6.89	Renaldo Nehemiah (A)	1-20-79	New York City
60-meter hurdles	7.30	Colin Jackson, Great Britain (W)	3-6-94	Sindelfingen, Germany
	7.36	Greg Foster (A)	1-16-87	Los Angeles
5,000-meter walk	18:07.08	Mikhail Shchennikov, Russia (W)	2-14-95	Moscow
	19:18.40	Tim Lewis (A)	3-7-87	Indianapolis
4 x 200-meter relay	1:22.11	Great Britain (W) (Linford Christie, Darren Braithwaite, Ade Mafe, John Regis)	3-3-91	Glasgow
	1:22.71	National Team (A) (Thomas Jefferson, Raymond Pierre, Antonio McKay Kevin Little)	3-3-91	Glasgow
4 x 400-meter relay	3:02.83	National Team (W, A) (Andre Morris, Dameon Johnson, Deon Minor, Milt Campbell)	3-7-99	Maebashi, Japan
4 x 800-meter relay	7:13.94	Global Athletics & Marketing (W, A) (Rich Kenah, Joel Woody, Karl Paranya, David Krummenacker)	2-6-00	Boston
High jump	7 ft 11½ in	Javier Sotomayor, Cuba (W)	3-4-89	Budapest
	7 ft 10½ in	Hollis Conway (A)	3-10-91	Seville
Pole vault	20 ft 2 in	Sergei Bubka, Ukraine (W)	2-21-93	Donetsk, Ukraine
	19 ft 9½ in	Jeff Hartwig (A)	3-10-02	Sindelfingen, Germany
Long jump	28 ft 10¼ in	Carl Lewis (W, A)	1-27-84	New York City
Triple jump	58 ft 6 in	Alicier Urrutia, Cuba (W)	3-1-97	Sindelfingen, Germany
	58 ft 3¼ in	Mike Conley (A)	2-27-87	New York City
Shot put	74 ft 4¼ in	Randy Barnes (W, A)	1-20-89	Los Angeles
Weight throw	84 ft 10¼ in	Lance Deal (W, A)	3-4-95	Atlanta
Pehtathlon	4478 pts	Steve Fritz, (W, A)	1-14-95	Lawrence, KS
Heptathlon	6476 pts	Dan O'Brien (W, A)	3-13/14-93	Toronto

*No recognized world record.

In or Out?

After sending tremors throught the track community with his declaration in the July 2002 issue of *Genre* magazine that he is homosexual, U.S. indoor 800-meter champ Derrick Peterson quickly reversed course. On Aug. 13 he issued a statement saying he's straight. What was going on? That's what Cyd Zeigler, the sports editor for *Genre*, a gay men's monthly, was wondering. "Having spent two days with him, I don't believe a word he's saying now," said Zeigler, who met Peterson when the runner was in L.A. to pose for photos that accompanied the story. In the article Peterson said that Adidas, his sponsor, supported his decision to come out. "I like men and women," he said, adding, "I am definitely not heterosexual." In his retraction—which came after a rush of media requests for interviews—Peterson said that he was going through an "experimental phase" at the time of the *Genre* interview and that he had now "determined with certainty that I am not homosexual." He also posted an explanation to the running website letsrun.com, saying that he'd lied (his word) to *Genre* because "I was upset that people of color were not getting equal representation in the 'alternative sexuality' areas." Peterson, who according to his agent was competing in Europe when SI attempted to contact him, was unavailable for comment.

Women

Event	Mark	Record Holder	Date	Site
50 meters	5.96	Irina Privolova, Russia (W)	2-9-95	Madrid
	6.02	Gail Devers (A)	2-21-99	Liévin, France
55 meters*	6.54	Evelyn Ashford (A)	2-26-82	New York
		Jeanette Bolden (A)	2-21-86	Inglewood, CA
60 meters	6.92	Irina Privalova, Russia (W)	2-11-93	Madrid
	6.92	Irina Privalova, Russia (W)	2-9-95	Madrid
	6.95	Gail Devers (A)	3-12-93	Toronto
	6.95	Marion Jones (A)	3-7-98	Maebashi, Japan
200 meters	21.87	Merlene Ottey, Jamaica (W)	2-13-93	Liévin, France
	22.33	Gwen Torrence (A)	3-2-96	Atlanta
400 meters	49.59	Jarmila Kratochvilová, Czech. (W)	3-7-82	Milan
	50.64	Diane Dixon (A)	3-10-91	Seville
800 meters	1:55.82	Jolanda Ceplak, Slovenia (W)	3-3-02	Vienna
	1:58.71	Nicole Teter (A)	3-2-02	New York
1,000 meters	2:30.94	Maria Mutola, Mozambique (W)	2-25-99	Stockholm
	2:35.29	Regina Jacobs (A)	2-6-00	Boston
1,500 meters	4:00.27	Doina Melinte, Romania (W)	2-9-90	East Rutherford, NJ
	4:00.80	Mary Slaney (A)	2-8-80	New York City
Mile	4:17.14	Doina Melinte, Romania (W)	2-9-90	East Rutherford, NJ
	4:20.5	Mary Slaney (A)	2-19-82	San Diego
3,000 meters	8:29.15	Berhane Adere, Ethiopia	2-3-02	Stuttgart
	8:39.14	Regina Jacobs (A)	3-7-99	Maebashi, Japan
5,000 meters	14:47.35	Gabriela Szabo, Romania (W)	2-13-99	Dortmund, Germany
	15:07.33	Marla Runyan (A)	2-18-01	New York
50-meter hurdles	6.58	Cornelia Oschkenat, E Germany (W)	2-20-88	Berlin
	6.67	Jackie Joyner-Kersee (A)	2-10-95	Reno
55-meter hurdles*	7.30	Tiffany Lott (A)	2-20-97	Air Force Academy, CO
60-meter hurdles	7.69	Lyudmila Narozhilenko, Russia (W)	2-4-90	Chelyabinsk, Russia
	7.81	Jackie Joyner-Kersee (A)	2-5-89	Fairfax, VA
3,000-meter walk	11:40.33	Claudia Iovan, Romania	1-30-99	Bucharest
	12:20.79	Debbi Lawrence (A)	3-12-93	Toronto
4 x 200-meter relay	1:32.55	SC Eintracht Hamm, W Gemany (W) (Helga Arendt, Silke-Beate Knoll, Mechthild Kluth, Gisela Kinzel)	2-20-88	Dortmund, W Germany
	1:33.24	National Team (A) (Flirtisha Harris, Chryste Gaines, Terri Dendy, Michele Collins)	2-12-94	Glasgow
4 x 400-meter relay	3:24.25	Russia (W) (Tatyanna Chebykina, Svetlana Goncharenko, Olga Kotlyarova, Natalya Nazarova)	3-7-99	Maebashi, Japan
	3:27.59	National Team (A) (Michelle Collins, Monique Hennagan, Zundra Feagin-Alexander, Shanelle Porter)	3-7-99	Maebashi, Japan
4 x 800-meter relay	8:18.71	Russia (W) (Natalya Zaytseva, Olga Kuvnetsova, Yelena Afanasyeva, Yekaterina Podkopayeva)	2-4-94	Moscow
	8:25.50	Villanova (A) (Gina Procaccio, Debbie Grant, Michelle DiMuro, Celeste Halliday)	2-7-87	Gainesville, FL
High jump	6 ft 9½ in	Heike Henkel, Germany (W)	2-8-92	Karlsruhe, Germany
	6 ft 7 in	Tisha Walker (A)	2-28-98	Atlanta
Pole vault	15 ft 7 in	Svetlana Feofanova, Russia (W)	3-3-02	Vienna
	15 ft 5 in	Stacy Dragila (A)	2-17-01	Pocatello, Idaho
Long jump	24 ft 2¼ in	Heike Drechsler, E Germany (W)	2-13-88	Vienna
	23 ft 4¾ in	Jackie Joyner-Kersee (A)	3-5-94	Atlanta
Triple jump	49 ft 9 in	Ashia Hansen, Great Britain (W)	2-28-98	Valencia, Spain
	46 ft 8¼ in	Sheila Hudson-Strudwick (A)	3-4-95	Atlanta
Shot put	73 ft 10 in	Helena Fibingerová, Czech. (W)	2-19-77	Jablonec, Czech.
	65 ft ¾ in	Ramona Pagel (A)	2-20-87	Inglewood, CA
Weight throw*	77 ft 5 in	Dawn Ellerbe (W, A)	3-4-00	Atlanta
Pentathlon	4991 pts	Irina Byelova, CIS (W)	2-14/15-92	Berlin
	4753	DeDee Nathan (A)	3-4/5-99	Maebashi, Japan

*No recognized world record.

World Track and Field Championships

Men

100 METERS

1983	Carl Lewis, United States	10.07
1987*	Carl Lewis, United States	9.93 WR
1991	Carl Lewis, United States	9.86 WR
1993	Linford Christie, Great Britain	9.87
1995	Donovan Bailey, Canada	9.97
1997	Maurice Greene, United States	9.86
1999	Maurice Greene, United States	9.80
2001	Maurice Greene, United States	9.82

200 METERS

1983	Calvin Smith, United States	20.14
1987	Calvin Smith, United States	20.16
1991	Michael Johnson, United States	20.01
1993	Frank Fredericks, Namibia	19.85
1995	Michael Johnson, United States	19.79
1997	Ato Boldon, Trinidad and Tobago	20.04
1999	Maurice Greene, United States	19.90
2001	Konstadínos Kedéris, Greece	20.04

400 METERS

1983	Bert Cameron, Jamaica	45.05
1987	Thomas Schoenlebe, E Germany	44.33
1991	Antonio Pettigrew, United States	44.57
1993	Michael Johnson, United States	43.65
1995	Michael Johnson, United States	43.39
1997	Michael Johnson, United States	44.12
1999	Michael Johnson, United States	43.18 WR
2001	Avard Moncur, Bahamas	44.64

800 METERS

1983	Willi Wulbeck, W Germany	1:43.65
1987	Billy Konchellah, Kenya	1:43.06
1991	Billy Konchellah, Kenya	1:43.99
1993	Paul Ruto, Kenya	1:44.71
1995	Wilson Kipketer, Denmark	1:45.08
1997	Wilson Kipketer, Denmark	1:43.38
1999	Wilson Kipketer, Denmark	1:43.30
2001	André Bucher, Switzerland	1:43.70

1,500 METERS

1983	Steve Cram, Great Britain	3:41.59
1987	Abdi Bile, Somalia	3:36.80
1991	Noureddine Morceli, Algeria	3:32.84
1993	Noureddine Morceli, Algeria	3:34.24
1995	Noureddine Morceli, Algeria	3:33.73
1997	Hicham El Guerrouj, Morocco	3:35.83
1999	Hicham El Guerrouj, Morocco	3:27.65
2001	Hicham El Guerrouj, Morocco	3:30.68

STEEPLECHASE

1983	Patriz Ilg, W Germany	8:15.06
1987	Francesco Panetta, Italy	8:08.57
1991	Moses Kiptanui, Kenya	8:12.59
1993	Moses Kiptanui, Kenya	8:06.36
1995	Moses Kiptanui, Kenya	8:04.16
1997	Wilson Boit Kipketer, Kenya	8:05.84
1999	Christopher Koskei, Kenya	8:11.76
2001	Reuben Kosgei, Kenya	8:15.16

5,000 METERS

1983	Eamonn Coghlan, Ireland	13:28.53
1987	Said Aouita, Morocco	13:26.44
1991	Yobes Ondieki, Kenya	13:14.45
1993	Ismael Kirui, Kenya	13:02.75
1995	Ismael Kirui, Kenya	13:16.77
1997	Daniel Komen, Kenya	13:07.38
1999	Salah Hissou, Morocco	12:58.13
2001	Richard Limo, Kenya	13:00.77

10,000 METERS

1983	Alberto Cova, Italy	28:01.04
1987	Paul Kipkoech, Kenya	27:38.63
1991	Moses Tanui, Kenya	27:38.74
1993	Haile Gebrselassie, Ethiopia	27:46.02
1995	Haile Gebrselassie, Ethiopia	27:12.95
1997	Haile Gebrselassie, Ethiopia	27:24.58
1999	Haile Gebrselassie, Ethiopia	27:57.27
2001	Charles Kamathi, Kenya	27:53.25

MARATHON

1983	Rob de Castella, Australia	2:10:03
1987	Douglas Wakiihuri, Kenya	2:11:48
1991	Hiromi Taniguchi, Japan	2:14:57
1993	Mark Plaatjes, United States	2:13:57
1995	Martín Fiz, Spain	2:11:41
1997	Abel Anton, Spain	2:13:16
1999	Abel Anton, Spain	2:13:36
2001	Gezahegne Abera, Ethiopia	2:12:42

110-METER HURDLES

1983	Greg Foster, United States	13.42
1987	Greg Foster, United States	13.21
1991	Greg Foster, United States	13.06
1993	Colin Jackson, Great Britain	12.91 WR
1995	Allen Johnson, United States	13.00
1997	Allen Johnson, United States	12.93
1999	Colin Jackson, Great Britain	13.04
2001	Allen Johnson, United States	13.04

400-METER HURDLES

1983	Edwin Moses, United States	47.50
1987	Edwin Moses, United States	47.46
1991	Samuel Matete, Zambia	47.64
1993	Kevin Young, United States	47.18
1995	Derrick Adkins, United States	47.98
1997	Stéphane Diagana, France	47.70
1999	Fabrizio Mori, Italy	47.72
2001	Felix Sánchez, Dominican Rep.	47.49

20-KILOMETER WALK

1983	Ernesto Canto, Mexico	1:20:49
1987	Maurizio Damilano, Italy	1:20:45
1991	Maurizio Damilano, Italy	1:19:37
1993	Valentin Massana, Spain	1:22:31
1995	Michele Didoni, Italy	1:19:59
1997	Daniel Garcia, Mexico	1:21:43
1999	Ilya Markov, Russia	1:23:34
2001	Roman Rasskazov, Russia	1:20:31

50-KILOMETER WALK

1983	Ronald Weigel, E Germany	3:43:08
1987	Hartwig Gauder, E Germany	3:40:53
1991	Aleksandr Potashov, USSR	3:53:09
1993	Jesus Angel Garcia, Spain	3:41:41
1995	Valentin Kononen, Finland	3:43:42
1997	Robert Korzeniowski, Poland	3:44:46
1999	German Skurygin, Russia	3:44:23
2001	Robert Korzeniowski, Poland	3:42:08

4 X 100-METER RELAY

1983	United States (Emmit King, Willie Gault, Calvin Smith, Carl Lewis)	37.86
1987	United States (Lee McRae, Lee McNeil, Harvey Glance, Carl Lewis)	37.90
1991	United States (Andre Cason, Leroy Burrell, Dennis Mitchell, Carl Lewis)	37.50 WR
1993	United States (Jon Drummond,	37.48

WR=World record.   *Ben Johnson, Canada, disqualified.

Men (Cont.)

4 X 100-METER RELAY (CONT.)

Andre Cason, Dennis Mitchell,
Leroy Burrell)
1995...............Canada (Robert Esmie,   38.31
Glenroy Gilbert, Bruny Surin,
Donovan Bailey)
1997...............Canada (Robert Esmie,   37.86
Glenroy Gilbert, Bruny Surin,
Donovan Bailey)
1999...............United States (Jon Drummond, 37.59
Tim Montgomery, Brian Lewis,
Maurice Greene)
2001...............United States (Mickey Grimes, 37.96
Bernard Williams, Dennis Mitchell,
Tim Montgomery)

4 X 400-METER RELAY

1983...............USSR (Sergei Lovachev,   3:00.79
Alecksandr Troschilo,
Nikolay Chernyetski, Viktor Markin)
1987...............United States (Danny Everett 2:57.29
Rod Haley, Antonio McKay,
Butch Reynolds)
1991...............Great Britain (Roger Black   2:57.53
Derek Redmond, John Regis,
Kriss Akabusi)
1993...............United States (Andrew   2:54.29 WR
Valmon, Quincy Watts, Butch
Reynolds, Michael Johnson)
1995...............United States (Marlon Ramsey, 2:57.32
Derek Mills, Butch Reynolds,
Michael Johnson)
1997...............United States (Jerome Young, 2:56.47
Antonio Pettigrew, Chris Jones,
Tyree Washington)
1999...............United States (Jerome Davis, 2:56.45
Antonio Pettigrew, Angelo
Taylor, Michael Johnson)
2001...............United States (Leonard Byrd, 2:57.54
Antonio Pettigrew, Derrick Brew,
Angelo Taylor)

HIGH JUMP

1983	Gennadi Avdeyenko, USSR	7 ft 7¼ in
1987	Patrik Sjoberg, Sweden	7 ft 9¾ in
1991	Charles Austin, United States	7 ft 9¾ in
1993	Javier Sotomayor, Cuba	7 ft 10½ in
1995	Troy Kemp, Bahamas	7 ft 9¼ in
1997	Javier Sotomayor, Cuba	7 ft 9¼ in
1999	Vyacheslav Voronin, Russia	7 ft 9¼ in
2001	Martin Buss, Germany	7 ft 8¾ in

POLE VAULT

1983	Sergei Bubka, USSR	18 ft 8¼ in
1987	Sergei Bubka, USSR	19 ft 2¼ in
1991	Sergei Bubka, USSR	19 ft 6¼ in
1993	Sergei Bubka, Ukraine	19 ft 8¼ in
1995	Sergei Bubka, Ukraine	19 ft 5 in
1997	Sergei Bubka, Ukraine	19 ft 8½ in
1999	Maksim Tarasov, Russia	19 ft 9 in
2001	Dmitri Markov, Australia	19 ft 10¼ in

LONG JUMP

1983	Carl Lewis, United States	28 ft ¾ in
1987	Carl Lewis, United States	28 ft 5¼ in
1991	Mike Powell, U.S.	29 ft 4½ in WR
1993	Mike Powell, United States	28 ft 2¼ in
1995	Ivan Pedroso, Cuba	28 ft 6½ in
1997	Ivan Pedroso, Cuba	27 ft 7½ in
1999	Ivan Pedroso, Cuba	28 ft 1 in
2001	Iván Pedroso, Cuba	27 ft 6¾ in

TRIPLE JUMP

1983	Zdzislaw Hoffmann, Poland	57 ft 2 in
1987	Khristo Markov, Bulgaria	58 ft 9½ in
1991	Kenny Harrison, United States	58 ft 4 in
1993	Mike Conley, United States	58 ft 7¼ in
1995	Jonathan Edwards, G.B.	60 ft ¼ in WR
1997	Yoelvis Quesada, Cuba	58 ft 6¾ in
1999	Charle Michael Friedek, Ger.	57 ft 8½ in
2001	Jonathan Edwards, G. Britain	58 ft 9½ in

SHOT PUT

1983	Edward Sarul, Poland	70 ft 2¼ in
1987	Werner Günthör, Switz.	72 ft 11¼ in
1991	Werner Günthör, Switz.	71 ft 1¼ in
1993	Werner Günthör, Switz.	72 ft 1 in
1995	John Godina, United States	70 ft 5¼ in
1997	John Godina, United States	70 ft 4¼ in
1999	C.J. Hunter, United States	71 ft 6 in
2001	John Godina, United States	71 ft 9 in

DISCUS THROW

1983	Imrich Bugar, Czechoslovakia	222 ft 2 in
1987	Juergen Schult, E Germany	225 ft 6 in
1991	Lars Riedel, Germany	217 ft 2 in
1993	Lars Riedel, Germany	222 ft 2 in
1995	Lars Riedel, Germany	225 ft 7 in
1997	Lars Riedel, Germany	224 ft 10 in
1999	Anthony Washington, U.S.	226 ft 8 in
2001	Lars Riedel, Germany	228 ft 9 in

HAMMER THROW

1983	Sergei Litvinov, USSR	271 ft 3 in
1987	Sergei Litvinov, USSR	272 ft 6 in
1991	Yuriy Sedykh, USSR	268 ft
1993	Andrey Abduvaliyev, Tajikistan	267 ft 10 in
1995	Andrey Abduvaliyev, Tajikistan	267 ft 7 in
1997	Heinz Weis, Germany	268 ft 4 in
1999	Karsten Kobs, Germany	263 ft 3 in
2001	Szymon Kiólkowski, Poland	273 ft 7 in

JAVELIN

1983	Detlef Michel, E Germany	293 ft 7 in
1987	Seppo Räty, Finland	274 ft 1 in
1991	Kimmo Kinnunen, Finland	297 ft 11 in
1993	Jan Zelezny, Czech Republic	282 ft 1 in
1995	Jan Zelezny, Czech Republic	293 ft 11 in
1997	Marius Corbett, S Africa	290 ft 0 in
1999	Aki Parviainen, Finland	293 ft 8 in
2001	Jan Zelezny, Czech Republic	304 ft 5 in

DECATHLON

1983	Daley Thompson, G. Britain	8666 pts
1987	Torsten Voss, E Germany	8680 pts
1991	Dan O'Brien, United States	8812 pts
1993	Dan O'Brien, United States	8817 pts
1995	Dan O'Brien, United States	8695 pts
1997	Tomás Dvorák, Czech Rep.	8837 pts
1999	Tomás Dvorák, Czech Rep.	8744 pts
2001	Tomás Dvorák, Czech Rep.	8902 pts

WR=World record.

Women

100 METERS

1983	Marlies Gohr, E Germany	10.97
1987	Silke Gladisch, E Germany	10.90
1991	Katrin Krabbe, Germany	10.99
1993	Gail Devers, United States	10.82
1995	Gwen Torrence, United States	10.85
1997	Marion Jones, United States	10.83
1999	Marion Jones, United States	10.70
2001	Zhanna Pintusevich-Block, Ukraine	10.82

200 METERS

1983	Marita Koch, E Germany	22.13
1987	Silke Gladisch, E Germany	21.74
1991	Katrin Krabbe, Germany	22.09
1993	Merlene Ottey, Jamaica	21.98
1995	Merlene Ottey, Jamaica	22.12
1997	Zhanna Pintusevich, Ukraine	22.32
1999	Inger Miller, United States	21.77
2001	Marion Jones, United States	22.39

400 METERS

1983	Jarmila Kratochvilova, Czech.	47.99
1987	Olga Bryzgina, USSR	49.38
1991	Marie-José Pérec, France	49.13
1993	Jearl Miles, United States	49.82
1995	Marie-José Pérec, France	49.28
1997	Cathy Freeman, Australia	49.77
1999	Cathy Freeman, Australia	49.67
2001	Amy Mbacke Thiam, Senegal	49.86

800 METERS

1983	Jarmila Kratochvilova, Czech.	1:54.68
1987	Sigrun Wodars, E Germany	1:55.26
1991	Lilia Nurutdinova, USSR	1:57.50
1993	Maria Mutola, Mozambique	1:55.43
1995	Ana Quirot, Cuba	1:56.11
1997	Ana Quirot, Cuba	1:57.14
1999	Ludmila Formanová, Czech Rep.	1:56.68
2001	Maria Mutola, Mozambique	1:57.17

1,500 METERS

1983	Mary Slaney, United States	4:00.90
1987	Tatyana Samolenko, USSR	3:58.56
1991	Hassiba Boulmerka, Algeria	4:02.21
1993	Dong Liu, China	4:00.50
1995	Hassiba Boulmerka, Algeria	4:02.42
1997	Carla Sacramento, Portugal	4:04.24
1999	Svetlana Masterkova, Russia	3:59.53
2001	Gabriela Szabo, Romania	4:00.57

3,000 METERS

1983	Mary Slaney, United States	8:34.62
1987	Tatyana Samolenko, USSR	8:38.73
1991	Tatyana Dorovskikh, USSR	8:35.82
1993	Qu Yunxia, China	8:28.71

5,000 METERS

1995	Sonia O'Sullivan, Ireland	14:46.47
1997	Gabriela Szabo, Romania	14:57.68
1999	Gabriela Szabo, Romania	14:41.82
2001	Olga Yegorova, Russia	15:03.39

10,000 METERS

1987	Ingrid Kristiansen, Norway	31:05.85
1991	Liz McColgan, Great Britain	31:14.31
1993	Wang Junxia, China	30:49.30
1995	Fernanda Ribeiro, Portugal	31:04.99
1997	Sally Barsosio, Kenya	31:32.92
1999	Gete Wami, Ethiopia	30:24.56
2001	Derartu Tulu, Ethiopia	31:48.81

*400 meters short.

MARATHON

1983	Grete Waitz, Norway	2:28:09
1987	Rosa Mota, Portugal	2:25:17
1991	Wanda Panfil, Poland	2:29:53
1993	Junko Asari, Japan	2:30:03
1995	Manuela Machado, Portugal	2:25:39*
1997	Hiromi Suzuki, Japan	2:29.48
1999	Jong Song-Ok, N Korea	2:26:59
2001	Lidia Simon, Romania	2:26.01

100-METER HURDLES

1983	Bettine Jahn, E Germany	12.35
1987	Ginka Zagorcheva, Bulgaria	12.34
1991	Lyudmila Narozhilenko, USSR	12.59
1993	Gail Devers, United States	12.46
1995	Gail Devers, United States	12.68
1997	Ludmila Engquist, Sweden	12.50
1999	Gail Devers, United States	12.37
2001	Anjanette Kirkland, United States	12.42

400-METER HURDLES

1983	Yekaterina Fesenko, USSR	54.14
1987	Sabine Busch, E Germany	53.62
1991	Tatyana Ledovskaya, USSR	53.11
1993	Sally Gunnell, Great Britain	52.74 WR
1995	Kim Batten, United States	52.61
1997	Nezha Bidouane, Morocco	52.97
1999	Daimi Pernia, Cuba	52.89
2001	Nezha Bidouane, Morocco	53.34

10-KILOMETER WALK

1987	Irina Strakhova, USSR	44:12
1991	Alina Ivanova, USSR	42:57
1993	Sari Essayah, Finland	42:59
1995	Irina Stankina, Russia	42:13
1997	Annarita Sidoti, Italy	42:56

20-KILOMETER WALK

1999	Hongyu Liu, China	1:30:50
2001	Olimpiada Ivanova, Russia	1:27.48

4 X 100-METER RELAY

1983	E Germany (Silke Gladisch, Marita Koch, Ingrid Auerswald, Marlies Gohr)	41.76
1987	United States (Alice Brown, Diane Williams, Florence Griffith, Pam Marshall)	41.58
1991	Jamaica (Dalia Duhaney, Juliet Cuthbert, Beverley McDonald, Merlene Ottey)	41.94
1993	Russia (Olga Bogoslovskaya, Galina Malchugina, Natalya Voronova, Irina Privalova)	41.49
1995	United States (Celena Mondie-Milner, Carlette Guidry, Chryste Gaines, Gwen Torrence)	42.12
1997	United States (Chryste Gaines, Marion Jones, Inger Miller, Gail Devers)	41.47
1999	Bahamas (Sevatheda Fynes, Chandra Sturrup, Pauline Davis-Thompson, Debbie Ferguson)	41.92
2001	United States (Kelli White, Chryste Gaines, Inger Miller, Marion Jones)	41.71

4 X 400-METER RELAY

1983	E Germany (Kerstin Walther, Sabine Busch, Marita	3:19.73

Women (Cont.)

4 X 400-METER RELAY (CONT.)

	Koch, Dagmar Rubsam)	
1987	E Germany (Dagmar Neubauer, Kirsten Emmelmann, Petra Müller, Sabine Busch)	3:18.63
1991	USSR (Tatyana Ledovskaya, Lyudmila Dzhigalova, Olga Nazarova, Olga Bryzgina)	3:18.43
1993	United States (Gwen Torrence, Maicel Malone, Natasha Kaiser-Brown, Jearl Miles)	3:16.71
1995	United States (Kim Graham, Rochelle Stevens, Camara Jones, Jearl Miles)	3:22.39
1997	Germany (Anke Feller, Uta Rohlander, Anja Rucker, Grit Breuer)	3:20.92
1999	Russia (Tatyana Chebykina, Svetlana Goncharenko, Olga Kotylarova, Natalya Nazarova)	3:21.98
2001	Jamaica (Sandie Richards, Catherine Scott, Debbie Ann Parris, Lorraine Fenton)	3:20.65

HIGH JUMP

1983	Tamara Bykova, USSR	6 ft 7 in
1987	Stefka Kostadinova, Bulgaria	6 ft 10¼ in
1991	Heike Henkel, Germany	6 ft 8¾ in
1993	Ioamnet Quintero, Cuba	6 ft 6¼ in
1995	Stefka Kostadinova, Bulgaria	6 ft 7 in
1997	Hanne Haugland, Norway	6 ft 6¼ in
1999	Inga Babakova, Ukraine	6 ft 6¼ in
2001	Hestrie Cloete, S Africa	6 ft 6¾ in

POLE VAULT

1999	Stacy Dragila, U.S.	15 ft 1 in EWR
2001	Stacy Dragila, United States	15 ft 7 in

LONG JUMP

1983	Heike Daute, E Germany	23 ft 10¼ in
1987	Jackie Joyner-Kersee, U.S.	24 ft 1¾ in
1991	Jackie Joyner-Kersee, U.S.	24 ft ¼ in
1993	Heike Drechsler, Germany	23 ft 4 in
1995	Fiona May, Italy	22 ft 10¾ in
1997	Lyudmila Galkina, Russia	23 ft 1¾ in
1999	Niurka Montalvo, Spain	23 ft 2 in
2001	Fiona May, Italy	23 ft ½ in

WR=World record. EWR=equals world record.

TRIPLE JUMP

1993	Ana Biryukova, Russia	49 ft 6 ¼ in WR
1995	Inessa Kravets, Ukraine	50 ft 10¼ in WR
1997	S. Kasparkova, Czech Rep.	49 ft 10½ in
1999	Paraskevi Tsiamita, Greece	48 ft 10 in
2001	Tatyana Lebedeva, Russia	50 ft ½ in

SHOT PUT

1983	Helena Fibingerova, Czech.	69 ft ¾ in
1987	Natalya Lisovskaya, USSR	69 ft 8¼ in
1991	Zhihong Huang, China	68 ft 4¼ in
1993	Zhihong Huang, China	67 ft 6 in
1995	Astrid Kumbernuss, Germany	69 ft 7½ in
1997	Astrid Kumbernuss, Germany	67 ft 11½ in
1999	Astrid Kumbernuss, Germany	65 ft 1½ in
2001	Yanina Korolchik, Belarus	67 ft 7½ in

HAMMER THROW

1999	Mihaela Melinte, Romania	246 ft 9 in
2001	Yipsi Moreno, Cuba	231 ft 9 in

DISCUS THROW

1983	Martina Opitz, E Germany	226 ft 2 in
1987	Martina Hellmann, E Germany	235 ft
1991	Tsvetanka Khristova, Bulgaria	233 ft
1993	Olga Burova, Russia	221 ft 1 in
1995	Ellina Zvereva, Belarus	225 ft 2 in
1997	Beatrice Faumuina, New Zeal.	219 ft 3 in
1999	Franka Dietzsch, Germany	223 ft 7 in
2001	Natalya Sadova, Russia	224 ft 11 in

JAVELIN

1983	Tiina Lillak, Finland	232 ft 4 in
1987	Fatima Whitbread, G.B.	251 ft 5 in
1991	Demei Xu, China	225 ft 8 in
1993	Trine Hattestad, Finland	227 ft
1995	Natalya Shikolenko, Belarus	221 ft 8 in
1997	Trine Hattestad, Norway	225 ft 8 in
1999	Mirela Manjani-Tzelili, Greece	220 ft 1 in
2001	Osleidys Menéndez, Cuba	228 ft 7 in

HEPTATHLON

1983	Ramona Neubert, E Germany	6714 pts
1987	Jackie Joyner-Kersee, U.S.	7128 pts
1991	Sabine Braun, Germany	6672 pts
1993	Jackie Joyner-Kersee, U.S.	6837 pts
1995	Ghada Shouaa, Syria	6651 pts
1997	Sabine Braun, Germany	6739 pts
1999	Eunice Barber, France	6861 pts
2001	Yelena Prokhorova, Russia	6694 pts

Track and Field News Athlete of the Year

Each year (since 1959 for men and since 1974 for women) *Track and Field News* has chosen the outstanding athlete in the sport.

Year	Athlete	Event	Year	Athlete	Event
1959	Martin Lauer, W Germany	110H/Decath	1973	Ben Jipcho, Kenya	1,500/5K/ST
1960	Rafer Johnson, United States	Decathlon	1974	Rick Wohlhuter, United States	800/1,500
1961	Ralph Boston, United States	Long jump	1975	John Walker, New Zealand	800/1,500
1962	Peter Snell, New Zealand	800/1,500	1976	Alberto Juantorena, Cuba	400/800
1963	C. K. Yang, Taiwan	Decath/PV	1977	Alberto Juantorena, Cuba	400/800
1964	Peter Snell, New Zealand	800/1,500	1978	Henry Rono, Kenya	5K/10K/ST
1965	Ron Clarke, Australia	5K/10K	1979	Sebastian Coe, Great Britain	800/1,500
1966	Jim Ryun, United States	800/1,500	1980	Edwin Moses, United States	400H
1967	Jim Ryun, United States	1,500	1981	Sebastian Coe, Great Britain	800/1,500
1968	Bob Beamon, United States	Long jump	1982	Carl Lewis, United States	100/200/LJ
1969	Bill Toomey, United States	Decathlon	1983	Carl Lewis, United States	100/200/LJ
1970	Randy Matson, United States	Shot put	1984	Carl Lewis, United States	100/200/LJ
1971	Rod Milburn, United States	110H	1985	Said Aouita, Morocco	1,500/5000
1972	Lasse Viren, Finland	5K/10K	1986	Yuri Syedikh, USSR	Hammer

MEN (CONT.)

Year	Athlete	Event
1987	Ben Johnson, Canada	100
1988	Sergei Bubka, USSR	Pole vault
1989	Roger Kingdom, United States	110H
1990	Michael Johnson, United States	200/400
1991	Sergei Bubka, CIS	Pole vault
1992	Kevin Young, United States	400H
1993	Noureddine Morceli, Algeria	1,500/mile/3K
1994	Noureddine Morceli, Algeria	1,500/mile/3K
1995	Haile Gebrselassie, Ethiopia	5K/10K
1996	Michael Johnson, United States	200/400
1997	Wilson Kipketer, Denmark	800
1998	Haile Gebrselassie, Ethiopia	5K/10K
1999	Hicham El Guerrouj, Morocco	1,500/Mile
2000	Virgilijus Alekna, Lithuania	Discus
2001	Hicham El Guerrouj, Morocco	1,500/Mile

WOMEN

Year	Athlete	Event
1974	Irena Szewinska, Poland	100/200/400
1975	Faina Melnik, USSR	Shot/Discus
1976	Tatyana Kazankina, USSR	800/1,500
1977	R. Ackermann, E Germany	High jump
1978	Marita Koch, E Germany	100/200/400
1979	Marita Koch, E Germany	100/200/400

WOMEN (CONT.)

Year	Athlete	Event
1980	Ilona Briesenick, E Germany	Shot put
1981	Evelyn Ashford, United States	100/200
1982	Marita Koch, E Germany	100/200/400
1983	J. Kratochvilova, Czechoslovakia	200/400/800
1984	Evelyn Ashford, United States	100
1985	Marita Koch, E Germany	100/200/400
1986	Jackie Joyner-Kersee, U.S.	LJ/Hept
1987	Jackie Joyner-Kersee, U.S	100H/LJ/Hept
1988	Florence Griffith Joyner, U.S.	100/200
1989	Ana Quirot, Cuba	400/800
1990	Merlene Ottey, Jamaica	100/200
1991	Heike Henkel, Germany	High jump
1992	Heike Drechsler, Germany	Long Jump
1993	Wang Junxia, China	1.5K/3K/10K
1994	Jackie Joyner-Kersee, U.S.	100H/LJ/Hept
1995	Sonia O'Sullivan, Ireland	1,500/3K/5K
1996	Svetlana Masterkova, Russia	800/1,500
1997	Marion Jones, United States	100/200/LJ
1998	Marion Jones, United States	100/200/LJ
1999	Gabriela Szabo, Romania	1,500/5,000
2000	Marion Jones, United States	100/200/LJ
2001	Stacy Dragila, United States	Pole vault

Marathon World Record Progression

Men

Record Holder	Time	Date	Site
John Hayes, United States	2:55:18.4	7-24-08	Shepherd's Bush, London
Robert Fowler, United States	2:52:45.4	1-1-09	Yonkers, NY
James Clark, United States	2:46:52.6	2-12-09	New York City
Albert Raines, United States	2:46:04.6	5-8-09	New York City
Frederick Barrett, Great Britain	2:42:31	5-26-09	Shepherd's Bush, London
Harry Green, Great Britain	2:38:16.2	5-12-13	Shepherd's Bush, London
Alexis Ahlgren, Sweden	2:36:06.6	5-31-13	Shepherd's Bush, London
Johannes Kolehmainen, Finland	2:32:35.8	8-22-20	Antwerp, Belgium
Albert Michelsen, United States	2:29:01.8	10-12-25	Port Chester, NY
Fusashige Suzuki, Japan	2:27:49	3-31-35	Tokyo
Yasuo Ikenaka, Japan	2:26:44	4-3-35	Tokyo
Kitei Son, Japan	2:26:42	11-3-35	Tokyo
Yun Bok Suh, Korea	2:25:39	4-19-47	Boston
James Peters, Great Britain	2:20:42.2	6-14-52	Chiswick, England
James Peters, Great Britain	2:18:40.2	6-13-53	Chiswick, England
James Peters, Great Britain	2:18:34.8	10-4-53	Turku, Finland
James Peters, Great Britain	2:17:39.4	6-26-54	Chiswick, England
Sergei Popov, USSR	2:15:17	8-24-58	Stockholm
Abebe Bikila, Ethiopia	2:15:16.2	9-10-60	Rome
Toru Terasawa, Japan	2:15:15.8	2-17-63	Beppu, Japan
Leonard Edelen, United States	2:14:28	6-15-63	Chiswick, England
Basil Heatley, Great Britain	2:13:55	6-13-64	Chiswick, England
Abebe Bikila, Ethiopia	2:12:11.2	6-21-64	Tokyo
Morio Shigematsu, Japan	2:12:00	6-12-65	Chiswick, England
Derek Clayton, Australia	2:09:36.4	12-3-67	Fukuoka, Japan
Derek Clayton, Australia	2:08:33.6	5-30-69	Antwerp, Belgium
Rob de Castella, Australia	2:08:18	12-6-81	Fukuoka, Japan
Steve Jones, Great Britain	2:08:05	10-21-84	Chicago
Carlos Lopes, Portugal	2:07:12	4-20-85	Rotterdam, Netherlands
Belayneh Dinsamo, Ethiopia	2:06:50	4-17-88	Rotterdam, Netherlands
Ronaldo Da Costa, Brazil	2:06:05	9-20-98	Berlin, Germany
Khalid Khannouchi, Morocco	2:05:42	10-24-99	Chicago
Khalid Khannouchi, United States	2:05:38	4-14-02	London

Women

Record Holder	Time	Date	Site
Dale Greig, Great Britain	3:27:45	5-23-64	Ryde, England
Mildred Simpson, New Zealand	3:19:33	7-21-64	Auckland, New Zealand
Maureen Wilton, Canada	3:15:22	5-6-67	Toronto
Anni Pede-Erdkamp, W Germany	3:07:26	9-16-67	Waldniel, W Germany

Women (Cont.)

Record Holder	Time	Date	Site
Caroline Walker, United States	3:02:53	2-28-70	Seaside, OR
Elizabeth Bonner, United States	3:01:42	5-9-71	Philadelphia
Adrienne Beames, Australia	2:46:30	8-31-71	Werribee, Australia
Chantal Langlace, France	2:46:24	10-27-74	Neuf Brisach, France
Jacqueline Hansen, United States	2:43:54.5	12-1-74	Culver City, CA
Liane Winter, W Germany	2:42:24	4-21-75	Boston
Christa Vahlensieck, W Germany	2:40:15.8	5-3-75	Dülmen, W Germany
Jacqueline Hansen, United States	2:38:19	10-12-75	Eugene, OR
Chantal Langlace, France	2:35:15.4	5-1-77	Oyarzun, France
Christa Vahlensieck, W Germany	2:34:47.5	9-10-77	Berlin, W Germany
Grete Waitz, Norway	2:32:29.9	10-22-78	New York City
Grete Waitz, Norway	2:27:32.6	10-21-79	New York City
Grete Waitz, Norway	2:25:41.3	10-26-80	New York City
Grete Waitz, Norway	2:25:29	4-17-83	London
Joan Benoit Samuelson, United States	2:22:43	4-18-83	Boston
Ingrid Kristiansen, Norway	2:21:06	4-21-85	London
Tegla Loroupe, Kenya	2:20:47	4-19-98	Rotterdam, Netherlands
Tegla Loroupe, Kenya	2:20:43	9-26-99	Berlin
Naoko Takahashi, Japan	2:19:46	9-30-01	Berlin
Catherine Ndereba, Kenya	2:18:47	10-7-01	Chicago

Boston Marathon

The Boston Marathon began in 1897 as a local Patriot's Day event. Run every year but 1918 since then, it has grown into one of the world's premier marathons.

Men

Year	Winner	Time	Year	Winner	Time
1897	John J. McDermott, United States	2:55:10	1939	Ellison M. (Tarzan) Brown, United States	2:28:51
1898	Ronald J. McDonald, United States	2:42:00	1940	Gerard Cote, Canada	2:28:28
1899	Lawrence J. Brignolia, United States	2:54:38	1941	Leslie Pawson, United States	2:30:38
1900	James J. Caffrey, Canada	2:39:44	1942	Bernard Joseph Smith, United States	2:26:51
1901	James J. Caffrey, Canada	2:29:23	1943	Gerard Cote, Canada	2:28:25
1902	Sammy Mellor, United States	2:43:12	1944	Gerard Cote, Canada	2:31:50
1903	John C. Lorden, United States	2:41:29	1945	John A. Kelley, United States	2:30:40
1904	Michael Spring, United States	2:38:04	1946	Stylianos Kyriakides, Greece	2:29:27
1905	Fred Lorz, United States	2:38:25	1947	Yun Bok Suh, Korea	2:25:39
1906	Timothy Ford, United States	2:45:45	1948	Gerard Cote, Canada	2:31:02
1907	Tom Longboat, Canada	2:24:24	1949	Karl Gosta Leandersson, Sweden	2:31:50
1908	Thomas Morrissey, United States	2:25:43	1950	Kee Yong Ham, Korea	2:32:39
1909	Henri Renaud, United States	2:53:36	1951	Shigeki Tanaka, Japan	2:27:45
1910	Fred Cameron, Canada	2:28:52	1952	Doroteo Flores, Guatemala	2:31:53
1911	Clarence H. DeMar, United States	2:21:39	1953	Keizo Yamada, Japan	2:18:51
1912	Mike Ryan, United States	2:21:18	1954	Veikko Karvonen, Finland	2:20:39
1913	Fritz Carlson, United States	2:25:14	1955	Hideo Hamamura, Japan	2:18:22
1914	James Duffy, Canada	2:25:01	1956	Antti Viskari, Finland	2:14:14
1915	Edouard Fabre, Canada	2:31:41	1957	John J. Kelley, United States	2:20:05
1916	Arthur Roth, United States	2:27:16	1958	Franjo Mihalic, Yugoslavia	2:25:54
1917	Bill Kennedy, United States	2:28:37	1959	Eino Oksanen, Finland	2:22:42
1918	No race		1960	Paavo Kotila, Finland	2:20:54
1919	Carl Linder, United States	2:29:13	1961	Eino Oksanen, Finland	2:23:39
1920	Peter Trivoulidas, Greece	2:29:31	1962	Eino Oksanen, Finland	2:23:48
1921	Frank Zuna, United States	2:18:57	1963	Aurele Vandendriessche, Belgium	2:18:58
1922	Clarence H. DeMar, United States	2:18:10	1964	Aurele Vandendriessche, Belgium	2:19:59
1923	Clarence H. DeMar, United States	2:23:37	1965	Morio Shigematsu, Japan	2:16:33
1924	Clarence H. DeMar, United States	2:29:40	1966	Kenji Kimihara, Japan	2:17:11
1925	Chuck Mellor, United States	2:33:00	1967	David McKenzie, New Zealand	2:15:45
1926	John C. Miles, Canada	2:25:40	1968	Amby Burfoot, United States	2:22:17
1927	Clarence H. DeMar, United States	2:40:22	1969	Yoshiaki Unetani, Japan	2:13:49
1928	Clarence H. DeMar, United States	2:37:07	1970	Ron Hill, England	2:10:30
1929	John C. Miles, Canada	2:33:08	1971	Alvaro Mejia, Colombia	2:18:45
1930	Clarence H. DeMar, United States	2:34:48	1972	Olavi Suomalainen, Finland	2:15:39
1931	James (Hinky) Henigan, United States	2:46:45	1973	Jon Anderson, United States	2:16:03
1932	Paul de Bruyn, Germany	2:33:36	1974	Neil Cusack, Ireland	2:13:39
1933	Leslie Pawson, United States	2:31:01	1975	Bill Rodgers, United States	2:09:55
1934	Dave Komonen, Canada	2:32:53	1976	Jack Fultz, United States	2:20:19
1935	John A. Kelley, United States	2:32:07	1977	Jerome Drayton, Canada	2:14:46
1936	Ellison M. (Tarzan) Brown, United States	2:33:40	1978	Bill Rodgers, United States	2:10:13
1937	Walter Young, Canada	2:33:20	1979	Bill Rodgers, United States	2:09:27
1938	Leslie Pawson, United States	2:35:34	1980	Bill Rodgers, United States	2:12:11

Year	Winner	Time	Year	Winner	Time
1981	Toshihiko Seko, Japan	2:09:26	1972	Nina Kuscsik, United States	3:10:36
1982	Alberto Salazar, United States	2:08:52	1973	Jacqueline A. Hansen, United States	3:05:59
1983	Gregory A. Meyer, United States	2:09:00	1974	Miki Gorman, United States	2:47:11
1984	Geoff Smith, England	2:10:34	1975	Liane Winter, W Germany	2:42:24
1985	Geoff Smith, England	2:14:05	1976	Kim Merritt, United States	2:47:10
1986	Rob de Castella, Australia	2:07:51	1977	Miki Gorman, United States	2:48:33
1987	Toshihiko Seko, Japan	2:11:50	1978	Gayle Barron, United States	2:44:52
1988	Ibrahim Hussein, Kenya	2:08:43	1979	Joan Benoit, United States	2:35:15
1989	Abebe Mekonnen, Ethiopia	2:09:06	1980	Jacqueline Gareau, Canada	2:34:28
1990	Gelindo Bordin, Italy	2:08:19	1981	Allison Roe, New Zealand	2:26:46
1991	Ibrahim Hussein, Kenya	2:11:06	1982	Charlotte Teske, W Germany	2:29:33
1992	Ibrahim Hussein, Kenya	2:08:14	1983	Joan Benoit, United States	2:22:43
1993	Cosmas N'Deti, Kenya	2:09:33	1984	Lorraine Moller, New Zealand	2:29:28
1994	Cosmas N'Deti, Kenya	2:07:15	1985	Lisa Larsen Weidenbach, United States	2:34:06
1995	Cosmas N'Deti, Kenya	2:09:22	1986	Ingrid Kristiansen, Norway	2:24:55
1996	Moses Tanui, Kenya	2:09:16	1987	Rosa Mota, Portugal	2:25:21
1997	Lameck Aguta, Kenya	2:10:34	1988	Rosa Mota, Portugal	2:24:30
1998	Moses Tanui, Kenya	2:07:34	1989	Ingrid Kristiansen, Norway	2:24:33
1999	Joseph Chebet, Kenya	2:09:52	1990	Rosa Mota, Portugal	2:25:24
2000	Elijah Lagat, Kenya	2:09:47	1991	Wanda Panfil, Poland	2:24:18
2001	Lee Bong-Ju, Korea	2:09:43	1992	Olga Markova, Russia	2:23:43
2002	Rodgers Rop, Kenya	2:09:02	1993	Olga Markova, Russia	2:25:27
			1994	Uta Pippig, Germany	2:21:45

Women

Year	Winner	Time	Year	Winner	Time
			1995	Uta Pippig, Germany	2:25:11
			1996	Uta Pippig, Germany	2:27:12
1966	Roberta Gibb, United States	3:21:40*	1997	Fatuma Roba, Ethiopia	2:26:23
1967	Roberta Gibb, United States	3:27:17*	1998	Fatuma Roba, Ethiopia	2:23:21
1968	Roberta Gibb, United States	3:30:00*	1999	Fatuma Roba, Ethiopia	2:23:25
1969	Sara Mae Berman, United States	3:22:46*	2000	Catherine Ndereba, Kenya	2:26:11
1970	Sara Mae Berman, United States	3:05:07*	2001	Catherine Ndereba, Kenya	2:23:53
1971	Sara Mae Berman, United States	3:08:30*	2002	Margaret Okayo, Kenya	2:20:43

Note: Over the years the Boston course has varied in length. The distances have been 24 miles, 1,232 yards (1897–1923); 26 miles, 209 yards (1924–1926); 26 miles, 385 yards (1927–1952); and 25 miles, 958 yards (1953–1956). Since 1957, the course has been certified to be the standard marathon distance of 26 miles, 385 yards. (*Unofficial.)

New York City Marathon

MEN			WOMEN		
Year	Winner	Time	Year	Winner	Time
1970	Gary Muhrcke, United States	2:31:38	1970	No finisher	
1971	Norman Higgins, United States	2:22:54	1971	Beth Bonner, United States	2:55:22
1972	Sheldon Karlin, United States	2:27:52	1972	Nina Kuscsik, United States	3:08:41
1973	Tom Fleming, United States	2:21:54	1973	Nina Kuscsik, United States	2:57:07
1974	Norbert Sander, United States	2:26:30	1974	Katherine Switzer, United States	3:07:29
1975	Tom Fleming, United States	2:19:27	1975	Kim Merritt, United States	2:46:14
1976	Bill Rodgers, United States	2:10:10	1976	Miki Gorman, United States	2:39:11
1977	Bill Rodgers, United States	2:11:28	1977	Miki Gorman, United States	2:43:10
1978	Bill Rodgers, United States	2:12:12	1978	Grete Waitz, Norway	2:32:30
1979	Bill Rodgers, United States	2:11:42	1979	Grete Waitz, Norway	2:27:33
1980	Alberto Salazar, United States	2:09:41	1980	Grete Waitz, Norway	2:25:41
1981	Alberto Salazar, United States	2:08:13	1981	Allison Roe, New Zealand	2:25:29
1982	Alberto Salazar, United States	2:09:29	1982	Grete Waitz, Norway	2:27:14
1983	Rod Dixon, New Zealand	2:08:59	1983	Grete Waitz, Norway	2:27:00
1984	Orlando Pizzolato, Italy	2:14:53	1984	Grete Waitz, Norway	2:29:30
1985	Orlando Pizzolato, Italy	2:11:34	1985	Grete Waitz, Norway	2:28:34
1986	Gianni Poli, Italy	2:11:06	1986	Grete Waitz, Norway	2:28:06
1987	Ibrahim Hussein, Kenya	2:11:01	1987	Priscilla Welch, Great Britain	2:30:17
1988	Steve Jones, Great Britain	2:20:20	1988	Grete Waitz, Norway	2:28:07
1989	Juma Ikangaa, Tanzania	2:08:01	1989	Ingrid Kristiansen, Norway	2:25:30
1990	Douglas Wakiihuri, Kenya	2:12:39	1990	Wanda Panfiil, Poland	2:30:45
1991	Salvador Garcia, Mexico	2:09:28	1991	Liz McColgan, Scotland	2:27:23
1992	Willie Mtolo, S Africa	2:09:29	1992	Lisa Ondieki, Australia	2:24:40
1993	Andres Espinosa, Mexico	2:10:04	1993	Uta Pippig, Germany	2:26:24
1994	German Silva, Mexico	2:11:21	1994	Tegla Loroupe, Kenya	2:27:37
1995	German Silva, Mexico	2:11:00	1995	Tegla Loroupe, Kenya	2:28:06
1996	Giacomo Leone, Italy	2:09:54	1996	Anuta Catuna, Romania	2:28:18
1997	John Kagwe, Kenya	2:08:12	1997	Franziska Rochat-Moser, Switzerland	2:28:43
1998	John Kagwe, Kenya	2:08:45	1998	Franca Fiacconi, Italy	2:25:17
1999	Joseph Chebet, Kenya	2:09:14	1999	Adriana Fernandez, Mexico	2:25:06
2000	Abdelkhader El Mouaziz, Morocco	2:10:09	2000	Ludmila Petrova, Russia	2:25:45
2001	Tesfaye Jifar, Ethiopia	2:07:43	2001	Margaret Okayo, Kenya	2:24:21

World Cross-Country Championships

Conducted by the International Amateur Athletic Federation (IAAF), this meet annually brings together the best runners in the world at every distance from the mile to the marathon to compete in the same cross-country race.

Men

Year	Winner	Winning Team	Year	Winner	Winning Team
1973	Pekka Paivarinta, Finland	Belgium	1989	John Ngugi, Kenya	Kenya
1974	Eric DeBeck, Belgium	Belgium	1990	Khalid Skah, Morocco	Kenya
1975	Ian Stewart, Scotland	New Zealand	1991	Khalid Skah, Morocco	Kenya
1976	Carlos Lopes, Portugal	England	1992	John Ngugi, Kenya	Kenya
1977	Leon Schots, Belgium	Belgium	1993	William Sigei, Kenya	Kenya
1978	John Treacy, Ireland	France	1994	William Sigei, Kenya	Kenya
1979	John Treacy, Ireland	England	1995	Paul Tergat, Kenya	Kenya
1980	Craig Virgin, United States	England	1996	Paul Tergat, Kenya	Kenya
1981	Craig Virgin, United States	Ethiopia	1997	Paul Tergat, Kenya	Kenya
1982	Mohammed Kedir, Ethiopia	Ethiopia	1998	Paul Tergat, Kenya	Kenya
1983	Bekele Debele, Ethiopia	Ethiopia	1999	Paul Tergat, Kenya	Kenya
1984	Carlos Lopes, Portugal	Ethiopia	2000	Mohammed Mourhit, Belgium	Kenya
1985	Carlos Lopes, Portugal	Ethiopia	2001	Mohammed Mourhit, Belgium	Kenya
1987	John Ngugi, Kenya	Kenya	2002	Bekele Kenenisa, Ethiopia	Kenya
1988	John Ngugi, Kenya	Kenya			

Women

Year	Winner	Winning Team	Year	Winner	Winning Team
1973	Paola Cacchi, Italy	England	1988	Ingrid Kristiansen, Norway	USSR
1974	Paola Cacchi, Italy	England	1989	Annette Sergent, France	USSR
1975	Julie Brown, United States	United States	1990	Lynn Jennings, United States	USSR
1976	Carmen Valero, Spain	USSR	1991	Lynn Jennings, United States	Kenya
1977	Carmen Valero, Spain	USSR	1992	Lynn Jennings, United States	Kenya
1978	Grete Waitz, Norway	Romania	1993	Albertina Dias, Portugal	Kenya
1979	Grete Waitz, Norway	United States	1994	Helen Chepngeno, Kenya	Portugal
1980	Grete Waitz, Norway	USSR	1995	Derartu Tulu, Ethiopia	Kenya
1981	Grete Waitz, Norway	USSR	1996	Gete Wami, Ethiopia	Kenya
1982	Maricica Puica, Romania	USSR	1997	Derartu Tulu, Ethiopia	Ethiopia
1983	Grete Waitz, Norway	United States	1998	Sonia O'Sullivan, Ireland	Kenya
1984	Maricica Puica, Romania	United States	1999	Gete Wami, Ethiopia	Ethiopia
1985	Zola Budd, England	United States	2000	Derartu Tulu, Ethiopia	Ethiopia
1986	Zola Budd, England	England	2001	Paula Radcliffe, Great Britain	Kenya
1987	Annette Sergent, France	United States	2002	Paula Radcliffe, Great Britain	Ethiopia

Notable Achievements

Longest Winning Streaks

MEN

Event	Name and Nationality	Streak	Years
100 meters	Bob Hayes, United States	49	1962–64
200 meters	Manfred Gemar, Germany	41	1956–60
400 meters	Michael Johnson, United States	58	1989–97
800 meters	Mal Whitfield, United States	40	1951–54
1,500 meters	Hicham El Guerrouj, Morocco	23	1996–00
1,500 meters/mile	Steve Ovett, Great Britain	45	1977–80
Mile	Herb Elliott, Australia	35	1957–60
Steeplechase	Gaston Roelants, Belgium	45	1961–66
5,000 meters	Emil Zátopek, Czechoslovakia	48	1949–52
10,000 meters	Emil Zátopek, Czechoslovakia	38	1948–54
Marathon	Frank Shorter, United States	6	1971–73
110-meter hurdles	Jack Davis, United States	44	1952–55
400-meter hurdles	Edwin Moses, United States	107	1977–87
High jump	Ernie Shelton, United States	46	1953–55
Pole vault	Bob Richards, United States	50	1950–52
Long jump	Carl Lewis, United States	65	1981–91
Triple jump	Adhemar da Silva, Brazil	60	1950–56
Shot put	Parry O'Brien, United States	116	1952–56
Discus throw	Ricky Bruch, Sweden	54	1972–73
Hammer throw	Imre Nemeth, Hungary	73	1946–50
Javelin throw	Janis Lusis, USSR	41	1967–70
Decathlon	Bob Mathias, United States	11	1948–56

Longest Winning Streaks (Cont.)

WOMEN

Event	Name and Nationality	Streak	Years
100 meters	Merlene Ottey, Jamaica	56	1987–91
200 meters	Irena Szewinska, Poland	38	1973–75
400 meters	Irena Szewinska, Poland	36	1973–78
800 meters	Ana Fidelia Quirot, Cuba	36	1987–90
1,500 meters	Paula Ivan, Romania	15	1988–91
1,500 meters/mile	Paula Ivan, Romania	19	1988–90
3,000 meters	Mary Slaney, United States	10	1982–84
10,000 meters	Ingrid Kristiansen, Norway	5	1985–87
Marathon	Katrin Dörre, E Germany	10	1982–86
100-meter hurdles	Annelie Ehrhardt, E Germany	44	1972–75
400-meter hurdles	Ann-Louise Skoglund, Sweden	18	1981–83
High jump	Iolanda Balas, Romania	140	1956–67
Long jump	Tatyana Shchelkanova, USSR	19	1964–66
Shot put	Nadezhda Chizhova, USSR	57	1969–73
Discus throw	Gisela Mauermeyer, Germany	65	1935–42
Javelin throw	Ruth Fuchs, E Germany	30	1972–73
Multi	Heide Rosendahl, W Germany	15	1969–72

Most Consecutive Years Ranked No. 1 in the World

MEN

No.	Name and Nationality	Event	Years
11	Sergei Bubka, Ukraine	Pole vault	1984–94
9	Viktor Saneyev, USSR	Triple jump	1968–76
8	Bob Richards, United States	Pole vault	1949–56
8	Ralph Boston, United States	Long jump	1960–67

WOMEN

No.	Name and Nationality	Event	Years
9	Iolanda Balas, Romania	High jump	1958–66
8	Ruth Fuchs, E Germany	Javelin	1972–79
7	Faina Melnick, USSR	Discus throw	1971–77

Major Barrier Breakers

MEN

Event	Mark	Name and Nationality	Date	Site
sub 10-second 100 meters	9.95	Jim Hines, United States	Oct. 14, 1968	Mexico City
sub 20-second 200 meters	19.83	Tommie Smith, United States	Oct. 16, 1968	Mexico City
sub 45-second 400 meters	44.9	Otis Davis, United States	Sept. 6, 1960	Rome
sub 1:45 800 meters	1:44.3	Peter Snell, New Zealand	Feb. 3, 1962	Christchurch, New Zealand
sub four minute mile	3:59.4	Roger Bannister, Great Britain	May 6, 1954	Oxford
sub 3:50 mile	3:49.4	John Walker, New Zealand	Aug. 12, 1975	Göteborg, Sweden
sub 13-minute 5,000 meters	12:58.39	Said Aouita, Morocco	July 22, 1986	Rome
sub 27:00 10,000 meters	26:58.38	Yobes Ondieki, Kenya	July 10, 1993	Oslo
sub 13-second 110-meter hurdles	12.93	Renaldo Nehemiah, United States	Aug. 19, 1981	Zurich
sub 50-second 400-meter hurdles	49.5	Glenn Davis, United States	June 29, 1956	Los Angeles
7' high jump	7' ⅝"	Charles Dumas, United States	June 29, 1956	Los Angeles
8' high jump	8'	Javier Sotomayor, Cuba	July 29, 1989	San Juan
60' triple jump	60' ¼"	Jonathan Edwards, Great Britain	Aug. 7, 1995	Göteborg, Sweden
20' pole vault	20'	Sergei Bubka, USSR	March 15, 1991	San Sebastian, Spain
70' shot put	70' 7¼"	Randy Matson, United States	May 5, 1965	College Station, Texas
200' discus throw	200' 5"	Al Oerter, United States	May 18, 1962	Los Angeles
300' (new) javelin	300' 1"	Steve Backley, Great Britain	Jan. 25, 1992	Auckland, New Zealand
9,000-pt decathlon	9026	Roman Sebrle, Czech Republic	May 27, 2001	Gotzis, Austria

Major Barrier Breakers (Cont.)

WOMEN

Event	Mark	Name and Nationality	Date	Site
sub 11-second 100 meters	10.88	Marlies Oelsner, E Germany	July 1, 1977	Dresden
sub 22-second 200 meters	21.71	Marita Koch, E Germany	June 10, 1979	Karl Marxstadt, E Germany
sub 50-second 400 meters	49.9	Irena Szewinska, Poland	June 22, 1974	Warsaw
sub 2:00 800 meters	1:59.1	Shin Geum Dan, N Korea	Nov. 12, 1963	Djakarta
sub 4:00 1,500 meters	3:56.0	Tatyana Kazankina, USSR	June 28, 1976	Podolsk, USSR
sub 4:20 mile	4:17.55	Mary Decker, United States	Feb. 16, 1980	Houston
sub 15:00 5,000 meters	14:58.89	Ingrid Kristiansen, Norway	June 28, 1984	Oslo
sub 30:00 10,000 meters	29:31.78	Wang Junxia, China	Sept. 8, 1993	Beijing
sub 2:30 marathon	2:27:33	Grete Waitz, Norway	Oct. 21, 1979	New York City
sub 2:20 marathon	2:19:46	Naoko Takahashi, Japan	Sept. 30, 2001	Berlin
sub 13-second 100-meter hurdles	12.9	Karin Balzer, E Germany	Sept. 5, 1969	Berlin
6' high jump	6'	Iolanda Balas, Romania	Oct. 18, 1958	Budapest
15' pole vault	15 ½''	Emma George, Australia	March 14, 1998	Melbourne
70' shot put	70' 4½''	Nadyezhda Chizhova, USSR	Sept. 29, 1973	Varna, Bulgaria
200' discus throw	201'	Liesel Westermann, W Germany	Nov. 5, 1967	Sao Paulo
200' javelin throw	201' 4''	Elvira Ozolina, USSR	Aug. 27, 1964	Kiev
first 7,000-point heptathlon	7,148	Jackie Joyner-Kersee, U.S.	July 6–7, 1986	Moscow

Olympic Accomplishments

Oldest Olympic gold medalist—Patrick (Babe) McDonald, United States, 42 years, 26 days, 56-pound weight throw, 1920.
Oldest Olympic medalist—Tebbs Lloyd Johnson, Great Britain, 48 years, 115 days, 1948 (bronze), 50K walk.
Youngest Olympic gold medalist—Barbara Jones, United States, 15 years 123 days, 1952, 4 x 100 relay.
Youngest gold medalist in individual event—Ulrike Meyfarth, W Germany, 16 years, 123 days, 1972, high jump.

World Record Accomplishments*

Most world records equaled or set in a day—6, Jesse Owens, United States, 5-25-35, (9.4 100 yards; 26' 8¼'' long jump; 20.3 200 meters and 220 yards; and 22.6 220-yard hurdles and 200-meter hurdles.
Most records in a year—10, Gunder Hägg, Sweden, 1941–42, 1,500 to 5,000 meters.
Most records in a career—35, Sergei Bubka, 1983–94, pole vault indoors and out.
Longest span of record setting—11 years, 20 days, Irena Szewinska, Poland, 1965–76, 200 meters.
Youngest person to set a set world record—Carolina Gisolf, Holland, 15 years, 5 days, 1928, high jump, 5' 3⅜''.
Youngest man to set a world record—John Thomas, United States, 17 years, 355 days, 1959, high jump, 7' 1¼''.
Oldest person to set world record—Carlos Lopes, Portugal, 38 years, 59 days, marathon, 2:07:12.
Greatest percentage improvement—6.59, Bob Beamon, United States, 1968, long jump.
Longest lasting record—long jump, 26' 8¼'', Jesse Owens, United States, 25 years, 79 days (1935–60).
Highest clearance over head, men—23¼'', Franklin Jacobs, United States (5' 8''), 1978.
Highest clearance over head, woman—12¾'', Yolanda Henry, United States (5' 6''), 1990.

*Marks sanctioned by the IAAF.

Swimming

Yankee Dandy

Led by 19-year-old Natalie Coughlin, U.S. swimmers thoroughly dominated the Pan Pacific Championships

BY MARK BECHTEL

After the 2000 Sydney Games, Jenny Thompson took her eight career Olympic medals and said goodbye to the sport of swimming. At 27, she didn't know when or if she'd be back. She had other things on her mind, like medical school, which she began at New York City's Columbia University in the fall of 2001. "After Sydney I felt done for the moment," she said.

Then on the morning of September 11th, 2001, she was in a computer lab on campus when she heard the news of the World Trade Center attacks. She returned to her apartment in time to see the second hijacked plane hit the South Tower. Like so many Americans, it made her stop and consider what she was doing with her life. "After 9-11 a lot of people took stock of their lives and what they should mean," said Thompson. "I definitely did that. I think maybe that had something to do with me wanting to swim again, because it is a platform I can use to help other people."

So after classes let out for the summer, Thompson returned to the pool in Dover, N.H. Her longtime coach, Mike Parratto, put her through eight weeks of weight training, yoga and two-a-day workouts in the pool. By August she was competing again, in the nationals, where she finished second in the 50-meter freestyle. That put her on the U.S. team for the Pan Pacific championships in Yokohama, Japan, where she set a personal best of 25.13 seconds en route to the gold.

Thompson's remarkable return was the highlight of a dominant performance by the U.S. at the Pan Pacs. Both the American men and women won the team points, total medal and gold medal counts. Thompson added a pair of silvers and two bronze medals to run her medal count to five, but that paled in comparison to Natalie Coughlin's take. The 19-year-old Cal junior, who weeks earlier at nationals became the first woman to break one minute in the 100 meter backstroke, won four golds, three in individual events. She also became the second woman ever to break 54 seconds in the 100 meter free, which she did in the finals. "I didn't think

Thorpe won six gold medals in Manchester.

I could swim much faster than I did in the semis," said Coughlin. "I was just hoping to do better than my nationals time of 54.6, but I can't believe I did that much better."

Coughlin had six medals overall, tying her with Australian Ian Thorpe for most at the meet. Thorpe's performance was magnificent, but it fell short of his accomplishments at the Commonwealth Games in Manchester, England, earlier in the month. The Thorpedo opened his account in Manchester by winning the gold medal and setting a world-record in the 400-meter freestyle, and he never slowed down. He won six gold medals and narrowly missed a seventh when countryman Matt Welsh, a backstroke specialist, swam a meet record time of 54.72 seconds to win the 100-meter backstroke. The win didn't come easy for Welsh, who felt the pressure of attempting to deprive Thorpe of a golden sweep. "In the last five meters it felt like a grand piano had been dropped on me," Welsh said. "The hardest thing is trying to deprive him of that sixth gold medal. But he came to my party."

The women's party in Manchester was hosted by Australian Petria Thomas, who swam in eight events and medaled in seven of them. At the Pan Pacs, she cut her load to six events—and won medals in five. The 10-year veteran of the Aussie team showed few signs of aging. In fact, after helping her team win the gold medal in the 4x100 meter freestyle relay she said, "I'm still enjoying what I'm doing. Someone compared me to a fine bottle of red wine."

But the next day Thomas lost in the 100-meter butterfly for the first time since winning the world championship in the event in 2001. Her conqueror? Coughlin, of course. And the upstart Californian beat Thomas on the champ's birthday, for good measure. It was typical of the Pan Pacs, as the Americans outswam everyone who dived into the pool with them. The meet ended with the U.S. men setting the meet's only world record, in the 400 meter medley relay. It was a fitting finale. Said Aaron Peirsol, who swam the first leg, "It was a great end to an excellent meet."

2001-2002 Major Competitions

Men

U.S Open
East Meadow, NY November 29–December, 1 2001

50 free	Julio Santos, Phoenix Swim Club	22.42
100 free	Romain Barnier, Auburn A	48.70
200 free	Romain Barnier, Auburn A	1:45.47
400 free	Robert Margalis	3:48.92
1,500 free	C. Thompson, Wolverine	14:55.12
100 back	Hong Zhe Sun, Iolani Swim Club	54.73
200 back	Hong Zhe Sun, Iolani Swim Club	1:57.74
100 breast	Glenn Moses, Curl-Burke	1:00.26
200 breast	Glenn Moses, Curl-Burke	2:10.26
100 fly	Thomas Malchow, Wolverine	53.68
200 fly	Thomas Malchow, Wolverine	1:53.48
200 IM	Michael Phelps, N Baltimore	1:59.07
400 IM	Michael Phelps, N Baltimore	4:11.95
400 m relay	Indiana University A	3:43.60
400 f relay	Penn State University A	3:22.70
800 f relay	Canada A	7:26.42

U.S. NATIONAL CHAMPIONSHIPS (SPRING)
Minneapolis, MN, March 19–23, 2002

50 free	Aaron Ciarla, Auburn	22.76
100 free	Jason Lezak, Novaquatics	48.89
200 free	Joshua Davis, Circle C	1:49.21
400 free	Scott Goldblatt, BAC	3:52.59
800 free	Francis Crippen, GAAC	7:57.04
1,500 free	Christopher Thompson, CW	15:24.97
100 back	Aaron Peirsol, Novaquatics	54.47
200 back	Aaron Peirsol, Novaquatics	1:55.15WR
100 breast	Henrique Barbosa, SRVL	1:03.55
200 breast	James Kibbe, ATAC	2:17.43
100 fly	Michael Cavic, Novaquatics	53.30
200 fly	Thomas Malchow, CW	1:55.13
200 IM	Nathaniel Dusing, Circle C	2:01.73
400 IM	Eric Shanteau, SA	4:21.60
400 m relay	Novaquatics A	3:53.15
400 f relay	Novaquatics A	3:31.17
800 f relay	Novaquatics A	7:44.42

FINA SHORT COURSE WORLD CHAMPIONSHIPS
Moscow, Russia, April 3–7, 2002

50 free	Jose Martin, Argentina	21.26
100 free	Ashley Callus, Australia	46.99
200 free	Klete Keller, United States	1:44.36
400 free	Grant Hackett, Australia	3:38.29
1,500 free	Grant Hackett, Australia	14:33.94
50 back	Matt Welsh, Australia	23.66
100 back	Matt Welsh, Australia	51.26
200 back	Aaron Peirsol, U.S.	1:51.17 WR
50 breast	Oleg Lisogor, Ukraine	26.42
100 breast	Oleg Lisogor, Ukraine	58.33
200 breast	Jim Piper, Australia	2:07.16
50 fly	Geoff Huegill, Australia	22.89
100 fly	Geoff Huegill, Australia	50.95
200 fly	James Hickman, Great Britain	1:54.16
100 IM	Peter Mankov, Slovenia	52.90
200 IM	Jan Sievinen, Finland	1:55.45
400 IM	Thomas Wilkens, United States	4:04.82*
400 m relay	United States	3:29.00 WR
400 f relay	United States	3:10.64*
800 f relay	Australia	7:00.36

FINA DIVING WORLD CUP
Sevilla, Spain, June 25–29, 2002

1-m spgbd	Xu Xiang, China	421.80
3-m spgbd	Dmitry Sautin, Russia	519.06
Platform	Tian Lang, China	558.84
3-m sync	Wang/Wang, China	363.24
10-m sync	Liang/Tong, China	353.21

U.S. NATIONAL CHAMPIONSHIPS (SUMMER)
Fort Lauderdale, FL, August 12–17, 2002

50 free	Jason Lezak, Novaquatics	22.34
100 free	Jason Lezak, Novaquatics	49.19
200 free	Nathaniel Dusing, Circle C	1:47.08
400 free	Klete Keller, Club Wolverine	3:48.60
800 free	John Cole, Gator SC	8:01.39
1,500 free	Erik Vendt, Trojan SC	15:03.49
100 back	Aaron Peirsol, Novaquatics	54.01
200 back	Aaron Peirsol, Novaquatics	1:56.21
100 breast	Glenn Moses, Curl-Burke	1:01.11
200 breast	Brendan Hansen, Circle C	2:13.05
100 fly	Michael Phelps, N Baltimore	51.88*
200 fly	Michael Phelps, N Baltimore	1:54.86
200 IM	Michael Phelps, N Baltimore	1:58.68*
400 IM	Michael Phelps, N Baltimore	4:11.09 WR
400 m relay	Circle C Swimming, TX A	3:38.37
400 f relay	Novaquatics, CA A	3:20.68
800 f relay	Minnesota, MN A	7:34.36

PAN PACIFIC CHAMPIONSHIPS
Yokohama, Japan, August 24–29, 2002

50 free	Jason Lezak, United States	22.22
100 free	Ian Thorpe, Australia	48.84
200 free	Ian Thorpe, Australia	1:44.75
400 free	Ian Thorpe, Australia	3:45.28
800 free	Grant Hackett, Australia	7:44.78
1500 free	Grant Hackett, Australia	14:41.64
100 back	Aaron Peirsol, United States	54.22
200 back	Aaron Peirsol, United States	1:56.88
100 breast	Kosuke Kitajima, Japan	1:00.36
200 breast	Brendan Hansen, United States	2:11.80
100 fly	Ian Crocker, United States	52.45
200 fly	Tom Malchow, United States	1:55.21
200 IM	Michael Phelps, United States	1:59.70
400 IM	Michael Phelps, United States	4:12.48
400 m relay	United States	3:33.48WR
400 f relay	Australia	3:15.15
800 f relay	Australia	7:09.00

*American record. WR World record.

Women

U.S. OPEN
East Meadow, NY November 29-December 1, 2001

50 free	Christina Swindle, Miami	25.08
100 free	Christina Swindle, Miami	54.70
200 free	Lindsay Benko, Trojan SC	1:59.28
400 free	Janelle Atkinson, Florida	4:05.39
800 free	Janelle Atkinson, Florida	8:20.13
100 back	Louise Ornstedt, Odense	1:00.82
200 back	Alenka Kejzar, SMU	2:09.01
100 breast	Megan Quann	1:07.40
200 breast	Masami Tanaka, Aqauzot SC	2:23.62
100 fly	Mary Descenza, Bullets	59.21
200 fly	Mary Descenza, Bullets	2:07.94
200 IM	Alenka Kejzar, SMU	2:13.10
400 IM	Alenka Kejzar, SMU	4:38.97
400 m relay	SMU A	4:06.27
400 f relay	Canada A	3:44.93
800 f relay	SMU A	8:06.04

U.S. NATIONAL CHAMPIONSHIPS (SPRING)
Minneapolis, MN March 19-23, 2002

50 free	Christina Swindle, MS	25.29
100 free	Gabrielle Rose, Novaquatics	55.82
200 free	Helene Muller, UN-01	2:00.85
400 free	Diana Munz, Lake Erie Silver	4:10.29
800 free	Diana Munz, Lake Erie Silver	8:33.06
1,500 free	Diana Munz, Lake Erie Silver	16:11.88
100 back	Diana MacManus, Novaquatics	1:01.32
200 back	Diana MacManus, Novaquatics	2:11.80
100 breast	Megan Quann, SST	1:03.55
200 breast	Megan Quann, SST	2:27.42
100 fly	Whitney Myers, MARO	1:00.84
200 fly	Mary Hill, DYNA	2:12.92
200 IM	Gabrielle Rose, Novaquatics	2:15.59
400 IM	Adrienne Binder, SBSC	4:44.65
400 m relay	Circe C Swimming A	4:14.16
400 f relay	Novaquatics B	3:49.76
800 f relay	Lake Erie Silver A	8:23.07

FINA SHORT COURSE WORLD CHAMPIONSHIPS
Moscow, Russia April 3-7, 2002

50 free	Therese Alshammar, Sweden	24.16
100 free	Therese Alshammar, Sweden	52.89
200 free	Lindse Benko, U.S.	1:54.04 WR
400 free	Yana Klochkova, Ukraine	4:01.26
800 free	Hua Chen, China	8:16.34
50 back	Jennifer Carroll, Canada	27.38
100 back	Haley Cope, United States	59.07
200 back	Lindsey Benko, United States	2.04.97
50 breast	Emma Igelstrom, Sweden	29.96 WR
100 breast	Emma Igelstrom, Sweden	1:05.38 WR
200 breast	Hui Qi, China	2:20.91
50 fly	A. Kammerling, Sweden	25.55
100 fly	Martina Moravcova, Slovakia	57:04
200 fly	Petria Thomas, Australia	2:05.76
100 IM	Martina Moravcova, Slovakia	59.91
200 IM	Yana Klochkova, Ukraine	2:08.82
400 IM	Yana Klochkova, Ukraine	4:30.63
400 m relay	Sweden	3:55.78 WR
400 f relay	Sweden	3:35.09
800 f relay	China	7:46.30 WR

*American record. WR World record.

FINA DIVING WORLD CUP
Sevilla, Spain June 25-29, 2002

1-m spgbd	Jingling Guo, China	312.84
3-m spgbd	Jingling Guo, China	355.08
Platform	Lishi Lao, China	377.88
3-m sync	Ilyina/Pakhalina, Russia	329.31
10-m sync	Lao/Li, China	317.16

U.S. NATIONAL CHAMPIONSHIPS (SUMMER)
Fort Lauderdale, FL August 12-17, 2002

50 free	Haley Cope, California Aquatics	25.48
100 free	Natalie Coughlin, Cal Aquatics	54.66
200 free	Natalie Coughlin, Cal Aquatics	1:58.20
400 free	Diana Munz, Lake Erie Silver	4:08.43
800 free	Diana Munz, Lake Erie Silver	8:29.02
1,500 free	Lauren Costello, Tigershark	16:29.16
100 back	Natalie Coughlin, Cal Aquatics	59.58
200 back	Natalie Coughlin, Cal Aquatics	2:08.53*
100 breast	Kristy Kowal, Athens Bulldog	1:08.53
200 breast	Amanda Beard, Tucson Ford	2:25.35
100 fly	Natalie Coughlin, Cal Aquatics	58.49WR
200 fly	Mary Descenza, Bullets	2:09.89
200 IM	Maggie Bowen, Auburn	2:14.07
400 IM	Maggie Bowen, Auburn	4:43.23
400 m relay	California Aquatics, PC A	4:07.78
400 f relay	Novaquatics, CA B	3:46.55
800 f relay	Aburn Aquatics, SE A	8:12.22

PAN PACIFIC CHAMPIONSHIPS
Yokohama, Japan, August 24-29, 2002

50 free	Jenny Thompson, United States	25.13
100 free	Natalie Coughlin, United States	53.99
200 free	Lindsay Benko, United States	1:58.74
400 free	Diana Munz, United States	4:09.50
800 free	Diana Munz, United States	8:30.45
1500 free	Diana Munz, United States	16:07.86
100 back	Natalie Coughlin, United States	59.72
200 back	Margaret Hoelzer, United States	2:11.0
100 breast	Amanda Beard, United States	1:08.22
200 breast	Amanda Beard, United States	2:26.31
100 fly	Natalie Coughlin, United States	57.88
200 fly	Petria Thomas, Australia	2:08.31
200 IM	Tomoko Hagiwara, Japan	2:13.42
400 IM	Jennifer Reilly, Australia	4:40.84
400 m relay	Australia	4:00.50
400 f relay	Australia	3:39.78
800 f relay	United States	7:56.96

World and American Records Set in 2002

Men

Event	Mark	Record Holder	Date	Site
200 back	1:55.15	Aaron Peirsol (W, A)	3-20-02	Minneapolis
400 free	3:40.08	Ian Thorpe, Australia (W)	7-30-02	Manchester, England
50 breast	27.18	Oleg Lisogor, Ukraine (W)	8-1-02	Berlin
200 IM	1:58.68	Michael Phelps, United States (A)	8-12-02	Fort Lauderdale
400 IM	4:11.09	Michael Phelps (W, A)	8-15-02	Fort Lauderdale
100 fly	51.88	Michael Phelps, United States (A)	8-16-02	Fort Lauderdale
800 free	7:52.05	Larsen Jensen, United States (A)	8-25-02	Yokohama, Japan
800 free relay	7:11.81	United States (A) (N. Dusing, K. Keller, M. Phelps, C. Carvin)	8-27-02	Yokohama, Japan
400 medley relay	3:33.48	United States (W, A) (Aaron Peirsol, Brendan Hansen, Michael Phelps, Jason Lezak)	8-29-02	Yokohama, Japan

Women

Event	Mark	Record Holder	Date	Site
400 free relay	3:36.00	Germany (W) (F. van Almsick, S. Vokler, P. Dallman, K. Meissner)	7-29-02	Berlin
50 breast	30.57	Zoe Baker, Great Britain (W)	7-30-02	Manchester, England
50 fly	25.57	A.K. Kammerling, Sweden (W)	7-30-02	Berlin
200 free	1:56.64	F. van Almsick, Germany (W)	8-3-02	Berlin
200 fly	2:05.78	Otylia Jedrejczak, Poland (W)	8-4-02	Berlin
100 back	59.58	Natalie Coughlin (W, A)	8-13-02	Fort Lauderdale
200 back	2:08.53	Natalie Coughlin, United States (A)	8-16-02	Fort Lauderdale
100 free	53.99	Natalie Coughlin, United States (A)	8-29-02	Yokohama, Japan

W= world record. A= American record.

du Toit Undeterred

Australian swimmer Ian Thorpe won six gold medals at the XVII Commonwealth Games in Manchester, England, in August 2002, but the honor for outstanding swimmer went to South Africa's Natalie du Toit, 18, who lost her left leg below the knee in a motor scooter accident in early 2000. Swimming in both the disabled and main programs, du Toit set world records in the 50- and 100-meter disabled freestyle and finished eighth in the standard 800 free.

World and American Records

MEN

Freestyle

Event	Time	Record Holder	Date	Site
50 meters	21.64	Alexander Popov, Russia (W)	6-16-00	Moscow
	21.76	Gary Hall Jr. (A)	8-15-00	Indianapolis
100 meters	47.84	Pieter van den Hoogenband (W) Netherlands	9-19-00	Sydney
	48.33	Anthony Ervin (A)	7-27-01	Fukuoka, Japan
200 meters	1:44.06	Ian Thorpe, Australia (W)	7-25-01	Fukuoka, Japan
	1:46.73	Josh Davis (A)	9-18-00	Sydney
400 meters	3:40.08	Ian Thorpe, Australia (W)	7-30-02	Manchester
	3:47.00	Klete Keller (A)	9-16-00	Sydney
800 meters	7:39.16	Ian Thorpe, Australia (W)	7-24-01	Fukuoka, Japan
	7:52.05	Larsen Jensen (A)	8-25-02	Yokohama, Japan
1,500 meters	14:34.56	Grant Hackett, Australia (W)	7-30-01	Fukuoka, Japan
	14.56.81	Chris Thompson (A)	9-23-00	Sydney

Backstroke

Event	Time	Record Holder	Date	Site
50 meters	24.99	Lenny Krayzelburg (W, A)	8-28-99	Sydney
100 meters	53.60	Lenny Krayzelburg (W, A)	8-24-99	Sydney
200 meters	1:55.15	Aaron Peirsol (W, A)	3-20-02	Minneapolis

Breaststroke

Event	Time	Record Holder	Date	Site
50 meters	27.18	Oleg Lisogor, Ukr (W)	8-1-02	Berlin
	27.39	Ed Moses (A)	3-31-01	Austin, TX
100 meters	59.94	Roman Sloudnov, Russia (W)	7-24-01	Fukuoka, Japan
	1:00.29	Ed Moses (A)	3-28-01	Austin
200 meters	2:10.16	Mike Barrowman (W, A)	7-29-92	Barcelona

Butterfly

Event	Time	Record Holder	Date	Site
50 meters	23.44	Geoff Huegill, Australia (W)	7-26-01	Fukuoka, Japan
	23.85	Ian Crocker (A)	7-26-01	Fukuoka, Japan
		Bryan Jones (A)	3-29-01	Austin, TX
100 meters	51.81	Michael Klim, Australia (W)	12-12-99	Canberra, Australia
	51.88	Michael Phelps (A)	8-16-02	Fort Lauderdale, FL
200 meters	1:54.58	Michael Phelps (W, A)	7-24-01	Fukuoka, Japan

Individual Medley

Event	Time	Record Holder	Date	Site
200 meters	1:58.16	Jani Sievinen, Finland (W)	9-11-94	Rome
	1:58.68	Michael Phelps (A)	8-12-02	Fort Lauderdale, FL
400 meters	4:11.09	Michael Phelps (W, A)	8-15-02	Fort Lauderdale, FL

Relays

Event	Time	Record Holder	Date	Site
400-meter medley	3:33.48	United States (W,A) (Aaron Peirsol, Brendan Hansen, Michael Phelps, Jason Lezak)	8-29-02	Yokohama, Japan
400-meter freestyle	3:13.67	Australia (W) (Ian Thorpe, Michael Klim, Ashley Callus, Chris Fydler)	9-16-00	Sydney
	3:13.86	United States (A) (Anthony Ervin, Neil Walker, Jason Lezak, Gary Hall Jr	9-16-00	Sydney
800-meter freestyle	7:04.66	Australia (W) (Ian Thorpe, Michael Klim, Bill Kirby, Grant Hackett)	7-27-01	Fukuoka, Japan
	7:12.51	United States (A) (Troy Dalbey, Matt Cetlinski, Doug Gjertsen, Matt Biondi)	9-21-88	Seoul

Note: Records through Sept. 1, 2002.

WOMEN

Freestyle

Event	Time	Record Holder	Date	Site
50 meters	24.13	Inge de Bruijn, Netherlands (W)	9-22-00	Sydney
	24.63	Dana Torres (A)	9-23-00	Sydney
100 meters	53.77	Inge de Bruijn, Netherlands (W)	9-20-00	Sydney
	53.99	Natalie Coughlin (A)	8-29-02	Yokohama, Japan
200 meters	1:56.64	Franziska van Almsick, Germany (W)	8-3-02	Berlin
	1:57.90	Nicole Haislett (A)	7-27-92	Barcelona
400 meters	4:03.85	Janet Evans (W, A)	9-22-88	Seoul
800 meters	8:16.22	Janet Evans (W, A)	8-20-89	Tokyo
1,500 meters	15:52.10	Janet Evans (W, A)	3-26-88	Orlando, FL

Backstroke

Event	Time	Record Holder	Date	Site
50 meters	28.25	Sandra Volker, Germany (W)	6-17-00	Berlin
	28.49	Natalie Coughlin (A)	7-23-01	Fukuoka, Japan
100 meters	59.58	Natalie Coughlin (W, A)	8-13-02	Fort Lauderdale, FL
200 meters	2:06.62	Krisztina Egerszegi, Hungary (W)	8-25-91	Athens, Greece
	2:08.53	Natalie Coughlin (A)	8-16-02	Fort Lauderdale, FL

Breaststroke

Event	Time	Record Holder	Date	Site
50 meters	30.57	Zoe Baker, Great Britain (W)	7-30-02	Berlin
	31.34	Megan Quann (A)	8-11-00	Indianapolis
100 meters	1:06.52	Penelope Heyns, Russia (W)	8-23-99	Sydney
	1:07.05	Megan Quann (A)	9-18-00	Sydney
200 meters	2:22.99	Hui Qi, China (W)	4-13-01	Hangzhou, China
	2:24.56	Kristy Kowal (A)	9-21-00	Sydney

Butterfly

Event	Time	Record Holder	Date	Site
50 meters	25.57	Anna-Karin Kammerling, Sweden (W)	7-30-02	Berlin
	26.50	Dana Torres (A)	8-9-00	Indianapolis
100 meters	56.61	Inge de Bruijn, Netherlands (W)	9-17-00	Sydney
	57.58	Dara Torres (A)	8-9-00	Indianapolis
200 meters	2:05.78	Otylia Jedrejczak, Poland (W)	8-4-02	Berlin
	2:05.88	Misty Hyman (A)	9-20-00	Sydney

Individual Medley

Event	Time	Record Holder	Date	Site
200 meters	2:09.72	Yanyan Wu, China (W)	10-17-97	Shanghai
	2:11.91	Summer Sanders (A)	7-30-92	Barcelona
400 meters	4:33.59	Yana Klochkova, Ukraine (W)	9-16-00	Sydney
	4:37.58	Summer Sanders (A)	7-26-92	Barcelona

Relays

Event	Time	Record Holder	Date	Site
400-meter medley	3:58.30	United States (W, A) (BJ Bedford, Megan Quann, Jenny Thompson Dana Torres)	9-23-00	Sydney
400-meter freestyle	3:36.00	Germany (W) (K. Meissner, P. Dallman, S. Volker, F. van Almsick)	7-29-02	Berlin
	3:36.61	United States (A) (Jenny Thompson, Courtney Shealy, Dara Torres, Amy Van Dyken)	9-16-00	Sydney
800-meter freestyle	7:55.47	E Germany (W) (Manuela Stellmach, Astrid Strauss, Anke Mohring, Heike Friedrich)	8-18-87	Strasbourg, France
	7:56.53	United States (A) (Natalie Coughlin, C. Teuscher, Julie Hardt, D. Munz)	7-25-01	Fukuoka, Japan

MEN

50-meter Freestyle

1986	Tom Jager, United States	22.49‡
1991	Tom Jager, United States	22.16‡
1994	Alexander Popov, Russia	22.17
1998	Bill Pilczuk, United States	22.29
2001	Anthony Ervin, United States	22.09

100-meter Freestyle

1973	Jim Montgomery, United States	51.70
1975	Andy Coan, United States	51.25
1978	David McCagg, United States	50.24
1982	Jorg Woithe, E Germany	50.18
1986	Matt Biondi, United States	48.94
1991	Matt Biondi, United States	49.18
1994	Alexander Popov, Russia	49.12
1998	Alexander Popov, Russia	48.93‡
2001	Anthony Ervin, United States	48.33‡

200-meter Freestyle

1973	Jim Montgomery, United States	1:53.02
1975	Tim Shaw, United States	1:52.04‡
1978	Billy Forrester, United States	1:51.02‡
1982	Michael Gross, W Germany	1:49.84
1986	Michael Gross, W Germany	1:47.92
1991	Giorgio Lamberti, Italy	1:47.27‡
1994	Antti Kasvio, Finland	1:47.32
1998	Michael Klim, Australia	1:47.41
2001	Ian Thorpe, Australia	1:44.06*

400-meter Freestyle

1973	Rick DeMont, United States	3:58.18‡
1975	Tim Shaw, United States	3:54.88‡
1978	Vladimir Salnikov, USSR	3:51.94‡
1982	Vladimir Salnikov, USSR	3:51.30‡
1986	Rainer Henkel, W Germany	3:50.05
1991	Joerg Hoffman, Germany	3:48.04‡
1994	Kieran Perkins, Australia	3:43.80*
1998	Ian Thorpe, Australia	3:46.29
2001	Ian Thorpe, Australia	3:40.17*

1,500-meter Freestyle

1973	Stephen Holland, Australia	15:31.85
1975	Tim Shaw, United States	15:28.92‡
1978	Vladimir Salnikov, USSR	15:03.99‡
1982	Vladimir Salnikov, USSR	15:01.77‡
1986	Rainer Henkel, W Germany	15:05.31
1991	Joerg Hoffman, Germany	14:50.36*
1994	Kieran Perkins, Australia	14:50.52
1998	Grant Hackett, Australia	14:51.70
2001	Grant Hackett, Australia	14:34.56*

100-meter Backstroke

1973	Roland Matthes, E Germany	57.47
1975	Roland Matthes, E Germany	58.15
1978	Bob Jackson, United States	56.36‡
1982	Dirk Richter, E Germany	55.95
1986	Igor Polianski, USSR	55.58‡
1991	Jeff Rouse, United States	55.23‡
1994	Martin Lopez Zubero, Spain	55.17‡
1998	Lenny Krayzelburg, United States	55.00‡
2001	Matt Welsh, Australia	54.31‡

200-meter Backstroke

1973	Roland Matthes, E Germany	2:01.87‡
1975	Zoltan Varraszto, Hungary	2:05.05
1978	Jesse Vassallo, United States	2:02.16
1982	Rick Carey, United States	2:00.82‡
1986	Igor Polianski, USSR	1:58.78‡
1991	Martin Zubero, Spain	1:59.52
1994	Vladimir Selkov, Russia	1:57.42‡

200-meter Backstroke (Cont.)

1998	Lenny Krayzelburg, United States	1:58.84
2001	Aaron Peirsol, United States	1:57.13‡

100-meter Breaststroke

1973	John Hencken, United States	1:04.02‡
1975	David Wilkie, Great Britain	1:04.26‡
1978	Walter Kusch, W Germany	1:03.56‡
1982	Steve Lundquist, United States	1:02.75‡
1986	Victor Davis, Canada	1:02.71
1991	Norbert Rozsa, Hungary	1:01.45*
1994	Norbert Rozsa, Hungary	1:01.24‡
1998	Frederik Deburghgraeve, Belgium	1:01.34
2001	Roman Sloudnov, Russia	1:00.16

200-meter Breaststroke

1973	David Wilkie, Great Britain	2:19.28‡
1975	David Wilkie, Great Britain	2:18.23‡
1978	Nick Nevid, United States	2:18.37
1982	Victor Davis, Canada	2:14.77*
1986	Jozsef Szabo, Hungary	2:14.27‡
1991	Mike Barrowman, United States	2:11.23*
1994	Norbert Rozsa, Hungary	2:12.81
1998	Kurt Grote, United States	2:13.40
2001	Brendan Hansen, United States	2:10.69‡

100-meter Butterfly

1973	Bruce Robertson, Canada	55.69
1975	Greg Jagenburg, United States	55.63
1978	Joe Bottom, United States	54.30
1982	Matt Gribble, United States	53.88‡
1986	Pablo Morales, United States	53.54‡
1991	Anthony Nesty, Suriname	53.29‡
1994	Rafal Szukala, Poland	53.51
1998	Michael Klim, Australia	52.25‡
2001	Lars Frolander, Sweden	52.10‡

200-meter Butterfly

1973	Robin Backhaus, United States	2:03.32
1975	Bill Forrester, United States	2:01.95‡
1978	Mike Bruner, United States	1:59.38‡
1982	Michael Gross, E Germany	1:58.85‡
1986	Michael Gross, E Germany	1:56.53‡
1991	Melvin Stewart, United States	1:55.69*
1994	Denis Pankratov, Russia	1:56.54
1998	Denys Sylantyev, Ukraine	1:56.61
2001	Michael Phelps, United States	1:54.58*

200-meter Individual Medley

1973	Gunnar Larsson, Sweden	2:08.36
1975	Andras Hargitay, Hungary	2:07.72
1978	Graham Smith, Canada	2:03.65*
1982	Aleksandr Sidorenko, USSR	2:03.30‡
1986	Tamás Darnyi, Hungary	2:01.57‡
1991	Tamás Darnyi, Hungary	1:59.36*
1994	Jani Sievin, Finland	1:58.16*
1998	Marcel Wouda, Netherlands	2:01.18
2001	Massimiliano Rosolino, Italy	1:59.71

400-meter Individual Medley

1975	Andras Hargitay, Hungary	4:32.57
1978	Jesse Vassallo, United States	4:20.05*
1982	Ricardo Prado, Brazil	4:19.78*
1986	Tamás Darnyi, Hungary	4:18.98‡
1991	Tamás Darnyi, Hungary	4:12.36*
1994	Tom Dolan, United States	4:12.30*
1998	Tom Dolan, United States	4:14.95
2001	Alessio Boggiatto, Italy	4:13.15

* World record. ‡Meet record.

MEN (Cont.)

400-meter Medley Relay

1973.....United States (Mike Stamm, John Hencken, Joe Bottom, Jim Montgomery)	3:49.49
1975.....United States (John Murphy, Rick Colella, Greg Jagenburg, Andy Coan)	3:49.00
1978.....United States (Robert Jackson, Nick Nevid, Joe Bottom, David McCagg)	3:44.63
1982.....United States (Rick Carey, Steve Lundquist, Matt Gribble, Rowdy Gaines)	3:40.84*
1986.....United States (Dan Veatch, David Lundberg, Pablo Morales, Matt Biondi)	3:41.25
1991.....United States (Jeff Rouse, Eric Wunderlich, Mark Henderson Matt Biondi)	3:39.66‡
1994.....United States (Jeff Rouse, Eric Wunderlich, Mark Henderson, Gary Hall)	3:37.74‡
1998.....Australia (Matt Welsh, Phil Rogers, Robin Backhaus, Rick Klatt, Jim Montgomery)	3:37.98
2001.....Australia (Matt Welsh, Ian Thorpe, Geoff Huegill, Regan Harrison)	3:35.35

400-meter Freestyle Relay

1973.....United States (Mel Nash, Joe Bottom, Jim Montgomery, John Murphy)	3:27.18
1975.....United States (Bruce Furniss, Jim Montgomery, Andy Coan, John Murphy)	3:24.85
1978.....United States (Jack Babashoff, Rowdy Gaines, Jim Montgomery, David McCagg)	3:19.74
1982.....United States (Chris Cavanaugh, Robin Leamy, David McCagg, Rowdy Gaines)	3:19.26*
1986.....United States (Tom Jager, Mike Heath, Paul Wallace, Matt Biondi)	3:19.89
1991.....United States (Tom Jager, Brent Lang, Doug Gjertsen, Matt Biondi)	3:17.15‡
1994.....United States (Jon Olsen, Josh Davis, Ugur Taner, Gary Hall Jr.)	3:16.90‡
1998.....United States (Bryan Jones, Jon Olsen, Bradley Schumacher, Gary Hall Jr.)	3:16.69†
2001.....Australia (Michael Klim, Ian Thorpe, Todd Pearson, Ashley Callus)	3:14.10†

800-meter Freestyle Relay

1973.....United States (Kurt Krumpholz, Robin Backhaus, Rick Klatt, Jim Montgomery)	7:33.22*
1975.....W Germany (Klaus Steinbach, Werner Lampe, Hans Joachim Geisler, Peter Nocke)	7:39.44
1978.....United States (Bruce Furniss, Billy Forrester, Bobby Hackett, Rowdy Gaines)	7:20.82
1982.....United States (Rich Saeger, Jeff Float, Kyle Miller, Rowdy Gaines)	7:21.09
1986.....E Germany (Lars Hinneburg, Thomas Flemming, Dirk Richter, Sven Lodziewski)	7:15.91‡
1991.....Germany (Peter Sitt, Steffan Zesner, Stefan Pfeiffer, Michael Gross)	7:13.50‡
1994.....Sweden (Christer Waller, Tommy Werner, Lars Frolander, Anders Holmertz)	7:17.34
1998.....Australia (Daniel Kowalski, Grant Hackett, Ian Thorpe, Anthony Rogis)	7:12.48†
1998.....Australia (Daniel Kowalski, Grant Hackett, Ian Thorpe, Anthony Rogis)	7:12.48†
2001.....Australia (Michael Klim, Ian Thorpe, William Kirby, Grant Hackett)	7:04.66*

WOMEN

50-meter Freestyle

1986....Tamara Costache, Romania	25.28*
1991....Zhuang Yong, China	25.47
1994....Le Jingyi, China	24.51*
1998....Amy Van Dyken, United States	25.15
2001....Inge de Bruijn, Netherlands	24.47

100-meter Freestyle

1973....Kornelia Ender, E Germany	57.54
1975....Kornelia Ender, E Germany	56.50
1978....Barbara Krause, E Germany	55.68‡
1982....Birgit Meineke, E Germany	55.79
1986....Kristin Otto, E Germany	55.05‡
1991....Nicole Haislett, United States	55.17
1994....Le Jingyi, China	54.01*
1998....Jenny Thompson, United States	54.95
2001:...Inge de Bruijn, Netherlands	54.18

200-meter Freestyle

1973.....Keena Rothhammer, United States	2:04.99
1975....Shirley Babashoff, United States	2:02.50
1978....Cynthia Woodhead, United States	1:58.53*
1982....Annemarie Verstappen, Netherlands	1:59.53‡
1986....Heike Friedrich, E Germany	1:58.26‡
1991....Hayley Lewis, Australia	2:00.48
1994....Franziska Van Almsick, Germany	1:56.78*
1998....Claudia Poll, Costa Rica	1:58.90
2001....Giaan Rooney, Australia	1:58.57

400-meter Freestyle

1973.....Heather Greenwood, United States	4:20.28
1975....Shirley Babashoff, United States	4:22.70
1978....Tracey Wickham, Australia	4:06.28*
1982....Carmela Schmidt, E Germany	4:08.98
1986....Heike Friedrich, E Germany	4:07.45
1991....Janet Evans, United States	4:08.63
1994....Yang Aihua, China	4:09.64
1998....Chen Yan, China	4:06.72
2001....Yana Klochkova, Ukraine	4:07.30

* World record; ‡ Meet record.

WOMEN (Cont.)

800-meter Freestyle

1973....Novella Calligaris, Italy — 8:52.97
1975....Jenny Turrall, Australia — 8:44.75‡
1978....Tracey Wickham, Australia — 8:24.94‡
1982....Kim Linehan, United States — 8:27.48
1986....Astrid Strauss, E Germany — 8:28.24
1991....Janet Evans, United States — 8:24.05‡
1994....Janet Evans, United States — 8:29.85
1998....Brooke Bennett, United States — 8.28.71
2001....Hannah Stockbauer, Germany — 8:24.66

100-meter Backstroke

1973....Ulrike Richter, E Germany — 1:05.42
1975....Ulrike Richter, E Germany — 1:03.30‡
1978....Linda Jezek, United States — 1:02.55‡
1982....Kristin Otto, E Germany — 1:01.30‡
1986....Betsy Mitchell, United States — 1:01.74
1991....Krisztina Egerszegi, Hungary — 1:01.78
1994....He Cihong, China — 1:00.57
1998....Lea Maurer, United States — 1:01.16
2001....Natalie Coughlin, United States — 1:00.37

200-meter Backstroke

1973....Melissa Belote, United States — 2:20.52
1975....Birgit Treiber, E Germany — 2:15.46*
1978....Linda Jezek, United States — 2:11.93*
1982....Cornelia Sirch, E Germany — 2:09.91*
1986....Cornelia Sirch, E Germany — 2:11.37
1991....Krisztina Egerszegi, Hungary — 2:09.15‡
1994....He Cihong, China — 2:07.40
1998....Roxanna Maracineanu, France — 2:11.26
2001....Diana Mocanu, Romania — 2.09.94

100-meter Breaststroke

1973....Renate Vogel, E Germany — 1:13.74
1975....Hannalore Anke, E Germany — 1:12.72
1978....Julia Bogdanova, USSR — 1:10.31*
1982....Ute Geweniger, E Germany — 1:09.14‡
1986....Sylvia Gerasch, E Germany — 1:08.11*
1991....Linley Frame, Australia — 1:08.81
1994....Samantha Riley, Australia — 1:07.96*
1998....Kristy Kowal, United States — 1:08.42
2001....Xuejuan Luo, China — 1:07.18‡

200-meter Breaststroke

1973....Renate Vogel, E Germany — 2:40.01
1975....Hannalore Anke, E Germany — 2:37.25‡
1978....Lina Kachushite, USSR — 2:31.42*
1982....Svetlana Varganova, USSR — 2:28.82‡
1986....Silke Hoerner, E Germany — 2:27.40*
1991....Elena Volkova, USSR — 2:29.53
1994....Samantha Riley, Australia — 2:26.87‡
1998....Agnes Kovacs, Hungary — 2:25.45†
2001....Agnes Kovacs, Hungary — 2:24.90

100-meter Butterfly

1973....Kornelia Ender, E Germany — 1:02.53
1975....Kornelia Ender, E Germany — 1:01.24*
1978....Joan Pennington, United States — 1:00.20‡
1982....Mary T. Meagher, United States — 59.41‡
1986....Kornelia Gressler, E Germany — 59.51
1991....Qian Hong, China — 59.68
1994....Liu Limin, China — 58.98‡
1998....Jenny Thompson, United States — 58.46†
2001....Petria Thomas, Australia — 58:27

200-meter Butterfly

1973....Rosemarie Kother, E Germany — 2:13.76‡
1975....Rosemarie Kother, E Germany — 2:15.92
1978....Tracy Caulkins, United States — 2:09.87*
1982....Ines Geissler, E Germany — 2:08.66‡
1986....Mary T. Meagher, United States — 2:08.41‡
1991....Summer Sanders, United States — 2:09.24
1994....Liu Limin, China — 2:07.25‡
1998....Susie O'Neill, Australia — 2:07.93‡
2001....Petria Thomas, Australia — 2:06.73‡

200-meter Individual Medley

1973....Andrea Huebner, E Germany — 2:20.51
1975....Kathy Heddy, United States — 2:19.80
1978....Tracy Caulkins, United States — 2:14.07*
1982....Petra Schneider, E Germany — 2:11.79
1986....Kristin Otto, E Germany — 2:15.56
1991....Li Lin, China — 2:13.40
1994....Lu Bin, China — 2:12.34‡
1998....Wu Yanyan, China — 2:10.88
2001....Martha Bowen, United States — 2:11.93

400-meter Individual Medley

1973....Gudrun Wegner, E Germany — 4:57.71
1975....Ulrike Tauber, E Germany — 4:52.76‡
1978....Tracy Caulkins, United States — 4:40.83*
1982....Petra Schneider, E Germany — 4:36.10*
1986....Kathleen Nord, E Germany — 4:43.75
1991....Lin Li, China — 4:41.45
1994....Dai Guohong, China — 4:39.14
1998....Chen Yan, China — 4:36.66
2001....Yana Klochkova, Ukraine — 4:36.98

400-meter Medley Relay

1973....E Germany (Ulrike Richter, Renate Vogel, Rosemarie Kother, Kornelia Ender) — 4:16.84
1975....E Germany (Ulrike Richter, Hannelore Anke, Rosemarie Kother, Kornelia Ender) — 4:14.74
1978....United States (Linda Jezek, Tracy Caulkins, Joan Pennington, Cynthia Woodhead) — 4:08.21‡
1982....E Germany (Kristin Otto, Ute Gewinger, Ines Geissler, Birgit Meineke) — 4:05.8*
1986....E Germany (Kathrin Zimmermann, Sylvia Gerasch, Kornelia Gressler, Kristin Otto) — 4:04.82
1991....United States (Janie Wagstaff, Tracey McFarlane, Crissy Ahmann-Leighton, Nicole Haislett) — 4:06.51
1994....China (He Cihong, Dai Guohong, Liu Limin, Lu Bin) — 4:01.67*
1998....United States (Kristy Kowal, Lea Maurer, Jenny Thompson, Amy Van Dyken) — 4:01.93
2001....Australia (Dyana Calub, Sarah Ryan, Petria Thomas, Leisel Jones) — 4:07.30

400-meter Freestyle Relay

1973....E Germany (Kornelia Ender, Andrea Eife, Andrea Huebner, Sylvia Eichner) — 3:52.45
1975....E Germany (Kornelia Ender, Barbara Krause, Claudia Hempel, Ute Bruckner) — 3:49.37

WOMEN (Cont.)

400-meter Freestyle Relay (Cont.)

1978....United States (Tracy Caulkins, 3:43.43*
Stephanie Elkins, Joan Pennington,
Cynthia Woodhead)
1982....E Germany (Birgit Meineke, 3:43.97
Susanne Link, Kristin Otto,
Caren Metschuk)
1986....E Germany (Kristin Otto, 3:40.57*
Manuela Stellmach, Sabine
Schulze, Heike Friedrich)
1991....United States (Nicole Haislett, 3:43.26
Julie Cooper, Whitney Hedgepeth,
Jenny Thompson)
1994....China (Le Jingyi, Ying Shan, 3:37.91*
Le Ying, Lu Bin)
1998.....United States (Catherine Fox, Lindsey 3:42.11
Farella, Melanie Valerio, B.J. Bedford)
2001....Germany (Petra Dallman, 3:39.58
Antje Buschschulter, Katrin Meissner,
Sandra Volkner)

* World record; ‡Meet record.

800-meter Freestyle Relay

1986....E Germany (Manuela 7:59.33*
Stellmach, Astrid Strauss,
Nadja Bergknecht, Heike Friedrich)
1991....Germany (Kerstin Kielgass, 8:02.56
Manuela Stellmach, Dagmar Hase,
Stephanie Ortwig)
1994....China (Le Ying, Yang Alhua, 7:57.96
Zhou Guabin, Lu Bin)
1998....Germany (Silvia Szalai, Antje 8:02.56
Buschschulte, Janina Goetz,
Franziska Van Almsick)
2001....Great Britain (Nicola Jackson, 7:58.69
Janine Belton, Karen Legg,
Karen Pickering)

World Diving Championships

MEN

1-meter Springboard

		Pts
1991	Edwin Jongejans, Netherlands	588.51
1994	Evan Stewart, Zimbabwe	382.14
1998	Yu Zhuocheng, China	417.54
2001	Wang Feng, China	444.03

3-meter Springboard

		Pts
1973	Phil Boggs, United States	618.57
1975	Phil Boggs, United States	597.12
1978	Phil Boggs, United States	913.95
1982	Greg Louganis, United States	752.67
1986	Greg Louganis, United States	750.06
1991	Kent Ferguson, United States	650.25
1994	Wu Zhuocheng, China	655.44
1998	Dmitry Sautin, Russia	746.79
2001	Dmitry Sautin, Russia	725.82

Platform

		Pts
1973	Klaus Dibiasi, Italy	559.53
1975	Klaus Dibiasi, Italy	547.98
1978	Greg Louganis, United States	844.11
1982	Greg Louganis, United States	634.26
1986	Greg Louganis, United States	668.58
1991	Sun Shuwei, China	626.79
1994	Dmitry Sautin, Russia	634.71
1998	Dmitry Sautin, Russia	750.90
2001	Tian Lang, China	688.77

3-meter Synchronized

		Pts
1998	China (Sun Shuwei, Tian Liang)	313.50
2001	China (Bo Peng, Kenan Wang)	342.63

10-meter Synchronized

1998	China (Xu Hao, Yu Zhuocheng)	326.34
2001	China (Jian Tian, Jia Bu)	361.41

WOMEN

1-meter Springboard

		Pts
1991	Gao Min, China	478.26
1994	Chen Lixia, China	279.30
1998	Irina Lashko, Russia	296.07
2001	Blythe Hartley, Canada	300.81

3-meter Springboard

		Pts
1973	Christa Koehler, E Germany	442.17
1975	Irina Kalinina, USSR	489.81
1978	Irina Kalinina, USSR	691.43
1982	Megan Neyer, United States	501.03
1986	Gao Min, China	582.90
1991	Gao Min, China	539.01
1994	Tan Shuping, China	548.49
1998	Yulia Pakhalina, Russia	544.62
2001	Jingling Guo, China	596.67

Platform

		Pts
1973	Ulrike Knape, Sweden	406.77
1975	Janet Ely, United States	403.89
1978	Irina Kalinina, USSR	412.71
1982	Wendy Wyland, United States	438.79
1986	Chen Lin, China	449.67
1991	Fu Mingxia, China	426.51
1994	Fu Mingxia, China	434.04
1998	Olena Zhupyna, Ukraine	550.41
2001	Mian Xu, China	532.65

3-meter Synchronized

		Pts
1998	Russia (Irina Lashko, Yulia Pakhalina)	282.30
2001	China (Minxia Wu, Jingjing Guo)	347.31

10-meter Synchronized

		Pts
1998	Ukraine (O. Zhupyna, S. Serbina)	278.28
2001	China (Qing Duan, Xue Sang)	329.94

Men

50-METER FREESTYLE

1988	Matt Biondi	22.14*
2000	Gary Hall Jr. and Anthony Ervin	21.98

100-METER FREESTLYE

1906	Charles Daniels	1:13.4
1908	Charles Daniels	1:05.6*
1912	Duke Kahanamoku	1:03.4
1920	Duke Kahanamoku	1:00.4
1924	John Weissmuller	59.0‡
1928	John Weissmuller	58.6‡
1948	Wally Ris	57.3‡
1952	Clarke Scholes	57.4
1964	Don Schollander	53.4‡
1972	Mark Spitz	51.22*
1976	Jim Montgomery	49.99*
1984	Rowdy Gaines	49.80‡
1988	Matt Biondi	48.63‡

200-METER FREESTYLE

1904	Charles Daniels	2:44.2
1906–1964	Not held	
1972	Mark Spitz	1:52.78*
1976	Bruce Furniss	1:50.29*

400-METER FREESTYLE

1904	Charles Daniels (440 yds)	6:16.2
1920	Norman Ross	5:26.8
1924	John Weissmuller	5:04.2‡
1932	Buster Crabbe	4:48.4‡
1936	Jack Medica	4:44.5‡
1948	William Smith	4:41.0‡
1964	Don Schollander	4:12.2*
1968	Mike Burton	4:09.0‡
1976	Brian Goodell	3:51.93*
1984	George DiCarlo	3:51.23‡

1,500-METER FREESTYLE

1920	Norman Ross	22:23.2
1948	James McLane	19:18.5
1952	Ford Konno	18:30.3‡
1968	Mike Burton	16:38.9‡
1972	Mike Burton	15:52.58‡
1976	Brian Goodell	15:02.40*
1984	Michael O'Brien	15:05.20

100-METER BACKSTROKE

1912	Harry Hebner	1:21.2
1920	Warren Kealoha	1:15.2
1924	Warren Kealoha	1:13.2‡
1928	George Kojac	1:08.2*
1936	Adolph Kiefer	1:05.9‡
1948	Allen Stack	1:06.4
1952	Yoshi Oyakawa	1:05.4‡
1976	John Naber	55.49*
1984	Rick Carey	55.79
1996	Jeff Rouse	54.10
2000	Lenny Krayzelburg	53.60‡

200-METER BACKSTROKE

1964	Jed Graef	2:10.3*
1976	John Naber	1:59.19*
1984	Rick Carey	2:00.23
1996	Brad Bridgewater	1:58.54
2000	Lenny Krayzelburg	1:56.76‡

100-METER BREASTSTROKE

1968	Donald McKenzie	1:07.7‡
1976	John Hencken	1:03.11*
1984	Steve Lundquist	1:01.65 *
1992	Nelson Diebel	1:01.50‡

200-METER BREASTSTROKE

1924	Robert Skelton	2:56.6
1948	Joseph Verdeur	2:39.3‡
1960	William Mulliken	2:37.4
1972	John Hencken	2:21.55
1992	Mike Barrowman	2:10.16*

100-METER BUTTERFLY

1968	Douglas Russell	55.9‡
1972	Mark Spitz	54.27*
1976	Matt Vogel	54.35
1992	Pablo Morales	53.32

200-METER BUTTERFLY

1956	William Yorzyk	2:19.3‡
1960	Michael Troy	2:12.8*
1968	Carl Robie	2:08.7
1972	Mark Spitz	2:00.70*
1976	Mike Bruner	1:59.23*
1992	Melvin Stewart	1:56.26
2000	Tom Malchow	1:55.35‡

200-METER INDIVIDUAL MEDLEY

1968	Charles Hickcox	2:12.0‡

400-METER INDIVIDUAL MEDLEY

1964	Richard Roth	4:45.4*
1968	Charles Hickcox	4:48.4
1976	Rod Strachan	4:23.68*
1996	Tom Dolan	4.:14.90
2000	Tom Dolan	4:11.76‡

3-METER SPRINGBOARD DIVING

1920	Louis Kuehn	675.4 points
1924	Albert White	696.4
1928	Pete Desjardins	185.04
1932	Michael Galitzen	161.38
1936	Richard Degener	163.57
1948	Bruce Harlan	163.64
1952	David Browning	205.29
1956	Robert Clotworthy	159.56
1960	Gary Tobian	170.00
1964	Kenneth Sitzberger	159.90
1968	Bernard Wrightson	170.15
1976	Philip Boggs	619.05
1984	Greg Louganis	754.41
1988	Greg Louganis	730.80

PLATFORM DIVING

1904	George Sheldon	12.66 points
1920	Clarence Pinkston	100.67
1924	Albert White	97.46
1928	Pete Desjardins	98.74
1932	Harold Smith	124.80
1936	Marshall Wayne	113.58
1948	Sammy Lee	130.05
1952	Sammy Lee	156.28
1960	Robert Webster	165.56
1964	Robert Webster	148.58
1984	Greg Louganis	576.99
1988	Greg Louganis	638.61

* World record. ‡Meet (Olympic) record.

Women

50-METER FREESTYLE

1996.....Amy Van Dyken	24.87

100-METER FREESTLYE

1920.....Ethelda Bleibtrey	1:13.6*
1924....Ethel Lackie	1:12.4
1928....Albina Osipowich	1:11.0‡
1932....Helene Madison	1:06.8‡
1968....Jan Henne	1:00.0
1972....Sandra Neilson	58.59‡
1984....Carrie Steinseifer	55.92
Nancy Hogshead	55.92

200-METER FREESTYLE

1968....Debbie Meyer	2:10.5‡
1984....Mary Wayte	1:59.23
1992....Nicole Haislett	1:57.90

400-METER FREESTYLE

1924....Martha Norelius	6:02.2‡
1928....Martha Norelius	5:42.8*
1932....Helene Madison	5:28.5*
1948....Ann Curtis	5:17.8‡
1960....Chris von Saltza	4:50.6
1964....Virginia Duenkel	4:43.3‡
1968....Debbie Meyer	4:31.8‡
1984....Tiffany Cohen	4:07.10‡
1988....Janet Evans	4:03.85*

800-METER FREESTYLE

1968....Debbie Meyer	9:24.0‡
1972....Keena Rothhammer	8:53.86*
1984....Tiffany Cohen	8:24.95‡
1988....Janet Evans	8:20.20‡
1992....Janet Evans	8:25.52
1996....Brooke Bennett	8:27.89
2000....Brooke Bennett	8:19.67

100-METER BACKSTROKE

1924....Sybil Bauer	1:23.2‡
1932....Eleanor Holm	1:19.4
1960....Lynn Burke	1:09.3‡
1964....Cathy Ferguson	1:07.7*
1968....Kaye Hall	1:06.2*
1972....Melissa Belote	1:05.78‡
1984....Theresa Andrews	1:02.55
1996....Beth Botsford	1:01.19

200-METER BACKSTROKE

1968....Pokey Watson	2:24.8‡
1972....Melissa Belote	2:19.19*

100-METER BREASTSTROKE

1972....Catherine Carr	1:13.58*
2000....Megan Quann	1:07.05

200-METER BREASTSTROKE

1968....Sharon Wichman	2:44.4‡

100-METER BUTTERFLY

1956....Shelley Mann	1:11.0‡
1960....Carolyn Schuler	1:09.5‡
1964....Sharon Stouder	1:04.7*
1984....Mary T. Meagher	59.26
1996....Amy Van Dyken	59.13

200-METER BUTTERFLY

1972....Karen Moe	2:15.57*
1984....Mary T. Meagher	2:06.90‡
1992....Summer Sanders	2:08.67
2000....Misty Hyman	2:05.88‡

200-METER INDIVIDUAL MEDLEY

1968....Sharon Wichman	2:44.4‡
1984....Tracy Caulkins	2:12.64‡

400-METER INDIVIDUAL MEDLEY

1964....Donna De Varona	5:18.7‡
1968....Claudia Kolb	5:08.5‡
1984....Tracy Caulkins	4:39.24
1988....Janet Evans	4:37.76

3-METER SPRINGBOARD DIVING

1920....Aileen Riggin	539.9 points
1924....Elizabeth Becker	474.5
1928....Helen Meany	78.62
1932....Georgia Coleman	87.52
1936....Marjorie Gestring	89.27
1948....Victoria Draves	108.74
1952....Patricia McCormick	147.30
1956....Patricia McCormick	142.36
1968....Sue Gossick	150.77
1972....Micki King	450.03
1976....Jennifer Chandler	506.19

PLATFORM DIVING

1924....Caroline Smith	33.2 points
1928....Elizabeth Becker Pinkston	31.6
1932....Dorothy Poynton	40.26
1936....Dorothy Poynton Hill	33.93
1948....Victoria Draves	68.87
1952....Patricia McCormick	79.37
1956....Patricia McCormick	84.85
1964....Lesley Bush	99.80
2000....Laura Wilkinson	543.75

* World record; ‡Meet (Olympic) record.

Barrier Breakers

MEN

Event	Barrier	Athlete and Nation	Time	Date
100 Freestyle	1:00	Johnny Weissmuller, United States	58.6	7-9-22
100 Freestyle	:50	James Montgomery, United States	49.99	7-25-76
200 Freestyle	2:00	Don Schollander, United States	1:58.8	7-27-63
200 Freestyle	1:50	Sergei Kopliakov, USSR	1:49.83	4-7-79
400 Freestyle	4:00	Rick DeMont, United States	3:58.18	9-6-73
400 Freestyle	3:50	Vladimir Salnikov, USSR	3:49.57	3-12-82
800 Freestyle	8:00	Vladimir Salnikov, USSR	7:56.49	3-23-79
1500 Freestyle	15:00	Vladimir Salnikov, USSR	14:58.27	7-22-80
100 Backstroke	1:00	Thompson Mann, United States	59.6	10-16-64
200 Backstroke	2:00	John Naber, United States	1:59.19	7-24-76
100 Breaststroke	1:00	Roman Sloudnov, Russia	59.97	6-28-01
200 Breaststroke	2:30	Chester Jastremski, United States	2:29.6	8-19-61
100 Butterfly	1:00	Lance Larson, United States	59.0	6-29-60
200 Butterfly	2:00	Roger Pyttel, E Germany	1:59.63	6-3-76

WOMEN

Event	Barrier	Athlete and Nation	Time	Date
100 Freestyle	1:00	Dawn Fraser, Australia	59.9	10-27-62
200 Freestyle	2:00	Kornelia Ender, E Germany	1:59.78	6-2-76
400 Freestyle	4:30	Debbie Meyer, United States	4:29.0	8-18-67
800 Freestyle	10:00	Jane Cederqvist, Sweden	9:55.6	8-17-60
800 Freestyle	9:00	Ann Simmons, United States	8:59.4	9-10-71
1500 Freestyle	20:00	Ilsa Konrads, Australia	19:25.7	1-14-60
	16:00	Janet Evans, United States	15:52.10	3-26-88
100 Backstroke	1:00	Natalie Coughlin, United States	59.58	8-16-02
200 Backstroke	2:30	Satoko Tanaka, Japan	2:29.6	2-10-63
100 Butterfly	1:00	Christiane Knacke, E Germany	59.78	8-28-77
400 Individual Medley	5:00	Gudrun Wegner, E Germany	4:57.51	9-6-73

Olympic Achievements

MOST INDIVIDUAL GOLDS IN SINGLE OLYMPICS

MEN

No.	Athlete and Nation	Olympic Year	Events
4	Mark Spitz, United States	1972	100, 200 Free; 100, 200 Fly

WOMEN

No.	Athlete and Nation	Olympic Year	Events
4	Kristin Otto, E Germany	1988	50, 100 Free; 100 Back; 100 Fly
3	Debbie Meyer, United States	1968	200, 400, 800 Free
3	Shane Gould, Australia	1972	200, 400 Free; 200 IM
3	Kornelia Ender, E Germany	1976	100, 200 Free; 100 Fly
3	Janet Evans, United States	1988	400, 800 Free; 400 IM
3	Krisztina Egerszegi, Hungary	1992	100, 200 Back; 400 IM
3	Michelle Smith, Ireland	1996	400 Free; 200, 400 IM
3	Inge de Bruijn, Netherlands	2000	50, 100 Free; 100 Fly

Olympic Achievements *(Cont.)*

MOST INDIVIDUAL OLYMPIC GOLD MEDALS, CAREER

MEN

No.	Athlete and Nation	Olympic Years and Events
4	Charles Meldrum Daniels, United States.	1904 (220, 440 Free); 1906 (100 Free) 1908 (100 Free)
4	Roland Matthes, E Germany	1968 (100, 200 Back); 1972 (100, 200 Back)
4	Mark Spitz, United States	1972 (100, 200 Free; 100, 200 Fly)

WOMEN

No.	Athlete and Nation	Olympic Years and Events
4	Kristin Otto, E Germany	1988 (50 Free; 100 Free, Back and Fly)
4	Janet Evans, United States	1988 (400, 800 Free; 400 IM); 1992 (800 Free)
4	Krisztina Egerszegi, Hungary	1992 (100, 200 Back; 400 IM); 1996 (200 Back)

Most Olympic Gold Medals in a Single Olympics, Men—7, Mark Spitz, United States, 1972: 100, 200 Free; 100, 200 Fly; 4 x 100, 4 x 200 Free Relays; 4 x 100 Medley Relay.

Most Olympic Gold Medals in a Single Olympics, Women—6, Kristin Otto, E Germany, 1988: 50, 100 Free; 100 Back; 100 Fly; 4 x 100 Free Relay; 4 x 100 Medley Relay.

Most Olympic Medals in a Career, Men—11, Matt Biondi, United States: 1984 (one gold), '88 (five gold, one silver, one bronze), '92 (two gold, one silver); 11, Mark Spitz, United States: 1968 (two gold, one silver, one bronze), '72 (seven gold).

Most Olympic Medals in a Career, Women—10, Jenny Thompson, United States: 1992 (two gold, one silver), 1996 (three gold), 2000 (three gold, one bronze); 8, Dawn Fraser, Australia: 1956 (two gold, one silver), '60 (one gold, two silver), '64 (one gold, one silver); 8, Kornelia Ender, E Germany: 1972 (three silver), '76 (four gold, one silver); 8, Shirley Babashoff, United States: 1972 (one gold, two silver); '76 (one gold, four silver).

Winner, Same Event, Three Consecutive Olympics—Dawn Fraser, Australia, 100 Freestyle, 1956, '60, '64; Krisztina Egerszegi, Hungary, 200 Back, 1988, '92, '96.

Youngest Person to Win an Olympic Diving Gold—Marjorie Gestring, United States, 1936, 13 years, 9 months, springboard diving.

Youngest Person to Win an Olympic Swimming Gold—Krisztina Egerszegi, Hungary, 1988, 14 years, one month, 200 backstroke.

World Record Achievements

Most World Records, Career, Women—42, Ragnhild Hveger, Denmark, 1936–42.

Most World Records, Career, Men—32, Arne Borg, Sweden, 1921–29.

Most Freestyle Records Held Concurrently—5, Helene Madison, United States, 1931–33; 5, Shane Gould, Australia, 1972.

Most Consecutive Lowerings of a Record—10, Kornelia Ender, E Germany, 100 Freestyle, 7-13-73 to 7-19-76.

Longest Duration of World Record—19 years, 359 days, 1:04.6 in 100 Free, Willy den Ouden, Netherlands.

Skiing

**Olympic champion
Janica Kostelic
of Croatia**

No Holding Back

Bode Miller's breakneck style won him two silver medals in Salt Lake City—and may have cost him a historic third

BY MARK BECHTEL

WHEN BODE Miller was two years old, his mom, Jo, took him skiing. All the way down the hill, as Jo held Bode between her legs, he fought to free himself from her grasp, yelling, "Let go! Let go!" Jo finally relented after two runs, letting her toddler go it alone. She hurtled for the base of the run, she says, "trying to get to the bottom before Bode got there and crashed into a fence."

Twenty-two years later, Bode Miller hadn't changed much. He only knew one way to ski: without restraint. He was an attacking skier—no one skied faster or straighter or carved earlier in the turns—whose style had been studied on tape by the mighty Austrian team. How, the Austrians wondered, could such an unorthodox style yield such results: Heading into the 2002 Winter Olympics, the laid-back Miller had won four World Cup races with his Type-A style. But the wins were more of an indication that Miller had matured than they were a vindication

of his aggressive style. Six times in his five previous years on the World Cup circuit he had won the first run of a two-run race, only to falter in the second run and fail to bring home a win.

In Salt Lake City, though, Miller proved that he had matured into a closer. His first event was the combined—a downhill run followed by two slaloms. He knew he would need a decent downhill to stay within striking range of the favorites in the race, Kjetil André Aamodt and Lasse Kjus of Norway. Instead, he nearly wiped out. "It was a crash," he said later. "My skis were not touching the ground and my ass was." He somehow bounced back up and saved the run, but the near-crash, combined with a bad first slalom run, left Miller 2.44 seconds behind Aamodt heading into the second slalom.

That set the stage for one of the most remarkable runs ever seen in the Olympics. Miller torched the course, finishing a second faster than two Austrian slalom specialists and forcing Aamodt, who could have been forgiven for thinking the gold medal

Miller produced a brilliant final run to take the silver medal in the combined.

was in the bag, to sweat. Aamodt won the gold by .28 of a second; Miller took the silver. (The victory gave Aamodt a record six career Olympic alpine medals. He would add another gold in the Super G.)

In the giant slalom, Miller again started slowly, placing seventh after the first run. But he passed five skiers on his second run to win another silver medal and enter the slalom with a chance to become the first American to win three alpine medals in a career, to say nothing of a single Olympics. He looked like a safe bet to achieve the distinction after his first run placed him second behind Jean-Pierre Vidal of France. If he played it safe, he would win another silver medal—but Miller had never played anything safe in his life. "That wasn't what I was thinking about at all," he said. "If it was, maybe I would have backed off."

Far from backing off, Miller attacked the course in his usual style, only to fall 15 seconds into his run. He climbed back onto the course and missed a gate, and by the time he reached the bottom, he was in 25th place, 12 seconds behind Vidal. "I put myself in a great position after the first run," said Miller after the race, sipping a beer. "That was the plan. To back off that, I think I would have been a lot more disappointed than I am now."

While Miller felt the sting of disappointment, Vidal, who held on to win the race, tasted an extra sweetness in his victory. He had severed ligaments in both knees in a training accident three years earlier and spent 45 days in a wheelchair before beginning his remarkable recovery.

And Vidal wasn't the only medical marvel to excel in Salt Lake. Janica Kostelic of Croatia, who underwent three surgeries on her left knee after winning the 2001 World Cup title, dominated the women's competition at the 2002 Games. She also had to contend with chronic back pain that developed during her rehabilitation from the knee operations. When she arrived in Utah, she was in 17th place in the World Cup standings and hadn't won a single race. But on Valentine's Day she won the combined gold medal, then came within .05 seconds of taking the Super G.

When the competition shifted to Park City for the slalom events, Kostelic had become the race favorite and, with her flying red pigtails and her *Dude, Where's My Car?* cadence, the crowd favorite as well. When asked if she could win the slalom and the giant slalom, she said, "No way, man, GS isn't my thing."

Turns out it was her thing after all. She won the giant slalom by a whopping 1.32 seconds, and that was two days after narrowly winning the slalom. Three gold medals and a silver wasn't a bad haul for someone who weeks earlier had looked, in the words of a fellow skier, "like an average skier. Just average, nothing more."

Indeed, Kostelic had been such a mess that when she was asked how she felt at the start of the Games, she jokingly said, "My right arm is okay, and my hair feels good."

Imagine if the rest of her had felt okay.

World Cup Alpine Racing Season Results

Men

Date	Event	Site	Winner
10-28-01	Giant Slalom	Sölden, Austria	Frederic Covili, France
11-25-01	Slalom	Aspen, Colorado	Ivica Kostelic, Croatia
11-26-01	Slalom	Aspen, Colorado	Mario Matt, Austria
12-7-01	Super G	Val D'Isere, France	Stephan Eberharter, Austria
12-8-01	Downhill	Val D'Isere, France	Stephan Eberharter, Austria
12-9-01	Giant Slalom	Val D'Isere, France	Bode Miller, United States
12-10-01	Slalom	Madonna di Campligio, Italy	Bode Miller, United States
12-14-01	Downhill	Val Gardena, Italy	Kristian Ghedina, Italy
12-15-01	Downhill	Val Gardena, Italy	Stephen Eberharter, Austria
12-16-01	Giant Slalom	Alta Badia, Italy	Frederic Covili, France
12-20-01	Giant Slalom	Kranjska Gora, Slovenia	Fredrik Nyberg, Sweden
12-21-01	Giant Slalom	Kranjska Gora, Slovenia	Benjamin Raich, Austria
12-22-01	Slalom	St. Moritz, Switzerland	Jean-Pierre Vidal, France
12-28-01	Downhill	Bormio, Italy	Christoph Gruber, Austria
12-29-01	Downhill	Bormio, Italy	Fritz Strobl, Austria
1-5-02	Giant Slalom	Adelboden, Switzerland	Didier Cuche, Switzerland
1-6-02	Slalom	Adelboden, Switzerland	Bode Miller, United States
1-13-02	Slalom	Wengen, Switzerland	Ivica Kostelic, Croatia
1-18-02	Super G	Kitzbühel, Austria	Stephan Eberharter, Austria
1-19-02	Downhill	Kitzbühel, Austria	Stephan Eberharter, Austria
1-20-02	Slalom	Kitzbühel, Austria	Rainer Schoenfelder, Austria
1-22-02	Slalom	Schladming, Austria	Bode Miller, United States
1-26-02	Super G	Garmisch-Partenkirchen, Germany	Fritz Strobl, Austria
1-27-02	Super G	Garmisch-Partenkirchen, Germany	Stephan Eberharter, Austria
2-2-02	Downhill	St. Moritz, Switzerland	Stephan Eberharter, Austria
2-3-02	Giant Slalom	St. Moritz, Switzerland	Stephan Eberharter, Austria
3-2-02	Downhill	Kvitfjell, Norway	Hannes Trinkl, Austria
3-3-02	Super G	Kvitfjell, Norway	Alessandro Fattori, Italy
3-7-02	Super G	Altenmarkt-Zauchensee, Austria	Didier Cuche, Switzerland
3-9-02	Slalom	Flachau, Austria	Ivica Kostelic, Croatia
3-10-02	Giant Slalom	St. Moritz, Switzerland	Michael von Brueningen, Switz

Women

Date	Event	Site	Winner
10-27-01	Giant Slalom	Sölden, Austria	Michaela Dorfmeister, Austria
11-21-01	Giant Slalom	Copper Mountain, United States	Andrine Flemmen, Norway
11-22-01	Slalom	Copper Mountain, United States	Laure Pequegnot, France
11-29-01	Downhill	Lake Louise, Alberta	Isolde Kostner, Italy
11-30-01	Downhill	Lake Louise, Alberta	Isolde Kostner, Italy
12-1-01	Super G	Lake Louise, Alberta	Petra Jaltmayr, Germany
12-9-01	Slalom	Sestriere, Italy	Anja Paerson, Sweden
12-15-01	Super G	Val D'Isere, France	Sonja Nef, Switzerland
12-16-01	Giant Slalom	Val D'Isere, France	Hilde Gerg, Germany
12-21-01	Downhill	St. Moritz, Switzerland	Sylviane Berthod, Switzerland
12-22-01	Super G	St. Moritz, Switzerland	Karen Putzer, Italy
12-28-01	Giant Slalom	Lienz, Austria	Lilian Kummer, Switzerland
12-29-01	Slalom	Lienz, Austria	Anja Paerson, Sweden
1-4-02	Giant Slalom	Maribor, Slovenia	Sonja Nef, Switzerland
1-5-02	Slalom	Maribor, Slovenia	Anja Paerson, Sweden
1-6-02	Slalom	Maribor, Slovenia	Anja Paerson, Sweden
1-11-02	Downhill	Saalbach-Hinterglemm, Austria	Hilde Gerg, Germany
1-12-02	Downhill	Saalbach-Hinterglemm, Austria	Hilde Gerg, Germany
1-13-02	Slalom	Saalbach-Hinterglemm, Austria	Laure Pequegnot
1-19-02	Giant Slalom	Berchtesgaden, Germany	Michaela Dorfmeister, Austria
1-20-02	Slalom	Berchtesgaden, Germany	Kristina Koznick, United States
2-2-02	Downhill	Are, Sweden	Renate Götschl, Austria
2-3-02	Slalom	Are, Sweden	Laure Pequegnot, France
3-2-02	Downhill	Lenzerheide, Switzerland	Corinne Rey-Bellet, Switzerland
3-6-02	Downhill	Altenmarkt-Zauchensee, Austria	Michaela Dorfmeister, Switz
3-7-02	Super G	Altenmarkt-Zauchensee, Austria	Michaela Dorfmeister, Switz
3-9-02	Giant Slalom	Flachau, Austria	Sonja Nef, Switzerland
3-10-02	Slalom	Flachau, Austria	Janica Kostelic, Croatia

World Cup Alpine Racing Final Standings

Men

OVERALL

	Pts
Stephan Eberharter, Austria	1,642
Kjetil André Aamodt, Nor	1,078
Didier Cuche, Switzerland	1,024
Bode Miller, United States	952
Fritz Strobl, Austria	846
Lasse Kjus, Norway	680
Ivica Kostelic, Croatia	648
Fredrik Nyberg, Sweden	534
Kristian Ghedina, Italy	505
Cristoph Gruber, Austria	477

DOWNHILL

	Pts
Stephan Eberharter, Austria	810
Fritz Strobl, Austria	520
Kristian Ghedina, Italy	381
Franco Cavegn, Switzerland	366
Hannes Trinkl, Austria	350
Kjetil Andre Aamodt, Norway	337
Christian Greber, Austria	329
Kurt Sulzenbacher, Italy	320
Michael Walchhofer, Austria	295
Ambrosi Hoffmann, Switz.	273

SLALOM

	Pts
Ivica Kostelic, Croatia	611
Bode Miller, United States	560
Jean-Pierre Vidal, France	456
Mitja Kunc, Slovenia	322
Rainer Schoenfelder, Austria	318
Kalle Palander, Finland	287
Giorgio Rocca, Italy	286
Mario Matt, Austria	267
Kjetil André Aamodt, Norway	232
Kilian Albrecht, Austria	226

GIANT SLALOM

	Pts
Frederic Covili, France	471
Benjamin Faich, Austria.	429
Didier Cuche, Switzerland	420
Fredrik Nyberg, Sweden	405
Michael von Gruenigen, Switz.	356
Stephan Eberharter, Austria	350
Bode Miller, United States	310
Sami Uotila, Finland	250
Joel Chenal, France	207
Christoph Gruber, Austria	202

SUPER G

	Pts
Stephan Eberharter, Austria	470
Didier Cuche, Switzerland	426
Fritz Strobl, Austria	326
Alessandro Fattori, Italy	294
Andreas Schifferer, Austria	214
Didier Defago, Switzerland	202
Christoph Gruber, Austria	193
Kjetil André Aamodt, Norway	177
Lasse Kjus, Norway	176
Fredrik Nyberg, Sweden	158

Women

OVERALL

	Pts
Michaela Dorfmeister, Austria	1,271
Renate Götschl, Austria	931
Sonja Nef, Switzerland	904
Hilde Gerg, Germany	847
Anja Paerson, Sweden	760
Isolde Kostner, Italy	641
Corinne Rey-Bellet, Switz.	618
Kristina Koznick, United States	592
Laure Pequegnot, France	552
Karen Putzer, Italy	535

DOWNHILL

	Pts
Isolde Kostner, Italy	568
Michaela Dorfmeister, Austria	469
Corinne Rey-Bellet, Switzer.	414
Hilde Gerg, Germany	412
Renate Götschl, Austria	408
Sylviane Berthod, Switzerland	346
Melanie Suchet, France	304
Selina Heregger, Austria	268
Brigette Obermoser, Austria	242
Pernilla Wiberg, Sweden	208

SLALOM

	Pts
Laure Pequegnot, France	597
Kristina Koznick, United States	518
Anja Paerson, Sweden	480
Sonja Nef, Switzerland	330
Ylva Nowen, Sweden	328
Christel Saioni, France	312
Tanja Poutiainen , Finland	301
Monika Bergmann, Germany	264
Marlies Oester, Switzerland	261
Sarah Schleper, United States	254

GIANT SLALOM

	Pts
Sonja Nef, Switzerland	574
Michaela Dorfmeister, Austria	494
Anja Paerson, Sweden	360
Andrine Flemmen, Norway	335
Stina Hofgard-Nilsen, Norway	330
Karen Putzer, Italy	324
Allison Forsyth, Canada	303
Tina Maze, Slovenia	224
Ylva Nowen, Sweden	223
Anna Ottosson, Sweden	219

SUPER G

	Pts
Hilde Gerg, Germany	355
Alexandra Meissnitzer, Austria	248
Michaela Dorfmeister, Austria	212
Renate Götschl, Austria	210
Karen Putzer, Italy	192
Caroline Lalive, United States	167
Daniela Ceccarelli, Italy	158
Stefanie Schuster, Austria	137
Carole Montillet, France	129
Tanja Schneider, Austria	122

FOR THE RECORD·Year by Year

Event Descriptions

Downhill: A speed event entailing a single run on a course with a minimum vertical drop of 500 meters (800 for men's World Cup) and very few control gates.
Slalom: A technical event in which times for runs on two courses are totaled to determine the winner. Skiers must make many quick, short turns through a combination of gates (55–75 gates for men, 40–60 for women) over a short course (140–220-meter vertical drop for men, 120–180 for women).
Combined: An event in which scores from designated slalom and downhill races are combined to determine finish order.

Giant Slalom: A faster technical event with fewer, more broadly spaced gates than in the slalom. Times for runs on two courses with vertical drops of 250–400 meters for men and 250–300 meters for women are combined to determine the winner.
Super Giant Slalom: A speed event that is a cross between the downhill and the giant slalom.
Parallel Slalom: A technical event that combines slalom and giant slalom turns.

FIS World Championships

Sites

1931	Mürren, Switzerland
1932	Cortina d'Ampezzo, Italy
1933	Innsbruck, Austria
1934	St. Moritz, Switzerland
1935	Mürren, Switzerland
1936	Innsbruck, Austria
1937	Chamonix, France
1938	Engelberg, Switzerland
1939	Zakopane, Poland

Men

DOWNHILL

1931	Walter Prager, Switzerland
1932	Gustav Lantschner, Austria
1933	Walter Prager, Switzerland
1934	David Zogg, Switzerland
1935	Franz Zingerle, Austria
1936	Rudolf Rominger, Switzerland
1937	Émile Allais, France
1938	James Couttet, France
1939	Hans Lantschner, Germany

SLALOM

1931	David Zogg, Switzerland
1932	Friedrich Dauber, Germany
1933	Anton Seelos, Austria
1934	Franz Pfnür, Germany
1935	Anton Seelos, Austria
1936	Rudi Matt, Austria
1937	Émile Allais, France
1938	Rudolf Rominger, Switzerland
1939	Rudolf Rominger, Switzerland

Women

DOWNHILL

1931	Esme Mackinnon, Great Britain
1932	Paola Wiesinger, Italy
1933	Inge Wersin-Lantschner, Austria
1934	Anni Rüegg, Switzerland
1935	Christel Cranz, Germany
1936	Evie Pinching, Great Britain
1937	Christel Cranz, Germany
1938	Lisa Resch, Germany
1939	Christel Cranz, Germany

SLALOM

1931	Esme Mackinnon, Great Britain
1932	Rösli Streiff, Switzerland
1933	Inge Wersin-Lantschner, Austria
1934	Christel Cranz, Germany
1935	Anni Rüegg, Switzerland
1936	Gerda Paumgarten, Austria
1937	Christel Cranz, Germany
1938	Christel Cranz, Germany
1939	Christel Cranz, Germany

FIS World Alpine Ski Championships

Sites

1950	Aspen, Colorado
1954	Are, Sweden
1958	Badgastein, Austria
1962	Chamonix, France
1966	Portillo, Chile
1970	Val Gardena, Italy
1974	St. Moritz, Switzerland
1978	Garmisch-Partenkirchen, W Germany
1982	Schladming, Austria
1985	Bormio, Italy
1987	Crans-Montana, Switzerland
1989	Vail, Colorado
1991	Saalbach-Hinterglemm, Austria
1993	Morioka-Shizukuishi, Japan
1996	Sierra Nevada, Spain
1997	Sestriere, Italy
1999	Vail, Colorado
2001	St. Anton, Switzerland

Men

DOWNHILL

1950.............Zeno Colo, Italy
1954.............Christian Pravda, Austria
1958.............Toni Sailer, Austria
1962.............Karl Schranz, Austria
1966.............Jean-Claude Killy, France
1970.............Bernard Russi, Switzerland
1974.............David Zwilling, Austria
1978.............Josef Walcher, Austria
1982.............Harti Weirather, Austria

1985.............Pirmin Zurbriggen, Switzerland
1987.............Peter Müller, Switzerland
1989.............Hansjörg Tauscher, W Germany
1991.............Franz Heinzer, Switzerland
1993.............Urs Lehmann, Switzerland
1996.............Patrick Ortlieb, Austria
1997.............Bruno Kernen, Switzerland
1999.............Hermann Maier, Austria
2001.............Hannes Trinkl, Austria

SLALOM

1950.............Zeno Colo, Italy
1954.............Christian Pravda, Austria
1958.............Toni Sailer, Austria
1962.............Karl Schranz, Austria
1966.............Jean-Claude Killy, France
1970.............Bernard Russi, Switzerland
1974.............David Zwilling, Austria
1978.............Josef Walcher, Austria
1982.............Harti Weirather, Austria

1985.............Pirmin Zurbriggen, Switzerland
1987.............Peter Müller, Switzerland
1989.............Hansjörg Tauscher, W Germany
1991.............Franz Heinzer, Switzerland
1993.............Urs Lehmann, Switzerland
1996.............Patrick Örtlieb, Austria
1997.............Bruno Kernen, Switzerland
1999.............Hermann Maier, Austria
2001.............Hannes Trinkl, Austria

GIANT SLALOM

1950.............Zeno Colo, Italy
1954.............Stein Eriksen, Norway
1958.............Toni Sailer, Austria
1962.............Egon Zimmermann, Austria
1966.............Guy Périllat, France
1970.............Karl Schranz, Austria
1974.............Gustavo Thoeni, Italy
1978.............Ingemar Stenmark, Sweden
1982.............Steve Mahre, United States

1985.............Markus Wasmaier, W Germany
1987.............Pirmin Zurbriggen, Switzerland
1989.............Rudolf Nierlich, Austria
1991.............Rudolf Nierlich, Austria
1993.............Kjetil André Aamodt, Norway
1996.............Alberto Tomba, Italy
1997.............Michael von Grünigen, Switzerland
1999.............Marco Büchel, Liechtenstein
2001.............Michael von Grünigen, Switzerland

COMBINED

1982.............Michel Vion, France
1985.............Pirmin Zurbriggen, Switzerland
1987.............Marc Girardelli, Luxembourg
1989.............Marc Girardelli, Luxembourg
1991.............Stefan Eberharter, Austria

1993.............Lasse Kjus, Norway
1996.............Marc Girardelli, Luxembourg
1997.............Kjetil André Aamodt, Norway
1999.............Kjetil André Aamodt, Norway
2001.............Kjetil André Aamodt, Norway

SUPER G

1987.............Pirmin Zurbriggen, Switzerland
1989.............Martin Hangl, Switzerland
1991.............Stefan Eberharter, Austria
1993.............Cancelled due to weather
1996.............Atle Skaardal, Norway

1997.............Atle Skaardal, Norway
1999.............Hermann Maier, Austria
              Lasse Kjus, Norway
2001.............Daron Rahlves, United States

Women

DOWNHILL

1950.............Trude Beiser-Jochum, Austria
1954.............Ida Schopfer, Switzerland
1958.............Lucile Wheeler, Canada
1962.............Christl Haas, Austria
1966.............Erika Schinegger, Austria
1970.............Annerösli Zryd, Switzerland
1974.............Annemarie Moser-Pröll, Austria
1978.............Annemarie Moser-Pröll, Austria
1982.............Gerry Sorensen, Canada

1985.............Michela Figini, Switzerland
1987.............Maria Walliser, Switzerland
1989.............Maria Walliser, Switzerland
1991.............Petra Kronberger, Austria
1993.............Kate Pace, Canada
1996.............Picabo Street, United States
1997.............Hilary Lindh, United States
1999.............Renate Götschl, Austria
2001.............Michaela Dorfmeister, Austria

Women (Cont.)

SLALOM

1950............Dagmar Rom, Austria	1985............Perrine Pelen, France
1954............Trude Klecker, Austria	1987............Erika Hess, Switzerland
1958............Inger Bjornbakken, Norway	1989............Mateja Svet, Yugoslavia
1962............Marianne Jahn, Austria	1991............Vreni Schneider, Switzerland
1966............Annie Famose, France	1993............Karin Buder, Austria
1970............Ingrid Lafforgue, France	1996............Pernilla Wiberg, Sweden
1974............Hanni Wenzel, Liechtenstein	1997............Deborah Compagnoni, Italy
1978............Lea Sölkner, Austria	1999............Trine Bakke, Norway
1982............Erika Hess, Switzerland	2001............Anja Paerson, Sweden

GIANT SLALOM

1950............Dagmar Rom, Austria	1985....................Diann Roffe, United States
1954............Lucienne Schmith-Couttet, France	1987....................Vreni Schneider, Switzerland
1958............Lucile Wheeler, Canada	1989....................Vreni Schneider, Switzerland
1962............Marianne Jahn, Austria	1991....................Pernilla Wiberg, Sweden
1966............Marielle Goitschel, France	1993....................Carole Merle, France
1970............Betsy Clifford, Canada	1996....................Deborah Compagnoni, Italy
1974............Fabienne Serrat, France	1997....................Deborah Compagnoni, Italy
1978............Maria Epple, W Germany	1999....................Anita Wachter, Austria
1982............Erika Hess, Switzerland	2001....................Sonja Nef, Switzerland

COMBINED

1982....................Erika Hess, Switzerland	1993....................Miriam Vogt, Germany
1985....................Erika Hess, Switzerland	1996....................Pernilla Wiberg, Sweden
1987....................Erika Hess, Switzerland	1997....................Renate Götschl, Austria
1989....................Tamara McKinney, United States	1999....................Pernilla Wiberg, Sweden
1991....................Chantal Bournissen, Switzerland	2001....................Martina Ertl, Germany

SUPER G

1987....................Maria Walliser, Switzerland	1996....................Isolde Kostner, Italy
1989....................Ulrike Maier, Austria	1997....................Isolde Kostner, Italy
1991....................Ulrike Maier, Austria	1999....................Alexandra Meissnitzer, Austria
1993....................Katja Seizinger, Germany	2001....................Regine Cavagnoud, France

Note: The 1995 FIS World Alpine Ski Championships were postponed to 1996 due to lack of snow.

King of the Hill

A year to the day after a horrific crash left him in a coma for three weeks, Bill Johnson returned on Friday, March 22, 2002, to ski the same slope at Montana's Big Mountain resort on which he had his near-fatal accident. Johnson, 42, still suffers from slurred speech and right side weakness, but he displayed the sleek form that won him a downhill gold in 1984. While Johnson doesn't remember the accident, Big Mountain's terrain struck him as familiar. The highlight of Johnson's weekend was his reunion with the ski patrol workers and doctors who treated him. "They were all very supportive," said Johnson. "I'd never known before how much I impressed people, but I really impressed people here."

Men

OVERALL

1967 ....Jean-Claude Killy, France	1985 ....Marc Girardelli, Luxembourg
1968 ....Jean-Claude Killy, France	1986 ....Marc Girardelli, Luxembourg
1969 ....Karl Schranz, Austria	1987 ....Pirmin Zurbriggen, Switzerland
1970 ....Karl Schranz, Austria	1988 ....Pirmin Zurbriggen, Switzerland
1971 ....Gustavo Thoeni, Italy	1989 ....Marc Girardelli, Luxembourg
1972 ....Gustavo Thoeni, Italy	1990 ....Pirmin Zurbriggen, Switzerland
1973 ....Gustavo Thoeni, Italy	1991 ....Marc Girardelli, Luxembourg
1974 ....Piero Gros, Italy	1992 ....Paul Accola, Switzerland
1975 ....Gustavo Thoeni, Italy	1993 ....Marc Girardelli, Luxembourg
1976 ....Ingemar Stenmark, Sweden	1994 ....Kjetil André Aamodt, Norway
1977 ....Ingemar Stenmark, Sweden	1995 ....Alberto Tomba, Italy
1978 ....Ingemar Stenmark, Sweden	1996 ....Lasse Kjus, Norway
1979 ....Peter Lüscher, Switzerland	1997 ....Luc Alphand, France
1980 ....Andreas Wenzel, Liechtenstein	1998 ....Hermann Maier, Austria
1981 ....Phil Mahre, United States	1999 ....Lasse Kjus, Norway
1982 ....Phil Mahre, United States	2000 ....Hermann Maier, Austria
1983 ....Phil Mahre, United States	2001 ....Hermann Maier, Austria
1984 ....Pirmin Zurbriggen, Switzerland	2002 ....Stephan Eberharter, Austria

DOWNHILL

1967 ....Jean-Claude Killy, France	1984 ....Urs Raber, Switzerland
1968 ....Gerhard Nenning, Austria	1985 ....Helmut Höflehner, Austria
1969 ....Karl Schranz, Austria	1986 ....Peter Wirnsberger, Austria
1970 ....Karl Schranz, Austria	1987 ....Pirmin Zurbriggen, Switzerland
Karl Cordin, Austria	1988 ....Pirmin Zurbriggen, Switzerland
1971 ....Bernhard Russi, Switzerland	1989 ....Marc Girardelli, Luxembourg
1972 ....Bernhard Russi, Switzerland	1990 ....Helmut Höflehner, Austria
1973 ....Roland Collumbin, Switzerland	1991 ....Franz Heinzer, Switzerland
1974 ....Roland Collumbin, Switzerland	1992 ....Franz Heinzer, Switzerland
1975 ....Franz Klammer, Austria	1993 ....Franz Heinzer, Switzerland
1976 ....Franz Klammer, Austria	1994 ....Marc Girardelli, Luxembourg
1977 ....Franz Klammer, Austria	1995 ....Luc Alphand, France
1978 ....Franz Klammer, Austria	1996 ....Luc Alphand, France
1979 ....Peter Müller, Switzerland	1997 ....Luc Alphand, France
1980 ....Peter Müller, Switzerland	1998 ....Andreas Schifferer, Austria
1981 ....Harti Weirather, Austria	1999 ....Lasse Kjus, Norway
1982 ....Steve Podborski, Canada	2000 ....Hermann Maier, Austria
Peter Müller, Switzerland	2001 ....Hermann Maier, Austria
1983 ....Franz Klammer, Austria	2002 ....Stephan Eberharter, Austria

SLALOM

1967 ....Jean-Claude Killy, France	1985 ....Marc Girardelli, Luxembourg
1968 ....Domeng Giovanoli, Switzerland	1986 ....Rok Petrovic, Yugoslavia
1969 ....Jean-Noël Augert, France	1987 ....Bojan Krizaj, Yugoslavia
1970 ....Patrick Russel, France	1988 ....Alberto Tomba, Italy
Alain Penz, France	1989 ....Armin Bittner, W Germany
1971 ....Jean-Noël Augert, France	1990 ....Armin Bittner, W Germany
1972 ....Jean-Noël Augert, France	1991 ....Marc Girardelli, Luxembourg
1973 ....Gustavo Thoeni, Italy	1992 ....Alberto Tomba, Italy
1974 ....Gustavo Thoeni, Italy	1993 ....Tomas Fogdof, Sweden
1975 ....Ingemar Stenmark, Sweden	1994 ....Alberto Tomba, Italy
1976 ....Ingemar Stenmark, Sweden	1995 ....Alberto Tomba, Italy
1977 ....Ingemar Stenmark, Sweden	1996 ....Sebastien Amiez, France
1978 ....Ingemar Stenmark, Sweden	1997 ....Thomas Sykora, Austria
1979 ....Ingemar Stenmark, Sweden	1998 ....Thomas Sykora, Austria
1980 ....Ingemar Stenmark, Sweden	1999 ....Thomas Stangassinger, Austria
1981 ....Ingemar Stenmark, Sweden	2000 ....Kjetil André Aamodt, Norway
1982 ....Phil Mahre, United States	2001 ....Benjamin Raich, Austria
1983 ....Ingemar Stenmark, Sweden	2002 ....Ivica Kostelic, Croatia
1984 ....Marc Girardelli, Luxembourg	

Men (Cont.)

GIANT SLALOM

1967 ....Jean-Claude Killy, France	1985 ....Marc Girardelli, Luxembourg
1968 ....Jean-Claude Killy, France	1986 ....Joël Gaspoz, Switzerland
1969 ....Karl Schranz, Austria	1987 ....Joël Gaspoz, Switzerland
1970 ....Gustavo Thoeni, Italy	Pirmin Zurbriggen, Switzerland
1971 ....Patrick Russel, France	1988 ....Alberto Tomba, Italy
1972 ....Gustavo Thoeni, Italy	1989 ....Pirmin Zurbriggen, Switzerland
1973 ....Hans Hinterseer, Austria	1990 ....Ole-Cristian Furuseth, Norway
1974 ....Piero Gros, Italy	Günther Mader, Austria
1975 ....Ingemar Stenmark, Sweden	1991 ....Alberto Tomba, Italy
1976 ....Ingemar Stenmark, Sweden	1992 ....Alberto Tomba, Italy
1977 ....Heini Hemmi, Switzerland	1993 ....Kjetil André Aamodt, Norway
Ingemar Stenmark, Sweden	1994 ....Christian Mayer, Austria
1978 ....Ingemar Stenmark, Sweden	1995 ....Alberto Tomba, Italy
1979 ....Ingemar Stenmark, Sweden	1996 ....Michael von Grünigen, Switzerland
1980 ....Ingemar Stenmark, Sweden	1997 ....Michael von Grünigen, Switzerland
1981 ....Ingemar Stenmark, Sweden	1998 ....Hermann Maier, Austria
1982 ....Phil Mahre, United States	1999 ....Michael von Grünigen, Switzerland
1983 ....Phil Mahre, United States	2000 ....Hermann Maier, Austria
1984 ....Ingemar Stenmark, Sweden	2001 ....Hermann Maier, Austria
Pirmin Zurbriggen, Switzerland	2002 ....Frederic Covili, France

SUPER G

1986 ....Markus Wasmeier, W Germany	1995 ....Peter Runggaldier, Italy
1987 ....Pirmin Zurbriggen, Switzerland	1996 ....Atle Skaardal, Norway
1988 ....Pirmin Zurbriggen, Switzerland	1997 ....Luc Alphand, France
1989 ....Pirmin Zurbriggen, Switzerland	1998 ....Hermann Maier, Austria
1990 ....Pirmin Zurbriggen, Switzerland	1999 ....Hermann Maier, Austria
1991 ....Franz Heinzer, Switzerland	2000 ....Hermann Maier, Austria
1992 ....Paul Accola, Switzerland	2001 ....Hermann Maier, Austria
1993 ....Kjetil André Aamodt, Norway	2002 ....Stephan Eberharter, Austria
1994 ....Jan Einar Thorsen, Norway	

COMBINED

1979 ....Andreas Wenzel, Liechtenstein	1992 ....Paul Accola, Switzerland
1980 ....Andreas Wenzel, Liechtenstein	1993 ....Marc Girardelli, Luxembourg
1981 ....Phil Mahre, United States	1994 ....Kjetil André Aamodt, Norway
1982 ....Phil Mahre, United States	1995 ....Marc Girardelli, Luxembourg
1983 ....Phil Mahre, United States	1996 ....Günther Mader, Austria
1984 ....Andreas Wenzel, Liechtenstein	1997 ....Kjetil André Aamodt, Norway
1985 ....Andreas Wenzel, Liechtenstein	1998 ....Werner Franz, Austria
1986 ....Markus Wasmeier, W Germany	1999 ....Kjetil André Aamodt, Norway
1987 ....Pirmin Zurbriggen, Switzerland	2000 ....Kjetil André Aamodt, Norway
1988 ....Hubert Strolz, Austria	Lasse Kjus, Norway
1989 ....Marc Girardelli, Luxembourg	2001 ....Lasse Kjus, Norway
1990 ....Pirmin Zurbriggen, Switzerland	2002 ....Kjetil André Aamodt, Norway
1991 ....Marc Girardelli, Luxembourg	

Women

OVERALL

1967 ....Nancy Greene, Canada	1985 ....Michela Figini, Switzerland
1968 ....Nancy Greene, Canada	1986 ....Maria Walliser, Switzerland
1969 ....Gertrud Gabl, Austria	1987 ....Maria Walliser, Switzerland
1970 ....Michèle Jacot, France	1988 ....Michela Figini, Switzerland
1971 ....Annemarie Pröll, Austria	1989 ....Vreni Schneider, Switzerland
1972 ....Annemarie Pröll, Austria	1990 ....Petra Kronberger, Austria
1973 ....Annemarie Pröll, Austria	1991 ....Petra Kronberger, Austria
1974 ....Annemarie Moser-Pröll, Austria	1992 ....Petra Kronberger, Austria
1975 ....Annemarie Moser-Pröll, Austria	1993 ....Anita Wachter, Austria
1976 ....Rosi Mitermaier, W Germany	1994 ....Vreni Schneider, Switzerland
1977 ....Lise-Marie Morerod, Switzerland	1995 ....Vreni Schneider, Switzerland
1978 ....Hanni Wenzel, Liechtenstein	1996 ....Katja Seizinger, Germany
1979 ....Annemarie Moser-Pröll, Austria	1997 ....Pernilla Wiberg, Sweden
1980 ....Hanni Wenzel, Liechtenstein	1998 ....Katja Seizinger, Germany
1981 ....Marie-Thérèse Nadig, Switzerland	1999 ....Alexandra Meissnitzer, Austria
1982 ....Erika Hess, Switzerland	2000 ....Renate Götschl, Austria
1983 ....Tamara McKinney, United States	2001 ....Janica Kostelic, Croatia
1984 ....Erika Hess, Switzerland	2002 ....Michaela Dorfmeister, Austria

Women (Cont.)

DOWNHILL

1967 ....Marielle Goitschel, France	1985 ....Michela Figini, Switzerland
1968 ....Isabelle Mir, France & Olga Pall, Austria	1986 ....Maria Walliser, Switzerland
1969 ....Wiltrud Drexel, Austria	1987 ....Michela Figini, Switzerland
1970 ....Isabelle Mir, France	1988 ....Michela Figini, Switzerland
1971 ....Annemarie Pröll, Austria	1989 ....Michela Figini, Switzerland
1972 ....Annemarie Pröll, Austria	1990 ....Katrin Gutensohn-Knopf, Germany
1973 ....Annemarie Pröll, Austria	1991 ....Chantal Bournissen, Switzerland
1974 ....Annemarie Moser-Pröll, Austria	1992 ....Katja Seizinger, Germany
1975 ....Annemarie Moser-Pröll, Austria	1993 ....Katja Seizinger, Germany
1976 ....Brigitte Totschnig, Austria	1994 ....Katja Seizinger, Germany
1977 ....Brigitte Totschnig-Habersatter, Austria	1995 ....Picabo Street, United States
1978 ....Annemarie Moser-Pröll, Austria	1996 ....Picabo Street, United States
1979 ....Annemarie Moser-Pröll, Austria	1997 ....Renate Götschl, Austria
1980 ....Marie-Thérèse Nadig, Switzerland	1998 ....Katja Seizinger, Germany
1981 ....Marie-Thérèse Nadig, Switzerland	1999 ....Renate Götschl, Austria
1982 ....Marie-Cecile Gros-Gaudenier, France	2000 ....Regina Haeusl, Germany
1983 ....Doris De Agostini, Switzerland	2001 ....Isolde Kostner, Italy
1984 ....Maria Walliser, Switzerland	2002 ....Isolde Kostner, Italy

SLALOM

1967 ....Nancy Greene, Canada	1985 ....Michela Figini, Switzerland
1968 ....Nancy Greene, Canada	1986 ....Maria Walliser, Switzerland
1969 ....Gertrud Gabl, Austria	1987 ....Maria Walliser, Switzerland
1970 ....Michèle Jacot, France	1988 ....Michela Figini, Switzerland
1971 ....Annemarie Pröll, Austria	1989 ....Vreni Schneider, Switzerland
1972 ....Annemarie Pröll, Austria	1990 ....Petra Kronberger, Austria
1973 ....Annemarie Pröll, Austria	1991 ....Petra Kronberger, Austria
1974 ....Annemarie Moser-Pröll, Austria	1992 ....Petra Kronberger, Austria
1975 ....Annemarie Moser-Pröll, Austria	1993 ....Anita Wachter, Austria
1976 ....Rosi Mitermaier, W Germany	1994 ....Vreni Schneider, Switzerland
1977 ....Lise-Marie Morerod, Switzerland	1995 ....Vreni Schneider, Switzerland
1978 ....Hanni Wenzel, Liechtenstein	1996 ....Katja Seizinger, Germany
1979 ....Annemarie Moser-Pröll, Austria	1997 ....Pernilla Wiberg, Sweden
1980 ....Hanni Wenzel, Liechtenstein	1998 ....Katja Seizinger, Germany
1981 ....Marie-Thérèse Nadig, Switzerland	1999 ....Alexandra Meissnitzer, Austria
1982 ....Erika Hess, Switzerland	2000 ....Renate Götschl, Austria
1983 ....Tamara McKinney, United States	2001 ....Janica Kostelic, Croatia
1984 ....Erika Hess, Switzerland	2002 ....Laure Pequegnot, France

GIANT SLALOM

1967 ....Nancy Greene, Canada	1986 ....Vreni Schneider, Switzerland
1968 ....Nancy Greene, Canada	1987 ....Vreni Schneider, Switzerland
1969 ....Marilyn Cochran, United States	Maria Walliser, Switzerland
1970 ....Michèle Jacot, France	1988 ....Mateja Svet, Yugoslavia
Françoise Macchi, France	1989 ....Vreni Schneider, Switzerland
1971 ....Annemarie Pröll, Austria	1990 ....Anita Wachter, Austria
1972 ....Annemarie Pröll, Austria	1991 ....Vreni Schneider, Switzerland
1973 ....Monika Kaserer, Austria	1992 ....Carole Merle, France
1974 ....Hanni Wenzel, Liechtenstein	1993 ....Carole Merle, France
1975 ....Annemarie Moser-Pröll, Austria	1994 ....Anita Wachter, Austria
1976 ....Lise-Marie Morerod, Switzerland	1995 ....Vreni Schneider, Switzerland
1977 ....Lise-Marie Morerod, Switzerland	1996 ....Martina Ertl, Germany
1978 ....Lise-Marie Morerod, Switzerland	1997 ....Deborah Compagnoni, Italy
1979 ....Christa Kinshofer, W Germany	1998 ....Martina Ertl, Germany
1980 ....Hanni Wenzel, Liechtenstein	1999 ....Alexandra Meissnitzer, Austria
1981 ....Marie-Thérèse Nadig, Switzerland	2000 ....Michaela Dorfmeister, Austria
1982 ....Irene Epple, W Germany	2001 ....Sonja Nef, Switzerland
1983 ....Tamara McKinney, United States	2002 ....Sonja Nef, Switzerland
1984 ....Erika Hess, Switzerland	
1985 ....Maria Keihl, W Germany	
Michela Figini, Switzerland	

SUPER G

1986 ....Maria Kiehl, W Germany	1991 ....Carole Merle, France
1987 ....Maria Walliser, Switzerland	1992 ....Carole Merle, France
1988 ....Michela Figini, Switzerland	1993 ....Katja Seizinger, Germany
1989 ....Carole Merle, France	1994 ....Katja Seizinger, Germany
1990 ....Carole Merle, France	1995 ....Katja Seizinger, Germany

Women (Cont.)

SUPER G (CONT.)

1996 ....Katja Seizinger, Germany	2000 ....Renate Götschl, Austria
1997 ....Hilde Gerg, Germany	2001 ....Regine Cavagnoud, France
1998 ....Katja Seizinger, Germany	2002 ....Hilde Gerg, Germany
1999 ....Alexandra Meissnitzer, Austria	

COMBINED

1979 ....Annemarie Moser-Pröll, Austria	1991 ....Sabine Ginther, Austria
Hanni Wenzel, Liechtenstein	1992 ....Sabine Ginther, Austria
1980 ....Hanni Wenzel, Liechtenstein	1993 ....Anita Wachter, Austria
1981 ....Marie-Thérèse Nadig, Switzerland	1994 ....Pernilla Wiberg, Sweden
1982 ....Irene Epple, W Germany	1995 ....Pernilla Wiberg, Sweden
1983 ....Hanni Wenzel, Liechtenstein	1996 ....Anita Wachter, Austria
1984 ....Erika Hess, Switzerland	1997 ....Pernilla Wiberg, Sweden
1985 ....Brigitte Oertli, Switzerland	1998 ....Hilde Gerg, Germany
1986 ....Maria Walliser, Switzerland	1999 ....Hilde Gerg, Germany
1987 ....Brigitte Oertli, Switzerland	2000 ....Renate Götschl, Austria
1988 ....Brigitte Oertli, Switzerland	2001 ....Janica Kostelic, Croatia
1989 ....Brigitte Oertli, Switzerland	2002 ....Renate Götschl, Austria
1990 ....Anita Wachter, Austria	

World Cup Career Victories

Men

DOWNHILL

25	Franz Klammer, Austria
19	Peter Müller, Switzerland
15	Franz Heinzer, Switzerland

SLALOM

40	Ingemar Stenmark, Sweden
35	Alberto Tomba, Italy
16	Marc Girardelli, Luxembourg

GIANT SLALOM

46	Ingemar Stenmark, Sweden
19	*Michael von Grünigen, Switz
15	Alberto Tomba, Italy

SUPER G

16	*Hermann Maier, Austria
10	Pirmin Zurbriggen, Switzerland
7	Marc Girardelli, Luxembourg

COMBINED

11	Phil Mahre, United States
	Pirmin Zurbriggen, Switzerland
	Marc Girardelli, Luxembourg

*Active in 2001.

Women

DOWNHILL

36	Annemarie Moser-Pröll, Austria
17	Michela Figini, Switzerland
16	Katja Seizinger, Germany

SLALOM

33	Vreni Schneider, Switzerland
21	Erika Hess, Switzerland
15	Perrine Pelen, France

GIANT SLALOM

21	Vreni Schneider, Switzerland
16	Annemarie Moser-Pröll, Austria
14	Anita Wachter, Austria
	Lise-Marie Morerod, Switzerland

SUPER G

16	Katja Seizinger, Germany
12	Carole Merle, France
4	Alexandra Meissnitzer, Austria
	Regine Cavagnoud, France

COMBINED

8	Hanni Wenzel, Lichtenstein
7	Annemarie Moser-Pröll, Austria
	Brigitte Oertli, Switzerland

U.S. Olympic Gold Medalists

Men

Year	Winner	Event
1980 ....Phil Mahre		Combined
1984 ....Bill Johnson		Downhill
1984 ....Phil Mahre		Slalom
1994 ....Tommy Moe		Downhill

Women

Year	Winner	Event
1948 ....Gretchen Fraser		Slalom
1952 ....Andrea Mead Lawrence		Slalom
1952 ....Andrea Mead Lawrence		Giant Slalom
1972 ....Barbara Ann Cochran		Slalom
1984 ....Debbie Armstrong		Giant Slalom
1994 ....Diann Roffe-Steinrotter		Super G
1998 ....Picabo Street		Super G

Figure Skating

Canada and Russia share the Olympic pairs gold medal

Ice Capades

A vote-swapping scandal marred the Olympic skating competition—and it didn't stop there

BY MERRELL NODEN

THIS WAS THE year the ice finally cracked wide open, revealing the cynical deal-making beneath figure skating's glittery surface. The sport has seen its share of nastiness before: In 1994, Tonya Harding conspired to hire a hitman to injure her rival, Nancy Kerrigan. But this scandal was different, involving, as it did, not a single bad egg, but the integrity of the sport itself. To those in the know, vote-swapping between competition judges hardly qualified as news, though it certainly was embarrassing to have it all revealed to the public, especially at an Olympics.

And unfortunately for the International Skating Union (ISU), the scandal came in the first event on the Olympic program, the pairs competition, and thereby cast an inescapable shadow across the rest of the events, including over Sarah Hughes's heartwarming, come-from-behind win in the ladies' final. The 16-year-old honor student's display of giddy joy upon learning she'd won restored some of the sport's innocence, but only some of it. Questions lingered into the late spring, when the ISU Congress gathered in Kyoto to devise a better way to pick its

winners, and into the summer as well, when damning new allegations surfaced and forced the ISU to reopen the case.

Here's how the scandal unfolded: Skating first, the Russian team of Anton Sikharulidze and Elena Berezhenaya performed somewhat tentatively and made one obvious mistake, a stumble by Sikharulidze. The Canadian team of Jamie Salé and David Pelletier made no mistakes and, gaining confidence as they fed off the appreciative crowd, also showed more joy in their skating.

Yet, apart from the Canadians' exuberance and the Russians' one mistake, there was little to separate the two pairs. "It was close," said referee Ronald Pfenning of the U.S. When the scores came up, they showed a 5–4 win for Sikharulidze and Berezhenaya. The crowd booed lustily, as did millions watching at home in the U.S. and Canada. The scoring split along old cold war lines, with the judges from Russia, China, the Ukraine and Poland voting for the Russians, and those from Canada, the U.S., Germany and Japan voting for the Canadians. The deciding vote fell to France, in the person of Marie-Reine Le Gougne, a 40-year-old for-

SIMON BRUTY

The ebullient Hughes vaulted from fourth place to first.

Marina Anissina and Gwendal Peizerat vehemently denied that their victory was rigged, though it was established that Anissina knew Tokhtakhounov. In early August 2002 the IOC announced it was considering wiping out the 2002 results as a solution to the mess.

After Alexei Yagudin of Russia took the men's gold medal (and Tim Goebel of the U.S. finished third), the ladies final temporarily restored the sport's dignity. Hughes, a junior at Great Neck North High School on Long Island, decided to go for broke after finishing fourth in the short program, behind the favorite, Michelle Kwan, their teammate Sasha Cohen and the woman many figured would battle Kwan for the gold, Irina Slutskaya, the 23-year-old Russian champ. Skating with abandon, Hughes landed all of her jumps in the long program. When she finished her final spin, she stared in wide-eyed disbelief at her coach, Robin Wagner, as flowers and stuffed animals and cheers rained down around her.

Each of the other three contenders succumbed to nerves in their long programs, and when an NBC cameraman told Hughes that she'd won, she lit up with joy and a hint of disbelief. The Russians protested, since, in this atmosphere, who knew what good might come of it? But Slutskaya, who barely held on to a triple flip and didn't attempt her two planned triple-triples, would have to content herself with silver. The delightful Hughes, whose next task was to study for the SAT, would keep her well-earned gold.

But even Hughes's surprising triumph could not erase the stain of scandal, which would only darken as 2002 progressed. Clearly, the ISU and the IOC had much work to do to restore the public's faith.

mer skater from Strasbourg. She cast her vote for the Russians.

That sour note might well have been the end of the affair, if not for Le Gougne's extraordinary, tearful confession at the mandatory judges' meeting the following day. She claimed that the head of the French federation, Didier Gailhaguet, had pressured her to vote for the Russians, in exchange for their vote in the ice dance competition. But Le Gougne later changed her story, claiming that almost from the day she was named a judge, she had been pressured to vote for the Canadians. The Canadians denied this, but the scandal remained the biggest Olympic story for almost a week.

In the end, the ISU's solution was to award a second pair of gold medals to Pelletier and Salé a full six days after the final. The Canadians were all smiles when they posed with their co-gold medalists, who, though they tried gamely to look magnanimous, succeeded only in looking a little bewildered. The ISU suspended both Le Gougne and Gailhaguet for three years.

Six months later, newspapers reported that Uzbek-born Alimzhan Tokhtakhounov, a reputed mobster, had contacted at least six judges in an effort to rig the pairs and dance competitions in Salt Lake City. The gold-medal-winnning French ice dance team of

FOR THE RECORD 2002

World Champions

Nagano, Japan, March 15–24

Women

1........Irina Slutskaya, Russia
2........Michelle Kwan, United States
3........Fumie Suguri, Japan

Men

1.........Alexei Yagudin, Russia
1.........Timothy Goebel, United States
3.........Takeshi Honda, Japan

Pairs

1........Xue Shen and Hongbo Zhao, China
2........Tatiana Totmianina and Maxim Marinin, Russia
3........Kyoko Ina and John Zimmerman, United States

Dance

1.........Irina Lobacheva and Ilia Averbukh, Russia
2.........Shae-Lynn Bourne and Victor Kraatz, Canada
3.........Galit Chait and Sergei Sakhnovski, Israel

World Figure Skating Championships Medal Table

Country	Gold	Silver	Bronze	Total
Russia	6	5	1	12
United States	1	2	2	5
Canada	1	2	0	3
France	1	1	1	3
China	1	1	1	3
Italy	1	1	0	2
Japan	0	0	2	2
Israel	0	0	1	1
Lithuania	0	0	1	1

Champions of the United States

Los Angeles, January 6-13

Women

1......................Michelle Kwan, Los Angeles FSC
2......................Sasha Cohen, Orange County FSC
3......................Sarah E. Hughes, SC of New York

Men

1........................Todd J. Eldredge, Los Angeles FSC
2........................Timothy Goebel, Winterhurst FSC
3........................Michael G. Weiss, Washington FSC

Pairs

1. ....Kyoko Ina and John Zimmerman,
SC of New York/Birmingham FSC
2......................Tiffany Scott and Philip Dulebohn,
Colonial FSC and Univeristy of Del FSC
3......................Stephanie Kalesavich and Aaron L.
Parchem, Detroit SC

Dance

1. ....Naomi Lang and Peter Tchernyshev,
American Academy FSC
2......................Tanith Belbin and Benjamin Agosto,
Detroit SC
3......................Melissa B. Gregory and Denis A.
Petukhov, Broadmoor SC and Skokie
Valley SC

Figuring it Out

In light of recent proposals to overhaul figure skating's scoring system, here is the sport's dirty little secret: The current judging system, flawed as it is, is great for figure skating's popularity. Part of the sport's appeal lies in the subjectivity of the scoring. Viewers delight in accusing the judges of being corrupt, idiotic or mean to cute Canadian kids. "What people love about this sport is they can all be experts," says Joe Inman, a U.S. judge. "The public will always want the score from the individual judges displayed. Many of my non-skating friends find this is one of the most exciting aspects of the sport." Nothing like an unpopular decision and a good conspiracy theory to make figure skating must-see TV.

—E.M. Swift

Skating Terminology*

Basic Skating Terms

Edges: The two sides of the skating blade, on either side of the grooved center. There is an inside edge, on the inner side of the leg; and an outside edge, on the outer side of the leg.

Free Foot, Hip, Knee, Side, etc.: The foot a skater is not skating on at any one time is the free foot; everything on that side of the body is then called "free." (See also "skating foot.")

Free Skating (Freestyle): A 4- or 5-minute competition program of free-skating components, choreographed to music, with no set elements. Skating moves include jumps, spins, steps and other linking movements.

Skating Foot, Hip, Knee, Side, etc.: Opposite of the free foot, hip, knee, side, etc. The foot a skater is skating on at any one time is the skating foot; everything on that side of the body is then called "skating."

Toe Picks (Toe Rakes): The teeth at the front of the skate blade, used primarily for certain jumps and spins.

Trace, Tracing: The line left on the ice by the skater's blade.

Jumps

Waltz: A beginner's jump, involving half a revolution in the air, taken from a forward outside edge and landed on the back outside edge of the other foot.

Toe Loop: A one-revolution jump taken off from and landed on the same back outside edge. This jump is similar to the loop jump except that the skater kicks the toe pick of the free leg into the ice upon takeoff, providing added power.

Toe Walley: A jump similar to the toe loop, except that the takeoff is from the inside edge.

Flip: A jump taken off with the toe pick of the free leg from a back inside edge and landed on a back outside edge, with one in-air revolution.

Lutz: A toe jump similar to the flip, taken off with the toe pick of the free leg from a backward outside edge. The skater enters the jump skating in one direction, and concludes the jump skating in the opposite direction. Usually performed in the corners of the rink. Named after inventor Alois Lutz, who first landed the jump in Vienna, 1918.

Salchow: A one-, two- or three-revolution jump. The skater takes off from the back inside edge of one foot and lands backwards on the outside edge of the right foot, the opposite foot from which the skater took off. Named for its originator and first Olympic champion (1908), Sweden's Ulrich Salchow.

Axel: A combination of the waltz and loop jumps, including one-and-a-half revolutions. The only jump begun from a forward outside edge, the Axel is landed on the back outside edge of the opposite foot. Named for its inventor, Norway's Axel Paulsen.

Spins

Spin: The rotation of the body in one place on the ice. Various spins are the back, fast or scratch, sit, camel, butterfly and layback.

Camel Spin: A spin with the skater in an arabesque position (the free leg at right angles to the leg on the ice).

Flying Camel Spin: A jump spin ending in the camel-spin position.

Flying Sit Spin: A jump spin in which the skater leaps off the ice, assumes a sitting position at the peak of the jump, lands and spins in a similar sitting position.

Pair Movements/Techniques

Death Spiral: One of the most dramatic moves in figure skating. The man, acting as the center of a circle, holds tightly to the hand of his partner and pulls her around him. The woman, gliding on one foot, achieves a position almost horizontal to the ice.

Lifts: The most spectacular moves in pairs skating. They involve any maneuver in which the man lifts the woman off the ice. The man often holds his partner above his head with one hand.

Throws: The man lifts the woman into the air and throws her away from him. She spins in the air and lands on one foot.

Twist: The man throws the woman into the air. She spins in the air (either a double- or triple-twist), and he catches her at the landing.

*Compiled by the United States Figure Skating Association.

World Champions

Women

1906	Madge Sayers-Cave, Great Britain
1907	Madge Sayers-Cave, Great Britain
1908	Lily Kronberger, Hungary
1909	Lily Kronberger, Hungary
1910	Lily Kronberger, Hungary
1911	Lily Kronberger, Hungary
1912	Opika von Meray Horvath, Hungary
1913	Opika von Meray Horvath, Hungary
1914	Opika von Meray Horvath, Hungary
1915–21	No competition
1922	Herma Plank-Szabo, Austria
1923	Herma Plank-Szabo, Austria
1924	Herma Plank-Szabo, Austria
1925	Herma Jaross-Szabo, Austria
1926	Herma Jaross-Szabo, Austria
1927	Sonja Henie, Norway
1928	Sonja Henie, Norway
1929	Sonja Henie, Norway
1930	Sonja Henie, Norway
1931	Sonja Henie, Norway
1932	Sonja Henie, Norway
1933	Sonja Henie, Norway
1934	Sonja Henie, Norway
1935	Sonja Henie, Norway
1936	Sonja Henie, Norway
1937	Cecilia Colledge, Great Britain
1938	Megan Taylor, Great Britain
1939	Megan Taylor, Great Britain
1940–46	No competition
1947	Barbara Ann Scott, Canada
1948	Barbara Ann Scott, Canada
1949	Alena Vrzanova, Czechoslovakia
1950	Alena Vrzanova, Czechoslovakia
1951	Jeannette Altwegg, Great Britain
1952	Jacqueline duBief, France
1953	Tenley Albright, United States
1954	Gundi Busch, W Germany
1955	Tenley Albright, United States
1956	Carol Heiss, United States
1957	Carol Heiss, United States

Women (Cont.)

1958	Carol Heiss, United States
1959	Carol Heiss, United States
1960	Carol Heiss, United States
1961	No competition
1962	Sjoukje Dijkstra, Netherlands
1963	Sjoukje Dijkstra, Netherlands
1964	Sjoukje Dijkstra, Netherlands
1965	Petra Burka, Canada
1966	Peggy Fleming, United States
1967	Peggy Fleming, United States
1968	Peggy Fleming, United States
1969	Gabriele Seyfert, E Germany
1970	Gabriele Seyfert, E Germany
1971	Beatrix Schuba, Austria
1972	Beatrix Schuba, Austria
1973	Karen Magnussen, Canada
1974	Christine Errath, E Germany
1975	Dianne DeLeeuw, Netherlands
1976	Dorothy Hamill, United States
1977	Linda Fratianne, United States
1978	Annett Poetzsch, E Germany
1979	Linda Fratianne, United States
1980	Annett Poetzsch, E Germany
1981	Denise Biellmann, Switzerland
1982	Elaine Zayak, United States
1983	Rosalynn Sumners, United States
1984	Katarina Witt, E Germany
1985	Katarina Witt, E Germany
1986	Debi Thomas, United States
1987	Katarina Witt, E Germany
1988	Katarina Witt, E Germany
1989	Midori Ito, Japan
1990	Jill Trenary, United States
1991	Kristi Yamaguchi, United States
1992	Kristi Yamaguchi, United States
1993	Oksana Baiul, Ukraine
1994	Yuka Sato, Japan
1995	Chen Lu, China
1996	Michelle Kwan, United States
1997	Tara Lipinski, United States
1998	Michelle Kwan, United States
1999	Maria Butyrskaya, Russia
2000	Michelle Kwan, United States
2001	Michelle Kwan, United States
2002	Irina Slutskaya, Russia

Men

1896	Gilbert Fuchs, Germany
1897	Gustav Hugel, Austria
1898	Henning Grenander, Sweden
1899	Gustav Hugel, Austria
1900	Gustav Hugel, Austria
1901	Ulrich Salchow, Sweden
1902	Ulrich Salchow, Sweden
1903	Ulrich Salchow, Sweden
1904	Ulrich Salchow, Sweden
1905	Ulrich Salchow, Sweden
1906	Gilbert Fuchs, Germany
1907	Ulrich Salchow, Sweden
1908	Ulrich Salchow, Sweden
1909	Ulrich Salchow, Sweden
1910	Ulrich Salchow, Sweden
1911	Ulrich Salchow, Sweden
1912	Fritz Kachler, Austria
1913	Fritz Kachler, Austria
1914	Gosta Sandhal, Sweden
1915–21	No competition
1922	Gillis Grafstrom, Sweden
1923	Fritz Kachler, Austria
1924	Gillis Grafstrom, Sweden
1925	Willy Bockl, Austria
1926	Willy Bockl, Austria
1927	Willy Bockl, Austria
1928	Willy Bockl, Austria
1929	Gillis Grafstrom, Sweden
1930	Karl Schafer, Austria
1931	Karl Schafer, Austria
1932	Karl Schafer, Austria
1933	Karl Schafer, Austria
1934	Karl Schafer, Austria
1935	Karl Schafer, Austria
1936	Karl Schafer, Austria
1937	Felix Kaspar, Austria
1938	Felix Kaspar, Austria
1939	Graham Sharp, Great Britain
1940–46	No competition
1947	Hans Gerschwiler, Switzerland
1948	Dick Button, United States
1949	Dick Button, United States
1950	Dick Button, United States
1951	Dick Button, United States
1952	Dick Button, United States
1953	Hayes Alan Jenkins, United States
1954	Hayes Alan Jenkins, United States
1955	Hayes Alan Jenkins, United States
1956	Hayes Alan Jenkins, United States
1957	David W. Jenkins, United States
1958	David W. Jenkins, United States
1959	David W. Jenkins, United States
1960	Alan Giletti, France
1961	No competition
1962	Donald Jackson, Canada
1963	Donald McPherson, Canada
1964	Manfred Schneldorfer, W Germany
1965	Alain Calmat, France
1966	Emmerich Danzer, Austria
1967	Emmerich Danzer, Austria
1968	Emmerich Danzer, Austria
1969	Tim Wood, United States
1970	Tim Wood, United States
1971	Andrej Nepela, Czechoslovakia
1972	Andrej Nepela, Czechoslovakia
1973	Andrej Nepela, Czechoslovakia
1974	Jan Hoffmann, E Germany
1975	Sergei Volkov, USSR
1976	John Curry, Great Britain
1977	Vladimir Kovalev, USSR
1978	Charles Tickner, United States
1979	Vladimir Kovalev, USSR
1980	Jan Hoffmann, E Germany
1981	Scott Hamilton, United States
1982	Scott Hamilton, United States
1983	Scott Hamilton, United States
1984	Scott Hamilton, United States
1985	Aleksandr Fadeev, USSR
1986	Brian Boitano, United States
1987	Brian Orser, Canada
1988	Brian Boitano, United States
1989	Kurt Browning, Canada
1990	Kurt Browning, Canada
1991	Kurt Browning, Canada
1992	Viktor Petrenko, CIS
1993	Kurt Browning, Canada
1994	Elvis Stojko, Canada
1995	Elvis Stojko, Canada

Men (Cont.)

1996..................Todd Eldredge, United States
1997..................Elvis Stojko, Canada
1998..................Alexei Yagudin, Russia
1999..................Alexei Yagudin, Russia

2000..................Alexei Yagudin, Russia
2001..................Evgeny Plushenko, Russia
2002..................Alexei Yagudin, Russia

Pairs

1908 ....Anna Hubler, Heinrich Burger, Germany
1909 ....Phyllis Johnson, James H. Johnson,
          Great Britain
1910 ....Anna Hubler, Heinrich Burger, Germany
1911 ....Ludowika Eilers, Walter Jakobsson,
          Germany/Finland
1912 ....Phyllis Johnson, James H. Johnson,
          Great Britain
1913 ....Helene Engelmann, Karl Majstrik,
          Germany
1914 ....Ludowika Jakobsson-Eilers, Walter
          Jakobsson-Eilers, Finland
1915–21 .....No competition
1922 ....Helene Engelmann, Alfred Berger,
          Germany
1923 ....Ludowika Jakobsson-Eilers, Walter
          Jakobsson-Eilers, Finland
1924 ....Helene Engelmann, Alfred Berger,
          Germany
1925 ....Herma Jaross-Szabo, Ludwig Wrede,
          Austria
1926 ....Andree Joly, Pierre Brunet, France
1927 ....Herma Jaross-Szabo, Ludwig Wrede,
          Austria
1928 ....Andree Joly, Pierre Brunet, France
1929 ....Lilly Scholz, Otto Kaiser, Austria
1930 ....Andree Brunet-Joly, Pierre Brunet-Joly,
          France
1931 ....Emilie Rotter, Laszlo Szollas, Hungary
1932 ....Andree Brunet-Joly, Pierre Brunet-Joly,
          France
1933 ....Emilie Rotter, Laszlo Szollas, Hungary
1934 ....Emilie Rotter, Laszlo Szollas, Hungary
1935 ....Emilie Rotter, Laszlo Szollas, Hungary
1936 ....Maxi Herber, Ernst Bajer, Germany
1937 ....Maxi Herber, Ernst Bajer, Germany
1938 ....Maxi Herber, Ernst Bajer, Germany
1939 ....Maxi Herber, Ernst Bajer, Germany
1940–46 ....No competition
1947 ....Micheline Lannoy, Pierre Baugniet,
          Belgium
1948 ....Micheline Lannoy, Pierre Baugniet,
          Belgium
1949 ....Andrea Kekessy, Ede Kiraly, Hungary
1950 ....Karol Kennedy, Peter Kennedy,
          United States
1951 ....Ria Baran, Paul Falk, W Germany
1952 ....Ria Baran Falk, Paul Falk, W Germany
1953 ....Jennifer Nicks, John Nicks, Great Britain
1954 ....Frances Dafoe, Norris Bowden, Canada
1955 ....Frances Dafoe, Norris Bowden, Canada
1956 ....Sissy Schwarz, Kurt Oppelt, Austria
1957 ....Barbara Wagner, Robert Paul, Canada
1958 ....Barbara Wagner, Robert Paul, Canada
1959 ....Barbara Wagner, Robert Paul, Canada
1960 ....Barbara Wagner, Robert Paul, Canada
1961 ....No competition
1962 ....Maria Jelinek, Otto Jelinek, Canada

1963 ....Marika Kilius, Hans-Jurgen Baumler,
          W Germany
1964 ....Marika Kilius, Hans-Jurgen Baumler,
          W Germany
1965 ....Ljudmila Protopopov, Oleg Protopopov,
          USSR
1966 ....Ljudmila Protopopov, Oleg Protopopov,
          USSR
1967 ....Ljudmila Protopopov, Oleg Protopopov,
          USSR
1968 ....Ljudmila Protopopov, Oleg Protopopov,
          USSR
1969 ....Irina Rodnina, Alexsei Ulanov, USSR
1970............Irina Rodnina, Alexsei Ulanov, USSR
1971 ....Irina Rodnina, Sergei Ulanov, USSR
1972 ....Irina Rodnina, Sergei Ulanov, USSR
1973 ....Irina Rodnina, Aleksandr Zaitsev, USSR
1974 ....Irina Rodnina, Aleksandr Zaitsev, USSR
1975 ....Irina Rodnina, Aleksandr Zaitsev, USSR
1976 ....Irina Rodnina, Aleksandr Zaitsev, USSR
1977 ....Irina Rodnina, Aleksandr Zaitsev, USSR
1978 ....Irina Rodnina, Aleksandr Zaitsev, USSR
1979 ....Tai Babilonia, Randy Gardner,
          United States
1980 ....Maria Cherkasova, Sergei Shakhrai,
          USSR
1981 ....Irina Vorobieva, Igor Lisovsky, USSR
1982 ....Sabine Baess, Tassilio Thierbach,
          E Germany
1983 ....Elena Valova, Oleg Vasiliev, USSR
1984 ....Barbara Underhill, Paul Martini, Canada
1985 ....Elena Valova, Oleg Vasiliev, USSR
1986 ....Ekaterina Gordeeva, Sergei Grinkov, USSR
1987 ....Ekaterina Gordeeva, Sergei Grinkov, USSR
1988 ....Elena Valova, Oleg Vasiliev, USSR
1989 ....Ekaterina Gordeeva, Sergei Grinkov, USSR
1990 ....Ekaterina Gordeeva, Sergei Grinkov, USSR
1991 ....Natalia Mishkutienok, Artur Dmitriev,
          USSR
1992 ....Natalia Mishkutienok, Artur Dmitriev, CIS
1993 ....Isabelle Brasseur, Lloyd Eisler, Canada
1994 ....Evgenia Shishkova, Vadim Naumov,
          Russia
1995 ....Radka Kovarikova, Rene Novotny,
          Czech Republic
1996 ....Marina Eltsova, Andrey Buskhov, Russia
1997 ....Mandy Wötzel, Ingo Steuer, Germany
1998 ....Jenni Meno, Todd Sand, United States
1999 ....Elena Berezhnaya, Anton Sikharulidze,
          Russia
2000 ....Maria Petrova and Aleksei Tikhonov,
          Russia
2001 ....Jamie Salé and David Pelletier, Canada
2002 ....Xue Shen and Hongbo Zhao, China

Dance

1950 ....Lois Waring, Michael McGean, United States	1973 ....Ljudmila Pakhomova, Aleksandr Gorshkov, USSR
1951 ....Jean Westwood, Lawrence Demmy, Great Britain	1974 ....Ljudmila Pakhomova, Aleksandr Gorshkov, USSR
1952 ....Jean Westwood, Lawrence Demmy, Great Britain	1975 ....Irina Moiseeva, Andreij Minenkov, USSR
1953 ....Jean Westwood, Lawrence Demmy, Great Britain	1976 ....Ljudmila Pakhomova, Aleksandr Gorshkov, USSR
1954 ....Jean Westwood, Lawrence Demmy, Great Britain	1977 ....Irina Moiseeva, Andreij Minenkov, USSR
1955 ....Jean Westwood, Lawrence Demmy, Great Britain	1978 ....Natalia Linichuk, Gennadi Karponosov, USSR
1956 ....Pamela Wieght, Paul Thomas, Great Britain	1979 ....Natalia Linichuk, Gennadi Karponosov,USSR
1957 ....June Markham, Courtney Jones, Great Britain	1980 ....Krisztina Regoeczy, Andras Sallai, Hungary
1958 ....June Markham, Courtney Jones, Great Britain	1981 ....Jayne Torvill, Christopher Dean, Great Britain
1959 ....Doreen D. Denny, Courtney Jones, Great Britain	1982 ....Jayne Torvill, Christopher Dean, Great Britain
1960 ....Doreen D. Denny, Courtney Jones, Great Britain	1983 ....Jayne Torvill, Christopher Dean, Great Britain
1961 ....No competition	1984 ....Jayne Torvill, Christopher Dean, Great Britain
1962 ....Eva Romanova, Pavel Roman, Czechoslovakia	1985.............Natalia Bestemianova, Andrei Bukin, USSR
1963 ....Eva Romanova, Pavel Roman, Czechoslovakia	1986.............Natalia Bestemianova, Andrei Bukin, USSR
1964 ....Eva Romanova, Pavel Roman, Czechoslovakia	1987.............Natalia Bestemianova, Andrei Bukin, USSR
1965 ....Eva Romanova, Pavel Roman, Czechoslovakia	1988.............Natalia Bestemianova, Andrei Bukin, USSR
1966 ....Diane Towler, Bernard Ford, Great Britain	1989.............Marina Klimova, Sergei Ponomarenko, USSR
1967 ....Diane Towler, Bernard Ford, Great Britain	1990.............Marina Klimova, Sergei Ponomarenko, USSR
1968 ....Diane Towler, Bernard Ford, Great Britain	1991.............Isabelle Duchesnay, Paul Duchesnay, France
1969 ....Diane Towler, Bernard Ford, Great Britain	1992.............Marina Klimova, Sergei Ponomarenko, CIS
1970 ....Ljudmila Pakhomova, Aleksandr Gorshkov, USSR	1993 ....Renee Roca, Gorsha Sur, United States
1971 ....Ljudmila Pakhomova, Aleksandr Gorshkov, USSR	1994 ....Oksana Grishuk, Evgeny Platov, Russia
1972 ....Ljudmila Pakhomova, Aleksandr Gorshkov, USSR	1995 ....Oksana Grishuk, Evgeny Platov, Russia
	1996 ....Oksana Grishuk, Evgeny Platov, Russia
	1997 ....Oksana Grishuk, Evgeny Platov, Russia
	1998 ....Anjelika Krylova and Oleg Ovsyannikov, Russia
	1999 ....Anjelika Krylova and Oleg Ovsyannikov, Russia
	2000 ....Marina Anissina and Gwendal Peizerat, France
	2001 ....Barbara Fusar-Poli and Maurizio Margaglio, Italy
	2002 ....Irina Lobacheva and Ilia Averbukh, Russia

Champions of the United States

The championships held in 1914, 1918, 1920 and 1921 under the auspices of the International Skating Union of America were open to Canadians, although the competitions were considered to be United States championships. Beginning in 1922, the championships have been held under the auspices of the United States Figure Skating Association.

Women

1914 ....Theresa Weld, SC of Boston	1931 ....Maribel Y. Vinson, SC of Boston
1915–17 .....No competition	1932 ....Maribel Y. Vinson, SC of Boston
1918............Rosemary S. Beresford, New York SC	1933 ....Maribel Y. Vinson, SC of Boston
1919 ....No competition	1934 ....Suzanne Davis, SC of Boston
1920 ....Theresa Weld, SC of Boston	1935 ....Maribel Y. Vinson, SC of Boston
1921 ....Theresa Weld Blanchard, SC of Boston	1936 ....Maribel Y. Vinson, SC of Boston
1922 ....Theresa Weld Blanchard, SC of Boston	1937 ....Maribel Y. Vinson, SC of Boston
1923 ....Theresa Weld Blanchard, SC of Boston	1938 ....Joan Tozzer, SC of Boston
1924 ....Theresa Weld Blanchard, SC of Boston	1939 ....Joan Tozzer, SC of Boston
1925 ....Beatrix Loughran, New York SC	1940 ....Joan Tozzer, SC of Boston
1926 ....Beatrix Loughran, New York SC	1941 ....Jane Vaughn, Philadelphia SC & HS
1927 ....Beatrix Loughran, New York SC	1942 ....Jane Vaughn Sullivan, Philadelphia SC & HS
1928 ....Maribel Y. Vinson, SC of Boston	1943............Gretchen Van Zandt Merrill, SC of Boston
1929 ....Maribel Y. Vinson, SC of Boston	1944............Gretchen Van Zandt Merrill, SC of Boston
1930 ....Maribel Y. Vinson, SC of Boston	

Women (Cont.)

1945...........Gretchen Van Zandt Merrill, SC of Boston	1975 ....Dorothy Hamill, SC of New York
1946...........Gretchen Van Zandt Merrill, SC of Boston	1976 ....Dorothy Hamill, SC of New York
1947...........Gretchen Van Zandt Merrill, SC of Boston	1977 ....Linda Fratianne, Los Angeles FSC
1948...........Gretchen Van Zandt Merrill, SC of Boston	1978 ....Linda Fratianne, Los Angeles FSC
1949 ....Yvonne Claire Sherman, SC of New York	1979 ....Linda Fratianne, Los Angeles FSC
1950 ....Yvonne Claire Sherman, SC of New York	1980 ....Linda Fratianne, Los Angeles FSC
1951 ....Sonya Klopfer, Junior SC of New York	1981 ....Elaine Zayak, SC of New York
1952 ....Tenley E. Albright, SC of Boston	1982 ....Rosalynn Sumners, Seattle SC
1953 ....Tenley E. Albright, SC of Boston	1983 ....Rosalynn Sumners, Seattle SC
1954 ....Tenley E. Albright, SC of Boston	1984 ....Rosalynn Sumners, Seattle SC
1955 ....Tenley E. Albright, SC of Boston	1985 ....Tiffany Chin, San Diego FSC
1956 ....Tenley E. Albright, SC of Boston	1986 ....Debi Thomas, Los Angeles FSC
1957 ....Carol E. Heiss, SC of New York	1987 ....Jill Trenary, Broadmoor SC
1958 ....Carol E. Heiss, SC of New York	1988 ....Debi Thomas, Los Angeles FSC
1959 ....Carol E. Heiss, SC of New York	1989 ....Jill Trenary, Broadmoor SC
1960 ....Carol E. Heiss, SC of New York	1990 ....Jill Trenary, Broadmoor SC
1961 ....Laurence R. Owen, SC of Boston	1991 ....Tonya Harding, Carousel FSC
1962 ....Barbara Roles Pursley, Arctic Blades FSC	1992 ....Kristi Yamaguchi, St Moritz ISC
1963 ....Lorraine G. Hanlon, SC of Boston	1993 ....Nancy Kerrigan, Colonial FSC
1964 ....Peggy Fleming, Arctic Blades FSC	1994 ....Tonya Harding, Portland FSC
1965 ....Peggy Fleming, Arctic Blades FSC	1995 ....Nicole Bobek, Los Angeles FSC
1966 ....Peggy Fleming, City of Colorado Springs	1996 ....Michelle Kwan, Los Angeles FSC
1967 ....Peggy Fleming, Broadmoor SC	1997 ....Tara Lipinski, Detroit SC
1968 ....Peggy Fleming, Broadmoor SC	1998 ....Michelle Kwan, Los Angeles FSC
1969 ....Janet Lynn, Wagon Wheel FSC	1999 ....Michelle Kwan, Los Angeles FSC
1970 ....Janet Lynn, Wagon Wheel FSC	2000 ....Michelle Kwan, Los Angeles FSC
1971 ....Janet Lynn, Wagon Wheel FSC	2001 ....Michelle Kwan, Los Angeles FSC
1972 ....Janet Lynn, Wagon Wheel FSC	2002 ....Michelle Kwan, Los Angeles FSC
1973 ....Janet Lynn, Wagon Wheel FSC	
1974 ....Dorothy Hamill, SC of New York	

Men

1914 ....Norman M. Scott, WC of Montreal	1952 ....Dick Button, SC of Boston
1915–17 .....No competition	1953 ....Hayes Alan Jenkins, Cleveland SC
1918 ....Nathaniel W. Niles, SC of Boston	1954 ....Hayes Alan Jenkins, Broadmoor SC
1919 ....No competition	1955 ....Hayes Alan Jenkins, Broadmoor SC
1920 ....Sherwin C. Badger, SC of Boston	1956 ....Hayes Alan Jenkins, Broadmoor SC
1921 ....Sherwin C. Badger, SC of Boston	1957 ....David Jenkins, Broadmoor SC
1922 ....Sherwin C. Badger, SC of Boston	1958 ....David Jenkins, Broadmoor SC
1923 ....Sherwin C. Badger, SC of Boston	1959 ....David Jenkins, Broadmoor SC
1924 ....Sherwin C. Badger, SC of Boston	1960 ....David Jenkins, Broadmoor SC
1925 ....Nathaniel W. Niles, SC of Boston	1961 ....Bradley R. Lord, SC of Boston
1926 ....Chris I. Christenson, Twin City FSC	1962 ....Monty Hoyt, Broadmoor SC
1927 ....Nathaniel W. Niles, SC of Boston	1963 ....Thomas Litz, Hershey FSC
1928 ....Roger F. Turner, SC of Boston	1964 ....Scott Ethan Allen, SC of New York
1929 ....Roger F. Turner, SC of Boston	1965 ....Gary C. Visconti, Detroit SC
1930 ....Roger F. Turner, SC of Boston	1966 ....Scott Ethan Allen, SC of New York
1931 ....Roger F. Turner, SC of Boston	1967 ....Gary C. Visconti, Detroit SC
1932 ....Roger F. Turner, SC of Boston	1968 ....Tim Wood, Detroit SC
1933 ....Roger F. Turner, SC of Boston	1969 ....Tim Wood, Detroit SC
1934 ....Roger F. Turner, SC of Boston	1970 ....Tim Wood, City of Colorado Springs
1935 ....Robin H. Lee, SC of New York	1971 ....John Misha Petkevich, Great Falls FSC
1936 ....Robin H. Lee, SC of New York	1972 ....Kenneth Shelley, Arctic Blades FSC
1937 ....Robin H. Lee, SC of New York	1973 ....Gordon McKellen Jr., SC of Lake Placid
1938 ....Robin H. Lee, Chicago FSC	1974 ....Gordon McKellen Jr., SC of Lake Placid
1939 ....Robin H. Lee, St Paul FSC	1975 ....Gordon McKellen Jr., SC of Lake Placid
1940 ....Eugene Turner, Los Angeles FSC	1976 ....Terry Kubicka, Arctic Blades FSC
1941 ....Eugene Turner, Los Angeles FSC	1977 ....Charles Tickner, Denver FSC
1942 ....Robert Specht, Chicago FSC	1978 ....Charles Tickner, Denver FSC
1943 ....Arthur R. Vaughn Jr., Philadelphia SC & HS	1979 ....Charles Tickner, Denver FSC
	1980 ....Charles Tickner, Denver FSC
1944–45 .....No competition	1981 ....Scott Hamilton, Philadelphia SC & HS
1946 ....Dick Button, Philadelphia SC & HS	1982 ....Scott Hamilton, Philadelphia SC & HS
1947 ....Dick Button, Philadelphia SC & HS	1983 ....Scott Hamilton, Philadelphia SC & HS
1948 ....Dick Button, Philadelphia SC & HS	1984 ....Scott Hamilton, Philadelphia SC & HS
1949 ....Dick Button, Philadelphia SC & HS	1985 ....Brian Boitano, Peninsula FSC
1950 ....Dick Button, SC of Boston	1986 ....Brian Boitano, Peninsula FSC
1951 ....Dick Button, SC of Boston	1987 ....Brian Boitano, Peninsula FSC

Men (Cont.)

1988 ....Brian Boitano, Peninsula FSC
1989 ....Christopher Bowman, Los Angeles FSC
1990 ....Todd Eldredge, Los Angeles FSC
1991 ....Todd Eldredge, Los Angeles FSC
1992 ....Christopher Bowman, Los Angeles FSC
1993 ....Scott Davis, Broadmoor SC
1994 ....Scott Davis, Broadmoor SC
1995 ....Todd Eldredge, Detroit SC

1996 ....Rudy Galindo, St Moritz ISC
1997 ....Todd Eldredge, Detroit SC
1998 ....Todd Eldredge, Detroit SC
1999 ....Michael Weiss, Washington FSC
2000 ....Michael Weiss, Washington FSC
2001 ....Timothy Goebel, Winterhurst FSC
2002 ....Todd Eldredge, Los Angeles FSC

Pairs

1914 ......Jeanne Chevalier, Norman M. Scott,
            WC of Montreal
1915–17.No competition
1918 ......Theresa Weld, Nathaniel W. Niles,
            SC of Boston
1919 ......No competition
1920 ......Theresa Weld, Nathaniel W. Niles,
            SC of Boston
1921 ......Theresa Weld Blanchard, Nathaniel W.
            Niles, SC of Boston
1922 ......Theresa Weld Blanchard, Nathaniel W.
            Niles, SC of Boston
1923 ......Theresa Weld Blanchard, Nathaniel W.
            Niles, SC of Boston
1924 ......Theresa Weld Blanchard, Nathaniel W.
            Niles, SC of Boston
1925 ......Theresa Weld Blanchard, Nathaniel W.
            Niles, SC of Boston
1926 ......Theresa Weld Blanchard, Nathaniel W.
            Niles, SC of Boston
1927 ......Theresa Weld Blanchard, Nathaniel W.
            Niles, SC of Boston
1928 ......Maribel Y. Vinson, Thornton L. Coolidge,
            SC of Boston
1929 ......Maribel Y. Vinson, Thornton L. Coolidge,
            SC of Boston
1930 ......Beatrix Loughran, Sherwin C. Badger,
            SC of New York
1931 ......Beatrix Loughran, Sherwin C. Badger,
            SC of New York
1932 ......Beatrix Loughran, Sherwin C. Badger,
            SC of New York
1933 ......Maribel Y. Vinson, George E. B. Hill,
            SC of Boston
1934 ......Grace E. Madden, James L. Madden,
            SC of Boston
1935 ......Maribel Y. Vinson, George E. B. Hill,
            SC of Boston
1936 ......Maribel Y. Vinson, George E. B. Hill,
            SC of Boston
1937 ......Maribel Y. Vinson, George E. B. Hill,
            SC of Boston
1938 ......Joan Tozzer, M. Bernard Fox, SC of Boston
1939 ......Joan Tozzer, M. Bernard Fox, SC of Boston
1940 ......Joan Tozzer, M. Bernard Fox, SC of Boston
1941 ......Donna Atwood, Eugene Turner, Mercury
            FSC/Los Angeles FSC
1942 ......Doris Schubach, Walter Noffke,
            Springfield Ice Birds
1943 ......Doris Schubach, Walter Noffke,
            Springfield Ice Birds
1944 ......Doris Schubach, Walter Noffke,
            Springfield Ice Birds
1945 ......Donna Jeanne Pospisil, Jean-Pierre Brunet,
            SC of New York
1946 ......Donna Jeanne Pospisil, Jean-Pierre Brunet,
            SC of New York

1947 ......Yvonne Claire Sherman, Robert J.
            Swenning, SC of New York
1948 ......Karol Kennedy, Peter Kennedy, Seattle SC
1949 ......Karol Kennedy, Peter Kennedy, Seattle SC
1950 ......Karol Kennedy, Peter Kennedy,
            Broadmoor SC
1951 ......Karol Kennedy, Peter Kennedy,
            Broadmoor SC
1952 ......Karol Kennedy, Peter Kennedy,
            Broadmoor SC
1953 ......Carole Ann Ormaca, Robin Greiner,
            SC of Fresno
1954 ......Carole Ann Ormaca, Robin Greiner,
            SC of Fresno
1955 ......Carole Ann Ormaca, Robin Greiner,
            St Moritz ISC
1956 ......Carole Ann Ormaca, Robin Greiner,
            St Moritz ISC
1957 ......Nancy Rouillard Ludington, Ronald
            Ludington, Commonwealth FSC/
            SC of Boston
1958 ......Nancy Rouillard Ludington, Ronald
            Ludington, Commonwealth FSC/
            SC of Boston
1959 ......Nancy Rouillard Ludington, Ronald
            Ludington, Commonwealth FSC
1960 ......Nancy Rouillard Ludington, Ronald
            Ludington, Commonwealth FSC
1961 ......Maribel Y. Owen, Dudley S. Richards,
            SC of Boston
1962 ......Dorothyann Nelson, Pieter Kollen,
            Village of Lake Placid
1963 ......Judianne Fotheringill, Jerry J. Fotheringill,
            Broadmoor SC
1964 ......Judianne Fotheringill, Jerry J. Fotheringill,
            Broadmoor SC
1965 ......Vivian Joseph, Ronald Joseph, Chicago FSC
1966 ......Cynthia Kauffman, Ronald Kauffman,
            Seattle SC
1967 ......Cynthia Kauffman, Ronald Kauffman,
            Seattle SC
1968 ......Cynthia Kauffman, Ronald Kauffman,
            Seattle SC
1969 ......Cynthia Kauffman, Ronald Kauffman,
            Seattle SC
1970 ......Jo Jo Starbuck, Kenneth Shelley,
            Arctic Blades FSC
1971 ......Jo Jo Starbuck, Kenneth Shelley,
            Arctic Blades FSC
1972 ......Jo Jo Starbuck, Kenneth Shelley,
            Arctic Blades FSC
1973 ......Melissa Militano, Mark Militano,
            SC of New York
1974 ......Melissa Militano, Johnny Johns,
            SC of New York/Detroit SC
1975 ......Melissa Militano, Johnny Johns,
            SC of NY/ Detroit SC

Pairs (Cont.)

1976 ......Tai Babilonia, Randy Gardner, Los Angeles FSC
1977 ......Tai Babilonia, Randy Gardner, LA FSC
1978 ......Tai Babilonia, Randy Gardner, Los Angeles FSC/Santa Monica FSC
1979 ......Tai Babilonia, Randy Gardner, Los Angeles FSC/Santa Monica FSC
1980 ......Tai Babilonia, Randy Gardner, Los Angeles FSC/Santa Monica FSC
1981 ......Caitlin Carruthers, Peter Carruthers, SC of Wilmington
1982 ......Caitlin Carruthers, Peter Carruthers, SC of Wilmington
1983 ......Caitlin Carruthers, Peter Carruthers, SC of Wilmington
1984 ......Caitlin Carruthers, Peter Carruthers, SC of Wilmington
1985 ......Jill Watson, Peter Oppegard, LA FSC
1986 ......Gillian Wachsman, Todd Waggoner, SC of Wilmington
1987 ......Jill Watson, Peter Oppegard, Los Angeles FSC
1988 ......Jill Watson, Peter Oppegard, Los Angeles FSC
1989 ......Kristi Yamaguchi, Rudy Galindo, St Mortiz ISC
1990 ......Kristi Yamaguchi, Rudy Galindo, St Mortiz ISC
1991 ......Natasha Kuchiki, Todd Sand, Los Angeles FSC
1992 ......Calla Urbanski, Rocky Marval, U of Delaware FSC/SC of New York
1993 ......Calla Urbanski, Rocky Marval, U of Delaware FSC/SC of New York
1994 ......Jenni Meno, Todd Sand, Winterhurst FSC/Los Angeles FSC
1995 ......Jenni Meno, Todd Sand, Winterhurst FSC/Los Angeles FSC
1996 ......Jenni Meno, Todd Sand, Winterhurst FSC/Los Angeles FSC
1997 ......Kyoko Ina, Jason Dungjen, SC of New York
1998 ......Kyoko Ina, Jason Dungjen, SC of New York
1999 ......Danielle Hartsell, Steve Hartsell, Detroit SC
2000 ......Kyoko Ina, John Zimmerman, SC of New York/Birmingham FSC
2001 ......Kyoko Ina, John Zimmerman, SC of New York/Birmingham FSC
2002 ......Kyoko Ina, John Zimmerman, SC of New York/Birmingham FSC

Dance

1914 ......Waltz: Theresa Weld, Nathaniel W. Niles, SC of Boston
1915–19..No competition
1920 ......Waltz: Theresa Weld, Nathaniel W. Niles, SC of Boston
       Fourteenstep: Gertrude Cheever Porter, Irving Brokaw, New York SC
1921 ......Waltz and Fourteenstep: Theresa Weld Blanchard, Nathaniel W. Niles, SC of Boston
1922 ......Waltz: Beatrix Loughran, Edward M. Howland, New York SC/SC of Boston
       Fourteenstep: Theresa Weld Blanchard, Nathaniel W. Niles, SC of Boston
1923 ......Waltz: Mr. & Mrs. Henry W. Howe, New York SC
       Fourteenstep: Sydney Goode, James B. Greene, New York SC
1924 ......Waltz: Rosaline Dunn, Frederick Gabel, New York SC
       Fourteenstep: Sydney Goode, James B. Greene, New York SC
1925 ......Waltz and Fourteenstep: Virginia Slattery, Ferrier T. Martin, New York SC
1926 ......Waltz: Rosaline Dunn, Joseph K. Savage, New York SC
       Fourteenstep: Sydney Goode, James B. Greene, New York SC
1927 ......Waltz and Fourteenstep: Rosaline Dunn, Joseph K. Savage, New York SC
1928 ......Waltz: Rosaline Dunn, Joseph K. Savage, New York SC
       Fourteenstep: Ada Bauman Kelly, George T. Braakman, New York SC
1929 ......Waltz and Original Dance combined: Edith C. Secord, Joseph K. Savage, SC of New York
1930 ......Waltz: Edith C. Secord, Joseph K. Savage, SC of New York
       Original: Clara Rotch Frothingham, George E. B. Hill, SC of Boston
1931 ......Waltz: Edith C. Secord, Ferrier T. Martin, SC of New York
       Original: Theresa Weld Blanchard, Nathaniel W. Niles, SC of Boston
1932 ......Waltz: Edith C. Secord, Joseph K. Savage, SC of New York
       Original: Clara Rotch Frothingham, George E. B. Hill, SC of Boston
1933 ......Waltz: Ilse Twaroschk, Frederick F. Fleishmann, Brooklyn FSC
       Original: Suzanne Davis, Frederick Goodridge, SC of Boston
1934 ......Waltz: Nettie C. Prantel, Roy Hunt, SC of New York
       Original: Suzanne Davis, Frederick Goodridge, SC of Boston
1935 ......Waltz: Nettie C. Prantel, Roy Hunt, SC of New York
1936 ......Marjorie Parker, Joseph K. Savage, SC of New York
1937 ......Nettie C. Prantel, Harold Hartshorne, SC of New York
1938 ......Nettie C. Prantel, Harold Hartshorne, SC of New York
1939 ......Sandy Macdonald, Harold Hartshorne, SC of New York
1940 ......Sandy Macdonald, Harold Hartshorne, SC of New York
1941 ......Sandy Macdonald, Harold Hartshorne, SCNY
1942 ......Edith B. Whetstone, Alfred N. Richards, Jr, Philadelphia SC & HS
1943 ......Marcella May, James Lochead Jr., Skate & Ski Club
1944 ......Marcella May, James Lochead Jr., Skate & Ski Club
1945 ......Kathe Mehl Williams, Robert J. Swenning, SC of New York
1946 ......Anne Davies, Carleton C. Hoffner Jr., Washington FSC
1947 ......Lois Waring, Walter H. Bainbridge Jr., Baltimore FSC/Washigton FSC
1948 ......Lois Waring, Walter H. Bainbridge Jr., Baltimore FSC/Washington FSC
1949 ......Lois Waring, Walter H. Bainbridge Jr., Baltimore FSC/Washington FSC
1950 ......Lois Waring, Michael McGean, Baltimore FSC
1951 ......Carmel Bodel, Edward L. Bodel, St Moritz ISC

Dance *(Cont.)*

1952 ......Lois Waring, Michael McGean,
Baltimore FSC
1953 ......Carol Ann Peters, Daniel C. Ryan,
Washington FSC
1954 ......Carmel Bodel, Edward L. Bodel, St Moritz ISC
1955 ......Carmel Bodel, Edward L. Bodel,
St Moritz ISC
1956 ......Joan Zamboni, Roland Junso,
Arctic Blades FSC
1957 ......Sharon McKenzie, Bert Wright,
Los Angeles FSC
1958 ......Andree Anderson, Donald Jacoby, Buffalo SC
1959 ......Andree Anderson Jacoby, Donald Jacoby,
Buffalo SC
1960 ......Margie Ackles, Charles W. Phillips Jr.,
Los Angeles FSC/Arctic Blades FSC
1961 ......Diane C. Sherbloom, Larry Pierce,
Los Angeles FSC/WC of Indianapolis
1962 ......Yvonne N. Littlefield, Peter F. Betts,
Arctic Blades FSC/ Paramount, CA
1963 ......Sally Schantz, Stanley Urban,
SC of Boston/Buffalo SC
1964 ......Darlene Streich, Charles D. Fetter Jr.,
WC of Indianapolis
1965 ......Kristin Fortune, Dennis Sveum,
Los Angeles FSC
1966 ......Kristin Fortune, Dennis Sveum, Los Angeles FSC
1967 ......Lorna Dyer, John Carrell, Broadmoor SC
1968 ......Judy Schwomeyer, James Sladky,
WC of Indianapolis/Genesee FSC
1969 ......Judy Schwomeyer, James Sladky,
WC of Indianapolis/Genesee FSC
1970 ......Judy Schwomeyer, James Sladky,
WC of Indianapolis/Genesee FSC
1971 ......Judy Schwomeyer, James Sladky,
WC of Indianapolis/Genesee FSC
1972 ......Judy Schwomeyer, James Sladky,
WC of Indianapolis/Genesee FSC
1973 ......Mary Karen Campbell, Johnny Johns,
Lansing SC/Detroit SC
1974 ......Colleen O'Connor, Jim Millns, Broadmoor
SC/ City of Colorado Springs
1975 ......Colleen O'Connor, Jim Millns, Broadmoor SC
1976 ......Colleen O'Connor, Jim Millns,
Broadmoor SC

1977 ......Judy Genovesi, Kent Weigle,
SC of Hartford/Charter Oak FSC
1978 ......Stacey Smith, John Summers,
SC of Wilmington
1979 ......Stacey Smith, John Summers,
SC of Wilmington
1980 ......Stacey Smith, John Summers,
SC of Wilmington
1981 ......Judy Blumberg, Michael Seibert,
Broadmoor SC/ISC of Indianapolis
1982 ......Judy Blumberg, Michael Seibert,
Broadmoor SC/ISC of Indianapolis
1983 ......Judy Blumberg, Michael Seibert,
Pittsburgh FSC
1984 ......Judy Blumberg, Michael Seibert,
Pittsburgh FSC
1985 ......Judy Blumberg, Michael Seibert,
Pittsburgh FSC
1986 ......Renee Roca, Donald Adair,
Genesee FSC/Academy FSC
1987 ......Suzanne Semanick, Scott Gregory,
U of Delaware SC
1988 ......Suzanne Semanick, Scott Gregory,
U of Delaware SC
1989 ......Susan Wynne, Joseph Druar,
Broadmoor SC/Seattle SC
1990 ......Susan Wynne, Joseph Druar,
Broadmoor SC/Seattle SC
1991 ......Elizabeth Punsalan, Jerod Swallow,
Broadmoor SC
1992 ......April Sargent, Russ Witherby,
Ogdensburg FSC/U of Delaware FSC
1993 ......Renee Roca, Gorsha Sur, Broadmoor SC
1994 ......Elizabeth Punsalan, Jerod Swallow,
Broadmoor SC/Detroit SC
1995 ......Renee Roca, Gorsha Sur, Broadmoor SC
1996 ......Elizabeth Punsalan, Jerod Swallow, Detroit SC
1997 ......Elizabeth Punsalan, Jerod Swallow, Detroit SC
1998 ......Elizabeth Punsalan, Jerod Swallow, Detroit SC
1999 ......Naomi Lang, Peter Tchernyshev, Detroit SC
2000 ......Naomi Lang, Peter Tchernyshev, Detroit SC
2001 ......Naomi Lang, Peter Tchernyshev, Detroit SC
2002 ......Naomi Lang, Peter Tchernyshev, American
Academy FSC

U.S. Olympic Gold Medalists

Women

1956 ....Tenley Albright
1960 ....Carol Heiss
1968 ....Peggy Fleming
1976 ....Dorothy Hamill

1992 ....Kristi Yamaguchi
1998 ....Tara Lipinski
2002 ....Sarah Hughes

Men

1948 ....Richard Button
1952 ....Richard Button
1956 ....Hayes Alan Jenkins

1960 ....David W. Jenkins
1984 ....Scott Hamilton
1988 ....Brian Boitano

Special Achievements

Women successfully landing a triple Axel in competition:
  Midori Ito, Japan, 1988 free-skating competition at Aichi, Japan.
  Tonya Harding, United States, 1991 U.S. Figure Skating Championship.
Men successfully landing three quadruple jumps in competition:
  Timothy Goebel, United States, 1999 Skate America, Colorado Springs (two Salchows and one toe loop).

Four-time Tour winner
Lance Armstrong

Miscellaneous Sports

Four in a Row

Cancer survivor Lance Armstrong won a fourth consecutive Tour de France, and stands poised for a record-tying fifth

BY MERRELL NODEN

THIS WAS THE year Lance Armstrong was supposed to be vulnerable, which, given what happened in the Tour de France in July, is bad news for the world's top cyclists. After stunning and inspiring the world by winning the world's most grueling bike race in 1999, slightly less than three years after being diagnosed with testicular cancer, Armstrong had won the last two Tours without permitting so much as a glimmer of hope to enter the minds of his unfortunate rivals. If you can call them rivals; heck, when crunch time arrived and spectators were craving a wee jolt of suspense, Armstrong proved to be utterly in control of things. The yellow jersey, on his back for days if not weeks by that time, would be going nowhere, and everyone knew it.

But the situation looked different going into the 2002 Tour. There appeared to be at least the prospect of a tight race. Armstrong had finished second in the Criterium International in March, and though he'd won several stage races since then, in each he had failed to win his specialty, the individual time trial. The Tour began in Luxembourg on July 6, and all the questions about Armstrong's fitness were resurrected on July 15, when he failed to win the 52-kilometer time trial that is the Tour's ninth stage, finishing second, 11 seconds behind Santiago Botero of Colombia. This was hugely encouraging to the so-called competition. "The Tour has changed," declared Igor González de Galdeano of Spain, who happened at the time to be wearing the yellow jersey.

Well, the Tour did not stay changed for long. Three days later, during the 11th stage, which runs up into the Pyrenees, from Pau to La Mongie in southwestern France, Armstrong and his U.S. Postal teammates rode down veteran Laurent Jalabert, a fearless climber who was determined to make his last Tour a memorable one. Armstrong was towed along by his teammate Roberto Heras before Heras moved aside with 200 meters to go, giving Armstrong the stage win and the yellow jersey. "Today Roberto Heras was the stage winner," said a grateful Armstrong.

That was one significant difference between the 2002 Tour and the past three. Armstrong's U.S. Postal Team was stronger than it had ever been. The multinational team protected Armstrong so perfectly in the peloton that it came to be known as the Blue Guard or the Lancemobile. (Such is Armstrong's fame that, off the course, he

Foreshadowing: Armstrong won the Tour's 7K prologue in Luxembourg.

also had to be accompanied everywhere he went by a bodyguard.)

When Armstrong won the next day's stage, the 12th, the race was essentially over. Galdeano's teammate Joseba Beloki narrowly beat him over the longest stage of the race, the 140.43-mile 15th, but rather than give Beloki even a few seconds Armstrong closed strongly to record the same time. "After the first two mountain stages, people realized Lance was as good as ever," said Team Rabobank's Levi Leipheimer, an American who would finish eighth in his first Tour. Armstrong won the final time trial, churning along at an average of 47 kilometers-per-hour (29+ m.p.h.). The following day, with a cushion of more than seven minutes, he rode into Paris and made his fourth consecutive triumphant passage down the Champs-Élysée.

One advantage Armstrong seems to give himself is that, for him, the Tour is all important. Those other races, which he enters sparingly, are merely preparation for his one clear goal each year, which is to win the Tour. Said five-time Tour champ Eddy Merckx of Belgium, "I raced 150 days of the year. Armstrong focuses on the Tour and arrived this year with only 21 days of racing in his legs."

Each year, Armstrong moves into a more exclusive club. With his first Tour victory, he joined Greg LeMond as the only U.S. riders ever to win what is surely one of the world's premiere sporting events, regardless of how much the average U.S. sports fan knows about it. With his 2002 win, his fourth, he becomes the fifth man to win the Tour four times. But Armstrong's wins have come in consecutive years, which only three men have managed: Jacques Anquetil of France in the early 1960s; Merckx of Belgium from 1969 through '72; and Spaniard Miguel Induráin in the '90s.

Armstrong's contract with U.S. Postal Service runs through 2004. If Armstrong wins again next year—and at this early date he rates as a strong favorite—he will tie Induráin for the record of five straight. Induráin's quest for a sixth ended when he failed to win the 1996 Tour. No one has won six, consecutively or otherwise. Armstrong "can win five, six or seven," said Bernard Hinault, who won five Tours in the eight years from 1978 to '85 and now serves as the race's technical director. "He's the best, and the only one who can beat him is himself."

If anything stands in Armstrong's way, it may be his own humanity, his need to spend time with his family. He has already had one brush with death. There's nothing like cancer to give one a pretty good sense of perspective. The child of a 17-year-old single mom who had to work two jobs to support herself and her son, Armstrong knows a good deal about family loyalty. He is a devoted dad, and is happy riding the family tandem with his wife, Kristin. The couple's son, Luke, turned three shortly after the Tour, and their twin daughters Grace and Isabelle were born in the fall of 2001. They seem to be the only ones with any chance of stopping Armstrong's historic streak.

Archery

National Men's Champions

1879...Will H. Thompson	1910...Henry Richardson	1947...Jack Wilson	1978...Darrell Pace
1880...L.L. Pedinghaus	1911...Dr. Robert Elmer	1948...Larry Hughes	1979...Rick McKinney
1881...F.H. Walworth	1912...George Bryant	1949...Russ Reynolds	1980...Rick McKinney
1882...D.H. Nash	1913...George Bryant	1950...Stan Overby	1981...Rick McKinney
1883...Col. Robert Williams	1914...Dr. Robert Elmer	1951...Russ Reynolds	1982...Rick McKinney
1884...Col. Robert Williams	1915...Dr. Robert Elmer	1952...Robert Larson	1983...Rick McKinney
1885...Col. Robert Williams	1916...Dr. Robert Elmer	1953...Bill Glackin	1984...Darrell Pace
1886...W.A. Clark	1919...Dr. Robert Elmer	1954...Robert Rhode	1985...Rick McKinney
1887...W.A. Clark	1920...Dr. Robert Elmer	1955...Joe Fries	1986...Rick McKinney
1888...Lewis Maxson	1921...James Jiles	1956...Joe Fries	1987...Rick McKinney
1889...Lewis Maxson	1922...Dr. Robert Elmer	1957...Joe Fries	1988...Jay Barrs
1890...Lewis Maxson	1923...Bill Palmer	1958...Robert Bitner	1989...Ed Eliason
1891...Lewis Maxson	1924...James Jiles	1959...Wilbert Vetrovsky	1990...Ed Eliason
1892...Lewis Maxson	1925...Dr. Paul Crouch	1960...Robert Kadlec	1991...Ed Eliason
1893...Lewis Maxson	1926...Stanley Spencer	1961...Clayton Sherman	1992...Alan Rasor
1894...Lewis Maxson	1927...Dr. Paul Crouch	1962...Charles Sandlin	1993...Jay Barrs
1895...W.B. Robinson	1928...Bill Palmer	1963...Dave Keaggy Jr.	1994...Jay Barrs
1896...Lewis Maxson	1929...Dr. E.K. Roberts	1964...Dave Keaggy Jr.	1995...Justin Huish
1897...W.A. Clark	1930...Russ Hoogerhyde	1965...George Slinzer	1996...Richard (Butch)
1898...Lewis Maxson	1931...Russ Hoogerhyde	1966...Hardy Ward	Johnson
1899...M.C. Howell	1932...Russ Hoogerhyde	1967...Ray Rogers	1997...Richard (Butch)
1900...A.R. Clark	1933...Ralph Miller	1968...Hardy Ward	Johnson
1901...Will H. Thompson	1934...Russ Hoogerhyde	1969...Ray Rogers	1998...Victor Wunderle
1902...Will H. Thompson	1935...Gilman Keasey	1970...Joe Thornton	1999...Victor Wunderle
1903...Will H. Thompson	1936...Gilman Keasey	1971...John Williams	2000...Richard (Butch)
1904...George Bryant	1937...Russ Hoogerhyde	1972...Kevin Erlandson	Johnson
1905...George Bryant	1938...Pat Chambers	1973...Darrell Pace	2001...Richard (Butch)
1906...Henry Richardson	1939...Pat Chambers	1974...Darrell Pace	Johnson
1907...Henry Richardson	1940...Russ Hoogerhyde	1975...Darrell Pace	2002...Victor Wunderle
1908...Will H. Thompson	1941...Larry Hughes	1976...Darrell Pace	
1909...George Bryant	1946...Wayne Thompson	1977...Rick McKinney	

National Women's Champions

1879...Mrs. S. Brown	1909...Harriet Case	1939...Belvia Carter	1972...Ruth Rowe
1880...Mrs. T. Davies	1910...J.V. Sullivan	1940...Ann Weber	1973...Doreen Wilber
1881...Mrs. A.H. Gibbes	1911...Mrs. J.S. Taylor	1941...Ree Dillinger	1974...Doreen Wilber
1882...Mrs. A.H. Gibbes	1912...Mrs. Witwer	1946...Ann.Weber	1975...Irene Lorensen
1883...Mrs. M.C. Howell	Tayler	1947...Ann Weber	1976...Luann Ryon
1884...Mrs. H. Hall	1913...Mrs. P, Fletcher	1948...Jean Lee	1977...Luann Ryon
1885...Mrs. M.C. Howell	1914...Mrs. B.P. Gray	1949...Jean Lee	1978...Luann Ryon
1886...Mrs. M.C. Howell	1915...Cynthia Wesson	1950...Jean Lee	1979...Lynette Johnson
1887...Mrs. A.M. Phillips	1916...Cynthia Wesson	1951...Jean Lee	1980...Judi Adams
1888...Mrs. A.M. Phillips	1919...Dorothy Smith	1952...Ann Weber	1981...Debra Metzger
1889...Mrs. A.M. Phillips.	1920...Cynthia Wesson	1953...Ann Weber	1982...Luann Ryon
1890...Mrs. M.C. Howell	1921...Mrs. L.C. Smith	1954...Laurette Young	1983...Nancy Myrick
1891...Mrs. M.C. Howell	1922...Dorothy Smith	1955...Ann Clark	1984...Ruth Rowe
1892...Mrs. M.C. Howell	1923...Norma Pierce	1956...Carole Meinhart	1985...Terri Pesho
1893...Mrs. M.C. Howell	1924...Dorothy Smith	1957...Carole Meinhart	1986...Debra Ochs
1894...Mrs. Albert Kern	1925...Dorothy Smith	1958...Carole Meinhart	1987...Terry Quinn
1895...Mrs. M.C. Howell	1926...Dorothy Smith	1959...Carole Meinhart	1988...Debra Ochs
1896...Mrs. M.C. Howell	1927...Mrs. R. Johnson	1960...Ann Clark	1989...Debra Ochs
1897...Mrs. J.S. Baker	1928...Beatrice	1961...Victoria Cook	1990...Denise Parker
1898...Mrs. M.C. Howell	Hodgson	1962...Nancy	1991...Denise Parker
1899...Mrs. M.C. Howell	1929...Audrey Grubbs	Vonderheide	1992...Sherry Block
1900...Mrs. M.C. Howell	1930...Audrey Grubbs	1963...Nancy	1993...Denise Parker
1901...Mrs. C.E.	1931...Dorothy	Vonderheide	1994...Judy Adams
Woodruff	Cummings	1964...Victoria Cook	1995...Jessica Carlson
1902...Mrs. M.C. Howell	1932...Ilda Hanchette	1965...Nancy Pfeiffer	1996...Janet Dykman
1903...Mrs. M.C. Howell	1933...Madelaine Taylor	1966...Helen Thornton	1997...Janet Dykman
1904...Mrs. M.C. Howell	1934...Desales Mudd	1967...Ardelle Mills	1998...Janet Dykman
1905...Mrs. M.C. Howell	1935...Ruth Hodgert	1968...Victoria Cook	1999...Denise Parker
1906...Mrs. E.C. Cook	1936...Gladys Hammer	1969...Doreen Wilber	2000...Karen Scavatto
1907...Mrs. M.C. Howell	1937...Gladys Hammer	1970...Nancy Myrick	2001...Kathie Loesch
1908...Harriet Case	1938...Jean Tenney	1971...Doreen Wilber	2002...Jessica Peterson

Chess

World Champions

FIDE

1866–94	Wilhelm Steinitz, Austria
1894–1921	Emanuel Lasker, Germany
1921–27	Jose Capablanca, Cuba
1927–35	Alexander Alekhine, France
1935–37	Max Euwe, Holland
1937–47	Alexander Alekhine, France
1948–57	Mikhail Botvinnik, USSR
1957–58	Vassily Smyslov, USSR
1958–59	Mikhail Botvinnik, USSR
1960–61	Mikhail Tal, USSR
1961–63	Mikhail Botvinnik, USSR
1963–69	Tigran Petrosian, USSR

FIDE

1969–72	Boris Spassky, USSR
1972–75	Bobby Fischer, United States
1975–85	Anatoly Karpov, USSR
1985–93	*Garry Kasparov, USSR
1994–98	Anatoly Karpov, Russia
1999–2000	Alexander Khalifman, Russia
2000–01	Anand Viswanathan, India
2000–02	Ruslan Ponomariov, Ukraine

*Kasparov stripped of title by FIDE in 1993.

Professional Chess Association

1993–	Garry Kasparov

United States Champions

1857–71	Paul Morphy
1871–76	George Mackenzie
1876–80	James Mason
1880–89	George Mackenzie
1889–90	Samuel Lipschutz
1890	Jackson Showalter
1890–91	Max Judd
1891–92	Jackson Showalter
1892–94	Samuel Lipschutz
1894	Jackson Showalter
1894–95	Albert Hodges
1895–97	Jackson Showalter
1897–1906	Harry Pillsbury
1906–09	Vacant
1909–36	Frank Marshall
1936–44	Samuel Reshevsky
1944–46	Arnold Denker
1946–48	Samuel Reshevsky
1948–51	Herman Steiner
1951–54	Larry Evans
1954–57	Arthur Bisguier
1957–61	Bobby Fischer

1961–62	Larry Evans
1962–68	Bobby Fischer
1968–69	Larry Evans
1969–72	Samuel Reshevsky
1972–73	Robert Byrne
1973–74	Lubomir Kavale
	John Grefe
1974–77	Walter Browne
1978–80	Lubomir Kavalek
1980–81	Larry Evans
	Larry Christiansen
	Walter Browne
1981–83	Walter Browne
	Yasser Seirawan
1983	Roman Dzindzichashvili
1983	Larry Christiansen
	Walter Browne
1984–85	Lev Alburt
1986	Yasser Seirawan
1987	Joel Benjamin
	Nick DeFirmian

1988	Michael Wilder
1989	Roman Dzindzichashvili
	Stuart Rachels
	Yasser Seirawan
1990	Lev Alburt
1991	Gata Kamski
1992	Patrick Wolff
1993	Alex Yermolinsky
	A. Shabalov
1994	Boris Gulko
1995	Patrick Wolff
	Nick DeFirmian
	Alexander Ivanov
1996	Alex Yermolinsky
1997	Alex Yermolinsky
1998	Alex Yermolinsky
1999	Boris Gulko
2000	Joel Benjamin
2001	Joel Benjamin
2002	Larry Christiansen

Curling

World Men's Champions

Year	Country, Skip	Year	Country, Skip	Year	Country, Skip
1972	Canada, Crest Melesnuk	1983	Canada, Ed Werenich	1994	Canada, Rick Folk
1973	Sweden, Kjell Oscarius	1984	Norway, Eigil Ramsfjell	1995	Canada, Kerry Burtnyk
1974	U.S., Bud Somerville	1985	Canada, Al Hackner	1996	Canada, Jeff Stoughton
1975	Switzerland, Otto Danieli	1986	Canada, Ed Luckowich	1997	Sweden, Peter Lindholm
1976	U.S., Bruce Roberts	1987	Canada, Russ Howard	1998	Canada, Wayne Middaugh
1977	Sweden, Ragnar Kamp	1988	Norway, Eigil Ramsfjell	1999	Scotland, Hammy McMillan
1978	U.S., Bob Nichols	1989	Canada, Pat Ryan	2000	Canada, Greg McAulay
1979	Norway, Kristian Soerum	1990	Canada, Ed Werenich	2001	Sweden, Peter Lindholm
1980	Canada, Rich Folk	1991	Scotland, David Smith	2002	Canada, Randy Ferbey
1981	Switzerland, Jurg Tanner	1992	Switzerland, Markus Eggler		
1982	Canada, Al Hackner	1993	Canada, Russ Howard		

World Women's Champions

Year	Country, Skip	Year	Country, Skip	Year	Country, Skip
1979	Switzerland, Gaby Casanova	1986	Canada, Marilyn Darte	1995	Sweden, Elisabet Gustafson
1980	Canada, Marj Mitchell	1987	Canada, Pat Sanders	1996	Canada, Marilyn Bodogh
1981	Sweden, Elisabeth Hogstrom	1988	Germany, Andrea Schopp	1997	Canada, Sandra Schmirler
1982	Denmark, Marianne Jorgenson	1989	Canada, Heather Houston	1998	Sweden, Elisabet Gustafson
1983	Switzerland, Erika Mueller	1990	Norway, Dordi Nordby	1999	Sweden, Elisabet Gustafson
1984	Canada, Connie Lallberte	1991	Norway, Dordi Nordby	2000	Canada, Kelley Law
1985	Canada, Linda Moore	1992	Sweden, Elisabet Johanssen	2001	Canada, Colleen Jones
		1993	Canada, Sandra Peterson	2002	Scotland, Jackie Lockhart
		1994	Canada, Sandra Peterson		

U.S. Men's Champions

Year	Site	Winning Club	Skip
1957	Chicago, IL	Hibbing, MN	Harold Lauber
1958	Milwaukee, WI	Detroit, MI	Douglas Fisk
1959	Green Bay, WI	Hibbing, MN	Fran Kleffman
1960	Chicago, IL	Grafton, ND	Orvil Gilleshammer
1961	Grand Forks, ND	Seattle, WA	Frank Crealock
1962	Detroit, MI	Hibbing, MN	Fran Kleffman
1963	Duluth, MN	Detroit, MI	Mike Slyziuk
1964	Utica, NY	Duluth, MN	Robert Magle Jr.
1965	Seattle, WA	Superior, WI	Bud Somerville
1966	Hibbing, MN	Fargo, ND	Joe Zbacnik
1967	Winchester, MA	Seattle, WA	Bruce Roberts
1968	Madison, WI	Superior, WI	Bud Somerville
1969	Grand Forks, ND	Superior, WI	Bud Somerville
1970	Ardsley, NY	Grafton, ND	Art Tallackson
1971	Duluth, MN	Edmore, ND	Dale Dalziel
1972	Wilmette, IL	Grafton, ND	Robert Labonte
1973	Colorado Springs, CO	Winchester, MA	Charles Reeves
1974	Schenectady, NY	Superior, WI	Bud Somerville
1975	Detroit, MI	Seattle, WA	Ed Risling
1976	Wausau, WI	Hibbing, MN	Bruce Roberts
1977	Northbrook, IL	Hibbing, MN	Bruce Roberts
1978	Utica, NY	Superior, WI	Bob Nichols
1979	Superior, WI	Bemidji, MN	Scott Baird
1980	Bemidji, MN	Hibbing, MN	Paul Pustovar
1981	Fairbanks, AK	Superior, WI	Bob Nichols
1982	Brookline, MA	Madison, WI	Steve Brown
1983	Colorado Springs, CO	Colorado Springs, CO	Don Cooper
1984	Hibbing, MN	Hibbing, MN	Bruce Roberts
1985	Mequon, WI	Wilmette, IL	Tim Wright
1986	Seattle, WA	Madison, WI	Steve Brown
1987	Lake Placid, NY	Seattle, WA	Jim Vukich
1988	St. Paul, MN	Seattle, WA	Doug Jones
1989	Detroit, MI	Seattle, WA	Jim Vukich
1990	Superior, WI	Seattle, WA	Doug Jones
1991	Utica, NY	Madison, WI	Steve Brown
1992	Grafton, ND	Seattle, WA	Doug Jones
1993	St. Paul, MN	Bemidji, MN	Scott Baird
1994	Duluth, MN	Bemidji, MN	Scott Baird
1995	Appleton, WI	Superior, WI	Tim Somerville
1996	Bemidji, MN	Superior, WI	Tim Somerville
1997	Seattle, WA	Langdon, ND	Craig Disher
1998	Bismarck, SD	Stevens Pt., WI	Paul Pustovar
1999	Duluth, MN	Superior, WI	Tim Somerville
2000	Ogden, UT	Wisconsin3	Craig Brown
2001	Madison, WI	Washington	Jason Larway
2002	Virginia, MN	Wisconsin2	Paul Pustovar

U.S. Women's Champions

Year	Site	Winning Club	Skip
1977	Wilmette, IL	Hastings, NY	Margaret Smith
1978	Duluth, MN	Wausau, WI	Sandy Robarge
1979	Winchester, MA	Seattle, WA	Nancy Langley
1980	Seattle, WA	Seattle, WA	Sharon Kozal
1981	Kettle Moraine, WI	Seattle, WA	Nancy Langley
1982	Bowling Green, OH	Oak Park, IL	Ruth Schwenker
1983	Grafton, ND	Seattle, WA	Nancy Langley
1984	Wauwatosa, WI	Duluth, MN	Amy Hatten
1985	Hershey, PA	Fairbanks, AK	Bev Birklid
1986	Chicago, IL	St Paul, MN	Gerri Tilden
1987	St Paul, MN	Seattle, WA	Sharon Good
1988	Darien, CT	Seattle, WA	Nancy Langley
1989	Detroit, MI	Rolla, ND	Jan Lagasse
1990	Superior, WI	Denver, CO	Bev Behnke
1991	Utica, NY	Houston, TX	Maymar Gemmell
1992	Grafton, ND	Madison, WI	Lisa Schoeneberg
1993	St Paul, MN	Denver, CO	Bev Behnke
1994	Duluth, MN	Denver, CO	Bev Behnke
1995	Appleton, WI	Madison, WI	Lisa Schoeneberg
1996	Bemidji, MN	Madison, WI	Lisa Schoeneberg

U.S. Women's Champions *(Cont.)*

Year	Site	Winning Club	Skip
1997	Seattle, WA	Arlington, WI	Patti Lank
1998	Bismarck, SD	Wilmette, IL	Kari Erickson
1999	Duluth, MN	Madison, WI	Patti Lank
2000	Ogden, UT	Nebraska	Amy Wright
2001	Madison, WI	Illinois	Kari Erickson
2002	Virginia, MN	Madison, WI	Patti Lank

Cycling

Professional Road Race World Champions

1927 ....Alfred Binda, Italy
1928 ....George Ronsse, Belgium
1929 ....George Ronsse, Belgium
1930 ....Alfred Binda, Italy
1931 ....Learco Guerra, Italy
1932 ....Alfred Binda, Italy
1933 ....George Speicher, France
1934 ....Karel Kaers, Belgium
1935 ....Jean Aerts, Belgium
1936 ....Antonio Magne, France
1937 ....Elio Meulenberg, Belgium
1938 ....Marcel Kint, Belgium
No competition 1939–45
1946 ....Hans Knecht, Switzerland
1947 ....Theo. Middelkamp, Holland
1948 ....Alberic Schotte, Belgium
1949 ....Henri Van Steenberger, Belgium
1950 ....Alberic Schotte, Belgium
1951 ....Ferdinand Kubler, Switzerland
1952 ....Heinz Mueller, Germany
1953 ....Fausto Coppi, Italy
1954 ....Louison Bobet, France
1955 ....Stan Ockers, Belgium
1956 ....Rik Van Steenbergen, Belg.

1957 ....Rik Van Steenbergen, Belgium
1958 ....Ercole Baldini, Italy
1959 ....Andre Darrigade, France
1960 ....Rik van Looy, Belgium
1961 ....Rik van Looy, Belgium
1962 ....Jean Stablenski, France
1963 ....Bennoni Beheyt, Belgium
1964 ....Jan Janssen, Holland
1965 ....Tommy Simpson, England
1966 ....Rudi Altig, West Germany
1967 ....Eddy Merckx, Belgium
1968 ....Vittorio Adorni, Italy
1969 ....Harm Ottenbros, Netherlands
1970 ....J.P. Monseré, Belgium
1971 ....Eddy Merckx, Belgium
1972 ....Marino Basso, Italy
1973 ....Felice Gimondi, Italy
1974 ....Eddy Merckx, Belgium
1975 ....Hennie Kuiper, Holland
1976 ....Freddy Maertens, Belgium
1977 ....Francesco Moser, Italy
1978 ....Gerri Knetemann, Holland
1979 ....Jan Raas, Holland
1980 ....Bernard Hinault, France

1981 ....Freddy Maertens, Belgium
1982 ....Giuseppe Saronni, Italy
1983 ....Greg LeMond, United States
1984 ....Claude Criquielion, Belgium
1985 ....Joop Zoetemelk, Holland
1986 ....Moreno Argentin, Italy
1987 ....Stephen Roche, Ireland
1988 ....Maurizio Fondriest, Italy
1989 ....Greg LeMond, United States
1990 ....Rudy Dhaenene, Belgium
1991 ....Gianni Bugno, Italy
1992 ....Gianni Bugno, Italy
1993 ....Lance Armstrong, United States
1994 ....Luc LeBlanc, France
1995 ....Abraham Olano, Spain
1996 ....Johan Museeuw, Belgium
1997 ....Laurent Brochard, France
1998 ....Oskar Camenzind, Switz
1999 .....Oscar Gomez Freire, Spain
2000 .....Romans Vainsteins, Latvia
2001 .....Oscar Gomez Freire, Spain

Tour DuPont Winners

Year	Winner	Time
1989	Dag Otto Lauritzen, Norway	33 hrs, 28 min, 48 sec
1990	Raul Alcala, Mexico	45 hrs, 20 min, 9 sec
1991	Erik Breukink, Holland	48 hrs, 56 min, 53 sec
1992	Greg LeMond, United States	44 hrs, 27 min, 43 sec
1993	Raul Alcala, Mexico	46 hrs, 42 min, 52 sec
1994	Viatcheslav Ekimov, Russia	47 hrs, 14 min, 29 sec
1995	Lance Armstrong, United States	46 hrs, 31 min, 16 sec
1996	Lance Armstrong, United States	48 hrs, 20 min, 5 sec

Note: Race not held since 1996.

Tour de France Winners

Year	Winner	Time
1903	Maurice Garin, France	94 hrs, 33 min
1904	Henry Cornet, France	96 hrs, 5 min, 56 sec
1905	Louis Trousselier, France	110 hrs, 26 min, 58 sec
1906	Rene Pottier, France	Not available
1907	Lucien Petit-Breton, France	158 hrs, 54 min, 5 sec
1908	Lucien Petit-Breton, France	Not available
1909	Francois Faber, Luxembourg	157 hrs, 1 min, 22 sec
1910	Octave Lapize, France	162 hrs, 41 min, 30 sec
1911	Gustave Garrigou, France	195 hrs, 37 min
1912	Odile Defraye, Belgium	190 hrs, 30 min, 28 sec
1913	Philippe Thys, Belgium	197 hrs, 54 min
1914	Philippe Thys, Belgium	200 hrs, 28 min, 48 sec
1915–18	No race	
1919	Firmin Lambot, Belgium	231 hrs, 7 min, 15 sec
1920	Philippe Thys, Belgium	228 hrs, 36 min, 13 sec
1921	Leon Scieur, Belgium	221 hrs, 50 min, 26 sec

Tour de France Winners (Cont.)

Year	Winner	Time
1922	Firmin Lambot, Belgium	222 hrs, 8 min, 6 sec
1923	Henri Pelissier, France	222 hrs, 15 min, 30 sec
1924	Ottavio Bottechia, Italy	226 hrs, 18 min, 21 sec
1925	Ottavio Bottechia, Italy	219 hrs, 10 min, 18 sec
1926	Lucien Buysse, Belgium	238 hrs, 44 min, 25 sec
1927	Nicolas Frantz, Luxembourg	198 hrs, 16 min, 42 sec
1928	Nicolas Frantz, Luxembourg	192 hrs, 48 min, 58 sec
1929	Maurice Dewaele, Belgium	186 hrs, 39 min, 16 sec
1930	Andre Leducq, France	172 hrs, 12 min, 16 sec
1931	Antonin Magne, France	177 hrs, 10 min, 3 sec
1932	Andre Leducq, France	154 hrs, 12 min, 49 sec
1933	Georges Speicher, France	147 hrs, 51 min, 37 sec
1934	Antonin Magne, France	147 hrs, 13 min, 58 sec
1935	Romain Maes, Belgium	141 hrs, 32 min
1936	Sylvere Maes, Belgium	142 hrs, 47 min, 32 sec
1937	Roger Lapebie, France	138 hrs, 58 min, 31 sec
1938	Gino Bartali, Italy	148 hrs, 29 min, 12 sec
1939	Sylvere Maes, Belgium	132 hrs, 3 min, 17 sec
1940–46	No race	
1947	Jean Robic, France	148 hrs, 11 min, 25 sec
1948	Gino Bartali, Italy	147 hrs, 10 min, 36 sec
1949	Fausto Coppi, Italy	149 hrs, 40 min, 49 sec
1950	Ferdi Kubler, Switzerland	145 hrs, 36 min, 56 sec
1951	Hugo Koblet, Switzerland	142 hrs, 20 min, 14 sec
1952	Fausto Coppi, Italy	151 hrs, 57 min, 20 sec
1953	Louison Bobet, France	129 hrs, 23 min, 25 sec
1954	Louison Bobet, France	140 hrs, 6 min, 5 sec
1955	Louison Bobet, France	130 hrs, 29 min, 26 sec
1956	Roger Walkowiak, France	124 hrs, 1 min, 16 sec
1957	Jacques Anquetil, France	129 hrs, 46 min, 11 sec
1958	Charly Gaul, Luxembourg	116 hrs, 59 min, 5 sec
1959	Federico Bahamontes, Spain	123 hrs, 46 min, 45 sec
1960	Gastone Nencini, Italy	112 hrs, 8 min, 42 sec
1961	Jacques Anquetil, France	122 hrs, 1 min, 33 sec
1962	Jacques Anquetil, France	114 hrs, 31 min, 54 sec
1963	Jacques Anquetil, France	113 hrs, 30 min, 5 sec
1964	Jacques Anquetil, France	127 hrs, 9 min, 44 sec
1965	Felice Gimondi, Italy	116 hrs, 42 min, 6 sec
1966	Lucien Aimar, France	117 hrs, 34 min, 21 sec
1967	Roger Pingeon, France	136 hrs, 53 min, 50 sec
1968	Jan Janssen, Netherlands	133 hrs, 49 min, 32 sec
1969	Eddy Merckx, Belgium	116 hrs, 16 min, 2 sec
1970	Eddy Merckx, Belgium	119 hrs, 31 min, 49 sec
1971	Eddy Merckx, Belgium	96 hrs, 45 min, 14 sec
1972	Eddy Merckx, Belgium	108 hrs, 17 min, 18 sec
1973	Luis Ocana, Spain	122 hrs, 25 min, 34 sec
1974	Eddy Merckx, Belgium	116 hrs, 16 min, 58 sec
1975	Bernard Thevenet, France	114 hrs, 35 min, 31 sec
1976	Lucien Van Impe, Belgium	116 hrs, 22 min, 23 sec
1977	Bernard Thevenet, France	115 hrs, 38 min, 30 sec
1978	Bernard Hinault, France	108 hrs, 18 min
1979	Bernard Hinault, France	103 hrs, 6 min, 50 sec
1980	Joop Zoetemelk, Netherlands	109 hrs, 19 min, 14 sec
1981	Bernard Hinault, France	96 hrs, 19 min, 38 sec
1982	Bernard Hinault, France	92 hrs, 8 min, 46 sec
1983	Laurent Fignon, France	105 hrs, 7 min, 52 sec
1984	Laurent Fignon, France	112 hrs, 3 min, 40 sec
1985	Bernard Hinault, France	113 hrs, 24 min, 23 sec
1986	Greg LeMond, United States	110 hrs, 35 min, 19 sec
1987	Stephen Roche, Ireland	115 hrs, 27 min, 42 sec
1988	Pedro Delgado, Spain	84 hrs, 27 min, 53 sec
1989	Greg LeMond, United States	87 hrs, 38 min, 35 sec
1990	Greg LeMond, United States	90 hrs, 43 min, 20 sec
1991	Miguel Induráin, Spain	101 hrs, 1 min, 20 sec
1992	Miguel Induráin, Spain	100 hrs, 49 min, 30 sec
1993	Miguel Induráin, Spain	95 hrs, 57 min, 9 sec
1994	Miguel Induráin, Spain	103 hrs, 38 min, 38 sec
1995	Miguel Induráin, Spain	92 hrs, 44 min, 59 sec

Tour de France Winners (Cont.)

Year	Winner	Time
1996	Bjarne Riis, Denmark	95 hrs, 57 min, 16 sec
1997	Jan Ullrich, Germany	100 hrs, 30 min, 35 sec
1998	Marco Pantani, Italy	92 hrs, 49 min, 46 sec
1999	Lance Armstrong, United States	91 hrs, 32 min, 16 sec
2000	Lance Armstrong, United States	92 hrs, 33 min, 8 sec
2001	Lance Armstrong, United States	86 hrs, 17 min, 28 sec
2002	Lance Armstrong, United States	82 hrs, 5 min, 12 sec

Sled Dog Racing

Iditarod

Year	Winner	Time	Year	Winner	Time
1973	Dick Wilmarth	20 days, 00:49:41	1988	Susan Butcher	11 days, 11:41:40
1974	Carl Huntington	20 days, 15:02:07	1989	Joe Runyan	11 days, 05:24:34
1975	Emmitt Peters	14 days, 14:43:45	1990	Susan Butcher	11 days, 01:53:23
1976	Gerald Riley	18 days, 22:58:17	1991	Rick Swenson	12 days, 16:34:39
1977	Rick Swenson	16 days, 16:27:13	1992	Martin Buser	10 days, 19:17:15
1978	Dick Mackey	14 days, 18:52:24	1993	Jeff King	10 days, 15:38:15
1979	Rick Swenson	15 days, 10:37:47	1994	Martin Buser	10 days, 13:02:39
1980	Joe May	14 days, 07:11:51	1995	Doug Swingley	9 days, 02:42:19
1981	Rick Swenson	12 days, 08:45:02	1996	Jeff King	9 days, 05:43:13
1982	Rick Swenson	16 days, 04:40:10	1997	Martin Buser	9 days, 08:30:45
1983	Dick Mackey	12 days, 14:10:44	1998	Jeff King	9 days, 05:52:26
1984	Dean Osmar	12 days, 15:07:33	1999	Doug Swingley	9 days, 14:31:19
1985	Libby Riddles	18 days, 00:20:17	2000	Doug Swingley	9 days, 00:58:06
1986	Susan Butcher	11 days, 15:06:00	2001	Doug Swingley	9 days, 19:55:50
1987	Susan Butcher	11 days, 02:05:13	2002	Martin Buser	8 days, 22:46:02

Fishing

Saltwater Fishing Records

Species	Weight	Where Caught	Date	Angler
Albacore	88 lb 2 oz	Gran Canaria, Canary Islands	Nov 19, 1977	Siegfried Dickemann
Amberjack, greater	155 lb 12 oz	Bermuda	Aug 16, 1992	Larry Trott
Amberjack, Pacific	104 lb	Baja California, Mexico	July 4, 1984	Richard Cresswell
Angler	126 lb 12 oz	Sognefjorden Hoyanger, Norway	July 4, 1996	Gunnar Thorsteinsen
Barracuda, great	85 lb	Christmas Island, Kiribati	April 11, 1992	John W. Helfrich
Barracuda, Mexican	21 lb	Phantom Isle, Costa Rica	Mar 27, 1987	E. Greg Kent
Barracuda, pickhandle	25 lb 5 oz	Scottburgh, Natal, South Africa	July 3, 1996	Demetrios Stamatis
Bass, barred sand	13 lb 3 oz	Huntington Beach, California	Aug 29, 1988	Robert Halal
Bass, black sea	10 lb 4 oz	Virginia Beach, Virginia	Jan 1, 2000	Allan P. Paschall
Bass, European	20 lb 14 oz	Cap d'Agde, France	Sept. 8, 1999	Robert Mari
Bass, giant sea	563 lb 8 oz	Anacapa Island, California	Aug 20, 1968	James D. McAdam Jr.
Bass, striped	78 lb 8 oz	Atlantic City, New Jersey	Sep 21, 1982	Albert R. McReynolds
Bluefish	31 lb 12 oz	Hatteras Inlet, North Carolina	Jan 30, 1972	James M. Hussey
Bonefish	19 lb	Zululand, South Africa	May 26, 1962	Brian W. Batchelor
Bonito, Atlantic	18 lb 4 oz	Faial Island, Azores	July 8, 1953	D.G. Higgs
Bonito, Pacific	21 lb 3 oz	Malibu, California	July 30, 1978	Gino M. Picciolo
Cabezon	23 lb	Juan De Fuca Strait, Washington	Aug 4, 1990	Wesley Hunter
Cobia	135 lb 9 oz	Shark Bay, Australia	July 9, 1985	Peter W. Goulding
Cod, Atlantic	98 lb 12 oz	Isle of Shoals, New Hampshire	June 8, 1969	Alphonse Bielevich
Cod, Pacific	35 lb	Unalaska Bay, Alaska	June 16, 1999	Jim Johnson
Conger	133 lb 4 oz	South Devon, England	June 5, 1995	Vic Evans
Dolphinfish	88 lb	Highbourne Cay, Bahamas	May 5, 1998	Richard D. Evans
Drum, black	113 lb 1 oz	Lewes, Delaware	Sep 15, 1975	Gerald M. Townsend
Drum, red	94 lb 2 oz	Avon, North Carolina	Nov 7, 1984	David Deuel
Eel, American	9 lb 4 oz	Cape May, New Jersey	Nov 9, 1995	Jeff Pennick
Eel, marbled	36 lb 1 oz	Durban, South Africa	June 10, 1984	Ferdie van Nooten
Flounder, southern	20 lb 9 oz	Nassau Sound, Florida	Dec 23, 1983	Larenza W. Mungin
Flounder, summer	22 lb 7 oz	Montauk, New York	Sep 15, 1975	Charles Nappi
Grouper, Warsaw	436 lb 12 oz	Destin, Florida	Dec 22, 1985	Steve Haeusler
Halibut, Atlantic	355 lb 6 oz	Valevag, Norway	Oct 20, 1997	Odd Arve Gunderstad

Saltwater Fishing Records (Cont.)

Species	Weight	Where Caught	Date	Angler
Halibut, California	58 lb 9 oz	Santa Rosa Island, California	June 26, 1999	Roger W. Borrell
Halibut, Pacific	459 lb	Dutch Harbor, Alaska	June 11, 1996	Jack Tragis
Jack, crevalle	58 lb 6 oz	Barro do Kwanza, Angola	Dec 10, 2000	Nuno A. P. da Silva
Jack, horse-eye	29 lb 8 oz	Ascencion Island, S Atlantic Ocean	May 28, 1993	Mike Hanson
Jack, Pacific crevalle	39 lb	Playa Zancudo, Costa Rica	Mar 3, 1997	Ingrid Callaghan
Jewfish	680 lb	Fernandina Beach, Florida	May 20, 1961	Lynn Joyner
Kawakawa	29 lb	Isla Clarion, Mexico	Dec 17, 1986	Ronald Nakamura
Lingcod	76 lb 9 oz	Gulf of Alaska, Alaska	Aug 11, 2001	Antwan D. Tinsley
Mackerel, cero	17 lb 2 oz	Islamorada, Florida	Apr 5, 1986	G. Michael Mills
Mackerel, king	93 lb	San Juan, Puerto Rico	Apr 18, 1999	Steve Perez Graulau
Mackerel, narrowbarred	99 lb	Natal, South Africa	Mar 14, 1982	Michael J. Wilkinson
Mackerel, Spanish	13 lb	Ocracoke Inlet, North Carolina	Nov 4, 1987	Robert Cranton
Marlin, Atlantic blue	1,402 lb 2 oz	Vitoria, Brazil	Feb 29, 1992	Paulo R.A. Amorim
Marlin, black	1,560 lb	Cabo Blanco, Peru	Aug 4, 1953	Alfred C. Glassell Jr.
Marlin, Pacific blue	1,376 lb	Kaaiwi Point, Hawaii	May 31, 1982	J.W. de Beaubien
Marlin, striped	494 lb	Tutukaka, New Zealand	Jan 16, 1986	Bill Boniface
Marlin, white	181 lb 14 oz	Vitoria, Brazil	Dec 8, 1979	Evandro Luiz Caser
Permit	56 lb 2 oz	Fort Lauderdale, Florida	June 30, 1997	Thomas Sebestyen
Pollock	50 lb	Salstraumen, Norway	Nov 30, 1995	Thor Magnus-Lekang
Pompano, African	50 lb 8 oz	Daytona Beach, Florida	Apr 21, 1990	Tom Sargent
Roosterfish	114 lb	La Paz, Mexico	June 1, 1960	Abe Sackheim
Runner, blue	11 lb 2 oz	Dauphin Island, Alaska	June 28, 1997	Stacey M. Moiren
Runner, rainbow	37 lb 9 oz	Isla Clarion, Mexico	Nov 21, 1991	Tom Pfleger
Sailfish, Atlantic	141 lb 1 oz	Luanda, Angola	Feb 19, 1994	Alfredo de Sousa Neves
Sailfish, Pacific	221 lb	Santa Cruz Island, Ecuador	Feb 12, 1947	Carl W. Stewart
Seabass, white	83 lb 12 oz	San Felipe, Mexico	Mar 31, 1953	Lyal C. Baumgardner
Seatrout, spotted	17 lb 7 oz	Ft. Pierce, Florida	May 11, 1995	Craig F. Carson
Shark, bigeye thresher	802 lb	Tutukaka, New Zealand	Feb 8, 1981	Dianne North
Shark, blue	528 lb	Montauk Point, New York	Aug 9, 2001	Joe Seidel
Shark, grter hammrhd	991 lb	Sarasota, Florida	May 30, 1982	Allen Ogle
Shark, Greenland	1,708 lb 9 oz	Trondheimsfjord, Norway	Oct 18, 1987	Terje Nordtvedt
Shark, porbeagle	507 lb	Caithness, Scotland	Mar 9, 1993	Christopher Bennet
Shark, shortfin mako	1,221 lb	Chatham, Massachusetts	July 21, 2001	Luke Sweeney
Shark, tiger	1,780 lb	Cherry Grove, South Carolina	June 14, 1964	Walter Maxwell
Shark, tope	72 lb 12 oz	Parengarenga Harbor, N.Z.	Dec 19, 1986	Melanie B. Feldman
Shark, white	2,664 lb	Ceduna, Australia	Apr 21, 1959	Alfred Dean
Skipjack, black	26 lb	Baja California, Mexico	Oct 23, 1991	Clifford K. Hamaishi
Snapper, cubera	121 lb 8 oz	Cameron, Louisiana	July 5, 1982	Mike Hebert
Snook, common	53 lb 10 oz	Parismina Ranch, Costa Rica	Oct 18, 1978	Gilbert Ponzi
Spearfish, Mediterr.	90 lb 13 oz	Madeira Island, Portugal	June 2, 1980	Joseph Larkin
Spearfish, longbill	127 lb 13 oz	Puerto Rico, Gran Canaria, Spain	May 20, 1999	Paul Cashmore
Spearfish, shortbill	74 lb 8 oz	Bay of Islands, New Zealand	Mar 16, 1999	Leonie Kai Patterson
Swordfish	1,182 lb	Iquique, Chile	May 7, 1953	Louis Marron
Tarpon	283 lb 4 oz	Sherbro Island, Sierra Leone	Apr 16, 1991	Yvon Victor Sebag
Tautog	25 lb	Ocean City, New Jersey	Jan 20, 1998	Anthony Monica
Tilapia, Mozambique	2 lb 8 oz	Delray Beach, Florida	Nov 10, 1997	Nick Cardella
Trevally, bigeye	31 lb 8 oz	Poivre Island, Seychelles	Apr 23, 1997	Les Sampson
Trevally, giant	145 lb 8 oz	Maui, Hawaii	Mar 28, 1991	Russell Mori
Tuna, Atlantic bigeye	392 lb 6 oz	Puerto Rico, Gran Caneria, Spain	July 25, 1996	Dieter Vogel
Tuna, blackfin	45 lb 8 oz	Key West, Florida	May 4, 1996	Sam J. Burnett
Tuna, bluefin	1,496 lb	Aulds Cove, Nova Scotia	Oct 26, 1979	Ken Fraser
Tuna, longtail	79 lb 2 oz	Montague Island, New South Wales, Australia	Apr 12, 1982	Tim Simpson
Tuna, Pacific bigeye	435 lb	Cabo Blanco, Peru	Apr 17, 1957	Russel Lee
Tuna, skipjack	45 lb 4 oz	Baja California, Mexico	Nov 16, 1996	Brian Evans
Tuna, southern bluefin	348 lb 5 oz	Whakatane, New Zealand	Jan 16, 1981	Rex Wood
Tuna, yellowfin	388 lb 12 oz	San Benedicto Is, Mexico	Apr 1, 1977	Curt Wiesenhutter
Tunny, little	35 lb 2 oz	Cape de Garde, Algeria	Dec 14, 1988	Jean Yves Chatard
Wahoo	158 lb 8 oz	Loreto, Baja California, Mexico	June 10, 1996	Keith Winter
Weakfish	19 lb 2 oz	Jones Beach Inlet, New York	Oct 11, 1984	Dennis Rooney
		Delaware Bay, Delaware	May 20, 1989	William E. Thomas
Yellowtail, California	88 lb 3 oz	Alijos Rocks, Baja Calif., Mexico	Jun 21, 2000	Ronald Fujii
Yellowtail, southern	114 lb 10 oz	Tauranga, New Zealand	Feb 5, 1984	Mike Godfrey

Freshwater Fishing Records

Species	Weight	Where Caught	Date	Angler
Barramundi	83 lb 7 oz	Lake Tinaroo, N Queensl'd, Aus.	Sept 23, 1999	David Powell
Bass, largemouth	22 lb 4 oz	Montgomery Lake, Georgia	June 2, 1932	George W. Perry
Bass, rock	3 lb	York River, Ontario	Aug 1, 1974	Peter Gulgin
Bass, shoal	8 lb 12 oz	Apalatchicola River, Florida	Jan 28, 1995	Carl W. Davis
Bass, smallmouth	10 lb 14 oz	Dale Hollow, Tennessee	April 24, 1969	John T. Gorman
Bass, Suwannee	3 lb 14 oz	Suwannee River, Florida	Mar 2, 1985	Ronnie Everett
Bass, white	6 lb 13 oz	Orange, Virginia	July 31, 1989	Ronald Sprouse
Bass, whiterock	27 lb 5 oz	Greers Ferry Lake, Arkansas	Apr 24, 1997	Jerald Shaum
Bass, yellow	2 lb 9 oz	Waverly, Tennessee	Feb 27, 1998	John Chappell
Bluegill	4 lb 12 oz	Ketona Lake, Alabama	Apr 9, 1950	T.S. Hudson
Bowfin	21 lb 8 oz	Florence, South Carolina	Jan 29, 1980	Robert Harmon
Buffalo, bigmouth	70 lb 5 oz	Bastrop, Louisiana	Apr 21, 1980	Delbert Sisk
Buffalo, black	63 lb 6 oz	Mississippi River, Iowa	Aug 14, 1999	Jim Winter
Buffalo, smallmouth	82 lb 3 oz	Athens Lake, Georgia	June 6, 1993	Randy Collins
Bullhead, brown	6 lb 1 oz	Waterford, New York	Apr 26, 1998	Bobby Triplett
Bullhead, yellow	4 lb 4 oz	Mormon Lake, Arizona	May 11, 1984	Emily Williams
Burbot	18 lb 11 oz	Angenmanalren, Sweden	Oct 22, 1996	Margit Agren
Carp, common.	75 lb 11 oz	Lac de St. Cassien, France	May 21, 1987	Leo van der Gugten
Catfish, blue	116 lb 12 oz	Mississippi River, Arkansas	Aug 3, 2001	Charles Ashley Jr.
Catfish, channel	58 lb	Santee-Cooper Reservoir, SC	July 7, 1964	W.B. Whaley
Catfish, flathead	123 lb	Elk City Reservoir, Indep., KS	May 14, 1998	Ken Paulie
Catfish, white	21 lb 8 oz	Gorton Pond, East Lime, CT	Apr 22, 2001	Thomas Urquhart
Char, Arctic	32 lb 9 oz	Tree River, Canada	July 30, 1981	Jeffrey Ward
Crappie, white	5 lb 3 oz	Enid Dam, Mississippi	July 31, 1957	Fred L. Bright
Dolly Varden	20 lb 14 oz	Wulik River, Alaska	July 7, 2001	Raz Reid
Dorado	51 lb 5 oz	Corrientes, Argentina	Sep 27, 1984	Armando Giudice
Drum, freshwater	54 lb 8 oz	Nickajack Lake, Tennessee	Apr 20, 1972	Benny E. Hull
Gar, alligator	279 lb	Rio Grande River, Texas	Dec 2, 1951	Bill Valverde
Gar, Florida	10 lb	Florida Everglades, Florida	Jan 28, 2002	Herbert Ratner Jr.
Gar, longnose	50 lb 5 oz	Trinity River, Texas	July 30, 1954	Townsend Miller
Gar, shortnose	5 lb 12 oz	Rend Lake, Illinois	July 16, 1995	Donna K. Willmert
Gar, spotted	9 lb 12 oz	Lake Mexia, Texas	Apr 7, 1994	Rick Rivard
Grayling, Arctic	5 lb 15 oz	Katseyedie River, Northwest Territories	Aug 16, 1967	Jeanne P. Branson
Inconnu	53 lb	Pah River, Alaska	Aug 20, 1986	Lawrence Hudnall
Kokanee	9 lb 6 oz	Okanagan Lake, Vernon, BC	June 18, 1988	Norm Kuhn
Muskellunge	67 lb 8 oz	Hayward, Wisconsin	July 24, 1949	Cal Johnson
Muskellunge, tiger	51 lb 3 oz	Lac Vieux-Desert, WI, MI	July 16, 1919	John Knobla
Peacock, speckled	27 lb	Rio Negro, Brazil	Dec 4, 1994	Gerald (Doc) Lawson
Perch, Nile	230 lb	Lake Nasser, Egypt	Dec 20, 2000	William Toth
Perch, white	3 lb 1 oz	Forest Hill Park, NJ	May 6, 1989	Edward Tango
Perch, yellow	4 lb 3 oz	Bordentown, New Jersey	May 1865	C.C. Abbot
Pickerel, chain	9 lb 6 oz	Homerville, Georgia	Feb 17, 1961	Baxley McQuaig Jr.
Pike, northern	55 lb 1 oz	Lake of Grefeern, W Germany	Oct 16, 1986	Lothar Louis
Redhorse, greater	9 lb 3 oz	Salmon River, Pulaski, New York	May 11, 1985	Jason Wilson
Redhorse, silver	11 lb 7 oz	Plum Creek, Wisconsin	May 29, 1985	Neal Long
Salmon, Atlantic	79 lb 2 oz	Tana River, Norway	1928	Henrik Henriksen
Salmon, Chinook	97 lb 4 oz	Kenai River, Alaska	May 17, 1985	Les Anderson
Salmon, chum	35 lb	Edye Pass, Canada	July 11, 1995	Todd A. Johansson
Salmon, coho	33 lb 4 oz	Pulaski, New York	Sep 27, 1989	Jerry Lifton
Salmon, pink	14 lb 13 oz	Monroe, Washington	Sep 30, 2001	Alexander Minerich
Salmon, sockeye	15 lb 3 oz	Kenai River, Alaska	Aug 9, 1987	Stan Roach
Sauger	8 lb 12 oz	Lake Sakakawea, North Dakota	Oct 6, 1971	Mike Fischer
Shad, American	11 lb 4 oz	Connecticut River, Massachusetts	May 19, 1986	Bob Thibodo
Sturgeon, white	468 lb	Benicia, California	July 9, 1983	Joey Pallotta III
Sunfish, green	2 lb 2 oz	Stockton Lake, Missouri	June 18, 1971	Paul M. Dilley
Sunfish, redbreast	1 lb 12 oz	Suwannee River, Florida	May 29, 1984	Alvin Buchanan
Sunfish, redear	5 lb 7 oz	Diverson Canal, Georgia	Nov 6, 1998	Amos M. Gay
Tigerfish, giant	97 lb	Zaire River, Kinshasa, Zaire	July 9, 1988	Raymond Houtmans
Trout, Apache	5 lb 3 oz	Apache Reservation, Arizona	May 29, 1991	John Baldwin
Trout, brook	14 lb 8 oz	Nipigon River, Ontario	July 1916	W.J. Cook
Trout, brown	40 lb 4 oz	Heber Springs, Arkansas	May 9, 1992	Howard (Rip) Collins
Trout, bull	32 lb	Lake Pond Oreille, Idaho	Oct 27, 1949	N.L. Higgins
Trout, cutthroat	41 lb	Pyramid Lake, Nevada	Dec 1925	John Skimmerhorn
Trout, golden	11 lb	Cook's Lake, Wyoming	Aug 5, 1948	Charles S. Reed

Freshwater Fishing Records (Cont.)

Species	Weight	Where Caught	Date	Angler
Trout, lake	72 lb	Great Bear Lake, Northwest Territories	Aug 19, 1995	Lloyd Bull
Trout, rainbow	42 lb 2 oz	Bell Island, Alaska	June 22, 1970	David Robert White
Trout, tiger	20 lb 13 oz	Lake Michigan, Wisconsin	Aug 12, 1978	Pete M. Friedland
Walleye	25 lb	Old Hickory Lake, Tennessee	Aug 2, 1960	Mabry Harper
Warmouth	2 lb 7 oz	Yellow River, Holt, Florida	Oct 19, 1985	Tony D. Dempsey
Whitefish, lake	14 lb 6 oz	Meaford, Ontario	May 21, 1984	Dennis Laycock
Whitefish, mountain	5 lb 8 oz	Elbow River, Calgary, Alberta	Aug 1, 1995	Randy Woo
Whitefish, broad	9 lb	Tozitna River, Alaska	July 17, 1989	Al Mathews
Whitefish, round	6 lb	Putahow River, Manitoba	June 14, 1984	Allan J. Ristori
Zander	25 lb 2 oz	Trosa, Sweden	June 12, 1986	Harry Lee Tennison

Greyhound Racing

Annual Greyhound Race of Champions Winners*

Year	Winner (Sex)	Affiliation/Owner	Year	Winner (Sex)	Affiliation/Owner
1982	DD's Jackie (F)	Wonderland Park/ R.H. Walters Jr.	1988	BB's Old Yellow (M)	Supplemental (Southland)/ Margie Bonita Hyers
1983	Comin' Attraction (F)	Rocky Mt. Greyhound Park/ Bob Riggin	1989	Osh Kosh Juliet (F)	Tampa Greyhound Track/ William F. Pollard
1984	Fallon (F)	Tampa Greyhound Track/ E.J. Alderson	1990	Daring Don (M)	Interstate Kennel Club/ Perry Padrta
1985	Lady Delight (F)	Lincoln Greyhound Park/ Julian A. Gay	1991	Mo Kick (M)	Flagler Greyhound Track/ Eric M. Kennon
1986	Ben G Speedboat (M)	Multnomah Kennel Club/ Louis Bennett	1992	Dicky Vallie (M)	Dairyland Greyhound Track/ George Benjamin
1987	ET's Pesky (F)	Supplemental (Flagler)/ Emil Tanis	1993	Mega Morris (M)	Jacksonville Kennel Club/ Ferrell's Kennel

* The Greyhound Race of Champions has not been held since 1993.

Gymnastics

World Champions
MEN
All-Around

Year	Champion, Nation	Year	Champion, Nation	Year	Champion, Nation
1903	Joseph Martinez, France	1938	Jan Gajdos, Czechoslovakia	1983	Dimitri Bilozertchev, USSR
1905	Marcel Lalue, France	1950	Walter Lehmann, Switzerland	1985	Yuri Korolev, USSR
1907	Joseph Czada, Czechoslovakia	1954	Valentin Mouratov, USSR Victor Chukarin, USSR	1987	Dimitri Bilozertchev, USSR
1909	Marcos Torres, France	1958	Boris Shaklin, USSR	1989	Igor Korobchinsky, USSR
1911	Ferdinand Steiner, Czechoslovakia	1962	Yuri Titov, USSR	1991	Grigori Misutin, CIS
1913	Marcos Torres, France	1966	Mikhail Voronin, USSR	1993	Vitaly Scherbo, Belarus
1922	Peter Sumi, Yugoslavia F. Pechacek, Czechoslovakia	1970	Eizo Kenmotsu, Japan	1994	Ivan Ivankov, Belarus
1926	Peter Sumi, Yugoslavia	1974	Shigeru Kasamatsu, Japan	1995	Li Xiaoshuang, China
1930	Josip Primozic, Yugoslavia	1978	Nikolai Andrianov, USSR	1997	Ivan Ivankov, Belarus
1934	Eugene Mack, Switzerland	1979	Alexander Ditiatin, USSR	1999	Nicolae Krukov, Russia
		1981	Yuri Korolev, USSR	2001	Feng Jing, China

Pommel Horse

Year	Champion, Nation	Year	Champion, Nation	Year	Champion, Nation
1930	Josip Primozic, Yugoslavia	1962	Miroslav Cerar, Yugoslavia	1981	Michael Mikolai, East Germany
1934	Eugene Mack, Switzerland	1966	Miroslav Cerar, Yugoslavia	1983	Dmitri Bilozertchev, USSR
1938	Michael Reusch, Switzerland	1970	Miroslav Cerar, Yugoslavia	1985	Valentin Moguilny, USSR
1950	Josef Stalder, Switzerland	1974	Zoltan Magyar, Hungary	1987	Zsolt Borkai, Hungary
1954	Grant Chaguinjan, USSR	1978	Zoltan Magyar, Hungary		Dmitri Bilozertchev, USSR
1958	Boris Shaklin, USSR	1979	Zoltan Magyar, Hungary		

World Champions (Cont.)
MEN (Cont.)
Pommel Horse (Cont.)

Year	Champion, Nation	Year	Champion, Nation	Year	Champion, Nation
1989	Valentin Moguilny, USSR	1993	Pae Gil Su, North Korea	1999	Alexei Nemov, Russia
1991	Valeri Belênki, USSR	1994	Marius Urzica, Romania	2001	Marius Urzica, Romania
1992	Pae Gil Su, North Korea	1995	Li Donghua, Switzerland		
	Vitaly Scherbo, CIS	1996	Pae Gil Su, North Korea		
	Li Jing, China	1997	Valeri Belenki, Germany		

Floor Exercise

Year	Champion, Nation	Year	Champion, Nation	Year	Champion, Nation
1930	Josip Primozic, Yugoslavia	1970	Akinori Nakayama, Japan	1989	Igor Korobchinsky, USSR
1934	Georges Miesz, Switzerland	1974	Shigeru Kasamatsu, Japan	1991	Igor Korobchinsky, USSR
1938	Jan Gajdos, Czechoslovakia	1978	Kurt Thomas, United States	1993	Grigori Misutin, Ukraine
1950	Josef Stalder, Switzerland	1979	Kurt Thomas, United States	1994	Vitaly Scherbo, Belarus
1954	Valentin Mouratov, USSR		Roland Brucker, GDR	1995	Vitaly Scherbo, Belarus
	Masao Takemoto, Japan	1981	Yuri Korolev, USSR	1996	Vitaly Scherbo, Belarus
1958	Masao Takemoto, Japan		Li Yuejui, Chi	1997	Alexei Nemov, Russia
1962	Nobuyuki Aihara, Japan	1983	Tong Fei, China	1999	Alexei Nemov, Russia
	Yukio Endo, Japan	1985	Tong Fei, China	2001	Marian Dragulescu, Rom
1966	Akinori Nakayama, Japan	1987	Lou Yun, China		

Rings

Year	Champion, Nation	Year	Champion, Nation	Year	Champion, Nation
1930	Emanuel Loffler, Czechoslovakia	1974	N. Andrianov, USSR	1992	Vitaly Scherbo, CIS
			D. Grecu, Rom.	1993	Yuri Chechi, Italy
1934	Alois Hudec, Czechoslovakia	1978	Nikolai Andrianov, USSR	1994	Yuri Chechi, Italy
1938	Alois Hudec, Czechoslovakia	1979	Alexander Ditiatin, USSR	1995	Yuri Chechi, Italy
1950	Walter Lehmann, Switzerland	1981	Alexander Ditiatin, USSR	1996	Yuri Chechi, Italy
		1983	Dimitri Bilozertchev, USSR	1997	Yuri Chechi, Italy
1954	Albert Azarian, USSR	1985	Li Ning, China	1999	Zhen Dong, China
1958	Albert Azarian, USSR		Yuri Korolev, USSR	2001	Jordan Jovtchev, Bulgaria
1962	Yuri Titov, USSR	1987	Yuri Korolev, USSR		
1966	Mikhail Voronin, USSR	1989	Andreas Aguilar, W Ger		
1970	Akinori Nakayama, Japan	1991	Grigory Misutin, USSR		

Parallel Bars

Year	Champion, Nation	Year	Champion, Nation	Year	Champion, Nation
1930	Josip Primozic, Yugoslavia	1979	Bart Conner, United States	1992	Li Jin, China
1934	Eugene Mack, Switzerland	1981	Koji Gushiken, Japan		Alexei Voropaev, CIS
1938	Michael Reusch, Switzerland		Alexandr Ditiatin, USSR	1993	Vitaly Scherbo, Belarus
1950	Hans Eugster, Switzerland	1983	Vladimir Artemov, USSR	1994	Huang Liping, China
1954	Victor Chukarin, USSR		Lou Yun, China	1995	Vitaly Scherbo, Belarus
1958	Boris Shaklin, USSR	1985	Sylvio Kroll, East Germany	1996	Rustam Sharipov, Ukraine
1962	Miroslav Cerar, Yugoslavia		Valentin Moguilny, USSR	1997	Zhang Jinjing, China
1966	Sergei Diamidov, USSR	1987	Vladimir Artemov, USSR	1999	Joo-Hyung Lee, S Korea
1970	Akinori Nakayama, Japan	1989	Li Jing, China	2001	Sean Townsend, U.S.
1974	Eizo Kenmotsu, Japan		Vladimir Artemov, USSR		
1978	Eizo Kenmotsu, Japan	1991	Li Jing, China		

High Bar

Year	Champion, Nation	Year	Champion, Nation	Year	Champion, Nation
1930	Istvan Pelle, Hungary	1978	Shigeru Kasamatsu, Japan	1994	Vitaly Scherbo, Belarus
1934	Ernst Winter, Germany	1979	Kurt Thomas, United States	1995	Andreas Wecker, Germany
1938	Michael Reusch, Switzerland	1981	Alexander Takchev, USSR	1996	Jesús Carballo, Spain
1950	Paavo Aaltonen, Finland	1983	Dimitri Bilozertchev, USSR	1997	Jani Tanskanen, Finland
1954	Valentin Mouratov, USSR	1985	Tong Fei, China	1999	Jesus Carballo, Spain
1958	Boris Shaklin, USSR	1987	Dimitri Bilozertchev, USSR	2001	Vlasios Maras, Greece
1962	Takashi Ono, Japan	1989	Li Chunyang, China		
1966	Akinori Nakayama, Japan	1991	Li Chunyang, China		
1970	Eizo Kenmotsu, Japan		R. Buechner, Germ		
1974	Eberhard Gienger, West Germany	1992	Grigori Misutin, CIS		
		1993	Sergei Kharkov, Russia		

World Champions (Cont.)
MEN (Cont.)
Vault

Year	Champion, Nation	Year	Champion, Nation	Year	Champion, Nation
1934	Eugene Mack, Switzerland	1978	Junichi Shimizu, Japan	1992	Yoo Ok Youl, South Korea
1938	Eugene Mack, Switzerland	1979	Alexander Ditiatin, USSR	1993	Vitaly Scherbo, Belarus
1950	Ernst Gebendinger, Switzerland	1981	Ralf-Peter Hemmann, East Germany	1994	Vitaly Scherbo, Belarus
1954	Leo Sotornik, Czechoslovakia	1983	Arthur Akopian, USSR	1995	G. Misutin, Ukraine A. Nemov, Russia
1958	Yuri Titov, USSR	1985	Yuri Korolev, USSR	1996	Alexei Nemov, Russia
1962	Premysel Krbec, Czechoslovakia	1987	Lou Yun, China Sylvio Kroll, East Germany	1997	Sergei Fedorchenko, Kazakhstan
1966	Haruhiro Yamashita, Japan	1989	Joreg Behrend, East Germany	1999	Xiaopeng Li, China
1970	Mitsuo Tsukahara, Japan	1991	Yoo Ok Youl, South Korea	2001	Marian Dragulescu, Rom
1974	Shigeru Kasamatsu, Japan				

WOMEN
All-Around

Year	Champion, Nation	Year	Champion, Nation	Year	Champion, Nation
1934	Vlasta Dekanova, Czechoslovakia	1970	Ludmilla Tourischeva, USSR	1991	Kim Zmeskal, United States
1938	Vlasta Dekanova, Czechoslovakia	1974	Ludmilla Tourischeva, USSR	1993	Shannon Miller, United States
1950	Helena Rakoczy, Poland	1978	Elena Mukhina, USSR	1994	Shannon Miller, United States
1954	Galina Roudiko, USSR	1979	Nelli Kim, USSR	1995	Lilia Podkopayeva, Ukraine
1958	Larissa Latynina, USSR	1981	Olga Bicherova, USSR	1997	Svetlana Khorkina, Russia
1962	Larissa Latynina, USSR	1983	Natalia Yurchenko, USSR	1999	Maria Olaru, Romania
1966	Vera Caslavska, Czechoslovakia	1985	Elena Shoushounova, USSR Oksana Omeliantchik, USSR	2001	Svetlana Khorkina, Russia
		1987	Aurelia Dobre, Romania		
		1989	Svetlana Bouguinskaia, USSR		

Floor Exercise

Year	Champion, Nation	Year	Champion, Nation	Year	Champion, Nation
1950	Helena Rakoczy, Poland	1979	Emilia Eberle, Romania	1992	Kim Zmeskal, United States
1954	Tamara Manina, USSR	1981	Natalia Ilenko, USSR	1993	Shannon Miller, United States
1958	Eva Bosakava, Czechoslovakia	1983	Ecaterina Szabo, Romania	1994	Dina Kochetkova, Russia
1962	Larissa Latynina, USSR	1985	Oksana Omeliantchik, USSR	1995	Gina Gogean, Romania
1966	Natalia Kuchinskaya, USSR	1987	Elena Shoushounova, USSR Daniela Silivas, Romania	1996	Gina Gogean, Romania
1970	Ludmilla Tourischeva, USSR	1989	Svetlana Bouguinskaia, USSR Daniela Silivas, Romania	1997	Gina Gogean, Romania
1974	Ludmilla Tourischeva, USSR	1991	Cristina Bontas, Romania Oksana Tchusovitina, USSR	1999	Andreea Raducan, Romania
1978	Nelli Kim, USSR Elena Mukhina, USSR			2001	Andreea Raducan, Romania

Uneven Bars

Year	Champion, Nation	Year	Champion, Nation	Year	Champion, Nation
1950	Gertchen Kolar, Austria Anna Pettersson, Sweden	1979	Ma Yanhong, China Maxi Gnauck, East Germany	1991	Gwang Suk Kim, North Korea
1954	Agnes Keleti, Hungary	1981	Maxi Gnauck, East Germany	1992	Lavinia Milosivici, Romania
1958	Larissa Latynina, USSR	1983	Maxi Gnauck, East Germany	1993	Shannon Miller, United States
1962	Irina Pervuschina, USSR	1985	Gabriele Fahnrich, East Germany	1994	Luo Li, China
1966	Natalia Kuchinskaya, USSR	1987	Daniela Silivas, Romania Doerte Thuemmler, East Germany	1995	Svetlana Khorkina, Russia
1970	Karin Janz, East Germany	1989	Fan Di, China Daniela Silivas, Romania	1996	Svetlana Khorkina, Russia
1974	Annelore Zinke, East Germany			1997	Svetlana Khorkina, Russia
1978	Marcia Frederick, United States			1999	Svetlana Khorkina, Russia
				2001	Svetlana Khorkina, Russia

World Champions (Cont.)
WOMEN (Cont.)

Balance Beam

Year	Champion, Nation	Year	Champion, Nation	Year	Champion, Nation
1950	Helena Rakoczy, Poland	1979	Vera Cerna, Czechoslovakia	1993	Lavinia Milosovici, Romania
1954	Keiko Tanaka, Japan	1981	Maxi Gnauck, East Germany	1994	Shannon Miller, United States
1958	Larissa Latynina, USSR	1983	Olga Mostepanova, USSR	1995	Mo Huilan, China
1962	Eva Bosakova, Czech.	1985	Daniela Silivas, Romania	1996	Dina Kochetkova, Russia
1966	Natalia Kuchinskaya, USSR	1987	Aurelia Dobre, Romania	1997	Gina Gogean, Romania
1970	Erika Zuchold, East Germany	1989	Daniela Silivas, Romania	1999	E. Zamolodchikova, Russia
1974	Ludmilla Tourischeva, USSR	1991	Svetlana Boguinskaia, USSR	2001	Andreea Raducan, Romania
1978	Nadia Comaneci, Romania	1992	Kim Zmeskal, United States		

Vault

Year	Champion, Nation	Year	Champion, Nation	Year	Champion, Nation
1950	Helena Rakoczy, Poland	1974	Olga Korbut, USSR	1992	Henrietta Onodi, Hungary
1954	T. Manina, USSR	1978	Nelli Kim, USSR	1993	Elena Piskun, Belarus
	Anna Pettersson, Sweden	1979	Dumitrita Turner, Romania	1994	Gina Gogean, Romania
1958	Larissa Latynina, USSR	1981	Maxi Gnauck, East Germany	1995	L. Podkopayeva, Ukraine
1962	Vera Caslavska,	1983	Boriana Stoyanova, Bulgaria		Simona Amanar, Rom.
	Czechoslovakia	1985	Elena Shoushounova, USSR	1996	Gina Gogean, Romania
1966	Vera Caslavska,	1987	Elena Shoushounova, USSR	1997	Simona Amanar, Romania
	Czechoslovakia	1989	Olesia Durnik, USSR	1999	Jie Ling, China
1970	Erika Zuchold, East Germany	1991	Lavinia Milosovici, Romania	2001	Svetlana Khorkina, Russia

National Champions
MEN
All-Around

Year	Champion	Year	Champion	Year	Champion
1963	Art Shurlock	1976	Kurt Thomas	1991	Chris Waller
1964	Rusty Mitchell	1977	Kurt Thomas	1992	John Roethlisberger
1965	Rusty Mitchell	1978	Kurt Thomas	1993	John Roethlisberger
1966	Rusty Mitchell	1979	Bart Conner	1994	Scott Keswick
1967	Katsuzoki Kanzaki	1980	Peter Vidmar	1995	John Roethlisberger
1968	Yoshi Hayasaki	1981	Jim Hartung	1996	Blaine Wilson
1969	Steve Hug	1982	Peter Vidmar	1997	Blaine Wilson
1970	Makoto Sakamoto	1983	Mitch Gaylord	1998	Blaine Wilson
	Mas Watanabe	1984	Mitch Gaylord	1999	Blaine Wilson
1971	Yoshi Takei	1985	Brian Babcock	2000	Blaine Wilson
1972	Yoshi Takei	1986	Tim Daggett	2001	Sean Townsend
1973	Marshall Avener	1987	Scott Johnson	2002	Paul Hamm
1974	John Crosby	1988	Dan Hayden		
1975	Tom Beach	1989	Tim Ryan		
	Bart Conner	1990	John Roethlisberger		

Floor Exercise

Year	Champion	Year	Champion	Year	Champion
1963	Tom Seward	1975	Peter Korman	1989	Mike Racanelli
1964	Rusty Mitchell	1977	Ron Galimore	1990	Bob Stelter
1965	Rusty Mitchell	1978	Kurt Thomas	1991	Mike Racanelli
1966	Dan Millman	1979	Ron Galimore	1992	Gregg Curtis
1967	Katsuzoki Kanzaki	1980	Ron Galimore	1993	Kerry Huston
	Ron Aure	1981	Jim Hartung	1994	Jeremy Killen
1968	Katsuzoki Kanzaki	1982	Jim Hartung	1995	Daniel Stover
1969	Steve Hug	1983	Mitch Gaylord	1996	Jay Thornton
	Dave Thor	1984	Peter Vidmar	1997	Jason Gatson
1970	Makoto Sakamoto	1985	Mark Oates	1998	Jason Gatson
1971	John Crosby	1986	Robert Sundstrom	1999	Jason Gatson
1972	Yoshi Takei	1987	John Sweeney	2000	Blaine Wilson
1973	John Crosby	1988	Mark Oates	2001	Sean Townsend
1974	John Crosby		Charles Lakes	2002	Morgan Hamm

National Champions (Cont.)

MEN (Cont.)

Pommel Horse

Year	Champion	Year	Champion	Year	Champion
1963	Larry Spiegel	1977	Gene Whelan	1990	Patrick Kirksey
1964	Sam Bailie	1978	Jim Hartung	1991	Chris Waller
1965	Jack Ryan	1979	Bart Conner	1992	Chris Waller
1966	Jack Ryan	1980	Jim Hartung	1993	Chris Waller
1967	Paul Mayer/Dave Doty	1981	Jim Hartung	1994	Mihai Begiu
1968	Katsuoki Kanzaki	1982	Jim Hartung	1995	Mark Sohn
1969	Dave Thor	1983	Bart Conner	1996	Josh Stein
1970	Mas Watanabe	1984	Tim Daggett	1997	John Roethlisberger
1971	Leonard Caling	1985	Phil Cahoy	1998	John Roethlisberger
1972	Sadao Hamada	1986	Phil Cahoy	1999	John Roethlisberger
1973	Marshall Avener	1987	Tim Daggett	2000	John Roethlisberger
1974	Marshall Avener	1988	Kevin Davis	2001	Brett McClure
1975	Bart Conner	1989	Kevin Davis	2002	Paul Hamm

Rings

Year	Champion	Year	Champion	Year	Champion
1963	Art Shurlock	1975	Tom Beach	1989	Scott Keswick
1964	Glen Gailis	1977	Kurt Thomas	1990	Scott Keswick
1965	Glen Gailis	1978	Mike Silverstein	1991	Scott Keswick
1966	Glen Gailis	1979	Bart Conner	1992	Tim Ryan
1967	Fred Dennis	1980	Jim Hartung	1993	John Roethlisberger
	Don Hatch	1981	Jim Hartung	1994	Scott Keswick
1968	Yoshi Hayasaki	1982	Jim Hartung	1995	Paul O'Neill
1969	Fred Dennis		Peter Vidmar	1996	Kip Simons
	Bob Emery	1983	Mitch Gaylord	1997	Blaine Wilson
1970	Makoto Sakamoto	1984	Jim Hartung	1998	Jeff Johnson
1971	Yoshi Takei	1985	Dan Hayden	1999	Blaine Wilson
1972	Yoshi Takei	1986	Dan Hayden	2000	Blaine Wilson
1973	Jim Ivicek	1987	Scott Johnson	2001	Sean Townsend
1974	Tom Weeder	1988	Dan Hayden	2002	Blaine Wilson

Vault

Year	Champion	Year	Champion	Year	Champion
1963	Art Shurlock	1977	Ron Galimore	1990	Lance Ringnald
1964	Gary Hery	1978	Jim Hartung	1991	Scott Keswick
1965	Brent Williams	1979	Ron Galimore	1992	Trent Dimas
1966	Dan Millman	1980	Ron Galimore	1993	Bill Roth
1967	Jack Kenan	1981	Ron Galimore	1994	Keith Wiley
	Sid Jensen	1982	Jim Hartung/Jim Mikus	1995	David St. Pierre
1968	Rich Scorza	1983	Chris Reigel	1996	Blaine Wilson
1969	Dave Butzman	1984	Chris Reigel	1997	Blaine Wilson
1970	Makoto Sakamoto	1985	Scott Johnson	1998	Brent Klaus
1971	Gary Morava		Mark Oates	1999	Guard Young
1972	Mike Kelley	1986	Scott Wilbanks	2000	Blaine Wilson
1973	Gary Morava	1987	John Sweeney	2001	Jason Furr
1974	John Crosby	1988	John Sweeney/Bill Paul	2002	Paul Hamm
1975	Tom Beach	1989	Bill Roth		

Parallel Bars

Year	Champion	Year	Champion	Year	Champion
1963	Tom Seward	1971	Brent Simmons	1981	Bart Conner
1964	Rusty Mitchell	1972	Yoshi Takei	1982	Peter Vidmar
1965	Glen Gailis	1973	Marshall Avener	1983	Mitch Gaylord
1966	Ray Hadley	1974	Jim Ivicek	1984	Peter Vidmar
1967	Katsuzoki Kanzaki	1975	Bart Conner		Mitch Gaylord
	Tom Goldsborough	1977	Kurt Thomas		Tim Daggett
1968	Yoshi Hayasaki	1978	Bart Conner	1985	Tim Daggett
1969	Steve Hug	1979	Bart Conner	1986	Tim Daggett
1970	Makoto Sakamoto	1980	Phil Cahoy/Larry Gerard	1987	Scott Johnson

National Champions (Cont.)

MEN (Cont.)

Parallel Bars (Cont.)

Year	Champion	Year	Champion	Year	Champion
1988	D. Hayden/K. Davis	1993	Chainey Umphrey	1998	Blaine Wilson
1989	Conrad Voorsanger	1994	Steve McCain	1999	Jason Gatson
1990	Trent Dimas	1995	John Roethlisberger	2000	Trent Wells
1991	Scott Keswick	1996	Jair Lynch	2001	Sean Townsend
1992	Jair Lynch	1997	Blaine Wilson	2002	Sean Townsend

High Bars

Year	Champion	Year	Champion	Year	Champion
1963	Art Shurlock	1979	Yoichi Tomita	1991	Lance Ringnald
1964	Glen Gailis	1980	Jim Hartung	1992	Jair Lynch
1965	Rusty Mitchell	1981	Bart Conner	1993	Steve McCain
1966	Katsuzoki Kanzaki	1982	Mitch Gaylord	1994	Scott Keswick
1967	Katsuzoki Kanzaki	1983	Mario McCutcheon	1995	John Roethlisberger
	Jerry Fontana	1984	Peter Vidmar	1996	Bill Roth
1968	Yoshi Hayasaki		Tim Daggett	1997	Douglas Stibel
1969	Rich Grisby		Mitch Gaylord	1998	Jason Gatson
1970	Makoto Sakamoto	1985	Dan Hayden	1999	Jamie Natalie
1971	Yoshi Takei	1986	D. Hayden/D. Moriel	2000	Trent Wells
1972	Tom Lindner	1987	David Moriel		Jamie Natalie
1973	John Crosby	1988	Dan Hayden	2001	Daniel Diaz-Luong
1974	Brent Simmons	1989	Tim Ryan	2002	Blaine Wilson
1975	Tom Beach	1990	Trent Dimas		
1977	Kurt Thomas		Lance Ringnald		
1978	Kurt Thomas				

WOMEN

All-Around

Year	Champion	Year	Champion	Year	Champion
1963	Donna Schanezer	1976	Denise Cheshire	1991	Kim Zmeskal
1965	Gail Daley	1977	Donna Turnbow	1992	Kim Zmeskal
1966	Donna Schanezer	1978	Kathy Johnson	1993	Shannon Miller
1968	Linda Scott	1979	Leslie Pyfer	1994	Dominique Dawes
1969	Joyce Tanac	1980	Julianne McNamara	1995	Dominique Moceanu
	Schroeder	1981	Tracee Talavera	1996	Shannon Miller
1970	Cathy Rigby McCoy	1982	Tracee Talavera	1997	Vanessa Adler
1971	Joan Moore Gnat	1983	Dianne Durham		Kristy Powell
	Linda Metheny	1984	Mary Lou Retton	1998	Kristen Maloney
	Mulvihill	1985	Sabrina Mar	1999	Kristen Maloney
1972	Joan Moore Gnat	1986	Jennifer Sey	2000	Elise Ray
	Cathy Rigby McCoy	1987	Kristie Phillips	2001	Tasha Schwikert
1973	Joan Moore Gnat	1988	Phoebe Mills	2002	Tasha Schwikert
1974	Joan Moore Gnat	1989	Brandy Johnson		
1975	Tammy Manville	1990	Kim Zmeskal		

Vault

Year	Champion	Year	Champion	Year	Champion
1963	Donna Schanezer	1976	Debbie Wilcox	1990	Brandy Johnson
1965	Gail Daley	1977	Lisa Cawthron	1991	Kerri Strug
1966	Donna Schanezer	1978	Rhonda Schwandt	1992	Kerri Strug
1968	Terry Spencer		Sharon Shapiro	1993	Dominique Dawes
1969	Joyce Tanac	1979	Christa Canary	1994	Dominique Dawes
	Schroeder	1980	J. McNamara/B. Kline	1995	Shannon Miller
	Cleo Carver	1981	Kim Neal	1996	Dominique Dawes
1970	Cathy Rigby McCoy	1982	Yumi Mordre	1997	Vanessa Atler
1971	Joan Moore Gnat	1983	Dianne Durham	1998	Dominique Moceanu
	Adele Gleaves	1984	Mary Lou Retton	1999	Vanessa Atler
1972	Cindy Eastwood	1985	Yolanda Mavity	2000	Kristen Maloney
1973	Roxanne Pierce	1986	Joyce Wilborn	2001	Mohini Bhardwaj
	Mancha	1987	Rhonda Faehn	2002	Elizabeth Tricase
1974	Dianne Dunbar	1988	Rhonda Faehn		
1975	Kolleen Casey	1989	Brandy Johnson		

National Champions (Cont.)
WOMEN (Cont.)
Uneven Bars

Year	Champion	Year	Champion	Year	Champion
1963	Donna Schanezer	1976	Leslie Wolfsberger	1991	Elisabeth Crandall
1965	Irene Haworth	1977	Donna Turnbow	1992	Dominique Dawes
1966	Donna Schanezer	1978	Marcia Frederick	1993	Shannon Miller
1968	Linda Scott	1979	Marcia Frederick	1994	Dominique Dawes
1969	Joyce Tanac Schroeder Lisa Nelson	1980	Marcia Frederick	1995	Dominique Dawes
		1981	Julianne McNamara	1996	Dominique Dawes
1970	Roxanne Pierce Mancha	1982	Marie Roethlisberger	1997	Kristy Powell
		1983	Julianne McNamara	1998	Elise Ray
1971	Joan Moore Gnat	1984	Julianne McNamara	1999	Jamie Dantzscher Jennie Thompson
1972	Cathy Rigby McCoy	1985	Sabrina Mar		
1973	Roxanne Pierce Mancha	1986	Marie Roethlisberger	2000	Elise Ray
		1987	Melissa Marlowe	2001	Katie Heenan
1974	Diane Dunbar	1988	Chelle Stack	2002	Tasha Schwikert
1975	Leslie Wolfsberger	1989	Chelle Stack		
		1990	Sandy Woolsey		

Balance Beam

Year	Champion	Year	Champion	Year	Champion
1963	Leissa Krol	1977	Donna Turnbow	1991	Shannon Miller
1965	Gail Daley	1978	Christa Canary	1992	Kerri Strug Kim Zmeskal
1966	Irene Haworth Linda Scott	1979	Heidi Anderson		
		1980	Kelly Garrison-Steves	1993	Dominique Dawes
1968	Linda Scott	1981	Tracee Talavera	1994	Dominique Dawes
1969	Lonna Woodward	1982	Julianne McNamara	1995	Doni Thompson Monica Flammer
1970	Joyce Tanac Schroeder	1983	Dianne Durham		
		1984	Pam Bileck Tracee Talavera	1996	Dominique Dawes
1971	Linda Metheny Mulvihill			1997	Kendall Beck
		1986	Angie Denkins	1998	Dominique Moceanu
1972	Kim Chace	1987	Kristie Phillips	1999	Vanessa Atler
1973	Nancy Thies Marshall	1985	Kelly Garrison-Steves	2000	Alyssa Beckerman Amy Chow
1974	Joan Moore Gnat	1988	Kelly Garrison-Steves		
1975	Kyle Gayner	1989	Brandy Johnson	2001	Tasha Schwikert
1976	Carrie Englert	1990	Betty Okino	2002	Tasha Schwikert

Floor Exercise

Year	Champion	Year	Champion	Year	Champion
1963	Donna Schanezer	1979	Heidi Anderson	1993	Shannon Miller
1965	Gail Daley	1980	Beth Kline	1994	Dominique Dawes
1966	Donna Schanezer	1981	Michelle Goodwin	1995	Dominique Dawes
1968	Linda Scott	1982	Amy Koopman	1996	Dominique Dawes
1970	Cathy Rigby McCoy	1983	Dianne Durham	1997	Lindsay Wing
1971	Joan Moore Gnat Linda Metheny Mulvihill	1984	Mary Lou Retton	1998	Vanessa Atler
		1985	Sabrina Mar	1999	Elise Ray
		1986	Yolanda Mavity	2000	Kristen Maloney
1972	Joan Moore Gnat	1987	Kristie Phillips	2001	Tabitha Yim
1973	Joan Moore Gnat	1988	Phoebe Mills	2002	Tasha Schwikert
1974	Joan Moore Gnat	1989	Brandy Johnson		
1975	Kathy Howard	1990	Brandy Johnson		
1976	Carrie Englert	1991	Kim Zmeskal Dominique Dawes		
1977	Kathy Johnson	1992	Kim Zmeskal		
1978	Kathy Johnson				

Handball

National Four-Wall Champions

MEN

1919.....Bill Ranft	1941.....Joe Platak	1963.....Oscar Obert	1985.....Naty Alvarado
1920.....Max Gold	1942.....Jack Clemente	1964.....Jimmy Jacobs	1986.....Naty Alvarado
1921.....Carl Haedge	1943.....Joe Platak	1965.....Jimmy Jacobs	1987.....Naty Alvarado
1922.....Art Shinners	1944.....Frank Coyle	1966.....Paul Haber	1988.....Naty Alvarado
1923.....Joe Murray	1945.....Joe Platak	1967.....Paul Haber	1989.....Poncho Monreal
1924.....Maynard Laswe	1946.....Angelo Trutio	1968.....Stuffy Singer	1990.....Naty Alvarado
1925.....Maynard Laswe	1947.....Gus Lewis	1969.....Paul Haber	1991.....John Bike
1926.....Maynard Laswe	1948.....Gus Lewis	1970.....Paul Haber	1992.....Octavio Silveyra
1927.....George Nelson	1949.....Vic Hershkowitz	1971.....Paul Haber	1993.....David Chapman
1928.....Joe Griffin	1950.....Ken Schneider	1972.....Fred Lewis	1994.....Octavio Silveyra
1929.....Al Banuet	1951.....Walter Plakan	1973.....Terry Muck	1995.....David Chapman
1930.....Al Banuet	1952.....Vic Hershkowitz	1974.....Fred Lewis	1996.....David Chapman
1931.....Al Banuet	1953.....Bob Brady	1975.....Fred Lewis	1997.....Octavio Silveyra
1932.....Angelo Trutio	1954.....Vic Hershkowitz	1976.....Fred Lewis	1998.....David Chapman
1933.....Sam Atcheson	1955.....Jimmy Jacobs	1977.....Naty Alvarado	1999.....David Chapman
1934.....Sam Atcheson	1956.....Jimmy Jacobs	1978.....Fred Lewis	2000.....David Chapman
1935.....Joe Platak	1957.....Jimmy Jacobs	1979.....Naty Alvarado	2001.....Vince Munoz
1936.....Joe Platak	1958.....John Sloan	1980.....Naty Alvarado	2002.....David Chapman
1937.....Joe Platak	1959.....John Sloan	1981.....Fred Lewis	
1938.....Joe Platak	1960.....Jimmy Jacobs	1982.....Naty Alvarado	
1939.....Joe Platak	1961.....John Sloan	1983.....Naty Alvarado	
1940.....Joe Platak	1962.....Oscar Obert	1984.....Naty Alvarado	

WOMEN

1980.....Rosemary Bellini	1986.....Peanut Motal	1992.....Lisa Fraser	1998.....Lisa Fraser
1981.....Rosemary Bellini	1987.....Rosemary Bellini	1993.....Anna Engele	1999.....Anna Christoff
1982.....Rosemary Bellini	1988.....Rosemary Bellini	1994.....Anna Engele	2000.....Priscilla
1983.....Diane Harmon	1989.....Anna Engele	1995.....Anna Engele	Shumate
1984.....Rosemary Bellini	1990.....Anna Engele	1996.....Anna Engele	2001.....Anna Christoff
1985.....Peanut Motal	1991.....Anna Engele	1997.....Lisa Fraser	2002.....Priscilla Shumate

National Three-Wall Champions

MEN

1950.....Vic Hershkowitz	1964.....Marty Decatur	1978.....Fred Lewis	1992.....John Bike
1951.....Vic Hershkowitz	1965.....Carl Obert	1979.....Naty Alvarado	1993.....Eric Klarman
1952.....Vic Hershkowitz	1966.....Marty Decatur	1980.....Lou Russo	1994.....David Chapman
1953.....Vic Herskkowitz	1967.....Carl Obert	1981.....Naty Alvarado	1995.....David Chapman
1954.....Vic Hershkowitz	1968.....Marty Decatur	1982.....Naty Alvarado	1996.....Vince Munoz
1955.....Vic Hershkowitz	1969.....Marty Decatur	1983.....Naty Alvarado	1997.....Vince Munoz
1956.....Vic Hershkowitz	1970.....Steve August	1984.....Naty Alvarado	1998.....Vince Munoz
1957.....Vic Hershkowitz	1971.....Lou Russo	1985.....Vern Roberts	1999.....Vince Munoz
1958.....Vic Hershkowitz	1972.....Lou Russo	1986.....Vern Roberts	2000.....Vince Munoz
1959.....Jimmy Jacobs	1973.....Paul Haber	1987.....Vern Roberts	2001.....Vince Munoz
1960.....Jimmy Jacobs	1974.....Fred Lewis	1988.....Jon Kendler	2002.....Vince Munoz
1961.....Jimmy Jacobs	1975.....Lou Russo	1989.....John Bike	
1962.....Oscar Obert	1976.....Lou Russo	1990.....Vince Munoz	
1963.....Marty Decatur	1977.....Fred Lewis	1991.....John Bike	

WOMEN

1981.....Allison Roberts	1987.....Rosemary Bellini	1993.....Anna Engele	1999.....Allison Roberts
1982.....Allison Roberts	1988.....Rosemary Bellini	1994.....Anna Engele	2000.....Priscilla Shumate
1983.....Allison Roberts	1989.....Rosemary Bellini	1995.....Allison Roberts	2001.....Anna Christoff
1984.....Rosemary Bellini	1990.....Rosemary Bellini	1996.....Anna Engele	2002.....Priscilla Shumate
1985.....Rosemary Bellini	1991.....Rosemary Bellini	1997.....Allison Roberts	
1986.....Rosemary Bellini	1992.....Anna Engele	1998.....Anna Christoff	

World Four-Wall Champions

1984...................Merv Deckert, Canada	1994...................David Chapman, United States
1986...................Vern Roberts, United States	1997...................John Bike Jr., United States
1988...................Naty Alvarado, United States	2000...................David Chapman, United States
1991...................Pancho Monreal, United States	

United States Club Lacrosse Association Champions

1960 ......Mt. Washington Club	1975 ......Mt. Washington Club	1990 ......Mt. Washington Club
1961 ......Baltimore Lacrosse Club	1976 ......Mt. Washington Club	1991 ......Mt. Washington Club
1962 ......Mt. Washington Club	1977 ......Mt. Washington Club	1992 ......Maryland Lacrosse Club
1963 ......University Club	1978 ......Long Island Athletic Club	1993 ......Mt. Washington Club
1964 ......Mt, Washington Club	1979 ......Maryland Lacrosse Club	1994 ......LI-Hofstra Lacrosse Club
1965 ......Mt. Washington Club	1980 ......Long Island Athletic Club	1995 ......Mt. Washington Club
1966 ......Mt. Washington Club	1981 ......Long Island Athletic Club	1996 ......LI-Hofstra Lacrosse Club
1967 ......Mt. Washington Club	1982 ......Maryland Lacrosse Club	1997 ......LI-Hofstra Lacrosse Club
1968 ......Long Island Athletic Club	1983 ......Maryland Lacrosse Club	1998 ......LI-Hofstra Lacrosse Club
1969 ......Long Island Athletic Club	1984 ......Maryland Lacrosse Club	1999 ......New York Athletic Club
1970 ......Long Island Athletic Club	1985 ......LI-Hofstra Lacrosse Club	2000 ......Team Toyota (Baltimore)
1971 ......Long Island Athletic Club	1986 ......LI-Hofstra Lacrosse Club	2001 ......LI Lacrosse Club
1972 ......Carling	1987 ......LI-Hofstra Lacrosse Club	2002 ......Sinlge Source Solutions
1973 ......Long Island Athletic Club	1988 ......Maryland Lacrosse Club	
1974 ......Long Island Athletic Club	1989 ......LI-Hofstra Lacrosse Club	

National Lacrosse League Champions*

1987 ......Baltimore Thunder	1993 ......Buffalo Bandits	1999 ......Toronto Rock
1988 ......New Jersey Saints	1994 ......Philadelphia Wings	2000 ......Toronto Rock
1989 ......Philadelphia Wings	1995 ......Philadelphia Wings	2001 ......Philadelphia Wings
1990 ......Philadelphia Wings	1996 ......Buffalo Bandits	2002 ......Toronto Rock
1991 ......Detroit Turbos	1997 ......Rochester Knighthawks	
1992 ......Buffalo Bandits	1998 ......Philadelphia Wings	

*Indoor league formerly known as the Eagle Pro Box Lacrosse League, and the Major Indoor Lacrosse League.

Major League Lacrosse*

2001 .....Long Island Lizards

*Outdoor league.

Little League World Series Champions

Year	Champion	Runner-Up	Score	Year	Champion	Runner-Up	Score
1947	Williamsport, PA	Lock Haven, PA	16–7	1975	Lakewood, NJ	Tampa, FL	4–3
1948	Lock Haven, PA	St. Petersburg, FL	6–5	1976	Tokyo, Japan	Campbell, CA	10–3
1949	Hammonton, NJ	Pensacola, FL	5–0	1977	Kao-Hsuing, Taiwan	El Cajun, CA	7–2
1950	Houston, TX	Bridgeport, CT	2–1	1978	Pin-Tung, Taiwan	Danville, CA	11–1
1951	Stamford, CT	Austin, TX	3–0	1979	Hsien, Taiwan	Campbell, CA	2–1
1952	Norwalk, CT	Monongahela, PA	4–3	1980	Hua Lian, Taiwan	Tampa, FL	4–3
1953	Birmingham, AL	Schenectady, NY	1–0	1981	Tai-Chung, Taiwan	Tampa, FL	4–2
1954	Schenectady, NY	Colton, CA	7–5	1982	Kirkland, WA	Hsien, Taiwan	6–0
1955	Morrisville, PA	Merchantville, NJ	4–3	1983	Marietta, GA	Barahona, D.Rep.	3–1
1956	Roswell, NM	Merchantville, NJ	3–1	1984	Seoul, S. Korea	Altamonte Sgs, FL	6–2
1957	Monterrey, Mex.	LaMesa, CA	4–0	1985	Seoul, S. Korea	Mexicali, Mex.	7–1
1958	Monterrey, Mex.	Kankakee, IL	10–1	1986	Tainan Park, Taiwan	Tucson, AZ	12–0
1959	Hamtramck, MI	Auburn, CA	12–0	1987	Hua Lian, Taiwan	Irvine, CA	21–1
1960	Levittown, PA	Ft. Worth, TX	5–0	1988	Tai-Chung, Taiwan	Pearl City, HI	10–0
1961	El Cajon, CA	El Campo, TX	4–2	1989	Trumbull, CT	Kaohsiung, Taiwan	5–2
1962	San Jose, CA	Kankakee, IL	3–0	1990	Taipei, Taiwan	Shippensburg, PA	9–0
1963	Granada Hills, CA	Stratford, CT	2–1	1991	Tai-Chung, Taiwan	San Ramon Vly, CA	11–0
1964	Staten Island, NY	Monterrey, Mex.	4–0	1992*	Long Beach, CA	Zamboanga, Phil.	6–0
1965	Windsor Locks, CT	Stoney Creek, Can.	3–1	1993	Long Beach, CA	David Chiriqui, Pan.	3–2
1966	Houston, TX	W. New York, NJ	8–2	1994	Maracaibo, Venez.	Northridge, CA	4–3
1967	West Tokyo, Japan	Chicago, IL	4–1	1995	Tainan, Taiwan	Sprint, TX	17–3
1968	Osaka, Japan	Richmond, VA	1–0	1996	Kao-Hsuing, Taiwan	Cranston, RI	13–3
1969	Taipei, Taiwan	Santa Clara, CA	5–0	1997	Guadalupe, Mex.	Mission Viejo, CA	5–4
1970	Wayne, NJ	Campbell, CA	2–0	1998	Toms River, NJ	Kashima, Japan	12–9
1971	Tainan, Taiwan	Gary, IN	12–3	1999	Osaka, Japan	Phenix City, AL	5–0
1972	Taipei, Taiwan	Hammond, IN	6–0	2000	Maracaibo, Venez.	Bellaire, TX	3–2
1973	Tainan City, Taiwan	Tucson, AZ	12–0	2001	Tokyo, Japan	Apopka, FL	2–1
1974	Kao-Hsuing, Taiwan	El Cajun, CA	7–2	2002	Louisville, KY	Sendai, Japan	1–0

*Long Beach declared a 6–0 winner after the international tournament committee determined that Zamboanga City had used players that were not within its city limits.

American Power Boat Association Gold Cup Champions

Year	Boat	Driver	Avg MPH	Year	Boat	Driver	Avg MPH
1904	Standard (June)	Carl Riotte	23.160	1955	Gale V	Lee Schoenith	99.552
1904	Vingt-et-Un II (Sep)	W. Sharpe Kilmer	24.900	1956	Miss Thriftaway	Bill Muncey	96.552
1905	Chip I	J. Wainwright	15.000	1957	Miss Thriftaway	Bill Muncey	101.787
1906	Chip II	J. Wainwright	25.000	1958	Hawaii Kai III	Jack Regas	103.000
1907	Chip II	J. Wainwright	23.903	1959	Maverick	Bill Stead	104.481
1908	Dixie II	E.J. Schroeder	29.938	1960	No race	—	—
1909	Dixie II	E.J. Schroeder	29.590	1961	Miss Century 21	Bill Muncey	99.678
1910	Dixie III	F.K. Burnham	32.473	1962	Miss Century 21	Bill Muncey	100.710
1911	MIT II	J.H. Hayden	37.000	1963	Miss Bardahl	Ron Musson	105.124
1912	P.D.Q. II	A.G. Miles	39.462	1964	Miss Bardahl	Ron Musson	103.433
1913	Ankle Deep	Cas Mankowski	42.779	1965	Miss Bardahl	Ron Musson	103.132
1914	Baby Speed Demon II	Jim Blackton & Bob Edgren	48.458	1966	Tahoe Miss	Mira Slovak	93.019
1915	Miss Detroit	Johnny Milot & Jack Beebe	37.656	1967	Miss Bardahl	Bill Shumacher	101.484
				1968	Miss Bardahl	Bill Shumacher	108.173
1916	Miss Minneapolis	Bernard Smith	48.860	1969	Miss Budweiser	Bill Sterett	98.504
1917	Miss Detroit II	Gar Wood	54.410	1970	Miss Budweiser	Dean Chenoweth	99.562
1918	Miss Detroit II	Gar Wood	51.619				
1919	Miss Detroit III	Gar Wood	42.748	1971	Miss Madison	Jim McCormick	98.043
1920	Miss America I	Gar Wood	62.022	1972	Atlas Van Lines	Bill Muncey	104.277
1921	Miss America I	Gar Wood	52.825	1973	Miss Budweiser	Dean Chenoweth	99.043
1922	Packard Chriscraft	J.G. Vincent	40.253				
1923	Packard Chriscraft	Caleb Bragg	43.867	1974	Pay 'n Pak	George Henley	104.428
1924	Baby Bootlegger	Caleb Bragg	45.302	1975	Pay 'n Pak	George Henley	108.921
1925	Baby Bootlegger	Caleb Bragg	47.240	1976	Miss U.S.	Tom D'Eath	100.412
1926	Greenwich Folly	George Townsend	47.984	1977	Atlas Van Lines	Bill Muncey	111.822
				1978	Atlas Van Lines	Bill Muncey	111.412
1927	Greenwich Folly	George Townsend	47.662	1979	Atlas Van Lines	Bill Muncey	100.765
				1980	Miss Budweiser	Dean Chenoweth	106.932
1928	No race						
1929	Imp	Richard Hoyt	48.662	1981	Miss Budweiser	Dean Chenoweth	116.932
1930	Hotsy Totsy	Vic Kliesrath	52.673				
1931	Hotsy Totsy	Vic Kliesrath	53.602	1982	Atlas Van Lines	Chip Hanauer	120.050
1932	Delphine IV	Bill Horn	57.775	1983	Atlas Van Lines	Chip Hanauer	118.507
1933	El Lagarto	George Reis	56.260	1984	Atlas Van Lines	Chip Hanauer	130.175
1934	El Lagarto	George Reis	55.000	1985	Miller American	Chip Hanauer	120.643
1935	El Lagarto	George Reis	55.056	1986	Miller American	Chip Hanauer	116.523
1936	Impshi	Kaye Don	45.735	1987	Miller American	Chip Hanauer	127.620
1937	Notre Dame	Clell Perry	63.675	1988	Miss Circus Circus	Chip Hanauer & Jim Prevost	123.756
1938	Alagi	Theo Rossi	64.340	1989	Miss Budweiser	Tom D'Eath	131.209
1939	My Sin	Z.G. Simmons Jr.	66.133	1990	Miss Budweiser	Tom D'Eath	143.176
1940	Hotsy Totsy III	Sidney Allen	48.295	1991	Winston Eagle	Mark Tate	137.771
1941	My Sin	Z.G. Simmons Jr.	52.509	1992	Miss Budweiser	Chip Hanauer	136.282
1942–45	—	No race	—	1993	Miss Budweiser	Chip Hanauer	141.195
1946	Tempo VI	Guy Lombardo	68.132	1994	Smokin' Joe Camel	Mark Tate	145.260
1947	Miss Peps V	Danny Foster	57.000	1995	Miss Budweiser	Chip Hanauer	149.160
1948	Miss Great Lakes	Danny Foster	46.845	1996	PICO American Dream	Dave Villwock	149.328
1949	My Sweetie	Bill Cantrell	73.612	1997	Miss Budweiser	Dave Villwock	129.366
1950	Slo-Mo-Shun V	Ted Jones	78.216	1998	Miss Budweiser	Dave Villwock	140.309
1951	Slo-Mo-Shun V	Lou Fageol	90.871	1999	Miss PICO	Chip Hanauer	152.591
1952	Slo-Mo-Shun IV	Stan Dollar	79.923	2000	Miss Budweiser	Dave Villwock	162.850
1953	Slo-Mo-Shun IV	Joe Taggart & Lou Fageol	99.108	2001	Miss Tubby's Subs	Michael Hanson	140.519
				2002	Miss Budweiser	Dave Villwock	143.093
1954	Slo-Mo-Shun IV	Joe Taggart & Lou Fageol	92.613				

Motor Boat Racing *(Cont.)*

Unlimited Hydroplane Racing Association Annual Champion Drivers

Year	Driver	Boat	Wins	Year	Driver	Boat	Wins
1947	Danny Foster	Miss Peps V	6	1976	Bill Muncey	Atlas Van Lines	5
1948	Dan Arena	Such Crust	2	1977	Mickey Remund	Miss Budweiser	3
1949	Bill Cantrell	My Sweetie	7	1978	Bill Muncey	Atlas Van Lines	6
1950	Dan Foster	Such Crust/DaphneX	2	1979	Bill Muncey	Atlas Van Lines	7
1951	Chuck Thompson	Miss Pepsi	5	1980	Dean Chenoweth	Miss Budweiser	5
1952	Chuck Thompson	Miss Pepsi	3	1981	Dean Chenoweth	Miss Budweiser	6
1953	Lee Schoenith	Gale II	1	1982	Chip Hanauer	Atlas Van Lines	5
1954	Lee Schoenith	Gale V	4	1983	Chip Hanauer	Atlas Van Lines	3
1955	Lee Schoenith	Gale V/Wha Hoppen	1	1984	Jim Kropfeld	Miss Budweiser	6
1956	Russ Schleeh	Shanty I	3	1985	Chip Hanauer	Miller American	5
1957	Jack Regas	Hawaii Kai III	5	1986	Jim Kropfeld	Miss Budweiser	3
1958	Mira Slovak	Bardah/Miss Buren	3	1987	Jim Kropfeld	Miss Budweiser	5
1959	Bill Stead	Maverick	5	1988	Tom D'Eath	Miss Budweiser	4
1960	Bill Muncey	Miss Thriftway	4	1989	Chip Hanauer	Miss Circus Circus	3
1961	Bill Muncey	Miss Century 21	4	1990	Chip Hanauer	Miss Circus Circus	6
1962	Bill Muncey	Miss Century 21	5	1991	Mark Tate	Winston/Oberto	3
1963	Bill Cantrell	Gale V	0	1992	Chip Hanauer	Miss Budweiser	7
1964	Ron Musson	Miss Bardahl	4	1993	Chip Hanauer	Miss Budweiser	7
1965	Ron Musson	Miss Bardahl	4	1994	Mark Tate	Smokin' Joe Camel	2
1966	Mira Slovak	Tahoe Miss	4	1995	Mark Tate	Smokin' Joe Camel	4
1967	Bill Schumacher	Miss Bardahl	6	1996	Dave Villwock	PICO American Dream	6
1968	Bill Schumacher	Miss Bardahl	4	1997	Mark Tate	Close Call	1
1969	Bill Sterett Sr.	Miss Budweiser	4	1998	Dave Villwock	Miss Budweiser	8
1970	Dean Chenoweth	Miss Budweiser	4	1999	Dave Villwock	Miss Budweiser	8
1971	Dean Chenoweth	Miss Budweiser	2	2000	Dave Villwock	Miss Budweiser	6
1972	Bill Muncey	Atlas Van Lines	6	2001	Dave Villwock	Miss Budweiser	1
1973	Mickey Remund	Pay 'n Pak	4	2002	Dave Villwock	Miss Budweiser	3
1974	George Henley	Pay 'n Pak	7				
1975	Billy Schumacher	Weisfield's	2				

Unlimited Hydroplane Racing Association Annual Champion Boats

Year	Boat	Owner	Wins	Year	Boat	Owner	Wins
1970	Miss Budweiser	Little-Friedkin	4	1987	Miss Budweiser	Bernie Little	5
1971	Miss Budweiser	Little-Friedkin	2	1988	Miss Budweiser	Bernie Little	4
1972	Atlas Van Lines	Joe Schoenith	6	1989	Miss Budweiser	Bernie Little	4
1973	Pay 'n Pak	Dave Heerensperger	4	1990	Miss Circus Circus	Bill Bennett	6
1974	Pay 'n Pak	Dave Heerensperger	7	1991	Miss Budweiser	Bernie Little	4
1975	Pay 'n Pak	Dave Heerensperger	5	1992	Miss Budweiser	Bernie Little	7
1976	Atlas Van Lines	Bill Muncey	5	1993	Miss Budweiser	Bernie Little	7
1977	Miss Budweiser	Bernie Little	3	1994	Miss Budweiser	Bernie Little	4
1978	Atlas Van Lines	Bill Muncey	6	1995	Miss Budweiser	Bernie Little	5
1979	Atlas Van Lines	Bill Muncey	7	1996	PICO Amer. Dream	Fred Leland	6
1980	Miss Budweiser	Bernie Little	5	1997	Miss Budweiser	Bernie Little	5
1981	Miss Budweiser	Bernie Little	6	1998	Miss Budweiser	Bernie Little	8
1982	Atlas Van Lines	Fran Muncey	5	1999	Miss Budweiser	Bernie Little	8
1983	Atlas Van Lines	Muncey-Lucero	3	2000	Miss Budweiser	Bernie Little	6
1984	Miss Budweiser	Bernie Little	6	2001	Miss Budweiser	Bernie Little	1
1985	Miller American	Muncey-Lucero	5	2002	Miss Budweiser	Bernie Little	3
1986	Miss Budweiser	Bernie Little	3				

United States Open Polo Champions

Year	Champion	Year	Champion	Year	Champion	Year	Champion
1904	Wanderers	1934	Templeton	1961	Milwaukee	1983	Ft. Lauderdale
1905–09	Not contested	1935	Greentree	1962	Santa Barbara	1984	Retama
1910	Ranelagh	1936	Greentree	1963	Tulsa	1985	Carter Ranch
1911	Not contested	1937	Old Westbury	1964	Concar Oak Brook	1986	Retama II
1912	Cooperstown	1938	Old Westbury			1987	Aloha
1913	Cooperstown	1939	Bostwick Field	1965	Oak Brook– Santa Barbara	1988	Les Diables Bleus
1914	Meadow Brook Magpies	1940	Aknusti	1966	Tulsa	1989	Les Diables Bleus
1915	Not contested	1941	Gulf Stream	1967	Bunntyco– Oak Brook	1990	Les Diables Bleus
1916	Meadow Brook	1942–45	Not contested	1968	Midland	1991	Grant's Farm Manor
1917–18	Not contested	1946	Mexico	1969	Tulsa Greenhill		
1919	Meadow Brook	1947	Old Westbury	1970	Tulsa Greenhill	1992	Hanalei Bay
1920	Meadow Brook	1948	Hurricanes	1971	Oak Brook	1993	Gehache
1921	Great Neck	1949	Hurricanes	1972	Milwaukee	1994	Aspen
1922	Argentine	1950	Bostwick	1973	Oak Brook	1995	Outback
1923	Meadow Brook	1951	Milwaukee	1974	Milwaukee	1996	Outback
1924	Midwick	1952	Beverly Hills	1975	Milwaukee	1997	Isla Carroll
1925	Orange County	1953	Meadow Brook	1976	Willow Bend	1998	Esque
1926	Hurricanes	1954	C.C.C.– Meadow Brook	1977	Retama	1999	Outback
1927	Sands Point			1978	Abercrombie & Kent	2000	Outback
1928	Meadow Brook	1955	C.C.C.			2001	Outback
1929	Hurricanes	1956	Brandywine	1979	Retama	2002	Team Coca Cola
1930	Hurricanes	1957	Detroit	1980	Southern Hills		
1931	Santa Paula	1958	Dallas	1981	Rolex A & K		
1932	Templeton	1959	Circle F	1982	Retama		
1933	Aurora	1960	Oak Brook– C.C.C.				

Top-Ranked Players

The United States Polo Association ranks its registered players from minus 2 to plus 10 goals, with 10-Goal players being the game's best. At present, the USPA recognizes ten 10-Goal and seven 9-Goal players:

10-GOAL

Mariano Aguerre (Greenwich)
Michael Azzaro (San Antonio)
Adolfo Cambiaso (Palm Beach)
Guillermo Gracida Jr. (Palm Beach)
Bautista Heguy (Palm Beach)
Ignacio Heguy (Palm Beach)
Eduardo Heguy (Palm Beach)
Marcos Heguy (Palm Beach)
Sebastian Merlos (Aiken)
Juan Ignacio Merlos (Aiken)
Carlos Gracida (Palm Beach)

9-GOAL

Javier Novillo Astrada (Palm Beach)
Miguel Novillo Astrada (Palm Beach)
Lucas Criado (Palm Beach)
Hector Galindo (Palm Beach)
Adam Snow (Langdon Road)
Santiago Chavanne (Everglades)
Fabio Diniz (Aspen)
Christian LaPrida (Equuleus)
Tomas Llorent (Everglades)

YET ANOTHER SIGN OF THE APOCALYPSE

*A U.S. table tennis team player,
Barney Reed Jr., was suspended after
testing positive for steroids.*

Professional Rodeo Cowboys Association World Champions

All-Around

1929....Earl Thode	1949....Jim Shoulders	1967....Larry Mahan	1985....Lewis Feild
1930....Clay Carr	1950....Bill Linderman	1968....Larry Mahan	1986....Lewis Feild
1931....John Schneider	1951....Casey Tibbs	1969....Larry Mahan	1987....Lewis Feild
1932....Donald Nesbit	1952....Harry Tompkins	1970....Larry Mahan	1988....Dave Appleton
1933....Clay Carr	1953....Bill Linderman	1971....Phil Lyne	1989....Ty Murray
1934....Leonard Ward	1954....Buck Rutherford	1972....Phil Lyne	1990....Ty Murray
1935....Everett Bowman	1955....Casey Tibbs	1973....Larry Mahan	1991....Ty Murray
1936....John Bowman	1956....Jim Shoulders	1974....Tom Ferguson	1992....Ty Murray
1937....Everett Bowman	1957....Jim Shoulders	1975....Tom Ferguson	1993....Ty Murray
1938....Burel Mulkey	1958....Jim Shoulders	1976....Tom Ferguson	1994....Ty Murray
1939....Paul Carney	1959....Jim Shoulders	1977....Tom Ferguson	1995....Joe Beaver
1940....Fritz Truan	1960....Harry Tompkins	1978....Tom Ferguson	1996....Joe Beaver
1941....Homer Pettigrew	1961....Benny Reynolds	1979....Tom Ferguson	1997....Dan Mortensen
1942....Gerald Roberts	1962....Tom Nesmith	1980....Paul Tierney	1998....Ty Murray
1943....Louis Brooks	1963....Dean Oliver	1981....Jimmie Cooper	1999....Fred Whitfield
1944....Louis Brooks	1964....Dean Oliver	1982....Chris Lybbert	2000....Joe Beaver
1947....Todd Whatley	1965....Dean Oliver	1983....Roy Cooper	2001....Cody Ohl
1948....Gerald Roberts	1966....Larry Mahan	1984....Dee Picket	

Saddle Bronc Riding

1929....Earl Thode	1949....Casey Tibbs	1967....Shawn Davis	1985....B. Gjermundson
1930....Clay Carr	1950....Bill Linderman	1968....Shawn Davis	1986....Bud Munroe
1931....Earl Thode	1951....Casey Tibbs	1969....Bill Smith	1987....Clint Johnson
1932....Peter Knight	1952....Casey Tibbs	1970....Dennis Reiners	1988....Clint Johnson
1933....Peter Knight	1953....Casey Tibbs	1971....Bill Smith	1989....Clint Johnson
1934....Leonard Ward	1954....Casey Tibbs	1972....Mel Hyland	1990....Robert Etbauer
1935....Peter Knight	1955....Deb Copenhaver	1973....Bill Smith	1991....Robert Etbauer
1936....Peter Knight	1956....Deb Copenhaver	1974....John McBeth	1992....Billy Etbauer
1937....Burel Mulkey	1957....Alvin Nelson	1975....Monty Henson	1993....Dan Mortensen
1938....Burel Mulkey	1958....Marty Wood	1976....Monty Henson	1994....Dan Mortensen
1939....Fritz Truan	1959....Casey Tibbs	1977....Bobby Berger	1995....Dan Mortensen
1940....Fritz Truan	1960....Enoch Walker	1978....Joe Marvel	1996....Billy Etbauer
1941....Doff Aber	1961....Winston Bruce	1979....Bobby Berger	1997....Dan Mortensen
1942....Doff Aber	1962....Kenny McLean	1980....Clint Johnson	1998....Dan Mortensen
1943....Louis Brooks	1963....Guy Weeks	1981....B. Gjermundson	1999....Billy Etbauer
1944....Louis Brooks	1964....Marty Wood	1982....Monty Henson	2000....Billy Etbauer
1947....Carl Olson	1965....Shawn Davis	1983....B. Gjermundson	2001....Tom Reeves
1948....Gene Pruett	1966....Marty Wood	1984....B. Gjermundson	

Bareback Riding

1932....Smoky Snyder	1951....Casey Tibbs	1968....Clyde Vamvoras	1985....Lewis Feild
1933....Nate Waldrum	1952....Harry Tompkins	1969....Gary Tucker	1986....Lewis Feild
1934....Leonard Ward	1953....Eddy Akridge	1970....Paul Mayo	1987....Bruce Ford
1935....Frank Schneider	1954....Eddy Akridge	1971....Joe Alexander	1988....Marvin Garrett
1936....Smoky Snyder	1955....Eddy Akridge	1972....Joe Alexander	1989....Marvin Garrett
1937....Paul Carney	1956....Jim Shoulders	1973....Joe Alexander	1990....Chuck Logue
1938....Pete Grubb	1957....Jim Shoulders	1974....Joe Alexander	1991....Clint Corey
1939....Paul Carney	1958....Jim Shoulders	1975....Joe Alexander	1992....Wayne Herman
1940....Carl Dossey	1959....Jack Buschbom	1976....Joe Alexander	1993....Deb Greenough
1941....George Mills	1960....Jack Buschbom	1977....Joe Alexander	1994....Marvin Garrett
1942....Louis Brooks	1961....Eddy Akridge	1978....Bruce Ford	1995....Marvin Garrett
1943....Bill Linderman	1962....Ralph Buell	1979....Bruce Ford	1996....Mark Garrett
1944....Louis Brooks	1963....John Hawkins	1980....Bruce Ford	1997....Eric Mouton
1947....Larry Finley	1964....Jim Houston	1981....J.C. Trujillo	1998....Mark Gomes
1948....Sonny Tureman	1965....Jim Houston	1982....Bruce Ford	1999....Lan LaJeunesse
1949....Jack Buschbom	1966....Paul Mayo	1983....Bruce Ford	2000....Jeffrey Collins
1950....Jim Shoulders	1967....Clyde Vamvoras	1984....Larry Peabody	2001....Lan LaJeunesse

Professional Rodeo Cowboys Association World Champions (Cont.)

Bull Riding

1929....John Schneider
1930....John Schneider
1931....Smokey Snyder
1932....John Schneider
1932....Smokey Snyder
      John Schneider
1933....Frank Schneider
1934....Frank Schneider
1935....Smokey Snyder
1936....Smokey Snyder
1937....Smokey Snyder
1938....Kid Fletcher
1939....Dick Griffith
1940....Dick Griffith
1941....Dick Griffith
1942....Dick Griffith
1943....Ken Roberts
1944....Ken Roberts
1947....Wag Blessing

1948....Harry Tompkins
1949....Harry Tompkins
1950....Harry Tompkins
1951....Jim Shoulders
1952....Harry Tompkins
1953....Todd Whatley
1954....Jim Shoulders
1955....Jim Shoulders
1956....Jim Shoulders
1957....Jim Shoulders
1958....Jim Shoulders
1959....Jim Shoulders
1960....Harry Tompkins
1961....Ronnie Rossen
1962....Freckles Brown
1963....Bill Kornell
1964....Bob Wegner
1965....Larry Mahan
1966....Ronnie Rossen

1967....Larry Mahan
1968....George Paul
1969....Doug Brown
1970....Gary Leffew
1971....Bill Nelson
1972....John Quintana
1973....Bobby Steiner
1974....Don Gay
1975....Don Gay
1976....Don Gay
1977....Don Gay
1978....Don Gay
1979....Don Gay
1980....Don Gay
1981....Don Gay
1982....Charles Sampson
1983....Cody Snyder
1984....Don Gay
1985....Ted Nuce

1986....Tuff Hedeman
1987....Lane Frost
1988....Jim Sharp
1989....Tuff Hedeman
1990....Jim Sharp
1991....Tuff Hedeman
1992....Cody Custer
1993....Ty Murray
1994....Daryl Mills
1995....Jerome Davis
1996....Terry West
1997....Scott Mendes
1998....Ty Murray
1999....Mike White
2000....Cody Hancock
2001....Blue Stone

Calf Roping

1929....Everett Bowman
1930....Jake McClure
1931....Herb Meyers
1932....Richard Merchant
1933....Bill McFarlane
1934....Irby Mundy
1935....Everett Bowman
1936....Clyde Burk
1937....Everett Bowman
1938....Burel Mulkey
1939....Toots Mansfield
1940....Toots Mansfield
1941....Toots Mansfield
1942....Clyde Burk
1943....Toots Mansfield
1944....Clyde Burk
1947....Troy Fort
1948....Toots Mansfield

1949....Troy Fort
1950....Toots Mansfield
1951....Don McLaughlin
1952....Don McLaughlin
1953....Don McLaughlin
1954....Don McLaughlin
1955....Dean Oliver
1956....Ray Wharton
1957....Don McLaughlin
1958....Dean Oliver
1959....Jim Bob Altizer
1960....Dean Oliver
1961....Dean Oliver
1962....Dean Oliver
1963....Dean Oliver
1964....Dean Oliver
1965....Glen Franklin
1966....Junior Garrison

1967....Glen Franklin
1968....Glen Franklin
1969....Dean Oliver
1970....Junior Garrison
1971....Phil Lyne
1972....Phil Lyne
1973....Ernie Taylor
1974....Tom Ferguson
1975....Jeff Copenhaver
1976....Roy Cooper
1977....Roy Cooper
1978....Roy Cooper
1979....Paul Tierney
1980....Roy Cooper
1981....Roy Cooper
1982....Roy Cooper
1983....Roy Cooper
1984....Roy Cooper

1985....Joe Beaver
1986....Chris Lybbert
1987....Joe Beaver
1988....Joe Beaver
1989....Rabe Rabon
1990....Troy Pruitt
1991....Fred Whitfield
1992....Joe Beaver
1993....Joe Beaver
1994....Herbert Theriot
1995....Fred Whitfield
1996....Fred Whitfield
1997....Cody Ohl
1998....Cody Ohl
1999....Fred Whitfield
2000....Fred Whitfield
2001....Cody Ohl

Steer Wrestling

1929....Gene Ross
1930....Everett Bowman
1931....Gene Ross
1932....Hugh Bennett
1933....Everett Bowman
1934....Shorty Ricker
1935....Everett Bowman
1936....Jack Kerschner
1937....Gene Ross
1938....Everett Bowman
1939....Harry Hart
1940....Homer Pettigrew
1941....Hub Whiteman
1942....Homer Pettigrew
1943....Homer Pettigrew
1944....Homer Pettigrew
1947....Todd Whatley
1948....Homer Pettigrew

1949....Bill McGuire
1950....Bill Linderman
1951....Dub Phillips
1952....Harley May
1953....Ross Dollarhide
1954....James Bynum
1955....Benny Combs
1956....Harley May
1957....Clark McEntire
1958....James Bynum
1959....Harry Charters
1960....Bob A. Robinson
1961....Jim Bynum
1962....Tom Nesmith
1963....Jim Bynum
1964....C.R. Boucher
1965....Harley May
1966....Jack Roddy

1967....Roy Duvall
1968....Jack Roddy
1969....Roy Duvall
1970....John W. Jones
1971....Billy Hale
1972....Roy Duvall
1973....Bob Marshall
1974....Tommy Puryear
1975....F. Shepperson
1976....Tom Ferguson
1977....Larry Ferguson
1978....Byron Walker
1979....Stan Williamson
1980....Butch Myers
1981....Byron Walker
1982....Stan Williamson
1983....Joel Edmondson
1984....John W. Jones

1985....Ote Berry
1986....Steve Duhon
1987....Steve Duhon
1988....John W. Jones
1989....John W. Jones
1990....Ote Berry
1991....Ote Berry
1992....Mark Roy
1993....Steve Duhon
1994....Blaine Pederson
1995....Ote Berry
1996....Chad Bedell
1997....Brad Gleason
1998....Mike Smith
1999....Mickey Gee
2000....Frank Thompson
2001....Rope Myers

Professional Rodeo Cowboys Association World Champions *(Cont.)*

Team Roping

1929....Charles Maggini	1950....Buck Sorrels	1971....John Miller	1992....Clay O. Cooper
1930....Norman Cowan	1951....Olan Sims	1972....Leo Camarillo	1993....Bobby Hurley
1931....Arthur Beloat	1952....Asbury Schell	1973....Leo Camarillo	1994....Jake Barnes
1932....Ace Gardner	1953....Ben Johnson	1974....H.P. Evetts	Clay O. Cooper
1933....Roy Adams	1954....Eddie Schell	1975....Leo Camarillo	1995....Bobby Hurley
1934....Andy Jauregui	1955....Vern Castro	1976....Leo Camarillo	Allen Bach
1935....Lawrence Conltk	1956....Dale Smith	1977....Jerold Camarillo	1996....Steve Purcella
1936....John Rhodes	1957....Dale Smith	1978....Doyle Gellerman	Steve Northcott
1937....Asbury Schell	1958....Ted Ashworth	1979....Allen Bach	1997....Speed Williams
1938....John Rhodes	1959....Jim Rodriguez Jr.	1980....Tee Woolman	Rich Skelton
1939....Asbury Schell	1960....Jim Rodriguez Jr.	1981....Walt Woodard	1998....Speed Williams
1940....Pete Grubb	1961....Al Hooper	1982....Tee Woolman	Rich Skelton
1941....Jim Hudson	1962....Jim Rodriguez Jr.	1983....Leo Camarillo	1999....Speed Williams
1942....Verne Castro	1963....Les Hirdes	1984....Dee Pickett	Rich Skelton
Vic Castro	1964....Bill Hamilton	1985....Jake Barnes	2000....Speed Williams
1943....Mark Hull	1965....Jim Rodriguez Jr.	1986....Clay O. Cooper	Rich Skelton
Leonard Block	1966....Ken Luman	1987....Clay O. Cooper	2001....Speed Williams
1944....Murphy Chaney	1967....Joe Glenn	1988....Jake Barnes	Rich Skelton
1947....Jim Brister	1968....Art Arnold	1989....Jake Barnes	
1948....Joe Glenn	1969....Jerold Camarillo	1990....Allen Bach	
1949....Ed Yanez	1970....John Miller	1991....Bob Harris	

Steer Roping

1929....Charles Maggini	1948....Everett Shaw	1967....Jim Bob Altizer	1986....Jim Davis
1930....Clay Carr	1949....Shoat Webster	1968....Sonny Davis	1987....Shaun Burchett
1931....Andy Jauregui	1950....Shoat Webster	1969....Walter Arnold	1988....Shaun Burchett
1932....George Weir	1951....Everett Shaw	1970....Don McLaughlin	1989....Guy Allen
1933....John Bowman	1952....Buddy Neal	1971....Olin Young	1990....Phil Lyne
1934....John McEntire	1953....Ike Rude	1972....Allen Keller	1991....Guy Allen
1935....Richard Merchant	1954....Shoat Webster	1973....Roy Thompson	1992....Guy Allen
1936....John Bowman	1955....Shoat Webster	1974....Olin Young	1993....Guy Allen
1937....Everett Bowman	1956....Jim Snively	1975....Roy Thompson	1994....Guy Allen
1938....Hugh Bennett	1957....Clark McEntire	1976....Marvin Cantrell	1995....Guy Allen
1939....Dick Truitt	1958....Clark McEntire	1977....Buddy Cockrell	1996....Guy Allen
1940....Clay Carr	1959....Everett Shaw	1978....Sonny Worrell	1997....Guy Allen
1941....Ike Rude	1960....Don McLaughlin	1979....Gary Good	1998....Guy Allen
1942....King Merrit	1961....Clark McEntire	1980....Guy Allen	1999....Guy Allen
1943....Tom Rhodes	1962....Everett Shaw	1981....Arnold Felts	2000....Guy Allen
1944....Tom Rhodes	1963....Don McLaughlin	1982....Guy Allen	2001....Guy Allen
1945....Everett Shaw	1964....Sonny Davis	1983....Roy Cooper	
1946....Everett Shaw	1965....Sonney Wright	1984....Guy Allen	
1947....Ike Rude	1966....Sonny Davis	1985....Jim Davis	

Note: In 1945–46 champions were crowned only in Steer Roping.

Rowing

National Collegiate Rowing Champions

MEN

1985 ....Harvard	1991 ....Pennsylvania	1997 ....Washington
1986 ....Wisconsin	1992 ....Harvard	1998 ....Princeton
1987 ....Harvard	1993 ....Brown	1999 ....California
1988 ....Harvard	1994 ....Brown	2000 ....California
1989 ....Harvard	1995 ....Brown	2001 ....California
1990 ....Wisconsin	1996 ....Princeton	2002 ....California

WOMEN

1979 ....Yale	1987 ....Washington	1995 ....Princeton
1980 ....California	1988 ....Washington	1996 ....Brown
1981 ....Washington	1989 ....Cornell	1997 ....Washington
1982 ....Washington	1990 ....Princeton	1998 ....Washington
1983 ....Washington	1991 ....Boston University	1999 ....Brown
1984 ....Washington	1992 ....Boston University	2000 ....Brown
1985 ....Washington	1993 ....Princeton	2001 ....Washington
1986 ....Wisconsin	1994 ....Princeton	2002 ....Brown

Rugby Union

National Men's Club Championship

Year	Winner	Runner-Up	Year	Winner	Runner-Up
1979	Old Blues (CA)	St. Louis Falcons	1992	Old Blues (CA)	Mystic River (MA)
1980	Old Blues (CA)	St. Louis Falcons	1993	Old Mission Beach AC	Milwaukee
1981	Old Blues (CA)	Old Blue (NY)	1994	Old Mission Beach AC	Life College (GA)
1982	Old Blues (CA)	Denver Barbos	1995	Potomac Athletic Club	Old Mission Beach
1983	Old Blues (CA)	Dallas Harlequins	1996	Old Mission Beach AC	Old Blues (CA)
1984	Dallas Harlequins	Los Angeles	1997	Gentlemen of Aspen	Old Blue (NY)
1985	Milwaukee	Denver Barbos	1998	Gentlemen of Aspen	Old Blue (NY)
1986	Old Blues (CA)	Old Blue (NY)	1999	Gentlemen of Aspen	Golden Gate (CA)
1987	Old Blues (CA)	Pittsburgh	2000	Gentlemen of Aspen	Hayward Griffins
1988	Old Mission Beach AC	Milwaukee	2001	San Mateo	New York AC
1989	Old Mission Beach AC	Philly/Whitemarsh	2002	San Mateo	Austin
1990	Denver Barbos	Old Blues (CA)			
1991	Old Mission Beach AC	Washington			

National Men's Collegiate Championship

Year	Winner	Runner-Up	Year	Winner	Runner-Up
1980	California	Air Force	1992	California	Army
1981	California	Harvard	1993	California	Air Force
1982	California	Life College	1994	California	Navy
1983	California	Air Force	1995	California	Air Force
1984	Harvard	Colorado	1996	California	Penn St
1985	California	Maryland	1997	California	Penn St
1986	California	Dartmouth	1998	California	Stanford
1987	San Diego State	Air Force	1999	California	Penn St
1988	California	Dartmouth	2000	California	Wyoming
1989	Air Force	Long Beach	2001	California	Penn St
1990	Air Force	Army	2002	California	Utah
1991	California	Army			

World Cup Championship

Year	Winner	Runner-Up	Year	Winner	Runner-Up
1987	New Zealand	France	1995	South Africa	New Zealand
1991	Australia	England	1999	Australia	France

Rugby League

American National Rugby League Champions

Year	Winner	Runner-Up
1998	Glen Mills Bulls	Philadelphia Bulldogs
1999	Glen Mills Bulls	New Jersey Sharks
2000	Glen Mills Bulls	Philadelphia Fight
2001	Glen Mills Bulls	Media Mantarays
2002	New York Knights	Glen Mills Bulls

World Cup Championship

Year	Winner	Runner-Up	Host
1954	Great Britain	France	France
1957	Australia	International Team	Australia
1960	Great Britain	International Team	England
1968	Australia	France	Australia–New Zealand
1970	Great Britain	Australia	England
1972	Australia	Great Britain	France
1975	Australia	England	Worldwide
1977	Australia	Great Britain	Australia–New Zealand
1985–88	Australia	New Zealand	Worldwide
1989–92	Australia	Great Britain	Worldwide
1995	Australia	England	Great Britain
2000	Australia	New Zealand	G Britain-Ireland-France

America's Cup Champions

SCHOONERS AND J-CLASS BOATS

Year	Winner	Skipper	Series	Loser	Skipper
1851	America	Richard Brown			
1870	Magic	Andrew Comstock	1–0	Cambria, Great Britain	J. Tannock
1871	Columbia (2–1)	Nelson Comstock	4–1	Livonia, Great Britain	J.R. Woods
	Sappho (2–0)	Sam Greenwood			
1876	Madeleine	Josephus Williams	2–0	Countess of Dufferin, Canada	J.E. Ellsworth
1881	Mischief	Nathanael Clock	2–0	Atalanta, Canada	Alexander Cuthbert
1885	Puritan	Aubrey Crocker	2–0	Genesta, Great Britain	John Carter
1886	Mayflower	Martin Stone	2–0	Galatea, Great Britain	Dan Bradford
1887	Volunteer	Henry Haff	2–0	Thistle, Great Britain	John Barr
1893	Vigilant	William Hansen	3–0	Valkyrie II, Great Britain	William Granfield
1895	Defender	Henry Haff	3–0	Valkyrie III, Great Britain	William Granfield
1899	Columbia	Charles Barr	3–0	Shamrock I, Great Britain	Archie Hogarth
1901	Columbia	Charles Barr	3–0	Shamrock II, Great Britain	E.A. Sycamore
1903	Reliance	Charles Barr	3–0	Shamrock III, Great Britain	Bob Wringe
1920	Resolute	Charles F. Adams	3–2	Shamrock IV, Great Britain	William Burton
1930	Enterprise	Harold Vanderbilt	4–0	Shamrock V, Great Britain	Ned Heard
1934	Rainbow	Harold Vanderbilt	4–2	Endeavour, Great Britain	T.O.M. Sopwith
1937	Ranger	Harold Vanderbilt	4–0	Endeavour II, Great Britain	T.O.M. Sopwith

12-METER BOATS

Year	Winner	Skipper	Series	Loser	Skipper
1958	Columbia	Briggs Cunningham	4–0	Sceptre, Great Britain	Graham Mann
1962	Weatherly	Bus Mosbacher	4–1	Gretel, Australia	Jock Sturrock
1964	Constellation	Bob Bavier & Eric Ridder	4–0	Sovereign, Australia	Peter Scott
1967	Intrepid	Bus Mosbacher	4–0	Dame Pattie, Australia	Jock Sturrock
1970	Intrepid	Bill Ficker	4–1	Gretel II, Australia	Jim Hardy
1974	Courageous	Ted Hood	4–0	Southern Cross, Australia	John Cuneo
1977	Courageous	Ted Turner	4–0	Australia	Noel Robins
1980	Freedom	Dennis Conner	4–1	Australia	Jim Hardy
1983	Australia II	John Bertrand	4–3	Liberty, United States	Dennis Conner
1987	Stars & Stripes	Dennis Conner	4–0	Kookaburra III, Australia	Iain Murray

60-FOOT CATAMARAN vs 133-FOOT MONOHULL

Year	Winner	Skipper	Series	Loser	Skipper
1988	Stars & Stripes	Dennis Conner	2–0	New Zealand	David Barnes

75-FOOT MONOHULL (IACC)

Year	Winner	Skipper	Series	Loser	Skipper
1992	America[3]	Bill Koch	4–1	Il Moro di Venezia, Italy	Paul Cayard
1995	Black Magic I	Russell Coutts	5–0	Young America, United States	Dennis Conner
2000	New Zealand	Russell Coutts	5–0	Luna Rossa, Italy	Francesco de Angelis

Note: Winning entries have been from the United States every year but three: In 1983 an Australian vessel won, and in 1995 and 2000 a vessel from New Zealand won.

Men

50M FREE RIFLE PRONE

1947 .....O. Sannes, Norway
1949 .....A.C. Jackson, U.S.
1952 .....A.C. Jackson, U.S.
1954 .....G. Boa, Canada
1958 .....M. Nordquist
1962 .....K. Wenk, W Germany
1966 .....D. Boyd, U.S.
1970 .....M. Fiess, S. Africa
1974 .....K. Bulan, Czechoslovakia
1978 .....A. Allan, Great Britain
1982 .....V. Danilschenko, USSR
1986 .....S. Bereczky, Hungary
1990 .....V. Bochkarev, USSR
1994 .....Venjie Li, China
1998 .....Thomas Tamas, U.S.
1999 .....Thomas Tamas, U.S.
2000 .....Siarhei Martynau, Belarus
2001 .....Matthew Emmons, U.S.

AIR RIFLE

1966 .....G. Kümmet, W Germany
1970 .....G. Kusterman, W Germ.
1974 .....E. Pedzisz, Poland
1978 .....O. Schlipf, W. Germany
1979 .....K. Hillenbrand
1981 .....F. Bessy, France
1982 .....F. Rettkowski, E Germ.
1983 .....P. Heberle, France
1985 .....P. Heberle, France
1986 .....H. Riederer, W Germany
1987 .....K. Ivanov, USSR
1989 .....J. P. Amet, France
1990 .....H. Riederer, W Germany
1994 .....Boris Polak, Israel
1998 .....Artem Khadjibekov, Russia
1999 .....Jozef Gonci, Slovakia
2000 .....Artem Khadjibekov, Russia
2001 ......Jason Parker, U.S.

MEN'S TRAP

1929 .....De Lumniczer, Hungary
1930 .....M. Arie, U.S.
1931 .....Kiszkurno, Poland
1933 .....De Lumniczer, Hungary
1934 .....A. Montagh, Hungary
1935 .....R. Sack, W Germany
1936 .....Kiszkurno, Poland
1937 .....K. Huber, Finland
1938 .....I. Strassburger, Hungary
1939 .....De Lumniczer, Hungary
1947 .....H. Liljedahl, Sweden
1949 .....F. Rocchi, Argentina
1950 .....C. Sala, Italy
1952 .....P.J. Grossi, Argentina
1954 .....C. Merlo, Italy
1958 .....F. Eisenlauer, U.S.
1959 .....H. Badravi, Egypt
1961 .....E. Mattarelli, Italy
1962 .....W. Zimenko, USSR
1965 .....J.E. Lire, Chile
1966 .....K. Jones, U.S.
1967 .....G. Rennard, Belgium
1969 .....E. Mattarelli, Italy
1970 .....M. Carrega, France
1971 .....M. Carrega, France
1973 .....A. Andrushkin, USSR
1974 .....M. Carrega, France
1975 .....J. Primrose, Canada
1977 .....E. Azkue, Spain
1978 .....E. Vallduvi, Spain
1979 .....M. Carrega, France
1981 .....A. Asanov, USSR
1982 .....L. Giovonnetti, Italy
1983 .....J. Primrose, Canada
1985 .....M. Bednarik,
          Czechoslovakia
1986.......M. Bednarik,
          Czechoslovakia

MEN'S TRAP (Cont.)

1987 .....D. Monakov, USSR
1989 .....M. Venturini, Italy
1990 .....J. Damne, E Germany
1994 .....Dmitriy Monakov, Ukraine
1995 .....Giovanni Pellielo, Italy
1998 .....Giovanni Pellielo, Italy
1999 .....Joao Rebelo, Portugal
2000 .....Michael Diamond, Australia
2001.......Michael Diamond, Australia

THREE POSITION RIFLE

1929 .....O. Ericsson, Sweden
1930 .....Petersen, Denmark
1931 .....Amundson, Norway
1933 .....De Lisle, France
1935 .....Leskinnen, Finland
1937 .....Mazoyer, France
1939 .....Steigelmann, Germany
1947 .....I.H. Erben, Sweden
1949 .....P. Janhonen, Finland
1952 .....Kongshaug, Norway
1954 .....A. Bugdanov, USSR
1958 .....Itkis, USSR
1962 .....G. Anderson, U.S.
1966 .....G. Anderson, U.S.
1970 .....Parkhimovitch, USSR
1974 .....L. Wigger, U.S.
1978 .....E. Svensson, Sweden
1982 .....K. Ivanov, USSR
1986 .....P. Heinz, W Germany
1990 .....E. C. Lee, S Korea
1994 .....P. Kurka, Czech Republic
1998 .....Jozef Gonci, Slovakia
1999 .....Jozef Gonci, Slovakia
2000 .....Jozef Gonci, Slovakia
2001 .....Marcel Bürge, Switz

Women

THREE POSITION RIFLE

1966 .....M. Thompson, U.S.
1970 .....M. Thompson Murdock, U.S.
1974 .....A. Pelova, Bulgaria
1978 .....W. Oliver, U.S.
1982 .....M. Helbig, E Germany
1986 .....V. Letcheva, Bulgaria
1990 .....V. Letcheva, Bulgaria
1994 .....A. Maloukhina, Russia
1998 .....Sonja Pfeilschifter, Germany
1999 .....Sonja Pfeilschifter, Germany
2000 .....Hong Shan, China
2001 .....Petra Horneber, Germany

AIR RIFLE

1970 .....V. Cherkasque, USSR
1974 .....T. Ratkinova, USSR
1978 .....W. Oliver, U.S.
1979 .....K. Monez, U.S.
1981 .....S. Romaristova, USSR
1982 .....S. Lang, W Germany
1983 .....M. Helbig, E Germany
1985 .....E. Forian, Hungary
1986 .....V. Letcheva, Bulgaria
1987 .....V. Letcheva, Bulgaria
1989 .....V. Letcheva, Bulgaria
1990 .....E. Joc, Hungary

AIR RIFLE (Cont.)

1994 .....Sonja Pfeilschifter, Germany
1998 .....Sonja Pfeilschifter, Germany
1999 .....Sonja Pfeilschifter, Germany
2000 ....Sonja Pfeilschifter, Germany
2001 ....Katerina Kurkova, Czech.

SPORT PISTOL

1966 .....N. Rasskazova, USSR
1970 .....N. Stoljarova, USSR
1974 .....N. Stoljarova, USSR
1978 .....K. Dyer, U.S.
1982 .....P. Balogh, Hungary
1986 .....M. Dobrantcheva, USSR
1990 .....M. Logvinenko, USSR
1994 .....Soon Hee Boo, S Korea
1998 .....Yieqing Cai, China
1999 .....Soon Hee Boo, S Korea
2000 .....Lalita Vauhleuskaya,
          Belarus
2001 .....Munkhbayar Dorjsuren,
          Germany

AIR PISTOL

1970 .....S. Carroll, U.S.
1974 .....Z. Simonian, USSR
1978 .....K. Hansson, Sweden
1979 .....R. Fox, U.S.

AIR PISTOL (Cont.)

1981 .....N. Kalinina, USSR
1982 .....M. Dobrantcheva, USSR
1983 .....K. Bodin, Sweden
1985 .....M. Dobrantcheva, USSR
1986 .....A. Völker, E Germany
1987 .....J. Brajkovic, Yugoslavia
1989 .....N. Salukvadse, USSR
1990 .....Jasna Sekaric, Yugoslavia
1994 .....Jasna Sekaric, IOP
1998 .....Dorisuren Munkhbayar,
          Mongolia
1999 .....Nino Salukvadze,
          Georgia
2000 .....Luna Tao, China
2001 .....Olena Kostevych, Ukraine

U.S. Champions—Men
MAJOR FAST PITCH

1933..........J.L. Gill Boosters, Chicago	1968..........Clearwater (FL) Bombers
1934..........Ke-Nash-A, Kenosha, WI	1969..........Raybestos Cardinals, Stratford, CT
1935..........Crimson Coaches, Toledo, OH	1970..........Raybestos Cardinals, Stratford, CT
1936..........Kodak Park, Rochester, NY	1971..........Welty Way, Cedar Rapids, IA
1937..........Briggs Body Team, Detroit	1972..........Raybestos Cardinals, Stratford, CT
1938..........The Pohlers, Cincinnati	1973..........Clearwater (FL) Bombers
1939..........Carr's Boosters, Covington, KY	1974..........Gianella Bros, Santa Rosa, CA
1940..........Kodak Park, Rochester, NY	1975..........Rising Sun Hotel, Reading, PA
1941..........Bendix Brakes, South Bend, IN	1976..........Raybestos Cardinals, Stratford, CT
1942..........Deep Rock Oilers, Tulsa	1977..........Billard Barbell, Reading, PA
1943..........Hammer Air Field, Fresno	1978..........Billard Barbell, Reading, PA
1944..........Hammer Air Field, Fresno	1979..........McArdle Pontiac/Cadillac, Midland, MI
1945..........Zollner Pistons, Fort Wayne, IN	1980..........Peterbilt Western, Seattle
1946..........Zollner Pistons, Fort Wayne, IN	1981..........Archer Daniels Midland, Decatur, IL
1947..........Zollner Pistons, Fort Wayne, IN	1982..........Peterbilt Western, Seattle
1948..........Briggs Beautyware, Detroit	1983..........Franklin Cardinals, Stratford, CT
1949..........Tip Top Tailors, Toronto	1984..........California Kings, Merced, CA
1950..........Clearwater (FL) Bombers	1985..........Pay'n Pak, Seattle
1951..........Dow Chemical, Midland, MI	1986..........Pay'n Pak, Seattle
1952..........Briggs Beautyware, Detroit	1987..........Pay'n Pak, Seattle
1953..........Briggs Beautyware, Detroit	1988..........TransAire, Elkhart, IN
1954..........Clearwater (FL) Bombers	1989..........Penn Corp, Sioux City, IA
1955..........Raybestos Cardinals, Stratford, CT	1990..........Penn Corp, Sioux City, IA
1956..........Clearwater (FL) Bombers	1991..........Guanella Brothers, Rohnert Park, CA
1957..........Clearwater (FL) Bombers	1992..........Natl Health Care Disc, Sioux City, IA
1958..........Raybestos Cardinals, Stratford, CT	1993..........Natl Health Care Disc, Sioux City, IA
1959..........Sealmasters, Aurora, IL	1994..........Decatur Pride, Decatur, IL
1960..........Clearwater (FL) Bombers	1995..........Decatur Pride, Decatur, IL
1961..........Sealmasters, Aurora, IL	1996..........Green Bay All-Car, Green Bay, WI
1962..........Clearwater (FL) Bombers	1997..........Green Bay All-Car, Green Bay, WI
1963..........Clearwater (FL) Bombers	1998..........Meierhoffer-Fleeman, St. Joseph, MO
1964..........Burch Tool, Detroit	1999..........Decatur Pride, Decatur, IL
1965..........Sealmasters, Aurora, IL	2000..........Meierhoffer, St. Joseph, MO
1966..........Clearwater (FL) Bombers	2001..........Frontier Players Casino, St. Joseph, MO
1967..........Sealmasters, Aurora, IL	2002..........Frontier Players Casino, St. Joseph, MO

SUPER SLOW PITCH

1981..........Howard's/Western Steer, Denver, NC	1992..........Ritch's Superior, Windsor Locks, CT
1982..........Jerry's Catering, Miami, FL	1993..........Ritch's Superior, Windsor Locks, CT
1983..........Howard's/Western Steer, Denver, NC	1994..........Bell Corp, Tampa, FL
1984..........Howard's/Western Steer, Denver, NC	1995..........Lighthouse/Worth, Stone Mt.., GA
1985..........Steele's Sports, Grafton, OH	1996..........Ritch's Superior, Windsor Locks, CT
1986..........Steele's Sports, Grafton, OH	1997..........Ritch's Superior, Windsor Locks, CT
1987..........Steele's Sports, Grafton, OH	1998..........Lighthouse/Worth, Stone Mt.., GA
1988..........Starpath, Monticello, KY	1999..........Team Easton, Wilmington, NC
1989..........Ritch's Salvage, Harrisburg, NC	2000..........Team TPS, Louisville, KY
1990..........Steele's Silver Bullets, Grafton, OH	2002..........Long Haul/Taylor Bros./Shen Corp./TPS,
1991..........Sunbelt/Worth, Centerville, GA	Albertville, MN

A Legend Retires

After 12 seasons in the National Lacrosse League, Paul Gait announced his retirement in April 2002. Paul, 35, and his twin brother, Gary, gained fame in the late 1980s and early '90s when they led Syracuse to three NCAA titles. In 2002 they played together for the Washington Power, and Paul had 54 goals in 16 games to win the league MVP award. He is the NLL's second alltime goal scorer, with 397. Gary, with 447, will play on.

U.S. Champions—Men *(Cont.)*

MAJOR SLOW PITCH

1953.........Shields Construction, Newport, KY	1978.........Campbell Carpets, Concord, CA
1954.........Waldneck's Tavern, Cincinnati	1979.........Nelco Mfg Co., Oklahoma City
1955.........Lang Pet Shop, Covington, KY	1980.........Campbell Carpets, Concord, CA
1956.........Gatliff Auto Sales, Newport, KY	1981.........Elite Coating, Gordon, CA
1957.........Gatliff Auto Sales, Newport, KY	1982.........Triangle Sports, Minneapolis
1958.........East Side Sports, Detroit	1983.........No. 1 Electric & Heating, Gastonia, NC
1959.........Yorkshire Restaurant, Newport, KY	1984.........Lilly Air Systems, Chicago
1960.........Hamilton Tailoring, Cincinnati	1985.........Blanton's, Fayetteville, NC
1961.........Hamilton Tailoring, Cincinnati	1986.........Non-Ferrous Metals, Cleveland
1962.........Skip Hogan A.C., Pittsburgh	1987.........Starpath, Monticello, KY
1963.........Gatliff Auto Sales, Newport, KY	1988.........Bell Corp/FAF, Tampa, FL
1964.........Skip Hogan A.C., Pittsburgh	1989.........Ritch's Salvage, Harrisburg, NC
1965.........Skip Hogan A.C., Pittsburgh	1990.........New Construction, Shelbyville, IN
1966.........Michael's Lounge, Detroit	1991.........Riverside Paving, Louisville, KY
1967.........Jim's Sport Shop, Pittsburgh	1992.........Vernon's, Jacksonville, FL
1968.........County Sports, Levittown, NY	1993.........Back Porch/Destin Roofing, Destin, FL
1969.........Copper Hearth, Milwaukee	1994.........Riverside RAM/Taylor Bros., Louisville, KY
1970.........Little Caesar's, Southgate, MI	1995.........Riverside/RAM/Taylor/TPS, Louisville, KY
1971.........Pile Drivers, Virginia Beach, VA	1996.........Bell 2/Robert's/Easton, Orlando, FL
1972.........Jiffy Club, Louisville, KY	1997.........Long Haul/TPS, Albertville, MN
1973.........Howard's Furniture, Denver, NC	1998.........Chase Mortgage/Easton, Wilmington, NC
1974.........Howard's Furniture, Denver, NC	1999.........Gasoline Heaven/Worth, Commack, NY
1975.........Pyramid Cafe, Lakewood, OH	2000.........Long Haul/TPS, Albertville, MN
1976.........Warren Motors, Jacksonville, FL	2001.........New Construction, Shelbyville, IN
1977.........Nelson Painting, Oklahoma City	2002.........Twin States/Worth, Montgomery, AL

Not-So-Little-Leaguer

Anyone who feared that the Little League scandal of 2001 might do irrevocable harm to the teenager caught in its vortex can rest easy. Ace pitcher Danny Almonte—whose Rolando Paulino All-Stars had to forfeit all of their Little League Tournament games after Almonte was found to be older than the maximum age of 12—is doing fine. Living with Paulino in the Bronx (Danny's parents are in his native Dominican Republic), he's starring in a youth league, and after a year of middle school his English has progressed so much that Almonte says if he doesn't make it to the majors, he'd like to become a lawyer in the U.S.

He certainly has experience in arguing his case. Last year, when he dominated the Little League World Series, Almonte and his father, Felipe, insisted that Danny was only 12. As recently as June 2002, Danny stuck to his story. But in August, after helping his Liga Paulino team go to the finals of the Under-19 Dominican League tournament in New York, the pitcher came clean to SI. Almonte, who is 15, said he knew that he was 14 during the controversy but insists that he found out after the tournament had begun. "What could I do then?" he says. "I was already playing."

In the summer of 2002, in a league dominated by older teams, Almonte went 2–0 with 21 strikeouts in 12⅔ innings and was to pitch in the league's title series. He also maintains a level of celebrity. During the summer of 2002 he was waiting to get autographs outside Shea Stadium when Astros pitcher Octavio Dotel, a Dominican, saw him and asked for his phone number. Almonte wasn't fazed; during an earlier autograph quest at Shea Brewers righthander Nelson Figueroa spotted Almonte, went back into the locker room and came out with a ball. "Could you sign this for my sister?" he asked.

—Luis Fernando Llosa

U.S. Champions—Women

MAJOR FAST PITCH

1933.........Great Northerns, Chicago	1968.........Raybestos Brakettes, Stratford, CT
1934.........Hart Motors, Chicago	1969.........Orange (CA) Lionettes
1935.........Bloomer Girls, Cleveland	1970.........Orange (CA) Lionettes
1936.........Nat'l Screw & Mfg., Cleveland	1971.........Raybestos Brakettes, Stratford, CT
1937.........Nat'l Screw & Mfg., Cleveland	1972.........Raybestos Brakettes, Stratford, CT
1938.........J.J. Krieg's, Alameda, CA	1973.........Raybestos Brakettes, Stratford, CT
1939.........J.J. Krieg's, Alameda, CA	1974.........Raybestos Brakettes, Stratford, CT
1940.........Arizona Ramblers, Phoenix	1975.........Raybestos Brakettes, Stratford, CT
1941.........Higgins Midgets, Tulsa	1976.........Raybestos Brakettes, Stratford, CT
1942.........Jax Maids, New Orleans	1977.........Raybestos Brakettes, Stratford, CT
1943.........Jax Maids, New Orleans	1978.........Raybestos Brakettes, Stratford, CT
1944.........Lind & Pomeroy, Portland, OR	1979.........Sun City (AZ) Saints
1945.........Jax Maids, New Orleans	1980.........Raybestos Brakettes, Stratford, CT
1946.........Jax Maids, New Orleans	1981.........Orlando (FL) Rebels
1947.........Jax Maids, New Orleans	1982.........Raybestos Brakettes, Stratford, CT
1948.........Arizona Ramblers, Phoenix	1983.........Raybestos Brakettes, Stratford, CT
1949.........Arizona Ramblers, Phoenix	1984.........Los Angeles Diamonds
1950.........Orange (CA) Lionettes	1985.........Hi-Ho Brakettes, Stratford, CT
1951.........Orange (CA) Lionettes	1986.........Southern California Invasion, Los Angeles
1952.........Orange (CA) Lionettes	1987.........Orange County Majestics, Anaheim, CA
1953.........Betsy Ross Rockets, Fresno	1988.........Hi-Ho Brakettes, Stratford, CT
1954.........Leach Motor Rockets, Fresno	1989.........Whittier (CA) Raiders
1955.........Orange (CA) Lionettes	1990.........Raybestos Brakettes, Stratford, CT
1956.........Orange (CA) Lionettes	1991.........Raybestos Brakettes, Stratford, CT
1957.........Hacienda Rockets, Fresno	1992.........Raybestos Brakettes, Stratford, CT
1958.........Raybestos Brakettes, Stratford, CT	1993.........Redding Rebels, Redding, CA
1959.........Raybestos Brakettes, Stratford, CT	1994.........Redding Rebels, Redding, CA
1960.........Raybestos Brakettes, Stratford, CT	1995.........Redding Rebels, Redding, CA
1961.........Gold Sox, Whittier, CA	1996.........California Commotion, Woodland Hills, CA
1962.........Orange (CA) Lionettes	1997.........California Commotion, Woodland Hills, CA
1963.........Raybestos Brakettes, Stratford, CT	1998.........California Commotion, Woodland Hills, CA
1964.........Erv Lind Florists, Portland, OR	1999.........California Commotion, Woodland Hills, CA
1965.........Orange (CA) Lionettes	2000.........Phoenix Storm, Phoenix
1966.........Raybestos Brakettes, Stratford, CT	2001.........Phoenix Storm, Phoenix
1967.........Raybestos Brakettes, Stratford, CT	2002.........Stratford Brakettes, Stratford, CT

MAJOR SLOW PITCH

1959.........Pearl Laundry, Richmond, VA	1981.........Tifton (GA) Tomboys
1960.........Carolina Rockets, High Pt, NC	1982.........Richmond (VA) Stompers
1961.........Dairy Cottage, Covington, KY	1983.........Spooks, Anoka, MN
1962.........Dana Gardens, Cincinnati	1984.........Spooks, Anoka, MN
1963.........Dana Gardens, Cincinnati	1985.........Key Ford Mustangs, Pensacola, FL
1964.........Dana Gardens, Cincinnati	1986.........Sur-Way Tomboys, Tifton, GA
1965.........Art's Acres, Omaha	1987.........Key Ford Mustangs, Pensacola, FL
1966.........Dana Gardens, Cincinnati	1988.........Spooks, Anoka, MN
1967.........Ridge Maintenance, Cleveland	1989.........Canaan's Illusions, Houston
1968.........Escue Pontiac, Cincinnati	1990.........Spooks, Anoka, MN
1969.........Converse Dots, Hialeah, FL	1991.........Kannan's Illusions, San Antonio, TX
1970.........Rutenschruder Floral, Cincinnati	1992.........Universal Plastics, Cookeville, TN
1971.........Gators, Ft. Lauderdale, FL	1993.........Universal Plastics, Cookeville, TN
1972.........Riverside Ford, Cincinnati	1994.........Universal Plastics, Cookeville, TN
1973.........Sweeney Chevrolet, Cincinnati	1995.........Armed Forces, Sacramento, CA
1974.........Marks Brothers Dots, Miami	1996.........Spooks, Anoka, MN
1975.........Marks Brothers Dots, Miami	1997.........Taylor's Major Slow Pitch, Glendale, MD
1976.........Sorrento's Pizza, Cincinnati	1998.........Lakerettes, Conneaut Lake, PA
1977.........Fox Valley Lassies, St. Charles, IL	1999.........Lakerettes, Conneaut Lake, PA
1978.........Bob Hoffman's Dots, Miami	2000.........Premier Motor Sports, Pittsboro, NC
1979.........Bob Hoffman's Dots, Miami	2001.........Shooters/Nike, Orlando, FL
1980.........Howard's Rubi-Otts, Graham, NC	2002.........Diamond Queens, Nashville, TN

Speed Skating

All-Around World Champions

MEN

1891 .....Joseph F. Donoghue, U.S.	1935 .....Michael Staksrud, Nor.	1973 .....Göran Claeson, Sweden
1893 .....Jaap Eden, Netherlands	1936 .....Ivar Ballangrud, Norway	1974 .....Sten Stensen, Norway
1895 .....Jaap Eden, Netherlands	1937 .....Michael Staksrud, Nor.	1975 .....Harm Kuipers, Netherlands
1896 .....Jaap Eden, Netherlands	1938 .....Ivar Ballangrud, Norway	1976 .....Piet Kleine, Netherlands
1897 .....Jack K. McCulloch, Can.	1939 .....Birger Wasenius, Finland	1977 .....Eric Heiden, U.S.
1898 .....Peder Ostlund, Norway	1947 .....Lassi Parkkinen, Finland	1978 .....Eric Heiden, U.S.
1899 .....Peder Ostlund, Norway	1948 .....Odd Lundberg, Norway	1979 .....Eric Heiden, U.S.
1900 .....Edvard Engelsaas, Nor.	1949 .....Kornel Pajor, Hungary	1980 .....Hilbert van der Duin, Neth.
1901 .....Franz F. Wathan, Finland	1950 .....Hjalmar Andersen, Nor.	1981 .....Amund Sjobrand, Norway
1904 .....Sigurd Mathisen, Norway	1951 .....Hjalmar Andersen, Nor.	1982 .....Hilbert van der Duin, Neth.
1905 .....C. Coen de Koning, Neth.	1952 .....Hjalmar Andersen, Nor.	1983 .....Rolf Falk-Larssen, Nor.
1908 .....Oscar Mathisen, Norway	1953 .....Oleg Goncharenko, USSR	1984 .....Oleg Bozhev, USSR
1909 .....Oscar Mathisen, Norway	1954 .....Boris Shilkov, USSR	1985 ......Hein Vergeer, Netherlands
1910 .....Nikolai Strunnikov, Russia	1955 .....Sigvard Ericsson, Swe.	1986 .....Hein Vergeer, Netherlands
1911 .....Nikolai Strunnikov, Russia	1956 .....Oleg Goncharenko, USSR	1987 .....Nikolai Guliaev, USSR
1912 .....Oscar Mathisen, Norway	1957 .....Knut Johannesen, Nor.	1988 .....Eric Flaim, U.S.
1913 .....Oscar Mathisen, Norway	1958 .....Oleg Goncharenko, USSR	1989 .....Leo Visser, Netherlands
1914 .....Oscar Mathisen, Norway	1959 .....Juhani Järvinen, Finland	1990 .....Johann Olav Koss, Nor.
1922 .....Harald Strom, Norway	1960 .....Boris Stenin, USSR	1991 .....Johann Olav Koss, Nor.
1923 .....Klas Thunberg, Finland	1961 .....Henk van der Grift, Neth.	1992 .....Roberto Sighel, Italy
1924 .....Roald Larsen, Norway	1962 .....Viktor Kosichkin, USSR	1993 .....Falko Zandstra, Neth.
1925 .....Klas Thunberg, Finland	1963 .....Jonny Nilsson, Sweden	1994 .....Johann Olav Koss, Nor.
1926 .....Ivar Ballangrud, Norway	1964 .....Knut Johannesen, Nor.	1995 .....Rintje Ritsma, Netherlands
1927 .....Bernt Evensen, Norway	1965 .....Per Ivar Moe, Norway	1996 .....Rintje Ritsma, Netherlands
1928 .....Klas Thunberg, Finland	1966 .....Kees Verkerk, Neth.	1997 .....Ids Postma, Netherlands
1929 .....Klas Thunberg, Finland	1967 .....Kees Verkerk, Neth.	1998 .....Ids Postma, Netherlands
1930 .....Michael Staksrud, Nor.	1968 .....Fred Anton Maier, Nor.	1999 .....Rintje Ritsma, Netherlands
1931 .....Klas Thunberg, Finland	1969 .....Dag Fornaes, Norway	2000 ....Gianni Romme, Netherlands
1932 .....Ivar Ballangrud, Norway	1970 .....Ard Schenk, Netherlands	2001 .....Rintje Ritsma, Netherlands
1933 .....Hans Engnestangen, Nor.	1971 .....Ard Schenk, Netherlands	2002 ....Jochem Uytdehaage, Neth.
1934 .....Bernt Evensen, Norway	1972 .....Ard Schenk, Netherlands	

WOMEN

1936 .....Kit Klein, U.S.	1964 .....Lidia Skoblikova, USSR	1985 .....Andrea Schöne, GDR
1937 .....Laila Schou Nilsen, Nor.	1965 .....Inga Artamonova, USSR	1986 .....Karin Kania-Enke, GDR
1938 .....Laila Schou Nilsen, Nor.	1966 .....Valentina Stenina, USSR	1987 .....Karin Kania, GDR
1939 .....Verné Lesche, Finland	1967 .....Stien Kaiser, Netherlands	1988 .....Karin Kania, GDR
1947 .....Verné Lesche, Finland	1968 .....Stien Kaiser, Netherlands	1989 .....Constanze Moser, GDR
1948 .....Maria Isakova, USSR	1969 .....Lasma Kauniste, USSR	1990 .....Jacqueline Börner, GDR
1949 .....Maria Isakova, USSR	1970 .....Atje Keulen-Deelstra, Neth.	1991 .....Gunda Kleemann, Ger.
1950 .....Maria Isakova, USSR	1971 .....Nina Statkevich, USSR	1992 .....Gunda Niemann-
1951 .....Eevi Huttunen, Finland	1972 .....Atje Keulen-Deelstra, Neth.	Kleemann, Germany
1952 .....Lidia Selikhova, USSR	1973 .....Atje Keulen-Deelstra, Neth.	1993 .....Gunda Niemann, Germany
1953 ....Khalida Shchegoleeva, USSR	1974 .....Atje Keulen-Deelstra, Neth.	1994 .....Emese Hunyady, Austria
1954 .....Lidia Selikhova, USSR	1975 .....Karin Kessow, GDR	1995 .....Gunda Niemann, Germany
1955 .....Rimma Zhukova, USSR	1976 .....Sylvia Burka, Canada	1996 .....Gunda Niemann, Germany
1956 .....Sofia Kondakova, USSR	1977 .....Vera Bryndzej, USSR	1997 .....Gunda Niemann, Germany
1957 .....Inga Artamonova, USSR	1978 .....Tatiana Averina, USSR	1997 ......Gunda Niemann, Germany
1958 .....Inga Artamonova, USSR	1979 .....Beth Heiden, U.S.	1998 .....Gunda Niemann, Germany
1959 .....Tamara Rylova, USSR	1980 .....Natalia Petruseva, USSR	1999 .....Gunda Niemann, Germany
1960 .....Valentina Stenina, USSR	1981 .,...Natalia Petruseva, USSR	2000 .....Claudia Pechstein, Ger.
1961 .....Valentina Stenina, USSR	1982 .....Karin Busch, GDR	2001 .....Anni Friesinger, Germany
1962 .....Inga Artamonova, USSR	1983 .....Andrea Schöne, GDR	2002 .....Anni Friesinger, Germany
1963 .....Lidia Skoblikova, USSR	1984 .....Karin Enke-Busch, GDR	

Squash

National Men's Champions

HARD BALL		HARD BALL (Cont.)		SOFT BALL	
Year	Champion	Year	Champion	Year	Champion
1907	John A. Miskey	1957	Henri R. Salaun	1983	Kenton Jernigan
1908	John A. Miskey	1958	Henri R. Salaun	1984	Kenton Jernigan
1909	William L. Freeland	1959	Benjamin H. Heckscher	1985	Kenton Jernigan
1910	John A. Miskey	1960	G. Diehl Mateer Jr.	1986	Darius Pandole
1911	Francis S. White	1961	Henri R. Salaun	1987	Richard Hashim
1912	Constantine Hutchins	1962	Samuel P. Howe III	1988	John Phelan
1913	Morton L. Newhall	1963	Benjamin H.	1989	Will Carlin
1914	Constantine Hutchins		Heckscher	1990	Syed Jafry
1915	Stanley W. Pearson	1964	Ralph E. Howe	1991	Hector Barragan
1916	Stanley W. Pearson	1965	Stephen T. Vehslage	1992	Phil Yarrow
1917	Stanley W. Pearson	1966	Victor Niederhoffer	1993	Phil Yarrow
1918–19	No tournament	1967	Samuel P. Howe III	1994	Roberto Rosales
1920	Charles C. Peabody	1968	Colin Adair	1995	A. Martin Clark
1921	Stanley W. Pearson	1969	Anil Nayar	1996	Mohsen Mir
1922	Stanley W. Pearson	1970	Anil Nayar	1997	A. Martin Clark
1923	Stanley W. Pearson	1971	Colin Adair	1998	A. Martin Clark
1924	Gerald Roberts	1972	Victor Niederhoffer	1999	David McNeely
1925	W. Palmer Dixon	1973	Victor Niederhoffer	2000	A. Martin Clark
1926	W. Palmer Dixon	1974	Victor Niederhoffer	2001	Damian Walker
1927	Myles Baker	1975	Victor Niederhoffer	2002	Damian Walker
1928	Herbert N. Rawlins Jr.	1976	Peter Briggs		
1929	J. Lawrence Pool	1977	Thomas E. Page		
1930	Herbert N. Rawlins Jr.	1978	Michael Desaulniers		
1931	J. Lawrence Pool	1979	Mario Sanchez		
1932	Beckman H. Pool	1980	Michael Desaulniers		
1933	Beckman H. Pool	1981	Mark Alger		
1934	Neil J. Sullivan II	1982	John Nimick		
1935	Donald Strachan	1983	Kenton Jernigan		
1936	Germain G. Glidden	1984	Kenton Jernigan		
1937	Germain G. Glidden	1987	Frank J. Stanley IV		
1938	Germain G. Glidden	1988	Scott Dulmage		
1939	Donald Strachan	1989	Rodolfo Rodriquez		
1940	A. Willing Patterson	1990	Hector Barragan		
1941	Charles M.P. Britton	1991	Hector Barragan		
1942	Charles M.P. Britton	1992	Hector Barragan		
1943–45	No tournament	1985	Kenton Jernigan		
1946	Charles M.P. Britton	1986	Hugh LaBossier		
1947	Charles M.P. Britton	1993	Hector Barragan		
1948	Stanley W. Pearson Jr.	1994	Hector Barragan		
1949	H. Hunter Lott Jr.	1995	W. Keen Butcher		
1950	Edward J. Hahn	1996	W. Keen Butcher		
1951	Edward J. Hahn	1997	Rob Hill		
1952	Harry B. Conlon	1998	Rob Hill		
1953	Ernest Howard	1999	Rob Hill		
1954	G. Diehl Mateer Jr.	2000	Thomas Harrity		
1955	Henri R. Salaun	2001	Rob Hill		
1956	G. Diehl Mateer Jr.	2002	Gary Waite		

National Women's Champions

HARD BALL		HARD BALL (Cont.)		SOFT BALL	
Year	Champion	Year	Champion	Year	Champion
1928	Eleanora Sears	1965	Joyce Davenport	1983	Alicia McConnell
1929	Margaret Howe	1966	Betty Meade	1984	Julie Harris
1930	Hazel Wightman	1967	Betty Meade	1985	Sue Clinch
1931	Ruth Banks	1968	Betty Meade	1986	Julie Harris
1932	Margaret Howe	1969	Joyce Davenport	1987	Diana Staley
1933	Susan Noel	1970	Nina Moyer	1988	Sara Luther
1934	Margaret Howe	1971	Carol Thesieres	1989	Nancy Gengler
1935	Margot Lumb	1972	Nina Moyer	1990	Joyce Maycock
1936	Anne Page	1973	Gretchen Spruance	1991	Ellie Pierce
1937	Anne Page	1974	Gretchen Spruance	1992	Demer Holleran
1938	Cecile Bowes	1975	Ginny Akabane	1993	Demer Holleran
1939	Anne Page	1976	Gretchen Spruance	1994	Demer Holleran
1940	Cecile Bowes	1977	Gretchen Spruance	1995	Ellie Pierce
1941	Cecile Bowes	1978	Gretchen Spruance	1996	Demer Holleran
1942–46	No tournament	1979	Heather McKay	1997	Demer Holleran
1947	Anne Page Homer	1980	Barbara Maltby	1998	Latasha Khan
1948	Cecile Bowes	1981	Barbara Maltby	1999	Demer Holleran
1949	Janet Morgan	1982	Alicia McConnell	2000	Latasha Khan
1950	Betty Howe	1983	Alicia McConnell	2001	Shabana Khan
1951	Jane Austin	1984	Alicia McConnell	2002	Latasha Khan
1952	Margaret Howe	1985	Alicia McConnell		
1953	Margaret Howe	1986	Alicia McConnell		
1954	Lois Dilks	1987	Alicia McConnell		
1955	Janet Morgan	1988	Alicia McConnell		
1956	Betty Howe Constable	1986	Alicia McConnell		
1957	Betty Howe Constable	1987	Alicia McConnell		
1958	Betty Howe Constable	1988	Alicia McConnell		
1959	Betty Howe Constable	1989	Demer Holleran		
1960	Margaret Varner	1990	Demer Holleran		
1961	Margaret Varner	1991	Demer Holleran		
1962	Margaret Varner	1992	Demer Holleran		
1963	Margaret Varner	1993	Demer Holleran		
1964	Ann Wetzel	1994	Demer Holleran		

Note: Tournament not held since 1994.

YET ANOTHER SIGN OF THE APOCALYPSE

Charles Mitchell, 34, a sporting goods store executive from Boca Raton, Fla., was charged with "aggravated battery on the elderly" after he choked a 74-year-old softball umpire into unconsciousness because the ump had ejected the profanity-shouting Mitchell from a game.

Triathlon

Ironman World Championship

	MEN			WOMEN	
Year	Winner	Time	Year	Winner	Time
1978	Gordon Haller	11:46	1978	No finishers	
1979	Tom Warren	11:15:56	1979	Lyn Lemaire	12:55
1980	Dave Scott	9:24:33	1980	Robin Beck	11:21:24
1981	John Howard	9:38:29	1981	Linda Sweeney	12:00:32
1982	Scott Tinley	9:19:41	1982	Kathleen McCartney	11:09:40
1982	Dave Scott	9:08:23	1982	Julie Leach	10:54:08
1983	Dave Scott	9:05:57	1983	Sylviane Puntous	10:43:36
1984	Dave Scott	8:54:20	1984	Sylviane Puntous	10:25:13
1985	Scott Tinley	8:50:54	1985	Joanne Ernst	10:25:22
1986	Dave Scott	8:28:37	1986	Paula Newby-Fraser	9:49:14
1987	Dave Scott	8:34:13	1987	Erin Baker	9:35:25
1988	Scott Molina	8:31:00	1988	Paula Newby-Fraser	9:01:01
1989	Mark Allen	8:09:15	1989	Paula Newby-Fraser	9:00:56
1990	Mark Allen	8:28:17	1990	Erin Baker	9:13:42
1991	Mark Allen	8:18:32	1991	Paula Newby-Fraser	9:07:52
1992	Mark Allen	8:09:09	1992	Paula Newby-Fraser	8:55:29
1993	Mark Allen	8:07:46	1993	Paula Newby-Fraser	8:58:23
1994	Greg Welch	8:20:27	1994	Paula Newby-Fraser	9:20:14
1995	Mark Allen	8:20:34	1995	Karen Smyers	9:16:46
1996	Luc Van Lierde	8:04:08	1996	Paula Newby-Fraser	9:06:49
1997	Thomas Hellriegel	8:33:01	1997	Heather Fuhr	9:31:43
1998	Peter Reid	8:24:20	1998	Natascha Badmann	9:24:16
1999	Luc Van Lierde	8:17:17	1999	Lori Bowden	9:13:02
2000	Peter Reid	8:21:01	2000	Natascha Badmann	9:26:17
2001	Tim DeBoom	8:31:18	2001	Natascha Badmann	9:28:37

Note: The Ironman Championship was contested twice in 1982.

Sites: Waikiki Beach (1978–79); Ala Moana Park (1980); Kailua-Kona (since 1981).

U.S. Triathlon National Champions*

MEN		MEN (CONT.)		WOMEN		WOMEN (CONT.)	
Year	Winner	Year	Winner	Year	Winner	Year	Winner
1984	Scott Molina	1995	Jeff Devlin	1984	Beth Mitchell	1992	Karen Smyers
1985	Scott Molina	1996	Jeff Devlin	1985	L. Buchanan	1993	Karen Smyers
1986	Scott Molina	1997	Cameron Wydoff	1986	Kirsten Hanssen	1994	Karen Smyers
1987	Mike Pigg					1995	Karen Smyers
1988	Mike Pigg	1998	Hunter Kemper	1987	Kirsten Hanssen	1996	Susan Latshaw
1989	Ken Glah	1999	Hunter Kemper			1997	Sian Welch
1990	Scott Molina	2000	Marcel Viffian	1988	Colleen Cannon Kaushansky	1998	Siri Lindley
1991	Mike Pigg					1999	Barb Lindquist
1992	Mike Pigg	2001	Hunter Kemper	1989	Jan Ripple	2000	Joanna Zeiger
1993	Bill Braun	2002	Seth Wealing	1990	Karen Smyers	2001	Karen Smyers
1994	Scott Molina			1991	Karen Smyers	2002	Barb Lindquist

*Olympic distances: 1.5 km swim, 40km bike, 10km run.

Volleyball

World Champions

	MEN		
Year	Winner	Runner-up	Site
1949	Soviet Union	Czechoslovakia	Prague
1952	Soviet Union	Czechoslovakia	Moscow
1956	Czechoslovakia	Soviet Union	Paris
1960	Soviet Union	Czechoslovakia	Rio de Janeiro
1962	Soviet Union	Czechoslovakia	Moscow
1966	Czechoslovakia	Romania	Prague
1970	East Germany	Bulgaria	Sofia, Bulgaria
1974	Poland	Soviet Union	Mexico City
1978	Soviet Union	Italy	Rome
1982	Soviet Union	Brazil	Buenos Aires
1986	United States	Soviet Union	Paris
1990	Italy	Cuba	Rio de Janeiro
1994	Italy	Netherlands	Athens
1998	Italy	Yugoslavia	Tokyo

World Champions (Cont.)

WOMEN

Year	Winner	Runner-up	Site
1952	Soviet Union	Poland	Moscow
1956	Soviet Union	Romania	Paris
1960	Soviet Union	Japan	Rio de Janeiro
1962	Japan	Soviet Union	Moscow
1966	Japan	United States	Prague
1970	Soviet Union	Japan	Sofia, Bulgaria
1974	Japan	Soviet Union	Mexico City
1978	Cuba	Japan	Rome
1982	China	Peru	Lima, Peru
1986	China	Cuba	Prague
1990	Soviet Union	China	Beijing
1994	Cuba	Brazil	Sao Paulo, Brazil
1998	Cuba	China	Osaka, Japan
2002	Italy	United States	Berlin

U.S. Men's Open Champions—Gold Division

Year	Champion	Year	Champion
1928	Germantown, PA YMCA	1966	Sand & Sea Club, CA
1929	Hyde Park YMCA, IL	1967	Fresno, CA VBC
1930	Hyde Park YMCA, IL	1968	Westside JCC, Los Angeles, CA
1931	San Antonio, TX YMCA	1969	Los Angeles, CA YMCA
1932	San Antonio, TX YMCA	1970	Chart House, San Diego
1933	Houston, TX YMCA	1971	Santa Monica, CA YMCA
1934	Houston, TX YMCA	1972	Chart House, San Diego
1935	Houston, TX YMCA	1973	Chuck's Steak, Los Angeles
1936	Houston, TX YMCA	1974	UC Santa Barbara, CA
1937	Duncan YMCA, IL	1975	Chart House, San Diego
1938	Houston, TX YMCA	1976	Malibu, Los Angeles
1939	Houston, TX YMCA	1977	Chuck's, Santa Barbara
1940	Los Angeles AC, CA	1978	Chuck's, Los Angeles
1941	North Ave. YMCA, IL	1979	Nautilus, Long Beach CA
1942	North Ave. YMCA, IL	1980	Olympic Club, San Francisco
1943–44	No championships	1981	Nautilus, Long Beach CA
1945	North Ave. YMCA, IL	1982	Chuck's, Los Angeles
1946	Pasadena, CA YMCA	1983	Nautilus Pacifica, CA
1947	North Ave. YMCA, IL	1984	Nautilus Pacifica, CA
1948	Hollywood, CA YMCA	1985	Molten/SSI Torrance, CA
1949	Downtown YMCA, CA	1986	Molten, Torrance, CA
1950	Long Beach, CA YMCA	1987	Molten, Torrance, CA
1951	Hollywood, CA YMCA	1988	Molten, Torrance, CA
1952	Hollywood, CA YMCA	1989	Not held
1953	Hollywood, CA YMCA	1990	Nike, Carson, CA
1954	Stockton, CA YMCA	1991	Offshore, Woodland Hills, CA
1955	Stockton, CA YMCA	1992	Creole Six Pack, Elmhurst, NY
1956	Hollywood, CA YMCA Stars	1993	Asics, Huntington Beach, CA
1957	Hollywood, CA YMCA Stars	1994	Asics/Paul Mitchell, Hunt. Beach, CA
1958	Hollywood, CA YMCA Stars	1995	Shakter, Belagarad, Ukraine
1959	Hollywood, CA YMCA Stars	1996	POL-AM-VBC, Brooklyn, NY
1960	Westside JCC, CA	1997	Canuck Stuff VBC, Calgary
1961	Hollywood, CA YMCA	1998	T-Town, Tulsa, OK
1962	Hollywood, CA YMCA	1999	Los Angeles Athletic Club,
1963	Hollywood, CA YMCA	2000	Paul Mitchell, Huntington Beach, CA
1964	Hollywood, CA YMCA Stars	2001	Los Angeles Athletic Club,
1965	Westside JCC, CA	2002	Paul Mitchell, Huntington Beach, CA

U.S. Women's Open Champions—Gold Division

Year	Champion
1949	Eagles, Houston
1950	Voit #1, Santa Monica, CA
1951	Eagles, Houston
1952	Voit #1, Santa Monica, CA
1953	Voit #1, Los Angeles
1954	Houstonettes, Houston, TX
1955	Mariners, Santa Monica, CA
1956	Mariners, Santa Monica, CA
1957	Mariners, Santa Monica, CA
1958	Mariners, Santa Monica, CA
1959	Mariners, Santa Monica, CA
1960	Mariners, Santa Monica, CA
1961	Breakers, Long Beach, CA
1962	Shamrocks, Long Beach, CA
1963	Shamrocks, Long Beach, CA
1964	Shamrocks, Long Beach, CA
1965	Shamrocks, Long Beach, CA
1966	Renegades, Los Angeles
1967	Shamrocks, Long Beach, CA
1968	Shamrocks, Long Beach, CA
1969	Shamrocks, Long Beach, CA
1970	Shamrocks, Long Beach, CA
1971	Renegades, Los Angeles
1972	E Pluribus Unum, Houston
1973	E Pluribus Unum, Houston
1974	Renegades, Los Angeles
1975	Adidas, Norwalk, CA
1976	Pasadena, TX
1977	Spoilers, Hermosa, CA
1978	Nick's, Los Angeles
1979	Mavericks, Los Angeles
1980	NAVA, Fountain Valley, CA
1981	Utah State, Logan, UT
1982	Monarchs, Hilo, HI
1983	Syntex, Stockton, CA
1984	Chrysler, Palo Alto, CA
1985	Merrill Lynch, AZ
1986	Merrill Lynch, AZ
1987	Chrysler, Pleasanton, CA
1988	Chrysler, Hayward, CA
1989	Plymouth, Hayward, CA
1990	Plymouth, Hayward, CA
1991	Fitness, Champaign, IL
1992	Nick's Kronies, Chicago
1993	Nick's Fishmarket, Chicago
1994	Nick's Fishmarket, Chicago
1995	Kittleman/Branfield's/Nick's, Chi.
1996	Pure Texas Nuts, Austin, TX
1997	Kittleman/Branfield's/Nick's, Chi.
1998	The Exterminators, Barrington, IL
1999	Dominican Dream Team, Santo Domingo, D.R.
2000	Dominican Dream Team II, Santo Domingo, D.R.
2001	Dominican Dream Team III, Santo Domingo, D.R.
2002	Team Trim, Long Beach, CA

Wrestling

United States National Champions
1983

FREESTYLE		FREESTYLE (Cont.)		GRECO-ROMAN (Cont.)	
105.5	Rich Salamone	220	Greg Gibson	136.5	Dan Mello
114.5	Joe Gonzales	Hvy	Bruce Baumgartner	149.5	Jim Martinez
125.5	Joe Corso	Team	Sunkist Kids	163	James Andre
136.5	Rich Dellagatta*			180.5	Steve Goss
149.5	Bill Hugent	**GRECO-ROMAN**		198	Steve Fraser*
163	Lee Kemp	105.5	T.J. Jones	220	Dennis Koslowski
180.5	Chris Campbell	114.5	Mark Fuller	Hvy	No champion
198	Pete Bush	125.5	Rob Hermann	Team	Minn. Wrestling Club

1984

FREESTYLE		FREESTYLE (Cont.)		GRECO-ROMAN (Cont.)	
105.5	Rich Salamone	220	Harold Smith	149.5	Jim Martinez*
114.5	Charlie Heard	Hvy	Bruce Baumgartner	163	John Matthews
125.5	Joe Corso	Team	Sunkist Kids	180.5	Tom Press
136.5	Rich Dellagatta*			198	Mike Houck
149.5	Andre Metzger	**GRECO-ROMAN**		220	No champion
163	Dave Schultz*	105.5	T.J. Jones	Hvy	No champion
180.5	Mark Schultz	114.5	Mark Fuller	Team	Adirondack 3-Style, WA
198	Steve Fraser	136.5	Dan Mello		

1985

FREESTYLE		FREESTYLE (Cont.)		GRECO-ROMAN (Cont.)	
105.5	Tim Vanni	220	Greg Gibson	136.5	Buddy Lee
114.5	Jim Martin	286	Bruce Baumgartner	149.5	Jim Martinez
125.5	Charlie Heard	Team	Sunkist Kids	163	David Butler
136.5	Darryl Burley			180.5	Chris Catallo
149.5	Bill Nugent*	**GRECO-ROMAN**		198	Mike Houck
163	Kenny Monday	105.5	T.J. Jones	220	Greg Gibson
180.5	Mike Sheets	114.5	Mark Fuller	286	Dennis Koslowski
198	Mark Schultz	125.5	Eric Seward*	Team	U.S. Marine Corps

United States National Champions (Cont.)

1986

FREESTYLE

105.5	Rich Salamone
114.5	Joe Gonzales
125.5	Kevin Darkus
136.5	John Smith
149.5	Andre Metzger*
163	Dave Schultz
180.5	Mark Schultz
198	Jim Scherr
220	Dan Severn

FREESTYLE (Cont.)

286	Bruce Baumgartner
Team	Sunkist Kids (Div. I)
	Hawkeye Wrestling Club (Div. II)

GRECO-ROMAN

105.5	Eric Wetzel
114.5	Shawn Sheldon
125.5	Anthony Amado

GRECO-ROMAN (Cont.)

136.5	Frank Famiano
149.5	Jim Martinez
163	David Butler*
180.5	Darryl Gholar
198	Derrick Waldroup
220	Dennis Koslowski
286	Duane Koslowski
Team	U.S. Marine Corps (Div. I)
	U.S. Navy (Div. II)

1987

FREESTYLE

105.5	Takashi Irie
114.5	Mitsuru Sato
125.5	Barry Davis
136.5	Takumi Adachi
149.5	Andre Metzger
163	Dave Schultz*
180.5	Mark Schultz
198	Jim Scherr
220	Bill Scherr

FREESTYLE (Cont.)

286	Bruce Baumgartner
Team	Sunkist Kids (Div. I)
	Team Foxcatcher (Div. II)

GRECO-ROMAN

105.5	Eric Wetzel
114.5	Shawn Sheldon
125.5	Eric Seward
136.5	Frank Famiano

GRECO-ROMAN (Cont.)

149.5	Jim Martinez
163	David Butler
180.5	Chris Catallo
198	Derrick Waldroup*
220	Dennis Koslowski
286	Duane Koslowski
Team	U.S. Marine Corp (Div. I)
	U.S. Army (Div. II)

1988

FREESTYLE

105.5	Tim Vanni
114.5	Joe Gonzales
125.5	Kevin Darkus
136.5	John Smith*
149.5	Nate Carr
163	Kenny Monday
180.5	Dave Schultz
198	Melvin Douglas III
220	Bill Scherr

FREESTYLE (Cont.)

286	Bruce Baumgartner
Team	Sunkist Kids (Div. I)
	Team Foxcatcher (Div. II)

GRECO-ROMAN

105.5	T.J. Jones
114.5	Shawn Sheldon
125.5	Gogi Parseghian*
136.5	Dalen Wasmund

GRECO-ROMAN (Cont.)

149.5	Craig Pollard
163	Tony Thomas
180.5	Darryl Gholar
198	Mike Carolan
220	Dennis Koslowski
286	Duane Koslowski
Team	U.S. Marine Corps (Div. I)
	Sunkist Kids (Div. II)

1989

FREESTYLE

105.5	Tim Vanni
114.5	Zeke Jones
125.5	Brad Penrith
136.5	John Smith
149.5	Nate Carr
163	Rob Koll
180.5	Rico Chiapparelli
198	Jim Scherr*
220	Bill Scherr

FREESTYLE (Cont.)

286	Bruce Baumgartner
Team	Sunkist Kids (Div. I)
	Team Foxcatcher (Div. II)

GRECO-ROMAN

105.5	Lew Dorrance
114.5	Mark Fuller
125.5	Gogi Parseghian
136.5	Isaac Anderson

GRECO-ROMAN (Cont.)

149.5	Andy Seras*
163	David Butler
180.5	John Morgan
198	Michial Foy
220	Steve Lawson
286	Craig Pittman
Team	U.S. Marine Corps (Div. I)
	Jets USA (Div. II)

1990

FREESTYLE

105.5	Rob Eiter
114.5	Zeke Jones
125.5	Joe Melchiore
136.5	John Smith
149.5	Nate Carr
163	Rob Koll
180.5	Royce Alger
198	Chris Campbell*
220	Bill Scherr

FREESTYLE (Cont.)

286	Bruce Baumgartner
Team	Sunkist Kids (Div. I)
	Team Foxcatcher (Div. II)

GRECO-ROMAN

105.5	Lew Dorrance
114.5	Sam Henson
125.5	Mark Pustelnik
136.5	Isaac Anderson

GRECO-ROMAN (Cont.)

149.5	Andy Seras
163	David Butler
180.5	Derrick Waldroup
198	Randy Couture*
220	Chris Tironi
286	Matt Ghaffari
Team	Jets USA (Div. I)
	California Jets (Div. II)

*Outstanding wrestler.

United States National Champions (Cont.)

1991

FREESTYLE

105.5 ......Tim Vanni
114.5 ......Zeke Jones
125.5 ......Brad Penrith
136.5 ......John Smith*
149.5 ......Townsend Saunders
163 ....Kenny Monday
180.5 ......Kevin Jackson
198 ....Chris Campbell
220 ....Mark Coleman

FREESTYLE (Cont.)

286 ....Bruce Baumgartner
Team ....Sunkist Kids (Div. I)
            Jets USA (Div. II)

GRECO-ROMAN

105.5 ......Eric Wetzel
114.5 ......Shawn Sheldon
125.5 ......Frank Famiano
136.5 ......Buddy Lee

GRECO-ROMAN (Cont.)

149.5 ......Andy Seras
163 ....Gordy Morgan
180.5 ......John Morgan*
198 ....Michial Foy
220 ....Dennis Koslowski
286 ....Craig Pittman
Team ....Jets USA (Div. I)
            Sunkist Kids (Div. II)

1992

FREESTYLE

105.5 ......Rob Eiter
114.5 ......Jack Griffin
125.5 ......Kendall Cross*
136.5 ......John Fisher
149.5 ......Matt Demaray
163 ....Greg Elinsky
180.5 ......Royce Alger
198 ....Dan Chaid
220 ....Bill Scherr

FREESTYLE (Cont.)

286 ....Bruce Baumgartner
Team ....Sunkist Kids (Div. I)
            Team Foxcatcher (Div. II)

GRECO-ROMAN

105.5 ......Eric Wetzel
114.5 ......Mark Fuller
125.5 ......Dennis Hall
136.5 ......Buddy Lee*

GRECO-ROMAN (Cont.)

149.5 ......Rodney Smith
163 ....Travis West
180.5 ......John Morgan
198 ....Michial Foy
220 ....Dennis Koslowski
286 ....Matt Ghaffari
Team ....NY Athletic Club (Div. I)
            Sunkist Kids (Div. II)

1993

FREESTYLE

105.5 ......Rob Eiter
114.5 ......Zeke Jones
125.5 ......Brad Penrith
136.5 ......Tom Brands
149.5 ......Matt Demaray
163 ....Dave Schultz*
180.5 ......Kevin Jackson
198 ....Melvin Douglas
220 ....Kirk Trost

FREESTYLE (Cont.)

286 ....Bruce Baumgartner
Team ....Sunkist Kids (Div. I)
            Team Foxcatcher (Div. II)

GRECO-ROMAN

105.5 ......Eric Wetzel
114.5 ......Shawn Sheldon
125.5 ......Dennis Hall*
136.5 ......Shon Lewis

GRECO-ROMAN (Cont.)

149.5 ......Andy Seras
163 ....Gordy Morgan
180.5 ......Dan Henderson
198 ....Randy Couture
220 ....James Johnson
286 ....Matt Ghaffari
Team ....NY Athletic Club (Div. I)
            Sunkist Kids (Div. II)

1994

FREESTYLE

105.5 ......Tim Vanni
114.5 ......Zeke Jones
125.5 ......Terry Brands
136.5 ......Tom Brands
149.5 ......Matt Demaray
163 ....Dave Schultz
180.5 ......Royce Alger
198 ....Melvin Douglas
220 ....Mark Kerr

FREESTYLE (Cont.)

286 ....Bruce Baumgartner*
Team ....Sunkist Kids (Div. I)
            Team Foxcatcher (Div. II)

GRECO-ROMAN

105.5 ......Isaac Ramaswamy
114.5 ......Shawn Sheldon
125.5 ......Dennis Hall
136.5 ......Shon Lewis

GRECO-ROMAN (Cont.)

149.5 ......Andy Seras*
163 ....Gordy Morgan
180.5 ......Dan Henderson
198 ....Derrick Waldroup

GRECO-ROMAN (Cont.)

220 ....James Johnson
286 ....Matt Ghaffari
Team ....Armed Forces (Div. I)
            NY Athletic Club (Div. II)

1995

FREESTYLE

105.5 ......Rob Eiter
114.5 ......Lou Rosselli
125.5 ......Kendall Cross*
136.5 ......Tom Brands
149.5 ......Matt Demaray
163 ....Dave Schultz
180.5 ......Kevin Jackson
198 ....Melvin Douglas
220 ....Kurt Angle

*Outstanding wrestler.

FREESTYLE (Cont.)

286 ....Bruce Baumgartner
Team ....Sunkist Kids (Div. I)
            Team Foxcatcher (Div. II)

GRECO-ROMAN

105.5 ......Isaac Ramaswamy
114.5 ......Shawn Sheldon
125.5 ......Dennis Hall*
136.5 ......Van Fronhofer

GRECO-ROMAN (Cont.)

149.5 ......Heath Sims
163 ....Matt Lindland
180.5 ......Marty Morgan
198 ....Michial Foy
220 ....James Johnson
286 ....Rulon Gardner
Team ....Armed Forces (Div. I)
            Sunkist Kids (Div. II)

United States National Champions (Cont.)

1996

FREESTYLE
105.5 ......Rob Eiter
114.5 ......Lou Rosselli
125.5 ......Kendall Cross
136.5 ......Tom Brands
149.5 ......Townsend Saunders
163 ....Kenny Monday
180.5 ......Les Gutches*
198 ....Melvin Douglas
220 ....Kurt Angle

FREESTYLE (Cont.)
286 ....Bruce Baumgartner
Team ....Sunkist Kids (Div. I)
　　　　　NY Athletic Club (Div. II)

GRECO-ROMAN
105.5 ......Mujaahid Maynard
114.5 ......Shawn Sheldon
125.5 ......Dennis Hall*
136.5 ......Shon Lewis

GRECO-ROMAN (Cont.)
149.5 ......Rodney Smith
163 ....Keith Sieracki
180.5 ......Marty Morgan
198 ....Michial Foy
220 ....John Oostendrop
286 ....Matt Ghaffari
Team ....Armed Forces (Div. I)
　　　　　Sunkist Kids (Div. II)

1997

FREESTYLE
110 ....Kanamti Soloman
119 ....Zeke Jones
127.75 ......Terry Brands
138.75 ......Carl Kolat
152 ....Lincoln McIlravy*
167.5 ......Dan St. John
187.25 .....Les Gutches
213.75 .....Melvin Douglas

FREESTYLE (Cont.)
275.5 ......Tom Erikson
Team ....Sunkist Kids (Div. I)
　　　　　NY Athletic Club (Div. II)

GRECO-ROMAN
110 ....Mark Yanagihara
119 ....Broderick Lee
127.75 .....Dennis Hall

GRECO-ROMAN (Cont.)
138.75 .....Kevin Bracken
152 ....Chris Saba
167.5 ......Miguel Spencer
187.25 .....Dan Henderson
213.75 .....Randy Couture*
275.5 ......Rulon Gardner
Team ....Armed Forces (Div. I)
　　　　　NY Athletic Club (Div. II)

1998

FREESTYLE
119 ....Sam Henson
127.75 .....Tony Purler
138.75 .....Shawn Charles
152 ....Lincoln McIlravy
167.5 ......Steve Marianetti
187.25 .....Les Gutches*
213.75 .....Melvin Douglas

FREESTYLE (Cont.)
286 ....Tolly Thompson
Team ....Sunkist Kids (Div. I)
　　　　　NY Athletic Club (Div. II)

GRECO-ROMAN
119 ....Shawn Sheldon
127.75 .....Dennis Hall
138.75 .....Shon Lewis

GRECO-ROMAN (Cont.)
152 ....Chris Saba
167.5 ......Matt Lindland
187.25 .....Dan Niebuhr*
213.75 .....Jason Klohs
286 ....Matt Ghaffari
Team ....Armed Forces (Div. I)
　　　　　Sunkist Kids (Div. II)

1999

FREESTYLE
119 ....Lou Rosselli
127.75 .....Terry Brands
138.75 .....Cary Kolat
152 ....Lincoln McIlravy
167.5 ......Joe Williams
187.25 .....Les Gutches
213.75 .....Dominic Black

FREESTYLE (Cont.)
286 ....Stephen Neal*
Team ....Sunkist Kids (Div. I)
　　　　　NY Athletic Club (Div. II)

GRECO-ROMAN
119 ....Steven Mays
127.75 .....Dennis Hall
138.75 .....Glen Nieradka

GRECO-ROMAN (Cont.)
152 ....David Zuniga
167.5 ......Matt Lindland
187.25 .....Quincey Clark
213.75 .....Randy Couture
286 ....Dremiel Byers*
Team ....Minnesota Storm (Div. I)
　　　　　Sunkist Kids (Div. II)

2000

FREESTYLE
119 ....Sammie Henson
127.75 .....Keyy Boumans
138.75 .....Cary Kolat
152 ....Lincoln McIlravy
167.5 ......Brandon Slay*
187.25 .....Les Gutches
213.75 .....Melvin Douglas

FREESTYLE (Cont.)
286 ....Kerry McCoy
Team ....Sunkist Kids (Div. I)
　　　　　NY Athletic Club (Div. II)

GRECO-ROMAN
119 ....Brandon Paulson
127.75 .....Dennis Hall
138.75 .....Kevin Bracken

GRECO-ROMAN (Cont.)
152 ....Heath Sims
167.5 ......Matt Lindland
187.25 .....Quincey Clark*
213.75 .....Jason Gleasman
286 ....Rulon Gardner
Team ....Armed Forces (Div. I)
　　　　　Sunkist Kids (Div. II)

*Outstanding wrestler.

United States National Champions (Cont.)
2001

FREESTYLE		**FREESTYLE** *(Cont.)*		**GRECO-ROMAN** *(Cont.)*	
119	Eric Akin	286	Kerry McCoy	152	Marcel Cooper
127.75	Eric Guerrero	Team	Sunkist Kids (Div. I)	167.5	Keith Sieracki
138.75	Bill Zadick		New York AC (Div. II)	187.25	Matt Lindland*
152	Ramico Blackmon	**GRECO-ROMAN**		213.75	Garrett Lowney
167.5	Joe Williams	119	Jeff Cervone	286	Rulon Gardner
187.25	Cael Sanderson*	127.75	Dennis Hall	Team	Army (Div. I)
213.75	Dominic Black	138.75	Kevin Bracken		Sunkist Kids (Div. II)

2002

FREESTYLE		**FREESTYLE** *(Cont.)*		**GRECO-ROMAN** *(Cont.)*	
121	Teague Moore	Team	Sunkist Kids (Div. I)	163	Keith Sieracki
132	Eric Guerrero		New York AC (Div. II)	185	Ethan Bosch
145.5	Bill Zadick	**GRECO-ROMAN**		211.75	Garrett Lowney
163	Joe Williams*	121	Brandon Paulson	264.5	Dremiel Byers
185	Cael Sanderson	132	Glenn Nieradka*	Team	Army (Div. I)
211.5	Tim Hartung	145.5	Kevin Bracken		New York AC (Div. II)
264.5	Kerry McCoy				

*Outstanding wrestler.

The Cover That Wasn't

Here at SI we've grown accustomed to receiving unsolicited suggestions from our readers on who should appear on the cover. (Yes, Lance Armstrong *would* have made a perfectly good cover subject for our 2001 Sportsman of the Year issue.) However, even longtime editors were taken aback at the flood of requests to put Iowa State wrestler Cael Sanderson, who finished an undefeated collegiate career in March 2002, on the cover of our April 1, 2002 issue. We received more than 100 e-mails from college wrestling fans across the nation asking for more respect for their sport. Many of the missives were the result of a campaign orchestrated by Tom Owens, founder of InterMat, an amateur wrestling website. "I welcome all of you to join me in pounding the staff at SI to get this kid on the cover," wrote Owens in a mass e-mail sent to wrestling aficionados. Although a feature on Sanderson did run inside the magazine's April 1 issue, wrestling fans were clearly looking for more. With respect to the matheads of the world, in our April 8 issue, we ran a photographic peek at what SI's cover might have looked like. Thankfully, they stopped pounding.

The Sports Market

Bernard Hopkins (left),
marketing innovator

Steady as She Goes

While the nation's economy sailed into rough waters, the business of sport found a surprising number of safe harbors

BY HANK HERSCH

KEYNOTE ADDRESS:
2002 Convention of Sports Executives
Panhandle Inn Conference Room, Ocala, Fla.
SPEAKER: Bart Fleece,
Former CEO, GetGo Intl.

"To begin with I want to thank you all for this very prestigious invitation to speak. I'd like to think that after 14 months at the helm of a multinational, diversified, high-tech company whose value increased by 700% in a period of six weeks, I have some light to shed on the current state of business in this great nation of ours. I also want to thank you for locating your meeting at my convenience. I know that you're accustomed to more luxurious surroundings when you get together, but officials at the prison were unwilling to let me travel beyond a 30-mile radius.

"To say the last year has been an economically challenging one—a time when even a normally ethical individual might feel pinched enough to siphon off a buck or two—is to put it mildly. Consider the trickle-down effect to consumers and sponsors of the tech bubble bursting, the Dow plummeting below 8,000, bankruptcies reaching record numbers and, yes, scandals dragging down myriad up-and-coming companies. Then factor in the terrorist attacks of Sept. 11, 2001, which not only shook us to our very roots but also made air travel unpalatable to many and the thought of merely going to a stadium pretty terrifying.

"In some respects, though, the worst fears of Sept. 11's economic impact were not realized in sports, and that is because sports contributed to the country's healing process. As Houston Astros infielder Geoff Blum said, 'What we do is fun. It's absolute joy. It's a great diversion from reality sometimes.'

"By the time the 2002 NFL season began, people were eager to get back to games. Robin Bachin, an assistant history

Selig and MLBPA head Donald Fehr staved off labor strife for a few more years.

matters in the post-9/11 world.'

One day, commissioner Bud Selig is claiming to Congress that teams suffered $519 million in losses in 2001. Two weeks later, the Boston Red Sox (along with the cable network that carries their games) were sold for $700 million. Players entered negotiations earning an average of $2.4 million a year, yet they were reluctant to help improve the game by making it more competitively balanced or by addressing the reportedly rampant use of steroids among their ranks.

"Ultimately, it doesn't matter who blinked. (Believe me. Had I perceived even the slightest flicker of an eyelid from federal prosecutors, I might not find myself so constrained today.) What matters is that the two sides settled and that there will be four years of labor peace. The players received a guarantee through 2006 that none of the 30 teams will be contracted, avoided the imposition of a hard salary cap and accepted a drug-testing plan that's essentially toothless. The owners got an increase in revenue sharing that will transfer $258 million from high-revenue to low-revenue clubs in 2006, up from $169 million in 2003. They also got a luxury tax ranging from 17.5% to 40% on teams with payrolls larger than $117 million in 2003, $120.5 million in '04, $128 million in '05 and $136.5 million in '06.

"Will the deal keep George Steinbrenner from buying the top players on the free-agent market even if it costs his New York Yankees an extra $50 mil in taxes?

professor at the University of Miami, told the *Miami Herald*, 'In our increasingly entertainment- and consumer-driven society, people look to sporting venues as places of community interaction. Stadiums have become sites where people share a sense of national identity.' That's a contribution, ladies and gentlemen, of which you should all be proud.

"Of course, just as sports influenced the public after the attacks, so too did the public influence sports. Does anyone believe our altered perspective didn't help prevent the sixth strike and ninth work stoppage in baseball since 1972? Again, Professor Bachin speaks: 'This time people were reluctant to feel any sympathy for what they perceived as the pettiness of the players and the owners compared to what really

JOHN BIEVER

Even Bryant (8) and Kidd (5) could not stop a huge ratings dip for the NBA Finals.

Does it mean a small-market team like the Pittsburgh Pirates—who suffered a 26% decrease in attendance one year after opening their new PNC Park—will spend its revenue-sharing windfall on keeping top young talent and not on servicing debt? Can it halt the declining viewership among kids 8 to 17? We won't know the answer to those and other questions for years, but we do know what reaching a settlement meant.

As David Carter of the Los Angeles-based Sports Business Group put it as the sides shook hands on Aug. 30, 'All they did today was avoid decimating the sport.'

"Still, financial decimation has taken place in the sports world, and I mean that in the global sense. The media giants that funded the soccer explosion in Europe fell on hard times, taking futbol with them. KirchMedia in Germany went bankrupt in April; three months later it renegotiated its $1.5 billion deal with the Bundesliga, cutting its annual payments by 25%. Around the same time Britain's ITV Digital collapsed, and with it went $271 million owed to British clubs. Instead of ITV's $160 million yearly payments, the teams will have to settle for $36 million from

News Corp.'s BSkyB. Hardest hit was the free-spending Serie A in Italy, where the pay-TV networks Stream and Telepiu—a subsidiary of debt-ridden, crisis-wracked Vivendi Universal in France—lost a combined $590 million last year and balked at paying hefty broadcast fees. The start of the season was delayed nine days until the richer clubs agreed to fork over $5.9 million to the poorer ones. And when the season did begin, it kicked off without World Cup hero Ronaldo of Brazil, who left Inter Milan and worked out a $44 million transfer to Real Madrid.

"The TV sports market in this country was a tough sell as well. In addition to an advertising market dip, there was the sense that event coverage has lost its grip on the crowd at home. According to research done by CBS, the average TV sports audience fell from 8.7 million viewers in 1990 to 6.8 million in 2000, a 22% drop. That decline was amply evident in the NBA, whose regular-season ratings dropped 35% from 1997–98 to 2000–01. The league's partnership with NBC ended after 12 years, concluding with a Finals sweep by the Los Angeles Lakers of the New Jersey Nets that drew the lowest prime-time average since the Boston Celtics defeated the Houston Rockets in 1981.

"Somehow, though, commissioner David Stern cobbled a new six-year, $4.6 billion deal with the Walt Disney Co. (ABC and ESPN) and AOL Time Warner (TNT and a possible new network). The average annual payout of $765 million was a 25% increase over the previous contract, but only 15 NBA games will air each year on network TV, as opposed to 33 in 2001–02. The NBA's arrival on ESPN will also decrease exposure there for the NHL, whose Stanley Cup ratings in 2002 were up 9% over the previous year's series.

"Not even the mighty NFL was immune to the changes in the marketplace. For their new stadium, the Super Bowl champion New England Patriots had signed a 15-year, $114 million naming rights contract with technology holding company CMGI. That was before the Internet bubble burst and CMGI's stock plunged from $163 a share in January 2000 to pocket change in 2002. Fortunately for New England, after a seven-month search Gillette came to the rescue, striking a 15-year deal only a few weeks before the 2002 NFL season started.

The St. Louis Rams, too, had one company, Edward Jones investments, pick up where another bankrupt one, TWA, left off. But the Baltimore Ravens (PSINet) and the Tennessee Titans (Adelphia) parted ways with their impoverished sponsors and have yet to find replacements. The Carolina Panthers announced that they will sever ties with struggling Ericsson, and have no new partner in sight; and the Seattle Seahawks and New Orleans Saints have failed to acquire even initial sponsorships. (I could go on at length about the ballpark formerly known as Enron Field, the Astros' Minute Maid Park, but, on the advice of counsel, I won't.)

"The one truly thriving sport in the United States is NASCAR, which continues to capitalize on its mix of high-intensity races, savvy public relations and ubiquitous decals. Retail sales of its licensed products have gone up from $80 million in 1990 to $1.34 billion in 2001, and only the NFL gets better TV ratings. NASCAR's emergence and new forms of sponsorship, such as virtual ads that appear only on TV, will help grease sports' engine in these troubled times. Not to mention more innovative approaches, such as the ink-drawn, washable tattoos appearing recently on boxers' torsos. As the architect of that idea, boxing agent Joe Lear, told the *Washington Times*, 'Sports is a much different business today. It's all changing. What I'm trying to do is give these boxers an opportunity to go out and tap into an untapped source of income, take more charge of themselves and, yes, build a business for myself.'

"That's the kind of entrepreneurship that should inspire us all, especially those of us who have mounting legal costs and a host of liens and are often asked to appear on TV to defend our case.... Hey, anybody here got a really thick felt-tip pen?"

Baseball Directory

Major League Baseball
Address: 245 Park Avenue
             New York, NY 10167
Telephone: (212) 931-7800
Commissioner: Bud Selig
Chief Operating Officer: Robert DuPuy
Senior VP, Public Relations: Richard Levin
www.majorleague baseball.com

Major League Baseball Players Association
Address: 12 East 49th Street, 24th Floor
             New York, NY 10017
Telephone: (212) 826-0808
Executive Director: Donald Fehr
Director of Communications: Greg Bouris
Director of Licensing: Judy Heeter
www.bigleaguers.com

Anaheim Angels
Address: P.O. Box 2000
             Anaheim, CA 92803
Telephone: (714) 940-2000
Stadium (Capacity): Edison International Field of
  Anaheim (45,050)
Owner: Walt Disney Company
General Manager: Bill Stoneman
Manager: Mike Scioscia
Vice President of Communications: Tim Mead
www.angelsbaseball.com

Arizona Diamondbacks
Address: 401 East Jefferson Street
             Phoenix, AZ 85004
Telephone: (602) 462-6500
Stadium (Capacity): Bank One Ballpark (49,033)
Managing General Partner: Jerry Colangelo
General Manager: Joe Garagiola Jr.
Manager: Bob Brenly
Director of Public Relations: Mike Swanson
www.azdiamondbacks.com

Atlanta Braves
Address: P.O. Box 4064
             Atlanta, GA 30302
Telephone: (404) 522-7630
Stadium (Capacity): Turner Field (50,091)
Vice Chrmn./Sr. Advisor of Time Warner/AOL: Ted Turner
Executive VP & General Manager: John Schuerholz
Manager: Bobby Cox
Director of Public Relations: Jim Schultz
www.atlantabraves.com

Baltimore Orioles
Address: Oriole Park at Camden Yards
             333 W Camden Street
             Baltimore, MD 21201
Telephone: (410) 685-9800
Stadium (Capacity): Oriole Park at Camden Yards
  (48,876)
Chairman of the Board/CEO: Peter G. Angelos
Vice Chairman/COO: Joseph E. Foss
Manager: Mike Hargrove
Director of Public Relations: Bill Stetka
www.theorioles.com

Boston Red Sox
Address: 4 Yawkey Way
             Fenway Park
             Boston, MA 02215
Telephone: (617) 267-9440
Stadium (Capacity): Fenway Park (33,993)
Principal Owner: John W. Henry
VP Baseball Operations/GM: Michael D. Port
Manager: Grady Little
Director of Communications/Baseball Info: Kevin Shea
www.redsox.com

Chicago Cubs
Address: Wrigley Field
             1060 West Addison
             Chicago, IL 60613
Telephone: (773) 404-2827
Stadium (Capacity): Wrigley Field (39,111)
President and CEO: Andrew B. MacPhail
Executive VP of Business Operations: Mark McGuire
Manager: TBA
Director of Media Relations: Sharon Panozzo
www.cubs.com

Chicago White Sox
Address: Comiskey Park
             333 West 35th Street
             Chicago, IL 60616
Telephone: (312) 674-1000
Stadium (Capacity): Comiskey Park (47,098)
Chairman: Jerry Reinsdorf
General Manager: Kenny Williams
Manager: Jerry Manuel
Director of Publc Relations: Scott Reifert
www.whitesox.com

Cincinnati Reds
Address: 100 Main Street
             Cincinnati, OH 45202
Telephone: (513) 765-7000
Stadium (Capacity): Great American Ball Park
  (42,000)
CEO/General Partner: Carl Lindner
COO: John L. Allen
General Manager: James G. Bowden
Managing Executive: John L. Allen
Manager: Bob Boone
Director of Media Relations: Rob Butcher
www.cincinnatireds.com

Cleveland Indians
Address: Jacobs Field
             2401 Ontario Street
             Cleveland, OH 44115-4003
Telephone: (216) 420-4200
Stadium (Capacity): Jacobs Field (43,368)
President and CEO: Lawrence J. Dolan
Executive VP and General Manager: Mark Shapiro
Manager: Joel Skinner
Vice President, Public Relations: Bob DiBiasio
www.indians.com

Colorado Rockies
Address: 2001 Blake Street
             Denver, CO 80205
Telephone: (303) 292-0200
Stadium (Capacity): Coors Field (50,449)
Chairman: Jerry D. McMorris
President: Keli McGregor
General Manager and Executive VP: Dan O'Dowd
Manager: Clint Hurdle
Senior Director of Communications/PR: Jay Alves
www.coloradorockies.com

Detroit Tigers
Address: Comerica Park
             2100 Woodward Avenue
             Detroit, MI 48201
Telephone: (313) 962-4000
Stadium (Capacity): Comerica Park (40,120)
Owner: Mike Ilitch
President and GM: Dave Dombrowski
Manager: Alan Trammell
Sr. V.P. of Marketing and Comm.: Mike Veeck
www.detroittigers.com

Florida Marlins
Address: 2267 Dan Marino Boulevard
             Miami, FL 33056
Telephone: (305) 626-7400
Stadium (Capacity): Pro Player Stadium (36,331)
Chairman, CEO and Managing General Partner:
Jeffrey H. Loria
President: David Samson
Senior VP and General Manager: Larry Beinfest
Manager: Jeff Torborg
VP of Communications/Broadcasting:P.J. Loyello
www.floridamarlins.com

Houston Astros
Address: P.O. Box 288
             Houston, TX 77001
Telephone: (713) 259-8000
Stadium (Capacity): Minute Maid Park (40,950)
Chairman: Drayton McLane
General Manager: Gerry Hunsicker
Manager: Jimy Williams
Director of Media Relations: Warren Miller
www.astros.com

Kansas City Royals
Address: P.O. Box 419969
             Kansas City, MO 64141
Telephone: (816) 921-8000
Stadium (Capacity): Kauffman Stadium (40,793)
Owner and Chairman of the Board: David D. Glass
General Manager: Allard Baird
Manager: Tony Peña
Vice President, Communications: Charlie Seraphin
www.kcroyals.com

Los Angeles Dodgers
Address: 1000 Elysian Park Avenue
             Los Angeles, CA 90012-1199
Telephone: (323) 224-1500
Stadium (Capacity): Dodger Stadium (56,000)
Managing Partner, Chairman and CEO: Robert Daly
President and COO: Bob Graziano
General Manager: Dan Evans
Manager: Jim Tracy
Director Media Relations/Publicity: John Olguin
www.dodgers.com

Milwaukee Brewers
Address: 1 Brewers Way
             Milwaukee, WI 53214
Telephone: (414) 902-4400
Stadium (Capacity): Miller Park (41,900)
President: Ulice Payne
General Manager: Doug Melvin
Manager: TBA
Director of Media Relations: Jon Greenberg
www.milwaukeebrewers.com

Minnesota Twins
Address: 34 Kirby Puckett Place
             Minneapolis, MN 55415
Telephone: (612) 375-1366
Stadium (Capacity): Hubert H. Humphrey
  Metrodome (48,678)
Owner: Carl Pohlad
General Manager: Terry Ryan
Manager: Ron Gardenhire
Manager of Media Relations: Sean Harlin
www.twinsbaseball.com

Montreal Expos
Address: P.O. Box 500 Station M
             Montreal, Quebec H1V 3P2 Canada
Telephone: (514) 253-3434
Stadium (Capacity): Olympic Stadium (46,500)
President: Tony Tavares

Montreal Expos *(Cont.)*
Vice President and General Manager: Omar Minaya
Manager: Frank Robinson
Director, Media Services: Monique Giroux
www.montrealexpos.com

New York Mets
Address: Shea Stadium
             123-01 Roosevelt Ave.
             Flushing, NY 11368
Telephone: (718) 507-6387
Stadium (Capacity): Shea Stadium (56,749)
Owner: Fred Wilpon
Senior VP and General Manager: Steve Phillips
Manager: TBA
VP of Media Relations: Jay Horwitz
www.mets.com

New York Yankees
Address: Yankee Stadium
             Bronx, NY 10451
Telephone: (718) 293-4300
Stadium (Capacity): Yankee Stadium (57,746)
Principal Owner: George Steinbrenner
Chief Operating Officer: Lonn Trost
VP/General Manager: Brian Cashman
Manager: Joe Torre
Director of Media Relations: Rick Cerone
www.yankees.com

Oakland Athletics
Address: 7000 Coliseum Way
             Oakland, CA 94621
Telephone: (510) 638-4900
Stadium (Capacity): Network Associates Coliseum
(43,662)
Owners: Steve Schott and Ken Hofmann
President: Michael Crowley
General Manager: Billy Beane
Manager: Art Howe
Baseball Information Manager: Mike Selleck
www.oaklandathletics.com

Philadelphia Phillies
Address: P.O. Box 7575
             Philadelphia, PA 19101-7575
Telephone: (215) 463-6000
Stadium (Capacity): Veterans Stadium (62,418)
Chairman: Bill Giles
President: David P. Montgomery
Vice President and General Manager: Ed Wade
Manager: Larry Bowa
Vice President, Public Relations: Larry Shenk
www.phillies.com

Pittsburgh Pirates
Address: P.O. Box 7000
             Pittsburgh, PA 15212
Telephone: (412) 323-5000
Stadium (Capacity): PNC Park (37,898)
CEO and Managing General Partner: Kevin McClatchy
Senior VP and General Manager: Dave Littlefield
Manager: Lloyd McClendon
Director of Media Relations: Jim Trdinich
www.pirateball.com

St. Louis Cardinals
Address: Busch Stadium/ 250 Stadium Plaza
             St. Louis, MO 63102
Telephone: (314) 421-3060
Stadium (Capacity): Busch Stadium (49,814)
President: Mark Lamping
Senior Vice President and GM: Walt Jocketty
Manager: Tony LaRussa
Director of Media Relations: Brian Bartow
www.stlcardinals.com

San Diego Padres
Address: P.O. Box 122000
             San Diego, CA 92112
Telephone: (619) 283-4494
Stadium (Capacity): Qualcomm Stadium (66,307)
Chairman: John Moores
General Manager: Kevin Towers
Manager: Bruce Bochy
Director of Media Relations: TBA
www.padres.com

San Francisco Giants
Address: 24 Willie Mays Plaza
             San Francisco, CA 94107
Telephone: (415) 972-2000
Stadium (Capacity): Pacific Bell Park (41,341)
President/Managing General Partner: Peter Magowan
General Manager: Brian Sabean
Manager: Dusty Baker
Manager of Media Relations: Jim Moorehead
www.sfgiants.com

Seattle Mariners
Address: P.O. Box 4100
             Seattle, WA 98104
Telephone: (206) 346-4000
Stadium (Capacity): SAFECO Field (47,116)
Chairman and CEO: Howard Lincoln
General Manager: Pat Gillick
Manager: TBA
Director of Baseball Information: Tim Hevly
www.seattlemariners.com

Tampa Bay Devil Rays
Address: One Tropicana Drive
             St. Petersburg, FL 33705
Telephone: (727) 825-3137
Stadium (Capacity): Tropicana Field (43,761)
Managing General Partner/CEO: Vincent J. Naimoli
Senior VP and General Manager: Chuck Lamar
Manager: TBA
Vice President, Public Relations: Rick Vaughn
www.devilray.com

Texas Rangers
Address: P.O. Box 90111
             Arlington, TX 76004
Telephone: (817) 273-5222
Stadium (Capacity): The Ballpark in Arlington (49,115)
Owner: Thomas O. Hicks
General Manager: John Hart
Manager: Buck Showalter
Senior VP, Communications: John Blake
www.texasrangers.com

Toronto Blue Jays
Address: SkyDome
             1 Blue Jays Way, Suite 3200
             Toronto, Ontario M5V 1J1 Canada
Telephone: (416) 341-1000
Stadium (Capacity): SkyDome (45,100)
President/CEO: Paul Godfrey
Senior Vice President/GM: J.P. Ricciardi
Manager: Carlos Tosca
Directo of Communications: Jay Stenhouse
www.bluejays.com

Pro Football Directory

National Football League
Address: 280 Park Avenue
             New York, NY 10017
Telephone: (212) 450-2000
Commissioner: Paul Tagliabue
www.nfl.com

NFL Players Association
Address: 2021 L Street, N.W.
             Washington, D.C. 20036
Telephone: (202) 463-2200
Executive Director: Gene Upshaw
Director of Communications: Carl Francis
www.nflpa.org

Arizona Cardinals
Address: P.O. Box 888
             Phoenix, AZ 85001
Telephone: (602) 379-0101
Stadium (Capacity): Sun Devil Stadium (73,377)
President and Owner: Bill Bidwill
General Manager: Bob Ferguson
Head Coach: Dave McGinnis
Director of Public Relations: Paul Jensen
www.azcardinals.com

Atlanta Falcons
Address: 4400 Falcon Park Way
             Flowery Branch, GA 30542
Telephone: (770) 965-3115
Stadium (Capacity): Georgia Dome (71,149)
Chairman, President and CEO: Arthur Blank
VP of Football Operations: Ron Hill
Coach: Dan Reeves
Director of Communications: Aaron Salkin
www.atlantafalcons.com

Baltimore Ravens
Address: 11001 Owings Mills Blvd.
             Owings Mills, MD 21117
Telephone: (410) 654-6200
Stadium (Capacity): Ravens Stadium (69,084)
Owner/CEO: Art Modell
President/COO: David Modell
Coach: Brian Billick
VP of Public Relations: Kevin Byrne
www.baltimoreravens.com

Buffalo Bills
Address: One Bills Drive
             Orchard Park, NY 14127
Telephone: (716) 648-1800
Stadium (Capacity): Ralph Wilson Stadium (73,967)
Chairman: Ralph C. Wilson Jr.
President and General Manager: Tom Donohoe
Coach: Gregg Williams
Vice President of Communications: Scott Berchtold
www.buffalobills.com

Carolina Panthers
Address:.   Ericsson Stadium
             800 South Mint St.
             Charlotte, NC 28202
Telephone: (704) 358-7000
Stadium (Capacity): Ericsson Stadium (73,250)
Founder and Owner: Jerry Richardson
President: Mark Richardson
General Manager: Marty Hurney
Coach: John Fox
Director of Communications: Charlie Dayton
www.panthers.com

Chicago Bears
Address: 1000 Football Drive
Lake Forest, IL 60045
Telephone: (847) 295-6600
Stadium (Capacity): Memorial Stadium (70,904)
Chairman: Michael McCaskey
President/CEO: Ted Phillips
Coach: Dick Jauron
Director of Public Relations: Scott Hagel
www.chicagobears.com

Cincinnati Bengals
Address: One Paul Brown Stadium
Cincinnati, OH 45202
Telephone: (513) 621-3550
Stadium (Capacity): Paul Brown Stadium (65,341)
President: Mike Brown
Executive Vice President: Katherine Blackburn
Coach: Dick LeBeau
Director of Public Relations: Jack Brennan
www.bengals.com

Cleveland Browns
Address: 76 Lou Groza Boulevard
Berea, OH 44017
Telephone: (440) 891-5000
Stadium (Capacity): Cleveland Browns Stadium (73,200)
Owner: Alfred Lerner
Director of Football Development: Pete Garcia
Coach: Butch Davis
Exec. Director of Publicity/Media Rel.: Todd Stewart
www.clevelandbrowns.com

Dallas Cowboys
Address: One Cowboys Parkway
Irving, TX 75063
Telephone: (972) 556-9900
Stadium (Capacity): Texas Stadium (65,639)
Owner, President and General Manager: Jerry Jones
Coach: Dave Campo
Public Relations Director: Rich Dalrymple
www.dallascowboys.com

Denver Broncos
Address: 13655 Broncos Parkway
Englewood, CO 80112
Telephone: (303) 649-9000
Stadium (Capacity): INVESCO Field at Mile High (76,125)
President and Chief Executive Officer: Pat Bowlen
General Manager: Ted Sundquist
Coach: Mike Shanahan
VP of Public Relations: Jim Saccomano
www.denverbroncos.com

Detroit Lions
Address: 222 Republic Drive
Allen Park, MI 48101
Telephone: (313) 216-4000
Stadium (Capacity): Ford Field (65,000)
Owner/Chairman: William Clay Ford
President/CEO: Matt Millen
Coach: Marty Mornhinweg
Director of Media Relations: Matt Barnhart
www.detroitlions.com

Green Bay Packers
Address: 1265 Lombardi Avenue
Green Bay, WI 54304
Telephone: (920) 496-5700
Stadium (Capacity): Lambeau Field (65,290)
President: Bob Harlan
Executive VP/GM/Coach: Mike Sherman
Executive Director of Public Relations: Lee Remmel
www.packers.com

Houston Texans
Address: Two Reliant Park
Houston, TX 77054
Telephone: (832) 667-2000
Stadium (Capacity): Reliant Stadium (69,500)
Chairman and CEO: Robert C. McNair
Senior VP and General Manager: Charley Casserly
Coach: Dom Capers
Director of Media Relations: Brent Williamson
www.houstontexans.com

Indianapolis Colts
Address: P.O. Box 535000
Indianapolis, IN 46253
Telephone: (317) 297-2658
Stadium (Capacity): RCA Dome (56,127)
Owner and Chief Executive Officer: Jim Irsay
President: Bill Polian
Senior Executive Vice President: Pete Ward
Coach: Tony Dungy
Vice President of Public Relations: Craig Kelley
www.colts.com

Jacksonville Jaguars
Address: One Alltel Stadium Place
Jacksonville, FL 32202
Telephone: (904) 633-6000
Stadium (Capacity): Alltel Stadium (73,000)
Owner: J. Wayne Weaver
Vice President and CFO: Bill Prescott
Senior VP of Football Operations: Paul Vance
Coach: Tom Coughlin
Executive Director of Communications: Dan Edwards
www.jaguars.com

Kansas City Chiefs
Address: One Arrowhead Drive
Kansas City, MO 64129
Telephone: (816) 920-9300
Stadium (Capacity): Arrowhead Stadium (79,451)
Founder: Lamar Hunt
CEO, President and General Manager: Carl Peterson
Coach: Dick Vermeil
Public Relations Director: Bob Moore
www.kcchiefs.com

Miami Dolphins
Address: 7500 S.W. 30th Street
Davie, FL 33314
Telephone: (954) 452-7000
Stadium (Capacity): Pro Player Stadium (75,540)
Chairman of the Board/Owner: H. Wayne Huizenga
Sr. VP Football Ops/Player Personnel: Rick Spielman
Head Coach: Dave Wannstedt
Senior VP Media Relations: Harvey Greene
www.miamidolphins.com

Minnesota Vikings
Address: 9520 Viking Drive
Eden Prairie, MN 55344
Telephone: (952) 828-6500
Stadium (Capacity): HHH Metrodome (64,121)
Owner: Red McCombs
President: Gary Woods
Coach: Mike Tice
Public Relations Director: Bob Hagan
www.vikings.com

New England Patriots
Address: Gillette Stadium
1 Patriot Place, Foxboro, MA 02035
Telephone: (508) 543-8200
Stadium (Capacity): Foxboro Stadium (68,436)
Owner and Chairman: Robert K. Kraft
Vice Chairman: Jonathan Kraft
Coach: Bill Belichick
VP of Corporate/Community Affairs: Meg Vaillancourt
www.patriots.com

New Orleans Saints
Address: 5800 Airline Highway
        Metairie, LA 70003
Telephone: (504) 733-0255
Stadium (Capacity): Louisiana Superdome (68,390)
Owner: Tom Benson
GM of Football Operations: Mickey Loomis
Head Coach: Jim Haslett
Director of Media Relations: Greg Bensel
www.neworleanssaints.com

New York Giants
Address: Giants Stadium
        East Rutherford, NJ 07073
Telephone: (201) 935-8111
Stadium (Capacity): Giants Stadium (79,469)
President and co-CEO: Wellington T. Mara
Chairman and co-CEO: Preston Robert Tisch
Senior VP and General Manager: Ernie Accorsi
Coach: Jim Fassel
Vice President of Communications: Pat Hanlon
www.giants.com

New York Jets
Address: 1000 Fulton Avenue
        Hempstead, NY 11550
Telephone: (516) 560-8100
Stadium (Capacity): Giants Stadium (80,062)
Owner: Robert Wood Johnson IV
Director of Player Personnel: Jesse Kaye
Coach: Herman Edwards
VP of Public Relations: Ron Colangelo
www.newyorkjets.com

Oakland Raiders
Address: 1220 Harbor Bay Parkway
        Alameda, CA 94502
Telephone: (510) 864-5000
Stadium (Capacity): Network Assoc. Coliseum (63,132)
President of the General Partner: Al Davis
Coach: Bill Callahan
Executive Assistant: Al LoCasale
Director of Public Relations: Mike Taylor
www.raiders.com

Philadelphia Eagles
Address: NovaCare Complex
        1 NovaCare Way
        Philadelphia, PA 19145
Telephone: (215) 463-2500
Stadium (Capacity): Veterans Stadium (65,352)
Chairman: Jeffrey Lurie
Exec. VP of Football Operations/Coach: Andy Reid
Football Media Services Coordinator: Derek Boyko
www.philadelphiaeagles.com

Pittsburgh Steelers
Address: 3400 South Water Street
        Pittsburgh, PA 15203
Telephone: (412) 432-7800
Stadium (Capacity): Heinz Field (64,350)
President: Dan Rooney
Director of Football Operations: Kevin Colbert
Coach: Bill Cowher
Director of Communications: Ron Wahl
www.steelers.com

St. Louis Rams
Address: One Rams Way
        St. Louis, MO 63045
Telephone: (314) 982-7267
Stadium (Capacity): Edward Jones Dome (66,000)
Owner and Chairman: Georgia Frontiere
President: John Shaw
Coach: Mike Martz
Director of Public Relations: Rick Smith
www.stlouisrams.com

San Diego Chargers
Address: Qualcomm Stadium
        4020 Murphy Canyon Road
        San Diego, CA 92123
Telephone: (858) 874-4500
Stadium (Capacity): Qualcomm Stadium (70,000)
Chairman: Alex G. Spanos
President and CEO: Dean A. Spanos
Executive VP and General Manager: John Butler
Coach: Marty Schottenheimer
Director of Public Relations: Bill Johnston
www.chargers.com

San Francisco 49ers
Address: 4949 Centennial Boulevard
        Santa Clara, CA 95054
Telephone: (408) 562-4949
Stadium (Capacity): 3Com Park (69,734)
Owner: Denise DeBartolo-York
President: Peter Harris
Director/Owner's Rep.: John York
General Manager: Terry Donahue
Coach: Steve Mariucci
Public Relations Director: Kirk Reynolds
www.49ers.com

Seattle Seahawks
Address: 11220 N.E. 53rd Street
        Kirkland, WA 98033
Telephone: (425) 827-9777
Stadium (Capacity): Seahawks Stadium (67,000)
Owner: Paul Allen
President: Bob Whitsitt
Coach/GM: Mike Holmgren
VP of Administration and Communications: Gary Wright
Director of Public Relations: Dave Pearson
www.seahawks.com

Tampa Bay Buccaneers
Address: One Buccaneer Place
        Tampa, FL 33607
Telephone: (813) 870-2700
Stadium (Capacity): Raymond James Stadium (66,321)
Owner: Malcolm Glazer
General Manager: Rich McKay
Coach: Jon Gruden
Communications Manager: Jeff Kamis
www.buccaneers.com

Tennessee Titans
Address: 460 Great Circle Road
        Nashville, TN 37228
Telephone: 615-565-4000
Stadium (Capacity): The Coliseum (68,804)
President: Jeff Diamond
General Manager: Floyd Reese
Coach: Jeff Fisher
Director of Media Relations: Robbie Bohren
www.titansonline.com

Washington Redskins
Address: 21300 Redskins Park Drive
        Ashburn, VA 20147
Telephone: (703) 726-7000
Stadium (Capacity): Fedex Field (86,484)
Owner: Daniel M. Snyder
VP of Football Operations: Joe Mendes
Coach: Steve Spurrier
Director of Public Relations: Michelle Tessier
www.redskins.com

Other Leagues

Canadian Football League
Address: 50 Wellington Street East - 3rd Floor
              Toronto, Ontario M5E1C8 Canada
Telephone: (416) 322-9650
Acting Commissioner: David Braley
Senior VP, Business Operations/Treasurer: James E.
Grundy
VP of Communications: Shawn Lackie
www.cfl.ca

NFL EUROPE
Address: 280 Park Avenue
              New York, NY 10017
Telephone: (212) 450-2000
Managing Directrors: John Beake and Jim Connolly
Chief Operating Officer: Dan Margoshes (London)
Director of Communications: David Tossel
www.nfleurope.com

Pro Basketball Directory

National Basketball Association

National Basketball Association
Address: 645 Fifth Avenue
              New York, NY 10022
Telephone: (212) 826-7000
Commissioner: David Stern
Deputy Commissioner: Russell Granik
Sr. VP of Communications: Brian McIntyre
www.nba.com

National Basketball Association Players Association
Address: 1700 Broadway
              Suite 1400
              New York, NY 10019
Telephone: (212) 655-0880
Executive Director: William Hunter
www.nbapa.com

Atlanta Hawks
Address: One CNN Center
              Atlanta, GA 30303
Telephone: (404) 827-3800
Arena (Capacity): Philips Arena (19,445)
Owner: AOL/Time Warner
President: Stan Kasten
VP and General Manager: Pete Babcock
Coach: Lon Kruger
VP of Communications: Arthur Triche
www.hawks.com

Boston Celtics
Address: 151 Merrimac Street
              Boston, MA 02114
Telephone: (617) 523-6050
Arena (Capacity): FleetCenter (18,624)
Owner and Chairman of the Board: Paul Gaston
General Manager: Chris Wallace
Coach: Jim O'Brien
Director of Media Relations: Bill Bonsiewicz
www.celtics.com

Chicago Bulls
Address: 1901 W. Madison Street
              Chicago, IL 60612
Telephone: (312) 455-4000
Arena (Capacity): United Center (21,711)
Chairman: Jerry Reinsdorf
Executive VP of Basketball Operations: Jerry Krause
Coach: Bill Cartwright
Senior Director of Media Services: Tim Hallam
www.bulls.com

Cleveland Cavaliers
Address: One Center Court
              Cleveland, OH 44115
Telephone: (216) 420-2000
Arena (Capacity): Gund Arena (20,562)
Chairman: Gordon Gund
Senior VP and GM: Jim Paxson
Coach: John Lucas
Sr. Director of Communications/PR: Bob Price
www.cavs.com

Dallas Mavericks
Address: 2500 Victory Avenue
              Dallas, TX 75219
Telephone: (214) 665-4660
Arena (Capacity): American Airlines Center (19,200)
Owner: Mark Cuban
General Manager and Head Coach: Don Nelson
President of Basketball Operations: Donn Nelson
Sr. VP of Marketing/Communications: Matt Fitzgerald
www.dallasmavericks.com

Denver Nuggets
Address: Pepsi Center
              1000 Chopper Circle
              Denver, CO 80204
Telephone: (303) 405-1100
Arena (Capacity): Pepsi Center (19,099)
Owner: E. Stanley Kroenke
Coach: Jeff Bzdelik
Media Relations Director: Tommy Sheppard
www.nuggets.com

Detroit Pistons
Address: The Palace of Auburn Hills
              Two Championship Drive
              Auburn Hills, MI 48326
Telephone: (248) 377-0100
Arena (Capacity): The Palace of Auburn Hills (22,076)
Owner: William M. Davidson
President of Basketball Operations: Joe Dumars
Coach: Rick Carlisle
VP of Public Relations: Matt Dobek
www.palacenet.com

Golden State Warriors
Address: 1011 Broadway
              Oakland, CA 94607-4019
Telephone: (510) 986-2200
Arena (Capacity): The Arena in Oakland
  (19,596)
Owner and CEO: Christopher Cohan
General Manager: Garry St. Jean
Coach: Eric Musselman
Director of Public Relations: Raymond Ridder
www.gs-warriors.com

National Basketball Association *(Cont.)*

Houston Rockets
Address: Two Greenway Plaza, Suite 400
              Houston, TX 77046
Telephone: (713) 627-3865
Arena (Capacity): Compaq Center (16,285)
Owner: Leslie Alexander
Chief Operating Officer: George Postolos
General Manager: Carroll Dawson
Coach: Rudy Tomjanovich
Director of Team Communications: Nelson Luis
www.rockets.com

Indiana Pacers
Address: 125 S. Pennsylvania Street
              Indianapolis, IN 46204
Telephone: (317) 917-2500
Arena (Capacity): Conseco Fieldhouse (18,345)
Owners: Melvin Simon and Herbert Simon
President: Donnie Walsh
General Manager: David Kahn
Head Coach: Isiah Thomas
Media Relations Director: David Benner
www.pacers.com

Los Angeles Clippers
Address: The Staples Center
              1111 S. Figueroa Street - St. 1100
              Los Angeles, CA 90015
Telephone: (213) 742-7500
Arena (Capacity): The Staples Center (18,964)
Owner: Donald T. Sterling
Vice President of Basketball Operations: Elgin Baylor
Coach: Alvin Gentry
Vice President of Communications: Joe Safety
www.clippers.com

Los Angeles Lakers
Address: 555 North Nash Street
              El Segundo, CA 90245
Telephone: (310) 426-6000
Arena (Capacity): The Staples Center (18,997)
Owner: Dr. Jerry Buss
General Manager: Mitch Kupchak
Coach: Phil Jackson
Director of Public Relations: John Black
www.lakers.com

Memphis Grizzlies
Address: 175 Toyota Plaza - Suite 150
              Memphis TN 38103
Telephone: (901) 888-4667
Arena (Capacity): The Pyramid (19,423)
Majority Owner: Michael E. Heisley
President of Basketball Operations: Jerry West
General Manager: Dick Versace
Coach: Sidney Lowe
Director of Media Relations: Kirk Clayborn
www.grizzlies.com

Miami Heat
Address: American Airlines Arena
              601 Biscayne Boulevard
              Miami, FL 33132
Telephone: (786) 777-4328
Arena (Capacity): American Airlines Arena (16,500)
Managing General Partner: Micky Arison
President and Coach: Pat Riley
President/GM of Basketball Operations: Randy Pfund
VP of Sports Media Relations: Tim Donovan
www.heat.com

Milwaukee Bucks
Address: The Bradley Center
              1001 N. Fourth Street
              Milwaukee, WI 53203
Telephone: (414) 227-0500
Arena (Capacity): The Bradley Center (18,717)
Owner: Herb Kohl
General Manager: Ernie Grunfeld
Coach: George Karl
Public Relations Director: Cheri Hanson
www.bucks.com

Minnesota Timberwolves
Address: 600 First Avenue North
              Minneapolis, MN 55403
Telephone: (612) 673-1600
Arena (Capacity): Target Center (19,006)
Owner: Glen Taylor
VP of Basketball Operations: Kevin McHale
Coach: Phil (Flip) Saunders
Director of Communications: Kent Wipf
www.timberwolves.com

New Jersey Nets
Address: 390 Murray Hill Parkway
              East Rutherford, NJ 07073
Telephone: (201) 935-8888
Arena (Capacity): Continental Airlines Arena (20,049)
Principal Owner: Lewis Katz
President/General Manager: Rod Thorn
Coach: Byron Scott
Director of Public Relations: Gary Sussman
www.njnets.com

New Orleans Hornets
Address: 1501 Girod Street
              New Orleans, LA 70113
Telephone: (504) 301-4000
Arena (Capacity): New Orleans Arena (18,500)
Majority Owner: George Shinn
Co-Owner: Ray Wooldridge
Coach: Paul Silas
VP of Public Relations: Harold Kaufman
www.hornets.com

New York Knicks
Address: Madison Square Garden
              Two Pennsylvania Plaza
              New York, NY 10121
Telephone: (212) 465-5867
Arena (Capacity): Madison Square Garden (19,763)
Owner: ITT/Sheraton and Cablevision
Chairman of MSG/President and CEO of Cablevision:
James Dolan
Team President/General Manager: Scott Layden
Coach: Don Chaney
Vice President of Public Relations: Joe Favorito
www.nyknicks.com

National Basketball Association (Cont.)

Orlando Magic
Address: Two Magic Place
8701 Maitland Summit Blvd.
Orlando, FL 32810
Telephone: (407) 916-2400
Arena (Capacity): TD Waterhouse Centre (17,248)
Owner: Rich DeVos
Senior Executive Vice President: Pat Williams
General Manager: John Gabriel
Coach: Glenn "Doc" Rivers
Director of Communications: Joel Glass
www.orlandomagic.com

Philadelphia 76ers
Address: First Union Center
3601 South Broad Street
Philadelphia, PA 19148
Telephone: (215) 339-7600
Arena (Capacity): First Union Center (20,444)
Head Coach and Vice President of Basketball
Operations: Larry Brown
General Manager: Billy King
Executive Vice President: Dave Coskey
Senior Director of Communications: Karen Frascona
www.sixers.com

Phoenix Suns
Address: 201 East Jeffreson Street
Phoenix, AZ 85004
Telephone: (602) 379-7900
Arena (Capacity): America West Arena (19,023)
Chairman/CEO and Managing General Partner: Jerry
Colangelo
President and General Manager: Bryan Colangelo
Coach: Frank Johnson
VP of Basketball Communications: Julie Fie
www.suns.com

Portland Trail Blazers
Address: One Center Court
Suite 200
Portland, OR 97227
Telephone: (503) 234-9291
Arena (Capacity): Rose Garden Arena (19,980)
Chairman of the Board: Paul Allen
President and General Manager: Bob Whitsitt
Coach: Maurice Cheeks
Executive Director of Communications: Mike Hanson
www.blazers.com

Sacramento Kings
Address: One Sports Parkway
Sacramento, CA 95834
Telephone: (916) 928-0000
Arena (Capacity): ARCO Arena (17,317)
Owners: Joe and Gavin Maloof
President of Basketball Operations: Geoff Petrie
Coach: Rick Adelman
Director of Media Relations: Troy Hanson
www.kings.com

San Antonio Spurs
Address: SBC Center
100 Montana
San Antonio, TX 78203
Telephone: (210) 554-7787
Arena (Capacity): SBC Center (18,500)
Chairman: Peter Holt
General Manager: R.C. Buford
Head Coach : Gregg Popovich
Director of Media Services: Tom James
www.spurs.com

Seattle SuperSonics
Address: 351 Elliott Avenue West
Suite 500
Seattle, WA 98119
Telephone: (206) 281-5847
Arena (Capacity): KeyArena (17,072)
Owner: The Basketball Club of Seattle, LLC
Chairman: Howard Schultz
President/CEO: Wally Walker
General Manager: Rick Sund
Coach: Nate McMillan
Director of Public Relations: Marc Moquin
www.supersonics.com

Toronto Raptors
Address: 40 Bay Street, Suite 400
Toronto, Ontario M5J 2X2 Canada
Telephone: (416) 815-5600
Arena (Capacity): Air Canada Centre (19,800)
Owner: Maple Leaf Sports and Entertainment, Ltd.
Senior VP and General Manager: Glen Grunwald
Coach: Lenny Wilkens
Director of Media Relations: Jim Labumbard
www.raptors.com

Utah Jazz
Address: 301 West So. Temple
Salt Lake City, UT 84101
Telephone: (801) 325-2500
Arena (Capacity): Delta Center (19,911)
Owner: Larry H. Miller
President: Dennis Haslam
VP of Basketball Operations: Kevin O'Connor
Coach: Jerry Sloan
Director of Media Relations: Kim Turner
www.utahjazz.com

Washington Wizards
Address: 601 F Street NW
Washington D.C. 20004
Telephone: (202) 661-5000
Arena (Capacity): MCI Center (20,173)
Owner: Abe Pollin
General Manager and Vice President: Wes Unseld
Coach: Doug Collins
Director of Public Relations: Nicole Hawkins
www.nba.com/wizards

Women's National Basketball Association

Women's National Basketball Association

Address: 645 Fifth Avenue
New York, NY 10022
Telephone: (212) 688-9622
President: Valerie B. Ackerman
Director of Sports Communications: Maureen Coyle
www.wnba.com

Charlotte Sting

Address: 100 Hive Drive
Charlotte, NC 29217
Telephone: (704) 357-0252
Arena (Capacity): Charlotte Coliseum (12,843)
Executive Vice President: Sam Russo
Coach: Anne Donovan
Vice President of Public Relations: Harold Kaufman
www.charlottesting.com

Cleveland Rockers

Address: Gund Arena
One Center Court
Cleveland, OH 44115
Telephone: (216) 420-2000
Arena (Capacity): Gund Arena (20,500)
Chairman: Gordon Gund
President, Business Division: James C. Boland
Coach: Dan Hughes
Director of Media Relations: Ed Markey
www.clevelandrockers.com

Detroit Shock

Address: 2 Championship Drive
Auburn Hills, MI 48326
Telephone: (248) 377-0100
Arena (Capacity): The Palace of Auburn Hills (19,000)
Managing Partner: William Davidson
President: Tom Wilson
Head Coach: Bill Laimbeer
Director of Media Relations: Dennis Sampier
www.detroitshock.com

Houston Comets

Address: Two Greenway Plaza, Suite 400
Houston, TX 77046-3865
Telephone: (713) 627-9622
Arena (Capacity): The Compaq Center (16,285)
President: Leslie L. Alexander
Coach and General Manager: Van Chancellor
Director of Media Relations: Nelson Luis
www.houstoncomets.com

Indiana Fever

Address: 125 S. Pennsylvania Street
Indianapolis, IN 46204
Telephone: (317) 917-2500
Arena (Capacity): Conseco Field House (18,345)
President: Donnie Walsh
Chief Operating Officer: Kelly Kraus Koupf
Coach: Nell Fortner
Director of Media Relations: Tom Savage
www.wnba.com/fever

Los Angeles Sparks

Address: 555 Nash Street
El Segundo, CA 90245
Telephone: (310) 330-2434
Arena (Capacity): Staples Center (19,282)
Chairman: Dr. Jerry Buss
General Manager: Virginia (Penny) Toler

Los Angeles Sparks (Cont.)

Coach: Michael Cooper
Media Relations Director: Kristal Shipp
www.lasparks.com

Miami Sol

Address: American Airlines Arena
601 Biscayne Blvd.
Miami, FL 33132
Telephone: (786) 577-4328
Arena (Capacity): American Airlines Arena (10,412)
Senior Director of Operations: Kim Stone
General Manager/ Coach: Ron Rothstein
Media Relations Manager: Alan Hancock
www.miami-sol.com

Minnesota Lynx

Address: Target Center
600 First Avenue North
Minneapolis, MN 55403
Telephone: (612) 673-8400
Arena (Capacity): Target Center (19,006)
Chief Operating Officer: Roger Griffith
Coach: Heidi Vanderveer
Public Relations Manager: Mike Cristaldi
www.wnba.com/lynx/

New York Liberty

Address: Two Penn Plaza
New York, NY 10121
Telephone: (212) 465-5867
Arena (Capacity): Madison Square Garden (19,763)
GM and Vice President: Carol Blazejowski
Coach: Richie Adubato
VP of Marketing and Communications: Amy Scheer
www.nyliberty.com

Orlando Miracle

Address: Two Magic Place
8701 Maitland Summit Boulevard
Orlando, FL 32810
Telephone: (407) 916-2400
Arena (Capacity): TD Waterhouse Centre (17,306)
Chairman: Rich DeVos
President: Bob Van der Weide
Coach: Dee Brown
Director of Media Relations: Katherine Wu
www.orlandomiracle.com

Phoenix Mercury

Address: 201 East Jefferson Street
Phoenix, AZ 85004
Telephone: (602) 514-8333
Arena (Capacity): America West Arena (10,746)
Chairman and CEO: Jerry Colangelo
President: Bryan Colangelo
Coach: Linda Sharp
Media Relations Director: Tami Scott
www.phoenixmercury.com

Portland Fire

Address: One Center Court
Suite 150
Portland, OR 97227
Telephone: (503) 234-9291
Arena (Capacity): The Rose Garden (19,980)
Chairman: Paul Allen
Vice President of Business Operations: Sandi Bittler
Coach: TBA
Director of Communications: Jill Wiggins
www.firebasketball.com

Women's National Basketball Association *(Cont.)*

Sacramento Monarchs
Address: One Sports Parkway
           Sacramento, CA 95834
Telephone: (916) 455-4647
Arena (Capacity): ARCO Arena (17,317)
Owner: Maloof Family
President: John Thomas
General Manager: Jerry Reynolds
Coach: Maura McHugh
Manager of Media Relations: Kimberly Williams
www.sacramentomonarchs.com

Seattle Storm
Address: 351 Elliott Avenue West
           Suite 500
           Seattle, WA 98119
Telephone: (206) 281-5800
Arena (Capacity): Key Arena (12,000)
Owners: The Basketball Club of Seattle LLC
Chairman: Howard Schultz
Coach: TBA
Director, Public Relations: Valerie O'Neil
www.wnba.com/storm

Utah Starzz
Address: 301 W. South Temple
           Salt Lake City, UT 84101
Telephone: (801) 325-7827
Arena (Capacity): Delta Center (8,916)
Owner: Larry H. Miller
President: Dennis Haslam
Coach: Candi Harvey
Media Relations Manager: Erin Bodily
www.utahstarzz.com

Washington Mystics
Address: MCI Center
           601 F Street, NW
           Washington, DC 20004
Telephone: (202) 661-5000
Arena (Capacity): MCI Center (19,093)
Chairman: Abe Pollin
President: Susan O'Malley
Coach: Marianne Stanley
Director, Public Relations: Dyani Gordon
www.washingtonmystics.com

Hockey Directory

National Hockey League
Address: 1251 Avenue of the Americas
           47th floor
           New York, NY 10020-1198
Telephone: (212) 789-2000
Commissioner: Gary Bettman
President of NHL Enterprises: Ed Horne
Executive VP and Dir. of Hockey Operations: Colin Campbell
VP of Media Relations: Frank Brown
www.nhl.com

National Hockey League Players Association
Address: 777 Bay Street, Suite 2400
           Toronto, Ontario M5G 2C8 Canada
Telephone: (416) 313-2300
Executive Director: Bob Goodenow
www.nhlpa.com

Mighty Ducks of Anaheim
Address: Arrowhead Pond of Anaheim
           2695 Katella Avenue
           Anaheim, CA 92806
Telephone: (714) 940-2900
Arena (Capacity): Arrowhead Pond of Anaheim (17,174)
Chairman and Governor: Jay Rasulo
Senior VP and General Manager: Bryan Murray
Coach: Mike Babcock
Manager of Communications: Alex Gilchrist
www.mightyducks.com

Atlanta Thrashers
Address: 1 CNN Center
           P.O. Box 15538
           Atlanta, GA 30348
Telephone: (404) 827-5300
Arena (Capacity): Philips Arena (18,545)
Owner: AOL/Time Warner

Atlanta Thrashers *(Cont.)*
President and Governor: Stan Kasten
VP and General Manager: Don Waddell
Coach: Curt Fraser
Director of Public Relations: Tom Hughes
www.atlantathrashers.com

Boston Bruins
Address: One Fleet Center Place, Suite 250
           Boston, MA 02114-1303
Telephone: (617) 624-1900
Arena (Capacity): FleetCenter (17,565)
Owner and Governor: Jeremy M. Jacobs
Alternative Governor and President: Harry Sinden
VP/General Manager and Alt. Governor: Mike O'Connell
Coach: Robbie Ftorek
Director of Media Relations: Heidi Holland
www.bostonbruins.com

Buffalo Sabres
Address: HSBC Arena
           One Seymour H. Knox III Plaza
           Buffalo, NY 14203
Telephone: (716) 855-4100
Arena (Capacity): HSBC Arena (18,690)
General Manager: Darcy Regier
Coach: Lindy Ruff
VP of Communications: Michael Gilbert
www.sabres.com

Calgary Flames
Address: Pengrowth Saddledome
             555 Saddledome Rise, SE
             Calgary, Alberta T2G 2W1
Telephone: (403) 777-2177
Arena (Capacity): Pengrowth Saddledome (17,409)
Owners: Harley N. Hotchkiss, N. Murray Edwards,
Alvin G. Libin, Allan P. Markin, J.R. "Bud" McCaig,
Byron J.Seaman, Daryl K. Seaman
President and CEO: Ken King
VP/General Manager: Craig Button
Coach: Greg Gilbert
Director of Communications: Peter Hanlon
www.calgaryflames.com

Carolina Hurricanes
Address: 1400 Edwards Mill Road
             Raleigh, NC 27607
Telephone: (919) 467-7825
Arena (Capacity): RBC Center (18,730)
Owner: Peter Karmanos
CEO and General Manager: Jim Rutherford
VP/Assistant General Manager: Jason Karmanos
Coach: Paul Maurice
Media Relations Manager: Mike Sundheim
www.carolinahurricanes.com

Chicago Blackhawks
Address: United Center
             1901 W. Madison Street
             Chicago, IL 60612
Telephone: (312) 455-7000
Arena (Capacity): United Center (20,500)
President: William W. Wirtz
Senior Vice President: Robert Pulford
General Manager: Mike Smith
Coach: Brian Sutter
Executive Director of Communications: Jim DeMaria
www.chicagoblackhawks.com

Colorado Avalanche
Address: Pepsi Center
             1000 Chopper Circle
             Denver, CO 80204
Telephone: (303) 405-1100
Arena (Capacity): Pepsi Center (18,007)
Owner and Governor: E. Stanley Kroenke
Alt. Governor, President and General Manager: Pierre
Lacroix
Coach: Bob Hartley
VP of Communications and Team Services:
  Jean Martineau
www.coloradoavalanche.com

Columbus Blue Jackets
Address: 200 West Nationwide Boulevard
             Columbus, OH 43215
Telephone: (614) 246-4625
Arena (Capacity): Nationwide Arena (18,136)
Owner: John H. McConnell
President and General Manager: Doug MacLean
Coach: Dave King
Director of Communications: Todd Sharrock
www.bluejackets.com

Dallas Stars
Address: 211 Cowboys Parkway
             Irving, TX 75063
Telephone: (972) 831-2401
Arena (Capacity): American Airlines Center (18,532)
Owner: Thomas O. Hicks
General Manager: Doug Armstrong

Dallas Stars *(Cont.)*
Coach: Dave Tippett
Director of Hockey Communications: Rob Scichili
www.dallasstars.com

Detroit Red Wings
Address: Joe Louis Arena
             600 Civic Center Drive
             Detroit, MI 48226
Telephone: (313) 396-7444
Arena (Capacity): Joe Louis Arena (20,056)
Owner and Governor: Mike Ilitch
Owner, Secretary and Treasurer: Marian Ilitch
Senior Vice President/Alt. Governor: Jim Devellano
General Manager: Ken Holland
Coach: Dave Lewis
Senior Director of Communications: John Hahn
www.detroitredwings.com

Edmonton Oilers
Address: 11230 110th Street
             Edmonton, Alberta T5G 3H7
Telephone: (780) 414-4000
Arena (Capacity): Skyreach Centre (16,839)
Owner: Edmonton Investors Group
Governor: Cal Nichols
President and Alt. Governor: Patrick LaForge
General Manager: Kevin Lowe
Coach: Craig MacTavish
VP of Public Relations, Hockey: Bill Tuele
www.edmontonoilers.com

Florida Panthers
Address: 1 Panther Parkway
             Sunrise, FL 33323
Telephone: (954) 835-7000
Arena (Capacity): Office Depot Center (19,250)
Chairman of the Board/CEO: Alan Cohen
Governor: William A. Torrey
General Manager: Rick Dudley
Coach: Mike Keenan
Director of Media Relations: Randy Sieminski
www.floridapanthers.com

Los Angeles Kings
Address: The Staples Center
             1111 South Figueroa Street
             Los Angeles, CA 90015
Telephone: (213) 742-7100
Arena (Capacity): The Staples Center (18,118)
Owners: Philip Anschutz and Edward P. Roske Jr.
President and Governor: Tim Leiweke
Vice President and GM: Dave Taylor
Coach: Andy Murray
Director of Media Relations: Mike Altieri
www.lakings.com

Minnesota Wild
Address: 317 Washington Street
             St. Paul, MN, 55102
Telephone: (651) 602-6000
Arena (Capacity): Excel Energy Center (18,064)
Chairman: Bob Naegele Jr.
General Manager: Doug Risebrough
Coach: Jacques Lemaire
VP of Communications/Broadcasting: Bill Robertson
www.wild.com

Montreal Canadiens

Address: Bell Centre
1260 de la Gauchetiere West
Montreal, Quebec H3B 5E8 Canada
Telephone: (514) 932-2582
Arena (Capacity): Bell Centre (21,273)
Owner: George N. Gillett Jr.
President and Governor: Pierre Boivin
General Manager: Andre Savard
Coach: Michel Therrien
Director of Communications: Donald Beauchamp
www.canadiens.com

Nashville Predators

Address: Gaylord Entertainment Center
501 Broadway
Nashville, TN 37203
Telephone: (615) 770-2300
Arena (Capacity): Gaylord Entertainment Center
(17,113)
Owner, Chairman and Governor: Craig Leipold
President, COO: Jack Diller
Executive VP of Hockey Operations/GM: David Poile
Coach: Barry Trotz
VP of Communications/Development: Gerry Helper
www.nashvillepredators.com

New Jersey Devils

Address: Continental Airlines Arena, PO Box 504
East Rutherford, NJ 07073
Telephone: (201) 935-6050
Arena (Capacity): Continental Airlines Arena (19,040)
Owners: Ray Chambers, Louis Katz and George
Steinbrenner
CEO, President and GM: Lou Lamoriello
Coach: Pat Burns
Director of Public Relations: Jeff Altstadter
www.newjerseydevils.com

New York Islanders

Address: 1535 Old Country Road
Plainview, NY 11803
Telephone: (516) 501-6700
Arena (Capacity): Nassau Coliseum (16,234)
Owners: Charles Wong and Sanjay Kumar
Senior VP of Operations and Alt. Governor: Michael J.
Picker
General Manager/Alt. Governor: Mike Milbury
Coach: Peter Laviolette
VP of Communications: Chris Botta
www.newyorkislanders.com

New York Rangers

Address: Madison Square Garden
2 Pennsylvania Plaza
New York, NY 10121
Telephone: (212) 465-6000
Arena (Capacity): Madison Square Garden (18,200)
Owner: Cablevision
President and General Manager: Glen Sather
Coach: Bryan Trottier
VP of Public Relations: John Rosasco
www.newyorkrangers.com

Ottawa Senators

Address: The Corel Centre
1000 Palladium Drive
Ottawa, Ontario K2V 1A5 Canada
Telephone: (613) 599-0250
Arena (Capacity): The Corel Centre (18,500)
Founder: Bruce M. Firestone
Chairman and Governor: Rod Bryden

Ottawa Senators (Cont.)

President and Chief Executive Officer: Roy Mlakar
General Manager: John Muckler
Coach: Jacques Martin
VP of Communications: Phil Legault
www.ottawasenators.com

Philadelphia Flyers

Address: First Union Center
3601 South Broad Street
Philadelphia, PA 19148
Telephone: (215) 465-4500
Arena (Capacity): First Union Center (19,523)
Majority Owner: Comcast Spectacor
Chairman: Ed Snider
President and General Manager: Bob Clarke
Coach: Ken Hitchcock
Director of Public Relations: Zack Hill
www.philadelphiaflyers.com

Phoenix Coyotes

Address: ALLTEL Ice Den
9375 East Belle Road
Scottsdale, AZ 85260
Telephone: (480) 473-5600
Arena (Capacity): America West Arena (16,210)
Chairman and Governor: Steve Ellman
Managing Partner and Alt. Governor: Wayne Gretzky
VP and General Manager: Michael Barnette
Coach: Bob Francis
VP of Media and Player Relations: Richard Nairn
www.phoenixcoyotes.com

Pittsburgh Penguins

Address: Mellon Arena
66 Mario Lemieux Place
Pittsburgh, PA 15219
Telephone: (412) 642-1300
Arena (Capacity): Mellon Arena (16,958)
Owner: Mario Lemieux (Lemieux Ownership Group)
General Manager: Craig Patrick
Coach: Rick Kehoe
Director of Media Relations: Steve Bovino
www.pittsburghpenguins.com

St. Louis Blues

Address: Savvis Center
1401 Clark Avenue
St. Louis, MO 63103
Telephone: (314) 622-2500
Arena (Capacity): Savvis Center (20,022)
President and Chief Executive Officer: Mark Sauer
Senior VP and General Manager: Larry Pleau
Coach: Joel Quenneville
Director of Media Relations: Frank Buomono
www.stlouisblues.com

San Jose Sharks

Address: HP Pavillion at San Jose
525 West Santa Clara Street
San Jose, CA 95113
Telephone: (408) 287-7070
Arena (Capacity): HP Pavillion at San Jose (17,496)
Owner: San Jose Sports And Entertainment
Enterprises
President and CEO: Greg Jamison
Executive VP and General Manager: Dean Lombardi
Coach: Darryl Sutter
Director of Media Relations: Ken Arnold
www.sjsharks.com

Tampa Bay Lightning

Address: 401 Channelside Drive
             Tampa, FL 33602
Telephone: (813) 301-6600
Arena (Capacity): Ice Palace (19,758)
Owner: Palace Sports & Entertainment/Bill Davidson and David Hermelin
CEO and Governor: Tom Wilson
President and Alt. Governor: Ron Campbell
General Manager: Jay Feaster
Coach: John Tortorella
VP of Public Relations: Bill Wickett
www.tampabaylightning.com

Toronto Maple Leafs

Address: Air Canada Centre
             40 Bay Street - St. 400
             Toronto, Ontario M5J 2X2 Canada
Telephone: (416) 815-5500
Arena (Capacity): Air Canada Centre (18,819)
Chairman of the Board: Steve A. Stavro
President: Ken Dryden
Coach/GM: Pat Quinn
Director of Media Relations: Pat Park
www.mapleleafs.com

Vancouver Canucks

Address: General Motors Place/800 Griffiths Way
             Vancouver, B.C. V6B 6G1
Telephone: (604) 899-4600
Arena (Capacity): General Motors Place (18,422)
Chairman and Governor: John E. McCaw Jr.
President and CEO: Stanley McCammon
Chief Operating Officer: David Cobb
President and GM: Brian Burke
Coach: Marc Crawford
Manager of Media Relations: Chris Brumwell
www.canucks.com

Washington Capitals

Address: 401 Ninth Street, NW
             Suite 750
             Washington, DC 20004
Telephone: (202) 266-2200
Arena (Capacity): MCI Center (18,672)
Majority Owner and Chairman: Ted Leonsis
Owner and President: Richard M. Patrick
VP and General Manager: George McPhee
Coach: Bruce Cassidy
Senior VP of Business Operations: Declan J. Bolger
www.washingtoncaps.com

Olympic Sports Directory

United States Olympic Committee

Address: Olympic House
             1 Olympic Plaza
             Colorado Springs, CO 80909
Telephone: (719) 632-5551
CEO: Lloyd Ward
Chief Communications Officer: Mike Moran
www.usolympicteam.com

U.S. Olympic Training Centers

Address: 1 Olympic Plaza
             Colorado Springs, CO 80909
Telephone: (719) 632-5551
Director: John Smith

Address: 421 Old Military Road
             Lake Placid, NY 12946
Telephone: (518) 523-2600
Director: Jack Favro

Address: 2800 Olympic Parkway
             Chula Vista, CA 91915
Telephone: (619) 656-1500
Director: Patrice Milkovich
www.olympic.org

International Olympic Committee

Address: Chateau de Vidy
             Case Postale 356
             CH-1007 Lausanne, Switzerland
Telephone: 41-21-621-6111
President: Jacques Rogge
Director General: Francois Carrard
www.olympic.org

Torino Olympic Organizing Committee for the 2006 Winter Games

Address: Via Nizza 262/58
             10126 Torino (Italy)
Telephone: 39 011 63 10 511
President: Valentino Castellani
Press Operations: Cristiano Carlutti
(XX Winter Games; Feb 10–26, 2006)
www.torino2006.org

Athens Olympic Organizing Committee for the 2004 Summer Games

Address: 7 Kifissias Avenue
             115 23 Athens, Greece
Telephone: 30 1 2004 000
President: Gianna Angelopoulos-Daskalaki
Head of Communications and Media: Serafim Kotrotsos
(XXVII Summer Games; Aug 11–29, 2004)
www.athens.olympic.org

U.S. Olympic Organizations

National Archery Association (NAA)

Address: 1 Olympic Plaza
             Colorado Springs, CO 80909
Telephone: (719) 866-4576
President: Mark Miller
Executive Director: Brad Camp
Media Relations: Desiree Freiherr
www.usarchery.org

USA Badminton (USAB)

Address: 1 Olympic Plaza
             Colorado Springs, CO 80909
Telephone: (719) 866-4808
President: Don Chew
Executive Director: Dan Cloppas
Media Contact: Barb Kissick
www.usabadminton.org

U.S. Olympic Organizations *(Cont.)*

USA Baseball
Address: Hi Corbett Field
            3400 East Camino Campestre
            Tucson, AZ 85716
Telephone: (520) 327-9700
Chairman: Lindsay Burbage
Executive Director/CEO: Paul V. Seiler
Director of Communications: David Fanucchi
www.usabaseball.com

USA Basketball
Address: 5465 Mark Dabling Blvd.
            Colorado Springs, CO 80918
Telephone: (719) 590-4800
President: Tom Jernstedt
Executive Director: Jim Tooley
Assistant Executive Director for Public Relations:
  Craig Miller
www.usabasketball.com

U.S. Biathlon Association (USBA)
Address: 29 Ethan Allen Avenue
            Colchester, VT 05446
Telephone: (802) 654-7833
President: Lyle Nelson
Executive Director: Stephen R. Sands
Media Contact: Anita Hall
www.usbiathlon.org

U.S. Bobsled and Skeleton Federation
Address: P.O. Box 828
            Lake Placid, NY 12946
Telephone: (518) 523-1842
President: Jim Morris
Executive Director: Matt Roy
Media and PR Director Director: Julie Urbansky
www.usabobsledandskeleton.org

USA Boxing, Inc.
Address: 1 Olympic Plaza
            Colorado Springs, CO 80909
Telephone: (719) 866-4506
President: Dr. Robert Voy
Executive Director: Eric Parthen
Director of PR and Media: Julie Goldsticker
www.usaboxing.org

U.S. Canoe and Kayak Team
Address: P.O. Box 789
            Lake Placid, NY 12946
Telephone: (518) 523-1855
Interim President: Anne Blanchard
Executive Director: Lisa Fish
Public Relations Director: Doug Haney
www.usacanoekayak.org

USA Cycling
Address: 1 Olympic Plaza
            Colorado Springs, CO 80909
Telephone: (719) 866-4581
President: Jim Ochowicz
Chief Executive Officer: Gerard Bisceglia
Director of Communications: Deborah Engen
www.usacycling.org

United States Diving, Inc. (USD)
Address: Pan American Plaza, Suite 430
            201 South Capitol Avenue
            Indianapolis, IN 46225
Telephone: (317) 237-5252
President: William Walker
Executive Director: Todd Smith
Director of Communications: Kelli Servizzi
www.usdiving.org

U.S. Equestrian Team (USET)
Address: Pottersville Rd.
            Gladstone, NJ 07934
Telephone: (908) 234-1251
Executive Director: Bonnie Jenkins
Director of Communications: Marty Bauman
www.uset.org

U.S. Fencing Association (USFA)
Address: 1 Olympic Plaza
            Colorado Springs, CO 80909
Telephone: (719) 866-4511
President: Stacey Johnson
Executive Director: Michael Massik
Media Relations Director: Cynthia Bent
www.usfencing.org

U.S. Field Hockey Association (USFHA)
Address: 1 Olympic Plaza
            Colorado Springs, CO 80909-5773
Telephone: (719) 866-4567
President: Sharon Taylor
Executive Director: Amy Frankenstein
Sport and Public Information Director:
  Howard Thomas
www.usfieldhockey.com

U.S. Figure Skating Association
Address: 20 First Street
            Colorado Springs, CO 80906
Telephone: (719) 635-5200
President: Phyllis Howard
Executive Director: John LeFevre
Communications Coordinator: Bob Dunlop
www.usfsa.org

USA Gymnastics
Address: Pan American Plaza, Suite 300
            201 South Capitol Avenue
            Indianapolis, IN 46225
Telephone: (317) 237-5050
Chairman of the Board: Ron Froehlich
President: Robert Colarossi
Director of Public Relations: Steve Penny
www.usa-gymnastics.org

USA Hockey
Address: 1775 Bob Johnson Drive
            Colorado Springs, CO 80906
Telephone: (719) 576-8724
President: Walter L. Bush, Jr.
Executive Director: Doug Palazzari
Manager of Media and PR: Heather Ahearn
www.usahockey.com

U.S. Olympic Organizations (Cont.)

United States Judo, Inc. (USJ)
Address:　1 Olympic Plaza Suite 202
　　　　　Colorado Springs, CO 80909
Telephone: (719) 866-4730
President: Dr. Ronald Tripp
Executive Director: William Rosenberg
www.usjudo.org

U.S. Luge Association (USLA)
Address:　35 Church Street
　　　　　Lake Placid, NY 12946
Telephone: (518) 523-2071
President: Doug Bateman
Executive Director: Ron Rossi
Public Relations Manager: Jon Lundin
www.usaluge.org

U.S. Modern Pentathlon Association
Address:　5407 Bandera Road - Suite 512
　　　　　San Antonio, TX 78238
Telephone: (210) 229-2004
President: Ralph Bender
Executive Director: Robert Marbut Jr.
www.usmpa.home.texas.net

U.S. Racquetball Association
Address:　1685 West Uintah
　　　　　Colorado Springs, CO 80904
Telephone: (719) 635-5396
President: Otto Dietrich
Executive Director: Jim Hiser
Public Relations Coordinator: Ryan John
www.usra.org

USA Roller Sports
Address:　4730 South Street
　　　　　P.O. Box 6579
　　　　　Lincoln, NE 68506
Telephone: (402) 483-7551
President: George Kolibaba
Communications Director: Bill Wolf
www.usacrs.com

U.S. Rowing
Address:　Pan American Plaza, Suite 400
　　　　　201 South Capitol Avenue
　　　　　Indianapolis, IN 46225
Telephone: (317) 237-5656/ 1 (800) 314-4769
Executive Director: John Dane
Press Contact: Brett Johnson
www.usrowing.org

U.S. Sailing Association
Address:　15 Maritime Drive
　　　　　P.O. Box 1260
　　　　　Portsmouth, RI 02871
Telephone: (401) 683-0800
President: Dave Rosekrans
Executive Director: Nick Craw
Communications Director: Penny Piva Rego
Olympic Yachting Director: Jonathan R. Harley
www.ussailing.org

USA Shooting
Address:　1 Olympic Plaza
　　　　　Colorado Springs, CO 80909
Telephone: (719) 866-4670
Chairman of the Board: Mike English
Executive Director: Robert K. Mitchell
Director of Marketing: Leaha Wirth
www.usashooting.com

U.S. Ski and Snowboard Association
Address:　P.O. Box 100
　　　　　Park City, UT 84060
Telephone: (435) 649-9090
Chairman: Jim McCarthy
President and CEO: Bill Marolt
V.P. of Communications and Media: Tom Kelly
www.usskiteam.com

U.S. Soccer Federation (USSF)
Address:　1801-1811 South Prairie Avenue
　　　　　Chicago, IL 60616
Telephone: (312) 808-1300
President: Robert Contiguglia
Secretary General: Dan Flynn
Director of Communications: Jim Moorhouse
www.us-soccer.com

Amateur Softball Association (ASA)
Address:　2801 N.E. 50th Street
　　　　　Oklahoma City, OK 73111
Telephone: (405) 424-5266
President: H. Franklin Taylor III
Executive Director: Ron Radigonda
Director of Communications: Brian McCall
www.softball.org

U.S. Speed Skating
Address:　P.O. Box 450639
　　　　　Westlake OH 44145
Telephone: (440) 899-0128
President: Fred Benjamin
Executive Director: Katie Marquard
Public Relations Director: Nick Paulenich
www.usspeedskating.org

U.S. Swimming, Inc. (USS)
Address:　1 Olympic Plaza
　　　　　Colorado Springs, CO 80909
Telephone: (719) 866-4578
President: Ron Van Pool
Executive Director: Chuck Wielgus
Public Relations Director: Mary Wagner
www.usa-swimming.org

U.S. Synchronized Swimming, Inc. (USSS)
Address:　Pan American Plaza, Suite 901
　　　　　201 South Capitol Avenue
　　　　　Indianapolis, IN 46225
Telephone: (317) 237-5700
President: Betty Hazle
Executive Director: Terry Harper
Media Relations: Brian Eaton
www.usasynchro.org

U.S. Table Tennis Association (USTTA)
Address:　1 Olympic Plaza
　　　　　Colorado Springs, CO 80909
Telephone: (719) 866-4583
Executive Director: TBA
President: Sheri Pittman
Director of Media and PR: Debbie Doney
www.usatt.org

U.S. Taekwondo Union (USTU)
Address:　1 Olympic Plaza, Suite 405
　　　　　Colorado Springs, CO 80909
Telephone: (719) 866-4632
President: Sang Lee
Executive Director: R. Jay Warwick
Media and Communications Director: Chris Condron
www.ustu.org

U.S. Olympic Organizations *(Cont.)*

USA Team Handball
Address: 1 Olympic Plaza
             Colorado Springs, CO 80909
Telephone: (719) 866-4036
President: Bob Djokovich
Executive Director: Mike Cavanaugh
www.usateamhandball.org

U.S. Tennis Association
Address: 70 West Red Oak Lane
             White Plains, NY. 10604
Telephone: (914) 696-7000
President: Mervin Heller
Executive Director: Richard D. Ferman
Director of Public Relations: Eric Handler
www.usta.com

USA Track & Field (formerly TAC)
Address: 1 RCA Dome, Suite 140
             Indianapolis, IN 46225
Telephone: (317) 261-0500
President: Bill Roe
Chief Executive Officer: Craig A. Masback
Director of Communications: Jill Geer
www.usatf.org

USA Volleyball
Address: 715 South Circle Drive
             Colorado Springs, CO 80910
Telephone: (719) 228-6800
President: Albert M. Monaco Jr.
Executive Director: Kerry Klostermann
Coordinator of Marketing and Comm.:Cecil Bleiker
www.usavolleyball.org

United States Water Polo (USWP)
Address: 1685 West Uintah
             Colorado Springs, CO 80904
Telephone: (719) 634-0699
President: Rich Foster
Executive Director: Bruce J. Wigo
Media Director: Eric Velazquez
www.usawaterpolo.com

USA Weightlifting
Address: 1 Olympic Plaza
             Colorado Springs, CO 80909
Telephone: (719) 866-4508
President: Dennis Snethen
Executive Director and Media Contact: Wesley
 Barnett
www.usaweightlifting.org

USA Wrestling
Address: 6155 Lehman Drive
             Colorado Springs, CO 80918
Telephone: (719) 598-8181
President: Bruce Baumgartner
Executive Director: Rich Bender
Director of Communications: Gary Abbott
www.usawrestling.org

Affiliated Sports Organizations

Amateur Athletic Union (AAU)
Address: Walt Disney World Resort; P.O. Box 22409
             Lake Buena Vista, FL 32830-1000
Telephone: (407) 934-7200
President: Bobby Dodd
Media Contact: Melissa Wilson
www.aausports.org

U.S. Curling Association (USCA)
Address: 1100 Center Point Drive
             P.O. Box 866
             Stevens Point, WI 54481
Telephone: (715) 344-1199
President: Jack McNelly
Executive Director: David Garber
Communications Director: Rick Patzke
www.usacurl.org

USA Karate Federation
Address: 1300 Kenmore Boulevard
             Akron, OH 44314
Telephone: (330) 753-3114
President: George Anderson
www.usakarate.org

U.S. Orienteering Federation
Address: P.O. Box 1444
             Forest Park, GA 30298
Telephone: (404) 363-2110
President: Chuck Ferguson
Executive Director: Robin Shannonhouse
Marketing and Public Relations VP: Sherry Litasi
Publicity telephone: (303) 694-4914
www.us.orienteering.org

U.S. Squash Racquets Association
Address: 23 Cynwyd Road
             P.O. Box 1216
             Bala Cynwyd, PA 19004
Telephone: (610) 667-4006
President: Eben Hardie III
Vice President: Kevin Jernigan
www.us-squash.org

USA Triathlon
Address: 616 West Monument Street
             Colorado Springs, CO 80905
Telephone: (719) 597-9090
President: Ray Plotecia
Executive Director: Steve Locke
Communications Director: B. J. Hoeptner Evans
www.usatriathlon.org

USA Waterski
Address: 1251 Holy Cow Road
             Polk City, FL 33868
Telephone: (863) 324-4341
President: Andrea Plough
Executive Director: Steve McDermeit
Public Relations Manager: Scott Atkinson
www.usawaterski.org

Championship Auto Racing Teams (CART)
Address: 5350 Lakeview Parkway South Drive
            Building 36 - Inner Park/Park 100
            Indianapolis, IN 46268
Telephone: (317) 715-4100
President and CEO: Christopher Pook
VP of Communications: Adam Saal
www.cart.com

Indy Racing League
Address: 4565 West 16th Street
            Indianapolis, IN 46222
Telephone: (317) 484-6526
President and Founder: Tony George
Director of Media Relations: Ron Green
www.indyracing.com

International Motor Sports Association
Address: 14175 Icot Blvd., Suite 300
            Clearwater, FL 33760
Telephone: (727) 533-0503
Managing Director: H. Doug Robinson
www.professionalsportscar.com

National Association for Stock Car Auto Racing (NASCAR)
Address: 1801 W International Speedway Blvd.
            Daytona Beach, FL 32114-1243
Telephone: (386) 253-0611
President: Mike Helton
VP of Corporate Communications: Jim Hunter
www.nascar.com

National Hot Rod Association
Address: 2035 East Financial Way
            Glendora, CA 91741
Telephone: (626) 914-4761
President: Tom Compton
VP of PR and Communications: Jerry Archambeault
www.nhra.com

Professional Women's Bowling Association
Address: 7171 Cherryvale Boulevard
            Rockford, IL 61112
Telephone: (815) 332-5756
Tournament Director: Fran Deken
Media Director: Gary Kohn
www.pwba.com

Professional Bowlers Association LLC
Address: 719 Second Avenue - Suite 701
            Seattle, WA 98104
Telephone: (206) 332-9688
Commissioner: TBA
Director of Corporate Communications: Beth Marshall
www.pba.com

U.S. Chess Federation
Address: 3054 Route 9 W
            New Windsor, NY 12553
Telephone: (845) 562-8350
President: R. John McCrary
Executive Director: George De Feis
Media Relations: Anne Ashton
www.uschess.org

International Game Fish Association
Address: 300 Gulf Stream Way
            Dania Beach, FL 33004
Telephone: (954) 927-2628
President: Mike Leech
www.igfa.org

Ladies Professional Golf Association
Address: 100 International Golf Drive
            Daytona Beach, FL 32124
Telephone: (386) 274-6200
Commissioner: Ty Votaw
Director of Media Relations: Connie Wilson
www.lpga.com

PGA Tour
Address: 112 PGA Tour Boulevard
            Ponte Vedra Beach, FL 32082
Telephone: (904) 285-3700
President: M.G. Orender
Senior VP of Communications: Bob Combs
www.pgatour.com

Professional Golfers' Association of America
Address: 100 Avenue of the Champions
            Box 109601
            Palm Beach Gardens, FL 33410-9601
Telephone: (561) 624-8400
President: Jack Connelly
Director of Public Relations: Julius Mason
www.pgaonline.com

United States Golf Association
Address: P.O. Box 708, Golf House
            Liberty Corner Road
            Far Hills, NJ 07931-0708
Telephone: (908) 234-2300
President: Dr. Trey Holland
Director of Communications: Craig Smith
www.usga.org

U.S. Handball Association
Address: 2333 North Tucson Boulevard
            Tucson, AZ 85716
Telephone: (520) 795-0434
President: Bob Hickman
Executive Director: Vern Roberts
Director of Public Relations: Mark Carpenter
www.ushandball.org

Breeders' Cup Limited
Address: 2525 Harrodsburg Road
            PO Box 4230
            Lexington, KY 40504
Telephone: (859) 223-5444
President: D. G. Van Clief Jr.
Media Relations Director: James Gluckson
Director of Marketing: Damon Thayer
www.breederscup.com

The Jockeys' Guild, Inc.
Address: P.O. Box 250
            Lexington, KY 40588-0250
Telephone: (859) 259-3211
Chairman of the Board: Tomey Swan
www.jockeysguild.com

Thoroughbred Racing Associations of America
Address: 420 Fair Hill Drive, Suite 1
            Elkton, MD 21921
Telephone: (410) 392-9200
President: Chris Scherf
www.tra-online.com

National Thoroughbred Racing Association

Address: 444 Madison Avenue, Suite 503
             New York, NY 10022
Telephone: (212) 907-9280
Senior VP/Mrkting & Industry Rels: Keith Chamblin
www.ntra.com

United States Trotting Association

Address: 750 Michigan Avenue
             Columbus, OH 43215
Telephone: (614) 224-2291
Executive Vice President: Fred J. Noe
Director of Publicity: John Pawlak
www.ustrotting.com

Iditarod Trail Committee

Address: P.O. Box 870800; Wasilla, AK 99687
Telephone: (907) 376-5155
Executive Director: Stan Hooley
Race Director: Joanne Potts
www.iditarod.com

U.S. Lacrosse

Address: 113 W University Parkway
             Baltimore, MD 21210
Telephone: (410) 235-6882
Executive Director: Steven B. Stenersen
www.lacrosse.org

Little League Baseball, Inc.

Address: P.O. Box 3485
             Williamsport, PA 17701
Telephone: (570) 326-1921
President & CEO: Stephen D. Keener
Communications & Marketing Director: Jud Rogers
www.littleleague.org

U.S. Polo Association

Address: 771 Corporate Drive, Suite 505
             Lexington, KY 40503
Telephone: (859) 219-1000
Executive Director: David Cummings
Media Contact: Merle Jenkins
www.uspolo.org

American Powerboating Association

Address: 17640 Nine Mile Road
             Eastpointe, MI 48021
Telephone: (586) 773-9700
Executive Administrator: Gloria Urbin
www.APBA.org

Professional Rodeo Cowboys Association

Address: 101 Pro Rodeo Drive
             Colorado Springs, CO 80919
Telephone: (719) 593-8840
Commissioner: Steven J. Hatchell
Director of Communications: Leslie King
www.prorodeo.com

USA Rugby Football Union

Address: 3595 East Fountain Boulevard
             Colorado Springs, CO 80910
Telephone: (719) 637-1022
President: Neal Brendel
Chair, Communications Committee: Patrick J. O'Connor
Chair, Collegiate & Membership Committee: Tam
  Breckenridge
www.usarugby.org

The United Soccer Leagues

Address: 14497 North Dale Mabry Highway, Ste 201
             Tampa, FL 33618
Telephone: (813) 963-3909
President and A-League Commissioner: Francisco
  Marcos
Director of Public Relations:Gerald Barnhart
www.unitedsoccerleagues.com

Major League Soccer

Address: 110 East 42nd Street, Suite 1000
             New York, NY 10017
Telephone: (212) 687-1400
Commissioner: Don Garber
Manager of Communications: Trey Fitzgerald
www.mlsnet.com

Major Indoor Soccer League

Address: 1175 Post Road East
             Westport, CT 06880
Telephone: (203) 222-4900
Commissioner: Steve Ryan
Director of Media Relations: Greg Bibb
www.misl.net

Women's United Soccer Association

Address: 6205 Peachtree Dunwoody Road
             Atlanta, GA 30328
Telephone: (678) 645-0800
Commissioner: Tony DiCicco
Director of Public Relations: Shaun May
www.wusa.com

Association of Tennis Professionals Tour

Address: 201 ATP Tour Boulevard
             Ponte Vedra Beach, FL 32082
Telephone: (904) 285-8000
Chief Executive Officer: Mark Miles
VP of Comm. and Media Relations: Greg Sharko
www.atptour.org

COREL WTA Tour (Women's Tennis)

Address: 133 First Street N.E.
             St. Petersburg, FL 33701
Telephone: (727) 895-5000
Chief Executive Officer: Kevin Wulff
Director of Communications: TBA
www.sanexwta.com

Association of Volleyball Professionals

Address: 1600 Rosecrans Avenue
             Suite 330, Building 7
             Manhattan Beach, CA 90266
Telephone: (310) 426-8000
Public Relations: Debbie Rubio, The Robbins Group
  (818) 776-1244
www.avptour.com

MINOR LEAGUES

Baseball (AAA)

National Association of Professional Baseball Leagues

Address: 201 Bayshore Drive S.E. - P.O. Box A
             St. Petersburg, FL 33731
Telephone: (727) 822-6937
President: Mike Moore
Director of Media Relations: Jim Ferguson
www.minorleaguebaseball.com

MINOR LEAGUES *(Cont.)*

Baseball (AAA) *(Cont.)*

International League
Address: 55 South High Street, Suite 202
           Dublin, OH 43017
Telephone: (614) 791-9300
President: Randy Mobley
www.ilbaseball.com

Pacific Coast League
Address: 1631 Mesa Avenue
           Colorado Springs, CO 80906
Telephone: (719) 636-3399
President: Branch Rickey
www.pclbaseball.com

Hockey

American Hockey League
Address: 1 Monarch Place Suite 2400
           Springfield, MA 01144
Telephone: (413) 781-2030
President, CEO & Treasurer: David A. Andrews
VP of Hockey Operations: Jim Mill
Director of Comm. & Media Relations: Bret Stothart
www.theahl.com

Halls of Fame Directory

National Baseball Hall of Fame and Museum
Address: P.O. Box 590/25 Main Street
           Cooperstown, NY 13326
Telephone: (607) 547-7200
President: Dale Petroskey
Senior Vice President: Bill Haase
V.P. of Communications and Education: Jeff Idelson
www.baseballhalloffame.org

Naismith Memorial Basketball Hall of Fame
Address: 1150 West Columbus Avenue
           Springfield, MA 01105
Telephone: (413) 781-6500
President and CEO: John L. Doleva
Senior Director of Marketing: Dan O'Keefe
www.hoophall.com

International Bowling Museum and Hall of Fame
Address: 111 Stadium Plaza
           St. Louis, MO 63102
Telephone: (314) 231-6340
Executive Director: Gerald Baltz
Communications Director: Jim Baer
www.bowlingmuseum.com

National Boxing Hall of Fame
Address: 1 Hall of Fame Drive
           Canastota, NY 13032
Telephone: (315) 697-7095
President: Donald Ackerman
Executive Director: Edward Brophy
www.ibhof.com

Professional Football Hall of Fame
Address: 2121 George Halas Drive NW
           Canton, OH 44708
Telephone: (330) 456-8207
Executive Director: John Bankert
Vice President of Public Relations: Joe Horrigan
www.profootballhof.com

LPGA Hall of Fame
Address: 100 International Golf Drive
           Daytona Beach, FL 32124
Telephone: (904) 274-6200
Commissioner: Ty Votaw
Director of Media Relations: Connie Wilson
www.lpga.com

Hockey Hall of Fame
Address: 30 Yonge Street BCE Place
           Toronto, Ontario Canada M5E 1X8
Telephone: (416) 360-7735
Chairman: William Hay
President & COO: Jeff Denomme
Director of Marketing and Facility Services: Craig Baines
www.hhof.com

National Museum of Racing and Hall of Fame
Address: 191 Union Avenue
           Saratoga Springs, NY 12866
Telephone: (518) 584-0400
Executive Director: Peter Hammell
Assistant Director: Catherine Maguire
Communications Officer: Richard Hamilton
www.racingmuseum.org

National Soccer Hall of Fame
Address: Wright Soccer Campus
           18 Stadium Circle
           Oneonta, NY 13820
Telephone: (607) 432-3351
President: Will Lunn
www.soccerhall.org

International Swimming Hall of Fame
Address: 1 Hall of Fame Drive
           Fort Lauderdale, FL 33316
Telephone: (954) 462-6536
President: Dr. Samuel J. Freas
Media Contact: Preston Levi
www.ishof.org

International Tennis Hall of Fame
Address: 194 Bellevue Avenue
           Newport, RI 02840
Telephone: (401) 849-3990
Executive Vice President and COO: Mark Stenning
Marketing Manager: Kat Anderson
www.tennisfame.com

National Track & Field Hall of Fame
Address: 216 Ft. Washington Avenue
           The Armory Foundation
           New York, NY 10032
Telephone: (317) 261-0500
Chief Executive Officer: Craig Masback
Director of Communications: Jill Geer
www.usatf.org
Note: New facility not yet opened.

Pro Football Venues

Arizona Cardinals

Sun Devil Stadium
ASU Campus Fifth Street,
Tempe, AZ 85281
(602) 379-0101
Capacity: · 73,377

Atlanta Falcons

Georgia Dome
One Georgia Dome Dr.
Atlanta, GA 30313
(770) 965-3115
Capacity: 71,149

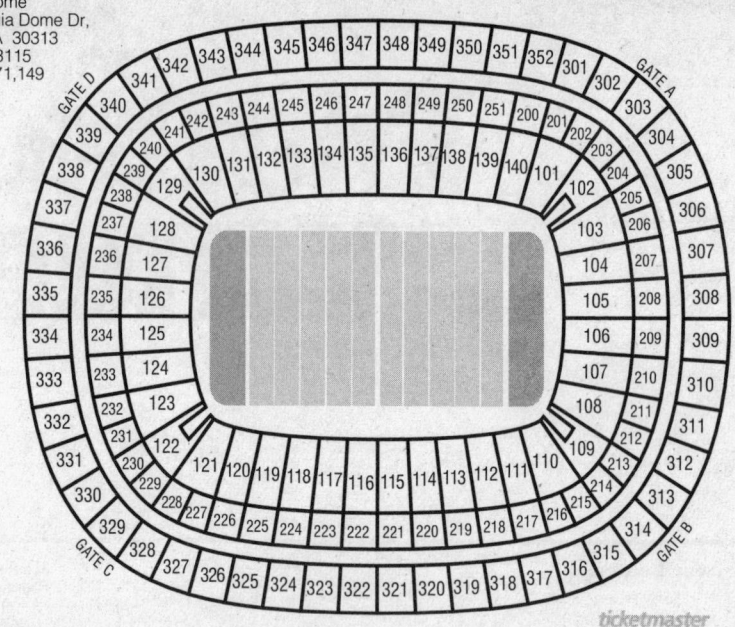

ticketmaster

Baltimore Ravens

Ravens Stadium
1101 Russell St.
Baltimore, MD 21230
(410) 654-6200
Capacity: 69,084

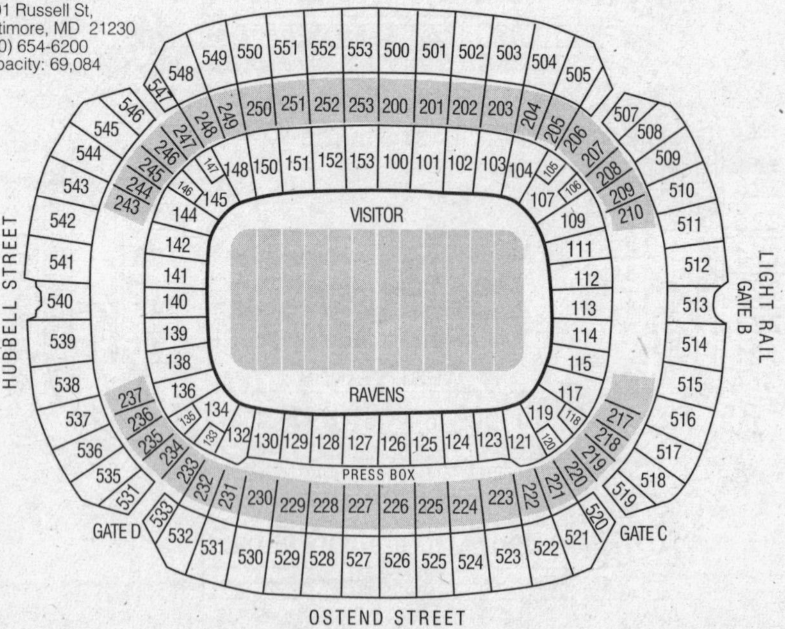

Buffalo Bills

Ralph Wilson Stadium
One Bills Drive
Orchard Park, NY 14127
(716) 648-1800
Capacity: 73,967

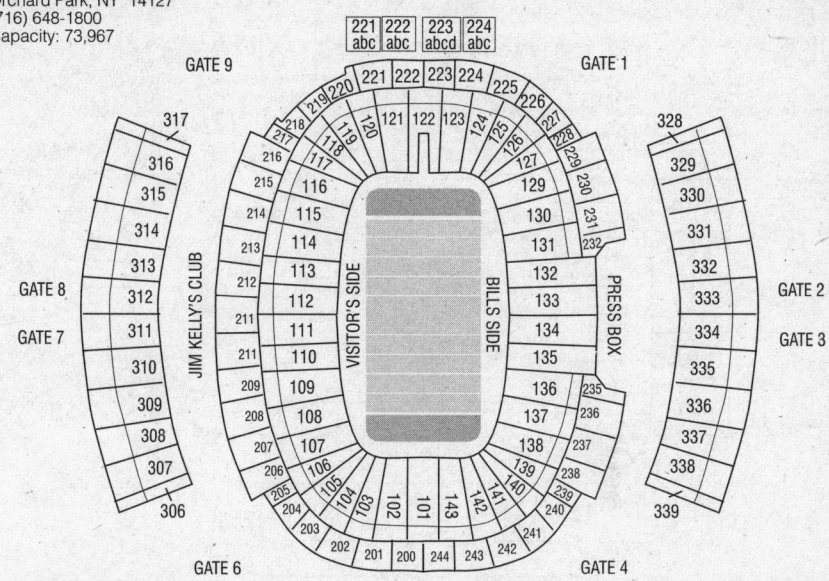

Carolina Panthers

Ericsson Stadium
800 South Mint St.
Charlotte, NC 28202
(704) 358-7000
Capacity: 73,250

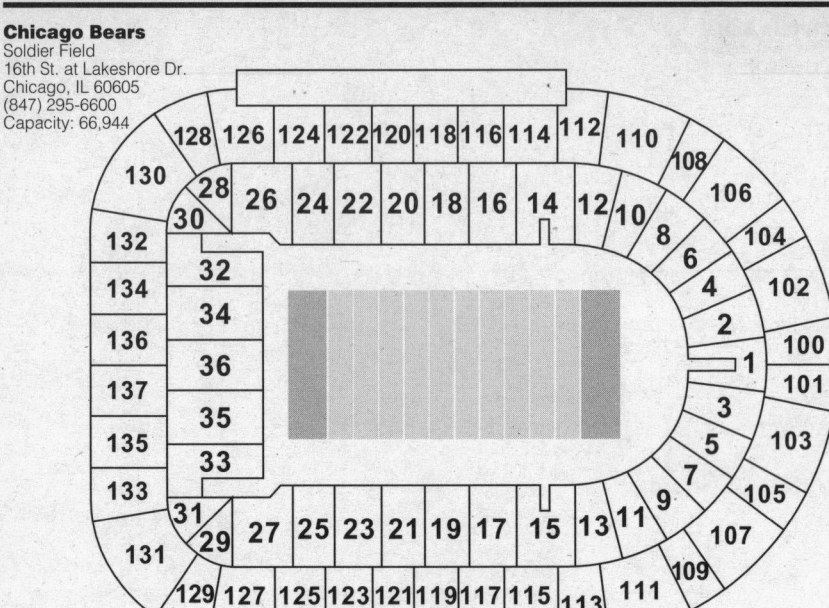

Chicago Bears
Soldier Field
16th St. at Lakeshore Dr.
Chicago, IL 60605
(847) 295-6600
Capacity: 66,944

Cincinnati Bengals
Paul Brown Stadium
One Paul Brown Stadium
Cincinnati, OH 45202
(513) 621-3550
Capacity: 65,341

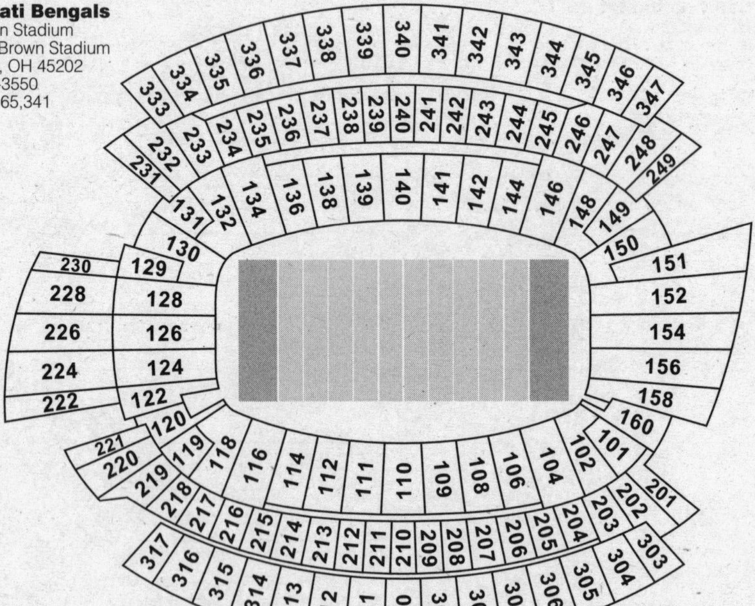

Cleveland Browns
Cleveland Browns Stadium
1085 W. 3rd St.
Cleveland, OH 44114
(440) 891-5000
Capacity: 73,200

Dallas Cowboys
Texas Stadium
2401 E. Airport Freeway
Irving, TX 75062
(972) 556-9900
Capacity: 65,639

Denver Broncos

INVESCO Field at Mile High
1701 Bryant St.
Denver, CO 80204
(303) 649-9000
Capacity: 76,125

EAST

GATE 5

527 528 529 530 531 532 533 534 535 536 537 538 539 540 541 542

GATE 9

526 525 524 523 522 521 520 519 518 517 516 515 514 513 512 511 510 509 508 507 506 505 504 503 502 501 500

GATE 10

GATE 4

GATE 3 WEST - GATE 2 GATE 1

329 328 330 331 332 333 334 335 336 337 338 339 340 341 342 343 344 345

327 326 325 324 323 322 321 320 319 318 317 316 315 314 313 312 311 310 309 308 307 306 305 304 303 302 301

228 229 230 231 232 233 234 235 236

118 119 120 121 122 123 124 125 126 127 128 129 130 131 132 133 134 135

117 116 115 114 113 112 111 110 109 108 107 106 105 104 103 102 101 100

VISITORS' BENCH

HOME BENCH

NORTH

SOUTH

ticketmaster

Detroit Lions

Ford Field
2000 Brush St.
Detroit, MI 48226
(313) 216-4000
Capacity: 65,000

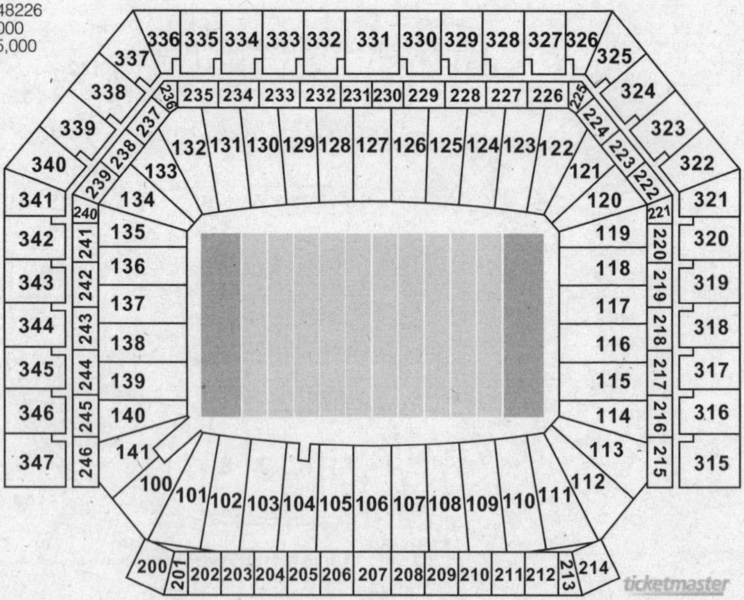

337 336 335 334 333 332 331 330 329 328 327 326 325 324 323 322 321 320 319 318 317 316 315

338 235 234 233 232 231 230 229 228 227 226 224 223 222 221 220 219 218 217 216 215

339 340 341 342 343 344 345 346 347

239 238 237 236

240 241 242 243 244 245 246

132 131 130 129 128 127 126 125 124 123 122 121 120 119 118 117 116 115 114 113 112

133 134 135 136 137 138 139 140 141

100 101 102 103 104 105 106 107 108 109 110 111

200 201 202 203 204 205 206 207 208 209 210 211 212 213 214

ticketmaster

Green Bay Packers
Lambeau Field
1265 Lombardi Avenue
Green Bay, WI 54304
Telephone: (920) 496-5700
Capacity: 65,290

Houston Texans
Reliant Stadium
One Reliant Park
Houston, TX 77054
(832) 667-2000
Capacity: 69,500

Indianapolis Colts

RCA Dome
200 S. Capitol Ave.
Indianapolis, IN 46225
(317) 297-2658
Capacity: 56,127

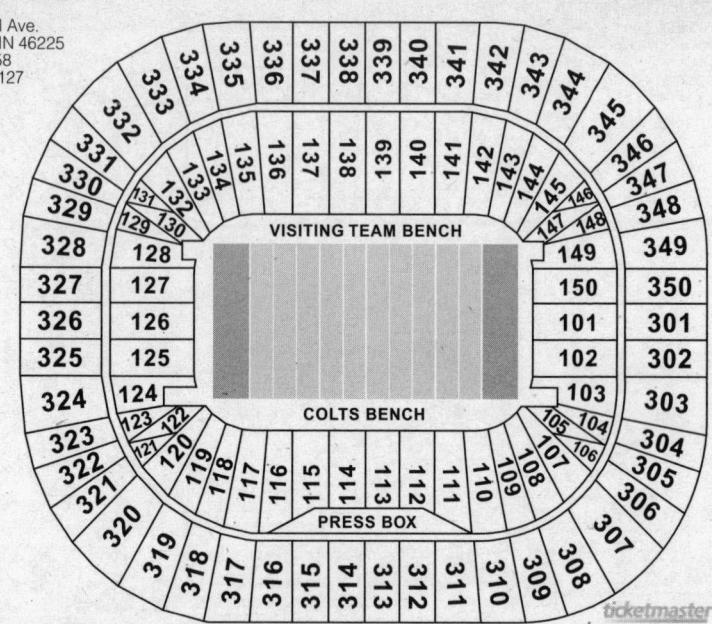

Jacksonville Jaguars

Alltel Stadium
1400 E. Duvall St.
Jacksonville, FL 32202
(904) 633-6000
Capacity: 73,000

Kansas City Chiefs
Arrowhead Stadium
One Arrowhead Drive
Kansas City, MO 64129
(816) 920-9300
Capacity: 79,451

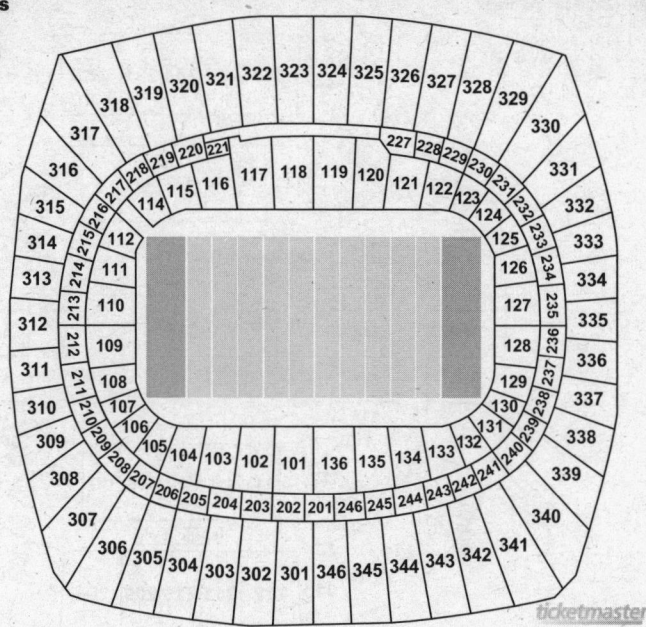

Miami Dolphins
Pro Player Stadium
2269 Dan Marino Blvd.
Miami, FL 33056
(954) 452-7000
Capacity: 75,540

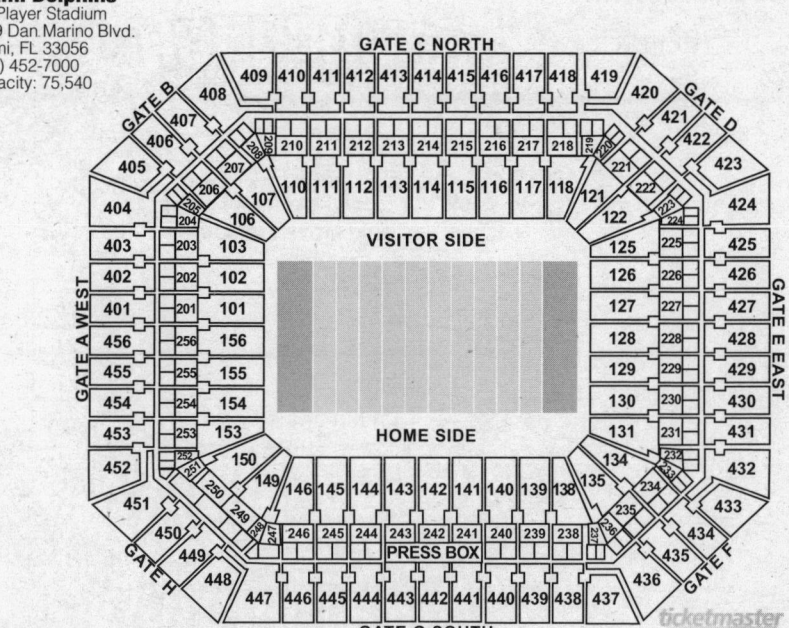

Minnesota Vikings
HHH Metrodome
500 11th Ave. South
Minneapolis, MN 55415
(952) 828-6500
Capacity: 64,121

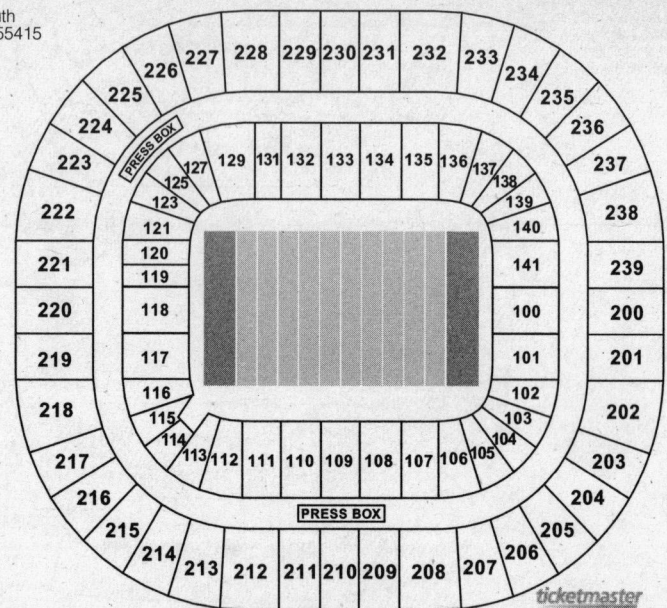

New England Patriots
Gillette Stadium
One Patriot Place
Foxborough, MA 02035
(508) 543-8200
Capacity: 68,436

New Orleans Saints

Louisiana Superdome
1500 Podyras St.
New Orleans, LA 70112
(504) 733-0255
Capacity: 68,390

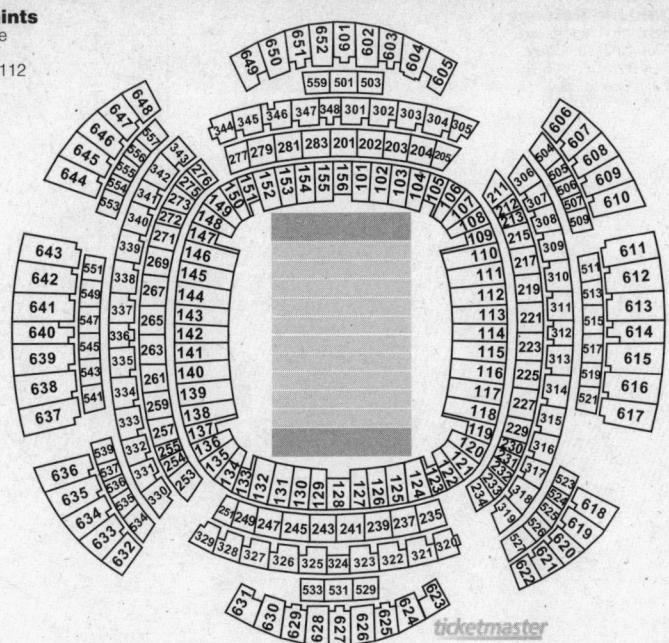

New York Giants
New York Jets

Giants Stadium
50 Route 120
East Rutherford, NJ 07073
(201) 935-8111
Capacity: 79,469

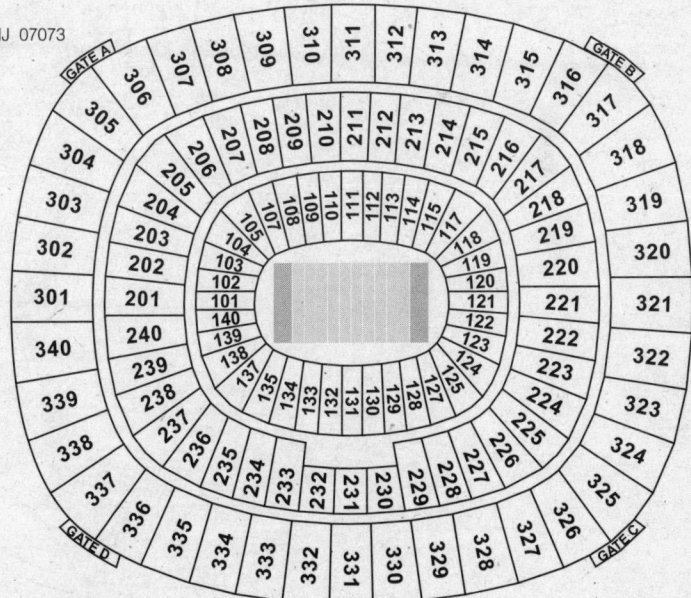

Oakland Raiders

Network Associates Coliseum
7000 Coliseum Way
Oakland, CA 94621
(510) 864-5000
Capacity: 63,132

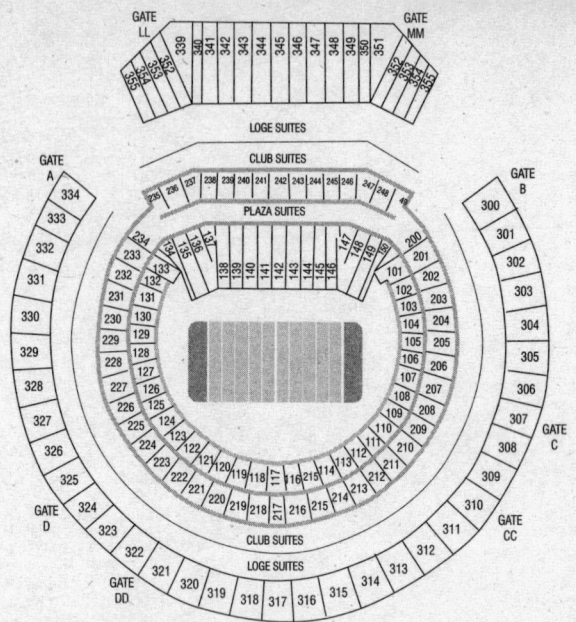

Philadelphia Eagles

Veterans Stadium
3551 Broad St.
Philadelphia, PA 19148
(215) 463-2500
Capacity: 65,352

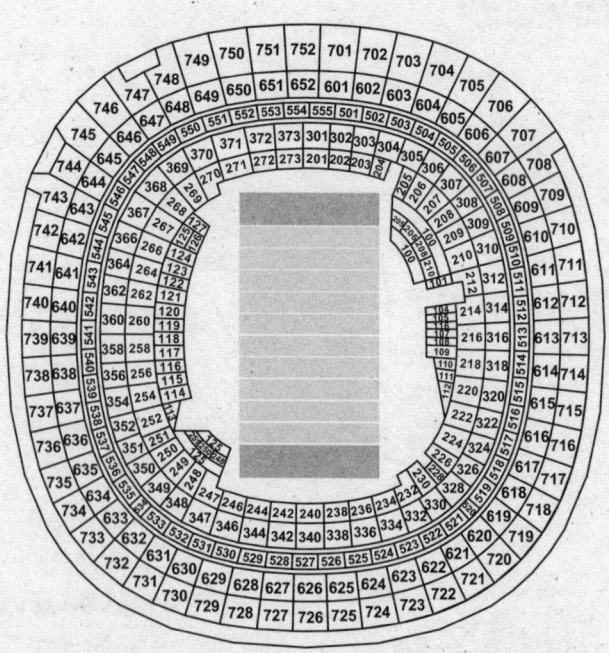

Pittsburgh Steelers

Heinz Field
100 Art Rooney Ave.
Pittsburgh, PA 15212
(412) 432-7800
Capacity: 64,350

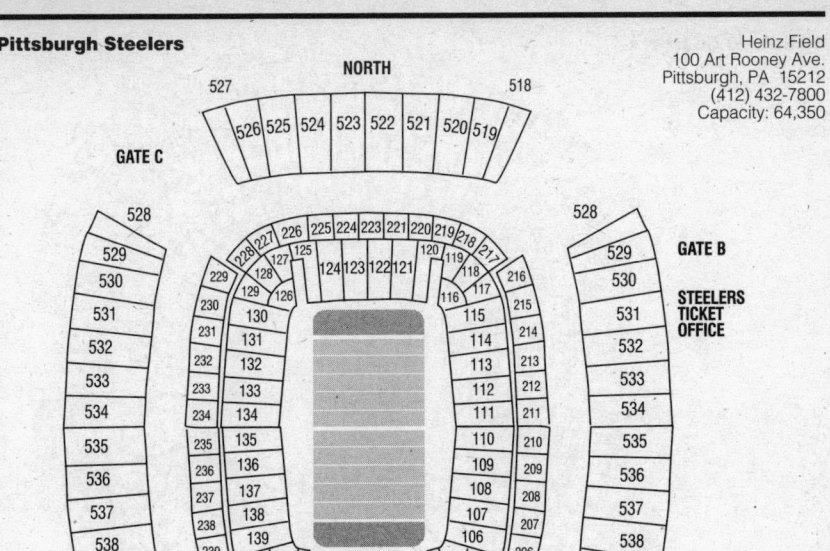

St. Louis Rams
Edward Jones Dome
701 Convention Plaza
St. Louis, MO 63101
(314) 982-7267
Capacity: 66,000

San Diego Chargers

Qualcomm Stadium
9449 Friars Rd.
San Diego, CA 92108
(858) 874-4500
Capacity: 70,000

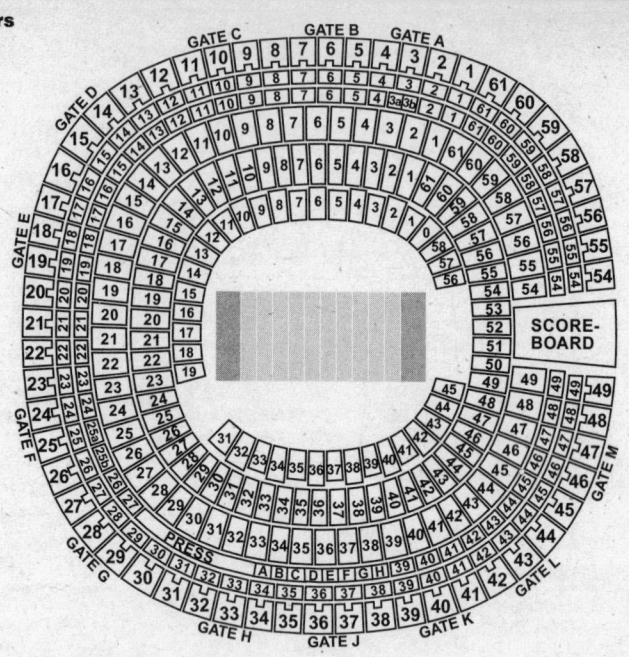

San Francisco 49ers

3Com Park
Jamestown and Harney Way
San Francisco, CA 94124
(408) 562-4949
Capacity: 69,734

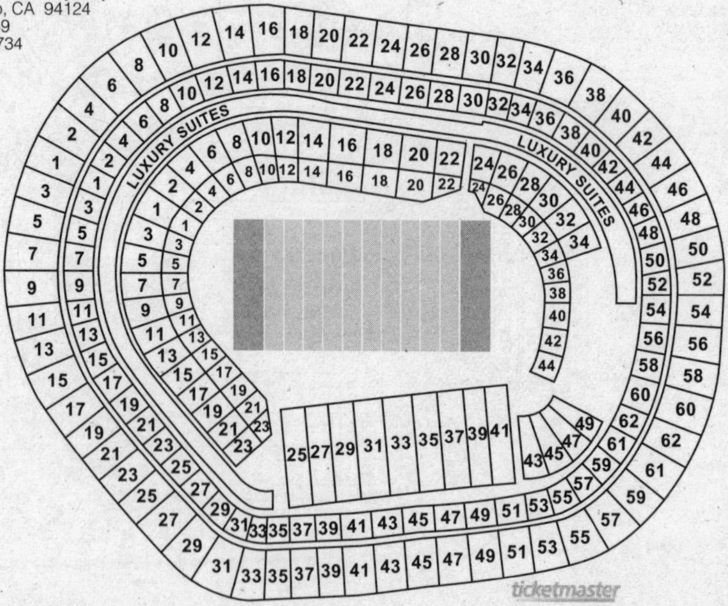

Seattle Seahawks

Seahawks Stadium
800 Occidental Ave. South
Seattle, WA 98104
(425) 827-9777
Capacity: 67,000

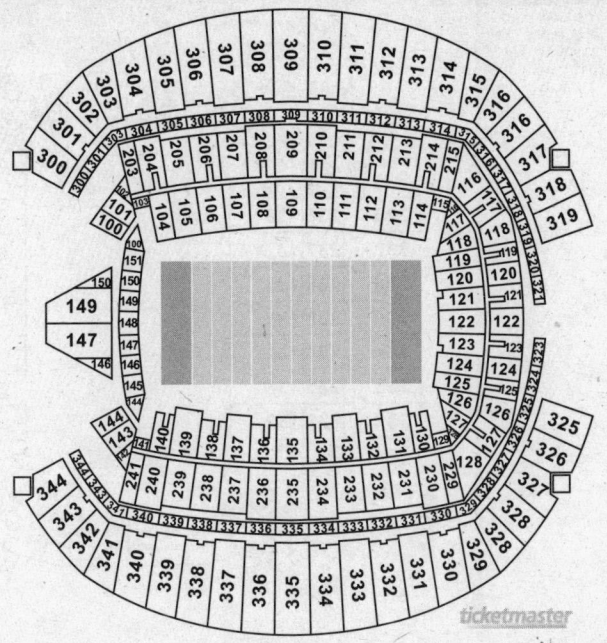

Tampa Bay Buccaneers

Raymond James Stadium
4201 N. Dale Mabry Hwy.
Tampa, FL 33607
(813) 870-2700
Capacity: 66,321

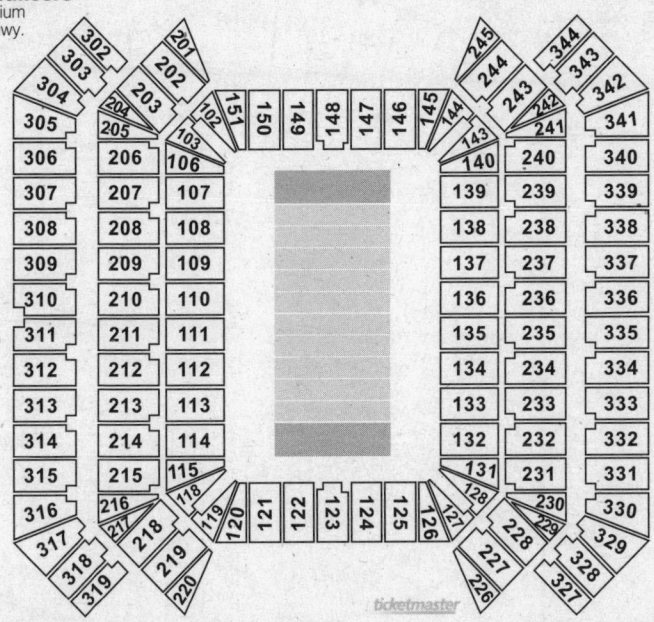

Tennessee Titans
The Coliseum
One Titans Way
Nashville, TN 37219
(615) 565-4000
Capacity: 68,804

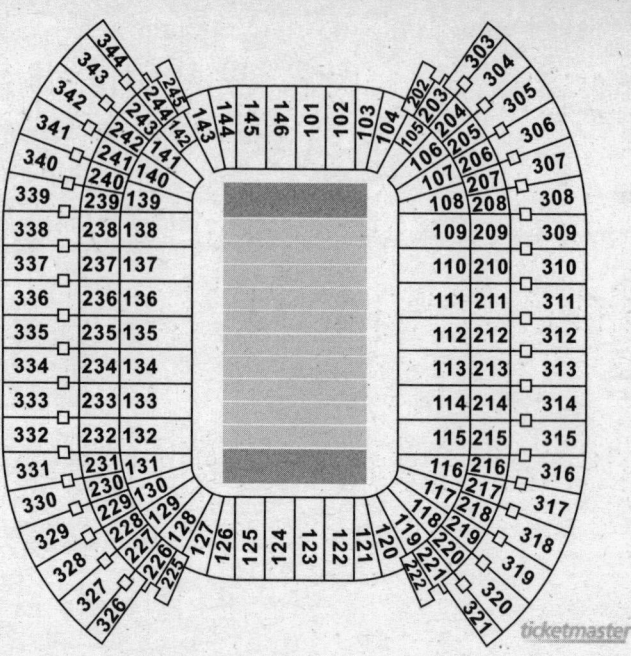

ticketmaster

Washington Redskins
Fedex Field
1600 Raljon Rd.
Landover, MD 20785
(703) 726-7000
Capacity: 86,484

Awards

SI Sportsmen of the Year Curt Schilling and Randy Johnson

Athlete Awards

Sports Illustrated Sportsman of the Year

1954	Roger Bannister, Track and Field
1955	Johnny Podres, Baseball
1956	Bobby Morrow, Track and Field
1957	Stan Musial, Baseball
1958	Rafer Johnson, Track and Field
1959	Ingemar Johansson, Boxing
1960	Arnold Palmer, Golf
1961	Jerry Lucas, Basketball
1962	Terry Baker, Football
1963	Pete Rozelle, Pro Football
1964	Ken Venturi, Golf
1965	Sandy Koufax, Baseball
1966	Jim Ryun, Track and Field
1967	Carl Yastrzemski, Baseball
1968	Bill Russell, Pro Basketball
1969	Tom Seaver, Baseball
1970	Bobby Orr, Hockey
1971	Lee Trevino, Golf
1972	Billie Jean King, Tennis
	John Wooden, Basketball
1973	Jackie Stewart, Auto Racing
1974	Muhammad Ali, Boxing
1975	Pete Rose, Baseball
1976	Chris Evert, Tennis
1977	Steve Cauthen, Horse Racing
1978	Jack Nicklaus, Golf
1979	Terry Bradshaw, Pro Football
	Willie Stargell, Baseball
1980	U.S. Olympic Hockey Team
1981	Sugar Ray Leonard, Boxing
1982	Wayne Gretzky, Hockey
1983	Mary Decker, Track and Field
1984	Mary Lou Retton, Gymnastics
	Edwin Moses, Track and Field
1985	Kareem Abdul-Jabbar, Pro Basketball
1986	Joe Paterno, Football
1987	Athletes Who Care:
	Bob Bourne, Hockey
	Kip Keino, Track and Field
	Judi Brown King, Track and Field
	Dale Murphy, Baseball
	Chip Rives, Football
	Patty Sheehan, Golf
	Rory Sparrow, Pro Basketball
	Reggie Williams, Pro Football
1988	Orel Hershiser, Baseball
1989	Greg LeMond, Cycling
1990	Joe Montana, Pro Football
1991	Michael Jordan, Pro Basketball
1992	Arthur Ashe, Tennis
1993	Don Shula, Pro Football
1994	Bonnie Blair, Speed Skating
	Johann Olav Koss, Speed Skating
1995	Cal Ripken Jr, Baseball
1996	Tiger Woods, Golf
1997	Dean Smith, College Basketball
1998	Mark McGwire, Sammy Sosa, Baseball
1999	U.S. Women's Soccer Team
2000	Tiger Woods, Golf
2001	Curt Schilling, Baseball
	Randy Johnson, Baseball

Associated Press Athletes of the Year

Year	MEN	WOMEN
1931	Pepper Martin, Baseball	Helene Madison, Swimming
1932	Gene Sarazen, Golf	Babe Didrikson, Track and Field
1933	Carl Hubbell, Baseball	Helen Jacobs, Tennis
1934	Dizzy Dean, Baseball	Virginia Van Wie, Golf
1935	Joe Louis, Boxing	Helen Wills Moody, Tennis
1936	Jesse Owens, Track and Field	Helen Stephens, Track and Field
1937	Don Budge, Tennis	Katherine Rawls, Swimming
1938	Don Budge, Tennis	Patty Berg, Golf
1939	Nile Kinnick, Football	Alice Marble, Tennis
1940	Tom Harmon, Football	Alice Marble, Tennis
1941	Joe DiMaggio, Baseball	Betty Hicks Newell, Golf
1942	Frank Sinkwich, Football	Gloria Callen, Swimming
1943	Gunder Haegg, Track and Field	Patty Berg, Golf
1944	Byron Nelson, Golf	Ann Curtis, Swimming
1945	Bryon Nelson, Golf	Babe Didrikson Zaharias, Golf
1946	Glenn Davis, Football	Babe Didrikson Zaharias, Golf
1947	Johnny Lujack, Football	Babe Didrikson Zaharias, Golf
1948	Lou Boudreau, Baseball	Fanny Blankers-Koen, Track and Field
1949	Leon Hart, Football	Marlene Bauer, Golf
1950	Jim Konstanty, Baseball	Babe Didrikson Zaharias, Golf
1951	Dick Kazmaier, Football	Maureen Connolly, Tennis
1952	Bob Mathias, Track and Field	Maureen Connolly, Tennis
1953	Ben Hogan, Golf	Maureen Connolly, Tennis
1954	Willie Mays, Baseball	Babe Didrikson Zaharias, Golf
1955	Hopalong Cassidy, Football	Patty Berg, Golf
1956	Mickey Mantle, Baseball	Pat McCormick, Diving
1957	Ted Williams, Baseball	Althea Gibson, Tennis
1958	Herb Elliott, Track and Field	Althea Gibson, Tennis
1959	Ingemar Johansson, Boxing	Maria Bueno, Tennis
1960	Rafer Johnson, Track and Field	Wilma Rudolph, Track and Field
1961	Roger Maris, Baseball	Wilma Rudolph, Track and Field
1962	Maury Wills, Baseball	Dawn Fraser, Swimming
1963	Sandy Koufax, Baseball	Mickey Wright, Golf
1964	Don Schollander, Swimming	Mickey Wright, Golf
1965	Sandy Koufax, Baseball	Kathy Whitworth, Golf
1966	Frank Robinson, Baseball	Kathy Whitworth, Golf
1967	Carl Yastrzemski, Baseball	Billie Jean King, Tennis

Associated Press Athletes of the Year (Cont.)

	MEN	WOMEN
1968	Denny McLain, Baseball	Peggy Fleming, Skating
1969	Tom Seaver, Baseball	Debbie Meyer, Swimming
1970	George Blanda, Pro Football	Chi Cheng, Track and Field
1971	Lee Trevino, Golf	Evonne Goolagong, Tennis
1972	Mark Spitz, Swimming	Olga Korbut, Gymnastics
1973	O.J. Simpson, Pro Football	Billie Jean King, Tennis
1974	Muhammad Ali, Boxing	Chris Evert, Tennis
1975	Fred Lynn, Baseball	Chris Evert, Tennis
1976	Bruce Jenner, Track and Field	Nadia Comaneci, Gymnastics
1977	Steve Cauthen, Horse Racing	Chris Evert, Tennis
1978	Ron Guidry, Baseball	Nancy Lopez, Golf
1979	Willie Stargell, Baseball	Tracy Austin, Tennis
1980	U.S. Olympic Hockey Team	Chris Evert Lloyd, Tennis
1981	John McEnroe, Tennis	Tracy Austin, Tennis
1982	Wayne Gretzky, Hockey	Mary Decker, Track and Field
1983	Carl Lewis, Track and Field	Martina Navratilova, Tennis
1984	Carl Lewis, Track and Field	Mary Lou Retton, Gymnastics
1985	Dwight Gooden, Baseball	Nancy Lopez, Golf
1986	Larry Bird, Pro Basketball	Martina Navratilova, Tennis
1987	Ben Johnson, Track and Field	Jackie Joyner-Kersee, Track and Field
1988	Orel Hershiser, Baseball	Florence Griffith Joyner, Track and Field
1989	Joe Montana, Pro Football	Steffi Graf, Tennis
1990	Joe Montana, Pro Football	Beth Daniel, Golf
1991	Michael Jordan, Pro Basketball	Monica Seles, Tennis
1992	Michael Jordan, Pro Basketball	Monica Seles, Tennis
1993	Michael Jordan, Pro Basketball	Sheryl Swoopes, Basketball
1994	George Foreman, Boxing	Bonnie Blair, Speed Skating
1995	Cal Ripken Jr, Baseball	Rebecca Lobo, Basketball
1996	Michael Johnson, Track and Field	Amy Van Dyken, Swimming
1997	Tiger Woods, Golf	Martina Hingis, Tennis
1998	Mark McGwire, Baseball	Se Ri Pak, Golf
1999	Tiger Woods, Golf	U.S. Women's Soccer Team
2000	Tiger Woods, Golf	Marion Jones, Track and Field
2001	Barry Bonds, Baseball	Jennifer Capriati, Tennis

James E. Sullivan Award

Presented annually by the AAU to the athlete who "by his or her performance, example and influence as an amateur, has done the most during the year to advance the cause of sportsmanship."

1930	Bobby Jones, Golf	1963	John Pennel, Track and Field
1931	Barney Berlinger, Track and Field	1964	Don Schollander, Swimming
1932	Jim Bausch, Track and Field	1965	Bill Bradley, Basketball
1933	Glenn Cunningham, Track and Field	1966	Jim Ryun, Track and Field
1934	Bill Bonthron, Track and Field	1967	Randy Matson, Track and Field
1935	Lawson Little, Golf	1968	Debbie Meyer, Swimming
1936	Glenn Morris, Track and Field	1969	Bill Toomey, Track and Field
1937	Don Budge, Tennis	1970	John Kinsella, Swimming
1938	Don Lash, Track and Field	1971	Mark Spitz, Swimming
1939	Joe Burk, Rowing	1972	Frank Shorter, Track and Field
1940	Greg Rice, Track and Field	1973	Bill Walton, Basketball
1941	Leslie MacMitchell, Track and Field	1974	Rich Wohlhuter, Track and Field
1942	Cornelius Warmerdam, Track	1975	Tim Shaw, Swimming
1943	Gilbert Dodds, Track and Field	1976	Bruce Jenner, Track and Field
1944	Ann Curtis, Swimming	1977	John Naber, Swimming
1945	Doc Blanchard, Football	1978	Tracy Caulkins, Swimming
1946	Arnold Tucker, Football	1979	Kurt Thomas, Gymnastics
1947	John B. Kelly Jr, Rowing	1980	Eric Heiden, Speed Skating
1948	Bob Mathias, Track and Field	1981	Carl Lewis, Track and Field
1949	Dick Button, Skating	1982	Mary Decker, Track and Field
1950	Fred Wilt, Track and Field	1983	Edwin Moses, Track and Field
1951	Bob Richards, Track and Field	1984	Greg Louganis, Diving
1952	Horace Ashenfelter, Track and Field	1985	Joan B. Samuelson, Track and Field
1953	Sammy Lee, Diving	1986	Jackie Joyner-Kersee, Track and Field
1954	Mal Whitfield, Track and Field	1987	Jim Abbott, Baseball
1955	Harrison Dillard, Track and Field	1988	Florence Griffith Joyner, Track
1956	Pat McCormick, Diving	1989	Janet Evans, Swimming
1957	Bobby Morrow, Track and Field	1990	John Smith, Wrestling
1958	Glenn Davis, Track and Field	1991	Mike Powell, Track and Field
1959	Parry O'Brien, Track and Field	1992	Bonnie Blair, Speed Skating
1960	Rafer Johnson, Track and Field	1993	Charlie Ward, Football, Basketball
1961	Wilma Rudolph, Track and Field	1994	Dan Jansen, Speed Skating
1962	Jim Beatty, Track and Field	1995	Bruce Baumgartner, Wrestling

James E. Sullivan Award (Cont.)

1996	Michael Johnson, Track and Field	1999	Kelly and Coco Miller, Basketball
1997	Peyton Manning, Football	2000	Rulon Gardner, Wrestling
1998	Chamique Holdsclaw, Basketball	2001	Michelle Kwan, Figure Skating

The Sporting News Sportsman of the Year

1968	Denny McLain, Baseball	1986	Larry Bird, Pro Basketball
1969	Tom Seaver, Baseball	1987	No award
1970	John Wooden, Basketball	1988	Jackie Joyner-Kersee, Track and Field
1971	Lee Trevino, Golf	1989	Joe Montana, Pro Football
1972	Charles O. Finley, Baseball	1990	Nolan Ryan, Baseball
1973	O.J. Simpson, Pro Football	1991	Michael Jordan, Pro Basketball
1974	Lou Brock, Baseball	1992	Mike Krzyzewski, Basketball
1975	Archie Griffin, Football	1993	Pat Gillick/Cito Gaston, Baseball
1976	Larry O'Brien, Pro Basketball	1994	Emmitt Smith, Pro Football
1977	Steve Cauthen, Horse Racing	1995	Cal Ripken Jr, Baseball
1978	Ron Guidry, Baseball	1996	Joe Torre, Baseball
1979	Willie Stargell, Baseball	1997	Michael Jordan, Basketball
1980	George Brett, Baseball	1998	Mark McGwire, Baseball
1981	Wayne Gretzky, Hockey	1999	New York Yankees, Baseball
1982	Whitey Herzog, Baseball	2000	Kurt Warner/
1983	Bowie Kuhn, Baseball		Marshall Faulk, Football
1984	Peter Ueberroth, LA Olympics	2001	Curt Schilling, Baseball
1985	Pete Rose, Baseball		

United Press International Male and Female Athlete of the Year

	MEN	WOMEN
1974	Muhammad Ali, Boxing	Irena Szewinska, Track and Field
1975	Joao Oliveira, Track and Field	Nadia Comaneci, Gymnastics
1976	Alberto Juantorena, Track and Field	Nadia Comaneci, Gymnastics
1977	Alberto Juantorena, Track and Field	Rosie Ackermann, Track and Field
1978	Henry Rono, Track and Field	Tracy Caulkins, Swimming
1979	Sebastian Coe, Track and Field	Marita Koch, Track and Field
1980	Eric Heiden, Speed Skating	Hanni Wenzel, Alpine Skiing
1981	Sebastian Coe, Track and Field	Chris Evert Lloyd, Tennis
1982	Daley Thompson, Track and Field	Marita Koch, Track and Field
1983	Carl Lewis, Track and Field	Jarmila Kratochvilova, Track and Field
1984	Carl Lewis, Track and Field	Martina Navratilova, Tennis
1985	Steve Cram, Track and Field	Mary Decker Slaney, Track and Field
1986	Diego Maradona, Soccer	Heike Drechsler, Track and Field
1987	Ben Johnson, Track and Field	Steffi Graf, Tennis
1988	Matt Biondi, Swimming	Florence Griffith Joyner, Track and Field
1989	Boris Becker, Tennis	Steffi Graf, Tennis
1990	Stefan Edberg, Tennis	Merlene Ottey, Track and Field
1991	Michael Jordan, Pro Basketball	Monica Seles, Tennis
1992	Mario Lemieux, Hockey	Monica Seles, Tennis
1993	Michael Jordan, Pro Basketball	Steffi Graf, Tennis
1994	Nick Price, Golf	Bonnie Blair, Speed Skating
1995	Cal Ripken Jr, Baseball	Steffi Graf, Tennis

Note: Award not given since 1995.

Dial Award

Presented by the Dial Corporation to the male and female national high school athlete/scholar of the year.

	BOYS	GIRLS
1979	Herschel Walker, Football	No award
1980	Bill Fralic, Football	Carol Lewis, Track and Field
1981	Kevin Willhite, Football	Cheryl Miller, Basketball
1982	Mike Smith, Basketball	Elaine Zayak, Skating
1983	Chris Spielman, Football	Melanie Buddemeyer, Swimming
1984	Hart Lee Dykes, Football	Nora Lewis, Basketball
1985	Jeff George, Football	Gea Johnson, Track and Field
1986	Scott Schaffner, Football	Mya Johnson, Track and Field
1987	Todd Marinovich, Football	Kristi Overton, Water Skiing
1988	Carlton Gray, Football	Courtney Cox, Basketball
1989	Robert Smith, Football	Lisa Leslie, Basketball
1990	Derrick Brooks, Football	Vicki Goetze, Golf
1991	Jeff Buckey, Football, Track and Field	Katie Smith, Basketball, Volleyball, Track
1992	Jacque Vaughn, Basketball	Amanda White, Track and Field, Swimming
1993	Tiger Woods, Golf	Kristin Folkl, Basketball
1994	Taymon Domzalski, Basketball	Shannon Miller, Gymnastics
1995	Brent Abernathy, Baseball	Shea Ralph, Basketball
1996	Grant Irons, Football	Grace Park, Golf
1997	Ronald Curry, Football	Michelle Kwan, Figure Skating

Note: Award not given since 1997.

Profiles

Ted Williams
1918–2002

Henry Aaron (b. 2-5-34): Baseball OF. "Hammerin' Hank." Alltime leader in HR (755) and RBI (2,297); third in hits (3,771). 1957 MVP. Led league in HR and RBI four times each, runs scored three times, hits and batting average twice. No. 44, he had 44 homers four times. Had 40+ HR eight times; 100+ RBI 11 times; .300+ average 14 times. All-Star 24 times . Career span 1954–76; jersey number retired by Atlanta and Milwaukee.

Kareem Abdul-Jabbar (b. 4-16-47): Born Lew Alcindor. Basketball C. Alltime leader points scored (38,387), field goals attempted (28,307), field goals made (15,837); second alltime blocked shots (3,189); third alltime rebounds (17,440). Won six MVP awards (1971–72, 1974, 1976–77, 1980). Career scoring average was 24.6, rebounding average 11.2. Ten-time All-Star, All-Defensive team five times. 1970 Rookie of the Year. Played on six championship teams; was playoff MVP in 1971, 1985. Career span 1969–88 with Milwaukee, Los Angeles. Also played on three NCAA championship teams with UCLA; tournament MVP 1967–69; Player of the Year two times.

Affirmed (b. 2-21-75, d. 1-12-01): Thoroughbred race horse. Triple Crown winner in 1978 with jockey Steve Cauthen aboard. Trained by Laz Barrera.

Andre Agassi (b. 4-29-70): Tennis player. Won 1999 French Open to become fifth man in history to win all four Grand Slams. Won '92 Wimbledon, '94 and '99 U.S. Opens and '95, '00 and '01 Australian Opens. Ranked No. 1 in 1995 and again in '99.

Troy Aikman (b. 11-21-66): Football QB. Quarterbacked Cowboys to three Super Bowl titles (XXVII, XXVIII, XXX). MVP of Super Bowl XXVII, in which he completed 22 of 30 passes for 273 yards and four TDs with no interceptions. Spent entire career (1989–2000) with Dallas Cowboys, passing for 32,942 yards and 171 TDs.

Michelle Akers (b. 2-1-66): Soccer player. Charter member of U.S. women's national team. Scored first goal ever for U.S. women's team on 8-21-85 against Denmark. Second alltime leading scorer in U.S. women's national team history (105 goals). Member of Women's World Cup champion team in 1991, '99, and third-place team in '95. Member of Olympic champion team in 1996. Battled chronic fatigue syndrome.

Tenley Albright (b. 7-18-35): Figure skater. Gold medalist at 1956 Olympics, silver medalist at 1952 Olympics. World champion two times (1953, 1955) and U.S. champion five consecutive years (1952–56).

Grover Cleveland Alexander (b. 2-26-1887, d. 11-4-50): Baseball RHP. Tied for third alltime in career wins (373), second in shutouts (90). Won 30+ games three times, 20+ games six other times. Set rookie record with 28 wins in 1911. Career span 1911–30 with Philadelphia (NL), Chicago (NL), St. Louis (NL).

Vasili Alexeyev (b. 1942): Soviet weightlifter. Gold medalist at two consecutive Olympics in 1972, 1976. World champion eight times.

Muhammad Ali (b. 1-17-42): Born Cassius Clay. Boxer. Heavyweight champion three times (1964–67, 1974–78, 1978–79). Stripped of title in 1967 because he refused to serve in the Vietnam War. Career record 56–5 with 37 KOs. Defended title 19 times. Also light heavyweight gold medalist at 1960 Olympics. Battles Parkinson Syndrome.

Phog Allen (b. 11-18-1885, d. 9-16-74): College basketball coach. Ninth alltime in coaching wins (746); .739 career winning percentage. Won 1952 NCAA championship. Spent most of his career from 1920 to '56 with Kansas.

Bobby Allison (b. 12-3-37): Auto racer. Third alltime in NASCAR victories (84). Won Daytona 500 three times (1978, 1982, 1988). NASCAR champion in 1983.

Naty Alvarado (b. 7-25-55): Mexican-born handball player. "El Gato (The Cat)." Won a record 11 U.S. pro four-wall handball titles, starting in 1977.

Lance Alworth (b. 8-3-40): Football WR. "Bambi" led AFL in receiving in 1966, '68 and '69. 200+ yards in a game five times in career, a record. Gained 100+ yards in a game 41 times. In 1965 gained 1,602 yards receiving. Career span 1962–70 with San Diego and 1971–72 with Dallas. Elected to Pro Football Hall of Fame 1978.

Gary Anderson (b. 7-16-59): Football K. Four-time Pro Bowl kicker (1983, '85, '93, '98). NFL's alltime leading scorer (2,133 pts). Made league record 40 consecutive FGs in 1997–98 season. Made every field goal and extra point attempt during the 1998–99 season.

Sparky Anderson (b. 2-22-34): Baseball manager. Only manager to win World Series in both leagues (Cincinnati, 1975–76, Detroit, 1984); only manager to win 100 games in both leagues. Elected to Hall of Fame in 2000.

Willie Anderson (b. 1880, d. 1910): Scottish golfer. Won U.S. Open four times (1901 and an unmatched three straight, 1903–05). Also won four Western Opens between 1902 and 1909.

Mario Andretti (b. 2-28-40): Auto racer. The only driver in history to win the Daytona 500 (1967), the Indy 500 (1969) and a Formula One world championship (1978). Second alltime in CART victories (52). Twelve career Formula One victories. USAC/CART champion four times (consecutively 1965–66, 1969, 1984).

Earl Anthony (b. 4-27-38, d. 8-14-01): Bowler. Won PBA National Championship six times, more than any other bowler (consecutively 1973–75, 1981–83) and Tournament of Champions two times (1974, 1978). First bowler to top $1 million in career earnings. Bowler of the Year six times (consecutively 1974–76, 1981–83). Won 41 career PBA titles.

Said Aouita (b. 11-2-60): Track and field. Moroccan set world records in 2,000 meters (4:50.81 in 1987), and 5,000 meters (12:58.39 in 1987). 1984 Olympic champion in 5,000; 1988 Olympic third place in 800.

Al Arbour (b. 11-1-32): Hockey D-coach. Led NY Islanders to four consecutive Stanley Cup championships (1980–83). Also played on three Stanley Cup champions: Detroit, Chicago and Toronto, from 1953 to 1971.

Eddie Arcaro (b. 2-19-16, d. 11-14-97): Horse racing jockey. The only jockey to win the Triple Crown two times (aboard Whirlaway in 1941, Citation in 1948). Rode Preakness Stakes winner (1941, 1948, consecutively 1950–51, 1955, 1957) and Belmont Stakes winner (consecutively 1941–42, 1945, 1948, 1952, 1955) six times each and Kentucky Derby winner five times (1938, 1941, 1945, 1948, 1952). 4,779 career wins.

Nate Archibald (b. 9-2-48): Basketball player. "Tiny" only by NBA standards at 6' 1", 160 pounds. Six-time All-Star. Led NBA in scoring (34.0) and assists (11.4) in 1972–73. First team, all-NBA in 1973, '75 and '76. MVP of NBA All-Star Game in 1981. Career span 1970–84 with six teams.

Alexis Arguello (b. 4-19-52): Nicaraguan boxer. Won world titles in three weight classes: featherweight, super featherweight and lightweight. Won first title, WBA featherweight, on 11-23-74 when he KO'd Ruben Olivares in 13. Career record: 88–8, 64 KO.

Henry Armstrong (b. 12-12-12, d. 10-24-88): Boxer. Champion in three different weight classes: featherweight, welterweight, and lightweight. Career record 145-20-9 with 98 KOs (27 consecutively, 1937–38) from 1931 to 1945.

Lance Armstrong (b. 9-18-71): Cyclist. Recovered from testicular cancer to win four straight Tour de France races (1999–02). Two-time winner of Tour DuPont (1995, '96). Won 1993 world championships.

Arthur Ashe (b. 7-10-43, d. 2-6-93): Tennis player. First black man to win U.S. Open (1968, as an amateur), Australian Open (1970) and Wimbledon singles titles (1975). 33 career tournament victories. Member of Davis Cup team 1963–78; captain 1980–85. Stadium at the United States Tennis Center, home of the U.S. Open, named in his honor.

Assault (b. 1943, d. 1971): Thoroughbred race horse. Horse of the Year for 1946 when he won the Triple Crown. Won Kentucky Derby by eight lengths, Preakness by a neck, and the Belmont by three lengths. Trained by Max Hirsch.

Red Auerbach (b. 9-20-17): Basketball coach-executive. 938 career wins. Coached Boston from 1946 to 1965, winning nine championships, eight consecutively. Had .662 career winning percentage, with 50+ wins eight consecutive seasons. Also won seven championships as general manager.

Hobey Baker (b. 1-15-1892, d. 12-21-18): Sportsman. Member of both college football and hockey Halls of Fame. College hockey and football star at Princeton, 1911–14. Fighter pilot in World War I, died in plane crash. College hockey Player of the Year award named in his honor.

Seve Ballesteros (b. 4-9-57): Spanish golfer. Notorious scrambler. Won British Opens in 1979, '84 and '88. Won Masters in 1980 and '83.

Ernie Banks (b. 1-31-31): Baseball SS-1B. "Mr. Cub." Won two consecutive MVP awards, in 1958–59. 512 career HR. League leader in HR, RBI two times each; 40+ HR five times; 100+ RBI eight times; career batting average of .274. Career span 1953–71 with Chicago.

Roger Bannister (b. 3-23-29): Track and field. British runner broke the four-minute mile barrier, running 3:59.4 on 5-6-54.

Red Barber (b. 2-17-08, d. 10-22-92): Sportscaster. TV-radio baseball announcer was the voice of Cincinnati, Brooklyn and NY Yankees. His expressions, such as "sitting in the catbird seat," "pea patch" and "rhubarb," captivated audiences from 1934 to 1966.

Charles Barkley (b. 2-20-63): Basketball F. "The Round Mound of Rebound." Eleven-time All-Star. One of only four NBA players to amass 20,000 points, 10,000 rebounds, and 4,000 assists. Named one of NBA's greatest 50 players. Leading scorer on the 1992 Olympic team. League MVP for 1992–93 season. Played for Philadelphia, Phoenix, Houston. Career averages: 22.2 ppg, 11.7 rpg.

Rick Barry (b. 3-28-44): Basketball F. Only player in history to win scoring titles in NCAA (Miami (FL), 1965), NBA (San Francisco, 1967) and ABA (Oakland, 1969). Five-time first-team All-NBA. 1966 Rookie of the Year. 1975 playoff MVP with Golden State. Eight-time NBA All-Star. Career scoring average 23.2. Career span 1966–79.

Carmen Basilio (b. 4-2-27): Boxer. Won titles as a welterweight and middleweight. Won welterweight title by TKO of Tony DeMarco in 12 rounds on 6-10-55. Won and then lost middleweight title in two 15-round fights with Ray Robinson. Made three unsuccessful bids to regain middle title. *The Ring* Fighter of the Year for 1957. Career record: 56–16–7, 27 KOs.

Sammy Baugh (b. 3-17-14): Football QB-P. Led NFL in passing six times and punting four times, a record. Holds record for highest career punting average (45.1) and highest season average (51.0 in 1940). Career span 1937–52 with Washington, passing for 21,866 yards and 186 TDs.

Elgin Baylor (b. 9-16-34): Basketball F. Fourth alltime highest scoring average (27.4) in NBA history. Averaged 30+ points three consecutive seasons (1960-63). 1959 Rookie of the Year. 11-time All-Star. Played in eight NBA Finals without winning championship. Career span 1958–71 with Lakers. MVP of 1958 NCAA Tournament with Seattle.

Bob Beamon (b. 8-29-46): Track and field. Gold medalist in long jump at 1968 Olympics with world record leap of 29' 2½" that stood until 1991.

Franz Beckenbauer (b. 9-11-45): West German soccer player. Captain of 1974 World Cup champions and coach of 1990 champions. Also played for NY Cosmos from 1977 to 1980.

Boris Becker (b. 11-22-67): German tennis player. The youngest male player (17, in 1985) to win a Wimbledon singles title. Won three Wimbledon titles (1985–86, 1989), one U.S. Open (1989) and one Australian Open title (1991). Led West Germany to consecutive Davis Cup victories (1988–89).

Chuck Bednarik (b. 5-1-25): Football C-LB. Last of the great two-way players, was named All-Pro at both center and linebacker. Missed only three games in 14 seasons with Philadelphia from 1949–62. Seven-time All-NFL. Two-time All-America at Pennsylvania.

Clair Bee (b. 3-2-1896, d. 5-20-83): Basketball coach. Originated 1-3-1 defense, helped develop three-second rule, 24-second clock. Won 82.7 percent of games as coach for Rider College and Long Island University. Coach, Baltimore Bullets, 1952–54. Author, 23-volume Chip Hilton series for children, 21 nonfiction sports books.

Jean Beliveau (b. 8-31-31): Hockey C. Won MVP award twice (1956, 1964), playoff MVP in 1965. Led league in assists three times, goals two times and points once. 507 career goals, 712 assists. All-Star six times. Played on 10 Stanley Cup champions with Montreal from 1950 to 1971.

Bert Bell (b. 2-25-1895, d. 10-11-59): Football executive. Second NFL commissioner (1946–59). Also owner of Philadelphia (1933–40) and Pittsburgh

(1941–46). Proposed the first college draft in 1936.

James (Cool Papa) Bell (b. 5-17-03, d. 3-7-91): Baseball OF. Legendary foot speed—according to Satchel Paige could flip light switch and be in bed before room was dark. Hit .392 in games against white major leaguers. Career span 1922–46 with many teams of the Negro Leagues, including the Pittsburgh Crawfords and the Homestead Grays. Inducted in the Hall of Fame in 1974.

Lyudmila Belousova/Oleg Protopov (no dates of birth available): Soviet figure skaters. Won Olympic gold medals in pairs competition in 1964 and 1968. Won four consecutive World and European championships (1965–68) and eight consecutive Soviet titles (1961–68).

Deane Beman (b. 4-22-38): Commissioner of the PGA Tour 1974–94. Won British Amateur title in 1959 and U.S. Amateur titles in 1960 and 1963.

Johnny Bench (b. 12-7-47): Baseball C. MVP in 1970, 1972; World Series MVP in 1976; Rookie of the Year in 1968. 389 career HR. League leader in HR two times, RBI three times. Career span 1967–83 with Cincinnati. Elected to Hall of Fame in 1989.

Patty Berg (b. 2-13-18): Golfer. Alltime women's leader in major championships (16), third alltime in career wins (57). Won Titleholders Championship and Western Open seven times each, the most of any golfer. Also won U.S. Women's Amateur (1938) and U.S. Women's Open (1946).

Yogi Berra (b. 5-12-25): Baseball C. Played on 10 World Series winners. Alltime Series leader in games, at-bats, hits and doubles. MVP in 1951 and consecutively 1954–55. 358 career HR. Career span 1946–63, '65. Managed pennant-winning Yankees (1964) and Mets (1973).

Jay Berwanger (b. 3-19-14): College football RB. Won the first Heisman Trophy and named All-America with Chicago in 1935.

Raymond Berry (b. 2-27-33): Football WR. Led NFL in receiving 1958–60. In 13-season career, caught 631 passes, 68 for TDs. Career span 1955–67, all with Baltimore Colts. Coached New England Patriots from 1984–89 with 51–41 record.

George Best (b. 5-22-46): Northern Ireland soccer player. Led Manchester United to European Cup title in 1968. Named England's and Europe's Player of the Year in 1968. Played in North American Soccer League from 1976–81. Frequent troubles with alcohol and gambling shadowed career.

Abebe Bikila (b. 8-7-32, d. 10-25-73): Track and field. Ethiopian barefoot runner won consecutive gold medals in the marathon at Olympics, in 1960 and 1964.

Fred Biletnikoff (b. 2-23-43): Football WR. In 14 pro seasons caught 589 passes for 8,974 yards and 76 TDs. In 1971 led NFL receivers with 61 catches; in '72 led AFC with 58. Career span 1965–78, all with Raiders. Elected to Pro Football Hall of Fame in 1988.

Dmitri Bilozerchev (b. 12-22-66): Soviet gymnast. Won three gold medals at 1988 Olympics. Made comeback after shattering his left leg into 44 pieces in 1985. Two-time world champion (1983, '87). At 16, became youngest to win all-around world championship title in 1983.

Dave Bing (b. 11-24-43): Basketball G. NBA Rookie of Year in 1967. Led NBA in scoring (27.1) in 1968.

MVP NBA All-Star game in 1976. In 12-year career from 1967–78, most of it with Detroit Pistons, averaged 20.3 points. Averaged 24.8 ppg in four years at Syracuse.

Matt Biondi (b. 10-8-65): Swimmer. Won five gold medals, one silver and one bronze at 1988 Olympics. Won one gold and one silver at 1992 Games.

Larry Bird (b. 12-7-56): Basketball F. Won three consecutive MVP awards (1984–86) and two playoff MVP awards (1984, 1986). Rookie of the Year (1980) and All-Star nine consecutive seasons. Led league in free throw percentage four times. Averaged 20+ points 10 times. Career span 1979–92 with Boston. Named College Player of the Year in 1979 with Indiana State. 1997–98 NBA Coach of the Year in first year as coach of Indiana Pacers.

Bonnie Blair (b. 3-18-64): Speed skater. Won gold medal in 500 meters and bronze medal in 1,000 meters at 1988 Olympics. Swept both Olympic events in 1992 and '94. 1989 World Sprint champion. Winner of 1992 Sullivan Award. *Sports Illustrated* 1994 Sportswoman of the Year.

Toe Blake (b. 8-21-12, d. 5-17-95): Hockey LW and coach. Second alltime highest winning percentage (.634) and eighth in wins (500). Led Montreal to eight Stanley Cup championships from 1955 to 1968 (consecutively 1956–60, 1965–66, '68). Also MVP and scoring leader in 1939. Played on two Stanley Cup champions with Montreal from 1932 to 1948.

Doc Blanchard (b. 12-11-24): College football FB. "Mr. Inside." Teamed with Glenn Davis to lead Army to three consecutive undefeated seasons (1944–46) and two consecutive national championships (1944–45). Won Heisman Trophy and Sullivan Award in 1945. All-America three times.

George Blanda (b. 9-17-27): Football QB-K. Alltime leader in seasons played (26), games played (340), and PAT's (943); third in points scored (2,002). kicked 335 field goals. Passed for 26,920 career yards and 236 touchdowns. Tied record with seven touchdown passes on Nov. 19, 1961. AFL Player of the Year (1961) when he threw 36 TDs. Played until age 48. Career span 1949–75 with Chicago, Houston, Oakland.

Fanny Blankers-Koen (b. 4-26-18): Track and field. Dutch athlete won four gold medals at 1948 Olympics, in 100 meters; 200 meters; 80-meter hurdles; and 400-meter relay. She also set world records in high jump (5' 7¼" in 1943), long jump (20' 6" in 1943) and pentathlon (4,692 points in 1951).

Wade Boggs (b. 6-15-58): Baseball 3B. Won five batting titles (1983, consecutively 1985–88); had .350+ average five times, 200+ hits seven times. Won World Series with 1996 Yankees. Career span 1982–99 with Boston, New York Yankees, Tampa Bay; .328 career average, 3,010 hits.

Nick Bolletieri (b. 7-31-31): Tennis coach. Since 1976, has run Nick Bolletieri Tennis Academy in Bradenton, Fla. Former residents of the academy include Andre Agassi, Monica Seles and Jim Courier.

Barry Bonds (b. 7-24-64): Baseball OF. Baseball's single-season home run king, with 73 in 2001. Also produced .863 slugging percentage and 177 walks in 2001, breaking two of Babe Ruth's records, the first of which had stood since 1920. One of three players to top 40 homers (42) and 40 steals (40) in same season (1996). Four-time National League MVP (1990, '92, '93,

'01); Career span 1986–92 with Pittsburgh; 1993– with San Francisco.

Bjorn Borg (b. 6-6-56): Swedish tennis player. Third alltime in Grand Slam singles titles (11—tied with Rod Laver). Set modern record by winning five consecutive Wimbledon titles (1976–80). Won six French Open titles (1974–75, 1978–81). Reached U.S. Open final four times, but title eluded him. 65 career tournament victories. Led Sweden to Davis Cup win in 1975.

Julius Boros (b. 3-3-20, d. 5-28-94): Golfer. Won U.S. Opens in 1952 at Northwood CC in Dallas and in 1963 at The Country Club in Brookline, Mass. Won 1968 PGA Championship at Pecan Valley CC, San Antonio, when 48 years old, making him oldest winner of a major ever. Led PGA money list in 1952 and '55.

Mike Bossy (b. 1-22-57): Hockey RW. Set NHL rookie scoring record of 54 goals in 1978. Scored 50 or more each of first nine seasons. Totaled 573 goals and 1,126 points in 10 seasons (1977–87) with New York Islanders. Elected to Hall of Fame in 1991.

Ralph Boston (b. 5-9-39): Track and field. Long jumper won medals at three consecutive Olympics: gold in 1960, silver in '64, bronze in '68.

Ray Bourque (b. 12-28-60): Hockey D. Highest scoring defenseman in NHL history (1,579 pts). Won five Norris Trophies as NHL's top defenseman. Played in 19 consecutive All-Star games. No. 77. Won first and only Stanley Cup in 2001.Career span 1979–00 with Boston; 2000–01 with Colorado.

Scotty Bowman (b. 9-18-33): Retired in 2002 after leading Detroit to his ninth Stanley Cup title. Alltime leader in regular-season wins (1,244) and playoff wins (223). Coached Montreal, St. Louis, Buffalo, and Detroit. Won Jack Adams Award, Coach of the Year, 1976–77, 1995–96.

Bill Bradley (b. 7-28-43): Basketball F. Played on two NBA championship teams with New York from 1967 to '77. Player of the Year and NCAA tournament MVP in 1965 with Princeton; All-America three times; Sullivan Award winner in 1965. Rhodes scholar. U.S. Senator (D-NJ) 1979–96.

Terry Bradshaw (b. 9-2-48): Football QB. Played on four Super Bowl champions (1974, '75, '78, '79). Named Super Bowl MVP two consecutive seasons (1978–79). 212 career touchdown passes; 27,989 yards passing. Player of the Year in 1978. Career span 1970–83 with Pittsburgh.

George Brett (b. 5-15-53): Baseball 3B-1B. Won batting titles in three different decades (1976, '80, '90). MVP in 1980 with .390 batting average. Hit .300+ 11 times. Led league in hits and triples three times. Career span 1973–93, with Kansas City. Career totals: 3,153 hits; 317 HR; 1,595 RBI; batting average .305. Elected to Hall of Fame in 1999.

Bret Hanover (b. 1962, d. 1993): Horse. Son of Adios. Won 62 of 68 harness races and earned $922,616. Undefeated as two-year-old. From total of 1,694 foals, he sired winners of $61 million and 511 horses that have recorded sub-2:00 performances.

Lou Brock (b. 6-18-39): Baseball OF. Second in career stolen bases (938); second highest single-season steals total (118) of modern era. Led league in steals eight times, with 50+ steals 12 consecutive seasons. Alltime World Series leader in steals (14—tied with Eddie Collins); hit .391 in World Series play. 3,023 career hits. Career span 1961–64 Chicago (NL), 1964–79 St. Louis.

Jim Brown (b. 2-17-36): Football FB. 126 career touchdowns; 12,312 career rushing yards. Led league in rushing a record eight times. His 5.2 yards per carry average is the best ever. Player of the Year four times (1957, '58, '63, '65) and Rookie of the Year in 1957. Rushed for 1,000+ yards in seven seasons, 200+ yards in four games, 100+ yards in 54 other games. Career span 1957–65 with Cleveland; never missed a game. All-America in both football and lacrosse at Syracuse.

Paul Brown (b. 9-7-08, d. 8-5-91): Football coach. Led Cleveland to 10 consecutive championship games. Won four consecutive AAFC titles (1946–49) and three NFL titles (1950, '54, '55). Coached Cleveland from 1946 to 1962; became first coach of Cincinnati, 1968–75, and then general manager. Career coaching record 222-113-9. Also won national championship with Ohio State in 1942.

Avery Brundage (b. 9-28-1887, d. 5-5-75): Amateur sports executive. President of International Olympic Committee 1952–72. Served as president of U.S. Olympic Committee 1929–53. Also president of Amateur Athletic Union 1928–35. Member of 1912 U.S. Olympic track and field team.

Paul (Bear) Bryant (b. 9-11-13, d. 1-26-83): College football coach. Third in Division I-A football history with 323 wins. Won six national championships (1961, '64, '65, '73, '78, '79) with Alabama. Career record 323–85–17, including four undefeated seasons. Won 15 bowl games. Career span 1945–82 with Maryland, Kentucky, Texas A&M, Alabama.

Sergei Bubka (b. 12-4-63): Track and field. Ukrainian pole vaulter was gold medalist at 1988 Olympics. Only five-time world outdoor champion in any event (1983, '87, '91, '93, '95). First man to vault 20 feet, set world indoor record of 20' 2" on 2-21-93 and world outdoor record of 20' 1½" on 9-20-92.

Don Budge (b. 6-13-15, d. 1-26-00): Tennis player. First player to achieve the Grand Slam, in 1938. Won two consecutive Wimbledon and U.S. singles titles (1937, '38), one French and one Australian title (1938).

Dick Butkus (b. 12-9-42): Football LB. Regarded as greatest middle linebacker in NFL history. Selected to eight Pro Bowls. Career span 1965–73 with Chicago. All-America two times with Illinois. Award recognizing the outstanding college linebacker named in his honor.

Dick Button (b. 7-18-29): Figure skater. Gold medalist at 1948 and 1952 Olympics. World champion five consecutive years (1948–52) and U.S. champion seven consecutive years (1946–52). Sullivan Award winner in 1949.

Walter Byers (b. 3-13-22): Amateur sports executive. First director of NCAA, served from 1952 to 1987.

Frank Calder (b. 11-17-1877, d. 2-4-43): Hockey executive. First commissioner of NHL, served from 1917 to 1943. Rookie of the Year award named in his honor.

Walter Camp (b. 4-7-1859, d. 3-14-25): Football pioneer. Played for Yale in its first football game vs. Harvard on Nov. 17, 1876. Proposed rules such as 11 men per side, scrimmage line, center snap, yards and downs. Founded the All-America selections in 1889.

Roy Campanella (b. 11-19-21; d. 6-26-93): Baseball C. MVP in 1951, '53, '55. Played on five pennant winners; 1955 World Series winner with

Brooklyn. Career span 1948–57, ended when paralyzed in car crash.

Earl Campbell (b. 3-29-55): Football RB. Led NFL in rushing three consecutive seasons. Rookie of the Year in 1978. Ran for 19 TDs in 1979 and 1,934 yards in 1980 when he was named league's Player of the Year twice. 9,407 career rushing yards. Career span 1978–85 with Houston, New Orleans. Won Heisman Trophy with Texas in 1977.

John Campbell (b. 4-8-55): Canadian harness racing driver. Alltime leading money winner with over $100 million in earnings. Leading money winner in 1986–90, 1992–95, '98, '00.

Billy Cannon (b. 2-8-37): Football RB. Led Louisiana State to national championship in 1958 and won Heisman Trophy in 1959. Signed contract with both NFL (Los Angeles) and AFL (Houston) teams. Houston won lawsuit for his services. Played in six AFL championship games with Houston, Oakland, Kansas City. Career span 1960–70. Served three-year jail term for 1983 conviction on counterfeiting charges.

Jose Canseco (b. 7-2-64): Baseball OF. One of three players to top 40 homers (42) and 40 steals (40) in same season (1988). AL MVP in 1988, when he also batted .307 with 124 RBI. AL Rookie of the Year in 1986. Career span 1985–01 with seven teams: 462 HRs, 1,407 RBIs, 1,942 K's.

Harry Caray (b. 3-1-17, d. 2-18-98): Sportscaster. TV-radio baseball announcer 1945–97 with St. Louis (NL), Oakland, Chicago (AL) and Chicago (NL). Achieved celebrity status on Cubs' superstation WGN by singing "Take Me Out to the Ball Game" with Wrigley Field fans.

Rod Carew (b. 10-1-45): Baseball 2B-1B. Won seven batting titles (1969, '72–75, '77, '78). Had .328 career average, 3,053 career hits, and .300+ average 15 times. 1977 MVP; 1967 Rookie of the Year. Career span 1967–85; jersey number (29) retired by Minnesota and Anaheim.

Steve Carlton (b. 12-22-44): Baseball LHP. Four Cy Young awards (1972, '77, '80, '82). Second in career strikeouts (4,136). 329 career wins; won 20+ games six times. League leader in wins four times, innings pitched and strikeouts five times each. Struck out 19 batters in one game in 1969. Career span 1965–88 primarily with St. Louis and Philadelphia.

JoAnne Carner (b. 4-21-39): Golfer. Won 42 titles, including U.S. Women's Opens in 1971 and '76 and du Maurier Classic in 1975 and '78. LPGA top earner in 1974, '82, '83. LPGA Player of the Year in 1974, '81, '82. Won five Vare Trophies (1974, '75, '81–83).

Joe Carr (b. 10-22-1880; d. 5-20-39): Football administrator. Instrumental in forming American Professional Football Association in 1920. President of AAFA from 1922 to '39.

Don Carter (b. 7-29-26): Bowler. Won All-Star Tournament four times (1952, '54, '56, '58) and PBA National Championship in 1960. Voted Bowler of the Year six times (1953, '54, '57, '58, '60, '62).

Alexander Cartwright (b. 4-17-1820, d. 7-12-1892): Baseball pioneer. Credited with setting the basic rules of baseball: bases 90 feet apart, nine men per side, three strikes per out and three outs per inning. On June 19, 1846, in what is often cited as the first baseball game, his New York Knickerbockers lost to the New York Nine 23–1 at Elysian Fields in Hoboken, NJ.

Billy Casper (b. 6-24-31): Golfer. Famed putter. Won 51 PGA tournaments. PGA Player of Year in both 1966 and '70. Won Vardon Trophy in 1960, '63, '64, '65 and '68. Won the U.S. Open twice, in 1959 at Winged Foot in Mamaronek, New York, and in 1966 in 18-hole playoff over Arnold Palmer at Olympic Club, San Francisco. Beat Gene Littler in 18-hole playoff to win 1970 Masters.

Tracy Caulkins (b. 1-11-63): Swimmer. Won three gold medals at 1984 Olympics. Won 48 U.S. national titles, more than any other swimmer, from 1978 to 1984. Also won Sullivan Award in 1978.

Steve Cauthen (b. 5-1-60): Jockey. In 1978 became youngest jockey to win Triple Crown, aboard Affirmed. First jockey to top $6 million in season earnings (1977). *Sports Illustrated* Sportsman of Year for 1977. Moved to England in 1979; rode Epsom Derby winners Slip Anchor (1985) and Reference Point (1987).

Evonne Goolagong Cawley (b. 7-31-51): Tennis player. Won four Australian Open titles from 1974 through '77; won 1971 French Open; won Wimbledon in 1971 and '80. Runner-up four straight years at U.S. Open (1973–76), which she never won.

Bill Chadwick (b. 10-10-15): Hockey referee. Spent 16 years as a referee despite vision in only one eye. Developed hand signals to signify penalties. Also former television announcer for the New York Rangers.

Wilt Chamberlain (b. 8-21-36, d. 10-12-99): Basketball C. "The Big Dipper." "The Stilt." Scored 100 points in a single game in 1962. Alltime leader in rebounds (23,924) and rebounding average (22.9). Third in career points (31,419). Alltime single-season leader in points scored (4,029 in 1962), scoring average (50.4 in 1962), rebounding average (27.2 in 1961) and field goal percentage (.727 in 1973). Set record for most rebounds in a game in 1960 (55). Four MVP awards (1960, '66–68); playoff MVP in 1972 and 1960 Rookie of the Year. 13-time All-Star. 30.1 career scoring average. Career span 1959–72 with Philadelphia/Golden State Warriors, Philadelphia 76ers, Los Angeles.

Colin Chapman (b. 1928, d. 12-16-83): Auto racing engineer. Founded Lotus race and street cars, designing the first Lotus racer in 1948. Introduced the monocoque design for Formula One cars in 1962 and ground effects in 1978.

Julio Cesar Chavez (b. 7-12-62): Mexican boxer. Held titles as junior welterweight, lightweight and super featherweight. Career record: 103-6-2 (83 KOs).

Gerry Cheevers (b. 12-7-40): Hockey goalie. Goaltender for Stanley Cup-winning Boston Bruins teams of 1970 and '72. In 12 seasons with Boston had 230-94-74 record with a goals against average of 2.89. Also coached Bruins from 1980–84, with 204-126-46 record. Elected to Hall of Fame 1985.

Cigar (b. 1990): Thoroughbred race horse. Tied Citation's American-record 16-race win-streak with a win on 7-13-96. Won $4 million Dubai World Cup on 3-27-96.

Citation (b. 4-11-45, d. 8-8-70): Thoroughbred race horse. Triple Crown winner in 1948 with jockey Eddie Arcaro aboard. Trained by Ben A. Jones.

King Clancy (b. 2-25-03, d. 11-6-86): Hockey D. Four-time All-Star. Coach, Montreal Maroons, Toronto. Also referee. Trophy named in his honor, recognizing leadership qualities and contribution to community.

Jim Clark (b. 3-4-36, d. 4-7-68): Scottish auto racer. Won 25 career Formula 1 races. Formula 1 champion two times (1963, 1965). Won Indy 500 in 1965. Named Indy 500 Rookie of the Year in 1963. Killed during competition in 1968 at age 32.

Bobby Clarke (b. 8-13-49): Hockey C. Won MVP award three times (1973, '75, '76). 358 career goals, 852 assists. Scored 100+ points three times. Played on two consecutive Stanley Cup champions (1974, '75) with Philadelphia. Career span 1969–84. Also general manager Philadelphia 1984–90, Minnesota 1991–92, Florida 1993–94, and Philadelphia 1994–.

Roger Clemens (b. 8-4-62): Baseball RHP. Won six Cy Young awards (1986, '87, '91, '97, '98, '01), most by any pitcher. Also 1986 MVP. Has struck out a record 20 batters in one game on two occasions. League leader in ERA six times, strikeouts four times, and wins four times. Won Triple Crown of pitching in 1997 and '98. Career span 1984–96 with Boston, 1997–98 with Toronto; 1999– with Yankees.

Roberto Clemente (b. 8-18-34, d. 12-31-72): Baseball OF. Killed in plane crash while still an active player. Had 3,000 career hits; .317 career average. Won four batting titles; .300+ average 13 times. 1966 MVP; 1971 World Series MVP. Twelve consecutive Gold Gloves; led league in assists five times. Career span 1955–72 with Pittsburgh.

Ty Cobb (b. 12-18-1886, d. 7-17-61): Baseball OF. Alltime leader in batting average (.366), second in runs scored (2,245) and hits (4,189), fourth in stolen bases (892). 1911 MVP and 1909 Triple Crown winner. Twelve batting titles. Had .400+ average three times, .350+ average 13 other times; 200+ hits nine times. Led league in hits seven times, steals six times and runs scored five times. Career span 1905–28 with Detroit and Philadelphia.

Mickey Cochrane (b. 4-6-03, d. 6-28-62): Baseball C. Second highest career batting average among catchers (.320). MVP in 1928, '34. Had .300+ average eight times. Career span 1925–37 with Philadelphia and Detroit.

Sebastian Coe (b. 9-29-56): Track and field. Two-time Olympic gold medalist in the 1,500 meters (1980, '84). Also won two silver medals in 800 meters at same two Olympics. Set world record in 800 meters (1:41.73 in 1981) and 1,000 meters (2:12.18 in 1981). Served in British Parliament after his running career.

Eddie Collins (b. 5-2-1887, d. 3-25-51): Baseball 2B. 3,311 career hits; .333 career average; .330+ average 12 times. 743 career stolen bases; alltime co-leader in World Series steals (14—tied with Lou Brock); alltime leader in single-game steals (six, twice). 1914 MVP. Career span 1906–30 with Philadelphia (AL), Chicago (AL).

Nadia Comaneci (b. 11-12-61): Romanian gymnast. First ever to score a perfect 10 at Olympics (on uneven parallel bars in 1976). Won three gold, two silver and one bronze medal at 1976 Olympics. Also won two gold and two silver medals at 1980 Olympics.

Dennis Conner (b. 9-16-42): Sailing. Captain of three America's Cup winners (1980, '87,'88).

Maureen Connolly (b. 9-17-34, d. 6-21-69): Tennis player. "Little Mo." First woman to achieve the Grand Slam, in 1953. Won the U.S. singles title in 1951 at age 16. Thereafter lost only four matches before retiring in 1954 after breaking her leg in a riding accident. Was never beaten in singles at Wimbledon, winning three

consecutive titles (1952–54). Won three consecutive U.S. singles titles (1951–53) and two consecutive French titles (1953–54). Also won Australian title (1953).

Jimmy Connors (b. 9-2-52): Tennis player. Alltime men's leader in tournament victories (109). Held men's No. 1 ranking a record 160 consecutive weeks (7-29-74 through 8-16-77). Won five U.S. Open singles titles on three different surfaces (grass 1974, clay 1976, hard 1978, '82, '83). Won two Wimbledon singles titles (1974, '82) further apart than anyone since Bill Tilden. Also won 1974 Australian Open title. Reached Grand Slam final seven other times.

Jim Corbett (b. 9-1-1866; d. 2-18-33): Boxer. "Gentleman Jim." Invented jab. Won heavyweight title on 9-7-1892 with a KO of John Sullivan in 21 rounds; it was first heavyweight title fight using gloves. Lost title when KO'd by Bob Fitzsimmons in 14 on 3-17-1897, then lost two bids to regain it against Jim Jeffries. Career record: 11-4-2, 7 KOs, 2 ND.

Angel Cordero (b. 11-8-42): Jockey. Seventh alltime in wins (7,057) and earnings ($164,561,227). Led yearly earnings three times, in 1976, '82, '83, winning Eclipse Awards in the last two years.

Howard Cosell (b. 3-25-18, d. 4-23-95): Sportscaster. Lawyer-turned–TV-radio sports commentator. Best known for his work on "Monday Night Football." His nasal voice and "tell it like it is" approach made him a controversial figure.

James (Doc) Counsilman (b. 12-28-20): Swimming coach. Coached Indiana from 1957 to 1990. Won six consecutive NCAA championships (1968–73). Career record 287-36-1. Coached U.S. men's team at Olympics in 1964, '76. Swam English Channel in 1979 at age 58.

Count Fleet (b. 3-24-40, d. 12-3-73): Thoroughbred race horse. Triple Crown winner in 1943 with jockey Johnny Longden aboard. Trained by Don Cameron.

Yvan Cournoyer (b. 11-22-43): Hockey RW. "The Roadrunner" had 428 goals and 435 assists during his 15-season career with the Montreal Canadiens. Had 25 or more goals in 12 straight seasons. Played on 10 Stanley Cup championship teams. Elected to Hall of Fame in 1982.

Margaret Smith Court (b. 7-16-42): Australian tennis player. Alltime leader in Grand Slam singles titles (24) and total Grand Slam titles (62). Achieved Grand Slam in 1970 and mixed doubles Grand Slam in 1963 with Ken Fletcher. Won 11 Australian singles titles (1960–66, 1969–71, '73), five French titles (1962, '64, '69, '70, '73), 5 U.S. titles (1962, '65, '69, '70, '73) and three Wimbledon titles (1963, '65, '70). Court also won 19 Grand Slam doubles titles and 19 mixed doubles titles.

Bob Cousy (b. 8-9-28): Basketball G. Led NBA in assists eight consecutive seasons. Averaged 18+ points and named to All-Star team 10 consecutive seasons. 1957 MVP. Played on six championship teams with Boston from 1950 to 1969. Finished career with 6,955 assists; in 1958 had 28 assists in a single game. Also played on 1947 NCAA title team with Holy Cross.

Dave Cowens (b. 10-25-48): Basketball C. NBA co-Rookie of Year in 1971. NBA MVP for 1973. All-Star game MVP in 1973. Career span 1970–71 through 1982–83, all but the last year with the Boston Celtics, averaging 17.6 points and 13.6 rebounds per game. Coached Charlotte 1996–99 and Golden State 2000–01. Elected to Hall of Fame in 1991.

Ben Crenshaw (b. 1-11-52): Golfer. Legendary putter. Won Masters in 1984 and '95. Captain of 1999 U.S. Ryder Cup team.

Johan Cruyff (b. 4-25-47): Dutch soccer player. Led Ajax Amsterdam to three European Cup titles, and guided the Netherlands to the 1974 World Cup final, a 2–1 loss to Germany.

Larry Csonka (b. 12-25-46): Football RB. In 11 seasons rushed for 8,081 yards and 64 TDs. MVP of Super Bowl VIII, when he rushed 33 times for a then Super Bowl–record 145 yards in Miami's 24–7 defeat of Minnesota. Career span 1968–74, '79 with Miami; 1976–78 with New York Giants. Elected to Hall of Fame in 1987.

Billy Cunningham (b. 6-3-43): Basketball player and coach. "Kangaroo Kid." In 11 pro seasons (1965–76) with Philadelphia 76ers and Carolina Cougars, averaged 21.2 points per game. Three-time first-team all-NBA selection (1969–71). 1973 ABA MVP. Coached 76ers to three NBA Finals and the 1983 NBA title. Elected to Hall of Fame in 1985.

Bjørn Dæhlie (b.6-19-67): Norwegian skier. Legendary cross-country skier won a Winter Olympics–record eight gold medals over three Games from 1992 to '98. Won a total of 12 Olympic medals and more than 40 World Cup races.

Chuck Daly (b. 7-20-30): Basketball coach. Coached the 1992 Olympic "Dream Team." Won two consecutive NBA titles with Detroit (1989, '90). Won 50+ games four consecutive seasons. Coached Detroit 1983–92, New Jersey 1992–94, and Orlando 1997–99.

Damascus (b. 1964, d. 1995): Thoroughbred race horse. After finishing third in 1967 Kentucky Derby, won the Preakness, the Belmont, the Dwyer, the American Derby, the Travers, the Woodward and others—12 of 16 starts. Unanimous Horse of the Year in 1967.

Stanley Dancer (b. 7-25-27): Harness racing driver. Only driver to win the Trotting Triple Crown two times (Nevele Pride in 1968, Super Bowl in 1972). Also won Pacing Triple Crown driving Most Happy Fella in 1970. Won The Hambletonian four times (1968, '72, '75, '83). Driver of the Year in 1968.

Tamas Darnyi (b. 6-3-67): Hungarian swimmer. Gold medalist in 200-meter and 400-meter individual medleys at 1988 and '92 Olympics. Won both events at World Championships in 1986 and '91. Set world records in these events at 1991 Championships (1:59.36 and 4:12.36).

Al Davis (b. 7-4-29): Football executive. Owner and general manager of Raiders since 1963. Team has won three Super Bowl championships (1976, '80, '83). Served as AFL commissioner in 1966; helped negotiate AFL–NFL merger. Famously moved Raiders to Los Angeles in 1982 and back to Oakland in 1995.

Ernie Davis (b. 12-14-39, d. 5-18-63): Football RB. Won Heisman Trophy in 1961, the first black man to win the award. All-America three times at Syracuse. First selection in 1962 NFL draft, but became fatally ill with leukemia and never played professionally.

Glenn Davis (b. 12-26-24): College football HB. "Mr. Outside." Teamed with Doc Blanchard to lead Army to three consecutive undefeated seasons (1944–46) and two consecutive national championships (1944, '45). Won Heisman Trophy in 1946. Named All-America three times.

John Davis (b. 1-12-21, d. 7-13-84): Weightlifter. Gold medalist at two consecutive Olympics, 1948, '52. World champion six times.

Terrell Davis (b. 10-28-72): Football RB. One of only four players to rush for more than 2,000 yards in a season (2,008 in 1998). MVP of Super Bowl XXXII, rushing for 157 yards and three TDs for Denver. Forced to retire in 2002 after several knee injuries.

Pete Dawkins (b. 3-8-38): Football RB. 1958 Heisman Trophy winner while at Army. Never played pro football. Attended Oxford on Rhodes scholarship, won two Bronze Stars in Vietnam, rose to brigadier general before leaving Army to become investment banker. Made unsuccessful run for Senate from New Jersey in 1988.

Len Dawson (b. 6-20-35): Football QB. MVP of Super Bowl IV, a 23–7 victory against Minnesota. Threw 239 TDs in his career. Career span 1957–75, the last 14 seasons with Kansas City Chiefs. Elected to Hall of Fame in 1987.

Dizzy Dean (b. 1-16-11, d. 7-17-74): Baseball RHP. 1934 MVP with 30 wins. League leader in strikeouts, complete games four times each. 150 career wins. Arm trouble shortened career after 134 wins by age 26. Career span 1930–41 and 1947 with St. Louis and Chicago (NL).

Dave DeBusschere (b. 10-16-40): Basketball F. NBA first-team All-Defensive Team six straight seasons, 1969–74. Member of NBA champion New York Knicks in 1970 and '73. Career span 1962–74 with Detroit and New York. Career stats: 16.1 ppg, 11.0 rpg. Youngest coach (24) in NBA history. Elected to NBA Hall of Fame in 1982.

Pierre de Coubertin (b. 1-1-1863, d. 9-2-37): Frenchman called the father of the Modern Olympics. President of International Olympic Committee from 1896 to 1925.

Oscar De La Hoya (b. 2-4-73): Boxer. Won title belts in five different weight classes between junior lightweight and junior middleweight divisions. 35–2 with 28 KOs. Won lightweight gold medal at 1992 Olympics in Barcelona.

Jack Dempsey (b. 6-24-1895, d. 5-31-83): Boxer. Heavyweight champ (1919–26), lost title to Gene Tunney and rematch in the famed "long count" bout in 1927. Career record 62-6-10 with 49 KOs from 1914–28.

Gail Devers (b. 11-19-66): Track and field sprinter-hurdler. Won 100 meters at 1992 and '96 Olympics. Successfully completed 100m/100h double at 1993 World Championships, winning 100 in 10.82 and 100 hurdles in American record 12.46. Also won '93 world indoor title in 60 (6.95). Battled Graves disease.

Klaus Dibiasi (b. 10-6-47): Italian diver. Gold medalist at three consecutive platform titles (1968, '72, '76) and silver medalist at 1964 Olympics.

Eric Dickerson (b. 9-2-60): Football RB. Alltime single-season record holder in yards rushing (2,105 in 1984). Fourth in career rushing yards (13,259). Led league in rushing four times. Rushed for 1,000+ yards in seven consecutive seasons; 100+ yards in 61 games, including 12 times in 1984. Rookie of the Year in 1983. Career span 1983–93 with Los Angeles Rams, Indianapolis, Los Angeles Raiders and Atlanta.

Bill Dickey (b. 6-6-07 d. 11-12-93): Baseball C. Lifetime average .313. Hit 202 career home runs. Played on 11 AL All-Star teams. In eight World Series, hit five homers with 24 RBI. Career span 1928–43 and 1946, all with New York (AL). Inducted to Hall of Fame 1954.

Harrison Dillard (b. 7-8-23): Track and field. Only man to win Olympic gold medal in sprint (100 meters in 1948) and hurdles (110 meters in 1952). Sullivan Award winner in 1955.

Joe DiMaggio (b. 11-25-14 d. 3-8-99): Baseball OF. "The Yankee Clipper." Hit safely in record 56 straight games in 1941. MVP in 1939, '41, '47. Had .325 career batting average; .300+ average 11 times; 100+ RBI nine times. League leader in batting average, HR, and RBI two times each. Played on 10 World Series winners with New York (AL). Career span 1936–51.

Mike Ditka (b. 10-18-39): Football TE–Coach. First TE elected to Hall of Fame (1988). NFL Rookie of the Year in 1961. Named to five Pro Bowls. Made 427 catches for 5,812 yards and 43 TDs. Career span 1961–72 with Chicago, Philadelphia and Dallas. Coached Chicago to 46–10 win against New England in Super Bowl XX. Recorded 127–101 record as head coach of Chicago and New Orleans.

Tony Dorsett (b. 4-7-54): Football RB. Fifth leading rusher in NFL history (12,739 yards). Set record for longest run from scrimmage with 99-yard TD run on 1-3-83. Scored 91 career TDs. Rushed for 1,000+ yards in eight seasons. Named Rookie of the Year in 1977. Career span 1977–88 with Dallas, Denver. Graduated from Pittsburgh as alltime NCAA leader in yards rushing (6,082) and won 1976 Heisman Trophy.

Abner Doubleday (b. 6-26-1819, d. 1-26-1893): Civil War hero incorrectly credited as the inventor of baseball in Cooperstown, NY, in 1839.

Clyde Drexler (b. 6-22-62): Basketball G. Nicknamed "The Glide" for his smooth play. Member of U.S. "Dream Team" that won 1992 Olympic gold medal. Career span 1984–1994 with Portland and 1995–98 with Houston, with whom he won his first NBA title in 1995. Career stats: 20.4 ppg, 5.6 apg. Head coach at University of Houston from 1998–00.

Ken Dryden (b. 8-8-47): Hockey G. Goaltender of the Year five times (1973, 1976–79). Playoff MVP as a rookie in 1971, maintained rookie status and named Rookie of the Year in 1972. Led league in goals against average five times. Career record 258-57-74, including 46 shutouts. Career 2.24 goals against average is the modern record. Four playoff shutouts in 1977. Played on six Stanley Cup champions with Montreal from 1970 to 1979.

Don Drysdale (b. 7-23-36, d. 7-3-93): Baseball RHP. Set the major league record—broken in 1988 by Orel Hershiser—of 58 consecutive scoreless innings in 1968. Led NL three times in strikeouts (1959, '60, '62) and once in wins (1962). Won 1962 Cy Young Award with 25–9 mark. Career record of 209–166, with 2,484 K's and 2.95 ERA. Career span 1956–69, all with Dodgers. Inducted into Hall of Fame 1984.

Tim Duncan (b. 4-25-76): Basketball C. 2001 NBA MVP. First-team All-NBA every season in the league (1998–02). 1998 Rookie of the Year. 1999 NBA Finals MVP, when he led San Antonio to the NBA title. Career span 1997– with San Antonio.

Roberto Duran (b. 6-16-51): Panamanian boxer. Champion in three different weight classes: lightweight (1972–79), welterweight (1980, lost rematch to Sugar Ray Leonard in famous "no más" bout) and junior middleweight (1983–84). Career record: 104–15 (69 KOs).

Leo Durocher (b. 7-27-05, d. 10-7-91): Baseball manager. "Leo the Lip." Said "Nice guys finish last." Managed three pennant winners and 1954 World Series winner. Won 2,008 games in 24 years. Led Brooklyn 1939–48; New York (NL) 1948–55; Chicago (NL) 1966–72; and Houston 1972–73.

David Duval (b. 11-9-71): Golfer. Won 2001 British Open. Set record for tour earnings in a single season with $2.6 million in 1998, when he also won Vardon Trophy for lowest scoring average (69.13). Four-time all-America at Georgia Tech.

Tomás Dvorák (b. 5-11-72): Czech decathlete. Broke Dan O'Brien's seven-year-old decathlon world record by 103 points on 7-4-99 in Prague, amassing 8,994 points. Won decathlon bronze medal at Atlanta in '96.

Eddie Eagan (b. 4-26-1898, d. 6-14-67): Only American athlete to win gold medal at Summer and Winter Olympic Games (boxing 1920, bobsled '32).

Alan Eagleson (b. 4-24-33): Hockey labor leader. Founder of NHL Players' Association and its executive director from 1967–92. Resigned from Hall of Fame 3-25-98 and served six months of an 18-month jail sentence for three counts of fraud and theft involving players' insurance premiums.

Dale Earnhardt (b. 4-29-52, d. 2-18-01): Auto racer. "The Intimidator." NASCAR champion seven times (1980, 1986–87, 1990–91, 1993–94). Won 1998 Daytona 500 and 75 other NASCAR races. Died in crash on the final lap of the 2001 Daytona 500.

Stefan Edberg (b. 1-19-66): Swedish tennis player. Won two Wimbledon singles titles (1988, '90), two Australian Open titles (1985, '87) and two U.S. Open titles (1991, '92). Led Sweden to three Davis Cup titles (1984, '85, '87).

Gertrude Ederle (b. 10-23-06): Swimmer. First woman to swim the English Channel, in 1926. Swam 21 miles from France to England in 14:39. Also won three medals at the 1924 Olympics.

Hicham El Gerrouj (b. 9-14-74): Track and field. Morrocan runner broke world record in mile on 7-7-99, clocking 3:43.13 to trim 1.26 seconds from six-year-old previous record. Performance was his fourth world records, in addition to indoor mile, indoor 1,500 and outdoor 1,500.

Herb Elliott (b. 2-25-38): Track and field. Australian runner was gold medalist in 1960 Olympic 1,500 meters in world record 3:35.6. Also set world mile record of 3:54.5 in 1958. Undefeated at 1,500 meters/mile in international competition. Retired at 22.

Ernie Els (b.10-17-69): South African golfer. Two-time U.S. Open winner (1994, '97); first foreign-born player to win the event twice since Alex Smith in 1910. 2002 British Open champion.

John Elway (b. 6-28-60): Football QB. First player taken in 1983 NFL draft. One of two NFL QBs with more than 50,000 passing yards (51,475). 300 career TD passes. Famous for last-minute drives. Won back-to-back Super Bowls (XXXII and XXXIII) after three previous Super Bowl losses. Career span 1983–99 with Denver.

Roy Emerson (b. 11-3-36): Australian tennis player. Second alltime in Grand Slam singles titles (12). Won six Australian titles, five consecutively (1961, 1963–67), two Wimbledon titles (1964, '65), two U.S. titles (1961, '64) and two French titles (1963, '67). Also won 13 Grand Slam doubles titles.

Kornelia Ender (b. 10-25-58): East German swimmer. Won four gold medals at 1976 Olympics and three silver medals at 1972 Olympics.

Julius Erving (b. 2-22-50): Basketball F. "Dr. J." His combined ABA and NBA career points (30,026) rank fifth alltime. Career scoring average of 24.2. Won four MVP awards (1974–76, '81); playoff MVP 1974, '76. All-Star 16 times. Led ABA in scoring three times. Played on three championship teams, with New York (ABA) and Philadelphia (NBA). Career span 1971–86. Elected to Hall of Fame in 1993.

Phil Esposito (b. 2-20-42): Hockey C. "Espo." First to break the 100-point barrier (126 in 1969). Led league in goals six consecutive seasons, points five times and assists three times. Won MVP award two times (1969, '74). 1,590 career points, 717 goals, and 873 assists. Scored 30+ goals 13 consecutive seasons and 100+ points six times. All-Star 10 times. Career span 1963–81 with Chicago, Boston, New York Rangers.

Tony Esposito (b. 4-23-43): Hockey goalie. Brother of Phil. A six-time All-Star during 16-season NHL career, almost all of it with the Chicago Blackhawks. Career GAA of 2.92. Won or shared Vezina Trophy three times. Elected to Hall of Fame in 1988.

Janet Evans (b. 8-28-71): Swimmer. Competed in 1988, '92 and '96 Olympics, winning three gold medals in '88 and one in '92. Set world record in 400-meter freestyle (4:03.85 in 1988), 800-meter freestyle (8:16.22 in 1989) and 1,500-meter freestyle (15:52.10 in 1988). Sullivan Award winner in 1989.

Lee Evans (b. 2-25-47): Track and field. Gold medalist in 400 meters at 1968 Olympics with world record time of 43.86, which stood until 1988.

Chris Evert (b. 12-21-54): Also Chris Evert Lloyd. Tennis player. Second alltime in tournament titles (157). Tied for fourth alltime in women's Grand Slam singles titles (18). Won at least one Grand Slam singles title every year from 1974–86. Won seven French Open titles (1974, '75, '79, '80, '83, '85, '86), six U.S. Open titles (1975–77, '78, '80, '82), three Wimbledon titles (1974, '76, '81) and two Australian Open titles (1982, '84). Reached Grand Slam finals 16 other times. Reached semifinals at 52 of her last 56 Grand Slams.

Weeb Ewbank (b. 5-6-07, d. 11-17-98): Football coach. Only coach to win titles in both the NFL and AFL. Coached Baltimore Colts to classic overtime defeat of New York Giants in 1958 and New York Jets to their stunning 16–7 win over Baltimore in Super Bowl III. Career record of 134-130-7. Career span 1954–62 with Colts and 1963–73 with Jets. Elected to Hall of Fame in 1978.

Patrick Ewing (b. 8-5-62): Basketball C. First NBA "lottery" pick. 1986 Rookie of the Year. A member of two gold-medal winning Olympic teams, including the 1992 "Dream Team." Career span 1985–02 with New York, Seattle, and Orlando; averaged 21.0 ppg, 9.8 rpg. Played in three NCAA title games with Georgetown (1982, '84, '85); tournament MVP in 1984.

Nick Faldo (b. 7-18-57): British golfer. Three-time winner of Masters (1989, '90, '96) and British Open (1987, '90, '92).

Juan Manuel Fangio (b. 6-24-11, d. 7-17-95): Argentine auto racer. 24 Formula 1 victories in just 51 starts. Formula 1 champion five times, the most of any driver (1951, '54–57). Retired in 1958.

Brett Favre (b.10-10-69): Football QB. Won NFL MVP award three years in a row (1995–97). Sixth on the alltime list for TD passes (287). Led Packers to victory in Super Bowl XXXI. Career span 1991– with Atlanta and Green Bay.

Bob Feller (b. 11-3-18): Baseball RHP. Pitched three no-hitters and 12 one-hitters. 266 career wins; 2,581 career strikeouts. Won 20+ games six times. League leader in wins six times, strikeouts seven times, innings pitched five times. Served four years in military during career. Career span 1936–41, 1945–56 with Cleveland.

Tom Ferguson (b. 12-20-50): Rodeo. First to top $1 million in career earnings. All-Around champion six consecutive years (1974–79).

Enzo Ferrari (b. 2-8-1898, d. 8-14-88): Auto racing engineer. Team owner since 1929, he built first Ferrari race car in Italy in 1947 and continued to preside over Ferrari race and street cars until his death. In 68 years of competition, Ferrari's cars have won over 5,000 races.

Herve Filion (b. 2-1-40): Harness racing driver. Alltime leader in career wins (more than 14,000). Driver of the Year 10 times, more than any other driver (consecutively 1969–74, '78, '81, '89).

Rollie Fingers (b. 8-25-46): Baseball RHP. Won 107 games in relief in his career; 341 career saves. 1981 Cy Young and MVP winner; 1974 World Series MVP. Saved six World Series games in his career. Career span 1968–85 with Oakland, San Diego, Milwaukee.

Bobby Fischer (b. 3-9-43): Chess. World champion from 1972 to 1975, the only American to hold title. Never played competitive chess during his reign. Forfeited title to Anatoly Karpov by refusing to play him.

Carlton Fisk (b. 12-26-47): Baseball C. Alltime HR leader among catchers (352) and second in games caught (2,226). 376 career HR, including a record 75 after age 40. Rookie of the Year in 1972 and All-Star 11 times. Hit dramatic 12th-inning HR to win Game 6 of 1975 World Series. Career span 1969–93 with Boston, Chicago (AL). Elected to Hall of Fame in 2000.

Emerson Fittipaldi (b. 12-12-46): Brazilian auto racer. Won Indy 500 in 1989 and '93. Won CART championship in 1989. Formula 1 champion two times (1972, '74).

James Fitzsimmons (b. 7-23-1874, d. 3-11-66): Horse racing trainer. "Sunny Jim." Trained two Triple Crown winners (Gallant Fox in 1930, Omaha in 1935). Trained six Belmont Stakes winners (1930, '32, '35, '36, '39, '55), four Preakness Stakes winners (1930, '35, '55, '57) and three Kentucky Derby winners (1930, '35, '39).

Peggy Fleming (b. 7-27-48): Figure skater. Olympic champion 1968. World champion (1966–68) and U.S. champion (1964–68).

Curt Flood (b. 1-18-38, d. 1-20-97): Baseball OF. Challenged baseball's reserve clause by refusing to be traded after 1969 season. Supreme Court rejected his plea, but baseball was eventually forced to adopt free agency system. Won seven consecutive Gold Gloves from 1963 to 1969. Career batting average of .293. Career span 1956–69 with St. Louis.

Whitey Ford (b. 10-21-26): Baseball LHP. Alltime World Series leader in wins, losses, games started, innings pitched, hits allowed, walks and strikeouts. 236 career wins, 2.75 ERA. Led league in wins and winning percentage three times each; ERA, shutouts, innings pitched two times each. 1961 Cy Young winner and World Series MVP. Career span 1950, 1953–67 with New York Yankees.

Forego (b. 1970, d. 8-27-97): Thoroughbred race horse. Horse of the Year in 1974 (won 8 of 13 starts); '75 (won 6 of 9); and '76 (won 8 of 8). Finished fourth in 1973 Kentucky Derby. Over six years won 34 of 57 starts and $1,938,957.

George Foreman (b. 1-22-48): Boxer. Heavyweight champion (1973–74). Retired in 1977, but returned to the ring in 1987. At age 45, KO'd Michael Moorer to regain heavyweight title. Also heavyweight gold medalist at 1968 Olympics.

Dick Fosbury (b. 3-6-47): Track and field. Gold medalist in high jump at 1968 Olympics. Introduced back-to-the-bar style of high jumping, called the "Fosbury Flop."

Jimmie Foxx (b. 10-22-07, d. 7-21-67): Baseball 1B. Won three MVP awards (1932–33, '38). Fourth alltime highest slugging average (.609), with 534 career HR; hit 30+ HR 12 consecutive seasons, 100+ RBI 13 consecutive seasons. Won Triple Crown in 1933. Led league in HR four times, batting average two times. Career span 1925–45 with Philadelphia, Boston (AL).

A.J. Foyt (b. 1-16-35): Auto racer. Alltime leader in Indy Car victories (67). Won Indy 500 four times (1961, '64, '67, '77), Daytona 500 one time (1972), 24 Hours of Daytona two times (1983, '85) and 24 Hours of LeMans one time (1967). USAC champion seven times, more than any other driver (1960, '61, '63, '64, '67, '75, '79).

William H.G. France (b. 9-26-09, d. 6-7-92): Auto racing executive. Founder of NASCAR and president from 1948–72. Builder of Daytona and Talladega speedways.

Dawn Fraser (b. 9-4-37): Australian swimmer. First swimmer to win gold medal in same event at three consecutive Olympics (100-meter freestyle in 1956, '60, '64). First woman to break the one-minute barrier at 100 meters (59.9 in 1962).

Joe Frazier (b. 1-12-44): Boxer. "Smokin' Joe." Heavyweight champion (1970–73). Best known for his three epic bouts with Muhammad Ali. Career record 32-4-1 with 27 KOs from 1965 to 1976. Also heavyweight gold medalist at 1964 Olympics.

Walt Frazier (b. 3-29-45): Basketball G. "Clyde." Point guard on championship Knick teams of 1970 and '73. First team All-NBA in 1970, '72, '74 and '75. First team All-Defense every year from 1969–'75. Averaged 18.9 points per game in 13-season NBA career. Elected to Hall of Fame in 1986.

Frankie Frisch (b. 9-9-1898, d. 3-12-73): Baseball IF. "The Fordham Flash." Led NL in hits in 1923 (223). NL MVP in 1931. Hit over .300 13 seasons. Scored 100+ runs seven times. Drove in 100+ runs three times. Career .316 batting average. Career span 1919–37 with New York (NL) and St. Louis (NL). Elected to Hall of Fame in 1947.

Dan Gable (b. 10-25-48): Wrestler. Gold medalist in 149–pound division at 1972 Olympics. Two-time NCAA champion (in 1968 at 130 pounds, in 1969 at 137 pounds). Coached Iowa to NCAA championship 15 times (1978–86, 1991–93 and 1995–97).

Clarence Gaines (b. 5-21-23): College basketball coach. "Bighouse." 828 career wins in 46 seasons at Division II Winston-Salem State from 1947–93.

John Galbreath (b. 8-10-1897, d. 7-20-88): Horse racing owner. Owner of Darby Dan Farms from 1935 until his death and of baseball's Pittsburgh Pirates from 1946 to 1985. Only man to breed and own winners of both the Kentucky Derby (Chateaugay in 1963 and Proud Clarion in 1967) and the Epsom Derby (Roberto in 1972).

Gallant Fox (b. 3-23-27, d. 11-13-54): Thoroughbred race horse. Triple Crown winner in 1930 with jockey Earle Sande aboard. Trained by James Fitzsimmons. The only Triple Crown winner to sire another Triple Crown winner (Omaha in 1935).

Don Garlits (b. 1-14-32): Auto racer. "Big Daddy." Has won 35 National Hot Rod Association Top Fuel events. Won three NHRA Top Fuel points titles (1975, 1985–86). First Top Fuel driver to surpass 190 mph (1963), 200 mph (1964), 240 mph (1973), 250 mph (1975) and 270 mph (1986). Credited with developing rear-engine dragster.

Haile Gebrselassie (b. 4-18-73): Track and field. Ethiopian distance runner has dominated long distance running since 1993. Holds world records in the 5,000 and 10,000 meters. Gold medalist in the 10,000 at the 1996 and 2000 Olympics.

Lou Gehrig (b. 6-19-03, d. 6-2-41): Baseball 1B. "The Iron Horse." Second alltime in consecutive games played (2,130), leader in grand slam HR (23), third in RBI (1,995) and slugging average (.632). MVP in 1927, '36; won Triple Crown in 1934. .340 career average; 493 career HR. 100+ RBI 13 consecutive seasons. Led league in RBI five times and HR three times. Played on seven World Series winners with New York (AL). Died of disease since named for him. Career span 1923–39.

Bernie Geoffrion (b. 2-16-31): Hockey RW. "Boom Boom" for his powerful slapshot. Won Hart Memorial Trophy for 1960–61. Scored 393 goals and 429 assists in 16 seasons (1950–68), the first 14 with Montreal, the final two with New York. Elected to Hall of Fame 1972.

Eddie Giacomin (b. 6-6-39): Hockey goalie. "Fast Eddie" led NHL goalies in wins for three straight seasons. Shared Vezina Trophy for 1970–71. Career GAA of 2.82. Career span 1965–78 with New York and Detroit.

Althea Gibson (b. 8-25-27): Tennis player. Won two consecutive Wimbledon and U.S. singles titles (1957, '58), the first black player to win these tournaments. Also won the French Open in 1956.

Bob Gibson (b. 11-9-35): Baseball RHP. 1968 Cy Young and MVP award winner with modern National League–best ERA (1.12). Also 1970 Cy Young award winner. Pitched no-hitter in 1971. Record holder for most strikeouts in a World Series game (17); Series MVP in 1964, '67. Won 20+ games five times. 251 career wins; 3,117 strikeouts. Career span 1959–75 with St. Louis.

Josh Gibson (b. 12-21-11, d. 1-20-47): Baseball C. "The Black Babe Ruth." Couldn't play in major leagues because of racial barrier. Credited with 950 HR (75 in 1931, 69 in 1934) and .350 batting average. Had .400+ average two times. Career span 1930–46 with Homestead Grays, Pittsburgh Crawfords.

Kirk Gibson (b. 5-28-57): Baseball OF. Played on two World Series champions (Detroit in 1984 and Los Angeles in 1988). Hit dramatic pinch-hit HR to win Game 1 of 1988 series. MVP in 1988. Career span

1979–94 with Detroit, Los Angeles, Kansas City, Pittsburgh. Also starred in baseball and football at Michigan State.

Frank Gifford (b. 8-16-30): Football RB. NFL Player of Year in 1956 when he rushed for 819 yards and caught 51 passes. Played in seven Pro Bowls. Retired for one season after ferocious hit by Chuck Bednarik. Career span 1952–60 and 1962–64, all with New York (N). Elected to Hall of Fame in 1977.

Rod Gilbert (b. 7-1-41): Hockey RW. Played 16 seasons, all with the New York Rangers (1960–78), and had 406 goals and 615 assists. Elected to Hall of Fame 1982.

Sid Gillman (b. 10-26-11): Football coach. Developed wide-open, pass-oriented style of offense, introduced techniques for situational player substitutions and the study of game films. Won AFL championship (1963) with San Diego Chargers. Career span 1955–59 Los Angeles; 1960–69 Los Angeles/San Diego Chargers; 1973–74 Houston. Lifetime record 123-104-7.

Pancho Gonzales (b. 5-9-28, d. 7-3-95): Tennis player. Won two consecutive U.S. singles titles (1948–49). In 1969, at age 41, beat Charlie Pasarell 22–24, 1–6, 16–14, 6–3, 11–9 in longest Wimbledon match ever (5:12).

Jeff Gordon (b. 8-4-71): Auto racer. NASCAR's alltime money winner. Four-time NASCAR Winston Cup champion (1995, '97, '98, '01). Youngest Winston Cup Series champion in the modern era, winning his first title at age 24. Won 1997 and '99 Daytona 500. Set NASCAR modern record with 13 wins in 1998.

Shane Gould (b. 11-23-56): Australian swimmer. Won three gold medals, one silver and one bronze at 1972 Olympics. Set 11 world records over 23-month period beginning in 1971. Held world record in five freestyle distances ranging from 100 meters to 1,500 meters in late 1971 and 1972. Retired at age 16.

Steffi Graf (b. 6-14-69): German tennis player. Achieved the Grand Slam in 1988. Won four Australian Open singles titles (1988–90, '94), seven Wimbledon titles (1988, '89, 1991–93, '95, '96), six French Open titles (1987, '88, '93, '95, '96, '99) and five U.S. Open titles (1988–89, '93, '95, '96). Held the No. 1 ranking for a record 186 weeks. Gold medalist at 1988 Olympics. Second in alltime Grand Slam singles titles (22).

Otto Graham (b. 12-6-21): Football QB. Led Cleveland to 10 championship games in his 10-year career. Played on four consecutive AAFC champions (1946–49) and three NFL champions (1950, '54, '55). Combined league totals: 23,584 yards passing, 174 touchdown passes. Player of the Year two times (1953, '55). Led league in passing six times. Career span 1946–55.

Red Grange (b. 6-13-03, d. 1-28-91): Football HB. "The Galloping Ghost." All-America three consecutive seasons with Illinois (1923–25), scoring 31 touchdowns in 20-game collegiate career. Signed by George Halas of Chicago in 1925, attracted sellout crowds across the country. Established the first AFL with manager C.C. Pyle in 1926, but league folded after one year. Career span 1925–34 with Chicago, New York.

Rocky Graziano (b. 6-7-22, d. 5-22-90): Boxer. Middleweight champion from 1947–48. Career record 67–13. Endured three brutal title fights against Tony Zale, with Zale winning by KO in 1946 and 1948, and Graziano winning by KO in 1947.

Hank Greenberg (b. 1-1-11, d. 9-4-86): Baseball 1B. 331 career HR (58 in 1938). MVP in 1935, '40. League leader in HR and RBI four times each. Fifth alltime highest slugging average (.605). 100+ RBI seven times. Career span 1933-41, 1945-47 with Detroit, Pittsburgh.

Joe Greene (b. 9-24-46): Football DT. "Mean Joe." Anchored Pittsburgh's famed "Steel Curtain" defense. Selected for Pro Bowl 10 times. Played on four Super Bowl champions (1974, '75, '78, '79). Career span 1969–81 with Pittsburgh.

Maurice Greene (b. 7-23-74): Track and field. Won Olympic gold medals in Sydney in the 100 meters and the 4x100 relay. Held world record for 100 meters for three years after running 9.79 in Athens on 6-16-99.

Forrest Gregg (b. 10-18-33): Football OT/G. Played in then-record 188 straight games from 1956–71. Named all-NFL eight straight years starting in 1960. Career span 1956–71, most of it with Green Bay Packers. Played on winning Packer team in first two Super Bowls. Inducted into Hall of Fame in 1977.

Wayne Gretzky (b. 1-26-61): Hockey C. "The Great One." No. 99. Most dominant player in NHL history. Alltime scoring leader in points (2,795), assists (1,910), and goals (885). Alltime single-season scoring leader in points (215 in 1986), goals (92 in 1982) and assists (163 in 1986). Won nine MVP awards (1980-87, '89). Led league in assists 16 times, scoring 11 times, goals five times. Scored 200+ points four times, 100+ points 10 other times; 70+ goals four consecutive seasons, 50+ goals five other times; 100+ assists 11 consecutive seasons. Playoff MVP two times (1985, '88). Played on four Stanley Cup champions with Edmonton from 1978 to 1988. Career span 1978–99 with Edmonton, Los Angeles, St. Louis, and New York Rangers.

Bob Griese (b. 2-3-45): Football QB. Led Miami to three straight Super Bowls (1971–73), including the 1972 Miami team that went 17–0. Career span 1967–80 with Miami, passing for 25,092 yards and 192 TDs. Elected to Hall of Fame in 1990.

Florence Griffith Joyner (b. 12-21-59, d. 9-21-98): Track and field. Won three gold medals (100 meters, 200 meters, 4x100-meter relay) at 1988 Olympics; Set world record in 100 (10.49) in 1988 and in 200 (21.34) at the 1988 Olympics. Sullivan Award winner in 1988.

Ken Griffey Jr. (b. 11-21-69): Baseball OF. Hit 56 home runs in back-to-back seasons (1997–98). Became youngest man (31 years 261 day) to reach 450 HRs when he connected on 8-9-01. Won AL MVP award in 1997, when he hit .304 with 56 HRs and 147 RBI. 10 Gold Glove Awards. Father Ken Sr. starred with Cincinnati Reds in 1970s.

Archie Griffin (b. 8-21-54): College football RB. Only player to win the Heisman Trophy two times (1974–75), with Ohio State. Eighth alltime NCAA career yards rushing (5,177). Professional career span 1976–83 with Cincinnati; totaled 2,808 yards rushing and 192 receptions.

Lefty Grove (b. 3-6-00, d. 5-22-75): Baseball LHP. 300 career wins and fifth alltime highest winning percentage (.680). League leader in ERA nine times, strikeouts seven consecutive seasons. Won 20+ games eight times. 1931 MVP. Career span 1925–41 with Philadelphia (AL), Boston (AL).

Tony Gwynn (b. 5-9-60): Baseball OF. Won eight batting titles (1984, 1987–89, 1994–97). League leader in hits six times, with .300+ average 16 times, 200+ hits five times. Career span 1982–01 with San Diego: .338 average, 3,141 hits.

Walter Hagen (b. 12-21-1892, d. 10-5-69): Golfer. Third alltime leader in major championships (11). Won PGA Championship five times (1921, 1924–27), British Open four times (1922, '24, '28, '29) and U.S. Open two times (1914, '19). Won 40 career tournaments.

Marvin Hagler (b. 5-23-54): Boxer. "Marvelous." Middleweight champion (1980–87). Career record 62-3-2 with 52 KOs from 1973–87. Defended title 13 times.

George Halas (b. 2-2-1895, d. 10-31-83): Football owner and coach. "Papa Bear." Alltime leader in seasons coaching (40) and second in wins (324). Career record 324-151-31 intermittently from 1920–1967. Remained as owner until his death. Chicago won a record seven NFL championships during his tenure.

Glenn Hall (b. 10-3-31): Hockey goalie. "Mr. Goalie" was an All-Star in 11 of his 18 seasons. Set record for consecutive games played by a goaltender (502) and ended career with goals against average of 2.51. Won or shared Vezina Trophy three times. Career span 1952–71 with Detroit, Chicago and St. Louis.

Charles Haley (b. 1-6-64): Football DE. Only player in NFL history to be a member of five Super Bowl champions, two with San Francisco (1989, '90) and three with Dallas (1993, '94, '96). Career span 1986–99. Recorded 100.5 career sacks.

Mia Hamm (b. 3-17-72): Soccer player. Alltime leading scorer in U.S. women's national team history. Member of Women's World Cup champion team in 1991, '99, and third-place team in '95. Member of 1996 Olympic champion team. Debuted with national team against China on 8-3-87 as its youngest player ever, at age 15.

Arthur B. (Bull) Hancock (b. 1-24-10, d. 9-14-72): Horse racing owner. Owner of Claiborne Farm and arguably the greatest breeder in history. For 15 straight years, from 1955–69, a Claiborne stallion led the sire list. Foaled at Claiborne Farm were four Horses of the Year (Kelso, Round Table, Bold Ruler and Nashua).

Tom Harmon (b. 9-28-19, d. 3-17-90): Football RB. Won Heisman Trophy in 1940 with Michigan. Triple-threat back led nation in scoring and named All-America two consecutive seasons (1939, '40). Awarded Silver Star and Purple Heart in World War II. Played in NFL with Los Angeles (1946–47).

Franco Harris (b. 3-7-50): Football RB. Holds Super Bowl record for career rushing yards (354), Super Bowl MVP in 1974. Made the "Immaculate Reception" to win 1972 playoff game against Oakland. Played on four Super Bowl champions (1974, '75, '78, '79) with Pittsburgh. Gained 1,000+ yards in nine seasons, 100+ yards in 47 games. Played in eight Pro Bowls. Rookie of the Year in 1972. Career span 1972–84 with Pittsburgh and Seattle. Rushed for 12,120 yards and scored 100 career touchdowns. Elected to the Hall of Fame in 1990.

Leon Hart (b. 11-2-28, d. 9-24-02): Football DE. Won Heisman Trophy in 1949, the last lineman to win the award. Played on three national championships with Notre Dame (1946, '47, '49), and the Irish went undefeated during his four years (36-0-2). Also played on three NFL champions with Detroit. Career span 1950–57.

Bill Hartack (b. 12-9-32): Horse racing jockey. Rode five Kentucky Derby winners (1957, '60, '62, '64, '69), three Preakness Stakes winners (1956, '64, '69) and one Belmont Stakes winner (1960).

Doug Harvey (b. 12-19-24, d. 12-26-90): Hockey D. Defensive Player of the Year seven times (1954–57, 1959–61). Led league in assists in 1954. All-Star 10 times. Played on six Stanley Cup champions with Montreal from 1947–68.

Dominik Hasek (b. 1-29-65): Czech hockey G. Two-time NHL MVP (1997, '98) with Buffalo; six-time Vezina Trophy winner (1994, '95, 1997–99, '01) as top goalie in league. Led NHL with a 1.95 goals-against average in 1993–94, the first sub-2.00 GAA since Bernie Parent in 1974. Topped that with 1.87 GAA in 1998–99. Guided Czech Republic to Olympic gold medal in 1998 at Nagano. Career span 1990–02 with Chicago, Buffalo and Detroit.

Billy Haughton (b. 11-2-23, d. 7-15-86): Harness racing driver. Won the Pacing Triple Crown driving Rum Customer in 1968. Won The Hambletonian four times (1974, '76, '77, '80).

John Havlicek (b. 4-8-40): Basketball F/G. "Hondo" averaged 20.8 points per game over 16-season NBA career, all with Boston. First team All-NBA (1971–74). Member of eight NBA championship teams. Playoff MVP 1974. Member of Ohio State team that won 1960 NCAA title. Elected to Hall of Fame in 1983.

Elvin Hayes (b. 11-17-45): Basketball C. Three-time first-team All-NBA selection (1975, '77, '79). 12-time All-Star (1969–80). Led NBA in scoring (1969) and in rebounding (1970, '74). Played from 1968–84 with San Diego/Houston Rockets and Baltimore/Washington Bullets, averaging 21.0 points and 12.5 rebounds per game. 1968 *Sporting News* College Player of Year as Houston senior. Elected to Hall of Fame in 1989.

Woody Hayes (b. 2-14-13, d. 3-12-87): College football coach. Won three national championship (1954, '57, '68) and four Rose Bowls. Career record 238-72-10, including four undefeated seasons, with Ohio State from 1951–1978. Forced to resign after striking an opposing player during 1978 Gator Bowl.

Marques Haynes (b. 10-3-26): Basketball G. Known as "The World's Greatest Dribbler." Beginning in 1946 barnstormed more than four million miles throughout 97 countries for the Harlem Globetrotters, Harlem Magicians, Meadowlark Lemon's Bucketeers, Harlem Wizards.

Thomas Hearns (b. 10-18-58): Boxer. "Hit Man." Champion in four weight classes: welterweight, super welterweight, middleweight and light heavyweight. Career record: 57–4–1 with 45 KOs.

Eric Heiden (b. 6-14-58): Speed skater. Won five gold medals at 1980 Olympics. World champion three consecutive years (1977–79). Won Sullivan Award in 1980.

Carol Heiss (b. 1-20-40): Figure skater. Gold medalist at 1960 Olympics, silver medalist at 1956 Olympics. World champion five consecutive years (1956–60) and U.S. champion four consecutive years (1957–60). Married 1956 gold medalist Hayes Jenkins.

Rickey Henderson (b. 12-25-57): Baseball OF. Career leader in stolen bases, walks and runs; modern single-season stolen base record holder (stole 130 bases in 1982). Led league in steals 11 times. 1990 MVP. Alltime leader in lead-off HRs. Career span 1979– with nine teams.

Sonja Henie (b. 4-8-12, d. 10-12-69): Norwegian figure skater. Gold medalist at three consecutive Olympics (1928, '32, '36). World champion 10 consecutive years (1927–36).

Orel Hershiser (b. 9-16-58): Baseball RHP. Alltime leader most consecutive scoreless innings pitched (59 in 1988). Cy Young Award winner in 1988 and World Series MVP. Career span 1983–00 with Los Angeles, Cleveland, San Francisco and New York (NL): 204–150, 3.48 ERA.

Foster Hewitt (b. 11-21-02, d. 4-22-85): Hockey sportscaster. In 1923, aired one of hockey's first radio broadcasts. Became the voice of hockey in Canada on radio and later television. Famous for the phrase, "He shoots ... he scores!"

Tommy Hitchcock (b. 2-11-00, d. 4-19-44): Polo. 10-goal rating 18 times in his 19-year career from 1922–40. Killed in plane crash in World War II.

Lew Hoad (b. 11-23-34): Australian tennis player. Won two Wimbledon singles titles (1956, '57). Also won French title and Australian title in 1956, but failed to achieve the Grand Slam when defeated at Forest Hills by countryman Ken Rosewall.

Ben Hogan (b. 8-13-12, d. 7-25-97): Golfer. Third alltime in career wins (63). Won U.S. Open four times (1948, '50, '51, '53), the Masters (1951, '53) and PGA Championship (1946, '48) two times each and British Open once (1953). PGA Player of the Year four times (1948, '50, '51, '53).

Marshall Holman (b. 9-29-54): Bowler. Won 21 PBA titles between 1975–88. Had leading average in 1987 (213.54) and was named PBA Bowler of the Year.

Nat Holman (b. 10-18-1896, d. 2-12-95): College basketball coach. Only coach in history to win NCAA and NIT championships in same season, in 1950 with CCNY; 423 career wins, a .689 winning percentage.

Larry Holmes (b. 11-3-49): Boxer. Heavyweight champion (1978–85). Career record 69–6 with 44 KOs from 1973–02. Defended title 21 times.

Lou Holtz (b. 1-6-37): Football coach. Has led four different programs to Top 20 seasons. Coached Notre Dame to national championship in 1988 and a 12–0 record with a 34–21 win over West Virginia in Fiesta Bowl. 12-8-2 career record in bowl games. Career span 1969–75 at William & Mary and N Carolina St; 1977–96 at Arkansas, Minnesota and Notre Dame; and 1999– at S Carolina. Career record: 233-113-7.

Evander Holyfield (b. 10-19-62): Boxer. Only man to win the heavyweight title four times. Won heavyweight crown Oct. 25, 1990 when he KO'd James (Buster) Douglas in Las Vegas. Fought three epic bouts with Riddick Bowe and two memorable fights with Mike Tyson (Tyson was disqualified in the rematch for biting Holyfield's ears.) Career record: 38–5–2, 26 KOs.

Red Holzman (b. 8-10-20; d. 11-13-98): Basketball coach. Led New York to NBA titles in 1970 and '73. NBA Coach of the Year in 1970. After two-year coaching stints with Milwaukee and St. Louis, coached New York from 1968–82. Career record: 696–604. Elected to Hall of Fame in 1985.

Harry Hopman (b. 8-12-06, d. 12-27-85): Australian tennis coach. As nonplaying captain, led Australia to 15 Davis Cup titles between 1950–69. Mentor to Lew Hoad, Ken Rosewall, Rod Laver and John Newcombe.

Willie Hoppe (b. 10-11-1887, d. 2-1-59): Billiards. Won 51 world championship matches from 1904–52.

Rogers Hornsby (b. 4-27-1896, d. 1-5-63): Baseball 2B. Second alltime in career batting average (.358), won seven batting titles, including with .424 average in 1924. Led league in slugging nine times. Triple Crown winner in 1922, '25; MVP award winner in 1925, '29. 2,930 hits and 1,584 RBI's from 1915–37 with five teams, including St. Louis (NL).

Paul Hornung (b. 12-23-35): Football RB–K. Led league in scoring three consecutive seasons, including a record 176 points in 1960 (15 touchdowns, 15 field goals, 41 extra points). Player of the Year in 1961. Career span 1957–66 with Green Bay. Suspended for 1963 season by Pete Rozelle for gambling. Also won Heisman Trophy in 1956 with Notre Dame.

Gordie Howe (b. 3-31-28): Hockey RW. Second alltime in goals (801), first in years played (26) and games (1,767). Finished career with 1,850 points and 1,049 assists. Won MVP award six times (1952, '53, '57, '58, '60, '63). Led league in scoring six times, goals five times and assists three times. All-Star 12 times. Played on four Stanley Cup champions with Detroit from 1946–71. Teamed with sons Mark and Marty in the WHA with Houston and New England from 1973–79, in NHL with Hartford in 1980.

Carl Hubbell (b. 6-22-03, d. 11-21-88): Baseball LHP. 253 career wins. MVP in 1933, '36. League leader in wins and ERA three times each. Won 24 consecutive games from 1936–37. Struck out Ruth, Gehrig, Foxx, Simmons and Cronin consecutively in 1934 All-Star game. Pitched no-hitter in 1929. Career span 1928–43 with New York (NL).

Sam Huff (b. 10-4-34): Football LB. Made 30 interceptions. Career span 1956–69 with New York Giants and Washington. Elected to Hall of Fame in 1982.

Bobby Hull (b. 1-3-39): Hockey LW. "The Golden Jet." Led league in goals seven times and points three times. 610 career goals. Won MVP award two consecutive seasons (1965, '66). Son Brett won MVP award in 1991, the only father and son to be so honored. All-Star 10 times. Career span 1957–72 with Chicago, 1973–80 with Winnipeg of WHA.

Brett Hull (b. 8-9-64): Hockey RW. Son of Bobby Hull. Won Hart Memorial Trophy for 1990–91 season. Scored Stanley Cup–winning goal for Dallas in third overtime of Game 6 against Buffalo in 1999. Career span 1986– with Calgary, St. Louis, Dallas and Detroit.

Jim (Catfish) Hunter (b. 4-8-46, d. 9-9-99): Baseball RHP. 1974 Cy Young award winner. Won 20+ games five consecutive seasons. Led league in wins and winning percentage two times each, ERA one time. 250+ innings pitched eight times. Pitched perfect game in 1968. Member of five World Series champions for Oakland and New York (AL). Career span 1965–79.

Don Hutson (b. 1-31-13, d. 6-26-97): Football WR. Fourth alltime in touchdown receptions (99). Led league in pass receptions eight times, receiving yards seven times and scoring five consecutive seasons. Caught at least one pass in 95 consecutive games. Player of the Year two consecutive seasons (1941, '42). Career span 1935–45 with Green Bay.

Hank Iba (b. 8-6-04; d. 1-15-93): College basketball coach. Coached Oklahoma A&M (which became

Oklahoma State) from 1934–70. Team won NCAA titles in 1945 and '46. 767 career wins is seventh alltime.

Jackie Ickx (b. 1-1-45): Belgian auto racer. Won the 24 Hours of LeMans a record six times (1969, 1975–77, '81, '82) before retiring in 1985.

Punch Imlach (b. 3-15-18, d. 12-1-87): Hockey coach. 467 wins. With Toronto from 1958–69. Won four Stanley Cup championships (1962–64, 1967).

Miguel Induráin (b. 7-16-64): Cyclist. Won an unprecedented five consecutive Tours de France (1991–95).

Juli Inkster (b.6-24-60): Golfer. 28 career victories. Became only the second woman ever to win all four of the LPGA's modern majors when she won the LPGA Championship on 6-27-99. Inducted to LPGA Hall of Fame in 1999.

Bo Jackson (b. 11-30-62): Baseball OF and Football RB. Only person in history to be named to baseball All-Star game and football Pro Bowl game. 1985 Heisman Trophy winner at Auburn. 1989 MLB All-Star game MVP. Signed with football's LA Raiders in 1988. Retired 1994 following hip replacement surgery.

Joe Jackson (b. 7-16-1889, d. 12-5-51): Baseball OF. "Shoeless Joe." Third alltime highest career batting average (.356), with .300+ average 11 times. One of the "Eight Men Out" banned from baseball for throwing 1919 World Series. Career span 1908–20 with Cleveland, Chicago (AL).

Phil Jackson (b. 9-17-45): Basketball F-Coach. Coached the Lakers to their third straight NBA Championship in 2002, his ninth as a coach. Won six titles as coach of Chicago (1991–93, 1996–98). Best winning percentage in NBA history (726–258, .738). Spent 13 years as a scrappy forward in the NBA, winning an NBA title with New York in 1973.

Reggie Jackson (b. 5-18-46): Baseball OF. "Mr. October." Alltime leader in World Series slugging percentage (.755). 1977 Series MVP, hit three HR in final game on three consecutive pitches. 563 career HR total is eighth best alltime. Led league in HR four times. 1973 MVP. Alltime strikeout leader (2,597). In a 12-year period played on 10 first-place teams, five World Series winners. Career span 1967–87 with Oakland, Baltimore, New York (AL) and California. Inducted to Baseball Hall of Fame in 1993.

Bruce Jenner (b. 10-28-49): Track and Field. Set decathlon world record (8,634) in winning gold medal at 1976 Olympics. Sullivan Award winner in 1976.

John Henry (b. 1975): Thoroughbred race horse. Sold as yearling for $1,100, the gelding was Horse of the Year in 1981 and 1984 and retired with then-record $6,597,947 in winnings.

Ben Johnson (b. 12-30-61): Track and field. Canadian sprinter set world record in 100 meters (9.83 in 1987). Won event at 1988 Olympics in 9.79, but gold medal revoked for failed drug test. Both world records revoked for steroid usage. Suspended for life after testing positive for elevated testosterone level at an indoor meet in Montreal on 1-17-93.

Earvin (Magic) Johnson (b. 8-14-59): Basketball G. Retired Nov. 7, 1991 after being diagnosed with HIV, the virus that causes AIDS. Returned to Lakers Feb '96 at age 36. Finished career second alltime in assists (10,141). MVP award three times (1987, '89, '90) and playoff MVP in 1980, '82 and '87. Played on five championship teams with Los Angeles. All-Star eight consecutive seasons. League leader in assists

four times, steals two times, free throw percentage once. Career stats: 19.5 ppg, 11.2 apg, 7.2 rpg. Also won NCAA championship and named tournament MVP in 1979 with Michigan State.

Jack Johnson (b. 3-31-1878, d. 6-10-46): Boxer. First black heavyweight champion (1908–15). Career record 78-8-12 with 45 KOs from 1897–28.

Jimmy Johnson (b. 7-16-43): Football coach. Won two straight Super Bowls (1993, '94) as Dallas coach. Career record of 89–66 with Dallas and Miami. Led Miami (FL) to collegiate national championship in 1987. One of only three men to win college and NFL championships.

Michael Johnson (b. 9-13-67): Track and field. First man to win gold medals in both the 200 and 400 at the Olympics (1996). Broke 17-year-old 200-meter world record (19.66) at 1996 U.S. Olympic trials, then further lowered mark to 19.32 at Atlanta. Repeated in the 400 meters at the 2000 Sydney Games. Anchored U.S. 4x400 team at 1993 World Championship to world record of 2:54.29.

Walter Johnson (b. 11-6-1887, d. 12-10-46): Baseball RHP. "Big Train." Alltime leader in shutouts (110), second in wins (416), fourth in losses (279) and third in innings pitched (5,914). His record of 3,509 career strikeouts lasted for 56 years. 2.17 career ERA. MVP in 1913, '24. Won 20+ games 12 times. League leader in strikeouts 12 times, ERA five times, wins six times. Pitched no-hitter in 1920. Career span 1907–27 with Washington.

Ben A. Jones (b. 12-31-1882, d. 6-13-61): Horse racing trainer. Trained Triple Crown winner (Whirlaway) in 1941). Trained six Kentucky Derby winners, more than any other trainer (1938, '41, '44, '48, '49, '52), two Preakness Stakes winners (1941, '44) and one Belmont Stakes winner (1941).

Bobby Jones (b. 3-17-02, d. 12-18-71): Golfer. Achieved golf's only recognized Grand Slam in 1930. Second alltime in major championships (13). Won U.S. Amateur five times, more than any golfer (1924, '25, '27, '28, '30), U.S. Open four times (1923, '26, '29, '30), British Open three times (1926, '27, '30) and British Amateur (1930). Also designed Augusta National course, site of the Masters, and founded the tournament. Winner of Sullivan Award in 1930.

K.C. Jones (b. 5-25-32): Basketball G-coach. Member of eight straight NBA-championship Boston teams in his nine season career from 1958–67. Averaged 7.4 points and 4.3 assists per game. Coached Celtics from 1983–88, with 308–102 regular season record and 65–37 playoff record with NBA titles in 1984 and '86.

Robert Trent Jones (b. 6-20-06, d. 6-14-00): English-born golf course architect designed or remodeled over 500 courses, including Baltusrol, Hazeltine, Oak Hill and Winged Foot. In the mid-60s five straight U.S. Opens were played on courses designed or remodeled by Jones.

Roy Jones Jr. (b.1-16-69): Boxer. Won titles as middleweight, super middleweight and light heavyweight. Career record: 47–1, 38 KOs. Won controversial silver medal at the 1988 Olympics in Seoul despite dominating his South Korean opponent in the final. Awarded Val Barker Trophy as outstanding boxer of '88 Games.

Sam Jones (b. 6-24-33): Basketball G. Played 12 seasons with Boston (1958–69), who won NBA title every year from 1959–66, plus 1968 and '69.

Averaged 17.7 points per game. Elected to Hall of Fame in 1983.

Michael Jordan (b. 2-17-63): Basketball G. "Air." Arguably greatest player of all time. Led Bulls to six NBA titles (1991–93; 1996–98). Alltime leader in scoring average (31.5 ppg) and record holder for most points scored in a playoff game (63 in 1986). Guided Bulls to an NBA-record 72 wins in 1995–96. Led league in scoring a record 10 seasons, steals three times. League MVP in 1988, '91, '92, '96 and '98; Finals MVP in 1991–93 and 1996–98; Rookie of the Year in 1985. Career span 1984–93, 1995–98 with Chicago; 2001– with Washington. College Player of the Year in 1984. Played on NCAA title team with North Carolina in 1982. Member of gold medal-winning 1984 and '92 Olympic teams. Played minor league baseball in 1994.

Jackie Joyner-Kersee (b. 3-3-62): Track and field. Gold medalist in heptathlon and long jump at 1988 Olympics and in the former at the 1992 Olympics. Set heptathlon world record (7,291 points) at 1988 Olympics. Also won silver medal in heptathlon at 1984 Games and bronze in long jump at 1992 and '96 Olympics. Sullivan Award winner in 1986.

Alberto Juantorena (b. 3-12-51): Track and field. Cuban was gold medalist in 400 and 800 meters at 1976 Olympics.

Wang Junxia (b. 1963): Chinese distance runner. Broke four world records in six days in Sept. 1993. Broke 10,000 (29:31.78) on Sept 8; ran 1,500 in 3:51.92 in finishing second to countrywoman Qu Yunxia's world record of 3:50.46 on Sept 11; ran 3,000 record of 8:12.19 in heats on Sept 12 and lowered it to 8:06.11 on Sept 13. Won gold in 5,000 and silver in 10,000 at 1996 Olympics.

Sonny Jurgensen (b. 8-23-34): Football QB. In 18 seasons, passed for 32,224 yards and 255 TDs. Led NFL in passing both 1967 and '69. Career span 1957–74 with Philadelphia and Washington. Elected to Hall of Fame in 1983.

Duke Kahanamoku (b. 8-24-1890, d. 1-22-68): Swimmer. Won a total of five medals (3 gold and two silver) at three Olympics in 1912, '20, '24. Introduced the crawl stroke to America. Surfing pioneer and water polo player. Later sheriff of Honolulu.

Al Kaline (b. 12-19-34): Baseball OF. 3,007 career hits and 399 career HR. As a 20-year-old in 1955, became youngest player to win batting title, with .340 average. Had .300+ average nine times. Played in 18 All-Star games. Career span 1953–74 with Detroit.

Anatoly Karpov (b. 5-23-61): Soviet chess player. First world champion to receive title by default, in 1975, when Bobby Fischer chose not to defend his crown. Champion until 1985 when beaten by Garry Kasparov. Recognized by FIDE as champion in 1994.

Garry Kasparov (b. 4-13-63): Born Garik Weinstein. Chess player. World champion from 1985 to 1993 when stripped of title by FIDE. Won six-game series against IBM computer, Deep Blue, in 1996. Lost to improved version of Deep Blue in 1997.

Kip Keino (b. 1-17-40): Track and field. Kenyan was gold medalist in 1,500 meters at 1968 Olympics and in steeplechase at 1972 Olympics.

Jim Kelly (b. 2-14-60): Football QB. Led Buffalo to four straight Super Bowls—all losses. Seventh-ranked passer of alltime (84.4). Led NFL in passing in 1990. In 11 NFL seasons passed for 35,467 yards and 237 TDs. Career span 1983–96 with Houston (USFL) and Buffalo Bills.

Kelso (b. 1957, d. 1983): Thoroughbred race horse. Gelding was Horse of the Year five straight years (1960–64). Finished in the money in 53 of 63 races. Career earnings $1,977,896.

Harmon Killebrew (b. 6-29-36): Baseball 3B-1B. 573 career HR total is seventh most alltime. 100+ RBI nine times, 40+ HR eight times. League leader in HR six times and RBI four times. 1969 MVP. 100+ walks and strikeouts seven times each. Career span 1954–75 with Washington and Minnesota.

Jean Claude Killy (b. 8-30-43): French skier. Won three gold medals at 1968 Olympics. World Cup overall champion two consecutive years (1967, '68).

Ralph Kiner (b. 10-27-22): Baseball OF. Led league in HR seven consecutive seasons. Third in alltime HR frequency (7.1 HR every 100 at bats). 369 career HR, with 50+ HR two times. 100+ RBI and runs scored in same season six times; 100+ walks six times. Career span 1946–55 with Pittsburgh, Chicago (NL), and Cleveland.

Billie Jean King (b. 11-22-43): Tennis player. Won a record 20 Wimbledon titles, including six singles titles (1966–68, '72, '73, '75). Won four U.S. singles titles (1967, '71, '72, '74), and singles titles at Australian Open (1968) and French Open (1972). Won 27 Grand Slam doubles titles—total of 39 Grand Slam titles is third alltime. Helped found the women's pro tour in 1970, serving as president of the Women's Tennis Association two times. Helped form Team Tennis.

Nile Kinnick (b. 7-9-18, d. 6-2-43): College football RB. Won the Heisman Trophy in 1939 with Iowa. Premier runner, passer and punter was killed in plane crash during routine Navy training flight. Stadium in Iowa City named in his honor.

Tom Kite (b. 12-9-49): Golfer. Winner of 19 career PGA Tour events, including the 1992 U.S. Open at Pebble Beach. Led PGA in scoring average in 1981 and '82. PGA Player of Year in 1989, when he won a then-record $1,395,278. Ryder Cup captain in 1997.

Franz Klammer (b. 12-3-54): Austrian alpine skier. Greatest downhiller ever. Gold medalist in downhill at 1976 Olympics. Also won four World-Cup downhill titles (1975–78).

Bob Knight (b. 10-25-40): College basketball coach. Won three NCAA championships with Indiana in 1976, '81, '87. Coached U.S. Olympic team to gold medal in 1984. Fired by Indiana in 2000 after a series of disputes with the media, ex-players, students, and the university. Hired by Texas Tech in 2001. 787 career wins and .725 career winning percentage. Career span since 1966 with Army, Indiana and Texas Tech.

Olga Korbut (b. 5-16-55): Soviet gymnast. First ever to complete backward somersault on balance beam. Won three gold medals at 1972 Olympics.

Johann Olav Koss (b. 10-29-68): Speed Skater. Norwegian won three gold medals at 1994 Olympics in Lillehammer, with world records in the 1,500, 5,000 and 10,000 meters. Won 1,500 meter gold medal and 10,000 meter silver medal in 1992 Games at Albertville.

Sandy Koufax (b. 12-30-35): Baseball LHP. Cy Young Award winner three times (1963, '65, '66); and MVP in 1963; World Series MVP in 1963, '65. Pitched four no-hitters, including one perfect game. League leader in ERA five consecutive seasons, strikeouts four times. Won 25+ games three times. Career record

165–87, with 2.76 ERA. Career span 1955–66 with Brooklyn/Los Angeles.

Jack Kramer (b. 8-1-21): Tennis player. Won two consecutive U.S. singles titles (1946, '47) and one Wimbledon title (1947). Also won six Grand Slam doubles titles. Served as executive director of Association of Tennis Professionals from 1972–75.

Ingrid Kristiansen (b. 3-21-56): Track and field. Norwegian runner is only person—male or female—to hold world records in 5,000 meters (14:37.33 set in 1986), 10,000 meters (30:13.74 set in 1986) and marathon (2:21:06 set in 1985). Also won Boston Marathon two times (1986, '89) and New York City Marathon once (1989).

Bob Kurland (b. 12-23-24): College basketball player. 6' 10¼" center on Oklahoma A&M teams that won NCAA titles in 1945 and '46. Consensus All-America and NCAA tournament MVP in both 1945 and '46. Led nation in scoring in 1946. His habit of swatting shots off rim led to creation of goaltending rule in 1945. Won gold medals in both 1948 and '52 Olympics. Turned down lucrative pro offers, playing instead for Phillips 66 Oilers AAU team.

Michelle Kwan (b. 7-7-80): Figure skater. Six-time U.S. champion (1996, 1998–02), four-time world champion (1996, '98, '00, '01); silver medalist in 1998 Olympics and bronze medalist in Salt Lake City in 2002.

Rene Lacoste (b. 7-2-05, d. 10-12-96): French tennis player. "The Crocodile." One of France's "Four Musketeers" of the 1920s. Won three French singles titles (1925, '27, '29), two consecutive U.S. titles (1926, '27) and two Wimbledon titles (1925, '28). Also designed casual shirt with embroidered crocodile that bears his name.

Marion Ladewig (b. 10-30-14): Bowler. Won All-Star Tournament eight times (1949–52, '54, '56, '59, '63) and WPBA National Championship once (1960). Also voted Bowler of the Year nine times (1950–54, 1957–59, '63).

Guy Lafleur (b. 9-20-51): Hockey RW. Won MVP award two consecutive seasons (1977, '78), playoff MVP in 1977. Scored 50+ goals and 100+ points six consecutive seasons. Led league in points scored three consecutive seasons, goals and assists one time each. 560 career goals, 793 assists. Played on five Stanley Cup champions with Montreal from 1971–85.

Curly Lambeau (b. 4-9-1898; d. 6-1-65): Football QB and coach. Quarterback for Packers team in early 1920s. Record of 212-106-21 in his 29 seasons (1921–49) as Packer coach, winning three NFL titles in 1929–31.

Jack Lambert (b. 7-8-52): Football LB. Anchored Pittsburgh's famed "Steel Curtain" defense. Selected for Pro Bowl nine times. Played on four Super Bowl champions (1974, '75, '78, '79) with Pittsburgh from 1974–84. Elected to Hall of Fame 1990.

Jake LaMotta (b. 7-10-21): Boxer. "The Bronx Bull." Subject of *Raging Bull*, a film by Martin Scorsese, starring Robert DeNiro. Won middleweight title by knocking out Marcel Cerdan in 10 on 6-16-49. Lost title to Ray Robinson, who KO'd him in 13 on 2-13-51. Career record: 83–19–4, 30 KOs.

Kenesaw Mountain Landis (b. 11-20-1866, d. 11-25-44): Baseball's first and most powerful commissioner from 1920–44. By banning the eight "Black Sox" involved in the fixing of the 1919 World Series, he restored public confidence in the integrity of baseball.

Tom Landry (b. 9-11-24, d. 2-12-00): Football coach. Third alltime in wins (270). The first coach in Dallas history, from 1960–88. Led team to 13 division titles, seven championship games and five Super Bowls. Won two Super Bowl championships (1971, '77). Career record 270-178-6.

Dick (Night Train) Lane (b. 4-16-28, d. 1-29-02): Football DB. Third alltime in interceptions (68) and second in interception yardage (1,207). Set record with 14 interceptions as a rookie in 1952. Career span 1952–65 with Los Angeles, Chicago Cardinals, Detroit.

Joe Lapchick (b. 4-12-00, d. 8-10-70): Basketball C–coach. One of the first big men in basketball, member of New York's Original Celtics. Coached St. John's (1936–47, 1956–65) to four NIT titles. Coached New York Knicks, 1947–56.

Steve Largent (b. 9-28-54): Football WR. Retired as alltime leader in pass receptions (819), and TD receptions (100). 177 consecutive games with reception, 10 seasons with 50+ receptions and eight seasons with 1,000+ yards receiving. Career span 1976–89 with Seattle. Oklahoma congressman from 1994–01.

Don Larsen (b. 8-7-29): Baseball RHP. Pitched only perfect game in World Series history, for New York (AL) on 10-8-56, beating the Dodgers 2–0; named World Series MVP. Career span 1953–67 for many teams.

Tommy Lasorda (b. 9-22-27): Baseball manager. Spent nearly his entire minor and major league career in Dodgers organization as a pitcher, coach and manager. Managed Dodgers 1977–96, winning four pennants and two World Series (1981, '88). Only three men managed one baseball team longer. Coached U.S. Olympic baseball team to the gold medal at the 2000 Sydney Games.

Rod Laver (b. 8-9-38): Australian tennis player. "Rocket." Only player to achieve the Grand Slam twice (as an amateur in 1962 and as a pro in 1969). Third alltime in men's Grand Slam singles titles (11—tied with Bjorn Borg). Won four Wimbledon titles (1961, '62, '68, '69), three Australian titles (1960, '62, '69), two U.S. titles (1962, '69) and two French titles (1962, '69). Also won eight Grand Slam doubles titles. First player to earn $1 million in prize money. 47 career tournament victories. Member of undefeated Australian Davis Cup team from 1959–62.

Andrea Mead Lawrence (b. 4-19-32): Skier. Gold medalist in slalom and giant slalom at 1952 Olympics.

Bobby Layne (b. 12-19-26; d. 12-1-86): Football QB. Led Detroit to NFL championships in both 1952 and '53. In 1952 led NFL in every passing category. Career span 1948–62, most with Detroit. Elected to Hall of Fame in 1967.

Sammy Lee (b. 8-1-20): Diver. Gold medalist at two consecutive Olympics (highboard in 1948, '52); bronze medalist in springboard at 1948 Olympics. Won the 1953 Sullivan Award. Also 1960 U.S. Olympic diving coach.

Jacques Lemaire (b. 9-7-45): Hockey C–Coach. As center for Montreal from 1967–79 was part of eight Stanley Cup winning teams. Over 12 seasons, all with Montreal, scored 366 goals and had 469 assists. Elected to Hall of Fame in 1984. Coached New Jersey to their first Stanley Cup in 1995.

Mario Lemieux (b. 10-5-65): Hockey C. Won MVP award in 1988, '93, '96. Playoff MVP in 1991. Led league in points five seasons and goals scored three seasons, assists one season. Rookie of the Year in 1985. Won 1992–93 scoring title despite sitting out six weeks to receive treatment for Hodgkin's disease, a form of cancer. Sat out 1994–95 season, returned in '95–96 to lead league in scoring and become second fastest player to score 500 career goals. Awarded ownership of Penguins in a settlement in 1999, and returned to the ice in 2001, when he scored 35 goals in 43 games. Career span 1984–94, 1995–97, 2001– with Pittsburgh.

Greg LeMond (b. 6-26-61): Cyclist. First American to win Tour de France; won event three times (1986, '89, '90). Recovered from hunting accident to win in 1989.

Ivan Lendl (b. 3-7-60): Tennis player. Second most alltime men's career tournament victories (94). Won three consecutive U.S. Open singles titles (1985–87) and three French Open titles (1984, '86, '87). Also won two Australian Open titles (1989, '90). Reached Grand Slam final nine other times.

Suzanne Lenglen (b. 5-24-1899, d. 7-4-38): French tennis player. Lost only one match from 1919–26. Won six Wimbledon singles and doubles titles (1919–23, '25). Won six French singles and doubles titles (1920–23, '25, '26).

Sugar Ray Leonard (b. 5-17-56): Boxer. Champion in five weight classes: welterweight, junior middle-weight, middleweight, super middleweight and light heavyweight. Career record 36-3-1 with 25 KOs from 1977–97, including comeback loss to Hector Camacho at the age of 41. Also light welterweight gold medalist at 1976 Olympics.

Carl Lewis (b. 7-1-61): Track and field. Held world record for 100 meters (9.86), set at 1991 World Championships in Tokyo. Duplicated Jesse Owens's feat by winning four gold medals at 1984 Olympics (100 and 200 meters, 4x100-meter relay and long jump). Won 1996 Olympic long jump gold at age 35, giving him nine career gold medals and making him just the second track and field athlete (along with Al Oerter) to win four Olympic golds in a single event. Sullivan Award winner in 1981.

Nancy Lieberman-Cline (b. 7-1-58): Basketball G. Three-time All-America at Old Dominion. Player of the Year (1979, '80). Olympian in 1976. Promoter of women's basketball: played in WPBL, WABA. First woman to play basketball in a men's professional league (USBL, 1986). Joined WNBA in 1997, retired in '98 to become GM/coach of the Detroit Shock.

Bob Lilly (b. 7-26-39): Football DT. Dallas Cowboys' first ever draft pick, first Pro Bowl player and first all-NFL choice. Made all-NFL eight times. Career span 1961–74, all with Dallas. Elected to Hall of Fame in 1980.

Tara Lipinski (b. 6-10-82): Figure skater. In 1998 at Nagano eclipsed Sonja Henie as the youngest individual Winter Olympic champion in history when, at 15, she won the women's figure skating gold medal. Also won U.S. and world championships in 1997.

Sonny Liston (b. 5-8-32, d. 12-30-70): Boxer. Heavyweight champion from 1962–64. Won title by KO of Floyd Patterson. Lost title when TKO'd by Cassius Clay (Muhammad Ali) and then lost rematch when KO'd in first round. Career record: 50-4, 39 KOs.

Vince Lombardi (b. 6-11-13, d. 9-3-70): Football coach. Highest alltime winning percentage (.740).

Career record 105-35-6. Won five NFL championships and two consecutive Super Bowl titles with Green Bay from 1959–67. Coached Washington in 1969. Super Bowl trophy named in his honor.

Johnny Longden (b. 2-14-07): Horse racing jockey. Rode Triple Crown winner Count Fleet in 1943. 6,032 career wins.

Nancy Lopez (b. 1-6-57): Golfer. 48 career LPGA Tour wins. LPGA Player of the Year four times (1978, '79, '85, '88). Winner of LPGA Championship three times (1978, '85, '89). Member of the LPGA Hall of Fame.

Greg Louganis (b. 1-29-60): Diver. Gold medalist in platform and springboard at two consecutive Olympics (1984, '88). World champion five times (platform in 1978, '82, '86; springboard in 1982, '86). Also Sullivan Award winner in 1984.

Joe Louis (b. 5-13-14, d. 4-12-81): Boxer. "The Brown Bomber." Longest title reign of any heavyweight champion (11 years, nine months) from 1937–49. Career record 63-3 with 49 KOs from 1934–51. Defended title 25 times.

Jerry Lucas (b. 3-30-40): Basketball F. Three-time first-team All-NBA (1965, '66, '68). Averaged 17.0 points and 15.6 rebounds per game from 1963–74 with Cincinnati, San Francisco and New York. Averaged over 20 points and 20 rebounds a game while at Ohio State. In 1960 member of both NCAA championship team and gold-medal winning U.S. Olympic team. Elected to Hall of Fame in 1979.

Sid Luckman (b. 11-21-16, d. 7-5-98): Football QB. Played on four NFL champions (1940, '41, '43, '46) with Chicago. Player of the Year in 1943. Tied record with seven touchdown passes in one game in 1943. All-Pro six times. 137 career touchdown passes. Career span 1939–50. Also All-America with Columbia.

Jon Lugbill (b. 5-27-61): Whitewater canoe racer. Won five world singles titles from 1979–89.

Hank Luisetti (b. 6-16-16): Basketball F. The first player to use the one-handed shot. All-America at Stanford three consecutive years from 1936–38.

D. Wayne Lukas (b. 9-2-35): Horse racing trainer. Former college basketball coach and quarter horse trainer. Won six straight Triple Crown races from 1994–96, including all three Triple Crown races in 1995, the first trainer to accomplish that feat with multiple horses (Thunder Gulch and Timber County). Trained horses that have won 13 Triple Crown races— four Kentucky Derbys, five Preakness' and four Belmonts—and three Horses of the Year (Lady's Secret in 1986, Criminal Type in 1990, and Charismatic in 1999).

Connie Mack (b. 2-22-1862, d. 2-8-56): Born Cornelius McGillicuddy. Baseball manager. Managed Philadelphia for 50 years (1901–50) until age 87. All-time leader in games (7,755), wins (3,731) and losses (3,948). Won nine pennants and five World Series (1910, '11, '13, '29, '30).

Greg Maddux (b. 4-14-66): Baseball P. Won 15 or more games in 15 straight seasons (1988–02). Four-time Cy Young Award winner (1992–95). Led league in wins three times, ERA four times. 12 Gold Gloves. Career span 1986– with Chicago (NL) and Atlanta.

Larry Mahan (b. 11-21-43): Rodeo. All-around champion six times (1966–70, '73).

Frank Mahovlich (b. 1-10-38): Hockey LW. Winner of Calder Trophy for top rookie for 1957–58 season. In 18 NHL seasons with Toronto, Detroit and Montreal, had 533 goals and 570 assists. Played for six Stanley Cup winners. Elected to Hall of Fame 1981.

Phil Mahre (b. 5-10-57): Skier. Gold medalist in slalom at 1984 Olympics (twin brother Steve won silver medal). World Cup champion three consecutive years (1981–83).

Joe Malone (b. 2-28-1890, d. 5-15-69): Hockey F. "Phantom Joe." Led the NHL in its first season, 1917–18, with 44 goals in 20 games with Montreal. Led league in scoring two times (1918, '20). Holds NHL record with most goals scored, single game (7) in 1920.

Karl Malone (b. 7-24-63): Basketball F. "The Mailman." Second in NBA history in points scored (34,707). Two-time NBA MVP (1997, '99). 11-time first-team All-NBA (1989–99). All-Star MVP, 1989, 1993 (shared with John Stockton). All-Rookie team, 1986. Member of 1992 and '96 Olympic teams. Career span 1985– with Utah.

Moses Malone (b. 3-23-55): Basketball C. Three-time NBA MVP (1979, '82, '83). Playoff MVP in 1983 when he led Philadelphia to the NBA title. Second alltime in free throws made (8,531), fifth in rebounds (16,212) and fifth in points scored (27,409). Four-time first-team All-NBA. Led league in rebounding six times, five consecutively. Went directly to pros from high school. Career span 1974–95 with nine teams, including Houston and Philadelphia.

Hermann Maier (b.12-7-72): Austrian skier. Recovered from spectacular crash in the downhill to win two gold medals at 1998 Olympics in Nagano. Won 1998 Super G, Giant Slalom and overall World Cup season titles.

Man o' War (b. 1917, d. 1947): Thoroughbred race horse. Won 20 of 21 races 1919–20. Only loss was in 1919 in Sanford Stakes to Upset. Passed up Derby but won both Preakness and Belmont. Winner of $249,465. Sire of War Admiral, 1937 Triple Crown winner.

Mickey Mantle (b. 10-20-31, d. 8-13-95): Baseball OF. Won three MVP awards (1956, '57, '62); won Triple Crown in 1956. 536 career HR. Greatest switch hitter in history. Played in 20 All-Star games. Alltime World Series leader in HR (18), RBI (40) and runs scored (42). No. 7 was a member of seven World Series winners with New York (AL). Career span 1951–68.

Diego Maradona (b. 10-30-60): Argentine soccer player. Led Argentina to 1986 World Cup victory and to 1990 World Cup finals. Led Naples to Italian League titles (1987, '90), Italian Cup (1987) and to UEFA Cup title (1989). Throughout 1980s often acknowledged as best player in the world. Tested positive for cocaine and suspended by FIFA and Italian Soccer Federation for 15 months in March 1991. Failed drug test in 1994 World Cup and suspended before second round.

Pete Maravich (b. 6-22-47, d. 1-5-88): Basketball G. "Pistol Pete." Alltime NCAA leader in points scored (3,667), scoring average (44.2) and games scoring 50+ points (28, including then Division I record 69 points in 1970). Alltime single-season leader in points scored (1,381) and scoring average (44.5) in 1970. NCAA scoring leader and All-America three consecutive seasons 1968–70 with Louisiana State. Averaged 20+ points eight times as a pro, leading the league in scoring in 1977. All-Star five times. Averaged 24.2 points per game from 1970–79 with Atlanta, New Orleans/Utah and Boston.

Gino Marchetti (b. 1-2-27): Football DE. Played in Pro Bowl every year from 1955–65, except 1958 when he broke right ankle tackling Frank Gifford in Colts' 23–17 win over the Giants. Career span 1952–66, almost all with Baltimore. Inducted into Hall of Fame in 1972.

Rocky Marciano (b. 9-1-23, d. 8-31-69): Boxer. Heavyweight champion (1952–56). Career record 49–0 with 43 KOs from 1947 to 1956. Only heavyweight to retire as undefeated champion.

Juan Marichal (b. 10-24-37): Baseball RHP. 243 career wins, 2.89 career ERA. Won 20+ games six times; 250+ innings pitched eight times; 200+ strikeouts six times. Pitched no-hitter in 1963. Career span 1960–75, mostly with San Francisco. Elected to Hall of Fame in 1983.

Dan Marino (b. 9-15-61): Football QB. Set alltime single-season record for yards passing (5,084) and touchdown passes (48) in 1984. Passed for 4,000+ yards five other seasons. Career totals: 61,361 yards passing, 420 touchdown passes, first alltime in both categories. Career span 1983–00 with Miami.

Roger Maris (b. 9-10-34, d. 12-14-85): Baseball OF. Broke Babe Ruth's alltime single-season HR record with 61 in 1961. Won consecutive MVP awards and led league in RBI 1960–61. Career span 1957–68 with Kansas City, New York (AL), St. Louis.

Billy Martin (b. 5-16-28, d. 12-25-89): Baseball 2B–manager. Volatile manager was hired and fired by Minnesota, Detroit, Texas, New York (AL) (five times!) and Oakland from 1969–88. Career record: 1253–1013. Won World Series with New York as manager in 1977 and as player four times.

Pedro Martinez (b. 10-25-71): Baseball P. Three Cy Young Awards (1997, '99, '00). Became second pitcher to win Cy Young Awards in both leagues in 1999. Became first pitcher in 25 years to have more than 300 Ks and ERA below 2.00 in 1997. Led league in ERA and strikeouts three times each. Started 1999 All-Star Game and was named MVP after striking out first four batters. Career span 1992– with Los Angeles, Montreal and Boston.

Eddie Mathews (b. 10-13-31, d. 2-18-01): Baseball 3B. 512 career HR and 30+ HR nine consecutive seasons. League leader in HR two times, walks four times. Career span 1952–68, mostly with Milwaukee.

Christy Mathewson (b. 8-12-1880, d. 10-7-25): Baseball RHP. Third alltime most wins (373, tied with Grover Alexander) and shutouts (79); career ERA 2.13. Led league in wins five times; won 30+ games four times and 20+ games nine other times. Led league in ERA and strikeouts five times each. Pitched two no-hitters. Pitched three shutouts in 1905 World Series. Career span 1900–16 with New York.

Bob Mathias (b. 11-17-30): Track and field. At age 17, youngest to win gold medal in decathlon at 1948 Olympics. First decathlete to win gold medal at consecutive Olympics (1948, '52). Also won Sullivan Award in 1948.

Ollie Matson (b. 5-1-30): Football RB. Versatile runner totalled 12,884 combined yards rushing, receiving and kick returning. Scored 73 career touchdowns, including a 105-yard kickoff return on 10-14-56, the second longest ever. Career span 1952–66 with Chicago Cardinals, Los Angeles, Detroit,

Philadelphia. Also won bronze medal in 400 meters at 1952 Olympics. Elected to Hall of Fame in 1972.

Roland Matthes (b. 11-17-50): German swimmer. Gold medalist in 100-meter and 200-meter backstroke at two consecutive Olympics (1968, '72). Set 16 world records from 1967–73.

Don Maynard (b. 1-25-37): Football WR. Retired in 1973 as the NFL's alltime leading receiver. In 15 seasons, 10 with the New York Jets, caught 633 passes for 11,834 yards and 88 TDs. Averaged 18.7 yards per catch for career. Elected to Hall of Fame in 1987.

Willie Mays (b. 5-6-31): Baseball OF. "Say Hey Kid." MVP in 1954, '65; Rookie of the Year in 1951. Third alltime most HR (660), with 50+ HR two times, 30+ HR nine other times. Led league in HR four times. 100+ RBI 10 times; 100+ runs scored 12 consecutive seasons. 3,283 career hits. Led league in stolen bases four consecutive seasons. 30 HR and 30 steals in same season two times and first man in history to hit 300+ HR and steal 300+ bases. Won 11 consecutive Gold Gloves; set record for career putouts by an outfielder and league record for total chances. His catch in the 1954 World Series off the bat of Vic Wertz called the greatest ever. Career span 1951–73 with New York/San Francisco and New York (NL).

Bill Mazeroski (b. 9-5-36): Baseball 2B. Hit dramatic ninth-inning home run in Game 7 to win 1960 World Series, first of only two Series' to end on a home run. Won eight Gold Gloves. Led league in assists nine times, double plays eight times and putouts five times. Inducted to Hall of Fame in 2001. Career 1956–72 with Pittsburgh; 2,016 hits, 138 HR, .260 avg.

Joe McCarthy (b. 4-21-1887, d. 1-3-78): Baseball manager. Alltime highest winning percentage among managers for regular season (.615). First manager to win pennants in both leagues (Chicago (NL), 1929, New York (AL), 1932). From 1926–50 his teams won seven World Series and nine pennants.

Mark McCormack (b. 11-6-30): Sports marketing agent. Founded International Management Group in 1962. Also author of best-selling business advice books.

Pat McCormick (b. 5-12-30): Diver. Gold medalist in platform and springboard at two consecutive Olympics (1952, '56). Also won Sullivan Award in 1956.

Willie McCovey (b. 1-10-38): Baseball 1B. Led NL in HRs three times (1963, '68, '69) and in RBI twice (1968, '69). 521 career homers. .270 career average. Hit 18 grand slams. Rookie of Year 1959. NL MVP in 1969. Career span 1959–80 with San Francisco, San Diego and Oakland. Elected to Hall of Fame in 1986.

John McEnroe (b. 2-26-59): Tennis player. Third alltime men's most career tournament victories (77). Won four U.S. Open singles titles (consecutively 1979–81, '84) and three Wimbledon titles (1981, '83, '84). Also won eight Grand Slam doubles titles. Led U.S. to five Davis Cup victories (1978, '79, '81, '82, '92).

John McGraw (b. 4-7-1873, d. 2-25-34): Baseball manager. Second alltime in games (4,801) and wins (2,784). Guided New York (NL) to three World Series titles and 10 pennants from 1902–32.

Mark McGwire (b. 10-1-63): Baseball 1B. Broke Roger Maris's 37-year-old single-season HR record with 70 in 1998. Rookie of the Year in 1987, when he

hit rookie record 49 home runs. Hit 30+ HR 12 times, 40+ HR six times, 50+ HR four straight years (1996–99). Member of 1984 U.S. Olympic baseball team. Had 583 career HRs and 1,414 RBIs with Oakland and St. Louis from 1986–01.

Denny McLain (b. 3-29-44): Baseball RHP. Last pitcher to win 30+ games in a season (Detroit, 1968); won 20+ games two other times. Won two consecutive Cy Young Awards (1968 '69). Led league in innings pitched two times. Served 2½-year jail term for 1985 conviction of extortion, racketeering and drug possession. Re-entered prison in 1997 on fraud conviction. Career span 1963–72, mostly with Detroit.

Mary T. Meagher (b. 10-27-64): Swimmer. "Madame Butterfly." Won three gold medals at 1984 Olympics (100-meter butterfly, 200-meter butterfly and 400-medley relay). In 1981 set world records in 100-meter butterfly (57.93) and 200-meter butterfly (2:05.96).

Rick Mears (b. 12-3-51): Auto racer. Has won Indy 500 four times (1979, '84, '88, '91) and been CART champion three times (1979, '81, '82). Named Indy 500 Rookie of the Year in 1978.

Eddy Merckx (b. 1945): Belgian cyclist. Won five Tours de France, including four in a row (1969–72).

Mark Messier (b. 1-18-61): Hockey C. Two-time Hart Trophy (MVP) winner. Won Stanley Cups with Edmonton (1984, '85, '87, '88, '90) and New York Rangers (1994). Third alltime in scoring (1,804 pts), fourth in assists (1,146) and seventh in goals scored (658). Career span 1979– with Edmonton, New York Rangers and Vancouver.

Cary Middlecoff (b. 1-6-21, d. 9-1-98): Golfer. Won 40 PGA tournaments, including 1955 Masters and U.S. Opens in 1949 and '56. Won 1956 Vardon Trophy. Also a dentist.

George Mikan (b. 6-18-24): Basketball C. The first dominant big man in professional basketball. Averaged 20+ points per game and named to All-Star team six consecutive seasons. Led league (NBA and NBL) in scoring six times. Played on five championship teams in six years (1949–54) with Minneapolis. Also played on 1945 NIT championship team with DePaul. All-America three times. Served as ABA Commissioner from 1968–69.

Stan Mikita (b. 5-20-40): Hockey C. Won MVP award two consecutive seasons (1967, '68). 926 career assists, 1,467 career points. Led league in assists four straight seasons and points four times. 541 career goals. All-Star six times. Career span 1958–80 with Chicago.

Del Miller (b. 7-5-13; d. 8-19-96): Harness racing driver. Raced in eight decades, beginning in 1929, the longest career of any athlete. Won The Hambletonian in 1950.

Marvin Miller (b. 4-14-17): Labor negotiator. Union chief of MLB Players Association from 1966–84. Led strikes in 1972 and '81. Negotiated five labor contracts that increased minimum salary and pension fund, allowed for agents and arbitration, and brought about the end of the reserve clause and the start of free agency.

Art Monk (b. 12-5-57): Football WR. Fourth alltime in pass receptions (940, for 12,721 and 68 TDs). Set NFL single season record with 106 catches in 1984. Career span 1980–95 with Washington, New York Jets and Philadelphia.

Earl Monroe (b. 11-21-44): Basketball G. "The Pearl" played 13 seasons (1967–80) with Baltimore and New York. NBA Rookie of Year in 1968. Four-time All-Star. Member of 1973 NBA championship Knicks team. Averaged 18.8 points a game. Elected to Basketball Hall of Fame 1989.

Joe Montana (b. 6-11-56): Football QB. Second alltime highest-rated passer (92.3); 40,551 career passing yards and 273 TD passes. Won four Super Bowl championships (1981, '84, '88, '89) with San Francisco. Named Super Bowl MVP three times (1981, '84, '89). Player of the Year in 1989. Voted to eight Pro Bowls. Led his teams to 31 fourth-quarter comebacks. Also led Notre Dame to national championship in 1977. Career span 1979–94 with San Francisco and Kansas City. Elected to Hall of Fame in 2000.

Carlos Monzon (b. 8-7-42, d. 1-8-95): Argentine boxer. Longest title reign of any middleweight champion (6 years, nine months) from 1970–77. Career record 89-3-9 with 61 KOs from 1963–77. Won 82 consecutive bouts from 1964–77. Defended title 14 times. Retired as champion.

Helen Wills Moody (b. 10-6-05, d. 1-1-98): Tennis player. Third alltime in women's Grand Slam singles titles (19). Her eight Wimbledon titles are second most alltime (1927–30, '32, '33, '35, '38). Won seven U.S. titles (1923–25, 1927–29, '31) and four French titles (1928–30, '32). Also won 12 Grand Slam doubles titles.

Archie Moore (b. 12-13-16 d. 12-9-98): Boxer. "The Mongoose." Longest title reign of any light heavyweight champion (9 years, one month) from 1952–62. Career record 199-26-8 with an alltime record 145 KOs from 1935–65. Retired at age 52.

Davey Moore (b. 11-1-33; d. 3-23-63): Boxer. Won featherweight title by KO of Kid Bassey in 13 on 3-18-59. Five successful defenses of title, before losing it on 3-21-63 to Sugar Ramos who KO'd him in 10. Died two days after fight of brain damage suffered during fight. Career record: 58-7-1, 30 KOs.

Noureddine Morceli (b. 2-20-70): Algerian track and field middle distance runner. Set world record for mile (3:44.39) in Rieti, Italy, on 9-5-93. Set world record for 1,500 (3:28.86) on 9-5-92. Won gold medal at 1,500 in 1991, '93 and '95. Won gold medal at 1996 Olympics in Atlanta. Only man ever to rank first in the world at 1,500/mile four straight years (1990–93).

Joe Morgan (b. 9-19-43): Baseball 2B. Sparkplug for Cincinnati's Big Red Machine in the 1970s. Won two MVP awards (1975, '76). 10-time All-Star. Fifth alltime in career walks (1,865). 689 stolen bases. 100+ walks and runs scored eight times each; 40+ stolen bases nine times. Won five Gold Gloves. Second alltime in games played by 2nd baseman (2,527). Career span 1963–84 with Houston, Cincinnati, San Francisco, Philadelphia and Oakland.

Willie Mosconi (b. 6-27-13; d. 9-16-93): Pocket billiards player. Won world title a record 15 straight times between 1941–57. Once pocketed 526 balls without a miss.

Edwin Moses (b. 8-31-55): Track and field. Gold medalist in the 400-meter hurdles at two Olympics (1976, '84); bronze medalist at 1988 Olympics. Won 122 consecutive races from 1977–87. Set four world records in 400-meter hurdles. Won the Sullivan Award in 1983.

Marion Motley (b. 6-5-20 d. 6-27-99): Football FB. All-time AAFC leader in yards rushing (3,024). Led NFL in rushing once. Combined league totals: 4,712 yards rushing, 39 touchdowns. Played for four consecutive AAFC champions (1946–49) and one NFL champion (1950). Career span with Cleveland 1946–1953.

Shirley Muldowney (b. 6-19-40): Drag racer. First woman to win the Top Fuel championship, which she won three times (1977, '80, '82).

Anthony Munoz (b. 8-19-58): Football OT. Probably the greatest offensive tackle ever. Made Pro Bowl a record-tying 11 times. Career span 1980–92 with Cincinnati. Elected to Hall of Fame 1998.

Isaac Murphy (b. 4-16-1861, d. 2-12-1896): Horse racing jockey. Top jockey of his era, Murphy, who was black, won three Kentucky Derbys (aboard Buchanan in 1884, Riley in 1890 and Kingman in 1891).

Eddie Murray (b. 2-24-56): Baseball 1B. One of greatest switch-hitters in baseball history. 100+ RBI six seasons and 30+ HRs five seasons. Retired with 3,255 hits, 504 HRs and 1,917 RBI—eighth alltime and most ever by switch hitter. Career span 1977–97 with Baltimore, Los Angeles, New York (NL), Cleveland and Anaheim.

Jim Murray (b. 12-29-19; d. 8-16-98): Sportswriter. Won Pulitzer Prize in 1990. Named Sportswriter of the Year 14 times. Columnist for *Los Angeles Times* 1961–98.

Ty Murray (b. 10-11-69): Rodeo cowboy. All-around world champion, 1989–94. Set single-season earnings record in 1990 ($213,771). Rookie of the Year in 1988. At 20, became youngest man ever to win national all-around title in 1989.

Stan Musial (b. 11-21-20): Baseball OF–1B. "Stan the Man." Had .331 career batting average and 475 career HR. MVP award winner (1943, '46, '48). Fourth alltime in hits (3,630) and third in doubles (725). Won seven batting titles. Led league in hits six times, slugging average five times, doubles eight times. Had .300+ batting average 17 times, 200+ hits six times, 100+ RBI 10 times, and 100+ runs scored 11 times. 24-time All-Star. Career span 1941–63 with St. Louis.

John Naber (b. 1-20-56): Swimmer. Won four gold medals and one silver medal at 1976 Olympics. Sullivan Award winner in 1977.

Bronko Nagurski (b. 11-3-08, d. 1-7-90): Football FB. Punishing runner played on three NFL champions (1932, '33, '43) with Bears. 2,778 career yards with Chicago from 1930–37 and 1943.

James Naismith (b. 11-6-1861, d. 11-28-39): Invented basketball in 1891 while an instructor at YMCA Training School in Springfield, Mass. Refined the game while a professor at Kansas from 1898–37. Hall of Fame is named in his honor.

Joe Namath (b. 5-31-43): Football QB. "Broadway Joe." Super Bowl MVP in 1968 after he guaranteed victory for New York. 173 career touchdown passes. Led league in yards passing three times, including 4,007 yards in 1967. Player of the Year,1968; Rookie of the Year, 1965. Career span 1965–77 with New York Jets and Los Angeles.

Ilie Nastase (b. 7-19-46): Romanian tennis player. "Nasty" for his unruly deportment on court. Beat Arthur Ashe to win 1972 U.S. Open title. Won 1973 French Open. Twice Wimbledon runner-up (to Stan Smith in 1972 and Bjorn Borg in 1976).

Martina Navratilova (b. 10-18-56): Tennis player. Fourth in women's Grand Slam singles titles (18—tied with Chris Evert). Won a record nine Wimbledon titles, including six consecutively (1978, '79, 1982–87, '90). Won four U.S. Open titles (1983, '84, '86, '87), three Australian Open titles (1981, '83, '85) and two French Open titles (1982, '84). Reached Grand Slam final 13 other times. Also won 38 Grand Slam doubles titles. Her total of 56 Grand Slam titles is second alltime to Margaret Court. Set mark for longest winning streak with 74 matches in 1984. Also won the doubles Grand Slam in 1984 with Pam Shriver. Won 109 consecutive doubles matches with Shriver from 1983–85.

Byron Nelson (b. 2-14-12): Golfer. Won 52 career tournaments, including 11 consecutively in 1945. Won the Masters (1937, '42) and PGA Championship (1940, '45) two times each and U.S. Open once (1939).

Ernie Nevers (b. 6-11-03, d. 5-3-76): Football FB. Set alltime pro single game record for points scored (40) and touchdowns (six) on 11-28-29. Career span 1926–31 with Duluth and Chicago. Also a pitcher with St. Louis (AL), surrendered two of Babe Ruth's 60 home runs in 1927. All-America at Stanford, earned 11 letters in four sports.

John Newcombe (b. 5-23-44): Australian tennis player. Won three Wimbledon singles titles (1967, '70, '71), two U.S. titles (1967, '73) and two Australian Open titles (1973, '75). Also won 17 Grand Slam doubles titles.

Pete Newell (b. 8-31-15): College basketball coach. Despite coaching only 13 seasons, 1947–60, was first coach to win NIT, NCAA and Olympic crowns. Led San Francisco to 1949 NIT title, Cal to 1959 NCAA title, and the 1960 U.S. Olympic basketball team that included Jerry Lucas, Oscar Robertson and Jerry West to gold medal. Overall collegiate coaching record of 234–123.

Jack Nicklaus (b. 1-21-40): Golfer. "The Golden Bear." Alltime leader in major championships (20). Second alltime in career wins (70). Won Masters six times, more than any golfer (1963, '65, '66, '72, '75, '86—at age 46, the oldest player to win event), PGA Championship five times (1963, '71, '73, '75, '80), U.S. Open four times (1962, '67, '72, '80), British Open three times (1966, '70, '78) and U.S. Amateur twice (1959, '61). PGA Player of the Year five times (1967, '72, '73, '75, '76). Also NCAA champion with Ohio State in 1961.

Ray Nitschke (b. 12-29-36 d. 3-8-98): Football LB. Defensive signal-caller for the great Green Bay teams of the '60s. Voted Packer MVP by teammates after 1967 season. MVP of the 1962 NFL title game. Career span 1958–72 with Green Bay.

Chuck Noll (b. 1-5-32): Football coach. Only coach to win four Super Bowls (1975, '76, '79, '80). Coaching career 1969–91 with Pittsburgh; 209-156-1.

Greg Norman (b. 2-10-55): Golfer. "The Shark" led PGA in winnings in 1986, '90, '95, '96. Won Vardon Trophy twice, 1989, '90. Won two British Opens (1986, '93) but is more famous for his heartbreaking losses. PGA Player of the Year 1996.

James D. Norris (b. 11-6-06, d. 2-25-66): Hockey executive. Owner of the Detroit Red Wings from 1933–43 and Chicago from 1946–66. Teams won four Stanley Cup championships (1936, '37, '43, '61). Defensive Player of the Year award named in his honor. Also a boxing promoter, operated International Boxing Club from 1949–58.

Paavo Nurmi (b. 6-13-1897, d. 10-2-73): Track and field. Finnish middle- and long-distance runner won a total of nine gold medals at three Olympics in 1920, '24, '28.

Matti Nykänen (b. 7-17-63): Finnish ski jumper. Three-time Olympic gold medalist. Won 90-meter jump (1984, '88) and 70-meter jump (1988). World champion on 90-meter jump in 1982. Won four World Cups (1983, '85, '86, '88).

Dan O'Brien (b. 7-18-66): Track and field decathlete. Won world decathlon title in 1991, '93, '95. Set world decathlon record of 8,891 in Talence, France, on 9-4/5-92, that stood for seven years. Heavily favored to win 1992 Olympic decathlon but missed making U.S. team when he no-heighted in pole vault at U.S. Olympic Trials. Redeemed himself with gold medal at 1996 Olympics in Atlanta.

Parry O'Brien (b. 1-28-32): Track and field. Shot-putter who revolutionized the event with his "glide" technique and won Olympic gold medals in 1952 and '56, silver in '60. Set 10 world records from 1953–59, topped by a put of 63' 4" in 1959. Sullivan Award winner in 1959.

Al Oerter (b. 8-19-36): Track and field. Gold medalist in discus at four consecutive Olympics (1956, '60, '64, '68), setting Olympic record each time. First to break the 200-foot barrier, throwing 200' 5" in 1962.

Sadaharu Oh (b. 5-20-40): Baseball 1B in Japanese league. 868 career HR in 22 seasons for the Tokyo Giants. Led league in HR 15 times, RBI 13 times, batting five times and runs 13 consecutive seasons. Awarded MVP nine times; won two consecutive Triple Crowns and nine Gold Gloves.

Hakeem Olajuwon (b. 1-21-63): Basketball C. From Nigeria. Alltime NBA career leader in blocked shots (3,830). Became the first player to be named NBA MVP, NBA Defensive Player of the Year and NBA Finals MVP in the same season as Houston won its first NBA championship in 1994. Led NCAA in FG %, rebounding and blocked shots in 1984 at Houston. Member of 1996 U.S. Olympic team. Career span 1984– with Houston and Toronto; 21.8 ppg, 11.1 rpg.

Merlin Olsen (b. 9-15-40): Fooball DT. Part of Los Angeles's "Fearsome Foursome" defensive line. Named to Pro Bowl 14 straight times. Career span 1962–76, all with the Los Angeles Rams. Elected to Hall of Fame 1982.

Omaha (b. 1932, d. 1959): Thoroughbred race horse. Won Triple Crown in 1935. Trained by Sunny Jim Fitzsimmons.

Mark O'Meara (b. 1-13-57): Golfer. Has 16 career PGA Tour victories, including the 1998 Masters and British Open, at age 41. Tour rookie of the year in 1981; won 1979 U.S. Amateur.

Shaquille O'Neal (b. 3-6-72): Basketball C. "Shaq." Three-time NBA Finals MVP after leading the Lakers to back-to-back-to-back NBA Finals victories (2000–02). Was named MVP of the regular season, All-Star game, and playoffs in 1999–2000. Nine-time All-Star selection (1993–98, 2000–02). Led league in scoring in 1995 and 2000, and in field goal percentage in 1994, 1998–02. Top pick of Orlando in 1992 NBA draft. NBA Rookie of the Year 1993. Member of 1996 U.S. Olympic team. Led NCAA in blocked shots in 1992 as an All-American at Louisiana State. Career span 1992– with Orlando and Los Angeles Lakers.

Bobby Orr (b. 3-20-48): Hockey D. Defensive Player of the Year more than any other player, eight consecutive seasons (1968–75). Won MVP award three consecutive seasons (1970–72), playoff MVP two times (1970, '72). Also Rookie of the Year in 1967. Led league in assists five times and scoring two times. Career span 1966–77 with Boston.

Mel Ott (b. 3-2-09, d. 11-21-58): Baseball OF. 511 career HR, 1,861 RBI, .304 batting average. League leader in HR and walks six times each. 100+ RBI nine times and 100+ walks ten times. Career span 1926–47 with New York (NL).

Jim Otto (b. 1-5-38): Football C. Number 00 started every game (210) in his 15-year career (1960–74) with Oakland. Inducted to Hall of Fame in 1980.

Kristin Otto (b. 1966): German swimmer. Won six gold medals for East Germany at 1988 Olympics.

Jesse Owens (b. 9-12-13, d. 3-31-80): Track and field. Gold medalist in four events (100 meters and 200 meters; 4x100-meter relay and long jump) at 1936 Olympics. At the 1935 Big 10 championship set or equaled six world record in 70 minutes, including 100 yards, long jump, 220-yard low hurdles and 220 dash.

Alan Page (b. 8-7-45): Football DT. First defensive player to be named NFL Player of the Year, in 1972. Played in 236 straight games, including four Super Bowls. Four-time NFC Defensive Player of Year. Career span 1967–81 with Minnesota and Chicago. Now sits on Minnesota Supreme Court.

Satchel Paige (b. 7-7-06, d. 6-8-82): Baseball RHP. Alltime greatest black pitcher, didn't pitch in major leagues until 1948 at age 42 with Cleveland. Oldest pitcher in major league history at age 59 with Kansas City in 1965. Pitched in the Negro leagues from 1926–50 with Birmingham Black Barons, Pittsburgh Crawfords and Kansas City Monarchs. Estimated career record is 2,000 wins, 250 shutouts, 30,000 strikeouts, 45 no-hitters.

Se Ri Pak (b. 9-28-77): South Korean golfer. 16 career LPGA Tour victories. 1998 LPGA Rookie of the Year for winning the first two majors she ever entered, the LPGA Championship and the U.S. Open.

Arnold Palmer (b. 9-10-29): Golfer. Fourth alltime in career wins (60). Won the Masters four times (1958, '60, '62, '64), British Open two consecutive years (1961, '62) and U.S. Open (1960) and U.S. Amateur (1954) once each. PGA Player of the Year two times (1960, '62). First golfer to surpass $1 million in career earnings. Also won Seniors Championship two times (1980, '84) and U.S. Senior Open once (1981).

Jim Palmer (b. 10-15-45): Baseball RHP. 268 career wins, 2.86 ERA. Won three Cy Young Awards (1973, '75, '76). Won 20+ games eight times. Led league in wins three times, innings pitched four times, ERA two times. Never allowed a grand slam HR. Pitched on six World Series teams with Baltimore, including shutout at age 20. Pitched no-hitter in 1969. Career span 1965–84 with Baltimore.

Bernie Parent (b. 4-3-45): Hockey G. Alltime leader for wins in a season (47 in 1974). Goaltender of the Year, playoff MVP, league leader in wins, goals against average and shutouts two consecutive seasons (1974–75). Career record 270-197-121, including 55 shutouts. Career 2.55 goals against average. Tied record of four playoff shutouts in 1975. Played on two consecutive Stanley Cup champions (1974–75). Career span 1965–79 with Philadelphia.

Brad Park (b. 7-6-48): Hockey D. Seven-time All-Star. In 17 seasons with the New York Rangers, Boston and Detroit (1968–85) scored 213 goals and had 683 assists. Elected to Hall of Fame 1988.

Jim Parker (b. 4-3-34): Football T/G. All-NFL four times at guard, four times at tackle. First full-time offensive lineman inducted to Hall of Fame, in 1973. Career span 1957–67, all with Baltimore. Winner of 1956 Outland Trophy as Ohio State senior.

Joe Paterno (b. 12-21-26): College football coach. First alltime in wins in Division I-A (327). Has won two national championships (1982, '86) with Penn State since 1966. Career record 327-96-3, including five undefeated seasons. Has also won 20 bowl games.

Lester Patrick (b. 12-30-1883, d. 6-1-60): Hockey coach. Led New York Rangers to three Stanley Cup championships (1928, '33, '40). Originated the NHL's farm system and developed playoff format.

Floyd Patterson (b. 1-4-35): Boxer. Heavyweight champion two times (1956–59, 1960–62). First heavyweight to regain title, in rematch with Ingemar Johansson. Career record 55-8-1 with 40 KOs from 1952–72. Also middleweight gold medalist at 1952 Olympics.

Walter Payton (b. 7-25-54, d. 11-1-99): Football RB. "Sweetness." Alltime leader in yards rushing (16,726). Gained 1,000+ yards rushing in 10 seasons. Third alltime in rushing touchdowns (110). 125 career touchdowns. Seven-time All-Pro. Player of the Year two times (1977, '85). Led league in rushing five consecutive seasons. Career span 1975–87 with Chicago.

Pelé (b. 10-23-40): Born Edson Arantes do Nascimento. Brazilian soccer player. Soccer's great ambassador. Played on three World Cup winners with Brazil (1958, '62, '70). Helped promote soccer in U.S. by playing with New York Cosmos from 1975–77. Scored 1,281 goals in 22 years.

Willie Pep (b. 9-19-22): Boxer. Featherweight champion two times (1942–48, 1949–50). Lost title to Sandy Saddler, won it back in rematch, then lost it to Saddler again. Master tactician: legend has it he once won a round without throwing a punch. Career record 230-11-1 with 65 KOs from 1940–66. Won 73 consecutive bouts from 1940–43. Defended title nine times.

Gil Perreault (b. 11-13-50): Hockey C. NHL Rookie of the Year in 1970–71. Five-time All-Star. Scored 512 goals and had 814 assists in career from 1970–87 with Buffalo. Elected to Hall of Fame in 1990.

Fred Perry (b. 5-18-09, d. 2-2-95): British tennis player. Won three consecutive Wimbledon singles titles (1934–36), the last British man to win the tournament. Also won three U.S. titles (1933, '34, '36), one French title (1935) and one Australian title (1934).

Gaylord Perry (b. 9-15-38): Baseball RHP. First pitcher to win Cy Young Award in both leagues (Cleveland 1972, San Diego 1978). 314 career wins, 3,534 strikeouts. 20+ wins five times; 200+ strikeouts eight times; 250+ innings pitched 12 times. Pitched no-hitter in 1968. Admitted to throwing a spitter. Career span 1962–83 with eight teams.

Bob Pettit (b. 12-12-32): Basketball F. First player in history to break 20,000-point barrier (20,880 career points scored). 26.4 career scoring average; 16.2 rebound avg. MVP in 1956 and 1959; Rookie of the Year in 1955. All-Star 10 consecutive seasons. Led league in scoring two times, rebounding once. Career span 1954–64 with St. Louis.

Richard Petty (b. 7-2-37): Auto racer. Alltime leader in NASCAR victories (200). Seven-time Daytona 500 winner (1964, '66, '71, '73, '74, '79, '81) and NASCAR season points champion (1964, '67, '71, '72, '74, '75, '79), the most of any driver in both categories. First stock car racer to reach $1 million in earnings. Son of Lee Petty, three-time NASCAR champion. Retired after 1992 season.

Laffit Pincay Jr. (b. 12-29-46): Jockey. Only jockey with more than 9,000 career victories. Among the top money-winners of all time, with more than $215,000,000 in career earnings. Won five Eclipse Awards as outstanding jockey. Rode one Kentucky Derby winner (Swale), and three Belmont winners (Conquistador Cielo, Cavaet, Swale).

Scottie Pippen (b. 9-25-65): Basketball F. Won six NBA titles with Chicago (1991–93, 1996–98). Three-time first-team All-NBA (1994–96). Named to NBA's first-team All-Defensive team six times. Named MVP of the 1994 NBA All-Star Game. Member of 1992 and '96 gold medal-winning U.S. Olympic basketball teams. Career span 1987– with Chicago, Houston and Portland.

Jacques Plante (b. 1-17-29, d. 2-27-86): Hockey G. First goalie to wear a mask. Third alltime in wins (435) and second lowest modern goals against average (2.38). Goaltender of the Year seven times, more than any other goalie (consecutively 1955–59, '61, '68). Won MVP award in 1961. Led league in goals against average eight times, wins six times and shutouts four times. Was on six Stanley Cup champions with Montreal from 1952–62 and played for four other teams until retirement in 1972.

Gary Player (b. 11-1-35): South African golfer. Won the Masters (1961, '74, '78) and British Open (1959, '68, '74) three times each, PGA Championship two times (1962, '72) and U.S. Open (1965). Also won Seniors Championship three times (1986, '88, '90) and U.S. Senior Open two consecutive years (1987, '88).

Sam Pollock (b. 12-15-25): Hockey executive. As general manager of Montreal from 1964–78 won nine Stanley Cup championships (1965, '66, '68, '69, '71, '73, '76, '78).

Denis Potvin (b. 10-29-53): Hockey D. Seven-time All-Star during 15-season career (1973–88), all with New York Islanders. Won Calder Trophy for 1973–74 season. Won Norris Trophy three times. Captained Islanders to four Stanley Cup championships. Elected to Hall of Fame in 1991.

Mike Powell (b. 11-10-63): Track and field. Long jumper broke Bob Beamon's 23-year-old world record at 1991 World Championships in Tokyo with a jump of 29' 4½". Won silver in 1992 Olympics.

Steve Prefontaine (b. 1-25-51, d. 5-30-75): Track and field. Distance runner killed in car accident at age 24. Held every American record from 2,000 meters to 10,000 meters at the time of his death. At age 21, finished fourth in the 5,000 meters at the 1972 Olympics in Munich after leading with less than 600 meters to go.

Annemarie Moser-Pröll (b. 3-27-53): Austrian skier. Gold medalist in downhill at 1980 Olympics. World Cup overall champion six times, more than any other skier (1971–75, '79).

Alain Prost (b. 2-24-55): French auto racer. Second

alltime in Formula 1 victories (51). Formula 1 champion four times (1985–86, '89, '93).

Jack Ramsay (b. 2-21-25): Basketball coach. Coached 11 seasons at St. Joseph's University, with 234–72 record. Overall record of 864–783 as NBA coach. Coach of NBA champion 1977 Portland Trail Blazers. Elected to Hall of Fame 1992.

Jean Ratelle (b. 10-3-40): Hockey C. In 21-season career (1960–81) with the New York Rangers and Boston, scored 491 goals and had 776 assists. Twice won Lady Byng Trophy. Elected to Hockey Hall of Fame in 1985.

Willis Reed (b. 6-25-42): Basketball C. Most noted for his dramatic return to the court on 5-8-70, in the seventh and deciding game of the 1970 NBA Finals against Los Angeles. Playoff MVP of both New York championship teams, in 1970 and '73. NBA Rookie of Year in 1965. NBA MVP in 1970. Played 10 seasons (1965–74), all with New York. Career average of 18.7 points a game. Elected to Hall of Fame in 1981.

Harold Henry (Pee Wee) Reese (b. 7-23-18 d. 8-14-99): Baseball SS. Played for six pennant-winning Brooklyn teams. Led NL in runs scored in 1949, with 132. Career span 1940–58 with Brooklyn; .269 avg., 2,170 hits, 1,338 runs, 232 SB. Elected to Hall of Fame in 1984.

Mary Lou Retton (b. 1-24-68): Gymnast. Won all-around gold with a perfect 10 on her final vault at the 1984 Olympics in Los Angeles. Also won one silver and two bronze medals at those Games.

Grantland Rice (b. 11-1-1880, d. 7-13-54): Sportswriter. Legendary figure during sport's Golden Age of the 1920s. Wrote "For when the one great Scorer comes/ To write against your name/ He writes not that you won or lost/ But how you played the game." Also named the 1924–25 Notre Dame backfield the "Four Horsemen."

Jerry Rice (b. 10-13-62): Football WR. Alltime leader in touchdowns (185), touchdown receptions (175), receptions (1,364), receiving yards (20,386) and in consecutive games with a TD reception (13 in 1988). Player of the Year in 1987 and led league in scoring (138 points on 23 touchdowns). Super Bowl MVP in 1989 with record 215 receiving yards on 11 catches. Also set Super Bowl record with three touchdown receptions in 1990 and in 1995. Career span 1985– with San Francisco and Oakland.

Henri Richard (b. 2-29-36): Hockey C. "The Pocket Rocket." Won 11 Stanley Cup championships with Montreal. Four-time All-Star. Career span 1955–75.

Maurice Richard (b. 8-4-21, d. 5-27-00): Hockey RW. "The Rocket." First player to score 50 goals in a season, in 1945. Led league in goals five times. 544 career goals. MVP in 1947. All-Star eight times. Tied playoff record for most goals in a game (five on March 23, 1944). Won eight Stanley Cups with Montreal 1942–59.

Bob Richards (b. 2-2-26): Track and field. The only pole vaulter to win gold medal at two consecutive Olympics (1952, '56). Also won Sullivan Award in 1951.

Branch Rickey (b. 12-20-1881, d. 12-9-65): Baseball executive. Integrated major league baseball in 1947 by signing Jackie Robinson to a contract with the Brooklyn Dodgers. Conceived of minor league farm system in 1919 at St. Louis; instituted batting cage and sliding pit.

Pat Riley (b. 3-20-45): Basketball coach. Coached Los Angeles to four NBA championships (1981, '85, '87, '88). Coach of the Year three times (1990, '93, '97) for three different teams. Led New York to NBA Finals in 1994. Coached teams to 50+ wins 13 years in a row. Coaching career 1984– with Los Angeles, New York and Miami; 1,085–512 (.679).

Cal Ripken Jr. (b. 8-24-60): Baseball SS–3B. Broke Lou Gehrig's record for most consecutive games played (2,131) on 9-5-95; streak ended at 2,632 games on 9-20-98. Two-time AL MVP (1983, '91). Rookie of the Year in 1982. 19-time All-Star. Set record for consecutive errorless games by a shortstop (95 in 1990). Hit 20+ HRs in 10 consecutive seasons. Career span 1981–01 with Baltimore; .276 avg., 431 HR, 1,695 RBI, 3,184 hits.

Glenn (Fireball) Roberts (b. 1-20-31, d. 7-2-64): Auto racer. Won 34 NASCAR races. Died as a result of a fiery accident in the World 600 at Charlotte Motor Speedway in May 1964. At the time of his death Roberts had won more major races than any other driver in NASCAR history.

Oscar Robertson (b. 11-24-38): Basketball G. "The Big O." Only player in NBA history to average a triple-double for an entire season (1962). Rookie of the Year in 1961, MVP in 1964, and nine-time first-team All-NBA (1961–69). Led league in assists eight times. Averaged 30+ points six times in seven seasons. MVP of NBA All-Star three times (1961, '64, '69). Career span 1960–74 with Cincinnati and Milwaukee; 9,887 career assists; 26,710 points, 25.7 ppg. Also College Player of the Year, All-America and NCAA scoring leader three consecutive seasons from 1958–60 with Cincinnati. Third all-time NCAA highest scoring average (33.8).

Brooks Robinson (b. 5-18-37): Baseball 3B. Alltime leader in assists, putouts, double plays and fielding average among 3rd basemen. Won 16 consecutive Gold Gloves. Led league in fielding average a record 11 times. MVP in 1964—led league in RBI—and MVP in 1970 World Series. Career span 1955–77 with Baltimore; .267 avg, 2,848 hits, 1,357 RBI.

David Robinson (b. 8-6-65): Basketball C. "The Admiral." Three-time Olympian (1988, '92, '96), and 1995 NBA MVP. One of only two players to win an NBA rebounding title (1991), a blocked shots title (1992) and a scoring title (1994). Four-time first-team All-NBA. All-American at Navy where he led the NCAA in both rebounding (13.0) and blocked shots (5.91) in 1986. 1990 NBA Rookie of the Year. Career span 1989– with San Antonio.

Eddie Robinson (b. 2-13-19): College football coach. Retired with alltime college record 408 career wins through 1941–97 at Division I-AA Grambling State.

Frank Robinson (b. 8-31-35): Baseball OF–manager. Only player to win MVP awards in both leagues (Cincinnati, 1961, Baltimore, 1966). Won Triple Crown and World Series MVP in 1966. Rookie of the Year in 1956. Fifth in career HR (586). Became first black manager in major leagues, with Cleveland in 1975. Career span 1956–76 with Cincinnati, Baltimore, Los Angeles, California and Cleveland; .294 avg., 1,812 RBI, 2,943 hits, 1,829 runs.

Jackie Robinson (b. 1-13-19, d. 10-24-72): Baseball 2B. Broke the color barrier as first black player in major leagues in 1947 with Brooklyn. 1947 Rookie of the Year; 1949 MVP with league-leading .342 batting average. Led league in stolen bases two times; stole home 19 times. Played on six pennant winners with Brooklyn, 1947–56; .311 avg., 137 HR, 947 runs, 197 SB. Elected to Hall of Fame in 1962. No. 42 retired by every team in the major leagues.

Larry Robinson (b. 6-2-51): Hockey D. Twice won Norris Trophy as NHL's top defenseman. Member of six Montreal teams that won Stanley Cup. Awarded Conn Smythe Trophy as MVP of 1978 Stanley Cup. Career span 1972–92, all but the last three with Montreal. Coached New Jersey to Stanley Cup in 2000.

Sugar Ray Robinson (b. 5-3-21, d. 4-12-89): Born Walker Smith Jr. Boxer. Called best pound-for-pound boxer ever. Welterweight champ (1946–51) and middleweight champ five times. Career record: 174-19-6 with 109 KOs from 1940–65. Won 91 consecutive bouts from 1943–51. Fifteen losses came after age 35.

Knute Rockne (b. 3-4-1888, d. 3-31-31): College football coach. Won national championship three times (1924, '29, '30). Alltime highest winning percentage (.881). Career record 105-12-5, including five undefeated seasons, with Notre Dame from 1918–30.

Bill Rodgers (b. 12-23-47): Track and field. Won the Boston and New York City marathons four times each between 1975–80.

Dennis Rodman (b. 5-13-61): Basketball F. Won seven consecutive NBA rebounding titles (1992–98). Won two NBA titles with Detroit (1989, '90) and three with Chicago (1996–98). NBA Defensive Player of the Year (1990, '91). Career span 1986–00, mostly with Detroit and Chicago; 7.3 ppg, 13.1 rpg.

Chi Chi Rodriguez (b. 10-23-35): Golfer. Led senior money list for 1987 ($509,145). Won eight events during PGA career that began in 1960.

Art Rooney (b. 1-27-01; d. 8-25-88): Owner of Pittsburgh Steelers. Bought team in 1933 and ran it until his death in 1988. Elected to Hall of Fame in 1964.

Murray Rose (b. 1-6-39) Australian swimmer. Won three gold medals (including 400- and 1,500-meter freestyle) at 1956 Olympics. Also won one gold, one silver and one bronze medal at 1960 Olympics.

Pete Rose (b. 4-14-41): Baseball OF-IF. "Charlie Hustle." Baseball's alltime hits leader (4,256), who was banned from the game for life in 1989 for his gambling activities and, thus, is ineligible for the Hall of Fame. Had 44-game hitting streak in 1978. 1963 Rookie of the Year; 1973 MVP; 1975 World Series MVP. Won three batting titles, and led the league in hits seven times, runs scored four times and doubles five times. Alltime leader in games played (3,562) and at bats (14,053); second in doubles (746); fifth in runs scored (2,165). Career span 1963–86 with Cincinnati, Philadelphia and Montreal; .303 avg., 160 HR, 1,314 RBI. Manager of Cincinnati from 1984–89. Served five-month jail term for tax evasion in 1990.

Ken Rosewall (b. 11-2-34): Australian tennis player. Won Grand Slam singles titles at ages 18 and 35. Won four Australian titles (1953, '55, '71, '72), two French titles (1953, '68) and two U.S. titles (1956, '70). Reached four Wimbledon finals, but title eluded him.

Art Ross (b. 1-13-1886, d. 8-5-64): Hockey D–coach. Improved design of puck and goal net. Manager-coach of Boston, 1924–45, won Stanley Cup, 1938–39. The Art Ross Trophy is awarded to the NHL scoring champion.

Donald Ross (b. 1873, d. 4-26-48): Scottish-born golf course architect. Trained at St. Andrews under Old Tom Morris. Designed over 500 courses, including Pinehurst No. 2 course and Oakland Hills.

Patrick Roy (b. 10-5-65): Hockey G. Alltime leader in career wins for a goalie (516). Won Vezina Trophy three times. Won Conn Smythe Trophy three times (1986, '93, '01). Career span 1984– with Montreal and Colorado.

Pete Rozelle (b. 3-1-26, d. 12-6-96): Football executive. Fourth NFL commissioner, served from 1960–89. During his term, league expanded from 12 to 28 teams. Created Super Bowl in 1966 and negotiated merger with AFL. Devised plan for revenue sharing of lucrative TV monies among owners. Presided during players' strikes of 1982 and '87.

Wilma Rudolph (b. 6-23-40, d. 11-12-94): Track and field. Gold medalist in three events (100 , 200 and 4 x100-meter relay) at 1960 Olympics. Also won Sullivan Award in 1961.

Adolph Rupp (b. 9-2-01, d. 12-10-77): College basketball coach. Second alltime in NCAA wins (876) and winning percentage (.822). Won four NCAA championships (1948, '49, '51, '58). Career span 1930–72 with Kentucky.

Amos Rusie (b. 5-3-1871, d. 12-6-42): Baseball RHP. Fastball was so intimidating that in 1893 the pitching mound was moved back 5' 6" to its present distance of 60' 6". Led league in strikeouts and walks five times each. Career record 246–174, 3.07 ERA with New York (NL) from 1889–1901.

Bill Russell (b. 2-12-34): Basketball C. Won MVP award five times (1958, 1961–63, '65). Played on 11 championship teams, eight consecutively, with Boston (1957, 1959–66, '68, '69). Player-coach 1968–69 (league's first black coach). Second alltime in career rebounds (21,620) and rebounding average (22.5); second-highest single-game rebounding total (51 in 1960). Led league in rebounding four times. Career span 1956–69 with Boston; 15.1 ppg, 4.3 apg. Also played on two NCAA championship teams with San Francisco in 1955–56; tournament MVP in 1955. Member of gold medal-winning 1956 Olympic team.

Babe Ruth (b. 2-6-1895, d. 8-16-48): Born George Herman Ruth. Baseball P–OF. "The Bambino," "The Sultan of Swat." Most dominant player in history. Alltime leader in slugging average (.690), HR frequency (8.5 HR every 100 at bats); second in career HR (714), RBI (2,211), and walks (2,056). Hit 54 HR in 1920, more than any other team in the American League. 1923 MVP. 60 HR in 1927, a record that stood for 34 years. Second alltime in World Series HR (15), including his "called shot" off Charlie Root in 1932. Began career as a pitcher: 94 career wins and 2.28 ERA. Won 20+ games two times; ERA leader in 1916. Played on 10 pennant winners, seven World Series winners (three with Boston, four with New York (AL)). Sold to Yankees in 1920 (Boston hasn't won World Series since). Career span 1914–35 with Boston, New York (AL) and Boston (NL); .342 avg., 2,873 hits.

Nolan Ryan (b. 1-31-47): Baseball RHP. Pitched seven no-hitters. Alltime leader in career strikeouts (5,714) and walks (2,795). League leader in strikeouts 11 times, shutouts three times, ERA two times. 300+ strikeouts six times, including season record of 383 in 1973. Career span 1966–93 with New York (NL), California, Houston and Texas; 324–292, 3.19 ERA. Elected to Hall of Fame 1999.

Jim Ryun (b. 4-29-47): Track and field. Youngest ever to run sub-four-minute mile (3:59.0 at 17 years, 37 days). Set two world records in mile (3:51.3 in 1966 and 3:51.1 in 1967) and one in 1,500 (3:33.1 in 1967). Plagued by bad luck at Olympics: won silver medal in 1968 1,500 meters despite mononucleosis; was bumped and fell in 1972. Won Sullivan Award in 1967.

Toni Sailer (b. 11-17-35): Austrian skier. Won gold medals in 1956 Olympics in slalom, giant slalom and downhill, the first skier to accomplish the feat.

Juan Antonio Samaranch (b. 7-17-20): Amateur sports executive. From 1980–01, Spaniard served as president of International Olympic Committee.

Pete Sampras (b. 8-12-71): Tennis player. Alltime leader in men's Grand Slam singles titles (14). First player in ATP rankings history to hold No. 1 ranking for six consecutive years. Has won 64 tournament titles.

Joan Benoit Samuelson (b. 5-16-57): Track and field. Gold medalist in first ever women's Olympic marathon (1984). Won Boston Marathon two times (1979, '83). Sullivan Award winner in 1985.

Barry Sanders (b. 7-16-68): Football RB. Third player in NFL history to rush for over 2,000 yards (2,053 in 1997). Led league in rushing four times (1990, '94, '96, '97). Rushed for 1,000+ yards in each of his 10 pro seasons. Retired abruptly in 1999, ranked second alltime in career rushing yards (15,269). NCAA single-season leader in yards rushing (2,628 in 1988), when he won the Heisman Trophy at Oklahoma State.

Gene Sarazen (b. 2-27-02 d. 5-13-99): Golfer. Won PGA Championship three times (1922, '23, '33), U.S. Open two times (1922, '32), British Open once (1932) and the Masters once (1935). His win at the Masters included golf's most famous shot, a double eagle on the 15th hole of the final round. Won 38 career tournaments. Also won Seniors Championship two times (1954, '58). Pioneered the sand wedge in 1930.

Glen Sather (b. 9-2-43): Hockey coach and general manager. 464 regular season wins. Led Edmonton to four Stanley Cup championships (1984, '85, '87, '88) from 1979–89 and 1993–94. Also played for six teams from 1966–76.

Terry Sawchuk (b. 12-28-29): Hockey G. Alltime leader in shutouts (103); second in wins (447). Career 2.52 goals against average. Goaltender of the Year four times (1951–52, '54, '64). Led league in wins and shutouts three times and goals against average two times. Rookie of the Year in 1950. Tied record of four playoff shutouts in 1952. Played on four Stanley Cup champions with Detroit and Toronto from 1949–69.

Gale Sayers (b. 5-30-43): Football RB. Alltime leader in kickoff return average (30.6). Scored 56 career touchdowns, including a rookie record 22 in 1965. Tied record with six touchdowns in one game on 12-12-65. Led league in rushing and gained 1,000+ yards rushing two times. Rookie of the Year in 1965. Career span 1965–71 with Chicago cut short due to knee injury. Also All-America two times with Kansas.

Dolph Schayes (b. 5-19-28): Basketball player. Retired as NBA's all-time leading scorer (19,249 pts). First-team All-NBA six times. Over stretch of 10 years played in 706 consecutive games. Career span 1948–64 with Syracuse and Philadelphia; 18.2 ppg. College star at NYU. Elected to Hall of Fame 1972.

Bo Schembechler (b. 4-1-29): Football coach. In 21 seasons at Michigan from 1969–89, had a 194-48-5 record. Overall college coaching record 234-65-8.

Mike Schmidt (b. 9-27-49): Baseball 3B. Won three MVP awards (1980, '81, '86). 548 career HR, ninth alltime. Led league in HR eight times, slugging average five times, and RBI and walks four times each. Won 10 Gold Gloves. Career span 1972–89 with Philadelphia; .267 avg., 1,506 runs, 1,595 RBI. Elected to the Hall of Fame in 1995.

Don Schollander (b. 4-30-46): Swimmer. Won four gold medals (including 100- and 400-meter freestyle) at 1964 Olympics; won one gold and one silver medal at 1968 Olympics. Also won Sullivan Award in 1964.

Dick Schultz (b. 9-5-29): Amateur sports executive. Second executive director of the NCAA, served from 1987–93. Also served as athletic director at Cornell (1976–81) and Virginia (1981–87).

Seattle Slew (b. 1974; d. 5-7-02): Thoroughbred race horse. Horse of the Year for 1977, when he won the Triple Crown, winning the Kentucky Derby by 1¾ lengths; the Preakness by 1½; and the Belmont by 4. In three-year career from 1976–78, won 14 of 17 starts.

Tom Seaver (b. 11-17-44): Baseball RHP. "Tom Terrific." 311 career wins. 2.86 ERA. Cy Young Award winner three times (1969, '73, '75) and Rookie of the Year 1967. Sixth alltime in career strikeouts (3,640). Led league in strikeouts five times, winning percentage four times and wins and ERA three times each. Won 20+ games five times; 200+ strikeouts 10 times. Struck out 19 batters in one game in 1970, including the final 10 in succession. Pitched no-hitter in 1978. Career span 1967–86 with New York (NL), Cincinnati, Chicago (AL), Boston.

Secretariat (b. 3-30-70, d. 10-4-89): Thoroughbred race horse. Triple Crown winner in 1973 with jockey Ron Turcotte aboard. Ran fastest Kentucky Derby and Belmont Stakes ever. Trained by Lucien Laurin.

Katja Seizinger (b. 5-10-72): German skier. Won downhill gold medals in 1994 at Lillehammer and '98 at Nagano. Won Giant Slalom bronze medal at Nagano. 1998 World Cup champion in downhill, Super G and overall. 32 World Cup victories in downhill and Super G.

Monica Seles (b. 12-2-73): Tennis player. Won three consecutive French Open singles titles (1990–92), four Australian Open titles (1991–93, '96) and two U.S. Open titles (1991, '92). Seles's 1993 season ended on 4-30 when she was stabbed in the back by Gunther Parche while seated during a changeover in a tournament in Hamburg, Germany; also missed 1994 season. Returned to tennis in 1995, reached U.S. Open final.

Bill Sharman (b. 5-25-26): Basketball G. First team All-Star four straight years 1956–59. Led NBA in free throw percentage every year from 1953–57, and in 1959 and '61. All-Star Game MVP in 1955. Career span 1950–61 with Washington and Boston; 17.8 ppg, 88.3 FT%. NBA Coach of the Year in 1972, when his Lakers won NBA title. Elected to Hall of Fame in 1974.

Wilbur Shaw (b. 10-31-02, d. 10-30-54): Auto racer. Won Indy 500 three times in four years (1937, '39, '40). AAA champion two times (1937, '39). Also pioneered the use of the crash helmet after suffering skull fracture in 1923 crash.

Patty Sheehan (b. 10-27-56): Golfer. Won back-to-back LPGA championships (1983, '84). Won 1992 and '94 U.S. Women's Opens, '93 LPGA title, '96 Nabisco. 1983 LPGA Player of Year. Vare Trophy winner in 1984. Qualified for Hall of Fame in 1993.

Fred Shero (b. 10-23-25, d. 11-24-90): Hockey coach. Fourth alltime highest winning percentage (.612). Led Philadelphia to two Stanley Cup championships (1974, '75). Former New York Rangers defender (1947–50) coached Philadelphia and New York from 1971–81; 390-225-119.

Bill Shoemaker (b. 8-19-31): Horse racing jockey. Second alltime in wins (8,833). Rode Belmont Stakes winner five times (1957, '59, '62, '67, '75), Kentucky Derby winner four times (1955, '59, '65, '86—at age 54, the oldest jockey to win Derby) and Preakness Stakes winner two times (1963, '67). Also won Eclipse Award in 1981.

Eddie Shore (b. 11-25-02, d. 3-16-85): Hockey D. Won MVP award four times (1933, '35, '36, '38). All-Star seven times. Played on two Stanley Cup champions with Boston from 1926–40.

Frank Shorter (b. 10-31-47): Track and field. Gold medalist in marathon at 1972 Olympics, the first American to win the event since 1908. Olympic silver medalist in 1976 marathon. Sullivan Award winner in 1972.

Jim Shoulders (b. 5-13-28): Rodeo. 16 career titles. All-Around champion five times (1949, 1956–59).

Don Shula (b. 1-4-30): Football coach. Alltime NFL leader in wins (347). Won two consecutive Super Bowl championships (1972, '73) with Miami, including NFL's only undefeated season in 1972. Also reached Super Bowl four other times. Career span 1963–95 with Baltimore and Miami.

Al Simmons (b. 5-22-02; d. 5-26-56): Baseball OF. "Bucketfoot Al" for hitting stance. Named AL MVP for 1929, when he led league with 157 RBI. Led league in batting average in 1930 (.381) and '31 (.390). Career span 1924–44 with several teams, including Philadelphia (AL); .334 avg., 307 HR. Elected to Hall of Fame in 1953.

O.J. Simpson (b. 7-9-47): Born Orenthal James. Football RB. "Juice." First man to top 2,000 yards rushing in one season (2,003 in 1973). 11,236 career yards rushing. Led league in rushing four times. Gained 1,000+ yards rushing five consecutive seasons. Player of the Year three times (1972, '73, '75). Gained 200+ yards rushing in a game a record six times. Scored 61 career touchdowns, including 23 in 1975. Also won Heisman Trophy with USC in 1968.

Sir Barton (b. 1916, d. 1937): Thoroughbred. In 1919, before they were linked as the Triple Crown, became first horse to win the Kentucky Derby, the Preakness and the Belmont. Won eight of 13 starts as 3-year-old.

George Sisler (b. 3-24-1893, d. 3-26-73): Baseball 1B. Set the alltime record in 1920 with 257 hits in one season. League leader in hits two times, banged out 200+ hits six times. Won two batting titles, including the 1922 crown with a .420 average; averaged .400+ two times and .300+ 11 other times. Career span 1915–30 with St. Louis (NL); .340 avg. and 2,812 hits.

Mary Decker Slaney (b. 8-4-58): Track and field. American record holder in five events ranging from 800 to 3,000 meters. Won 1,500 and 3,000 meters at World Championships in 1983. Lost chance for medal at 1984 Olympics when she tripped and fell after contact with Zola Budd. Won Sullivan Award in 1982. Competed in 1996 Olympics at age 37.

Bruce Smith (b. 6-18-63): Football DE. Second alltime in NFL sacks (186). Played in four consecutive

Super Bowls with Buffalo (1991–94), all losses. Career span 1985– with Buffalo and Washington.

Dean Smith (b. 2-28-31): College basketball coach. Alltime leader in wins (879); seventh alltime highest winning percentage (.776). Alltime most NCAA tournament appearances (27), reached Final Four 11 times. Won NCAA championship in 1982 and '93. Coached 1976 Olympic team to gold medal. Career span 1962–97 with North Carolina. 1997 *Sports Illustrated* Sportsman of the Year.

Emmitt Smith (b. 5-15-69): Football RB. Led NFL in rushing four times (1991, '92 , '93, '95). Set NFL record with 25 TDs in 1995. Named MVP of Super Bowl XXVIII, when he ran for 132 yards in a 30–13 Dallas victory over Buffalo. Career span 1990– with Dallas; poised to pass Walter Payton as the NFL's alltime leading rusher.

Ozzie Smith (b. 12-26-54): Baseball SS. "The Wizard of Oz." May be the best defensive shortstop in history. Holds alltime record for most assists in a season among shortstops (621 in 1980). Career double-play and assist leader among shortstops. 14-time All-Star. Won 13 consecutive Gold Gloves. Career span 1978–96 with San Diego and St. Louis; .262 avg., 2,460 hits, 580 SB.

Red Smith (b. 9-25-05, d. 1-15-82): Sportswriter. Won Pulitzer Prize in 1976. After Grantland Rice, the most widely syndicated sports columnist. His literary essays appeared in the *New York Herald Tribune* from 1945–71 and the *New York Times* from 1971–82.

Stan Smith (b. 12-14-46): Tennis. Won 39 tournaments in career, including 1972 Wimbledon in five sets over Ilie Nastase. Won 1971 U.S. Open over Jan Kodes and amateur version of U.S. Open in 1969. 1970 won inaugural Grand Prix Masters. Inducted to Tennis Hall of Fame in 1987.

Tommie Smith (b. 6-5-44): Track and field. Won 1968 Olympic 200 meters in world record of 19.83, then was expelled from Olympic Village, along with bronze medalist John Carlos, for raising black-gloved fist and bowing head during playing of national anthem to protest racism in U.S.

Conn Smythe (b. 2-1-1895, d. 11-18-80): Hockey executive. As general manager with Toronto from 1929–61 won seven Stanley Cup championships (1932, '42, '45, '47–49, '51). Award for playoff MVP named in his honor.

Sam Snead (b. 5-27-12): Golfer. Alltime leader in career wins (81). Won the Masters (1949, '52, '54) and PGA Championship (1942, '49, '51) three times each and British Open (1946). Runner-up at U.S. Open four times, but title eluded him. PGA Player of the Year in 1949. Won Seniors Championship six times, more than any golfer (1964, '65, '67, '70, '72, '73).

Peter Snell (b. 12-17-38): Track and field. New Zealand runner was gold medalist in 800 meters at two consecutive Olympics (1960 and 1964). Also gold medalist in 1,500 meters at 1964 Olympics. Twice broke world mile record; broke world 800 record once.

Duke Snider (b. 9-19-26): Baseball OF. Holds NL record with 11 home runs and 26 RBI in World Series play. Played on six pennant winners with Brooklyn. Hit 40+ HR five consecutive seasons and 100+ RBI six times. Career span 1947–64 with Brooklyn/LA, New York (NL) and San Francisco; .295 average, 407 HR and 1,333 RBI.

Sammy Sosa (b. 11-12-68): Baseball RF. Followed Mark McGwire in eclipsing Roger Maris's single-season HR mark in 1998. Lost HR race to McGwire that season but won MVP with .308 average, 66 HR, 134 runs, 158 RBI. In 2001, became first man to hit 60+ home runs in three seasons. Career span 1989– with Texas, Chicago (AL) and Chicago (NL).

Javier Sotomayor (b. 10-13-67): Track and field. Cuban high jumper broke the 8-foot barrier with world record jump of 8' 0" in 1989. Set record of 8' ½" in 7-27-93 in Salamanca, Spain.

Warren Spahn (b. 4-23-21): Baseball LHP. Alltime leader in wins by a lefthander (363); 20+ wins 13 times. League leader in eight times, complete games nine times, strikeouts four consecutive seasons, innings pitched four times and ERA three times. 1957 Cy Young award. 63 career shutouts. Pitched two no-hitters after age 39. Career span 1942–65, all but last year with Boston/Milwaukee Braves.

Tris Speaker (b. 4-4-1888, d. 12-8-58): Baseball OF. Alltime leader in doubles (792), fifth in hits (3,514) and fifth in batting average (.345). One batting title (.386 in 1916), but .375+ average six times. League leader in doubles eight times, hits two times and HR and RBI one time each. 200+ hits four times; 40+ doubles 10 times and 100+ runs scored seven times. MVP in 1912. Career span 1907–28, mostly with Boston (AL) and Cleveland.

Michael Spinks (b. 7-13-56): Boxer. Defeated Larry Holmes for the heavyweight championship of the world on 9-22-85. Lost title to Mike Tyson in 91 seconds on 6-27-88. Won world light heavyweight title on 7-18-81 and defended it nine times before moving up to heavyweight division. 1976 Olympic middleweight champion.

Mark Spitz (b. 2-10-50): Swimmer. Won a record seven gold medals (two in freestyle, two in butterfly, three in relays) at 1972 Olympics, setting world record in each event. Also won two gold medals, one silver and one bronze medal at 1968 Olympics. Sullivan Award winner in 1971.

Amos Alonzo Stagg (b. 8-16-1862, d. 3-17-65): College football coach. 314 career wins. Won national title with Chicago in 1905. Coach of the Year with Pacific in 1943 at age 81. Five undefeated seasons. Career span 1892–46. Only person elected to both college football and basketball Halls of Fame. Played in the first basketball game in 1891.

Willie Stargell (b. 3-6-40, d. 4-9-01): Baseball OF–1B. "Pops" achieved a 1979 MVP triple crown, winning NL regular season, playoff and World Series MVP awards. Led NL in homers in 1971 and '73. Career span 1962–82 with Pittsburgh; .282 avg., 475 HR, 1,540 RBI. Elected to Hall of Fame in 1988.

Bart Starr (b. 1-9-34): Football QB. Played on three NFL champions (1961, '62, '65) and first two Super Bowl champions (1966, '67) with Green Bay. Also named MVP of first two Super Bowls. Player of the Year in 1966. Led league in passing three times. Career span 1956–71 with Green Bay; 24,718 passing yards, 152 TDs. Also coached Green Bay to 53-77-3 record from 1975–83.

Roger Staubach (b. 2-5-42): Football QB. Led Dallas to six NFC Championships, four Super Bowls and two Super Bowl titles (1971, '77). Player of the Year and Super Bowl MVP in 1971. Also led league in passing four times. Won Heisman Trophy with Navy as a junior in 1963. Served four-year military obligation before turning pro. Career span 1969–79 with Dallas; 22,700 passing yards, 153 TDs passing.

Jan Stenerud (b. 11-26-42): Football K. Scored 1,699 career NFL points. Converted 373 field goals in 558 attempts. Career span 1967–85 with Kansas City, Green Bay and Minnesota. First pure kicker inducted to Hall of Fame, 1991.

Casey Stengel (b. 7-30-1890, d. 9-29-75): Baseball manager. "The Ol' Perfesser." Managed New York (AL) to 10 pennants and seven World Series titles (five consecutively) in 12 years from 1949–60. Alltime leader in World Series games (63), wins (37) and losses (26). Platoon system was his trademark strategy, Stengelese his trademark language ("You could look it up."). Managed New York (NL) from 1962–65. Jersey number (37) retired by Yankees and Mets. Career mark: 1,905-1,842 (.508).

Ingemar Stenmark (b. 3-18-56): Swedish skier. Gold medalist in slalom and giant slalom at 1980 Olympics. World Cup overall champion three consecutive years (1976–78).

Woody Stephens (b. 9-1-13 d. 8-22-98): Horse racing trainer. Trained two Kentucky Derby winners · (Cannonade, who won the 100th Derby in 1974 and Swale in 1984) and five straight Belmont winners from 1982–86, starting with 1982 Horse of the Year Conquistador Cielo.

David Stern (b. 9-22-42): Fourth NBA commissioner. Has served since 1984. Oversaw unprecedented growth of league. Owners rewarded him with five-year, $40-million contract extension in 1996.

Jackie Stewart (b. 6-11-39): Scottish auto racer. Fifth alltime in Formula 1 victories (27); Formula 1 champion three times (1969, '71, '73). Also Indy 500 Rookie of the Year in 1966. Retired in 1973.

Payne Stewart (b. 1-3-57, d. 10-25-99): Golfer. Two-time U.S. Open champion (1991, '99), also won 1989 PGA Championship. Killed in plane crash.

John Stockton (b. 3-26-62): Basketball G. Alltime leader in assists (15,177) and steals (3,128). Set single-season assist record (1,164) in 1990–91. Led NBA in assists a record nine consecutive times (1988–96). 10-time All-Star, consecutively 1989–97, 2000. Co-MVP (with Karl Malone) of 1993 All-Star Game. Member of 1992 and '96 Olympic teams. Career span 1984– with Utah; 13.2 ppg, 10.7 rpg.

Picabo Street (b. 4-3-71): Skier. Won silver medal in downhill at 1994 Olympics in Lillehammer and gold in Super G at '98 Games in Nagano. World Cup downhill champion in 1995 and '96. Nine career World Cup victories.

John L. Sullivan (b. 10-15-1858, d. 2-2-18): Boxer. Last bareknuckle champion. Heavyweight title holder (1882–92), lost to Jim Corbett. Career record 38-1-3 with 33 KOs from 1878–92.

Paul Tagliabue (b. 11-24-40): Football executive. Fifth NFL commissioner, has served since 1989.

Anatoli Tarasov (b. 1918, d. 6-23-95): Hockey coach. Orchestrated Soviet Union's emergence as a hockey power. Won nine consecutive world amateur championships (1963–71) and three Olympic gold medals in 1964, '68, '72.

Fran Tarkenton (b. 2-3-40): Football QB. Hall of Famer retired with 342 touchdown passes, 47,003 yards passing, 6,467 pass attempts and 3,686 pass completions. Player of the Year in 1975. Career span 1961–78 with Minnesota, New York Giants.

Lawrence Taylor (b. 2-4-59): Football LB. Revolutionized the linebacker position. Retired as the alltime leader in sacks. Named to Pro Bowl a record 10 consecutive seasons. Player of the Year in 1986. Played on two Super Bowl champions with New York Giants (1986, '90). Career span 1981–93 with New York. Elected to Hall of Fame 1999.

Isiah Thomas (b. 4-30-61): Basketball G. Point guard for Detroit team that won NBA title in 1989 and '90. All-NBA First Team 1984–86. NBA All-Star Game MVP in 1984 and '86. Led NBA in assists (13.9) in 1984–85. Fifth alltime in assists (9,061). Career span 1981–94 with Detroit; 19.2 ppg, 9.3 apg. GM of Toronto Raptors 1995–97. Coached Indiana Pacers 2000–. Member of Indiana University team that won 1981 NCAA title.

Thurman Thomas (b. 5-15-66): Football RB. Rushed for 1,000+ yards eight years in a row (1989–96). Led AFC in rushing in 1990 and 1991. Career span 1988–01 with Buffalo and Miami; 12,074 yards, 88 TDs.

Daley Thompson (b. 7-30-58): Track and field. British decathlete was gold medalist at two consecutive Olympics in '80 and '84. At 1984 Olympics set world record (8,847 points) that lasted eight years.

John Thompson (b. 9-2-41): College basketball coach. Former Boston Celtic coached at Georgetown (1973–99), where he mentored Patrick Ewing, Alonzo Mourning and Dikembe Mutombo. Won NCAA title in 1984, runner-up in '82 and '85. Career record: 596–239.

Bobby Thomson (b. 10-25-23): Baseball OF. Three-time All-Star who hit dramatic "shot heard 'round the world" off of Ralph Branca to win NL pennant for New York (NL) in 1951. The Giants had come from 13½ games behind to tie Brooklyn and force a three-game playoff. Career span 1946–60 with New York (NL), Milwaukee, Chicago (NL), Boston and Baltimore; .270, 264 HR, 1,026 RBI.

Jim Thorpe (b. 5-28-1888, d. 3-28-53): Sportsman. Gold medalist in decathlon and pentathlon at 1912 Olympics. Played pro baseball with New York (NL) and Cincinnati 1913–19, and pro football with several teams 1919–26. Stripped of gold medals when it was discovered he had played pro baseball, and they were restored only after his death. Also All-America two times with Carlisle.

Dick Tiger (b. 8-14-29; d. 12-14-71): Nigerian boxer. Born Richard Ihetu. Two-time middleweight champ, also won light heavyweight title. Fighter of the Year for 1962 and '65. Elected to Boxing Hall of Fame 1974.

Bill Tilden (b. 2-10-1893, d. 6-5-53): Tennis player. "Big Bill." Won seven U.S. singles titles, six consecutively (1920–25, '29) and three Wimbledon titles (1920, '21, '30). Also won six Grand Slam doubles titles. Led U.S. to seven consecutive Davis Cup victories (1920–26).

Ted Tinling (b. 6-23-10, d. 5-23-90): British tennis couturier. The premier source of women's tennis fashion, from Suzanne Lenglen to Steffi Graf—most notable creation: the frilled lace panties worn by Gorgeous Gussy Moran at Wimbledon in 1949.

Y.A. Tittle (b. 10-24-26): Football QB. Two-time NFL Most Valuable Player (1961, '63). Set NFL record with 36 TD passes in 1963. Career span 1948–64 with Baltimore, San Francisco and New York Giants; 33,070 yards, 242 TD. Inducted into Hall of Fame 1971.

Jayne Torvill/Christopher Dean (b. 10-7-57/ b. 7-27-58): British figure skaters. Won four consecutive ice dancing world championships (1981–84) and Olympic ice dancing gold medal (1984). Won world professional championships in 1985. Won Olympic ice dancing bronze in 1994.

Vladislav Tretiak (b. 4-25-52): Hockey G. Led USSR to gold medals at Olympics in 1972, '76, '84. Played on 13 world amateur champions from 1970–84.

Lee Trevino (b. 12-1-39): Golfer. Won U.S. Open (1968, '71), British Open (1971, '72) and PGA Championship (1974, '84) two times each. PGA Player of the Year in 1971. Also won U.S. Senior Open in 1990. First Senior $1 million season.

Emlen Tunnell (b. 3-29-25, d. 7-23-75): Football S. Alltime leader in interception return yardage with 1,282 and second in interceptions (79). All-Pro nine times. Career span 1948–61 with New York Giants and Green Bay.

Gene Tunney (b. 5-25-1897, d. 11-7-78): Boxer. Heavyweight champion (1926–28). Defeated Jack Dempsey two times, including famous "long count" bout. Career record 65-2-1 with 43 KOs from 1915–28. Retired as champion.

Ted Turner (b. 11-19-38): Sportsman. Skipper who successfully defended the America's Cup in 1977. Also owner of the Atlanta Braves since 1976 and Hawks since '77. Founded the Goodwill Games in 1986.

Mike Tyson (b. 6-30-66): Boxer. Became boxing's youngest heavyweight champion (20 years, 144 days) by knocking out Trevor Berbick in 1986. Lost crown in devastating upset to James (Buster) Douglas in 1990. Served three years in prison (1992–95) for rape. Regained piece of heavyweight title but lost it to Evander Holyfield in 1997. He "lost it" again in their rematch in 1997, when he was disqualified for biting Holyfield's ears. Career record: 49–4, 43 KOs.

Johnny Unitas (b. 5-7-33, d. 9-11-02): Football QB. Set record for throwing TD passes in 47 consecutive games (1956–60). Three-time NFL MVP (1959, '64, '67). Led league in TD passes four consecutive seasons. Career span 1956–72 with Baltimore and San Diego; 290 TD passes, 40,239 passing yards.

Al Unser Sr. (b. 5-29-39): Auto racer. Won Indy 500 four times (1970, '71, '78, '87). Retired with 39 career CART victories. USAC/CART champion three times (1970, '83, '85). Brother of Bobby.

Bobby Unser (b. 2-20-34): Auto racer. Won Indianapolis 500 three times (1968, '75, '81). Retired with 35 career victories. USAC champion twice (1968, '74). Brother of Al Sr.

Harold S. Vanderbilt (b. 7-6-1884, d. 7-4-70): Sailor. Owner and skipper who successfully defended the America's Cup three consecutive times, in 1930, '34 and '37.

Glenna Collett Vare (b. 6-20-03, d. 2-2-89): Golfer. Won U.S. Women's Amateur six times, more than any golfer (1922, '25, '28–30, '35).

Bill Veeck (b. 2-9-14, d. 1-2-86): Baseball owner. From 1946–80, owned ballclubs in Cleveland, St. Louis (AL) and Chicago (AL). In 1948, Cleveland became baseball's first team to draw two million in attendance. That year Veeck integrated AL by signing Larry Doby and Satchel Paige. A brilliant promoter, Veeck sent midget Eddie Gaedel up to bat for St. Louis in 1951.

Guillermo Vilas (b. 8-17-52): Tennis. Argentine won 50 straight matches in 1977. In '77 won French Open, where he beat Brian Gottfried, and the U.S. Open, where he beat Jimmy Connors. Also won Australian Open twice, 1978–79.

Lasse Viren (b. 7-22-49): Track and field. Finnish runner was gold medalist in 5,000 and 10,000 meters at two consecutive Olympics (1972, '76).

Virginia Wade (b. 7-10-45): Tennis. Beloved in Britain, Wade won three major titles, most notably Wimbledon in 1977, its centenary year, where she triumphed over Betty Stove. Also won 1968 U.S. Open, '72 Australian Open, and doubles titles in '73 at the Australian, French and U.S. Opens, all with Margaret Smith Court.

Honus Wagner (b. 2-24-1874, d. 12-6-55): Baseball SS. Had .327 career batting average, 3,415 hits and eight batting titles. Averaged .300+ 15 consecutive seasons. Led league in RBI four times, with 100+ RBI nine times. Third alltime in triples (252) and league leader in doubles eight times. 703 career stolen bases, league leader in steals five times. Career span 1897–1917 with Pittsburgh.

Grete Waitz (b. 10-1-53): Track and field. Norwegian runner won New York City Marathon a record nine times (1978–80, '82–86, '88). Won the women's marathon at the 1983 World Championship.

Jersey Joe Walcott (b. 10-31-14, d. 2-25-94): Boxer. Heavyweight champion from 1951–52. Won title at age 37 on fifth attempt before surrendering it to Rocky Marciano. Later became sheriff of Camden, NJ.

Doak Walker (b. 1-1-27, d. 9-27-98): Football HB. Led NFL in scoring two times, his first and final seasons. All-Pro five times. Played on two consecutive NFL champions (1952–53) with Detroit. Career span 1950–55. Also won Heisman Trophy as a junior in 1948. All-America three consecutive seasons with SMU.

Herschel Walker (b. 3-3-62): Football RB. 1982 Heisman Trophy winner signed with the New Jersey Generals of the USFL in '83. Gained 5,562 rushing yards and scored 61 touchdowns in three seasons before league folded. Entered NFL in 1986 with Dallas and led league in rushing yards in 1988. Career span 1983–97 with New Jersey (USFL), Dallas, Minnesota, Philadelphia and New York Giants; 13,787 rushing yards and 143 TD (both leagues).

Bill Walsh (b. 11-30-31): Football coach. "The Genius." Led San Francisco to three Super Bowl wins, after the 1981, '84, '88 seasons. Career record with 49ers from 1979–88, 102-63-1. Perfected short-passing game.

Bill Walton (b. 11-5-52): Basketball C. College Player of the Year three consecutive seasons (1972–74). Played on two NCAA championship teams (1972, '73) with UCLA; tournament MVP twice (1972, '73). Sullivan Award winner in 1973. NBA MVP in 1978, playoff MVP in '77. Led league in rebounding and blocks in 1977. Career span 1974–86 with Portland, San Diego and Boston; 13.3 ppg, 10.5 rpg.

War Admiral (b. 1934, d. 1959): Thoroughbred race horse. A son of Man o' War, won Triple Crown and Horse of the Year honors in 1937.

Paul Warfield (b. 11-28-42): Football WR. Five-time All-NFL, averaged sensational 20.1 yards per catch during his career. Played on two Super Bowl–winning Miami teams. Career span 1964–77 with Cleveland

and Miami; 427 receptions for 8,565 yards and 85 TDs. Inducted to Hall of Fame 1983.

Glenn (Pop) Warner (b. 4-5-1871, d. 9-7-54): College football coach. Fourth alltime in wins (319). Won three national championships with Pittsburgh (1916, '18) and Stanford (1926). Career record 319-106-32 with six teams from 1896–38.

Tom Watson (b. 9-4-49): Golfer. Winner of British Open five times (1975, '77, '80, '82, '83), the Masters two times (1977, '81) and U.S. Open once (1982). PGA Player of the Year six times, more than any golfer (1977–80, '82, '84).

Dick Weber (b. 12-23-29): Bowler. Won All-Star Tournament four times (1962, '63, '65, '66). Voted Bowler of the Year three times (1961, '63, '65). Won 31 career PBA titles.

Johnny Weismuller (b. 6-2-04, d. 1-21-84): Swimmer. Won three gold medals (including 100- and 400-meter freestyle) at 1924 Olympics and two gold medals at the 1928 Olympics. Also played Tarzan in the movies.

Jerry West (b. 5-28-38): Basketball G. "Mr. Clutch." 10 time first-team All-NBA; All-Defensive Team four times; 1969 playoff MVP. Led league in assists and scoring one time each. Career span 1960–72 with Los Angeles; 27.0 ppg, 6.7 apg. All-America two times with West Virginia. Played on 1960 gold medal-winning Olympic team. Guided the Lakers to seven NBA championships as either a general manager or a consultant from 1980 to 2001.

Whirlaway (b. 4-2-38, d. 4-6-53): Thoroughbred race horse. Triple Crown winner in 1941 with jockey Eddie Arcaro aboard. Trained by Ben A. Jones.

Byron (Whizzer) White (b. 6-8-17, d. 4-15-02): Football RB. Led NFL in rushing two times (Pittsburgh in 1938, Detroit in '40). Led NCAA in scoring and rushing with Colorado in 1937; named All-America. United States Supreme Court justice 1962–93.

Reggie White (b. 12-19-62): Football DE. "Minister of Defense." Alltime leader in sacks (198). Set a Super Bowl record with three sacks against New England in Super Bowl XXXI. He played in 13 Pro Bowls. Career span: 1984–01 with Memphis Showboats (USFL), Philadelphia, Green Bay and Carolina.

Charles Whittingham (b. 4-13-13 d. 4-20-99): Thoroughbred race horse trainer. "Bald Eagle" after losing hair to tropical disease in World War II. Led yearly earnings list for trainers in 1970–73, '75, '81, '82. Won three Eclipse Awards and trained two Horses of the Year (Ack Ack in 1971 and Ferdinand in '87).

Kathy Whitworth (b. 9-27-39): Golfer. Alltime LPGA leader with 88 tour victories, including six majors. Won LPGA Championship in 1967, '71 and '75. Won Titleholders Championship (extinct major) in 1965 and '66. Won Western Open (extinct major) in 1967. Won Vare Trophy every year from 1965–72, except '68. LPGA Player of Year from 1966–69 and 1971–73.

Hoyt Wilhelm (b. 7-26-23): Baseball RHP. Hall of Famer. Threw knuckleball until age 48. Career 2.52 ERA, 227 saves. Hit home run in his first at bat (never hit another) and pitched no-hitter in 1958. Career span 1952–72 with nine teams.

Bud Wilkinson (b. 4-23-15 d. 2-9-94): Football coach. Coached Oklahoma to NCAA record 47 consecutive wins (1953–57). Won three national championships (1950, '55, '56) with Oklahoma, where

he coached from 1947–1963. Won Orange Bowl four times and Sugar Bowl two times. Career record 145-29-4, including four undefeated seasons. Also coached St. Louis of NFL in 1978–79.

Billy Williams (b. 6-15-38): Baseball OF. "Sweet Swinging." Six-time All-Star and the 1961 NL Rookie of the Year. Career span 1959–76 with Chicago (NL) and Oakland; .290 avg., 426 HR, 1,475 RBI. Elected to Hall of Fame in 1987.

Ted Williams (b. 8-30-18, d. 7-5-02): Baseball OF. "The Splendid Splinter." Last player to hit .400 (.406 in 1941). MVP in 1946, '49 and Triple Crown winner in 1942, '47. Sixth in career batting average (.344), third in walks (2,019) and second in slugging average (.634). Won six AL batting titles, and led the league in HR and RBI four times each. Had .300+ average 15 consecutive seasons; 100+ RBI and runs scored nine times each; 30+ HR eight times; and 100+ walks 11 times. Lost nearly five seasons to military service. Career span 1939–42 and 1946–60 with Boston; 521 career HR.

Hack Wilson (b. 4-26-1900; d. 11-23-48): Baseball OF. Stood 5' 6" but weighed 210. Had five astounding seasons 1926–30, before alcohol ruined his career. Best was 1930 when he hit .356, scored 146 runs, hit a NL record 56 homers and drove in 190, which is still the major league record. Career span 1923–34 with several teams. Elected to Hall of Fame in 1979.

Dave Winfield (b. 10-3-51): Baseball OF. Drafted out of Univ. of Minnesota by baseball, basketball and football teams. Drove in 100+ runs eight times, and led the NL in 1979 with 118. Derided by George Steinbrenner as "Mr. May," but hit clutch double to win 1992 World Series for Toronto. Career span 1973–95 with San Diego, New York (AL), California, Toronto, Minnesota and Cleveland; .283 avg., 465 HR, 3,110 hits, 1,833 RBI and 1,669 runs. Inducted into Hall of Fame in 2001.

Major W.C. Wingfield (b. 10-16-1833, d. 4-18-12): British tennis pioneer. Credited with inventing the game of tennis, which he called "Sphairistike" or "sticky" and patented in February 1874.

Colonel Matt Winn (b. 6-30-1861, d. 10-6-49): General manager of Churchill Downs from 1904 until his death; made Kentucky Derby premier U.S. race.

Katarina Witt (b. 12-3-65): East German figure skater. Gold medalist at 1984 and '88 Olympics. Also world champion four times (1984, '85, '87, '88).

John Wooden (b. 10-14-10): College basketball coach. Coached UCLA to 10 NCAA championships in 12 years (1964, '65, '67–73, '75). Record winning streak of 88 games (1971–74). 664 career wins and fourth highest career winning percentage (.804). First member of basketball Hall of Fame as coach and player. Career span 1949–75 with UCLA. 1932 College Player of the Year at Purdue.

Tiger Woods (b. 12-30-75): Golfer. Produced the Tiger Slam in 2000–01, an unofficial Grand Slam during which he won four consecutive professional majors. Holds the tournament record for best scores at the Masters, the U.S. Open, the PGA Championship and the British Open. Became the youngest winner of the Masters in 1997, when he shot a record-270 to win by a record 12 strokes. Became the youngest player to win all four major tournaments ('99 PGA, '00 U.S. Open, '00 British Open). Also won three straight U.S. Junior Amateur titles (1991–93) and three straight U.S. Amateur titles (1994–96). Then took the PGA tour by storm, winning six of his first 21 tournaments. Already has 34 PGA Tour victories (including eight majors) and has won more money ($32,687,252) than any golfer in history. 1996 and 2000 *Sports Illustrated* Sportsman of the Year.

Mickey Wright (b. 2-14-35): Golfer. Second alltime in career wins (82) and major championships (13; tied with Louise Suggs). Won the U.S. Open four times (1958, '59, '61, '64), the LPGA Championship four times (1958, '60, '61, '63), and the Western Open three times (1962, '63, '66).

Kristi Yamaguchi (b.7-12-71): Figure skater. Olympic champion in 1992. Back-to-back world champion (1991, '92).

Cale Yarborough (b. 3-27-40): Auto racer. Won Daytona 500 four times (1968, '77, '83, '84). 83 career victories. NASCAR champion three consecutive years (1976–78).

Carl Yastrzemski (b. 8-22-39): Baseball OF. "Yaz." 1967 MVP and Triple Crown winner. Three batting titles. Second alltime in games played (3,308) and sixth in walks (1,845). Career span 1961–83 with Boston; .285 avg., 3,419 hits, 452 HR and 1,844 RBI.

Cy Young (b. 3-29-1867, d. 11-4-55): Baseball RHP. Alltime leader in wins (511), innings pitched (7,354⅔) and complete games (749); fourth in shutouts (76). Had 2.63 career ERA. Pitched three no-hitters, including a perfect game in 1904. Career span 1890–1911 with Cleveland and Boston (AL).

Steve Young (b. 10-11-61): Football QB. Highest rated passer in NFL history, with 96.8 rating. Led the league in passing six times. Led 49ers to victory in Super Bowl XXIX of which he was MVP for tossing a record six TD passes. Two-time NFL MVP (1992 and '94). Repeated concussions forced his retirement in 2000. Career span 1984–00 with Los Angeles Express (USFL), Tampa Bay and San Francisco; 33,124 yards, 232 TD passes; rushed for 43 TD.

Robin Yount (b. 9-16-55): Baseball OF–SS. Won AL MVP as a shortstop (1982) and a centerfielder (1989). Became Milwaukee's shortstop at 18. Career span 1974–93 with Milwaukee; .285 avg., 3,142 hits, 251 HR and 583 2B. Elected to Hall of Fame 1999.

Steve Yzerman (b. 5-9-65): Hockey C. Won three Stanley Cups with Red Wings (1997, '98, '02). Won Conn Smythe trophy in 1998. Scored 100+ points six consecutive seasons (1987–93). Career span 1983– with Detroit.

Babe Didrikson Zaharias (b. 6-26-14, d. 9-27-56): Sportswoman. Commonly called the greatest female athlete of all time, Zaharias was the Gold medalist in the 80-meter hurdles and javelin throw at the 1932 Olympics; she also won the silver medal in the high jump (her gold medal jump was disallowed for using the then-illegal western roll). Became a golfer in 1935 and won 12 major titles, including U.S. Open three times (1948, '50, '54—a year after cancer surgery). Also helped found the LPGA in 1949.

Tony Zale (b. 5-29-13, d. 3-20-97): Boxer. Born Anthony Zaleski. "The Man of Steel." Two-time middleweight champ. Fought Rocky Graziano for title three times in 21 months, winning twice. 67-18-2 with 44 KOs. Elected to Boxing Hall of Fame 1958.

Emil Zatopek (b. 9-19-22): Track and field. Czech runner became only athlete to win gold medal in 5,000 and 10,000 meters and marathon, at 1952 Olympics. Also gold medalist in 10,000 meters at '48 Olympics.

Zinedine Zidane (b. 6-23-72): French soccer player. "Zizou." Led France to 1998 World Cup title; scored two goals in 3–0 win over Brazil in the final. Led Juventus to 1998 Italian League title and to '98 European Cup final. 1998 FIFA World Player of the Year. Led France to 2000 European Championship.

Obituaries

John Unitas
1933–2002

Bob Akin, 66, race car driver. Akin, who won the prestigious 12 Hours of Sebring in 1979 and 1986, was a standout in sports car racing in the International Motor Sports Association (IMSA) during his professional driving career. He also made six starts in the 24 Hours of Le Mans with a best finish of fourth in 1984. He won the IMSA World Endurance Championship in 1986.

He started racing in 1957 in dragsters, then switched to road racing in 1959. He retired from driving in 1961 to concentrate on his business, but returned to racing in 1973. Mr. Akin was also a member and former president of the Road Racers Drivers Club. Akin devoted his time to the management of Bob Akin Motorsports, which specializes in the restoration and race preparation of historic race cars. He was a writer and frequent contributor to *Road & Track* magazine, and did on-air commentary for Speedvision, TBS and ESPN.

In Atlanta, of injuries caused by an automobile accident, April 29, 2002.

Alice Bauer, 74, golf pioneer. Bauer was one of the original founders of the LPGA. She gained attention after winning the South Dakota Amateur title at the age of 14. In the 1940s and '50s, she and her sister Marlene toured the country as the famous "Bauer Sisters" and were regarded as two of the most glamorous women in sports. Bauer turned pro in 1950 and helped create the LPGA the same year.

She had two children by the age of 22 and only competed occasionally after that, although she did become one of the first golfers to bring her children on tour. "As a founder of the LPGA, Alice's passion and love for the game and the association provided the foundation for the LPGA of today," said LPGA Commissioner Ty M. Votaw.

In Palm Springs, Calif., of colon cancer, March 6, 2002.

Bo Belinsky, 64, baseball player. Belinsky had a 28–51 record in eight seasons with five different teams. As an Angels rookie in 1962, he threw the first major league no-hitter on the West Coast, but he was better known for his hard partying and his dalliances with such starlets as Mamie Van Doren, Ann-Margret and Tina Louise. "You know, I've probably gotten more mileage winning 28 games in the majors than most guys who've won 200," Belinsky told the *Las Vegas Review-Journal* in 2000.

In Las Vegas, of a heart attack, Nov. 23, 2001.

Jay Berwanger, 88, football player. The first winner of what became known as the Heisman Trophy, Berwanger was an All-America at the University of Chicago in 1936. A triple-threat, Berwanger had 577 rushing yards, 406 passing yards, 359 yards on kickoff returns and six touchdowns. Berwanger was also the first player ever selected in the NFL draft. Chicago Bears owner and coach George Halas acquired Berwanger's signing rights but balked at meeting the player's demand for $25,000 over two years. Berwanger subsequently passed on pro football and took a job as a foam-rubber salesman.

In Oak Brook, Ill., of lung cancer, June 26, 2002.

Prince Ahmed bin Salman, 43, Saudi thoroughbred owner. A nephew of King Fahd of Saudi Arabia and chairman of a publishing empire, bin Salman became the first Arab owner to win the Kentucky Derby when his War Emblem won in 2002. War Emblem went on to win the 2002 Preakness Stakes, but he stumbled at the start of the Belmont Stakes and missed out on the Triple Crown, The Prince also owned the 2001 horse of the year, Point Given. "He had major flair and loved the game and was continuing to grow in the sport," said jockey Gary Stevens. "At 43, everybody was looking forward to him having a long, long career in the industry and he was definitely a boost to thoroughbred racing."

In Riyadh, Saudi Arabia, of a heart attack, July 22, 2002.

Peter Blake, 53, New Zealand yachtsman. Blake, who began sailing at age five, was considered one of the most successful yachtsmen in history. He led Team New Zealand to victory in 1995 in the America's Cup, yachting's most prestigious team competition. In 2000, he became the first non-American entry to retain the America's Cup in 149 years.

Blake was the head of the Jacques Cousteau Foundation and had recently been appointed a goodwill ambassador of the United Nation's environment program. He was on a research expedition up the Amazon River when his boat *Seamaster* was attacked by pirates. He was shot and killed in an exchange of gunfire.

SI's E.M. Swift writes:

"A national hero in New Zealand, Blake wasn't accustomed to failure. He was the most accomplished sailor of his time. A charismatic leader whose fairness, work ethic and sense of humor engendered fierce loyalty in his crews, he won all the major ocean races. Blake was the only man to complete the first five Whitbread Round-the-World races, and he dominated that event in 1989–90, when he skippered *Steinlager 2* to line, handicap and overall honors on each of the race's six legs. In '94 Blake and Robin Knox-Johnston broke the nonstop round-the-world sailing record by four days in a 92-foot catamaran, completing the 27,000-mile circumnavigation in 74 days, 22 hours and 17 minutes. . . .

"Aboard *Seamaster* he planned, as his website blakeexpeditions.com, said, 'to undertake voyages to those parts of the world that are key to the planet's ecosystem.' When he was killed, Peter—who is survived by his wife, Pippa, and their two teenage children—was in the first year of a five-year odyssey to study the waters of the earth and raise awareness of changes that were affecting them. It was the latest and most noble of his voyages that cost him his life."

Near Macapá, Brazil, of gunshot wounds, Dec. 5, 2001.

Jack Buck, 77, broadcaster. Buck began calling St. Louis Cardinals games on radio in 1954 and he continued as the voice of the Cardinals until 2001. Nationally, Buck called Super Bowls, World Series and even pro bowling for CBS, ABC and NBC. Some of his most memorable calls are permanently etched in the collective sports consciousness: After a gimpy Kirk Gibson hit a game-winning two-run homer off Oakland's Dennis Eckersley in Game 1 of the 1988 World Series, Buck was incredulous: "I don't believe what I just saw!"

Buck was also behind the microphone for the first

telecast of the AFL and at the NFL championship "Ice Bowl" in 1967. Inducted into the Baseball Hall of Fame's broadcaster's wing in 1987, Buck later became a member of both the broadcasters and radio halls of fame.

In St. Louis, Mo., of complications following lung cancer surgery, June 18, 2002.

Chris Campbell, 21, football player. Campbell had been a starter for the Miami Hurricanes at strongside linebacker since midway through the 1999 season, starting 30 consecutive games before missing the 2002 Rose Bowl after suffering an infection to his left knee following minor surgery. Campbell finished third on the team with 68 tackles in 2001 and was expected to be drafted by an NFL team. He finished his career at Miami with 221 tackles and six sacks in 41 games. "When Chris shook your hand, he meant he was Chris Campbell and he was glad to meet you," safety James Lewis said, referring to the crushing handshake that earned Campbell the nickname "The Grip." "It got to the point that you didn't want to shake his hand," fullback Najeh Davenport said. "Chris will be missed but not forgotten. No matter what Chris did he went full speed."

In Coral Gables, Fla., of injuries caused by an automobile accident, Feb. 16, 2002.

Regine Cavagnoud, 31, French skier. Cavagnoud had long been a strong competitor in the downhill and giant slalom. After a string of injuries, she won her first race in January 1999—the 10th year of her career. The win broke a 17-year downhill drought for French women. She won the 2001 super G World Cup and was third overall in the World Cup standings. She also won the super G title at the 2001 World Championships in St. Anton, Austria.

"My passion for skiing carried me through all the injuries and doubts," Cavagnoud said after winning her world championship. "I had many injuries but I was brave enough to come back each time."

"French sport has lost one of its great champions today," French President Jacques Chirac said. "Regine has made her mark on world skiing with her boundless generosity and her unusual courage in the face of difficulties."

Cavagnoud died two days after slamming into a German coach while training on a glacier. She had just cleared a slight hump on the Pitztal glacier and was hurtling down the mountain at about 40 mph when Markus Anwander, a coach from the German team, crossed into her path, witnesses told authorities.

In Vienna, of injuries caused by a skiing collision, Oct. 31, 2001.

Frank Crosetti, 91, baseball player. Nicknamed "The Crow," Crosetti was known for his steady play at shortstop during a 17-year career with the New York Yankees from 1932 to '48. He was a teammate of Yankee greats Babe Ruth, Lou Gehrig and Joe DiMaggio and had a career batting average of .245 with 98 home runs and 649 RBI.

In Stockton, Calif., of complications from a fall, Feb. 11, 2002.

Tommy Joe Crutcher, 60, football player. Crutcher helped the Packers win three straight NFL titles and the first two Super Bowls during his nine-year NFL career. He lettered at TCU from 1961 to '63, playing both fullback and linebacker. He was a key figure in the Horned Frogs' 6–0 upset of No. 1 Texas in 1961 and earned All-America honors at fullback in 1963. The *Fort Worth Star-Telegram* selected Crutcher to its all-time TCU team as a linebacker in 1995.

In McAllen, Texas, of natural causes, Feb. 16, 2002.

Kevin Dare, 19, pole vaulter. A sophomore on Penn State's track and field team, Dare won the pole vault at the United States Track and Field Junior National Championships in June 2001, winning the event by clearing 16-6¾. Dare also competed for the United States at the Pan American Junior Championships in Argentina and placed fifth in the pole vault at the IC4A Championships, helping seal the team title for Penn State, in 2001.

He was competing in the Big Ten's indoor championships when his injury occurred. Witnesses said Dare tumbled backward, headfirst, onto the metal "box," the area 8 inches deep that is used to plant the pole. He was attempting a vault of 15 feet, 7 inches, well below his personal best.

In Minneapolis, of head injuries, Feb. 28, 2002.

Mike Darr, 25, baseball player. Darr was San Diego's opening day centerfielder in 2001, his first full season in the big leagues. He batted .277 with 34 RBIs. "He had a pretty good year last year," San Diego manager Bruce Bochy said. "He could run, he could throw, he could hit. Here's a 25-year-old kid with his future ahead of him, and it's a shame it happened." Darr was the Padres' minor league player of the year in 1997 after being obtained from Detroit. "My immediate thoughts were of his family, his two young children," teammate Trevor Hoffman said. "Michael was a free spirit. He was a happy-go-lucky guy. He embraced life. He embraced everybody in a special way. He always had a smile that lit up the clubhouse."

SI's Tom Verducci writes:

"Darr left behind a wife, Natalie, and two young sons, Mike Jr. and Matthew. A fourth outfielder blessed with speed and boundless enthusiasm, the 6'3", 205-pound Darr hit .277 with two home runs and 34 RBIs in 289 at bats last season, his third with the Padres. During his five years in the organization he personified the spirit of a youthful, scrappy outfit. Once, in the minor leagues, an injured Darr was sitting in the training room wearing only sliding shorts hiked to his hips, ice packs strapped on his hamstrings and shower sandals when a brawl erupted on the field. A nearly naked Darr bolted onto the field to join the fray. 'At one point the fight just kind of came to a halt because nobody could believe what he was doing,' former teammate Ben Davis says."

In Peoria, Ariz., of injuries from an automobile accident, Feb. 15, 2002.

Willie Davenport, 59, hurdler. Davenport equaled the Olympic record when he ran the 110-hurdles in 13.3 seconds at Mexico City in 1968. Nicknamed "Breeze," he won a bronze in the same event at the 1976 Games at the age of 33, and he also competed at the 1964 and 1972 Games. In 1980, Davenport competed in his fifth Olympics as a member of the U.S. four-man bobsled team that finished 12th at the Winter Olympics in Lake Placid. Davenport and Jeff Gadley were the first black Olympic bobsledders, and Davenport became one of eight Americans to compete in both the Summer and Winter Games. He joined the National Guard in 1981, and logged 27 years of military service. Davenport was honored as one of this country's 100 Golden Olympians before the 1996 Centennial Olympics in Atlanta, and he was a vice president of the U.S. Olympic Alumni Association.

In Chicago, of a heart attack, June 17, 2002.

Dan Devine, 77, football coach. Devine replaced legendary coach Ara Parseghian at Notre Dame and led the Irish to a national championship in 1977. In five seasons under Devine, the Irish were 53-16-1 and won three bowl games. During 22 seasons in the college ranks, Devine went 172-57-9 (a .742 winning percentage) at Arizona State, Missouri and Notre Dame, suffering only one losing season. He also coached the Green Bay Packers for four seasons, going 25-27-4.

SI's Tim Layden writes:

"Devine was more commonly a soft-spoken technician who delegated responsibility to assistant coaches and revealed little of himself to the public. 'He was a low-key man of great dignity and talent, but he lacked Ara's charisma, and for that reason he was never fully accepted by the Subway Alumni,' says Rev. Edmund Joyce, Executive Vice President Emeritus at Notre Dame, the man who hired Devine. Indeed, despite averaging nearly nine victories per season at Notre Dame, Devine rarely comes up when the Irish faithful discuss their most revered coaches. ...

"'He was private and introverted, and maybe that hurt him,' says former NFL safety Dave Duerson, who played for Devine at Notre Dame. 'But you have to know that Coach was a man who touched many lives. He always said, 'Be a better player every day when you leave the field than when you stepped onto it.' I still live my life by those words,'"

In Tempe, Ariz., of complications following heart surgery, Dec. 21, 2001.

Bob Hayes, 59, sprinter/football player. "Bullet" Bob Hayes earned the title of "World's Fastest Human" and had such blazing speed as a receiver that he redefined the way pass defense is played in the NFL. At the 1964 Tokyo Olympics, Hayes won the gold medal in the 100 meters, tying the world record of 10.05 seconds, and he anchored the U.S. 400-meter relay team to victory in a world-record 39.06. As a receiver for the Dallas Cowboys, Hayes forced opposing defenses to use zone pass coverage. When Dallas won the Super Bowl in 1972, Hayes became the only athlete to win an Olympic gold medal and a Super Bowl ring. He finished his 11-year NFL career with 76 touchdowns, a 20-yard average per catch, and three trips to the Pro Bowl.

SI's Paul Zimmerman writes:

"Speed is what Hayes brought into the league in 1965, more speed than anyone had ever seen on a football field. And when the rest of the NFL saw how he stretched defenses and forced them to go to all sorts of zones to try to stop him, general managers pored over copies of *Track & Field News* and sent out their invites.

"Hayes differed from the sprinters who would follow him into and out of the NFL, because he was not merely a sprinter who happened to play football. He was, as he liked to put it, 'a football player first, then a runner.'"

In Jacksonville, Fla., of kidney failure, Sept. 18, 2002.

Chick Hearn, 85, broadcaster. The only play-by-play announcer the Los Angeles Lakers ever had, Hearn introduced phrases such as "slam dunk" and "air ball" to the sport lexicon. Before temporarily leaving the booth in December 2001 for heart surgery, Hearn had broadcast 3,338 consecutive Lakers games. "His colorful descriptions of the game transcended the sport and have had an indelible influence on basketball and broadcasting itself," NBA commissioner David Stern said. He was best known for his prodigious work with the Lakers, but Hearn also broadcast NCAA and NFL football, UNLV basketball, PGA golf tournaments, the first Ali-Frazier fight and Los Angeles Sparks games.

In Los Angeles, after a fall, Aug. 5, 2002.

Jerry Heidenreich, 52, swimmer. Heidenreich won two gold medals, a silver and a bronze swimming for the United States at the 1972 Olympics in Munich. His Olympic exploits were overshadowed by Mark Spitz's record haul, but his own feats were remarkable. He was a four-time All-America at SMU and set a world record in the 200-meter freestyle. He is a member of the Texas Sports Hall of Fame and the International Swimming Hall of Fame as the only Texan to win four Olympic medals.

In Paris, Texas, of an apparent suicide following a stroke, April 18, 2002.

Thor Heyerdahl, 87, Norwegian adventurer. Heyerdahl was one of the great individualistic standard-bearers of mid-20th-century adventure. In 1947, he and his five-person crew climbed aboard *Kon-Tiki*, an experimental balsa raft, and swept atop the Pacific's Humboldt current from Peru to the Tuamotu islands to prove that it was possible that many of the islands of the South Pacific were settled by pre-Incan inhabitants of South America. After 101 days at sea in the South Pacific, he arrived in French Polynesia, after a journey of over 4,900 miles. His achievement, Heyerdahl believed, proved that New World mariners from the east might have sailed into Polynesia, contradicting the general assumption that it had been populated from the west. Heyerdahl documented his journey in the best-selling book *Kon-Tiki*, which has sold 30 million copies in 37 languages. The book was also made into an Academy Award–winning documentary.

Following his first voyage, Heyerdahl made several subsequent voyages, including a 3,200-mile crossing of the Atlantic Ocean from Morocco to Barbados. Heyerdahl's voyages forever laid to rest questions of the abilities of the ancients to travel long distances to spread their culture.

Before Heyerdahl made his voyage on the *Kon-Tiki*, he had to overcome a major obstacle: "If you had asked me as a 17-year-old whether I would go to sea on a raft, I would have absolutely denied the possibility. At that time, I suffered from fear of the water," Heyerdahl once said. At Oslo's Kon-Tiki Museum in 1998, a visiting schoolchild asked Heyerdahl if he ever got scared in his expeditions. "Oh, yes. On every single expedition," the explorer replied. "Everything was planned to the last detail. I haven't survived by good luck, but rather by the absence of bad luck."

In Colla Muchari, Italy, of a brain tumor, April 18, 2002.

Darryl Kile, 33, baseball player. Kile was the unquestionned leader of the St. Louis Cardinals pitching staff. An 11-year veteran and three-time All-Star, he had revitalized his career in St. Louis after two bumpy seasons with the Rockies in the thin air of Colorado. In 2000, he joined the Cardinals and won 20 games. A 30th-round draft choice, Kile was 133–119 in his career, and he pitched a no-hitter against the New York Mets in 1993.

SI's Stephen Cannella writes:

"Kile kept a low profile with the media, but he was one of the leaders in the St. Louis clubhouse. Although he was only a 30th-round draft pick by the Houston Astros in 1987, out of Chaffey College, a two-year school in his native Southern California, Kile earned a spot in the rotation by '91. While back in California in '88 he met Flynn Behrens, and they were married four years later. . . . After going 19–7 with a 2.57 ERA in '97, he landed a three-year, $24 million free agent contract with the Colorado Rockies. Kile quickly became the poster boy for the difficulties of pitching at Coors Field: His trademark pitch, a sharp, overhand curve, flattened out in the thin Colorado air, and in two seasons he was a combined 21–30 with a 5.84 ERA. Despite his struggles Kile won respect for his gutsy attempts to tame the Coors beast—and he never made excuses for his poor performance.

"Kile was rejuvenated by a trade to St. Louis before the 2000 season. The bite returned to his curveball, and he won 20 games that year, followed by 16 last season, helping the Cardinals into the playoffs both years. He was also a mentor to the team's young pitchers. Last year he worked closely with lefthander Rick Ankiel, who was trying to regain the control that mysteriously abandoned him late in 2000. Kile also took righthander Matt Morris, a 20-game winner last season, under his wing. The two hung out together on the road, and Morris credits Kile with helping him mature into a successful pitcher. 'My numbers might look better, but Kile's the best guy on our staff,' Morris said late last year. 'He's the ace.'"

In Chicago, of coronary arteriosclerosis, June 22, 2002.

Dick Lane, 73, football player. One of the hardest-hitting players in football history and a member of the NFL's 75th anniversary team in 1994, "Night Train" Lane made 68 career interceptions in 14 years in the league. He was a Pro Bowl selection seven times, was named to the NFL's 50th anniversary team in 1969 and to the Pro Football Hall of Fame in 1974. He developed a clothesline tackle, dubbed the "Night Train Necktie," which the NFL subsequently banned.

SI's Paul Zimmerman writes:

"He came up in an era when cornerbacks were still called defensive halfbacks. He played a style of football that was born of poverty and desperation. Years later Night Train Lane's technique would acquire the catchy name bump and run, but when he came into the NFL, in 1952, his approach was as elemental as the game itself. Lock on a receiver, rough him up down the field, try to knock him off his pattern, and if he still caught the ball, take his head off."

In Austin, Tex., of a heart attack, Jan. 29, 2002.

Abe Lemons, 79, basketball coach. Lemons was as well known for his sense of humor as for his coaching ability. He compiled a 599–343 record in 34 years in stops at Texas, Oklahoma City (twice) and Pan American. Lemons' personality and up-tempo style of play revitalized the program at Texas beginning in the late 1970s. The Longhorns went 110–63 in six seasons, winning a share of two Southwest Conference titles and the 1978 NIT. He retired after the 1989–90 season, one win shy of 600 wins. "Damn referees," he said after losing his final game by one point. "I'll miss them less than anybody."

In Oklahoma City, of Parkinson's disease, Sept. 2, 2002.

Harvey Martin, 51, football player. A four-time Pro Bowl player, Martin was the co-MVP of the 1978 Super Bowl as a member of the Dallas Cowboys. He set team records with 114 career sacks, including 20 in 1977.

In Grapevine, Tex., of pancreatic cancer, Dec. 24, 2001.

Wahoo McDaniel, 63, football player/wrestler. McDaniel bounced around the AFL for much of his eight-year career, spending time with the Houston Oilers, Denver Broncos, New York Jets and, finally, the Miami Dolphins. He capitalized on the stardom from his gridiron days to become one of the country's most popular and beloved pro wrestlers. Over the course of his 30-year wrestling career, McDaniel—as Chief Wahoo— had memorable battles with foils such as Ric Flair, Roddy Piper and Sgt. Slaughter. He "won" several titles before retiring in 1989.

In Houston, Texas, of complications from renal failure and diabetes, Apr. 18, 2002.

Tom Moore, 88, hurdler/track official. Moore tied the world record in the 120-yard high hurdles in 1935, but his greatest contribution to his sport came in 1942, when he organized the Modesto Relays, which evolved into one of the biggest track meets in the world. During that first meet in 1942, Moore fired the starting gun for all the races except one, the hurdles, which he won. Sixty years later, the Modesto Relays remain one of the premier events in all of track and field. Moore was inducted into the National Track & Field Hall of Fame in 1988. As one of the finest race starters in the world, Moore worked 18 national championships and the 1984 Olympic Games in Los Angeles.

In Modesto, Calif., of bone cancer, May 10, 2002.

Ogden Phipps, 93, court-tennis player/throroughbred owner. Phipps was actively involved with thoroughbred racing for approximately 70 years, racing stakes winners such as Buckpasser, Easy Goer and the undefeated Personal Ensign. He won Breeders' Cup races with Personal Ensign in 1988, Dancing Spree in 1989, and My Flag in 1995, and won Eclipse Awards as the nation's leading owner and leading breeder in 1988 and as the nation's leading owner in 1989. His greatest moment was the 1989 Belmont Stakes, when Easy Goer spoiled Sunday Silence's bid for the Triple Crown. "I had waited a long time to win the Belmont Stakes," Phipps said.

"I was not only blessed to have trained for Mr. Phipps, but I was also blessed to have known him as a person," Easy Goer's trainer Shug McGaughey said. "He was not only an icon in this sport, but in this country as well. There are not many people like him left in our world. He was a great man."

Phipps was also a seven-time United States Court Tennis champion in the mid-1930s and mid-1940s and won the British Amateur championship in 1949. He was inducted into the International Court Tennis Hall of Fame in 2001.

In West Palm Beach, Fla., after a short illness, April 22, 2002.

Darrell Porter, 50, baseball player. Porter was an All-Star catcher with the Kansas City Royals and the 1982 World Series Most Valuable Player with the St. Louis Cardinals, but drug addiction plagued his career. He checked himself into an Arizona drug rehab center in 1980 and later wrote a book, "Snap Me Perfect! The Darrell Porter Story," about overcoming drug abuse with the help of religion. During his 17-year major league career, Porter hit 188 home runs, played in three World Series and four All-Star games.

In Kansas City, Mo., of a violent reaction to drug use, Aug. 5, 2002.

Umer Rashid, 26, British cricket player. Rashid was a left-handed batsman with the English County cricket club in Sussex. He made his debut for Middlesex at 19 before switching to Sussex in 1999.

Reports indicate that his 18-year-old brother Burhan got into trouble while swimming in a pool below Concord Falls, a popular tourist spot. Rashid attempted to rescue his brother but both men drowned.

In Concord Falls, Grenada, of drowning, April 1, 2002.

John Roseboro, 69, baseball player. Roseboro, who succeeded Roy Campanella as the Dodgers' full-time catcher, was a four-time All-Star and the starting catcher in the 1959, 1963, 1965 and 1966 World Series. Roseboro had a lifetime batting average of .249 in 14 seasons with the Dodgers, Minnesota Twins and Washington Senators. But he is also remembered as the victim of one of the most frightening attacks in baseball history. On Aug. 22, 1965, San Francisco pitcher Juan Marichal clubbed Roseboro over the head with a bat, inciting a 14-minute brawl between the National League rivals. Roseboro later sued Marichal for $110,000 in damages, but they became good friends in the 1980s.

In Los Angeles, of a stroke, Aug. 16, 2002.

Kyle Rote, 74, football player. Rote, an All-America at Southern Methodist and the No. 1 pick of the New York Giants in the 1951 NFL Draft, retired as the franchise's alltime leading receiver. In 11 seasons with the Giants, Rote caught 300 passes for 4,797 yards and 48 touchdowns. Later he became the first president of the NFL Players Association. "To me the most remarkable thing about him from a football standpoint was that he had 14 teammates who named sons after him," said his son, Kyle, Jr.

In Baltimore, of cardiopulmonary complications, Aug. 14, 2002.

Dick Schaap, 67, journalist. Tabbed "The Leonardo da Vinci of multimedia journalism," Schaap worked in television, radio, newspapers, magazines and books for more than 50 years. He wrote 33 books, but younger audiences recognized him as the host ESPN's Sunday morning show, *The Sports Reporters*. His co-star Mitch Albom once wrote about Schaap: "He has walked with kings, ridden shotgun with legends, dined with the power elite and gotten drunk with some of the biggest sports stars of our time. And what he comes away with is not a swelled head, an inflated sense of his own importance, or a need to lecture the world with an opinion much richer than ours. What he comes away with are stories." Schaap once wrote, "I have gotten to know the heroes of my youth, and the villains, and I have learned how thin the line is between them."

In New York City, of complications following hip replacement surgery, Dec. 21, 2001.

Seattle Slew, 28, thoroughbred. Slew won 14 of 17 races—including the 1977 Triple Crown—and earned $1,208,726 in his brief racing career. An awkward-looking yearling that was purchased at auction for only $17,500, Slew blossomed as a three-year old, developing a "body so bulged with muscles that it always looked like his coat was cut a size too

small," according to SI's William Nack. Retired after his four-year-old season, he proved even more valuable as a stud, siring 102 stakes winners that won more than $75 million in purses. The big, black stallion's death came on the 25th anniversary of his Kentucky Derby victory.

SI's William Nack writes:

"Few horses of any era made such a powerful, lasting impression as Slew—and this from the moment he first strode on the track. Hall of fame trainer LeRoy Jolley recalls the colt on the day he made his second start—on Oct. 5, 1976, in a seven-furlong allowance race at Belmont Park—and of how Slew materialized in the paddock like some black Baryshnikov, exuding radiant energy and bouncing to the track on the tips of his toes. 'I don't think I ever saw that horse walk,' Jolley says. 'He danced everywhere he went.'"

In Lexington, Ky, of complications from a spine operation, May 7, 2002.

Jack Shea Sr., 91, speedskater. Shea was the patriarch of the first family with three generations of Olympians, and the winner of two gold medals at the 1932 Winter Games. At 91, he was America's oldest living Winter Olympics gold medalist. As a 22-year-old speedskater, Shea won gold in the 500 and 1,500 meter events in front of his home crowd at Lake Placid. His son, Jim Sr., was a cross-country skier at the 1964 Winter Olympics, and his grandson, Jim Jr., won the gold medal in the skeleton in Salt Lake City just weeks after his grandfather's death.

In Lake Placid, N.Y., of injuries sustained in an automobile accident, Jan. 22, 2002.

Wayne Simmons, 32, football player. A 1993 first-round pick out of Clemson, Simmons won a Super Bowl ring with the 1996 Green Bay Packers. His best season came in 1995 when he had 68 tackles, 23 assists and four sacks.

In Kansas City, Mo., of injuries from an automobile accident, Aug. 23, 2002.

Enos Slaughter, 86, baseball player. A 10-time All-Star, "Country" Slaughter was one of the St. Louis Cardinals' most beloved players. In the 1946 World Series against Boston, he scored the go-ahead run in Game 7 with what became known as a "Mad Dash" from first base on a single by Harry Walker. In 19 seasons, Slaughter had a lifetime batting average of .300 and played in five World Series. He was elected to the Hall of Fame in 1985 and his No. 9 was retired by the Cardinals.

In Durham, N.C., of complications following stomach and colon surgery, Aug. 12, 2002.

Sam Snead, 89, golfer. Famous for his straw hat, cocky grin and homespun humor, "Slammin' Sammy" Snead won a record 81 tournaments on the PGA Tour. "Watching Sam Snead practice hitting golf balls is like watching a fish practice swimming," said John Schlee, a U.S. Open runner-up in 1973, of Snead's effortless swing. Snead won three PGA Championships, three Masters Tournaments (including a playoff victory over Ben Hogan in 1954), and the 1946 British Open.

SI's John Garrity writes:

"No golfer between Bobby Jones and Tiger Woods—not even Arnold Palmer, whose swing was too much a wild swipe to inspire imitation—was as iconic as Snead. With his coconut-straw hat and long, syrupy swing, Snead was the only golfer that casual fans could identify at a distance or in silhouette. His follow-through spoke like poetry; the club face finished parallel to his shoulders, and his balance was so exquisite that he could hold the pose indefinitely. . . .

"Snead's reputation rested on conventional measures of greatness—he won the Masters and the PGA Championship three times each, the British Open once, was the Tour's leading money winner three times and played on seven U.S. Ryder Cup teams—but his appeal transcended the records. He had an alliterative name, like Mickey Mantle, and a marketable swagger, like his friend Ted Williams. 'Any guy who would pass up a chance to see Snead on a golf course,' Jim Murray wrote, 'would pull the shades driving past the Taj Mahal.' . . .

"Above all, he was voluble. Snead would kill an hour swapping blue jokes or debating the best way to skin a deer. He'd even jaw at his golf ball ('Now stay put, you little fooler, this ain't gonna hurt none at all.')"

In Hot Springs, Va., following a series of strokes, May 23, 2002.

Sunday Silence, 16, Thoroughbred. Sunday Silence won the Kentucky Derby, Preakness Stakes and Breeder's Cup Classic and was the 1989 Horse of the Year before going to stud in Japan in 1991. He was named the leading sire in Japan for seven straight years from 1995, but it was his pursuit of the Triple Crown in 1989 that most racing fans will remember. Sunday Silence's battles with Easy Goer during his Triple Crown chase stirred memories of Affirmed's duels with Alydar 11 years earlier. Easy Goer ended Sunday Silence's quest for the Triple Crown at the Belmont, but Silence exacted some revenge by winning the Breeder's Cup Classic later that year by a neck.

In Hokkaido, Japan, of heart failure, Aug. 19, 2002.

Fred Taylor, 77, basketball coach. Taylor coached an Ohio State team that featured Jerry Lucas, John Havlicek and a seldom-used sub named Bobby Knight to the 1960 NCAA championship. Twice the national college coach of the year, Taylor led his alma mater to seven Big Ten titles during his 18 years as coach. In 1960, '61 and '62 he guided Ohio State to the national title game, winning in 1960 and losing twice to Cincinnati. Taylor's .778 winning percentage in NCAA tournament games is the eighth highest, and his teams were 14–4 in the tournament. His career record was 297–158. "Fred Taylor was an absolute giant in coaching," Knight said. "You could have no way played for a better coach in college from whom you learned more and in no way could have had a better friend."

In Hilliard, Ohio, of natural causes, Jan. 6, 2002.

Johnny Unitas, 69, football player. Unitas broke nearly every NFL passing record and won three championships with the Baltimore Colts. With his trademark crewcut and black hightops, Johnny U captured the public's imagination and helped drive the growing popularity of professional football. Unitas was the NFL's Most Valuable Player in 1964 and 1967 and played in 10 Pro Bowls. He led Baltimore to the NFL championship in 1958 and 1959 and the Super Bowl in 1970. Unitas was the first to throw for 40,000 career yards, and his record of completing at least one touchdown pass in 47 straight games has never been threatened. His toughness and leadership came to define the quarterback position, and his skill and guile as a passer and play-caller set the standard for all those who followed him. John Mackey, the Colts' tight end during the Unitas years, once said of his teammate, "It's like being in a huddle with God."

SI's Frank Deford writes:

"Johnny U was an American original, a piece of work like none other, excepting maybe Paul Bunyan and Horatio Alger.

"Part of it was that he came out of nowhere, like Athena springing forth full-grown from the brow of Zeus, or like Shoeless Joe Hardy from Hannibal, Mo., magically joining the Senators, compliments of the devil. But that was a myth, and that was fiction. Johnny U was real, before our eyes. . . .

"Certainly he didn't look the part of a hero. This is how his teammate Alex Hawkins described Unitas when Hawkins first saw him in the locker room: 'Here was a total mystery. [Unitas was from Pennsylvania, but he looked so much like a Mississippi farmhand that I looked around for a mule. He had stooped shoulders, a chicken breast, thin bowed legs and long, dangling arms with crooked, mangled fingers.' . . .

"In those halcyon days, quarterbacks were field generals, not field lieutenants. And there was Unitas after he called a play (and probably checked off and called another play when he saw what the ruffians across the line were up to), shuffling back into the pocket, unfazed by the violent turbulence all around him, standing there in his hightops, waiting, looking, poised. I never saw war, so that is still my vision of manhood: Unitas standing courageously in the pocket, his left arm flung out in a diagonal to the upper deck, his right cocked for the business of passing, down amidst the mortals."

In Timonium, Md., of a heart attack, Sept. 11, 2002.

Art Wall, 77, golfer. A quiet champion who won 14 times on the PGA Tour in a career that spanned six decades. At the 1959 Masters, Wall birdied five of the last six holes for a 6-under-par 66 and a one-shot victory over Jimmy Demaret. An 11-foot birdie putt on the 72nd hole made Wall the first champion in Masters history to take his first lead of the tournament on the final hole. The comeback—Wall was five shots down with seven to play—is the fourth-best in Masters history.

In Scranton, Pa., of respiratory failure, Oct. 31, 2001.

Mike Webster, 50, football player. During his career from 1974–90 with the Pittsburgh Steelers and Kansas City Chiefs, Webster made the Pro Bowl nine times and won four Super Bowls. With the Steelers, he protected Terry Bradshaw and paved the way for Franco Harris. In 2000, he was chosen as the center on the All-Time NFL team.

SI's Paul Zimmerman writes:

"I talked to Webster in that Steeler locker room many times, and he never lied or sugarcoated. And after I'd interview him, he'd thank me, then smile and point to the crowded section of the locker room and say, 'Better go talk to the superstars.' In his mind he was just a workingman who played center. Many people feel no one ever played it better."

In Pittsburgh, of a heart attack, Sept. 24, 2002.

Byron White, 84, football player. An All-America halfback at Colorado in the 1930's, White's greatest contributions were made in Washington, where he served on the Supreme Court for 31 years before retiring in 1993. In the court's history, only eight justices served longer. White was known as one of the high court's clearest thinkers—a centrist who often provided key votes on divisive issues.

As a football player, "Whizzer" White was one of the best players of his era. He postponed his studies at Oxford to become the NFL's leading rusher in the 1938–39 season, a feat he repeated the following year.

In Denver, Colo., of complications from pneumonia, Apr. 15, 2002.

Hoyt Wilhelm, 79, baseball player. Wilhelm wielded a physics-defying knuckleball and became the first reliever elected to the Hall of Fame. A five-time All-Star, he played mostly for the Giants, Baltimore and the Chicago White Sox, going 143–122 with 227 saves and a 2.52 ERA. When he retired in 1972, at age 48, he held the major league record for games pitched at 1,070. His knuckleball was so difficult to catch that after the Orioles catchers allowed 49 passed balls in 1959, the team introduced an oversized catcher's mitt specifically designed to handle Wilhelm. "He was a great teammate and obviously an outstanding pitcher," said Bobby Valentine, who played with Wilhelm on the Dodgers. "He had humor, work ethic, and camaraderie that I will always remember."

In Sarasota, Fla., of heart failure, Aug. 23, 2002.

Curtis Williams, 24, football player. Williams, who played safety for the University of Washington, was injured in a helmet-to-helmet hit in a game against Stanford in 2000. He had spinal-cord surgery and was left with no voluntary muscle movement. The Huskies dedicated their victory over Purdue in the Rose Bowl in January 2001 to Williams, wearing his initials on their jerseys. Williams played in 24 games, starting every one as a junior and senior before his injury. He finished his career with 142 tackles and one interception.

In Fresno, Calif., of complications associated with his paralysis, May 6, 2002.

Ted Williams, 83, baseball player. "All I want out of life," Williams once told a friend, "is that when I walk down the street, folks will say, 'There goes the greatest hitter that ever lived.'" In a playing career that spanned four decades with the Boston Red Sox and was interrupted by two military tours of duty that cost him nearly five full seasons, the "Splendid Splinter" hit .344 with 521 home runs, 1,839 RBI, 2,019 walks, a slugging percentage of .634 that remains second only to Babe Ruth's .690, and an on-base percentage of .483 that is second to no one. Williams was a two-time MVP who twice won the Triple Crown. His greatest achievement came in 1941 when he batted .406, getting six hits in a doubleheader on the final day of the season. Williams led the league in hitting six times, the last in 1958, when, at age 40, he became the oldest batting champ in major league history.

Williams was only 20 when he joined the Red Sox in 1939, beginning a tempestuous, colorful career. He had 145 RBIs as a Red Sox rookie and closed out his career—fittingly—by hitting a home run at Fenway Park in his final major league at-bat in 1960. A 28-year-old John Updike immortalized the moment: "Our noise for some seconds passed beyond excitement into a kind of immense open anguish, a wailing, a cry to be saved. But immortality is nontransferable. The papers said that the other players, even the umpires on the field, begged him to come out and acknowledge us in some way, but he never had and did not now. Gods do not answer letters."

He had several nicknames: Thumpin' Ted, Teddy Ballgame and The Kid. But none stuck like The Splendid Splinter. "Ted Williams was what John Wayne would have liked us to think he was," said sportswriter Robert Lipsyte. "Williams was so big, and handsome, and laconic, and direct, and unafraid in that uniquely American cowboy way. To me he epitomized the sense of the athlete as gunslinger."

SI's Leigh Montville writes:

"If you grew up watching Ted Williams hit a baseball, well, you simply kept watching, even after he stopped hitting. That was the way it was. From the day he arrived at Fenway Park in Boston in 1939 as a slender 20-year-old outfielder with a swing for the ages until last Friday, when he died of cardiac arrest in Inverness, Fla., at age 83, he was part of your life. As years passed, he might have changed, and you might have changed, and times might have changed, but he always was a fascinating character. He was a superstar before the word was invented. He was a man's man, icon of all icons. . . .

"Williams was a mythical figure, a creation of radio words and black-and-white newspaper pictures. He had the purity of Sir Lancelot, the strength of Paul Bunyan, the tenacity of, say, Mighty Mouse. Distance, to be sure, made heroes much more heroic than they ever can be today."

In Inverness, Fla., of cardiac arrest, July 5, 2002.

Mamo Wolde, 69, Ethiopian runner. Wolde won the Olympic marathon in 1968 in Mexico City, and then came back to claim the bronze four years later—at age 40—in Munich. He also won the silver medal in the 10,000 meters in Mexico City. The rest of his life, however, was not nearly as glorious. An army officer during Marxist dictator Mengistu Haile Mariam's regime, Wolde was imprisoned in 1993 after Mariam was ousted, and he was accused of the 1978 murder of a 15-year-old boy. Wolde always maintained that he was innocent but he was never officially cleared. A court finally found him formally guilty in January 2002 and sentenced him to six years. However, he was released because he had already spent nine years behind bars.

SI's Kenny Moore writes:

"The last four months of his life were filled with bliss and honor. He lived in Addis Ababa with his wife, Aberash Wolde-Semhate, and their two children, ages 12 and 10. 'The children hug me all the time,' Wolde said, laughing. 'If I go to the store, we all have to go, kids and wife and me, in a big tangle of love.' . . .

"It's heart-wrenching that after enduring so much, he has gone so quickly. I can only imagine that when he reached his finish, in the embrace of his family, he was completely spent. I have no doubt he went at pace, as befits a marathoner, knowing the rightness of all things physical having an end."

In Addis Ababa, Ethiopia, of a liver condition, May 26, 2002.

George Young, 71, football executive. Young turned the floundering New York Giants into Super Bowl champions and was named NFL Executive of the Year five times during his 19 years with the Giants, beginning in 1979. He drafted Phil Simms and Lawrence Taylor and promoted Bill Parcells to head coach to create a football powerhouse. "I never draft anyone too smart," Young said. "If he's smart, he can find something to do other than to play this dumb game." Commissioner Paul Tagliabue said, "He was in essence a teacher, both in the history class and in football, who helped people at all levels."

In Baltimore, of a rare brain illness, Dec. 8, 2001.

2003 Major Events

JANUARY

Major College Bowl Games	Jan 1 & 2
Fiesta Bowl/National Championship	Jan 3
NFL Wild-Card Playoffs	Jan 4 & 5
NFL Divisional Playoffs	Jan 11 & 12
U.S. Figure Skating Championships	Jan 12–19
Australian Open Tennis	Jan 13–26
NFL Conference Championships	Jan 19
Super Bowl XXXVII	Jan 26

FEBRUARY

NHL All-Star Game	Feb 2
AFC-NFC Pro Bowl	Feb 2
Millrose Games	Feb 7
NBA All-Star Game	Feb 9
Daytona 500	Feb 16

MARCH

U.S. Indoor Track and Field Championships	Feb 28–Mar 2
PBA World Championship	March 3–9
The Players Championship	March 27–30
Baseball Opening Day	March 31

APRIL

Major League Soccer Season Begins	April 5*
NCAA Men's Basketball Final Four	April 5–7
NCAA Women's Basketball Final Four	April 6–8
Stanley Cup Playoffs Begin	April 9
Masters Tournament	April 10–13
NBA Playoffs Begin	April 19
NFL Draft	April 19–20
Boston Marathon	April 21

MAY

Kentucky Derby	May 3
Preakness	May 17
Indianapolis 500	May 25
Stanley Cup Finals Begin	May 26

JUNE

French Open Tennis	May 26–June 8
NBA Finals Begin	June 4
Belmont Stakes	June 7
U.S. Open Golf	June 12–15
NBA Draft	June 26

JULY

Wimbledon Tennis	June 23–July 6
Baseball All-Star Game	July 8
British Open Golf	July 17–20
Tour de France	July 5–27

AUGUST

Brickyard 400	Aug 3
PGA Championship	Aug 14–17
College Football Season Begins	Aug 23

SEPTEMBER

U.S. Open Tennis	Aug 25–Sept 7
NFL Season Begins	Sept 4*

OCTOBER

NHL Season Begins	Oct 2*
World Series Begins	Oct 18*
Breeders' Cup	Oct 25*
NBA Regular Season Begins	Oct 28
2003 Women's World Cup	Sept 28–Oct 16

NOVEMBER

Women's Tennis Tour Championships	Oct 27–Nov 2*
New York Marathon	Nov 2
The President's Cup	Nov 6–9*
MLS Cup 2003	Nov 9*
Tennis Masters Cup	Nov 10–16

DECEMBER

Heisman Trophy Presentation	Dec 13
Major College Bowl Games Begin	Dec 18*

* Approximate date.